P9-EED-149

JANUARY — DECEMBER 1997

Published by Congressional Quarterly Inc. 1414 22nd Street, N.W., Washington, D.C. 20037
Congressional Quarterly offers a complete line of publications and research services.
For subscription information, call (202) 887-6279 or (800) 432-2250 ext. 279.

ISBN 1-56802-257-3
ISSN 1056-2036

...nts of The CQ Researcher

(...rmerly Editorial Research Reports)

Subscribers to *The CQ Researcher* receive 48 reports per year. Each report provides background on a current topic of widespread interest. Designed as a starting place for research, the reports define the issues and include a chronology and extensive bibliographies. A feature called "At Issue," which quotes opposing viewpoints from two experts, also is a part of each report.

The publication is available in various formats.

The Report

The report, about 12,000 words in length, is issued on Friday four times a month. Each report treats a subject that is in the news or likely to be in the news in the near future.

Bound Reports

The weekly reports are bound into quarterly paperback editions and an annual hardbound cumulation.

Index

A subject index to the reports is published each quarter and cumulated annually. The latest index may be found (in the blue pages) at the back of this volume.

Citation

Recommended format for citing these reports in a bibliography, based on The Modern Language Association of America's *Handbook for Writers of Research Papers,* 3rd edition, follows.

Clark, Charles S. "The Obscenity Debate." *The CQ Researcher* 20 Dec. 1991: 969-992.

THE CQ Researcher
formerly Editorial Research Reports

CONTENTS

JANUARY - DECEMBER 1997

THE CQ Researcher©

PUBLISHED BY CONGRESSIONAL QUARTERLY INC.

Combating Scientific Misconduct

Are government investigations unfair?

Increasing concern that some scientists were faking their experiments led the government in 1989 to create a special office to investigate fraud among recipients of biomedical research grants. Recently, however, several of the office's most sensational guilty verdicts have been reversed, raising questions about the fairness of the government's investigations. Critics within the scientific community charge the office conducted witch hunts, denying due process to accused scientists and unfairly tarring careers. Meanwhile, reformers are urging the government to expand its oversight of research misconduct, arguing that untrustworthy data — even if not the product of outright fraud — can mislead other scientists searching for medical cures. Responding to widespread dissatisfaction, a White House panel is developing new guidelines for dealing with research misconduct.

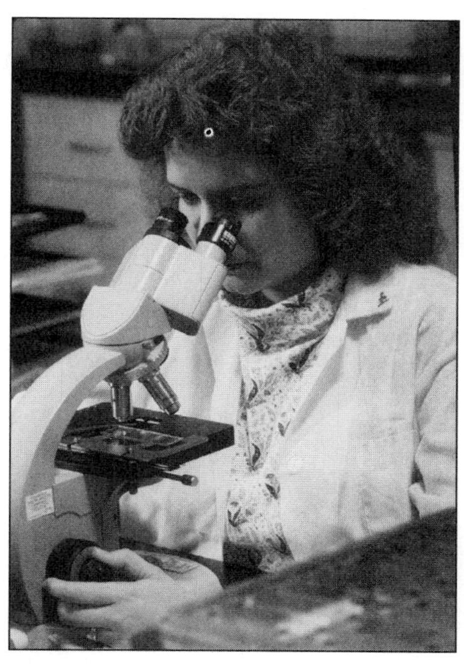

INSIDE THIS ISSUE

CQ Jan. 10, 1997 • Volume 7, No. 1 • Pages 1-24

Formerly Editorial Research Reports

THE ISSUES

BACKGROUND

CURRENT SITUATION

OUTLOOK

SIDEBARS AND GRAPHICS

FOR MORE INFORMATION

COVER: © 1992 CHARLES GUPTON, PICTURE NETWORK INTERNATIONAL

Jan. 10, 1997
Volume 7, No. 1

EDITOR
Sandra Stencel

MANAGING EDITOR
Thomas J. Colin

ASSOCIATE EDITORS
Sarah M. Magner
Richard L. Worsnop

STAFF WRITERS
Charles S. Clark
Mary H. Cooper
Kenneth Jost

EDITORIAL ASSISTANT
Vanessa E. Furlong

PUBLISHED BY
Congressional Quarterly Inc.

CHAIRMAN
Andrew Barnes

VICE CHAIRMAN
Andrew P. Corty

EDITOR AND PUBLISHER
Neil Skene

EXECUTIVE EDITOR
Robert W. Merry

ASSISTANT EXECUTIVE EDITOR/DEVELOPMENT
David Rapp

The CQ Researcher (ISSN 1056-2036). Formerly Editorial Research Reports. Published weekly (48 times per year, not printed Jan. 3, May 30, Aug. 29, Oct. 31) by Congressional Quarterly Inc., 1414 22nd St., N.W., Washington, D.C. 20037. Annual subscription rate for libraries, businesses and government is $340. Additional rates furnished upon request. Periodicals postage paid at Washington, D.C. POSTMASTER: Send address changes to The CQ Researcher, 1414 22nd St., N.W., Washington, D.C. 20037.

Combating Scientific Misconduct

BY SARAH GLAZER

THE ISSUES

The case had all the elements of high drama: the idealistic junior researcher who accused a respected senior scientist of fabricating data, the aggressive chairman of a congressional investigating committee and the indignant Nobel Prize-winning biologist.

The Nobel laureate was David Baltimore of the Massachusetts Institute of Technology (MIT), a co-author of the paper with the questionable data. [1] He not only defended the accused scientist, Thereza Imanishi-Kari, also an MIT biologist, but denounced the congressional probe as an audacious attack on scientific freedom by politicians with little understanding of the complex science involved. Baltimore, in turn, was roundly criticized for refusing to take a junior researcher's legitimate questions seriously and for his stance toward Congress.

Yet last summer, almost 10 years after whistleblower Margot O'Toole leveled her charge, a government appeals board exonerated Imanishi-Kari and portrayed the federal Office of Research Integrity (ORI), which investigated the case, as bumbling and overly zealous. *

The appeals panel's decision appears to have changed few minds in a scientific community that was already deeply polarized over the fundamental question raised by the case: Does the blame for 10 years of charges and countercharges lie with government zealots who unfairly hounded an innocent scientist, or with senior scientists who turned a blind eye to possible fraud in their midst?

* The ORI is part of the Department of Health and Human Services (HHS), which funds biomedical research through its National Institutes of Health. The Research Integrity Adjudications Panel, which decided the case on appeal, is part of the HHS Departmental Appeals Board.

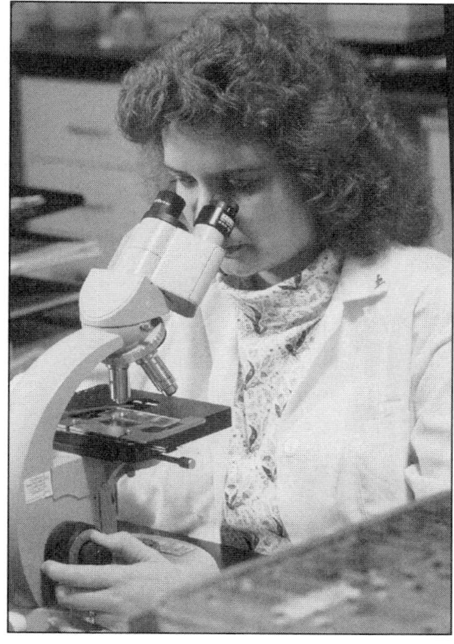

While scientists and their government funders remain divided over the answer, all agree on one thing: The case raised important questions about the extent of misconduct in the scientific community and the effectiveness and fairness of the response when charges are made.

The "Baltimore case," as it is known, probably would not have sustained media attention for so many years had it not been for two strong personalities pitted against one another: Rep. John D. Dingell, D-Mich., then the powerful chairman of the House Energy and Commerce Committee, who openly sided with O'Toole, and the equally forceful Baltimore.

"Baltimore wrapped the mantle of the science community around himself," says Nicholas Wade, science editor of *The New York Times.* "He framed the issue as if the scientific community was under attack, which in a sense it was."

The fearsome Dingell had become legendary for his quarter-century battle to uncover waste, fraud and abuse among defense contractors and other recipients of federal funds. He expressed suspicion that the academic community also was abusing taxpayers' money and set out to use the Baltimore case as an example. (*See story, p. 4.*) But while his investigation raised important issues, it also left bad feelings throughout the scientific community, and wrecked careers.

To scientists who objected to the government's involvement in the first place, the case has only confirmed their view that the government should be more judicious in pursuing scientists. "The main lesson is that the scientists have to be given an opportunity to cross-examine their accusers early on — which they don't have today — and be given the ability to present their own witnesses," says Joseph Onek, Imanishi-Kari's lead attorney.

In the hands of an academic rival, a charge of fraud or research misconduct can become an effective weapon for destroying the career of a scientist. If the fraud finding had been upheld, Imanishi-Kari would have been barred from receiving federal research grants for 10 years, one of the harshest penalties ever levied against a scientist. "Hopefully, universities will be a little more skeptical about charges as a result of the Imanishi-Kari case," Onek says.

For critics of the scientific establishment, who tend to be skeptical of the appeals panel's finding of innocence, the case remains an example of scientific hubris. They point to Baltimore's arrogant response to Dingell's investigators, his seeming refusal to take O'Toole's charges seriously and his failure to issue an immediate correction.* Many scientists had hailed O'Toole for courageously pursuing her convictions in a hierarchical system where junior researchers rarely dare to question se-

* Baltimore and other authors of the paper later did publish several corrections under pressure from government panels that found errors in the paper.

Did Investigators Push Too Hard . . .

In 1985, Margot O'Toole, a young postdoctoral researcher, began working in the laboratory of Thereza Imanishi-Kari, then an assistant professor of biology at the Massachusetts Institute of Technology (MIT). O'Toole was hired to perform a set of experiments on mice replicating and extending Imanishi-Kari's findings in the field of immunology. The findings had important implications for how genes could affect antibodies and the immune system in humans.

O'Toole started a major controversy in 1986 when she questioned some of the claims made in a paper published that year in the journal *Cell* by a team of MIT and Tufts University scientists, including Imanishi-Kari and Nobel laureate David Baltimore. The paper was based in part on O'Toole's experiments.

Nobel laureate David Baltimore

The paper's conclusions, O'Toole said, were at odds with some of her findings in the laboratory. She said she had not been able to replicate Imanishi-Kari's results. Imanishi-Kari, she later testified, had directed her to prepare some of the experiments in ways that manipulated the data to conform to her hypothesis.

In meetings with senior faculty members at MIT and Tufts in 1986, O'Toole urged a public correction of the errors she saw in the paper. As she testified at congressional hearings held in 1988 by Rep. John D. Dingell, D-Mich., senior faculty told her that "a retraction or correction might be very detrimental to Imanishi-Kari [and] it was best for all concerned to drop the matter." O'Toole said she *had* dropped the matter and "left science saddened and disillusioned." [1]

But the senior scientists involved remembered it differently. Although they had discovered two errors, they believed the problems were minor and that "neither error determined the central claim of the paper," according to historian Daniel J. Kevles. Baltimore, who had little hands-on experience with the tests under discussion, also considered the errors minor and suggested further experimentation as a way of testing O'Toole's questions. [2]

From 1986 to 1989, three separate panels at MIT, Tufts and the National Institutes of Health (NIH) found errors in the paper but no misconduct. Each panel concluded the dispute had to do with differing interpretations of research results.

At the urging of Dingell, however, NIH reopened the case in May 1989 under its newly formed Office of Scientific Integrity (OSI). In 1992, the office was reorganized within the Department of Health and Human Services (HHS) and named the Office of Research Integrity (ORI).

Dingell continued to hold hearings from 1988 to 1990 and directed the Secret Service to conduct a forensic ink analysis of several of Imanishi-Kari's laboratory notebooks. The Secret Service concluded that Imanishi-Kari had fabricated data for experiments she had not conducted. After seeing the notebooks, O'Toole formally changed her charge to fraud in November 1989.

Based largely on the Secret Service findings and a statistical analysis of Imanishi-Kari's data, the research integrity office found Imanishi-Kari guilty of fraud on Oct. 26, 1994. The office recommended she be barred from federal research funds for 10 years, one of the harshest penalties ever imposed on a scientist. The office concluded that she had committed 19 counts of fraud including falsification and fabrication of data. Imanishi-Kari appealed the finding to the HHS agency's appeals board.

On June 21, 1996, the appeals panel exonerated Imanishi-Kari of fraud. The panel concluded that the evidence on which ORI had based its case was "irrelevant, had limited probative value, was internally inconsistent, lacked reliability or foundation, was not credible or not corroborated or was based on unwarranted assumptions."

The Secret Service data "provided no independent or convincing evidence that the data or documents were not authentic or could not have been produced during the time in question," the appeals panel concluded.

While the panel called the *Cell* paper "rife with errors" and said Imanishi-Kari's record-keeping could be faulted for sloppiness, it found no evidence that she had falsified data. The pages that had been questioned as falsified often had "bizarre and conflicting results" that would not have supported her conclusions, the panel found. Most of the allegedly fabricated data were not even included in the *Cell* paper, the panel noted. [3]

How did two agency panels reach such different conclusions? According to the appeals panel, the Secret Service based its conclusions on the "erroneous assumption" that Imanishi-Kari's notebook was a chronological record in

nior scientists.

Some scientists say the government was justified in pursuing the Baltimore case as vigorously as it did even if what was involved was sloppy science rather than actual forgery. The case "didn't rise to the certainty of fraud, but the way the notebooks were kept left something to be desired," says Kenneth J. Ryan, professor emeritus of obstetrics, gynecology and reproductive biology at Harvard University and chair of a congression-

. . . to Find Misconduct in the Baltimore Case?

which experiments were recorded as they occurred. In fact, the panel said, Imanishi-Kari had cobbled together loose pages at the advice of her lawyer to comply with a subpoena from Dingell's subcommittee in 1988. The "notebook," it concluded, was organized by topic, with data from experiments performed at different times sometimes pasted onto the same page. [4] The Secret Service evidence, like the Imanishi-Kari case, contained enough ambiguities that it could lead to more than one conclusion, the panel said.

The Secret Service, says Imanishi-Kari's lead attorney, Joseph Onek, "didn't understand how the notebook was compiled. They didn't understand the science. They were under a lot of pressure from Dingell's committee to find falsification."

But the parties who pursued the investigation against Imanishi-Kari say the appeals decision has not changed their minds. "The decision in this case is no more consistent with reality in my view than the decision in the O.J. Simpson criminal case," says Suzanne Hadley, who was acting director of OSI until the summer of 1992, when she was detailed to Dingell's committee for two years. She maintains that the Secret Service analysis, together with a statistical analysis of the data, constitute "compelling" evidence that "those data were not real."

Peter Stockton, who served as Dingell's lead investigator in the case, insists that ORI was "outlawyered" by Imanishi-Kari's experienced attorneys.

O'Toole said she believed the case proves that lawyers are not qualified to judge science misconduct. The appeals panel was composed of two lawyers and one scientist. [5]

It's virtually impossible for a layman to reconcile the accounts of both sides. Many observers, including Dingell, believe the case would never have gotten as far as it did if senior scientists had taken O'Toole's questions seriously in the first place. In the story as told by Kevles, O'Toole moved from frustration to anger as the scientists with the power to issue a correction appeared to stonewall her. Some blame political pressure from Dingell's committee, which used the case to critique the way federally funded scientists resolve charges of misconduct.

A recent investigative article in *Science* magazine describes Dingell's subcommittee staff as pushing the Secret Service and ORI at each stage of the process to come up with the findings it needed to keep the charges of fraud alive. [6] "The only pressure I'm aware of was based on the overwhelming evidence for fraud," maintains Walter Stewart, an NIH scientist who has made a career of pursuing fraud and who worked for Dingell on the case.

In an editorial written after the appeals decision, Dingell defended his hearings from charges of bullying. Unapologetic, he took issue with the panel's conclusion that because certain data were "inexplicable," it was unlikely they were fabricated. He portrayed O'Toole as a victim of retaliation "driven from science." Lost in the midst of the controversy, he argued, was a "serious public policy issue . . . the inability of science to police itself and correct itself." [7]

Amid mounting negative publicity over the case, Baltimore resigned as president of Rockefeller University, one of the nation's top biomedical research institutions. He is now a professor of molecular biology and immunology at MIT. Last month, Baltimore was appointed to head a new national initiative to develop an AIDS vaccine, a sign that his reputation may be on the mend. The appointment as chairman of the AIDS Vaccine Research Committee at NIH is Baltimore's first position outside the university since the resolution of the Imanishi-Kari fraud case, *The New York Times* noted. [8]

O'Toole was unable to find a job in science research for several years and at one point found herself answering phones at a relative's moving company. Some scientists hailed her as a hero for standing up to prominent scientists. In 1993, the American Institute of Chemists gave O'Toole its ethics award. She has been working at a pharmaceutical company since 1990.

As for Imanishi-Kari, she was reinstated as an assistant professor at the Tufts School of Medicine. Later work by other scientists bore out Imanishi-Kari's observations in the laboratory but came up with different interpretations of their significance, according to Kevles, who is writing a book on the case.

"If you probe Imanishi-Kari's and Baltimore's work prior to the mid-1980s, it's really implausible that there was fabrication," he says. "It flows so naturally from everything she was doing and he was doing."

---

[1] The hearings were held before the House Energy and Commerce Subcommittee on Oversight and Investigations. For background, see "Combating Science Fraud," *Editorial Research Reports*, Aug. 5, 1988, p. 395.

[2] Daniel J. Kevles, "The Assault on David Baltimore," *The New Yorker*, May 27, 1996, p. 98.

[3] Research Integrity Adjudication Panel, "Decision; Subject: Thereza Imanishi-Kari," June 21, 1996, pp. 11, 13, 15.

[4] *Ibid.*, p. 24.

[5] Quoted in Paulette V. Walker, "A Dramatic End to a Misconduct Case," *The Chronicle of Higher Education*, July 5, 1996.

[6] Jock Friedly, "How Congressional Pressure Shaped the 'Baltimore Case,'" *Science*, Aug. 16, 1996, pp. 873-875.

[7] John D. Dingell, "The Elusive Truths of the Baltimore Case," *The Washington Post*, July 18, 1996, p. A27.

[8] Warren Leary, "Nobel Laureate to Head Panel Pushing for AIDS Vaccine," *The New York Times*, Dec. 13, 1996, p. B15.

ally mandated panel that has suggested changes in the government's approach to investigating research misconduct. "We're talking about whether the government is interested in the quality of the work when they fund it," Ryan says. "It goes beyond just, 'Am I lying.'"

If researchers are to be supported by taxpayers' dollars, critics often say, they must pay the price of public investigation into the use of that money. The federal government sup-

Dealing With Threats to Whistleblowers

While the case of Thereza Imanishi-Kari has focused scientists' attention on the rights of the accused, the congressional hearings and the legislation that followed them were prompted largely by sympathy for whistleblowers. Margot O'Toole, the young researcher who charged initially that Imanishi-Kari had manipulated and fabricated data, testified in 1988 that challenging Imanishi-Kari's work had "halted my career, disrupted my social milieu and had a devastating effect on my life." [1]

The Ryan Commission heard testimony during its 1994-95 hearings from other whistleblowers who described receiving threats, being subjected to retaliatory investigations and being expelled from academia. The commission recommended additional protection for whistleblowers, including holding hearings in cases of retaliation to give whistleblowers an opportunity to present witnesses and confront those they charge with retaliation.

Walter Stewart, a National Institutes of Health scientist who with NIH scientist Ned Feder has made a reputation as a self-appointed and controversial "fraud-buster," says whistleblowers still face serious risk of damaging their careers if they make an allegation. "We tell most whistleblowers, 'Forget completely about your case; it's a complete waste of time in the current atmosphere.' " He adds that university administrations still often regard allegations of fraud as a taboo. "It's like civil rights workers challenging segregation in the 1950s," he says. "You could get your teeth kicked in."

But several scientific groups, taking the viewpoint of accused scientists, have blasted the Ryan Commission for leaning over backwards to protect accusers. In a recent letter to the Department of Health and Human Services (HHS), Bruce Alberts, president of the National Academy of Sciences, and six other members of the academy's governing council charged that the commission ignores the fact that "whistleblowers can be wrong or even malicious and that the rights of the accused must be preserved. There is no such balance in the . . . report." [2]

The Ryan Commission recommended that whistleblowers be allowed to object to those appointed to investigate their allegations and have a chance to comment on the accuracy of information reviewed. Those recommendations "make the accuser part of the investigating team and create an asymmetric relationship with the accused," said Ralph A. Bradshaw, former president of the Rockville, Md.-based Federation of the American Societies for Experimental Biology (FASEB), in a letter signed by 50 scientific societies. [3]

A survey conducted for HHS in 1995 found a majority of people who blow the whistle on scientific misconduct face some kind of retaliation, but only a few have their careers destroyed. Among those who reported serious negative consequences, about 12 percent reported being fired after they lodged their complaints. But a substantial majority said they were able to go on with their careers. The most common consequence was pressure to drop the allegations, followed by countercharges. [4]

A follow-up report looked at what happens to scientists who are accused of research misconduct but found innocent. A majority of those surveyed reported suffering negative consequences, such as additional allegations, ostracism or reduction in research support. Seventeen percent reported such severe consequences as losing their jobs or being denied promotions or salary increases. While a sizable majority said negative effects often persisted after they were exonerated, 57 percent said the allegations had a neutral effect on their careers. The vast majority were continuing to work in research. [5]

---

[1] Quoted in Daniel J. Kevles, "The Assault on David Baltimore," *The New Yorker*, May 27, 1996, p. 106. Also see "Combating Science Fraud," *Editorial Research Reports*, Aug. 5, 1988, p. 394.

[2] Letter to William Raub, science adviser, Department of Health and Human Services, March 15, 1996.

[3] Letter to William F. Raub, science adviser, Department of Health and Human Services, May 13, 1996.

[4] James S. Lubalin et al., *Consequences of Whistleblowing for the Whistle blower in Misconduct in Science Cases*, prepared by Research Triangle Institute for Office of Research Integrity, Oct. 2, 1995, pp. 18-21.

[5] *Survey of Accused but Exonerated Individuals in Research Misconduct Cases*, prepared for Office of Research Integrity by Research Triangle Institute, June 30, 1996.

plies some $9 billion annually to the National Institutes of Health (NIH) alone for biomedical research.

"Scientists like to say, 'Trust us, and leave to us the quality control, and we'll take care of it,' " says Daryl Chubin, division director for research, evaluation and communication at the National Science Foundation (NSF), a federal agency that funds a broad range of science research. "The problem is that taxpayers' money is being spent," and scientists' own methods for detecting errors can take years to uncover a fraud. "If you have misleading information in the literature that others in the research community are trying to build upon, you're diverting scarce resources" to false leads, Chubin adds.

The debate over the Baltimore case harks back to perennial questions about the scientific community's ability to police itself. The two traditional mechanisms are peer review, in which scientists review grant proposals and articles submitted for publication, and replication of other researchers' experiments.

This fall, a peer reviewer's suspicions about an article submitted to a scientific journal led to a stunning announcement by Francis S. Collins, director of the National Center for Human Genome

Research, an NIH project to map all human genes.[2] Collins announced in October that he was retracting five already published papers on leukemia because a junior colleague had fabricated data. Collins said he had been unaware that there was any problem with the data until the journal's editor alerted him to the reviewer's suspicions about a sixth paper on leukemia that had been submitted.

Some hailed the incident as a classic example of the scientific community policing itself, but others asked how such significant articles could have remained in publication for as long as two years before questions were raised about the research.

Few scientists argue today that peer review eliminates the need for government oversight. But they differ over how aggressively the government should go after fraud, largely because they differ over how much there is. Some see the scientific research climate as inherently conducive to cheating; others blame instances of fraud on a few isolated offenders.

Wade argued 15 years ago in *Betrayers of the Truth* that the "roots of fraud lie in the barrel, not in the bad apples that occasionally roll into public view."[3] Today, he still believes that "the structure of the system encourages fraud." He points to the competitive environment of major research laboratories, where junior researchers do the drudge work for senior scientists rushing to publish articles before their academic rivals. "The people who do most of the work in the system are the graduate students," Wade says. "They can become cynical and take to producing results that are wanted."

Wade strongly favors some government oversight of research, but not too much. "I always thought it was worth doing something about science fraud," he says, "but not an enormous amount since its impact on science progress isn't that great." He thinks all research notes should be kept in central repositories, so any scientist could check them, and that every scientist listed as an author of a journal article should say what their part was in the research.

While many scientists call for some oversight by government, they look at the Imanishi-Kari case and question the fairness of the government machinery for investigating and penalizing fraud that Dingell's investigation spawned. Almost no one on either side of the debate is happy with the current system.

"We created a monster, and now it's time to bury it," said Robert P. Charrow, a former deputy general counsel at the Department of Health and Human Services (HHS).[4]

But some observers see today's approach to oversight as an improvement. Following the first Dingell hearings in 1988, HHS and the NSF required universities that receive federal funds to set up formal procedures for investigating fraud cases. "Institutions up to that point were very reluctant to have any standing apparatus to investigate fraud," Chubin notes. "Now most do."

Critics of the scientific establishment fear that ORI will back off because of the black eye it received in the Imanishi-Kari case, which in turn will make scientists complacent once again. "We've gone 10 steps backward," says Peter Stockton, who was an investigator for Dingell. "After the Baltimore case, they can ridicule the system and say, 'Government shouldn't be doing investigations; Congress shouldn't be doing it.' "

In an effort to improve the fairness of agency investigations, HHS Secretary Donna E. Shalala is considering recommendations from the congressionally created Commission on Research Integrity (*see p. 19*). And a White House panel is expected to recommend governmentwide guidelines for resolving research misconduct cases and a new definition of research misconduct applicable to all government agencies. The panel is currently briefing federal agencies on the recommendations before issuing a final policy.

As governmental and scientific groups debate the handling of science fraud, these are some of the questions being asked:

Is the current system of investigating and judging science fraud fair?

In addition to the Baltimore case, several other cases have stimulated the government's move to change its science fraud oversight system, notably the case involving famed AIDS researchers Robert Gallo and Mikulas Popovic. (*See story, p. 18.*)

Key recommendations made by the Commission on Research Integrity in 1995 called for HHS to separate the function of investigating charges from the judgment of guilt. The director of ORI, who decides an accused scientist's fate, "cannot be considered a disinterested party to the success of the investigative effort," said the commission, which is known as the Ryan Commission after its chairman, Ryan of Harvard.[5] The commission favors the approach taken by the NSF, where the foundation's inspector general investigates misconduct allegations and the agency's deputy director renders a verdict.

However, an HHS study group has recommended that Shalala reject the Ryan Commission approach. The so-called implementation group, chaired by William Raub, Shalala's science policy adviser, noted that more than 85 percent of misconduct cases are investigated by the researcher's home institution, generally a university, and then reviewed by ORI for a final verdict. That process, the group maintained, already constitutes a separation between investigation and judgment. In only about 15 percent of cases does ORI take responsibility for the investigation.[6]

Imanishi-Kari's lawyers argue that defense attorneys should get a chance to face down their clients' accusers in a formal forum earlier in the process. Onek says due process is particularly crucial if the government has the power to impose potentially career-wrecking punishments like barring scientists from receiving federal research funds.

At the university level, where most misconduct allegations are handled initially, lawyers may accompany an accused scientist to a hearing, Onek notes, but often may not speak on behalf of their clients. "In general, most [faculty tribunals] are not capable of handling these cases, largely because they don't permit cross-examination," Onek says. "In many cases, science is not the only issue. You have 'He said, she said' issues. How can a scientist decide that without the benefit of cross-examination?"

When the HHS integrity office was created, scientists argued that their colleagues could reach rational consensus on technical grounds alone. One of the first directors, Jules Hallum, championed a "scientific dialogue" model, much like editorial peer review. "ORI was set up as an agency of scientists — and keep the lawyers out of it. That was a big mistake," says Daniel J. Kevles, a historian of science at the California Institute of Technology, whose long *New Yorker* account of the Baltimore case supports Imanishi-Kari.[7]

But the "scientific dialogue" model was widely criticized, even by scientists. The office was criticized for being easily influenced by outside political forces and for being both too secretive and too prone to leaks. In answer to these criticisms, HHS in 1992 altered procedures to allow those found guilty to contest the finding with a trial-like hearing before its appeals board.

These days, the Imanishi-Kari appeals decision has many scientists looking more favorably on lawyers. "I think there needs to be more due process," says biochemist John Suttie, president of the Rockville, Md.-based Federation of the American Societies for Experimental Biology (FASEB), representing some 44,000 research scientists. "The Imanishi-Kari case should give the federal office some concern," Suttie adds, "because when we finally got down to the point where both sides had their own legal counsel and presented the evidence, they [ORI] were not able to prove a case."

Everyone agrees that the Imanishi-Kari case took too long to resolve, whether counting the 10 years from O'Toole's original questions or the eight years from HHS' first investigation. The longer ORI takes to investigate something, the longer it takes before accused scientists get their first chance for a full-fledged hearing before the appeals board. "You need due process a lot earlier than four to 10 years down the road," says Washington attorney Barbara Mishkin, who represented AIDS researcher Popovic.

By regulation, universities receiving HHS grants are supposed to start a fact-finding inquiry immediately after an allegation is made, finish the initial inquiry within 60 days after it starts, then launch a full-fledged investigation within the next 30 days, and complete the investigation within 120 days.

In 1991, the Public Health Service, an HHS agency, published a policy in the *Federal Register* saying the integrity office should abide by the same time limits for its own investigations. But, ORI Acting Director Chris B. Pascal says that goal was "unrealistic" and "hasn't been met."

"I've got cases [that ORI] has been sitting on for two years," Onek says. "If it's a hard case, ORI is just sitting on it, so everyone's in limbo for years." (Since the Imanishi-Kari decision was handed down, Onek says ORI has dropped charges in two of his languishing cases, which he takes as a sign of improvement.)

Pascal says the Imanishi-Kari case is not typical. "Frankly, there was no good justification for how long it took other than the fact that it had a very roundabout procedural history where there were several separate looks at the allegations," he says. "ORI doesn't believe that's the way we want to do business in the future or the way we're doing it now." The average duration of a case at ORI was 12 months as of Nov. 1, 1996, according to Pascal, but ORI's goal is to close all future cases within 12 months.

Universities are worried by what they see as a trend toward more adversarial proceedings, which tend to insulate institutions against countersuits by accused scientists.

"The trend is full-blown legalization, and I don't think that's healthy," says C.K. "Tina" Gunsalus, associate provost at the University of Illinois in Champaign-Urbana. "You bring in a high-powered lawyer, and that can unbalance the proceeding . . . blow witnesses out of the water. You can very easily get the wrong answer. Perry Mason is not the right approach in a university."

The University of Michigan, one of the nation's largest research universities, does not permit attorneys for an accused party to cross-examine witnesses, according to Judith Nowack, assistant vice president for research. The investigation, she explains, is "not intended to be legal. We're trying to determine the integrity of the scientific record as well as culpability. In the courtroom setting, investigators focus on culpability. Even if we couldn't find someone guilty, if we find the scientific record is faulty, we'll want to correct it."

Gunsalus suggests a better alternative might be a European-style system where the judge conducts the investigation. Advocates of this approach argue that the American adversarial system sets up dueling witnesses and encourages lawyers to distort the truth in favor of their clients without getting to the bottom of the matter. Howard Anderson, a Washington lawyer who has conducted independent investigations of science misconduct for government laboratories, describes one case where the lawyers for a whistleblower and the institution settled the allegations by agreeing the whistleblower's job should be restored, and there should be a cash settlement.

"The problem [with the resolution] was the whistleblower had pointed out some institutional failures that raised safety implications," Anderson says. But these were not looked into as part of the resolution. Because the goal of lawyers is primarily to reach a resolution agreeable to their clients, he says, "the lawyers get up from the table, stuff their briefcases and say, 'We don't need to know what caused the O-ring to blow up.' "

Walter Stewart and Ned Feder, NIH scientists who have made reputations as self-appointed and controversial "fraud-busters," argue that universities have a vested interest in finding that there's no truth to misconduct allegations. A finding of fraud at a university is likely to hurt the institution's reputation, they say. They have argued that an outside investigative body should be appointed for university-level investigations, a recommendation that the Ryan Commission rejected.

Anderson can testify to the problems in university settings. "You ought to see what happens when a panel of academics starts questioning a Nobel laureate," he says. "Unless they have skills in questioning, it turns into an open-ended seminar. There are holes in the answers, nothing gets pinned down, the witnesses' misleading answers are not followed up. It's very difficult for a colleague to confront another colleague like that."

Scientists and academics are also at odds over how public the proceedings and decisions in misconduct cases should be. Feder and Stewart argue that all of ORI's hearing records should be open to the public as a way of ensuring that the decision reached is a fair one. Currently, ORI does not publish the names of people found innocent of misconduct unless they specifically ask to have their names printed as a form of exoneration.

The Ryan Commission has also proposed systematic public disclosure of federal research-misconduct case results. But science groups like FASEB see this recommendation as a threat to the confidentiality of the current system. "The Ryan report would give new regulatory authority to go back and publish the names of people who were not guilty," Suttie objects. "A charge of misconduct is so disastrous, whether it's true or not. It's like a sexual misconduct case that's eventually proven not guilty. It's never believed." [8]

Should science misconduct be defined more broadly?

When the Ryan Commission proposed in November 1995 that HHS broaden the kinds of unethical research conduct it investigates, many scientists reacted with outrage. The governing body of the National Academy of Sciences urged the department to reject the commission's new definitions, saying they would turn "normal research procedures" into "federal offenses" and stifle the "creative process." [9]

To a layman, the debate over definitions can seem esoteric. However, "To the extent that you can limit the definition, you can limit the scope of government involvement," notes Mark S. Frankel, director of the program in Scientific Freedom, Responsibility and Law at the American Association for the Advancement of Science (AAAS). And many scientists are outspoken in their desire to keep the federal presence out of their laboratories.

Under the federal regulations currently applied to HHS grantees, misconduct is defined primarily by three crimes: fabrication, falsification and plagiarism. [10] The Ryan Commission proposed to replace this definition with a new trio of crimes — misappropriation, misrepresentation and interference. The new definition, the commission argued, would cover a broader range of clearly unethical behavior.

"The Ryan Commission found out the [existing] definition doesn't work on the ground in real cases," commission member Gunsalus says. Under the current definition, "You get to the end of the process and you want to sanction someone, and the lawyer says, 'Where's the rule against that?' "

Several of the commission's examples are based on real cases in which ORI refused to penalize a form of misconduct that did not fit into its trilogy of offenses. In one case cited by Gunsalus, a junior researcher at Michigan State University walked off with important data she had developed under a lab chief's supervision after the chief fired her. After 11 months of unsuccessful attempts to get the data returned, the professor, microbiologist Jeffrey Williams, asked ORI to take formal action against the student so he could get the data back. But the office told him that withholding data didn't fit into its definition of research misconduct. [11] The commission's newly minted term "interference" would cover sequestering or sabotaging raw data, according to its report.

Similarly, by replacing the term plagiarism with "misappropriation," Gunsalus argues, the stealing of ideas as well as words would be proscribed. Supporters say this has become a growing problem among peer reviewers who steal ideas from grant proposals they are reviewing and use them to apply for grants of their own.

"Misrepresentation" would cover an omission of information that "significantly distorts the truth," the report proposes, as well as direct lies covered by the existing term "falsification."

FASEB President Suttie says his organization opposes a broadened definition because it would replace "rather clear statements that everyone understands" with words that people don't understand. Under the new definition's emphasis on crimes of omission, he fears, a scientist could be accused of misrepresentation for failing to reference another scientist's contribution to the field in a published article. "Everyone has to make a judgment about what papers to cite," he says. "Failure to do that may not be right, but it's not fraud."

Howard Schachman, a molecular biologist at the University of California-Berkeley, says a broadened definition could lead to "a tremendous enlargement of the machinery being used to investigate problems of fraud." When coupled with another Ryan Commission recommendation that HHS make regular on-site visits to universities, the Big Brother-style threat looms even larger from his perspective. "Do you want policemen coming and saying, 'Let me look at your lab notes for the last 10 years?' " Schachman asks. Government monitors won't understand them, he objects, and may read evil intent into common practices.

The biggest ethical disagreement centers around how much scientists need to tell their readers about problems they've had in the lab or with data. John C. Bailar III, chair of the Department of Health Studies at the University of Chicago, condemns efforts to "beautify" data.

"I think it's very common and probably becoming more common to engage in uncollegial and anti-scientific behavior," says Bailar, a former statistical consultant for *The New England Journal of Medicine*. Examples he cites are "not telling readers everything they need to know to evaluate the data, repeating experiments until you get what you think is the right answer and fishing through a great big data set till something interesting turns up and reporting it as if it's what you set out to look for." In Bailar's eyes, "all of these involve deception, but they do not require any misstatement of fact. I would regard them as scientific misconduct."

Schachman sees it differently. "Misrepresentation to a lawyer means I can't select data," he says. As a scientist, he maintains, "You know which experiments are better than others or when equipment is faulty. You know when a cell culture is contaminated — in which case you throw away the data. I'd argue every great scientist does it."

Science historian Kevles draws a parallel to the government attack on Imanishi-Kari, which he says stemmed in large part from government officials' "mechanistic" view of science. The investigators, he says, condemned Imanishi-Kari because they allowed little room for scientists' different interpretations of the same data. "The data doesn't always speak clearly as to what it means; you inevitably have to use judgment," he says.

In the Imanishi-Kari case, the appeals board criticized ORI for trying to expand its charges against Imanishi-Kari from fabrication to "bad practice or bad interpretations or judgments" in the material she published. Kevles believes that ORI was encouraged in this direction because of a clause in the regulations that scientists have long found objectionable.

The phrase says that in addition to fabrication, falsification and plagiarism, misconduct includes "other practices that seriously deviate from those that are commonly accepted within the scientific community for proposing, conducting or reporting research."

One of ORI's charges against Imanishi-Kari was that she failed to report the difficulties she was having getting a particular chemical sensor to perform as expected. "Where does it say you have to report difficulties with data?" asks Kevles, who is writing a book on the case. "I don't see how you could support the charge unless you take it as a deviation."

Some scientists have long objected to the deviation phrase as too vague. Who is to say what "commonly accepted practice" is anyway? But Pascal disputes Kevles' view of its importance, saying, "I don't recall a single time when ORI has made a finding based on the 'other practices' clause." Suttie concedes that the phrase has been much less of a problem than scientists originally feared.

The NSF has a similar "deviations" clause in its definition of research misconduct. Deputy Assistant Inspector General for Oversight Donald E. Buzzelli has defended the phrase as a crucial, if rarely used, element of the agency's work.

In one case, the foundation declared a senior researcher guilty of research misconduct after he was accused of sexually harassing and assaulting undergraduates studying primates with him in Mexico under an NSF-funded program. NSF determined that the incident "deviated" from commonly accepted scientific practice.

Schachman sees the case as an extreme example of the problems with a broad definition. "If a scientist committed murder this wouldn't be a practice that seriously deviated from scientific practice," he says indignantly.

The project in question had received grants under a program intended to give research experiences to undergraduates to attract talented students to research careers. Even though the researcher had not committed fabrication, falsification or plagiarism, this was a "genuine instance of misconduct in science," Buzzelli has written. The NSF barred the researcher from receiving any federal grants for five years.

"Science is harmed," Buzzelli wrote, when undergraduates in such a program "are taught to advance themselves by submitting to a research director's sexual demands." He added, "The important thing is that government agencies must not adopt a definition that is limited to the common run of the cases so that they prevent themselves in advance from being able to deal with unexpected cases like this one." [12]

Marcel LaFollette, a research professor of international science and technology policy at George Washington University, agrees that research crimes in the future may not fit neatly into a restricted definition. The power of computers to cut and paste texts invisibly, to alter photographic data in experiments and to transmit information of dubious origin to entire scientific communities instantaneously presents new temptations, she suggests.

"It seems easier to manipulate data in deceitful ways," LaFollette says. "In 1996, we're able to morph, and it's difficult to detect that," she adds. "You could see new forms of unethical conduct, deception and deceit that the person inclined to do that will find a whiz-bang way to do."

Schachman counters that while open-ended definitions of crimes satisfy lawyers' needs, "The very principle of due process is to define a crime before you convict people of doing it."

Scientists are disturbed by definitions that include gray areas of scientific practice in part because "what they would like to see as a scientific discussion becomes a legal proceeding that involves a lot of people outside of science," says Chubin of NSF. But public involvement is unavoidable, he believes. His advice to scientists who receive federal grants: "The string attached with this is, 'You accepted public money. You open yourself to this kind of examination that drags on forever and may be embarrassing.' " ■

BACKGROUND

Early Investigations

Historians have uncovered instances of fraud dating back to ancient times and to some of the most revered scientists in history. [13] A contemporary of Galileo's who attempted to reproduce one of his experiments expressed doubts that the experiments had ever been performed. Galileo described an experiment on gravity in which he rolled a brass ball down a groove in a long board "near a hundred times." Today's historians say the experiment never would have yielded an exact law and just shows how firmly Galileo had made up his mind beforehand.

Francis Bacon, the 17th-century father of the scientific method, understood the temptations for scientists to make observations in line with their theories. "In general," he advised, "let every student of nature take this as a rule, that whatever his mind seizes and dwells upon with particular satisfaction is to be held in suspicion." [14]

The seeds of the modern debate over science fraud date back to the 1940s, when the federal government created new agencies to provide generous funding for scientific research. In exchange for the promise of scientific advances and expanded employment opportunities, scientists were given a relatively free hand in running a decentralized system of university and medical laboratories. With their contributions to the successful war effort fresh in the public's mind, faith in scientists was at a high point. [15]

Aside from occasional hoaxes in archaeology, public attention was not focused on science fraud until a few spectacular incidents in the 1970s and early '80s. In 1974, William Summerlin, an immunologist at Sloan-Kettering Institute in New York, used a felt-tip pen to fake a successful skin transplant from a black mouse to two white ones.

It was not until 1981 and the front-page case of John Darsee, a young medical researcher at Harvard, that the first congressional hearings were held on science fraud. An NIH committee later concluded that Darsee, who worked in the laboratory of noted cardiologist Eugene Braunwald, had fabricated his experiments with dogs, which he claimed demonstrated that certain drugs reduced damage to the heart during the early phase of heart attacks. Perhaps most shocking, the investigation invalidated most of the 109 papers Darsee had published, many of them in prestigious journals with eminent co-authors.

At congressional hearings in 1981 chaired by then-Rep. Albert Gore, D-Tenn., NAS President Philip Handler called the issue of science fraud "grossly exaggerated." But members of Congress, startled to find that the NIH had continued to fund scientists accused of wrongdoing, warned that there was no political entitlement to federal funding. [16]

With those hearings, the debate was joined over two issues that have continued to divide scientists and public officials today: the seriousness of science fraud and the government role in policing it.

Science fraud became an even bigger issue in April 1988, when Rep. Dingell launched hearings on the Baltimore case before his Energy and Commerce Subcommittee on Oversight and Investigations. Researcher O'Toole testified she had questioned research conducted in Imanishi-Kari's MIT lab but had been rebuffed by senior scientists, including Baltimore. Thus began Dingell's relentless investigation of how NIH handled cases of science fraud.

"We have been shocked to find that the NIH relies completely upon the universities to investigate themselves," Dingell declared at the first day's hearing, on April 12, noting that the $5 billion allocated annually by the government for biomedical research grants was at stake. [17] Dingell and other members of Congress concluded that the handful of staff people NIH employed to look into the cases was insufficient.

In 1989, with Congress considering legislation to tighten up federal oversight of science research, HHS preempted Congress by creating a new Office of Scientific Integrity (OSI) within NIH. New HHS regulations that year required universities applying for NIH grants to set up formal procedures for investigating fraud and to report allegations and investigative results to the new office. But the new OSI, operated exclusively by scientists, ran into criticism from scientists for being too prosecutorial toward defendants and from congressional investigators for not being aggressive enough.

In 1992, responding to the critics, HHS moved the office from NIH to its parent agency and renamed it the Office of Research Integrity (ORI). For the first time, scientists were given the option of appealing the office's verdict to the departmental appeals board. Congress codified the ORI in legislation signed into law by President Clinton on June 10, 1993.* The measure, originally developed by Dingell and Rep. Ted Weiss, D-N.Y., was part of a larger bill vetoed by President George Bush in 1992 because it would have allowed fetal-tissue research. The legislation also created the Ryan Commission to improve HHS handling of fraud allegations and to develop regulations protecting whistleblowers.

The NSF took a different approach to handling possible science misconduct. In 1989, the foundation set up an inspector general's office to handle mismanagement of all kinds, including research misconduct. By handling science misconduct much like any other kind of waste, fraud and abuse, NSF appears to have escaped the high-visibility controversies that have plagued NIH. Some critics of ORI consider NSF investigations superior to those handled by ORI, which is still staffed entirely by scientists. At NSF, an investigator with a law enforcement background is assigned to each case along with a scientist. (Some investigators have both scientific and legal/law enforcement backgrounds.)

How Much Fraud?

No one knows if the cases of research misconduct reported by universities to their funding agencies are the tip of the iceberg or all that's there. Approximately 70 percent of the cases of scientific misconduct that come to the attention of the ORI result in exoneration. [18]

Of the cases reported to government agencies and universities, pettiness and infighting stand out more than brilliant forgeries. "In 1988, everyone thought that making up data would be the problem," says LaFollette. But "the fastest-growing type of accusation at NSF by the mid-1990s was plagiarism."

Between 1989, when the inspector general's office was established at NSF, and 1992, only 10 of the 124 misconduct cases received involved fabrication or misrepresentation of data. About 70 of the cases involved disputes over intellectual property — plagiarism, theft of research ideas or failure to give credit. Most of the cases that were closed by 1992 did not lead to a formal finding of misconduct or a sanction because, according to Deputy Assistant Inspector General Buzzelli, the allegations were not really about misconduct or the offense was "trivial." [19]

University officials report similar trends. "Seventy percent of the complaints that came to me had to do with authorship and attribution of credit," says Gunsalus of the University of Illinois. Often, notes science historian Judith P. Swazey, plagiarism accusations start out as disputes between scientists over who should get credit for the research.

Historian Kevles says the handful of misconduct cases received by ORI among the tens of thousands of research grants the agency gives out each year indicates that relatively little fraud plagues biomedical research. Last year, for example, ORI found misconduct in only 24 out of 41 cases it investigated. Twenty-two of the misconduct cases involved fabrication of data, falsification of information or a combination of both; two involved plagiarism. [20]

To determine how widespread research misconduct is, Swazey surveyed 2,000 doctoral candidates and 2,000 of their teachers from 99 graduate departments in chemistry, civil engineering, microbiology and sociology in 1990 and 1991. Between 6 and 9 percent of the students and faculty reported that they had direct knowledge of faculty who had plagiarized or falsified data. Nearly a third of the faculty members said they had observed student plagiarism. [21] A *New York Times* article on the study in November 1993 announced, "Her Study Shattered the Myth that Fraud in Science is a Rarity." [22]

After the 1993 Times article, Swazey said she received hundreds of letters and calls from people who had knowledge of research misconduct seeking advice on whether to report it. (In 1978, together with other faculty members at Boston University, Swazey blew the whistle on researcher Marc Strauss, who fabricated data in clinical trials of drug treatments for cancer. He was the first scientist to be barred from receiving federal funds from NIH.)

"Misconduct is not an epidemic problem," says Swazey, now president of the Acadia Institute in Bar Harbor, Maine, which studies ethical issues, "but it's not the astronomically small number that people like [*Science* Editor Daniel E.] Koshland Jr. claimed." Koshland wrote in an oft-cited editorial published Jan. 9, 1987, that "99.9999 percent of [scientific] reports are accurate and truthful."

Swazey's survey has been criticized for several methodological weaknesses. As she herself acknowledges, it's not clear how many of those surveyed are reporting on the very same incidents of misconduct. In addition, the survey responses could be biased toward those who have witnessed misconduct and are anxious to report it on a questionnaire.

Nonetheless, more recent surveys have found even higher percentages of scientists who have experienced research misconduct when it is defined more broadly than Swazey does. In a 1995 survey of some 1,000 postdoctoral fellows training for careers in biomedi-

Continued on p. 14

* The law is the NIH Revitalization Act of 1993. HHS is in the process of developing whistleblower regulations for public notice and comment.

Chronology

1970s *Aside from occasional archaeological forgeries, research scientists consider their profession immune from fraud, despite one prominent case of fakery in medical research.*

1974
William Summerlin, an immunologist at the Sloan-Kettering Institute, fakes a transplantation in mice using a felt-tipped pen.

1980s *In the wake of several highly publicized cases of science fraud, Congress pressures federal agencies and universities to investigate fraud cases aggressively.*

1981
John R. Darsee, a Harvard research worker in cardiology, is caught falsifying data in the laboratory. Because Darsee had published more than 100 papers in prestigious journals with many eminent co-authors, the case raised questions about the profession's ability to detect fraud in its midst.

1981
Prompted by the Darsee scandal, Rep. Albert Gore, D-Tenn., holds hearings on science fraud before his investigations and oversight subcommittee of the House Committee on Science and Technology.

1985
Congress passes the Health Research Extension Act, directing the Department of Health and Human Services (HHS) to issue regulations requiring institutions applying for research funds to report allegations of fraud and investigations to the government.

April 12, 1988
Margot O'Toole, a junior researcher working in a lab at the Massachusetts Institute of Technology, testifies that senior scientists, including Nobel laureate David Baltimore, dismissed questions she raised about inconsistencies in research conducted by Thereza Imanishi-Kari, an assistant professor of biology at MIT. O'Toole later charged fraud.

Sept. 19, 1988
Psychologist Stephen J. Breuning pleads guilty to federal charges he falsified data in research reports to the federal government. His articles affected the treatment of hundreds of retarded children. He was barred from practicing psychology for five years and sentenced to five years' probation.

1989
HHS creates the Office of Scientific Integrity to investigate science fraud and issues regulations requiring universities to set up formal procedures for investigating fraud. The National Science Foundation establishes an Office of Inspector General to investigate science misconduct along with other types of waste, fraud and abuse.

1990s *HHS reorganizes the Office of Science Integrity in an effort to afford more due process to scientists accused of fraud. However, criticism of the department continues.*

1992
Responding to criticisms that the Office of Scientific Integrity is insufficiently impartial, HHS pulls the office out of the National Institutes of Health and offers scientists accused of fraud the right to appeal. The office is renamed the Office of Research Integrity.

Nov. 3, 1993
An HHS departmental appeals panel overturns ORI's finding that Mikulas Popovic, a scientist in Robert C. Gallo's NIH laboratory, falsified statements in a seminal AIDS article. ORI drops its charges against Gallo of stealing an AIDS culture from a French laboratory.

1994
The Office of Research Integrity concludes that Thereza Imanishi-Kari fabricated and falsified data.

1995
The congressionally mandated Commission on Research Integrity, known informally as the "Ryan Commission," issues a report urging that the role of investigating fraud be separated from adjudication and that the definition of science misconduct be broadened.

June 21, 1996
An appeals panel at the Department of Health and Human Services overturns the finding of fraud against Imanishi-Kari, finding insufficient evidence for any of the charges.

December 1996
Immunologist Baltimore is picked to head a new effort by the Office of AIDS Research to develop a preventive vaccine for AIDS.

Top Scientist Reveals Student's Fraud . . .

This fall, even as scientists were delivering post-mortems in the Baltimore-Imanishi-Kari case, a spectacular new incident of data fabrication exploded on the scene.

In an Oct. 1 letter to a hundred colleagues, Francis S. Collins, chief of the National Institutes of Health's National Center for Human Genome Research, wrote that he was retracting five already published papers on leukemia because a graduate student in his lab had fabricated data. In the letter, Collins said his junior colleague "had confessed to a stunning series of data misrepresentations and outright fabrications, extending over a period of at least two years." [1]

Francis S. Collins
Director, National Center for Human Genome Research

Based on an examination of the papers Collins had co-authored and retracted, *The New York Times* identified the student as Amitov Hajra, who worked under Collins first at the University of Michigan and then at NIH. [2]

The fraud was discovered in mid-August, Collins said, when an editor of the journal *Oncogene* told him a scientist reviewing a manuscript submitted by Collins and the student had raised questions about data that "suggested intentional deception."

Collins said he began a clandestine, two-week investigation of the student's work, pulling genetic samples out of the freezer and cloning them to compare his results with the student's findings. At that point the scope of the fabrication "began to be very apparent," he told the Times. [3]

The incident was reminiscent of the 1981 case involving John R. Darsee (*see p. 11*) in the scope and brilliance of the fraud, the number of papers published and the involvement of an apparently unwitting senior lab chief.

To some scientists, the Collins case was a classic example of how the scientific community can effectively police its own, since the suspicion of fraud was aroused by a peer reviewer.

The fabrication in the Collins case "got picked up in the normal course of science. It did not need a congressional committee, an ORI [the federal Office of Research Integrity] or an inspector general," says microbiologist Howard Schachman at the University of California-Berkeley. "This is a classic example of how scientific advances will cause scrutiny of existing work."

But editors of scientific journals consider the Collins case a rarity. Peer reviewers are asked to judge a manuscript's quality, not to look for fraud, most say. "If we get a manuscript that's logical and internally consistent and seems to be well done, it could be made up of whole cloth, and we wouldn't know it," says Marcia Angell, executive editor of *The New England Journal of Medicine,* which published several of Darsee's papers. "The design can be second-guessed, but peer review is not designed to say, 'You didn't see 10 patients, you only saw five.' That's a mistake about what peer review does."

In some highly visible cases, fraud or mistaken conclusions may be detected quickly by other scientists trying to replicate the results. The widely publicized announcement a few years ago that two scientists had discovered a way of generating energy through "cold fusion" was quickly demolished as scientists around the world were unable to duplicate the results. [4]

But for less visible areas of science, it may take much longer for attempts at replication to be made, or the results to be published. Moreover, "when you get into clinical research in large-scale trials, they're not going to replicate that," notes Judith Swazey, president of the Acadia Institute in Bar Harbor, Maine, which studies ethical issues in science. That's because clinical trials involving human volunteers can cost millions of dollars and take years of recruiting and study.

Swazey cites the National Surgical Adjuvant Breast and Bowel Project, a large federally funded cancer study costing some $8 million a year and involving thousands of patients. [5] In 1994, newspaper reports revealed that one of the doctors

Continued from p. 12

cal research, more than half said they had observed what they considered unethical research practices. [23]

Few of the recent reported frauds appear to have influenced medical treatment of humans, according to LaFollette. In an infamous exception from the days before government-required reporting, University of Pittsburgh psychologist Stephen E. Breuning faked data claiming that in retarded children stimulant drugs were more effective and had fewer side effects than the standard treatment with tranquilizers. His publications in the 1980s were said to have influenced the treatment of hundreds of children. * ■

* In 1988, Breuning pled guilty in federal court to charges of making false statements to the federal government on federal grant applications. He was sentenced to serve 60 days in a halfway house, 250 hours of community service and five years of probation. He was also required to stay out of psychology for five years and to return $11,352 in salary from the grants to the university.

Correcting the Problem

In the wake of the Dingell hearings, federal regulations were written set-

. . . Raising Doubts About Efficacy of Peer Review

participating in the study, Roger Poisson of Montreal, Canada, had falsified patient records.

Initially, the revelation prompted a wave of anxiety across the country. The study's conclusion that lumpectomy is as effective as mastectomy in treating breast cancer had been the basis for treating tens of thousands of women. The National Cancer Institute eventually concluded that Poisson's fabrications, involving a minority of patients, did not change the study's conclusions.

Nevertheless, the failure of federal officials to publicize the fraud attracted harsh criticism from *The New England Journal of Medicine*, which had published the original study. The government was alerted to the fabrication in 1990 and concluded Poisson was guilty of scientific misconduct in 1993, but the editors were not aware of the fraud until 1994, when a newspaper reporter tipped them off. Over that four-year period, "The *Journal's* readers and the public at large were left in the dark, and the flawed reports remained uncorrected," a journal editorial charged.[6]

Many students of science fraud blame the exalted status of lab chiefs for failing to catch or discourage fraud by their junior colleagues and students. "By the time you get to be a successful lab director, you don't have much time to be in the lab," Swazey observes. "You're on the road, writing proposals to keep funding going. Unless you have a very small lab, there really isn't a lot of supervision from the head of the lab."

Many scientists have praised Collins for publicly admitting the fraud by his grad student. "I really admire Collins for sending out that letter to geneticists, rather than saying we have to sit back and let the university investigate and let it go to ORI for so many years," Swazey says. The University of Michigan is expected to complete an investigation of the case shortly.

But Lowell M. Greenbaum, vice president emeritus for research at the Medical College of Georgia, argues that Collins should bear more blame for failing to discover the fraud earlier. Collins should have been particularly wary since the student's findings were a "bombshell" that could have led to a new understanding of leukemia, Greenbaum says.

"When a student makes such a finding, this is all the more reason to express some doubt, because students have a way of wanting to ingratiate themselves," Greenbaum says. "I think most lab directors would be wary of a major finding by a student and spend a lot of time trying to verify it."

When research results are too good to be true, even experienced scientists can lose their sense of skepticism, according to Paul Friedman, professor of radiology at the University of California-San Diego. Friedman served on an academic committee that investigated a notorious case of fabrication at his university involving Robert Slutsky, a resident in cardiological radiology.

In 1986, the university announced that Slutsky had not performed patient and animal studies in heart research that he had published in respected journals. Over a 10-year period, Slutsky was extraordinarily prolific, publishing more than 130 articles. During one spell, he was churning out one paper every 10 days.

The fraud was detected by a referee who questioned identical statistical results for two different sets of data in consecutive articles he read upon Slutsky's application for a promotion. Several of Slutsky's colleagues had happily accepted "gift" authorship on papers for which they had done no work and could not have done work since the experiments were never performed.[7]

"People were so delighted to have a very productive guy, they didn't look critically at the details. That's probably a universal weakness of senior people," Friedman says.

[1] Quoted in John Crewdson, "Disclosures of Fraud Rock Gene Project; Leukemia Research Dealt Setback," *Chicago Tribune*, Oct. 29, 1996, p. 1.

[2] Lawrence K. Altman, "Falsified Data Found in Gene Studies," *The New York Times*, Oct. 30, 1996, p. A12.

[3] *Ibid.*

[4] For background, see "Nuclear Fusion," *The CQ Researcher*, Jan. 22, 1993, pp. 49-72.

[5] For background, see "Advances in Cancer Research," *The CQ Researcher*, Aug. 25, 1995, pp. 753-776.

[6] Marcia Angell and Jerome P. Kassirer, "Setting the Record Straight in the Breast-Cancer Trials," *The New England Journal of Medicine*, May 19, 1994, pp. 1448-1449.

[7] See Stephen Lock and Frank Wells, *Fraud and Misconduct in Medical Research* (1996), p. 22.

ting out specific procedures for universities to follow in investigating allegations of misconduct. Despite these changes, Swazey says, "too many institutions still have a proclivity to sweep things under the rug."

Prompted by the Darsee scandal on its own campus, Harvard Medical School was one of the first universities, starting in 1988, to issue guidelines aimed at preventing science fraud. The guidelines require that responsibility for supervising each junior researcher be specifically assigned to a faculty member in the research unit and that supervisors oversee the actual experiments — not just edit the manuscript reporting the experiment. Because the lack of original notebooks has often plagued fraud investigations, it has become more common for universities to adopt requirements like Harvard's that all primary data remain in the custody of the laboratory that perform the research.

In some of the most spectacular cases of fraud, such as those involving prolific authors like Darsee, investigators have blamed the highly competitive climate. Research jobs, grants and promotions depend primarily on a scientist's ability to publish frequently and be the first to make a discovery.

"The fundamental problem is in the reward structure for science," says Bailar of the University of Chicago.

"It is compounded now by the inadequacy of funds to support all the good investigators or all of the good ideas," he adds, because of tightening federal budgets for biomedical research.

A surprising percentage of students say they would be willing to cheat to get something published. A 1990 survey conducted at the University of California-San Diego found that 13 percent of the respondents would be willing to select or omit data to boost their chance of receiving a grant and 7 percent to get a paper published. [24]

"Everybody will lie or cheat if you make the stakes high enough," said the survey's author.

Two years later, a survey of biomedical postdoctoral fellows at the University of California-San Francisco, found an even higher proportion were willing to cut corners to advance their career. Twenty-seven percent said they were willing to select or omit data to improve their chances of getting a grant application funded. Fifteen percent said they would select or omit data to make publication of their article more likely, and 37 percent said they would list an undeserving author. The authors suggest the decline in NIH funding of science and increased competition among post-doctoral fellows may explain the rising percentage of students who say they would cheat. [25]

In an effort to stress quality over quantity, Harvard and the University of California-San Diego now limit the number of publications they accept when considering researchers for promotions. But Marcia Angell, executive editor of *The New England Journal of Medicine,* who originally proposed the approach in 1983 as one way of eliminating deception, says universities honor the change more in letter than in spirit. [26]

"What they do is say, 'Let's have your 10 best articles for a full professorship, but attach a list of all the other ones you've published.' When the promotion committee sees the list of all the articles, it still says, 'Wow, 600 articles!' Working on 594 of the articles would be a distraction from the six that mattered," Angell contends.

Some journals have taken steps aimed at correcting problems of the past, most notably the glut of honorary authorships. The issue first became hot when several co-authors on Darsee's papers, notably eminent scientists, admitted they had taken no part in the actual experiments and in some cases had not even read the articles carefully enough to catch obvious errors.

New York Times science editor Wade believes honorary authorship is an important contributor to fraud, particularly in cases where the lab chief is the lead author but his students do most of the laboratory work. "When grad students know the lab chief will take most of the credit anyway and wants a certain result, they tend to give him what he wants," Wade says, up to and including fraudulent data.

A dramatic rise in big collaborative science projects has given rising visibility to authorship questions. A study of 4,000 scientific journals found that the number of articles with more than 50 authors grew from 49 in 1981 to 407 in 1994, while those with more than 100 authors grew from just one to 182 over the same period. [27]

As Harvard's guidelines observe, the trend toward multiple authorship has led to the publication of papers in which "no single author was prepared to take full responsibility." [28]

Several journals, including *The New England Journal of Medicine,* now require authors to send letters vouching that they have made a substantial contribution to the article they submit. But some question whether these have become just another formality. "I think there's a lot of fraud in those letters," Bailar says. "I have seen multiple statements in the same pen and same handwriting. Someone is signing them all and sending them back."

Teaching Ethics

NIH now requires that young research scientists funded by its training grants receive education in research ethics. However, experts say that the quality of these programs varies greatly and there are few evaluations of their effectiveness. "It ranges from serious programs running a semester or a year to half-day dog and pony shows," says Swazey, who supports education in research ethics.

At the Medical College of Georgia, all Ph.D candidates must pass a six-hour course on research ethics in which they act out plays based on real cases of misconduct. In "The Presentation," for example, a student must tell his adviser that he cannot verify the results of their joint experiment — a triumph that they are about to present to a national conference.

The American Association for the Advancement of Science (AAAS) has produced several videotapes dramatizing moral dilemmas that scientists often face. In one, a young graduate student is under pressure to turn in favorable results on his experiments so his lab chief can get his article into a journal before researchers from another university. But two of his 10 experiments have failed to perform as expected. His girlfriend suggests he delete any mention of the two failed experiments in his write-up.

Most teachers of such courses admit they can't change an evil person into a good one, but they argue they can clarify questions students have about gray areas like "cooking data."

The University of Michigan is highly regarded in the field for taking research ethics seriously. It offers young researchers six optional sessions each year in research misconduct, is developing a for-credit course and is planning to integrate research ethics across the engineering curriculum. Yet it was also the site of this season's most

Continued on p. 19

At Issue:

Should the Department of Health and Human Services adopt the Ryan Commission's recommendations?

yes

KENNETH J. RYAN
Professor emeritus, Harvard Medical School

FROM "SCIENTIFIC CONDUCT IN PERSPECTIVE: THE NEED TO IMPROVE ACCOUNTABILITY," *THE CHRONICLE OF HIGHER EDUCATION,* JULY 19, 1996.

In 1993 . . . Congress . . . created a 12-member Commission on Research Integrity to propose new procedures for addressing scientific misconduct. . . . The report proposed a new definition of scientific misconduct, which we believe describes the types of violations that occur far more precisely than the current definition does.

We also proposed additional protections for whistle-blowers who expose research misconduct. . . . And further. . . we suggested improvements in the administrative practices that both research institutions and the federal government follow in handling allegations of misconduct.

Now that the [Robert] Gallo and [Thereza] Imanishi-Kari cases are closed, scientists might be tempted to declare victory for the cause of scientific freedom and ignore the commission's recommendations, which many scientists feel would impede them unnecessarily in their work. But this would be a mistake, because, beyond the high-profile cases, widespread problems in the conduct of research remain. . . .

Our commission ultimately defined scientific misconduct as "significant misbehavior that improperly appropriates intellectual property or contributions of others, that intentionally impedes the progress of research or that risks corrupting the scientific record or compromising the integrity of scientific practices." Instead of relying on the current federal categories of misconduct — falsification, fabrication and plagiarism — the commission proposed new categories that it considered more specific. . . .

I believe some scientists find the commission's definition of misconduct threatening because it covers new ground, such as actions that interfere with research. Further, some scientists have misinterpreted the definition to include all cases of omissions of data, when in fact the commission included only omissions that would falsify a researcher's conclusions. . . .

[Under our proposal], the Office of Research Integrity (ORI) [in the Department of Health and Human Services] would continue to investigate allegations of misconduct in research conducted at NIH, or in cases involving more than one institution. It would also investigate cases in which it decided that the institution could not conduct a proper investigation. . . .

Scientists now must respond constructively to the issues that the commission has identified. The problems will not go away by themselves, and both the government and the public will continue to expect scientists to be accountable for the federal money they receive.

no

COUNCIL OF THE NATIONAL ACADEMY OF SCIENCES

FROM LETTER TO WILLIAM RAUB, SCIENCE ADVISER, DEPARTMENT OF HEALTH AND HUMAN SERVICES, MARCH 15, 1996.

The [Commission on Research Integrity] recommendations differ radically from the recommendations of a previous blue-ribbon panel that addressed the same issues. This panel was convened in 1989 by the National Academies of Sciences and Engineering and the Institute of Medicine under the auspices of the Committee on Science, Engineering and Public Policy (COSEPUP). . . . In general, we are convinced that the guidelines in the COSEPUP report are adequate to meet the needs of federal oversight agencies in dealing with scientific misconduct. . . .

The CRI report differs from the COSEPUP report in four ways that endanger the scientific enterprise: It adopts a vague and open-ended definition of scientific misconduct; it offers specific "examples" of scientific misconduct that threaten to inhibit legitimate types of scientific inquiry; it transfers much of the responsibility for oversight of scientific misconduct from the research institutions to the federal government, thereby creating an intrusive bureaucracy; and it fails to protect adequately the rights of scientists who are accused of misconduct. . . .

The original COSEPUP report adopted a definition of scientific misconduct that limited federal involvement to three precisely defined categories: fabrication, falsification and plagiarism. . . . The COSEPUP report acknowledged that there are other questionable practices and forms of misconduct in science, but it concluded that these practices do not require new types of sanctions at the federal level. . . .

The CRI report calls for an increased roll for federal agencies in oversight of scientific conduct through departments such as the Office of Research Integrity [ORI]. The COSEPUP report restricted the roles of such agencies to the investigation of charges of fabrication, falsification and plagiarism, and only when problems failed to be resolved at the institutional level. . . . Although the [CRI] report repeatedly states that the primary investigative responsibility rests with the research institutions, the report also gives ORI the right, and even the obligation, to enforce the regulations, which would require the office to review the results of all institutional investigations of scientific misconduct. Since the scope of scientific misconduct has been expanded, this will necessarily mean an expanded role for the ORI. We do not dispute the authority of the ORI to oversee institutional compliance, but we believe that this oversight should be restricted to charges of fabrication, falsification or plagiarism as outlined in COSEPUP report.

When Fraud-Busters Went After Mikulas Popovic

In 1984, Mikulas Popovic, a Czechoslovakian-born scientist at the National Institutes of Health (NIH), published a seminal paper in *Science*. Based on work described in the paper, Popovic developed a technique for growing the AIDS virus in large enough quantities to permit the commercial development of a blood test to detect HIV in the blood. By preventing HIV-contaminated blood from entering the nation's blood banks, the blood test is credited with saving hundreds of thousands of lives over the last decade.[1]

Within a few years, however, Popovic's life had become a nightmare. On Dec. 29, 1992, the federal Office of Research Integrity (ORI) issued a report concluding that Popovic had falsified one sentence and seven data points in the 1984 paper. But a Department of Health and Human Services (HHS) appeals board exonerated Popovic, ruling that the statements that ORI considered intentional falsifications were merely ambiguous, in part because of Popovic's poor English skills.

From the start of the investigation in 1989 until the appeals board exonerated him in 1993, Popovic was prevented from working in science, his lawyers charge. Now a professor of medical virology at the University of Maryland in Baltimore, Popovic has filed a $5 million lawsuit against the U.S. government and against Suzanne W. Hadley, former acting director of the Office of Scientific Integrity (OSI), which handled the initial investigation.[2] The suit charges denial of due process, negligence, invasion of privacy, refusal to hire for reasons contrary to public policy and intentional infliction of emotional distress.

"Popovic was damaged more than anyone else who went through that system during those years," says Washington attorney Barbara Mishkin, who represented Popovic before the appeals board. "He became unemployed and unemployable for four years." Between being unemployed and paying an estimated $350,000 in legal fees, Popovic "wiped out his savings going into retirement," Mishkin says.

The Popovic case raises questions about the fundamental fairness of the government's system for investigating and judging misconduct in biomedical research. Under the current system, the ORI not only investigates allegations of misconduct but also makes the determination as to whether misconduct was actually committed. If ORI finds a scientist guilty, it publishes the scientist's name, offense and penalty in its annual report. After scientists have received ORI's final judgment, they can appeal to the HHS Departmental Appeals Board.

The appeals panel hearing is typically the first and only time accused scientists can cross-examine government witnesses and present witnesses and evidence of their own.

Indeed, until Popovic's appeals hearing, ORI investigators "refused to tell him what the charges were, what the evidence was or who the witnesses were against him," says Washington attorney Lars H. Liebeler, who represents Popovic in his lawsuit. "It really was a star chamber."

Popovic's lawyers contend the OSI and ORI staffs were badly trained in basic principles of unprejudiced investigation, burden of proof and due process. OSI Acting Director Hadley "came to the conclusion he was guilty of scientific misconduct long before she knew what the facts were," Liebeler says. "She was prosecutor, judge and jury. There was no sense of impartiality at all." Moreover, the lawyers say, the investigators leaked Popovic's name to the press.

Hadley, now on loan from NIH to George Washington University as a visiting associate professor in psychiatry, responds, "I am quite confident that we were really scrupulous about protecting people's rights during the investigation." While it's true that Popovic did not have the opportunity to cross-examine witnesses, Hadley acknowledges, "There is a system for cross-examination during a separate process" — the appeals board hearing. She adds, "I am absolutely convinced of the accuracy of the findings of the [OSI] draft report."

ORI Acting Director Chris B. Pascal, sounds more chastened. "ORI accepts the decision of the Departmental Appeals Board, and we have for three years. We feel that decision has restored Dr. Popovic's reputation. To the extent he feels he is still harmed by this process, I'm sorry to hear that."

In what most observers consider a poor reflection on ORI's staff, the departmental appeals panel has overturned three of the five ORI decisions it has heard. The appeals panel decisions exonerating Popovic and Tufts University biologist Thereza Imanishi-Kari in another high-profile case drip with disdain for the investigations that found the two scientists guilty.[3]

In exonerating Popovic, the panel asked: "How could it happen that such a massive effort produced no substantial evidence of its premise?" The answer, it surmised, lay in a larger controversy: At the time, ORI was pursuing misconduct charges against Popovic's lab chief at NIH, virologist Robert C. Gallo. ORI's case against Gallo in turn was prompted by a 1989 *Chicago Tribune* article by reporter John Crewdson suggesting that Gallo had stolen the virus for the lab's AIDS breakthrough from the Pasteur Institute in Paris.[4]

Following the reversal in the Popovic decision, ORI withdrew its case against Gallo.

---

[1] For background, see "Blood Supply Safety," *The CQ Researcher*, Nov. 11, 1994, pp. 985-1008.

[2] Popovic was initially found guilty of misconduct by the OSI, which later became the ORI. In its draft report issued June 25, 1991, the OSI recommended as a penalty that Popovic be subjected to "close supervision" in his laboratory work over the next three years. Popovic's lawyers argued that this "effectively precluded" Popovic from employment as a scientist.

[3] Department of Health and Human Services, Departmental Appeals Board, Research Integrity Adjudications Panel, "Mikulas Popovic Decision," Nov. 3, 1993, p. 2.

[4] *Ibid.*, pp. 2-3.

Continued from p. 16

spectacular fraud — the announcement by Collins that a graduate student working under him had fabricated data.

"I don't think anyone believes an educational program will expunge certain kinds of human behavior from the planet," Nowack says.

It's not clear whether ethics education changes students' behavior, since few evaluations have been performed. But several experts in the field suggest formal courses are likely to have little effect if senior faculty are giving students conflicting signals with their own research style. Some surveys suggest research ethics courses make little difference in students' attitudes about what they have to do to succeed. Among postdoctoral fellows surveyed at the University of California, San Francisco, those who had taken a research ethics course were just as likely to say they were willing to fabricate data in the future as researchers who had not. [29]

"I know such behavior is not honest," said one young researcher, commenting on his willingness to select or omit data, "but more and more people are doing these kinds of things to increase their chances of publication." [30] ■

OUTLOOK

Redefining the Problem

HHS Secretary Shalala is currently considering recommendations from the Ryan Commission to improve the department's handling of research misconduct allegations. However, it has been over a year since the commission's report, and progress on the recommendations appears to be moving slowly.

According to Ryan, the congressional interest in science fraud that led to the commission's creation largely evaporated after the Republicans took control of Congress. In addition, he adds, "It's very hard for legislators to respond when the National Academy of Sciences says, 'This will kill science.' "

An internal working group appointed by Shalala has recommended that the department implement 23 of the commission's 33 regulations. In its recommendations, the group generally sided with biological researchers, who strongly criticized the Ryan Commission's most controversial recommendations as stifling to scientific creativity. The internal group headed by Shalala's science adviser William Raub rejected the commission's recommendations that investigations be separated from findings of guilt and that the agency disclose more information about investigations.

But Ryan says the "most important recommendation" made by his commission, in his view, would require university recipients of federal grants to run educational programs in the responsible conduct of research. The proposed requirement, which was endorsed by Shalala's internal committee, would expand the existing educational requirement for recipients of NIH training grants to all students as well as more senior researchers and technicians serving on research groups.

As Ryan sees it, the educational programs would reinforce the basic principles distinguishing scientific thinking from non-scientific thinking: recording data, making accurate measurements and trying to avoid biased conclusions by using control groups. Asked if universities aren't teaching these basic elements of the scientific method already, Ryan recalls that he was "appalled" when several scientists told him after a talk he gave that they always leave some data out of their final reports. "How could I repeat your work without knowing what you drop out?" he asked.

The White House, meanwhile, has gotten involved in the issue, appointing a panel to develop a definition of science misconduct that would be applicable to all government agencies. If the White House comes up with a governmentwide definition, HHS is expected to defer to it.

Members of the scientific community anticipate that the White House definition will be more restrictive than the Ryan Commission's, thus ceding more control to scientists. "We've been told we'll be happy with it," says FASEB President Suttie, whose organization has protested the broadened definition.

No matter what recommendations the panel makes, it is unlikely to end the debate over how fraud and misconduct should be judged. Nobody seems happy with the current system, but there's little consensus about what to replace it with. The proposed solutions divide starkly between those who think the main problem is ferreting out fraud and protecting whistleblowers and those preoccupied with defending scientists from frivolous charges.

The debate over retooling the legal machinery of fraud oversight continues to share some of the same unsatisfactory qualities as the debate over the facts in the Baltimore case. "We don't know whether the truth came out," says Horace Freeland Judson, a research professor at George Washington University. "There was no way the truth could have come out fully." At the root of the problem, Judson says, is his belief that science and the legal system are "two different worlds incommensurable with each other."

Attorneys who have defended scientists see things differently. Mishkin, who early in her career argued that the government should be more vigorous in ferreting out science fraud, agrees with Charrow that the ORI became a persecuting monster. But she thinks publicity about the lack of due process and the addition of better trained staff

FOR MORE INFORMATION

Federation of American Societies for Experimental Biology, 9650 Rockville Pike, Bethesda, Md. 20814-3998; (301) 530-7090. This federation of 10 scientific and education groups serves as a support group for member societies and some 44,000 scientists.

American Association for the Advancement of Science, 1200 New York Ave., N.W. Washington, D.C. 20005; (202) 326-6640. The AAAS, composed of scientists, scientific organizations and individuals interested in science, fosters scientific education and seeks to influence public policy and public understanding of science and technology.

Association of American Medical Colleges, 2450 N St. N.W., Washington, D.C. 20037-1126; (202) 828-0400. The association administers the Medical College Admissions Test; its members include councils of deans, teaching hospitals and U.S. schools of medicine.

National Academy of Sciences, 2101 Constitution Ave. N.W. Washington, D.C. 20418; (202) 334-2000. The NAS is a congressionally chartered independent organization that advises the federal government on questions of science, technology and health.

Office of Research Integrity, 5515 Security Lane, Suite 700, Rockville, Md. 20852; (301) 442-3400. ORI is the Health and Human Services agency that investigates allegations of science misconduct by federal grant recipients.

could still salvage the office. "The question," she says, "is whether the monster has been contained." ■

Sarah Glazer is a free-lance writer in the New York City area who writes about health and social-policy issues.

Notes

[1] D. Weaver, M. Reis, C. Albanese, F. Constantini, D. Baltimore and T. Imanishi-Kari, "Altered Repertoire of Endogenous Immunoglobulin Gene Expression in Transgenic Mice Containing a Rearranged Mu Heavy Chain Gene," *Cell,* April 25, 1986, pp. 247-259.

[2] For background, see "Gene Therapy," *The CQ Researcher,* Oct. 18, 1991, pp. 777-800.

[3] William Broad and Nicholas Wade, *Betrayers of the Truth* (1982).

[4] Quoted in Paulette V. Walker, "A Dramatic End to a Misconduct Case," *The Chronicle of Higher Education,* July 5, 1996.

[5] *Integrity and Misconduct in Research: Report of the Commission on Research Integrity,* Department of Health and Human Services, 1995, p. 28.

[6] Implementation Proposals on Recommendations by the Commission on Research Integrity, June 14, 1996, p. 15.

[7] Daniel J. Kevles, "The Assault on David Baltimore," *The New Yorker,* May 27, 1996, p. 94.

[8] A recent survey of scientists accused of misconduct but later exonerated by ORI found that 33 percent of the scientists said the institution handling their investigations failed to maintain confidentiality, and 75 percent said they were unsatisfied with their institution's efforts to restore their reputations after the investigations were closed. See Research Triangle Institute, *Survey of Accused but Exonerated Individuals in Research Misconduct Cases,* June 30, 1996, p. ii.

[9] Letter from the Council of the National Academy of Sciences to Dr. William Raub, science adviser to HHS, March 15, 1996.

[10] Quoted from a 1989 Public Health Service regulation in *Integrity and Misconduct in Research, op. cit.,* p. 50.

[11] See Gary Taubes, "The Devil's Data: The Intellectual Property that Possessed a University," *Lingua Franca,* April 1994, pp. 1, 24-35.

[12] Donald E. Buzzelli, "The Definition of Misconduct in Science: A View from NSF," *Science,* Jan. 29, 1993, pp. 584-648. The case was the only one of 67 closed cases between 1989 and June 1992 that fell under the "serious deviation" clause.

[13] See "Combating Science Fraud," *Editorial Research Reports,* Aug. 5, 1988, pp. 389-404.

[14] *Ibid.,* p. 392.

[15] See Marcel C. LaFollette, "Paycheques on Saturday Night: A Brief History and Analysis of the Politics of Integrity in the United States," in Stephen Lock and Frank Wells, eds., *Fraud and Misconduct in Medical Research* (1996), p. 1.

[16] Hearings on "Fraud in Biomedical Research," House Committee on Science and Technology Subcommittee on Investigations and Oversight, March 31-April 31, 1981.

[17] Editorial Research Reports, *op. cit.,* p. 401.

[18] Research Triangle Institute, *op. cit.,* p. i.

[19] Buzzelli, *op. cit.,* p. 584. This is the NSF's most recent analysis of misconduct cases by type of case received.

[20] Office of Research Integrity, *Annual Report 1995* (1996), pp. 11-23.

[21] Judith P. Swazey et al., "Ethical Problems in Academic Research," *American Scientist,* November-December 1993, pp.542-553.

[22] "Lawrence K. Altman, "Her Study Shattered the Myth that Fraud in Science is a Rarity, *The New York Times,* Nov. 23, 1993.

[23] Susan Eastwood et al., "Ethical Issues in Biomedical Research: Perceptions and Practices of Postdoctoral Research Fellows Responding to a Survey," *Science and Engineering Ethics,* Vol. 2, No. 1, 1996.

[24] Cited in Eastwood, *op. cit.,* p. 100.

[25] *Ibid.,* p. 89.

[26] Angell made the proposal in an editorial, "Editors and Fraud," *The New England Journal of Medicine,* summer 1983, pp. 3-8.

[27] Lock and Wells, *op. cit.,* p. 10.

[28] Faculty of Medicine, *Harvard University Faculty Policies on Integrity in Science,* February 1996, p. 5.

[29] Eastwood, *op. cit.,* p. 89.

[30] *Ibid.,* p. 100.

Bibliography

Selected Sources Used

Books

Kohn, Alexander, *False Prophets*, Basil Blackwell, 1986.
A professor of virology at Tel Aviv Medical School in Israel discusses famous cases of science fraud — proven and otherwise — starting with Claudius Ptolemy, the ancient Greek astronomer.

LaFollette, Marcel C., *Stealing into Print: Fraud, Plagiarism, and Misconduct,* University of California Press, 1996.
LaFollette, a research professor of international science and technology policy at George Washington University, reviews recent cases of science fraud and their implications for the field as a whole.

Lock, Stephen, and Frank Wells, eds., *Fraud and Misconduct in Medical Research,* BMJ Publishing Group, 1996.
This collection of essays reviews the recent history of science fraud in the United States, Canada and Europe and compares various government responses.

Sarasohn, Judy, *Science on Trial: The Whistleblower, the Accused and the Nobel Laureate,* St. Martin's Press, 1993.
In this detailed account of the fraud case against biologist Thereza Imanishi-Kari, published before an appeals panel exonerated her, *Legal Times* reporter Sarasohn found the evidence against Imanishi-Kari "more persuasive" than that supporting her innocence.

Articles

Beardsley, Tim, "Profile: Imanishi-Kari," *Scientific American,* November 1996, pp. 50-52.
Scientific American interviews Thereza Imanishi-Kari following her exoneration from charges of fraud and finds the biologist, recently reinstalled as an assistant professor at the Tufts University School of Medicine, "remarkably unbitter."

Friedly, Jock, "How Congressional Pressure Shaped the 'Baltimore Case,' " *Science,* Aug. 16, 1996, pp. 873-875.
In an investigative article, reporter Friedly describes how Rep. John D. Dingell's, D-Mich., investigative subcommittee took an active part in helping the Secret Service and a government agency to find Thereza Imanishi-Kari guilty of fraud.

Kevles, Daniel J., "The Assault on David Baltimore," *The New Yorker*, May 27, 1996, pp.94-109.
Making clear his sympathies for biologist David Baltimore, science historian Kevles writes a fascinating account of the fraud case against Baltimore co-author Thereza Imanishi-Kari.

Marshall, Eliot, "Fraud Strikes Top Genome Lab," *Science*, Nov. 8, 1996, pp. 908-910.
The recently announced fabrication of data by a graduate student working under National Institutes of Health genome research chief Francis Collins is described in detail along with its implications for the study of leukemia.

Weiss, Rick, "After Misconduct Probes, Some Scientists are Fighting Back in Court," *The Washington Post*, Nov. 29, 1996, p. A29.
This article describes several cases in which scientists accused of fraud are suing the federal government for damaging their reputations.

Reports and Studies

Office of Inspector General, National Science Foundation, *Semiannual Report to the Congress, No. 14, Oct. 1, 1995-March 31, 1996,* April 30, 1996.
The inspector general office, which is responsible for investigating scientific misconduct at the National Science Foundation, describes selected cases in its semi-annual reports but does not reveal the names of those found guilty.

Office of Research Integrity, Department of Health and Human Services, *Annual Report 1995*, July 1996.
In this annual report, the office charged with investigating and resolving scientific fraud and misconduct in biomedical research summarizes the cases it has resolved in 1995 along with the names of scientists found guilty.

Research Triangle Institute, *Consequences of Whistleblowing for the Whistleblower in Misconduct in Science Cases,* Submitted to Office of Research Integrity, Department of Health and Human Services, Oct. 2, 1995.
Most people who report scientific misconduct say they experienced some negative effects, such as pressure to drop their allegations, but fewer than one in eight suffer such serious consequences as being fired or denied promotion.

Research Triangle Institute, *Survey of Accused but Exonerated Individuals in Research Misconduct Cases,* Submitted to Office of Research Integrity, Department of Health and Human Services, June 30, 1996.
About 70 percent of scientific misconduct cases that come to the investigative arm of HHS are exonerated, but most say their career suffered even after their reputations were cleared.

The Next Step

Additional information from UMI's Newspaper & Periodical Abstracts™ database

Thereza Imanishi-Kari

Beardsley, Tim, "Profile: Thereza Imanishi-Kari," *Scientific American,* November 1996, pp. 50-52.
Geneticist Thereza Imanishi-Kari was cleared of all charges of scientific misconduct arising from a tangled, decade-old controversy. The controversy concerned antibodies produced by genetically engineered mice.

Dingell, John D., "The elusive truths of the Baltimore case," *The Washington Post,* July 18, 1996, p. A27.
Rep. John D. Dingell, D-Mich., former chairman of the House Energy Subcommittee on Oversight and Investigations, explains why the committee targeted Thereza Imanishi-Kari with allegations of scientific misconduct.

Kolata, Gina, "Inquiry Lacking Due Process," *The New York Times,* June 25, 1996, p. C3.
As scientists absorb the decision by a federal appeals panel the week of June 16, 1996, dismissing all charges of scientific misconduct against Theresa Imanishi-Kari, many are asking how the process for handling allegations of fraud in science could have gotten so badly off track.

Marshall, Eliot, "Disputed results now just a footnote," *Science,* July 12, 1996, pp. 174-175.
The ruling of the appeals board that dismissed misconduct charges against Thereza Imanishi-Kari last month with a withering indictment of the case against her spoke volumes about the way misconduct cases are handled. Many immunologists have said that for the field of immunology, any verdict on the integrity of the paper has turned out to be largely irrelevant.

Singer, Maxine, "Assault on science," *The Washington Post,* June 26, 1996, p. A21.
Singer comments that the Housing and Urban Development Department's (HUD) announcement in June 1996 vindicating Thereza Imanishi-Kari, and thus indirectly David Baltimore, from charges of falsification of scientific data in a paper they co-authored in 1986, was a welcome end to a decade-long assault on their integrity.

Weiss, Rick, "Researcher absolved of data fraud," *The Washington Post,* June 22, 1996, p. A1.
One of the longest and most torturous investigations into scientific misconduct came to a close on June 21, 1996, when an appeals board at HHS cleared Tufts University scientist Thereza Imanishi-Kari of all charges that she had fabricated data.

David Baltimore

Friedly, Jock, "How congressional pressure shaped the 'Baltimore case'," *Science,* Aug. 16, 1996, pp. 873-875.
The so-called "Baltimore affair," a 10-year ordeal in which Nobel Prize winner David Baltimore testified before Congress and was linked to research fraud, is recounted. The ways in which Congress is able to influence such hearings are examined.

Kevles, Daniel J., "The assault on David Baltimore," *The New Yorker,* May 27, 1996, pp. 94-104.
Whistleblower Margot O'Toole's accusations of fraud brought down Massachusetts Institute of Technology (MIT) Nobel Prize-winning biologist David Baltimore and his colleague Thereza Imanishi-Kari. Kevles discusses the case and argues that the evidence supports Imanishi-Kari's innocence.

Lewis, Anthony, "Tale Of A Bully," *The New York Times,* June 24, 1996, p. A15.
Lewis criticizes the record of Rep. John D. Dingell, D-Mich., the former chairman of the House Energy and Commerce Committee, and highlights the "savage and prolonged attacks" that Dingell carried out on David Baltimore and Thereza Imanishi-Kari in the late 1980s over their research into the immune system.

Stone, Richard, "Baltimore defends paper at center of misconduct case," *Science,* July 14, 1995, p. 157.
David Baltimore is staunchly defending Thereza Imanishi-Kari on charges of scientific misconduct. Baltimore testified that Imanishi-Kari's research has stood the test of scientific scrutiny and that her results were not fabricated.

Warsh, David, "The fortune that never was," *The Boston Globe,* June 30, 1996, p. 71.
Warsh describes the end of the public skirmish over the reputations of Massachusetts Institute of Technology Professor David Baltimore and Tufts University researcher Thereza Imanishi-Kari with a report deeply embarrassing to the federal government.

Commission on Research Integrity

Burd, Stephen, "Federal panel will seek tougher rules on scientific misconduct," *The Chronicle of Higher Education,* Nov. 3, 1995, p. A42.
The 12-member Commission on Research Integrity is ready to recommend tougher penalties for universities that are not diligent in preventing scientific misconduct or in dealing with cases that do arise.

Healy, Bernadine, "The Dangers of Trial by Dingell," *The New York Times,* July 3, 1996, p. A23.
Former NIH Director Healy discusses how the unfair system of justice meted out by Rep. John D. Dingell, D-Mich., the

powerful former chairman of the House Energy and Commerce Committee and its investigative subcommittee, and the Office of Research Integrity trampled the system of due process in their efforts to expose scientific fraud at NIH.

Kaiser, Jocelyn, "HHS is still looking for a definition," *Science,* June 21, 1996, p. 1735.
The HHS' top officials have mixed views concerning the Commission on Research Integrity's sweeping proposals for changing the way the federal government handles allegations of scientific misconduct. A new definition of misconduct has been criticized.

Kaiser, Jocelyn, "Panel urges new approach to inquiries," *Science,* Dec. 1, 1995, p. 1431.
The Commission on Research Integrity has recommended that the Office of Research Integrity (ORI) rid itself of some of its enforcement responsibilities. The ORI currently investigates, adjudicates and recommends punishment for biomedical researchers funded by the federal government.

Macilwain, Colin, "Problems of integrity are 'pervasive,'" *Nature,* June 27, 1996, p. 719.
Kenneth Ryan, professor emeritus at Harvard Medical School and chairman of the Commission on Research Integrity, warns that problems of integrity are now pervasive in U.S. science. He says that the scientific community has ignored recommendations by the National Academy of Sciences for extensive self-regulation of scientific conduct.

Ryan, Kenneth J., "Scientific misconduct in perspective: The need to improve accountability," *The Chronicle of Higher Education,* July 19, 1996, pp. B1-B2.
Scientists have failed to set standards for the proper conduct of research, and the Office of Research Integrity has had little success in resolving the misconduct cases it has investigated. If scientific researchers want to maintain public trust, they must be more accountable for their use of federal funds.

Walker, Paulette V., "Scientists step up attack against proposals on research misconduct," *The Chronicle of Higher Education,* May 17, 1996, p. A32.
Scientists believe that a federal panel's proposals for fighting scientific misconduct are too broad and invasive. Many scientists oppose the proposals outlined by the Commission on Research Integrity .

Federal Oversight

Flint, Anthony, "U.S. curbs on data fraud not expected," *The Boston Globe,* April 11, 1995, p. 3.
Despite disturbing cases of fraud and scientific misconduct in the academic research community, it is unlikely that the government will propose vast new layers of regulation to try to control the problem, said Kenneth J. Ryan, chairman of the federal Commission on Research Integrity.

Stone, Richard, "Federal panel recommends universities play bigger role," *Science,* Jan. 27, 1995, p. 449.
A congressional panel has recommended that universities take the lead in defining and investigating scientific misdeeds. Universities, said the panel, should be responsible for transgressions less serious than misconduct.

Walker, Paulette V., "Federal panel endorses most of plan for new policies on scientific misconduct," *The Chronicle of Higher Education,* June 28, 1996, p. A24.
An HHS panel has accepted most of the 33 recommendations that the 12-member Commission on Research Integrity made to improve integrity in scientific research.

Monitoring of Misconduct by Universities

Abelson, Philip H., "Impact of regulations on universities," *Science,* March 3, 1995, p. 1247.
Institutions of higher learning are particularly vulnerable to a growing burden of mandates because of their dependence on federal funds. As a result, student aid, research grants and hazardous material become problem areas.

Burd, Stephen, "Federal panel will seek tougher rules on scientific misconduct," *The Chronicle of Higher Education,* Nov. 3, 1995, p. A42.
The 12-member Commission on Research Integrity is ready to recommend tougher penalties for universities that are not diligent in preventing scientific misconduct or in dealing with cases that do arise.

Rights of Scientists Accused of Misconduct

Kaiser, Jocelyn, "Societies back Fisher," *Science,* Oct. 18, 1996, p. 331.
University of Pittsburgh cancer surgeon Bernard Fisher has gained the backing of three organizations as he sues the federal government for identifying him as guilty of scientific misconduct. The lawsuit is discussed.

Weiss, Rick, "After misconduct probes, some scientists are fighting back in court," *The Washington Post,* Nov. 29, 1996, p. A25.
The possibility of a scientists' backlash against the federal government's decade-long crackdown on scientific fraud following suits filed by researchers Mikulas Popovic and Bernard Fisher is discussed.

Weiss, Rick, "Proposed shifts in misconduct reviews unsettle many scientists," *The Washington Post,* June 30, 1996, p. A6.
The dramatic June 1996 exoneration of Tufts University immunologist Thereza Imanishi-Kari and her senior collaborator, David Baltimore, of scientific fraud charges has done little to mollify those two and other researchers who feel that the government's system for dealing with accused scientists is unfair.

Back Issues

Great Research on Current Issues Starts Right Here...Recent topics covered by The CQ Researcher are listed below. Before May 1991, reports were published under the name of Editorial Research Reports.

JUNE 1995
Combating Infectious Disease
Property Rights
Repetitive Stress Injuries
Regulating the Internet

JULY 1995
War Crimes
Highway Safety
Combating Terrorism
Preventing Teen Drug Use

AUGUST 1995
Job Stress
Organ Transplants
United Nations at 50
Advances in Cancer Research

SEPTEMBER 1995
Catholic Church in the U.S.
Northern Ireland Cease-Fire
High School Sports
Teaching History

OCTOBER 1995
Quebec's Future
Revitalizing the Cities
Networking the Classroom
Indoor Air Pollution

Back issues are available for $5.00 (subscribers) or $10.00 (non-subscribers). Quantity discounts apply to orders over ten. To order, call Congressional Quarterly Customer Service at (202) 887-8621.

Binders are available for $18.00. To order call 1-800-638-1710. Please refer to stock number 648.

NOVEMBER 1995
The Working Poor
The Jury System
Sex, Violence and the Media
Police Misconduct

DECEMBER 1995
Teens and Tobacco
Gene Therapy's Future
Global Water Shortages
Third-Party Prospects

JANUARY 1996
Emergency Medicine
Punishing Sex Offenders
Bilingual Education
Helping the Homeless

FEBRUARY 1996
Reforming the CIA
Campaign Finance Reform
Academic Politics
Getting Into College

MARCH 1996
The British Monarchy
Preventing Juvenile Crime
Tax Reform
Pursuing the Paranormal

APRIL 1996
Centennial Olympic Games
Managed Care
Protecting Endangered Species
New Military Culture

MAY 1996
Russia's Political Future
Marriage and Divorce
Year-Round Schools
Taiwan, China and the U.S.

JUNE 1996
Rethinking NAFTA
First Ladies
Teaching Values
Labor Movement's Future

JULY 1996
Recovered-Memory Debate
Native Americans' Future
Crackdown on Sexual Harassment
Attack on Public Schools

AUGUST 1996
Fighting Over Animal Rights
Privatizing Government Services
Child Labor and Sweatshops
Cleaning Up Hazardous Wastes

SEPTEMBER 1996
Gambling Under Attack
The States and Federalism
Civic Journalism
Reassessing Foreign Aid

OCTOBER 1996
Political Consultants
Insurance Fraud
Rethinking School Integration
Parental Rights

NOVEMBER 1996
Global Warming
Clashing Over Copyright
Consumer Debt
Governing Washington, D.C.

DECEMBER 1996
Welfare, Work and the States
The New Volunteerism
Implementing the Disabilities Act
America's Pampered Pets

Future Topics

- ***Restructuring the Electric Industry***
- ***The New Immigrants***
- ***Biochemical Weapons***

THE CQ Researcher

PUBLISHED BY CONGRESSIONAL QUARTERLY INC.

Restructuring the Electric Industry

Will competition help or hurt consumers?

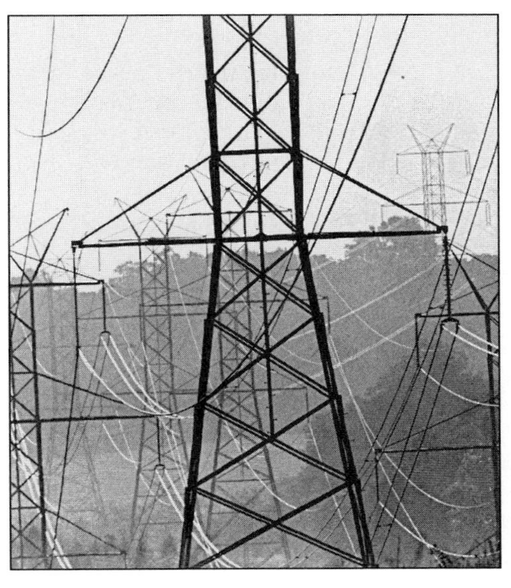

Competition is coming to one of the last remaining government-regulated monopolies: the electric power industry. Seven states have adopted policies within the past year that give electric customers the right to choose between competing suppliers. Many other states are considering similar moves, and Congress is being urged to make competition national policy. Advocates say competition will bring lower prices, but critics fear the savings will only go to big industrial customers. Most electric utilities are resisting the change; they fear that competition may weaken their customer base. They also want to be compensated for the costs of power plants that may not be competitive in a free market. The issues are complex, the stakes are high and lobbying is likely to be intense in Washington and in state capitals.

INSIDE THIS ISSUE

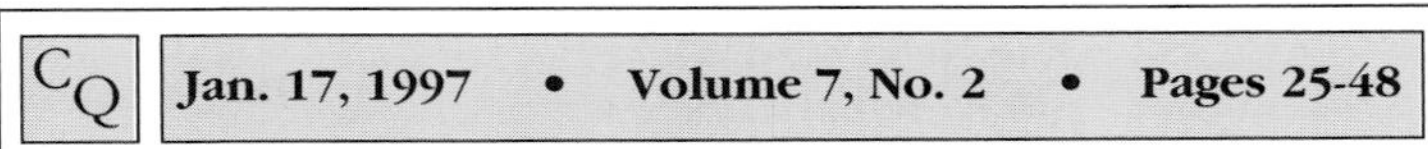
CQ Jan. 17, 1997 • Volume 7, No. 2 • Pages 25-48

Formerly Editorial Research Reports

THE ISSUES

BACKGROUND

CURRENT SITUATION

OUTLOOK

SIDEBARS AND GRAPHICS

FOR FURTHER RESEARCH

COVER: R. MICHAEL JENKINS

Jan. 17, 1997
Volume 7, No. 2

The CQ Researcher (ISSN 1056-2036). Formerly Editorial Research Reports. Published weekly (48 times per year, not printed Jan. 3, May 30, Aug. 29, Oct. 31) by Congressional Quarterly Inc., 1414 22nd St., N.W., Washington, D.C. 20037. Annual subscription rate for libraries, businesses and government is $340. Additional rates furnished upon request. Periodicals postage paid at Washington, D.C. POSTMASTER: Send address changes to The CQ Researcher, 1414 22nd St., N.W., Washington, D.C. 20037.

Restructuring the Electric Industry

By Kenneth Jost

The Issues

In a simpler time, there was "the phone company." When it came to telephone service and equipment, the vast, national monopoly was the only game in town. Today, a host of telephone companies hustle to sell long distance service at "special" rates and telephones in every imaginable color and design.

The telephone company may be gone, but in most communities the monolithic utility known as "the electric company" still survives. If consumers want electricity for their homes, businesses or factories, they have to buy it from a government-protected monopoly at rates determined not by the market but by government regulators.

But now, competition is coming even to the electric power industry. Some 17,000 customers in New Hampshire already have the freedom to choose from among 33 companies offering to sell electricity for less than the state's notoriously high rates. Soon, customers in six other states from Rhode Island to California will have the same privilege. Other states seem likely to follow their lead, and Congress is being urged to make "retail competition" for electric power a national policy.

"Retail competition in the electric utility industry is inevitable," says Robert Frank, a staff attorney with the New Hampshire Public Utility Commission. "It's just a matter of how long it takes to get there."

In New Hampshire, the start of a two-year experiment in retail competition last May touched off a marketing blitz. Power companies that did not even exist a decade ago wooed customers with marketing gimmicks ranging from bird feeders, energy-efficient showerheads and spruce saplings to cash rebates (*see p. 40*). "People have been overwhelmed," says Karen Hicks, executive director of the New Hampshire chapter of the consumer group Citizen Action.

In Peterborough (population 5,200), the board of selectmen took competitive bids from about a dozen companies on behalf of 600 customers selected for the state-sponsored pilot program. The tactic worked. Participating townsfolk and businesses are paying some of the lowest rates in the state.

But Charles Leedham, the Peterborough selectman who took the lead on the issue, says deregulating the electric power industry is about more than just lower rates. "You and I have been paying electric bills all our lives, and, if we didn't like it, there wasn't much we could do," he says. "Here we are, for the very first time, in a position to reward or punish a [power] provider."

Supporters of the drive to introduce competition into the electric power market insist that consumers will be the principal beneficiaries. "Consumers will have choice as well as lower prices," says Steven Burton, president of Sithe Energies Inc., a New York-based power producer, who also serves as president of the Electric Power Supply Association, the trade group for independent power providers. "They will be able to choose the type of service they want, how they want it delivered, and there will be a wider range of services."

Despite such claims, many consumer advocates remain highly skeptical. "In theory, it sounds very good," says Edwin Rothschild, Citizen Action's energy policy director in Washington. "The question is whether it will work in practice."

Certain segments of the utility industry itself also are urging lawmakers to take a cautious approach to competition. Private, investor-owned utilities — which currently provide about three-fourths of the electricity sold in the United States — fear not only that they will lose many of their customers to upstart competitors but also that they will be stuck paying the bills for outmoded but expensive nuclear power plants and high-priced, long-term power contracts.

The nuclear behemoths, constructed primarily in the 1970s and '80s under a regulatory system that set rates to cover the utilities' costs plus a "reasonable" rate of return, cannot compete with the small-scale, natural-gas-fired turbine plants being operated by many of the emerging power providers of the '90s. Utilities also were required by a 1978 federal law to pay above-market rates for power from suppliers using renewable resources like solar or wind energy (*see p. 38*).

Utility industry officials say they should be reimbursed for what they call "stranded costs" — costs that they cannot recover in a fully competitive market. The companies "have promises on the books from the regulators that they would get back the costs that they have incurred," says David K. Owens, senior vice president of the

The Cost of Electric Power

The nation's highest electric rates are in the Northeast, California, Alaska and Hawaii. Rates are below the national average in 32 states and above in 18 states and the District of Columbia.

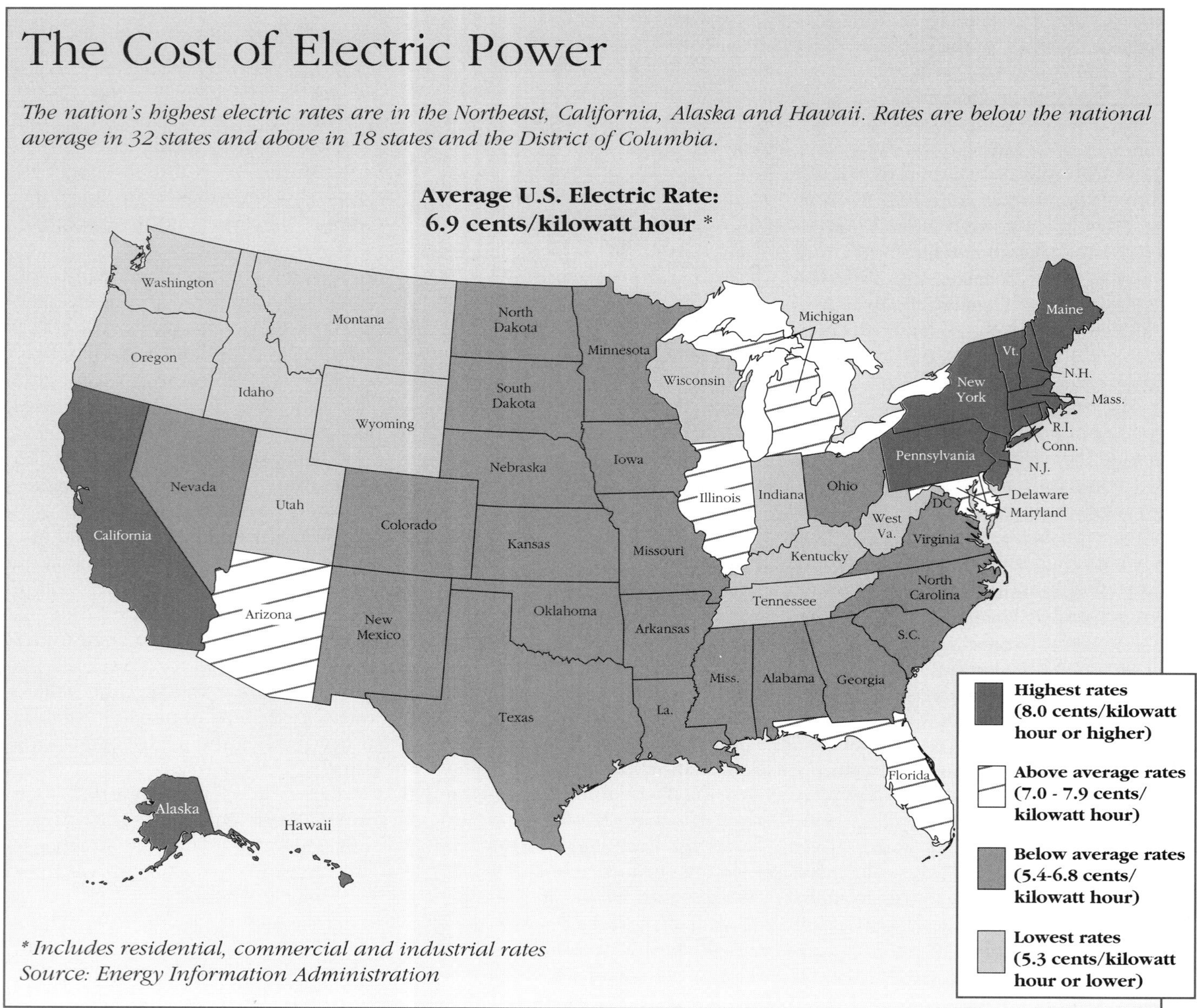

** Includes residential, commercial and industrial rates*
Source: Energy Information Administration

Edison Electric Institute, the trade association for the nation's largest investor-owned utilities.

Consumer groups insist that the utilities are simply asking for a government bailout. "You have utilities with very high-cost power, particularly the nuclear power plants, that say, 'If we enter this world of retail competition, then someone's going to have to pay off those costs,'" says Rothschild. "We shouldn't be paying for mismanagement."

Electric industry leaders insist, however, that they are not trying to stymie the move toward competition. "We're working hard to get the right issues in the debate," Owens says. "Those who may not be in agreement with us may perceive that as slowing down the debate."

The utilities have amassed a multimillion-dollar war chest to lobby on the issue in Washington and in state capitals around the country. On many issues, they will find common ground with traditional adversaries that also have a powerful lobbying presence in Washington: public power systems and rural electric cooperatives, which together provide power to about 25 percent of the country's electric customers. Like the investor-owned utilities, municipal-owned systems and electric cooperatives fear that competition may weaken their customer base.

Arrayed against the utilities, however, are some equally powerful lobbying forces: business and industry groups that buy electricity by the megawatt and hunger for the chance to bargain with competing power suppliers. "We think competition in any industry brings about not only lower prices but also increased innovation and technological stimulation," says John Anderson, executive director of the Electricity Consumers Resource Council.

The council — known as "Elcon" — includes some 30 major industrial companies, such as General Motors Corp., E.I. du Pont de Nemours & Co. and Bethlehem Steel Corp. Founded 20 years ago, Elcon is now pushing hard in Washington for legislation to mandate competition in the electric industry.

In addition, the new breed of electric power suppliers are themselves lobbying to open up the market. Among the most aggressive in pushing the issue is Enron Corp., a Houston-based natural gas pipeline company that has diversified to become the country's largest private marketer of electricity. Enron's chairman, Kenneth L. Lay, says that consumers could save $60 billion-$80 billion per year if the electric power market were completely opened to competition.

The forces sweeping through the $207 billion electric power industry are similar to those that transformed the telecommunications industry over the past two decades. Technological changes, market forces and political trends have combined to discredit the public utility philosophy that governed the generation, transmission and distribution of electricity for most of this century (*see p. 33*).

But most experts and advocates agree that federal and state regulators will maintain an important role in the electric industry for the foreseeable future. "This is not going to be a deregulated business, believe me," says Thomas R. Kuhn, president of the Edison Electric Institute.

Still, restructuring is moving rapidly, in large measure due to the Federal Energy Regulatory Commission (FERC), which monitors interstate electricity transmission. It issued an order in April 1996 requiring utilities to allow competing power providers to use their transmission lines to sell electricity to other utilities — a practice known as wholesale competition. Seven states — Arizona, California, Massachusetts, New Hampshire, New York, Pennsylvania and Rhode Island — have adopted laws or regulatory orders providing for retail competition in electricity statewide next year or soon thereafter.

"I'm amazed at how fast this is moving," says Jim Conran, president of the California group Consumers First and a critic of some of the restructuring measures. "I would expect that within a decade we will see massive deregulation or restructuring throughout the country."

In Congress, Rep. Dan Schaefer, a Colorado Republican from suburban Denver, last year introduced legislation to require states to permit retail competition by Dec. 15, 2000. Schaefer plans to introduce a similar bill in the new Congress, and many other lawmakers are likely to come up with their own restructuring proposals.

The Clinton administration also is expected to submit comprehensive energy restructuring legislation early this year. "This is our most vital industry," said Deputy Energy Secretary Charles B. Curtis. "It's important to get it right." [1]

For supporters, competition cannot come soon enough. "We should work through it very carefully, but that doesn't require four years," says Elcon's Anderson.

But others say that given the importance of electricity to the economy and to Americans' daily lives, Congress should move slowly. "We're not in a crisis situation where Congress must act quickly and risk errors that it can correct two years down the line," says Alan Richardson, executive director of the American Public Power Association.

As the debate proceeds, consumers and policy-makers alike will have to educate themselves quickly about the complexities of an industry that most people have taken largely for granted. Here are some of the issues that figure in the discussions:

Will retail competition result in price savings for most electric power customers?

Retail competition — also known as "retail wheeling" * — won't bring about dramatic, visible changes in the way most people use electricity. Most customers — residential or business — will still get electricity delivered over wires owned by a regulated public utility. They probably will still send their monthly payments to the same public utility, although the bill will be broken up to show separate charges by the company that provides the power and the utility that distributes it to the home or business.

But advocates of competition contend that customers will see the price of electricity come down as a result of freer markets and consumer choice. "Competition in the electric industry is something that has the potential to benefit all customers," says Anderson of the industrial users group Elcon.

"The large electricity users know very well that if they can choose between providers, they're going to get the lowest price," says Burton of the Electric Power Supply Association. "The same thing is true of customers down to the residential level."

Opponents and skeptics warn, however, that price reductions may be enjoyed only by big commercial and industrial users and that most residential and small business customers may re-

* "Wheeling" refers to the practice of a utility using its own transmission network to take in and pass along electricity produced by another utility or generator. "Wholesale wheeling" allows a local utility to buy energy from competing electric generators but does not affect the utility's government-granted monopoly in the retail market. "Retail wheeling" allows competing electric power generators to use the local utility's transmission lines to provide retail customers with a choice of providers besides the local utility.

A Profile of U.S. Electric Utilities

Americans get their electricity from both public and private utilities. Only 250 of the 3,204 electric utilities in the United States are **investor-owned,** *but they provide about three-fourths of the electricity sold in the United States. This segment includes giant utilities like Pacific Gas & Electric, Southern California Edison, Consolidated Edison in New York and Commonwealth Edison in Chicago, which serve 3 million or more customers each, as well as a handful of small companies serving fewer than 1,000 customers. The 2,005 state and local* **publicly owned** *power systems range from the Los Angeles Department of Water and Power, which serves 1.3 million customers, to small systems serving 500 or fewer customers. (There also are 10 federal power systems, including the Tennessee Valley Authority and the Bonneville Power Administration in the Pacific Northwest.)* **Rural electric cooperatives** *serve about 30 million customers in 46 states. Most of the co-ops are owned and controlled by the people they serve.*

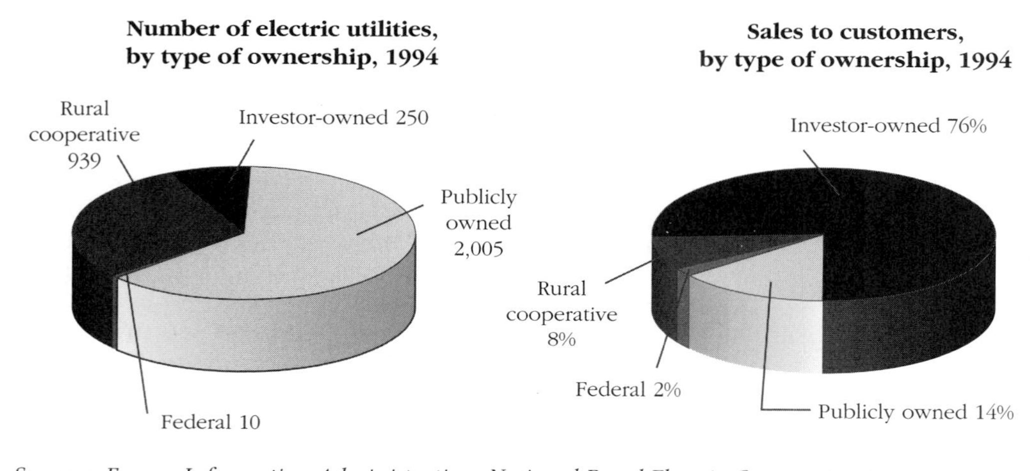

Sources: Energy Information Administration, National Rural Electric Cooperative Association

alize few, if any, savings.

"There have to be major changes in the way the system is regulated to have real competition," says Charlie Higley, senior policy analyst for Public Citizen, a public interest group affiliated with consumer activist Ralph Nader. "You have to make sure that there is real open access to the transmission system. You have to make sure that customers have the option of different suppliers. If utilities are allowed to keep their monopolies intact, that won't do anybody any good."

Consumer groups also worry about the wave of mergers and consolidations in the electric and gas power industries. (*See story, p. 42.*) "If we're going to have competition, let's have it with lots of companies, lots of players and lots of choice," Higley says.

More immediately, though, consumer groups are complaining that utility companies' efforts to recover stranded costs will negate the benefits of competition by saddling consumers with big financial bills for the utilities' past financial mistakes.

The issue of stranded costs creates a tension between the utility companies and the industrial users that are pushing for competition. Elcon's Anderson says there should be "a sharing of costs between shareholders and customers," while electric utilities say they should be able to recover all costs.

The investor-owned utilities also raise the prospect of higher rates for some customers by calling for a "level playing field" between private companies and public power companies and rural electric cooperative systems. They complain that the public and rural co-op systems have benefits — including exemption from federal income taxes and tax-exempt financing — that give them a competitive advantage over investor-owned utilities.

The public power systems and rural co-ops say that their lower rates — about 24 percent lower on average than investor-owned utilities — result not primarily from tax benefits but from their nonprofit status, lower administrative costs and access to federally produced hydroelectric power. So far, most restructuring proposals leave their tax status unchanged.

Even if retail competition does lower prices for electricity in the marketplace, many residential customers may see no savings because, out of choice or habit, they simply stick with their existing utility. "If given an opportunity, a small customer may decide it's not in their best interests to take the time and effort to shop" for a new supplier, Anderson says. "That's freedom of choice, and that's perfectly OK."

But some experts say that customers will see benefits even if they do not take advantage of price reductions. "The real benefits of deregulation and competition are going to be in technological changes that are induced as a result of competition," says Douglas Bohi, director of the energy and natural resources division of the nonpartisan environmental group Resources for the Future.

Will deregulation lead to more power outages and "brown-outs"?

Twice last year, high-voltage electric lines that sagged in the summer heat and brushed against trees set off an improbable series of short circuits on the Western electric power grid, leaving millions of customers without electricity for hours. Critics of electric power deregulation seized on the July 2 and Aug. 10 incidents to warn that similar outages may occur more often under deregulation. But supporters of competition insist that such fears are groundless and contend that competition may, in fact, enhance the reliability of the nation's electric power distribution systems.

The electric industry took steps to strengthen the reliability of the "grid" in the wake of the "great Northeast blackout" of 1965 and a lesser power outage in 1967. To ward off federal legislation, private utilities set up the North American Electric Reliability Council, which coordinates with nine regional councils to oversee planning and operation of the electric power interconnections.

In its report on the Aug. 10 power outage, the Western regional council, based in Salt Lake City, blamed the incident on the lack of a contingency plan to deal with an overload on one of the circuits. It also faulted the Bonneville Power Administration, the federal public utility responsible for the power line, for "inadequate tree-trimming" and for delays in informing other utilities about the short circuit once it developed. [2]

Critics of deregulation say that the increase in competition will add to the risk of outages simply because the system is moving into uncharted territory, with unanswered questions about how the grid will operate and be maintained. In addition, some experts warn that a competitive market may hamper the cooperation between electric power suppliers that is needed to ensure a reliable transmission system.

"Utilities can't cooperate when they're also becoming competitive enemies," explains Bohi, an advocate of restructuring. "When they have to start sacrificing investments in their systems, the place where they're likely to sacrifice is the transfer capability between one system and another."

Robert K. Johnson, executive director of the Electric Consumers' Alliance, a group representing residential and small business customers, says that short-term economic considerations may also lead utilities to make similar decisions about what power sources to use — natural gas, for example, instead of coal. If that happens, he says, the country would "lose a diverse resource mix" needed to "absorb the shock from different fuel price changes."

But supporters of deregulation insist that competition poses no threat to reliability. "There's absolutely nothing from a technological standpoint that should cause a problem in reliability under competition," Anderson says.

Indeed, Anderson says, the incentives for maintaining the power grid may increase when utilities separate the power-generating function from transmission and distribution. "When you get your revenues from generation, it doesn't surprise me that your focus is not on tree-trimming," Anderson says. When those functions are separate, he says, "management responsible for the wires is going to give that more attention, not less."

The utility industry similarly voices confidence that reliability will not be a problem under competition. "We will get the cooperation that is necessary," says Gene Gorzelnik, a spokesman for the reliability council in Princeton, N.J. "We're working on that to see that it does happen."

For his part, Bohi says the reliability problem is being addressed with proposals to create "independent system operators," or ISOs, that would operate the transmission system but have no responsibility for generation or distribution. California's restructuring law calls for an ISO to be operational by 1998. "That's how it has to play out," Bohi says.

Will deregulation hurt the environment?

Environmentalists were among the early advocates of competition for electric power, but today many raise concerns that competition will disadvantage renewable resource technologies — chiefly solar and wind energy. Some proponents of competition respond that renewable energy technologies should be left to the marketplace — to live or die strictly based on their ability to compete for customers. But most restructuring proposals include some measures to help renewable technologies survive the transition to greater competition.

"There are both opportunities and risks to renewable energy development in opening up the market to greater competition," explains Alan Nogee, an environmental activist with the Union of Concerned Scientists in Cambridge, Mass. "The opportunity will be that individuals would be allowed to choose renewable energy sources in their supply." The risk, Nogee says, is that commercial and industrial users "will choose dirtier [energy] sources if they're cheaper." He notes that commercial and industrial users account for about two-thirds of electric power consumption.

"I'm not against any of these [renewable] resources," responds Anderson of Elcon. But, he adds, "We should let the market decide which of these resources is best. We should not try to artificially adjust the market."

Environmental advocates, however, contend that head-to-head competition would be unfair for renewable technologies. They say that solar and wind energy suppliers are still too small to enjoy the kind of economies of scale that can enable them to bring prices down to a competitive level. In addition, they say, the market does not yet account for the environmental costs of fossil fuels and nuclear generating plants. [3]

"Left to itself, the market doesn't include the cost to the environment that's imposed by various power sources," says Rothschild of Citizen Action. "And that's a serious problem."

Environmentalists also worry that any reduction in the price of electricity will lead to increased consumption and, as a result, increased emissions from existing power plants. But advocates of restructuring say that with or without competition, existing federal antipollution laws limit the emissions from electric power plants.

"All power plants have to meet the Clean Air Act requirements," Anderson says. "That's the law of the country and will be the law of the country with increased competition."

The new power suppliers add that competition benefits the environment by bringing on line newer, cleaner sources of electricity. "The environment has benefited because all these new power plants have had to meet maximum environmental standards," says Burton of the Electric Power Supply Association.

Some environmental advocates agree that antipollution laws provide the best assurance of reducing emissions from electric power plants. "The emissions problem need not detract either from the objectives of competition in the market or the way in which those objectives are arranged," says Bohi.

In any event, the governmental support for renewable resources that began in the 1970s appears likely to continue as competition is introduced. The four states that have passed restructuring legislation — California, New Hampshire, Pennsylvania and Rhode Island * — have included provisions for so-called clean energy trust funds, funded either from ratepayers or from general revenues, to provide support for research and demonstration of renewable resources.

In Congress, the bill introduced by Rep. Schaefer last year included a provision — expected to be included again this year — to encourage development of renewable energy sources. The provision would require all generators of electricity either to produce a specified minimum percentage of power from renewable sources or to buy "renewable energy credits" from other producers that exceed the minimum level. The level would be set initially at 2 percent and rise to 4 percent by 2010.

Some experts believe market forces may in the long run help hold down consumption of electricity and therefore reduce environmental impacts. "You're going to see the development of technologies that use power more efficiently," Bohi says. "In some ways, a lot less power needs to be used than right now because people are going to be a lot more inclined toward conservation in the brave new world than they are now."

Should regulators allow electric utilities to recover "stranded costs" from outmoded power plants?

The issue of stranded costs sounds at first like an abstruse regulatory dispute, but the question carries a multibillion dollar price tag for electric utilities. "No other restructuring issue stacks up against stranded costs for . . . dollar signs with lots of zeros attached," notes a primer on restructuring published by Resources for the Future. [4]

The estimates of "stranded costs" vary widely — from a low of $20 billion (the American Public Power Association) to as much as $200 billion or even higher. [5] Whatever the exact figure, utilities insist that they should be allowed to recover these costs because of what they call the "regulatory compact" that has governed the electric power industry for most of the 20th century.

"There ought to be an opportunity to recover the sunk costs that we invested in order to serve our customers," says Thomas J. Dennis, a Washington-based vice president of Edison International, the parent company of Southern California Edison.

"It's a question of honoring past commitments," says Owens of the Edison Electric Institute.

Lining up with the utilities on the issue are the emerging independent power producers, who fear that stranded costs could derail competition proposals or tie up restructuring in protracted litigation. "I think it's a deal-breaking issue," says Burton of the Electric Power Supply Association. "If it's not properly resolved, you're going to see litigation for the next 10 years."

Some consumer groups counter that the utilities are simply asking for a "bailout." They say utilities made colossal mistakes in building billion-dollar nuclear plants and in overestimating the generating capacity needed. "We don't favor the bailout of any [operation] that can't stand on its own feet in this competitive market," says Public Citizen's Higley.

Industrial users are taking a middle ground, saying utilities should bear some but not all of the costs. "The only way to move from the regulated monopoly system to a competitive system is to look at each of these uneconomic assets and ask who is responsible," says Elcon's Anderson. "If the utility was responsible for those mistakes, most of those costs should fall on the utility," Anderson says. But customers should bear at least some of the costs, he says, "if it's demonstrated that [a public utility commission] or federal law required a utility to make an investment that was later shown to be uneconomic."

So far, consumer groups that oppose stranded cost recovery are disappointed with state action and federal proposals on the issue. The Clinton administration called for stranded cost recovery in the president's 1996 economic report. [6] The Federal Energy Regulatory Commission's ruling in April 1996, which required utili-

* Retail competition proposals were adopted by public utility commissions in three other states: Arizona, New York and Massachusetts.

ties to allow wholesale competition, authorizes the states to permit recovery of stranded costs. Rep. Schaefer's bill in the last session of Congress also would have left the question to state regulators.

At the state level, all four states that have passed restructuring legislation have included provisions to permit some stranded cost recovery. "So far, the way it's been resolved is that stranded costs are being passed through" to consumers, says Rothschild of Citizen Action. "The shareholders aren't paying dime one."

Some state laws come close to giving the utilities a blank check. Rhode Island's law, for example, mandates full stranded cost recovery; California's provides for a surcharge on electric rates for five years to recover the costs. But the New Hampshire and Pennsylvania laws both give the state public utility commissions authority to determine what "just and reasonable" stranded costs the utilities will be allowed to recover. "We are authorized in the statute to award [the utilities] anything from zero to 100 percent," said Pennsylvania PUC member John Hanger. [7]

Still, utility companies insist they are entitled to recover the costs and warn that the issue could stymie any moves toward competition in the industry. "Without some position on stranded recovery, there is not going to be a deal," says Edison International's Dennis. "Utilities are going to fight for the right to recover costs for the investments they made on behalf of their customers." ■

BACKGROUND

Politics and Electricity

Electricity became a politically charged issue in the United States from the moment it began to move out of the laboratory and into America's streets, businesses and homes. Initially, private electric lighting companies competed vigorously — and often corruptly — for municipal markets. At the same time, some cities moved to provide electric power themselves, initiating the long political battle between private and public power companies. The combined threats of economic competition and public power then led the industry itself to call for the system of state regulation that has prevailed since the early 1900s, accepting public oversight in return for a government-protected territorial monopoly. [8]

The father of the U.S. electric industry was Thomas Alva Edison, a prolific inventor and shrewd businessman. Edison followed his invention of the incandescent light bulb in 1879 with the building of a central power station in New York's financial district in 1882. Although other electric pioneers had built street lighting systems in London in 1878, Cleveland in 1879 and San Francisco in 1880, Edison's Pearl Street station was the first to demonstrate the use of electricity to illuminate offices. And with Edison's fame and financial backing, the Edison Electric Illuminating Co. — forerunner of today's Consolidated Edison Co. in New York — became the model of the electric utility industry: a central power station transmitting electric current to thousands of customers, generating reliable and growing revenue for the operating company.

Edison's administrative assistant, Samuel Insull, was as significant as Edison for the industry's development. In the mid-1880s, Insull used his financial and political skills to win contracts for the Edison company to build power stations in some 20 cities and towns. But the Edison company had a rival: municipal power systems, urged by reform-minded leaders who saw electricity as a public good that should be publicly controlled and provided to the public at the lowest possible cost. The idea proved politically appealing. By the late 1890s, public power systems were growing much faster than private power companies.

To counter the trend, Insull in 1898 put forth an audacious proposal: eliminate competition through government regulation. Speaking to a power industry convention, he declared that competition was "economically wrong." Electricity was a natural monopoly, he said, and competition only drove up costs. The best service for the lowest possible cost, he said, could be achieved only through "exclusive control of a given territory" — to be guaranteed by a state regulatory body.

Insull's proposal was first scorned but then embraced by the industry. It also fit in well with the Progressive Era's belief in government decision-making by supposedly politically neutral experts. In 1907, Wisconsin and New York became the first states to create state utility commissions. By 1921, all the states except Delaware had followed suit. The result matched Insull's hopes: The growth of public power was stunted, competition between private companies all but ended and regulators proved to be either unable or unwilling to control rates charged to customers.

But Insull's ambition brought about his downfall. He had established in Chicago the first model for a web of holding companies that by the end of the 1920s controlled 85 percent of the country's electric power. The companies aggressively marketed stock to small investors, but they were speculative bubbles waiting to burst. Insull had overextended, and when the banks called his loans, his companies collapsed, touching off a wave of failures that left investors with nearly worthless stock, threw 90 electric or gas companies into receivership and forced the companies to write down $600 million in debt. Insull himself fled the country.*

* Insull was brought back to the United States in 1934, tried for mail fraud and embezzlement, and acquitted on all counts.

Insull's failure was seized on by the Democratic Party's 1932 presidential nominee, Franklin D. Roosevelt, a long-time proponent of public power. In a campaign speech in Portland, Ore., he said Insull's failure demonstrated the need for more effective regulation of utility companies and for government ownership and operation of electric power systems. As president, Roosevelt made good on both promises.

In his first 100 days, he won Congress' approval to create the Tennessee Valley Authority, a quasi-public corporation that grew from a handful of hydroelectric dams to become the country's leading producer of electricity. In 1937, Congress approved Roosevelt's proposal to create the Bonneville Power Administration in the Pacific Northwest to sell the electricity produced by federally constructed dams on the Columbia River. Two years earlier, Roosevelt had created by executive order the Rural Electrification Administration (REA) to provide financing for rural electric cooperatives to bring electricity to unserved areas in the country's farmlands.

Roosevelt also fought for the passage of two centerpieces of federal regulation of electric utilities. The Public Utility Holding Company Act of 1935 forced the breakup of the interlocking electric power concerns. The law essentially gave the Securities and Exchange Commission power to require utilities to confine themselves to electric power transmission and distribution within a defined geographic area and to limit transactions with any parent company. In addition, the Federal Power Act of 1935 gave the Federal Power Commission, the forerunner of the FERC, authority to oversee interstate transmission of electricity and to regulate wholesale electric power rates.

The two laws resulted in the pattern of vertically integrated companies operating within a state's boundaries facing state regulation of rates to retail customers and limited federal regulation of rates for bulk power sales between utilities. Into the 1960s, the pattern was thought to be serving the country well. Electricity was abundant, the companies appeared to be well managed and prices were thought to be low — in fact, were low by comparison with other countries.

Confidence in the electric power industry was so great that when science brought forth a new power source — nuclear energy — Congress hesitated only a moment before turning it over to private industry. Despite a few skeptics, the public generally appeared to believe nuclear power advocates' promises that the new technology could provide cheap and abundant power, safely and reliably, for years to come. And confidence remained unshaken even when the country experienced a series of blackouts in the 1960s, including the "great Northeastern blackout" of 1965, which left much of New York and New England without electricity for up to 13 hours. "Live Better Electrically," the industry's advertising campaign promised, and the country seemed to agree.

Shocks to the System

The golden era of electricity ended in the 1970s, when the system suffered a series of shocks, some external and some of the industry's own making. The combined effects drove up costs while consumer prices were already increasing, made regulators more wary of approving rate increases, created new environmental hurdles for utilities and provoked more critical public scrutiny of utility management.

The most dramatic of the changes was the 1973 oil embargo by the Organization of Petroleum Exporting Countries (OPEC), which caused a sudden and unanticipated tripling in oil prices within the United States. Since oil fueled many electric power plants, utilities began filing for rate increases; there were a record 212 requests totaling $4.5 billion in 1974 alone. State public utility commissions typically reduced the amounts requested, but the resulting increases still rankled inflation-weary consumers and depressed demand for electricity.

But increased demand had been the strategy, indeed, the prerequisite, for the industry's economic well-being ever since Edison. Demand growth was especially significant given the industry's increased reliance on larger and more expensive power plants. And the interest rate hikes of the early 1970s made financing all the more expensive, adding to the economic pressures on an ever more capital-intensive industry.

The major reason for the industry's increased capital needs was its nuclear power program. Spurred by presidents belonging to both political parties, the electric utility industry had been aggressively pursuing and promoting nuclear energy since the 1950s. The public, lulled by such reassuring media messages as Walt Disney Co.'s documentary "Our Friend the Atom," looked on with general approval. But as the utilities moved to build nuclear reactors, they encountered local and then nationwide resistance. Opposition from New York City residents in the early 1960s forced Consolidated Edison to drop plans for one of its first reactors, which had been planned for a site in Queens. California utilities met stiff opposition from residents who feared for the safety of the plants in the event of earthquakes.

The anti-nuclear campaigns did not have an immediate effect. President Richard M. Nixon in 1970 called for 1,000 nuclear plants to produce 50 percent of the nation's electricity by 2000. A record 41 new plants were begun in 1973. But opposition on a variety of environmental, safety and economic grounds grew and became more tenacious. Nuclear plant opponents brought a steady stream of regulatory and legal challenges, forcing utilities to justify and often to make expensive

Continued on p. 38

Chronology

1800s *Scientists in Europe and the United States master the basic principles of electricity. Inventors begin using electricity to light streets and offices, power factories and run streetcars.*

1882
Thomas A. Edison builds the Pearl Street electric power station in New York City.

1898
Samuel Insull, Edison's administrative assistant and a financial "pioneer" of the electric industry, proposes state regulation of power companies to eliminate "vicious competition."

1900-1965 *The states establish public utility regulatory plans, giving electric power companies territorial monopolies in exchange for rate regulation.*

1907
Wisconsin and New York become the first states to establish public commissions to regulate private power companies. All the states except Delaware follow by 1921.

1935
Congress passes Public Utilities Holding Company Act, which forces the breakup of interlocking electric power concerns, and the Federal Power Act, which gives the Federal Power Commission authority to regulate wholesale electric power rates.

1954
Congress passes Atomic Energy Act, permitting private power companies to use nuclear energy.

1965
Much of New York State and New England lose electricity for up to 13 hours in the country's worst power blackout.

1966-1979 *Energy prices rise in the wake of an international oil embargo; the federal government pushes conservation and the development of "renewable resources."*

1973
Electric utilities face sudden cost increases after a worldwide embargo by the Organization of Petroleum Exporting Countries.

1978
The Public Utilities Regulatory Policies Act (PURPA) includes a provision requiring utilities to buy power from producers using renewable energy sources.

1979
Accident at Three Mile Island nuclear plant in Pennsylvania shakes public confidence in nuclear power.

1980s *Independent electric power companies establish a toehold in the market. Free-market advocates push for deregulation.*

1988
Federal Energy Regulatory Commission (FERC) proposes to widen competition in wholesale electric power sales but backs off after widespread opposition.

1990s *The drive for competition in electric power expands.*

1992
Energy Policy Act allows power producers to seek approval from the FERC to compete to sell large quantities of electricity to utilities.

April 24, 1996
The FERC issues Order 888 requiring utilities to open transmission lines to competing wholesale electric generators.

May 16, 1996
New York State Public Service Commission orders state's utilities to introduce retail access to all customers by early 1998.

May 28, 1996
New Hampshire launches two-year program to allow competition in residential and business markets for electricity. One week earlier, Gov. Stephen Merrill signs legislation mandating retail competition statewide by Jan. 1, 1998 — prior to completion of pilot program.

July 11, 1996
Rep. Dan Schaefer, R-Colo., introduces bill to require states to permit retail competition by Dec. 15, 2000. No action is taken, but similar bill is planned for new Congress.

Sept. 23, 1996
Gov. Pete Wilson, R-Calif., signs measure to permit retail competition for electricity beginning Jan. 1, 1998. Rhode Island adopts similar measure Aug. 7; Pennsylvania follows Dec. 3.

December 1996
Regulators in Arizona and Massachusetts adopt rules to phase in retail competition.

Electric Industry Restructuring: State by State

Alabama	Law signed May 6, 1996, discourages competition by authorizing Public Service Commission to impose costs on any retail customer that switches suppliers
Alaska	Public Utilities Commission studying plans for more efficient power pooling; retail competition on back burner
Arizona	Corporation Commission adopted rule Dec. 23 to phase in retail competition over four-year period beginning Jan. 1, 1999; rule does not guarantee stranded cost recovery
Arkansas	No activity
California	Restructuring law signed Sept. 23 requires retail competition beginning Jan. 1, 1998; provides 10 percent rate reduction but also assures stranded cost recovery; requires three major utilities to divest 50 percent of generating capacity; establishes independent system operator; preserves energy conservation and low-income assistance programs through 2001
Colorado	Legislature likely to consider issue this session; retail competition bill withdrawn last year
Connecticut	Legislative task force on restructuring issued background report in late December
Delaware	Public Service Commission has held public forums on restructuring and competition
District of Columbia	Public Service Commission is studying merger of Potomac Electric Power Co. and Baltimore Gas & Electric Co.; restructuring and competition on back burner
Florida	Legislative subcommittee on March 13, 1996, defeated bill to require state regulators to study "retail wheeling"
Georgia	Retail wheeling bill died in legislative committee March 8, 1996
Hawaii	No activity
Idaho	Public Utility Commission on Aug. 16 rejected competition proposal as "not feasible or desirable at this time"
Illinois	Commerce Commission authorized two limited retail wheeling pilot programs in March 1996; legislature likely to consider rival proposals this spring
Indiana	Utility Regulatory Commission on Sept. 27 denied request by largest utility to allow some commercial and industrial customers to choose suppliers
Iowa	Utilities Board due to issue report on restructuring in late January after series of public meetings last year; board not expected to submit restructuring legislation this session
Kansas	Legislative task force issued interim informational report on Jan. 13; law signed in April 1996 provides for three-year moratorium on retail wheeling
Kentucky	No formal activity
Louisiana	Public Service Commission is conducting inquiry on restructuring and competition, but no hearings have been held or scheduled
Maine	Public Utilities Commission adopted report on Dec. 31 calling on legislature to introduce retail choice for all customers beginning in 2000
Maryland	Public Service Commission on Oct. 9 initiated new study of restructuring; report due May 31
Massachusetts	Department of Public Utilities issued proposal Dec. 30 that would permit retail competition to begin Jan. 1, 1998, and called for authorizing legislation; rules would allow stranded cost recovery, but would require utilities to get rid of all generating facilities
Michigan	Public Service Commission is holding hearings on plan introduced Dec. 19 to phase in competition, beginning in 1997
Minnesota	Report by Public Utilities Commission work group on restructuring due in late January; legislature expected to consider issue this session, but action viewed as unlikely
Mississippi	Public Service Commission opened restructuring inquiry in August after rejecting proposal by biggest utility to go slow on competition; public hearings scheduled in April

Missouri	No current activity; Public Service Commission may open restructuring inquiry soon
Montana	Montana Power is backing bill to phase in retail competition 1998-2001
Nebraska	Legislative committee opening three-year study of competition issues; Nebraska is only state that has no investor-owned utilities and no statewide regulation of electric rates
Nevada	Public Service Commission adopted report June 13 saying retail competition could benefit Nevada but issue was for legislature to decide; lawmakers may take up issue this session
New Hampshire	Law signed May 21, 1996, requires retail customer choice statewide by Jan. 1, 1998; limited, two-year pilot program instituted May 28; Public Utility Commission holding hearings on stranded cost recovery, with report due in late February
New Jersey	Board of Public Utilities was to act on Jan. 16 on plan that calls for full-scale wholesale competition and phased-in retail competition
New Mexico	Public Utility Commission received staff report on restructuring on Jan. 10; retail competition bills have previously failed in legislature, but new effort likely in upcoming session
New York	Public Service Commission on May 16, 1996, ordered state's utilities to introduce retail access by 1998; utilities have filed plans but are also challenging commission's authority in court
North Carolina	Public Utility Commission in July 1995 rejected petition to open inquiry on retail competition
North Dakota	Public Service Commission opened general restructuring inquiry in September
Ohio	Retail competition bill introduced in March 1996, but failed to advance; Public Utilities Commission has approved limited restructuring steps
Oklahoma	Legislative task force on restructuring revived in fall 1996 after period of inactivity; competition proposal failed previously
Oregon	Public Utility Commission has asked utilities to submit plans for retail choice pilot programs
Pennsylvania	Law signed Dec. 3 provides for retail competition for all customers to be phased in from 1999 to 2001; Public Utility Commission to determine stranded cost recovery; no divestiture
Rhode Island	Law signed Aug. 7 mandates retail competition to begin July 1 and to be completed by July 1, 1998; act allows full recovery of stranded costs; requires utilities to divest 15 percent of generating capacity; preserves environmental and low-income assistance programs
South Carolina	Industrial users' group will lobby for legislation this session; Public Service Commission in 1995 rejected proposal to study retail competition
South Dakota	No current activity
Tennessee	No activity
Texas	Public Utility Commission report on restructuring, due Jan. 15, was to lay out range of options for legislature to consider in upcoming session; 1995 law opened up wholesale competition
Utah	Public Service Commission restructuring work group recommends go-slow approach on retail competition in report due Jan. 17; industrial users will lobby legislature for retail access
Vermont	Public Service Board on Dec. 30 adopted report calling on legislature to permit retail competition for all customers beginning in 1998; legislature to take up issue this session
Virginia	State Corporation Commission report adopted on Aug. 5 recommended moving slowly on restructuring and customer choice
Washington	Utilities and Transportation Commission has approved proposals for direct-access pilot programs from state's three investor-owned utilities; no full-scale retail competition proposals pending
West Virginia	No activity
Wisconsin	Public Service Commission is pressing utilities to create statewide independent system operator; legislature has urged commission to go slow on retail competition
Wyoming	Public Service Commission approved white paper on Nov. 12 calling for creation of broad-based steering committee to study economic impact of restructuring

Note: Information in chart is current through mid-January 1997

U.S. Electric Industry Depends Heavily on Coal

More than half of the electricity generated in the U.S. comes from coal-fired plants. Nuclear power, natural gas and hydroelectric power all provide significant amounts, but less than 1 percent comes from wind, solar and other alternative energy sources.

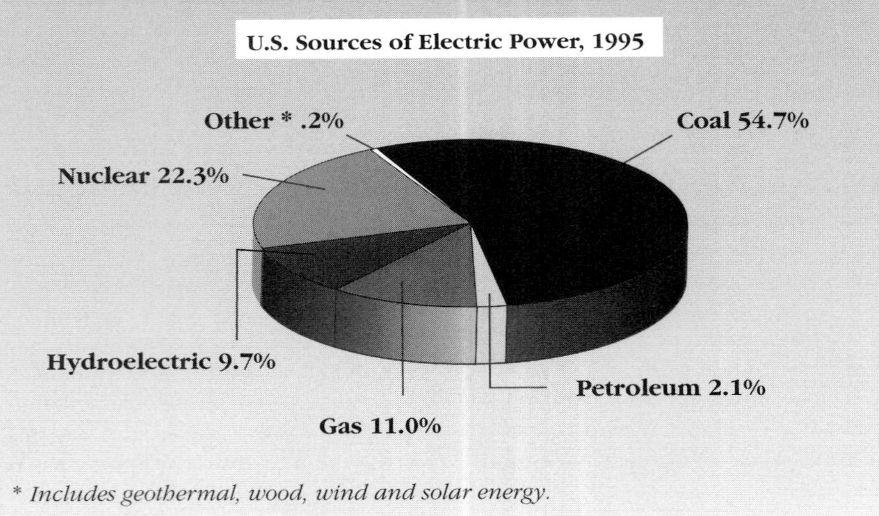

* *Includes geothermal, wood, wind and solar energy.*

Source: Energy Information Administration

Continued from p. 34

modifications to nuclear plants. Costs of building and operating nuclear plants rose sharply, especially after the mishap at the Three Mile Island plant in Pennsylvania in 1979, which heightened regulatory oversight even further. [9] The industry continued to defend nuclear power, but it also began to back away. More than 100 nuclear plant projects were canceled between 1972 and 1984, and no new plants were started after 1978.

The economic pressures revealed that the industry was by no means as well-managed or as well-regulated as had been thought. "Some utilities did a very good job of coping with those factors while others didn't," Anderson says. "Their prices went up and went up dramatically. And the common knowledge was that it didn't matter because the customers had nowhere to go."

Conservation Moves

President Jimmy Carter came to the White House in 1977 determined to "solve" the energy crisis by reducing the country's dependence on foreign oil, promoting energy conservation and efficiency, and encouraging the development of new energy sources — including the so-called renewable resources: solar, wind and geothermal. Congress rejected many parts of Carter's legislative program and weakened many others. But three of the measures it approved helped lay the groundwork for opening up the electric power industry.

The most important of the new laws was the Public Utilities Regulatory Policies Act of 1978 (PURPA). The law requires utilities to buy power produced by small projects using renewable sources of power and by co-generators, industrial plants that use steam to produce electricity. The law also props up the price paid to these so-called "qualifying facilities" by requiring utilities to pay what it would cost them to generate the same amount of power at their own plants. In effect, the law forced the major utilities to create a favorable market for a new class of electric power generators.

The effect of the law was strengthened by two other measures also passed in 1978. In the name of energy independence, the Power Plant and Industrial Fuel Use Act forbade the use of oil or natural gas in new power plants. And the Energy Tax Act provided a 10 percent credit to generators using geothermal, wind, solar or other renewable energy sources.

Combined with the economic pressures utilities faced in constructing new power plants, the laws helped stimulate the growth of a new electric power sector: independent generators. While the non-utility generators provide only about 7 percent of total U.S. output, they have been the industry's fastest growing sector. In 1994, they accounted for 60 percent of new capacity. [10]

Opening Up the System

The drive for competition in the electric power industry began gathering steam in the 1980s, fueled by politics and by economics. But opposition from utility companies thwarted federal regulators' first attempt to permit competition in the wholesale market. With growing political support, however, Congress in 1992 set the stage for mandating wholesale competition. And the states were also moving on the issue, with several states adopting plans to permit retail competition and many others seriously considering it.

The movement toward deregulation and competition gained visibility and influence under President Ronald Reagan, who appointed free-market advocates to posts in his administration and at regulatory agencies, including the Federal Energy Regulatory Commission. Equally important for the electric industry, utility companies themselves encouraged the birth of a competitive power production sector. The big utilities faced rising construction costs for new plants, and state regulators were reviewing those costs more carefully, and in some instances disallowing them. As a result, utility companies turned increasingly to non-utility generators, buying power to sell to their retail customers rather than producing it themselves.

In 1988, the FERC proposed a rule to allow utilities to sell power on a wholesale basis outside their service areas. The rule was strongly pushed by Martha Hesse, a free-market advocate named by Reagan to head the commission in 1986. "Electric generation may no longer be a monopoly in all markets," Hesse told a congressional committee in September 1987. [11] But the rule, formally issued in 1988, was shelved after utility companies and many other groups filed what Elcon's Anderson recalls today as "roomfuls of comments" in opposition.

Four years later, however, the political climate in Congress was more favorable toward competition. Environmentalists as well as the public power and rural electric co-op lobbies shifted to favor competition in the wholesale market, leaving the utility companies almost alone in their resistance. So Congress included in the omnibus Energy Policy Act of 1992 two provisions to foster competition in the electric industry. One provision lifted restrictions contained in the 1935 holding-company law in order to allow new, independent electricity-generating companies, called "exempt wholesale generators," to sell power to utilities. In addition, the law directed the FERC to adopt a regulation requiring utilities to open their electrical transmission lines to all sellers of electricity.

The commission adopted the rule (Order 888) on April 24, 1996, after three years of sorting out an array of technical and substantive issues. Independent power generators were satisfied with the provisions to ensure access to transmission lines on a nondiscriminatory basis. But utilities won an important victory on the stranded-cost issue. The order provides that utilities can recover any "prudently incurred" costs on power plants if their customers move to other suppliers.

As for consumers, the commission's chair, Elizabeth A. Moler, said the move to permit competition in the wholesale power market could mean "billions of dollars" in savings every year. [12] The commission went out of its way to stress, however, that its order left the question of permitting retail competition up to the states.

Movement in the States

By the time of the federal action, most states were already at least looking at the issue. And a few states — all with higher than average electric rates — were moving decisively toward opening up their electric power markets to direct competition for customers.

In New Hampshire, the move toward competition came against a background of simmering discontent with high rates and a protracted battle over the Seabrook nuclear power plant, owned by the state's dominant utility, Public Service Co. of New Hampshire (PSNH). [13] The state legislature and the Public Utility Commission (PUC) both began moving to permit retail competition in 1995. With bipartisan support, the legislature adopted a law in June 1995 directing the PUC to set up a retail competition experiment by May 1996. Meanwhile, the PUC was fighting a court battle with PSNH, which claimed the commission had no authority to permit new power suppliers to enter the market.

The state Supreme Court rejected the utility's plea in a ruling on May 13. In the meantime, the legislature had gone further and passed a law mandating retail competition statewide, beginning Jan. 1, 1998. The state's Republican governor, Stephen Merrill, signed the bill into law on May 21. A week later, after obtaining approval from the FERC, the state PUC initiated its retail competition pilot program, inviting 17,000 of the state's electric customers to participate in the country's first broad-scale experiment in a competitive electric power marketplace. ■

CURRENT SITUATION

Growing Competition

When the Maryland Public Service Commission first looked at the idea of retail competition for electricity, it decided to pass up the opportunity. Electric power rates were so low in the state, the five-member commission said in its August 1995 report, that there was "no need for dramatic fixes at this time."

But the commission is now planning to take a second look. In a six-page order issued Oct. 9, 1996, the commission directed its staff to "study and make recommendations as to how Maryland electric customers can best benefit from developing competitive markets for electric services."

"Things are moving very quickly," Commissioner Gerald Thorpe explains. "There's a very strong current, almost of inevitability, for deregulation of the electric industry."

Maryland now joins the vast majority of states to have some kind of active proceeding or study relating to opening up electric power markets to competition. But supporters of competition who depict the trend as inevitable are, at best, premature. Most states that have examined the issue so far have either rejected moves toward competition, adopted half-steps or put the issue on hold while waiting to see what happens in other states. (*See chart, pp. 36-37.*)

Seven states, however, have acted within the past year to permit retail competition for electric power on a statewide basis. Besides New Hampshire, four others are in the Northeast. Rhode

Island and Pennsylvania both enacted laws mandating retail competition, to begin in July in Rhode Island and Jan. 1, 1999, in Pennsylvania. In New York, the state's Public Utility Commission in May approved a plan calling for retail competition to begin early next year. And the Massachusetts Department of Public Utilities issued a detailed proposal Dec. 30 that calls for retail competition to begin on Jan. 1, 1998.

Meanwhile, California is scheduled to open its $20 billion electric power market — the country's largest — to retail competition over the next five years. The complex plan, signed into law by Republican Gov. Pete Wilson on Sept. 23, won unanimous approval in the legislature in late August after negotiations that gave the state's big utilities a big victory on stranded costs while promising residential and small commercial customers a 20 percent rate reduction by 2002.

The law imposes a three-year surcharge on electricity — called a "competitive transition charge" — on all customers to allow utilities to recover about $30 billion in stranded costs. Residential and small commercial customers will get a 10 percent rate reduction beginning in 1998, but it will be financed by so-called "rate reduction bonds" to be paid off as part of their rates over a 10-year period.

The state's big utilities — Pacific Gas & Electric, Edison International and Enova — all voiced satisfaction with the plan. But consumers' groups were less pleased. Elcon's Anderson said it was unfair to require consumers to pay 100 percent of stranded costs. Robert Finkelstein, attorney for the California consumer group Toward Utility Rate Normalization (TURN), called the rate cut for smaller customers "a sham." "We'll still be paying the same amount overall" as larger customers, Finkelstein says, "just under different financing terms — 10 years instead of five years."

The California plan also calls for the establishment of an "independent system operator" (ISO) to run the electric power grid within the state. That feature is designed to ensure all electric power producers non-discriminatory access to the grid, which will nonetheless still be owned by the established utilities. The plan also continues funding for energy conservation, low-income programs and development of renewable resources such as solar power.

Three other states acted on restructuring plans in December. In Arizona, the state's Corporation Commission on Dec. 23 approved a plan to phase in retail competition over a four-year period beginning on Jan. 1, 1999. Parts of the plan require implementing legislation — notably, how to include the Salt River Project, a big public utility that serves Phoenix and surrounding areas, in the new competitive marketplace. Later in the month, state regulators in Vermont and Maine adopted reports calling on their state legislatures to pass legislation to introduce retail competition — beginning Jan. 1, 1998, in Vermont, and in the year 2000 in Maine.

Elsewhere around the country, however, restructuring proposals are moving at a slower pace. Some states have rejected competition outright, at least for the time being. In Florida, for example, a legislative subcommittee killed a restructuring proposal in March 1996, fearful that "upsetting" the electric power market could disrupt the state's economic growth. In other states — including Oregon and Washington — regulators are approving plans for utilities to test competition on a small scale while they continue to study the issue.

In many states, the major electric utilities are helping to slow the process. Owens of the Edison Electric Institute says restructuring should proceed on a gradual, state-by-state basis. "We can gain a lot of insight from what's happening" in the states that have already approved restructuring plans, he says. "We can learn a lot from those experiences."

Despite the delays, however, a Washington lobbyist for the organization of state regulators says competition is sure to come. "It's an inevitable fact that restructuring at the retail level is going to happen," says John Gawronski, director of congressional relations for the National Association of Regulatory Utility Commissioners (NARUC). "Customers want cheaper power, and regulators want to give it to them."

Power Marketing

For newly emerging independent power providers, New Hampshire's two-year experiment in retail competition offers a low-cost opportunity to learn how to reach and win customers in the new electricity marketplace. For participating customers — who prior to the experiment faced average rates of 11.7 cents per kilowatt hour, highest in the nation [14] — the experiment has produced real savings. Residential and small business consumers have seen savings of 15-20 percent, according to Frank at the state Public Utility Commission, while some industrial users have saved more than 20 percent.

But consumer advocates, state officials and some electric power marketers caution that the experiment may give residential and small business customers an unrealistic picture of the cost savings that are likely to be seen as retail competition spreads. "We're seeing a market in the pilot [program] that's not going to be indicative of the prices in full competition," Frank says.

As part of the pilot program, the state commission negotiated an agreement with the existing four electric utilities that effectively gave participants in the experiment an assured 10 percent rate cut on top of any savings from competition. The power suppliers then offered rates that company officials themselves acknowledge are below market price.

George Gantz, president of Unitil

Continued on p. 43

At Issue:

Should Congress require the states to permit competition in providing electric power to all customers, including residential users?

JOHN ANDERSON
Executive Director, Electricity Consumers Resource Council, which represents large industrial users of electricity. It has lobbied for competition in the electric power industry at the federal and state levels.

WRITTEN FOR *THE CQ RESEARCHER*, JANUARY 1996.

yes

Of all the claims and assertions made in the debate on electric restructuring, perhaps none has less merit than the charge that the issue is one solely of state jurisdiction, that the federal government has no (or only a minimal) role, and that there should not be a federal date certain by which all states have to adopt a plan embodying customer choice.

We might as well make the national highway system, and everything on it, exclusively the states' to own and operate.

In a very simple way, the evolution of the electricity market mirrors the evolution of the overall economy of our nation. When Thomas Edison first started his Pearl Street generating station in 1882, the electricity was generated in New York and it stayed in New York. As electricity spread across the country, utilities operated within the bounds of one state. Gradually the industry grew, and utilities operated in more than one state with several large holding companies operating virtually across the nation.

It soon became clear that electricity was interstate commerce, that companies operated in more than one state and that electrons generated in one state were used to light up homes and businesses in another.

Utilities have historically been regulated by both state and federal bodies, providing a hodge-podge of sometimes ambiguous rules as to what aspects of electricity are considered interstate — and theoretically subject to federal rules — and which aspects are intrastate, and therefore subject to state regulations. This confusing web of regulation is one reason that prices for electricity vary so tremendously, sometimes producing 70 percent or 80 percent price differentials within a single state.

Electricity for the most part is clearly interstate commerce. If electricity consumers in each and every state are to benefit from restructuring, consumers in each state must be given the right to choose their supplier of electricity and electricity services. Certainly, each state should have the right to develop its own regulations. But, if a state fails to act, should the customers in that state be penalized? Should they be denied the right to choose? Or, put more crassly, should they be beholden to a monopoly that has no incentive whatsoever to provide lower rates and better service? Of course not.

ROBERT K. JOHNSON
Executive Director, Electric Consumers' Alliance, which represents a wide range of consumer groups on electric industry restructuring issues. It was founded in 1994 with start-up funds from the Edison Electric Institute, the trade association representing private, investor-owned utilities.

WRITTEN FOR *THE CQ RESEARCHER*, JANUARY 1996.

no

Geography is not all that separates Idaho from New Hampshire. The two states are miles apart when it comes to electric restructuring policy as well. But from their differing experiences emerges a valuable lesson for those promoting a federal preemptive approach.

New Hampshire has embraced — and is in the process of implementing — a retail access structure. Idaho, on the other hand, has determined that retail access is not in the best interests of its consumers at this time because of the likelihood that it would lead to increased rates and diminished service quality.

The cases of New Hampshire and Idaho provide a real-world illustration of the potentially disparate impact of any federal decision to preempt the states on electric industry restructuring. In New Hampshire, like most of the Northeast, consumers pay electric rates that are much higher than the country on average.

By contrast, Idaho regulators find their state on the opposite end of the curve. Idaho enjoys the country's lowest rates, largely because of abundant hydroelectric resources and low-cost coal supplies. If Idaho consumers were suddenly forced to pay electric rates based upon a national average or some other market index, there would be dramatic rate increases.

New Hampshire and Idaho are a microcosm of the nation as a whole. Their experiences confirm that a decision by Congress to mandate competition in all states by some specific date would prevent some states from making decisions that are in the best interests of their consumers. It is much too early to determine whether one state's conclusions are right while the others are wrong, much less to mandate a given result to the nation as a whole.

It would be a tragedy if Congress were to dismiss the vital role of states in experimenting and developing electric restructuring policy. These issues are complex and cannot be addressed through simplistic approaches. Hopefully, in the coming months, those who think they have the answer will begin asking the right questions and, hopefully, they will begin by looking at New Hampshire and Idaho.

'Merger Mania' in Electric Utilities: What Effect on Consumers?

When Baltimore Gas & Electric Co. and Potomac Electric Power Co. announced plans to merge in September 1995, officials of the two companies said the marriage could help the utilities hold down rates and improve service. But consumer representatives and federal and state regulators are holding up the merger, questioning the claimed benefits and warning of its impact on future competition in the electric power industry.

The proposed merger of the two neighboring utilities — Pepco serves Washington, D.C., and the Maryland suburbs, BG&E serves Baltimore and the surrounding area — exemplifies the wave of corporate marriages that has been sweeping the electric power industry over the past decade. Investor-owned utilities are merging with other electric utilities, sometimes with a partner in an adjoining area, sometimes with a company farther away. Electric utilities are also attractive merger partners for other energy companies — in particular, companies in the booming natural gas industry.

For the companies, the mergers are viewed as a way of combining strengths and shaving costs as the industry braces for the anticipated arrival of retail competition in the electric power marketplace. Smaller utilities seek out desirable merger partners to avoid being taken over in less friendly acquisitions.

For consumers, proponents say the mergers will bring about lower rates by promoting efficiency in an industry that they say has too many companies.

The current structure "makes no sense," says Edward Tirello, a longtime electric industry analyst with the New York-based brokerage firm NatWest Securities. "Except for the United States, nowhere else do we have so many integrated companies so closely connected. In most countries of the world, there is a national grid and a national power company."

But opponents and critics say the wave of mergers is more likely to hurt than to help consumers. "I think you need more [companies] rather than less," says Charlie Higley, a policy analyst with Public Citizen, a public interest group affiliated with Ralph Nader. "If you look at each piece of the market, it's dominated by a monopoly. Right now, customers don't have choice, and the question is whether you will have true choice in the future."

"A lot of the people are skeptical of the benefits of merging," says Mark Frankena, an economist and former antitrust official in the Federal Trade Commission (FTC), who is now a Washington-based consultant with the firm Economists, Inc. "If there are benefits, a lot of them could be achieved by merging utilities that are not close competitors — for example, utilities in different parts of the country."

Some mergers do combine utilities from distant locations — like the proposed combination a few years ago of Sierra Pacific Power in Nevada and Washington Water Power (WWP). More commonly, however, mergers involve utilities that serve adjacent areas — like the proposed Pepco-BG&E merger or a series of mergers since 1990 that have reduced the number of utilities in Iowa from seven to three.

Most recently, electric utilities and natural gas companies have moved to join forces to better position themselves for the anticipated arrival of competition in electric power. Enron Corp., a Houston-based company that has evolved from a natural gas pipeline concern into an aggressive wholesale electric power marketer, inked a deal in July to merge with the Oregon-based electric utility Portland General Corp. Three big electric-gas mergers were announced over the next four months: Houston Industries Inc., with Houston-based NorAm Energy Corp., in August; Southern California Gas with San Diego Gas & Electric in October; and Duke Power Co., the giant North and South Carolina utility, with PanEnergy Co., a natural gas pipeline concern, in November.

Utility mergers typically require approval both from state regulators and from the Federal Energy Regulatory Commission (FERC). Regulators have blocked a few proposed mergers — notably, the planned consolidation a few years ago of Southern California Edison, which serves Los Angeles and surrounding areas, and San Diego Gas & Electric Co. Some others have been abandoned because of questions or delays in the regulatory process. The Sierra Pacific-WWP merger, for example, was dropped after the FERC announced plans to hold hearings on the combination.

Industry leaders have complained about the regulatory delays for a long time. Last month, in a long-awaited move, the FERC acknowledged the criticisms as it adopted new guidelines for reviewing utility mergers. The changes were designed, the commission said in a news release describing the Dec. 18 action, "to simplify and expedite the processing of merger applications in the new competitive era."

The FERC's year-long review of its merger policy helped hold up action on nine proposed deals valued collectively at $25 billion, including the Enron-Portland General and BG&E-Pepco combinations.[1] Officials of some of the companies involved voiced optimism afterward that the deals would now gain speedy approval. Steven Ross, a lawyer representing BG&E and Pepco, told *The New York Times* he expected the proposed merger "will not raise any problems" under the commission's new guidelines.[2]

But FERC staff previously said the proposed merger posed "a serious threat to competition at both the wholesale and retail levels."[3] And the government office set up to represent consumers before the D.C. Public Service Commission is continuing to oppose the merger. In a letter to *The Washington Post* this month, Elizabeth Noel, People's Counsel for the District of Columbia, said the merger would "stall efforts to introduce competition and lower rates to D.C. utility customers."[4]

---

[1] See *The Wall Street Journal*, Dec. 18, 1996, p. A1.

[2] *The New York Times*, Dec. 19, 1996, p. D5.

[3] See Martha M. Hamilton, "Power Merger Resistance," *The Washington Post*, Dec. 9, 1996, Business Section, p. 1.

[4] *The Washington Post*, Jan. 5, 1996, p. E8.

Continued from p. 40

Resources, an independent power retailer established by the parent company of the state's two smallest utilities, says the result is that consumers were given an unrealistic picture of their own role in a fully competitive market. "The way this played out, with consumers being offered a risk-free opportunity to get a 10 percent cost savings off this bill and maybe some other savings, reinforced the sense that the consumer didn't really have to take any responsibility for this as they will have to do in a real competitive market," Gantz says.

Gantz is also critical of what he calls "the carnival atmosphere" created by the power suppliers' marketing blitz as the pilot program opened in May. Green Mountain Energy Partners, a company that billed itself as environmentally friendly, sent a blue spruce sapling to customers who signed up with it for the pilot. Another "green power" marketer, Working Assets Green Power, promised to donate 1 percent of its revenue to unspecified environmental organizations. Two other companies offered free bird feeders or low-flow showerheads.

Other companies offered a more conventional inducement to lure customers: money. Northeast Utilities, the multistate holding company that owns the state's dominant utility, Public Service Co. of New Hampshire, set up two independent subsidiaries to market power in the pilot program. One of the two, NorthEast Utilities Wholesale Power, offered to waive customers' first month's service charge if they signed up by May 20, eight days before the start of the program. The other, PSNH Energy, mailed out $25 checks as a bonus for signing up. Gantz's own company offered free power for the entire pilot program to 10 of the first 1,000 customers to sign up.

The pilot program has yielded ambiguous evidence about the relative effectiveness of the two marketing pitches expected to emerge in retail competition: green power vs. cheaper power. Dorothy Schnure, a spokesperson for Green Mountain Power, which joined with the government-owned utility Hydro-Quebec and two U.S. and Canadian natural gas companies to market electricity in the pilot program, says the company is satisfied with its strategy of offering environmentally friendly electricity. "What we were offering was not necessarily the lowest price at any cost, but a competitive price and using power in a way that people could feel good about," she says.

But Gantz says his company chose instead to focus on low rates. "We said this was going to be a market price, just as you buy other commodities," Gantz explains. One reason, he adds, is that power suppliers rely on a variety of sources, thus making "green power" pitches inherently misleading. "Every supplier has a portfolio [of power sources]," he explains.

The pilot program is also giving uncertain indications about the potential effectiveness of "aggregating" smaller customers into a single buying unit to try to negotiate lower rates. In Peterborough, the town received bids from a dozen companies when its board of selectmen decided to represent residents chosen to participate in the pilot program. Enron offered the lowest bid for power (not including the cost of transmission): 2.29 cents per kilowatt hour for residential customers, 2.25 cents per kilowatt hour for businesses. The rates are among the lowest being offered in the pilot program. [15] "Aggregation is the only way to go," selectman Leedham says.

The state's Retail Merchants Association similarly acted as "aggregator" for its members and helped secure relatively low rates. But Gantz thinks aggregation will not be widespread. "It worked for Peterborough, and the reason it worked was you had a town and a selectman [Leedham] who invested a great deal of time and energy and thoughtfulness into the process," Gantz says. "The ability of organizations like that to add value without being compensated is an interesting question."

Despite the disagreements about the meaning of the pilot program, state officials say the experiment is yielding one clear lesson: the importance of consumer education in a fully competitive marketplace for electric power. "Just hearing the questions that customers have and the concerns that they have has emphasized the need for broader public education in our restructuring efforts," says PUC attorney Frank.

But Frank quickly adds that the pilot program is also showing that the state's consumers favor competition. "The pilot's been a success given the prices we're seeing and the level of interest we're seeing," he says. "The level of participation says that the customers want this." ■

OUTLOOK

Power Politics

The advocates of competition in the electric power industry envision a flourishing of new services for customers. Electric wires, they say, can be used to provide home security systems or access to the Internet. They also say that competition can bring about more efficient use of electricity — for example, by establishing time-sensitive pricing that encourages customers to reduce their consumption of electricity at peak times of day. And they say that the companies that provide these comfort- and efficiency-enhancing services can make money in the process.

"When you have a situation where a competitor can take away customers, then you have the incentives for providing not only a new set of services, but a better set of services," says Bohi, who in mid-February will become a vice president of Charles River Associates, an economics consulting firm based in Cambridge, Mass. "You have the incentive to establish a system where power is not the entity that is important to the customer, but what the customer derives from the power."

"The incentives for true conservation, for true innovations in the use of power, are yet to come," Bohi concludes, "and they're going to come with retail access."

These 21st-century innovations will not be widely realized, however, until and unless the advocates of competition succeed in some late 20th-century politics. The process of deregulating and restructuring the electric industry has made gains in some states, but the prospects for quick action to create competition on a nationwide basis are at best uncertain.

In Washington, some advocates of competition are retreating from their earlier predictions about the pace of legislation. [16] Given the complexity of the issue, and the array of other matters for Congress to work on, many say broad legislation is unlikely in the new Congress. "I would love to say yes, but realistically I would have to say no," says Anderson of the industrial users' group Elcon.

Others, however, continue to profess guarded optimism about legislation in the current Congress — and determined confidence in the eventual outcome. "I'm comfortable that we will ultimately get legislation," says Burton of the Electric Power Supply Association. "There's a reasonable shot that we will get it out of this Congress."

Around the country, state lawmakers and regulators are opening inquiries, holding hearings and issuing reports about competition for electric power. But the only states to approve competition proposals so far have been those with unusually high rates for electricity.

"Some states have decided it's not such a great idea because they have low-cost rates for power," says Gawronski of the National Association of Regulatory Utility Commissioners. "But those states that have high rates are moving forward — and moving forward pretty boldly."

But Gawronski stresses that state regulators will continue to resist a federal mandate to permit competition. "State regulators want the same benefits, but they just want to look at this," he says. "It is inconceivable to see how a decision in Washington on how to restructure the market anywhere from New Mexico to Oregon to New Hampshire or California can be made without prejudice."

In New Hampshire itself, regulators are rushing to complete the restructuring process by a legislatively imposed deadline of Jan. 1, 1998 — several months before the scheduled end of the current pilot program on retail competition. The state's Public Utility Commission is holding hearings this January on how to deal with the stranded cost issue.

"Some people are arguing that utilities are entitled to no recovery," says staff attorney Frank. "Utilities are arguing they're entitled to full recovery."

The commission's decision is due in late February. Frank says any surcharges imposed to cover the utilities' past costs will take effect next year and last for two years. The ruling will have an impact on how much savings consumers see from retail competition, but Frank has no doubts that customers will benefit from opening up the marketplace.

"For customers, I think that you will see lower prices than ratepayers pay under the current regulatory regime," Frank says. "That will be the result of customers' gaining access to a competitive market where you see efficiency gains."

Suppliers make similar predictions, but Gantz of Unitil Resources cautions that the process will be messy. "We're going to see a very competitive market," Gantz says. "It's going to be very aggressive. It's going to be very active and confused for a period of time." ■

Notes

[1] Quoted in Jonathan Weisman, "Drive To Open Power Industry To Competition Gains Steam," *Congressional Quarterly Weekly Report,* Oct. 12, 1996, p. 2911.

[2] Western Systems Coordinating Council, "Disturbance Report for the Power System that Occurred on the Western Interconnection, August 10, 1996," Oct. 18, 1996. For background, see *Los Angeles Times,* Aug. 22, 1996, p. A1; *The New York Times,* Aug. 19, 1996, p. A14.

[3] For background, see "Alternative Energy," *The CQ Researcher,* July 10, 1992, pp. 573-596.

[4] Timothy J. Brennan et al., *A Shock to the System: Restructuring America's Electricity Industry* (1996), p. 95.

[5] *Ibid.,* p. 100.

[6] Council of Economic Advisers, *1996 Economic Report of the President,* pp. 186-188. The report estimated stranded costs at $135 billion.

[7] Quoted in *The Pittsburgh Post Gazette,* Dec. 4, 1996, p. C1.

[8] Much of the historical background is drawn from Richard Rudolph and Scott Ridley, *Power Struggle: The Hundred-Year War over Electricity* (1986). See also Brennan, *op. cit.,* pp. 15-35; Richard Munson, *The Power Makers: The Inside Story of America's Biggest Business . . . and Its Struggle to Control Tomorrow's Electricity* (1985).

[9] For background, see "Will Nuclear Power Get Another Chance?" *Editorial Research Reports,* Feb. 22, 1991, pp. 113-128.

[10] Brennan, *op. cit.,* p. 30.

[11] Quoted in "Deregulating Electric Power," *Editorial Research Reports,* Nov. 20, 1987, p. 603.

[12] Quoted in *The New York Times,* April 25, 1996, p. A1.

[13] See Jonathan Weisman, "Nuclear Power's Fate on the Line in Utility Deregulation Debate," *Congressional Quarterly Weekly Report,* Jan. 11, 1997, pp. 123-126.

[14] Energy Information Administration table, "Estimated Electric Utility Average Revenue per Kilowatt Hour by Sector, January Through September 1996 and 1995."

[15] Rates for power only — not including the cost of transmission — range from 2.29 cents per kilowatt hour to 3.50 cents per hour for customers using at least 750 kilowatt hours per month, according to a compilation in October by George Gantz of Unitil Resources.

[16] See Jonathan Weisman, "Chances for Quick Action on Deregulation Fading," *Congressional Quarterly Weekly Report,* Nov. 23, 1996, pp. 3307-3308.

Bibliography

Selected Sources Used

Books

Brennan, Timothy J., *et al., A Shock to the System: Restructuring America's Electricity Industry,* Resources for the Future, 1996.
This book-length primer, published by a nonprofit environmental research organization, gives a balanced, step-by-step explanation of the major issues in the debate over restructuring the U.S. electric power industry.

Frankena, Mark W., and Bruce M. Owen, *Electric Utility Mergers: Principles of Antitrust Analysis,* Praeger, 1994.
The authors, who served as antitrust enforcers in, respectively, the Federal Trade Commission and the U.S. Department of Justice, provide a critical analysis of the effects of electric utility mergers on competition and efficiency. The book includes a 12-page bibliography.

Munson, Richard, *The Power Makers: The Inside Story of America's Biggest Business . . . and Its Struggle to Control Tomorrow's Electricity,* Rodale Press, 1985.
Munson, a former solar energy lobbyist, depicts electric utilities as beset by financial and managerial problems and confronting new challenges from "a new generation" of independent power producers using renewable resources. The book includes detailed source notes.

Nye, David E., *Electrifying America: Social Meanings of a New Technology, 1880-1940,* MIT Press, 1990.
Nye, of Copenhagen University, traces the social impact of electricity in the U.S. from the industry's beginnings in the 1880s through the coming of near-universal service in 1940. The book includes a 25-page bibliography.

Rudolph, Richard, and Scott Ridley, *Power Struggle: The Hundred-Year War Over Electricity,* Harper & Row, 1986.
Journalists Rudolph and Ridley provide a critical overview of the history of the electric power industry from the days of Thomas Edison and Samuel Insull through the middle years of the Reagan administration. The book includes detailed source notes.

Articles

Glazer, Sarah, "Deregulating Electric Power," *Editorial Research Reports,* Nov. 20, 1987, pp. 600-615.
The report examines the proposals to deregulate the electric power industry being put forward in the middle of the Reagan years.

Kriz, Margaret, "A Jolt to the System," *National Journal,* Aug. 31, 1996, pp. 1631-1636.
Kriz provides an overview of the current lobbying drive in Congress to require states to permit retail competition for electricity.

Weisman, Jonathan, "Drive to Open Power Industry to Competition Gains Steam," *Congressional Quarterly Weekly Report,* Oct. 12, 1996, pp. 2911-2917.
This package of articles includes a comprehensive overview of the effort in the states and in Congress to permit retail competition in electric power, as well as separate stories focusing on the debates over "stranded costs" and renewable resources.

FOR MORE INFORMATION

American Public Power Association, 2301 M St., N.W., 3rd floor, Washington, D.C. 20037; (202) 467-2900. The association represents local, publicly owned utility companies.

Edison Electric Institute, 701 Pennsylvania Ave., N.W., Washington, D.C. 20004; (202) 508-5000. The institute is the trade association for private, investor-owned utility companies.

Electric Consumer Alliance, First Indiana Plaza, Suite 2700, 135 North Pennsylvania St., Indianapolis, Ind. 46204; 1-800-585-8208; (317) 684-5346. The alliance, founded with start-up funds from the Edison Electric Institute, represents a variety of consumer groups on electric industry restructuring issues.

Electricity Consumers Resource Council, 1333 H St., N.W., 8th floor, West Tower, Washington, D.C. 20005; (202) 682-1390. The council represents about 30 large industrial and commercial users of electricity.

Electric Power Supply Association, 1401 H St., N.W., Suite 760, Washington, D.C. 20005; (202) 789-7200. The association represents independent power producers and suppliers of goods and services to the competitive power generation industry.

National Rural Electric Cooperative Association, 4301 Wilson Blvd., Arlington, Va. 22303; (703) 907-5500. The association represents rural electric cooperatives.

Public Citizen, 1600 20th St., N.W,, Washington, D.C. 20009; (202) 588-1000. The public interest group, a longtime critic of nuclear power, has worked on electric industry restructuring issues relating to stranded costs and consolidations and mergers.

Resources for the Future, 1616 P St., N.W., Washington, D.C. 20036; (202) 328-5000. The nonpartisan research organization has published several reports on electric industry restructuring.

The Next Step

Additional information from UMI's Newspaper & Periodical Abstracts™ database

Deregulating Electric Utilities

Levinson, Marc, "Monopoly unplugged," ***Newsweek,*** **Sept. 9, 1996, pp. 54-56.**

The impending deregulation of the electric power industry is discussed. The push for competition is greatest where electricity costs most — the Northeast and California.

Moyer, Charles R., "The Future of Electricity," ***Business Economics,*** **October 1996, pp. 13-18.**

An overview of the current state of electric utility regulation in the U.S. and how deregulation has shaped the industry in other countries is presented. Electric power users will, in the future, see moderating pressures for rate increases, and, in the longer term, real reductions in rates.

Navarro, Peter, "Electric utilities: The argument for radical deregulation," ***Harvard Business Review,*** **January 1996, pp. 112-125.**

Six steps for the radical restructuring of electric utilities are presented. Deregulation, vertical deintegration, direct access between buyers and sellers, aggregation of small consumers, denial of full recovery of stranded costs and performance-based rate making are detailed.

Passell, Peter, "A makeover for electric utilities," ***The New York Times,*** **Feb. 3, 1995, p. D1.**

The prospect of lower utility bills and the likelihood of deregulation are powering a drive to introduce real competition to electric production around the U.S. However, transforming the industry will require wrenching changes and challenge a variety of interests, from environmental groups to utility stockholders and power plant builders.

Restructuring and Deregulation Proposals in the States

Berenson, Alex, "Utility deregulation debate sparks critics, supporters," ***Denver Post,*** **Feb. 14, 1996, p. C3.**

A bill that would deregulate Colorado's electric power industry was debated by representatives of utilities, natural gas producers and consumer groups at a committee meeting at the state capitol on Feb. 13, 1996. The bill, HB 1234, would end utility monopolies and give electric consumers the right to pick their power suppliers.

"Electricity deregulation: A nasty shock," ***The Economist,*** **Jan. 6, 1996, pp. 20-21.**

On Dec. 20, 1995, the California Public Utilities Commission voted to let the state's power-generating industry set electricity rates according to market forces. Electricity is the last of the U.S.' monopoly industries to be deregulated.

"Electric utilities told to begin deregulating in New York by 1997," ***The Wall Street Journal,*** **May 17, 1996, p. A9.**

The New York Public Service Commission has ordered the state's electric utilities to create a competitive wholesale power market in early 1997 and introduce retail competition in 1998. New York is one of several states moving toward deregulated electrical service for industrial and residential users.

Marshall, Jonathan, "Power reform started here," ***San Francisco Chronicle,*** **Dec. 21, 1995, p. D1.**

Even as California regulators seize the initiative to bring about competition in the electric power industry, as many as 36 other states have a regulatory process under way to investigate ways of replacing traditional monopoly utilities with a system that would let electricity users choose their supplier.

Mutch, David, "Electric utilities brace for new state rules," ***The Christian Science Monitor,*** **April 4, 1996, p. 8.**

There is a serious move underway in the United States to unplug electric utilities from the monopoly status they have held since the 1930s and allow customers to choose their power company with the idea that it would drive electricity rates down.

Skilling, Jeffrey, "Consumers should cut off electric utilities' monopoly," ***Houston Chronicle,*** **May 5, 1996, p. D2.**

Skilling discusses proposals to deregulate Texas utilities, stating that we must not delay the day when businesses and homeowners can exercise a measure of control over their electricity costs.

"The buzz on electric utilities," ***Amicus Journal,*** **fall 1996, p. 6.**

Some people in the U.S. may be able to choose their electric utility suppliers by January 1998 due to a dramatic transformation of the industry. New York and California have emerged as leaders in responsible utility restructuring, as their state public utilities have recently arranged happy marriages between environmental protection and increased competition.

Economic Issues

Baumol, William J., and Gregory J. Sidak, "Stranded costs," ***Harvard Journal of Law & Public Policy,*** **summer 1995, pp. 835-849.**

The authors argue that consumers will benefit if utilities are allowed to recover "stranded costs."

Bryce, Robert, "Why a merger wave zaps electric utilities," *The Christian Science Monitor,* Aug. 15, 1996, p. 9.

Mergers and acquisitions among electric utilities are spreading like wildfire. Analysts say the moves will lead to lower costs for consumers, uncertainty for investors and chaos in an industry that, since it was heavily regulated in the 1930s, has been characterized by stability, even stodginess.

Jones, Cate, "Inside utility mergers: Trends within the trend," *Electrical World,* January 1996, pp. 59-62.

The impending deregulation of the electric power industry has increased the number of utility mergers in efforts to improve competitive positions. Current trends in utility mergers are discussed.

Quinn, Matthew C., "$135 billion in losses possible for electric utilities, study says," *Atlanta Constitution,* Aug. 8, 1995, p. F3.

Moody's Investor Service said that 87 of the nation's largest 114 investor-owned utilities will be stuck with "stranded costs," forcing them to lose $135 billion during the next decade as deregulation of the industry drives prices for electricity down.

Competition in Electric Power Industry

Lubove, Seth, "Electric utilities," *Forbes,* Jan. 2, 1995, pp. 154-157.

New competition is the biggest worry for electric utilities. Ways that utilities are dealing with competition are discussed.

Moorhouse, John C., "Competitive markets for electricity generation," *Cato Journal,* winter 1995, pp. 421-441.

The feasibility of replacing regulation or state ownership with market competition in electric power generation is examined. Current policy reflects growing support for a move to competitive electricity markets.

Retail Wheeling

Bryce, Robert, "Foes become friends over electricity deregulation," *The Christian Science Monitor,* Jan. 31, 1995, p. 9.

The electric power industry and consumer groups have banded together to fight "retail wheeling," which would allow customers to choose their electricity provider in the same way they choose a long-distance telephone company. Big companies favor the practice as a way to foster competition and reduce electricity rates.

Chadwick, Kyle, "Crossed wires: Federal preemption of states' authority over retail wheeling of electricity," *Administrative Law Review,* spring 1996, pp. 191-212.

Many state regulators are considering launching retail competition by requiring utilities to transmit, or "wheel," to retail consumers electricity generated by third parties. The article argues that wheeling falls under federal jurisdiction.

Miller, William H., "Power-ful change," *Industry Week,* Feb. 19, 1996, pp. 65-68.

As competition creeps into the electric power industry, industrial users are seeking the regulatory authority to shop for electricity. The impact that this scenario would have on utility rates is examined.

Steyer, Robert, "Competition sparks utility changes," *St. Louis Post-Dispatch,* May 5, 1996, p. E1.

Illinois Power Co. of Decatur and Central Illinois Light Co. of Peoria are the first utilities in the U.S. to try "retail wheeling," which means that users of electricity buy power from sources outside their home utility's territory.

Electric Power Generation

Bergstrom, Stephen W., and Terry Callender, "Gas and power industries linking as regulation fades," *Oil & Gas Journal,* Aug. 12, 1996, pp. 59-62.

As the natural gas and electricity markets merge, the two once-distinct industries will become much more alike. The changes occurring in light of deregulation are discussed.

Flavin, Christopher, and Nicholas Lenssen, "The unexpected rise of natural gas," *Futurist,* May 1995, pp. 34-37.

Despite reports of its early demise in the mid-1980s, natural gas has enjoyed an industrial comeback that could significantly shape the world's energy future.

Pospisil, Ray, "Nuclear plants under deregulation," *Electrical World,* January 1995, pp. 56-57.

One of the biggest issues in deregulation of the electric power industry is the fate of stranded utility investments. Nuclear power plants represent the biggest of these investments. The fate of nuclear plants under deregulation is discussed.

Saunders, Barbara, "Oil/gas firms take lead among new breed of energy megamarketers," *Oil & Gas Journal,* Sept. 16, 1996, pp. 16-19.

Oil and natural gas companies in the U.S. are increasing their efforts to make the most of policy reforms opening the electricity market to competition. These companies are among the strongest players in a new breed of energy megamarketers that is evolving in response to continuing power deregulation.

Stover, Dawn, "The forecast for wind power," *Popular Science,* July 1995, pp. 66-72.

Advanced turbine technology has made wind power economically competitive with fossil fuels and nuclear energy. Columbia River Gorge is the site of three planned wind power plants.

Back Issues

Great Research on Current Issues Starts Right Here...Recent topics covered by The CQ Researcher are listed below. Before May 1991, reports were published under the name of Editorial Research Reports.

JULY 1995
War Crimes
Highway Safety
Combating Terrorism
Preventing Teen Drug Use

AUGUST 1995
Job Stress
Organ Transplants
United Nations at 50
Advances in Cancer Research

SEPTEMBER 1995
Catholic Church in the U.S.
Northern Ireland Cease-Fire
High School Sports
Teaching History

OCTOBER 1995
Quebec's Future
Revitalizing the Cities
Networking the Classroom
Indoor Air Pollution

NOVEMBER 1995
The Working Poor
The Jury System
Sex, Violence and the Media
Police Misconduct

Back issues are available for $5.00 (subscribers) or $10.00 (non-subscribers). Quantity discounts apply to orders over ten. To order, call Congressional Quarterly Customer Service at (202) 887-8621.

Binders are available for $18.00. To order call 1-800-638-1710. Please refer to stock number 648.

DECEMBER 1995
Teens and Tobacco
Gene Therapy's Future
Global Water Shortages
Third-Party Prospects

JANUARY 1996
Emergency Medicine
Punishing Sex Offenders
Bilingual Education
Helping the Homeless

FEBRUARY 1996
Reforming the CIA
Campaign Finance Reform
Academic Politics
Getting Into College

MARCH 1996
The British Monarchy
Preventing Juvenile Crime
Tax Reform
Pursuing the Paranormal

APRIL 1996
Centennial Olympic Games
Managed Care
Protecting Endangered Species
New Military Culture

MAY 1996
Russia's Political Future
Marriage and Divorce
Year-Round Schools
Taiwan, China and the U.S.

JUNE 1996
Rethinking NAFTA
First Ladies
Teaching Values
Labor Movement's Future

JULY 1996
Recovered-Memory Debate
Native Americans' Future
Crackdown on Sexual Harassment
Attack on Public Schools

AUGUST 1996
Fighting Over Animal Rights
Privatizing Government Services
Child Labor and Sweatshops
Cleaning Up Hazardous Wastes

SEPTEMBER 1996
Gambling Under Attack
The States and Federalism
Civic Journalism
Reassessing Foreign Aid

OCTOBER 1996
Political Consultants
Insurance Fraud
Rethinking School Integration
Parental Rights

NOVEMBER 1996
Global Warming
Clashing Over Copyright
Consumer Debt
Governing Washington, D.C.

DECEMBER 1996
Welfare, Work and the States
The New Volunteerism
Implementing the Disabilities Act
America's Pampered Pets

JANUARY 1997
Combating Scientific Misconduct

Future Topics

- ***The New Immigrants***
- ***Biochemical Weapons***
- ***Refugees***

The CQ Researcher

Published By Congressional Quarterly Inc.

The New Immigrants

Do they threaten the American identity?

The history of the American "melting pot" reflects alternating tensions and accommodations between newcomers and the old guard. No country on Earth, it is said, has absorbed immigrants in greater numbers or variety, or has done more to incorporate immigrants into the national culture. But in today's era of globalizing trade and mass communications, immigrants coming to the U.S. are more diverse in appearance and language than earlier generations of newcomers, more prosperous and more assertive about seeking changes in the cultural and political landscape. Critics charge that the American identity is threatened by the government's overly accommodating immigration policy. Defenders of new immigrants say that putting roadblocks to citizenship in the path of patriotic foreign-born residents is unnecessary and unjust.

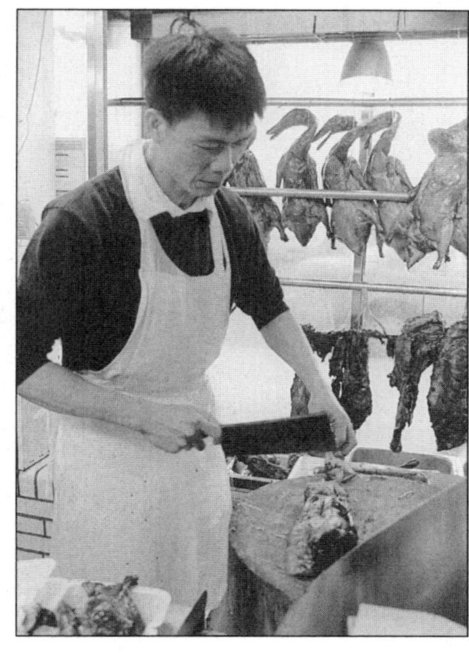

Inside This Issue

CQ Jan. 24, 1997 • Volume 7, No. 3 • Pages 49-72

Formerly Editorial Research Reports

THE ISSUES

BACKGROUND

CURRENT SITUATION

OUTLOOK

SIDEBARS AND GRAPHICS

FOR FURTHER RESEARCH

COVER: PEKING DUCK IS CHOPPED INTO FAST-FOOD SNACKS AT EDEN CENTER, A SPRAWLING VIETNAMESE-AMERICAN SHOPPING CENTER IN FALLS CHURCH, VIRGINIA. (THOMAS J. COLIN)

THE CQ Researcher

Jan. 24, 1997
Volume 7, No. 3

The CQ Researcher (ISSN 1056-2036). Formerly Editorial Research Reports. Published weekly (48 times per year, not printed Jan. 3, May 30, Aug. 29, Oct. 31) by Congressional Quarterly Inc., 1414 22nd St., N.W., Washington, D.C. 20037. Annual subscription rate for libraries, businesses and government is $340. Additional rates furnished upon request. Periodicals postage paid at Washington, D.C. POSTMASTER: Send address changes to The CQ Researcher, 1414 22nd St., N.W., Washington, D.C. 20037.

The New Immigrants

By Charles S. Clark

The Issues

The bustling mall, with a tire store at one end and a variety store at the other, seems typical of shopping centers in affluent American suburbs — save one key detail: Almost all the shops and restaurants display neon signs in Vietnamese. Restaurants advertise *pho*, a traditional Asian noodle soup; travel agents specialize in trans-Pacific flights and currency transfers; nightclubs blare the latest pop hits in Saigon; and posters in video stores promote sexy Asian film stars.

Welcome to Eden Center in Falls Church, Va., just outside Washington. The site that just a decade ago housed a quintessentially American retail arcade — complete with a paint store, greeting card shop and ice cream parlor — is now said to be the largest Vietnamese shopping center in the United States.

"I'd like to take credit, but it really just happened by itself," says owner Norman Ebenstein, of Boca Raton, Fla. "It just grew bigger, the place became a meeting center, so we sort of fell into the plan."

Today, 70 percent of the customers at the 250,000-square-foot shopping center are Asian, Ebenstein says. He credits his success to his tenants, and their "homogeneous, hard-working, family-oriented society."

Ebenstein "gets a kick" out of his involvement in Vietnamese small business. He flies the South Vietnamese and American flags in the parking lot. He and the merchants are erecting Oriental archways at the center's entrance, and they built a replica of a landmark clock tower in Saigon. Ebenstein also contributes to Vietnamese charities, organizes checkers tournaments for Asian senior citizens and joins in celebrations of Vietnam's Armed Forces Day.

Eden Center reflects the dramatic

impact of immigrants in modern America, an impact that affects both the new arrivals and long-time residents. In the 1990s, Americans who grew up in a historically white, Anglo-Saxon society are having to adjust to a Polish-born chairman of the Joint Chiefs of Staff, John Shalikashvili; to Spanish-language editions of *People* magazine on Seven-11 shelves; and to Buddhist temples and Islamic mosques rising in their communities. [1]

Today's America contains nearly 23 million foreign-born residents, or about 8.4 percent of the population, and about 32 million residents whose primary language is not English. Los Angeles, the Census Bureau says, is now about 40 percent foreign-born, while 88 percent of its Monterey Park neighborhood is Asian and Hispanic.

The impact of immigration is not spread evenly across the country, notes George Vernez, director of the Center for Research on Immigration Policy at the RAND Corp. For example, most Cubans stream to Miami; people from the Caribbean and Central America flock to New York City; and Asians make Seattle a prime destination. California is home to fully 45 percent of the nation's Mexican immigrants, which strains California schools because Mexicans tend to have lower education levels than other immigrants.

Though earlier historical periods have seen as much or more immigration, many of today's immigrants differ from their 19th- and early 20th-century counterparts. The classic stories of American immigrants have focused on the "tired and poor," but many modern immigrants are well-educated and even wealthy — witness the 12,000 Chinese technicians working in Silicon Valley computer firms or the well-heeled Iranian expatriots so visible in Beverly Hills.

Over the past three decades, Asians, Latinos and Caribbean immigrants have outpaced the numbers of Irish, Italian and Eastern European immigrants so familiar at the turn of the century, sometimes prickling racial tensions among native-born Americans. And Hispanics and Asians, in particular, have become politically more influential, as evidenced by the important political races in 1996 that turned on the Latino vote (*see p. 66*) and by the current concern over Asian involvement in President Clinton's campaign financing. (*See story, p. 56.*)

"Political loyalty has dropped in weight due to globalization, the end of the Cold War and the rise of the United Nations," says Harvard University sociologist Nathan Glazer, author of the forthcoming book *We Are All Multiculturalists Now*. "The world of today's immigrants has two main differences from the immigrants' world of the 1920s. One is the rise of the welfare state that offered a safety net for immigrants, having replaced the [modest] private welfare efforts of the 1920s that prompted many immigrants to give up and return home. Secondly, the whole thrust toward Americanization in language and culture that used to be common in this country has weakened."

Saigon in the Suburbs

Flying the U.S. and South Vietnamese flags, sprawling Eden Center in suburban Falls Church, Va., boasts dozens of shops and restaurants catering to Vietnamese-Americans.

Thomas J. Colin

Thomas J. Colin

Perhaps because of their daily encounters in the new "melting pot," many Americans have grown weary of high immigration, viewing it as a drain on jobs and government social spending. Indeed, an NBC News/*Wall Street Journal* survey of 2,000 Americans in December found that 72 percent want the number of immigrants reduced, a huge increase from the 33 percent who wanted reductions in 1965. For several years now, states and the federal government have been planning cutbacks in welfare, health and education benefits for immigrants both legal and illegal. [2]

The new immigrants have not stood by idly. Taking advantage of newly streamlined procedures at the Immigration and Naturalization Service (INS), thousands who have been in the country the required five years have been applying for citizenship. "Since welfare reform," says Vilay Chaleunrath, executive director of the Indochinese Community Center in Washington, D.C., "there's been a surge of applications, especially among the elderly, who used to think they would one day go back and die in the old country."

In 1996, an estimated 1.1 million people took the citizenship oath, up from an average of only 200,000 in the early 1990s. The increase in part reflects newly eligible illegal aliens who won amnesty following the 1986 Immigration Reform and Control Act. The INS predicts 1.7 million applications in fiscal 1997.

"Naturalization builds bridges between new immigrant groups and the existing society, much as labor unions, political parties and public schools have done in the past," says INS Commissioner Doris Meissner. [3] That's one reason that Hungarian-born billionaire George Soros last September set up his $50 million Emma Lazarus Fund to help immigrants become citizens.

The rush to citizenship, however, is not welcomed by all. In her recent book, *Americans No More: The Death of Citizenship,* journalist Georgie Anne Geyer blasts immigrants and government policies that encourage immigrants to view citizenship as an opportunity for economic benefits rather than civic responsibility.

Indeed, she says, immigrants take naturalization about as seriously as "joining a health club." And, she told a Senate panel, Americans seem reluctant to assert their national identity. If not countered, she warns, the trend "will destroy America as we have known it and substitute a very different country, one that is spiritually incoherent, humanly conflict-ridden and economically hobbled." [4]

John Fonte, a visiting scholar at the American Enterprise Institute, denounces immigrant demands for ethnic-group rights, such as multicultural education and bilingual ballots. "Today we face a crisis of citizenship," he told the Senate panel. "Our goal should be Americanization, stated clearly without apology and without embarrassment. . . . Americanization does not mean giving up our ethnic traditions, customs, cuisine or birth languages. It means patriotic assimilation." [5]

Finally, a perception that immigrants tend to vote Democratic has led some Republicans in Congress to charge that the Clinton administration's INS was partisan and even corrupt in its efforts to streamline the naturalization process so that new citizens could vote in the last elections (*see p. 64*).

Immigration supporters — including many who belong to the Republican Party, which is split over immigration — argue that new immigrants traditionally have been among the most patriotic Americans and that all they want is help in making the transition. Some accuse immigration "restrictionists" of veiled racism and xenophobia, of scapegoating immigrants for many social ills.

John Kromkowski, president of the National Center for Urban Ethnic Affairs, challenges the notion of a fixed and superior American identity. "America itself is a history of changes, of developments, not of static categories," he says. "The nativists are out of touch with the real situation and the process. And their whole anti-immigrant hysteria has recently done what the League of Women Voters never could do: produce record voter registration and citizenship."

Today, says a 1993 Ford Foundation study, "America's story is no longer one simply of 'coming to America.' It is also an account of the places where immigrants settle and how those already there change." [6]

As policy-makers and everyday citizens consider the nation's immigration policies, these are some of the questions being asked:

Are immigrants doing enough to fit into American life?

"There is a central American culture that goes beyond our legal institutions," writes former State Department official Francis Fukuyama. "America was founded with liberal political institutions, but it is the sectarian nature of American Protestantism that set the cultural tone." [7]

How newcomers fare at picking up on this "cultural tone" is the focus of much anxiety among Americans who look askance at the immigration influx from places such as Latin America and the Caribbean. "Successful" societies value education, says Massachusetts Institute of Technology international studies Professor Lawrence Harrison, citing Western Europe, North America, East Asia and Australia as examples. In Latin America, by contrast, "the tradition has been a focus not on the future, not on progress, but on the present, or on the past. Work has been seen as a necessary evil, importantly informed by the slavery experience. Education is something which has been made available principally to the elite. . . . Merit plays a relatively unimportant role in how people get ahead. Connections — family — are much more important. - . . . The idea of fair play is not well-developed." [8]

Immigrants from such societies, the argument goes, inevitably produce the kind of tensions that arose, for example, in Mount Kisco, N.Y., recently, when citizens complained that Latino day laborers who gather every morning in parking lots were too often publicly intoxicated. "We want our town back," longtime residents wrote to the local paper. [9]

Complaints are not limited to whites. "A for-sale sign in our neighborhood causes panic," writes an African-American of the arrival of Hispanic immigrants in South-Central Los Angeles. "We know who will get that house. There will be 20 to 30 people living in it, they will keep goats, they will grow corn in their front yard, they will hang their wash on the front fence." [10]

Critics such as Geyer cite examples of immigrant crime, singling out the Middle Eastern terrorists convicted of the 1993 World Trade Center bombing, or Ethiopians who seek to import the practice of female genital mutilation. *Forbes* magazine writer Peter Brimelow, himself a U.S.-naturalized Briton, warns of the day when America is no longer majority white. "This unprecedented demographic mutation," he writes of current immigration levels, is creating an America in which people are "alien to each other." [11]

What has disappeared, says Daniel A. Stein, executive director of the Federation for American Immigration Reform (FAIR), "is the old immigrants' idea that you would never go home, that you were so proud to learn English that you would be insulted if someone spoke your old language. Immigrants are no longer grateful to be here."

It is the high level of immigration itself that prevents many immigrants from assimilating, adds Yeh Ling-Ling, founder of the Diversity Coalition for an Immigration Moratorium, in San Francisco. "In schools in places like Monterey [Calif.], many immigrants are surrounded only by other immigrants while they receive bilingual education and multiculturalism. I get calls from immigrants saying they're angry at the ethnic activists who tell them, 'You'll never be an American. Your yellow skin will never turn white.' "

According to an Urban Institute report, the number of immigrants who told 1990 census takers that they "don't speak English well" totaled about half the population of Miami, a fifth of New York and a third of Los Angeles. [12]

Polls, however, show that immigrants do not see themselves so ghettoized. Fifty-eight percent of immigrants who have been in the U.S. less than 10 years report that they spend time with "few or none of their fellow countrymen," according to a May-June 1995 *USA Today*/CNN/Gallup survey. An identical 58 percent felt it is important to blend into American culture, compared with only 27 percent who said it was important to maintain their own culture. (Surprisingly, a higher portion of native-born Americans — 32 percent — said the immigrants should maintain their own culture.)

Studies show that many of the most visible immigrant enclaves are con-

Naturalizations on the Rise

During the 1990s, the number of immigrants who became naturalized American citizens skyrocketed. Several factors caused the rise, including efforts to deny public assistance to non-citizens and the large group of illegal immigrants who became eligible for citizenship through the 1986 amnesty law.

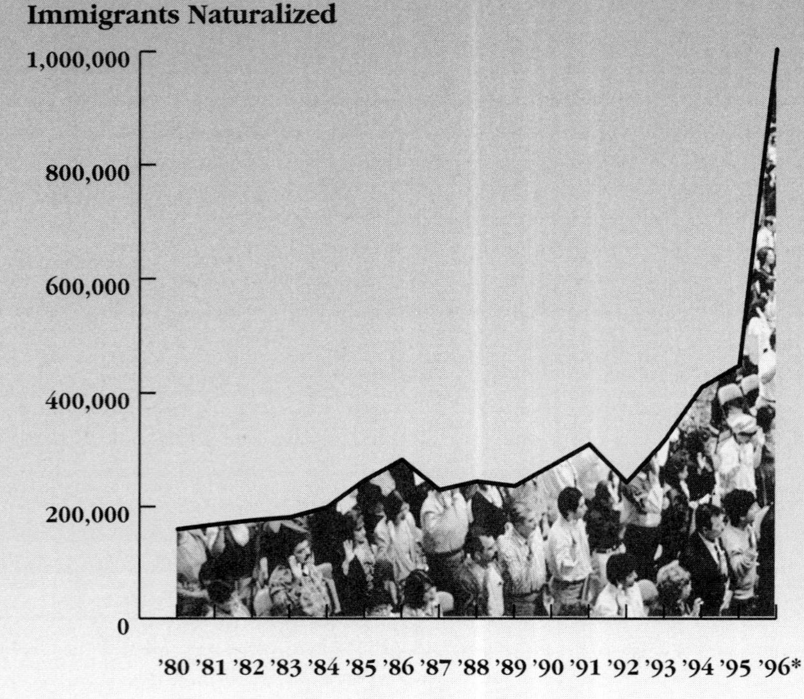

* *Estimated*

Source: Immigration and Naturalization Service

stantly turning over, with new arrivals replacing veterans who acquire education and skills that permit them a better job and housing. The 1995 annual housing survey by the Federal National Mortgage Association (Fannie Mae) found that 55 percent of immigrants who are renters are more likely to see themselves as foreigners temporarily living in America; among immigrants who own a home, the percentage with that feeling drops to 41. The Commerce Department, meanwhile, recently reported that the number of Hispanic-owned businesses jumped 76 percent from 1987 to '92. [13]

"Walk into any Latino neighborhood and you see all the American icons, from Dallas Cowboys posters to the New York Yankees to rock and roll," says Raul Yzaguirre, president of the National Council of La Raza, the nation's largest Latino civil rights group. "Hispanics are learning English faster than previously, and there are 50,000 waiting for night classes in Los Angeles alone. Latinos are hard-working and patriotic, and in the armed forces they win more medals proportionately than their numbers."

Rather than generalizing about a whole continent and culture, Yzaguirre adds, critics should understand that persistent Hispanic poverty has to do with job discrimination, which he says has been documented time and again in controlled studies.

Other immigrants' spokesmen stress the importance to transplants of maintaining their self-esteem by staying in touch with their cultural roots, even if that means disguising it. "Concealing one's real emotional feelings was particularly useful while dealing with the white majority," wrote a Japanese immigrant woman in 1981. "To show a 'good face' as a representative of the Japanese in general insured greater acceptance by the majority society." [14]

Critics of new immigrants, says Frank Sharry, executive director of the National Immigration Forum, a lobbying and research group, "overlook that there's a tremendous desire to belong, to participate, to embrace America, to love it and wrestle with it while maintaining one's own sense of identity. This is a good thing. Citizenship is a classic example of how dynamic and vibrant American democracy is. But in the public mind, it is largely the Latino population that seems not to have embraced America the way average Joes want them to."

But Linda Chavez, president of the Center for Equal Opportunity and a critic of ethnic lobbies that cry racism, says "the first generation that is born here is the dividing line. If they fully take part in American life, then all is fine, and it is not impossible for the country to absorb large numbers of immigrants. Unless you're too old, you must learn English to take part. The foreign-language newspapers that many immigrants read are too concentrated on news from the old country."

Speaking foreign languages creates barriers, she adds, which produce frustration among Americans that leads to the anti-immigrant backlash and the debate over English as the official language.

The language debate, though often discussed in the context of government administration and official documents, has an emotional undercurrent relating to political domination.[15] Recently retired Rep. Toby Roth, R-Wis., one of the leaders of the official-English legislation movement in Congress, told a press conference in December that new Americans were some of his biggest supporters because they see learning English as the key to economic opportunity. "One tells me that Spanish is the language of bellhops and busboys, while English is the language of doctors and lawyers," he says.

Yzaguirre finds such views "suggestive of the offensive, ugly-American attitude that has gotten us in trouble all over the world. We've got to stop having America be the world's most linguistically ignorant country."

Dennis Gallagher, executive director of the Refugee Policy Group, acknowledges that there are limits to how much new immigrants should assert their native cultures. "My [Indian-born] wife is appalled by the garish show some Hindu groups make in building temples in prominent places in the United States, some of which would be extreme even in their own countries," he says. But, Gallagher adds, having a group of 100,000 Iranians, some of whom succeed or fail only within boundaries of that community, is not a threat to our overall society. They won't get us to learn Farsi. They're a part of America now.

"Immigrants bring different attitudes and values and perceptions of who the good and bad guys are in international affairs," he adds. "That's both the benefit and cost of diversity. We're getting more frightened of that. We shouldn't be, because in the longer term, it makes us stronger."

Should immigrants be permitted to hold dual citizenship?

"American citizenship is more precious than any other status a man or woman can have," recently retired Sen. Alan K. Simpson, R-Wyo., told the Senate Judiciary hearing in October. "Not only does it guarantee membership in the society that offers the most political and civil liberty of any nation . . . and the opportunity to participate in choosing the government and therefore in crafting the laws that will help shape its future — in addition, it provides the immense emotional satisfaction of being part of a nation with a very special and wonderful history."[16]

Immigration and Naturalization Service/Rick Kenney

Attorney General Janet Reno administers the oath of citizenship to 3,000 new citizens at a 1995 ceremony at the U.S. Air Arena in Maryland, near Washington, D.C.

Given the allure of U.S. citizenship, Simpson and others question an increasingly common practice among immigrants: dual citizenship. Commonplace among Britons who emigrate to the United States and American Jews who move to Israel, dual citizenship in recent years has become popular among Central American and Asian immigrants as well, in part due to advances in worldwide mass communication. In New York City, seven of the 10 largest immigrant groups come from countries that permit it, said Linda Basch, author of a 1985 book on transnationalism. "Many people live an existence that's transnational," she wrote. "They have families in both places. They invest in both places. They get involved in politics in both places."[17]

By law, the United States does not recognize dual citizenship, says an INS spokesman, though the Supreme Court has ruled that a foreigner need not renounce foreign citizenship to apply for U.S. citizenship. When a qualified immigrant takes the oath of U.S. citizenship, the State Department notifies the government of his native country, and it is up to that government to determine whether to revoke citizenship.

Critics question the loyalty of dual citizens, warning of wartime defections and the risk of the proverbial "fifth column" of espionage agents. They point to dual citizens who have become pawns in international aggression, as in the late-1930s, when Adolf Hitler cited the presence of German nationals in Czechoslovakia as a pretext for launching an invasion.

"Dual nationality with Britons or Israelis at least involves a shared cultural legacy," says Stein of FAIR. "But now, with immigration from neighboring countries such as Mexico and Latin America, it involves huge income differentials and claims to ancestral territory" within the United States.

Efforts to discourage dual citizenship have put new pressure on immigrants who have been willing to forgo such privileges as government employment opportunities and security clearances in order to maintain links with

Clinton Troubles Over Campaign Finance . . .

Foreign money. Immigrants' money. Money from citizens with foreign-sounding names. Such distinctions have been blurred by the current controversy over foreign money contributed to U.S. political campaigns. Among many of America's immigrants, the issue has brought a discomfiting feeling that they are regarded with new suspicion.

"In the last few weeks," President Clinton told a post-election press conference on Nov. 8, "a lot of Asian-Americans who have supported our campaign have come up to me and said, 'You know, I'm being made to feel like a criminal.' " Their reports of harassing calls from reporters and "disparaging comments" about people with Asian last names prompted Clinton to "remind" the public that "our country has been greatly enriched by the work of Asian-Americans. They are famous for working hard for family values and for giving more than they take."

Reuters

Democratic fund-raiser John Huang

Since then, however, the press, Clinton's Republican opponents and his own fund-raising officials have documented a growing array of apparent violations of U.S. campaign finance law and custom, most involving Asian-Americans, Indonesians, Thais and Chinese.

The scandal broke during the final weeks of the election with news reports that a Democratic fund-raiser named John Huang, an Indonesian-American, had raised what eventually was estimated at $3.4 million from Asian-Americans, some $1.2 million of which had to be returned because the true donors were apparently foreigners. Huang's previous employment as a mid-level Commerce Department official and with the Lippo Group, an Indonesian financial conglomerate, provoked suspicion that his fund-raising and dozens of visits to the White House might constitute illegal lobbying on behalf of Indonesian interests.

The story expanded with reports that $140,000 had been raised during a Democratic fund-raiser held last April at a Los Angeles-area Buddhist temple attended by religious devotees of modest means. Many of the donations had to be returned when it was ascertained that they were actually from non-citizens. [1]

Then came reports that a Chinese-American entrepreneur from Torrance, Calif., Johnny Chung, had given $366,000 to the Democratic Party and had made 49 visits to the White House over two years, sometimes bringing Chinese business leaders with him. [2]

Next, there were problems at the legal defense fund set up to raise money for President Clinton's defense against the sexual harassment case filed by Paula Corbin Jones. Fund officials revealed that they were returning some $400,000 raised by Little Rock, Ark., restaurateur Charles Yah Lin Trie, a friend of Clinton, because the money had come from non-citizens, mainly followers of a Buddhist sect leader. Trie was later shown to have made numerous visits to the White House, including one in which he escorted a Communist Chinese arms dealer to meet with Clinton, apparently without the president's knowledge. [3]

Soon after, it was revealed that Pauline Kanchanalak, a legal, non-citizen U.S. resident originally from Thailand, had brought five business associates to a White House coffee to meet the president after having given some $253,000 to the Clinton campaign. The money was later returned when it came out that it belonged to her mother. [4]

Though the Clinton campaign was able to delay the most embarrassing disclosures until after the election (in part by using a public relations strategy that dismissed the charges as racism and Asian-bashing), the damage is still being determined. Besides an internal review by the Democratic National Committee (after which it made a confession of laxness), a probe is under way by the Justice Department (including the FBI). And in February, the Senate Government Affairs Committee is set to open hearings on fund-raising abuses of the 1996 campaign, just as Congress as a whole is under pressure to take up campaign finance reform. [5]

The impact of the disclosures on Asian-Americans, meanwhile, has already been dramatic. "The image of Asian-Americans has been tarnished by a perception that they are foreigners and are illegally participating in campaign finance," says Stewart Kwoh, executive director of the Asian Pacific American Legal Center of Southern California, an immigrant-advocacy group. "The media coverage has been one-sided. Only 10 or 12 contributions have had to be returned out of thousands given legally by Asian-Americans.

"I'm not saying the alleged improprieties are not serious, or that they don't need investigating," Kwoh continues. "But the press has not been reporting the other ways in which Asians participate politically, such as our voter registration drive," he adds. "The public has not tuned into the fact that Congress [in the early 1970s] permitted campaign donations from permanent residents and from foreign

their native land. "My wife is not quite comfortable giving up her ties [to India] because of tax advantages and the loss to her identity," Gallagher says. "Even some of our non-xenophobic but well-traveled friends tell her that after 25 years, what's so bad about having to make up your mind? And she could probably get her Indian citi-

. . . Put Spotlight and Suspicions on Asian-Americans

subsidiaries that earn money here. Overall, Asian companies gave less than European and Canadian subsidiaries, but reporters didn't care. They knew that the scandal about 'the yellow peril' would attract more readers."

The suggestion that the scandal was fueled by an age-old fear of inscrutable Asians was picked up by columnist Russell Baker, who ridiculed "Fu Manchu's latest incarnation" in an age of globalized trade. [6]

But many observers see genuine cultural differences that have contributed to the problem. "This idea of racism is ludicrous," says Daniel A. Stein, executive director of the Federation for American Immigration Reform (FAIR). "These are orchestrated transactions by people outside the country. The way things are done in Japan and China is antithetical to the tradition of openness in the United States. Clinton needs to reread George Washington's farewell address, where it says be vigilant about pernicious foreign influences."

Similarly, efforts by Clinton and other Democrats to paint the issue in racial terms strike many as a diversion. "Clinton will do anything to deflect discussion from what is really an old-fashioned corruption scandal that people can understand," says Linda Chavez, president of the Center for Equal Opportunity.

Chavez acknowledges, however, that many Asian cultures view the giving of gifts to high officials as a sign of respect. "A lot of the Asians are probably mystified at what they have done wrong," she says, "and this is the kind of thing that immigrants learn during the assimilation process. But Clinton himself knows the rules of the game. If he really wants to be sensitive to Asians, he should make sure they know them, too."

Kwoh, however, says that what traditions of gift-giving exist in Asian cultures are hardly different from American campaign finance laws, which permit unlimited donations of soft, or unregulated, money and allow millionaires to fund their own rise to power. "I personally believe in campaign finance reform across the board, but it shouldn't come from scapegoating Asians," he says, citing a remark made by former independent presidential candidate Ross Perot. In a jab at Clinton fund-raiser Huang, the Texas billionaire asked an audience, "Wouldn't you like to have someone named O'Reilly out there?" [7]

"Asians are not going to change their last names," Kwoh promises.

Francey Lim Youngberg, executive director of the Congressional Asian Pacific American Caucus Institute, worries that the press' focus on the Asian money connection will "be to the detriment of the Asian-American community because it comes at a time when we are coming of age politically, with more Asian candidates running for office than ever before. I am scared it will have a chilling effect on participation because it has now evolved into a witch hunt for anyone who is connected to someone who's mentioned in one of the media's stories."

The Clinton administration, meanwhile, argues that no one has found evidence that any Asian or Asian-American donor won a quid pro quo in terms of policy changes. At his press conference, Clinton pointed out that many Asian-Americans vote Republican, and that Republicans have their own campaign-finance and foreign-money issues to confront. (Indeed, last month, Rep. Jay C. Kim, R-Calif., who is the first Korean-American in Congress, saw his campaign treasurer indicted following a four-year FBI investigation into fraud involving money allegedly funneled from five South Korean companies. [8])

In January, the DNC announced it would no longer take money from resident non-citizens and U.S. subsidiaries of foreign companies.

As for press coverage of Asians, several newspapers, as preparations were under way for Clinton's second inauguration, have been reporting on Asians both here and abroad who have been jockeying for inaugural tickets. They see it as a chance to get their photo taken with Clinton, a proven reputation enhancer for doing business in Asia. [9]

Tom McCarthy, deputy bureau chief of the *Los Angeles Times* in Washington, who has managed the paper's campaign finance stories, disagrees with the charge that Asian-American donors have been unfairly singled out by reporters. "It is apparent why we have written about the donors we have," he says. "As a normal part of the process, we methodically scrub all campaign finance reports. We see some perennial names and some new ones. Not a lot of people give sums as high as $250,000, so we don't have a lot of discretion as to who we contact. What you do in journalism is follow the money."

---

[1] *The Washington Post*, Dec. 6, 1996.

[2] *Los Angeles Times*, Nov. 28, 1996.

[3] *The New York Times*, Dec. 19, 1996.

[4] *The Washington Post*, Dec. 27, 1996.

[5] See "Campaign Finance Reform," *The CQ Researcher*, Feb. 9, 1996, pp. 121-144.

[6] Russell Baker, "Yellow Peril's Return," *The New York Times*, Dec. 7, 1996.

[7] *Philadelphia Inquirer*, Oct. 30, 1996.

[8] *Los Angeles Times* [Washington edition], Dec. 4, 1996.

[9] See *The Wall Street Journal*, Dec. 27, 1996.

---

zenship back later if it were withdrawn when she became an American."

"But it's not a trivial thing, psychologically," he adds. "She told me when we married that she had to give up a lot when she moved here, and now has to give up that last remaining link to home. Americans don't seem to understand. Their nationalism is so strong, they don't seem to respect it in other countries."

The legal arguments against dual citizenship, says Douglas Klusmeyer, editor of the *Stanford Humanities Review,* "more often than not are red herrings. The modern trend in international law and in state practice has been to acknowledge that in today's mobile world, the phenomenon of dual citizenship is simply going to increase." Moreover, says Klusmeyer, who testified before the Senate panel, banning it in the United States will simply perpetuate a fiction, because "if their countries of origin are willing to issue new passports, there's no way you can stop it."

The country whose dual citizenship policy raises the most concern is Mexico. In December its Parliament voted to allow dual citizenship so that Mexicans who naturalize in the United States could still go back to Mexico to own property and get a Mexican passport, but not to vote. This move was alarming to some Americans, particularly those in Southern California who worked on the 1994 measure passed by California to halt public benefits to immigrants (since blocked by courts). The fear is that dual citizenship openly encourages Mexicans to move to the U.S. and try to influence U.S. policy toward Mexico. Latino college students and the occasional state legislator often talk of banning English in parts of the United States gained from Mexico under the 1848 Treaty of Guadalupe Hidalgo.

"This is not immigration, this is colonization," Stein says. "If at some point down the line Mexico were to decide to run its [boundary] across parts of the southern United States, which side of the conflict would these dual nationals fall on? The Mexican mythology that the Americans stole their land," Stein adds, "means that a time could come when Southern California will say we need a regional Hispanic council and then become as fragmented and confused as the Weimar Republic" was in Germany.

The large number of Mexican immigrants in the Southwest gives new credence to the theory of Mexican irredentism known as the "reconquista," agrees historian David M. Kennedy. "There is no precedent in American history for these possibilities. No previous immigrant group had the size and concentration and easy access to its original culture that the Mexican immigrant group in the Southwest has today." [18]

Such theories are "crazy," says La Raza's Yzaguirre. "Even if there were too many Mexican-Americans in the Southwest, I know of no serious movement that talks about seceding. Being American is one of the most prized attributes — there has never been a Mexican-American turncoat in U.S. history."

Are Americans doing enough to ease the transition of new immigrants?

In New York City, 90 percent of the 45,000 cab drivers are foreign-born. So last year, when the city's Taxi and Limousine Commission was looking to boost the industry, it decided to provide new business opportunities for immigrants. For the first time since 1937, it increased the number of licensed cabs, adding 400 "medallions" to the 12,000 coveted plaques already in use.

"Many drivers in the past put their kids through college by owning a medallion," says Allan Fromberg, the taxi authority's assistant commissioner for public affairs. "But today it means more because it also means freedom, whether from religious persecution or an absence of economic opportunity. We're proud to have a part in it."

In the hotel industry, Marriott International Inc. has been leading a trend toward stabilizing corporate work forces by offering day care and social service referrals to the Bosnian, Chinese and Mexican immigrants who staff its cleaning and kitchen crews. [19]

The federal government aids immigrants with money provided by the 1982 Job Training Partnership Act and by State Legalization Impact Assistance Grants, as well $262 million annually for bilingual education programs for Asian and Hispanic students.

On the religious front, the Council of Jewish Organizations in Brooklyn recently launched its Business Outreach Center to help ethnic small businesses. And the Catholic Legal Immigration Network (CLINIC) has long provided legal aid, mentoring and training to indigent immigrants. "In many ways, the human condition is that of an immigrant," says John Swenson, executive director of migration and refugee services for the U.S. Catholic Conference. "Yes, some national limits on immigration are reasonable, but Catholic social policy emphasizes what is necessary for the preservation of individual dignity, even for illegal immigrants."

Public schools have an interest in being effective for immigrants, says Michael A. Resnick, senior associate executive director of the National School Boards Association. "Immigrants are an investment because the chances are they will be here the rest of their lives. Many of them come from countries with higher poverty rates and are illiterate even in their native language. And they require help not just with language transition problems but also with the larger cultural context. Some children from Mexico, for example, sometimes stay home for several weeks during the Christmas season because they're not used to having just a week off."

According to the 1995 Fannie Mae survey, 35 percent of immigrants say that native-born Americans are warm and welcoming, while 14 percent say they are cold and negative.

And just as there are extremes of antisocial immigrants, there are examples of home-grown misbehavior. South Asian newcomers settling on Staten Island, N.Y., for example, were recently greeted with graffiti reading "Indians go home. Leave or Die." [20] And in Houston, a Vietnamese immigrant was beaten to death by skinheads.

To accuse average Americans of xenophobia, however, is unfair, says Yeh of the diversity coalition. "In Minnesota or Iowa, where immigration numbers are low, Americans will help newcomers, even if they don't speak English," she says. "But in a high-impact state like California or New York City, most people think immigration has made life worse. You don't have an obligation to adopt your neighbor's children. It's a burden. And if there are high numbers, it doesn't matter what color the people are. People in Oregon, Idaho and Montana are getting up in arms about the high numbers of white Californians coming to their states."

Immigration restriction advocates also argue that offering generous social services merely makes the United States a magnet for immigrants who are either illegal or too numerous. FAIR's Stein believes that America does not have to have a diverse society if it doesn't want to. "If we as a nation choose to believe it's better, more productive of human happiness not to be, then it's our own business.

"Most Americans don't see why we have immigration," he says. "They're told by *The Wall Street Journal* that it's a free lunch, but then they're told that immigrants are getting on welfare. How far can we stretch it without social turmoil? We could admit Moslems or Buddhists at rates that would overwhelm us, but why? Would it be the same country? I won't pass judgment on whether it would be for better or for worse, but it *would be* different. The old ties that bind are easy to ignore when the economic pie is growing, but the test is in periods of crisis."

The same arguments against racial and ethnic diversity "were made early in this century against Jews, Italians and Greeks, who were even called 'blacks' then because of their dark hair," Chavez says. "But I don't disagree that we have to have an American common culture and that the largest part of it is not merely European but in fact English. People adjust to it."

Such talk of preserving American culture is fine, "but which culture?" asks Gregory Fossedal, chairman of the Alexis de Tocqueville Institute, a pro-immigrant think tank in Arlington, Va. "When I drive along Wilson Boulevard in Arlington and see it teeming with hard-working Koreans and Vietnamese, I see the teamwork of new Americans. No one has established that difficulties are economic or culturally due to immigrants. There may be cultural limits, but we don't know where those limits are, and they would be at least three-to-five-times the current immigration levels because we handled that amount in the past with the Irish and Italians."

If immigration critics "can find an America that doesn't include these foreign influences," Fossedal says, "I'd like to see it." ■

Newly arrived European immigrants gather at the processing facility at Ellis Island, N.Y., in 1910.

BACKGROUND

A Nation of Immigrants

"Once I thought to write a history of the immigrants of America," wrote renowned Harvard University historian Oscar Handlin. "Then I discovered that the immigrants *were* American history." [21]

INS records show that since 1820, the earliest year records were kept, fully 60.7 million immigrants have come to America, plus uncounted others who came illegally. [22]

This vital component of the American society has been expressed in an array of metaphors — mosaic, rainbow, kaleidoscope, melting pot, simmering cauldron, necklace of varied stones and "jazz ensemble, with each member improvising as an individual but having to play together under the agreed-on framework of a song." [23]

From the beginning of the Republic, most new Americans had a strong romantic sense of themselves as a unique, fresh slate of a nation. As French writer J. Hector St. John de Crevecoeur put it: "He is an American, who, leaving behind him all his ancient prejudices and manners, receives new ones from the new mode of life he has embraced, the new government he obeys and the new rank he holds. He becomes an American by being received in the broad lap of our great Alma Mater. Here, individuals of all nations are melted into a new race of men, whose labors and posterity will one day cause great changes in the world." [24]

Founding Fathers' Nationalism

Yet the Founding Fathers were overwhelmingly British in their outlook, and were hardly what today might be called world citizens. It was Thomas Jefferson who insisted on the five-year residency requirement for citizenship, and Benjamin Franklin who worried that German immigrants were arriving at such rates that they were "shortly to be so numerous as to Germanize us instead of us Anglifying them." [25] (Indeed, *The Federalist Papers* were published in German as well as English, and a 1794 proposal from some German settlers in Virginia to have federal laws translated into German was defeated in committee by just one vote.)

The Founding Fathers were careful to equip the president, under the 1798 Alien and Sedition Act, with the power to deport immigrants deemed dangerous to security. Colonists "held the view that somehow the good people had come here and the bad people had stayed home in Europe," says Yale University historian John Morton Blum. [26]

In the early 19th century, famed French political writer Alexis de Tocqueville marveled at America's capacity for absorbing foreigners: "As they mingle, the Americans become assimilated," he wrote. "They all get closer to one type." But precisely because de Tocqueville is cited by American immigration enthusiasts, immigration critic Brimelow argues that de Tocqueville actually hated many of the immigrants he saw in America, blaming them for an urban riot and calling them part of a "rabble more dangerous even than that of European towns. [They carry] our worst vices to the United States without any of those interests which might counteract their influence." [27]

Rising Hostility

By the mid-19th century, when the Irish potato famine had brought more than a million new immigrants to the U.S., hostility toward them was formalized in the political party that took the name Know-Nothings. With the slogan "Nationalize, Then Naturalize," the group wanted to impose a 25-year waiting period for the foreign-born to become citizens, and it wanted Catholics (most of the Irish) prohibited altogether.

After running Millard Fillmore unsuccessfully for president in 1856, the Know-Nothings prompted Abraham Lincoln to comment: "As a nation, we began by declaring that 'All men are created equal.' We now practically read it 'All men are created equal, except negroes.' When the Know-Nothings get control, it will read 'All men are created equal, except negroes, and foreigners, and Catholics.' " [28]

As the Civil War approached, the subsequent debates over slavery, black citizenship and the 14th Amendment prompted soul-searching comments among members of Lincoln's Cabinet, one of whom acknowledged that they themselves enjoyed citizenship by a mere "accident of birth." The language amending the Constitution in 1868 would read: "All persons born or naturalized in the United States and subject to jurisdiction thereof, are citizens of the United States and of the State wherein they reside."

The phrase "subject to the jurisdiction thereof," modern interpreters argue, was inserted to exclude self-governing American Indians (who would become U.S. citizens by statute in 1924) and to exclude the children of diplomats who happened to be born while their parents resided in the United States. It would figure in current-day debates over the citizenship status of children born in the U.S. to illegal aliens. [29] (*See "At Issue," p. 65.*)

In the latter 19th century, the waves of immigration continued at such a pace that in 1886, when the French government presented Americans with the world's largest statue to celebrate the American Revolution, they quickly converted the Statue of Liberty to a celebration of America's "open gates." Its famous poem by Emma Lazarus, a wealthy German Jew —"Give me your tired, your poor, your huddled masses yearning to breathe free" — is gently mocked by some modern-day descendants of immigrants, who point out that many of those masses were actually brimming with pluck and marketable skills. [30]

Fear of Foreigners

The phrase "the melting pot" was first popularized in a play written and produced in 1908 in Washington, D.C., by an immigrant named Israel Zangwill. The plot, which revolved around a Russian Jew and a Russian Christian who fall in love in New York City, included such universalist dialogue as: "East and west, and north and south, the palm and the pine, the pole and the equator, the crescent and the cross, how the Great Alchemist melts and fuses them with his purging flame!" [31]

Such transcendental ideals, however, were resisted by a prominent Jewish-American philosopher, Horace Kallen, who thought it more realistic to speak of "cultural pluralism." He wrote of "a federation or commonwealth of national cultures . . . a democracy of nationalities, cooperating voluntarily and autonomously through common institutions . . . a multiplicity in a unity." [32]

The issue was of no small consequence in the first decades of the 20th century. Statesmen such as Theodore Roosevelt and Woodrow Wilson expressed worry over the loyalties of what already were termed "hyphenated Americans." Roosevelt warned against becoming "a tangle of squabbling nationalities," and Wilson argued that "a man who thinks of himself as belonging to a particular national group in America has not yet

Continued on p. 62

Chronology

1800s *U.S. gains reputation as world's most welcoming immigrant society.*

1845-49
Ireland's potato famine sends more than a million Irish immigrants to the United States.

1886
President Grover Cleveland dedicates Statue of Liberty, a gift from France.

1898
Supreme Court rules in *United States v. Wong Kim Ark* that a man born in California to Chinese parents is a U.S. citizen.

1900s *The white Anglo-Saxon Protestant establishment grows concerned about open immigration by Irish, Italians, Greeks and Jews.*

1908
Opening of Israel Zangwill's play "The Melting Pot" in Washington.

1910
Census shows 13.5 million Americans out of a total population of 92 million are foreign-born.

1920s-1950s

Growing concern about immigration leads to restrictions.

1924
Congress tightens immigration, implementing quotas that favor Northern Europeans.

1941
Japanese attack on Pearl Harbor prompts U.S. to hold Japanese-Americans in internment camps.

1952
Immigration and Nationality Act limits non-Western Hemisphere immigrants and gives preference to high-skill workers.

1960s-1970s

Government "Great Society" programs lay groundwork for aid to immigrants.

1965
Immigration and Nationality Act Amendments increase immigration, invite more non-Europeans and stress family unification.

1972
Congress passes Ethnic Heritage Studies Programs Act.

1980s *Debate over high immigration levels produces compromise legislation.*

1980
Refugee Act calls for refugees to be processed separately from immigrants and offers social services.

1986
Immigration Reform and Control Act gives amnesty to illegal aliens, who in early 1990s will become eligible for citizenship.

1988
Immigration amendments promote diversity by allowing visas for countries that have sent few immigrants to the U.S. in recent years.

1990s *Efforts to streamline citizenship processing cause controversy.*

1990
Immigration Act (IMMACT) streamlines citizenship process for 4 million eligible citizens.

1994
Census reports that 22.3 million Americans are foreign-born. Jordan Commission on Immigration Reform recommends reducing number of immigrants. California voters pass Proposition 187 ("Save Our State") in November, denying school and health benefits to non-citizens including children; courts later block its implementation.

August 1995
Immigration and Naturalization Service (INS) launches Citizenship USA drive.

Aug. 1, 1996
House votes 259-169 to declare English the official language of the federal government.

September 1996
Financier George Soros sets up $50 million fund to help immigrants become citizens. President Clinton signs continuing resolution containing immigration bill beefing up border security. Congress holds hearings on whether INS and Vice President Al Gore sought to pressure INS to speed naturalizations to create Democratic voters.

Dec. 4, 1996
Supreme Court agrees to hear *Arizonans for Official English v. Arizona* on whether government services must be in English.

Should the Test for U.S. Citizenship Be...

Question: *A proper test for aspiring citizens should be (choose one):*
a) a solemn ritual that inculcates deep patriotic feelings;
b) a routine indicator that the applicant has mastered a minimum of American civics.

For a decade now, the Immigration and Naturalization Service (INS) has required every foreign-born person seeking U.S. citizenship to pass a written test. (In earlier decades, the tests were less formal, with administering attorneys merely requiring the applicant to write a few dictated sentences as proof of some knowledge of English.)

Today's test, typically comprised of a dozen questions drawn from nearly 300 that the INS has available, is a factually oriented review of Civics 101. It has simple queries about political history, the structure of the U.S. government and the design of the American flag. To prepare test takers, the INS publishes paperback books, such as "Citizenship Education and Naturalization Information," "United States History: 1600-1987" and "U.S. Government Structure."

Due in part to variations in how the test is administered in each of the 33 INS districts, it has become the object of political feuding between those who consider the questions laughably shallow and those concerned that new immigrants not be tripped up over challenges that are beyond the ken of many native-born citizens.

Journalist Georgie Anne Geyer, in her recent book bemoaning what she views as the "death of citizenship" in this country, sees the test as part of a general laxness she calls "the great American citizenship dumb-down." To the question, "Name one benefit of being a citizen of the United States," a thoughtful would-be citizen, she says, might reflect on French writer Hector Saint John de Crevecoeur's 18th-century notion of the American "who is a new man, who acts upon new principles." [1] Instead, she notes, the answers the INS accepts focus on such personal benefits as "vote for the candidate of your choice, travel with a U.S. passport, serve on a jury, apply for federal employment opportunities."

Other critics complain that only 5-10 percent of the test takers fail, largely, they argue, because local test officials in the districts sometimes spoonfeed applicants the answers. "We try to administer the test in line with the applicant's capacity," an assistant INS district director in Puerto Rico told two researchers from the Center for Equal Opportunity. [2]

"There is an overemphasis on memorization, which is one-dimensional, and the facts are not presented in context," says center President Linda Chavez. "But the test shouldn't be a Ph.D. dissertation."

Finally, many observers object to reports that the INS conducts some citizenship tests in Spanish, Thai or Vietnamese. "It is sad that they would give the test in multiple languages," says Yeh Ling-Ling, founder of the Diversity Coalition for an Immigration Moratorium, in San Francisco. "Why become a citizen if you can't speak the language of the land? They should make the test tougher, because now people call it a joke."

Proposals to require more of test takers are resisted by Dennis Gallagher, executive director of the Refugee Policy Group in Washington, D.C. "The critics ought to go out to some high school that has lower-middle-class whites and give them the test, and see how many of them know the name of the vice president," he says. "You can't impose on immigrants higher standards than you impose on your own people who already speak good English."

Indeed, surveys of average American students show startling gaps in their knowledge of civics. Results of a "grade-school-level" questionnaire given to 500 college seniors by the Roper

Sample Naturalization Questions

What do the stripes on the flag mean?

What country did we fight during the Revolutionary War?

Who elects the President of the U.S.?

How many changes or amendments are there to the Constitution?

What are the duties of Congress?

Can you name the two Senators from your state?

Who becomes President if both the President and Vice President die?

Can you name the 13 original states?

Who said, "Give me liberty or give me death?"

Which countries were our Allies during World War II?

Who helped the Pilgrims in America?

Name one amendment which guarantees or addresses voting rights?

Which President freed the slaves?

Continued from p. 60

become an American." [33]

During the first decades of the 20th century, America was home to a (then and still) unequalled proportion of foreign-born residents — mainly Irish, Italians, Greeks and European Jews. Many of them were seeking what Jewish writer Irving Howe called "an interval of equilibrium." For Russian Jews, this meant "a structure of values neither strictly religious or rigidly secular" for use in adapt-

. . . a Patriotic Ritual or a Routine Drill?

Center for Public Opinion Research last year showed that only 44 percent correctly answered such questions as, Which political party is currently in the majority in Congress? and How many United States senators are there?

One proposal now under debate would eliminate the test for any applicant with a U.S. high school diploma or anyone who has passed a course in U.S. history or political science at any American college or INS-approved facility. [3]

Defenders of offering the test in foreign languages point out that by law, the INS permits it only for applicants who are at least 50 years old and who have been in the United States for at least 20 years. (Those at least 55 years old need only to have been in the country 15 years.)

About 90 percent of those who take the test pass on the first try, according to a 1992 survey by the Los Angeles-based National Association of Latino Elected and Appointed Officials. Of the test takers, 49.5 percent described the test as very easy, 28 percent as somewhat easy and just 25 percent as hard. Fully 97 percent of those surveyed thought the questions were fair.

Complaints that the citizenship test should be more standardized around the country were first addressed in the early 1990s. Following a set of streamlining procedures passed as part of the 1990 Immigration Act, the Educational Testing Service (ETS), in Princeton, N.J., was asked to create a uniformly worded set of questions that test givers can choose from. At the same time, however, the INS agreed to contract out about a quarter of its citizenship testing to six private firms, including ETS and American College Testing. Some offer courses in how to pass the test, charging up to $215, and many boast a 98 percent pass rate.

"Many of the outside groups that are administering the test or are working closely with the INS on regulations are the same organizations that reject Americanization, work hard at obliterating all distinctions between citizens and non-citizens and promote multicultural separatism," complains American Enterprise Institute scholar John Fonte. [4]

One licensee, Florida-based Naturalization and Assistance Services Inc., last year was the target of television news exposés that captured test proctors on videotape coaching paying applicants as to which questions would be on the company-administered test. A subsequent INS investigation resulted in the company losing its contract (a decision it is challenging in court), and the INS rethinking its policy of hiring outside firms to conduct tests.

Rep. Lamar Smith, R-Texas, chairman of the Judiciary Subcommittee on Immigration and Claims, is planning oversight hearings early this year that will focus, in part, on the conduct of citizenship test licensees. It's part of an overall look at charges that the INS in the Clinton administration has accelerated the naturalization process to create more Democratic voters. "We will ask very probing questions on whether the INS had begun to investigate Naturalization and Assistance Services before the news media called attention to it," Smith spokesman Allen Kay says.

David Rosenberg, INS director of program initiatives, explains that the reason for the variations in different INS districts is that the decision to qualify someone for citizenship is a judgment call made by an immigration official after a face-to-face interview and a separate oral test for spoken English. "There is no requirement that a certain number of the civics questions be answered," he says. "The test is just one tool."

The INS is seeking to develop a new, more standardized test, Rosenberg adds, working with the Center for Applied Linguistics and soliciting suggestions from the public. "We are not saying that the test is either too hard or too easy. We're focusing on what people use. I mean, to ask which was the 49th state is a test of whether the applicant completely read the study book, but is it really something that all Americans must know?

"We would like to get at something more substantive, such as the concept of government limited by the people," he says. "But the written test was never envisioned as a knowledge test — imagine the language sophistication that would be needed."

Rosenberg envisions the ideal test as one that encourages the "minimum knowledge needed to participate in the body politic so one can become part of the mainstream and not be open to demagoguery." At this stage, he says, "it doesn't have to be more than a basis on which to build."

But still, the test does represent "our stamp of approval," Rosenberg adds, which is one reason the INS sponsors a public television series called "Cafe Crossroads," a sort of "adult Sesame Street" for the basics of American civic life. "The INS feels an obligation not just to test the applicants, but a duty to help them prepare."

---

1 Georgie Anne Geyer, *Americans No More: The Death of Citizenship* (1996), p. 3.

2 John J. Miller and William James Muldoon, "Citizenship for Granted: How the INS Devalues Naturalization Testing," Center for Equal Opportunity Policy Brief, October 1996.

3 Arnold Rochvarg, "Reforming the Administrative Naturalization Process: Reducing Delays While Increasing Fairness," *Georgetown Immigration Law Journal*, Vol. 9, No. 3, summer 1995, p. 428.

4 Testimony at hearings before Senate Judiciary Subcommittee on Immigration and Claims, Oct. 22, 1996.

ing American ideas, style, manners and language to be "transformed by their absorption" into Yiddish culture. [34]

The blending, however, was not always smooth. A contemporary observer described the new arrivals at the dock as "hirsute, low-browed, big-faced persons of obviously low mentality. . . . They simply look out of place in black clothes and stiff collar, since clearly they belong in skins, in wattled huts at the close of the Great

Ice Age." [35] And in the infamous Red Scare of 1920, Attorney General A. Mitchell Palmer raided immigrant homes looking for anarchists and Bolsheviks, arguing that Fourth Amendment bans on search and seizure did not apply to foreigners. [36]

In the 1920s, with Congress having enacted a crackdown on unchecked immigration, the rise of presidential candidate Al Smith, a New York Democrat and the first Catholic to run nationally, became an emblem of the country's divisions over immigration. Influential columnist Walter Lippmann was moved to comment: "Here are the new people, clamoring to be admitted to America, and there are the older people defending their household gods. The rise of Al Smith has made the conflict plain, and his career has come to involve a major aspect of the destiny of American civilization." [37]

Ethnic Pride

Mainstream culture, meanwhile, clearly celebrated the superiority of native-born Americans. As author Sanford Ungar argues, patriotic lyrics by early-20th century songwriter George M. Cohan contained a gentle jab at naturalized citizens: "This is my country; *land of my birth*. This is my country, the greatest on Earth." [38]

Many immigrants would compensate by becoming superpatriots, among them Sol Feinstone, a Lithuanian Jew who came to America in 1902. Working his way up in New York City sweatshops, he became a chemist and then a real estate investor. The fortune he amassed allowed him to become a philanthropist and major collector of books and 18th-century manuscripts relating to the American Revolution. He would found a well-known library in Washington Crossing, Pa. [39]

As second and third generations were launched, however, there arose a new phenomenon of ethnic pride. In the oft-quoted words of immigration historian Marcus Lee Hansen, "What the son wishes to forget, the grandson wishes to remember." [40] The post-World War II period brought popular ethnic novels and Broadway plays (such as "Fiddler on the Roof" and novels by Philip Roth and Saul Bellow), while the 1960 election of Irish-Catholic John F. Kennedy, one historian wrote, "reinvigorated the idea that being an American also meant being a member of one ancestral group or another." [41]

By the 1970s, Democratic Rep. Roman Pucinski of Chicago was holding hearings on ethnicity, criticizing the tendency to "homogenize 200 million human beings into a single monolith, instead of recognizing that America is a magnificent mosaic, made up of many cultures." [42]

In 1972, Congress enacted the Ethnic Heritage Studies Programs Act, and the Ford Foundation and other philanthropic groups began giving out ethnic-studies grants. The American Jewish Committee and the U.S. Catholic Conference began serving as mediators in tensions between ethnics and American blacks. By 1988, when Greek-American Michael S. Dukakis became the first major ethnic candidate in modern times to seek the presidency, his campaign theme song was Neil Diamond's "Coming to America."

Modern immigrants and their descendants were not only proud of their ethnic identity, but — unlike their predecessors — they could count on government policies designed to help them along. "The civic incorporation of newcomers," wrote the late Barbara C. Jordan, chair of the 1994 U.S. Commission on Immigration Reform, "is an essential part of immigration policy."

As Jordan later told a congressional hearing, "It was immigration that taught us that, in this country, it does not matter where you came from, or who your parents were. What counts is who you are." [43] ■

CURRENT SITUATION

Immigration Politics?

Last fall, thousands of new Americans gave up foreign allegiances by taking the citizenship oath in courtrooms, sports stadiums and even historic sites such as Mount Vernon, George Washington's stately Virginia home. By law, each candidate must be at least 18 years of age; have lived in the U.S. legally for five years; be of good moral character; be able to speak, read, write and understand ordinary English words and phrases; and be able to demonstrate knowledge and understanding of the fundamentals of U.S. history and principles of government. Also required are $95, two photos and a fingerprint card.

In return, citizenship bestows on citizens the right to vote, serve on a jury, hold office, apply for government jobs that require security clearance, bring immediate relatives to the U.S. without a waiting period and travel abroad for an unlimited time.

For years, applicants have found themselves thwarted by INS backlogs. In 1994, the wait for citizenship processing was 390 days in the Detroit district, 360 days in San Francisco and 300 days in Milwaukee, according to the National Immigration Forum.

When Meissner, a veteran INS official, appeared at her confirmation hearings in 1993, she and a bipartisan group in Congress agreed that the agency should seek ways to reduce its backlog. Following a 1995 report on "Reengineering the Naturalization Process," the INS added 1,000 new staffers. At the same time, the National Performance Review, the government

Continued on p. 66

At Issue:

Should children born to illegal immigrants in the United States be denied birthrights to U.S. citizenship?

yes

REP. ELTON GALLEGLY, R-CALIF.
FROM TESTIMONY BEFORE A JOINT HEARING OF THE HOUSE JUDICIARY SUBCOMMITTEE ON IMMIGRATION AND CLAIMS AND THE SUBCOMMITTEE ON THE CONSTITUTION, DEC. 13, 1995.

Since 1991, I have sponsored legislation to amend our Constitution to abolish automatic citizenship to children born in this country to illegal alien parents. . . . I have long championed this change to the 14th Amendment because it is my belief that our current law encourages widespread illegal immigration and costs American taxpayers billions of dollars each year.

I expect that opponents of this change in our citizenship law will decry this proposal as radical. However, far from being radical, such restrictions on citizenship are the norm around the world. Only a handful of countries — Argentina, Canada and Mexico — still grant automatic birthright citizenship. . . .

Nearly every nation in Europe, Africa and Asia does not permit automatic citizenship to children of illegal immigrants. In fact, both the United Kingdom and even Australia, a country which shares a long immigration tradition similar to ours, both repealed their U.S.-style citizenship policies during the 1980s. My proposed amendment is much more limited. It would confer automatic citizenship to children of legal residents as well as citizens, denying it only to children of illegal alien parents.

This change in our citizenship laws is long overdue, as there are a growing number of women who illegally enter the United States for the sole purpose of giving birth to an American citizen. . . . [T]hese children are eligible for federal, state and local benefit programs, and having a child is a virtual guarantee against deportation. In addition, under our current legal immigration system, the citizen child can sponsor [his] illegal parents, or any other close relative, for permanent resident status. . . .

Some will argue that the reform would violate the spirit of the 14th Amendment. That amendment was drafted after the Civil War to guarantee that recently freed slaves did not lose their citizenship rights based on action by the states. When that amendment was enacted in 1868, there were no illegal immigrants in the United States because there were no illegal-immigration laws until 1875.

Other advocates of maintaining the status quo argue that reforming citizenship policies would create a permanent subclass of residents, as is found in some parts of the world. I reject that analogy because our nation continues to encourage assimilation and citizenship of those who are here legally. Our proposal only aims at illegal immigrants.

no

REP. LUIS V. GUTIERREZ, D-ILL.
FROM TESTIMONY BEFORE A JOINT HEARING OF THE HOUSE JUDICIARY SUBCOMMITTEE ON IMMIGRATION AND CLAIMS AND THE SUBCOMMITTEE ON THE CONSTITUTION, DEC. 13, 1995.

Should we deny citizenship to an entire group of people — people born in America? Let me answer by quoting a Republican. A Republican leader who also had to consider whether we should deny citizenship to an entire group of people, born in America. A Republican leader who faced a decision — how to respond to a Supreme Court that wanted to deny those rights.

How did that Republican leader respond to the idea that America should deny citizenship to an entire group of people? He said that idea, quote, "does obvious violence to the plain, unmistakable language of the Declaration of Independence. It leaves the Declaration assailed, and sneered at, and construed, and hawked at, and torn — till, if its framers could rise from their graves, they could not at all recognize it."

That Republican was Abraham Lincoln. The idea was Justice Roger Taney's *Dred Scott* decision — which denied the right of citizenship to all blacks, merely because they were black. Our greatest president answered that idea with courage. And because he did, the 14th Amendment was born, and America became a greater, stronger nation. That Republican, faced with exclusion, chose unity. Lincoln took a stand — a stand that our nation should not abandon the words of the Declaration of Independence . . . that "We hold these truths to be self-evident, that all Men are created equal."

Now, the proposals before this committee make a very different declaration: that today "We hold these truths to be self-evident, that all Men — except those born to non-citizens — are created equal." The proposals that we consider today suggest that where Lincoln chose brotherhood, we should choose division. . . .

Lincoln was right: Denying citizenship to an entire group of people at our whim leaves the Declaration of Independence assailed. It leaves the Constitution frayed. And it steals from the American people a principle that is at the foundation of what makes our nation great — a commitment to equality.

Unfortunately, this stab at the heart of the Constitution and the Declaration of Independence is wrapped in rhetoric concerning a serious national problem. Sponsors of these proposals want us to believe that by punishing children, our nation's immigration problems will somehow magically disappear. Unfortunately, absolutely no evidence exists that supports these claims. . . .

FOR MORE INFORMATION

Congressional Asian Pacific American Caucus Institute (CAPACI), 1301 K St. N.W., Suite 400, East Tower, Washington, D.C. 20005; (202) 289-0355. This group collects statistics, provides forums, informs citizens on legislation, runs an intern program and presses for Asian-Pacific Americans to win government appointments.

Federation for American Immigration Reform, 1666 Connecticut Ave. N.W., Suite 400, Washington, D.C. 20009; (202) 328-7004. Founded in 1979, FAIR is a national advocacy group that works for "new and realistic approaches to immigration law and border security."

National Council of La Raza, 810 First St. St. N.E., Suite 300, Washington, D.C. 20002; (202) 785-1670. La Raza, the nation's largest Hispanic civil rights group, monitors legislative and regulatory policies affecting Hispanics and provides technical assistance in such areas as language, housing, community development and immigration.

National Immigration Forum, 220 I St. N.E., Suite 220, Washington, D.C. 20002; (202) 544-0004. Founded in 1982, this coalition of 200 organizations promotes "fair and generous immigration policies in the United States."

Continued from p. 64

efficiency effort led by Vice President Al Gore, became interested. In August 1995, the INS launched "Citizenship USA," a centralized paperwork-tracking center that President Clinton called "the most ambitious citizenship effort in history." As the election drew nearer, Gore stepped in to further "cut red tape" after hearing complaints from immigrant groups that INS "incompetence" might deprive thousands of aspiring citizens of a chance to vote in the 1996 elections. [44]

Republican political strategists, however, became wary that the Clinton administration was seeking to pad the electoral rolls with new immigrants, who, they believe, tend to vote Democratic. The accelerated efforts became the subject of political accusations. "Aren't you outraged that Vice President Gore with his staff would push the INS to naturalize as many people as possible?" presidential candidate Bob Dole thundered last fall. He accused the INS of rushing through over a million applicants "so they could be ready for the election, even if they have criminal records." [45]

In late October, the INS released a review saying it had found no evidence that applicants with criminal records had had their background checks waived. But after the elections, current and former INS employees told a House panel that FBI background checks had been skipped for more than 10,000 applications. [46] The INS again reported that it had tightened procedures but that it had not waived checks for anyone. Attorney General Janet Reno rejected a Republican request for an independent counsel to look into the INS.

David Rosenberg, the INS director of program initiatives, said the issue was not a new policy instituted by the Democrats but problems with the existing policy. The FBI, he said, partly because it was short-staffed following the move of its fingerprint center to West Virginia, fell behind in processing citizenship applications, but that only 2 percent of the year's applications were affected. When critics refer to criminal "rap sheets" they must be careful, he added, because not all charges against someone resulted in a conviction, and while a homicide conviction automatically disqualifies one for citizenship, a drunken-driving offense might not, depending on the circumstances.

Still, Rosenberg says, the INS is double-checking all the cases in question, using an outside auditor. "None of this was political or a last-minute election-year policy," he says. "Yes, there are always local pressures from community groups who have political intent, but from a social and governmental standpoint, it is still a positive thing to try to get people to become citizens and exercise suffrage."

Ethnics for Democrats

The Republican assumption that immigrants vote Democratic seemed to have been partially borne out in the November elections. Republicans took a beating in many high-immigrant areas, and 72 percent of Latino votes went Democratic. (Democrats took only 43 percent of the Asian vote, however.) Most notable was the defeat of conservative Rep. Robert K. Dornan, R-Calif., by Loretta Sanchez, the daughter of Mexican immigrants, by less than a thousand votes.

"I don't want to be the first person in history, man or woman, House or Senate, to be voted out of office by felons, by people voting who are not U.S. citizens, who are felons or children or people not allowed to vote," Dornan told C-SPAN in early December after demanding a recount and filing a fraud complaint with House officials. Orange County records studied by the National Immigration Forum showed that voter registration went up by 9,000 among Latinos, and by 7,000 among Vietnamese, but down 17,000 among whites. Approximately the same changes were recorded for voter turnout, a clear sign of immigrant impact on Dornan's race.

The Republicans brought it on themselves, says the forum's Sharry. "If you stand in line at the naturalization bureau, the name on all the immigrants' lips is [Republican California Gov.] Pete Wilson," he says.

"He and lots of GOP politicians after him have used the language issue, bilingual education and citizenship to blur the line between legal and illegal immigrants. He tried to ride the tiger of Proposition 187, but the GOP ended up in the tiger's belly," referring to the 1994 ballot referendum that would have cut off public health and welfare aid to all California immigrants. "Immigrants felt attacked, and feared government was after them," Sharry says, "so they did what people in a democracy do — they expressed power at the ballot box.

"What's wrong with this picture?" he asks. "Nothing. Most immigrants seem to have voted for Clinton, but party affiliation is up for grabs. Our polls show the Cubans went mostly for Dole. Immigrants don't just vote on the immigration issue; they're concerned about crime, education and jobs, and tend to be socially conservative. The Democrats benefited this time only."

Chavez, a Republican, said the "GOP made a big mistake by going hog wild on immigration. But Pete Wilson is a smart politician who had an uphill battle, and immigration gave him an issue that he had hoped would take him national. He's not a racist. He probably wanted to walk the line but attracted some folks who are motivated for the wrong reasons. It's an old problem of being a politician."

A Changed Congress?

The recently departed 104th Congress passed an immigration bill in 1996 that sponsors originally had hoped would include broad language reducing legal immigration. But a coalition of immigrant advocacy groups and business interests blocked it. Instead, the legislation only provides new funding for a border fence between the U.S. and Mexico and new INS inspectors. [47]

Though many in the new Republican-controlled Congress are wary of taking on immigrant issues because of their 1996 losses, several are talking of changing the law on the birthright of babies born to illegals. And the effort begun in the House last year to declare English as the nation's official language is expected to be renewed.

Clinton, meanwhile, is hoping to use executive authority to block some of the provisions of last year's welfare reform bill that halt aid to legal immigrants. Wilson, in a reversal, recently announced that he would allow children of legal immigrants to still get some public welfare and health benefits. [48] ■

OUTLOOK

Weaving New Fabric

In November, the New York state Legislature passed a bill requiring every public and private school in the state to teach about the devastation inflicted on the Irish by the 19th-century potato famine, including discussion of charges that British agricultural and trade policies deliberately caused the tragedy. [49]

That demonstration of political clout by a well-entrenched ethnic group was followed the next month by a sign of coming immigrant clout. Shanghai-born computer mogul Charles B. Wang announced that he was giving nearly $25 million to establish an Asian-American cultural center at the State University of New York at Stony Brook to create a little "touch of home" for students from Asia.

The Census Bureau, meanwhile, forecasts 9 million new immigrants to the U.S. this decade, the most since the 1900s.

Will we all get along? The Ford Foundation study says it will take leadership in bridge-building by teachers, clergy, social workers and police. And it recommends shared activities such as sports and public festivals, which "create opportunities for interaction and improve the general level of tolerance. Festivals often reduce tension because they celebrate symbols of diversity, such as food and dance, that do not directly threaten day-to-day American beliefs about culture and identity," the study says. [50]

In California, trade analyst and demographer Joel Kotkin notes that 20 percent of the marriages are interracial, and that nearly half of the Mexican-Americans intermarry. [51] "No nation in history had proved as successful as the United States in managing ethnic diversity," historian Lawrence Fuchs said. "No nation before had ever made diversity itself a source of national identity and unity." [52]

Harvard's Glazer recommends that policy-makers "concentrate on a few problems, such as the language issue, and not focus on the general resistance to assimilate. As a country, we made political errors," he said. "We allowed language rights in voting, which became mere rallying points for militants, and we allowed foreign languages to become the way to get federal money. We should withdraw from our errors, even though that creates the impression that we're anti-immigrant. They were only mistakes."

FAIR's Stein warns that "we're changing into a country that lacks a coherent civic culture. There's more to civic life than cuisine. We must balance immigration with the natural desire to remain a family as defined by natural boundaries. We have to reassert our national and religious identity out of civic defense. That means building a sense in immigrants that there's a country worth dying for. Being an American is a set of core virtues, and values. It is not ethnically defined."

To Chavez, "There is such a thing as American exceptionalism, with the hegemony of our vibrant pop culture. We're a wonderful country, but we risk losing that. We have enormous problems in crime, the family, city decay."

Many of the perceptions of the

problems, however, have to do with fear of the unknown and preconceived notions. In 1992, the American Jewish Committee surveyed Americans on their perception of the social standing of 58 ethnic groups. At the top of the ladder were Germans, Irish and Scandinavians, followed by Italians, Greeks, Poles, Russians and Jews. Yet the lowest score went to a fictional group the researchers created and named the Wisians." Fully 39 percent of Americans believed that Wisians as a class were not doing well. [53]

"New immigrants have always been hated, and xenophobia and insecurity are hardly new," says Gallagher of the Refugee Policy Group. "We're in one cycle now, and it will lift over the years. But the danger is, once we start to legislate against some of the negative things about immigration, the laws become harder to change later, even if public attitudes have changed." ■

Notes

[1] See "Asian Americans," *The CQ Researcher,* Dec. 13, 1991, pp. 945-968, and "Hispanic Americans," *The CQ Researcher,* Oct. 30, 1992, pp. 929-952.

[2] See "Cracking Down on Immigration," *The CQ Researcher,* Feb. 3, 1995, pp. 97-120; "Illegal Immigration," *The CQ Researcher,* April 24, 1992, pp. 361-384; and "Welfare, Work and the States," *The CQ Researcher,* Dec. 6, 1996, pp. 1057-1080.

[3] National Conference of State Legislatures, *America's Newcomers: An Immigrant Policy Handbook,* September 1994, p. 57.

[4] Testimony before the Senate Judiciary Subcommittee on Immigration, Oct. 22. 1996.

[5] *Ibid.*

[6] Ford Foundation, "Changing Relations" (1993), p. 4.

[7] Manhattan Institute and Pacific Research Institute, *Strangers at Our Gate: Immigration in the 1990s* (1994), p. 76.

[8] Senate Judiciary hearing, *op. cit.*

[9] *The New York Times,* Dec. 1, 1996.

[10] Terry Anderson, "The Culture Clash in South-Central L.A." *Los Angeles Times,* May 29, 1996.

[11] Peter Brimelow, *Alien Nation* (1995), p. xix.

[12] National Conference of State Legislatures, *op. cit.,* p. 60.

[13] *The Wall Street Journal,* July 11, 1996.

[14] Quoted in National Endowment for the Humanities, "A National Conversation: How We Act in Private and in Public," 1994.

[15] See "Debate Over Bilingualism," *The CQ Researcher,* Jan. 19, 1996, pp. 49-72.

[16] Senate Judiciary hearings, *op. cit.*

[17] Quoted in *The New York Times,* Dec. 30, 1996.

[18] David M. Kennedy, "Can We Still Afford to be a Nation of Immigrants?" *The Atlantic Monthly,* November 1996, p. 58.

[19] See "Low-Wage Lessons," *Business Week,* Nov. 11, 1996, p. 109.

[20] See Juan F. Perea (ed.), *Immigrants Out! The New Nativism and the Anti-Immigrant Impulse in the United States* (1997), p. 13.

[21] Quoted in National Conference of State Legislatures, *op. cit.,* p. 49.

[22] Sanford Ungar, *Fresh Blood: The New American Immigrants* (1996), p. 98. Ungar is dean of the School of Communications at American University.

[23] National Endowment for the Humanities, *op. cit.*

[24] Arthur M. Schlesinger Jr., *The Disuniting of America* (1991), p. 1.

[25] Perea, *op. cit.,* p. 18.

[26] Interviewed in *Los Angeles Times,* June 12, 1994.

[27] Brimelow, *op. cit.,* p. 213.

[28] Schlesinger, *op. cit.,* p. 9.

[29] See House Judiciary Committee hearings, Dec. 13, 1995.

[30] Column by A.M. Rosenthal, *The New York Times,* Dec. 3, 1996.

[31] Arthur Mann, *The One and the Many: Reflections on the American Identity* (1979), p. 100.

[32] Schlesinger, *op. cit.,* p. 13.

[33] *Ibid.,* pp. 12, 69.

[34] Irving Howe, *World of Our Fathers* (1976), p. 169.

[35] Kennedy, *op. cit.,* p. 52.

[36] Ungar, *op. cit.,* p. 107.

[37] Mann, *op. cit.,* p. 131.

[38] Ungar, *op. cit.,* p. 106.

[39] David J. Fowler, *Guide to the Sol Feinstone Collection of the David Library of the American Revolution* (1994).

[40] Schlesinger, *op. cit.,* p. 16.

[41] Mann, *op. cit.,* p. 5.

[42] *Ibid.,* p. 37.

[43] Statement to House Judiciary Committee hearings, Dec. 13, 1995.

[44] Dick Kirschten, "The Politics of Citizenship," *Government Executive,* January 1997, p. 36.

[45] Quoted in *National Journal,* Nov. 30, 1996, p. 2622.

[46] *The Washington Times,* Dec. 13, 1996. The House panel was the Government Reform and Oversight Subcommittee on National Security, International Affairs and Criminal Justice.

[47] *CQ Weekly Report,* Dec. 14, 1996, p. 3397.

[48] *Los Angeles Times* [Washington edition], Dec. 23, 1996.

[49] *The New York Times,* Nov. 21, 1996.

[50] Ford Foundation, *op. cit.,* p. 56.

[51] Manhattan Institute and Pacific Research Institute, *op. cit.,* p. 92.

[52] Schlesinger, *op. cit.,* p. 79.

[53] National Conference of State Legislatures, *op. cit.,* p. 51.

Bibliography

Selected Sources Used

Books

Peter Brimelow, *Alien Nation: Common Sense About America's Immigration Disaster,* Random House, 1995.
A British-born, U.S.-naturalized, conservative writer for *Forbes* and *National Review* magazines lays out his ideological and historical case for curbing immigration.

Chavez, Linda, *Out of the Barrio: Toward a New Politics of Hispanic Assimilation,* Basic Books, 1991.
The president of the Center for Equal Opportunity criticizes Hispanic ethnic lobbies in the United States that pursue a separate culture and government benefits.

Geyer, Georgie Anne, *Americans No More: The Death of Citizenship,* Atlantic Monthly Press, 1996.
A longtime syndicated columnist in international affairs outlines her case that promiscuous immigration policies and what she sees as a lax approach to processing citizenship applications pose disturbing questions about the future of the country.

Mann, Arthur, *The One and the Many: Reflections on the American Identity,* University of Chicago Press, 1979.
A University of Chicago historian offers this historical overview of the forces that shaped the American immigrant experience, offering a paradigm for group affiliation in the United States that leaves room for ethnic loyalty while creating an American whole.

Juan F. Perea (ed.), *Immigrants Out!: The New Nativism and the Anti-Immigrant Impulse in the United States,* New York University Press, 1997.
A University of Florida law professor assembled these interdisciplinary essays providing history and analysis of political and behavioral issues that the authors regard as nativistic and xenophobic, including the official English movement.

Arthur M. Schlesinger Jr., *The Disuniting of America: Reflections on a Multicultural Society',* Whittle Direct Books, 1991.
A noted historian now at the City University of New York surveys the literature and history of the American "melting pot," asking whether the 'E Pluribus" is in danger of overshadowing the "unum."

Ungar, Sanford J., *Fresh Blood: The New American Immigrants,* Simon & Schuster, 1995.
A journalist and foreign affairs analyst now the dean of American University School of Communications traces his own Eastern European ancestry, interviews dozens of immigrants across the United States and argues that many of the tensions involving new American immigrants result from misunderstanding.

Reports

Bouvier, Leon, *Embracing America: A Look at Which Immigrants Become Citizens,* Center for Immigration Studies, 1996.
A demographer for a Washington-based research and policy group examines the numbers and trends within different immigrant nationalities to determine which factors—education and language skills, for example—make residents more likely to seek citizenship.

Ford Foundation, *Changing Relations: Newcomers and Established Residents in U.S. Communities,* 1993.
A multidisciplinary team of scholars from the State University of New York examined which programs and approaches are best for integrating new immigrants into the American mainstream, emphasizing the responsibilities both of immigrants and native-born Americans.

National Conference of State Legislatures, *America's Newcomers: Am Immigrant Policy Handbook,* September 1994.
This anthology of articles assembled by the immigrant policy division of a state legislatures group examines federal, state and local programs designed to ease the transition of new immigrants.

Manhattan Institute and Pacific Research Institute, *Strangers at Our Gate: Immigration in the 1990s,* 1994.
Two conservative think tanks teamed up to collect these essays, debating statements and data advancing the argument for slowing the current rate of immigration to the United States.

National Endowment for the Humanities, *A National Conversation on American Pluralism and Identity,* 1994.
As part of NEH Chairman Sheldon Hackney's "conversation starter" series to promote American discourse, this packet provides essays, quotations, histories and provocative questions surrounding immigration, ethnicity, race and patriotism.

The Next Step

Additional information from UMI's Newspaper & Periodical Abstracts™ database

Immigration as a Political Issue

Branigin, William, "Immigration issues await new Congress," *The Washington Post,* Nov. 18, 1996, p. A5.
The far-reaching immigration law that took effect in October 1996 has left many issues festering, and legislators on both sides of the political divide agree that renewed debates are likely to occur when Congress reconvenes in 1997.

Dine, Philip, "Immigrants enter a volatile environment," *St. Louis Post-Dispatch,* Dec. 17, 1995, p. B5.
The nature and size of the stream of newcomers to the U.S. propel the expanding debate over immigration. Domestic changes that lend much of the edge are examined.

Dugger, Celia W., "Immigrant voters reshape politics," *The New York Times,* March 10, 1996, p. 1.
Largely because of their numbers, new immigrant citizens are reshaping the politics of New York City and the nation's highly charged debate about immigration. The phenomenal increase in the number of immigrants who are becoming citizens and voters in the city and across the nation is discussed.

Holmes, Steven A., "Influx of Immigrants Is Changing Electorate," *The New York Times,* Oct. 30, 1996, p. A16.
The growing influence of immigrants in politics is examined. Since the 1992 election, the Immigration and Naturalization Service (INS) says more than 2.3 million immigrants have been naturalized, the largest number of new citizens over a four-year presidential election cycle since 1924.

"Immigration 'reform' looks a lot like politics," *Los Angeles Times,* Sept. 25, 1996, p. B8.
An editorial criticized planned changes in Congress to U.S. immigration law.

Rosenfeld, Stephen S., "Getting a grip on immigration," *The Washington Post,* Oct. 18, 1996, p. A27.
Rosenfeld discusses the tangled issues involved in U.S. immigration policy and the political skirmishes over it in 1996.

Schmitt, Eric, "Milestones and Missteps on Immigration," *The New York Times,* Oct. 26, 1996, p. A1.
An analysis of the Clinton administration's immigration record is presented. The administration has poured more money and political capital into addressing immigration problems than any other administration in recent times. It has doubled the budget for the INS, increased the number of border patrol agents by about 45 percent, weeded out abuse in the political-asylum process and passed a bill that imposes tough measures against illegal immigration.

"Stop Attacking Immigrants," *Business Week,* Oct. 14, 1996, p. 142.
Although there are definite problems with immigration, the current actions of politicians to stigmatize immigrants cannot be tolerated. The U.S. is dependent on immigrants, who form a very important part of every industry.

Immigration and Naturalization Service

"Black immigrant says INS singled him out," *Los Angeles Sentinel,* May 23, 1996, p. A13.
Michael Williams, a 42-year-old rock musician who flew to Seattle, Wash., to reunite with his family before flying to London, was held for five days in an immigration detention center. Williams believes he was singled out by the INS either because he is a black man or because he complained of his treatment.

Branigin, William, "Immigrant job checks to expand," *The Washington Post,* Aug. 9, 1996, p. A15.
The Clinton administration is pushing ahead with a computerized pilot program to verify employment eligibility of immigrant job-seekers.

Dine, Philip, "U.S. joins with poultry firms to deny jobs to illegal immigrants," *St. Louis Post-Dispatch,* Aug. 16, 1996, p. C7.
Dine discusses how several poultry companies in Missouri and six other states have joined a pioneer program of the INS. According to Dine, the poultry industry was selected because the work requires little training or language ability and hence attracts many newcomers.

McDonald, Greg, "54,362 illegal immigrants, many of them felons, deported," *Houston Chronicle,* Aug. 30, 1996, p. A25.
More than 54,000 illegal immigrants, many of them convicted felons, have been deported in 1996, after being rounded up by U.S. immigration officials in operations focused on removing those who committed crimes after entering the U.S.

Schmitt, Eric, "Immigration Aides Deceived Lawmakers, Inquiry Finds," *The New York Times,* June 21, 1996, p. A14.
A Justice Department investigation has concluded that in 1995 top INS managers released detainees, including some with criminal records, to deceive a group of visiting House members about overcrowding and security problems at the agency's Miami facility.

Sullivan, John, and Clifford Levy, "Immigration Service Keeps a Wary Eye on its Newark Office," *The New York Times,* Aug. 18, 1996, p. 43.

When agents from the INS's office in Newark, N.J., swooped down on a private cleaning company at Newark International Airport in March 1995, they detained scores of illegal immigrants, recovering more than 60 fraudulently issued green cards and other work papers. But the striking success of the raid was quickly tempered by a sobering realization; at least some of those faked documents appeared to have been smuggled out of the immigration service's own office in Newark.

Sun, Lena H., "Immigration agency's geographical distinctions," *The Washington Post,* July 8, 1996, p. B1.

Baltimore's office of the INS, which handles immigrants living in Maryland, has earned a reputation as a responsive, smoothly run operation. The Washington, D.C., office, which handles immigrants in the District and Virginia, is known for just the opposite.

Williams, Lena, "A Law Aimed at Terrorists Hits Legal Immigrants," *The New York Times,* July 17, 1996, p. A1.

In the three months since a tougher new counterterrorism bill was signed into law, many immigrants who have been living legally in the U.S. for years have been placed in detention by the INS and are facing deportation. Under provisions in the new law, any resident immigrant who is not a naturalized citizen and has been convicted of a crime in the U.S. can be detained without appeal and is not eligible for release on bond.

Learning English

Hinojosa, Tish, "Immigrants add a rich flavor to the American stew," *Denver Post,* Oct. 27, 1996, p. F3.

Hinojosa comments on the development of Ignacio, a Mexican immigrant, and a friend in her son's bilingual class at school.

McKay, Sandra Lee, and Sau-Ling Cynthia Wong, "Multiple discourses, multiple identities: Investment and agency in second-language learning among Chinese adolescent immigrant students," *Harvard Educational Review,* fall 1996, pp. 577-608.

McKay and Wong argue for a revision of code-based and individual learner-based views of second-language learning. Their position is based on a two-year qualitative study of adolescent Chinese-immigrant students conducted in California in the early 1990s.

McKim, Jennifer, "Immigrants fear aid cuts as deadline looms," *The Boston Globe,* Nov. 10, 1996, Sec. WKC, p. 1.

The struggle of elderly immigrants to learn English in order to keep federal benefits which they will lose in 1997 due to the controversial welfare reform legislation passed by Congress and signed by President Clinton in 1996, is examined.

Parsekian, Penny, "English and Today's Young Immigrants," *The New York Times,* Dec. 31, 1995, Sec. CN, p. 3.

In an interview, James Connelly, superintendent of schools in Bridgeport, Conn., discusses the problems of dealing with a multilingual student body. Connelly says that about 44 percent of his students come from homes where English is not the first language.

Pyle, Amy, "Debate focuses on school standards for immigrants," *Los Angeles Times,* Nov. 21, 1996, p. A3.

The plight of immigrant students dominated discussion over proposed statewide high school graduation standards at the first of two Southern California hearings on those standards, with the state's two largest advocacy groups for bilingual students taking dramatically different stands.

Walters, Laurel Shaper, "U.S. immigrants join rebellion to topple bilingual education," *The Christian Science Monitor,* May 23, 1996, p. 1.

Though criticism of bilingual education dates back to its earliest days in the 1960s, the latest backlash against such education is coming from immigrant parents. Parents across the U.S. have complained that their children are held too long in bilingual classes and have been unable to master English.

Naturalization Issues

Brenner, Elsa, "Changes in Laws Spur Immigrants to Citizenship," *The New York Times,* Nov. 24, 1996, Sec. WC, p. 1.

Many immigrants in Westchester County, N.Y., are feeling a sense of urgency to attain legal status in the U.S. to protect themselves from changes in federal and local laws that are expected to make the lives of many immigrants more difficult.

DeSipio, Louis, "Making citizens or good citizens? Naturalization as a predictor of organizational and electoral behavior among Latino immigrants," *Hispanic Journal of Behavioral Sciences,* May 1996, pp. 194-213.

DeSipio draws on the Latino National Public Survey to contrast the political behaviors of naturalized and native-born Latino U.S. citizens.

Schneider, William, "Massive immigrant vote for Clinton?" *National Journal,* Sept. 14, 1996, p. 1986.

A speedup in naturalization procedures, combined with anger over Republican initiatives that hurt immigrants, could help President Clinton in his re-election bid. Clinton's Citizenship U.S.A. program is discussed.

Back Issues

Great Research on Current Issues Starts Right Here...Recent topics covered by The CQ Researcher are listed below. Before May 1991, reports were published under the name of Editorial Research Reports.

JULY 1995
War Crimes
Highway Safety
Combating Terrorism
Preventing Teen Drug Use

AUGUST 1995
Job Stress
Organ Transplants
United Nations at 50
Advances in Cancer Research

SEPTEMBER 1995
Catholic Church in the U.S.
Northern Ireland Cease-Fire
High School Sports
Teaching History

OCTOBER 1995
Quebec's Future
Revitalizing the Cities
Networking the Classroom
Indoor Air Pollution

NOVEMBER 1995
The Working Poor
The Jury System
Sex, Violence and the Media
Police Misconduct

Back issues are available for $5.00 (subscribers) or $10.00 (non-subscribers). Quantity discounts apply to orders over ten. To order, call Congressional Quarterly Customer Service at (202) 887-8621.

Binders are available for $18.00. To order call 1-800-638-1710. Please refer to stock number 648.

DECEMBER 1995
Teens and Tobacco
Gene Therapy's Future
Global Water Shortages
Third-Party Prospects

JANUARY 1996
Emergency Medicine
Punishing Sex Offenders
Bilingual Education
Helping the Homeless

FEBRUARY 1996
Reforming the CIA
Campaign Finance Reform
Academic Politics
Getting Into College

MARCH 1996
The British Monarchy
Preventing Juvenile Crime
Tax Reform
Pursuing the Paranormal

APRIL 1996
Centennial Olympic Games
Managed Care
Protecting Endangered Species
New Military Culture

MAY 1996
Russia's Political Future
Marriage and Divorce
Year-Round Schools
Taiwan, China and the U.S.

JUNE 1996
Rethinking NAFTA
First Ladies
Teaching Values
Labor Movement's Future

JULY 1996
Recovered-Memory Debate
Native Americans' Future
Crackdown on Sexual Harassment
Attack on Public Schools

AUGUST 1996
Fighting Over Animal Rights
Privatizing Government Services
Child Labor and Sweatshops
Cleaning Up Hazardous Wastes

SEPTEMBER 1996
Gambling Under Attack
The States and Federalism
Civic Journalism
Reassessing Foreign Aid

OCTOBER 1996
Political Consultants
Insurance Fraud
Rethinking School Integration
Parental Rights

NOVEMBER 1996
Global Warming
Clashing Over Copyright
Consumer Debt
Governing Washington, D.C.

DECEMBER 1996
Welfare, Work and the States
The New Volunteerism
Implementing the Disabilities Act
America's Pampered Pets

JANUARY 1997
Combating Scientific Misconduct
Restructuring the Electric Industry

Future Topics

- ***Biochemical Weapons***
- ***Refugees***
- ***Alternative Medicine's Next Phase***

THE CQ Researcher

PUBLISHED BY CONGRESSIONAL QUARTERLY INC.

Chemical and Biological Weapons

Should the U.S. sign the new treaty?

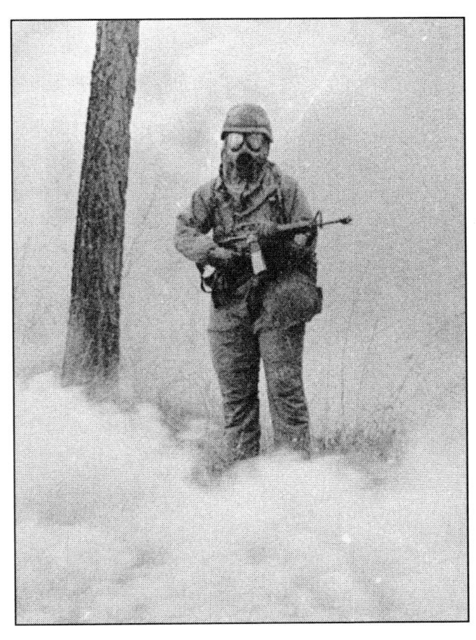

A global treaty banning the production, stockpiling and deployment of lethal agents will go into effect in April, but U.S. participation is questionable. Ratification of the Chemical Weapons Convention has been held up by senators who say the agreement lacks adequate verification provisions and would be too costly. Recent events are adding new elements to the debate over ways to curb chemical and biological weapons. New studies of Gulf War Syndrome are considering whether these weapons may cause disabling chronic illnesses as well as death. And the release of deadly sarin nerve gas in the Tokyo subway by members of a religious cult demonstrates the devastating impact these easily produced weapons of mass destruction can have on civilian targets as well.

INSIDE THIS ISSUE

CQ Jan. 31, 1997 • Volume 7, No. 4 • Pages 73-96

Formerly Editorial Research Reports

THE ISSUES

BACKGROUND

CURRENT SITUATION

OUTLOOK

SIDEBARS AND GRAPHICS

FOR FURTHER RESEARCH

COVER: SMOKE BILLOWS AROUND A MEMBER OF THE 82ND CHEMICAL BATTALION DURING TRAINING EXERCISES AT FORT MCCLELLAN, ALA. (U.S. ARMY/ARMS CONTROL ASSOCIATION)

Jan. 31, 1997
Volume 7, No. 4

The CQ Researcher (ISSN 1056-2036). Formerly Editorial Research Reports. Published weekly (48 times per year, not printed Jan. 3, May 30, Aug. 29, Oct. 31) by Congressional Quarterly Inc., 1414 22nd St., N.W., Washington, D.C. 20037. Annual subscription rate for libraries, businesses and government is $340. Additional rates furnished upon request. Periodicals postage paid at Washington, D.C., and additional mailing offices. POSTMASTER: Send address changes to The CQ Researcher, 1414 22nd St., N.W., Washington, D.C. 20037.

Chemical and Biological Weapons

By Mary H. Cooper

The Issues

In the heady days following the allied victory over Iraq in the Persian Gulf War in 1991, Brian Martin received the kind of order that combat engineers relish. Martin and his unit from the 37th Engineer Battalion had stumbled onto a vast ammunition depot, abandoned by fleeing Iraqi soldiers. Blow it up, they were ordered.

"Witnessing these awesome explosions was a remarkable sight," the 27-year-old Martin told a House panel recently. "The explosions blew straight into the air, and then would spread at the top. Many of us joked that this would be the closest thing to a nuclear mushroom cloud that we would . . . ever hope to see." [1]

The awe turned to horror, however, when missiles from the exploding bunkers and warehouses in Kamisiyah began raining down on Martin's unit. "Men were running everywhere for cover," he said. "Hiding behind our vehicles for safety, we felt all hell had broken loose."

The battalion retreated to a safer location, but for Martin's unit, the nightmare had just begun.

Actually, Martin told lawmakers, he had been suffering a variety of symptoms even before the ammo dump explosion. "Since just before those days at Kamisiyah, I have suffered from symptoms and ailments that have altered everything about me and my family's lives," he said. "It started in early 1991 with blood in [my] vomit and stools, blurred vision, shaking and trembling like I was on a caffeine high." Martin was diagnosed with multiple chemical sensitivity, inflammatory bowel disease, brain damage and other ailments and was discharged in December 1991 with permanent and total disability.

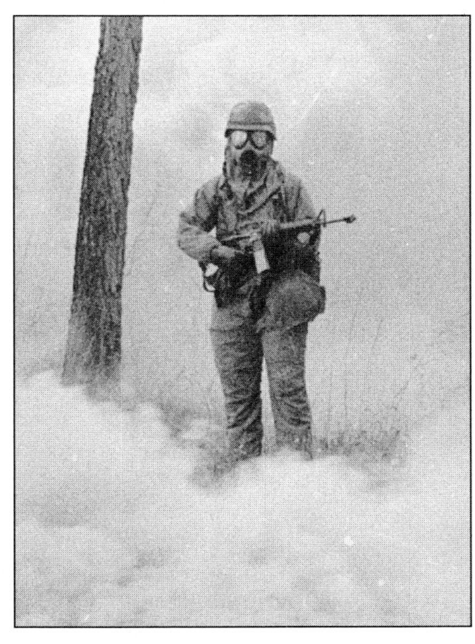

About 80,000 of the 697,000 American men and women who served in the Persian Gulf during Operations Desert Shield and Desert Storm say they suffer from the broad range of ailments known collectively as Gulf War Syndrome. The most common symptoms include joint pain, fatigue, headache and memory loss.

From the first deployment of U.S. troops in the region in August 1990 until their pullout in June 1991, the operation was initially hailed as a resounding victory, a "clean" war that had achieved its objective at a relatively low cost of 293 American deaths and 467 wounded.

But returning servicemen soon started complaining of sickness. Iraq was known to have stockpiled chemical and biological weapons. But because the Defense Department initially denied that personnel had been exposed to such agents, the symptoms were attributed to unknown causes or to post-traumatic shock, a mental disorder caused by stress.

Amid growing criticism of the government's response to the veterans' complaints, the Pentagon last June revealed that the Kamisiyah ammunition facility had indeed contained chemical weapons. But the official government position continued to be that the exposure to chemical agents had been insufficient to cause physical symptoms. (*See story, p. 80*)

At the White House on Jan. 7, a presidential advisory committee presented its 16-month study of Gulf War Syndrome. The 13-member panel said it found no conclusive evidence that the reported symptoms were caused by chemical or biological weapons and recommended further research.

The panel also offered scathing criticism of the government's handling of its investigations and its treatment of sick veterans. "Investigatory efforts have been slow and superficial, and no credible attempts to communicate with the public on these investigations have been made," they concluded. "Our most severe criticisms are reserved for this issue. Regrettably, [the Defense Department] did not act in good faith in this regard." [2]

Many gulf war veterans were frustrated by the panel's failure to link their illnesses to chemical weapons. Some senators, meanwhile, have been reluctant to act on a treaty to outlaw the very chemical agents that the veterans say cause Gulf War Syndrome. Indeed, the Chemical Weapons Convention failed to even reach the Senate floor for debate.

The Chemical Weapons Convention, the result of a draft treaty drawn up by the administration of Ronald Reagan in 1984 and signed by President George Bush in 1993, would ban the production of chemical weapons, as well as their use. Building on the 1925 Geneva Protocol for the Prohibition of the Use in War of Asphyxiating, Poisonous or Other Gases, and of Bacteriological Methods of Warfare, which only bans the actual use of chemical weapons, the new treaty also contains exhaustive provisions for verifying compliance. Signed by more

The Deadliest Chemical and Biological Agents

The Chemical Weapons Convention (CWC) that goes into effect April 29 lists three categories of chemicals that would be banned or regulated. The deadliest 25 chemicals, grouped in Schedule 1, are banned altogether and cannot be produced, sold or stored. Thirty other chemicals, mostly materials that have commercial use but could be transformed into weapons, are in schedules 2 and 3 and come under the treaty's monitoring regime, which allows for inspections of plants and storage facilities. These chemicals include:

Mustard gas: First used by Germany in World War I, mustard gas causes blistering over the entire body, including the eyes and lungs, blinding victims and often causing death by respiratory failure. Easy to produce and long-lasting, mustard and other so-called blistering agents make ideal chemical weapons because they force targeted soldiers to wear cumbersome protective gear. Blistering agents are all banned by the CWC and include nitrogen mustard and Lewisite.

Phosgene gas: Also used in World War I, phosgene is a choking agent, damaging the respiratory system and causing the lungs to fill with water and choke the victim. Because they dissipate quickly in the wind, choking agents, which also include chlorine gas, are less useful as weapons than blistering agents. Because they have broad commercial use, these agents either fall into Schedule 3, the least restrictive CWC category, or are unlisted.

Cyanogen chloride: When this Schedule 3 blood agent is inhaled, it destroys tissues by interrupting the supply of oxygen to the cells. Like choking agents, it dissipates quickly in the atmosphere.

Sarin: Developed in the 1930s, Sarin is one of several so-called G-series nerve agents that quickly paralyze and kill victims after minuscule amounts come in contact with the skin or lungs. Death is caused by respiratory paralysis. Similar nerve gases include soman, tabun and GF. All nerve agents are banned under the CWC.

VX: Developed in the 1950s, VX belongs to a class of chemicals called V-series nerve agents, which act by inhibiting a nervous system enzyme. Others are VE, VG, VM and VS.

Biological Agents and Toxins

The 1925 Geneva Protocol and the 1972 Biological and Toxin Weapons Convention ban the production, stockpiling and use of any biological agents as weapons. The most common agents used in weapons are anthrax, botulinum toxin and ricin. Other pathogens that are potential ingredients include emerging infectious agents, as well as a virtually endless range of microorganisms that may be produced through bioengineering. The broad range of potentially deadly pathogens includes:

Anthrax: Produced by a fermentation process similar to that used to make beer, anthrax, or the spores of the bacterium *Bacillus anthracis,* will kill if even minute quantities are inhaled or ingested. Death typically comes within five days of exposure if penicillin is not administered before the onset of symptoms. Death results from pneumonia, general infection and organ failure. One gram of anthrax would be enough to kill more than a third of the U.S. population.

Botulinum toxin: Produced by the common bacterium *Botulinum clostridium,* this toxin blocks the transmission of nerve impulses, causing paralysis and death, usually within two days, unless antitoxin is administered. One form of the toxin requires only one microgram to kill a person.

Ricin: This toxin, easily made from castor beans, is lethal when inhaled, usually within two hours. It attacks the circulatory system, causing fluid buildup in the lungs.

Q fever: This is one of several microorganisms known as rickettsiae, or intracellular parasites, that are similar in structure to bacteria. Others that are suitable for weapons include typhus and Rocky Mountain spotted fever.

Plague: A well-known but rare bacterial disease caused by contact with *Yersinia pestis,* plague was widespread in medieval Europe. A highly contagious form, pneumonic plague, broke out in India in 1994. The theory, later discounted, was that it was caused by a biological attack. Plague usually kills within five days unless antibiotics are administered.

Ebola virus: One of a number of "emerging" viruses unknown until recent outbreaks, Ebola has no known cure. It has killed about 90 percent of the infected people in natural outbreaks, usually within days. Death occurs as a result of "bleed-out," when organ systems break down. Because they cannot be controlled, emerging viruses are considered to be relatively poor candidates for weapons production.

Sources: Central Intelligence Agency, Business Executives for National Security

than 160 countries and already ratified by 67, the convention will enter into force on April 29, whether the United States ratifies it or not. Although the convention is strongly supported by the Clinton administration, its passage is uncertain.

The new treaty was prompted by the proliferation of chemical-weapons use in recent years. The Germans used deadly mustard gas on allied soldiers in World War I, but chemical weapons weren't used again in combat until Iraq turned them against Iran during their 1980-1988 war, as well as against dissident Kurdish communities in Iraq itself. Today, the number of countries believed to have chemical weapons programs has grown from about a dozen in 1980 to about 20.[3]

Concern over chemical weapons mounted in March 1995, when members of Aum Shinrikyo, a fanatical Japanese religious cult, released deadly sarin gas in the Tokyo subway system, killing 12 people and injuring more than 5,000. This first known use of chemical weapons by a terrorist group raised the specter of further terrorism using lethal chemicals, which are relatively easy to obtain and fashion into weapons of mass destruction.

"We have learned from the study of terrorism in the past that when a highly publicized incident occurs, it is more likely to be repeated," says Brian M. Jenkins, a terrorism expert and deputy chairman of Kroll Associates, an international investigative and consulting firm in Los Angeles. "I don't believe that chemical, Tokyo-type attacks are going to become the truck bombs of the second half of the 1990s. But I would assert that an event like the Tokyo attack is more probable than it was before March 1995."

Biological weapons could cause even more widespread devastation than chemical weapons. Lethal pathogens like anthrax bacilli and botulinum toxin are even easier to produce and conceal than deadly chemicals because they exist freely in nature. (*See story, p. 76.*) And unlike the Tokyo sarin attack, which affected the victims immediately, some biological weapons could kill long after they come into contact with people.

"Because of incubation periods, diseases take a while to develop after exposure," says James M. Hughes, director of the National Center for Infectious Diseases, a branch of the Centers for Disease Control and Prevention (CDC) in Atlanta. "That's what makes this type of weapon particularly insidious. It allows for the geographic dissemination of infected people, and some of these agents, such as pneumonic plague, are transmissible from person to person."

The 1972 Biological Weapons Convention bans the production, stockpiling and use of biological agents. The United States, a signatory, says it stopped all production of biological weapons in 1969, though it continues to conduct research on lethal pathogens. Amid evidence that the Soviet Union and as many as 14 other countries were continuing or establishing biological-weapons programs, the parties to the treaty have tried to strengthen its verification provisions, but to little avail.[4] The most recent conference on the treaty, held last November, yielded no significant progress.

Reuters

Japanese army chemical warfare specialists decontaminate a Tokyo subway car after the March 20, 1995, sarin gas attack that killed 12 and injured more than 5,000.

For now, however, the Tokyo attack and uncertainties surrounding Gulf War Syndrome have focused the arms control debate on chemical weapons. Critics of the current treaty charge that for all its provisions to ensure compliance, the Chemical Weapons Convention is no improvement over the existing ban on the use of such weapons established by the Geneva Protocol.

"It would be very nice to rid the world of chemical weapons if we could," says Frank J. Gaffney Jr., director of the Center for Security Policy. Gaffney, formerly deputy assistant Defense secretary for arms control during the Reagan administration, stresses that chemical weapons are much easier to make and conceal than nuclear arms, the target of most existing arms-control initiatives. "But as a practical matter," Gaffney says, "that cannot be done, considering that any high school student can whip up a chemical agent if he wants to. Therefore, we should concentrate on what's practical, and what's practical here is ensuring that nobody uses the stuff and stipulating what we will do to them if they do."

Proponents of the Chemical Weapons Convention agree that production and even deployment of chemical agents are hard to monitor. "The worst part about all this is that the methods for making sarin gas and other nerve gases have been in the open scientific literature since the 1950s," says Leonard Cole, a political science professor at Rutgers University and an expert on biological and chemical agents. "The ultimate question is, 'What can we do to stop this?' I say you can't do much more than you can to prevent somebody from throwing a grenade or spraying somebody with gunshots."

But Cole and other proponents of the treaty insist it has value as a statement by the world community that chemical weapons will not be tolerated. "Verification is not going to be foolproof, but I think it will create a substantial disincentive," Cole says. "More than that, though, the treaty is a renewal of an old, international contract that chemical weapons are wrong and that we ought to get them off the table."

The Clinton administration has placed ratification of the convention near the top of its foreign policy agenda. "As we continue to investigate gulf war illnesses," the president said in accepting the panel's report on Jan. 7, "let me again take this opportunity to urge the Congress to ratify the Chemical Weapons Convention, which would make it harder for rogue states to acquire chemical weapons in the future and protect the soldiers of the United States and our allies in the future."

As the debate unfolds over the treaty's implications for U.S. defense against weapons of mass destruction, these are some of the issues under consideration:

Will the Chemical Weapons Convention slow the spread of chemical weapons?

Chemical weapons are one of three categories of so-called weapons of mass destruction. The other two, nuclear and biological weapons, are regulated by separate multilateral treaties, both signed by the United States. The 1968 Nuclear Non-Proliferation Treaty prohibits the transfer or manufacture of nuclear weapons outside the five recognized nuclear powers and ensures that all 168 signatory countries have access to civilian nuclear technology.[5] The 1972 Biological Weapons Convention bans the production, possession and use of biological weapons.

Until this year, the only constraint on chemical weapons was the ban on their use in combat under the 1925 Geneva Protocol. Efforts to ban their production and deployment as well began in the 1960s but were held up by disagreements among negotiating countries over verification.

Iraq's use of chemical weapons in its eight-year war against Iran lent new urgency to the task of drawing up a tougher chemical weapons ban. The momentum picked up after the 1991 gulf war, during which civilians and soldiers alike often donned gas masks in fear of chemical attacks by Iraq. When United Nations Secretary General Boutros Boutros-Ghali presented the Chemical Weapons Convention for signature in January 1993, 131 countries signed, including the United States.

Unlike nuclear weapons, whose production and deployment can be monitored by spy satellites, chemical weapons are relatively easy to hide. For this reason, the convention includes extensive inspection measures and limits on trade in commercially used chemicals — known as dual-use chemicals — that can be transformed into weapons.

In order to be ratified by the United States, the Chemical Weapons Convention must be approved by two-thirds of the Senate. Treaty opponents, who derailed efforts to bring the agreement to a vote in September, cite two main reasons for their stance — the "ineffectiveness" of its verification provisions and its potential cost to American businesses.

Although most of the 186-page treaty is devoted to verification measures — chiefly inspections of suspected chemical weapons facilities on short notice — opponents say it can't begin to stop production of chemical arms.

"As the proponents are wont to say, this has got to be the most intrusive, complex and comprehensive verification regime of any arms control treaty ever drafted," Gaffney says. "The problem is that it still won't work. At the end of the day, you can have an enormously complex, intrusive and comprehensive verification regime, and if it does not materially increase the chances that you'll be able to detect — let alone ensure enforcement in instances of non-compliance — it isn't worth a hill of beans."

Senate Foreign Relations Chairman Jesse Helms, R-N.C., a leading congressional opponent to the treaty, agrees. "The thing that bothers me most, I suppose, about the way this convention is being presented is the psychology of it, where people are assuming things are going to be all right just so we ratify this treaty," Helms said. "And I think we all know that's not so."[6]

Helms points to evidence that many of the 14 countries believed to have chemical weapons programs have not ratified the treaty. * "Russia, the country that possesses the largest and most sophisticated chemical weaponry in the world," Helms said, "has signaled that it has no intention of abiding by our bilateral agreement to get rid of the chemical weapons stockpile. To the contrary, over the past six years Russia consistently has refused to come clean about the true size of its chemical weapon stockpile and about the status of its binary chemical weapons program."

Proponents of the convention agree that it will be hard or even impossible to prevent the development of chemical weapons. But they claim that the treaty will allow for the early detection of violations by governments and terrorist groups alike. "The CWC would make it more difficult and more costly for terrorists to acquire or use chemical weapons," wrote Sen. Richard G. Lugar, R-Ind., a senior member of the Senate Foreign Relations and Intelligence committees, in a Sept. 11, 1996, letter to Senate colleagues. "The CWC will provide access to international declaration and inspection information and will strengthen the intelligence links between the United States and the international community that will help us detect and prevent chemical attacks."

Treaty supporters also warn that the Senate's failure to ratify would deny the United States any say in the treaty's enforcement. "It's far better . . . that we have some of our people in the inspec-

* The U.S. government does not provide an officially acknowledged list of states with chemical weapons. Helms mentioned Libya, Syria, Iraq, Egypt, Taiwan, North Korea, Russia, China, Iran and India.

CHEMIC

The

Two
che
an
fo

tion teams to conduct these inspections in various countries than we have no participation at all," Defense Secretary William Cohen said Jan. 26 on ABC's "This Week." The former Republican senator from Maine became the new Pentagon chief on Jan. 24.

Chemical weapons often are made of substances commonly used in commercial manufacturing. For example, thiodoglycol, a chemical used as a solvent in ball-point pen ink, is a key ingredient of mustard gas. To ensure that these dual-use chemicals are not diverted to make weapons, the treaty requires manufacturers to document their production and, if necessary, to open their facilities to international inspection.

Though these requirements would increase the cost of producing chemicals, the Chemical Manufacturers Association and the Synthetic Organic Chemical Manufacturers Association, representing the bulk of U.S. producers, both have endorsed the treaty. They say failure to ratify the treaty would be costlier than not ratifying it because it bars signatory countries, including some of the United States' biggest trading partners, from importing many dual-use chemicals from non-signatory countries. The chemical industry estimates that the cost of that provision to its members would be as much as $600 million a year in lost sales — the value of current imports and exports of these items.

But treaty critics say the bulk of the cost will fall on other U.S. manufacturers, including firms with valuable proprietary information that would be easy targets, under the treaty's inspection provision, for economic espionage by foreign competitors. "While the chemical manufacturers are quite satisfied that the costs to them are manageable," Gaffney says, "there are costs to everybody else in the country who is going to be subjected to this, whether they use chemicals, whether they happen to produce chemicals as part of their production process, or whether they just happen to be on the target list of French intelligence or anybody else who can use the inspection provision as an opportunity to get in and find out what they're doing."

Gaffney also charges that the chemical manufacturers stand to actually gain business if the United States ratifies the treaty. That's because of a little-noticed provision requiring industrialized signatory countries to provide signatory countries in the developing world with advanced technology to produce chemicals for commercial use. Modeled on the Atoms for Peace provision of the Nuclear Non-Proliferation Treaty, this provision — dubbed "poisons for peace" by tı
inducei.
ons ban.
ogy, chemica
to offensive use
or obvious warni
fertilizer plant, you c
a switch change it ove
phosphates for fertilizer
deadly phosgene gas," Gaffn.

Chemical manufacturers strong ject Gaffney's cont tion that they have a financial stake in selling chemicals to potential weapons proliferators. "It is not true that we're going to gain financially because of the Chemical Weapons Convention," says Michael Walls, senior assistant general counsel for the Chemical Manufacturers Association. "In fact, if the United States stays out of this convention, we stand to lose." He says the clause in the treaty that calls for providing technological assistance to signatory countries in no way erodes existing U.S. export controls barring the sale of dual-use chemicals and equipment that could be used to make weapons.

U.N. photo 159089/H. Arvidsson/Arms Control Association

Iraqi rockets filled with sarin nerve agents are readied for destruction by members of a United Nations team in Kamisiyah, Iraq, in March 1991.

"The so-called debate on the Chemical Weapons Convention has been nothing but a string of distortions from opponents like Mr. Gaffney about what the convention's impact will be on the commercial sector," Walls says. "The chemical industry has supported this treaty because it's the right thing to do. We don't want to see our legitimate products diverted to illegal uses. That's the principal motivation here."

Treaty supporters also insist that ratification by the world's strongest military

Continued on p. 81

Pentagon's Handling of Gulf War Syndrome

undamental questions have been raised by the 80,000 chronically ill gulf war veterans: Were they exposed to nical and/or biological weapons during the 1991 conflict? And did that exposure sicken them? To many observers, equally troubling question is whether the Pentagon held back information on Iraq's use of chemical weapons. The llowing chronology was culled from a wide range of media, government and think tank sources.

Jan. 16, 1991
The 39-day air war against Iraq begins. Most chemical-weapons factories and storage depots are destroyed.

Feb. 24, 1991
The four-day ground war begins.

March 4-15, 1991
U.S. blows up ammunition facility in Kamisiyah, Iraq, which contained chemical weapons.

June 13, 1991
The last U.S. ground troops return home.

Fall 1991
Gulf veterans begin seeking treatment for combat-related illnesses.

August 1992
Veterans Affairs Department (VA) sets up Persian Gulf Registry to provide medical examinations to all veterans.

May 1993
CIA reports that Iraq did not use chemical agents during the war and had removed chemical weapons from the war zone before the fighting.

September 1993
Senate Banking Committee report contains testimony from veterans describing exposure to chemicals.

June 7, 1994
Pentagon sets up Comprehensive Clinical Evaluation Program to evaluate care for gulf veterans.

May 26, 1995
President Clinton establishes a panel of independent experts to assess the government's response to veterans' health complaints.

June 21, 1996
Pentagon announces that it now has evidence that 300-400 U.S. troops near Kamisiyah may have been exposed to chemicals.

Oct. 8, 1996
Pentagon discloses log books on biological and chemical warfare compiled during the war for Gen. H. Norman Schwarzkopf, the allied commander, which show no entries for the period when the Kamisiyah facility was destroyed.

Oct. 22, 1996
A new Pentagon estimate says that up to 20,000 troops were near the Kamisiyah depot when it was destroyed.

Dec. 10, 1996
British Defense Ministry launches study of possible link between chemicals and chronically ill British veterans.

Dec. 19, 1996
Defense Secretary William J. Perry calls perceptions of a Pentagon cover-up of evidence linking veterans' illnesses to chemical weapons "dead wrong."

Jan. 7, 1997
Presidential Advisory Committee on Gulf War Veterans' Illnesses reports no conclusive evidence linking illnesses to chemical or biological weapons, but that the Pentagon "did not act in good faith" in its investigation of Gulf War Syndrome.

Jan. 9, 1997
Senate Veterans' Affairs Committee wins permission to examine Gen. Schwarzkopf's personal notes. Secretary Perry again denies knowledge of a Pentagon cover-up.

Jan. 21, 1997
VA study suggests a direct link between severe joint pain, a symptom of Gulf War Syndrome, and chemical weapons released at Kamisiyah. This is the first official acknowledgment by a federal agency of such a link.

Jan. 29, 1997
Gen. Schwarzkopf tells Veterans' Affairs Committee he never received information about Iraqi use of chemical weapons "before, during or after hostilities."

Sarah M. Magner

Continued from p. 79

power would constitute a persuasive deterrent to anyone contemplating the use of chemical weapons. Military leaders who support the treaty cite the gulf war to bolster this argument. Although Iraq was known to have a chemical arsenal, it refrained from using it against U.S. troops after then-Defense Secretary Dick Cheney repeatedly vowed to retaliate against any chemical attack with "absolutely overwhelming" and "devastating" force.

Even in the absence of such an immediate threat of retaliation, supporters say the treaty is likely to reduce the risk of further chemical weapons proliferation because it allows for the use of sanctions and even force to stop it — even against countries that are not parties to the agreement. "No one is claiming that this treaty will be foolproof or that it will guarantee 100 percent that no country will cheat," Cole says. "But most everybody who has an interest in the issue recognizes that it will lower the chance that anybody is going to cheat."

In the end, treaty proponents say, the United States would be better off with the Chemical Weapons Convention than without it. "If we refuse to ratify, some governments will use our refusal as an excuse to keep their chemical weapons," writes retired Adm. Elmo R. Zumwalt Jr., who served as chief of naval operations from 1970-1974. "At the bottom line, our failure to ratify will substantially increase the risk of a chemical attack against American service personnel." [7]

U.N. photo 159097/H. Arvidsson/Arms Control Association

Members of a U.N. chemical weapons team monitor air contamination in Kamisiyah, Iraq, after destroying hundreds of Iraqi rockets filled with sarin nerve agents.

Is it feasible to protect Americans from the threat of biological or chemical attack?

Because biological and chemical weapons are easy to produce and conceal, civilians have few defenses against potential attackers. All it took for the Aum Shinrikyo terrorists to turn the Tokyo subway system into a deadly gas chamber were holes poked in a few plastic bags of strategically placed sarin. Closer to home, the truck containing the bomb that devastated the World Trade Center in 1993 was later found to have contained sodium cyanide. Had the device containing the cyanide not malfunctioned, it would have released a cloud of deadly cyanide vapor into the skyscraper, causing many more casualties. [8]

Although biological and chemical weapons have been readily available for many years, there are few defenses in place to protect civilians against an attack. In 1995, an Ohio man, Larry Harris, a former member of the white supremacist group Aryan Nations, had no trouble ordering by mail three vials of *Yersinia pestis,* the bacterium that causes bubonic plague, from a laboratory supply house. However, a company employee became suspicious about the order and alerted the Federal Bureau of Investigation. Harris was apprehended before he could carry out his alleged plan to make a biological weapon out of the material. But because there were no laws prohibiting the distribution of *Yersinia pestis* and other potentially lethal pathogens, Harris was released after serving a brief sentence for mail fraud for providing false information on the order form. [9]

"When we called in the authorities on the plague incident, CDC's response was that there was nothing they could do about it because Mr. Harris had done nothing illegal by having it in his possession or using it," says Kaye Breen, a vice president of American Type Culture Collection, the Rockville, Md., firm that provided the pathogen. "All of our requirements to have detailed information in writing are voluntary."

Later this year, however, tough, new regulations that were included in anti-terrorism legislation passed last April will go into effect, limiting the availability of many pathogens. The regulations impose penalties for the illegal possession and distribution of dangerous biological agents. But Breen says the new rules may do little to deter a terrorist or madman bent on conducting biological mayhem. "Even if you took all the 450 major [pathogen] culture collections around the world, they still collectively represent about 20 percent of the distribution of biologicals," Breen says. "The bulk of it is from researcher to researcher, and anyway, every single one of these biologicals is available in nature. If you're a true terrorist, why go where you have to leave a paper trail?"

Given the limits of effective defense, some experts say important steps are being taken to protect civilians against biochemical attack. "We're working on it," says Hughes of the National Center for Infectious Diseases. He offers as a model a detailed plan of action drawn up by various agencies to intervene quickly in case of an infectious-disease outbreak, whether by natural causes or as the result of a biological attack.

During last summer's Olympic Games in Atlanta, he says, "We set up a special infectious-disease surveillance system in which hospitals, emergency rooms and outpatient centers reported daily on disease encounters. The key to surveillance is the alert clinician or health-care worker who recognizes and reports."

Biological attacks, unlike those using chemicals, can be indistinguishable from spontaneous outbreaks if no one claims responsibility for the act. "Otherwise, it is going to present exactly like any other infectious-disease epidemic," Hughes says. "That's the reason we argue that we need, first and foremost, to strengthen surveillance and response capacity at the local, state, federal and even global levels so that these incidents can be detected early and a response can be rapidly mounted."

The CDC has drawn up a strategy for dealing with outbreaks that follows these suggestions. But even Hughes acknowledges the limits of civilian defenses against bioterrorism. "Another aspect to this issue is the availability of agents to treat these things should they occur on large numbers of people," he says. "You could easily overwhelm the health-care delivery system and exhaust available supplies of antibiotics or antisera that aren't used very often. They're adequate to deal with things that you could anticipate occurring in a natural setting.

"But if somebody should put botulinum toxin in the New York City water supply, there's not enough botulinum antitoxin in the world to treat the people who would be exposed."

Arms Control Association

Security police at the U.S. air station in Sola, Norway, participate in chemical warfare exercises.

Did exposure to chemical weapons cause Gulf War Syndrome?

For more than five years, the Defense Department denied that — with one small exception — U.S. military personnel serving in the gulf war had come into contact with any Iraqi chemical or biological weapons. The only officially recognized case of exposure involved an Army sergeant who received superficial mustard burns on his arms while he was near an Iraqi bunker. [10]

Last June, the Pentagon acknowledged that 150 soldiers might have been exposed to low-level amounts of chemicals that were released into the air when American troops blew up the Iraqi ammunition storage facility at Kamisiyah shortly after the war's end. With mounting evidence that winds may have carried the resulting poison cloud farther south toward the bulk of U.S. troops, the official count of potentially exposed personnel grew. By October, the Pentagon had raised the official estimate of troops who were exposed to as many as 20,000.

While acknowledging the possibility that U.S. service personnel were exposed to chemical weapons at Kamisiyah, however, the Pentagon holds firm to its position that the exposure cannot be positively linked to Gulf War Syndrome. "The current orthodox, scientific view is that with exposure to a chemical agent, if you do not get enough exposure to become ill at the time, you will not have chronic symptoms or symptoms down the road," said Stephen P. Joseph, assistant secretary of Defense for health affairs. "There really is no basis at the present time, beyond cocktail chatter, to say that a low-level exposure at Kamisiyah below the level that would give acute symptoms, is responsible for a whole series of symptoms that we're seeing now [several] years later." Following repeated accusations by veterans and some lawmakers that it had ignored veterans' reports linking chemical exposure to their illnesses, however, the Pentagon announced in November that it was expanding its investigation into the issue. [11]

The official Pentagon view is supported by many experts in the field, including the Presidential Advisory Committee on Gulf War Veterans' Illnesses. Though it is known that allied air strikes in January and February 1991 damaged two Iraqi storage facilities containing sarin and mustard gas, the panel concluded: "The best evidence available indicates theaterwide contamination with chemical warfare agent fallout from the air war is highly unlikely." [12]

The committee based its conclusion on the fact that chemical agents known as organophosphates, such as sarin, when delivered in doses suitable for weapons, immediately cause convulsions, neuromuscular blockage, airway obstruction and ultimately death from respiratory paralysis — all within one to two minutes of exposure. Mustard agents can take a couple of hours to work, but a victim of a mustard-gas attack has unmistakable symptoms: severe blistering of the eyes, skin, lungs and digestive tract. Neither sarin nor mustard are known to have long-term health effects at low concentrations, such as those the gulf veterans probably experienced. [13]

Numerous gulf veterans, health professionals and other researchers dispute these findings. "Chemical agents had clearly been detected — repeatedly — by U.S., U.K., French and Czech forces during and after the war," said Patrick G. Eddington, a former CIA analyst who began investigating the government's handling of veterans' claims two years ago. "There were credible reports of a sublethal chemical and/or biological agent attack against coalition units at the Saudi port of Al Jubayl in the early morning hours of Jan. 19, 1991.

"Additionally, eyewitness accounts of several Iraqi SCUD [missile] attacks on American units in Saudi Arabia described symptoms consistent with low-dose chemical or biological agent exposure during or immediately after those attacks." Eddington claims that "tens of thousands of Desert Storm veterans" may suffer the ill effects of chemical or biological weapons exposure. [14]

The most recently published non-governmental studies leave open the possibility that at least some sufferers of Gulf War Syndrome were indeed injured by chemical weapons. [15] A small group of gulf war veterans who complained of confusion and impaired balance were found to have abnormalities in nerve and brain function that the researchers said may have been caused by exposure to harmful chemicals, such as pesticides and possibly poison gas. This same group included soldiers who reported they were exposed to a cloud of nerve gas that blew over northeastern Saudi Arabia early in the war.

At least one expert claims that some of the veterans' symptoms may be the result of exposure to biological weapons, which Iraq is suspected of having deployed since before the war. Biochemist Garth Nicholson, director of the Institute for Molecular Medicine in Irvine, Calif., says he successfully treated some of his gulf war patients with antibiotics and suspects that the culprit in those cases may be a genetically altered form of a disease-causing bacterium, *Mycoplasma fermentans*.

Other infectious-disease experts are skeptical, however. Hughes, whose CDC institute has helped investigate this hypothesis, says Nicholson's findings have not been replicated elsewhere. "Obviously, the Gulf War Syndrome is a complicated thing, and I don't know how it will play out," Hughes says. "But I'm not persuaded that there's any significant evidence for the role of biological agents in this syndrome."

The Pentagon, the Department of Veterans Affairs and non-governmental researchers will continue to study the possibility of long-term effects of exposure to chemical and biological warfare agents. But widespread skepticism surrounding the Pentagon's investigations to date prompted President Clinton to extend the presidential panel's term, which would have expired in December, at least through the end of fiscal 1997, ending Sept. 30. ■

BACKGROUND

Early Horrors

Poison has been used to assassinate enemies and wipe out communities — often by contaminating well water — since the beginning of recorded history. But modern biochemical warfare dates to April 22, 1915, when German troops entrenched at Ypres, Belgium, opened 6,000 chlorine cylinders, releasing a cloud of deadly gas into the wind blowing toward their French adversaries. Thousands perished in this first large-scale use of chemical warfare.

Two years later, Germany introduced another deadly chemical to the battlefield as well: mustard gas. By the war's end, chemical weapons had inflicted 1.3 million casualties, including almost 100,000 deaths. [16] Germany also introduced biological agents during the conflict, reportedly using anthrax to kill the allied forces' horses and mules. [17]

The horrifying images of soldiers dying blistered and gagging on the battlefield led to the 1925 Geneva Protocol. The United States was among the signatories, though it did not ratify the agreement until 1975 because of senators' concerns that it might constrain the use of non-lethal chemical herbicides and tear gas. The Senate ratified the treaty on Jan. 22, 1975, after President Gerald Ford affirmed that the United States would renounce the first use of herbicides in war except for uses "applicable to their domestic use" and the first use of tear gas except for riot-control use in "defensive military modes to save lives."

Because the agreement did not prohibit the development of biological or chemical arsenals, it lacked verification or enforcement provisions. The agreement served rather as a statement that it is morally contemptible to use these weapons in combat.

By World War II, nonetheless, all the major combatants — Germany, Japan, the United States, Britain, Canada and the Soviet Union — had developed biochemical arsenals. Violations of the Geneva Protocol occurred throughout the war: Soviet soldiers reportedly spread typhus and typhoid fever in eastern Germany, Italy used chemical weapons against Ethiopia and Japan dropped bombs carrying plague germs as well as chemical agents over China, raising concern that U.S. forces in the Pacific might also come under biochemical attack.

The United States began its biological and chemical weapons programs during World War II on the premise that they would be used to retaliate in kind against an enemy attack. Such attacks never occurred. During the 1950s and '60s, the programs were expanded and revised. Up until the late 1950s, the Army even tested its biological and chemical readiness by releasing supposedly harmless agents over populated areas of the United States to see how widely they dispersed. [18]

At the height of the biochemical warfare programs in the 1960s, the United States developed chemical herbicides as well as munitions armed with organisms that cause Q fever and tularemia. A product of this research was Agent Orange, the controversial defoliant used to expose enemy hideouts during the Vietnam War that later was linked to cancer and other serious illnesses among Vietnam veterans. [19]

Arms Control Efforts

The development of a U.S. biochemical arsenal drew much of its urgency from the Cold War-era arms race with the Soviet Union, which also was building up its own supplies. But President Richard M. Nixon, arguing that it was not necessary to retaliate in kind against a biological or chemical attack, ended that policy in November 1969 when he unilaterally dismantled the U.S. biological weapons program. In February 1970, he also suspended development of weapons made with toxins produced from living organisms, such as staphylococcal enterotoxin.

By 1973, all U.S. stocks of bacteriological weapons and anti-crop substances had been destroyed, according to the Pentagon. All that was left of the U.S. biological weapons program were military and civilian laboratories used for research and the development of substances and systems for use in defensive measures. These include decontamination agents and vaccines and antibiotics against specific pathogens, as well as detection systems, gas masks and protective clothing designed for battlefield use.

During this period, the United States signed the 1972 Biological and Toxin Weapons Convention. By prohibiting the "development, production, stockpiling, acquisition or retention" of biological weapons, and not just their use, the new treaty went far beyond the Geneva Protocol. The Senate ratified the treaty on Dec. 16, 1974, and President Ford signed the ratification on Jan. 22, 1975.

Biological weapons are very hard to detect, and the Biological Weapons Convention contained no provisions to ensure compliance. This weakness became clear in the wake of an anthrax outbreak in Sverdlovsk, Russia, in April 1979. Though the Soviet government at the time claimed the outbreak was caused by contaminated meat, there was widespread suspicion that it stemmed from an accidental leak at a munitions complex. That was recently confirmed by Russian President Boris N. Yeltsin, who in April 1992 announced he was discontinuing biological programs being operated by Russia in violation of the treaty.

The anthrax outbreak prompted signatory countries to the Biological Weapons Convention to hold a series of review conferences to try to strengthen the treaty. Most changes have involved so-called confidence-building measures, notably agreements to exchange information on national programs to defend against biological attack and immediately notify the World Health Organization of any infectious-disease outbreaks.

Iran Offensive Prompts Chemical Weapons Treaty

Throughout the Cold War, international control of chemical weapons remained limited to the Geneva Protocol's ban on their use. Until the 1980s, the treaty appeared to have been successful in deterring poison gas attacks. In 1983, however, Iraq began launching chemical attacks against Iran that continued until the war between the two nations ended in 1988. During the 1980s, the Iraqi government also used poison gas to kill Kurdish civilians in northern Iraq. The United States and its NATO allies knew about Iraq's repeated violations of the Geneva Protocol — including the genocide of its own countrymen — but failed to strongly denounce the breaches. They had been reluctant to take sides in a war between two countries that had been hostile to the West during the oil embargoes of the 1970s and to Israel, the United States' main ally in the Middle East,

Confronted by the Geneva Protocol's loss of deterrent value, the United States

Continued on p. 86

Chronology

1910s-1920s

The first use of chemical and biological weapons in combat leads to efforts to ban their use.

April 22, 1915
The first use of chemical weapons in combat occurs in World War I when Germany releases chlorine gas onto the battlefield near Ypres, Belgium. Two years later, Germany launches mustard gas attacks as well. By the war's end, the death toll from chemical weapons approaches 100,000 people.

1925
The Geneva Protocol prohibits the use of biological and chemical weapons in war. The United States signs, but fails to ratify, the treaty.

1950s-1970s

As the United States and the Soviet Union build arsenals of biological and chemical weapons, international pressure mounts to draw up new treaties to curb such weapons.

Nov. 25, 1969
President Richard M. Nixon unilaterally renounces the use of biological weapons in war by the United States and restricts research to immunization and safety efforts. Three months later, he extends the ban to include toxins.

1972
The Biological and Toxin Weapons Convention enters into force, banning the production and stockpiling of these weapons.

Jan. 22, 1975
The United States ratifies the Biological and Toxin Weapons Convention as well as the 1925 Geneva Protocol.

April 1979
An outbreak of anthrax occurs in Sverdlovsk, Russia. The incident, initially described as a natural outbreak, is later found to be the result of a leak from a Soviet biological-weapons facility.

1980s

Arms control initiatives fail to curb biological and chemical weapons proliferation.

1980-88
Iraq uses chemical weapons in its eight-year war against Iran as well as against dissident Kurdish communities in Iraq — the first use of chemical agents in combat since World War I.

1984
The Reagan administration presents a draft treaty to ban the production and storage of chemical weapons to the Conference on Disarmament in Geneva.

1990s

Concern over exposure to chemical and biological weapons during the Persian Gulf War increases support for international treaties.

May 13, 1991
Shortly after the allied victory against Iraq, President George Bush announces that the United States will renounce the use of chemical weapons for any reason once an international treaty banning them takes effect.

April 1992
Russian President Boris N. Yeltsin declares that Russia's biological weapons programs is being discontinued.

January 1993
President Bush signs the Chemical Weapons Convention banning the production and use of chemical weapons.

March 20, 1995
In the first terrorist attack using chemical weapons, members of Aum Shinrikyo, a Japanese religious cult, release sarin nerve gas in the Tokyo subway, killing 12 people and injuring more than 5,000.

1995
Larry Harris, a white supremacist from Ohio, obtains three vials of deadly plague bacteria by mail order from a laboratory supply house. Alleged white supremacist Thomas Lewis Lavy is apprehended while trying to smuggle the toxin ricin across the Canadian border.

Jan. 7, 1997
The Presidential Advisory Committee on Gulf War Veterans' Illnesses finds no conclusive evidence linking Gulf War Syndrome to exposure to chemical or biological weapons.

April 15, 1997
New regulations aimed at limiting access to chemicals and pathogens that could be made into weapons go into effect under the 1996 Antiterrorism and Effective Death Penalty Act.

April 29, 1997
The Chemical Weapons Convention goes into effect. As of late January, it had more than 160 signatories and 65 ratifications.

Continued from p. 84

and other Western countries pressed for a stronger chemical weapons treaty. On May 13, 1991, shortly after the gulf war against Iraq ended, President Bush announced that the United States would renounce the use of chemical weapons for any reason once such a treaty took effect. The Army has already begun destroying its stockpiles of sarin and other chemicals used in weapons.

In January 1993, the Chemical Weapons Convention was presented for signature at the United Nations. Unlike the treaty banning biological weapons, the chemical convention contains extensive provisions for monitoring compliance with the ban, including intrusive inspection rights and allowance for sanctions and the use of force against violators.

Arsenals Proliferate

Efforts to rid the world of biological and chemical weapons have thus far failed to halt the global demand for their lethal ingredients. In the absence of aggressive verification measures, it is impossible to say exactly how many governments — or terrorist groups, religious fanatics and otherwise deranged individuals — actually possess workable chemical arsenals. But all estimates suggest a significant proliferation over the past two decades. Since 1980, the number of countries known or suspected to possess biological weapons has grown from one — the Soviet Union — to 17. [20] Chemical arsenals are even more widespread, numbering about 20, up from about a dozen in 1980. Many of the governments that have these weapons are hostile to Western interests — in particular the United States. [21]

Iraq — said to be the most blatant offender of existing biochemical accords — has maintained and openly used both types of weapons since before the gulf war. The Iraqi arsenal was long believed to include anthrax, botulinum, mustard and sarin, as well as VX, one of the most lethal forms of nerve gas. [22] The United Nations Special Commission on Iraq (UNSCOM), set up after the gulf war to conduct on-site inspections of Iraq's weapons of mass destruction, has confirmed their existence.

Since the gulf war, evidence of chemical weapons proliferation has mounted. Yugoslavia, Bosnia and Croatia had access to, and may have used, chlorine-filled shells during fighting in the region in the early 1990s. [23] And Russia, which inherited the vast chemical and biological arsenals built up by the Soviet Union, has recently weakened its commitment to disarm. Last fall, Prime Minister Viktor S. Chernomyrdin suggested that his government may no longer abide by a bilateral agreement with the United States to destroy existing arsenals.

Japanese Cult Raises Specter of Terrorism

Arms control treaties, of course, primarily serve to restrict governments' deployment of biological or chemical weapons. They do little, however, to curb access of groups or individuals to the lethal agents of which they are made. This reality became abundantly clear on March 20, 1995, when members of the Aum Shinrikyo cult released sarin gas in the Tokyo subway system at the height of the morning rush hour. Police investigating the incident discovered that the cult had bought air-filtration equipment, lasers and other sophisticated equipment in the United States to make its weapons. Members even bought a sheep station in Australia where they tested nerve gas. They also used chemicals to assassinate several people in Japan and sent representatives to Zaire during the 1992 outbreak of Ebola virus in search of samples of the deadly pathogen to use in future attacks. [24]

To date, no other group is known to have developed as lethal a biochemical capability as Aum Shinrikyo. But several incidents in the United States demonstrate this country's vulnerability to similar attacks. They include the mail-order sale of bubonic plague virus to white supremacist Harris in May 1995 and, later that year, the arrest of Thomas Lewis Lavy, another alleged white supremacist with ties to survivalist groups, who was apprehended as he tried to smuggle 130 grams of the deadly toxin ricin — enough to kill thousands of people — across the Canadian border. [25] ■

Current Situation

Gulf War Studies

The health effects of most poisons used in biological or chemical weapons have long been known. Chemical weapons act immediately or within hours. Nerve gases, for example, kill almost as soon as they are inhaled. Most biological weapons act more slowly. Deadly viruses have incubation periods as long as several weeks. But the potential for longer-term effects of these agents on human health is only beginning to be investigated in earnest, largely in response to the complaints of chronic health problems by thousands of gulf war veterans.

More than 100 studies of Gulf War Syndrome have been carried out or are currently in progress. Even more investigations are expected to begin as a result of the Pentagon's recent decision to expand its own research into the problem. On Nov. 12, Pentagon spokesman Kenneth Bacon announced that the Defense Department would spend $27 million in fiscal 1997 on research into the effects of low-level exposures to chemical weapons and other potential causes of the syndrome, doubling the 1996 budget for this research.

The most recent non-governmental studies, released Jan. 8 by a team of researchers at Southwestern Medical Center at the University of Texas in Dallas, suggest that the main cause of the syndrome in at least some veterans is damage to the nervous system due to exposure to one or more of a class of toxic chemicals called organophosphates, such as sarin and mustard. These chemicals were also present in the war zone as pesticides contained in flea collars many soldiers wore around their ankles to ward off insects or sprayed around their encampments. [26]

The Presidential Advisory Committee on Gulf War Veterans' Illnesses concluded its 16-month study with disappointing news for veterans eager for confirmation that their illnesses were the direct result of exposure to chemical or biological weapons. The panel also failed to link the syndrome to the wide range of other toxins present in the war zone, including pesticides, vaccines, pyridostigmine bromide (an antidote to nerve gas distributed to soldiers), infectious diseases, depleted uranium, smoke from oil-well fires and petroleum products.

But the panel's scientists were careful not to dismiss the veterans' claims and stressed the need for more research. "Prudence requires further investigation of some areas of uncertainty," the panel concluded, "such as the long-term effects of low-level exposure to chemical warfare agents and the synergistic effects of exposure to pyridostigmine bromide and other risk factors." [27]

In addition to extending the life of the panel, President Clinton has announced that he supports making disability aid available to more sick gulf war veterans. Current rules require veterans who claim their "undiagnosed" illnesses can be traced to military service to prove the symptoms began within two years of leaving the gulf area. Many veterans who say they did not fall ill until several years after Desert Storm have been denied disability benefits by the Department of Veterans Affairs. VA Secretary Jesse Brown is expected to issue new time limits for these cases in March. [28]

U.S. Marine Corps/Arms Control Association

Officer candidates wearing gas masks prepare for a mock assault at the Marine Corps training facility at Quantico, Va.

Defense Strategies

The now-recognized fact that at least some U.S. military personnel were indeed exposed to Iraqi chemical weapons has raised concern over the United States' preparedness for attacks using these as well as biological agents. Some critics of the Chemical Weapons Convention even question the wisdom of abandoning the U.S. chemical capability, citing its deterrent value. "We've got to try to make the use of chemical weapons as unattractive an option as possible," says Gaffney, who calls for more evaluation of the question. "Historically, it has been the case that the threat of retaliation in kind is a powerful disincentive. Hitler is widely believed to have refrained from using large quantities of chemical weapons that he had at his disposal because he feared retaliation in kind. It is also the case that most, if not all, uses of chemical weapons have been against people who didn't have the means to retaliate in kind."

But reestablishing a chemical, much less a biological, capability seems highly unlikely. Shortly after the gulf war, President Bush announced that the United States was formally forswearing the use of chemical weapons for any reason — including retaliation against a chemical attack — as soon as the treaty enters into force. Indeed, Gen. John M. Shalikashvili, chairman of the Joint Chiefs of Staff, said the gulf war showed that eliminating chemical weapons from the U.S. arsenal in no way made the United States more vulnerable to chemical attack. "Desert Storm proved that retaliation in kind is not required to deter the use of chemical weapons," he said. [29]

Meanwhile, Congress has acted to

strengthen U.S. defenses, especially against biological weapons, in the wake of incidents such as the 1995 mail order sale of plague bacteria. The 1996 Antiterrorism and Effective Death Penalty Act, passed last April, includes new regulations aimed at limiting access to chemicals and pathogens that could be made into offensive weapons. Under the new rules, which will take effect April 15, the Health and Human Services Department will regulate the transfer of 36 lethal viruses, toxins and other biological agents by mail.

Improving Global Surveillance

But the main emphasis of new defensive efforts against biological weapons has been on improving global surveillance of and response to infectious disease outbreaks. Ironically, the scientific community's success in combating infectious diseases in recent decades has eroded its ability to deal with outbreaks. When plague broke out in two cities in India in 1994, for example, there was only one World Health Organization lab with the ability to respond to the disease. According to Hughes of the NCID, the CDC's plague branch had been reduced from 16 researchers to just one. "Because of all this complacency that's developed over the years," he says, "the number of experts who work with these agents is relatively limited. So there is a vulnerability. There's no doubt about that."

Recognizing that most U.S. cities are within 36 hours by commercial airliners of any area of the world, President Clinton issued a new policy directive on June 12 that would strengthen federal, state and local health agencies' ability to identify and combat disease outbreaks. The new policy covers all outbreaks, whether they arise from a biological weapons attack or natural causes, such as the recent outbreaks of Ebola in Zaire and hantavirus in the Southwestern United States. [30]

The new policy also would enhance U.S. cooperation with other countries to quell outbreaks wherever they may occur. "Emerging infectious diseases present one of the most significant health and security challenges facing the global community," said Vice President Al Gore in announcing the policy. "Through President Clinton's leadership, we now have the first national policy to deal with this serious international problem." [31]

There are limits, however, to what the U.S. government, or any government, can do to prevent a biological or chemical attack from taking place once a country, group or individual has decided to launch one. "Certainly, the government is paying more attention to this issue than before," says terrorism expert Jenkins. "This in part is a result of fears raised during the gulf war, which I think have been exacerbated by the events in Tokyo. Having said that, one has to recognize the difficulty in this area of prevention. This is not a problem that can be as easily addressed as airplane hijackings or keeping bombs and guns off airplanes." ■

OUTLOOK

Treaty Debate

Opponents of the Chemical Weapons Convention surprised most observers last September when they garnered enough support to force the treaty's backers to postpone the scheduled Senate discussion and vote on its ratification. The new 105th Senate is expected to take up the treaty once again early this year. A vote is expected before April 29, when the agreement will go into effect — with or without the United States as a party — and backers are urging its prompt approval.

"I urge my colleagues to support ratification of this treaty, which establishes an important international organization to suppress the threat of chemical warfare and terrorism," Sen. Lugar said in response to the Jan. 7 statement of support for the treaty by the Clinton administration. "The CWC would require other countries to destroy their chemical weapons, as the U.S. is already doing. Unless the U.S. ratifies the treaty by April 29, we will have no input in its rules and administration."

According to some experts, the Senate's action on the convention will also affect the United States' ability to curb the threat from biological weapons. "I think that chemical and biological agents — the way they're perceived and in some ways the way they behave — are similar enough that if one of the conventions isn't successful, it will drag the other treaty down, and if one is successful it will pull the other up," Cole says.

The detailed verification measures included in the chemical weapons treaty offer a model for monitoring lethal biological agents that could be added to the Biological Weapons Convention, Cole says. "But even without verification measures, these treaties have value as a kind of moral statement, and I see these two weapons systems as sufficiently linked that as one goes, so will the other."

Even in the absence of stronger international controls, some experts offer hope that the threat of biological or chemical weapons may be less immediate than the widely publicized incidents of the past few years may suggest. "Outside a few criminal extortionists and incidents involving fanatical cults such as Aum Shinrikyo, there is little evidence that other types of terrorists have done anything more than express a modest interest in chemical or biological agents," Jenkins says. Because of their objectives, he says, terrorists are unlikely to unleash a wave of mass killings using these weapons. "Terrorism is not about killing people," he says. "It is aimed at the people watch-

Continued on p. 90

At Issue:

Does exposure to chemical weapons explain Gulf War Syndrome?

yes

MAJ. RANDY LEE HEBERT
United States Marine Corps

FROM TESTIMONY BEFORE THE GOVERNMENT REFORM AND OVERSIGHT SUBCOMMITTEE ON HUMAN RESOURCES AND INTERGOVERNMENTAL RELATIONS, DEC. 10, 1996.

In December 1990 I was assigned to the 2nd Combat Engineer Battalion, 2nd Marine Division, in Saudi Arabia. . . . On 23 February 1991, the eve prior to our ground attack, we moved into our attack position approximately . . . three miles from the border of Kuwait. . . . On G-day, 24 February 1991, we were to link up with a section of tanks; this never happened. . . . I decided to halt my men south of the berm dividing Saudi Arabia and Kuwait. I proceeded . . . to a traffic control point.

As we approached, we received the hand and arm signal for chemical attack. We put on our masks and gloves. In doing so, I recall my right hand feeling cool and tingling. I was mad because we were just starting and already receiving the sign for chemicals. I jumped from the vehicle and asked the Marine MP in strong Marine Corps language who had told him to go to (MOPP) Level 4. . . .

We drove back and radioed to my Marines to get to MOPP Level 4. When we arrived, some were, others were not. The driver and I jumped from the vehicle giving the sign for chemicals. I approached the MP controlling traffic to ask why he wasn't in MOPP Level 4. He told me the alarm was false. I was angry and removed my mask. I now feel that was a mistake. I radioed to Battalion Three and told him, "We are rolling and we have not made contact with the tanks." He said, "OK." Within a minute of rolling he called back saying that, "Your lane is dirty, chemical mine has gone off, go to MOPP 4. . . ."

Around the 22nd of February, I started taking pyrostigmine bromide pills for anti-nerve agent protection. I believe I took the pills for 11-14 days. Once we returned to Saudi Arabia in early April, I began to have some difficulty with sleep. This continued upon my return home on 15 May 1995 until early July, at which time I have having difficulty reading and remembering what I had read. I was extremely aggressive, moody and excitable. I had headaches, vomiting and diarrhea. I was also diagnosed with moderate depression. . . .

In October 1995 I was diagnosed with ALS (amyotrophic lateral sclerosis, also known as Lou Gehrig's Disease). I believe the medical problems I have discussed are due to low-level chemical exposure over an extended period.

I learned after the war that the chemical mine detonated in Lane Red One was confirmed for the nerve agent sarin and also the agent Lewisite mustard gas by a FOX vehicle in the lane. It has been brought to my attention that there have been at least seven other cases of ALS in service members who served in the gulf. To me, this is more than mere chance or coincidence.

no

PRESIDENTIAL ADVISORY COMMITTEE ON GULF WAR VETERANS' ILLNESSES

FROM "FINAL REPORT," DECEMBER 1996.

Iraq successfully used chemical weapons in its war with Iran, with massive casualties not seen in the gulf war.

A Department of Defense (DOD) review of U.S. Army hospital admissions records identified no admissions for chemical warfare (CW) agent exposures during the gulf war. The U.S. Army officer responsible for chemical-biological warfare (CBW) agent medical surveillance during the war has testified to the committee that only one accidental casualty was treated. Additionally, UNSCOM * reported to us that Iraqi officials have denied to them any use of chemical weapons during the war. Lastly, veterans groups testifying before this committee concede there were no widespread chemical attacks. Based on the information compiled to date, there is no persuasive evidence of intentional Iraqi use of CW agents during the war. . . .

During the gulf war, Coalition forces conducted air attacks on suspected Iraqi CW agent manufacturing and storage facilities. Some veterans and independent researchers have suggested that fallout from Coalition bombing of these sites led to large-scale nerve agent contamination in [the Kuwait theater of operations]. The committee looked at evidence of the effects of Coalition airstrikes on Iraqi chemical munitions storage sites to examine this hypothesis. In late January and February 1991, Coalition forces conducted aerial bombings that damaged chemical munitions stored at two sites in central Iraq: Muhammadiyat and Al Muthanna. Subsequent UNSCOM investigations indicate these are the only sites (among 11 known storage sites) where Coalition airstrikes actually damaged or destroyed chemical agents. . . .

To assess possible hazards to U.S. forces from CW agent releases at Muhammidiyat and Al Muthanna, atmospheric modeling was conducted for the [Central Intelligence Agency] for all possible bombing dates at each site. This modeling indicates that on the bombing date . . . Muhammadiyat releases, at worst, would have resulted in downwind contamination for up to 300 kilometers (km) at general population exposure levels established by DOD. This modeling also indicates that on the bombing date when southerly winds were most pronounced, Al Muthanna releases, at worst, would have resulted in downwind contamination for up to 160 km. . . . During the air war, the nearest U.S. personnel were in Rafha, Saudia Arabia — more than 400 km from Muhammadiyat and Al Muthanna. . . .

The best evidence available indicates theaterwide contamination with CW agent fallout from the air war is highly unlikely.

** UNSCOM, the United Nations Special Commission on Iraq, carries out on-site inspections of Iraqi biological, chemical and missile capabilities.*

FOR MORE INFORMATION

AMERICAN LEGION, 1608 K St. N.W., Washington, D.C. 20006; (202) 861-2700. The legion's Persian Gulf Task Force is among the most vocal critics of the Pentagon's treatment of U.S. servicemen who say they suffer from Gulf War Syndrome.

ARMS CONTROL AND DISARMAMENT AGENCY, 320 21st St. N.W., Washington, D.C. 20451; (202) 647-4800. The ACDA advises the president and secretary of State on arms control policy and develops verification procedures for arms control agreements, such as the Chemical and Biological Weapons conventions.

CENTER FOR SECURITY POLICY, 1250 24th St. N.W., Suite 350, Washington, D.C. 20037; (202) 466-0515. This defense and foreign-policy research organization opposes ratification of the Chemical Weapons Convention.

CHEMICAL AND BIOLOGICAL ARMS CONTROL INSTITUTE, 2111 Eisenhower Ave., Suite 302, Alexandria, Va. 22314; (703) 739-1538. The institute promotes arms control and the elimination of chemical and biological weapons.

Continued from p. 88

ing, and at creating psychological reactions." To avoid undermining all sympathy for their political agendas, Jenkins expects most terrorists to continue exercising a certain degree of restraint. "Terrorists have always had the capacity to kill more people than they have actually killed. Moreover, if you want to kill a lot of people, exotic weaponry is not required." ■

Notes

[1] Martin testified Sept. 19, 1996, before the House Government Reform and Oversight Subcommittee on Human Resources and Intergovernmental Affairs.

[2] Presidential Advisory Committee on Gulf War Veterans' Illnesses, *Final Report,* December 1996, p. 7.

[3] U.S. Arms Control and Disarmament Agency, "The Chemical Weapons Convention, Fact Sheet," Dec. 17, 1996. See also Leonard A. Cole, *The Eleventh Plague* (1997), pp. 4-5. See "War Crimes," *The CQ Researcher,* July 7, 1995, pp. 585-608.

[4] Office of Technology Assessment, *Proliferation of Weapons of Mass Destruction,* August 1993, p. 82.

[5] For background, see "Non-Proliferation Treaty at 25," *The CQ Researcher,* Jan. 27, 1995, pp. 73-96. The five nuclear powers are the United States, China, France, Russia and Great Britain.

[6] Helms spoke March 28, 1996, at Senate Foreign Relations Committee hearings on chemical and biological defense capabilities.

[7] E.R. Zumwalt Jr., "A Needless Risk for U.S. Troops," *The Washington Post,* Jan. 6, 1997.

[8] See Laurie Mylroie, "WTC Bombing — The Case of 'Secret' Cyanide," *The Wall Street Journal,* July 26, 1996.

[9] See Robert Ruth, "Judge Who Nixed Deal in Plague Case May Step Down," *The Columbus Dispatch,* Nov. 20, 1996.

[10] Presidential Advisory Committee, *op. cit.,* p. 96.

[11] Joseph spoke Nov. 12, 1996, at a Pentagon news briefing.

[12] Presidential Advisory Committee, *op. cit.,* pp. 40-41.

[13] *Ibid.,* p. 107.

[14] Eddington, who is writing a book about Gulf War Syndrome, testified Dec. 10, 1996, before the House Government Reform and Oversight Subcommittee on Human Resources and Intergovernmental Relations. See also Patrick G. Eddington and Mark S. Zaid, "The True Costs of the Gulf War Syndrome," *The Washington Post,* Jan. 1, 1997.

[15] Robert W. Haley, "Is There a Gulf War Syndrome: Searching for Syndromes by Factor Analysis of Symptoms," *Journal of the American Medical Association,* Jan. 15, 1997, pp. 215-222.

[16] See Cole, *op. cit.,* pp. 1-2. Unless otherwise noted, information in this section is based on Cole's book.

[17] See W. Seth Carus, "The Proliferation of Biological Weapons," in Brad Roberts, ed., *Biological Weapons: Weapons of the Future?* (1993), p. 20.

[18] See Cole, *op. cit.,* pp. 17-41.

[19] See Thomas Dashiell, "A Review of U.S. Biological Warfare Policies," in Roberts, *op. cit.,* p. 3.

[20] See Leonard A. Cole, "The Specter of Biological Weapons," *Scientific American,* December 1996, p. 62. The 17 countries cited by Cole are Iran, Iraq, Libya, Syria, North Korea, Taiwan, Israel, Egypt, Vietnam, Laos, Cuba, Bulgaria, India, South Korea, South Africa, China and Russia.

[21] The Arms Control and Disarmament Agency does not identify chemical weapons states, but says it suspects "some 20 countries have or may be developing chemical weapons." See ACDA, *Fact Sheet: The Chemical Weapons Convention,* Dec. 17, 1996. Countries most often cited are Israel, Libya, Iraq, Egypt, Iran, Syria, Taiwan, North Korea, Vietnam, Myanmar, China, Pakistan, South Korea, India and Ethiopia. See Office of Technology Assessment, *Proliferation of Weapons of Mass Destruction: Assessing the Risks,* 1993, p. 80.

[22] See John F. Sopko, "The Changing Proliferation Threat," *Foreign Policy,* winter 1996-97, p. 4.

[23] See "Bosnia Produced Chemical Arms, Report Says," *The New York Times,* Dec. 4, 1996.

[24] Cole, "The Specter of Biological Weapons," *op. cit.,* p. 60.

[25] Sopko, *op. cit.,* p. 6.

[26] See David Brown, "New Studies Indicate 6 Patterns of Gulf 'Syndrome'," *The Washington Post,* Jan. 9, 1997.

[27] Presidential Advisory Committee, *op. cit.,* p. 125.

[28] See David Brown, "Liberalized Rules Weighed for Gulf Disability Aid," *The Washington Post,* Jan. 8, 1997.

[29] Cited by Arms Control and Disarmament Agency, *op. cit.*

[30] For background, see "Combating Infectious Diseases," *The CQ Researcher,* June 9, 1996, pp. 489-512.

[31] Gore spoke on June 12, 1996, before the National Council for International Health in Crystal City, Va.

Bibliography

Selected Sources Used

Books

Cole, Leonard A., *The Eleventh Plague: The Politics of Biological and Chemical Warfare*, W. H. Freeman, 1997.
The author, a Rutgers University professor of science and public policy, outlines the history and potential dangers of biological and chemical weapons proliferation. He argues that arms control agreements can provide an imperfect but necessary protection against these weapons.

Roberts, Brad, ed., *Biological Weapons: Weapons of the Future?*, The Center for Strategic and International Studies, 1993.
A strong defense in nuclear and conventional weapons and strengthening of the Biological Weapons Convention are needed to counter the growing danger of biological weapons attack, concludes the editor of this collection of essays on biological warfare.

Weinberger, Caspar, and Peter Schweizer, *The Next War*, Regnery, 1996.
Weinberger, Defense secretary during the Reagan administration, and Schweizer, an analyst at the conservative Hoover Institution, offer several hypothetical war-game scenarios to illustrate their contention that defense spending cuts have left the United States vulnerable to biological, chemical and nuclear attack.

Articles

Newman, Richard J., Mike Tharp and Timothy M. Ito, "Gulf War Mysteries," *U.S. News & World Report*, Nov. 25, 1996, pp. 36-38.
Recent congressional testimony suggests that Iraqi chemical weapons may be responsible for many gulf war veterans' health complaints, but the link may never be fully established.

Sopko, John F., "The Changing Proliferation Threat," *Foreign Policy*, winter 1996-97, pp. 3-20.
According to Sopko, a counsel for Sen. Sam Nunn, D-Ga., before the senator's recent retirement, the United States is dangerously unprepared to counter attacks using biological, chemical or nuclear weapons by rogue states or terrorists.

Thompson, Mark, "The Silent Treatment," *Time*, Dec. 23, 1996, pp. 33-34.
The author reviews investigations into Gulf War Syndrome, which thus far have failed to satisfy veterans' claims that they were sickened by exposure to chemical or biological weapons.

Reports and Studies

Business Executives for National Security, *Twelve Myths about the Chemical Weapons Convention*, January 1997.
A group of business leaders concerned about U.S. defense policy rebuts the main arguments presented by critics who oppose Senate ratification of the 1993 treaty aimed at curbing chemical-weapons proliferation.

Central Intelligence Agency, *The Chemical and Biological Warfare Threat*, undated.
This primer includes a review of the technology, proliferation and arms control efforts involving biological and chemical weapons, as well as a description of the main substances and microorganisms used to produce them.

National Science and Technology Council, Committee on International Science, Engineering, and Technology Working Group on Emerging and Re-emerging Infectious Diseases, *Infectious Disease — A Global Health Threat*, September 1995.
The NSTC, a Cabinet-level council charged with coordinating federal science policies, identifies the microorganisms involved in recent infectious disease outbreaks and offers a plan for responding more effectively to them, whether they result from natural causes or from deliberate use of biological weapons.

Presidential Advisory Committee on Gulf War Veterans' Illnesses, *Final Report*, December 1996.
This 13-member panel of experts commissioned in 1995 by President Clinton finds no conclusive evidence that Gulf War Syndrome is linked to exposure to chemical or biological weapons during the 1991 conflict.

Rodrigues, Leslie A., "The Emerging Threat of Chembio Terrorism: Is the United States Prepared?" *The Arena*, Chemical and Biological Arms Control Institute, November 1996.
The 1995 release of sarin gas by terrorists in the Tokyo subway system raises questions about vulnerability to similar attacks in the United States, according to this report by a group that supports tighter arms control in the area of chemical and biological weapons.

Selden, Zachary, *Assessing the Biological Weapons Threat*, Business Executives for National Security, January 1997.
This study analyzes the technology of biological warfare, proliferation of these weapons and recent efforts to strengthen the 1972 Biological Weapons Convention.

U.S. Arms Control and Disarmament Agency, *Convention on the Prohibition of the Development, Production, Stockpiling and Use of Chemical Weapons and on Their Destruction*, October 1993.
The federal agency that advises the president on arms control analyzes in detail the Chemical Weapons Convention, due to go into effect April 29.

The Next Step

Additional information from UMI's Newspaper & Periodical Abstracts™ database

Biological Weapons

Cole, Leonard A., "The specter of biological weapons," ***Scientific American,*** **December 1996, pp. 60-64.**
States and terrorists alike have shown a growing interest in germ warfare with the use of biological weapons. More stringent arms-control efforts are needed to discourage attacks.

"Human Rights Watch Arms Project — Chemical and biological weapons program," ***Politics & the Life Sciences,*** **March 1996, pp. 114-115.**
A chemical and biological weapons program was initiated by the Human Rights Watch Arms Project in 1995.

"Information on biological weapons program reported hidden," ***U.N. Chronicle,*** **December 1995, pp. 24-25.**
Iraq hid information on its biological weapons program from the U.N. Special Commission (UNSCOM) set up under Security Council Resolution 687. Sanctions remain in place against Iraq.

Mathews, Jessica, "Doom and gloom and biological weapons," ***The Washington Post,*** **Oct. 7, 1996, p. A21.**
Mathews questions whether biological weapons are becoming the poor man's atomic bomb, asserting that biological agents are lousy battlefield weapons.

McMahon, Scott K., "Unconventional nuclear, biological and chemical weapons delivery methods: Whither the 'smuggled bomb'," ***Comparative Strategy,*** **April 1996, pp. 123-134.**
McMahon examines the threat of rogue state nuclear, biological or chemical (NBC) weapons attacks on the U.S. homeland using terrorist methods. In contrast to missile-delivered NBC weapons, the military utility of terrorist attacks would be limited because the U.S. could marshal effective defenses.

Shaw, Russell, "Bio-bombs are biggest threat," ***Insight on the News,*** **Oct. 7-14, 1996, p. 41.**
Experts are preparing for the "when, rather than the if" of nuclear or biological terrorism in the U.S. More than 15,000 law-enforcement officials, security consultants, entrepreneurs and chemists met to discuss this problem at the recent American Society for Industrial Security convention.

Chemical Weapons Convention

Cole, Leonard A., "U.S. should have signed chemical weapons treaty," ***The Christian Science Monitor,*** **Sept. 20, 1996, p. 19.**
Cole criticizes the Senate's decision the week of Sept. 9, 1996, to postpone a vote on ratification of the Chemical Weapons Convention.

Helms, Jesse A., "Why this chemical weapons treaty is badly flawed," ***USA Today,*** **Sept. 12, 1996, p. A15.**
Sen. Jesse Helms, R-N.C., says the Chemical Weapons Convention treaty before the Senate would improve rogue states' access to chemical agents while imposing massive new regulations on thousands of U.S. businesses, compromising their trade secrets and exposing them to inspections by international regulators.

"A Ban on Chemical Weapons," ***The New York Times,*** **Sept. 3, 1996, p. A14.**
An editorial says that by voting to ratify the Chemical Weapons Convention, the Senate can make it harder for a future dictator to endanger American troops with chemical weapons, and harder for future terrorists to unleash lethal gases on subway commuters.

"An overdue chemical weapons ban," ***The Boston Globe,*** **Sept. 11, 1996, p. A18.**
An editorial comments on the Senate's overdue acceptance of its responsibility to vote on ratification of the Chemical Weapons Convention.

Batsanov, Serguei, "Preparing for the entry into force of the Chemical Weapons Convention," ***NATO Review,*** **September 1996, pp. 16-20.**
The 1993 Chemical Weapons Convention is a unique global accord that will prohibit all chemical weapons. Batsanov argues that the situation is now at a critical juncture and that the major players who have not yet ratified the Convention should do so in order to ensure the success of this new approach to arms control and nonproliferation.

Cassata, Donna, "Chemical weapons treaty nears climactic vote," ***Congressional Quarterly Weekly Report,*** **Sept. 7, 1996, p. 2534.**
The Senate is poised for a historic vote on the Chemical Weapons Convention, which will outlaw most chemical weapons. Proponents of the treaty are cautiously optimistic about the prospects of garnering the two-thirds vote necessary to approve ratification.

"Chemical weapons pact must be ratified," ***San Francisco Chronicle,*** **Sept. 3, 1996, p. A16.**
An editorial states that Congress should ratify the international Chemical Weapons Convention — which would totally ban chemical weapons — when it comes up for a vote on Sept. 15, 1996. The editorial criticizes Sen. Jesse Helms, R-N.C., for waging a "dishonest" campaign to defeat the measure.

Landay, Jonathan S., "Senate may nix chemical weapons ban," ***The Christian Science Monitor,*** **Nov. 21, 1996, p. 4.**
The Clinton administration says that it will seek Senate approval of the Chemical Weapons Convention — which would require nations to eliminate their chemical weapons stocks or face targeted international sanctions — as soon as the 105th Congress opens in January 1997. Congressional conservatives, however, do not support the ban, saying that it cannot be enforced and that the U.S. will lose jobs.

Meselson, Matthew S., "Ratify the chemical weapons treaty as a force against terrorism," ***Los Angeles Times,*** **Sept. 11, 1996, p. B9.**
Meselson calls for U.S. ratification of the Chemical Weapons Convention as an anti-terrorism measure.

Moodie, Michael, "Ratifying the Chemical Weapons Convention: Past time for action," ***Arms Control Today,*** **February 1996, pp. 3-9.**
The importance of ratifying the Chemical Weapons Convention (CWC) is addressed. If the U.S. fails to ratify the CWC, it will be a crushing blow for countries committed to ridding the world of chemical weapons.

Robinson, Perry J.P., "Implementing the Chemical Weapons Convention," ***International Affairs,*** **January 1996, pp. 73-89.**
Robinson examines the essential underpinnings of the Chemical Weapons Convention established during the 24 years of its construction and the forms and safeguards arrived at by negotiators in order to make it acceptable to the 159 states that have so far signed it. The erosion of these safeguards and underpinnings in the process of implementation risks endangering the success of the convention, he writes.

Towell, Pat, "Administration begins new drive for chemical weapons treaty," ***Congressional Quarterly Weekly Report,*** **March 30, 1996, pp. 893-894.**
On March 28, 1996, top Clinton administration officials made a strong pitch for Senate approval of a treaty to outlaw most chemical weapons a month before the Senate Foreign Relations Committee completes deliberations on the treaty.

Weinberger, Caspar W., "Hyping the Chemical Weapons Convention," ***Forbes,*** **Oct. 7, 1996, p. 35.**
President Clinton's claim that the Chemical Weapons Convention will help "banish poison gas from the Earth" is as hollow a boast as any of his other false promises. The treaty is not verifiable or enforceable and does not include some of the world's worst offenders.

Chemical Weapons Disposal

"Army Begins Burning Chemical Weapons," ***The New York Times,*** **Aug. 23, 1996, p. A18.**
On Aug. 22, 1996, the U.S. Army began a seven-year program to destroy a huge stockpile of chemical weapons in a chemical weapons incinerator at Tooele Army Depot in Utah, 50 miles southwest of Salt Lake City. An M-55 rocket containing the nerve agent sarin (GB) was the first to be incinerated. Opponents who fear the plant is unsafe and will spew out toxic gases are challenging the burn permit.

Brooke, James, "At Chemical Weapons Depot, the Target Is Tenants," ***The New York Times,*** **Nov. 24, 1996, p. 24.**
The attempts to find renters of the warehouses at the old Pueblo Chemical Depot in Colorado, which holds 10 percent of the nation's chemical weapons, are discussed.

Campbell, Velma L., and Ross J. Vincent, "Chemical weapons destruction: A window of opportunity," ***Social Justice,*** **winter 1995, pp. 114-125.**
Modern chemical weapon stockpiles in the U.S. had reached about 36,000 tons by the time U.S. production ceased in 1969. Congress authorized the army to dispose of the existing stockpile nearly 20 years ago, but the program scheduled for completion a year ago has barely begun. The army intended to incinerate chemical weapons, but there have been sharp criticisms against such a plan.

"Getting rid of chemical weapons," ***Science News,*** **Oct. 5, 1996, p. 218.**
The controversy continues over the chemical weapons incinerator at the U.S. Army's Tooele Depot in Utah. It was shut down to fix internal leaks for a second time in its first full month of operation. Tooele is the first full-scale facility to eliminate deadly nerve and mustard agents.

Stern, Bill, "Chemical weapons disposal dilemma," ***Earth Island Journal,*** **winter 1995, p. 21.**
Despite problems, the U.S. Army continues to assure Congress that the incineration of its aging stockpile of chemical weapons is safe and effective. Research on disposal alternatives is discussed.

"U.S. to Start Destroying Chemical Weapons," ***The New York Times,*** **Aug. 21, 1996, p. B6.**
The Defense Department said a chemical weapons incinerator will start destroying its stockpile of nerve and blister agents in the Utah desert beginning on Aug. 22. The work, at the Tooele disposal facility, will cost $12.4 billion.

Vartabedian, Ralph, "Chemical weapons burial sites: Risks, if any, remain unknown," ***Los Angeles Times,*** **March 4, 1996, p. A12.**
After years of environmental research on chemical weapons, much remains unknown about potential hazards lurking at the bottom of the world's seas and oceans and in burial pits across the United States. No monitoring of the known sea burial sites of chemical weapons from World War II

has occurred for two decades.

Controlling Proliferation

Clinton, William J., "Letter to congressional leaders on weapons of mass destruction," *Weekly Compilation of Presidential Documents,* Nov. 18, 1996, p. 6.
In a letter to congressional leaders, President Clinton discusses the dangers stemming from the proliferation of weapons of mass destruction and urges Congress to extend the national emergency pertaining to such weapons.

Landay, Jonathan S., "Nuclear test ban talks fizzle but pact on chemical weapons may win nod," *The Christian Science Monitor,* Aug. 15, 1996, p. 18.
For more than two years, delegates from 61 nations have labored in Geneva, Switzerland, to negotiate a treaty banning nuclear weapons tests for all time. There appeared little chance, however, that they would succeed by the Aug. 15, 1996, deadline. With the United Nations Conference on Disarmament required to approve all issues by consensus, India appeared determined to use its veto to block the proposed Comprehensive Test Ban Treaty from being sent to the U.N. General Assembly for approval before it dissolves in September.

Reiss, Tom, "Chemical Weapons, Made in the U.S.A.," *The New York Times,* Aug. 23, 1996, p. A27.
Reiss accuses the U.S. of having "an erratic policy" on chemical warfare, piously calling for non-proliferation while producing a huge arsenal of chemical weapons and failing to protect its troops adequately. Reiss cites the case of the gulf war veterans who were probably exposed to chemical weapons in Iraq, according to the Pentagon's recent concession, and the U.S.'s delay in ratifying the Chemical Weapons Convention, which was signed by 158 nations in 1993.

Shenon, Philip, "Perry, in Egypt, Warns Libya to Halt Chemical Weapons Plant," *The New York Times,* April 4, 1996, p. A6.
Former Defense Secretary William J. Perry said on April 3, 1996, that the U.S. would not allow Libya to complete an underground chemical weapons plant and would not rule out a military attack if Libya does not halt its chemical weapons program. Perry issued the warning after presenting Egyptian President Hosni M. Mubarak with a detailed report on the plant, which is under construction in Tarhuna.

Smithson, Amy E., and Laurie H. Boulden, "Chemical weapons: Neglected menace," *Issues in Science & Technology,* spring 1996, pp. 75-81.
While the world has been preoccupied with containing the number of nuclear arms produced in the world, chemical weapons have been quietly proliferating in massive numbers. Federal policy-makers must recognize and deal with the problem of chemical weapons before a tragedy occurs in the U.S.

Weymouth, Lally, "Chemical weapons fraud," *The Washington Post,* Sept. 12, 1996, p. A27.
Weymouth says that if the Clinton administration succeeds in persuading the Senate to ratify the Chemical Weapons Convention, the mere fact of a new treaty will not help the U.S. combat the spread of such weapons of mass destruction.

Gulf War Syndrome

Block, Herb, "Gulf War syndrome," *The Washington Post,* Nov. 15, 1996, p. A30.
A Herb Block editorial cartoon satirizes the Pentagon for portraying everything as rosy in the face of the Gulf War Syndrome.

"Britain Studies Pesticides In Gulf War Syndrome," *The New York Times,* Oct. 5, 1996, p. A2.
Britain said on Oct. 4, 1996, that pesticides used in the 1991 Persian Gulf war could be linked to the crippling illnesses known as Gulf War Syndrome suffered by many of its veterans.

Brown, David, and Dana Priest, "Report finds no evidence of Gulf War Syndrome," *The Washington Post,* Nov. 9, 1996, p. A1.
The preliminary report of a special panel appointed by President Clinton has found no support for the myriad theories proposed as causes of illnesses among Persian Gulf War veterans, or even evidence that there is a Gulf War Syndrome.

"Chemical weapons suspect in Gulf Syndrome," *Veterans of Foreign Wars Magazine,* September 1996, p. 9.
The Department of Defense (DOD) has admitted that chemical weapons may be responsible for Gulf War Syndrome. The DOD previously denied that U.S. troops were exposed to chemical weapons.

Fairhall, David, "Cabinet in about-turn on Gulf War syndrome," *The Guardian,* Dec. 11, 1996, p. 1.
The UK government on Dec. 10, 1996, buckled under six years of pressure from veterans' organizations when it announced a major investigation into the Gulf War Syndrome, the condition it previously refused to acknowledge.

Fairhall, David, "Flea treatments 'linked to Gulf war syndrome,'" *The Guardian,* Oct. 31, 1996, p. 13.
Dangerous chemicals suspected as a cause of the mysterious Gulf War Syndrome are also present in everyday treatments for children with head lice and flea-ridden pets. UK Liberal Democratic MP Paul Tyler called for a ban on organophosphate pesticides.

Greenberg, Daniel S., "Distrust and more studies of Gulf War Syndrome in U.S.A.," *Lancet,* Dec. 7, 1996, p. 1577.
The final report from the White House committee ap-

pointed to restore the government's credibility on the subject of illness among Gulf War veterans is expected soon. A majority of the committee is expected to emphasize stress as the principal cause of the symptoms labeled Gulf War Syndrome.

"Gulf War Syndrome," *St. Louis Post-Dispatch,* Sept. 28, 1996, p. C6.
An editorial discusses the Pentagon's reluctance to deal with the illnesses collectively known as Gulf War Syndrome.

"Gulf War Syndrome remains unproven," *Lancet,* Jan. 20, 1996, p. 182.
A U.S. Institute of Medicine committee has concluded that there is no clinical evidence for a previously unknown, serious illness among the veterans of the gulf war.

Hilts, Philip J., "Panel doubts Gulf War Syndrome is new," *The New York Times,* Jan. 5, 1996, p. D19.
On Jan. 4, 1996, a panel of experts working on behalf of the Institute of Medicine reported that soldiers who served in the Persian Gulf War do not appear to have any new or unique illness, but added that medical studies done so far cannot rule out mild or rare illnesses associated with service there.

Krauthammer, Charles, "What Gulf War syndrome?" *The Washington Post,* Dec. 20, 1996, p. A27.
Charles Krauthammer asserts that Gulf War Syndrome is a fiction.

McAllister, Bill, "Gulf War Syndrome gets new diagnosis," *The Washington Post,* Sept. 26, 1996, p. A29.
Faced with mounting bipartisan criticism, on Sept. 25, 1996, the Pentagon promised to reassess its response to mysterious illnesses affecting several thousand Persian Gulf War veterans.

O' Kane, Maggie, "Cure claim for Gulf war syndrome," *The Guardian,* Jan. 3, 1996, p. 3.
Leading U.S. AIDS expert Howard Urnovitz will tell a gathering of scientists in London on Jan. 3, 1996, that he has found the cause and a potential treatment for Gulf War Syndrome, a debilitating condition with multiple symptoms that 4,000 British veterans claim they contracted during the war.

Pennisi, Elizabeth, "Chemicals behind Gulf War Syndrome?" *Science,* April 26, 1996, pp. 479-480.
A privately funded team of epidemiologists and toxicologists may have found an answer to some of the problems faced by veterans from the gulf war. The problems may stem from the soldiers being exposed to combinations of chemicals that are harmless when used by themselves.

Shellenberger, Michael, "The answer to Gulf War Syndrome," *San Francisco Chronicle,* April 9, 1996, p. A19.
Shellenberger criticizes the Pentagon's report on Gulf War Syndrome, released on April 2, 1996, which contended that the variety of ailments associated with the disorder are more the result of psychological and physical exertion than everything else.

Schnabel, Jim, "Spurious premise behind Gulf War Syndrome," *Houston Chronicle,* Nov. 19, 1996, p. A19.
Schnabel discusses Gulf War Syndrome in light of leaks from a panel of experts that indicate that they found no evidence that the syndrome even exists.

Schnabel, Jim, "The real causes of 'Gulf War syndrome'," *The Washington Post,* Nov. 15, 1996, p. A31.
Schnabel examines the divide between the scientific culture and the popular culture over Gulf War Syndrome, asserting that it is not a syndrome in search of an explanation, but is an explanation in search of a syndrome.

Streeter, Michael, "More Gulf War Syndrome revelations in Britain," *Lancet,* Oct. 12, 1996, p. 1023.
Official doubts that Gulf War Syndrome exists are being undermined by the revelation that more pesticides containing organophosphates were used by British troops during the Persian Gulf War than what had previously been stated. Veterans' campaigners feel the government has been incompetent or even was indulging in a conspiracy about the extent to which troops were poisoned.

"Study of 19,000 Finds No 'Gulf War Syndrome'," *The New York Times,* April 4, 1996, p. B11.
A clinical study of 18,924 veterans of the Persian Gulf War has found frequent cases of headaches, fatigue, memory loss and depression but no single cause or mystery ailment to support suspicions about the existence of a Gulf War Syndrome. The survey said 36 percent of the patients suffered from psychological or ill-defined ailments in a wide variety of diagnoses.

"The Gulf War Syndrome," *San Francisco Chronicle,* Sept. 23, 1996, p. A20.
An editorial calls for the Pentagon to turn over its investigation into the cause of Gulf War Syndrome to an independent body that has the unquestioned trust and confidence of veterans and the public.

Warden, John, "Pesticide link with Gulf War syndrome," *British Medical Journal* (International), Oct. 12, 1996, p. 897.
Britain's minister of defense has admitted a possible link between gulf war sickness and exposure to organophosphate insecticides. It seems that these organophosphate pesticides were used more widely in the gulf than was previously realized.

Back Issues

Great Research on Current Issues Starts Right Here...Recent topics covered by The CQ Researcher are listed below. Before May 1991, reports were published under the name of Editorial Research Reports.

JULY 1995
War Crimes
Highway Safety
Combating Terrorism
Preventing Teen Drug Use

AUGUST 1995
Job Stress
Organ Transplants
United Nations at 50
Advances in Cancer Research

SEPTEMBER 1995
Catholic Church in the U.S.
Northern Ireland Cease-Fire
High School Sports
Teaching History

OCTOBER 1995
Quebec's Future
Revitalizing the Cities
Networking the Classroom
Indoor Air Pollution

NOVEMBER 1995
The Working Poor
The Jury System
Sex, Violence and the Media
Police Misconduct

Back issues are available for $5.00 (subscribers) or $10.00 (non-subscribers). Quantity discounts apply to orders over ten. To order, call Congressional Quarterly Customer Service at (202) 887-8621.

Binders are available for $18.00. To order call 1-800-638-1710. Please refer to stock number 648.

DECEMBER 1995
Teens and Tobacco
Gene Therapy's Future
Global Water Shortages
Third-Party Prospects

JANUARY 1996
Emergency Medicine
Punishing Sex Offenders
Bilingual Education
Helping the Homeless

FEBRUARY 1996
Reforming the CIA
Campaign Finance Reform
Academic Politics
Getting Into College

MARCH 1996
The British Monarchy
Preventing Juvenile Crime
Tax Reform
Pursuing the Paranormal

APRIL 1996
Centennial Olympic Games
Managed Care
Protecting Endangered Species
New Military Culture

MAY 1996
Russia's Political Future
Marriage and Divorce
Year-Round Schools
Taiwan, China and the U.S.

JUNE 1996
Rethinking NAFTA
First Ladies
Teaching Values
Labor Movement's Future

JULY 1996
Recovered-Memory Debate
Native Americans' Future
Crackdown on Sexual Harassment
Attack on Public Schools

AUGUST 1996
Fighting Over Animal Rights
Privatizing Government Services
Child Labor and Sweatshops
Cleaning Up Hazardous Wastes

SEPTEMBER 1996
Gambling Under Attack
The States and Federalism
Civic Journalism
Reassessing Foreign Aid

OCTOBER 1996
Political Consultants
Insurance Fraud
Rethinking School Integration
Parental Rights

NOVEMBER 1996
Global Warming
Clashing Over Copyright
Consumer Debt
Governing Washington, D.C.

DECEMBER 1996
Welfare, Work and the States
The New Volunteerism
Implementing the Disabilities Act
America's Pampered Pets

JANUARY 1997
Combating Scientific Misconduct
Restructuring the Electric Industry
The New Immigrants

Future Topics

- ***Assisting Refugees***
- ***Alternative Medicine's Next Phase***
- ***Independent Counsels***

The CQ Researcher

Published By Congressional Quarterly Inc.

Assisting Refugees

Do current aid policies add to the problems?

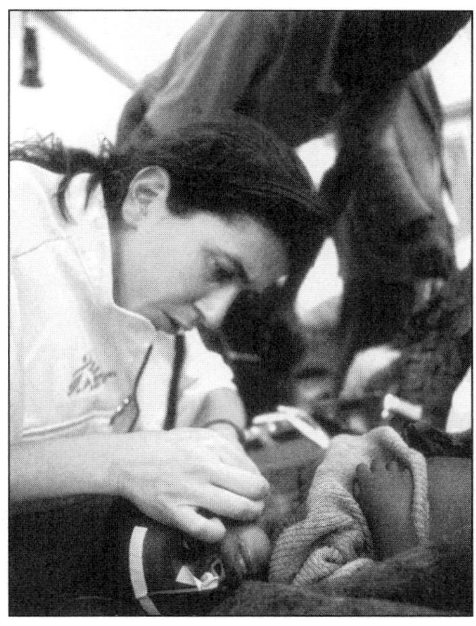

The refugee crisis in Zaire and Rwanda has once again focused world attention on displaced people. Affecting more than 5 million people, the crisis has forced refugee-aid groups, governments and others to reassess the way aid to refugees is now rendered. For the U.N. High Commissioner for Refugees and other humanitarian relief organizations, the situation raises fundamental questions about aiding refugees: Can efforts to help actually make matters worse? And how can tragedies like the one in Central Africa be prevented or at least mitigated in the future? For the United States and other developed nations, the crisis has reopened the debate over whether using soldiers to assist humanitarian relief efforts is appropriate, and whether dramatic media coverage of crises can lead to bad policy decisions.

Inside This Issue

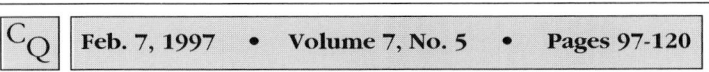

CQ | Feb. 7, 1997 • Volume 7, No. 5 • Pages 97-120

Formerly Editorial Research Reports

THE ISSUES

BACKGROUND

CURRENT SITUATION

OUTLOOK

SIDEBARS AND GRAPHICS

FOR MORE INFORMATION

COVER: A PHYSICIAN FROM THE RELIEF GROUP DOCTORS WITHOUT BORDERS TREATS A SICK BABY ON THE ROAD FROM GOMA, ZAIRE, TO GISENYI, RWANDA, LAST NOVEMBER. © REMCO BOHLE

THE CQ Researcher

Feb. 7, 1997
Volume 7, No. 5

PUBLISHED BY
Congressional Quarterly Inc.

The CQ Researcher (ISSN 1056-2036). Formerly Editorial Research Reports. Published weekly (48 times per year, not printed Jan. 3, May 30, Aug. 29, Oct. 31) by Congressional Quarterly Inc., 1414 22nd St., N.W., Washington, D.C. 20037. Annual subscription rate for libraries, businesses and government is $340. Additional rates furnished upon request. Periodicals postage paid at Washington, D.C., and additional mailing offices. POSTMASTER: Send address changes to The CQ Researcher, 1414 22nd St., N.W., Washington, D.C. 20037.

Assisting Refugees

BY DAVID MASCI

THE ISSUES

On the dusty road to Gisenyi, just inside Rwanda, 200,000 bedraggled people were at last nearing home.

"You could see this river of humanity, with all of their belongings on their heads and their kids straggling along," recalls Samantha Bolton, an aid worker. "Most of them were barefoot and exhausted."

The next day, says Bolton, communications director for Doctors Without Borders USA, another 150,000 people made the trek.

The people returning to Rwanda last November were Hutus. In 1994, by the hundreds of thousands, they had been chased out of Rwanda by an army of rebel Tutsis, a rival ethnic group. Now the Tutsis were pushing the Hutus back into Rwanda by forcibly closing the refugee camps in Zaire.

Thousands of refugees who had fled to Zaire would never come home. Many children and older people had died of starvation or cholera during the exodus from Rwanda. Others had been killed in the camps by thugs and extremists from their own tribe. Tens of thousands more had died in Hutu-Tutsi fighting that flared up last year in Zaire. *

Throughout the crisis, the United Nations High Commissioner for Refugees (UNHCR) and other aid groups scrambled, often with questionable success, to help. Many of the world's most powerful nations seemed in a quandary about whether to get involved at all, fearful of becoming too entangled in the horrific chaos.

As shocking and tragic as it has been, the situation in Rwanda and

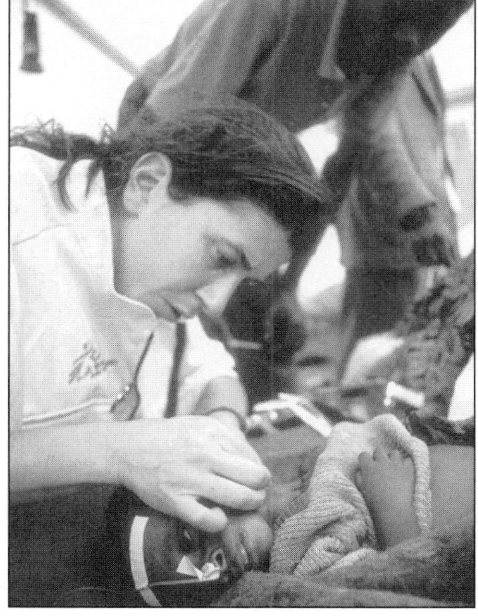

Zaire represents nothing more than the planet's latest refugee crisis, sandwiched between the festering upheavals in Bosnia and the next catastrophe yet to appear on the evening news.

Actually, many international experts say, the world is experiencing a level of conflict and population displacement rarely seen in human history. And, they warn, crises are becoming so commonplace that the world community can ignore them only at its own peril. Georgetown University Professor Charles Keeley predicts that multiethnic strife will force many states to collapse in coming decades, leading to still greater chaos.

The last decade has been especially volatile. While the United States, China, Germany and other global powers have been at peace through most of the post-World War II era, the developing world has seen a steady rise in war and civil strife. With the Cold War coming to an end, human misery and displacement became increasingly common in poorer countries, such as Somalia, Liberia and Burma. Since 1980, the estimated number of refugees in the world has roughly tripled, rising from 5.7 million to 15.3 million in 1996. The number of people displaced within their own countries is even higher, topping 20 million by most estimates. [1] (*See story, p. 108.*)

The refugee increases generally have not been tied to one cause. In the past, a cataclysm on the scale of World War II or the partitioning of India would create millions of refugees for a relatively short period of time. But today, refugee crises are a series of small, constant blips on the world's radar screen, with many crises being precipitated by old ethnic conflicts that flare up periodically.

The growing plight of refugees has generated an unprecedented increase in the size and number of aid groups. The UNHCR, once a small agency that provided legal assistance to refugees seeking asylum in post-World War II Europe, aided more than 27 million people in 1995. (*See graph, p. 109.*) In addition, there are now hundreds of non-governmental relief organizations (NGOs) — including CARE, the Red Cross and Doctors Without Borders.

Besides trying to provide food and shelter, UNHCR and other organizations are searching for new and innovative ways to prevent or at least mitigate the number of refugees. They also are focusing more attention on aiding displaced peoples after they have been repatriated, to decrease the chance that they will leave their homes again.

But some observers find fault with the aid efforts, and even question the motives of the aid groups themselves. A number of refugee experts argue that UNHCR may have done more harm than good in Rwanda and Zaire by blindly providing assistance to all Hutus who crossed into Zaire in 1994. The problem, they say, is that among the refugees was a large group of militants who were responsible for the genocidal slaughtering — often by machete — of more than 500,000

* By early December, more than 1 million of the 1.5 million Hutu refugees in Zaire had returned to Rwanda. Many of the half-million Hutus who had sought refuge in Tanzania also returned.

Tracking the World's Refugees

There are an estimated 35 million displaced people around the world, including 15 million refugees and 20 million displaced within their own countries, according to the United Nations High Commissioner for Refugees. The major refugee crises are highlighted on the map.

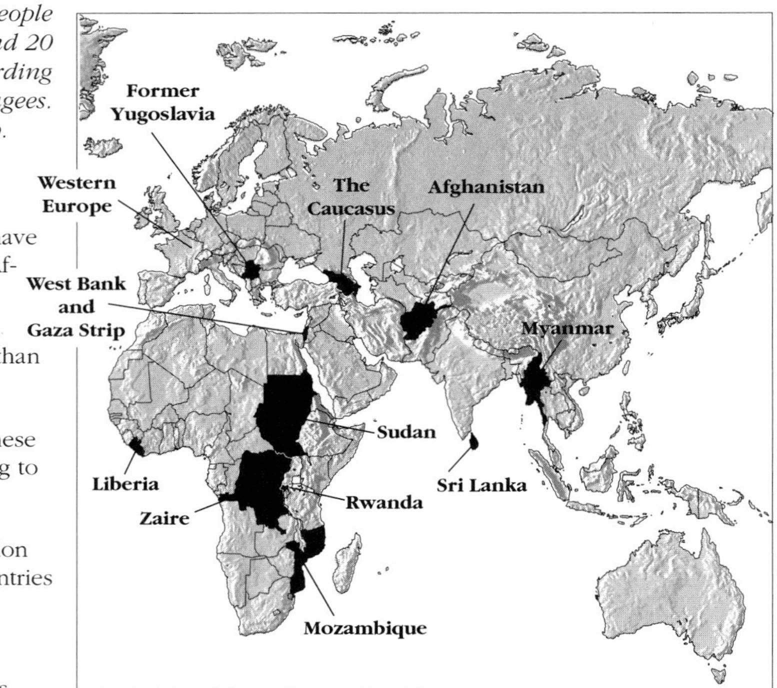

Major Displaced Populations

Afghanistan: More than half of all Afghan refugees have been repatriated since 1992, but roughly 2.5 million Afghans remain in Pakistan and Iran.

The Caucasus: Within the Russian Federation, more than 1.5 million people have been displaced in Armenia, Azerbaijan, Georgia and Chechnya in recent years. Although an uneasy peace has returned to some of these areas, many displaced persons are unable or unwilling to return to their homes.

Liberia: Civil war has displaced an estimated 1.5 million Liberians, half of whom have fled to neighboring countries such as Sierra Leone and Guinea.

Mozambique: About 1.7 million refugees have returned to Mozambique from six neighboring nations following the end of civil war in 1992. Millions of land mines hinder efforts to rebuild Mozambique.

Myanmar: Fewer than 50,000 of the 250,000 people who fled from Myanmar (formerly Burma) in 1991 and 1992 remain in Bangladesh, which has closed its borders to further refugee flows.

Rwanda/Zaire: In late 1996, about 1.5 million Rwandan Hutus returned to their homeland after spending more than two years in refugee camps in Tanzania and Zaire. Estimates vary widely, but it is believed that more than 200,000 Rwandans remain in Zaire. These refugees fled east into the jungles of Zaire, largely out of the reach of most aid groups.

Sri Lanka: Most of the more than 100,000 refugees who fled to India have returned since 1992. But hundreds of thousands of Sri Lankans continue to be displaced internally as a result of the continuing civil war.

Sudan: Due to the continuing civil war between the Muslim north and largely Christian south, almost 500,000 Sudanese remain refugees in Uganda, Zaire and other nations. Another 4 million Sudanese have been internally displaced by the conflict.

Former Yugoslavia: More than 2.5 million people were displaced by the civil wars that rocked the republics of the former Yugoslavia. The vast majority of these displaced persons come from the republic of Bosnia-Herzegovina, where most have not been able to return home despite a peace agreement between the warring sides negotiated in November 1995 in Dayton, Ohio.

West Bank and Gaza Strip: Around 2.8 million people are registered with the United Nations Relief and Works Agency, which cares for Palestinian refugees. Whether they will return to the West Bank and Gaza Strip must be addressed in upcoming negotiations between Israel and the Palestinian Authority.

Western Europe: Since the early 1980s, more than 5 million applications for refugee status have been submitted in Western Europe. Recent tightening of asylum laws in most European countries has led to a marked decrease in applications. In 1995, for instance, fewer than 300,000 persons applied for asylum, compared with 700,000 in 1992.

Note: Displaced persons are defined as those who have been forced from their homes; refugees are displaced persons who have fled across international borders. More than 27 million displaced people are being assisted by UNHCR.

Tutsis and moderate Hutus. The Hutu extremists used the refugee camps as de facto military bases and treated the refugees as hostages.

Some cynics among the critics even say that UNHCR and the NGOs see it in their interest to create and perpetuate refugee crises. More starving children with bloated bellies on the evening news means more donations and government funding.

Aid groups call such views ridiculous. But they admit to owing their increased visibility, in no small part, to the news media, even as they fault the media for their short attention span and for ignoring many countries in turmoil. In the final analysis, they acknowledge, the media play the key role in making the global community aware of humanitarian needs.

Citizen awareness is crucial, aid experts say, and not just because it leads to charitable donations. Governments are more inclined to address a problem halfway around the world, they say, if their citizens call for action. Even then, nations in a position to help are often loath to do more than offer money. Many U.S. lawmakers, among others, are apprehensive about sending soldiers into harm's way to aid refugees or others in need, unless a key American interest is threatened. For example, they say, the Persian Gulf War was really about protecting U.S. access to Saudi Arabian oil, not saving Kuwait from Saddam Hussein's plundering troops.

Aid officials argue that affluent world powers like the United States should, in the interests of humanity and global peace, send troops to protect refugees and aid workers. UNHCR officials say they were rebuffed when they asked the major powers to send soldiers to the refugee camps in Zaire to separate the Hutu extremists from the legitimate refugees. UNHCR officials also say the international community's refusal to help left the agency with no choice but to assist everyone, good and bad, in the camps, in order to prevent innocent refugees from starving.

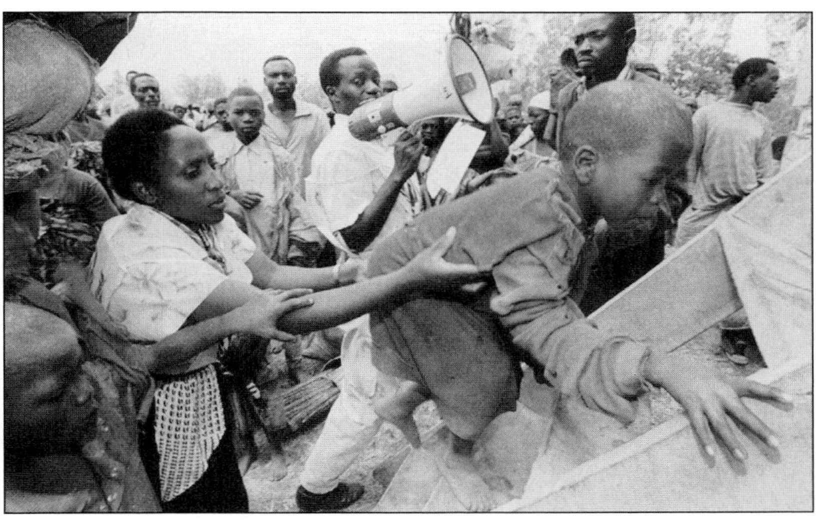

Reuters/Corinne Dufka

A young Rwandan Hutu refugee climbs into a truck for a ride back to Rwanda from Burundi in August 1996.

"If we had not started feeding them immediately, many people would have starved to death," says Soren Jessen-Petersen, director of UNHCR's New York City office.

As refugee advocates, politicians and others debate how to best respond to crises like the one in Zaire, these are some of the questions being asked:

Do the methods used by UNHCR and private relief organizations to help refugees actually make matters worse?

The crisis in the great lakes region of Eastern Africa has rocked the UNHCR to its foundations. Never before has the agency faced such a difficult and chaotic situation on such a vast scale.

In the second half of 1994, an estimated 2 million Rwandans, mainly from the Hutu tribe, fled into Zaire and Tanzania. The flight was triggered by a rebel army of Tutsis, which unseated the country's Hutu-led government.

The coup by the Rwandan Patriotic Front (RPF) was triggered, in turn, by the massacre earlier in 1994 of Tutsis and some moderate Hutus by Hutu extremists. The death toll in what has come to be known as the "Rwandan genocide" is estimated at about 800,000. [2]

When the RPF took control of Rwanda, the Hutus involved in the killings fled. Hundred of thousands of innocent Hutus followed the extremists into exile after being told that they would be targets of Tutsi retribution despite their innocence.

Critics of UNHCR say that it made egregious strategic mistakes at almost every step during the crisis in Zaire, revealing the organization's outmoded, institutional mindset. In particular, they say, UNHCR and the NGOs that support its work immediately moved to feed and care for all the Rwandan refugees streaming across the border, without considering the consequences.

Michael Maren, the author of a recent book highly critical of international aid efforts, contends that UNHCR, however unintentionally, provided aid and comfort to the perpetrators of the genocide when it set up camps for the Hutus. [3] "The Hutu leaders ran the camps and essentially controlled the distribution of aid," he says. In addition, says Maren, a former field worker for the U.S. Agency for Inter-

UNHCR to the Rescue

The United Nations High Commissioner for Refugees (UNHCR) coordinates the world community's efforts to assist and resettle refugees. Based in Geneva, Switzerland, the High Commissioner is nominated by the Secretary-General of the United Nations and elected by the General Assembly every five years. Sadako Ogata of Japan, the agency's eighth High Commissioner, took office on Jan. 1, 1991, but served a foreshortened three-year term. Her mandate was renewed for the full five years in 1994 and will expire at the end of 1998.

The UNHCR's budget and activities are monitored by a group of 50 U.N. member governments, including all of the major powers, known as the Executive Committee.

Roughly 2 percent of UNHCR's $1.4 billion budget, or $25 million, is provided by the U.N. to cover the agency's administrative costs. The remainder of the agency's funding is provided voluntarily by U.N. member states. Last year, 32 of the more than 170 U.N. members contributed.

Until recently, UNHCR worked largely to aid refugees after they had found asylum, often by providing legal assistance. In some cases, the agency aided the repatriation of displaced persons back to their country of origin after the danger that had forced them to flee had subsided.

Today, the agency's mandate is much broader. Since the 1970s, UNHCR has worked around the world to provide assistance to people who have recently been displaced, instead of waiting for them to reach a third country of asylum. As of last year, UNHCR maintained 255 offices in 118 countries.

national Development, the legitimate refugees were completely controlled by the Hutu killers, giving them enormous leverage with the international community. "The aid groups weren't feeding refugees," he says, "they were feeding hostages."

Instead of setting up camps, Maren says, the UNHCR and the NGOs should have provided services to Hutus in Rwanda. "The agencies should have told them: 'You cross the border, you're on your own,' " he says.

Stephen Stedman, a professor of African Studies at Johns Hopkins University's School of Advanced International Studies, agrees. He argues that if UNHCR had not assisted the Hutu refugees, they ultimately would have returned to Rwanda. This in turn would have denied the Hutu extremists the benefits they derived from the refugee camps.

Stedman also criticizes UNHCR and the NGOs for ignoring their own guidelines. "There are international conventions on what a refugee is, and it is very clear that they cannot be fleeing a country because they committed crimes; cannot be armed; and cannot use their refugee status to reconstruct an armed force," he says. [4]

But others say that the UNHCR made the best of a bad situation. They argue the Hutus so feared for their lives that they would not have returned to Rwanda. If they had stayed, and UNHCR had remained aloof, mass starvation and disease would have resulted.

"What could we have done?" asks Harlan Hale, assistant director for food and logistics at Atlanta-based CARE. "Our humanitarian imperative is to minister to people who are at risk." Those who think that it would have been better in the long run to let some Hutus starve wouldn't feel that way "if it was one of their kids out there," Hale adds.

It is easy to ponder better strategies after the fact, when you don't have to make snap decisions, says Jessen-Petersen. "More than 1 million people fled, and we had to provide life-saving assistance within 72 hours, something that is not very easy when you're in the African bush," he says.

Jessen-Petersen says that it took UNHCR four to six weeks just to stabilize the situation to the point where his agency could begin considering issues beyond providing basic assistance. "Once we got our head above water, we understood that we had a monster on our hands," he says.

UNHCR decided that the only way to tame the monster — the Hutu militants — was to disarm them or drive them from the camps. "The UNHCR knew that the camps contained a lot of killers, and they advocated a police force to separate out the killers from the refugees," says Jeff Drumtra, a policy analyst at the U.S. Committee for Refugees, an advocacy group in Washington. But the appeal fell on deaf ears, according to Drumtra and others. "There was simply no interest in doing this."

UNHCR supporters say that the unwillingness of the United States and other donor nations to commit the forces necessary to separate the extremists left the agency with limited options. "It was a horrible situation, and we faced it alone," says Marie Okabe, a senior UNHCR liaison officer in New York.

Others say that the donor countries' inaction allowed them to blame the UNHCR for anything that went wrong. Instead of taking action, Drumtra says, donor nations assuaged their consciences by pouring money into UNHCR to run the refugee camps in Zaire and Tanzania. UNHCR became "a fig leaf for their own lack of political will," he says.

After it became apparent that no military help was forthcoming, UNHCR officials say they tried to exert more control over the camps by breaking them down into smaller, more manageable units and by distributing food directly to those deemed to be legitimate refugees. But these efforts were stymied by the Hutu militants, who retained a firm hold on the populations in the camps.

Finally, UNHCR hired 1,500 members of the notoriously corrupt Zairian military to provide security in the camps. The intention, Jessen-Peterson says, was to create "a minimum of security" for legitimate refugees inside the camps. But the tiny force proved ineffective against the estimated 50,000-60,000 members of the Hutu militia. "In the end," Jessen-Peterson says, "nothing worked."

Bolton at Doctors Without Borders agrees that UNHCR was in a difficult situation after the refugee camps in Zaire had been established. But she also says the agency made other, big mistakes before the refugee crisis even occurred. "We had two weeks notice before the refugees crossed the border," she says, but "when they arrived no camps had been set up yet."

Bolton says UNHCR should have used the two-week window to set up many small camps, making it harder for militant Hutus to organize and control the refugees. "They had camps with 250,000 people, which you never do," she says, "because you're always going to have militarization."

But Jessen-Petersen and others say that with so many refugees crossing into Zaire at the same time, it was not logistically possible to break them into small groups while providing food and medical assistance.

Some critics also charge that many of the aid groups that responded to the crisis in Zaire can be criticized for more than shortsightedness. For instance, Maren says, UNHCR and other aid groups perpetuated this and other crises largely out of institutional self-interest. "NGOs don't want to shut down camps because they have a bureaucratic structure built up around these projects," he charges, adding that "there is very little accountability in the aid business, and that leaves lots of room for fat."

This is not true, Hale says. While he admits that groups like his receive more money — in the form of outside donations and UNHCR payments — during well-publicized crises, NGOs do not try to perpetuate disasters in order to improve their balance sheets, nor do they focus only on those situations that catch the public's eye. "It's not a question of helping some refugees and not others," he says, referring to those disasters that receive media attention and those that do not. "We distribute assistance based solely on need."

Reuters

Iraqi Kurds enter a refugee camp in Silopi, Turkey, in September 1996 after being evacuated from North Iraq.

Should American military personnel be sent overseas to help refugees if it exposes them to danger?

The use of American troops to provide food and other aid to displaced people has become relatively common. In the last few years, U.S. soldiers have been sent to help people in Somalia, Haiti and Bosnia. In November, President Clinton said he would send American troops to Zaire and only reversed that decision after he determined that the situation had improved.

Still, Americans and their leaders are generally wary of committing troops to humanitarian missions in far-off lands. (*See "At Issue," p. 113.*) As chairman of the Joint Chiefs of Staff, Gen. Colin L. Powell was an influential advocate for sending American forces rarely, and only when the mission's goals were clear and the use of overwhelming force made the chances of success high.

Much of the reluctance about using force stems from the nation's painful experience in Vietnam, where a small number of American military advisers grew to a half-million combat troops in a matter of years. More recently, Americans watched in horror in 1993 as news reports showed a dead American serviceman in Somalia being dragged through the streets of Mogadishu.

The incident produced what has been dubbed the "Somalia Syndrome," or lawmakers' and the military's fear of sending troops overseas if the possibility exists for even a few casualties.[5] "They really got burned in Somalia, and they don't want to see any more body bags coming home," Bolton says.

Still, many refugee advocates argue that there are times when troops simply must be sent, particularly to protect refugees and aid workers. For instance, it is widely thought that the

Africa Now Has the Most Refugees

Far more displaced persons in Africa than Asia are being assisted by the U.N. High Commissioner for Refugees, mainly due to recent civil wars in Africa and the resolution of refugee problems in Asia stemming from the Vietnam War and upheavals elsewhere in the region. In the decade from 1985-95, the number of UNHCR-assisted refugees and other displaced persons in Africa increased nearly fourfold; the number increased almost tenfold in Europe, primarily because of the crisis in the Balkans.

Number of People Assisted by the UNHCR

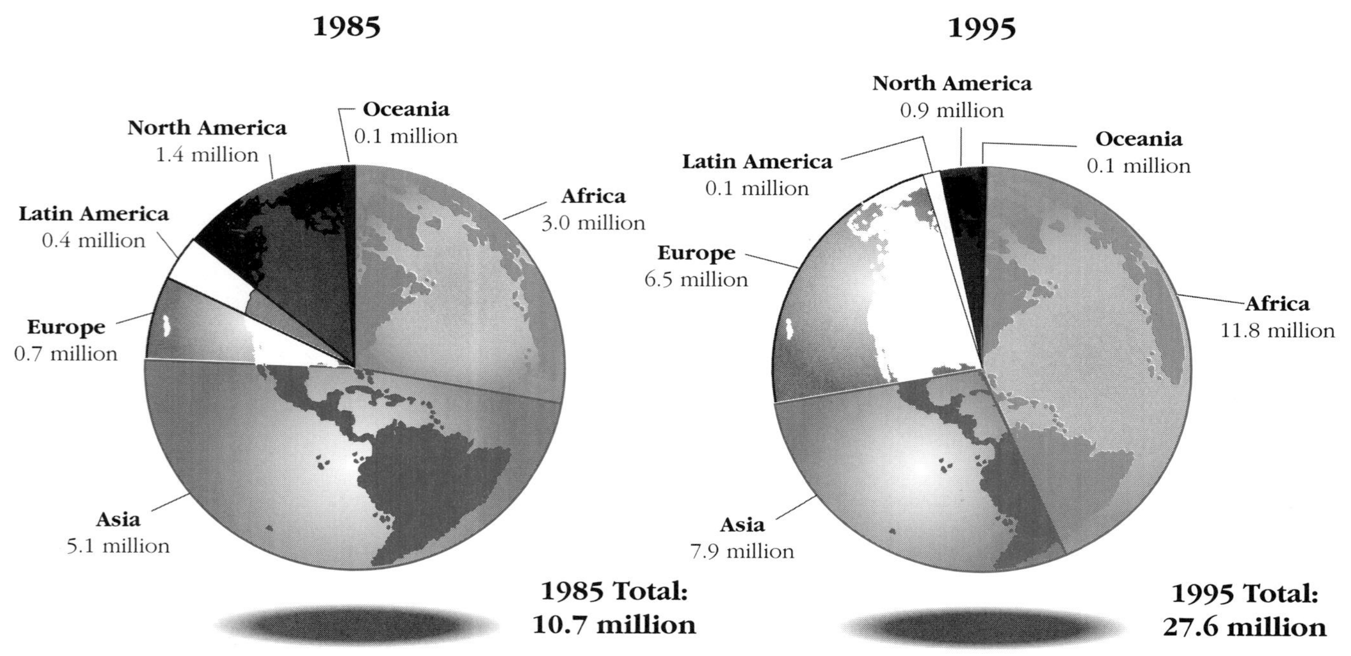

Source: United Nations High Commissioner for Refugees, The State of the World's Refugees, 1995

international community should have sent solders to drive Hutus who had participated in the Rwandan genocide out of the refugee camps.

"We had situations where Hutu soldiers just came into hospitals in the camps and shot patients dead," Bolton says. And, Bolton points out, refugees are not the only victims of such violence. Over the last five years, scores of aid workers have been killed in Somalia, Burundi and other hot spots. As recently as Feb. 4, five U.N. workers investigating human rights abuses in Rwanda were ambushed on a country road and shot to death. And in December, six International Red Cross workers in Chechnya were murdered in their beds.

While refugee advocates generally favor multiethnic forces, they argue that some situations demand a U.S. military presence if the intervention is to be effective. CARE's Hale notes that the U.S. has more heavy-lifting capacity, access to intelligence and sheer firepower than any other nation on Earth. Steven Hansch, a senior program officer at the Refugee Policy Group, agrees: "In certain circumstances, our armed forces are the only ones who can do the job."

But, Hansch says, the Somalia syndrome has set "such a conservative threshold of pain" that the nation won't send soldiers anywhere unless the mission is risk free. "We are chickens about this," Hansch says.

According to many refugee advocates, this attitude has soured other nations on working with the U.S. to resolve international problems. "We need to show that we are willing to be a player, that we stand for something," Hale says.

But others argue that the United States military has done more than its share in humanitarian crises, pointing to the deployments in Haiti in 1994 and in Bosnia the following year. "We're doing this too routinely, and it's starting to become the norm," says Eugene B. McDaniel, president of the American Defense Institute, a Washington think tank.

Others question sending American soldiers under any circumstances. "Why should it always be the United States that answers the global 911 call?" asks Lionel Rosenblatt, executive director for Refugees International. Rosenblatt and others say that military leaders should be especially wary of sending troops into countries where warring factions are still fighting and civil society has broken down.

In addition, McDaniel says, "Our troops are for defending our country and its national interests," not feeding refugees in a country halfway around the world. This means defending the industrial world's access to oil — as was done during the 1991 Persian Gulf War — but not protecting combatants in Bosnia from each other, McDaniel says. "It's degrading to send our soldiers to those places on those missions," he says.

But Michael Clough, a research associate at the Institute of International Studies at the University of California-Berkeley, calls the argument put forward by McDaniel and others "nonsense." Clough says the United States and other industrialized countries have a clear interest in solving humanitarian and refugee crises around the world. "First, we have an interest in ensuring that places like Africa don't collapse," he says, adding that "by 2025, 30 percent of the world's population will live in Africa, and you just can't write off a part of the world that big."

Another reason rich countries cannot ignore poorer states, Clough says, stems from the fact that large numbers of refugees will eventually reach the shores of European nations and the United States. In addition, he argues, there needs to be stability in the developing world if the global economy is to continue to expand.

But there may be a way to satisfy both McDaniel and Clough. Rosenblatt is among those who propose the establishment of a permanent United Nations rapid deployment force to intervene in humanitarian crises. While the proposal has received some tepid support from the United States and other powers, no action has been taken on the idea, and its prospects are uncertain, at best. [6]

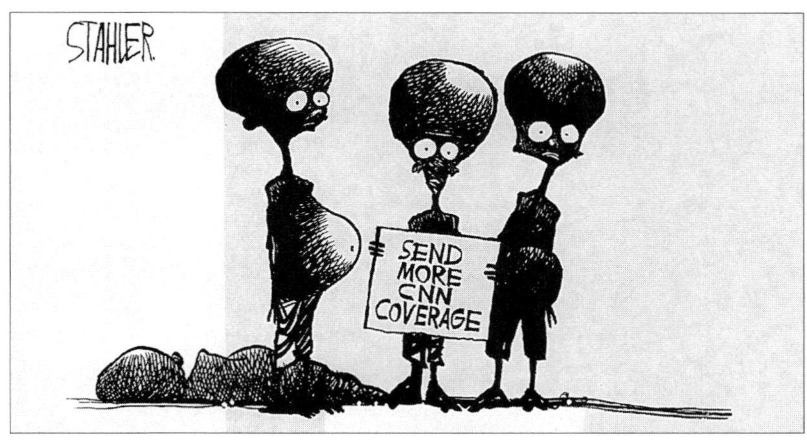

© JEFF STAHLER reprinted with permission of Newspaper Enterprise Association, Inc.

Does media coverage of refugee crises lead to aid decisions based on emotion and public opinion rather than reasoned policies?

Many in the refugee community argue that the media, despite their flaws, have served refugees well. They say that few people would ever learn about the plight of refugees anywhere if it were not for journalists on the scene, and the dramatic, heart-wrenching images they bounce off satellites and into homes around the world. Such publicity is vital, they say, because the U.S. and other developed nations are typically reluctant to respond to an overseas crisis unless a sizable number of its own citizens call for action.

"On balance, I'd say that the media are a positive force, because when CNN or some other news crew is there, governments will follow," Rosenblatt says.

Drumtra of the U.S. Committee for Refugees agrees. "CNN drives policy simply by deciding where they are going to set up the cameras," he says.

By the same token, Drumtra adds, the media have a responsibility to do more than just show up at the occasional disaster. In general, he says, print and broadcast media outlets need to broaden their coverage to include more parts of the world. "The mission of journalists is to inform people about their world," he says, "and if they don't inform people of the activities of all the countries around the world, then they are failing in that mission."

In fact, others say, many catastrophes are simply ignored. For example, while the world in October and November was given repeated updates on the crisis in Zaire, few media outlets reported on a veritable roll call of other African nations with huge numbers of displaced persons. Among the most severely afflicted were Sudan, where a civil war has been raging since 1983 and an estimated 4 million people are internally displaced; another half-million Sudanese refugees were believed to be living in Uganda, Zaire, Ethiopia and other neighboring nations. Another victim of civil war, Liberia, had an estimated 120,000 refugees and 1 million internally displaced persons. [7]

Critics also say that the media's short-term coverage of situations leads to poorly considered policy that often seems designed only to assuage the conscience of the viewing public. "You get a very selective coverage of the worst disasters at a time when nothing constructive can be done about them," says Stedman at Johns Hopkins. "People say, 'Make the pictures go away,' and policy-makers respond to that," he says, adding that "when the pictures go away, everyone thinks that the problem must be solved."

But others say that it is unrealistic to expect the news media to cover so many stories for so long. Newspapers and television stations "only have so many columns or minutes on the air," says CARE's Hale, "and there are over 100 conflicts in the world." Instead, "it's our job to keep awareness of issues alive by doing more outreach and public education." ■

BACKGROUND

Modern Aid Movement

For as long as there have been wars, persecutions and natural disasters, people have been forced to flee their homes. One of the first great works of ancient literature, the Bible, is replete with stories of people being displaced, from Adam and Eve, who were cast out of Eden, to the 40-year wanderings of the ancient Hebrews after slavery in Egypt to the Babylonian Captivity.

The fall of Rome in the 5th century AD led to 500 years of displacement on a scale never before seen. Waves of invaders swept through Western Europe and the Mediterranean basin scattering millions of people. Arab and Mongol invasions followed, also uprooting millions. [8]

Massive population displacements often have driven important historical events. The early European settlement of North America, for example, was precipitated by groups like Quebec's Huguenots, New England's Puritans and Maryland's Catholics, all of whom fled religious persecution in their homelands.

While refugees have always been a part of history's landscape, it was not until the 20th century that institutions were created to ease their plight. The first such organization was established in 1921, when the League of Nations named Norwegian explorer Fridjof Nansen as High Commissioner for Refugees to assist those fleeing the Russian Revolution. [9]

Impact of World War II

The modern refugee movement, like much of today's world, grew from the ashes of World War II. The allies actually began assisting displaced persons even before the war ended. In 1943, they established the United Nations Relief and Rehabilitation Administration, which for the next four years aided citizens of occupied countries who were liberated by the allies as they pushed the Germans back. [10]

By the time the war in Europe was over in May 1945, millions of people had been displaced. Millions more became refugees in the months following the war's end after ethnic German populations were expelled from Poland, Czechoslovakia, Hungary and other Eastern European countries.

The war's end also brought the beginning of decolonization, creating new refugee crises. For example, in 1947, the British pulled out of India. The subsequent division between Muslim Pakistan and largely Hindu India led to the displacement of more than 10 million people. [11]

During this period, a number of temporary refugee agencies were established by the great powers under the auspices of the United Nations, including the International Refugee Organization in 1947. But it was not until 1951 that the UNHCR came into being.

U.N. Involvement

On Jan. 1, 1951, the United Nations High Commissioner for Refugees (UNHCR) began operations. With a budget of just $300,000, the agency was given a mandate to seek "permanent solutions for the problems of refugees." In practice, this meant providing mostly legal assistance to persons who had reached a country of asylum. [12]

The scope of the work actually undertaken by UNHCR in those early years was far more limited than that of its immediate predecessors. The United States and other great powers had spent billions of dollars repatriating and resettling refugees during and directly after World War II. A far-reaching UNHCR, they feared, could become an expensive proposition, especially if refugee problems in the developed world ever mirrored those of Europe during the 1940s.

In addition to establishing UNHCR in 1951, the U.N. also adopted the Convention Relating to the Status of Refugees, which created the legal underpinnings for the new agency's work. The convention defined refugees as people who left their homeland "owing to a well-founded fear of being persecuted for reasons of race, religion, nationality, membership in a particular social group or political opinion." [13] The all-encompassing definition grew out of a desire to protect the kinds of victims who had been persecuted by the Nazis, such as Jews and communists.

While the convention obligated sig-

Continued on p. 108

Chronology

1920s-1940s

The first organized efforts to aid refugees are launched following international crises such as the Russian Revolution and World War II.

1921
League of Nations appoints a High Commissioner for Refugees to assist people fleeing the Russian Revolution.

1943
United Nations Relief and Rehabilitation Agency is created to aid the millions of people displaced by the allies as they push the Germans out of occupied Europe.

1947
British withdrawal from India leads to division between Muslim Pakistan and largely Hindu India, displacing at least 10 million people.

1948
The United Nations adopts the Universal Declaration of Human Rights, giving all persons the right to "life, liberty and the security of person."

1950s-1970s

The modern refugee regime is established with the creation of the United Nations High Commissioner for Refugees (UNHCR) and the adoption of the Convention Relating to the Status of Refugees.

1950
U.N. General Assembly creates the UNHCR to provide legal assistance to European refugees seeking asylum. The organization begins operation on Jan. 1, 1951.

1951
The Convention Relating to the Status of Refugees is adopted, requiring signatory nations to offer haven to refugees displaced from Europe before 1951.

1967
U.N. protocol is adopted applying the 1951 Refugee Convention to all refugees, regardless of their country of origin or the date of their displacement.

1975
The end of the Vietnam War sparks the beginning of a huge outflow of refugees from Indochina that will continue into the 1990s.

1979
Soviet Union invades Afghanistan, sending 3 million refugees into Pakistan. UNHCR helps to coordinate food and other emergency assistance to the displaced Afghans.

1980s-1990s

Large-scale refugee assistance and resettlement programs become more commonplace as the Cold War winds down. UNHCR expands its mandate beyond providing emergency assistance to trying to prevent or mitigate refugee flows.

1980
Congress passes the Refugee Act of 1980, overhauling U.S. refugee admissions policy.

1989
Berlin Wall, the pre-eminent symbol of the Cold War, falls. Less than two years later, the Soviet Union disintegrates into 15 independent and often chaotic states.

1991
Kurdish rebellion in northern Iraq displaces 1.5 million people. The international community responds by creating a Kurdish "safe haven" in Iraq. UNHCR expands its mandate to provide aid beyond traditional emergency assistance to include the reconstruction of villages.

1992
Civil war breaks out in the former Yugoslavian state of Bosnia-Herzegovina, displacing millions. Use of the "safe haven" strategy in 1995 fails to protect Bosnian Muslims from Serbian persecution.

1994
Two million Rwandan Hutus flee into Zaire and Tanzania. UNHCR efforts to assist the refugees are hampered by Hutu extremists, who dominate refugee camps set up by the agency.

1995
Immigration and Naturalization Service (INS) issues regulations calling for a larger, better trained staff to handle asylum cases and requiring the INS to handle cases within six months.

1996
Thousands of Hutus who fled from Rwanda are forced to return home after rival Tutsis disband the refugee camps. Immigration Control Act of 1996 revamps procedures to handle asylum requests more quickly and requires applicants to file requests for asylum within a year of arriving in the United States.

Internal Displacement Now Gets More Attention

Today, in a recent turnabout in refugee affairs, there are more people displaced within their own countries than beyond the borders of their homelands. Estimates of the number of internally displaced persons run as high as 30 million, or roughly twice the number of refugees in the world.

But the United Nations High Commissioner for Refugees (UNHCR) devotes the bulk of its time and resources to assisting refugees, who are defined as those displaced outside of their own countries. The agency's legal mandate requires it to care for refugees, not internally displaced people.

Under the UNHCR's charter, the High Commissioner has the authority to act on its own to assist refugees without seeking further U.N. permission. But UNHCR can help internally displaced persons only after the General Assembly, Security Council or some other principal body of the United Nations requests its assistance. [1]

Even when the agency gets U.N. permission, protecting the internally displaced can be difficult, because UNHCR and other aid organizations must often obtain the permission of the host government to intervene. In Sudan, for example, where a brutal 13-year civil war has internally displaced an estimated 4 million people, aid agencies often have had trouble receiving permission from the government and the rebels to help the victims of the conflict. Other countries with large populations of internally displaced citizens, notably Turkey and Burma, also limit international access by aid agencies.

Despite the obstacles, UNHCR is becoming more and more involved in assisting the internally displaced. "Most of the world's conflicts are now internal," says Soren Jessen-Petersen, director of UNHCR's New York office. "We would be totally irrelevant in today's world if we weren't involved in these internal conflicts."

An internal displacement problem of immense scale has been presented by the countries of the former Yugoslavia, where most displaced people remained within state boundaries. UNHCR was asked by then-U.N. Secretary-General Javier Perez de Cuellar to coordinate relief efforts throughout that shattered country. In Bosnia, the agency provided assistance to many who had never left their homes. "This was a real departure for us because we were dealing with besieged people," says Marie Okabe, a UNHCR spokesperson in New York.

In the future, experts predict, an even greater share of the world's displaced persons will remain within their own countries. Roberta Cohen, a guest scholar at the Brookings Institution, traces the internal displacements to the fact that more and more countries will be unraveling internally in the post-Cold War world.

But Cohen and others worry that UNHCR may not be adequately positioned to deal with the new challenge. "UNHCR has stretched its mandate to help the internally displaced," she says, "but it's not enough." To be as effective as possible, she says, the agency must expand its mandate to directly cover the internally displaced, so that it can act rapidly on its own.

Many refugee advocates, Cohen among them, say that a state actually forfeits its right to be left alone when it neglects or abuses its people. "[S]tate sovereignty can no longer be defined negatively as a barricade against external involvement," writes Francis M. Deng, former Sudanese ambassador to the United States. "It must be recast as primarily a positive concept of responsibility toward the citizens and all those falling under the jurisdiction of the state. It is precisely by discharging those responsibilities that a state can legitimately claim sovereignty." [2]

Cohen, who is an expert on the problems facing the internally displaced, agrees. "The international community is moving toward the notion that sovereignty does not give you carte blanche to do whatever you want to your own people," she says. "There is a growing acceptance of the idea that when there is a humanitarian crisis, the international community must come in."

[1] United Nations High Commissioner for Refugees, "International Legal Standard Applicable to the Protection of Internally Displaced Persons: A Reference Manual for UNHCR Staff," 1996, p. 1.

[2] Francis M. Deng, "These Borders Are Not Sacred," Op. Ed. article in *The Washington Post*, Dec. 20, 1996.

Continued from p. 106

natory states to offer haven to refugees, it covered only those persons who had been displaced before 1951. In addition, signatories were given the option of ignoring refugees outside of Europe. The U.N. removed those limits in 1967.

The 1967 change came in response to a trend that had been accelerating since the mid-1950s: the decline of the refugee problem as a uniquely European phenomenon. By the 1970s, European refugees, with the exception of occasional escapees from the Soviet bloc, were a thing of the past. Most refugees were now coming from Africa and Southeast Asia. [11]

UNHCR's New Mandate

Until the late 1970s, the agency dealt with refugee movements after they had happened. In other words, once a group had left their country and become refugees, UNHCR would then step in to try to help them either settle in the asylum country, resettle elsewhere or return to their country of origin. Little was done to aid refugees as they were fleeing their homeland. For example, UNHCR played no role in resettling the 7 million refugees that flowed into India from Bangladesh when that nation was created in 1972.

In the late 1970s though, things began to change. During that time, the world witnessed three large refugee crises simultaneously in Thailand, Afghanistan and Ethiopia. In Afghanistan, the 1979 Soviet invasion forced 3 million Afghans into Pakistan. The agency, in conjunction with the Pakistani government, provided food and other assistance to the refugees.

The magnitude of the Afghan crisis and others led the international community to look increasingly to UNHCR for leadership in organizing the care and protection of such huge, displaced populations. With the new responsibility came growth. From 1970 to 1980, UNHCR's budget ballooned from $8 million to almost $500 million — with 1,700 employees and more than 80 field offices around the world. [15]

Throughout the 1980s, the agency continued to grow. In addition, UNHCR solidified its role as the lead refugee agency by helping to coordinate relief to refugees around the world, from Central America to the horn of Africa.

Refugee Profile Undergoes Change

In the early 1990s, the number of refugees being aided by the U.N. High Commissioner for Refugees (UNHCR) began dropping while the number of other displaced people rose dramatically, particularly in the Balkans, Central Africa and parts of the former Soviet Union. Displaced persons are those who have been forced from their homes, including people displaced within their own countries and war-affected populations; refugees are displaced persons who have fled across international borders.

People Being Assisted by UNHCR, 1975-1995

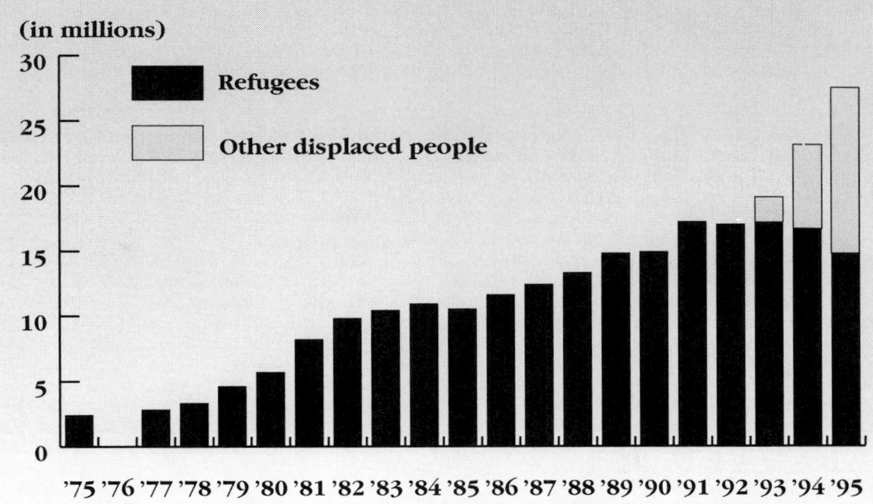

Note: No figure is available for 1976.

Source: United Nations High Commissioner for Refugees, The State of the World's Refugees, 1995

Rise in Refugees

The number of people cared for by UNHCR has risen dramatically in recent years. In 1990, for example, 15 million refugees and other displaced persons were receiving some sort of help from the agency. That number had almost doubled, to 27.5 million, by 1995. * [16]

Much of the increase in refugees is linked to the end of the Cold War. Before the Soviet Union collapsed in 1989, many nations were held together, albeit tenuously, by the struggle between the two superpowers. The rivalry pushed the superpowers to give massive amounts of arms and aid to states that would not have been considered strategically important under different circumstances. When the aid was reduced, and in many cases eliminated, in the early 1990s, many countries quickly began unraveling, allowing ethnic, religious and political tensions that had been held in check to burst into the open. In the former Soviet Union alone, there were conflicts or civil wars in the republics of Georgia, Armenia, Azerbaijan, Tajikistan and Moldova and the Russian province of Chechnya.

"Conflicts spiraled out of control," says the Refugee Policy Group's Hansch, because "the hatreds, animosities and weapons were still there without the puppet masters to rein them in." Liberia, Yugoslavia, Somalia and other hotbeds of conflict virtually disintegrated as nation states. The resulting chaos displaced millions.

The first real post-Cold War test for UNHCR and other aid agencies came early in 1991 in northern Iraq. An uprising by ethnic Kurds following Saddam Hussein's defeat in the Persian Gulf War led to reprisals by the Iraqi government that displaced 1.5 million people, most of whom were trying to cross into neighboring Tur-

* There are a total of 35 million refugees and other displaced people throughout the world, including those being aided by UNHCR, according to the U.S. Committee for Refugees.

key or Iran. In an effort to stop the exodus as well as to prevent Iraq's brutal suppression of the Kurdish revolt, the United States and some of its allies against Saddam established a "safety zone" over part of the Kurdish area. UNHCR coordinated efforts to provide emergency relief for the displaced. In addition, the agency immediately began a massive reconstruction program to ensure that people would have adequate shelter by the time cold weather arrived. [17]

"Iraq was a real watershed," says Kathleen Newland, a senior associate at the Carnegie Endowment for International Peace. By setting up the safe haven and focusing on reconstruction, she says, the international community "was trying to be more proactive. There was a new attitude here: We need to do more than just try to feed people." ■

CURRENT SITUATION

Preventive Action

Throughout the early 1990s, the new, proactive policy known as preventive action became the cornerstone of UNHCR's strategy. So far, however, it has enjoyed only limited success. In Bosnia, for example, the use of safe havens failed to protect the Muslim population from the genocidal killing known as "ethnic cleansing."

Even in northern Iraq, where the safe haven enabled the Kurds to establish a de facto state, the area has been riven by internal strife. In late 1996, in fact, Iraqi government troops actually invaded the safe haven — albeit briefly.

Since the 1970s, UNHCR has worked to assist refugees after they flee their homelands. But recently, the agency has been trying to change its approach to dealing with humanitarian crises.

"For many years, UNHCR and its operational partners waited for refugees to cross an international border before providing them with protection and assistance," High Commissioner Sadako Ogata wrote in 1995. By shifting some of its focus to preventive action, Ogata continues, the agency is becoming "equally concerned with conditions in actual and potential refugee-producing states." [18]

Preventive action is predicated on the notion that UNHCR can stop refugee flows before they start by closely monitoring tense situations; using diplomacy and conflict resolution to defuse pending crises; and providing more economic and social assistance to improve conditions in poor areas.

Countries Taking the Most Refugees

Country of asylum	Number of Refugees (in thousands)
Iran	2,236.4
Zaire	1,724.4
Pakistan	1,055.0
Germany	1,004.6
Tanzania	883.3
Sudan	727.2
USA	591.7
Guinea	553.2
Cote d'Ivoire	360.1
Ethiopia	348.1
Armenia	304.0
Burundi	300.3
China	287.1
Uganda	286.5

"In areas where there are obvious danger signals and risks for population movements, we have tried to go in and work with the authorities and private organizations to analyze the risks and find ways to prevent them," Jessen-Petersen says. "If we can't manage the risks, then we set up structures to manage such movements, should they happen."

In Somalia in 1992, for example, "We went into villages where people were at risk and provided aid to prevent them from moving," he says, rather than "allowing people to move hundreds of kilometers under horrendous conditions in which they will die, just to find food."

Preventive action also entails paying more attention to refugees after they are repatriated. "Our task is to help people feel a level of confidence that they can reconstruct their lives without feeling like they're living on the edge any more, with one foot over the border," says Anita Parlow, a UNHCR spokesperson.

By working closely with other U.N. entities and NGOs, UNHCR helps restore basic services, such as roads, schools and hospitals, to the areas where refugees will be returning. In addition, Parlow says, the agency tries to create and sustain international support for the repatriation to give returnees a sense that they are not facing their challenges alone. "This means a lot to people," she adds.

But many observers outside UNHCR think that for the time being, preventive action is often little more than a nice idea when efforts are not backed by the broader international community, which they say is often the case. "It's good that UNHCR raises the issue," Drumtra says. "But ultimately, it comes down to the political will of the big powers."

Drumtra and others say that the UNHCR and other aid organizations do not have the resources and clout to take the unilateral actions required to really make preventive action workable. "UNHCR has very little running room of its own," Drumtra says, adding that "their budget and staff are already stretched to the limit."

U.S. Refugee Policy

The United States long has prided itself on being a haven for those in need. But many refugee advocates say that when it comes to taking in displaced persons, the U.S. doesn't live up to its self-image. [19]

Refugees can enter the United States either by being processed through the refugee admissions system or by requesting asylum. If a refugee's application for admission to the U.S. is approved, the refugee is provided with assistance by federal, state and private agencies. Each year, the president sets a limit on the number of refugees who can be admitted under this procedure. In fiscal 1996, the cap was set at 90,000, down from 110,000 the year before. This fiscal year, the number has dropped even further, to 78,000. [20]

The current system of annual refugee caps was established under the Refugee Act of 1980. The law requires the president each year to consult with Congress on the proposed number of refugees to be admitted. This is more than a formality since Congress in turn appropriates funds needed to help resettle the refugees.

The act also requires the administration to set, within the overall number, an admissions ceiling by region. Traditionally, the lion's share of refugee admissions has come from Eastern Europe (particularly countries of the former Soviet Union) and Southeast Asia. For instance, in fiscal 1997, 48,000, or more than half the total refugee admissions to the U.S., will come from Eastern Europe. By contrast, only 7,000 refugees from Africa will be admitted. [21] The policy, established during the Cold War, is intended to help Jews and other religious minorities from the former Soviet Union as well as those persecuted by the authoritarian regimes in Vietnam and other parts of Indochina.

Many refugee and immigration experts argue that the current admissions system is outmoded and needs to be changed. "We're doing it for domestic reasons [to satisfy] ethnic politics and because we still have a Cold War mentality," says Georgetown's Keeley. He and others say that the current system, which is vigorously defended by powerful ethnic lobbies, is too rigid and numbers-oriented. "We need to be more flexible about the numbers," he says, adding that refugee admissions should be dictated more by circumstances than politics.

Others say that regional ceilings should be done away with entirely and replaced with a system based on need alone. "We need to restrict refugee resettlement to those people who have no other options," says Mark Krikorian, executive director of the Center for Immigration Studies. Krikorian points out that most of the Jews from the former Soviet Union and the Southeast Asians being admitted today as refugees are not really refugees as defined by international law. For example, he notes, Jews in the former Soviet republics no longer face institutional prejudice, and they have the option of emigrating to Israel.

But the Carnegie Institute's Newland warns against making hasty policy changes. While she wants a more flexible refugee admissions system that "can better respond to refugee flows," she is not entirely ready to scrap the current rules. In the case of Soviet Jews, for instance, "there is still a tremendous amount of anti-Semitism in the former Soviet countries," Newland says. She adds that "many [Jewish] people coming to the United States have relatives here, and so going to Israel is more difficult."

Where Most Refugees Are From

Country of Origin	Number of Refugees (in thousands)
Afghanistan	2,743.6
Rwanda	2,257.0
Liberia	794.2
Iraq	702.1
Somalia	535.9
Eritrea	422.4
Sudan	398.6
Burundi	389.2
Bosnia-Herzegovina	321.2
Vietnam	307.0
Azerbaijan	299.0
Angola	283.9
Sierra Leone	275.1
Mozambique	234.5
Chad	211.9

Asylum Policy Changes

Someone fearing persecution can also enter the United States by requesting asylum. In such cases, the person arrives in the United States either legally or illegally and asks for asylum. That request will be granted if the person can demonstrate a well-founded fear of being persecuted at home due to race, religion, nationality, political opinion or membership in a particular social group. [22]

Unlike refugee admissions, there is no limit to the number of people who can be granted asylum. In 1996, 22 percent of all adjudicated cases (13,368 persons) were granted asylum. [23]

U.S. asylum policy, which is based on the Immigration and Nationality Act of 1952, has been altered several times. The most recent changes, in 1995 and 1996, were aimed at both streamlining procedure and stiffening requirements.

The Immigration and Naturalization Service (INS) issued regulations, effective Jan. 1, 1995, that mandated a larger, better trained staff to handle asylum cases and required the agency to rule on an asylum request within six months. In addition, the Immigration Control Act of 1996 provided for expedited procedures at points of entry in an effort to quickly reject and send back those without a solid claim. In addition, the new law required those applying for asylum to do so within one year of arriving in the United States.

INS officials say the new rules have substantially reduced the number of new claims for asylum. In fiscal 1996, the number of asylum applications fell sharply to 49,447, from 74,888 the year before.[24]

Changes in the asylum law are also coming from the courts. Refugee advocates have succeeded in expanding the number of categories for refugee status to include people suffering from discrimination based on their gender, sexual orientation or resistance to coercive population-control methods. For instance, in June 1996, the Board of Immigration Appeals granted asylum to a woman from Togo who had fled to avoid genital mutilation, a common practice throughout much of Africa.[25] People who have been persecuted because they are homosexual and those who refuse to obey China's one-child policy have also been granted asylum in the last few years.

The trend toward flexibility troubles Krikorian, who argues that the concept of asylum is being extended way beyond its traditional boundaries by feminist, gay rights and other advocacy groups. Such organizations are interested in using asylum as a legal tool to help "their favorite class of victims," Krikorian says, whether they deserve asylum or not. "Political asylum can't simply be a way for people in unfortunate circumstances to come to the United States," he says.

Instead, Krikorian says, asylum needs to be reserved for those who are being persecuted based on their beliefs. "If there is a basis for claiming that all women in the Third World who are suffering from [discrimination] deserve asylum, then this could apply to all Muslim women, all African women and all Chinese women and could potentially turn into a flood of people," Krikorian adds. That would ultimately turn the American people against the idea of asylum, he says, and force Congress to impose severe limits on the practice that would hurt legitimate asylum seekers.

But Newland argues that there is a difference between genital mutilation and more common forms of discrimination against women in the Third World. "It's absurd to think that, say, all Saudi Arabian women will be eligible for asylum because they are not allowed to drive," she says.

In addition, Newland says, "the United States is not in any danger of being overrun by any one group," because, contrary to Krikorian, it is very hard to make a case for entering the country under the asylum laws. Georgetown's Keeley agrees, adding that the asylum laws would likely be changed if there were any signs that huge numbers of people were going to be able to use them to enter the country.

"Asylum and refugee policy is done for the state," he says, "and if that policy weakens the state, then it will be changed." ■

Reuters

Russian refugees from Grozny, Chechnya, flee the city last August after Russian troops threatened to renew bombing.

Outlook

More Refugees Likely

Journalist Robert Kaplan has predicted that more and more people will be displaced both inside and outside of their countries in the coming decades. According to Kaplan, the chaos and anarchy that now permeate much of the developing world today will only spread, further destroying civil society in many countries and uprooting millions of people.[26]

While most refugee experts consider Kaplan to be overly pessimistic, many do agree that in some places, particularly Africa, things are likely to get worse before they get better.

"I'm afraid we're going to see more foreign crises," says CARE's Hale, adding that the developed world is helping to lay the groundwork for future tragedies by reducing foreign aid and by requiring many Third World governments to impose economic austerity on their people in the name of free market reform.

Others blame at least part of the problem on the nation-state system, which is becoming harder and harder to sustain in many parts of the post-Cold War world. "We assume that once a state is founded, it will always

Continued on p. 114

At Issue:

Should American military personnel be used to help provide assistance to refugees?

yes

STEVEN HANSCH
Senior program officer, Refugee Policy Group, Washington, D.C.

WRITTEN FOR *THE CQ RESEARCHER*, JANUARY 1996.

The U.S. armed forces often can provide critical assistance in refugee and emergency situations that complements the efforts of less well-equipped private voluntary agencies. Because of its tremendous infrastructure of equipment, the military can save lives in situations where the rest of the international humanitarian community falls short.

In recent years the efforts of our Army, Air Force, Navy and Coast Guard have saved tens of thousands of innocent civilians abroad, through rescue at sea (for example, Bangladesh), evacuation (Iraq), airlift of water pumps (Zaire) and assistance in delivery of food aid (Somalia).

Far too much is made of the perceived risks to our military personnel in humanitarian emergencies. Most humanitarian operations proceed quietly and without risk. Specific incidents in Lebanon and in Somalia are the exceptions, repeatedly abused by isolationists as grounds for retreating from any effort to provide aid — in effect, conceding victory to terrorists. Far less publicized are the military's numerous successes — in rescuing boat people at sea, providing security in complex emergencies, rehabilitating roads and wells, designing telecommunications systems and providing laboratory facilities in tropical epidemics.

Oddly, of all the agencies involved in emergency relief, only the military is routinely kept back because of concerns about security threats: It is ironic that those Americans who voluntarily enlist in the military and are paid to be prepared to accept combat risks are claimed by some to be less expendable than the American doctors, nurses and other humanitarians who are so much more routinely involved in the world's problem spots and incur significantly higher casualty rates per person than do military personnel.

Per capita, more American and European civilians were injured or killed in Somalia than the troops that were sent in. But the killing of the heroic civilian trying to save lives rarely makes headlines. Casualties to Americans volunteering with charitable groups like CARE, Catholic Relief Services and the International Rescue Committee count for little among isolationist policy analysts, but they count for a lot among millions of Americans who sponsor their heroic efforts.

Of course, we should deploy our foreign aid and diplomatic resources to facilitate resolution of problems. And flexing our military might will rarely be pivotal in these long-term arrangements. But that's a different matter. If lives are immediately at stake, most Americans would agree that the military should be involved and, where appropriate, lead the charge.

no

DOUG BANDOW
Senior fellow, Cato Institute, Washington, D.C.

WRITTEN FOR *THE CQ RESEARCHER*, JANUARY 1996.

Yet another crisis has flared overseas. The images never change — starving people fleeing murder, rape and war. Only the victims are different.

Such conflicts cry out for Western involvement. Some people propose military intervention to stop conflict. A few even advocate de facto colonialism to remake failed societies. All treat their proposal as the only moral course of action.

However, none of these strategies is likely to succeed. At least not at a cost acceptable to the American people, who would be doing the paying and dying.

First, sending in the Marines would not automatically bring peace to shattered lands. This is a lesson that we should have learned from Lebanon and Somalia. Bitter conflicts around the world are not a consequence of, say, sunspots. Rather, they grow out of ethnic, religious and tribal hatreds, many of which go back centuries.

Of course, some people merely hope to stop the killing, obviously a worthy goal. But treating symptoms rather than causes is unlikely to save many lives. At best, intervention would create a temporary cease-fire likely to break down once the outside forces depart. Far worse is the possibility of Americans finding themselves dying in a civil war, as they did in Lebanon a decade ago. And, if Washington followed a consistent policy of humanitarian intervention in today's world of tragedy, U.S. soldiers could end up involved in a dozen or more conflicts simultaneously.

Moreover, the long-term Western occupation of poorer lands is no option. Remaking failed societies is an extraordinarily ambitious task for even the most arrogant social engineer. Casualties among the occupying forces would be inevitable, as warring factions coalesced against outsiders. Even average foreign citizens, the supposed "beneficiaries" of U.S. intervention, would likely grow to resent their new overlords.

Finally, for Washington to become Globocop would violate the government's duty toward the 18-year-old Americans who actually have to enforce a de facto empire. What right have Washington policy-makers to risk the lives of soldiers who joined the military in order to defend the U.S. when that nation's security is not at stake? There is nothing humanitarian about sending other people off to fight and possibly die, however attractive the end.

Americans like to solve problems, but not every crisis, however tragic, is soluble. Unfortunately, we simply aren't capable of putting dissolving nations back together. Nor would it be right to compound foreign tragedies by making casualties of our fellow citizens.

UNHCR Scores a Win in Mozambique

With no end in sight to refugee crises in so many places — Rwanda, Bosnia and Afghanistan to name just three — stories of successful repatriations may seem like an aid worker's faraway dream. But not every refugee problem remains unresolved. In Guatemala, Lebanon and, most dramatically, in Mozambique, many displaced citizens have been able to return to their homes.

Since 1992, in the largest organized repatriation ever undertaken in Africa, an estimated 1.7 million refugees and 4 million internally displaced people have returned home to Mozambique.

Refugee experts say that things went right in Mozambique because a number of pieces fell into place. Most important, the civil war that had been raging for 16 years ended in 1992, giving refugees their first reason to go home. That conflict, between the Marxist government and the RENAMO rebel group, had killed more than 500,000 people and displaced roughly one-quarter of Mozambique's 16.5 million people. [1]

The war wound down in part because the primary supporters of the government and the rebels, the Soviet Union and South Africa, respectively, withdrew their patronage. In addition, according to Samantha Bolton, communications director for the aid group Doctors Without Borders USA, everyone was ready for peace. "The sides were just so exhausted that they stopped fighting," she says. Another reason for the truce, she says, was Mozambique's limited natural resources. "In Mozambique there is nothing to fight over, unlike Angola, where the war has dragged on because there are gold and diamonds," Bolton says.

After the fighting had stopped in Mozambique, the situation further improved after both sides agreed to a peace treaty that allowed for power sharing within a democratic framework. "This was very important in terms of the assurances it gave refugees who were thinking of returning," says Soren Jessen-Petersen, director of the United Nations High Commissioner for Refugees' New York office. The public reconciliation convinced many displaced people that the peace would hold, he says. (By contrast, many people displaced as a result of the conflict in Bosnia did not return to their homes, because the peace accord signed by the warring factions in December 1995 was perceived as tenuous.)

Once the peace accord was signed in Mozambique, UNHCR and other aid groups began repatriating the nearly 2 million refugees who had fled the country. According to Jessen-Petersen, the task was daunting for a number of reasons. First, the refugees were displaced throughout six countries: South Africa, Tanzania, Malawi, Zambia, Zimbabwe and Swaziland. [2] Such widespread dispersion required UNHCR to deploy 41 heavy trucks to help transport refugees who were particularly far from their villages. [3] Others returned by rail and boat, but most Mozambicans went home on foot.

To make matters worse, Mozambique, a poor country to begin with, had been ravaged by the prolonged war. It was extremely important that the refugees' return be accompanied by the rehabilitation of their communities, Jessen-Petersen says. To aid the rehab work, UNHCR funded more than 800 small-scale development projects throughout the country, ranging from efforts to repair roads, bridges and other infrastructure to meeting basic community health and education needs. In addition, returnees were given enough food for 10 months as well as basic supplies like plastic sheeting for temporary shelter. UNHCR also distributed 190,000 seed kits and more than 900,000 agricultural tools to help the 90 percent of the refugees who were returning to farms to become self-sufficient. [4]

The repatriation reached its peak in 1994, when UNHCR estimates that some 17,000 refugees were returning home each week. The two-and-a-half-year operation cost almost $1.2 billion. The refugee agency has largely pulled out of Mozambique, and its mandate there now is to provide emergency assistance, not long-term development.

But if UNHCR's success in the country is to be sustained, the land-mine problem will have to be solved. During the war, both sides placed a vast number of mines throughout the country — possibly as many as 10 million. According to the U.S. Committee for Refugees, land mines still kill at least 40 people and injure scores more each month in Mozambique. Efforts by the United Nations and others to remove the mines continue, but progress is painstakingly slow. [5]

Another challenge is the economy. Decades of war and mismanagement have left Mozambique the world's poorest nation, with an annual per capita income of $60.

These and other remaining problems leave refugee experts cautiously optimistic. "I'd say things have gone right there, so far," Bolton says.

---

[1] United Nations High Commissioner for Refugees, *The State of the World's Refugees 1995,* p. 174.

[2] *Ibid.*

[3] Andrew Meldrum, "Repatriating the Refugees," *Africa Report,* March-April 1994, p. 46.

[4] U.S. Committee for Refugees, "World Refugee Survey 1996," p. 59.

[5] *Ibid.*

Continued from p. 112

exist, and that is simply not true," says Keeley. Multiethnic states, such as those in Africa, are "a recipe for disaster." He predicts that "there will be a lot of weak, imploding states in the near future," which will lead to further population displacement.

At the same time, Hale says, the humanitarian-relief community is getting better at assisting those in need. "NGOs are now specializing in providing specific services — Doctors Without Borders for medicine, Oxfam with supplying water and CARE with food distribution and camp management." The new division of labor, he says, is making NGOs faster and much more efficient providers of relief.

"We're seeing attempts to consolidate the lessons of the past," says Bolton of Doctors Without Borders. But while she believes that UNHCR and other groups will continue to hone their technical skills, the politics of each new situation will continue to prove challenging. "There are no formulas with this because the dynamic is always different," she says.

But one factor will remain constant, Keeley says ruefully: "Like the poor, refugees will always be with us." ■

David Masci is a freelance writer in Washington, D.C.

FOR MORE INFORMATION

United Nations High Commissioner for Refugees, New York Liaison Office, United Nations, United Nations Plaza, New York, N.Y. 10017; (212) 963-6200. As the world's leading refugee aid organization, UNHCR coordinates relief efforts in scores of countries.

Doctors Without Borders USA, 11 East 26th St., Suite 1904, New York, N.Y. 10010; (212) 679-6800. This organization provides medical assistance to refugees and others in need, ranging from surgery to nutrition and sanitation programs.

U.S. Committee for Refugees, 1717 Massachusetts Ave., N.W., Suite 701, Washington D.C. 20005; (202) 347-3507. The committee monitors refugee crises and reports its findings to the public.

CARE, 151 Ellis St. N.E., Atlanta, Ga. 30303; (404) 681-2552. CARE aids refugees and other displaced persons through the delivery of food and other emergency assistance.

Refugees International, 21 Dupont Circle, N.W., Washington, D.C. 20036; (202) 828-0110. This group lobbies on behalf of refugees and works with the U.N., governments and humanitarian relief organizations to assess refugee crises and come up with workable solutions.

Notes

[1] U.S Committee for Refugees, "World Refugee Survey 1996," pp. 4-6.

[2] "Death Shadows Africa's Great Lakes," *The Economist,* Oct. 19, 1996, pp. 45-47.

[3] Michael Maren, *The Road to Hell: The Ravaging Effects of Foreign Aid and International Charity* (1996). Maren served as a field worker in Somalia for the U.S. Agency for International Development. He also has worked overseas for Catholic Relief Services and as a Peace Corps volunteer.

[4] For background, see "War Crimes," *The CQ Researcher,* July 7, 1995, pp. 585-608.

[5] For background, see "Foreign Policy and Public Opinion," *The CQ Researcher,* July 15, 1994, pp. 601-624.

[6] See Walter Clarke and Jeffrey Herbst, "Somalia and the Future of Humanitarian Intervention," *Foreign Affairs,* March/April 1996, p. 84.

[7] U.S Committee for Refugees, *op. cit.,* pp. 4-6.

[8] See Brian Tierney and Sidney Painter, *Western Europe in the Middle Ages,* 300-1475 (1983), p. 66.

[9] Gil Loescher, *Beyond Charity: International Cooperation and the Global Refugee Crisis* (1993), pp. 37-40.

[10] *Ibid.,* pp. 46-51.

[11] See Paul Johnson, *Modern Times, From the Twenties to the Nineties* (1991), p. 474.

[12] Loescher, *op. cit.,* pp. 87-88. For background, see "United Nations at 50," *The CQ Researcher,* Aug. 18, 1995, pp. 729-752.

[13] United Nations, *Treaties and International Agreements Registered or Filed and Recorded with the Secretariat of the United Nations,* Vol. 189 (1954), p. 137.

[14] For background, see "New Era in Asia," *The CQ Researcher,* Feb. 14, 1992, pp. 121-144; and "Democracy in Africa," *The CQ Researcher,* March 24, 1995, pp. 241-264.

[15] Loescher, *op. cit.,* pp. 87-88.

[16] United Nations High Commissioner for Refugees, *The State of the World's Refugees* (1995), p. 247.

[17] *Ibid.,* pp. 117-118.

[18] *Ibid.,* p. 8.

[19] For background, see "The New Immigrants," *The CQ Researcher,* Jan. 24, 1997, pp. 49-72.

[20] "FY 95 & 96 Refugee Admissions and FY 96 & 97 Ceilings," *Refugee Reports,* Sept. 30, 1996, p. 16.

[21] *Ibid.*

[22] Bill Frelick and Barbara Kohnen, "Filling the Gap: Temporary Protected Status," *Journal of Refugee Studies,* December 1995, p. 340.

[23] Immigration and Naturalization Service, Asylum Division.

[24] *Ibid.*

[25] David Wheeler, "Harvard Program Helps Change the Law," *The Chronicle of Higher Education,* July 5, 1996.

[26] Robert Kaplan, "The Coming Anarchy," *The Atlantic Monthly,* February 1994, p. 44.

Bibliography

Selected Sources Used

Books

Harrell-Bond, B.E., *Imposing Aid: Emergency Assistance to Refugees,* Oxford University Press, 1986.

Though somewhat dated, the author's dissection of the international community's response to refugee crises is still pertinent. In addition, she examines many aspects of refugee situations that are rarely discussed, ranging from fertility rates among displaced women to the practice of taxing refugees.

Loescher, Gil, *Beyond Charity: International Cooperation and the Global Refugee Crisis,* Oxford University Press, 1993.

Loescher, a professor of international relations at Notre Dame University, traces the development of the modern refugee movement around the world. In addition, he focuses on more recent attempts by the international community to aid refugees, from efforts to provide emergency assistance to current asylum policies.

Maren, Michael, *The Road to Hell: The Ravaging Effects of Foreign Aid and International Charity,* Free Press, 1996

Maren, a former aid worker turned free-lance writer, asserts that humanitarian aid generally does more harm than good. In addition, he accuses private aid organizations of perpetuating refugee and other crises in order to continue to attract private donations and government grants.

United Nations High Commissioner for Refugees, *The State of the World's Refugees 1995: In Search of Solutions,* Oxford University Press, 1995.

This is the most recent edition of UNHCR's annual reports on its accomplishments for the year before and its goals for the future. The book details the agency's efforts to assist refugees around the world, including case studies of some of the countries where UNHCR is currently operating.

Articles

Clarke, Walter, and Jeffrey Herbst, "Somalia and the Future of Humanitarian Intervention," *Foreign Affairs,* March/April, 1996.

The authors explore the failed military intervention in Somalia and its impact on the willingness of developed nations to send soldiers on future relief missions.

"Death Shadows Africa's Great Lakes," *The Economist,* Oct. 19, 1996.

The history and issues behind the ethnic strife that has led to so much death and displacement in Rwanda and Burundi are examined in detail. Of special interest, the article explains how German colonization in the late 19th century reinforced the existing dominance of the Tutsi tribe over the more populous Hutus and sowed the seeds for inter-tribal conflict in the two nations.

Krikorian, Mark, "Who Deserves Asylum?" *Commentary,* June 1996.

Krikorian, executive director of the Center for Immigration Studies, criticizes recent efforts by feminists, gay rights activists and others to expand the definition of a refugee for purposes of qualifying for asylum. Krikorian argues that letting more people enter the country under the asylum laws will undermine the entire system and ultimately hurt refugees entitled to protection in the United States.

Rieff, David, "Camped Out: Why Rwanda Invaded Zaire," *The New Republic,* Nov. 25, 1996.

Rieff, a senior fellow at the World Policy Institute at the New School for Social Research, argues that UNHCR and other aid agencies made huge mistakes when they set up refugee camps for Rwandan Hutus streaming into Zaire. Rieff asserts that the situation in Rwanda may alter the international community's opinion on the efficacy of humanitarian aid.

Reports and Studies

U.S. Committee for Refugees, *World Refugee Survey 1996,* Immigration and Refugee Services of America, 1996

An invaluable resource guide, compiled by a refugee advocacy group, that assesses the situation for refugees and other displaced people in almost every country in the world. In addition to the nations directly affected by human displacement, the book also examines the refugee policies of the United States and other developed countries.

The Next Step

Additional information from UMI's Newspaper & Periodical Abstracts™ database

Assisting Refugees

"Armed Tanzanians hurry refugees home," ***San Francisco Chronicle,*** **Dec. 17, 1996, p. B2.**
Tanzanian officials on Dec. 16, 1996, fired guns into the air to move more Rwandan refugees homeward, and Red Cross workers bound children to their mothers with yellow twine to keep them from getting lost on the road.

"Contraceptives to go to Rwanda Refugees," ***The New York Times,*** **Nov. 20, 1996, p. A10.**
The United Nations (U.N.) says that aid destined for Rwandan refugees from U.N. agencies and the International Federation of Red Cross and Red Crescent Societies will be the first to include contraceptives.

Drogin, Bob, "Aid groups seek access to refugees in Zaire war zone," ***Los Angeles Times,*** **Nov. 8, 1996, p. A14.**
U.N. agencies and other aid groups scrambled on Nov. 7, 1996, to prepare emergency cross-border relief operations, but international diplomatic efforts again failed to gain access to more than 1 million Hutu refugees cut off in embattled eastern Zaire.

"Humanitarian aid plan for refugees in Zaire approved," ***San Francisco Chronicle,*** **Nov. 30, 1996, p. A12.**
A Canadian-led international force to assist the hundreds of thousands of refugees still believed to be in eastern Zaire finally won approval on Nov. 29, 1996, from ambassadors of the U.S. and 13 other countries. About 20 countries, including the U.S., Britain, France and Japan, are expected to provide support to the force.

Ogata, Sadako, "Refugees: A challenge to humanity," ***World Health,*** **November 1995, p. 3.**
Refugee emergencies pose new challenges for the providers of humanitarian relief. The common approach of the World Health Organization and the United Nations High Commissioner for Refugees to meet the urgent health needs of refugees and migrants is discussed.

"Who'll rescue the refugees of Zaire?" ***Chicago Tribune,*** **Nov. 9, 1996, p. 22.**
An editorial calls for the "international community" to respond to the predicament of refugees from the Hutu-Tutsi bloodbaths in Rwanda and Burundi who are trapped in eastern Zaire.

Bosnia

Hundley, Tom, "Fate of refugees in Bosnia true test of Dayton accord," ***Chicago Tribune,*** **Dec. 10, 1995, p. 11.**
The fate of Bosnian refugees will be the true test of the success or failure of the Dayton peace agreement. The plight of the refugees and the murder of 6,000 to 8,000 Muslim men by Bosnian Serb troops is examined.

Hundley, Tom, "In a Bosnia filled with refugees, home is where the hardship is," ***Chicago Tribune,*** **June 12, 1996, p. 1.**
Until March 1996, Ilidza, Bosnia-Herzegovina, was a suburb in the Serb-held part of Sarajevo, but under the terms of the Dayton peace agreement, control was transferred to the Muslim-dominated Bosnian government. This triggered an exodus by panicky Bosnian Serbs.

O'Connor, Mike, "New Refugee Conflict Points Up Flaw in Bosnia Pact," ***The New York Times,*** **April 29, 1996, p. A3.**
Hundreds of Muslims were expected to return on April 28, 1996, to their homes in the shelled-out Bosnian village of Mahala, where hundreds of Bosnian Serbs were expected to try to keep them away. Fearing bloodshed, American troops barred cars and buses from entering the area. That tactic proved successful in preventing violence on April 29, but it also underscored the fragility of the peace and exposed what appears to be a serious deficiency in the Dayton peace agreement.

Woodard, Colin, "Few welcome mats out for Bosnia's refugees," ***The Christian Science Monitor,*** **Sept. 26, 1996, p. 6.**
In attempting to return to their homes, Bosnia's 3 million war refugees and displaced persons face either total desolation of their homes or the ardent antipathy of people of different ethnic groups who have settled in the villages they vacated. And thus far, the international community's efforts to return them to their homes continue to yield few results.

Military Intervention

Black, Ian, "Zaire aid force on hold as jets seek refugees," ***The Guardian,*** **Nov. 21, 1996, p. 16.**
Scaled-down plans for an international military mission to Central Africa were put on hold Nov. 20, 1996, awaiting information from British and U.S. aerial reconnaissance on the whereabouts of between 500,000 and 700,000 displaced Rwandans whom aid agencies maintain are still stranded in eastern Zaire.

Crossette, Barbara, "U.S. Sets Conditions for Using Troops to Aid Refugees in Zaire," ***The New York Times,*** **Nov. 15, 1996, p. A7.**
Plans for an international military mission to support

relief efforts for a million refugees in eastern Zaire bogged down on Nov. 14, 1996, as Canadian and American officials haggled over the duration and conditions of the operation, which involves 15,000 troops.

Posen, Barry R., "Military responses to refugee disasters," *International Security,* summer 1996, pp. 72-111.
New concern about the problem of refugees has prompted a greater inclination to consider and apply military remedies. Posen argues that the application of military power to this set of problems will often prove politically and militarily difficult.

Political Asylum

Geiger, Eric, "Germany to send back Bosnia refugees," *San Francisco Chronicle,* April 11, 1996, p. A8.
Determined to reduce the costly and politically unpopular presence of asylum-seekers, the German government has decided to begin a three-phase program of repatriation for the 320,000 Bosnians who found sanctuary in Germany during their homeland's civil war. The repatriation program will begin in July 1996, and calls for the refugees to return home by mid-1997.

"Not So Harsh on Refugees," *The New York Times,* April 22, 1996, p. A12.
An editorial says that Congress should follow the lead of Sen. Patrick J. Leahy, D-Vt., who plans to offer an amendment that would not only override the "harsh exclusion provisions" in the immigration bill but also supersede the same provisions in the anti-terrorism bill for those seeking political asylum in the U.S.

"Refugees from Mutilation," *The New York Times,* May 2, 1996, p. A22.
An editorial calls for a favorable ruling in the case of Fauziya Kasinga, a woman from Togo seeking asylum in the U.S. after being threatened with female genital mutilation in her country, saying that more needs to be done to end the practice around the world.

Schrag, Philip G., "Deporting refugees who miss asylum deadline is dangerous," *The Christian Science Monitor,* June 20, 1996, p. 19.
Schrag comments on an immigration bill introduced in the House that would deny asylum to any refugee who asks for it more than 180 days after entering the U.S., with exceptions only for applications based on changed circumstance. Schrag calls the Senate's version of the bill, which imposes no deadline for affirmative applications for asylum, fairer.

Refugee Camps

McKinley, James C. Jr., "Exodus From Zairian Camps Left Many Refugees Behind," *The New York Times,* Nov. 19, 1996, p. A1.
The once-teeming refugee camps around Goma, Zaire, have been emptied, with the river of refugees returning to Rwanda from Zaire dwindling to a trickle on Nov. 18, 1996. But another half-million remained cut off from international aid, somewhere in the hills and valleys around Bukavu in the south.

Straus, Scott, "A million without a home: Refugees find little refuge, too much suffering in camps," *Houston Chronicle,* Nov. 15, 1996, p. A32.
The plight of the Rwandan Hutu refugees is highlighted as they await help from an international force in their efforts to return home after a Tutsi-led rebel movement began in October 1996, closing in on the major towns of eastern Zaire and attacking the refugee camps where they have been living since 1994.

"Zaire plans to close Rwanda refugee camps," *The New York Times,* Feb. 11, 1996, p. 6.
The government of Zaire said on Feb. 10, 1996, that it would gradually begin closing 40 camps holding a million Rwandan refugees, prompting some refugees to leave the camp at Kibumba, which is expected to be shut down first.

Zarembo, Alan, "Zaire's refugee camps — Bad idea got worse," *San Francisco Chronicle,* Nov. 8, 1996, p. A2.
The November 1996 closing of Hutu refugee camps in eastern Zaire, due to heavy expenses and Tutsi forces, may indicate that a peaceful resolution to the situation is unlikely. International response to the situation, which has been sporadic, is discussed.

U.S. Refugee Policy

Baker, Peter, "U.S. near approval of mission to aid Central Africa refugees," *The Washington Post,* Nov. 28, 1996, p. A44.
The U.S. inched closer to a humanitarian mission to rescue ill and hungry refugees in central Africa Nov. 27, 1996, endorsing a Canadian plan to establish a multinational headquarters in the region and putting troops on alert for possible airdrops of food and medicine into Zaire.

Estrada, Richard, "Resettlement plan fails refugees and communities," *Chicago Tribune,* May 14, 1996, p. 19.
Estrada examines efforts to convince the federal government to change its refugee resettlement policies.

"Food aid, but no relief, for refugees," *Chicago Tribune,* Nov. 15, 1996, p. 30.
An editorial says President Clinton did the right thing by giving a conditional go-ahead to U.S. participation in a refugee relief effort in Zaire, but questions what will be the future for those refugees once U.S. troops leave.

Marcus, David L., "Aid groups fault U.S. on refugees," *The Boston Globe,* Nov. 23, 1996, p. A1.

A dispute over the numbers of Rwandan refugees in Zaire is leading some international aid agencies to charge that the U.S. government is downplaying the crisis in order to abandon a commitment to send troops to Central Africa.

Myers, Steven Lee, "U.S. to Help Free Refugees in Iraq," *The New York Times,* Sept. 13, 1996, p. A1.
The Clinton administration said on Sept. 12, 1996, that the U.S. would help evacuate more than 2,000 refugees who had worked with its military and relief operations in northern Iraq and grant many of them asylum. However, the administration all but ruled out a dramatic rescue operation for the refugees.

Zaire

Byrne, Nicola, "A terrifying trail home for Hutu refugees in Zaire," *The Boston Globe,* Nov. 16, 1996, p. A8.
The massacre of some 30 Hutu refugees by Tutsi rebels near Mugunga, Zaire, and the death, disease and violence accompanying refugees as they head home to Rwanda in mid-November 1996 are detailed.

DePalma, Anthony, "Ottawa Talks Set for Aiding Zaire Refugees," *The New York Times,* Nov. 29, 1996, p. A18.
Diplomats and senior officials from at least 15 nations committed to supporting a Canadian proposal to provide aid to refugees in Central Africa will meet in Ottawa on Nov. 29, 1996, to discuss the framework for a scaled-down mission to aid refugees in Zaire.

Drogin, Bob, "Missing Zaire refugees leave trail of death," *Los Angeles Times,* Nov. 7, 1996, p. A10.
The first eyewitness accounts of more than 1 million refugees missing in the maelstrom of eastern Zaire's bitter civil war paint a horrific picture of suffering and deprivation, with people dying of hunger, thirst, exhaustion and exposure in remote rain forests.

French, Howard W., "Zaire Sets Stringent Terms for Effort to Help Refugees," *The New York Times,* Nov. 7, 1996, p. A12.
Still reeling form the loss of several important cities to Rwandan-backed rebels, the Zairian government on Nov. 6, 1996, set stringent conditions for any Western-led intervention on its soil, and vowed to recapture the lands it had lost, whatever the cost.

McGreal, Chris, "West plans air drop for Zaire refugees," *The Guardian,* Nov. 28, 1996, p. 23.
Plans for a multinational force to aid hundreds of thousands of Rwandan refugees fleeing fighting in eastern Zaire have been revived in the form of a Canadian proposal for an airlift to drop food to the wandering Hutus.

McKinley, James C. Jr., "Efforts to Help Refugees in Zaire Are Blocked by Shelling," *The New York Times,* Nov. 14, 1996, p. A14.
Efforts to help Rwandan refugees in Zaire were blocked by the shelling of a hospital in Goma by Hutu militias on Nov. 13, 1996. The attack was evidence that the conflict, which has kept aid workers from reaching 400,000 trapped refugees, has not eased.

McKinley, James C Jr., "Refugees Say Fighting Continues in Zaire," *The New York Times,* Nov. 28, 1996, p. A8.
While officials in the U.S. and Canada considered a plan to air-drop food to Rwandan refugees in eastern Zaire, several thousand refugees came out of the war-torn region on Nov. 27, 1996, saying the Zairian rebels had Hutu militias on the run and were herding refugees back to Rwanda by force.

O'Loughlin, Ed, "Refugees on the run: Settle them in Zaire, or send them to Rwanda?" *The Christian Science Monitor,* Nov. 7, 1996, p. 7.
Recent advances in eastern Zaire by the rebel group Alliance of Democratic Forces for the Liberation of Congo-Zaire displaced hundreds of thousands of mostly Hutu refugees from Rwanda and Burundi. The refugees' condition can only be guessed at, as the rebels have refused to allow aid workers to cross into Zaire

O'Loughlin, Ed, "Thousands of hungry refugees trickle in from Zaire's forests," *The Christian Science Monitor,* Nov. 25, 1996, p. 7.
A week after the massive return of refugees to Rwanda, small groups of desperate humanity continue to file down from the thickly forested volcanoes of northeastern Zaire. The International Committee of the Red Cross estimated on Nov. 22, 1996, that 3,000 Rwandan Hutus had appeared out of the forest above the Mugunga camp.

Straus, Scott, "Fighting closes in on Zaire refugees," *Houston Chronicle,* Nov. 9, 1996, p. A1.
On Nov. 8, 1996, Freddy Mbabakata, a medical coordinator at the Muganga refugee camp who fled with thousands of refugees when Zairian rebels took Goma from government troops, provided the first account of the growing tragedy in eastern Zaire.

"Zaire Refugees' Lack of Food Grows Acute," *The New York Times,* Nov. 10, 1996, p. 18.
With food shortages in eastern Zaire already acute, a U.N. relief official warned on Nov. 9, 1996, that thousands of refugees faced death by starvation. The warning came after the U.S. blocked a move by the U.N. Security Council to authorize the immediate deployment of a force to help feed the refugees.

Back Issues

Great Research on Current Issues Starts Right Here...Recent topics covered by The CQ Researcher are listed below. Before May 1991, reports were published under the name of Editorial Research Reports.

JULY 1995
War Crimes
Highway Safety
Combating Terrorism
Preventing Teen Drug Use

AUGUST 1995
Job Stress
Organ Transplants
United Nations at 50
Advances in Cancer Research

SEPTEMBER 1995
Catholic Church in the U.S.
Northern Ireland Cease-Fire
High School Sports
Teaching History

OCTOBER 1995
Quebec's Future
Revitalizing the Cities
Networking the Classroom
Indoor Air Pollution

NOVEMBER 1995
The Working Poor
The Jury System
Sex, Violence and the Media
Police Misconduct

Back issues are available for $5.00 (subscribers) or $10.00 (non-subscribers). Quantity discounts apply to orders over ten. To order, call Congressional Quarterly Customer Service at (202) 887-8621.

Binders are available for $18.00. To order call 1-800-638-1710. Please refer to stock number 648.

DECEMBER 1995
Teens and Tobacco
Gene Therapy's Future
Global Water Shortages
Third-Party Prospects

JANUARY 1996
Emergency Medicine
Punishing Sex Offenders
Bilingual Education
Helping the Homeless

FEBRUARY 1996
Reforming the CIA
Campaign Finance Reform
Academic Politics
Getting Into College

MARCH 1996
The British Monarchy
Preventing Juvenile Crime
Tax Reform
Pursuing the Paranormal

APRIL 1996
Centennial Olympic Games
Managed Care
Protecting Endangered Species
New Military Culture

MAY 1996
Russia's Political Future
Marriage and Divorce
Year-Round Schools
Taiwan, China and the U.S.

JUNE 1996
Rethinking NAFTA
First Ladies
Teaching Values
Labor Movement's Future

JULY 1996
Recovered-Memory Debate
Native Americans' Future
Crackdown on Sexual Harassment
Attack on Public Schools

AUGUST 1996
Fighting Over Animal Rights
Privatizing Government Services
Child Labor and Sweatshops
Cleaning Up Hazardous Wastes

SEPTEMBER 1996
Gambling Under Attack
The States and Federalism
Civic Journalism
Reassessing Foreign Aid

OCTOBER 1996
Political Consultants
Insurance Fraud
Rethinking School Integration
Parental Rights

NOVEMBER 1996
Global Warming
Clashing Over Copyright
Consumer Debt
Governing Washington, D.C.

DECEMBER 1996
Welfare, Work and the States
The New Volunteerism
Implementing the Disabilities Act
America's Pampered Pets

JANUARY 1997
Combating Scientific Misconduct
Restructuring the Electric Industry
The New Immigrants
Chemical and Biological Weapons

Future Topics

- ***Alternative Medicine's Next Phase***
- ***Independent Counsels***
- ***Future of Feminism***

THE CQ Researcher

PUBLISHED BY CONGRESSIONAL QUARTERLY INC.

Alternative Medicine's Next Phase

Are unconventional treatments joining the mainstream?

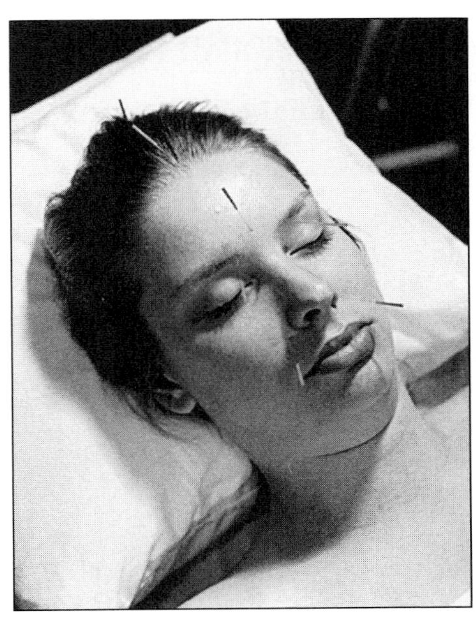

Many Americans prefer non-traditional medicine to "intrusive" modern treatments based on drugs and surgery. Others dismiss alternative approaches as dubious, if not outright quackery. But a nationwide study found that a surprising 34 percent of all Americans have tried such alternative treatments as homeopathy and chiropractic. Indeed, many physicians foresee a growing convergence of mainstream and alternative healing practices. Medical schools increasingly offer courses in alternative therapies, some of which are now covered by health insurance. Meanwhile, efforts are under way at the state level to sanction the use of marijuana for certain medical purposes. The federal government opposes the idea, but it has agreed to an 18-month, $1 million study of whether marijuana has therapeutic value.

INSIDE THIS ISSUE

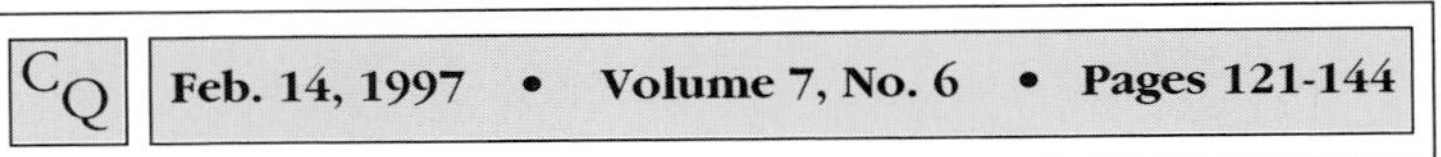

CQ Feb. 14, 1997 • Volume 7, No. 6 • Pages 121-144

Formerly Editorial Research Reports

COVER: ONCE CONSIDERED EXOTIC IN THE UNITED STATES, ACUPUNCTURE IS NOW ALMOST MAINSTREAM. (AMERICAN ASSOCIATION OF ORIENTAL MEDICINE)

Feb. 14, 1997
Volume 7, No. 6

EDITOR
Sandra Stencel

MANAGING EDITOR
Thomas J. Colin

ASSOCIATE EDITORS
Sarah M. Magner
Richard L. Worsnop

STAFF WRITERS
Charles S. Clark
Mary H. Cooper
Kenneth Jost

EDITORIAL ASSISTANT
Vanessa E. Furlong

PUBLISHED BY
Congressional Quarterly Inc.

CHAIRMAN
Andrew Barnes

VICE CHAIRMAN
Andrew P. Corty

PRESIDENT AND PUBLISHER
Robert W. Merry

EXECUTIVE EDITOR
David Rapp

The CQ Researcher (ISSN 1056-2036). Formerly Editorial Research Reports. Published weekly (48 times per year, not printed Jan. 3, May 30, Aug. 29, Oct. 31) by Congressional Quarterly Inc., 1414 22nd St., N.W., Washington, D.C. 20037. Annual subscription rate for libraries, businesses and government is $340. Additional rates furnished upon request. Periodicals postage paid at Washington, D.C., and additional mailing offices. POSTMASTER: Send address changes to The CQ Researcher, 1414 22nd St., N.W., Washington, D.C. 20037.

Alternative Medicine's Next Phase

BY RICHARD L. WORSNOP

THE ISSUES

Julie Jones, an artist in New York's Hudson Valley, didn't know much about non-traditional medicine back in 1993, but she knew she didn't much like doctors. After a midwife delivered her first child, she gave Jones a quick education in the healing properties of echinacea, chamomile and other herbal remedies.

When 7-month-old Lily began teething, Jones gave her tablets containing chamomile and a touch of belladonna. "They soothed her and made her go to sleep," she recalls. "I never even considered giving her Tylenol or Anbusol."

Henry L. Heyward, a computer programmer in Bethesda, Md., for years had blamed his arthritis pain on a high school basketball injury. Heyward didn't put much stock in chiropractors, but when a local practitioner offered free consultations last August, Heyward figured it was worth a try.

The routine office visit turned out to be anything but routine. After taking and analyzing X-rays, the chiropractor told Heyward he did not have rheumatoid arthritis, as he thought, but osteoarthritis. "I was shocked," Heyward says. "It was as if he knew my whole medical history just from looking at an X-ray." Heyward's medical doctor concurred with the new diagnosis, which led to a pair of orthopedic shoes for Heyward — and relief for his painful feet.

Jones and Heyward are among the millions of Americans who have tried — and benefited from — alternative medicine in recent years. Neither is about to cast mainstream medicine aside, however. Jones, who like many people favors a blend of folk-based and conventional healing techniques, has progressed beyond chamomile to Ayurveda, a system of healing developed in ancient India that uses combinations of herbs, oils and purgatives. "I like Ayurveda as a form of preventive care," she says, "but when traumatic injury hits, I'm glad we also have Western medicine and hospitals."

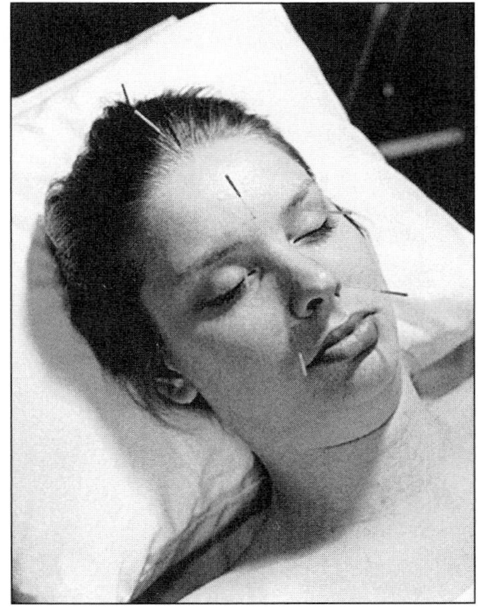

Increasing numbers of Americans feel the same way, judging from a much-cited study published in 1993 by the prestigious *New England Journal of Medicine*. Based on more than 1,500 telephone interviews, the study sought to determine the extent to which Americans used 16 "unconventional" therapies judged to be commonly available. * The results startled the medical profession. (*See graph, p. 124.*)

Extrapolating their data to the entire U.S. population, the authors declared that "Americans made an estimated 425 million visits to providers of unconventional therapy" in 1990, compared with 388 million visits to primary-care physicians. Moreover, the study estimated the expenditures for unconventional treatment in 1990 at $13.7 billion, of which patients paid three-quarters ($10.3 billion) out-of-pocket. "This figure is comparable to the $12.8 billion spent out-of-pocket annually for all hospitalizations in the United States," the study said. [1]

Other survey findings also challenged conventional wisdom. For instance, "use of unconventional therapy was significantly less common among blacks (23 percent) than among members of other racial groups (35 percent). It was significantly more common among persons with some college education (44 percent) than among those with no college education (27 percent) and significantly more common among people with annual incomes above $35,000 (37 percent) than among those with lower incomes (31 percent)."

Mainstream medical practitioners doubtless were pleased that 83 percent of the users of alternative therapy for a serious health condition also sought treatment from a physician for the same disorder. But a related finding must have sparked dismay among traditional physicians: "72 percent of the respondents who used unconventional therapy did not inform their medical doctor that they had done so."

The type of alternative treatment received made a significant difference. "Medical doctors were most likely to be informed about the use of homeopathy (73 percent), megavitamin therapy (72 percent) and self-help groups (61 percent) and least likely to be informed about folk remedies (11 percent), religious or spiritual healing by others (17 percent) or imagery (19 percent)."

The findings prompted the survey's authors to conclude that "Medical doctors should ask about their patients' use of unconventional therapy whenever they obtain a medical history." They also advised medical schools to "include information about unconventional therapies and the clinical social sciences (anthropology and

* The study defined unconventional therapies as "medical interventions not widely taught at U.S. medical schools or generally available at U.S. hospitals."

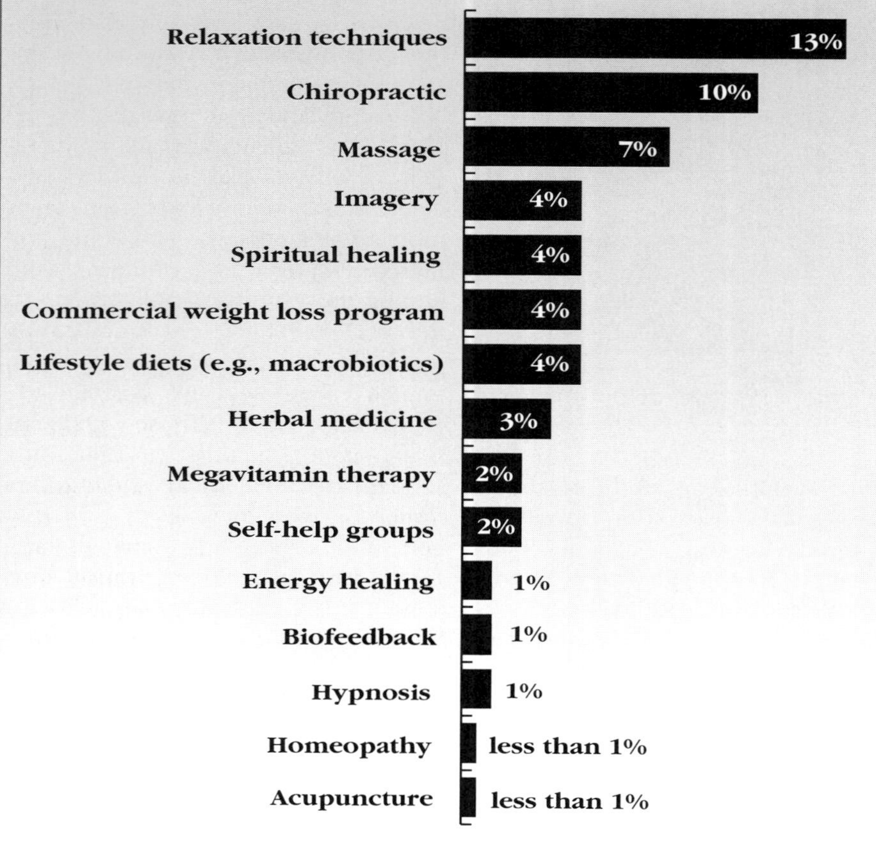

Many Americans Use Alternative Therapies

More than a third of American adults have used alternative therapies for health problems, according to a recent study. Relaxation techniques and chiropractic were the most popular treatments. Most respondents sought help for chronic, rather than life-threatening conditions.*

* *Respondents to the 1990 study said they had used at least one unconventional therapy in the past year.*

Source: "Unconventional Medicine in the United States," The New England Journal of Medicine, *Jan. 28, 1993.*

sociology) in their curriculums."

Marc S. Micozzi, executive director of the College of Physicians of Philadelphia, the nation's oldest medical society, agrees. Medical students should "take fewer courses in the subspecialties of conventional medicine and spend more time working directly with patients, learning to appreciate their different cultures and attitudes toward health and disease," he wrote recently. "Teaching health-care professionals more about alternative medicine, with its emphasis on healing instead of technology, may do as much to improve the health of our citizens as any scientific discovery about the many diseases that still plague us." [2]

Health-care professionals seem to be listening. Increasing numbers of U.S. medical schools are revamping course offerings to make students more aware of unconventional therapies (*see p. 139*). And insurers are beginning to cover alternative treatments. Indeed, insurers are finding that unconventional therapies often cost a lot less than the usual drug-surgery model.

Still, controversy is never far from center stage in the alternative medicine field. Voters in Arizona and California caused the latest flap last fall, when they approved ballot proposals sanctioning the therapeutic use of marijuana, still an illegal drug under federal law. After the votes, U.S. drug policy officials promptly warned that doctors who prescribed marijuana for medicinal purposes could face legal sanctions (*see p. 136*). That set the stage for a spirited national debate on the benefits and hazards of cannabis.

In a Jan. 30 editorial, *New England Journal of Medicine* Editor in Chief Jerome P. Kassirer assailed the federal policy banning doctors from prescribing pot for "seriously ill patients" as "misguided, heavyhanded and inhumane." Kassirer acknowledged that marijuana "may have long-term adverse effects, and its use may presage serious addictions, but neither long-term side effects nor addiction is a relevant issue in such patients." [3]

The U.S. Office of National Drug Control Policy responded that the health benefits claimed for marijuana have not been demonstrated through rigorous clinical testing. "[U]p to this point, smoke is not a medicine," the office declared. "Other treatments have been deemed safer and more effective than a psychoactive burning carcinogen self-induced through one's throat." [4]

More established forms of alternative medicine are also taking hits from critics, who condemn them as quackery at worst, unproven at best. Occasional news stories about purveyors of beyond-the-fringe therapies who prey on desperate, terminally ill people lend substance to the charge. But as *The New England Journal of Medicine* study indicates, alternative medicine holds great appeal for Americans, much as it does for the rest of the world. As Micozzi notes, "What we call alternative or complementary medicine in this country is primary care for 80 percent of the world's people."

As consumers, health experts and lawmakers seek to understand alternative medicine and put it into practice, these are among the questions being asked:

Will traditional medicine and alternative medicine reach an accommodation?

Despite the doubters, some health experts contend that conventional and alternative systems of medicine are surprisingly close to reconciling their differences. The boundaries between "establishment doctors and their less conventional colleagues . . . have dissolved considerably, and the critics have managed to stimulate much-needed change," physician Oscar Janiger and Philip Goldberg wrote in their 1993 book on alternative medicine. They noted, for instance, that the "ideological conflict between the non-traditional camp and the mainstream" had sparked new research "on diet, the immune system, the brain's role in mediating health and the impact of noxious elements in the environment." [5]

James S. Gordon, director of the Center for Mind-Body Medicine in Washington, D.C., holds similar views. In his 1996 book, he detailed the emergence of "a larger, more generous kind of medicine, one that combines conventional and alternative therapies, alternative treatment with respectful care." [6]

The new medicine, Gordon wrote, "is a synthesis of modern technology and perennial wisdom, of powerful and definitive treatment and compassionate care, of Western and Eastern, high technology and indigenous and folk-healing traditions." Further, it "insists that healing be a fully collaborative partnership in which teaching is as important as treatment, and it regards self-care — particularly through self-awareness, relaxation, meditation, nutrition and exercise — as the true 'primary care.' "

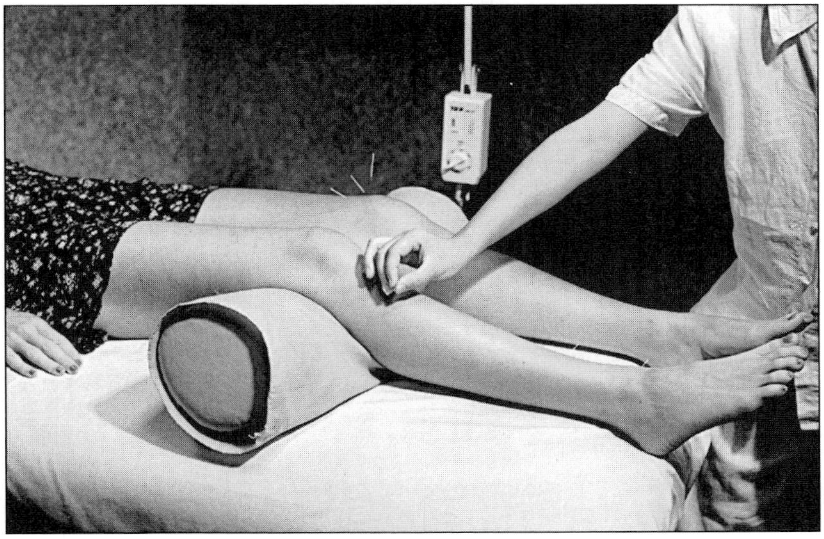

American Association of Oriental Medicine

The ancient practice of acupuncture, in which hair-thin needles are inserted into predetermined points in the body, has become increasingly mainstream in the United States.

Critics of alternative medicine often say that much of its purported effectiveness stems from the "placebo effect," in which a sick person credits his recovery to the preparation he took, even though it may have had no active ingredients. Often, critics say, the patient had a mild illness that would have gone away without intervention, or the person's determination to get well sparked recovery.

Believers in alternative medicine dismiss such comments as quibbles. They point out that many ancient healing techniques, and modern holistic medicine as well, respect the mind's role in maintaining health and combating illness. "Research suggests that hope stimulates our immune functioning," Gordon wrote, "and helps protect us against the onset of illness of all kinds." [7]

Psychologist David Bresler, co-founder of the Academy for Guided Imagery, in Mill Valley, Calif., also sees mainstream medicine as starting to acknowledge the mind's contribution to bodily health. "Unfortunately, one of the most common uses of imagery is for worry," he says. "People tend to worry about things that aren't happening, except in their imagination. And these negative thoughts have physiologic implications, because people can literally worry themselves sick."

But can they also think themselves well? According to Bresler, guided-imagery therapists strive to motivate people to "use their minds to find positive images within themselves. Instead of envisioning all the most horrible things that can happen to them, they are encouraged to think how wonderful it would be if they were able to heal themselves."

Many of the alternative therapies that seem closest to winning the medical establishment's seal of approval involve no herbs or medications of any kind. Barrie R. Cassileth, an adjunct professor of medicine at the University of North Carolina-Chapel Hill, is especially high on massage and two Chinese exercise regimens, t'ai chi and qi gong.

"Those techniques are particularly good for people who are frail or elderly or sick, because they are so gentle," she says. "Also, studies have

Continued on p. 127

Homeopathy Sales Defy Critics

Judging by product sales, homeopathy is on a roll. Sales of homeopathic remedies have climbed by 20-25 percent a year since the late 1980s, according to the American Homeopathic Pharmaceutical Association (AHPA). Satisfied users extol homeopathy as safe, gentle, "natural" and, above all, effective. Remedies may be derived from such plants as dandelion and plantain; from minerals such as iron phosphate, arsenic oxide and sodium chloride; from animal substances such as snake venom, cuttlefish ink and duck liver; and from drugs such as penicillin and streptomycin.

To medical historians, all this smacks of dèjá vu. They note that the German physician Samuel Christian Hahnemann founded homeopathic medicine 200 years ago out of disgust with such standard therapies of the time as bloodletting and purging the body of toxins with mercury compounds. During his search for less invasive ways of treating illness, Hahnemann took a dose of quinine, the drug of choice then as now for malaria. He was intrigued to find himself developing chills and a fever — malaria's best-known symptoms.

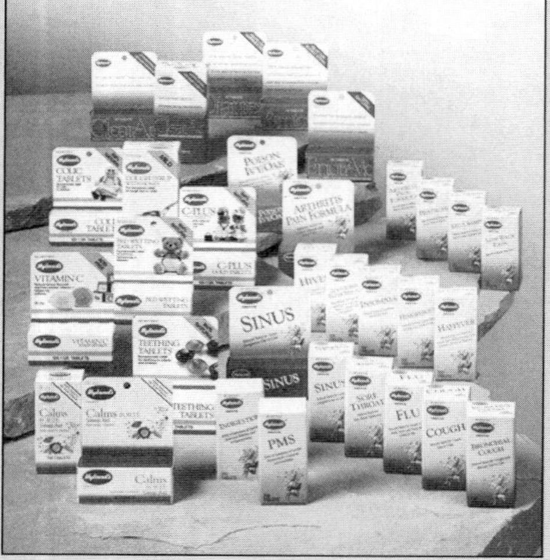

Standard Homeopathic Co.

The experience inspired Hahnemann to propound his Law of Similars, which holds that a substance known to produce certain symptoms in a healthy individual should be prescribed for an individual suffering from a disease exhibiting the same symptoms. However, under Hahnemann's Law of Infinitessimals, the more a homeopathic remedy is weakened, the more powerful its effect.

Consequently, the active ingredients in homeopathic preparations undergo repeated dilution — often as many as 30 times in all. The National Center for Homeopathy describes the process as follows: "A plant substance, for example, is mixed in alcohol to obtain a tincture. One drop of the tincture is mixed with 99 drops of alcohol (to achieve a ratio of 1:100) and the mixture is strongly shaken." [1] At the end of the third such dilution, the active ingredient constitutes only one molecule of every million in the solution.

Can such a diluted solution have any effect? "Almost no one, including homeopaths, quarrels with the chemical principle that says a substance can only be diluted so far before it statistically disappears altogether," Leah R. Garnett wrote in the *Harvard Health Letter*. [2]

Nonetheless, homeopaths insist that their remedies are effective. Their potency, they say, is imparted by vigorous shaking after each step of the dilution process. Hahnemann believed that these "succussions" left behind a "spirit-like" essence of the active ingredient, and that this sufficed to trigger the body's innate self-healing mechanism.

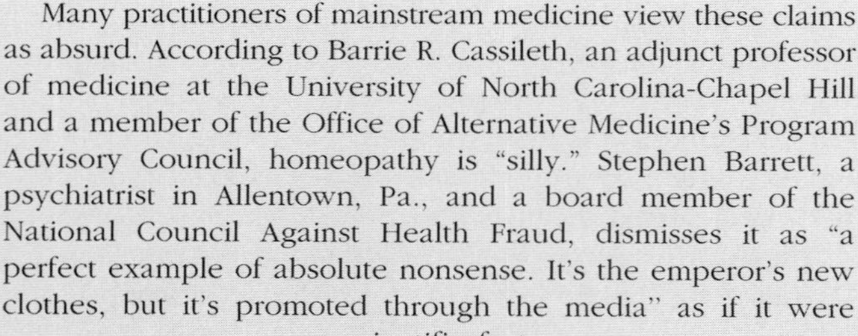

Many practitioners of mainstream medicine view these claims as absurd. According to Barrie R. Cassileth, an adjunct professor of medicine at the University of North Carolina-Chapel Hill and a member of the Office of Alternative Medicine's Program Advisory Council, homeopathy is "silly." Stephen Barrett, a psychiatrist in Allentown, Pa., and a board member of the National Council Against Health Fraud, dismisses it as "a perfect example of absolute nonsense. It's the emperor's new clothes, but it's promoted through the media" as if it were scientific fact.

Homeopaths respond by citing studies published in reputable medical journals. For instance, the May 1994 issue of *Pediatrics* reported on a randomized, double-blind clinical trial indicating that homeopathy was effective for treating acute childhood diarrhea. And the Dec. 10, 1994, issue of *The Lancet*, the leading British medical journal, reported on a similar trial that suggested homeopathic preparations helped relieve allergic asthma. [3]

Small wonder, then, that sales of homeopathic remedies have been booming. Jay Bornemann, a spokesman for the AHPA, estimates total retail sales at $200 million in 1996, or about 20 percent more than the 1995 total of $165 million. [4] Bornemann cautions, however, that reliable data are hard to come by because almost all producers of homeopathic medicines are small, privately owned companies.

For similar reasons, he adds, it's almost impossible to pinpoint the best-selling homeopathic preparation. "The consensus is that the top-selling products are clustered," he says. Heading the list, industry officials believe, are flu medications, sleeping aids and teething remedies.

"Homeopathy doesn't exist in a vacuum," Bornemann says. "Americans are becoming more pro-active about their health care and their lifestyles. The increase in health-club memberships also shows that people are trying to take better care of themselves." In addition, he feels that people are turning to homeopathic remedies out of concern that mainstream medications "may have side-effects and contraindications that are unacceptable to them on a daily basis."

---

[1] National Center for Homeopathy, "Homeopathy: Natural Medicine for the 21st Century," 1993, p. 3.

[2] Leah R. Garnett, "Is Less Really More?" *Harvard Health Letter*, May 1995, p. 1.

[3] National Center for Homeopathy, *op. cit.*, p. 5.

[4] Bornemann also is executive vice president of the Standard Homeopathic Co., which makes homeopathic remedies.

Continued from p. 125

shown that t'ai chi helps improve balance and thus reduces the number of falls and hip fractures among the elderly. It's more effective in that regard than the approaches medicine has traditionally used for the purpose," such as medication.

Cassileth also looks with favor on meditation, whether in the form of relaxation therapy, yoga or some other variation. "Meditation can create or induce very positive physiologic changes and enhance well-being," she says. "I don't know that I'd call it alternative or complementary medicine any more, because it has been brought so fully into mainstream practice."

So-called therapeutic touch, a fixture of many Eastern healing approaches, in Cassileth's view only has "some placebo benefit. I don't believe energy goes from the therapist into the patient at all," Cassileth says. "As I see it, any benefit achieved comes from the therapist's presence in the room. I suspect that if another person came into that room, sat down near the patient, and did not perform any therapeutic touch, the outcome would be the same. In other words, just having a nice, warm body sitting next to you helps."

Stephen Barrett, a psychiatrist in Allentown, Pa., and board member of the National Council Against Health Fraud, doesn't anticipate any wholesale crumbling of the wall between alternative and mainstream medicine. In his critical view, very few alternative therapies merit inclusion in conventional medical practice. Homeopathy, he says, doesn't come close. "There's no point in investigating homeopathy with the idea you might learn something useful," he says, "because the whole thing is nonsensical. It lacks investigative data, for one thing." Other experts cite studies challenging Barrett. (*See story, p. 126.*)

Another difficulty with alternative therapies, Barrett says, is that some of them "don't fit into just one category," such as the many forms of relaxation therapy. For example, he says, biofeedback "has been shown to be useful for bladder control in incontinent people." But biofeedback also has applications of dubious value, he says: "If someone starts talking to you about biofeedback as an aid to expanding your mind, that's quackery!"

Barrett even sees little room for herbal preparations in conventional medicine, despite the growing popularity of health food. "The vast majority of herbal products are already known to be worthless," he contends. "Another problem is that the largest group of people prescribing herbal remedies are chiropractors, who aren't trained to recognize many of the diseases they try to treat. Herbologists are no better. In fact, the number of people in this country who know how to prescribe herbs properly may well be zero."

Posters supporting medicinal marijuana were distributed during last fall's campaign for California's Proposition 215.

Do marijuana's claimed health benefits outweigh its hazards?

Marijuana is suddenly the topic of the moment, but in many ways America's marijuana debate still seems stuck in a 60-year-old time warp. Until the mid-1930s, cannabis was used to treat many ailments. But popular attitudes rapidly began to shift with the 1936 release of "Reefer Madness," a lurid, low-budget docudrama purporting to show how a puff or two of pot could transform clean-cut teenagers into spaced-out junkies. [8]

"Reefer Madness" led to the Marijuana Tax Act of 1937, which made pot a federally proscribed drug, a status it still retains. But last fall's passage of ballot initiatives in Arizona and California legalizing marijuana for medicinal use portends another upheaval in popular opinion over marijuana's health benefits, and whether they are compelling enough to justify pot's partial re-legalization.

The medical establishment approaches the question gingerly. In a Dec. 30 statement, the American Medical Association (AMA) said it "will continue" to work closely with federal agencies "to combat the use of illicit drugs." At the same time, it urged "federal funding of research to deter-

Glossary of Terms and Treatments

Acupuncture: In this ancient Chinese technique, hair-thin metal needles are inserted into key points in the body to balance "energy flow" and stimulate the body's natural healing mechanisms; used to relieve physical and emotional pain and nausea.

Ayurveda: Originated in India some 5,000 years ago, Ayurvedic medicine uses "natural" diet, herbs, exercise and "rejuvenation" therapies, such as massage and use of aromatic scents, as preventive health care tailored to each person's body type. Ayurvedic practitioners regard disease either as an imbalance in the life force ("prana") or, in some cases, as karmically preordained.

Biofeedback: Patients suffering from headaches, insomnia, high blood pressure, anxiety, incontinence and other problems use electronic sensors to monitor their involuntary functions, such as temperature, brain waves and blood flow. They attempt to relieve their symptoms by using mental energy to raise or lower the readings.

Chiropractic: Manipulation of the spinal column and other areas of the body is said to relieve symptoms caused by misalignments of vertebrae, including internal ailments, stress, poor nutrition and emotional problems. A 1994 study by the U.S. Department of Health and Human Services concluded that spinal manipulation was not only effective in relieving acute lower-back pain but also worked better than surgery, drug therapy and other conventional medical treatments.

Echinacea: An herb widely used by Native Americans and others, echinacea "has been demonstrated to have both immune-stimulating and antiviral properties," writes James S. Gordon, director of the Center for Mind-Body Medicine in Washington, D.C.[1] Many users take it to lessen the severity of colds and flu.

Energy Healing: Practitioners view the body as an "energy system" whose energy must circulate freely. They seek to correct imbalances in energy flow by using touch therapy (see below) and other similar techniques.

Guided Imagery: Patients suffering from heart disease, cancer and many stress-related illnesses are guided in trying to visualize their immune systems actually fighting the disease or problem. Psychiatrists employ guided imagery to help patients "recover" long-suppressed memories of childhood trauma as a first step toward emotional recovery.[2]

Homeopathy: A system of medicine based on the Law of Similars, which postulates that a substance that triggers certain symptoms in a healthy person can cure similar symptoms in a sick person. Homeopathy also teaches that an extremely weak dose of the appropriate substance is the most effective in restoring a patient to health.

Naturopathy: Naturopaths believe that disease reflects the body's effort to purify itself. Thus naturopathic treatments include vitamins, herbs, natural-food diets, minerals and salts, massage and exercise, enemas, acupuncture and homeopathy.

Oriental Medicine: This ancient system of health care is grounded in the concept of qi (pronounced "chee," and loosely translated as "energy"), and the effect of qi on health. The overall goal is to promote self-healing. In addition to acupuncture, the armamentarium of Oriental medicine comprises heat therapy, massage, exercise and diet and lifestyle-management techniques.

Osteopathy: Widely regarded as the forerunner of holistic medicine, osteopathy adopts an integrated mind-body-spirit approach to treating patients. It originated in the 1870s as a technique for manipulating the spine to treat muscle spasms, pain or bone disease.

Relaxation Techniques: Practitioners seek to teach users how to train their minds to ease the tension in skeletal and internal muscles.

Spiritual Healing: Advocates generally ascribe healing to divine power or to doctors residing in the spirit world. Examples include Christian Science, exorcism, shamanism, Christian evangelical healing and Sufi healing.

Touch Therapy: Despite its name, touch therapy entails no physical contact between practitioner and patient. Therapists hold their hands about two inches above the patient's body in an effort to restore balance to the energy field that supposedly envelops all living things.

---

[1] James S. Gordon, *Manifesto for a New Medicine* (1996), pp. 158-159.

[2] For background on guided imagery and recovered memory, see "Recovered-Memory Debate," *The CQ Researcher*, July 5, 1996, pp. 577-600.

mine the validity of marijuana as an effective medical treatment."

Advocates of medicinal marijuana retort, in effect, "What's left to determine?" They contend that clinical tests have established that pot suppresses nausea in patients undergoing cancer chemotherapy. They also cite anecdotal evidence suggesting that marijuana controls AIDS-related nausea and appetite loss and reduces the abnormal pressure in the eye that leads to glaucoma and, in extreme instances, blindness. [9]

At the five-year-old Office of Alternative Medicine (OAM), a branch of the National Institutes of Health (NIH), no research is being funded on marijuana. Indeed, the marijuana question is such a sticky subject that the new director of the OAM declined to be interviewed by *The CQ Researcher.* Wayne B. Jonas, a respected family practitioner and alternative medicine enthusiast, said that because medicinal marijuana was being included in this report, he would not discuss any of the OAM's research efforts (*see p. 134*).

But the Center for Mind-Body Medicine's Gordon, who until recently was chairman of OAM's Program Advisory Council, was happy to address the subject. "We've just begun to explore the therapeutic applications of marijuana," he says. "It may have many uses, particularly in the psychological area. For instance, it could be extremely helpful to people undergoing certain kinds of emotional crises, provided it's used appropriately. We know that other cultures use it that way."

Going beyond the immediate issue of marijuana, Gordon adds: "We need to open up, once again, the whole area of psychedelic plants and psychedelic compounds. We need, as a culture, to re-examine our phobic mindset regarding drugs and start developing a much more intelligent attitude. I hope that [the Arizona and California] initiatives mark the beginning of a kind of openness to the therapeutic possibilities of these substances."

Many health professionals say there are compelling reasons for keeping the lid on pot. Donald Tashkin, a medical researcher at the University of California-Los Angeles, has been studying the effect of marijuana on the lungs of regular pot users for more than a decade. His preliminary findings suggest that those who smoke three or four joints a day develop chronic bronchitis as often as cigarette smokers who consume a pack or more daily. The reason, he says, is that a self-rolled, loosely packed joint delivers far more tar and carcinogens to the lungs than a machine-made cigarette. [10]

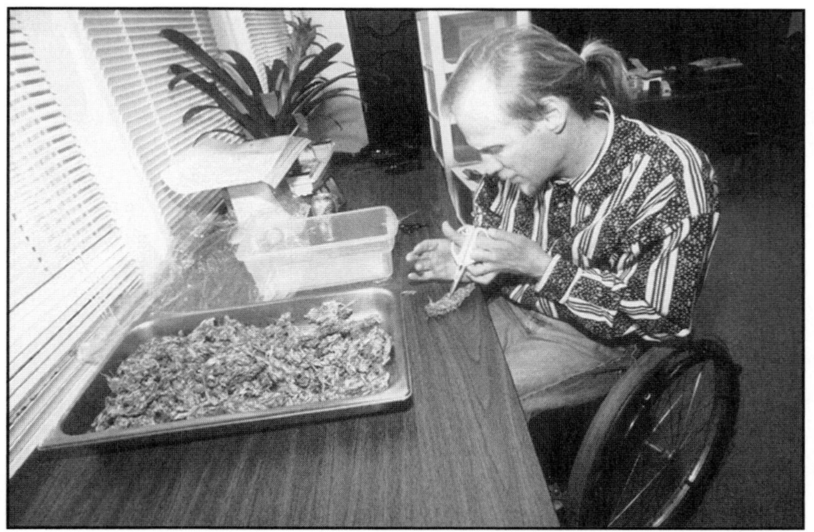

Marijuana is processed at the Cannabis Buyers' Club in Oakland, Calif.

Paul Consroe, a professor of pharmacology and toxicology at the University of Arizona-Tucson, says the likelihood of lung damage makes marijuana an iffy therapeutic option in some situations. "You wouldn't want to use it for trivial things," he says. "You'd only choose it when you had nothing else likely to do any good, or you were going to use it for a relatively short time, or you had a terminal patient who just wanted to get away from pain and stress."

Efforts to remove the tars and carcinogens from marijuana plants have made scant headway so far, Consroe says. He notes, however, that smoking is not the only way to ingest the drug. "You can swallow it as an extract or a tincture, as people did in the 19th century. But making it go through the digestive system delays the effect. You don't get the fast result most patients are looking for when they talk about marijuana relief."

At the American Holistic Medical Association (AHMA), Communications Director David Perlmutter argues that "Marijuana is not completely safe — but then neither is aspirin or Tylenol, which are sold over-the-counter. I'm not suggesting marijuana should be similarly available, because we know it has detrimental effects. Still, it's a plant-derived natural substance with relatively low health risks. I think it should be added to the armamentarium so that physicians can prescribe it in certain circumstances."

Micozzi agrees that marijuana "is a natural product, which can make it an appealing option for the herbal and nutritional approaches often included in complementary medicine." Many doctors, he adds, "would like to take advantage of this, but they worry about the legal and regulatory complications they could face by doing that." ■

BACKGROUND

Rise of Alternatives

Alternative therapies occupied a prominent place in American health care only a century ago. Modern medicine "has only recently graduated as a scientific (or partly scientific) discipline embracing a central corps of accepted philosophy, rules and regulations," the authors of a 1995 book on healing and healers wrote. In the 19th century, they noted, U.S. medical practitioners "were an ill-assorted group, comprising a few scientists, a few skillful and observant bedside physicians and a larger motley collection of hopefuls, enthusiasts, evangelic believers, snake-oil salesmen, mountebanks, quacks, plain frauds and con men, all of whom can trace their ancestry back beyond alchemists, herbalists, priests and nuns to tribal shamans and magicians." [11]

Well into the 20th century, doctors in America and Europe routinely treated their patients with hoary folk remedies. Their approach typically was purgative. Enemas and laxatives were freely prescribed to rid the body of toxins, while vacuum cups and leeches helped to draw off "bad" blood. Many "medicines" consisted mainly of herbs, spices, floral extracts and even tinctures of substances such as pearls. Many people of the period doubtless would have agreed with the Roman sage Publilius Syrus, who observed in the first century B.C., "There are some remedies worse than the disease."

Indeed, Oliver Wendell Holmes Sr., the author and physician, voiced similar thoughts in 1860. "I firmly believe," he declared, "that if the whole *materia medica,* as now used, could be sunk to the bottom of the sea, it would be all the better for mankind — and all the worse for the fishes." [12]

At the time Holmes spoke, efforts already were under way to make medicinal practice less invasive. Homeopathy was the product of one such initiative. The German doctor Samuel Christian Hahnemann originated the practice in 1796 with his "Law of Similars." In brief, Hahnemann held that a substance that can cause certain symptoms in healthy individuals can cure similar symptoms in a sick person. (*See story, p. 126.*)

A second, more controversial, tenet of homeopathy was that the smallest effective dose of a remedy was always preferable, since the body needed only a medicinal nudge to rev up its self-healing engine. In an age when many potentially lethal substances were used as medicines, such as mercury, few observers disputed Hahnemann's contention that large doses of medicine often produced toxic side effects; experience had shown this to be true in all too many instances.

Two subsequent developments also were premised on the homeopathic notion that sick people could be made well with minimal resort to potions, elixirs and nostrums. The first was osteopathy, a school of medicine based upon the principle that the body, when healthy and in "correct adjustment," is a machine capable of manufacturing its own remedies against infections and other toxic conditions.

Osteopathy was founded in 1874 by Andrew Taylor Still, a largely self-taught medical practitioner. In his autobiography, Still wrote that "a natural flow of blood is health; and disease is the effect of local or general disturbance of blood [and that] the bones could be used as levers to relieve pressure on nerves, veins and arteries." Physicians should study disease prevention as well as cure, he believed, and treat "patients," not "symptoms." [13]

Today, osteopaths employ the diagnostic and therapeutic techniques of conventional medicine in addition to the bone manipulations championed by Still. Osteopathic students receive training similar to that of medical students and earn a doctor of osteopathy (D.O.) degree, which enables them to practice on an equal footing with medical doctors.

A doctor of chiropractic (D.C.), however, has much less freedom than an osteopath. In essence, chiropractic has not evolved significantly from the precepts of its founder, Daniel David Palmer, a grocer in Davenport, Iowa, with some knowledge of osteopathy and spinal adjustment. Palmer experienced his life's epiphany in September 1895, when he manipulated the vertebrae of Harvey Lillard, a deaf janitor. "Palmer's maneuver restored the hearing that Lillard had lost 17 years before," according to Gordon, "and provided the basis for a new profession, which he named chiropractic (from the Greek words *cheir* (hand) and *praxis* (practice or action)." [14]

Ironically, Palmer's triumph laid the groundwork for the controversy that dogs chiropractic to this day. Then as now, the medical establishment scoffed at the idea that spinal misalignments — "subluxations," in chiropractic jargon — are the primary cause of disease. This doctrine is now soft-pedaled, if not repudiated outright, by many chiropractors. Nonetheless, it is still cited by alternative medicine's critics to buttress the charge that chiropractic is nothing more than quackery.

By 1900, many alternative therapies had carved out what seemed a secure niche in American medicine. For instance, an estimated 10 percent of the nation's practitioners were doctors of homeopathy. "They were trained in 22 homeopathic medical schools," Gordon writes, "practiced in more than 100 homeopathic hospitals, published their studies in 29 journals and prescribed remedies that were dispensed by more than 1,000 homeopathic pharmacies." [15]

Fall and Resurrection

A decade later, however, homeopaths and practitioners of other alternative therapies found themselves struggling desperately for professional survival. They were the chief targets of a scathing report on medical schools

Continued on p. 132

Chronology

Pre-1900 ***Efforts are made to bring order and the scientific method to haphazard health-care practices.***

1796
German physician Samuel Hahnemann, the father of homeopathy, devises his Law of Similars, postulating that drugs that produce certain disease symptoms in healthy individuals can cure the same symptoms in sick people.

1895
Daniel David Palmer, the founder of chiropractic, manipulates the spine of a deaf janitor, reportedly restoring the man's hearing.

1910s-1930s ***Scientifically based allopathic medicine becomes dominant in advanced Western countries, as many traditional folk remedies fall from favor.***

1910
A scathing report by educational reformer Abraham Flexner leads to wholesale upgrading of U.S. medical schools, and the demise of many institutions that specialized in alternative therapies.

1937
President Franklin D. Roosevelt signs the Marijuana Tax Act, which prohibits the use or sale of marijuana except for approved research.

1938
Congress exempts all substances in the *Homeopathic Pharmacopoeia of the United States* from the safety and efficacy tests required of conventional drugs under the Food, Drug and Cosmetic Act of 1938, thus placing homeopathic remedies beyond the regulatory reach of the Food and Drug Administration (FDA).

1970s ***The holistic health movement, which stresses the interaction of the body and the mind, gains adherents in the U.S.***

July 1971
New York Times correspondent James Reston describes how acupuncture relieved his postoperative discomfort following an emergency appendectomy in China.

1975
Responding to lawsuits by chiropractors, the American Medical Association (AMA) abolishes its Committee on Quackery, established in 1962.

1976
Congress amends the Food, Drug and Cosmetic Act to curb FDA enforcement authority, thus making it easier to market new nutritional supplements.

1977
Four chiropractors sue the AMA, charging it with trying to destroy the chiropractic profession.

1990s ***New federal agency becomes a forum for advocates of alternative and complementary medicine.***

1991
Congress establishes Office of Alternative Medicine (OAM).

Jan. 13, 1992
AMA says it is ethical for doctors to refer patients to chiropractors.

September 1993
OAM announces its first 30 pilot projects to identify promising areas of research into alternative therapies. Each project receives $30,000.

July 1995
Wayne B. Jonas, director of the Medical Research Fellowship program at Walter Reed Army Institute of Research, succeeds Joseph Jacobs as director of OAM.

October 1995
OAM funds research into alternative medicine at eight major medical centers.

January 1996
Washington state requires health plans to cover treatment by all state-licensed health-care providers, including acupuncturists, chiropractors, naturopaths and other alternative practitioners.

Nov. 5, 1996
Voters in Arizona and California approve ballot proposals legalizing the use of marijuana for medicinal purposes, provided a physician gives prior authorization.

Jan. 7, 1997
Federal drug policy Director Barry R. McCaffrey announces a $1 million, 18-month study of marijuana and its potential therapeutic applications.

Jan. 8, 1997
San Francisco Superior Court judge allows Cannabis Cultivators Club to provide marijuana to its members for medical purposes under the recently approved California voter initiative.

Does Melatonin Really Work?

Melatonin is hot. A natural bodily hormone sold in synthetic form by health-food stores, it is the latest self-therapy craze to sweep a country that has experienced many such crazes in recent years.

Why all the fuss? Insomniacs and frequent flyers swear that melatonin helps them fall asleep and counteract the effects of jet lag. But some enthusiasts make much more extravagant claims, asserting that melatonin can retard aging, protect against cancer and heart disease, enhance sexual performance and strengthen the immune system. These purported benefits, none of which have been proven, have gained wide currency through a number of recent books on the subject, including *The Melatonin Miracle*, by Dr. Walter Pierpaoli and William Regelson.

"My guess is that if you did a profile of the buyers of *The Melatonin Miracle*, they'd be between 37 and 57," said Robert Butler, a gerontologist at New York's Mount Sinai Medical Center. "Baby boomers want a more vital middle age and old age than what they've seen their parents go through." [1]

First identified in 1958, melatonin is produced in the body after dark, attaining peak concentrations in the body between the ages of 1 and 3. As a person ages, the brain's pineal gland releases progressively less of the hormone at night, when its apparent sleep-inducing properties come into play. Commercial marketing of synthetic melatonin was made possible by the 1994 Dietary Supplement Health and Education Act, which sanctioned the sale of natural dietary supplements without a prescription as long as no health claims were made for them. [2]

The craze for melatonin troubles many medical experts, who caution that people may be ingesting much more of it than they need. "Even one milligram, the smallest available commercial dose, is at least three times higher than the normal amount in the body," said Margarita Dubocovich, a neuropharmacologist at Northwestern University. "Does the body need so much melatonin? Maybe adults produce less [than children] for some reason." [3]

According to a workshop sponsored by the National Institutes of Health (NIH) last August, scientists don't known how much melatonin the body needs. In a widely quoted paper presented at the Bethesda, Md., meeting, researchers Fred Turek of Northwestern University and Charles Czeisler of Brigham and Women's Hospital in Boston declared that "carefully controlled clinical trials that focus on the possible beneficial effects of melatonin on specific sleep disorders are urgently needed." They added that "chronic use of melatonin cannot be justified for any sleep disorder at this time, since neither the therapeutic [nor] potential toxic effects of long-term use of this hormone — which has profound effects on the reproductive system of other mammals — are known."

At present, NIH is funding five small-scale studies of melatonin and sleep. The most ambitious is a five-year, 60-subject clinical trial at Massachusetts Institute of Technology in which patients suffering from insomnia receive doses of the hormone. An unrelated study at the Oregon Health Sciences University in Portland, Ore., reported successfully using melatonin to restore normal sleep-wake cycles in blind persons. [4]

Pending completion of more studies, physicians generally advise prudence in taking commercial preparations of melatonin. "As far as using melatonin to extend longevity, I really don't think we have a clue as to what difference it's going to make for human beings," says James S. Gordon, director of the Center for Mind-Body Medicine in Washington, D.C., and former chair of the Program Advisory Council of NIH's Office of Alternative Medicine.

What is needed above all, in Gordon's view, is "some studies that will take a look at melatonin's potential long-term side effects. I think it may have significant use for treating lupus, and perhaps other autoimmune illnesses as well. It does seem to do something in terms of balancing the immune system."

Gordon adds that there are "promising melatonin studies under way involving people with advanced cancer, especially in combination with conventional treatment. Also, some of the benefits that people get from meditation may be mediated through increases in melatonin."

"It's a very interesting compound, but I would be very, very wary about prescribing long-term use of it," Gordon says.

[1] Quoted by Elizabeth DeVita, "Melatonin: The Hottest Hormone of All," *American Health*, January-February 1996, p. 72.

[2] For background, see "Dietary Supplements," *The CQ Researcher*, July 8, 1994, pp. 577-600.

[3] Quoted by Geoffrey Cowley, "Melatonin Mania," *Newsweek*, Nov. 6, 1995, p. 62.

[4] "More Research Needed to Confirm Melatonin Benefits, Examine Possible Harm, NIH Workshop Told," *Council for Responsible Nutrition News*, January 1997, p. 6.

Continued from p. 130

issued in 1910 by educational reformer Abraham Flexner. [16] In the course of his research, Flexner visited all 155 U.S. and Canadian medical schools and described each in detail. The vast majority, he concluded, fell far short of the high standards set by the medical school of his alma mater, Johns Hopkins University in Baltimore. Flexner recommended that 120 of the schools be closed, and within the next few years most of them were.

Homeopathic institutions were especially hard hit. Their number declined from 22 to two in 1923; none remained by 1950. Allopathic medicine, with its reliance on pharmaceutical drugs and surgery, had become entrenched by then as the nation's dominant system of health care.

Most historians of American medicine hailed the ascendancy of science-based health care. But some expressed misgivings.

"[In] throwing out the proverbial dirty bathwater of quacks and charlatans, the healing arts also lost a few babies that might have been worth salvaging," Janiger and Goldberg wrote. "Instead of objectively seeking out what might be valuable in osteopathy, chiropractic, naturopathy, homeopathy and the like, authorities lumped them together with the dangerous and dispensable. Thus, alternatives that might have contributed something worthwhile were stigmatized and relegated to the sidelines of medicine.

"Further, the criteria for what constitutes acceptable medicine and who shall be granted the status of legitimate physician began to be defined along political and jurisdictional lines. The issue became who is entitled to do what as opposed to who and what is good at helping sick people get better." [17]

Though marginalized, alternative medicine did not completely fold its tent. Indeed, homeopathy received a new lease on life when the Food, Drug and Cosmetic Act of 1938 exempted all substances in the *Homeopathic Pharmacopeia of the United States* from the rigorous safety and efficacy testing required of conventional drugs. Crafted by Sen. Royal S. Copeland, D-N.Y., the only physician then serving in the Senate, the exemption gave homeopathic preparations a marketing edge over undiluted herbal products and dietary supplements.

Holistic Revival

More than 30 years were to pass, however, before alternative medicine re-emerged as a major component of health care in the United States. The revival coincided with rising interest in holistic medicine, which Gordon defines as "a synthesis of modern technology and perennial wisdom, of powerful and definitive treatment and compassionate care, of Western and Eastern, high technology and indigenous and folk healing traditions." [18]

Holistic medicine's popularity also reflected popular disenchantment with mainstream health care. Conventional medicine, Gordon wrote, "is inadequate to explain the origins or treat the consequences of the chronic illnesses, the disabilities and the distresses that afflict more than 80 percent of those who seek medical attention. Its overuse and misuse have produced a deadly host of mutated bacterial and viral life-forms and an epidemic of iatrogenic — physician-and-treatment-caused — illnesses. Its economic cost — almost $1 trillion a year and close to 15 percent of our gross national product — has become insupportable." [19]

In contrast to most conventional treatments, alternative therapies are promoted as cost-effective and less invasive. A prime example is the ancient Chinese practice of acupuncture, in which hair-thin needles are inserted into the body at predetermined sites to relieve pain, nausea and other symptoms. Many Americans were introduced to acupuncture by *New York Times* correspondent James Reston, who underwent the procedure to relieve pain after an emergency appendectomy in Peking in 1971.

The insertion of needles into his right elbow and below both knees, Reston reported in a Page One story, initially "sent ripples of pain racing through my limbs and, at least, had the effect of diverting my attention from the distress in my stomach." However, he felt "noticeable relaxation of the pressure and distension within an hour and no recurrence of the problem thereafter." [20]

It did not take acupuncture long to make the transition from an exotic to an almost prosaic therapy. But many alternative approaches remain largely unfamiliar, among them guided imagery, used by psychiatrists to help patients "recover" long-suppressed memories of traumatic events. [21]

However, imagery has other applications as well. According to Bresler, "It's used to treat many stress-related illnesses, including those that originate in the workplace. It also can enhance performance, especially in athletes. And schools can use it to enhance students' memory and learning."

Bresler says a doctor treating an ill patient with guided imagery would "have them close their eyes and visualize all their symptoms and everything else associated with the illness, and allow an image to form." At that point, the doctor would tell the patient to confront the symptoms by asking them, as if they were persons: "Why are you doing this? What do you want?" The rationale for this approach is that "the symptoms are there for a reason, so why not tap the wisdom of the body to find out its point of view?"

Physicians employing guided imagery, Bresler notes, must take care "not to contaminate the patient's thought process. That means using content-free language during therapy. What we like to say is that the guide provides the setting, but the client provides the jewel. In other words, it's the client's imagery experience, not the guide's."

Practitioners of holistic medicine rarely use alternative therapies like acupuncture and guided imagery in isolation. More typically, they assemble a menu of approaches tailored to the individual patient's needs.

"Combined use of conventional medicine and one or more vernacular strategies is extremely common," writes Bonnie Blair O'Connor, an assistant professor of community and preventive medicine at the Medical College of Pennsylvania in Philadelphia. She notes, for example, that a cancer patient "may be following a course of chemotherapy while simultaneously using prayer for healing, together with the application of sacred

Wide Range of Alternative Therapies Being Studied

Research on alternative health treatments ranging from music therapy to Chinese herbal remedies is being funded at 10 U.S. medical research centers by the Office of Alternative Medicine.

Facility	Specialty	Alternative Treatment	Grant
University of Virginia School of Nursing, Center for the Study of Complementary and Alternative Therapies, Charlottesville, Va.	Pain	Chiropractic, massage, therapeutic touch, sound (binaural beats)	$1.1 million
Kessler Institute for Rehabilitation, West Orange, N.J., and the University of Medicine and Dentistry, Newark, N.J.	Stroke and neurological conditions	Music, pets, chiropractic, applied kinesthesiology	$1.1 million
Columbia University College of Physicians and Surgeons, Center for Complementary and Alternative Medical Research in Women's Health, New York, N.Y.	Women's health	Traditional Chinese medicine (fibroid tumors); Tibetan medicine (metastatic breast cancer); biofeedback (menopausal hot flashes)	$1.1 million
University of Texas Health Science Center, Houston, Texas	Cancer	Herbal medicine, shark and bovine cartilage, melatonin	$1.0 million
Beth Israel Deaconess Medical Center, Harvard Medical School, Boston, Mass.	General medical conditions	Chiropractic and acupuncture (lower back pain); homeopathy (ear infections); diet, yoga, exercise and support groups (heart disease)	$935,696
Minneapolis Medical Research Center, Minneapolis, Minn.	Addictions	Acupuncture, herbal medicine (including Kudzu extract)	$924,000
Bastyr University, Seattle, Wash.	HIV/AIDS	Nutrition, traditional and ethno-medicine, energetic therapies	$920,000
University of Maryland School of Medicine, Baltimore, Md.	Pain	Acupuncture	$900,088
University of California, Davis, Calif.	Asthma, allergy and immunology	Homeopathy (wheat grass juice for hay fever); manipulations and biofeedback (asthma)	$899,021
Stanford University, Palo Alto, Calif.	Aging	Traditional Chinese medicine; herbal medicine	$864,150

Source: Office of Alternative Medicine, National Institutes of Health; individual research centers

relics to the afflicted part(s) of the body; following a natural-foods diet and taking large doses of vitamins and minerals in an effort to eliminate toxins and bolster the immune system; practicing meditation to reduce stress, and visualization to mobilize the body's healing forces; using botanical or homeopathic medicines to combat the side effects of chemotherapy; and seeing a chiropractor to help restore vitality and proper functioning, or an acupuncturist for pain control or restoration of critical internal balance."[22]

Practitioners of chiropractic took a giant step toward professional respectability in the 1980s, when a long-standing civil court case was settled in their favor. In 1977, several chiropractors charged the AMA with antitrust violations and engaging in a conspiracy to destroy the chiropractic profession.

A 1987 U.S. District Court decision favoring the chiropractors was upheld in 1990 by an appellate court. After the Supreme Court declined to hear the AMA's appeal, the doctors ended their policy of unbending hostility to chiropractic. In a Jan. 13, 1992, statement, the AMA announced that it was ethical for doctors of medicine to refer patients to doctors of chiropractic. But the association stressed that physicians were not obligated to make such referrals.

OAM and Its Critics

Establishment of the OAM in 1992 served notice that, along with chiropractic, other unconventional health treatments also were gaining respectability. In fact, the AMA supports the OAM because it promises to subject alternative therapies to scientific scrutiny.

OAM was the brainchild of Sen. Tom Harkin, D-Iowa, chairman of the Senate Appropriations Subcommittee on Labor, Health and Human Services, and Education. Harkin's interest in alternative therapies stemmed in large part from his own health history; he credited large doses of bee pollen with curing his hay fever.

Harkin had been influenced by fellow Iowa Democrat Berkeley W. Bedell, who served in the House from 1975 to 1987. Bedell attributed his return to good health after cancer surgery in 1987 to injections of 714-X, an untested camphor-derived treatment developed by Gaston Naessens, a controversial Quebec physician. Bedell subsequently was appointed to OAM's Program Advisory Council.

OAM seemed to be off to a promising start with the appointment of Joseph Jacobs as its first director. A Native American, Jacobs had served as a pediatrician in the Indian Health Service, and later as a medical director with the Aetna Life Insurance Co. At OAM, he saw his role as that of "broker between the alternative medicine community and the orthodox medicine community." [23]

Instead, Jacobs soon found himself caught in a three-way crossfire involving the alternative and traditional medicine communities as well as Harkin and his allies. The climax came at a congressional hearing convened by Harkin on June 24, 1993. Bedell, appearing as a witness, urged OAM to hire staffers to identify anyone claiming to have an effective alternative therapy, examine the relevant files and "just simply find out whether what he claims is correct." Bedell called this approach "outcomes research." [24]

Harkin essentially agreed, underscoring the need to "investigate and validate" specific therapies. Jacobs commented afterward that it was clear to him that OAM "had to do field investigations" because Harkin was saying, "'This is what you've got to do.' " [25]

Not surprisingly, OAM's initial grant awards were criticized in some quarters for being too narrowly focused. The 42 awards, announced in fiscal 1993 and 1994, each involved only one therapy technique and one health condition — dance as a treatment for cystic fibrosis, acupuncture for osteoarthritis, guided imagery for asthma, and so on.

The highly focused approach left some proponents of holistic medicine feeling left out, among them members of the American Holistic Medical Association (AHMA). "When the OAM first opened," recalls AHMA President Rob Ivker, "they were looking for research projects to support. So I asked if they would be interested in funding the program I described in my book, *Sinus Survival.* Their first question was, 'Well, what do you use? Is it diet, homeopathy, acupuncture, herbs?' I said, 'All of the above.' And then they told me, 'We can't study that — it's not acceptable for a research project.' It seems that specific modalities was what they were looking for."

Other medical experts faulted OAM for insufficient rigor in evaluating alternative therapies. The University of North Carolina's Cassileth said she tried without success to convince fellow members of the OAM's Program Advisory Council that unconventional treatments should be subjected to the same kind of clinical testing required of experimental drugs that pharmaceutical companies submit to the Food and Drug Administration for marketing approval.

Outcomes research can be misleading, Cassileth says, because many people who undergo alternative therapies don't even have the targeted disease. Moreover, "most people with serious illnesses who seek unproven methods have already received conventional care." And finally, many such people have minor disorders that would go away even without therapy. Unless persons in the treated group are compared with those in a second, untreated group, "you never know" if the treatment actually made patients get better. [26]

However, some proponents of alternative medicine argue that unconventional therapies are not always amenable to clinical testing. Gordon, for instance, says that "double-blind, randomized, placebo-controlled studies * can be used completely appropriately for herbal remedies and perhaps even for homeopathic remedies." On the other hand, "You can't do a double-blind study on meditation. That's because you're either meditating or not meditating, and you know if you are or are not."

Perlmutter of the AHMA cites another difficulty. Pharmaceutical trials "are generally very revenue-intensive," he notes. "But the things that many alternative practitioners are engaged

* In a double-blind clinical test, patients are randomly assigned to an experimental group that gets treated or to a control group that receives a visually identical but chemically inert substance (a placebo), and neither researchers nor subjects know which group is which.

in are therapies that don't involve pharmaceuticals. As a result, there's no profit motive to justify the sort of time-consuming clinical studies that are the gold standard of medical research. The therapies we're interested in aren't patentable."

Jacobs resigned as OAM director in September 1994, charging that political interference from Harkin's subcommittee had made his position untenable. "Supporting a program is one thing, but telling you how to run it is something else," he said. "It puts you in a situation where you have congressional staff people telling you how to do research." [27] ■

Current Situation

New OAM Director

In July 1995, Wayne Jonas took over as the new OAM director.* Jonas, a lieutenant colonel in the Army, had headed the Medical Research Fellowship program at Walter Reed Army Institute of Research in Washington. Alternative-medicine advocates noted with satisfaction that he had received training in bioenergetics, homeopathy, acupuncture and spiritual healing, among other therapies, and used such treatments in his family medical practice.

By the time Jonas took command, Sen. Arlen Specter, R-Pa., had replaced Harkin as chairman of the Senate Appropriations subcommittee with jurisdiction over OAM funding.

*Alan Trachtenberg, a physician who had worked at the National Institute on Drug Abuse, served as acting director during the interregnum between Jacobs and Jonas.

Jonas said he accepted the OAM directorship because he saw it as "a win-win situation." The office, he predicted, "will provide the public with more choices in their health care, it will provide scientists with new and exciting areas to explore and it will hopefully lead to better health and reduced health-care costs." [28]

Soon after settling in, Jonas addressed the first International Congress on Alternative and Complementary Therapy, in Arlington, Va. He cautioned his listeners against accepting anecdotal reports about the efficacy of alternative treatments without getting corroborating data from trials in which individuals were not allowed to select one therapy over another.

"If patients are given a choice, there will be improvements that are not due to the actual treatment but occur because a certain type or group of patients received the treatment," Jonas declared. "The randomized, controlled trial in which patients are assigned to one therapy or another is an attempt to balance this out. From the start, you have a comparable group that is likely to get better or likely to get worse at the same rate as another group that is not receiving the treatment being tested." [29]

In October 1995, OAM announced that it was funding eight centers for alternative medicine research, each specializing in a designated area. Two similar centers had received OAM grants in September 1994. (*See table, p. 134.*)

As it approaches its fifth anniversary, OAM receives mixed performance reviews. Gordon believes it "has done extremely well, on a limited budget." At the outset, he notes, there was "virtually total unfamiliarity at NIH with the concepts, principles and practices of alternative medicine. And so I think the office has done a very good job of educating the rest of NIH and beginning the process of funding significant research."

In contrast, Perlmutter only gives OAM a grade of "fair." The office's mandate was "to evaluate alternative medicine in a disciplined way so the public would have the information it needed," he says. "Has OAM done that so far? Not to any significant degree, in my opinion."

Barrett, typically, is even more dismissive. Consumer protection rests on the premise "that if you can't prove it, you shouldn't be allowed to sell it," he reasons, but "OAM has fostered the marketing of unproven and invalid treatments."

Marijuana Controversy

However, OAM has distanced itself from what may be the most controversial alternative therapy of all — marijuana. Though not generally regarded as addictive, marijuana is classified as a Schedule I drug (along with heroin, mescaline and peyote) under the Comprehensive Drug Abuse Prevention and Control Act of 1970, meaning the government views such drugs as having no accepted medicinal value.

In his recent *New England Journal of Medicine* editorial, Kassirer urged the federal government to move marijuana to Schedule II "and regulate it accordingly." Schedule II drugs, which include cocaine, morphine and liquid injectable methamphetamine ("speed"), may be prescribed by doctors under certain restricted conditions.

The marijuana issue came to the fore last Nov. 5, when voters in Arizona and California approved ballot proposals sanctioning marijuana's use for medicinal purposes.* Barry R. McCaffrey, director of the White House Office of National Drug Control Policy, condemned the measures at a Dec. 30 news conference as "hoax initiatives" that were "not about compassion" but about "legalizing dangerous drugs."

Continued on p. 138

* The vote was 56 percent to 44 percent in California and 65 percent to 35 percent in Arizona.

At Issue:

Is marijuana appropriate for medicinal use?

PAUL ARMENTANO
Publications Director, National Organization for the Reform of Marijuana Laws (NORML)

FROM "MAKING THE CASE FOR MEDICINAL MARIJUANA," ***NORML REPORTS,*** **OCTOBER 1996.**

yes

Marijuana has been used for thousands of years to treat a wide variety of ailments. Marijuana was legal in the United States and prominent in the pharmacopoeia until 1937, when possession and use of marijuana was outlawed by the federal government. Today, eight patients receive marijuana legally from the government; for all other Americans who could benefit from its therapeutic value, it remains a forbidden medicine. The time has come to amend this injustice.

Contrary to our popular belief, there have been hundreds of studies on the medical uses of cannabis since its introduction to Western medicine in the mid-19th century. The best established medical use of smoked marijuana is as an anti-nauseant for cancer chemotherapy. During the 1980s, smoked marijuana was shown to be an effective anti-emetic in six . . . state-sponsored clinical studies. . . . Currently, many oncologists are recommending marijuana to their patients despite its prohibition.

In addition to its usefulness as an anti-emetic, there exists evidence — both scientific and anecdotal — that marijuana is a valuable aid in reducing pain and suffering for patients with a variety of other serious ailments, and that it is less toxic and costly than the conventional medicines for which it may be substituted. For example, marijuana alleviates the nausea, vomiting and the loss of appetite caused by the AIDS wasting syndrome and by treatment with AZT and other drugs without accelerating the rate at which HIV-positive individuals develop clinical AIDS or other illnesses.

It is generally accepted — by the National Academy of Sciences and others — that marijuana reduces intraocular pressure (IOP) in patients suffering from glaucoma, the leading cause of blindness in the United States. . . . There also exists historical evidence that marijuana is effective in treating a variety of spastic conditions such as multiple sclerosis, paraplegia, epilepsy and quadriplegia.

Evidence in support of marijuana's medical value has existed for centuries and has been validated by numerous studies, researchers, committees, health organizations and even the Drug Enforcement Agency's chief administrative law judge, Francis L. Young, who in 1988 declared marijuana to be "one of the safest therapeutically active substances known to man." Unfortunately, patients who could benefit from marijuana's therapeutic value have been held hostage by a federal government that continues to treat the issue as a political football. . . . American medical patients deserve better, and it is time for the federal government to begin addressing their needs.

DAN QUAYLE
Vice President of the United States, 1989-1992

FROM "LIBERAL DRUG MEASURES ARE UNSAFE MEDICINE," ***THE ARIZONA REPUBLIC,*** **NOV. 29, 1996.**

no

Several years ago, when then-Surgeon General Joycelyn Elders suggested that we consider legalizing drugs, she was widely (and properly) criticized. While most of the country continued to talk about the importance of fighting drugs, proponents of drug legalization were busy developing a strategy to accomplish their goal. Their first step: legalizing marijuana for medical use. . . .

On Nov. 5, when voters in California approved Proposition 215 and those in Arizona gave their nod to Proposition 200, supporters of drug legalization won two important battles. On the surface, these initiatives seem to make sense. They were presented to voters as an act of compassion for those suffering from diseases such as cancer, AIDS, glaucoma and multiple sclerosis. . . . Pretty straightforward, right? A simple act of compassion? Well, not exactly.

California's Proposition 215, which passed 55 percent to 45 percent and is now state law, legalized the use of marijuana for medicinal purposes. But the measure was so poorly written (perhaps intentionally) that it is riddled with loopholes and essentially legalized the use of marijuana in California.

Arizona's proposition, which passed 64 percent to 36 percent, was a bit more complicated. Cloaked in the garb of waging a tougher war on drugs, it legalized all Schedule I drugs for medicinal purposes. For those unfamiliar with the term, Schedule I drugs are those having a high potential for abuse, not currently accepted for medicinal use and unable to be prescribed. . . .

There are numerous problems associated with both of these initiatives, but two main issues are paramount. First, to put it bluntly, there is no scientific evidence that marijuana, or any other Schedule I drug, is safe or effective. That is why both propositions were opposed by virtually every doctors' organization in the country including the American Medical Association, American Cancer Society, National Multiple Sclerosis Association and American Academy of Ophthalmology. . . .

The propositions also skirted the FDA approval process. I have often been critical of the FDA's method of approving drugs, and I will no doubt continue to be so, but there is no scientific evidence to suggest that marijuana . . . is beneficial in treating illnesses. As a result, the FDA has not sanctioned it. . . .

The champions of these propositions are already taking their successful strategy to other states. All Americans, from the president on down, need to be ready to help convey the message that marijuana is a dangerous drug that is not appropriate for medicinal use.

How to Spot a Snake-Oil Salesman

Is the latest alternative therapy or preparation really effective, or is it just snake oil? Though it's often difficult to tell whether an unfamiliar health treatment is worth trying, or even safe, medical experts say it's best to avoid them if any of these red flags appear:

• Promotion of the product or therapeutic technique is through pulp magazines, newspaper ads employing a news-story format, direct-mail, telephone marketing or TV infomercials. Reputable treatments, such as those reported on in professional journals, do not advertise in such media.

• A "secret formula" is involved. Research scientists freely share their knowledge so that their peers can test the clinical results by trying to duplicate them.

• "Amazing" or "miraculous" medical breakthroughs are claimed that will produce a "quick, painless cure." Genuine breakthroughs, which are extremely rare, never are touted as such by bona fide researchers.

• Testimonials from "satisfied customers" are cited. Invariably, they either do not exist or are paid representatives who never had the problem claimed.

Continued from p. 136

A Clinton administration strategy disclosed the same day as the vote warned doctors that if they advised patients to take marijuana for therapeutic use they could be barred from participation in Medicare and Medicaid. They might even lose the right to prescribe drugs, crippling them professionally. But Attorney General Janet Reno said later that decisions on whether to bring criminal charges in such cases would be decided on an individual basis.

Some doctors took the White House to task for trespassing on what they regarded as their exclusive turf. "They can't go after the voters in California and Arizona, so they go after the medical profession," said David C. Lewis, director of the Center for Alcohol and Addiction Studies at Brown University. "Now the federal government is entering the practice of medicine, placing itself in the physician's office between the doctor and the patient." [30]

The Arizona and California measures differed in key respects. California's Proposition 215 provided that "patients or defined caregivers, who possess or cultivate marijuana for medicinal treatment recommended by a physician, are exempt from general provisions of law which otherwise prohibit possession or cultivation of marijuana." Moreover, Proposition 215 provided that physicians "shall not be punished or denied any right or privilege for recommending marijuana to a patient for medical purposes."

Arizona's Proposition 200 stated that non-violent offenders no longer would face jail for a first or second conviction on marijuana-possession charges. Instead, they would have to undergo drug treatment or education. The measure also established a Parents Commission on Drug Education and Prevention and medicalized not only marijuana but also all the other Schedule I drugs as well.

Most post-mortems on the referendums focused on Prop. 215, tacitly recognizing that California often launches nationwide trends. The provision sanctioning cultivation of marijuana for therapeutic purposes drew particular notice, including a week-long sequence in the comic strip "Doonesbury."

In turn, the cultivation issue focused the media spotlight on a San Francisco "club" that sells medicinal marijuana to its owner-members. The club, which reopened for business on Jan. 15 as the Cannabis Cultivators Club, sells the smokable variety of pot as well as such pot-imbued products as brownies, pesto sauce, gel capsules and tincture of rum.

The club, previously known as the Cannabis Buyers Club, was shut down by California Attorney General Dan Lungren during last fall's initiative campaign. On Jan. 8, Judge David A. Garcia of San Francisco Superior Court ordered the club reopened, saying it was protected under Proposition 215.

The Clinton administration, meanwhile, retreated somewhat from its initial hard-line stance on the two initiatives. In a Jan. 7 statement, the White House said that it had asked the National Academy of Sciences' Institute of Medicine to conduct an 18-month, $1 million study to "provide a comprehensive assessment of the state of scientific knowledge and to identify gaps in the knowledge base about marijuana."

Speaking in Los Angeles three days later, McCaffrey elaborated on the announcement. "There are some doctors, respected ones, who think smoked marijuana is beneficial," he said. "We need to look into it. We need to respect their opinions, too." He added, "If a scientific, medical process establishes that marijuana has a medical benefit, we will move . . . to make it available in America." [31]

Unimpressed by the administration's assurances, a group of doctors and patients supporting the medicinal use of marijuana sued senior Clinton administration officials on Jan. 14. They are seeking to block federal sanctions against doctors who recommend the drug under Prop. 215.

"The lawsuit doesn't deal with whether marijuana is efficacious as a medicine or not, or whether people should be smoking it or taking it," said one of the plaintiffs, Marcus A. Conant, an AIDS specialist in San Francisco. "The suit is all about [doctors'] freedom of speech." [32]

Action in Other States

With California hogging the marijuana spotlight, it's easy to lose sight of the fact that many other states also are trying to ease curbs on therapeutic use of the drug. Last August, for instance, Massachusetts approved a law that authorizes persons arrested for marijuana possession to present their medical histories in court as exculpatory evidence. The law also provides for a registry and research office in the state Department of Public Health that would enable registered medicinal marijuana users to use marijuana now being grown by the federal government.[33]*

"There will be some opponents who will say we're succumbing to the drug culture," Massachusetts Public Health Commissioner David Mulligan said on Jan. 20. "But we shouldn't enforce the drug laws by making the ill patients suffer. We feel people are suffering now, and we want to bring them as much comfort as we can." Mulligan and Republican Gov. William F. Weld have both urged Washington to provide their state with medicinal marijuana.

Since 1978, according to the National Organization for the Reform of Marijuana Laws (NORML), 36 states and the District of Columbia have enacted legislation similar to Massachusetts' recently passed law. The laws typically set up state-sponsored programs of therapeutic research into controlled substances, amend existing laws to permit physicians to prescribe marijuana for specified disorders or generally express support for marijuana's medicinal value.

California's Proposition 215, in NORML's view, "meets the needs of patients and doctors living in today's political climate." Moreover, the measure could "benefit more patients than any other state marijuana law to date and . . . serve as a model for other states to address the medical marijuana crisis."[34] ■

*Marijuana is grown legally at the University of Mississippi-Oxford under contract with the National Institute on Drug Abuse. Researchers there cultivate different varieties of pot under different growing conditions and also analyze batches of marijuana confiscated by federal law enforcement agencies.

FOR MORE INFORMATION

American Holistic Medical Association, 4101 Lake Boone Trail, Suite 201, Raleigh, N.C. 27607; (919) 787-5146. The association promotes holistic health care, which stresses the integration of physical, mental, emotional and spiritual concerns.

National Center for Homeopathy, 801 North Fairfax St., Suite 306, Alexandria, Va. 22314, (703) 548-7790. The center fosters the study of homeopathy by the medical and allied health professions and promotes an understanding of homeopathy among the lay public.

National Organization for the Reform of Marijuana Laws, 1001 Conn. Ave. N.W. Suite 1010, Washington, D.C. 20036; (202) 483-5500. NORML advocates eliminating all criminal penalties for personal possession, use and cultivation of marijuana.

Office of Alternative Medicine/NIH Information Center, P.O. Box 8218, Silver Spring, Md. 20907-8218; 1-888-644-6226. OAM was established in 1992 to "facilitate the evaluation of alternative medical treatment modalities" with a view to determining their efficacy and to help integrate effective treatments into mainstream medical practice.

OUTLOOK

Growing Acceptance

Medical experts generally believe that popular interest in alternative medicine, and sales of related products and services, will continue to grow for the foreseeable future. "This has been a classic consumer movement, really," says the College of Physicians' Micozzi. "The whole thing has been driven by consumers."

He hastens to add, however, that alternative medicine also is developing a firm academic base. Nearly 50 U.S. medical schools now offer instruction in alternative therapies, though most of the courses are electives. "And it's the high-caliber schools — Columbia, Harvard, Stanford, Yale — that are doing this," he says.

How doctors are taught is critical, Micozzi notes, citing the root-and-branch transformation of U.S. medical education sparked by the 1910 Flexner report. "That study gave a strong rationale to what we now call mainstream medical education," he says. "And it all stemmed from the example of just one institution, Johns Hopkins, which stressed the germ theory of disease. Within a single generation, Hopkins had become the model for educating medical students all across the country." Knowledge of alternative medicine also will spread through the continuing-education courses that doctors routinely take, Micozzi predicts.

Meanwhile, alternative medicine is winning broader acceptance by health insurers. "It's always the bottom line that drives change in this country," says Ivker of the holistic medical association. "Managed-health-care companies are looking for physicians who treat chronic disease effectively while keeping costs under control. Conventional medicine can't do either of those things, but alternative and holistic medicine can."

Alternative therapies now covered

by some insurance plans include Ayurveda, chiropractic and naturopathy. Perhaps the best-known example is a lifestyle-oriented regimen designed not only to prevent but also to reverse heart disease — without recourse to drugs or surgery. Developed by Dean Ornish, director of the Preventive Medicine Research Institute in Sausalito, Calif., the yearlong program comprises exercise, meditation, a vegetarian diet and group support. Mutual of Omaha agreed to insure patients enrolled in the Ornish program after funding a two-year study.

"To me, [heart] bypass surgery is literally bypassing the problem," said Ornish. His patients, "by addressing the cause of the problem, the lifestyle choices they make every day, are tending to actually get better and better, rather than have the problem keep coming back." [35]

Using a similar regimen, Ivker reports non-surgical results comparable to Ornish's in eliminating sinus problems. "The problem with sinus surgery is that it's not a cure," he says. "Experience shows that most people who have a sinus operation get better for only six months to a year, and then end up having surgery recommended again. I've seen many people with multiple sinus surgeries, just as you come across people who have had more than one coronary bypass procedure."

Doctors, patients and insurers are by no means the only ones who stand to profit from alternative medicine in coming years. Drug stores, supermarkets and health-food stores that stock alternative remedies also are well-positioned. Many independent and chain retailers are increasing their stocks of homeopathic medicines, herbal preparations and dietary supplements because managed-care providers are squeezing stores' profit margins on prescription drugs.

Growing popularity may well mean that alternative medicine will receive harder scrutiny in coming years. Media reports about quack remedies, many related to cancer and AIDS, serve as constant reminders of the need for care in choosing health-care providers. But the American Homeopathic Pharmaceutical Association doesn't mind the skepticism. "Good critics make good scientists think harder," says spokesman Jay Bornemann. ■

Notes

[1] David M. Eisenberg et al., "Unconventional Medicine in the United States — Prevalence, Costs, and Patterns of Use," *The New England Journal of Medicine,* Jan. 28, 1993, p. 246. Eisenberg is a member of the U.S. Office of Alternative Medicine's Program Advisory Council.

[2] Marc S. Micozzi, "The Need to Teach Alternative Medicine," *The Chronicle of Higher Education,* Aug. 16, 1996, p. A48.

[3] Jerome P. Kassirer, "Federal Foolishness and Marijuana," *The New England Journal of Medicine,* Jan. 30, 1997, p. 366.

[4] Statement issued through Executive Office of the President, Jan. 29, 1997.

[5] Oscar Janiger and Philip Goldberg, *A Different Kind of Healing* (1993), p. 40.

[6] James S. Gordon, *Manifesto for a New Medicine* (1996), p. 17.

[7] *Ibid.,* p. 285.

[8] The film was originally titled "The Burning Question," and later, "Tell Your Children." For background, see "Preventing Teen Drug Use," *The CQ Researcher,* July 28, 1995, pp. 657-680.

[9] See "Advances in Cancer Research," *The CQ Researcher,* Aug. 25, 1995, pp. 753-776; "Combating AIDS," *The CQ Researcher,* April 21, 1995, pp. 345-368.

[10] David Ferrell, "Scientists Unlocking Secrets of Marijuana's Effects," *Los Angeles Times* (Washington edition), Dec. 19, 1996, pp. A4-A5.

[11] Robert Buckman and Karl Sabbagh, *Magic or Medicine? An Investigation of Healing and Healers* (1995), pp. 9-10. See also "Alternative Medicine," *The CQ Researcher,* Jan. 31, 1992, pp. 73-96.

[12] Address before the Massachusetts Medical Society, Boston, May 30, 1860.

[13] Quoted in *Encyclopedia Americana,* Vol. 25, p. 714.

[14] Gordon, *op. cit.,* p. 170.

[15] *Ibid.,* p. 182.

[16] Flexner's 1910 study was "Medical Education in the United States and Canada." In 1930, Flexner became the first director of the Institute for Advanced Study at Princeton University.

[17] Janiger and Goldberg, *op. cit.,* p. 24.

[18] Gordon, *op. cit.,* p. 17.

[19] *Ibid.,* p. 22.

[20] James Reston, "Now, About My Operation in Peking," *The New York Times,* July 26, 1971, p. A1.

[21] For background, see "Recovered Memory Debate," *The CQ Researcher,* July 5, 1996, pp. 577-600.

[22] Bonnie Blair O'Connor, *Healing Traditions: Alternative Medicine and the Health Professions* (1995), p. 26.

[23] Quoted by Sally Satel and James Taranto, "Bogus Bee Pollen," *The New Republic,* Jan. 8, 1996, p. 24.

[24] Quoted by Eliot Marshall, "The Politics of Alternative Medicine," *Science,* Sept. 30, 1994, pp. 2000-2001.

[25] *Loc. cit.*

[26] Quoted by Stephen Budiansky, "Cures or 'Quackery': How Sen. Harkin Shaped Federal Research on Alternative Medicine," *U.S. News & World Report,* July 17, 1995, p. 48.

[27] Quoted by Charles Marwick, "Time for New Head, New Approach at OAM," *The Journal of the American Medical Association,* Dec. 21, 1994, p. 1806.

[28] Interview with Bonnie Horrigan, *Alternative Therapies,* January 1996, p. 85.

[29] Quoted by Charles Marwick, "Complementary Medicine Congress Draws a Crowd," *The Journal of the American Medical Association,* July 12, 1995, p. 106.

[30] Quoted by Christopher S. Wren, "Doctors Criticize Move Against State Measures," *The New York Times,* Dec. 31, 1996, p. D18.

[31] Remarks at luncheon sponsored by Town Hall Los Angeles, a nonprofit business group, Jan. 10, 1997.

[32] Quoted by Tim Golden, "Marijuana Advocates File Suit to Stop U.S. Sanctions," *The New York Times,* Jan. 15, 1997, p. A10.

[33] "Chemist is USA's guardian of grass," *USA Today,*" Feb. 10, 1997, p. 3A.

[34] Paul Armentano, "A Closer Look at State Efforts to Allow Marijuana as a Medicine (And How They Relate to Proposition 215)," *NORML Reports,* October 1996.

[35] Quoted in Paul Trachtman, "NIH Looks at the Implausible and the Inexplicable," *Smithsonian,* September 1994, p. 122.

Bibliography

Selected Sources Used

Books

Barrett, Stephen, and the editors of "Consumer Reports," ***Health Schemes, Scams and Frauds,*** **Consumers Union, 1990.**

Barrett, a psychiatrist in Allentown, Pa., and a board member of the National Council Against Health Fraud, has little positive to say about most alternative therapies.

Buckman, Robert, and Karl Sabbagh, ***Magic or Medicine? An Investigation of Healing & Healers,*** **Prometheus Books, 1995.**

Buckman and Sabbagh, like many other writers on alternative medicine, draw a distinction between "doctors" and "healers." A healer, by their definition, is "any person who offers help to sick people, whether trained in any branch or discipline of health care or lacking any training whatsoever." Diseases, they conclude, "need treatment, but human beings need a healer. The healer may or may not give medicine, but in virtually every situation, he or she has to give some magic as well."

Gordon, James S., ***Manifesto for a New Medicine,*** **Addison-Wesley, 1996.**

Gordon, director of the Center for Mind-Body Medicine in Washington, draws upon his own health experiences as well as those of his patients to show how he came to believe that conventional Western medicine should adopt alternative therapeutic techniques, many of which date from antiquity.

Janiger, Oscar, and Philip Goldberg, ***A Different Kind of Healing: Doctors Speak Candidly About Their Successes With Alternative Medicine,*** **G.P. Putnam's Sons, 1993.**

Janiger, a physician, and Goldberg, a writer, provide a useful overview of alternative medicine since ancient times. Numerous contemporary doctors, who unfortunately are not identified, testify to the effectiveness of the therapies highlighted by the authors.

O'Connor, Bonnie Blair, ***Healing Traditions: Alternative Medicine and the Health Professions,*** **University of Pennsylvania Press, 1995.**

Earlier in this century, O'Connor notes, the Western medical establishment assumed that modernization would crush "folk and popular systems of health beliefs and practices." She explains why the resurgence of interest in alternative medicine has been led by affluent members of society.

Articles

Budiansky, Stephen, "Cures or 'Quackery': How Senator Harkin Shaped Federal Research on Alternative Medicine," ***U.S. News & World Report,*** **July 17, 1995.**

Budiansky documents how Sen. Tom Harkin, D-Iowa, played a pivotal role in establishing the Office of Alternative Medicine and pressured it to take research shortcuts.

Cowley, Geoffrey, "Melatonin Mania," ***Newsweek,*** **Nov. 6, 1995.**

Cowley analyzes the sudden craze for melatonin, a synthetic replica of a naturally occurring hormone that is thought to hasten sleep and counterract the effects of jet lag.

Eisenberg, David M., et al., "Unconventional Medicine in the United States — Prevalence, Costs, and Patterns of Use," ***The New England Journal of Medicine,*** **Jan. 28, 1993.**

This widely cited 1990 study found that 34 percent of the respondents "reported using at least one unconventional therapy in the past year, and a third of these saw providers of alternative therapy."

Maxwell, Joe, "Nursing's New Age?" ***Christianity Today,*** **Feb. 5, 1996.**

Maxwell reports that some Christian nursing professionals are troubled by the increasing popularity of Eastern-based healing therapies, such as therapeutic touch. There are, he says, "deep divisions on, first, whether the method works, and, second, whether it is incurably tainted by non-Christian religious ideas."

Stehlin, Isadora B., "An FDA Guide to Choosing Medical Treatments," ***FDA Consumer,*** **June 1995.**

Stehlin focuses mainly on alternative therapies that either have no demonstrated benefits or have been proved dangerous, including Laetrile and coffee enemas for cancer treatments and snake venom for arthritis.

Reports and Studies

Council for Responsible Nutrition, ***The Role of Oxidants and Other Nutritional Supplements in Health Promotion and Disease Prevention,*** **December 1996.**

This paper is the transcript of a presentation by Annette Dickenson, director of scientific and regulatory affairs for the Council for Responsible Nutrition (CRN), at a scientific conference in October 1996 in Cairo, Egypt. It reaffirms CRN's position that nutritional supplements can enhance health and seeks to blunt the impact of studies suggesting that beta carotene, an anti-oxidant, may be harmful rather than beneficial to health.

Workshop on Alternative Medicine, ***Alternative Medicine: Expanding Medical Horizons,*** **1992.**

"One of the simplest and most effective ways to significantly lower health-care costs . . . is through a major focus on preventive medicine," the so-called Chantilly Report concludes. "In this clinical arena, many of the alternative health-care systems may have much to offer."

The Next Step

Additional information from UMI's Newspaper & Periodical Abstracts™ database

Alternative Medicine

Abbott, Alison, and Gabor Stiegler, "Support for scientific evaluation of homeopathy stirs controversy," *Nature,* Sept. 26, 1996, p. 285.

The German government has given a positive signal to supporters of homeopathic medicine. The European Commission also conducted a study that concluded that the efficacy of homeopathic products can indeed be proved using conventional methodology.

Dolby, Victoria, "Homeopathic treatments can help ease childhood tension & anxiety," *Better Nutrition,* September 1996, p. 24.

Many children face as much, if not more, stress than their adult counterparts. Six homeopathic ingredients that provide a convenient and effective remedy for children suffering from stress are discussed.

Gordon, James S., "How I learned to love alternative medicine," *Self,* August 1996, pp. 138-141.

Gordon, a Harvard Medical School graduate, explains how traditional Western medicine can coexist and thrive with alternative therapies such as acupuncture and hypnosis.

Griffin, Katherine, "The best of both worlds," *Health,* October 1996, p. 67.

Three options for people who are interested in alternative medicine but wary of hopping from homeopath to herbalist to hypnotist and don't want to give up the benefits of mainstream medical care are presented.

"Homeopathy gaining greater acceptance," *USA Today,* October 1996, p. 15.

The mainstream medical establishment is taking a closer look at homeopathic medicine. Homeopathy involves the use of natural substances to boost the body's own immune system.

Murray, Carolyn Kresse, "Herbal remedies," *Nursing,* December 1996, pp. 58-59.

Various herbal remedies and alternative therapies are quickly becoming mainstream medicine. Some of the popular herbal remedies and some precautions that should be taken when using them are discussed.

Murray, Frank, "A variety of children's ills often respond to homeopathic treatment," *Better Nutrition,* March 1996, p. 20.

Homeopathy, developed at the end of the 18th century by physician Samuel Hahnemann, is a complete system of medicine that aims to promote general health by reinforcing the body's own natural healing capacity. Childhood problems that may respond to various homeopathic remedies are discussed.

Sebastian, Matt, "Alternative medicine touted," *Denver Post,* June 23, 1996, p. B2.

The sixth annual alternative medicine conference held in Boulder, Colo., brought together nearly 400 doctors, nurses and healers to discuss holistic medicine.

Shelton, Deborah L., "Physicians should be aware of alternative medicine," *American Medical News,* Jan. 1, 1996, p. 21.

The American Medical Association's policy-making body recently stated that the growing popularity of alternative medicine necessitates that physicians become better informed about the unconventional treatments their patients are undergoing.

Education Programs

Langone, John, "Challenging the mainstream," *Time,* fall 1996, pp. 40-43.

An estimated 3,000 American physicians have begun to incorporate acupuncture into their practices, and hundreds more are taking courses in its use. In Europe, 62,000 medical doctors are also acupuncturists. Physicians are also learning biofeedback and meditation techniques.

Micozzi, Marc S., "The need to teach alternative medicine," *The Chronicle of Higher Education,* Aug. 16, 1996, p. A48.

Teaching students in the health professions what is known as alternative medicine is becoming increasingly necessary in the U.S. More and more people are turning to alternative medicine as they become dissatisfied with conventional health care.

Weiss, Rick, "Alternative medicine textbook is available," *The Washington Post,* Feb. 6, 1996, Sec. WH, p. 5.

Suggesting that alternative medicine is not an alternative anymore, Churchill Livingstone, a major publisher of medical texts, has released the first textbook on alternative medicine for use by students in American medical schools.

Insurance Coverage of Alternative Medicine

Hube, Karen, "More insurers pick up the tab for alternative medicine," *Money,* October 1996, p. 25.

Small and large health insurers around the U.S. are beginning to cover alternative medicine treatments, prompted by the recent turnaround in attitudes toward these forms of treatment. Tips on getting the best and most affordable care from alternative specialists are presented.

"Oxford Health Plans to Cover Alternative Care," *The New York Times,* Oct. 9, 1996, p. A11.

Oxford Health Plans said on Oct. 8, 1996, that it would add alternative medicine coverage to some of its health plans, making it the first company to form a network of practitioners offering chiropractic and massage therapy services. Oxford, which provides care to 1.4 million people through HMOs and other plans, said only practitioners who met its standards would qualify to treat members.

Whitaker, Barbara, "Now in the H.M.O.: Yoga Teachers and Naturopaths," *The New York Times,* Nov. 24, 1996, p. 11.
Alternative medicine, long on the fringes of medical care, is slowly being offered by more health plans. While most states require health insurers to cover chiropractic care, some states have gone further, requiring many insurers to cover treatments like acupuncture and naturopathy. In October 1996, Oxford Health Plans, a managed-care company based in Norwalk, Conn., announced that it would become the first medical insurer to have a network of alternative-care providers.

Medical Use of Marijuana

Brookhiser, Richard, "Lost in the weed," *U.S. News & World Report,* Jan. 13, 1997, p. 9.
Brookhiser discusses the referendums in California and Arizona that have made it legal to use marijuana as a medicine and comments on his own use of marijuana to deal with the nausea caused by his chemotherapy treatments for cancer. He asserts that opponents to the medical use of marijuana typically make three arguments, all of which are faulty.

"Government to Spend $1 Million Studying Marijuana as Medicine," *The New York Times,* Jan. 9, 1997, p. B10.
White House drug czar Gen. Barry R. McCaffrey said on Jan 7, 1997, that his office would spend up to $1 million gathering scientific evidence on the effectiveness of marijuana as medical treatment. The announcement came one week after the White House denounced the approval of laws in California and Arizona that permit the medical use of marijuana.

Manning, Anita, "Is marijuana good medicine?" *USA Today,* Jan. 3, 1997, p. D8.
In an interview, University of Arizona professor of pharmacology and toxicology Paul Consroe addresses questions regarding the legalization of medicinal marijuana.

Martin, Glen, "Medical pot sales resume in S.F.," *San Francisco Chronicle,* Sept. 14, 1996, p. A13.
Sales of medical marijuana resumed in San Francisco, Calif., on Sept. 13, 1996, — after more than a month's hiatus — through the efforts of the Healing Alternatives Foundation, which specializes in providing non-traditional medicines to AIDS sufferers.

McCaffrey, Barry, "Proposition 215 is bad medicine," *San Francisco Chronicle,* Oct. 7, 1996, p. A18.
Director of the Office of National Drug Control Policy Barry McCaffrey urges California voters to vote "no" on Proposition 215, which would legalize marijuana for medicinal use. McCaffrey believes that the legalization would bypass FDA safety regulations and put the public at risk.

Simmons, Michael "Give pot a chance," *Rolling Stone,* Dec. 26, 1996, pp. 111-113.
The war on drugs was dealt a devastating blow when Arizona and California passed ballot initiatives that will lead to major reforms in their states' marijuana laws. These initiatives may shift the debate on drugs to a realistic middle ground.

Office of Alternative Medicine

Elias, Marilyn, "Aiming acupuncture at depression," *USA Today,* March 7, 1996, p. D8.
A pioneering pilot study funded by the NIH's Office of Alternative Medicine suggests acupuncture might offer some surprising benefits for those who are clinically depressed.

Park, Robert L., and Ursula Goodenough, "Buying snake oil with tax dollars," *The New York Times,* Jan. 3, 1996, p. A15.
Park and Goodenough criticize the NIH for cloaking alternative medicine "in a mantle of NIH respectability." They argue the NIH 's Office of Alternative Medicine was created by Congress in 1992 to evaluate "unconventional medical practices." However, rather than debunking "superstition masquerading as science," it has elevated magical notions to matters of serious scientific debate.

Satel, Sally, and James Taranto, "Bogus bee pollen," *The New Republic,* Jan. 8, 1996, pp. 24-26.
The Office of Alternative Medicine is supposed to determine if the variety of unconventional remedies prescribed by alternative medicine are safe and actually effective. The agency's rejection of scientific scruples, however, may result in ineffective medicines slipping past its scrutiny, the authors write.

Friend, Tim, "Go slow on melatonin use, experts advise," *USA Today,* Aug. 13, 1996, p. D1.
Experts at a meeting sponsored by the National Institute on Aging on Aug. 12, 1996, cautioned that people should think twice about taking melatonin until scientists determine who should take it, what doses are safest and when it should be taken. Tens of millions of people take melatonin — a potent hormone secreted by the brain's pineal gland — based on unsubstantiated health claims that it alleviates sleep problems and jet lag, improves sex and extends life.

"Melatonin popular, but still unproven," *American Medical News,* Sept. 2, 1996, p. 18.
Melatonin, which has been widely publicized as a sleep aid, remains very popular even though the hormone has not been proven scientifically safe or effective. Some physicians worry about this trend since the possible negative effects of the hormone are unknown.

Back Issues

Great Research on Current Issues Starts Right Here...Recent topics covered by The CQ Researcher are listed below. Before May 1991, reports were published under the name of Editorial Research Reports.

AUGUST 1995
Job Stress
Organ Transplants
United Nations at 50
Advances in Cancer Research

SEPTEMBER 1995
Catholic Church in the U.S.
Northern Ireland Cease-Fire
High School Sports
Teaching History

OCTOBER 1995
Quebec's Future
Revitalizing the Cities
Networking the Classroom
Indoor Air Pollution

NOVEMBER 1995
The Working Poor
The Jury System
Sex, Violence and the Media
Police Misconduct

DECEMBER 1995
Teens and Tobacco
Gene Therapy's Future
Global Water Shortages
Third-Party Prospects

Back issues are available for $5.00 (subscribers) or $10.00 (non-subscribers). Quantity discounts apply to orders over ten. To order, call Congressional Quarterly Customer Service at (202) 887-8621.

Binders are available for $18.00. To order call 1-800-638-1710. Please refer to stock number 648.

JANUARY 1996
Emergency Medicine
Punishing Sex Offenders
Bilingual Education
Helping the Homeless

FEBRUARY 1996
Reforming the CIA
Campaign Finance Reform
Academic Politics
Getting Into College

MARCH 1996
The British Monarchy
Preventing Juvenile Crime
Tax Reform
Pursuing the Paranormal

APRIL 1996
Centennial Olympic Games
Managed Care
Protecting Endangered Species
New Military Culture

MAY 1996
Russia's Political Future
Marriage and Divorce
Year-Round Schools
Taiwan, China and the U.S.

JUNE 1996
Rethinking NAFTA
First Ladies
Teaching Values
Labor Movement's Future

JULY 1996
Recovered-Memory Debate
Native Americans' Future
Crackdown on Sexual Harassment
Attack on Public Schools

AUGUST 1996
Fighting Over Animal Rights
Privatizing Government Services
Child Labor and Sweatshops
Cleaning Up Hazardous Wastes

SEPTEMBER 1996
Gambling Under Attack
The States and Federalism
Civic Journalism
Reassessing Foreign Aid

OCTOBER 1996
Political Consultants
Insurance Fraud
Rethinking School Integration
Parental Rights

NOVEMBER 1996
Global Warming
Clashing Over Copyright
Consumer Debt
Governing Washington, D.C.

DECEMBER 1996
Welfare, Work and the States
The New Volunteerism
Implementing the Disabilities Act
America's Pampered Pets

JANUARY 1997
Combating Scientific Misconduct
Restructuring the Electric Industry
The New Immigrants
Chemical and Biological Weapons

FEBRUARY 1997
Assisting Refugees

Future Topics

- ***Independent Counsels***
- ***Future of Feminism***
- ***New Air Quality Standards***

THE CQ Researcher

PUBLISHED BY CONGRESSIONAL QUARTERLY INC.

Independent Counsels

Should Congress make major changes in the law?

Independent counsel Kenneth W. Starr may be at a critical stage in the Whitewater investigation. The special prosecutor reportedly is weighing evidence to decide whether to bring criminal charges against President Clinton or the first lady stemming from their involvement in the failed Arkansas development. Starr has been criticized for his outside legal work and political activities. In addition, the Whitewater investigation has provoked new criticism of the independent counsel law. Critics say the post-Watergate law costs too much, hurts innocent people and reduces public confidence in government. But supporters say the law is needed to ensure impartial investigations of misconduct by top officials. Congress is being urged to rewrite the law, and Clinton himself has said the act's costs outweigh its benefits.

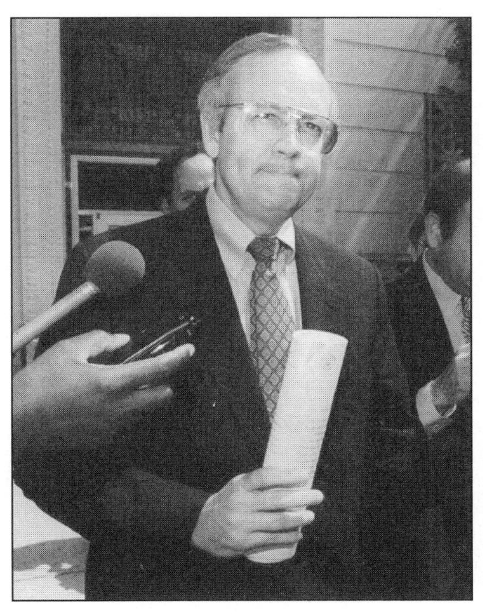

INSIDE THIS ISSUE

CQ Feb. 21, 1997 • Volume 7, No. 7 • Pages 145-168

Formerly Editorial Research Reports

COVER: WHITEWATER INDEPENDENT COUNSEL KENNETH W. STARR (REUTERS)

Feb. 21, 1997
Volume 7, No. 7

The CQ Researcher (ISSN 1056-2036). Formerly Editorial Research Reports. Published weekly (48 times per year, not printed Jan. 3, May 30, Aug. 29, Oct. 31) by Congressional Quarterly Inc., 1414 22nd St., N.W., Washington, D.C. 20037. Annual subscription rate for libraries, businesses and government is $340. Additional rates furnished upon request. Periodicals postage paid at Washington, D.C., and additional mailing offices. POSTMASTER: Send address changes to The CQ Researcher, 1414 22nd St., N.W., Washington, D.C. 20037.

Independent Counsels

BY KENNETH JOST

THE ISSUES

The blockbuster announcement came on Feb. 17, Presidents' Day: Kenneth W. Starr would leave his post as Whitewater independent counsel this summer to become dean of Pepperdine University Law School in California.

Starr had become a controversial figure since August 1994, when he began investigating President Clinton's involvement in a failed land development while governor of Arkansas and White House handling of the investigation after he became president. Clinton's supporters, and the president himself, had suggested the former Republican official was engaged in a partisan witch hunt against the president and first lady Hillary Rodham Clinton.

"There's joy in Mudville," one unidentified Clinton administration official exulted after the surprise announcement. [1]

But Starr, who reportedly had been nearing a decision on whether to file charges against the president or Mrs. Clinton, played down speculation that his resignation meant the investigation had come up empty-handed. "I would read nothing into this except it is an extraordinary opportunity for me," Starr told reporters. "I had no control over the timing," he added. [2]

Earlier in the day, Starr's office had issued a statement in his name stressing that the investigation was "proceeding without interruption." Still, legal observers could not resist the immediate speculation that Starr was unlikely to be leaving his office on the eve of a precedent-setting criminal prosecution of either the president or first lady.

Starr's departure for the post at the mid-sized Southern California law school will come after recurrent accusations that he had skirted legal ethics and pursued a political agenda while directing the Whitewater probe. Starr had largely kept a low profile, giving only a few speeches or interviews to deny wrongdoing and to stress that the investigation was continuing.

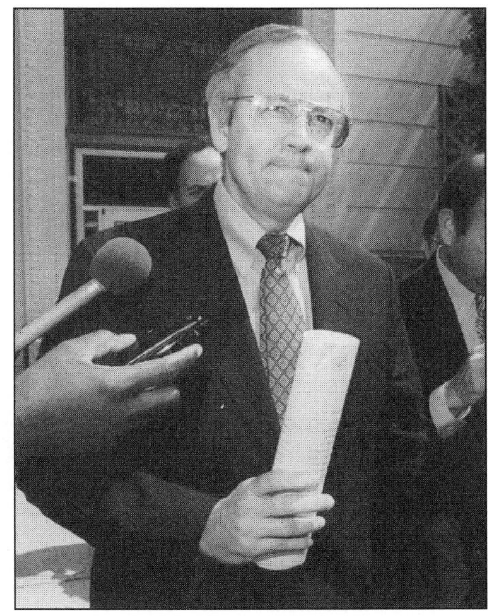

But a few days after President Clinton was re-elected for a second term, Starr sought out the public spotlight. In a speech at the prestigious Detroit Economic Club on Nov. 11, he again denied he had any partisan ax to grind. But he also laid out in more detail than ever before his view of the Whitewater case.

The Whitewater investigation, Starr told the friendly audience of business executives, centered on what he depicted as a sorry tale about "lying" and "fraud" that began with tangled financial transactions in Arkansas and may have extended to Washington. The case, he concluded, was "about the integrity of the official processes of government in Washington. . . . It is, in short, about public trust." [3]

Starr's speech did nothing to silence the Clinton partisans who had emerged as the independent counsel's loudest critics. Appearing on NBC-TV's "Meet the Press" two weeks later, Clinton's sometime political adviser James Carville vowed to start a media campaign to publicize what he called Starr's "right-wing agenda." The investigation, Carville said in the Nov. 23 broadcast, "is an entirely political thing being conducted by a partisan politician, and the American people need to know that." [4]

But Starr's continuing investigation was also contributing to a broader, less sharply partisan debate over the independent counsel law itself. Nearly two decades after its enactment, the Watergate-era law is under fire from a growing number of legal experts, journalists and public officials from both parties. The 1978 law was enacted to ensure impartial investigations of accusations of criminal misconduct by the president or other high officials. Instead, critics say, the law has spawned costly, uncontrollable scandalmongering that hurts innocent people and ultimately reduces rather than increases public trust in government.

"It's structurally flawed and has been from the beginning," says former independent counsel Joseph E. diGenova, who investigated Bush administration officials involved in searching Clinton's passport file during the 1992 campaign.

"It is now readily apparent, even to the law's staunchest original supporters," says diGenova, a former U.S. attorney, "that its triggering mechanism is too low, the number of covered persons is too great, the power of the attorney general during the preliminary investigation is too weak and the attorneys' fees provisions are not sufficient."

"The lack of checks and balances is too great," adds Abbe Lowell, a Washington lawyer who has represented public officials in misconduct cases. "The system needs to be changed."

But liberal public interest groups say the law is vital, even if changes are needed. "We need the assurance that in cases where there is going to be a clear conflict of interest in having the

'Special Counsels' Play Key Congressional Ethics Role

Their names are virtually unknown outside legal circles, but Richard J. Phelan and James M. Cole will go down in history for helping to topple one powerful Speaker of the House and to severely wound another.

It was Phelan, a Chicago trial lawyer, who laid out the financial deals that ended the political career of Jim Wright, D-Texas, in 1989. Last month, it was Cole, a former Justice Department prosecutor, who dissected the web of political fund-raising that earned Newt Gingrich, R-Ga., an ethical reprimand.

The two attorneys were serving as special counsels to the House ethics committee, brought in to investigate complex misconduct charges. In the past two decades, the use of special counsels has become standard in high-profile congressional ethics cases. And, even though they have less power than independent counsels appointed to prosecute high-level executive branch officials, the special ethics counsels have made it harder for lawmakers to ignore or ride out misconduct charges.

"It's like a breath of fresh air," Phelan says today. "It also brings to bear certain pressures that wouldn't have occurred otherwise."

"They have considerable influence in our current political and public climate," says Abbe Lowell, a Washington defense lawyer and special counsel for a House ethics case in the 1980s, "because neither a Republican or Democratic segment of Congress can afford special counsels to come out saying they have been prevented from following their course."

Unlike independent counsels in criminal cases, the special counsels used by both the House and the Senate ethics panels cannot issue subpoenas or bring charges on their own. A subpoena needs the approval of the chairman and ranking minority member of the panel; a formal charge needs the vote of the full committee.

But both Phelan and Cole are credited with critical roles in shaping the course of events for Wright, who resigned, and Gingrich, who masterminded the GOP's takeover of the House in 1994.[1] Phelan won the ethics committee's go-ahead midway through the Wright probe to expand the investigation into a wide-ranging look at his dealings with one of his key financial backers. Cole methodically documented the ties between Gingrich's political fund-raising and his ostensibly non-political activities.

Phelan and Cole had to concentrate more on behind-the-scenes negotiating skills with ethics committee members of both parties than on the courtroom lawyer's more visible abilities of arguing a case. They also had to learn to accept being overruled by the committee. Phelan wanted to charge Wright with abusing his office by intervening with federal regulators on behalf of Texas businesses, but the committee refused. Cole wanted to say Gingrich had violated tax laws and "knew" that he had provided inaccurate information to the committee. The panel opted instead to say that Gingrich should have consulted a tax lawyer and "knew or should have known" about the inaccurate information.

Both lawyers prepared lengthy reports documenting their findings of misconduct against the two Speakers. Phelan's April 1989 report concluded that Wright violated House ethics rules by accepting unreported gifts in the form of investments or loans from two financial backers and bulk purchases of his autobiography from interest groups. The report helped erode Wright's support within his own party; he resigned a month later.

In Gingrich's case, Cole laid out his findings during a five-hour ethics committee hearing on Jan. 18. The panel then voted 7-1 to recommend that Gingrich be reprimanded and fined $300,000; the full House concurred three days later.

[1] For background, see *The Washington Post*, May 22, 1989, p. A4 (Phelan); Jan. 14, 1997, p. C1 (Cole).

---

attorney general conduct an investigation, there is a mechanism for the appointment of an outside person to conduct a complete and impartial investigation," says Donald Simon, executive vice president of Common Cause.

"The law is fundamentally sound and has to be retained in some form," says Alan Morrison, a lawyer with the Public Citizen Litigation Group. "There's just no way that the Clinton administration would have investigated Whitewater [fully], just as there is no way the Reagan administration was going to investigate Iran-contra" *(see p. 158)*.

The law has long been unpopular among Republicans, who chafed under a flurry of investigations during the presidencies of Ronald Reagan and George Bush. Now, these conservative critics have been joined by Democrats who are rankled by the Whitewater probe as well as by three other independent counsel investigations of Clinton Cabinet members.

On Capitol Hill, two bills were introduced in the House on the first day of the new Congress calling for substantial changes in the law. Both measures — one from a Democrat, the other from a Republican — would make it easier for the attorney general to reject calls for a court-appointed prosecutor to take over a Justice Department probe. Both also seek to limit investigations once an independent counsel is appointed.

President Clinton himself has said the law, which expires in 1999, needs to be re-examined. "This special counsel thing ought to be reviewed," Clinton said at a Dec. 20 news conference, "because the costs outweigh the benefits."[5]

Despite the criticism, the law appears in no immediate danger of repeal. Republicans, who control both houses of Congress, are loath to be seen as criticizing Starr's investigation, which has netted a number of convictions and guilty pleas in Arkansas and has turned to examining questions about the handling of the Whitewater investigation by the White House. Starr's mandate also has widened to include possible mishandling of investigations into the 1993 firing of seven White House travel office employees and into the White House's collection of FBI files on former Republican officeholders.

In addition, administration critics are continuing to call for an independent counsel to investigate charges of illegal fund-raising in connection with President Clinton's re-election campaign. Common Cause and a number of Republican lawmakers called for an independent counsel in October, but Attorney General Janet Reno in November turned them down.

Still, Starr's investigation ensures that the role of independent counsels in examining allegations of high-level misconduct in Washington will stay in public view as President Clinton moves into his second term. As the issue is debated in Washington and elsewhere, here are some of the questions being considered:

Should Congress make it harder to appoint an independent counsel?

The independent counsel law gives the attorney general only limited discretion to refuse to apply for an outside prosecutor once an allegation of wrongdoing has been made against an official. As a result, critics say, independent counsels have been appointed in several cases where accusations were too flimsy to warrant further investigation. Supporters of the law, however, insist the investigations so far generally have been justified. In any event, they say, the limits on the attorney general's discretion protect against a politically motivated decision to quash allegations of high-level misconduct.

As originally enacted, the special prosecutor law required the attorney general to seek an outside lawyer unless a limited investigation by the Justice Department showed that the matter was "so unsubstantiated that no further investigation is warranted." Today, the standard is not quite so strict: The attorney general is required to apply for an independent counsel if a preliminary, 90-day inquiry shows there are "reasonable grounds" for further investigation.

But the law severely limits the attorney general's initial inquiry by prohibiting the use of subpoenas to obtain testimony or documents. Consequently, diGenova says, outside prosecutors are virtually inevitable whenever an accusation is made against officials covered by the act. Relying on a voluntary investigation, he says, means "no credible preliminary investigation is possible, and referral to a court is almost automatic."

In fact, attorneys general have rejected independent counsels in a few cases. When Attorney General Edwin L. Meese III asked for an independent counsel to investigate former Assistant Attorney General Theodore B. Olson in 1985 for allegedly lying to Congress during a probe of the Environmental Protection Agency (EPA), Meese refused to include two other officials in the request, saying the accusations against them were too flimsy. [6]

More recently, Attorney General William P. Barr in 1992 sidetracked a request for an independent counsel to investigate whether Bush administration officials had been involved in making U.S.-insured loans to Iraq's military for arms purchases. Instead, Barr appointed retired federal Judge Frederick B. Lacey as a "special counsel" to look into the matter; Lacey found no crime was committed. [7] And late last year, the Justice Department rejected two requests for independent counsels — one for the Democratic National Committee campaign fund-raising investigation and a second to determine whether Clinton administration officials improperly exploited immigration programs for political purposes. [8]

Still, the Justice Department's limited leeway has resulted in some independent investigations that critics say would have been less time-consuming and less expensive for all concerned if handled through normal procedures. For example, Attorney General Reno asked for an independent probe into the personal finances of the late Secretary of Commerce, Ronald H. Brown, despite doubts about evidence of criminal intent on one of the matters to be investigated. And when an independent counsel was named to investigate whether Housing and Urban Development (HUD) Secretary Henry G. Cisneros lied during his confirmation process about money he paid to a former mistress, some government lawyers said the matter would not have warranted a further inquiry under normal Justice Department policies.

Supporters of the law, however, deny that there have been too many independent investigations. "I have not seen any examples of frivolous investigations," says Charles Lewis, executive director of the Center for Public Integrity. "Has there been too much misconduct? That's my answer back."

Both bills introduced in Congress this year to rewrite the law would make it easier for attorneys general to reject calls for an independent counsel by expanding their authority during the preliminary inquiry and by giving them added leeway to conclude that no criminal intent was involved. But both bills retain the existing "reasonable grounds" standard rather than adopting a more stringent requirement to trigger a request for an independent counsel.

Critics say that changing the mechanism for appointing an independent

Continued on p. 151

A Status Report on Whitewater Cases

The Office of Independent Counsel for Whitewater and other matters has convicted three defendants and obtained guilty pleas from nine others. Three defendants pleaded guilty while Robert E. Fiske Jr. was counsel; the other cases were concluded under Kenneth W. Starr. One indictment is pending; other investigations are ongoing.

David Hale
Arkansas businessman and former municipal judge pleaded guilty March 22, 1994, to two counts of conspiring to defraud the Small Business Administration (SBA); sentenced March 28, 1996, to 28 months in prison; testified in trial of James McDougal that Clinton pressured him to make improper loan to Susan McDougal; Clinton denied accusation

Eugene Fitzhugh
Charles Matthews
Hale's associates pleaded guilty June 23, 1994, to misdemeanor bribery counts; Fitzhugh received 10 months in prison, Matthews 16 months

Robert Palmer
Madison Guaranty accountant pleaded guilty Dec. 5, 1994, to creating back-dated appraisal; probation

Webster Hubbell
Former U.S. associate attorney general pleaded guilty Dec. 6, 1994, to mail fraud and tax evasion for fraudulent billing practices at Rose Law Firm; sentenced June 28, 1995, to 21 months in prison

Neal Ainley
Ex-banker pleaded guilty May 2, 1995, to two misdemeanor counts for filing fraudulent financial documents; probation

Lawrence Kuca
Former Madison financial director pleaded guilty July 13, 1995, to one misdemeanor count for misapplying funds from Hale's company, Capital Management Services; probation

Christopher Wade
Main real estate agent for Whitewater Development Corp. pleaded guilty March 21, 1995, in unrelated bankruptcy fraud case; 15-month prison sentence. Ex-Clinton aide Stephen A. Smith pleaded guilty in June 1995 to conspiring to misuse $65,000 SBA loan; probation

James McDougal
Susan McDougal
Jim Guy Tucker
The McDougals, partners with the Clintons in Whitewater venture, were convicted May 28, 1996, along with Arkansas Gov. Tucker, of fraud and conspiracy charges tied to loans from Madison Guaranty, the now-defunct thrift owned by James McDougal; Tucker resigned as governor and was placed on probation Aug. 19 for four years; James McDougal was convicted of 18 counts, including conspiracy, fraud and false statements; sentencing delayed to April 14 because he is cooperating with prosecutors; Susan McDougal convicted on 4 felony counts and given a two-year prison term on Aug. 20; she has been in jail since Sept. 9 for contempt of court for refusing to testify before a grand jury

John Haley, William Marks Sr.
Jim Guy Tucker
Tucker, his business associate Marks and his lawyer Haley were indicted for allegedly making false statements to get SBA loans for cable-television venture; trial set for March 17 has been postponed to Sept. 22; motion for continuance pending

White House Travel Office Firings
Starr's office received authority March 22, 1996, to investigate allegations that ex-White House aide David Watkins lied about Hillary Rodham Clinton's role in May 1993 dismissals of seven travel office employees

James McDougal

Jim Guy Tucker

Herby Branscum Jr., Robert Hill
Arkansas bankers acquitted on Aug. 1, 1996, of four counts of concealing illegal contributions to Clinton's 1990 gubernatorial campaign; jury deadlocked on seven other counts; no retrial

FBI Files
Starr's office received authority Oct. 25, 1996, to investigate whether former White House counsel Bernard Nussbaum lied to congressional panel probing improper White House possession of FBI files on former Republican officials and others

Sarah M. Magner

Continued from p. 149

counsel would be a step forward, and some supporters of the law say they are open-minded on the issue. But Common Cause's Simon says any changes should not detract from the law's main objective — "to protect the public interest where there is a serious threat that an investigation by an appointee of the president will not have the credibility required."

Should Congress change the law to limit the scope of independent counsel investigations?

The independent counsel law currently requires an outside prosecutor for investigations of the president or vice president; Cabinet officers; top White House aides and officials in the Justice Department, Central Intelligence Agency and Internal Revenue Service; and officers of a president's campaign committee. The law gives independent counsels jurisdiction over all but the most minor federal crimes. And, in practice, independent counsels have expanded their investigations well beyond the original accusations.

Critics say the law is too broad, that it gives independent counsels an unrestricted hunting license that rakes in too many people and sweeps in too much of the federal criminal code. Even the law's supporters call for limiting the number of officials and crimes covered. And the Whitewater investigation has prompted calls from many observers to limit independent counsel investigations to conduct while in office — a restriction that would have severely limited the Whitewater probe.

Other supporters of the law, however, oppose these limits. They say an administration has an inevitable conflict of interest in investigating any ranking officials even those not in the top positions. And they want the independent counsel to have the same power as other prosecutors to pursue any suspected crimes uncovered during an investigation.

Several former special prosecutors are among those calling for limits. Former Watergate special prosecutor Archibald Cox says the law should apply only to the president, vice president, "key" Cabinet officers and "high-ranking" White House staff. [9] DiGenova would limit the law only to the president and vice president and their families, the attorney general and possibly other top Justice Department officials. "There is no reason to cover anybody outside the Justice Department," diGenova says.

But Lewis says that the risk of political favoritism extends to any Cabinet-level agency. "Some of our biggest political hacks wind up in the minor [departments]," Lewis says.

In their legislation, Reps. Jay Dickey, R-Ark., and John Conyers Jr., D-Mich., propose no change in the officials covered by the law. But both of their bills limit the independent counsel to the initial allegations and any charges directly related to them, such as perjury or destruction of evidence. Both bills also would require an independent counsel to obtain specific approval of additional funding after two years in office. *

Dickey notes that the 17 independent counsel investigations conducted since 1978 have cost about $115 million. "We need to treat this program just like all others," Dickey says. "It's a budget-buster if we don't."

Limiting an independent counsel's authority over ancillary offenses has broad appeal. "There is a tendency in every independent counsel investigation to have more investigations of more people than you would otherwise have," says Terry Eastland, a fellow at the conservative Ethics and Public Policy Center and author of a 1989 book on independent counsels.

Theodore Blanton, executive director of the liberal National Security Archive, defends independent counsel Lawrence W. Walsh's handling of the Iran-contra case. He nonetheless complains about the scope of the Whitewater investigation. "Why is it you need an independent counsel to try two local bankers in Arkansas?" he asks.

In a congressional hearing on the independent counsel law last February, Walsh endorsed limiting the independent counsel to conduct committed while in office. But he opposed restricting an independent counsel to matters originally referred by the attorney general. He noted that the court gave him broad jurisdiction in the Iran-contra case even though Attorney General Meese had referred only the Iran arms deal and only one individual: Oliver L. North. "To have tried to do the job with only jurisdiction over half of it would have been wasteful and very unsatisfactory," Walsh said. [10]

Walsh also opposed limits on the independent counsel's funding. He told the panel that the costs — he spent nearly $48 million during the seven-year investigation — were inevitable in assembling a separate legal staff to handle a broad-ranging, high-profile investigation.

DiGenova strongly opposes fixed limits on the length or cost of an investigation. "No self-respecting investigator will accept one of these positions with one of those types of limitations," he says.

But Eastland says costs can be reduced, and other concerns addressed, by creating a special counsel's office within the Justice Department, with a director appointed for a 10-year term just like the FBI director. "When you create [an independent counsel office] anew" for each probe, Eastland says, "you don't have what the Justice Department has now: the ability to contrast and compare cases. That would be more likely with an office that has continuity, people working from year to year, case to case."

Is Kenneth Starr conducting a fair or partisan investigation of the Whitewater case?

Since he was chosen independent counsel in August 1994, Starr has been faulted for not devoting full time to the position and for allowing some of

* Independent counsels currently have unlimited funding from the Justice Department's permanent appropriation.

Paula Jones: Clinton's Other Legal Headache

Whatever the outcome of the Whitewater investigation, President Clinton faces another legal problem left over from his days as governor of Arkansas: a sexual harassment suit.

Paula C. Jones, a former state employee, claims that Clinton made a crude sexual advance to her in a Little Rock hotel room on May 8, 1991. But Clinton has managed to delay the federal civil rights suit Jones filed nearly three years later by claiming that he is immune from civil suit as long as he is in office.

Clinton's attorneys argue that requiring a president to defend himself in a civil suit would distract him from his duties, open the door to a floodgate of litigation and allow the courts to intrude on presidential prerogatives. They want all proceedings in the suit, including the taking of depositions in pretrial discovery, delayed until after Clinton leaves the White House.

When the case was argued before the U.S. Supreme Court on Jan. 13, several of the justices were skeptical. "The notion that he doesn't have a minute to spare is not credible," Justice Antonin Scalia told Clinton's private attorney, Robert S. Bennett, early in the hour-long argument.

Acting Solicitor General Walter Dellinger also faced rough questioning when he argued in support of Clinton's plea. Justice Anthony M. Kennedy told Dellinger the president's position was unfair to Jones. "The imbalance here is very substantial," Kennedy said.

Jones, then unmarried, was working at the registration desk of a state-sponsored conference in Little Rock on the day of the alleged incident. She says that after an Arkansas state trooper asked her to come to Clinton's suite. Clinton made verbal and physical advances, including asking for oral sex. She says she refused and that, as she left the room, Clinton warned her not to tell about the incident.

When Jones first made her accusation publicly, at a news conference in January 1994, legal and political observers were generally skeptical. Three months later, when she sued Clinton in federal court in Little Rock for allegedly violating her civil rights, Bennett dismissed the allegations as "tabloid trash."

Ordinarily, plaintiffs in civil suits can take depositions from witnesses, including the defendant, before trial. But Clinton's attorneys asked to stay the litigation until Clinton leaves office.

U.S. District Judge Susan Webber Wright gave Clinton a partial victory in December 1994. She ruled that any trial would be delayed until after Clinton leaves the White House, but also held that pretrial discovery could proceed. In January 1996, the 8th U.S. Circuit Court of Appeals took away Clinton's half-victory. In a 2-1 decision, the court said discovery could proceed and that the trial need not be postponed.

The Supreme Court's decision to hear Clinton's appeal effectively put the case on hold until after the presidential election. In the meantime, however, journalistic and public opinion about the case appeared to be shifting.

On the eve of the election, Stuart Taylor Jr., senior writer for *The American Lawyer*, concluded that the evidence in support of Jones' claim was "highly persuasive." [1] In January, *Newsweek* said Jones had "believable evidence" that she had been in the room alone with Clinton. [2]

In his argument before the Supreme Court, Bennett emphasized that Clinton was not seeking to dismiss Jones' suit altogether. "All we're saying," Bennett told the justices, "is we'll give Ms. Jones her day in court, but let's not do it now." Jones' attorney, Gilbert K. Davis, countered that the president "has the same rights and responsibilities as all other citizens, including the duty to answer a lawsuit filed against him."

While several of the justices were skeptical of Clinton's position, some also worried about subjecting the president to the scheduling demands of a civil lawsuit. The arguments left many Supreme Court-watchers predicting a possible compromise decision that would allow Jones to begin gathering evidence but also limit the demands on the president. A decision is expected before the court takes a break this summer.

But legal and political observers were also predicting that any ruling short of a complete victory for Clinton's position would raise the pressure on him to settle the case rather than risk a potentially embarrassing trial.

[1] Stuart Taylor Jr., "Her Case Against Clinton," *The American Lawyer*, November 1996.

[2] Evan Thomas with Michael Isikoff, "Clinton v. Paula Jones," *Newsweek*, Jan. 13, 1997, p. 26.

his outside legal work and activities to cast doubt on his impartiality. * Critics charge specifically that:

- A month before the election, Starr spoke at an event hosted by TV evangelist Pat Robertson, one of Clinton's fiercest political opponents.
- While serving as independent counsel, Starr did legal work for groups opposed to the administration, including the tobacco industry.
- Before his appointment, Starr opposed Clinton's bid for limited immunity in Paula Jones' sexual harassment suit.
- Before accepting the appointment, Starr failed to disclose a seeming conflict of interest: the high-stakes suit against his law firm by the banking agency that started the Whitewater investigation.
- Perhaps above all, Starr, a former Republican official, was thought to harbor political ambitions that could only be enhanced, some said, by visiting misfortune on a Democratic White House.

But Starr and his supporters maintain

* Starr was chosen by the panel of three federal judges responsible for appointing independent counsels. The panel was appointed by Chief Justice William H. Rehnquist. As independent counsel, Starr receives a per diem rate equivalent to $115,700 per year.

he has done nothing to violate legal ethics rules or to taint the investigation.

Starr assumed responsibility for the Whitewater probe after the three-judge panel unexpectedly replaced the "special counsel" then handling the case, Robert B. Fiske Jr. A well-regarded Wall Street lawyer and moderate Republican, Fiske had been designated in January 1994 by Attorney General Reno to direct the investigation during the period while the independent counsel law had lapsed. * When the law was re-enacted, the panel of federal judges decided to replace Fiske, saying that his appointment by Reno created a "perceived" conflict.

A week after Starr's selection, *The Washington Post* disclosed that the judge who heads the selection panel, David B. Sentelle, had lunched the previous month with North Carolina's two conservative Republican senators: Jesse Helms and Lauch Faircloth. Faircloth, who had been one of Clinton's strongest critics on the Senate Whitewater Committee, said the two senators and Sentelle, a fellow North Carolinian, had not discussed Whitewater. But critics insisted the meeting created the appearance of a political conflict. *The New York Times* called on Starr to resign. [11]

Controversy erupted again last spring when two magazine articles raised questions about Starr's private practice and potential political conflicts. Writing in *The New Yorker,* reporter Jane Mayer stressed Starr's work for conservative organizations and corporations with interests opposed to President Clinton. [12] Mayer reported that Starr had been retained in summer 1995 by the Bradley Foundation to work on a school choice case in Wisconsin; the foundation, she noted, supports "many of Clinton's most virulent critics." She also reported that Starr's private clients included two major tobacco companies and the fruit company Chiquita Brands International; the tobacco industry was a major contributor to the Republican Party, she noted, and Chiquita Chairman Carl H. Lindner was a major contributor to Bob Dole's presidential campaign.

A few weeks earlier, investigative reporters Joe Conason and Murray Waas had disclosed what they described as a "stark" legal conflict of interest. Writing in the leftist magazine *The Nation,* they reported that when Starr accepted appointment as independent counsel, his law firm — Kirkland & Ellis — was facing a potentially costly negligence suit by the Resolution Trust Corporation (RTC) for work the firm did for a Colorado savings and loan institution. As independent counsel, Conason and Waas emphasized, Starr would be reviewing the RTC's enforcement activities in Whitewater. Even though the suit involved events before Starr joined the firm, as a partner he faced potential financial liability in the case. And while Starr served as independent counsel, the firm negotiated a settlement with the RTC, paying $700,000 on Jan. 2, 1996. [13]

The articles appeared as Starr was already in the spotlight for his outside legal work. In late February, he argued the school choice case before the Wisconsin Supreme Court; in early April, he represented the tobacco industry before the federal appeals court in New Orleans. With the controversy raging, Starr defended himself before a San Antonio lawyers' group, pointing out that almost all of the independent counsels had served part-time and maintained private practices. [14]

Later, in a detailed interview for *The ABA Journal,* Starr denied point by point that his outside legal work posed any conflict. [15] He acknowledged that he had discussed filing a brief opposing immunity for President Clinton in the Paula Jones suit, but stressed that he had dropped the idea after being named independent counsel. As for the RTC suit, Starr said that he had not known about it before accepting the counsel's position and that an outside legal adviser had concluded it posed no ethical conflict.

Many legal experts disagreed with each of Starr's rebuttals. They said that the RTC suit posed a clear conflict of interest and that Starr's political and legal work created at least an appearance of a conflict. And they noted that in the two previous investigations of a president — Watergate and Iran-contra — special prosecutors had worked full time, just as Fiske had been doing before he was replaced in the Whitewater case.

Again, *The New York Times* urged Starr to resign. [16] Again, he declined. The controversy faded, only to erupt again last fall. The new criticisms, led by Clinton adviser Carville, recapped the old complaints, including Starr's $1,750 contribution to his law firm's political action committee, which then gave money to a number of Republican candidates, including Clinton's eventual challenger, Dole. [17] In addition, Carville criticized Starr's Oct. 4 appearance at an event at the Regent University law school in Virginia Beach, Va., hosted by Robertson, a onetime Republican presidential contender and harsh critic of Clinton. [18]

Again, Starr insisted he had done nothing wrong. He told *Newsweek* that the law school speech was apolitical and that he played no role in deciding on his law firm's political contributions. [19]

Clinton himself has obliquely accused Starr of excessive partisanship. "Isn't it obvious?" Clinton replied when public TV anchorman Jim Lehrer asked him in an interview last fall whether Starr was "out to get you and Mrs. Clinton." [20] But the president did not elaborate. Starr did raise eyebrows in January 1996 when he summoned Hillary Clinton before a grand jury to answer questions about billing records from her former law firm, the Rose Law Firm in Little Rock, that were mysteriously and belatedly discovered in the White House living quarters. In

* The statute lapsed for 18 months after Republicans blocked re-enactment in December 1992, but the Democratic-controlled Congress put the law back on the books in June 1994.

the fall, Carville complained that Starr was harassing witnesses, and other critics suggested Starr was dragging out the investigation.

Starr implied that any delays resulted from uncooperative witnesses, particularly Susan McDougal, who with her former husband had been a partner in the Whitewater venture with the Clintons and who was jailed in September for refusing to testify before a grand jury. "It would have been very helpful, frankly, if each person with relevant information had simply come forward — honestly, truthfully assisted the prosecution in seeking to get at the facts, get at the truth," Starr told the Nov. 10 news conference.

Still, Starr said the investigation was making "good progress." And *The New York Times* agreed. In a December editorial defending the independent counsel statute, the paper said Starr "seems to be running an orderly investigation aimed at finding the truth." [21]

In Congress, however, both Dickey and Conyers included provisions in their bills to deal with some of the issues raised about Starr. Dickey's bill calls for the independent counsel to be full time. Conyers' directs the three-judge panel to consider possible conflicts of interest before selecting an independent counsel and also requires that at least one judge be appointed by a president of a different political party than the other two. Neither bill would apply to Starr. ■

BACKGROUND

Lessons of Watergate

Before Watergate, using private lawyers to investigate high-level government corruption was rare. According to Eastland, presidents or their attorneys general turned to special prosecutors in five previous cases, including two of the nation's most notorious political scandals: the Whiskey Ring bribery scheme under President Ulysses S. Grant and the Teapot Dome scandal of the 1920s. [22]

Those early episodes brought no proposals for regularly bypassing the Justice Department in government corruption cases. But the work of special prosecutors Cox and Leon Jaworski in breaking open the Watergate case led Congress in 1978 to enact a special prosecutor law.

Democratic National Committee Chairman Lawrence F. O'Brien called for a special prosecutor just eight days after the break-in at the party's Watergate Hotel headquarters on June 17, 1972. But President Richard M. Nixon refused. "We are doing everything we can to take this incident and to investigate it and not to cover it up," he told a news conference Aug. 29. [23]

In fact, as shown later, the president and his aides worked feverishly to contain the investigation during the 1972 presidential campaign. Later, Nixon directed a scheme of paying hush money to the Watergate burglars to try to prevent them from implicating the White House. But the scheme failed. By April 1973, the U.S. attorney's office in Washington had learned some of the details of the coverup both from some of the original defendants and from White House counsel John W. Dean III.

Nixon made a final effort to contain the scandal with his April 30, 1973, speech announcing that he had fired his two closest aides, H.R. Haldeman and John D. Ehrlichman, along with Dean. At the same time, Nixon forced Attorney General Richard G. Kleindienst to resign, ostensibly because Kleindienst would be compromised by his prior service under former Attorney General John N. Mitchell, who was also being implicated in the break-in and coverup.

With Kleindienst's resignation, Nixon was essentially forced to accept the appointment of a special prosecutor for the case. His new attorney general, Elliott L. Richardson, compiled a list of 100 candidates and — after being turned down by several candidates, including Jaworski — picked Cox, a Harvard law professor and former solicitor general under President John F. Kennedy.

The Senate Judiciary Committee closely questioned both Richardson and Cox during Richardson's confirmation hearing in May to try to guarantee Cox's independence. Cox pronounced himself satisfied that he would have full authority to investigate the scandal "wherever the trail might lead." Only five months later, however, Nixon ordered Cox fired because he refused to back away from his effort to subpoena secret tape recordings from the White House.

The Oct. 20, 1973, firing — immediately labeled "the Saturday night massacre" — touched off a firestorm of protest. But it failed to disrupt the special prosecutor's work. Less than two weeks later, Acting Attorney General Robert H. Bork — who took over after Richardson and his deputy, William D. Ruckelshaus, resigned rather than carry out Nixon's order — appointed a new prosecutor: Jaworski.

The former president of the American Bar Association (ABA) took up where Cox had left off, pursuing the fight over the tapes to the Supreme Court. Jaworski argued the case himself, and on July 24, 1974, the court unanimously ordered Nixon to turn over the recordings. The tapes disclosed Nixon's deep, personal involvement in the coverup, and on Aug. 9, 1974, Nixon resigned.

The Watergate prosecutors compiled an impressive record. More than 50 individuals and 19 corporations were convicted or pleaded guilty to charges in connection with the break-in, coverup, campaign misconduct or other activities. On Jan. 1, 1975, following the most dramatic of the trials, Haldeman, Ehrlichman, Mitchell and Robert C. Mardian of Nixon's re-election committee were con-

Continued on p. 158

Chronology

Before 1970

Private lawyers are named as special counsels in five cases of high-level misconduct, but no proposals are made for a permanent special prosecutor.

1875
President Ulysses S. Grant names special prosecutor in the St. Louis Whiskey Ring case.

1924
President Calvin Coolidge nominates and Senate confirms special counsel to investigate corruption allegations against Interior Secretary Albert B. Fall in the Teapot Dome scandal.

1970s

Watergate scandal results in enactment of first special prosecutor statute.

Oct. 20, 1973
President Richard M. Nixon orders the firing of Watergate special prosecutor Archibald Cox in the "Saturday Night Massacre." Public outcry forces Nixon to appoint Leon Jaworski as new special prosecutor on Nov. 1.

Oct. 15, 1975
Watergate special prosecutor's office issues final report after winning convictions or guilty pleas against more than 50 individuals and 19 corporations on charges relating to the Watergate break-in and coverup and illegal fund-raising in the Nixon 1972 re-election campaign.

Oct. 26, 1978
Special prosecutor provisions are signed into law by President Jimmy Carter as Title VI of Ethics in Government Act.

1980s

Independent counsel statute is invoked against more than a dozen Reagan administration officials; law is reauthorized twice by Congress and upheld by Supreme Court.

Sept. 20, 1984
White House counselor Edwin L. Meese is cleared of criminal conduct charges after independent counsel probe; Meese is confirmed as attorney general in second Reagan administration.

Dec. 19, 1986
Lawrence E. Walsh, a former federal judge, is named by appeals court panel as special prosecutor in Iran-contra case.

Dec. 15, 1987
President Ronald Reagan signs bill reauthorizing independent counsel statute while expressing doubts about its constitutionality.

June 29, 1988
Supreme Court upholds constitutionality of independent counsel statute in *Morrison v. Olson.*

1990s

Independent counsel statute is reauthorized after 18-month lapse, but then draws bipartisan criticism as Democrats join in criticizing Whitewater investigation and use of statute against three Clinton administration Cabinet members.

Dec. 15, 1992
Independent counsel statute lapses after Senate Republicans block action on reauthorization.

Jan. 13, 1994
President Clinton asks Attorney General Janet Reno to appoint an outside counsel for the Whitewater investigation; Reno on Jan. 20 selects New York lawyer Robert B. Fiske Jr.

Jan. 18, 1994
Walsh issues final report on Iran-contra case; office won seven guilty pleas and four convictions after trial, but two convictions were overturned on appeal and two others withdrawn after pardons by President Bush.

June 21, 1994
Congress completes action on reauthorization of independent counsel statute; President Clinton signs bill on June 30.

August 5, 1994
Appeals court panel chooses former Solicitor General Kenneth W. Starr as Whitewater independent counsel, replacing Fiske.

May 28, 1996
Starr wins convictions of former Clinton business partners James and Susan McDougal and Arkansas Gov. Jim Guy Tucker on 24 felony counts in first Whitewater-related trial; Clinton, in videotaped testimony, denied pressuring bankers to make illegal loan.

Nov. 29, 1996
Reno rejects requests to name independent counsel to investigate allegations of illegal fund-raising by the Democratic Party.

Feb. 18, 1997
Starr says he will leave Whitewater post by Aug. 1 to become dean of Pepperdine University Law School.

Investigations by Independent Counsels

There have been at least 17 investigations since the 1978 Ethics in Government Act authorized the use of court-appointed special prosecutors (known as independent counsels after 1982) to probe allegations of wrongdoing by high-ranking federal officials. [1]

	Subject and Dates of Investigation	Counsel	Issue	Outcome	Cost (Through March 31, 1996) [2]
Carter Administration	**Hamilton Jordan** White House chief of staff (1979-1980)	Arthur Hill Christy	Cocaine use	No charges	$182,000
Carter Administration	**Timothy Kraft** White House aide (1980-81)	Gerald J. Gallinghouse	Cocaine use	No charges	$3,300
Reagan Administration	**Raymond J. Donovan** Secretary of Labor (1981-82)	Leon Silverman	False testimony about ties to organized crime	No charges [3]	$326,000
Reagan Administration	**Edwin L. Meese III** White House counselor and attorney general designate (1984)	Jacob A. Stein	Incomplete personal financial disclosures	No charges	$312,000
Reagan Administration	**Theodore B. Olson** Assistant attorney general (1986-89)	Alexia Morrison [4]	Lying to Congress during probe of EPA	No charges	$2.1 million
Reagan Administration	**Michael K. Deaver** White House deputy chief of staff (1986-89)	Whitney North Seymour Jr.	Lying about his lobbying activities	Conviction	$1.6 million
Reagan Administration	**Iran-contra** (1986-94) Oliver L. North	Lawrence E. Walsh	Destroying documents, lying to Congress, aiding the obstruction of a congressional investigation and other matters	14 indictments: 7 guilty pleas and 4 convictions after trials [2 convictions overturned on appeal (Oliver L. North, John Poindexter) and 4 convictions nullified by pardons]; 2 indictments nullified by pardons; 1 dismissal	$47.9 million
Reagan Administration	**Wedtech** (1987-90)	James C. McKay	Illegal lobbying of White House officials (Lyn Nofziger); official actions on Wedtech's behalf (Meese)	Two indictments; one conviction (Nofziger), overturned on appeal; one acquittal; (Nofziger's partner); no charges against Meese	$2.8 million
Reagan Administration	**Confidential** (1986-1987)	Carl S. Rauh James R. Harper [5]	Confidential	No charges	$50,000

	Subject and Dates of Investigation	Counsel	Issue	Outcome	Cost (Through March 31, 1996) [2]
Bush Administration	**Confidential** (1989)	Confidential	Confidential	No charges	$15,000
	Dept. of Housing and Urban Development (1990-1996)	Arlin M. Adams, Larry D. Thompson	Perjury; conspiracy to defraud the U.S. government, obstructing a federal grand jury; illegal gratuities, false statements	13 indictments; 12 guilty pleas [11 individuals, 1 corporation;] 4 convictions after trial; 1 acquittal	$25.8 million
	Confidential (1991-1992)	Confidential	Confidential	No charges	$93,000
	Clinton passport search (1992-1995)	Joseph E. diGenova Michael Zeldin	Privacy act violation (search of passport files)	No charges	$2.8 million
Clinton Administration	**Mike Espy** Secretary of Agriculture (1994-present)	Donald C. Smaltz	Illegal gratuities	4 guilty pleas (2 individuals, 2 corporations); 2 convictions; 1 acquittal; 4 trials ongoing or pending	$5.9 million
	Whitewater (1994-present)	Robert B. Fiske Jr., Kenneth W. Starr [6]	Financial, official misconduct	Nine guilty pleas; 3 jury convictions; 2 defendants partly acquitted, mistrial on other counts; 1 trial pending; other investigations pending	$6.1 million (Fiske); $17.3 million (Starr)
	Henry G. Cisneros Secretary of Housing and Urban Development (1995-present)	David M. Barrett	False statements during confirmation process	Ongoing	$902,000
	Ronald H. Brown Secretary of Commerce (1995-1996)	Daniel S. Pearson	Personal financial improprieties	Case closed after Brown's death	$1.3 million

Total cost: $114.5 million

Note: Some indictments included more than one defendant.

1 The independent counsel law lapsed in December 1992 and was re-enacted in June 1994.

2 Cost figures are from the Congressional Research Service before 1985 and from the General Accounting Office (GAO) through March 31, 1996.

3 Donovan was later indicted by a state grand jury in New York and acquitted.

4 James McKay was originally named for this investigation but resigned a month later due to a conflict of interest.

5 Rauh served nine months and was replaced by Harper, who served two months; they were named in GAO report.

6 President Clinton ordered the appointment of a special counsel to investigate the Whitewater affair in January 1994. Attorney General Janet Reno appointed Fiske. After the independent counsel law was re-enacted, the three-judge panel replaced Fiske with Starr.

Sources: Senate Governmental Affairs Committee; General Accounting Office; Congressional Research Service

Continued from p. 155

victed of obstructing justice, and later sentenced to prison. [24]

Jaworski returned to Texas in October 1974 and was succeeded by Henry S. Ruth Jr., who had been second-in-command under both Cox and Jaworski. Ruth oversaw the office through the issuance of its final report in October 1975. Despite the office's record, the report advised against creating a permanent special prosecutor. "An independent prosecutor reports directly on prosecutions to no one, takes directions from no one and could easily abuse his power with little chance of detection," the report stated. [25]

Despite the warning, Democratic lawmakers began pushing for a permanent mechanism for appointing special prosecutors. The Senate passed a special prosecutor bill in 1976, but a House bill failed to get to the floor for a vote. The Justice Department opposed the measure under President Gerald R. Ford but shifted its stance with the election of a Democratic president, Jimmy Carter. With the administration's support, the measure cleared Congress in October 1978; Carter signed it into law on Oct. 26.

Today, legal scholars and advocates disagree on the importance of the special prosecutor in resolving the Watergate scandals. A few — most notably, Bork — argue that the U.S. attorney's office in Washington would have cracked the case by itself. "Watergate would have played out about the way it did had the U.S. attorney's office been allowed to continue," Bork wrote recently. [26]

But most legal experts say the Watergate special prosecutor was justified. "I don't think that any of us would disagree with the notion that given the constitutional crisis that confronted this country during Watergate that the independent counsel or the use of a special prosecutor was appropriate," diGenova told the House Judiciary Subcommittee on Crime last February. "I don't think anyone who ever has studied Watergate would think differently."

Other Investigations

Dozens of people have been targets or subjects of investigations by independent counsels since 1978 — ranging from high-ranking White House officials and Cabinet members to mid-level political appointees and private citizens. Most of the 17 investigations ended without indictment; six have resulted in convictions. *(See chart, p. 156.)*

The first two independent counsel investigations were straightforward and short-lived. Carter Chief of Staff Hamilton Jordan and Appointments Secretary Tim Kraft were investigated separately for cocaine use on the basis of flimsy accusations. Both men were cleared; Jordan's investigation lasted seven months, Kraft's six.

In sharp contrast, most of the 11 independent counsel investigations during the Reagan and Bush presidencies originated with diffuse accusations of misconduct, often with political overtones. The targets included some of the most important figures of the Reagan administration: Meese; senior White House aide Michael M. Deaver; and national security advisers John Poindexter and Robert C. McFarlane, among others, in connection with the Iran-contra investigation.

The investigations were also more protracted. Five of the probes spanned at least three years. The longest, Iran-contra, lasted seven. Nonetheless, seven of the 11 investigations ended with no indictments, including three confidential cases where the subjects and underlying allegations were never publicly disclosed. Other officials cleared of criminal wrongdoing included Labor Secretary Raymond J. Donovan, investigated for improper ties to organized crime figures; Assistant Attorney General Theodore B. Olson, charged with lying to Congress; and three mid-level State Department aides, among others, investigated for their role in the search of Clinton's passport file during the 1992 presidential campaign.

Meese was cleared of criminal conduct twice — once on a variety of allegations of financial misconduct while awaiting Senate confirmation as attorney general in 1984. Meese asked for the independent counsel investigation himself. The report clearing him of any criminal wrongdoing was crucial in clearing the way for Meese's confirmation to head the Justice Department in Reagan's second term. Two years later, Meese was a secondary target in a tangled financial probe centering around a New York-based defense contractor, Wedtech; the final report said Meese "probably violated the criminal law" but concluded prosecution was not warranted because Meese had no corrupt motive.

The Wedtech investigation did result in the conviction of another onetime Reagan aide: Lyn Nofziger, who was found guilty in February 1988 of violating the 1978 ethics act by lobbying on Wedtech's behalf less than a year after leaving government. But a federal appeals court overturned the conviction in June 1989, terming the lobbying restrictions too vague. Deaver also ran afoul of the post-employment lobbying restrictions. He was indicted in March 1987 for lying to Congress about his lobbying after leaving the White House and convicted in December.

Deaver received a suspended three-year prison sentence. The indictment, conviction and sentence were the first to be imposed under the independent counsel law.

Iran-contra Investigation

The criticism of the independent counsel law that simmered in the early 1980s heated up during the Iran-contra investigation. President Reagan called for an independent counsel on Dec. 2, 1986, a week after he and Attorney General

Meese confirmed reports that the administration had sold arms to Iran in an effort to free U.S. hostages and diverted proceeds from the sales to the U.S.-backed Nicaraguan rebels known as contras. The plot had been hatched by Oliver North, a Marine lieutenant colonel assigned to the White House national security staff, with the approval of McFarlane and later Poindexter.

The three-judge panel turned to a respected lawyer: Lawrence E. Walsh, who had previously been a deputy attorney general, federal judge and ABA president. Walsh, a Republican, began his work as Congress was gearing up for its own investigation.

The congressional investigation complicated, and eventually frustrated, Walsh's task. Over his objections, the joint House-Senate committee granted immunity to both Poindexter and North for their testimony. Since any use of their immunized testimony could taint a later prosecution, Walsh went to elaborate lengths to insulate his investigation from the hearing. All staff working on the North and Poindexter part of the probe were instructed to avoid any exposure to the hearings or any of the saturation media coverage of the proceedings. [27]

Walsh eventually obtained multicount indictments of both North and Poindexter and convicted both men after separate trials in 1989 and '90. By that time, he had also won convictions or guilty pleas from six other men involved in the arms deal, including McFarlane.

But the federal appeals court in Washington reversed the convictions of North and Poindexter. Despite Walsh's precautions, separate appeals panels ruled in 1990 and '91 that the trials had violated North's and Poindexter's privilege against self-incrimination because government witnesses had been — as one court put it — "thoroughly soaked" in the immunized congressional testimony.

Walsh continued with his investigations, even as conservatives said he was dragging out the probe. But President Bush dealt the investigation a final blow with a Christmas Eve 1992 pardon of six former Reagan administration officials charged in the probe, including McFarlane and former Assistant Secretary of State Elliott Abrams, who had both pleaded guilty to withholding information from Congress, and former Defense Secretary Caspar W. Weinberger, who was awaiting trial on charges of withholding his personal diaries from investigators.

Influence-Peddling at HUD

Walsh's investigation was at its midway point when an independent counsel was appointed in 1990 for another multifaceted probe: an investigation of alleged influence-peddling at HUD. The investigation was touched off by disclosures that HUD had appeared to steer contracts for building low-income housing to politically connected Republican contractors.

Over the course of six years, the investigation netted a total of 16 convictions — more than in all the previous probes combined. Those convicted included three former assistant HUD secretaries as well as Deborah Gore Dean, executive assistant to HUD Secretary Samuel R. Pierce Jr. She was convicted in October 1993 of 12 felony counts of defrauding the government, taking a bribe and lying to Congress.

Pierce himself was never charged, but independent counsel Arlin Adams later obtained an out-of-court admission from him that he created an atmosphere at HUD that permitted influence-peddling. The probe ended last year with a final conviction of former Interior Secretary James G. Watt for lying to Congress about his work as a consultant for housing contractors after leaving office.

Attacks on the Law

The HUD and Iran-contra scandals showed that independent counsels could obtain convictions in politically sensitive cases where the public might not have confidence in a Justice Department prosecution. But Walsh's spotty record in upholding convictions and the repeated use of the statute in politically charged cases fed a growing backlash against the law itself.

The law had been renewed twice during the Reagan years. In 1982, with a Republican-controlled Senate, Congress somewhat narrowed the act. In 1987, a Democratic-controlled Congress went the other way and somewhat broadened the statute. In signing the 1987 measure, President Reagan voiced doubts about its constitutionality but said he would await a court ruling on the issue.

The next year, the Supreme Court disappointed critics of the law with a decisive 7-1 ruling upholding the statute. A federal appeals court, ruling in a challenge brought by Olson against independent counsel Alexia Morrison, deemed the law an improper invasion of the president's appointment power and a violation of the separation-of-powers principle.

But in an opinion written by Chief Justice William H. Rehnquist, the Supreme Court said the Constitution's "appointments clause" allows Congress to provide for "inferior officers" to be named by lower-level executive officials or by the courts. Rehnquist also rejected the separation of powers argument, saying that Congress had not acted to enhance its own authority at the expense of the executive. [28]

In a lone dissent, Justice Antonin Scalia insisted the law infringed on the president's constitutional powers. And he warned of the risk of "irresponsible conduct" against the subjects of an investigation because of the independent counsel's single-minded focus. "How frightening it must be," Scalia wrote, "to have your own independent counsel and staff appointed, with nothing else to do but to investigate you until investigation is no longer worthwhile."

As the Iran-contra investigation dragged on, Republican lawmakers and officials stepped up their criticism of the statute. When the law came up for renewal in 1992, the Bush administration opposed reauthorization. The bills moved through the House and the Senate slowly as GOP lawmakers offered amendments aimed at curbing costs while also seeking to broaden the statute to cover members of Congress as well. On Sept. 29, in the final days before adjournment, then Senate GOP Leader Bob Dole of Kansas blocked consideration of the bill. Two months later, on Dec. 15, the law expired.

Clinton and Whitewater

Democratic lawmakers resumed work on reauthorizing the independent counsel measure in 1993, but it took 18 months to get the law back on the books. Re-enactment came only after some Republicans had a change of heart because of President Clinton's own problems with an independent counsel investigation: Whitewater.

The initial Whitewater stories linking Clinton to a failed real estate venture while governor of Arkansas generated limited interest during the 1992 campaign. But the story gathered new strength just six months into Clinton's first term after the suicide of Deputy White House Counsel Vincent W. Foster Jr. on July 20, 1993. Foster was a personal friend of the Clintons, had been a law partner of Hillary Clinton in Little Rock and had done legal work on the Whitewater venture.

The personal tragedy was transformed into a political issue after disclosures that Foster had kept Whitewater files in his White House office and that U.S. Park Service police investigating the death were denied access to his office until White House lawyers had examined the files. White House lawyers also delayed for 30 hours turning over a note in which Foster had indicated anguish about the acrimonious atmosphere in Washington. Administration critics publicly speculated that the White House was attempting to contain damaging information about the Clintons.

The controversy grew when *The Washington Post* reported on Oct. 31, 1993, that the RTC had asked the U.S. attorney's office in Little Rock to investigate whether Madison Guaranty Savings & Loan had used depositors' funds to benefit local politicians, including Clinton in his 1984 re-election campaign. [29] Then in November, Arkansas banker David Hale claimed that Clinton, while governor, had pressured him to make a federally backed $300,000 loan to Susan McDougal, one of the Whitewater partners.

Even though the independent counsel law had lapsed, Republican lawmakers began calling for an outside counsel to investigate Whitewater. Clinton and Attorney General Reno resisted, but the issue refused to go away. On Jan. 12, 1994, Clinton acceded to the pressure and instructed Reno to appoint a special counsel. Reno picked Fiske, who had been considered for the Justice Department's second-ranking post in the Bush administration but blocked by conservatives.

Fiske quickly replaced the Justice lawyers working on the case with his own staff. Two months later, Fiske won the first Whitewater-related conviction when Hale pleaded guilty to conspiring to defraud the Small Business Administration (SBA). Hale admitted that during the 1980s he had obtained SBA funding for loans made by his company, Capital Management Services, to business associates by fraudulently claiming that the loans were intended for economically disadvantaged entrepreneurs. Hale's sentencing was delayed; the plea agreement stipulated that he would cooperate with prosecutors.

Starr Takes Over

Fiske appeared to be proceeding smoothly, if slowly. But after the independent counsel statute was renewed on June 30, the three-judge panel decided on its own to replace Fiske with a prosecutor appointed under the law. Since Congress had specifically included a provision to permit Fiske's appointment under the law, the court's decision on Aug. 5 to name Starr in his place caught everyone by surprise. The puzzlement turned to controversy after the disclosure of the lunch between Sentelle and the North Carolina senators.

Starr rode out the controversy, spurning the scattered calls then — and again last spring — for him to resign. Then, with the second round of attacks ebbing, Starr's office won its first major courtroom victory in Little Rock. A federal court jury on May 28 convicted the Clintons' partners in the Whitewater venture, James and Susan McDougal, and Arkansas Gov. Jim Guy Tucker on fraud and conspiracy charges. The charges concerned loans made by the thrift owned by James McDougal, Madison Guaranty Savings & Loan, as well as by Hale's company.

The trial included Hale's first in-court accusation that Clinton had pressured him to make loans to Susan McDougal — accusations that Clinton denied in videotaped testimony used in the trial. Many jurors said they believed Clinton's denial, but the dispute had little to do with the major charges against the three defendants.

Other Officials Probed

As the Whitewater case continued, independent counsels were also appointed to investigate three Clinton Cabinet members. Agriculture Secretary Mike Espy came under investigation in September 1994 following allegations he had accepted gifts from people or companies with business before his

Continued on p. 162

At Issue:

Should Congress make major changes in the independent counsel law?

Terry Eastland
Fellow, Ethics and Public Policy Center
Author, **Ethics, Politics and the Independent Counsel**

WRITTEN FOR *THE CQ RESEARCHER,* FEBRUARY 1997

yes

The independent counsel law, I am convinced, is unconstitutional and unwise. But the Supreme Court has upheld the law, and Congress is unlikely to repeal it. So, when the law is up for renewal in 1999, the question will be whether the law can be usefully reformed or, if not, what can be put in its place.

If we are going to keep the statute, the number of "covered" persons (there are now roughly 70) should be greatly reduced. Only the most important executive figures should be covered: the president, vice president and a few key Cabinet officers, such as the attorney general. There is no good reason to suppose that the Justice Department would fail to investigate and prosecute most of the other officials now covered.

Also, the attorney general should have more discretion in deciding whether to refer a case for appointment. The A.G. should have subpoena power during the preliminary investigation to be able to make that decision on the basis of better information. The A.G. should not have to refer an allegation that, even if true, the Justice Department would not normally prosecute. And the standard for referral — the A.G. must ask for a special counsel unless there are no reasonable grounds to believe that further investigation is warranted — should be loosened.

Reforms that try to micromanage the work of a counsel — such as Archibald Cox's proposal to limit an independent counsel investigation to one year subject to court extension — have much less merit. Requiring independent counsels to work on their assignments full-time is worth consideration. But it must be noted that investigations move according to their own pace, and there may be some dead time for a full-time counsel even as the FBI or others conduct interviews and gather evidence.

My preference would be to replace the independent counsel with a new Office of Special Counsel within the Justice Department to handle allegations against many of those now covered by the law. The office would be headed by someone nominated by the president subject to Senate confirmation and given a 10-year term like the FBI director's.

This proposal would do away with many of the issues now drawing the attention of reformers. The judiciary would not have to be involved, and the counsel would be full time. He or she would have the power needed to make better informed decisions at every stage of an investigation. Most important, such an office, staffed with attorneys working on a broader range of cases, would be able to make the critical decision whether actually to seek an indictment in a more well-considered fashion.

Donald J. Simon
Executive vice president, Common Cause

WRITTEN FOR THE CQ RESEARCHER, FEBRUARY 1997

no

The underlying purpose and structure of the independent counsel — enacted as part of the comprehensive Ethics in Government Act of 1978 — remain sound. Experience under the statute has revealed the need for some refinements to be made, but the law should not be fundamentally disturbed.

The law is premised on a recognition that the attorney general is both the chief federal law enforcement official and a high-level political appointee. As the House Judiciary Committee observed when the law was enacted, these dual roles "present a fundamental conflict of interest."

It is important to recall the origin of the law. The reform flowed directly from the Watergate scandal, which generated an extraordinary crisis of public confidence in the integrity of our government. The Senate Watergate investigation that culminated in President Nixon's resignation not only exposed gross misconduct by top officials but also raised serious questions about the Justice Department's investigation of that misconduct.

The Senate Watergate report concluded, for instance, that the chief of the Justice Department's Criminal Division served as a "conduit for a constant flow of information from the grand jury and the prosecutors" to President Nixon and his counsel. Based on this evidence, the Senate Watergate Committee questioned "whether high Department of Justice officials can effectively administer criminal justice when White House personnel, or the president himself, are the subjects of the investigation."

Even if the attorney general acts with complete probity, public confidence in the investigation will never be complete because of the attorney general's inherent conflict of interest. By providing for an independent prosecutor, the law safeguards the perception, as well as the fact, of impartial justice.

No prosecutorial mechanism located within the Department of Justice and subject to the attorney general's direct control could serve these purposes as well. The public can never be sure that any office within the department would be free from the taint of political interference.

Although the law should be retained, it should also be improved. It is important to ensure that the independent counsels are free from the appearance of political conflicts. Reasonable questions have been raised about whether compensation should be paid to targets of investigations who are subsequently cleared. And Congress should review whether judicial supervision of independent counsels should be improved to ensure that investigations do not extend beyond a reasonable time, scope or cost.

But the fundamentals of the law are sound. To dismantle it would be to forget the lessons of Watergate.

Continued from p. 160

department; Espy resigned two months later, but the probe continued.

In March 1995, an independent counsel was appointed to investigate whether HUD Secretary Cisneros had lied about payments to his former mistress during his confirmation background check. Two months later, Commerce Secretary Brown also came under scrutiny. The investigation focused on suggestions that a former business partner had overpaid Brown for his share of the business, possibly to curry favor with him in his new position.

The Brown investigation was closed after he died in a plane crash in the former Yugoslavia last April. The Cisneros investigation remained largely out of public view. But the Espy probe produced its first conviction in October 1995 when Washington lobbyist James H. Lake pleaded guilty to making illegal campaign contributions to Espy's brother, Henry, when he ran for Congress from Mississippi. Almost a year later, Sun Diamond Growers, a major agricultural firm that Lake had represented, was convicted in Washington of parallel charges of making illegal contributions to Henry Espy and bestowing illegal gifts on Mike Espy while he was Agriculture secretary.

The flurry of independent counsel probes provoked a number of Democrats, including Clinton, to have second thoughts about the law. News stories in late 1995 quoted unidentified White House aides criticizing Attorney General Reno for being too willing to seek independent counsel probes; Reno responded that she was only following the law. After weeks of speculation, Clinton finally announced on Dec. 13 that he was keeping Reno in her post. At the same time, though, he called for a reassessment of the independent counsel law by people who "understand the enormous costs of the law" as well as "whatever benefits might come through it." ■

Current Situation

Waiting for Starr

When he spoke with *Newsweek* reporters shortly after the presidential election, Whitewater prosecutor Starr joked that he had "no intention of this [investigation] going into the next millennium." [30] But the protracted investigation was no joke for Clinton, who began his second term with a raft of legal problems: Whitewater itself, dual investigations by the Justice Department and a congressional committee into campaign-funding irregularities and the prospect of renewed legal action on the sexual harassment suit brought against him by Paula Jones, a former Arkansas state employee. (*See story, p. 152.*)

Despite Starr's claim in November that his office had made "very substantial progress," some observers wondered whether the investigation will end without a dramatic climax. "I think it's going to fizzle," Bob Woodward, *The Washington Post* editor who helped break the Watergate story two decades earlier, said on NBC-TV's "Meet the Press" on Jan. 26.

Both the Little Rock and Washington investigations appeared to be centering on whether the White House violated any laws in its handling of the various investigations. The three-judge panel gave Starr expanded authority last year to determine whether former White House aides had lied to federal investigators in connection with the White House travel office firings or to Congress in its probe of the FBI files scandal.

In addition, Starr was examining whether Hillary Clinton herself had tried to conceal her legal work on one of the Arkansas land deals under investigation, the Castle Grande real estate development. Mrs. Clinton had disclaimed any role in the transactions, but Rose Law Firm billing records that were discovered in the White House living quarters last August show she had at least 12 conversations about the project.

Starr's office was reported this month to be preparing a detailed memorandum summarizing the evidence against both Clintons in order to make a decision on bringing charges against either or both of them. *The Washington Post,* quoting "sources close to the investigation," said Starr had planned to begin making decisions by the end of January, but postponed any decision for several weeks after asking for revisions in the memorandum. The Post noted that Starr's office had asked for a delay in James McDougal's scheduled Feb. 24 sentencing because of "new and important information" he had provided investigators. [31]

The two other independent counsel investigations appear to pose little if any danger for the president. Independent counsel Donald C. Smaltz is continuing with his investigations of alleged influence-peddling involving former Agriculture Secretary Espy. Two top executives of a large crop-insurance company, Crop Growers Corp., went on trial in federal court in Washington on Jan. 28 on charges of trying to curry favor with Espy by funneling illegal campaign contributions to his brother's congressional campaign. But the trial ended with an acquittal on Feb. 13.

Meanwhile, independent counsel David M. Barrett is drawing criticism for taking so long to determine whether to charge Cisneros with lying about the payments to his mistress. "It does seem very long for as simple as the case appears to be," said Katy J. Harriger, a professor of politics at Wake Forest University and author of a book on independent counsels. [32] In any event, Cisneros left office in January.

Weighing the Costs

Whatever their outcome, the flurry of independent counsel investigations has provoked the broadest attacks on the law in its history. Critics from President Clinton down maintain that the act has resulted in huge costs in terms of money, time and adverse effects on politics and justice — costs that far outweigh any benefits to law enforcement or public trust in government.

Some critics emphasize the financial costs of the law, both to the government and to the people caught up in independent counsel investigations. "I saw the independent counsel running rampant, out of control, with a blank check," says Rep. Dickey, a member of the House Appropriations Committee, "and I said something's wrong."

The financial impact is especially painful for targets and witnesses in independent counsel investigations. Legal fees can quickly reach into six figures. State Department aides Janet Mullins and Steven Berry, who were cleared of wrongdoing in the Clinton passport search case, said their legal bills totaled more than $400,000 each. Bruce Lindsey, the presidential adviser who was named an unindicted co-conspirator in one of the Whitewater cases, has put his legal fees at more than $250,000. Margaret Williams, chief of staff to Hillary Clinton, claims legal fees of $250,000. [33]

President Clinton, whose own legal fees for Whitewater are now put at $3 million, vowed in a CNN interview last August to help officials in his administration pay off their bills "if it's the last thing I do." [34] The Clintons' own legal defense trust fund has raised somewhat over $1 million thus far.

"There is a problem here about financial ruin, and we don't have a solution to it," says Lewis of the Center for Public Integrity. "But it's not a function of the independent counsel law. [The same thing] can occur with an FBI or Justice Department investigation."

In one respect, however, unindicted independent counsel targets are better off than subjects of other investigations. They can apply for government reimbursement of legal fees. Mullins and Berry did and each got about $200,000.

In other respects, though, independent counsel targets are said to fare worse than subjects of ordinary prosecutions. One unique provision of the independent counsel law calls for a final report on the investigation. Some reports have criticized the target of an investigation even though no charges were brought — for example, both reports on Attorney General Meese in the 1980s.

"There have been a lot of complaints about the report provision," says diGenova, "and there will probably be more after the Whitewater investigation is over."

Most broadly, critics say the law is hurting the political system itself by discouraging people from entering government service and reducing rather than increasing public confidence in their officials. "It can be used, and occasionally has been used, as a weapon in policy disputes," Wake Forest's Harriger says.

Supporters of the law acknowledge the need to reassess some of its provisions but insist that the statute is worthwhile. "The cost of the statute," Simon of Common Cause says, "is a price we have to pay to preserve the integrity of government and to instill public confidence in investigations of high-level public officials." ■

OUTLOOK

Talk or Action?

Jacob A. Stein is a superb courtroom litigator and a knowledgeable observer of the legal scene. As an independent counsel for the first of the Meese investigations, he won high praise for a professional job in an intensely partisan atmosphere.

Today, Stein joins the critics of the independent counsel law. "The criticisms have all been established," Stein says. "The investigations go on too long. There are too many crimes covered. Too many people covered. And they appear to be incredibly expensive."

But Stein stops short of advocating repeal of the law. "It's a very close call whether it should be repealed," Stein says. He thinks the Justice Department would conduct investigations properly if the statute were wiped off the books. But, he acknowledges, "Thoughtful people think the appearance of a neutral person is important."

For much of the past two decades, critics of the independent counsel law have hoped to see it eliminated entirely, either by Congress for policy reasons or by the Supreme Court on constitutional grounds. But today even the strongest critics appear to accept the law as a fact of political life.

"It is now a fixture of American law," diGenova says. "I don't think it's feasible to repeal it."

The focus instead is on rewriting the law. But the critics also acknowledge that the calendar does not favor revision this year. "The practical fact is that the statute doesn't expire until 1999," Eastland says. "There may be hearings this year. But I don't think we'll get much serious movement."

Republicans have an additional reason for going slow on the issue: They do not want to be seen as criticizing Starr at a critical juncture of his Whitewater investigation. "Republicans view any attempt to amend the law as a slap against Ken Starr," says a Democratic legislative aide working on the issue.

The go-slow approach is somewhat ironic since even supporters of the law, including the former independent counsels who defend the law

FOR MORE INFORMATION

American Bar Association, 750 N. Lake Shore Dr., Chicago, Ill. 60611; 312-988-5000. The ABA supports continuation of the independent counsel statute with some changes.

Common Cause, 1250 Connecticut Ave., N.W., Washington, D.C. 20036; 202-833-1200. The citizens' lobbying group has been a major supporter of the independent counsel statute since its enactment.

Ethics and Public Policy Center, 1015 15th St., N.W., Suite 900, Washington, D.C. 20005; 202-682-1200. Fellow Terry Eastland is a major critic of the independent counsel law.

Public Citizen Litigation Group, 1600 20th St., N.W., 20009; 202-588-1000. The public interest law firm supports the independent counsel law.

against the critics, are calling for revisions. Iran-contra prosecutor Walsh says there have been too many independent counsels; he would limit the procedure to serious misconduct committed while in office. Watergate prosecutor Cox wants to limit the number of officials covered and to establish a presumptive time limit for investigations of one year. James McKay, who directed the Wedtech investigation, wants to limit the scope of investigations. "My basic problem is the whole things gets to snowballing," McKay says. "One allegation leads to another allegation. It can go on forever."

The two bills introduced in the House this year would address some but not all of these problems. Neither Dickey, the Republican, nor Conyers, the Democrat, included provisions to change the number of officials or the number of crimes covered by the independent counsel law. "I'm afraid if we got into that," Dickey says, "we'd get into more factions." In addition, neither bill would limit investigations to crimes committed while in office.

Instead, both bills would seek to reduce the number of independent counsel investigations indirectly by giving the attorney general power to issue subpoenas during the preliminary inquiry and more discretion to decide that accusations did not rise to the level of a crime. And — in a change opposed by even some of the critics of the law — Dickey would require independent counsels to get a specific congressional appropriation to continue an investigation after two years in office.

Supporters of the law are willing to entertain some changes as long as they do not go too far. "I don't think that revisiting the law to fine-tune it should be used as an excuse for repealing what is fundamentally a sound and important measure for assuring the integrity of criminal law enforcement," says Common Cause's Simon.

Moreover, supporters say that Congress' decision to reauthorize three times despite the increasing chorus of criticisms indicates that the measure enjoys considerable public support.

"The public is quite comfortable and satisfied with the result," says Irvin Nathan, a Washington lawyer who follows the issue for the ABA, "even though it is quite painful to the subject of an investigation." ■

Notes

[1] *The Washington Post*, Feb. 18, 1997, p. A1.
[2] Quoted in *The New York Times*, Feb. 18, 1997, p. A1.
[3] For excerpts from Starr's speech, see *The Wall Street Journal*, Nov. 13, 1996, p. A22.
[4] See *The Washington Post*, Nov. 25, 1996, p. A8.
[5] Quoted in Terry Eastland, "Democrats Change Their Mind on Independent Counsel Law," *The Wall Street Journal*, Jan. 22, 1997, p. A15.
[6] See Suzanne Garment, *Scandal: The Culture of Mistrust in American Politics* (1991), p. 104.
[7] See *The Washington Post*, Jan. 9, 1994, p. A6.
[8] See *The Washington Post*, Nov. 30, 1996, p. A1, and Dec. 5, 1996, p. A19.
[9] Archibald Cox, "Curbing Special Counsels," *The New York Times*, Dec. 12, 1996, p. A37.
[10] Walsh testified before the House Judiciary Subcommittee on Crime, Feb. 29.
[11] *The New York Times*, Aug. 18, 1994, p. A22.
[12] Jane Mayer, "How Independent Is the Counsel," *The New Yorker*, April 22, 1996, pp. 56-65.
[13] Joe Conason and Murray Waas, "Troubled Whitewater: The Dual Roles of Kenneth W. Starr," *The Nation*, March 18, 1996, pp. 13-18.
[14] See *The New York Times*, April 9, 1996, p. A19.
[15] Kenneth Jost, "Navigating the Shoals," *The ABA Journal*, July 1996, pp. 20-21. The interview with Starr was on May 28.
[16] *The New York Times*, April 17, 1996, p. A22.
[17] *The Washington Post*, March 19, 1996, p. A5.
[18] *The Washington Post*, Oct. 4, 1996, p. A2, and Oct. 5, 1996, p. A12.
[19] *Newsweek*, Dec. 2, 1996, p. 31.
[20] PBS, "The NewsHour with Jim Lehrer," Sept. 24, 1996.
[21] *The New York Times*, Dec. 20, 1996, p. A34.
[22] See Terry Eastland, *Ethics, Politics and the Independent Counsel: Executive Power, Executive Vice, 1789-1989* (1989), pp. 7-16. Outside counsel were appointed to prosecute corruption charges during Theodore Roosevelt's administration, and a special prosecutor served briefly under President Harry S Truman.
[23] Cited in Stanley Kutler, *The Wars of Watergate: The Last Crisis of Richard Nixon* (1990), pp. 191, 222.
[24] Mardian served as assistant attorney general.
[25] *Watergate Special Prosecution Force Report* (October 1975), p. 138. Ruth was succeeded by Charles Ruff, who served as special prosecutor until the closing of the office in June 1977. In December 1996, Ruff was named President Clinton's White House counsel.
[26] Robert H. Bork, "Against the Independent Counsel," *Commentary*, February 1993, p. 22.
[27] See Jeffrey Toobin, *Opening Arguments: A Young Lawyer's First Case: United States v. Oliver North* (1991), pp. 60-62.
[28] The name of the case is *Morrison v. Olson*, June 29, 1988.
[29] *The Washington Post*, Oct. 31, 1993, p. A1. This account is drawn from James B. Stewart, *Blood Sport: The President and His Adversaries* (1996), pp. 312-346.
[30] *Newsweek*, op. cit., p. 31.
[31] *The Washington Post*, Feb. 6, 1997, p. A7. The Associated Press broke the story on Feb. 5, quoting "several lawyers familiar with the probe."
[32] Quoted in *Legal Times*, Jan. 27, 1997, p. 18.
[33] See Judy Bachrach, "They Who Serve and Suffer," *Vanity Fair*, December 1996, p. 148.
[34] See *The New York Times*, Aug. 26, 1996, p. A13.

Bibliography

Selected Sources Used

Books

Eastland, Terry, *Ethics, Politics and the Independent Counsel: Executive Power, Executive Vice, 1789-1989*, National Legal Center for the Public Interest, 1989.
Eastland, who served in the U.S. Justice Department from 1983 to 1988, provides a detailed examination of the independent counsel law from its origins in the Watergate scandals through its second reauthorization in 1987. The book includes source notes and the text of the independent counsel statute as of 1987.

Garment, Suzanne, *Scandal: The Culture of Mistrust in American Politics*, Times Books, 1991.
Garment, a resident scholar at the American Enterprise Institute, argues that the use of independent counsels has been unfair to officials under investigation and has lowered rather than raised public confidence in government.

Harriger, Katy J., *Independent Justice: The Special Prosecutor in American Politics*, University of Kansas Press, 1992.
Harriger, a political science professor at Wake Forest University, discusses special prosecutors from Teapot Dome and Watergate through the independent counsel appointed under the current law. The book includes detailed source notes and a 12-page bibliography.

Jaworski, Leon, *The Right and the Power: The Prosecution of Watergate*, Reader's Digest Press, 1976.
Jaworski provides a personal memoir of his service as Watergate special prosecutor from November 1973 to October 1974. The book includes a complete status report on cases as of 1976. For other accounts of the Watergate prosecutions, see Richard Ben-Veniste and George Frampton Jr., *The Real Story of the Watergate Prosecution*, and James Doyle, *Not Above the Law*, both published in 1976.

Kutler, Stanley, *The Wars of Watergate: The Last Crisis of Richard Nixon*, Knopf, 1990.
Kutler, a historian at the University of Wisconsin, provides good accounts of the hiring and firing of special prosecutor Archibald Cox and the hiring of Leon Jaworski to succeed him in his exhaustive history of the Watergate scandals. Detailed source notes guide readers to the rest of the extensive literature on the scandals.

Stewart, James B., *Blood Sport: The President and His Adversaries*, Simon & Schuster, 1996.
After being allowed wide access to information and individuals connected to the Whitewater case, legal affairs author Stewart drew a portrait of President Clinton and Hillary Rodham Clinton widely viewed as unflattering but less than damning. The book includes a four-page listing of other published sources.

Toobin, Jeffrey, *Opening Arguments: A Young Lawyer's First Case: United States v. Oliver North*, Viking, 1991.
Toobin, now a staff writer on legal affairs for *The New Yorker*, has written a highly personalized memoir of his two years as a junior member of the Office of Independent Counsel for the Iran-contra case.

Articles

Bachrach, Judy, "They Who Serve and Suffer," *Vanity Fair*, December 1996, p. 28.
The article examines the impact of independent counsel investigations on high-level aides in the Bush and Clinton administrations.

Kladiman, Daniel, and Michael Isikoff, "The Most Dangerous Man in Washington," *Newsweek*, Dec. 2, 1996, pp. 28-34.
The article, based in part on an exclusive, three-hour interview with Whitewater independent counsel Kenneth Starr, recounts the current status of the case and outlines some of the major questions under investigation.

Spencer, Scott, "Lawrence Walsh's Last Battle," *The New York Times Magazine*, July 4, 1993, p. 11.
The 5,400-word article, based in part on interviews with Iran-contra independent counsel Lawrence Walsh, gives a detailed account of the case as Walsh was preparing his final report on the scandal.

Reports and Studies

***Final Report of the Independent Counsel for Iran/Contra Matters*, Aug. 4, 1993.**
The three-volume report includes a status report on cases, a chronology, the text of indictments issued in the case, and — in the final volume, dated Dec. 3, 1993 — formal comments by some of the subjects of the investigation or their attorneys.

House Judiciary Subcommittee on Crime, *Independent Counsel Statute and Independent Counsel Accountability and Reform Act*, Feb. 29, 1996.
The one-day hearing included testimony from nine witnesses, including: Iran-contra prosecutor Lawrence Walsh and Joseph diGenova, who investigated the State Department's search of Clinton's passport files.

***Watergate Special Prosecution Force Report*, October 1975.**
The 277-page report details the work of the Watergate special prosecutor's office. It includes a status report on cases, a comprehensive chronology and a bibliography of Watergate source materials.

The Next Step

Additional information from UMI's Newspaper & Periodical Abstracts™ database

FBI Files

Duffy, Brian, and Edward T. Pound, "Summer on the grill," *U.S. News & World Report*, July 1, 1996, pp. 24-26.
President Clinton and his aides are scrambling to explain how summaries of 407 secret FBI background files came to be in the possession of the White House.

Lardner, George Jr., "Chairman wants Starr to review testimony," *The Washington Post*, Oct. 16, 1996, p. A3.
Rep. William F. Clinger Jr., R-Pa., asked independent counsel Kenneth W. Starr on Oct. 15, 1996, to review "vague and often conflicting testimony" by seven key witnesses during House investigations of the White House travel office firings and the FBI files controversy.

Independent Counsel Law

Cox, Archibald, "Revise job description for independent counsel," *Houston Chronicle*, Dec. 13, 1996, p. A47.
Cox discusses the functions of independent counsels, recommending changes in the implementation of the independent counsel law and the scope of investigations.

Eastland, Terry, "Rule of law: Democrats change their mind on independent counsel law," *The Wall Street Journal*, Jan. 22, 1997, p. A15.
Eastland analyzes the history of the independent counsel law, which was a product of Watergate, and observes that few Democrats were critical of the law, so long as it was directed at Republican presidencies. Eastland asserts that President Clinton's comments indicating his interest in revising the statute would be more credible if he admitted his party's role in establishing the very system he now complains about.

"Keep the Independent Counsel," *The New York Times*, Dec. 21, 1996, p. A24.
An editorial argues that the 105th Congress should not pass legislation that would fundamentally weaken the independent counsel law, noting that the issue has become hot again after Attorney General Janet Reno expanded independent counsel Kenneth W. Starr's Whitewater portfolio.

Independent Counsel Probes

"A case against independent counsel," *Chicago Tribune*, May 26, 1996, p. 20.
An editorial discusses the cost of the special prosecutor investigation of the Housing and Urban Development Department (HUD), which has run up a tab of almost $21 million, saying that it is better to let normal legal processes work in such governmental investigations.

Lewis, Neil A., "Judges Allow New Inquiry Of Agriculture Officials," *The New York Times*, April 3, 1996, p. D19.
On April 2, 1996, a panel of federal judges ruled that the prosecutor investigating bribery allegations against former Agriculture Secretary Mike Espy could look into new evidence that other department officials may have done favors for industry officials in return for gifts. Attorney General Janet Reno had challenged the authority of prosecutor Donald Smaltz contending that the new evidence was beyond his charter as independent counsel .

Locy, Toni, "Fees paid in passport inquiry," *The Washington Post*, June 1, 1996, p. A6.
Taxpayers have to pay nearly $240,000 in legal bills for two former Bush administration officials, Janet G. Mullins and Elizabeth M. Tamposi, who were investigated but not indicted, in an independent counsel investigation into the search of then-presidential candidate Bill Clinton's passport records in 1992.

Locy, Toni, "Major agricultural co-op charged with trying to influence Espy," *The Washington Post*, June 14, 1996, p. A27.
Sun Diamond Growers, a large Pleasanton, Calif., agricultural cooperative, was charged with trying to illegally influence former Agriculture Secretary Mike Espy by plying him with more than $9,000 in expensive gifts. Independent counsel Donald C. Smaltz is investigating whether Espy misused his Cabinet-level position.

Kenneth W. Starr

"Clinton suggests Starr is pursuing vendetta," *San Francisco Chronicle*, Sept. 24, 1996, p. A1.
In an interview on Sept. 23, 1996, President Clinton suggested that Whitewater independent counsel Kenneth W. Starr is out to get him and first lady Hillary Rodham Clinton. His comments, meanwhile, came on a day when a federal inspector general concluded that Mrs. Clinton drafted a real estate document that was used by Madison Guaranty Savings & Loan to "deceive" federal regulators in 1986.

Jackson, Robert L., "Starr's probe expands to include travel office statements," *Los Angeles Times*, March 23, 1996, p. A11.
Events leading up to the 1993 firing of White House travel office employees took on added significance on March 22, 1996, when Whitewater independent counsel Kenneth W. Starr assumed control of an investigation to determine whether former presidential aide David Watkins made false statements to cover up the role of first lady Hillary Rodham Clinton.

Mikva, Abner J., "Whitewater's Starr is taking some things too far," *Houston Chronicle,* Aug. 21, 1996, p. A31.
Mikva asserts that the allegations in the Whitewater investigation against presidential aide Bruce Lindsey demonstrate how far independent counsel Kenneth W. Starr has strayed from appropriate limits on his duty and discretion and make clear the need to reform the independent counsel statute.

Nelson, Jack, "Carville resumes campaign against Starr," *Los Angeles Times,* Dec. 11, 1996, p. A21.
Presidential adviser James Carville renewed his blistering campaign on Dec. 10, 1996, to discredit independent counsel Kenneth W. Starr, despite earlier indications that he would back away in the face of heated GOP criticism and concern by some Democrats that the campaign is counterproductive.

Oliphant, Thomas, "Starr's unsavory smearing of a White House aide," *The Boston Globe,* June 25, 1996, p. 15.
Oliphant decries the application of the label "unindicted co-conspirator" to White House aide Bruce Lindsey by independent counsel Kenneth W. Starr in the Whitewater case, asserting that such labels are bad enough in politics and have no place in law enforcement.

Olson, Theodore B., "No 'taint' in Starr's appointment," *The Wall Street Journal,* Nov. 4, 1996, p. A23.
Olson responds to Al Hunt's Oct. 24, 1996, Politics & People article "Why the Character Issue Doesn't Cut Against Clinton." Olson defends the appointment of Kenneth W. Starr as independent counsel in the Whitewater case.

Schmidt, Susan, "Starr answers White House criticism," *The Washington Post,* Nov. 16, 1996, p. A6.
After months of public silence in the face of White House criticism, Whitewater independent counsel Kenneth W. Starr drew a parallel between himself and Watergate prosecutor Archibald Cox, who was fired on orders from President Richard M. Nixon. Starr has been criticized for being a partisan Republican.

Schmidt, Susan, "Starr given authority to widen probe," *The Washington Post,* March 23, 1996, p. A1.
Whitewater independent counsel Kenneth W. Starr was given new authority to investigate whether former presidential aide David Watkins lied about first lady Hillary Rodham Clinton's role in the White House travel office firings and whether Clinton officials obstructed justice by covering up facts.

Whitewater Investigations

Duffy, Brian, "Whitewater on the Rise," *U.S. News & World Report,* June 10, 1996, pp. 32-34.
The current state of the Whitewater investigation and how new evidence may cause trouble for first lady Hillary Rodham Clinton is discussed.

Fritz, Sarah, "Susan McDougal takes different tack in Whitewater case," *Los Angeles Times,* Sept. 21, 1996, p. A17.
Susan McDougal's refusal to testify before the grand jury or cooperate with Whitewater independent counsel Kenneth W. Starr is discussed. McDougal has been held in contempt of court and jailed for her stance.

Hohler, Bob, "Whitewater churning continues," *The Boston Globe,* June 5, 1996, p. 1.
Fallout from the Whitewater affair hit the White House from multiple fronts on June 4, 1996; convicted former Gov. Jim Guy Tucker, D-Ark., sought to strike a deal with independent counsel Kenneth W. Starr to avoid a second criminal trial, and a Senate panel released an FBI analysis that found Hillary Rodham Clinton's fingerprints on her long-missing legal bill records.

Labaton, Stephen, "Two Acquitted by Whitewater Jury; Mistrial Declared on Other Counts," *The New York Times,* Aug. 2, 1996, p. A1.
On Aug. 1, 1996, a federal jury handed a major setback to Whitewater independent counsel Kenneth W. Starr when it acquitted two Arkansas bankers of four felony counts, including charges that they conspired to conceal large cash withdrawals made during Bill Clinton's 1990 campaign for governor of Arkansas.

Pooley, Eric, "Guilty, guilty, guilty," *Time,* June 10, 1996, p. 56.
In the fraud and conspiracy trial brought by Whitewater independent counsel Kenneth W. Starr, a jury in Arkansas returned 24 guilty verdicts against former Gov. Jim Guy Tucker, D-Ark., James McDougal and Susan McDougal. Pooley discusses what effect the verdicts will have on President Clinton's re-election chances.

Simpson, Glen R., "Legal beat; McDougal is now cooperating with prosecutor on Whitewater," *The Wall Street Journal,* Aug. 16, 1996, p. B2.
Convicted Whitewater figure James McDougal is cooperating with independent counsel Kenneth W. Starr in exchange for a recommendation of leniency at his sentencing.

"Whitewater focus shifts to possible perjury," *The New York Times,* March 23, 1996, p. A9.
Whitewater independent counsel Kenneth W. Starr received formal legal authority on March 22, 1996, to investigate whether former presidential aide David Watkins lied about Hillary Rodham Clinton's role in the White House travel office affair.

Back Issues

Great Research on Current Issues Starts Right Here...Recent topics covered by The CQ Researcher are listed below. Before May 1991, reports were published under the name of Editorial Research Reports.

AUGUST 1995
Job Stress
Organ Transplants
United Nations at 50
Advances in Cancer Research

SEPTEMBER 1995
Catholic Church in the U.S.
Northern Ireland Cease-Fire
High School Sports
Teaching History

OCTOBER 1995
Quebec's Future
Revitalizing the Cities
Networking the Classroom
Indoor Air Pollution

NOVEMBER 1995
The Working Poor
The Jury System
Sex, Violence and the Media
Police Misconduct

DECEMBER 1995
Teens and Tobacco
Gene Therapy's Future
Global Water Shortages
Third-Party Prospects

Back issues are available for $5.00 (subscribers) or $10.00 (non-subscribers). Quantity discounts apply to orders over ten. To order, call Congressional Quarterly Customer Service at (202) 887-8621.

Binders are available for $18.00. To order call 1-800-638-1710. Please refer to stock number 648.

JANUARY 1996
Emergency Medicine
Punishing Sex Offenders
Bilingual Education
Helping the Homeless

FEBRUARY 1996
Reforming the CIA
Campaign Finance Reform
Academic Politics
Getting Into College

MARCH 1996
The British Monarchy
Preventing Juvenile Crime
Tax Reform
Pursuing the Paranormal

APRIL 1996
Centennial Olympic Games
Managed Care
Protecting Endangered Species
New Military Culture

MAY 1996
Russia's Political Future
Marriage and Divorce
Year-Round Schools
Taiwan, China and the U.S.

JUNE 1996
Rethinking NAFTA
First Ladies
Teaching Values
Labor Movement's Future

JULY 1996
Recovered-Memory Debate
Native Americans' Future
Crackdown on Sexual Harassment
Attack on Public Schools

AUGUST 1996
Fighting Over Animal Rights
Privatizing Government Services
Child Labor and Sweatshops
Cleaning Up Hazardous Wastes

SEPTEMBER 1996
Gambling Under Attack
The States and Federalism
Civic Journalism
Reassessing Foreign Aid

OCTOBER 1996
Political Consultants
Insurance Fraud
Rethinking School Integration
Parental Rights

NOVEMBER 1996
Global Warming
Clashing Over Copyright
Consumer Debt
Governing Washington, D.C.

DECEMBER 1996
Welfare, Work and the States
The New Volunteerism
Implementing the Disabilities Act
America's Pampered Pets

JANUARY 1997
Combating Scientific Misconduct
Restructuring the Electric Industry
The New Immigrants
Chemical and Biological Weapons

FEBRUARY 1997
Assisting Refugees
Alternative Medicine's Next Phase

Future Topics

- ***Future of Feminism***
- ***New Air Quality Standards***
- ***Alcohol Advertising***

THE CQ Researcher

PUBLISHED BY CONGRESSIONAL QUARTERLY INC.

Feminism's Future

Is the women's movement growing or losing power?

Thirty years of modern feminism have shattered old barriers in employment, education, sports and military service, bringing uncounted changes in American life. Most Americans endorse the progress, but many women resist the term "feminist." They fear being stereotyped as strident, humorless and anti-male, or worry that feminists downgrade the importance of motherhood. The women's movement, meanwhile, has spawned an array of competing organizations that disagree over such issues as abortion, pornography and the proper role for government in American life. Most attacks on feminism nowadays are heard from conservative females. But feminist leaders say that an electoral "gender gap" and high levels of political activism show that the movement is alive and even growing.

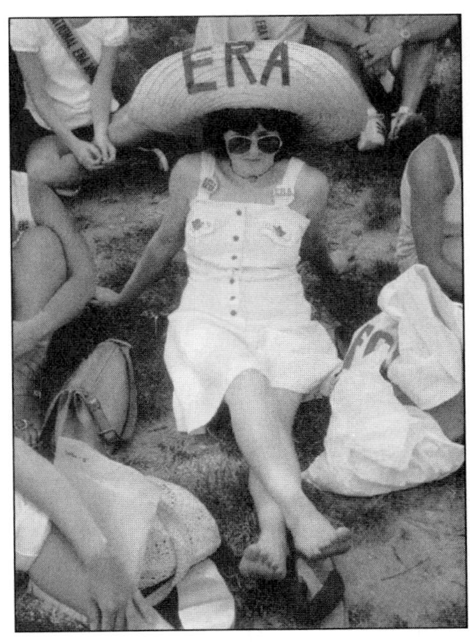

INSIDE THIS ISSUE

CQ Feb. 28, 1997 • Volume 7, No. 8 • Pages 169-192

Formerly Editorial Research Reports

COVER: A SUPPORTER OF THE EQUAL RIGHTS AMENDMENT AT THE 1978 ERA RALLY IN WASHINGTON, D.C. (© 1978 FRANK JOHNSTON, BLACK STAR, PICTURE NETWORK INTERNATIONAL)

THE *CQ Researcher*

Feb. 28, 1997
Volume 7, No. 8

EDITOR
Sandra Stencel

MANAGING EDITOR
Thomas J. Colin

ASSOCIATE EDITORS
Sarah M. Magner
Richard L. Worsnop

STAFF WRITERS
Charles S. Clark
Mary H. Cooper
Kenneth Jost
David Masci

EDITORIAL ASSISTANT
Vanessa E. Furlong

PUBLISHED BY
Congressional Quarterly Inc.

CHAIRMAN
Andrew Barnes

VICE CHAIRMAN
Andrew P. Corty

PRESIDENT AND PUBLISHER
Robert W. Merry

EXECUTIVE EDITOR
David Rapp

The CQ Researcher (ISSN 1056-2036). Formerly Editorial Research Reports. Published weekly (48 times per year, not printed Jan. 3, May 30, Aug. 29, Oct. 31) by Congressional Quarterly Inc., 1414 22nd St., N.W., Washington, D.C. 20037. Annual subscription rate for libraries, businesses and government is $340. Additional rates furnished upon request. Periodicals postage paid at Washington, D.C., and additional mailing offices. POSTMASTER: Send address changes to The CQ Researcher, 1414 22nd St., N.W., Washington, D.C. 20037.

Feminism's Future

BY CHARLES S. CLARK

THE ISSUES

At Feminist Majority headquarters in Arlington, Va., security cameras monitor the entrance for anti-abortion protesters. Posters celebrate efforts to elect more women to political office. The library stocks *Off Our Backs, Skirt!* and other feminist journals. And the mail-order service offers such products as T-shirts that proclaim "Feminism is the radical notion that women are people."

At the Independent Women's Forum, just five blocks away on the same street of this Washington suburb, the ambience — and the politics — couldn't be more different. The "virtual organization," as members describe it, is just a back room at a forum leader's law firm. Copies of the conservative *Weekly Standard* lie about, along with announcements for an upcoming anti-Clinton administration speech and *Ex Femina,* a forum publication.

Leaders of the 1,500-member forum are scattered around the nation's capital in jobs as attorneys, business owners and — last but definitely not least — stay-at-home moms. Communicating often by e-mail, they spend their energies researching, publishing and testifying against affirmative action, federal mandates for women's college sports and funding for the 1994 Violence Against Women Act.

"We concentrate on deconstructing feminism," says Executive Vice President and General Counsel Anita K. Blair. "Feminism began as a movement to improve the status of women, but it ended up as just another political interest group. A lot of what passes for feminism today is a few leaders consolidating economic power in their own interests, not the interests of a majority of women."

Blair's neighbor down the street, Eleanor Smeal, president of the 90,000-

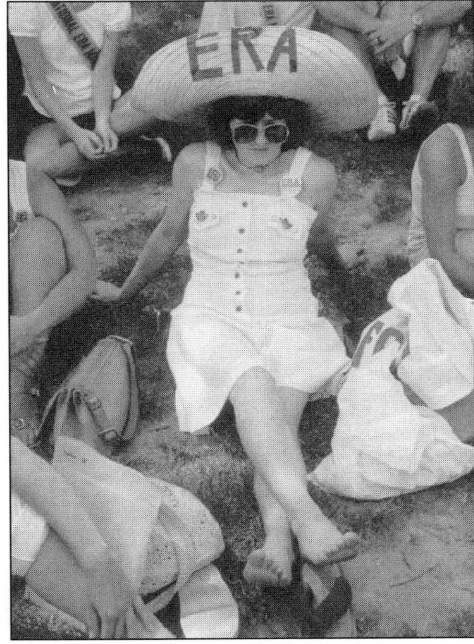

member Feminist Majority, dismisses such views as predictable from an "inside the Beltway" group of women who, in many cases, are married to prominent Republicans. "No one can attack our message of pay equity, breaking the [workplace] glass ceiling and preserving abortion rights, so they attack the messenger," she says. "And I would prefer that they attack the messenger, because even with all the darts they throw, we're registering higher in the polls." (*See table, p. 173.*)

Three decades after its birth in the 1960s, modern American feminism finds itself at a peculiar crossroads. Enthusiasts point to its undeniable improvements in the status of American women — the breaking of gender barriers in employment, education, law, sports and military service. But a steady chorus of criticism is heard from political conservatives and traditional women's and men's groups, who portray feminists as elitist, negative and out of touch with ordinary women. (*See "At Issue," p. 185.*)

There are plentiful signs that today's women's movement is mainstream and vibrant. First lady Hillary Rodham Clinton was saluted this month at a career women's luncheon organized by *Working Mother* magazine. [1] *The New Yorker* devoted a special double issue to feminist topics last year. Also in 1996, 3,000 supporters flocked to the "Feminist Expo" in Washington, D.C., where they heard pop singer and feminist icon Helen Reddy perform her 1970s anthem "I Am Woman."

But other indicators point to a movement that has stalled. "What Happened to the Women's Movement?" asked *Newsweek* in a 1994 eulogy. [2]

A recent trend among career women — staying home to raise children — has encouraged a spate of books by feminists who've had second thoughts. Anne Roiphe, author of last year's *Fruitful: A Real Mother in the Modern World,* explained her new enthusiasm for traditional motherhood by declaring that "the feminist in me says that we have failed at bringing men into the home. We have failed at sharing the experience with them." [3] As another writer recently lamented, the once symbolically assertive practice of keeping one's maiden name has been adopted by only one-fourth of married American women. [4]

A hefty 76 percent of Americans believe the women's movement has had a positive impact, according to a December NBC News/*Wall Street Journal* poll. But only 42 percent described themselves as "a supporter of the women's movement."

Such wariness is evidence of "a self-destructive chasm that exists in mainstream American women between what they believe and how they act on those beliefs," writes feminist Sherrye Henry, a Democratic Party activist who analyzed focus groups discussing the topic for her 1994 book *The Deep Divide.* [5]

One reason for the discomfort, according to Emory University historian

Who Claims the Term 'Feminist'?

"American feminism is currently dominated by a group of women who seek to persuade the public that American women are not the free creatures we think we are," writes Clark University philosophy Professor Christina Hoff Sommers.[1]

The recent attacks on feminism by conservative women have added baggage to a term that many women already hesitate to use, fearing a stereotype of strident women with unshaven legs who are lesbians or unhappy in love. "There are those who feel it has a narrow and pejorative connotation and shy away for fear of being labeled a radical, deviant person," says Susan McGhee Bailey, executive director of the Wellesley College Centers for Research on Women. "But others see it as a positive, clear description of a set of beliefs in the inherent equality of men and women and ensuring the widest range of opportunities for women and men. That's the understanding of most who use it."

Back in 1989, a poll by Yankelovich Clancy Shulman for *Time*/CNN found that only 33 percent of American women considered themselves feminists (even though 77 percent said the women's movement since the 1960s had made things better for women). A 1990 poll by Voter Research and Surveys found women more likely to consider themselves feminists if they had a postgraduate degree (32 percent) compared with 7 percent of those with only a high school degree. Similarly, women earning more than $100,000 were more likely to claim feminism (31 percent) compared with only 19 percent of those earning less than $100,000 and 14 percent of those earning $30,000-$49,000.

More recently, however, the term shows signs of gaining favor. A poll by *Redbook* magazine in 1992 found that 77 percent of its readers agreed that a woman can be both feminine and a feminist. A 1995 Harris poll for The Feminist Majority found that 51 percent approved of "feminism." "That's more than liberals, conservatives, Democrats or Republicans get," says Eleanor Smeal, the group's president. "I'll take it."

[1] Christina Hoff Sommers, *Who Stole Feminism? How Women Have Betrayed Women* (1994), p. 16.

Elizabeth Fox-Genovese, is that "most women still hope to fit their new gains at work and in the public world into some version of the story of marriage and family that they have inherited from their mothers. Thus, many women who shudder at the mounting reports of sexual abuse and violence favor a strengthening of marriage and family rather than an increase in sexual permissiveness. And the growing numbers of working mothers especially worry about what is happening to children in a world in which most mothers work outside the home." [6]

A source of frustration for women's advocates is the widespread appropriation of the word feminism — defined by *Webster's* as "organized activity on behalf of women's rights and interests" — by a feuding multitude of narrower interests. Proposals to ban pornography by University of Michigan law Professor Catherine MacKinnon appear in her 1987 book *Feminism Unmodified*. Efforts to protect First Amendment rights of the mass media are championed by the New York City-based Feminists for Free Expression. Anti-abortion activists take on the name Feminists for Life, while Christian feminists in divinity school rally around Hildegaard of Bingen, a 12th-century German abbess who struggled against the male-dominated church. [7]

Feminist theoreticians debate an array of subcategories. "Difference feminists" emphasize how men and women are born to miscommunicate, writer Katha Pollitt notes in *The Nation*. [8] "Equity feminists" concentrate on parity with men in all pursuits. "Gender feminists" rail against male hegemony. "Victim feminists," who blame a sexist society for all their problems, need to become "power feminists" who take responsibility for themselves, advises author Naomi Wolf. [9]

For many women, feminism brought the realization — especially during the 1980s — that striving to live as the "superwoman" who gives her all to career and family can mean a hectic, treadmill existence. "The idea of 'having it all' was a perversion of feminism," says Marcia Ann Gillespie, editor in chief of *Ms.*, which is celebrating its 25th anniversary this year. "What we were always talking about was having choices. Some can have the job, some have the family, but the expectation of both didn't meet the reality because there was no support system. As a result, there is a new call to activism, a rising sense that we have to do something to create a woman-friendly family and a family-friendly workplace."

Last November's elections have encouraged women's-rights advocates who believe that women make a powerful — even decisive — political force. An 11-point gender gap showed up in the vote that re-elected President Clinton. And women appear more than men to favor government solutions to problems, according to a pre-election poll sponsored by the Center for Policy Alternatives.

"The word 'feminism' has fallen into disfavor, but so will 'liberal' and 'conservative' sometime soon," says Ellen R. Malcolm, founder and president of Emily's List, a Washington group that raises funds for female Democratic candidates. But feminism's core concepts are not out of favor, she adds. "We hear lots of women talking about equality, about helping women become full and equal participants in the country."

Others say the fact that feminism provoked counter-feminism is actually a sign of the movement's maturity. "That groups such as the Independent Women's Forum feel compelled to call themselves feminists is a tribute to the women's movement," says Patricia Ireland, president of the 250,000-member National Organization for Women (NOW). "Women of all political stripes have moved to elect politicians and speak out in the press. We always said when we called for more women in power that there would be some we disagree with. But overall there is a very appealing image of many strong women working for themselves, their families and their communities."

Students of history know that "feminism had never been a tranquil movement, or a cheerfully anarchic one," writes Wendy Kaminer, a public policy fellow at Radcliffe College. "It has always been plagued by bitter civil wars over conflicting ideas." [10]

How those feminism civil wars play out in the future may be decided on the following issues:

'Women's Movement' Scores High

Nearly three-quarters of Americans approve of "The Women's Movement" but only about half view "The Feminist Movement" favorably, according to a 1995 survey of 16 key institutions and public figures.

	Favor	Oppose
The Civil Rights Movement	78%	14%
The movement to strengthen women's rights	71%	21%
The Women's Movement	69%	19%
The Pro-Choice Movement	58%	30%
The Right-to-Life Movement	57%	30%
TV news	58%	35%
The Feminist Movement	51%	34%
Those running major companies	49%	32%
The gun lobby	45%	42%
Congress	41%	48%
Anti-Abortion Movement	38%	52%
Conservative TV preachers	28%	57%

Note: Percentages do not add to 100 because some people answered "not sure" in each category.

Source: "Women's Equality Poll 1995"; poll by Louis Harris for The Feminist Majority Foundation based on interviews with 1,364 adults from March 1 to April 3, 1995.

Is sexism still a big problem for most women?

Support for feminism boils down to whether or not one feels that females in society get a raw deal. Complexity comes, however, from the fact that for most women, the picture is mixed. "We have made great strides, and that excites me," says Judith L. Lichtman, president of the Women's Legal Defense Fund. "There is a world of difference since the early 1970s, when the classified ads still divided jobs between women and men — and guess which ones paid more. There were back-alley abortions, no sexual harassment laws and you could be fired if you got pregnant. Many of these changes were instigated by the women's movement.

"And though we have come far, we have far to go," Lichtman says. "Just look at today's headlines: sexual harassment at Mitsubishi [auto plant in Illinois] and grocery store chains paying large settlements for job discrimination." [11] Lichtman says she hears from women around the country who are struggling to "make a decent living and balance life with their families. They are worried about how to provide health care and security in retirement."

Women still earn an average of only 71 cents on the dollar earned by men, according to the Labor Department's Women's Bureau. And the number of women age 19 and over who live in poverty is 14.1 million, vs. only 8.6 million men.

In the executive suites, women still constitute only 5 percent of senior managers at the top 2,000 companies, according to the federal government's Glass Ceiling Commission Report in 1995. [12] And only 50 of the nation's 2,500 top-earning executives are women, according to a study released last fall. [13]

In academia, the percentage of female tenured professors stands at only 24 percent, up from 18 percent in 1975, according to Ernest Benjamin, director of research at the American Association of University Professors. (He cautions, however, that full tenure nowadays is being granted to progressively fewer candidates overall, and that women have accounted for a dramatic two-thirds of the rise in the number of untenured professors.)

In politics, women currently make up just 11 percent of Congress (nine senators and 51 House members). On the state level, they hold 1,584 legislative seats, or 21.3 percent of the total, though their numbers have increased fivefold since 1969, according to the Center for the American Woman and Politics at Rutgers University.

In the news media, according to liberal-leaning Fairness and Accuracy

U.S. Women Making Progress

The number of female-owned businesses rose from less than a half-million in 1972 to nearly 8 million last year. Nearly half of all law degrees awarded in 1994 went to women, compared with less than 7 percent in 1992.

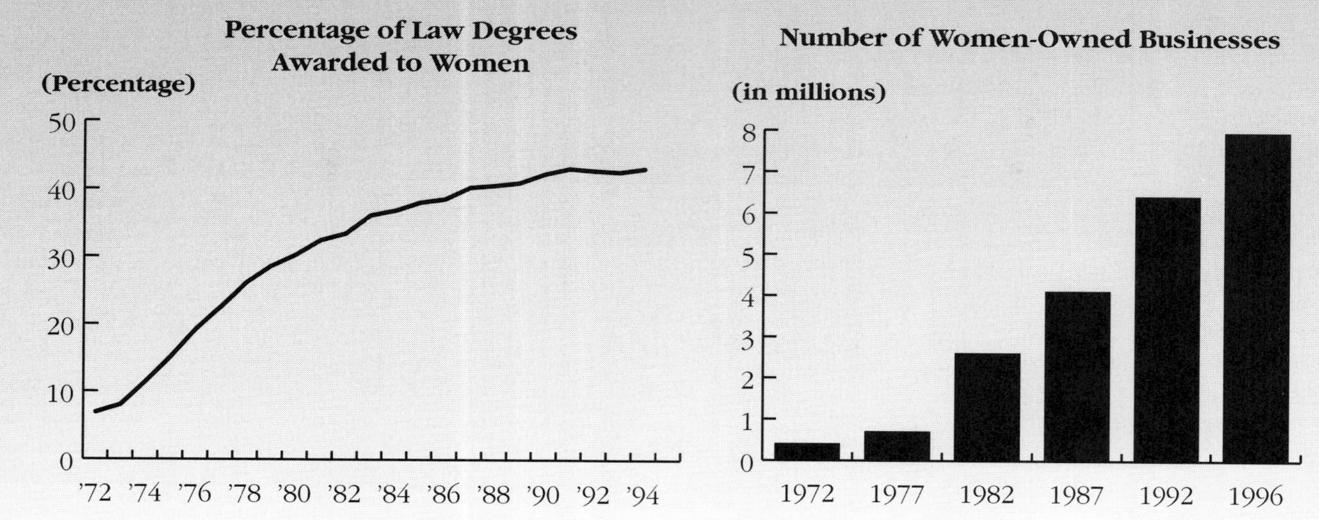

Sources: "Women's Figures: The Economic Progress of Women in America," Independent Women's Forum, 1996, based on data from U.S. Department of Education and U.S. Bureau of the Census

in Reporting (FAIR), of 185 leading independent journalists and syndicated columnists, only 39, or 21 percent, are women. A count of six months' worth of non-staff opinion pieces printed by *The New York Times* in 1995 showed that "men wrote 93 percent of all the columns on the nation's most prestigious op-ed page," the group says. [14]

To this portrait of a glass less than full can be added data on women's successes. An Independent Women's Forum compendium released last fall argues that "women are quickly closing in." It asserts that:

- women are now earning more than half of all college degrees — and nearly 40 percent of the medical school degrees (Last year 54 percent of the class admitted to Yale University Medical School were women);
- among wage-earners ages 27-33 who have never had children, women's earnings approach 98 percent of men's, according to data from the federal government's National Longitudinal Survey of Youth;
- From 1920-1980, women's wages grew at a rate 20 percent faster than men's, says the Labor Department. [15]

The scarcity of women in top corporate jobs is explained by some as understandable — at least for the time being — given that women with the requisite education and job experience are still too few, and too young, in comparison with men; one survey showed that the average age of senior corporate women was only 44, while the average age of CEOs was 56. [16]

"Women have the opportunity to earn as much as men . . . but they often have different goals and values," says the 500,000-member conservative group Concerned Women for America. "The fact that more women are in lower-paying professions is not due to rampant discrimination, as the feminists charge. . . . Many women chose such professions voluntarily because they have decided to keep their families the top priority in their lives."

But many of the reports showing women on par with men are based on one-sided studies designed to "show that government action is no longer necessary," says Heidi I. Hartmann, director of the Institute for Women's Policy Research. "They misleadingly say 'Government data show,' as if you could call up the government and get the data, when in fact, the study in question was a manipulation of the data by two researchers."

There is some truth, Hartmann says, to the notion that single, childless women earn more than the average 71 cents on the male's dollar, but that's been true among younger people for 50 years. "The question is what happens when those young women become old. The jury is still out on that. In fact, there has been little change in that 71-cent figure over the past five years, which is a reason why feminists are concerned. Women are becoming more like men in their education and career skills, so the two should be drawing steadily closer."

Blair counters that much of the data suggesting disadvantages for women are "exaggerated by feminists who want more government programs. As women get more into business ownership, they won't feel so warm and fuzzy about government," she says.

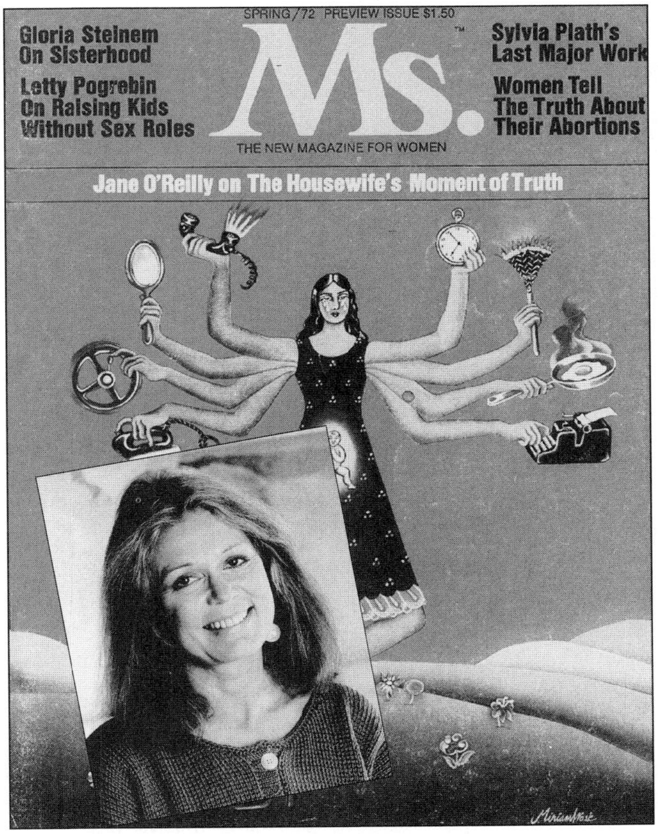

Polling data on sexism is contradictory. A November survey of 1,200 adults by The Polling Company for the Independent Women's Forum showed that only 26 percent agreed that society has a gender bias against women; 62 percent said the opportunities for both men and women are the same.

Yet a survey and questionnaire sent to 250,000 workers by the Labor Department in 1994 showed that 61 percent of working women said they had little or no ability to advance; 65 percent said improving pay scales is their top priority; 56 percent of those with young children have problems finding child care; and 14 percent of white women and 26 percent of women of color reported losing a job or promotion on the basis of gender or race. [17]

Closer to home is the eternal question of sharing housework. Three out of four women in a 1996 poll for the Center for Policy Alternatives said they do most of the family chores, while fully half of married women said they do them all.

Betty Friedan, the feminist pioneer who authored *The Feminine Mystique* in 1963, is no longer troubled by the housework issue. Nowadays, "there are more variations among families, and among people at different times of their lives," she says. "The strengths of a marriage are based on equality in job, child care and housework, but it doesn't have to be 50-50. The rubrics that were once defined by men are now also defined by women, so life is more interesting. Instead of the men all barbecuing while the wife cleans the toilet, men are more hands-on — they can diaper as well as women. My son is a successful physicist, and he's in charge of all the cooking." Friedan also acknowledges that "some women may be leery of giving up the power" they've long had in running their own households.

Efforts to measure sexism can be colored by the investigator's predispositions. Laura Flanders, who analyzes women in media for FAIR, says that she must do more than merely "count beans" in deciding whether women get a fair shake in news coverage. "We look at how a story is told and whether there is a consciousness of women's rights," she says. The new visibility of various right-wing women among pundits and opinion-givers "hasn't moved us forward, except that there are more women in the debate."

The Women's Freedom Network, a group of libertarian-leaning men and women, argues against "special protections" for women in employment, child care, the justice system and personal relations. "Too many feminists cry victim all the time, when actually women should be celebrating how well we're doing," says President Rita J. Simon, a sociologist at American University. "Feminists say that most crime against women is what is called 'intimate crime,' perpetrated by lovers and husbands. But that represents only 13 percent of crime, whereas the main victims of crime are young, black men."

Finally, today's conservative feminists appear more willing to accept gender differences as a fact of life. The common complaint that women are charged more for dry cleaning, for example, was investigated by a member of the Independent Woman's Forum, who asked her local Korean laundress about it. "Men's shirts," she explained, "could be done by machine. But because the women's shirts were smaller and constantly differed in style and fabric, they had to be done by hand." [18]

The first issue of Ms. magazine, spring 1972, and co-founder Gloria Steinem (inset)

Has the feminist movement lost touch with younger women?

Females growing up today have no memory of the 1960s and '70s, when there were few women TV anchors, clergy, stockbrokers or lawyers, when the few women visible in the workplace were often expected — without being asked — to pour coffee for their male colleagues.

"The gains we've made since then

Women's Magazines May Soft-Pedal Feminism . . .

"Hey girls, you've got the power of control," exhorts the Clairol hair care ad in *Cosmopolitan*. The message — at once belittling and empowering — embodies the ambivalence toward feminism reflected in women's magazines today.

The booming industry (five of the 10 highest-circulation magazines in the country target women) has for decades been a reflector of female wants, needs and preoccupations. But in serving up monthly doses of fashion, sex, celebrity, health, careers, relationships and homemaking, most of the grocery-store checkout favorites avoid overt discussion of feminism.

"We don't use the term 'feminist' because our assumption is that men and women are quite equal, and that now is a given," says Betsy Carter, editor in chief of *New Woman* (circulation 1.2 million). "It would be like saying, 'Are you an integrationist or a segregationist?' — that part of the dialogue is over."

Actually, says Myrna Blyth, editor in chief of *Ladies' Home Journal* (circulation 4.7 million), "Women in general do not like the word 'feminist.' They say they're not feminist, even though they like its results, such as equal pay for them and their daughters. But most don't think about it, according to our focus groups, surveys and gut feelings."

A study of seven months of *Cosmopolitan* (circulation 2.6 million) in 1993 found that more than 50 percent of its pages were devoted to body image, fashion, marriage and relationships, health and leisure, but less than 5 percent dealt with career and work, only 1 percent on feminist issues. [1]

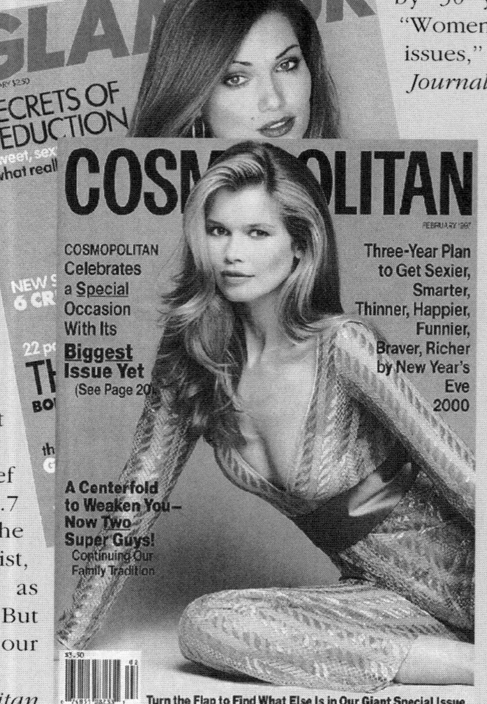

An exception to this unstated industry policy is *Glamour* (circulation 2.1 million), where editors are "not shy or reluctant to discuss feminism," notes Editor in Chief Ruth Whitney. "The attitudes of feminists run in every page of *Glamour*, from fashion, to mascara, to sex. The core of it is that we never address our readers as victims," she says. "Another difference with our magazine is that we also run an editorial page every month discussing such issues as affirmative action and pay equity."

Avoiding the F-word, however, hardly means that the magazines ignore the revolution wrought by 30 years of the women's movement. "Women's issues have become the [nation's] issues," Blyth says, noting that *Ladies' Home Journal* has commissioned public-policy polls and cooperated on a voter-turnout project with the League of Women Voters. "The country is talking about [television] V-chips instead of Stealth bombers and family issues more than international issues. The personal has become political in a way never seen before."

Perhaps the greatest change reflected in the magazines, Blyth adds, is enhanced coverage of women's health. "Twenty years ago, women were ashamed of the topic of breast cancer. Now they march at rallies to win more money for research, and men's magazines are focusing on health as well," she says.

Another major change is the fact that with women in the work force, domestic pursuits such as cooking, gardening and raising kids have become "more fun," for both women and men, "because there's real pleasure in private life while public life is mostly stress," Blyth says.

Others note that the magazines have become more sophisticated, less predictable and less prone to stereotyping. At *New Woman*, Carter looks for writers with a personal voice. "And I try to assign topics about which I don't know the answers, such as our recent story 'What makes a woman cry.' *New Woman* is not instructive or chiding. We try to have the dialogue and the self-discovery rather than just giving you 10 tips for making you a better person."

are considered irrelevant by young women," says Shawn Leary, a feminist, mother of three and attorney in Lenox, Mass. "Now that employment protections are the law, now that women are not being denied admission to medical school and now that women have been educated to know that they don't have to be sexually harassed, the young don't feel they have to fight."

Indeed, many twentysomething women of so-called Generation X have startled older baby boomers with their assertive individuality: the wish by some to opt out of the Social Security program, the new woman's fad of cigar-smoking and reports of young women's up-front demands during job interviews that their working hours permit a personal life. [19]

"Baby boomers think the young see them as the be-all and end-all, but the young are sick of us," says Betsy Carter, editor in chief of *New Woman*. "They see boomers who've been divorced and remarried, and who're constantly

. . . But It Shows Up in Every Issue

The topic that in recent years has fairly oozed from women's magazines is the once subdued subject of sex. Nearly every issue boasts a lusty cover teaser offering tips on seduction, oral sex, orgasm, or as *Redbook* (circulation 2.9 million) recently promised, "The Simple Move that Makes Sex Shockingly Great."

Glamour's Whitney sees no contradiction. "You can be a feminist and a flirt," she says. "*Glamour* talks to the whole woman, and while our readers in their 20s and 30s are just starting their careers, they're deep into male-female relationships. They enjoy sex, but that doesn't mean they lose interest in getting ahead in the world." The attractive models who wear bathing suits on her pages, Whitney says, "are good-looking women, not sex objects," though she acknowledges occasional complaints from readers who expect women to be "portrayed with respect."

Women's magazines have long been criticized for holding up standards of beauty that are unattainable to average women, and for encouraging women to devote lots of time and money to making themselves attractive to men. Carter recalls working on a women's magazine that conducted focus groups to see how readers would respond to more average-looking women as photographic models. "We found that the women readers didn't want to see themselves, but wanted to see a better version of themselves," she says. "Women now dress sexy for themselves, and are no longer worried if it's not politically correct. [Pop singer] Madonna and feminism gave us that. Political correctness got boring. Now you see women who are overtly sexual, who wear soft, colorful clothes that cling to the body. These women are happy to be women, and no longer have to fight that battle."

Readers of *Ladies' Home Journal*, where many advertisements emphasize motherhood and children, "come to marriage sexually experienced," says Blyth, "but they are more conservative than the women portrayed in some of these magazines. Because of the threat of AIDS, most don't embrace a free-flowing sexuality."

The sexual frankness that pervades women's magazines has offended religious conservatives. Discussions of lesbianism in *Glamour* and *New Woman* brought angry letters and complaints to supermarket managers. And in the late 1980s, a now-defunct magazine for teenage girls called *Sassy* was targeted with a letter-writing campaign to its advertisers organized by Christian groups concerned about its articles on birth control, incest and lesbianism. [2]

Editorial pressure from advertisers was a big reason why *Ms.* (circulation 200,000) was relaunched in 1990 as an ad-free bimonthly, says Editor in Chief Marcia Ann Gillespie. "It's a double-edged sword. Our coverage of abortion would cause five advertisers to pull out, and then if we printed a [suggestive] Calvin Klein advertisement, readers would complain" about sexism. "We think it is a very important part of feminism to be up-front about sex, to express a feminist ownership of sexuality, with all the lusty, zestful and humorous sides to sex. And there's a whole world of sexual pleasure beyond just intercourse," she adds, citing masturbation. "The problem is that part of the bargain is that there's a message sent by some multimillion-dollar industries telling the woman that she has to be fixed and made better. Most people enjoy the idea of looking good — I'm a makeup-wearing feminist — but what that unfortunately means in the end is that you must buy something, whether it's larger breasts or lipstick."

Observers of women's magazines took note this month of the changing of the guard at the controversial old standby, *Cosmopolitan*. Legendary Helen Gurley Brown, author of the 1960s classic *Sex and the Single Girl*, stepped down after 33 years at the helm of *Cosmo*, during which she made the sight of exposed cleavage acceptable in American households. Her final issue was a whopping 375 pages that promised a centerfold featuring two men "that will weaken you" and a "Three-Year Plan to Get Sexier, Smarter, Thinner, Happier, Braver, Richer by New Year's Eve 2000."

"She deserves credit for having introduced the sexuality into women's magazines," said *Ms.* co-founder Gloria Steinem. "But then it became the unliberated women's survival kit, with advice on how to please a man, lover or boss under any circumstances and also — in a metaphysical sense — how to smile all the time. The *Cosmo* girl needs to become a woman." [3]

---

[1] Elizabeth Fox-Genovese, *Feminism Is Not the Story of My Life* (1996), p. 53.

[2] Christina Kelly, "Sassy Postscript," *Ms.*, January-February 1997, p. 96.

[3] *The New York Times*, Jan. 13, 1997.

feeling the pressure of balancing babies and work, and they don't want to be like that. They are more conservative and conventional. They want to get family right before career."

To Blair, this reliance on personal pluck rather than collectivist politics is a rejection of mainstream feminism. "A lot of baby boomer women exaggerate the difficulties women have," she says. "It's a misdirected altruism that sympathizes not with the self but with others. But the young know they have to take care of themselves. They were the latchkey kids. They don't just jump on the bandwagon like the boomers, or like the older people who take their cue from [the activist government of President Franklin Delano] Roosevelt."

Such views are echoed by conservative pollster Kellyanne Fitzpatrick. She sees evidence that younger women are shifting rightward and voting Republican because they are more concerned with macroeconomic issues than the social issues associated with feminism. "A twentysomething female college graduate wondering why she pays for entitlements she'll never receive may have more in common with men her own age than with older women who rely upon these entitlements," she writes. [20]

Smeal of The Feminist Majority reaches precisely the opposite conclusion. "We've never been more popular among young women, especially in the polls, which bodes well for the future," she says, citing large turnouts when she speaks on college campuses, the thousands of college women who attended the 1992 abortion rights march on Washington and the more than 1,000 volunteers her group signed up last summer to fight the California ballot question on rolling back affirmative action.

"Feminism registers with the young due to the facts of their lives," Smeal says. "They plan to match their brothers in terms of careers, and they care about pay and family planning. If they take [the efforts of earlier feminists] for granted, then I say 'Thank God.' If we had opened all those doors, and no one had walked through, it would have been a calamity. Instead they flooded through those doors, and for me there is no greater joy than seeing these new opportunities and knowing that I was a part."

One indicator of feminist spark in the young is the continuing growth of campus women's-studies programs. It is a field sometimes derided as doctrinaire, lacking in rigor and less than useful in terms of career enhancement. But interest is strong enough to support a growth of women's studies that went from 78 programs nationwide in 1973 to 519 in 1988 to an estimated 670 in 1996, according to the Association of American Colleges and Universities.

"Those who felt women's studies was a flash in the pan have been proven wrong," says Susan McGhee Bailey, executive director of the Wellesley College Centers for Research on Women. "While women's studies is an indicator of feminism, studying it does not necessarily identify one as a feminist. Gender affects society so much, you can study it from any perspective. But the way women's roles are underportrayed or misrepresented is important to understanding what feminists are talking about in terms of institutional and individual change."

Friedan, now teaching at Mount Vernon College in Washington, says the fact that young women take women's gains for granted is a "tribute to what we've done. The world is their oyster, and I say Hallelujah! This is a result of 30 years of this marvelous transformative movement from a time when their mothers couldn't and didn't aspire to these things. I am stopped on the street by young women who say, 'Thanks, my mother says you changed her life,' but that's not the point."

NOW's Ireland, who is organizing an April conference in Washington for young feminists, says that in terms of sophistication, today's 17-year-olds are "light years ahead of where we were at that age; they are standing on the shoulders of giants." Ireland does note a generation gap between women who have young children and those whose kids are grown, and between young women interested in birth control and older ones more concerned about 20 years of their lives." [21]

BACKGROUND

Roots of Sisterhood

"Women are told from their infancy," wrote early British feminist Mary Wollstonecraft, "that outward obedience, and a scrupulous attention to a puerile kind of propriety, will obtain for them the protection of man; and should they be beautiful, everything else is needless, for, at least, 20 years of their lives." [21]

This passage from the seminal *A Vindication of the Rights of Woman* was published more than two centuries ago. Yet it contains — as do many feminist tracts that would follow — the themes that show up in modern-day feminist debates: resistance to strict gender roles, to female economic and legal dependency on men and to an overemphasis on physical attractiveness.

The assertion of rights for women equal to men's and, indeed, as urgent to the good of society as the emancipation of slaves, was the major theme of a celebrated 1848 convention in Seneca Falls, N.Y. Here America's early feminists gathered with luminaries such as black leader Frederick Douglass to push for expanded suffrage and the "social, civil and religious condition and rights of woman."

The notion of sexual independence for women was asserted as early as 1870, when free-love advocates Victoria Woodhull and Tennessee Claflin published the first feminist weekly paper and urged women to "take the sting out" of such words as "mistress" and "courtesan."

The vision of the female as the more peaceful, "less-tainted half of the race," was advanced in the 19th century by Women's Christian Temperance Union President Frances Willard. The practice of mocking male expectations goes back to novelist Virginia Woolf's statement in the 1920s that women's role is to use their eyes for "reflecting men at twice their natural size." And the critique of misogyny found its voice when French feminist Simone de Beauvoir wrote that "in the mouth of a man the epithet female has the sound of an insult." [22]

Yet the tendency of modern feminists to view feminist pioneers as models does not guarantee consensus. To Smeal, the gathering of 1848 was "a movement for dynamic social reform just like we are today. The women then, she said, held views that differed from those of men because their

Continued on p. 180

Chronology

1940s-1960s

First stirrings of modern feminism.

1948
United Nations' "Universal Declaration of Human Rights" calls for all nations to gauge the status of women.

1949
French feminist Simone de Beauvoir publishes *The Second Sex.*

1961
President John F. Kennedy appoints President's Commission on Status of Women headed by former first lady Eleanor Roosevelt.

1963
Congress passes Equal Pay Act; Betty Friedan publishes *The Feminine Mystique.*

1964
Civil Rights Act outlaws sex discrimination.

1966
Founding of National Organization for Women (NOW).

Sept. 7, 1968
TV coverage of feminists protesting Miss America pageant in Atlantic City.

1970s ***Spread of sexual revolution; movement launched to enact Equal Rights Amendment (ERA)***

1970
Kate Millet publishes *Sexual Politics.*

1971
Germaine Greer publishes *The Female Eunuch*; Norman Mailer critiques feminism in *Prisoner of Sex*; National Women's Political Caucus co-founded by Bella S. Abzug.

1972
Founding of *Ms.* magazine by Gloria Steinem and others; Feminists for Life launched after anti-abortion women expelled from NOW; Title IX law provides equal funding for women's sports; Congress passes ERA.

1973
Publication of Mary Daly's Beyond God the Father and Erica Jong's sexual-freedom novel *Fear of Flying*; Supreme Court legalizes abortion.

1975
Marabel Morgan publishes *The Total Woman* as antidote to feminism.

1976
First issue of *Working Woman* magazine.

1977
National Women's Conference in Houston, Texas, marks International Women's Year.

1978
Congress passes law preventing employer discrimination against pregnant women; pro-ERA march draws 100,000 to Washington.

1980s ***Women combining work with motherhood are labeled "superwomen."***

1981
Betty Friedan's *The Second Stage* emphasizes motherhood.

1982
Psychologist Carol Gilligan's *In a Different Voice* published; time limit expires for ratifying ERA.

1984
Rep. Geraldine A. Ferraro, D-N.Y., becomes first woman to run for vice president on major party ticket.

1990s ***Rise of conservative women's groups***

1991
Law Professor Anita F. Hill accuses Supreme Court nominee Clarence Thomas of sexual harassment; Congress passes civil rights act calling for study of workplace "glass ceiling" on women's advancement; publication of Susan Faludi's *Backlash: The Undeclared War Against American Women.*

1992
Marilyn Quayle, wife of Vice President Dan Quayle, tells Republican convention that "nothing offends me more than attempts to paint Republicans as looking to turn back the clock for women."

1994
Congress passes Violence Against Women Act.

1995
U.N. Fourth World Conference on Women meets in Beijing.

Jan. 13, 1997
Conservative pickets at Supreme Court call feminists hypocrites for not backing Paula C. Jones in her sexual harassment suit against President Clinton.

Anti-Feminist Men's Groups Fight to Be Heard

"Men are simply not joiners," laments Frank Bertels, founder, director and self-proclaimed "world leader" of the Men's Liberation Foundation in Miami, Fla. "It's biological. Men don't help men; they fight other men and help women," he says. "Ten years ago, there were 1,000 men's organizations put together by practically anyone who got clipped in some divorce. But most couldn't pay their phone bills, so now there's fewer than half left."

For three decades, men's-rights group's have come and gone in an inevitable reaction to feminism. And what they have lacked in membership growth, they have made up for in angry rhetoric about unfair child custody rulings, women entering traditionally male professions and women who use sex to manipulate men.

"The radical feminists' 30-year war against men, family, housewives and children, while promoting lesbianism and other world ills, has caused the decline of the family, with irresponsible single 'moms' for the first time in 5,000 years raising 12-year-old murderers," reads one of Bertel's photocopied diatribes.

Equally scathing are dispatches from the New York City-based National Organization for Men (NOM), said to be the largest male-rights group, with 14,000 members. Its newsletter notes that "when women learn there is a grass-roots men's movement, they become hostile. . . . The man-hating feminist fringe has been very effective in getting its message out and twisting the reality."

Lawyer Sydney Siller, who founded NOM in 1983, believes "the feminist movement has outlived its usefulness and has become counterproductive. It is destroying our military forces with its equal rights. If you throw hot-blooded males and females together in a barracks or tent, what will you get? The feminists don't care, just as long as it's politically correct."

Siller also says that feminists have a hammerlock on President Clinton — "the biggest wimp in the country" — as evidenced by his appointment of Madeleine K. Albright as the first female secretary of State and by speculation that he might appoint Supreme Court Associate Justice Ruth Bader Ginsburg as chief justice of the United States when William H. Rehnquist retires.

Another group, Men's Rights Inc., in Sacramento, Calif., is less critical of feminism and more concerned with the new needs of men. "Male sex roles have been just as damaging and dehumanizing and have limited men in ways as serious and pervasive as the reproducer (sex object) and child socializer (housewife) roles have done to women," writes Fred Hayward, executive director of the group, which was founded in 1977 and claims 1,000 contributors. "We are not here to win the battle of the sexes. We are here to end it."

Anti-feminist blasts from men's groups — along with the "feminazi" label popularized by conservative radio commentator Rush Limbaugh — are dismissed by many feminists. But ironically, the attacks actually may help the women's movement, says Eleanor Smeal, president of The Feminist Majority. "By saying things one would think no one would possibly say, they make other men and women furious, so there's a backlash that helps us gain support," she says.

Others point to a genuine need among men to join forces with their own gender, as seen in the recent growth of the Promise Keepers Christian religious revivals and in the male-bonding, drum-beating rituals popularized by author Robert Bly. "Men feel they don't know who they are," says Shawn Leary, an attorney, feminist and mother of three in Lenox, Mass. "Perhaps because they're no longer forced to join the Army, there's no rite of passage for men anymore. If they want to get in touch with their inner little boy or their cave man, if they need to prove their manhood by sitting around the fire with Robert Bly, that is better than raping women."

Other feminists point out that many men choose to ally themselves with feminists. The number of male feminists has moved well beyond such well-known "sensitive" figures as talk-show host Phil Donahue (now retired) and actor Alan Alda. "We work with lots of great men who are experts in such things as child abuse and psychotherapy," says Marcia Ann Gillespie, editor in chief of *Ms.* magazine. "Nowadays we get lots of regular guys who are living with women and interacting with women, as well as young men who grew up hearing about feminism from their mothers."

But when it comes to an organized movement, the male population — which dominates so much of politics in general — finds itself reduced to a novelty act. "The radical, liberal media and the liberal feminists support each other," complains Bertels, who launched his group in 1965, "but there's never been a feature story on me even though I've done 2,000 electronic media interviews. I charge $2,000 a lecture, but Gloria Steinem gets $20,000. I've been on the Sally Jesse Raphael, Montel Williams and Geraldo Rivera shows, but I just can't get [speech] bookings."

Bartels, who authored *The First Book on Male Liberation and Sex Inequality* in 1975, says his men's rights message has been better received in England, where a speech he gave in 1989 started a movement that changed Britain's retirement law so that men can retire as early as women. It is also catching on among men in Japan, he adds. But in the United States, "We're going to have mass feminism for the next 50 or 100 years. When will the slumbering giant awaken?"

Continued from p. 178

life's experiences were different. "It took them 72 years to get suffrage, which men resisted because they knew the women would vote differently from men."

The lesson of Seneca Falls, writes Clark University philosophy Professor Christina Hoff Sommers, is that "its goals were clearly stated, finite and practicable." But the offensive feminist tendency toward "misandrism (hostility to men, the counterpart to misogyny) was not a notable feature of the women's movement until our own times." [23]

Divisions on Abortion

The modern women's movement came of age in the 1960s amid virtually nonstop controversy. The phrase "male chauvinist pig" was gaining currency, and housewives seeking to enter the work force told themselves that "the personal is political." In September 1968, 200 feminists made national news when they protested the Miss America pageant, symbolically dumping bras, girdles, false eyelashes and copies of *Playboy* in a trash can. (Though the event gave rise to the term "bra-burning," witnesses say no undergarments were actually burned. [24])

But the issue that would bring the most passionate controversy was abortion. In 1967, NOW became the first national group to advocate the legalization that would come with the Supreme Court's *Roe v. Wade* decision in 1973. That led to a walkout by pro-life women and the founding of Feminists for Life, who continue to oppose abortion by citing the works of 19th-century founding feminists. Elizabeth Cady Stanton viewed abortion as "infanticide," the group says, and Susan B. Anthony, in her weekly feminist newspaper *Revolution,* proclaimed, "No matter what the motive, love of ease, or a desire to save from suffering the unborn innocent, the woman is awfully guilty who commits the deed."

"Feminism is based on the premise that we all have human rights, not at the expense of blacks, children or women who couldn't own land or vote," says Serrin M. Foster, executive director of Feminists for Life of America. "We are proud to be part of that heritage, and we have more grounding in history than anyone else." Foster says that women's rights shouldn't come at the expense of men's or fathers' rights, and that "women who are truly in control of their bodies wouldn't have an abortion." The group's 5,000 members work with a variety of groups on other women's issues such as welfare reform and domestic violence, she says. "The conservatives see us as radical, the feminists see us as conservative."

To many feminists, however, the right to an abortion is a core belief. "The overwhelming majority of women and men don't see any way to be anti-abortion because for a women to control her own life, she must control when she has children," Ireland says. "We all remember our grandmothers who had eight or 12 births that physically drained them. The feminists in the 19th century were still fighting for birth control, and any surgical procedure then was dangerous because there were no antibiotics. We don't believe it makes sense to lock into a way of thinking and say we can't evolve."

Ireland adds that mainstream feminists would "be more respectful of Feminists for Life if we saw them standing with us on the welfare and income issues."

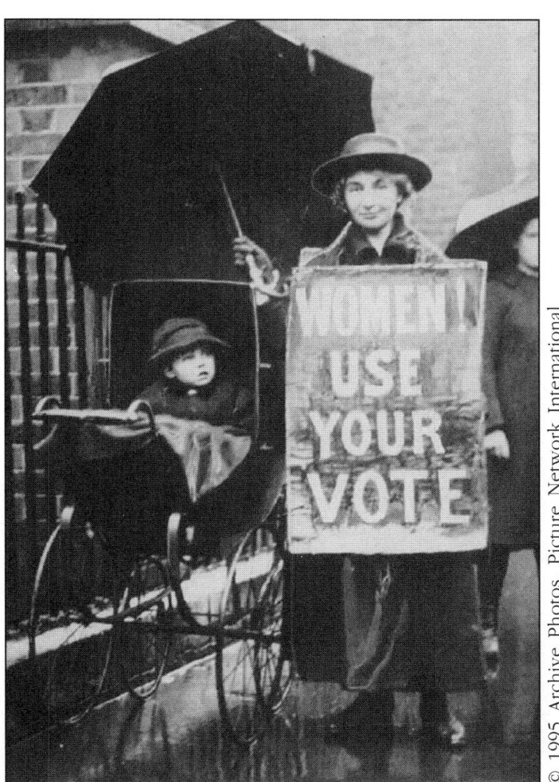

A suffragette pickets for the vote in 1918.

ERA and Homemakers

"Equality of rights under the law shall not be denied or abridged by the United States or by any state on account of sex." That was the text of the Equal Rights Amendment to the Constitution, first introduced in 1923 and finally pried loose from a reluctant, mostly male Congress in the early '70s. For nearly a decade, the ERA dominated women's issues as efforts were made to win ratification from the necessary three-fourths of states.

Why it failed, even after winning an extension, is still debated by feminists. A report by The Feminist Majority lays the blame on sexist male lawmakers. Among state legislators in general, 75 percent of women and 50 percent of men backed the amendment, it says. But in the 15 states that declined to ratify the ERA, it was backed by only 36 percent of male legislators. [25]

Anita Perez Ferguson, president of the National Women's Political Caucus, which is seeking to resurrect the ERA, says the "elements of the text are things that everyone can get behind — it's the issues of how to spend tax dollars and implement business regulations where we see a political separation." She believes that "equality with men is the most healthy thing we all could do for the economy because we all need partners economically." But she acknowledges that the text "can be in-

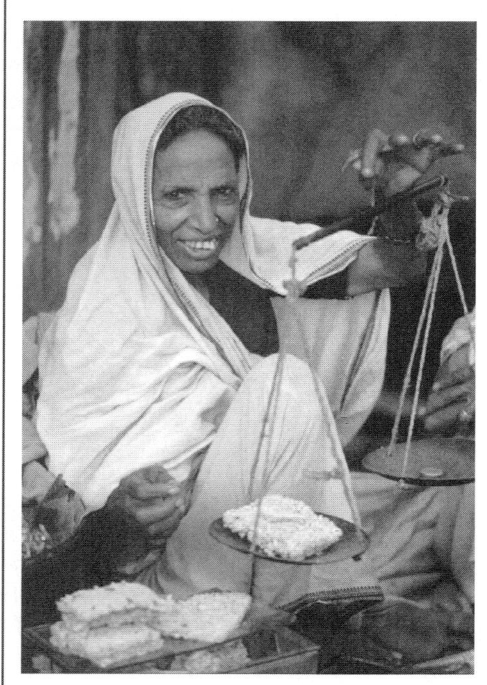

Fruits of Labor Elude World's Women

Women perform two-thirds of the world's work, but their share of the income and land is comparatively minuscule. Among other factors, women head more than three-quarters of the single-parent families and account for two-thirds of the world's illiterate adults.

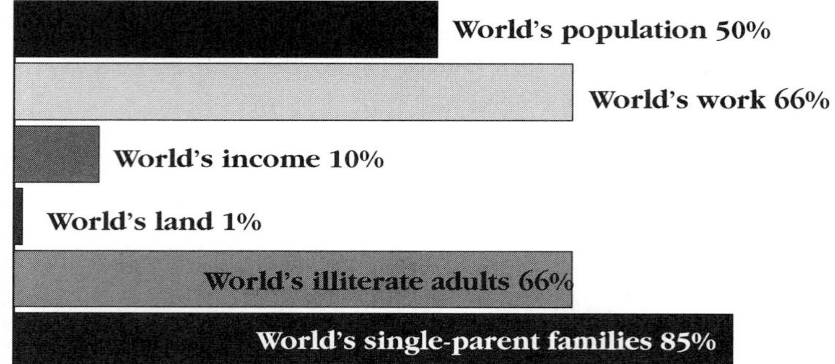

Source: The Center for Policy Alternatives; Pew Global Stewardship/Population Reference Bureau

terpreted more broadly than what is written, and conservatives thought it threatened the nuclear family."

A key exponent of that view was Sylvia Ann Hewlett, a former Barnard College economics professor. In her 1986 book *A Lesser Life: The Myth of Women's Liberation in America,* she wrote: "In a profound way, feminists have failed to connect with the needs and aspirations of ordinary American women. Many homemakers did not want to be treated equally. When you add in the legitimate fears of blue-collar women that they would lose their hard-won protective benefits, you have a powerful constituency ranged against the ERA." [26]

Henry wrote of "the dirty little secret" that many women see housewives as living "inconsequential lives." [27] What's more, while 68 percent of the women she asked felt there is inequality, only 53 percent said this inequality was important, and only 25 percent felt concerned enough to fight it.

During the 1980s and '90s, as more women struggled at "having it all," polls showed a new interest in getting off the career treadmill. A Roper Starch Worldwide Poll done for Virginia Slims cigarettes showed that the number of women wishing to stay at home had shrunk from 60 percent in 1974, to 51 percent in 1980, down to 45 percent in 1985, but that it was back up to 51 percent in 1990 before tipping down to 47 in 1994. A recent Wirthlin poll for Concerned Women for America showed that 80 percent agree with the statement "If I could afford it, I would like to stay home and be a full-time mother." Actual labor force participation for women, except for a small dip among young women, has been steadily rising and stands at 59.2 percent, according to the Bureau of Labor Statistics. [28]

Rape and Victimhood

In critiquing feminism, philosophy Professor Sommers accuses various authors and women's magazines of misusing statistics, of exaggerating, for example, the number of females who die of anorexia, or the rise in wife beatings that supposedly occurs on the day of the Super Bowl. A certain type of movement feminist needs this psychologically as a way of demonizing men, she argues, so they "can point to one victim and say, 'In wronging her, he has betrayed his contempt for us all.' " [29]

No issue brings home the victimhood debate as dramatically as rape and date rape, issues discussed widely during the late 1980s and '90s as campus feminists organized protest marches under the banner Take Back the Night. [30]

In a study published by the *Ms.* Foundation for Women, Robin Warshaw explained "how men are taught to rape" and cited statistics alleging that 15 percent of campus women had been raped, and that another 14.5 percent had been touched sexually against their will. [31]

More recently, however, other women have criticized such approaches as a paranoid way of casting women in the role of collective victims when what is called for is individual responsibility.

Scholar and author Camille Paglia, a politically conservative but sexually adventuresome feminist, has rattled feminists with her view that women should quit denying the naturalness of "male sexual energy." [32] "We shouldn't need to be reminded that the rigidly conformist '50s were not the heyday of women's power," writes Katie Roiphe, daughter of novelist Anne Roiphe. "Rape-crisis feminists threaten the progress that's been made. They are chasing the same stereotypes our mothers spent so much energy running away from." [33]

Smeal points out, however, that Take Back the Night marches were intended to pressure colleges to spend more money on lighting and security precautions so that women could study in the library at night. "It was the parents as much as feminists who wanted it because the colleges were sweeping the problem under the rug to protect their reputations," she says. "We're not damsels in distress. Feminists are the first to say that people should take individual responsibility."

But many conservatives reply that the best way to avoid rape is the set of common-sense rules used by women for generations. Fox-Genovese writes with puzzlement of the attitude of a sexually active student she encountered: "How could this intelligent young woman not understand that there were likely to be consequences if she exercised her right by engaging in heavy petting with a young man, going to his room, removing her clothes, initiating sexual foreplay and then just saying no?" [34]

Divided Over Sex

Feminists are also divided over sex itself. There are clearly two historical traditions — both in evidence today — between the extremes of prudishness and promiscuity. In one culture are "The New Victorians," as author Rene Denfeld calls them in his 1995 book of the same name. They range from anti-porn crusader MacKinnon to the female University of Nebraska graduate students who insisted that a male colleague put away desktop photos of his wife in a bikini.

In another culture are "joy of sex" advocates such as Nancy Friday, whose 1996 book *The Power of Beauty* counsels women (and certain feminists) to stop viewing sex as dirty. There is also author Wolf, who has written that she became a feminist because orgasm felt so good and was hence "the natural call to feminine politics." [35]

Author Kate Fillion recently scrutinized the stereotype that many females grow up with: that men are "sex-crazed bad boys" while women are "good girls" whose lives are built around long-term relationships. But she concludes that such oversimplifications come less from feminists than from politicians and the media. [36]

The split over sex is acknowledged by Blair, whose Independent Woman's Forum last year drew hisses from feminists when it circulated a tasteful nude drawing as a play on words to promote its economic report "Women's Figures." "Ever since the arrival of the birth control pill [in the early '60s], there's been a movement for sexual freedom, for sex without consequences while most of us are still brain-wired for sex with consequences," she says. "But we should all be more careful about sex. Women once had power to control sex until they gave it up. Now it's tough to replace that."

NOW's Ireland agrees that sex is a "loaded issue" for feminists, creating a tension between a woman's desire not to "capitulate to the culture," but not to come across as anti-sex. "Our culture still views a good woman as one who doesn't have sex, that sex is an idea that must be punished and that sex inevitably connects to pregnancy," she says. "Women have a responsibility to be clear when they want sex and with whom, and have the courage to insist on using birth control, which can be hard to do. But not having sex is antithetical to human nature. Women will have sex. Get over it." ■

CURRENT SITUATION

The Gender Gap

"Women re-elected Bill Clinton President," shouted the headlines in women's group newsletters following last November's Democratic victory over Republican Bob Dole. The reason, they say, is the so-called gender gap. Based on exit polling of voters' presidential preferences, women apparently voted differently from men by either 11 points or 17 points, depending on the analysis methodology. *

From the 1950s, when women began voting in significant numbers, through the '70s, women basically leaned Republican (women have been a majority of voters since 1964). But in the 1980 election won by Ronald Reagan, exit polls for the first time showed women leaned toward the Democrats. Smeal, who says she was devastated by Reagan's victory, recalls how she was poring through data looking for a "silver lining" when the gender gap leapt out at her. Primarily male political scientists and pundits resisted her unique analysis (though Reagan's pollster Richard B. Wirthlin

* Analysts at The Feminist Majority and National Women's Political Caucus arrive at 11 points by subtracting the percentage of men who voted for Clinton (43) from the percentage of women who voted for Clinton (54). Analysts at Emily's List and the American Enterprise Institute compare those same two percentages against the percentages of women and men who voted for Dole (38 and 44, respectively), producing an overall gap of 17 points.

says he used the phrase "gender gap" during his extensive polling among female voters in the late 1970s).

What was clear, however, is that women, who are more likely to be swing voters, were emerging as a new variable. "Political science had masked the importance of the women's vote because everyone assumed women didn't like politics and voted like their husbands," Smeal says. "But look at their life's experiences: Social Security? More women are dependent on it. Abortion? Nearly half of all women have one. Why do women care more about education? Women tend to be teachers."

The gender gap also shows up among office-seekers, notes Ferguson of the Women's Political Caucus. "Research on state legislatures shows that women office-holders over the past 25 years have shared with other women a high priority for funding education, health care and anti-crime efforts."

Malcolm of Emily's List says that during the 104th Congress, women were the first to start moving away from the "extremist" Republicans who were talking about bringing back orphanages. "Women have a sense of community and are angry when others such as children are being hurt," she says, "whereas men are more concerned with their own situations."

Karlyn Bowman, a polling analyst at the American Enterprise Institute, agrees that the gender gap is "now a permanent feature of the landscape." It was given new visibility by the arrival of more women candidates and female reporters. she says. "People pay attention to it because women are more than 50 percent of the electorate. But the gap between men and women voters is not as large as the marriage gap, the racial gap or the low-income or low-education gap."

"Publicity about the gender gap creates false expectations that there's a bloc of votes because of chromosomes," Blair says. "But married women tend to vote more like men because they feel security with a husband, whereas it's the singles and women who rely on government programs." Nor, she adds, do female politicians behave differently from men. Politicians of either gender, "the kind of people who go out and raise money and get votes, are very different from the average person."

"The feminists' silence on Paula Jones is deafening. The Jones case is more egregious, yet they were all pushing for Anita Hill even though she had waited 10 years to come forward. I guess sisterhood only extends so far."

—Rita J. Simon
President,
The Women's Freedom Network

Republican Angst

This past election season, a series of public musings by major Republican strategists revealed deep worry over the apparent disaffection of women from the party. In January, outgoing Republican National Committee Chairman Haley Barbour wrote a public criticism of his party for failing to communicate effectively to women and minorities. "Men want to talk, women want to be heard," GOP pollster Frank Luntz said in a memo to his party's faithful. "Bill Clinton listened. The Dole campaign talked." [37]

Barbour drew a scathing rebuttal from fellow Republican Selwa Roosevelt, formerly Reagan's chief of protocol. "You still don't get it," she said in an attack on the anti-abortion wing of the GOP. "'We women cannot be lured back as long as the extreme right is in control." [38]

Myrna Blyth, editor in chief of *Ladies' Home Journal,* says the Republicans' problems are a "combination of their agenda and the way they communicate. When they'd say, 'Let's get rid of the Education Department,' women went crazy. But if they were to say, 'Let's combine Education with Labor to assure jobs in the 21st century,' women would have thought it was good."

There have been indications the Republican-controlled Congress is responding to the concerns of women. On Jan. 29, Sen. Alfonse M. D'Amato, R-N.Y., joined with Sens. Olympia J. Snowe, R-Maine, and Dianne Feinstein, D-Calif., to introduce a bill to stop hospitals from the early dismissal of patients who've had mastectomies. And shortly before last fall's election, Congress passed a resolution moving the 75-year-old statue of 19th-century feminist icons Anthony, Stanton and Lucretia Mott from the Capitol basement up to the Rotunda.

The Paula Jones Case

In January, the Supreme Court heard arguments in the sexual harassment

Continued on p. 186

At Issue:

Are feminists out of touch with the majority of women?

yes

Elizabeth Powers
Author and lecturer, Manhattan School of Music

FROM "A FAREWELL TO FEMINISM," *COMMENTARY,* JANUARY 1997

My coming of age in the early 1970s was inextricably linked with what is variously known as feminism, the women's movement, women's liberation. It is a link by which I am much puzzled and troubled. The passing years have brought me a closer look at, so to speak, the fine print, and I shiver now when I observe the evolution that some of my closest friends from the era have undergone, spouting phrases about comparable worth and voicing most fantastic bureaucratic visions of the future. . . .

[O]ne of the peculiar results of the reign of feminism is that women have actually become unimportant, indeed non-essential. This has come about by feminism's making radically suspect the influence that women . . . have traditionally exercised on the souls of those with whom they have come into contact. The first effective thrust was to deny that any of the endless tasks performed by women within the marriage union contributed in any way to its spiritual wholeness. Housekeeping and child-raising were transformed into a purely material operation, consisting of the kind of mindless, mechanical steps that characterize the assembly of an automobile or computer. It is no surprise that the most ambitious women of my generation fled this scenario of drudgery, and, by extension, also avoided traditional women's occupations as they would the plague. . . .

This abandonment of the female realm has also led to the production of a class that appears to be in the vanguard of the nanny state: women who "have it all," whose marriages are not so much unions as partnerships of two career paths, and whose children, once assembled and produced, are willingly turned over by them to caretakers. . . .

Whether such women really do have it all is for them, perhaps, to say. Even so, there remains a lack of synchronicity between the highest levels of feminist achievers and ordinary women. Housework and the raising of children, denigrated by the movement and by so many elite women, is looked upon very differently by my unmarried friends, even those who call themselves feminists. They sense that the struggle to form one's life in conjunction with another . . . is a spiritual enterprise of the highest sort. . . . And they sense acutely that, in declining or refusing to make those compromises of daily living-with-another, they have missed out on the greatest of human challenges. . . .

The tragic part is the egocentrism of their current existence, the days and years devoted to self-maintenance, with minimal effect on the lives of others. Women now get to fulfill themselves . . . but they do so in the most resolute solitude.

no

Eleanor Smeal
President, The Feminist Majority

FROM A SPEECH AT THE NATIONAL PRESS CLUB, FEB. 13, 1997.

The feminist movement has one powerful, peaceful weapon: the gender gap in voting. Now we see even this powerful tool is being devalued, distorted and dismissed. Yet there is a story to be told about the strength of the women's movement and the power of the gender gap. Not for historical purposes, but to empower women to counter these assaults on women's rights and women's lives and to affect the future agenda of the nation. . . .

The gender gap in voting is based on gender gaps in public issues primarily in three cluster areas: violence, health and human services and women's rights. Virtually since public opinion polling began, women have registered different opinions from men on a whole host of significant public-policy issues. . . .

The gender gap will continue to expand because young women are the most consistent supporters of gender gap issues. The gender gap also will be expanded by older women who fear social-spending programs upon which they depend will be cut. And, most importantly, the gender gap will continue to expand as long as women's groups continue to make women's issues salient to women voters.

Today more women — especially young women — identify as feminists than identify as Republican, Democrat, independent, conservative or liberal. Our challenge is empowering that majority that already exists for women's rights. . . .

Right now in the United States, we are experiencing a backlash against women's rights and civil rights. Women who are venturing into heretofore male-dominated territory are experiencing organized sexual harassment, be it in the military, in police forces, in shipyards or on Wall Street. . . .

Some reactionary male want-to-be-patriarchs — the so-called Promise Keepers — are preaching to football stadiums of men that men must resume their rightful place at the head of their household. The submission of women is at the core of all these attacks on women's rights and is a backlash to the changed role of women in every facet of our society.

But wish as they might, women are not and cannot go back. One of the ironic twists of the current debate to re-segregate women in the military is that when asked if the modern military could exist without women, the answer is a resounding "NO" by most military experts. Women can't go back, the military can't go back and neither can the nation.

As long as the reality of women's lives continues to be denied, there will be a boomerang effect to the reactionaries, and the gender gap will continue to grow into a gender gulf.

FOR MORE INFORMATION

Center for Women Policy Studies, 1211 Connecticut Ave. N.W., Suite 312, Washington, D.C. 20036; (202) 872-1770. Founded in 1972, this "multiethnic and multicultural feminist policy" research and advocacy organization produces research, analysis and strategies for empowering women.

The Feminist Majority, 1600 Wilson Blvd., Suite 801, Arlington, Va. 22209; (703) 522-2214. Founded in 1987, this group promotes feminist candidates for public office while organizing a nationwide feminist agenda.

Independent Women's Forum, 2111 Wilson Blvd., Arlington, Va. 22201; (703) 243-8989. Founded in 1992, this group of women and men seeks to promote individual responsibility, strong families, freedom and opportunity. It conducts litigation, publishes periodicals, maintains a speakers bureau and monitors legislation.

Institute for Women's Policy Research, 1400 20th St. N.W., Suite 104, Washington, D.C. 20036; (202) 785-5100. Founded in 1987, this independent nonprofit group provides women-centered, policy-oriented research. It works with policy-makers, scholars and advocacy groups nationwide to disseminate findings.

National Organization for Women, 1000 16th St. N.W., Suite 700, Washington, D.C. 20036; (202) 331-0066. Founded in 1966, this feminist civil rights group for women and men uses traditional and non-traditional forms of political activism, including civil disobedience, to improve the status of women regardless of age, income, sexual orientation or race.

Women's Freedom Network, 4410 Mass. Ave. N.W., Suite 179, Washington, D.C. 20016; (202) 885-6245. The network was founded in 1993 by women "seeking alternatives to both extremist ideological feminism and anti-feminist traditionalism." The WFN believes in "empowering individual women rather than the state and its bureaucracies."

suit brought by Paula C. Jones against President Clinton. At issue was not whether the charges brought by Jones, a former Arkansas state employee, are true, but whether a lawsuit against a sitting president must wait until after the president leaves office. Outside the courtroom, demonstrators from the Independent Women's Forum carried signs charging feminist groups with hypocrisy for not backing Jones.

"Where are the women's groups?" echoed Jones' attorney Joseph Cammarata. Even liberal feminist Barbara Ehrenreich wrote an op-ed piece castigating the "Beltway feminists" for not rallying to the cause of sexual harassment as they had in 1991 when law Professor Anita F. Hill accused Supreme Court nominee Clarence Thomas of sexual harassment. [39]

"The feminists' silence on Paula Jones is deafening," says Simon of the Women's Freedom Network. "The Jones case is more egregious, yet they were all pushing for Anita Hill even though she had waited 10 years to come forward. I guess sisterhood only extends so far."

All the major feminist spokeswomen, however, point out that Jones went public with her case with the firm backing of an array of conservative activist groups — anti-Clinton muckraker Floyd Brown and the Christian Defense Coalition, for instance — none of whom have supported laws against sexual harassment. According to Smeal, feminist groups had scarcely heard about the case before they were being pounced on by Jones' backers.

"The conservatives are out to make a political point and tear down the image of the women's movement," says Lichtman of the Women's Legal Defense Fund. "We see it for the political hocus-pocus and the bait-and-switch that it is. Allegations of sexual harassment always have to be taken seriously, and Paula Jones will have her day in court after the president leaves office. We haven't heard from any of these conservatives on current sexual harassment controversies such as the scandal at [the Army's] Aberdeen Proving Ground. Who's being hypocritical?"

NOW's Ireland points out that she tried to meet with Jones but was told she was busy, and that NOW has shown its willingness to break with President Clinton as it did when he signed last fall's welfare reform bill. "Paula Jones picked her forum, and she picked her friends," reads a NOW statement. "We wouldn't force ourselves on an unwilling plaintiff anymore than any man should force himself on a woman."

Women in Action

At George Washington University this winter, the undergraduate group Womyn's Issues Now (it uses the altered spelling preferred by some feminists) held a Take Back the Night rally and vigil targeting a fraternity house. They assert that the fraternity's ritual of hanging pairs of shoes from a campus tree is an offensive symbol of their sexual conquests.

Also on the protest front, NOW members spent Valentine's Day picketing *The Washington Post* for its policy of not printing wedding announcements for gay couples.

In the legislative arena, the Center for Women Policy Studies is working with women in state legislatures to implement the power-sharing and economic security principles articulated at the 1995 United Nations Conference on Women.

In the workplace, the Labor Department's Women's Bureau is planning a national working women's summit with satellite broadcasts this summer to all regions of the country to inform women of their rights in the workplace.

Among conservatives, the Independent Women's Forum recently convened experts to its "Women's Health Law and the Junking of Science" conference to discuss feminist charges that science is "tainted by male dominance" and whether the consumer alarms over the safety of silicone breast implants have spread "needless fear and anxiety." [40]

The five-year-old group RENEW (Republican Network to Elect Women) plans a "Women Leaders Summit" in May in Washington at which representatives from business, local government and community organizations will offer advice to Congress.

Concerned Women for America has organized opposition to ratification of the United Nations Convention on the Elimination of All Forms of Discrimination Against Women (CEDAW), signed by President Jimmy Carter in 1980. The group charges that the treaty would "supersede the Constitution of the United States."

Perhaps the best-known feminist action that takes place yearly is Take Your Daughter to Work Day. Scheduled for April 24 this year, the event is intended not as a career day but as a response to research showing that the self-confidence of girls plummets suddenly as they reach adolescence. "At the very moment appearances take on inordinate importance for girls, our culture bombards them with unrealistic and dangerous images of women's beauty," says the event's planners at the *Ms.* foundation.

A Roper poll shows that seven in 10 Americans are aware of Take Your Daughter to Work Day, and that 132 million feel it is a positive experience. Participation last year was 16.6 million, or 7.6 million more than in 1995.

To feminism critics such as Simon, the whole project is "silly," an example of special treatment of women that trivializes their individual accomplishments. Frank Bertels, founder of the Male Liberation Foundation, says Take Your Daughter to Work Day is unconstitutional. He would ask the women who participate, "Don't you have any sons?" ■

"*Playboy* has always encouraged feminism ever since the birth control pill."

—Cindy Rakowitz
Vice President,
Playboy Enterprises Inc.

OUTLOOK

Playboy and Sexism

While the women's movement is firmly established from a legal standpoint, says attorney Leary, there is still much to be done in the area of media and culture. "So many of the TV movies and advertisements show men as predators and women as thin and beautiful victims who get punished for that," she complains. "What is required is not legal redress but a sense of shame." [41]

Also frustrating to feminists is the trend, reported this February by TV's "Entertainment Tonight," that more Hollywood actresses are being denied work because their breasts are too small.

Cultural issues, however, are famous for eluding consensus. Witness the irony in the fact that one of the perennial targets of feminist wrath, *Playboy* (circulation 3.4 million), considers itself a backer of the cause. "*Playboy* has always encouraged feminism ever since the birth control pill," says Cindy Rakowitz, vice president for public relations at Playboy Enterprises Inc. "We're for non-discrimination," and half of *Playboy* employees and nearly half of all managers are women. Founder Hugh Hefner "has said he was surprised when the feminist left turned against *Playboy*. They argue that if a woman poses nude, she's exploited and is responsible for others' exploitation. But we don't chain women to the wall. We get bombarded with letters saying, 'I've always dreamed of posing,' or 'I need money for college.' Our women are paid $25,000, are given new career opportunities and are made to look beautiful."

As for the charge that *Playboy* encourages men to view women as sex objects, Rakowitz says: "We're probably the most healthy way to be introduced to the female body. And there are other elements in the magazine besides nudity."

Leary says it may be laudable for *Playboy* to support women who want to take their clothes off, but that this affects society in general. "Hefner should have invested in the breast-implant industry for all the attempts to emulate *Playboy* models," she says. "We can't choose to live in a society where *Playboy* doesn't exist." NOW, meanwhile, has a new committee on media issues.

Alienation From Men

"Sexism is dying out," says Blair of Independent Women's Forum. "It is an artifact of people raised in a different time and with different sensibilities. Younger people now see it as natural for women to be leaders, unlike earlier times when women leaders were flukes and even reflected badly on their men because they were seen as not taking care of their families."

Too many feminists, she says, perhaps because they've had bad experiences with men, fall victim to the stereotype of being "strident or screechy. Most would say men are better at conducting reasoned, unemotional disputation, and women should acknowledge this and learn from it. It may be more difficult to be a man than a woman," she adds, citing men's duty to fight in wars, their work in dangerous occupations and their shorter lifespans. "Many of us plan to have long-term relationships with men. We don't regard them as a separate race."

The goal of understanding men is seconded by feminist author Wolf, who writes that "a lot of sexism . . . is not the stubbornness of a pig or the oppressiveness of a born monster so much as the basic math of politics, a natural human response to a threatened and real loss of status. Women would certainly exhibit it themselves were the roles reversed." [42]

Simon goes further. "I would be happy if we did away with all women's groups and simply concentrated on issues," she says.

But feminists such as Lichtman counter that without women's groups, no one would be fighting such issues as family leave from work. What's more, "our accomplishments of yesterday are under attack. The movement has pushed the envelope, but it also fights a defensive battle for things already in place."

Ireland says that in grass-roots organizing, it is still important to "link up with identity groups" such as the women's bar, women's medical caucuses as well as ethnic and racial groups in order to "bring strength to the whole." She says NOW would like to make new alliances with homemakers over such issues as retirement income. "What could be more shocking to the Senate," she asks, "than to have the Concerned Women for America and NOW on the same side of an issue?"

Friedan says the movement must move beyond men vs. women. "The women's movement must enlarge its vision. It can't disband any more than unions can. And it needs new alliances with labor and civil rights groups to fight for such things as a French-style national child care program and a Canadian-style single-payer government health plan." She is concerned that men might become angry if the "masters of the universe" — as macho business types were called in the 1980s — fall victim to corporate downsizing. "If the stock market burst its bubble, there could be a reversion to the feminine mystique that seeks to push women into the home again."

Smeal says she has never viewed feminists as alienated from their men, their sons or their husbands. "All people should want to correct injustice," she says. "And those who fight for justice are always a minority." ■

Notes

[1] See "First Ladies," *The CQ Researcher,* June 14, 1996, pp. 505-528.

[2] "Sisterhood Was Powerful," *Newsweek,* June 20, 1994, p. 68.

[3] Quoted in *USA Today,* Sept. 24, 1996.

[4] Jenny McPhee, "A Mother's Name," *The New York Times Magazine,* Feb. 2, 1997, p. 68.

[5] Sherrye Henry, *The Deep Divide* (1994), p. 1.

[6] Elizabeth Fox-Genovese, *Feminism Is Not the Story of My Life* (1996), p. 16.

[7] *McLean's,* April 8, 1996, p. 46.

[8] Katha Pollitt, "Are Women Morally Superior to Men?" *The Nation,* Dec. 28, 1992, p. 799.

[9] Naomi Wolf, *Fire with Fire* (1994), p. 251.

[10] Wendy Kaminer, "Feminism's Identity Crisis," *The Atlantic Monthly,* October 1993, p. 56.

[11] The grocery chains were Publix and Lucky's. See "Supermarket to Pay $81 Million in Bias Suit," *The New York Times,* Jan. 25, 1997. For background, see "Crackdown on Sexual Harassment," *The CQ Researcher,* July 19, 1996, pp. 625-648.

[12] See "The Glass Ceiling," *The CQ Researcher,* Oct. 29, 1993, pp. 937-960.

[13] *Business Week,* Oct. 28, 1996, p. 55.

[14] Laura Flanders, "How Many Women and Which Ones?" *Extra,* September-October 1995.

[15] Diana Furchtgott-Roth and Christine Stolba, "Women's Figures: The Economic Progress of Women in America," Independent Woman's Forum, 1996.

[16] *The Economist,* Aug. 10, 1996, p. 50.

[17] "Working Women Count!" Labor Department, 1994.

[18] Danielle Crittenden, "The Shirt Gap," *The Women's Quarterly,* summer 1996, p. 2.

[19] Sue Shellenbarger, "Work and Family," *The Wall Street Journal,* Jan. 29, 1997.

[20] *The Wall Street Journal,* May 17, 1996.

[21] Miriam Schneir (ed.), *Feminism: The Essential Historical Writings* (1992), p. 6.

[22] Simone de Beauvoir, *The Second Sex* (1989 edition), p. 3.

[23] Christina Hoff Sommers, *Who Stole Feminism? How Women Have Betrayed Women* (1994), p. 35.

[24] Henry, *op. cit.,* p. 44.

[25] Toni Carabillo and Judith Meuli, "The Feminization of Power," Fund for the Feminist Majority, 1988. p. 13.

[26] Quoted in Susan Faludi, *Backlash: The Undeclared War Against American Women* (1991), p. 312.

[27] Henry, *op. cit.,* pp. 151, 155.

[28] See Peter Brimelow, "The New Stay-at-Homes?" *Forbes,* Jan. 13, 1997. See "Work, Family and Stress," *The CQ Researcher,* Aug. 14, 1992, pp. 869-892.

[29] Sommers, *op. cit.,* p. 42. See "Violence Against Women," *The CQ Researcher,* Feb. 26, 1993, pp. 169-182.

[30] See "Sex on Campus," *The CQ Researcher,* Nov. 4, 1994, pp. 961-982.

[31] Robin Warshaw, *I Never Called it Rape, The Ms. Report on Recognizing, Fighting and Surviving Date and Acquaintance Rape* (1988, 1994), p. 92.

[32] Quoted in "Face to Face," *Working Woman,* March 1992, p. 79.

[33] Katie Roiphe, *The Morning After: Sex, Fear and Feminism* (1993), p. 84.

[34] Fox-Genovese *op. cit.,* p. 164.

[35] *The Nation,* March 16, 1992, p. 24.

[36] Kate Fillion, *Lip Service: The Truth About Women's Darker Side in Love, Sex and Friendship* (1996).

[37] Barbour's column appeared in *The Washington Post,* Jan. 19, 1997. Luntz was quoted in a column by Amy E. Schwartz, *The Washington Post,* Nov. 20, 1996.

[38] *The Washington Post,* Jan. 26, 1997.

[39] *The New York Times,* Jan. 17, 1997.

[40] See "Women's Health Issues," *The CQ Researcher,* May 13, 1994, pp. 416-438.

[41] See "Sex, Violence and the Media," *The CQ Researcher,* Nov. 17, 1995, pp. 1017-1040.

[42] Wolf, *op. cit.,* p. 14.

Bibliography

Selected Sources Used

Books

Faludi, Susan, Backlash: *The Undeclared War Against American Women*, Crown Publishers, 1991.
A former *Wall Street Journal* reporter analyzes media coverage of feminism to argue that the modern women's anxieties and the widely reported "failures" of feminism are purposefully exaggerated by conservatives.

Fox-Genovese, Elizabeth, *"Feminism is Not the Story of My Life": How Today's Feminist Elite Has Lost Touch with the Real Concerns of Women*, Doubleday, 1996.
An Emory University historian combines personal recollections with social commentary to describe how she thinks modern feminism has gone astray.

Henry, Sherrye, *The Deep Divide: Why American Women Resist Equality*, MacMillan, 1994.
A Democratic political activist describes her personal journey in feminism while summarizing results of focus groups exploring why average women have not flocked to the feminist label.

Smeal, Eleanor, *Why and How Women Will Elect the Next President*, Harper & Row, 1984.
The current president of The Feminist Majority presents the election data that led her to popularize "the gender gap" following the 1980 elections.

Schneir, Miriam (ed.), *Feminism: The Essential Historical Writings*, Vintage Books, 1992.
This collection of essays, memoirs, fiction and letters offers samplings of the works of such seminal feminist thinkers as Elizabeth Cady Stanton, Emma Goldman, Abigail Adams, Friedrich Engels and Virginia Woolf.

Sommers, Christina Hoff, *Who Stole Feminism?: How Women Have Betrayed Women*, Simon and Schuster, 1994.
A Clark University philosophy professor lays out the argument of contemporary conservative feminists who say that mainstream feminist leaders are out of touch with average women and misuse sociological and scientific data to exaggerate the extent to which women are victimized by sexism.

Wolf, Naomi, *Fire With Fire: The Female Power and How to Use It*, Fawcett Columbine, 1993.
A feminist author who takes brickbats from the left and right outlines her vision of how modern feminists can abandon "victim feminism" and get comfortable with "power feminism."

Reports and Studies

Center for Policy Alternatives, *"A Matter of Simple Justice: Women's Rights Are Human Rights,"* 1996.
This follow up to the 1995 United Nations World Conference on Women held in Beijing summarizes the social and economic conditions of women's lives worldwide. It contains numerous advocacy positions and a forward from President Clinton.

Furchtgott-Roth, Diana, and Stolba, Christine, *Women's Figures: The Economic Progress of Women in America*, Independent Women's Forum, 1996.
This compendium from a conservative group critical of feminism offers data and analysis on women's progress in earnings, education, business ownership and voting patterns.

Institute for Women's Policy Research, *The Status of Women in the States*, 1996
This compendium from a Washington research and advocacy group offers state-by-state rankings, charts and maps detailing the status of women in politics, economics and health.

Mattox, William R. Jr., "Gender Politics: Is America Really a House Divided?" *Family Policy*, Family Research Council, December 1994
A conservative, pro-family research and advocacy group challenges common media depictions of the gender gap, arguing that husbands and wives vote alike on most major issues.

Women's Bureau, U.S. Labor Department, *1993 Handbook on Women Workers: Trends and Issues,* 1994
This compendium of data, analysis and contacts surveys demographic trends and summarizes policy histories in such as areas as employment discrimination, poverty and minority advancement.

Women's Bureau, U.S. Labor Department, *What Works!: The Working Women Count Honor Roll Report*, 1996.
This follow-up to a 1994 survey of women in the workplace highlights private and public employer policies that help women advance economically and balance family with career.

The Next Step

Additional information from UMI's Newspaper & Periodical Abstracts™ database

Feminism

Baker, Christina Looper and Christina Kline, "Mothers & daughters: Honest talk about feminism and real life," *Ms.,* May 1996, pp. 45-63.

In an excerpt from "The Conversation Begins," three pairs of mothers and daughters discuss the struggles and joys of growing up in the midst of the feminist revolution.

Denfeld, Rene, "Feminism 2000: What does it really mean (to you)?" *Sassy,* May 1996, pp. 60-61.

Individuals need to figure out what feminism means to them right now. A lot of young women call themselves feminists without a solid understanding of what they actually mean. A quiz is presented to find out if one is a secret sexist.

Farnham, Christie, "Male bashing or what's in a name? Feminism in the United States Today," *Journal of Women's History,* summer 1996, pp. 6-9.

There are various broad definitions of feminism today, including domestic feminism, socialist feminism, radical feminism and cultural feminism. Farnham discusses what it means to be a feminist today.

Merida, Kevin, "Feminist Expo '96 billed as rebirth of the women's movement," *The Washington Post,* Feb. 4, 1996, p. A22.

The "Feminist Expo '96 for Women's Empowerment" is described. Women from 300 organizations and 46 states joined to defend affirmative action and other programs under assault that benefit them. Some are calling it the rebirth of the feminist movement.

Poster, Winifred R., "The challenges and promises of class and racial diversity in the women's movement: A study of two women's organizations," *Gender & Society,* December 1995, pp. 659-679.

Based on a comparative study of two feminist organizations, the formation of divergent types of gender politics was charted. Differences in the class and racial backgrounds of the memberships were found to create distinct organizational needs, and these divergent political interests also motivate contrasting organizational ideologies.

Walker, Rebecca, "Changing the face of feminism," *Essence,* January 1996, p. 123.

Walker discusses the strictures involved in being a feminist and the amount of devotion that many people perceive it must take. She urges many feminists to find a common ground with their own lives and feminism.

Wetzel, Janice Wood, "On the road to Beijing: The evolution of the international women's movement," *Affilia,* summer 1996, pp. 221-232.

Wetzel traces the evolution of the international women's movement through the four international conferences on women that have been held since 1975, paying special attention to the fourth conference, held in China in 1995.

Gender Gap

Baker, Peter, "Clinton aims to translate the gender gap into votes," *The Washington Post,* Oct. 31, 1996, p. A15.

In the days before the Nov. 5, 1996, election, the Clinton re-election campaign dispensed with subtlety to maximize its gender-gap advantage with a series of campaign messages and policy pronouncements that explicitly appeal to women to vote.

"Closing the merit test gender gap," *Chicago Tribune,* Oct. 26, 1996, Sec. 1, p. 18.

An editorial comments on the College Board agreeing to change the qualifying test for National Merit Scholarships. The College Board stated that as long as the tests fail to reflect or predict fairly the academic performance of young women who take them, their merit as a measure of merit will remain under a cloud.

Hasson, Judi, "GOP can't close the 'gender gap,'" *USA Today,* Nov. 6, 1996, p. A1.

Women gave President Clinton his biggest re-election boost on Nov. 5, 1996, — Clinton got 55 percent of their vote, and Republican challenger Bob Dole got 37 percent — according to an exit poll by Voter News Service.

Kelly, Katy, "Survey measures teens' gender gap," *USA Today,* Sept. 4, 1996, p. D4.

The results of *USA Weekend's* ninth annual "The Great Divide: Teens & the Gender Gap Survey," released Sept. 7, 1996, are discussed. Teenagers of both sexes worry more about finding a job than a spouse, many believe a woman will be president in their lifetime and a majority expect to share equally with their spouse in the care of children they may have in the future.

Ryan, Joan, "The Rice Krispies gender gap," *San Francisco Chronicle,* Aug. 25, 1996, p. S8.

Ryan discusses the "gender gap" that is within the family and asserts that where boys are concerned she believes much of their behavior is the result of a "special imprint on their DNA."

Shea, Lois R., "Gender gap gives edge to Shaheen," *The Boston Globe,* Oct. 6, 1996, Sec. WKNH, p. 1.

In the 1996 election cycle, where the in-vogue target voter is the "soccer mom" — 40ish, white, suburban, professional, pressed for time and determined to make it to her kids' ball games — New Hampshire gubernatorial candidate Jeanne Shaheen, a "soccer mom," has excited these voters.

Glass Ceiling

Blair, Anita K., "Why women are breaking through glass ceiling," *Houston Chronicle,* July 8, 1996, p. A15.

Blair analyzes the progress made by women in the U.S. over the last 30 years, asking whether affirmative action policies should receive the credit for their success.

Groves, Martha, "Women still bumping up against glass ceiling," *Los Angeles Times,* May 26, 1996, p. D1.

The fact that Jill Elikann Barad of Mattel Inc. is the sole woman on the *Los Angeles Times*' list of 100 executives with the highest cash compensation in California for 1995 illustrates how a glass ceiling still exists for women executives. A federal report on the problem is detailed.

Kimelman, John, "Greco, CoreStates' president, considers 'glass ceiling' from above," *American Banker,* Oct. 10, 1996, p. 6.

Rosemarie B. Greco, named president of CoreStates Financial Corp. in May 1996 talks about the problems women face in breaking into the top echelons of the banking industry.

Silverstein, Stuart, "Female execs — In the pipeline or still hitting the glass ceiling?" *Los Angeles Times,* Nov. 3, 1996, p. D5.

Silverstein discusses whether women still need help in breaking through barriers that have unfairly kept them from reaching the top of the corporate world.

Neuborne, Ellen, "Glass ceiling still in place," *USA Today,* Oct. 18, 1996, p. B2.

A census of women in corporate America, conducted by the research firm Catalyst, found women make up 46 percent of the work force but just 10 percent of corporate officers at Fortune 500 companies.

Sward, Susan, "Chevron's glass ceiling suit settled," *San Francisco Chronicle,* Nov. 7, 1996, p. A1.

In a move legal observers call a "wake-up call" for corporate America, Chevron agreed on Nov. 6, 1996, to pay more than $8 million to settle a case in which hundreds of its female employees argued that the company discriminated against them in pay, promotions and assignments.

Sex Discrimination

Chemerinsky, Erwin, and Laurie Levenson, "Sex discrimination made legal," *Los Angeles Times,* Jan. 10, 1996, p. B9.

The authors criticize a provision of the proposed "California civil rights initiative," an anti-affirmative action initiative which they claim would legalize sex discrimination by government agencies.

Gutek, Barbara A., Aaron Groff Cohen and Anne Tsui, "Reactions to perceived sex discrimination," *Human Relations,* June 1996, pp. 791-813.

Independent samples of psychologists and managers were examined to assess the relationship of perceived discrimination to an individual's reactions to the job and the organization. For women, perceptions of discrimination against women were associated with lower feelings of power and prestige on the job, more hours spent on paid work activities and more work conflict.

Mills, Steve, "County to pay $440,000 in sex discrimination case," *Chicago Tribune,* Dec. 9, 1995, Sec. 1NW, p. 5.

The McHenry County Board of Illinois has agreed to pay $440,000 and make dramatic changes in how the Sheriff's Department hires its patrol deputies to settle a sex discrimination lawsuit filed in 1994 by the Justice Department. Not a single woman was hired as a patrol officer in 17 years.

"OfficeMax Inc.: Sex discrimination charge is withdrawn by official," *The Wall Street Journal,* Aug. 27, 1996, p. B6.

OfficeMax Inc. said its vice president of human resources, Suzanne V. Forsythe, withdrew her sex discrimination charges against the company. The discount retailer of office products said it did not make any cash settlement in connection with Forsythe's decision, though in connection with her termination she will be allowed to exercise certain stock options.

Stay-at-Home Moms

Downey, Maureen, "Stay-at-home moms stay in touch," *Atlanta Constitution,* May 14, 1996, p. F1.

Without the traditional cornerstones of family and neighbors, more stay-at-home mothers around the country are plugging into technology to find one another. Moms are also flocking to support networks such as FEMALE (Formerly Employed Mothers at the Leading Edge). Formed in 1995, the Atlanta chapter of FEMALE is the second largest in the country.

Salmon, Jacqueline L., "It's lonely for moms at home office," *The Washington Post,* Dec. 14, 1996, Sec. PWE, p. 1.

Stay-at-home moms in Prince William County, Va., may have a bigger challenge than their counterparts in other areas because many of their husbands have long commutes to jobs in Washington, D.C., leaving the mothers with 14-hour days in which most of the family responsibilities fall on them.

Schwab, Robert, "Live-at-home moms take ideas to market," *Denver Post,* Oct. 5, 1996, p. D1.

Several stay-at-home moms, including Millie Thomas, founder of RGT Enterprises in Fort Collins, Colo., are profiled for their entrepreneurial products that cater to child-care needs.

Back Issues

Great Research on Current Issues Starts Right Here...Recent topics covered by The CQ Researcher are listed below. Before May 1991, reports were published under the name of Editorial Research Reports.

AUGUST 1995
Job Stress
Organ Transplants
United Nations at 50
Advances in Cancer Research

SEPTEMBER 1995
Catholic Church in the U.S.
Northern Ireland Cease-Fire
High School Sports
Teaching History

OCTOBER 1995
Quebec's Future
Revitalizing the Cities
Networking the Classroom
Indoor Air Pollution

NOVEMBER 1995
The Working Poor
The Jury System
Sex, Violence and the Media
Police Misconduct

DECEMBER 1995
Teens and Tobacco
Gene Therapy's Future
Global Water Shortages
Third-Party Prospects

JANUARY 1996
Emergency Medicine
Punishing Sex Offenders
Bilingual Education
Helping the Homeless

FEBRUARY 1996
Reforming the CIA
Campaign Finance Reform
Academic Politics
Getting Into College

MARCH 1996
The British Monarchy
Preventing Juvenile Crime
Tax Reform
Pursuing the Paranormal

APRIL 1996
Centennial Olympic Games
Managed Care
Protecting Endangered Species
New Military Culture

MAY 1996
Russia's Political Future
Marriage and Divorce
Year-Round Schools
Taiwan, China and the U.S.

JUNE 1996
Rethinking NAFTA
First Ladies
Teaching Values
Labor Movement's Future

JULY 1996
Recovered-Memory Debate
Native Americans' Future
Crackdown on Sexual Harassment
Attack on Public Schools

AUGUST 1996
Fighting Over Animal Rights
Privatizing Government Services
Child Labor and Sweatshops
Cleaning Up Hazardous Wastes

SEPTEMBER 1996
Gambling Under Attack
The States and Federalism
Civic Journalism
Reassessing Foreign Aid

OCTOBER 1996
Political Consultants
Insurance Fraud
Rethinking School Integration
Parental Rights

NOVEMBER 1996
Global Warming
Clashing Over Copyright
Consumer Debt
Governing Washington, D.C.

DECEMBER 1996
Welfare, Work and the States
The New Volunteerism
Implementing the Disabilities Act
America's Pampered Pets

JANUARY 1997
Combating Scientific Misconduct
Restructuring the Electric Industry
The New Immigrants
Chemical and Biological Weapons

FEBRUARY 1997
Assisting Refugees
Alternative Medicine's Next Phase
Independent Counsels

Back issues are available for $5.00 (subscribers) or $10.00 (non-subscribers). Quantity discounts apply to orders over ten. To order, call Congressional Quarterly Customer Service at (202) 887-8621.

Binders are available for $18.00. To order call 1-800-638-1710. Please refer to stock number 648.

Future Topics

▶ ***New Air Quality Standards***

▶ ***Alcohol Advertising***

▶ ***Civic Renewal***

THE CQ Researcher

PUBLISHED BY CONGRESSIONAL QUARTERLY INC.

New Air Quality Standards

Should U.S. pollution regulations be stricter?

The proposed tightening of federal air quality regulations has sparked bitter debate between businesses and public-health professionals as well as entire regions of the country. At issue are the maximum levels of smog and soot permitted under the 1990 Clean Air Act. Affected industries say the stricter regulations would impose intolerable financial burdens while providing negligible health benefits. Environmentalists and many health professionals say enforcing stricter air standards would save lives at relatively low cost and improve everyone's quality of life. The Environmental Protection Agency must make its final decision on the new standards this summer. Meanwhile, disagreement over the need for new standards is developing into one of the most acrimonious environmental debates in decades.

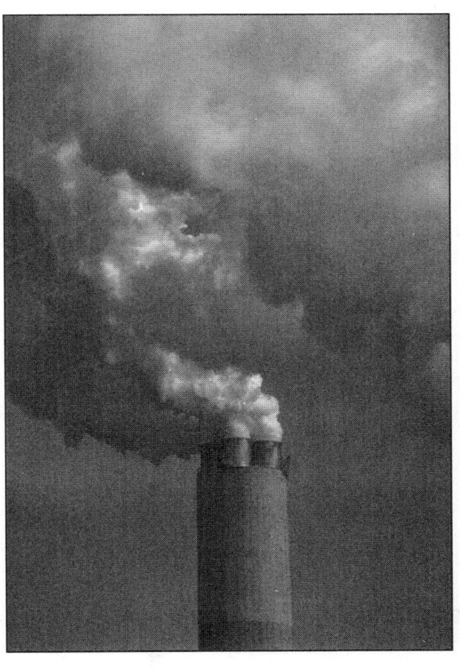

INSIDE THIS ISSUE

CQ March 7, 1997 • Volume 7, No. 9 • Pages 193-216

Formerly Editorial Research Reports

COVER: SMOKE BILLOWS FROM AN ELECTRIC GENERATING PLANT IN PENNSYLVANIA. (© ROBERT VISSER/GREENPEACE)

THE CQ Researcher

March 7, 1997
Volume 7, No. 9

The CQ Researcher (ISSN 1056-2036). Formerly Editorial Research Reports. Published weekly (48 times per year, not printed Jan. 3, May 30, Aug. 29, Oct. 31) by Congressional Quarterly Inc., 1414 22nd St., N.W., Washington, D.C. 20037. Annual subscription rate for libraries, businesses and government is $340. Additional rates furnished upon request. Periodicals postage paid at Washington, D.C., and additional mailing offices. POSTMASTER: Send address changes to The CQ Researcher, 1414 22nd St., N.W., Washington, D.C. 20037.

New Air Quality Standards

By Mary H. Cooper

The Issues

Fifty years ago, Pittsburgh was a city cloaked in gray. Coal-fired steel mills ran around the clock, spewing plumes of black, soot-laden smoke thick enough to blot out the sun.

Today, most of the city's mills are shuttered, and the remainder have been fitted with smokestack "scrubbers" that filter out much of the noxious pollution. Sunshine and blue skies have returned to western Pennsylvania.

Pittsburgh's success in cleaning its air has been repeated throughout the industrial Midwest and other manufacturing regions. Much of the progress can be attributed to the 1970 Clean Air Act, the country's first sweeping environmental law. Amended several times since, the act authorizes the federal government to set air quality standards and requires the states to devise ways to meet them.

"Thus far, when you consider how the country has grown since the act was first passed, it has been a tremendous success," said Carol M. Browner, administrator of the Environmental Protection Agency (EPA). "Since 1970, while the U.S. population is up 28 percent, vehicle miles traveled are up 116 percent and the gross domestic product has expanded by 99 percent, emissions of the six major pollutants or their precursors [regulated by the EPA] * have dropped by 29 percent." [1]

But many Americans — notably residents of Southern California and the East Coast between Boston and Washington — continue to live with high levels of air pollution. The worst offenders in these regions are motor vehicles. The compounds they emit form ozone and other pollutants, turning the air into an unhealthy, yellow haze. Factories in the Midwest contribute to the East Coast's problems. While they are markedly cleaner, they still emit pollutants, which are borne eastward by prevailing winds.

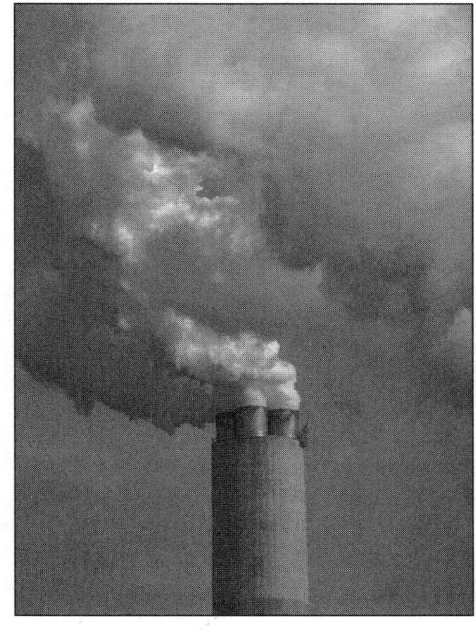

To remedy these lingering problems, Browner last November proposed strengthening the air quality standards for two harmful pollutants — ozone and particulate matter (PM). She based her decision on an exhaustive review of environmental and health studies by the EPA and outside experts. "I am satisfied that our decision-making process . . . has been thorough, complete and based on extensive peer-reviewed science," she said.

According to some studies, very low amounts of ground-level ozone, the main component of smog, can cause acute respiratory problems, aggravate asthma and damage lung tissue, impairing the body's resistance to disease. Children and outdoor workers are especially vulnerable.

Other studies indicate that "fine particulate matter" — a mixture of solid particles and droplets produced by industrial fuel combustion, wood stoves and agricultural burning — is more dangerous than previously believed. Able to penetrate the deepest recesses of the lungs, the tiny particles have been linked to premature death and increased hospitalizations related to asthma, bronchitis and decreased lung function. Children, the elderly and adults with heart or lung diseases are especially vulnerable.

Browner's proposal sparked instant controversy, although she will not make a final decision on the new standards until July 19, after a public-comment period ends. Industries that would be affected by the stricter standards accused the EPA of basing the proposals on "junk science" and charged that the costs of tougher standards would far outweigh any benefits to public health.

"The statistical models have been clearly manipulated, and the costs appear to be understated," said Richard Klimisch, vice president of the American Automobile Manufacturers Association and inventor of the catalytic converter used to reduce vehicle tailpipe emissions. "This is a recipe for disaster, putting states in a bureaucratic trap that will require them to regulate barbecue grills and lawn mowers." [2]

Browner strongly denies these charges. "While the ultimate decisions as to what programs are needed to meet air quality standards are up to the state and local governments, I would like to state categorically that there will not be any new federal mandates eliminating backyard barbecues or requiring car pooling," she testified Feb. 12. "These kinds of claims are merely scare tactics designed to shift the debate away from the critical, complex public health issues we are attempting to address."

For some environmentalists, strengthening the air quality standards for smog and soot would amount to an acknowledgment that the nation has a long way to go before victory can be declared in the war on air pollution.

*The six pollutants regulated by the EPA are carbon monoxide, lead, nitrogen dioxide, ozone, particulate matter and sulfur dioxide.

Six Major Air Pollutants Are Monitored . . .

The Clean Air Act identifies six major air pollutants and directs the Environmental Protection Agency (EPA) to set national standards for each to protect human health and the environment. The states are responsible for devising and implementing plans to meet those standards, subject to EPA oversight.

Ozone: Ground-level ozone (O_3), the main component of smog, is the most pervasive and hardest to control of the six major air pollutants regulated by the EPA. Unlike the others, ozone is not emitted directly into the air but is the result of a chemical reaction when sunlight acts on nitrogen oxides and volatile organic compounds (VOCs) in the air. Ozone and its chemical precursors can be carried by wind hundreds of miles to affect regions far from the sources of emission.

Sources: VOCs and nitrogen oxides are emitted by thousands of sources, including gasoline vapors, chemical solvents, fuel combustion and consumer products. Some VOCs are also hazardous air pollutants in their own right.

Health Effects: Ozone causes breathing problems and reduced lung function, irritated eyes, stuffy nose, reduced resistance to colds and other infections, and may speed up aging of lung tissue. Recent studies link high ozone levels and increases in hospital admissions for respiratory problems. Animal studies show permanent structural damage of the lungs from exposure to high ozone levels.

Environmental Effects: Ozone can damage trees and other plants, costing up to $2 billion a year in reduced crop yields and damaging forest ecosystems in California and the Eastern U.S. Smog can reduce visibility.

Property Damage: Ozone damages rubber, fabrics and other materials.

Trends: Levels vary with weather conditions and changes in emissions. Ozone concentrations fell 6 percent from 1986 to 1995, but rose 4 percent from 1994 to 1995 because of the hot, dry summer in 1995 in the eastern half of the country. VOC emissions fell 9 percent from 1986-95.

Particulate Matter: Suspended liquid or solid particles that can be visible as dust, smoke and soot, depending on their size and chemical composition. PM can be emitted directly or formed in the atmosphere when gaseous pollutants such as sulfur dioxide and nitrogen oxides react to form fine particles.

Sources: A wide variety of sources, including burning of wood, diesel and other fuels; industrial plants; agriculture (plowing and burning of fields); unpaved roads.

Health Effects: PM causes nose and throat irritation, lung damage, bronchitis, early death, especially among the elderly, children and people with chronic lung disease, influenza or asthma.

Environmental Effects: Particulates are the main source of regional haze, which reduces visibility.

Property Damage: Ashes, soot, smoke and dust can dirty and discolor buildings, clothes, furniture and other property.

Trends: From 1988 (when monitoring began) to 1995, PM-10 concentrations fell by 22 percent.

Nitrogen Dioxide: NO_2 is one of a group of highly reactive gases called nitrogen oxides (NOx), which form when fuel is burned at high temperatures. NO_2 is a suffocating, brownish gas that reacts in the air to form corrosive nitric acid and toxic organic nitrates. It plays a major role in the formation of ground-level ozone, or smog.

Sources: burning of gasoline, natural gas, coal and other fossil fuels. Most emissions come from vehicles and stationary sources such as electric utilities and industrial boilers.

Health Effects: Irritates the lungs and can lower resistance to respiratory diseases such as influenza. High exposure can cause acute respiratory illness in children.

"This is a truth-in-labeling issue," says Jeff Bocan, an environmental quality analyst at the Sierra Club. "We are backing the proposed standards because our kids are breathing dirty air, and it could be cleaner. Tighter standards will affect power plants, buses and trucks. There will be no change in the lifestyles of the average American because of these standards."

Under the EPA's existing standards for ozone, 106 of the nation's more than 3,000 counties already are not in compliance. (*See map, p. 200.*) Under the new ozone standard, however, an additional 229 counties would fall out of "attainment," or compliance. The number of counties that wouldn't meet the revised particulate standards would rise from 41 to 168 counties. (*See map, p. 206.*)

Many areas, especially ozone-ridden Los Angeles, have already imposed sweeping measures in a thus-far fruitless effort to meet national clean air standards. But critics say these areas need to do much more. "Lawn mowers are not the problem," says A. Blakeman Early, an environmental consultant for the American Lung Association (ALA). "Obviously, you start with the largest sources first."

Early points to some 700 coal-burning power plants in use around the country that were built before the Clean Air Act. All were exempted from the law's ozone standards in the erroneous expectation that they eventually would be replaced with less-polluting facilities. Most are located in the Ohio River Valley, which, ironically, meets current ozone standards, in large part because emissions created

. . . by the EPA Under the Clean Air Act

Environmental Effects: NO_2 is an ingredient of acid rain, which can damage trees and lakes and reduce visibility. NO_2 reduces oxygen content of coastal waters such as the Chesapeake Bay, destroying fish and other aquatic animals.

Property Damage: Acid rain can erode stone used in buildings, statues, monuments.

Trends: After remaining steady in the 1980s, NO_2 concentrations recently began to fall as a result of lower emissions from the two main sources, transportation and industrial fuel combustion; 1995 marked the fourth consecutive year that all areas, including smog-ridden Los Angeles, met the federal NO_2 air quality standard.

Lead: A heavy, soft metal used in batteries, pipes, solder and protective shields against radiation exposure.

Sources: Smelters (metal refineries) and lead battery plants are the main sources of airborne lead; other sources are leaded gasoline and house paint (being phased out).

Health Effects: Lead inhaled or ingested in contaminated food, water or soil accumulates in the blood, bone and soft tissues of the body. Children are especially vulnerable to exposure, which can cause anemia, kidney disease, reproductive disorders and nervous system damage such as seizures, mental retardation and behavioral disorders. Even low doses can interfere with basic processes in fetuses and children, causing nervous system damage or slowed growth. Recent studies link lead exposure to osteoporosis, high blood pressure and heart disease. Lead-containing chemicals cause cancer in animals.

Environmental Effects: Harms wildlife when ingested.

Trends: The introduction of unleaded gasoline led to a 78 percent fall in average lead concentrations in urban areas and a 32 percent fall in total lead emissions from 1986 to 1995.

Carbon Monoxide: CO is a colorless, odorless, poisonous gas formed when carbon in fuels is not burned completely.

Sources: Most emissions come from vehicle exhaust; industrial boilers; incinerators.

Health Effects: Reduces oxygen supply to organs and tissues, posing greatest threat to people with cardiovascular disease. In healthy people, exposure to high levels can cause visual impairment, reduced work capacity, reduced manual dexterity, poor learning ability and difficulty in performing complex tasks.

Trends: Emissions were down 16 percent from 1986-1995, despite a 31 percent increase in vehicle miles traveled over the period. Transportation sources account for 81 percent of total CO emissions.

Sulfur Dioxide: The gas SO_2 is formed when fuel containing sulfur — mainly coal and oil — is burned, and during metal smelting and other industrial processes.

Health Effects: SO_2 causes respiratory illness, reduced lung defenses against disease, worsening of existing cardiovascular disease, especially among children, the elderly and people with asthma, cardiovascular disease or chronic lung disease such as emphysema and bronchitis.

Environmental Effects: Sulfur dioxide produces sulfates, which cause acid rain and reduce visibility.

Property damage: Sulfates corrode buildings and monuments.

Trends: Thanks largely to the EPA's Acid Rain Program, launched in 1994, SO_2 concentrations decreased 37 percent from 1986 to 1995.

Source: Environmental Protection Agency, *The Plain English Guide to the Clean Air Act,* Jan. 15, 1996; *Brochure on National Air Quality: Status and Trends,* October 1996.

by local mills are blown eastward to Pennsylvania, New York, New Jersey and New England. In fact, only one Ohio county currently exceeds the ozone standard, but 26 counties would top it under the new standard.

"Why do you suppose that [Ohio Republican] Gov. [George V.] Voinovich is among the most vocal opponents of EPA's new standards?" Early asks. "Because coal-fired facilities in his state are going to get nailed if we approach the implementation phase with any kind of rationality. The bottom line is that the politicians in Ohio don't give a rat's ass about the people who live in Pennsylvania, New York and New Jersey because those people don't vote in Ohio."

Whatever Secretary Browner decides on tougher standards, wind-blown pollution appears likely to play a key role in future anti-pollution efforts. "There is a strong, though not unanimous, recognition that regional controls are necessary and even paramount to curbing air pollution," says S. William Becker, executive director of the Association of Local Air Pollution Control Officials. "There seems to be strong support now for this concept of not only areas of violation, or non-attainment areas, but also areas of influence," such as the Ohio River Valley.

As Browner moves toward a final decision on the new air quality standards, these are some of the questions being asked:

Is the EPA moving too hastily to tighten air quality standards?

The Clean Air Act requires the EPA

Continued on p. 199

Emissions of Major Pollutants Dropped From 1986-1995

Emissions of the six major pollutants monitored by the EPA fell in the past decade despite increases in population, vehicle miles traveled and the gross domestic product. However, studies indicating that serious health problems result from exposure to particulate matter and ground-level ozone (formed when sunlight heats volatile organic compounds) prompted the EPA to propose tougher standards for those two pollutants.

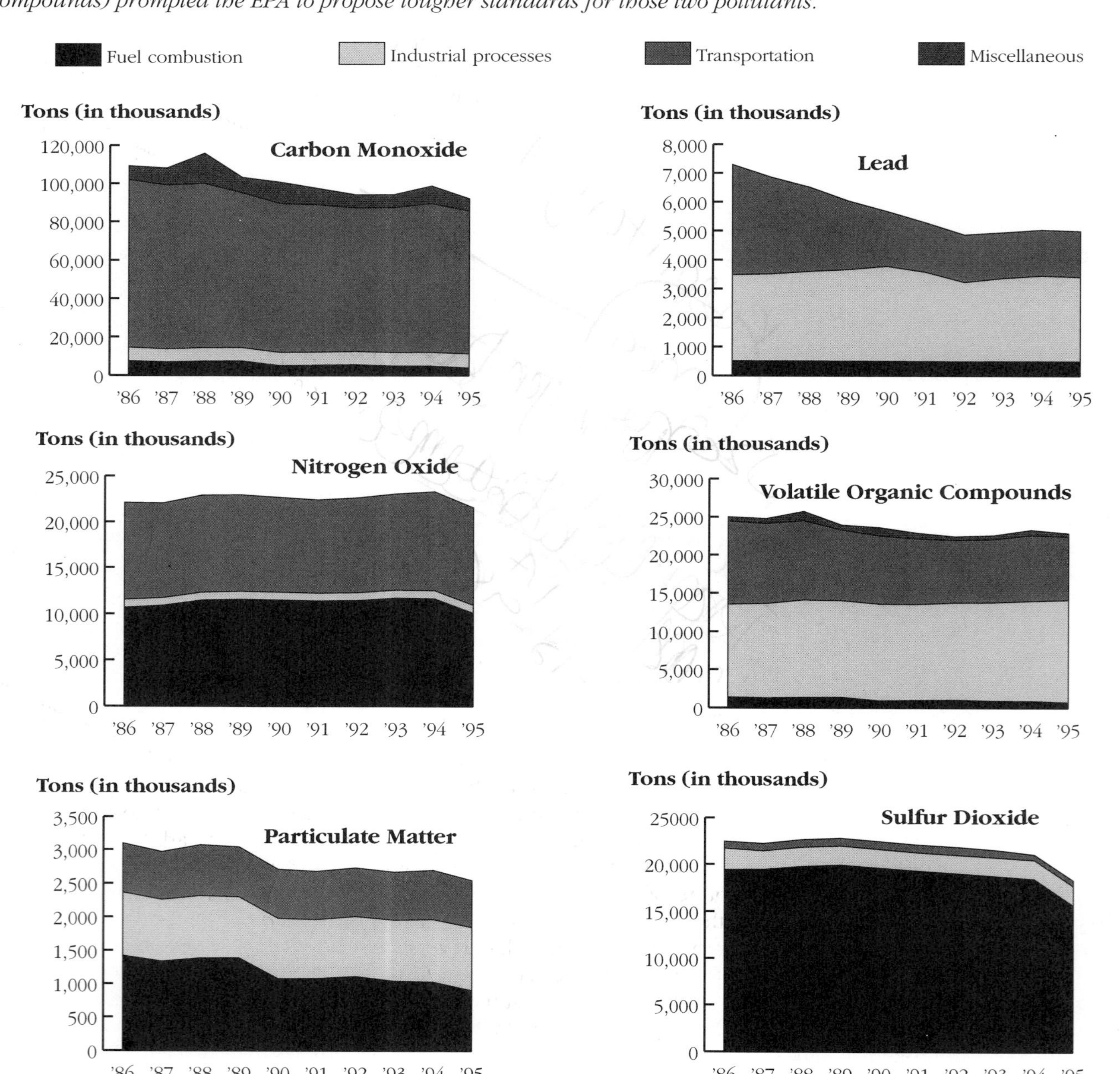

To read graphs: The top line of each graph indicates total emissions. For example, total emissions of lead dropped from 7.3 million tons in 1986 to 5.0 million tons in 1995, including lead emissions from fuel combustion (dropped from 516,000 tons to 493,000 tons), industrial processes (remained level at about 3.0 million tons) and transportation (dropped from 3.8 million tons to 1.6 million tons). Tonnages are given in short tons (2,240 pounds).

Source: Environmental Protection Agency, National Air Quality and Emissions Trends Report, 1995, *October 1996.*

Continued from p. 197

to review the latest scientific literature on pollutants every five years and to revise national air quality standards based on the best available science "with an adequate margin of safety."

Charging that the agency had failed to review the evidence in a timely manner, the lung association sued the EPA in 1993 for missing the required deadline for reviewing studies on particulate matter. In October 1994, a U.S. District Court in Arizona agreed with the ALA. That forced the EPA to launch an accelerated scientific review of the available literature that resulted in Browner's proposal last November to tighten the standards. (*See story, p. 204.*)

Browner recommended lowering the standard for allowable ozone in the air from 0.12 to 0.08 parts per million. This would be the first change in the ozone standard since 1979. She also proposed tightening the existing standard for particulate matter because studies indicated that tiny particles penetrate deeply into the lungs, where they can remain and cause disease.

Under the EPA's current particulate standard, set in 1987, areas are not in compliance with the regulations if they have higher-than-allowable concentrations of particles less than 10 microns in diameter — about one-seventh the diameter of a human hair. This so-called PM10 standard would continue to apply. A proposed, new standard sets a specific allowable level for "fine" particles, smaller than 2.5 microns. PM2.5 particles result from fuel combustion by utilities and factories, fireplaces and wood stoves and agricultural burning. Fine particles also can be formed in the atmosphere from gases such as sulfur dioxide, nitrogen oxides and volatile organic compounds (VOCs).

While many environmentalists and health professionals charge the EPA with foot-dragging in administering the Clean Air Act, some critics — including the chairman of the EPA's health advisory committee — say it is moving too fast, basing the new proposals on inadequate scientific evidence. In particular, the critics say the agency is relying excessively on epidemiological data, which show that the number of people who are hospitalized or die in certain areas rises during periods of high pollution levels. That may be true, the critics say, but it does not prove that air pollution actually caused the observed diseases and deaths.

Reuters

EPA Administrator Carol M. Browner

"The EPA has been forced to rush to judgment," said Roger McLellan, president of the Chemical Industry Institute of Toxicology and chairman of the Clean Air Scientific Advisory Committee, the panel that reviewed the literature and advised the EPA on its findings. "I have an asthmatic child, but unfortunately we do not know what causes asthma." [3]

The EPA rejects these charges. "This is a solid, science-based foundation on which to build public policy," said Mary Nichols, assistant EPA administrator and head of the Office of Air and Radiation. [4] Early of the ALA agrees. "We've got more information and probably better information than in any other previous review," he says. "In our view, the claim that EPA is moving too fast is a rather obvious attempt on the part of industry to raise the burden of proof that EPA must meet before it takes action."

Many clinicians and public health officials agree with Nichols that the scientific evidence justifies changing the standards, even though the causes of disease and death are still unclear. Epidemiological studies conducted by Morton Lippmann, a professor of environmental medicine at New York University's Norton Institute of Medicine, found that asthmatic children attending summer camp reported to the camp clinic more often when ozone levels had risen.

"We can't find any alternative explanation, such as changes in the weather," Lippmann said. "Sometimes the more prudent way to address policy is to protect the public, even if we don't have all the information we would like." [5] He emphasized that stricter ozone and particulate standards would be especially crucial for asthmatic children and the elderly. "More healthy people won't die on a dirty day," he said. "But if you're already on the edge, you might."

But McLellan voted against the proposed standard for fine particles, arguing that it was arbitrary. "Particulate matter is everywhere, and you can't reduce it to zero." he said. "There is no so-called bright line, so it is a policy call where you put that standard." In McLellan's view, the agency needs to do more research before changing the regulations limiting particulate matter. "I don't think we have a science base today to set a PM2.5 standard," he said. "In fact, it might be better at PM1.0," or more than twice as stringent.

Will the costs of the proposed standards outweigh their benefits?

When the Senate Environment and

New Ozone Standards Would Trip 335 Counties

*Under the new ozone-pollution standards proposed by the Environmental Protection Agency, the number of counties not complying with ozone regulations would rise from 106 to 335.**

* *Based on 1993-95 pollution data.*

Source: Environmental Protection Agency

Public Works Committee held hearings last month on Browner's air quality proposals, Chairman John H. Chafee, R-R.I., surprised many people by siding with the critics. Chafee is widely regarded as one of his party's strongest environmentalists and a key ally of those who favor stringent air quality standards in the Republican-majority Congress.

"These are very complex and far-reaching proposals," Chafee said. "After careful review, I am concerned that they may be too far-reaching. Even in the name of public health, it is possible to press too far, too fast." [6]

Implicit in the senator's misgivings about the proposed standards is concern that their expected benefits might be outweighed by the costs required to comply with them — one of the critics' main arguments against the new standards.

But the EPA is under seemingly conflicting mandates on evaluating the cost of environmental regulations. The Clean Air Act requires the agency to consider only the potential health and environmental effects of pollutants when setting air quality standards. "Under the law, we are not to take costs into consideration when setting these standards," Browner said. "This has been the case through six presidential administrations and 14 Congresses, and has been reviewed by the courts. We believe that approach remains appropriate." [7]

But regulatory agencies like the EPA also are required by law to conduct periodic cost-benefit analyses of regulations they issue, outside the standard-setting process.

Browner emphasizes the benefits of keeping cost out of the calculation when setting air quality standards. "Sensitive populations like children, the elderly and asthmatics deserve to be protected from the harmful effects of air pollution," she said. "And the American public deserves to know whether the air in its cities and counties is unsafe or not; that question should never be confused with the separate issues of how long it may take or how much it may cost to reduce pollution to safe levels." By law, cost calculations only come into play after a standard is adopted, as states devise strategies for cleaning the air.

Industry opponents are under no such legal constraints regarding costs. Steven Ziman, a staff scientist at Chevron Corp., cites studies prepared by the American Petroleum Institute that predict it would cost from $2.5 billion to $7 billion a year in the Chicago area alone just to meet the stricter standard for ozone. "At least 13 major areas are similar to the lower Lake Michigan region comprising Chicago in terms of the difficulty" they would have in meeting the standards, he said. [8]

But costs of complying with air quality standards are notoriously hard to predict. In 1990, when the EPA strengthened its standard for sulfur dioxide, the main pollutant that causes acid rain, the electric power industry predicted that complying would cost power plants and other factories an extra $1,500 per ton of emissions — about three times the cost predicted by the EPA at the time and about 15 times what it actually costs today.

One reason for the lower cost is that air quality standards often drive down compliance costs over time as industries develop new technologies to cope with the stricter standards. The development of new coatings for glossy paper used in publications, for example, largely eliminated emissions of volatile organic compounds (VOCs) — an ozone precursor.

"Everybody knows tighter regulations will cost a lot of money," the ALA's Early says. "But it costs a lot of money if we don't regulate, too. If we relied on costs for taking action, we wouldn't have taken the lead out of gasoline or done many other things to improve air quality. These things are always very difficult to judge because we're talking about activities that won't actually be taking place for another 10 years. It's very difficult to know what the opportunities for reduction will be and what they will cost 10 years from today."

Supporters of tighter standards say the improvement in job productivity they would bring would immediately outweigh the costs of implementing them. "Asthma is the No. 1 cause of absences from school," Bocan says. "Often when a child stays home from school, a parent has to stay home, too. If the proposed standards are adopted, there will be far fewer absenses from work as well."

Would states and localities be able to meet tougher standards for smog and soot?

Quite apart from the costs involved, many experts wonder whether some states could ever meet tighter standards for ozone and particulates. Today, 106 counties in 25 states, plus the District of Columbia, fail to meet the current ozone standard. Under tighter standards, the number of deficient counties would rise by 229 counties in 31 states.

"Everybody knows tighter regulations will cost a lot of money. But it costs a lot of money if we don't regulate, too. If we relied on costs for taking action, we wouldn't have taken the lead out of gasoline or done many other things to improve air quality."

— A. Blakeman Early
Environmental Consultant
American Lung Association

Some areas would find it extremely difficult to meet new standards. The Baltimore, New York City and Philadelphia areas are "severely" out of compliance with the current ozone standard, despite the introduction of cleaner-burning gasoline, car-pooling incentives and other steps to reduce emissions of ozone-producing compounds, especially from cars and trucks.

The ability of Eastern cities to make further headway against ozone pollution will depend largely on the outcome of efforts to establish a regional approach to air-quality programs. In some experts' view, tightening the ozone standard will promote regionalism by bringing many areas that currently meet the ozone standard into non-compliance, thereby forcing the states involved to reduce their ozone levels. With tougher ozone standards, the number of counties in non-compliance would rise in Ohio from one to 26, in West Virginia from zero to four and in Tennessee from one to 16, according to EPA estimates based on 1993-95 data. [9] Forcing these areas to curb emissions of ozone-producing compounds, mostly from industrial plants, would reduce the amount of ozone carried eastward by wind.

Wind-borne pollution, or pollution transport, also makes it hard for other areas, such as Chicago and other communities along Lake Michigan, to reduce their ozone levels. "It's impossible for the Lake Michigan [non-compliance] areas to correct the problem as required under current law," said Donald Theiler, director of Wisconsin's Bureau of Air Management. "The area of violation covers the Lake Michigan lakefront northward past Green Bay [Wis.] and across to the lower peninsula of Michigan." But the region that actually generates the Chicago area's ozone pollution covers parts of nine states, mostly to the south. "Northern Lake Michigan does not contribute to the pollution at all," Theiler said. [10]

Strengthening the particulate matter standard also poses daunting challenges to the 41 areas in 18 states, mostly in the West, that currently exceed permissible limits. By regulating finer particles, which are produced by a broader range of sources than bigger particles, the number of areas required to reduce their particulate matter would soar from 41 to

168, spread among 37 states, the EPA estimates.

A regional approach to reducing particulates as well as ozone may be necessary because winds also carry PM far from the source. The haze that obstructs visibility in Arizona's Grand Canyon, for example, is composed largely of particulates generated in Southern California.

"Particulate matter transport may be even a bigger issue than ozone transport," said Alan Krupnick, a senior fellow at the environmental group Resources for the Future and a member of the EPA's Subcommittee for Ozone, Particulate Matter and Regional Haze Implementation Programs. "Midwestern emissions are making their way all the way down to Florida. So the 'area of influence' may stretch from Florida to Massachusetts." [11]

No place in the country faces a bigger pollution challenge than the Los Angeles Basin, the only area to receive an "extreme" rating for ozone pollution and one of the areas with the worst particulate matter pollution as well. "Unfortunately, [meeting] ozone and particulate matter standards will be very difficult for Los Angeles, even under current standards," said Robert Wyman, a Los Angeles attorney active in anti-pollution efforts. [12] Many local industries have already adopted costly emission-control measures, while others decided to leave Los Angeles rather than comply, adding to the area's high unemployment.

But hard-pressed areas, including Los Angeles, will be able to meet stricter standards, Wyman said, if the EPA changes the way it regulates air pollution to rely on a more flexible, less punitive approach. "If the [new] standards are adopted, how can we implement them? EPA should not penalize non-attainment areas if they take steps to curb pollution, set reasonable deadlines for them to comply and allow the states complete discretion in crafting programs if they meet federal targets." ■

BACKGROUND

A Slow Beginning

The air we breathe, known as ambient air, is a fairly constant mixture of gases held by the force of gravity within the seven-to-10-mile space above Earth's surface known as the troposphere. It is largely made up of nitrogen (78 percent), oxygen (21 percent) and carbon dioxide (.03 percent) — all essential to plant and animal life. Pollution occurs when harmful chemical compounds are not quickly dissipated by wind or precipitation or not broken down by solar energy. [13]

Volcanic eruptions, rotting vegetation and other natural processes release gases such as ammonia, methane and sulfur dioxide into the air. But these natural emissions rarely cause lasting and widespread damage to plants or animals. Pollution as we know it is a byproduct of human activity, which accelerated following the Industrial Revolution in 19th-century Europe and North America. London, New York and other heavily industrialized cities were blanketed with soot and smoke belched from coal-fired factories.

By the 1880s, U.S. cities had begun passing ordinances aimed at curtailing sulfur oxides and particulates, contained in coal smoke. But coal-burning continued to spew clouds of smog that sowed disease and death. As recently as 1948, 20 residents of Donora, Pa., died and hundreds fell ill during a two-day bout with "killer smog." Coal-polluted air had become trapped over the town by a temperature inversion — a blanket of cold air that impedes air movement and often contributes to winter pollution alerts. A similar lethal incident occurred in London four years later.

By the 1940s, coal was no longer the only major source of U.S. pollution. The widespread use of automobiles powered by gasoline, another fossil fuel, created pollutants of a different sort wherever roads were built. Cities already fouled by industrial pollutants came under further assault by hydrocarbons, carbon monoxide and nitrogen oxides released from vehicle tailpipes.

Scientific studies had linked air pollution to sickness and death since the 1940s. In 1955, the Public Health Service launched the first federal efforts to study and remedy the problem.

In 1963, Congress passed the first Clean Air Act, a modest initiative that boosted funding for research and enabled states, localities and the federal government to issue regulations to curb emissions from sources of pollution. In 1965, Congress authorized the Department of Health, Education and Welfare (HEW, the forerunner of today's Department of Health and Human Services) to set standards for emissions of hydrocarbons and carbon monoxide by new cars. These first auto emission standards took effect in the 1968 model year.

Congress was loath, however, to expand federal authority in the fight against air pollution. But after the repeated failure of states to issue and enforce meaningful air quality standards, lawmakers passed the 1967 Air Quality Act. It authorized the department to set up metropolitan air quality regions and to issue and enforce federal standards in them if the states failed to do so. By 1970, however, no state had issued standards for any pollutant, and no more than a few air quality regions had been created.

Clean Air Act

Leaving air pollution regulation to the states threatened to create a

Continued on p. 204

Chronology

1950s-60s *The first federal efforts to curb air pollution take effect.*

1955
The Public Health Service launches the first federal efforts to study and remedy the problem of air pollution, produced mainly by coal-fired industrial plants and vehicle exhaust.

1963
Congress passes the first Clean Air Act, funding research and enabling federal, state and local governments to issue regulations to curb harmful emissions.

1965
The Department of Health, Education and Welfare is authorized to set standards for hydrocarbons and carbon monoxide emitted by new cars. The first auto emission standards take effect for the 1968 model year.

1967
The Air Quality Act authorizes the federal government to identify metropolitan air quality regions and to issue and enforce federal pollution standards if the states fail to do so.

1970s *Congress strengthens legislation to curb air pollution.*

April 1970
Earth Day is held in Washington, D.C., and throughout the country, launching the environmental movement.

December 1970
Congress passes a tougher Clean Air Act, the country's first sweeping environmental law. The law authorizes the government to set air quality standards for six major air pollutants and requires the states to devise plans to meet them.

1979
The Environmental Protection Agency (EPA) sets the standard for allowable ozone at 0.12 parts per million of air.

1980s *Environmental regulation takes a back seat to free-market priorities during the Reagan administration.*

1987
The EPA changes its standard for particulate matter (PM). Instead of covering all suspended particles, the new standard focuses on smaller particles, measuring no more than 10 microns in diameter (PM10).

1990s *Lawsuits force the EPA to review air quality standards for soot and smog.*

1990
The Clean Air Act Amendments strengthen the EPA's enforcement powers and provide greater flexibility for meeting air-quality standards.

1991
The American Lung Association (ALA) files the first of three lawsuits against the EPA for missing deadlines required under the Clean Air Act to review the air quality standard for ozone.

Oct. 10, 1993
The ALA sues the EPA for failing to review the air quality standard for particulate matter.

Oct. 6, 1994
A U.S. District Court in Arizona requires the EPA to review its particulate matter standard.

1995
The EPA and 37 states east of Colorado set up the Ozone Transport Assessment Group (OTAG) to determine how much ozone pollution is attributable to out-of-area sources and to recommend regional solutions to the problem.

1996
The Small Business Regulatory Enforcement Fairness Act strengthens lawmakers' ability to block federal regulations.

Nov. 27, 1996
EPA Administrator Carol M. Browner proposes tightening the standards for ozone, unchanged since 1979, and for particulate matter, in effect since 1987.

Dec. 5, 1996
General Motors' EV1, the first electric car sold by a big U.S. automaker in 80 years, goes on sale in Southern California.

March 12, 1997
The last day of public comment on the proposed new air quality standards.

July 19, 1997
Deadline for Browner to make her final decision on new standards.

Lung Association's Lawsuit Forced EPA to Act

When EPA Administrator Carol M. Browner proposed tightening air pollution standards last November, opponents portrayed her as a radical activist who would sacrifice business interests for questionable health benefits. But a closer look at the circumstances surrounding the proposals suggests that the Environmental Protection Agency was a reluctant activist. In fact, the American Lung Association (ALA) had to take the agency to court before it would even begin to review the scientific evidence on which the standards are based, much less make them more stringent.

The lung association, which promotes research and treatment of respiratory diseases such as asthma and emphysema, brought suit Oct. 12, 1993. For years, the group has pressed the EPA, in and out of court, to review federal air quality standards, as Congress requires it to do every five years. But the agency had reviewed the standards for particulate matter (PM) only once, in December 1982. On the basis of that review, which found that smaller particles pose the greatest threat to human health, the EPA in 1987 changed the soot standard, which had applied to all suspended particles, to cover only those measuring no more than 10 microns in diameter.

But the ALA contended in its suit that later scientific studies showed the soot standard was still too lax to protect the public health, as required by the Clean Air Act. When the EPA let the review deadline slip yet again, the association sued the agency in U.S. District Court in Arizona. "We filed in Arizona because the Arizona Center for Law and the Public Interest agreed to represent us on a pro bono basis," says Ron White, ALA deputy director of national programs. "Also, the Tucson and Phoenix areas both have significant particulate matter problems."

The EPA admitted to the court that it had failed to meet the deadlines for reviewing the particulate standard. At issue was the time needed to complete the review process. The agency wanted to have until the end of 1998.

"We certainly felt that it was unconscionable to wait [that long]," White says, "especially given the information that we had even at that point on the health effects of particulate matter." In fact, White says, studies since 1993 have shown that particulates are even more harmful than was thought then.

In fairness, even critics concede that the EPA is hard-pressed to meet its obligations under the law because the same Congress that requires the agency to protect the environment has failed to appropriate adequate funding to meet all its obligations.

"The EPA has been given too much to do and too few resources to do it with," says A. Blakeman Early, an environmental consultant to the ALA. "Essentially, the only way you get them to pay attention is through a lawsuit. There is substantial evidence to support the fact that the Office of Management and Budget will allow EPA to proceed with an activity where a lawsuit is involved and will typically ignore activities where there isn't a lawsuit involved."

In 1994, a year after its suit was filed, the court decided in the ALA's favor. Declaring that the EPA's proposed review schedule "frustrates congressional intent," Senior U.S. District Judge Alfredo C. Marquez ruled: "Because almost 12 years have passed since 1982 when PM criteria were last reviewed and almost seven years have passed since 1987 when [the standard] was last reviewed and revised, the EPA has not merely missed a deadline, it has nullified the congressional scheme for a fixed interval review and revision process."

As part of its ruling, the court required the EPA to review and revise the particulate standard by Jan. 31, 1997. Following a period of public comment, the agency was to issue its final decision by June 28. The court later extended EPA's deadline for issuing final rules on the particulate matter standard to July 19.

The EPA decided on its own to review the ozone air quality standard at the same time as the particulate standard. But here, too, the agency acted under pressure from the courts. The American Lung Association had sued EPA three times since 1991 over its failure to re-examine the ozone standard, last reviewed in 1979.

Continued from p. 202

patchwork system in which regulated industries would migrate to more lenient jurisdictions. To avoid such economic disruption, President Richard M. Nixon called for amendments to the Air Quality Act authorizing HEW to establish national ambient air quality standards for harmful pollutants. Once uniform national standards were set, it would remain up to the states to devise implementation plans to meet them.

The debate over ways to combat the country's growing air pollution problem was at the heart of a grass-roots campaign to combat environmental degradation that culminated in April 1970 with the first Earth Day. Massive demonstrations were held in Washington, D.C., and around the country, launching the environmental movement as a major, new voice in American politics. One of the movement's first victories was the creation that year of the EPA to enforce the country's environmental laws. [14]

The debate over new air pollution legislation was marked by automakers' claims that stricter tailpipe emission standards would be too costly, as well as technologically unattainable. While the industry accepted the concept of national, rather than state, air quality standards, it opposed allowing the states to adopt their own stricter regulations. An exception was granted to California, which already had launched aggressive auto emission and fuel standards in an effort to clean up Los Angeles, fast emerging as the country's most heavily polluted region.

After months of debate, Congress in December 1970 passed a tough, new version of the Clean Air Act, the first of a series of landmark environmental laws. It set an ambitious deadline of five years to bring all areas of the country into compliance with national ambient air quality standards to be established by the EPA. The states retained the authority to develop and implement plans to satisfy the new standards; they would have nine months to submit their plans to the EPA once the standards were set. Factories, power plants and other stationary sources of air pollution had to comply with the state plans by 1975 and were allowed a two-year extension if needed.

Cars and trucks and other modes of transportation also were subject to inspection for compliance with emission standards. The law mandated a 90 percent reduction in motor vehicle emissions of carbon monoxide and hydrocarbons over the five-year period, with a similar cut in nitrogen oxides by 1976. New vehicles were required to meet the new standards for five years or 50,000 miles, and the removal of automobile pollution-control devices was punishable by a $10,000 fine.

To give the law teeth, lawmakers authorized the EPA to seek injunctions to curtail emissions deemed harmful to human health. It also allowed citizens to sue the agency for failure to enforce the law and polluters for violating the standards. Each willful violation of the law was punishable by a fine of up to $25,000 a day and up to a year in prison.

Because both stationary and mobile pollution sources failed to comply with the new standards, the Clean Air Act was amended several times during the 1970s to extend the deadlines. Despite the compliance delays, the decade saw lower concentrations of particulates and sulfur dioxide — thanks in large part to the installation of "scrubbers," or filters, in factory smokestacks. There also were declines in concentrations of carbon monoxide, produced mainly by motor vehicles. Levels of ozone and nitrogen dioxide, however, remained high.

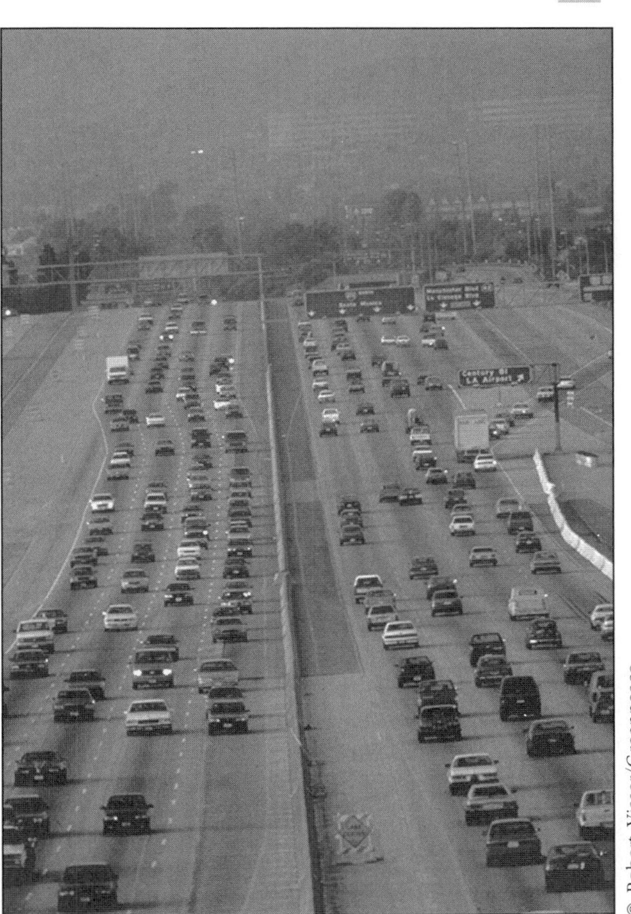

© Robert Visser/Greenpeace

Sweeping measures by smog-ridden Los Angeles to meet clean air standards have not been successful.

During the 1980s, enforcement of air quality regulations was weakened under pressure from affected industries and their allies in the two administrations of President Ronald Reagan (1981-88). Allowable tailpipe emissions were doubled, and other steps were taken to relax enforcement of air pollution regulations.

Tough Amendments

With the support of President George Bush, Congress passed sweeping amendments to the original Clean Air Act in 1990. While leaving the law's basic provisions intact, the amendments added new programs found to be needed by research during the 1980s but thwarted by the Reagan administration's emphasis on deregulation.

The main additions were programs to combat acid rain and erosion of stratospheric ozone.[15] For decades, residents of the Northeastern United States and Canada had observed a progressive die-out of fish in local streams and lakes as well as widespread defoliation of forests. The cause was found to be sulfur dioxide from industrial plants in the Midwest, borne east by winds and then falling to Earth after mixing with rain or snow.

The Clean Air Act amendments created an acid rain program that allowed affected industries to earn "emission credits" for reducing their sulfur dioxide emissions below the minimum allowable levels, usually by installing smokestack filters. They could later sell any credits they earned to other businesses that were unable to curb their emissions, helping to defray the cost of the scrub-

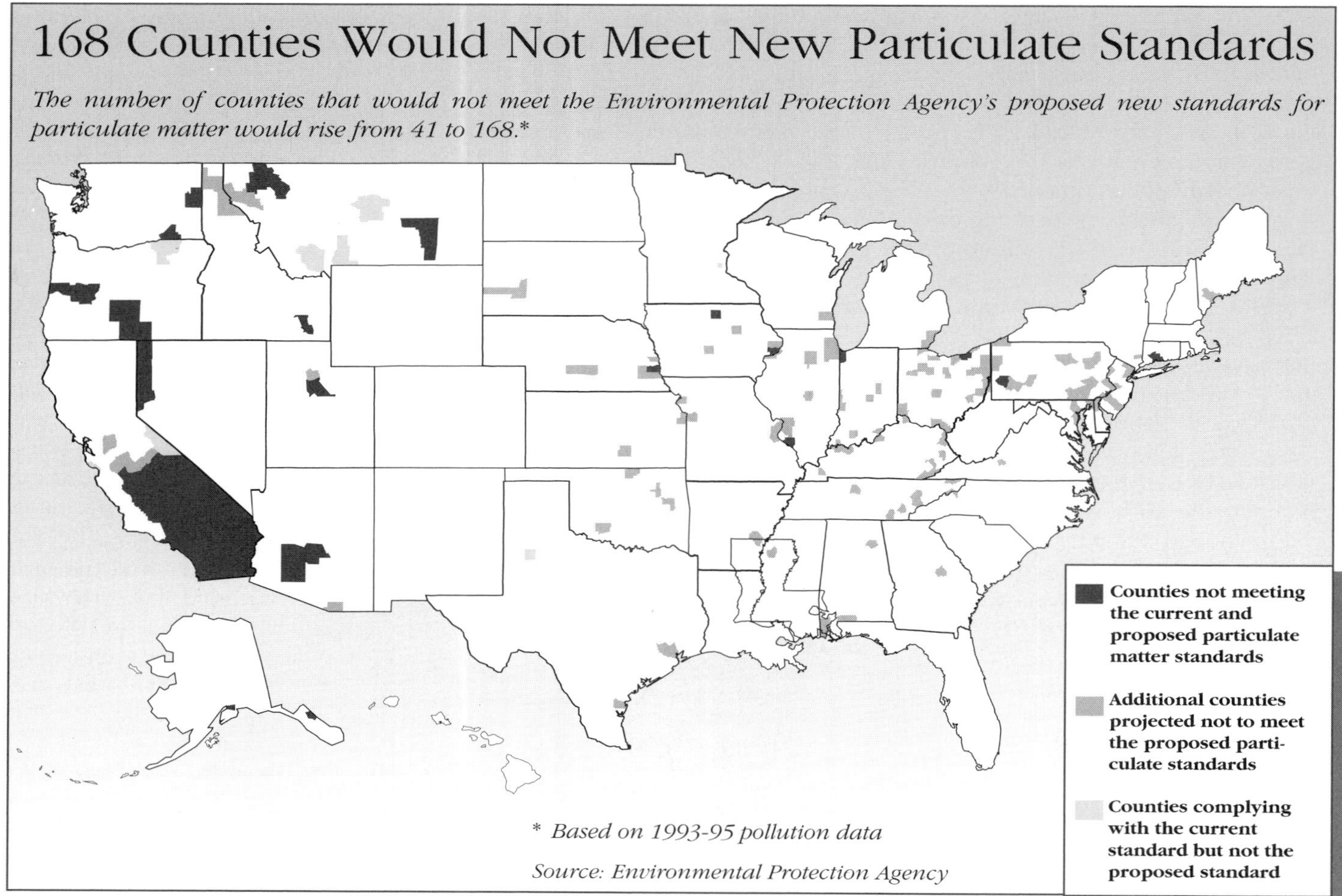

168 Counties Would Not Meet New Particulate Standards

*The number of counties that would not meet the Environmental Protection Agency's proposed new standards for particulate matter would rise from 41 to 168.**

* *Based on 1993-95 pollution data*

Source: Environmental Protection Agency

bers. The emissions-trading program was highly successful in financing cleanup costs. Today, companies that aren't reducing their emissions to legal limits can buy credits for less than $100 per ton of pollutants not removed, a fraction of earlier estimates of the cost of complying with the new sulfur dioxide standard.

The Clean Air Act amendments also targeted chlorofluorocarbons (CFCs) and other compounds used as refrigerants and solvents, which had been found to cause an alarming erosion of stratospheric ozone. Unlike ground-level ozone, which is harmful to human health, ozone high above the Earth's surface forms an essential shield protecting plants and animals from the sun's ultraviolet radiation, the main cause of skin cancer in humans. The new program forced industries to find alternative chemicals, enabling the U.S. to comply with the 1987 Montreal Protocol on Substances That Deplete the Ozone Layer. [16]

In addition to establishing new programs, the amendments made major changes in the existing programs covering the six pollutants regulated under the act. A more elaborate system of classifying pollutants was created that distinguished between areas of marginal and extreme pollution and set deadlines for meeting standards according to the severity of pollution. More sources of ground-level ozone, which has proved the most difficult pollutant to curb over the years, were brought under regulation, and states for the first time were required to reach ozone target levels.

The amendments targeted mobile sources of pollution, growing as a source of ozone and other pollutants as the number of cars and miles travelled continued to rise. The new provisions tightened tailpipe emissions, required oil companies to produce alternative formulations of gasoline for sale in the most polluted areas and required service stations to install devices on gasoline pumps to capture vapors released during fueling.

The 1990 amendments granted the EPA greater enforcement powers by allowing it to issue fines directly to violators — much as policemen can issue a fine for speeding (or littering) — instead of having to seek court-imposed fines. The changes also provided greater flexibility in meeting air quality standards, using market approaches such as the emissions credit trading system set up under the acid rain program. Other economic incentives included giving credits to gasoline refiners for producing greater quantities of cleaner gasoline than required; the credits could be used to avoid penalties when their gasoline failed to meet clean-up requirements. ■

CURRENT SITUATION

Air Quality Today

Thanks to the Clean Air Act, the nation's air is much cleaner than it was 27 years ago. According to a 1996 EPA report, emissions of five of the six pollutants regulated under the act decreased between 1970 and 1995.

By far the biggest improvement has been in lead emissions. After researchers discovered that lead causes nerve damage in children, lead was removed from gasoline, paint and other products, and lead emissions fell 98 percent. Nitrogen dioxide, the only regulated pollutant that did not fall over the 25-year period, rose by 6 percent. But since 1986, that trend has been reversed, and these emissions, too, have fallen slightly. [17]

"Clearly, we do not need to choose between our health and our job," Browner said recently. "Economic growth and environmental protection can go hand in hand. A healthy economy helps us achieve a healthier environment; a healthy environment helps us to build a stronger economy." [18]

But the nation's growing population, coupled with industrial expansion and the continuing discovery of adverse effects of air pollution, have bolstered support for further anti-pollution efforts. The EPA estimates that about 80 million people in the United States lived in counties that failed to meet at least one EPA air quality standard in 1995. The worst offender, in terms of both the number of polluted areas and the population living in them, is ozone. In 1995, 71 million people lived in counties that exceeded the standard for ozone. [19]

"In Southern California, which is unique in some ways, manufacturing companies are now responsible for only 8 percent of nitrogen dioxide and volatile organic compounds. Industry has done an awful lot already and is very heavily regulated."

— Robert Wyman
Los Angeles attorney

In many jurisdictions, finding affordable means to further reduce nitrogen dioxide and VOCs — the main contributors to ozone pollution — poses a daunting challenge. Areas such as Southern California, Chicago and cities along the Atlantic seaboard have already tried the least expensive and intrusive steps to curtail emissions. "In Southern California, which is unique in some ways, manufacturing companies are now responsible for only 8 percent of nitrogen dioxide and volatile organic compounds," Los Angeles attorney Wyman said Feb. 10. "Industry has done an awful lot already and is very heavily regulated."

Cost concerns have forced the EPA to retreat from several ozone-reduction measures mandated by the 1990 Clean Air Act amendments. Rules calling for an ambitious federal vehicle-inspection and maintenance program in areas with "serious" or worse ozone pollution were dropped, with the states assuming responsibility for inspection. A second program, aimed at reducing commuting in areas with "extreme" ozone levels, also has been dropped in the face of cost concerns and doubts about its effectiveness. The EPA also has withdrawn a rule calling for the sale of cleaner-burning fuel — gasoline with an ethanol additive — in areas classified as serious or worse for ozone pollution. [20]

The lack of readily accessible local measures to reduce pollution levels in areas that are subject to wind-borne pollution has raised interest in a regional approach to the problem. Although particulate matter also is carried far from its source of emission, the main focus of concern over pollution transport has been ozone, especially in the eastern half of the country. In 1995, 37 states east of Colorado joined with the EPA to create the Ozone Transport Assessment Group (OTAG) to determine how much ozone pollution is attributable to out-of-area sources and to recommend solutions.

Browner's Proposal

The changes the EPA has proposed in the ozone and particulate matter standards involve both pollution levels and the ways they are measured. Under the current standards, an area is in violation when ozone exceeds 0.12 parts per million (ppm) of air over one hour.* The agency recommends lowering the limit to 0.08 ppm, averaged over eight hours. Three "exceedances" every three years would be excused, and a more complex averaging system would replace the current system for allowable exceedances.

Because all ozone molecules are identical, ozone is generally easier to measure than particulate matter, which can be made up of a variety of substances. The 1970 law originally covered "total suspended particles," but was changed in 1987 to exclude coarse particles, so that it covered only those no bigger than 10 microns (PM10).

Most violations of the PM10 standard occur in the West, where arid weather conditions make it easier for dust and smoke — the main constituents of particles that size — to linger in the air. The new standard would continue to cover PM10, though at concentrations that would make it easier for areas to comply. But many more areas would fail to meet the proposed standard for much finer particles (PM2.5). Singling out such tiny particles would require new emission controls because they are produced mainly by fuel combustion and are contained in vehicle exhaust and the sulfur emissions of power plants and factories.

Currently there are only about 50 PM2.5 monitors in place around the country. Once they are fully installed throughout the country, areas would be deemed in compliance if they measured no more than an average of 15 micrograms of PM2.5 per cubic meter over three years. But "hot spots" of high particulate pollution within an area would be in compliance only if they measured no more than 50 micrograms per cubic meter under a complex, 24-hour averaging scheme for the entire area.

After Browner proposed the new air quality standards for ozone and particulate matter last November, the EPA began holding hearings around the country to solicit public comments on the standards. "Don't take my barbecue away!" screamed a banner at a Chicago meeting in January, where opponents of the new regulations brandished bags of charcoal and a hibachi, warning that such totems of American life would become bygones under new standards. [21]

'Does the right hand know what the left hand is doing? One agency is shutting jobs down, and another agency is creating jobs."

— Gov. George V. Voinovich, R-Ohio

With many industries claiming, along with state and local government officials, that the new regulations would cost billions of dollars, the EPA sought to extend the May deadline for issuing its final decision. The court-ordered deadline grew out of the ALA lawsuit against the EPA. On Feb. 10, a federal court in Arizona granted the agency a 60-day extension. As a result, the public comment period was extended to March 12, and the deadline for the EPA's final decision was bumped to July 19.

Browner has launched an unprecedented campaign to involve the public in the ongoing debate over the proposed new rules. In addition to hearings, the agency set up a Web site where people can voice their opinions on the proposals. [22] "Although we would have preferred more time, we will obviously comply with the court's order . . . by March 12," she said following the ruling.

Opposition Builds

The public comment period has placed the EPA in the middle of a tug of war between health professionals and environmentalists, who have long pressed for tougher pollution regulations, and the electric and automobile industries, among others, which are most likely to be affected by stricter standards.

The ALA and others who support new regulations fault the EPA for not going far enough to fulfill its obligation to protect public health and the environment."We believe that the agency should be proposing a standard of 0.07 ppm for ozone, and not 0.08," consultant Early says. "On particulate matter, we believe that the standard should be 10 micrograms and not 15, and that the 24-hour standard [for hot spots] ought to be between 18 and 20 micrograms instead of 50."

Early cites studies reviewed by the ALA showing that 17 million children, 12 million elderly, 5 million sufferers of chronic obstructive lung disease, 5 million asthmatics and 3 million victims of ischemic heart disease would be exposed to unhealthy levels of particulate matter under the EPA's proposals. [23]

The ALA is particularly critical of

Continued on p. 210

*Monitoring instruments stationed around the nation produce measurements every hour during the ozone season, which typically runs from May through September.

At Issue:

Does scientific evidence support the tightening of air quality standards?

yes

GEORGE D. THURSTON
Professor of Environmental Medicine, New York University School of Medicine

FROM TESTIMONY BEFORE SENATE ENVIRONMENT AND PUBLIC WORKS SUBCOMMITTEE ON CLEAN AIR, WETLANDS, PRIVATE PROPERTY AND NUCLEAR SAFETY, FEB. 5, 1997.

Ozone (O_3) is a highly irritant gas which is formed in our atmosphere in the presence of sunlight from other air pollutants, including nitrogen oxides and hydrocarbons. These "precursor" pollutants, which cause the formation of ozone, are emitted by pollution sources including automobiles, electric power plants and industry.

The adverse health consequences of breathing ozone at levels below the current U.S. National Ambient Air Quality Standard (NAAQS) of 120 parts per billion (ppb) are serious and well-documented. This documentation includes impacts demonstrated in controlled chamber exposures of humans and animals, and observational epidemiology showing consistent associations between ozone and adverse impacts across a wide range of human health outcomes. . . .

Observational epidemiology studies have shown compelling and consistent evidence of adverse effects by ozone below the current U.S. standards. . . .

In my own research, I have found that ozone air pollution is associated with increased numbers of respiratory hospital admissions in New York City, Buffalo, N.Y., and Toronto [Canada], even at levels below the current standard of 120 ppb. My ozone-hospital admissions results have been confirmed by other researchers considering locales elsewhere in the world. . . . [C]onsidering the published results from various cities, the EPA analysis underpredicts the respiratory hospital admission benefits of their proposed regulations by about a factor of two. . . .

Airway inflammation in the lung is among the serious effects that have been demonstrated by controlled human studies of ozone at levels typically experienced by most Americans. Airway inflammation is especially a problem for children and adults with asthma, as it makes them more susceptible to having asthma attacks. . . .

In addition, increased inflammation in the lungs can make the elderly more susceptible to pneumonia, a major cause of illness and death in this age group.

In conclusion, I would like to reiterate the key messages contained in the letter that I and 26 other air pollution researchers and physicians sent to President Clinton last month:

Please listen to the medical and scientific community on this issue. Exposures to O_3 and particulate matter air pollution have been linked to medically significant adverse health effects. The current NAAQS for these pollutants are not sufficiently protective of public health.

no

DANIEL B. MENZEL
Chairman, Department of Community and Environmental Medicine, University of California-Irvine

FROM TESTIMONY BEFORE SENATE ENVIRONMENT AND PUBLIC WORKS SUBCOMMITTEE ON CLEAN AIR, WETLANDS, PRIVATE PROPERTY AND NUCLEAR SAFETY, FEB. 5, 1997.

Both the ozone and particulate matter standards have vast implications for the quality of life and the economy of the United States. It is my opinion that the vast majority of Americans support improving and enhancing the quality of their life by eliminating or decreasing air pollution. Americans are quite willing to shoulder the burden of cleaner air, cleaner water and cleaner food if they can understand clearly the benefits to be gained by these activities. . . .I am very concerned that the Environmental Protection Agency and the Congress maintain the confidence of the U.S. public and demonstrate to the public their vigorous support for a better quality of life and clean air. . . .

It is my opinion that we will have achieved only marginal effects by decreasing the current ambient air quality standards for ozone from 120 parts per billion to 90 parts per billion. The nature of the dose-response relationship is such that . . . reduction to much lower levels may be necessary to result in the abolition of detectable health effects from ozone. . . . How much would one have to reduce the ozone concentration in the air in order to be able to find a detectable advance in public health? Because the data are so sparse, a multitude of different kinds of theoretical treatments are possible. None of them, however, are sufficiently sensitive that one could lead to a clear prediction of a health benefit. . . .

Continued research into the health effects of ozone is urgently needed. Further reductions in the ozone standard may be indicated in the near future. Because of the economic impact of ozone standards and strategies, the highest quality research is needed. . . .

I do not doubt that the particulate matter problem is a very serious problem indeed. We need to place a very strong, active and progressive research program into place in order for us to cope with this problem. It is my view that too little is known. . . .

I am not in favor of the use of a PM2.5 [particulate matter of 2.5 micrometers in diameter or less] standard. . . . We lack information on the actual PM2.5 in the atmosphere of our cities. We do not know the duration of exposure of people to PM2.5. The chemical nature of the PM2.5 fraction is poorly known. We lack a plausible biological mechanism for particulate matter. We do not know if regulation of PM2.5 will be of benefit. A strong, aggressive, long-term research program is essential to address the current data deficiencies if we are to convince people that this is a major problem. . . .

FOR MORE INFORMATION

American Lung Association, 1726 M St. N.W., Suite 902, Washington, D.C. 20036-4502; 202-785-3355. A lawsuit by this group, which supports research and public awareness campaigns to fight lung disease, prompted the Environmental Protection Agency's review and ultimate recommendation to tighten air quality standards for smog and soot.

Association of Local Air Pollution Control Officials, 444 N. Capitol St. N.W., Suite 307, Washington, D.C. 20001; 202-624-7864. This group is composed of the local officials who are responsible for implementing provisions of the Clean Air Act.

Environmental Protection Agency, Office of Air and Radiation, 401 M St. S.W., West Tower, MC 6101, Washington, D.C. 20460; 202-260-7400. The office administers air quality standards under the Clean Air Act and oversees state implementation of plans to meet them.

Resources for the Future, 1616 P St. N.W., Washington, D.C. 20036; 202-328-5000. This independent think tank studies public and private costs of environmental policy decisions, including revisions to federal air quality standards.

Continued from p. 208

changes in the way PM10 levels are measured. "This is a dramatic weakening of that standard," Early says. "Particularly in the West, this weakening may be a very critical matter in terms of increasing the exposure of people living in places like Denver, Phoenix and Seattle, not only to PM10 but also to PM2.5."

"One of the things that has gotten lost in the discussion," Early adds, "is that the agency has chosen standards that are in the middle of the range. These are not by any means, from our point of view, radical standards."

This is hardly the picture portrayed by the lung association's opposite number in the air quality debate, the industry-funded Air Quality Standards Coalition. Klimisch of the automobile manufacturers association, a coalition member, testified Feb. 10 that, "It's going to be very difficult to comply" with the proposed standards. "We're already controlling all the things that contribute to fine particulate emissions."

To tighten standards even further, Klimisch said, the states will have to begin requiring Americans to car pool to work and make other radical changes to their personal habits. "We're moving toward regulating behavioral change," he said. "I hope EPA will come to its collective senses."

The coalition's 500 member companies and trade groups are joined by a number of state and local officials, who would be required to impose new anti-pollution measures in areas that would come into non-compliance under new standards. One of the harshest critics is Gov. Voinovich, who complains that the proposals threaten the economy at the same time President Clinton is seeking new ways to promote economic growth.

"As the former mayor of a city who tried to keep jobs in the city and who worked for years to try and [meet] ambient air standards so that businesses wouldn't move, this new proposal will take Ohio from five counties that are not in attainment and put 52 of them in non-attainment," Voinovich said. "Does the right hand know what the left hand is doing? One agency is shutting jobs down, and another agency is creating jobs." [24]

But the governor's complaints may fall on deaf ears. For one thing, the nation's governors are hardly united in their opposition. East Coast governors, including Christine Todd Whitman, R-N.J., strongly support the new standards because they would force Voinovich and other Midwestern governors to curb the emissions that contribute to their pollution problems.

Further undermining governors' complaints of excessive federal regulation is evidence that some states are evading their responsibility under the Clean Air Act. The EPA reports that a number of states, including Pennsylvania, Michigan and Idaho, not only have failed to comply with existing standards but also have devised ways to skirt federal law by protecting companies that voluntarily report pollution violations to state enforcement agencies. Unless they report serious violations to the EPA and strictly enforce compliance, the agency warns, those states may lose federal financing of their air quality programs. [25] ■

OUTLOOK

If Browner Says No

The debate over the proposed smog and soot standards will only intensify with the approach of the mid-July decision deadline. If the EPA opts for the stronger standards, it may face a congressional challenge later this year.

Such a possibility surfaced last month when Sen. Chafee openly questioned the wisdom of tightening the standards. As a result, support may be building for lawmakers to test the new powers they acquired last year under the 1996 Small Business Regulatory Enforcement Fairness Act. Under the act, Congress can issue a joint resolution disapproving a federal regulation within 60 legislative days of its publication. Such a resolution would be subject, however, to a presidential veto, which would require a two-thirds vote of Congress to override. [26]

With just over four months to go before Browner must make a final decision on the proposed standards, even the industry-supported Air Quality Standards Coalition may find it hard to drum up enough public opposition to force the agency to back down. Because the Clean Air Act allows the EPA to give areas up to 12 years to meet new standards after they are found to be in violation, the public is unlikely to feel the effects of any new air quality programs any time soon.

"From the time the standards are adopted this summer — if they are — until the first pound of pollution is required to be reduced as a result of a control strategy, it could be years," says Becker of the air pollution control officials association. "Depending on how quickly the monitoring infrastructure is installed and the decisions for designating compliance take place, we're talking about up to 2012 or later."

Change may be in store for many areas no matter what the outcome of this summer's debate. Even if the EPA decides to maintain existing standards for ozone and particulate matter, Midwestern states that contribute to pollution problems outside their jurisdiction may well be forced to adopt stricter emission controls. The OTAG's recommendations for ways to address the problem of pollution transport, expected this spring, likely will stress the need for some kind of regional approach to air pollution.

The air pollution control officials association will not take sides in the debate over revised standards, but it does foresee stricter controls in some areas, no matter how the EPA decides to set the standards. "Almost everyone supports the notion that areas upwind, including possibly areas [in compliance with regulations] that are contributing to violations elsewhere, would be regulated as well," Becker says. "So clearly, there is a need for regional controls. As a result of the OTAG process, even if the standards are not changed, it is very likely that additional controls will still be required" in areas that meet current standards.

The news is not all bad for the states that "export" pollution. Becker predicts that the ultimate result of the debate will be innovative ways to meet air quality standards, such as systems of tradable emissions credits for ozone and particulates similar to the acid rain program.

"This is a tremendous opportunity for everyone," he says, "including those states and industries that are not excited about tougher standards, to craft the most cost-effective, flexible approach that they can to make implementation as easy as possible." ■

Notes

[1] Browner testified Feb. 12, 1997, before the Senate Environment and Public Works Committee.

[2] Klimisch addressed a symposium on the proposed air quality standards held Feb. 10, 1997, by Resources for the Future, a nonprofit group in Washington, D.C., that studies environmental issues.

[3] McLellan addressed the Feb. 10 Resources for the Future symposium.

[4] Nichols addressed the Feb. 10 symposium.

[5] Lippmann spoke at the Feb. 10 symposium.

[6] Chafee spoke at the hearing on Feb. 12, 1997.

[7] Browner testified at the Environment and Public Works Committee's Feb. 12 hearing.

[8] Ziman addressed the Feb. 10 Resources for the Future symposium.

[9] See Environmental Protection Agency, *National Air Quality and Emissions Trends Report*, 1995, October 1996, pp. 1-2.

[10] Theiler spoke at the Feb. 10 symposium held by Resources for the Future.

[11] Krupnick addressed the Feb. 10 symposium.

[12] Wyman spoke at the Feb. 10 symposium.

[13] Unless otherwise noted, material in this section is based on Gary C. Bryner, *Blue Skies, Green Politics* (1995).

[14] For background, see "Environmental Movement at 25," *The CQ Researcher*, March 31, 1995, pp. 273-296.

[15] For background, see "Acid Rain: New Approach to Old Problem," *Editorial Research Reports*, March 8, 1991, pp. 129-144.

[16] For background, see "Ozone Depletion," *The CQ Researcher*, April 3, 1992, pp. 289-312.

[17] Environmental Protection Agency, *loc. cit.* For background, see "Lead Poisoning," *The CQ Researcher*, June 19, 1992, pp. 537-560.

[18] Browner spoke at a news conference on Dec. 17, 1996.

[19] Environmental Protection Agency, *op. cit.*, p. 2.

[20] See Alan J. Krupnick and Deirdre Farrell, *Six Steps to a Healthier Ambient Ozone Policy*, Natural Resources Defense Council, March 1996, p. 3.

[21] See Joby Warrick, "Factions Ratchet Up Rhetoric Over Tougher Air Standards," *The Washington Post*, Jan. 24, 1997.

[22] Comments on the ozone and particulate matter proposals can be made via the Web at http://www.epa.gov/tellepa/.The EPA's special Web site for information on the proposals is http://ttnwww.rtpnc.epa.gov.

[23] American Lung Association, *Gambling With Public Health II: Who Loses Under New Health Standards for Particulate Matter*, January 1997. Ozone was covered by an earlier ALA study, *Gambling With Public Health: Who Loses Under New Health Standards for Ozone*, September 1996.

[24] Voinovich spoke Feb. 3, 1997, after meeting with President Clinton on behalf of the National Governors' Association, of which he is vice chairman. For background, see "Jobs vs. Environment," *The CQ Researcher*, May 15, 1992, pp. 422-445.

[25] See John H. Cushman Jr., "States Neglecting Pollution Rules, White House Says," *The New York Times*, Dec. 16, 1996.

[26] See Allan Freedman, "Congress' New Tool May Not Fix Much," *CQ Weekly Report*, Jan. 18, 1997, p. 169.

Bibliography

Selected Sources Used

Books

Bryner, Gary C., *Blue Skies, Green Politics: The Clean Air Act of 1990 and Its Implementation,* Congressional Quarterly, 1995.

The author, a professor of political science at Brigham Young University, recounts the political story behind passage of laws to combat air pollution. The book focuses on problems related to implementing the vast array of amendments to the Clean Air Act passed in 1990.

Rajan, Sudhir Chella, *The Enigma of Automobility: Democratic Politics and Pollution Control*, University of Pittsburgh Press, 1996.

The author, an air pollution engineer in India who once served on the California Air Resources Board, argues that by requiring emission testing and costly equipment to curb the major source of air pollution — motor vehicles exhaust — current policy blames individual car owners for a problem whose causes are rooted in the economic system.

Articles

Litvan, Laura M., "A Breath of Fresh Air," *Nation's Business*, May 1995, pp. 50-51.

An innovative program allows some 400 businesses in Southern California to buy and sell emissions credits as a way to meet air quality standards in the most polluted area of the country.

Miller, William H., and Anthony Garvin, "Clean-Air Confusion," *Industry Week*, April 1, 1996, pp. 11-14.

A requirement that companies obtain operating permits for plants that emit pollutants has made it hard for them to comply with the 1990 Clean Air Act Amendments.

Milloy, Steven J., and Michael Gough, "The EPA's Clean Air-ogance," *The Wall Street Journal*, Jan. 7, 1997.

Milloy, publisher of the Junk Science Home Page on the World Wide Web, and Gough, director of science and risk studies at the Cato Institute, argue that the EPA's proposal to tighten smog and soot air quality standards this year is based on faulty scientific evidence of the likely benefits the changes will bring.

O'Connell, Kim A., "Commission Votes to Limit Haze on Colorado Plateau," *National Parks*, September-October 1996, pp. 11-12.

A special commission created under the 1990 Clean Air Act Amendments has required a power plant in Nevada to curb sulfur dioxide emissions in an effort to improve visibility in the Grand Canyon.

Reports and Studies

American Lung Association, *Health Effects of Outdoor Air Pollution*, 1996.

Despite improvements in air quality over the past 40 years, the association warns that the young, elderly and chronically ill, as well as people who are active out of doors, remain vulnerable to the health effects of pollution.

Anderson, J.W., *Revising the Air Quality Standards: A Briefing Paper on the Proposed National Ambient Air Quality Standards for Particulate Matter and Ozone,* Resources for the Future, Feb. 4, 1997.

The author outlines the issues involved in EPA's proposal to tighten air quality standards and argues that the change is more clearly warranted for the soot standard than for the ozone standard.

Antonelli, Angela, *Needed: Aggressive Implementation of the Congressional Review Act*, The Heritage Foundation, Feb. 19, 1997.

The director for economic policy studies at a conservative think tank argues that a subtitle of the 1996 Small Business Regulatory Enforcement Fairness Act hands lawmakers a powerful weapon for blocking regulations, including the EPA's proposed changes to air quality standards.

Environmental Protection Agency, *Brochure on National Air Quality: Status and Trends*, October 1996.

The agency responsible for administering the Clean Air Act examines the emissions and concentrations of the six pollutants covered by the law over the past 10 years.

Environmental Protection Agency, *National Air Quality and Emissions Trends Report, 1995*, October 1996.

EPA's latest annual report on air quality describes a gradual improvement in most areas of the country. The publication provides a pollution status report card for every county in the United States.

Krupnick, Alan J., and Deirdre Farrell, *Six Steps to a Healthier Ambient Ozone Policy*, Resources for the Future, March 1996.

The authors argue that changes in the Clean Air Act and the EPA's regulatory approach, such as recognizing costs in setting standards and focusing on more dangerous pollutants such as particulate matter rather than ozone, would reduce the costs involved in meeting air quality standards.

The Next Step

Additional information from UMI's Newspaper & Periodical Abstracts™ database

Air Quality Status

"Air quality issues continue to confuse," ***Denver Post,*** **Oct. 4, 1996, p. B6.**
An editorial clarifies two air quality issues that many in Denver, Colo., may find confusing. The first issue concerns whether Denver's pollution is getting worse or better, and the second concerns why so much money is being spent on the PM-10 project, described as a marginally beneficial program to reduce the carbon monoxide.

Dawson, Bill, "Air quality in the area looking up," ***Houston Chronicle,*** **Nov. 2, 1996, p. A1.**
Air quality in and around Houston, Texas, took a dramatic turn for the better in 1996, with a 10-year low in the number of days with readings above the federal health standard for ground-level ozone.

Fialka, John J., "EPA's Browner says air quality has been improved," ***The Wall Street Journal,*** **Dec. 18, 1996, p. C19.**
EPA Administrator Carol M. Browner said the use of reformulated gasolines and cleaner-burning power plants has helped clear the nation's air pollution. In an annual statement on air quality, Browner noted that over the last 25 years the levels of six major air pollutants have declined 29 percent.

Hatcher, Carolyn Boyd, "Air quality and roads," ***Atlanta Journal Constitution,*** **June 22, 1996, p. A11.**
In a letter to the editor, Georgia Conservancy CEO Carolyn Boyd Hatcher says her organization wasn't surprised to learn that the Atlanta Regional Commission's transportation improvement program failed to meet federal air quality goals; focusing on road projects is no way to improve air quality, she says.

Lindecke, Fred W., "Air quality 'grim'," ***St. Louis Post-Dispatch,*** **June 22, 1996, p. A1.**
Air pollution violations in St. Louis, have already passed 1995 levels, raising the possibility that the EPA will impose industrial-development restrictions or cut federal highway aid.

Clean Air Act and 1990 Amendments

Anderson, Will, "Officials: Clean Air Act won't affect road plans," ***Atlanta Constitution,*** **Jan. 2, 1997, Sec. XJR, p. 1.**
While some suburban counties are clamoring for changes in the federal Clean Air Act, county officials in Rockdale, Ga., say the law won't have much effect on road improvements in this area for several years. As one of 13 metropolitan Atlanta counties where air quality does not meet the standards set by the federal law, Rockdale must look at ways to improve its air or face losing federal transportation dollars.

Ashcraft, Michael, "Commentary: Speaking up would be a breath of fresh air for many Americans," ***Detroit News,*** **Jan. 22, 1997, p. E3.**
The Environmental Protection Agency is taking public comment on the issue of new air quality standards. The 1970 Clean Air Act mandates that air quality and clean air standards be reviewed at least every five years. In the 26 years since, those standards have been reviewed four times. The two biggest issues right now are particulate matter and ozone levels.

Bukro, Casey, "Clean Air Act ahead of schedule," ***Chicago Tribune,*** **March 27, 1996, p. 4.**
Market forces of supply and demand are working for the environment, and far faster than anyone expected. The 1990 Clean Air Act mandated a 10.9 million-ton cut by 2010 in emissions that cause acid rain. Instead of the expected 2.2 million-ton reduction, emissions are down by 5.6 million tons.

Connery, Robert T., "Overhaul of Clean Air Act rules dismays industry," ***National Law Journal,*** **June 10, 1996, p. C6.**
The EPA's proposed reform of new source review rules under the Clean Air Act may subject manufacturing facilities undergoing minor modifications to years of costly re-evaluation as a "new source" of pollution. Details of the proposed review rules and industry's negative reaction to them are discussed.

Crimmins, Jerry, "Car pool law of Clean Air Act left for dead," ***Chicago Tribune,*** **Dec. 26, 1995, Sec. 2C, p. 1.**
With little fanfare or public notice, Congress has ditched the so-called car pool law of the federal Clean Air Act, a law that would have required employers to devise plans aimed at reducing the number of employees who drive solo to work.

Guilford, Dave, "Clean Air Act ushers in era of heavy regulation," ***Automotive News,*** **June 26, 1996, p. 130.**
The Clean Air Act of 1970 ushered in a new era of sharply increased federal regulation of the automobile industry. Information about the increasing federal regulation of the auto industry in the 1970s is presented.

Johnson, Jeff, "EPA readies study of future costs, benefits of implementing 1990 Clean Air Act," ***Environmental Science & Technology,*** **January 1997, pp. A16-17.**
The EPA anticipates that next month it will have preliminary results from a prospective study of the expected costs and benefits of the 1990 Clean Air Act Amendments for the years 2000 and 2010.

"Proposed changes to Clean Air Act standards," *Nation's Cities Weekly,* Dec. 16, 1996, p. 15.
The EPA proposed new standards under the Clean Air Act for ozone and particulate matter on Nov. 27, 1996. Information about these proposals and their potential impact on cities is presented.

Proposed Air Quality Standards

"Air quality: New standards would make important progress," *Detroit News & Free Press,* Dec. 1, 1996, p. F2.
An editorial discusses the new air quality standards proposed in November 1996 by the EPA for ozone levels and particulate control, saying that the proposed EPA regulations appear affordable and practical and perhaps even a bit weak for a country with such a record of environmental concern.

Fialka, John J., "Group gears up to block EPA proposals on national air quality standards," *The Wall Street Journal,* Nov. 29, 1996, p. B3.
A coalition of large industry groups, governors and big-city mayors is lining up to block two proposed national air quality standards on small-particle soot and ozone levels that were announced on Nov. 27, 1996, by EPA Administrator Carol M. Browner.

Figura, Susannah Zak, "EPA proposes major new air standards," *Occupational Hazards,* January 1997, p. 31.
The EPA has proposed sweeping new standards that are designed to strengthen protections against particulate matter and ground-level ozone .

Hanson, David, "Conflict over air quality rules," *Chemical & Engineering News,* Dec. 16, 1996, pp. 27-28.
Chemical industry groups are angry over the EPA's proposed ozone and particulate standards. They say the proposals have high compliance costs and little perceived benefit.

"Industry steps up fight over EPA's new air rules," *Oil & Gas Journal,* Dec. 9, 1996, p. 34.
Industry groups are stepping up the battle over the air quality standards for smog and soot that the EPA is proposing.

Lambrecht, Bill, "EPA targets air pollution in new rules," *St. Louis Post-Dispatch,* Nov. 28, 1996, p. A1.
On Nov. 27, 1996, the EPA proposed strict new standards for air quality that could force Americans to pay more to breathe better and live longer. After reviewing more than 250 health studies, the EPA proposed separate rules to control ozone and the microscopic particles that people take into their lungs unknowingly each day.

"Proposed changes to Clean Air Act standards," *Nation's Cities Weekly,* Dec. 16, 1996, p. 15.
The EPA proposed new standards under the Clean Air Act for ozone and particulate matter on Nov. 27, 1996. Information about these proposals and their potential impact on cities is presented.

Walker, Roger, "New Clean-Air Rules Ignore Common Sense," *St. Louis Post-Dispatch,* Dec. 27, 1996, p. B7.
Walker criticizes the EPA's decision, in late 1996, to raise air standards for ozone and fine particulate matter, asserting that the action was taken by the EPA with virtually no evidence that the change in standards would result in significant health benefits and with no analysis of the costs and benefits.

Warrick, Joby, "Panel Seeks Cease-Fire on Air Quality but Gets a War," *The Washington Post,* Feb. 6, 1997, p. A21.
Dueling experts in the air pollution debate testified for three hours before the Senate's clean air subcommittee in the first congressional review of the Environmental Protection Agency's proposals for tightening air standards for urban smog and soot. But instead of yielding a consensus on the scientific evidence for the new rules, the hearing succeeded only in showing how different experts — with different backgrounds and funding sources — can draw different conclusions from the same data.

Wood, Daniel B., "Heat rises over clean-air proposal," *The Christian Science Monitor,* Nov. 29, 1996, p. 1.
Tighter clean air standards, proposed by the EPA on Nov. 27, 1996, are the most far-reaching environmental initiative of the Clinton administration to date. The proposed standards for ozone and particulate emissions that make up smog are scheduled to become permanent in June 1997, but in the meantime an intense political battle is expected. At issue is whether the benefits — measured primarily by lower health-care costs — exceed the plan's multibillion-dollar price tag.

Regional Differences and Initiatives

"Agency Seeks a Move Because of Air Quality," *The New York Times,* April 4, 1996, p. A17.
Following complaints that the air in its headquarters was making workers sick, the Transportation Department said on April 3, 1996, that it would ask its landlord to spend $5 million to relocate employees and overhaul the ventilation system in the summer. The ventilation system was found to be the cause of workers' complaints that the building's air had caused nausea, headaches and sore throats.

Brandon, Karen, "As California goes, so goes the nation in fighting pollution," *Chicago Tribune,* Dec. 2, 1996, p. 7.
The pervasive measures taken by Southern California to reduce air pollution are unparalleled by any other place on the planet; confrontations that are likely on a national scale when the EPA seeks to set new standards will likely begin there.

Burke, Maria, "United Kingdom to set air quality emission standards," ***Environmental Science & Technology,*** **October 1996, p. 436.**

The United Kingdom has announced a national air quality strategy that may lead to legislation, as early as April 1997, to regulate eight pollutants.

Burtraw, Dallas, "Call it 'pollution rights,' but it works," ***The Washington Post,*** **March 31, 1996, p. C3.**

Burtraw comments that an innovative approach to regulating sulfur dioxide emissions was implemented by the EPA under a key provision in the 1990 Clean Air Act, dispelling the belief that Congress foils everything it touches and that the EPA is too intrusive.

Cushman, John H. Jr., "States Neglecting Pollution Rules, White House Says," ***The New York Times,*** **Dec. 15, 1996, p. 1.**

Worried that some state governments are neglecting federal environmental laws, the Clinton administration is investigating several states' performances, officials said. EPA officials say they have found that Pennsylvania and some other big industrial states are reporting only a handful of major pollution violations. Also, a number of states have passed laws that may conflict with federal policies by protecting companies that report their own violations.

Hans, Mick, "EPA's 33/50 Program: Companies cooperate to reduce pollution," ***Safety & Health,*** **August 1996, pp. 42-46.**

The EPA's 33/50 Program targeted 17 widely used chemicals for voluntary emissions reductions. A total of 1,290 companies pledged voluntary participation in the project

Huppke, Rex W., "Air quality group pushes car pools, mass transit," ***St. Louis Post-Dispatch,*** **p. B3.**

The Regional Clean Air Partnership of St. Louis, Mo., announced new air quality initiatives on June 10, 1996. Partnership members hope to increase the use of car pools and mass transportation.

Jones, Cynthia L., and Anna K. Harding, "Pollution prevention practices in Oregon's electronics industry," ***Journal of Environmental Health,*** **January 1997, pp. 21-27.**

A study was conducted to identify pollution prevention strategies that are currently being used by the electronics industry in Oregon and to assess the industry's interest in switching to less hazardous practices. A survey was distributed to 180 businesses, including all companies affiliated with the Oregon Electronic Association, and additional electronics corporations listed in Oregon phone directories.

Miles, Katrina, "Manufacturing pollution down sharply," ***The Boston Globe,*** **June 27, 1996, p. 30.**

Massachusetts manufacturers reduced the amount of pollutants emitted into the environment by 68 percent between 1988 and 1994, according to an EPA survey released on June 26, 1996.

Tyson, Rae, "Report: Industry spewing less pollution," ***USA Today,*** **June 27, 1996, p. A7.**

Spurred by aggressive pollution-cutting efforts in Louisiana, industry is making good on its promise to reduce toxic emissions nationwide, an EPA report shows. Industries released 2.2 billion pounds of toxic wastes in 1994, down 9 percent from 1993. Louisiana is responsible for 98 percent of the reduction.

Soot and Smog

Allen, Scott, "Industries mount fight against EPA's move to tighten standards of air pollution," ***The Boston Globe,*** **Nov. 19, 1996, p. A3.**

Industries from carmakers to electric utilities in 1996 have launched a multimillion-dollar campaign to derail federal rules — expected to be proposed by the EPA in December — that would set tough new standards for pollution caused by smog and tiny airborne particles.

Alvarez, Ramon, "Tougher pollution standards vital," ***USA Today,*** **Dec. 4, 1996, p. A14.**

In a letter to the editor, Alvarez of the Environmental Defense Fund says opposition to tighter urban smog and haze standards proposed by the EPA is resulting in scare tactics about the new regulation.

Barnum, Alex, "Air pollution rules sure to draw fire," ***San Francisco Chronicle,*** **Nov. 28, 1996, p. A1.**

Setting the stage for an epic environmental battle, the Clinton administration proposed tough new standards for smog and soot on Nov. 27, 1996, that it said are aimed at protecting the health of millions of Americans. EPA Administrator Carol M. Browner said the new standards would cut the number of premature deaths from air pollution by 20,000 and reduce the suffering of people with asthma and other respiratory diseases.

Overberg, Paul, "Counties choking on pollution-reduction standards," ***USA Today,*** **Nov. 25, 1996, p. A8.**

The EPA is set to announce strict limits on ozone in an effort to reduce levels of urban smog. U.S. counties that are not meeting current ozone standards, not likely to meet new standards and those not meeting current standards but expected to meet new standards are listed by state.

"Rule will reduce air pollution from landfills," ***Safety & Health,*** **June 1996, p. 16.**

The EPA has issued a rule that will reduce smog-causing emissions and toxic air pollutants from municipal solid-waste landfills by 50 percent. The rule applies to approximately 280 large landfills that emit more than 55 tons of volatile organic compounds per year.

Back Issues

Great Research on Current Issues Starts Right Here...Recent topics covered by The CQ Researcher are listed below. Before May 1991, reports were published under the name of Editorial Research Reports.

AUGUST 1995
Job Stress
Organ Transplants
United Nations at 50
Advances in Cancer Research

SEPTEMBER 1995
Catholic Church in the U.S.
Northern Ireland Cease-Fire
High School Sports
Teaching History

OCTOBER 1995
Quebec's Future
Revitalizing the Cities
Networking the Classroom
Indoor Air Pollution

NOVEMBER 1995
The Working Poor
The Jury System
Sex, Violence and the Media
Police Misconduct

DECEMBER 1995
Teens and Tobacco
Gene Therapy's Future
Global Water Shortages
Third-Party Prospects

JANUARY 1996
Emergency Medicine
Punishing Sex Offenders
Bilingual Education
Helping the Homeless

FEBRUARY 1996
Reforming the CIA
Campaign Finance Reform
Academic Politics
Getting Into College

MARCH 1996
The British Monarchy
Preventing Juvenile Crime
Tax Reform
Pursuing the Paranormal

APRIL 1996
Centennial Olympic Games
Managed Care
Protecting Endangered Species
New Military Culture

MAY 1996
Russia's Political Future
Marriage and Divorce
Year-Round Schools
Taiwan, China and the U.S.

JUNE 1996
Rethinking NAFTA
First Ladies
Teaching Values
Labor Movement's Future

JULY 1996
Recovered-Memory Debate
Native Americans' Future
Crackdown on Sexual Harassment
Attack on Public Schools

AUGUST 1996
Fighting Over Animal Rights
Privatizing Government Services
Child Labor and Sweatshops
Cleaning Up Hazardous Wastes

SEPTEMBER 1996
Gambling Under Attack
The States and Federalism
Civic Journalism
Reassessing Foreign Aid

OCTOBER 1996
Political Consultants
Insurance Fraud
Rethinking School Integration
Parental Rights

NOVEMBER 1996
Global Warming
Clashing Over Copyright
Consumer Debt
Governing Washington, D.C.

DECEMBER 1996
Welfare, Work and the States
The New Volunteerism
Implementing the Disabilities Act
America's Pampered Pets

JANUARY 1997
Combating Scientific Misconduct
Restructuring the Electric Industry
The New Immigrants
Chemical and Biological Weapons

FEBRUARY 1997
Assisting Refugees
Alternative Medicine's Next Phase
Independent Counsels
Feminism's Future

Future Topics

- ***Alcohol Advertising***
- ***Civic Renewal***
- ***Educating Gifted Children***

THE CQ Researcher

PUBLISHED BY CONGRESSIONAL QUARTERLY INC.

Alcohol Advertising

Should liquor be advertised on radio and TV?

Liquor ads began running on television last year for the first time in nearly a half-century. Many public health groups and government officials reacted with alarm, arguing that distilled spirits ads inevitably would be seen by young, impressionable viewers — and in fact deliberately were aimed at youth. The major networks say they won't run liquor commercials. But distillers argue that a standard serving of wine or beer contains approximately the same volume of alcohol as a mixed drink, and that they are only seeking a level playing field with wine and beer, which have advertised on radio and television for decades. Critics retort, however, that the liquor industry's actual goal is to boost liquor sales, which have been declining for years.

INSIDE THIS ISSUE

CQ March 14, 1997 • Volume 7, No. 10 • Pages 217-240

Formerly Editorial Research Reports

Alcohol Advertising

The Issues

Background

Current Situation

Outlook

Sidebars and Graphics

For Further Research

Cover: Photo Illustration By Sarah Magner and Rick Rose (Photos © Photodisc and V&S Vin & Sprit AB.)

March 14, 1997
Volume 7, No. 10

Editor
Sandra Stencel

Managing Editor
Thomas J. Colin

Associate Editors
Sarah M. Magner
Richard L. Worsnop

Staff Writers
Charles S. Clark
Mary H. Cooper
Kenneth Jost
David Masci

Editorial Assistant
Vanessa E. Furlong

Published By
Congressional Quarterly Inc.

Chairman
Andrew Barnes

Vice Chairman
Andrew P. Corty

President and Publisher
Robert W. Merry

Executive Editor
David Rapp

The CQ Researcher (ISSN 1056-2036). Formerly Editorial Research Reports. Published weekly (48 times per year, not printed Jan. 3, May 30, Aug. 29, Oct. 31) by Congressional Quarterly Inc., 1414 22nd St., N.W., Washington, D.C. 20037. Annual subscription rate for libraries, businesses and government is $340. Additional rates furnished upon request. Periodicals postage paid at Washington, D.C., and additional mailing offices. POSTMASTER: Send address changes to The CQ Researcher, 1414 22nd St., N.W., Washington, D.C. 20037.

Alcohol Advertising

BY RICHARD L. WORSNOP

THE ISSUES

Two telegenic dogs made advertising history recently in Corpus Christi, Texas. The canines were depicted as "obedience school graduates" in a commercial aired last June on KRIS-TV, the local NBC affiliate. One pooch was shown holding a newspaper in its jaws; then the class "valedictorian" trotted into view, not with a paper but a pouch containing a bottle of Seagram's Crown Royal whiskey.

From a creative standpoint, the commercial may not have been ready for prime time. Nor did many viewers realize they were watching a broadcasting milestone. But the ad marked the first time that a liquor company had broken a 60-year-old voluntary industry ban on broadcast advertising of distilled spirits — hard liquor.

Not surprisingly, the ad sent tremors through the alcoholic beverage industry, which has long been dominated by beer makers. It also attracted the concerned attention of the public health and federal regulatory communities, raising new questions about the need for tighter government curbs on alcohol advertising.

In Corpus Christi, calm prevailed. According to KRIS owner F. Frank Smith Jr., there was "very little" viewer reaction to the commercials. "They ran through June, were off for a while and then they ran again during the Olympics and during the holidays." Other liquor companies have inquired about Seagram's deal with KRIS, Smith reports, but so far, "No one else has said to us, 'Would you like to take our order?' "

At the same time, Smith is aware of the media stir his station caused. "All the comment seems to come from Washington," he says. "I think people up there are just looking for some kind of a national controversy to latch onto."

It seemed, at first, that the controversy was destined for an early fade. The four major TV broadcasters — NBC, ABC, CBS and Fox — quickly announced they would not show liquor ads on network programs or individual stations owned and operated by them. They noted, however, that they had no control over the advertising practices of their affiliates.

The flap took a new turn Nov. 7, when the Distilled Spirits Council of the United States (DISCUS) announced that it was lifting the voluntary ban on broadcast advertising adopted by the liquor industry in 1936. "For decades, beer and wine have been advertised on television and radio while the distilled spirits industry has upheld its own voluntary ban," said DISCUS President and CEO Fred A. Meister. "The absence of spirits from television and radio has contributed to the mistaken perception that spirits are somehow 'harder' or worse than beer or wine and thus deserving of harsher social, political and legal treatment." [1]

Meister added that advances in broadcast technology had contributed to the policy change. "The extensive growth of cable, computer and broadcast communications continues to fragment audiences," he explained. "Audience fragmentation enables the distilled spirits industry to direct its messages more precisely to adult audiences than would have been possible when we first voluntarily decided not to advertise on radio or television. At that time there were only a few channels."

Among broadcasters, reaction to the DISCUS decision was muted. Edward O. Fritts, president and CEO of the National Association of Broadcasters (NAB), cited the organization's "staunch support of the First Amendment rights of broadcasters to advertise legal products." Nonetheless, he said, the NAB was "disappointed with DISCUS' decision to end its voluntary code." Fritts added that "individual stations have adopted their own standards regarding the acceptability of hard liquor advertising," and he expressed confidence that they "will continue to make judgments every day on what is most appropriate for their local audiences." [2]

The Cabletelevision Advertising Bureau (CAB) said it would continue to adhere to its advertising guidelines, which call for decisions about advertising distilled spirits "on a case-by-case basis."

But President Clinton and other top government officials lambasted DISCUS. It was "simply irresponsible" of the liquor industry to reverse its longstanding broadcast advertising ban, Clinton said Nov. 9 in his weekly radio address to the nation. "We've worked so hard here to warn our children about the dangers of drugs [and] we also have a duty to protect our families from the consequences of alcohol abuse," the president said. "Now the American liquor industry has made a decision that will make this hard work even harder."

Sounding a bipartisan note, Senate Majority Leader Trent Lott, R-Miss.,

A Drink Is a Drink Is a Drink

Although the percentage of alcohol is lower in beer and wine than in distilled spirits, standard servings of beer (12 ounces), wine (five ounces) and cocktails (1 1/2 ounces of scotch, vodka etc.) all contain the same amount of absolute alcohol. According to the National Council on Alcoholism and Drug Dependence, "Beer, wine and liquor have the same effect if the person drinks them in a standard size serving and at the same rate."

Note: Low-fat or "lite" beers have the same alcohol content as regular beer.

Source: National Coalition on Alcoholism and Drug Dependence

said on NBC's "Meet the Press" the next day, "I think that [advertising alcohol on TV] is a big mistake. I think it would have a bad impact on our children and young people and society as a whole."

Federal Communications Commission (FCC) Chairman Reed E. Hundt also berated DISCUS, calling its decision "disappointing for parents and dangerous for kids." Hundt has argued that the FCC shares authority with the Federal Trade Commission (FTC) over radio and television advertising for liquor — a position challenged by trade groups representing advertisers and ad agencies. Indeed, 26 Democratic and Republican members of Congress wrote to the FCC in November urging a formal investigation of liquor ads on television. The lawmakers said they feared a flood of liquor ads on television, "leaving our children to drown in images of academic and athletic success that is to be gained by drinking liquor."

But Rep. John D. Dingell, D-Mich., the ranking minority member of the House Commerce Committee, has challenged the FCC's authority. In a Jan. 2 letter to Hundt, he said that "Congress has never given the [FCC] the ability to censor specific programming or advertising; to prohibit or limit broadcasters' ability to air commercial advertising; or to prohibit or limit particular advertising of products or services legally sold in interstate commerce." He added, "It is unclear that Congress could give the commission the ability to do any of those things in a manner consistent with the First Amendment."

Former Sen. George S. McGovern, D-S.D., wants the FCC "to conduct a careful investigation of the actual impact of alcohol advertising on young people." McGovern, the 1972 Democratic presidential nominee, is national spokesman for the National Council on Alcohol and Drug Dependence (NCADD).* "To what extent does advertising cause young people to turn to drinking — even more seriously, uncontrolled drinking?" McGovern asks. Moreover, he wants to "know more about what happens to the 15-20 million alcoholics in this country — some of whom are in recovery, most of whom are not — under the influence of these seductive television ads on alcoholic beverages."

To McGovern and others seeking tighter curbs on advertising alcoholic beverages, the First Amendment could be a major obstacle. As many commentators have noted, Seagram's break with liquor industry tradition last year was announced shortly after the Supreme Court struck down a Rhode Island law that barred print advertisement of retail liquor prices except at the point of sale. The court held that the law abridged retailers' constitutionally protected right of free speech (*see p. 229*).

There is speculation that the distilled spirits industry will cite its First Amendment rights if future broadcast liquor advertising comes under court challenge. The industry says it simply wants to compete with beer and wine on a level playing field, exercising the same right to advertise on TV and

*McGovern's daughter Theresa froze to death at age 45 in 1994 while acutely intoxicated. McGovern's book, *Terry: My Daughter's Life-and-Death Struggle With Alcoholism*, was published in 1996.

Minorities Object to Targeted Alcohol Ads

Marketing to minorities has long been among the most sensitive issues confronting alcoholic beverage makers. A decade ago, the Center for Science in the Public Interest (CSPI) published two highly critical reports on the subject.[1] And in 1992, the introduction of Crazy Horse Malt Liquor drew widespread criticism.[2]

Crazy Horse "is only the latest in a string of offensive malt liquor campaigns," Patricia Taylor, former director of CSPI's alcohol policies project, testified at a congressional hearing. "We condemn Crazy Horse's manufacturer for the way in which the company has appropriated a spiritual and cultural figure to promote a product responsible for such much devastation to Native Americans."[3]

Crazy Horse remains on the market despite persistent efforts by Native American groups and their supporters to force Hornell Brewing Co. to halt its production. "To the people who put this out, it's nothing but a way to make money," said Big Crow, a descendant of Crazy Horse. "For them, everything is there to make money off of. But there are many things that we honor and cherish, and we are going to defend them."[4]

CSPI and other critics of malt liquor marketing object in particular to the fact that it is often sold in 40-ounce cans. "Singles of that size enhance the user's ability to become intoxicated," says George A. Hacker, current director of the group's alcohol policies project. (Malt liquors typically contain as much as 20 percent more alcohol than regular beers.)

Jeff Becker, the Beer Institute's vice president for alcohol issues, acknowledges that malt liquor advertising often is placed in African American and Hispanic communities. But he rejects claims that the ads promote alcohol abuse, noting that studies show lower rates of alcohol consumption among blacks and Hispanics than among whites. And he says it is insulting to intimate that members of minority groups are less able to assess the content of alcohol advertising than other people.

Malt liquor marketing practices remain an area of concern for CSPI, says Hacker. "But it hasn't been as high-level an issue in the last couple of years," he says, "because other things have arisen that seem more urgent right now." He cites liquor advertising on television and radio and concerns about alcohol's impact on health as prime examples.

Though no clear pattern has yet emerged, there are indications that liquor companies may find radio and TV stations in minority areas especially receptive to their advertising. Broadcasting and alcohol industry observers note that the only two national cable TV networks to accept liquor commercials to date are Black Entertainment Television, oriented toward African Americans, and Telemundo, a Spanish-language service that has run spots for Presidente Brandy. And it may be more than coincidence that the first liquor ads to run on U.S. television appeared on a station in Corpus Christi, a southern Texas city with a large Hispanic population.

As the CSPI reported in its report on marketing to Hispanics, "Today, the Hispanic community is paying the price for the marketing savvy of the alcohol and tobacco companies with increased levels of drinking and smoking."

---

[1] "Marketing Booze to Blacks" (1987) and "Marketing Disease to Hispanics" (1989).

[2] Crazy Horse is the Sioux chief whose forces defeated Col. George A. Custer at the 1876 Battle of Little Bighorn in Montana. Custer and all the members of his regiment died in the battle.

[3] Testimony before House Select Committee on Children, Youth and Families, May 19, 1992.

[4] Quoted by Michael A. Fletcher, "Crazy Horse Again Sounds Battle Cry," *The Washington Post*, Feb. 18, 1997, p. A3.

radio. After all, the liquor industry stresses, beer, wine and hard liquor are equal in that typical servings of beer and wine contain approximately the same volume of ethyl alcohol as hard liquor.

There's no argument that the distilled spirits industry hopes to revive its sagging fortunes. Liquor sales have been declining for years, a trend that the industry itself expects to continue at least through the year 2000. (*See graphs, p. 224.*)

Whether liquor producers will turn to radio and television commercials — and whether broadcast ads can spark a sales turnaround — remain to be seen. As industry officials, government regulators and consumers ponder the influence of alcohol advertising on American society, here are some of the questions being asked:

Does alcohol advertising encourage underage or excessive drinking?

The alcohol industry, like the tobacco industry, says it doesn't pitch its products specifically at young people. Consumer and public health groups scoff at the claim, noting that beer is heavily advertised on televised sports events, which are popular with high school and college students. They also argue that commercials featuring real or cartoon animals, such as Seagram's obedience school dogs or Budweiser's talking frogs, are designed expressly to catch the eye of young viewers.[3] (*See story, p. 230.*)

Actually, says the Coors Brewing Co., "Advertising and other marketing practices promote competition, resulting in higher quality and lower-priced products for consumers. Restrictions on advertising will not reduce the misuse of alcohol. . . . Advertising does what it is designed to do — promote consumer

Drinkers and Advertisers Are Hooked on Beer

Nearly three-fourths of the more than $1 billion spent to advertise alcoholic beverages in the U.S. in 1995 promoted beer, while less than one-quarter of the total was spent on distilled spirits. American consumers spent an estimated $104 billion on alcoholic beverages in 1995, nearly two-thirds of it on beer and slightly less than one-third on spirits.

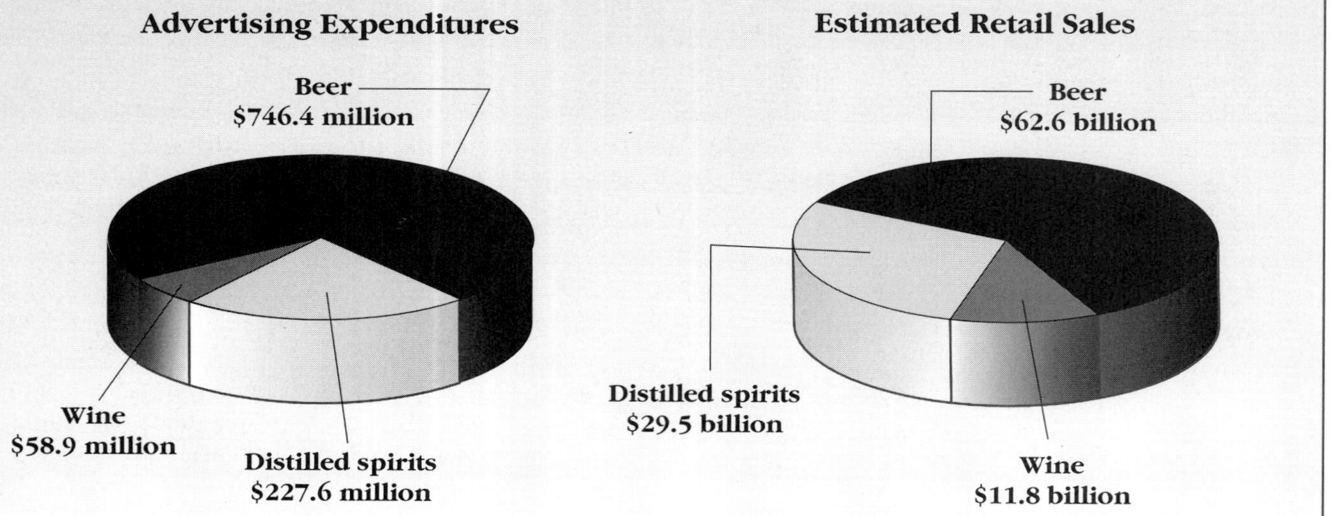

Advertising Expenditures

Beer
$746.4 million

Wine
$58.9 million

Distilled spirits
$227.6 million

Estimated Retail Sales

Beer
$62.6 billion

Distilled spirits
$29.5 billion

Wine
$11.8 billion

Sources: CMR and Impact Databank (advertising); Distilled Spirits Council of the United States (retail sales)

loyalty and encourage brand shifting." [4]

Adds Francine Katz, vice president of consumer awareness and education at Anheuser-Busch: "Awareness of an ad does not cause drinking any more than ignorance causes abstinence." [5]

Advertising executive Joseph C. Fisher makes a similar claim in a 1993 book often cited by alcohol industry officials. "Advertising appears to have a very weak positive influence on consumption and no impact on experimentation with alcohol or abuse of it," he wrote. "Moreover, there is no evidence that changes in regulations regarding permissible advertising that either increase or decrease it affect consumption patterns." [6]

Alcohol industry critics disagree. McGovern, for instance, believes young people decide to sample alcohol mainly because of peer pressure — but "advertising reinforces" the decision. "I'm not a big television watcher, but I am a sports fan," he says. "And I'm struck by how seductive those beer commercials are. You see these healthy, attractive young men and women drinking beer, and at the end someone says, 'It just doesn't get much better than this.'

"Well, it can get a hell of a lot worse if you drink too much of that stuff. That's the side of the story that needs to be told. I think the net impact of alcohol advertising is to convince people that drinking produces fun, relaxation, sex, social advancement — that it's the thing to do if you want to take part in the real joys of life."

McGovern adds that he is a firm believer "in truth in advertising and truth in labeling. I've had an interest in that ever since my days as chairman of the Senate Select Committee on Nutrition. I always favored more labeling of the content of products, and also the possible side effects."

Morris E. Chafetz, president of the Health Education Foundation and the first director of the National Institute on Alcohol Abuse and Alcoholism, doubts whether there is a connection between alcohol ads and alcohol consumption. "[O]pponents of TV advertising for distilled spirits (or any other alcoholic beverage, for that matter) assert a connection between the ads and the altering of behavior that, scientifically speaking, just isn't there," he wrote recently. [7]

"As a father and grandfather, I've noticed through the years that young people are not Pavlovian in their responses," Chafetz added. "Billions of dollars are spent each year bombarding young people with ads for all kinds of products, some of which they covet and some of which they ignore." *(See "At Issue," p. 233.)*

But Sarah Kayson, director of public policy at the NCADD, argues that alcohol advertising "leads to the normalization and glamorization of alcohol use in just about any situation in American society — and for anybody. We don't believe it has a Pavlovian dog effect, where someone watches a beer commercial and then immediately gets up and downs a six-pack.

"Our concern is about ads giving an unrealistic view of what alcoholic beverages are, and what they do. You know, 'If you drink, then you're more attractive to the opposite sex.' We find that approach to be very problematic, to say the least. The same goes for ads that portray drinking as a reward for a hard day's work."

Jeff Becker, the Beer Institute's vice president for alcohol issues, retorts that alcohol ads reflect and encourage popular desires for healthier lifestyles. "The best example of that is [low-calorie] 'lite' beer, which now comprises more than 35 percent of the total beer market," he says.

Art DeCelle, the institute's general counsel, stresses that advertising is just part of an internal beer industry struggle for market share. "People from the Federal Trade Commission and the Bureau of Alcohol, Tobacco and Firearms come to our office all the time to look at industry publications that track beer advertising," he says. "And when they see that beer advertising is tracked by brand, they ask us, 'Don't you have anything else? Isn't this monitored any other way?' Well, the fact is that beer advertising is all about brands, and that is how it is followed in the industry."

George A. Hacker, director of the alcohol policies project of the Center for Science in the Public Interest (CSPI), dismisses the industry denials. "It's just ludicrous that the industry contends advertising has no effect on consumption, or that alcohol companies only advertise to shift people from one brand to another."

"Of course they go after new users," Hacker says. "And the new users happen to be kids. Let's face it: Old drinkers die, and new drinkers grow up. The industry would say new users start drinking at 21, but that's absurd. In this country, new alcohol users start at 13. And the industry knows that very well."

Hacker also notes that beer, wine and liquor producers "are interested in increasing the consumption of those who already use alcohol. It's the same impulse as with any other product, whether it's laundry detergent or chocolate pudding. You just want people to use your product more frequently.

"So, it's ridiculous for this industry to claim it doesn't seek to increase consumption of what it makes, and that it spends millions of dollars a year just trying to shift people from one brand to another. That simply doesn't happen, and a person has to be incredibly naive — or incredibly rich from contributions from industry political action committees — to believe something like that."

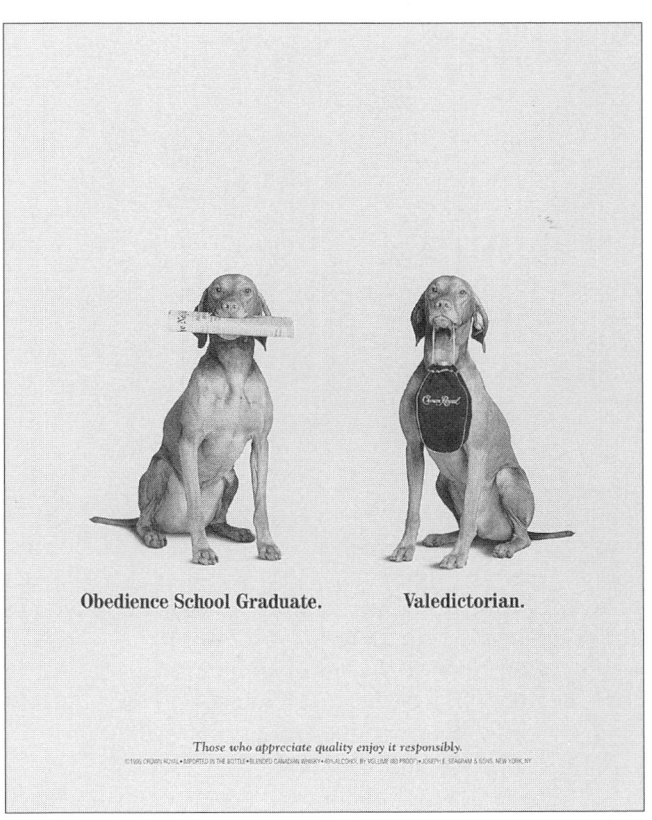

Obedience School Graduate. Valedictorian.

Those who appreciate quality enjoy it responsibly.

This print advertisement for Seagram's Crown Royal whiskey is similar to the Seagram's ad first broadcast on KRIS-TV in Corpus Christi, Texas, in June 1996, breaking the liquor industry's voluntary ban on broadcast liquor ads.

Are beer, wine and liquor essentially identical products?

"Although 'alcohol is alcohol is alcohol,' that doesn't mean that beer and liquor and wine are all the same," Hacker says. "They're consumed in different situations. The alcohol in liquor is much more concentrated, particularly given the thoughtless way in which many young people drink. Persuading them to drink liquor instead of beer would increase the level and the severity of alcohol-related problems."

"When you read about alcohol poisonings on college campuses," Hacker adds, "that doesn't occur when kids are drinking only beer or wine. It occurs when they are drinking liquor, either alone or in combination with other substances."

But McGovern feels it's "a mistaken view that hard liquor is more dangerous than beer and wine. There's just as much alcoholism in this country stemming from beer and wine as there is from vodka and bourbon and scotch. In fact, as beer and wine consumption increased, they have become more of a danger in terms of producing addiction, auto accidents

Liquor Drinking Declines While Beer Flows Freely

The decline of U.S. hard liquor consumption in the past 15 years has fueled the concern that liquor companies will turn to TV and radio advertising to try to take market share away from beer and wine.

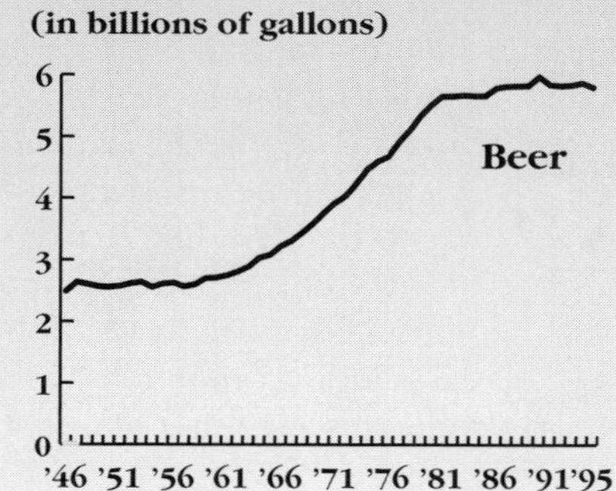

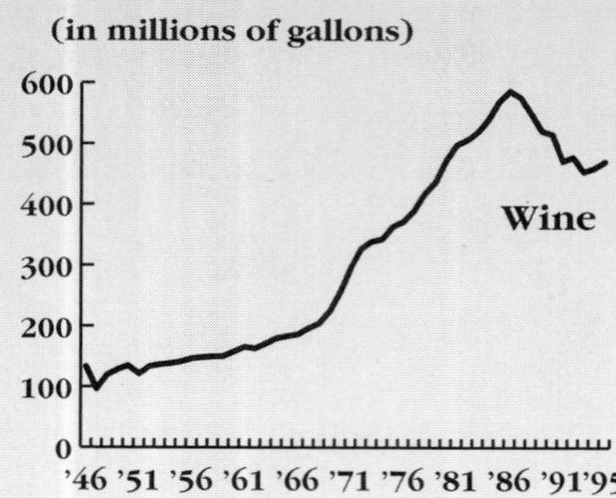

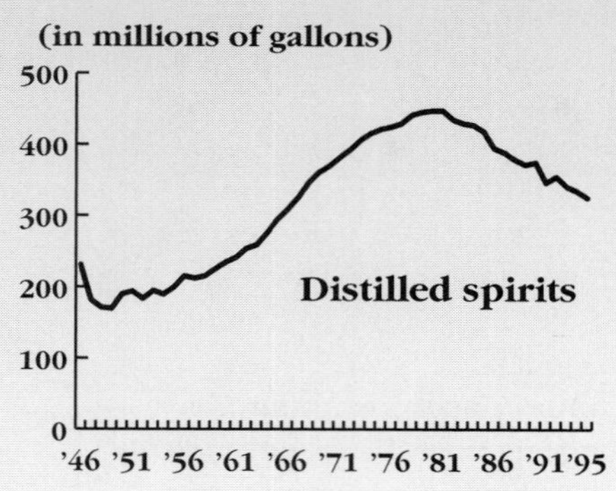

Source: Distilled Spirits Council of the U.S., Feb. 18, 1997; based on data from the Beer Institute, Wine Institute, National Alcoholic Beverage Control Association and Steve Barsby & Associates Inc.

and so on."

In McGovern's view, "The distillers have a point when they say that if we're going to permit the advertising of beer and wine, why not allow them to advertise their products, too? It's hard to refute them in any scientifically sound way."

Sarah Ward, president of the National Woman's Christian Temperance Union (WCTU), regards all alcoholic beverages as basically identical for the simple reason that "we are opposed to all of them." She notes that, on a per-serving basis, "there's the same amount of ethyl alcohol in each drink. The only difference is whether you want to get the poison in your system with a couple of gulps, or you want to take a little longer — it all has the same ultimate effect."

But Gladys Horiuchi, communications manager for the Wine Institute, a San Francisco-based trade group, points out that many vintners prefer to target affluent consumers rather than the larger market sought by beer and liquor advertisers. "People who buy wine tend to be upper-income and college-educated," she says. Consequently, many wineries "feel they are able to precisely target that market by placing print ads in *Smithsonian* or *Runner's World*, or similar niche magazines. They often feel television is a waste of their advertising money, because you are reaching out to people who do not drink fine table wines. And don't forget that TV is an enormously expensive advertising medium."

For Kayson, the key issue is not the distinctiveness of various alcoholic beverages or their marketing niches but the combined volume of advertising used to market all alcoholic beverages. "We're concerned that $600 million worth of beer ads already appears on TV every year," she says. "Who knows how much the distilled spirits companies would be willing to spend on commercials?

"We're not concerned simply because the distilled spirits industry is becoming involved. The problem is that kids will be exposed to many more alcohol ads, and there will be a doubling of the normalization and glamorization of alcohol in our country."

But to DISCUS chief Meister, the issue comes down to parity. "There is simply no justifiable social, political or scientific basis for treating spirits differently than other alcoholic beverages." ■

BACKGROUND

Temperance Movement

Americans have had mixed feelings about alcohol since Colonial times. "In the period immediately after the American Revolution, a generally favorable view of alcoholic beverages coincided with rising levels of consumption that far exceeded any in modern times," wrote Yale University's David F. Musto, an authority on attitudes toward alcohol and other drugs. "By the early decades of the

19th century, Americans drank roughly three times as much alcohol as they do in the 1990s." [8]

They viewed alcoholic beverages as "important and invigorating foods, whose restorative powers were a natural blessing," Musto noted in a historical survey. People in all regions and of all classes drank heavily — and at all hours. They imbibed wine with sugar at breakfast, took a work break for "bitters" (strongly hopped ale) around 11 a.m., downed beer and cider at lunch, drank more bitters at about 4 p.m., and then consumed toddies (brandy or other liquor mixed with hot water, sugar and spices) at supper and during the remainder of the evening. [9]

Conventional wisdom held alcohol to be superior to water, which in fact was often hazardous to drink. Alcohol also acted as a social lubricant. "Hired farm workers were supplied with spirits as part of their pay and generally drank with their employer," Musto noted. "Stores left a barrel of whiskey or rum outside the door from which customers could take a dip."

Though strong drink was freely available, there was little tolerance for drunkenness, which was blamed not on the alcohol but on the irresponsibility of those who drank to excess.

Indeed, public drunkenness was a punishable offense in many places. The earliest law to address the problem was a 1619 Virginia statute that decreed that a person found drunk for the first time was to be reproved privately by a minister, the second time publicly and the third time made to "lye in halter" for 12 hours as well as to pay a fine. In the Massachusetts Bay Colony, drunkenness was punishable by whipping, fines and confinement in stocks. Still, even the Puritans never outlawed drinking entirely.

The Coors Brewing Co. and Anheuser-Busch Companies sponsor programs to prevent underage drinking, including the use of posters and print and broadcast ads.

Organized temperance groups emerged in the early 19th century, primarily in reaction against excessive drinking on the frontier and in cities. The earliest statewide group was the Massachusetts Society for the Suppression of Intemperance, founded in 1812. Though many temperance advocates merely sought to reduce consumption of alcohol, their goal eventually became total abstinence.

The temperance movement's first great period of success occurred in the 1850s. In 1851, Maine became the first state to enact a prohibition law. It barred the manufacture, storage and sale of intoxicating liquors and imposed heavy penalties on violators, including imprisonment upon conviction for a third offense. By the end of 1855, 12 more states had passed similar laws.

But then the temperance movement hit a wall. After 1855, not another state was to adopt prohibition for a quarter-century. Reasons were not hard to find. During the late 1850s and all of the next decade, the country was preoccupied by slavery, secession and the Civil War. A series of unfavorable court decisions, declaring certain parts of state anti-liquor legislation unconstitutional, also slowed the temperance bandwagon. In addition, law enforcement problems in dry states persuaded many people that prohibition was inherently infeasible.

The 'Noble Experiment'

The temperance movement responded to the problems not by folding its tent but by regrouping, often under the leadership of women. The Woman's Christian Temperance Union (WCTU), the largest and most influential group of its kind, dates from Dec. 23, 1873, when Eliza Jane Thompson led 70 women on a march through Hillsboro, Ohio, urging tavern owners to close. Preaching, praying and singing about the evils of alcohol, Thompson's group, originally known as the Woman's Temperance Crusade, shuttered 150 bars during one 50-day campaign.

The crusade reorganized in November 1874 under Frances E. Willard and became known as the WCTU. It was subsequently joined by the Anti-Saloon League, which formed in Ohio in 1893 and went national two years later as the Anti-Saloon League of America. Soliciting aid from Protestant evangelical churches, the league grew rapidly and came to regard itself as the "Church in Action Against the Saloon." Working in tandem, the league and the WCTU transformed the temperance movement into a potent campaign for nationwide prohibition by the beginning of the 20th century.

One of the campaign's most colorful figures was Carry Moore Nation, who came to national notice in 1900 when she began wrecking saloons in Kansas. Nation, then 54, said that God had directed her to do her work, typically performed with a hatchet. Although she gained wide notoriety, Nation was never embraced by the mainstream temperance groups. Nonetheless, historians credit her with helping to create a public mood conducive to the passage of a national prohibition law.

That goal was finally reached in 1919 with the ratification of the 18th Amendment to the Constitution.* It barred the "manufacture, sale, or transportation of intoxicating liquors" within the United States as well as all imports and exports of alcoholic beverages. The measure took effect a year later, on Jan. 16, 1920.

Even if the 18th Amendment had fallen short of ratification, most of the country still would have been dry. By January 1920, 19 states had written prohibition into their constitutions, while 14 others had enacted statutes outlawing traffic in alcohol. With the exception of Maryland, the 15 states still "wet" when national prohibition took effect all subsequently passed enforcement laws of their own.

*The amendment ultimately was adopted by all states except Connecticut and Rhode Island. The total vote in the senates of the various states was 1,310 in favor (84.6 percent) and 237 against. In the lower houses of the states, the vote was 3,782 for prohibition (78.5 percent) and 1,035 against.

Despite the massive popular support Prohibition enjoyed at the outset, the "noble experiment"* soon ran into trouble. "Evasion of the law began almost immediately . . . and strenuous and sincere opposition to it — especially in the large cities of the North and East — quickly gathered force," historian Frederick Lewis Allen wrote. "The results were the bootlegger, the speakeasy and a spirit of deliberate revolt which in many communities made drinking 'the thing to do.' "[10]

Prohibition, Allen noted, also wrought significant changes in the way Americans regarded alcohol. These included "the increased popularity of distilled as against fermented liquors, the use of the hip-flask, the cocktail party and the general transformation of drinking from a masculine prerogative to one shared by both sexes together. The old-time saloon had been overwhelmingly masculine; the speakeasy usually catered to both men and women." Prohibition formally ended when the states repealed the 18th Amendment in 1933.

Limiting Alcohol Ads

Post-mortems on Prohibition tend to dwell on the boost it provided to organized crime. But in an influential essay published in 1968, Ohio State University historian John C. Burnham argued that the national ban on alcohol helped improve Americans' health. Death rates from liver cirrhosis fell from 29.5 per 100,000 men in 1911 to 10.7 in 1929, he wrote, while admissions to state mental hospitals for treatment of alcoholic psychosis also declined markedly. In Burnham's view, moreover, the "crime wave" linked to Prohibition was more a newspaper creation than a reality.[11]

* During the 1928 presidential campaign, Republican nominee Herbert Hoover called Prohibition "a great social and economic experiment, noble in motive and far-reaching in purpose."

In any event, the re-legalization of alcoholic beverages occurred at the depth of the Great Depression. Consequently, repeal "was brought about as much by the need for [tax] revenue as by the desire to eradicate the evils that grew out of that social experiment," a study of liquor control observed in 1936. The study added, " 'Turn the bootlegger's profits into public revenues' became a watchword."[12]

Shortly before repeal became official, President Franklin D. Roosevelt had met with members of an interdepartmental committee to develop a federal plan for alcohol control under the terms of the National Industrial Recovery Act. They agreed to create a Federal Alcohol Control Administration (FACA) with authority to set production and price limits and to enforce fair trade practices, including advertising and labeling.

FACA, however, fell victim to a May 27, 1935, Supreme Court decision striking down the National Industrial Recovery Act as unconstitutional. Congress plugged the gap three months later by passing the Federal Alcohol Administration (FAA) Act, which incorporated FACA's advertising and labeling provisions.

Under the 1935 law, the FAA was authorized to regulate the advertising of alcoholic beverages to prevent deception of consumers; provide adequate information on the identity and quality of the products advertised, their alcoholic content and the person responsible for the ad; prohibit language disparaging a competitor's products or making false, misleading, obscene or indecent statements; and bar statements inconsistent with those on product labels.

For the brewing industry, restrictions on labeling and advertising only applied in states with similar laws on their books. This provision represented a compro-

Continued on p. 228

Chronology

19th Century

In response to heavy drinking throughout society, a temperance movement emerges in the early 1800s.

1812
The Massachusetts Society for the Suppression of Intemperance is founded.

1851
Maine becomes the first state to enact a prohibition law. Twelve additional states approve similar legislation over the next five years.

1867
The Prohibition Party is founded for the purpose of outlawing alcoholic beverage production and consumption on a national scale.

1874
The Woman's Christian Temperance Union (WCTU) is established.

1895
The Anti-Saloon League of America is founded and soon assumes a leading role in the burgeoning national Prohibition movement.

1910s-1920s

In the aftermath of World War I, the American temperance movement records its greatest triumph.

Dec. 18, 1917
The 18th Amendment, outlawing the use of alcoholic beverages nationwide, is submitted to the states for ratification.

Jan. 16, 1920
The 18th Amendment takes effect. It prohibits the "manufacture, sale, or transportation of intoxicating liquors within . . . the United States" as well as all imports and exports of such products.

1930s-1940s

Prohibition is repealed, but controls on the alcohol industry are established.

Nov. 26, 1933
President Franklin D. Roosevelt signs the Code of Fair Competition for the Distilled Spirits Industry, which establishes the Federal Alcohol Control Administration (FACA).

Dec. 5, 1933
Prohibition ends as the 21st Amendment is ratified, repealing the 18th Amendment.

May 27, 1935
The Supreme Court declares the National Industrial Recovery Act unconstitutional, thus casting doubt on the legitimacy of FACA.

Aug. 24, 1935
Congress approves (and President Roosevelt later signs) the Federal Alcohol Administration (FAA) Act, which incorporates FACA's advertising and labeling provisions.

1936
The Distilled Spirits Institute adopts a voluntary ban on radio advertising. In 1948, the ad ban is amended to include television.

1980s-1990s

Congress and the courts become more deeply involved in the debate on alcoholic beverage advertising.

1988
President Ronald Reagan signs a bill into law that requires all alcoholic beverage containers to carry health warnings.

1993
Sen. Strom Thurmond, R-S.C., and Rep. Joseph P. Kennedy II, D-Mass., introduce bills requiring that all advertising for alcoholic beverages carry one of seven health warnings on a rotating basis. The legislation fails to reach the floor of either chamber of Congress.

May 13, 1996
Ruling in the case of *44 Liquormart v. Rhode Island*, the Supreme Court strikes down a 40-year-old state law that prohibits liquor retailers from citing liquor prices in their advertisements.

June 1996
Seagram America Co. begins running commercials for its Crown Royal brand of whiskey on KRIS-TV, an NBC affiliate in Corpus Christi, Texas.

Nov. 7, 1996
The Distilled Spirits Council of the United States (DISCUS), successor to the Distilled Spirits Institute, ends its decades-old ban on broadcast advertising.

Nov. 13, 1996
A federal appeals court in Baltimore upholds the constitutionality of the city's ordinance banning outdoor display advertising of alcoholic beverages near schools and playgrounds.

March 6, 1997
The Center for Media Education releases a report outlining efforts by alcohol and tobacco companies to market their products to youth via the Internet.

Continued from p. 226

mise between House and Senate supporters of the FAA Act. Brewers had lobbied hard to be completely excluded from the law, contending that beer was a "non-intoxicating" beverage.

Taking the initiative, the alcoholic beverage industry decided to adopt voluntary advertising and marketing codes with a view to winning popular approval and forestalling stricter federal regulation. The Distilled Spirits Institute (forerunner of DISCUS) led the way in 1936 by banning all liquor advertising on radio, a policy extended to television after World War II. The code also discouraged ads on the comic pages and in school, college or religious publications and ads featuring women or children.

The beer and wine industry advertising codes, formulated somewhat later, were broadly similar in purpose and approach. For example, beer advertisements were "not to encourage overindulgence, depict scenes of drunkenness or loss of control, or associate beer drinking with activities and situations that require a high degree of alertness." Taverns, moreover, "should not be depicted as unkempt, but rather as well-kept neighborhood gathering places." [13]

Wine industry guidelines urge advertisers to portray the product as an appropriate mealtime beverage. At the same time, though, the code advises vintners to avoid suggesting that wine contributes to personal success or achievement. It also frowns upon the use of rock stars, past or present sports celebrities and models who appear under age 25.

In some respects, the alcohol industry advertising codes go further than federal regulations. But consumer advocacy groups note that "good taste" in advertising is subject to wide interpretation and that the voluntary codes lack enforcement mechanisms.

As a result, there have been repeated efforts over the years to ban or curb national (as opposed to local) advertising of alcoholic beverages. The arguments supporting such action have become familiar through repetition.

"The deceptive glamour of alcoholic beverages is vastly intensified by the extremes to which their advertising now goes," Samuel McCrea Cavert, general secretary of the Federal Council of the Churches of Christ in America, testified in 1950 at congressional hearings on a federal ban on alcohol ads. "Unlike most advertising, it is less directed to showing the consumer the merits of a certain brand, as compared with others, than to building good will among those who are not yet consumers. More particularly, and most dangerously, it exerts a constant and powerful pressure upon each new generation of youth to acquire habits of drinking." [14]

Subsequent campaigns to ban or restrict beer and wine commercials on television and radio featured similar arguments. The anti-alcohol initiatives have produced few results, however. In November 1983, for example, a CSPI-led coalition of 28 consumer, women's, health, religious and other organizations petitioned the FTC for a ban on beer and wine commercials or, failing that, a requirement that such ads be balanced by public service announcements warning of the risks of excessive drinking. The petition also asked the FTC to require alcohol advertisements in magazines and newspapers to contain health warnings and to prohibit beer companies from sponsoring rock music concerts and beer-tasting parties on college campuses.

The commission rejected the coalition's requests for tighter ad controls and for an industrywide probe of alcohol marketing practices.

Project SMART

In response, the coalition targeted Congress with its 1985 campaign Project SMART (Stop Marketing Alcohol on Radio and Television). The coalition argued that alcohol commercials, by featuring former athletes and other celebrities, encouraged excessive drinking by young people and others without cautioning potential purchasers that alcohol can impair health.

Though Project SMART's goal was a complete ban on alcohol ads, supporters indicated they would be satisfied with a law requiring broadcasters to air public service announcements warning of the dangers of excessive drinking as a condition for running beer and wine commercials. Observers noted that when Congress banned cigarette commercials beginning in 1971, tobacco companies almost welcomed the move because of existing "counter-advertising" requirements that filled the airwaves with graphic messages that cigarettes cause cancer.

To counter Project SMART, broadcasting and alcohol industry officials claimed that an advertising ban would do little to curb abusive drinking. Moreover, they said, they already funded public service announcements and other educational programs to discourage excessive alcohol consumption.

Professional and college sports leagues also have a vested interest in televised alcohol ads. That's because the networks pay millions of dollars a year for the right to televise college and pro football, baseball, basketball and hockey games as well as major events such as the Olympics and the Masters golf tournament. In turn, the networks earn millions from alcoholic beverage companies, which account for an estimated 20 percent of all advertising shown during sports telecasts. It follows that restrictions on beer and wine revenue could force the networks to scale back their sports coverage.

But opponents of Project SMART insisted that money was not the only reason for their stance. They argued, in addition, that the First Amendment right of free speech protects beer and wine advertising. And they heatedly denied the existence of any scientific link between advertising and alcohol abuse. (The FTC made the same point in rejecting the CSPI coalition's petition.) Though Project SMART received extensive media coverage, it produced no legislation. ■

CURRENT SITUATION

Action in Congress

The campaign for stricter regulation of alcohol advertising now centers on the proposed Sensible Advertising and Family Education (SAFE) Act, first introduced in 1993 by Sen. Strom Thurmond, R-S.C., and Rep. Joseph P. Kennedy II, D-Mass. The legislation would have required all advertising for alcoholic beverages to include one of seven health warnings on a rotating basis. The Health and Human Services Department, moreover, would have had to maintain toll-free telephone numbers cited in some of the warnings, which would caution against underage drinking, drunken driving and drinking while pregnant, among other topics.

"We need these messages — especially for our underage drinkers," Kennedy said in introducing the SAFE bill in 1993. "By the time most American children reach the age of 18, they will have seen tens of thousands of alcohol ads bombarding them with misinformation about how beer or wine will make them fit in with their peers, get that new job or meet that special someone. Things have got to change — and we know the alcohol industry isn't going to change voluntarily."

Thurmond has advocated alcohol health warnings for years, pushing a bill through Congress in 1988 to require a health warning from the U.S. surgeon general on all alcoholic beverage containers.* His crusade became more personal in April 1993, when his 22-year-old daughter was killed by a drunken driver just weeks after he introduced his version of the SAFE Act. Neither the Thurmond bill nor the Kennedy bill was reported out of committee during 1993 or 1994.

Kennedy introduced an expanded version of the SAFE Act in May 1996. In addition to the health warning and toll-free-number provisions, it would institute drug- and alcohol-prevention programs in universities, curtail alcohol advertising to children and on college campuses, ban most alcohol ads on TV from 7 a.m. to 10 p.m. and eliminate the tax deductibility of alcohol ads and promotions. The bill languished in committee in 1996, though it is expected to be reintroduced this year.

Court Decisions

Federal courts also have been drawn into the alcohol advertising controversy. On May 13, 1996, for example, the Supreme Court unanimously struck down a 1956 Rhode Island law that prohibited liquor retailers from including liquor prices in their advertisements. The state had argued that banning price advertising kept liquor prices high by preventing increased competition among retailers. The state further contended that higher liquor prices served a valid public interest — discouraging alcohol consumption.

However, the court unanimously rejected that reasoning, declaring that the ban amounted to "an abridgement of speech protected by the First Amendment." That amendment, the court continued, "directs us to be especially skeptical of regulations that seek to keep people in the dark for what the government perceives to be their own good." [15]

The court said it could agree with Rhode Island's argument "that demand, and hence consumption throughout the market, is somewhat lower whenever a high, non-competitive price level prevails." But it went on to state that, "without any findings of fact, or indeed any evidentiary support whatsoever, we cannot agree with the assertion that the price advertising ban will significantly advance the state's interest in promoting temperance." By the same token, "any conclusion that elimination of the ban would significantly increase alcohol consumption would require us to engage in the sort of 'speculation or conjecture' that is an unacceptable means of demonstrating that a restriction on commercial speech directly advances the state's asserted interest."

In any event, said the court, "It is perfectly obvious that alternative forms of regulation that would not involve any restriction on speech would be more likely to achieve the state's goal of promoting temperance." It cited increased taxes, per capita limits on liquor purchases and educational campaigns on the hazards of drinking as possibilities. Rhode Island, in sum, had "failed to establish a 'reasonable fit' between its abridgement of speech and its temperance goal."

The *44 Liquormart* ruling was followed within a month by Seagram's decision to break with the liquor industry's longstanding voluntary ban on advertising distilled spirits on radio and television. At the same time, tobacco and advertising industry officials hailed the ruling as a potential boost to their campaign against proposed federal curbs on cigarette advertising. Wally Snyder, president and CEO of the American Advertising Federation, said on May 13 that "Alcohol is also a product that is off-

*The message states: "GOVERNMENT WARNING: (1) According to the Surgeon General, women should not drink alcoholic beverages during pregnancy because of the risk of birth defects. (2) Consumption of alcoholic beverages impairs your ability to drive a car or operate machinery, and may cause health problems."

Combating Alcohol Abuse by Young Drinkers . . .

When it comes to combating alcohol abuse, major concern focuses on young drinkers. Teenagers are thought to be more susceptible than adults to alcoholic beverage advertising, especially on radio and television. And there is increasing concern about alcohol ads on the Internet being targeted at youths (*see p. 232*). Moreover, statistics indicate that young people are at high risk of becoming involved in alcohol-related traffic accidents.

A surge in drunken driving by teenagers led Congress in 1984 to approve legislation prodding states to raise the minimum drinking age to 21. The law penalized states that permitted drinking under age 21 by withholding a portion of their federal highway funds. Though conservatives denounced the measure as infringing on states' rights and discriminating on the basis of age, every state fell into line by 1988. [1]

Statistics suggest the law has been effective. According to figures released in December by the Centers for Disease Control and Prevention (CDC) in Atlanta, fatal auto crashes involving teenage drivers fell by 24 percent in the past eight years. But the CDC said crashes still were the leading cause of death for youths between ages 15 and 20.

Two months earlier, Mothers Against Drunk Driving (MADD) had announced that it was focusing its programs more narrowly on drinking by teenagers. Alarmed by data showing high school students drinking more and at younger ages, MADD said it planned to urge states to reduce alcohol advertising that targets young consumers and impose more restrictions on licenses issued to drivers under 21, such as barring newly licensed drivers from driving after midnight.

MADD was among the groups that pressed for the 1984 minimum drinking age law. It also campaigned successfully for the 1995 "zero tolerance" amendment to the statute, which made it illegal for under-21 drivers to have any measurable alcohol in their blood.

Are the efforts having any success? The latest annual survey in the University of Michigan's ongoing Monitoring the Future Study cited data on youth drinking that was both reassuring and discouraging, depending on one's point of view. "Alcohol use among American secondary students [in the 8th, 10th and 12th grades] has remained fairly stable in the past few years, though at rates which most adults would probably consider unacceptably high," the university said. "This remains true in 1996. The measures of self-reported drunkenness and occasions of having five or more drinks in a row during the prior two weeks, however, have inched up by 2 to 4 percentage points at all three grade levels in recent years." [2]

Hundreds of high schools around the country have instituted alcohol testing in an effort to curb student drinking. Since autumn 1995, for example, Piedmont (Calif.) High School has required students attending school dances to undergo breath testing. A similar program that began recently in Arlington, Texas, goes further. If students headed for the senior prom flunk the Breathalyzer test, their parents will be called to take them home. Moreover, the students will be transferred to an alternative school and banned from extracurricular activities for the remainder of the school year and from graduation ceremonies. [3]

Colleges also have taken steps to curtail student drinking.

limits to teenagers. . . . This decision transfers the focus back to speech and the First Amendment and away from the product." [16]

White House spokesman Michael D. McCurry said the same day that Clinton administration hopes to use the FDA to restrict tobacco ads targeting minors were not likely to be affected by *44 Liquormart*. He said the proposals were not as sweeping as the Rhode Island advertising ban because they concerned tobacco advertising aimed specifically at minors, who may not legally purchase cigarettes. [17]

Baltimore Judge Acts to Protect Children

On Nov. 13, exactly six months after the *44 Liquormart* ruling, the U.S. Court of Appeals in Baltimore upheld the constitutionality of a local ordinance restricting stationary, outdoor advertising of alcoholic beverages in certain parts of the city. The ordinance was designed to promote the welfare and temperance of minors by banning alcohol ads within view of children going to or from neighborhood schools or playgrounds.

In upholding the Baltimore measure, Judge Paul V. Niemeyer noted how it differed from the state law at issue in *44 Liquormart*. "Baltimore's ordinance expressly targets persons who cannot be legal users of alcoholic beverages, not legal users as in Rhode Island," he declared. "More significantly, Baltimore does not ban outdoor advertising of alcoholic beverages outright but merely restricts the time, place and manner of such ads. And Baltimore does not foreclose the plethora of newspaper, magazine, radio, television, direct mail, Internet and other media." [18]

Niemeyer pointed to another difference between the two cases. "In contrast to Rhode Island's desire to enforce adult temperance. . . . Baltimore's interest is to protect children who are not yet independently able to assess the value of the message presented. This decision thus conforms to the Supreme Court's repeated recognition that children deserve special solicitude in the First Amendment balance because they lack the ability to assess and analyze fully the information presented through commercial media."

. . . Draws Efforts by MADD and Other Groups

Last August, for example, the University of California-Los Angeles suspended the Zeta Beta Tau fraternity for the fall quarter because members had violated campus alcohol policies by serving underage youths at a party where three fraternity members were accused of sexually assaulting a sorority woman. The previous February, Virginia's Radford University suspended two fraternities after a female student was found dead of alcohol poisoning in her dormitory room the day after she attended the fraternities' keg parties.

Some campus officials are especially disturbed that alcohol abuse seems to be significantly higher among athletes. That was the main finding of a study released last year by the Harvard School of Public Health. Among the students involved in athletics, 61 percent of the male respondents and 50 percent of the female respondents said they had engaged in "binge drinking" in the previous two weeks. The corresponding figures for non-athletes were 43 percent and 36 percent, respectively.[4]

George W. Dowdall, a professor of sociology at St. Joseph's University in Philadelphia and an author of the Harvard study, said sports-linked factors may be responsible for the higher levels of alcohol abuse among college athletes. "Many of the student athletes I've taught over the years feel they are under a great deal of pressure," he said. "It is almost like they have two full-time jobs."[5]

Some colleges have dealt with the substance-abuse issue by establishing dormitories where alcohol, drug and tobacco use are strictly forbidden. "Students want a clean environment around them, not just a clean lifestyle for themselves," said Karla Shepherd, coordinator of programs and orientation at the University of Maryland, which operates a substance-free program. "In the morning, they don't want to look in the sink and find the results of someone's drinking too much the night before."[6] Last year, about 1,000 of the school's 8,000 on-campus residents opted for the special dorms.

However, some campus officials are ready to throw in the towel. Roderic Park, chancellor of the University of Colorado-Boulder, calls current drinking laws "an enormous hypocrisy." He favors amending the law to permit youths 18, 19 and 20 to drink alcohol in bars and restaurants provided they have successfully completed a short course on the risks and responsibilities of drinking.

In Park's view, "Prohibition doesn't work. Teenage drinking is as common now as it's always been." He added, "I'm approaching this from a risk-management point of view, not a prohibitionist point of view."[7]

[1] For background, see "Highway Safety," *The CQ Researcher*, July 14, 1995, pp. 609-632.

[2] University of Michigan news release, Dec. 19, 1996.

[3] Mark Potok, "Texas City to Give Students Pre-Prom Breath Tests," *USA Today*, Feb. 10, 1997, p. 3A.

[4] Henry Wechsler, et al, "Binge Drinking, Tobacco and Illicit Drug Use and Involvement in College Athletes: A Survey of Students at 140 American Colleges," *Journal of American College Health* (in press). The study was based on a survey conducted in 1993 that covered 17,251 students at 140 colleges and universities.

[5] Quoted by Jim Naughton, "Alcohol Abuse by Athletes Poses Big Problems for Colleges," *The Chronicle of Higher Education*, Sept. 20, 1996, p. A47.

[6] Fern Shen, "These Dorms a Study in Sobriety," *The Washington Post*, September 3, 1996, p. A1.

[7] Quoted by Ben Gose, "A License to Drink," *The Chronicle of Higher Education*, May 31, 1996, p. A29.

Regulatory Agencies

Concern for children's welfare also was the stated reason for an FTC investigation that came to light in late November. According to *The Wall Street Journal,* the regulatory agency is studying the TV liquor ads launched by Seagram last June as well as a Stroh Brewery Co. campaign for Schlitz malt liquor. At issue are the content of the commercials as well as the time slots in which they ran. If the FTC concludes that the companies were deliberately targeting younger viewers, it could try to take the commercials off the air.[19]

At the FCC, Chairman Hundt, who is eager to probe broadcast liquor advertising, may soon find himself with less commission support for such a move. Up to four of the commission's five seats could become vacant this year.[20]

Meanwhile, Hundt received a letter last Nov. 19 from 26 members of Congress seeking FCC involvement in alcohol advertising. "We believe cable and broadcast advertising of hard liquor is detrimental to our children and the public interest," they wrote. "Therefore, we urge you to issue a notice of inquiry to gather data and information on the effects of distilled spirits advertisements on our nation's youth, and to explore avenues of possible commission action."

But DISCUS' Meister strongly opposes FCC involvement. "One individual in Washington has knighted himself as the savior on the issue of alcohol advertising — and that's Chairman Hundt," Meister says. "He does not have any authority on the issue. The FTC has the authority. Committee chairman have publicly said this to Mr. Hundt. But in fact he keeps threatening the stations that if they run our ads, he will be very upset. And since he is the person who holds the license of the broadcasters, he's had a very chilling effect on their ability and their desire, in many instances, to run our ads. Somebody has to rein Mr. Hundt in."

Despite the uncertain regulatory climate, some broadcasters and cable operators have followed KRIS in Corpus Christi and broken with tradition by accepting liquor ads. At least 25 independently owned TV stations across the country have done so, according to *Broadcasting & Cable* magazine. The Black Entertainment Television (BET) cable network also agreed to take the ads, while Continental Cablevision and Cox Cable Communications said they will allow their regional operating units "discretion" to make their own decisions on the basis of guidelines supplied by the parent company. [21] (*See story, p. 221.*)

"Liquor is a legal product, and one that is no [more] damaging to society than wine or beer," said Robert L. Johnson, BET's chief executive. "For some reason, there's been this historical attitude toward demon rum. It's something people frown on. But I see no reason why liquor ads, during the right time slots, aren't appropriate for television." [22]

Indeed, advertising executives view cable TV as prime marketing territory for liquor producers. "I think we'll see more and more of it [liquor advertising] in cable because it gives you more of an opportunity to do narrow targeting," said Donny Deutsch, chief executive of the New York ad agency Deutsch Inc. "Responsible targeted television makes a lot of sense." [23]

On the other hand, the nation's leading beer advertiser had second thoughts about placing commercials on a youth-oriented cable network. Anheuser-Busch, the maker of Budweiser and Michelob, in December pulled its ads from MTV. The company said it was moving the spots to MTV's sister network, VH1, which draws a somewhat older group of viewers. Anheuser-Busch's move amounted to "head 'em off at the pass self-censorship," said beverage industry consultant Tom Pirko. [24] ■

OUTLOOK

Voluntary Curbs?

Decades of experience suggest that current efforts to tighten federal curbs on broadcast alcohol ads may not go far. Numerous hearings on proposed regulations have been held over the years, but few of the bills were even reported out of committee.

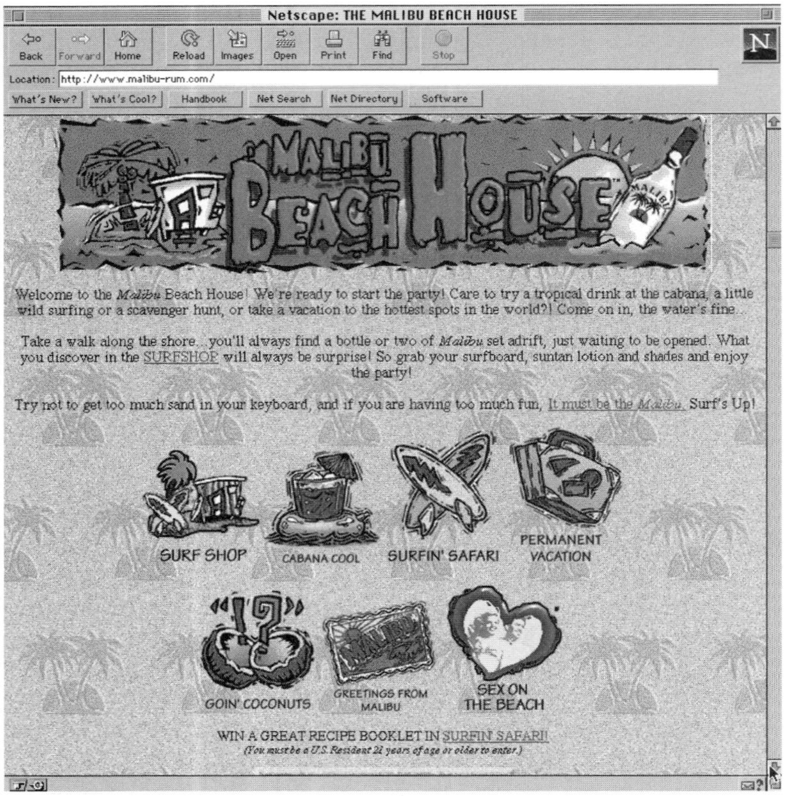

A study by the Center for Media Education released March 6 reported that 14 liquor companies and 10 large breweries have corporate World Wide Web sites, such as this one for Malibu rum, that use marketing techniques attractive to youths, including sports scores, interactive games and chat rooms.

Indeed, supporters of new curbs on liquor commercials have even run into difficulty scheduling a hearing in the current session of Congress. The Senate Commerce Committee shelved a hearing originally planned for Feb. 25, reportedly because of disagreement on whether to focus mainly on liquor ads or to cover beer and wine commercials as well.

Nonetheless, CSPI's Hacker says he's "not discouraged" because, ultimately, "there'll be some changes." He foresees "voluntary retrenchment" on the industry's part, "just to avoid the potential for further legislative action. We may not be able to keep liquor advertising off the air, though I don't look for it to spread like wildfire, either. We'll see the development of a voluntary agreement that sets a more level playing field for beer, wine and liquor advertising. And that may mean that the beer industry will have to give up" some market share.

Proponents of alcohol advertising curbs have learned not to expect quick or easy victories, Hacker says. "We do have health warnings on alcoholic beverage containers now; that was one small step forward 10 years ago. And how many years did we wait for real progress on cigarettes? It took a very long time to move against a product that is not nearly as ambiguous or as longstanding — or as attractive — as alcohol. Alcohol is a much more complicated issue than tobacco. So these battles on alcohol advertising

Continued on p. 234

At Issue:

Should liquor commercials be banned from television?

YES

JOHN LEO
***Columnist,* U.S. News & World Report**

FROM "SCOTCH THE ADS? ABSOLUT-LY!,"* U.S. NEWS & WORLD REPORT, *DEC. 9, 1996.

It could be a put-on, but *Adweek* magazine says liquor ads on television may be good for society. The magazine noted that the first booze ad shown on American TV in nearly 50 years celebrated fundamental American values. It was a Seagram commercial, placed on a station in Corpus Christi, Texas, and it featured two dogs.

One dog, labeled "obedience school graduate," carried a newspaper in its mouth. The other, carrying a bottle of Crown Royal, was labeled "valedictorian." *Adweek* said this positioned liquor as a reward for achievement and delayed gratification in a world sadly governed by instant gratification. Liquor flourished in the pre-'60s culture of self-restraint, said *Adweek,* and the impact of televised liquor ads "could well be salutary."

Maybe. But it's possible to doubt that the rapid spread of self-restraint is what the distillers have in mind. The more likely long-term result is a set of psychologically clever ads aimed at young people and resulting in another upward tick or two each year in the death rate from drunk driving. . . .

Among the egregious magazine ads for liquor, my favorite is the Bacardi Black "Taste of the night" campaign with its unmistakable theme of night and liquor as the liberators of the real you (and your darker side) from the bonds of civilized society. Just what we need in this troubled culture — more promotion of everyone's darker side. . . .

In dropping their self-imposed ban on TV ads, the distillers said they wouldn't target the young. We should be dubious. The liquor executives fear they won't be able to sell their brown drinks anymore — bourbon, Scotch and brandy have not caught on among boomers or post-boomers. The trend is toward white drinks — vodka and gin — and sweet-tasting or healthy-looking drinks that disguise alcoholic content. . . .

The distillers' argument about beer ads has more merit. They say a can of beer has about as much alcohol as a mixed drink, so either ban beer from TV or let liquor ads on. In fact, some conspiracy theorists think the distillers' real goal is to drive beer off TV. That's extremely unlikely. Beer is so entrenched in TV economies that it's hard to imagine the sort of social upheaval necessary to drive it away.

But if beer and liquor ads are going to be on TV, the ads should be regulated in the public interest. Alcohol is really a drug, and we have a long history of regulating drug ads to protect the public. The makers of Rogaine and Prozac aren't permitted to say whatever they wish in ads. Why should the good-tasting narcotics be exempted?

NO

MORRIS E. CHAFETZ
***President, Health Education Foundation, and author of* The Tyranny of Experts**

FROM "FACTS ABOUT KIDS, BOOZE AND TV,"* CHICAGO TRIBUNE, *DEC. 23, 1996.

Critics are raising the specter that television liquor advertising will increase alcohol abuse and underage drinking. If I believed that banning these ads from TV would keep a bottle out of the hands of a child or a person with an alcohol-abuse problem, I would lead the charge against lifting the moratorium.

Instead, I find myself asking an important question: Where in the name of science is there any proof? If alcohol ads will end society as we know it, shouldn't there be some science to say it's so?

I come to this issue as a psychiatrist and a scientist, nothing more. It's not my business whether manufacturers of distilled spirits should or should not advertise on TV. That is — quite literally — their business, something more appropriate for an MBA than an M.D. to decide. What I can say is that opponents of TV advertising for distilled spirits (or any other alcohol beverage for that matter) assert a connection between ads and the altering of behavior that, scientifically speaking, just isn't there.

As I've written in *The New England Journal of Medicine,* there is not a single study . . . that credibly connects advertising with an increase in alcohol use or abuse. . . .

The hypocrisy concerning advertising is reflected in a recent newspaper editorial against liquor ads in the name of protecting the health of youngsters. So far as I know, no newspaper is ready to forgo liquor ads and the revenue liquor advertisements bring. Members of the print media rationalize their hypocrisy by calling television "the medium most likely to reach most members of potential underage drinking." The old adage that it's easy to give advice one does not have to take operates here. . . .

The public ought to stop worrying about the power of ads and focus on the power of prohibition: the unintended consequence of demonizing a product or behavior. Never underestimate the seductive power of a "Thou Shalt Not."

The natural impulse to go against the grain is a reality of adolescent life. Forbidden fruit is an old story, but it's one with enduring power. I ponder the question countless times: Are anti-drinking advocacy groups — unintentionally or not — the most effective marketers for underage drinking?

As we debate the issues of advertising distilled spirits on TV, let's do it with open eyes. We need to respect young people more than we now do. They will take their risks as we did when we were adolescents. Ignorance does not lead to abstinence.

FOR MORE INFORMATION

Beer Institute, 1225 Eye St. N.W., Suite 825, Washington, D.C. 20005; (202) 737-2337. The institute monitors legislation and regulations on behalf of domestic and international brewers and their suppliers.

Center for Media Education, 1511 K St. N.W., Suite 518, Washington, D.C. 20002; (202) 628-2620. The center is a nonpartisan research and educational organization that studies media coverage of social and political issues.

Center for Science in the Public Interest, 1875 Connecticut Ave. N.W., Suite 300, Washington, D.C. 20009; (202) 332-9110. CSPI's alcohol policies project focuses on the marketing, labeling and taxation of alcoholic beverages.

Distilled Spirits Council of the United States, 1250 Eye St. N.W., Suite 900, Washington, D.C. 20005-3998; (202) 628-3544. DISCUS represents producers and marketers of distilled spirits sold in the United States.

National Council on Alcoholism and Drug Dependence, 12 West 21st St., New York, N.Y. 10010; (212) 206-6770. The center works for the prevention and control of alcoholism through programs of public and professional education, medical and scientific information and public policy advocacy.

National Woman's Christian Temperance Union, 1730 Chicago Ave., Evanston, Ill. 60201, (847) 864-1396. The WCTU is the nation's oldest group advocating complete abstinence from alcohol.

Wine Institute, 425 Market St., Suite 1000, San Francisco, Calif. 94105; (415) 512-0151. The institute supports public policies promoting the responsible consumption of wine.

will, I think, continue for a long time."

Some observers suspect that DISCUS revised its longstanding broadcast ad policy to restore the liquor industry's sagging economic fortunes. In 1980, distilled spirits consumption in the United States totaled 190,903 cases. In 1995, the most recent year for which complete data are available, the number had fallen to only 137,810 cases. Moreover, the industry projects a further decline to 125,450 cases by the year 2000.

Hacker believes liquor producers will find it hard to stage a comeback because liquor costs considerably more than beer and most table wines. In addition, he says, "Beer, you can buy almost anywhere. Liquor, in most states, you can only buy in liquor stores."

The Beer Institute's DeCelle feels that the alcohol industry as a whole is moving into an era whose outlines still are unclear. Until fairly recently, he says, "a rough sense of balance existed among the lawmakers and the agencies and the industry. Periodically, Congress reviewed the industry, and the FTC reviewed advertising. Before the distillers decided to go on TV, we were in a state of relative equilibrium. If problems arose, the agencies mentioned them — and most of the time, the problems were very quickly remedied."

In DeCelle's opinion, broadcasters hold the key to the future. "It will be influenced heavily by the way television — both the broadcast and cable networks — responds to the spirits industry's initiative."

More Internet Ads?

Some media commentators see the Internet as a promising new advertising and marketing tool for the alcohol industry. The Beer Institute's Becker disagrees, at least for now. "It's hard for people who have lives and jobs and families to spend an awful lot of time on the Internet," he says. "So I'm not sure the Internet is going to provide all the vast marketing opportunities that some folks thought it might."

A report issued March 6 by the Center for Media Education (CME), however, called attention to the "growing commercial presence" on the World Wide Web of advertising and other promotional material for alcohol. "The Internet will supplant TV and become more powerful than TV has ever been" as a tool for marketing alcohol and tobacco, CME President Kathryn C. Montgomery told a press conference. [25]

CME "found 14 liquor companies and 10 large breweries with corporate Web sites that use techniques attractive to youth." [26] These techniques include up-to-the-minute sports scores, interactive games and contests, chat rooms and bulletin boards, online magazines and recipes for "bridge drinks," or sweetened concoctions that are likely to appeal to novice drinkers.

"The combination of these new Web marketing technologies gives marketers of alcohol . . . an arsenal of powerful new weapons," the CME report said. "Urgent action is needed to ensure that effective safeguards are put in place to protect young people." Among other things, the report called for congressional hearings and an FTC investigation of possible deceptive advertising practices.

In response to the CME report, Elizabeth Board, public issues director of DISCUS, notes that the organization has a code of good practice for advertising and all forms of marketing, including the Web. "The major tenet of the code is to avoid targeting advertising to individuals below the legal purchase age. And I believe that all of these [liquor] Web sites are absolutely in concert with our code."

Besides, Board adds, "Adults who

like the Web like games and interactive elements, too. So a Web site with such features is not inherently appealing just to young people." And, she adds with a laugh, "I just came back from the islands with a group of 45-to-50-year-olds. We drank a lot of sweet drinks. Sweet drinks have been around forever."

DeCelle, meanwhile, discerns great growth potential in a recently developed system for purchasing alcoholic beverages either electronically or by the traditional mail-order method. The system's central feature is sophisticated bar-coding that contains much more information than the product codes used in supermarkets. The additional data capacity enables all coding to be customized, permitting the shipper to sort and track orders and minimize the chance of misdelivery.

Though limited at present to wine and spirits, the technology could easily accommodate beer, DeCelle says.

Such marketing possibilities leave Ward of the WCTU apprehensive. "I'm not a prophet, so it's hard for me to say what the future holds," she says. "But in my ideal world, each individual would make the very best choices for themselves and for society in general. If that happened, we in the WCTU believe that Prohibition would return — not by law, but by individuals making wise decisions. Well, we can always dream of Utopia." ■

Notes

[1] DISCUS news release, Nov. 7, 1996.

[2] NAB news release, Nov. 7, 1996.

[3] For background, see "Underage Drinking," *The CQ Researcher*, March 13, 1992, pp. 217-240.

[4] Coors Brewing Co., "Does Advertising Cause Abuse?" (1993 company brochure).

[5] Quoted in "Youths Aren't Buying the Cute and Flashy Beer Images," *USA Today*, Jan. 31, 1997, p. 4B.

[6] Joseph C. Fisher, *Advertising, Alcohol Consumption and Abuse: A Worldwide Survey* (1993), p. 150.

[7] Morris E. Chafetz, "Facts About Kids, Booze and TV," *Chicago Tribune*, Dec. 23, 1996, p. 17.

[8] David F. Musto, "Alcohol in American History," *Scientific American*, April 1996, p. 78.

[9] Paul Aaron and David F. Musto, "Temperance and Prohibition in America: A Historical Overview," in Mark H. Moore and Dean R. Gerstein, eds., *Alcohol and Public Policy: Beyond the Shadow of Prohibition* (1981), p. 131.

[10] Frederick Lewis Allen, *Only Yesterday: An Informal History of the 1920s* (1964), p. 82.

[11] John C. Burnham, "New Perspectives on the Prohibition 'Experiment' of the 1920s," in *Burnham, Paths Into American Culture* (1988), pp. 175-176.

[12] L.V. Harrison and E. Laine, *After Repeal: A Study of Liquor Control Administration* (1936), p. 73.

[13] Robert Gerald Laforge, *Misplaced Priorities: A History of Federal Alcohol Regulation and Public Health Policy* (1987), p. 278.

[14] Testimony before Senate Commerce Committee, Jan. 13, 1950.

[15] The case was *44 Liquormart Inc. and Peoples Super Liquor Stores Inc. v. Rhode Island and Rhode Island Liquor Stores Association.*

[16] Quoted in *Facts on File*, May 16, 1996, p. 339.

[17] For background, see "Advertising Under Attack," *The CQ Researcher*, Sept. 13, 1991, pp. 657-680, "Regulating Tobacco," *The CQ Researcher*, Sept. 30, 1994, pp. 841-864 and "Teens and Tobacco," *The CQ Researcher*, Dec. 1, 1995, pp. 1065-1083.

[18] *Anheuser-Bush Inc. v. Schmoke.*

[19] *The Wall Street Journal*, Nov. 27, 1996, p. A3. FTC spokeswoman Vicki Streitfeld would neither confirm nor deny that an investigation is taking place.

[20] Chris McConnell, "New Faces Head for FCC," *Broadcasting & Cable*, Nov. 4, 1996, p. 7.

[21] Chris McConnell and Heather Fleming, "Spirited Debate Over Liquor," *Broadcasting & Cable*, Nov. 25, 1996, p. 8.

[22] Quoted in *The Washington Post*, Nov. 9, 1996, p. H1.

[23] Quoted in *The Wall Street Journal*, June 12, 1996, p. B5.

[24] Quoted in *USA Today*, Dec. 24, 1996, p. 1A.

[25] See "On the Web, This Bud's for Your Chilidren," *The New York Times*, March 7, 1997, p. A1.

[26] Center for Media Education, "Alcohol and Tobacco on the Web: New Threats to Youth," March 1997, p. 13. The center is a national, nonprofit organization "dedicated to improving the quality of the electronic media." The CME report also "identified 11 distilled spirits companies with Web sites [that] do not appear to target youth [but] appeal to people interested in a particular brand or type of alcoholic beverage and focus on information about the product, such as microbreweries and wineries."

Bibliography

Selected Sources Used

Books

Aerts, Erik, et al., eds., *Production, Marketing and Consumption of Alcoholic Beverages Since the Late Middle Ages*, Leuven University Press, 1990.
Wide-ranging in both time and geography, this collection of studies looks at the rum trade in 19th-century Venezuela, the global brandy trade from 1600 to 1760, the export marketing of Scotch whiskey from 1870 to 1939 and much more.

Fisher, Joseph C., Advertising, *Alcohol Consumption, and Abuse: A Worldwide Survey*, Greenwood Press, 1993.
Fisher, an advertising agency executive, is often cited by alcohol industry representatives. He writes that "Advertising appears to have a very weak positive influence on consumption and no impact on experimentation with alcohol or abuse of it."

Harris, Moira F., *The Paws of Refreshment: The Story of Hamm's Beer Advertising*, Pogo Press, 1990.
The cutesy title refers to the cartoon bear that was the advertising symbol of Hamm's Beer, the brewing pride of St. Paul, Minn. ("Land of the sky-blue waters," according to Hamm's). The illustrations of old-time Hamm's newspaper ads make one yearn for a past that most living Americans never experienced.

Laforge, Robert Gerald, *Misplaced Priorities: A History of Federal Alcohol Regulation and Public Health Policy*, University Microfilms International, 1987.
In this doctoral dissertation for Johns Hopkins University, Laforge surveys key developments in federal regulation of alcohol, most of which date from the onset of nationwide Prohibition in 1920.

Articles

Musto, David F., "Alcohol in American History," *Scientific American*, April 1996.
Musto, a professor of child psychiatry and the history of medicine at Yale University, reviews the swings between binges and abstinence that have been an enduring feature of the history of U.S. alcohol consumption. "Those who oppose alcohol doubt that it might have any value in the diet; those who support it deny any positive effect of Prohibition," he writes. "Compromise seems unthinkable for either side."

Reports and Studies

Alexander, Barton, *The Role of the Alcohol Beverage Industry in Preventing Abuse*, paper presented at the 37th International Congress on Alcohol and Drug Dependence, San Diego, Calif., August 1995.
Alexander, public affairs director for the Coors Brewing Co. in Golden, Colo., notes that both sides in the alcoholic beverage advertising controversy typically "enlist researchers, advocacy organizations, political organizations and public relations experts to fight their battles. Often, considerable expertise and resources produce nothing but a stalemate."

Center for Science in the Public Interest, *Marketing Booze to Blacks*, 1987.
"For years, the special devastation that alcohol use and abuse wreak among blacks has been largely ignored by both blacks and whites, researchers and educators," says this report from CSPI, which has studied the impact of alcoholic beverage advertising for years. It adds: "Black drinking habits are not, however, being ignored by alcohol producers, who have implemented ambitious marketing campaigns that target blacks."

Center for Science in the Public Interest, *Marketing Disease to Hispanics*, 1989.
This CSPI report, similar to the 1987 study on marketing of alcohol to African Americans, has a somewhat broader field of vision. In addition to alcohol, it examines tobacco and junk-food advertising campaigns targeting the Hispanic community.

U.S. House Select Committee on Children, Youth, and Families, *Confronting the Impact of Alcohol Labeling and Marketing on Native American Health and Culture*, published proceedings of hearing held May 19, 1992.
Federal officials, representatives of Indian tribes and public health advocates air their views on the effects of alcoholic beverages on Native American communities.

U.S. House Select Committee on Children, Youth and Families, *Preventing Underage Drinking: A Dialogue With the Surgeon General*, published proceedings of hearing held Nov. 15, 1991.
Antonia C. Novello, U.S. surgeon general during the Bush administration, testifies: "The kinds of ads that appeal to our young people are appealing to some degree to all of us, but our young people, in their search for identity, their doubts about their own popularity and sexual attractiveness, are particularly vulnerable. And that is the part that worries me."

The Next Step

Additional information from UMI's Newspaper & Periodical Abstracts™ database

Advertising Aimed at Kids

Fleming, Heather, "Ad Council eyes liquor ad probe," *Broadcasting & Cable,* Dec. 16, 1996, p. 28.
The National Advertising Review Council (NARC) will consider creating a board to examine whether advertising for tobacco and alcohol targets underage consumers. NARC frequently investigates ads for truthfulness and accuracy, and the industry has complied with 95 percent of the group's decisions.

Horovitz, Bruce, "Critics say Bud ads too ribbet-ing for kids," *USA Today,* April 25, 1996, p. B1.
According to a survey of 221 fourth- and fifth-graders by the Center on Alcohol Advertising, elementary school kids are more familiar with Budweiser's cartoon frogs than they are with Tony the Tiger or Smokey Bear. The group asked Anheuser-Busch to stop airing advertisements that appeal to minors.

Kreck, Dick, "Do frogs sell beer to kids?" *Denver Post,* April 27, 1996, p. E8.
Kreck discusses a study by the Center on Alcohol Advertising that examines the influence that alcohol advertising on TV has on children.

Scherer, Ron, and Nicole Gaouette, "Critics Take Aim at the Effect of Hip Commercials on Kids," *The Christian Science Monitor,* Dec. 26, 1996, p. 1.
In a debate similar to the one over cigarette advertising, the liquor industry is coming under fire for its TV ads and jingles that appeal to children. Critics of the alcohol industry believe there are links between advertising and teenage alcoholism. The industry argues that children drink because of peer pressure and parental practices, not because of the ads. The underlying issues include basic questions about sales psychology and First Amendment rights. (Pt 1 of 2).

Stamborski, Al, "Wise-Er? under Pressure, A-B Drops Frog Commercials," *St. Louis Post-Dispatch,* Jan. 15, 1997, p. C1.
Anheuser-Busch is apparently scrapping its wildly popular and controversial ad campaign using the lifelike Bud-Weis-Er frogs in January 1997. The Center on Alcohol Advertising and other child advocates such as Mothers Against Drunk Driving say the advertisements encourage children to drink beer.

Strausberg, Chinta, "Pfleger warns Clinton to keep an eye on alcohol," *Chicago Defender,* Oct. 14, 1996, p. 10.
On Oct. 13, 1996, Father Michael L. Pfleger of St. Sabina Church in Chicago, Ill., urged President Clinton "not to take his eyes off" the alcohol industry, which Pfleger says is aggressively escalating its advertising campaigns to seduce women and youth.

Advertising Aimed at Minorities

Bell, Kim, "Troupe backs ban on alcohol ads," *St. Louis Post-Dispatch,* May 7, 1996, Sec. A, p. 13.
State Rep. Quincy Troupe, D-Mo., argued in the House on May 6, 1996, that billboards advertising alcohol targeted black men and contributed to the decline of the city's most dangerous neighborhoods. Troupe wants the state to ban such advertising in high-crime areas.

Thornton, Jerry, "Priest has message for negative ads on billboards," *Chicago Tribune,* July 11, 1996, Sec. 2C, p. 3.
For over a decade, Michael L. Pfleger has been waging a war against alcohol and tobacco billboard advertising in African-American and Hispanic neighborhoods in Chicago, Ill. Pfleger's campaign recently got a boost when President Clinton made comments against such advertising.

Health Warning Labels

Chapman, Stephen, "Alcohol labels and the uninformed consumer," *Chicago Tribune,* Jan. 28, 1996, p. 21.
Chapman comments on the United States Department of Agriculture's dietary guidelines, which note "current evidence suggests that moderate drinking is associated with a lower risk of coronary heart disease in certain individuals." He notes that the Bureau of Alcohol, Tobacco and Firearms (BATF) doesn't want the news to be released to the public because the agency believes that an ignorant consumer is a good consumer.

Jacoby, Jeff, "Feds slow to wake up to alcohol's healthful effects," *The Boston Globe,* Jan. 9, 1996, p. 15.
Jacoby comments on health benefits of moderate alcohol consumption and argues that "Big Brother's federal bully boys" want to keep any mention of it from the public and off of labels.

Wood, Valerie D., "The precarious position of commercial speech: *Rubin v. Coors Brewing Co.,*" *Harvard Journal of Law & Public Policy,* winter 1996, pp. 612-625.
The Supreme Court's decision in *Rubin v. Coors Brewing Co.* is examined. The court extended commercial speech protection to labels on alcoholic beverages but failed to define the scope of that protection.

Industry Advertising Codes

"Ad industry group rejects alcohol, tobacco system," *The Wall Street Journal,* Dec. 23, 1996, p. B5.

The National Advertising Review Council, the advertising industry's main voluntary review body, said it will not set up a separate system for reviewing the impact of alcohol and tobacco ads on children, in a move following fierce opposition from brewers to such a plan.

Beatty, Sally Goll, "Advertising: Group weighs alcohol, tobacco ad rules," *The Wall Street Journal,* Dec. 9, 1996, p. B7.

The American Association of Advertising Agencies is considering adopting limits on alcohol and tobacco advertising by setting up a self-regulatory body that would review ads for adult-only products — a reversal of strategy amid mounting industry fears of a government crackdown. The proposed body would look at all ads for "products that cannot be sold or consumed by minors" legally, said O. Burtch Drake, the association's president.

Klahr, Sharon, "Where do you draw the line?" *Graphis,* November 1996, pp. SS2-SS3.

There are those in advertising who struggle to maintain certain personal and professional standards of integrity, with regard to politics, sex and particularly products such as cigarettes and alcohol. Ethics in advertising is discussed.

Spain, William, "Media are the message for 2 alcohol marketers," *Advertising Age,* Oct. 7, 1996, p. S2.

Arthur Shapiro, an advertising executive at Seagram Americas, , and August A. Busch IV, an advertising executive at Anheuser-Busch, are profiled. Their marketing strategies are discussed.

State and Local Regulation

Barrington, Stephen, "Canada eases alcohol-ad rules," *Advertising Age,* Sept. 9, 1996, p. 53.

The Canadian Radio-Television & Telecommunications Commission has decided to loosen restrictions on alcoholic beverage advertisers. This decision could result in increased advertising spending and a freer rein on creativity.

Crumley, Bruce, "Ad restrictions back under fire," *Advertising Age,* March 11, 1996, p. I6.

The French law that severely restricts alcohol advertising and virtually bans tobacco advertising appears set to be overturned by the European Commission on the grounds that it is incompatible with European Union (E.U.) rules. While the law has good intentions, the E.U. feels that it has no effect diminishing alcohol and tobacco consumption.

Enrico, Dottie, "High court cracks lid on alcohol ads," *USA Today,* May 21, 1996, p. B1.

On May 20, 1996, the Supreme Court set aside a ruling that upheld a Baltimore, Md., law barring billboards that advertise alcoholic beverages, sending the matter back to the 4th Circuit Court of Appeals in Richmond, Va. Baltimore adopted the ordinance to discourage underage drinking.

Hassell, Greg, "Don't blame ads for alcohol's ills," *Houston Chronicle,* June 12, 1996, p. C1.

Hassell discusses the Comprehensive Alcohol Abuse Prevention Act of 1996 proposed by U.S. Rep. Joseph P. Kennedy II, D-Mass., which would ban alcohol ads in publications with a youth readership unless the ads are text only with black-and-white print. The author argues that there's not much evidence that advertising drives people to drink abusively.

Hershey, Robert D. Jr., "U.S. Expands Inquiry Into Alcohol Ads," *The New York Times,* Nov. 28, 1996, p. D1.

In an investigation into the beer industry, the Federal Trade Commission (FTC) is looking at whether Stroh Brewing Co. is running TV ads that are aimed at underage viewers, officials said on Nov. 27, 1996. The FTC is also looking into the marketing and advertising practices of Seagram Co., a Canadian distiller. Earlier in the month, distillers ended a self-imposed ban on liquor ads on TV and radio.

"High court bars limits on alcohol advertising," *San Francisco Chronicle,* May 14, 1996, p. A3.

Bolstering the free-speech rights of advertisers, the U.S. Supreme Court on May 13, 1996, ruled that the government cannot bar the promotion of lawful products it deems undesirable, a decision that casts doubt on President Clinton's campaign to ban cigarette ads aimed at young people.

Ingersoll, Bruce, "FTC opens investigation of TV alcohol advertising," *The Wall Street Journal,* Nov. 27, 1996, p. A3.

In the first action of its kind, the FTC has opened an investigation into alcoholic-beverage advertising on TV, focusing initially on ads being run by Joseph E. Seagram & Sons Inc. and by Stroh Brewery Co. In a unanimous vote, the FTC authorized its consumer-protection staff to use its subpoena powers in the inquiry. One objective is to determine the advertising's effect on underage viewers.

"Kennedy unveils ad limits to combat underage drinking," *Alcoholism & Drug Abuse Weekly,* May 20, 1996, pp. 1-3.

Rep. Joseph P. Kennedy II, D-Mass., has introduced a much-anticipated bill to curb alcohol advertisements in an attempt to deter underage drinking. Kennedy is a long-time critic of alcohol advertising campaigns.

McConnell, Chris, "FCC to study liquor ads," *Broadcasting & Cable,* Nov. 4, 1996, p. 6.

The Federal Communications Commission (FCC) has requested that copies of Seagram distillery's TV advertisements be sent to it so that these ads can be studied by the agency. Whether or not the FCC has the authority to regulate alcohol advertising, however, is unclear.

Robins, Max J., "Current ads may be alcohol's last call," *TV Guide,* Jan. 25, 1997, pp. 65-66.

A major battle brewing in Washington, D.C., could result

in the virtual prohibition of liquor commercials on TV. Robins discusses the challenges alcohol advertising is getting from Congress and the FCC.

Weinstein, Henry, "Ruling may boost FDA's ad crackdown," *Los Angeles Times,* Nov. 15, 1996, p. D3.
A federal appeals court has upheld a ban by the city of Baltimore that prohibits billboards from advertising tobacco and alcohol in most parts of the city. The ruling could significantly bolster the FDA's efforts to keep alcohol and cigarette ads away from children.

Temperance Movement

"Celebrating sobriety," *The Boston Globe,* July 3, 1996, p. 14.
An editorial supports a multifront effort of advertising to curb underage alcohol use, stressing that ads for alcoholic beverages should be restricted to some degree while ads stressing personal responsibility should continue.

Cohen, Deborah A., "Restrict alcohol as well," *Times-Picayune,* Sept. 1, 1996, p. B6.
In a letter to the editor, Cohen of the Louisiana State University Medical Center's 21-Proof Coalition calls for the federal government to regulate and limit advertising for alcoholic beverages.

Grayson, George W., "Striking a blow against booze peddlers," *The Washington Post,* Nov. 24, 1996, p. C8.
Rep. George W. Grayson D-Va., comments that with liquor producers poised to take to the airwaves to advertise alcohol, Virginia can do something to protect its youth: Its state-operated ABC stores can discontinue the sale of any hard liquor advertised on TV or radio.

Komro, Kelli A., Cherly L. Perry, David M. Murray and Sara Veblen-Mortenson et al, "Peer-planned social activities for preventing alcohol use among young adolescents," *Journal of School Health,* November 1996, pp. 328-334.
The Project Northland peer participation program tested the feasibility of involving students in the planning and promotion of alcohol-free social activities for their peers and to determine whether such participation was associated with reduced alcohol use. The peer program was offered in 20 northeastern Minnesota schools when the study cohort was in seventh grade.

Peele, Stanton, "Getting wetter?" *Reason,* April 1996, pp. 58-61.
After several decades of anti-alcohol crusading, it now appears that the U.S. is swinging back toward a more positive attitude. Peele provides an overview of the temperance movement in the U.S. and its waning power.

Youth Drinking

Aiken, Doris, "Alcohol in academe," *Chicago Tribune,* June 1, 1996, p. 17.
In a letter to the editor, Doris Aiken of Remove Intoxicated Drivers U.S.A. Inc. suggests that parents looking into selecting a college for their child also examine the school's policy in relation to alcohol and its abuse.

Chaloupka, Frank J., and Henry Wechsler, "Binge drinking in college: The impact of price, availability, and alcohol control policies," *Contemporary Economic Policy,* October 1996, pp. 112-124.
A study estimates the effects of beer prices, alcohol availability and policies related to drunk driving on drinking and binge drinking among youths and young adults.

Chassin, Laurie, and Christian DeLucia, "Drinking during adolescence," *Alcohol Health & Research World,* 1996, pp. 175-180.
Experience with drinking alcohol often begins in adolescence, and research has associated a variety of serious health risks with adolescent drinking. Risk factors for adolescent drinking encompass sociocultural factors, parental behavior and drinking patterns, the influence and drinking habits of peers and siblings, personality traits and positive beliefs about the effects of alcohol.

"Eight Charged In Alcohol Death," *The New York Times,* Feb. 11, 1997, p. A19.
Eight students at Frostburg State University in Maryland have been charged with manslaughter in the alcohol poisoning death of a freshman who got drunk at a fraternity party. The freshman, John Eric Stinner, 20, consumed at least six beers and 12 shots of vodka in two hours at the off-campus party held by Kappa Beta Zeta, said the Allegany County State's Attorney, Lawrence V. Kelly.

Naughton, Jim, "Alcohol abuse by athletes poses big problems for colleges," *The Chronicle of Higher Education,* Sept. 20, 1996, pp. A47-48.
A number of universities have been forced to deal with players or coaches who violate drinking laws or get into trouble while drunk. Alcohol abuse by college athletes and coaches and efforts by universities to deal with this problem are discussed.

Webb, E., and C. H. Ashton, and P. Kelly, and F. Kamali, "Alcohol and drug use in U.K. university students," *Lancet,* October 5, 1996, pp. 922-925.
The authors report on a survey concerning alcohol and drug use among university students from the United Kingdom. Information about drinking, use of cannabis and other illicit drugs, other lifestyle variables and subjective ratings of anxiety and depression was obtained by questionnaire in a sample of 3,075 second-year university students.

Back Issues

Great Research on Current Issues Starts Right Here...Recent topics covered by The CQ Researcher are listed below. Before May 1991, reports were published under the name of Editorial Research Reports.

SEPTEMBER 1995
Catholic Church in the U.S.
Northern Ireland Cease-Fire
High School Sports
Teaching History

OCTOBER 1995
Quebec's Future
Revitalizing the Cities
Networking the Classroom
Indoor Air Pollution

NOVEMBER 1995
The Working Poor
The Jury System
Sex, Violence and the Media
Police Misconduct

DECEMBER 1995
Teens and Tobacco
Gene Therapy's Future
Global Water Shortages
Third-Party Prospects

JANUARY 1996
Emergency Medicine
Punishing Sex Offenders
Bilingual Education
Helping the Homeless

Back issues are available for $5.00 (subscribers) or $10.00 (non-subscribers). Quantity discounts apply to orders over ten. To order, call Congressional Quarterly Customer Service at (202) 887-8621.

Binders are available for $18.00. To order call 1-800-638-1710. Please refer to stock number 648.

FEBRUARY 1996
Reforming the CIA
Campaign Finance Reform
Academic Politics
Getting Into College

MARCH 1996
The British Monarchy
Preventing Juvenile Crime
Tax Reform
Pursuing the Paranormal

APRIL 1996
Centennial Olympic Games
Managed Care
Protecting Endangered Species
New Military Culture

MAY 1996
Russia's Political Future
Marriage and Divorce
Year-Round Schools
Taiwan, China and the U.S.

JUNE 1996
Rethinking NAFTA
First Ladies
Teaching Values
Labor Movement's Future

JULY 1996
Recovered-Memory Debate
Native Americans' Future
Crackdown on Sexual Harassment
Attack on Public Schools

AUGUST 1996
Fighting Over Animal Rights
Privatizing Government Services
Child Labor and Sweatshops
Cleaning Up Hazardous Wastes

SEPTEMBER 1996
Gambling Under Attack
The States and Federalism
Civic Journalism
Reassessing Foreign Aid

OCTOBER 1996
Political Consultants
Insurance Fraud
Rethinking School Integration
Parental Rights

NOVEMBER 1996
Global Warming
Clashing Over Copyright
Consumer Debt
Governing Washington, D.C.

DECEMBER 1996
Welfare, Work and the States
The New Volunteerism
Implementing the Disabilities Act
America's Pampered Pets

JANUARY 1997
Combating Scientific Misconduct
Restructuring the Electric Industry
The New Immigrants
Chemical and Biological Weapons

FEBRUARY 1997
Assisting Refugees
Alternative Medicine's Next Phase
Independent Counsels
Feminism's Future

MARCH 1997
New Air Quality Standards

Future Topics

- ***Civic Renewal***
- ***Educating Gifted Children***
- ***Declining Crime Rates***

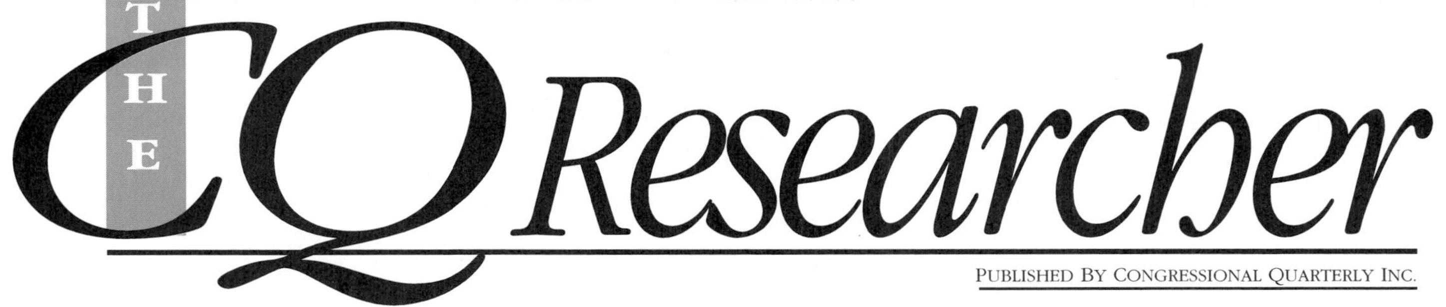

PUBLISHED BY CONGRESSIONAL QUARTERLY INC.

Civic Renewal

Do America's problems stem from a lack of morality?

The perception that civil society is declining has gained currency in recent years. With increasing frequency, politicians and scholars talk about the need for Americans to pay more attention to values and individual responsibility. Meanwhile, many people long for the tranquillity and prosperity of the 1950s and blame many of today's social ills, including poverty and crime, on a dearth of morality and common courtesy. Concern for the nation's moral health has sparked a movement of ideologically diverse thinkers who are linked by the belief that institutions like family and community must be strengthened if America is to thrive. But others wonder whether the positive aspects of the past can be resurrected without also bringing back the conformity and discrimination that flourished in the "good old days."

INSIDE THIS ISSUE

CQ **March 21, 1997 • Volume 7, No. 11 • Pages 241-264**

Formerly Editorial Research Reports

THE ISSUES

BACKGROUND

CURRENT SITUATION

OUTLOOK

SIDEBARS AND GRAPHICS

FOR MORE INFORMTION

COVER: © ARCHIVE PHOTOS/PICTURE NETWORK INTERNATIONAL

March 21, 1997
Volume 7, No. 11

EDITOR
Sandra Stencel

MANAGING EDITOR
Thomas J. Colin

ASSOCIATE EDITORS
Sarah M. Magner
Richard L. Worsnop

STAFF WRITERS
Charles S. Clark
Mary H. Cooper
Kenneth Jost
David Masci

EDITORIAL ASSISTANT
Vanessa E. Furlong

PUBLISHED BY
Congressional Quarterly Inc.

CHAIRMAN
Andrew Barnes

VICE CHAIRMAN
Andrew P. Corty

PRESIDENT AND PUBLISHER
Robert W. Merry

EXECUTIVE EDITOR
David Rapp

The CQ Researcher (ISSN 1056-2036). Formerly Editorial Research Reports. Published weekly (48 times per year, not printed Jan. 3, May 30, Aug. 29, Oct. 31) by Congressional Quarterly Inc., 1414 22nd St., N.W., Washington, D.C. 20037. Annual subscription rate for libraries, businesses and government is $340. Additional rates furnished upon request. Periodicals postage paid at Washington, D.C., and additional mailing offices. POSTMASTER: Send address changes to The CQ Researcher, 1414 22nd St., N.W., Washington, D.C. 20037.

Civic Renewal

BY DAVID MASCI

THE ISSUES

Freshman Rep. Kenny Hulshof, a Missouri Republican, had his epiphany after chatting with Lynn Rivers, a two-term Michigan Democrat. It was their first conversation, he realized with amazement, although they occupy nearby offices. Rep. Karen L. Thurman, D-Fla., drew her insight from a friendly game of hearts between two children whose parents belong to opposing parties. It showed her the pointlessness of political partisanship.

Children were also on the mind of House Speaker Newt Gingrich, R-Ga. "They reminded all of us, first of all, to act like adults and, second, that everybody around us had human relationships," he said.

Such insights were just what organizers had hoped for when they lured 200 House members and their families to Hershey, Pa., in early March to promote a kinder and gentler Congress.

Promoting greater civility might seem redundant in a place where members address each other as "The Gentleman (or "Gentle lady") from New York" or "My good friend and colleague," even in the heat of debate. But the retreat was deemed necessary because of a deepening sense that, despite the institutional decorum on Capitol Hill, name calling, rudeness and general incivility have become too common in the nation's legislature.

Indeed, a new report by the Annenberg Public Policy Center at the University of Pennsylvania charts a noticeable decline in civility in the House in recent years. The number of accusations of dishonesty and similar personal attacks rose from three in 1993 to 23 in 1995. [1]

During the retreat, members tried to find ways "to unpoison the well," in the words of Rep. David E. Skaggs, D-Colo., who organized the get-away with Rep. Ray LaHood, R-Ill. Gingrich, for example, suggested that holding Republican and Democratic party caucuses together — occasionally — would promote greater understanding and reduce partisan bickering. [2]

But members quickly learned that creating a more civil environment entailed more than just changing procedures and rules. Many said the retreat's greatest value was simply allowing members to spend three days with their colleagues away from Washington, gaining insights into the whys and ways they conduct themselves as human beings as well as legislators.

"We came together in the right frame of mind, realizing, to our own surprise, that we are our own adult supervisors and are responsible for any changes that are going to happen," Skaggs says.

Congress tends to mirror the nation at large, and indeed words like "civility" and "courtesy" increasingly are being invoked far from Capitol Hill. "What has been going on in Congress has been going on in the country as a whole," says Rep. Tom Sawyer, D-Ohio, who also attended the retreat. To many observers, this new attitude reflects a more general feeling among Americans that the nation's tangible problems, like crime or poverty, can in part be linked to a decline in morality and a decrease in the importance of basic institutions like family, church and community. There is a sense that the oft-quoted maxim of President Clinton's 1992 campaign no longer holds true. It's no longer, "the economy stupid." It's more the lament of Los Angeles beating victim Rodney King: "We can all get along. We've just got to."

"I think most Americans know that our problems are not material," says Marshall Wittman, a fellow at the Heritage Foundation, a conservative think tank. "The issue is one of spiritual and moral poverty," he adds.

Polls seem to bear Wittman out. According to a survey last spring, 59 percent of all Americans believe that the nation's major problems result from a lack of morality. [3]

Another indicator of the national mood is a declining sense of trust in fellow citizens and institutions. A 1996 poll found that only 35 percent of all Americans believed that most people could be trusted.[4] In 1964, 56 percent of Americans were trusting. Moreover, only 25 percent of the respondents in 1996 said that they trust the federal government to "do the right thing," compared with 76 percent of those polled in 1964. (*See poll, p. 248.*)

They may be looking through rose-colored glasses, but when many Americans look back 30 or 40 years, they see a better, more wholesome country. There was less crime, they say, and lower rates of drug use and divorce. There is also the pervasive feeling that the essentials of a good society were in greater abundance in those bygone days — that people treated each other with greater courtesy and respect; that families were stronger, and worked harder, to stay

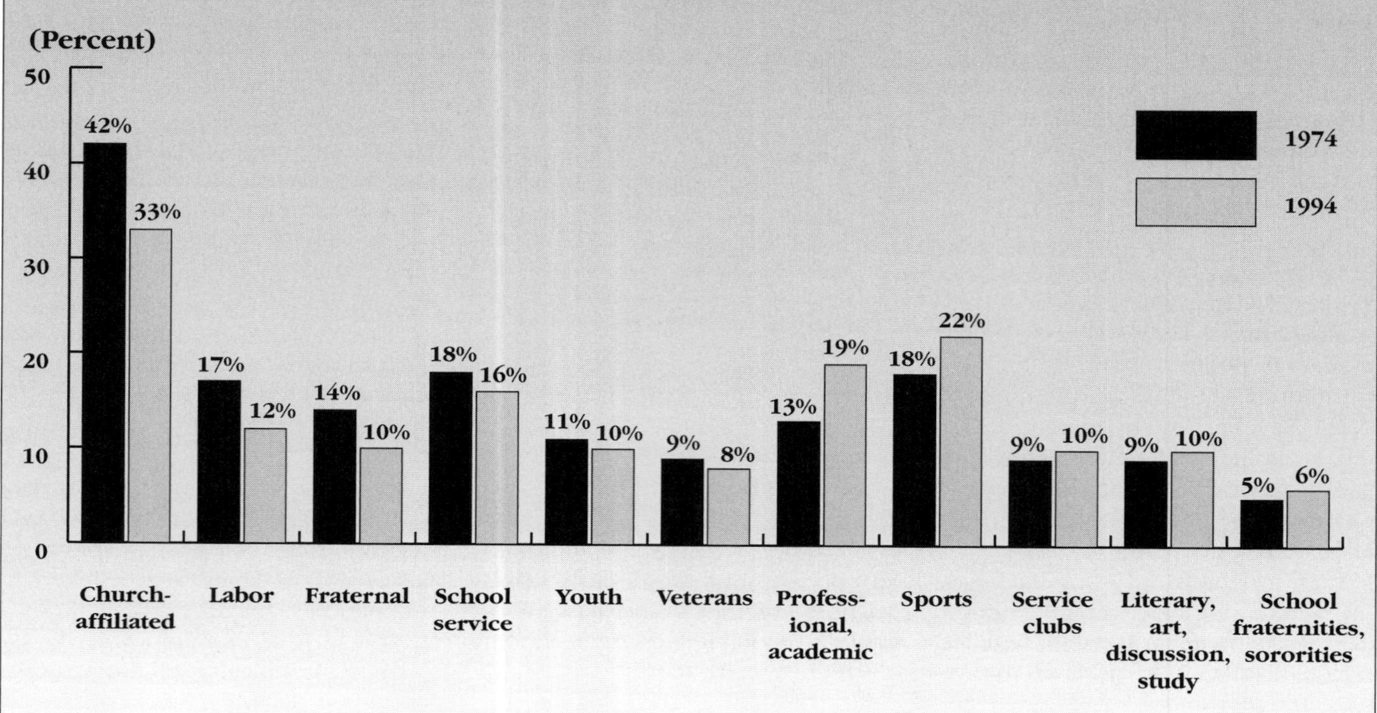

together; and that citizens felt closer to their neighborhoods and communities, through relationships built around churches, civic organizations and local businesses.

"The 1950s is America's favorite decade," says William Galston, a professor of political science at the University of Maryland-College Park and executive director of the Commission on Civic Renewal. "There's this image of what life was like, and it is very positive. This is the perception people have — and perceptions are important."

But does this idyllic view of America's past reflect reality? Certainly not for all Americans, observers say. The lives of minorities, women, the disabled and others were very restricted in the 1950s, they note. And there is more prosperity and freedom for everyone today than 40 years ago, they say.

Still, the idea that a civil society once flourished, and can once again, has gained increasing currency in recent years. Politicians from President Clinton on down talk about "values," "personal responsibility" and "community." During last year's presidential campaign, as *Time* magazine's Robert Wright pointed out, the Republican and Democratic party conventions "were virtuefests, four-day parades of people conspicuously devoted to their families." [5]

At the same time, a virtual cottage industry has sprung up around the notion that civil decline must be reversed. Some mark its beginning with former Education Secretary William J. Bennett's popular 1993 *Book of Virtues*, which eventually became a television show for children. Since then, similar titles have been turned out like clockwork, including Amitai Etzioni's *The New Golden Rule* and Gertrude Himmelfarb's *The De-Moralization of Society: Life From Victorian Virtues to Modern Values.*

Underpinning the new focus on civil decline is a broad, almost nebulous movement, comprised of thinkers of all ideological perspectives.

Some, like Bennett, have become prominent simply by raising the issue and stoking the fires of the national debate. Others, like George Washington University's Etzioni, who aims to foster a greater sense of community in America, have gained attention within academic and political circles. Invariably, they all have different notions of how best to bring about a renewal of community and civil society.

Given such diversity of opinion, it's not surprising that the movement isn't easily described by a single label or name, though "Restoring Civil Society," "Return to Civility" and "Civic Renewal" are often heard. But the aims are generally the same: to restore civic virtue and to rebuild those institutions, like family and community, that serve as conduits between people and society.

In addition, the movement to restore civil society has, of late, begun to take on more form, due in part to the creation within the last year or so of several groups devoted to studying and reversing civic decline. (*See story, p. 247.*)

But while politicians, pundits and scholars see much work to be done, others wonder whether the solutions that have been proposed are realistic — or if there really is a problem at all.

In search of answers, many scholars look to the past, especially the 1950s, for inspiration, eying the decade's stronger families and more closely knit communities. They argue that there must be a greater emphasis on personal responsibility, whether it means trying to preserve a troubled marriage or fulfilling one's duty to civic institutions, such as serving on a jury when called.

Whatever solutions are chosen, they say, must be linked by a strong system of common values. And while supporters of civic renewal disagree about what these values are, or how they should be determined, almost all agree that Americans need more moral education.[6]

But others wonder whether the positive aspects of the past can be resurrected without also bringing back the conformity and discrimination that flourished not so long ago. When, they ask, will encouraging responsibility turn into coercion? And who will choose the values Americans are supposed to embrace?

Many of these same skeptics also question the value of another cornerstone of the civility movement: the perceived need for greater courtesy. A greater emphasis on civil behavior, supporters of civil society argue, will pay dividends by allowing people from different walks of life to better understand each other and hence work more closely together.

But the skeptics worry that encouraging civil behavior will muffle the voices of less powerful groups in society who traditionally have had to resort to aggressive, "in your face" tactics just to be heard.

Another source of disagreement is the role of free market capitalism – in particular consumerism and corporate downsizing – which is often blamed for much of the decline of community life in the United States. For example, the argument goes, rampant, rapacious consumerism has brought sprawling suburban shopping malls, which have sucked the retail life from once vibrant downtown areas. As a result, critics say, one of the foundations of a good community — the place where people congregated and met their neighbors — has disappeared.

Others dismiss this view as misguided nostalgia for the past. For instance, they argue, local retailers on Main Street charged higher prices and offered less choice, which is why most consumers today shop at larger chain stores in suburban malls.

As strategies to restore civil society are debated, these are some of the questions being asked:

Can the "good" aspects of pre-1960s American society be recaptured without sacrificing individual and civil rights?

Compared with life in the 1990s, the '50s conjure up images of more community involvement, stronger families and greater individual courtesy. But the '50s also were characterized by rigid conformity, McCarthyism and a widespread lack of opportunity for minorities and women, as well as outright discrimination.

Still, many observers believe that much of what was perceived as worthwhile about the 1950s can be recaptured without bringing back the decade's more negative aspects. "I don't think the two are mutually exclusive," says Bruno Manno, executive director of the Commission for Philanthropy and Civil Society. Positive change can come without conformity, Manno says, because attitudes are dramatically different today. "People are a lot more tolerant than they were in the '50s," he says, adding that tolerance will allow people to find ways to strengthen their families and communities even though society is much more diverse than it was 40 years ago.

Manno's contention is born out by recent polls, which indicate strong support among all segments of society for tolerance. For example, a 1996 poll conducted by the Gallop Organization found that eight out of 10 Americans looked favorably on increased cultural and ethnic diversity.[7]

Etzioni agrees, arguing that "a moral revival ... is possible without Puritanism; that is, without busybodies meddling into our personal affairs, without thought police controlling our intellectual life."[8]

According to Etzioni, Americans have more common values than the "elites" in the media and academia are willing to give them credit for. Americans need to rediscover these values, Etzioni says, and begin instituting non-coercive policies that further them (*see p. 256*).

For instance, he says, there is widespread concern that America's high rate of divorce is hurting a whole generation of children. But instead of legally restricting divorce, Etzioni fa-

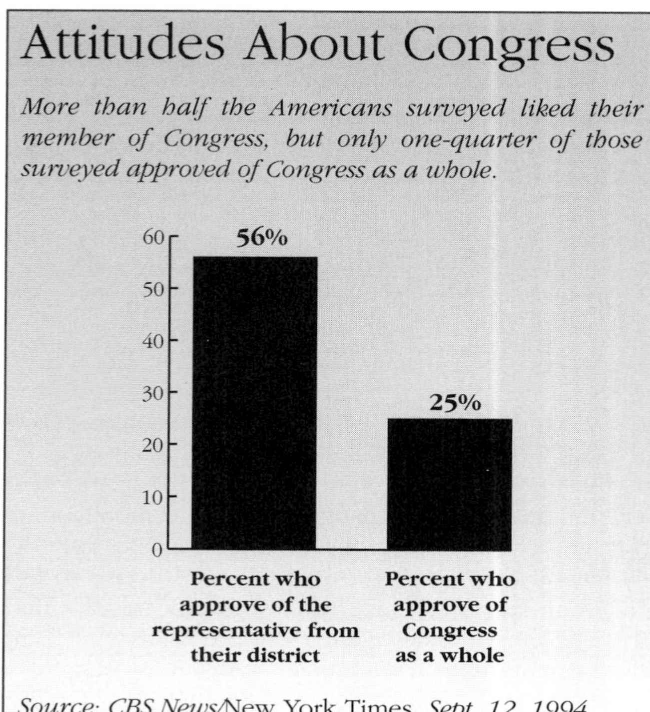

Source: CBS News/New York Times, Sept. 12, 1994

vors a preventive and less coercive approach. "Today, there are churches and synagogues that will not marry anyone unless the couple comes at least four times to discuss basic marital issues, such as who will control the money and how many children will they have," he said. "We can slow the rush to divorce by slowing the rush to marriage." [9]

But others say that Manno and Etzioni, while well-intentioned, have an unrealistic sense of what is possible. "We want to keep the safe streets, the friendly grocers and the milk and cookies, while blotting out the [reality of] political bosses, the tyrannical headmasters, the inflexible rules and the lectures on 100 percent Americanism and the sinfulness of dissent," writes Alan Ehrenhalt, executive editor of *Governing* magazine and author of *The Lost City: Discovering the Lost Virtues of Community in Chicago of the 1950s.* [10]

Ehrenhalt is among those who say it is not possible to bring back the best parts of America's past without also reviving many of its darker aspects as well. "There is no easy way to have an orderly world without somebody making the rules by which order is preserved," he writes. "Every dream we have about re-creating community in the absence of authority will turn out to be a pipe dream in the end." [11]

Ehrenhalt believes that Americans, regardless of what they say, are unwilling to make the sacrifices necessary to recapture the virtues of the '50s. "There are likely to be times in which we are more willing to accept some restraints in the name of order and stability than we've been in the last 20 years, but I don't think we're quite ready for that now," he says.

In addition, he argues, it is unlikely that the one of the pillars of the 1950s — the housewife — will reappear any time soon. Having a stay-at-home wife (or husband) presumes "a level of prosperity that would allow families to live on one income," he says.

But other observers are optimistic that Americans are already finding a middle ground between '50s and '90s values. "Many people have found a balance," says Alan Wolfe, a professor of sociology at Boston University. For instance, "Many people today only want to work part time when they have kids."

Is the "return to civility" movement elitist?

Civility has become part of the cultural zeitgeist. Political leaders like President Clinton and Speaker Gingrich talk of the need for greater forgiveness and courtesy in the political arena. "This town [Washington] is gripped with people who are self-righteous, sanctimonious and hypocritical" Clinton said at a Feb. 6 prayer breakfast. "We're in a world of hurt [and] we need help," the president added. [12]

Meanwhile, a growing number of commentators bemoan the loss of civility in America's cities and towns. Others attack basketball badboy Dennis Rodman, radio personality Howard Stern and other celebrities for their shocking public behavior.

Those who support a push for greater civility, like University of Maryland political scientist Eric M. Uslaner, say that it is vitally important "because it takes the rough edges off political and social life." [13]

According to Uslaner, smoothing out society's rough edges translates into a number of tangible benefits. First, he says, "it makes it easier for us to compromise with each other." In addition, less civility leads to weaker community ties, since people tend to withdraw more from society when their fellow citizens are discourteous. "This leads people to stay at home more and makes them less likely to participate in outside organizations," he says.

But for all of the perceived benefits of increased civility, there are those who question the motivation of Americans who are urging their fellow citizens to be nicer to each other. Some, like author Camille Paglia, a humanities professor at the University of the Arts in Philadelphia, say that efforts to promote civility are actually an attempt by society's haves to stifle its have-nots. "I am very much opposed to people constantly invoking old standards of middle-class propriety," she told National Public Radio, because working-class people often have to scream the loudest to be heard. [14]

Others, while not as adamant in their criticism, agree that efforts to promote civility could have a negative impact on weaker elements in society. "One

Restoring Civil Society Is a Group Effort

America is on the way to becoming the most civil society on Earth, judging by the plethora of organizations working on the problem.

Many were established in just the last year or so. Several — like the Institute for Civil Society, the Council on Civil Society and the Civil Society Project — sound so similar that it's hard not to confuse them.

Some of the groups are small and obscure. Others have attracted the support of political heavyweights and substantial foundation underwriting.

Among the most notable of the new crop is the National Commission on Civic Renewal (NCCR), launched last November by a $1 million grant from the Pew Charitable Trusts to "study and promote civic participation across the country." The NCCR is chaired by two of Washington's most respected figures: former Sen. Sam Nunn, D-Ga., and former Education Secretary William J. Bennett, author of the bestselling *Book of Virtues*. Other well-known members of the group's 23-person board include former GOP presidential hopeful Lamar Alexander, Harvard University Professor Henry Louis Gates and Cardinal Bernard Law of Boston.

The commission kicked off its efforts with a conference in Washington in late January to hear testimony on topics such as social trust and civic engagement. Two similar conferences will be held later in the year, culminating in a report on the state of the nation's civil and civic society.

Another well-known group, the National Commission on Philanthropy and Civic Renewal, has a similar name but a different mandate. Rather than broad trends, the commission will focus on encouraging Americans to give more time and money to charity. Formed in September 1996 and chaired by Alexander, the group is holding a series of meetings around the country to debrief scholars and community leaders. It plans to issue a report in June to "offer recommendations suggesting how giving can strengthen community institutions."

Those looking for the liberal view on moral decline can turn to the Institute for Civil Society, established last December. Headed by former Rep. Patricia Schroeder, D-Colo., and backed by a $35 million grant from an anonymous donor, the institute supports local groups that are working to build stronger families and communities around the country. The institute already has funded a program, run by black churches, aimed at reducing the crime rate in Boston's poorer neighborhoods.

Public officials are also addressing the problem. In Congress, a group of 20 House and Senate Republicans has formed the Renewal Alliance to promote non-governmental solutions to society's ills. One of the group's leaders, Sen. Daniel R. Coats, R-Ind., has introduced no less than 19 bills that offer proposed solutions to the decline of civil society, from additional tax credits for charitable giving to seed money for single-sex schools.

President Clinton has organized an April "summit" on community service and volunteerism that will include former Presidents Jimmy Carter, Gerald R. Ford and George Bush.

All the recent activities, private and public, have drawn praise from a variety of observers. "These groups are great, and they do great work," says George Washington University's Amitai Etzioni. Etzioni founded his own group, The Communitarian Network, in 1991 to find ways to bolster the nation's values, institutions and communities without oppressive standards or authoritarianism. Communitarian ideas have been embraced by a broad range of politicians and political thinkers from Clinton to 1996 Republican vice presidential nominee Jack F. Kemp.

The efforts to restore civil society even have elicited an upbeat response from Harvard's Robert B. Putnam, whose 1995 article on the decline of civic involvement garnered wide attention. [1] "The whole civic society movement is the beginning of a national social movement focused on rebuilding American communities," Putnam said. [2]

[1] See Robert B. Putnam, "Bowling Alone: America's Declining Social Capital," *Journal of Democracy*, January 1995.

[2] Quoted by Debbie Reichmann, "Let's Be Civil: One by One and In Groups, Americans Searching for Civic Spirit," The Associated Press, Feb. 5, 1997.

of the ways to keep women in line is to encourage 'ladylike behavior,'" says Susan McGee Bailey, director of the Centers for Research on Women at Wellesley College. "Sometimes, we cannot reach a point of understanding unless we have a conflict that at times is uncomfortable," she adds.

Many in the women's and civil rights community agree with Bailey, pointing out that "in-your-face" tactics are often needed to get people's attention and effect change. "Uncivil speech has been the main agent of social change in America, whether it's race, women or gay rights," says Sam Walker, a professor of criminal justice at the University of Nebraska-Omaha.

That's essentially the approach that Rep. Maxine Waters, D-Calif., took when she was not invited to a 1992 meeting between members of Congress and President George Bush after rioting in Los Angeles, even though her district was affected by the turmoil. Only by showing up uninvited at the White House and pushing her way into the meeting did she get a seat at the table. [15]

Even some conservative thinkers say that incivility in the political arena serves a valuable purpose. "When politicians say that they want the tone of the debate to be sober and quiet, they're really saying that the people should quiet down and let them run things," says David Boaz, executive

Confidence in Government Plummets, 1964-1992

More than half of all Americans in 1992 felt ignored by public officials compared with about a third of Americans surveyed in 1964. More than three-quarters of all Americans said they trusted government most of the time or always in 1964, compared with less than a third in 1992.

How much of the time do you think you can trust the government in Washington to do what is right?

	1964	1968	1972	1976	1980	1984	1988	1992
Just about always	14.3	7.1	5.3	3.4	2.0	3.5	4.2	3.2
Most of the time	62.1	52.3	47.7	29.7	23.0	39.0	36.3	25.7
Only some/none of the time	21.9	35.3	44.8	63.1	72.6	52.2	57.9	69.8

Would you say government is pretty much run by a few big interests looking out for themselves or that it is run for the benefit of all the people?

	1964	1968	1972	1976	1980	1984	1988	1992
Few big interests	28.4	38.2	53.0	65.6	69.5	52.5	63.1	74.7
Benefit of all	63.7	49.4	37.5	23.8	20.8	37.2	30.7	20.1

I don't think public officials care much what people like me think.

	1964	1968	1972	1976	1980	1984	1988	1992
Agree	35.9	41.4	48.8	51.0	51.7	41.9	50.5	51.7
Disagree	61.2	53.4	48.6	44.0	43.1	56.3	37.2	37.4

How much attention do you feel the government pays to what the people think when it decides what to do?

	1964	1968	1972	1976	1980	1984	1988	1992
A good deal	31.8	22.4	17.3	10.5	8.4	14.7	12.8	12.2
Some	38.0	40.6	56.0	54.2	48.9	53.6	57.0	60.9
Not much	23.7	28.2	24.0	32.6	40.8	29.5	28.1	25.5

And how much do you feel that having elections makes the government pay attention to what the people think?

	1964	1968	1972	1976	1980	1984	1988	1992
A good deal	64.6	57.7	54.4	51.7	50.6	42.0	36.8	46.7
Some	24.6	27.6	35.6	35.4	34.6	36.4	44.1	41.0
Not much	6.5	8.1	7.5	10.3	12.5	19.9	17.2	11.1

Source: American National Election Studies, 1964-1992, *in Stephen C. Craig,* The Malevolent Leaders: Popular Discontent in America

vice president of the CATO Institute, a libertarian think tank.

But others argue that uncivil behavior is really only valued by the cultural elite, who exhort others to follow their example. "There has been a contempt for middle-class morality [among artists and others] since the early 19th century," Galston says. "There is this notion that free expression and artistic genius are at war with bourgeois restraints." As a result, he says, there is a constant effort to revere anything that flies in the face of these restraints. "It's profoundly troubling when the cultural elite can think of nothing better to do than to make a film glorifying [*Hustler* Publisher] Larry Flint."

Have corporate downsizing and consumerism contributed to the decline of communal loyalties?

In the 1950s, with most industrialized nations still recovering from the destruction of World War II, the United States dominated the world economy. The nation's phenomenal prosperity lifted millions of blue-collar families into the middle class.

Today, the U.S. is not quite the economic behemoth of old. Competition from Europe and Asia has become fierce, and American corporations often have responded by cutting workers at all levels and shifting many jobs to foreign countries where labor costs are much lower. [16]

At the same time, a new global economy has given Americans unprecedented access to goods and services. Recent innovations, like discount superstores, supermalls and cable TV, which would have seemed unbelievable just a generation ago, are the norm today.

Many scholars think that such innovations have contributed to the overall decline in community in the United States. Corporate downsizing is viewed as particularly destructive, with societal consequences that go far beyond the economic well-being of affected workers and their families.

"Threatening to move a profitable company out of its historic home wasn't done in the 1950s mostly because it wasn't thinkable, in the same way it wasn't thinkable to cancel employees' vacations or fire them at 50 or 55 when their productivity began to slow down," Ehrenhalt writes. Such actions "were gross infringements on the enduring relationship between worker and manager [and were] not on the menu of options." [17]

© Photodisc

Life was more congenial in the 1950s, many observers say, because merchants on main street knew their customers personally and took an interest in the community, but today suburban superstores are elbowing out the small retailer.

But the unthinkable is now reality. According to Ehrenhalt, Uslaner and others, downsizing has eroded the sense of trust that many people used to have in their institutions, both private and public. It has supplanted communal loyalty with an environment dominated by fear and insecurity. "When you're less optimistic and feel insecure, you only want to stick with your own kind," Uslaner says.

"When you live in fear of getting a pink slip every day that you walk into work," Ehrenhalt adds, "it makes you a much more suspicious, inward and selfish kind of person."

The decline of loyalty, in turn, has created an increasingly mobile society, where people are forced to move from city to city in search of the next job. "To what extent can we maintain social cohesiveness in an economy where mobility is increasingly the norm?" Galston asks.

But other observers say that corporate downsizing is a red herring when it comes to its effect on communities. "The economy is always dynamic," CATO's Boaz says, noting that since the Industrial Revolution began in the mid-1700s, two-thirds of the jobs that existed at the start of each century had disappeared when the century ended. "If you want an economy where people don't get laid off, you're not talking about the '50s, you're talking about the Soviet Union."

CATO Chairman William Niskanen argues that the impact of corporate downsizing has been blown out of proportion by the media and others. "There really isn't any significant increase in job turnover rates," says Niskanen, who notes that it's simply fashionable these days to talk — and write — about anxieties. In addition, he contends that the fear Americans are supposed to have about their future is not reflected by their behavior. "If there were real anxiety," he says, "you'd expect an increase in the personal savings rate, and yet it's dropped over the last five years; you'd expect a lowering of credit card debt, but credit card bankruptcies are at an all-time high." [18]

Ehrenhalt and others also bemoan the rise in consumer culture. In the last 30 years, all over the United States, sterile superstores built on the edge of town have elbowed out the local retailers on main streets, he says. It was local business people, many argue, who took an interest in the community because they lived there, too. But with the changes in retailing, they say, daily commerce no longer reinforces community bonds the way it once did. Going to the store is just another impersonal act, another transaction. "Today, you can walk into a bank where you've had an account for 20 years and be asked for identification, because the teller hasn't been there long enough," Ehrenhalt says.

In Ehrenhalt's view, it's easy to underestimate the value of knowing people who provide you with goods and services, like the manager of the bank or barkeep at your local tavern. "These local institutions are a part of what gives life its texture," he says. "Life is difficult without anchors and roots."

Harvard University government Professor Michael Sandel, author of the 1996 book *Democracy's Discontent*, agrees that replacing downtown shopping with suburban malls has had a devastating effect on society. "These downtown areas were public spaces where men and women from different walks of life and different classes came together," he says. "When people don't come together, they think of themselves less and less as a participant in a common venture, undermining our whole sense of community."

But others say such thinking is rooted in misguided nostalgic yearnings. "We hear about all of these small towns that don't want Wal-Mart," Boaz says, "but when Wal-Mart comes in, people go there because prices are lower."

Niskanen agrees, adding that the opposition to big chain stores usually comes from upper-middle-class Americans, who can afford to pay more for their needs. "People who buy food at Sutton Place Gourmet have no idea why people shop at Food Lion," he says.

But Ehrenhalt says the big retailers get support because shoppers don't consider the long-term consequences of their actions. "People don't shop at Wal-Mart thinking, 'This is great, I'm going to destroy the main street of my community,'" he says. ■

BACKGROUND

In Search of Utopia

Trying to improve communal life is nothing new. In ancient Greece, the philosopher Plato asked how society should be ordered. In the *Republic*, he envisioned a state where a small group of enlightened thinkers would rule to the benefit of the mass citizenry. In another dialogue, the *Crito*, Plato concludes that each individual has a duty to the community, even when that community is wrong.

Nearly two millennia later, the philosophers of the Enlightenment asked many of the same questions and came up with very different answers. They considered the protection of individual liberty as society's main function. Thomas Jefferson later expressed the idea in the Declaration of Independence, writing that the new American Republic should guarantee its citizens the right to "life, liberty and the pursuit of happiness."

But Europeans had been living in North America for more than 150 years before Jefferson wrote those immortal words. And during that time, other notions of community had come to the continent's shores. The Puritans, for instance, arrived in New England early in the 17th century and built a rigid community where conformity was a way of life.

By the 19th century, many of the values of the Puritans and the Enlightenment had been inculcated into American communal life. The push westward, which began in the late 18th century, allowed a level of freedom hitherto unimagined in most other countries. At the same time, the Industrial Revolution was urbanizing more settled areas. Factory labor, railroads and other trappings of the industrial age pulled millions from rural areas, creating a more mobile and prosperous society.

And yet Americans still yearned for the structure of community and for civil society in general. The French statesman and author Alexis de Tocqueville, when he traveled through the United States in the early 1830s, noted that Americans, for all of their love of individualism, differed from other people because of their tendency to organize into civic and other groups to achieve common goals.

The desire for a sense of community often manifested itself in more far-reaching ways than merely joining civic organizations. The history of 19th-century America is littered with utopian communities that sought in different ways to perfect humanity. Some were religious, like those founded by the Shakers. Others, like the socialist community established in New Harmony, Ind., in 1825, simply sought a better way to organize society. [19]

The Fabulous '50s?

Barely 100 years after de Tocqueville, the United States was a transformed land. The West, no longer a wild wilderness, had been tamed and brought into the Union. The federal government, once a minor player in people's lives, controlled many spheres of public life.

By 1945, the United States had helped to win two world wars and had become the globe's premier nation state, with unparalleled political, military and economic power. The fruits of what came to be known as "Pax Americana" were never more abundant or, many argue, sweeter than they were in the 1950s.

Whatever the reality, the 1950s is remembered as a time when economic prosperity and domestic tranquillity were the norm. Recent polls indicate that a majority of adults, regardless of age, see that decade as a much better time to be alive than the 1990s.

And indeed, by many social indices, things were better in the 1950s. The divorce rate was one-third today's rate. Only 5 percent of all births were out-of-wedlock, compared with roughly one-third of the births today. And crime was far below contemporary rates.

Society was more white, more overtly Christian and hence more homogeneous and more at peace with itself. This perception was heightened by the fact that minority groups either were pushed into the background or were striving to conform to majority ideas and values in an effort to fit in. And what those ideas and values were was clear to the average citizen. Fam-

Continued on p. 252

Chronology

1800s American society struggles to find a balance in what political philosopher Edmund Burke calls the tension of order and freedom.

1825
Englishman Robert Owen tries, unsuccessfully, to establish a socialist community in New Harmony, Indiana. Other reformers later attempt to establish other "utopian" communities throughout the century.

1835
French thinker Alexis de Tocqueville publishes the first volume of *Democracy in America*, a ground-breaking treatise on the nature of society in the United States. De Tocqueville noted the tendency of Americans to organize into civic and other groups to achieve common goals.

1847
Under the leadership of Brigham Young, the Mormons establish a new community in Utah.

1854
Henry David Thoreau publishes *Walden*, which celebrates the uniqueness of all individuals, regardless of their standing in the community. A similar theme is echoed by Walt Whitman and other American writers.

1900s-1940s

The United States grows into an economic and military giant. New prosperity brings with it new opportunities and the consumer culture.

1901
Theodore Roosevelt becomes president following the assassination of William McKinley. Roosevelt, a progressive reformer, seeks to control the power of big business over the democratic process.

1932
Franklin Roosevelt is elected president. Roosevelt's New Deal dramatically increases the role of the federal government in citizens' lives.

1945
World War II ends, heralding a period of unparalleled economic prosperity in the United States.

1950s The United States settles into post-war prosperity and relative social calm. The decade is characterized by an emphasis on family, community and conformity.

1950
Sen. Joseph R. McCarthy, R-Wis., begins his fulminations against communists and communist sympathizers in the State Department.

1954
The Supreme Court, in *Brown v. Board of Education*, ends legal segregation. The historic decision forms the legal pillar of the civil rights movement over the next 15 years.

1954
The United States, with 6 percent of the world's population, contains 60 percent of all the cars.

1960s-1980s

The U.S. undergoes sweeping changes, ranging from the civil rights and women's rights movements to rising crime and illegitimacy.

1964
Congress passes the Civil Rights Act.

1966
The National Organization for Women is founded.

1968
Protests over the war in Vietnam disrupt the Democratic National Convention in Chicago.

1980
Ronald Reagan is elected president, calling for smaller government as a way to expand individual opportunity.

1990s The movement to restore civil society begins to emerge.

1993
Amitai Etzioni publishes *The Spirit of Community*, a manifesto for the Communitarian movement.

1995
Harvard University's Robert B. Putnam argues in a provocative article, "Bowling Alone: America's Declining Social Capital," that Americans have lost much of the "propensity for civic association" that so impressed de Tocqueville.

1996
The National Commission on Civic Renewal, the Institute for Civil Society and several other similar groups are formed.

Sentencing Lawbreakers to a Dose of Shame

Stocks and pillories aren't making a comeback, but less severe forms of public humiliation are gaining favor as judges seek alternatives to jailing non-violent lawbreakers.

In one Texas jurisdiction, people convicted of driving under the influence of alcohol must put "DUI" bumper stickers on their cars. [1]

In Port St. Lucie, Fla., a judge ordered a child molester to post a sign on his property warning children away. The same judge required a woman convicted of buying drugs in front of her children to put a notice in the local newspaper that described the details of her crime. [2]

And in one of the most inventive alternative sentences, a judge in Tennessee ordered convicted burglars to allow their victims to go through their homes and take whatever items they wanted. [3]

"We rely too heavily on imprisonment for white-collar crimes, property offenses and other non-violent crimes," says Dan M. Kahan, a constitutional and criminal law professor at the University of Chicago Law School. Shame offers an effective alternative to the expense of sending miscreants to prison, Kahan says, because it allows society to express its reproach for the criminal and his crime.

But others worry that shame may do more harm than good. "I'm very skeptical when criminologists and sociologists say that the best way to rehabilitate someone is to isolate him and put some sort of scarlet letter on him," says Nadine Strossen, president of the American Civil Liberties Union (ACLU). "We need to integrate criminals back into our communities."

Another potential problem with public shaming, according to Sam Walker, a professor of criminology at the University of Nebraska, is that it could "incite people in the community to engage in some sort of vigilantism."

But Kahan argues that someone who is given a shame-based sentence is more likely to reintegrate into society than a person who went to prison. "People who come out of prison have a hard time because other people won't deal with" ex-convicts, he says. On the other hand, shame-based sentences do not trigger the same life-changing disruptions inevitably caused by prison. "You can still do your job and stay with your family," he says.

The use of shame by the state has a long history in many societies. In Europe, until the 19th century, branding was frequently employed to punish criminal offenders. Today, in many countries, particularly in the Islamic world, public forms of physical punishment, like flogging, are still common.

In Colonial America, a variety of public humiliations from the stocks to tarring and feathering were used. By the mid-19th century though, shame as a social tool was viewed as an anachronism in the United States. It was replaced by incarceration, which came into vogue as the notion took hold that society could remold criminals into law-abiding citizens.

Although there are no long-term studies on the impact of shame-based sentences, Kahan and other experts are hopeful that it will deter future bad behavior. "Sociologists and criminologists tell us that shame, and not the threat of punishment, is the reason people obey the law in the first place," Kahan says, "because they are afraid of how their peers will perceive them if they are caught."

But Walker argues that Kahan's reasoning is flawed because people only worry about being embarrassed within their close social circle. "Shame could be a powerful tool in the workplace, where everyone knows everyone else," he says, "but I can't see it having much effect in society at large."

---

[1] The jurisdiction is Fort Bend County. See Dan Kahan, "What Do Alternative Sanctions Mean?" *The University of Chicago Law Review*, spring 1996, p. 635.

[2] See Jan Hoffman, "Crime and Punishment: Shame Gains Popularity," *The New York Times*, Jan. 16, 1997.

[3] See Kahan, *op. cit.*, p. 635, and Penny Bender, "Break the Law? Shame on You," *Tennessean*, Dec. 15, 1996.

Continued from p. 250

ily, country and God were, at least ostensibly, paramount. Civility was not only prized but expected.

People who lived in the same communities "really had a set of values about life, and they could assume that their neighbors had the same values," Ehrenhalt says, to the extent that "if a kid was doing something wrong, any parent on the street could discipline him, something you can't do today because you can't assume your next-door neighbor has the same ideas about child rearing that you do."

All of this produced a society that, by most accounts, ran much more smoothly than it does today, with few non-conformists to roil the surface. "It was a period of great social restraint," Galston says.

But not everyone has such a rosy view. "It's much easier to say, 'Let's go back to the wonderful values of the '50s,' when you don't look at things too carefully," says Wellesley's Bailey, arguing that women were essentially forced to stay at home or choose from a limited number of career options.

For minorities, especially African-Americans, the 1950s were a time of great oppression. Jim Crow laws were still in effect throughout the South, segregating blacks from general society and denying them many basic human, political and economic rights. And in the rest of the country, de facto segregation was a way of life.

But even if the obvious defects of the decade are removed, the notion of the '50s as a golden age is more fuzzy-headed nostalgia than clear recollection, Boaz says. "This whole idea that there was a common set of shared values is exaggerated," he says. Rather than "a nation of Christian prayer and the pledge of allegiance, in reality we were much less homogeneous."

When viewed from a distance, the past has often been found more appealing than one's own age. As the British historian Thomas Babington Macaulay wrote more than 150 years ago, "Those who compare the age in which their lot has fallen with a golden age which exists only in imagination may talk of degeneracy and decay; but no man who is correctly informed as to the past will be disposed to take a morose or desponding view of the present."

Post-1950s America

In his 1996 bestseller *Slouching Towards Gomorrah: Modern Liberalism and American Decline*, former federal Judge Robert H. Bork sounds a now-common theme among conservatives in the United States: During the 1960s, America lost its way, replacing the values that had served society so well with a hedonistic and even nihilistic form of individualism. [20]

The Heritage Foundation's Wittmann agrees. "The 1960s called into question a lot of ways we order society that had worked for millennia, like the family unit," he says.

That such sentiments spring from conservatives like Bork or Wittmann is not surprising. But lately, criticism of the 1960s has come from liberals as well. Etzioni, among others, also believes that in many ways the United States took a turn for the worse during that decade. [21]

Critics of the 1960s say that the cult of the individual fostered during the decade ultimately undermined responsibility among today's young and middle-aged adults. Men's movement founder Robert Bly, in his 1996 book *The Sibling Society*, says that many Americans who came of age in the 1960s and after are "half-adults" who have never entirely shaken the selfish and capricious nature that they had as children. Instead of assuming responsibility for what they already have and trying to genuinely better themselves, he says, these half-adults are consumed by greed and an almost childlike desire for fame and recognition.

Some critics of the '60s also believe that the decade's self-absorption was exacerbated during the 1970s and, especially, the 1980s. The election of Ronald Reagan as president in 1980, they say, heralded a new national mindset that glorified rugged individualism. And while the prototypical hero of the 1980s did not break the rules (at least openly) like his counterpart in the 1960s, the result, many say, was the same: further damage to communal loyalties.

But to other observers, the period after the 1950s brought an improved American society, when landmark court decisions and legislation nourished a flowering of individual liberty. "Before the 1960s, whole categories of people — minorities, women, children, mentally handicapped and prisoners — were not entitled to protection under the Constitution," says Nadine Strossen, president of the American Civil Liberties Union (ACLU).

Others view the 1980s as a decade of conservative triumph, marked by the fall of the Soviet Union and the beginning of efforts to shrink the size of the federal government. In addition, they say, the economy grew at a faster rate than it had during the tumultuous 1970s, benefiting all Americans. "Wealth was diffused throughout the system much more than it had been before," says Manno of the Commission for Philanthropy and Civil Society.

But Ehrenhalt sees a more insidious legacy of post-1950s America. In the last three and a half decades, Americans have become addicted to choice, he says, which has fundamentally weakened our society's anchors. "What makes a community is not people making all sorts of individual choices for themselves," he says, "but sharing values and sharing what they do and how they live."

Harvard's Sandel also sees choice, or what he calls "the consumerist idea of freedom," as a major obstacle in restoring civil society. The consumerist impulse, he argues, has altered the nation's mindset. Progressive politicians like President Theodore Roosevelt, he says, developed an antitrust policy to ensure that big business did not become too powerful and subvert the democratic process.

"By the 1940s, we still had an antitrust policy, but its purpose had changed," he says. "It was now about keeping consumer prices low by avoiding monopolies." In other words, the government's purpose shifted from protecting political rights to safeguarding consumer rights. The reason, Sandel says, is that "today we think of ourselves as consumers first and citizens second."

Similarly, Harvard sociologist Daniel Bell argues that America's consumer culture has destroyed the values of work and family that made communities strong in the 19th and early 20th centuries. In his widely read 1976 book *The Cultural Contradictions of Capitalism*, Bell noted that Americans had replaced such values with "play, fun, display and pleasure." [22]

But choice is attractive, even to those who regard it as a source of civil decline. "I must admit, I find Wal-Mart alluring," says Ehrenhalt.

But for CATO's Niskanen, choice is more than a temptation. "I grew up in a town in Oregon where everyone worked for the lumber mill or for someone who provided services for the mill," says Niskanen, who is in his 60s. "For most people, there was no choice then, and I think that's bad. Most Americans value choice." ■

Disney Tries to Create the Perfect Community ...

Just a few miles south of the Magic Kingdom near Orlando, Fla., the Walt Disney Co. has set out to build America's ideal community.

When completed in about 10 years, Celebration, as it is called, will have a Norman Rockwell look, complete with front porches, white picket fences and a cozy town center. At the same time, the community will also have one foot firmly in the future. For instance, every house in Celebration will be wired with fiber-optic cable to ensure that residents are fully capable of participating in every new wave of the communications revolution.

"We looked at what made communities great in our past, added what we've learned from the best practices of today, and combined that with a vision and hope for strong communities in the future," Disney Chairman Michael Eisner said recently.

Homes in Celebration feature small-town amenities like picket fences and front porches.

Celebration is a reaction against haphazard suburban sprawl and the development of so-called "edge cities," which increasingly evolve at the edges of major metropolitan areas.[1]

"Over the last 40 years or so, real estate developers have focused on just building place, not community," says Chris Corr, manager of community business development at the Celebration Co., a subsidiary of Disney. At Celebration, Disney hopes to create the "sense of security and belonging . . . that was part of the close-knit communities of the past," Corr says.

Many of the ideas behind Celebration are not new. Other planners have tried to create a modern, small-town environment in places like Seaside, Fla., Harbor Town, Tenn., and Reston, Va. But the Disney project, when complete, hopes to be the largest and most comprehensive of such "planned" communities ever built.

Disney's design team includes two of the world's most famous architects, Philip Johnson and Robert A.M. Stern. The aim, says Corr, is to create designs that encourage a sense of community by bringing residents physically together. The recently opened downtown district features wide, pedestrian-friendly streets that encourage residents to stroll or shop. Built beside a lake, the commercial area contains restaurants and shops as well as a nine-acre waterfront park. "It's all structured to drain people out of their homes," Corr says.

CURRENT SITUATION

Call for Responsibility

In his second inaugural address, on Jan. 20, President Clinton returned to a theme he has been sounding repeatedly since he spoke of the need for a "new covenant" between the people and their government at the Democratic National Convention in 1992. "Our Founders taught us that the preservation of our liberty and our Union depends upon responsible citizenship," he said, "and we need a new sense of responsibility."

The call for a renewed emphasis on responsibility is one of the intellectual cornerstones of almost every effort to restore civil society. Most thinkers, regardless of their politics, say that there is too much emphasis on rights at the expense of responsibility. For instance, while Americans cherish the right to trial by a jury of their peers, many seek to avoid jury duty.

This imbalance must be restored, they say, if society is to right itself. People must be made responsible for themselves and their communities in tangible ways. "If you really can't serve on the jury," Etzioni says, "I would favor some sort of alternative community service that would be more burdensome than jury duty."

Etzioni blames part of the problem on groups like the ACLU, which he says continually try to expand the boundaries of individual liberty as an end in itself. According to Etzioni, the ACLU has fought many proposals, like metal detectors at airports and drug-testing of bus drivers, that did not greatly restrict liberty and were clearly in the public interest.[23]

But civil libertarians, among others, worry that the rush to make citizens more responsible will lead to, at best, a more

. . . Blending Old and New in Celebration, Fla.

Houses are clustered around small, common areas in order to encourage residents to mix with their immediate neighbors. And each home is linked to a computer network — an electronic common area — accessible only to those living and working in Celebration. It enables residents to read about upcoming events and communicate with each other.

Finally, Disney has created institutions within the town designed to foster community spirit. The Celebration Foundation, for example, helps residents to set up volunteer and civic organizations like the Boy Scouts. And the combined elementary and high school will offer educational opportunities to adults as well as children.

The town imposes a large number of restrictions on its residents, ranging from limits on when you can resell your house (to prevent real estate speculation) to what colors you can paint it. But, says Corr, those who move into Celebration know what they want and what they're getting. "We are promoting certain values, like community, and that's appealing to people who share those values," he says.

But some observers say that residents may be looking for a utopia that will never exist. "The notion that you can get away from social conflict and crime [is] not possible," says Evan McKenzie, author of the 1994 book *Privatopia: Homeowners Associations and the Rise of Residential Private Government*. The idea behind Celebration is "escapist and secessionist," McKenzie says. "It says, 'I'm going to be leaving America and going into this fantasy kingdom where there is no crime, with only people like me.' " [2]

It will be some time before Celebration can be judged a success or failure. Currently, only 350 of a projected 8,000 homes are built and occupied. But, Corr says, Disney sees Celebration as a "laboratory" for developing real communities. It is not, he says, a movie-set, ersatz version of a 1950s town. "We definitely want to be able to share what we learn from Celebration with other communities," he says.

The "pedestrian friendly" downtown mixes stores and apartments beside a lake and a public park.

[1] For background, see "Revitalizing the Cities," *The CQ Researcher*, Oct. 13, 1995, pp. 897-920.

[2] Quoted in "Celebration Puts Disney in Reality's Realm," *USA Today*, Oct. 18, 1995.

conformist environment or, at worst, a more coercive one. "They haven't thought things through at all," Walker says. "The minute you put the rights of society above the rights of the individual, you start doing a lot of unsavory things," he adds, "like excluding black people from certain neighborhoods."

Moreover, Walker says, the whole push to "make people more responsible" is a red herring. "Rights and responsibilities are mutually reinforcing concepts because when you entrust people with rights you are implying responsibility. If I can't keep a black person out of my neighborhood because he has the right to be there, that imposes some responsibility on me," he says.

But those who support efforts to promote greater responsibility say that it is needed precisely to protect citizens' rights. According to the University of Maryland's Galston, prized individual liberties will be threatened if communities and government institutions are not maintained properly by the citizenry. "Rights are not self-actualizing or self-sustaining," Galston says. "We all have to contribute something to sustain the institutional framework that sustains these rights."

Harvard's Sandel adds that, unfortunately, fostering civic virtue is no longer a priority in American life, having long ago been replaced by the drive to expand prosperity and personal choice. While conservatives and liberals may have different policies, Sandel says, they have the same fundamental goal: enhancing the citizenry's capacity "to choose their own ends." He adds: "To deliberate about the common good requires more than the capacity to choose one's ends and to respect others' rights to do the same. It requires a knowledge of public affairs and also a sense of belonging, a concern for the whole, a moral bond with the community whose fate is at stake." [24]

To accomplish this, Sandel says, "we need to rejuvenate our political discourse and direct it to citizenship and away from individual gratitude and economics." But, he argues, "it will be very difficult to rejuvenate this debate until we rebuild the institutions of civil society that are between the individual and society, like family, congregations and civic groups."

Yet others see a different problem and a different solution. "Of course people feel a loss of responsibility when the [federal] government has taken away many of the responsibilities once held by local communities and individuals," says libertarian Boaz. Many of the government programs created during the 1960s and thereafter have encouraged irresponsible behavior on many levels, he says. For instance, by providing welfare benefits to single mothers, the government has, in a sense, given its blessing to the establishment of one-parent households, Boaz contends. "As a result, we have an illegitimacy rate that has gone from 5 percent in 1950 to 32 percent today," he says.

Boaz also sees big government as the reason for the decline of communal loyalty. He points, for example, to the increased role of the federal government in local education. By displacing many of the functions once held by local school boards, Boaz says, the government has created a disincentive for citizens to involve themselves in their community schools.

But others argue that the average citizen will probably not know or even care whether a particular government service comes from Washington, the state capital or town hall. "If a particular governmental service devolved from the federal government to the government of the state of New York, do you think anyone would notice?" Ehrenhalt asks. "I don't think so."

Seeking Common Values

Finding and instilling common values is another important item on the agenda of those seeking to restore civil society. But in a nation with so much diversity — political, ethnic and economic — how much common ground can be found?

"There are things that virtually all of us agree on," Etzioni says, such as tolerance of those of different races or religions. It is imperative, he says, that communities teach and encourage these common values to those of all ages and at every level of society.

In addition, he contends, there is more common ground than most people realize, even on divisive issues such as abortion, with its anti-abortion and abortion-rights lobbies. In Etzioni's view, 95 percent of all Americans would accept a middle-ground position that would allow abortion in the first trimester and gradually add restrictions in the later stages of pregnancy. "On this issue, you have two groups who scream," he says, "but if it weren't for these two groups, the American people would have settled it already."

Boston University's Wolfe agrees. "Among the cultural elites, there is a very deep conflict on many of these issues," he says. "But among the common people, there really are common values." For instance, Wolfe says, on an issue like affirmative action, polls indicate that most blacks and whites agree that jobs should be awarded primarily on the basis of merit. "So our differences on this issue are not really that great," he says.

In order to find more of these common values, Etzioni and others say that the nation must engage in more of what he calls "moral dialogue." Only after such a dialogue, which he says "is often a long and messy process," can we make sound public policy. "There are two kinds of laws — those that are backed by moral dialogue and those that are not," he argues. "For example," he says, "we had a moral dialogue about smoking, and about drinking and driving, and now we regulate them, and people accept this."

But some say that very little can be done to speed up the national debate on morals and values. "I am somewhat skeptical as to what we can do," Ehrenhalt says. "People have a moral debate when they're ready to try on some new ideas," but not before.

Others say that little really needs to be done to instill values in the American people. "The values are already there," says Andrea Camp, a senior fellow at the Institute for Civil Society, in Newton, Mass. The challenge, according to Camp, is for groups like hers to help the tens of thousands of Americans who are turning their values into action in communities all over the nation.

Still others say that all the talk about instilling some kind of moral code in citizens is entirely unnecessary. "The shared values society needs are minimal: a respect for basic rights, the law and property," Boaz says. "When our society isn't threatened by Nazi Germany or Soviet Russia, we really don't have common goals except living together in peace." ■

OUTLOOK

No Overnight Changes

Many observers believe that the effort to restore civil society in its many forms has already gathered a head of steam that few could have imagined in the 1980s. "If President Clinton had spoken out about school uniforms — as he recently did — 10 years ago, it would not have resonated nearly so much," Galston says. "People are worried more than ever about the aggregate consequences of individual choices."

Manno agrees. "There seems to be a yearning for a return to personal responsibility and a sense that there is more to life than material success."

Manno, Galston and others believe that these factors will create more momentum in the years ahead for confront-

Continued on p. 258

At Issue:

Should Americans be willing to give up some of their privacy to advance policies that are generally perceived to be in society's best interest?

AMITAI ETZIONI
Professor at George Washington University; founder and chairman of the Communitarian Network

FROM "THE PRICE OF PRIVACY," *LEGAL TIMES*, SEPT. 23, 1996

yes

At first, you are horrified. Your remaining shreds of privacy are being peeled off as if you are in some nightmarish forced striptease. Neighbors listen in on your cellular phone. Your boss taps into your e-mail and medical records. . . . Furiously, you seek new laws to protect yourself from data rape.

Not so fast. Our ability to restore old-fashioned privacy is about the same as our ability to vanquish nuclear weapons. Once the genie of high-powered computers and communication technologies has been let out of the bottle, no one can cork it again. We must either return to the Stone Age — pay cash, use carrier pigeons, forget insurance — or learn to live with shrunken privacy. . . . Most important, giving up some measure of privacy is exactly what the common good requires. . . .

Does it make sense, in the hallowed name of privacy, to allow both deadbeat fathers and students who default on their loans to draw a salary from a government agency, just to avoid use of computer cross-checks? Would you rather allow banks to hide the movements of large amounts of cash or curb drug lords' transactions? . . .

Will all these new knowledge technologies lead to a police state, as civil libertarians constantly warn us? As I see it, the shortest way to tyranny runs the other way around: If we do not significantly improve our ability to reduce violent crime and sexual abuse, and to stem epidemics, an even larger number of Americans will demand strong-arm tactics to restore law and order. Already too many desperate fellow citizens are all too ready to "suspend the Constitution until the war against drugs is won. . . ."

Once one accepts that privacy is not an absolute value, we must look for the criteria that will guide us when additional trimming of this basic good is suggested. Basic guidelines include the following: tolerate new limitations on privacy only when there is a compelling need (e.g., to reduce the spread of contagious disease); minimize the entailed intrusion (e.g., measure the temperature of a urine sample for drug tests, rather than observe as it is being produced); double-check that there is no other way of serving the same purpose; and minimize the side effects (e.g., insist that we be allowed to refuse junk mail).

Frankly, most of us would rather prevent others from peeping into our records, but we can readily see the merits of tracking data about other people. Well, they feel the same way about us.

NADINE STROSSEN
President, American Civil Liberties Union; professor at New York Law School

WRITTEN FOR *THE CQ RESEARCHER*, MARCH 1997

no

Technological advances are a double-edged sword when it comes to civil liberties: The same advances that promote the First Amendment right of access to information pose a serious threat to another fundamental right — privacy.

For every convenient shopper's check cashing card, there is a marketing research firm tracking what you buy and sending you unsolicited offers. For every visit to your doctor, there is a host of people accessing your record — including employers with the power to hire or fire, and insurance companies with the power to deny you services based on your health "risk factors."

Government officials and others who seek to curb our privacy claim that it must yield to countervailing concerns, such as efficiency or safety, or the communitarian's vision of "the common good." Their assumption is that any potential social benefit should automatically outweigh the individual rights at stake. But if our precious individual freedoms could so readily be sacrificed, we would have turned the Constitution upside down. Contrary to the communitarian credo, "[t]hose who won our independence by revolution . . . did not exalt order at the cost of liberty," to quote Supreme Court Justice Louis Brandeis. In contrast, they "believed that the final end of the state was to make men free."

Accordingly, the government must show that any measure that restricts a fundamental right, such as privacy, is "necessary" to advance a countervailing interest of "compelling" importance. While protecting our safety is certainly an important interest, invasions of privacy still cannot be justified on law enforcement grounds unless they are necessary, and no less invasive measure would suffice. For example, if the government decided to compile a massive genetic databank on all Americans, it would be hard to dispute that this would promote law enforcement efforts. But what is highly debatable is whether an adequate level of crime control couldn't be assured through some less drastic measure.

At bottom, this analysis calls for a kind of balancing, but with a thumb on the scales in favor of individual rights. After all, it's well-known that totalitarian countries often have much lower crime rates than free societies. Yet most of us are unwilling to make that trade-off.

As Thomas Jefferson noted: "A society that will give up a little liberty to gain a little security will deserve neither and lose both."

FOR MORE INFORMATION

The National Commission on Civic Renewal, 3111 Van Munching Hall, University of Maryland, College Park, Md. 20742; (301) 405-2790. Founded in November 1996, the commission studies and promotes civic participation across the country.

The Communitarian Network, 2130 H St. N.W. Suite 714J, Washington, D.C. 20052; (202) 994-7997. Founded in 1991 by George Washington University Professor Amitai Etzioni, the network is dedicated to bringing values and responsibility back to American life without "intolerance or oppression."

Institute for Civil Society, 53 Langley Rd., Suite 250, Newton, Mass. 02159; (617) 928-3408. Founded in 1996, the institute supports local groups that are working to building stronger families and communities.

The Heritage Foundation, 214 Massachusetts Ave. N.E., Washington, D.C. 20002; (202) 546-4400. The conservative think tank studies ways to reverse moral and civic decline.

National Commission on Philanthropy and Civic Renewal, 1150 17th St., N.W. Suite 201, Washington, D.C. 20031; (202) 463-1460. Founded in 1996, the commission focuses on encouraging Americans to become more involved in charitable and other civic organizations.

ing the ills that plague civil society. "It may be the central social discussion in the next decade," Galston says.

But Walker believes that this, like many other movements before it, is simply a fad that will be forgotten in a few years. The reason, he says, is that "there are no substantive ideas here, and so they haven't been able to translate them into a real program of action."

In the meantime, Walker says, there is very little chance that those who want to restore civil society will be able to stop the continued expansion of individual liberties. "I've lived through three so-called conservative revolutions — Nixon, Reagan and Newt [Gingrich] — and yet individual rights have expanded during those years," he says. "There is something very appealing about individual rights."

Others say that the renewed emphasis on responsibility and community put forth by civil society supporters will not suit America at this time in its history. The United States, unlike the nations of Western Europe, is still "an ambitious, dynamic power," writes conservative journalist David Brooks. "We're still a country too young to settle down." [25]

But civil society supporters say that in the future, society will be more, not less, open to their ideas. Still, there is no sense that changes will come fast and furious. "It took us 30 years to get into this mess," Galston says. "We won't get out of it overnight."

And yet, some observers already see signs that the situation is improving. "I look at the growth of charter schools, where parents and teachers come together to create community-based schools, as an example of where civil society is really coming alive," Manno says. [26]

But other supporters are less sanguine. "I'm not optimistic, because the obstacles to rejuvenating our civic life are powerful," Sandel says, referring to political and business interests. Still, there are grounds for hope, Sandel says, "a growing awareness that in the face of the global economy, our only hope for active, engaged citizenship is to rebuild the in-between institutions, beginning with families and neighborhoods." ■

Notes

[1] "Civility in the House of Representatives," March 1997. The report was prepared for the retreat by the Annenberg Center.

[2] See E.J. Dionne Jr., "Anything but Being 'Nice,'" *The Washington Post*, March 14, 1997, A27.

[3] The survey was taken by Chilton Research Services in April and May 1996 for ABC-TV.

[4] *General Social Surveys*, National Opinion Research Center, 1996.

[5] Robert Wright, "The False Politics of Values," *Time*, Sept. 9, 1996, p. 42.

[6] See "Teaching Values," *The CQ Researcher*, June 21 1996, pp. 529-552.

[7] See James Davison Hunter and Carl Bowman, *The State of Disunion: 1996 Survey of American Culture* (1996), p. 7.

[8] Amitai Etzioni, *The Spirit of Community: Rights, Responsibilities, and the Communitarian Agenda* (1993), p. 1.

[9] Quoted in "Making America Better: A Hometown Responsibility," *American Legion Journal*, August 1994, pp. 22-23. For background, see "Marriage and Divorce," *The CQ Researcher*, May 10, 1996, pp. 409-432.

[10] Alan Ehrenhalt, *The Lost City: Discovering the Lost Virtues of Community in Chicago of the 1950s* (1995), p. 21.

[11] *Ibid.*

[12] Quoted in Laura Blumenfeld, "Our President Begs Your Pardon," *The Washington Post*, Feb. 10, 1997, p. D1.

[13] Eric M. Uslaner, "Civility Matters," unpublished paper.

[14] Quoted on "Morning Edition," National Public Radio, Eric Westervelt, "More Manners Please," Jan. 15, 1997.

[15] See Phil Duncan, ed., *Politics in America: The 103rd Congress* (1994), p. 205.

[16] For background, see "Downward Mobility," *The CQ Researcher*, July 23, 1993, pp. 625-648.

[17] Ehrenhalt, *loc. cit.*

[18] For background, see "Consumer Debt," *The CQ Researcher*, Nov. 15, 1996, pp. 1009-1032.

[19] See Peter N. Carroll and David W. Noble, *The Restless Centuries, A History of the American People* (1979), pp. 217-18.

[20] Robert Bork, *Slouching Towards Gomorrah: Modern Liberalism and American Decline* (1996), p. 5.

[21] Amitai Etzioni, *The New Golden Rule: Community and Morality in a Democratic Society* (1996), pp. 64-73.

[22] Daniel Bell, *The Cultural Contradictions of Capitalism* (1976), p. 70.

[23] Etzioni, *The New Golden Rule, op. cit.*, pp. 19-20.

[24] Michael Sandel, "America's Search for a New Public Philosophy," *The Atlantic Monthly*, March 1996, p. 58.

[25] David Brooks, "Civil Society and its Discontents," *The Weekly Standard*, Feb. 5, 1996, p. 21.

[26] For background on charter schools, see "Attack on Public Schools," *The CQ Researcher*, July 26, 1996, p. 656.

Bibliography

Selected Sources Used

Books

Bell, Daniel, *The Cultural Contradictions of Capitalism*, BasicBooks, 1976.
Bell examines the roots of the capitalist system in the United States and argues that it has destroyed the hardworking and austere culture that created the nation's wealth in the first place and replaced it with a hedonistic society.

Bork, Robert, *Slouching Towards Gomorrah: Modern Liberalism and American Decline*, Harper Collins, 1996.
Bork, a legal scholar and former federal judge, argues that the United States is in a state of moral and cultural decline due to a triumph of modern liberalism. This ruinous creed, he says, which emphasizes group and individual rights regardless of their impact on society, is in large part the fruit of the 1960s radicalism that evolved on college campuses around the country.

Ehrenhalt, Alan, *The Lost City: Discovering the Lost Virtues of Community in the Chicago of the 1950s*, BasicBooks, 1995.
Ehrenhalt, the executive editor of *Governing* magazine, recreates the neighborhoods and communities of Chicago in the 1950s. He argues that while the past may have offered people fewer choices and less privacy, stronger families and communities made life more fulfilling than it is today.

Etzioni, Amitai, *The New Golden Rule: Community and Morality in a Democratic Society*, BasicBooks, 1996.
Etzioni, the founder of the Communitarian movement, argues that it is possible to successfully balance the need for order and autonomy, if that order is based on moral rather than legal authority. The United States needs to foster this moral authority by engaging in moral dialogues, he says.

Wattenberg, Ben, J., *Values Matter Most: How Republicans or Democrats or a Third Party Can Win And Renew the American Way of Life*, The Free Press, 1995.
Wattenberg, a senior fellow at the American Enterprise Institute, argues that the nation's greatest problem is a decline in values. He believes that the government has caused much of this "values deficit" through policies based on guilt rather than a search for rational solutions. According to the author, government's response to poverty, crime and other important problems has worked to create an environment that strikes "at the heart of a decent life."

Articles

Brooks, David, "Civil Society and Its Discontents," *The Weekly Standard*, Feb. 5, 1996.
Brooks explores the intellectual underpinnings of the civic renewal movement. He argues that for conservatives, the movement to restore civil society is a worthy challenger to the philosophy of the Reagan years, with its emphasis on rugged individualism.

"Freedom and Community," *The Economist*, Dec. 24, 1994.
This article examines and disputes some of the core ideas of the Communitarian movement. Etzioni and other communitarians are accused of being overly optimistic in their belief that it is possible to restore some of the societal order of the past without any unwanted restrictions.

Merida, Kevin, and Barbara Vobejda, "Promoting a Return to 'Civil Society," *The Washington Post*, Dec. 15, 1996.
Reporters Merida and Vobejda give a broad overview of the groups and prominent thinkers in the recently formed movement to restore civil society.

Sandel, Michael, "America's Search for a New Public Philosophy," *The Atlantic Monthly*, March 1996.
Sandel, a professor of government at Harvard University, argues that civic virtue, once a central point of political debate, has all but been forgotten in the United States. In its place, he says, politicians pander to a new consumerist ideology, centered around expanding people's choices in life.

Wright, Robert, "The False Politics of Virtues," *Time* magazine, Sept. 9, 1996.
Wright examines the recent inclusion of "morality" in the national political and cultural debate. According to Wright, talking about virtue is popular because it is easy and generally popular. But, he argues, both conservatives and liberals will run up against contradictions in their core ideology if they attempt to put these words into action.

Reports

Jamieson, Kathleen Hall, *Civility in the House of Representatives*, Annenberg Public Policy Center, March 1997.
Jamieson, dean of the Annenberg School of Communication at the University of Pennsylvania, documents a decline in civility in the House of Representatives during the 104th Congress. She argues that much of this decline can be traced to the 1994 election, when the Republicans gained control of the House for the first time in 40 years and both parties reacted to the their new status with less than gracious behavior.

The Next Step

Additional information from UMI's Newspaper & Periodical Abstracts™ database

Citizens' Disengagement From Civic Life

Alperovitz, Gar, "The reconstruction of community meaning," ***Tikkun,*** **May 1996, pp. 13-16.**

The continuing depth of American discontent with contemporary society demonstrates capitalism's subversion of the basis of community integration and wholeness in the U.S. Alperovitz examines the work of Martin Buber to gain perspective on the deepening crisis in the U.S.

Bloomfield, Lincoln P., "'Civil society' strengthens the fabric of peace," ***The Christian Science Monitor,*** **April 8, 1996, p. 19.**

Lincoln P. Bloomfield comments on the concept of civil society, which he contends lies at the heart of the historic struggle between self-government and tyranny. Bloomfield defines civil society as what occupies the space between government at the top and the atomized mass of individuals at the bottom, and details several examples of how civil society promotes democracy, as well as several in which civil society is stifled.

Brooks, David, "Civil society and its discontents," ***The Weekly Standard,*** **Feb. 5, 1996, pp. 18-21.**

Although proponents of civil society see it as a way of returning morality to communities, they also want individual choice to be exercised inside a thick web of local bonds. Civil society supporters' emphasis on stability and small communities doesn't suit an ambitious, dynamic power like the United States.

DeMott, Benjamin, "Seduced by civility: Political manners and the crisis of democratic values," ***The Nation,*** **Dec. 9, 1996, pp. 11-19.**

Lately, the leading political classes have declared that the major cause of the U.S.' current malaise is the decline of civility. However, the incivility that the elite bemoan should be seen as a protest by Americans outside the ranks of the publicly articulate against the conduct of their presumed betters.

Fost, Dan, "Farewell to the lodge," ***American Demographics,*** **January 1996, pp. 40-45.**

Fraternal organizations that were once quite popular have suffered membership decline and are fighting for survival because the baby boomer generation never joined such clubs. Most boomers who want a connection to their communities seek it in new ways.

Heller, Scott, "'Bowling alone'," ***The Chronicle of Higher Education,*** **March 1, 1996, pp. A10-12.**

Harvard government and international affairs Professor Robert D. Putnam's "Bowling Alone: America's Declining Social Capital," has vaulted him to the forefront of experts worried about the loss of community in American life.

Lipman, Joanne, "Newspapers Dissect Negative Political Ads," ***The Wall Street Journal,*** **July 27, 1990, p. B3.**

In a response to negative political ads, a number of newspapers around the country have started new columns devoted to fact-checking and critiquing such commercials.

Marks, Alexandra, "Backlash grows against negative political ads," ***The Christian Science Monitor,*** **Sept. 28, 1995, p. 1.**

Polls show that Americans are increasingly critical of negative campaigning by politicians, and more than a dozen states have laws against intentionally false political ads.

Putnam, Robert D., "Tuning in, tuning out: The strange disappearance of social capital in America," ***PS,*** **December 1995, pp. 664-683.**

In the 1995 Ithiel de Sola Pool Lecture, Putnam outlines his theory of "social capital" and how its recent decline in U.S. society is leading to civic disengagement, social isolation and a coarsening of societal discourse. The term "social capital" refers to social connections and the trust they generate, which is the glue of society.

Shillinger, Kurt, "The Quest To Restore Common Decency to Uncivil Society," ***The Christian Science Monitor,*** **Dec. 20, 1996, p. 1.**

A growing number of people think America has lost all semblance of civility, and their concerns are spurring a new field of research and activism into the causes of unruliness. The civility movement gained fresh momentum the week of Dec. 16, 1996, with an anonymous $35 million contribution to the Institute for Civil Society in Boston, Mass., one of a handful of new commissions founded by retiring members of Congress.

Wallis, Allan D., "Toward a paradigm of community-making," ***National Civic Review,*** **winter 1996, pp. 34-47.**

Efforts in the U.S. to address the problems of communities living in persistent poverty have been guided by two rival paradigms. The paradigm based on the assumption that communities had to be empowered to define and solve their own challenges is discussed, and its six defining principles-of-practice are examined.

Weil, Marie O., "Community building: Building community practice," ***Social Work,*** **September 1996, pp.**

481-499.

As downsizing of the federal government's role in social programs continues, social workers will be called on to respond to local concerns for the economic and social development that sustains and supports families and communities. Ideas to strengthen and expand community practice and community building are presented.

Government Efforts to Restore Civility

Bradley, Bill, "Our fragmented civil society," *St. Louis Post-Dispatch,* March 6, 1995, p. B7.

Excerpts from a speech by former Sen. Bill Bradley, D-N.J., on the deterioration of U.S. civil society and the need to revitalize the democratic process are presented.

Coats, Dan, Gertrude Himmelfarb, Don Eberly and David Boaz, "Can Congress revive civil society?" *Policy Review,* January 1996, pp. 24-33.

Coats discusses his legislative proposals to help renew civil society in the U.S. Himmelfarb, Eberly and Boaz critique his proposals.

Keigher, Sharon M., "Speaking of personal responsibility and individual accountability," *Health & Social Work,* November 1996, pp. 304-311.

Keigher discusses two recent pieces of legislation — the Personal Responsibility and Work Opportunity Reconciliation Act of 1996, and the Health Insurance Reform Act — and how the National Association of Social Workers and other social work organizations will respond to them.

"Nation revives the value of personal responsibility," *Atlanta Journal,* Aug. 2, 1996, p. A14.

An editorial says that although it may be hyperbole to say that the welfare reform bill Congress is sending to the White House ends welfare as Americans know it, it is unquestionably historic. For one thing, it ends any legal entitlement to welfare.

Groups Promoting Civic Renewal

Ambrose, Jay, "A study of consequence," *Atlanta Journal Constitution,* Nov. 24, 1996, p. C7.

Ambrose discusses the objectives of a study by the National Commission on Civic Renewal that is scheduled for completion at the end of 1997.

Black, Chris, "$35m gift to push civility," *The Boston Globe,* Dec. 15, 1996, p. A1.

An unnamed New England family has donated $35 million to create a Institute for a Civil Society in Newton, Mass. The society is aimed at exploring and encouraging a civil society.

Gigot, Paul A., "Potomac watch: Rethinking the politics of charity," *The Wall Street Journal,* Dec. 20, 1996, p. A16.

Gigot discusses the announcement by Sen. Daniel R. Coats, R-Ind., that he will not seek re-election in 1998, and the impact of the National Commission on Philanthropy and Civic Renewal, which will study how charity can once again do a better job of renewing civil society in an era of smaller government, a goal shared by Coats.

Healy, Melissa, "Civic Renewal: New money, old values. The U.S. is awash with national commissions being set up to promote 'active citizenship,' Melissa Healy reports," *Guardian,* Jan. 8, 1997, p. 6.

Amitai Etzioni, a George Washington University sociology professor and founder of the fledgling Communitarian Movement, was a kind of cult figure to intellectually minded political centrists and scholars interested in the growing lack of civility in American life in the late 1980s. Now, Etzioni has to shout over a crowd. In recent months, the notion that American society is in need of renewal has spread nationwide. National commissions, their letterheads weighted down with the gravitas of distinguished former lawmakers, have begun sprouting at a rate of almost one a week. Fueled by a surge of interest — and money — from the nation's philanthropic foundations, there has been a spate of conferences convened, studies commissioned and books penned.

"Marching to a civic beat," *The Boston Globe,* Dec. 17, 1996, p. A30.

An editorial lauds the anonymous donation of $35 million to fund a new Institute for a Civil Society in Newton, Mass., stating that such an institute is welcome in late 1996, when essential social networks nationwide are losing their connections.

Merida, Kevin, and Barbara Vobejda, "Promoting a return to 'civil society'," *The Washington Post,* Dec. 15, 1996, p. A1.

Amid widespread disillusionment with government and its ability to solve the nation's most pervasive problems, a loosely formed social movement promoting a return to "civil society" has emerged in 1996, drawing a powerful and ideologically diverse group of political leaders.

"Troubled nation," *Houston Chronicle,* Nov. 16, 1996, p. A36.

An editorial discusses the efforts of the National Commission on Civic Renewal to understand why Americans are so angry, dissatisfied and distrustful.

Incivility in Public Life

Berkow, Ira, "A Solution To a Rodman Problem," *The New York Times,* Jan. 17, 1997, p. B9.

Berkow compares a Jan. 15, 1997, incident in which Chicago Bulls basketball star Dennis Rodman kicked a cameraman in or near the groin after falling out of bounds while in pursuit of a rebound with the unlikely act of civility he showed on Dec. 30, 1996, when he was on his best behavior because his 8-year-old daughter, Alexis, was in the crowd as the Bulls played the Indiana Pacers. Berkow urges that Rodman receive a "meaningful punishment" for bad behavior, and even suggests having his daughter watch all his games in order to prevent further incidents.

Herbert, Wray, "The revival of civic life," *U.S. News & World Report,* Jan. 29, 1996, pp. 63-67.
Although there is little disagreement over the decline in civic engagement, there is much discussion over the causes and cures for it. The infrastructure of civic life remains intact.

Kreyche, Gerald F., "The debasing of American culture," *USA Today,* May 1996, p. 82.
The U.S. is caught up in a vulgar morass, as evidenced by "cyberporn," four-letter words flaunted on bumper-stickers, T-shirts and caps, and contemporary music. If one is critical, one is accused of intolerance.

Marks, John, "The American uncivil wars," *U.S. News & World Report,* April 22, 1996, pp. 66-72.
Crude, rude and obnoxious behavior has replaced good manners in the U.S. This behavior is hurting both the U.S.' culture and its politics.

Leo, John, "The private parts of Don Imus," *U.S. News & World Report,* April 8, 1996, p. 14.
While Don Imus is very funny, well-informed and doesn't take himself too seriously, he does have a nasty streak and does trivialize politicians who appear on his show by demanding that they be entertaining. His tendency to viciously attack his critics looks a lot like an enforcement policy to keep other potential critics in line.

Lincicome, Bernie, "Rodman's Points Too Delicious to Ignore," *Chicago Tribune,* Feb. 2, 1997, p. 1.
Since Dennis Rodman merely talked to National Basketball Association (NBA) Commissioner David Stern, this ought to be proof of Rodman's improved civility, considering the usual options. Apparently impressed, Stern now will consider whether Rodman is fit to rejoin the NBA.

Nostalgia/Return to Traditional Values

Beem, Christopher, "Civic virtue and civil society," *Los Angeles Times,* May 27, 1996, p. B5.
Beem discusses calls for strengthening America's civil society arguing that it would require articulating and enforcing America's core of values and beliefs, including acknowledging and accommodating the religious language and imagery that is abundant in the nation's moral heritage.

Bivins, Ralph, "Nostalgic by design," *Houston Chronicle,* June 2, 1996, p. E1.
Celebration, the new housing community in Orlando, Fla., by Disney Design & Development, is highlighted. Houston home builder David Weekley, who is building homes in Celebration and has incorporated some of the traditional influences learned from the project into some Houston houses, says "It's the Disneyland of the housing industry.

Flanagan, Barbara, "Cause to celebrate?" *Metropolitan Home,* Sept. 1996, pp. 54-60.
Information about Celebration, a new planned community near Orlando, Fla., is presented. The project, being developed by Disney, could popularize New Urbanism.

Galston, William A., "Divorce American style," *Public Interest,* summer 1996, pp. 12-26.
Galston discusses the current state of divorce in the U.S. No-fault divorces have hit women and children especially hard, and now some are considering whether no-fault divorce laws should be reformed.

Goodman, Ellen, "A vow of civility for the new year," *The Boston Globe,* Jan. 2, 1997, p. A15.
Goodman discusses the numerous calls for increased civility in public life in the U.S. in 1997, stating that a return to the small daily conversations that are so trivially labeled as "mere pleasantries" is a good starting point for a strengthened sense of community.

Grunwald, Henry, "Jane Austen's civil society," *The Wall Street Journal,* Oct. 2, 1996, p. A16.
Grunwald links the popularity of films based on the novels of Jane Austen to an appreciation of the good manners and correct English displayed by her characters, in contrast to much of modern daily life. Grunwald wonders whether informality, one of the blessings of America, must lead to "an all-around rudeness and snarling hostility" or the "verbal acid rain of obscenities."

Guttman, Monika, "The split over divorce," *USA Today,* June 21, 1996, Sec. USW, p. 4.
The debate over reforms designed to make it harder to divorce is examined. As many as 18 states are introducing such requirements as proving fault, family therapy, planning for the financial future of any children, and marriage counseling. A table lists the state-by-state divorce rates per thousand residents.

Langdon, Philip, "The new, neighborly architecture," *American Enterprise,* pp. 41-46.
Langdon examines whether traditional buildings can bolster traditional values. Traditional community designs are being revived and given an opportunity to do battle against contemporary social ills.

Lester, David, "Trends in divorce and marriage around the world," *Journal of Divorce & Remarriage,* 1996, pp. 169-171.
A study of 27 nations indicated that divorce rates rose in 25 of the nations between 1950 and 1985 while marriage rates declined in 22 of the nations. Nations with higher divorce rates in 1950 had steeper increases in the divorce rate subsequently, supporting a critical-mass hypothesis.

Rymer, Russ, "Back to the future," ***Harper's,*** **October 1996, pp. 65-78.**
Disney is in the process of reinventing the concept of the company town with its latest Florida-based project, "Celebration." Information about the conception and construction of Disney's model town is presented.

Spaid, Elizabeth Levitan, "Disney turns its dream machine to building real-life community," ***The Christian Science Monitor,*** **March 11, 1996, p. 1.**
On 4,900 acres of piney woods just south of Orlando, Fla., the Walt Disney Co. is building what it conceives of as the ideal American town. Called Celebration, it is billed as a place of cozy neighborhoods, picket fences and porches, with schools, offices and a downtown all within walking distance. The creation symbolizes a new trend in urban design modeled on early 20th-century communities. Nationwide, more than 100 similar projects labeled "new urbanism" are being planned.

Vitek, William, "Building community," ***The Denver Post,*** **Sept. 15, 1996, p. E1.**
Vitek highlights Celebration, a 4,900-acre town being built near Orlando, Fla., by Celebration Co., a subsidiary of the Walt Disney Co. The town features a pedestrian oriented downtown for 20,000 residents, complete with office park, public schools, medical center, extensive parks and recreational facilities.

Vobejda, Barbara, "Critics, seeking change, fault 'no-fault' divorce laws for high rates," ***The Washington Post,*** **March 7, 1996, p. A3.**
Alarm over high divorce rates is propelling efforts to tighten the laws again. Determined to discourage divorce, legislators in several states have suggested "cooling-off" periods and mandatory counseling and are trying to restrict no-fault divorce.

Promoting Personal Responsibility

Balz, Dan, "At Penn State, Clinton stresses personal responsibility," ***The Washington Post,*** **May 11, 1996, p. A9.**
Returning to themes that were at the center of his 1992 campaign, President Clinton at a Pennsylvania State University commencement on May 10, 1996, encouraged all Americans to become personally involved in helping to strengthen their communities, saying "government alone cannot solve" the country's problems.

Goodman, Ellen, "When politicians push personal responsibility, they mean ours, not theirs," ***The Boston Globe,*** **Dec. 31, 1995, p. 85.**
Goodman asserts that when politicians start talking about personal responsibility, they mean individual citizens' responsibility, not theirs. Goodman says the GOP Congress is not just trying to balance the budget, they want to end the idea of government as an agent of mutual responsibility.

Firestone, David, "Mayor's New Theme: Personal Responsibility," ***The New York Times,*** **Sept. 10, 1996, p. B3.**
Responding to days of questions about the needs of the city's children, Rudolph W. Giuliani, R-N.Y., began to sound a theme on the relationship between New Yorkers and their government. He argued with exasperation that it is time that individuals, families and neighborhoods assume more responsibility for the city's well-being. Giuliani suggested that the public too often looks to government to solve problems it is better able to solve itself.

Hurst, Blake, "Entitlements are corroding personal responsibility," ***American Enterprise,*** **January 1997, pp. 44-45.**
Hurst discusses how entitlements, such as Medicaid and Social Security, are corroding people's sense of personal responsibility. The U.S. needs to move toward a more rational and sustainable way of dealing with retirement.

Kruh, Nancy, "Public journalism and civic revival: A reporter's view," ***National Civic Review,*** **winter 1996, pp. 32-34.**
Rather than relying on experts or public officials to solve community problems, citizens are increasingly becoming involved in arriving at solutions themselves. Public journalism, an accompaniment to this trend of civic renewal, has the potential to open up an entirely new way of developing communities.

O' Connell, Brian, "Impact of nonprofits on civil society," ***National Civic Review,*** **spring 1995, pp. 126-129.**
While nonprofits exist technically in the private sector, their voluntary character renders them the "most public" of organizations, and thus the agents of maintenance and continuous renewal of civil society.

"Summer 1993 meeting addresses 'civil society' and service," ***Educational Record,*** **fall 1993, p. 58.**
The importance of building a strong "civil society" at home in the U.S. and abroad and the value of community service were the chief topics addressed at this summer's meeting of the Business-Higher Education Forum. Highlights of the meeting are presented.

Back Issues

Great Research on Current Issues Starts Right Here...Recent topics covered by The CQ Researcher are listed below. Before May 1991, reports were published under the name of Editorial Research Reports.

SEPTEMBER 1995
Catholic Church in the U.S.
Northern Ireland Cease-Fire
High School Sports
Teaching History

OCTOBER 1995
Quebec's Future
Revitalizing the Cities
Networking the Classroom
Indoor Air Pollution

NOVEMBER 1995
The Working Poor
The Jury System
Sex, Violence and the Media
Police Misconduct

DECEMBER 1995
Teens and Tobacco
Gene Therapy's Future
Global Water Shortages
Third-Party Prospects

JANUARY 1996
Emergency Medicine
Punishing Sex Offenders
Bilingual Education
Helping the Homeless

FEBRUARY 1996
Reforming the CIA
Campaign Finance Reform
Academic Politics
Getting Into College

MARCH 1996
The British Monarchy
Preventing Juvenile Crime
Tax Reform
Pursuing the Paranormal

APRIL 1996
Centennial Olympic Games
Managed Care
Protecting Endangered Species
New Military Culture

MAY 1996
Russia's Political Future
Marriage and Divorce
Year-Round Schools
Taiwan, China and the U.S.

JUNE 1996
Rethinking NAFTA
First Ladies
Teaching Values
Labor Movement's Future

JULY 1996
Recovered-Memory Debate
Native Americans' Future
Crackdown on Sexual Harassment
Attack on Public Schools

AUGUST 1996
Fighting Over Animal Rights
Privatizing Government Services
Child Labor and Sweatshops
Cleaning Up Hazardous Wastes

SEPTEMBER 1996
Gambling Under Attack
The States and Federalism
Civic Journalism
Reassessing Foreign Aid

OCTOBER 1996
Political Consultants
Insurance Fraud
Rethinking School Integration
Parental Rights

NOVEMBER 1996
Global Warming
Clashing Over Copyright
Consumer Debt
Governing Washington, D.C.

DECEMBER 1996
Welfare, Work and the States
The New Volunteerism
Implementing the Disabilities Act
America's Pampered Pets

JANUARY 1997
Combating Scientific Misconduct
Restructuring the Electric Industry
The New Immigrants
Chemical and Biological Weapons

FEBRUARY 1997
Assisting Refugees
Alternative Medicine's Next Phase
Independent Counsels
Feminism's Future

MARCH 1997
New Air Quality Standards
Alcohol Advertising

Back issues are available for $5.00 (subscribers) or $10.00 (non-subscribers). Quantity discounts apply to orders over ten. To order, call Congressional Quarterly Customer Service at (202) 887-8621.

Binders are available for $18.00. To order call 1-800-638-1710. Please refer to stock number 648.

Future Topics

- ***Educating Gifted Children***
- ***Declining Crime Rates***
- ***The FBI***

THE CQ Researcher

PUBLISHED BY CONGRESSIONAL QUARTERLY INC.

Educating Gifted Students

Are U.S. schools neglecting the brightest youngsters?

Public schools have gone to great lengths in recent years to improve educational services for students who had previously been neglected, such as low-income pupils or youngsters with disabilities. But they have paid less attention to providing special instruction and programs for gifted students. Advocates of gifted and talented education say schools are failing in their responsibility to help their brightest pupils achieve their full potential and are squandering a valuable national resource needed to compete in a global economy. But critics of gifted education say special programs for gifted youngsters benefit only a small, predominantly white and middle-class minority of students and divert resources and political support from broader educational reform.

INSIDE THIS ISSUE

CQ March 28, 1997 • Volume 7, No. 12 • Pages 265-288

Formerly Editorial Research Reports

EDUCATING GIFTED STUDENTS

COVER: COUNCIL FOR EXCEPTIONAL CHILDREN

March 28, 1997
Volume 7, No. 12

EDITOR
Sandra Stencel

MANAGING EDITOR
Thomas J. Colin

ASSOCIATE EDITORS
Sarah M. Magner
Richard L. Worsnop

STAFF WRITERS
Charles S. Clark
Mary H. Cooper
Kenneth Jost
David Masci

EDITORIAL ASSISTANT
Vanessa E. Furlong

PUBLISHED BY
Congressional Quarterly Inc.

CHAIRMAN
Andrew Barnes

VICE CHAIRMAN
Andrew P. Corty

PRESIDENT AND PUBLISHER
Robert W. Merry

EXECUTIVE EDITOR
David Rapp

The CQ Researcher (ISSN 1056-2036). Formerly Editorial Research Reports. Published weekly (48 times per year, not printed Jan. 3, May 30, Aug. 29, Oct. 31) by Congressional Quarterly Inc., 1414 22nd St., N.W., Washington, D.C. 20037. Annual subscription rate for libraries, businesses and government is $340. Additional rates furnished upon request. Periodicals postage paid at Washington, D.C., and additional mailing offices. POSTMASTER: Send address changes to The CQ Researcher, 1414 22nd St., N.W., Washington, D.C. 20037.

Educating Gifted Students

BY KENNETH JOST

THE ISSUES

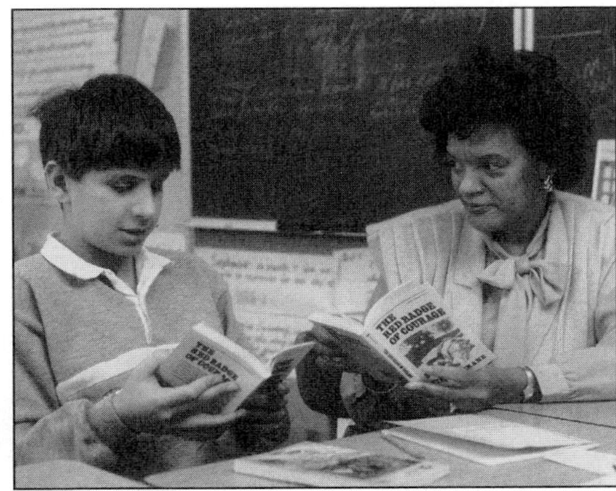

From the outside, Stratford Landing Elementary School looks like a typical suburban public school: a rambling one-story, brick building on a grassy campus ensconced in a leafy middle-class neighborhood. But Carol Horn's sixth-graders at the Alexandria, Va., school aren't getting a typical sixth-grade education.

They're reading Greek and Roman literature, making cameras out of cardboard boxes and doing mathematics that many of their friends won't study until eighth grade. And they're having fun.

"It's a lot harder, but it's really worth it," says 12-year-old Carolyn Amole.

Before coming to Stratford Landing, these Fairfax County youngsters attended neighborhood schools with classmates of wide-ranging abilities and interests. But by qualifying for Stratford's "gifted and talented center," they get to spend most of their school time with other high-ability kids and learn at a more challenging pace.

To advocates of gifted education, the experiences these youngsters had at their former schools demonstrate the need for special programs for very bright students. "I used to get most of my work done before everybody else," Carolyn says. "So most of my school day was spent waiting on them — or helping them."

"I was bored to tears," says Simon Gershman. "I made up stuff to do, but I still wasn't extremely happy."

Now, the students appear fully engaged. On a recent visit, they told a visitor about their coming class production of Aeschylus' play *Prometheus Unbound*. They demonstrated the rudimentary camera they made in science class in a two-week photography session added after they finished the regular sixth-grade material ahead of schedule.

The class appears to be a model of modern education, but gifted education also has its critics. Many educators and academics doubt that establishing separate educational paths for brighter pupils benefits any students. They also say that "gifted education" inevitably creates divisions among students, among families, even among staff. And they complain that gifted programs primarily benefit white and middle-class students, with youngsters from minority groups or disadvantaged backgrounds grossly underrepresented.

"I want school systems that meet the needs for all kids," says Mara Sapon-Shevin, a professor at Syracuse University and author of the 1994 book *Playing Favorites*. The advocates of gifted education, she says, are impeding broader reforms: "They have become part of the problem by siphoning off resources, attention and students to a separate system."

In Fairfax County, Stratford Landing principal Claudia Chaille stresses, gifted students get no extra resources and no extra teachers. The classrooms for Stratford's "G/T center" — which serves about 120 pupils out of a total enrollment of 560 — are interspersed with the "general education" classrooms, not set off in a separate part of the school. Students from both programs mix in music, art and physical education classes, and at lunch and recess. "We try real hard for them to get to know each other," she says.

Chaille also says that all of Stratford's teachers are moving away from lecture-drill instruction and toward the kind of active, hands-on learning seen in gifted classes. "My goal is for you to walk into any classroom and not know whether you're in a G/T class," she says.

Still, in Horn's class many youngsters say they feel a lot of resentment from their non-G/T schoolmates. "They don't like us because we're so much smarter," Simon says. A visit to several classrooms shows that the G/T center indeed has far fewer minority students than the regular classes.

The county's overall statistics reflect the same underrepresentation of minority youngsters. African-Americans make up about 11 percent of the system's 145,000 pupils, but only 5 percent of the 25,000 students enrolled in gifted classes. Hispanic students constitute 10 percent of the overall population, but only 3 percent of the gifted class enrollment.

Nationwide, figures from a 1992 survey of school districts by the Department of Education's Office of Civil Rights paint a similar picture. [1] Based on statistical projections, whites were said to comprise about 68 percent of total school enrollment, but 77 percent of students enrolled in gifted-and-talented programs. Blacks accounted for 16 percent of the total enrollment, but only 9 percent of the gifted classes; Hispanics were 12 percent of total enrollment, but 6 percent of students in gifted classes.

No one has an authoritative count, however, of the total number of students around the country enrolled in gifted programs, which vary from

About Half the States Require Gifted Education Programs

Programs to identify gifted students and provide educational services for them are required in 24 states, while 18 states and the District of Columbia have no such mandates. Eight states only require the identification of gifted students. About two-thirds of the states provided funds to local school systems in 1996 for gifted students (list at left).

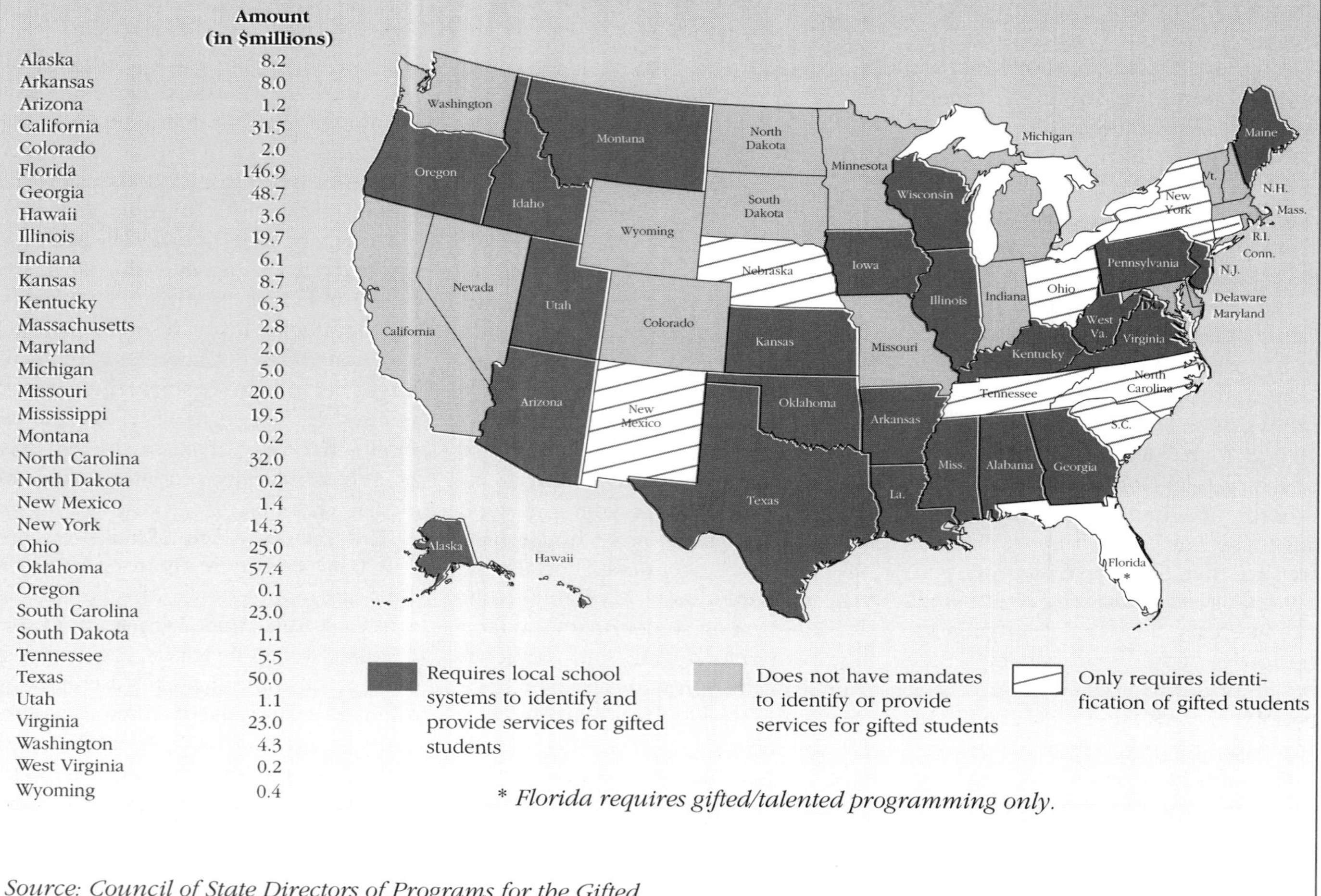

	Amount (in $millions)
Alaska	8.2
Arkansas	8.0
Arizona	1.2
California	31.5
Colorado	2.0
Florida	146.9
Georgia	48.7
Hawaii	3.6
Illinois	19.7
Indiana	6.1
Kansas	8.7
Kentucky	6.3
Massachusetts	2.8
Maryland	2.0
Michigan	5.0
Missouri	20.0
Mississippi	19.5
Montana	0.2
North Carolina	32.0
North Dakota	0.2
New Mexico	1.4
New York	14.3
Ohio	25.0
Oklahoma	57.4
Oregon	0.1
South Carolina	23.0
South Dakota	1.1
Tennessee	5.5
Texas	50.0
Utah	1.1
Virginia	23.0
Washington	4.3
West Virginia	0.2
Wyoming	0.4

* *Florida requires gifted/talented programming only.*

Source: Council of State Directors of Programs for the Gifted

completely separate schools or classes to "pull-out" classes that provide enrichment or acceleration for as little as an hour a week. Advanced-placement courses in high school are also usually counted as gifted classes.

The Department of Education has estimated that about 5 percent of U.S. students are enrolled in gifted classes of some sort, or about 3 million youngsters nationwide based on current enrollment. But the figure is only an estimate. The label "gifted" is itself controversial, and the definitions used by school systems or by researchers vary widely. (*See box, p. 271.*)

Whatever their number, gifted students are today not the country's highest educational priority. Special classes or programs for them are the exception, rather than the rule. "Most gifted kids spend all day in regular classrooms," says Peter Rosenstein, executive director of the National Association for Gifted Children.

Funding for gifted programs is also meager. The federal government spent just $5 million last year on the only educational program targeted specifically at gifted and talented students — less than .02 percent of the Department of Education's $31 billion budget. About two-thirds of the states provide specific appropriations for gifted education, but the most recent report from state directors for gifted and talented education shows an average of only $17 million alloted to gifted education among the states providing figures. (*See list, p. 268.*)

"For the most part, we're a pretty low priority," says Barbara Clark, a professor at California State University in Los Angeles and author of the college-level textbook for teachers *Growing Up Gifted*. "There always seem to be quite a few needs that people will take up and champion, but the gifted are very seldom among the groups that people champion. People seem to think that if they're really gifted, they'll get along whatever we do."

Critics, however, view gifted education as anything but politically powerless. "The advocates for the gifted are very well-organized, very effective," says Professor Robert Slavin, director of Johns Hopkins University's Center for Research on the Education of Students Placed at Risk. "That's partly because they are often the affluent and better-educated parents themselves and partly because it's so much more fun to go to a meeting and rave about the needs of your incredibly gifted child than to go to a meeting and say, 'My average child has needs too.'"

Still, gifted education appears to be on the defensive in much of the country. Gifted programs that serve only a fraction of the school population are an easy target for budget-cutters. Intelligence testing used to identify gifted students is under attack. [2] And many education groups favor mixed grouping of students in the same classroom rather than separating students by ability (*see p. 274*).

To gifted education advocates, these trends ignore the difficulties that bright students face. "Yes, the majority of gifted kids will get good grades, but we also know that there are large numbers of gifted kids who spend years in schools without learning anything," says Professor Carolyn Callahan of the University of Virginia, president of the National Association for Gifted Children.

Moreover, the advocates say, failing to help the brightest students reach their full potential wastes a valuable resource and threatens the nation's position in the global economy. "If our brightest are not competitive with the brightest in other countries, there are implications for global competition and for global cooperation as well," says Sandra Berger, director of the gifted education division at the Council for Exceptional Children, which also lobbies on behalf of students with disabilities.

As gifted education advocates seek more programming for the country's ablest students, here are some of the questions being debated:

Do gifted youngsters need separate classes or programs?

Highly intelligent youngsters need to have curricula and instruction adapted to their abilities and knowledge, gifted education advocates contend. Without advanced or enriched programs, they say, gifted students will fall short of their potential or, worse, lose interest in school altogether.

"These kids have distinct educational needs because their ability exceeds that of the normal range," says Michael Hall, gifted education specialist in the Montana Office of Public Instruction and current president of the Council of State Directors of Programs for the Gifted. "If we don't educate to that level, we're not living up to our responsibility to educate people to the best of their abilities."

The critics of gifted education insist that they also want the best quality education for the ablest students. But they argue that the best teaching techniques for gifted youngsters are also well-suited to the general student population.

"I have difficulty with most gifted education programs as being appropriate only for" the gifted, says Jeannie Oakes, a professor of education at the University of California-Los Angles (UCLA). "Much of what I see takes the form of activities from which all children could benefit a great deal."

But California State's Clark says gifted students do have special needs distinct from other youngsters: "a tremendous need for complexity," which requires additional materials, and "an accelerated rate of learning," which means they may be as much as four years ahead of the standard curriculum. "It requires a lot more material, it requires sophistication of experience, it requires advanced levels of work," Clark says.

Within a general classroom, some advocates of gifted education say, teachers are likely to treat exceptional students with indifference or even hostility. "A highly gifted child is not [the teacher's] most serious problem," Callahan says. "That kid can wait because that kid has already learned it." The fundamental problem, Callahan says, is that classes typically have students with a wide range of needs, including those who are learning-disabled, competing for the teacher's attention. "There's simply not enough time in the day to prepare for every child in that classroom."

"There is not the feeling that the gifted have needs," Clark says. "The egalitarian movement seems to think that these youngsters don't need more, that they already have more, and that's not fair."

In fact, critics sometimes do paint a picture of gifted students as enjoying educational advantages over other students thanks to well-to-do-families and well-off school districts. "Many children who are labeled as gifted have economic resources behind them — not all of them, but many of them," says Syracuse's Sapon-Shevin.

But she also says that the picture that gifted education advocates draw of the typical classroom sounds unfit for any kind of student. "I find it very hard to believe that a classroom that makes a gifted child feel miserable is a good classroom for everybody else," she says.

To these critics, gifted programs represent a political response to general school problems more than a carefully designed educational strategy. "Politically, gifted education programs often mollify a very powerful parent constituency who might otherwise be more activist about improving the quality of education generally," Oakes says.

Still, even the critics of gifted education see some arguments for giving special attention to exceptionally bright students. Oakes approves of accelerated programs for true "prodigies" — students who have demonstrated "quite unusual abilities" in specific subjects. Slavin also approves of accelerated curricula for exceptionally bright students but says that most gifted education consists instead of "enrichment" — adding activities such as experiments, oral history or extended writing projects specifically for the brightest students.

"My concern is that a lot of those activities, perhaps all, are activities that would be equally beneficial to anybody else," Slavin says. "And they tend to be very expensive. These are extra teachers, extra resources, to serve only a portion of the population."

Gifted education advocates continue to argue, however, that the brightest students have needs that cannot be met in the regular classroom with the ordinary curriculum. "They need a differentiation in the curriculum and instruction so that they can maximize their potential," says Kathleen Beattie, administrator of gifted and talented education in Fairfax County.

"I have no problem with differentiation if every child is being treated with the same quality of educational programming," responds Sapon-Shevin. "It's not that everybody has to have the same thing, but everybody has to be treated with the same care in quality of educational programming."

Do gifted education programs help or hurt opportunities for other students?

The advocates of gifted education believe that special programs for the brightest youngsters ultimately benefit all students by introducing new teaching techniques and generally raising the quality of classroom instruction. Some, but not all, of the critics acknowledge that gifted education has introduced techniques that are proving valuable in regular classrooms. But the critics strongly argue that gifted education hurts the broader student population by taking away resources — students, teachers and money — from the general classroom.

Council for Exceptional Children

Highly intelligent youngsters need to have curricula and instruction adapted to their abilities and knowledge, gifted education advocates contend.

"Gifted education has always been a laboratory for general education," says Berger at the Council for Exceptional Children. "What gets developed in the gifted laboratory has often been used by general ed as good education methods."

For example, Berger says, the teaching of critical thinking skills — emphasizing analysis and evaluation rather than rote learning — began in gifted education in the 1950s and in the past decade has been adopted in regular classrooms.

"When you talk about educating all children, gifted children are part of that population," says Clark at California State. "It doesn't necessarily take away from anybody else. In fact, the data indicate that if you're giving appropriate education to the gifted youngster, you have established a program that raises the quality of education for your whole school."

But Slavin scoffs at the idea that gifted education programs typically benefit the whole school population. "That's silly on its face," he says. "The notion that you provide something to a small group of kids and then somehow it's going to magically transfer to the rest of the school seems implausible to me."

In practice, Slavin says, gifted education techniques often do not "trickle down" to regular classrooms: "I've heard some teachers say, 'We don't do that. They do that in the gifted program.' "

The critics also contend that labeling some students as gifted inevitably reduces the educational experiences of other students. "It perpetuates a notion that we can judge ahead of time which children will benefit from enriching experiences," says UCLA's Oakes, "and then restricts the access to those experiences to the children that we predict can benefit."

Slavin also stresses that students who are not included in gifted classes often feel stigmatized, especially if the special classes grow to accommodate more students and become, in his view, a form of tracking. "You may have schools where one-third of the kids are in gifted classes," Slavin says. "When it's that many, it has an effect on other kids because the other two-

What's in a Name: 'Gifted' Label Adds to Emotional Debate

Advocates and experts on both sides of the debate dislike labeling very bright youngsters as "gifted," but the term lives on — helping to polarize the question of how best to educate the country's best students.

"I hate the word," says Susan Schneider, an advertising writer in New York City whose daughter is in a public school "gifted and talented" program. "The word itself says if my child is gifted, then your child must not be."

"The problem of being labeled as gifted is that once you're labeled, that's it, and once you're not labeled, that's it," says Mara Sapon-Shevin, a professor at Syracuse University and critic of gifted education.

For its part, the U.S. Department of Education officially disapproves of the label. "The term 'gifted' connotes a mature power rather than a developing ability and, therefore, is antithetic to recent research findings about children," Pat O'Connell Ross wrote in her 1993 report, "National Excellence." [1]

Nonetheless, the federal program that Ross directs is still entitled the Javits Program for Gifted and Talented Education. Schools around the country talk of "gifted and talented programs" — G/T for short — and pull out youngsters for special classes in the "gifted cabin" or "gifted trailer." And kids themselves learn the label at an early age.

The sixth-graders in the G/T center at Stratford Landing Elementary School in Alexandria, Va., casually used the jargon in talking with a recent visitor. Carolyn Amole, 12, said she had previously gone to a school with "G/T pullouts." "It wasn't nearly the same," she said, "as doing G/T all day."

Experts on both sides of the debate worry about the effect that labeling students as gifted can have on the youngsters themselves. James Delisle, a professor of education at Kent State University and co-director of the group Supporting the Emotional Needs of the Gifted, says that even in an age of "computer geeks" it is still far from fashionable to be smart in school.

"Look at the media stereotypes: Steve Urkel on television," Delisle says, referring to the brainy but awkward preadolescent on the situation comedy "Family Matters." "The role models that gifted kids see are often not what you want to be."

As for other students, critic Sapon-Shevin says the effects of in-school labeling can be demoralizing. "What does it do to a group of children," she asks, "to say there's another group of children who are smarter than they are and get to have experiences that they don't get to have?"

Despite the unease, the gifted label still sticks. The National Association for Gifted Children considered changing its name a few years ago, but decided not to. And Ross says that any other term would take on negative connotations after a few years anyway. "I think that if you were to change the name," she says, "that name, whatever it would be, would eventually evoke the same level of discomfort."

[1] U.S. Department of Education, "National Excellence: A Case for Developing America's Talent," October 1993.

---

thirds are in the lower tracks."

Most concretely, critics believe that gifted education is taking away money and other resources at a time of severe budget problems for many schools. But gifted education advocates scoff at the idea that the limited funding earmarked for gifted programs is draining resources away from general education purposes. "Given the minuscule funding for gifted programs," Berger says, "the competition is more on paper than real."

"There's probably a lot more money to spend on kids than we're spending," adds Callahan. "We ought to be asking 'Where is the money for instruction?' and not pitting kids against kids."

But the critics are less hopeful about the schools' funding problems. And they say that as long as resources are limited, many parents of abler students will be pressing for special classes and programs to benefit their children.

"Everybody wants to have a gifted child, and that's understandable," says Jacqueline Ancess, a senior research associate at the National Center for Restructuring Education, Schools and Teaching at Columbia University's Teachers College in New York. "But if we could ensure that all kids get a challenging education, then we would not have to worry about gifted programs."

Do gifted education programs discriminate against youngsters from minority or disadvantaged backgrounds?

Critics of gifted education forcefully complain that students in special academic programs are predominantly and disproportionately white and middle-class. Advocates of gifted education acknowledge the accusation but insist that they are working with teachers and administrators to increase the number of minority and disadvantaged youngsters.

"Generally speaking, 'gifted' in urban areas often is a kind of a code for upper-middle-class and white," says Ancess, who spent 23 years teaching and supervising gifted programs in New York City schools.

"When I came into this field, that was true," says Callahan, who began teaching in 1969. "In certain places, it probably still is. But no field has devoted itself more wholeheartedly to trying to deal with that" imbalance.

"Even though the numbers are not what we would like to see," Callahan continues, "we've certainly made many, many efforts to turn that around, to make the identification process fairer, to create more opportunities for kids and to make up for some of the disadvantages that they come to school with."

Gifted education advocates are eager to tell about their outreach efforts. In an initial conversation, Berger at the Council for Exceptional Children rattled off the names of contacts the council is working with in the African-American, Hispanic and Native American communities to identify gifted minority youngsters. A staff person at the National Association for Gifted Children urged a reporter to speak with Mary Frasier, a former president of the association and a professor at the University of Georgia at Athens.

Frasier, who is black, was instrumental in changing state board of education guidelines in Georgia on identifying youngsters for gifted programs (*see p. 280*). The new guidelines deemphasize the use of standardized intelligence tests, which many educators say are biased against minority groups. But Frasier says overreliance on IQ scores is not the only reason why minority youngsters are underrepresented in gifted programs.

"People don't expect that gifted children are going to be found in minority populations and poor populations as often as in majority population," she explains. "People tend not to look as aggressively for talent in minority and disadvantaged groups as they do in other populations."

Civil rights groups that work on education issues voice similar complaints. "To some extent, the assumption is that some children can learn and others can't," says Nona Smith, director of education for the National Association for the Advancement of Colored People in New York state.

In a recent study, a community-organizing group in New York City documented a common complaint among minority group parents — that they are not given the same kinds of information and encouragement about special academic programs that white parents receive. The Association of Community Organizations for Reform Now (ACORN) sent white and minority "testers" into several New York City schools, posing as parents of entering kindergarten students and asking for information about gifted education programs. The whites were typically given information and allowed to see classes or meet with an administrator, while the minority visitors were not.

"People tend not to look as aggressively for talent in minority and disadvantaged groups as they do in other populations."

— Mary Frasier, Former President, National Association for Gifted Children

"Institutional racism curtails the amount and quality of information made available to parents of color compared to what is provided for white parents," the study, "Secret Apartheid," said. [3]

The ACORN report prompted New York City Schools Chancellor Rudy Crew to initiate a review of the city's gifted-and-talented programs. In February, he announced plans to ensure that minority groups get better information about and access to the programs (*see p. 280*).

Some gifted education advocates point to other factors to explain the low numbers of minority or disadvantaged youngsters in special programs. Giftedness "doesn't happen in a vacuum," Clark says. "You have genetics and the environment working together in a nurturing way, and very few socioeconomically deprived areas are nurturing in that way."

Whatever the cause or causes, advocates and critics alike agree on the importance of looking for gifted students among minority and disadvantaged families. "We were very concerned when we looked around the classroom and saw that it didn't have the same mix as the local community," says Bernard Cotton, a former president of the Fairfax County Association for Gifted Children and a parent of two children enrolled in gifted programs.

"There ought to be this kind of education for every single child," Ancess says. "What happens is that good education tends to be rationed, and it tends to be rationed in a way that deprives the neediest kids in our nation." ■

BACKGROUND

Cultivating Talents

Societies from ancient Greece and China up to the present have looked for ways to identify their most intelligent youngsters, give them the best education and prepare them for leadership roles in government, science or other fields. But in the United States, the impulse to educate the best and brightest has competed with a strong egalitarian imperative to try to provide the best quality education not

Gifted Children's Special Emotional Needs

Gifted youngsters often receive too little attention in schools because teachers and administrators simply assume they can learn on their own, according to gifted education advocates. A similar misperception often results in slighting the emotional needs of very bright youngsters, some experts say.

"A lot of people think that because you're a smart kid, you can make it on your own," says James Delisle, a professor of education at Kent State University. "Any crisis that comes along, you can take care of it."

In fact, Delisle continues, gifted youngsters often have greater emotional needs than other children. "Gifted children may not have different specific emotional needs, but they seem to come to them at a much earlier age and with much greater intensity," Delisle says.

Very bright youngsters develop a sensitivity to others at an earlier age than other children, Delisle says. As a result, they may feel greater pain than other youngsters at times of personal tragedies, such as a divorce or death in the family. In addition, since their minds are "racing so fast," it may be difficult for them to communicate with adults — or for adults to communicate with them — about their feelings.

Delisle is the co-director of Supporting the Emotional Needs of the Gifted (SENG), a group that tries to help parents, educators and health-care professionals understand the special emotional problems of very bright youngsters. The organization was founded in 1982 through the efforts of a Dayton, Ohio, couple whose 16-year-old son committed suicide after dropping out of Michigan State University.

Through a mutual friend, the family contacted James Webb, then a psychologist at Wright State University in Dayton, looking for a group that could help them work through their grief. When Webb found out that no such organization existed, the family agreed to help start one.

Webb, who is now retired and living in Scottsdale, Ariz., says that the group has worked to counter misimpressions about gifted youngsters. "Psychologists knew very little about gifted children," he recalls. Oftentimes, he says, gifted youngsters were being misdiagnosed as suffering from psychological problems such as attention-deficit-hyperactivity disorder (ADHD) or obsessive-compulsive disorder.

In a similar vein, pediatricians often asked parents why they were putting so much pressure on their children. In fact, many gifted youngsters have an innate tendency toward perfectionism, Webb says. He recalls one mother who told him, "My child has one motto: 'Anything worth doing is worth doing to excess.' "

Webb says his group helped prompt the National Association of Gifted Children to establish a division of parent and community involvement to address emotional issues affecting gifted children. Webb, who co-authored a book, *Guiding the Gifted Child*, also helped organize a national conference for health-care professionals in 1987 on gifted children's emotional needs. "We have made some difference there," Webb says, "but there's a lot more to be done."

Webb and Delisle both say that gifted youngsters are susceptible to depression and thoughts of suicide. "Some 10-year-olds seem to be going through an existential crisis, asking themselves, 'Why am I here?' " Delisle says. "These kids seem to ask themselves questions like that at an early age."

Most research studies conclude that depression and suicidal tendencies are not abnormally high among gifted youngsters, Webb acknowledges.[1] But he says the studies may be flawed because they overlook underachieving gifted youngsters, whose failure to perform up to their abilities is itself a sign of an emotional problem.

In his 1996 book *The Gifted Kids' Survival Guide* (co-authored with Judy Galbraith), Delisle says giftedness may contribute to thoughts of suicide because bright youngsters have a heightened perception of failure and because their intellectual abilities are outpacing their emotional development and their ability to affect the world around them. He advises teenagers who find themselves thinking about suicide: "Try to remember that life isn't always fair, winning isn't always best and many questions don't have one 'right answer.' "

Schools can contribute to gifted youngsters' emotional problems, Delisle says, by failing to give them a challenging curriculum. "That has an intellectual effect, but also a social effect," he says, "because if you're being challenged, you'll feel more worthwhile."

As for parents of gifted students, Delisle suggests they should organize with each other to urge schools to give greater attention to their children's needs. He also warns that many parents do set too high standards for gifted children. He advises youngsters to talk frankly with parents about the need to be supportive without pushing too hard or demanding too much.

Above all, Delisle and Webb both say, people who deal with gifted children — and gifted children themselves — need to recognize that exceptional intelligence is no guarantee against emotional problems. Too many people, Delisle says, "still have the misperception that life [for gifted children] is a breeze. Sometimes it is, but sometimes it's not."

---

[1] Jean A. Baker, "Depression and Suicidal Ideation Among Academically Gifted Adolescents," *Gifted Child Quarterly*, fall 1995, p. 218.

for a select few, but for all youngsters.[4]

Public schools have moved between these two impulses since the spread of universal compulsory education in the late 19th and early 20th centuries. A few school systems — most notably, Cambridge, Mass. — established the equivalent of tracking systems, with different classes and curricula for students with different abilities. Most schools, however, coped with increasing enrollment by designing curricula aimed at the abilities of the average pupil — a policy explicitly recommended by an influential report in 1909 on how to reduce the high rate of school failure. [5]

The idea of specialized education for gifted students also clashed with prevailing views of precocious youngsters. Many educators viewed highly gifted students as deviants whose exceptional abilities were liabilities rather than assets. It was thought that giftedness as a youngster would not last into adulthood: "Early ripe, early rot," it was said. Many educators also believed that gifted youngsters developed social and emotional problems — the so-called "mad genius syndrome" — that continued into adulthood.

The shift in American attitudes toward giftedness began with the studies of psychologist Lewis Terman, a pioneer in intelligence testing. Beginning in the 1920s, Terman traced the life histories of exceptionally intelligent youngsters. He showed that their abilities continued to grow into adulthood and that they had no unusual incidence of social or emotional problems as adults.

Some gifted education advocates credit Terman's work with promoting development of school curricula aimed at gifted youngsters. But others say that Terman's emphasis on heredity rather than schooling as an explanation for exceptional intelligence discouraged specialized curricula. Terman's goal, according to Professors Daniel Resnick and Madeline Goodman at Carnegie-Mellon University, was "to place students of different abilities with their peers. Education became involved more with recognizing talents than with developing them." [6]

Federal Aid Initiatives

The first nationwide push to improve education for gifted students came in the 1950s in the early years of the Cold War. The Soviet Union's launching of the sputnik satellite in 1957 — ahead of the then hapless U.S. space effort — created a national panic about the quality of the country's schools. To alleviate the perceived shortage of scientists and engineers, Congress in 1958 approved the first ever direct federal aid to education: the National Defense and Education Act. While the law specifically provided funds for training in math, science and foreign languages, it was more generally seen as a spur to school systems around the country to devote greater attention to educating their brightest students. The nation's survival, it was thought, was at stake.

The Soviet challenge to U.S. technological superiority produced a revealing debate in America about the priorities to be given to educating gifted youngsters. Adm. Hyman G. Rickover called in 1958 for establishing 25 "elite" high schools to train students who were especially talented in mathematics and science. The suggestion drew a sharp retort from the then leading expert on gifted youngsters, A. Harry Passow of Columbia University's Teachers College. Passow had written an influential article four years earlier, "Are We Short-Changing the Gifted?" But he blasted Rickover's plan as a "perversion of democracy," noting that "Quality education for the academically talented can and must be provided within the framework of universal education." [7]

The goal of educating gifted students took a back seat in the 1960s to concerns about educational equity. The civil rights and anti-poverty movements focused attention on the poor quality of education being provided to youngsters in urban ghettos and centers of rural poverty. When Congress passed the first broad federal aid to education bill in 1965, its major provisions included aid for disadvantaged students: Head Start and the so-called Chapter 1 program providing special assistance to school systems in poverty areas. As Joseph Renzulli, director of the federally funded National Research Center on the Gifted and Talented at the University of Connecticut, writes, improving the schooling of "at-risk" students became "the driving force in American education" — and has been ever since. [8]

While the needs of gifted students took a back seat to this egalitarian movement, they were not completely ignored. In 1970, Congress included a provision in an omnibus aid to education bill calling for the commissioner of Education to conduct a study on the needs of gifted students. The 1971 report by Commissioner Sidney P. Marland Jr. depicted gifted students as a neglected minority of at least 2.5 million pupils, languishing in the country's public schools amid apathy or even hostility. Only a small percentage of the gifted students received any special services, Marland reported, and the lack of services resulted in psychological damage and permanent impairment of the abilities of the country's brightest youngsters. [9]

The report provided the impetus for the federal government's first direct assistance to gifted education. The Office of Gifted and Talented Education was established — tellingly housed under the Bureau of Education for the Handicapped. One Office of Education staff member in each of 10 regional offices was designated as an advocate for gifted students. And in 1974, Congress appropriated the first program of aid to states for gifted students — about $2.5 million for fiscal 1975.

A follow-up study commissioned by the Office of Education in 1976 found that services for gifted and talented had improved. The study, done by the Council for Exceptional Children in 1978, reported that more gifted students were receiving services than before and that most states had written policies for providing services and

Continued on p. 276

Chronology

Before 1950
Researchers study best way to educate gifted students.

1891
Cambridge, Mass., adopts "double-track plan" that allows abler students to complete six years' work in four.

1925
Psychologist Lewis Terman publishes first results of three-decade-long study of 1,500 gifted persons, indicating giftedness develops from childhood into adulthood without high incidence of emotional problems.

1950s ***The Soviet Union's Sputnik satellite creates national panic about U.S. education.***

1954
A. Harry Passow of Columbia University Teachers College publishes influential article, "Are We Short-Changing the Gifted?"

1958
Congress responds to Soviet Union's launch of Sputnik satellite in 1957 by enacting National Defense Education Act to provide federal aid for math, science and foreign language instruction.

1960s ***Federal aid to education is expanded, emphasizing programs to help the disadvantaged.***

1965
Congress passes Elementary and Secondary Education Act, providing funds for preschool program Head Start and for aid to low-income students (Title I).

1968
President Lyndon B. Johnson creates White House Task Force on the Gifted and Talented, which completes a 50-state survey but never publishes formal report.

1970s ***First federal office on gifted education is established.***

1971
U.S. Commissioner of Education Sidney P. Marland Jr. submits report to Congress decrying lack of programs for gifted students.

1974
Congress creates Office of the Gifted and Talented and establishes national clearinghouse on the gifted; funding, initially set at $2.5 million, rises to $6.2 million by end of decade.

1980s ***Reagan administration virtually eliminates federal aid for gifted education, but Congress later creates new program to aid research on gifted. Many states mandate services for gifted students, but educational-equity movement mounts attack on "tracking."***

1981
Under President Ronald Reagan, federal program for gifted education is consolidated with other programs, and overall education funding is cut more than 40 percent.

1988
Congress passes Javits Act, re-establishing federal Office of Gifted and Talented, creating research center on gifted education, and providing grants for research and demonstration projects.

1990s ***Gifted education movement struggles against budget cutbacks and educational-equity advocates as it continues to argue for more funding and better services.***

1990
National Governors' Association adopts report urging states to abolish "tracking" and "grouping" of students.

October 1993
U.S. Department of Education's "National Excellence" report says gifted students continue to receive inadequate attention in U.S. public schools.

November 1996
U.S. students score above average in science and slightly below average in math among 41 countries included in the Third International Math Science Study. Advocates of gifted education stress that U.S. pupils were underrepresented among top-scoring students.

Jan. 1, 1997
New regulations take effect in Georgia requiring local school systems to use multiple criteria to identify gifted students instead of relying solely on IQ test scores.

February 1997
President Clinton requests $7 million for Javits Act funding in budget for fiscal 1998.

Continued from p. 274

assigned at least one staff member to gifted and talented education. Total state and federal funding for gifted education had risen to $27.4 million. Despite the progress, the report concluded that gifted education still suffered from inadequate funding, a shortage of trained personnel and problems in identifying gifted students.

Federal funding for gifted education increased to $6.2 million under President Jimmy Carter, but a change of administration resulted in the virtual abolition of federal aid for gifted programs. President Ronald Reagan ordered the consolidation of most specific education programs, including gifted education, into a single block grant, with an overall 42 percent cut in funding. States continued to give more attention to gifted education through the 1980s — funding rose to $175 million in 1985 — but with essentially no assistance from the federal government.

National advocacy groups for gifted education continued to press their cause with Congress, however. By the mid-1980s, they had coalesced around the proposal that Congress eventually approved in 1988 as the Jacob K. Javits Gifted and Talent Student Education Act, named after the longtime New York Republican senator (*see p. 274*). At the same time, though, a major debate was breaking out among educators and policy-makers on the widespread practice in the schools of assigning students to different "tracks" based on their abilities, usually as indicated by IQ test scores. That debate once again put the issue of equity at the forefront of education policy discussions and served as a direct challenge to many of the tenets espoused by advocates for gifted education.

Tracking and Grouping

The rise of gifted education beginning in the 1950s was accompanied by increased use of tracking practices in American schools. As critic Oakes describes it, tracking began in the early 20th century as public high schools coped with the influx of students from immigrant families. [10] The practice gained strength from an influential report in 1959 by James Bryant Conant, the president of Harvard University, who advocated grouping of students subject-by-subject according to their abilities as the common sense response to the Sputnik challenge.

By the mid-1980s, according to Oakes, most schools used tracking even if they did not acknowledge the practice by name. Students were separated into groups by their perceived learning abilities — fast, average or slow — or by their own selected interests — vocational, general or academic. The practice of sorting students into homogeneous groups made eminent good sense to many educators as well as to the families of students sorted into the higher tracks. But Oakes and other critics contended the practice had no significant educational benefits for most students, including those in the high tracks. And they said it resulted in alienation and high dropout rates among students in the lower tracks.

Council on Exceptional Children

Critics of gifted education argue that the best teaching techniques for gifted youngsters are also well-suited to the general student population.

Today, Oakes says tracking is "in decline, but with lots of kicking and screaming." But gifted education advocates continue to push what they call "ability grouping" or sometimes simply "grouping." As Renzulli explains the distinction, tracking is the "usually permanent" assignment of students to classes that are taught at a certain level. Grouping is a "more flexible arrangement," he says, that takes into consideration such factors as motivation, specific skills and career aspirations "in addition to ability, and sometimes in place of ability." [11]

In these more flexible arrangements, students can supposedly be grouped into more advanced classes in some subjects and less advanced classes in others. But the tracking critics view the distinction between grouping and tracking as theoretical at best. "People play with language a lot," says Slavin at Johns Hopkins. "In practice, the flexibility that people talk about doesn't happen." Scheduling conflicts, in particular, make it difficult to move students in and out of different course paths, Slavin says.

The research on the effects of

Head of U.S. Gifted Program Sees 'Long Way to Go'

As head of the Javits Gifted and Talented Education Program in the U.S. Department of Education since its establishment in 1989, Pat O'Connell Ross presides over the federal government's only program targeted at gifted youngsters. She is the author of the 1993 report, "National Excellence: A Case for Developing America's Talent," which decried the "quiet crisis" in education for gifted students in American schools. Before assuming her current position, Ross served as director of Maine's program for gifted and talented students. The following are excerpts from an interview staff writer Kenneth Jost conducted with Ross at her office in Washington on March 7, 1997:

Q: Is there still a "quiet crisis" in education for gifted youngsters?

A: The Third International Math and Science Study published its first results on eighth-graders last fall. If you look at the top 10 percent of students across the 41 countries, only 5 percent of American students are in the top 10 percent. If it were evenly distributed, it would be 10 percent. Something like 40 percent of Singaporean children are in the top 10 percent; 30 percent of Japanese children are in the top 10 percent. That's hard data that we have. We have a long way to go.

Q: Should gifted students be taught in separate classes and programs?

A: I would rather not focus on the structural issue: where they should be taught. I would rather focus on what they should learn. In a lot of the programs, even if they are separated, the actual substance is not appreciably different. In other programs, it's substantially different. So the issue is not where they are, but what they're taught.

Q: Do gifted programs siphon away resources from the general student population?

A: It's pretty hilarious when you think about how much money goes to gifted programs vs. how much money is actually spent on education today: it's like two cents out of every hundred dollars. So I don't think in the aggregate it's taking away from what's available for other children.

The more troubling part of that is that there becomes a notion that the high level of learning — conceptual work, creative thinking, problem solving — and the more interesting curriculum and instruction are being reserved somehow for bright kids, and less bright kids get remediation and drill and practice. That's a dichotomy that I don't think is true in most school systems, yet it's the ancillary to the resource question. So that's why there is a large push for many of the strategies and curricula that have been developed for gifted students to be adapted to a larger population.

Q: Do gifted programs divert potential support for broader changes in public schools?

A: I don't know if it's true or not. The problem is that some of the reformers have used gifted programs as the straw dog [for] what's wrong. A lot of the reformers could have brought parents of the gifted into the conversation and helped them understand how the reforms that are being proposed would or would not impact on their children. They missed an opportunity to not create an enemy to their reforms. It's been a big mistake because the parents [of gifted students] have been vociferous in many places.

Q: Why are minority and disadvantaged youngsters underrepresented in gifted programs?

A: There's a link between poverty and school achievement and parental expectations. The more enrichment children have, the more they can learn; the more they can make connections with other things, the more they know. So if children are deprived at an early age of those kinds of experiences those are real discrepancies. But it doesn't mean that with the right kind of educational intervention children from minority backgrounds cannot achieve.

Q: Your report cites Alexis de Tocqueville's reference in the 19th century to America's "middling standards" for education. Is that still true?

A: As a culture, that's probably still true. We still have ambivalence about intellectuals. Intellectuals in this country are not something we revere. Kids who care passionately about their education are still an oddity.

grouping practices is voluminous, but the conclusions are disputed. Two professors at the University of Michigan — James A. Kulik and his wife Chen-Lin C. Kulik — have produced a series of studies since 1982 based on reviews of previous research on grouping. Their meta-analyses discern positive educational benefits, especially for higher-ability students, in some but not all grouping practices. Specifically, they find that simply sorting students of the same age into classes by ability — so-called "multilevel classes" — has no statistically significant effect. But other techniques — such as grouping across grades for specific subjects, grouping within the same class by ability or providing high-ability students with enriched or accelerated curricula — do have measurable benefits. American schools, they conclude, "would be harmed" by eliminating all grouping practices. [12]

Slavin draws similar findings from the various grouping studies. He says the research shows no evidence of benefits from assigning students to "self-contained classes" according to ability but some benefits from cross-grade or within-class grouping. [13] But in his conclusion, he emphasizes the limitations of grouping. Ability grouping, he says, is "maximally effective when done for only one or two subjects, with students remaining in heterogeneous classes most of the day."

Whatever the research shows, critics of tracking and grouping appear to have the advantage in policy debates. The National Governors' Association since 1990 has been urging states to "eliminate ability grouping and tracking," with no distinction between the two. In many school systems around the country, "heterogeneous grouping" and "cooperative learning" are viewed as the best educational practices. Students are assigned to classes with no special regard for differing abilities and, within the classroom, often work together rather than apart on course material and projects.

To gifted education advocates, these practices are a disservice to the needs of the ablest students. While they acknowledge some role for cooperative learning, they say it often amounts to asking the brightest students to tutor other youngsters, to the detriment of their own educational development. "You don't have anybody to challenge that bright person," Clark says.

As for ability grouping, Renzulli insists that as long as teachers adapt the curriculum and instructional techniques for the kinds of students in the classroom, the practice simply reflects common sense. "Go ask any teacher," he says. "They will tell you that when you shorten the range of abilities, you are able to do more for any and all individuals in the classroom."

'The Quiet Crisis'

Despite the developing controversy over grouping, gifted education advocates won an important victory in Washington in 1988 with congressional approval of a new educational assistance program specifically designated for gifted and talented students. The Javits program provided grants for demonstration projects and teacher training to help schools identify and meet the special educational needs of gifted children. Up to 30 percent of the funding was earmarked for the establishment of a research center on gifted children, now operated by a five-university consortium at the University of Connecticut in Storrs.

Funding for the Javits program, however, has been minimal. Initially set at $7.9 million for fiscal 1989, funding rose to nearly $10 million a year for the next five years, but has fallen as low as $3 million since 1994. For the current fiscal year, President Clinton is requesting $7 million, an increase of $2 million over the previous year.

Clinton's election cheered the gifted education community, which viewed the one-time Rhodes scholar, his Ivy League-educated wife and their precocious daughter as natural allies. "Having three gifted people in the White House has been a very definite plus for us," says Clark. And in the administration's first year, the Department of Education put out a new report on gifted students that served as a rallying cry for devoting more attention to educating the country's brightest youngsters.

The 1993 report by Pat O'Connell Ross, the administrator of the Javits program, began by complaining that the U.S. was "squandering one of its most precious resources — the gifts, talents and high interests of many of its students." [14] Most gifted students, Ross wrote, "spend their school days without attention paid to their special learning needs." Many have mastered up to half of the curriculum to be offered in basic subjects before they begin their school year. Regular assignments provide little challenge for gifted students, Ross wrote, and specialized services are available for only a few hours a week. The result, she concluded, is that America's brightest youngsters are less well-prepared than their counterparts in other countries.

In a foreword to the 1993 report, Education Secretary Richard W. Riley said it highlighted the "quiet crisis that continues in how we educate top students." Riley, who as governor of South Carolina opened two schools for gifted students, said the report showed that "youngsters with gifts and talents . . . are still not challenged to work to their full potential." "Our neglect of these students," he continued, "makes it impossible for Americans to compete in a global economy demanding their skills." [15]

Gifted education advocates were delighted. The report "represented a real turnaround for gifted education," says Rosenstein of the National Association for Gifted Children. At the same time, though, the Clinton administration proposed to shift the Javits program's focus away from gifted students. Instead, the administration called for using the money to apply research on gifted education to benefit all students. Gifted education advocates complained about diverting the focus of the federal government's only program for gifted children. The proposal was dropped.

Today, Ross says little has changed for gifted youngsters in the United States. America's brightest students still compare unfavorably with the best students in other countries. [16] *(See interview, p. 277.)* Gifted and talented programs are being eliminated in many places, sometimes because of opposition from educational reformers, sometimes for budget reasons. "We still have a long way to go," she concludes. ■

CURRENT SITUATION

Fighting for Resources

With school systems around the country facing budget problems, advocates of gifted education face a difficult time winning additional funds for programs specifically targeted for only the brightest youngsters. Many states report increased funding for gifted education programs in recent years, but the sums generally are modest. And a significant minority of states provide no targeted assistance to local school systems for gifted and talented education.

"Gifted education in most places is way underfunded at the state level," says Frank Rainey, Colorado's director of gifted and talented education and vice president of the nationwide council of state directors. "Considering that there are probably as many gifted kids as there are kids with disabilities, there's a huge difference."

Billions for Some Students, But Not the Gifted

The federal government provided billions of dollars for programs for disabled and low-income students in fiscal 1997 but only $7 million for gifted education.

	Fiscal 1997 appropriations	Estimated number of students affected
Title I (low-income students)	$7.2 billion	6 million
Special education (students with disabilities)	$4.0 billion	2.5 million
Gifted students	$7.0 million	3 million

Source: U.S. Department of Education, March 7, 1997

Still, Rainey is encouraged by the recent trends. He notes that about two-thirds of the states require local schools to identify gifted students and nearly half mandate special services for them. (*See map, p. 268.*) In its most recent report — covering fiscal 1996 — the council found that a majority of states had increased spending on gifted programs over the previous year.

Leaders of state advocacy groups express similarly mixed feelings about funding levels and educational services for gifted students. In California, local school systems that receive state aid are required to provide at least 200 minutes a week of special services for gifted students. And the state Board of Education increased funding for gifted programs for fiscal 1997 to $40 million — a one-third increase. "We feel relatively secure," says Margaret Gosfield, president of the California Association for the Gifted.

In Maryland, local school systems are encouraged but not required to provide special services to gifted students. "No one takes it very seriously," says Joan Roache, treasurer of the Maryland Coalition for Gifted and Talented Education. A state Board of Education task force issued a report in late 1994 recommending a service mandate. But mandates are unpopular among Maryland lawmakers, and the state's Democratic governor, Parris N. Glendening, is pushing instead a $500,000 incentive grant system to encourage local schools to do more for gifted students.

Thirteen states provide no targeted funds for gifted students, according to the state directors' 1996 report. Renzulli recalls that his state, Connecticut, eliminated funding for gifted programs several years ago because of the combined effects of a budget squeeze and anti-grouping sentiment. "Getting rid of gifted programs was a good way to tighten up on the budget," Renzulli says, "and it was nice to have a rationale."

Critics view the gifted education advocates' efforts to get more money for their programs as a disservice to other students. "When resources are focused on gifted programs to the exclusion of anybody who's not in them, those [other] kids wind up having inferior educational experiences," says Ancess in New York.

In addition, these critics view the fights as a diversion from the broader issue about what they view as inadequate spending for education. "What we have is schools fighting over meager resources," says Sapon-Shevin. "You pit people against each other in a hierarchy of the oppressed: If you have only $5, should you give it to the kid with Down's syndrome instead of to the child who is gifted?"

For his part, Rosenstein advises his state counterparts to look to other federal grant programs — such as the Title I grants for low-income students or the Eisenhower grants for math and science teaching — to help meet the needs of gifted students. "What people in gifted ed have to learn to do better is to access that funding for programs for gifted and talented students," Rosenstein says. "That funding is meant to serve the needs of all students, and that includes gifted and talented students."

In addition, gifted education advocates call for some changes that do not require additional money. They join other education critics, for example, in complaining about the "dumbing down" of textbooks. And they say that all teachers need better training in how best to educate gifted youngsters. The typical teacher-education course, they say, deals with gifted education only at the end in abbreviated fashion.

"The key issue is providing gifted education training to all teachers," says Roache, "because every teacher has gifted kids in her classroom."

'Multiple Criteria'

Gifted education advocates and administrators recognize that the historic underrepresentation of poor and minority students is a major political liability as well as an educational challenge. They are concentrating on efforts to remedy the problem but face a recurrent criticism in doing so that they may be lowering the standards for gifted and talented programs.

The efforts are mainly focused on changing the criteria for entry into gifted classes. Historically, teachers and administrators relied almost exclusively on IQ test scores. "There was a certain tidiness in saying, '130, you're in; 129, you're out,' " explains Renzulli.

Intelligence tests, however, are now being widely criticized not only for a claimed bias against minorities but also for creating a misleadingly restrictive definition of intelligence. Advocates of so-called multiple intelligences — such as Robert Sternberg at Yale University and Howard Gardner at Harvard — argue that traditional IQ tests take account only of cognitive ability and ignore other kinds of intelligence, such as creativity, task commitment and motivation. [17]

Many gifted education advocates, administrators and teachers accept these criticisms as proving the need to look at "multiple criteria" in identifying students for gifted programs. Besides traditional IQ or achievement tests, they say that students also should be evaluated on the basis of tests that measure creativity and motivation or on the basis of work or performances by the student.

The new identification techniques are controversial among some people within the gifted education community and, even more so, among teachers, administrators and parents accustomed to using IQ tests alone. "For folks that are used to looking at percentiles, they just don't like many of those things," says Evelyn Hiatt, director of the Division of Advanced Academic Studies at the Texas Education Agency.

Texas and Georgia are among the states that have recently adopted guidelines calling on local school systems to use multiple criteria in identifying students for gifted programs. Sally Krisel, coordinator of gifted education for the Georgia Board of Education, says the change, which went into effect at the start of the year, was viewed by some parents and teachers as "watering down" the standards for admission. "There was certainly a concern of some folks that the multiple criteria would be a lowered standard," she says.

The Atlanta Journal reflected that concern in an editorial that gave a qualified endorsement to the change. "The new, broader criteria ought not swing the doors open so wide that the notion of 'giftedness' loses its meaning," the editorial stated. It went on to warn against any "politically correct effort to 'include' sufficient numbers of all ethnic groups." [18]

Frasier, the University of Georgia professor who helped push through the change, rejects the insinuation that the change amounts to lower standards for gifted programs. "The perception is that it is watering down the criteria," Frasier says. "But when you think about it, having to meet multiple criteria is more difficult."

In New York City, Crew recently began urging individual school districts to adopt a wider range of criteria. In announcing the new policy, Crew hinted that he may use a new law that gives him added powers over the traditionally decentralized school system to press school districts to adopt the change. [19]

Gifted education advocates make clear that one major purpose of adopting multiple criteria is to remedy the underrepresentation of minority students in gifted programs. "Whenever a state relies on a test score to make a final decision, we tend to have less participation of minority students," Frasier says.

But Hiatt says there are other reasons why minority or disadvantaged youngsters are underrepresented. "Parents in low-income areas often don't ask the question, 'Is my kid advanced?' " Hiatt explains. "We do get that question from middle-class parents." In addition, Hiatt notes that language-based testing disadvantages students with limited proficiency in English — like many Hispanic youngsters in Texas and elsewhere in the Southwest.

Frasier says 35-40 states have "some information about using multiple criteria," but she also says local school systems are moving more slowly to adopt the change. "We still find at the local level that [the use of] cutoff scores for acceptance tends to be more true than we'd like it to be," she says. In Georgia, the legislature approved the change in 1994, but the Board of Education delayed implementation until this year to meet some of the criticisms.

For the liberal critics of gifted edu-

Continued on p. 282

At Issue:

Should public schools devote more resources to special programs for gifted students?

James J. Gallagher
William Rand Kenan Jr. Professor of Education, University of North Carolina-Chapel Hill

WRITTEN FOR *THE CQ RESEARCHER,* MARCH 1997.

yes

One of the most cherished principles of American education is equality of opportunity. All students should have the right to exercise their talents to their fullest potential. We have honored that principle through our vigorous financial support for children with disabilities and for children from low-income families who need special help to reach their potential. Should we ignore this principle when it comes to children who learn faster than others, remember more, solve problems more efficiently? All students should have the right to develop and exercise all of their talents fully.

We have accepted that principle in higher education. We support entire schools for gifted students like the UCLA Medical School or the University of Virginia Law School or graduate schools everywhere. We do that because we recognize that we might need a good lawyer or surgeon someday and that we want the very best.

But in many public schools around the country, we are allowing our eight-cylinder students to perform on four cylinders. They "learn" in class what they have already mastered, sometimes years earlier. We teach them that learning is "easy" and that you don't have to work hard on problems. We are told that special programs enhancing the talents of bright students are unfair because there are ethnic disproportions in the membership of such programs. Even though the federal Javits Act and major professional organizations are working to include more diverse and economically disadvantaged students in gifted programs.

Should we shut down these special programs of excellence until our society is truly equal? That is a recipe for educational mediocrity and decay. For many years programs for gifted students have upheld the banner of high standards and encouraged outstanding performance in our schools. What we have learned from our programs for gifted students has been put to use with good effect in the general education programs. We support the educational philosophy of Excellence for All, but that does not mean identical education for all. One size does *not* fit all.

The cost of providing a differentiated program for these bright students is much less than the cost of not providing it. What is the cost of the medical discovery never made or the symphony never written?

Our true opponents are not those who disagree; rather, they are ignorance, disease, war, poverty and discrimination, and it will take all of our intellectual resources to defeat these foes. We don't need to hold back those students who might accomplish what this generation has been unable to do.

Mara Sapon-Shevin
Professor of education, Syracuse University

WRITTEN FOR *THE CQ RESEARCHER,* MARCH 1997.

no

If the question is really, "Should schools be devoting more resources to all students, making sure that every student has access to qualified teachers, adequate resources, excellent curricula and effective pedagogy?" then the answer would be a resounding "yes." But if the question is, "Given our current insufficient resources, our lack of commitment to public education and the reality that many children in our nation do not receive even a minimally adequate education, should education of the gifted be our first priority?" then the answer must be "no."

Students identified as "gifted" have legitimate educational needs that should be met. But every child has the potential to learn and perform better given appropriate support and teaching; we have an entire nation of "underachieving gifted" students. All students deserve to be in classrooms in which their educational and social-emotional needs are met. All students are entitled to be part of learning communities that are safe, caring and supportive.

How will providing special services to students identified as "gifted" propel us to systematic, structural school reform? Won't concentrating our energies on "gifted" students actually pull our attention *away* from more general school reform by placating the vocal, vehement, often privileged parents of students identified as "gifted?" Is our commitment to quality public education, or will we create privatized education within the public schools by funding segregated gifted programs and services?

The question at hand is not differentiation; the same bland, one-size-fits-all, lock-step, teacher-talk curriculum is not appropriate for "gifted children" or for anyone else. But let's make sure that curriculum differentiation is providing high-quality opportunities and options for all students.

Most of what is provided for students identified as "gifted" is simply good teaching: participatory, exploratory, child-centered, constructivist curricula and pedagogy provided by enthusiastic teachers in well-resourced classrooms. Where is the research showing that only students identified as "gifted" profit from mentorships in the community, chances to engage in real science with working scientists, opportunities to participate in theater and music productions or be coached by community leaders?

How dare we as a nation engage in educational triage — deciding, a priori, which of our students "count" and which of them don't? Let's act as if we really believed in high-quality, democratic, public schooling. Let's guarantee first-class educational nutrition for all these students, not peanut butter and Kool-Aid to the majority and haute cuisine to a precious few.

Continued from p. 280

cation, the moves to include more minority and disadvantaged youngsters are welcome but not enough to answer all their concerns. "In our country, education is still a sorting game," Ancess says. "You have to get through certain hurdles to enable you to get into the right college so that you have the right connection to get into the right graduate school or the right job. What I have a problem with is when we don't make sure that all kids, especially kids who are poor or kids of color, have the same opportunity to take that route." ■

OUTLOOK

Equity and Excellence

When he addressed state gifted association leaders in Washington recently, Gerald Tirozzi, the assistant secretary of Education for elementary and secondary education, gave a lengthy recitation of President Clinton's initiatives to improve the nation's schools. But he made only glancing references to gifted youngsters.

The audience at the March 10 meeting was less than pleased. "We consider our kids to be at-risk," one of the state advocates said in the question-and-answer session. Tirozzi tried to deflect the point: "We're saying all children can learn to high levels." But the effort at reassurance failed. "When all you talk about is raising the bar," another of the state advocates said, "you're not talking about our kids."

The exchange encapsulates the issue that has plagued the advocates of gifted education since the birth of the movement: the perceived conflict between excellence and equity. Critics see gifted education advocates as striving for excellence among the few exceptionally bright students at the expense of the broader student population. But gifted education advocates insist that the best students deserve nothing less than any other youngsters: a school system that provides the opportunity to achieve their full potential.

At times, the debate can be harsh. Clark at Cal State has nothing but scorn for the critics of gifted education, such as UCLA's Oakes. "She's ruining it for gifted kids," Clark says. "There are these people who have other agendas and don't realize what they're doing to kids who are very bright."

Oakes responds that she has all children's interests at heart. "I am very much in favor of [children] learning as much as they can, as quickly as they can, with all the assistance we can give them," she says. "I'm very concerned about all children's learning, and I am no less interested in children who are identified as gifted."

But Oakes also pointedly criticizes the motivations of many of the parents in the gifted education movement. She says that even though new theories about human intelligence are undermining some of the arguments for classifying students as "gifted," the advocates of gifted education are still pushing for special classes and programs. "To the extent that the gifted education movement is a political movement and an effort to garner special status and some additional resources for a small group of children, that may very well continue," she says.

Gifted education advocates have been working in recent years to counteract the political liability of being viewed as elitist — most notably, through the efforts to identify and serve more minority and disadvantaged youngsters. "That's the No. 1 issue they've had to deal with," critic Slavin says. But their efforts to find more minority kids are hampered by the living conditions that many of those youngsters face before arriving at school.

"We work at a considerable disadvantage when we work with kids who have not been provided the kind of health care, the kind of stimulation, the kind of school readiness that kids from other environments get," the University of Virginia's Callahan says.

The educational reformers also say they are confronting a problem larger than the narrow debate over gifted education: the difficulty of providing adequate and equitable funding for the country's schools despite the public's professed support for raising educational standards. Sapon-Shevin at Syracuse says the gifted education movement is only part of a growing trend that threatens to relegate many of the country's youngsters to an inferior education.

"I do not see a commitment to public education," Sapon-Shevin says. "I see increased privatization of schools. I see a day when public schools will be the exclusive domain of poor kids, and everybody else will be in voucher schools or charter schools or private schools."

Gifted education advocates insist that their conflicts with education reformers are not inevitable. "We have tried so hard to reach out to equity that we have done it at the expense of excellence, as though they were contradictory, which they are not," says James Webb, a retired family psychologist in Scottsdale, Ariz., and founder of the organization Supporting the Emotional Needs of the Gifted. (*See story, p. 271.*)

"A lot of the reformers could have brought parents of the gifted into the conversation," says Ross at the Department of Education, "and helped them understand how the reforms that were being proposed could have impact on their children. They missed an opportunity to not create an enemy."

As these policy debates swirl, teachers and students around the country are going about the daily business of education. In gifted programs, teachers have special rewards in guiding exceptionally bright youngsters, but they also face special challenges. "The children are highly motivated," says Horn, the sixth-grade teacher at Stratford Landing Elementary. "They think much more abstractly. They have a lot of energy. You have to challenge them."

To Horn, those youngsters' abilities call for special attention. "It's a need they have," she says, "and if we weren't meeting those [needs] well, we'd be doing a disservice to them." But Horn thinks her efforts do not detract from the education that the other students at Stratford Landing are getting. In fact, despite the gloom voiced by many of the experts and advocates, Horn is hopeful about the quality of education in the U.S. "Education is getting better for everyone," she says. "I see education improving across the board." ■

FOR MORE INFORMATION

Center for Research on the Education of Students Placed at Risk, Johns Hopkins University, Baltimore, Md. 21218; (410) 516-8809. Robert Slavin, the center's director, is one of the major critics of the gifted education movement.

Council for Exceptional Children, 1920 Association Dr., Reston, Va. 22091; (703) 620-3660. The council's gifted education division is an information clearinghouse and advocacy group for gifted students.

National Association for Gifted Children, 1707 L St. N.W., Suite 505, Washington, D.C. 20036; (202) 785-4268. The association represents about 7,500 parents, educators and administrators in conducting research and advocacy on behalf of gifted children. The executive director is Peter Rosenstein.

National Research Center on the Gifted and Talented, University of Connecticut, Storrs, Conn. 06269-0067; (860) 486-5279. The federally funded research center is operated by a consortium of five universities: the Universities of Connecticut and Virginia; City University of New York's Hunter College; and Stanford and Yale Universities. The director is Joseph Renzulli.

Supporting the Emotional Needs of the Gifted, 404 White Hall, Kent State University, Kent, Ohio 44242; (330) 672-4450. The organization was founded in 1982 to address the emotional needs of gifted children.

Notes

[1] U.S. Department of Education, Office of Civil Rights, "1992 Elementary and Secondary School Civil Rights Compliance Report: Reported and Projected Enrollment Data for the Nation," March 1994.

[2] For background, see "Intelligence Testing," *The CQ Researcher*, July 30, 1993, pp. 649-672.

[3] New York ACORN Schools Office, "Secret Apartheid: A Report on Racial Discrimination Against Black and Latino Parents and Children in the New York City Public Schools," April 15, 1996. See *The New York Times*, April 16, 1996, p. B4.

[4] For background, see Robert F. DeHaan and Robert J. Havighurst, *Educating Gifted Children* (1961, rev. ed.); Abraham J. Tannenbaum, "History of Giftedness and 'Gifted Education' in World Perspective," in Kurt A. Heller et al. [eds.], *International Handbook of Research and Development of Giftedness and Talent* (1993), pp. 12-23.

[5] The study by former school Superintendent Leonard Ayres was supported by the Russell Sage Foundation.

[6] Daniel P. Resnick and Madeline Goodman, "American Culture and the Gifted," in U.S. Department of Education, *National Excellence: A Case for Developing America's Talent: An Anthology of Readings* (1994), pp. 109-121.

[7] Cited in Passow's obituary, *The New York Times*, March 29, 1996, p. D19.

[8] Joseph S. Renzulli and Sally M. Reis, "The Reform Movement and the Quiet Crisis in Gifted Education," in *Gifted Child Quarterly*, winter 1991, p. 28. Reis, Renzulli's wife, is also a professor of education at the University of Connecticut.

[9] U.S. Commissioner of Education, *Education of the Gifted and Talented*, October 1971. See Barbara Clark, *Growing Up Gifted: Developing the Potential of Children at Home and at School* (1992, 4th ed.), pp. 159-162.

[10] See Jeannie Oakes, *Keeping Track: How Schools Structure Inequality* (1985).

[11] Renzulli and Reis, *op. cit.*, p. 31.

[12] See James A. Kulik and Chen-Lin C. Kulik, "Meta-analytic Findings on Grouping Programs," *Gifted Child Quarterly*, spring 1992, pp. 73-77.

[13] See Robert E. Slavin, "Ability Grouping and Student Achievement in Elementary Schools: A Best-Evidence Synthesis," *Review of Educational Research*, fall 1987, pp. 293-336.

[14] U.S. Department of Education, "National Excellence: A Case for Developing America's Talent," October 1993.

[15] See *Newsweek*, Nov. 15, 1993, p. 67.

[16] See Rene Sanchez, "Math-Science Study Faults U.S. Teaching, Curricula," *The Washington Post*, Nov. 21, 1996, p. A1, and Peter Applebome, "Americans Straddle the Average Mark in Math and Science," *The New York Times*, Nov. 21, 1996, p. B14..

[17] See Howard Gardner, *Frames of Mind: The Theory of Multiple Intelligences* (1983) and Robert J. Sternberg, *Beyond IQ: A Triarchic Theory of Human Intelligence* (1985).

[18] *The Atlanta Journal*, Aug. 27, 1996, p. 8A.

[19] See *The New York Times*, Feb. 28, 1997, p. A1.

Bibliography

Selected Sources Used

Books

Clark, Barbara, *Growing Up Gifted: Developing the Potential of Children at Home and at School* [4th ed.], Macmillan, 1992.

This college-level textbook includes chapters on such issues as identifying gifted youngsters, developing curricula for gifted students in schools and promoting their intellectual and emotional development at home. Clark, a professor at California State University in Los Angeles, ends each chapter with her personal answers to "questions often asked." The book also includes a 36-page listing of references. A new edition was to be published this month.

Galbraith, Judy, and Jim Delisle, *The Gifted Kids' Survival Guide: A Teen Handbook*, Free Spirit Publishing, 1996.

The book provides a practical guide for gifted teenagers in dealing with educational, social and emotional issues. A three-page list of references is included. Galbraith is a guidance counselor in Minneapolis; Delisle is a professor of education at Kent State University.

Oakes, Jeannie, *Keeping Track: How Schools Structure Inequality*, Yale University Press, 1985.

Oakes, a professor of education at UCLA, writes a strongly argued critique of the practice of "tracking" students in elementary and secondary schools. The book includes 12 pages of source notes.

Sapon-Shevin, Mara, *Playing Favorites: Gifted Education and the Disruption of Community*, State University of New York Press, 1994.

Sapon-Shevin, a professor of education at Syracuse University, writes an impassioned critique of gifted education derived in part from a case study of practices in one community in North Dakota. The book includes an eight-page listing of references.

Webb, James T., *Guiding the Gifted Child: A Practical Source for Parents and Teachers*, Ohio Psychology Publishing, 1982.

Webb, a retired professor of psychology from Wright State University in Dayton, Ohio, provides practical advice for parents and teachers on guiding gifted children. Webb founded the organization Supporting the Emotional Needs of the Gifted, now based at Kent State University in Kent, Ohio.

Articles

***Journal for the Education of the Gifted*, Vol. 19, No. 2, winter 1996.**

This issue includes articles by seven leading experts broadly debating from a variety of perspectives the role of gifted education in U.S. schools.

Kulik, James A., and Chen-Lin C. Kulik, "Meta-analytic Findings on Grouping Programs," *Gifted Child Quarterly*, spring 1992, pp. 73-77.

The Kuliks — professors at the University of Michigan — argue that ability grouping has clear positive effects on students if accompanied by substantial adjustments in curriculum.

Slavin, Robert E., "Ability Grouping and Student Achievement in Elementary Schools: A Best-Evidence Synthesis," *Review of Educational Research*, fall 1987, pp. 293-336.

Slavin, a professor at Johns Hopkins University, says ability grouping has positive effects only when accompanied by curricular changes not adopted by most schools using the practice.

Reports and Studies

Council of State Directors of Programs for the Gifted, *The 1996 State of the States Gifted and Talented Education Report*, 1996.

The 105-page report includes state-by-state information on programs for gifted and talented students, including service mandates and funding.

U.S. Commissioner of Education, *Education of the Gifted and Talented*, October 1971.

The 74-page report to Congress by then Commissioner of Education Sidney P. Marland Jr. concluded that providing educational services for gifted and talented youngsters was "a very low priority" at all levels of government. The report was published by the Senate Education and Labor Committee in March 1972.

U.S. Department of Education, *National Excellence: A Case for Developing America's Talent*, October 1993.

The 33-page report by Pat O'Connell Ross, director of the Javits gifted and talented education program, concludes that most gifted youngsters spend their school days "without special attention to their special learning needs." The report includes a two-page listing of references.

U.S. Department of Education, *National Excellence: A Case for Developing America's Talent: An Anthology of Readings*, 1994.

The anthology, edited by Javits program Director Pat O'Connell Ross, includes five articles on various aspects of gifted education, including state issues and international comparisons.

The Next Step

Additional information from UMI's Newspaper & Periodical Abstracts™ database

Curriculum and Instruction

Asin, Stefanie, "HISD to decide enrollment issue at River Oaks school," *Houston Chronicle*, March 20, 1996, p. A1.

HISD trustees were to decide March 21, 1996, if River Oaks Elementary School in Texas, the only all-Vanguard — or gifted school — in the district, will open its doors for neighborhood children to attend regular classes there. Parents fear opening the school would dilute its unique ethnic mix.

Bower, Carolyn, "Gifted children pose problem for parents, schools," *St. Louis Post-Dispatch*, Dec. 8, 1995, p. C1.

The issue of how much to spend on gifted education has become a thorny one as school districts struggle to find enough money to cover the many educational programs.

Meador, Karen, "Meeting the needs of young gifted students," *Childhood Education*, fall 1996, pp. 6-9.

Meador focuses on the organization of early childhood classrooms that strive to be individually appropriate for all children. She writes from her own perspective as a mother of two gifted children, a gifted education specialist and a regular classroom teacher.

Mosteller, Frederick, Richard J. Light and Jason Sachs, "A Sustained inquiry in education: Lessons from skill grouping and class size," *Harvard Educational Review*, winter 1996, pp. 797-842.

The authors examine the nature of the empirical evidence that can inform school leaders' key decisions.

Naylor, Janet, "Gifted students may share school space with dropouts," *Detroit News*, Aug. 14, 1996, p. D1.

About 280 students from schools in Macomb County, Mich., who were selected for the nationally recognized Macomb Mathematics and Science Technical Center, may attend classes in the same facility as teens who could not handle the work in a regular high school, under a plan before the Warren Consolidated school board.

Osin, Luis, and Alan A. Lesgold, "A proposal for the reengineering of the educational system," *Review of Educational Research*, winter 1996, pp. 621-656.

Osin and Lesgold propose a reengineering of the educational system that focuses on mastery and on more substantial learning activities and eliminates the constraints on learning that arise from the current insistence on grouping children by age. They argue that modern information systems allow richer educational activities, research-based methods and multiage schooling to proceed efficiently and effectively.

Shields, Carolyn M., "To group or not to group academically talented or gifted students?" *Educational Administration Quarterly*, April 1996, pp. 295-323.

Shields identifies the administrative implications of the findings from the first year of a longitudinal study that compares the performance and attitudes of academically talented or gifted fifth-grade students in homogeneous classes with gifted students in heterogeneous classes.

Winner, Ellen, "The miseducation of our gifted children," *Education Week*, Oct. 16, 1996, pp. 35 & 44.

Research indicates that gifted children are usually unengaged and bored in school and are highly critical of their teachers. Standards need to be raised for all children, although profoundly gifted children will still be out of sync with what schools can offer. "Advanced" classes should be created, and admission to the classes should be based not on IQ, but on what the child has actually achieved.

Growing Up Gifted

Coles, Joanna, "Eleven into 147 will go," *Guardian*, Dec. 21, 1996, p. 3.

Coles describes life in the family of Ruth Davies, a 7-year-old girl with an IQ of 147 who lives in Belper, England. Davies learned how to use a word processor at age 2, wrote her first book at 4 and currently attends special classes at Warwick University.

Corrigan, Patricia, "Boy wonder." *St. Louis Post-Dispatch*, April 19, 1996, p. C1.

Nick Gass, a whiz kid at the age of 6, began reading at 3 and likes to keep journals. His parents, Dan and Kim Gass of Grover, Mo., are concerned about educating him and keeping him from being bored in school.

Lindstrom, Pia, "Itzhak Perlman Discusses Child Prodigies and Handicap Access," *The New York Times*, Dec. 1, 1996, Sec LI, p. 1.

Violinist Itzhak Perlman is interviewed about the difficulties that child prodigies encounter.

Loupe, Jo Ann, "Different talents keep brothers busy," *Times-Picayune*, May 2, 1996, Sec. OTR, p. 1.

The different styles of Mike and Ryan Harvey of Luling La., two of Hahnville High School's most talented students, complement each other, both in life and in music. Mike is the artist; whereas, Ryan is a technology guru. Their relationship is explored.

Nieves, Evelyn, "Being a Genius Can Be Tough, and Costly," *The New York Times*, Nov. 29, 1996, p. B1.

Nieves discusses the efforts of 7-year-old Jonathan Estrada's family to ensure that their gifted son receives a quality education. Nieves says that Jonathan's dad works 12 hours a day, seven days a week, to pay his son's $6,400 tuition at the Long Island School for the Gifted.

Pogrebin, Robin, "Portrait of a gifted child," ***The New York Times*****, Feb. 25, 1996, Sec. CY, p. 1.**

The difficulties that 8-year-old Sheria Mattis faces as a gifted child in the Bedford-Stuyvesant neighborhood of Brooklyn, N.Y., are examined. At Public School 308, Sheria's intellect can be isolating, cloaking her in a sense of otherness, inviting occasional ridicule. Her mother, Velma Stoner, says she wants Sheria to respect and feel comfortable in the community she comes from, but also to rise above it. She says these dual loyalties necessitate something of a double life.

Strauss, Robert, "Top of the heap," ***Los Angeles Times*****, June 10, 1996, p. E1.**

The phenomenon of child prodigies is examined. Critics decry pushy parents, but some people believe certain gifted children fare well when allowed to develop their talents early.

Identifying Gifted Students

Feldhusen, John F., "How to identify and develop special talents," ***Educational Leadership*****, February 1996, pp. 66-69.**

Talent-oriented education builds a strong sense of self-efficacy, effective goal-setting and a personal commitment that can enhance students' specific achievements. Six strategies for helping teachers to develop the talents of their gifted students are discussed.

"How reliable are IQ tests?, ***Parents*****, September 1996, p. 60.**

Many educators question the validity and fairness of IQ tests, which are used to identify gifted individuals.

"Identify, nurture gifts in each child," ***Atlanta Constitution*****, Aug. 29, 1996, p. A22.**

An editorial notes the use of doodling prowess in Atlanta,Ga., schools as a measure of whether a child is "gifted" or not, saying that the goal of schools should not be to identify which child is gifted, but to identify the gifts in each child.

"The right kind of discrimination," ***Atlanta Journal*****, Aug. 27, 1996, p. A8.**

An editorial notes a change to include academic achievement, creativity and motivation along with IQ scores in considering students for Georgia's gifted program, expressing the hope that officials will avoid a politically correct effort to "include" sufficient numbers of all ethnic groups.

Towns, Gail H., "New giftedness criteria coming into play early," ***Atlanta Constitution*****, Oct. 3, 1996, Sec. XJD, p. 3.**

A 20-year-old policy that determines who gets into gifted classes in Atlanta, Ga., schools is on its way out, and local officials aren't wasting any time making up for lost students or lost time. Atlanta educators are not waiting until Jan. 1, 1997, to implement the new criteria, and expect the number of children in gifted classes to go from about 1,700 students to nearly 2,900.

"Watch 'gifted' definition to maintain real meaning," ***Atlanta Journal*****, Jan. 2, 1997, p. A8.**

An editorial urges the state of Georgia to conduct a thorough review of the new methods used by school districts to determine which students qualify for gifted education, to make sure the door hasn't been opened too wide. If there are excesses, they should be reined in.

White, Betsy, "Doodling assignment gives intelligence insight," ***Atlanta Journal Constitution*****, Aug. 25, 1996, p. D2.**

The Torrance Tests of Creative Thinking, which asks test takers to prove their intellectual firepower by doodling, will be given by most metro Atlanta, Ga., public schools as they switch to a new method of determining who gets into special classes for the gifted. A state mandate requires schools to measure creativity, achievement and motivation instead of just IQ.

Minority Groups

"Fair Access to Public Schools," ***The New York Times*****, May 18, 1996, p. A18.**

An editorial discusses a study carried out in New York City that reveals dramatic differences in how black or Hispanic parents are treated in contrast with whites when they seek information about public schools and their programs for gifted students.

Lloyd, Jean, "Sacrificing kids on the alter of equality," ***The Wall Street Journal*****, Aug. 7, 1996, p. A12.**

Lloyd criticizes teachers and school administrators who don't support a gifted program for minority children from economically disadvantaged families at the Harlem, N.Y., school where she works. Lloyd argues that these gifted youngsters are unable to perform to their full potential.

Nabonne, Rhonda, "Orleans gifted classes under federal scrutiny," ***Times-Picayune*****, March 2, 1996, p. A1.**

Three Louisiana school systems are being probed by the Office of Civil Rights to find out why it appears that African-Americans and other minorities are not getting equal access to special programs for gifted and talented students.

Pogrebin, Robin, "Gifted programs: Necessary elitism?" ***The New York Times*****, Feb. 25, 1996, Sec. CY, p. 10.**

The controversy over schools for gifted and talented children in New York City is examined. Supporters argue that such schools are important for low-income children, who would not otherwise be able to obtain a caliber of education comparable to what is available to their middle-class counterparts. Opponents say such schools drain off the smartest students from neighboring schools that are struggling to stay afloat.

Scott, Marcia Strong, Lois-Lynn Stoyko, Beda Jean-Francois and Richard C. Urbano, "Identifying cognitively gifted ethnic minority children," ***Gifted***

***Child Quarterly*, summer 1996, pp. 147-153.**

Scott and others presented 400 kindergarten children in regular education and 31 kindergarten children identified as gifted with a cognitive battery consisting of nine different tasks. Using a child's performance on a cognitive battery could be effective for identifying gifted minority children who have not previously been identified as having superior cognitive abilities.

Sengupta, Somini, "School Disparities Cited in Gifted Programs," *The New York Times*, April 16, 1996, p. B4.

The Association of Community Organizations for Reform Now (ACORN) released a report asserting that minority children are denied equal access to programs for gifted students in New York City schools. The group sent volunteers posing as parents into schools and found that blacks and Hispanics were much less likely than whites to be allowed to speak to school administrators and obtain information about gifted programs for their children.

Programs for the Gifted

Anders, Gigi, "Summer's the season for studying: Enrichment program gives gifted students learning boost," *The Washington Post*, Aug. 1, 1996, Sec. DC, p. 1.

Summerbridge, a free summer enrichment program at Sidwell Friends School in Washington, D.C., where highly motivated 12-, 13- and 14-year-olds from local public schools come to learn, is discussed.

Davis, Stephania H., "Being known for a high IQ no longer has to smart," *Chicago Tribune*, Oct. 6, 1996, Sec. 4C, p. 1.

Over the years, America has exhibited a love-hate relationship with intelligence in general and with intellectuals such as those belonging to the Mensa Society in particular. Several Mensans in the Chicago, Ill., area tell how they handled growing up as gifted students.

Delaney, Yvonne, "Music school for gifted students opens at Goodman House," *Amsterdam News*, Sept. 28, 1996, p. 24.

The development and opening of the Special Music School of America in New York City is detailed.

Kaufman, Marc, "The Best For The Brightest; Accelerated learning programs help gifted students achieve. But they may also compound inequalities," *The Washington Post*, Feb. 2, 1997, Sec. WMAG, p. 18.

Jason Monaco, Jack Dobbyn and Laura Wells were among the 350 or so students enrolled in the John Hopkins University Center for Talented Youth's (CTY) second session last summer at Dickinson College in Carlisle, Pa., one of six college campuses where CTY sets up camp. Many Washingtonians know Carlisle only as the Redskins' former training home, but since 1982 it has offered hundreds of local teenagers very different associations: It's where they go to learn about molecular structures, free verse and logic, and to be surrounded by other kids excited by learning.

Librach, Phyllis Brasch, "Gifted pupils' creative work goes to dogs of the future," *St. Louis Post-Dispatch*, March 6, 1996, p. B1.

Over 200 hand-picked elementary school students from the St. Louis, Mo., area built three-dimensional doghouses from recycled materials for the year 2996 as part of a "creative convention" sponsored by the Gifted Resource Council.

Librach, Phyllis Brasch, "Gifted students taken up a PEG," *St. Louis Post-Dispatch*, April 15, 1996, p. B1.

Missouri's St. Louis Regional Program for Exceptionally Gifted Students, known as PEGS, is featured. Educators hand-pick the students, who must be tested, interviewed and recommended to attend the school. To even be considered, a student must have an IQ of 140, although many score higher.

McCarthy, Elizabeth Altick, "Advocates for the gifted," *Chicago Tribune*, Dec. 31, 1995, Sec. 17NW, p. 3.

Supporters and Advocates of Gifted Education of Mt. Prospect is a volunteer organization in Illinois that aims to develop an information network, to act as an advocate for gifted children and to support one another.

Towns, Gail Hagans, "Newspaper salutes Mays math program," *Atlanta Journal Constitution*, May 18, 1996, p. C1.

While most ninth-graders in metro-Atlanta, Ga., spend their first year tackling physical science, Helen Carithers' students in the Benjamin E. Mays High School Math and Science Academy are initiated into the culture of filing abstracts for summer university fellowships, finding internships in local laboratories and producing substantive mathematical and scientific research. It's an equation that works, according to *USA Today*, which salutes the program in its May 17, 1996, edition.

Walker, Jennie, "Learning gets new dimension for gifted kids. Decisions in human chess match fortify school's special approach," *The Denver Post*, Feb. 6, 1997, p. B8.

Little kings and queens met for a battle of human chess yesterday at the Ricks Center for Gifted Children at the University of Denver in Colorado. The center was created in 1984 "to serve a need," said founder Norma Lu Hafenstein. "There were no services for gifted preschool kids." Lu Hafenstein believes that gifted schools are important in ensuring that gifted children stay in school. She said gifted students often do poorly in traditional schools because they have different methods of learning. That is why the Ricks Center offers interactive programs, such as human chess.

Walker, Reagan, "Best of the brightest," *Atlanta Journal Constitution*, Oct. 6, 1996, p. H1.

The Advanced Academy of Georgia, located at the State University of West Georgia, is a one-of-a-kind program in the state that allows gifted high school students to live in a residence hall on campus and take college-level courses that count toward both a high school diploma and a college degree.

Back Issues

Great Research on Current Issues Starts Right Here...Recent topics covered by The CQ Researcher are listed below. Before May 1991, reports were published under the name of Editorial Research Reports.

SEPTEMBER 1995
Catholic Church in the U.S.
Northern Ireland Cease-Fire
High School Sports
Teaching History

OCTOBER 1995
Quebec's Future
Revitalizing the Cities
Networking the Classroom
Indoor Air Pollution

NOVEMBER 1995
The Working Poor
The Jury System
Sex, Violence and the Media
Police Misconduct

DECEMBER 1995
Teens and Tobacco
Gene Therapy's Future
Global Water Shortages
Third-Party Prospects

JANUARY 1996
Emergency Medicine
Punishing Sex Offenders
Bilingual Education
Helping the Homeless

Back issues are available for $5.00 (subscribers) or $10.00 (non-subscribers). Quantity discounts apply to orders over ten. To order, call Congressional Quarterly Customer Service at (202) 887-8621.

Binders are available for $18.00. To order call 1-800-638-1710. Please refer to stock number 648.

FEBRUARY 1996
Reforming the CIA
Campaign Finance Reform
Academic Politics
Getting Into College

MARCH 1996
The British Monarchy
Preventing Juvenile Crime
Tax Reform
Pursuing the Paranormal

APRIL 1996
Centennial Olympic Games
Managed Care
Protecting Endangered Species
New Military Culture

MAY 1996
Russia's Political Future
Marriage and Divorce
Year-Round Schools
Taiwan, China and the U.S.

JUNE 1996
Rethinking NAFTA
First Ladies
Teaching Values
Labor Movement's Future

JULY 1996
Recovered-Memory Debate
Native Americans' Future
Crackdown on Sexual Harassment
Attack on Public Schools

AUGUST 1996
Fighting Over Animal Rights
Privatizing Government Services
Child Labor and Sweatshops
Cleaning Up Hazardous Wastes

SEPTEMBER 1996
Gambling Under Attack
The States and Federalism
Civic Journalism
Reassessing Foreign Aid

OCTOBER 1996
Political Consultants
Insurance Fraud
Rethinking School Integration
Parental Rights

NOVEMBER 1996
Global Warming
Clashing Over Copyright
Consumer Debt
Governing Washington, D.C.

DECEMBER 1996
Welfare, Work and the States
The New Volunteerism
Implementing the Disabilities Act
America's Pampered Pets

JANUARY 1997
Combating Scientific Misconduct
Restructuring the Electric Industry
The New Immigrants
Chemical and Biological Weapons

FEBRUARY 1997
Assisting Refugees
Alternative Medicine's Next Phase
Independent Counsels
Feminism's Future

MARCH 1997
New Air Quality Standards
Alcohol Advertising
Civic Renewal

Future Topics

- ***Declining Crime Rates***
- ***The FBI Under Fire***
- ***Gender Equity in Sports***

THE CQ Researcher©
PUBLISHED BY CONGRESSIONAL QUARTERLY INC.

Declining Crime Rates

Does better policing account for the reduction?

Crime has been going down in the United States since 1991. In New York, Fort Worth and other cities, police are cracking down on quality-of-life offenses like public drinking and aggressive panhandling and claiming credit for the big drops in violent crime that follow. But New York, traditionally a high-crime city, is responsible for a big chunk of the nationwide decline. Skeptics credit the declining statistics to the improving economy, the fading of the crack wars and the maturing of the baby boomers, rather than new policing tactics. The only way to drive down crime in the long run, these experts argue, is to mend the nation's social fabric, especially racial and class disparities in education and employment.

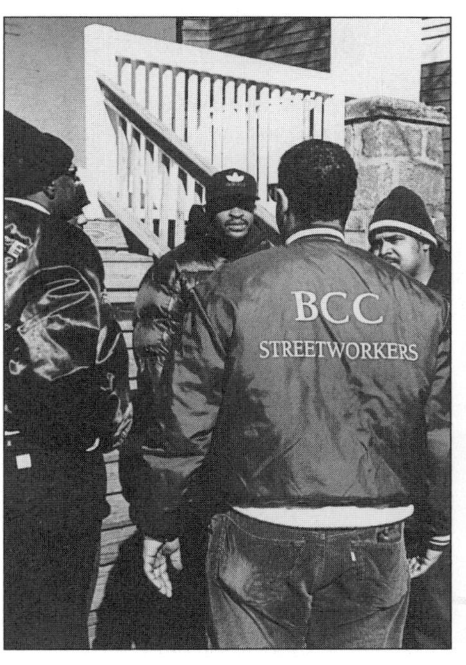

INSIDE THIS ISSUE

CQ April 4, 1997 • Volume 7, No. 13 • Pages 289-312

Formerly Editorial Research Reports

DECLINING CRIME RATES

COVER: AN INNOVATIVE GANG OUTREACH PROGRAM IN BOSTON, MASS., CLAIMS DRAMATIC RESULTS (BOSTON COMMUNITY CENTERS)

April 4, 1997
Volume 7, No. 13

The CQ Researcher (ISSN 1056-2036). Formerly Editorial Research Reports. Published weekly (48 times per year, not printed Jan. 3, May 30, Aug. 29, Oct. 31) by Congressional Quarterly Inc., 1414 22nd St., N.W., Washington, D.C. 20037. Annual subscription rate for libraries, businesses and government is $340. Additional rates furnished upon request. Periodicals postage paid at Washington, D.C., and additional mailing offices. POSTMASTER: Send address changes to The CQ Researcher, 1414 22nd St., N.W., Washington, D.C. 20037.

Declining Crime Rates

BY SARAH GLAZER

THE ISSUES

Real estate agent Laurie Bloomfield used to leave her Upper West Side brownstone in the morning and find the sidewalk shimmering with glass from smashed car windows. Not anymore. In fact, it has been two years since her own car was broken into.

Like many New Yorkers, Bloomfield has her own theories for why things improved. "It was the crack addicts," she says. "They were looking for radios." She often found empty crack cocaine vials amid the glass shards.

Today, however, fewer drug addicts seem to be hitting the neighborhood, a favorite with upscale professionals. Bloomfield sees more police patrolling — on bicycles in the summer. And just a few blocks away, prosecutors crushed several drug-selling gangs whose turf wars led to shooting in the streets.

Crime statistics bear out Bloomfield's perceptions. In the 24th Precinct, which encompasses Bloomfield's neighborhood as well as the run-down area known as Manhattan Valley, overall crime has dropped 50 percent since 1993, according to the New York City Police Department. There were just seven murders last year, compared with 23 in 1993.

In previous years, most of the victims were members of gangs with names like Red Top and Yellow Top, named for the color of the cap on the vials of crack they peddled. The shooting also claimed some innocent victims: 14-year-old Lamont Williams, killed while sitting on a park bench, and 9-year-old John Paul Valentine, wounded by crossfire on the way to school. [1]

Nationwide, crime began dropping in 1992. But nowhere has the drop been as dramatic as in New York City. Serious crimes as measured by the Federal Bureau of Investigation dropped 3 percent across the country in the first six months of 1996, compared with 1995. In New York City, the drop was 10.5 percent, according to the FBI.

New York's double-digit drops since Republican Mayor Rudolph W. Giuliani instituted a campaign against "quality-of-life" crimes have dwarfed national declines. (*See tables, p. 294.*) Between 1993 and 1996 in New York City, murder dropped 49 percent and auto theft 47 percent, according to the NYPD. So far this year murder and auto theft dropped 27 percent and 20 percent, respectively. [2]

Like Bloomfield, the experts also have their theories to explain the decreases. Some criminologists believe the nation's downward trend is largely driven by what's happening in New York City. Several other big cities — Los Angeles and Dallas among them — are also experiencing drops in crime, but none has been as fast or as large as New York's.* The Big Apple accounted for nearly three-quarters of the nation's decrease in serious crimes last year.

New York City's police department has been quick to claim credit for the drops. "One of the reasons we've been able to decrease crime is a complete focus on minor crimes — quality-of-life crimes that drive people crazy," says department spokesman Lenny Alcivar. "Aggressive panhandling, people acting as doormen at the automatic teller machine (ATM), squeegee men at the intersection, graffiti, public urination — all these problems New Yorkers have been told they have to put up with are out the window."

The quality-of-life campaign launched by Giuliani and former Police Chief William Bratton embraced the "broken windows" theory put forward by criminologists James Q. Wilson and George L. Kelling in a 1982 *Atlantic Monthly* article. They argued that broken windows in a neighborhood convey the message that nobody is in charge. The sense of disorder becomes an invitation to delinquents to break more windows, causes citizens to abandon the streets and eventually leads to more serious crimes.

Until recently, it was common in New York to see unkempt men with styrofoam cups standing guard at night over isolated ATM lobbies. Some New Yorkers shrugged and went inside. But others, fearful of getting ripped off, were reluctant to enter. Now New York outlaws aggressive panhandling near ATM machines.

"The notion is if you affect signs of crime and disorder, people feel more comfortable about using public

* According to the FBI, murders in Dallas dropped 23 percent from the first half of 1995 to the first half of 1996, but serious crime overall increased. In Los Angeles, serious crime dropped 9 percent, but murders increased.

National Crime Rate Began Falling in 1992

The FBI's index of seven serious crimes more than doubled from 1960 to 1970, when today's middle-aged baby boomers were in their young, crime-prone years (graph). The index's rise slowed after the 1970s, and by 1992 the rate had begun dropping. From 1960-1995, rates for burglary and murder rose relatively slowly, while rape, robbery and assault at least quadrupled (table).

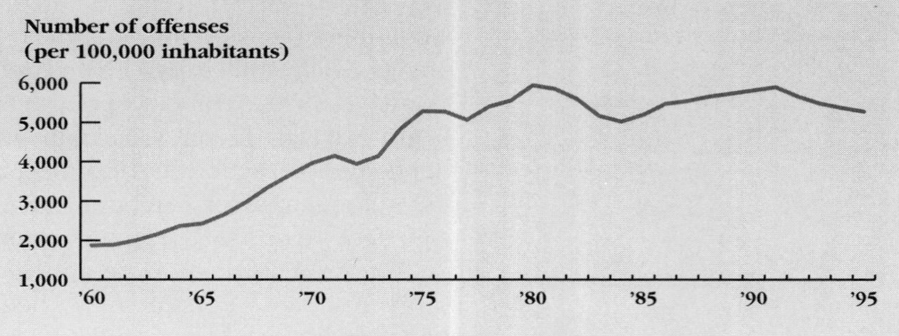

U.S. Crime Index, 1960-1995

	Murder	Forcible rape	Robbery	Aggrav. assault	Burglary	Larceny theft	Motor vehicle theft
1960	5.1	9.6	60.1	86.1	508.6	1,034.7	183.0
1962	4.6	9.4	59.7	88.6	535.2	1,124.8	197.4
1964	4.9	11.2	68.2	106.2	634.7	1,315.5	247.4
1966	5.6	13.2	80.8	120.3	721.0	1,442.9	286.9
1968	6.9	15.9	131.8	143.6	932.3	1,746.6	393.0
1970	7.9	18.7	172.1	164.8	1,084.9	2,079.3	456.8
1972	9.0	22.5	180.7	188.6	1,140.8	1,993.6	426.1
1974	9.8	26.2	209.3	215.8	1,437.7	2,489.5	462.2
1976	8.8	26.6	199.3	233.2	1,448.2	2,921.3	450.0
1978	9.0	31.0	195.8	262.1	1,434.6	2,747.4	460.5
1980	10.2	36.8	251.1	298.5	1,684.1	3,167.0	502.2
1982	9.1	34.0	238.9	289.2	1,466.8	3,084.8	458.8
1984	7.9	35.7	205.4	290.2	1,263.7	2,791.3	437.1
1986	8.6	37.9	225.1	346.1	1,344.6	3,010.3	507.8
1988	8.4	37.6	220.9	370.2	1,309.2	3,134.9	582.9
1990	9.4	41.2	257.0	424.1	1,235.9	3,194.8	657.8
1991	9.8	42.3	272.7	433.3	1,252.0	3,228.8	659.0
1992	9.3	42.8	263.6	441.8	1,168.2	3,103.0	631.5
1994	9.0	39.3	237.7	427.6	1,042.0	3,026.7	591.3
1995	8.2	37.1	220.9	416.3	987.6	3,044.9	560.5

Source: Federal Bureau of Investigation

spaces, and the opportunity for crime is less," says Deputy Police Commissioner Michael Farrell. The other dividend, he says, is a reduction in serious crimes. Stopping someone for a minor offense like aggressive panhandling or public drinking allows police to check outstanding warrants for other crimes, to frisk the individual and confiscate illegal guns. [3]

"We've had a reduction in the number of shootings and even in the number of gun arrests, although overall arrests have increased," Farrell says. "The fact that there are fewer gun charges means [suspects] are not carrying them. In the past, murders would be the result of spontaneous disputes. Shooting is way down."

The declines have caught some experts by surprise. Andrew Karmen, a sociologist at John Jay College of Criminal Justice at the City University of New York, sees an "ideological war" surrounding the decreases: "One side is saying you can't bring crime to its lowest levels without attacking the social roots of crime: limited educational opportunities, poverty. The other side is saying you can suppress crime with tough police tactics, and you don't have to tackle poverty, discrimination and the schools."

Karmen says he's squarely on the side of the social-roots school. But he concedes that his skeptical investigation of New York's declining murder rate indicates the police "deserve some of the credit." He's found that gun-related murders began declining sharply in 1994 after Giuliani's approach had a year to work. He also found that a drop in killings in outdoor locations visible to officers on patrol accounts for most of the decline in murders. [4] The police department credits its strategy of saturating specific high-crime neighborhoods with police officers as another reason for sharp crime drops in neighborhoods like drug-infested Washington Heights, north of Harlem.

Assistant Manhattan District Attorney Walter M. Arsenault, who specializes in gang cases, has noticed fewer shootouts on the street and more murders in stairwells or elevators. "Mostly it's because police do patdown frisks, and people are not carrying their weapons out," he says. "We've had dozens of people say they're keeping their guns in their hubcaps or the sunroof of their cars. So they don't have the opportunity to reach in and start blasting. By the time they go get the gun, their heads may have cooled."

Kelling, who teaches at Rutgers University, believes New York-style approaches are helping to decrease crime in some other cities, though he says few cities have seen New York's drops in virtually all crimes and all precincts. In downtown Dallas, he says "order maintenance" along the lines he recommends has reduced serious crime 60 percent in a little over a year. But he adds, "Very few chiefs have been willing to push across the board like Bratton did."

One confirmed skeptic, criminology and sociology Professor Richard Moran of Mount Holyoke College, contends that a new factory does more to reduce crime in a bad neighborhood than anything police do. He believes New York's crime drops, like other cities', should be attributed to three broad social trends: an improving economy that sent thousands of idle, young men back to work; the winding down of the crack wars among gangs; and the increased incarceration of young criminals — at a rate that has almost doubled over the last 10 years.

"When you talk about new policing tactics [Giuliani and Bratton] have no scientific, solid evidence that what they did made a difference," Moran says. "They did a rain dance and it rained." He adds, "We have over 30 years of research that shows police tactics don't make any difference in the rates of crime."

Unfortunately, counters Kelling, "a lot of police adopted the Moran position as well: crime is caused by poverty, social injustice, racism. Ergo, police can't do anything about crime."

Now, however, the downward trend in crime has given police departments across the country new confidence that they can affect crime. As a vigorous debate continues over whether police action or social trends are more important in driving crime down, these are key questions being asked:

Are get-tough policing initiatives more effective than programs to address root causes?

In the late 1980s, "lawlessness reigned" in the subways of New York, according to Kelling. [5] In his 1996 book *Fixing Broken Windows*, he describes aggressive panhandlers demanding money from passengers, indigents sprawled full length on the seats and young people jumping the turnstiles without paying. During rush hour, intimidating youths stood at subway gates extorting money from confused passengers and creating general chaos. Petty crimes, robbery and felonies started a steep increase in 1987.

In April 1990, Bratton was recruited to lead the Transit Police Department. He started cracking down on fare beating, disorder and robbery. One development of arresting fare beaters was unexpected, writes Kelling, who was a consultant to the New York City Transit Authority during this period. One arrestee out of seven either had an outstanding warrant for a felony charge or was carrying an illegal weapon. Would-be robbers, it appeared, had been interrupted on the way to victimizing subway passengers. The increasing arrests of fare beaters brought crime down and, Kelling adds, police morale soared. (Felonies in the subway system are down by 80 percent since 1990.) [6]

The subway experience provided the "blueprint for restoring order on the streets of New York," Kelling writes, when Bratton was appointed police commissioner in early 1994 by the newly elected Giuliani. [7] Police began handing out summonses for minor offenses like urination and public drinking, which they had once routinely ignored, and made follow-up arrests for offenders who didn't show up in court.

The breakthrough in attacking quality-of-life crimes on city streets actually occurred under Bratton's predecessor as police commissioner, Raymond Kelly, according to Kelling. In 1993, in a highly publicized initiative, Kelly focused on the problem of the "squeegee" men.

Groups of these window-washers had taken to congregating at the entrances to tunnels and bridges where traffic was backed up. As Kelling recalls, some worked hard at washing windshields to earn money or retreated politely when drivers declined their services. But others had a more menacing style, spitting on the windshields of drivers who turned them down or draping themselves over the hoods of cars to prevent them from moving, even after traffic lights changed.

Obstructing traffic, the squeegeemen's main offense under the law, was a minor infraction punishable only by a fine or community service. Officers could not make arrests, they could only give out "Desk Appearance Tickets."

"Youths would sneer at [the officers] and say 'I've got plenty of these,' " Kelling recalls. Offenders generally failed to appear or pay their fines. They could be arrested for failure to appear, but warrants for non-appearance would generally disappear into a "black hole" — the warrant room of the police department — and were never served. Working with the Manhattan district attorney, the Transit Authority arranged to have warrants for non-appearance served by the officer who had written the squeegee ticket in the first place. Finally, officers could say to the squeegeemen, "You're going to jail tonight for not appearing." Within a few weeks, the squeegeeing epidemic died out.

According to Kelling, about half of the squeegeemen arrested had previous arrests for serious felonies like robbery, assault or carrying a gun, and almost half had arrests for drug-related offenses.

Kelling argues that stopping

Big Apple Took Biggest Bite Out of Crime

New York City posted double-digit decreases in major crimes from 1993-95 — dwarfing nationwide declines. Nearly three-quarters of the nationwide drop in total index crimes from 1994-95 was due to New York's steep decline. Police officials credit the city's dramatic declines to the campaign against "quality-of-life" crimes begun by Mayor Rudolph Giuliani in 1993.*

New York City

	Number of offenses			Percent change	Percent change
	1993	**1994**	**1995**	**(1993-1995)**	**(1994-1995)**
Murder/non-negligent manslaughter	1,946	1,561	1,177	-39.5%	-24.6%
Forcible rape	2,818	2,666	2,374	-15.8%	-11%
Robbery	86,001	72,540	59,280	-31.1%	-18.3%
Aggravated assault	62,778	59,755	52,322	-16.7%	-12.4%
Burglary	99,207	88,370	73,889	-25.5%	-16.4%
Larceny/theft	235,132	209,808	183,037	-22.2%	-12.8%
Motor vehicle theft	112,464	95,421	72,679	-35.4%	-23.8%
Total crime index	600,346	530,121	444,758	-25.9%	-16.1%

U.S.

	Number of offenses			Percent change	Percent change
	1993	**1994**	**1995**	**(1993-1995)**	**(1994-1995)**
Murder/non-negligent manslaughter	24,530	23,300	21,600	-11.9%	-7.3%
Forcible rape	106,010	102,220	97,460	-8.1%	-4.7%
Robbery	659,870	618,950	580,550	-12.0%	-6.2%
Aggravated assault	1,135,610	1,113,180	1,099,180	-3.2%	-1.3%
Burglary	2,834,800	2,712,800	2,595,000	-8.5%	-4.3%
Larceny/theft	7,820,900	7,878,800	8,000,600	+2.3%	+1.5%
Motor vehicle theft	1,563,100	1,539,300	1,472,700	-5.8%	-4.3%
Total crime index	14,144,820	13,989,550	13,867,090	-2.0%	-0.9%

* *New York's decline of 86,363 index crimes from 1994-95 represents 70 percent of the nationwide decline of 122,460 index crimes.*

Source: Federal Bureau of Investigation

people for minor crimes actually prevents them from escalating to more serious crimes. "Once the word got out about squeegeeing, we didn't have to prosecute," he says. "This is to warn people, to alert people to set boundaries earlier. . . . We don't wait till they're committing violent crimes to intervene."

He also sees the order-maintenance strategy as sending a warning to young criminal "wannabees" who are getting the "wrong message" about how much society will look the other way. Creating more orderly neighborhoods, he argues, makes it possible for basic social institutions like families and schools to operate normally, thus attacking root causes of criminality.

"We've created an environment in which the streets are out of control," Kelling asserts. "Youths are in charge of the streets. There are kids carrying guns and joining gangs because they're afraid. This [get-tough strategy] is saying, 'Adults will control the streets.' "

Other criminologists are unconvinced. Mount Holyoke's Moran says it's mere coincidence that crime dropped as Giuliani mounted his quality of life campaign. Indeed, crime in some categories had started to turn down as early as 1989, four years before Giuliani took office.

The lively economy, increasing use of imprisonment and shriveling crack market have produced similar decreases in cities without the hoopla of New York City's creative policing, Moran argues.

He points out that East St. Louis, Ill., one the nation's poorest cities, experienced an even sharper drop in murders than New York City — 60 percent between 1991 and 1996. (New York City murders dropped 55 percent.) Yet East St. Louis introduced no new policing strategies during this period, according to Moran. Because of a budget crisis, the department often lacked enough gas to run all its police cars or keep its two-way radios in repair, he says.

Los Angeles, long the target of criticism for its slowness to shift from patrol-car-based military-style policing to community policing, also experienced a decrease in serious crimes last year — 9 percent in the first six months of 1996 compared with the first six months of 1995, according to the FBI. [8]

"The most fuddy-duddy, old-fashioned police departments in the country are now able to claim that whatever they are doing is making crime drop," says Michael Tonry, a professor of law and public policy at the University of Minnesota, who strongly advocates attacking the social roots of crime in his 1995 book *Malign Neglect*. [9] "If you want to change crime rates, you have to get at underlying social and economic realities."

New York Police Department officials counter that East St. Louis is a poor comparison statistically. Because the number of murders involved is relatively small — it dropped from 67 in 1991 to 27 in 1996, Moran says — there could easily be questions about the margin of error, they say. (By comparison, New York City had more than 2,000 murders in 1991.)

Moreover, although New York's crime started to decline in 1991, it accelerated dramatically after Giuliani took over in 1993, moving into double-digit declines in every category and in every precinct, notes Deputy Commissioner Farrell. Most social trends, such as increased imprisonment, would have taken effect more gradually, he argues.

Other criminologists point to the maturing of drug markets over the last 10 years, arguing that a few remaining large players now dominate the market in big cities and do not have to resort to violence over turf.

But Farrell is not convinced by that explanation either. "We're unaware of any summit meeting where all these groups got together and said, 'We will stop fighting among ourselves' and carved up the territory," he says.

In a recent op-ed column, New York University School of Law criminologist Jerome H. Skolnick asserted that "no social scientist, liberal or conservative, really knows the answer" to why crime is declining. He went on to suggest it could be a combination of New York-style quality-of-life policing and long-term social trends. [10]

"The argument that it's a matter of root causes and has nothing to do with policing is as silly as saying it's a matter of sanctions and has nothing to do with families and school and community," agrees Lawrence Sherman, chairman of the criminology department at the University of Maryland-College Park. "We've got to work on both."

Sherman argues that New York's most effective tactic has been getting guns off the street through its crackdown on minor violations. At the same time, he points to studies calculating that most of the nation's gun homicides are concentrated in areas where a majority of the residents live in single-parent households below the poverty line.

"I think it suggests, like AIDS prevention, [that we should] put most of the resources where the problem is concentrated," Sherman says, speaking both of increased police and social programs. "We have proven programs of early-infancy home visitation, preschool Head Start with parental involvement. If we were to concentrate these expensive but effective programs in neighborhoods with high concentrations of poverty and gun violence — both the criminal justice side and social service side working together — we'll get both a short- and long-term payoff in terms of lower levels of gun violence in America."

Investment banker Andrew M. Silberstein, 29, expresses pleasure mixed with moral pangs over New York's recent improvements. "It's a different city. I feel safe walking the streets now," he says. "But I can't help wondering: What have they done with all the homeless people?"

According to Norman Siegel, executive director of the New York Civil Liberties Union (ACLU), the homeless have simply moved to less visible parts of the city where police are less likely to hassle them. A recent *New York Times* account described homeless people who now sleep at the New Jersey end of the Lincoln Tunnel. Squeegee cleaners and panhandlers, who have dwindled markedly in Manhattan, now approach commuters in Newark. [11]

New York's police have "won the war on sqeegeeing and panhandling, but I'm not sure they've won much," Siegel says. "They haven't addressed the underlying issue of why we have people living out on the streets."

During the police department's war on squeegeemen, Siegel says he suggested that Bratton gather the men in a midtown hotel room and offer them jobs in lieu of tickets. But Kelling says viewing these men as "homeless" was a misnomer. During a 60-day experiment, the city discovered that approximately three-quarters of the men resided at legitimate addresses, and half had criminal records. Because of their criminal backgrounds, he argues, squeegeers "were not merely a troubled population, they were capable of considerable mayhem." [12]

"To say we can't enforce the law because we don't have a solution to poverty is ridiculous," argues Deputy Commissioner Farrell. "Squeegeemen are stopping and interfering with traffic. It may be helpful to get them into the mainstream of society and get them employment and so on, but that's not what we're set up to do." He adds, "We're not clear on how to eliminate poverty. Frankly, it's not particularly productive for a police agency to pretend that it's able to solve these problems."

Civilian complaints of police abuse

Boston Gang Members Were Offered a Choice . . .

No youngsters under 17 have been shot and killed since July 1995 in Boston, Many experts credit an innovative campaign aimed at youth gangs in the city, which suffered a spate of youth shootings in recent years. The campaign combined threats of stiff federal prison sentences for gun violence with the offer of summer jobs to gang members.

Boston city officials teamed up with federal law enforcers in summer 1995 in an effort funded by the National Institute of Justice at Harvard University. David M. Kennedy, a youth violence specialist at Harvard's Kennedy School of Government, said there was general agreement that most youth murders could be traced to active gang members, numbering about 1,300, many of whom had outstanding warrants or previous criminal records.

"We were convinced a lot of gang violence is driven by fear and vulnerability," Kennedy says. "If you don't stand up for yourself, you make yourself vulnerable. Violence made people join gangs and get guns. We believed if we made the street safer, people would behave differently."

Members of the law enforcement group met with gang members and sent the word out through Boston's 40 gang outreach workers that violence among the gangs would be subject to federal prosecution and penalties. They told the youths they would be arrested for minor violations like public drinking and that a new spate of gang violence would produce a crackdown on outstanding warrants and a shutdown of gang drug markets. Probation officers, who normally oversee paper files from a desk, rode with police in patrol cars at night in gang neighborhoods and visited youths' homes to arrest youths violating their curfews.

Boston Community Centers

Gang outreach workers in Boston told gang members they had the choice of summer jobs or possible prosecution for violence under tough federal penalties.

One arrest made a particularly big impression, says Tracy Litthcut, director of Youth Services for Boston Community Centers, who oversees gang out-reach workers. Eddie Cardoza of Roxbury, who had 15 previous convictions, was sentenced to 20 years in a federal penitentiary for carrying a single bullet in his pocket.

"We talked to the gang members and said, 'Listen, the federal government is here, they're going to be making arrests, prosecuting people and will be giving federal time if you don't take advantage of the opportunities that we're here to give you,' " Litthcut says. In contrast to state prisons, where gang members can hang out with their friends and get visits from their families, the mention of federal penitentiaries hundreds of miles from home with no hope of parole strikes fear in even the most toughened youths, Boston's gang experts say.

have risen about 50 percent since the start of Giuliani's administration, Siegel notes, and he says he personally gets calls about police hassling minorities and young people. Farrell counters that the increase in complaints has been minimal viewed in the context of the increasing number of arrests and summonses by New York City's enlarged police force, which grew from about 25,000 to 38,000 officers between 1990 and 1996.

But the new attack on minor offenses has created tension between the police and minority communities, Siegel contends. Officers targeted drivers in predominantly black Harlem in summer 1995, Siegel says, pulling over drivers for changing lanes without signaling as a pretext for stop-and-frisks. "I didn't know we had lanes in Manhattan," Siegel comments dryly in a reference to New York's predominantly two-lane streets.

Yet Siegel concedes that Giuliani's crime-fighting efforts have been enormously popular. In TV appearances, Siegel has offered to represent citizens who want to mount a constitutional challenge to the increased police searches, but he says no one has stepped forward claiming their rights were violated (*see p. 306*).

Has crime peaked?

A majority of Americans don't believe that crime is going down, but most criminologists say the trend is real. If anything, crime statistics have been getting more accurate in recent years (*see p. 299*).

The question that divides experts is whether the downward trend can be sustained or whether new crime spikes hover in the future. Many criminologists attribute the current lull in crime to the small proportion of young men now in their crime-prone years

. . . Federal Prison or a Summer Job

In summer 1996, Litthcut's group offered gang members jobs ranging from landscaping to working with youngsters at community centers. "When we provided this economic resource, it gave the kids the opportunity to step off the street corners and stop selling crack," he says. "Not one of those gang members got arrested over the summer."

As part of its anti-violence effort, Boston's police department has made a concerted effort to track down gun traffickers by questioning arrestees about the source of their guns, Kennedy says. Using gun serial numbers in a gun-tracing study, Kennedy found that one-third of the guns from youths under 22 had been sold in Massachusetts, and many of those could be traced to adults who purchased the guns new in retail stores, then sold them on the street. Since summer 1995, gun homicides in Boston have dropped 70 percent for males under 27 and 50 percent for males 25 and over, according to Kennedy.

Boston Community Centers

During the summer, gang-involved and at-risk youth in Boston play basketball in the city's Peace League.

Last July, 17 cities began participating in a federal effort to trace guns using the Boston approach and help from the Justice Department. Legislation introduced by President Clinton Feb. 25 would increase penalties for gun dealers and individuals who transfer guns to juveniles.

But two aspects of the program may be unique to Boston. "The fact that Boston has those links to gangs is very impressive evidence of community policing. I'm not sure a lot of other police departments are able to communicate in that way," says Lawrence Sherman, chairman of the criminology department at the University of Maryland-College Park.

Sherman's own research indicates that enforcing laws against carrying concealed weapons, which police have been lax about in the past, is the single most effective tactic for reducing gun homicides.

Boston is relatively unusual in being able to squeeze its gun supply by going after local suppliers because it has an unusually concentrated black market in guns, Sherman says. It also has a relatively low number of juvenile gun murders compared with other large cities. The high-est number recorded in recent years was 10 in 1991 and '93. [1]

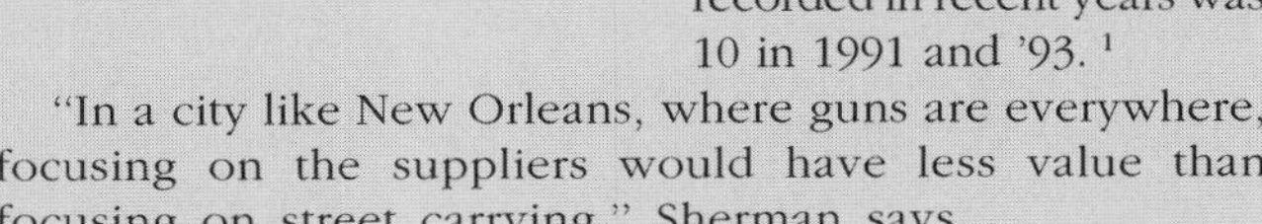

"In a city like New Orleans, where guns are everywhere, focusing on the suppliers would have less value than focusing on street carrying," Sherman says.

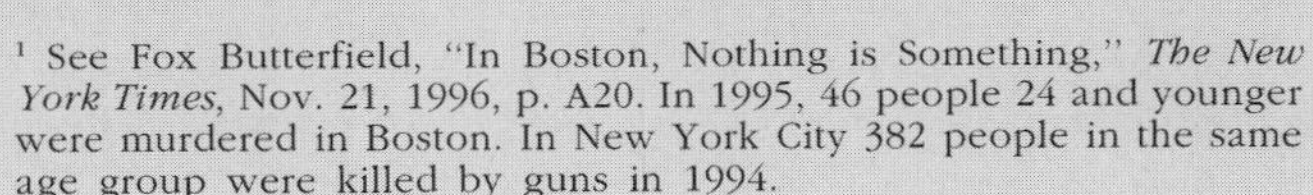

[1] See Fox Butterfield, "In Boston, Nothing is Something," *The New York Times*, Nov. 21, 1996, p. A20. In 1995, 46 people 24 and younger were murdered in Boston. In New York City 382 people in the same age group were killed by guns in 1994.

— currently at its lowest point since 1980. Traditionally, the peak age for committing violent crime is 17. Today's baby boomers, born between 1947 and 1964, were 16-33 in 1980, when crime hit a peak. Now they are 33-50, the years when the focus is on raising families, not sowing wild oats.

James Alan Fox, a professor at Northeastern University's College of Criminal Justice in Boston, sees a new threat on the horizon as baby boomers' children — an "echo boom" — reach the prime years for criminality over the next 10 years. He has warned against a future juvenile crime wave so bad that "we will look back at the '90s and call them the good old days." [13]

Even as crime rates among adults have been dropping, violent crime rates among youths have been increasing exponentially, and younger teens have become more involved in gun violence. Since 1985, the rate of homicides committed by adults 25 and older declined 25 percent as the baby boomers matured. At the same time, the homicide rate among 18-to-24-year-olds increased 61 percent. Among younger teens 14 to 17, the rate of homicide more than doubled. [14]

Ironically, Fox had predicted in 1978 that crime would drop in the late 1980s as the traditionally crime-prone group of boomers aged and the number of teens declined. [15] Instead crime rose to a new peak. What he hadn't counted on, he now says, was an unprecedented rate of violence among teens — and increasingly younger teens — even though they were dwindling as a proportion of the population.

"What happened in 1986 is teens started picking up guns and shooting one another in record numbers," Fox says. "While historically 15-to-16-year-olds rarely committed homicides, that has all changed. A lot of that has to do with the crack market. It included a larger number of teens in the drug-selling business, and they had to protect themselves with guns."

Arrest rates show that 14-to-17-year-olds have now surpassed 18-to-24-year-olds in violent crimes like murder, rape and robbery. Even if the per-capita rate of teen homicide remains the same, the number of 14-to-17-year-olds who commit murder will increase from 4,000 now to nearly 5,000 annually in 2005 because of population growth alone, Fox predicts. [16]

Last year, the Justice Department announced that the violent-crime rate among juveniles 10-17 had turned down slightly for the first time in seven years. The announcement raised questions about Fox's dire predictions. The decline was 4 percent from 1994-95. [17]

Fox dismisses the downturn with the comment, "We're having a warm day in December, and people think spring is here." He points to worsening social indicators — millions of children living in poverty and a growing percentage of teens without parental supervision during after-school hours, when most juvenile crime is committed.

"If anything, I believe juvenile crime has plateaued," he says. "Even if we stay at the same rate [of crime] we have now, the future expansion of the teenage population would mean more crime. What I can say for sure is we'll have more kids at risk. Whether these kids commit more muggings and murders partly depends on us — whether we invest in the next generation of teenagers."

Alfred Blumstein, a professor of urban systems at Carnegie Mellon University, is skeptical of Fox's predictions. He calculates the population of young men at crime-prone ages will be increasing at a rate of only about 1 percent a year. "Certainly a demographic story of 1 percent a year shouldn't give us a blood bath," he says, especially if policing and social conditions improve.

Fox concedes that teen growth over the next 10 years does not look that dramatic compared with the baby boomer bulge. But he sees the danger concentrated in the growing numbers of at-risk black children. White baby boomers have had fewer children or had them later than demographers predicted, so growth in the white teen population is going to be modest. "But growth in the black teen population will be much sharper," he says. "Black teens have 10 times the rate of violence of white teens. If you have a disproportionate growth among black teens, you will have a disproportionate impact on the crime problem."

According to the U.S. Census, 46 percent of black teenagers live below the federal poverty level. Criminologists like Fox expect that number to increase. Studies show a strong correlation between living in poverty and entering a life of crime. [18]

John J. DiIulio Jr., a professor of politics and public affairs at Princeton University, joins Fox in predicting a ticking demographic time bomb among young, mostly male criminals he dubs "super-predators."

In a recent interview, he describes them as a "small fraction of kids who are simply surrounded by deviant, delinquent, criminal adults in fatherless, godless and jobless settings. . . . They are remorseless, radically present-oriented and radically self-regarding." An important predictor for the future, he says, is the rising rate of child abuse and neglect, which increases the chances of delinquency by 40 percent. While the super-predators may be a small percentage of delinquents, he says, the "most radically impulsive and violent kids tend to be the ones who are leading the more than 200,000 kids who are organized into gangs in this country today." [19]

But the University of Minnesota's Tonry says he has been skeptical of the predictions of a youth crime wave from the beginning. "In the long term, this country has been becoming a more socially and culturally conservative country with greater concerns about personal responsibility for 20 years," he asserts, "and it's been showing up in [decreasing] crime."

While it's true, for example, that the proportion of children born out of wedlock to teens has been rising, Tonry notes, the fertility rate of teens has been declining, yielding a smaller overall number of such children. Having an unmarried, teenage mother is another social factor that has been correlated with criminality.

Other experts agree with Tonry that "demography isn't destiny." One factor that could make a difference for the better in the future is the declining popularity of crack among 18-to-21-year-olds, Karmen notes. Heroin may be replacing crack among some young users, but street experts suggest heroin users are slower to commit crimes and less violent under the sedating influence of heroin than crack addicts.

Another major factor is the extent of gun carrying among juveniles. Boston and several other cities have been working to reduce the glamour of owning a gun by cracking down on concealed weapons and traffickers. (*See story, p. 296.*) In Charleston, police have offered a bounty of $100 for any report of an illegal gun, which tends to discourage youngsters from brandishing guns in public, Blumstein notes.

"The hula hoop went out, and maybe gun carrying is going to go out," the University of Maryland's Sherman suggests. "If that happens, we're not going to see a blood bath."

"Changes in values among young people" could be explaining the downturn in crime we're starting to see, Karmen says, as AIDS and inner-city funerals bring home the price of drug use and gang involvement. "Young people are learning that life in the fast lane of drugs and gangs is counterproductive." Perhaps, says

Karmen, "They've learned from older brothers and sisters and decided not to take that road." ■

BACKGROUND

Crime Rate Soars

Many Americans over 45 remember a childhood when their neighborhoods and cities seemed much safer. [20] It's not just their imagination: From 1960 to 1970, the rate of the seven serious crimes measured by the FBI more than doubled. *(See chart, p. 292.)*

"There was a tranquillity that got shattered in the mid-1960s with the arrival of the baby boomers," Blumstein says. Between the first wave born in 1947 and the last group continuing until 1964, millions of young people were coming of age in an anti-authoritarian environment starting with the civil rights movement and the Vietnam War.

"Large masses of people were going through their typical teenage rebellion accompanied by much greater mobility than the country had seen before," Blumstein says. "With mobility comes diminished social control."

In 1964, when conservative Republican Sen. Barry Goldwater of Arizona made crime in the streets the major theme of his presidential campaign, the first wave of baby boomers born in 1947 was reaching 17, traditionally the peak age of criminality.

Experts like Blumstein and Fox predicted that as these baby boomers matured into adulthood during the 1980s, taking on families and jobs, the violent crime rate would subside.

A downturn in the violent crime rate did occur in 1980, but it was short-lived. By 1986, the crime rate began to surge, despite the declining proportion of 18-to-24-year-olds. Crack, guns and younger teens who were more crime-prone than in the past confounded criminologists' predictions of crime declines lasting through the late 1980s. The lock-step relationship between demography and crime had been broken.

According to Blumstein, one unanticipated effect of the federal government's continuing effort to fight drug dealing was that older criminals were now behind bars and unavailable to sell drugs. [21] So younger teens became recruits. Kids carrying drugs or drug money felt obliged to carry guns to protect themselves from robberies. As other teens saw their peers carrying weapons to school, gun acquisition among youngsters escalated as a form of protection.

Perception vs. Reality

Americans have been generally incredulous at reports that crime rates have been declining since 1991. A recent *Washington Post* survey ranked crime second among the top 20 worries confronting voters. [22]

The discrepancy between perception and reality is an old story, according to E. Mark Warr, a sociologist and criminologist at the University of Texas-Austin.

"We have done surveys for decades in which we ask people, 'Do you think crime is going up or down?' Invariably people say it's going up," Warr reports. "That occurs regardless of what actual crime rates are doing. There's a tendency to think the world is getting worse all the time." Historically, he notes, the 19th century and the 1930s were more dangerous eras to live in than the 1990s.

Local news coverage is a major factor behind the perception that crime is both getting worse and more violent, according to Warr. Crime often composes fully a third of local news content, he says. In many cities he has studied, about half the news stories are homicide reports, even though homicide is but a fraction of 1 percent of all the crime in the United States.

"If I came from another planet and knew about our society from watching TV and reading newspapers, I would think the most common crimes are homicide, rape and robbery, when in fact those are the least common crimes," Warr says. "It creates a reverse mirror image of what's going on in the world.

In addition, the big decreases in crime, particularly violent crime, have generally been in the larger cities and in the poorest inner-city neighborhoods of those metropolitan centers, notes Lawrence Greenfield, deputy director of the Bureau of Justice Statistics. New York City's more than 2,200 murders in 1990 accounted for almost 10 percent of the nation's total, so much of the national decline was attributable to New York's plunge to under 1,000 murders last year.

"The declines are less dramatic for suburban areas and for many cities," Greenfield notes. [23] While the lowered murder rates reported on the news may be impressive, people tend to more fearful of being burglarized than being shot, Warr reports. That's rational, since property crimes like thefts and burglaries make up 12 million of the approximately 14 million serious crimes reported to the FBI. In addition, the FBI's crime index picks only seven crimes intended to serve as an indicator of overall crime — murder, forcible rape, robbery, aggravated assault, burglary, theft and auto theft. It leaves out other crimes, like vandalism and auto break-ins, that may be more likely to brush the lives of families.

Recent focus groups in New York have led Mayor Giuliani to target property crimes in the city's new policing initiative. Despite a sharp decline in violent crime rates since 1990, most public opinion polls show only a marginal improvement in New Yorkers' appraisal of the city's safety. Giuliani told *The New York Times* that focus group studies of New Yorkers conducted for the police department and polls showed that many city residents do not feel the crime reduction has affected them personally.

In a new initiative, the police department said it would crack down on fencing rings, thieves who sell stolen bicycles and "chop shops" that dispose of stolen cars. [24]

Experts have long known that more crime occurs than is reported to police. "We know that only about a third of crimes people experience are reported to the police," Greenfield says. The evidence for this gap comes from the higher number of crimes that households report to the Bureau of Justice Statistics' National Crime Victimization Survey, a national survey of 50,000 households. But Greenfield says the number of crimes the FBI reports, which are collected from police departments around the country, has moved much closer to what victims say they have experienced in his agency's surveys.

One reason, statisticians suggest, is that people are more willing to contact police about crimes like rape and assaults, once viewed as shameful. In addition, police departments have become better at keeping statistics through the use of computers and increasingly take a more professional approach to victims of crimes like domestic abuse.

When researchers ask whether crime has increased, people tend to think the nation is in much worse shape than their own neighborhood or city, Warr says. Even people who live in very dangerous neighborhoods will say their neighborhood is safe simply because it's familiar, according to Warr. For most Americans, the perception that violent crime is happening to other people is correct.

In fact, "Criminals are the most victimized members of society," Moran notes. "They're more likely to get shot and murdered and more likely to be victims of armed robbery than anyone else." It's often said that the murder epidemic in this country is one of young inner-city men killing one another. To the extent that increased incarceration has removed would-be criminals from the street, it has also removed the most likely victims.

New York City may be one of the few places in the country where inhabitants are conscious of crime even in upscale areas, such as midtown or the Upper East Side. There, well-dressed women sling their purses across their chests and clutch them tightly as they stride the sidewalks. "No radio" signs, which made their appearance during the crime rise of the 1970s, seem permanently affixed to many cars, despite the recent drop in auto thefts. Some experts say the increased vigilance simply reflects decades of conditioning. But others say it's a reaction to a changed reality.

"I want to cheer the decrease in New York," DiIulio has said, but the crime rate is still unacceptable. "We ought not be happy that New York City may only have a thousand or so murders this year when in the 1940s with a population as large and with paramedics who weren't as fast, we had 44 gunshot murders in a typical year." [25] ■

CURRENT SITUATION

New Strategies

Claiming credit for the national drop in crime during the last presidential campaign, President Clinton often cited his anti-crime bill and its plan to put 100,000 new cops on the street. His Republican opponent, former Sen. Bob Dole, R-Kan., argued that New York's Giuliani had more to do with the drop than any federal program.

Under the legislation that Clinton signed in 1994, $8.8 billion is authorized over six years for grants to policing agencies to hire new cops. [26] To qualify for the grants, police departments must show they are committed to community policing, where police try to get acquainted with residents and neighborhoods through foot patrols, storefront stations and similar approaches. As of January 1997, the Clinton program, dubbed COPS (Community Oriented Policing Services) was halfway to its hiring goal, having awarded grants to hire more than 54,000 police officers.

But some criminologists doubt that the program has had much to do with the declines in crime. By law, half the funds must go to police departments serving populations under 150,000. "They're policing Montana and Wyoming — places that have gun violence for shooting at rattlesnakes but not teenagers looking at each other sideways," quips University of Maryland criminologist Sherman.

Even if all the money went to inner cities, Sherman argues, it would not be effective unless police forces concentrated their manpower during the prime times when gun crimes occur — between 9 p.m. and 3 a.m. — and in the hot spots where crimes are committed. Police patrol patterns in most cities generally don't match those patterns because nobody wants to work the late shift, Sherman says.

New York Sets the Pace

The exception is New York, where the police department's computer mapping approach, known as Compstat,

Continued on p. 304

Chronology

1960s *The baby boom generation starts to enter the crime-prone adolescent years amid protests against the Vietnam War and the beginning of the drug revolution. Crime starts to rise, although it remains less than one-half of today's level.*

1964
Crime in the streets is the theme of conservative Republican Barry Goldwater's presidential campaign as the first wave of baby boomers reaches 17, traditionally the peak age for criminality.

1970s *Crime continues to rise. Police officials and academics shift their strategies on gangs from social work to suppression and control. Loitering and vagrancy laws are struck down in the courts.*

1972
In *Papachristou v. City of Jacksonville*, the Supreme Court strikes down a city ordinance against loitering as an overly vague prohibition on innocent acts like strolling.

1973
The National Crime Survey is initiated by the Law Enforcement Administration to survey households and uncover the extent of crimes not reported to the police. This survey is later overhauled by the Bureau of Justice Statistics.

Aug. 21, 1974
Congress passes Juvenile Justice and Delinquency Prevention Act.

1975
Justice Department's first attempt to survey U.S. gang problem.

1978
James Alan Fox publishes *Forecasting Crime Data*, predicting that violent crime will subside in the 1980s as the baby boom matures into adulthood.

1980s *Crime declines in the early 1980s, but contrary to predictions it soars again in the mid-1980s as crack reaches the inner city. The Reagan administration declares war on drugs.*

1981
Police Foundation publishes "Newark Foot Patrol Experiment," which shows that fear of crime drops dramatically wherever there was a foot patrol.

1983
In *Kolender v. Lawson*, the Supreme Court invalidates a California statute under which a man walking late at night was stopped repeatedly and detained or arrested. The court said the statute was vague and encouraged arbitrary enforcement by police.

1985
After falling steadily for four years, crime turns up again, surprising criminologists like Fox. Most attribute the rise to a more crime-prone teen population with deadlier weapons than ever before.

1988
President Reagan signs Anti-Drug Abuse Act; California convenes a task force on gangs and drugs.

1990s *Crime begins a gradual national decline with big decreases in New York.*

April 1990
William Bratton becomes head of New York Transit Authority and begins cracking down on fare beating and disorder.

1993
New York City Police Department starts campaign against squeegee men during Dinkins-Giuliani mayoral campaign. On Jan. 10, 1994, newly elected Republican Mayor Rudolph Giuliani appoints Bratton as police commissioner. Bratton intensifies campaign against quality-of-life offenses.

Sept. 13, 1994
President Clinton signs into law the Violent Crime Control and Enforcement Act of 1994 authorizing $8.8 billion over six years for grants to police departments to put 100,000 additional police officers on the street.

January 1997
California Supreme Court upholds a San Jose city ordinance that prohibited suspected gang members from standing together on street corners, wearing beepers and other activities that would be legal for ordinary citizens. The court held that individual rights cannot be protected at the expense of a community's right to security.

Feb. 25, 1997
Clinton sends Congress proposed legislation (the Anti-Gang and Youth Violence Act of 1997), toughening penalties for violent gang activity and witness intimidation.

New York City's 'Nasty Boys' Got Busted . . .

On an unseasonably warm day in late February, April Wilson sat in front of her South Bronx apartment building lunching on French fries and fried chicken. It's something she says she never would have done a year and a half ago, when drug gangs were fighting over the neighborhood.

"It's quiet here now," says Wilson, 27, gesturing to the schoolchildren with backpacks playing in front of the apartment buildings and corner bodegas. "There used to be shooting and everything else. You can sit outside and enjoy the weather. The cops have cleaned it up."

By middle-class standards, the impoverished Hunt's Point neighborhood still has a long way to go. A block from where Wilson's three children played, two prostitutes cruised the sidewalk near deserted warehouses and empty lots surrounded by barbed wire. Still, it is one of several New York City neighborhoods where crime has plummeted since drug gangs were arrested en masse in a predawn raid in 1995.

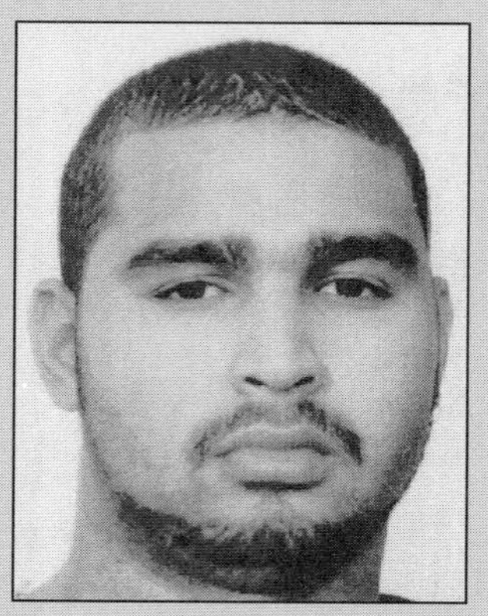

Julio Beniquez was among more than 30 South Bronx gang members arrested on Halloween 1995 and charged with drug trafficking and other crimes under sweeping federal racketeering laws.

Before then, Wilson would not let her children walk to school by themselves because of the danger from crossfire. Wilson's building on Seneca Avenue was one of several centers for gang drug dealing. Crack vials littered the lobby. Crack and heroin were sold openly on the front steps. On a wall next to the building, an elaborate mural testifies to the death of a gang member, Chaz, and pleads for peace among the gangs.

The gang violence that had terrorized the neighborhood since the mid-1980s reached a crescendo on Sunday afternoon, April 24, 1994. In broad daylight, two rival Puerto Rican drug gangs — the Bryant Boys and the Nasty Boys — shot it out across Bryant and Seneca avenues. A 2-year-old girl was grazed by a bullet, her mother was hit in the arm and Porfirio Ortiz, a bystander, was killed.

Joining forces, the U.S. Attorney's Office for the Southern District of New York, the Drug Enforcement Administration and the New York City Police Department launched a major investigation of the gangs. More than a year later, on Halloween 1995, they rounded up leading members of the two gangs. More than 30 members were charged with drug trafficking, firearms violations and other crimes under sweeping federal racketeering laws.

Following the arrests, murders in the local 41st Precinct dropped dramatically — from 42 in 1994 to 17 last year. As of late March, only one homicide had been recorded in the precinct this year.

Det. Joseph Marrero of the Bronx Homicide Task Force noticed the difference within days of the arrests. "I wouldn't say it's dead, but it's not the way it used to be," he says. The lines of 10 or 20 customers waiting to buy drugs from the gangs' multimillion-dollar operations have disappeared, as have the double- and triple-parked cars of local and out-of-town drug buyers, Marrero says. The 'Hole," the abandoned building where the Bryant Boys used to sell drugs, has been renovated for families.

Williams College sociologist Robert Jackall believes that targeted gang strikes by federal and state prosecutions have been a major factor in New York City's declining murder rate. Police "finally arrested a lot of these people in a fairly short time and got them off the street," Jackall says. "Suddenly, the most violent predators are gone." Jackall is finishing a book about the Wild Cowboys, a drug gang of American-born Dominicans that operated in the Bronx from 1986-1993, when key leaders were arrested. [1]

The 1995 crackdown in Hunt's Point reflects a continuing effort by federal prosecutors to bust gangs using the federal Racketeer Influenced and Corrupt Organizations Act (RICO), which was originally designed to fight the Mafia. Prosecutions of gangs under those laws have more than doubled over the past four years, according to Attorney General Janet Reno. [2]

Marrero calls RICO "the greatest weapon against these gangs." Unlike state murder laws, RICO requires proof only that a suspect was part of an enterprise that committed a murder, not that he pulled the trigger. Under state law, Marrero says, "We can arrest the shooter, but the person who ordered it is still out there." In addition, federal law gives greater credence to the testimony of accomplice gang members than New York state law, which requires corroborating testimony from neighborhood witnesses.

New York gang members arrested under RICO typically are not offered bail because of their presumed threat to the community, according to Steven M. Cohen, chief of the Violent Gangs Unit in the U.S. Attorney's Office. Taking them off the street immediately means they can't threaten potential witnesses. That was a crucial distinction in Hunt's Point, where fear of retaliation kept terrorized residents from talking to Marrero and his partner, Det. Linda Alicea.

According to a Justice Department report released in January, witness intimidation by gang members is a "pervasive and insidious problem." Prosecutors and police investigators in eight jurisdictions said that violence against

...But Now Other Cities Have Gang Problems

witnesses, including homicide, drive-by shootings and physical assault occurs on a daily or weekly basis.[3]

President Clinton on Feb. 25 proposed new legislation to prevent members of gangs from intimidating witnesses and to make it easier for U.S. attorneys to prosecute them under RICO. The bill would allow a judge to hold a defendant without bail pending trial when there was probable cause that he had been involved in criminal gang activity. In addition, conspiracy to intimidate or retaliate against a witness would be punishable with the same federal penalties that attach to the underlying crime.[4]

The big break for Marrero and Alicea came when they joined forces with federal prosecutors, which enabled them to use RICO. "We can use the managers, the bosses, the pitchers [sellers] against each other," Alicea says. "To be effective in cleaning up an area, you have to get everybody."

In the Wild Cowboys case, Jackall says, local prosecutors got around the problem of neighborhood residents who were "terrified out their wits" to testify. After numerous attempts, they found a judge willing to deny bail and lock up the leaders until their trials. With the threat of gang retaliation largely removed, residents who had suffered gang beatings and sexual abuse came forward to testify. Fifty gang members were arrested, and all but nine pleaded guilty. In June 1995, the convicted gang members received prison sentences ranging from 20 years to life.

Many criminologists question how long a single prosecution, no matter how successful, can keep the peace in a neighborhood plagued by poverty, broken families and the lure of drug money. "The problem with police crackdowns is the same with crash diets: They don't get sustained," says Richard Moran, a professor of sociology and criminology at Mount Holyoke College.

Marrero is aware of the social pressure on neighborhood youngsters. "At a young age, kids can see: 'Why get $5 an hour at McDonalds and kill yourself for eight hours when you can make $120 a day selling drugs?'" Marrero says. Many of the gang members started as early as age 12 or 13 earning $80 a day warning dealers when police were coming, Marrero and Alicea say. Older gang members can earn $1,000-$2,000 as enforcers for making "hits" on rival or disloyal gang members.

At the intersection of Bryant and Seneca, young men in their 20s who had been on the fringes of the warring gangs appear to be trying to regroup, according to Marrero and Alicea.

"It is depressing because they don't learn their lesson," says Alicea, who describes several of the would-be leaders as intelligent and personable. "They know 30 people were arrested and are facing life imprisonment, but they want easy money. They're wiling to risk it all for a little extra flamboyance." Several residents of the neighborhood told a recent visitor they were still fearful in the neighborhood, even though they knew the gang leaders were behind bars awaiting trial. "Things are better now," said a woman who wouldn't give her name, but she still does not let her five children play outside. During the height of the gang warfare, she found a slain man on her doorstep and got caught in a shootout at the local bodega. Her 13-year-old daughter recalled ducking outside the store to dodge the bullets.

Some experts think that cleaning up gangs in one location simply forces them to move to another. According to a recent White House report, 95 percent of the nation's largest cities and 88 percent of the smaller ones suffer gang-related crime, compared with fewer than half of American cities a generation ago.[5]

Jackall predicts further migration of gang activity outside New York because the city is increasingly "inhospitable to crime." Part of the lure is the higher prices that can be commanded in less competitive drug markets. A vial of crack that sells for $5 in New York costs $20 in sleepy Pittsfield, Mass., Jackall says. The town, which once only had one or two murders a year, has had "an explosion of drug-related violence in the last three years," Jackall says. Another lure to gang migration, according to police, is the opportunity for buying cheap guns and selling them for double and triple the price back in the big city.

Migrations of this kind have been spotted in cities like Dallas since the late 1980s and early '90s. Jamaican gangs from New York City "moved in on us because they could make a lot of money," Dallas Det. Charles Storey says. Gang leaders would go to the black slums of Crown Heights, Brooklyn, "hire four kids ages anywhere from 15-22 from an impoverished family and say, 'We'll fly you to Dallas and pay you $500 cash per week.' You put them in a crack house, they've got a gun and more money than they've ever had."

Drug-related shootings exploded as the young gang recruits attempted to defend their $5,000-$10,000-a-day sales operations from crack addicts and rival drug entrepreneurs.

Now, Storey says, dealers in Dallas are "more or less using local talent rather than workers from New York."

---

[1] *Wild Cowboys: Urban Marauders and the Forces of Order* is slated for publication by Harvard University Press in late summer/early fall.

[2] Written testimony before House Education and Workforce Subcommittee on Early Childhood, Youth and Families and the Judiciary Subcommittee on Crime, Feb. 26, 1997, p. 4.

[3] Dan Morgan, "Clinton Wants to Gang up on Gangs," *The Washington Post*, Jan. 12, 1997, p. A6.

[4] The Anti-Gang and Youth Violence Act was introduced Feb. 25 in the House as HR 810 and Feb. 26 in the Senate as S 362. The bill also authorizes $200 million over two years in grants to state, county and local prosecutors to hire new prosecutors and develop special units aimed at targeting gangs.

[5] "*The President's Anti-Gang and Youth Violence Strategy*," The White House, Feb. 25, 1997, p. 9.

Continued from p. 300

shows precinct commanders when and where crimes are occurring almost instantaneously. Sherman describes sitting in on one of the twice weekly morning meetings where the hours of arrests in a precinct were displayed on a wall graph next to the hours most crimes were committed. New York police officials have used these meetings to ask precinct commanders why arrests aren't being made when the crime is happening and to pressure them to come up with improved crime-fighting strategies.

"That's what's impressive about New York," Sherman says. "They've worked relentlessly to change a century of practice that treated police like a factory, where you had to have equal numbers of workers in every shift — which is not the way criminals work."

The other highly touted aspect of New York's strategy — on-foot policing of quality-of-life crimes — grows out of the community policing concept, according to Kelling. The predominant approach of the 1970s, in which police mainly answered 911 emergency calls, kept officers tied to their patrol cars and radios.

As a result, officers were prevented from getting to know residents on the street, Kelling argues, and were relatively ineffective in cutting crime. Even where police speeded up their response times to 911 calls, a study in Kansas City in the 1970s found, it led to arrest in only 3 percent of serious crimes. The primary reason is that citizens generally do not call police immediately after a crime is committed because they are still in shock, because they know the offender or they want to be certain the criminal is gone from the scene.[27]

Also in the 1970s, Kelling studied the reintroduction of foot patrols in Newark, N.J. He found that "wherever there was a foot patrol, fear of crime dropped enormously." Police had taken to enforcing the neighborhood's informal rules, Kelling found: You could drink alcohol outside, but you had to do it in a back alley out of a brown paper bag; you could sit but not lie down on the stoops of stores, you could panhandle from people moving down the street but you could not harangue those standing still — at a bus stop, for example.

To critics of community policing, the Newark study supports their contention that it was a public relations tool, not a crime-fighting strategy. "You didn't get much of an impact on crime at the time," Kelling concedes. But he says Bratton went the next step, seeing these street contacts as a way to gather information that might lead to arrests for serious crime.

In New York City, officers now routinely question citizens they have stopped on minor violations about who is dealing drugs in the neighborhood and other criminal activity, according to Deputy Commissioner Edward T. Norris. "Each one is a wealth of information," he says. Earlier this year, police checks on two people given summonses for sleeping on a bench and for jumping a turnstile led to the discovery that both were wanted for murder, Norris reports.

Optimism in Fort Worth

Converts to community policing among chiefs in other cities are convinced that they've also made the Bratton leap from simply improving community relations to cutting crime.

"I have to believe our drop in crime is almost totally due to neighborhood policing," says Chief Thomas R. Windham, of Fort Worth. The Texas city started aggressively pursuing community policing in 1992. Since then, serious crimes as measured by the FBI have dropped 49 percent, according to Windham. Last year, Fort Worth's murder rate dropped 39 percent from the previous year.

Windham points to the transformation of J.A. Cavile Place, a predominantly black public housing complex, where a white officer, Jim Smith, runs a storefront police office opened in 1991. In the late 1980s and early '90s, the complex was infested with open drinking, gambling and narcotics selling.

In the summer, the central parking area, known as the alley, "looked like a sea of glass because of broken whiskey bottles and 40-ounce beer bottles," recalls Smith. "There would be 100 people carousing at night who didn't live there."

At a meeting with distressed tenants, Smith helped draft changes in the housing authority's lease agreements barring alcohol consumption in common areas and glass containers on the property. He also helped tenants develop visitor parking restrictions to prevent non-residents from hanging out. According to Smith, "there's no carousing in the alley now, no gambling and no dope dealers hanging out."

Resident Callie Pollard, 61, who raised her two grown children in the complex, agrees that the neighborhood patrolling and the presence of officers eight hours a day helped "a lot" to reduce crime. "We had numerous gangs. People were shot down and killed just like animals. There were drug sales day and night. People were afraid to come out. It was just horrible," she says. "Things have changed dramatically."

Pollard points to the Boys and Girls Club and public library the city has installed in the complex as well as the police storefront, where residents drop by to chat. "When people really get to know a police officer, it's like a partnership where everyone knows Jim, and Jim knows everybody," Pollard says.

One sign of that relationship was the neighborhood's reaction in June 1993, when Smith was shot by a man he was trying to arrest for drug possession. Smith says when he cried for help, "There was never doubt in my

Continued on p. 306

At Issue:

Does fighting "quality-of-life" crimes reduce murder and other more serious crimes?

GEORGE KELLING
Professor of criminology, Rutgers University

FROM *THE WASHINGTON POST,* FEB. 9, 1997

yes

Two months ago, Mayor Marion Barry and Police Chief Larry D. Soulsby said that Washington would begin replicating some of the successful law enforcement techniques developed in New York, Boston and other cities. In each case, an emphasis on . . . restoring order in public spaces by cracking down on seemingly minor infractions such as graffiti and public drinking was central to reducing violent crime.

Order, however, will not be restored, nor crime reduced, by political declarations. The solution may sound simple, but it's a complicated business requiring fundamental changes in the . . . philosophy of the police department. . . .

Commitment means taking the time to plan a strategy. In New York City's subways, it took a year of planning, in which I was involved, before William Bratton arrived to lead a reluctant Transit Police Department and began to restore order. When we discovered, for instance, that 1 out of 7 subway fare beaters was either carrying a weapon or had an outstanding warrant for a serious felony, officers learned firsthand the value of restoring basic order. . . .

Mayor Rudolph Giuliani and Bratton, building on the subway experience, implemented aggressive order maintenance in the city itself, and the results are equally impressive — homicide has dropped to the lowest rate in 30 years. The results came quickly, but not overnight.

If similar results are to be obtained in Washington, the same concern for doing it right will have to guide Mayor Barry and Chief Soulsby. . . .

First, leadership will be required to change how police do their business. For generations, police "business" has been "sending a car" when there's a problem. But what police should do when, for instance, they get to a park that has been taken over by drinking youths is not immediately apparent. "Rousting" them is no answer; they have probably been rousted for years with no effect. . . .

Second, police must figure out what the problems really are. Everyone . . . "knew" that the problem in New York's subway was homelessness. In fact, the problem was illegal disorderly behavior by troublemakers, only some of whom were homeless. . . .

While crime, poverty and injustices are linked, it is wrong to presume that police can do nothing about crime. When troublemakers, gangs and criminals rule the streets, they block the basic institutions of society — family, church, schools, commerce — from functioning. Reclaiming public spaces is the first step to restoring neighborhoods.

RICHARD MORAN
Professor of criminology, Mount Holyoke College

FROM *THE WASHINGTON POST,* FEB. 9, 1997

no

New York Mayor Rudolph Giuliani and his former police commissioner, William Bratton, have seized credit for the abrupt drop in New York City's murder rate. . . . But while the argument that the police deserve all the credit for the drop in homicides sounds plausible, no solid scientific evidence supports their claims of omnipotence. . . .

The "broken windows" theory is a cornerstone of New York City's policing strategy. It purports to explain how disorder, incivility and urban decay lead to crime: If a window is broken, and remains unfixed, before long more windows will be broken. Because such transgressions proclaim that no one is in charge, official tolerance for nuisances such as graffiti and panhandling hastens a neighborhood's decline and animates serious crime. . . .

The contention that "grime leads to crime by attracting slime" is a seductive hypothesis. The empirical support for it, however, is weak. Improving a neighborhood's economic profile is at least as important. . . .

A close and careful look at the data, however, reveals one indisputable fact that cannot be reconciled with the argument that the change in police methods is solely responsible. The decline in the murder rate began in 1991, three years before Giuliani and Bratton took office. . . .

Not surprisingly, experienced criminologists have been reluctant to endorse the claims of Giuliani and Bratton. More than 30 years of criminological research has shown that the ability of the police to influence crime is extremely limited. . . . In 1991, San Diego and Dallas had about the same ratio of police to population, yet twice as many crimes were reported in Dallas. Meanwhile Cleveland and San Diego had comparable crime rates even though Cleveland had twice as many police officers per capita. . . .

If more police do not mean less crime, what about foot patrols? . . . The most thorough study ever done, a 1981 analysis of police beats in Newark, N.J., found that foot patrols had virtually no effect on crime rates. . . . Poverty, lack of education, addiction and the paucity of jobs for unskilled workers are the real causes of crime and neighborhood deterioration.

Most seasoned criminologists have a more plausible explanation for the decline in murder in New York City. They point to a twofold increase in the number of criminals sent to jail over the past 10 years, an improving economy that has summoned idle young men back to full-time work and, most importantly, the waning of murderous crack wars. . . .

Continued from p. 304

mind the residents would call the police. The switchboards lit up with people telling the police I needed help." Chief Windham credits the neighborhood with saving Smith's life.

Community Policing in Tampa

Skeptics of community policing like Mount Holyoke's Moran insist there's no evidence that community policing brings crime down; it's mainly a way of improving relations with residents.

That could be the conclusion drawn in Florida's Hillsborough County, a suburban-rural area around Tampa where crime increased 3 percent last year despite the introduction of community policing in 1993. But it's not the conclusion drawn by Sheriff Cal Henderson. Through federal COPS grants, the county added 26 deputies to do community policing two years ago and 22 more this year.

Henderson says he became an enthusiast of community policing because he saw a major improvement in relations with residents after he created two community police stations in 1993 — one in a migrant workers area and another in a high-crime area outside Tampa.

Henderson believes crime may have increased because residents are now more willing to report crimes to officers they know on a first-name basis. "It takes a year or two until you get a new baseline," Henderson says. "You can't base it all on the crime rate [initially] or you will give up a good program."

Order vs. Civil Rights

Practically every city that has aggressively implemented the "order maintenance" strategies advocated by criminologist Kelling in New York City has been sued for civil rights violations.

In most cities over the past 20 years, loitering and vagrancy laws ceased to be enforced by police or prosecuted by city attorneys after they came under constitutional challenge. Two landmark Supreme Court cases in 1972 and 1983 dealt a fatal blow to loitering and vagrancy statutes.

In *Papachristou v. City of Jacksonville* (1972), eight individuals were charged with "prowling by auto" and loitering. The court invalidated the Jacksonville ordinance as "void for vagueness" and said it made criminal an innocent act such as "wandering or strolling." The 1983 case, *Kolender v. Lawson,* involved a man who had been stopped by police in California and asked for identification, detained or arrested 15 times between 1975 and 1977 while walking late at night on an isolated street near a high-crime area. The court found the California statute vague under the 14th Amendment and said it encouraged arbitrary enforcement by police.

Other courts overturned many such local laws under the due process clause of the 14th Amendment. The statutes were generally criticized for failing to provide guidelines specific enough so people could avoid unlawful behavior and for giving too much discretion to officers.

Civil libertarians continue to see such laws as a pretext for discrimination. "The people stopped and frisked are those who don't have a voice in the system," says Mark Kappelhoff, legislative counsel at the ACLU. "We're seeing increasing incidences of minorities being stopped and searched."

In a recent test case, the California Supreme Court in January upheld a San Jose city ordinance that prohibited suspected gang members from standing together on street corners, wearing beepers and other activities that would be legal for ordinary citizens. The case had been challenged by the ACLU of Northern California, which charged the injunction violated constitutional rights to free speech and free association. [28]

Specifically, the injunction prevented 38 Hispanic men and women suspected of membership in a street gang from frequenting a four-block neighborhood that police said the gang had terrorized.

Catherine M. Coles, a lawyer at the Kennedy School of Government at Harvard University and co-author with Kelling of *Fixing Broken Windows,* says the case "represents a sea change in thinking by the courts." The court held that individual rights cannot be protected at the expense of a community's right to security and protection. "One thing that was missing in a lot of court decisions was a recognition of the importance of order maintenance" and the link between these low-level problems and "overall crime and neighborhood deterioration," Coles says.

Kelling and Coles advise cities to avoid antiquated loitering laws, which can be challenged as discriminating against people on the basis of their status, such as homelessness or race. They urge cities to draft laws that outlaw specific disruptive behavior, such as disorderly conduct or aggressive panhandling in a particular area, and to be prepared to defend those laws in court.

But the distinction between someone's down-and-out status and disorderly behavior can be blurry. NYU's Skolnick guesses that New York City police "probably are exceeding the constitutional limits of the law" in frisking people arrested for low-level crimes. But even when the police are acting within the law, poor people are more likely to be stopped for minor violations, he says.

"People don't drink beer on the street in Sutton Place," he says. "They drink beer in the South Bronx and Brooklyn. Their houses are lousy; it's more pleasant to be on the street. They don't play loud music in Sutton Place. In rich people's cars, the light isn't busted." ■

OUTLOOK

Whither Society?

Despite the good news about policing, conservatives continue to see the root cause of crime as a collapse of moral values in the inner city, much as liberals see poverty and inequality in education as the root cause.

In a recent report on preventing juvenile crime, the Council on Crime in America, co-chaired by conservative William J. Bennett, former secretary of Education, praises New York-style policing tactics and harsher imprisonment policies as effective tools against crime. But the council, which includes conservative thinker DiIulio and former Police Commissioner Bratton among its members, urges that more efforts be put into helping America's most disadvantaged children through inner-city church and mentoring programs.

"Even if, for example, we succeeded in depriving tomorrow's would-be juvenile felons of access to high-tech weapons and thereby averted many shootings and murders, we would still be left with the tragedy of youngsters whose social and spiritual conditions were such that they would use guns to commit crimes if they could get them," the report says. The council cites a study of predominantly low-income children from single-parent homes whose participation in Big Brothers/Big Sisters programs appears to offer one bulwark against delinquency. The study found that the children were less likely than their peers to start using drugs or to cut school. [29]

But other experts say that providing more jobs and closing the income disparities between whites and blacks would ultimately do more to shape the extent of crime in America.

"It isn't rocket science," says NYU's Skolnick, who sees future crime rates as dependent largely on the economy. "You know that a very small proportion of the people who grow up in Sutton Place will end up as street criminals."

The New York City Police Department's insight that prevention is more effective than retribution should be expanded to the broader social realm to create more opportunities for at-risk youths, Skolnick recently urged. [30] "A lot of kids don't want to be in gangs," he says. "If there are more opportunities for work, they won't be in gangs."

In *Malign Neglect*, Tonry argues that America's imprisonment and crime-control policies are decimating the black community. He puts the blame squarely on the racially inequitable world in which he sees young black men growing up. Tonry points to a famous study that compared a group of Philadelphia youths who became teens in the 1950s with those who reached adolescence in the 1960s. [31] About the same percentage of both birth cohorts got into trouble, but the later generation committed more offenses.

"It's because the world had changed," asserts Tonry. "We had increasing ghettoization and high poverty rates." Even in a socially tranquil country like the Netherlands, Tonry reports that crime rates are rising as the country experiences — American-style — an influx of foreigners, widening disparities in income, higher unemployment and the beginning of ethnic ghettos.

But journalist James Traub recently questioned Tonry's socially oriented prescription after hanging around Washington Heights, where crime plummeted after New York police saturated the area. In a recent *New Republic* piece, Traub argued that "root-cause liberalism . . . stigmatizes the idea of law enforcement by insisting that inner-city criminals are the true victims of crime." The Tonry outlook ignores the fact that innocent bystanders who live in the same bad neighborhoods but lead law-abiding lives are the true victims of crime,

FOR MORE INFORMATION

American Civil Liberties Union, 122 Maryland Ave. N.W., Washington, D.C. 20002; (202) 544-1681. The American Civil Liberties Union has challenged the constitutionality of laws aimed at panhandlers and loiterers, which growing numbers of police departments are enforcing to reduce crime on the streets.

Bureau of Justice Statistics Clearinghouse, Box 179, Annapolis Junction, Md. 20701-0179; (800) 732-3277. The BJS, an arm of the Justice Department, produces a variety of reports on crime rates, including an annual household survey, "The National Crime Victimization Survey."

Federal Bureau of Investigation, Criminal Justice Information Services Division, Communications Division\Module D-3, 1000 Custer Hollow Road, Clarksburg, W. Va 26306; (304) 625-4995. This branch of the FBI provides statistical information on crime rates for the nation and for individual cities.

Office of Community Oriented Policing (COPS), 1100 Vermont Ave. N.W., Washington, D.C. 20530; (800) 421-6770. This office within the Justice Department promotes community policing and oversees grants to police departments for the hiring of new officers under President Clinton's "100,000 cops" legislation.

Traub contended.

"It is in fact precisely because drug dealers and muggers are not simply impelled by overwhelming social forces — but like other people, respond rationally to changes in circumstances — that concentrated police action can alter their behavior," Traub wrote.[32]

The debate over how much — if at all — policing can change a society fraught with racial tensions and pockmarked with wastelands of joblessness is not likely to be resolved soon. But both conservatives and liberals agree much will depend on how the fabric of American society evolves. When it comes to predicting future crime rates, "The question," says Tonry, is "what the world will be like in 2005." ■

Sarah Glazer is a freelance writer in New York who specializes in social policy and health issues.

Notes

[1] David Kocieniewski, "Nasty Boys," *Newsday*, June 23, 1994, p. A04, and Lizette Alvarez, "Police Patrols to Increase where Child was Shot," *The New York Times*, Jan. 25, 1996, p. B4. See "Youth Gangs," *The CQ Researcher*, Oct. 11, 1991, pp. 753-776

[2] Clifford Krauss, "Reported Crimes Continue to Show Decline, *The New York Times*, Oct. 2, 1996, p. B3; Office of the Mayor, press release, Dec. 31, 1996. The reductions cited in murder, robbery and auto theft in New York are based on New York City statistics for 1996. Michael Cooper, "Crime Reports Drop Sharply in New York," *The New York Times*, April 1, 1997, p. B1. The 1997 decreases were for the first quarter of the year compared with the first quarter of 1996.

[3] See "Gun Control," *The CQ Researcher*, June 10, 1994, pp. 505-528.

[4] Andrew Karmen, "Why is New York City's Murder Rate Dropping so Sharply?" unpublished paper, October 1996, p. 1.

[5] George L. Kelling and Catherine M. Coles, *Fixing Broken Windows* (1996), p. 117.

[6] George Kelling, "Restore Order and You Reduce Crime," *The Washington Post*, Feb. 9, 1997, p. C3.

[7] Kelling and Coles, *op. cit.*, p. 137.

[8] See "Community Policing," *The CQ Researcher*, Feb. 5, 1993, pp. 97-120.

[9] Michael Tonry, *Malign Neglect* (1995).

[10] Jerome H. Skolnick, "Making Sense of the Crime Decline," *Newsday*, Feb. 2, 1997.

[11] Evelyn Nieves, "Chased Out of New York Into a Hole," *The New York Times*, March 13, 1997, p. B1.

[12] *Ibid.*, p. 143.

[13] Quoted in Rebecca Carr, "Crime," *Congressional Quarterly Weekly Report*, Oct. 5, 1996, p. 2810.

[14] James Alan Fox, *Trends in Juvenile Violence: A Report to the United States Attorney General on Current and Future Rates of Juvenile Offending*, March 1996. Prepared for the Bureau of Justice Statistics, U.S. Department of Justice, pp. 1-2.

[15] James Alan Fox, *Forecasting Crime Data* (1978).

[16] Fox, *Trends in Juvenile Violence, op. cit.*, pp. 1-3.

[17] Roberto Suro, "Violent Crime Drops Among Young Teens," *The Washington Post*, Dec. 13, 1996, p. A1.

[18] Carr, *op. cit.*

[19] Quoted in Michael Cromartie, "Kids Who Kill," *Books and Culture*, January/February 1997, p. 10. The magazine reviews books and ideas from an evangelical Christian point of view.

[20] See "Civic Renewal," *The CQ Researcher*, March 21, 1997, pp. 241-264.

[21] See "War on Drugs," *The CQ Researcher*, March 19, 1993, pp. 241-264.

[22] Carr, *op. cit.* More than half of shoppers polled in another recent survey are still afraid to shop at night. Most thought crime would get worse over the next two years. See Robert Langreth, "Optimistic FBI Reports, Mall-Security Efforts Fail to Quell Concerns," *The Wall Street Journal*, May 13, 1996, p. B4.

[23] See "Suburban Crime," *The CQ Researcher*, Sept. 3, 1993, pp. 769-792.

[24] David Kocieniewski, "Police to Press Property-Crime Fight and Install Cameras," *The New York Times*, Feb. 5, 1997, p. B4.

[25] Quoted in Cromartie, *op. cit.*

[26] President Clinton signed the Violent Crime Control and Law Enforcement Act of 1994 on Sept. 13, 1994, authorizing the grant program.

[27] Kelling and Coles, *op. cit.*, p. 92.

[28] Maura Dolan and Alan Abrahamson, "State High Court Allows Injunctions to Restrict Gangs," *Los Angeles Times* [Washington Edition], Jan. 31, 1997, p. 1.

[29] "Preventing Crime, Saving Children, Monitoring, Mentoring and Ministering: Second Report of the Council on Crime in America," February 1997, pp. 2, 4.

[30] Skolnick, *op. cit.*

[31] Marvin Wolfgang et al, "Delinquency in a Birth Cohort" (1972).

[32] James Traub, "New York Story," *The New Republic*, Jan. 27, 1997, pp. 12-15.

Bibliography

Selected Sources Used

Books

Kelling, George L., and Catherine M. Coles, *Fixing Broken Windows: Restoring Order and Reducing Crime in Our Communities,* The Free Press, 1996.
Kelling, a professor of criminal justice at Rutgers University, and Coles, a lawyer at the Kennedy School of Government at Harvard University, describe efforts by New York and other cities to fight crime by going after neighborhood disorder and minor lawbreakers.

Tonry, Michael, *Malign Neglect: Race, Crime and Punishment in America,* Oxford University Press, 1996.
For crime rates to decline in the long run, major social policy changes will have to made in areas like job creation, argues University of Minnesota Professor of Law and Public Policy Tonry. In the meantime, he maintains, the nation's current crime control policies are decimating black communities.

Articles

Anderson, David C., "Crime Stoppers," *The New York Times Magazine,* Feb. 9, 1997, pp. 47-48, 51-52.
This article discusses the strategy of going after small crimes to stop big ones in New York City.

Benson, Jyl, et al., "Crime," *Time,* Jan. 15, 1996, pp. 48-54.
This article reviews the debate over why crime is declining around the nation.

Lardner, James, "Better Cops, Fewer Robbers," *The New York Times Magazine,* Feb. 8, 1997, pp. 45-54, 62.
To find out how the culture of the New York City Police Department has changed, the author accompanies a rookie cop on the job.

Remnick, David, "The Crime Buster," *The New Yorker,* Feb. 24/March 3, 1997, pp. 94-113.
Remnick profiles a colorful former New York subway cop, Jack Maple, who came up with some of the central ideas that helped clean up New York. The article looks at Maple's attempt to adapt his crime-fighting approach to New Orleans.

Richardson, John H., "Secrets of the Kings," *New York,* Feb. 17, 1997, pp. 28-37.
In tracking the Latin Kings' public relations effort to transform themselves from a violent gang to a force for peace, a reporter asks whether the shooting has really stopped.

Traub, James, "New York Story," *The New Republic,* Jan. 27, 1997, pp. 12-15.
Traub observes police efforts to cut crime in Washington Heights, an upper Manhattan neighborhood once known as the crack capital of New York, and finds that residents consider the neighborhood safer. He argues that "root-cause liberalism" "stigmatizes the idea of law enforcement by insisting that inner-city criminals are the true victims of crime" while neglecting the innocent bystanders who suffer the consequences of crime in their neighborhoods.

Reports and Studies

Fox, James Alan, *Trends in Juvenile Violence: A Report to the United States Attorney General on Current and Future Rates of Juvenile Offending,* prepared for the Bureau of Justice Statistics, U.S. Department of Justice, March 1996.
Fox, dean of criminal justice at Northeastern University, predicts continuing increases in juvenile crime as the teen population swells.

Federal Bureau of Investigation, *Crime in the United States — 1995,* Oct. 13, 1996.
This annual report provides statistics on the FBI's seven index crimes — murder, rape, robbery, aggravated assault, burglary, theft and auto theft — both nationally and by city.

The White House, *The President's Anti-Gang and Youth Violence Strategy,* February 1997.
This report lays out President Clinton's proposed Anti-Gang and Youth Violence Act, submitted to Congress on Feb. 25, and presents three cities' "success stories" in combating youth violence.

***Preventing Crime, Saving Children: Monitoring, Mentoring and Ministering, Second Report of the Council on Crime in America,* Manhattan Institute, February 1997.**
The council, which is co-chaired by former Education Secretary William J. Bennett and former Attorney General Griffin B. Bell, lays out its conservative agenda for preventing youth crime through inner-city churches, Big Brother/Big Sister programs and alternative youth courts.

The Next Step

Additional information from UMI's Newspaper & Periodical Abstracts™ database

Community Policing

"Community policing can make a difference," ***San Francisco Chronicle,*** **July 14, 1996, p. S6.**
An editorial notes that community policing has led to increased crime reporting by citizens and has cut down on urban flight. While police departments should continue to expand their commitment to this effective form of law enforcement, other public agencies also would do well to apply the strategies of community policing to their jobs.

Cortez, Angela, "Littleton seeking grant for community policing," ***The Denver Post,*** **Jan. 20, 1997, p. B2.**
Police Chief Gary Maas of Littleton, Mass., is applying for a $450,000 federal grant that would put six more police officers on the streets and create a citywide community policing program. The program, which is part of President Clinton's promise to put 100,000 more police officers on the nation's streets, would give Littleton enough money to pay slightly more than half the officers' salaries for three years. After that, the city would have to determine whether it could continue to pay for the positions.

Cytrynbaum, Pamela, "A passion for community policing," ***Chicago Tribune,*** **May 21, 1996, Sec. 2SW, p. 1.**
Chicago, Ill., and its suburbs all include elements of community policing programs, and one of its strongest and most well-known local proponents is Orland Park Police Chief Tim McCarthy. With 20 new officers increasing the staff to 83, the resources afforded by a generous property and sales tax base, McCarthy has instituted programs including a Citizens Police Academy, bike patrols and two tactical teams.

Recktenwald, William, "Community policing gets mixed grade after 3 years," ***Chicago Tribune,*** **Dec. 6, 1996, Sec. 2C, p. 3.**
In 1996, three years after an ambitious community-policing program began in Chicago, Ill., a new study says it needs improvements in several areas, including better problem solving by police and residents. Chicago's version of community policing, called the Chicago Alternative Policing Strategy, seeks to team up police and citizens to fight crime and improve neighborhoods.

Crime Rates/Statistics

Browne, J. Zamgba, "Fudged crime statistics no surprise, says Al Sharpton," ***Amsterdam News,*** **Nov. 2, 1996, p. 33.**
The October 1996 removal of Police Capt. Louis Vega, a South Bronx, N.Y., police commander, on charges he fudged crime statistics in the area is discussed.

"Crime statistics can mislead," ***St. Louis Post-Dispatch,*** **April 5, 1996, p. C14.**
An editorial comments on how crime statistics can be misleading, citing statistics released in 1996, that the crime rate in St. Louis, Mo., dropped 4.5 percent in 1995.

Carroll, Matt, "Crime rates seen in decline," ***The Boston Globe,*** **May 12, 1996, Sec. WW, p. 1.**
Crime is down overall in the cities and towns in suburban areas west of Boston, Mass., following a nationwide trend. However, burglaries increased 10 percent or more in nine area communities, according to statistics supplied by local police departments.

DiIulio, John J. Jr., and Anne Morrison Piehl, "What the crime statistics don't tell you," ***The Wall Street Journal,*** **Jan. 8, 1997, p. A22.**
The authors call for an adjustment in the "crime index," arguing that the two main ways that the federal government counts crimes, the Federal Bureau of Investigation's (FBI) Uniform Crime Reports and the Bureau of Justice Statistics' National Crime Victimization Survey, undercount crime in the U.S.

Gladstone, Mark, "California Crime Rate Declines; Statistics: Lungren sees three strikes, more prisons, community policing as factors," ***Los Angeles Times,*** **Jan. 30, 1997, p. A3.**
On Jan. 26, state Atty. Gen. Dan Lungren delivered more good news to Californians fearful for their personal safety: Major crimes plunged more than 12 percent in the first nine months of 1996, to rates not seen since the late 1960s. The preliminary crime figures, reflecting the continuation of a much-publicized four-year downward trend in major cities and counties, are especially encouraging to Lungren because they provide him a ready-made platform from which to launch his 1998 bid for governor.

Marquand, Robert, "Good news on crime rates may be lull before the storm," ***The Christian Science Monitor,*** **Jan. 9, 1996, p. 3.**
Urban crime figures across the U.S. indicate that the overall U.S. crime rate fell sharply in 1995, leading criminologists to offer a variety of explanations. On Jan. 5, 1996, a national council of prosecutors and police officials made public a report arguing that the country is in a "lull before the storm," which it says will hit as the number of 14- to 17-year-olds increases in the next 10 years.

"Will crime wave good-bye?" ***The Economist,*** **Jan. 6,**

1996, pp. 19-20.
Criminologists the world over are struggling to explain a fairly recent decline in urban crime. It just might be that diligence, rather than demographics, has wrought the change.

Get-Tough Initiatives vs. Addressing Root Causes of Crime

Fagan, Patrick F., "Disintegration of the family is the real root cause of violent crime," *USA Today,* May 1996, pp. 36-38.
The link between family and violent crime deserves attention. A focus on the importance of marriage, stable communities and families is vital to reducing violent crime. Fagan outlines a five-step process to becoming a criminal. This process begins when a child is neglected and abandoned during the critical early years.

Villafranca, Armando, "Cities urged to focus on fighting root causes of crime," *Houston Chronicle,* Nov. 10, 1996, p. A37.
Urban crime experts believe efforts to fight crime should focus on the root causes of violent crime, especially since building more prisons did not produce the results expected 20 years ago. In late November, a panel of experts will meet at the James A. Baker III Institute for Public Policy's second annual conference on Domestic Challenges at the End of the Century to discuss urban crime and violence.

New York City

Browne, J. Zamgba, "Despite drop in crime rate New Yorkers feel 'unsafe'," *Amsterdam News,* Nov. 9, 1996, p. 3.
While New Yorkers generally are pleased by the statistical decline in serious crime, they do not believe that it has eased significantly in their own neighborhoods, according to Manhattan Borough President Ruth Messinger. A recent *New York Daily News* poll reported that only 30 percent of New Yorkers feel safer today than they did six years ago.

"Drop in crime is reported," *The New York Times,* Jan. 15, 1996, p. B3.
On Jan. 14, 1996, Mayor Rudolph W. Giuliani, R-N.Y., and Police Commissioner William J. Bratton announced that the city had seen a 27.4 percent drop in the number of major felonies committed in the two-year period ending on Dec. 31, 1995.

Haberman, Clyde, "Crime Down, But Courts Are Clogged," *The New York Times,* Jan. 3, 1997, p. B1.
Haberman says that the New York City court system has become clogged by low-level offenders but that police are unlikely to change from their current course of making arrests for quality-of-life crimes because of the impressive drop in serious crime in the city.

"In NYC, 'taking back streets' curbed crime," *USA Today,* Oct. 25, 1996, p. A7.
William Bratton, New York City's police commissioner from 1994 to 1996, discusses the drop in crime under his community policing policy and its relevance for drug prevention.

Kocieniewski, David, "2 Polls Give Bratton Major Credit for Drop in Crime," *The New York Times,* April 21, 1996, p. 41.
New York City voters approve of Republican Mayor Rudolph Giuliani's handling of crime, but they believe that former Police Commissioner William J. Bratton deserves most of the credit for the city's historic drop in crime rates, according to two new polls focusing on crime-fighting.

Myers, Linnet, "Big Apple takes big bite out of crime — But how?" *Chicago Tribune,* Jan. 11, 1996, p. 1.
The New York Police Department seems to be gaining ground against crime. Figures for 1995 show that in two years crime has fallen about 27 percent. Although New York, with its newly aggressive police force, is leading the way, criminologists contend that much of the decline in crime comes from demographics.

Youth Gangs

Holleman, Joe, "Youth gangs: Suburban teens are joining up, experts say," *St. Louis Post-Dispatch,* Oct. 28, 1996, p. A1.
Experts say that the nation's gang problem is spreading into suburbs from its original home in urban centers. Gang experts with police departments in St. Charles and Jefferson counties in Missouri say that gangs are not just black, and they're not just in the city.

Nguyen, Lan, "Va. survey finds 260 youth gangs," *The Washington Post,* Oct. 22, 1996, p. E1.
A statewide survey of law enforcement agencies indicated there are 260 youth gangs in Virginia, more than half of them based in the Washington, D.C., suburbs. Results of the survey were released Oct. 21, 1996.

Wilson, Melinda, "New police details target Detroit's youth gangs," *Detroit News & Free Press,* Nov. 17, 1996, p. E4.
Wayne County, Mich., Prosecutor Douglas Baker plans to use information received at the trial of Detroit gang member Scott Younes to help two new Detroit police gang units infiltrate and neutralize youth gangs in Detroit neighborhoods. The new six-member units will concentrate on educating would-be gang members and arresting those already involved in gang activity.

Back Issues

Great Research on Current Issues Starts Right Here...Recent topics covered by The CQ Researcher are listed below. Before May 1991, reports were published under the name of Editorial Research Reports.

SEPTEMBER 1995
Catholic Church in the U.S.
Northern Ireland Cease-Fire
High School Sports
Teaching History

OCTOBER 1995
Quebec's Future
Revitalizing the Cities
Networking the Classroom
Indoor Air Pollution

NOVEMBER 1995
The Working Poor
The Jury System
Sex, Violence and the Media
Police Misconduct

DECEMBER 1995
Teens and Tobacco
Gene Therapy's Future
Global Water Shortages
Third-Party Prospects

JANUARY 1996
Emergency Medicine
Punishing Sex Offenders
Bilingual Education
Helping the Homeless

Back issues are available for $5.00 (subscribers) or $10.00 (non-subscribers). Quantity discounts apply to orders over ten. To order, call Congressional Quarterly Customer Service at (202) 887-8621.

Binders are available for $18.00. To order call 1-800-638-1710. Please refer to stock number 648.

FEBRUARY 1996
Reforming the CIA
Campaign Finance Reform
Academic Politics
Getting Into College

MARCH 1996
The British Monarchy
Preventing Juvenile Crime
Tax Reform
Pursuing the Paranormal

APRIL 1996
Centennial Olympic Games
Managed Care
Protecting Endangered Species
New Military Culture

MAY 1996
Russia's Political Future
Marriage and Divorce
Year-Round Schools
Taiwan, China and the U.S.

JUNE 1996
Rethinking NAFTA
First Ladies
Teaching Values
Labor Movement's Future

JULY 1996
Recovered-Memory Debate
Native Americans' Future
Crackdown on Sexual Harassment
Attack on Public Schools

AUGUST 1996
Fighting Over Animal Rights
Privatizing Government Services
Child Labor and Sweatshops
Cleaning Up Hazardous Wastes

SEPTEMBER 1996
Gambling Under Attack
The States and Federalism
Civic Journalism
Reassessing Foreign Aid

OCTOBER 1996
Political Consultants
Insurance Fraud
Rethinking School Integration
Parental Rights

NOVEMBER 1996
Global Warming
Clashing Over Copyright
Consumer Debt
Governing Washington, D.C.

DECEMBER 1996
Welfare, Work and the States
The New Volunteerism
Implementing the Disabilities Act
America's Pampered Pets

JANUARY 1997
Combating Scientific Misconduct
Restructuring the Electric Industry
The New Immigrants
Chemical and Biological Weapons

FEBRUARY 1997
Assisting Refugees
Alternative Medicine's Next Phase
Independent Counsels
Feminism's Future

MARCH 1997
New Air Quality Standards
Alcohol Advertising
Civic Renewal
Educating Gifted Students

Future Topics

- ***FBI Under Fire***
- ***Gender Equity in Sports***
- ***Space Program's Future***

THE CQ Researcher

PUBLISHED BY CONGRESSIONAL QUARTERLY INC.

The FBI Under Fire

How serious are the bureau's recent problems?

For decades, the FBI has ruffled feathers as it sought to balance tough law enforcement with sensitivity toward civil liberties. But today's bureau operates in a climate vastly altered from the days when agents in J. Edgar Hoover's virtually unchecked empire could burglarize homes and keep files on political opponents. With stepped-up scrutiny from Congress and the press, the modern FBI under Louis Freeh has demonstrated new willingness to admit its mistakes. Currently, the bureau is under fire for, among other things, alleged misconduct in its famous forensics lab and possible political favoritism toward the White House. The FBI's defenders, nonetheless, say the agency's record-high budgets are needed more than ever to fight high-tech criminals in globalized drug-running, terrorism, espionage and organized crime.

INSIDE THIS ISSUE

CQ April 11, 1997 • Volume 7, No. 14 • Pages 313-336

Formerly Editorial Research Reports

THE FBI UNDER FIRE

THE ISSUES

BACKGROUND

CURRENT SITUATION

OUTLOOK

SIDEBARS AND GRAPHICS

FOR MORE INFORMATION

COVER: FBI DIRECTOR LOUIS J. FREEH (REUTERS)

April 11, 1997
Volume 7, No. 13

The CQ Researcher (ISSN 1056-2036). Formerly Editorial Research Reports. Published weekly (48 times per year, not printed Jan. 3, May 30, Aug. 29, Oct. 31) by Congressional Quarterly Inc., 1414 22nd St., N.W., Washington, D.C. 20037. Annual subscription rate for libraries, businesses and government is $340. Additional rates furnished upon request. Periodicals postage paid at Washington, D.C., and additional mailing offices. POSTMASTER: Send address changes to The CQ Researcher, 1414 22nd St., N.W., Washington, D.C. 20037.

The FBI Under Fire

BY CHARLES S. CLARK

THE ISSUES

"A whole generation of people like me grew up believing the FBI could do no wrong," Sen. Charles E. Grassley, R-Iowa, declared in an impassioned speech on the Senate floor recently. "Now, that confidence, that trust, has been shaken." [1]

The conservative lawmaker's wrath was triggered by the steady drumbeat of allegations last winter of corruption and mismanagement in the FBI's world-famous forensics laboratory. Each year the 65-year-old lab helps police departments and prosecutors from around the country to analyze more than a half-million pieces of evidence — from paint chips to blood droplets and shoe prints. An FBI lab analyst-turned-whistle-blower has charged that evaluations of evidence by the lab were subject to manipulation by FBI officials. Critics deride the secretive facility as "the last redoubt of Hooverism," after the bureau's iron-fisted founding director, J. Edgar Hoover.

Controversy over the lab prompted the 63-year-old Grassley to warn that the "integrity of the American criminal justice system is at stake." But it is not the only problem that has beset the FBI in recent days.

Last June came revelations that the FBI acceded to Clinton White House security officers when they improperly sought and obtained FBI background files on 900 Republican former White House staffers. Then in July, the FBI's investigation of a fatal bombing during the Olympics in Atlanta was marred when security guard Richard Jewell was identified to news media as the prime suspect, only to be exonerated later.

Most recently, the politically neutral FBI became embroiled with the White House in a clash of conflicting statements over Chinese campaign

donations (*see p. 327*).

The way the agency has handled the mud on its image says much about today's FBI. During Hoover's 48-year reign, the agency was loath to admit a mistake. Contrast that with the mea culpas by Director Louis J. Freeh. Since he took over the bureau in September 1993, he has continued to answer for the FBI's conduct in, among other things, the 1992 shootout at a tax-resister's isolated cabin in Ruby Ridge, Idaho, which killed a federal agent, an unarmed woman and her teenage son.

The FBI's performance was "terribly flawed," Freeh told a congressional panel in 1995, referring not only to the deaths but also to slanted reports on the FBI's conduct and his own "blind spot" in later promoting his friend Larry Potts, who was criticized for his role in the controversial affair. [2]

"I am not saying that I approve of" the gunshot that killed Vicky Weaver, Freeh told the lawmakers. "I am not trying to justify it. . . . I am certainly not saying that in a future similar set of circumstances, FBI agents or law enforcement officers could take such a shot. . . . But on careful balance," he said, the shot was "constitutional" under the circumstances.

Freeh also reminds his inquisitors of the FBI's recent successes — the arrests of suspect Timothy McVeigh in the 1995 Oklahoma City bombing, of Unabomber suspect Ted Kaczynski, of CIA spy Aldrich Ames and of the Muslim terrorists who bombed the World Trade Center in 1993. And there was last year's arrest of the Mountaineer Militia, which was planning to blow up the FBI's fingerprint analysis facility in West Virginia. [3]

But the FBI still takes heat for unsolved cases, such as the still mysterious crash last summer of TWA Flight 800 into Long Island Sound and the terrorist bombing of the U.S. Air Force barracks in Saudi Arabia. And the arrest of Earl Edwin Pitts, the highest FBI official ever accused of spying, sullied the bureau's image, though the sting operation that nabbed him was praised.

During the Clinton administration, the FBI's annual budget (currently $2.8 billion) has grown by 25 percent. Freeh has persuaded Congress to pay for 3,600 new employees (among them more than 1,000 agents), and he has moved 500 agents out of headquarters and into the field. He is beefing up the fingerprint operation (recently criticized for being slow in performing naturalization background checks). He is hiring staff to trim the FBI's backlog of 16,000 Freedom of Information Act requests (*see p. 328*). And he is setting up two new computer systems intended to streamline the collection and retrieval of nationwide information on crime.

Critics, however, see remnants of what they view as arrogance from the Hoover era (nearly 6,200 current FBI employees worked under Hoover). "Hoover was so focused on protecting his own position in government that in a funny way he actually had a rather narrow understanding of what a police agency could do," says Marcus Raskin, a distinguished fellow at the left-leaning Institute for Policy Studies. The forensics lab troubles and the FBI's handling of the Olympic Park bombing case, he says, "show that this new notion of a professionalized FBI that has cleaned up its act is just not so."

Other critics, who were tough on the FBI for domestic civil liberties violations in the 1970s, argue that the bureau's insensitivity toward privacy and free speech has not changed, only its political targets. "Their focus has shifted from left-wing groups to supporters of right-wing militia, pro-lifers and Arab-Americans," says Kate Martin, director of the Center for National Security Studies.

Indeed, the FBI's storming of the Branch Davidian cult's compound near Waco, Texas, in 1993 has guaranteed an ongoing barrage of accusations on talk radio and on the Internet. Rightist critics such as the John Birch Society claim that federal agents knew in advance of the Oklahoma City bombing.

"This hostility toward the FBI and the government nowadays is kind of a weird twist from the situation of 25 years ago," when the bureau's targets were anti-Vietnam War activists, says former Sen. George S. McGovern, D-S.D., on whom Hoover opened a secret FBI file after the one-time presidential nominee criticized his firing of an agent. [4] "Hoover ran the FBI as sort of a personal fiefdom, but the type of director we have today is much better."

Surveys indicate that most Americans actually backed the FBI's handling of Waco. According to a Harris Poll, 71 percent believed that defiant religious leader David Koresh was more to blame for the deaths than the FBI and other federal agencies. [5]

FBI veterans say today's agents deserve all the respect the country can muster. "The work they do is more dangerous now," says security consultant Sean McWeeney, a 24-year FBI veteran. "I probably drew my gun about six times in my whole career. But now agents are facing drug traffickers in flak vests and all these street gangs and Mafia from Colombia, Russia and Mexico who are armed to the teeth." [6]

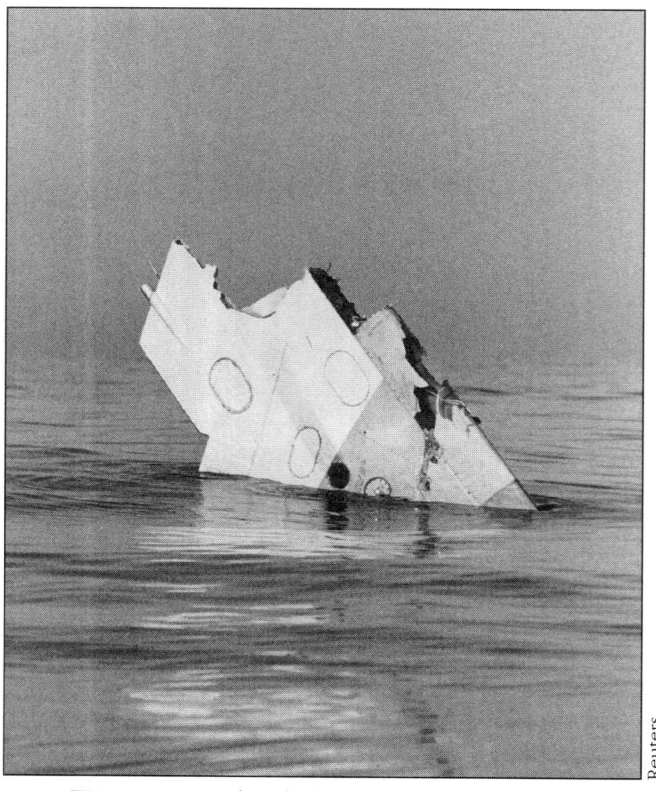
Reuters

FBI critics note that the bureau has failed to solve several big cases, among them the crash of TWA Flight 800 into Long Island Sound in July 1996.

Heroics aside, the controversy over the forensics lab could seriously damage the FBI's worldwide reputation, and possibly decide what happens to Freeh, who prosecuted some of the cases being questioned.

"I doubt the lab was ever on the up-and-up," says media consultant John Kelly, who is writing a book on the lab. "But under Freeh, the corruption and abuse have become institutionalized."

As scrutiny of the FBI continues, these are some of the key questions being asked:

Does the FBI lab need major reforms?

The crime lab controversy reaches back to 1989, when federal Judge Robert S. Vance was killed by a mail bomb at his home in Birmingham, Ala. Walter Leroy Moody Jr., a scam artist and known bomb maker, was convicted in Vance's death. The prosecutor in the highly publicized case was future FBI Director Freeh, who used evidence analyzed by the FBI lab.

Actually, the forensics lab had been under scrutiny since a 1988 internal review (following a 1980 General Accounting Office critique) had raised concerns about lab methodology. There were charges of sloppy handling of specimens, analytical procedures biased in favor of prosecutors and pressure on analysts from higher-ups to modify their findings.

One employee who shared such concerns was chemist Frederic Whitehurst, who in June 1991 wrote a memo to his superiors with the goal of documenting "fabrications of evidence" in Moody's trial. Whitehurst wrote of the "bullying ways" of his immediate superior (not Freeh) that "circumvented the established protocols and procedures of the FBI laboratory in order to get the answer that he wanted for the residue analysis of the explosive in the pipe" bomb used to kill the judge. Whitehurst cited numerous other cases for which he felt results were being manipulated.

Whitehurst's complaints did not become public until after another internal review of the lab in 1994. Soon after, an in-depth investigation by the Justice Department's inspector general had gotten under way. Having fed material to the I.G. and gone public with his complaints, Whitehurst was abruptly suspended by the FBI this January. Other lab employees who deny misconduct in the lab have dismissed him as unstable.[7] The Justice Department, however, found Whitehurst's statements credible and possibly exculpatory enough to warrant sending them to Moody, who sits on death row in Alabama.

Whitehurst was not the only lab employee to make charges, as was indicated in excerpts from a draft of the inspector general's report that were leaked to the media in January. The FBI immediately transferred four key employees out of the lab. In February, the Justice Department made the startling announcement that misconduct in the lab had jeopardized as many as 50 recent or pending cases — including the Oklahoma City, Olympic Park and World Trade Center bombings and the 1989 impeachment of then-Judge Alcee Hastings, now a Democratic House member from Florida.[8]

Criminal defense attorneys from around the country immediately began planning new strategies to discredit evidence used to convict their clients. They unsuccessfully sought the inspector general's 500-page draft report; the final report is expected to be released this month.

To add to the mess, Freeh in mid-March had to back off key statements he had made to skeptical members of Congress when he said that he was on top of the lab situation — that none of the transferred supervisors had altered evidence and that his actions against lab personnel had been in accordance with the inspector general's wishes.[9] "Mr. Freeh totally rejects any contention that he deliberately misled the Congress or the public," the FBI said in a March 17 statement.

Reuters

The Branch Davidian cult compound near Waco, Texas, burns April 19, 1994. Seventy-five adults and children died in the fire, which erupted after the FBI began pouring tear gas into the building.

Questions of Freeh's credibility, given his personal stake in the cases, were followed by debate about the overall purpose of the FBI lab: whether, for example, it should be required to be more open about its methodologies and whether defense attorneys should have access to analyses currently available only to the prosecution.

"We think it is in the public interest to have lab information available for academics, litigation, habeas corpus appeals and preparing pending cases for cross-examination," says G. Jack King Jr., public affairs director of the National Association of Criminal Defense Lawyers. "The reason we wanted the draft report was that we'd like to know who has done sloppy work or shaded the truth, so that people can judge for themselves or use exculpatory evidence to reopen their cases. The people best qualified to judge are the defendant and his lawyer, not the prosecutors," he adds. "It saddens me to think that the Justice Department is more concerned with the FBI's image than with innocent people who might be in prison."

To James E. Starrs, a professor of forensic sciences and law at George Washington University — Hoover's alma mater — and a longtime critic of the FBI lab, "There is no doubt that Whitehurst is onto something; the only question is whether the problems are deliberate or reckless. The real issue is the lab's mind-boggling secrecy. In a sample report on, say, paint analysis, there is no method identified. There are vague, uncertain conclusions, but no indicator of who did the tests," he says. "The FBI might say a certain fingerprint is less than a month old, when in fact there is no science that says that. The FBI waits until it is challenged, and if it is not challenged, it doesn't have to do the necessary research and get the supportive data. And it doesn't ever back down."

In general, Starrs adds, "the more secrecy, the less reliability and integrity. The FBI puts itself on a pedestal with its untouchable forensic science. The requirements for scientific candor don't apply because these cops in lab coats generally favor prosecut-

New Thriller Reveals Love-Hate Relations . . .

After watching the new hit movie "Donnie Brasco," a retired FBI official wrote an angry letter to FBI Director Louis J. Freeh. "The film is disgraceful," said security consultant Sean McWeeney, a 24-year veteran of the FBI's organized crime and anti-drug divisions.

The crime thriller, starring Johnny Depp and Al Pacino, is based on the true story of Joseph D. Pistone, who in the 1970s spearheaded the FBI's longest and most successful undercover operation against the Mafia. [1] But far from being thrilled by the film's portrayal of FBI derring-do (as many FBI employees were), McWeeney was appalled at what he sees as the film's numerous inaccuracies. "I supervised many of these cases, and Pistone was never present at murders in Brooklyn or at the killing of informants," he says. "He never sawed the legs off of any body, and never would have slapped his wife. He did a tremendous job."

© 1997 Mandalay Entertainment

Johnny Depp (left) is an undercover FBI agent and Al Pacino is a Mafia member in "Donnie Brasco."

Many FBI employees were also upset, McWeeney adds, by the scene in which "Brasco," the undercover agent, offers $300,000 to the Mafia hitman he befriended "so he can get on a boat and sail off into the sunset. That's a figment of Hollywood's imagination," McWeeney says, "yet my [teenage] son saw 'Brasco' and asked me whether the FBI really did those things."

There is some irony in complaints from FBI loyalists about the bureau's treatment by the entertainment media. That's because the FBI's reputation for crime-fighting heroics was built with sizable assistance from popular portrayals (some of them FBI-instigated) in radio, film, comic books, magazines and television.

Beginning in the early 1930s, before the young FBI Director J. Edgar Hoover had become a household name, the bureau's success stories were dramatized on the popular radio program "The Lucky Strike Hour." [2] Then followed numerous knockoffs with names like "Gangbusters," "This is Your FBI" and "The FBI in War and Peace." Even more influential were movies such as the 1935 James Cagney smash "G-Men." It and such follow-ups as "Persons in Hiding" and "Queen of the Mob" spawned a nationwide craze of Junior G-Men Clubs and a popular song that went, "I Wanna Be a G-man and Go Bang, Bang, Bang, Bang." [3]

According to former FBI Assistant Director Ray Wannall, who appeared in the 1952 espionage movie "Walk East on

ing." (*See "At Issue," p. 329.*)

Some in the FBI resist the notion of an FBI lab that could be used equally by defense attorneys. The ideal lab specialist "stands in the shoes of the investigator in the field, whom he is serving," said John J. McDermott, a senior FBI official. [10] Defenders also argue that lab analysts have no incentive to cook their conclusions because they often know very little about the case surrounding the piece of evidence they're handling.

"Obviously," says former special agent McWeeney, "if the lab has specific problems, they should be fixed — and perhaps the lab should be opened up. I'm not a guy who says 'Hey, the FBI's perfect.' But hundreds of men and women work in the lab, and only a handful work in that bombing analysis area where there are questions. And Whitehurst, from what I've seen on TV, doesn't seem very sharp to me."

In response to the lab furor, Freeh released a statement on Jan. 27 outlining recent changes the bureau had made to improve performance. By 2000, the lab will have moved from Washington to a larger facility at Quantico, Va. A new director, possibly an outside expert, is being sought. A panel of experts — including a British specialist on terrorism in Northern Ireland — has been assembled to review lab methodology. Some $30 million will be spent on technological improvements. For the first time, the lab will seek accreditation with the American Society of Crime Laboratory Directors.

Finally, Freeh recused himself from deciding the fate of Whitehurst and other whistleblowers, given his own stake in the cases. "I pledge to you," he told a House Appropriations subcommittee on March 5, "that I will do everything in my power to ensure that the FBI lab remains, as I believe it is, the foremost forensic laboratory in the world."

Meanwhile, members of a violent

. . . Between the FBI and Hollywood

Beacon," Hoover "had been critical of Hollywood for glorifying gangsters, so our Los Angeles office had someone go over to the studios to make sure the filmmakers got it right. Hoover had influence on Hollywood, and Hollywood in turn had an influence on the public."

Historians disagree over whether it was Hoover, Hoover's boss in the 1930s (Attorney General Homer Cummings), or a public relations man he hired named Henry Suydam who did the most to shine a spotlight on Hoover and his G-Men. What was clear, though, was the explosion of Hoover appearances on magazine covers and in newsreels and FBI-orchestrated movies. They were justified, as a pair of criminologists wrote, because "public opinion is a strong deterrent, and when you have the public conscience and public opinion well-organized, there is bound to be progress." [4]

Yet even then, the Hollywood image of the FBI was at variance with the prosaic reality. "Pop culture creates audience identification with action heroes like the G-Man by using them as embodiments of the public's most cherished cultural fantasies: absolute freedom, irresistible power, total self-reliance," cultural critic Richard Gid Powers wrote. "On the contrary, the special agent in the FBI formula was the antithesis of the action hero. He was faceless and anonymous, and repelled the sort of projective fantasies that the G-Man formula encouraged." [5]

The FBI's efforts to mold its reputation through entertainment reached their peak in 1965, when the bureau created and supervised what became the popular TV show "The FBI," starring Efram Zimbalist Jr. (It was followed in 1981 by a short-lived imitation, "Today's FBI.")

But by the early 1970s, the rise of a counterculture and revelations about FBI abuses of domestic civil liberties made the popular image of the stout-hearted G-Man passé. The Hoover long revered as every boy's role model was caricatured by a black actress in Woody Allen's movie "Bananas." The 1980s and '90s would offer the public idiosyncratic FBI agents in surreal TV shows such as "Twin Peaks" and "The X-Files."

FBI officials today are as conscious as ever of the power of popular media. They cooperated extensively to show off the bureau's serial-killer profiling operations for the 1991 hit movie "The Silence of the Lambs." They cooperate regularly with producers of reality crime shows such as the Fox network's "America's Most Wanted" and NBC's "Unsolved Mysteries." They also work closely with the producers of ABC's fictionalized "The FBI: The Untold Stories."

But the most common portrayals can be offensive to FBI veterans such as McWeeney. The ABC drama "NYPD Blue" showed an FBI agent "so frightened he urinated in his pants, which is disgraceful," McWeeney says. "What is the media's problem with the bureau? Real agents are out there being killed, and yet Hollywood is portraying agents as either nerdy stiffs or turf-grabbing bureaucrats. It drives me insane."

---

[1] Pistone was profiled in *The Washington Post*, Feb. 28, 1997.

[2] Ronald Kessler, *The FBI* (1993), p. 363.

[3] Diarmuid Jeffreys, *The Bureau: Inside the Modern FBI* (1995), p. 60.

[4] Richard Gid Powers, *G-Men: Hoover's FBI in Popular Culture* (1983), p. 110.

[5] *Ibid.*, p. 112.

paramilitary group went on trial in February in Seattle, Wash., marking the first case in which evidence from the FBI lab has actually been questioned in court. [11] "It's time the bureau stopped its narcissistic infatuation with its own image," thundered Sen. Grassley.

"It's time to stop selling an inferior product with false advertising. The American people deserve from [their] chief law enforcement agency a product with integrity. . . . This is an issue of leadership."

Can the FBI be trusted with expanded powers?

"To my amazement, there are voices that . . . claim repression by government — and fear of government," Freeh said in May 1995. He was immediately pounced on by libertarian author James Bovard, who wrote: "It is especially ludicrous for an FBI chief to express amazement at people's fear of the government when the FBI itself trampled many citizens' rights in the 1950s and '60s with burglaries, illegal wiretaps, character assassination and intimidation." [12]

Right-wingers' smoldering resentment of the FBI's role in the 1993 Waco tragedy is revisited in a new book, *No More Wacos: What's Wrong With Federal Law Enforcement and How to Fix It*. The authors argue that the FBI lied when it said it didn't expect Branch Davidian cult members to commit suicide, and that bureau agents tricked Attorney General Janet Reno about the lack of progress of negotiations to win approval for a gas attack (*see p. 326*). [13]

From the left, Martin of the Center for National Security Studies expresses concern over how the FBI in the Clinton era has accelerated its efforts to win new powers. In the name of investigating terrorism, it has been reinterpreting and loosening the Justice Department's guidelines (handed

Continued on p. 321

FBI Tours End With a Bang

"Inside the FBI" is a snappy phrase for a reporter's exposé. It is also a ready-made boast for postcards sent by the tourists who flock to FBI headquarters — a half-million every year.

The thousands who line up daily to tour the J. Edgar Hoover FBI Building on Washington's Pennsylvania Avenue were anticipated when the imposing building — detractors describe the architectural style as "fascist" — opened in 1975. Visitors wait in a comfortable lounge before being guided around the building's two lowest floors on a tour designed by Disney to avoid disrupting the facility's 7,300 employees.

Tours of FBI headquarters in Washington were designed by Disney.

Observers have suggested that the tourist-friendly layout is just another of the FBI's Hoover-era public relations techniques. But former Assistant Director Ray Wannall points out that Hoover was already dead when the building was under construction in the early 1970s and that there was little room to splurge on tourists. He recalls how pressed they were for space when the employees first moved in, and how concerned his colleagues were that the open access to the first two floors would permit an intruder to plant a bomb.

Engraved in the courtyard is a quotation from Hoover: "The most effective weapon against crime is cooperation." A gift from the Society of Former Special Agents of the FBI, the engraving was actually a second choice. They had originally proposed this Hooverism: "Law and order are the pillars of democracy on which our safety and welfare rest," but then-FBI Director William H. Webster thought it too militant. [1]

Walls along the FBI tour are covered with portraits of past directors as well as Attorney General Janet Reno. There are posters promoting the many movies made with the FBI's blessing, among them "G-Men" and "Federal Agent at Large." Also on display is a blow-up of the FBI seal, with its motto of "fidelity, bravery, integrity."

Visitors are told that the FBI employs 10,089 agents, of whom 1,500 are women. Only 611 agents work at headquarters, where the majority of employees are civil servants toiling in administrative services, criminal justice information services, technical services, criminal investigations, the laboratory and training.

To enforce the laws against more than 250 categories of federal crimes, the bureau maintains 56 field offices and 400 smaller satellite offices, as well as 23 offices overseas. It has a total work force of 25,750.

The FBI maintains a fingerprint facility near Clarksburg, W. Va., and its famous training academy 35 miles south of Washington, in Quantico, Va. Along with a police academy on the same grounds, the FBI participates in the training of some 14,000 law enforcement personnel annually.

The headquarters tour emphasizes the FBI's successes. A series of photos shows the 1994 arrest of CIA spy Aldrich Ames near his Arlington, Va., home. A display of the FBI's 10 Most Wanted criminals reports that 446 names have been on the list since it was started in 1950, and that 418 fugitives have been caught. Ten of those arrests were made following appeals on the TV show "America's Most Wanted," two came after their cases were dramatized on "Unsolved Mysteries" and one arrest, last year, was made after a fugitive's picture appeared on the FBI's Internet home page.

The tour includes a stop at the memorial to agents who have died in the line of duty: 33 from gunfire and 13 others in automobile or training accidents. Signs discussing the FBI's mission explain that anti-terrorism efforts were made a priority in 1982, along with illegal drugs. [2]

Upstairs, visitors can peer through windows to see work being performed in the famous forensics laboratory, established in 1932. The tourguide describes how technicians perform "materials analysis" of paint, glass, or metal from cars, and how they analyze shoe-sole patterns to identify footprints. An exhibit on microscopic analysis of fibers from carpeting or bedding tells how crucial pieces of evidence can rub off invisibly from one person to another when there is close human contact. Technicians analyzing a human hair can tell which part of body it came from, visitors are told, and whether the hair is its original color.

Visitors can also get a glimpse of the FBI's 5,000-piece firearms reference collection, which contains samples of every known firearm used by criminals in this country as well as 12,000 specimens of test-fired ammunition. There also is an exhibit of the bureau's National DNA Index, which preserves semen samples from each of the country's released sex offenders, in case one is again suspected of an offense.

Following an agent's ear-splitting demonstration of three different firearms at the shooting range — including a vintage tommy gun — the tour ends with a visit to the gift store, which offers T-Shirts, hats and mugs celebrating the FBI.

[1] Ronald Kessler, *The FBI* (1993), p. 30.

[2] See "War on Drugs," *The CQ Researcher*, March 19, 1993, pp. 241-264.

Continued from p. 319
down in 1976 and modified in the early 1980s) for determining when it is appropriate to conduct surveillance on a domestic group.

During debate on the 1994 crime bill and the 1996 anti-terrorism bill, Martin says, the Democrats, who long opposed such powers, were "mushy, and have been rolling over ever since the 1993 World Trade Center bombing. Now the FBI can break in and photograph all your papers and replicate everything on your computer, and you won't know it unless you were later indicted."

Civil libertarians on the right continue objecting to the FBI's success in molding the 1994 Communications Assistance in Law Enforcement Act. The so-called "digital telephony law" is designed to prevent the telephone industry from making technological improvements that block the FBI's capacity to install wiretaps.

Barry Steinhardt, associate director of the American Civil Liberties Union (ACLU) in New York City, warns that current FBI proposals for implementing the law pose an unprecedented burden on a national industry, tantamount to "requiring all home builders to include an electronic bug in every new home." There is also a fear that the FBI, which so infamously wiretapped civil rights leader the Rev. Dr. Martin Luther King Jr. in the 1960s, will misuse information gleaned serendipitously during authorized wiretaps to pursue other investigations.

"Wiretapping is the worst sort of general search, precisely what the Fourth Amendment was intended to prevent," Steinhardt told a March conference at the Cato Institute. The FBI, he says, has only a 17 percent efficiency rate in using wiretaps to convict criminals, and yet wiretapping has reached record highs under the Clinton administration. The question, he said, "is whether we can trust the FBI not to abuse these powers."

The ACLU and Martin's group also object to the FBI's longstanding practice of keeping files on the political activities of Americans suspected of disloyalty. For decades, FBI files have been the subject of countless investigations, legal battles and rumors. (Excerpts from the FBI's once confidential files on former Beatle John Lennon and the late poet Allen Ginsberg can be found on the World Wide Web.) "Are we now to assume that an FBI file doesn't constitute an invasion of privacy, that having an FBI file is somehow part of civic life, like having a driver's license?" columnist Andrew Cockburn asked during the White House files controversy. [14]

Last December, however, the District of Columbia Circuit Court affirmed the FBI's right to determine on its own whether it should keep files on a domestic group or individual under suspicion. The case, brought in 1988 by the Center for National Security Studies, was prompted by a Freedom of Information Act request the group had made for FBI files on an academic named Lance Lindbloom, then president of the Chicago-based J. Roderick MacArthur Foundation. Citing national security concerns, the FBI had refused to release its complete files on Lindbloom, who had met several times with South Korean dissident Kim Dae Jung and accompanied Kim, along with a member of Congress and former State Department officials, when he returned to South Korea from exile in 1985.

One group with particular reasons to fear the FBI is Arab-Americans, many of whom received visits from FBI agents during the 1991 Gulf War. According to James Zogby, president of the Arab American Institute, "the FBI sent out a press release saying they had questioned 200 Arab leaders. Many were longtime city council members, small-town mayors or state senators. It was a nightmare until we got support from the editorial pages of about 50 newspapers that condemned it."

Zogby describes the FBI's interviews as "harassment," in which Arab-Americans were questioned in front of their employers or customers or neighbors. His own experience with the bureau began as far back as 1980, when the FBI interrogated fellow members of a church-based group called the Palestinian Human Rights Campaign after it had been firebombed. "The FBI was using the occasion to find out about the Arab community, which was just getting organized, in order to create a political chill by saying, 'We're watching you,' " he says.

FBI spokesmen emphasize that the bureau's law enforcement powers are determined by the checks and balances in the Constitution, Congress and the Supreme Court. Alan McDonald, general counsel for the FBI's Information Resources Division, says wiretaps are always used in accordance with the amended 1968 electronic surveillance law. It requires police to obtain court-ordered warrants before tapping a criminal suspect's phone, and warrants can only be obtained when police have "probable cause" and specific suspicions. Further, the number of wiretaps must be tabulated and reported annually to Congress.

Wiretaps are executed "in a surgical fashion," McDonald says, in only about 1 percent of investigations. "The FBI and prosecutors must convince courts that other means are not available or are too dangerous. The situation is far from some tantalizing prospect of a pervasive Big Brother." Wiretaps are not used against political dissidents or those with unpopular opinions. In fact, 70 percent of them are against people suspected of dealing illegal drugs, he says. "But the high-quality, unbiased evidence that wiretaps furnish can allow law enforcement to react promptly to head off heinous crimes."

As for secret files, McWeeney points out that agents are constantly receiving information from multiple sources, and the procedure is to write it up for a file in case the subject is later investigated. "But just because there's a file doesn't mean there's an active investigation," he says. "If someone calls in and says a certain guy is in the Mafia, we document it."

The FBI can be trusted with new anti-terrorism powers, argues social scientist James Q. Wilson. Justice Department guidelines on infiltrating domestic groups are clear enough, he writes, but the FBI has trouble interpreting them. "FBI agents have learned to be politically risk-averse," he writes. "The intelligence guidelines under which the FBI operated would not have barred infiltration of the group responsible for the Oklahoma bombing, assuming that anybody had heard of it in advance. But the bureau has been whipsawed so many times by contrary political pressures — 'Stop terrorism!' 'Protect civil liberties!' — that many of its top officials have adopted a perfectly understandable bureaucratic reaction: 'Who needs the trouble?' " [15] ■

BACKGROUND

Flawed First Steps

The world's most famous law enforcement agency was created in 1908, the brainchild of Charles Joseph Bonaparte, who was attorney general during the administration of Theodore Roosevelt. A descendent of Emperor Napoleon of France, Bonaparte had authority under the 1870 act that created the Justice Department to launch a new federal investigative unit — and he would need that authority. Many in Congress steadfastly opposed the idea, warning that any sort of federal police force would degenerate into a "secret police" operation like the one that terrorized czarist Russia. [16]

Bonaparte was undaunted, and the following year his plan to switch 10 Secret Service agents from Treasury to join several others from elsewhere at Justice was implemented in the Taft administration by Attorney General George W. Wickersham. The new Bureau of Investigation was to pursue crimes on the high seas, violations of neutrality laws, crimes on Indian reservations, narcotics trafficking, violations of anti-peonage (slave labor) law and violations of antitrust laws. Within a year, Congress passed the Mann Act, making it a federal crime to transport women across state lines for immoral purposes. [17]

For the next decade and a half, the bureau would confirm the fears of its congressional detractors. Headed by William Burns, whom many saw as a self-aggrandizing union-buster obsessed with wiretapping, the bureau focused on ferreting out Bolsheviks, anarchists and German sympathizers during World War I. Congressional hearings at the time, one historian notes, revealed that the bureau had found suspects "in all walks of American life." Among those guilty of pro-Germanism, the public learned, were members of the Senate, judges, mayors and former Secretary of State William Jennings Bryan. [18]

The bureau ended this era of its history, says former FBI Assistant Director Ray Wannall, as "a dumping ground for political hacks, alcoholics, ex-cons and procurers of women."

The Young Hoover

By 1924, the situation had moved Attorney General Harlan Fiske Stone to action. He had noticed J. Edgar Hoover, then a 29-year-old assistant attorney general who had been active in the Justice Department's "Red Scare" raids. Stone charged him with reinvigorating the bureau.

A devout Presbyterian, Hoover was the son and grandson of civil servants and still lived with his mother. Hoover set out to retrain the bureau's 650 employees in order to "merit the respect of the public." That meant no foul language, and everyone clean-shaven and wearing a white shirt. Hoover encouraged citizens to "refrain from making private investigations" but to "report the information you have [to the bureau] and leave the checking of data to trained investigators." [19] It was Hoover's professionalization, says veteran McWeeney, that led the bureau to "memorialize information in reports instead of just jotting it on the back of matchbooks."

As Prohibition and the Depression enveloped America, the rise of notorious gangsters — such as Al Capone, Bonnie and Clyde and Baby Face Nelson — gave Hoover's bureau its big chance. "Racketeering has got to a point where the government [must] stamp out this underworld army," declared Attorney General Homer S. Cummings soon after Franklin D. Roosevelt's administration came to power. On July 30, 1933, Cummings tapped Hoover to head a new unit combining the Justice Department's Prohibition Bureau, Bureau of Identification and Bureau of Investigation. He was handed 226 new agents and vast amounts of publicity, partly as psychological warfare against the famous criminals he was up against. Hoover's appearances on multiple magazine covers made him a household name. [20]

In 1935, the rejuvenated agency was renamed the Federal Bureau of Investigation. Congress throughout

Continued on p. 324

Chronology

1900s-1940s

First federal anti-crime unit focuses on anarchists and Bolsheviks, then expands to deal with gangsters during the Great Depression.

July 26, 1908
Bureau of Investigation created within Justice Department.

1924
Young J. Edgar Hoover appointed head of bureau.

1930
Bureau begins publishing national crime statistics.

1932
Bureau's forensics laboratory created.

1933
Hoover named to head expanded bureau.

1935
Bureau renamed FBI. National Academy created to train law enforcement personnel.

1940
Wartime federal law gives FBI authority to investigate domestic subversives.

1950s-1960s

FBI focuses on anti-Communism, corruption of American youth.

1968
Congress passes crime bill limiting FBI directors to 10 years and requiring Senate confirmation.

1970s ***FBI criticized for civil liberties violations.***

1970
Passage of Racketeer Influenced and Corrupt Organizations (RICO) law, giving FBI more power to investigate organized crime.

1972
Hoover dies; L. Patrick Gray named acting director.

1973
Kansas City Police Chief Clarence Kelley named FBI director.

1975
Senate Select Committee on Intelligence Activities exposes FBI civil liberties abuses.

1976
Attorney General Edward Levi issues guidelines on FBI surveillance.

1978
William H. Webster becomes director.

1980s ***FBI focuses on drugs, white-collar crime and international terrorism.***

1980
FBI's ABSCAM undercover operation convicts 12 public officials of bribery.

1987
William S. Sessions named director.

1988
Revelation that FBI inappropriately targeted domestic activists on human rights in El Salvador.

1990s ***FBI acknowledges mistakes.***

August 1992
FBI involved in shootout at Ruby Ridge, Idaho, in which an unarmed woman and her teenage son are killed.

April 19, 1993
FBI assault on the Branch Davidian complex near Waco, Texas, leaves 75 adults and children dead.

Sept. 1, 1993
Louis J. Freeh becomes director.

1994
Congress passes communications law preserving FBI wiretap capabilities.

1995
FBI chemist Frederic Whitehurst sets off inquiry by complaining of sloppiness and misbehavior in FBI lab.

April 24, 1996
Congress passes Anti-Terrorism and Effective Death Penalty Act broadening FBI powers.

June 1996
FBI captures anti-government "Freeman" after three-month standoff in Montana.

Feb. 28, 1997
FBI agent Earl Edwin Pitts pleads guilty to spying for Moscow.

March 1997
FBI and White House clash over investigation of Chinese efforts to influence U.S. elections.

Continued from p. 322
the 1930s would expand its charter with new laws making federal crimes of such offenses as kidnapping, while Secretary of State Cordell Hull authorized Hoover to investigate fascists and communists within the U.S.

Hoover responded with many crime-fighting coups, notably his agents' shooting of murderer and bank robber John Dillinger in 1934 as he emerged from a Chicago cinema. Hoover also made a big splash that year by helping to collar kidnapper Alvin Karpis, "Public Enemy No. 1," following criticism that Hoover himself had never made an arrest.

But as FBI agents who became disgruntled with Hoover would later reveal, many of the successes were exaggerated. Former agent William W. Turner charged that the famous "Lady in Red" who betrayed Dillinger was actually working with the private Hargrave Secret Service, not the FBI. The 1934 capture of Lindbergh baby kidnapper Bruno Richard Hauptmann was accomplished by Treasury agents rather than the FBI, and the German saboteurs who landed in the U.S. by submarine in the early 1940s were betrayed by one of their own, not nabbed by the FBI. [21]

In fact, the FBI agent who shot Dillinger, Melvin Purvis, saw his career dead-end, apparently because Hoover was jealous of the credit he received, and he later committed suicide. [22]

Hoover loyalists chalk up much of the myth-busting to the resentment of disgraced agents. "Hoover was a staunch disciplinarian," Wannall recalls. "Some agents couldn't live with that so they became dissidents. We who stayed recognized that the head of law enforcement and intelligence has to rule with a pretty strong hand."

Making Enemies

By the early 1940s, Hoover had assembled a staff of 13,000, including 4,000 agents, and the power to go after foreign spies and draft evaders. All the while, he put out word of steadily worsening crime statistics, warning once of "a horde larger than any of the barbarian hosts that overran Europe and Asia in ancient times." [23]

FBI

Portrait of a G-man: Legendary J. Edgar Hoover ran the FBI for 48 years until his death in 1972.

But the rapid growth was not always welcomed by local law enforcement, who viewed the FBI as stingy in sharing information and too eager to take over their cases. "Despite a public facade of normality, relations between the FBI and local police departments have also been tense for years," wrote ex-agent Turner. "It is only natural that the police seethe under the bureau's air of superiority and the way the bureau is pampered by Congress and the public." [24]

Others faulted the bureau for emphasizing statistics at the expense of selectivity in tackling the crime problem. "When I came into the bureau, we used to go to the Metropolitan Police Department [in Washington] every day and check the stolen-car list," said one ex-agent. "If the car was recovered, we took credit; if it was stolen in Washington and recovered in Maryland, we would claim that as a stat, interstate theft." [25]

Still, Hoover continued building on his status as an American hero. His most famous book, a 1958 anti-communist tract called *Masters of Deceit*, is said to have been ghostwritten on government time, and the bureau also had a hand in Don Whitehead's 1956 celebratory chronicle *The FBI Story*. Through the 1950s and '60s, Hoover's byline was familiar in *Reader's Digest*, Sunday supplements and PTA magazines, in the later period warning of the impending corruption of youth by a new type of "conspiracy" characterized by "non-conformity in dress and speech, even by obscene language, rather than by formal membership in a specific organization." [26]

The seeds for the subsequent disillusionment with Hoover among many members of the public were sown by critics, particularly on the left. Fred Cook, writing first in *The*

Nation and *Ramparts* and later in a book, *The FBI Nobody Knows*, accused the FBI of ignoring organized crime.[27] After the 1963 assassination of President John F. Kennedy, Turner wrote that Hoover had withheld information from the investigating Warren Commission showing that the FBI had received advance word that alleged assassin Lee Harvey Oswald had made violent threats against the government.[28] By the mid-1970s, explosive revelations about FBI and CIA misconduct were being investigated by a special Senate committee headed by Sen. Frank Church, D-Idaho. They led to a 1975 *Time* magazine cover story, "The Truth About Hoover," and later a 1981 book by David Garrow, *The FBI and Martin Luther King Jr.*

Hoover's Secrets

Only now was the public learning about Hoover as a master bureaucrat who was often able to hide his actual budget from prying congressional oversight. "One of Hoover's regular practices was to turn off many [FBI wiretaps] just before his annual appearance in front of the House Appropriations Committee, to avoid . . . having to lie to Congress about the huge number of illicit taps that were in place," one historian wrote.[29]

It emerged that Hoover had not only wiretapped Martin Luther King Jr.'s phones (with authorization from Attorney General Robert F. Kennedy) because he suspected him of being a communist, but that he had amassed secret files on celebrities and politicians, such as Marilyn Monroe and John F. Kennedy. The story is told of how the aging Hoover blackmailed Kennedy into reappointing him by flaunting his evidence of Kennedy's extramarital affairs. ("You don't fire God," Kennedy would say.[30])

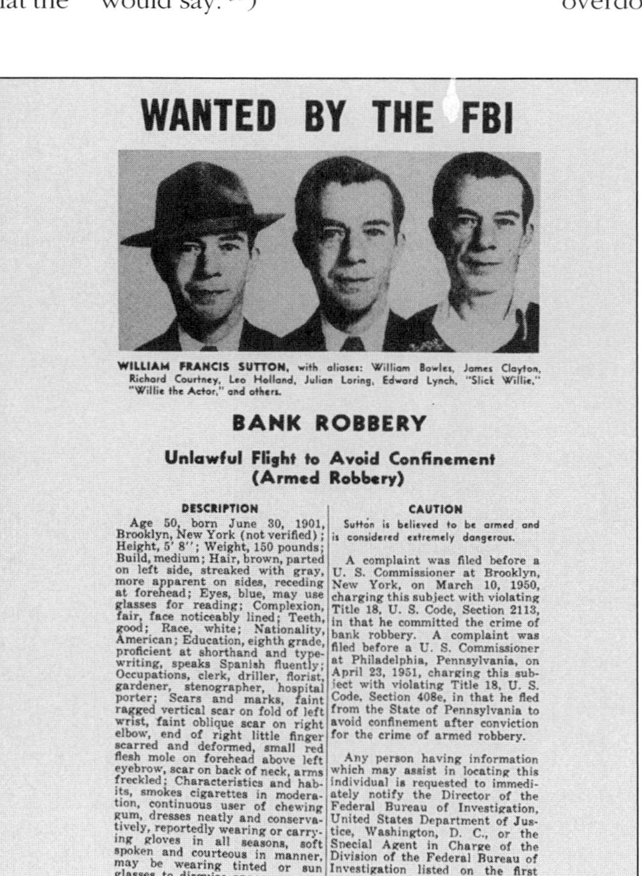

WANTED BY THE FBI

WILLIAM FRANCIS SUTTON, with aliases: William Bowles, James Clayton, Richard Courtney, Leo Holland, Julian Loring, Edward Lynch, "Slick Willie," "Willie the Actor," and others.

BANK ROBBERY

Unlawful Flight to Avoid Confinement (Armed Robbery)

DESCRIPTION

Age 50, born June 30, 1901, Brooklyn, New York (not verified); Height, 5' 8''; Weight, 150 pounds; Build, medium; Hair, brown, parted on left side, streaked with gray, more apparent on sides, receding at forehead; Eyes, blue, may use glasses for reading; Complexion, fair, face noticeably lined; Teeth, good; Race, white; Nationality, American; Education, eighth grade, proficient at shorthand and typewriting, speaks Spanish fluently; Occupations, clerk, driller, florist, gardener, stenographer, hospital porter; Scars and marks, faint ragged vertical scar on fold of left wrist, faint oblique scar on right elbow, end of right little finger scarred and deformed, small red flesh mole on forehead above left eyebrow, scar on back of neck, arms freckled; Characteristics and habits, smokes cigarettes in moderation, continuous user of chewing gum, dresses neatly and conservatively, reportedly wearing or carrying gloves in all seasons, soft spoken and courteous in manner, may be wearing tinted or sun glasses to disguise appearance.

CAUTION

Sutton is believed to be armed and is considered extremely dangerous.

A complaint was filed before a U. S. Commissioner at Brooklyn, New York, on March 10, 1950, charging this subject with violating Title 18, U. S. Code, Section 2113, in that he committed the crime of bank robbery. A complaint was filed before a U. S. Commissioner at Philadelphia, Pennsylvania, on April 23, 1951, charging this subject with violating Title 18, U. S. Code, Section 408e, in that he fled from the State of Pennsylvania to avoid confinement after conviction for the crime of armed robbery.

Any person having information which may assist in locating this individual is requested to immediately notify the Director of the Federal Bureau of Investigation, United States Department of Justice, Washington, D. C., or the Special Agent in Charge of the Division of the Federal Bureau of Investigation listed on the first page of your telephone directory.

Dramatic "Wanted by the FBI" posters helped catch notorious criminals and raise the bureau's public image. Bank robber Willie Sutton was among the bureau's most celebrated cases.

Histories being published in the 1990s have revealed more detail about Hoover's special files, some of which were marked "Personal and Confidential" and others "Official and Confidential" and kept in Hoover's own office so that ordinary FBI clerks would not have access. Some of these files are said to contain information on the bureau's illegal domestic burglaries, and others reputedly are filled with surveillance data on sexual deviancy.[31] Many are thought to have been destroyed by his secretary, Helen Gandy, or other aides.

Former Assistant Director Wannall says all the talk about secret files is overdone. "I have 85 pages of them, and any member of the public can get them," he says. "Most of the files kept in his office were personal correspondence about his investments in oil. One file was simply a survey of what electronic equipment the FBI owned at the time. We agents had access to the files in Hoover's office. We just went to Miss Gandy."

Domestic Surveillance

The most controversial Hoover secret to emerge in the 1970s was the bureau's 14-year counterintelligence program to monitor the political activities of leftists and anti-Vietnam War protesters. COINTELPRO, as it was known, was launched in 1956 when the FBI was instructed to go after the Communist Party USA, and ended in 1970, when activists calling themselves the Citizens Committee to Investigate the FBI stole documents from the FBI office in Media, Pa., and leaked them to the press.[32]

The exposure of COINTELPRO prompted Ford administration Attorney General Edward H. Levi to issue guidelines as to when the FBI can infiltrate or conduct surveillance on domestic groups. Litigation against the FBI for civil liberties abuses went on into the 1980s, and two top bureau officials, Mark Felt and Edward S. Miller, were convicted of ordering illegal burglaries. The Society of Former Special

Agents of the FBI raised more than $1 million to defend them and others; Felt and Miller were pardoned by President Ronald Reagan in 1981.

Wannall, who testified before Congress in defense of COINTELPRO, says the program was fully authorized by the presidents and attorneys general of each administration. "Lyndon Johnson spoke to the nation on July 24, 1967, at the time of the race riots in Detroit, saying that we must use 'every means at our command' and that 'no American has the right to loot,' " he says. "Johnson made it clear that we couldn't do business in our usual way, that he expected more than what was being done."

When bombs started to go off on American college campuses a few years later, Wannall continues, "there were real American people looking to their government and the FBI to protect their rights and property."

Post-Hoover Era

Hoover's death in 1972 (he was the first civil servant to lie in state in the Capitol Rotunda), heralded a new era for the FBI. The 1968 crime bill had already required future FBI directors to be confirmed by the Senate and limited their terms to 10 years. For the first time, amid considerable unease, black and female agents were recruited. Training was updated to emphasize "quality over quantity," as a director put it, to place less emphasis on mere statistics. The FBI also began taking advantage of undercover techniques. It enjoyed great successes against organized crime in New York, Cleveland and other cities, McWeeney notes.

Under Acting Director L. Patrick Gray and later under former Kansas City Police Chief Clarence Kelley, the FBI also demonstrated the kind of political neutrality that the public expected. Gray, despite his desire to ingratiate himself with President Richard M. Nixon to win a permanent appointment, refused to conduct wiretapping and break-ins against White House enemies, and wouldn't help Nixon cover up the Watergate scandal. Indeed, FBI agents took pride in ferreting out White House misdeeds committed during Watergate, staying a couple of months ahead of *Washington Post* reporters Bob Woodward and Carl Bernstein, who got the credit. [33]

Under the firm leadership of Judge William H. Webster, who became director in 1978, the bureau took on the international Mafia, foreign counterintelligence, world terrorism and white-collar crime, such as the savings and loan abuses.

It was under Webster and Reagan Attorney General William French Smith that Justice Department guidelines for domestic surveillance were relaxed in the hope that the bureau would "anticipate crime." What occurred, however, was considered by many as another FBI abuse.

From 1984-86, the FBI conducted extensive surveillance against leftist opponents of U.S. policy toward El Salvador. The primary target was the Committee in Solidarity with the People of El Salvador (CISPES), whose associates included such "subversives" as former U.S. Ambassador Robert White, musician Jackson Browne, actor Charlie Sheen and 10 members of Congress. When media attention forced the project's demise, new FBI Director William S. Sessions was required to apologize for a policy he called "an unfortunate aligning of mistakes . . . of which the FBI is not proud." [34]

Though Sessions had merely inherited the CISPES policy, it may have been a factor in President Clinton's decision in 1993 to fire him following a series of controversies over his reported misuse of government perks and the alleged involvement of his wife in policy matters.

Standoff at Waco

The Clinton era began with the FBI's botched standoff against the Branch Davidian cultists outside Waco. An official post-mortem criticized the bureau after the deadly tank assault, tear gassing and fire on April 19, 1993, that killed 75 adults and children. The bureau was faulted for being impatient in negotiations with the religious group; for employing dangerous CS gas of which it had little understanding; and for failing to adequately consult religious experts concerning the potential for mass suicide.

In addition, recalls Alan Stone, the Harvard University law and psychiatry professor who headed the review, "The FBI and the Justice Department did not help our panel to get the necessary information until I made a terrible fuss and insisted. Then, after we filed the report, the FBI condemned it." (The FBI insisted it did consult experts, and several months after Waco the FBI's Active Agents Association issued a special award to hostage rescue team members.)

After Republicans took control of Congress in 1995, they conducted new hearings on the Waco and Ruby Ridge episodes and reiterated the critiques. "FBI officials on the ground had effectively ruled out a negotiated end long before April 19, and had closed minds when presented with evidence of a possible negotiated end following completion of Koresh's work on interpreting the Seven Seals of the Bible," a House report said. [35]

Stone says he was impressed with the FBI's successful, non-violent resolution of the 1996 standoff in Jordan, Mont., against the anti-government Freemen group. "The FBI has taken the criticism to heart," he says. "I wrote letters of congratulation to both Louis Freeh and Janet Reno. I have great respect for Freeh." ■

CURRENT SITUATION

Political Independence?

"I don't see how Louis Freeh can survive this confrontation with the president," newsman Sam Donaldson said March 16 on ABC's "This Week." He was referring to the clash between the FBI and the White House over what the White House said was the FBI's failure to tell Clinton that the FBI was investigating whether the Chinese government was funneling money illegally into Democratic campaigns. Though Attorney General Reno subsequently attributed the conflict to a "misunderstanding," it later emerged that Freeh may have been withholding information on his 30-agent probe into Chinese funding because of earlier charges that the FBI was too cozy with the White House. [36]

The situation only dramatizes the political tightrope Freeh must walk these days. For nearly two years, Republicans have been blasting the FBI for, among other things, allegedly allowing itself to be used by the White House after Clinton aides fired White House travel office employees in 1993, and then sought an FBI probe to prove their criminality. [37]

Last year, the bureau's counsel was criticized for providing the White House with an advance copy of former special agent Gary Aldrich's titillating memoir, *Unlimited Access: An FBI Agent at the White House*. And last month, Rep. Charles H. Taylor, R-N.C., told Freeh at a hearing that "it seems like the FBI is acting like Stepin Fetchit for the White House and giving up its role as a respected law enforcement agency." Moreover, Rep. Dan Burton, R-Ind., who is chairing a major probe into Clinton fund-raising improprieties, dismissed as "a blatant political move" the report that he had become the target of an FBI investigation into charges that he shook down a Democratic lobbyist for campaign cash.

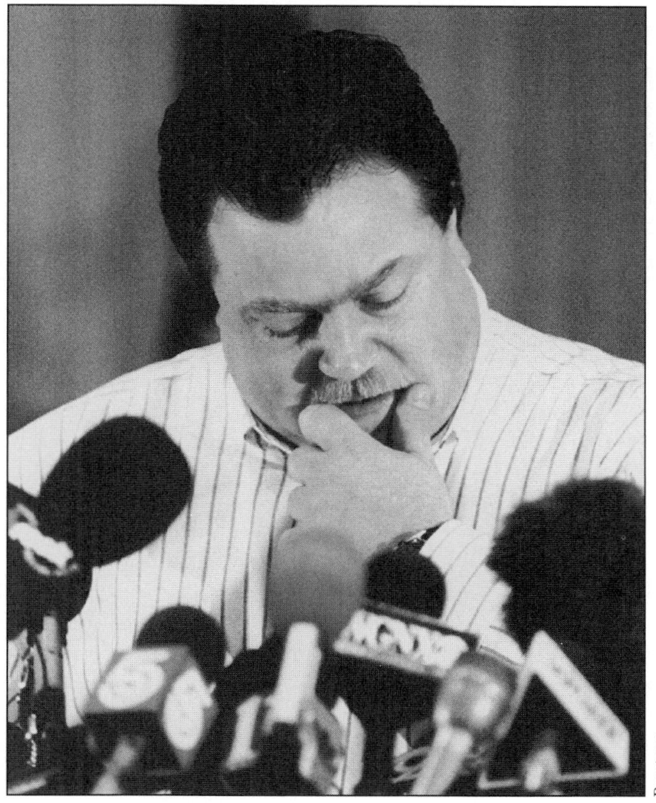

Reuters

The FBI's investigation of a fatal bombing during the Olympics in Atlanta was marred when security guard Richard Jewell was identified to news media as a suspect, only to be exonerated later.

Freeh has replied to the Republicans by citing the pride he takes in the fact that his identity as either a Republican or Democrat has never been made public. He said his only conditions for accepting Clinton's offer to elevate him from federal judge to FBI director was that there be no White House interference with his work. [38]

Freeh also said that he takes "full responsibility" for the problems on his watch, noting that he has introduced new procedures to avoid a repeat of allowing partisan White House staffers to obtain FBI files on political opponents. "I did not call it an administrative snafu," he said. "I called it an egregious violation of privacy, and I said it was the result of the abdication of management responsibility in the FBI."

Freeh is not a pawn of the White House, McWeeney says. "Those charges are just the Republicans trying out their own political agenda. Freeh is a decent man with integrity who is now faced with issues in the media spotlight that years ago would have been kept quiet."

The Jewell Case

An area where Freeh has also been promising action is the FBI's investigation of the Olympic Games bombing, in which someone, apparently in law enforcement, leaked the name of security guard Richard Jewell as a suspect, and the FBI may have tricked Jewell into giving interviews under the guise of coming to help make a training video. In March, senior FBI official David Tubbs and others were reported to be facing disciplinary action in the Jewell affair.

Freeh said he has "zero tolerance" for leaks by agents, but he noted that "over 500 FBI agents, local detectives and other people" knew [Jewell's] identity. "They reported up 10 organizational chains. It was much too many people to be aware of a subject's identity in a case where you had 15,000 reporters in town."[39]

Tom Rosenstiel, director of the Project for Excellence in Journalism, says "the press in this case was used by the FBI to try to squeeze Jewell. This violates the first tenet of journalism, which is don't become an arm of government." The press in the future should return to the old code of waiting until a suspect has been officially charged to report his name, and to require the police to offer evidence as to why someone is a suspect, he says. "The FBI's reliability has been tarnished, too, and perhaps that's good, because the press had gotten too cozy with it." Jewell later sued several news organizations for naming him as a suspect.

Reuters

The FBI counts the capture of CIA spy Aldrich Ames among its biggest recent successes.

Freedom of Information

Last summer's "Filegate" controversy at the White House produced a surge in requests from journalists, academics, prison inmates and average citizens for FBI files under the Freedom of Information Act.[40] Kevin O'Brien, chief of the FBI's FOIA and Privacy Acts section, last June reminded Congress that "FBI files contain very sensitive information, and [reviewing requests] is necessarily time-consuming, and the analysis cannot be done properly if it is done in haste. We are critically understaffed."[41]

In February, the FBI began sending letters to all requesters explaining the backlog. "If we do not receive a response within 30 days of the date of this communication," it said, "we will conclude that you are no longer interested and close your request (s) administratively."

The FBI generally handles FOIA requests on a first-come, first-served basis, though it does have a special track for requests that can be filled in one day. In balancing citizen rights against the FBI's need to protect national security and confidential sources, courts have ruled that action on FOIA requests must be accelerated if their topics are newsworthy, or if they involve possible government misconduct.

Recent court rulings have backed the FBI's right to keep certain information (such as the file on murdered Teamster boss Jimmy Hoffa) secret if officials judge that the case could still be reopened. Courts have also ruled that the FBI may not withhold documents if they have already been reviewed for other FOIA requests. FBI exemptions from FOIA requirements must be justified case by case.

Harry Hammitt, editor-publisher of *Access Reports*, a biweekly on the FOIA, says that the FBI receives far more FOIA requests than other agencies. "The law and intelligence agencies have the worst time because they are overly cautious, and the reviews are labor-intensive," he says. But the common notion that most requests are from outraged average citizens seeking suspected files on themselves is overblown. "There are an awful lot of people in jail or in the justice system who make requests, as well as reporters and researchers and public interest groups," he says. "I'll bet the FBI doesn't think it's being too secretive, but I say they apply too much caution, and that more could be disclosed. They spend huge amounts of time and money in court defending their policies." In the FBI's defense, a single request from a journalist can amount to 3,000 pages, he adds, and require a staff of 60 to handle.[42]

By 1999, the bureau plans to have an electronic imaging system installed at FBI headquarters and at all field offices for the tracking and processing of information requested under the FOIA and the Privacy Acts.[43] The FBI's track record on new computer systems in general, however, has been flagging. There have been delays and cost overruns in its effort to upgrade its National Crime Information Center, a computerized system designed to handle 100,000 inquiries a day from law enforcement officials. The bureau's planned Integrated Automated Fingerprint Identification System, which will allow police in squad cars to check fingerprints via portable computers, is also behind schedule.[44]

Continued on p. 330

At Issue:

Is the FBI forensics laboratory too secretive?

yes

JAMES E. STARRS
Professor of law and forensic sciences, George Washington University

FROM "UNINVITED AND UNWELCOME GUESTS: BIASES IN THE HOUSE OF FORENSIC SCIENCES," SPEECH PRESENTED TO AMERICAN ACADEMY OF SCIENCES, FEB. 20, 1997.

Forensic scientists are expected to keep abreast of the times, especially when the times are changing under the impetus of judicial decisions and statutory revisions. As the front-runner in the field of forensic science, the FBI lab could be expected to take the lead in accommodating the old ways to the new rules.

Ruefully, that has not been the policy at the FBI lab. Change resulting in more open and reviewable practices . . . seems to cut against the establishment mentality of the FBI laboratory. The hidebound attitude at the FBI laboratory seems to be saying out with the new and on with the old.

In this regard, the FBI lab suffers from a very acute case of mural dyslexia, by which I mean it has failed to see the handwriting on the wall. It is no wonder that it is steeped in controversy at the present time. To be hidebound is no guarantee that the slings and arrows of criticism will be aimed elsewhere. Quite to the contrary.

Closed doors, I would submit, lead to closed minds, and closed minds are a substantial opening to inefficiency and ineptitude and possibly worse . . . .

External proficiency testing is the norm for responsible and accredited laboratories, but not for the FBI lab. Its internal proficiency testing best serves its fixation with bolting its doors to the peer review of outsiders, even outsiders who are preeminent in their scientific fields.

The studied refusal of the FBI lab . . . to countenance a second opinion is indicative of the FBI's negative posture toward peer review. Of course, it could be said that the FBI's unwillingness to accept evidence that has been or will be analyzed elsewhere is just a matter of sensible conservation of its resources. In light, however, of the determined refusal of the FBI lab to stand the criticism of peer review in other circumstances, it would appear that resource conservation is a secondary motive against second opinions of, or at, the FBI lab. . . .

Everything in the FBI lab is being played by the adversarial book. All disclosures are made grudgingly, and only when and in the terms required by the rules. The forensic scientists at the FBI lab seem to be more scrupulously lawyerlike in their close-to-the-vest view of pretrial discovery than even lawyers would be. All the better to squelch peer review and to advance the cause of the prosecution, which, from every viewpoint, seem to be the dual purposes of the FBI lab.

no

DAVID FISHER
***Author,* Hard Evidence: Inside the FBI Sci-Crime Lab**

FROM "FBI CRIME LAB RECEIVES UNFAIR CRITICISM FROM WHISTLE-BLOWER," *CONTRA COSTA TIMES,* MARCH 5, 1997.

For some of us who naturally believe whistle-blowers, it was a source of great confusion to read allegations by FBI Special Agent Fred Whitehurst that the bureau's criminal laboratory had mishandled or fabricated evidence in many cases.

Whitehurst's loud whistle led to a Justice Department investigation, and parts of the resulting inspector general's report recently leaked to the media seemed to support some of his complaints.

Newspaper headlines criticized the lab and stated that hundreds of cases might have been reopened. On "Nightline," Sen. Charles Grassley, R-Iowa, suggested that work done by the lab was so poor that the lab could not even be accredited by forensic organizations . . . .

Having spent more than six months inside the FBI lab, where I conducted more than 180 hours of interviews, Whitehurst's claims made little sense to me. And, while it is certainly possible that there are serious problems inside the lab about which I know nothing, the evidence thus far made public has confirmed my belief that this story is only slightly more accurate than recent news coverage of Richard Jewell in Atlanta and Michael Irvin in Dallas. . . .

Grassley is correct that the FBI lab has not been accredited. But not because, as the senator seems to suggest, the work done there is substandard. The FBI lab established the American Society of Crime Lab Directors, the parent of the accrediting organization, many years ago to standardize procedures used by crime labs.

Smaller state and local labs had little difficulty conforming to these standards, but problems faced by the bureau are considerably different. Until recently, for example, the bureau's lab has not been a restricted facility, which is mandatory for accreditation; that the entire building was a restricted facility was not acceptable.

Most of the reasons the lab has not been accredited . . . are structural or mechanical, rather than quality-based, and will be resolved when the lab moves to a new facility. . . .

There simply is no reason for FBI agents to falsify data. In many cases their tests simply provide lead information, rather than trial evidence. Examiners and technicians rarely know any more than is necessary about the materials they are examining, and most often never learn how an investigation or trial ended. . . .

Unlike J. Edgar Hoover's FBI, where the publicity was far greater than its accomplishments, in this instance the crime lab is much better than these headlines.

FOR MORE INFORMATION

Center for National Security Studies, Gelman Library, Suite 701, 2130 H St. N.W., Washington, D.C. 20037; (202) 994-7060. Sponsored by the Fund for Peace, the center conducts research and performs legislative and legal advocacy to ensure that civil liberties and human rights are not eroded in the name of national security.

Federal Bureau of Investigation, 10th St. and Pennsylvania Ave. N.W., Washington, D.C. 20535; (202) 324-2614. The FBI maintains a headquarters in Washington as well as 56 field offices nationwide, 400 smaller local offices and 23 overseas offices.

Freedom of Information Center, 127 Neff Annex, University of Missouri, Columbia, Mo. 65211; (573) 882-4856. Founded in 1958, this nonprofit group maintains files that document actions by government, media and society affecting the flow and content of information. It monitors FBI policy on Freedom of Information Act requests.

Society of Former Special Agents of the FBI Inc. P.O. Box 1027, Building 715, Quantico, Va., 22134; (800) 527-7372. Founded in 1937, the 8,000-member group holds annual conferences and social events, maintains a memorial to slain agents and raises funds for scholarships, members' families in need and agents' legal fees.

Continued from p. 328

"The bureau has not delivered vital law enforcement systems . . . anywhere near within budget or on time," House Appropriations Subcommittee on Commerce, Justice, State and Judiciary Chairman Harold Rogers, R-Ky, told Freeh recently. [45] ■

OUTLOOK

FBI Ethics

Working for the FBI, makes for a stressful life, and the bureau employs two full-time counselors to work with troubled agents. Despite the danger and frequent travel, some 10,000 men and women apply to become agents every year; 400 are chosen. About 10 percent drop out during the tough training course at the FBI Academy, where Freeh recently added new courses in ethics.

To further bolster the agency's moral fiber, Freeh announced in March that he was creating an expanded and newly independent Office of Professional Responsibility to investigate and adjudicate internal misconduct allegations. To speed up the handling of cases, Freeh said he had doubled the number of employees assigned to internal investigations.

For some, the decades-old fear of the FBI has not disappeared. In March, attorneys in Northern California revived a lawsuit on behalf of Judi Bari, a member of the radical environmental group Earth First!, who was injured in a 1990 car bombing in Oakland, Calif. Police arrested her and accused her of carrying the bomb, while she accused the FBI of portraying her as a suspect to smear her group. The suit on behalf of Bari, who recently died of cancer, is another one likely to challenge the credibility of the FBI's forensics lab.

The influence of J. Edgar Hoover persists at the modern bureau, Wannall says. "His policies haven't changed," even if there are people at the FBI now who get in situations that require them to apologize for mistakes.

Hoover loyalists were especially irked at the bizarre reports by a British journalist in 1993 asserting that Hoover and his top aide, Clyde Tolson, were gay lovers, that Hoover had been seen in the late 1950s wearing a dress and makeup, and that the Mafia used its knowledge of these hypocritical behaviors to prevent Hoover from going after the mob. [46]

There is "no cogent evidence" that such stories are true, says A.J. McFall, executive director of the former special agents society. The source for them, he notes, is Susan Rosenstiel (no relation to Tom Rosenstiel), the ex-wife of a wealthy former bootlegger with contacts both in the mob and the FBI. "She had gone through a divorce and was bitter at the property settlement, and she blamed the former FBI agents that her ex-husband had hired as private eyes," McFall says. "FBI agents who worked with Hoover every day were pretty straight types, and if Hoover had done anything like this, someone would have come forward," McFall adds. "To say that Hoover and Tolson were anything more than professional and above board is absolute slander."

Global Reach

Efforts by Freeh and the FBI to become more active overseas have raised some concerns. Last winter, Freeh traveled to Jordan to discuss the extradition of a Muslim militant wanted in Israel. He also recently traveled to Saudi Arabia in connection with the U.S. barracks bombing. "It seems that Mr. Freeh and Ms. Reno hadn't bothered to consult the Clinton foreign policy team before rattling around in one of Washington's most sensitive bilateral relationships," complained columnist George Melloan. [47]

Martin of the Center for National Security Studies worries about new powers the FBI acquired under last year's intelligence appropriations bill. In the course of going after terrorists overseas, the FBI will now be allowed to be guided by intelligence-gathering rules that apply to the CIA, which are looser about protecting civil liberties than the rules for law enforcement. "There used to be a wall between the two which Congress used to protect civil liberties," she says. [48]

The FBI is expected to continue seeking expanded powers for "roving" wiretaps using satellite technology, and to require airlines, courier services and hotels to give the FBI information it seeks. Such new capabilities are needed as a matter of survival, says former agent McWeeney. "You have to grow with the criminal element with all these state-of-the-art digital telephones and wire transfers. If the FBI doesn't keep up with the bad guys, who will?"

"We're living now in a society of surveillance," says Raskin of the Institute for Policy Studies. "You must show a picture ID when you enter a government or corporate building, or when you board an airplane. The police and the FBI are one piece of this apparatus, and it's a very scary picture."

Zogby of the Arab American Institute says the FBI has become a bit more sensitive to the hurt caused by some of its investigations of ethnic Americans, particularly after years of surveillance that reached almost comic proportions have yielded so little in crime fighting. "But the FBI is still more feared than trusted because of what happened in the 1970s and '80s," he says. "Perhaps they could make an affirmative effort at confidence building, and say they are sorry for what happened during the Gulf War."

"The American public trusts the FBI," says FBI counsel McDonald, "when they look at what it has done and not what it has been accused of doing. It hasn't been running afoul of the law. It has a good record."

Moreover, the old feeling that the FBI runs over local law enforcement is no longer the case, says Daniel N. Rosenblatt, executive director of the International Association of Chiefs of Police. "The cooperation today is stellar. Freeh has the right kind of attitude. He's a courageous man who has made no secret about the problems of the FBI, which he's trying to address. The evaluation of an agency head is not whether he's free of problems but what he is doing about the problems."

But Freeh's days at the FBI may be numbered. "I have wondered about leaving," he says in the current issue of *Newsweek*. The magazine also quoted friends saying they have heard Freeh wonder aloud, "Am I hurting the FBI?" [49] ■

Notes

[1] *Congressional Record*, Feb. 25, 1997, p. S1547.

[2] *The Washington Post*, Oct. 20, 1995.

[3] See "Combating Terrorism," *The CQ Researcher*, July 21, 1995, pp. 633-656.

[4] Athan Theoharis, *From the Secret Files of J. Edgar Hoover* (1991), p. 80.

[5] See "Cults in America," *The CQ Researcher*, May 7, 1993, pp. 385-408.

[6] See "Mafia Crackdown," *The CQ Researcher*, March 27, 1992, pp. 265-288.

[7] *The Washington Post*, Feb. 15, 1997.

[8] *The Washington Post*, Feb. 14, 1997.

[9] *Los Angeles Times* [Washington edition], March 18, 1997.

[10] Quoted in *The Washington Post*, Feb. 14, 1997.

[11] *The New York Times*, Feb. 13. 1997.

[12] James Bovard, "The New J. Edgar Hoover," *The American Spectator*, August 1995.

[13] David B. Kopen and Paul H. Blackman, *No More Wacos: What's Wrong with Federal Law Enforcement and How to Fix It* (1997).

[14] *Los Angeles Times* [Washington edition], June 28, 1996.

[15] James Q. Wilson, *Time*, May 1, 1995, p. 73.

[16] Max Lowenthal, *The Federal Bureau of Investigation* (1950), p. 3.

[17] Harry and Bonaro Overstreet, *The FBI in Our Open Society* (1969), p. 73.

[18] Lowenthal, *op. cit.*, p. 36.

[19] Overstreet, *op. cit.*, p. 37.

[20] Richard Gid Powers, *G-Men: Hoover's FBI in Popular Culture* (1983), p. 97.

[21] Pat Watters and Stephen Gillers (eds.), *Investigating the FBI* (1973), p. 88.

[22] Diarmuid Jeffreys, *The Bureau: Inside the Modern FBI* (1995), pp. 61-62.

[23] Max Lowenthal, *The Federal Bureau of Investigation* (1950), p. 394.

[24] Watters and Gillers, *op. cit.*, p. 118.

[25] Ronald Kessler, *The FBI* (1993), p. 2.

[26] Powers, *op. cit.*, p. 265.

[27] Overstreet, *op. cit.*, p. 354.

[28] Gentry, *op. cit.*, p. 544.

[29] Jeffreys, *op. cit.*, p. 200.

[30] Gentry, *op. cit.*, p. 472.

[31] Athan Theoharis, *From the Secret Files of J. Edgar Hoover* (1991), p. 7.

[32] Jeffreys, *op. cit.*, p. 67.

[33] Kessler *op. cit.*, p. 269.

[34] Jeffreys, *op. cit.*, p. 267.

[35] House Judiciary and Government Reform and Oversight committees, "*Investigation into the Activities of Federal Law Enforcement Agencies Toward the Branch Davidians*," Aug. 2, 1996.

[36] *The New York Times*, March 25, 1997; *The Washington Post,* April 9, 1997.

[37] House Government Reform and Oversight Committee, "*Investigation of the White House Travel Office Firings and Related Matters*," Sept. 26, 1996.

[38] Testimony before House Appropriations Subcommittee on Commerce, Justice, State and Judiciary, March 5, 1997.

[39] *Ibid.*

[40] *Privacy Times*, Oct. 17, 1996, p. 10.

[41] *Insight*, Aug. 19, 1996, p. 20.

[42] See Carl Stern, "Journalists Could do a Lot to Make Their Requests Easier to Fill," *The American Editor*, July-August 1995, p. 14.

[43] *FOIA Update*, winter 1996, p. 1.

[44] *The Washington Post*, March 16, 1997.

[45] *The Washington Post*, March 16, 1997.

[46] Anthony Summers, *Official and Confidential: The Secret Life of J. Edgar Hoover* (1993), p. 248.

[47] "Is the FBI Making Foreign Policy?" *The Wall Street Journal*, Feb. 3, 1997.

[48] See "Reforming the CIA," *The CQ Researcher*, Feb. 2, 1996, pp. 97-120.

[49] *Newsweek*, April 14, 1997.

Bibliography

Selected Sources Used

Books

Gentry, Curt, *J. Edgar Hoover: The Man and the Secrets*, Penguin, 1991.
An author of popular works of American history produced this less-than-flattering biography of the legendary FBI director using newly released classified documents and more than 300 interviews.

Jeffreys, Diarmuid, *The Bureau: Inside the Modern FBI*, Houghton Mifflin, 1995.
A British television producer and author offers an in-depth portrait of today's FBI and its longstanding "myths" based on dozens of interviews with current and former employees.

Kessler, Ronald, *The FBI: Inside the World's Most Powerful Law Enforcement Agency — by the Award-Winning Journalist Whose Investigation Brought Down FBI Director William S. Sessions*, Simon and Schuster, 1993.
A former *Washington Post* reporter produced this thorough history and profile of the FBI's successes and failures, with an emphasis on the bureau's internal culture and its interface with Washington politics.

Lowenthal, Max, *The Federal Bureau of Investigation*, William Sloane Associates, 1950.
In one of the earliest full-length works to critique the FBI, Lowenthal explores the bureau's early failures and successes, with a special emphasis on its role in countering espionage.

Overstreet, Harry and Bonaro, *The FBI in Our Open Society*, W.W. Norton, 1969
Two authors of popular psychology works trace the history of the FBI with an emphasis on the bureau's chartered powers and its clashes with critics.

Powers, Richard Gid, *G-Men: Hoover's FBI in American Popular Culture*, Southern Illinois University Press, 1983.
A cultural historian at the College of Staten Island traces the history of the FBI with an emphasis on its public relations efforts and its portrayal in film, television and popular press.

Summers, Anthony, *Official and Confidential: The Secret Life of J. Edgar Hoover*, G.P. Putnam's Sons, 1993.
A British author and television correspondent made worldwide headlines with this biography's assertion that Hoover was a homosexual transvestite who allowed the Mafia to blackmail him.

Theoharis, Athan, *From the Secret Files of J. Edgar Hoover*, Ivan R. Dee, 1991.
An author specializing in intelligence and security issues filed numerous Freedom of Information Act requests to produce these annotated selections from FBI personal files on such notables as President John F. Kennedy, Attorney General Robert F. Kennedy and Sen. George S. McGovern.

Watters, Pat, and Stephen Gillers, *Investigating the FBI*, Doubleday, 1973.
These proceedings from a 1971 Princeton University conference on the FBI in American life contain some of the most critical commentary on the bureau's conduct in such areas as domestic surveillance, budgetary gamesmanship and public-image manipulation.

Articles

Bovard, James, "The New J. Edgar Hoover," *The American Spectator*, August 1995.
Bovard writes that FBI Director Louis J. Freeh runs an agency "inclined to destroy evidence of its botched investigations."

"FBI's Freeh: About to bolt?" *National Journal*, July 20, 1996, p. 1563.
Rumors are circulating that FBI Director Louis J. Freeh may leave his position. Sources say a law firm has offered Freeh an $800,000-a-year salary.

Klaidman, Daniel, and Evan Thomas, "The FBI: The Victim of His Virtues," *Newsweek*, April 14, 1997.
The authors argue that FBI Director Louis J. Freeh's biggest problem may be his pride.

The Next Step

Additional information from UMI's Newspaper & Periodical Abstracts™ database

Campaign Finance Investigations

Duffy, Brian, and Bob Woodward, "FBI Probes China-Linked Contributions; Task Force Examines Influence on Congress," *The Washington Post*, Feb. 28, 1997, p. A1.

A witness interviewed by FBI agents assigned to the task force said he was told that one focus of the Justice Department inquiry is to determine whether members of both parties in Congress had been improperly influenced by Chinese representatives who may have made illegal payments to them.

Duffy, Brian, "Senator Says FBI Warned of Chinese Influence-Buying Plans in 1995," *The Washington Post*, March 17, 1997, p. A6.

The FBI told the State Department, the CIA, the Justice Department and some members of Congress in 1995 that China as planning to make illegal campaign contributions to members of Congress, Sen. Orrin G. Hatch, R-Utah, said March 16, 1997.

Mathis, Nancy, "Clinton says he should've been told of briefing/ FBI denies agents demanded confidentiality on China probe," *Houston Chronicle*, March 11, 1997, p. A1.

In a stunning public spat between the White House and the FBI, President Clinton said Monday he should have been informed last June of the agency's suspicions that China wanted to influence congressional elections. The White House told reporters that FBI agents provided two National Security Council staff members with information on China's interest in political races, but insisted that no one else be told. White House spokesman Mike McCurry stood by his earlier account of the June meeting, maintaining the FBI was "in error."

Civil Liberties

"A Reasonable Response to Terror," *The New York Times*, July 30, 1996, p. A16.

An editorial urges that Congress not give in to pressure in the wake of the terrorist bombing in Atlanta, Ga., in considering the anti-terrorism bill. The editorial argues that a plan to make explosives easier to trace should have been approved long ago, but the proposal to extend the government's wiretapping authority is excessive, given the "proven need" to watch the FBI for invasion of civil liberties.

McGee, Jim, "Heightened tensions over digital taps," *The Washington Post*, Oct. 27, 1996, p. H1.

Tensions between the FBI and the U.S. telecommunications industry came to a boil in late 1996 because of new efforts by the FBI and other intelligence agencies to monitor cellular telephones and other mobile communications systems. Civil liberties groups contend the surveillance is too broad.

Newton, Jim, "ACLU seeks review of pepper spray," *Los Angeles Times*, Feb. 29, 1996, p. A3.

The American Civil Liberties Union asked state and federal officials to overhaul methods of testing police weapons and to stop using a brand of pepper spray in the wake of FBI Special Agent Thomas Ward's admission that he took $57,500 from the spray's manufacturer as he conducted research that eventually endorsed its use.

"World-wide: The FBI suspended," *The Wall Street Journal*, Jan 28, 1997, p. A1.

The FBI suspended a crime laboratory supervisor who in 1995, alleged that pro-prosecution bias and mishandling of evidence may have tainted testimony in several big cases, including the World Trade Center and Oklahoma City bombings.

"Filegate"

"Filegate flap," *Houston Chronicle*, July 14, 1996, p. C2.

An editorial comments on the "Filegate " controversy in which White House security personnel have been caught with hundreds of confidential FBI files on various persons of the opposite political persuasion, and asserts that no matter to whatever degree misuse of the files eventually is proved, the mere fact that the files were there is cause for public outrage.

"Filegate scandal begins to develop a strong odor," *Atlanta Journal*, July 9, 1996, p. A6.

An editorial opines that of all the scandals and reports of scandals that have touched the Clinton administration, the most troubling is the still-developing story of official snooping into the personal FBI files of potential enemies.

McGrory, Brian, "FBI report condemns file requests," *The Boston Globe*, June 15, 1996, p. 1.

FBI officials on June 14, 1996, condemned the Clinton administration's acquisition of bureau background files as "egregious violations of privacy," while FBI Director Louis J. Freeh ordered strict new controls over access to the agency's files.

McGrory, Brian, "Panetta apologizes on FBI files," *The Boston Globe*, June 10, 1996, p. 1.

White House Chief of Staff Leon Panetta issued a formal and blanket apology on June 9, 1996, to the hundreds of people, including many former Republican officials, whose classified FBI personnel files were obtained by the Clinton administration and reviewed by an Army security officer.

Forensics Lab

"Is the FBI Going Downhill?" *The Washington Post*, Jan. 30, 1997, p. A18.

The FBI's world-renowned crime laboratory is less than the reliable operation it was once thought to be. Indications of evidence mishandling have turned up in dozens of cases, according to the Justice Department's inspector general. That may not seem like many for a laboratory that conducts hundreds of thousands of evidence examinations a year. But hundreds of state and federal courts annually rely on the testimony of FBI experts.

Jackson, Robert L., and David G. Savage, "FBI Warns of Possible Flaws in Lab Evidence; Courts, Prosecutors, defense counsel nationwide are told of potential problems due to alleged misconduct," *Los Angeles Times*, Jan. 31, 1997, p. A1.

Fearing that an undetermined number of federal prosecutions could be put in jeopardy, Justice Department officials said Thursday that they have been telling prosecutors and defense attorneys across the country in recent weeks about potential flaws in evidence caused by serious problems at the FBI crime laboratory here.

Serrano, Richard A., "Workers Portray FBI Lab as a Shoddy Shop; Probe: Some current, former employees tell investigators of shortcomings, including possible contamination of tests by tour groups," *Los Angeles Times*, Jan. 31, 1997, p. A16.

Public tour groups filed through a hallway, kicking up dust, as delicate experiments were conducted nearby. Agents, fresh from the FBI's gun range or bomb unit, passed through — perhaps unwittingly spreading residue that could jeopardize tests. Lab technicians sometimes ignored or violated scientific protocols, some examiners were unqualified to issue test reports and, in one case, an analyst enhanced his scientific knowledge by "viewing videos." Throughout the history of the FBI, the lab on the third floor of the J. Edgar Hoover Building here has enjoyed a reputation for precision and expertise. But for more than a year now, the Justice Department's inspector general has been reviewing widespread allegations of abuse and shortcomings at the lab.

Serrano, Richard A., "FBI Lab Hasn't Jeopardized Cases, Freeh Tells Panel," *Los Angeles Times*, March 6, 1997, p. A1.

FBI Director Louis J. Freeh testified Wednesday that no criminal cases will be jeopardized by widespread reports of sloppy and incompetent work at the bureau's crime laboratory in Washington, D.C. Freeh's comments to a House Appropriations subcommittee suggested that the government's high-profile cases against the Oklahoma City bombing defendants and the accused Unabomber, plus as many as 50 other criminal cases, had not been compromised.

Suro, Roberto, and Pierre Thomas, "FBI Lab Woes Put 50 Cases In Jeopardy," *The Washington Post*, Feb. 14, 1997, p. A1.

The Justice Department has identified at least 50 criminal cases where evidentiary problems created by questionable forensic analysis at the FBI laboratory may have resulted in improper prosecutions, Deputy Attorney General Jamie S. Gorelick said yesterday, acknowledging that the number of problem cases could go higher.

Louis J. Freeh

Cannon, Angie, and Robert A. Rankin, "FBI curbs White House access to personal files," *Detroit News & Free Press*, June 15, 1996, p. A6.

FBI Director Louis J. Freeh on June 14, 1996, ordered new measures to protect sensitive agency background files from White House misuse while also disclosing that the White House wrongly obtained 408 files, more than was previously known.

"More trouble at the FBI," *The Washington Post*, Dec. 20, 1996, p. A26.

An editorial states that FBI Director Louis J. Freeh needs to do some hard introspection in relation to the number of scandals that have involved the agency in 1996.

Nelson, Jack, "Memo by Freeh denies rumors he'll quit FBI," *Los Angeles Times*, Oct. 26, 1996, p. A27.

FBI Director Louis J. Freeh, battered by a cross-fire of partisan politics and widely rumored to be planning to resign, has sent a memorandum to bureau employees assuring them that he intends to remain on the job.

Nichols, Bill, "FBI enters travel office controversy," *USA Today*, June 6, 1996, p. A1.

FBI Director Louis J. Freeh on June 5, 1996, ordered an inquiry into who at the White House asked the FBI for travel office chief Billy Dale's background file seven months after Dale was fired along with six other White House travel office workers in 1993. The request stated Dale was being considered for renewed White House access, but Dale said he had not sought the access.

Suro, Roberto, "FBI chief finds himself under microscope," *The Washington Post*, Nov. 18, 1996, p. A1.

FBI Director Louis J. Freeh's judgments in several high-profile episodes, such as the deadly 1992 Ruby Ridge standoff, are coming under increased scrutiny that is likely to escalate as 1996 comes to a close.

Montana Freemen

Freemantle, Tony, "After Waco tragedy, FBI stays low-key in Montana case," *Houston Chronicle*, April 3, 1996, p. A1.

The FBI is staying low-key in the case of the Montana Freemen after the disastrous confrontations between federal law enforcement teams and members of extremist groups at Ruby Ridge in Idaho and the Branch Davidian compound near Waco, Texas. The Freemen have been holed up since March 25, 1996.

Thomas, Pierre, and George Lardner, "FBI ponders mediation offer in Montana standoff," *The Washington Post*, March 31, 1996, p. A10.

The FBI is considering whether to accept an offer from Randy Weaver, whose wife was killed by an FBI agent in 1992 in a bloody standoff near Ruby Ridge, Idaho, to mediate an end to the siege with anti-government Freemen holed up on a remote ranch in Jordan, Mont., officials said March 30, 1996.

Smith, Wes, "Militants test FBI's resolve," *Chicago Tribune*, March 31, 1996, p. 1.

The 1,500 residents of Jordan, Mont., have asked the FBI to rid their town of the anti-government group known as Freemen. The problems facing the government officials, remembering the Waco, Texas, fiasco, are noted.

Olympics Bombing Incident

"FBI ends surveillance of Jewell," *Chicago Tribune*, Oct. 8, 1996, Sec. EVENING, p. 1.

The FBI questioned former security guard Richard Jewell over the Oct. 5, 1996, weekend and has dropped the surveillance it started after the Olympic Park bombing in Atlanta, Ga., his lawyer said on Oct. 8. All of Jewell's private property that had been seized by bombing investigators has been returned.

"Hyde vows probe of FBI, Jewell leak," *Atlanta Constitution*, Dec. 27, 1996, p. E2.

U.S. Rep. Henry J. Hyde, R-Ill., says his House Judiciary Committee will scrutinize the FBI, including its handling of a news leak in the 1996 Olympic bombing in Atlanta, Ga., after the new Congress convenes in January 1997.

"Jewell has his say about the FBI, media," *Houston Chronicle*, Oct. 29, 1996, p. A1.

Leveling a blistering attack on the FBI and the news media on Oct. 28, 1996, Richard Jewell held an emotional news conference that laid the groundwork for lawsuits against those who portrayed him as the leading suspect in the bombing at Centennial Olympic Park in July 1996

Johnson, Kevin, and Gary Fields, "Jewell investigation unmasks FBI 'tricks'," *USA Today*, Nov. 8, 1996, p. A13.

The FBI investigation of Richard Jewell in the July 1996, bombing of the Atlanta Centennial Park in Georgia is examined in light of the Justice Dept.'s investigation of whether the FBI's treatment of Jewell crossed the line.

Ruby Ridge

Jackson, Robert L., "FBI official pleads guilty in Ruby Ridge case," *Los Angeles Times*, Oct. 31, 1996, p. A16.

Suspended FBI official E. Michael Kahoe pleaded guilty on Oct. 30, 1996, to obstructing justice by destroying a critical report on the ill-fated shoot-out at Ruby Ridge, Idaho. Kahoe pledged to cooperate in the continuing investigation into an alleged cover-up of FBI actions in the 1992 incident.

"The FBI tries to clean its tarnished reputation," *San Francisco Chronicle*, Nov. 4, 1996, p. A24.

An editorial comments on the tarnished image that the FBI suffered the week of Oct. 28, 1996, with the announcement that a senior FBI official, E. Michael Kahoe, has pleaded guilty to obstructing justice in the 1992 Ruby Ridge siege and the disclosure of possible misconduct in the agency's investigation of Richard Jewell as a possible suspect in the July 1996 bombing at Olympic Park in Atlanta, Ga.

Potok, Mark, "Ruby Ridge: FBI official charged," *USA Today*, Oct. 23, 1996, p. A1.

Ranking FBI agent E. Michael Kahoe was charged Oct. 22, 1996, with obstructing justice amid indications he'll testify against others in a probe of a cover-up of events surrounding the deadly siege at Ruby Ridge, Idaho, in 1992. Kahoe is charged in a one-count criminal information filed by federal prosecutors in Washington, D.C.

Waco

Pankratz, Howard, "FBI avoided Waco's pitfalls," *Denver Post*, June 16, 1996, p. A11.

According to U.S. Deputy Attorney General Philip B. Heyman's lengthy report assessing the Waco tragedy, the multiple deaths of federal agents limited what negotiators could do with David Koresh and the Branch Davidians while the Freemen standoff in Jordan, Mont., presented the FBI with considerably more options.

Nealon, Patricia, "Critic of Waco praises 'landmark' FBI effort," *The Boston Globe*, June 15, 1996, p. 8.

Harvard Professor Alan Stone, who sharply criticized the FBI for its tactics after the deadly Waco, Texas, Branch Davidian standoff, said on June 14, 1996, that the FBI should be congratulated for orchestrating the peaceful surrender of the anti-government Freemen at their Montana ranch.

Back Issues

Great Research on Current Issues Starts Right Here...Recent topics covered by The CQ Researcher are listed below. Before May 1991, reports were published under the name of Editorial Research Reports.

SEPTEMBER 1995
Catholic Church in the U.S.
Northern Ireland Cease-Fire
High School Sports
Teaching History

OCTOBER 1995
Quebec's Future
Revitalizing the Cities
Networking the Classroom
Indoor Air Pollution

NOVEMBER 1995
The Working Poor
The Jury System
Sex, Violence and the Media
Police Misconduct

DECEMBER 1995
Teens and Tobacco
Gene Therapy's Future
Global Water Shortages
Third-Party Prospects

JANUARY 1996
Emergency Medicine
Punishing Sex Offenders
Bilingual Education
Helping the Homeless

Back issues are available for $5.00 (subscribers) or $10.00 (non-subscribers). Quantity discounts apply to orders over ten. To order, call Congressional Quarterly Customer Service at (202) 887-8621.

Binders are available for $18.00. To order call 1-800-638-1710. Please refer to stock number 648.

FEBRUARY 1996
Reforming the CIA
Campaign Finance Reform
Academic Politics
Getting Into College

MARCH 1996
The British Monarchy
Preventing Juvenile Crime
Tax Reform
Pursuing the Paranormal

APRIL 1996
Centennial Olympic Games
Managed Care
Protecting Endangered Species
New Military Culture

MAY 1996
Russia's Political Future
Marriage and Divorce
Year-Round Schools
Taiwan, China and the U.S.

JUNE 1996
Rethinking NAFTA
First Ladies
Teaching Values
Labor Movement's Future

JULY 1996
Recovered-Memory Debate
Native Americans' Future
Crackdown on Sexual Harassment
Attack on Public Schools

AUGUST 1996
Fighting Over Animal Rights
Privatizing Government Services
Child Labor and Sweatshops
Cleaning Up Hazardous Wastes

SEPTEMBER 1996
Gambling Under Attack
The States and Federalism
Civic Journalism
Reassessing Foreign Aid

OCTOBER 1996
Political Consultants
Insurance Fraud
Rethinking School Integration
Parental Rights

NOVEMBER 1996
Global Warming
Clashing Over Copyright
Consumer Debt
Governing Washington, D.C.

DECEMBER 1996
Welfare, Work and the States
The New Volunteerism
Implementing the Disabilities Act
America's Pampered Pets

JANUARY 1997
Combating Scientific Misconduct
Restructuring the Electric Industry
The New Immigrants
Chemical and Biological Weapons

FEBRUARY 1997
Assisting Refugees
Alternative Medicine's Next Phase
Independent Counsels
Feminism's Future

MARCH 1997
New Air Quality Standards
Alcohol Advertising
Civic Renewal
Educating Gifted Students

Future Topics

- ***Gender Equity in Sports***
- ***Space Program's Future***
- ***The Stock Market***

THE CQ Researcher

PUBLISHED BY CONGRESSIONAL QUARTERLY INC.

Gender Equity in Sports

Does federal law help female athletes by hurting men?

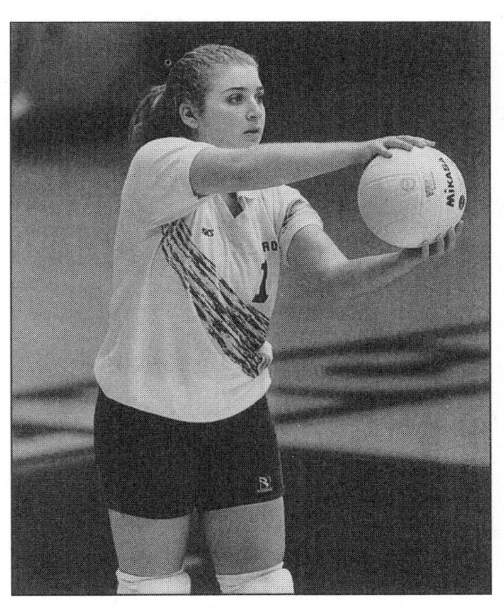

Title IX of the Education Amendments of 1972 required gender equity in school and college sports. Now, 25 years later, American women athletes are on a roll: They collected nearly half the 44 gold medals won by the U.S. at the 1996 Olympics; the 1997 women's college basketball championship game was seen by a record TV audience and not one but two women's pro basketball leagues have been formed. Title IX is widely credited with igniting the women's sports boom, but critics say the progress has been at the expense of men's programs, because Title IX is too rigidly enforced. In a case being watched closely by sports programs around the nation, Brown University has asked the Supreme Court to review lower court rulings that said its sports program discriminated against women in violation of Title IX.

INSIDE THIS ISSUE

CQ April 18, 1997 • Volume 7, No. 15 • Pages 337-360

Formerly Editorial Research Reports

Gender Equity in Sports

Cover: Christy Mumm plays varsity volleyball for Brown University, which is seeking Supreme Court review of lower court rulings that its sports program discriminated against women. (Brown University)

April 18, 1997
Volume 7, No. 15

The CQ Researcher (ISSN 1056-2036). Formerly Editorial Research Reports. Published weekly (48 times per year, not printed Jan. 3, May 30, Aug. 29, Oct. 31) by Congressional Quarterly Inc., 1414 22nd St., N.W., Washington, D.C. 20037. Annual subscription rate for libraries, businesses and government is $340. Additional rates furnished upon request. Periodicals postage paid at Washington, D.C., and additional mailing offices. POSTMASTER: Send address changes to The CQ Researcher, 1414 22nd St., N.W., Washington, D.C. 20037.

Gender Equity in Sports

BY RICHARD L. WORSNOP

THE ISSUES

When 17-year-old Linnea Bloom scored her first varsity soccer goal recently for West Potomac High School in Alexandria, Va., exuberant teammates showered her with high-fives. The Wolverines went on to beat Jeb Stuart High, 5-2, and the celebrating continued.

Linnea pays special tribute to her coach, Becky Bonzano, who she says is warm, supportive and low-key. But across the nation, the unsung hero of women's athletics is the law known as Title IX, now celebrating its 25th birthday.

Title IX. It's not a ringing, memorable name, like the Civil Rights Act. But there's wide agreement that the astounding progress of U.S. women's sports in recent years — and the increasing opportunities for female athletes like Linnea — is due to Title IX of the Education Amendments of 1972.

Title IX's impact was evident on March 30, when a capacity crowd and millions of television viewers across the nation watched the University of Tennessee beat Old Dominion University for the National Collegiate Athletic Association's women's basketball championship. It was, says ESPN, the sports network's "most-watched" NCAA basketball game — men's or women's — since 1990.

Title IX outlaws sex discrimination in all federally funded education programs, but it has always been linked in the public mind with high school and college athletics, where its impact has been most visible. [1] In 1971, the year before Title IX, fewer than 300,000 girls played high school sports nationwide; in 1996 there were more than 2.4 million participants. (*See graphs, p. 340.*)

The impressive performance of American women at last summer's

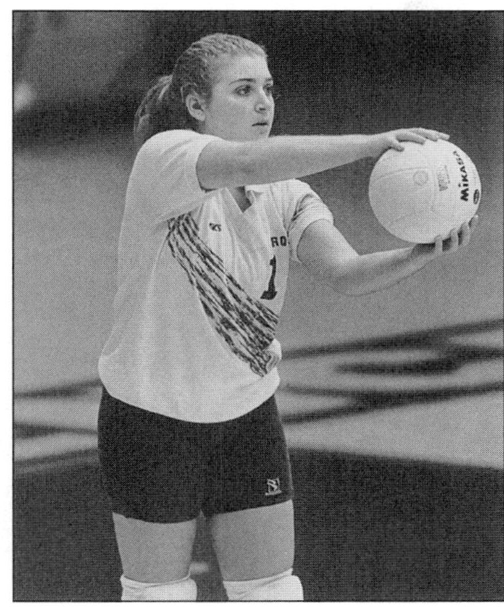

Olympics also is credited by many analysts to Title IX. Of the 44 gold medals won by the U.S. in Atlanta, women captured 19, including four by swimmer Amy Van Dyken and team medals in basketball, softball, gymnastics, synchronized swimming and soccer.

Soccer is one of Title IX's greatest success stories, women's sports officials say. In 1977, only 11,534 girls nationwide played high school soccer. By 1996, there were 209,287. [2] Title IX is credited with helping to nurture the players that won the first women's World Cup soccer championship in 1990 as well as the soccer gold medal in Atlanta.

"We are seeing for the first time a generation of women who grew up with sporting opportunities that were at least somewhat comparable to their brothers'," says Christine H.B. Grant, women's athletic director at the University of Iowa. "I think we are walking away from the rest of the world in this area."

But Grant is still steamed about the skimpy TV time given to U.S. women in Atlanta. "We had very poor coverage of women's basketball," she says, "and for women's soccer and softball, almost none. I don't know what else young women can do. Win the gold medal, and you still don't get on camera."

That may change thanks to what many observers say is yet another legacy of Title IX — the recent emergence of professional female sports leagues, including fast-pitch softball, ice hockey and basketball.

"What that says is something we all knew — you cannot make a professional league overnight," says Donna Lopiano, executive director of the Women's Sports Foundation in East Meadow, N.Y. "It takes 15-20 years to make a pro ball player. The women playing for these new pro teams all grew up under Title IX."

Marcia Saneholtz, senior associate athletic director at Washington State University, says, "More attention needs to be focused on gender-equity issues at the grass-roots level," including junior high school sports and community youth activities. "We're not going to be any more equitable at the collegiate level than we are at those lower levels, which is where our student-athletes come from." (*See story, p. 346.*)

Saneholtz points to the increasing number of gender-equity lawsuits being filed on behalf of female athletes in high school and junior high sports programs. "The girls' parents are saying, 'Hey, this isn't right! Our daughters deserve the same kinds of opportunities and support that our sons are getting,'" she says. "It's unfortunate that change often has to be driven by litigation, but that seems to be the one thing that gets people moving in the right direction."

When it comes to women's sports litigation — and criticism of Title IX — all eyes are on Brown University. Five years ago, 11 women sued Brown for sex discrimination under Title IX. The plaintiffs were former

Girls' Participation Soared After Title IX

Eight times as many women played high school sports in 1996 as in 1971, the year before passage of Title IX. At the college level, where fewer women participate in athletics, the rise was less dramatic.

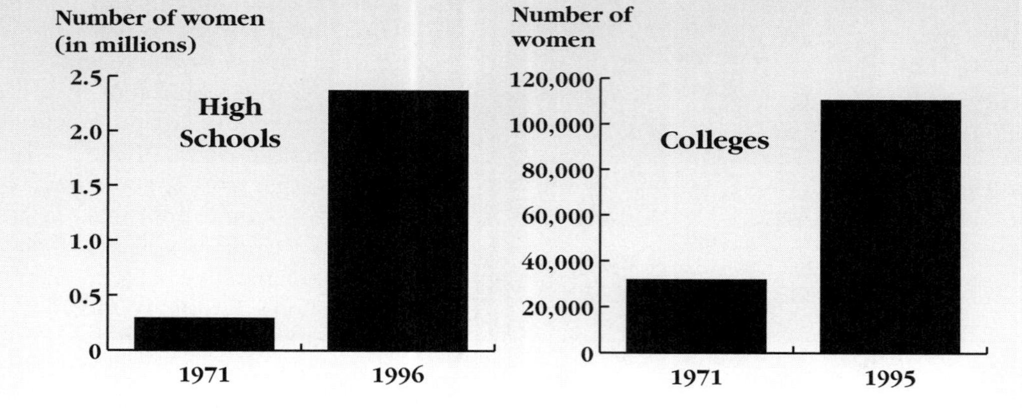

Sources: National Collegiate Athletic Association; National Federation of State High School Associations

members of Brown's women's gymnastics and volleyball teams, which had lost university funding as part of an overall belt-tightening effort (*see p. 348*). (Today Brown still operates a large athletic program — 18 varsity sports for men and 19 for women.)

Sports administrators across the country are following *Cohen v. Brown* closely because it centers on the core issue in the Title IX debate: how to determine whether sports programs are in compliance with the law. To arrive at an answer, the Education Department's Office of Civil Rights (OCR) applies a three-part test asking:

- whether men's and women's sports participation opportunities are "substantially proportionate" to their share of student enrollment;
- whether the institution can show "a history and continuing practice of program expansion" for the underrepresented sex; and
- whether "the interests and abilities of the members of [the underrepresented] sex have been fully and effectively accommodated by the present program."

A passing grade in any of the three areas is tantamount to Title IX compliance, OCR says. But Brown, which has flunked at both the District and Appeals court levels, contends that the courts and OCR have adopted such a rigid proportionality standard for female sports participation that it amounts to an illegal quota system. Brown has appealed *Cohen v. Brown* to the U.S. Supreme Court, which has yet to announce whether it will accept the case for review. (*see p. 349*).

Brown President Vartan Gregorian * defends his school against the Title IX suit. "[W]hat is happening here is an assault against common sense," he told lawmakers. "If Brown with its robust program of women's sports is not in compliance with Title IX, it is hard to imagine how any institution is today. . . . Brown supports Title IX. But the government, it seems to me, must find ways to make it work. . . . Such a solution should also permit institutions of higher learning to meet the respective interests of men and women to participate in sports fairly and equally without resorting to blunt and arbitrary measurements, such as those called for by a District Court judge and seemingly also by OCR's regulations." [3]

T.J. Kerr, president of the National Wrestling Coaches Association, is among the administrators of sports programs for men who argue that ending discrimination against women is a worthy goal but that Title IX accomplishes that end by discriminating against men. "We are particularly concerned about the tens of thousands of young men whose athletic careers have already been cut short by the OCR rules," he told lawmakers. "While we firmly agree with the letter and spirit of Title IX, we are firmly committed to the proposition that it is unconscionable to eliminate male programs or male athletes to satisfy a gender quota." [4]

Former Sen. Birch Bayh, D-Ind., who was the chief Senate sponsor of Title IX, said the struggle for gender equity "goes beyond just the basketball court or the soccer field." Bayh added that there are now nine women in the Senate and 51 in the House, "proving that [women] can succeed, not on the basis of their sex, but on what they have to offer." [5]

While the Supreme Court considers taking *Cohen v. Brown* for review, these are some of the questions about Title IX being asked by parents, coaches and athletic program administrators:

---

* Gregorian is leaving Brown University and in July will become president of The Carnegie Corp. of New York, a philanthropic organization.

Do gains in women's sports under Title IX come at the expense of men's sports?

The overriding goal of Title IX is equality of opportunity for men and women in all federally funded school and college programs. Supporters of the law say it has gone far toward achieving that aim — though not far enough.

But critics say the participation gains posted by female athletes often have been achieved by trimming opportunities for males. College wrestling, an exclusively male sport, often is cited. "In its heyday in the early 1970s . . . more than 9,000 wrestlers competed on 400 college teams," sports reporter Kimberly Jones recently noted. But "Last year, just over 6,000 wrestlers competed at the college level, according to the NCAA," at only 251 schools. [6]

Kerr of the wrestling coaches association blames the decline in college wrestling programs and other "minor" men's sports such as gymnastics on what he derisively termed OCR's "gender-quota" system. [7]

"Nationally, there are about 190,000 male college athletes and about 105,000 female athletes," Kerr told lawmakers in 1995. "Since female students outnumber male students nationally (53 percent vs. 47 percent), OCR's gender quota requires that there be more female athletes than male athletes. So educational administrators must either add 100,000 female athletes, eliminate 100,000 male athletes or some combination thereof. If administrators continue to choose 'elimination' — even in combination with adding female sports programs — all male Olympic athletic programs will be destroyed before the gender quota can be satisfied." [8]

Kerr's complaints about proportionality cut no ice with Lopiano, who helped draft the Title IX regulations. "Women didn't set those rules," she says. "Men did. Back in the early 1970s, 60 percent of college students were male. So the men on the drafting panel thought, 'Well, gee, why don't we promote proportionality? That way, we can make sure we'll have more male athletes than females.' That's where that idea came from." Lopiano adds: "I think it's the epitome of bad sportsmanship to say, 25 years into the game, ' I'm losing, and I want to change the rules.' Come on!"

Reuters

Amy Van Dyken claimed four of the 19 Olympic gold medals won by U.S. women in Atlanta in 1996.

Many sports commentators point to football as the No. 1 speed-bump on the road to gender equity. NCAA Division I-A football, which includes perennial gridiron powers such as Notre Dame, Penn State and Nebraska, consumes a disproportionate share of athletic budgets, critics say. For one thing, uniforms and equipment are far more expensive in football than in other sports, notably basketball. But the main reason college football costs so much is the size of the squads — typically more than 100 players — most of them on athletic scholarship.

In Lopiano's view, "college presidents are eliminating men's sports rather than telling the football coach to share program resources and then blaming cuts on Title IX and gender equity. The school/college community is unwilling to take many actions short of cutting programs because they fear reducing the competitiveness of football." [9]

But football can prosper even after sports programs are downsized, says Diana Everett, executive director of the National Association for Girls and Women in Sport in Reston, Va. "You can certainly have winning programs in men's football, in men's basketball, without spending exorbitant amounts of money. The problem is that we've developed those particular sports into games where 'bigger is better, more is better.' But there are lots of successful college sports programs with balanced opportunities for men and women."

Measures that purportedly can create additional sports opportunities for women without reducing those for men include cutting back on air travel and hotel accommodations, adding

Top High School Girls' Sports

	Participants in 1995-96
Basketball	445,869
Track and Field (outdoor)	379,060
Volleyball	357,576
Softball (fast pitch)	305,217
Soccer	209,287
Tennis	146,573
Cross-Country	140,187
Swimming and Diving	111,360
Field Hockey	56,142
Golf	39,634

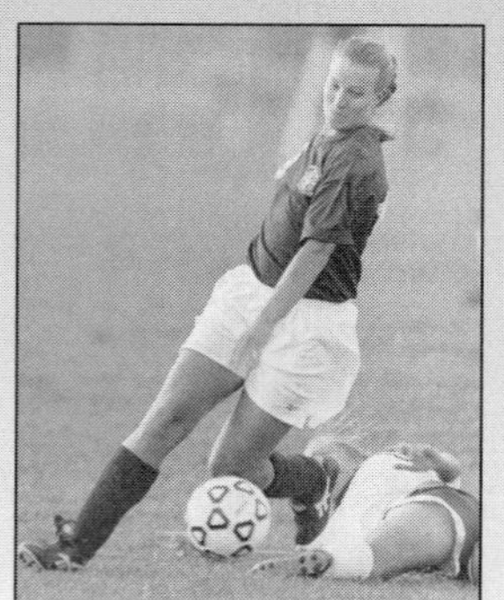

National Federation of State High School Associations, 1996

an extra game to the schedule to increase revenue, trimming recruiting efforts and basing all athletic scholarships on financial need. And since football squads are so large, some reformers see roster limits as a promising remedy.

No way, said Tom Osborne, head football coach at the University of Nebraska. "Opponents of college football maintain that 85 scholarships exceed what is necessary, since pro football teams have fewer numbers [of players]," he said. "What they fail to recognize is that pro players are already fully developed. Approximately a third of each college football squad is still in a developmental stage. Most football players are not able to compete at a Division I level until they get bigger, faster or stronger than when they first enroll in school." [10]

The resultant risk of injury justifies ample football squads, Osborne claimed. "Five to 10 players are hurt and can't play at any given time — we do not have an injured reserve squad or a waiver wire that enables us to acquire players when injuries occur, as [professional] teams do."

But the main argument made in defense of football and the other "revenue sport" — men's basketball — is that they support not only themselves but also women's and men's teams in so-called minor sports.

"Big-time football makes money," says Charles M. Neinas, executive director of the College Football Association (CFA), which comprises a majority of the nation's Division I-A football powers. "Below the level of the CFA, the Big 10 and the Pacific 10 conferences, football doesn't make money. Ironically, the targets of the women's activist groups are the more prominent football institutions. And yet, those are the very institutions that have the most visible, well-funded women's sports programs."

In Lopiano's opinion, "Football isn't an issue in the gender-equity debate because Title IX does not mandate that an institution develop a women's program that is a mirror image of the men's. It simply says, in effect, 'Men are interested in certain sports, and women are interested in certain sports.' So, if you have 200 participation opportunities for men, they can play football, basketball, whatever they want." By the same token, women "should have a similar number of opportunities and the same freedom to choose what they want to play."

The name or the nature of the sport is beside the point, Lopiano says. "Men should have the right to pick a sport that has 100 players," she says, "if they want to use up their opportunities that way. And if women want to use up their opportunities by picking a sport with 50 players, or 20, that's up to them."

Are women less interested in playing interscholastic and intercollegiate sports than men?

The Title IX issues of "proportionality" and "interests and abilities" are closely linked, but nowhere more so than in *Cohen v. Brown.* In its brief asking the Supreme Court to review the case, the university acknowledges that "the percentage of women participating in Brown's varsity athletic program did not mirror the percentage of women in its student body" when the lawsuit was filed in 1992. Brown argued then, as it does today, that it "had not engaged in discrimination by allocating more than 50 percent of its varsity opportunities to men because men represented substantially more than half of the pool of interested and able athletes."

Mark Nickel, director of the university's news bureau, says the university "has been told it should have a gender ratio in intercollegiate sports participation matching that of the entire undergraduate student body. The only way that makes sense is if it can be indisputably proven that men and women, at this point in time, exhibit the same level of interest in intercollegiate competition. And that's not so."

Nickel hastens to add that "It's never been Brown's argument that men are inherently more interested in sports than women. We don't believe that. But we do have to deal with the

Coaching Women's Teams: It's a Guy Thing

Viewers of this year's National Collegiate Athletic Association women's basketball championship no doubt noticed that all the Final Four teams had female coaches. Just what one would expect, right? Not necessarily.

Actually, it was the first time since 1982 — the inaugural year of the NCAA-sponsored event — that women held all the head coaching jobs on the final weekend.

The situation points up one of the ironies of Title IX, the 25-year-old law that vastly expanded sports participation opportunities for millions of high school and college women. Contrary to expectations, the law also sharply reduced college coaching opportunities for women. In 1972, the year Title IX was enacted, women coached more than 90 percent of female college teams. The proportion has since dropped below 50 percent.

The trend is easily explained, according to Vivian Acosta and Linda Jean Carpenter of Brooklyn College, who have tracked the issue for 20 years. One of the first things many college presidents did to comply with Title IX, they said, was to eliminate separate athletic departments for men and women. In almost all cases, the incumbent male athletic director was handed the reins of the merged sports program.

"When the male directors looked for people to fill jobs in the women's programs, they turned to their male friends," Acosta said. "They'd get Joe instead of Josie to fill the basketball job. It wasn't deliberate. They were just using their natural networking skills." [1]

In a report issued last year, Acosta and Carpenter reported little change in the percentage of coaching jobs held by women at NCAA member institutions over the past five years. [2] Women coaches accounted for 49.4 percent of the total in 1994 but only 47.7 percent in 1996 — the second lowest representation level since Title IX was enacted in 1972.

"It's really important for girls to see females as coaches and athletic directors at the high school level," says Helen E. Upton, assistant director of the National Federation of State High School Associations, the national governing body for high school sports. "Women in those jobs can serve as great advocates for female athletes — and, of course, many male coaches can, too."

Debbie Ryan, women's basketball coach at the University of Virginia, agrees. "Men definitely deserve to be in the profession." she says. "Lots of kids come from single-parent homes, and it's good for them to have the role models." [3]

To increase college coaching opportunities for women, says Christine H.B. Grant, women's athletic director at the University of Iowa, there has to be "active recruitment of qualified women. You can't just put an ad in the *NCAA News* and hope you're going to land a woman who's suited for the job."

Women are reticent about applying for college coaching jobs, Grant says, "because they often feel they're not going to have a fair shot. So the athletic director has got to get on the phone and, if necessary, go to see qualified women and encourage them to submit an application. That's what we do at Iowa." All but one of the 12 varsity women's teams at Iowa have female coaches.

Diana Everett, executive director of the National Association for Girls and Women in Sport in Reston, Va., says it's all a matter of networking. "There certainly are women out there, maybe in assistant-coaching positions, who are head-coaching material. The difficulty is that the people doing the hiring usually are men. And generally speaking, men don't have as effective a network for finding female coaches as they do for male coaches."

Charles M. Neinas, executive director of the College Football Association, has his own explanation for the gender imbalance. "I assume there are not as many female coaches as male coaches in the pipeline," he says, "because it takes a while to develop a backlog of coaches. I also assume that as more women enter the profession and gain experience, they'll move on" up the coaching ladder.

Donna Lopiano, executive director of the Women's Sports Foundation in East Meadow, N.Y., says that "It's a question of institutional leadership. If the college president tells the athletic director, 'You had better choose somebody from an underrepresented group when you make a new hire,' it will happen. That's the kind of leadership we need — a statement that says, in effect, 'This situation is out of whack; I expect you to correct it, and I want a report card every year.' "

Lopiano is less sanguine about swelling the thin ranks of female athletic directors. "We know from experience that the higher-paying the job, and the higher the competitive division, the more likely it is that the athletic director will be male," she says. "It's easier for a woman to become a college president than it is to become a college athletic director."

---

[1] Quoted by Mary Collins, "And the Men Shall Lead Them," *Women's Sports and Fitness*, April 1997, p. 19.

[2] Vivian Acosta and Linda Jean Carpenter, "Women in Intercollegiate Sport, a Longitudinal Study, 19-Year Update, 1977-1996," unpublished study, 1996.

[3] Quoted in Collins, *op. cit.*, p. 20.

---

student body that we have right here and now in designing our athletic program. And right now, there is a difference between the interest level displayed by women and men."

Women scoff at such reasoning. "Girls and boys are equally interested in playing sports," Women's Sports Foundation (WSF) President

Benita Fitzgerald Mosely recently wrote. "Saying that girls are not as sports-oriented as boys is similar to saying that girls are not as good at math and science as boys. These sorts of faulty assumptions result from gender stereotypes — it's the assumptions themselves that often limit opportunities for our daughters." [11]

Also, Everett argues, opinion surveys of female college undergraduates produce unreliable data on sports-participation interest. "Let's say the University of Virginia was thinking of forming a women's ice hockey team," she says. "If people from the athletic department walked around campus and asked women students if they were interested in playing on the team, the majority obviously would say no. If Virginia women were interested in playing ice hockey, they would have gone to a university that already had a women's team."

Wendy Hilliard, Mosley's predecessor as WSF president, argued that "There is also a double standard in the application of an 'interests and ability' requirement for girls and women in athletics. No such standard has ever been imposed for men. For men, there is an assumption of interest. If a men's sport is unsuccessful, there is no presumption of lack of ability or interest. Rather, the coach is blamed for being an unsuccessful teacher and motivator, his employment is terminated and a new and often better-paid coach is obtained." [12]

Those who argue that men are more interested than women in playing sports often cite "walk-ons" in college athletics to bolster their case. A walk-on is a student without an athletic scholarship who tries to win a spot on a varsity team. "It's a significant fact," Neinas says, "that women do not walk on and try out for the team like men will do."

Graham Spanier, chancellor of the University of Nebraska, agrees. "We have tried to interest young women to 'walk on' for varsity competition," he said, "but despite our efforts, still about four times the number of men vs. women walk on." [13]

Women sports officials roll their eyes at such remarks. Helen E. Upton, assistant director of the National Federation of State High School Associations, responds that the country needs "a youth-based level of female sports that can provide a pool of participants for high schools. Then, female high school athletes should be able to see that they can continue playing their sport in college. And now, with women's pro leagues arriving on the scene, female athletes can see that they also have a place to play after college."

The evolving situation reminds Upton of the 1989 movie "Field of Dreams," in which an Iowa farmer (played by Kevin Costner) builds a baseball diamond in his cornfield in hopes that the legendary Shoeless Joe Jackson will materialize to play on it. Jackson does just that in the movie, and Upton says today's women athletes will do the same, given the chance. "If you build it," she says, echoing a line from the film, "they will come." ■

BACKGROUND

Crashing the Men's Club

Americans' attitudes toward women's sports have long been ambivalent, if not openly disapproving. Though female athletes have competed in every Olympics beginning in 1900, their participation was limited that year to the socially acceptable women's events of golf and lawn tennis. Archery was added in 1904.

Women athletes of the time hardly constituted a cross-section of society. Indeed, "The seven American women who entered the 1900 Paris Olympic Games matched the profile of late 19th-century scions of wealth," wrote women's sports experts Paula Welch and D. Margaret Costa. "They belonged to social clubs; studied art, music, literature and language; and, through their country club affiliations, entered sport from an acceptable realm." [14]

The choice of golf, tennis and archery as the charter Olympic sports for women spoke volumes about turn-of-the-century notions of propriety. Competitors wore long, loosely fitting garments, thus sparing them the embarrassment of exposing their bodies to crowds of mostly male strangers.

The sports boom of the 1920s, which also witnessed a reappraisal of relations between the sexes, led some U.S. colleges to develop athletic programs for women. However, a reaction against women's basketball by people who thought female athletes in shorts should not perform before male spectators led to the elimination of many college programs by decade's end. During the 1930s, women's basketball was played mainly in industrial leagues.

But conflicted male feelings held sway even in this egalitarian milieu. Consider, for example, the decision by the Elks Club in Wichita, Kan., to have players in the 1930 Amateur Athletic Union (AAU) women's basketball championship take part in a beauty contest held in conjunction with the tournament. J. Lyman Bingham, chairman of the AAU Basketball Committee, reported afterward: "I will admit I . . . fully expected to see fainting girls carried away in ambulances, others laced in [strait-] jackets after severe cases of hysteria and some in complete collapse after extreme cases of melancholia, the air permeated with smelling salts, etc., but I was agreeably

Continued on p. 346

Chronology

1900s-1930s

The Olympics help to reshape popular opinion about women in sports.

1900
Seven American women compete in golf and lawn tennis at the Paris Olympic Games, the first to feature female sports.

1932
Mildred "Babe" Didrickson wins three track and field medals at the Los Angeles Olympics, gaining renown as the top U.S. female athlete of her generation.

1970s

The women's and civil rights movements inspire women to rebel against male monopoly control of the nation's sports establishment.

1971
The Association for Intercollegiate Athletics for Women (AIAW) challenges the male-dominated National Collegiate Athletic Association (NCAA).

1972
Title IX of the Education Amendments outlaws sex discrimination by all recipients of federal education funds.

July 21, 1975
Title IX takes effect, but high schools and colleges are given three additional years to comply with the equal-athletic-opportunity provisions.

Dec. 11, 1979
The Education Department's Office of Civil Rights (OCR) sets forth a three-part test for determining whether an institution is providing non-discriminatory participation opportunities.

1980s

Legal uncertainties about the scope of Title IX temporarily stall further progress toward gender equity in athletics.

1982
With membership plummeting, the AIAW disbands, leaving the NCAA as the dominant group representing women in college sports.

Feb. 28, 1984
Ruling in *Grove City College v. Bell*, the U.S. Supreme Court narrows the scope of Title IX by holding that the law applies only to specific programs receiving direct federal funding.

1987
Washington's Supreme Court finds that Washington State University treated women unfairly in its sports programs.

March 22, 1988
Congress passes the Civil Rights Restoration Act over President Ronald Reagan's veto. In effect, the measure strikes down *Grove City* by barring sex discrimination throughout educational institutions receiving federal aid.

1990s

An Ivy League college never known as a sports powerhouse becomes the focus of Title IX debate.

April 29, 1991
To help close a budget deficit, Brown University withdraws funding from four varsity teams: men's water polo and golf, and women's gymnastics and volleyball.

Feb. 26, 1992
Ruling in *Franklin v. Gwinnett County Public Schools*, the Supreme Court says students may sue for monetary damages for sexual harassment and other forms of sex discrimination.

March 11, 1992
The NCAA discloses that men's and women's enrollments are roughly equal at member institutions, but that men's programs constitute 70 percent of the participants in intercollegiate sports.

April 9, 1992
Members of the two unfunded women's teams at Brown file suit in U.S. District Court in Providence, R.I., alleging violation of Title IX. Gymnast Amy Cohen is the lead plaintiff.

March 29, 1995
U.S. District Judge Raymond S. Pettine finds for the plaintiffs in *Cohen v. Brown* and gives the university 120 days to file a compliance plan.

Aug. 18, 1995
Pettine rejects Brown's compliance proposal. He orders the university to fully fund three donor-supported women's varsity teams and to elevate one intercollegiate club team to fully funded varsity status.

Nov. 21, 1996
The U.S. Court of Appeals in Boston reverses Pettine's order that Brown fund four additional women's varsity teams. However, it upholds his other findings.

Feb. 18, 1997
Brown announces it has petitioned the U.S. Supreme Court to review the appellate court ruling.

Equity Is the Name of the Game at WSU

Sooner or later, most discussions of gender equity in sports turn to Washington State University. The percentage of women on WSU's varsity teams almost precisely matches the percentage of women in the undergraduate student body, typically 46-48 percent.

And yet Washington State didn't deliberately set out to become a Title IX poster child, notes Senior Associate Athletic Director Marcia Saneholtz. "We restructured our athletic program as a result of litigation based on state law — the Washington equal rights amendment and other anti-discrimination measures," she says. "We're in compliance with Title IX because of that process, although that wasn't our initial goal. The orders we had to comply with from the state courts were more stringent than what Title IX requires."

The university's struggle with gender equity began in 1982, when a group of WSU athletes and coaches of women's teams filed suit against the university in state Superior Court, claiming the school discriminated against women. The court ruled that Washington State had to provide greater opportunities for women athletes. "It was probably the first court to use undergraduate female enrollment as the standard against which to measure equitable opportunities in athletics," Saneholtz says. Significantly, though, the Superior Court order did not include football in the calculations on which it based its decision.

In response to the ruling, the WSU athletic department cleaned house. Varsity women's teams in field hockey, skiing, gymnastics and rifle and men's varsity teams in wrestling and rifle were dropped, along with all men's and women's junior varsity teams. The only addition to the program was women's varsity golf. The overall goal, said WSU Athletic Director Rick Dickson, was to enhance "the quality of the programs offered for women in regard to equipment, facilities, services, coaching, publicity, scheduling and other areas." [1]

But that was only the beginning. In 1987, the state Supreme Court overturned WSU's football exemption, stating that "The exclusion of football would prevent sex equity from ever being achieved, since men would always be guaranteed many more participation opportunities than women."

After further deliberation, the university decided in 1988 to fully fund all of its women's sports to the maximum number of scholarships allowed by the NCAA. It also added a women's soccer team in 1989 and women's crew in 1990.

At the same time, the university successfully lobbied the Washington Legislature to enact three laws designed to promote sports gender-equity throughout the state. One measure required the state Higher Education Coordinating Board and the state superintendent of public instruction to sponsor a sports gender-equity conference for coaches, administrators, teachers and others involved in athletics. A companion bill required colleges to evaluate all of their programs from a gender-equity perspective and to eliminate any problem areas. The third law allowed four-year colleges and universities to withhold 1 percent of their revenue from undergraduate tuition and fees and use the money to help achieve gender equity in athletics.

From the beginning, Saneholtz says, Washington State administrators "took the position that, 'We're not doing this because we have to do. We're doing it because it's right, and we should be doing it.' They didn't say one thing to one audience and something else to another audience."

Commitment was the key to success, Saneholtz says. "It's the same in education as in business," she says. "You can find ways to achieve the goals you are committed to. If you don't have that commitment, then you find excuses for doing nothing."

[1] Statement submitted to House Committee on Economic and Educational Opportunities Subcommittee on Postsecondary Education, Training and Life-long Learning, May 9, 1995.

pleased that none of these things happened.

"What I actually did see was a group of girls at the end of the game, rush to the center of the floor to cheer their opponents and then go arm in arm with them off the floor to appear later at a dance where a number of well-behaved University of Wichita boys had been selected to dance with them." [15]

Even after World War II, interscholastic and intercollegiate athletics was widely held to be a male preserve. Until the early 1970s, "Men at the intercollegiate level enjoyed all of the varsity participation slots in the nation, opportunities often financially supported by both institutional funds as well as student fees from both male and female students," Iowa's Grant observed. "Thus, at many institutions, women were not only denied the opportunity to participate in varsity sports, they were also required to financially support the athletic opportunities for men! Any women who desired to participate in club sports . . . had to pay for these opportunities out of their pockets again." [16]

Norma V. Cantú, head of the OCR, has cited a specific instance of unequal treatment: "After winning two swimming gold medals in the 1964 Olympics, Donna de Varona was, in effect, forced to retire at the age of 17; scholarships at colleges for women in swimming did not exist. Meanwhile, her best friend, a fellow gold medalist in swimming, Don Schollander, got a full scholarship to Yale." [17]

Correcting such inequities was a prime objective of the Association for Intercollegiate Athletics for Women (AIAW), founded in 1971. AIAW "assumed the leadership role for women's athletics in the United States," Jennifer Hargreaves wrote, "embodying a student-centered, education-oriented approach and resisting the professionalized model of men's college athletics." [18] From 278 institutions at the outset, AIAW's membership rose to a peak of 970 in 1979.

Title IX

Meanwhile, pressure from the civil rights and women's movements finally resulted in congressional approval of Title IX. The title simply states that "No person in the United States shall, on the basis of sex, be excluded from participation in, be denied the benefits of, or be subject to discrimination under any education program or activity receiving federal financial assistance."

Though the provision applied to all programs in elementary, secondary and higher education, it soon became closely identified with athletics in particular. Perceiving a threat to its authority, the male sports establishment launched a campaign to clip Title IX's wings.

In 1974, Congress debated but rejected an amendment to exempt revenue-producing sports (football and men's basketball) from Title IX coverage. Instead, it adopted compromise language directing the Department of Health, Education and Welfare to draft Title IX regulations including "reasonable provisions considering the nature of particular sports." The regulations, which took effect on July 21, 1975, established a three-year transition period to give high schools and colleges time to comply with the equal-athletic-opportunity requirements. [19]

Even then, however, uncertainty lingered. OCR issued a policy interpretation of Title IX responsibilities with respect to sports financial aid, athletic benefits and opportunities and accommodation of the interests and abilities of student athletes. Testifying before a House subcommittee, Cantú said the regulations "required that the total amount of athletic financial assistance awarded to men and women be proportionate to their respective participation rates in intercollegiate athletic programs," though temporary disparities "may be justified by legitimate, non-discriminatory factors." [20]

Similarly, she added, the compliance standard for athletic benefits and opportunities was that "male and female athletes should receive equivalent [as opposed to identical] benefits, treatment, services and opportunities." Here again, certain disparities were permissible. "Generally, these differences will be the result of unique aspects of particular sports, such as the nature of equipment and maintenance of facilities required for competition."

In this connection, Cantú asserted: "Those who have argued that OCR does not consider the unique aspects of football programs in its enforcement of Title IX are, simply, misinformed." She noted that her office "has found that the size of the football team and the nature of the sport justify an apparent imbalance that favors the football team in the provision of medical and training facilities and services."

As for accommodation of interests and abilities, said Cantú, an institution would be found in compliance if it provided men and women both non-discriminatory opportunities to participate in sports and competitive team schedules that equally reflect their abilities.

Further, she said, a school or college could meet the OCR standard for non-discriminatory participation opportunities by meeting any part of the OCR's three-part test, which gauges whether a school offers sports participation opportunities in numbers that are "substantially proportionate" to enrollment by gender; by establishing a "history and continuing practice of program expansion" for members of the underrepresented sex; or by "fully and effectively accommodating the interests and abilities" of the underrepresented sex.

"No one part of the three-part test is preferred by OCR or used exclusively by OCR over another as a method of ensuring compliance with the law," Cantú said. [21] "Rather, the three-part test furnishes three individual avenues for compliance." Despite its brevity and apparent simplicity, the test was to become the focal point of debate on how to apply Title IX to interscholastic and intercollegiate sports.

Setbacks in the '80s

Though Title IX seemed firmly entrenched by the early 1980s, the cause of gender equity in sports suffered two key setbacks, in the eyes of many supporters. The first dates from 1980, when the NCAA announced it would offer collegiate championships in a variety of women's sports. AIAW leaders interpreted the move as a thinly disguised takeover attempt. However, the NCAA said it was only living up to its "obligations" under Title IX: If it sponsored men's championships, it must also sponsor women's.

"This was a transparently false

claim," Susan K. Cahn wrote in her 1994 book, *Coming on Strong: Gender and Sexuality in 20th-Century Women's Sport*, "since the NCAA itself received no federal funds and had never mentioned this obligation before." [22]

Be that as it may, the NCAA initiative effectively assured AIAW's extinction. "When the NCAA sponsored its first set of women's championships in the 1981-82 school year, the vast majority of women's programs switched their affiliation to the NCAA," Cahn noted. "The AIAW faded quickly from the scene, closing down operations in 1982 and conceding final defeat in 1984, when it lost an antitrust suit against the NCAA, a last-ditch effort to use the courts to halt the takeover." [23]

The Supreme Court dealt a second blow to Title IX in 1984 with its ruling in *Grove City [Pa.] College v. Bell.* Until then, the law had been interpreted to mean that a college found to have practiced sex discrimination in one of its programs risked a cutoff of federal funds to the entire institution. But in *Grove City*, the court held that Title IX applied only to the specific "program or activity" of an institution receiving federal aid. This interpretation effectively placed school sports beyond the law's reach, since few athletic departments received federal aid directly.

The impact of *Grove City* was immediate. Soon after the decision, OCR dropped its investigation of 64 Title IX complaints, including several against college athletic departments. Moreover, much of the progress achieved under Title IX was lost as schools and colleges began cutting back on women's programs.

Four years later, though, Congress came to the rescue by passing the Civil Rights Restoration Act over President Ronald Reagan's veto. The law voided *Grove City* by redefining "program or activity," making it clear that entire institutions must not discriminate if any of their components receive federal funding.

The Supreme Court issued another opinion with Title IX implications on Feb. 26, 1992. Ruling in *Franklin v. Gwinnett County [Ga.] Public Schools*, the court held that Title IX gave students the right to sue for monetary damages for sexual harassment and other forms of sex discrimination at schools and colleges. Women's sports officials predicted a rash of lawsuits making such claims.

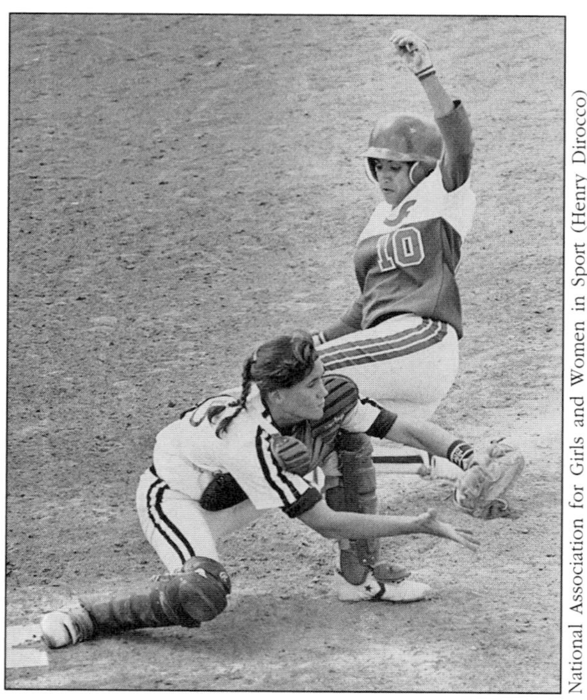

National Association for Girls and Women in Sport (Henry Dirocco)

It's a close play at the plate during the women's college fast-pitch softball championship game between California State University-Fullerton and Texas A&M.

Two weeks later, the NCAA released a long-awaited study on gender equity in the sports programs of its member institutions. [24] The findings confirmed suspicions that female college athletes still were a long way from achieving equality with their male counterparts.

"While the study was not designed to gauge Title IX compliance," said NCAA Executive Director Cedric W. Dempsey, "much of the data, in fact, indicated problems with compliance: Undergraduate enrollment was roughly evenly divided by gender, but men constituted 69.5 percent of the participants in intercollegiate athletics, and their programs received approximately 70 percent of the athletic scholarship funds, 77 percent of operating budgets and 83 percent of recruiting money." [25]

Women Athletes Sue Brown University

It was in this atmosphere of Title IX ferment that several former female athletes at Brown filed a class-action lawsuit in U.S. District Court in Providence, R.I., in April 1992, alleging sex discrimination. [26] A year earlier, Brown had stopped funding four varsity teams — men's water polo and golf and women's gymnastics and volleyball — to help close a budget deficit.*

"Even with these cuts, we will be operating a quality, broad-based program with 27 men's and women's sports at the varsity level," Brown Athletic Director David Roach said at the time. "We will be slightly smaller now, but more focused. It leaves us with the resources to do a good job with the sports we continue to support and remain competitive at the national level." [27]

In a partial settlement of the case announced on Sept. 28, 1994, Brown and the plaintiffs agreed to remove from the table all issues involving

*The teams continued to compete at the intercollegiate varsity level and remained eligible for postseason play, but they had to raise their own funds.

equal treatment of men's and women's varsity teams funded by the university. In other words, both sides agreed that Brown's treatment of men's and women's teams was nondiscriminatory with respect to locker rooms, practice and competition venues, game and practice schedules, access to the weight room and trainers, equipment and supplies, travel arrangements and other sports-related policies and practices. [28]

When the treatment of men's and women's teams "is evaluated on a programwide basis as Title IX requires," said Brown Executive Vice President Robert A. Reichley, "there is absolutely no suggestion of discrimination against women's teams. In this settlement, the university is only agreeing to continue its current policies and practices, maintaining its historical role as a national model for women's intercollegiate varsity athletics." [29] ■

CURRENT SITUATION

The Brown Case

Subsequent developments in *Cohen v. Brown* centered on proportionality, and by this OCR measure the university was found wanting. On March 29, 1995, U.S. District Judge Raymond S. Pettine ruled for the plaintiffs, observing that "far more male athletes are being supported at the university varsity level than are female athletes, and thus, women receive less benefit from their intercollegiate varsity program as a whole than do men." At the time, women represented about 51 percent of Brown's enrollment, but only 40 percent of all varsity athletes.

Brown immediately announced it would appeal the ruling to the U.S. Court of Appeals in Boston. Pettine, in turn, stayed his order while giving the university 120 days to present a plan for Title IX compliance. This could be done in any one of several ways, he suggested. An institution seeking to comply with the law "may eliminate the athletic program altogether, it may elevate or create the requisite number of women's positions, it may demote or eliminate the requisite number of men's positions or it may implement a combination of these remedies."

Pettine's ruling was "extremely disappointing," Reichley declared: "Brown University continues to believe that strict numerical proportionality — that is, a conformance of gender ratios between the athletic and general undergraduate student bodies — is neither fair to the student body nor required by Title IX." Brown's position, he added, is that "any fully compliant athletic program must accommodate the interests and abilities of all students, regardless of gender," and that "Title IX was never intended to be a quota bill for athletes." [30]

Six weeks after Pettine's ruling, Brown President Gregorian argued the university's case before a House subcommittee. Title IX guidelines, he asserted, "are so ambiguous, so inconsistent and so imprecise that they leave judges with total discretion and rob institutions of any flexibility in meeting OCR's tests." [31]

Insistence upon strict proportionality, Gregorian suggested, intrudes upon an institution's right to manage its own affairs. "Brown, which for the first time is 51 percent female, must have in place an athletic program which matches exactly that percentage, or apparently it loses its right to determine the size and content of its program." He added that, "While the proportion of males and females changes from year to year, teams cannot be turned on and off like hot and cold running water."

Moreover, Gregorian argued, it was unfair to hold Brown to a narrow interpretation of OCR's "continuous improvement" guideline. The university's female sports program came into being shortly after the merger in 1971 with all-female Pembroke College. Over the next six years, Brown added 14 fully funded women's varsity teams to its intercollegiate sports program. Thus, "because we chose to undertake early, rapid expansion, our rate of increase slowed after 1980, and it was decided that we could not, therefore, demonstrate 'continuous improvement' " [32]

Gregorian's reasoning finds scant support among women involved in Title IX issues. Deborah L. Brake, senior counsel for the National Women's Law Center, dismisses the "continuous improvement" argument as specious. "Brown wants to get credit for creating a women's sports program out of thin air," she says. "A lot of colleges around the country are in the same position. Before Title IX, colleges weren't required to operate intercollegiate sports teams for women."

The University of Iowa's Grant agrees. "All of us greatly expanded our offerings in the 1970s," she says. "Before that, we had nothing but club sports for women. The Ivy League colleges have a historic tradition, for their men's sports programs, of offering innumerable opportunities — way above those available at other Division I schools. I should think Brown would want to do the same for their women. And really, that's all they're being asked to do by the court."

More Setbacks for Brown

In any event, the university suffered additional setbacks as *Cohen v.*

Brown made its way through the federal court system. In July 1995, Brown submitted its compliance proposal to Pettine's court. The plan called for limiting the size of men's teams while seeking to increase female participation by establishing minimum squad sizes and creating junior varsity squads in five existing women's sports. Pettine rejected the arrangement six weeks later, ordering Brown to provide full funding for three donor-funded varsity teams and to elevate one intercollegiate women's club team to fully funded varsity status.

Gregorian reacted bitterly. "Judge Pettine has done what he said he would not do," he declared. "He has told the university which teams it must offer and has defined the level at which the university must support them financially. This is precisely the kind of micromanagement Judge Pettine said he would avoid. . . . Rather than adopt the university's full plan or request revisions, he has acceded to the plaintiffs' demands, willingly embraced micromanagement and sent the case on to [the 1st U.S. Circuit Court of Appeals in] Boston." [33]

The appellate court's ruling, handed down on Nov. 21, 1996, reversed in part and affirmed in part Pettine's August 1995 opinion. Rejecting the order that Brown provide full funding for four additional women's teams, U.S. senior Circuit Judge Hugh H. Bownes declared that the District Court had "erred in substituting its own specific relief in place of Brown's statutorily permissible proposal to comply with Title IX by cutting men's teams until substantial proportionality was achieved."

Laura Freid, Brown's executive vice president for external affairs, hailed this part of Bownes' decision because it "recognized Brown's autonomy in determining its budget and in designing the scope of its athletic program. The court has confirmed that Brown has the right to determine which teams will receive university-funded status, as long as the plan comports with the requirements of the law." [34]

Women's National Basketball Association

Former University of Southern California standout Lisa Leslie plays for the Los Angeles Sparks in the new eight-team Women's National Basketball Association, which starts play June 21.

However, Bownes also found that Brown had failed to meet any of the three OCR criteria that determine whether a college is in compliance with Title IX. For instance, Brown had presented statistics demonstrating, it claimed, that women were less interested in athletics than men were, and that Brown's support for women's sports was commensurate with the interests and abilities of its female undergraduates.

The court viewed this argument with "great suspicion," Bownes wrote. "There exists the danger that, rather than providing a true measure of women's interest in sports, statistical evidence purporting to reflect women's interest instead provides only a measure of the very discrimination that is, and has been, the basis for women's lack of opportunity to participate in sports."

Attorneys for the plaintiffs were elated by this part of Bownes' opinion. "The courts have created a very important trend in terms of stopping what was a developing trend of cutting women's sports teams to balance the budget," said Lynette Labinger, lead counsel for Trial Lawyers for Public Justice, a Washington-based group representing the plaintiffs. [35] Added Arthur H. Bryant, the group's executive director: "The decision is clearly a wake-up call to colleges and to the country: Sex discrimination against women in athletics had better stop." [36]

On Feb. 18, Brown formally petitioned for Supreme Court review. In doing so, it contended that Title IX had been misinterpreted not only by the appellate court but also by OCR and four other federal appeals courts that had ruled on similar cases.

Brown "designed its athletic program to accommodate the interests and abilities of all students, without regard to gender," Freid said. "The athletic program was ruled out of compliance with Title IX because the ratio of men to women athletes reflected the gender ratio of all qualified athletes. The lower court required the gender ratio of athletes to mirror that of the undergraduate student body." [37]

In its brief to the Supreme Court,

Brown argued that "virtually every institution must now do what Brown has been ordered to do: Find the funds necessary to continue expanding women's teams, or eliminate opportunities for men. . . . Universities that dismantle men's athletic programs to comply with the standards at issue [will not be able to] turn back the clock when those standards are later found to conflict with Title IX."

As Brake of the women's law center sees it, Brown's case "falls flat" unless one accepts the premise that men are more interested in playing sports than women are. "[W]hat Brown misses is that opportunity is what drives interest," she said. "Universities, in determining what sports they are going to offer, are also determining the proportions of men and women in their athletics programs." [38]

Women's sports officials at other institutions also show scant sympathy for Brown's stance. "I just wish they had spent a fraction of what they've given to lawyers on their women's program," Iowa's Grant says. "If they had, they would have been in compliance with Title IX five or six years ago. What a waste of money! And what a sad commentary on an otherwise fine university. Shouldn't they be standing up for what's right for young women?"

Patchy Progress

The gender-equity lawsuit against Brown tended to overshadow a similar case involving Colgate University, which was quietly settled out of court in January. Agreement was reached three weeks before the suit, dating from 1990, was scheduled to go to trial for the second time. In the settlement, Colgate agreed to promote its women's ice hockey team to varsity status.

Colgate had contested the suit because it believed Title IX could not be used to compel a university to add a specific sport to its women's program. Further, it contended that the ability of its female ice hockey players fell short of varsity standards. Although the trial was decided in favor of the players, an appeals court struck down the verdict a year later because all the plaintiffs had graduated in the interim. Faith A. Seidenberg, the plaintiffs' attorney, thereupon rounded up a second group of female hockey players and filed the suit again.

After a pretrial settlement, she said: "My personal preference was that we should go to court. I like to get these things on the books. But if we had done that, no one on this team would ever have seen varsity play." [39]

Colgate Athletic Director Mark Murphy said it was no longer true that women are not skilled enough to play intercollegiate varsity hockey. "At the collegiate level, as well as at the high school level," he said, "women's hockey is a growing sport." [40]

Nationwide, progress toward gender equity in intercollegiate women's athletics seems patchy at best. So concluded a report published last fall by the General Accounting Office (GAO), the investigative arm of Congress. After reviewing eight recent studies on gender equity at colleges across the country, GAO found that "women's athletic programs have made slight advances since 1992 toward gender equity as measured by the number of sports available to female students, the number of females participating in athletics and the percentage of scholarship expenditures for women's sports." [41]

Specifically, the GAO said the studies had shown a 6 percent increase from 1992 to 1996 in the average number of women's sports offered by colleges. Moreover, an almost equal number of men's and women's sports now use marketing and promotional campaigns to increase attendance at games.

On the other hand, reported the GAO, "women's programs remain behind men's programs as measured by the percentage of female head coaches, comparable salaries for coaches and the ratio of student athletes to undergraduate enrollment." In fact, the report said, "Women often constituted half of all undergraduates in 1995, while constituting only 37 percent of all student athletes." [42] ■

OUTLOOK

Bright Future Seen

Supporters of U.S. women's sports foresee a bright future, citing continued Title IX progress and the sparkling performance of American female athletes at the 1996 Olympics. Also significant, they say, is the emergence of professional women's sports leagues and the willingness of major advertisers to fund them.

Basketball is leading the way toward hoped-for acceptance and financial viability. The all-female American Basketball League completed its inaugural season in mid-March. The Women's National Basketball Association (WNBA), an offshoot of the men's National Basketball Association, will begin its first season June 21, with championship playoffs scheduled for Aug. 28-30. General Motors is the WNBA's exclusive automotive sponsor.

It remains to be seen whether the country will support two women's pro basketball leagues — or even one — over the long haul. But as *Working Woman* noted recently, the existence of two leagues "creates an

FOR MORE INFORMATION

College Football Association, 6688 Gunpark Dr., Suite 201, Boulder, Colo. 80301; (303) 530-5566. CFA represents colleges and universities committed to major football programs.

National Association for Girls and Women in Sport, 1900 Association Dr., Reston, Va. 22091; (703) 476-3450. The association represents teachers, coaches, athletic trainers, officials, athletic administrators and students.

National Collegiate Athletic Association, 6201 College Blvd., Overland Park, Kan. 66211; (913) 339-1906. The NCAA is the governing body for men's and women's sports programs at most four-year colleges and universities.

National Federation of State High School Associations, 11724 N.W. Plaza Circle, P.O. Box 20626, Kansas City, Mo. 64195-0626; (816) 464-5400. The federation represents governing bodies for sports and other extracurricular activities at the secondary-school level.

Office of Civil Rights, U.S. Education Department, 330 C St. S.W., Suite 5000, Washington, D.C. 20202; (202) 205-5413. OCR is in charge of interpreting Title IX of the Education Amendments of 1972.

Women's Sports Foundation, Eisenhower Park, East Meadow, N.Y. 11554; (516) 542-4700. The WSF encourages women to participate in sports activities for their health, enjoyment and mental development.

unheard-of seller's market" for top female hoops stars. "At about 10 slots per team, there will be over 160 paying jobs for female basketball players in the U.S. this year. A year ago, there were none." [43]

Basketball is not the only women's sport with a professional future. The AT&T Wireless Services Professional Fastpitch softball league, based in six Southern cities, is due to start play in June. And if current plans materialize, the Women's Elite Soccer League will kick off sometime this fall.

In the next 10 years, Lopiano says, there should be substantial progress toward closing the gender-equity gap in women's athletics. "We're about halfway there now," she says. "But I would hope we get to 80 or 90 percent compliance by then. It's going to take a while, because institutions are so hard to change. One reason is that many of today's decision-makers grew up not really respecting women's ability in sports. That makes it a real slow, hard go."

Neinas of the College Football Association, in contrast, doesn't expect a "satisfactory resolution" of the gender-equity debate "until a more reasonable test for Title IX compliance is adopted." Division I-A college football programs, he argues, don't get the credit they deserve for keeping many women's sports afloat. "Football is criticized," he says, "and yet if it weren't for football, you wouldn't see the type of women's sports programs they've got at Tennessee, Florida, Alabama, Texas, Notre Dame, Penn State and the like."

Everett agrees with Lopiano that the nation is "on a good track for reaching a much higher percentage of Title IX compliance in 10 years." Sounding a cautionary note, however, she recalls that sports programs "were on this same track in the early 1980s. And then, because of the *Grove City* ruling, progress stalled. *Grove City* set us back for years."

Though Executive Director Grant Teaff of the American Football Coaches Association has been on the receiving end of Title IX brickbats for his staunch support of football programs, he says he remains supportive of gender equity. "We've got to keep looking for a middle ground and to make it all work," he says, "and I feel a lot of progress has been made already. I'm not uptight about it anymore. I served on the gender equity task force of the NCAA, and so I could see a lot of this stuff coming."

Back then, he adds, "There was a tendency to get panicky or uptight, but I honestly don't feel that way any more. As I see it, cool heads are in charge, and people are beginning to understand that football is not out to cheat women out of opportunities to participate in sports."

Grant says that the Equity in Athletics Disclosure Act, which took effect Oct. 1, will do much to increase sports opportunities for women in coming years. The law requires colleges to release data on expenditures for their men's and women's sports programs on an annual basis.

"Universities are going to find that their reputations will be damaged unless they start making some progress" toward gender equity in sports, Grant predicts. "Would a young woman who is committed to excelling in sports go to a university that isn't committed to equal athletic opportunities for both sexes?"

"Whenever you have a gender-equity report card, whenever you have public embarrassment as a result, it creates incentives to do better the next time around," Lopiano adds. "Institutions don't like being portrayed in a bad light. Gender-equity report cards are also going to encourage more litigation, because the data will be right in front of everybody."

Upton of the Federation of State High School Associations believes some future Title IX disputes will center on women's activities not currently recognized as sports by OCR. For instance, she notes, "Cheerleading

Continued on p. 354

At Issue:

Does federally mandated "gender equity" in sports discriminate against male athletes?

yes

T.J. Kerr
Wrestling coach, California State University-Bakersfield; President, National Wrestling Coaches Association

FROM TESTIMONY BEFORE HOUSE EDUCATION SUBCOMMITTEE ON POSTSECONDARY EDUCATION, TRAINING AND LIFE-LONG LEARNING, MAY 9, 1995

All-male sports programs are at risk because of the proportionality rule/gender quota which the Office of Civil Rights, U.S. Education Department, has drafted. There are about 190,000 male college athletes in Divisions I, II and III. There are about 105,000 female athletes. How can proportionality be achieved when the present male to female [enrollment] ratio is 47-53? If the trend continues, administrators will have to eliminate about 100,000 male athletes to reach proportionality.

In 1972, when Congress enacted Title IX, the college enrollment ratio nationally was 55 percent-plus male. By the 21st century, 55 percent of the college population may well be female. The 55-45 female-to-male ratio sets up a gender quota which is impossible to achieve, in no small part because females do not tend to compete in sports — particularly those like football and wrestling. . . .

Elimination of male athletes occurs in two ways — administrators eliminate programs and/or they eliminate non-scholarship/walk-on athletes from those programs. Both are anathema. We have one goal — we seek to end the elimination or reduction of male sports programs to achieve a quota.

School administrators believe that they must achieve proportionality. Many are unable, because of budget constraints, to add female sports programs, so these administrators drop male programs or "cap" sports by dropping the non-scholarship or walk-on athlete.

Both of these approaches to achieving "gender equity" are wrong. Programs should not be eliminated because athletes matriculate at a school in the good faith belief that the administration will honor its commitment to provide a program for their four years of college. . . .

The capping of male sports is equally discriminatory and destructive. In this circumstance a young man pays tuition, walks onto a team, works as hard as a first-teamer, but simply does not have the skills to compete at the highest levels. . . . The school dumps them because they are the most expendable. . . .

I have sought in my program to work with the many young men who otherwise would not be able to attend college, and I know I speak for the coaches of all male programs when I say that the elimination of male opportunities will greatly affect the future generation of young men.

no

Former Rep. Cardiss Collins, D-Ill.

FROM TESTIMONY BEFORE HOUSE EDUCATION SUBCOMMITTEE ON POSTSECONDARY EDUCATION, TRAINING AND LIFE-LONG LEARNING, MAY 9, 1995

I am sure that during the course of your hearings you will hear the same arguments that you hear against affirmative action — namely that Title IX is taking opportunities away from men, or that Title IX establishes quotas for women. Most of these arguments come from school administrators or football coaches who fear that the increasing opportunities for women will come out of their hides.

The reality is the exact opposite. Athletic directors and coaches are the ones who establish quotas at the schools. They decide, often arbitrarily, how many men and how many women get to play sports. Schools, not the Department of Education, are responsible for quotas assuring that men receive over two-thirds of all opportunities, and 75 cents out of every dollar spent on sports. The purpose of Title IX is to eliminate these artificial quotas, and permit opportunities to be based upon student interest, without gender bias. . . .

The law does not require fixed quotas. The law has been interpreted to mean that if schools have participation rates equal to enrollment rates, the school is automatically considered in compliance. However, even if the numbers are not the same, the regulations allow a school to show compliance either through a history of expanding opportunities in women's programs, or by showing that the interests of women have been fully accommodated. . . .

Suppose a family has a son, and he enjoys playing ball in the backyard, basketball at the gym, or soccer at the park. A second child comes along, but the family's income does not change. Do we assume that the second child's interests in the same sports can only be accommodated at the expense of the first child? Of course not. It may become necessary for the two children to learn to share the baseball bat or the basketball. We don't give one child some artificial priority over supplies, or even the use of the backyard. You would be surprised that many of the Title IX cases boil down to little more than the need for men's teams to share resources, share playing fields and share prime times with the women's teams.

In summary, when you get to know the facts, you find out that the issue is simply how do schools accommodate the growing interest in women's sports. If schools stick to quotas to ensure an artificial advantage for men, the courts will strike them down. However, if schools take steps to accommodate this interest, everyone's child will benefit. It is time for schools to share their resources fairly, and eliminate their self-imposed quotas.

Continued from p. 352

doesn't count as part of a sports program under Title IX. Well, the whole concept of cheerleading has changed in the last 25 years. Today's cheerleaders definitely are athletes."

"Competitive cheer," involving intricate tumbling and gymnastic routines, is a recognized interscholastic activity in many states, Upton points out. "Members of those squads are subject to the same eligibility standards as any other athletes. They have practices as well as competitions that culminate in a state championship event — the whole ball of wax." Still, competitive cheer and competitive aerobics — another interscholastic activity gaining in popularity — don't yet qualify as OCR-sanctioned sports.

Washington State's Saneholtz says she expected a greater degree of Title IX compliance by now than has actually occurred. One reason for the slow pace, she says, is that "there haven't been any sanctions for noncompliance." Without that prod, she says, it's much easier to maintain the status quo than it is to change things.

"There's still a prevailing attitude out there that sports participation is a right for men and a privilege for women," Saneholtz says. "But whatever it is — a right or a privilege — it should be the same for both." ■

Notes

[1] See "College Sports," *The CQ Researcher*, Aug. 26, 1994, pp. 745-768; "High School Sports," *The CQ Researcher*, Sept. 22, 1995, pp. 825-848, and "Women in Sports," *The CQ Researcher*, March 6, 1992, pp. 193-216.

[2] National Federation of State High School Associations, *National Federation Handbook 1996-97* (1996), p. 42. For background, see "Soccer in America," *The CQ Researcher*, April 22, 1994, pp. 337-360.

[3] Testimony before House Economic and Educational Opportunities Subcommittee on Postsecondary Education, Training and Life-long Learning, May 9, 1995.

[4] Testimony before House Economic and Educational Opportunities Subcommittee on Postsecondary Education, Training and Life-long Learning, May 9, 1995.

[5] Remarks on "The Diane Rehm Show," National Public Radio, March 18, 1997.

[6] Kimberly Jones, "College Wrestling Grapples to Keep a Foot on the Mat," *Centre Daily Times*, March 19, 1997, p. 1B, published in State College, Pa.

[7] In 1976, 138 NCAA member institutions offered varsity men's gymnastics programs. In 1996, only 28 such programs remained.

[8] Testimony before House Economic and Educational Opportunities Subcommittee on Postsecondary Education, Training and Life-long Learning, May 9, 1995.

[9] Statement submitted to Senate Commerce, Science and Transportation Subcommittee on Consumer Affairs, Foreign Commerce and Tourism, Oct. 18, 1995.

[10] Statement submitted to House Economic and Educational Opportunities Subcommittee on Postsecondary Education, Training and Life-long Learning, May 9, 1995.

[11] Benita Fitzgerald Mosley, "No Question About It," *Women's Sports and Fitness*, April 1997, p. 27.

[12] Statement submitted to House Economic and Educational Opportunities Subcommittee on Postsecondary Education, Training and Life-long Learning, May 9, 1995.

[13] Quoted by Nebraska head football coach Tom Osborne in 1995 congressional testimony, *op. cit.*

[14] Paula Welch and D. Margaret Costa, "A Century of Olympic Competition," in Costa and Sharon R. Guthrie, eds., *Women and Sport: Interdisciplinary Perspectives* (1994), p. 124.

[15] Quoted by Lynne Emery, "From Lowell Mills to the Halls of Fame: Industrial League Sport for Women," in Costa and Guthrie, *op. cit.*, p. 115.

[16] Statement submitted to House Economic and Educational Opportunities Subcommittee on Postsecondary Education, Training and Life-long Learning, May 9, 1995.

[17] *Loc. cit.*

[18] Jennifer Hargreaves, *Sporting Females: Critical Issues in the History and Sociology of Women's Sports* (1994), pp. 179-180.

[19] In 1975 and 1977, the Senate failed to act on bills to bar enforcement of Title IX athletics regulation in cases where participation in those sports activities was not a required part of the curriculum.

[20] Statement submitted to House Economic and Educational Opportunities Subcommittee on Postsecondary Education, Training and Life-long Learning, May 9, 1995.

[21] *Loc. cit.*

[22] Susan K. Cahn, *Coming on Strong: Gender and Sexuality in 20th-Century Women's Sport* (1994), p. 344.

[23] *Ibid.*, p. 257.

[24] National Collegiate Athletic Association, "NCAA Gender-Equity Study," March 1992.

[25] Statement submitted to House Economic and Educational Opportunities Subcommittee on Postsecondary Education, Training and Life-long Learning, May 9, 1995.

[26] Gymnast Amy Cohen was the lead plaintiff in *Cohen v. Brown.*

[27] Brown University News Bureau release, April 29, 1991.

[28] Brown University News Bureau release, Sept. 30, 1994.

[29] *Loc. cit.*

[30] Brown University News Bureau release, March 29, 1995.

[31] Testimony before House Economic and Educational Opportunities Subcommittee on Postsecondary Education, Training and Life-long Learning, May 9, 1995.

[32] *Loc. cit.*

[33] Brown University News Bureau release, Aug. 18, 1995.

[34] Brown University News Bureau release, Nov. 21, 1996.

[35] Quoted by Christina Nifong, "Ruling on Brown University Boosts Women's Sports Teams," *The Christian Science Monitor*, Nov. 25, 1996, p. 4.

[36] Quoted by Jim Naughton, "Appeals Court Affirms Ruling That Brown U. Discriminated Against Female Athletes," *The Chronicle of Higher Education*, Nov. 29, 1996, p. A41.

[37] Brown University News Bureau release, Feb. 19, 1997.

[38] Quoted by Jim Naughton, "Brown University Appeals Ruling on Women's Sports to Supreme Court," *The Chronicle of Higher Education*, Feb. 28, 1997, p. A45.

[39] Quoted by Jim Naughton, "Colgate U. Settles Gender-Equity Lawsuit," *The Chronicle of Higher Education*, Jan. 31, 1997, p. A32.

[40] *Loc. cit.*

[41] U.S. General Accounting Office, "Intercollegiate Athletics: Status of Efforts to Promote Gender Equity," October 1996, p. 13.

[42] A recent study by *The Chronicle of Higher Education* reached conclusions similar to those in the GAO study. It found that women received only 38 percent of the athletic scholarships awarded by colleges and universities in NCAA Division I in 1995-96. Those schools, moreover, spent almost three times as much money recruiting players and sponsoring competitions for men's teams (about $407 million) as they did for women's teams ($137 million). See Jim Naughton, "Women in Division I Sports Programs: The Glass is Half Empty and Half Full," *The Chronicle of Higher Education*, April 11, 1997, p. A39.

[43] Daniel Green, "Toss-Up," *Working Woman*, April 1997, p. 29.

Bibliography

Selected Sources Used

Books

Costa, D. Margaret, and Sharon R. Guthrie, eds., *Women and Sport: Interdisciplinary Perspectives, Human Kinetics*, 1994.

This collection of studies views women's sport from a variety of perspectives. Among the issues covered are "Women, Sport and Exercise in the 19th Century," "Cardiovascular Fitness," "Ideological Control of Women in Sport" and "The Contributions of Feminist Psychology."

Guttmann, Allen, *Women's Sports: A History*, Columbia University Press, 1991.

Guttmann traces the evolution of women's sports from ancient Egypt to the present day.

Hargreaves, Jennifer, *Sporting Females: Critical Issues in the History and Sociology of Women's Sports*, Routledge, 1994.

Hargreaves treats the history of women's sports as a long, still-unfinished struggle for recognition. One of her most insightful chapters is titled "Femininity or 'Musculinity'? Changing Images of Female Sports." Both women and men, she writes, have trouble reconciling notions of femininity with the masculine aura of competitive sports: "The idealized male sporting body — strong, aggressive and muscular — has been a popular symbol of masculinity against which women, characterized as relatively powerless and inferior, have been measured."

Salter, David F., *Crashing the Old Boys' Network: The Tragedies and Triumphs of Girls and Women in Sports*, Praeger, 1996.

Salter's commitment to gender equity in sports stems from his perspective as a father. "Marriage and children can enlighten a man in a hurry, especially when his children are daughters whom he loves like nothing else on the planet," he writes. "I thought, if there is anyone who thinks my daughters will be denied fair and equitable treatment, they are going to have one angry, vocal and resourceful father to deal with."

Articles

Collins, Mary, "And the Men Shall Lead Them," *Women's Sports and Fitness*, April 1997.

Title IX did more than expand opportunities for female athletes, Collins writes. By upgrading women's sports programs across the country, it also made head-coaching jobs in those programs more appealing to men. As a result, more than 50 percent of women's college teams are now coached by men, as against less than 10 percent in 1972.

Green, Daniel, "Toss Up," *Working Woman*, April 1997.

Perhaps the surest sign that women's sports have arrived, Green writes, is the recent emergence of professional female leagues in basketball, soccer and fast-pitch softball.

Reports and Studies

National Collegiate Athletic Association, *NCAA Gender Equity Study*, March 1992.

In this widely discussed study, the NCAA acknowledges that women still have a long way to go before achieving gender equity in college athletics.

National Federation of State High School Associations, *National Federation Handbook 1996-97*, 1996.

This survey contains detailed data on boys' and girls' participation in high school sports from 1971 to 1995-96. The nationwide totals are broken down state-by-state and sport-by-sport.

Subcommittee on Postsecondary Education, Training and Life-Long Learning, House Committee on Economic and Educational Opportunities, *Hearing on Title IX of the Education Amendments of 1972* (published proceedings of hearing held May 9, 1995).

Sports officials, coaches and college administrators debate the merits of Title IX and offer suggestions on how it might be improved.

Subcommittee on Consumer Affairs, Foreign Commerce and Tourism, U.S. Senate Committee on Commerce, Science and Transportation, *Amateur Sports Act* (published proceedings of hearing held Oct. 18, 1995).

Officials of major U.S. sports organizations discuss the effect of Title IX on the development of elite athletes and the promotion of grass-roots sports opportunities under the Amateur Sports Act of 1978.

U.S. General Accounting Office, *Intercollegiate Athletics: Status of Efforts to Promote Gender Equity*, October 1996.

This report by GAO, the independent watchdog agency for Congress, contains the results of eight national gender-equity studies issued in recent years. According to GAO, they show increases in the number of women's college teams between 1992 and 1996 as well as a rise in the share of athletic scholarship money allocated to women's teams in NCAA Division I, the most competitive level.

The Next Step

Additional information from UMI's Newspaper & Periodical Abstracts™ database

Cohen v. Brown

Lazerson, Marvin, and Ursula Wagener, "Missed opportunities," *Change*, July 1996, pp. 46-52.

Lazerson and Wagener discuss the battle over Title IX at Brown University in Providence, R.I., which has been sued for non-compliance by nine women student athletes. Reducing the Title IX controversy to a battle over women and sports overlooks several opportunities, including the chance for higher education to embrace athletics as part of its educational responsibilities.

Naughton, Jim, "Brown University appeals ruling on women's sports to Supreme Court," *The Chronicle of Higher Education*, Feb. 28, 1997, p. A45.

Brown University is asking the Supreme Court to overturn its defeat in a case involving the school's decision to stop funding women's volleyball and gymnastics. The university contends all previous appeals courts failed to take into account relative interest of men and women in participating in intercollegiate sports.

Nifong, Christina, "Brown University lawsuit will color the future of women's sports," *The Christian Science Monitor*, May 9, 1996, p. 1.

The U.S. Court of Appeals in Boston, Mass., will soon decide a landmark case involving gender equality in collegiate athletics. Former Brown University students sued the college four years ago after it eliminated funding for women's gymnastics and volleyball. The decision will have major implications for both sides of the issue.

Nifong, Christina, "Ruling on Brown University boosts women's sports teams," *The Christian Science Monitor*, Nov. 25, 1996, p. 4.

Women athletic teams across the U.S. have been given a boost in the wake of a federal court's ruling that said Brown University had violated federal Title IX regulations, which require schools to provide equal sports opportunities for women. Under the decision, colleges must calculate that the number of male and female athletes is strictly proportional to their enrollments at the school rather than use proportionality as a general guideline.

Srisavasdi, Rachanee, "Athlete who sued Brown is happy with outcome," *The Chronicle of Higher Education*, Dec. 6, 1996, pp. A60-61.

Amy Cohen was the lead plaintiff in the gender-equity suit in "*Cohen v. Brown University*." Cohen discusses her involvement in the lawsuit.

Dembner, Alice, "Court upholds ruling on sports at Brown," *The Boston Globe*, Nov. 22, 1996, p. B2.

A federal appeals court in Boston, Mass., on Nov. 21, 1996, upheld a landmark ruling by a U.S. District Court judge that Brown University discriminated against female athletes in violation of Title IX, the federal law that mandates gender equity in education.

Female Athletes

Becker, Debbie, "More women athletes head for Atlanta," *USA Today*, Jan. 18, 1996, p. C12.

The history of women in the Olympics is examined, including Joan Benoit Samuelson's win in the first Olympic women's marathon in 1984. A record 3,779 women will compete in 97 events in the 1996 Olympics. A graph shows the number of women and men competing in Olympics from 1896 to 1996.

Conley, Steve, "Magazine counts female athletes," *The Denver Post*, Nov. 29, 1996, p. A53.

A 1996 summer Olympics tailwind has magazine publishers racing to introduce more publications targeted at serious female athletes. *Women's Sports on Campus*, a new magazine for college women by Sports and Fitness Publishing, will debut in March 1997. The semi-annual publication will feature top athletes, provide instructional stories and analyze fitness trends and products.

Dupont, Kevin Paul, "Women athletes equal to the task," *The Boston Globe*, Aug. 6, 1996, p. C1.

A look is taken at women in the Olympics.

Lopiano, Donna, "The year of the woman in sports," *Sporting News*, Dec. 30, 1996, p. S18.

A look at the achievement of women in sports during 1996 is offered. High school, college, professional sports and the 1996 Olympics are discussed.

Miklasz, Bernie, "Female athletes near cloud nine, thanks to their Title IX," *St. Louis Post-Dispatch*, July 19, 1996, p. D1.

Miklasz comments on how nearly 40 percent of all athletes in the 1996 summer Olympics are women, and notes that much of the success of women in the U.S. is due to the passage of Title IX in 1972, which mandated full equality for women's intercollegiate sports.

"Olympics show progress but not yet equality," *USA*

***Today*, July 23, 1996, p. A14.**

An editorial says that while women are making progress in sports equality at the 1996 Olympics in Atlanta, Ga., male athletes still dominate Olympic events 2-to-1, and women remain barred from several events. Further, the International Olympic Committee (IOC) has ignored requests to take action against countries that discriminate against women.

Patrick, Dick, "Danish star paved way for top female athletes," *USA Today*, Feb. 8, 1996, p. C3.

Inge Nissen of Denmark, who played basketball for Old Dominion University in the late 1970s, was the first prominent international player in the college ranks. Twenty years after Nissen's arrival, there are 166 international women players in Division I exercising considerable influence.

Rosen, Karen, "96 is year for female athletes to take spotlight," *Atlanta Constitution*, July 9, 1996, p. SS1.

The 1996 Atlanta Olympics will surely have a woman's touch. Shut out of the first Games in 1896, women pushed to get in. Now women make up about 35 percent of the athletes. At the Atlanta Games, men will outnumber women by an estimated 6,582 to 3,779. However, this will be the greatest showcase for women in Olympic history.

Female Sports Coaches

Barnhart, Tony, "Fired West Georgia coach may file Title IX suit," *Atlanta Constitution*, March 7, 1996, p. E5.

The attorney for fired West Georgia College women's basketball coach Sheila Collins would not rule out the possibility of a Title IX sex discrimination suit against the school and its athletics director, Ed Murphy.

Durando, Stu, "Women Wanted. Girls Sports Still Growing But Female Coaches Scarce," *St. Louis Post-Dispatch*, Jan. 16, 1997, p. D1.

A look is taken at the small number of female coaches involved in high school sports. As more girls sports have been added, the percentage of female coaches has failed to grow proportionately.

Kulfan, Ted, "Special Report: Women in Sports: Closing the gap: Despite inroads in achieving gender equity, women's athletic programs still suffer from a lack of officials, coaches and role models," *Detroit News*, Jan. 30, 1997, Sec. B, p. 1W.

When she hears the kind words, Nikita Lowry diverts the praise. The University of Detroit Mercy women's basketball coach would rather talk about her team, or people who have helped her along the way. Lowry will talk of former coaches, such as Brenda Gatlin, who touched Lowry's life deeply while playing at Detroit Cass Tech in Michigan. Talk to anyone who knows Lowry and they'll say Gatlin did very well. Hard-working, energetic, knowledgeable and personable are adjectives that are used to describe Lowry. She's a rookie head coach, who has driven U-D to a 12-6 record (6-2 in the Midwest Collegiate Conference).

Palombo-McCallie, Joanne, "A Lot of People Talk About Sports as an Extra. I Find That Sad," *The Boston Globe*, Jan. 5, 1997, p. C1.

Palombo-McCallie, coach of the University of Maine's women's basketball team, relates her philosophy that sports are an essential part of the educational process and of the life of communities.

Will, Ed, "Rec. center coach molds record-setting women athletes," *The Denver Post*, April 8, 1996, p. F1.

The Colorado Flyers track club at the Skyland Recreation Center in Denver, Colo., is featured, and their coach Tony Wells is profiled. The team may well be Colorado's most consistent sports success story with all its club records representing one-time national records.

Gender Equity

Haworth, Karla, "Report notes progress in women's sports," *The Chronicle of Higher Education*, Nov. 8, 1996, p. A40.

According to a report by the General Accounting Office (GAO), college sports programs have not yet achieved gender equity, but they are making progress. The report states that 100,000 American women are now participating in intercollegiate athletics.

Naughton, Jim, "Higher education weighs the impact of a ruling on gender equity in sports," *The Chronicle of Higher Education*, Dec. 6, 1996, pp. A57-58.

Legal experts expect more pressure on colleges to add women's teams or cut men's teams and more debate over the concept of "proportionality" in measuring sports equity.

Naughton, Jim, and Rachanee Srisavasdi, "Data on funds for men's and women's sports become available as new law takes effect," *The Chronicle of Higher Education*, Oct. 25, 1996, pp. A45-46.

Under a new federal law that went into effect on Oct. 1, 1996, data on athletics expenditures for men's and women's college sports programs must be made public. Implications of the Equity in Athletics Disclosure Act of 1995 are discussed.

Navratilova, Martina, "Men and women in sports: The playing field is far from level," *USA Today: The Magazine of the American Scene*, November 1996,

pp. 33-34.
There is a double standard in the world of sports between male and female athletes. The double standard exists in terms of gay issues, but it certainly goes way beyond this.

Women's Basketball

Klein, Frederick C., "On sports: Women's hoops takes long shot at scoring big," *The Wall Street Journal*, Jan. 17, 1997, p. B9.
Klein comments on the Women's National Basketball Association (WNBA), which is scheduled to begin a 28-game series on June 21, 1997. Klein discusses the issues facing the new women's basketball league.

Wieberg, Steve, "U.S. women charging into sports spotlight," *USA Today*, July 31, 1996, p. A1.
While the Olympics traditionally have spawned female stars and role models in such individual sports as gymnastics, swimming and track, the 1996 Olympics in Atlanta, Ga., are the games of women's dream teams. Teams such as the women's basketball, softball and soccer teams have made 1996 a successful year for women's sports.

Women's Soccer

DeSimone, Bonnie, "U.S. — Or part of it, at least — Gets '99 Women's Cup soccer meet," *Chicago Tribune*, May 31, 1996, p. 5.
Officials from Federation Internationale de Football Association (FIFA), soccer's international governing body, will on May 31, 1996, award the 1999 Women's World Cup to the U.S., which was the only nation to complete a formal bid. The women will compete in small stadiums concentrated in the Northeast and Mid-Atlantic regions.

Eisenbath, Mike, "Big 12 women's soccer grows in big hurry," *St. Louis Post-Dispatch*, Nov. 7, 1996, p. D4.
A look is taken at the rising popularity of college women's soccer in preview of the Big 12 Tournament at the A-B Conference & Sports Centre in Fenton, Mo., on Nov. 7, 1996.

Gildea, William, "U.S. defeats China, wins first women's soccer gold," *The Washington Post*, Aug. 2, 1996, p. A1.
The U.S. women's soccer team defeated China 2-1 on Aug. 1, 1996, to win the gold medal in the first Olympics to include women's soccer.

Hollan, Elizabethe, "Illinois Elevates Women's Soccer from Club to Varsity Standing," *St. Louis Post-Dispatch*, Jan. 31, 1997, p. D2.
The University of Illinois has added a women's sport to its lineup for the first time in two decades, promoting soccer from club status to a full-fledged National Collegiate Athletic Association (NCAA) program.

Jordan, Ray, "Everything's even as women's soccer debuts," *St. Louis Post-Dispatch*, Aug. 19, 1996, p. C1.
The women's soccer programs launched at the University of Missouri, St. Louis University and Southwest Missouri State University in 1996 are described.

Jordan, Ray, "Soccer gold bolsters what Title IX began," *St. Louis Post-Dispatch*, Aug. 13, 1996, p. C1.
Part three of a four-part series discusses how Title IX, the federal push toward gender equity in sports, boosted women's soccer even before the Olympic Games in Atlanta, Ga., began. Colleges with scholarships are heavily recruiting good high school players.

Vecsey, George, "Women's Soccer: 76,481 Fans, 1 U.S. Gold," *The New York Times*, Aug. 2, 1996, p. B9.
By beating a spirited and talented China, 2-1, in an Aug. 1, 1996, Olympics match in Atlanta, Ga., the U.S. team won a gold medal in the first women's soccer tournament in Summer Games history.

Wojciechowski, Gene, and Andrew Gottesman, "A Golden era for women," *Chicago Tribune*, Aug. 4, 1996, p 1.
It was apparent that Title IX had grown up when the U.S. women's soccer team defeated Norway in the semifinals of the 1996 Olympic Games in Atlanta, Ga., July 28. The medals won by female athletes are evidence that women are finally getting a shot at sports equality.

Title IX

Brady, Erik, "Disclosure deadline to give Title IX a boost," *USA Today*, Feb. 1, 1996, p. C3.
Title IX, the 1972 federal law that prohibits sex discrimination at schools receiving federal funds, will get a boost in coming months. New Department of Education rules will require colleges to make public by Oct. 1, 1996, what they spend on men's and women's sports, including coaching and recruiting costs, as well as participation rates and other information.

Brady, Erik, and Tom Witosky, "Title IX improves women's participation," *USA Today*, March 3, 1997, p. C4.
Title IX was supposed to change the world. And it has: The number of women participating in college sports has jumped fourfold since the law was enacted 25 years ago. But the world changes slowly. *USA Today* surveyed 303 Division I schools to see where Title IX has taken us in its 25 years and found that men still get most of the money.

Danziger, Lucy S., "Title IX Scores Rewards, On and Off the Field; Sports: A generation of women have gained self-esteem and pride in achievement along with the medals," *Los Angeles Times*, March 17, 1997, p. B5.

This year marks the 25th anniversary of the passage of Title IX, the 1972 law mandating equal opportunity for girls and boys in education, including sports. "Almost by accident," the author recalls, "my high school was one of the first to be affected by the intent of Title IX. It was a private boys school that was going coed at almost the exact moment the law was signed. I feel as if I had a sneak preview of what Title IX could be, were it taken to its fullest potential. The biggest impact is not felt during the hour and a half when sports are actually happening, but in the downtime between practices. It's the self-esteem built through taking up a new sport (in my case, crew) and doing it as well as possible."

Jensen, Rita Henley, "Endurance test for Title IX," *The Denver Post*, July 21, 1996, p. E1.

Jensen discusses Title IX of the Education Amendments of 1972, which has paved the way for American female athletes, and notes that only 10 percent of U.S. colleges fully comply with the law.

Kleinpeter, Jim, "LSU has meeting set on Title IX matters," *Times-Picayune*, Feb. 27, 1996, p. E6.

Officials and attorneys from both sides of the Title IX case involving Louisiana State University (LSU) will meet March 1, 1996, in Lafayette, La., for an informal conference with Judge Rebecca Doherty, who will go over LSU's compliance plan and advise of changes and additions she wants.

Lewis, Ted, "LSU's Corum calls Title IX suit a plus," *Times-Picayune*, Sept. 23, 1996, p. D9.

Debbie Corum accepted a position with Louisiana State University as assistant athletic director for Olympic sports. Since LSU went through a Title IX lawsuit, Corum is confident the program is now in compliance.

Lewis, Ted, "LSU responds in Title IX case, *Times-Picayune*, Feb. 2, 1996, p. D3.

Louisiana State University will upgrade its planned facilities for softball and soccer significantly and implement an extensive plan to assess the athletic interests and abilities of its students in response to a federal judge's ruling that the school is not in compliance with Title IX.

McKinzie-Lechault, Pat, "Title IX must be enforced for the sake of all girls," *Chicago Tribune*, March 17, 1996, Sec. 13, p. 6.

McKinzie-Lechault says that more than a decade after the Title IX law was implemented in 1972, she's appalled to see that women across the U.S. are still being denied equal opportunity in athletics. She believes it gives girls the impression that they aren't as important as boys when it comes to athletics.

"Title IX proves itself," *The Boston Globe*, Aug. 19, 1996, p. A12.

An editorial asserts that the prominence of women athletes on the 1996, U.S. Olympic team owes much to the 1972 passage of Title IX, which prohibits sex discrimination in schools, and states that the components of Title IX on sexual harassment need stronger enforcement in the nation's schools.

White, Carolyn, "USA celebrates Title IX 25th anniversary," *USA Today*, Feb. 5, 1997, p. C2.

The 25th anniversary of Title IX is in 1997, and a contingent of world champions, Olympic heroes and professional athletes will gather in Washington, D.C. on Feb. 6, 1997 to celebrate National Girls and Women in Sports Day.

Back Issues

Great Research on Current Issues Starts Right Here...Recent topics covered by The CQ Researcher are listed below. Before May 1991, reports were published under the name of Editorial Research Reports.

OCTOBER 1995
Quebec's Future
Revitalizing the Cities
Networking the Classroom
Indoor Air Pollution

NOVEMBER 1995
The Working Poor
The Jury System
Sex, Violence and the Media
Police Misconduct

DECEMBER 1995
Teens and Tobacco
Gene Therapy's Future
Global Water Shortages
Third-Party Prospects

JANUARY 1996
Emergency Medicine
Punishing Sex Offenders
Bilingual Education
Helping the Homeless

FEBRUARY 1996
Reforming the CIA
Campaign Finance Reform
Academic Politics
Getting Into College

MARCH 1996
The British Monarchy
Preventing Juvenile Crime
Tax Reform
Pursuing the Paranormal

APRIL 1996
Centennial Olympic Games
Managed Care
Protecting Endangered Species
New Military Culture

MAY 1996
Russia's Political Future
Marriage and Divorce
Year-Round Schools
Taiwan, China and the U.S.

JUNE 1996
Rethinking NAFTA
First Ladies
Teaching Values
Labor Movement's Future

JULY 1996
Recovered-Memory Debate
Native Americans' Future
Crackdown on Sexual Harassment
Attack on Public Schools

AUGUST 1996
Fighting Over Animal Rights
Privatizing Government Services
Child Labor and Sweatshops
Cleaning Up Hazardous Wastes

SEPTEMBER 1996
Gambling Under Attack
The States and Federalism
Civic Journalism
Reassessing Foreign Aid

OCTOBER 1996
Political Consultants
Insurance Fraud
Rethinking School Integration
Parental Rights

NOVEMBER 1996
Global Warming
Clashing Over Copyright
Consumer Debt
Governing Washington, D.C.

DECEMBER 1996
Welfare, Work and the States
The New Volunteerism
Implementing the Disabilities Act
America's Pampered Pets

JANUARY 1997
Combating Scientific Misconduct
Restructuring the Electric Industry
The New Immigrants
Chemical and Biological Weapons

FEBRUARY 1997
Assisting Refugees
Alternative Medicine's Next Phase
Independent Counsels
Feminism's Future

MARCH 1997
New Air Quality Standards
Alcohol Advertising
Civic Renewal
Educating Gifted Students

APRIL 1997
Declining Crime Rates
The FBI Under Fire

Back issues are available for $5.00 (subscribers) or $10.00 (non-subscribers). Quantity discounts apply to orders over ten. To order, call Congressional Quarterly Customer Service at (202) 887-8621.

Binders are available for $18.00. To order call 1-800-638-1710. Please refer to stock number 648.

Future Topics

- ***Space Program's Future***
- ***The Stock Market***
- ***Cloning Controversy***

THE CQ Researcher

PUBLISHED BY CONGRESSIONAL QUARTERLY INC.

Space Program's Future

Is NASA putting safety at risk to cut costs?

The National Aeronautics and Space Administration was plagued by cost overruns, lengthy program delays and weak public support when Daniel Goldin took over NASA in 1992. Goldin set out to expand the agency's space missions while reducing its overall budget. Thanks to such recent achievements as the joint U.S.-Russian mission aboard the *Mir* space station and the discovery of evidence of primitive life forms on Mars, public support for space missions seems to be on the upswing. But the Russian government's failure to fund its share of the International Space Station has put a cloud over the space program. Moreover, some critics say NASA's cost-cutting strategy is compromising human flight safety as well as robotic missions.

INSIDE THIS ISSUE

CQ April 25, 1997 • Volume 7, No. 16 • Pages 361-384

Formerly Editorial Research Reports

COVER: LIKE A GIANT MOSQUITO, THE RUSSIAN SPACE STATION MIR STANDS OUT AGAINST THE DARKNESS OF SPACE AND EARTH'S CLOUD-COVERED HORIZON AS IT PREPARES TO RENDEZVOUS WITH THE U.S. SPACE SHUTTLE DISCOVERY. (NATIONAL AERONAUTICS AND SPACE ADMINISTRATION PHOTOGRAPH)

THE CQ Researcher

April 25, 1997
Volume 7, No. 16

The CQ Researcher (ISSN 1056-2036). Formerly Editorial Research Reports. Published weekly (48 times per year, not printed Jan. 3, May 30, Aug. 29, Oct. 31) by Congressional Quarterly Inc., 1414 22nd St., N.W., Washington, D.C. 20037. Annual subscription rate for libraries, businesses and government is $340. Additional rates furnished upon request. Periodicals postage paid at Washington, D.C., and additional mailing offices. POSTMASTER: Send address changes to The CQ Researcher, 1414 22nd St., N.W., Washington, D.C. 20037.

Space Program's Future

BY MARY H. COOPER

THE ISSUES

Are we alone in the universe? Since time immemorial, humans have wondered and — lacking solid evidence to the contrary — concluded that life exists only here on Earth.

Last summer, that assumption was seriously challenged for the first time when a small meteorite from Mars was found to contain evidence of a primitive life form. The discovery has sparked intensive research to determine if the bacterialike structures in the rock are indeed fossilized remains of ancient Martian life.

"We've got some clues, but we're not sure, and we want to subject this to the most intense peer review by the world that any science project has seen," says Daniel S. Goldin, administrator of the National Aeronautics and Space Administration (NASA). "The most wonderful thing is the fact that we could have front-page news about a scientific debate that's so esoteric. Isn't this great for our young people? That there is national interest in this rekindles my appreciation of Americans as pioneers."

The Mars meteorite discovery, by a group of NASA-led planetary scientists, was just one of the space agency's successes in the last year. NASA also:

- Played a key role in the discovery of organisms living near underwater thermal vents at depths and temperatures that had been thought impossible;
- Launched two spacecraft to Mars that could answer questions about the existence of ancient life on the red planet;
- Received satellite images suggesting that water may lie under the ice covering Jupiter's moon Europa, prompting speculation that it, too, may harbor evidence of life; and
- Celebrated a new duration record for an American in space when astronaut Shannon Lucid spent 179 days aboard the Russian space station *Mir*.

The accomplishments have been a welcome balm to the troubled space agency's public image. Established in the 1950s during the Cold War, NASA won broad support as it competed with the Soviet Union in the highly visible "space race" that eventually put men on the Moon.

But the public's enthusiasm for the program turned to horror in January 1986, when the space shuttle *Challenger* exploded shortly after liftoff, killing New Hampshire schoolteacher Christa McAuliffe and the six other crew members and halting manned U.S. space flights for nearly three years.

The space program came under further scrutiny in December 1991, when the Soviet Union's demise brought the Cold War to an end, leaving NASA overstaffed and guided by an outdated mandate. By 1990, when the trouble-plagued Hubble Space Telescope was launched, NASA was being described by *Time* magazine as an agency "under siege, its reputation tarnished, its programs in disarray, its future clouded." [1]

Goldin, appointed in 1992 by then-President George Bush, launched an ambitious program to revamp NASA for the post-Cold War era. "People had been able to see the shuttle going up and relate it to the defense of the nation, so there was never a doubt about why we had a NASA," Goldin says. "Now that we didn't have this common enemy, we had to connect more to the American public.

"If you look at the elections of 1992-96, it is clear that the American people are sending a message: 'The Cold War is over. We want government that's much more efficient, that costs less, but that also is relevant to our lives.' "

Goldin proposed to cut the number of agency personnel as well as the cost of missions. The savings in space science would come by building "cheaper, faster, better" robotic, or unmanned, spacecraft; by reducing the high cost of launching satellites and shuttles through management and technical improvements; and by developing a single-stage, reusable launch vehicle for the shuttle instead of the three-stage rocket now used to send it into Earth orbit. (*See interview, p. 364.*)

Five years into his tenure, Goldin gets high marks for his efforts. "NASA may not be perfect, but it's a hell of a lot better off in the public's estimation," says John Logsdon, director of the Space Policy Institute at George Washington University. "It's happened through a combination of good management, programs that the public wants and some luck, like the Mars meteorite and the beautiful images from the Hubble Space Telescope. I think the program has been downsized to a level that seems to feel right in political terms and at the same time can be extremely productive for the country

NASA Chief Goldin Sets His Sights . . .

Daniel S. Goldin laid out an ambitious agenda for reforming the troubled National Aeronautics and Space Administration when he became NASA administrator in April 1992. He promised to end its notorious cost overruns by finding "faster, better and cheaper" ways to run the nation's space program without compromising safety. He gave high-priority status to several programs, including environmental monitoring from space through the Mission to Planet Earth program; redesign of the space station and integration of Russia into the program; and revitalization of the agency's aeronautics program. In an interview with CQ Researcher *staff writer Mary H. Cooper, Goldin discusses the space program's prospects:*

Daniel S. Goldin

How close have you come to meeting your goals for NASA?

Before I talk about myself, let me tell you, it's an easy job because the people at NASA and our contractors are the smartest, most dedicated group of people I've ever been exposed to in my life. I'm a facilitator: The NASA people made everything happen. I really am just overwhelmed by the capacity of this organization.

I set some very challenging goals, and I thought that the revolution to transition NASA from a Cold War agency into a go-getter, 21st-century agency would take five years. I feel I'm two years off that pace. I came from corporate America, and I underestimated the time it takes to communicate to all our stakeholders. It is a very, very time-intensive process. If you have a board of directors in a corporation, you deal with 20 to 25 people, then maybe you deal with some tens of investment banking people, and then you deal with some finite numbers of customers. We have 535 members on our board of directors in the Congress — 435 in the House and 100 in the Senate — and then we have the folks at the White House. And then we have all of the companies and universities that we deal with, the grass-roots groups that support the space programs and the people who are the beneficiaries of our technology.

And then we have the press. NASA has more sunshine than I think almost any organization in the world because of the intense interest in the space program. When we do something, 2 billion people watch. How'd you like to go into the laboratory and have 200 people peering over your shoulder? When you get done, it's a wonderful product. But I underestimated that process by about two years.

How serious are Russia's financial problems in completing the space station?

There is a very serious problem in Russia, and it's well beyond the control of the people at the Russian Space Agency. They want so hard to perform, and they are highly frustrated. I have empathy for them because they're so proud of this relationship they have with us, and they're not getting the funding that they need. What's going on in Russia is gripping. They went from totalitarianism to attempted democracy, and from a controlled economy to an open economy overnight. So in that sense, I have a concern for the Russian people. But they have to do what they said they were going to do.

Do you plan to postpone the scheduled launches of U.S. space station components to accommodate the Russian delay?

This is my second frustration. Our people and our contractors have been pouring their hearts out. They've been working seven days a week, three shifts a day to hold the schedule, and we would have been ready to launch on time. We wanted to deliver this as a present to the American people, to meet their expectations by getting the space station up on time. This is a condition beyond our control, and so we're all frustrated. We're not angry, we're just frustrated.

Is the space station the centerpiece of NASA's current agenda?

I see it as one of the legs of the stool on which NASA stands. It is an essential leg because we have to see how people can live and work safely in space. And we want to have a unique laboratory in Earth orbit to do biomedical, biotechnical, advanced materials and combustion research. The space station will also open the space frontier, not just for NASA astronauts but for commerce and people. And we're developing radical, new launch vehicles that hopefully will be servicing the space station and providing us with translunar transportation. Remember the Pan Am shuttle to the space station in the movie "2001: A Space

over the next decade."

According to a recent poll, Americans think the government has been more successful in promoting space exploration than any other major federal mission, including providing for the national defense. [2]

But trouble looms on the horizon for the U.S. space program. The International Space Station, the centerpiece of NASA efforts over the next decade, is threatened by the Russian

. . . on Mars, Jupiter and Beyond

Odyssey?" I want to see that in my lifetime.

Another leg of the stool is fundamental science. We announced the Origins program this year, which, when we get our results back, I believe is going to change the beliefs that people have as to who they are and how they relate to this planet. In the Origins program, we're trying to answer such questions as, "Is life of any form — single-celled or higher, carbon-based or not — unique to planet Earth?" We're also trying to understand how galaxies, stars, solar systems and planets form and evolve and how this knowledge can help us rewrite chemistry, physics and biology textbooks. This Origins program is going to reach out 100 light-years to see if we can identify any Earth-like planets, directly detect them and remotely sense their atmospheres to see if they contain water vapor, carbon dioxide and oxygen. We're also going to try to understand how the universe formed, starting with the Big Bang. It will help our understanding of physics and chemistry and will allow us to do unbelievable things in the future.

The third leg of the stool is understanding our own planet. We have been on Earth for thousands of years, and in 1997 the best weather model we have is five days. If we're ever to have sustainable development on this planet, to get the yields we're going to need out of our farms and agriculture, we're going to need predictive climate and environmental models that are good from seasonal to interannual and ultimately to decades so that we can be much more predictive and can help in the process of sustainable development, managing resources and getting foodstuffs. This is an unbelievable program, and NASA is making major contributions to the knowledge base of America.

There's actually a fourth leg on the stool. It's not a space leg, it's an aeronautics leg. I don't think that people recognize that the first "A" in NASA stands for aeronautics. You can't fly on a plane today that hasn't been tested in a NASA facility or fly on that plane without having NASA technology in it. NASA is leading the charge for the renaissance of flight through the air. We have committed to cutting the accident rate on planes by a factor of five in 10 years and by a factor of 10 in 20 years. If you consider the fact that for the past 20 years the crash rate of planes has been constant, that is a bold goal. For the next five years, we've reprogrammed a half-billion dollars to do it, and we're doing it in cooperation with the Federal Aviation Administration and the industry. I'd like Americans to be able to get on planes and not worry. And we've taken a number of other goals that are all just as challenging. A four-legged stool kind of wobbles, but sometimes a little wobble is good.

Given the state of knowledge provided by existing space programs, what do you hope NASA may produce in the future?

Within 10 to 15 years, if they exist within 100 light-years of Earth, I hope that the agency will have directly detected Earth-sized planets and sampled their atmospheres. Within 10 to 15 years, we will have had the most comprehensive robotic reconnaissance of the planet Mars, and we will have brought back samples of material from Mars. We will have generated resources robotically — breathing gas and fuel — to sustain human life on the surface of Mars, and we will have proved that it's safe and cost-effective to send people to Mars. We will have sent probes to our key planetary bodies, and by that point in time, if we did find a liquid-water ocean on Europa, a moon of Jupiter, we will have planted a robotic submarine in that ocean.

Within 15 years, I think we'll have a lunar base. I won't guarantee it, but I think we have a good chance within 15 years of having a seasonal-to-interannual model of our weather, so we will be able to do predictive farming. We'll be able to do a much better job of predicting natural disasters, like torrential downpours and drought, which is crucial to the survival of U.S. agriculture. Perhaps in 15 years we will have a more complete understanding of the evolution of our universe, from the time of the Big Bang, and we will have peered out to the very edge of time. And certainly, within my lifetime we will start sustained presence on Mars.

Can NASA accomplish these goals with federal funding alone?

One of the things we're exploring is teaming with industry and bringing in commercial interests to broaden the funding base. We'd also like to see if it's possible to form a space venture-capital fund, because I worry about the future funding for this agency. So we are now experimenting not just in having NASA lead the nation in technological prowess, but in beginning to help lead in managerial and financial prowess and offload the American people of some of the financial burden. I don't know if we're going to be successful, but I'm not afraid to say we're trying.

government's failure to provide the money needed to complete a vital component that the Russians are building: a service module containing living quarters and powered by rockets to keep the spacecraft at the proper altitude.

Russia was brought into the space station project by President Clinton to cement relations with the United States' former Cold War enemy and to profit from its expertise. But the funding delay has forced NASA to postpone the first construction flight, originally set for November, to October 1998, and jeopardizes the station's planned completion by June 2002.

To reduce the program's vulnerability to Russia's uncertain political and economic future, NASA has said that an existing module built by the Naval Research Laboratory for another project could be adapted and used if Russia drops out of the program. But substituting key components at this stage would undoubtedly delay the space station's construction and possibly undermine public support for the project, which includes Canada, Japan and 11 members of the European Space Agency. *

To avoid a Russian pullout from the project, some observers say the United States should help the Russians stay on schedule. "I happen to be one of the few people who feel that it's worth a couple of hundred million bucks off the reserves on the space station to give it to Russia to get the job done," says Jerry Grey, public policy director of aerospace and science policy at the American Institute of Aeronautics and Astronautics, in Reston, Va. "The Russians can build the logistics module. They just don't have the money. And I'd rather just give them the money and tell them we'll tide them over this time while warning them not to let it happen again."

Other space policy experts are less sanguine about NASA's ability to aid the Russians, let alone deliver on all the agency's promises, given the space program's shrinking budget. After declining in real terms for the first time in two decades in fiscal 1995, to $14 billion, NASA's budget has continued to fall, reaching $13.7 billion in fiscal 1997; it is projected to stabilize at $13.2 billion by fiscal 2000.

For all their savings, NASA's new robotic spacecraft, such as the recently launched *Mars Pathfinder* and *Mars Global Surveyor,* pose certain risks. "Things are smaller, cheaper and faster; the question is whether or not they are better," says Marcia S. Smith, a space policy analyst at the Congressional Research Service (CRS), a branch of the Library of Congress. "When you build satellites faster and better and cheaper, they may not be as successful technically," because they may not have been built with redundant, or backup, systems. "So far, things are going very well for NASA in terms of this faster, better, cheaper philosophy. But if *Mars Pathfinder* gets to Mars on July 4, 1997, as scheduled, and doesn't land properly or doesn't send back data, I'm not sure that NASA will view this as having been successful."

Analysts generally agree that NASA has taken many of the steps necessary to adapting the space program to the budgetary and political realities imposed by the Cold War's end. But they also stop short of declaring Goldin's new strategy an unqualified success.

"I think it is too soon to say whether the cheaper, faster, better model of robotic missions is actually going to turn out better," says John Pike, director of the Federation of American Scientists' Space Policy Project. "It's also too soon to say whether they have been simply cutting costs or also cutting corners on the shuttle. And, until they are well along in the space station assembly sequence, there is always the possibility that the collaboration with the Russians could come unglued and that the whole house of cards could get knocked over."

As lawmakers and NASA officials contemplate further changes in the American space program, these are some of the questions being asked:

NASA

Astronauts Shannon Lucid and John Blaha reunite after the U.S. space shuttle Atlantis *docked with the Russian space station* Mir *last year. Lucid spent a record 179 days aboard* Mir *before Blaha replaced her.*

Would the billions of dollars now being spent on space programs be better used to solve problems on Earth?

Since the U.S. space program began in the late 1950s, it has attracted both impassioned support and opposition. Early U.S. successes were considered vital in winning the space race with the Soviet Union, such as John Glenn's 1962 orbit around the

* The 11 members participating in the space station project are Belgium, Denmark, France, Germany, Italy, The Netherlands, Norway, Spain, Sweden, Switzerland and the United Kingdom.

Earth and the *Apollo* program, which put U.S. astronauts on the Moon.

But public support for space missions plummeted after the *Challenger* tragedy. That was followed by the disappointing performance of the Hubble telescope in 1990. The criticism mounted when the Soviet Union's breakup in 1991 effectively ended the Cold War space race, and mounting concern over the budget deficit prompted heated debates over which federal programs lawmakers should target for spending cuts.

"I can't see voting monies to find out whether or not there is some microbe on Mars," said former New York City Mayor Ed Koch, "when in fact I know there are rats in the Harlem apartments." [3]

Despite NASA's recent successes, critics continue to debate the value of spending billions of dollars each year on space programs when poverty, disease and other social ills at home remain unresolved. The issue was raised once again last year during congressional debate over legislation funding several federal agencies, including NASA, which was seeking $5.7 billion in fiscal 1997 for manned space-flight programs. (NASA is seeking $5.3 billion for fiscal 1998.) Rep. Joseph P. Kennedy II, D-Mass., offered two amendments that would have diverted $471 million from 1997 NASA programs — including $297 million earmarked for the space station — to grants for the homeless and assisted-housing programs. Kennedy is a nephew of President John F. Kennedy, who championed the U.S. human space-flight program.

"All of our members know about *Apollo 13* and Tom Hanks," said Rep. Tim Roemer, D-Ind., in support of the amendment. "We like to go see those fun movies. We all know about the excitement [of] going to see a space launch down in Florida, and we feel pride in our space program. How many of us go into the homeless centers? . . . This space station does not deserve $297 million. It is $80 billion over budget from when it was first designed in 1984. It has gone from eight scientific missions to one scientific mission, and we are cutting our homeless centers by 25 percent since 1995. Now that is not justice, and that is not fair choices. That is the easy way out."

"When we look at space station development and other programs related to man in space, and look at $5.3 billion, the homeless program is only 20 percent of that amount," said Rep. Bruce F. Vento, D-Minn., who co-sponsored the amendment. "Where are our priorities? If we have to make tough choices, let us not make them and take them from the poorest of the poor." The Kennedy-Vento amendment went down to defeat by a 138-277 vote margin. [4]

NASA's Goldin views efforts to cut the agency's funding as shortsighted. "If we only live in the present, where we worry about the food we have today, the shelter we have today, the jobs we have today, we are ignoring the future of our children," he says. "Things that you take advantage of today happen because NASA 25 years ago had the courage to do things."

Goldin cites a spinoff from the Hubble telescope that enables physicians to perform high-resolution mammograms and needle biopsies of potential tumors in a single sitting, reducing the cost of breast cancer prevention and treatment.

"People tell me that because we have problems here on Earth, I should convince them of the technology transfers coming from each and every project," Goldin continues. "Should I have testified before Congress that I wanted to fix the Hubble telescope so we could get a better breast biopsy? Sometimes you don't even know. In our personal lives, if we don't have long-term savings our retirements are not pleasurable. And in a similar manner, a nation has to make long-term investments without always being able to define the benefits." *(See story, p. 372.)*

Supporters of space exploration say that NASA, accounting for less than 1 percent of the federal budget, is a bargain. "The space programs are a very important contribution to being able to solve some of our problems here on Earth," says Pike of the Federation of American Scientists. "The space station budget is about 1 percent of the defense budget, and that 1 percent that we're spending on the space station is contributing a lot more toward helping prevent the Cold War from coming back than all those submarines, bombers and other stuff the military's using."

Is the space station an appropriate use of public funds?

During last year's congressional debate over NASA funding, critics zeroed in on the space station as their chief target for budget cuts. "We are spending multibillions for a space station, a motel in the heavens, and we do not have money here on Earth for affordable housing," Rep. Carolyn B. Maloney, D-N.Y., said on June 26, 1996. "So I certainly support wholeheartedly shifting funds from a motel in space to needed housing here on Earth."

Such criticism has plagued the costly space station almost since its inception. First proposed by President Ronald Reagan in 1984, the program was designed to provide a permanent platform in space for astronauts and scientists to perform long-term experiments and space-based manufacturing projects.

The often-redesigned space station became a symbol of NASA mega-projects and earned the space agency a reputation as a black hole that gobbled taxpayers' dollars with little to show for the effort. Since 1991, lawmakers have tried 15 times to terminate the project. Once, in 1993, it

With Expenses Out of This World . . .

The high cost of delivering crews and equipment into Earth orbit has long posed a major impediment to scientific and commercial activities in space. Early spacecraft, including those used for the *Apollo* missions, could only make one trip. The rockets used to blast the craft aloft were jettisoned and burned up during re-entry into Earth's atmosphere; cargo was left in orbit; and the crew capsules were irreparably damaged by re-entry heat and the impact of splashdown.

In an effort to cut costs, President Richard M. Nixon in 1972 launched a program to design a reusable spacecraft, the space shuttle. In 1981, the first shuttle flight took place, and the following year the program was declared operational. The shuttle resembled a civilian aircraft, complete with a cockpit, stubby wings and landing gear. Thick, heat-resistant tiles lent the craft a bulky silhouette.

A computer-generated rendering depicts the X-33, the prototype for the next generation of reusable launch vehicle. Designed to deliver commercial or military payloads to low Earth orbit at low cost, it will use a single-stage rocket to liftoff vertically and then glide to a conventional landing.

While the shuttle still jettisoned the three stages, or rockets, required to lift the heavy craft into orbit, the shuttle itself could survive re-entry, make a dry landing and undergo repairs for repeated trips to space.

Designed to carry people as well as payloads, the shuttle incorporated countless safety features, and the craft operated smoothly for several years. But the shuttle program came to an abrupt halt after the January 1986 explosion of the shuttle *Challenger*, killing all seven people on board. For 32 months, NASA engineers worked to redesign the shuttle and build-in new safety features. The effort has paid off: Since returning to service in 1988, the shuttle has performed without serious flaws. In early April, NASA decided to cut short the shuttle *Columbia's* planned 16-day mission because of a malfunctioning electrical generator, but it planned to relaunch the craft this summer to complete the mission.

But cost remains a serious obstacle to space activities. Each shuttle flight costs about $400 million, and that doesn't include the cost of engine overhaul and repair. Pressure also has mounted for the U.S. to maintain its leading role in space exploration by designing a replacement for the 35-year-old craft before another country does. In the late 1980s, NASA and the Defense Department began a joint program to design a new launch vehicle called the national launch system. Congress terminated this program in 1993, however, citing budget concerns. [1]

To resolve the ongoing debate over space launch costs, the Clinton administration in 1994 ordered the Pentagon and NASA to design two new shuttle replacements. The Defense Department, which developed the *Delta, Atlas* and *Titan* rockets, was charged with developing a new expendable launch vehicle. NASA was to continue operating the shuttle and at the same time develop a new, reusable launch vehicle (RLV) to eventually replace the shuttle.

came within one vote of cancellation. [5]

In 1988, to help defray the station's cost, the U.S. brought several international partners into the project. In 1993, President Clinton invited Russia aboard, which helped restore support for the project. No longer a Cold War adversary, Russia offered invaluable expertise in space science, including operating the space station Mir.

But as Maloney made clear, some lawmakers still feel the space station is a waste of federal dollars that could be put to better use. "There is certainly very strong support for the space station, both in Congress and the White House, the strongest I've seen in many years," says Smith of the CRS. "But there continue to be concerns by some members who feel that it is not affordable by the country at this time and will not be worth the money that's being spent on it when it's ultimately built."

Supporters say the station is a necessary step toward further human exploration of space. "It is the only thing that makes sense if we're going to continue our long-term progress in human space flight," says Logsdon of the Space Policy Institute. "If we want one-shot trips to Mars or back to the

. . . NASA Seeks a Reusable Launch Craft

The quest to replace the shuttle took a decisive turn last July, when NASA chose Lockheed Martin Corp., a leading defense and space contractor, to help design a prototype for the next generation of launch vehicles. To reduce the three-year project's cost, the firm agreed to invest $220 million, with NASA putting up the remaining $941 million.

"We have to have an attitudinal change in America," says NASA Administrator Daniel S. Goldin. "If you have a policy of everyone living off of Uncle Sugar, you will continue to go on living that way. The worst that will happen is that we'll fail and continue to have federal funding. But what if we succeed? We can come back and ask the American people for less money."

Saving federal dollars is only one advantage of involving private industry in the new design, Goldin says. "Better than that, Lockheed Martin is risking $220 million of their own money," he says. "I've got to believe that their executives are really gripped about making this project successful. So it's no longer just a question of NASA pulling; Lockheed Martin is pushing. I think it's worth the risk, and I'm not afraid of failure."

NASA and Lockheed Martin engineers chose a revolutionary design for the sub-scale vehicle, known as the *X-33*. Like the shuttle, the *X-33* is designed to launch vertically and land horizontally. But unlike the shuttle, which requires three stages, the *X-33* would reach orbit with an innovative, single-stage "linear aerospike engine." [2]

Experts are divided over the degree of risk Goldin has assumed with the *X-33*. The improvements may be so great that space transportation costs could fall to one-tenth the current level, according to David Brandt, executive director of the National Space Society.

"Everybody says this aerospike engine is going to work," Brandt says. "Technically, there are many issues that have yet to be settled. But there is a high degree of probability that it will all work."

Other experts are less sanguine about the *X-33's* prospects. "The single-stage-to-orbit technology may or may not work," says Jerry Grey, public policy director for aerospace and science policy at the American Institute of Aeronautics and Astronautics. "It's a very high-risk approach, and there is no funding going into backups at this point. I'd like to see some money supporting a slightly simpler operational vehicle, two-stage-to-orbit, maybe."

After 15 suborbital test flights of the *X-33*, scheduled to begin in 1999, NASA will decide whether to use the model as the basis of a new reusable launch vehicle, dubbed the *VentureStar*. Because the agency has already decided to turn over the development and operation of the shuttle's replacement to private industry, the decision to proceed also will depend on industry's willingness to assume the financial risk.

While NASA is seeking a revolutionary departure from existing technology for the shuttle replacement, the Pentagon is taking a less radical approach with its Evolved Expendable Launch Vehicle (EELV). On Dec. 20, the Defense Department chose Lockheed Martin and McDonnell Douglas Corp. to collaborate on developing the new vehicle. Next May, one of the two companies is expected to be chosen to produce the EELV. [3]

Whatever design is eventually chosen, the shuttle's familiar silhouette will not fade from view anytime soon. "There's a lot of misunderstanding about the RLV," says John Logsdon, director of the Space Policy Institute at George Washington University. "It is only going to carry cargo in its first years. Therefore, obviously it's not going to be a replacement for the shuttle as a people carrier. I think at some point the shuttle will be transitioned out of service, but I don't expect it in the next decade."

---

[1] See Marcia S. Smith, "U.S. Space Programs," *CRS Issue Brief*, Congressional Research Service, March 17, 1997, p. 11.

[2] For more on the X-33's aerospike engine, see Kathy Sawyer, "Bargain-Hunting NASA Picks Blast From Past," *The Washington Post*, Feb. 3, 1997.

[3] Smith, *op. cit.*, p. 11.

Moon, we don't need a station. But if we really want to learn to live and work in space and to move outwards, it's necessary to have it."

The space station is expected to yield new information on the effects of long-term space travel on human health. Deprived of the force of gravity, astronauts suffer from bone loss and muscle atrophy as well as impaired immune and endocrine function, problems that biological research aboard the space station may help resolve. Microgravity conditions on the station may also enable manufacturers to come up with more efficient ways to produce metal alloys and other products.

"It's hard to define exactly what you're going to get from this research," says David Brandt, executive director of the National Space Society. "But from our past experience with the [NASA] program, it has phenomenal payoff. If we want to continue our prosperity into the future, we have to continue to play a major role in this."

But some scientists say the space station is a poor way to spend the nation's dwindling federal support for basic science. "The annual cost of the space station is going to be about the same as the annual research budget of the National Science Foundation," Pike says. "I don't care if you cloned Albert Einstein and stuffed [the clones] into the station, I can't believe the work that can be done by a handful of people in that one laboratory module could be as productive as all the basic science funded by the National Science Foundation."

Supporters of the station contend that its main value stems from Clinton's decision to include Russia, thereby turning a former military enemy into a commercial partner.

"If you think of this as a science project, it's a ferocious waste of money," Pike says. "If you think of it as a foreign policy or national security project, it's one of the best things we've got going."

Pike emphasizes the dangers inherent in Russia's economic morass, which has cost the jobs of thousands of scientists formerly employed by the Soviet weapons industry.

"This gives the Russian aerospace industry something to do besides move into North Korea," he says. "Figure that we're spending half as much for the space station as we are on Star Wars. I think the space station program has had a much bigger impact on halting missile proliferation than anything Star Wars has done."

Should robotic space programs take priority over human space flight?

During the early years of space exploration, public interest focused on human flight. Soviet cosmonaut Yuri Gagarin ignited the interest on April 12, 1961, when he became the first person to orbit the Earth, quickly followed in February 1962 by Glenn. President Kennedy's goal of landing a man, not a robot, on the Moon was reached with the July 20, 1969, lunar landing of Neil Armstrong and Edwin "Buzz" Aldrin; over the next three years, six lunar landings followed.

Some scientists say space exploration's biggest payoffs are likely to come from robotic missions, such as the Mars probes; the Origins program, which focuses on such fundamental questions as how the universe was formed and the potential for life beyond Earth; and Mission to Planet Earth, which is studying weather patterns and global warming.

Although it is attracting far less public attention than earlier manned missions to the Moon, the robotic *Lunar Prospector,* scheduled for launch Sept. 27, is expected to yield information far beyond the scope of any manned lunar mission. It will map the Moon's surface and try to determine the accuracy of recent evidence of polar ice.

At the same time, experts say, political and budget realities are forcing NASA to focus more on popular human flight programs rather than potentially more productive robotic science missions.

"We've got to fund the space station because the president wants it," Pike says. "And there are probably limits to our ability to cut back on the shuttle without blowing the dang thing up. Since there seems to be a bipartisan consensus to balance the budget on NASA's back, we're seeing a lot of the robotics science and the small science stuff really getting squashed. We're seeing a lot of good new ideas — like global network telescopes to look for comets and asteroids that could kill us all — that just can't get new funding at all."

In fact, achieving a better balance between human and robotic missions has been one of NASA's goals. Since he took over the agency five years ago, Goldin says, the portion of NASA's budget used to fund human space flight has fallen from 50 percent to 38 percent, while the portion used for science, aeronautics and technology has grown from 31 percent to 44 percent.

"What's amazing is that the shuttle has higher reliability now," Goldin says, "and instead of talking about the space station, we're building it." Goldin points to the recent opening of a NASA-supported biomedical institute and a new center for microgravity research in combustion and fluids. "So in addition to having a human space-flight program that costs less and does more," he says, "it's richer in its scientific content, which is what the American public wanted."

Pike acknowledges the value of human missions as well. "The formulation that the piloted stuff might be fun and exciting but that the robotics stuff is what has the real payoff is a formulation that appreciates the price of everything and the value of nothing," Pike says. "Fun is a serious payoff. What price tag do you want to put on the American flag?"

Many space enthusiasts feel that human space flight should continue to play a leading role in the space program.

"I think the American people, who after all pay for the program, expect human involvement," Logsdon says. "The scientific community might like to have more of their plaything — which I don't mean in a trivial way — but that's serving a relatively narrow set of scientific interests rather than a broader segment of the population who like the drama of humans in space and like the identification with the astronauts." ■

BACKGROUND

NASA's Launch

U.S. space exploration began as perhaps the most visible manifestation of the Cold War that con-

Continued on p. 372

Chronology

1950s *The United States and the Soviet Union take pioneering steps in the quest to explore space.*

Oct. 4, 1957
The Soviet Union launches *Sputnik I,* the first satellite to orbit the Earth.

Oct. 1, 1958
The National Aeronautics and Space Act creates the National Aeronautics and Space Administration (NASA) to oversee civilian space activities.

Jan. 31, 1959
The United States launches its first satellite, *Explorer I.*

1960s-1970s *The space race gets under way as a highly visible aspect of the Cold War between the U.S. and U.S.S.R.*

April 12, 1961
Soviet cosmonaut Yuri Gagarin becomes the first person to orbit the Earth. The following month, President John F. Kennedy announces plans to land an American astronaut on the Moon within 10 years.

February 1962
John Glenn becomes the first American to orbit Earth.

July 20, 1969
Americans Neil Armstrong and Edwin "Buzz" Aldrin become the first humans to land on the Moon.

1972
President Richard M. Nixon launches the shuttle program to develop the first reusable spacecraft to deliver people and cargo into Earth orbit.

1975
U.S. and Soviet spacecraft in the *Apollo-Soyuz* Test Project dock for two days of joint experiments by three astronauts and two cosmonauts.

1980s *Support for the U.S. human space flight program plummets after a devastating accident.*

Jan. 25, 1984
President Ronald Reagan announces plans to develop a permanently occupied space station within 10 years. Congress directs NASA to encourage commercialization of its activities in an amendment to the 1958 law creating the space agency.

Jan. 28, 1986
The space shuttle *Challenger* blows up 74 seconds after liftoff, killing all seven crew members aboard. NASA suspends shuttle flights for the next 32 months.

1990s *NASA undertakes ambitious reforms to improve efficiency while reducing costs.*

April 1990
The Hubble Space Telescope is lifted into orbit aboard the shuttle *Discovery*, but a faulty mirror prevents the costly instrument from working properly.

September 1990
NASA comes under heavy criticism from the Advisory Committee on the Future of the U.S. Space Program for undertaking excessively risky and costly projects and for putting too much emphasis on human space flight without sufficient safety.

April 1992
Daniel S. Goldin becomes the ninth administrator of NASA and launches a new strategy to expand space missions with a greatly reduced budget.

1993
President Clinton invites Russia to join the United States and other countries in building the International Space Station.

1995
For the first time in two decades, NASA's budget declines, to $14 billion, beginning a downward trend expected to stabilize at $13.2 billion in 2000.

1996
The Clinton administration issues a space policy directive that emphasizes shifting control of some NASA operations, including the space shuttle, to the private sector.

July 4, 1997
Mars Pathfinder, one of NASA's newly designed downsized satellites, is scheduled to land on Mars.

March 1999
NASA is scheduled to begin test flights of the *X-33,* a scaled-down prototype of a new reusable launch vehicle designed to replace the space shuttle.

Feet Don't Ache? Thank an Astronaut

Most of us know that the U.S. space program helped develop the satellites orbiting the Earth that relay TV images and phone connections around the world.

But countless other commercial products and innovations we use daily also were spawned by space-age technology, including sneakers that let you walk off the tennis court without aching feet. They are made with shock-absorbing materials developed for the boots astronauts wore on the moon. Other spinoffs from space, developed by scientists from private industry and the National Aeronautics and Space Administration (NASA) include:

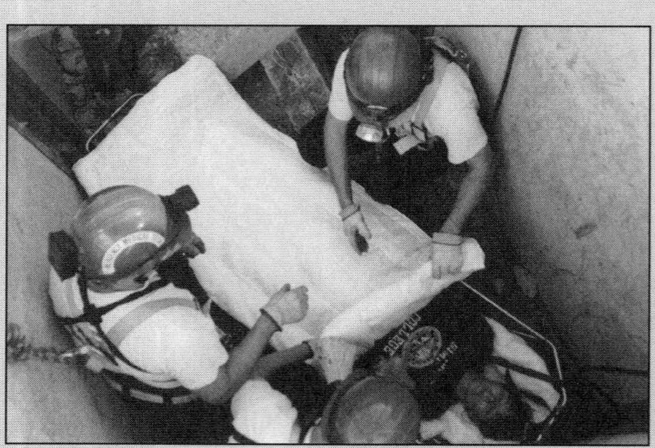

Tom Trower/NASA Ames Home Page

Rescue blankets made of recycled plastic milk bottles are a new spin-off from NASA research into the development of lightweight metal insulation for spacecraft.

- Pacemakers to regulate heartbeat and remote monitoring devices for intensive-care patients, derived from telemetry systems to monitor astronauts and spacecraft.
- Portable medical equipment carried aboard ambulances, developed by NASA for use aboard manned spacecraft.
- Survival blankets, insulating covers for water heaters and home insulation, inspired by aluminized insulation for satellites.
- Beta Glass, a fireproof cloth used in firefighters' suits, designed to protect astronauts in the pure-oxygen air of early spacecraft.
- Helmets, tennis rackets and other sporting goods made of lightweight composite materials, devised for many types of equipment in space.
- Home smoke detectors, originally developed for NASA's early 1970s Skylab spacecraft.
- Quartz timing crystals in wristwatches and small clocks, first designed as a highly accurate timing device for *Apollo* spacecraft.
- Cordless screwdrivers, drills and other rechargeable power tools, developed to enable astronauts to take rock samples from the Moon.
- Supermarket bar codes, first developed by NASA to keep a highly accurate inventory of millions of spacecraft parts.
- Baby formula containing Formulaid, an algae-based, nutrient-rich additive derived from NASA research into algae as recycling agents.
- Foot warmers for ski boots, from heating elements used to keep astronauts warm in the extreme temperatures of the Moon.

Continued from p. 370

sumed Russia and the U.S. for 45 years. The space race began Oct. 4, 1957, when the Soviet Union successfully launched *Sputnik I,* the first satellite, into Earth orbit. [6] Less than four months later, on Jan. 31, 1958, the United States launched its first satellite, *Explorer I.*

Explorer I had been propelled by military rockets, prompting concern over potential conflicts of interest between military and civilian uses of space exploration. Shortly after *Explorer's* orbit, then-President Dwight D. Eisenhower proposed separating military and civilian space programs. Congress responded with the 1958 National Aeronautics and Space Act, which created NASA as a civilian agency and left military space missions to the Defense Department.

The early years of the space race saw the most dramatic advances in human space flight. Again, the Soviet Union led the way, with cosmonaut Gagarin's pioneering 1961 Earth orbit. Less than a month later, on May 5, Alan Shepard made the first suborbital flight by an American, followed in 1962 by Glenn.

President Kennedy's 1961 pledge to land a man on the Moon within the decade led to the *Apollo* program and the 1969 Moon landing by Armstrong and Aldrin. The U.S. sent 12 more astronauts to the Moon over the next three years. Also in the early 1970s, three crews of astronauts manned the experimental *Skylab* space station.

Surprisingly, not all the early space missions were adversarial in nature. In 1975, at the height of the Cold War, the United States and the Soviet Union collaborated on the *Apollo-Soyuz* Test Project, in which three U.S. astronauts and two Soviet cosmonauts docked their crafts for two days of joint experiments.

The shuttle emerged as the next milestone in U.S. space exploration. President Richard M. Nixon launched the program in 1972 to develop the first reusable spacecraft. Using three rockets, or stages, to escape Earth's gravitational pull, the shuttle made its first flight in 1981. But after the Challenger tragedy in 1986, NASA suspended shuttle operations — and human space flight — for nearly three years.

Although the shuttle resumed flight in 1988 and suffered no subsequent accidents, NASA's image had been tarnished. In 1990, its setbacks in human space flight were compounded by the discovery of a crippling defect in a key robotic program, the Hubble Space Telescope. Designed to provide astronomers with a view of the universe unobstructed by Earth's atmosphere, the telescope could not send back clear images because of flaws in its primary mirror.

In September 1990, a blue-ribbon panel was convened to assess NASA's failings and offer a blueprint for future space exploration. Headed by Norman Augustine *, then chairman and chief executive officer of Martin Marietta Corp., the Advisory Committee on the Future of the U.S. Space Program concluded that NASA had undertaken excessively costly and risky projects. Moreover, the committee staff said NASA had placed too much emphasis on human space flight, without first establishing the technological base to adequately ensure safety.

The Augustine committee charged that the agency had relied excessively on the shuttle program to carry the civilian space program and recommended that the agency shift its main focus from human flight to robotic missions and space science. [7]

Goldin's Challenge

In April 1992, 15 months after the Augustine committee's scathing assessment, Goldin became the agency's new administrator. Appointed by then-President George Bush, Goldin brought to the post extensive knowledge of space technology gained from a long career managing the development and production of advanced spacecraft and space instruments at TRW Space & Technology Group, in Redondo, Calif. He immediately laid out an ambitious agenda for NASA, addressing many of the Augustine committee's concerns.

From the outset, Goldin proposed cutting a billion dollars from the shuttle program's annual operating budget and shifting resources from human flight missions to robotic flight and space science. To reduce risks and costs in the satellite program, Goldin promised to build more "faster, better, cheaper" spacecraft designed to meet limited goals while undertaking fewer big, multipurpose projects, such as the Hubble telescope, which set back the entire space program when they fail. NASA would accomplish all this, Goldin promised, with less money and fewer employees.

Goldin also pledged to reduce the cost of the space station and put it into operation faster than planned by reducing its complexity. After President Reagan first directed NASA to build a permanently occupied space station in 1984, the craft — originally named *Freedom* — underwent repeated design changes. In 1988, the program became an international venture, with members of the European Space Agency, Canada and Japan as partners.

In 1993, shortly after becoming president, Clinton called for yet another redesign. The following year, Russia was brought into the project. NASA agreed to pay the Russian Space Agency $472 million to start work on construction of the new craft, now called the *International Space Station,* as well as for the use of *Mir,* Russia's existing space station, to study the effects of weightlessness and conduct other experiments.

The object of repeated delays, the space station quickly became one of NASA's most expensive programs ever. It is expected to cost NASA $17.4 billion from 1994 to 2002, when construction is scheduled to be completed, and $13 billion for operational costs for the next decade.

If all launch and earlier design costs are included in the price tag, according to a General Accounting Office estimate, the station will cost the United States a total of $94 billion. The original international partners of the U.S. were to spend at least $9 billion, and Russia was to contribute about $3.5 billion, though Russia's economic crisis placed that amount in doubt from the beginning. [8]

According to the Congressional Budget Office, cancellation of the program would have saved about $10 billion from 1998-2002. [9] Because of its high cost, the space station was targeted by budget-conscious lawmakers for elimination. But after repeated proposals to kill the program, the space station gained congressional support with Russia's inclusion and with the designation of Boeing Corp. in 1994 as its prime contractor.

In 1995, the turnaround in congressional sentiment over the space station was demonstrated by a unanimous House vote authorizing up to $13.1 billion to complete the project by NASA's target date of June 2002.

"Passage of this bill by unanimous consent confirms America's leadership responsibility in space exploration to carry us into the next millennium and America's commitment to the people of this nation to enhance commercialization opportunities for all," said then-House Science Committee Chairman Robert S. Walker, R-Pa., a leading supporter of the space station until his retirement last fall. ■

* Augustine, who is now chairman and chief executive of Lockheed Martin Corp., recently announced he will retire as chief executive to teach engineering at Princeton University. He will remain board chairman.

CURRENT SITUATION

'Faster, Better, Cheaper'

Many space experts give Goldin high marks for his efforts to downsize NASA and improve the efficiency of civilian space programs. "We think very highly of him and what he's managed to do, especially given the political climate that he's had to work in on the Hill," says Brandt of the National Space Society. "He really took up this mantra that he's associated with — 'faster, better, cheaper' — and changed the whole space station from a U.S.-centered program to an international activity. We can't imagine who else could have tackled that and done a better job."

One of the most controversial ways Goldin has coped with a shrinking budget has been to reduce NASA's work force — from 25,000 employees in 1993 to fewer than 20,000 today. An additional 2,000 jobs are to be eliminated by 2000. Most of the reductions have come through $25,000 buy-out incentives rather than unpopular reductions-in-force, or RIFs, that government workers have suffered since government downsizing began in earnest in the early 1990s.

"Goldin is making some tough cuts at various NASA centers, including headquarters, which is a very difficult subject," Brandt says. "No one wants to see their center cut, and many complain that he shouldn't be letting go of these employees because they're a national asset."

One result of NASA's downsizing has been a shift of responsibility from the agency's Washington headquarters to the 10 space centers around the country, such as the Kennedy and Johnson centers in Florida and Houston. The centers' authority had eroded over the years as NASA headquarters tried to get a grip on schedule delays and cost overruns by assuming more oversight over the programs.

"Dan Goldin has said again and again that he's going to cut people, not programs, and that's what he's been doing," the CRS' Smith says. "Goldin has made a policy decision that he's just going to have a very small corporate headquarters in Washington and let the authority go back to the centers. The jury is out, however, on whether the pendulum will swing the other way 10 years from now."

The quest to downsize satellites also remains a subject of some debate. Of course, the space station is a huge project involving several countries, tens of billions of dollars and multiple launches of components just to get it built. There is also one robotic megaproject still in the works — the *Cassini* mission to Saturn, scheduled to be launched on Oct. 6. But *Cassini* is an exception. The average cost of building spacecraft is falling — from $590 million in the first half of the 1990s to a projected $190 million in the second half and just $77 million after 2000.

"You just don't see [big] missions in the space science area beyond Cassini," Smith says. Some of the very first robotic missions using smaller designs are the two Mars probes and the *NEAR* (Near Earth Asteroid Rendezvous), another spacecraft launched last year to study asteroids. "NASA is only now starting to launch these spacecraft," Smith says. "There's a whole slew of them scheduled, and this may really be good news, because if you look at the number of scientific missions NASA is mounting, it's really quite impressive."

Even for robotic missions, however, downsizing has its limits. "Goldin certainly has scaled down the costs of many missions that formerly would have been done with big spacecraft and now are being done very effectively with small ones," says Grey of the Institute of Aeronautics and Astronautics. "But if you're trying to collect light with a telescope, you can't shrink the size of the telescope. You can only collect so much light per square meter. So in some cases, going smaller is not necessarily better. It's certainly cheaper, but it may not be better."

Some scientists fault the agency for still preferring big-ticket, visible projects over smaller projects that nonetheless have enormous potential for expanding our knowledge of the universe. When a team of astronomers from the University of California-Santa Cruz undertook a project to seek new planets outside our solar system, they had trouble obtaining agency funding.

"As someone who has submitted a proposal to NASA through the Origins program, I have a sense that there is an awful lot of talk and not very much money," says Steven Vogt, a member of the team. "I can only conclude that expensive missions are really where their interest lies. The really cut-rate stuff that also provides very good science is a lot less visible and of a lot less interest to whomever it is who controls the purse strings up there." [10]

Vogt acknowledges the need for long-term, big-ticket projects to hold public interest in space exploration. "You've always got to have the mission that's out there 10 years from now that brings in the billions of dollars," he says. "But when you find that, gee, we can do this for [only] $200,000, it's very hard to get someone's attention." Vogt's team finally did receive their NASA grant to search for extrasolar planets using the immense Keck telescope complex in Hawaii.

Despite his difficulties in receiving support from NASA, Vogt gives Goldin high marks for channeling agency efforts into long-term scientific projects like his own. "I think the Origins mission is a very good mission," he says. "Goldin has a great vision there that I haven't seen come out of any previous NASA director. Support from the Origins program will keep our planet search going, probably for the next 10 years or so, which is the kind of commitment you really need to be able to find planetary systems like our own."

Long-term research projects such as the search for extrasolar planets are vulnerable to political developments, however. "I'm sure that if Goldin stepped down this could all dry up immediately," Vogt says. "If somebody decided it was more interesting to build power stations on the Moon, support for our work could disappear."

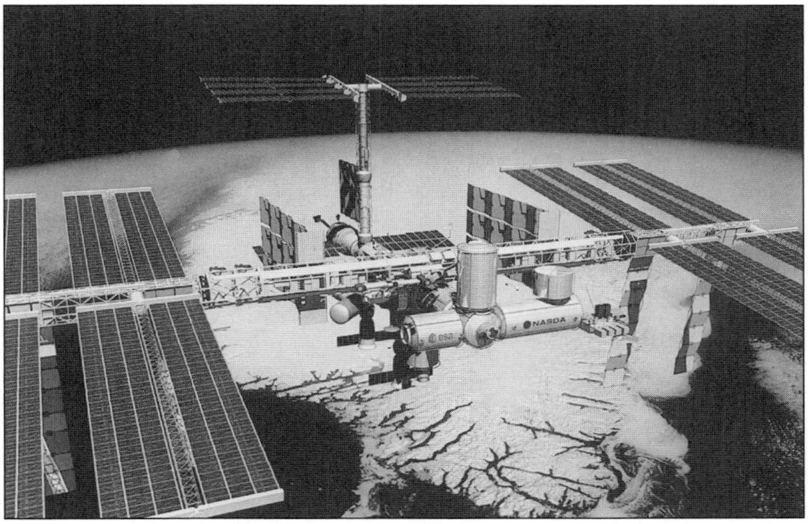

Commercializing Space

Private industry has assumed some of the risks and reaped the profits from space involvement for decades. The 1962 Communications Satellite Act, for example, ushered in the era of commercial satellite communications, which has produced improved telephone communications and spun off new technologies. More recently, budget cuts are forcing NASA to take commercialization to a new level.

One way to reduce the taxpayers' burden of supporting space exploration is to turn it over to the private sector. Indeed, Congress directed NASA to encourage commercialization of its activities in a 1984 amendment to the 1958 National Aeronautics and Space Administration Act.

NASA/John Frassanito and Associates

A rendering illustrates the International Space Station as it will look when operational. It is being built by the U.S., Canada, Japan, Russia and 11 members of the European Space Agency.

Under Goldin's direction, NASA has taken steps to privatize certain elements of the space program.

Last year, for example, a consortium of companies called the United Space Alliance assumed responsibility for operating the shuttle program. "The concept of turning shuttle operations over to a private contractor is an excellent concept," says Grey. "It should have been done years ago."

Brandt, whose organization strongly supports commercialization of space programs, agrees. "The company that now has the contract to operate the shuttle program is essentially the same people who were doing this before, when NASA was acting as the manager, so to speak," he says. "These people have vast stores of experience doing this. Besides, it's in their best interest to make sure that the thing flies safe. They've got to do this successfully or they're not going to get another flight."

But other experts fear that commercialization may jeopardize safety, especially with regard to human space flight programs like the shuttle.

"I'm unconvinced that the shuttle is nearly as safe as they have said," says Pike of the federation of scientists. "I think that they found it to be politically convenient to claim that the shuttle was no longer a test vehicle and could be turned over to a private contractor. But that sounds like a lot of that big talk they had back before the *Challenger* accident. Of course, it hasn't blown up yet, but. . . ."

Pike's biggest concern about privatization of shuttle operation involves the loss of NASA's oversight. "They've had a lot of safety problems," he says. "The anxiety, obviously, is that if you have fewer people trying to do the same amount of work with less safety and quality-assurance oversight, there's a greater opportunity for something to go wrong. It's not so much that there's an identifiable safety problem that I wish they would fix, but rather the recognition that the thing that will lead to the next accident is a problem that nobody knew about because it was overlooked or misunderstood."

The National Space Society fully supports NASA's efforts to commercialize its programs and calls for even more. "One of the problems of the space station program, the space shuttle and a whole lot of other endeavors that NASA was involved in before Mr. Goldin's time was that it was becoming this huge operational agency," Brandt says. "After 35 years in the space era, we should have gotten to the point where we can begin to spin some of this off to the nation's commercial providers of services. Now it's moving in that direction."

But NASA still has an essential role to play in space exploration, Brandt says. "We are very supportive of this effort to commercialize not only the space shuttle program but also other activities that NASA does as an operational agency. Get NASA back to being a [research and development] agency. R and D is what it can do best."

Even though commercialization is a high priority for NASA, some critics fault the agency for failing to shift the financial burden to the private sector fast enough. In 1996, then-Science Committee Chairman Walker introduced legislation aimed at leading NASA to privatize some of its operation and promoting the development of space by commercial companies.

Walker's bill failed to become law, but support for commercial development of space remains strong, especially among lawmakers whose districts depend heavily on space technology for jobs and economic growth. Rep. George E. Brown Jr., D-Calif., for example, has long supported commercialization of space as a key to jobs in his San Bernardino district, home to many aerospace and electronics firms.

"One of the best examples of how space commercialization can create jobs is in my district," he said. "Kelly Space and Technology is offering companies a new and innovative way to launch satellites. They already have significant contracts with major corporations, which will mean more jobs for my constituents in the future. As more companies venture into this field, we will see accelerated job growth nationwide." [11]

NASA

The space shuttle Columbia *touches down July 7, 1996, at the Kennedy Space Center after a 17-day flight.*

According to a recent study by the Potomac Institute for Policy Studies, NASA falls short of its mandate to commercialize. Part of the problem, the study says, lies with the agency's current emphasis on the space station's potential as a platform for scientific research rather than on its promise for future commercial ventures.

The report also says that the agency should strengthen its commercialization program by allowing more non-astronauts on shuttle flights; identifying companies with potential interest in space manufacturing; and providing free transport for a broad range of commercial ventures. The *International Space Station,* the report concludes, offers the greatest potential for further commercialization efforts in the near term.

"Our failures to commercially leverage our nation's superior science and technology in areas such as the television, the VCR and the compact disc led to large industries and profits — in Japan," the report states. "The [space station] and other space assets should be used to our advantage, not only for scientific interests but also for commercial gain. [12]

A major obstacle to commercializing space programs is the high cost involved. NASA is currently trying to consolidate spacecraft mission communications operations from the four NASA field centers * that currently provide this service to a single private contractor and a single NASA manager by Aug. 1, 1998. Last July, following a 1996 Clinton administration directive to privatize space communications operations by 2005, NASA put the contract out for bid.

But the number of companies that initially expressed interest in bidding for the contract, worth up to $600 million a year over the next 10 years, quickly dwindled from 40 to just two — Boeing Corp. and Lockheed Martin — in the face of concerns over the

Continued on p. 378

* The four facilities are the Goddard, Johnson and Kennedy space centers and the Jet Propulsion Laboratory.

At Issue:

Should the Russian government be involved in building the International Space Station?

yes

Daniel S. Goldin
Administrator, National Aeronautics and Space Administration

FROM TESTIMONY BEFORE THE HOUSE SCIENCE COMMITTEE, FEB. 12, 1997.

In 1993, under President Clinton's leadership, we were asked to redesign the space station one last time and to consider bringing in the Russians as partners. Our evaluation showed that it made sense then, and it makes sense now. . . .

We would gain enormously from the Russians' expertise, and it would give us critical redundancy in the functions of life support, attitude control, extra-vehicular activity and launch support. . . . It is also giving America the opportunity to learn about assembling a large, highly technical project in space and to learn from the only country in the world that has spent 10 continuous years in space on *Mir.*

When the Russians joined the partnership, estimates were that $2 billion and approximately 18 months of schedule would be saved. We committed to building the station within a level annual funding cap of $2.1 billion and to complete International Space Station assembly for $17.4 billion. So far, we have met these commitments and intend to continue to perform to them in the future. . . .

The Russians are going through dramatic changes, unlike anything we have ever experienced. They went from totalitarianism to democracy overnight. From a controlled economy to an open one. They have been presented with serious challenges. They are struggling to meet their commitments under harrowing circumstances. Still, the Russian-produced [Functional Cargo Block] is the most mature piece of hardware we have. And it's on time and on budget. Russian industry has demonstrated that they can deliver when adequate funding is provided. . . .

I commit to you that the International Space Station will be built. I believe Russia will continue to be an important part of this international partnership. Let us not forget why we brought the Russians into the program. It is in the best interest of the American people — we could gain incredible scientific capabilities; we could develop cutting-edge technology; we could have the knowledge that Russia is focusing its technological expertise to benefit humanity and promote world peace.

Yet we have to hold the Russians accountable for holding up their end of the bargain. And we are. . . . With your support, the International Space Station can be . . . a symbol and the reality of a new, hard-won partnership that broke all the rules of history to find a new course, a new way, for two former Cold War enemies and the world.

no

Rep. Dana Rohrabacher, R-Calif.
Chairman, House Science Subcommittee on Space and Aeronautics

FROM TESTIMONY BEFORE THE HOUSE SCIENCE COMMITTEE, FEB. 12, 1997.

I was an early supporter of involving the former Soviet Union in our space program generally, and in the space station specifically. Indeed, in my first meeting with newly appointed NASA Administrator [Daniel S.] Goldin in 1992, I urged him to avail the U.S. space program of the capabilities Russia had built up during the Cold War. . . .

What especially excited me, though, was that the Russians wanted to privatize these abilities and resources and earn commercial revenues through foreign trade. In short, they wanted to be like us; they wanted to be capitalists.

So what have we done since 1992 with our new comrades? In the space station program, we've gone from buying things of value from their industry (the approach under the Bush administration) to creating a governmental partnership with their bureaucracy. So they then have to tax their weak economy to fund their industry to do something with us. Instead of practicing capitalism with them, we've been the ones favoring a state-controlled approach.

Doesn't that seem crazy? Shouldn't we be encouraging them to liberate their economy? Was it so important that our government feel comfortable by working with their government, rather than simply urging our industry to create commercial alliances with theirs. . .?

Today, we are finally beginning to face up to the schedule and cost risk introduced into this program by depending on the Russian government (as opposed to industry) to help build the space station. But I would argue that even ignoring the Russian government's failure to deliver on their promises, the whole idea of a government-government partnership wasn't very good to start with. . . .

Like all of us, I cheered and wept at the end of the Cold War. If we have learned anything, we've learned that it is free peoples working together, trading together and profiting together that can win a "warm peace" by fostering freedom and promoting prosperity. I strongly recommend that we pursue those approaches in space cooperation that build and strengthen real ties between private initiatives in Russia and the U.S., rather than depending on the artificial and highly political relationships of diplomats and bureaucrats.

FOR MORE INFORMATION

American Institute of Aeronautics and Astronautics, 370 L'Enfant Promenade S.W., Washington, D.C. 20024-2518; (202) 646-7432. This organization of scientists, engineers and students provides information on technical issues related to space flight.

National Aeronautics and Space Administration (NASA), NASA Headquarters, Mail Code A, Washington, D.C. 20546; (202) 358-0000. The U.S. space agency is responsible for all non-military space activities, including the shuttle program, the International Space Station and scientific probes within and beyond the solar system.

National Space Society, 922 Pennsylvania Ave. S.E., Washington, D.C. 20003; (202) 543-1900. This organization of individuals interested in space exploration provides information on NASA and commercial space activities and policy issues.

Space Policy Institute, George Washington University, 2130 H St. N.W., Suite 714, Washington, D.C. 20052; (202) 994-7292. The institute conducts research on space policy issues and organizes seminars on civilian space activities, including commercial space ventures and international competitiveness in space technology.

risks and broad range of expertise the job would require. Last month, even Boeing dropped out, leaving Lockheed Martin as the sole bidder.[13] ■

OUTLOOK

Crisis in Russia

NASA's immediate priority is resolving the threat of delays to construction of the space station posed by Russia's failure to fund its part of the international project. The funding delay is but one sign of Russia's difficulty in supporting its space programs at a time of economic crisis resulting from the Soviet Union's collapse five years ago. After 11 years in service, Russia's existing space station, *Mir,* is showing signs of wear. On Feb. 28, a fire destroyed an oxygen-generating canister and endangered *Mir's* crew of six, including U.S. astronaut Jerry Linenger. Two weeks later *Mir's* main oxygen-generating system broke down, further reducing the craft's oxygen supply. The funding crisis has forced the Russian Space Agency to put most of its other programs on hold and NASA to postpone space station construction by 11 months.

For Goldin, the delay poses a dilemma: Should he wait out the Russians in hopes that the Russian government will come through with funds, justifying the Clinton administration's gamble to bring them aboard in the first place? Or should he go ahead with contingency plans to replace the Russian module with the Navy's component?

"We are having very long, deep discussions about this," Goldin says. "We now are beginning to execute our contingency plans so that we can continue the assembly of the space station. This is not to preclude the Russians, because when they [resume funding] they'll certainly still be involved."

Space station construction had been scheduled to begin in November with the launch of a Russian-built, NASA-financed module on a Russian rocket. The so-called functional cargo block would provide temporary altitude control for the spacecraft. The first U.S.-made component, a pressurized node that would link other modules on the space station, was to be launched aboard the shuttle *Endeavor* in December. Because funding of the third component, Russia's service module, has been delayed, the entire schedule has been pushed back.[14]

NASA announced its decision to delay construction on April 9. Before making a final decision, Goldin sent Gen. Thomas Stafford, a former astronaut who flew on the 1975 *Apollo-Soyuz* mission, speaks Russian and is familiar with Russian space technology, to determine first-hand from Russian officials and scientists the status of their country's collaboration on the space station.

"If there's one thing I can tell you, it is that we are going to build the space station," Goldin says. "We are determined to do it."

Replacing the Shuttle

While the space station's construction remains an immediate priority, NASA also is developing a new launch vehicle intended to replace the shuttle. Despite recent improvements in the 15-year-old shuttle program, engineering advances are rendering the design obsolete.

"The space shuttle is a wonderful vehicle and ought to keep flying for 10 or 15 more years," Brandt says. "But we're flying with vehicles that were designed 35 years ago, and at some point in time we've got to replace it."

Also spurring the redesign effort are the shuttle's high freight costs, a major obstacle both to space exploration as well as the long-awaited commercialization of space.

"Whether you want to place commercial communications or remote-sensing satellites, send scientific satellites to outer planets or send up crews and equipment to the space station, we've got to get the cost down," Brandt says. "At $10,000 or more a pound today, it's almost prohibitive."

If the costs can be reduced to $500 a pound, Brandt predicts, "not only will people be going into space for tourism, but you'll be able to send small packages from the United States to Europe or the Orient in an hour's time" via highly maneuverable orbiting shuttles.

The first step toward developing a replacement for the shuttle is well under way. NASA-sponsored research has produced a revolutionary design for a reusable launch vehicle that can reach space using a single-stage rocket rather than the three now required to propel the shuttle into Earth orbit. (*See story, p. 368.*) The *X-33,* a scaled-down prototype of the new design, is expected to begin sub-orbital test flights in March 1999. If it's successful, construction will proceed with a full-scale version, to be called the *VentureStar.*

While Goldin remains optimistic about NASA's ability to proceed with its ambitious programs under current spending limits, some experts see trouble down the road. The agency expects to develop the reusable launch vehicle, for example, for around $5 billion.

"That's less money than Boeing spent on the 777" jetliner, Pike says. "Something's wrong with this picture. They're basically claiming that the reusable launch vehicle is going to be everything that the shuttle was originally supposed to be, but wasn't, and that they're going to achieve this for a fraction of the cost of what they spent on developing the shuttle to begin with. I just don't believe that."

Other experts are guardedly optimistic about NASA's ability to pursue all its ambitious goals in an era of federal budget cuts.

"Partly as a result of what Goldin has instituted in the way of cost reduction measures, I think NASA can afford its programs," Grey says. "But NASA always has a success-oriented budget. If we were to lose a shuttle carrying something like the habitation module, of which we have only one, we would be unable to complete the launching of the space station effectively. A bad accident could really totally wipe out the program." ■

Notes

[1] Leon Jaroff, "Spinning Out of Orbit," *Time,* Aug. 6. 1990, p. 26.

[2] The research firms of Peter D. Hart and Robert M. Teeter conducted the nationwide poll in February for the Council for Excellence in Government,

[3] Quoted in Charles P. Cozic, ed., *Space Exploration: Opposing Viewpoints* (1992), p. 13.

[4] Roemer and Vento addressed the House on June 25, 1996.

[5] On June 23, 1993, the House rejected, by a vote of 215-216, an amendment to kill the space station project, sponsored by Reps. Tim Roemer, D-Ind., and Dick Zimmer, R-N.J.

[6] Unless otherwise noted, information in this section is from Marcia S. Smith, "U.S. Space Programs," Congressional Research Service, March 17, 1997. For background, see "Space Program's Future," *The CQ Researcher,* Dec. 24, 1993, pp. 1129-1152.

[7] Report of the Advisory Committee on the Future of the U.S. Space Program, December 1990.

[8] Smith, *op. cit.,* p. 2.

[9] Congressional Budget Office, *Reducing the Deficit: Spending and Revenue Options,* March 1997, pp. 104-105.

[10] For background on the extrasolar planetary search, see Kathy Sawyer, "Hunting New Worlds Far Afield," *The Washington Post,* Dec. 25, 1996.

[11] Brown spoke at the 35th Goddard Memorial Symposium of the American Astronautical Society held on March 5, 1997, where he received the group's John F. Kennedy Astronautics Award for his support of the space program.

[12] Potomac Institute for Policy Studies, *The International Space Station Commercialization (ISSC) Study,* March 20, 1997, p. 3.

[13] See Anne Eisele, "Boeing Declines to Bid on $6 Billion Contract," *Space News,* March 17-23, 1997.

[14] See William Harwood, "Station Delays Fuel NASA's Search for Shuttle Payloads," *Space News,* March 17-23, 1997.

Bibliography

Selected Sources Used

Books

Chaikin, Andrew, *A Man on the Moon: The Voyages of the Apollo Astronauts,* Penguin, 1994.

This detailed history of U.S. lunar exploration examines the technological advances as well as the personalities involved in what is widely viewed as the high point of the human space flight program.

Cozic, Charles P., ed., *Space Exploration: Opposing Viewpoints,* Greenhaven Press, 1992.

This collection of essays by a broad range of experts presents arguments for and against space exploration, the use of space for military purposes and various civilian space programs.

Gump, David P., *Space Enterprise Beyond NASA,* Praeger, 1990.

Writing in the wake of the *Challenger* disaster, the author describes a brave new world in which private enterprise will take over NASA's leading role in space exploration.

McCurdy, Howard E., *The Space Station Decision: Incremental Politics and Technological Choice,* Johns Hopkins University Press, 1989.

This history of the space station program sheds light on ways this complex scientific effort has been shaped by political, as well as scientific, decisions.

Shipman, Harry L., *Humans in Space: 21st Century Frontiers,* Plenum Press, 1989.

A physicist examines the long-term scientific and cultural value of establishing a continuing human presence in space, from constructing a space station, to establishing a lunar base, to setting up a colony on Mars.

Articles

Dickey, Beth, "The Final Frontier," *Government Executive,* March 1997, pp. 12-21.

NASA's attempts to downsize and transfer shuttle operations to a private contractor, the author writes, may threaten not only jobs for NASA employees but also spacecraft safety.

Logsdon, John M., "Creating a Goldin Report Card," *Space News,* March 10-16, p. 13.

The author, director of the Space Policy Institute at George Washington University, applauds NASA Administrator Daniel S. Goldin's success in reforming the agency over the past five years, but he cautions that the changes are only beginning to take effect and must continue if NASA is to become an effective space agency.

Newcott, William R., "Time Exposures," *National Geographic,* April 1997, pp. 3-7.

For more than three years after its 1990 launch, the Hubble Space Telescope, with its faulty mirror, was cited by NASA critics as an example of waste and inefficiency in the space program. Stunning photographs of far-off galaxies and other cosmic marvels taken after the telescope's mirror was repaired in December 1993 may help dispel that negative image.

Schine, Eric, and Peter Elstrom, "The Satellite Biz Blasts Off," *Business Week,* Jan. 27, 1997, pp. 62-70.

Over the next decade, 1,700 satellites are scheduled for launch, more than 10 times the number of commercial satellites now in orbit. Consumers can expect sharper TV images, global wireless phone service and fast, cheap access to the Internet as a result.

Reports and Studies

National Aeronautics and Space Administration, *NASA Strategic Plan,* February 1996.

As part of his effort to make NASA more efficient at lower cost, Administrator Goldin revamped the agency's goals and streamlined its organization. Goldin also identified six strategic enterprises, including the Mission to Planet Earth, space science and human exploration, that will comprise the focus of its activities.

Potomac Institute for Policy Studies, *The International Space Station Commercialization Study,* March 20, 1997.

A panel of experts, including former NASA Administrator James Beggs, criticizes NASA for taking insufficient steps to attract private industry participation to the U.S. space program and offers suggestions on how to boost the commercialization of space activities.

Smith, Marcia S., "U.S. Space Programs," *CRS Issue Brief,* Congressional Research Service, March 17, 1997.

This excellent overview of current U.S. space programs and plans for future development includes background on the space station, commercialization of space activities and development of a replacement for the shuttle. CRS briefs are prepared for members of Congress and are available to the public only from them.

The Next Step

Additional information from UMI's Newspaper & Periodical Abstracts™ database

International Space Station

"Astronauts say space station work is feasible," *The New York Times,* Jan. 20, 1996, p. A24.
The astronauts on the shuttle *Endeavour* said on Jan. 19, 1996, that their work during two excursions into the spacecraft's cargo bay showed that the work needed to build a space station could be done. Three astronauts went on space walks to test the tools and techniques that are expected to be used to build an international space station in a few years. Nearly every task and tool got a good review.

Carreau, Mark, "Russians make new vow to supply funding for space station venture," *Houston Chronicle,* April 17, 1996, p. A8.
The Russians have offered new assurances of their financial commitment to the International Space Station, a development that could ease the threat of a production delay, a White House official said on April 16, 1996.

Carreau, Mark, "Russia wants NASA to include Mir components in space station," *Houston Chronicle,* Dec. 16, 1995, p. A8.
The Russian Space Agency formally proposed that NASA change plans for a new international space station by incorporating major components of Russia's 10-year-old orbiting *Mir* outpost.

Carreau, Mark, "Space station flaw seems to be resolved, NASA engineers say," *Houston Chronicle,* Aug. 29, 1996, p. A25.
Amid mounting budget and schedule threats, NASA announced Aug. 28, 1996, that engineers appear to have successfully corrected a structural flaw in the first shuttle-launched component of the planned U.S.-led International Space Station.

Clayton, William E. Jr., "NASA chief still hopeful about Russian contribution to space station," *Houston Chronicle,* March 21, 1996, p. A8.
NASA Administrator Daniel S. Goldin said on March 20, 1996, that he is "cautiously optimistic" that Russia can overcome budget problems threatening its participation in the International Space Station project.

Hines, Cragg, "Russia pledges to pay its share of space station; Gore reviews funding details with prime minister, NASA," *Houston Chronicle,* Feb. 9, 1997, p. A1.
With Russian Prime Minister Viktor Chernomyrdin at his side, Vice President Al Gore said Saturday he had secured in "intricate detail" reassurances of the Kremlin's commitment to pay its share of the International Space Station program.

Leary, Warren E., "Space Station Faces a Delay Over Russia's Lack of Money," *The New York Times,* Feb. 27, 1997, p. A16.
The start of construction of the International Space Station will probably be delayed until next year because of trouble Russia is having in financing its share of the project, the head of NASA said today. Daniel S. Goldin, the administrator of the space agency, told a congressional panel that he believed the schedule for launching the first components of the orbiting laboratory might be put off from November until mid-1998 because a vital Russian segment was behind schedule.

Toner, Mike, "Space Station May Have to Dodge Flying Debris," *Atlanta Constitution,* Jan. 9, 1997, p. A3.
The International Space Station, due to be assembled in space starting later in 1997, may be more vulnerable than expected to speeding meteoroids and space debris, the National Research Council warned January 8.

Vartabedian, Ralph, "Russian plan would hike international space station cost," *Los Angeles Times,* Dec. 27, 1995, p. A4.
A Russian proposal to redesign the International Space Station would cause up to a one-year construction delay and boost the project's cost by as much as $2 billion, according to a space agency analysis provided to Congress.

Mission to Planet Earth

Leary, Warren E., "NASA Plans to Study Forests and Global Gravity," *The New York Times,* March 19, 1997, p. B10.
NASA announced today that it would sponsor two low-cost satellite projects to study the distribution of Earth's forests and provide a detailed map of the planet's gravity field. NASA officials said the new projects, part of the agency's Mission to Planet Earth program (MTPE), were intended to complement more expensive space missions to study the planet's environment. The first is expected to be the Vegetation Canopy Lidar mission, a satellite that would orbit 250 miles above Earth, firing energy pulses from five lasers to the ground. The mission would spend two years accumulating three-dimensional details of 98 percent of the world's forests. The satellite is scheduled for launching in January 2000.

Reichhardt, Tony, "Panel seeks 'fundamental' shift

in handling of observation data," *Nature,* March 20, 1997, p. 203.
The U.S. Mission to Planet Earth (MTPE) is undergoing yet another major review that may complete the program's evolution from the use of large, centralized spacecraft to a smaller and more distributed system. The MTPE includes a multibillion-dollar series of satellites to observe the planet, oceans and atmosphere.

Mars Probe

Chandler, David L., "Mars probe fell in Pacific a day earlier, Russian agency says," *The Boston Globe,* Nov. 19, 1996, p. A13.
Russian space officials on Nov. 18, 1996, said that the Mars 96 spacecraft, initially believed to have plunged back to Earth on Nov. 17 off the coast of Chile, had in fact crashed 24 hours earlier.

Hoversten, Paul, "Russia Mars probe crashes," *USA Today,* Nov. 18, 1996, p. A1.
A failed Russian Mars probe carrying four small plutonium batteries crashed into the Pacific Ocean on Nov. 17, 1996, about 900 miles east of Easter Island.

Sawyer, Kathy, "Craft? What craft? Russian Mars probe already had fallen before dire warnings," *The Washington Post,* Nov. 19, 1996, p. A3.
The U.S. Space Command on Nov. 17, 1996, apparently mistook the upper stage of a booster rocket for a spacecraft carrying deadly plutonium, prompting what turned out to be an unnecessary scare for the Australian people.

MIR

Carpenter, Dave, "Drifting to disaster or resourceful? Mir space station's mixed signals," *Chicago Tribune,* Feb. 20, 1996, p. 2.
As the *Mir* space station floats toward its implausible 10th year in orbit on Feb. 20, 1996, Russian officials are emitting mixed signals about the state of their troubled, still-secretive program. The cash-strapped program is characterized as either remarkably resourceful or drifting toward disaster.

Carreau, Mark, "Russia launches final, major Mir component," *Houston Chronicle,* April 24, 1996, p. A7.
Russia successfully launched the final major component of its decade-old *Mir* space station from Central Asia early on April 23, 1996, a large science module bearing a ton of U.S. experimental gear for guest NASA astronaut Shannon Lucid.

"Fire on Russian Space Station Doused, but Raises Concern," *The New York Times,* Feb. 25, 1997, p. C9.
Fire broke out on the *Mir* space station on Sunday night, Russian and American space officials said today, and though the blaze was quickly extinguished, it raised new questions about the health of the Russian space program. Russian officials said the fire, which occurred in a faulty air purification unit, caused no serious damage to the space station. But it highlighted concern about Russia's space program, which has been starved of funds even as it becomes more deeply involved in projects with the American and European space programs.

"For American, Wait in Space On Mir Craft May Be Over," *The New York Times,* Sept. 16, 1996, p. A11.
Russian space officials have only the highest praise and affection for Shannon Lucid, the NASA astronaut who has spent the last six months aboard their orbiting station *Mir*. Lucid, whose return to Earth has been delayed three times, is expected to return on Sept. 26, 1996.

Sawyer, Kathy, "Astronaut spends a Mir 5 months in orbit," *The Washington Post,* Aug. 30, 1996, p. A1.
Shannon Lucid is now the most experienced astronaut of either sex in the NASA corps, with five space flights and several orbital records to her credit. Lucid is the first U.S. woman to fly aboard the Russian space station *Mir,* a 136-ton facility somewhat resembling a flying trailer park.

"U.S. Woman Begins 5-Month Stay on Russian Space Station," *The New York Times,* March 25, 1996, p. B9.
Shannon Lucid became a member of Russia's space station *Mir* on March 24, 1996, beginning her five-month stay with hugs, camera flashes and chocolate Easter bunnies. Lucid is the first American woman to live on *Mir,* and her mission signals the beginning of a permanent American presence in space for the next two years.

NASA

Aldinger, Charles, "NASA, Pentagon work on asteroid-tracking project," *USA Today,* Feb. 19, 1997, p. A5.
The U.S. military on Feb. 18, 1997, said that it was working with NASA to improve the ability to forecast asteroid strikes on Earth, such as one 65 million years ago that might have led to the extinction of dinosaurs.

Carreau, Mark, "Debate over life on Mars waxes passionate at NASA conference; More than three dozen research papers are presented at annual JSC event," *Houston Chronicle,* March 20, 1997, p. A19.
Seven months after NASA made its claims public, an often passionate debate continues over the possibility that a Martian meteorite in the agency's custody contains fossil evidence of primitive life. In early August, the Johnson Space Center team led by geologist David McKay announced it had found evidence for the tiny fossilized bacteria in a meteorite recovered in 1984 from the Antarctic.

Carreau, Mark, "NASA chooses astronauts to help build international space station," *Houston Chronicle,* Aug. 17, 1996, p. A9.
NASA on Aug. 16, 1996, selected the first crew of astronauts that will tackle the five-year assembly of the planned International Space Station. Two additions also

were named to the ranks of U.S. astronauts to visit the Russian *Mir* orbital outpost.

Carreau, Mark, and Ruth SoRelle, "NASA sets its sights on Med. Center; Institute will study health, space life," *Houston Chronicle,* March 15, 1997, p. A9.

A new NASA-sponsored research institute created to investigate health issues associated with human space exploration will join the ranks of the Texas Medical Center in June, officials said Friday. The space agency announced formally Friday that Baylor College of Medicine had won a lengthy competition to lead the new National Biomedical Research Institute, the most highly organized effort yet in this country to address the medical obstacles confronting humankind as it prepares for a permanent leap into space.

Causey, Mike, "Soft Landing at NASA," *The Washington Post,* March 7, 1997, p. D2.

Hundreds of National Aeronautics and Space Administration headquarters staffers can breathe easier these days. NASA has scrubbed plans that at one time had called for a layoff of nearly half its downtown workers.

Crenson, Matt, "New Hubble Should Really Open Some Eyes. Its Orbiting Telescope Has Been Dazzling, But NASA Says We Haven't Seen Anything Yet," *Chicago Tribune,* Feb. 13, 1997, p. 8.

It's been three years since astronauts turned the crippled Hubble Space Telescope into the most powerful astronomical instrument ever — a telescope that has dazzled astronomers by detecting the faintest galaxies ever seen, chronicling a comet's collision with Jupiter and revealing Pluto's surface. By replacing two of the telescope's four instruments, astronauts will change Hubble's character as an astronomical observatory, turning a telescope designed to detect and characterize extremely faint points of light into one better able to make detailed images and analyses of complex structures.

Hoversten, Paul, "NASA seeks $75 million for another eye in the sky," *USA Today,* Feb. 6, 1997, p. A3.

President Clinton is asking Congress for money to begin building the last of NASA's four space-based telescopes known as the "Great Observatories." Included in NASA's budget request, to be released Feb. 6, 1997, is at least $75 million to design and develop the Space Infrared Telescope Facility, which would allow scientists to see the glowing embers from the explosive birth of the universe.

Spotts, Peter N., "NASA Plots How to Handle 'Alien' Invasion," *The Christian Science Monitor,* March 7, 1997, p. 4.

The potential visitants aren't Martians or meteorites but microscopic organisms that could be brought back to earth in rock and soil samples collected during U.S. missions to other parts of the solar system. But today, with a series of flights planned to Mars and proposed for other celestial bodies that are considered more likely homes for microscopic life forms, the need to take precautionary steps is becoming more acute.

Space Shuttle

"Atlantis Heads to Space Station," *San Francisco Chronicle,* Jan. 13, 1997, p. A4.

The space shuttle *Atlantis* took off on Jan. 12, 1997, and began chasing the Russian space station *Mir* to pick up John Blaha, an American astronaut. The $2 billion spaceship lifted off from Kennedy Space Center in Florida.

"2 astronauts circle Russian space station," *Chicago Tribune,* March 27, 1996, p. 1.

Two U.S. astronauts floated back inside the space shuttle *Atlantis* early March 27, 1996, after their historic six-hour space walk around the Russian space station *Mir.*

Harwood, William, "Atlantis Roars Into Orbit, Begins Chasing Mir for Tuesday Linkup; American on Space Station Will Get Shuttle Lift Home," *The Washington Post,* Jan. 13, 1997, p. A4.

The shuttle *Atlantis* streaked into orbit today and set off after the Russian *Mir* space station for a planned Tuesday linkup to pick up American astronaut John Blaha, who will be ending a 128-day voyage.

"Shuttle Atlantis Successfully Docks With Russian Space Station," *The New York Times,* March 24, 1996, p. 33.

The space shuttle *Atlantis* on March 23, 1996, docked with Russia's *Mir* space station 245 miles above Earth, despite some earlier worry about a leak in a steering system that was found the day before. It was NASA's third docking with *Mir* in less than a year.

X-33 Reusable Launch Vehicle

Becker, Pamela, "X-33 program signals new approach for NASA," *Mechanical Engineering,* September 1996, p. 50.

NASA has selected Lockheed Martin to design, build and conduct the first flight test of the *X-33* technology demonstration vehicle by March 1999. Lockheed must raise private funds for the final development phase.

Sweetman, Bill, "VentureStar: 21st century space shuttle," *Popular Science,* October 1996, pp. 42-44.

Lockheed Martin's Skunk Works had the winning design for NASA's rocket competition. The *X-33* relies on a number of technologies that ostensibly have never been tested in flight. Lockheed decided that the vehicle would lift off like a rocket and land like an airplane.

Wilson, Jim, "Cheap rides into space," *Popular Mechanics,* September 1996, p. 24.

Lockheed Martin's X-33 VentureStar reusable launch vehicle will take off like a rocket but land like an airplane. NASA hopes the research vehicle will lead to a new generation of cheap space transportation.

Back Issues

Great Research on Current Issues Starts Right Here...Recent topics covered by The CQ Researcher are listed below. Before May 1991, reports were published under the name of Editorial Research Reports.

OCTOBER 1995
Quebec's Future
Revitalizing the Cities
Networking the Classroom
Indoor Air Pollution

NOVEMBER 1995
The Working Poor
The Jury System
Sex, Violence and the Media
Police Misconduct

DECEMBER 1995
Teens and Tobacco
Gene Therapy's Future
Global Water Shortages
Third-Party Prospects

JANUARY 1996
Emergency Medicine
Punishing Sex Offenders
Bilingual Education
Helping the Homeless

FEBRUARY 1996
Reforming the CIA
Campaign Finance Reform
Academic Politics
Getting Into College

MARCH 1996
The British Monarchy
Preventing Juvenile Crime
Tax Reform
Pursuing the Paranormal

APRIL 1996
Centennial Olympic Games
Managed Care
Protecting Endangered Species
New Military Culture

MAY 1996
Russia's Political Future
Marriage and Divorce
Year-Round Schools
Taiwan, China and the U.S.

JUNE 1996
Rethinking NAFTA
First Ladies
Teaching Values
Labor Movement's Future

JULY 1996
Recovered-Memory Debate
Native Americans' Future
Crackdown on Sexual Harassment
Attack on Public Schools

AUGUST 1996
Fighting Over Animal Rights
Privatizing Government Services
Child Labor and Sweatshops
Cleaning Up Hazardous Wastes

SEPTEMBER 1996
Gambling Under Attack
The States and Federalism
Civic Journalism
Reassessing Foreign Aid

OCTOBER 1996
Political Consultants
Insurance Fraud
Rethinking School Integration
Parental Rights

NOVEMBER 1996
Global Warming
Clashing Over Copyright
Consumer Debt
Governing Washington, D.C.

DECEMBER 1996
Welfare, Work and the States
The New Volunteerism
Implementing the Disabilities Act
America's Pampered Pets

JANUARY 1997
Combating Scientific Misconduct
Restructuring the Electric Industry
The New Immigrants
Chemical and Biological Weapons

FEBRUARY 1997
Assisting Refugees
Alternative Medicine's Next Phase
Independent Counsels
Feminism's Future

MARCH 1997
New Air Quality Standards
Alcohol Advertising
Civic Renewal
Educating Gifted Students

APRIL 1997
Declining Crime Rates
The FBI Under Fire
Gender Equity in Sports

Back issues are available for $5.00 (subscribers) or $10.00 (non-subscribers). Quantity discounts apply to orders over ten. To order, call Congressional Quarterly Customer Service at (202) 887-8621.

Binders are available for $18.00. To order call 1-800-638-1710. Please refer to stock number 648.

Future Topics

- ***The Stock Market***
- ***Cloning Controversy***
- ***Expanding NATO***

THE CQ Researcher

PUBLISHED BY CONGRESSIONAL QUARTERLY INC.

The Stock Market

How high is too high?

The U.S. stock market has climbed to record heights in the 1990s, driven by a prolonged economic expansion and explosive growth in mutual funds. The growing number of investors — more than 40 percent of U.S. households — are delighted. But the Federal Reserve Board is worried that stock prices have gone too high. Fed Chairman Alan Greenspan warned in December of "irrational exuberance" in the market, and the Federal Reserve raised interest rates in late March to try to cool the economy and ward off inflation. The move caused the markets to slide, but blue-chip stocks began climbing again in April. Now the markets are waiting to see whether the Fed will raise interest rates again.

INSIDE THIS ISSUE

CQ May 2, 1997 • Volume 7, No. 17 • Pages 385-408

Formerly Editorial Research Reports

COVER: THE TRADING FLOOR AT THE NEW YORK STOCK EXCHANGE

May 2, 1997
Volume 7, No. 17

EDITOR
Sandra Stencel

MANAGING EDITOR
Thomas J. Colin

ASSOCIATE EDITORS
Sarah M. Magner
Richard L. Worsnop

STAFF WRITERS
Charles S. Clark
Mary H. Cooper
Kenneth Jost
David Masci

EDITORIAL ASSISTANT
Vanessa E. Furlong

PUBLISHED BY
Congressional Quarterly Inc.

CHAIRMAN
Andrew Barnes

VICE CHAIRMAN
Andrew P. Corty

PRESIDENT AND PUBLISHER
Robert W. Merry

EXECUTIVE EDITOR
David Rapp

The CQ Researcher (ISSN 1056-2036). Formerly Editorial Research Reports. Published weekly (48 times per year, not printed Jan. 3, May 30, Aug. 29, Oct. 31) by Congressional Quarterly Inc., 1414 22nd St., N.W., Washington, D.C. 20037. Annual subscription rate for libraries, businesses and government is $340. Additional rates furnished upon request. Periodicals postage paid at Washington, D.C., and additional mailing offices. POSTMASTER: Send address changes to The CQ Researcher, 1414 22nd St., N.W., Washington, D.C. 20037.

The Stock Market

BY KENNETH JOST

THE ISSUES

Daniel Tully stands on the balcony overlooking the football-field-size trading floor of New York Stock Exchange. Wall Street has been in a slump, but Tully is upbeat: He got a 40 percent raise last year, earning more than $10 million. That's not all: To mark his retirement as chairman of Merrill Lynch, he gets to ring the Big Board's opening bell.

Surrounded by his wife, children and grandchildren, the white-haired Tully looks more like a small-town mayor than the head of Wall Street's biggest investment firm. With 15 seconds to go before the market opens at 9:30, Tully pushes a button to start the bells clanging. Traders turns away from computer screens and portable phones to give Tully a cheer. Then the bells stop, and amid much uncertainty, trading on April 14 begins.

The big worry is whether the record 6-1/2-year rise on the world's largest stock exchange is about to end. Since the Federal Reserve notched up interest rates on March 25, the market has fallen to a point where it is just 15 points away from its first so-called "correction" — a drop of 10 percent — since late 1990.

Tully, however, is still bullish. "I feel we're pretty close to the bottom of this particular correction," he tells a CNBC reporter.

Some of Tully's colleagues think otherwise. In fact, Merrill Lynch's chief market analyst, Richard McCabe, says, "You just don't correct six years of no decline . . . with a little drop of two months."

Until recently, predicting the market was largely an insider's game. But today, following the stock market is a national pastime. About 41

percent of all U.S. households now own shares in corporate America — compared with 32 percent in 1989 and only 1-1/2 percent when the market crashed in 1929. Stocks also account for a growing share of consumer wealth — about 40 percent today, compared with 26 percent in 1989. (*See chart, p. 392.*)

Many new investors are workers saving for retirement by using payroll deductions to buy stock-holding mutual funds. [1] "In the past, companies took the risk of investing in pension plans," says Michael Goldstein, a professor of corporate finance at the University of Colorado-Boulder. "Now we all are investing as individuals. We've tied our retirement to the stock market."

For these new stock market investors, the recent "bull market" has been a heady experience. The Dow Jones Industrial Average — an average of 30 so-called blue-chip stocks widely used as a stock market barometer — has more than doubled since the market began rising after the Persian Gulf War in 1990. (*See graph, p. 388.*) Even though the Dow has fallen from its record peak of 7,085 on March 11, the market has gone a record 78 months since its last 10 percent correction: The previous record was 37 months following the stock market's 1987 crash. [2]

Many market professionals warn, however, that the experience has been a bit too heady. The low-inflation economic expansion of the decade has been an exception to the typical pattern of business cycles, they say. The stock market, they caution, necessarily goes both up and down, and investors need to appreciate both the risks and the rewards of owning stock.

"You have people investing in mutual funds as though they are variable rate [certificates of deposit], as though they're guaranteed rates of return of anywhere from 6 percent to 25 percent," says James Stack, an investment adviser in Whitefish, Mont. "With those kinds of lofty expectations, it doesn't take much to upset the apple cart."

For the past five months, the country's most powerful economic regulator has added his voice to those cautionary sentiments. Alan Greenspan, chairman of the Federal Reserve System's Board of Governors, first hinted in December that he believed the stock market had reached unsustainable heights.

"How do we know when irrational exuberance has unduly escalated asset values, which then become subject to unexpected and prolonged contractions as they have in Japan over the past decade?" Greenspan asked in a speech to the American Enterprise Institute on Dec. 5.

The remark was buried in a scholarly discussion of central banks, but it sent shock waves to markets around the world. Then, in late February, Greenspan stiffened his warning. Appearing before the Senate Banking Committee on Feb. 25, Greenspan challenged the prediction by some market

Market's Record Climb Began in 1982

The Dow Jones Industrial Average — the widely cited index of 30 blue-chip industrial companies — climbed in the decade after World War II, fluctuated in the 1960s and '70s and then began its current record 15-year climb in 1982. Standard and Poor's broader index of 500 stocks (not shown) reflects a similar pattern.

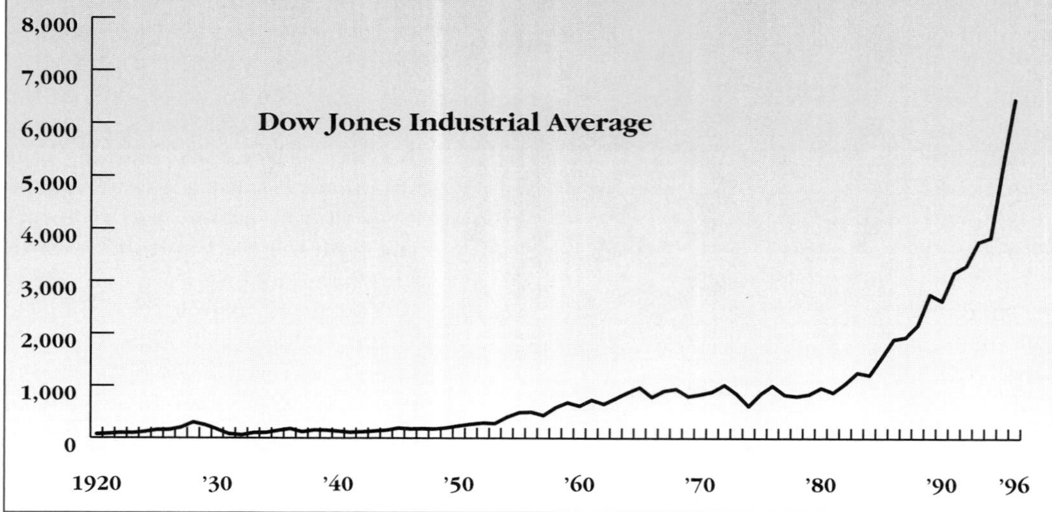

analysts that the country was entering a "new era" of low-risk investing.

"History is strewn with visions of such 'new eras' that in the end have proven to be a mirage," Greenspan said. "In short," he added, "history counsels caution."

Greenspan's remarks rankled many Wall Streeters. "We wish once in a while he'd keep his opinions to himself," Vincent Fazzi, a mutual fund trader, said in early March. [3] But Stack, who has been advising investors to shift from stocks to cash, welcomed Greenspan's warnings. "The longer you go without healthy corrections," he says, "the greater the risk in the next downturn."

The downturn appeared finally to have arrived after the Fed's major policy-making body — the Federal Open Market Committee — decided March 25 to raise its principal short-term interest rate by one-quarter of a percentage point. The action marked the first rise since 1994 in the Fed's "federal funds target rate" for overnight loans between banks. Many analysts expected the Fed to try to slow the economy a bit more with another rate hike at the open market committee's next scheduled meeting on May 20.

The March hike was widely blamed for the stock market's near 10 percent slide over the next three weeks. But then, just as Tully was being feted on Wall Street, the markets turned back up.

Analysts continue to disagree, however, about whether the bull market is nearing its end. "Bull markets are over when profits peak and are declining, when you have excess valuation and when you have an increase in inflation," says Richard Cripps, a market strategist at the Baltimore-based investment firm of Legg Mason. Without any of those factors, he says, "the fundamentals have not changed enough that you would say this bull market is over."

But Stack says rosy forecasts could themselves signal a coming downturn or bear market. "Bull markets peak when optimism is highest," Stack says. And he warns that new investors will be among those hit hardest by an eventual decline: "They don't have the profits [built up] to cushion the loss, and their expectations are most out of touch with reality."

Whatever direction stock prices take, the nation's stock markets are today widely regarded as efficient and well-regulated marketplaces that each day handle hundreds of millions of shares of stocks. (*See story, p. 390.*)

"We have the most successful securities markets in the world at this point," says Joel Seligman, a securities law expert and dean of the University of Arizona College of Law.

But abuses do occur, ranging from fraudulent stock sales and trading by corporate insiders to manipulative practices by stockbrokers and dealers. In one of the most dramatic instances of abuse, the National Association of Securities Dealers (NASD) agreed last summer to take steps to eliminate collusive pricing practices by dealers on its electronic marketplace, the Nasdaq stock market. (*See story, p. 396.*)

Some regulators and consumer groups want additional measures to protect investors, such as beefed up enforcement by the Securities and Exchange Commission (SEC). In addition, some lawmakers want the stock markets to stop pricing stocks fractionally, in eighths, and shift to decimals. They say the move will

What Goes Up Also Goes Down

Stocks have been on a roller coaster this year, according to major stock price indexes. The Dow Jones Industrial Average and the Standard & Poor's 500 both began falling in March amid speculation that the Federal Reserve Board would raise interest rates, continued to fall for three weeks after rates were raised on March 25 and then began climbing. The Nasdaq stock market index has been falling for most of the year.

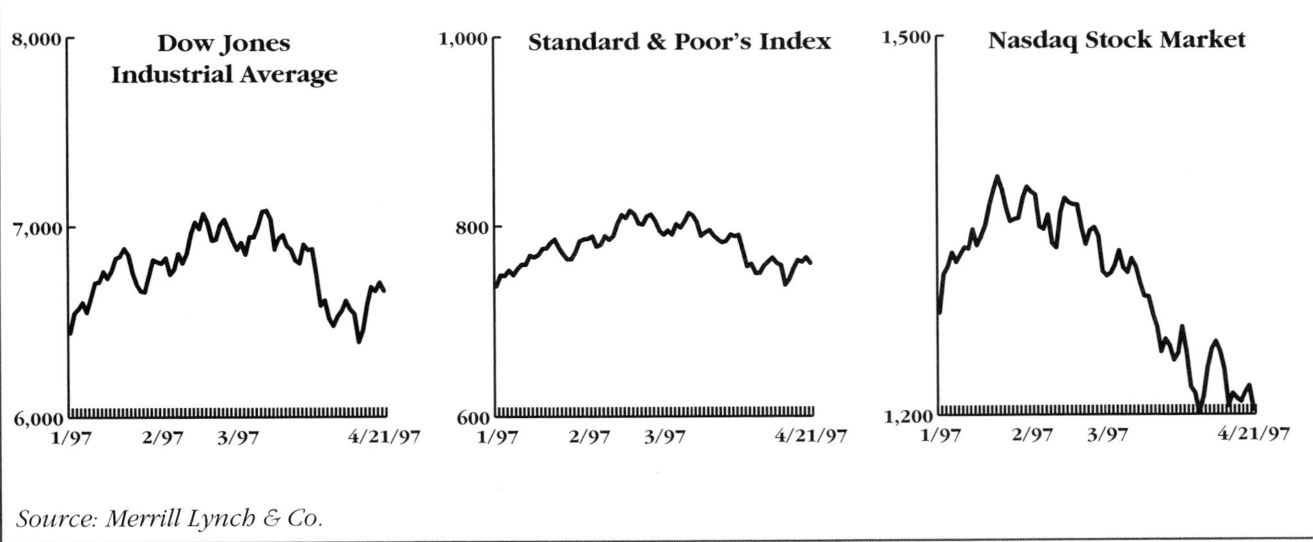

Source: Merrill Lynch & Co.

save investors as much as $1 billion or more annually. (*See story, p. 398.*)

The calls for tighter regulation collide, however, with the general laissez faire climate on Capitol Hill. In the past two years, the securities industry has won two important victories in Congress. In 1995, it succeeded in enacting, over President Clinton's veto, a measure to limit fraud suits by shareholders in federal court. [4] And last year, Congress overwhelmingly approved a measure to eliminate what securities firms called duplicative regulation by state and federal agencies. [5]

For now, however, regulatory debates are not a primary focus for policy-makers or investors. From Wall Street to Main Street, and from the financial capital to the nation's Capitol, everyone is closely monitoring the market and waiting to see what the Federal Reserve will do later this month. Meanwhile, these are some of the questions everyone is asking:

Are stock prices too high?

Billionaire investment guru Warren Buffet likes to give shareholders in his Berkshire Hathaway Co. an annual report laced with homespun assessments of the stock market. This year, Buffet opines, the market has risen so high that investors are likely overpaying for "virtually all stocks." [6]

Indeed, many experts and analysts have been warning that stock prices cannot be sustained. "Today's thrilling stock market ride depends on economic growth that is sufficient to lift profits, while the inflation rate is flat," financier Henry Kaufman wrote last November. "The ride will end either because growth will slow a lot more than optimistic estimates foretell or because inflation moves up." [7]

Other market-watchers, however, say that the favorable economic climate for the past decade justifies the high prices. The 1990s have seen the lowest inflation cycle since World War II and the strongest corporate earnings in modern history, according to Bruce Steinberg, chief economist at Merrill Lynch.

"Rational exuberance is the term for describing what happened," Steinberg says. "There were things to be exuberant about."

Bearish analysts note that stock prices are at historic highs according to a common measure: the ratio of stock prices to corporate earnings. Today, the price-earnings ratio for the 500 stocks in the widely used Standard and Poor's index is near its highest level since 1960. (*See chart, p. 391.*)

In addition, these bears note, stock dividend yields are relatively low compared with levels of the recent past. "Historically, a dividend yield below 3 percent was considered the danger zone for the S&P 500 index," Stack says. "Today, we're down under 1.9 percent. That means you could see the market drop by 35 percent

U.S. Stock Markets at a Glance

Shares of stock in U.S. corporations can be traded in a number of ways.

The United States has two major national auction stock exchanges — the New York Stock Exchange (NYSE) — and the American Stock Exchange (Amex) — and five regional exchanges. Trading among all the exchanges is possible because they are linked through the Intermarket Trading System (ITS), established under a 1975 federal law. (Stocks in major U.S. companies can also be traded on a number of foreign exchanges.)

In an auction exchange, a floor trader — known as a "specialist" — is designated for each individual stock listed on that exchange. The specialist maintains an electronic book of unfilled buy and sell orders from public investors and arranges trades by matching those orders at the best possible price for buyers and sellers. The specialist is also required to "maintain an orderly market" in the stock by buying when there are no willing buyers or selling when there are no willing sellers.

The New York exchange — also called the Big Board — is the world's largest stock market in dollar volume. Companies listed on the Big Board must have pretax earnings of at least $2.5 million and at least 1.1 million shares of publicly held stock with a minimum capitalization value of $40 million. The Amex, also in New York, has a lower minimum capitalization requirement: $4 million. Some stocks listed on the NYSE or Amex can also be traded on one or more of the regional exchanges.

The Nasdaq stock market — originally, an abbreviation for National Association of Securities Dealers Automated Quotation System — is an electronically interconnected market of independent dealers. For each listed company, there are a number of competing securities firms that "make a market" in its stock by posting "bid" and "asked" prices. Nasdaq has grown to become the largest U.S. stock market in number of shares traded and second largest after the NYSE in value of shares traded.

The regional exchanges have small trading volumes but contend that they offer competitive prices and lower transaction costs for trading in the NYSE-listed companies that they handle. Stocks in smaller and new companies may be bought from brokers "over the counter." Brokers obtain quotes on OTC stocks from prices published by dealers in daily "pink sheets" or on an electronic service, the "OTC Bulletin."

Name	Founded	Number of companies listed	Average 1997 daily trading volume	Average 1997 daily dollar volume
New York Stock Exchange	1792	2,917	514 million	$22 billion
Nasdaq Stock Market	1971	5,500	638.3 million	$17.5 billion
American Stock Exchange	1849	748	21.4 million	$387.7 million
Pacific Exchange	1882	517	13.5 million	$400 million
Chicago Stock Exchange	1882	288	19.7 million	$600 million
Cincinnati Stock Exchange [1]	1885	578	8.2 million	$389.8 million
Boston Stock Exchange	1834	182	7.1 million	$300 million
Philadelphia Stock Exchange	1790	300	5.8 million	$270 million

[1] The Cincinnati exchange, a floorless, electronic market, moved to Chicago in 1986.

just to bring the dividend yield back to where the level might be considered more normal."

Other analysts, however, say that yields and price-earnings ratios are less valid indicators of stock values today than in the past.

"Dividend yields are low, yes," the University of Colorado's Goldstein says. "But business schools have been turning out MBAs for years who have been telling companies that investors would rather have an increase in [a stock's] price than a dividend."

As for corporate earnings, Goldstein says changes in accounting procedures give more accurate earnings figures today than in the past. "If your earnings estimate is more accurate, [investors] are willing to pay a higher price" for the stock, he says.

Are Today's Stocks Overvalued?

One measure used to gauge stock value is the price-earnings ratio, which compares the price of a stock to the company's earnings. A high ratio indicates possible overvalue, a low ratio undervalue. The price-earnings ratio for the Standard & Poor's index of 500 stocks has been high throughout the 1990s.

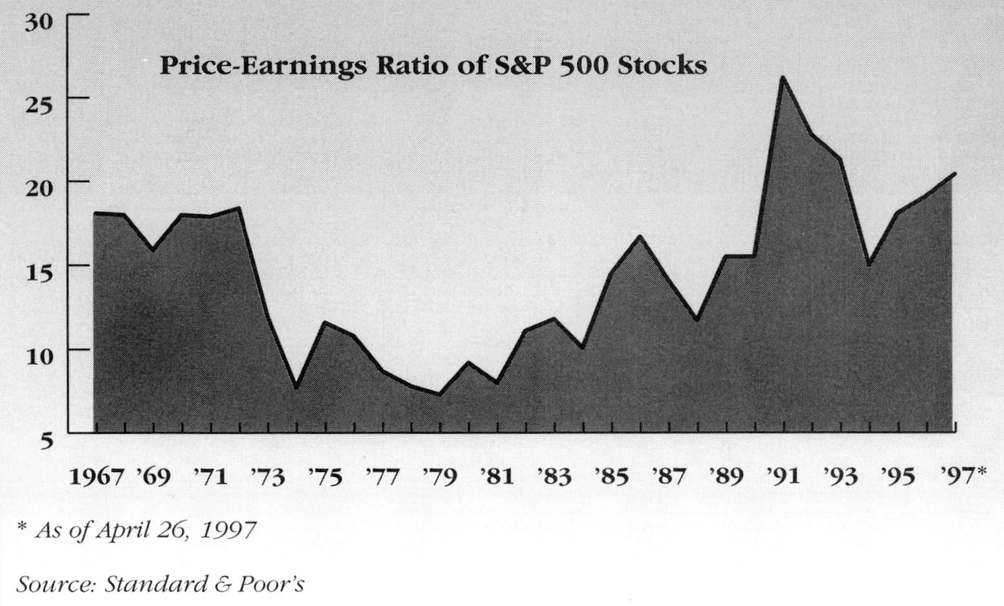

** As of April 26, 1997*

Source: Standard & Poor's

The debate over stock values continued even after the major market indexes fell nearly 10 percent following the interest rate hike in March. Abby Joseph Cohen, a managing director of the investment firm of Goldman Sachs & Co. and a prominent "bull," sticks to her predictions of a rising market despite the Fed's action. "We think that in a few months, the market will reach new highs," Cohen said in early April. "The fundamentals have not changed very much." [8]

But Merrill Lynch chief investment strategist Charles Clough warns investors to expect the market to head South, as they say on Wall Street. "We don't see a lot of opportunity in the U.S. market," Clough said a week after the Fed's action. "We see more risks than rewards." [9]

For the nation's growing number of investors — many of them newcomers to the stock market — the disagreements among experts may seem as unsettling as the market fluctuations themselves. For them, Goldstein and others emphasize that historically, stocks have yielded higher returns over time than either of the "safer" investments, bonds or cash.

"The little dips and turns, even if they're a 20 percent dip, are never good news," Goldstein says. "But over time, you'll make it up."

Has the Federal Reserve overreacted by trying to drive stock prices down?

In his 10 years as Federal Reserve chairman, Greenspan has gained power perhaps unmatched by any previous head of the nation's central bank. [10] When he testifies on Capitol Hill, the former adviser to two Republican presidents is typically accorded deferential treatment.

In March, however, just after Greenspan's blunt warning about stock prices, he fielded some unusually tough questioning, from a Republican lawmaker no less, Rep. Jim Bunning of Kentucky. "My question to you," Bunning asked during a House Budget Committee hearing, "is why have you, on two occasions, taken to jawboning the U.S. stock market and the U.S. bond market with your comments to affect a free and open market?" [11]

Greenspan, who is described by his biographer as a one-time libertarian, insisted he had no intention to affect stock market prices — and no power to do so either. "These are very thick, elaborate, international markets which are driven by decisions of mil-

Stock Ownership on the Rise

The percentage of U.S. families that own stocks increased by more than 30 percent from 1989 to 1995, according to the Federal Reserve Board. Moreover, the portion of the average family's financial assets represented by stocks increased to more than 40 percent during the same period.

	Families with stock holdings			Median value, among families with holdings (1995 dollars)			Share of family's financial assets in stocks		
	1989	**1992**	**1995**	**1989**	**1992**	**1995**	**1989**	**1992**	**1995**
All families	31.7%	37.2%	41.1%	$10,400	$11,500	$13,500	26.3%	34.4%	40.4%
Income (1995 dollars)									
Less than $10,000	2.3	6.9	6.0	*	5.9	4.0	10.0	15.2	21.1
$10,000-$24,999	13.1	19.4	25.3	9.2	4.3	5.0	10.0	18.6	21.6
$25,000-$49,999	33.1	41.6	47.7	5.5	7.6	8.0	20.3	25.4	33.0
$50,000-$99,999	54.0	64.1	66.7	10.4	14.6	21.3	25.6	35.1	39.9
$100,000 and more	79.7	79.1	83.9	47.9	74.6	90.8	31.4	40.2	47.6

* *Sample size too small to provide representative data.*

Source: Federal Reserve Bulletin, *January 1997*

lions of people," Greenspan told Bunning. "Nobody can affect them in a fundamental way." [12]

Despite his protestations, many Wall Street-watchers believe the Fed chairman was trying to drive stock prices down with his "irrational exuberance" speech in December and his Senate Banking Committee testimony in February. And clearly, these analysts agree, the Fed raised interest rates in late March knowing a market slide was likely.

Some investment analysts welcome the Fed's action. "The Federal Reserve is trying to let some of the exuberant air out of the Wall Street bubble without popping it or risking an economic recession," Stack says.

Other analysts, however, accept the Fed's move begrudgingly. Cohen likens it to a "flu shot" — unpleasant but necessary. Bernard Schaeffer, president of the Investment Research Institute, in Cincinnati, says the Fed "overreacted" to signs of an overheated economy, but he predicts the move will not chill the market much.

"Taking a quarter-point step is not going to kill the economy," Schaeffer says. Even another quarter-point rise in May only would have minimal effects, he continues. "There's room for the Fed doing not quite the right thing."

In fact, the market did fall for three weeks after the Fed's interest rate move. "Alan Greenspan has seen happen what he probably wanted to happen," analyst Cripps says. The slide hit bottom on April 11, as investors responded to Labor Department statistics showing signs of future inflation — which they saw as likely to lead to another interest hike in May.

For his part, economist Steinberg says Greenspan's major concern about the stock market was to make sure that any move away from its peak levels was gradual rather than abrupt. He believes Greenspan is especially worried about a repeat of the 1987 crash, when the stock market fell more than 20 percent in a single day, and the Fed felt obliged to expand credit the next day in order to stabilize the market.

"What he definitely didn't want to see was the market go down 15-20 percent in one day," Steinberg says, "because then the Fed would have to do what it had to in 1987, whatever its inflationary consequences."

The Fed's interest rate move provoked grumbling on Wall Street and drew criticism in Washington from a handful of liberal Democrats and pro-growth conservative Republicans: They found the signs of inflation too weak to justify the action. Sympathetic Fed-watchers regard the criticisms as inevitable.

Interest rate moves "always have some political consequences," says John Coffee, a professor of corporate and securities law at Columbia University. But, Coffee adds: "Almost everyone recognizes that the Fed has to play some moderating function so that we don't go into some roller coaster boom-and-bust cycle."

Are more regulations needed to protect investors or prevent a market panic?

The 1929 crash spawned a web of federal laws and regulations and stock exchange rules designed to protect investors from fraud and other market abuses. The century's second great crash, in 1987, prompted several smaller, additional steps aimed at preventing panic in the stock markets.

Nowadays, efforts to protect investors are generally applauded. "Investors today are pretty safe," says Robert Sobel, a business historian at Hofstra University, in Hempstead, N.Y.

"There have been constant increases in protection over the years," agrees James Cloonan, president of the American Association of Individual Investors.

Not surprisingly, stock market officials voice confidence in the protections accorded investors. "The U.S. securities market is the most liquid, efficient and well-regulated securities market in the world," New York Stock Exchange President William R. Johnston says.

The Nasdaq market, meanwhile, is currently implementing a far-reaching agreement with the SEC to clean up abuses. "We're light-years ahead of where we were 10 years ago," says Richard Ketchum, chief operating officer of the NASD, Nasdaq's parent organization.

Some consumer groups, however, are less satisfied with current regulations and enforcement. "We're more exposed to the market than we've ever been before," says Barbara Roper, director of investor protection for the Consumer Federation of America. "There are reams of evidence showing that the vast majority of Americans don't have even the basic knowledge they need to make sound investment decisions. They're very vulnerable to fraud, and to making bad choices."

Headlines in the press frequently attest to the impact of laws passed in the New Deal-era to protect investors. The SEC has concentrated in the past two decades on illegal insider trading — the buying or selling of stock by corporate insiders based on financial information that has not been publicly disclosed. Self-regulatory organizations such as Nasdaq and the New York exchange discipline brokers and dealers for account "churning," or excessive trading on a customer's account to earn more commissions; or for violating "suitability" rules designed to protect small investors from making inappropriate investments.

With the growing number of Americans invested in stocks, Roper says the SEC's powers and resources are inadequate. "The markets have boomed, and as a result their workload boomed, but their budget was kept essentially flat through most of the 1980s," Roper says. The agency's budget nearly doubled from 1987-1995 but has been flat in succeeding years.

The 1987 crash disclosed a different danger in the country's securities markets: the risk of simply being overwhelmed by the combined effects of technological advances and sophisticated market strategies. In the 1980s, professional traders developed computer programs to capitalize on differences between stock prices and the prices for so-called stock index futures — contracts specifying the right to buy or sell a specified package of stocks at a specified price at a given date.

"Program trading," as it is known, caused volatile price swings in stock prices. It was widely blamed for "Black Monday" — Oct. 19, 1987 — when the Dow average dropped 508 points, or 22.6 percent of its value. The next day, the Federal Reserve took the dramatic step of promising expanded credit for banks to shore up brokerage houses' strained capital reserves.

Goldstein credits the Fed for "managing the 1987 crash" so as to minimize its impact. "They told banks that they would supply credit purchasing power," Goldstein says. "No one walked around worrying that Merrill Lynch was going to go bankrupt."

Later, the SEC and the stock markets adopted rules aimed at preventing a sharp market swing from triggering an investor panic. One rule — a so-called circuit breaker — calls for a one-hour halt in trading if the Dow falls 350 points and two hours if the average falls 550 points.

Thus far, the circuit-breaker has never been triggered, but it is nonetheless credited with helping to keep markets relatively calm. "It seems to have reduced investor anxiety," says the University of Arizona's Seligman.

The New York exchange adopted a separate rules change after the 1987 crash to retard wild price swings. The so-called "collar" limits program trading whenever the Dow industrial average rises or falls 50 points in a given day.

Both the circuit-breaker and the 50-point collar go against the basic idea of maintaining an open market even during price swings. The circuit-breaker was almost triggered in March 1996 when the Dow fell 218 points; as a result, the SEC pressured the New York exchange to raise the trigger from the original 250 points to 350 points.

The Big Board is also being pressured to raise the 50-point collar, which was rarely triggered when introduced in 1990 but was set off more than 100 times during 1996. The Chicago Mercantile Exchange, the primary market for stock index futures, say the collar hurts trading. But the New York exchange, reflecting the insurance it offers to its traders against losses when prices plummet, is resisting. [13]

For investors, the major question left from the 1987 crash is whether another sudden price swing could be caused by technological or other factors besides general economic conditions. The New York exchange has dealt with one of the problems identified in the 1987 crash by dramatically expanding trading capacity: It can now process 2.5 billion shares a day, five times the current average daily volume.

New York exchange officials also say that the collar and circuit-breaker have helped smooth price swings. They note, for example, that the market declined 500 points during 1990, but the fall was gradual and did not create the turmoil seen during the one-day crash in 1987.

Still, experts agree that a dramatic price drop can never completely be prevented. "If there really was a general panic, I don't think the rules on program trading would be more than a modest barrier," says Howard Kramer, senior associate director for market regulation at the SEC.

Experts also caution that neither legal regulations nor favorable market conditions should lull investors into thinking that stocks are risk-free.

Investors "have a market that's fairly well-regulated in terms of fairness," says Columbia's Coffee. "But a market that's gone up is a market that is going someday to experience a correction." ■

BACKGROUND

Booms and Busts

The country's first stock exchange was founded in Philadelphia, in 1790, but New York's stock markets began their rise to pre-eminence shortly thereafter. The New York exchange traces its history to a 1792 agreement by traders in federal bonds and New York bank stocks to operate jointly, with a minimum commission of one-quarter of 1 percent on trades. The dealers held their auctions under a buttonwood tree in good weather and inside when it rained. Later, they built a coffeehouse as their headquarters at the corner of Wall and Water streets — now the heart of New York's financial district. [14]

By 1817, the stock traders had adopted a formal name: the New York Stock and Exchange Board, shortened during the Civil War to the New York Stock Exchange. Brokers who were not members operated precariously on its periphery. Since they conducted their trades on the streets, the exchange dealers dubbed them "curbstone brokers." Eventually, they adopted the appellation themselves: the New York Curbstone Agency. They continued trading out of doors until 1921, when they began operating indoors; in 1953, they adopted the current name, the American Stock Exchange. [15]

Through the 19th century, these exchanges dealt primarily in bonds rather than stocks, and their principal customers were banks rather than individuals. They helped finance the construction of the railroads, the North's victory over the South in the Civil War and the country's accelerating industrialization.

But the exchanges also operated with virtually no oversight. The corporations that issued securities were not required to disclose any financial information until 1895, when the New York Stock Exchange itself decided that listed companies should file annual reports. The exchange itself was regulated neither by the federal government nor New York state.

With no assurance of accurate, timely information, investors had few protections against the ordinary risks of the marketplace, much less against the many techniques of manipulation and fraud that flourished in the age of robber barons. The stock exchanges operated much like private clubs, and big banks — such as J.P. Morgan and Co. — used inside information to buy the most valuable securities. Speculative manias were recurrent and resulted in periodic "panics" touched off by various corporate calamities, usually compounded by adverse economic conditions.

One such panic — in 1907 — led to the federal government's first legislated effort to impose discipline on the country's financial system. J.P. Morgan himself stepped in to stave off financial disaster when stock prices began to plummet in October, personally commanding New York's leading bankers to lend the stock exchange $27 million to prop up prices. In Washington, policy-makers decided the country's financial system should not be so dependent on one individual. Six years later, Congress created the Federal Reserve System, the country's central bank.

The most wrenching of the stock market panics, of course, was the Great Crash of 1929. What began as a slide in September turned into panic when the Dow industrial average fell nearly 13 percent on Oct. 28 and another 12 percent the next day, "Black Tuesday." All told, stocks listed on the New York Stock Exchange lost $30 billion out of $80 billion in value before prices stopped falling in mid-November. The bear market was to last, however, for nearly another three years. [16]

The crash came at the end of a decade of investor euphoria and speculative frenzy, and market mania was surely one of the causes. But the Federal Reserve itself has also been blamed. In a recent op-ed article, Wayne Angell, a former Federal Reserve governor and now chief economist at the investment firm of Bear Stearns, says the Fed adopted a "misguided monetary policy" of contracting the money supply even

Continued on p. 397

Chronology

1700s-1800s

Stock markets develop from rudimentary auction houses and curbstone bazaars into more formal exchanges.

1790
The first stock exchange in the U.S. is organized in Philadelphia.

1817
New York Stock and Exchange Board is adopted as the name of Wall Street stock traders on lower Manhattan; name is changed to New York Stock Exchange in 1863.

1895
New York Stock Exchange requires listed companies to file annual financial reports.

1900-1930

The stock market helps finance America's growth into an industrial superpower but crashes dramatically in 1929.

1921
New York's curbstone brokers move inside and adopt the name American Stock Exchange.

Oct. 29, 1929
Dow Jones Industrial Average drops 30 points or nearly 12 percent on "Black Tuesday," following a 38-point drop the day before. The crash kicks off a 34-month-long bear market.

1930s-1940s

Federal regulation of stock markets is established.

May 27, 1933
Securities Act of 1933 is signed into law, requiring detailed financial disclosure by companies issuing stock.

June 6, 1934
Passage of Securities Exchange Act creates Securities and Exchange Commission to oversee operation of exchanges and requires ongoing financial disclosures by companies.

1950s-1970s

Americans invest heavily in the stock market.

Jan. 25, 1954
New York Stock Exchange launches "Monthly Investment Plan" for average Americans.

1970s

The stock market falls or stays flat during double-digit inflation.

Feb. 8, 1971
National Association of Securities Dealers begins operating the "automated" Nasdaq stock market.

Feb. 11, 1971
Securities and Exchange Commission orders New York Stock Exchange to eliminate fixed commissions on stock transactions over $500,000. Four years later, the exchange agrees to eliminate fixed fees altogether.

Nov. 14, 1972
Dow Jones Industrial Average closes above 1,000 for first time.

1980s

The stock market rises for much of the decade — interrupted dramatically by the 1987 crash.

Oct. 19, 1987
In the stock market's worst single-day loss, the Dow falls 508 points, or 22.6 percent.

1990s

Stock prices soar in record-setting, six-year bull market.

1995
The Dow passes 4,000 on Feb. 23 and 5,000 on Nov. 21 — the only year in which it breaks two 1,000-point milestones.

Dec. 5, 1996
Federal Reserve Chairman Alan Greenspan warns of "irrational exuberance" by investors.

Feb. 13, 1997
Dow closes above 7,000 for the first time in history.

Feb. 26, 1997
Dow drops 55 points after Greenspan tells Senate Banking Committee that the "sharp rise in equity prices" raises "questions of sustainability."

March 25, 1997
The Federal Reserve's Open Market Committee raises its federal funds target rate; Dow falls 514 points over the next three weeks before rebounding.

May 20, 1997
Federal Reserve is scheduled to meet; many observers predict another rate hike to slow the economy a bit more.

Nasdaq Promises to End Trading Abuses

The Nasdaq stock market grew into the country's second-largest equity trading center under the slogan "the stock market for tomorrow — today." But these days, the Nasdaq — short for National Association of Securities Dealers Automated Quotation System — is struggling with the short-term task of regaining public confidence after three years of controversy.

Investigations by the Justice Department and the Securities and Exchange Commission (SEC) documented evidence of price fixing and trading abuses by dealers, as well as lax supervision by the self-regulatory organization the National Association of Securities Dealers (NASD). To stem the controversies, the NASD and many of the biggest Nasdaq dealers agreed last summer to precedent-setting settlements.

The NASD itself, which polices the nation's 5,400 securities firms and 513,000 registered brokers and dealers, agreed to improve oversight of the Nasdaq stock market by separating its regulatory functions from its marketing functions. It also agreed to provide a newly created regulatory arm with an additional $100 million over the next five years to beef up enforcement.

Some two dozen dealers — including such major brokerage houses as Merrill Lynch and Goldman Sachs — settled a two-year price-fixing probe by the Justice Department by agreeing to randomly tape traders' telephone calls in order to prevent trading abuses. In announcing the settlement last July 17, Attorney General Janet Reno said the investigation had uncovered "substantial evidence of coercion and misconduct" by dealers aimed at keeping price spreads and thus their profits high.

The dual investigations were launched after a study raising suspicions of Nasdaq price-fixing was publicized in May 1994. [1] The study — by William Christie of the Owen Graduate School of Management at Vanderbilt University and Paul Schultz of Ohio State University's Max Fisher College of Business — compared the Nasdaq's price competitiveness with the New York Stock Exchange.

They found a statistically improbable pattern: Prices on Nasdaq were typically quoted in even eighths, hardly ever in odd eighths. In effect, as Christie explains today, the pattern "ensured a minimum price spread of 25 cents."

Christie and Schultz said the only plausible explanation for the pattern appeared to be "tacit collusion" by Nasdaq dealers. The article stirred immediate controversy when the professors issued a press release about their findings prior to actual publication. News stories appeared in May 1994, and almost immediately prices in major Nasdaq stocks began to be quoted in odd eighths — prompting Christie, Schultz and a third colleague to conclude in a new article that the change reinforced the inference of price-fixing. [2]

The study triggered an investigation by the Justice Department's Antitrust Division and also fed into the SEC's ongoing oversight of the NASD. Over the next two years, both investigations turned up solid evidence that traders had a widespread practice of manipulating prices to the disadvantage of investors. "Investors paid too much, and received too little, when they bought and sold stock on Nasdaq," SEC Chairman Arthur Levitt Jr. said in announcing the settlement last August.

For Nasdaq, the controversy came after two decades of relatively steady growth from its founding in 1971 as an interconnected quotation system for the over-the-counter (OTC) securities market. By permitting simultaneous, nationwide display of quoted prices in a given security, the new system immediately enhanced competition and helped narrow spreads. One study found the spread on a sample of OTC stocks fell to about 40 cents from 48 cents from 1970-1972. [3]

Over time, Nasdaq evolved into a dealer stock market with more than 5,000 listed companies and a daily volume that surpassed the New York Stock Exchange. It was promoted as the market for emerging companies, especially high-technology companies like Microsoft or Intel. And Nasdaq officials maintained that their market, with multiple dealers in individual stocks, provided more competitive prices than the New York exchange with its system of designating a single market-maker ("specialist") in a given stock.

The government investigations cast a pall over those claims. The NASD began responding even while the probes were being conducted. In September 1995, an NASD commission headed by former Sen. Warren Rudman, R-N.H., recommended separating the organization's broker-regulation functions from its market operation functions. As recommended, NASD's regulatory arm was created in January 1996, headed by Mary L. Schapiro, a former SEC commissioner who also served as chair of the Commodity Futures Trading Commission.

The negative publicity climaxed last summer with the Justice and SEC settlements. The Justice settlement covered 24 firms that accounted for 70 percent of Nasdaq trading. It required the firms to hire "antitrust compliance officers" to randomly tape and listen to traders' telephone calls and report possible violations to the Justice Department.

Today, NASD officials acknowledge responsibility for the abuses and promise they will not recur. "The SEC has properly chastised us," says Richard Ketchum, NASD president and chief operating officer. "It will never happen again."

---

[1] William G. Christie and Paul H. Schultz, "Why Do NASDAQ Market Makers Avoid Odd-Eighth Quotes," *Journal of Finance*, December 1994, pp. 1813-1840.

[2] See William G. Christie, Jeffrey H. Harris and Paul H. Schultz, "Why Did NASDAQ Market Makers Stop Avoiding Odd Eighth Quotes," *Journal of Finance*, December 1994, pp. 1841-1860.

[3] See Joel Seligman, *The Transformation of Wall Street: A History of the Securities and Exchange Commission and Modern Corporate Finance* (1982), pp. 490-497.

though the economy was already slowing down.[17]

From an opposite political perspective, liberal Harvard economist John Kenneth Galbraith also scorns the Fed's performance. In his history of the crash, Galbraith depicts the Fed as sitting by idly in the face of wild market speculation — failing, for example, to ask Congress to limit the purchase of stock on margin (bought using credit), or even to denounce the speculation in any but the weakest terms.[18]

Policing the 'Street'

The role of the stock market crash in the Great Depression has been and remains a subject of great debate. With so few stock owners at that time, many people both then and now have minimized the crash's impact on the overall economy. But the crash at least added to the economic crisis by reducing wealth and disposable income and sapping public confidence.

Whatever its impact on the Depression, the crash undoubtedly spurred Congress, at the start of the New Deal, to regulate the stock market. The two cornerstones of the federal regulatory system — the Securities Act of 1933 and the Securities Exchange Act of 1934 — imposed pervasive disclosure requirements on issuers of securities and required the stock exchanges to adopt regulations governing their members. In addition, the Glass-Steagall Act forced banks to give up their investment affiliates. Wall Street was — as Seligman writes — "fundamentally transformed."[19]

The Securities Act replaced Wall Street's buyer-beware philosophy with a new premise: that disclosure was needed to protect investors. Companies had to disclose detailed financial records as well as information about their business, need for capital and officers. The Federal Trade Commission — later, the SEC — could block the sale of any security if the statement were inaccurate or incomplete, and corporate officers or directors could be held civilly liable.

A year later, the Securities Exchange Act gave the new SEC ongoing oversight over the markets. Companies that issued securities were required under the act to file annual and quarterly reports with the SEC. The stock exchanges themselves had to adopt rules subject to SEC approval.

The business community opposed both bills and accused the patrician President Franklin D. Roosevelt of being a "traitor to his class." Six decades later, however, the securities industry has largely come to terms with the regulatory regime. Indeed, many observers credit the legal protections, along with post-World War II prosperity, with helping draw increasing numbers of Americans into the stock market.

The growth in the number of investors, along with the rise of large institutional investors such as pension funds, transformed Wall Street a second time.

In the 1950s, the stock market began becoming less a private club and more like a consumer-oriented industry. The trend can be dated from 1954, when the president of the New York Stock Exchange, Keith Funston, unveiled his "Monthly Investment Plan," aimed at getting "Joe Public" to buy at least $40 worth of stock every three months. Despite skepticism from many brokers, the plan attracted many new investors.[20]

Meanwhile, the postwar boom in mutual funds was also beginning. As of 1940, there were fewer than 80 funds with about $500 million in assets; by 1960, the number of funds had tripled and assets reached $50 billion.

The growth of mutual funds along with the growing role of institutional investors helped introduce a measure of competition into the investment industry. One pivotal issue was the industry's insistence on its 170-year old tradition of fixed commission rates.[21] But in the new world of large-volume transactions executed for mutual funds or institutional investors, fixed commission rates premised on small-volume sales for individual investors were clearly unjustifiable.

The New York Stock Exchange, however, resisted pressure from the SEC and the Justice Department through the late 1960s to permit volume discounts or negotiated rates. Finally, the SEC itself acted, forcing the exchanges to eliminate fixed rates first for large trades in 1971, and then altogether in 1975.

The Crash of '87

The Dow industrial average closed above 1,000 for the first time ever on Nov. 14, 1972. It stood at around the same level a decade later when the country began climbing out of the 1982 recession. Since then, the Dow has increased sixfold, and other stock price measures have similarly risen as the market enjoyed an unprecedented 15-year climb with only a few interruptions.

The most dramatic of those interruptions, however, shook Wall Street to its very foundations.[22] On Oct. 19, 1987 — "Black Monday" — the New York Stock Exchange suffered a virtual meltdown. The Dow's 508-point plunge — representing 22.6 percent of its value — was the exchange's worst single-day trading loss ever, on a then-record volume of more than 604 million shares.

Rumors swirled that the market might temporarily shut down for the first time since before World War I.

Lawmakers Urge Markets to Get Rid of Fractions

Investors who read the daily stock tables had better know their fractions. Stock prices in the United States — but nowhere else in the world — are quoted in eighths, a tradition dating to the 18th century, when Spanish gold was divided into "pieces of eight."

Now, say several members of Congress, it's time for a change — to the 20th century. Backed by institutional investors, academic experts and at least one member of the Securities and Exchange Commission (SEC), the bipartisan group wants to require U.S. stock markets to move to decimals in order to reduce both confusion and costs for investors.

Fractional stock pricing "prevents competition from bringing better stock prices to investors," says Rep. Michael G. Oxley, an Ohio Republican who chairs the House Commerce Subcommittee on Finance and is the prime sponsor of a bill aimed at introducing decimals into U.S. stock markets.

But the move is being strongly opposed by the New York Stock Exchange. Exchange officials and member firms say the change is unnecessary and costly and would benefit professional traders rather than the investing public.

"We believe there is no real evidence that decimal trading will benefit investors," New York Stock Exchange President William R. Johnston testified before an April 16 hearing of the Subcommittee on Finance.

Proponents say decimal pricing would bring U.S. stock markets into line with other monetary transactions in this country and with markets in the rest of the world. More important, they say, the change would lower the cost of investing by ultimately reducing stock dealers' "spread" on trading — the difference between the price bid for a stock and the price asked.

The spread determines the dealer's income. When one investor offers stock for $20 a share and another offers to buy for $20-1/4, the dealer makes 25 cents per share on the trade. Currently, the New York Stock Exchange requires that the difference between the bid and ask prices — the "tick" — be at least one-eighth.

Proponents of decimalization say the minimum tick size is an anti-competitive device that benefits traders and hurts investors. The change, SEC Commissioner Steven Wallman told an April 10 subcommittee hearing, will "enhance competition among markets" and "lead to more efficient pricing of securities."

Opponents of decimalization, however, say the effects of the change would not be as simple as the proponents claim. A reduction in the minimum tick size, they say, would actually help professional traders by making it easier for them to "step in front of" a public investor.

In the above example, a dealer could raise the $20 bid to $20-1/8. That would net the selling investor more money, but the dealer could suffer a loss if it could not later sell the stock for at least $20-1/8. If the minimum tick size were reduced, however, the dealer could raise the bid by a nickel, for example. The seller would realize only a negligible price improvement, and the dealer would be taking only a slight risk.

"Exchange markets protect investors from this front-running strategy through their minimum price increment rules," Lawrence Harris, a professor of business at the University of Southern California, told the lawmakers on April 16. "Any trader who wants to go before another trader must offer a non-trivial improvement in price. This is not only good economics; it is also fair."

In fact, Oxley's bill — cosponsored by, among others, Rep. Edward J. Markey, D-Mass., a longtime supporter of the change — would not mandate any change in minimum tick sizes. The bill would only require the SEC to adopt a rule, within one year of enactment, to eliminate any barriers to the use of decimals on U.S. stock markets. But supporters of the legislation expect that competition between markets would inevitably result in lower spreads. They note that both the American Stock Exchange and the Nasdaq stock market already allow trading in smaller increments of sixteenths — or "teenths."

The New York exchange was virtually alone in its opposition to decimalization during the two days of hearings. Johnston's opposition was echoed by a representative from the association of exchange specialists, the trading firms that serve as "market-makers" for stocks on the New York exchange. Harris, who acknowledged financial support for his research from the New York exchange, was the only academic to testify in opposition. But several lawmakers voiced skepticism about the change, including two New Yorkers — Republican Rick Lazio and Democrat Thomas Manton.

For their part, officials from the American and Pacific stock exchanges said they could support or accept a change to decimals, though Amex President Thomas F. Ryan Jr. opposed a congressional mandate. A representative from the Nasdaq stock market called for a study of decimalization. Stock prices are still quoted in eighths on the Nasdaq, but traded in smaller price increments.

Meanwhile, at least one U.S. newspaper is not waiting for the markets to act. The *San Francisco Chronicle* began reporting stock quotes in decimals instead of fractions last November. Business Editor Lois Kazakoff acknowledged to the committee that the quotes are less accurate because space constraints force the newspaper to round fractions to two places: one-eighth becomes 13 cents instead of 12.5 cents.

But Kazakoff also said most readers appeared to welcome the move. Before the change was adopted, about 1,650 readers answered a poll asking whether they preferred fractions or decimals. Kazakoff said 62 percent of those responding "wanted to see prices listed in the plain terms of everyday life: dollars and cents."

In fact, the market stayed open, but only the Federal Reserve's dramatic intervention the next day prevented a "liquidity crisis" by making sure that banks could provide the credit needed for brokers and exchange specialists to keep trading going.

Familiar factors could be cited in partial explanation of the sell-off. The market was said to be due for a correction after a five-year climb, especially in the face of bad economic news: the federal budget deficit, the trade deficit, rising interest rates and low consumer confidence. In addition, news of a proposal in Congress to eliminate a tax benefit for corporate mergers had sent shivers through the Street the previous week, triggering a 235-point collapse in the Dow over four days.

But many experts also saw another cause: the rise of "program trading," the computer-driven trading strategies that sought to capture profits with little or no risk by taking advantage of price differentials between the stock market and the options and stock index futures markets. As *The Wall Street Journal's* Tim Metz has noted, brokerage firms loved program trading, but the sudden waves of programmed buy or sell orders could produce wide swings in stock prices. [23]

Within the previous year, program trading had twice been blamed for wild swings in the Dow: an 86-point drop on Sept. 11, 1986, and an 115-point plunge within an hour on Jan. 23, 1987. But New York exchange President John J. Phelan Jr. had failed to win support for any controls on the practice.

The crash disclosed serious weaknesses in the market system and prompted a raft of studies aimed at remedying them. The most sweeping recommendations were not adopted — notably, the proposed consolidation of the stock market and the Chicago-based futures markets. But the SEC sought to limit the impact of program trading by adopting the circuit-breaker, and the stock exchanges worked to expand trading capacity and improve communication between the Chicago and New York markets.

With a decade's perspective, the crash is remembered today as far less harrowing than it appeared at the time. The market began a rebound the very next day and regained about half of the loss by year's end.

"If you bought stocks on Jan. 1, 1987, and sold them on Dec. 31, 1987, you made money," says Goldstein of the University of Colorado. The crash "was a Wall Street crisis. It wasn't a Main Street crisis."

The Soaring '90s

The 1990s have been a joy for investors. Driven by a six-year economic expansion and explosive growth in mutual funds, the market obliterated previous price and trading records. At the Federal Reserve, however, the climb was unnerving evidence of speculative excesses that could trigger inflation and threaten, instead of promote, economic growth.

As the Dow reached record heights at the end of 1993, Chairman Greenspan was among those worried about the rapid climb. To slow things down, the Fed began raising interest rates in February 1994 — boosting the federal funds target rate from 3 percent to 6 percent in a series of hikes over the span of a year.

At the time, Greenspan acknowledged wanting to temper the stock market's enthusiasm. Investors had been "lured by consistently high returns in capital markets," he told the Senate Banking Committee on May 27, but "some" of them "perhaps did not fully appreciate the exposure of their new investments to the usual fluctuations in bond and stock prices." [24]

The market responded as Greenspan hoped. It fell with the first of the rate hikes, stabilized, then fell again and stayed flat for the rest of the year. The Dow's 1994 year-end close of 3,834 was only 80 points — or 2.1 percent — above the 1993 close.

When Greenspan told Congress in February 1995 that the Fed was through raising interest rates for the time being, the market responded again, this time with a renewed and accelerated climb. It rose 30 points that day to break the 4,000-point barrier for the first time, pushed past 5,000 later that year and then broke the 6,000-point record last October. [25]

By then, Greenspan was again worried, but not yet talking. "The watchword among Fed officials," *The Wall Street Journal* noted on Nov. 25, "is: Don't use the words 'stock' and 'market' in the same sentence. No one wants the blame for a crash." [26]

Just 10 days later, however, Greenspan delivered his "irrational exuberance" warning. The late-night address jolted the Tokyo stock market as it opened, and traders began selling stocks in anticipation of a U.S. interest rate hike. The sell-off spread to markets in Sydney and London and reached New York at daybreak. The Dow dropped 145 points in its first half-hour. But the dive was halted by the release of monthly unemployment figures showing a rise in the jobless rate that, presumably, would deter the Fed from raising interest rates.

The market languished through December but began climbing in January. By Feb. 13, the Dow industrials had risen nearly 575 points to top 7,000 for the first time. Greenspan responded with his more explicit warning about stock prices to the Senate Banking Committee on Feb. 25. Over the next week, the Dow dropped 185 points, prompting Greenspan to temper his remarks in another congressional appearance March 5. "We don't view monetary policy as a tool . . . to prick the stock market bubble or something like that," he told the House Banking Committee.

Meanwhile, the Fed was conducting a behind-the-scenes debate over actively intervening in the economy by raising interest rates. [27] Regional banks were urging an increase in the discount rate — the interest rate the Fed charges to member banks — through much of last year, according to Fed documents released in late March. But Greenspan opposed the move, saying that expansion was slowing and inflation was not worsening. By December, most of the banks had stopped lobbying for the hike.

In February, the Fed's chief policy-making group, the Federal Open Market Committee, seriously debated the Fed's other interest rate: the federal funds target rate. But the committee adopted what the minutes, released in March, called a "wait-and-see attitude." Committee members were not yet convinced that inflation was worsening, the minutes showed. In addition, the Fed policy-makers were worried that the stock market was not ready for an interest rate increase. Without a forewarning, the minutes said, the rate hike "could have exaggerated repercussions." ■

Current Situation

The Fed Acts

Greenspan returned to Capitol Hill on March 20 to give the markets an unmistakable warning. The Federal Reserve's policy, he told the Joint Economic Committee, calls for "acting promptly — ideally pre-emptively — to keep inflation low."

Five days later, the Fed acted. The Federal Open Market Committee announced it was raising the federal funds target rate one-quarter of a percentage point to 5.5 percent.

The Fed's move went unappreciated by either business or labor. "The Federal Reserve has sacrificed the economic interest of America's working families on the basis of a hunch," AFL-CIO President John J. Sweeney said. "The Fed had room to wait," the U.S. Chamber of Commerce said. Over the next few days, populist-minded Democrats such as Sen. Tom Harkin of Iowa and pro-growth conservative Republicans such as former vice presidential nominee Jack E. Kemp joined in criticizing the rate hike. [28]

On Wall Street, the immediate reaction was no reaction. Having been forewarned, the stock market actually rose 100 points on the eve of the Fed's Tuesday meeting and fell a mere 29 points on the day of the decision. But on the next two trading days the Dow fell nearly 300 points. Many investors, it appeared, had come to believe that what the Fed described as a "slight firming of monetary conditions" was only the first step to slow the economy and cool the climate on Wall Street.

At week's end, some analysts were still shrugging off the market's slide. "The market finds itself hiccuping," Edwin Walczack, manager of the U.S. Value Fund, remarked on PBS' "Wall Street Week." Others, however, viewed the events more bearishly. "As long as the direction of interest rates is upward, the stock market is going to stall and probably correct," Michael Metz, chief investment strategist for Oppenheimer & Co. told *USA Today*. [29]

The fall hit bottom on April 11, when the Dow dropped 148 points after signs of inflation added to investors' fears of another interest rate hike. By then, however, the market had reached what insiders call an "oversold condition." Investors were ready to buy again. In addition, a new government report on April 15 indicated only mild inflation, and quarterly corporate earning reports released during the week generally met or exceeded analysts' expectations. For the week, the Dow industrial average rose more than 300 points, regaining more than half of its loss during the post-Fed slide.

The week's trading encouraged a new round of bullish forecasts. "The earnings are pretty terrific," Frank Cappiello, head of McCullough, Andrews & Cappiello, a Baltimore-area investment firm, told "Wall Street Week." He forecast a rising stock market for the year unless the Fed raised interest rates not just once but twice. Agreeing, John Dessauer, editor of *Dessauer's Investors' World*, a Massachusetts-based investment newsletter, said an interest rate hike seemed unlikely.

"With inflation coming down," Greenspan "doesn't have much latitude to raise rates," Dessauer said. [30]

A Changing Industry

Three days after Tully's retirement as chairman of Merrill Lynch, the investment house reported its first-quarter earnings: a record $465 million, 13.6 percent higher than the previous year and about 15 percent higher than analysts had estimated. But the earnings mainly reflected performance during the stock market's rise in January and February rather than the decline of late March. Tully's successor, David Komansky, candidly said that with a sagging market, higher earnings would be "more difficult to achieve" for the rest of the year. [31]

A weak stock market hurts brokers by depressing trading volume and thus

Continued on p. 402

At Issue:

Should Congress require stock markets to set prices by decimals instead of fractions?

yes

Rep. Michael G. Oxley, R-Ohio
Chairman, House Commerce Subcommittee on Finance
Co-sponsor, Common Cents Stock Pricing Act

FROM OPENING STATEMENT TO HOUSE SUBCOMMITTEE ON FINANCE, APRIL 10, 1997

The current stock pricing system in the U.S. is based on a tradition that dates back to the 1700s. . . . Age is not good enough to continue a practice . . . And I believe there are many good reasons to change the practice. . . .

First, fractions are more confusing than decimals. . . . It will be easier for average investors to understand stock prices in the common language of American commerce. . . .

Second, the U.S. fractional pricing system is out of step with the rest of the world. . . . There must be a reason that every other major market in the world prices in decimals. . . .

Third, and most important, fractional stock pricing is anti-competitive. It prevents competition from bringing better stock prices to investors. . . . [A] dealer making a market in a stock will sell you a stock for 12 and a half cents more than he'll buy it from you for — and pocket the difference, or "spread." If the spread were determined by competitive forces, rather than regulatory requirements, it would be narrower in many cases and investors would be able to get more stock for their money. . . .

Rep. Edward J. Markey, D-Mass.
Co-sponsor, Common Cents Stock Pricing Act

FROM OPENING STATEMENT, APRIL 10, 1997

Some might ask, why are we bothering about a few pennies? The answer is the "golden crumbs" that Wall Street firms can extract from the "spread" adds up to billions of dollars in costs to consumers each year. Estimates of the savings resulting from a move to decimal pricing range widely — from $4 billion to $9 billion a year. . . .

[This bill] . . . directs the Securities and Exchange Commission to . . . adopt a rule, within one year after the date of enactment, that would transition the stock and options markets away from trading in fractions to trading in dollars and cents. We give the SEC the flexibility to implement it in a fashion that does not impose undue burdens on trading and information systems.

Some have suggested that we shouldn't legislate in this area at this time, but merely study the issue. . . . [T]his issue has already been studied quite thoroughly. At this point, we don't need to be nickeled and dimed to death with foot-dragging studies and delaying tactics. . . .

no

William R. Johnston
President, New York Stock Exchange

FROM TESTIMONY TO HOUSE COMMERCE SUBCOMMITTEE ON FINANCE, APRIL 16, 1997

The New York Stock Exchange has carefully studied the issue of decimal pricing of securities quotations. We find no real evidence at this time that it would be of net benefit to investors, and we have concerns that in the long run it would make our market less transparent and less liquid.

The U.S. securities market is the most liquid, efficient and well-regulated securities market in the world. Congress should not mandate changes without clear benefit to all investors, large and small, and to the capital-formation process. Competitive market forces are preferable to a government mandate.

The supposed benefits of decimal trading do not withstand careful scrutiny. Estimates of investor savings are speculative at best. There is no evidence that bid-asked spreads will narrow under decimal pricing. Even if they do narrow in some stocks, over 80 percent of our volume represents customer-to-customer trades, where reduced spreads will not result in investor savings. . . .

Professional front-running is another hazard which could result from decimal pricing. Under current rules, professional traders must improve the bid or offer by a meaningful amount to establish priority over a customer. Reducing this amount to a penny would facilitate the ability of professional traders to step in front of other orders. Decimal pricing could result in a significant shift of power away from public customers to professional traders, undermining the very basis of the market.

Globalization and the use of decimal pricing in other world markets is not a deterrent to non-U.S. companies listing in our market. The biggest obstacle to listing in the U.S. remains the requirement of U.S. accounting standards. If the U.S. securities market believed that decimalization were necessary for international competitiveness, it could convert without government direction.

The costs of converting to decimals could be significant. At a minimum, it would affect all stock and options exchanges, the National Association of Securities Dealers, all securities firms, market data vendors and participants in the national clearance and settlement systems.

Market forces are working. The strength of our market is based on freedom of competition. Investors and other market participants, not the government, should determine the wisdom of any move to decimal pricing.

Did Illegal Insider Trading Yield Millions?

Minneapolis attorney James O'Hagan made a $4.3 million killing in the stock market nine years ago. The secret to his success? A crucial tidbit of information from one of his law partners about a planned takeover of the locally based Pillsbury Co.

O'Hagan used the so-called insider information to invest heavily in Pillsbury stock before the acquisition and then liquidated his holdings at a whopping profit after the takeover was announced. But the Securities and Exchange Commission (SEC) took a dim view of O'Hagan's trading. It won criminal convictions of O'Hagan in 1994 on 57 counts of securities fraud and related charges.

Now O'Hagan's case is before the U.S. Supreme Court in a closely watched test of the SEC's broad definition of illegal insider trading. The government wants the justices to overturn a federal appeals court decision last year that threw out O'Hagan's conviction and that the government says weakens the SEC's authority to police the stock market.

"Investors in the securities market rely on the fact that the markets are essentially honest," Deputy Solicitor General Michael Dreeben told the justices on April 16. "Investors do assume that they are not dealing with someone who has acquired an informational advantage by fraud."

O'Hagan's attorney, however, insisted that the government was stretching securities law too far. "What's wrong with the government's theory," John French argued, "is that it doesn't have anything to do with taking advantage of any participant in the stock market."

The case comes at a time when stock market regulators are reporting an increase in suspected illegal insider trading. The National Association of Securities Dealers (NASD) referred a record 121 such cases to the SEC last year, while the New York Stock Exchange sent 48 — significantly higher than the average of 28 for the last three years. [1] But the case also comes at a time of increased uncertainty about the theory the SEC has used to extend insider trading rules beyond traditional "insiders" — directors, officers or employees of a company.

Insider trading is not per se illegal. An employee shows confidence in a company's financial condition by buying stock and may have any number of valid reasons later for selling it — for example, to pay for a child's college vacation. But the SEC has for many years crafted rules that make it illegal for company insiders to trade on the basis of material information not available to public investors — for example, by buying in advance of good news or selling before the release of bad news about the company.

In the 1970s and early '80s, the SEC devised what it called a "misappropriation theory" to extend illegal trading rules to people outside a company who fraudulently obtain non-public information and use it to trade the company's stock. Although the theory has been accepted by the federal appeals court in New York — a leading forum for securities cases — the Supreme Court has never squarely ruled on it.

The high court skirted a direct ruling on the theory in a 1981 case involving a financial printer who used information in a stock prospectus for trading. Later, in 1987, the justices divided 4-4 in a case brought against a *Wall Street Journal* reporter who traded on the basis of information he obtained in writing a column. The split decision left the reporter's conviction standing but established no legal precedent.

In O'Hagan's case, the SEC contends that he misappropriated confidential information when he confirmed information about the tender offer in a conversation with one of his partners. Some justices, however, questioned whether O'Hagan's actions violated securities law. "He didn't deceive anybody who sold him the securities," Chief Justice William H. Rehnquist said.

Some of the justices appeared more receptive to the government's arguments on a narrower charge based on a more recent SEC rule that prohibits anyone from trading in stock on the basis of non-public information during a tender offer. French argued that the SEC first had to prove that O'Hagan had committed a fraud, but Justice Antonin Scalia disagreed. The law, Scalia said, "allows [the SEC] to prohibit other things to prevent fraud. That's how the statute reads."

O'Hagan was sentenced to 18 months in prison, fined $150,000 and in a separate civil proceeding ordered to disgorge his $4.3 million in profits plus $3 million in interest. He has not begun his federal sentence, but he did serve two years in state prison after being convicted of theft. (He was also disbarred.) His crime in that case was taking about $3 million from client accounts. Federal prosecutors said O'Hagan used the profits from his Pillsbury investment to try to cover up the theft.

[1] See *The New York Times*, April 16, 1997, p. D1.

commissions. Daily trading volume on the New York Stock Exchange, which had been averaging above 500 million shares during January and February, fell below 450 million shares following the Federal Reserve's interest rate hike in late March.

In addition, a weak market hurts another part of the business: underwriting new stock offerings. Some new offerings are being postponed, and those that are going to market are bringing in less money than underwriters were estimating, *The Wall Street Journal* reported.

"It's a pretty tough environment," Richard Smith, director of equity syndication at Montgomery Securities in San Francisco, told the Journal.

Securities firms are also facing the prospect of stiffened competition from commercial banks, which are now being given greater leeway to get into the investment business. Banks have generally been barred from selling securities since Congress passed the Glass-Steagall Act in 1933. But since 1987, the Federal Reserve Board has allowed bank holding companies to set up separate subsidiaries to deal in securities as long as the subsidiary accounted for no more than 10 percent of the parent company's business. Some 20 banks had taken advantage of the rule by last summer. Then, last fall, the Fed opened the door wider by raising the limit on bank security activities to 25 percent.

In the first major use of the new rule, Bankers Trust New York Corp. announced plans on April 7 to acquire the nation's oldest brokerage firm, Baltimore-based Alex. Brown & Co. Bankers Trust said it anticipated no regulatory problems for the proposed $1.7 billion deal. Industry analysts say they expect more such deals in the future.

"We will probably see more banks buying securities firms once prices get a bit more sensible," said Raphael Soifer, an analyst at Brown Brothers Harriman, a New York investment bank. [32]

Meanwhile, dealers on the Nasdaq market are adjusting to the prospect of reduced margins on trading under new SEC rules. The rules allow investors in Nasdaq-listed stocks to make "limit orders" — an order to buy or sell at a price specified by the investor instead of at the prevailing market price. Limit orders, already permitted on the New York and other auction exchanges, help investors by allowing a voice in setting price, but they can hurt dealers by reducing the "spread" between bid and ask prices — and thus cut into their profit. The new rules are being phased in gradually, but some traders are complaining that their spreads are being reduced just as their business is being hurt by the slump in trading and underwriting. [33]

Despite the general deregulatory climate in Washington, there have been some calls for new rules to help protect investors. One SEC official recently urged mutual funds to expand their quarterly reports to investors to include individualized valuations of how their personal investments are doing in addition to an overall report on the fund's performance. [34] The Consumer Federation's Roper calls for other steps to improve information for investors — for example, more explicit disclosure by brokers of commissions and other fees.

The industry's most far-reaching change, however, may not be financial or regulatory, but technological. Computers now provide instantaneous links between stock markets and investors around the country — indeed, around the world. "We're all wired," Merrill Lynch's Steinberg says.

With everybody getting information so quickly, the communications revolution creates additional pressures both for investors and for investment firms. But Steinberg says it also creates opportunities for a better-functioning market.

"For years, economists have talked about the ideal of a market with perfect information," Steinberg says. "Now you're getting a lot closer to having adequate information than ever was the case. Information now gets to everyone at the same time." ■

OUTLOOK

Stay Put?

J.P. Morgan once was asked what stocks were going to do next. "They will fluctuate, young man, they will fluctuate," the legendary financier replied tersely. Wall Street professionals today evince the same acceptance of market risks. "It's the business," says Michael LaBranche of LaBranche & Co., a veteran Big Board floor trader. "You have your good days and your bad days."

This truism may be lost, however, on many investors today. Some stock market experts fear that new investors have been lulled by the market's record rise since 1990 into thinking that stock prices move in only one direction. In a poll conducted last year, mutual fund investors were asked how they thought prices would move over the next decade in view of the fact that prices had risen about 14 percent a year for the past decade. Only 14 percent of the respondents thought that prices would not continue rising at the same rate. [35]

Many mutual fund investors were shaken, however, when they received their first-quarter reports last month. Mutual funds averaged only a 2 percent gain for the first quarter of 1997 — their worst performance in two years, according to Morningstar Inc., a Chicago-based service that tracks funds' performance. [36] Some of the leading funds lost money; Fidelity Magellan, the biggest fund with $53.8 billion in assets, lost 0.27 percent.

The poor performance was accompanied by a decline in net investment in mutual funds. Mutual stock funds last year reported a record $221.6 billion in net inflows — new sales minus redemptions by departing shareholders. But figures from the Investment Company Institute, the mutual funds' trade association, indicated that after a seasonal peak in January, sales slumped to $18.5 billion in February and sank to $10.5 billion in March — about half the level in March 1996. [37]

Despite the discouraging returns, mutual fund managers — and many analysts — were advising investors to stay put. "The global economic situation couldn't be brighter for long-term holders of financial assets," John Cleland, chief investment strategist at the Security Benefit Group, a Topeka, Kan., investment company, said. [38]

But some bears disagreed. "I would advise investors to recognize that this is a time for a different strategy, with a higher allocation to cash and bonds or undervalued stocks," says Montana adviser Stack.

In the short term, the funds' sagging returns would hurt the investors, mainly retirees, who use the funds for income rather than growth. The stock market's sagging performance has other ripple effects. A weak market may reduce the value of employee stock options, which a growing number of companies are giving to executives as well as to rank-and-file workers as an incentive to improve productivity.

In addition, the stock market's decline came as policy-makers in Washington were debating proposals aimed at shoring up the Social Security system either by allowing the government to invest trust funds in stocks or by permitting individuals to control more of their retirement savings and direct funds into stocks. [39] As the stock market rose in the '90s, the proposals seemed a sure way of improving returns on Social Security funds. But the sagging market underlines the risk of flat returns or even losses, at least in the short term.

For consumer groups, a sliding market may bring to the surface problems obscured by a rising market. "You don't know what the real problems are in the market while the market is going up and up," says the Consumer Federation's Roper. "But once the market corrects, we'll know where the problems are."

But the University of Colorado's Goldstein says that Americans should feel good about the stock market even if it fails to match the soaring gains from 1995 and 1996.

"All in all, we're the world's strongest economy," Goldstein says. "If stock markets only go up 10 percent this year, everybody would think that's terrible, but in fact it's pretty good — a little below the historical average, but still pretty good." ■

Notes

[1] For background, see "Mutual Funds," *The CQ Researcher*, May 20, 1994, pp. 433-456.

[2] For background on the 1987 crash, see "Spotlight on Wall Street," *Editorial Research Reports*, Dec. 18, 1987, pp. 657-672.

[3] Quoted in *The Wall Street Journal*, March 7, 1997, p. C1.

[4] See *1995 Congressional Quarterly Almanac*, pp. 2-90 to 2-92..

[5] See *Congressional Quarterly Weekly Report*, Nov. 2, 1996, p. 3139.

[6] The annual report is on the company's home page at www.berkshirehathaway.com. See *The Wall Street Journal*, March 17, 1997, p. C1.

[7] Henry Kaufman, "Today's Financial Euphoria Can't Last," *The Wall Street Journal*, Nov. 25, 1996, p. A18.

[8] Quoted in *The Washington Post*, April 6, 1997, p. H4.

[9] *The Wall Street Journal*, April 1, 1997, p. C1.

[10] For a recent profile of Greenspan, see Linton Weeks and John M. Berry, "The Shy Wizard of Money," *The Washington Post*, March 24, 1997, p. A1.

[11] See *The New York Times*, March 5, 1997, p. D10.

[12] Steven K. Beckner, *Back From the Brink: The Greenspan Years* (1996), p. vii.

[13] See *The Wall Street Journal*, April 16, 1997, p. C1; *The Washington Post*, Dec. 15, 1996, p. H1.

[14] For background, see Robert Sobel, *The Big Board: A History of the New York Stock Market* (1965).

[15] For background, see Robert Sobel, *The Curbstone Brokers: The Origins of the American Stock Exchange* (1970).

[16] See William K. Klingman, *1929: The Year of the Great Crash* (1989).

[17] See Wayne Angell, "Understanding 1929," *The Wall Street Journal*, March 7, 1997, p. A14.

[18] John Kenneth Galbraith, *The Great Crash: 1929* (1988 edition), pp. 29-35.

[19] Seligman, *op. cit.*, p. x.

[20] See Robert Sobel, *N.Y.S.E.: A History of the New York Stock Exchange*, 1935-1975 (1975), pp. 199-203.

[21] See Seligman, *op. cit.*, pp. 398-406, 443-450.

[22] For background, see Tim Metz, *Black Monday: The Catastrophe of October 19, 1987 . . . and Beyond* (1988). For a comparison of the 1929 and 1987 crashes, see John R. Dorfman, "Crash Courses," *The Wall Street Journal*, May 28, 1996, p. R12.

[23] Metz, *op. cit.*, pp. 44-45.

[24] Cited in Beckner, *op. cit.*, pp. 364-365.

[25] John R. Dorfman, "Greenspan: 'Dow 4000' Hero," *The Wall Street Journal*, Nov. 18, 1996, p. C1.

[26] David Wessel, "Worried Fed Watches Stock Market's Climb," *The Wall Street Journal*, Nov. 25, 1996, p. C1.

[27] See *The Wall Street Journal*, March 28, 1997, p. A2; *The Washington Post*, March 28, 1997, p. A1.

[28] See Tom Harkin, "Fed's tax hikes hurt," *USA Today*, April 7, 1997, p. 14A; Jack Kemp, "The Fed's Retreat on Principles," *The Wall Street Journal*, April 2, 1997, p. A14.

[29] PBS, "Wall Street Week," March 28, 1997; *USA Today*, March 31, 1997, p. 1B.

[30] PBS, "Wall Street Week," April 18, 1997.

[31] Quoted in *The Wall Street Journal*, April 16, 1997, p. C1.

[32] Quoted in *The New York Times*, April 15, 1997, p. D2.

[33] See *The Wall Street Journal*, April 21, 1997, p. C1.

[34] *The Wall Street Journal*, April 7, 1997, p. C1.

[35] Cited in *The New York Times*, Jan. 2, 1997, p. C21. The poll, conducted in September for Liberty Financial, a Boston mutual fund investment firm, consisted of a telephone survey of 1,014 investors who owned mutual funds not provided as part of an employer-sponsored plan.

[36] See *The New York Times*, April 1, 1997, p. D1; *The Wall Street Journal*, April 2, 1997, p. C1.

[37] See *The New York Times*, April 11, 1997, p. D1.

[38] Quoted in *The New York Times*, April 6, 1997, p. C1.

[39] For background, see "Overhauling Social Security," *The CQ Researcher*, May 12, 1995, pp. 417-440.

Bibliography

Selected Sources Used

Books

Beckner, Steven K., *Back From the Brink: The Greenspan Years,* Wiley, 1996.
Beckner's admiring biography traces Greenspan's career from his early days as an adviser to Richard M. Nixon through his decade as Federal Reserve chairman. Beckner is a reporter with Market News Service. For a more critical examination of the Fed, prior to Greenspan's chairmanship, see William Greider, *Secrets of the Temple: How the Federal Reserve Runs the Country.*

Metz, Tim, *Black Monday: The Catastrophe of October 19, 1987 . . . and Beyond,* William Morrow, 1988.
Metz, a writer with *The Wall Street Journal,* provides an hour-by-hour, day-by-day account of the 1987 crash and its aftermath from the perspective of five individuals who played critical roles in the events.

Morris, Kenneth M., Alan M. Siegel and Virginia B. Morris, *Your Guide to Understanding Investing,* Lightbulb Press, 1996.
This illustrated 191-page primer, prepared for the Securities Industry Association, explains the basics of investing in clear and understandable terms. The book also includes practical advice on financial planning and planning for retirement.

***The NASDAQ Handbook: The Stock Market of Tomorrow — Today,* Probus Publishing, 1987; *The NASDAQ Handbook: The Stock Market for the Next 100 Years* [rev. ed.], Probus Publishing, 1992.**
The earlier 572-page primer and the shorter revised edition both include articles by a number of experts aimed at providing an overview of the history, operation and role of the Nasdaq stock market.

Seligman, Joel, *The Transformation of Wall Street: A History of the Securities and Exchange Commission and Modern Corporate Finance,* Houghton Mifflin, 1982.
Seligman, dean of the University of Arizona College of Law, traces the history of the Securities and Exchange Commission from its birth in the aftermath of the stock market crash of 1929 through the mid-1970s. The book includes detailed source notes.

Sobel, Robert, *N.Y.S.E.: A History of the New York Stock Exchange, 1935-1975,* Weybright and Talley, 1975; *Amex: A History of the American Stock Exchange, 1921-1971,* Weybright and Talley, 1972; *The Curbstone Brokers: The Origins of the American Stock Exchange,* Macmillan, 1970; *The Big Board: A History of the New York Stock Market,* Free Press, 1965.
Works by the proflific Sobel chronicling the history of the American stock markets include four broad surveys detailing the development of the New York and American exchanges. Sobel is a professor at Hofstra University.

FOR MORE INFORMATION

American Association of Individual Investors, 25 N. Michigan Ave., Suite 1900, Chicago, Ill. 60611; (312) 280-0170. The association, founded in 1978, represents about 170,000 individual investors.

Consumer Federation of America, 1424 16th St. N.W., Suite 604, Washington, D.C. 20036; (202) 387-6121. The federation, founded in 1967, lobbies on a variety of consumer issues, including banking, credit, insurance and investing.

Investment Company Institute, 1401 H St. N.W., 12th floor, Washington, D.C. 20005; (202) 326-5800. The trade association represents mutual fund investment companies.

National Association of Investors Corp., 711 W. 13 Mile Road, Madison Heights, Mich. 48071; (810) 583-6242. The association represents about 500,000 members of investment clubs around the country.

National Association of Securities Dealers, 1735 K St. N.W., Washington, D.C. 20006; (202) 728-8000. The NASD is the self-regulatory organization for the 5,400 securities firms and 513,000 registered brokers and dealers in the U.S. It is also the parent organization for the Nasdaq stock market.

North American Securities Administrators Association, 1 Massachusetts Ave. N.W., Suite 310, Washington, D.C. 20001; (202) 737-0900. The association represents state, provincial and territorial agencies in the United States and Canada responsible for investor protection.

Securities and Exchange Commission, 450 5th St. N.W., Washington, D.C. 20549; (202) 942-8088. The SEC was established in 1934 to regulate securities markets.

Securities Industry Association, 120 Broadway, New York, N.Y. 10271-0080; (212) 608-1500; 1401 I St. N.W., Washington, D.C. 20005-2225; (202) 296-9410. The trade association represents 760 securities firms, including investment banks, broker-dealers and specialists.

The Next Step

Additional information from UMI's Newspaper & Periodical Abstracts™ database

Federal Reserve System

"Federal Reserve sets risk—capital standard for trades by banks," ***The Wall Street Journal,*** **Aug. 8, 1996, p. B10.**

Aiming to reduce risks from foreign exchange, commodities and derivatives trading, the Federal Reserve Board adopted "risk-based" capital guidelines for banks. Under the new standard, banks are required to set aside capital for general market risk and for specific market risks associated with debt and equity positions in certain circumstances.

McGee, Suzanne, "Bond prices fall after Federal Reserve officials say they see signs of inflationary pressure," ***The Wall Street Journal,*** **May 30, 1996, p. C21.**

Bond prices fell on May 29, 1996, after several Federal Reserve Board officials indicated signs of inflationary pressure. The benchmark 30-year Treasury bond fell more than a point to 88 2/32, pushing the yield to 6.94 percent from 6.85 percent on May 28.

Wessel, David, "Federal Reserve policy makers continue to see risk of inflation pushing higher," ***The Wall Street Journal,*** **Nov. 18, 1996, p. A6.**

Although Federal Reserve Board policy-makers agreed to hold short-term interest rates steady at their Sept. 24, 1996, meeting, they "generally agreed" that "the risks continued to be tilted . . . in the direction of rising price inflation," according to a summary of the meeting released on Nov. 15, 1996.

Alan Greenspan

"Greenspan Stops Nagging and Acts," ***Chicago Tribune,*** **March 26, 1997, Sec. 1, p. 24.**

For months, Federal Reserve Chairman Alan Greenspan has been warning about overvalued stock prices and the inflationary dangers of a stronger-than-expected economy, but he and his colleagues at the central bank have patiently refrained from taking any action to tighten the money supply and slow growth. Greenspan stopped admonishing Tuesday and acted. The Federal Reserve raised the overnight bank lending rate by a quarter of a point, the first short-term interest rate increase in more than two years.

Kuttner, Robert, "The cost of Greenspan's phobia," ***The Boston Globe,*** **March 31, 1997, p. A15.**

Kuttner comments with dismay on the anti-inflation interest rate hikes implemented by the Federal Reserve Board and Chairman Alan Greenspan.

Novak, Robert D., "Papa Greenspan," ***The Washington Post,*** **March 31, 1997, p. A21.**

Novak comments on Federal Reserve critics' belief that Alan Greenspan prematurely pulled the trigger in calling for a rise in interest rates in March 1997.

Investment Trends

Causey, Mike, "Stock market magnetism," ***The Washington Post,*** **Sept. 6, 1996, p. B2.**

Causey notes that in August 1996, civil servants invested more money in the stock fund of their 401(k) plan than they did in either the Treasury or bond fund.

Crenshaw, Albert B., "If you know when to say when on the stock market," ***The Washington Post,*** **Feb. 18, 1996, p. H1.**

Crenshaw comments on the concern among stock market investors about whether they should cash in their winnings and head for safer ground after the dramatic rise in the Dow Jones Industrial Average.

Dugas, Christine, "Couple target stock market," ***USA Today,*** **Oct. 7, 1996, p. B3.**

The investment goals and tactics of the Calvin and Annette Johnson family in St. Louis, Mo., are featured in connection with their hopes of retiring in 20 years.

Fromson, Brett D., "Investment Stars Bet on the Bull; Experts Expect Stock Market to Stay Strong, But Some Warn of a Reversal of Fortune," ***The Washington Post,*** **Feb. 15, 1997, p. B1.**

Top hedge fund managers such as Stanley Druckenmiller of the Soros Organization look for the party to continue, even as they keep one eye on the door. One of the few bears among the financial superstars is billionaire investor Laurence Tisch, a friend of Alan Greenspan who compares today's market with 1929. For his part, Tisch said he holds few stocks, with the significant exception of his nearly $2 billion holding in Loews Corp.

Kapiloff, Howard, "Bankers fear fallout when the skyrocketing stock market falters," ***American Banker,*** **March 1, 1996, p. 10.**

The stock market's phenomenal rise is giving some bankers cause for concern over how to keep customers calm when the market turns bearish, a problem now that many banks have shifted from selling mostly bond mutual funds to the more risky stock funds. The views of those attending the annual conference in Palm Desert, Calif., of the Bank Securities Association are discussed.

Nocera, Joseph, "Playing the Stock Market Lotto," ***The New York Times,*** **Jan. 14, 1997, p. A15.**

Nocera says that 1997 marks the 14th year of the greatest sustained bull market in history and without question it has changed America. Middle-class Americans, especially baby boomers, who used to fear the stock market now view it as an ordinary part of life, Nocera adds.

Mutual Funds

Waggoner, John, "Stock market sell-off pressures mutual funds," ***USA Today,*** **July 16, 1996, p. B1.**

Mutual fund companies said phone calls from investors, some wanting to know why stocks were falling and others just wanting out, rose from 10 percent to 35 percent July 15, 1996, as the Dow Jones Industrial Average lost 161 points.

Wyatt, Edward, "Fund investors hold key to health of stock market," ***The New York Times,*** **March 11, 1996, p. A1.**

The importance of mutual fund investors in insuring the health of the stock market is discussed. On March 8, 1996, — as on three other occasions in seven years — the Dow Jones Industrial Average fell more than 120 points, but Main Street investors usually step in to stem the selling tide and market panic.

Stock Exchanges

Halverson, Guy, "Nasdaq stock market is risky, analysts say," ***The Christian Science Monitor,*** **May 6, 1996, p. 9.**

The Nasdaq market, the bastion of small-company stocks, has been on an upward roll in 1996, and no major slump is yet in sight, which makes some analysts in conservative investment houses nervous. The Nasdaq has long been a center of financial speculation, with share prices moving up and down with greater volatility than America's other major stock exchanges.

Baker, Molly, "Small stock focus: Nasdaq Stock Market hits 25th birthday but don't expect any big celebrations," ***The Wall Street Journal,*** **Feb. 5, 1996, p. C1.**

The Nasdaq Stock Market is celebrating its 25th anniversary the week of Feb. 5, 1996. Nasdaq was launched in 1971 as a tiny network of 100 or so securities firms to trade Over The Counter (OTC) stocks, at a time when OTC stocks were not traded by "nice people." Its growth over a quarter-century is detailed.

Podd, Ann, "NYSE discloses disciplinary actions against eight individuals and a firm," ***The Wall Street Journal,*** **Aug. 12, 1996, p. 5.**

The NYSE disclosed disciplinary measures against one firm and eight individuals for violations of NYSE rules and federal securities laws. The actions taken are listed in alphabetical order.

Puri, Shafali, "Nasdaq vs. NYSE," ***Fortune,*** **March 31. 1997, pp 26-28.**

A fight has broken out between Nasdaq and NYSE over which stock exchange will list Concert, the company created from the $25 billion merger of MCI Communications and British Telecommunications. The new listing battle is discussed.

Stock Market Conditions

Halverson, Guy, "Nagging Concerns Put Chill On U.S. Stock Market's Rise," ***The Christian Science Monitor,*** **Jan. 27, 1997, p, 8.**

For the past three weeks, the Dow Jones Industrial Average has been bounding upward toward the 7000 point level. On Jan. 23, the Dow almost broke through the 6900 point level. "There just doesn't seem to be any real hard news" explaining current market instability, says Arnold Kaufman, editor of *The Outlook,* a newsletter published by Standard & Poor's Corp.

Hylton, Richard D., "Is the stock market too pricey?" ***Fortune,*** **April 1, 1996, pp. 151-152.**

The Dow Jones' steep climb is causing worrisome valuations and falling dividend yields. These stock market indicators suggest that stock prices are getting out of hand. Stock market signals are discussed.

Myers, Randy, "Stock market shows little inclination to pause," ***Nation's Business,*** **August 1996, pp. 65-66.**

The stock market is now in its record sixth year without a correction of at least 10 percent from its recent peak, prompting concern in some quarters that a reversal is overdue. Financial analysis for small businesses is presented.

Sivy, Michael, "Beat the stock market jitters," ***Money,*** **September 1996, pp. 58-61.**

Financial columnist Sivy provides a strategy to help investors calmly sail to double-digit investing profits. Potential high-returning stocks and mutual funds are discussed.

Wyatt, John, "The incredible, death — defying stock market: Love it and fear it," ***Fortune,*** **Dec. 23, 1996, pp. 110-118.**

The bullish stock market is on its last stampede. It could collapse soon, or it could keep running. Since 1990, the Dow has pushed through four 1,000-point barriers on its way to 6500.

Back Issues

Great Research on Current Issues Starts Right Here...Recent topics covered by The CQ Researcher are listed below. Before May 1991, reports were published under the name of Editorial Research Reports.

OCTOBER 1995
Quebec's Future
Revitalizing the Cities
Networking the Classroom
Indoor Air Pollution

NOVEMBER 1995
The Working Poor
The Jury System
Sex, Violence and the Media
Police Misconduct

DECEMBER 1995
Teens and Tobacco
Gene Therapy's Future
Global Water Shortages
Third-Party Prospects

JANUARY 1996
Emergency Medicine
Punishing Sex Offenders
Bilingual Education
Helping the Homeless

FEBRUARY 1996
Reforming the CIA
Campaign Finance Reform
Academic Politics
Getting Into College

MARCH 1996
The British Monarchy
Preventing Juvenile Crime
Tax Reform
Pursuing the Paranormal

APRIL 1996
Centennial Olympic Games
Managed Care
Protecting Endangered Species
New Military Culture

MAY 1996
Russia's Political Future
Marriage and Divorce
Year-Round Schools
Taiwan, China and the U.S.

JUNE 1996
Rethinking NAFTA
First Ladies
Teaching Values
Labor Movement's Future

JULY 1996
Recovered-Memory Debate
Native Americans' Future
Crackdown on Sexual Harassment
Attack on Public Schools

AUGUST 1996
Fighting Over Animal Rights
Privatizing Government Services
Child Labor and Sweatshops
Cleaning Up Hazardous Wastes

SEPTEMBER 1996
Gambling Under Attack
The States and Federalism
Civic Journalism
Reassessing Foreign Aid

OCTOBER 1996
Political Consultants
Insurance Fraud
Rethinking School Integration
Parental Rights

NOVEMBER 1996
Global Warming
Clashing Over Copyright
Consumer Debt
Governing Washington, D.C.

DECEMBER 1996
Welfare, Work and the States
The New Volunteerism
Implementing the Disabilities Act
America's Pampered Pets

JANUARY 1997
Combating Scientific Misconduct
Restructuring the Electric Industry
The New Immigrants
Chemical and Biological Weapons

FEBRUARY 1997
Assisting Refugees
Alternative Medicine's Next Phase
Independent Counsels
Feminism's Future

MARCH 1997
New Air Quality Standards
Alcohol Advertising
Civic Renewal
Educating Gifted Students

APRIL 1997
Declining Crime Rates
The FBI Under Fire
Gender Equity in Sports
Space Program's Future

Back issues are available for $5.00 (subscribers) or $10.00 (non-subscribers). Quantity discounts apply to orders over ten. To order, call Congressional Quarterly Customer Service at (202) 887-8621.

Binders are available for $18.00. To order call 1-800-638-1710. Please refer to stock number 648.

Future Topics

- ***Cloning Controversy***
- ***Expanding NATO***
- ***Libraries' Changing Role***

THE CQ Researcher

PUBLISHED BY CONGRESSIONAL QUARTERLY INC.

The Cloning Controversy

Should the U.S. ban human cloning research?

The world was stunned in February with the announcement that an adult mammal had produced an offspring without an egg being fertilized by a sperm. The "Dolly" story ignited a global media storm, in large part because of its chilling implication that human cloning was possible. There was deep disagreement, however, over the ethics of cloning humans. Opponents called for a ban on human cloning research, arguing that cloning offers few benefits to science while requiring unacceptable risks and undermining our very concept of humanness. But many scientists argued that cloning research could open the door to better understanding of how cells work and thus help battle cancer and other diseases. Others said its benefits could range from duplicating embryos for in vitro fertilization to replacing a dying child.

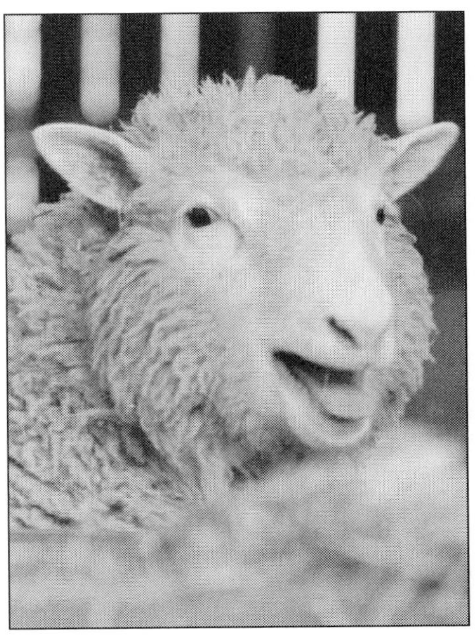

INSIDE THIS ISSUE

CQ May 9, 1997 • Volume 7, No. 18 • Pages 409-432

Formerly Editorial Research Reports

THE CLONING CONTROVERSY

THE ISSUES

BACKGROUND

CURRENT SITUATION

OUTLOOK

SIDEBARS AND GRAPHICS

FOR MORE INFORMATION

COVER: "DOLLY" WAS ANNOUNCED TO THE WORLD ON FEB. 22, 1997. FOR THE FIRST TIME IN HISTORY, AN ADULT MAMMAL PRODUCED AN OFFSPRING WITHOUT AN EGG BEING FERTILIZED BY A SPERM. (REUTERS)

THE CQ Researcher

May 9, 1997
Volume 7, No. 18

PUBLISHED BY
Congressional Quarterly Inc.

The CQ Researcher (ISSN 1056-2036). Formerly Editorial Research Reports. Published weekly (48 times per year, not printed Jan. 3, May 30, Aug. 29, Oct. 31) by Congressional Quarterly Inc., 1414 22nd St., N.W., Washington, D.C. 20037. Annual subscription rate for libraries, businesses and government is $340. Additional rates furnished upon request. Periodicals postage paid at Washington, D.C., and additional mailing offices. POSTMASTER: Send address changes to The CQ Researcher, 1414 22nd St., N.W., Washington, D.C. 20037.

The Cloning Controversy

BY DAVID MASCI

THE ISSUES

To those terrified by *Frankenstein* and other such cautionary tales, the recent breakthrough in cloning research must have been a letdown. Far from a frightening monster, the sensational experiment brought forth . . . a little lamb.

But despite appearances, Dolly was anything but ordinary. The little ewe's arrival on the world stage signaled the rewriting of the rules of reproduction. For the first time in history, an adult mammal had produced offspring without an egg being fertilized by a sperm.

Dolly's impact was heightened by the fact that she was so unexpected. The scientific community was almost as shocked as the general public at the Feb. 22 announcement by Ian Wilmut, the English scientist who led Scotland's Roslin Institute to its historic achievement. Indeed, replicating an adult mammal through cloning was considered so unlikely that the work being done at Roslin had been largely ignored — until Dolly.

Wilmut and his colleagues "proved the dogma wrong," said James Murray, a professor of reproductive biology at the University of California-Davis. [1]

Dolly's story set off a media frenzy. Images of Wilmut and the 6-month-old ewe appeared on TV and in newspapers around the globe. ("Hello Dolly," said one headline.

Ultimately, of course, the hoopla was not about a rather endearing ewe, but Dolly's potentially chilling implications for mankind. Amid references to *Frankenstein, Brave New World* and other tales of science run amok, two simple questions emerged: Could Dolly lead to the cloning of a human being? And if so, was it morally permissible?

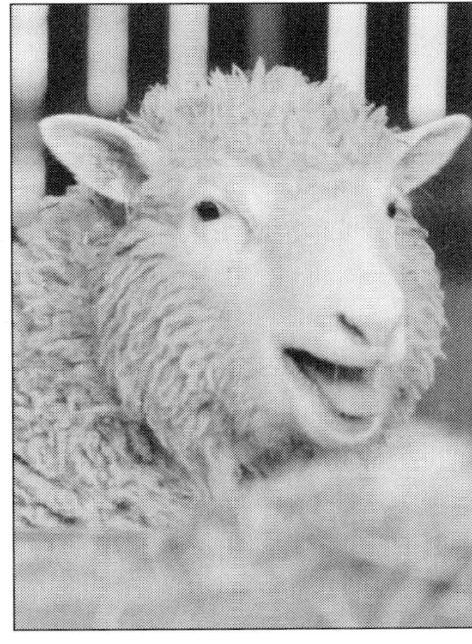

Most scientists agree that cloning a human will be possible; some have predicted it is as close as a decade away.

But as to the ethics of human cloning, there is deep disagreement. Wilmut and many others want human cloning research banned. Cloning will offer few if any benefits to science, they argue, while requiring unacceptable ethical and medical risks. In the worst-case scenario, women carrying cloned fetuses could suffer miscarriages or give birth to severely malformed babies.

Opponents also argue that cloning would undermine our fundamental concept of humanness. What, for example, would become of individuality in a world where another person could be copied not once but an infinite number of times? And what would happen to the fundamental assumption that children — human beings — are created by the union of a man and a woman, by two parents?

"The bottom line is, cloning a person would change the definition of what it means to be human," says George Annas, a professor of health law at Boston University's School of Public Health — "and who has the right to do that for the rest of us?"

But many scientists warn against moving too quickly to stop human cloning research. Such work should be encouraged, they say, because it could provide invaluable insight into how cells work, opening the door to treating cancer and other diseases.

Others favor going beyond basic research, arguing that the benefits of human cloning could range from duplicating embryos for in vitro fertilization to replacing a dying child with an identical baby.

Regardless of their differences over the feasibility or ethics of human cloning, scientists and ethicists agree that Wilmut's achievement ranks with other groundbreaking scientific discoveries through the ages.

"In terms of its ultimate importance for humanity, [Dolly] has only one rival in our century and perhaps in all of history: the development of the atomic bomb," wrote Millsaps College Professor Robert S. McElvaine. [2]

Dolly's birth is indeed an immense achievement. But researchers actually had begun replicating sheep and other mammals in 1984, using cells taken from fertilized embryos in the early stages of development. What made Dolly unique was that an *adult* cell was used to activate and program the egg from which she grew.

Scientists had failed in the past to replicate animals using adult cells because most of the trait-bearing genes in adult cells are genetically "turned off." Thus, they cannot be used as a genetic blueprint to produce a clone. Rather, adult cells only activate those genes they need to fulfill their specialized function, such as carrying oxygen (blood cells) or transmitting electric impulses (nerve cells). (*See story, p. 413.*)

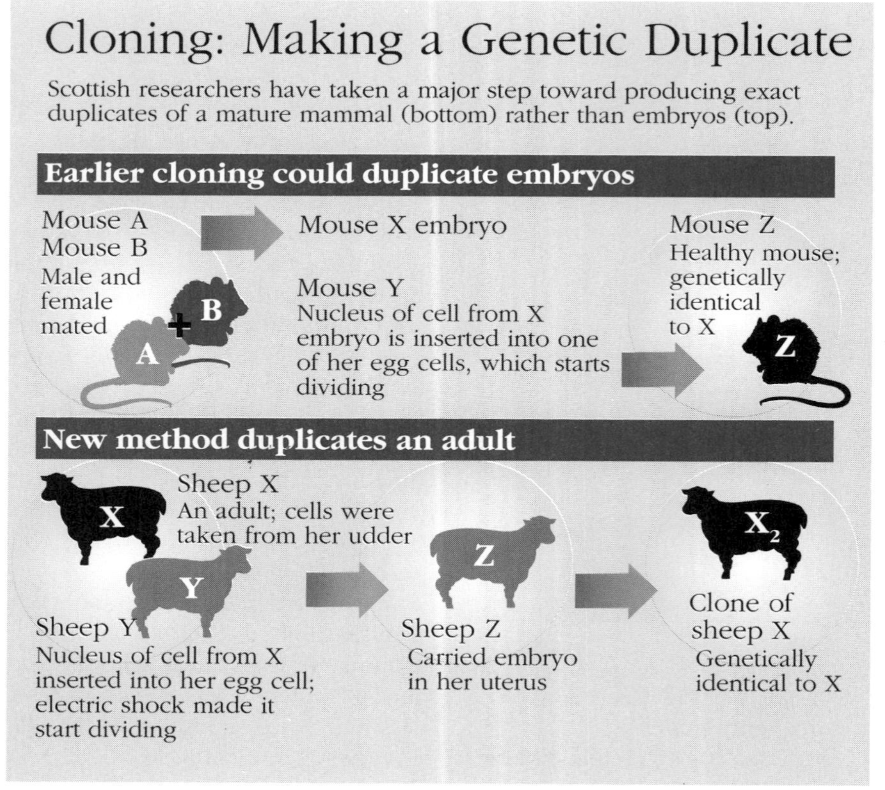
Cloning: Making a Genetic Duplicate
Scottish researchers have taken a major step toward producing exact duplicates of a mature mammal (bottom) rather than embryos (top).
Earlier cloning could duplicate embryos
Mouse A
Mouse B
Male and female mated
A
B
Mouse X embryo
Mouse Y
Nucleus of cell from X embryo is inserted into one of her egg cells, which starts dividing
Mouse Z
Healthy mouse; genetically identical to X
Z
New method duplicates an adult
Sheep X
An adult; cells were taken from her udder
X
Y
Sheep Y
Nucleus of cell from X inserted into her egg cell; electric shock made it start dividing
Z
Sheep Z
Carried embryo in her uterus
X2
Clone of sheep X
Genetically identical to X

Knight-Ridder Tribune/TIM GOHEEN

Wilmut and his colleagues found a way to activate all of the genes in adult cells so that when the cell's genetic material was transferred to a sheep egg cell, it was able to pass on its genetic blueprint. After a viable embryo was produced, it was implanted in a surrogate mother, which gave birth to Dolly, an almost identical twin of the ewe that had donated the original cell. (*See diagram above.*)

Before Dolly, arguments for and against cloning had been rare, primarily because the feasibility of cloning adult mammals, let alone humans, seemed so unlikely. [3]

So when Wilmut announced his breakthrough, the implications of human cloning had been little considered. "We had always thought: 'Why waste our time on something that's not going to happen; let's turn our attention to other more important issues,'" says Nancy Duff, an associate professor at Princeton Theological Seminary.

Still, the issue has been debated occasionally. In the 1960s, Nobel Prize-winning geneticist Joshua Lederberg argued publicly in favor of replicating humans. Among other things, he said, cloning would allow humanity to better direct the development of the species.

Lederberg's declaration sparked a variety of negative responses, including theologian Paul Ramsey's 1970 book, *Fabricated Man*, which warns that humanity will not have the wisdom to manage the power that comes with gaining total control over its own destiny. [4]

Surveys indicate that the American public solidly opposes cloning, human or otherwise. According to a *Time*/CNN poll taken just days after Wilmut's announcement, 93 percent of Americans said cloning a human was a bad idea, and 66 percent also opposed cloning animals. [5]

Not surprisingly, politicians have attempted to reassure the public that cloning will be approached with the utmost caution. Indeed, in Congress and a host of state legislatures, bills limiting or banning cloning research have already surfaced.

And President Clinton has imposed a temporary moratorium on the use of federal funds for human cloning research. He also commissioned a study of current and future ethical ramifications of the new technology (*see p. 422*).

As the newly intensified debate on cloning continues, these are some of the questions being asked:

Do ethical concerns outweigh any benefits that might be derived from human cloning?

The debate over cloning has been marked by hyperbole, especially in the popular culture. News stories often seem to refer to armies of Hitlers (or Mozarts) to illustrate the potential dangers or benefits of cloning.

The reality is far less dramatic, says Ruth Macklin, a professor of bioethics at the Albert Einstein College of Medicine in New York City. "All of this herds of Hitlers stuff — these are not realistic warnings," she says.

For one thing, scientists explain, it's highly unlikely that clones of Hitler would grow up to be tyrants.

"Producing a clone of a human being would not amount to creating a 'carbon copy' — an automaton of the sort familiar from science fiction," writes Robert Wachbroit, a research scholar at the Institute for Philosophy and Public Policy at the University of Maryland. "It would be more like producing a delayed identical twin." And like identical twins, a donor and a clone would have different person-

How Scientists Created "Dolly"

Researchers have been using embryonic cells to clone sheep, cows and other mammals for more than a decade. But attempts to use adult cells had always ended in failure — until the birth of a lamb named Dolly was announced in February.

Each cell of a mammal, say a sheep, contains thousands of genes, which together form its genetic blueprint. In the early stages of development, after an egg has been fertilized and begins to divide, all the genes in the dividing cells are functional, or "turned on," because they are needed to pass on the genetic blueprint to the developing animal. At this point in the embryo's development, it is too small and primitive for cells to have specialized functions.

As the embryo grows into a fetus, cells begin taking on special functions. Some, for example, become nerve cells, or skin, or bones, and so on. When cell specialization, or differentiation, begins to occur, the genes not being used for specialization — all of which had been functional in the embryonic stage — are turned off because they are no longer needed.

Until Dolly, cloning with an adult cell had been impossible because most of the genes of adult cells were genetically turned off, and thus could not pass on the donor's entire genetic blueprint. Moreover, scientists thought that once differentiation began, the cell could not be reprogrammed to turn all of its genes back on.

Ian Wilmut and his colleagues at the Roslin Institute in Scotland found a way to turn on all the genes in adult cells. To do that, they first had to artificially induce quiescence, or hibernation, early in the embryo's development. Quiescence normally occurs briefly after a cell has divided. During hibernation, all of the cell's genes are turned off. Wilmut and the others found that by starving cells of serum — a source of hormonelike growth factors — for a few days in a petri dish, they could artificially induce quiescence.

After inducing quiescence in the udder cell of a 6-year-old ewe, Wilmut's team removed its nucleus, which contains almost all of its genetic material, and implanted it into a sheep egg cell which had had its nucleus removed. After the transfer, the egg was placed in a nutrient broth and subjected to an electric shock, which fused the new nucleus to it.

The combination of nutrients and electricity reversed the cell's quiescent state. But, instead of reactivating only those genes needed to fulfill a specialized function, as might have been expected, the process turned on all the genes, enabling the nucleus to give the egg a complete genetic blueprint.

The electric shock also "tricked" the egg into believing that it had been fertilized, allowing it to begin dividing and growing into an embryo. After about six days, the researchers implanted the embryo in a surrogate mother, which later gave birth to Dolly.

So far, Dolly appears to be a healthy, normal ewe. But the process used to create her was anything but seamless. In their attempt to clone an adult sheep, Wilmut and the others fused 277 cells to eggs. Of these, only 29 developed into embryos that could be implanted in surrogate mothers. And only one of these 29 embryos developed into a healthy lamb. Many of the implanted embryos were stillborn or born deformed or with other problems.

alities, even though their physical appearance was the same. [6]

While the dangers of human cloning may be exaggerated, supporters of cloning research do not argue that it will bring immediate, untold benefits to humanity. Instead, they say, human cloning research would probably only produce modest societal gains, at least at first. Still, they argue, work on human cloning should not be prohibited simply because it does not guarantee immediate substantial benefits.

"There are many things that don't provide societal benefits," Macklin says, and yet they're not prohibited."

Nonetheless, Macklin and others say, some benefits probably would be derived from human cloning once the technology became available. For example, cloning research might improve the effectiveness of in vitro fertilization, in which an egg is removed from a woman's uterus, fertilized with a donated sperm and then implanted in her uterus. However, in vitro fertilization only results in pregnancy about 10 percent of the time. In addition, the procedure is painful for the woman and expensive. Moreover, couples often can't provide enough eggs and sperm to produce even one embryo. By cloning the embryo before implanting it in the woman, doctors could dramatically improve the in vitro success rate, they say, especially for couples having difficulty producing enough embryos for more than one try.

"Even if they only produced three or four embryos [by cloning,] it could greatly improve the odds that it will work," says John Robertson, an authority on reproductive technology and the law at the University of Texas School of Law in Austin.

Cloning also might offer new options for couples who cannot have children — even using in vitro or other artificial techniques — and do not want to use a surrogate mother or father. "This could be a great benefit to those who want genetically related progeny," Macklin says. In this case, of course, the child would be a replica of only one parent.

Another possible use might involve cloning a dying son or daughter, which might appeal to parents too old to produce another child on their own. Or they simply may prefer to replace a lost child with one that looks exactly like it.

In addition to aiding reproduction, human cloning research also might help combat certain diseases. Scientists know that an adult cell deactivates all of its genes, except those needed to maintain itself and to fulfill its special function in the body.

For instance, in a liver cell, only those genes concerned with liver function and cell maintenance are operational. All remaining genes in the cell are dormant. Since adult cells must activate all of their genes in order to be used in cloning, researchers would need to learn the hows and whys of this cellular process.

According to Jon Gordon, an obstetrics researcher at Mount Sinai Hospital in New York City, discovering how cells turn genes off and on might lead to the development of effective treatments for a variety of diseases, including many cancers. Liver and colon cancer, for example, are thought to occur when cells malfunction by turning on genes that are supposed to be dormant. If scientists can determine how genes turn on and off, they may be able stop or even eliminate the growth of tumors.

Cloning research might also allow scientists to replicate certain tissues for transplantation. Some researchers say it will be possible someday to clone healthy organs and bone marrow. If the genetic material used in the cloning came from the patient, the chance that the body would reject the new organ or other tissue would be greatly reduced, if not eliminated.

But many scientists, Wilmut among them, argue that the tangible benefits of human cloning, if any, are outweighed by ethical and moral considerations.

Douglas Graham

Ian Wilmut, who led the team of scientists who created Dolly, told the Senate Public Health and Safety Subcommittee on March 12, 1997, that he opposed attempts to clone humans.

"I personally still have not heard of a potential use of this technique to produce a person that I would find ethical or acceptable," Wilmut told the Senate Labor and Human Resources Subcommittee on Public Health and Safety on March 12.

"There's simply no justification for it," says Randall Prather, an associate professor of animal sciences at the University of Missouri-Columbia. Prather and others say that duplicating a person for any reason — whether to indulge someone's ego, produce a genetically related child or replicate a dying child — does not justify the potential problems that cloning would cause.

"It's not bad to say that there are going to be certain things that we just won't do," says Karen Rothenberg, a professor at the University of Maryland School of Law in Baltimore.

According to Rothenberg, human cloning would challenge a number of "concepts basic to our humanness." For instance, she says, cloning would remove the fundamental and crucial interdependence associated with reproduction by requiring only one, as opposed to two, parents. "The fact that the propagation of the species takes two — whether in a test tube or a bedroom — humbles us because it means that practically and symbolically human survival is dependent upon human connectedness," she told the Senate panel.

In addition, Rothenberg argued, by allowing the possibility of producing endless copies of one person, cloning would shatter our concept of individuality, even though none of the replicas would be exactly the same.

"While I feel unique if I have one twin sister, I do not if I have 50 or 100," she said. "I no longer understand myself as a creation but as a copy."

Others say that humans have no business perverting God's method of creation. "The human body is God's property, not man's laboratory," writes Munawar Ahmad Anees, an Islamic scholar and author of the 1989 book *Islam and Biological Futures.* For Anees, the body should not be replicated by any means other than that given to humanity by God: namely sexual reproduction.[7]

This view is widely shared by Christians and Jews. Pope John Paul II, in his 1995 encyclical "Evangelium Vitae" ("The Gospel of Life") writes: "It is precisely in their role as co-workers with God who transmits his image to the new creature that we see the greatness of couples who are ready to cooperate with the love of the Creator and the Savior, who through them will enlarge and enrich his own family day by day."[8]

In addition to the moral and ethical concerns associated with human cloning, opponents also argue that there are other ways to obtain the knowledge needed to fight cancer and other diseases.

"I can't at the moment honestly see anything in this that's going to tell us something about humans that we can't find out in experimentally more acceptable animals like mice and sheep," says Colin Stewart, director of the Laboratory for Cancer Developmental Biology at the government's Advanced Biosciences Laboratories in Frederick, Md.

Some scientists also say that cloning tissue for organ transplants would probably be largely unnecessary and once again fraught with ethical concerns. For example, Gordon says, cloning would not be needed to create bone marrow for transplantation because it is already possible to take a sample of existing marrow and "grow these cells in a dish" until there is enough. In addition, Gordon says, the creation of human embryos for the purpose of growing organs or other tissue "would be very objectionable to many people."

Ron Sachs/CNP/Archive Photo

Sen. Bill Frist, R-Tenn. (left), chairman of the Public Health and Safety Subcommittee and the only physician in the Senate, held hearings on the ethics of cloning in March to "get the dialogue going." Subcommittee member Sen. Edward M. Kennedy, D-Mass., also urges more discussion before banning cloning research.

But others say that objections to cloning, whether ethical or pragmatic, are simply a reaction to something that is different. "These are the same arguments that people used against [in vitro fertilization]," Robertson says. In other words, he argues, it's just another case of people fearing what they don't know.

"When one thinks about how cloning might be used," it loses its capacity to scare people," he says. For example, Robertson says, if a cloned child were raised by a loving family, "It's hard for me to see how that child would be any different" from any other child.

Many cloning advocates see efforts to ban research as simply the latest round in the age-old struggle between the seekers of knowledge and those who would preserve the status quo.

"Some say that cloning is demeaning to human nature, but I say that to stop the quest for knowledge is demeaning to human nature" Sen. Tom Harkin, D-Iowa, said at the March 12 Senate subcommittee hearing. "I want to be on the side of the Galileos who say that the human mind knows no limits," he added, referring to the 17th century Italian astronomer who, under torture, recanted his then controversial view that the Earth was not the center of the universe.

But cloning opponents say that some knowledge carries certain responsibilities that cannot be ignored. "We cannot permit scientists to do something that changes our definition of what it means to be human and put the burden on society to prove that it is wrong," Annas says. "The burden of proof should be on the scientists to show that it is beneficial," he adds.

Will scientists be able to clone a human in the next decade or so?

Cornell University animal sciences Professor W. Bruce Currie is among the optimists. "We could be there in 10 years, if we really decided to do

Questions and Answers About Human Cloning

Is it possible to make a genetically exact copy of another person?

Cloning a human being would not produce an exact genetic replica. The nucleus of the donor cell, which is used to make the clone, contains only 98 percent of a person's genetic material. The remaining 2 percent is contained in the cell's mitochondria, which process energy for cell functions. Since the mitochondria are not contained in the nucleus, they are not transferred from the donor. Instead, the clone would receive genetic material from the mitochondria contained in the egg in which the donor's nucleus has been implanted.

Biologists believe that when life first began more than 3 billion years ago, mitochondria were separate organisms, which may explain why they contain genetic material apart from the genes in the nucleus. Yet scientists say their effect on the physical outcome of the clone would not be significant, and that physical differences between a clone and its donor would not be detectable to the naked eye.

Could a dinosaur or other extinct or dead animal be cloned?

In Michael Crichton's best-selling novel *Jurassic Park*, scientists clone dinosaurs by extracting their DNA from fossilized blood.

While Crichton's idea is intriguing, scientists say it is unlikely to move into the realm of reality. According to Randall Prather, an associate professor of animal sciences at the University of Missouri-Columbia, it might be possible to clone animals that have just died. But soon after death, he says, cells begin to degenerate, making them unsuitable for cloning.

Would a clone have the personality of its donor?

No. Even identical twins do not share personalities, although they can share some personality traits. But unlike twins, who grow up at the same time and are usually raised in the same household, a clone would be reared in a different age, in a different environment and probably by different people. Thus, any personality differences between a clone and its donor would likely, on average, be greater than those between identical twins.

Would a human clone enjoy full legal rights?

Some ethicists and lawyers say that courts would likely accord clones the same rights enjoyed by other American citizens. "The legal rights of these people are going to be the rights of any human being," says Ruth Macklin, a professor of bioethics at the Albert Einstein College of Medicine in New York City. According to Macklin, legal rights "kick in" when people are born, regardless of how they were conceived.

But others say that a human clone might have a different legal status. "Our whole legal system is based on human reproduction," says Jeremy Rifkin, president of the Foundation on Economic Trends. For example, Rifkin asks, "Who will get custody of the clone?" after its birth, the mother or the person who donated the cell?

Would the clone's donor be its parent or sibling?

Neither definition is an exact fit. Traditionally, a parent provides only half of the DNA needed to create a person as opposed to the 98 percent that the donor would pass on to the clone.

On the other hand, siblings share the same mother and father. Still, says John Robertson, a law professor at the University of Texas-Austin, a donor and clone are more like siblings because they are essentially twins.

it," he says. "How long did it take to put a man on the moon?" *

Gordon agrees. "I think that if you could use humans in your research and set up a very aggressive set of experiments, it could be done in 10 years."

According to Currie, who opposes cloning humans, the great discovery by Wilmut and his colleagues — how to reactivate all of an adult cell's genes — probably would prove helpful in cloning a human because there are no "obvious differences between human and sheep cells."

In fact, a small step toward cloning humans already has been taken. In 1993, scientists at George Washington University in Washington, D.C., cloned human embryos, although not by the usual method of transferring the genetic material of a cell to an egg. Instead, researchers separated cells from existing embryos, putting each of them into a lab dish. Some of these cells began developing into embryos on their own before dying.

But other scientists say that there are profound differences between humans and other mammals that make predictions such as Currie's unlikely. For one thing, Stewart says, sheep and human embryos turn on their DNA at different times. DNA is comprised of billions of molecules within the cell that contain almost all of its genetic information. In normal human reproduction, immediately after an egg is

* Neil Armstrong and Edwin "Buzz" Aldrin landed on the moon in 1969, eight years after President John F. Kennedy made landing on the moon in 10 years a national goal.

fertilized the resulting embryonic cells run on a sort of auto-pilot until the DNA activates and begins to direct the synthesis of proteins and other crucial cellular activities.

In sheep, the DNA does not activate until the embryo has divided three or four times to form eight or 16 cells. On the other hand, Stewart argues that in humans, the DNA begins functioning earlier, after the embryo has divided only twice to form four cells. According to Stewart, the extra time the DNA has in the sheep embryo may allow it to reprogram the nucleus that was taken from the adult sheep into one that is suitable for embryonic growth.

The earlier DNA activation in human cells may not leave the embryo enough time to reprogram the new nucleus. If the nucleus is not reprogrammed when the embryo's DNA activates, the embryo will die very quickly, he says, which could prevent all attempts at human cloning for the foreseeable future.

But Currie argues that the hurdle is imaginary. "To the best of my knowledge, [DNA activation] occurs in farm animals and humans at the same time," he says. In addition, he says, "We don't even know if the adult nucleus needs to be reprogrammed."

While scientists may disagree about the feasibility of cloning humans, most feel that something much more fundamental will stand in the way of successful experimentation: the need to use human test subjects.

"Until you get the technique 100 percent reliable, you're going to have lots of miscarriages, still births and abnormal babies," Stewart says. He points out that Dolly was the only healthy ewe produced among the 277 sheep eggs used in the experiment. "The [uproar] that would come out of this would be tremendous," he adds.

Others agree. "What happens when someone is born with two heads or three eyes or with fur all over their body?" asks Nancy Kass, an associate professor of health policy and management at the Johns Hopkins University Bioethics Institute. "That's a horrible use of a human being."

A related problem would be finding women who understood the risks associated with the experiments and still would be willing to participate.

"I personally still have not heard of a potential use of this technique to produce a person that I would find ethical or acceptable."

— Ian Wilmut, Dolly's creator

"I don't think we would have enough information on hand to really explain the risks they would be facing by taking one of these embryos," Gordon says. Thus, "it will be very hard to get real 'informed consent.' "

Should researchers continue to clone animals to produce better livestock breeds or medical breakthroughs?

Cloning animals is widely considered both ethical and useful. Scientists and ethicists argue that if researchers can improve upon the techniques developed in Scotland, cloned animals will help provide the world with better and cheaper food and medicine.

Researchers have been cloning farm animals from embryonic cells, as opposed to the adult cell used to make Dolly, since 1984, when a multicell sheep embryo was used to create a clone of the donor embryo. Since then, many animals have been successfully cloned using embryonic cells, including pigs, cattle and goats.

Animal cloning research will probably have its greatest impact in two broad areas, experts say. First, it will enable livestock breeders to replicate an almost unlimited number of copies of the specific animal wanted.

"For example, you could implant identical embryos [of a cow] with more meat, less fat and greater resistance to disease," Prather says. In other words, once breeders found the "perfect cow," they could simply copy it, instead of trying to breed it with less "perfect" cows.

The advantages to this kind of uniformity would be felt at every stage of an animal's journey from the farm to the dinner table, according to Prather. Feed lots, for example, would soon learn how to care for these identical animals and apply the techniques to successive generations of clones. And since the animals always would be roughly the same size, they would be easier to slaughter and process. In addition, Prather argues, consumers would know exactly what they were buying every time they went to the supermarket.

But some observers view the creation of "designer animals" as unethical and dangerous.

"Every creature that comes into

being ought to have the right to its individual genetic makeup," says Jeremy Rifkin, president of the Foundation on Economic Trends. According to Rifkin and others, it is morally wrong to alter the genetic makeup of an animal simply to make it produce more meat or milk or wool. "It's a lack of basic respect for the intrinsic value of life," he says.

In addition, Rifkin and others argue, replacing all of the cows or sheep in the world with a "perfect" breed could easily cause the species to weaken or die off.

"We've been monoculturing domesticated plants and animals to the point where there are only several breeds of many species left, which is bad enough," he says, referring to the practice of eliminating less efficient breeds in favor of those that produce the highest yields.

Maintaining different breeds is important because the diversity guarantees that the gene pool of a particular species will be varied, and thus more resilient, says Bernard Rollin, a professor of philosophy at the University of Colorado. Without variety, Rollin says, animals become more susceptible to a host of bacterial and viral infections. [9]

Rifkin agrees, pointing out that farmers already must feed animals with unusually high doses of antibiotics to keep them healthy. These existing problems associated with monoculturing will "increase exponentially" if all the animals of one breed were genetically identical, he says.

But cloning supporters say that it is simply a more efficient way to do what is already being accomplished through reproductive breeding. Moreover, they say, cloning could become even more important in the future.

"We have an ever-growing world population," Prather adds. "So if we can improve agricultural production, we can make feeding those people that much easier."

Medical researchers are also excited about cloning animals. PPL Therapeutics PLC, which aided Wilmut's work with Dolly, is among many firms that breed transgenic, or genetically engineered, animals. [10] Genetic engineering has created animals that produce substances in their milk to treat diseases. For example, goats have been patented that produce anti-clotting drugs for heart attack and stroke victims, and sheep are used to make an enzyme inhibitor to combat cystic fibrosis.

Using transgenic animals to produce drugs is already a multibillion-dollar industry. But current methods used to create such creatures are very inefficient. In essence, scientists inject many copies of the gene that will make the desired change into a recently fertilized egg and then implant it in a surrogate mother.

But the procedure results in the successful birth of a transgenic animal less than 1 percent of the time, Wilmut says. Cloning would be infinitely more efficient, he says, since it is easy to genetically modify adult cells, as opposed to fertilized eggs. [11]

In addition, cloning will allow easy replication of a transgenic animal after the first one is successfully produced. "If you succeed in making that [first] transgenic cloned sheep, you are essentially home free," said Viren Mehta, a financial analyst in New York specializing in biotechnology. "You just keep making them." [12]

Cloning also can aid in the development and production of animals to provide organs for xenotransplantation, or animal transplants, to human beings. As with transgenics, scientists say, cloning will allow researchers to modify animals to make their organs or tissue more acceptable to the human immune system and less likely to be rejected. And, once again, cloning will allow scientists to essentially mass produce those animals that are successfully bred as xenotransplant donors.

But Rifkin urges caution. Introducing biological material from animals directly into a patient's body, either as a drug or organ transplant, might expose the person to diseases that are harmless to the animal (and thus hidden from researchers) but deadly to humans, he says.

"When you start breaking the species barrier," he says, "you get dangerous organisms in new forms where there may be no cure." ■

BACKGROUND

An Ancient Quest

The idea of skirting the rules of reproduction has tantalized human beings since the beginning of recorded time. Four millennia ago, a Mesopotamian story told of the god Enki, who tried to create life using only his semen. [13]

More than 1,500 years later, the Greek playwright Euripedes had a similar notion. In his play *Hippolytus* (428 BC), the male protagonist speculates on the benefits of being able to have children without women. And in the Bible, of course, Adam and Eve and Jesus Christ are created using means other than sexual reproduction.

Humans also have devoted much thought to the idea of "playing God." The notion that hubris, scientific or otherwise, will lead to trouble dates back to ancient times. From the Greek myth of Prometheus to the hit movie *Jurassic Park,* the idea that there are limits to what man should know is repeated over and over again in literature. In Mary Shelley's classic tale, *Frankenstein,* a doctor, learns the

Continued on p. 420

Chronology

1850s-1950s

Scientists make great strides in the science of genetics and cell biology. Cloning is first proposed and attempted.

1866
Gregor Mendel, an Austrian monk, publishes an article explaining basic laws of genetic inheritance. The discovery goes virtually unnoticed until 1900.

1932
German scientist Hans Spemann proposes transferring the nucleus from the cell of an adult animal into an egg in order to replicate that animal.

1952
Two scientists fail in attempt to clone a frog by transferring the nucleus from a cell to an egg.

1953
James Watson and Francis Crick discover the structural model for deoxyribonucleic acid (DNA), the chemical basis for heredity.

1960s-1980s

Initial success in cloning frogs is followed by two decades of little progress. But in the 1980s, scientists begin cloning mammals.

1962
In the first successful cloning experiment, Oxford University zoologist John Gurdon transfers the nucleus from a frog cell to a frog egg, resulting in embryos that develop into tadpoles.

1970
Theologian Paul Ramsey argues against cloning humans in his book, *The Fabricated Man*.

1978
The Boys from Brazil, a film that concerns the cloning of Hitler, is released.

1981
Researchers Karl Illmensee and Peter Hoppe announce that they have cloned mice using embryonic cells. But the experiment cannot be duplicated and an inquiry reveals that Illmensee, of the University of Geneva, faked his results.

1984
Steen Willadsen, a Danish embryologist, clones a sheep using embryonic cells. Over the next decade, other scientists duplicate Willadsen's experiment with sheep and other farm animals.

1985
A genetically engineered, or transgenic, pig is created that produces a human growth hormone in its milk.

1990s

The first animal cloned from an adult, rather than an embryonic cell, is born.

1993
Scientists at the George Washington University clone human embryo cells.

1994
Scientists led by Neil Furst at the University of Wisconsin induce quiescence, or hibernation, in a cell, the first step toward using adult cells in cloning.

1995
Scientists at the Roslin Institute in Scotland, led by Ian Wilmut, repeat Furst's experiment using mature embryonic cells from sheep.

January 1996
Wilmut and his colleagues plant 29 embryos cloned from adult sheep cells into surrogate ewes. In July, one of the ewes gives birth to Dolly, the first mammal ever cloned from an adult cell.

Feb. 22, 1997
Wilmut announces the cloning of Dolly to a stunned world.

Feb. 24, 1997
President Clinton asks the National Bioethics Advisory Commission (NBAC) to study the implications of cloning.

March 4, 1997
President Clinton issues an executive order barring the use of federal money for human cloning reasearch. Also in early March, researchers at the Oregon Regional Primate Research Center announce the cloning of Rhesus monkeys using embryonic cells — the first time primates have been cloned.

May 29, 1997
The NBAC's report containing recommendations on cloning humans is due.

Cloning Goes to the Movies

In the race between fantasy and reality, filmmakers are still far ahead of the scientists.

Since the 1950s, Hollywood has produced a string of films and television shows that have dealt with efforts to replicate humans. The rich dramatic possibilities of cloning make Tinseltown's longstanding fascination with the subject understandable .

But while many of these efforts have been entertaining, few if any have tried to paint an accurate picture of cloning or its likely uses. Instead, cloning has either been used as a comic device, or enlisted as the latest prop in a long line of yarns about the dangers of new technology.

In last year's film *Multiplicity*, Michael Keaton plays a married man who is cloned not once but three times — into a tough guy; a sensitive, caring man; and a buffoon.

Another comedy, Woody Allen's *Sleeper* (1973), also pokes fun at the idea of making copies of someone. In this case, an assassinated president is to be brought back to life by using his nose to clone him.

A second and much larger genre of cloning films explores the darker theme of "playing God." The latest and most popular of these movies is *Jurassic Park,* directed by Steven Spielberg and based on Michael Crichton's best-selling novel.

In the film, scientists find well-preserved dinosaur blood in mosquitoes and other insects that were trapped in amber, and use it to clone tyrannosaurs, veloraptors and other fierce dinosaurs. The purpose of the enterprise is purely commercial — *Jurassic Park* is for vacationers. But before the venture's owners can open for business, everything goes haywire, and the animals, so to speak, begin to run the zoo (and dispatch quite a few of the film's characters in the process.)

Jurassic Park is a direct descendant of cautionary tales like Frankenstein, its underlying message being that humans should have respect for the unknown. And predictably, as in Frankenstein and other such works, the scientists in *Jurassic Park* learn that when you play with fire, you're likely to get your fingers burned.

A film that also deals with cloning, but in a different way, is *The Boys from Brazil* (1978), based on Ira Levin's novel about an attempt to make multiple clones of Adolph Hitler. Here, the mad scientist is Joseph Mengele, the notorious, real-life Nazi doctor who was responsible for conducting inhumane experiments on concentration camp inmates during World War II. Unlike the researchers who make the dinosaurs in *Jurassic Park,* Mengele is already damned to hell when the story opens. His enterprise does not "go wrong," it is wrong from the very beginning.

All of these movies, even the comedies, share a common theme: Cloning is too risky to pursue responsibly. This sentiment mirrors society's ingrained and widespread fear of the new, a fact that has not been lost on Hollywood.

As with cloning, there have been a host of films about other dangerous technologies, ranging from nuclear weapons (*Failsafe*) to biological research (*Outbreak*). In each case, humanity learns the valuable lesson that with some things, it is better to leave well enough alone.

But the idea that there are lines that we are not supposed to cross was not invented by screenwriters. Indeed, it is as old as literature itself, tracing its beginning to the Old Testament story of Adam and Eve and the forbidden fruit.

Throughout the ages, the story of man's expulsion from Eden has been recast and retold. One reason, of course, is that it's entertainment; watching someone fall from grace is riveting.

Yet fall-from-grace stories, in a way, are comforting. Just as comedy has fun at someone else's expense, these cautionary tales are a way to ease our anxiety about the unknown, for in almost all such stories, those who try to unlock forbidden secrets usually fail, restoring the sense of balance that existed in the universe before the tale began.

Or, to quote Christopher Marlowe, in his play *Dr. Faustus*, "the wise only . . . wonder at unlawful things whose deepness doth entice such forward wits to practice more than heavenly power permits."

Continued from p. 418

secret of bringing the dead back to life, only to unleash a monster who ultimately destroys him.

But no story goes to the heart of what it means to play God better than the legend of Faust. Great writers from Christopher Marlowe to Goethe to Thomas Mann have been drawn to the tale of a man who is overwhelmed by his thirst for knowledge and power.

Science Marches On

By the beginning of the Enlightenment, biology, and science in general, were catching up with the literature. An early development occurred in the late 17th century when Englishman Robert Hooke used a microscope to discern separate compartments in a piece of cork. He called them cells.

Over the next 200 years, biologists built on Hooke's work, discovering the basic parts of the cell as well as the process of mitosis, or reproduction through cell division. By the end of the 19th century, scientists had theorized that chromosomes were the agents of inheritance. But proof of how traits were passed from parent to offspring proved elusive. [14]

In 1866, however, the Austrian monk Gregor Mendel laid out the basic laws of genetic inheritance after observing different varieties of peas in his monastery garden. Mendel realized that inherited traits, such as eye color (or in the case of peas, seed color,) came in pairs, one of which was dominant and the other recessive. Through observation, he discovered that parents were three times more likely to pass on a dominant trait than a recessive one. [15]

Mendel's groundbreaking work on inherited traits was not accepted until 1900, when three other scientists reached the same conclusions independently.

Thereafter, the study of genetics progressed rapidly. Scientists realized that chromosomes, and the genes within them, were responsible for passing on traits. In addition, Mendel's ideas were refined to take into account differences in gender and other factors.

A big breakthrough came in 1953, when researchers James Watson and Francis Crick discovered the structural model for deoxyribonucleic acid (DNA), the chemical basis for heredity. Watson and Crick won the Nobel Prize for their discovery that each gene contains chains of four simple molecules. Each of these DNA chains contain hundreds or thousands of these molecules, the order of which, like letters in a word, determines the information contained in the chain. When taken together, these DNA chains form a person's genetic blueprint. [16]

Fiction to Reality

The idea of cloning first surfaced in the scientific community in 1938, when a German scientist, Hans Spemann, proposed transferring the nucleus from the cell of an adult animal into an egg. The challenge was not taken up until 1952, when scientists added the nucleus from a frog cell to an egg. But the experiment did not produce a cloned frog. [17]

Ten years later, the first cloning experiment was successfully performed. Oxford University zoologist John Gurdon transferred the nucleus from a frog cell into a frog egg with its nucleus removed. The resulting embryos developed into tadpoles, though they died before reaching adulthood. Other attempts at the nuclear transfer of frog cells also produced death in the tadpole stage.

The work of Gurdon and others led to speculation that cloning would never work. Then in 1981, Karl Illmensee of the University of Geneva and Peter Hoppe of the Jackson Laboratory in Bar Harbor, Maine, stunned the scientific community by announcing that they had cloned mice using embryonic cells. There was only one problem: The results could not be duplicated by other scientists, and it was later revealed that Illmensee had faked his data.

AFP Photo/Philippe Huguen

Members of the European Parliament belonging to the Green Party wear masks to protest cloning during the Parliament's session on March 11, 1997.

The Illmensee/Hoppe fiasco renewed the conviction that cloning mammals would remain in the realm of science fiction. In 1984, however, Steen Willadsen of Denmark cloned a sheep using embryonic cells. This time, others were able to duplicate the experiment, and not only with sheep. In the last decade, researchers have cloned a variety of mammals ranging from cattle to pigs. But in each case, embryonic cells were used. [18]

The next step was cloning with adult cells. But there was a big barrier to overcome. In early embryonic cells, all of the genes in the nucleus are functioning, which means they can be used as a genetic blueprint to create a new duplicate animal. In adult cells, many genes have been genetically "turned off," making the blueprint incomplete. The key to success was finding a way to make adult cells act like embryonic cells and turn all of their genes on.

The first clues to how to tackle this problem came from a team of scientists led by the University of Wisconsin's Neil Furst. By accidentally depriving embryonic cells of serum — a source of hormonelike growth factors usually needed to grow cells in culture — Furst discovered that they could be put into a state of quiescence, or hibernation, with their genes turned off. But when the nuclei of these cells were removed and fused with an egg, all of the genes turned on, resulting in the birth of healthy calves. [19]

In 1995, Wilmut successfully repeated Furst's experiment using mature embryonic cells from sheep. The big question was what would happen with adult cells? Would they turn on all of their genes when fused with an egg or just those that had been functional before hibernation?

In January 1996, Wilmut and his colleagues fused adult sheep nuclei onto 277 eggs whose nuclei had been removed. Thirty eggs developed into embryos, proving that quiescent adult cells could reactivate all of their genes.

Twenty-nine embryos were implanted in surrogate ewes, but only one healthy lamb was produced — 15-pound Dolly.

A week after Wilmut's historic announcement, researchers at the Oregon Regional Primate Research Center announced that they had successfully cloned Rhesus monkeys. Although embryonic cells had been used, the experiment was still important: For the first time, scientists had cloned primates, taking the technology one step closer to human beings. [20] ■

CURRENT SITUATION

Government Responds

Many developed countries, including Germany, Denmark and the United Kingdom, ban human cloning. But in the United States, the world's leading biotechnology research center, cloning was never even debated as a matter of public policy.

That changed this year on Feb. 22. The announcement of Dolly's birth may have caught government officials and members of Congress off guard. But it did not take long for President Clinton to react.

"Science often moves faster than our ability to understand its implications."

— President Bill Clinton

On Feb. 24, Clinton formally asked the National Bioethics Advisory Commission (NBAC) to "undertake a thorough review of legal and ethical issues associated with the use of this technology and report back to me within 90 days with recommendations on possible use of this technology to clone human embryos." The 18-member panel had been created by the president in October 1995.

On March 4, Clinton issued an executive order barring the use of federal money for human cloning experiments.

"Science often moves faster than our ability to understand its implications," Clinton said. He also urged private institutions to voluntarily stop human cloning research until "our entire nation [has] had a real chance to understand and debate the profound ethical implications of the latest advances."

According to Kass of Johns Hopkins, a moratorium is appropriate both ethically and politically. "We need to make people confident that we will not go forward until we're sure about this," she says.

But others feared that Clinton's order could make federal agencies wary of funding any related research.

"I think he acted politically and reflexively," says Cornell's Currie, who works on embryo cell biology and thinks Clinton "should have kept his mouth shut until he understood what this was all about."

In Congress, Rep. Vernon J. Ehlers, R-Mich., has proposed an outright ban on all cloning research, regardless of its funding source. Two other measures, one also sponsored by Ehlers and another introduced by Sen. Christopher S. Bond, R-Mo., would permanently ban funding for human cloning research. [21]

Most members of Congress probably would oppose any attempt to clone a human being. But there is no rush to impose substantial limits on general cloning research, in part because lawmakers worry that a ban on research would shut off possible agricultural and medical advances.

"My fear is that someone, in their haste . . . will deny my family and other families important medical research," said Sen. Connie Mack, R-Fla., whose wife is a breast cancer survivor. [22]

Mack's concern was echoed by Sen. Bill Frist, R-Tenn., chairman of the Labor and Human Resources Sub-

Continued on p. 424

At Issue:

Should the United States ban human cloning?

GEORGE J. ANNAS
Professor of health law, Boston University School of Law, Medicine and Public Health

FROM *ABA JOURNAL*, MAY 1997

yes

Human cloning should be banned because it would radically alter our very definition of ourselves by producing the world's first human with a single genetic parent. This manufacture of a person made to order undermines human dignity and individuality, and encourages us to treat children like commodities.

Prior discussion of the ethics of human cloning was interrupted in 1978 by the birth of Louise Brown, the world's first baby conceived through in vitro fertilization. . . .

We still have not answered any of the questions of parental identity, embryo disposition and posthumous reproduction that in vitro fertilization has spawned. In vitro fertilization is no precedent for cloning; the child is still conceived by the union of the egg and sperm from two separate persons, and the child is genetically unique. Cloning is replication, not reproduction, and represents a difference in kind, not in degree, in the way humans continue the species.

Novels such as *Frankenstein* and *Brave New World*, and films such as *Jurassic Park* and *Bladerunner* have prepared the public to discuss deep ethical issues in human cloning.

Victor Frankenstein never named his creature, repudiating parental responsibility. . . . Naming the cloned sheep "Dolly" was done for the public to suggest an individual, or a least a pet or a doll, not for the scientific article (in which she is referred to simply as 6LL3). The strategy was meant to distance her from Frankenstein myth by making her appear to be more normal than she is. . . .

Rather than look deeply into ethics and world literature, supporters of human cloning have tried to come up with extreme and improbable hypotheticals to sell this technique to the American public. . . . The most popular suggestion is that parents of a dying child should be able to clone the child for a replacement. But when a child is cloned, it is not the parents who are replicated, but the child. No one should have such dominion over a child as to be allowed to use its genes to create the child's child. . . .

Humans have a basic right not to reproduce, and human dignity requires that human reproduction not be equated with that of farm animals or even pets. We could only discover whether cloning is even feasible in humans by unethically subjecting the planned child to the risk of serious genetic and physical injury. Congress and states should take a stand at this boundary.

JOHN A. ROBERTSON
Vinson & Elkins chair in law, University of Texas School of Law

FROM *ABA JOURNAL*, MAY 1997

no

The successful cloning of an adult sheep has startled the public in the speed of its arrival, and in the potential it offers to control the genome of people. Although nurture and environment are crucially important in making people who they are, there is also truth in the claim that "who designs the plan, controls the product."

The prospect of human cloning elicits fears of abuse — visions of power-hungry tycoons cloning themselves or a class of permanent servants. But we should hesitate to act on initial reactions. . . .

A ban on cloning now is both imprudent and unjustified because there are potentially valid uses, and the potential harms have not yet been clearly identified. . . .

A key moral fact is that cloning will not necessarily harm anyone. In the most likely cloning scenarios, parents will be seeking a child whom they love for itself. Any resulting child would be a person with all the rights of persons, and no more would be the property or subject of the person who commissions or carries out the cloning than any other child. . . .

Consider some reasons for choosing to replicate a human genome. At the embryo level, it may be to assure that an infertile couple produces enough embryos available to achieve pregnancy. In that case cloning an embryo could lead to the birth of a twin. Even if the birth of the twins is temporarily separated, this is not necessarily harmful, and may lead to a special form of sibling bonding. There may be other situations of merit, such as creating embryos from which a child may be able to obtain needed organs or tissue, or creating a twin of a previous child who died. . . .

These uses vary in their appeal, in the existence of alternatives to the same goal and in their potential impact on persons providing the DNA and persons born with that genome. As a result, all cases of cloning need not be treated similarly. Self-cloning, which many would find to be the height of narcissism, may create problems for offspring that do not exist when cloning occurs to enhance the fertility or the health of the children.

Cloning raises challenging questions about human liberty, dignity and identity. At this early stage in the development process, however, enough good uses can be imagined that it would be foolish to ban all cloning and cloning research because of vague and highly speculative fears. As with the other technological developments, science fiction should not drive science policy.

Continued from p. 422

committee on Public Health and Safety, which would play a key role in crafting any cloning legislation. Frist, the only physician in the Senate, said that the public's fear of cloning research was similar to its initial reaction to heart and lung transplants. "It's ultimate acceptance required a rational discourse among scientists, ethicists and the general public." [23]

But Ehlers predicts that if Congress does not move to limit or ban human cloning research, states will act on their own. Indeed, legislators in many states, including California and New York, already have raised the issue. State Sen. Patrick Johnston, D-Calif., for instance, has proposed a five-year moratorium on human cloning and a fine of up to $100,000 for violators.

Whether the federal and state governments ultimately decide to limit cloning research or not, their decisions will likely be influenced by the NBAC's report, which is due May 29.

"My guess is that they will recommend some limited research," Kass says. Maryland's Rothenberg agrees. "We may ban the cloning of an entire human being but allow research to go forward on the cellular level," she says.

Some observers see only a limited value in the commission because they suspect it will tell the decision-makers what it thinks they want to hear. Instead of relying on a commission that can only recommend policy, Boston University's Annas favors the creation of a new agency, like the Food and Drug Administration, which would issue and enforce regulations. Annas would give the new body authority over "issues like genetic engineering, artificial organs and other similar things that alter our basic view of ourselves."

As for the NBAC, "They'll come up with a political compromise because the nature of these organizations is to be more political than ethical," Annas says. ■

OUTLOOK

Consumer Cloning?

If scientists are allowed to go ahead with human cloning experiments, and if they succeed, there could still be problems in the offing.

Some researchers worry that clones may age prematurely since their genetic material will have been based on the nucleus of an adult cell. While scientists have much to learn about cells and how they affect aging, there is some evidence that there is a biological "clock" in human genes that causes aging and, eventually, death.

Will a clone with the genetic material of a 40-year-old be born with a reduced life span? Some scientists say it's a possibility. But Gordon disagrees, pointing out that the children of women in their 40s do not age faster than those born to teenagers.

A related concern is that clones may be much more susceptible to life-threatening diseases at a very early age. Over time, according to this theory, radiation and other environmental factors damage cell DNA. As the radiation accumulates, it increases the risk for cancer and other diseases. If the cell of a 40-year-old is used to clone another person, some scientists theorize, the clone may end up receiving damaged genetic material, increasing the risk of contracting diseases at an earlier age than normal.

Even with these and other concerns, many see human cloning research as inevitable, arguing that technological advances, once launched, cannot be stopped. And yet the developed world has had some success in limiting the proliferation of nuclear and other weapons of mass destruction.

Some thinkers believe that, like nuclear weapons, cloning will be seen as a potentially dangerous technology that has to be controlled.

"I don't think we'll clone a whole human being in our lifetime," Rothenberg says, pointing out that most people are repulsed by the idea of cloning another person and that no one, including biotechnology companies, "is clamoring to do this." Instead, she says, governments will probably allow some limited human cloning research to go forward with the aim of using it for medical purposes and to enhance existing reproductive technologies.

Like Rothenberg, Annas agrees that cloning a human being will probably not come to pass in the foreseeable future because it is not an appealing reproductive option.

"Hardly anyone wants to reproduce themselves," he says, adding that, "Most people want to produce something better than themselves."

And yet, there always will be people interested in cloning themselves. "There are always people who want to be remembered," says Mount Sinai's Gordon. In addition, Gordon and others say, the facilities needed to conduct cloning experiments would not be terribly expensive to set up, making it easy for a wealthy person to sponsor such work. "The hardest part would probably be getting [specialists] together to do the research," he says.

But others argue that far from being for narcissist billionaires, cloning will be developed for average consumers.

"What I see is not social eugenics, but commercial eugenics," Rifkin says, adding that companies will use cloning in conjunction with other developments in genetics to offer consumers a range of products and services. "Cloning is on a parallel track with the mapping of the human and animal genome and developments in our ability to intervene in

FOR MORE INFORMATION

Center for Biomedical Ethics, 701A Welch St., Suite 1105, Palo Alto, Calif. 94304; (415) 723-5760. The center conducts a broad range of research on biomedical issues.

Council for Responsible Genetics, 5 Upland Rd., Suite 3, Cambridge, Mass. 02140; (617) 868-0870. The council supports more stringent government regulation of genetic research.

Foundation on Economic Trends, 1130 17th St. N.W., Suite 630, Washington, D.C. 20036; (202) 466-9602. Jeremy Rifkin, the foundation's president, is among the nation's most outspoken critics of cloning and many forms of genetic engineering.

Kennedy Institute of Ethics, Georgetown University, 1437 37th St. N.W., Washington, D.C. 20057; (202) 687-8099. The institute sponsors research on issues concerning medical ethics, including recombinant DNA and human gene therapy.

the gene line, which will allow us to change the specific genes of an organism," he says.

Rifkin envisions a world in which parents will be able to produce and "replicate" children who are smarter, better-looking and healthier than babies born today.

"The importance of cloning is replication, so that you can have precise quality control, quantifiable standards of measurement and the efficiency associated with being able to replicate something over and over," Rifkin says, drawing a parallel with manufacturing techniques developed during the Industrial Revolution.

Rifkin and others say that in our consumerist society, "the market for cloning will blossom." Duff of Princeton Theological Seminary agrees, predicting that once people realize the commercial potential of cloning "money will dictate policy."

The commercialization of cloning may be aided by a shift in public attitudes, making public opposition to human cloning less intense over time. "Our natural reaction to things that are new is to be scared of them and to think they are wrong," Kass says.

And yet some believe that, regardless of ethical debate or commercial potential, researchers will ultimately be driven to replicate a human being simply because it hasn't been done.

"Sure they'll make noise — 'Oh the horror' — but they'll do it," says Macklin, the bioethics professor.

Robert Oppenheimer, who led the effort to develop the atomic bomb, said much the same: "When you see something that is technologically sweet, you go ahead and do it." [24]

Daniel Callahan, a bioethicist at the Hastings Center in Briarcliff Manor, N.Y., agrees that scientists won't stop with cloning animals.

"We are at the mercy of these technical developments," he says. "Once they're here, it's hard to turn back." ■

Notes

[1] Thomas Maugh II, "Brave New World," *Los Angeles Times,* Feb. 27, 1997, p. B2.

[2] Quoted in "Cloning: How Do We Morally Navigate the Uncharted Future?" *Los Angeles Times,* March 5, 1997.

[3] *The New York Times,* March 8, 1997, p. NE 15.

[4] Paul Ramsey, *Fabricated Man* (1970), p. 96.

[5] The poll was conducted on Feb. 26-27.

[6] Robert Wachbroit, "Should We Cut This Out?" *The Washington Post,* March 2, 1997, p. C1.

[7] Munawar Ahmad Anees, "Cloning: How Do We Morally Navigate the Uncharted Future?" *Los Angeles Times,* March 5, 1997.

[8] Pope John Paul II, *The Gospel of Life* (1995), p. 76.

[9] Terence Monmaney, "Prospect of Human Cloning Gives Birth to Volatile Issues," *Los Angeles Times,* March 3, 1997, p. A3.

[10] See "Gene Therapy's Future," *The CQ Researcher,* Dec. 8, 1995, pp. 1089-1112.

[11] Bruce Wallace, "The Dolly Debate," *Maclean's,* March 10, 1997, p. 57.

[12] Quoted in Lawrence M. Fisher, "Cloned Animals Offer Companies a Faster Path to New Drugs," *The New York Times,* Feb. 24, 1997, p. A 15.

[13] Robert S. McElvaine, "Cloning: How Do We Morally Navigate the Uncharted Future?" *Los Angeles Times,* March 5, 1997.

[14] Edward Edelson, *Genetics and Heredity* (1990), pp. 16-18.

[15] *Ibid.* pp. 18-20.

[16] Christopher Lampton, *DNA and the Creation of Life* (1983), pp.13-19.

[17] Michael Specter and Gena Kolata, "After Decades and Many Missteps, Cloning Succeeds," *The New York Times,* March 3, 1997, p. A1.

[18] *Ibid.*

[19] *Ibid.*

[20] Rick Weiss and John Schwartz, "Monkeys Cloned for the First Time," *The Washington Post,* March 2, 1997, p. A4.

[21] Dan Carney, "Most Adopting Cautious Approach as Congress Confronts Cloning," *Congressional Quarterly's Weekly Report,* March 15, 1997, p. 641.

[22] Testimony before Senate Labor and Human Resources Subcommittee on Public Health and Safety, March 12.

[23] *Ibid.*

[24] Quoted in Kirkpatrick Sale, "Ban Cloning? Not a Chance?" *The New York Times,* March 2, 1997.

Bibliography

Selected Sources Used

Books

Alpern, Kenneth, D., ed., *The Ethics of Reproductive Technology,* Oxford University Press, 1992.
The ethical issues surrounding surrogate motherhood and in vitro fertilization are examined in detail by several authors. In addition, the writers discuss fundamental legal questions, such as, When is someone a child's parent?

Carmen, Ira H., *Cloning and the Constitution: An Inquiry into Government Policymaking and Genetic Experimentation,* University of Wisconsin Press, 1985.
Carmen examines cloning in the context of America's legal traditions, asking questions such as, Is scientific experimentation a form of expression that is protected by the Constitution?

Grace, Eric, *Biotechnology Unzipped: Promises and Realities,* Trifolium, 1997.
Grace, a well-known science writer, presents a good overview of recent developments in biotechnology, including cloning. He warns against imposing limits on research simply to soothe public anxieties. At the same time, he argues that scientists should also pursue new research with caution, especially since no one can be sure of the long-term effects of many developments.

Ramsey, Paul, *Fabricated Man: The Ethics of Genetic Control,* Yale University Press, 1970.
Ramsey, a leading medical ethicist and theologian, argues against cloning, warning that humanity will not have the wisdom to go along with the power that comes with gaining total control over one's destiny.

Articles

Begley, Sharon, "Little Lamb, Who Made Thee?" *Newsweek,* March 10, 1997.
Newsweek takes a comprehensive look at cloning in the wake of Dolly, focusing on the science of cloning farm animals and the ethics of attempting to clone humans.

Carey, John, Julia Flynn, Naomi Freundlich and Neil Gross, "The Biotech Century," *Business Week,* March 10, 1997.
The article looks at the future of the biotechnology industry in light of the recent advances in cloning research. The writers predict that advances in biotechnology will come fast and furious and that "advances in genetics and biology will define progress in the 21st century."

Carney, Dan, "Most Adopting Cautious Approach as Congress Confronts Cloning," *Congressional Quarterly Weekly Report,* March 15, 1997.
Carney gauges the mood on Capital Hill following the announcement of Dolly's birth. While a number of bills banning human cloning in the United States have already been introduced, he says, many members of Congress are wary of shutting down cloning research because it could lead to advances in the war against cancer and other terrible diseases.

"Cloning: How Do We Morally Navigate the Uncharted Future?" *Los Angeles Times,* March 5, 1997
This piece collects short essays by four thinkers on the ethics of cloning. Some, like Oxford University law Professor Ronald Dworkin, argue that government has no business banning human cloning, since the decision to replicate oneself is highly personal. Others, like Italian politician Rocco Buttiglione, say that nature dictates that children should "be procreated, not produced."

Garvey, John, "The Mystery Remains: What Cloning Can't Reproduce," *Commonweal,* March 28, 1997.
Garvey, a *Commonweal* columnist, argues that human cloning violates the sacredness and mystery of life. This in turn, takes us closer to "the idea of human beings as product or property."

Wachbroit, Robert, "Should We Cut This Out? Human Cloning isn't as Scary As it Sounds," *The Washington Post,* March 2, 1997.
Wachbroit, a research scholar at the University of Maryland's Institute for Philosophy and Public Policy, says that much public fear about cloning stems from ignorance. He argues that human cloning may have real societal benefit and that the government should not rush to ban it.

"Whatever Next," *The Economist,* March 1, 1997.
The article gives a clear explanation of the science behind adult cell cloning. It also explains some of the medical concerns, such as premature aging, that may arise if human cloning is ever permitted.

The Next Step

Additional information from UMI's Newspaper & Periodical Abstracts™ database

Ban on Cloning

"Cloning Begets Questions," *Times-Picayune,* March 10, 1997, p. B6.

President Clinton this week announced a ban on the use of federal funds to research human cloning and has asked scientists whose work is privately financed to refrain from such research until a national bioethics commission reviews the many implications. Britain already has such a ban. In this country, laws regulating human embryo research may have some bearing on cloning research. President Clinton signed an executive order in 1994 forbidding the use of federal funds for human embryo research, but he said the administration thinks there may be loopholes that would allow cloning research, hence the specific ban. Nine states regulate human embryo research, including Louisiana, which passed a law in 1986 that prohibits any experiments on human embryos outside the uterus.

Haworth, Karla, and Kim Strosnider, "Controversy grows over cloning research as scientists report new breakthroughs," *The Chronicle of Higher Education,* March 14, 1997, p. A14.

Amid numerous reports of successful cloning of mammals, President Clinton banned the use of federal grants for research on cloning human beings and called for private companies and universities to adopt a similar moratorium. National Institutes of Health Director Harold E. Varmus, even though he agrees with the president, said that more discussion among researchers was needed before laws permanently banning cloning are enacted.

Poor, Tim, "Ban Human Cloning Research, Bond Says," *St. Louis Post-Dispatch,* Feb. 26, 1997, p. A9.

Sen. Christopher S. Bond, R-Mo., said Tuesday he would propose a government-wide ban on federal funding for research on human cloning. He said he wanted to look into the possibility of barring private research as well. A ban on funding for research on human embryos has been in federal spending bills since 1994. Bond said the prohibition should be extended in light of the successful cloning of a sheep by Scottish scientist Ian Wilmut. "I don't think we should be playing God in trying to produce humans by cloning," said Bond, a member of the Senate subcommittee that oversees spending for the Department of Health and Human Services, including the National Institutes of Health.

Sneider, Daniel, "Rush by States to Ban Cloning Draws Ire, Again and Again," *The Christian Science Monitor,* March 21, 1997, p. 1.

The debate over human cloning, provoked by recent scientific breakthroughs, is suddenly echoing through statehouses from Florida to California. The announcement last month that a Scottish scientist had succeeded in cloning a sheep has prompted legislators in at least seven states to offer bills to ban experiments to clone human beings.

Williams, Nigel, "Cloning sparks calls for new laws," *Science,* March 7, 1997, p. 1415.

Officials and scientists around the world are calling for new laws after the successful cloning of a sheep. President Clinton has banned federal funding for human cloning research and asked for a moratorium on non-federally funded efforts.

Bioethics

Dorning, Mike, "U.S. Panel Examines Morality of Cloning; Children Should Be 'a Gift, Not a Product,' Church Scholar Says," *Chicago Tribune,* March 14, 1997, p. 12.

With its chairman declaring that "the very nature of what it means to be human" is at issue, a presidential bioethics panel on Thursday began an examination of cloning that is expected to shape the government's response to the first successful cloning of an adult animal. Protestant and Catholic theologians who appeared before the 18-member panel uniformly opposed the creation of new human beings through biotechnology. Bills to ban human cloning have been introduced in Congress, as well as in several state legislatures and foreign parliaments, prompting some scientists to express concern that overly broad bans could deny society beneficial medical uses of cloning techniques.

Kolata, Gina, "Little-Known Panel Challenged to Make Quick Cloning Study," *The New York Times,* March 18, 1997, p. C1.

The National Bioethics Advisory Commission, was directed by President Clinton on Feb. 24 to deliver a report to him within 90 days on legal and ethical issues involved in cloning techniques and "possible federal actions to prevent its abuse." But the panel that is looking at cloning was never intended to take on such a momentous topic, and no national ethics commission has ever had to work so quickly to get out a report. "Nothing has been analogous to this," said R. Alta Charo, a commission member who is a law professor at the University of Wisconsin. The 15-member group began its crash course in cloning on Thursday, meeting in an L-shaped room on the ground floor of the Watergate Hotel in Washington, D.C. Dr. Shirley Tilghman, a molecular biologist at Princeton University, informed them of the science behind the recent cloning report. In that report, by Dr. Ian Wilmut of the Roslin Institute in Edinburgh, Scotland, researchers described how they had merged an udder cell from a six-year-old sheep with a specially prepared sheep egg. The genetic material from the udder cell directed the egg to grow and develop into a lamb that was born last July, the identical twin of the sheep whose udder cell was used. Dr. Wilmut's feat shocked the world, for even most scientists had assumed that the cloning of adults was biologically impossible and was merely the stuff of science fiction.

Tye, Larry, "Lawmakers want panel on ethics of cloning," *The Boston Globe,* March 11, 1997, p. B1.
Massachusetts legislators agreed yesterday to push for creation of a bioethics commission to study controversial high-tech issues like cloning, and one influential senator said he will propose that this state become the first to ban the cloning of humans. Those moves grew out of a legislative hearing on last month's announcement that Scottish scientists had, for the first time, cloned an animal from adult cells. There was a surprising consensus among scientists, businessmen, ethicists, religious representatives and others testifying yesterday that while government should be wary about regulating science, it should set limits on cloning humans.

Wallace, Bruce, "The Dolly debate," *Maclean's,* March 10, 1997, pp. 54-58.
A sheep cloned in Scotland has raised hopes and fears about eugenics. Ethical questions surrounding the issue of genetic cloning and the research that led to this startling breakthrough are discussed.

Warrick, Pamela, "Have a Moral Dilemma? Relax, the Ethicist Is In; Philosophy: Arthur Caplan, Ph.D., has an answer for everything, from cloning to physician-assisted suicide to health care rationing," *Los Angeles Times,* March 13, 1997, p. E1.
Since the birth of modern bioethics 35 years ago, few practitioners have been so high-profile, so aggressive or so self-promoting as the 46-year-old Arthur Leonard Caplan, Ph.D. Even the scholarly father of bioethics, Daniel Callahan, who hired Caplan to join his bioethics research at the famed Hastings Center in Briercliff Manor, N.Y., risks being eclipsed by Caplan's spotlight. During the first week of "clone fever," about 10,000 people per day were checking into Caplan's University of Pennsylvania Web site (http://www.med.upenn.edu/bioethics) for a look at his special cloning page.

Dolly

Craig, Charles, "Near-Term Benefits of Cloning Likely to Be Medical; Scottish Firm Hopes to Create Sheep for Therapeutic Proteins," *The Washington Post,* March 29, 1997, p. F1.
The routine genetic modification of animals to create healthier food products may be the most dramatic legacy of the remarkable cloning experiment in Scotland that produced Dolly, the world's first mammal cloned from an adult cell. But that is at best decades away, many geneticists say. In the nearer term, Dolly's creation is likely to bring less visible but nonetheless profound changes in medicine, where advances increasingly depend on understanding and manipulating the genetic process.

Nolan, Bruce, "Humans Grapple with New Way of Coming to Be; Debate Begins After Cloning of Large Mammal," *Times-Picayune,* March 1, 1997, p. A20.
Grown from a single cell donated by her mother, Dolly was conceived without a father and nurtured in a dish before being planted in the womb of another ewe. At stake, as the Catholic theologian Rev. William Maestri of Covington pointed out, is nothing less than human dignity: whether modern man, ever impatient with physical imperfection, will remain willing "to accept and love each of us for who we are, flaws and all, as a unique gift from God." The first reports of Dolly 's birth summoned the horrors of Aldous Huxley's 1932 novel "Brave New World," in which humans, all cloned replicas designed for various jobs in society, were "decanted" from test tubes in a de-sexualized industrial process.

Vogt, Amanda, "Is Cloning Baaaaaaaad?" *Chicago Tribune,* March 4, 1997, p. 3.
The idea of cloning an animal once seemed like the stuff of mad scientists. But last week Scottish researchers announced that they had done it. Taking a single cell from an adult ewe (a female sheep), they produced a lamb that was her exact genetic twin. "Dolly," the clone, raises many issues.

Dr. Ian Wilmut

Dorning, Mike, "Human Cloning Curbs Urged; Scottish Pioneer Tells Senators It's Ethically Wrong," *Chicago Tribune,* p. 4.
Although he held out hope that the cloning techniques he developed would lead to readily available organs for transplants and cures for genetic diseases, Dr. Ian Wilmut emphatically stated his opposition to the creation of cloned humans, even to save or replace a dying child. The now-familiar image of Dolly, the cloned sheep that Wilmut produced, has put that possibility within sight, at least in the popular imagination. It has lent a sense of immediacy to the emotionally charged possibility that people could recreate themselves in their own genetically precise image.

Friend, Tim, "Getting to the nucleus of cloning concerns," *USA Today,* March 12, 1997, p. D7.

As Congress seeks the views of Dr. Ian Wilmut, creator of Dolly the sheep, and the National Bioethics Advisory Commission prepares for a hearing on Thursday, three experts offer their own opinions. Wilmut and his colleagues in Scotland stunned the world when they announced they had successfully cloned a sheep from the cells of another adult sheep — something never done before with mammals. Now the world is trying to decide what it means and whether cloning a sheep might be the precursor to cloning a human. Wilmut appears before Congress today to give his views. The National Bioethics Advisory Commission holds hearings on the topic Thursday in Washington, D.C.

Kevles, Daniel J., "Study Cloning, Don't Ban It," *The New York Times,* Feb. 26, 1997, p. A23.

Dr. Ian Wilmut and his colleagues at the Roslin Institute near Edinburgh, Scotland, created Dolly, a cloned sheep. Her birth marks a milestone in our ability to engineer animals for food and medicine. It also signals that humans can, in principle, be cloned too. That prospect troubles many people, but they ought not be too concerned about it at the moment. Dolly has provoked widespread ethical foreboding: The Church of Scotland suggested that cloning animals runs contrary to God's biodiversity; Dr. Wilmut himself said that cloning humans would be "ethically unacceptable;" and Carl Feldbaum, president of the Biotechnology Industry Organization, urged that human cloning be prohibited in the United States."

Kolata, Gina, "Congress Is Cautioned Against Ban on Human-Cloning Work," *The New York Times,* March 13, 1997, p. B11.

Scientists and ethicists testifying at a Senate hearing on cloning urged Congress today not to rush to ban research on the cloning of human beings. Among the witnesses today was Dr. Ian Wilmut, the Scottish scientist who stunned the world last month when he announced that he had cloned an adult sheep. Dr. Wilmut told the senators that talk of cloning humans was premature because the technique was too inefficient. At the same time, he said, society should not lose the opportunity to develop new treatments based on cloning techniques. The hearing, before the Senate Labor Subcommittee on Public Health and Safety, also featured testimony by Dr. Harold Varmus, director of the National Institutes of Health, three ethicists and three scientists from the biotechnology industry. Only one, George Annas, a health law professor and ethicist at Boston University, was ready for an immediate ban on human-cloning research.

Saltus, Richard, "Scientist against human cloning; Embryologist backs curb on his discovery," *The Boston Globe,* March 13, 1997, p. A3.

Scottish embryologist Ian Wilmut, whose laboratory created Dolly the cloned lamb, said at a Senate hearing yesterday that he supports a ban on the use of his cloning technique to create people, saying it would be "quite inhuman." Witnesses from various fields including science, government and industry testified at the hearing of the Public Health and Safety subcommittee of the Committee on Labor and Human Resources, the first event to bring together Wilmut, bioethicists and lawmakers in a formal discussion of the cloning breakthrough's implications. Testimony at the hearing, which was held to weigh the need for legislation to ban human cloning, reflected a general distaste for copying whole people, but there were conflicting views on whether a ban would hamper opportunities to exploit cloning technology for human benefits.

Human Cloning

Casscell, Ward, "Human cloning should — and will — become a reality," *Houston Chronicle,* March 30, 1997, p. C4.

The recent announcement of the cloning of a lamb from an udder cell of a sheep has raised the possibility of human cloning. President Clinton has banned the use of federal funds for human cloning research, pending a commission's review. His staff, including Harold Varmus, director of the National Institutes of Health, and Donna Shalala, secretary of the Health and Human Services Department, back this action. Scientists are focused now on the inefficiency of the current method of cloning (though Dolly succeeded, 276 other eggs did not) and the potential of damaged DNA (due to aging of the donor DNA or damage during the cloning itself). The silence of the scientific community on the ethical aspects probably derives in part from the traditional reluctance of scientists to involve themselves in issues where data are insufficient.

Friend, Tim, "Scientist calls for limited human cloning," *USA Today,* March 13, 1997, p. A1.

The scientist who stunned the world by cloning an adult sheep told a Senate hearing Wednesday that limited human cloning should be allowed, but only to create pre-embryos for basic research. Ian Wilmut of the Roslin Institute near Edinburgh, Scotland, testified he is opposed to human cloning but believes research using pre-embryos — balls of about 250 cells — would dramatically enhance knowledge of how genes are turned on and off in the body. Wilmut, who announced two weeks ago that he had cloned a lamb named Dolly using the cells of a 6-year-old ewe, was the star attraction at a hearing led by Sen. Bill Frist, R-Tenn., to determine whether the Senate should legislate cloning research.

Marshall, Eliot, "Mammalian cloning debate heats up," *Science,* March 21, 1997, p. 1733.

The controversy over the cloning of a sheep in Scotland refuses to let up. The debate on cloning other mammals continues, with researchers saying they see no good reason to clone humans.

Monmaney, Terence, "Prospect of Human Cloning Gives Birth to Volatile Issues; Ethics: Twins scoff at notion of creating duplicate personalities, but possibilities are troublesome to many," *Los Angeles Times,* March 2, 1997, p. A1.

As identical twins reared together in Minneapolis, Minn., the Robinson brothers are nature's virtual clones, and yet their point of view has been largely overlooked in the current outbreak of clone mania. Contrary to many prominent and ordinary singletons (as non-twins are sometimes called), they do not believe that cloning people would undermine the cherished human trait of individuality.

Syed, Ibrahim B., "Human cloning," *Muslim Journal,* March 28, 1997, p. 1.

Syed details the announcement by Dr. Ian Wilmut on Feb. 22, 1997, that he had created the first animal cloned from an adult, a lamb named Dolly. Syed also notes that on March 14, President Clinton barred the spending of federal money on human cloning.

Travis, John, "Ewe again? Cloning from adult DNA," *Science News,* March 1, 1997, p. 132.

A genetic duplicate of an adult mammal was created when a healthy lamb named Dolly was born in July 1996. It has been proven that at least some adult cells prepared in the same manner as Dolly's cells can generate a viable human clone when their nuclei are transferred to eggs.

Joshua Lederberg

Bruni, Frank, "Experts Urge No Hasty Curbs on Cloning," *The New York Times,* March 14, 1997, p. B2.

Nearly a dozen witnesses, including fertility specialists, medical ethicists, Nobel Prize winner Joshua Lederberg and John Cardinal O'Connor, the Roman Catholic Archbishop of New York, urged New York State legislators yesterday not to act hastily in curtailing or regulating research into cloning. At a hearing in lower Manhattan held by State Sen. Roy M. Goodman, chairman of the Senate Investigations Committee, Cardinal O'Connor said that while he opposed the cloning of human beings, lawmakers need to be careful "not to cut off potentially valuable research." For the most part, the physicians, researchers and medical ethicists who testified yesterday said that it was too soon to weigh the plausibility or implications of human cloning. "By all means, keep a critical eye on the developments," said Lederberg, emeritus president of Rockefeller University, who won a Nobel Prize in 1958 for his research in bacterial genetics.

Lederberg, Joshua, "The flu's lethal future," *The New York Times,* Jan. 27, 1996, p. A21.

Lederberg discusses the lethal history of influenza viruses, asserting that there will be future confrontations with deadly flu strains.

Radford, Tim, "Animal viruses 'could threaten humans through transplants,'" *Guardian,* June 25, 1996, p. 6.

Viruses which could incorporate themselves into human genes, possibly during transplant operations from wild animals, could threaten the future of mankind, according to Joshua Lederberg of Rockefeller University in New York.

"These germs mean business," *Atlanta Journal Constitution,* Jan. 21, 1996, p. G4.

An editorial discusses Joshua Lederberg's warning that humankind has never been more vulnerable to infectious diseases and notes some ways to fight dangerous microbes, from good hygiene to adequate funding for the Centers for Disease Control and Prevention.

National Bioethics Advisory Committee

Clinton, William J., "Memorandum on the prohibition on federal funding for cloning of human beings," *Weekly Compilation of Presidential Documents,* March 10, 1997, p. 281.

In a memorandum, President Clinton notes he has asked the National Bioethics Advisory Commission to review the legal and ethical issues associated with use of cloning technology. He says that federal funds should not be used for cloning of human beings.

Weiss, Rick, "Ethics Board to Review Cloning's Implications; Human Embryo Research to Be Reconsidered," *The Washington Post,* Feb. 25, 1997, p. A4.

Yesterday, President Clinton asked a national ethics board to review the "troubling" implications of the cloning of an adult sheep by Scottish researchers, a biological feat that might allow the mass production of identical people. Clinton asked the 18-member National Bioethics Advisory Commission to consider whether federal policies relating to human embryo research should be reconsidered in the light of the weekend's startling revelation. Among other things, the commission is to consider whether privately funded human embryo research in the United States — which today is largely unregulated — ought to be more "sensitive" to the ban on such research imposed on federally funded researchers.

Wadman, Meredith, "U.S. senators urge caution on cloning ban," *Nature,* March 20, 1997, p. 204.

Several U.S. congressmen are urging their colleagues to take a calmer approach to human cloning, after an initial burst of support for restrictive legislation that followed last month's announcement that a sheep had been cloned. The 18-member National Bioethics Advisory Commission was asked by President Clinton to draw up policy recommendations on human cloning.

Weiss, Rick, "Issues of Cloning Research to Be Placed Under Microscope; Bioethics Commission Will Aim to Help Clarify Federal Role in Dealing With a Rap-

idly Changing Field," ***The Washington Post,*** **March 3, 1997, p. A17.**

Last week President Clinton asked the commission to put aside its current work on genetic privacy and the protection of human research subjects to conduct an emergency analysis of the legal and ethical implications of the recent cloning work. The task is enormous and represents the first true test of the commission, which has suffered from a lack of funds and an uncertain future since Clinton created it in 1995. Because of the commission's arcane funding apparatus, which relies on an atypical degree of coordination among several different federal agencies, money for its staff and research expenses was not forthcoming until early this year — more than a year into the group's two-year mandate from Congress. Meanwhile, uncertainty about whether Congress will extend the commission's life beyond its current expiration date of October 3, has forced the group to organize its work in a cumbersome dual-track agenda. One track assumes a close of business this fall, the other looks ahead to what the commission might do if it gets budgeted for another term. The first national bioethics commission, created in 1974, quickly issued its first report (addressing research on human fetuses) and its recommendations were codified immediately as federal regulations. Before expiring in 1978, it created widely respected reports on the protection of human research subjects, including prisoners and children, which also became law.

Transgenic Animal

Colman, Alan, "Production of proteins in the milk of transgenic livestock: Problems, solutions and successes," ***American Journal of Clinical Nutrition,*** **April 1996, pp. S639-645.**

The milk of livestock can be modified dramatically by introducing foreign DNA into the germline. Exclusive expression of DNA is ensured by the presence of regulatory sequences from mammary gland-specific genes.

Shuldiner, Alan R., "Transgenic animals," ***The New England Journal of Medicine,*** **March 7, 1996, pp. 653-655.**

Shuldiner describes how transgenic animals are produced and used in medical research. The initial step in constructing a transgenic animal is to construct the DNA to be transferred.

Xenotransplantation

Baker, Beth, "Experts ponder the ethics of xenotransplantation," ***Bioscience,*** **October 1996, p. 643.**

Two new reports on the ethics of xenotransplantation indicate that the potential benefits of animal-to-human organ transplantation outweigh the risks involved. A shortage of human organ donors has created a need for xenotransplantation.

Barnett, Alicia Ault, "U.S. agencies issue proposals for xenotransplantation," ***Lancet,*** **Oct. 5, 1996, p. 953.**

The Health and Human Services Department has issued a new draft guideline to encourage xenotransplantation without introducing potentially deadly new pathogens into the human species.

Walker, Paulette V., "Regulating research on xenotransplantation proves difficult for government," ***The Chronicle of Higher Education,*** **Jan. 31, 1997, pp. A24-25.**

Interest in xenotransplantation — the implanting of animal organs, tissues or cells into humans — has grown sharply due to the inadequate supply of organs from human donors. Last fall, the Food and Drug Administration published guidelines designed to protect the public without impeding research efforts in xenotransplantation that show promise.

Koechlin, Florianne, "The animal heart of the matter: Xenotransplantation and the threat of new diseases," ***Ecologist,*** **May 1996, pp. 93-97.**

Xenotransplantation — the transplantation of animal organs into humans — is being promoted as the solution to a "shortage" of human organs for medical operations. To prevent the human immune system from rejecting these organs, researchers intend to engineer pigs genetically so as to trick the immune system into reacting to the animal's organs as if they were human. The risks of xenotransplantation include creating new diseases.

Marwick, Charles, "British, American reports on xenotransplantation," ***JAMA: The Journal of the American Medical Association,*** **Aug. 28, 1996, pp. 589-590.**

The U.S. Institute of Medicine and the United Kingdom's Nuffield Council on Bioethics recently presented reports on the current status of xenotransplantation and the circumstances under which it can safely proceed.

"New science of xenotransplantation sparks fierce debate," ***The CQ Researcher,*** **Aug. 2, 1996, p. 684.**

Animal rights groups and some scientists are protesting xenotransplantation — the transferring of tissue from one species to another. Other scientists say that xenotransplantation is needed, if the organ shortage problem continues.

Wise, Jacqui, "New authority to monitor xenotransplantation experiments," ***British Medical Journal,*** **Jan. 25, 1997, p. 247.**

A British advisory committee report, "Animal Tissue into Humans," indicates that pigs would be an acceptable source of material for xenotransplantation, provided there is only limited genetic modification. It recommends more research on transplant function, organ growth, the functioning of the recipient's immune system and other aspects of immunological rejection. The Xenotransplantation Interim Regulatory Authority has been established.

Back Issues

Great Research on Current Issues Starts Right Here . . . Recent topics covered by The CQ Researcher are listed below. Before May 1991, reports were published under the name of Editorial Research Reports.

OCTOBER 1995
Quebec's Future
Revitalizing the Cities
Networking the Classroom
Indoor Air Pollution

NOVEMBER 1995
The Working Poor
The Jury System
Sex, Violence and the Media
Police Misconduct

DECEMBER 1995
Teens and Tobacco
Gene Therapy's Future
Global Water Shortages
Third-Party Prospects

JANUARY 1996
Emergency Medicine
Punishing Sex Offenders
Bilingual Education
Helping the Homeless

FEBRUARY 1996
Reforming the CIA
Campaign Finance Reform
Academic Politics
Getting Into College

MARCH 1996
The British Monarchy
Preventing Juvenile Crime
Tax Reform
Pursuing the Paranormal

APRIL 1996
Centennial Olympic Games
Managed Care
Protecting Endangered Species
New Military Culture

MAY 1996
Russia's Political Future
Marriage and Divorce
Year-Round Schools
Taiwan, China and the U.S.

JUNE 1996
Rethinking NAFTA
First Ladies
Teaching Values
Labor Movement's Future

JULY 1996
Recovered-Memory Debate
Native Americans' Future
Crackdown on Sexual Harassment
Attack on Public Schools

AUGUST 1996
Fighting Over Animal Rights
Privatizing Government Services
Child Labor and Sweatshops
Cleaning Up Hazardous Wastes

SEPTEMBER 1996
Gambling Under Attack
The States and Federalism
Civic Journalism
Reassessing Foreign Aid

OCTOBER 1996
Political Consultants
Insurance Fraud
Rethinking School Integration
Parental Rights

NOVEMBER 1996
Global Warming
Clashing Over Copyright
Consumer Debt
Governing Washington, D.C.

DECEMBER 1996
Welfare, Work and the States
The New Volunteerism
Implementing the Disabilities Act
America's Pampered Pets

JANUARY 1997
Combating Scientific Misconduct
Restructuring the Electric Industry
The New Immigrants
Chemical and Biological Weapons

FEBRUARY 1997
Assisting Refugees
Alternative Medicine's Next Phase
Independent Counsels
Feminism's Future

MARCH 1997
New Air Quality Standards
Alcohol Advertising
Civic Renewal
Educating Gifted Students

APRIL 1997
Declining Crime Rates
The FBI Under Fire
Gender Equity in Sports
The Stock Market

Back issues are available for $5.00 (subscribers) or $10.00 (non-subscribers). Quantity discounts apply to orders over ten. To order, call Congressional Quarterly Customer Service at (202) 887-8621.

Binders are available for $18.00. To order call 1-800-638-1710. Please refer to stock number 648.

Future Topics

- ***Expanding NATO***
- ***Libraries' Changing Role***
- ***FDA Reform***

THE CQ Researcher

PUBLISHED BY CONGRESSIONAL QUARTERLY INC.

Expanding NATO

Does adding new members pose serious risks?

The U.S., Canada and the 14 European members of the North Atlantic Treaty Organization are expected to invite three Eastern European countries to join the alliance in July. Hailed as the most successful military alliance in history, NATO is credited with preventing the Soviet Union from invading Western Europe during the Cold War, speeding the U.S.S.R.'s demise and encouraging the subsequent development of democratic institutions throughout Eastern Europe. With no apparent enemies to defend against, NATO is focusing on promoting stability throughout Europe, which includes extending membership to former Soviet allies. The Clinton administration has led the call for expansion amid growing concern that an enlarged NATO would cost too much and threaten world peace by alienating Russia.

INSIDE THIS ISSUE

CQ May 16, 1997 • Volume 7, No. 19 • Pages 433-456

Formerly Editorial Research Reports

THE ISSUES

BACKGROUND

CURRENT SITUATION

OUTLOOK

SIDEBARS AND GRAPHICS

FOR MORE INFORMATION

COVER: U.S. SOLDIERS MAN A SELF-PROPELLED HOWITZER IN BOSNIA AS PART OF THE NATO IMPLEMENTATION FORCE TRYING TO MAINTAIN PEACE IN THE FORMER YUGOSLAVIA. (DEPARTMENT OF DEFENSE)

THE CQ Researcher

May 16, 1997
Volume 7, No. 19

EDITOR
Sandra Stencel

MANAGING EDITOR
Thomas J. Colin

ASSOCIATE EDITORS
Sarah M. Magner
Richard L. Worsnop

STAFF WRITERS
Charles S. Clark
Mary H. Cooper
Kenneth Jost
David Masci

EDITORIAL ASSISTANT
Vanessa E. Furlong

PUBLISHED BY
Congressional Quarterly Inc.

CHAIRMAN
Andrew Barnes

VICE CHAIRMAN
Andrew P. Corty

PRESIDENT AND PUBLISHER
Robert W. Merry

EXECUTIVE EDITOR
David Rapp

The CQ Researcher (ISSN 1056-2036). Formerly Editorial Research Reports. Published weekly, except Jan. 3, May 30, Aug. 29, Oct. 31, by Congressional Quarterly Inc., 1414 22nd St., N.W., Washington, D.C. 20037. Annual subscription rate for libraries, businesses and government is $340. Additional rates furnished upon request. Periodicals postage paid at Washington, D.C., and additional mailing offices. POSTMASTER: Send address changes to The CQ Researcher, 1414 22nd St., N.W., Washington, D.C. 20037.

Expanding NATO

BY MARY H. COOPER

THE ISSUES

On May 14, Russia and the North Atlantic Treaty Organization came to an historic agreement, paving the way for NATO expansion.

By all accounts, expanding the powerful alliance is the most crucial foreign policy issue since the Cold War ended. But there consensus ends.

"[T]he fundamental goal of [expanding NATO] is to build, for the first time, a peaceful, free and undivided trans-Atlantic community," said Secretary of State Madeleine K. Albright. "It is to extend eastward to Central Europe and the former Soviet Union the peace and prosperity that Western Europe has enjoyed for the last 50 years." [1]

But George F. Kennan, a key U.S. architect of the postwar international order, takes an almost apocalyptic view of the initiative.* "[E]xpanding NATO would be the most fateful error of American policy in the entire post-Cold War era," he wrote recently. [2]

The effort to add new members to NATO is expected to reach fruition this summer. The 16-member alliance is expected to invite three Eastern European countries — Poland, Hungary and the Czech Republic — to join NATO during its special summit in Madrid on July 8.

The U.S.-dominated alliance, which also includes 14 European countries and Canada, is widely hailed as the most successful military alliance in history. Since its inception

in the wake of World War II, NATO is credited with preventing the Soviet Union's expansion into Western Europe and the likely outbreak of yet another conflagration on the European continent. In fact, some observers see a link between the alliance's strength and the Soviet Union's breakup in December 1991.

Ironically, the U.S.S.R.'s demise called into question NATO's very mission. No sooner had the Cold War ended then the former members of the Soviet-led Warsaw Pact introduced democratic and free-market institutions and called for closer ties with their former adversaries to the west, including membership in NATO.

Under U.S. leadership, NATO initially responded to the requests for NATO membership by creating the Partnership for Peace (*see p. 444*). A less-binding arrangement than the North Atlantic Treaty, the partnership allows for joint military exercises and peacekeeping missions between the alliance and the former Warsaw Pact countries, including Russia.

But Russia's Eastern European neighbors, mindful of the control the Soviet Union once had over the region, want the guarantee against external attack that NATO membership would bring. Last year, in response, President Clinton called on NATO to invite new members into the alliance no later than summer 1997. Clinton's goal was to obtain approval of NATO expansion by members' legislatures in time for the alliance's 50th anniversary in 1999.

Russia strongly objects to NATO's eastward march, however, arguing that expansion would reduce the buffer zone that now exists between NATO territory and the Russian border. During his March 20-21 summit meeting with President Clinton in Helsinki, Finland, Russian President Boris N. Yeltsin appeared to admit partial defeat on the issue by implicitly accepting Poland, the Czech Republic and Hungary as the first new members.

But Yeltsin later warned that any further eastward movement by NATO or the placement of nuclear or other offensive forces beyond current alliance territory would be considered an act of aggression.

The United States "will make a rude and serious mistake if it implements the plan for NATO's eastward enlargement," Yeltsin declared at the summit's conclusion. "Our diplomacy has made enough concessions to the United States. To concede further is no longer possible."

Some experts dismiss Russia's objections and blast the Clinton administration for handing Moscow too many concessions to win its grudging acceptance of NATO enlargement. At the Helsinki summit, for example, Clinton formally offered to create a new NATO-Russian Council to give Russia a consultative place at NATO's table and pledged more U.S. economic aid to Russia. The May 14 agreement removed remaining obstacles to the council's creation.

"Until now, NATO has been a

* Kennan played a key role in shaping the postwar U.S. policy of "containment" toward the Soviet Union. He served as ambassador to Moscow in the 1950s and is a recipient of the Presidential Medal of Freedom and a founder of the Kennan Institute for Advanced Russian Studies in Washington.

Will the NATO Alliance Expand?

Twelve countries in Eastern Europe are seeking membership in the 16-member North Atlantic Treaty Organization. Poland, Hungary and the Czech Republic are considered the most likely to be invited to join on July 8, when NATO meets for a special summit in Madrid, Spain.

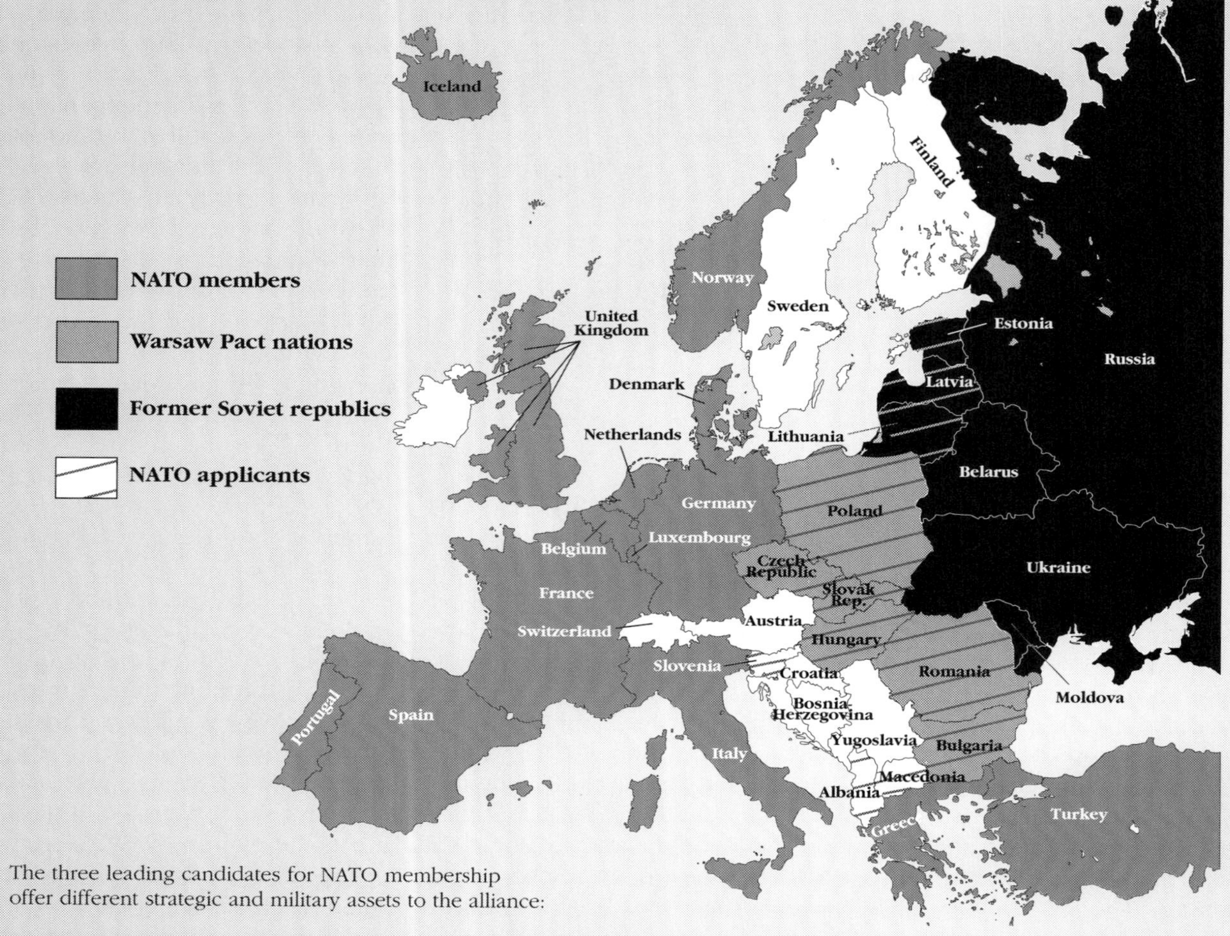

The three leading candidates for NATO membership offer different strategic and military assets to the alliance:

Poland — Poland's flat, open terrain and exposed borders with seven countries would make it hard to defend. Poland has been a favored invasion route between Western Europe and Eastern Europe and Russia, making it the most strategically located of the three leading candidates. Poland has the largest military of the three and hopes to increase defense spending from 2.4 percent of gross domestic product ($2.4 billion) in 1995 to 3 percent. Poland produces tanks, helicopters, radar equipment and small arms.

Hungary — Two of Hungary's seven neighbors, Croatia and Serbia, pose the greatest security risk to Hungary because of their involvement in the recent Balkan wars. Indeed, a Hungarian border town came under fire from Serbian forces during the hostilities. Tensions have arisen between Hungary and neighboring Serbia, Slovakia and Romania over the rights of Hungarian minorities in those countries. The absence of Slovakia in the first group of new NATO members will make it hard to defend Hungary, which will have no common borders with an allied country. NATO forces would have to arrive by air in case of an attack on Hungary. In 1995, Hungary spent just 1.5 percent of its GDP, or $600 million, for defense, and has little possibility of raising defense spending in the foreseeable future. It produces communication and electronic systems, but no major weapons systems.

Czech Republic — With mostly highlands and mountainous terrain, the Czech Republic is the least vulnerable of the three NATO candidates to external attack. The republic is bordered by current NATO member Germany, likely new member Poland and neutral Austria, enhancing its security. Tensions have arisen recently with another neighbor, Slovakia, from which the republic split peacefully in 1993, but a serious security threat is not seen as likely. Defense spending is expected to remain stable at 2.5 percent of GDP, or $1.1 billion in 1995. The republic produces electronic warfare equipment, training aircraft and small arms.

Source: Congressional Budget Office, "The Costs of Expanding the NATO Alliance," CBO Papers, *March 1996.*

family club where — even with occasional backsliding — common purposes were taken for granted," wrote former Secretary of State Henry A. Kissinger, a strong supporter of expansion but an equally strong critic of the administration's handling of the matter. "This is bound to end with Russia's de facto participation. The Europeans will want to prevent a Russo-American condominium; Russia will try to play the allies off against each other; and American energies will be absorbed in navigating these turbulent waters." [3]

But the loudest criticism of expansion is coming from a growing number of experts who say NATO is giving Russia too little, not too much. Russia's transition to free-market, democratic institutions, they point out, is far from complete. Indeed, they say, the country is in the midst of a profound economic crisis that is fanning support for a return to communism and eroding the military's control over the vast arsenals it inherited from the Soviet Union.

To help Yeltsin's government weather the crisis, the United States and other Western countries have provided billions of dollars in aid to promote trade, shore up Russia's faltering economy and help destroy nuclear weapons in compliance with arms control agreements. Critics warn that NATO expansion, by risking a breakdown in U.S.-Russian cooperation, may expose the allies to the very instability expansion is designed to prevent.

"It's not too hard to figure out that a breakdown within the Russian military command system is far and away the No. 1 danger to the United States and the world," says John Steinbruner, senior fellow in foreign policy studies at the Brookings Institution. "The problem is not that they're going to rise up and attack us. It's that they are going to disintegrate from the inside. What we really want to do is back them out of their rapid-reaction, mass-attack deterrent operation, because they can't handle it safely. That means we have to back out ourselves, and NATO expansion is going in exactly the wrong direction."

Department of Defense/Andrew McGalliard

U.S. Army Sgt. Faith Morris, a member of the NATO Implementation Force in Bosnia, passes out crayons and coloring books in Visegrad, in July 1996.

Critics also dispute the immediate benefits that expansion is supposed to provide Eastern Europe as a whole. Although NATO has yet to formally announce which of the 12 countries that have applied for membership will be invited to join at Madrid, the three most likely candidates — Poland, the Czech Republic and Hungary — lie closer to existing allied territory than to Russia. Because Russia vehemently opposes the inclusion of countries closer to its borders, applications from the small Baltic states of Estonia, Lithuania and Latvia are all but certain to be ignored.

"NATO expansion, as it has been conceived, is not a good way to contain Russia because Russia is not now a threat," says Michael Mandelbaum, a professor of American foreign policy at Johns Hopkins University's School of Advanced International Studies. "And if Russia should become a threat, it won't threaten the countries that are scheduled to join NATO. So there's an irony, in that the countries that need NATO don't get it, and the countries that get it don't need it."

The cost of enlarging NATO is as controversial as its potential impact on security in Europe. The Clinton administration estimates that it will cost up to $37 billion and take 13 years to integrate and modernize the militaries of new and existing NATO members, but that the bulk of these costs will fall to the European members. The Congressional Budget Office, however, predicts that expansion will cost as much as $125 billion and cost American taxpayers as much as $1.3 billion a year. (*See story, p. 438.*)

Meanwhile, the American public appears oblivious to NATO's planned expansion and its potential implications. Congress is just beginning to hold hearings on NATO expansion, and there are few signs of broad grass-roots interest. [4]

"I think the American public has checked out of security issues,"

How Much Will NATO Expansion Cost the U.S.?

To win U.S. support for NATO expansion, President Clinton will have to convince a budget-conscious Senate that the move will come at minimal cost to American taxpayers. Because the addition of new alliance members entails changing the North Atlantic Charter, two-thirds of the Senate must approve the move before the United States can ratify the change.

Twelve countries of Eastern Europe have applied for membership in the Atlantic alliance, but only three — Poland, Hungary and the Czech Republic — are expected to be invited to join during a NATO summit to be held this July in Madrid. The Clinton administration claims that these and subsequent additions to NATO's membership will come at little cost to Americans.

"[B]ecause we are already the world's premier power-projection-capable nation, and because we intend to retain strong forces in Europe," said Defense Secretary William S. Cohen, "the costs to the United States of enlargement are quite modest." [1]

The administration estimates that NATO enlargement would take 13 years and cost from $27 billion to $35 billion. But because the United States has already restructured its forces to contend with expected threats in post-Cold War Europe, Cohen said, the bulk of the costs would fall to the European allies. The 14 current European NATO members will be restructuring their own military forces, at an annual cost of $600 million to $800 million, from now until 2009, when the changes are expected to be complete. "They're getting more flexible, developing force-projection capability," Cohen said. "Those costs will have to be borne in any event."

New alliance members also will bear a heavy financial burden, according to the administration's estimate — about $800 million a year until 2009. "They understand they have got to also restructure their militaries to make them more compatible, interoperable, with NATO," Cohen said. "So they will have direct enlargement costs as well."

Cohen hastened to add that the United States would not be expected to help the European allies pay for force modernization unless Congress appropriated funds for that purpose.

"We're under no obligation to do so," he said. But Uncle Sam would be expected to pay up to $200 million a year in "direct enlargement costs" for 10 years following the admission of new members. These would help cover upgrades, such as broadened communications and air-defense surveillance systems to incorporate the new members, that would not be necessary if NATO membership remained unchanged.

Even if the cost to Americans is $2 billion, Cohen says, NATO enlargement would be a bargain for the United States because it would cost taxpayers far more to go it alone on defense. "Adequate defense is always expensive," he said. "But alliances make it cheaper because the costs are shared and the countries join together to meet the challenges. And, more importantly, the alliance defense is stronger than the alternative."

Not everyone shares Cohen's upbeat assessment of the costs of NATO expansion, however. The Congressional Budget Office (CBO) a year ago said the costs could range from $61 billion to $125 billion, almost four times the administration's estimate. [2] The low-cost scenario calls for a limited program of defense upgrades in the new member states and restructuring of the other European allies' capabilities. The costliest scenario would also include the permanent deployment of NATO ground forces and equipment in the new member states.

The CBO is less optimistic than the Clinton administration about the ability of the U.S. to shift the cost of NATO enlargement to its allies.

"Existing NATO members seem reluctant to increase their defense budgets to finance expansion," the agency concludes. "The defense budgets of the [Eastern European candidate] nations are small, their economies are in transition from communism to capitalism and public opinion polls show that their populations do not support increases in the proportion of government spending devoted to defense."

If Uncle Sam is indeed left holding the bag once expansion begins, the CBO continues, it can ill afford to refuse to pay up: "If basic tasks needed for an adequate defense were left uncompleted, a viable NATO security guarantee would be questionable." [3]

A third study places the cost of NATO expansion somewhere between these two extremes. Researchers at RAND Corp., a research organization based in Santa Monica, Calif., estimate the cost over 10-15 years at $10 billion to $110 billion, depending on the type of military deployments NATO adopts. A realistic scenario, the authors predict, would cost $42 billion — or $3 billion to $4 billion a year. Of that total, the United States could be expected to pay $420 million to $1.4 billion annually, depending on how great a military and political role the United States decides to play in Europe in coming years.

"While the costs of enlargement are not trivial, they are also not overwhelming, when placed in context," the RAND analysts conclude. "Indeed, the entire programme's costs are only about one-quarter of what NATO's European members currently spend on defence in any given year." [4]

---

[1] Cohen addressed the Senate Armed Services Committee on April 23, 1997.

[2] Congressional Budget Office, "The Costs of Expanding the NATO Alliance," *CBO Papers*, March 1996.

[3] *Ibid.*, p. xiii.

[4] Ronald D. Asmus, Richard L. Kugler and F. Stephen Larrabee, "What Will NATO Enlargement Cost?" *Survival*, autumn 1996, p. 25.

Steinbruner says. "They want to believe the Cold War is over. They don't want to be told the actual fact, which is that, with regard to nuclear weapons operations, we are not out of the Cold War. It's still the same as it ever was, and we've got a long way to go before we transcend it."

Many critics are calling on the Clinton administration to reconsider its support of NATO expansion before committing to it at the July summit.

"What would be the actual, objective consequences of stopping and thinking twice and taking a wiser course?" Mandelbaum asks. "Is it really conceivable that the 'Soviet' army would march into Berlin? The argument that it's too late to change course on NATO enlargement is specious."

But it may be too late for the administration to reverse course, even if it wanted to. "I am convinced that there's no way to pull out of it now," says Sherman Garnett, a senior associate at the Carnegie Endowment for International Peace and a former deputy assistant secretary of Defense for Russia and Ukraine. "For all those who argue that we ought to stop all this nonsense and madness, there are just as many people in Europe who think this expansion is something that will guarantee a kind of a U.S. presence."

Because of the administration's strong leadership in the push for NATO enlargement, Garnett says, changing course at this point would come at too high a diplomatic price. "U.S. fingerprints are all over this," he says. "If we were to take the advice of the critics and pull out, I think we would suffer a defeat."

Far from considering reversal, some supporters of expansion urge NATO to pick up the pace after the July summit. "While I agree that NATO must proceed cautiously after Madrid and take time absorbing the new members, it is essential that the alliance make clear at Madrid that the first new members will not be the last," said Sen. Richard G. Lugar, R-Ind., a member of the Senate Foreign Relations Committee. "Such a pledge would be particularly important for the Baltic states, which were, after all, also captive nations throughout the Cold War."[5]

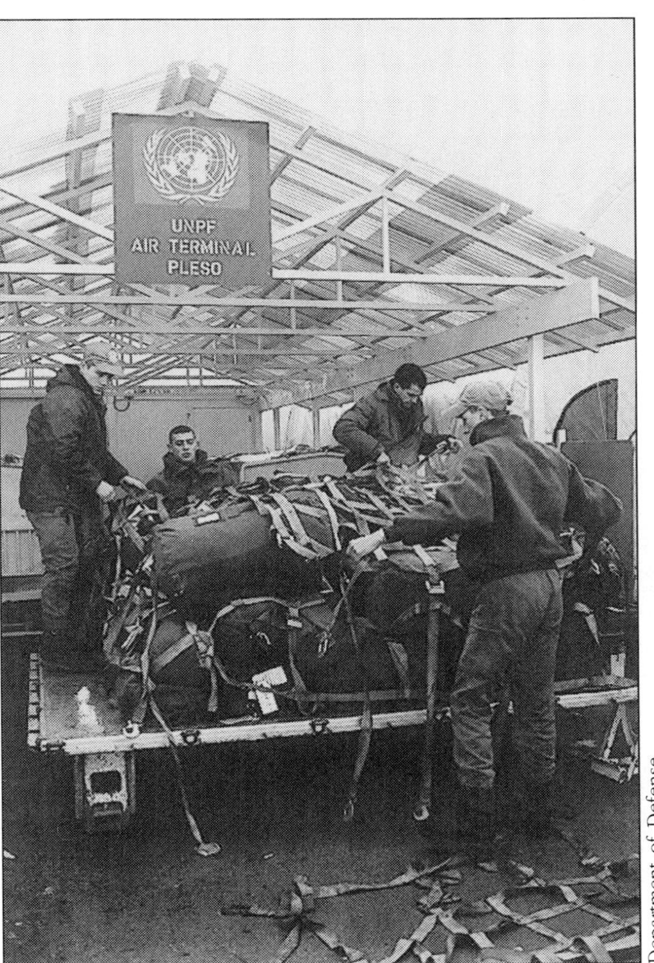

U.S. troops serving with the U.N. Implementation Force (IFOR) await transfer from Zagreb, Croatia, to Sarajevo, Bosnia.

As the July summit draws near and members of Congress focus more closely on NATO enlargement, these are some of the issues they will consider.

Does NATO still serve a useful purpose?

From its beginnings in the wake of World War II, NATO's mandate was unmistakable: "to keep the Americans in, the Russians out and the Germans down," in the words of Britain's Lord Ismay, NATO's first secretary-general. Europe was just emerging from the rubble of the second cataclysmic world war in this century, both sparked by German aggression. The United States had played a vital role in both conflicts, especially in defeating Nazi Germany's quest to overrun the continent.

After World War II, the Soviet Union refused to end its occupation of Poland and East Germany, posing a new threat to Western Europe from the east. A strong military alliance, whose ultimate defense was the U.S. nuclear umbrella, was deemed the surest way to prevent history from repeating itself in Western Europe.

The heart of the 1949 North Atlantic Treaty is Article V, which obliges all NATO members to defend any other members that come under attack. This provision, which made it clear to Moscow that any incursion into NATO territory would be answered by the military might of the United States, is widely credited with keeping the peace in Europe during the

Cold War.

But the Cold War's end lifted the "iron curtain" that had separated East from West. The breakup of the Soviet Union and its military alliance, the Warsaw Pact, eliminated the focus of NATO's defensive strategy and the very reason for its creation. Some experts say these developments have eliminated the need for NATO, in particular the United States' leading role in Europe's defense. In this view, regional defense structures such as the 10-member Western European Union (WEU), should assume responsibility for its members' defense. *

"I think NATO is basically an alliance whose time has come and gone,'' says Ted Galen Carpenter, director of foreign policy studies at the Cato Institute, a policy research group that advocates a limited role for government. "There is an argument for a long-term strategic counterweight in Europe in the event that Russia does recover politically, economically and militarily. But I think that a somewhat more robust Western European Union would serve that purpose. NATO is really not necessary."

Carpenter's view that NATO has outlived its purpose is not widely shared. Despite frequent tiffs over U.S. domination of the alliance, the European allies find comfort in the United States' continued commitment to keeping peace on the continent. In the United States, most arguments over NATO concern how it should adapt to Europe's changing environment, not its merits as a permanent alliance.

"I think NATO as it stands now is neither as central to keeping the peace in Europe as it was during the Cold War nor a readily discardable relic of that period," Mandelbaum says. "I think it is still useful as a way to keep the United States engaged in European security, as a way of relieving Germany of the need to conduct an independent security policy and as insurance in case at some point in the future Russia should pose a threat to Europe's security. So I am very much in favor of the status quo in NATO and very much opposed to expansion."

Expansion, Mandelbaum believes, would jeopardize NATO's usefulness while bringing no discernible benefits.

"I think it's a dangerous idea because it will certainly have costs and, although those costs are unpredictable, they may be very steep," he says. "I do not believe that an expanded NATO will enhance democracy in Europe because the countries that are slated to join are already democracies. It will not prevent future Bosnias because these counties have no conceivable potential for ethnic conflict.

"Finally, expansion will not fill a security vacuum between Germany and Russia because there is already a new, improved and highly desirable security system in place, an important component of which is the series of arms treaties signed between 1987 and 1993." *

Other experts say the alliance should abandon its focus on the Article V guarantee of defense against foreign attack and turn its energies toward enhancing the kinds of confidence-building measures that have helped keep the peace among its members over the years.

"NATO is needed, but it's a different conception of NATO than the one that is associated with the Article V guarantee," Steinbruner says. "The biggest achievement of the Cold War is that NATO resolved the tensions in Western Europe and enabled the German military establishment to develop a very large capability without any-

* Members of the WEU are Belgium, France, Germany, Greece, Italy, Luxembourg, the Netherlands, Portugal, Spain and the United Kingdom. Austria, Denmark, Finland, Ireland and Sweden are "observers"; Iceland, Norway and Turkey are "associate members" and the former Soviet and Warsaw Pact states of Bulgaria, the Czech Republic, Estonia, Hungary, Latvia, Lithuania, Poland, Romania and Slovakia are "associate partners."

* The 1987 Intermediate-Range Nuclear Forces Treaty called for the elimination of all intermediate-range U.S. and Soviet nuclear missiles from Europe. The strategic arms reduction treaties, START I (signed in 1991) and START II (signed in 1993), called for deep cuts in U.S. and Soviet nuclear weapons and the destruction of all multiple warheads on ballistic missiles.

Department of Defense

Elements of the 1st Armored Division serving with U.N. forces in the former Yugoslavia cross the Sava River into Bosnia on a bridge constructed by Army Engineers.

body being worried about it. It did this by making it clear that nobody is intending to attack anyone else.

"If you could somehow redefine NATO in this sense, so that the expansion of NATO would be the expansion of this kind of integration and reassurance, not only would NATO be relevant, it's vital."

By failing to shift its focus from external threats to confidence-building, Steinbruner says, NATO is courting disaster. "Obviously, this kind of expansion has to include the Russians to make any sense at all," he says. "Instead, NATO is taking the classic Article V notion and extending that eastward. I think that is an unbelievable disaster, a strategic misjudgment of historic proportions."

Mary Iuvone

Secretary of State Madeleine K. Albright is greeted by Senate Foreign Relations Committee Chairman Jesse Helms, R-N.C., at Albright's confirmation hearings in January. Former Secretary Warren Christopher looks on.

Will NATO's expansion enhance security in Eastern Europe?

The Clinton administration cites two main reasons for wanting to add new members to NATO from Eastern Europe. The chief justification is that NATO's eastward move would enhance security in what has been Europe's most volatile region and thereby diminish the main threat on the continent today: regional instability. Supporters of expansion say that NATO's requirements for admission — the adoption of democratic political institutions, free-market economic reforms and civilian control over the military — have already spurred reform in most of Eastern Europe.

"All countries who are seeking to get in now, I think, are trying to cooperate . . . to basically aspire to the same democratic principles that those members in NATO currently have," said Defense Secretary William S. Cohen. "And so we're seeing remarkable efforts under way. We ought to try to consolidate those efforts by having them gain admission." [6]

The other big reason for including Eastern European countries in NATO, the administration says, is that they deserve it. "[T]here is a basic injustice to perpetuating a dividing line down the center of Europe which was created by force and where the countries that were a part of it never voted for being in the Warsaw Pact," said Albright, who fled her native Czechoslovakia following the 1948 Soviet-backed communist takeover there. "[T]hey now, as sovereign nations, have the right to choose their security alliance. . . ." [7]

While no one disputes the second motive for admitting new members into NATO, there is widespread disagreement over the notion that enlarging the alliance would actually enhance security in Eastern Europe. While it is true that expansion would erase the old dividing line between East and West, skeptics say it would simply draw a new line along the eastern borders of new members.

"I'm concerned that the course we're on here may . . . validate the notion that there is going to be a dividing line," said Sen. Jeff Bingaman, D-N.M. "And instead of eliminating the dividing line, it essentially sets out to move it." [8]

Critics also charge that current plans to admit only a few new members to the alliance in July will undermine, not enhance, the region's security by dividing the 12 applicant countries into NATO "ins" and "outs."

"When you go to a group of 12 nations and try and determine eligibility and select some, in my judgment you're breeding that very instability between those selected and those not selected," said Sen. John W. Warner, R-Va., the second-ranking Republican on the Senate Armed Services Committee. "And indeed, some of the earliest confrontations, as occasioned by this expansion, could well be NATO having to come in to settle the instability between those selected and those not selected." [9]

The situation is particularly grave, critics say, for the three countries that have applied for NATO membership even though they once were part of the Soviet Union and lie adjacent or close to the Russian border — Estonia, Latvia and Lithuania. Citing its own security interests, Russia has declared unequivocally that it will not tolerate admission of these countries or Ukraine into NATO, and the alliance is unlikely to challenge Russia on this issue in the foreseeable future.

"NATO enlargement creates a new gray area," Mandelbaum says. "It makes more vulnerable than they otherwise would be these new, fragile democracies that are important to us for moral and strategic reasons. So we have created a problem where none existed before."

As a military organization, NATO requires new members to spend precious resources to upgrade their military capabilities to satisfy alliance standards. Some observers say Eastern European countries could establish strong links with the West by joining the region's economic and political institutions at far less risk and cost than NATO membership entails.

"I think a better approach would be to push for the rapid enlargement of the European Union * eastward," Carpenter says. "That would give the Central and East European countries a stake in being part of the Western community, but do so in a way that is not threatening to Russia, instead of having a powerful alliance perched on Russia's western frontier."

Does NATO enlargement undermine Russia's move toward democracy and a market economy?

The Soviet Union became one of the two most powerful countries in the world on the strength of a rigidly controlled political and economic system developed over three-quarters of a century. Russia's rejection of its past and embrace of democratic reforms may be the most remarkable transformation of the post-Cold War period. But the conversion is far from complete, and the severe economic hardship that has accompanied reform has fanned considerable public support for a return to communism. Indeed, a coalition of communists and nationalists won the majority of seats in the State Duma, the lower house of Russia's parliament, in December 1995.

Western observers of NATO's plans to expand appear divided between those who are confident in Russia's commitment to democratic institutions and those who fear the move may torpedo the reform process. The Clinton administration says NATO's enlargement will actually strengthen the Yeltsin government's hand against its communist opponents.

"NATO's enlargement will benefit Russia, above all by increasing stability in Central and Eastern Europe, where Russia twice has been pulled into world war in this century," writes Samuel R. Berger, Clinton's national security adviser. "As NATO and Russia work together, we believe the advantages of cooperation for both sides will be apparent."

Skeptics say the administration's push to expand NATO is an unacceptable gamble. "It is, of course, unfortunate that Russia should be confronted with such a challenge at a time when its executive power is in a state of high uncertainty and near-paralysis," Kennan writes, alluding to Yeltsin's precarious health and questionable political future. "And it is doubly unfortunate considering the total lack of any necessity for this move. Why, with all the hopeful possibilities engendered by the end of the Cold War, should East-West relations become centered on the question of who would be allied with whom and, by implication, against whom in some fanciful, totally unforeseeable and most improbable future military conflict?" [10]

Even some supporters of NATO enlargement worry about its impact on Russia. "I'm in favor of it," says Garnett, who dismisses worries about a sudden collapse of the reform process. "I don't think NATO is the straw that will break the camel's back. The Russian reaction I worry about is different, that Russia will become alienated from Europe. Objectively, we have a very good opportunity with Russia now, but the psychology of this relationship seems to be going the wrong way on both sides."

Some critics fault the Clinton administration for failing to appreciate Russia's sensitivity to expanding NATO. Russia has endured repeated invasions from the West for centuries, most recently barely a half-century ago at the hands of Nazi Germany. Albright tried to assuage Russian suspicions of NATO motives during her first trip to Moscow as secretary of State last February.

"It is no longer you vs. us, or us vs. you," she told Foreign Minister Yevgeny Primakov. "We are on the same side." [11]

Some critics say Albright's assurances rang hollow because NATO is proceeding with its plan in the face of repeated objections from Yeltsin that it threatens Russia's security.

"I don't doubt her sincerity, but her remarks debase the currency of reassurance," Steinbruner says. "The implication of using reassuring rhetoric to cover what is objectively a confrontational policy is, in my view, flat-out irresponsible because it diminishes our credibility with the Russians and with everyone else in between." ■

BACKGROUND

Cold War Origins

In June 1945, as World War II ground to a close, representatives

Continued on p. 444

* The European Union is comprised of Austria, Belgium, Denmark, Finland, France, Germany, Greece, Ireland, Italy, Luxembourg, the Netherlands, Portugal, Spain, Sweden and the United Kingdom.

Chronology

1940s *World War II ends amid new struggles for the control of Europe.*

June 1945
Fifty countries sign the United Nations Charter as World War II comes to an end.

March 1948
A month after a Soviet-backed communist government takes power in Czechoslovakia, Belgium, France, Luxembourg, the Netherlands and the United Kingdom sign the Brussels Treaty establishing the Western Union Defense Organization — later named the Western European Union — to provide a regional defense system.

April 4, 1949
The United States, Canada, the Brussels Treaty signatories, Denmark, Iceland, Italy, Norway and Portugal sign the North Atlantic Treaty creating the North Atlantic Treaty Organization (NATO) and promise to defend any member that is attacked.

1950s-1960s *The East-West divide deepens with the U.S.-Soviet arms race.*

February 1952
Greece and Turkey join NATO after efforts to bring the countries into the Soviet orbit fail.

1955
After signing the 1954 Paris Agreements resolving outstanding disputes with France, West Germany joins NATO.

1967
French President Charles de Gaulle withdraws from NATO's integrated military command.

1980s *U.S. and Soviet negotiators agree to curb the spiraling arms race.*

1982
Spain becomes NATO's 16th member and the last country to join during the Cold War.

1985
Upon assuming the Kremlin leadership, Mikhail S. Gorbachev launches gradual political and economic reforms.

1987
The Intermediate-Range Nuclear Forces Treaty calls for the elimination of all intermediate-range U.S. and Soviet nuclear missiles from Europe.

1990s *The Cold War's end brings calls for new security arrangements in Europe.*

Oct. 3, 1990
A year after the Berlin Wall falls, Germany is united.

1991
The U.S. and the Soviet Union sign START I, the first of two strategic arms reduction treaties calling for deep cuts in both countries' nuclear arsenals.

November 1991
NATO creates the North Atlantic Cooperation Council to improve the exchange of defense information between NATO and the former Soviet and Warsaw Pact states. NATO shifts from heavy armored deployments along the eastern flank to more flexible forces. War breaks out in the Balkans.

Dec. 25, 1991
The Soviet Union dissolves, and with it the Warsaw Pact.

January 1994
NATO establishes the Partnership for Peace enabling Russia and the other former Warsaw Pact states to develop military cooperation with the alliance. President Clinton announces that NATO is open to new members.

1995
NATO deploys 60,000 troops in Bosnia to enforce the Dayton peace accords.

April 23, 1997
The Senate Armed Services Committee holds the first of an expected series of hearings on NATO expansion.

May 14, 1997
NATO and Russia agree to create a permanent council in which Russia will have a voice in such NATO activities as peacekeeping, arms control and counter-terrorism.

July 8, 1997
Poland, Hungary and the Czech Republic are expected to be invited to join NATO at a special summit in Madrid.

1999
President Clinton aims to win approval of NATO's first group of new members by the alliance's 50th anniversary.

of 50 countries met in San Francisco to sign the United Nations Charter. The hope: to establish a new world order that would prevent future global conflicts.

Germany's surrender did not, however, end the threat of invasion in Europe. During the war, the Soviet Union had annexed Estonia, Latvia and Lithuania, as well as Romania, Poland, northeastern Germany and eastern Czechoslovakia. After Germany's surrender, Soviet leader Josef Stalin used political pressure to bring Albania, Bulgaria, Romania, East Germany, Poland, Hungary and Czechoslovakia into the sphere of Soviet control.

While the United States and the other wartime allies proceeded to demobilize their forces, the Soviet military remained on a war footing, prompting British Prime Minister Winston Churchill to warn that an "iron curtain" was being lowered across Central Europe. [12]

By 1947, pro-Soviet forces had gained support in Greece and Turkey. In response, President Harry S Truman declared that the United States would send economic and military aid to Athens and Ankara "to support free peoples who are resisting attempted subjugation by armed minorities or by outside pressure."

The Truman Doctrine was followed by the Marshall Plan, a massive U.S. economic-assistance program for Europe named for its principal author, then Secretary of State Gen. George C. Marshall.

In March 1948, a month after a communist coup ended Czechoslovakia's attempt to resist Soviet domination, representatives of Belgium, France, Luxembourg, the Netherlands and the United Kingdom signed the Brussels Treaty promising closer economic ties and creating a common defense system, the Western Union Defense Organization.

To prevent further Soviet inroads on the continent, the United States and Canada expressed interest in bringing these and other Western European countries together in a broader "Atlantic alliance." Denmark, Iceland, Italy, Norway and Portugal were invited to join the effort.

On April 4, 1949, representatives of the 12 countries met in Washington to sign the North Atlantic Treaty creating NATO. The treaty, of indefinite duration, contains a framework for preventing or repelling military aggression from outside its territory. It also provides for extensive political and economic cooperation and consultation among the members in an effort to keep the peace within the alliance.

Of the treaty's 14 articles, Article V contains the essence of NATO's strength during the Cold War. This is the "all-for-one-and-one-for-all" clause that firmly commits all member countries to treat an armed attack against any NATO member, in Europe or North America, as an attack against them all. Although it allows each signatory to take whatever action it deems appropriate, the article states that the member countries must take steps to restore and maintain security.

Tension, Resentment

Current plans to expand NATO are not without precedent. Article X of the North Atlantic Treaty expressly provides for the accession of any other European state in a position to further its principles, provided all current members agree. In September 1951, after Soviet efforts to bring Greece and Turkey into the Soviet orbit failed, NATO invited both countries to join the alliance, which they did in February 1952.

Two years later, alliance members invited the successor to their former enemy, the Federal Republic of Germany, to join NATO. As a preliminary step, West Germany signed the 1954 Paris Agreements, resolving outstanding disputes with France and naming Gen. Dwight D. Eisenhower as NATO's first Supreme Allied Commander Europe. The next year, Germany became the 15th member of the alliance. Almost three decades were to pass before NATO again expanded. In 1982 Spain became the 16th and last country to join the alliance during the Cold War.

As U.S.-dominated NATO assumed the leading military role in postwar Europe, other, strictly European institutions emerged to promote economic and political ties on the continent. The European Community was established in 1957 as a customs union regulating trade within the Common Market, comprised then of Belgium, France, Italy, Luxembourg, the Netherlands and West Germany.

Although it got off to a slow start, the EC later moved closer to its ultimate goal of creating a United States of Europe by removing customs barriers, establishing a common passport and enhancing the powers of the European Parliament. Known today as the European Union (EU), it counts 15 members and is moving toward establishing a common currency, the euro.

European countries also participate in a number of defense organizations outside the Atlantic alliance. The Western European Union (WEU), established by the 1954 Paris Agreements, grew out of the early postwar Western Union Defense Organization and promotes increased military cooperation among its members. As a military body, however, the WEU has been largely overshadowed by NATO.

NATO's European allies have been ambivalent about the United States' dominant role in Western Europe's security structure almost from the beginning. The United States' overwhelming military superiority, especially its nuclear forces, offered welcome protection from a feared Soviet attack. Freed from the need to build extensive military forces of their own, the European allies could use their resources to rebuild their economies, fueling the continent's postwar economic boom.

But U.S. dominance also sparked resentment among some countries, especially France. In 1967, President Charles de Gaulle withdrew his country from NATO's integrated military command, leaving France with only a political role in the alliance.

As the nuclear arms race between the United States and the Soviet Union heated up in the 1980s, tensions mounted among NATO members required to host the growing number of short- and medium-range nuclear weapons aimed at Warsaw Pact countries bordering NATO's eastern flank. An active peace movement in West Germany and other NATO countries called for the withdrawal of all U.S. forces in Europe. Meanwhile, West Germany conducted a policy of détente with the Soviet Union in an effort to improve East-West relations and thus reduce the risk of war.

Mikhail S. Gorbachev's ascent to Kremlin leadership in 1985 marked the beginning of what came to be Russia's second revolution. As Moscow's last communist leader, Gorbachev relaxed the country's rigid political controls and introduced limited market reforms to revive the moribund Soviet economy. Even before the Soviet Union broke up in December 1991, its Warsaw Pact allies interpreted "perestroika," Gorbachev's reform program, as a signal to shed their repressive political systems.

In 1989, East Germans tore down the Berlin Wall, the Cold War's most visible symbol. On Oct. 3, 1990, East Germany ceased to exist when it merged with the Federal Republic. Taking the lead from Georgia, Moldova and the Baltic republics, the other Soviet republics declared their independence. By 1992, the map of Central and Eastern Europe had been redrawn.

Partnership for Peace

The early years of the post-Cold War era presented fresh challenges to Europe's security system. With the Warsaw Pact's dissolution, the greatest risks of conflict came not from within NATO territory, but at its periphery. No longer reined in by strict state controls, longstanding ethnic tensions in Central and Eastern Europe flared, from Russia's breakaway province of Chechnya to the Balkans.

To prepare for this new security threat, NATO in November 1991 adopted a new strategic concept. Instead of deploying forces along a well-defined front to defend against attack from a known adversary, the alliance directed its members to develop forces that could be quickly transported to meet emergencies, including out-of-area missions, crisis management and peacekeeping operations.

The 1991 outbreak of war in the successor republics of Yugoslavia found Europe unwilling to halt the hostilities. Armed to the teeth by NATO and organized through regional security bodies such as the WEU, the allies nonetheless stood by for months in the face of relentless Serbian massacres of Muslims in Bosnia-Herzegovina.

Bosnia eventually provided NATO with its first out-of-area mission and its first involvement in combat. In 1992 NATO and the WEU agreed to help enforce U.N. sanctions barring arms deliveries to Serbian forces in Bosnia. But a proposed WEU mission to send ground forces to protect humanitarian efforts in Bosnia was vetoed by the United Kingdom. NATO ships helped enforce the arms embargo, and NATO warplanes patrolled a U.N.-defined no-fly zone over Bosnia as well as so-called safe areas inside the country.

In 1995 NATO planes also conducted strikes against Serb military positions on the ground. At the end of 1995, NATO led 60,000 troops from 34 countries, a third of them American, to enforce a settlement to the conflict, the Dayton peace accords. NATO's mission in Bosnia is due to end in June 1998. [13]

Apart from its involvement in the Balkans, NATO has emphasized confidence-building as a key role for the alliance in the post-Cold War era. First introduced as a formal tool of diplomacy in the 1975 Helsinki Accords, confidence-building measures are intended to make surprise attacks increasingly difficult and thus remove the need for large standing forces. The measures include:

- advance notification of military maneuvers to neighboring countries;
- lengthening the time required between notification and the maneuvers;
- decreasing the size of maneuvers over time;
- arms-control agreements; and
- providing information about weapons and other military assets. [14]

In November 1991, NATO created the North Atlantic Cooperation Council to encourage the free exchange of military information between NATO members and the former communist states, including Russia. In January 1994, NATO established the Partnership for Peace, enabling these countries to develop military cooperation with the alliance.

Participants in the Partnership for Peace were invited to send ambassadors to NATO, conduct joint exercises, integrate the alliance's technical standards into their own equipment and participate in NATO's peacekeeping mission in Bosnia. By the end of 1996, 27 countries had joined the partnership and engaged in 27 joint military exercises. Thirteen partner states had contributed to the NATO-led peacekeeping operations in the Balkans.

"The significance of these programs lies not in any joint task that they involve, such as peacekeeping, but in reassurance about intentions and capabilities that the process of interaction engenders," writes Mandelbaum. "Among former adversaries, familiarity of this kind, its participants hope, will breed not contempt but confidence." [15] ■

CURRENT SITUATION

Clinton's Gambit

The Partnership for Peace reflected the view that NATO could adapt to Europe's changed environment by establishing ties with non-member countries, not by expanding the alliance. But no sooner did the partnership take shape than pressures emerged to undermine it. Some former Warsaw Pact countries wanted a guarantee against future Russian incursions, which only NATO membership, with its Article V commitment, could provide. The greatest pressure came from Poland, the Czech Republic (which split off from Slovakia in 1993) and Hungary.

Another factor that enhanced the allure of NATO membership was the European Union's reluctance to admit the newly democratic countries of Central and Eastern Europe into its fold. To strengthen itself politically and economically, the union decided to create a common currency among its existing members instead of broadening it by adding new members. But this goal already was hampered by some EU members' difficulties in meeting the strict monetary and fiscal standards required for adoption of the euro. With the EU closed to new members, NATO was seen as a back door for Eastern European countries to enter the West's political and economic establishment.

Another push to expand NATO came from Germany, Europe's leading economic power. "The Germans wanted to have NATO move eastward to increase overall ties with the Central European countries in a multilateral framework," Carpenter says. "They also have a very selfish reason — namely, they want a security buffer to their east, in the event of a deterioration of relations with Russia."

But the strongest impetus for expanding NATO came from the United States, where advocates of expansion began pushing to admit new members even before the Partnership for Peace was established.

"During the fall of 1993, even as the bureaucracy and senior levels of government agreed to the Partnership for Peace, there was still this bubbling idea, both outside and apparently inside the government, that we ought to go farther," says Garnett, then a deputy assistant secretary of Defense. "One of the most interesting historical questions about the Clinton administration's foreign policy is what happened, who decided, and why the president didn't lay the groundwork for expansion very well. Immediately the Russians felt betrayed."

Some experts say the answer lies with Clinton's domestic policy priorities.

"Clinton came into office with a largely domestic agenda to reinvigorate the American economy," Steinbruner says. "There was a sense that he was going to take on the conservatives on that agenda and basically concede security policy to the conservatives. There's a small group of people who are promoting NATO expansion, and their underlying agenda is unmistakably to stick it to the Russians. I don't know if the Clinton administration has literally bought into it or whether they are simply mollifying what they consider to be the strongest blowing wind."

Contributing to the pressure to expand NATO was the Central and East European Coalition, an alliance of 18 grass-roots organizations representing some 21 million Americans who trace their roots to the region. Led by the Chicago-based Polish American Congress, the coalition began pressing for NATO enlargement in 1993.

"We were concerned that fall that Russia was starting to show signs of neo-imperialism and exert influence on the newly independent countries of Central and Eastern Europe," says Casimir I. Lenard, national director of the Polish American Congress. "At the time, Clinton was not in favor of NATO expansion and was pushing instead for the Partnership for Peace. But we did not accept that as a substitute."

Whatever the impetus for the policy shift, on his first European trip as president in January 1994, Clinton announced that NATO remained open to new members and told an audience in Prague that Czech membership was no longer a question of "if" but "when." By the fall, a timetable for NATO enlargement had been adopted. [16]

Europe's Response

Of course, the United States is not the only NATO ally that supports enlargement. The North Atlantic Treaty stipulates that admission of new members must have the unanimous consent of existing alliance members. But apart from Germany, the European allies have taken a back seat in the campaign to expand NATO eastward.

"No existing NATO member has

any interest in this whatsoever, except the United States and Germany," Mandelbaum says. Even the Germans, in his view, are ambivalent about expansion, wanting to further their own interests in Eastern Europe but avoid offending Russia.

NATO enlargement may become a pawn in a game the Europeans arguably care more about: strengthening the EU. Although the 15-member union is resisting calls to add new members before it adopts a common currency, several outsiders are clamoring to come on board now. Turkey has already threatened to use its veto power over NATO expansion if the EU — which includes 11 NATO members — does not let it in.

But some countries in Eastern Europe have achieved greater economic growth than Turkey and thus may stand a better chance of gaining admission to the EU. [17] "Turkey is not going to be admitted to the EU, and the Turks presumably understand that," Mandelbaum says. "So I interpret their message to be that NATO is going to have to pay them for their vote to enlarge. But if we have to pay them, we'll have to pay the Greeks, the Spanish and the Portuguese, none of whom cares in the slightest about NATO expansion. And who's going to pay? The Europeans will turn to us and say, 'Uncle Sam.' "

Arguments over NATO burden-sharing between the United States and European allies is hardly new, having plagued Atlantic relations for years. But this time the struggle is taking place in a rapidly changing political environment in Europe. France, for example, wants to return to NATO's military command structure, but insists on having a European officer appointed to head NATO's Southern Command in Naples. The United States has refused to relinquish its hold on that post, which U.S. admirals have held since 1949.

Regional concerns also are coloring an emerging debate over the most likely challenges NATO will face in the future. France and other southern allies are concerned about potential threats from radical Islamic movements in Northern Africa; Italy is leading a multinational force to oversee humanitarian efforts in Albania; and the United States and Germany continue to worry most about the eastern flank.

"We all cared about the Soviet Union, even though everybody had their own practical, regional perspective on security," Garnett says. "Now the regional perspective is much more important. The big debate in NATO right now is whether a problem in Algeria is going to be seen as a Bosnia or as something too far away to care about. With all of these changes, NATO members are asking, 'Are we so changing the alliance's character that it starts to erode because it no longer fits what people are used to? Or is this change what's needed to keep it vital?' " [18]

NATO's regional differences are already becoming apparent. The alliance rejected calls from Albania, championed by Italy and Greece, to intervene in a government crisis earlier this year that sent thousands of refugees to Italy. Regionalism also is coloring the debate over which of the 12 applicants should be admitted in July. Italy wants to include its neighbor Slovenia as a way to extend NATO's stabilizing influence into the troubled Balkans. France, wary of U.S.-German favoritism toward northeastern Europe, is championing Romania's bid.

Helsinki Summit

NATO expansion topped the agenda when Clinton and Yeltsin met in Helsinki in March. With the United States firmly committed to inviting new members this year, Yeltsin continued to call the move "a mistake, and a serious one at that." Nonetheless, he was seen as accepting the move in exchange for a NATO-Russian charter that would spell out Russian relations with the alliance.

Clinton also promised more economic aid to Moscow, endorsed Russia's bid to join the World Trade Organization and agreed to give Russia a prominent place in the G-7 meeting of the world's leading industrial powers to be held this summer in Denver, Colo.

Yeltsin called for the NATO-Russian charter to be signed well before the alliance invites new members, preferably at a May 27 meeting in Paris to be attended by Clinton and other NATO leaders. The main obstacles to agreement were the terms of troop and weapons deployments on the territory of new NATO states.

Russia rejected NATO's assurances that it has "no intention, no plan and no reason" to deploy nuclear weapons or "substantial" combat troops outside the alliance's current territory. But the alliance stopped short of making further concessions to Russia.

Under the May 14 agreement, Russia dropped its insistence on a formal charter granting it veto power over NATO decisions in return for the creation of a permanent council in which Russia will have a voice on alliance activities, such as peacekeeping, arms control and counter-terrorism. The agreement also included assurances that NATO would not build or adapt storage facilities for nuclear weapons on the territory of new member states.

A compromise solution to the impasse on acceptable non-nuclear forces on new NATO territory may be the inclusion of troop and weapons levels in a separate agreement, now under negotiation in Vienna, to revise the 1990 treaty on Conventional Forces in Europe. Signed before the Soviet Union's demise, the treaty is being rewritten to reflect the current needs of European countries for non-nuclear forces. [19]

The Helsinki summit did little to assuage critics' concerns. Kissinger and some other avid supporters of

NATO's eastward move charged the Clinton administration with caving in excessively to Russian demands. [20] In Steinbruner's view, however, Clinton gave Yeltsin what amounted to a dangerous slap in the face.

"Helsinki gave Yeltsin no material relief to the underlying military pressures whatsoever," Steinbruner says, "and no basis for going to his own political system and saying, 'We have [received] reasonable terms of accommodation [from NATO].' If our political system were facing terms of this sort, we would be in massive, screaming rebellion over it. Yet we expect him to turn around and make their political process absorb what ours wouldn't even think of absorbing."

To some supporters of NATO's expansion, both views miss the mark. Garnett, who met with officials in Moscow earlier this year, says the opposition to NATO's plans is far less entrenched than the official rhetoric would suggest.

"There are a lot of divisions within the Russian elite about what to do about it," he says. "The people who still want to have a positive relationship with the West fear this move is destructive of momentum by pushing Russia away. In other words, the effects are more psychological, whereas another group in the foreign policy community thinks it is a sort of geopolitical thrust against Russia that requires some sort of military response."

Russia's Lebed Voices Support for Expansion

Although nationalists and communists in the Duma are calling on the government to beef up Russia's military deployments along its western border in response to NATO's expansion, other prominent political leaders are taking a decidedly moderate stance. Aleksander I. Lebed, the popular retired general who brokered last year's political settlement to the Chechen crisis, dismisses the notion that NATO's expansion poses a threat to Russia.

An outspoken law-and-order candidate, Lebed contested Yeltsin's successful bid for re-election in June 1996 until the president brought Lebed into his administration in return for his support. After brokering the cease-fire with the breakaway province of Chechnya in October, Lebed was dismissed as Yeltsin's national security adviser, but he remains a popular political figure and has clearly been testing the waters for a political comeback in recent months. [21]

"Those in the government who attack NATO expansion are trying to recreate the atmosphere they are used to," Lebed said in an interview earlier this year. "They must have somebody as a 'foreign enemy' to distract attention from their failures at home." [22]

"Lebed's position is that expansion will become a tremendous fiscal burden for the West," Garnett says. "In his view, NATO will discover that the Poles and other Central Europeans are not the desirable allies it thought they would be and will find itself in a position of imperial overstretch. In Lebed's view, in the end it will all work out if Russia remains calm and concentrates on its internal development." ■

OUTLOOK

Debate Heats Up

Applicants for NATO membership are eagerly awaiting details of the May 14 agreement amid fears that the alliance may be weakening its commitment in the face of Russian demands. Any agreement to bar NATO equipment and forces from new members' lands, applicants fear, would relegate the new members to second-class citizenship in the alliance. The Clinton administration assures the East Europeans that they will enjoy all the benefits of alliance participation.

"The United States and NATO have emphasized that the new members of the alliance will be full members, not second-class citizens," Defense Secretary Cohen said. "In other words, there will be no Potemkin village that we will construct and call an enlarged NATO." [23]

Some observers say this is an empty promise, however. "The Central and Eastern European countries are very eager to get NATO security protection, but I wonder how serious the United States and the other members of NATO are about actually fulfilling those commitments if they are challenged," Carpenter says. "And we can't just proceed down the road on the assumption that they'll never be challenged. That's a real Pollyanna attitude. I think there's a danger that we're leading the Central European countries down the garden path, that we're pretending to offer security commitments that we're not serious about. That's a bluff, and potentially a very dangerous bluff."

As the July summit nears, tensions are mounting between the likely NATO candidates and their neighbors, throwing into doubt the stabilizing nature of NATO enlargement. In April, Slovak Prime Minister Vladimir Meciar blamed Czech President Vaclav Havel for thwarting Slovakia's bid to join the alliance. Havel dismissed the claim as an expression of Meciar's "customary paranoia," and Meciar called off a planned official visit to Prague. [24]

Later in April, the Parliament of Lithuania made a desperate appeal to NATO to reconsider its apparent acquiescence to Russia's opposition to the Baltic states' admission to the alliance. Adding further uncertainty to the region, the authoritarian government of Belarus has entered into a security agreement with Russia.

Continued on p. 450

At Issue:

Does NATO enlargement serve U.S. interests?

yes

SECRETARY OF STATE MADELEINE K. ALBRIGHT
FROM TESTIMONY BEFORE THE SENATE ARMED SERVICES COMMITTEE, APRIL 23, 1997

NATO enlargement involves the most solemn commitments one nation can make to another. Let me explain exactly why it is in our interests to do this.

First, to protect against Europe's next war. Three times in this century, American troops have had to go to Europe in two hot wars and one cold one to end conflicts that arose in Central Europe. And yet, in the last half-century, America has never been called upon to go to war to defend a treaty ally.

We have learned that alliances make the threat of force more credible, and therefore, the use of force less likely; that by promising to fight if necessary, we can make it less necessary to fight. . . .

The second reason is to defend Europe's gains toward democracy, peace and integration. Just the prospect of enlargement has given Central and Eastern Europe greater stability than it has seen in this century. Old disputes are melting away as nations align themselves with NATO. Democracy is advancing. Country after country has made sure soldiers take orders from civilians. These nations are fixing exactly the problems that could have led to future Bosnias.

What's more, NATO's prospective members know they will not have to go it alone if peace is threatened. This means they have less incentive to pursue arms buildups. It means confidence within the region will grow, allowing ties with Russia to improve.

The third reason . . . is to right the wrongs of the past. If we do not enlarge NATO, we will be validating the dividing line Stalin imposed. With the Cold War over, there is just no moral or strategic basis for saying to the American people, "We must be allied with Europe's old democracies forever, but with Europe's new democracies never."

That would create a permanent injustice mocking a half-century of sacrifices on both sides of the Iron Curtain, and it would create a permanent source of tension in the heart of Europe.

The final reason for enlargement is that it will strengthen NATO by adding capable new allies. . . . The nations we are considering share our most fundamental values and aspirations. Many shared risks with our soldiers in the Gulf War. Without hesitation, they provided troops and bases for NATO's mission in Bosnia. They are heeding our call to stop dealing with rogue states. And they have lent their support to the expansion of democracy and respect for human rights around the globe.

Our future allies will bear the cost of defending freedom because they know the price of losing freedom.

no

REP. DAVID R. OBEY, D-WIS.
FROM COMMENTS BEFORE THE HOUSE APPROPRIATIONS SUBCOMMITTEE ON COMMERCE, JUSTICE, STATE, JUDICIARY AND RELATED AGENCIES, MARCH 5, 1997

I have worked with this administration and previous administrations in the area of foreign affairs for a long time, as you know, on budgets, on Russia, on Central Europe, on peacekeeping, on development issues, you name it.

But I have profound misgivings about the administration's intentions with respect to expansion of NATO. I think you're going to get a deal with Mr. Yeltsin, but I'm concerned about what that means in the future. Because based on my understanding of the way Russia works . . . I think that we run a grave risk that future Russian nationalists, under worse economic and political conditions than we have in Russia today, will be able to exploit any Russian government decision to accept a movement east of the military borders of NATO.

And I think that could have profoundly negative consequences long-term.

Secondly, I don't think the American people have heard anything about this issue. And if we do proceed, I think they're going to wake up one morning and discover that we have provided a guarantee to defend Central Europe, three or four more new countries, they didn't know about it and I doubt that they're going to be very thrilled about it. . . .

Thirdly, I'm concerned they will, in fact, create a more tense no-man's land between the newly defined NATO and Russia, putting under [more] pressure than you have right now, countries like the Baltics and Ukraine, countries who don't get in in the first slice.

And lastly, I find it very difficult to believe that we are not going to have more difficulty getting the Russians to ratify in the Duma the arms control treaties which are now before them, or arms control treaties that might be before them in the future.

And so I guess I would simply ask, do you really have evidence that shows that the arms control ratification by the Duma will not be made more difficult? Can you really tell us that the intelligence agencies conclude that this would result in a stronger U.S.-Russian relationship?

Are we really going to be committed to defend Central Europe, either with conventional forces or with our nuclear weapons, if Russia attacks Central Europe in the distant future? And if not, what does that do to the confidence that other parties have had in our commitment to NATO countries over the years that we will, in fact, do so?

FOR MORE INFORMATION

Council on Foreign Relations, 58 East 68th St., New York, N.Y. 10021; (212) 434-9400. A task force set up by this nonprofit research group recently endorsed NATO expansion.

Polish American Congress, 5711 N. Milwaukee Ave., Chicago, Ill. 60646-6294; (312) 763-9944. This grass-roots organization leads a coalition of 18 groups representing 21 million Americans of Eastern European descent in support of NATO expansion.

RAND Corp., 1700 Main St., P.O. Box 2138, Santa Monica, Calif. 90407-2138; (310) 451-6913. This research organization has issued estimates of the costs of NATO enlargement to American taxpayers.

Continued from p. 448

The Central and East European Coalition has intensified its campaign in favor of NATO expansion, including a mailgram campaign last fall in which constituents pressed their representatives and President Clinton to facilitate the admission of new members to the alliance.

"We had to fight tooth and nail," says Lenard of the Polish American Congress. "But finally, in 1996, we convinced the White House that NATO enlargement was an issue that would not go away."

Apart from Americans of Eastern European descent, however, there is little sign that the American public has taken notice of NATO's plans for expansion or of the critical situation in Russia.

"The polls show that most people don't care or even know anything about it," Mandelbaum says. Among those who do, he says, "people approve of NATO expansion because they regard it as an inclusive gesture. And most of those assume that the Russians will be included in NATO as well." [25]

These views may change if NATO extends its invitations to new members in July and the Clinton administration begins in earnest to try to win public support of the move. The Senate must approve, by a two-thirds majority, any additions to NATO's membership. At the Senate Armed Services Committee's April 23 hearing, members grilled both Albright and Cohen on the move's potential dangers of alienating Russia, committing U.S. troops to defend a historically unstable region and placing a new burden on the shoulders of American taxpayers. But committee members appeared more interested in gathering information than in opposing NATO expansion.

"Today we begin deliberation of what may be the most important issue that will face the Senate in the postwar era," said Sen. Carl Levin, D.-Mich., the committee's ranking member. "I only hope that this hearing and others . . . will encourage the discussion throughout our nation that this subject deserves, but has not yet received."

Some critics of NATO expansion also look forward to the coming debate in hopes that it will spur Americans to scrutinize the issues at stake.

"Hopefully," Steinbruner says, "this whole debate will stimulate a very sleepy country into recognizing what the real problem is — massive deterioration going on in the Russian military establishment and the very serious set of dangers that are associated with it. If the whole fuss about NATO enlargement gets us to recognize the risks involved, it may be worth it." ■

Notes

[1] Albright testified April 23, 1997, before the Senate Armed Services Committee.

[2] George F. Kennan, "A Fateful Error," *The New York Times,* Feb. 5, 1997.

[3] Henry A. Kissinger, "Helsinki Fiasco," *The Washington Post,* March 30, 1997.

[4] See "NATO Expansion Forges Ahead With Little Hill Scrutiny," *Congressional Quarterly Weekly Report,* March 15, 1997, pp. 648-652.

[5] Sen. Lugar chaired a recent Council on Foreign Relations task force on NATO. The group's May 5 report supports expansion.

[6] Cohen testified April 23, 1997, before the Senate Armed Services Committee.

[7] Albright testified April 23, 1997, before the Senate Armed Services Committee. For more on her family background, see Michael Dobbs, "Out of the Past," *The Washington Post Magazine,* Feb. 9, 1997.

[8] Bingaman is a member of the Senate Armed Services Committee and spoke at the April 23 hearing.

[9] Warner spoke at the April 23 Senate Armed Services Committee hearing.

[10] Kennan, *op. cit.*

[11] Albright spoke Feb. 21 at a joint news conference in Moscow. See Michael Dobbs and David Hoffman, "Yeltsin Stands Firm Against Larger NATO," *The Washington Post,* Feb. 22, 1997.

[12] Unless otherwise noted, information in this section is based on "The North Atlantic Treaty Organisation: Facts and Figures," NATO Information Service, 1989.

[13] For a detailed discussion of NATO's involvement in Bosnia, see Michael Mandelbaum, *The Dawn of Peace in Europe* (1996), pp. 28-44.

[14] Mandelbaum, *op. cit.,* pp. 98-102.

[15] *Ibid.,* p. 101.

[16] See Tyler Marshall, "NATO's Eastern Growth a Giant Step or Stumble?" *Los Angeles Times,* April 13, 1997.

[17] See "Eastern Promise," *The Economist,* April 12, 1997, p. 77.

[18] For background, see "NATO's Changing Role," *The CQ Researcher,* Aug. 21, 1992, pp. 713-736.

[19] From NATO statements issued last December and on March 14, 1997. See Michael Dobbs, "U.S.-Russia Talks on NATO Charter Stall," *The Washington Post,* May 2, 1997.

[20] Kissinger, *op. cit.*

[21] For background see "Russia's Political Future," *The CQ Researcher,* May 3, 1996, pp. 385-408.

[22] See Jim Hoagland, "A Look at Lebed," *The Washington Post,* Feb. 9, 1997.

[23] Cohen testified April 23, 1997, before the Senate Armed Services Committee.

[24] See Christine Spolar, "Bids to Join NATO Put Czech and Slovak at Odds," *The Washington Post,* April 13, 1997.

[25] For polling data, see Mandelbaum, *op. cit.,* pp. 163-164.

Bibliography

Selected Sources Used

Books

Mandelbaum, Michael, *The Dawn of Peace in Europe,* Twentieth Century Fund, 1996.
NATO continues to play a vital role in maintaining Europe's security, writes Mandelbaum, a professor of American foreign policy at Johns Hopkins University. But if peace is to reign on the continent, any changes to the existing order must include Russia, he contends.

North Atlantic Treaty Organisation, *Facts and Figures,* NATO, 1989.
Though dated, this official guide to the Atlantic alliance provides valuable information on NATO's history and mandate.

Articles

Albright, Madeleine, "Enlarging NATO: Why Bigger Is Better," *The Economist,* Feb. 15, 1997, pp. 21-23.
The secretary of State argues that NATO expansion is the key to achieving security in Europe and dismisses Russian objections to the move as inappropriate, in light of the alliance's peaceful intentions.

Asmus, Ronald D., Richard L. Kugler and F. Stephen Larrabee, "What Will NATO Enlargement Cost?" *Survival,* autumn 1996, pp. 5-26.
RAND Corp. analysts conclude that the costs of expanding the alliance are not overwhelming when viewed in the context of overall defense spending and the important strategic benefits the move will bring its members.

Bailes, Alyson, "Europe's Defense Challenge," *Foreign Affairs,* January/February 1997, pp. 15-20.
From this Briton's viewpoint, the United States is presenting an ambivalent stance to its allies by asking the Europeans to assume greater responsibility for their own defense while at the same time rebuffing British, French and German attempts to have a greater say in security decisions.

Brzezinski, Zbigniew, "A Plan for Europe," *Foreign Affairs,* January/February 1995, pp. 26-42.
The former national security adviser supports a two-track policy toward Europe that includes the expansion of NATO as well as independent steps to include Russia in a system of collective security stretching from the Atlantic to the Urals.

Judt, Tony, "New Germany, Old NATO," *The New York Review of Books,* May 29, 1997, pp. 38-45.
In this review of five new books on post-Cold War Europe, the author warns that inclusion of some, but not all, the Eastern European countries that want to join NATO would destabilize the region.

Kamp, Karl-Heinz, "The Folly of Rapid NATO Expansion," *Foreign Policy,* spring 1995, pp. 116-129.
A German foreign policy expert writes that NATO's plan to expand will only humiliate Russia and offer new members a less than credible guarantee that the alliance will defend them if they come under attack.

Kull, Steven, "The American Public, Congress and NATO Enlargement," *NATO Review,* January 1997, pp. 9-11.
A poll conducted last September by the Program on International Policy Attitudes found that a large majority of Americans support NATO expansion, especially if it eventually includes Russia.

Rosner, Jeremy D., "NATO Enlargement's American Hurdle," *Foreign Affairs,* July/August 1996, pp. 9-16.
The author, recently appointed to head the Clinton administration's effort to win support for NATO enlargement, predicts that the American public will stand behind the initiative if the president strongly supports it.

Reports and Studies

Congressional Budget Office, *The Costs of Expanding the NATO Alliance,* March 1996.
The CBO estimates that NATO expansion will cost up to $125 billion — about four times as much as the Clinton administration predicts.

Council on Foreign Relations, *Russia, Its Neighbors, and an Enlarging NATO,* May 5, 1997.
An independent task force chaired by Sen. Richard G. Lugar, R-Ind., concludes that NATO enlargement is urgently needed and should not stop with the expected admission of Poland, Hungary and the Czech Republic this summer.

U.S. Department of State, Bureau of European and Canadian Affairs, *Report to the Congress on the Enlargement of the North Atlantic Treaty Organization: Rationale, Benefits, Costs and Implications,* Feb. 24, 1997.
In this report to Congress, the State Department estimates that NATO enlargement will come at a modest cost to the United States while improving stability in Europe by removing remaining divisions imposed during the Cold War.

The Next Step

Additional information from UMI's Newspaper & Periodical Abstracts™ database

Czech Republic

"Is a Bigger NATO a Better NATO?" *St. Louis Post-Dispatch,* Dec. 16, 1996, p. B6.
An editorial discusses plans to expand NATO to include the Czech Republic, Poland and Hungary, asserting that the U.S. must ensure that Russia is treated as an important partner in ensuring European security, not division.

Kitfield, James, "NATO's new horizons," *National Journal,* Sept. 14, 1996, p. 7.
NATO is redefining itself and its future. NATO forces in Bosnia are conducting the alliance's first "out of area" operation, and it is expected to offer membership to the Czech Republic, Hungary and Poland next spring.

Spolar, Christine, "Bids to Join NATO Put Czech and Slovak at Odds; With Prague Favored, Bratislava's Angry Meciar Demands Apology for Havel Remark," *The Washington Post,* April 13, 1997, p. A26.
The push to join NATO has touched off a dispute between the sibling nations of Slovakia and the Czech Republic in the former Eastern Bloc. In surprisingly personal blasts, Czech President Vaclav Havel and Slovak Prime Minister Vladimir Meciar have sparred through the media over Slovakia's apparently declining chances for early inclusion in the alliance. The leading candidates to be added to NATO this year are Poland, Hungary and the Czech Republic.

European Union

Abarinov, Vladimir, "Turkey blackmails its NATO allies," *Current Digest of the Post-Soviet Press,* March 5, 1997, p. 22.
Turkey's Deputy Prime Minister and Foreign Minister Tansu Ciller threatened to block NATO expansion unless Ankara's application for full membership in the European Union is put back on the agenda. Turkey has been threatening the European Union for six months.

Cornish, Paul, "European security: The end of architecture and the new NATO," *International Affairs,* October 1996, pp. 751-769.
Cornish examines the three institutions that lie at the heart of the debate about European security after the Cold War: NATO, the WEU and the EU. Seven years after the end of the Cold War, Europe's defense and security requirements are still not entirely clear.

Palmer, John, "EU urged to take in states left out by NATO," *Guardian,* Nov. 25, 1996, p. 8.
The European Commission was under pressure from the U.S. and NATO in November 1996, to drop plans for phasing the enlargement of the EU and to begin talks with almost all would-be members in central and Eastern Europe by the end of next year.

Ruggie, John Gerard, "Consolidating the European pillar: The key to NATO's future," *Washington Quarterly,* winter 1997, pp. 109-124.
Deepening the relationship between NATO and the EU is more critical to maintaining a vital U.S. role in Europe than immediate NATO expansion. A European-led eastward expansion would pose fewer risks and be more beneficial to the U.S.

Staunton, Dennis, and Alex Smith Duval "Upbeat French hail 'new NATO'," *Guardian,* June 4, 1996, p. 12.
NATO foreign ministers agreed to a new command structure in June 1996, which theoretically enables European alliance members to mount military operations independently of the U.S. It allows for combined joint task forces to be deployed in troubled regions under the command of the Western European Union.

Helsinki Summit

Albright, Joseph, and Marcia Kunstel, "Russia rumbles stubbornness on NATO; Helsinki summit opens amid reports of Cold War-style military maneuvering," *Atlanta Constitution,* March 21, 1997, p. A7.
Against a backdrop of renewed Russian military muscle-flexing, President Clinton began a summit Thursday in which he hopes to persuade President Boris Yeltsin to drop his opposition to eastward expansion of NATO. Clinton did not address recent assertions by Yeltsin and other Russian officials that they strongly oppose Western plans to invite former Soviet satellites Poland, Hungary and the Czech Republic to join the North Atlantic Treaty Organization.

"Clinton, Yeltsin to discuss economics, NATO expansion at summit this week," *The Wall Street Journal,* March 17, 1997, p. A14.
While expansion of NATO promises to dominate the Helsinki summit between President Clinton and Russian President Boris Yeltsin the week of March 17, 1997, economic issues will be important playing cards. The two leaders will discuss Russia's desire to join the World Trade Organization, the Paris Club of creditor nations and even the Group of Seven, which brings together the world's leading industrialized nations.

Harris, John F., and Michael Dobbs, "Clinton, Yeltsin to Meet in Helsinki; March Summit Designed to Allay Russia's Fears Over NATO Expansion," *The Washington Post*, Feb. 8, 1997, p. A17.

President Clinton will meet with Russian President Boris Yeltsin next month in Helsinki, Finland, for a summit designed to allay Moscow's fears about the expansion of NATO, the administration said yesterday in an announcement that had been delayed for weeks because of concerns about the Russian leader's frail health. Clinton, speaking with reporters before an Oval Office meeting with Russian Prime Minister Viktor Chernomyrdin, said he hopes when he meets with Yeltsin next month to "make it clear that no one has any intention of providing any increased threat to the security of Russia." The 16-member North Atlantic Treaty Organization, an alliance formed to thwart feared aggression in Europe by the Soviet Union after World War II, will meet in Madrid, Spain, in July to invite three Warsaw Pact nations to join NATO. The nations, while officially undecided, are Poland, Hungary and the Czech Republic, U.S. officials said.

Kempster, Norman, "Summit Underscores Intent to Proceed With NATO Expansion; Diplomacy: Russia remains opposed, but it apparently accepts fact that it cannot thwart alliance," *Los Angeles Times*, March 22, 1997, p. A19.

Despite Russian President Boris Yeltsin's opposition to the expansion of NATO, the Helsinki summit virtually guarantees that the alliance — originally created to block Soviet ambitions — will enter the 21st century with some of Moscow's former satellites as full members. At a post-summit news conference Friday, President Clinton was succinct: "NATO enlargement in the Madrid summit will proceed." Although Yeltsin continued to object to NATO's expansion plans, the two presidents called for accelerated negotiations on a new charter between Russia and NATO that would establish a forum for military and political cooperation between Moscow and the 16-nation alliance.

"NATO on the Cheap," *Detroit News*, March 20, 1997, p. A10.

President Bill Clinton is gamely setting off today for his Helsinki summit meeting with Russian President Boris Yeltsin. What the administration wants at Helsinki is Russian approval of a deal to allow expansion of the North Atlantic Treaty Organization to Poland, Hungary and the Czech Republic. The administration is offering some questionable concessions in hopes of gaining Mr. Yeltsin's agreement. The Clinton team already has agreed not to station Western troops or nuclear weapons on the soil of the new NATO members. But a hollow alliance would be the worst of both worlds — a pledge to come to the aid of allies without providing the means to do so. And a NATO without troops in Central Europe wouldn't be much help in discouraging border conflicts and ethnic tensions among the Central Europeans.

Neikirk, William, "NATO Expansion to Dominate Summit; Clinton's Task: Assure Yeltsin a Wider Alliance Will Not Threaten Russia," *Chicago Tribune*, March 19, 1997, p. 3.

President Bill Clinton and Russian President Boris Yeltsin meet in Helsinki on Thursday for a summit on enlarging NATO and controlling nuclear arms that could help heal or fester old Cold War suspicions. Clinton will seek to break down Yeltsin's sharp opposition to NATO expansion with promises to expand Russia's role in the Western economic system and to refrain from putting nuclear weapons and troops in the new NATO countries.

Walker, Martin, "Helsinki summit: Russia may climb down over NATO," *Guardian*, March 21, 1997, p. 15.

Russia yesterday signaled its readiness to drop its long-standing demand for a veto on NATO's future, as the Helsinki summit opened with a formal dinner last night. Weeks of tough Russian rhetoric eased into the softer tones of conciliation as the two presidents arrived in the cold but sunny Finnish capital yesterday. President Boris Yeltsin predicted a mood of "friendliness and compromise" despite American insistence on enlarging NATO into Eastern Europe. Russian and American officials said they expected "to do serious business, despite agreeing to disagree." "No one has a right to a veto, but no one has the right to spring surprises," said Kremlin spokesman Sergei Yastrzhembsky, who gave the first hint that Moscow was bowing to the inevitable over NATO's expansion plans. He added that the Russian goal at the summit was "to minimize the possible damage to Russian-U.S. and Russian-West relations if NATO expands eastwards."

Hungary

Erlanger, Steven, "U.S. Pushes Bigger NATO Despite Qualms on Russia," *The New York Times*, Oct. 10, 1996, p. A16.

Despite new uncertainties about the possible Russian reaction and the qualms of some NATO allies, the U.S. is pushing ahead with its plan to bring several former Soviet satellites into NATO in 1999. The list of prospective new members will likely include Hungary, Poland and the Czech Republic

Hornbeck, Mark, and Phil Linsalata, "Clinton wants NATO to grow," *Detroit News*, Oct. 23, 1996, p. A1.

In a major foreign policy address on Oct. 22, 1996, at the Fisher Theater in Detroit, Mich., President Clinton set 1999 as the target date for admitting former Eastern bloc countries to NATO. Clinton did not specify in his campaign speech which nations he wants to add, but foreign affairs experts said Poland, Hungary and the

Czech Republic are likely first choices.

Landay, Jonathan S., "E. Europe acts like a bloc to win NATO membership," *The Christian Science Monitor,* Nov. 4, 1996, p. 8.

When 16-member NATO opens its doors in 1997 to its first members from the former communist bloc, Hungary, Poland and the Czech Republic are considered shoo-ins for invitations. Other East European countries like Romania, Slovakia and Slovenia say they should be included also, and they're starting to put aside age-old rivalries and support each other in an effort to convince the U.S. and its allies to accept them in the opening round.

Robbins, Carla Anne, "Initiation rites: Hungary's NATO bid illustrates the hopes, risks in Central Europe," *The Wall Street Journal,* Jan. 2, 1997, p. A1.

While politicians from Bosnia to Russia are exploiting nostalgic passions, Hungary's prime minister, Gyula Horn, has other priorities. Foremost among them is winning admission into NATO. The Czech Republic and Poland are also expected to be invited to join the alliance when NATO leaders meet in Madrid, Spain, in July 1997.

"World-wide: Clinton urged NATO," *The Wall Street Journal,* Oct. 23, 1996, p. A1.

During a swing among Midwestern voters of Eastern European ancestry, President Clinton urged NATO to admit a first group of Eastern European states by 1999. The president's plan was immediately criticized as too timid by former presidential candidate Robert Dole, who wanted Poland, Hungary and the Czech Republic admitted by 1998.

NATO Enlargement

Asmus, Ronald D., Richard L. Kugler and Stephen F. Larrabee, "What will NATO enlargement cost?" *Survival,* autumn 1996, pp. 5-26.

Determining how much NATO enlargement will cost requires a political and strategic calculus. The costs of enlargement will depend on who joins the alliance, how defense strategies in both new and old members are adjusted and how the financial burdens are distributed among NATO members.

Cohen, Elliott A., "NATO: Dissolution, enlargement or neither?" *International Journal on World Peace,* June 1995, pp. 13-15.

NATO was formed in 1949 to deter Soviet expansion and political subversion. The end of the Cold War has many people rethinking its mission.

Cortright, David, "NATO's new frontier," *Nation,* March 31, 1997, pp. 21-22.

NATO expansion threatens to poison relations between the West and Russia and re-divide Europe, and will be a rebuff to the fragile stirrings of democracy in Russia. NATO is an anachronism, and an alternative strategy for European security is needed.

"Five into NATO won't go," *The Economist,* April 5, 1997, pp. 18-19.

An editorial notes that enlarging too far and too fast could ruin NATO. NATO officials hope Russia will sign a special partnership with the alliance, paving the way for Eastern European countries to join the alliance.

Garfinkle, Adam, "NATO enlargement: What's the rush?" *National Interest,* winter 1996/1997, pp. 102-111.

The question of enlarging NATO has become the most important foreign policy debate in the U.S. since the end of the Cold War. Garfinkle examines the arguments for and against the enlargement of NATO.

Mann, Paul, "Clinton Soft-Sells Cost Of NATO's Enlargement," *Aviation Week & Space Technology,* Oct. 28, 1996, pp. 70-71.

President Clinton made a recent campaign pitch to enlarge the NATO alliance by 1999; however, he failed to tell taxpayers it might cost them as much as $19 billion. The American public has not yet realized the cost.

Robbins, Carla Anne, "Devil is in details of NATO expansion," *The Wall Street Journal,* Aug. 9, 1996, p. A6.

By early 1997, NATO is expected to announce plans to admit the Czech Republic, Poland and Hungary. But the membership list is about all the U.S. and its allies have agreed upon. The impact of adding the new members to NATO is examined.

Voigt, Karsten, "NATO enlargement: Sustaining the momentum," *NATO Review,* March 1996, pp. 15-19.

Sustaining the impetus of the enlargement process is essential to the future role and relevance of NATO. Some of the issues that must be covered in order to expand the alliance, especially with regard to Russia, are discussed.

von Moltke, Gebhardt, "NATO moves toward enlargement," *NATO Review,* January 1996, pp. 3-6.

NATO recently completed its internal study on enlargement. The study provides the basis of a framework that will be gradual, deliberate and transparent, and contribute to overall European stability. An analysis of the expansion study considers Russia's contribution to the European security architecture.

Walker, Martin, "Clinton pushes ahead on NATO enlargement," *Guardian,* Oct. 22, 1996, p. 11.

U.S. President Bill Clinton on Oct. 22, 1996, will present a "concrete timetable" for the enlargement of NATO, putting the prestige of his office behind a firm deadline for the completion of negotiations by 1999.

Partnership for Peace

Gorka, Sebestyen, "Waiting for NATO," *World Policy Journal,* spring 1996, pp. 119-124.

The Partnership for Peace (PFP) has emerged as one of the pillars of U.S.-Central European cooperation. The PFP, conceived originally as a substitute for full NATO membership, has helped address the primary security needs of the Central and East European states.

"NATO Foreign Minister meeting: Progress in ensuring peace in an undivided Europe," *U.S. Department of State Dispatch,* June 10, 1996, pp. 297-301.

The goals of the North Atlantic Cooperation Council and the Partnership for Peace are discussed. The North Atlantic Council reaffirms the steady, gradual and deliberate path of NATO enlargement.

Poland

Cimoszewicz, Wlodzimierz, "Building Poland's security: Membership of NATO a key objective," *NATO Review,* May 1996, pp. 3-7.

Poland's key foreign policy issues are outlined. Poland wants to be an active member of NATO while also engaging in talks with Russia.

Drozdiak, William, "Poland Urges NATO Not to Appease Russia; 'The Smell of Yalta Is Always With Us'," *The Washington Post,* March 17, 1997, p. A13.

As President Clinton prepares to discuss the fate of NATO expansion with Russian President Boris Yeltsin, senior officials from Poland and other eastern states say they are fearful their own security interests could be jeopardized by the quest for compromise between Washington and Moscow. With Poland, Hungary and the Czech Republic anxiously awaiting invitations to join the Western alliance this summer, the United States and its partners are striving to soften Russia's antagonism by offering Moscow a permanent consultative link with NATO and limits on the forward deployment of allied troops and nuclear weapons. Polish officials are particularly alarmed that NATO and Russia might agree on the creation of a consultative forum that could begin operating as early as this year, while the new members would have to complete entry negotiations and await ratification by NATO legislatures — a process likely to last until 1999, at least.

Hale, David D., and Anna Hejka-Arczynska, "Poland and NATO," *National Review,* June 3, 1996, pp. 36-39.

The debate about NATO expansion in Central Europe centers around Poland because it has the potential to alter the balance of power in Europe in ways that the other countries do not. As a result of economic and demographic trends, Poland could become a highly valuable member of the NATO alliance in the 21st century.

Hundley, Tom, "Amid spy scandal, Poland tries to salvage NATO membership bid," *Chicago Tribune,* Feb. 8, 1996, p. 11.

Poland is still reeling from the resignation of Prime Minister Jozef Oleksy amid allegations that he may have been passing state secrets to the Russians for more than a decade. The main concern is how the scandal will affect Poland's chances for early membership in NATO.

Perlez, Jane, "Poland's Top Commander Resists Terms for NATO," *The New York Times,* Jan. 22, 1997, p. A3.

As Poland gears up to convince Washington that it meets one of the conditions for joining NATO — having its military under civilian control — the top commander, a Moscow-trained general, is resisting the reduction in his authority, a senior Polish defense official and Western diplomats say. The senior defense official, Deputy Defense Minister Andrzej Karkoszka, acknowledged in an interview that the Chief of General Staff, Gen. Tadeusz Wilecki, was fighting rules that give civilians in the ministry the final say.

Western European Union

Art, Robert J., "Why Western Europe needs the United States and NATO," *Political Science Quarterly,* spring 1996, pp. 1-39.

Art analyzes the six-year political struggle that took place within Western Europe to define its post-Cold War security arrangements. He shows why the military presence of NATO and the U.S. remains an essential ingredient of Western Europe's stability.

Palmer, John, and Ian Black and David Fairhall, "NATO changes pose questions for role of WEU," *Guardian,* May 6, 1996, p. 9.

NATO's U.S.-dominated military command structure will be radically recast to make room for the return of the French, prompting new questions in May 1996, about how EU nations will organize security operations on their own. European NATO commanders may be mandated to run separate missions for the Western European Union using NATO resources.

Palmer, John, "French NATO move gives EU new role," *Guardian,* Dec. 6, 1995, p. 15.

An agreement to let the Western European Union use NATO troops and equipment in its peace missions may rapidly follow France's decision to play a greater military role in the Atlantic alliance.

Back Issues

Great Research on Current Issues Starts Right Here . . . Recent topics covered by The CQ Researcher are listed below. Before May 1991, reports were published under the name of Editorial Research Reports.

NOVEMBER 1995
The Working Poor
The Jury System
Sex, Violence and the Media
Police Misconduct

DECEMBER 1995
Teens and Tobacco
Gene Therapy's Future
Global Water Shortages
Third-Party Prospects

JANUARY 1996
Emergency Medicine
Punishing Sex Offenders
Bilingual Education
Helping the Homeless

FEBRUARY 1996
Reforming the CIA
Campaign Finance Reform
Academic Politics
Getting Into College

MARCH 1996
The British Monarchy
Preventing Juvenile Crime
Tax Reform
Pursuing the Paranormal

APRIL 1996
Centennial Olympic Games
Managed Care
Protecting Endangered Species
New Military Culture

MAY 1996
Russia's Political Future
Marriage and Divorce
Year-Round Schools
Taiwan, China and the U.S.

JUNE 1996
Rethinking NAFTA
First Ladies
Teaching Values
Labor Movement's Future

JULY 1996
Recovered-Memory Debate
Native Americans' Future
Crackdown on Sexual Harassment
Attack on Public Schools

AUGUST 1996
Fighting Over Animal Rights
Privatizing Government Services
Child Labor and Sweatshops
Cleaning Up Hazardous Wastes

SEPTEMBER 1996
Gambling Under Attack
The States and Federalism
Civic Journalism
Reassessing Foreign Aid

OCTOBER 1996
Political Consultants
Insurance Fraud
Rethinking School Integration
Parental Rights

NOVEMBER 1996
Global Warming
Clashing Over Copyright
Consumer Debt
Governing Washington, D.C.

DECEMBER 1996
Welfare, Work and the States
The New Volunteerism
Implementing the Disabilities Act
America's Pampered Pets

JANUARY 1997
Combating Scientific Misconduct
Restructuring the Electric Industry
The New Immigrants
Chemical and Biological Weapons

FEBRUARY 1997
Assisting Refugees
Alternative Medicine's Next Phase
Independent Counsels
Feminism's Future

MARCH 1997
New Air Quality Standards
Alcohol Advertising
Civic Renewal
Educating Gifted Students

APRIL 1997
Declining Crime Rates
The FBI Under Fire
Gender Equity in Sports
Space Program's Future

MAY 1997
The Stock Market
The Cloning Controversy

Back issues are available for $5.00 (subscribers) or $10.00 (non-subscribers). Quantity discounts apply to orders over ten. To order, call Congressional Quarterly Customer Service at (202) 887-8621.

Binders are available for $18.00. To order call 1-800-638-1710. Please refer to stock number 648.

Future Topics

- ***Libraries' Changing Role***
- ***FDA Reform***
- ***China After Deng***

THE CQ Researcher

PUBLISHED BY CONGRESSIONAL QUARTERLY INC.

The Future of Libraries

Is the rush to high technology misguided?

As more and more libraries retool to get on the "information superhighway," library users and professional librarians alike have been rethinking the mission of libraries. Fans of technology and long-distance communication envision a day when printed books play only marginal roles, and the once cherished public reading room loses its allure. Library patrons of the future, they say, will depend heavily on Internet browsers and vast electronic databases. But bibliophiles and old-school library devotees decry the new technology as overrated and full of inconveniences. Library professionals, for the most part, foresee a hybrid future that combines the strengths of electronics with those of the traditional print media. What is undeniable is that today's librarians are at the center of the information debate.

INSIDE THIS ISSUE

CQ May 23, 1997 • Volume 7, No. 20 • Pages 457-480

Formerly Editorial Research Reports

THE FUTURE OF LIBRARIES

COVER: SURFING THE WORLD WIDE WEB AT THE NEW SAN FRANCISCO PUBLIC LIBRARY (© STEVE FISCH)

May 23, 1997
Volume 7, No. 20

The CQ Researcher (ISSN 1056-2036). Formerly Editorial Research Reports. Published weekly, except Jan. 3, May 30, Aug. 29, Oct. 31, by Congressional Quarterly Inc., 1414 22nd St., N.W., Washington, D.C. 20037. Annual subscription rate for libraries, businesses and government is $340. Additional rates furnished upon request. Periodicals postage paid at Washington, D.C., and additional mailing offices. POSTMASTER: Send address changes to The CQ Researcher, 1414 22nd St., N.W., Washington, D.C. 20037.

The Future of Libraries

BY CHARLES S. CLARK

THE ISSUES

Several years ago, farsighted citizens in historic Alexandria, Va., approached city officials with a futuristic proposal: They wanted to "wire up" the town surveyed by George Washington. They envisioned an "electronic community" network linking home computers with each other and with the mayor's office, the Chamber of Commerce and the police and fire departments.

When the network was launched in 1994, however, only one city department was ready to hook up: the library system. Indeed, library users had been surfing the Internet for two years. The library system's home page on the World Wide Web provided easy access to the network, dubbed "ALEX." And ALEX also dovetailed with the library's 24-hour telnet service, which lets patrons with computers consult library catalogs from home. The Web site also informs Alexandrians about civic happenings, including expansion plans that will give local libraries a total of 32 computer terminals and 56 laptop data ports.

"This new world of information makes me feel like I'm reborn in my profession," Library Director Patrick M. O'Brien says. "Five years ago, most libraries were in the throes of budget cutbacks. Now, whether it's the overall economy or libraries positioning themselves better, the decline in budgets for the most part has stopped, and libraries have reinvented themselves. Having always dragged behind in technology, libraries are now smack dab in the middle of it." [1]

Not all of O'Brien's modernization efforts have been well-received. There is opposition, for example, to his plan to move the city's collection of rare books and manuscripts from an 18th-century house to a newer, and roomier, facility. But the move would place the old and the modern under the same roof. The collection is best appreciated, its overseers say, in a period setting, not sharing space with CD-ROMS.

But overall, O'Brien's embrace of technological change is at the cutting edge of libraries across the United States.

From 1994-96, the percentage of American public libraries offering Internet service rose 113 percent, to about half of all libraries, according to the National Commission on Libraries and Information Science. [2]

State and local library systems are becoming interconnected, enabling previously isolated rural libraries to share resources and eliminate redundancy in reference works and magazine subscriptions. [3] The Library of Congress, which on March 1 ended its 96-year-old practice of selling printed catalog cards, has watched the percentage of its budget spent on Internet transactions rise more than 2,000 percent over the past five years. (The percentage of its budget spent on maintaining reading room hours, in the same period, shrank 17 percent.)

Though trained librarians can still recite Dewey Decimal System classifications, most can now be found checking the Web site for "Hot Flashes/Library News" or various news feeds and "listservs" offered by commercial and nonprofit Internet access providers. Graduates of library schools today "are finding a lot of different kinds of roles they can play, such as being a Web master, in addition to helping people find information they need," says Jean Preer, associate dean at the School of Library and Information Science at Catholic University in Washington. "The Internet is a vast universe of information waiting to be organized. Librarians are the professionals who can do it."

The Information Age is also shaking up the working habits of researchers and scholars, whose patronage is the lifeblood of libraries.

"There used to be a four-year time frame for publication of work in journals, but now, with listservs on the Internet, people learn about things immediately," notes Richard Hill, executive director of the American Society for Information Science. "What's more, biologists are talking to physicists, and sociologists are talking with mathematicians on the same problem, often across international borders."

The Clinton administration's goal of connecting every school and library to the Internet by 2000 — plus the discounted online telephone rates for libraries authorized by last year's telecommunications reform bill — led the American Library Association (ALA) to set up an Office for Information Technology Policy in Washington. Given that not all American children have a home computer, "the ALA realized that we were needed as an advocate for libraries in important policy issues concerning the information superhighway," explains the office's director, J. Andrew

Magpantay. [4]

Yet the American library's rapid evolution from a quiet temple of books to a dynamic, high-tech mall has also produced a backlash. A movement that some describe as made up of "technophobes" and Luddites worries that the "virtual library" that chases information more than knowledge is a library that is losing its soul. (*See "At Issue," p. 473.*)

"Hordes of academics, engineers, cyberpunks and self-advertised 'infonauts' roam the Net looking for treasure troves of information, like so much gold," writes author Stephen L. Talbott. "It's almost as if the 'electrons' themselves exuded a certain fascination — a kind of spell or subliminal attraction. . . . The dissonance occurs only when one tries to imagine these same adventurers standing in a library, surrounded in three dimensions by records of human achievement far surpassing what is now Net-accessible. Would there, in these surroundings, be the same breathless investigation?" [5]

Courtesy of Alexandria Public Library

The newly renovated main library in Alexandria, Va., marries high-technology and traditional media.

Critics of Internet-worship point out that despite the free news, data and graphics online, most substantive information not in the public domain is still withheld from the Internet by commercial copyright holders. [6] Other critics — particularly parents — worry that sending young people onto the Internet exposes them to indecent material (*see p. 472*). Then there is the question of how to pay for all the new hardware, software and training.

A body of literature has emerged complaining about the hassles involved in online catalog searching. (*See story, p. 462.*) Researchers and journalists complain of the eyestrain of reading from a terminal, and about the adjustment to using computer printouts cluttered with coding rather than full-color, tactile copies of newspapers and magazines. They especially dislike the fact that printouts of articles don't come with layouts and graphics, and that all headlines are the same size. (A massive earthquake gets a head the same size as a recipe in the food section.)

Finally, it has become common for people to predict that the book is dead, or that libraries are doomed by the ability of patrons to easily access information from the convenience of their homes. At the ALA's annual conference in San Francisco next month, a sociologist, a scientist and a humanities scholar will speak on a topic that is anxiety-provoking for librarians: "The New Generation of Scholars: Do They Really Need Us? (Maybe/Maybe Not!)"

So far, such anxieties have not proved justified. In a 1995 Gallup Poll for *U.S. News & World Report*/CNN, 67 percent of the respondents reported that they had used a library in the past year, up from 51 percent in 1978. And fully 91 percent of those who used computerized libraries felt confident that libraries will still be needed in the future.

"I can understand the fear" of digital technology, says George Farr, director of the Division of Preservation and Access at the National Endowment for the Humanities (NEH), which is overseeing the development of a policy on digital preservation of books and manuscripts. (*See story, p. 470.*) "But the Luddites eventually had to lay down their weapons." Too many critics, including many "apostles of digital technology, see the whole thing as an either/or situation, when it's not."

What is gaining ground in the library profession is a notion of balance between the tradition of the library as a democratic, community-service provider and the new vision of an up-to-the-minute, speed-of-light, electronic information nexus.

"We believe in the enduring mission of libraries," two librarians write in a study for the ALA. "Clinging to the past for the sake of the past is as futile as sweeping away the past for the sake of a delusionary future. We advocate a straight and narrow path between the librarianship of nostalgia and the ill-informed embrace of any technology that happens to capture the magpie fancy of the moment." [7]

How libraries will arrive at such a balance in the future will hinge on the following issues:

Will electronic information technology render libraries obsolete?

"Just like a hurricane, the Internet is sweeping away many long-established practices, procedures and traditions," Donald T. Hawkins writes in "Technotrends," a column about the computer industry. "The Internet has made it possible for anyone to become a publisher." [8]

In libraries, such enthusiasm for things digital has raised the possibility of "the virtual library." Spurred by futuristic predictions of the demise of the book, techno-soothsayers in the past decade have played out ever-expanding visions of an everyman's desktop communications center that pulls in limitless quantities of up-to-date, verified, custom-tailored information from around the globe. [9]

Some observers have gone so far as to say that this information utopia will prompt society to stop spending tax dollars on the quaint, old, reading rooms we call libraries and convert those familiar buildings to homeless shelters. "I don't think libraries as places to store physical-information containers have a terribly lengthy future," says John Perry Barlow, the former lyricist for the "Grateful Dead," who co-founded the Internet-boosting Electronic Frontier Foundation. "The library is becoming an increasingly dumb place to store information." [10]

The consensus in recent years, however, is that while the library's physical plant may well change and modernize, there is one key ingredient in a library that is likely to stay as vital as ever: the librarian. "We're now in a world where people need more data faster, and knowledge work has become the backbone of our economy," O'Brien says. "All these electronic search engines are wonderful" in how they access data far outside the local library, "but they don't give the patrons exactly what they're looking for. There's nothing that can replace librarians using their expertise to sift through the vast amount of stuff coming in."

James Billington, Librarian of Congress

Others emphasize the enduring importance of librarians as educators rather than mere data clerks. Public libraries were always a "unifying force in the communities . . . a communal tribute to the culture and values of the books, which have in many ways undergirded our democratic system," writes Librarian of Congress James H. Billington. The Internet's current "flood of unsorted, unverified information will not replace knowledge in the country if librarians can transform themselves from information dispensers to knowledge navigators." [11]

Demand for career librarians is only going up, according to Linda McKell, president of Advanced Information Management, a "headhunting" firm for librarians in Mountain View, Calif., that reported 1996 as its best year yet. [12] And though the job titles may change (library aides and media specialists have given way to library technicians and computer specialists), the onslaught of new technology may have created more personnel needs than it has eliminated.

Take CD-ROMs, for example. Surveys of library patrons show that they are very popular for their search capability and the way they group back issues of a publication on the same disk. But "the introduction of CD-ROMS in academic libraries has created an increase in demand for point-of-use assistance by the reference staff," notes one study. With the technology explosion in libraries, the number of workstations, databases and queries for assistance has multiplied in reference departments, but the number of staff has not increased accordingly." [13]

Perhaps most important, in the view of the ALA, is the role libraries play in assuring that the blessings of technology are not confined to a wealthy few. "Libraries are still needed to make sure that all Americans will have access to specialized information sources, which is important in a democracy," Magpantay says. Pooling of information, he adds, has always been good economics, because each person probably does not need to own a personal copy of a world atlas or the *Oxford English Dictionary*. "Now we're in a time of transition with the electronic industry. Print is still the prime media, but electronics is becoming important. What will we do if certain information is available only electronically? What will the [non-computer-literate] do? Some people still aren't comfortable navigating the Internet and can't

Continued on p. 464

In an Age of Terminals, Cursors and 'Mice' . . .

The "conversation piece" in Andrew Pace's living room has shiny brass fittings and a familiar walnut finish. Pace and his wife use the old-fashioned card catalog cabinet to store everything from bottles of wine to flashlight batteries.

Pace spotted the relic at a consignment shop when he was studying for his master's degree in library science, and it's a daily reminder of how libraries are changing. But even though he misses the handsome card catalog of bygone days, as a systems librarian at a library automation firm in Emeryville, Calif., he says "the online system that replaced it is better."

Douglas Graham

Nothing in the world of libraries has heralded the Information Age so dramatically as the evolutionary sequence that has been unfolding in libraries across the country over the past decade: First, the venerable card catalog is declared "frozen," and new entries are barred; then new acquisitions are catalogued only by computer; and finally, once all card entries for the standing collection have been transferred to electronic format, the space-hogging cabinet is hauled from its time-honored spot in the reading room.

A catalog, of course, is a library's *sine qua non.* (The ancient Sumerians, in fact, referred to catalogs as "ordainers of the universe." [1]) So it's no surprise that some lovers of libraries have greeted the conversion to computerized cataloging as a harrowing experience.

Few in the library profession missed the fusillade of criticism aimed at them three years ago by best-selling author Nicholson Baker in *The New Yorker* magazine. [2] Describing with bitterness the elaborate parties being thrown by libraries to celebrate the demise of the card catalog, Baker wrote of a "national paroxysm of shortsightedness and anti-intellectualism." The villains, he said, are not "book-banners or Saracen sackers" but "smart, well-meaning library administrators, quite certain that they are doing what is right for their institutions."

Baker's diatribe was echoed a year later by Clifford Stoll, a self-described former computer addict. In his book blasting the "hype" of the information revolution, Stoll describes the frustrations of popping into the library in search of a few books and watching instead as a computer screen offers a not-so-handy list of 622 possibilities.

"Computerized subject searches can't discriminate between Saturn the planet, Saturn the God and Saturn the car," he writes. "So researchers learn a logic system to express their needs — library patrons become computer programmers." [3]

Critics of online searching acknowledge some clear advantages: Computers permit library patrons to consult catalogs from the comfort of home, including out-of-town catalogs; they can check which branches have a copy of the book they want and whether it is checked out or on the shelf. Computerized catalogs, they agree, are more wheelchair-accessible, and less vulnerable to damage from mildew, theft and defacement, which have long been frustrating to librarians. In libraries where access to stacks is not permitted, an online catalog can even tell a browser which books are shelved right next to a given book.

But such progress also has introduced new hassles. Often, a patron must learn new software when using an unfamiliar library. Computer systems crash, and there are often long lines at working terminals. The formats of many of the varying catalog designs require the reader to wade through scads of confusing and peripheral information — the call number, for example, often isn't supplied until the third page of a record, in a location on the screen that varies by library.

Baker has other complaints. He writes of a high error rate on the part of computer clerks who keyboard bibliographical information; he bemoans the loss of decades of handwritten corrections and elaborations that professional librarians contributed to the old card catalogs; he laments the loss of ancient cards that document the history of the library itself.

What's more, Baker complains that a computer can't tell when an author's name has changed due to marriage or knighthood, for example. They have a "low tolerance for deviation," he says, noting that tiny differences in punctuation or capitalization in a search might cause relevant items to be missed. He gripes that many search systems reject a lot of key words that are just common sense, and that after wafting off in a cyberspace search, it is too easy to lose one's place. Finally, he cites a 1989 study showing that schoolchildren had a lower success rate in finding a book on a computer than in a traditional card catalog.

Jerry Campbell, dean of the library at the University of Southern California, replies that many of Baker's technical criticisms are "just plain wrong." Baker's argument "is

. . . Some Miss the Old, Wooden Card Catalogs

equivalent to saying the printing press was a failure because the folio [the large books common in Elizabethan times] wouldn't work," he says. "Online is still in its first generation, and it currently mimics the card catalog. It's getting better all the time."

There is a certain "nostalgia attached to the card catalog, particularly among patrons with socio-historical and cultural leanings," says Liz Bishoff, vice president for member services at the Dublin, Ohio-based Online Computer Library Center (OCLC), the nonprofit consortium of thousands of libraries worldwide that creates the massive Union Catalog, which contains 36 million separate titles in nearly 400 languages. Bishoff explains the limits of the old card catalog: "In the early 20th century, catalog cards were handwritten or typed. To minimize the workload, many libraries had policies that permitted only, say, two subject headings, or no descriptions from the book's contents page. One benefit of going online," she says, "is that we're no longer so constrained. We add more than a million new titles a year, so yes, there is bound to be a percentage of typographical errors, but we are looking at ways to curb them through training."

A skilled librarian, Bishoff adds, can help a researcher by structuring a search with effective key words and cross references that guide the user from his own subject headings to headings that the catalog recognizes. An online librarian can also create new combinations, such as biographies of an individual published only within a certain time frame, which ultimately allows the patron more independence in research. Those annoying variations in where different libraries place the call number, she says, stem from the fact that different branches of a library system may keep several copies of a book, one in the juvenile section, one in reference and one in general circulation, for example, each of which requires a slightly different number.

Robert Zich, director of electronic programs at the Library of Congress, which once boasted the largest card catalog in the world, acknowledges that online systems have shortcomings.

"That is why there are the Nicholson Bakers of the world," he says. "But most of those problems will be solved. I try not to be a fanatic on either side of the question."

Zich points out that he regularly found errors in the LC's old card catalog back in the 1960s and reported them to his superiors. "They were from filer inattention, or typos, different names for, say, the Russian czars, or foreign names that the filer didn't understand. And the errors all came from the same source data and went out to OCLC as well. But with the card catalog, the errors were hidden and discovered only inadvertently, whereas with online errors, the mistakes are easily highlighted. With machine-readable data, we can run it through a spell check."

What favored the old card catalog, Zich adds, was that a user could size up a large collection of drawers and get an instant intuitive sense of how much material was available on a topic. (The U.S. government section, for example, comprised hundreds of drawers, which sent many researchers scurrying away.) Experienced researchers, for example, knew that there were about 1,000 cards in each drawer, or 100 cards to an inch.

In addition, the old card catalog allowed for more physical control, he adds. "You could place a little piece of paper to mark your place in the drawer and get a feeling of making progress." In the digital environment, you lose the ability to form a quick impression, and adjustments are needed. "A digital watch, for example, is more accurate than a traditional watch, but your brain must process it differently," he says.

The advantage of online, Zich continues, is that the catalog can be instantly and quickly updated with a previously non-existent search term, such as "Mudbikes." With the card catalog, by contrast, it took months for librarians working by hand to change "European War" to "World War I" after World War II changed history. "And with all the opportunities for advanced searches nowadays, we've gone so far beyond the old catalog, there's hardly any comparison."

(Indeed, the Library of Congress Web site offers home users round-the-clock choice of four types of searches, using varying combinations of linked words, browsing by subject, custom-tailored commands and more experimental methods that rank catalog records by relevance and permit the user to E-mail results to a home computer.)

"The challenge of online," Zich says, "is to find out what it was people liked and found effective about the card catalog and make the accommodation."

The transition to the new catalogs is "intimidating to some patrons, particularly the older generation — the kids have no problem with it," says Patrick O'Brien, director of public libraries in Alexandria Va. At first, library patrons got confused when he supplied computers that mixed Windows programs with all-text programs, or mixed a keyboard with the mouse or trackball. So he made operations more uniform.

The next step in online catalog searching appears to lie on the Internet's World Wide Web, he notes. Ironically, the way the information is displayed on a Web site is very much like it was on an old card catalog.

---

[1] Alberto Manguel, *A History of Reading* (1996), p. 191.

[2] Nicholson Baker, "Discards," *The New Yorker*, April 4, 1994, p. 64.

[3] Clifford Stoll, *Silicon Snake Oil: Second Thoughts on the Information Highway* (1995), p. 201.

Continued from p. 461

yet think critically about how to evaluate sites on the Web."

Libraries and librarians will "continue their critical role in providing access as we marry the worlds of print and electronic media," says Liz Bishoff, vice president for member services at the Dublin, Ohio-based Online Computer Library Center (OCLC), whose huge Union Catalog over the past 25 years has made 36 million titles in 370 languages available to 23,000 member libraries around the world. "Librarians bring skills to organizing information according to the user's interest or personal slant."

The modern electronic library, far from atomizing patrons by sending them home to their private terminals, can actually increase onsite use. Jerry Campbell, dean of the library at the University of Southern California, says that the school's new Leavey Library "has become a symbol of the digital age: It was so popular that as soon as it opened we made it a 24-hour building." The library has an "information commons" and peer learning rooms in addition to the 100,000 new books recently ordered for its undergraduates. "I don't think the college student's ideal is working all alone in one's room," Campbell says. "We make certain that our constituency has what it wants."

Those who assume a future in which all citizens cruise the market as independent database clients may be surprised to learn that commercial information marketers do not — at least not yet — expect to eclipse the role of public libraries. "Libraries now are more of a customer than a competitor, and we're very comfortable with them," says Daniel C. Duncan, vice president for government relations at the Information Industry Association. "Librarians are efficient information brokers who respect copyright law, limit redistribution and copying and are willing to sign an information licensing agreement. Most information content providers want a trusted relationship and an agreement that's enforceable, as opposed to the Internet, where the general public has no understanding of this and often wants only a one-time buy."

Duncan adds that librarians play a key role in designing information systems and deciding what providers should put on them. "We're happy when there's more of a hunger for quality information," he says. And though he can see commercial providers taking over for libraries eventually, "we're a long way from having computers as ubiquitous as televisions in every home. No one knows how fast technology will develop."

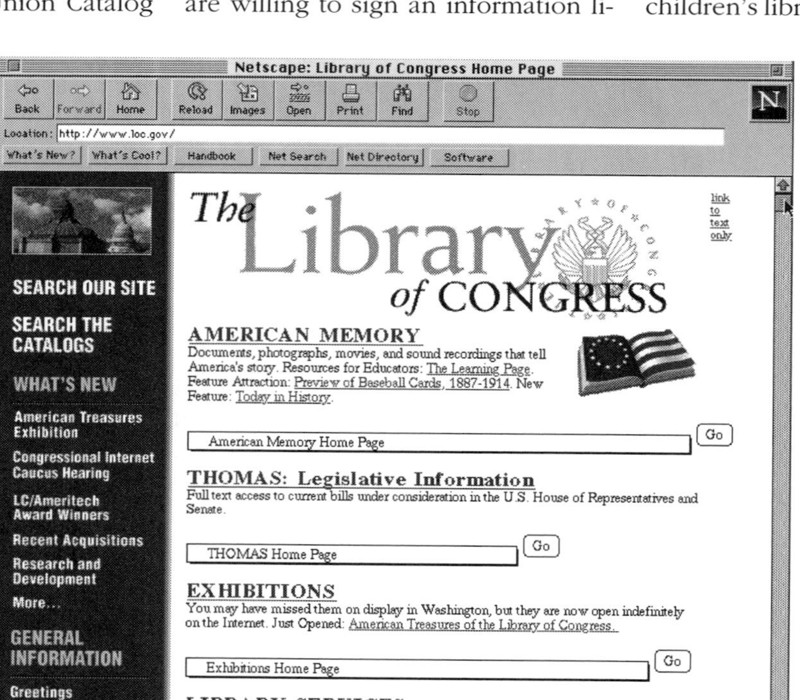

The Library of Congress' home page on the World Wide Web.

Are libraries embracing technology at the expense of their traditional mission?

"The difficulty with the Internet is knowing when to stop!" warns a children's librarian in explaining how to manage a search on the World Wide Web.[14]

Some would say the same applies to the headlong rush of many in the library profession to go high-tech. Most who tout the blessings of the digital library are careful to be concrete about the advantages. Hence computer scientist Michael Lesk notes that the French National Library in Paris has 100,000 books online that can be read by multiple readers and take up practically zero shelf space, compared with the two huge buildings the library needs for its 22 million conventional volumes.[15]

Hill of the Information Science Society gives the example of a new software technology, "DR-LINK," manufactured by Manning & Napier Information Services, which will search for companies that have become profitable under new management: "You simply couldn't find that in an old library," he says.

Public librarians explain how computers allow patrons to scan the past borrowings in their library records online or check out their own books.

Though only a true Luddite would

deny any benefits from digital, the number of people who are uneasy with the changes technology has brought is growing, and vocal. Last year, author Nicholson Baker went so far as to file a lawsuit against the newly modernized San Francisco Public Library, demanding to inspect the card catalog it had dismantled.

Some worry that fascination with technology encourages short-term attention spans and a preference for entertainment rather than a deep quest for knowledge. "Transitions like the one from print to electronic media do not take place without rippling or, more likely, reweaving the entire social and cultural web," writes literary critic Sven Birkerts. "We don't need to look far to find their effects. We can begin with the newspaper headlines and the millennial lamentations sounded in the op-ed pages: that our educational systems are in decline; that our students are less and less able to read and comprehend their required texts. . . . Tagline communication, called 'bite-speak' by some, is destroying the last remnants of political discourse." [16]

The joy that technology-lovers take in customized research and personalized Internet news feeds is troublesome to many. "I worry that the reader of the 'electronic books' of the future will choose to sample only the information that he knows he wants to know. In many cases that's probably not the information he most needs to know," complains physicist and public policy adviser Lewis M. Branscomb. [17]

Finally, there are many who chafe at proposals to turn libraries into "expert-driven" systems in which engineers and artificial-intelligence specialists design software that automatically guides patrons sitting at terminals through complicated problems.

This bookless library is a "hallucination of online addicts, network neophytes and library automation insiders," complains astronomer and one-time computer addict Clifford Stoll. "Let me describe my idealized library of the future. There are lots of books, a card catalog, a children's section with a story hour, a reading room with this morning's newspapers, plenty of magazines, a box of discarded paperback books (selling for a quarter each), a cork bulletin board stapled over with community announcements, a cheap photocopier and a harried, smiling librarian. I'll see a couple of library volunteers shelving volumes. Oh yes, locate this library smack in my neighborhood." [18]

Contrary to popular impression, conventional books, newspapers and periodicals still make up the vast majority of library holdings: 71 percent of the holdings in public libraries and 63 percent in academic facilities, according to a recent survey. [19] The average library last year spent about $15,000 for print acquisitions vs. $6,400 for online services and $5,300 for CD-ROMs. The trend for the future, however, has swung dramatically in favor of electronic products.

"I haven't heard many librarians say it's an either/or situation," says OCLC's Bishoff. "You can still get access to print at the New York Public Library, and many libraries still give browsers direct access to the stacks. But the real advantage of this online world is how it offers access to collections regardless of the time or day or the place."

The ALA's Magpantay points out that "whenever a technology is still new, some people will question its place or its use. Is the Internet a broadcast or a private medium? Is it for graphics or text? We need to have these discussions for the technology to mature. Radio was supposed to be killed by television, and movies were supposed to be killed by the VCR, but each of these technologies now has its proper niche. The book is portable, can be read in the bathtub and does not require a machine. A computer has the advantage of the key word search, which is what you'd want if you are analyzing, say, the role of nature vs. nurture in the works of Shakespeare. But you wouldn't take a CD-ROM to the beach."

Besides, Magpantay adds, "libraries don't have the power to dictate what the market wants. Some local libraries still offer old 78 rpm records."

Others point out that the book-publishing industry is still flourishing. Witness the power of talk-show host Oprah Winfrey to launch a best-seller; witness the crowds at superstores such as Borders and Barnes & Noble; and witness the recent public stock offering by Internet-based Amazon.com, which enables online customers to order from some 1.5 million book titles.

"In the foreseeable future, we won't have a satisfactory replacement for the book, because there's nothing as convenient," says Robert Zich, director of electronic programs at the Library of Congress. "But certain reference books, like the *Britannica,* which are usually read non-consecutively, are being transformed in order to compete with $40 electronic encyclopedias."

In addition, Zich says, "more pure information is becoming available online, such as Census Bureau data and tourist information on bed and breakfasts. But right now we still need books in order to interpret the raw materials," and many online offerings — the Library of Congress' digital photographs from the Civil War, for example — send people into the stacks to learn more. "At some point, however, there will be much more online, and we will have portable computers to replicate the convenience of the book."

USC's Campbell speaks effusively of "the extraordinary love affair that a great portion of humankind has had with the particular medium called the book. It's a legitimate love affair, and I love rare books. But after all, people used to read and write on rocks," he notes. "The next generation will have its love affair with something, and we don't know what that medium will be."

Clearly, Alexandria's O'Brien adds, Internet technology would not have emerged the way it has without "tremendous numbers of people getting into it," a popularity that exploded not from efforts by commercial entities but from users who expect the free and open access one gets from a public library. "But I don't believe in the death of the book. I don't want to sit at my computer and read a whole book, or even a long magazine article. The first thing I do is hit the print button."

One area where many battles over technology will be fought is cost. Boosters such as Lesk point out, for example, that it costs only about $2 to store a 300-page book on a disk, compared with about $30 for the actual book. Others emphasize that much government information is now free on the Web or through specialized agency services that have replaced expensive private services. They also brag that libraries that can't afford to subscribe to hundreds of magazines and journals can sign licensing agreements with periodical databases that permit patrons to pay only for single articles they actually need.

The problem with this apparent bounty, however, is that publications that lose all their steady subscribers to libraries and individuals on the Net will no longer have the revenue to pay their writers, editors, designers and business staffs. They could sink. This sobering reality has recently become more apparent to people who previously assumed the Internet was a bottomless sea of comprehensive information, according to Anne Caputo, senior director of information professional development for Knight-Ridder Information, which sells the Dialog electronic article service to libraries across the country. "Yes, we are in the business of providing selective needs, but part of our responsibility is to the publications," she says. "They bring expertise and value to the mix, too."

Those designing the library of the future do not consider it realistic to digitize every book or periodical that future patrons might request. Selectivity is inevitable, so libraries should coordinate to share costs and start with the best-sellers to create interest in lesser works, according to Clifford Lynch, librarian for the University of California's Office of the President. If too many books are left undigitized, he warns, "visitors to a library 20 years hence may find everything online except a strange pile of books published from 1920-1990, a kind of Sargasso Sea of publishing relegated to the stacks." [20]

The most important thing is for libraries to avoid losing sight of their mission, says Edwin S. Clay, the library director for Fairfax County, Va. "We're not a movie theater or a bookstore. And not everyone in the community wants to use the same media as the others. If a person wants to hold a book and have no sounds around him, then you provide him a quiet study room. If someone else does not, you must accommodate them. I hope there's lots of freedom and latitude to carry out the mission."

Perhaps in a few years, when the novelty of the Internet settles down, there will be less friction about which is the best technology.

"What's exciting on the Web is how easily you can get its information, not how great the information is once you get it," observes *Washington Post* cultural writer Amy E. Schwartz. "At the risk of sounding technophobic, it may also be useful to remember that the proposition also holds when run the other way; old, slow, creaky ways of getting your data may still be the secret to finding really exciting information." [21] ■

BACKGROUND

Shudder of Doom?

"There are numerous men and women perambulating the earth — in appearance much like ordinary respectable citizens — who have warm, loving, passionate — even sensuous — feelings about libraries." [22]

This wry observation from a journalist in 1970 goes a long way toward explaining the sound and the fury that have accompanied the recent transformation of America's libraries. For centuries, the emblematic image of a library was as a temple for the book, a community-scale version of the personal collections that are bound up in the identities of many avid readers. Note the caressing imagery in this passage from a noted book-lover:

"As I build pile after pile of familiar volumes (I recognize some by their color, others by their shape, many by a detail on the jackets whose titles I try to read upside down or at an odd angle) I wonder, as I have wondered . . . why I keep so many books I know I will not read again. I tell myself that, every time I get rid of a book, I find a few days later that this is precisely the book I'm looking for. . . . I delight in knowing that I'm surrounded by a sort of inventory of my life, with intimations of my future. I like discovering, in almost forgotten volumes, traces of the reader I once was — scribbles, bus tickets, scraps of paper with mysterious names and numbers, the occasional date and place on the book's flyleaf which take me back to a certain cafe." [23]

Lovers of creamy-paged books and wood-paneled libraries can't help but sense a shudder of doom in the past decade's explosion of computer communications. They worry that "infor-

Continued on p. 468

Chronology

1960s *Library of Congress develops machine-readable cataloging (MARC).*

1967
Ohio College Library Center (OCLC) founded in Dublin, Ohio, to computerize state academic libraries to share costs.

1969
Pentagon's Defense Advanced Research Projects Agency embarks on ARPANET, precursor to Internet designed for fail-safe communications in nuclear war.

1970s *Rise of private information brokers as "alternatives to libraries"; early Internet connections in academia.*

1970
OCLC begins developing machine-readable catalog techniques and takes over national cataloging from Library of Congress.

1973
MARC format becomes international standard for communicating bibliographic information.

1974
Pentagon embraces Internet protocol, giving all members common method of transmitting data.

1980s *Use of personal computers explodes for long-distance communication, E-mail; rise of online databases for information on demand.*

1981
OCLC changes name to Online Computer Library Center. Library of Congress stops adding entries to manual card catalog.

1985
Office of Preservation created at National Endowment for the Humanities.

1986
CD-ROMS (compact disc-read-only memory) appear in libraries.

1990s *Libraries and schools connect to Internet; arrival of World Wide Web, library telnet services.*

1990
Library of Congress launches American Memory project to make audio and visual materials accessible electronically at 44 computer stations around the country.

1991
High-Performance Computing Act helps link computer networks around the country.

1993
Clinton administration proposes Telecommunications and Information Infrastructure Assistance Program to match private grants to schools and libraries.

1994
Library of Congress launches National Digital Library.

June 1995
American Library Association (ALA) sets up Office for Information Technology Policy. Congress debates Communications Decency Act.

Feb. 8, 1996
President Clinton signs Telecommunications Reform Act, which includes crackdown on Internet indecency and discount phone rates for school, library and hospital online communications.

Sept. 30, 1996
Clinton signs appropriations bill containing Library Services and Construction Act with largest appropriation ever, changing name to Library Services and Technology Act. Some Education Department programs transferred to Institute for Museum and Library Services.

November 1996
Federal-State Joint Board of Regulators established by telecom act recommends 20-90 percent discount for libraries.

Feb. 11, 1997
Clinton creates Advisory Committee on High-Performance Computing and Communications, Information Technology, and the Next Generation Internet.

March 19, 1997
Supreme Court hears oral arguments in *Reno v. American Civil Liberties Union* on constitutionality of Communications Decency Act.

April 16, 1997
National Library Log-On Day spotlights role of libraries in connecting children to Information Superhighway.

April 19, 1997
Second annual "Net Day" marked by Clinton administration.

May 7, 1997
Federal Communications Commission mandates discounted telephone rates for online communication by libraries, schools and hospitals.

Continued from p. 466

mation" and "data" have been elevated above "knowledge" and "wisdom." And, like all consumers in the modern era, they have watched as new products and formats come and go with ever-shorter half-lives.

"For every new technology that today functions beside an old one (e.g. television and radio), it is possible to identify a new technology that actually was replaced by a new one (e.g. teletype by radio, typewriters by printers)," notes a report on preservation issues in digital technology. [24]

In their enthusiasm for working online, many of today's librarians may lack a proper skepticism, says Fairfax librarian Clay. But the notion of librarians taking an active role in helping society incorporate new communications technologies is nothing new. "We've been techno-dudes since before there was such a thing," he adds, citing the public library's applications of electricity and the telephone early in the century. "We've been in this business a long time."

Road to Automation

The groundwork for today's electronic library was laid in the 1960s, on a variety of fronts. First, the concept of "information science" was emerging in industry and in academe. In 1962, economist Fritz Machlup identified more than 50 information-oriented activities in education, communications media, research and development and machinery. [25]

In 1963, a conference of librarians in Great Britain developed PRECIS, a new cataloging system that formulated rules for a new indexing system that could be manipulated by computer. In 1964, the U.S. National Library of Medicine was already running on-demand information services, and a year later, abstracts of technical articles about chemistry were available through the miracle of magnetic tape.

It didn't take long for the consumer angle to take shape. In 1965, *Popular Science* published an article that asked: "How would you like to have the Library of Congress, occupying 270 miles of bookshelves, in your house? Sounds impossible? Well through a new microphotography process, you may, one day, be able to have the entire contents of the great library in your den on film — all contained in about six filing cabinets." [26]

By 1968, computer scientists at a Cambridge, Mass., consulting firm had won the first federal contract to build "interface message processors" for the Defense Department, which led to the birth of the Internet. One of the firm's earliest ideas was to create computer networks that would wire up hospitals and libraries. [27]

On campus, meanwhile, computerized card catalogs began their takeover, gaining a first toehold at research libraries such as the one at Northwestern University. By 1973, the machine-readable cataloging (MARC) format had become the international standard for communicating bibliographic information. OCLC, the consortium of college libraries in Ohio, was soon expanding its computerized cataloging at such a rate that it overtook the Library of Congress in the number of cards provided to libraries. [28]

By 1981, the Library of Congress had ceased updating its traditional card catalog, and a new set of Anglo-American Cataloging Rules prompted reconsideration of the old systems. The only reason automated cataloging didn't happen faster, argues one history, was the "absence of a sense of permanence or stability" of any one system that would give library administrators enough confidence to invest in them. [29] Even so, they argued, eventual arrival of the computer did not alter cataloging's basic logic: "The fundamental principles of catalog organization have been in evidence in catalogs produced in a variety of forms for at least three centuries. A close examination of these principles reveals that they exist independently of any medium."

The 1970s brought several other changes that would mold today's information revolution. An "Alternatives to Libraries" trend appeared among profit-seeking information entrepreneurs catering to researchers, beginning in the San Francisco area. [30] Michael Hart, a professor at Illinois Benedictine College, launched Project Gutenberg, an effort to make 10,000 public-domain classic works of literature available on computer. (It currently is up to 624 volumes.) [31] And most dramatically, long-distance communication using the Internet began to spread from a select few users in the military and scientific communities to the popular consumer medium it has become today.

San Francisco Shootout

Though countless library patrons have expressed frustration at all the newfangled machinery, the inevitable clash between "the tekkies" and "the technophobes" came to a head most dramatically last fall in San Francisco. Author Baker had received a cry for help from unionized staff members at the San Francisco public library. The new headquarters facility had just opened to crowds who came to bask in its ultra-modern, high-tech atmosphere and community meeting rooms. But the architecture's lack of emphasis on books and stacks, and the names of corporate donors on its walls, also brought out critics who called it "anti-book." "The new main is a betrayal of what a public library is supposed to be about," said Tille Olson, a poet and short-story author. The rush into technology has meant that it has "left its soul behind." [32]

Word came out that while creating the new building, the library had discarded some 100,000-200,000 old books in a landfill, and that poor records had been kept of which were discarded. This prompted action from San Francisco locals such as the Grey Panthers, who organized a salvage operation to rescue some of the books.

Baker took his case to the pages of *The New Yorker*, asserting that many of the discarded books were "old, hard to find, out of print and valuable" and that the new building was short on storage space for books. [33] "The real story is a case study of what can happen — what to a greater or lesser degree is happening in a number of cities around the country — when telecommunications enthusiasts take over big old research libraries and attempt to remake them, with corporate help, as high-traffic showplaces for information technology," Baker wrote.

But that wasn't all. Library Director Kenneth Dowlin, who'd been planning the new library since 1987, announced that a $1.2 million deficit was forcing him to cut 93 staff positions and reduce hours for part-timers. That was too much for Mayor Willie Brown, who announced, "I will take it over, if necessary, to prevent cuts." [34] Dowlin resigned in January amid charges of bad management and overspending on computers. (He is running for president of the American Library Association.)

Defenders of the new library point out that much of the fear of vanishing books is belied by the fact that book acquisitions in the San Francisco system rose from 61,000 in 1991-92 to 238,000 in 1995-96. They point out that books were buried in a landfill because of a city ordinance against selling them. They also note that the new library was drawing huge crowds. Dowlin says that an outside audit of the library released in May confirms the steps he took.

To librarians around the country, the episode provided several lessons — the public relations sensitivities in computerization, and the need for library managers to avoid getting too far out in front of their staffs. But the main lesson revolved around the standard practice of "deaccessioning," or "weeding" books that are out-of-date, damaged, obscure or duplicative. "When I was in library school," says Zich of the Library of Congress, "I had a professor who stood in front of the class and tore up a book and threw it in the trash. One of the most important tasks is getting past the idea that we must keep everything forever. The Library of Congress is the library of permanent record, but the public libraries are not. Most are constantly weeding."

To O'Brien, "the least understood aspect of public education on libraries is weeding. It's not a sexy issue, but it gets people excited in that 99 percent usually agree on 99 percent of what to weed, but that 1 percent will raise a ruckus. It's a judgment call, and a librarian has to be judicious. It's a fact of life that all libraries at some point hit capacity. You can't have a zero-growth collection." ■

CURRENT SITUATION

Optimistic Budgets

When it comes to funding, "Public libraries by and large are doing OK," says Mary Jo Lynch, director of research and statistics at the ALA. "The number of new library buildings in cities indicates something about how city and county governments feel about libraries in general, though it depends on the region and the local economy." Still, with the arrival of new Internet technology, she adds, there's never enough for equipment, installing lines, maintenance and constant training.

Public library budgets are up by 6.4 percent over last year, according to a *Library Journal* survey. [35] About half the nation's libraries are engaging in fund-raising, up from 42 percent last year. Of those that have trimmed jobs, 25 percent cited budget cuts, while only 3 percent cited technological advances.

At the federal level, prospects are also favorable. President Clinton is a library booster (he mentioned libraries twice in his last State of the Union address). House Speaker Newt Gingrich, R-Ga., also has lent his support, having countered an outside consultant's recommendation last year and recommended increased funding for the Library of Congress.

The Clinton administration is seeking $137 million for aid to the nation's libraries. Though the ALA would favor a $150 million appropriation, it says it is pleased with recent hikes. The Library of Congress, meanwhile, says it needs $388 million, a 7.1 percent boost.

"Technology is the area where this Congress is willing to see federal money spent," says Carol Henderson, executive director of the ALA's Washington office. The Federal Communications Commission's ruling this month in favor of unprecedented discounted telephone rates for libraries for use online is also greeted as good news.

One new way that public libraries are solidifying their funding is to share a building with "house mates" such as seniors centers, police stations, schools and government offices. [36] Others, such as the public

Digital Revolution Offers New Way . . .

In the 1970s and '80s, America's libraries and archives took stock of a daunting threat. The crisis, explains Jan Merrill-Oldham, the preservation librarian at Harvard University, was — and still is — the decay over time of millions of valuable books, manuscripts, photographs and sound recordings. "Throughout most of the 19th and 20th centuries, information was recorded on highly ephemeral media, including acidic paper, unstable film and short-lived magnetic tape," she says. "Think about the cultural and intellectual output of this period — the scientific findings, great fiction, the critical records of government. Do we believe that future generations can do without this legacy?"

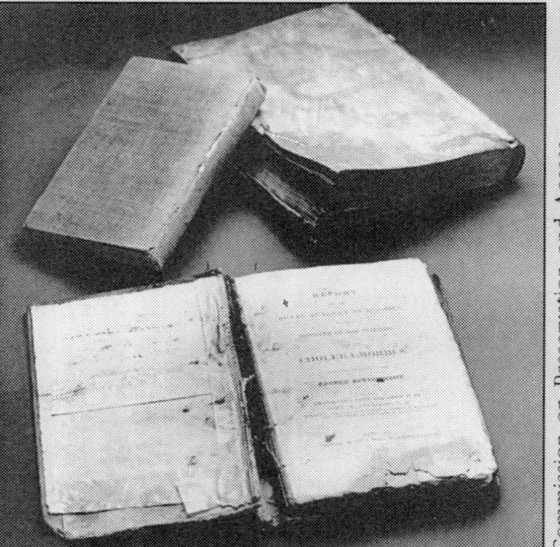
Commission on Preservation and Access

Surveys of North American libraries showed as many as 80 million books threatened with destruction, primarily because they were printed on acidic paper. (Modern publishers have converted to more durable alkaline paper.) In testimony before Congress, historian James McPherson recalled that in the course of reading original books and pamphlets in his research on slavery and the Civil War, "I turned these precious but highly acidic pages, [and] some of them tore and crumbled in my hands no matter how carefully and delicately I handled them. I was horrified by the experience of damaging, perhaps destroying the very sources that nurtured my knowledge." [1]

In 1985, the National Endowment for the Humanities (NEH) stepped in and set up its Office of Preservation. Two years later, a documentary on the crisis, "Slow Fires," was funded by NEH, the Library of Congress and the Council on Library Resources and shown on public television. And in 1989, the NEH announced a 20-year plan to reproduce the pages of 3 million of the nation's most important brittle books and serial publications on microfilm. In 1990, the endowment launched a new program of grants for improvements in climate control for collections held by museums, historical societies and other cultural repositories. At the same time, the NEH increased its support for the efforts of states and territories to catalog and microfilm endangered 19th-century U.S. newspapers.

As a result, NEH Chairman Sheldon Hackney recently told Congress, the NEH "is the acknowledged national leader" in the effort to preserve cultural resources made from high-acid paper. With NEH grants and private funding, some 750,000 brittle books and 55 million newspapers have been microfilmed, and 27 million objects of archaeological, ethnographic and historical importance have been preserved through improved housing and environmental control. [2]

Yet just as the microfilming movement was proceeding apace, the world of books and manuscripts was swept by new digital technology. "Digitization may ultimately become an effective means of preserving as well as enhancing access to cultural resources," says George Farr, director of the NEH's Division of Preservation and Access. "But these new technologies also present a tremendous preservation challenge due to the incompatibility and rapid obsolescence of computer software and hardware. The nation's cultural institutions must therefore arrive at a shared understanding of the strategies that will be necessary to ensure access to electronic resources as far forward into the future as possible."

Information specialists have been wary of the risks of incompatible technologies for decades. In the mid-1970s, the National Archives decided that data from the 1960 decennial census had long-term historical value, but was bewildered to learn that all of that data was accessible only with a 1960-vintage UNIVAC type II-A computer. The only two machines capable of reading the data were eventually found in Japan and in the Smithsonian Institution. [3]

Another problem peculiar to digital technology is "fixity" — using computer graphics programs to alter text and visual images of documents, raising opportunities for untold mischief. "You can put trees on a landscape where they did not exist; you can show Forrest Gump with John F. Kennedy," Farr says. "The authenticity of the original is open to question in the absence of some method of protecting the original version as it is transmitted and used." (Indeed, this spring, Kideo Productions Inc. patented an inexpensive technique for placing images of people into existing photographs, for entertainment or educational videos. [4]

Digital enthusiasts, notes Merrill-Oldham, often overlook the new challenges inherent in the digital environment. "There is this notion that once something is digitized, it

library in San Leandro, Calif., are opening cafes as revenue-raisers. Libraries also are tapping increasingly into money from corporations and foundations, coordinated by the ALA's Fund for America's Libraries, which has raised $8 million in two years.

Since November 1995, Microsoft Corp. has been working with the

. . . to Preserve Decaying Books and Papers

leaves the material world. But digitized information resides on tapes and disks, which present greater preservation problems than paper. They must be read by complex machinery and require significant ongoing maintenance," she says. "What's more, technology is not as advanced as people are led to believe by the popular press. Try scanning in a page from a 19th-century text that has small, light, spidery text and many broken characters. The results will be pretty disappointing." Nor, she adds, can you buy low-cost equipment that can capture images at high resolution from bound volumes.

The problems of digitization, however, may well be dwarfed by the medium's advantages in expanding access. The NEH, for example, has been instrumental in digitizing the Dead Sea Scrolls, Egyptian papyri, an array of ancient Greek texts and the original works of Shakespeare for use by limitless researchers online. "One of the wonderful things about digitizing is that it enables the juxtaposition of materials that heretofore have been separate," Merrill-Oldham says. "You can gather together virtual collections from different sources, be they huge libraries or local historical societies — some of which have incredible collections. You can distribute widely and use them in new ways. Tiny details on an illuminated manuscript, when scanned at high resolutions and enlarged on a computer screen, really come to life."

To meet the challenges of digital preservation, the National Digital Library Federation was established last August. A combined effort of 12 universities, the Library of Congress, the National Archives, the New York Public Library and the Washington-based Commission on Preservation and Access, the group intends to formulate "best practices" for discovery, retrieval and archiving of digital information as well as create models to clarify economic and intellectual property issues.

A preview of possible solutions to digital preservation conundrums appeared in a pair of reports this spring, both of which assigned a central role to public-sector information specialists. "Librarians and archivists can influence vendors and manufacturers to develop new systems that are 'backwardly compatible' with existing ones," wrote the Commission on Preservation and Access. "Librarians and archivists can help exercise control over the integrity of digital image files by authenticating access procedures and documenting successive modifications to a given digital file." [5]

Not everyone is convinced that digital technology is worthy of high-priority effort. The National Archives' National Historical Publication and Records Commission, for example, in addition to its traditional funding of document preservation is currently exploring the problems involved in preserving electronic records. But it was recently criticized in print by a Yale University historian for neglecting longstanding projects such as publication of the private papers of Benjamin Franklin, Thomas Jefferson and George Washington. "The new head of the National Archives has decided that it is more important to preserve modern electronic records in local and state archives than it is to publish the papers of the dead white males who created the government for which he works," he complained. [6]

"Given the costs of digital technology," notes the NEH's Farr, "it will be some time before there's a decisive body of culturally significant material in digital form available for shared use around the country. That means that digitized resources will exist within a larger library of traditional books, microfilm, manuscripts, photographs, sound recording and film." And though digitizing manuscripts and archives will protect them from excessive handling, there will always be cases where people must consult the original document.

"Finding enough money will remain a major obstacle to broadly based digital conversion," Farr continues, "in addition to the problem of standardizing procedures among hundreds of libraries and archives. "It is somehow appropriate that the cultural patrimony of our democracy is lodged not in one or two large institutions, but in a variety of smaller libraries, museums and historical societies across the country." He notes that the Mellon Foundation is supporting a series of projects that seek to determine whether digital will in fact save libraries money in the long run.

"The amount of valuable information held in U.S. repositories calls for funding that goes far beyond the means of any individual research library," adds Merrill-Oldham. "When are we going to make a reasonable investment in the survival of our history? When it comes to a broad, national commitment to preservation, we're simply not there yet."

---

[1] Testimony to House Interior Appropriations Subcommittee, April 18, 1991.

[2] Testimony before Senate Interior Appropriations Subcommittee, April 24, 1997.

[3] Commission on Preservation and Access, "Preserving Digital Information: Report of the Task Force on Archiving of Digital Information," May 1, 1996, p. 2.

[4] The New York Times, April 21, 1997, p. D2.

[5] Commission on Preservation and Access, "Preservation in the Digital World," March 1996, pp. 16-17. See also *ibid.*

[6] Edmond S. Morgan, "Honor The Founding Fathers," The Wall Street Journal, April 23, 1997.

Seattle Public Library and the ALA on "Libraries Online!," a program in which the computer giant is funneling more than $16.5 million in software, technical assistance and grants to 43 libraries around the country. Christopher Hedrick, senior program manager for corporate contributions at Microsoft, says the project is "designed as a sustained effort to expand access in disadvantaged communities so that there won't be two classes of people in America. We think the public library is a great place to do that because it is staffed by people who help lead the way to knowledge."

Preservation Funding

Another budget debate in Washington is being watched closely in the library community. Funding for preservation efforts and digital policy research by the NEH will depend on larger issues: Congress' efforts to reduce the federal deficit, as well as the tactics of some Republicans who have vowed to eliminate the endowment, along with its sister agency, the National Endowment for the Arts (NEA). It is the NEA, headed by actress Jane Alexander, that has drawn the most criticism, due to its past funding of certain artists whom some consider indecent or sacrilegious. [37]

But the NEH has also provoked skepticism among Republicans who saw waste in its "National Conversation" program, which over the past four years has organized some 3 million Americans in a dialogue about being an American.

For fiscal 1998, Clinton has requested $136 million for the NEH, which would include $21 million for preservation. That would be $26 million more than last year's budget, and $3 million more than last year's preservation allotment. At a March 24 Senate Interior Appropriations Subcommittee meeting, NEH Chairman Sheldon Hackney (who is retiring in July) remarked that the budget request is still far below the $172 million that the NEH was given in 1994, the year before the Republicans took over Congress and slashed NEH spending by 36 percent.

"We made the transition with pain, but with imagination, by seeking private-sector help as we enter the digital age," Hackney said. He also said he had learned the importance of telling Congress and the public the story of the NEH's "unglamorous but necessary work of keeping the culture alive."

Sheldon Hackney
Chair, National Endowment for the Humanities

John Hammer, director of the Washington-based National Humanities Alliance, which advocates more NEH spending, points out that the impact of Republican cuts in the fiscal 1996 budget was softened in the preservation area, out of deference to the preservation program's original patron, Rep. Sydney R. Yates, D-Ill. It was cut only by 25 percent, which meant that other research areas at NEH took a 60 percent cut, a pattern not likely to be repeated, Hammer says. [38] "We expect flat funding in 1998," an expectation echoed by a spokeswoman at NEH.

A spokeswoman for Rep. Ralph Regula, R-Ohio, chairman of the House Interior Appropriations Subcommittee, said that once Congress enacts a budget resolution and resolves the question of abolishing the NEA, the panel is likely to approve either the $110 million the NEH received last year, or the $99 million that the House backed last year.

Sen. Slade Gorton, R-Wash., chairman of the Senate Interior Appropriations Subcommittee, recently complimented Hackney on his handling of controversies at the NEH. But Clinton's request for $136 million, he said, "does not have a snowball's chance in hell."

Policing Indecency

In addition to all the treasures on a library's Internet hookup have come the real-world bugaboos of pornography, hate literature and sexually oriented material that may be suitable for adults but not for children. In June, the Supreme Court is expected to rule on the constitutionality of the Communications Decency Act, a Clinton-backed attempt to regulate Internet content passed by Congress in February 1996 but struck down by a panel of judges. In the meantime, many libraries have responded to complaints from parents by subscribing to filtering services that block texts that contain a prescribed list of sexually oriented words and images. In Orange County, Fla., for example, the public library spent $6,000 to subscribe to such a service. [39]

Continued on p. 474

At Issue:

Are high-tech libraries losing their soul?

Sallie Tisdale
From *Harper's* Magazine, March 1997

When I entered the library as a child, I walked up several imposing steps to a door of respectful size, through a small foyer — and through the looking glass. . . . The rooms were close, filled with big, heavy tables that had dictionaries open on reading stands; tall, sweet-smelling, precarious shelves; leather armchairs; rubber-coated wheeled step stools; and other readers, silent and absorbed. . . .

This was a place set outside the ordinary day. Its silence — outrageous, magic, unlike any other sound in my life — was a counterpoint to the interior noise in my crowded mind. . . .

In the library, I could hunker down in an aisle, seeing only the words in my lap, and a stranger would simply step over me and bend down for his book with what I now think of as a rare and touching courtesy. That place was then, and remains, the library; what Jorge Luis Borges knew all along was more than that: it was "the Universe (which others call the library)". . . .

I am disabled by this memory. I still show up at 10 in the morning at the central branch of the Multnomah County Library, in Portland, Ore., where I now live, impatient for the doors to open. I always find people ahead of me, waiting on the wide stone steps, and I wait with them, knowing better. The library I knew, the one I remember, is almost extinct.

In the last few years, I have gone to the library to study or browse or look something up, and instead have found myself listening to radios, crying babies, a cappella love songs, puppet shows, juggling demonstrations, CD-ROM games and cellular telephone calls. . . .

Children run through the few stacks still open to patrons, spinning carts and pulling books off shelves, ignored by parents deep in conversation with one another. A teenager Rollerblades through, playing crack-the-whip by swinging himself around the ends of the shelves. . . . Patrons hum along with their earphones, stand in line for the Internet screens, clackety-clack on keyboards. Silence, even a mild sense of repose, is long gone.

Today's library is trendy, up-to-date, plugged in and most definitely not set outside the ordinary day. It's a hip, fun place, the library. You can get movies there and Nintendo games, drink cappuccino and surf cyberspace, go to a gift shop or a cafeteria, rent a sewing machine or a camera. There is a library in a Wichita supermarket and a Cleveland shopping mall. But the way things are going, in a few years it's going to be hard to tell the difference between the library and anything, everything, else.

yes

Francine Fialkoff
***Executive Editor,* Library Journal**

From *Library Journal*, December 1996

PETCO, a huge chain pet-supply store, opened on my block recently. It joins HMV, the humongous music store, Staples, the stationery chain, Starbucks, the coffeehouse chain, and Barnes & Noble, the you-know-what chain. . . .

There's another "chain" in my neighborhood, though, a not-for-profit chain: three branches of the New York Public Library (NYPL). It aims to be a model of diversity, providing materials in many formats and in numerous areas of knowledge to its multiethnic populations in an uncensorious way. . . .

Newsweek recently scrutinized a handful of new libraries, including NYPL's own technology showplace. . . . *Newsweek* found out what librarians already know: The new technology that draws people in or allows them dial-in access to the library's collection has also led to substantial increases in . . . circulation. . . .

The move toward information technology is not a threat to books and other materials libraries traditionally provide but a spur to their usage. . . .

Diversity of information, in whatever format it may be available, has been the long suit of public libraries. Some 20 years ago, an anti-technology diatribe might have been about books being replaced by audiovisual materials; 10 years ago it might have homed in on feature film videos or abridged audiobooks. More recently, it might protest the library's collection of CD-ROMs. Yet audiovisual departments are thriving in their multiplicity of formats, and library circulation figures for books continue to be strong.

The slew of classics on film this past year — from the teen-throb version of *Romeo and Juliet* to movie and cable TV makeovers of *Sense and Sensibility*, *Pride and Prejudice*, *Emma*, *Jane Eyre* and *Richard III* — has people buzzing about some of the best that English literature has to offer and has sent many of them back to the books. . . .

There is no doubt that people have format preferences. Indeed some . . . might be described as format-obsessed. They are threatened by the translation of codex books or even 3 x 5 catalog cards into newer formats. . . .

Yes, sometimes quality and substance are diminished in the translation from one format to another. But sometimes, as in the case of novels like *Love Story* or that tear-jerker *The Bridges of Madison County*, the translation from print to another format like the movies is an improvement on the original. . . .

As for the chains in my neighborhood, they, too, provide the occasional service when I find an item there not stocked in the local specialty store. But, no, there's no chain that can replace my nonprofit chain.

no

FOR MORE INFORMATION

American Library Association, Office for Information Technology Policy, 1301 Pennsylvania Ave. N.W., Suite 403, Washington, D.C. 20004; 202-628-8421; (headquarters in Chicago, 800 545-2433); E-mail: oitp@alawash.org. This new section of the association's Washington office promotes the development and utilization of electronic access to information as a means to ensure the public's right to a free and open information society.

Commission on Preservation and Access, 1400 16th St. N.W., Suite 715, Washington, D.C. 20036; 202-939-3400. Founded in 1986, this nonprofit group supports collaboration among libraries and allied organizations to ensure the preservation of the published and documentary record in all formats and to provide enhanced access to scholarly information. (The commission will merge July 1 with the Council on Library Resources and become the Council on Library and Information Resources.)

OCLC (Online Computer Library Center Inc.), 6565 Frantz Rd., Dublin, Ohio, 43017; (614) 761-5002; home page, http://www.oclc.org/ Founded in 1967, this nonprofit consortium of more than 23,000 libraries worldwide produces the world's largest online catalog and promotes computerization of libraries to share costs and materials.

National Endowment for the Humanities, Nancy Hanks Center, 1100 Pennsylvania Ave. N.W., Washington, D.C. 20506; (202) 682-5400. Founded in 1965, this federal agency provides grants for research, scholarship, educational and public programs, including preservation of books, newspapers and historical documents.

National Commission on Libraries and Information Science, 1110 Vermont Ave. N.W., Suite 820, Washington, D.C. 20005. This permanent, independent federal agency advises the president and Congress on national and international issues affecting library and information policy.

In Alexandria, the library posts a disclaimer reminding patrons that if they link to Web sites outside of the library's home page, the library can no longer control the suitability of the content. In Fairfax, most computers do not carry filters, except for a few that were donated, according to librarian Clay. "We think it's the adults' responsibility to monitor their children," he says. "But we're realistic, so we place all computers in open areas within eyesight of staff."

Judith Krug, director of the ALA's Office of Intellectual Freedom, opposes filtering devices, saying it is mostly the large libraries that are getting them. "My theory is that the smaller libraries have more of a sense of community, and the kids, as with books, mostly stick to what they came for," she says. Krug sees filters as censorship. And as she and many librarians have pointed out, a program that blocks the word "breast" will censor material on breast cancer or on how to cook chicken breasts, while a program blocking "sex" will also block "sex education" and "Mars exploration." "It's the adults who want to protect the children, and they're the ones accessing the raunchiest sites and then complaining," she says. "They're transferring adult interests, concerns and even desires to children that really aren't there." She predicts that the problem might be solved in a couple of years with individualized filtering software that will erase itself when a new Internet user logs on. ■

OUTLOOK

Librarians Needed

At a Smithsonian Institution panel discussion in April, several of the scientists who helped create the Internet looked into the mind-boggling future of computers. They envisioned telephone lines being replaced by wireless networks, and computers everywhere — even an Internet address for every light bulb to sound an alert when it burned out.

"Everyone will have access to as much information as they can use, and then some," said former National Science Foundation researcher Steve Wolff. But all the panelists predicted that individuals would always prefer their reading with a book, and that humanity's social and community needs ensured the survival of libraries. [40]

Evidence that the Net is around for the long haul can be found in the establishment of the Internet Archive. Run by a staff of 10 in San Francisco, it is preserving for posterity important Web sites such as those that affected debate during the 1996 presidential campaign. [41]

The same can be said for all the library digitization projects being launched around the country. Research scientist Lesk predicts that by 2000, half of the material accessed in major libraries will be in digital format. Such a pace may be necessitated by space limitations — futurists estimate that scientific knowledge is now doubling every 12 years. [42]

But more and more naysayers point out that the Internet is still a library without librarians, that its World Wide Web and its search engines are littered with expired sites, disappointing links and incomplete indexes. [43]

"Some say libraries or information

systems should be designed to make using them more self-evident, so you can find what you want without intervention," says the ALA's Magpantay. "Libraries are ideally suited to provide someone to show you. The two systems can coexist, they're not opposites. Whether the library means a good building with good signage or interfacing with a computer, there will still be a need for experts on information."

And though thousands of librarians have plunged into mid-career computer training, there appears little danger that their old-fashioned concept of serving patrons will fade away.

"Total, cataclysmic change is not coming," writes John N. Berry III, editor in chief of *Library Journal*. "We have learned, once again, that most people don't want to be experts in what we do, they don't want to be librarians. They will want what we offer, even though they may not always understand how much expertise it takes to provide it." [44]

"This is a very challenging time for libraries, a time of dynamic change that is driven partly by technology and partly by the needs of users in the information age," says OCLC's Bishoff. "But libraries are well-positioned for it, even if we have to re-evaluate ourselves and continually educate our users. Libraries won't be all online. There will still be a need for a place to meet, a community place, even as more people telecommute. The Post Office just can't play that role. Only libraries can." ■

Notes

[1] See "Hard Times for Libraries" *The CQ Researcher*, June 26, 1992, pp. 549-572.

[2] John Carlo Bertot, Charles R. McClure and Douglas L. Zweizig, "The 1996 National Survey of Public Libraries and the Internet: Progress and Issues," *National Commission on Libraries and Information Science, Final Report*, July 1996.

[3] Ron Chepesiuk, "Where the Information Superhighway Meets the Back Roads," *American Libraries*, November 1996, p. 42. See also, Ron Chepesiuk,"The Future is Here: America's Libraries Go Digital," *American Libraries*, January 1997, p. 47.

[4] See "Computers in Schools," *The CQ Researcher*, Oct. 20, 1995, pp. 921-944.

[5] Stephen L. Talbott, *The Future Does Not Compute* (1995), p. 195.

[6] See "Clashing Over Copyright" *The CQ Researcher*, Nov. 8, 1996, pp. 985-1008. See also "Regulating the Internet," *The CQ Researcher*, June 30, 1995, pp. 561-584.

[7] Walt Crawford and Michael Gorman, *Future Libraries: Dreams, Madness & Reality* (1995), p. 1.

[8] *Online*, January/February 1997, p. 30.

[9] See "The End of the Book?" D.T. Maxx, *The Atlantic Monthly*, September 1994, p. 61.

[10] Ron Chepesiuk, "Librarians as Cyberspace Guerrillas," *American Libraries*, September 1996, p. 49.

[11] James H. Billington, "Libraries, the Library of Congress, and the Information Age," *Daedalus*, September 1996, p. 35.

[12] Andrea Neighbours, "From the Stacks to the Internet, Librarians Still Keep Up the Search," *The Christian Science Monitor*, Nov. 19, 1996, p. 13.

[13] Cheryl A. McCarthy, Sylvia C. Krausse and Arthur A. Little, "Expectations and Effectiveness Using CD-ROMS: What Do Patrons Want and How Satisfied Are They?" *College & Research Libraries*, March 1997, Vol. 58, No. 2, p. 128.

[14] Dr. Julie Todaro, "The New Tools of the Trade," *School Library Journal*, November 1996, p. 24.

[15] Michael Lesk, "Going Digital," *Scientific American*, March 1997, p. 58.

[16] Sven Birkerts, *The Gutenberg Elegies: The Fate of Reading in an Electronic Age* (1994), p. 123.

[17] Lewis M. Branscomb, *Confessions of a Technophile* (1995), p. 140.

[18] Clifford Stoll, *Silicon Snake Oil* (1995), p. 175.

[19] Norman Oder, "Online References Emerge," *Library Journal*, Nov. 15, 1996, p. S74.

[20] Clifford Lynch, "Searching the Internet," *Scientific American*, March 1997, p. 52.

[21] Amy E. Schwartz, "The Information Laundromat," *The Washington Post*, March 22, 1997.

[22] Paul Dickson, *The Library in America: A Celebration in Words and Pictures* (1986), p. x.

[23] Alberto Manguel, *A History of Reading* (1996), p. 237.

[24] Commission on Preservation and Access, "*Preservation in the Digital World*," March 1996, p. 10.

[25] Alice Jane Holland Johnson, *Information Brokers: Case Studies of Successful Ventures* (1994), p. 3.

[26] Stoll, *op. cit.,* p. 177.

[27] Katie Hafner and Matthew Lyon, *Where Wizards Stay Up Late: The Origins of the Internet* (1996), p. 85.

[28] Nicholson Baker, "Discards," *The New Yorker*, April 4, 1994, p. 64.

[29] Michael Malinconico, and Paul J. Fasana, *The Future of the Catalog: The Library's Choices* (1979), pp. v, 43.

[30] Johnson, *op. cit.,* p. 5.

[31] David Nicholson, "Exploring On-Line Libraries," *The Washington Post Book World*, April 6, 1997, p. 15.

[32] *Los Angeles Times*, Feb. 2, 1997.

[33] Nicholson Baker, "The Author vs. the Library," *The New Yorker*, Oct. 14, 1996, p. 50.

[34] *San Francisco Chronicle*, Jan. 9, 1997.

[35] Evan St. Lifer, "Public Library Budgets Brace for Internet Costs," *Library Journal*, January 1997, p. 44.

[36] Bette-Lee Fox with Erin Cassin, "Beating the High Cost of Libraries," *Library Journal*, December 1996, p. 43.

[37] See "Arts Funding," *The CQ Researcher*, Oct. 21, 1994, pp. 913-936.

[38] See joint written statement from the Association of Research Libraries, Commission on Preservation and Access and the National Humanities Alliance to the House Interior Appropriations Subcommittee, March 7, 1997.

[39] *The Wall Street Journal*, April 23, 1997.

[40] The other speakers at the April 16 panel were David Clark, senior research scientist at Massachusetts Institute of Technology, George Strawn, division director for networking and communications research, National Science Foundation, and Sid Karin, director of the Center for Advanced Computational Science and Engineering at the University of California, San Diego.

[41] Brewster Kahle, "Preserving the Internet," *Scientific American*, March 1997, p. 82.

[42] "Information Technology Revolution: Boon or Bane?" *The Futurist*, January/February 1997, p. 10.

[43] Margot Williams, "Interfacing Reality: The Net Isn't Living Up to Its Promise," *The Washington Post*, March 10, 1997.

[44] Editorial, *Library Journal*, January 1997, p. 6.

Bibliography

Selected Sources Used

Books

Birkerts, Sven, *The Gutenberg Elegies: The Fate of Reading in an Electronic* Age, Faber and Faber, 1994.

An author and critic of English fiction meditates on society's fascination with electronic communications, lamenting what he sees as a decline in patience and depth of knowledge that he associates with the printed word.

Branscomb, Lewis M., *Confessions of a Technophile*, American Institute of Physics, 1995.

A physicist and public policy adviser weighs the pros and cons of the Information Revolution, arguing that true benefits of science flow not from laboratories but from people in industry, universities and government who cooperate to achieve desired ends.

Crawford, Walt, and Michael Gorman, *Future Libraries: Dreams, Madness & Reality*, American Library Association, 1995.

A senior analyst at the Research Libraries Group and the dean of library services at California State University, Fresno, weigh the arguments in the debate over the role of libraries in the electronic age.

Dickson, Paul, *The Library in America: A Celebration in Words and Pictures*, Facts on File Publications, 1986.

The rich social history of the library's role in American history, education and community life is dramatized in this compilation.

Malinconico, S. Michael, and Paul J. Fasana, *The Future of the Catalog: The Library's Choices*, Knowledge Industry Publications, 1979.

Two New York Public Library technical specialists produced this analysis of the history, structure and outlook for library cataloging, weighing the early versions of electronic cataloging against the card catalog that has been vanishing.

Johnson, Alice Jane Holland, *Information Brokers: Case Studies of Successful Ventures*, Haworth Press, 1994.

A practitioner of private-sector information service (so-called alternatives to libraries) examines the history and profiles of businesses that sell information to customers.

Manguel, Alberto, *A History of Reading*, Viking, 1996.

A Canadian author and translator penned this lyrical examination of the joys of reading, discussing the role of libraries through history. He writes, "At one magical instant in your early childhood, the page of a book — that string of confused, alien ciphers — shivered into meaning."

Stoll, Clifford, *Silicon Snake Oil: Second Thoughts on the Information Highway*, Doubleday, 1995.

An author and "early adapter" to computer technology who has since given it up lays out his case for why the electronic revolution may be bringing more troubles than it is worth.

Talbott, Stephen L., *The Future Does Not Compute: Transcending the Machines in Our Midst*, O'Reilly & Associates, 1995.

An editor and scholar critiques the claims of pundits who "tell you that the computer is ushering us toward a new Golden Age of Information." He examines whether the Internet is an instrument for social dissolution.

Articles

Baker, Nicholson, "Discards," *The New Yorker*, April 4, 1994, p. 64.

A novelist and scholar offers a history of the card catalog, bemoaning its demise and finding fault with online electronic searching as its replacement.

Baker, Nicholson, "The Author vs. the Library," *The New Yorker*, Oct. 14, 1996, p. 50.

Baker attacks the new public library in San Francisco, which has been controversial for its emphasis on computers and for discarding thousands of old books that some thought valuable.

Reports and Studies

Bertot, John Carlo, Charles R. McClure and Douglas L. Zweizig, *The 1996 National Survey of Public Libraries and the Internet: Progress and Issues*, National Commission on Libraries and Information Science, Final Report, July 1996.

This survey of the nation's public libraries found that library connections to the Internet rose 113 percent from 1994-1996, so that nearly 50 percent of libraries are now online. The survey will be updated in 1997.

The Next Step

Additional information from UMI's Newspaper & Periodical Abstracts™ database

Filtering

Anand, Geeta, "New library chief, Menino clash on Internet censoring; Filtering software would limit adults, invite tampering, BPL president argues," ***The Boston Globe,*** **March 12, 1997, p. A28.**

The new president of the Boston Public Library and Democratic Mayor Thomas M. Menino appeared to be on a collision course yesterday over whether to censor Internet access at library computers. A library spokesman said yesterday that Bernard Margolis, the library president who began work Monday, would try to persuade the mayor not to use the software because it would limit adults from pursuing legitimate research and make the library's computer system vulnerable to tampering.

Baldauf, Scott, "Parents Push For Libraries Free Of Internet Porn," ***The Christian Science Monitor,*** **Feb. 19, 1997, p. 15.**

Some kids don't known much about pornography until they find it on the Internet — at the public library. The issue recently caused a stir in Boston, Mass., when officials at the Boston Public Library admitted they had no way of keeping children from stumbling onto X-rated sections of the Internet on library computers. Boston Mayor Thomas Menino last week ordered the city to install software on library computers to filter out "adult-only" information. Many, including officials in the American Library Association in Washington, D.C., say that restricting adult Web sites could be the first step toward a cyberspace book burning.

Brown, Diana, "Filtering the net: Libraries eye Boston compromise," ***The Boston Globe,*** **March 30, 1997, Sec. WKNW, p. 1.**

As many suburban libraries in Massachusetts prepare to give patrons access to graphic images over the Internet and World Wide Web, librarians are being forced to choose between using software to block pornography and violence or remaining true to their ideals of uncensored access to information.Suburban librarians are watching the results of Boston Public Library's decision to use the filtering software.

Kramer, Art, "Libraries Online; What about pornography?" ***Atlanta Constitution,*** **March 27, 1997, p. F1.**

Libraries in Georgia's metro-Atlanta area accept varying degrees of responsibility for protecting library patrons from Internet content that many find objectionable. But even libraries that use Internet filtering software advise concerned parents to supervise their children at all times.

McLeod, Ramon G., and Carolyne Zinko, "Online Smut in the Reading Room; Net access poses library dilemma," ***San Francisco Chronicle,*** **March 1, 1997, p. A1.**

Even though most school children are regularly blocked from browsing X-rated Web sites in class, they can access pornography on the Internet in the most public of places — the local library. Some library patrons are upset at the free-access policy, which is followed by most public libraries and goes along with a policy set by a national library association that fiercely opposes any form of censorship.

Wheeler, Sheba R. "Internet addicts pose library dilemma; Restrictions weighed as porn appears," ***Denver Post,*** **March 13, 1997, p. A2.**

Internet addicts are hogging the computers for hours — sending electronic mail, talking with anonymous friends in "chat rooms" and leering at Internet porn. On Saturday in Denver, Colo., officials at the city library will begin restricting access to chat rooms and E-mail to free up computer time for bona fide research. In Weld County, the public library is looking at ways to install software to block access to pornographic Web sites after one patron recently left obscene pictures on a public computer terminal. The person also "bookmarked" World Wide Web sites containing X-rated pictures, leading curious viewers directly to the images.

Funding

Allen, Frank R., "Materials budgets in the electronic age: A survey of academic libraries," ***College & Research Libraries,*** **March 1996, pp. 133-143.**

Academic libraries have a host of expenditures for products and services. A survey of the extent to which academic libraries fund these services through materials budgets found that most librarians are continuing to allocate materials budgets in a traditional manner.

Page, Susan, "Clinton: Give schools, libraries free Internet," ***USA Today,*** **Oct. 11, 1996, p. A2.**

The Clinton administration on Oct. 10, 1996, urged federal and state regulators, who are scheduled to meet in November, to give all schools and libraries free access to basic Internet services. President Clinton also announced he would propose spending $100 million in 1997 on the software and wiring to begin connecting 100 major universities and national laboratories to the "next generation" Internet.

St. Lifer, Evan, "Public library budgets brace for Internet Costs," ***Library Journal,*** **January 1997, pp. 44-47.**

Strong national news and encouraging numbers locally are helping public libraries deal with their greatest challenge — finding a way to pay for their new role as the community access point to the Internet. The costs of plugging into the Internet and ways that public libraries are adjusting their budgets are discussed.

St. Lifer, Evan, and Michael Rogers, "Discard charges roil Dowlin's 21st-century library," *Library Journal,* August 1996, pp. 14-15.
The new Main Library in San Francisco, Calif., has been subjected to heated criticism for discarding approximately 100,000 books, its ties to corporate and special interests and its planned disposal of its old card catalog.

Wiley, Peter Booth, "The library: Tradition vs. technology," *San Francisco Chronicle,* Nov. 26, 1996, p. A19.
Wiley comments on the budgetary problems that confront San Francisco's new Main Library, and the trade-off between spending funds for new media vs. print collections.

Internet

"Ideas for our Community Libraries' online challenge," *Atlanta Constitution,* April 7, 1997, p. A6.
A May 1996 survey by the U.S. National Commission on Libraries and Information Science, a presidential advisory group, found that one public library in four provided free Internet access. To boost that figure, the Federal Communications Commission next month will reveal details of a plan to help set up low-cost Internet access at libraries.

Gentili, Kathleen, "School library media specialists new to the Internet ask: Where do I begin?" *School Library Media Activities Monthly,* January 1997, pp. 25-27.
One school library media specialist found it difficult and very time-consuming to locate useful professional resources on the Internet, but she was finally able to build a list of worthwhile sites to use at school. Advice on using the Internet is given.

Pack, Thomas, "A guided tour of the Internet Public Library," *Database,* October 1996, pp. 52-56.
The Internet Public Library at http://www.ipl.org/ receives 50,000 to 60,000 hits a day. Once online, a user can go into several divisions, rooms and services.

Wilson, David L., "Colleges welcome plan to make Internet access cheaper for libraries and schools," *The Chronicle of Higher Education,* Nov. 22, 1996, p. A22.
A plan to make Internet access less expensive has been hailed by educators as a first step toward directing the information highway to libraries and schools. The program involves government subsidies and discounts.

Libraries' Role

Billington, James H. "Libraries, the Library of Congress and the information age," *Daedalus,* fall 1996, pp. 35-54.
Billington examines the history of the American library system and the effect of the information age on the Library of Congress. The Library of Congress has worked to integrate electronic information into traditional sources.

Kent, Susan Goldberg, "American public libraries: A long transformative moment," *Daedalus,* fall 1996, pp. 207-220.
Kent examines the future of public libraries, stating that while libraries will need to change to accommodate the information age, they will not disappear in favor of cyberinformation filtered in by cyberlibrarians.

Lang, Brian, "Bricks and bytes: Libraries in flux," *Daedalus,* fall 1996, pp. 221-234.
Lang examines the future of libraries, including what new responsibilities they will need to meet. A national library is key in insuring comprehensive collection and recording of the nation's published archive.

Marcum, Deanna B., "Redefining community through the public library," *Daedalus,* fall 1996, pp. 191-205.
Marcum examines how public libraries have developed and how they have been maintained in the community. A delicate balancing act between the information-providing purposes, the social purposes and the cultural purposes of the institution is visible in public library systems.

"President Clinton on libraries, funding, the Internet and the CDA," *American Libraries,* December 1996, pp. 34-37.
In an interview, President Clinton discusses some issues facing the library community and his administration's plans for a second term. Topics examined include the Internet, the Communications Decency Act and the government's movement toward converting to nonprint formats.

Stearns, Susan, "The Internet-enabled virtual public library," *Computers in Libraries,* September 1996, pp. 54-57.
Virtual libraries, their use of the Internet and their prospects for the future are discussed. One way libraries are forming a global virtual library is through the use of Web sites.

Online Cataloging

Akst, Daniel, "The Internet lends itself to searching library catalogs," *Los Angeles Times,* Feb. 21, 1996, p. D4.
Akst comments on Internet access to online library catalogs.

Lee, Claire, "Cataloging a small library collection

with a bibliographic database management system," ***Library Software Review,*** **summer 1996, pp. 82-87.**

Lee demonstrates how a bibliographic database manager such as Library Master can be used successfully as an online catalog.

Online Libraries

Apple, R. W. Jr., "Library of Congress is an Internet Hit," ***The New York Times,*** **Feb. 16, 1997, p. 18.**

Exactly a hundred years ago, in 1897, the Library of Congress's Jefferson building opened, inaugurating a new, populist era in the history of one of the world's great repositories of knowledge. For the first time, the library's books were available not just to members of Congress and their staffs, not just to scholars and specialists, but to everyone. Now the library is doing the same thing with its special collections, the more than 70 million items in non-book format that it holds, such as the papers of eminent men and women, including those of the first 23 presidents of the United States, Mathew Brady's Civil War photographs, newspaper cartoons, maps — 6 million of them — Gershwin scores and theatrical posters. The goal is to put 5 million items on the Internet by 2000. Already, the library has raised $23.5 million from private sources and has won commitments of $15 million more from Congress, more than half way toward a goal of $60 million. A foundation started by the late David Packard, the California computer magnate, and the telecommunications billionaire John W. Kluge have each given more than $5 million.

Cibbarelli, Pamela, "IOLS software for special libraries: An overview of Today's best options," ***Computers in Libraries,*** **June 1996, pp. 32-39.**

An overview of the top-selling software for integrated online library systems for special libraries is presented.

Fox, Robert, "Tomorrow's library today," ***Communications of the ACM,*** **January 1997, pp. 20-21.**

Cyber-age form and function combined with public Internet access, electrically operated movable stacks and vast electronic data resources update the old paper-based library model. A list of library and research Web sites is presented.

St Lifer, Evan, "Born-again Brooklyn: Gates wires the library," ***Library Journal,*** **Nov. 1, 1996, pp. 32-34.**

Microsoft Chairman Bill Gates and New York City's political elite announced the launch of Libraries Online!, a program that provides low-income communities with access to online information by wiring public libraries to the Internet. Microsoft will give grants to link 41 libraries nationwide to the Internet.

Reidy, Chris, "Infomercial touts Electric Library," ***The Boston Globe,*** **Feb. 14, 1997, p. E2.**

For 16 cents a day, parents can help their children get straight A's in school, a perky pitchwoman says in an infomercial now airing locally for a student online data service called the Electric Library. In the 30-minute infomercial for Electric Library, the supporting cast includes educators from Massachusetts schools in Boston, Cambridge, Newton and Wellesley. Along with books, the Electric Library database includes hundreds of magazines and newspapers. Once known as Homework Helper, Electric Library has won awards and the endorsement of the American Federation of Teachers.

Technology

Balas, Janet, "Selecting Internet resources for the library," ***Computers in Libraries,*** **January 1997, pp. 44-46.**

As information technologies mature, librarians are struggling to apply their skills in materials selection to the vast world of the Internet. Balas discusses the impact of technology on library collections.

Lyman, Peter, "What is a digital library? Technology, intellectual property and the public interest," ***Daedalus,*** **fall 1996, pp. 1-33.**

Lyman examines how the past and future will come together in the concept of the digital library. Digital libraries can balance the needs of the market and the polity, intellectual property and the public interest.

Lynch, Mary Jo, "How wired are we? New data on library technology," ***College & Research Libraries News,*** **February 1996, pp. 97-100.**

Key findings of a survey of 1,000 higher education institutions concerning the instructional uses of communications technology are presented.

World Wide Web

Balas, Janet, "Library systems information on the World Wide Web," ***Computers in Libraries,*** **February 1997, pp. 34-36.**

Balas discusses the move of library automation products and systems to the Internet. The Web sites of several library automation vendors are examined to learn how familiar library systems and products are evolving onto the Internet.

Saunders-McMaster, Laverna , "The 'coolest' job in the library," ***Computers in Libraries,*** **February 1997, p. 37.**

The emerging role of "Webmaster" for librarians is examined. Librarians who have accepted the challenge of managing a Web site have seen their jobs explode with new tasks.

Back Issues

Great Research on Current Issues Starts Right Here . . . Recent topics covered by The CQ Researcher are listed below. Before May 1991, reports were published under the name of Editorial Research Reports.

NOVEMBER 1995
The Working Poor
The Jury System
Sex, Violence and the Media
Police Misconduct

DECEMBER 1995
Teens and Tobacco
Gene Therapy's Future
Global Water Shortages
Third-Party Prospects

JANUARY 1996
Emergency Medicine
Punishing Sex Offenders
Bilingual Education
Helping the Homeless

FEBRUARY 1996
Reforming the CIA
Campaign Finance Reform
Academic Politics
Getting Into College

MARCH 1996
The British Monarchy
Preventing Juvenile Crime
Tax Reform
Pursuing the Paranormal

Back issues are available for $5.00 (subscribers) or $10.00 (non-subscribers). Quantity discounts apply to orders over ten. To order, call Congressional Quarterly Customer Service at (202) 887-8621.

Binders are available for $18.00. To order call 1-800-638-1710. Please refer to stock number 648.

APRIL 1996
Centennial Olympic Games
Managed Care
Protecting Endangered Species
New Military Culture

MAY 1996
Russia's Political Future
Marriage and Divorce
Year-Round Schools
Taiwan, China and the U.S.

JUNE 1996
Rethinking NAFTA
First Ladies
Teaching Values
Labor Movement's Future

JULY 1996
Recovered-Memory Debate
Native Americans' Future
Crackdown on Sexual Harassment
Attack on Public Schools

AUGUST 1996
Fighting Over Animal Rights
Privatizing Government Services
Child Labor and Sweatshops
Cleaning Up Hazardous Wastes

SEPTEMBER 1996
Gambling Under Attack
The States and Federalism
Civic Journalism
Reassessing Foreign Aid

OCTOBER 1996
Political Consultants
Insurance Fraud
Rethinking School Integration
Parental Rights

NOVEMBER 1996
Global Warming
Clashing Over Copyright
Consumer Debt
Governing Washington, D.C.

DECEMBER 1996
Welfare, Work and the States
The New Volunteerism
Implementing the Disabilities Act
America's Pampered Pets

JANUARY 1997
Combating Scientific Misconduct
Restructuring the Electric Industry
The New Immigrants
Chemical and Biological Weapons

FEBRUARY 1997
Assisting Refugees
Alternative Medicine's Next Phase
Independent Counsels
Feminism's Future

MARCH 1997
New Air Quality Standards
Alcohol Advertising
Civic Renewal
Educating Gifted Students

APRIL 1997
Declining Crime Rates
The FBI Under Fire
Gender Equity in Sports
Space Program's Future

MAY 1997
The Stock Market
The Cloning Controversy
Expanding NATO

Future Topics

- ***FDA Reform***
- ***China After Deng***
- ***Line-Item Veto***

THE CQ Researcher

PUBLISHED BY CONGRESSIONAL QUARTERLY INC.

Reforming the FDA

Does the agency act too slowly?

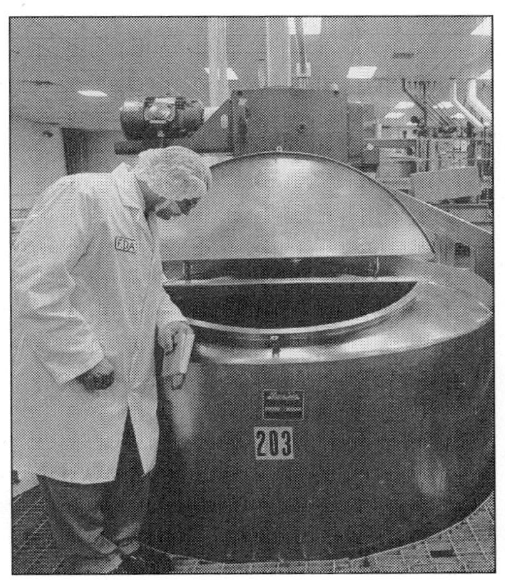

The Food and Drug Administration rarely has a shortage of critics. That's not surprising considering the agency's extraordinary role in American life: 25 cents of every consumer dollar is spent on FDA-regulated products. Much of the criticism leveled at the agency in recent years centered on its activist chief, David A. Kessler, who recently resigned to head the Yale University Medical School. Just before leaving, Kessler refocused the spotlight on the FDA with his bid to regulate tobacco. Whoever is chosen as Kessler's successor likely will face close scrutiny during Senate confirmation hearings. Other FDA issues before Congress include reauthorization of the Prescription Drug User-Fee Act, credited with speeding approval of proposed new drugs, and bills to streamline other FDA procedures.

INSIDE THIS ISSUE

CQ June 6, 1997 • Volume 7, No. 21 • Pages 481-504

Formerly Editorial Research Reports

Reforming the FDA

The Issues

Background

Current Situation

Outlook

Sidebars and Graphics

For Further Research

Cover: An FDA Inspector Checks The Cleanliness Of A Compounding Tank At A Baltimore Drug Plant. (Food and Drug Administration)

June 6, 1997
Volume 7, No. 21

The CQ Researcher (ISSN 1056-2036). Formerly Editorial Research Reports. Published weekly, except Jan. 3, May 30, Aug. 29, Oct. 31, by Congressional Quarterly Inc., 1414 22nd St., N.W., Washington, D.C. 20037. Annual subscription rate for libraries, businesses and government is $340. Additional rates furnished upon request. Periodicals postage paid at Washington, D.C., and additional mailing offices. POSTMASTER: Send address changes to The CQ Researcher, 1414 22nd St., N.W., Washington, D.C. 20037.

Reforming the FDA

BY RICHARD L. WORSNOP

THE ISSUES

The new drug was called thalidomide. Thousands of pregnant women in Europe who took the anti-nausea/sleeping medication in the late 1950s and early '60s gave birth to babies with flipperlike limbs and other deformities. But American women were spared. A skeptical U.S. government inspector refused to approve the drug for use in the United States.

Back then, Frances O. Kelsey helped win plaudits for the Food and Drug Administration. (*See story, p. 493.*) In recent years, however, the FDA's drug-approval process has not fared so well.

"Industry grouses that it over-regulates," *Fortune* noted. "Consumers complain that it under-protects. Victims of unsafe drugs and medical devices howl that it approves products willy-nilly, while AIDS activists agonize over its glacial testing procedures." [1]

Strictly from an economic standpoint, the spotlight on the FDA is understandable: Americans spend an extraordinary 25 cents of every U.S. consumer dollar on FDA-regulated products — chiefly drugs, medical devices, foods and cosmetics.

David A. Kessler, who recently stepped down as FDA chief to become dean of the Yale University Medical School, did much to focus intense scrutiny on FDA performance. During Kessler's controversial six-year tenure, his activism helped restore agency morale, but it also made the agency a lightning rod for anti-regulatory sentiment.

Because Kessler alienated many key figures in Congress and FDA-regulated industries, the appointment of a successor sharing his activist proclivities could provoke fierce opposition. Indeed, some lawmakers have vowed to block the confirmation of any nominee from the FDA.

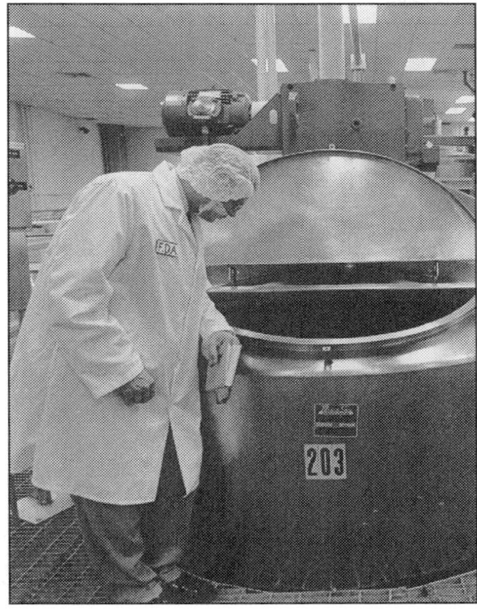

Kessler himself received mixed reviews. "He made some good moves, and some not-so-good moves," says Louis Lasagna, dean of Tufts University's Sackler School of Biomedical Sciences. "He deserves a lot of credit for meeting the goals of the Prescription Drug User-Fee Act, which shortened the time required for approval of new-drug applications. That's a plus.

"Also, the role he played in bringing about mandatory nutrition labeling — secondary though his role was — made a lot of Americans feel grateful to him. However, I think his handling of the breast implant issue was a negative — probably the worst thing he did as commissioner." (*See story, p. 487.*)

It still may be too early to pass judgment on another hotly debated Kessler effort — his claim that the FDA had authority to regulate tobacco. A federal district judge in North Carolina recently upheld the agency's tobacco initiative. However, he rejected FDA proposals to control youth-oriented advertising and marketing of tobacco products (*see p. 496*).

Cynthia A. Pearson, executive director of the National Women's Health Network, applauds Kessler's decision to go after tobacco. "It shows that the FDA is not a pushover," she says. "It's willing to take on a tough issue and try to act in the best interests of the public. And that's what my group wants. The tobacco initiative was great for the FDA's future. It showed that they're keeping themselves alive as an important and respected consumer watchdog."

But Lasagna sees the tobacco initiative as "a burden that was needlessly assumed by the FDA" because cigarettes don't fit the standard drug profile. "Traditionally, drugs are [substances] that can harm you on occasion, but that also deliver good effects. I don't look on cigarettes as being in that category." Tobacco regulation, he believes, "will just distract the FDA from tasks I'd rather see it concentrate on."

Under legislation now pending in Congress, those tasks could include faster evaluation of new products, especially medical devices. Many of the proposals would require the FDA to allow experts employed by outside organizations to participate in the review process. But critics contend outside review would raise conflict-of-interest problems without necessarily saving the agency any time or money.

The FDA launched a pilot program last year to test the feasibility of using third parties to streamline agency reviews of medical devices. If successful, the program could be extended to drugs and food additives, both for humans and animals. The agency already has more than 40 advisory committees of outside experts that provide policy and technical assistance linked to product development and evaluation. The committees have no independent decision-making power, and their recommendations are not binding on the FDA.

Approval Time Dropped for New Drugs

*The FDA's average approval time for new drugs dropped by nearly half from 1987 to 1992, according to the General Accounting Office. **

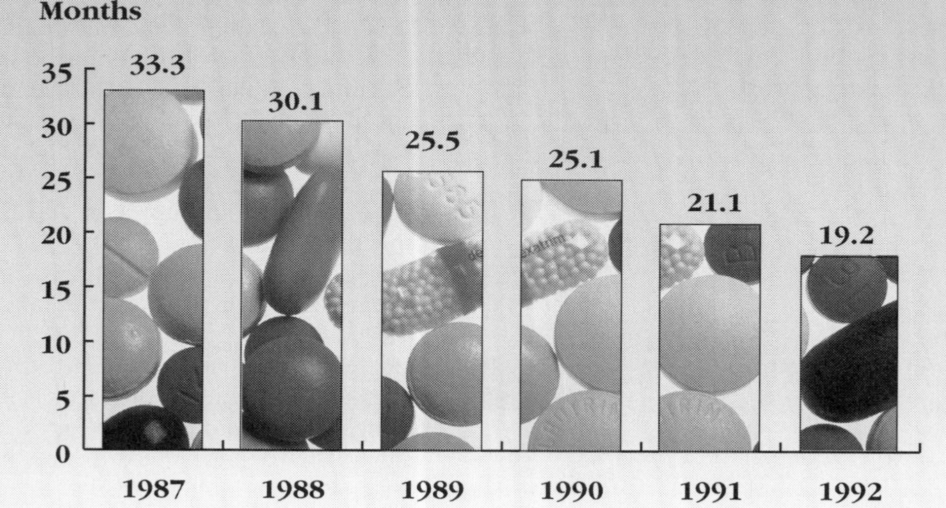

** Number of approved new drug applications: 1987 (80), 1988 (70), 1989 (65), 1990 (53), 1991 (64), 1992 (53).*

Source: General Accounting Office, "FDA Drug Approval: Review Time Has Dropped in Recent Years," October 1995

Kessler urged lawmakers to go slowly before allowing third-party reviews, based on the agency's past performance.

"Unfortunately, too many of our critics justify the call for 'reform' based on how the FDA did its job in the 1980s, or earlier," he told a House subcommittee last year. "They have missed the substantial progress that the dedicated doctors, nurses, engineers, chemists, microbiologists, biostatisticians, nutritionists and others at the FDA have achieved over the past several years. . . . Those who fail to recognize the agency's performance and achievements threaten to undermine the real progress the agency has made." [2]

As debate on third-party review and other FDA-related issues continues, these are some of the questions being asked:

Does the FDA take too long to review drugs and medical devices?

Industry critics contend the agency takes far too long to evaluate new products, thus blocking the public's access to advances in health care. The agency concedes that its performance in reviewing applications for medical devices needs upgrading. But it notes substantial reductions in the average time required to approve or disapprove new-drug applications in recent years.

Most observers credit the reductions to the Prescription Drug User-Fee Act of 1992 (PDUFA), which requires producers of brand-name pharmaceuticals to pay fees to the FDA to expedite federal safety and efficacy reviews. Under the law, which expires Sept. 30, companies must pay the FDA a fee for each drug submitted for evaluation. Moreover, companies making prescription drugs for which no generic copies are available must give the FDA an additional yearly fee.

But FDA argues that streamlining was well under way before PDUFA, a claim supported by a 1995 report by the General Accounting Office (GAO). "It took an average of 33 months for NDAs [new-drug applications] submitted in 1987 to be approved but only 19 months on average to approve NDAs submitted in 1992," the GAO found. [3]

The GAO also looked into claims by FDA critics that drug reviews conducted by Britain's Medicines Control Agency are equivalent in quality to the FDA's and performed more quickly. Although comparisons of the two regulatory bodies were hard to make, the GAO stated, "overall approval times are actually somewhat longer in the United Kingdom than they are in this country." [4]

Kessler and four FDA colleagues came to similar conclusions in a study published last December focusing on four major drug-manufacturing countries — the United States, Britain, Germany and Japan. The study examined marketing approval dates for 214 drugs that entered the world market between January 1990 and December 1994.*

* The four countries account for 60 percent of worldwide pharmaceutical sales.

The study contends "that no single country gets all drugs [approved] first, but that the United States and Great Britain have similar patterns of availability and that the United States is faster than either Germany or Japan in approving 'global' drugs — those important enough ultimately to be approved in more than one of the countries under study." [5] (*See graphs, p. 488.*)

"The results of FDA efforts to speed drug development and availability are most dramatically apparent for priority drugs," the study added. "The United States approved the first major antiviral drug available for use against HIV at the same time as Great Britain and approved all seven other anti-HIV drugs well ahead of every country in the world." [6]

The study went on to note that, "None of these accomplishments would be impressive if the FDA were not ensuring that approved drugs are safe and effective. Keeping products whose benefits do not outweigh their risks off the market is as important as ensuring that the U.S. public have access to significant therapies." [7]

Lasagna is less impressed with the FDA's record on reducing drug-approval times than Kessler. "While it's true that, on average, the U.S. patient is about as likely as the British patient to get useful new drugs," Lasagna says, "that means we're ahead of the British half of the time and the British are ahead of us the rest of the time. So we haven't completely solved the drug lag, as far as I'm concerned."

Lasagna also wishes Kessler had devoted more time as FDA commissioner "to what, if anything, the agency can do to cut the long period between drug discovery and drug approval. It's true that the time for handling new-drug applications has been shortened. But as far as the pharmaceutical industry is concerned, or patients are concerned, the important thing is how long it takes from discovery to getting the drug on the market."

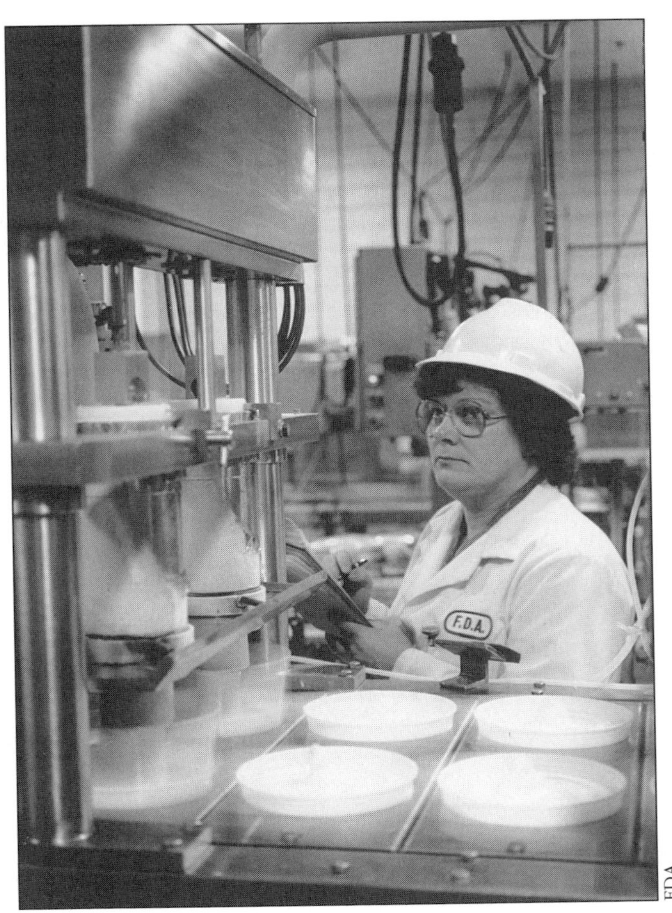

An FDA investigator inspects an ice cream-manufacturing plant during an on-site visit, required at least once every two years.

Lasagna adds that "it's not at all clear to anybody, including me, how much of that time lag is due to unreasonable FDA requirements or unreasonable judgments on the part of FDA staff. But somebody ought to be looking into what could be fixed to make drugs available more quickly and at less expense to the sponsors."

Experts generally agree that medical-device manufacturers have more reason for complaining about FDA review, especially compared with reviews by the 15-country European Union (EU). "The U.S. and EU medical-device regulatory systems share the goal of protecting public health, but the EU system has the additional goal of facilitating EU-wide trade," GAO noted in a report issued last year. "Another distinction between the two systems pertains to the criteria for reviewing devices. Devices marketed in the EU are reviewed for safety and performing as the manufacturer intended; devices marketed in the United States are reviewed for safety and effectiveness. Effectiveness includes the additional standard of providing benefit to patients." [8]

The proof-of-efficacy requirement means that the FDA has more testing before passing judgment on a particular device. Consequently, review times are considerably longer than in the EU. Indeed, a study issued last year by the Health Industry Manufacturers Association (HIMA) found that higher-risk, breakthrough medical devices were approved in Europe up to three times as fast as in the U.S. [9] (*See graphs, p. 486.*)

As a result, U.S. device makers increasingly are shifting their operations to Europe. "This is an industry in which 98 percent of the manufacturers employ less than 500 people, and many are leaving the industry or moving production overseas because of the regulatory system in the United States," said Stephen L. Ferguson, CEO of the Cook Group Inc., a major

U.S. Lags on Medical Device Approvals

New medical devices are approved in Europe up to three times faster than in the United States, according to a study released by the Health Industry Manufacturers Association.

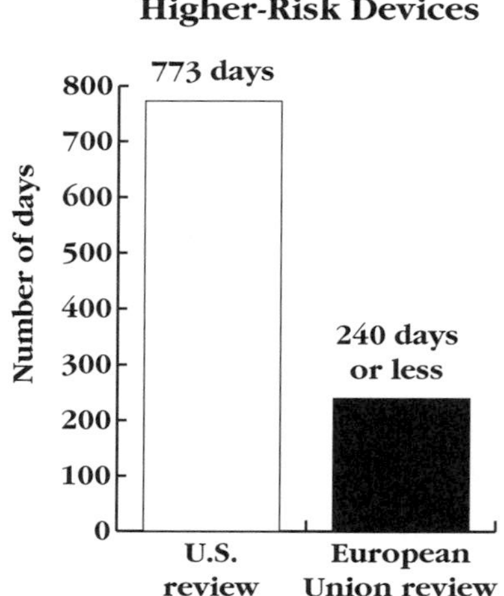

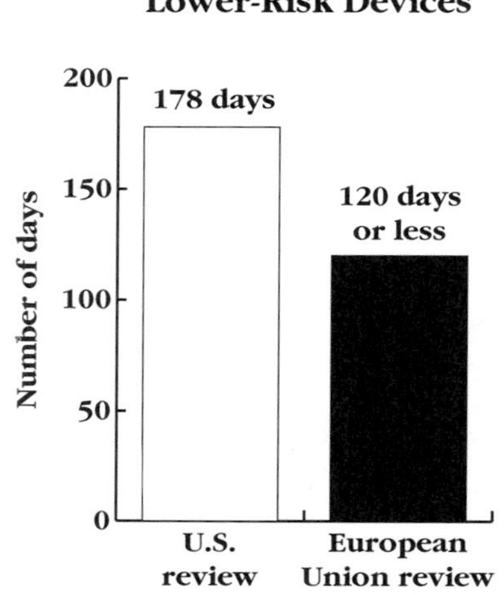

Source: Medical Technology Consultants Europe Ltd./Health Industry Manufacturers Association, February 1996.

U.S. medical-device company. "Many small, innovative companies cannot withstand the long waiting periods with attendant costs and the lack of predictability that result from the regulatory process in the United States. As they go out of business, Americans are losing the benefits of new technologies that come from their creativity." [10]

According to Jeffrey J. Kimbell, executive director of the Medical Device Manufacturers Association (MDMA), the ongoing trend "creates a really scary scenario for the future of the device industry in the United States. First of all, our companies are introducing their most innovative products in Europe. Affluent Americans can go there to make use of these state-of-the-art technologies, but Medicare and Medicaid patients won't have access to them."

However, a survey conducted last fall by *Medical Device & Diagnostic Industry,* a trade journal, indicated that industry executives are bullish about current and future marketing prospects. Editor John Bethune cited "the impact of FDA's internal reforms and review-time improvements" as a key factor. "The agency has not only reduced the product approval delays that slowed new product introductions, but perhaps more importantly, has also greatly reduced both executives' and investors' uncertainty about the timeliness of future product introductions."

Bruce Burlington, director of the FDA's Center for Devices and Radiological Health, credits improvements in the agency's medical-device review times to an internal program called "process improvement." He defines it as an attempt to make medical-device evaluation "accommodate budget reality and position us to do the right job for consumers, health professionals and the device industry. Process improvement is something we need to build into our way of doing business for the indefinite future." [11]

Should medical-device and generic-drug companies pay "user fees" to the FDA?

Since PDUFA slashed the average time taken by the FDA to review applications for new brand-name drugs, some public-health activists have suggested that user fees also could expedite the processing of applications for generic drugs, as well as medical devices.

Broadening PDUFA to cover generics would be "a natural extension of this successful legislation," argues the Patients' Coalition, a national network of more than 100 patient and consumer-advocacy groups. In addition, the coalition noted, "Many concerns voiced by the medical device industry regarding FDA performance would be resolved through the implementation of a similar [user-fee] program for medical devices." [12]

The generic-drug and medical-device industries, however, are not interested. "We don't want to be part of PDUFA," says Diane E. Dorman, vice president for public affairs at the Generic Pharmaceutical Industry Association. "That's strictly a brand-name thing. What we're fighting for is full [congressional] funding for FDA's Office of Generic Drugs [OGD]. That's our biggest concern right now."

Kimbell of MDMA also is cool to the user-fee idea. "Drugs and medical devices are very, very different in terms of both average company size

Continued on p. 488

David Kessler's Wild Ride at FDA

David A. Kessler, who recently stepped down after six years as commissioner of the U.S. Food and Drug Administration (FDA), was unusually qualified for the job. He is both a doctor and a lawyer. Indeed after graduating from Amherst College in 1973, Kessler studied at Harvard Medical School for two years, and then at the University of Chicago Law School for two years. He completed his third year of both law and medical school simultaneously at Harvard. He later worked on food and drug legislation for Sen. Orrin G. Hatch, R-Utah, chairman of the Senate Labor and Human Resources Committee.

This background gave Kessler insights into Americans' ambivalent feelings about government regulation in general — and by the FDA in particular. "Ask whether government should get off the backs of business, get out of our lives, and the answer is a resounding yes," he told an interviewer. "Then ask whether government has a role to play in protecting the food supply and the blood supply, and you get a resounding yes. That's the American way." [1]

Scott Ferrell

Former FDA Commissioner David A. Kessler

Kessler took command of the FDA at a low point in the agency's history. In November 1989, Commissioner Frank Young had resigned during a scandal in which generic-drug manufacturers were found to have tampered with test results and to have bribed FDA employees to expedite drug approvals. Five agency officials were convicted of bribery as a result.

In April 1991, after just two months on the job, Kessler ordered U.S. marshals to seize 24,000 gallons of Citrus Hill Fresh Choice orange juice from a warehouse outside Minneapolis. Kessler said he acted because Procter & Gamble, the producer of Citrus Hill, had labeled the juice "fresh" even though it was made from concentrate. Within days, he also forced the maker of Ragu tomato sauce to remove the word "fresh" from its label because it was heat-processed.

Kessler's hard-nosed approach to food labeling set the tone for his stewardship of the FDA. In June 1991, for example, he launched a crackdown on drug companies that promote and advertise their products for non-approved uses — a practice known as "off-label" marketing. After a drug wins FDA approval, doctors may prescribe it for any purpose. But drug companies may promote it solely for the use sanctioned by the FDA.

In this connection, it should be noted that the FDA's initial decisions on drug use are open to revision. Last November, for instance, the agency said Prozac, the world's top-selling antidepressant, also could be used to treat the eating disorder bulimia. The decision allowed Eli Lilly Co. to advertise Prozac for that purpose.

The most common complaint against the FDA, whether under Kessler or his predecessors, is that it takes too long to process applications for promising new drugs. But the agency blunted some of that criticism early in Kessler's tenure by giving conditional approval to experimental drugs for Alzheimer's disease and AIDS. Manufacturers of the drugs were required to continue research on their effectiveness.

Occasionally, the FDA is accused of acting prematurely. In January 1992, for example, critics claim the agency acted too quickly in calling for a voluntary moratorium on the use of silicone breast implants. The FDA acted, officials said, because of evidence that the implants were linked to immune-system and connective-tissue disorders. But the agency lifted the moratorium three months later, saying limited use of the devices would be permitted for women who agreed to take part in clinical studies on their safety. The action echoed an earlier recommendation by an agency advisory panel.

Asked last December about the FDA's flip-flop on breast implants, Kessler noted that they "were one of the devices that came to market before the Medical Devices Act of 1976" made them subject to federal regulation. As a result of studies conducted since then, "We now know that although the implant may cause local pain, swelling or deformity, the patient is not at significant risk for systemic tissue disease." [2]

Kessler leaves the FDA without regrets. "The one thing I discovered about Washington is that while it's important to serve, it's also important to leave. I didn't want to spend my entire career within the Beltway." [3]

In a sense, Kessler added, his new post is a continuation of his former one. "At the FDA, we were only as good as the applications that came into the agency. Medical schools like Yale are where the real work gets done. Over the next 10 to 15 years, we'll see staggering advances in medical knowledge. We will know more in the next 10 years about human biology than we learned in decades — and that knowledge will result in new therapies that will help people." [4]

---

[1] Quoted by Jeffrey Goldberg, "Next Target: Nicotine," *The New York Times Magazine*, Aug. 4, 1996, p. 25.

[2] Quoted in "FDA Commissioner Sees No Special Deal Ahead for Tobacco Companies," *Barron's*, Dec. 30, 1996, p. 29 (interview with David A. Kessler).

[3] Quoted by Katherine S. Mangan, "Controversial FDA Chief Moves to Yale," *The Chronicle of Higher Education*, May 2, 1997, p. A9.

[4] *Loc. cit.*

U.S. Approved More New Drugs First, 1990-1994

The United States outpaced three big foreign drug producers in approving major, new drugs from 1990-1994. Compared with Germany, for example, the U.S. was first to approve 31 of the 44 new drugs available to both countries, while 13 new drugs were available first in Germany.*

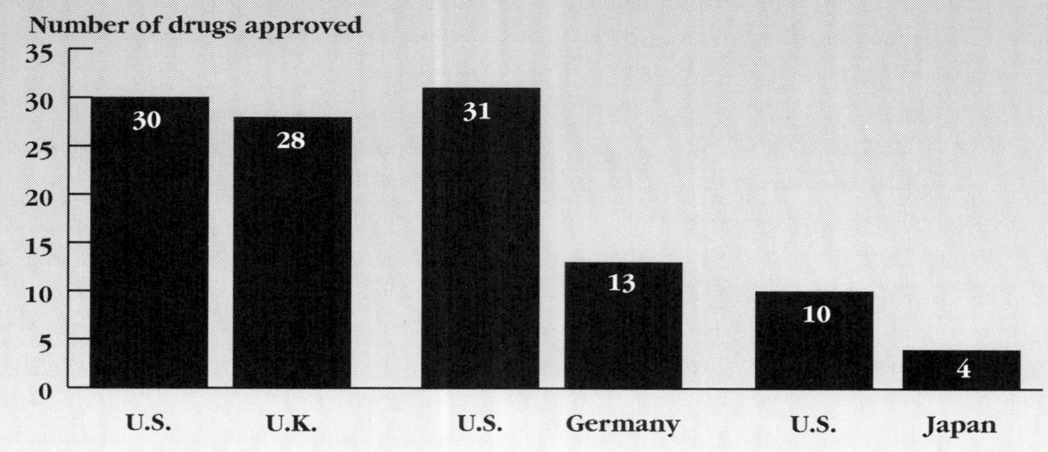

* *A total of 214 new drugs were newly introduced to world markets from 1990-1994.*

Source: David A. Kessler, et al, "Approval of New Drugs in the United States," The Journal of the American Medical Association, *Dec. 11, 1996.*

Continued from p. 486

and the nature of the product," he says. "Eighty percent of the companies in our industry have fewer than 50 employees. They are entrepreneurial, innovative firms with a few product lines and a few million dollars in annual sales. The drug industry, on the other hand, is mainly composed of multinational, multibillion-dollar corporations. Those corporations can easily afford user fees, but most of our members can't."

Moreover, Kimbell notes, a manufacturer that wins FDA approval of a new brand-name drug receives a patent giving it 17 years of exclusive marketing rights. During that period, the makeup of the drug never changes.

"But with medical devices," he says, "as soon as a company gets FDA approval for a new or improved device, it may start tinkering with the technology with a view to improving it still further — something as simple as shortening the length of a syringe needle."

Such improvements can put device manufacturers at a disadvantage, Kimbell says: "Under any user-fee proposal, device makers would have to pay additional money to the government every time they sought FDA approval of a product that was modified even slightly." The marketing life of a typical medical device, industry officials say, is only two to three years.

Pearson of the Women's Health Network says she understands why generic-drug and medical-device companies oppose user fees, but she still feels "consumers would benefit" from such an arrangement. "It works on the pharmaceutical side, so why not give it a try on the device side?" she reasons. The women's network wants new medical products to "go to market every bit as quickly as the industry does. We want FDA to have enough funding to do a thorough job and not miss anything they should have found during the review process."

Opinion within the generic-drug and device industries on user fees is by no means monolithic. "It's essentially a big business vs. small business issue," Kimbell says. "There are some multinational, multibillion-dollar medical-device companies that might actually welcome user fees." That's because a fee system "would eliminate a lot of the ankle-biters that are eating away at their market share in each particular product area."

Similarly, generic-drug producers also might accede to user fees under certain conditions, says Bruce Downey, president and CEO of Barr Laboratories, in Pomona, N.Y.

"Ultimately, to be embraced by the generic pharmaceutical industry, any user-fee proposal would have to be based on two essential assumptions," Downey told a House subcommittee in April. "First, the [Office of Generic Drugs] budget would have to be fully funded, and the FDA would have to provide services that meet all statutory requirements.

"Second, user fees would have to be clearly tied to some incremental improvements in timeliness of the review and approval process, such as making available additional or higher-

The Drug-Approval Process

Drugs go through a painstaking approval process before reaching American consumers.

When a company develops a new drug, it first conducts "preclinical testing," during which the compound is given to animals to determine whether it would be safe for human consumption. If the tests are successful, the company drafts a plan for clinical trials on humans, known as a protocol.

Preapproval process — With animal test data and its protocol in hand, the company files an investigational New Drug Application with the FDA. If the agency accepts both the test results and the protocol, the company conducts a three-phase clinical trial.

During the first phase, the drug is tested on 20-80 healthy volunteers to determine its safety, dosage range and how it is absorbed, metabolized, distributed and excreted by the body.

The second phase uses 100-300 volunteers afflicted with the disease targeted by the proposed drug. The aim is to evaluate effectiveness and monitor side effects.

The third phase is similar, but involves some 1,000-3,000 patients in clinics and hospitals. Doctors try to verify effectiveness and track reactions to long-term use. The developmental and preapproval stages typically last six or more years.

Approval process — After the third phase, the drug company assembles its data and presents its case to the agency in a New Drug Application, asserting that the new product is both safe and at least as effective as comparable drugs already on the market.

The FDA is required by law to review new drug applications within six months, but usually takes much longer. If the application is approved, the drug goes to market and the agency continues to monitor it.

Adapted from Steve Langdon, "Drug Approval Process," *CQ Weekly Report*, Jan. 27, 1996, p. 224.

level reviewers or statisticians for particularly complex applications. In this way, additional fees would provide clearly defined benefits for the generic industry, in the same way that PDUFA benefits the brand companies, rather than simply replacing appropriations from previous years." [13]

Should the FDA turn to third parties for review of new-product applications?

One of the most hotly debated FDA reform issues is product review by third parties — standard practice in much of Europe. FDA-regulated industries argue that outside experts could accelerate the review process without sacrificing thoroughness or integrity. FDA officials tend to be skeptical, mainly citing the potential for conflicts of interest.

But the "monopolized and centralized" review system in place now is hopelessly overburdened, the MDMA's Kimbell argues. "Essentially, Congress has asked FDA to do the impossible — maintain the best expertise in every product area in the medical device field," he says. "It's absolutely impossible for any institution in the world to do that."

Instead, he contends, companies should have the option of submitting their product-approval applications to a "leading, independent, scientific review organization," possibly based at a top-flight university. The FDA itself would accredit those institutions and prescribe conflict-of-interest safeguards, Kimbell says, adding that violations could bring loss of accreditation.

In congressional testimony last year, Kessler said he found third-party review "problematic for a number of reasons." For instance, "FDA's reviewers have extensive knowledge about all of the similar products that are made by different companies around the country. When a reviewer looks at all of the drugs for arthritis and other inflammatory diseases, or all of the heart valves, what that reviewer learns . . . increases his/her understanding of that group of drugs or devices and their effect on the body. As a result, FDA reviewers see problems that [independent] reviewers with less information might not see."

Kessler also addressed the conflict-of-interest issue. "[B]ecause there is a risk that only third parties that err on the side of approving applications and petitions will succeed in this market, there is a risk that the incentive will be for third parties to approve applications and petitions — not to critically review them." [14]

Advocates of third-party review claim it would be more economical than the present system. For instance, the National Electrical Manufacturers Association says it "will result in a competitive framework for the review of new-product submittals, thus leading to greater efficiency in the product-review process and a reallocation of FDA resources to focus on those products most likely to pose the greatest risk to the public safety and health." [15]

Pearson, for one, dismisses the association's argument. "There is no proof that third-party review is more timely or cost-efficient or even feasible," she told lawmakers in April. "Indeed, this system could well prove more expensive, slower and less safe. Additionally, even if direct conflict of financial interest is prohibited, indirect conflicts may be equally detrimental. Many universities or their staffs, who could serve as third-party reviewers, have significant financial and academic links to industry. Will such parties be willing to act independently and potentially risk losing a source of significant funds?" [16]

Gordon M. Binder, chairman and CEO of Amgen Inc., a biotechnology firm in Thousand Oaks, Calif., says that third-party testing actually is widespread, if not widely acknowledged. "For example, Amgen's toxicology studies for . . . Epogen and Neupogen were primarily conducted in Japan," he told lawmakers in 1996. "These products were approved in Europe and here in the United States by the FDA based in part upon these third-party toxicology studies. Furthermore, every clinical trial in the United States is conducted by third parties in collaboration with the sponsor and FDA."

Binder emphasized, however, that third-party involvement occurs before submission of a product-review application to the FDA. "The third parties have no authority to approve a drug or device, and no one in industry is suggesting they should have such authority." [17]

Carl B. Feldbaum, president of the Biotechnology Industry Organization, believes that the FDA now would accept third-party review in cases where it lacked in-house expertise — provided it retained the power of final approval.

"Judging from our talks late last year and early this year," he says, "I think there's consensus between FDA and industry that third-party review should be in place without any further ado. There doesn't seem to be any disagreement at all on that." ■

BACKGROUND

'Embalmed Beef'

Food regulation in the United States dates from 1785, when Massachusetts approved the nation's first food-adulteration law. More than a half-century later, in 1848, Congress passed the Drug Importation Act, requiring U.S. Customs inspectors to block the entry of adulterated drugs from overseas.

Some historians date the birth of modern U.S. food and drug regulation to President Abraham Lincoln's naming of Charles M. Wetherill to head a Division of Chemistry in the new Department of Agriculture in 1862. The appointment eventually led to the formation of the department's Bureau of Chemistry, forerunner of the FDA.

A bill introduced in 1879 by Rep. Hendrick Bradley Wright, D-Pa., was the first to seek federal regulation of the entire field of food and drugs. The measure was never reported out of committee, however. Indeed, only eight of approximately 190 bills proposing to regulate specific commodities were passed by Congress between 1879 and 1906. Among them was a law requiring inspection of meat intended for export and barring the importation of adulterated food and beverages. Other commodities subjected to some degree of federal control during this period included glucose, cheese, canned fish and baking powder.

Before 1900, proposals for federal regulation of food and drugs were widely dismissed as unnecessary. Moreover, Southern Democrats in Congress charged that such measures intruded on the autonomy of the states. Not surprisingly, manufacturers of the targeted products also were strongly opposed.

In the 19th century, families generally grew their own produce, chemicals were little used in foodstuffs and the effects of bacteria and common chemicals on human health were only dimly understood. It was assumed that consumers were capable of detecting filth, impurities, poisonous ingredients and other adulterants in food and medicines without government intervention.

However, popular opinion began to shift around the turn of the century. U.S. soldiers in the Spanish-American War claimed that the canned meat issued to them was "embalmed beef" that had been in storage since the Civil War.* The meatpacking industry also came under fire in *The Jungle,* the muckraking 1906 novel by journalist Upton Sinclair. In a celebrated passage, he described sausage-making in a typical Chicago packinghouse:

"There would be meat stored in great piles in rooms; and the water from leaky roofs would drip over it, and thousands of rats would race about on it. . . . These rats were nuisances, and the packers would put poisoned bread out for them, they would die and then rats, bread and meat would go into the hoppers together."

Sinclair was hardly alone in his crusade to expose industrial abuses. Other muckrakers assailed companies that used harmful chemicals to preserve food; produced "rectified" whiskey from artificially flavored and colored alcohol; made patent medicines; and misbranded and mislabeled food and drug products.

Congress Acts

The public outcry that greeted such exposés prompted Congress to en-

Continued on p. 492

* After the war, a presidential board of inquiry exonerated the War Department of the charge that it had supplied troops with contaminated beef.

Chronology

19th Century

The nation's concern about wholesome foods and drugs predates the Civil War.

1848
Congress passes the Drug Importation Act, directing U.S Customs to block entry of adulterated drugs from overseas.

1850
The first federal law to protect consumers against unwholesome foods excludes certain brands of imported tea.

1862
President Abraham Lincoln taps chemist Charles M. Wetherill to head the Division of Chemistry, forerunner of the Food and Drug Administration (FDA).

1900s

Abuses uncovered by muckraking journalists inspire legislation.

1902
The Biologics Control Act is passed to ensure the purity and safety of serums and vaccines.

1906
Congress enacts the Food and Drug Act, barring interstate commerce in misbranded and adulterated foods and medicines, and the Meat Inspection Act.

1930s-1950s

During the Depression, new safeguards protect against unsafe foods and drugs.

1938
President Franklin D. Roosevelt signs the Food, Drug and Cosmetic Act. The law extends federal regulatory control to cosmetics and therapeutic devices and requires manufacturers to show new drugs to be safe.

1954
The Pesticide Chemical Amendments details procedures for setting safety standards for pesticide residues on raw produce.

1958
The Food Additives Amendments require manufacturers to demonstrate the safety of additives. The Delaney Clause bars any food additive shown to induce cancer in humans and animals.

1960s-1970s

New food and drug products necessitate additional laws.

1960
President Dwight D. Eisenhower signs the Color Additive Amendments, which require manufacturers to establish the safety of color additives in foods, drugs and cosmetics.

1962
Europe is hit by birth defects caused by thalidomide, an anti-nausea and sleeping medicine taken by many pregnant women. The tragedy prompts Congress to pass the Drug Amendments, requiring manufacturers to prove the effectiveness — not just the safety — of new drugs before marketing them.

1976
Congress enacts the Medical Device Amendments, which are designed to ensure the safety and effectiveness of medical devices.

1980s-1990s

Though often criticized by industry and consumer groups, the FDA continues to gain more responsibilities.

1985
The FDA approves an AIDS blood test, its first major action to protect patients from donors infected with fatal diseases.

1990
Congress approves the Nutrition Labeling and Education Act, which requires packaged foods to carry nutrition labeling and health claims. The Safe Medical Devices Act requires hospitals and nursing homes to report any incidents that suggest a medical device caused a patient's death or serious injury.

1992
President George Bush signs the Prescription Drug User-Fee Act (PDUFA), requiring makers of drugs and biologics to pay fees for drug and biologics applications and supplements.

1994
President Clinton signs the Dietary Supplement Health and Education Act, authorizing the FDA to issue good manufacturing practice regulations for dietary supplements.

Continued from p. 490

act the landmark Federal Food and Drug Act in 1906.* Covering products shipped in foreign or interstate commerce, it sought to eliminate adulteration and misbranding. The law also required labels on medicines to indicate the presence of narcotics, stimulants or other such potentially dangerous ingredients.

Although the Food and Drug Act initially seemed far-reaching, it soon proved inadequate. The legislation "was, in fact, quite weak," writes reporter Philip J. Hilts of *The New York Times*. "Manufacturers did not have to prove that their drugs were safe in order to get them on the market; rather, the FDA had to prove they were unsafe before they could be taken *off* the market." [18]

To toughen the law, Congress in 1912 added penalties for "false and fraudulent" statements about the curative qualities of drugs, and in 1913 it required labels on packaged foods to indicate the net weight. In 1923, Congress revised the law yet again to prohibit the interstate shipment of "filled" milk — skim milk whose fat content had been increased by the addition of vegetable oils.

FDA's Powers Expanded

In 1938, Congress greatly expanded FDA's powers and responsibilities by passing the Federal Food, Drug and Cosmetic Act (FDCA).** The law brought cosmetics and medical devices under federal regulation for the first time and applied to both fresh and processed foods, including poultry and fish. (Meat was largely regulated by the Agriculture Department under the 1906 Meat Inspection Act.)

The FDA could prevent the sale of adulterated or misbranded food through seizure and condemnation and through federal injunctions against the manufacturer, shipper or seller. Criminal penalties were provided for violations of the act.

These enforcement provisions fell short of what was needed, many commentators said. Except for coal-tar dyes and drugs introduced after the 1938 act, FDCA did not provide for the automatic establishment of safety standards, or require inspection or testing, before individual products could be placed on the market. Thus, drugs introduced before the law was passed were allowed to remain on store shelves unless the FDA could prove they were dangerous.

After World War II, Congress moved to strengthen federal controls over food additives, as well as over drugs and pesticides. The Food Additives Amendments of 1958 shifted the burden of proof from FDA to manufacturers, who were ordered to submit additive formulas to the agency along with evidence of their safety. In 1960, color additives in food, drugs and cosmetics were made subject to the same procedure.

The Delaney Clause

The 1958 amendments contained the famous Delaney Clause, named for Rep. James J. Delaney, D-N.Y., which stated: "No additive shall be deemed to be safe if it is found to induce cancer when ingested by man or animal." The clause stipulated that any substance found in laboratory tests to cause cancer in humans or animals was to be banned — even if a "safe" level for human food could be established.

The clause resulted from concern in the 1950s about the rising incidence of cancer and its possible causes. It sparked controversy at the time among some scientists and food-industry spokesmen, who said it was not valid scientifically to bar use of a food additive at safe levels merely because the same substance at much higher levels of use could cause cancer in laboratory animals. Debate over the clause's merit continues today.

Another controversial aspect of the 1958 amendments concerned additives already in use. The food industry asked that they be exempt from licensing. When backers of the legislation protested that hazardous products might be left untested, a compromise was reached. Additives previously approved under old procedures were exempted, but they could be forced off the market through the courts if the FDA later found them to be dangerous. Additives designated in 1958 as "generally regarded as safe" (GRAS) included sugar, salt and spices that had been used for centuries. But some of the items originally on the GRAS list, such as the artificial sweetener cyclamate, were later found to be carcinogenic and were banned by the FDA. *

Response to Thalidomide

A medical tragedy that swept Western Europe in the early 1960s, but spared the U.S., inspired legislation that significantly strengthened the FDA's drug-regulation powers. The incident centered on thalidomide, the generic name for a sleeping and anti-nausea medication developed in West Germany and put on the market there in 1957. Doctors liked to prescribe it because clinical trials had shown no risk of accidental death from an overdose. But Frances O. Kelsey, an FDA medical officer, refused to approve the drug for the U.S. market, suspecting that it might have some

Continued on p. 494

* The act is also known, incorrectly, as the Pure Food and Drug Act. A comparable law, the Biologics Control Act of 1902, was designed to ensure the purity and safety of serums, vaccines and similar products used to prevent or treat diseases in humans.

** FDCA was enacted a year after 107 people died from ingesting an untested drug, sulfanilimide.

* In 1977, Congress passed the Saccharin Study and Labeling Act, which stopped the FDA from banning the chemical sweetener. But the law also required product labels warning that saccharin had been found to cause cancer in laboratory animals.

A Stubborn FDA Inspector Saves the Day

In the late 1950s and early '60s, an anti-nausea and sleeping medication came on the market that quickly developed the aura of a wonder drug. Thalidomide not only did what it was supposed to do, but it carried no risk of death from overdose. European doctors enthusiastically prescribed the new drug to their patients, including thousands of pregnant women.

Eager to get in on the action, Cincinnati-based William S. Merrell Co. asked the Food and Drug Administration (FDA) in September 1960 for permission to market thalidomide in the United States under the trade name Kevadon. Merrell's application was assigned to Frances O. Kelsey, a physician who had been working at the agency for less than a month. Under FDA regulations, she had 60 days to evaluate the request.

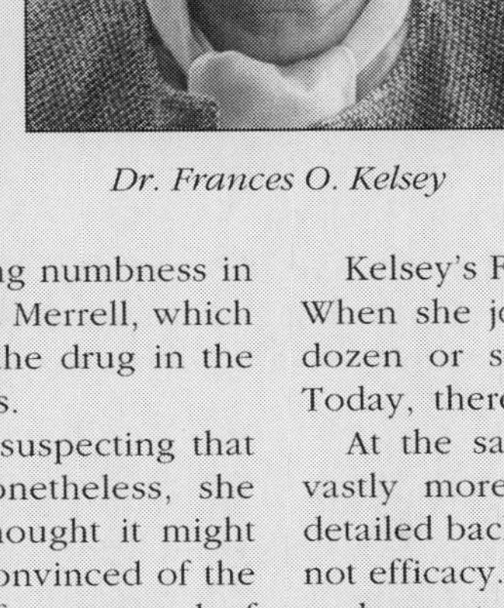

Dr. Frances O. Kelsey

While poring over data supplied by the company, Kelsey, who specialized in pharmacology, was struck by the fact that thalidomide did not put animals to sleep, and that it acted differently than drugs it chemically resembled. With the backing of her FDA superiors, she withheld approval of the application and asked Merrell for more information on how thalidomide worked.

Then, in February 1961, Kelsey happened to see a letter in the *British Medical Journal* from a doctor who suggested that thalidomide might be causing numbness in the arms and legs. Kelsey promptly notified Merrell, which in turn alerted doctors who were testing the drug in the United States to watch out for side effects.

At that time, Kelsey had no reason for suspecting that thalidomide could cause deformities. Nonetheless, she informed Merrell in May 1961 that she thought it might have some effect on unborn babies. Still convinced of the drug's safety, Merrell continued to press for approval of its application. Meanwhile, reports of Kelsey's reluctance to certify thalidomide began to appear in the press, which generally portrayed her as a stubborn bureaucrat.

Six months later, she was being hailed as a savior. The turnaround came in November 1961, when German scientist Widukind Lenz cited thalidomide as the probable cause of an epidemic in his country of phocomelia, the medical term for malformed arms and legs in newborn babies. In some severe cases, the limbs resembled rudimentary flippers. Similar birth-defect reports soon surfaced in other countries where thalidomide had been widely used. [1]

Kelsey, meanwhile, had become a celebrity. In a July 1962 floor speech, Sen. Estes Kefauver, D-Tenn., praised her "great courage and devotion to the public interest" and suggested she be given the Award for Distinguished Federal Civilian Service. President John F. Kennedy presented her with the gold medal the following month, accompanied by a citation stating that her refusal to certify thalidomide had "prevented a major tragedy of birth deformities in the United States."

Galvanized by the thalidomide scare, Congress approved legislation requiring manufacturers to prove to the FDA the effectiveness — not just the safety — of new drugs before marketing them. Kennedy invited Kelsey to the White House signing ceremony that October. Two months later, she was named to head a new in-vestigational drug branch within the agency.

Kelsey, who will be 83 in July, still works for the FDA — as deputy director for science and medicine in the Office of Compliance. Looking back, she credits the 1962 Drug Amendments for a number of improvements, including "better communications and better adverse-action reporting" within the agency, as well as "advances in the science of teratology," the study of malformations.

"A few human teratogens were recognized in 1962," Kelsey says, "but thalidomide really made people familiar with the problem. Quite a lot of research work got under way as a result. And it is still being done now."

Kelsey's FDA career spans a period of explosive growth. When she joined the agency in 1960, she recalls, only a dozen or so persons reviewed new-drug applications. Today, there are hundreds.

At the same time, the reviewing process has become vastly more complex. "Applications weren't nearly so detailed back then, since sponsors only had to show safety, not efficacy. A lot of sophisticated clinical trials are needed to demonstrate efficacy. So the information we were looking at then wasn't nearly as extensive as it is now."

Drugs themselves also have grown more complex. "When I joined the FDA, really exciting new drugs were few and far between," Kelsey says. "Many of them actually were mixtures of old drugs with minor modifications. Tranquilizers and antibiotics still were relatively new, and I don't think antiviral agents even existed."

Though Kelsey will always be remembered for having kept a particular drug off the market, that isn't a characteristic posture for the FDA, she says. "There's an eagerness here to get new drugs into the marketplace as quickly as possible. And I'm sure that effort won't relax."

[1] Thalidomide was developed in West Germany in the early 1950s and marketed there since 1957.

effect on unborn babies. (*See story, p. 493.*)

Congress responded to the thalidomide tragedy by passing the Drug Amendments of 1962, which extended the FDA's time limit for deciding whether to grant "new drug" applications to at least a year in most cases.* The amendments also permitted the secretary of Health, Education and Welfare to bar any drug from the market, even if already approved, if it was thought to pose an imminent danger to public health; and effectiveness, not just safety, was made a criterion for approving a new drug application. **

Medical Devices

During the 1970s, the FDA took on additional duties, while a number of existing ones were shifted to other agencies. In 1971, for example, the Bureau of Radiological Health, which regulates human exposure to radiation, was transferred to the FDA. The FDA's National Center for Toxicological Research was established the same year in Pine Bluff, Ark., to monitor the biological effects of chemicals in the environment. In 1972, the FDA assumed responsibility for regulating biologics, including serums, vaccines and blood products.

Congress focused on medical devices in 1976, the first time it had addressed the subject in depth since approving FDCA 38 years earlier. Lawmakers enacted a bill giving the federal government clear-cut power to regulate the safety and effectiveness of medical devices ranging from tongue depressors to heart pacemakers. Key provisions of the law barred the sale of life-supporting devices, including implants, until they received FDA approval. Existing law had empowered the FDA to regulate medical devices only if they were misbranded or adulterated.

Two federal regulatory agencies created in the 1970s took control of functions previously handled by the FDA. The Environmental Protection Agency, founded in 1970, was put in charge of pesticide research and standards. Three years later, Congress gave the newly established Consumer Product Safety Commission control of programs pioneered by the FDA under the 1927 Caustic Poison Act, the 1960 Hazardous Substances Labeling Act and the 1966 Child Protection Act.

Sweeping New Laws

After months of difficult negotiations between drug companies and public-interest groups, Congress in 1984 approved landmark legislation aimed at making generic drugs, or cheaper versions of many widely prescribed brand-name drugs, available to consumers while giving manufacturers additional patent protection for new brand-name pharmaceuticals. The FDA estimated that under the 1984 law, more than 150 brand-name drugs could be quickly made available in cheaper generic form, saving consumers $1 billion over 12 years. [19]

A key section of the 1984 measure directed the FDA to expand its use of a fast-track procedure for approving generic drugs, which retail for 50-80 percent less than brand drugs in many cases.

Until 1984, FDA had been using the expedited procedure only for drugs approved before 1962. This meant that so-called "post-1962" drugs still could be marketed exclusively, even after their patents had expired, largely because the expense of the regular FDA approval procedure generally discouraged generic versions of post-1962 drugs.

A second section of the 1984 measure, intended to reward pharmaceutical innovation, gave manufacturers up to five additional years of patent protection for new drugs, as well as certain other exclusive marketing rights. Companies had complained that a significant part of the standard 17-year patent period was lost to time-consuming regulatory reviews.

Crackdown on Claims

In 1990, Congress responded to consumer groups' calls for a crackdown on advertising claims about the health benefits of processed foods. Lawmakers enacted legislation that for the first time ordered manufacturers to display detailed nutritional data on most packaged food items and some seafood. The measure required labels listing such information as calorie content and levels of fat and cholesterol.

In addition, the Nutrition Labeling and Education Act barred manufacturers from making certain nutritional claims on product labels — such as promoting a product as "high-fiber" or "low-sodium" — when other equally important nutritional information had not been mentioned. Companies also were prohibited from making health claims about a product — for instance, saying that high-fiber diets prevented cancer — if the claim had not been fully tested or endorsed by the FDA.

A second 1990 law sought to overhaul federal regulation of medical devices. The Safe Medical Devices Act required hospitals and nursing homes to report promptly to the FDA any incidents suggesting that a medical device caused or contributed to a death or serious illness or injury. In addi-

* Under the 1938 FDCA, an application for a "new drug" approval became effective automatically in 60 days (the FDA could extend the limit to 180 days if it needed more time), unless disapproved.

** To be certified as "effective" by the FDA, a drug must be shown to be equal to or better than comparable drugs already on the market.

tion, it directed manufacturers to monitor devices that are permanently implanted in the body and whose failure could cause serious health impairment or death. For its part, the FDA was authorized to order product recalls of suspect medical devices.

Prescription Drug User-Fees Act of 1992

One of the most successful drug-regulation laws of recent years has been the Prescription Drug User-Fees Act of 1992 (PDUFA), which required producers of brand-name pharmaceuticals and biologics to pay a separate fee for each drug submitted to the FDA for approval. The law is credited with substantially reducing the average length of FDA review by enabling the FDA to hire more personnel.

After two years of intense lobbying, manufacturers and consumers of vitamins, minerals and herbal remedies persuaded Congress in 1994 to curtail the federal government's power to regulate dietary supplements. Passage of the Dietary Supplement Health and Education Act created an independent commission to set labeling guidelines for vitamins and other health supplements. However, the measure allowed the FDA to enforce existing regulations while the commission completed its work. [20]

In an unanticipated development last year, food industry representatives and environmental activists overcame their longstanding impasse over the 1958 Delaney Clause, which had barred processed food from containing even minute amounts of cancer-causing chemicals. Under the Food Quality Protection Act, they agreed to change the "no risk" Delaney standard to one based on "a reasonable certainty of no harm." Applying to raw as well as processed food, the revised standard meant there could be as much as one chance in a million that pesticide residue would cause cancer. ■

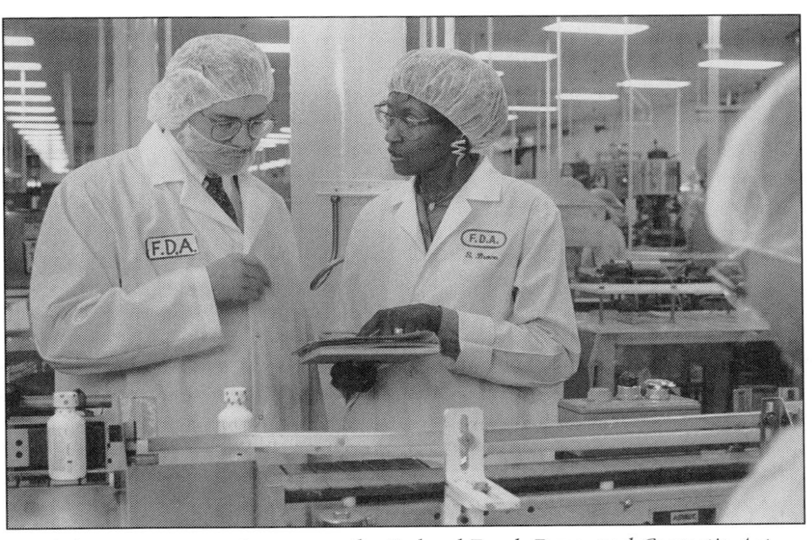

At least once every two years, the Federal Food, Drug and Cosmetic Act requires the FDA to inspect each of the approximately 15,000 U.S. facilities that manufacture, test, pack and label drug products for humans.

CURRENT SITUATION

'Reforms' Fizzle

Efforts to pass legislation "reforming" the FDA fizzled in 1996, despite seemingly broad bipartisan support. The proposed Food and Drug Administration Performance and Accountability Act, approved in March 1996 by the Senate Labor and Human Resources Committee, sought to speed up the review process for drugs, food products and medical devices. It reduced the amount of supporting data that manufacturers had to submit with their applications. The measure also would have required the agency to use third parties to help with product reviews.

Three reform bills were introduced in the House, dealing separately with pharmaceuticals, medical devices and food. All took the same general approach as the Senate bill, but none advanced beyond committee. Although Republicans had enough votes to move the House bills, they chose to negotiate with Democratic lawmakers and the Clinton administration before proceeding. Industry support weakened as Republicans made concessions to Democratic concerns, with the result that time ran out before Congress adjourned in early October.

Efforts to streamline FDA operations have resumed in the current session of Congress. Amgen's Binder told lawmakers in April that the drug industry had trimmed its legislative wish list to make it more politically palatable. The industry "dropped provisions that would have expedited FDA action on [new-drug applications] that had been approved abroad, required mandatory third-party reviews and established a Policy and Performance Panel to oversee agency activities," he said. [21]

FDA Funding

At the same time, Binder stressed that "industry believes it is essential that FDA be funded in fiscal year 1998 at the level of appropriations enacted for the current fiscal year [$820 million], adjusted for inflation, and designating similar-level funding for the human drug development and review process." He added that drug manufacturers are "concerned" that the administration's fiscal 1998 budget proposal for the FDA "would reduce budget authority by over $68 million — an 8 percent reduction in federal appropriations and a 13 percent cut in the budget for human-drug approvals." [22]

The FDA funding issue also troubles public-interest groups. Bruce Silverglade, director of legal affairs for the Center for Science in the Public Interest, told another Senate panel in late April that the FDA's Center for Food Safety and Applied Nutrition (CFSAN) is seriously overburdened.

"[T]he size of the food industry has been increasing while the FDA's staffing levels for food programs have been decreasing," he said. "From 1989-1994 alone, the value of food products under FDA's jurisdiction grew by almost $50 billion. That means that although CFSAN staff levels have declined, there are more facilities for the FDA to inspect, more food labels for the FDA to check and more food standards to issue and update. . . . By failing to halt, and then reverse, this trend, Congress and the administration are seriously jeopardizing the health and welfare of the American people." [23]

Funding worries also figure in the debate over reauthorization of the Prescription Drug User-Fee Act. According to Binder, FDA and the drug industry "have developed a legislative framework for Congress to consider that would renew PDUFA for five more years and not only continue to reduce the FDA review times but also for the first time address the drug-development phase, in exchange for which the industry would pay at least 21 percent more in user fees." This arrangement, he said, "would allow the agency to continue PDUFA without interruption and implement new performance goals, enabling patients to receive medicine 10 to 16 months earlier." [24]

But these prospective gains could be jeopardized, Binder warned, unless funding for the FDA remains at the current level, adjusted for inflation. "[W]ithout level funding," he said, "the [user] fees would just be used for general deficit reduction — not to benefit patients. . . . With industry spending $19 billion on R&D to develop new cures and U.S. taxpayers providing $13 billion to [the National Institutes of Health] for biomedical research, it makes no sense to cut FDA's budget . . . and slow down approval of these new cures." [25]

Kessler's Successor

Kessler's departure for the Yale Medical School means the FDA needs to fill a leadership void. The agency's acting commissioner is Michael Friedman, who Kessler persuaded in 1995 to become deputy commissioner for operations and to energize the FDA science board, which coordinates in-house research. In Friedman's view, the FDA would benefit from more frequent consultations with experts in other government agencies and academic institutions.

"We need more effective linkages with scientists outside the agency," he said. [26] Friedman and FDA deputy commissioners Mary K. Pendergast and William B. Schultz have been cited in media reports as leading candidates to succeed Kessler.

However, some observers feel it is much more likely that the job will go to someone with no current ties to the agency. Possibilities include Myron Weisfeldt, a former American Heart Association president who heads the Medical Department at Columbia University's Presbyterian Hospital; Gilbert Omenn, dean of the University of Washington's School of Public Health; and Randy Juhl, dean of the University of Pittsburgh's School of Pharmacy. All three reportedly have been interviewed by Health and Human Services Secretary Donna E. Shalala.

Administration officials also are said to have talked with Janet Woodcock, director of the FDA's Center for Drug Evaluation and Research, and Steven Phillips, an Iowa heart surgeon whose candidacy is backed by Sen. Tom Harkin, D-Iowa, a member of the Senate Labor and Human Resources Committee.

Taking on Tobacco

Whoever succeeds Kessler may well be preoccupied with the consequences of his decision to assert FDA's authority to regulate tobacco. The initiative dates from Aug. 2, 1994, when an agency advisory panel rejected claims by the tobacco industry that its products were not addictive, asserting that the nicotine content of cigarettes produced and marketed by the companies was sufficient to cause addiction in most smokers.

A year later, on Aug. 10, 1995, the FDA published proposed regulations in the *Federal Register* curbing tobacco advertising and promotional activities directed at youngsters and requiring manufacturers to establish a $150-million-a-year education cam-

Continued on p. 498

At Issue:

Should the FDA privatize its product-review process?

NATIONAL ELECTRICAL MANUFACTURERS ASSOCIATION

FROM TESTIMONY SUBMITTED TO THE SENATE LABOR AND HUMAN RESOURCES COMMITTEE, APRIL 11, 1997

Specific elements of FDA modernization for which NEMA believes a statutory remedy is necessary include empowering the agency to expand upon its existing enterprise by making use of its independent scientific review organizations as a means of enhancing the product review process. . . . Fundamentally, delegating product review to independent scientific review organizations will result in a competitive framework for the review of new product submittals, thus leading to greater efficiency in the product review process and a re-allocation of FDA resources to focus on those products most likely to pose the greatest risk to the public safety and health.

Moreover, delegating FDA's product review functions to independent scientific review organizations will enhance the scientific and technical expertise available to the agency. . . . This, in turn, holds the potential to re-focus the product review process on product safety and performance. Finally, delegating product review and inspection responsibilities to independent scientific review organizations would result in considerable savings to the taxpayer. . . .

Although the agency's third-party pilot program represents a positive initial step toward the utilization of independent scientific-review organizations, NEMA continues to maintain that the scope and structure of the third-party pilot is insufficient, and that additional statutory changes are necessary to promote greater agency reliance on independent scientific review organizations. . . .

Second, just as the FDA needs the statutory authority to delegate its product review process to independent scientific review organizations, so does the agency need the statutory authority to utilize independent scientific experts to conduct good manufacturing practices inspections. Currently, FDA inspectors are required to inspect not only medical device manufacturing facilities but also factories engaged in the manufacture of foods, biologics, pharmaceuticals and animal drugs. As a result, oftentimes FDA inspectors lack the expertise necessary to offer constructive suggestions on improving the quality of the manufacturing process. . . .

Third, FDA needs the authority to recognize and permit manufacturer certifications of compliance to consensus standards as a means of expediting the product review process. Consensus standards, developed with the input of industry, government and medical professionals, represent state-of-the-art norms for ensuring the safety and performance of safety devices. . . .

Fourth, FDA needs to be provided with the flexibility to streamline reporting requirements so that the emphasis is on product safety, rather than paperwork. . . .

DAVID A. KESSLER
Commissioner, Food and Drug Administration (FDA) *

FROM TESTIMONY BEFORE THE HOUSE COMMERCE SUBCOMMITTEE ON HEALTH AND THE ENVIRONMENT, MAY 1, 1996.

The concept of privatization of product application reviews is problematic for a number of reasons. First, FDA's scientific and clinical experts are charged with exercising independent unbiased judgment. They comply with stringent financial disclosure and conflict-of-interest requirements designed to protect the decision-making process against bias. It is not clear how or whether this independence can be maintained with the private sector, particularly since the sponsor gets to choose and pay the private party, and repeat business may depend on the sponsor's satisfaction with the private party's decision.

Second, FDA's reviewers have extensive knowledge about all of the similar products that are made by different companies around the country. When a reviewer looks at all of the drugs for arthritis and other inflammatory diseases, or all of the heart valves, what the reviewer learns from each review increases his/her understanding of that group of drugs or devices and their effect on the body. As a result, FDA reviewers see problems that reviewers with less information might not see.

The third problem with privatization is the lack of continuity. For example, FDA's reviewers are able to work with the same drug over time. By staying involved in a drug's development, reviewers can build on what they already know. Third-party reviewers may have little knowledge of the specific development process for the product and/or of the development agreements made during the process.

We believe that contracting out product review to third parties should be done only if there is evidence that it can be done safely. A pilot study is essential to determine if that can be done. That is why FDA is conducting its pilot program for low-risk medical devices. We are trying to determine whether third parties can accomplish the goal of getting safe and effective products to the American public.

Finally, because there is a risk that only third parties that err on the side of approving applications and petitions will succeed in this market, there is a risk that the incentive will be for third parties to approve applications and petitions — not to critically review them.

* Kessler stepped down in February as FDA commissioner to become dean of the Yale University School of Medicine.

FOR MORE INFORMATION

Biotechnology Industry Organization (BIO), 1625 K St. N.W., Suite 1100, Washington, D.C. 20006-1604; (202) 857-0244. Members are manufacturing and research companies. BIO favors the contracting out of many FDA activities.

Generic Pharmaceutical Industry Association, 1620 I St. N.W., Suite 800, Washington, D.C. 20006; (202) 833-9070. The association represents the generic pharmaceutical industry in legislative, regulatory, scientific and health-care policy matters.

Grocery Manufacturers of America, 1010 Wisconsin Ave. N.W., Suite 900, Washington, D.C. 20007; (202) 337-9400. The GMA comprises companies that manufacture products sold in retail groceries. Many of the products are regulated by the FDA.

Health Industry Manufacturers Association, 1200 G St. N.W., Suite 400, Washington, D.C. 20005; (202) 783-8700. HIMA represents manufacturers of medical devices, diagnostic products and health-care information systems.

Medical Device Manufacturers Association, 1900 K St. N.W., Suite 100, Washington, D.C. 20006; (202) 496-7150. MDMA represents about 130 mostly small- and medium-sized U.S. device manufacturers.

National Women's Health Network, 514 10th St. N.W., Suite 400, Washington, D.C. 20004; (202) 347-1140. The network acts as an information clearinghouse on women's health issues. It also is a member of the Patients' Coalition, a national network of more than 100 patient and consumer advocacy groups, (202) 347-1140.

Pharmaceutical Research and Manufacturers Association of America, 1100 15th St. N.W., Suite 900, Washington, D.C. 20005; (202) 835-3400. The association's members are companies that develop and manufacture prescription drugs.

paign to discourage children and adolescents from smoking. Coalitions of tobacco companies and national advertisers quickly sued in U.S. District Court in Greensboro, N.C., to block implementation of the FDA's rulemaking package.

Because North Carolina is the nation's largest tobacco-producing state, some observers said the industry might get a more sympathetic hearing there than elsewhere. But the court's ruling, issued this April 25 by Judge William L. Osteen Sr., was widely seen as a sharp setback for tobacco producers. Osteen agreed that the FDA had authority to regulate tobacco as a drug, since nicotine alters bodily functions, and cigarettes are expressly designed to deliver it to smokers. At the same time, however, he held that the FDA lacked authority to regulate youth-oriented tobacco advertising.*

Osteen's ruling left intact FDA proposals to ban tobacco sales nationwide to persons under 18, require photo identification checks of all cigarette purchasers under 27, restrict the placement of cigarette vending machines and bar free samples or single cigarette sales. But Osteen rejected proposals to restrict the placement and format of print advertising and outdoor signs and billboards; prohibit giveaways of clothing and other products bearing tobacco brand names or logos; and require that entertainment or sporting events be sponsored under the corporate rather than cigarette brand name.

"It's a victory for the nation, for the public health," Kessler said. "A small group of very committed people at the agency took on the impossible. The president of the United States supported them and a federal judge in North Carolina in very large measure agreed. . . . It will change forever the way tobacco products are viewed." [27]

Indeed, a product recently approved by the FDA could be regarded as an indirect form of tobacco regulation. On May 5, the agency cleared for prescription sale the Nicotrol Inhaler, a device manufactured by McNeil Consumer Products Co., a unit of Johnson & Johnson.

According to McNeil, the inhaler is the first form of nicotine replacement therapy to help control a smoker's cravings for cigarettes while satisfying the need for a key behavioral aspect of smoking, the hand-to-mouth ritual. The device delivers nicotine to the user, but at a lower level than cigarettes.

Pilot Programs

The FDA is approaching the midpoint of a two-year pilot program that could improve relations with the companies it regulates. The program, which began last Aug. 1, seeks to determine whether third-party review of medical devices will trim review times and whether strong conflict-of-interest safeguards can be maintained throughout the process.

"The program applies only to low- and moderate-risk devices for which the FDA does not require clinical data on safety and effectiveness — products such as electronic thermometers and surgical gloves," an article in the *FDA*

* In another blow to the tobacco industry, the Federal Trade Commission charged on May 28 that the R.J. Reynolds Tobacco Co. illegally aimed its Joe Camel advertising campaign at minors in violation of federal fair trade practice laws.

Consumer explained. "A manufacturer must show in a premarket notification application that such a product's safety and effectiveness are comparable to a device already legally marketed." [28]

The FDA receives about 1,500 applications a year from makers of devices eligible for the pilot program. Participation is voluntary. A firm may choose to have a third party conduct most of the review, or turn the entire job over to the agency.

A second FDA pilot program changes the ground rules for inspections of firms with a good history of compliance with agency regulations. During the experiment, targeted firms are to receive advance notice from the FDA, presumably giving them ample time to prepare for the visit. Ordinarily, FDA inspectors arrive at a plant unannounced.

FDA Under Fire

Two recent incidents demonstrated yet again that FDA decisions on new-drug applications often create hard feelings, either immediately or years later. On May 8, for instance, an agency advisory panel voted to reject a new drug for treating amyotrophic lateral sclerosis (ALS), or Lou Gehrig's disease, which kills about 10,000 Americans a year. More than 20 ALS sufferers, some in wheelchairs, tearfully pleaded with panel members to recommend FDA approval of the drug, Myotrophin. [29] But a majority of panelists concluded that the manufacturer, Cephalon Inc., had failed to present persuasive evidence that Myotrophin was effective against ALS. The next day, Cephalon stock lost $7 a share, or 35 percent of its value, in trading on the Nasdaq exchange.

Also on May 8, FDA came under heavy fire for deciding in 1990 to let the Defense Department require U.S. troops in the Persian Gulf War to take an experimental drug intended to protect them against exposure to nerve gas. The drug, pyridostigmine bromide, is now suspected as a possible cause of the array of disorders called Gulf War Syndrome. Consequently, the FDA is now being assailed for allowing the Pentagon to administer the drug without first telling those who took it about potential side effects and obtaining their informed consent.

"It was feasible to inform them, and that's the least they could do," said Rep. Christopher Shays, R-Conn. "I have no sympathy whatever that they could not inform the soldiers." FDA Deputy Commissioner Pendergast acknowledged that the agency had extended "considerable deference" to the Defense Department. She added, "This was war. This was the first time, and it didn't work out particularly well." [30] ■

OUTLOOK

Era of Cooperation?

With a new commissioner waiting in the wings, and reform legislation unclear, the agency's future remains uncertain. But one thing is clear: The torrent of data pouring into the FDA will continue.

Pearson says she has listened to agency officials "discuss what they need to do over the next 10 years, and they talk about information management — getting on the electronic superhighway. They're wondering, as many business people are, how to take advantage of the ability to communicate more quickly and access huge amounts of information?"

Years ago, Pearson notes, "that was real easy. The agency handled only food, drugs and cosmetics. Then Congress gave it authority over medical devices, radiological health and other areas. But I don't think the agency adapted its thinking to the evolving product mix. FDA reviewers are now dealing with more medical devices than they used to, as well as genetically engineered foods. And I foresee even more dramatic changes down the road."

Changes to date in this area already are dramatic. "It's not unusual for [a new-drug application] to run to hundreds of thousands of pages," Hilts noted. "Drug companies used to deliver their applications to the FDA in trucks; now they're sent on CD-ROMs." [31]

Feldbaum of the Biotechnology Industry Organization expects continuation of formal and informal contacts between the FDA and industry representatives. These meetings "have proven to be very useful for both the regulators and the regulated," he says, because medical technology "changes kaleidoscopically." And since the situation is so fluid, Feldbaum says, "it requires a great deal of responsiveness from the regulating agencies — on an almost monthly basis, in fact. The idea is to acquaint the regulators with changes that are occurring in the science."

Tufts University's Lasagna agrees with Feldbaum on the desirability of more frequent FDA-industry communication. He adds, however, that "a lot will depend on the new commissioner — how supportive he or she will be of attempts to improve relationships between the regulators and the regulated." Lasagna believes there is evidence "suggesting that where early and collegial relations exist between the agency and sponsors, new-drug applications would turn out to be self-reviewing. The reason is that all the important questions would have been asked and answered in the course of the product's development."

But so far, Lasagna says, no "systematic and agencywide approach" to bilateral contacts has been established. "To my knowledge, no drug has ever benefited, all the way through its history, from this kind of early and continuing relationship between the regulator and the regulated."

Some sort of continuing relationship may be emerging, however, between the FDA and the medical-device industry. At MDMA's May 16 annual meeting, several company representatives voiced appreciation for the work done by Burlington of the FDA Center for Devices and Radiological Health to improve agency-industry relations in recent years. Burlington, in turn, acknowledged industry's help in bringing about change at the center and expressed hope that future contacts would remain cordial and productive.

The unyielding reality that government agencies face today, Burlington said, is that "discretionary domestic spending is not headed up. You're lucky if you're getting constant dollars. Everybody in business knows constant dollars get eroded by inflation. It's just as true in the government."

To cope with the fund squeeze, Burlington says, the center examined several options. User fees and higher funding from Congress were discarded as "rescue fantasies." The most promising approach, it was agreed, was to "refocus priorities to match resources and re-engineer processes for efficiency."

That means, Burlington says, that "FDA is going to be more involved in high-risk, high-consumer-benefit areas" in coming years. "We're going to redirect work where it can optimize consumer benefits. Conversely, our direct role in low-risk products will be greatly decreased." And that may open the way to third-party review of FDA-related products, with the FDA retaining overall direction of the process.

Change could come as early as the current session of Congress. But, he cautions, "Legislative reform takes time to develop," and experience "tells us that if we're going to do it this year, we ought to make sure we do it right." ■

Notes

[1] Andrew E. Serwer, "SOS for the FDA?" *Fortune*, April 4, 1994, p. 142.

[2] Testimony before House Commerce Subcommittee on Health and the Environment, May 1, 1996.

[3] U.S. General Accounting Office, "*FDA Drug Approval: Review Time Has Decreased in Recent Years*," October 1995, p. 4.

[4] *Ibid.*, pp. 10-11.

[5] Kessler, David A., et al., "Approval of New Drugs in the United States: Comparison With the United Kingdom, Germany, and Japan," *The Journal of the American Medical Association*, Dec. 11, 1996, p. 1826.

[6] *Ibid.*, p. 1831.

[7] *Loc. cit.*

[8] U.S. General Accounting Office, "*Medical Device Regulation: Too Early to Assess European System's Value as Model for FDA*," March 1996, pp. 5-6.

[9] Gordon R. Higson, Medical Technology Consultants Europe Ltd., "*Medical Device Approval Times in Europe*," February 1996.

[10] Testimony before Senate Labor and Human Resources Committee, April 11, 1997.

[11] Remarks at the annual meeting of the Medical Device Manufacturers Association, Washington, D.C., May 16, 1997.

[12] The Patients' Coalition, "Agenda for Effective Change at FDA" (undated policy paper).

[13] Testimony before House Commerce Subcommittee on Health and the Environment, April 23, 1997.

[14] Testimony before House Commerce Subcommittee on Health and the Environment, May 1, 1996.

[15] Statement submitted to Senate Labor and Human Resources Committee, April 11, 1997.

[16] Testimony before Senate Labor and Human Resources Committee, April 11, 1997.

[17] Testimony before House Commerce Subcommittee on Health and the Environment, May 1, 1996.

[18] Philip J. Hilts, "Doing Drugs," *George*, September 1996, p. 81.

[19] See "Generic Drug Legislation Cleared by Congress," *1984 CQ Almanac*, pp. 451-453.

[20] For background, see "Dietary Supplements," *The CQ Researcher*, July 8, 1994, pp. 577-600.

[21] Testimony before Senate Labor and Human Resources Committee, April 11, 1997. Binder testified on behalf of the Biotechnology Industry Organization and the Pharmaceutical Research and Manufacturers of America.

[22] *Loc. cit.*

[23] Testimony before Senate Appropriations Subcommittee on Agriculture, Rural Development and Related Agencies, April 29, 1997.

[24] Testimony before Senate Labor and Human Resources Committee, April 11, 1997.

[25] *Loc. cit.*

[26] Quoted by Richard Stone, "Kessler's Legacy: Unfinished Reform," *Science*, Dec. 6, 1996, p. 1604.

[27] Quoted by John Schwartz, "Judge Rules That FDA Can Regulate Tobacco," *The Washington Post*, April 26, 1997, p. A14.

[28] Dixie Farley, "Agency Changes Include Medical Device Review," *FDA Consumer*, November 1996, p. 30.

[29] The FDA is not bound to accept the findings of its advisory panels, but it usually does so.

[30] Quoted by Sheryl Gay Stolberg in *The New York Times*, May 9, 1997, p. A26. Shays and Pendergast spoke at a May 8 hearing of the House Committee on Government Reform and Oversight.

[31] Hilts, *op. cit.*, p. 82.

Bibliography

Selected Sources Used

Books

Burkholz, Herbert, *The FDA Follies*, Basic Books, 1994.
Burkholz revisits some of the FDA's misadventures of the 1980s, which included its hesitant response to the AIDS crisis, its fumbling of the Shiley heart valve and silicone breast implant cases and a generic-drug bribery scandal. He concludes on a hopeful note, however, citing reforms instituted by Commissioner David A. Kessler, then relatively new on the job.

Morgenthaler, John, and Steven Wm. Fowkes, eds., *Stop the FDA: Save Your Health Freedom*, Health Freedom Publications, 1992.
Making no claim to evenhandedness, the editors of this collection of articles lash out at the FDA for being "alone among federal institutions in its anti-vitamin, anti-nutrient and anti-health agenda." The authors include Sen. Orrin G. Hatch, R-Utah, and Linus C. Pauling, the late Nobel Prize-winning chemist and Vitamin C enthusiast.

Articles

Annas, George J., "Cowboys, Camels and the First Amendment — The FDA's Restrictions on Tobacco Advertising," *The New England Journal of Medicine*, Dec. 5, 1996.
The author, a lawyer with a master's degree in public health, analyzes the main legal issues involved in the FDA's challenge to the tobacco industry.

Farley, Dixie, "Agency Changes Include Medical Device Review," *FDA Consumer*, November 1996.
Farley describes an FDA pilot program allowing private organizations to take part in the agency's evaluation of medical devices.

Goldberg, Jeffrey, "Next Target: Nicotine," *The New York Times Magazine*, Aug. 4, 1996.
Goldberg, a regular contributor to the Times magazine, uses the FDA's thus-far successful bid to regulate tobacco as the focal point of an analysis of the many controversies surrounding the agency.

Kessler, David A., et al., "Approval of New Drugs in the United States: Comparison With the United Kingdom, Germany, and Japan," *The Journal of the American Medical Association*, Dec. 11, 1996.
Kessler and four of his FDA colleagues present the results of a study of 214 new drugs introduced into the world market from January 1990 through December 1994. They found that the United States outpaced both Germany and Japan in approving important new drugs and that it ranked slightly ahead of Britain.

Mahar, Maggie, "FDA Commissioner Sees No Special Deal Ahead for Tobacco Companies" (an interview with David A. Kessler), *Barron's*, Dec. 30, 1996.
Noting that morale at the FDA "was rock-bottom" when he assumed command in 1992, Kessler reviews the highlights of his stewardship, including the confrontation with the tobacco industry and streamlining of the process for reviewing proposed new drugs.

Reports and Studies

U.S. General Accounting Office, *FDA Drug Approval: Review Time Has Decreased in Recent Years*, October 1995.
GAO, the investigative arm of Congress, concludes that it took FDA an average of 33 months to approve new drug applications in 1987, but only 19 months in 1992.

U.S. General Accounting Office, *Medical Devices: FDA Review Time*, October 1995.
Surveying FDA review times for medical device applications between 1988 and 1995, GAO finds that median review times were stable from 1989 to 1991, rose sharply in 1992 and 1993 and then dropped in 1994.

U.S. General Accounting Office, *Medical Device Regulation: Too Early to Assess European System's Value as Model for FDA*, March 1996.
According to the GAO, "Meaningful comparison of the length of review time in the United States and the EU [European Union] is not possible because there are no data documenting review times under the new EU system comparable to data describing FDA's experience."

U.S. General Accounting Office, *Blood Supply: FDA Oversight and Remaining Issues of Safety*, February 1997.
GAO finds that the blood industry "has made many positive changes in collecting and processing blood in response to FDA initiatives." But it recommends that blood facilities be required to take several additional steps, including viral testing of all blood given for the donor's exclusive use.

U.S. Senate Committee on Labor and Human Resources, Assessing the FDA's Performance, Efficiency and Use of Resources (published proceedings of hearing held April 11, 1997).
Industry officials and representatives of public-interest groups present their views on proposed FDA reform legislation. Also examined is reauthorization of the expiring Prescription Drug User-Fee Act (PDUFA), which is credited with substantially trimming the time it takes for FDA review of new drug applications.

The Next Step

Additional information from UMI's Newspaper & Periodical Abstracts™ database

Criticism of the FDA

Barnett, Alicia Ault, "Kessler replies to FDA's critics," ***Lancet,*** **Dec. 21-Dec. 28, 1996, p. 1729.**

Outgoing U.S. FDA Commissioner David Kessler has been criticized over the years for being in charge of a slow and cumbersome agency. However, in his final address last week, Kessler may have silenced critics with his recitation of vastly improved performance.

Duplantier, F R , "FDA is stifling medical innovation," ***Chicago Defender,*** **Aug. 28, 1996, p. 12.**

Duplantier criticizes the FDA for stifling medical technology by taking years to approve new medical devices.

Hunt, Albert R, "Politics & people: How the FDA bureaucracy hurt needy kids," ***The Wall Street Journal,*** **Sept. 19, 1996, p. A23.**

Albert R. Hunt, whose teenage son has spina bifida, discusses the FDA bureaucracy that has prevented the approval of a medical device used to treat children who because of neurogenic bladders are incontinent.

Manders, Dean Wolfe, "The FDA ban of L-Tryptophan: Politics, profits and Prozac," ***Social Policy,*** **winter 1995, p. 55-58.**

The FDA's ban of L-Trypthophan means that millions of Americans who suffer from depression, anxiety and PMS will have to use drugs that are highly addictive or expensive, or use no drugs to relieve their symptoms. Political considerations that prompted the decision are criticized.

Drug Approvals

"Alpharma, Lemmon get FDA approval to sell OTC Rogaine," ***The Wall Street Journal,*** **April 9, 1996, p. B6.**

The FDA said two companies, Alpharma Inc. and Lemmon Co., received approval to sell generic, nonprescription versions of Rogaine, the hair-regrowth solution.

"FDA approves a device for treating back pain," ***The Wall Street Journal,*** **Sept. 24, 1996, p. B6.**

The FDA approved a new medical device called the BAK Interbody Fusion System made by Spine-Tech Inc, for the treatment of lower back pain caused by degenerative disk disease.

"FDA cleared 139 products in 1996, a record increase," ***The Wall Street Journal,*** **Jan. 15, 1997, p. B5.**

The FDA approved 139 new drugs and biological products in 1996, a record one-year jump of 63 percent in approvals. FDA spokesman Donald McLearn attributed the record-setting results to the Prescription Drug User-Fee Act, under which drug manufacturers have been paying fees to the government to cover the cost of additional drug reviewers. The agency cleared 131 new drugs for marketing in 1996—up 60 percent from 1995.

"FDA shortened drug approval time in 1995," ***Public Health Reports,*** **July 1996, p. 290.**

The FDA's approval of 85 new drugs and biological products in 1995 was highlighted by the continuing decline in median drug approval times. Seven drugs for AIDS and other life-threatening diseases were approved in six months or less.

Ingersoll, Bruce, "Premarin maker ties up FDA to fight rivals," ***The Wall Street Journal,*** **Jan. 24, 1997, p. B1.**

Premarin, a hormone-replacement product that is one of the most widely prescribed drugs in the U.S., looks natural for generic competition. However, generic drug makers are finding that they are no match for Wyeth-Ayerst, a unit of American Home Products Inc, which has proved highly skilled at using the FDA regulatory process to thwart its rivals.

"Medtronic Inc.: FDA marketing approval is granted for defibrillator," ***The Wall Street Journal,*** **May 13, 1996, p. B3.**

Medtronic Inc. said the FDA granted marketing approval for the medical -device maker's Jewel Plus model inplantable defibrillator.

New FDA Programs and Procedures

Algeo, David, "Medical- device makers hail new FDA approach," ***Denver Post,*** **April 17, 1996, p. C2.**

The FDA's new pilot programs designed to minimize the adversarial relationship between the agency and manufacturers of medical devices are described.

McGinley, Laurie, "FDA orders addition of folic acid to grain foods to cut birth defects," ***The Wall Street Journal,*** **March 1, 1996, p. B2.**

The FDA issued new rules on Feb. 29, 1996, that would require enriched breads, flour, pasta and other grains to be fortified with folic acid to reduce the risk of spina bifida and other birth defects.

Henkel, John, "FDA, states collaborate for safety's

sake," *FDA Consumer,* March 1996, p. 27-30.
The FDA and the states are working in a collaborative effort to keep people safe. Programs between the FDA and states work to protect radiological health, retail food, milk and shellfish.

Reform Efforts

Barnett, Alicia Ault, "Conflict continues over plans for FDA reform," *Lancet,* Feb. 17, 1996, p. 464.
A plan to reform the FDA was announced on Feb. 7. The Progress and Freedom Foundation, a think tank, claims that FDA interference forces U.S. companies to do more clinical work overseas, thereby taking jobs away from Americans.

Carey, John , "Revamping the FDA — Without the Stridency," *Business Week,* 484, July 15, 1996, p. 41.
Rep. James C. Greenwood, R-Pa., is authoring FDA reform legislation without a lot of the partisanship that has doomed previous efforts. Greenwood is showing Republicans how they should have gone about their conservative revolution.

Cimons, Marlene, "FDA faces new pressure to speed approval process," *Los Angeles Times,* April 14, 1996, p. A1.
As Congress prepares to take up legislation aimed at accelerating FDA procedures for approving drugs and medical devices , it is being inundated with emotional pleas, including advertising. The FDA says the ads are deceptive and ignore the good it has done by keeping dangerous products off the market.

Goldberg, Robert, "The ethical mess at the FDA," *The Wall Street Journal,* Jan. 16, 1997, p. A18.
Robert Goldberg accuses the FDA of playing politics during the tenure of Commissioner David Kessler, citing the case of Summit Technology Inc, which Goldberg alleges made campaign contributions in return for expedited FDA approval of a laser surgery device. Goldberg says Kessler's departure provides an opportunity for Congress to reform the FDA and urges Congress to delay action on renewing the Prescription Drug User-Fee Act until the FDA addresses its ethical problems.

Kuttner, Robert, "Hampering the FDA," *Boston Globe,* July 8, 1996, p. 11.
Robert Kuttner describes the latest assault on federal regulation in the form of three proposed bills before the House Commerce Committee that would weaken FDA regulation of drugs, medical devices and food additives.

"Prodding the FDA," *The Washington Post,* March 17, 1996, p. C6.
An editorial describes FDA reform legislation in the Senate that would make changes in the FDA approval process.

Schwartz, John, "FDA reforms have momentum as hearings open," *The Washington Post,* May 1, 1996, p. A8.
Under proposals for FDA reform being considered by both houses of Congress in May 1996, companies seeking approval of new drugs and medical devices would be able to pay contractors of their choosing to conduct the safety and effectiveness reviews that until now have been the responsibility of the FDA.

Schwartz, John, "With leadership in transition, FDA to face many challenges in new congress," *The Washington Post,* Dec. 1, 1996, p. A30.
Getting a new commissioner in place is only one of the challenges ahead in 1997 for the FDA, which regulates a seemingly endless assortment of controversial products including drugs, medical devices such as artificial heart valves and silicone breast implants, and cosmetics and blood.

Serafini, Marilyn Werber, "Confronting the future of the FDA," *National Journal,* Dec. 14, 1996.
Some of the challenges the successor of FDA Commissioner David A. Kessler will face are discussed. Congress has already embarked on efforts to rein in the agency.

Shenk, Joshua Wolf, "Warning: Cutting the FDA could be hazardous to your health," *Washington Monthly,* January 1996, p. 17-23.
In Congress, a coalition of conservatives has set its sights on slashing the budget of the FDA. Although the FDA isn't perfect, it can be improved only through tough, fair scrutiny and analysis, not major budget cuts.

"The House and the FDA, "*The Washington Post,* May 5, 1996, p. C6.
An editorial comments that a disconnection persists between the goals expressed by proponents of FDA reform legislation, which is beginning its trek through the House, and the more sweeping and problematic measures that are actually being proposed in regard to safety reviews of drugs and medical devices.

"What price FDA reform?" *National Review,* Sept. 30, 1996, p. 18.
While FDA reform legislation goes down to the wire, the agency is poised to rush through the approval of the French abortion pill RU-486, ignoring studies that have linked the drug to breast cancer. Pro-life members of Congress are willing to let RU-486 be approved rather than hurt the chances of FDA reform.

Back Issues

Great Research on Current Issues Starts Right Here . . . Recent topics covered by The CQ Researcher are listed below. Before May 1991, reports were published under the name of Editorial Research Reports.

NOVEMBER 1995
The Working Poor
The Jury System
Sex, Violence and the Media
Police Misconduct

DECEMBER 1995
Teens and Tobacco
Gene Therapy's Future
Global Water Shortages
Third-Party Prospects

JANUARY 1996
Emergency Medicine
Punishing Sex Offenders
Bilingual Education
Helping the Homeless

FEBRUARY 1996
Reforming the CIA
Campaign Finance Reform
Academic Politics
Getting Into College

MARCH 1996
The British Monarchy
Preventing Juvenile Crime
Tax Reform
Pursuing the Paranormal

APRIL 1996
Centennial Olympic Games
Managed Care
Protecting Endangered Species
New Military Culture

MAY 1996
Russia's Political Future
Marriage and Divorce
Year-Round Schools
Taiwan, China and the U.S.

JUNE 1996
Rethinking NAFTA
First Ladies
Teaching Values
Labor Movement's Future

JULY 1996
Recovered-Memory Debate
Native Americans' Future
Crackdown on Sexual Harassment
Attack on Public Schools

AUGUST 1996
Fighting Over Animal Rights
Privatizing Government Services
Child Labor and Sweatshops
Cleaning Up Hazardous Wastes

SEPTEMBER 1996
Gambling Under Attack
The States and Federalism
Civic Journalism
Reassessing Foreign Aid

OCTOBER 1996
Political Consultants
Insurance Fraud
Rethinking School Integration
Parental Rights

NOVEMBER 1996
Global Warming
Clashing Over Copyright
Consumer Debt
Governing Washington, D.C.

DECEMBER 1996
Welfare, Work and the States
The New Volunteerism
Implementing the Disabilities Act
America's Pampered Pets

JANUARY 1997
Combating Scientific Misconduct
Restructuring the Electric Industry
The New Immigrants
Chemical and Biological Weapons

FEBRUARY 1997
Assisting Refugees
Alternative Medicine's Next Phase
Independent Counsels
Feminism's Future

MARCH 1997
New Air Quality Standards
Alcohol Advertising
Civic Renewal
Educating Gifted Students

APRIL 1997
Declining Crime Rates
The FBI Under Fire
Gender Equity in Sports
Space Program's Future

MAY 1997
The Stock Market
The Cloning Controversy
Expanding NATO
The Future of Libraries

Back issues are available for $5.00 (subscribers) or $10.00 (non-subscribers). Quantity discounts apply to orders over ten. To order, call Congressional Quarterly Customer Service at (202) 887-8621.

Binders are available for $18.00. To order call 1-800-638-1710. Please refer to stock number 648.

Future Topics

- ***China After Deng***
- ***Line-Item Veto***
- ***Breast Cancer***

THE CQ Researcher

PUBLISHED BY CONGRESSIONAL QUARTERLY INC.

China After Deng

Will Deng Xiaoping's dramatic changes survive?

As China's paramount leader for nearly 20 years, Deng Xiaoping guided the Middle Kingdom toward a future that combined market-oriented economic reforms and authoritarian rule. But his death in February raised many questions for the world's most populous country, including how long President Jiang Zemin and other Communist leaders are likely to hold power. In addition, China's fast-growing economy may slow down significantly. The nation also is preparing for China's historic takeover of British Hong Kong, which reverts to Chinese rule on July 1. Whether the Western-oriented city state will retain its uniqueness — and whether it will influence mainland China's tepid steps toward a more pluralistic society or cause problems for Jiang — are questions that only time will answer.

INSIDE THIS ISSUE

CQ June 13, 1997 • Volume 7, No. 22 • Pages 505-528

Formerly Editorial Research Reports

CHINA AFTER DENG

COVER: WORLD BANK

The CQ Researcher

June 13, 1997
Volume 7, No. 22

PUBLISHED BY
Congressional Quarterly Inc.

The CQ Researcher (ISSN 1056-2036). Formerly Editorial Research Reports. Published weekly, except Jan. 3, May 30, Aug. 29, Oct. 31, by Congressional Quarterly Inc., 1414 22nd St., N.W., Washington, D.C. 20037. Annual subscription rate for libraries, businesses and government is $340. Additional rates furnished upon request. Periodicals postage paid at Washington, D.C., and additional mailing offices. POSTMASTER: Send address changes to The CQ Researcher, 1414 22nd St., N.W., Washington, D.C. 20037.

China After Deng

BY DAVID MASCI

THE ISSUES

It was a remarkably simple funeral, considering that Deng Xiaoping had been the undisputed leader of one-fifth of the world's population. Only his family, friends and important Chinese officials were invited to the Feb. 24 ceremony in the Great Hall of the People in Beijing. In just over an hour, it was over.

The public mood was muted, too, which was clearly in accord with the government's wishes. Those few citizens who tried to leave wreaths or flowers for Deng in Tiananmen Square were stopped and even arrested.

By contrast, the deaths in 1976 of Deng's predecessors, Mao Zedong and Zhou Enlai, had drawn tens of thousands of mourning Chinese into the streets. Zhou and especially Chairman Mao — the founder of Communist China — were memorialized with unrestrained pomp and circumstance. Their passing marked the end of an era and triggered more than a year of political chaos before Deng emerged as China's new leader.

By staging a relatively modest service for the 92-year-old Deng, President Jiang Zemin signaled to the nation and the world that despite Deng's death, things would continue in China without interruption. Indeed, in his eulogy, Jiang pledged that he would preserve the legacy that Deng had left to China.

Much of that legacy, in fact, embodied the dramatic changes Deng had inspired since he became the nation's paramount leader in 1978. He had introduced market-oriented economic reforms that had transformed the so-called Middle Kingdom from a backward socialist state into arguably the most dynamic economy in the world. He had also shaken off his

predecessors' obsession with isolation, opening up China to foreign goods, tourists, international investment and even Western ideas in areas like economics and science.

But Deng had also left in place an authoritarian regime that suppressed dissent. And although he had permitted some experiments with limited democracy, especially in the countryside, Jiang gave no indication that further changes in China's political system were in the offing.

Jiang's apparent desire not to rock the boat is likely due to apprehension over what lies ahead. For all the talk of continuity, Deng's death inevitably will change China, presenting Jiang and other leaders with both opportunities and problems.

Officially, Deng's death will have no impact on the makeup of China's leadership. For one thing, Deng had become virtually incapacitated in the last two or three years of his life. But even before his health deteriorated severely, he had given up all of his official posts to Jiang, his handpicked successor, and others. So Jiang and other members of China's leadership, which is centered around the powerful seven-member politburo, essentially had been running the country for years by the time Deng died.

While Deng was alive, Jiang and other leaders he had anointed were secure. "No one would touch Jiang as long as Deng was alive," says Winberg Chai, a professor of political science at the University of Wyoming in Laramie.

With Deng gone, the competition for power is almost certain to heat up. "I think there are about 50 to 75 commissars, political party hacks [and] generals who are going to be jockeying for influence," said Jim Hoagland, an associate editor at *The Washington Post.* [1] The question is whether the jockeying by these less important leaders will affect Jiang.

The future is likely to become clearer at the 15th Communist Party Congress, expected to take place in October. Held every five years, the Congress has traditionally been a forum for top-level personnel changes.

Many China-watchers, like Chai, predict that Jiang will remain, at least for the time being, as China's leader. But some say he could be weakened by the Congress or by other upcoming events.

One such test, even before the party Congress, will come on July 1, when Britain turns over control of Hong Kong to China. (*See story, p. 510.*) If the transition does not go smoothly, Jiang could lose some power.

Another major test for Jiang could be the economy, which has grown tremendously in the last two decades but could be headed for a severe slowdown. That could happen, many experts say, because the government crippled the banking industry by forcing it over the years to lend money to China's large and inefficient state industrial sector. Most of the loans probably will never be paid back, leaving the banks with a huge portfolio of

China at a Glance

With a land area of nearly 4 million square miles and a burgeoning economy, the People's Republic of China has become a powerful force in East Asia. The transfer of Hong Kong from the British back to China in July could cause problems for President Jiang Zemin. And the Republic of China (Taiwan) has long been an irritant to the mainland.

Land area:	3.7 million square miles (excluding Taiwan)
Population:	1.2 billion (1994)
Population growth (1990-94):	1.2 percent
Life expectancy:	69 years
Literacy:	male, 90 percent female, 73 percent
Gross national product per capita (1995):	$660
Economic growth (1995):	10.2 percent

Source: World Bank

bad loans. In addition, many of the state-run companies that owe the money are not profitable and are a further drag on economic growth.

Some economists predict that China's economy is dynamic enough to continue growing at a healthy clip in spite of these problems. Others warn that if Jiang does not deal with the problems in the banking and state industrial sectors, the economy could go into a tailspin. But meaningful reform of the banks and state-owned companies would be expensive and probably exacerbate an already huge unemployment problem.

Still other headaches for Jiang are likely to stem from China's relations with the United States, which have been strained in recent years over issues ranging from Taiwan to human rights to trade.

Tensions are high on a number of trade fronts. Even though President Clinton renewed China's most-favored-nation (MFN) trading status on May 19, the administration is putting ever-greater pressure on the Chinese to find ways to reduce their growing trade surplus with the United States. In addition, many members of Congress, as well as various interest groups, want to block China's access to U.S. markets to force China to improve its record on human rights, weapons proliferation and other issues.

There is also increasing talk, in both countries, of Sino-American rivalry in the Pacific region. Concern about competition between the two countries intensified last year, when the Chinese harassed Taiwan by firing missiles close to its coast during training maneuvers, and the United States responded by dispatching two aircraft carriers to the area.

Experts differ over China's likely concerns about the American presence in Asia. According to some, China is bent on dominating the region and it views the United States as an obstacle to these plans. As evidence, they point to China's recent military buildup and to its aggressive posturing with others in the area, such as Taiwan. In the view of these experts, the United States should maintain a strong military presence in Asia and work to strengthen its alliances with Japan, Taiwan, South Korea and other nations to keep China's ambitions in check.

Some experts contend, however, that China is not trying to dominate the region but is merely taking its rightful place as a great Asian power. In addition, they say, China's military remains relatively toothless despite its efforts at modernization. Given these limitations, they argue, the United States should be encouraging China to integrate into the world community instead of working to "contain" what is largely an imaginary threat.

Whether or not China "threatens" the United States, few would dispute that it will play a significant global role in the coming years. As the Middle Kingdom enters the post-Deng era, these are some of the questions being asked:

Is China trying to become the dominant power in East Asia, and if so, how should the United States respond?

In their recent and much discussed book, *The Coming Conflict with China,* journalists Richard Bernstein and Ross H. Munro predict that China and the United States are headed toward ever-worsening relations, possibly war. [2] There are many potential sources of friction between the two countries, including trade, weapons sales and human rights. But the real problem, the authors say, is simply that China believes the time has come for it to take its rightful place in Asia as the continent's dominant power.

"And that puts the United States and China on a collision course," Munro says, "because the United States has had a single foreign policy toward Asia for more than 100 years, and that has been to oppose the domination of Asia by any single power." [3]

Robert Kagan, a professor of history at American University, agrees, adding: "[The Chinese] cast us as the enemy because when they look around them they see a chain of our allies surrounding them." This alliance system, which includes Japan, South Korea and other Asian nations, is a direct threat to China's ambitions, Kagan argues. "China wants to be sure that all countries in the region are heeding its wishes," he says.

Kagan, Munro and others say that China's actions in the recent past reflect its desire to push the United States out of Asia and dominate its neighbors.

First, they argue, China has embarked on a massive program to modernize its military. While the United States and other Western powers decrease defense spending each year, China's military budget is growing. For instance, in 1996, military spending was 11.3 percent higher than in 1995, according to Bernstein and Munro. The year before, it increased by 14.6 percent. [4] Purchases have focused on advanced weapons (including the recent acquisition of 72 SU-27 fighter planes from Russia) and technology with military applications, such as supercomputers and specialized machine tools.

Reuters

Zhu Lin, the widow of Deng Xiaoping, grieves at his funeral as his three daughters look on.

In addition, China has shown an increasing willingness to take an aggressive, even threatening, stance against its neighbors. For example, the Chinese are pressing several territorial claims, some of which are hundreds of miles from the mainland, like the Spratley Islands chain in the South China Sea. This pugnacious posturing has brought China into conflict with a number of Asian countries — among them Japan, Vietnam, Malaysia and the Philippines — which have accused their giant neighbor of bullying. Moreover, last year, China fired missiles near the Taiwan coast, apparently to underscore its strong opposition to anything resembling a declaration of

Continued on p. 511

Saying Goodbye to 'British' Hong Kong

In Beijing's Tiananmen Square, a huge clock is counting down the days, hours, minutes and seconds remaining until midnight on June 30. At that moment, 155 years of British rule and Chinese ignominy will come to an end in the coastal city of Hong Kong. Britain's Prince Charles, U.S. Secretary of State Madeleine K. Albright and an estimated 9,000 journalists will be on hand to watch as the Union Jack is lowered for the last time, amid fireworks and revelry.

But for all the expected hoopla, the transfer of rule in Hong Kong has produced a measure of anxiety among many of the city's 6.3 million residents. Hong Kong, after all, is not just the most open business environment in the world. It also is a free city in other ways, with an elected legislature, civil liberties and a style of life more akin to Los Angeles than Beijing. Western freedoms are largely unknown in mainland China and, more importantly, are frowned upon by Chinese leaders.

"Hong Kong is cosmopolitan, integrated into the world, [while] China is insular, self-absorbed and not integrated into the international system," says David Shambaugh, a professor of international relations at George Washington University.

These differences were supposedly taken into account when Britain and China negotiated the transfer of power in 1984. The agreement, known as the Joint Declaration, required China to maintain Hong Kong's basic economic and political freedoms for 50 years. In essence, Hong Kong and China would, in an oft-quoted phrase, be "one country with two systems."

But the 1989 crackdown on pro-democracy protesters in Tiananmen Square cast doubts on China's commitment to honor the Joint Declaration.

The fears were not unfounded. Beijing has already established an unelected provisional legislature that will replace Hong Kong's elected council.

In addition, the Chinese-appointed chief executive, Hong Kong shipping magnate Tung Chee-hwa, in April announced a package of measures that would restrict the rights of citizens to assemble and protest. Limits would also be imposed on political parties. In particular, political organizations would not be able to raise money abroad, a proposal aimed at powerful overseas Chinese communities, many of which have supported pro-democracy activists in Hong Kong. (*See story, p. 519.*)

Tung has defended the new proposals, calling them "the right balance" between individual liberty and social order. [1] In addition, he says, the Bejing-appointed legislature is only an interim body and will be replaced with an elected parliament in 1998.

But Martin Lee, who heads the largest party in Hong Kong's legislature, says that "we already have the proper balance" between order and freedom. According to Lee, protests in Hong Kong have never been anything but peaceful. "We do not throw Molotov cocktails." [2] In addition, Lee worries that China's promise to allow elections will result in a rigged process that ultimately produces a group of pro-Chinese lawmakers.

Politics is not the only aspect of city life that may change under the new regime. Even Hong Kong's much-vaunted economy may be tinkered with a bit, a surprising development given the city's reputation as a haven for business. In fact, Hong Kong, with its low tax rates and highly regarded bureaucracy, is often considered to be the best place in the world to do business. Hong Kong is Asia's leading financial center and the world's busiest port. If Hong Kong were a country, it would be the eighth-largest trading nation in the world.

But recently, economic advisers to Tung have proposed steps that would inject the government into the economy. One proposal would encourage, through direct spending and tax breaks, the development of certain industries in the city, notably high-technology manufacturing. Some experts fear that if that happens, Hong Kong's largely service-oriented economy will no longer be such a rich source of wealth and jobs. [3]

For all of China's proposed changes, Hong Kong's future remains unclear. But one thing is certain: China views the handover of Hong Kong as a highly important event. "The return symbolizes the end of what the Chinese like to call the end of the century of shame and humiliation," Shambaugh says. "This is not simply getting back a wayward territory that happened to get away," he adds, but the final chapter in China's long experience with Western imperialism.

Many China-watchers think that, by and large, the Chinese understand that Hong Kong's success is tied to its uniqueness. "On the whole, China will try to keep its commitments," writes Frank Ching, an editor at the *Far Eastern Economic Review*. After all, China did not spend years ironing out the Joint Declaration and other Sino-British agreements over Hong Kong "with the idea that it would tear them all up on July 1." [4]

---

[1] Quoted on "The NewsHour with Jim Lehrer," April 10, 1997.

[2] *Ibid.*

[3] "Is Hong Kong Ripe for a Bit of Central Planning?" *The Economist*, April 12, 1997.

[4] Frank Ching, "Misreading Hong Kong," *Foreign Affairs*, May/June, 1997.

Continued from p. 509
Taiwanese independence. *

But other China-watchers say that Kagan, Munro and their colleagues are reading too much into China's recent actions. The Middle Kingdom, they say, lacks the capability, and the desire, to challenge the United States in Asia. "I don't think China wants to be 'the' dominant power in Asia," says A. Doak Barnett, a professor emeritus at the Johns Hopkins School of Advanced International Studies in Washington. "I think it wants to be a major power among major powers."

Kenneth Lieberthal, a professor at the University of Michigan, agrees. "China has no 'Monroe Doctrine' in Asia," he says, referring to President James Monroe's 1823 declaration that Latin America was within the U.S. sphere of influence. Instead of dominating Asia, Lieberthal says, China cares more about pressing what it sees as historic territorial claims in places like Hong Kong, Taiwan and even the Spratley Islands. "There is no expansionist ideology in China," he says.

As for the military buildup, Barnett and others argue that it is understandable, given the condition of China's armed forces. "They are gradually building up — very gradually in my assessment — their military power because they have felt inferior to all the major powers, and still are."

In fact, says David Shambaugh, a professor of international relations at George Washington University, "They are at least 20 years away from becoming a regional power. There is categorically no 'China threat.' "

Thomas Christensen, an assistant professor of government at Cornell University, says that the Chinese military is so outmoded that even with a crash modernization program, it would be decades before China could hope to challenge the United States in the Pacific. "China is not going to replace the Soviet Union for a very long time — if ever," he says.

And yet, Lieberthal, Barnett and others warn, treating China like the next Soviet Union, as Kagan and others want, could become a self-fulfilling prophecy. "If we keep saying that we are convinced that China is going to be our adversary, that has got to produce a response on their part," Lieberthal says.

Others say that ever since the fall of the Soviet Union, the United States has cast about for a country to replace it as a rival. "Since the end of the Cold War, many Americans have been suffering from enemy-deprivation syndrome," writes Owen Harries in the *National Review*. [5] Attempts to replace the Soviets with the Japanese in the late 1980s collapsed, he says, when Japan failed to become the economic juggernaut that was supposed to dominate the United States.

But Kagan and others say it is foolish to draw parallels between U.S.-Japan friction and the current state of Sino-American relations. "Japan is an economic [as opposed to military] power that is firmly within the U.S. alliance system," he says. "China, on the other hand, is not only not in that alliance system, but is challenging it."

As a result, Kagan and others say, the United States must maintain and strengthen its military presence in Asia. American armed forces in the Pacific must always be vastly superior to China's in order to deter the Chinese from seriously considering policies that could lead to a military conflict with the United States, they argue.

In addition, the U.S. must strengthen its links with key allies in the region, particularly Japan, South Korea and Taiwan, Kagan says. The best way for the United States to keep this alliance system strong, he says, is to show, time and again, that the U.S. is committed to standing by its friends when they are intimidated by China. "When you create uncertainty as to your staying power, it encourages these countries to accommodate China," he says.

Finally, Kagan and others say, by standing up to China when it becomes overly aggressive, the U.S. will help deter China from acting belligerently in the future. In addition, notes *Washington Post* columnist Fred Hiatt, displays of American resolve will reassure its allies in Asia that it can be relied upon to "press China to play by the rules." [6] For example, many of these countries applauded last year's decision by the United States to send two aircraft carrier battle groups to Taiwan in response to China's provocations.

But others argue that "get tough" policies will simply lead to another Cold War. While the United States should maintain its security alliances in Asia, they say, it should not unnecessarily antagonize China by creating a huge anti-Chinese coalition.

Maintaining good relations with the most dynamic country in the most dynamic part of the world is "a necessity, not a luxury," writes *Newsweek* contributing editor Fareed Zakaria. [7] Besides, Zakaria and others argue, China will never become a more pluralistic and open society without continued expansion of trade and information, which would be greatly hindered if the U.S. and its allies tried to contain the Middle Kingdom.

"Containment is folly," Shambaugh says. Besides, he points out, trying to hem in China would be impossible because the surrounding nations ultimately would refuse to allow the United States to build its own iron curtain around China.

Instead, Shambaugh and others say, the United States should be working to bring China into the world community.

"We need to manage the relationship in a way that tries to bring China into multilateral arrangements," says

* Although Taiwan enjoys de facto independence, it is still considered part of China by both governments. Mainland China considers it a renegade province; the Nationalist Party in Taiwan considers itself to be the legitimate government of all China.

Lucian Pye, a professor of political science at the Massachusetts Institute of Technology (MIT). According to Pye, the best way to make China behave like a responsible power is to integrate it into multilateral organizations and treaties that require it to work within a structure to resolve international disputes.

Joseph S. Nye Jr., dean of the John F. Kennedy School of Government at Harvard University, agrees and credits recent improvements in China's behavior with regard to nuclear nonproliferation and testing in part to its signing of international treaties in those areas. "As China sees its interests in a larger context, the prospects for conflict diminish," he recently wrote. [8]

Will China, in the near future, continue to enjoy the very high rate of economic growth that has characterized the last two decades?

In the almost 20 years since Deng instituted the first market-oriented reforms, China's economy has grown at a tremendous rate. During the decade of the 1980s, the gross domestic product (GDP) increased at an average of more than 9 percent per year. So far, GDP growth in the 1990s has been even faster, running at an average annual rate of better than 10 percent. [9]

By contrast, developed countries grew at an almost anemic pace of 2.6 percent in the 1980s and 2.3 percent during the first seven years of this decade. China has even outpaced the other dynamic economies of Asia, such as Indonesia, Singapore and South Korea. [10]

China's galloping economic growth was and is fueled by cheap labor, a high savings rate and large dollops of foreign investment. What was a poverty-stricken, largely agrarian society in 1978 (the year the reforms began) has been transformed into an increasingly urban country that exports hundreds of billions of dollars in goods every year.

By some estimates China's economy is already the world's second largest, ahead of Japan and Germany. And if current growth rates continue, by the end of the first decade of the 21st century, China's GDP could be as large if not larger than that of the United States.

Yet it is by no means assured that China's economy will continue to grow at the breakneck pace that has characterized the last two decades. Indeed, many economists are predicting that the Middle Kingdom's economy will slow significantly. "I think it is highly unlikely that they will be able to sustain their current rate of growth over the next decade," says Nicholas Lardy, a fellow at the Brookings Institution who specializes in China's economy.

World Bank

Market-oriented reforms introduced by Deng Xiaoping transformed China from a backward socialist state into a global economic powerhouse.

One worry for China, Lardy and others say, is its banking system. China's banks, which are owned by the state, have been lending billions of dollars each year to government-owned enterprises, many of which are unprofitable and unlikely to ever repay the money. According to Lardy, 83 percent of all existing bank loans are to these state enterprises. The only thing that keeps the system afloat, he says, is that ordinary Chinese people keep depositing a high percentage of their income into the banking system. "It's essentially a huge pyramid scheme," Lardy says, adding: "You can't keep operating an insolvent banking system forever."

As it is, the banking system is already an increasing drain on economic growth because money that could be lent to private businesses is instead being diverted to prop up the more inefficient public sector.

But there is a greater problem. According to Dominic Zeigler of *The Economist* magazine, the bad loans in China's banks equal roughly one-third of the country's GDP. By comparison, the bad loans associated with the U.S. savings and loan crisis of the late 1980s and early '90s equaled 2 percent of the American GDP. [11]

"There is a consensus that [the banking system] needs to be fixed," Lardy says of China's leaders. "But," he adds, "there is no consensus as how to pay to recapitalize the system" because the cost would be tremendous. Even when banks are privatized, he says, they are still required to lend money to state industries.

This inaction, Lardy and others say, makes a massive banking crisis and a run on the banks inevitable. And if such a crisis occurred, hundreds of millions of people would lose their money and faith in the country's financial system. This in turn would lead to drastic reductions in investment (because the banks would not have money) and consumer spending (because the people would have lost their savings). As a result, Lardy says, the buoyant economy would come to a screeching halt.

Another economic headache for China, Lardy and others say, is the state-owned industries that are taking the bank loans in the first place.

China's state industrial sector is not as important as it once was. In 1978, for instance, state companies accounted for 78 percent of the country's industrial output. Today that figure is 42 percent, as the number of private businesses in China, both domestic and foreign, has grown exponentially. [12]

Still, the state sector cannot be neglected. For example, nearly one in five Chinese workers is employed at a state-owned company. [13] And for most of these employees, the company is more than a place to work. Many state industries provide a host of essential social services, like housing, education and health care, to workers and their families. Many "companies in the state sector are designed to control workers, not make money," says Steven Yates, a fellow at the Heritage Foundation.

This social function has been costly and, coupled with bad management, has made many state-owned companies unprofitable. According to the Chinese government, 37 percent of all state firms lose money. Many economists believe that the number of money-losing enterprises is actually much higher. If the banks had not provided these companies with easy money, many of them would have gone bankrupt years ago, Yates, Lardy and many others say.

In addition to draining the lion's share of money from the banking system, the state sector is also inefficiently using workers and factories that could be put to more productive use in the private sector. "This is a terrible waste of human and other resources," Yates says.

But, as with the banking system, China's leaders are only making cosmetic changes, Lardy and others say. For example, companies are privatized or sold off. But often the state is the largest or the only shareholder, leaving the bad management and other inefficiencies in place.

One big reason for the government's reluctance to let go of many of these companies is a fear of widespread unemployment. If a lot of firms were allowed to go bankrupt or to substantially shrink their work forces, tens of millions of workers could become jobless. This is a sensitive issue in China, where 100 million people are already jobless or underemployed.

But despite these and other problems, some are optimistic about China's economic prospects over the next decade. For instance, the World Bank estimates that China's GDP will grow at roughly 8 percent over the next 10 years or just shy of its current phenomenal growth rate.

Gary Jefferson, a professor of economics at Brandeis University, agrees with this more upbeat assessment, arguing that the problems cited by Lardy and others are not as grave as they say they are.

First, he argues, the banking system, while in trouble, is also showing signs of changing for the better. For instance, banks are becoming more competitive as they respond to the limited entry into the Chinese market of foreign financial institutions and home-grown private savings and loans.

In addition, he believes that as state-sponsored companies play less of a role in the economy (some economists estimate that publicly owned businesses will make up only 30 percent of industrial output by 2000), banks will have more money to loan to profitable private businesses.

Jefferson also sees signs of real hope in the state industrial sector. "They are already restructuring [the state sector] by giving company managers more autonomy and selling all or part of firms to private investors," he says. In addition, he says, many state-owned companies are working more closely with international firms, which are providing them with technical and management assistance.

In addition, Jefferson and others say, increased competition from domestic and foreign firms is forcing the Chinese government to finally address the state sector's problems. "These pressures are either going to force the state sector to disappear or substantially restructure," he says.

Indeed, Chinese officials are now indicating that they are serious about privatizing huge numbers of state-owned companies. Other companies will be allowed to issue stock or sell a share of their business to domestic or foreign investors. Although there has been no formal statement of policy, "there's now a unified view" among the leadership, says Fan Hengshan, a deputy director at the State Commission for Restructuring Economic Systems. [14]

Do China's recent limited experiments with the democratic process represent a trend toward greater political openness?

At the very top, China is ruled by a small clique of unelected leaders who maintain their grip on power, in part, by suppressing dissent. But at the lowest level of government, the situation is quite different.

In 1988, the first rural villages began electing their local leaders. Today, the head of almost every village has been voted into office. And while these elections do not have all of the trappings of Western-style democracy — for instance, there are no competing parties — they are generally fair and conducted by secret ballot. In addition, this practice has given a taste of the democratic process to the roughly three-quarters of all Chinese who still live in rural villages. [15] Democracy may touch even more people if a proposal to expand local elections to larger towns is adopted.

Surprisingly, most of the winners of local elections are not members of the Communist Party but simply traditional clan leaders. Even more surprising, the elections have not only the consent but also the blessing of China's top leaders.

"The motivation behind this is not some kind of love of democracy but a recognition that the place is too big and complicated to be run from the center," says Lieberthal. According to Lieberthal and others, these elected officials have authority over local issues, like zoning laws or water rights. Questions of national import are still decided by the leadership in Beijing.

But democratic stirrings are not limited to the local level. The National People's Congress (NPC), for decades a mere rubber stamp of leadership decisions, has begun showing an independent streak. In 1992, for instance, 841 of the body's 3,000 delegates abstained from voting to show their opposition to a plan to build the environmentally controversial Three Gorges dam on the Yangtze River. An even greater surprise came in 1995, when 37 percent of the delegates voted against one of President Jiang's key appointments. [16]

Despite these and other protest votes, the NPC is still largely subservient to the Communist Party and the leadership. It has never, for example, rejected a directive from the top.

Still, many China-watchers see the NPC's recent actions and the elections at the village level as part of broader trend toward a more democratic society. This trend, they argue, is a response to the increasing wealth and education of the citizenry. And just as in Taiwan and South Korea, where pressure from a growing middle class forced authoritarian regimes to democratize, China will slowly liberalize its political system. "Unless China is unique in history, the political system will take into account the wishes of the citizenry," Lieberthal says.

Barnett agrees, arguing that although democratization suffered a "major setback" after the democracy movement was crushed in Tiananmen Square in 1989, new pressures from all levels of society within China as well as internationally will lead to more political openness. "I think the process of political liberalization will continue," he says.

But other experts on China are not as sanguine. "If democracy is going to come, it's going to have to come from the top," Pye says, adding that the changes made so far only came because the leadership saw them in their interest. "I don't see anyone at the top having an interest in doing this anymore," he says.

According to Pye, change would only come "if there were a crisis at the top" and someone within the leadership saw democratic reform to be in his interest.

In addition, Pye argues, other segments of Chinese society are not really pushing for political reform. For example, he says, there are no significant interest groups trying to effect change. "In China," he explains, "you don't say, 'Let's change the policy I don't like.' You say, 'Just don't apply it to me.' "

Yates is also pessimistic about the prospects for democracy. China's future middle class may choose stability over individual freedom, Yates says, adding that "the Chinese people have a very real fear of chaos."

In addition, he says, comparing China to South Korea or Taiwan is dangerous because they were allies of the United States, which eventually pressured them to democratize. "China is different because it is not a U.S. ally," he says.

Another factor may be political apathy. "The average man on the street just wants to be left alone," says Jim Shinn, a senior fellow for Asia at the Council on Foreign Relations. "The Chinese have been subjected to so much strife and brutality in their lifetimes, and that produces a pacifism toward their political masters." ■

Background

East Meets West

Until recently, China rarely took an interest in the outside world. Secure in its venerable culture and society, the Middle Kingdom usually ignored the world beyond its borders.

Even when the Chinese did venture out, they acted in ways that would have seemed alien to the explorers, conquistadors and adventurers from the West. For example, in the early 15th century, Adm. Cheng Ho launched a series of naval expeditions that took the Chinese navy as far as East Africa. But Cheng was not seeking new lands to conquer or even plunder. His mission was "to make 'the whole world' into voluntary admirers of the one and only center of civilization." [17]

But China could not remain closed to the outside world forever. And when European powers took an interest in China in the 19th century, the Middle Kingdom was wholly

Continued on p. 516

Chronology

1840-1939

Internal strife and Western imperialism weaken China, toppling the last imperial dynasty.

1840
Britain and China go to war after the Chinese close their market to opium sales.

1842
The Opium War ends in China's defeat. A peace treaty cedes Hong Kong to Britain and opens five ports to foreigners.

1912
The last Ch'ing emperor abdicates the throne. Nationalist Party leader Sun Yat-sen becomes the president of the new Republic of China. Sun soon resigns, and by 1915 China is ruled by regional warlords.

1921
The Communist Party of China is founded.

1927
Civil war begins between the Communists and Nationalists (now led by Chiang Kai-shek).

1934
The Communists are defeated and forced on "The Long March" into northern China, where they regroup.

1940-1974

The Communists defeat the Nationalists for control of China. Mao's early alliance with the Soviet Union breaks down, leading to friendlier relations with the United States.

1949
After routing the Nationalists, the Communists proclaim the People's Republic of China on Oct. 1. Chiang and the Nationalists escape to Taiwan and establish a parallel seat of government.

1958
Mao Zedong launches "The Great Leap Forward" to accelerate socialism.

1960
Mao taps Deng Xiaoping and other pragmatists to reverse the economic damage caused by the Great Leap.

1966
Mao launches "The Cultural Revolution" to eliminate Western influence. Millions are killed and millions more, including Deng, are purged from their jobs or positions.

1972
President Richard M. Nixon visits China; the United States recognizes the Communist government.

1973
With the assistance of Premier Zhou Enlai, Deng is rehabilitated and made vice premier.

1975-1997

Mao passes from the scene and is replaced by Deng, who institutes sweeping reforms of the economy and other sectors of Chinese society.

1976
Mao dies, leaving no clear successor.

1978
After a brief power struggle, Deng becomes China's paramount leader and launches "The Four Modernizations," which include economic reform.

1979
Under President Jimmy Carter, the United States resumes full diplomatic relations with the People's Republic of China and breaks ties with Taiwan.

1984
Britain agrees to return Hong Kong to China on July 1, 1997.

1989
Pro-democracy protests in Tiananmen Square in Beijing are brutally suppressed by Deng. Jiang Zemin becomes Deng's handpicked successor.

1994
Deng is seen in public for the last time. Rumors begin circulating that he is incapacitated.

1996
China fires missiles off the coast of Taiwan, leading the United States to dispatch two aircraft carriers to the area.

February 1997
Deng dies; Jiang takes over as first among equals.

July 1, 1997
Britain is scheduled to turn over Hong Kong to China.

October 1997
The 15th Communist Party Congress is expected to be held.

Did China Try to Buy Influence?

It may take months to determine if the Chinese government tried to illegally influence U.S. policy by making campaign contributions before the 1996 elections.

But if the allegations of Chinese involvement in the American political process are true, Sino-U.S relations could suffer tremendously. It is, after all, against U.S. law for foreign governments to contribute to American political campaigns.

More importantly, evidence of illegal or secret campaign contributions could turn into a public-relations nightmare for the Chinese.

Already, the charges have soured moods on Capitol Hill, helping to kill what was previously thought to be a good chance for the United States and China to negotiate an agreement allowing China to join the World Trade Organization (*see p. 519*). In addition, the allegations have helped to generate fear in some quarters that Chinese influence is growing and is dangerous.

The Chinese have flatly denied any wrongdoing. China "has never been involved in or supported any contributions," said Chinese President Jiang Zemin last month.

But the May 19 issue of *Newsweek* quotes federal investigators as saying that there is "strong evidence" that the Chinese funneled nearly $1 million to their consulates in the United States. Chinese diplomats then reportedly passed the money to Asian and Asian-American businesses or individuals who contributed to a variety of political candidates, including President Clinton and Vice President Al Gore. [1] *The Washington Post* reported that the contributions had been approved by the top leaders in Beijing. [2]

In addition, there is evidence to suggest that these political contributions may have totaled more than $1 million. For instance, the Democratic National Committee (DNC) has already returned or pledged to return about $3 million (almost all from Asian donors). [3] Reports also have surfaced alleging that a company with links to China extended a $2 million loan to a GOP think tank and gave $122,000 to the Republican National Committee. [4]

These allegations have stoked fears that Beijing may be trying to corrupt American democracy. Questions have arisen over what impact the contributions might have had on President Clinton, who benefited from some of the questionable money given to the DNC.

The president did meet with businessmen who, it was later learned, had connections to the Chinese government. But, so far, no firm evidence has been found that indicates that the administration worked on behalf of the contributors or changed its policy toward China as a result of any gifts.

Still, many observers say that, if true, the allegations against China add up to more than just a few illegal campaign contributions. "This was an intelligence operation," says Robert Kagan, a professor of history at American University. "[The Chinese] were trying to covertly influence the outcome of an election," he adds.

But others urge caution. "It seems to me that we should not leap to the conclusion that China is simply trying to subvert our political system in order to promote its own agenda," says Kenneth Lieberthal, a professor at the University of Michigan.

Still others worry that all of the talk of scandal could lead Americans to cast China as the nation's great enemy. Indeed, many see a parallel in the growing fear of China and the way Japan was perceived until the early 1990s. "Just as Japan's investments touched a nerve about American economic impotence, the ethnic Chinese money has fed into today's anxiety that Greater China poses the next great challenge to America," *New York Times* reporter David E. Sanger wrote earlier this year. [5]

---

[1] Daniel Klaidman, "A Break in the Case," *Newsweek*, May 19, 1997.

[2] Bob Woodward, "Top Chinese Linked to Plan to Buy Favor," *The Washington Post*, April, 25, 1997.

[3] Howard Fineman and Mark Hosenball, "A Hobbled President," *Newsweek*, March 24, 1995.

[4] Michael Weisskopf, "Manna from Hong Kong," *Time*, May 12, 1997.

[5] David E. Sanger, "'Asian Money,' American Fears," *The New York Times*, Jan. 5, 1997.

Continued from p. 514

unprepared to deal with the threat.

The first major disaster came in 1840, when a British fleet arrived in southern China to force the Chinese to repeal measures that had outlawed the lucrative, British-controlled opium trade. Outgunned by the English on sea and land, the Chinese swallowed a peace treaty that not only permitted the opium trade but ceded Hong Kong to the British and opened five ports in China to foreigners.

The rest of the 19th century was equally difficult for China. Forays by France, Russia and Japan, in addition to Britain, were common. This foreign meddling, coupled with internal strife weakened the state tremendously.

In 1912, China's last imperial dynasty, the Ch'ing, fell, and a republic was proclaimed under the leadership of Sun Yat-sen, a Western-educated reformer. But Sun's republic quickly disintegrated into dictatorship and chaos, as independent warlords fought for control of the country.

After World War I, Sun's Nationalist Party, known as the Kuomintang, began working to reunite China. Under Sun's successor, Chiang Kai-shek, and aided by the growing Communist Party, the Nationalists began creating a unified Chinese state.

In 1927, Chiang broke with his Communist allies. While the Nationalists controlled most of the country, the Communists established a substantial military and even administrative presence in parts of China.

Japanese aggression in Manchuria beginning in 1931 distracted the Nationalists. But in 1934, Chiang refocused his attention on the Communists, routing them from most of the areas under their control. The scattered Communist army retreated for nearly two years, fighting its way through western China to Shensi Province in summer 1936. Known as "The Long March," the odyssey established Mao Zedong as the leader of the Communists. [18]

In 1937, Japanese aggression turned into a full-scale invasion of northern and eastern China. The Nationalists and Communists buried their differences and fought the Japanese together. But Japan, with its modern military, quickly occupied much of the country.

Chairman Mao

Both the Nationalists and Communists knew that their alliance was merely one of convenience. After World War II ended with Japan's defeat at the hands of the United States and its allies, Chiang and Mao began fighting again. This time, the Communists were stronger than they had been during the days of the Long March. Mao's genius for organizing had enabled the party and its military wing, now called the People's Liberation Army (PLA), to grow tremendously during the war years. [19]

By 1948, the Nationalists were in severe trouble. Chiang's undisciplined army was no match for the well-organized PLA. The following year, Chiang and about 200,000 followers fled to Taiwan, and on Oct. 1, the Communists formally established the People's Republic of China.

During the first decade of his rule, Mao turned China into a socialist state. Agriculture was collectivized and industry was nationalized. China's first five-year plan, in 1953, set out to develop heavy industry, using the Soviet Union as a model. At the same time, Chinese society became more structured and, for some, more inhospitable. For example, peasants and workers were organized into brigades, while many artists, professionals and businessmen were persecuted as enemies of the party. In 1958, the transformation was accelerated in what came to be known as "The Great Leap Forward," which lasted for two years.

Throughout the first decade of Communist rule, China maintained close relations with the Soviet Union. China's entry into the Korean War against the United States in 1950 strengthened the tie. But as the 1950s came to a close, Sino-Soviet relations grew colder; the freeze would last for three decades.

By 1960, Mao and others in the Chinese leadership recognized that the Great Leap had been a failure. The economy and other sectors of society were in a state of crisis. In response to these difficulties, a new group of pragmatic leaders arose, including Deng. They improved the economy by allowing farm and factory managers more control over production. At the same time, Deng strengthened the Communist Party. [20]

But Mao, sensing that he was being edged from power, began a campaign against what he said were China's increasingly "capitalist" tendencies. During what became known as "The Cultural Revolution" (1966-1968), Mao used the PLA to purge and harass his political opponents, including Deng. Millions of people were killed, including many of China's leading thinkers, politicians and professionals. Many other educated people were sent to remote parts of China to be "re-educated" through manual labor.

Secure once again as undisputed leader, Mao, during his remaining years, eschewed the bold and often disastrous steps that characterized the first 20 years of his rule. One major exception was the building of better relations with the United States. The process officially started in 1972, when President Richard M. Nixon made a historic trip to China. Each country saw the other as a valuable ally against the Soviet Union.

Deng's Reforms

By the time Mao died in 1976, Deng had been rehabilitated. Mao's trusted lieutenant, Premier Zhou Enlai — himself a pragmatic modernizer — had brought Deng back in 1973 to once again help restructure Chinese society.

But Zhou had died eight months before Mao, leaving a huge leadership vacuum. After a relatively brief struggle for power with Mao's widow and her supporters (known as The Gang of Four), Deng became China's paramount leader.

Almost immediately after assuming power, Deng began a series of ambitious reforms. Collective agriculture was scrapped in favor of the old system of family-run farms. Private enterprise, once illegal, was encouraged, leading to the rapid creation of a new business class. China's market was opened to foreign trade and investment.

Important non-economic changes were also undertaken. Couples were restricted to one child to reduce China's huge population. In addition, diplomatic relations were established with the United States and other Western countries.

In the political arena, though, there was a marked absence of change. The Communist Party retained control of the government, and individual liberties remained very limited. The limits on freedom of speech and assembly were dramatically revealed to the world in 1989, when tens of thousands of democracy supporters assembled in Tiananmen Square to demand change. After vacillating for a number of weeks, the government violently crushed the protest, killing thousands, according to some reports. [21]

Tiananmen tarnished the regime's image abroad and at home but had little impact on China's reforms. In the years both preceding and following the debacle, China's economy has grown at an almost unbelievable rate.

When Deng died earlier this year, he left a country that had been transformed from an isolated state with an inefficient command economy into an economic powerhouse that many say will be a superpower in the next century. ■

CURRENT SITUATION

Trade With China

In the 1990s, trade replaced human rights and other issues to become the greatest source of friction between China and the United States. The reason is simple: In the last decade, the U.S. trade deficit with China has increased by a factor of more than 10. If current trends continue, the deficit with China, which stood at $39.5 billion in 1996, will top the current imbalance with Japan, which had a $47.7 billion surplus with the United States in 1996. [22]

Following the path laid by other Asian success stories, such as Japan and South Korea, China is relying on exports to grow and modernize its economy. Access to the U.S. market, the world's largest, is crucial if this export-led growth is to continue. [23]

Currently, China enjoys most-favored-nation (MFN) trading status with the United States. MFN is a slightly misleading term since China's low-tariff access to the American market is roughly the same as that enjoyed by all but a few nations, among them North Korea and Cuba, that are restricted for political reasons.

Yet China is in a different category than, say, Britain, which enjoys permanent MFN treatment. Congress is required as part of the Trade Act of 1974 to review China's trade status each year. This review has rarely been a mere formality. For example, after the crackdown in Tiananmen Square, an outraged Congress revoked China's MFN status twice in 1992, only to have President George Bush veto the measures.

That same year, then-Gov. Bill Clinton promised, if elected president, to use MFN renewal to punish the Chinese leadership for human rights abuses. But by 1994, President Clinton, under pressure from U.S. corporations, had adopted Bush's tactic, delinking China's trade status from its human rights record and other issues.

But while China has enjoyed open access to the U.S. market, it has not offered similar benefits to American exporters. The reason, Chinese leaders say, is that their country is just developing economically. China's industries need protection for a time from untrammeled competition in order to rise to international standards, they argue.

But as China's trade surplus with the United States has ballooned, this argument has fallen on less sympathetic ears among U.S. policy-makers. At the same time, there is a renewed push on Capitol Hill to punish China for its record on human rights and weapons proliferation. And this time, former supporters of free trade with China, such as House Majority Leader Dick Armey, R-Texas, are saying their position on the issue could change.

On May 19, Clinton announced that he was renewing China's MFN status for another year. Congress now has until Aug. 31 to revoke the president's order. But with Clinton and the U.S. business community firmly in favor of renewal, supporters of revoking MFN stand little chance of success. For one thing, revocation does not enjoy the support of two-thirds of both houses, which would be needed to override a promised presidential veto.

China Eyes World Trade Organization

Instead, the debate over trade has shifted to negotiations over China's desire to join the World Trade Organization (WTO). The WTO is an international free-trading club whose members agree to reduce tariffs, quotas and other barriers to world commerce. The organization has 130 members, including the United States.

Over the past few years, China has mounted a vigorous campaign to enter the WTO. But China's entry into the organization would require current members to grant it permanent MFN status, something the U.S. Congress is not likely to do this year. Still, the MFN requirement has given the United States tremendous leverage over China, forcing it to negotiate the terms under which it will enter the WTO.

Among other things, the Clinton administration has been pressing China to change its trade and investment laws as a condition for entering the WTO. The United States wants China to remove many of the quotas and high tariffs currently in place on foreign goods, like automobiles. The Chinese agree in prin-

Big Business in the Chinese Diaspora

In a roll call of the greatest entrepreneurs and tycoons of the 20th century, Yue-Che Wang and Li Kas-shing may not spring immediately to mind; but they should. Like Bill Gates, Ted Turner and other obvious candidates from the West, they have built huge business empires and made billions of dollars through perseverance and vision.

But Wang and Kas-shing are not entirely like their fiercely independent Western counterparts. They are part of a network, almost an informal family, of other ethnic Chinese businessmen that has come to dominate the commerce of East Asia.

The "Bamboo Network," as it is known, grew out of the Chinese migrations of the late 19th and early 20th centuries that established Chinese communities in nearly every country in East Asia. Today, less than 100 years later, the 55 million descendants of these invariably poor immigrants play a major role in Asia's spectacular economic growth.

Beyond the borders of the People's Republic of China, ethnic Chinese make up less than 10 percent of the population of East Asia. And yet they control two-thirds of the region's retail trade and represent nine out of every 10 billionaires in Asia.[1] In addition, overseas Chinese businessmen are responsible for more than two-thirds of the $140 billion that has been invested in mainland China by foreigners since market reforms were instituted in 1978. By some estimates, the combined economic output of businesses controlled by ethnic Chinese equals or exceeds that of mainland China.

Half the population of the entire Chinese diaspora is located in Taiwan, Hong Kong and Singapore. They became Asian business hubs after World War II, protected from Mao's disastrous economic experiments and the general turmoil that has wracked China for much of this century.

But even in countries where Chinese migrants are a small and often persecuted minority, they have succeeded brilliantly. In Indonesia, for example, ethnic Chinese make up 4 percent of the population and control 50 percent of the economy. In the Philippines, Chinese-owned businesses produce 40 percent the gross domestic product even though ethnic Chinese comprise less than 1 percent of the population.

Most Chinese entrepreneurs in the diaspora engage in a host of businesses. The typical group might be involved in real estate development (almost always part of the mix since it has been so lucrative in Asia), food packaging and electronic manufacturing.

These conglomerates are also firmly in the hands of the family that founded them, no matter how large they become. Subsidiaries are usually run by the children or grandchildren. Managers who are not family members rarely make big decisions without the approval of the patriarch.

Much of the success of China's overseas population is due to their reliance on *guanxi,* or "connections." On its most basic level, this system functions as a mutual-assistance network. For instance, one business will lend the other money or assist it in gaining entry into a new market.

Guanxi allows entrepreneurs to base their dealings with each other on trust, a decidedly un-Western concept. A handshake is usually good enough to seal even large deals. "If a business owner violates an agreement, he is blacklisted," according to Murray Weidenbaum and Samuel Hughes, authors of *The Bamboo Network: How Expatriate Chinese Entrepreneurs Are Creating a New Superpower in Asia.* "This is far worse than being sued, because the entire Chinese network will refrain from doing business with the guilty party."[2]

Connections are also important outside the network. In particular, overseas Chinese businessmen work diligently to establish ties to political leaders. This is especially important in countries such as Indonesia and Thailand, where resentment of the tremendous economic power enjoyed by the tiny Chinese communities has led to discrimination and persecution. "It is not greed that drives the overseas Chinese," said Simon Murray, head of Deutsche Bank's Asia Pacific operation, "it's fear — and the yearning for the protection that money will give you."[3]

---

[1] "Inheriting the Bamboo Network," *The Economist,* Dec. 23, 1995.

[2] Murray Weidenbaum and Samuel Hughes, "Asia's Bamboo Network," *The American Enterprise,* September/October 1996.

[3] Quoted in "Business in Asia," *The Economist,* March 9, 1996.

ciple but are demanding long timetables in order to protect what they regard as nascent industries.

In addition, Washington has demanded that foreign firms be able to import and export goods in China as they see fit and to be able to sell goods in China directly to the Chinese — practices that are currently prohibited.

Some politicians and China-watchers applaud White House efforts to pry open the Chinese market. But human rights, religious and labor groups are among those who want Clinton to require China to improve its human rights record as the price of entry into the WTO. Others want to link membership with China's actions in Hong Kong after Chinese rule begins on July 1.

But others say that trying to wring substantial trade and other concessions out of China could backfire terribly. "We're already demanding more of the Chinese than is politically feasible" for them to grant, Lardy says, adding that "China has almost nothing to gain from WTO membership." In reality, Lardy and others say, the United States and other developed economies will be the winners if China joins the WTO because China will be forced to make its markets much more open.

According to Lardy and others, China's reputation as a closed and hostile market is undeserved. "If you count U.S. trade with Hong Kong [much of which goes on to the mainland], China is now our eighth largest export market," he says. Indeed, he notes, American exports to China "are growing faster than any of our other top 20 export markets."

Lardy and others also argue that China's growth as an exporter has not come at the expense of American workers. According to Jefferson of Brandeis, most of the goods coming from China are low-technology products such as toys, footwear and clothing. They had been manufactured elsewhere in Asia, notably Taiwan and South Korea, due to low labor costs but moved to China to take advantage of its even lower costs. "Most of those [American] jobs were lost to Asia 20 years ago," Lardy says.

Instead of trying to squeeze concessions out of China, Lardy recommends allowing the Chinese to maintain import quotas for years to come in a few industries that they determine are crucial to their long-term growth.

But others say that just getting China into the WTO won't solve any big trade problems, and that the only way to level the trade playing field with China is to deny them access to the U.S. market.

"People place too much emphasis on the WTO," Shinn says. "Japan and Korea have been members of GATT [the General Agreement on Tariffs and Trade, which is the WTO's predecessor], and how much has it opened their markets?" he asks. ■

Xinhua/Reuters

Chinese President Jiang Zemin is greeted by workers during an inspection tour at a woolen mill.

OUTLOOK

Challenges for Jiang

Deng Xiaoping's death probably will have little immediate impact on China's leadership.

But President Jiang is no Deng, nor is he likely ever to be. Deng, with his unassailable credentials as a founding member of the Communist Party, was indisputably China's paramount leader. Like Mao before him, Deng could take bold steps (instituting market-based economic reforms, for instance) without worrying about his job.

Jiang, on the other hand, is merely first among equals in a collective leadership, and must consider how each decision will affect his position within that leadership.

According to some China experts, however, Jiang is probably secure in his position for the next few years. "I don't think anyone will challenge him, because none of his potential rivals are really in a position to replace him right now," says Barnett of Johns Hopkins.

Henry Harding, dean of the Elliot School of International Relations at George Washington University, agrees. "Jiang Zemin's position as president and general secretary of the [Communist] Party is not being questioned [because] there is no alternative at this point."

Barnett is among those who say Jiang has some natural advantages that make him hard to topple. First, he says, as Deng's protégé, "Jiang has Deng's imprimatur, which is still valuable."

Moreover, he points out, Jiang did not make any major blunders during the last few years, when he essentially held the reins of power as Deng grew increasingly incapacitated. This can only strengthen his position as leader, Barnett argues.

In addition, Jiang has shown himself adept at solidifying his base of support. "Deng's long survival allowed Jiang to consolidate and strengthen his position," Harding testified on March 18 before the Senate Foreign Relations Committee.

Continued on p. 522

At Issue:

Should the United States grant permanent most-favored-nation trade status to China?

John Howard
Director, International Policy and Programs, U.S. Chamber of Commerce

WRITTEN FOR *THE CQ RESEARCHER*, MAY 1997.

yes

Continued most-favored-nation (MFN) status is good not only for commerce between our two countries. It is also critical to sustained U.S. influence, as well as to the cause of economic, political and religious freedom in China.

MFN is a misnomer because there is nothing "most-favored" about that status. MFN status is the normal tariff treatment the United States provides to all but a small handful of its trading partners.

Simply put, the MFN principle stipulates that a nation will manage its basic commercial relationships with any other single nation the way it manages its commercial relationships with all other nations. As such, MFN status is fundamental and necessary to international commerce in the modern global economy. Neither the United States nor any other nation can afford to reject this reality as it relates to the world's largest and one of its most rapidly growing nations. And no other major nation is even contemplating such rejection.

U.S. national interests clearly lie in expanding trade with China. In 1996, U.S. companies exported nearly $12 billion in merchandise to China. These exports supported over 170,000 high-wage jobs in a variety of high-value-added sectors. Many thousands of additional jobs depend on services related to China trade. These jobs would be at substantial risk if China's MFN status was ended. But that is not all.

On May 6, Hong Kong Gov. Chris Patten urged House Speaker Newt Gingrich, R-Ga., to delink the MFN debate from Hong Kong's upcoming transition to Chinese rule. Recognizing China MFN's critical importance to Hong Kong's continued viability and its people, Gov. Patten wrote, "There is no comfort in the proposition that if China reduces their freedoms, the United States will take away their jobs." And Christian advocacy organizations are increasingly concerned that ending China's MFN status will set back, rather than advance, the cause of religious freedom in China.

Support for permanent MFN status for China does not suggest uncritical approval of China's policies or practices. Various U.S. trade laws and continued engagement with China's leadership provide ample opportunities to challenge those policies and practices we don't like. However, to terminate or annually rethink a fundamental commercial relationship recognized worldwide as normal is to cast doubt on U.S. reliability, harm forces for progress we profess to support and ultimately hinder U.S. objectives across the board.

Rep. Nancy Pelosi, D-Calif.
Ranking Democrat, House Foreign Operations Appropriations Subcommittee

WRITTEN FOR *THE CQ RESEARCHER*, MAY 1997.

no

President Clinton is again asking Congress to extend most-favored-nation (MFN) trade status to China. Since the president delinked trade from human rights three years ago, the human rights situation in China and Tibet has deteriorated, the U.S. trade deficit with China has soared and China's authoritarian government has continued its sale of nuclear, chemical, missile and biological weapons technology to dangerous countries, including Iran.

The administration's policy of so-called "constructive engagement" is neither constructive nor true engagement. It has brought us to a status quo that is not sustainable in terms of trade, the proliferation of weapons of mass destruction and human rights. The U.S. trade deficit with China is projected to be $50 billion for 1997; the piracy of our intellectual property continues, costing the U.S. economy $2.3 billion in 1996; and Chinese demands for technology and production are increasing, at the expense of American workers.

Those who espouse the current policy of so-called constructive engagement characterize those who disagree with them as advocating containment. I take issue with that characterization. I believe the current U.S.-China policy is a policy of containment. By following a policy that bolsters the Chinese government, the United States is actually supporting the containment of the Chinese people, their hopes and aspirations. China's authoritarian rulers are engaged in active containment of the thoughts, beliefs and statements of its population because full engagement by Chinese people with the outside world is a direct threat to their hold on power.

The president's decision signals business as usual in U.S-China policy. It runs counter to the concerns of a growing number of Americans, who in a May 1 *Wall Street Journal*/NBC/Hart & Teeter Poll said, by a margin of 67 percent to 27 percent, that China should improve human rights or lose its current trade status.

Unfortunately, once again, the administration has chosen to hold U.S.-China policy hostage to the profits of a few exporting elites at the expense of most products made in America. Instead, we should have a policy of sustainable engagement, an engagement that sustains our economy, our values and the safety of our world.

For More Information

Council on Foreign Relations, 58 East 68th St. New York, N.Y. 10021; (212) 734-0400. The council is a nonpartisan organization devoted to the study of international issues.

Embassy of the People's Republic of China, 2300 Connecticut Ave., N.W. Washington, D.C. 20008; (202) 328-2500. The embassy represents the interests of the People's Republic in the United States.

Heritage Foundation, Asian Studies Center, 214 Massachusetts Ave. N.E., Washington, D.C. 20002; (202) 546-4400. The center conducts research and provides information on trade, military policy and other issues that concern the United States and Asia.

U.S.-Asia Institute, 232 E. Capitol St. N.E., Washington, D.C. 20003; (202) 544-3181. The institute conducts research and sponsors conferences in an effort to foster greater cooperation and understanding between the United States and Asian countries.

Continued from p. 520

Jiang has prevailed, Harding says, by placing allies in key posts throughout the government. Jiang also has assiduously courted the all-important People's Liberation Army by granting large increases in their budget and promoting supporters to key military posts. [24]

But others say that Jiang, for all his skill as a political operator, is vulnerable. "I think he will be threatened" by rivals waiting for him to make a big mistake, Pye says.

"He could be in trouble if he mishandled a crisis," Shambaugh agrees.

Jiang's first test may come this summer, when Britain hands Hong Kong back to China. If the turnover results in strained relations between the mainland government and the island, Jiang could be blamed.

The 15th Communist Party Congress, expected to be held in October, will be another big hurdle. "This will be his baptism of fire," Pye says.

During the Congress, the party will fill a number of important leadership posts. An obvious question is how to handle Prime Minister Li Peng, who is required by the Chinese Constitution to relinquish his post in early 1998. Li, 68, is probably the most powerful man in the leadership, after Jiang. If he is not given a satisfactory new job, Li could make trouble for Jiang.

Li reportedly wants to head the National People's Congress, whose current chairman, the powerful Qiao Shi, is not anxious to turn over his post, especially to the more conservative Li.

When it comes to Jiang's future, China-watchers agree on one thing. As Shambaugh puts it: "He certainly has his work cut out for him this year." ■

Notes

[1] Quoted on "The NewsHour with Jim Lehrer," Feb. 19, 1997.

[2] Richard Bernstein and Ross H. Munro, *The Coming Conflict with China* (1997), pp. 4-5.

[3] Quoted on "The NewsHour with Jim Lehrer," April, 16, 1997.

[4] Bernstein and Munro, *op. cit.,* p. 73.

[5] Owen Harries, "How Not to Handle China," *National Review,* May 5, 1997.

[6] Fred Hiatt, "Counterweight to China," *The Washington Post,* May 5, 1997.

[7] Fareed Zakaria, "Hedging It," *Newsweek,* March 3, 1997.

[8] Joseph S. Nye Jr., "We Can't Afford to Lose China Again," *Los Angeles Times,* Jan. 6, 1997.

[9] "The Asian Miracle: Is It Over?" *The Economist,* March 1, 1997.

[10] *Ibid.*

[11] Dominic Zeigler, "Ready to Face the World?" *The Economist,* March 8, 1997.

[12] Kathy Chen, "Chinese President Ratchets Up Reforms," *The Wall Street Journal,* April 7, 1997.

[13] *Ibid.*

[14] *Ibid.*

[15] "China's Grassroots Democracy," *The Economist,* Nov. 2, 1996.

[16] "China's Government-in-Waiting," *The Economist,* Nov. 2, 1996.

[17] Daniel J. Boorstin, *The Discoverers* (1983), p. 192.

[18] Frederica M. Bunge and Rinn-Sup Shinn, eds., *China: A Country Study* (1981), p. 27.

[19] *Ibid.,* pp. 27-30.

[20] *Ibid.*

[21] Harry Harding, *A Fragile Relationship: The United States and China Since 1972* (1992), pp. 216-224.

[22] U.S. Census Bureau, cited in David E. Sanger, "China Faces Test of Resolve to Join Global Economy," *The New York Times,* March 2, 1997.

[23] Carroll J. Doherty, "U.S. Agonizes Over China Policy: Engagement or Confrontation?" *Congressional Quarterly Weekly Report,* April 26, 1997.

[24] "Price of Power," *The Economist,* March 8, 1997.

Bibliography

Selected Sources Used

Books

Bernstein, Richard, and Ross Munro, *The Coming Conflict with China,* Alfred A Knopf, 1997.

Veteran journalists Bernstein and Munro argue that China and the United States are headed toward ever-worsening relations and possibly war. There are many potential sources of friction between the two countries, including trade, weapons sales and human rights. But the real problem, according to the authors, is that China wants to become the dominant power in Asia and it sees the American presence in the region as its primary obstacle.

Harding, Harry, *A Fragile Relationship: The United States and China Since 1972,* Brookings Institution, 1992.

Harding, dean of the Elliot School of International Affairs at George Washington University, traces the history of Sino-American relations from President Richard M. Nixon's historic trip to China in 1972 to the early 1990s. Harding points out that since the early 1970s, U.S. relations with China have been characterized by cycles of "progress, stalemate and crisis."

Huntington, Samuel P., *The Clash of Civilizations and the Remaking of World Order,* Simon & Schuster, 1996.

Huntington, director of the John M. Olin Institute for Strategic Studies, argues that fault lines in geopolitics are increasingly being drawn according to culture, as opposed to ideology. Huntington believes that Sino-American friction is likely, as the standard bearers of East Asian and Western culture vie for hegemony in the Pacific. The author also says that other Asian countries, like Japan and South Korea, have shown a greater willingness of late to cast their lot with China, their cultural cousin.

Shinn, James, ed., *Weaving the Net: Conditional Engagement with China,* Council on Foreign Relations, 1996.

Shinn, a senior fellow at the Council on Foreign Relations, and the other contributors to the book argue that the United States should pursue a policy of "conditional engagement" with China. Conditional engagement, according to Shinn and the others, entails setting and sticking to some basic principles in order to encourage China to integrate into the international economic and political order.

Articles

"America's Dose of Sinophobia," *The Economist,* March 29, 1997.

This article shows how China has replaced Japan as America's chief overseas worry. While much of this fear is misplaced, the article says, it should not be entirely dismissed.

Doherty, Carroll J., "U.S. Agonizes Over China Policy: Engagement or Confrontation?" *Congressional Quarterly's Weekly Report,* April 26, 1997.

Doherty examines the growing movement on Capitol Hill to "get tough" with China over issues like trade, human rights and Taiwan.

Elliott, Dorinda, and Michael Elliott, "Why the World Watches," *Newsweek,* May 19, 1997.

The Elliotts gauge the mood in Hong Kong as the city prepares to merge with mainland China. While many are excited about the change, "there's an undercurrent of anxiety," they write. In particular, advocates for democracy expect the new regime to be unsympathetic to their desire to preserve political and other freedoms.

Harries, Owen, "How Not to Handle China," *National Review,* May 5, 1997.

Harries, editor of *The National Interest,* argues that if the United States insists on viewing China as an enemy, "it is likely to become one." He says the evidence suggests that on issues ranging from human rights to China's intentions in East Asia, the Middle Kingdom is probably not as bad as the United States thinks it is.

Ziegler, Dominic, "Ready to Face the World?" *The Economist,* March 8, 1997.

This special report looks at the state of China as it enters the post-Deng era. According to Ziegler, severe economic and political weaknesses coupled with nationalism, could make the Middle Kingdom more troublesome for other powers, especially the United States.

Reports and Studies

Jost, Kenneth, "Taiwan, China and the U.S.," *The CQ Researcher,* May 24, 1996, pp. 457-480.

Jost argues that Taiwan's surging economic self-confidence and China's increasing assertiveness pose difficult policy choices for the United States, with significant implications for peace, stability and trade in the Asia-Pacific region. The report includes a sidebar on Hong Kong.

The Next Step

Additional information from UMI's Newspaper & Periodical Abstracts™ database

Campaign Contributions

Brauchli, Marcus W., Phil Kuntz and Leslie Chang, "Vying for influence: Fund-raising flap has roots in bitter rivalry between China, Taiwan," *The Wall Street Journal,* April 3, 1997, p. A1.

The Democratic Party has had to return about $3 million in foreign or otherwise questionable donations raised mostly by its ethnic-Chinese loyalists. Some of its fund-raisers, steadfast supporters of President Clinton, are under criminal investigation. The FBI is looking into the activities of both China and Taiwan, having advised some in Congress that China might have tried to funnel illegal foreign money to their campaigns. This controversy is examined.

"China connection," *The Wall Street Journal,* March 28, 1997, p. A1.

FBI agents probing donations to the Democratic National Committee in March 1997 are searching for Xue Haipei, former director of the little-known Council for U.S.-China Affairs. Xue, whose group got $10,000 from Boeing to work on China trade issues, strategized with DNC fund-raiser John Huang on influencing Congress.

Hamblin, Ken, "China's foothold in California," *Denver Post,* March 16, 1997, p. D3.

Liberal media and political pundits are running in circles trying to determine whether President Clinton cut a deal with the communist Chinese to peddle a portion of the American dream in exchange for so-called soft campaign contributions. Meanwhile, Californians living near the historic Long Beach Naval Shipyard have little if any doubt what the Chinese financial subsidy purchased from the Democratic National Committee and the Clinton administration, Hamblin explains.

Harris, John F., and Bob Woodward, "White House Looks Inward On FBI Flap; Error Acknowledged On China Briefing," *The Washington Post,* April 9, 1997, p. A1.

Despite President Clinton's public rebuke of the FBI, senior administration officials say they have concluded that the White House's own personnel and procedures bear significant responsibility for a breakdown in communications that left Clinton unaware of an investigati into suspected Chinese influence on U.S. elections.

Harris, John F., "Freeh Briefs Clinton Adviser On China Probe; More Frequent Meetings Are Being Considered," *The Washington Post,* May 1, 1997, p. A6.

After complaints from the White House, FBI Director Louis J. Freeh briefed President Clinton's national security adviser on the status of a Justice Department investigation into possible attempts by China to influence U.S. elections. Freeh and Attorney General Janet Reno gave what administration officials called "a highly general overview of the controversy" to National Security Adviser Samuel R. "Sandy" Berger and his deputy, James Steinberg. The previous week, according to sources, Berger called Reno to ask why she and Freeh had given a briefing to senior members of the Senate Select Committee on Intelligence but not offered a similar meeting to the White House.

Lacey, Marc, and Jack Nelson, "Clinton Tries to Quell China Funds Impact," *Los Angeles Times,* April 26, 1997, p. A1.

President Clinton and his White House struggled Friday to contain the foreign policy fallout from intelligence reports suggesting that China's top leaders have been involved in an effort to covertly funnel money into the U.S. electoral system. The revelations were particularly awkward for the White House because it appeared that Clinton had not received a similar briefing. In the past, the FBI has been wary of providing investigative updates because the probe is exploring, in part, whether fund-raisers for the Democratic National Committee who have ties to China were among the conduits of illegal Chinese money. While skirting questions about what he had been told, Clinton asserted that the White House must not be cut out of the information loop on important foreign policy matters. "I believe that the president and secretary of State and the national security adviser should have access to whatever information is necessary to conduct the foreign policy and to protect the national interest of the country," he said.

Lynch, April, and Marshall Wilson, "China's interest in U.S. politics may start here; California lawmakers play roles in key issues," *San Francisco Chronicle,* March 14, 1997, p. A1.

From high-tech piracy and international trade to democracy and human rights, the controversy over China's influence in U.S. politics that began at the White House has spread to one of the places it will have the most impact — California. Earlier this week, it was disclosed that California Democratic Senators Dianne Feinstein and Barbara Boxer and two Bay area members of the House of Representatives received warnings about China's activities from the FBI . Only one of the members of Congress known to have been briefed by the FBI is from another state.

Taylor, Jeffrey, "Little Windmere, with China connections, sees bounty from company's generosity to the DNC," *The Wall Street Journal*, March 24, 1997, p. A20.

Since 1993, Windmere Corp., a manufacturer and distributor of hair dryers and other personal-care appliances, has showered the Democratic National Committee with donations totaling $290,000. The reason: to plug most-favored-nation trading status for China, which keeps tariffs low on Windmere's products, virtually all of which come from its 2-million-square-foot factory in Guangdong province.

Deng Xiaoping

Burdman, Pamela, "Upheaval in China Seen as Unlikely; Academics, politicians assess future after Deng," *San Francisco Chronicle*, Feb. 20, 1997, p. A1.

Although Chinese leader Deng Xiaoping was a pivotal figure on China's political scene for much of the 20th century and the country's modernizer since the late '70s, his death yesterday is not expected to provoke major upheaval, say China experts and political leaders. Deng's handpicked successor, Communist Party General Secretary Jiang Zemin, may withstand political maneuvering and stay in place after China's 15th Party Congress in October. His standing was bolstered yesterday by the announcement that he will chair Deng's funeral committee. Still, Jiang will continue to share power with a team of technocrats, including Premier Li Peng, that Deng helped install.

Cox, James, "Deng Xiaoping: — 20th century 'emperor' molded modern China," *USA Today*, Feb. 20, 1997, p. A1.

Deng Xiaoping was, in his final days, Communist China's most revered political figure. In a span of nearly 20 years, he helped rid his country of destructive ideological schisms and propelled China on its long march from a starving, backward nation to a growing economic power. It was Deng, China's so-called "red emperor," who ordered the violent crackdown in Tiananmen Square in 1989. But it was also Deng, joking in cowboy hats, chain-smoking cigarettes and inviting Westeners to marvel at China's wonders, who risked his standing by embracing free market economics and a measure of social freedoms for his people. It will be Deng's heirs who deal with problems such as the widening gap between China's nouveau rich and rural poor, a massive and ailing state industrial sector and signs of unrest among peasants and workers. China's post-Mao, post-Deng generation also must prove to the United States and other nations that China will play by established rules in trade, human rights, arms proliferation and other spheres.

"Deng Xiaoping: Leader secure in history; China's future uncertain," *Houston Chronicle*, Feb. 20, 1997, p. A32.

Many Houstonians remember the striking image of the diminutive Deng Xiaoping, who has died at the age of 92, in a 10-gallon Stetson hat during a visit here in 1979. Former President Bush said Thursday that Deng will be remembered as one of the world's great leaders. "Although he was a committed totalitarian," Bush said, "I will always respect the changes he brought to China. It is important to remember just how bad things in China were before Deng came to power."

McGeary, Johanna, "The next China," *Time*, March 3, 1997, pp. 48-56.

Deng Xiaoping set off seismic changes in China, liberating it from the most self-defeating precepts of Marxist economics, but his revolution left much undone. Deng's successors must now struggle to solve the political and economic problems he ignored.

Overholt, William H., "China after Deng," *Foreign Affairs*, May 1996, pp. 63-78.

At age 92, Deng Xiaoping's role as China's leader is nearly over. The architect of China's economic reforms is long past effective leadership and participation in China's governance. Overholt previews Chinese Communist leadership and politics in the post-Deng era.

"The Notable Legacy of Deng Xiaoping; 'Paramount leader' brought China into the mainstream," *Los Angeles Times*, Feb. 20, 1997, p. B8.

Mao Zedong led a revolution that brought epochal social and economic change to China at a terrible human cost. The death toll from state-induced famine and state-sanctioned brutality numbered in the tens of millions. Deng Xiaoping led a revolution no less history-changing for China, but one with consequences far more lasting and vastly more beneficial to the Chinese masses.

Hong Kong

"Clinton sends China a signal on Hong Kong," *San Francisco Chronicle*, April 19, 1997, p. A10.

President Clinton met with Martin Lee on April 18, 1997, and assured the Hong Kong democratic leader that freedom "should and must continue" after China takes over the British colony on July 1.

Cox, James, "Hong Kong's new restrictions defended; Designated leader denies that China is forcing changes," *USA Today*, May 6, 1997, p. A8.

Hong Kong's leader-in-waiting denied Monday that China is forcing him to limit public protests and foreign political support. He said the new restrictions are his ideas. Tung Chee-hwa, who takes office when the British colony is reunited with China July 1, is reviewing about 5,000 comments he received on his plans to ban demonstrations advocating independence for Taiwan and foreign contributions to political parties in Hong Kong.

Cox, James, "Hong Kong faces a wave of illegals from China; Rumors of a general amnesty fuel an influx from mainland," *USA Today,* April 30, 1997, p. A8.

Thousands of people from mainland China have slipped illegally into Hong Kong in recent weeks or are overstaying their visas. Many have paid smugglers, called snakeheads, to bring them across so they can join fathers or husbands residing legally in Hong Kong. The sudden surge was unleashed by rumors in China that illegal immigrants with parents or spouses in Hong Kong will be given amnesty after Britain returns the territory to Chinese rule on July 1.

Crowell, Todd, "Britain, China can't agree on rite of passage for Hong Kong in 1997," *The Christian Science Monitor,* June 26, 1996, p. 7.

Relations are so sour between Britain and China over Hong Kong that the two sides can't agree on how to commemorate the July 1, 1997 "remarriage" of Hong Kong and China. So far the two have agreed only that any ceremony will be "dignified." Britain would prefer it to be "grand," while China would rather it be "modest." This lack of agreement, along with reports that China would prefer that the role of British-appointed Hong Kong Gov. Christopher Patten be minimized, is further damaging confidence in the territory's future as the handover date approaches.

Erlanger, Steven, "Clinton and Gingrich View Hong Kong as Test for China," *The New York Times,* May 1, 1997, p. A8.

President Clinton pronounced himself "quite satisfied'" with the assurances on the future of Hong Kong he received today from Chinese Foreign Minister Qian Qichen, but said he was waiting to see if China's words matched its actions. Clinton administration officials have said repeatedly that they regard the way China handles its reassertion of sovereignty over Hong Kong on July 1 as an "important benchmark" for the larger U.S.-China relationship. Qian met Clinton for 40 minutes, discussing issues ranging from Hong Kong to China's growing trade surplus with the United States, now nearing $40 billion by some accounts.

Stein, Peter, and Marcus W. Brauchli, "China may ease curbs on liberty for Hong Kong," *The Wall Street Journal,* May 16, 1997, p. A14.

Following a barrage of public criticism, Hong Kong's next government appeared to back away from planned harsh measures that were aimed at limiting liberties when China regains sovereignty July 1, 1997.

Tsang, Steve, "Maximum flexibility, rigid framework: China's policy towards Hong Kong and its implications," *Journal of International Affairs,* winter 1996, pp. 413-433.

Chinese policy-makers are very aware of Hong Kong's economic value to the People's Republic of China (PRC). Tsang outlines the structure of the PRC's relevant policy-making apparatus, examines the forces that determine the PRC's policy toward Hong Kong and explains it in terms of maximum flexibility within a rigid framework.

Human Rights

Palmer, John, "E.U. divided on China policy; Human rights groups have denounced 'capitulation' to Beijing," *Guardian,* April 5, 1997, p. 15.

France, Germany and Italy have withdrawn their backing for a United Nations resolution on China's human rights violations sponsored by the European Union. The decision has infuriated the Dutch government, which holds the presidency of the European Union. The row could develop into an open foreign policy split when E.U. foreign ministers meet informally here this weekend. In an irate letter to other E.U. governments, Dutch Foreign Minister Hans van Mierlo called the French decision "a serious setback for the prospects of the European Union developing its own common foreign and security policy." He added: "More serious is the fact that the essence of the human rights policy of the European Union is at stake."

Dobbs, Michael, "Clinton Attends Meeting With Hong Kong's Lee; President Reminds China of Rights Assurances," *The Washington Post,* April 19, 1997, p. A1.

Clinton told Hong Kong Democratic Party leader Martin Lee that a political crackdown by Beijing could seriously damage U.S.-Chinese relations, the White House said. With time running out before China assumes control over the former British colony, Hong Kong has emerged as a potential threat to the Clinton administration's strategy of "engaging" China. Any attempt by the communist authorities in Beijing to stifle the freedoms enjoyed by the 6 million people of Hong Kong could lead to an anti-China backlash in the United States. The president called on Beijing to abide by the terms of a 1984 agreement with Britain that, in his words, "commits China to respect not only the economic liberties but also the political and civil liberties" of Hong Kong's people.

Gittings, John, "China moves on human rights," *Guardian,* March 4, 1997, p, 12.

China has said it will resume talks with the International Committee of the Red Cross (ICRC) as part of an apparent new drive to improve its human rights image. Talks on allowing access to China's political prisoners began in 1994, but lapsed within a year. The ICRC says China indicated that the talks were not a priority, and no progress was made. China's agreement to resume "expert level" meetings comes before next week's opening of the annual United Nations Human Rights Commission in Geneva, Switzerland. Beijing is anxious to head off

Washington's sponsorship of a resolution calling for China's human rights record to be investigated.

"Gore Calls China 'More Receptive' on Human Rights; Greater Access to Markets Promised," ***Chicago Tribune,*** **March 26, 1997, p. 1.**

After two days of intensive talks, Vice President Al Gore said China is promising greater access to its markets and listening with a "more receptive" ear to U.S. complaints about its human rights record. Gore called Wednesday's meeting with President Jiang Zemin and earlier talks with Premier Li Peng "productive, friendly, searching" and said they elevated U.S.-China relations to a new level of trust. Gore offered no specifics, however, and America's leaders have heard such promises before. They have often come away convinced they had won Chinese concessions, only to complain later that Beijing was not keeping its end of the deal.

Jiang Zemin

Mufson, Steven, "China's Deng Xiaoping is Dead at 92; Party Chief Jiang Zemin, 70, Holds Reins but Faces Tests," ***The Washington Post,*** **Feb. 20, 1997, p. A1.**

To the new Chinese President Jiang Zemin and all of China, Deng bequeaths the central paradox of his 18-year reign: While he undertook economic emancipation and an "open-door" policy, Deng protected the sclerotic Communist Party's monopoly on political power. Given China's history of policy dictated from above, people in search of direction will look to Jiang, hailed by the official Chinese media as the "core" of the next generation of Chinese leadership.

Lakshmanan, Indira A.R., "China bids Deng Xiaoping farewell; Albright raises issues to nation's leadership," ***The Boston Globe,*** **Feb. 25, 1997, p. A1.**

In a somber hour-long ceremony this morning full of superlatives and symbolism, China's President Jiang Zemin vowed to follow the path toward economic modernization and Chinese reunification started by his predecessor, Deng Xiaoping. Jiang's funeral oration before 10,000 invited Communist Party members capped a remarkable 24 hours that saw the cremation of Deng's remains, an emotional funeral procession attended by tens of thousands and a visit by U.S. Secretary of State Madeleine K. Albright to underscore the continuing importance of Sino-U.S. ties.

"Exchange with reporters prior to discussions with President Jiang Zemin of China in Manila, Philippines," Weekly Compilation of Presidential Documents, Dec. 2, 1996, p. 2431.

President Clinton fields reporters' questions on the differences he wants to raise in his discussion with President Jiang Zemin of China when they meet in Manila, Philippines.

Most-Favored-Nation Status

Butterton, Glenn R., "Renew MFN for China? Right decision, wrong reasons," ***Chicago Tribune,*** **July 3, 1996, p. 27.**

Butterton examines the decision to extend most-favored-nation trading privileges for China, and contends that President Clinton made the right decision but for the wrong reasons.

Lachica, Eduardo, "House instructs panels to probe abuses in China despite allowing MFN status," ***The Wall Street Journal,*** **July 1, 1996, Sec. B, p. 7F.**

Despite defeat of a bill that would have denied China its most-favored-nation trading status, the House isn't about to let the Chinese off that easily. Shortly after rejecting that bill the week of June 24, 1996, the House passed a companion resolution instructing its committees to investigate China's alleged human-rights abuses, illicit arms transfers and unfair trade practices and to report on "appropriate legislation" by the end of September.

Murray, William J., "Rubin warns China that MFN debate is likely to be more difficult this year," ***The Wall Street Journal,*** **April 7, 1997, p. A16.**

Treasury Secretary Robert Rubin, steering clear of the controversy over Chinese political contributions, focused on U.S. concerns about Hong Kong and human rights during an April 6, 1997, meeting with Chinese Finance Minister Liu Zhongli.

Back Issues

Great Research on Current Issues Starts Right Here . . . Recent topics covered by The CQ Researcher are listed below. Before May 1991, reports were published under the name of Editorial Research Reports.

DECEMBER 1995
Teens and Tobacco
Gene Therapy's Future
Global Water Shortages
Third-Party Prospects

JANUARY 1996
Emergency Medicine
Punishing Sex Offenders
Bilingual Education
Helping the Homeless

FEBRUARY 1996
Reforming the CIA
Campaign Finance Reform
Academic Politics
Getting Into College

MARCH 1996
The British Monarchy
Preventing Juvenile Crime
Tax Reform
Pursuing the Paranormal

APRIL 1996
Centennial Olympic Games
Managed Care
Protecting Endangered Species
New Military Culture

Back issues are available for $5.00 (subscribers) or $10.00 (non-subscribers). Quantity discounts apply to orders over ten. To order, call Congressional Quarterly Customer Service at (202) 887-8621.

Binders are available for $18.00. To order call 1-800-638-1710. Please refer to stock number 648.

MAY 1996
Russia's Political Future
Marriage and Divorce
Year-Round Schools
Taiwan, China and the U.S.

JUNE 1996
Rethinking NAFTA
First Ladies
Teaching Values
Labor Movement's Future

JULY 1996
Recovered-Memory Debate
Native Americans' Future
Crackdown on Sexual Harassment
Attack on Public Schools

AUGUST 1996
Fighting Over Animal Rights
Privatizing Government Services
Child Labor and Sweatshops
Cleaning Up Hazardous Wastes

SEPTEMBER 1996
Gambling Under Attack
The States and Federalism
Civic Journalism
Reassessing Foreign Aid

OCTOBER 1996
Political Consultants
Insurance Fraud
Rethinking School Integration
Parental Rights

NOVEMBER 1996
Global Warming
Clashing Over Copyright
Consumer Debt
Governing Washington, D.C.

DECEMBER 1996
Welfare, Work and the States
The New Volunteerism
Implementing the Disabilities Act
America's Pampered Pets

JANUARY 1997
Combating Scientific Misconduct
Restructuring the Electric Industry
The New Immigrants
Chemical and Biological Weapons

FEBRUARY 1997
Assisting Refugees
Alternative Medicine's Next Phase
Independent Counsels
Feminism's Future

MARCH 1997
New Air Quality Standards
Alcohol Advertising
Civic Renewal
Educating Gifted Students

APRIL 1997
Declining Crime Rates
The FBI Under Fire
Gender Equity in Sports
Space Program's Future

MAY 1997
The Stock Market
The Cloning Controversy
Expanding NATO
The Future of Libraries

JUNE 1997
FDA Reform

Future Topics

- ***Line-Item Veto***
- ***Breast Cancer***
- ***Transportation Policy***

THE CQ Researcher

PUBLISHED BY CONGRESSIONAL QUARTERLY INC.

Line-Item Veto

Can it control wasteful federal spending?

Nearly a dozen presidents have sought the power to eliminate individual spending items from money bills approved by lawmakers. Now, the Republican-controlled Congress has given a modified line-item veto to a Democratic president, Bill Clinton. Signed last year, the new law authorizes the president to "cancel" any spending item after signing a bill into law. Clinton and congressional supporters in both parties say the procedure will help control wasteful spending, especially the kind of "pork-barrel" expenditures that individual members of Congress like to bestow on their districts. Opponents say the law will have little fiscal impact, and that it infringes on Congress' constitutional power over federal spending. A legal challenge is before the Supreme Court, which should rule on the case soon.

INSIDE THIS ISSUE

CQ June 20, 1997 • Volume 7, No. 23 • Pages 529-552

Formerly Editorial Research Reports

THE ISSUES

BACKGROUND

CURRENT SITUATION

OUTLOOK

SIDEBARS AND GRAPHICS

FOR MORE INFORMATION

COVER: PRESIDENT CLINTON SIGNS THE LINE ITEM VETO ACT IN THE OVAL OFFICE ON APRIL 9, 1996, AS REP. JOHN M. SPRATT JR., D-S.C., AND SEN. DON NICKLES, R-OKLA., LOOK ON. (REUTERS)

THE CQ Researcher

June 20, 1997
Volume 7, No. 23

The CQ Researcher (ISSN 1056-2036). Formerly Editorial Research Reports. Published weekly, except Jan. 3, May 30, Aug. 29, Oct. 31, by Congressional Quarterly Inc., 1414 22nd St., N.W., Washington, D.C. 20037. Annual subscription rate for libraries, businesses and government is $340. Additional rates furnished upon request. Periodicals postage paid at Washington, D.C., and additional mailing offices. POSTMASTER: Send address changes to The CQ Researcher, 1414 22nd St., N.W., Washington, D.C. 20037.

Line-Item Veto

By Kenneth Jost

The Issues

When the Clinton administration listed federal programs and projects it wants to eliminate this year, the compilation looked like the hit list from an anti-government waste advocacy group.

The 254 items the administration hopes to ax include an Agriculture Department research grant for peach tree short life; a smattering of corporate-welfare programs at the Department of Commerce; a dozen or so weapons systems; and a miscellany of programs at the Energy, Health and Human Services and Transportation departments.

All told, the administration said it could save almost $3.4 billion for the coming fiscal year if the 254 items were left on the budget-cutting floor. In a $1.7 trillion budget, the savings were modest, perhaps. Still, one might have expected a cheer — however muted — from Republicans on Capitol Hill who had been pressuring the administration to control federal spending and bring down the budget deficit.

There was no cheering. Instead, Republicans zeroed in on two GOP initiatives the administration put on the hit list: a $310 million educational assistance block grant for the states and $523 million in block grants for local law enforcement. The two programs represented key Republican initiatives designed to give the states and local governments greater control over financial assistance from Washington.

Not surprisingly, when the Republican chairman of the House Appropriations Committee saw the hit list, he saw red.

"A slap in the face at Republican initiatives," Rep. Robert L. Livingston of Louisiana said after prying the list

from a reluctant Office of Management and Budget (OMB). "Suggesting we eliminate these programs, is simply not helpful." [1]

In years past, a president would have been hard-pressed to eliminate the kind of spending items on the administration's hit list. Congress would have included the items as relatively small entries in omnibus appropriations bills sent from Capitol Hill to the White House for the president to sign or veto on an all-or-nothing basis. In practical terms, presidents didn't want to snarl up a Cabinet department's entire funding just to knock out a few million dollars — or even a few hundred million dollars — in a multibillion-dollar bill.

Now, however, President Clinton has been given a power that no previous chief executive enjoyed: the authority to reject a single spending item in a massive appropriations bill.

The new Line Item Veto Act gives the president the power to "cancel" a spending item within five days after signing a bill into law. If Congress wants to force the president to approve the expenditure, lawmakers must pass a "disapproval" bill, send it to the president, and — if he vetoes the new measure — muster two-thirds majorities in the House and the Senate to override the veto. (*See box, p. 533.*)

The law includes a so-called "lockbox" provision, aimed at making sure that any savings are applied only to deficit reduction. The measure also allows the president to cancel newly approved mandatory entitlement provisions as well as certain limited tax benefits. In the current fiscal climate, however, Congress is thought unlikely to approve any new entitlements. And the tax-benefit provision is viewed as unlikely to have great impact either. (*See story, p. 543.*)

Proponents of the line-item veto say the measure gives the president a valuable tool in controlling federal spending, especially the kind of "pork-barrel" expenditures that individual members of Congress like to bestow on their states or districts. "We've advocated this as a great opportunity to eliminate pork-barrel spending in the budget," says Jim Campi, a spokesman for Citizens Against Government Waste.

"Americans are understandably outraged when we spend $2 million on a study of the effects on the ozone layer of flatulence in cows, or $4.5 million to study desert shrimp in Arizona," says Sen. John McCain, R-Ariz., the primary congressional sponsor of line-item veto legislation for several years. The new law, he says, will allow the president to eliminate many of these wasteful programs. "There's not a doubt in my mind," he says.

The new law cleared the Republican-controlled Congress last year with nearly unanimous support from GOP lawmakers and the backing of a substantial majority of Democratic members, too. Clinton also backed the proposal, following the example of at least 10 other chief executives who have sought a line-item veto since President Ulysses S. Grant first proposed it in 1873.

More recently, Clinton's two Republican predecessors, Ronald Reagan and George Bush, both urged Democratic-controlled Congresses to give them a line-item veto. They noted that 43 out of 50 governors have the power to veto individual budget items. (*See story, p. 536, and map, p. 540.*) Proponents also have noted that polls indicate popular approval of the idea. An ABC News poll taken in January 1995, just as the Republicans were assuming control of Congress, found that 64 percent of those responding favored a line-item veto for the president, while 31 percent opposed the idea.

But an array of lawmakers, constitutional law experts and policy advocates fought the line-item veto and continue to oppose it. The lawmakers, mostly Democrats, say the item veto infringes on Congress' constitutionally bestowed power over federal spending and gives the president a too-formidable weapon to use in lobbying individual members of Congress not only on the budget but also on other issues.

Many legal experts contend that the law passed by Congress violates the Constitution. "It fundamentally alters the balance of power in the area of appropriation and budgeting," says Michael Gerhardt, a constitutional law expert and dean of Case Western Reserve law school in Cleveland. In addition, many experts on congressional budget policies, as well as some budget-reduction advocacy groups, maintain that the line-item veto will yield little, if anything, in actual budget savings.

The most prominent of the opponents has been Sen. Robert C. Byrd, a West Virginia Democrat first elected in 1958, who prides himself on his command of constitutional law and congressional procedure as well as his unremitting defense of congressional power.

For more than a decade, Byrd led the fight in the Senate against line-item veto proposals. In 1992, he denounced the line-item veto on the Senate floor as "demagoguery" — and specifically included in his criticism Clinton and two other Democratic presidential aspirants who were supporting the idea.

Last year, as he finally lost the fight on Capitol Hill, Byrd was both somber and bitter. "The Senate, you mark my words, is on the verge of making a colossal mistake," Byrd said in the March 27 debate. "We are about to adopt a conference report which will upset the constitutional system of checks and balances and separation of powers." [2]

Byrd did not surrender, however. On Jan. 3, 1997, he joined with five other lawmakers in filing a challenge to the law in federal court in Washington. The lawmakers — four other Democrats and one Republican, Oregon Sen. Mark O. Hatfield, now retired — claimed the law infringed on their constitutional responsibilities. [3]

Three months later, U.S. District Judge Thomas Penfield Jackson agreed. "The Act effectively permits the President to repeal duly enacted provisions of federal law," Jackson, a Reagan appointee, wrote in his April 10 ruling. "This he cannot do."

The administration promptly appealed the ruling to the Supreme Court, which agreed to hear the case on an expedited basis. The arguments before the justices on May 27 featured a truncated debate on the policy arguments for and against a line-item veto. Instead, the justices appeared to focus primarily on an important preliminary question: whether the lawmakers have legal "standing" to challenge the law in court before it has even been used (*see p. 544*).

Clinton has had no chance to use the line-item veto yet. The court challenge to the law was proceeding as Congress was just starting to work on appropriations bills for fiscal 1998. White House officials and GOP congressional leaders opened the budget season by negotiating a tenuous agreement designed to balance the federal budget by 2002 (*see p. 546*). But the agreement already has begun to fray. And some congressional experts warn that even if the high court upholds the line-item veto, Clinton may hesitate to

The Presentment Clause

Every Bill which shall have passed the House of Representatives and the Senate, shall, before it become a Law, be presented to the President of the United States; If he approve he shall sign it, but if not he shall return it, with his Objections to that House in which it shall have originated . . . . If . . . two thirds of that House shall agree to pass the Bill, it shall be sent . . . to the other House, . . . and if approved by two thirds of that House, it shall become a Law.

— U.S. Constitution (Article I, Sec. 7, clause 2)

use it for fear of jeopardizing already fragile relations with members of Congress on both sides of the aisle.

As the justices ponder the constitutional issues, and the White House and Congress jockey for position in shaping the federal budget, here are some of the questions being debated:

How the Line-Item Veto Works

The Line Item Veto Act does not give the president the power to "veto" a line item in a spending bill before it becomes law. Instead, the act authorizes the president, after he signs a bill into law, to "cancel" any of three types of provisions: a discretionary spending item contained in an appropriations bill, a new mandatory entitlement ("direct spending") or a targeted tax break benefiting 100 or fewer taxpayers. Under a "sunset" provision in the act, the law expires after eight years, on Jan. 1, 2005.

Step 1: Congress sends a bill to the president.

Step 2: President signs the bill into law.

Step 3: President has five days to notify Congress of his decision to "cancel" a spending item (or limited tax benefit provision) in the law. Under the law's "lockbox" provision, any resulting savings must go toward deficit reduction.

Step 4: Congress can "disapprove" the president's cancellation within the next 30 days in session by passing a new bill, by a simple majority in both houses, containing the canceled item.

Step 5: President can veto the disapproval bill.

Step 6: Congress can override the president's veto of the disapproval bill — and thus enact the original item into law — only by a two-thirds majority vote in both the House and the Senate.

Will a line-item veto significantly reduce federal spending?

The General Accounting Office (GAO) estimated in 1992 that President Reagan could have reduced federal spending by $70 billion over a six-year period if he had had the power to cut out all the spending items his administration had formally opposed during congressional consideration. Six months later, however, the head of the GAO, Comptroller General Charles Bowsher, largely disavowed the report. In an apologetic letter in response to criticism of the report from Sen. Byrd, then head of the Senate Appropriations Committee, Bowsher conceded that the report used a number of wrong assumptions in deriving the figure. In fact, Bowsher wrote, use of the line-item veto most likely would have yielded "substantially" lower savings — and might actually have resulted in increased spending. [4]

Today, the debate over how much spending — if any — will be eliminated under the line-item veto continues to be shaped by speculative assumptions rather than concrete facts. House Speaker Newt Gingrich, R-Ga., has predicted savings of $10 billion a year, while other congressional supporters speak more modestly of savings in the range of a few billion dollars a year. President Clinton vowed in a letter to Congress in 1995 that he would use the item veto if the power was granted to him. But a senior White House aide who attended a law school symposium on the subject in April said privately that budget officials expected little if any use of the item veto in the immediate future, according to one of the participants.

Proponents of the line-item veto insist that congressional appropriations bills are rife with unjustifiable pork-barrel spending. In its recent compilation, *The 1997 Congressional Pig Book,* Citizens Against Government Waste claims to have found more than $14.5 billion in "pork" in the 13 appropriations measures for fiscal 1997. [5]

The list includes, for example, 14 agricultural research items totaling about $8.5 billion that the group says the administration did not include in its budget request and tried to block during congressional consideration. The group also lists a host of energy and transportation projects, many of them added by lawmakers of both parties who serve on the House or Senate Appropriations committees, as well as $8.9 billion in defense spending, mostly on military construction projects.

"We've been able to identify billions of dollars of this kind of spending," says Campi, a former aide to a Republican House member. "This kind of spending goes in at the last minute. Most members don't even know about it, much less the public."

Some other groups working to control the budget deficit, however, minimize the significance of the line-item veto. Martha Phillips, executive director of the Concord Coalition, a bipartisan balanced-budget advocacy group founded in 1992, says the impact is likely to be "exceedingly modest."

"We have never thought that squeezing out waste, fraud and abuse — or even pork-barrel spending — is the answer to deficit reduction," Phillips says.

"As a taxpayer, you don't want to see your money wasted on projects

President Finally Gets the 'Veto' . . .

At least 11 presidents since the Civil War have asked Congress for the power to reject individual spending items in appropriations bills: Ulysses S. Grant, Rutherford B. Hayes, Chester A. Arthur, Franklin D. Roosevelt, Harry S Truman, Dwight D. Eisenhower, Richard M. Nixon, Gerald R. Ford, Ronald Reagan, George Bush and Bill Clinton. Members of Congress from both parties have joined to defeat or block line-item veto proposals until last year, when Congress passed the Line Item Veto Act.

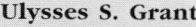

Ulysses S. Grant

A constitutional amendment to permit the president to veto individual parts of any bill, Grant said, "would protect the public against the many abuses and waste of public moneys which creep into appropriations bills and other measures passing during the expiring hours of Congress, to which otherwise due consideration can not be given."
(Dec. 1, 1873)

Rep. Robert M. McLane, D-Md.

"I understand very well that the Executive is called upon from time to time to make recommendations to Congress. . . . But I also understand that when the Executive makes these recommendations . . . he ought not to criticize the legislation of the country in a way to place the legislators at a discredit."
(House floor debate, River and Harbor Appropriations Bill, Feb. 28, 1883)

Franklin D. Roosevelt

"A respectable difference of opinion exists as to whether [an] item veto power could be given to the president by legislation or whether a constitutional amendment would be necessary," Roosevelt wrote in his annual budget message. "I strongly recommend that the present Congress adopt whichever course it may deem to be the correct one."
(Jan. 3, 1938)

Rep. Fontaine M. Maverick, D-Texas

"It is said the single-item veto is intended to stop pork-barrel practices, but, as a matter of fact, the Executive can use it to dominate Congress completely and more or less make us a sort of company union of messenger boys."
(House floor debate, Jan. 11, 1938)

Dwight D. Eisenhower

"I strongly urge the House," Eisenhower wrote Speaker Sam Rayburn, D-Texas, "to help assure continuing economy on the part of Congress as well as the executive branch, [to] take action which will grant the president the power now held by many state governors to veto specific items in appropriation bills."
(April 18, 1957)

Rep. Clarence A. Cannon, D-Mo.

"[T]he item-veto on appropriation bills would be tantamount to permitting the president to tell the Congress what to include in appropriation bills. It would in substance let the Executive appropriate rather than the Legislative."
(House Judiciary subcommittee hearing, May 27, 1957)

that aren't efficacious," Phillips adds. "If an item veto helps prevent that, that's all well and good. But that's not the answer to deficit reduction."

Independent budget experts also minimize the possibility of any significant spending reductions from the line-item veto. "The impact on the deficit was always going to be relatively small," says Stanley Collender, a former congressional budget committee staffer and now director of the federal budget consulting group at Burson-Marsteller, a lobbying-public relations firm.

"With respect to the overall deficit, you'd probably need an electron microscope to find the impact," says Robert D. Reischauer, a senior fellow

. . . After a Century-long Fight with Congress

Ronald Reagan

"As governor [of California], I found this 'line-item veto' was a powerful tool against wasteful or extravagant spending," Reagan said in his 1984 State of the Union address. "It works in 43 states. Let us put it to work in Washington for all the people."
(Jan. 25, 1984)

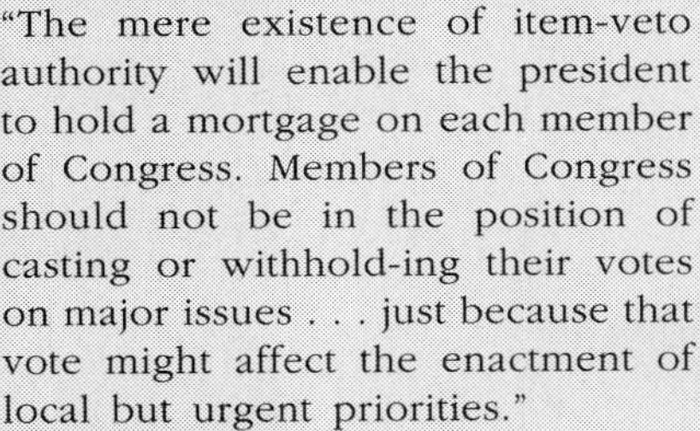

Sen. Mark O. Hatfield, R-Ore.
"The mere existence of item-veto authority will enable the president to hold a mortgage on each member of Congress. Members of Congress should not be in the position of casting or withhold-ing their votes on major issues . . . just because that vote might affect the enactment of local but urgent priorities."
(Senate floor debate, July 22, 1985)

George Bush
"I call upon Congress to adopt a measure that will help put an end to the annual ritual of filling the budget with pork-barrel appropriations," Bush said in his 1992 State of the Union address. "Give me the same thing 43 governors have — the line-item veto — and let me help you control spending."
(Jan. 28, 1992)

Sen. Robert C. Byrd, D-W.Va.
"[W]e, as members of the legislative branch, should oppose any proposal to shift the power over the purse from the legislative to the executive branch. Why? Because it would radically unbalance the delicate system of checks and balances that are the very heart of our republican form of government."
(Senate floor debate, Feb. 27, 1992)

Bill Clinton

"If the members of Congress from both parties are serious about cutting the deficit, give me this line-item veto, and I will get started right away," Clinton said in a prepared statement issued after the House had passed a line-item veto and the Senate was considering its own version. "This is one area where both parties can, and should, come together."
(March 20, 1995)

Sen. Robert C. Byrd, D-W.Va.
"The so-called Line-Item Veto Act should be more appropriately labeled 'The President Always Wins Bill.' . . . It is difficult to imagine why this body would want to deal such a painful blow, not only to itself, but to this basic structure of our constitutional form of government and to the interests of the people we represent."
(Senate floor debate, March 27, 1996)

Graphic by Sarah M. Magner

at the Brookings Institution and former head of the Congressional Budget Office.

Both Collender and Reischauer stress that even if appropriations bills contain dubious spending items, presidents may be reluctant to use the power.

"There is this desire to maintain civil relations between the president and Congress," Reischauer says. "Full-blown exercise of the line-item veto is not likely to do that."

Collender and some other observers even predict that the line-item veto could backfire by increasing pork-barrel spending through a new form of log-rolling between the White House and Congress. "The president says, 'If

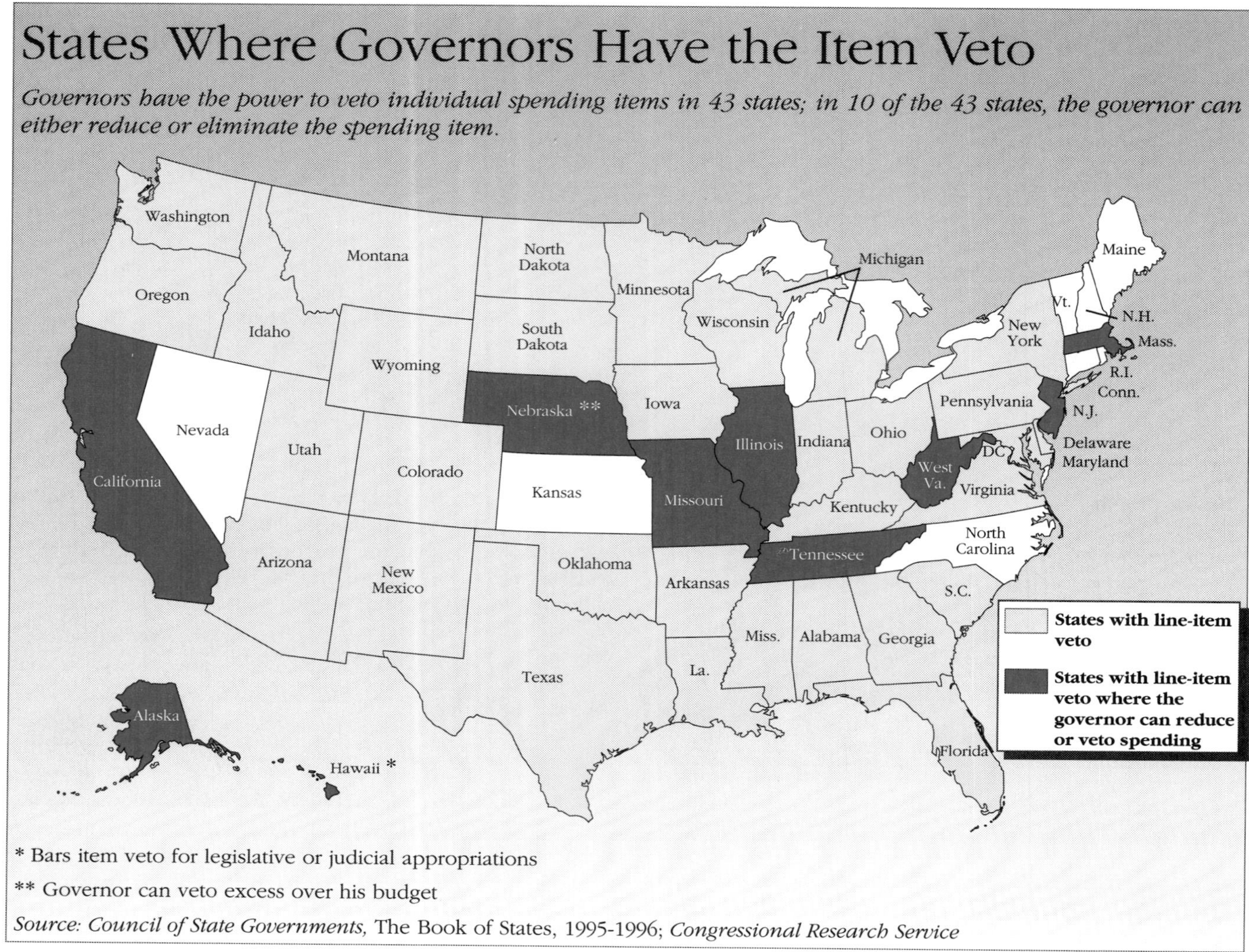

Source: Council of State Governments, The Book of States, 1995-1996; *Congressional Research Service*

you vote for my Supreme Court nominee, I won't veto your project,'" Collender explains. "You'll end up trading dollars for votes on other things."

Still, proponents insist that the item veto would improve accountability whatever its ultimate impact on federal spending. "The line-item veto reduces the power of individual congressmen to bury their projects in an entire bill," says Ronald Rotunda, a conservative law professor at the University of Illinois. Without the veto, Rotunda says, "we've got money spent that neither the president nor a majority of Congress want to spend, but they're not given the choice" to eliminate it.

Is the Line Item Veto Act unconstitutional?

When President Reagan urged Congress to pass a line-item veto, he said it would be "better" if it were adopted through a constitutional amendment. Some conservatives were arguing at the time, however, that the Constitution already gave the president power to block individual spending items. The Justice Department rejected the theory. "Article I of the Constitution does not vest the president with the inherent power to veto portions of a bill while signing the remainder of it into law," the department's Office of Legal Counsel concluded (*see p. 544*).

The Line Item Veto Act poses a subtler constitutional issue: whether Congress, by statute, can delegate to the president the power to "cancel" an individual spending item in a bill he has already signed into law. Many political and legal experts say the law is blatantly unconstitutional. But a seemingly growing number of legal experts, are predicting the law may pass constitutional muster, including some who oppose the line-item veto on policy grounds.

"The proposal's most likely constitutional," says Johnny Killian, senior specialist in American constitutional law at the Library of Congress. "It's an exercise by Congress of its power to delegate. It's a typical delegation in the sense that Congress has provided standards. That's the only thing that the Supreme Court has required, and it hasn't required very much."

"The president is being given criteria" for exercising the veto, agrees Neil Devins, a constitutional law professor at the College of William and Mary law school in Williamsburg, Va. "And the fact that the money has to go into the 'lockbox' creates a limitation on the delegation."

Experts who view the law as unconstitutional maintain that it gives the president a legislative power that the Constitution explicitly gives to Congress, not the chief executive. "He's literally rewriting the law," says Gerhardt at Case Western Reserve.

These experts also insist that the "delegation" of power in the line-item veto law is completely different from other provisions giving the president power to carry out congressionally approved functions.

"What's unique about the line-item veto," says Lawrence Lessig, a law professor at the University of Chicago, "is that the relationship between the president's means and Congress' ends is basically negation. It's basically saying, 'I'm not going to do what you say here.' And that is not a relationship that fits between any means-end relationship."

As for the criteria in the line-item veto law, Lessig dismisses them as "just formulaic."

Apart from the specifics of the legislation, those who view the law as unconstitutional also say that it overrides the separation of powers that is central to the constitutional framework for the government.

"It's increasing the president's policy-making role at the expense of Congress' policy-making role in an area that is constitutionally committed to Congress," Lessig says.

But some proponents of the law insist that it actually gives Congress more rather than less power in conflicts with the president over spending issues. They contend that the president has the power under the Constitution to "impound" money appropriated by Congress and that the line-item veto law puts a limit on that power.

"The impoundment authority gave the president authority to decide not just the whole amount or zero, but any amount in-between," says Michael B. Rappaport, an assistant law professor at the University of San Diego and a former Justice Department official in the Reagan administration. "This gives the president less authority. If you think that impoundment authority is legal, then it's odd to say this is illegal because it's narrower."

Will the federal budget deficit be controllable if the line-item veto is struck down?

A little over a year after enactment of the Line Item Veto Act, President Clinton and Republican congressional leaders reached another bipartisan milestone in budget politics: agreement on a plan designed to balance the federal budget by 2002. Administration officials and GOP lawmakers hailed the May 2 accord — combining unspecified reductions in entitlements, domestic spending curbs and tax cuts — as "historic."

In the many hours of White House and Capitol Hill briefings that day, the line-item veto went unmentioned — mute testimony to its apparent insignificance in bringing the federal budget deficit under control. "This budget deal is happening with or without the line-item veto," says budget expert Collender. "You're going to get more deficit reduction by far [under the agreement] than you ever would with the line-item veto."

The budget deal came after intensive negotiations, conducted largely behind closed doors, between Clinton's newly assembled budget team — headed by Chief of Staff Erskine Bowles, OMB Director Franklin D. Raines and Gene Sperling, deputy assistant to the president for economic policy — and the leaders of the House and Senate Budget committees. But the deal was only the first step. Most of the details remained to be filled in by legislative committees that were not party to the negotiations. And even the broad outlines of the agreement were questioned by maverick lawmakers in both parties and by a number of political observers and budget experts (*see p. 546*).

The five-year plan calls for $58 billion in unspecified domestic program cuts, to be offset by about $34 billion in new spending urged by the Clinton administration, and about $85 billion in unspecified military spending cuts. It envisions $115 billion in savings in Medicare — the government health insurance program for the elderly — and about $16 billion in savings in federal spending on Medicaid, the health insurance program for the indigent. And it calls for $135 billion in tax cuts over five years — including the administration's child tax credit and some Republican-backed reductions in capital gains and estates taxes. The tax cuts would be offset by about $50 billion in revenue enhancements from renewing expired taxes and closing loopholes.

In the next few days, the plan drew predictable reactions: Republicans and conservative advocacy groups viewed the spending and tax cuts as too modest; Democrats and liberal organizations called the domestic spending cuts inequitable and the tax cuts unnecessary and regressive. But observers from across the political spectrum joined in faulting the budget negotiators for failing to tackle what they described as the looming, long-term budget problem: the prospect of dramatically increasing entitlement bills in the next century as retiring baby boomers increase the demands on Social Security and Medicare.

The plan "does very, very little to solve the structural problems of changing demographics that will send our entitlement payments for the middle-class far beyond the ability of working-age citizens to pay for them," says Phillips of the Concord Coalition. "That hasn't even been addressed."

"Is it significant and substantial deficit reduction? The answer is no," says James Thurber, director of the Center for Congressional and Presidential Studies at American University in Washington. "The real issue is mandatory spending in the 'out' years, beyond 2002. All the predictions show that [the deficit] starts climbing back up after then."

Thurber, however, says the deficit was already being brought under control before the Clinton-Congress accord. "We're getting deficit reduction primarily because of more controls over discretionary spending," he says. "We're getting it in addition because of the 1994 elections. And we're getting it because of the good performance of the economy, and that depends on the Federal Reserve" rather than Congress or the president.

Congressional expert Dennis Ippolito of Southern Methodist University in Dallas also says the prospects for deficit reduction are more favorable than some of the critics are predicting. And he says those critics are "right" but "unrealistic" in criticizing the government for putting off the entitlement problem.

"What you're asking the government to do is to solve something that everybody understands doesn't become critical for another 15 years," Ippolito says. "I would simply challenge those people to find some historical examples of when governments were able to do that." ■

BACKGROUND

Power of the Purse

The Constitution gives the power of the purse to Congress. "No money shall be drawn from the Treasury, it provides, "but in Consequence of Appropriations made by Law." [6] As James Madison wrote in *The Federalist Papers,* the "legislative department alone has access to the pockets of the people." [7] The president's spending power was not spelled out in the Constitution.

For more than a century, the president played a limited role on spending issues even within the executive branch. [8] Until 1921, the president did not submit a unified budget to Congress for its consideration. Instead, each department or agency sent its budget request directly to Congress.

Despite the limited role in initiating budget requests, presidents early on established the practice on occasion of authorizing spending on their own or withholding expenditures approved by Congress. President Thomas Jefferson, for example, withheld money Congress appropriated in 1803 to buy gunboats to patrol the Mississippi River. Four years later, he authorized military spending after British gunships fired on a U.S. craft. Congress did not protest on either occasion.

Congress also had no effective centralized budget process until after the Civil War, when the growth of federal spending prompted both the Senate and the House to create appropriations committees to handle spending bills. [9] The increase in federal spending on public works projects also led lawmakers to try to steer money to their own states or districts. Presidents Ulysses S. Grant and Chester A. Arthur both protested congressional parochialism on federal river and harbor improvements projects.

Grant was the first president, in 1873, to ask Congress to approve a line-item veto constitutional amendment. After Congress failed to act on the proposal, Grant vowed three years later to unilaterally block congressionally approved expenditures on river and harbor projects that he viewed as "purely of private or local interest" rather than "national" concern.

Six years later, Arthur vetoed a public works bill while complaining about lawmakers' penchant for including dubious public works projects. When citizens from one state learned that money was being used elsewhere, they insisted on projects for themselves. "Thus," Arthur said, "as the bill becomes more objectionable it secures more support." [10]

The growth of federal spending in the 20th century forced both the president and Congress to seek greater control over the budget. In 1921, Congress passed the Budget and Accounting Act, requiring the president to submit a unified budget to Congress and creating the Bureau of the Budget — predecessor of the current OMB. Congress tried after World War II to devise its own procedure for creating a unified legislative budget, but the effort was less than successful.

Meanwhile, Congress and the president were coming into conflict more often on specific spending items. Presidents Harry S Truman and John F. Kennedy both refused to spend defense funds appropriated by Congress that the administration had opposed. President Lyndon B. Johnson in 1966 said he would withhold some federal spending on anti-inflation grounds, though he released much of the money the next year in the face of criticism from the states. These precedents helped prompt President Richard M. Nixon to assert a broader authority to impound money

Continued on p. 541

Chronology

Before 1900

Congress and the president begin to sort out their respective powers over spending.

1787
Constitution gives Congress primary power over spending by national government; president's powers are not spelled out.

1873
President Ulysses S. Grant asks Congress to approve constitutional amendment to permit president to reject individual budget items.

1901-1950

President's budget power grows as federal spending on defense and social welfare grows.

1921
Congress approves Budget and Accounting Act, requiring president to submit unified budget to lawmakers each year.

1938
President Franklin D. Roosevelt asks Congress to approve "item veto" for president. House approves proposal by voice vote.

1951-1970

Federal spending continues to grow, as do conflicts between Congress and president.

1957
President Dwight D. Eisenhower urges Congress to approve "item veto," but proposal does not advance beyond hearings.

1970s

Congress acts to control presidential "impoundments" and put its own budget process in order.

1972
President Richard M. Nixon asserts broad power to "impound" funds appropriated by Congress.

1974
Congressional Budget and Impoundment Control Act establishes new budget procedure in Congress; act also bars president from suspending or terminating federal programs except by rescission legislation approved by Congress.

1980s

Federal budget deficit soars under President Ronald Reagan, who calls for line-item veto and balanced-budget constitutional amendment.

1984
Reagan asks for line-item veto in State of the Union address.

1985
Senate Majority Leader Bob Dole, R-Kan., drops effort to bring line-item veto constitutional amendment to vote.

1990s

Modified line-item veto is enacted and promptly challenged as unconstitutional.

1992
President George Bush and Democratic nominee Bill Clinton both endorse line-item veto in presidential campaign.

1993
House passes bill to force vote on presidential requests for rescissions; measure dies in Senate.

1994
More than 300 Republican candidates for House endorse line-item veto as part of "Contract With America."

Feb. 6, 1995
Republican-controlled House passes legislative line-item veto — or enhanced rescissions — bill, 294-134.

March 23, 1995
Senate passes a form of line-item veto bill requiring items in appropriations bills to be unbundled and separately enrolled for president to sign or veto.

March 1996
House and Senate conferees agree on bill along lines passed by House and send measure to president for his signature.

April 9, 1996
President Clinton signs Line Item Veto Act.

Jan. 2, 1997
Sen. Robert C. Byrd, D-W.Va., and five other lawmakers file suit challenging line-item veto.

April 10, 1997
U.S. District Judge Thomas Penfield Jackson rules line-item veto unconstitutional.

May 27, 1997
Supreme Court hears arguments in *Raines v. Byrd;* decision is due before justices' summer recess.

States Report Varied Experiences With 'Veto'

Gov. Tommy G. Thompson, R-Wis., says he used the line-item veto to knock out $143 million in spending and nearly $1.5 billion in taxes during his first eight years in office. His Republican colleague in Massachusetts, William F. Weld, says he has used his line-item veto more than 1,000 times while doing battle with a Democratic-controlled legislature.

Ronald Reagan cited his use of the line-item veto as governor of California in pushing hard for the proposal while in the White House. When he signed the Line Item Veto Act into law last year, Bill Clinton claimed the power had helped him as governor of Arkansas to balance the state's budget.

In most of the 43 states with a line-item veto, however, the governor's power to kill spending items "is not used at all," according to political scientist Neil Berch.

"There is very little effect on overall spending," says Berch, an assistant professor at West Virginia University in Morgantown. "Even in extreme cases, you're dealing with maybe 2 percent of the state budget."

Instead, Berch says, governors use the line-item veto most often to impose their own political priorities on the legislature or to impose political retribution on individual lawmakers. "The governor uses it to punish legislators," Berch says.

By all accounts, the combative Thompson holds the individual record for invoking the line-item veto. He told a Senate Judiciary subcommittee two years ago that he had exercised the "partial veto" provided in the state constitution more than 1,500 times on 81 separate pieces of legislation. Among the legislative provisions Thompson boasted of killing were "special tax loopholes for windmills" and "funding to clean a statue in a specific park in one of Wisconsin's cities." [1] But Thompson also said he used his power on bigger-ticket items, like a $500 million tax increase. And the state constitution allowed him to wield his partial-veto pen on non-budget items as well.

Other Republican chief executives have also used their line-item vetoes on big budget items in addition to individual pork-barrel programs or projects. Weld told the Senate Governmental Affairs Committee that he used his line-item veto to cut a pay raise for state employees and to reduce welfare payments under the state's "general assistance" program. [2] In Michigan, Republican Gov. John Engler credits the line-item veto with allowing him to cut $1.7 billion in spending — including an entire state department. [3]

But other Republican governors have made far less use of the line-item veto. Rep. Michael N. Castle, who served as governor of Delaware, says he used the power "only a few times." [4] In New Jersey, Christine Todd Whitman exercised the power about 15 times in her first year in office, but with little fiscal impact.

Clinton himself appears to have an exaggerated recollection of the importance of the line-item veto in his years in the Arkansas statehouse. Despite Clinton's statement when he signed the federal law, he is reported to have used the line-item veto during his almost 11 years as governor fewer than 10 times. [5]

In his research, Berch examined the impact of the line-item veto on the rate of growth in welfare and highway construction spending over a 16-year period, 1970-1986. He concluded the line-item veto had no effect on welfare spending and only slight impact on the growth in highway construction expenditures. [6]

In an earlier study, two proponents of the item veto — W. Mark Crain, a professor at George Mason University in Fairfax, Va., and James C. Miller III, President Reagan's former budget director and now president of Citizens for a Sound Economy — concluded that the procedure has somewhat greater impact. They said that when budget figures were controlled for other factors, the veto cut the rate of growth in spending from 2.8 percent to 1 percent. [7] But Crain and Miller acknowledge that the impact is felt mostly in the minority of states where the governor has the power to reduce a spending figure, rather than having to choose between approving the spending item or eliminating it altogether.

Most experts agree with the narrower view of the line-item veto's impact. Berch notes that one reason for the limited impact is that legislatures in most states are required to balance the budget. Thus, the governor has little incentive to use the power for purposes of fiscal restraint.

The differences between budget procedures in the states and those in Washington caution against using the states' experiences to predict how the federal law will play out. As for the states themselves, Berch predicts that the item veto will prove to have even less impact in the future.

"The big change in states is that they're taking on so much of the federal responsibility, and most of that is not pork-barrel stuff," Berch says. "My guess is that if anything it will have less impact in states in coming years."

[1] Senate Judiciary Subcommittee on the Constitution, Federalism, and Property Rights, "The Line-Item Veto: A Constitutional Approach," 104th Congress, 1st session, Jan. 24, 1995, pp. 87-88.

[2] Senate Committee on Governmental Affairs, S. 4 and S. 14, Line-Item Veto, 104th Congress, 1st session, Feb. 23, 1995, pp. 76-78.

[3] *The Wall Street Journal,* Nov. 15, 1995, p. A22.

[4] House Committee on Government Reform and Oversight, and Senate Committee on Governmental Affairs, Line-Item Veto, 104th Congress, 1st session, Jan. 12, 1995, pp. 33-35.

[5] See Paul Magnusson, "Put This Budget Scalpel in the President's Hands," *Business Week,* April 3, 1995, p. 50. Magnusson says Clinton used the veto nine times; Rep. Castle put the figure at eight in his testimony to the joint congressional committee hearing.

[6] Neil Berch, "The Item Veto in the States: An Analysis of the Effects Over Time," *The Social Science Journal,* spring 1992, pp. 335-346.

[7] W. Mark Crain and James C. Miller III, "Budget Process and Spending Growth," *William and Mary Law Review,* spring 1990, pp. 1021-1046.

Continued from p. 538

approved by Congress — touching off a bitter constitutional conflict that resulted in new controls on presidential power and new budget procedures in Congress itself.

Nixon's Impoundments

Nixon withheld billions of dollars in domestic spending approved by Congress by claiming a broad presidential impoundment power that he and his supporters traced to Jefferson. Critics in Congress and elsewhere, however, insisted that the president had gone beyond previous practice in asserting a right to substitute his judgment for that of Congress on spending issues. [11]

Nixon, a Republican, confronted a Democratic-controlled Congress that challenged him on a variety of domestic, economic and foreign policy issues, including his policies in the Vietnam War. As he campaigned for re-election in 1972, Nixon blamed Congress for profligate spending and called for a budget ceiling of $250 billion. The House and the Senate agreed on the overall ceiling, but could not agree on the details. After the election, however, Nixon relied on the spending ceiling to justify withholding billions of dollars in funds Congress had appropriated in such areas as farm programs, public housing and aid to local water- and sewer-treatment plants.

In many instances, Nixon acted in the face of statutory language that appeared to require him to allot the appropriated funds. In one case, Nixon withheld over a three-year period half of the $18 billion that Congress had approved under the Federal Water Pollution Control Act Amendments of 1972 — a bill that Congress enacted over Nixon's veto.

Several lower federal courts ruled Nixon had exceeded his authority. In 1975, the Supreme Court agreed. But the ruling was closely tied to the clean water law and, in the eyes of Nixon's sympathizers, left unresolved the question whether the president has the power to impound funds in the absence of congressional directive. [12]

While losing in the courts, Nixon had put Congress on the defensive. Lawmakers in both houses recognized a need to establish a more orderly budget process to regain control from the president over spending priorities. A joint study committee in 1973 recommended that each house create a separate budget committee to set overall spending ceilings that would be adopted in a joint budget resolution to be acted on before actual appropriations measures. The proposal, which also called for moving the start of the fiscal year from July 1 to Oct. 1, moved through Congress in 1973 and 1974 as Nixon found himself entangled in the Watergate scandal.

Lawmakers also saw the bill as a vehicle for restricting presidential impoundments. In its final form, the bill provided that the president could curtail total spending or terminate a program only by asking Congress to rescind its earlier action appropriating the funds. Without rescission legislation, the president would have to spend the money. The House and the Senate gave final approval to the measure, entitled the Congressional Budget and Impoundment Control Act, in June 1974. Nixon signed the measure on July 12, only four weeks before he resigned from office to avoid impeachment.

Hopes that the new budget procedure would result in either orderly or disciplined congressional spending policies have proved somewhat illusory. Congress often fails to pass the budget resolution by April 15, as the procedure requires.

More important, federal budget deficits rose in the years immediately after enactment of the change and remained persistently high through the 1980s.

Critics of congressional spending view the 1974 act — with its reassertion of congressional prerogatives — itself as a cause of the deficits. "The era of runaway spending and deficits began right there," *The Wall Street Journal* said in a recent editorial. [13] But observers more sympathetic to Congress say the budget process has in fact helped control deficits that resulted from other causes.

"All of the modern industrial democracies wound up with structural deficits in the 1980s for the same reasons — expansion of social insurance programs and the assumption of economic growth that didn't occur," Ippolito says. "What [the budget procedure] has allowed us to do, under Ronald Reagan and George Bush, is to ratchet those deficits down to a point where they're not very significant anymore."

Reagan's Deficits

President Reagan presided over record peacetime federal budget deficits that nearly tripled the national debt in eight years. At the same time, he pushed — unsuccessfully — for two constitutional amendments aimed at controlling the federal budget: a line-item veto and a so-called balanced-budget amendment. [14]

Reagan inherited a deficit of $79 billion from his Democratic predecessor, Jimmy Carter. The deficit jumped to $128 billion in Reagan's first full year in office, thanks to increased defense spending and a first-year tax cut. Despite a series of tax increases, the deficit continued to rise to a peak of $221.2 billion in 1986.

As journalists George Hager and Eric Pianin note in their new book on federal budget policies, Reagan backed away on two pivotal occasions from politically dangerous moves to challenge the deficit. [15] In drawing up the first Reagan budget in 1981, Reagan's top adviser, Edwin L. Meese III, overrode the opposition of Budget Director David A. Stockman to declare Social Security, Medicare and five other social welfare programs safe from any cuts.

Then in 1985, Reagan pulled the rug out from under Senate Republicans after they had pushed through by the narrowest of margins a $33 billion deficit-reduction plan that included a politically explosive freeze in cost-of-living increases in Social Security benefits. After the proposal reached the House, Reagan changed his mind on the plan, and it died. [16]

Instead of actual budget cuts, Reagan called for constitutional cures to the deficit problem. Beginning in his 1984 State of the Union message, Reagan repeatedly urged Congress to approve a line-item veto. "It works in 43 states," Reagan said, referring to the number of states that allow governors to veto budget items. "Let us put it to work in Washington for all the people." In the same address, he also urged Congress to pass a constitutional amendment requiring a balanced budget unless deficit spending was approved by a two-thirds majority in each house of Congress.

Neither of the budget changes won approval in Congress while Reagan or his Republican successor George Bush was in the White House. In 1985, for example, then-Senate GOP Leader Bob Dole of Kansas brought the line-item veto proposal to the floor but could not muster the 60 votes needed to cut off a filibuster. Among those leading the filibuster were West Virginia Democrat Robert C. Byrd and Oregon Republican Mark O. Hatfield, two of the plaintiffs in the suit challenging the current line-item veto law.

Later in 1985, however, Congress approved a different approach to deficit reduction: the Gramm-Rudman-Hollings law. The act — named after GOP cosponsors Phil Gramm of Texas and Warren B. Rudman of New Hampshire and South Carolina Democrat Ernest F. Hollings — sought to impose gradually declining deficit ceilings in order to reach a balanced budget by 1990.

The plan was politically and constitutionally controversial. Although the law survived a constitutional challenge largely intact, it proved to have less force than expected. "Congress and the White House conspired to ignore the deficit targets," Hager and Pianin note. And to avoid spending cuts in 1988, Congress simply extended the deadline for a balanced budget to 1993.

Meanwhile, frustrated line-item veto supporters were urging Reagan and later Bush to claim an inherent authority to excise individual spending items without a constitutional amendment or congressional statute. The theory — first aired prominently in an op-ed article in *The Wall Street Journal* in December 1987 — relied on an interpretation of the Constitution's provision requiring that "every order, resolution, or vote" requiring approval by both houses of Congress "shall be presented" to the president for approval or disapproval. [17]

Glazier argued that the provision meant that any individual spending item was subject to the same kind of presidential veto over bills approved by Congress. But the Justice Department rejected the theory in an exhaustive legal opinion in July 1988. "Historically, 'bills' have been made by Congress to include more than one subject," Charles J. Cooper, then head of the department's Office of Legal Counsel, wrote in the opinion, "and no president has viewed such instruments as constituting more than one bill for purposes of the veto." [18]

Bush's Gamble

President Bush followed Reagan in urging Congress to approve a line-item veto and in declining to claim such power without congressional action. Like Reagan, he also pushed unsuccessfully for a balanced-budget constitutional amendment. Unlike Reagan, however, Bush also staked his personal prestige and political fortune on a concrete deficit-reduction plan. [19]

Under pressure from congressional Democrats, Bush in June 1990 backed off his 1988 campaign pledge never to raise taxes. Then, White House and congressional leaders negotiated a budget agreement in an 11-day summit held at Andrews Air Force Base, outside Washington. The late-September agreement included tax increases, gradually reduced caps on spending and new congressional procedures that set up a so-called "firewall" between defense and domestic discretionary spending. Although the agreement failed in the House, a hastily assembled substitute along similar lines won approval from Congress in late October. [20]

Today, the 1990 budget deal is given credit for substantial deficit reduction: about $482 billion of the $500 billion originally claimed by negotiators. The new budget procedures have also imposed a straitjacket on congressional spending by making it impossible to shift defense spending cuts over to domestic programs.

Bush, however, paid a heavy price. He never recovered the standing he lost among Republican conservatives or the general public by going back on his no-new-taxes pledge. Campaigning for reelection with a sour economy, Bush lost in 1992 to a five-term Democratic governor from Arkansas, Bill Clinton.

Congressional Passage

As a presidential candidate in 1992, Clinton echoed Bush in urging enactment of a line-item veto. Clinton called it "one of the most powerful

Impact on Tax Breaks May Be Limited

Former Sen. Bill Bradley, D-N.J., opposed the line-item veto when he entered Congress in 1981, but he switched positions in 1992 after watching years of soaring deficits and rampant pork-barreling on Capitol Hill. Bradley, who retired at the end of the last Congress, insisted, however, that the line-item veto should extend not only to traditional congressional pork-barrel spending but also to special-interest tax breaks.

"Whatever line-item veto bill we approve must authorize the president to veto wasteful spending not just in appropriations bills, but also in the Tax Code," Bradley told a Senate Governmental Affairs Committee hearing on Feb. 23, 1995. Otherwise, Bradley continued, "we would simply find the special-interest lobbyists who work the appropriations process simply turning themselves into tax lobbyists and pushing for the same kind of spending through the Tax Code."

Some line-item veto supporters, such as Sen. John McCain, R-Ariz., were lukewarm at best toward the added provision. But they acceded to the political appeal of giving the president power to close tax loopholes.

Still, the tax-benefit provision included in the Line Item Veto Act that Congress and President Clinton finally approved last year is far more limited than Bradley and others envisioned. The law authorizes the president to cancel a newly enacted revenue-losing provision — tax exemption, deduction or credit — only if it is a permanent change that affects 100 or fewer taxpayers or a transitional rule that affects 10 or fewer taxpayers in any fiscal year.

In a further limitation, the provision would not apply to a tax break that provided equal treatment for all companies or individuals engaged in the same industry or activity. Thus, the president could not knock out a tax provision affecting five companies if those were the only companies in a given line of work.

As the law was nearing enactment, tax-writers and tax lawyers braced for significant changes. Kenneth Kies, chief of staff of Congress' Joint Tax Committee, warned the proposal would make it "more difficult" to enact narrow tax provisions "no matter how meritorious they might be." [1] But today several leading tax experts, including a longtime tax reform advocate, say the provision is likely to have slight impact at most.

"I thought it was basically window-dressing," says Robert McIntyre, director of Citizens for Tax Justice. "It would be hard to find its use in any significant number of cases."

Donald Alexander, who served as commissioner of the Internal Revenue Service from 1973 to 1977, agrees. He says the once-common practice in Congress of inserting special tax breaks benefiting only a handful of taxpayers into big revenue bills has largely disappeared.

"It doesn't happen much any more," Alexander says. "I think the [tax-writing] committees are very nervous about helping out only one or two taxpayers."

While the line-item veto bill was moving through Congress, however, Kies prepared a memorandum listing 11 tax provisions in the Balanced Budget Act of 1995 that would have fallen within the act's definition if it had been on the books at the time. The provisions included, for example, an extension of a tax credit for pharmaceutical companies for testing and manufacturing so-called "orphan drugs" for certain rare diseases.

The tax-benefit provision got little attention as the line-item veto bill moved through Congress. Clinton mentioned it only briefly when he signed the law on April 9, 1996. And when the administration defended the law before the Supreme Court last month, Acting Solicitor General Walter Dellinger described the provision as "quite minor."

One of the justices, however, was particularly troubled by the discretion the law gives to the president in deciding what tax benefits to cut out. "What do we do about the fact that it says that the president can simply set aside a tax law, any tax law that affects fewer than a certain number of people?" Justice Stephen G. Breyer asked Dellinger. "I mean, how is there a sufficient intelligible principle for that?"

Even if the law is upheld, Alexander says tax lawyers will learn to work around the definitions in the act — for example, by making sure that any limited tax provision benefits more than 100 taxpayers. "Bring in some other folks," Alexander says, "just enough to get over 100."

In his argument, Dellinger himself anticipated the likelihood that tax-writers' ingenuity would triumph over the provision. "We may never see a limited tax benefit" that the line-item veto applies to, Dellinger said.

[1] Quoted in *The Wall Street Journal,* March 27, 1996, p. A1.

---

weapons we could use in our fight against out-of-control deficit spending" and estimated it could save $2 billion a year. But Byrd vowed to keep up his fight against the idea even with a Democrat in the White House.

"I'm opposed to any legislation that would diminish the Congress' constitutional role with respect to the power of the purse," Byrd said just two weeks after Clinton's popular-vote victory. [21]

Clinton did move toward congressional Democrats by endorsing a so-called enhanced rescissions proposal — requiring Congress to vote on presidential requests to rescind appropriations — as an alternative to a line-item veto. Twice, the Democratic-controlled House passed such proposals, in April 1993 and July 1994. But the Senate let both bills languish. And Republican-backed line-item veto proposals failed in both chambers. McCain tried to attach a line-item veto to a White House-backed bill aimed at increasing voter registration in March 1993, but he lost on a largely party-line vote of 45-52. Similarly, the House in July 1994 rejected a GOP line-item veto proposal, 205-218.

Republicans Capture Congress

Then, in the fall, House GOP candidates included the line-item veto in their 10-point campaign charter, the "Contract With America." After capturing control of both the House and the Senate, Republicans in both chambers moved on the issue with dispatch — though not in accord.

The House acted first, approving a so-called modified legislative line-item veto on Feb. 6, 1995 — which Republicans emphasized was Reagan's 84th birthday. House Speaker Gingrich said the measure "would allow the president to cut out some of the worst of the spending, to set some fiscal discipline." Seventy-one Democrats joined 223 Republicans in the 294-134 vote for the bill, which gave the president power after signing a bill to rescind spending items as well as targeted tax breaks unless Congress acted to block the cuts within 20 days.

The Senate adopted a very different approach. After the Senate Budget Committee in February sent to the floor two different proposals to strengthen the president's rescission power, Majority Leader Dole brokered a compromise unlike any of the other plans. The proposal required items in appropriations bills and some tax and entitlement measures to be "unbundled" and sent to the president separately for him to sign or veto. It passed by a 69-29 vote on March 23, with 50 Republicans and 19 Democrats voting in favor.

After the speedy start, Republicans paused to weigh the politics of the situation. Neither chamber appointed conferees to resolve the differences between the two bills, and McCain and other supporters complained that some GOP lawmakers had lost enthusiasm for giving a Democratic president power to ax spending approved by a Republican-controlled Congress.

Meanwhile, Clinton was chiding Republicans on the issue. When he vetoed a spending measure in June, he complained that Republicans had loaded the bill with "pork-barrel" projects but were refusing to give him the line-item veto to block the spending.

"They talked about what an urgent thing it was," Clinton said. "Now they say they don't think they ought to give it to me this year because I might use it." [22]

Presidential politics ultimately intervened to break the impasse. Having clinched the GOP nomination to run against Clinton, Dole in early 1996 urged Republicans in both chambers to resolve their differences and give him a legislative victory to take into the presidential campaign. Still wary of Clinton, however, Republicans decided to delay the new presidential budget power until after the next president was sworn in.

Byrd maintained his opposition to the end, warning in a final speech on March 27 that Congress was about to commit "a colossal mistake" by passing what he called "the President Always Wins Bill." The speech was stirring, but changed no votes. The Senate approved the final measure 69-31; the House followed suit the next day after clearing the way for the measure to be considered on a 232-177 vote.

Clinton signed the measure in an Oval Office ceremony on April 9. "For years, presidents of both parties have pounded this very desk in frustration at having to sign necessary legislation that contained special-interest boondoggles, tax loopholes and pure pork," Clinton said. "The line-item veto will give us a chance to change that, to permit presidents to better represent the public interest by cutting waste, protecting taxpayers and balancing the budget." ■

CURRENT SITUATION

Supreme Court Test

Both before and after entering the White House, Clinton strongly backed the line-item veto as an important tool for the president to help control federal spending and reduce the budget deficit. But when the administration's top lawyer defended the Line Item Veto Act before the U.S. Supreme Court, he took a much more modest view of the law's importance and the shift in power from Congress to the chief executive. [23]

Acting Solicitor General Walter Dellinger told the justices on May 27 that despite the new law, Congress can still include provisos in any appropriations bill to force the president to spend money on budget items he personally opposes.

"A simple majority of Congress retains full authority to make mandatory any item of spending," Dellinger declared at the opening of his 35-minute argument.

But the attorney representing the lawmakers challenging the law insisted that it "fundamentally alters the federal lawmaking process" in viola-

Continued on p. 546

At Issue:

Is the Line Item Veto Act constitutional?

FROM THE GOVERNMENT'S BRIEF IN *RAINES V. BYRD*, U.S. SUPREME COURT

yes

The Line Item Veto Act gives the President conditional authority to cancel certain spending and revenue items within five days after a bill containing such items has been enacted into law. The Act is the latest in a series of statutes, dating from 1789 to the present, in which Congress has given the Executive Branch discretion over the expenditure of appropriated funds. . . .

Its title notwithstanding, the Act does not authorize the President to sign into law some provisions of an appropriations bill while "returning" other provisions to Congress. The President remains subject to the constitutional obligation to sign or return, in its entirety, an appropriations bill presented to him by Congress. His cancellation authority under the Act comes into existence only after an appropriations bill has been passed by both Houses of Congress and approved, *in toto*, by the President.

The effect of the Line Item Veto Act is to vest the President with authority to determine, in accordance with statutorily prescribed standards and procedures, whether items of spending that Congress has appropriated will in fact be spent. That grant of authority is fully consistent with historical practice. . . . The settled historical practices of Congress and the Executive Branch regarding spending discretion strongly support the political Branches' shared judgment that the Line Item Veto Act is constitutional.

This Court has repeatedly recognized that Congress may vest the Executive Branch with considerable discretion in the administration of federal laws. The Line Item Veto Act places constitutionally sufficient limits on the President's exercise of discretion over federal spending. The President must cancel items "in whole" rather than in part and must devote any cancelled amounts to deficit reduction. The Act also provides significant guidance to the President in his decision whether particular items should be cancelled.

Finally, the Line Item Veto Act does not vest the President with the power to repeal any portion of an appropriations law. This Court has repeatedly upheld federal statutes authorizing the President to suspend their provisions, grant exemptions from their requirements, or otherwise modify their operation. Like the statutes previously upheld, the Line Item Veto Act permissibly vests the President with executive rather than legislative power. The fact that the President's cancellation of a particular item is irrevocable unless overturned by Congress does not alter the constitutional analysis. Indeed, that feature of the Act limits rather than expands the scope of the President's authority.

FROM THE BRIEF FOR THE LAWMAKERS IN *RAINES V. BYRD*, U.S. SUPREME COURT *

no

Article I [of the Constitution] vests the responsibility for enacting, amending, and repealing federal statutes in two Houses of Congress. . . . Article I gives the President only a qualified check on the process: the power to veto a bill *in toto*, subject to congressional override. It denies him the power to modify the law unilaterally, either by item vetoing provisions of a bill as he signs it, so that only the portions he selects become law, or by striking and thus repealing provisions after the bill has become law. These limitations . . . preserve the constitutional role of each House of Congress and its Members in determining what federal law will be.

The [Line Item Veto] Act is an unconstitutional attempt to do indirectly what the text of Article I forbids. The Act's purpose, indicated by its title and repeatedly stated throughout its legislative history, is to give the President the line item veto power that the Constitution denies him, and that is exactly its effect. It authorizes the President to cancel items the instant after signing a bill, conceivably in the same breath (and in no event more than five days later). There is no practical difference between giving the President power to strike items at the same time he signs a bill and giving him power to strike them immediately afterwards.

The mechanism chosen to evade the *in toto* requirement is unconstitutional. To "cancel" an item is to repeal it, and the Constitution requires bicameral passage and presentment to the President for repeals of laws, no less than for enactments. The Act defines "cancel" to mean "rescind" and "prevent . . . from having legal force or effect." The effect of a cancellation under the Act is to eliminate a provision permanently and irretrievably. . . .

The Act does not . . . merely delegate in a new manner a discretionary power to decline to spend. The Act contains provisions dealing with entitlement and tax benefits to which this explanation is wholly inapplicable. Moreover, the Act gives the President a virtually unfettered power to alter statutes themselves at their enactment, not the continuing discretion to carry out the law as circumstances mandate. . . . The Act does not resemble any prior statute examined by this Court granting such discretionary power over spending (or any other activity), because its purpose is not to give the President any form of executive discretion, but rather to give him the line item veto that the Constitution denies him.

** The brief was filed on behalf of Sens. Robert C. Byrd, D-W.Va., Daniel Patrick Moynihan, D-N.Y., and Carl Levin, D-Mich., former Sen. Mark O. Hatfield, R-Ore., and Reps. David E. Skaggs, D-Colo., and Henry A. Waxman, D-Calif.*

Continued from p. 544

tion of the constitutional principle of separation of powers. The new law, veteran public-interest lawyer Alan B. Morrison declared, gives the president "the power to extinguish the law and not to enforce the law."

The administration's minimalist posture seemed to catch some of the justices by surprise. Was he contending that Congress could simply render the law "a nullity," Chief Justice William H. Rehnquist asked Dellinger.

"It could," Dellinger responded, "though we doubt that it will."

Justice Anthony M. Kennedy voiced doubts about Dellinger's stand. "It does seem to me that there is some point to the fact that it does change the legislative design," Kennedy remarked.

The new law "changes the equation to some extent," Justice Sandra Day O'Connor added. She pointed out that under the Line Item Veto Act, lawmakers would need a two-thirds majority in both houses of Congress to overcome the president's decision to disapprove a budget item.

The arguments over the law were obscured somewhat by a preliminary legal question: whether the lawmakers could challenge the law in court and — even if they could — whether the suit was nonetheless premature. In his ruling, Judge Jackson had held that the lawmakers had "standing" to bring the case because the law "infringes upon their lawmaking powers" under the Constitution.

And, Jackson said that the suit was "ripe," or not premature, even though Clinton had not yet exercised his new veto power. "[P]laintiffs now find themselves in a position of unanticipated and unwelcome subservience to the President before and after they vote on appropriation bills," Jackson wrote.

Morrison was closely questioned by the justices on both points.

"I can't think of a case in which an individual federal officer in 200 years has brought suit to claim a derogation of his powers as a federal officer," Justice Antonin Scalia told Morrison. As a federal appeals court judge in Washington, Scalia had previously written an opinion opposing the idea of granting members of Congress legal standing to challenge the constitutionality of laws. The Supreme Court had never ruled on the issue. [24]

Some other justices also voiced doubts that the lawmakers have the right to challenge a law that they unsuccessfully opposed in Congress. "So far, they're only injured by their own actions," Justice Ruth Bader Ginsburg said. "The president's done absolutely nothing."

The arguments over the standing and ripeness issues left Dellinger and Morrison with only limited time to address the second major issue in the case: whether the new law gives the president sufficient guidance in canceling budget items to qualify as a proper "delegation of authority" from Congress to the president.

Dellinger pointed to the law's provisions allowing the president to cancel a budget item if the cancellation will "reduce the federal budget deficit," "not impair any essential government functions" and "not harm the national interest."

O'Connor was openly skeptical of the provisions. "They appear to be so general that they seem to apply to anything," she told Dellinger.

Morrison tried to pick up on the issue, describing the law as giving the president "unfettered discretion" to block individual items. But his time expired as he was midway through the point.

After the arguments, Byrd and his named adversary in the case — OMB Director Raines — stood side by side as they answered reporters' questions, repeating arguments their lawyers had made in the courtroom.

"This is not a shift or delegation of authority," Byrd declared. "It is a transfer of power to the president."

But Raines insisted the law was in line with other laws passed by Congress that "limit the ability of members to spend money."

Constitutional law expert Fisher, who attended the arguments, faulted both lawyers on their performance. He said Dellinger "got off on a very ragged start by claiming that the shift in power was not very significant.

"I don't think he ever crystallized for the court why this statute, if you get to the merits, is OK," Fisher said.

But Fisher said Morrison had failed to satisfy the justices' doubts about taking on the case at all. "I think every justice was anxious, understandably anxious, about taking on cases that ought to be resolved through the political process," he said.

A Budget Deal

As the justices pondered the legal arguments in the line-item veto case, Congress and the Clinton administration were working to implement the May 2 budget agreement between the White House and GOP leaders on Capitol Hill. But the agreement was proving to be more controversial, and more difficult to put into effect, than the White House and Republican leaders originally suggested it would be.

The carefully woven budget agreement, announced on a Friday, began to unravel as soon as the critics could get to the weekend talk shows. Sen. Phil Gramm, the conservative Texas Republican, complained on CNN's "Late Edition" on May 4 that the agreement relied too much on favorable economic assumptions and too little on "fiscal restraint." On the same program, Sen. Paul Wellstone, a liberal Democrat from Minnesota, said the agreement called for excessive tax cuts and too little for education and job training.[25]

Two weeks later, more formidable opposition emerged when House Minority Leader Richard A. Gephardt, D-Mo., declared that he could not vote for the budget agreement. "This budget just isn't fair," he told a May 20 news conference.[26] But the criticisms failed to derail the accord. The House and the Senate voted to approve budget resolutions based on the agreement before going home for the Memorial Day recess — the House by a 333-99 margin in the early morning hours of May 21, the Senate by a 78-22 tally on May 23.

As lawmakers turned to translating the agreement into concrete legislation, however, differences emerged between the White House and Republican leaders on Capitol Hill. Administration officials said the agreement called for restoring welfare benefits for legal immigrants, but the House Ways and Means Committee on June 10 refused. On the same day, President Clinton denounced the GOP's tax plan offered by Ways and Means Chairman Bill Archer of Texas — which emphasized a capital gains tax cut — as violating the budget agreement. Republicans responded that the agreement allowed for more flexibility than the White House was claiming and that the administration needed to compromise with GOP lawmakers.

The disputes presaged a long summer of conflicts between the administration and congressional Republicans in shaping the final budget for the new fiscal year that begins Oct. 1. Beyond the coming year, however, many budget experts warned that the five-year plan was itself built on spending reductions that may not materialize and economic assumptions that may prove unfounded.

"No one should ever believe a five-year forecast," Collender says. "Anything beyond two years starts to approach science fiction."

With tens and hundreds of billions of dollars at stake in some of the tax and spending disputes, budget politicians were giving virtually no attention to the line-item veto. For its part, the White House was trying to play down the likelihood of confrontations with Congress on the issue.

"I believe that if the [Supreme Court] sustains the line-item veto, the president will not have to use it very much because Congress will be more restrained in its willingness to simply add [spending] provisions," OMB Director Raines said as he emerged from the high court arguments May 27.

"But if it is necessary," he continued, "I believe the president will use it to avoid needless spending. I believe that's what Congress meant when they passed this — that their own procedures were insufficient to prevent this needless spending, and they wanted to delegate it to the president." ■

OUTLOOK

Defining 'Pork'

In 18 years in the Senate until his retirement two years ago, Dennis DeConcini, an Arizona Democrat, counted himself a fiscal conservative. But he also opposed the line-item veto. When his Republican colleague, John McCain, was pushing the proposal in 1992, DeConcini argued against it by recalling the history of the Central Arizona Project, a federally financed water development project strongly supported by Arizona lawmakers of both parties.

Describing the water project as "our lifeblood," DeConcini reminded senators in the Feb. 27, 1992, debate that President Jimmy Carter had called for killing the project in 1977 along with 17 other water projects around the country. The Arizona project survived, DeConcini said, only because Congress repeatedly insisted on full funding for it. With a line-item veto, he concluded, Carter could easily have killed it along with all the others on his administration's hit list.

DeConcini's argument illustrates the difficulty of identifying pork-barrel projects in the federal budget. "One person's pork is another person's sacred cow," says budget expert Collender. "There is no generally accepted definition of pork barrel."

Moreover, as other budget experts say, trying to remove the pork-barrel instinct from Congress may be a futile exercise. "There are a lot of projects that don't make a lot of programmatic sense," says Ippolito of the University of Texas. "But beyond a certain point, it's hard to take that sort of distributional politics out of a Congress whose members are supposed to represent districts and states."

For his part, McCain insists that the Central Arizona Project survived because it was supported by members from a number of Western states. But he maintains that he is willing to hold projects in his own state to the same standard as any other. "If any project in any state, including Arizona, cannot undergo the scrutiny that all projects should undergo," McCain says, "then it shouldn't be funded."

McCain believes the line-item veto law, if upheld, will temper some lawmakers' support for dubious projects. "It will have a very cautionary effect on the pork-barrelers," he says. Collender agrees, saying the law would make Congress "more leery about doing some pork-barrel things than they have been in the past."

But Collender and other experts also say the line-item veto will complicate presidential relations with Congress. "Projects that are taken out will really upset some members," Collender says. "And other members will complain that it's not being used enough."

Opponents of the measure fear most that presidents will use the budget-cutting power not just to cut spending but to enhance their power vis-à-vis Congress across the board. "It will give the president the power to leverage, to extort legislative acts to serve his purposes," says Rep. David E. Skaggs, D-Colo., one of the plaintiffs in the court challenge. "Americans should be trembling at that prospect."

McCain, however, dismisses the likelihood of presidential abuse of the item veto. A senator has "enormous powers of retaliation" if a president tried to link approval of a specific spending item to the senator's vote on an unrelated matter, McCain says. "There's a whole range of tools that a senator has if that sort of behavior were embarked on."

For the moment, speculation about the likely impact of a line-item veto is premature. The fate of the law hangs in the balance at the Supreme Court. The court's decision in the current challenge will be known soon: The justices are due to begin their summer recess before the Fourth of July. But legal observers are offering differing predictions on whether the justices will rule on the validity of the law or postpone a resolution by holding that the lawmakers contesting the measure had no legal standing to bring their suit. [27]

For his part, McCain hopes the court will defer a decision. "I'd like to see some judicious use of the line-item veto so that the court can see the enormous use of the line-item veto in eliminating unnecessary and wasteful spending and also see that there's not some huge shift in power from Congress to the president," he says.

But House Appropriations Committee Chairman Livingston hopes the court will rule in the current case. "I would hope they would address the issue," Livingston says. "It's one that should be discussed seriously by the Supreme Court."

If the measure is struck down, some lawmakers may fall back on the alternative of separate enrollment of budget items, which the Senate approved in 1995. But that procedure would pose a host of practical as well as constitutional problems if adopted. Another option would be a line-item veto constitutional amendment, but that route would be both difficult and time-consuming.

McCain himself doubts that the issue could be revived after an adverse Supreme Court ruling. "We'd have difficulty resurrecting it," he says. "I don't think Congress would want to go through it again."

Opponents, naturally, would cheer a Supreme Court ruling to strike the law down. But, in addition, they believe that taking the line-item veto off the table will help Congress and the president focus on bigger and more important budget issues.

"They're going to be dealing with budget issues that dwarf anything they've ever dealt with before," says Ippolito. "To add this complication seems unnecessary in a practical sense as well as raising all sorts of constitutional problems." ■

Notes

1 *The Washington Post,* March 14, 1997, p. A25.

2 See *1996 Congressional Quarterly Almanac,* p. 2-29.

3 The case is now before the U.S. Supreme Court under the name *Raines v. Byrd.* Besides Byrd and Hatfield, the other plaintiffs are Democratic Sens. Daniel Patrick Moynihan, N.Y., and Carl Levin, Mich., and Reps. David E. Skaggs, Colo., and Henry A. Waxman, Calif.

4 See U.S. General Accounting Office, "Line Item Veto: Estimating Potential Savings," January 1992. For a critique of the GAO report by Louis Fisher of the Congressional Research Service, see *Congressional Record,* April 30, 1992, pp. S5882-5884.

5 Citizens Against Government Waste, *1997 Congressional Pig Book: The Book Washington Doesn't Want You to Read* (1997).

6 Article I, section 9, clause 7.

7 *The Federalist No. 48.*

8 For background on presidential powers, see Louis Fisher, *Presidential Spending Power* (1975).

9 See Dennis S. Ippolito, *Congressional Spending: A Twentieth Century Fund Report* (1991), pp. 38-48.

10 Quoted in Fisher, *op. cit.,* p. 165 (Grant), p. 25 (Arthur).

11 Much of this section is derived from Fisher, *op. cit.,* pp. 175-201.

12 The case is *Train v. City of New York* (Feb. 18, 1975).

13 *The Wall Street Journal,* April 1, 1996, p. A14.

14 Some of this section is drawn from George Hager and Eric Pianin, *Mirage: Why Neither Democrats Nor Republicans Can Balance the Budget, End the Deficit, and Satisfy the Public* (1997), pp. 99-155.

15 *Ibid.*

16 See *ibid.,* pp. 103-106 (1981), 137-145 (1985).

17 Stephen C. Glazier, "Reagan Already Has a Line-Item Veto," *The Wall Street Journal,* Dec. 4, 1987, p. A14. See *Congressional Quarterly Weekly Report,* May 14, 1988, p. 1284.

18 The opinion can be found in Senate Judiciary Subcommittee on the Constitution, "Line-Item Veto: The President's Constitutional Authority," 103rd Congress, 2nd session, June 15, 1994, pp. 123-176. Cooper, now in private practice in Washington, is one of the attorneys for the lawmakers challenging the Line Item Veto Act.

19 For background on the Bush administration, see Hager and Pianin, *op. cit.,* pp. 156-187.

20 See *1990 Congressional Quarterly Almanac,* pp. 173-178.

21 Quoted in *The Washington Post,* Nov. 18, 1992, p. A.17.

22 *Congressional Quarterly Weekly Report,* June 10, 1995, p. 1627.

23 For coverage of the arguments, see *Congressional Quarterly Weekly Report,* May 31, 1997, p. 1266; *The New York Times,* May 28, 1997, p. A17; *The Washington Post,* May 28, 1997, p. A8.

24 See Kenneth Jost, "Line-Item Case May Hinge on Standing," *Legal Times,* May 19, 1997, p. 2.

25 See *The Washington Post,* May 5, 1997, p. A8; *The Washington Times,* May 5, 1997, p. A4; *Congressional Quarterly Weekly Report,* May 10, 1997, p. 1051.

26 See *Congressional Quarterly Weekly Report,* May 24, 1997, p. 1180.

27 See Marcia Coyle, "Line-Item Veto: Who'll Vote How," *The National Law Journal,* June 9, 1997, p. A1.

Bibliography

Selected Sources Used

Books

Fisher, Louis, *The Politics of Shared Power: Congress and the Executive* (3rd ed.), Congressional Quarterly, 1993.
This broad survey includes a chapter discussing congressional-presidential relations on budget issues. Fisher is a senior specialist in separation of powers at the Library of Congress.

Fisher, Louis, *Presidential Spending Power*, Princeton University Press, 1975.
Fisher's history details the development of presidential spending power from George Washington through the impoundment controversies under Richard M. Nixon. The book includes detailed source notes.

Hager, George, and Eric Pianin, *Mirage: Why Neither Democrats Nor Republicans Can Balance the Budget, End the Deficit, and Satisfy the Public*, Times Books, 1997.
The book traces the recent history of efforts to control the federal budget deficit. Hager and Pianin covered budget issues in Congress for the *Congressional Quarterly Weekly Report* and *The Washington Post,* respectively. The book includes 10 pages of source notes.

Ippolito, Dennis S., *Uncertain Legacies: Federal Budget Policy from Roosevelt Through Reagan*, University of Virginia Press, 1990.
Ippolito, a professor of political science at Southern Methodist University, critically examines the role of Congress and the president in federal budget policy. The book includes detailed source notes.

Ippolito, Dennis S., *Congressional Spending: A Twentieth Century Fund Report*, Cornell University Press, 1981.
Ippolito critically assesses Congress' role on spending and budget issues seven years after enactment of the 1974 Congressional Budget Act. The book includes detailed source notes.

Reports and Studies

House Committee on Government Reform and Oversight, and Senate Committee on Governmental Affairs, *Line-Item Veto*, 104th Congress, 1st session, Jan. 12, 1995.
The 12 witnesses who testified before this joint hearing at the beginning of the 104th Congress included the administration's budget director, several lawmakers and representatives of two spending-reduction advocacy groups, all in support of the line-item veto. The outgoing director of the Congressional Budget Office was one of two witnesses who opposed the measure.

National Legal Center for the Public Interest, *Pork Barrels and Principles: The Politics of the Presidential Veto*, 1988.
The essays in the 62-page booklet, published by a conservative public interest legal center, include essays by six contributors setting forth opposing views on the historical, legal and policy arguments relating to the line-item veto.

Senate Judiciary Subcommittee on the Constitution, *Line-Item Veto: The President's Constitutional Authority*, June 15, 1994.
The hearing focused on the question of whether the president has an inherent line-item veto power without statutory authorization or constitutional amendment. Legal experts testified on both sides of the issue.

FOR MORE INFORMATION

Center on Budget and Policy Priorities, 810 1st St., N.E., Suite 510, Washington, D.C. 20002; (202) 408-1080. The liberal advocacy group analyzes federal, state and local budget policies as they affect low- and moderate-income persons.

Citizens Against Government Waste, 1301 Connecticut Ave., N.W., Suite 400, Washington, D.C. 20036; (202) 467-5300. The advocacy group publishes an annual report, *The Congressional Pig Book,* listing what it regards as "pork-barrel" spending by Congress.

Concord Coalition, 1019 19th St., N.W., Suite 810, Washington, D.C. 20036; (202) 467-6222. The bipartisan interest group promotes tax and spending policies intended to eliminate the federal budget deficit.

Council of State Governments, 444 N. Capitol St., N.W., Washington, D.C. 20001; (202) 624-5460. The council's semiannual *Book of the States* includes compilations of state statutory and constitutional provisions regarding the appro-priation and budget process. The council's headquarters is P.O. Box 11910, Lexington, Ky. 40578; (606) 244-8000.

National Taxpayers Union, 108 N. Alfred St., Alexandria, Va. 22314; (703) 683-5700. The advocacy group, which testified in favor of line-item veto proposals in Congress, promotes tax and spending reduction at all levels of government.

The Next Step

Additional information from UMI's Newspaper & Periodical Abstracts™ database

Balancing the Budget

Clayton, William E. Jr., "Line-item ruling not likely to affect budget fight," *Houston Chronicle,* April 13, 1997, p. A27.

A federal judge's ruling against presidential line-item veto powers removed a potential White House bargaining chip from the touchy balanced-budget negotiations with Capitol Hill.

Lambro, Donald, "The line-item veto will not end deficit spending but it's a start," *Atlanta Journal,* April 15, 1996, p. A11.

Lambro discusses the federal budget fight between President Clinton and the Republican Congress, saying that the line-item veto, which gives the president power to strike spending provisions, is a start in a better direction for the budget process.

"Read between lines," *Houston Chronicle,* Jan. 4, 1997, p. A32.

An editorial discusses the impact that the line-item veto is likely to have on the balancing of the federal budget.

History

"History of line-item veto effort," *Congressional Quarterly Weekly Report,* April 12, 1997, p. 834.

A history of the line-item veto effort in the White House and Congress since Jan. 25, 1984, when then-President Reagan called for a constitutional amendment giving the president this power, is presented.

Welch, William M., "Line-item veto: A long time in the works," *USA Today,* Jan. 3, 1997, p. A6.

Since Ulysses S. Grant was in the White House, presidents have wanted a line-item veto. It wasn't until Ronald Reagan, however, that it was actively pursued.

Line-Item Veto

Barone, Michael, "A new way to say no," *U.S. News & World Report,* April 22, 1996, p. 17.

It was originally thought that presidents would veto bills they believed to be unconstitutional. It remains to be seen what presidents will do with the line-item veto that President Clinton recently signed into law.

Cohen, Richard E., *National Journal,* March 23, 1996, p. 663.

Bipartisan support for a line-item veto is discussed. Proponents say it would be used primarily to kill spending on pork-barrel projects that have powerful legislative patrons.

Gettinger, Stephen, "More bargaining chip than budget knife," *Congressional Quarterly Weekly Report,* Oct. 12, 1996, p. 2938.

Gettinger discusses the line-item veto. He says it will be used primarily not to ratchet spending down, but to force Congress to spend money on presidential priorities.

"Kicking a slat from pork-barrel," *Los Angeles Times,* March 18, 1996, p. B4.

An editorial supports a congressional proposal to give the president line-item veto privileges.

Kramer, Michael, "New power for the pen," *Time,* April 8, 1996, p. 32.

Kramer discusses how presidents can use or abuse the line-item veto. Last week, Congress approved a modified line-item veto bill.

Taylor, Andrew, "Line-Item Veto Act," *Congressional Quarterly Weekly Report,* April 13, 1996, p. 5.

President Clinton signed the Line Item Veto Act into law on April 9, 1996, giving presidents the authority to strike individual items from bills. The text of the legislation is presented.

Line-Item Veto Debate

"Keep the line-item veto," *Denver Post,* April 14, 1997, p. B9.

An editorial calls for retaining the power of line-item veto for the president in the wake of a federal court ruling against it citing violation of the separation of powers.

Schoenbrod, David, and Marci A. Hamilton, "The Constitution and the line-item veto," *The Wall Street Journal,* May 21, 1997, p. A15.

Schoenbrod and Hamilton assert that Congress and President Clinton did the people a disservice by casting the much-needed line-item veto in a decidedly unconstitutional form. They state that the benefits of controlled spending pale in comparison to the harm that it does to the Constitution.

Taylor, Andrew, "Administration seeks to kill line-item veto challenge," *Congressional Quarterly Weekly Report,* Jan. 18, 1997, p. 167.

The Justice Department's Jan. 16, 1997, motion to dismiss a lawsuit, *Byrd v. Raines,* that challenges the constitutionality of a new line-item veto law is the first of several motions and briefs that will be filed in advance of oral arguments before

U.S. District Judge Thomas Penfield Jackson on March 21.

"The line-item veto," *The Wall Street Journal,* Jan. 3, 1997, p. A1.
The line-item veto was challenged in court by six members of Congress, who argued that the law, which took effect Jan. 1, 1997, represents an unconstitutional shift in power from the legislative to the executive branch.

"Value of the Line-Item Veto," *San Francisco Chronicle,* April 12, 1997, p. A20.
An editorial criticizes a U.S. District judge's decision to strike down the new law giving the president line-item veto power. The editorial claims that the veto adhered to the Constitution and offers a promising tool for progress on deficit reduction.

President's Spending Powers

Grier, Peter, "Republicans grumble over how president will wave veto wand," *The Christian Science Monitor,* Dec. 3, 1996, p. 1.
The rise of the line-item veto may soon cause a profound change in the balance of power between the Oval Office and Capitol Hill. Republican lawmakers are watching closely to see how President Clinton intends to use his new tool. Some party leaders are already warning Clinton that they believe he is interpreting line-item veto power too broadly.

Joyce, Philip G., and Robert D. Reischauer, "The Federal Line-Item Veto: What is it and what will it do?" *Public Administration Review,* March 1997, pp. 95-104.
The new presidential line-item veto is an expansion of the president's authority to rescind appropriated funds. The authors say it will have a profound effect on the relationship between Congress and the president in the budget process.

Welch, William M., "Power of the pen taken to another level," *USA Today,* Jan. 3, 1997, p. A6.
President Clinton has begun 1997 with a weapon many of his predecessors longed for: the line-item veto. The line-item veto is intended to permit the president to carve wasteful spending out of the government's budget. Proponents hope it will help reduce the budget deficit.

Supreme Court Hearing

Baker, Peter, "Clinton Plans Quick Line-Item Veto Appeal; Supreme Court Will Be Asked to Rule Before New Budget Year," *The Washington Post,* April 12, 1997, p. A6.
President Clinton announced yesterday that he will ask the Supreme Court to restore his newly established line-item veto power, calling for an expedited hearing so a ruling can be handed down before the next fiscal year's budget takes effect this fall.

Greenhouse, Linda, "High Court Grants Prompt Hearing on Line-Item Veto," *The New York Times,* April 24, 1997, p. B7.
The Supreme Court today granted an accelerated hearing to the Clinton administration's defense of the president's new line-item veto authority, which was declared unconstitutional by a U.S. District judge barely two weeks ago.

Savage, David G., "High Court Plans Quick Ruling on Line-Item Veto," *Los Angeles Times,* April 24, 1997, p. A26.
Moving to decide quickly whether the president can cancel wasteful spending items that are part of larger bills, the Supreme Court announced Wednesday that it will hear arguments and issue a ruling by July on the constitutionality of the Line-Item Veto Act.

Taylor, Andrew, "Court will rule on line-item veto," *Congressional Quarterly Weekly Report,* April 26, 1997, p. 949.
The Clinton administration's attempt to defend the line-item veto law has been accepted for review by the Supreme Court. The law was declared unconstitutional by a U.S. District judge.

U.S. District Court Decision

Jacoby, Mary, "U.S. Judge Rules Line-Item Veto is Unconstitutional; Yielding Such Power to President Upsets Balances, He Says," *Chicago Tribune,* April 11, 1997, p. 1.
One year after the enactment of a law giving the president line-item veto power over congressional spending bills, a federal judge ruled Thursday that the law is unconstitutional. Sen. Robert C. Byrd, D-W.Va., who along with five other lawmakers filed a lawsuit challenging the legislation as an unconstitutional abrogation of congressional powers, called U.S. District Judge Thomas Penfield Jackson's decision "a great victory for the American people . . . and our constitutional system of checks and balances."

Pear, Robert, "Odd Team Goes to Bat for New Power to Veto Budget Items," *The New York Times,* March 22, 1997, p. A10.
Republican congressional leaders defended the new presidential power, known as the line-item veto, as a legitimate way to achieve an overarching national purpose: reduction of the federal budget deficit. U.S. District Judge Thomas Penfield Jackson hinted that he had reservations about the new law. He is not expected to rule for several weeks. Justice Department lawyer Neil H. Koslowe defended the new veto power as a routine delegation of authority to the president.

Taylor, Andrew, "Judge voids line-item veto law; Backers look to high court," *Congressional Quarterly Weekly Report,* April 12, 1997, p. 833.
A key plank of the "Contract With America" and a major presidential goal, the line-item veto law was ruled unconstitutional on April 10, 1997, by U.S. District Judge Thomas P. Jackson. The law would have enhanced presidential power.

Back Issues

Great Research on Current Issues Starts Right Here . . . Recent topics covered by The CQ Researcher are listed below. Before May 1991, reports were published under the name of Editorial Research Reports.

DECEMBER 1995
Teens and Tobacco
Gene Therapy's Future
Global Water Shortages
Third-Party Prospects

JANUARY 1996
Emergency Medicine
Punishing Sex Offenders
Bilingual Education
Helping the Homeless

FEBRUARY 1996
Reforming the CIA
Campaign Finance Reform
Academic Politics
Getting Into College

MARCH 1996
The British Monarchy
Preventing Juvenile Crime
Tax Reform
Pursuing the Paranormal

APRIL 1996
Centennial Olympic Games
Managed Care
Protecting Endangered Species
New Military Culture

MAY 1996
Russia's Political Future
Marriage and Divorce
Year-Round Schools
Taiwan, China and the U.S.

JUNE 1996
Rethinking NAFTA
First Ladies
Teaching Values
Labor Movement's Future

JULY 1996
Recovered-Memory Debate
Native Americans' Future
Crackdown on Sexual Harassment
Attack on Public Schools

AUGUST 1996
Fighting Over Animal Rights
Privatizing Government Services
Child Labor and Sweatshops
Cleaning Up Hazardous Wastes

SEPTEMBER 1996
Gambling Under Attack
The States and Federalism
Civic Journalism
Reassessing Foreign Aid

OCTOBER 1996
Political Consultants
Insurance Fraud
Rethinking School Integration
Parental Rights

NOVEMBER 1996
Global Warming
Clashing Over Copyright
Consumer Debt
Governing Washington, D.C.

DECEMBER 1996
Welfare, Work and the States
The New Volunteerism
Implementing the Disabilities Act
America's Pampered Pets

JANUARY 1997
Combating Scientific Misconduct
Restructuring the Electric Industry
The New Immigrants
Chemical and Biological Weapons

FEBRUARY 1997
Assisting Refugees
Alternative Medicine's Next Phase
Independent Counsels
Feminism's Future

MARCH 1997
New Air Quality Standards
Alcohol Advertising
Civic Renewal
Educating Gifted Students

APRIL 1997
Declining Crime Rates
The FBI Under Fire
Gender Equity in Sports
Space Program's Future

MAY 1997
The Stock Market
The Cloning Controversy
Expanding NATO
The Future of Libraries

JUNE 1997
FDA Reform
China After Deng

Back issues are available for $5.00 (subscribers) or $10.00 (non-subscribers). Quantity discounts apply to orders over ten. To order, call Congressional Quarterly Customer Service at (202) 887-8621.

Binders are available for $18.00. To order call 1-800-638-1710. Please refer to stock number 648.

Future Topics

- ***Breast Cancer***
- ***Transportation Policy***
- ***Executive Pay***

THE CQ Researcher

PUBLISHED BY CONGRESSIONAL QUARTERLY INC.

Breast Cancer

How should research funds be spent?

Diagnoses of breast cancer, the disfiguring disease most dreaded by American women, rose steadily during the 1980s and now appear to have leveled off. But death rates from the disease have changed little since the 1930s. To some experts, the data indicate that modern medicine is conquering the disease through treatments like chemotherapy and regular screening with mammograms, which can catch the disease at an earlier, more curable stage. But to skeptics, the statistics mean that breast cancer remains an intractable disease and that scientists have yet to find a cure for its most virulent forms. As politically savvy breast cancer activists push for increased federal spending to find a cure, they are asking increasingly skeptical questions about how the money should be spent.

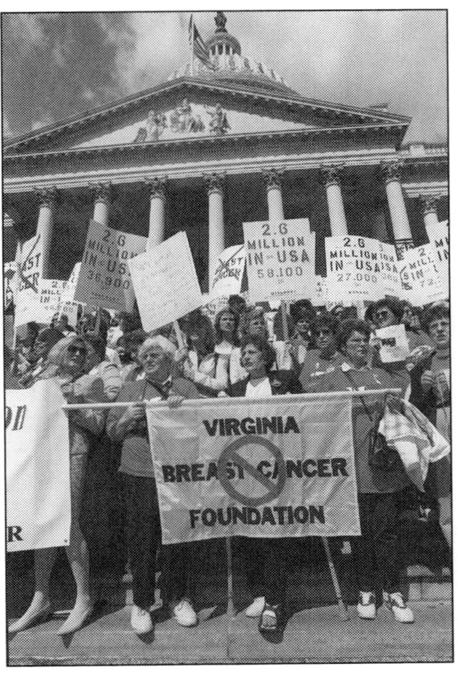

INSIDE

THIS ISSUE

CQ June 27, 1997 • Volume 7, No. 24 • Pages 553-576

Formerly Editorial Research Reports

COVER: WOMEN URGE MORE FUNDING FOR BREAST CANCER RESEARCH AT A RALLY AT THE CAPITOL ON MAY 6, 1997, SPONSORED BY THE NATIONAL BREAST CANCER COALITION. (SCOTT J. FERRELL/CONGRESSIONAL QUARTERLY)

THE CQ Researcher

June 27, 1997
Volume 7, No. 24

The CQ Researcher (ISSN 1056-2036). Formerly Editorial Research Reports. Published weekly, except Jan. 3, May 30, Aug. 29, Oct. 31, by Congressional Quarterly Inc., 1414 22nd St., N.W., Washington, D.C. 20037. Annual subscription rate for libraries, businesses and government is $340. Additional rates furnished upon request. Periodicals postage paid at Washington, D.C., and additional mailing offices. POSTMASTER: Send address changes to The CQ Researcher, 1414 22nd St., N.W., Washington, D.C. 20037.

Breast Cancer

By Sarah Glazer

The Issues

Frances M. Visco was a lawyer and the mother of a 14-month-old son when a routine mammogram discovered her breast cancer. She was 39.

But Visco, who has been cancer-free for 10 years, knows the limits of mammography. Earlier this year, she lost two close friends to breast cancer. Both were under 50.

Visco was "appalled" when the National Cancer Institute (NCI) recommended in March that all women in their 40s get regular mammograms.* Mammography saved neither of her friends, Visco told a Senate committee recently. "Where was the outrage over that fact?" she asked, urging the committee not to sell women "false hope" by endorsing mammography screening. [1]

"We reduced breast cancer to a soundbite in past years: It was 'Early detection saves lives,' and the new guideline is just more soundbite medicine," charges Visco, president of the National Breast Cancer Coalition.** "It's not based on the evidence. It's based on emotion and a desire to make this simplistic."

The loudest applause from the 600 activists at the coalition's conference last month in Washington, D.C., came when Visco urged, "We need to move the debate about breast cancer beyond mammography."

Visco and other activists charge that years of public health messages promoting mammograms as the solution to breast cancer have distracted public attention from a disturbing reality — the inability of modern medicine to prevent or cure breast cancer. Despite the advent of mammography and treatments like chemotherapy, death rates from breast cancer have changed surprisingly little since the 1930s.

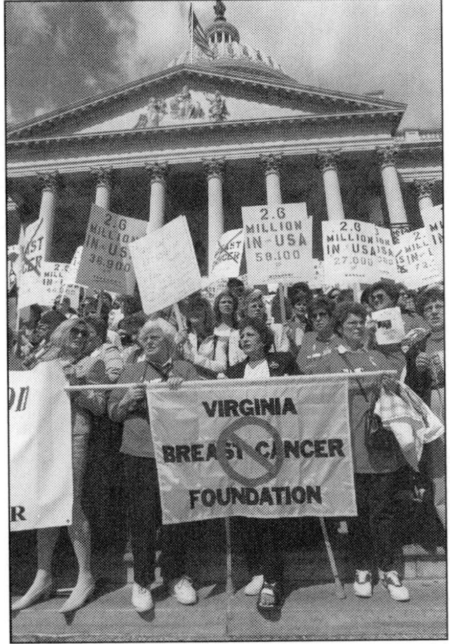

This year, 180,200 women will be identified with new breast cancer and 43,900 will die of it, according to American Cancer Society (ACS) estimates. At least one-third of the women diagnosed with the disease die of it. *

Visco's views represent a sea change from five years ago, when breast cancer survivors often proselytized for mammography as their salvation. Today, the coalition is training survivors of breast cancer to read scientific studies with skepticism and to agitate for innovative research attacks on the intractable disease.

Yet the decade-old public health campaign promoting mammography has been so successful that many politicians instantly took up the banner when its scientific basis was questioned in January by a panel appointed by the National Institutes of Health (NIH) to evaluate the scientific benefits of routine mammograms for women in their 40s. After three days of listening to presentations and sifting through data, the so-called consensus panel * found insufficient evidence to recommend populationwide screening for that age group, although it recognized solid benefits for women 50 and older.

The panel urged that women and their doctors be given information about the benefits and the risks, such as surgery for abnormalities that may not be cancer, so that they could make a decision for themselves.

Politicians and cancer specialists were among those who reacted with outrage to the panel's decision. One radiologist called the panel's refusal to recommend widespread screening "tantamount to a death sentence" for women in their 40s. [2] The cancer society, a longtime promoter of mammography, quickly issued its own recommendations for yearly screening. Sen. Olympia J. Snowe, R-Maine, charged that the scientists had produced "muddled recommendations" that "ultimately endanger women's lives." [3] *(See "At Issue," p. 569.)*

Within a week of the January meeting, the Senate voted 98-0 to endorse a "sense of the Senate" resolution sponsored by Snowe urging populationwide screening for younger women. A month later, the NCI * rejected the panel's advice, adopting instead its advisory

* A mammogram is an X-ray used to find tumors in women's breasts.

* *The coalition represents more than 350 grass-roots groups lobbying for more visibility and research funding for breast cancer.

* Sixty-five percent of women diagnosed with breast cancer survive 10 years after their original diagnosis, according to the American Cancer Society; 56 percent survive 15 years after the original diagnosis.

* The NIH appoints outside scientists, physicians and patient representatives to "consensus" panels to review current science and develop a consensus on issues where there is significant controversy.

Incidence and Mortality Rates

In the early 1980s, when mammography became more widespread, breast cancer rates among U.S. women began increasing about 4 percent per year. Now the incidence rate has begun to level off (top line). Breast cancer mortality (bottom line) has been relatively stable overall, but between 1989 and 1993 the rate declined about 6 percent, possibly due to improvements in breast cancer treatment and increases in cancer awareness and screening.

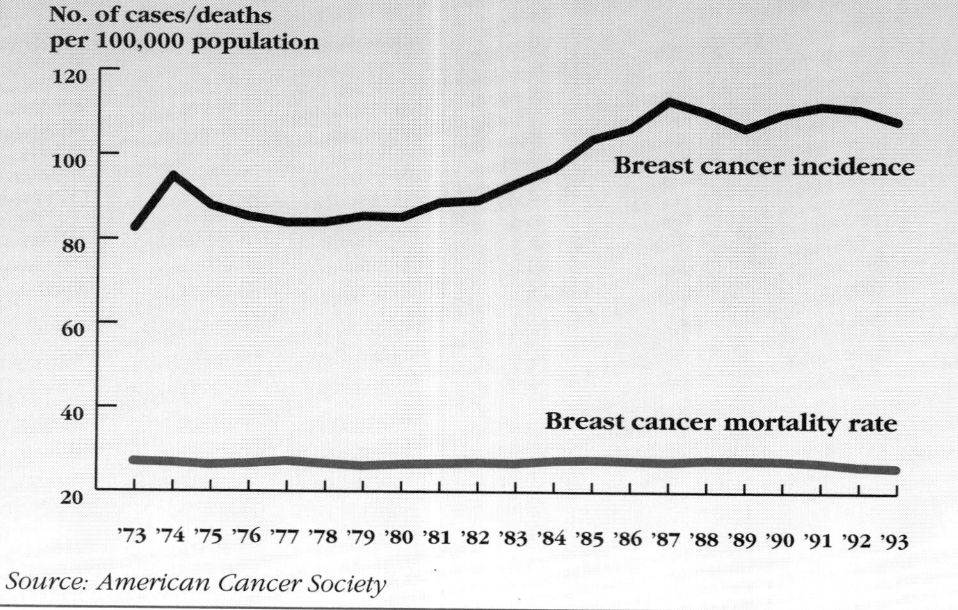

Source: American Cancer Society

board's recommendation that women in their 40s have mammograms every one to two years.

Some consumer activists say the senators had been "pandering" to their female constituents, but misread them. "I don't think women will pay attention to any guidelines, because we've been oversold on mammography," says Maryann Napoli, associate director and founder of the Center for Medical Consumers in New York City.

Several cancer survivors attending the coalition's conference agreed. The senators were "just looking for votes," and "the swing vote is the women's vote," says Marlene C. McCarthy, chair of the Rhode Island Breast Cancer Coalition.

"[The senators] thought they were doing the right thing. They're clueless," McCarthy adds. "Can you imagine if we said, 'We're going to screen all women 40-49, but we can't tell you what benefit or what risk they have?' They could have taken the same energy and voted for research for more appropriate screening tools."

However, the downsides of screening appear to be of less concern to the general public. A *New York Times*/CBS News poll released June 22, 1997, indicates most U.S. women favor aggressive screening: 44 percent said regular mammograms should start at age 40; another 40 percent said they should start earlier.

Sounding like the more skeptical experts, consumer groups increasingly express disappointment in mammography's results even for older women, despite its broadly advertised benefits. Studies demonstrate 30 percent fewer deaths from breast cancer among women who received regular mammograms in their 50s than among women who had not received regular mammograms. That means that even among women 50 and over who are regularly screened, 70 percent of those deaths occurred in spite of regular screening.

"What has been lost in this whole debate is the fact that mammography remains an imperfect tool even for women 50 and above," says Robert S. Lawrence, professor of health policy at the Johns Hopkins University School of Hygiene and Public Health. "The way it was being touted as a benefit being denied women 40-49, you'd think it was virtually a guarantee against dying from breast cancer — and it's far from that." By the time even the most sophisticated mammography machine detects a tumor, Lawrence observes, the tumor has often been growing for five years, spreading the cancer through the body.

"The benefit of mammography overall is small," acknowledges Barbara K. Rimer, a Duke University cancer expert who chaired the NCI advisory board that recommended mammograms for all women in their 40s. "That doesn't mean we don't do something when it's the best we have."

But breast cancer activists say it's

* The National Cancer Institute, the federal government's premiere agency funding cancer research, is part of the federally funded National Institutes of Health in Bethesda, Md.

time to demand something better than the current treatment choices of "slash, burn and poison," as California breast surgeon Susan M. Love, a coalition founder, dubs surgery, chemotherapy and radiation.

What treatments do exist often have horrendous side effects. Visco says she was treated with "regulated poison," her term for chemotherapy. "One of the most dreadful things that happened to me was that chemotherapy put me into premature menopause, and I was unable to have any more children," she says. Through research, Visco says, her coalition hopes scientists will discover a cure that can kill cancer cells without attacking healthy cells, too, as chemotherapy does.

The focus of the coalition's recent gathering, which was followed by a day of lobbying Congress, indicates that grass-roots breast cancer groups are developing a better understanding both of the science and the politics of cancer research.

Even Diane Swandel, director of the mammography center at St. Joseph's Hospital in Bangor, Maine, and a passionate advocate of mammography for younger women, acknowledged the new sophistication.

At the start of the conference, she had said: "I see women 32-40 coming through our center all the time. To say having that mammogram did not save their life and offer more opportunities for treatment is ridiculous."

But after hearing several activists' presentations, Swandel acknowledged, "I hear them loud and clear: We need a cure. They're saying, 'Let's get more sophisticated, get beyond detection.' "

Since organizing in 1991, the coalition has succeeded in boosting federal funding for breast cancer research more than fivefold. Flush with victory, the coalition has succeeded in winning a "seat at the table" with government panels to evaluate grants for funding. It is also pushing for $2.7 billion in funding over the next three years, representing a 54 percent increase for next year alone. And with President Clinton's blessing, the coalition has launched an effort to identify neglected areas of breast cancer research at the NIH.

The coalition's early funding successes drew criticism for politicizing breast cancer, Visco reminded coalition conferencegoers last month. But that's "a good thing," she said.

"Breast cancer is a political issue," Visco says, noting that most research is paid for with taxpayers' dollars. "You don't take your entire biomedical budget, give it to the scientific community and say 'Go play.' There have always been decisions made on how much money should go here and how much should go there. This is really an issue of power and who gets to decide that."

As activists, scientists and lawmakers confront breast cancer, these are some of the questions being debated:

Is the mammogram question settled once and for all?

The recent National Cancer Institute guidelines urging women in their 40s to get regular mammograms may give the general public the impression that science is united on the question. But vigorous and angry debate continues inside the scientific community.

The guidelines emanated from the National Cancer Advisory Board, a presidentially appointed committee that advises the NCI. On March 27, the board announced it had voted 17-1 to recommend that the NCI advise women ages 40-49 to get screening mammograms every one to two years if they are at average risk for breast cancer. The board said that women at higher than average risk should seek expert medical advice about beginning mammography before age 40 (*see p. 568*). The institute endorsed the recommendations the same day. [4]

Critics charge that the NCI's new guidelines were the result of political pressure. "I don't think [the debate] will go away, because it's clear there was politics and not science involved in this whole process," says Karla M. Kerlikowske, an assistant professor in the department of medicine, epidemiology and biostatistics at the University of California in San Francisco. Kerlikowske co-authored a 1995 analysis of 13 studies that found no benefit from mammography for women in their 40s. [5] Kerlikowske says other studies under way in Great Britain and elsewhere will support her findings.

Critics have pointed to a number of instantaneous reactions to the consensus panel's report as evidence that politics was at work. NCI Director Richard D. Klausner said he was "shocked" that the panel had found no convincing benefit of screening. [6]

At hearings in February and again in March, Sen. Arlen Specter, R-Pa., who heads the Appropriations subcommittee responsible for NIH funding, urged NIH to recommend mammography screening for women in their 40s.

Two physicians recently argued in *The Washington Post* that there had been "political tampering" with the NCI's decision-making process. Specter had demanded that the board speed up its deliberations — presumably to favor screening — in a series of "stern letters and phone calls" to the heads of NIH, NCI and the cancer advisory board, the doctors charged. [7]

"Scientific integrity is a fragile thing, and when your funding committee tells you that you haven't yet come up with the right answer, it's pretty tough not to be influenced in some subtle unconscious or conscious way," says Lawrence, one of the co-authors of the column in the Post. Lawrence headed a government-appointed panel, the U.S. Preventive Services Task Force, which

The Raging Controversy Over Hormones . . .

Dressed informally in a button-down shirt and slacks, breast surgeon Susan M. Love bounds onto the podium and cheerfully confides to her audience that she has just removed her suit jacket in response to a "hot flash."

Love, author of the best-selling *Dr. Susan Love's Hormone Book* and an adjunct professor at the University of Southern California, has recently gone on a campaign to counter the prevailing wisdom that women should routinely take hormones after menopause.

"Just as the baby-boomers are hitting menopause, it's become a disease — estrogen deficiency disease," she told 600 breast cancer activists at the National Breast Cancer Coalition conference in Washington, D.C., in May. But Love ridicules that idea, suggesting instead that evolution has programmed a shifting-down in hormone levels once women reach an age when high hormone levels are no longer necessary for reproduction. She tells her audience she's worried by the evidence that hormones increase the risk of breast cancer and isn't convinced by the studies showing it reduces the risk of heart disease.

Love's contention has plunged her into a controversy over the pros and cons of hormone replacement therapy. The largest study done to date, published in June, found that the chance of dying was 37 percent lower among women who were using hormones than among women who did not, primarily because of fewer deaths from heart disease. However, the mortality benefit dropped to 20 percent after 10 or more years of hormone use as the women's risk of breast cancer mortality rose. The study of 60,000 post-menopausal women is the latest report from the Nurses' Health Study, which has followed more than 100,000 female registered nurses on their health-related behavior starting in 1976. [1]

For women with family histories of breast cancer or who are otherwise at higher risk for breast cancer, the implications of the new study are more complicated. The study found a 43 percent increase in deaths from breast cancer among women who had used the hormones for 10 or more years. A counterintuitive finding is that short-term hormone users had a reduced risk of death from breast cancer.

Francine Grodstein, an epidemiologist at Brigham and Women's Hospital in Boston who directed the study, suspects that's because those women who took hormones for a few years were health-conscious women who were likely to see their doctors often, were diagnosed with breast cancer at an early, more curable stage and were taken off hormones as soon as they were diagnosed. The main hormone given to menopausal women, estrogen, is thought to promote breast cancer.

In a surprising finding, women with a family history of breast cancer had the same reduction in overall mortality risk (from all causes) as other women in the study, once the benefits of reduced heart disease deaths were factored in.

But Grodstein cautions that this study looked only at the risk of *dying*, not the risk of getting a disease like breast cancer. An earlier study she published in *The New England Journal of Medicine* found an increase in the occurrence of breast cancer starting after five years of hormone use.

"There's a difference between having a disease and dying from it. This [study] doesn't mean women with a

has recommended against screening women in their 40s.

"I think in the scientific community there's very little confidence left that (the advisory board members) were really able to speak independently and arrive at [their recommendation] dispassionately," Lawrence says.

Advisory board Chairman Barbara Rimer denies that the board's recommendation was the result of political pressure.

"Yes, we were pressured. Does that mean we came out with what we did because we were pressured? No," says Rimer, who is director of cancer prevention, detection and control research at Duke University Medical School.

As Rimer points out, debate over mammography has tended to divide by professional specialty. Radiologists and clinical oncologists tend to favor screening. But "evidence-based" scientists — epidemiologists and statisticians who examine large bodies of data — have been more doubtful that mammography provides a benefit.

Increasingly, consumer activists regard radiologists' views skeptically because of the profession's vested financial stake in frequent use of mammographic facilities and services. Surgeons, who see firsthand the suffering of their breast cancer patients, are more likely to push for whatever tools are available even if imperfect, critics say.

"I believe we've allowed surgeons and radiologists to set the agenda," says Napoli. "If other specialties were setting guidelines, perhaps we'd have a different understanding of breast cancer."

The advisory board looked at the same studies as the consensus panel but apparently found the evidence of benefit for women in their 40s more convincing. The benefit of mammography, it said, is detecting cancer early, when it is more easily treated with a better outcome. Regular screening mammography in average-

. . . Should All Women Take Them?

family history should be told to take hormones," she says. "Having breast cancer and not dying of it is not an acceptable option."

As for other women, Grodstein says, "Overall, in terms of mortality, they're likely to get a benefit [from taking hormones], particularly if they have risk factors for heart disease" like smoking or high cholesterol levels.

Since the mid-1960s, doctors have prescribed the female hormone estrogen to relieve some of the temporary symptoms that accompany the onset of menopause — hot flashes, headaches, vaginal dryness, sleeplessness and mood swings among them. In response to research suggesting that estrogen also protects against heart disease and the bone-thinning disease osteoporosis, doctors have increasingly distributed the hormone for its preventive properties.

Starting in 1975, studies have shown that estrogen given alone increases the risk of uterine cancer. The increased risk can be countered by giving estrogen in combination with progestin — a synthetic form of the natural hormone progesterone.

But what worries many women is the possibility that the hormones will increase their risk of breast cancer. The evidence on this issue is conflicting, with some studies showing no effect or even decreased effect on breast cancer.

However, one of the most publicized studies — a 1995 report from the Nurses' Health Study — found an increased incidence of breast cancer among women who take estrogen or estrogen-progestin combinations.

It's these findings that Love, who has treated thousands of breast cancer patients, focuses on. Love argues that the medical community is underestimating the risk of breast cancer and overestimating the benefits for heart disease.

Love observes that in studies so far, women who took hormones tended to be higher-income, thinner and better educated than those who did not. As a result, it's not clear if healthier women are taking hormones or the hormones made them healthy, she says. Grodstein contends this is less of a concern in the Nurses' Health Study, since nurses tend to have similar knowledge when it comes to health.

Love's most powerful argument is that breast cancer is more of a concern for younger women than heart disease or osteoporosis. The average age for death from breast cancer among women in the U.S. is 68; for heart disease it's 79.3. The average age at which women get their first hip fracture because of osteoporosis is 79, according to Love.

But in a recent article in *The New Yorker*, science writer Malcolm Gladwell said one statistic that is central to Love's argument is dead wrong. In her book on hormones, she writes that among women younger than age 75, there are actually three times as many deaths from breast cancer as there are from heart disease. In fact, the figures from the government's National Center for Health Statistics shows the reverse, Gladwell notes. About three times as many women in that age bracket die from heart disease as from breast cancer. [2]

---

[1] Francine Grodstein et al., "Postmenopausal Hormone Therapy and Mortality," *The New England Journal of Medicine,* June 19, 1997, pp. 1769-1775.

[2] Malcolm Gladwell, "The Estrogen Question: How Wrong is Dr. Susan Love?" *The New Yorker,* June 9, 1997, pp. 54-60.

---

risk women 40-49 reduces deaths from breast cancer by about 17 percent, the board said.

But, the board also noted, hinting at its differences with the consensus panel, "not all experts [find] this statistically significant." [8]

"Everyone is saying there's a benefit, but it's a small benefit," Rimer says, commenting on why the two panels came to different conclusions. "What people disagree about is whether that justifies a universal recommendation [for mammography]. That percentage reduction is greater than most of what we see in chemotherapy trials. Our board felt it justified a recommendation as long as you tell people what the benefits and limitations are."

But several members of the consensus panel, whose report had cited a similar benefit in terms of reduced deaths, said they did not find the reduction compelling, and they were more disturbed by the risks of unnecessary surgery. They noted that the mortality statistic was arrived at by combining eight different studies in a method known as meta-analysis.

The analysis was authored by a group of scientists, including a researcher at the pro-mammography American Cancer Society, who had argued in 1995 that death rates were lower for women in their 40s screened with mammography. To get this result, the authors had excluded the influential Canadian National Breast Screening Study, the first trial specifically designed to look at younger women separately. That study found no benefit for women in their 40s. The authors argued that the study was flawed. [9]

In January, the authors told the consensus panel that by including new, longer-term data from Swedish studies they could show for the first time that mammography produced a statistically significant benefit for women in their 40s.

The meta-analysis method has

Is the Environment to Blame . . .

Virginia Regnante remembers her children racing their bikes to keep up with the poisonous DDT fog that billowed from trucks spraying for mosquitoes. Mary Ann Varvaro wonders if contaminated water rotted out the hot water heater. Karen Miller recalls her neighbor's pet rabbit dying the day the lawn was sprayed.

All three women have been treated for breast cancer. All suspect that environmental pollution caused their disease. All three live on Long Island.

In 1980, when Regnante was diagnosed with breast cancer at age 47, she says,

"I had none of the risk factors. I was very trim, I had my first child at 24, I played tennis four or five days a week."

Regnante and her husband moved to Long Island in 1959 because it offered a convenient rail commute to New York City and wide-open spaces close to Atlantic Ocean beaches. Today, the suburban streets fit America's ideal of healthy, pesticide-assisted living with their neatly trimmed lawns and shade trees.

Long Island's Nassau and Suffolk counties have traditionally had among the highest breast cancer rates in the state. Between 1988 and 1992, women in Nassau developed breast cancer at a rate of 117 for every 100,000 women and in Suffolk at a rate of 109, considerably above the state average of 100, according to the New York State Department of Health.

That has long made activists like Regnante, who is president of the West Islip Breast Cancer Coalition, suspect Long Island's environment. "What is the common denominator here?" she asks. "We're all eating the same foods, breathing the same air and drinking the same water."

On a recent tour, Regnante pointed to lush golf course greens treated with herbicides and pesticides, a construction dump site adjoining yards where children play and a factory that until recently spewed waste into a nearby stream. In May, the federal government fired the managers of Long Island's Brookhaven National Laboratory, charging that low-level radioactive tritium had been allowed to leak from its nuclear reactors into the groundwater. [1]

Under pressure from Long Island activists, Congress voted in 1993 to fund a study of the possible relationship between the environment and breast cancer on Long Island and two other counties in New York and in Connecticut. The Long Island Breast Cancer Study Project is examining everything from electromagnetic fields to air pollution. The cornerstone is a case-control study that is recruiting the 2,000 Long Island women who were expected to be newly diagnosed with breast cancer between Aug. 1 1996, and July 31 of this year. The study will compare them to area women who do not have breast cancer.

Sarah Glazer

Virginia Regnante (second from right) and fellow Long Island breast cancer activists.

The primary aim of the study is to determine if organochlorines, commonly used in such pesticides as DDT (now banned in the U.S.) and polycyclic aromatic hydrocarbons (PACs), which are found in car exhaust, cigarette smoke and charcoal-broiled food, are linked to breast cancer. Researchers are also collecting dust, water and soil samples from the homes of some of the women who have lived in their houses for at least 15 years.

Some critics have noted that Long Island does not have the highest breast cancer rates in the nation. Marin County, Calif., an affluent suburb of San Francisco, holds that record. Moreover, many other areas of the country have shared an agricultural history like Long Island's, including its heavy use of pesticides.

But Marilie D. Gammon, an epidemiologist at the Columbia University School of Public Health who is heading up the case-control study, points out that Long Island residents get their water from a shallow, narrow aquifer, rather than wells, which makes it hard for nature to flush pollutants out of the water supply.

"It's possible that even if exposures are not as high as in other parts of the country, this lack of a natural cleaning system may have exposed them to higher levels than

come under criticism, however, from some experts on the grounds that it can be jiggled to represent the biases of the author. A consensus panel member who is wary of the method, Dartmouth Medical School Professor John Wasson, points out that of the eight studies analyzed together, only six included women as young as 40. And only three of the six found that mammograms reduced breast cancer deaths among women in their 40s.

"That is three to three. It doesn't sound too convincing to me," says Wasson, an internist. "When you start doing statistical manipulation and adding different types of patient populations, you can make it look like a decrease."

Donald A. Berry, another panel member, said it's not clear that one

. . . for Long Island's High Breast Cancer Rate?

other people," she says. The study may also offer clues to explain breast cancer in similar suburban areas, Gammon and other experts suggest.

Gammon chose organochlorines like DDT to study because laboratory studies have shown them to increase mammary tumors in animals, and small studies show an association in humans. "This is a way of looking at it in a much larger group of women," she says.

One theory is that organochlorines mimic estrogen in the body, which has been linked to breast cancer. Similar studies are under way in North Carolina and California. As for hydrocarbons, studies in highly polluted regions of Eastern Europe have shown an association between PACs and DNA damage, Gammon says.

Many of the Long Island activists are disappointed that the study is not examining a broader list of pollutants, such as pesticides currently used on their neighborhood lawns.

Since most cancers take as long as 20 years to show up, Gammon responds, it's harder to study the effects of pesticides applied recently. By contrast, exposures to DDT were very high 20-30 years ago, before the pesticide was banned. Moreover, the chemical is long-lasting in body tissue.

Steven Stellman, an epidemiologist at the American Health Foundation, a research organization in New York City, says he's finding that older women tend to have higher concentrations of organochlorines in their body than younger women. He is looking at blood and tissue samples from patients at two hospitals serving Long Island as part of the study.

"We think as people get older, they've been exposed longer and tend to accumulate these things," he says. "Organochlorine pesticides and PCBs (another organochlorine formerly used as insulating fluid for electrical transformers) are pretty indestructible compounds, and once they get in your body they tend to accumulate."

The Long Island breast cancer activists started their movement in 1990. Several were outraged by a government study which concluded that Long Island's high rates of breast cancer were attributable to the residents' high socioeconomic status. Being middle or upper class and highly educated is a risk factor associated with breast cancer, largely because higher income women tend to have children later in life, researchers believe, and thus have longer lifetime exposure to estrogen.

"We didn't like the 'Blame the victim' syndrome," says Fran Kritchek, who was one of the founders of the breast cancer group "1 in 9," named after the one in nine Long Island women who were developing breast cancer. Several activists said they were appalled at the suggestion that "We were fat, rich and Jewish." Barbara Balaban, former director of a breast cancer hot line at Adelphi University in Garden City, observes that Long Island includes areas of poverty as well as wealth.

Gammon notes that known risk factors, including social class and a family history of the disease, account at most for half of breast cancer cases. "That means we need to be more creative in looking at why these women are getting breast cancer," she says, adding that the environmental factors she is studying are "biologically plausible."

The first piece of evidence vindicating the activists was a 1994 New York State Health Department Study that found women who once lived near large chemical plants on Long Island ran a 62 percent higher risk of developing breast cancer after menopause. [2]

But Gammon says the study was "a crude way of trying to establish a connection" between chemicals and breast cancer. Researchers plotted on a grid how close someone lived to a plant rather than determining their actual exposure.

Devra Lee Davis, an epidemiologist at the World Resources Institute, a research organization in Washington, D.C., has argued that estrogen-like synthetics in pesticides, drugs, fuels and plastics could account for some of the unexplained cases of breast cancer. [3] She calls the Long Island study "a good effort" but says it's unlikely to prove conclusively whether pollutants contribute to cancer. "One epidemiological study seldom is definitive," Davis observes.

Nevertheless, she says, "Long Island is a natural laboratory, just as any group of women is, because we don't know why women there get breast cancer."

She adds, "We do know that a woman who lives on Long Island 40 years has four times the risk of developing breast cancer as a woman living there 10 years. That's suggesting there's something about living on Long Island."

[1] Dan Barry, "U.S. Energy Chief Removes Manager for Brookhaven," *The New York Times*, May 2, 1997, p. A1.

[2] Diana Jean Schemo, "L.I. Breast Cancer is Possibly Linked to Chemical Sites," *The New York Times*, April 13, 1994, p. A1.

[3] Devra Lee Davis and H. Leon Bradlow, "Can Environmental Estrogens Cause Breast Cancer?" *Scientific American*, October 1995, pp. 144-149.

can "glump together" the data from studies that used different populations, different mammogram techniques and different kinds of comparison groups. "I think the biggest issue is we don't know it's 17 percent; this is an estimate. The question of whether it's statistically significant does come into the recommendation," says Berry, a professor at the Institute of Statistics and Decision Sciences and the Comprehensive Cancer Center, both at Duke University.

In addition, Berry points out, women in those studies who received mammograms in their 40s did not start to show a trend toward reduced breast cancer mortality until 10 or more years after they received mammograms. As a result, the panel noted, "one cannot determine" if the women showed a

Risk Factors for Breast Cancer

Cancer risk factors can be conditions that directly cause the disease (such as exposure to radiation) or personal characteristics that are indirectly associated with the cause (such as age). Established risk factors for breast cancer include:

Increasing age — The single most important risk factor for breast cancer is age.

Family history of breast cancer — Although any family history of breast cancer is associated with an increase in the risk, the history of breast cancer in a first-degree relative (mother, sister or daughter) is associated with the largest increase.

A personal history of breast cancer — Invasive and in situ breast cancers increase the lifetime risk of developing a new breast cancer in any remaining tissue in either breast.

History of benign breast disease — Biopsy-confirmed benign-breast disease is associated with an increased risk of breast cancer.

Hormonal factors — Early age at menarche, late at menopause, late age at first live birth and few pregnancies all may increase a woman's risk of breast cancer by affecting her lifetime exposure to hormones. Oral contraceptive use may be related to breast cancer diagnosed at young ages, and long-term estrogen replacement therapy also may increase risk.

In addition, white race, high socioeconomic status and exposure to ionizing radiation are risk factors for breast cancer.

Source: American Cancer Society

benefit because of the breast cancer diagnosis they got in their 50s rather than their 40s. [10] It may be that they would have received the same benefit if they had started mammogram screening at 50.

Furthermore, only the Canadian study was organized to look specifically at women in their 40s, and it found no benefit for that age group, notes Kerlikowske. The 1995 meta-analysis that she co-authored reaching the same conclusion included the Canadian study. [11]

By contrast, all the other studies have included older women as well, and later analyzed the data for women in their 40s separately. Because that reduces the numbers of women being analyzed overall, it reduces the statistical power of the analysis and makes it difficult to rule out the possibility that chance may have played a role, experts say.

The mammogram test is much less reliable in women in their 40s than in their 50s. As many as 25 percent of breast cancers for women in their 40s will be missed by the test, as opposed to 10 percent for women in their 50s, the advisory board noted. In addition, women in this age group are far more likely to get "false positive" results — abnormalities found on a mammogram that turn out not to be cancer upon further testing through biopsies, additional mammograms or ultrasound. If a woman got mammograms every year between 40 and 49, she would have about a 30 percent chance of having a "false positive" mammogram result.

Experts generally have presented the downside of getting a mammogram for younger women as very minor surgery — a biopsy to test breast tissue if abnormalities are found, followed by temporary anxiety while a woman waits for tests to determine if a lump found by a mammogram really is cancerous.

But in presentations to the consensus panel, several experts stressed an additional risk — mastectomy for something that is not cancer at all. About 45 percent of women in their 40s whose cancers are detected by mammogram are diagnosed with abnormalities or small cancers known as ductal carcinoma in situ (DCIS), abnormal cells confined to the milk ducts of the breast, according to Kerlikowske. Pathologists do not yet have a standard technique to tell which of these lesions will become invasive cancer. Although estimates vary, it is generally agreed that anywhere from 30-75 percent will not become harmful. Yet 45 percent of these cases are treated with mastectomy, says Kerlikowske, "and no one knows if that's good or not. You're clearly overtreating some of those women."

The concern about DCIS has mounted because it has turned into a small epidemic. Detection of DCIS has increased about 400 percent since the 1980s, when mammography screening became widespread, Kerlikowske says.

John C. Bailar III, chairman of the department of health studies at the University of Chicago, is convinced that many women are getting mastectomies for tiny lesions like DCIS that are harmless. "I'm sure they were always there, but they didn't cause any trouble when you just left them alone," he says.

As more women get screened, and

improved mammography technology detects smaller abnormalities, Bailar argues, pathologists are increasingly likely to tag an abnormality as cancer, especially with malpractice suits hanging over them like a sword of Damocles.

"Every thinking pathologist has to be terrified of missing a diagnosis of cancer, so they keep pushing the boundaries further and further out," he says.

At its root, the decision for a woman comes down to a question of values. Rimer explains how her board weighed the pros and cons: "People on the board decided that because, with the present level of knowledge, we can't say which cases of DCIS are going to become invasive and which aren't . . . we have to treat it as cancer."

But some women are horrified at the thought of removing their breasts for what could be a small probability of danger. That kind of woman had better think twice before setting the screening process in play, Wasson warns. Once abnormalities are detected, "Do you think in the medical-legal framework of the U.S., the doctor isn't going to play it safe" and operate? Wasson asks. "So once you start down the slippery slope of getting a mammogram, you have to be prepared to get full treatment for anything that's found."

Within the scientific community, another round of debate could be stimulated when the meta-analysis presented to the consensus panel in January is published. "With the latest follow-up data" from trials involving women in their 40s, "there is now convincing evidence of benefit from screening mammography to women of this age group," Denver radiologist R. Edward Hendrick and three colleagues wrote recently.

They note it is the first time a statistically significant benefit for women in their 40s has been found. The authors calculate that among women with breast cancer, 18 percent fewer will die of the disease if they get mammograms in their 40s. [12]

On the basis of the new data, the cancer society in March upped its screening recommendation to every year for women in their 40s, rather than every one to two years.

Hendrick and his co-authors suggest that mammography benefits are likely to be even greater than the studies suggest. The technology of mammography has improved since the studies were conducted, and not all women in the studies who were invited to have mammograms had them, the authors wrote. Women in the comparison groups who went outside the study to get mammograms could have diluted the benefit of mammograms shown in the studies, they add.

But not everyone finds the study as convincing as the authors. "What we have now is a set of studies that show the random wobbles up and down you would expect in any collection of studies," Bailar says. "I think it's outrageous to take the one study that shows what somebody likes and pretend like that's the whole of the evidence."

Women under 50 have denser breasts than older women, making it harder to distinguish tumors on a mammogram X-ray picture, since both tumors and dense breast tissue show up as white areas.

In addition, several experts speculate, breast cancer in younger women appears to be of a particularly virulent, faster-growing variety. "In younger women, it tends to be a systemic disease from the start," suggests Kerlikowse. "A lot of people think that when we find a small tumor there are malignant cells that have gone to the bone, the liver and lung already."

As for why there should be such stark differences between age 49 and 50, Kerlikowske suggests it's related to the differences between pre-menopausal and post-menopausal women. The median age for menopause in the United States, she notes, is 51.2. The studies conducted so far have not collected data on women's menopausal status, but age 50 has probably served as a rough dividing line.

"I still think they're two different diseases, and you can't expect the same test to work well for two different diseases," Kerlikowske says. "It definitely has something to do with hormones."

But experts at the cancer society say that if cancer grows faster in young women, the solution is to screen them more frequently. They note that in some of the trials, mammograms were done at intervals as long three years. Thus, they reason, the trials missed many of the fast-growing tumors in women in their 40s and mainly caught the slower-growing ones, which is why the benefit was delayed so long.

In the Swedish studies, where young women were screened every two years on average, younger women developed twice as many cancers between mammograms, says Robert A. Smith, senior director for detection at the ACS. "This has led people to say if you screen women under 50, you must do it every year, otherwise it's an empty exercise."

Notwithstanding the fact that the new guidelines emanate from the prestigious National Cancer Institute, advisory board Chair Rimer expects to see little effect on current practice. In her own surveys, Rimer has found that most physicians follow the guidelines either of their health-care organization or their medical specialty.

The majority of women in their 40s who get mammograms — and over half do, according to Rimer — get them as a result of seeing their gynecologists. Gynecologists tend to follow the guidelines of the American College of Obstetricians and Gynecologists, which favors routine screening. By contrast, internists, who are more likely to see older women past menopause, tend to follow the guidelines of their specialty organization, the American College of Physicians, or the Preventive Services Task Force. The College of Physicians does not recommend mammography

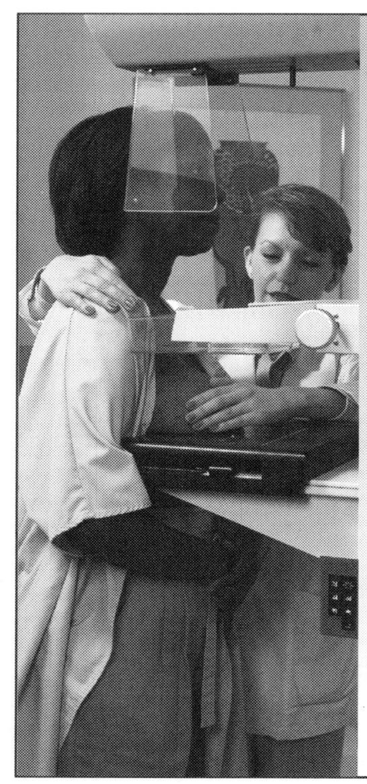

Mortality Rate Falls

In recent years there has been about a 6 percent decrease in the overall breast cancer mortality rate. Some ascribe the decline to the success of mammography and chemotherapy, but others note that the highest decrease in mortality is among younger women, who are less likely to get mammography. At the same time, there is a troubling increase in the mortality rate among African-American women, possibly because breast cancer in black women may be diagnosed at later stages and may be more aggressive and difficult to treat.

Breast Cancer Mortality Rates, 1989-93

Age	White	African American
30-39	-13%	-5%
40-49	-9%	-2%
50-59	-9%	<-1%
60-69	-6%	<-1%
70-79	-3%	+5%
80+	+2%	+5%
Total	**-6%**	**+1%**

Source: American Cancer Society, Surveillance Research, 1997

screening until 50 unless the patient has symptoms, a family history of breast cancer or is otherwise at increased risk. The task force recommends screening starting at 50. Most health insurers have been willing to pay for mammograms in both age groups because of fear of lawsuits, Rimer notes.

Meanwhile, the Canadian government is sticking by its recommendation, in place since 1988, to start screening at age 50. Starting then, most Canadian women receive a letter inviting them to get a mammogram screening every two years. (However, women in their 40s are assured of a free mammogram under Canada's national health insurance system if they desire one, government officials say.)

"Women hear what happens in the States," says Lise Mathieu, program manager in the disease prevention division of Canada's federal department of health. "There are lots of questions being asked. Some women are demanding it. Our position is let's wait till it's peer-reviewed."

Is breast cancer research getting the appropriate level of funding?

Grass-roots activists have been enormously successful in increasing federal research funding for breast cancer. Since 1991, the federal research budget for the disease has risen from $100 million to $510 million. One of the breast cancer coalition's biggest coups was persuading Congress to initiate a $210 million research program at the Department of Defense (DOD) in 1993, practically doubling annual government spending in one stroke. Sen. Tom Harkin, D-Iowa, who has lost two sisters to the disease, initially proposed an outright transfer of the $210 million from DOD to NIH. Failing that, he succeeded in passing an amendment authorizing DOD to fund the research.

The coalition wants even more in the future. In May, it gathered 2.6 million signatures — symbolizing the 2.6 million women living with breast cancer in the United States — to present to members of Congress in support of a $2.6 billion breast cancer research budget for the next three years.

The breast cancer cause has been so well-received on Capitol Hill that Senate Appropriations Committee staff don't foresee strong opposition to new increases. However, overall budget constraints on discretionary spending could dampen the coalition's expectations.

For fiscal year 1998, the coalition is proposing a 44 percent increase in breast cancer research at the NIH alone. But Sen. Specter, an avowed supporter of breast cancer research, has introduced a bill to increase the agency's overall funding for medical research by only about 7.5 percent in 1998.

Critics have questioned why breast cancer should take such a big chunk of a shrinking biomedical pie, considering that other diseases — lung cancer and cardiovascular disease — kill more women every year. Joan I. Samuelson, founder of the Parkinson's Action Network, questions why the federal government spends only $78 on research for each person suffering from Parkinson's disease compared with almost $200 for every breast cancer victim. [13] (About 1 million Americans have Parkinson's, compared with 2.6 million with breast cancer.) Privately, some women's health activists say it's a disturbing reality that the loudest voice and most powerful lobbying machine is determining which disease gets the big increases.

Last year, *The New York Times* cited breast cancer as "This year's hot charity." Glitzy fund-raisers to raise money for research have lured such corporate contributors as J.C. Penney and Pier 1 Imports along with Ralph Lauren and Estée Lauder. [14]

By contrast, congressional observers note that prostate cancer, which claims about as many men's lives each year and poses similar risks in detection and treatment, lacks breast cancer's high-visibility campaigning for funding. The federal government is spending $133 million on prostate cancer research this year. Prodded by lobbying from former junk bond trader Michael Milken, who was diagnosed with prostate cancer in 1993, Congress allocated about $38 million in new research funds in fiscal 1997. [15]

Breast cancer activists say the success of the AIDS movement helped spur them to action. In 1989, AIDS was killing an estimated 22,000 people a year and receiving $1.6 billion in research funds from the federal government. Breast cancer was killing about 43,000 each year and receiving only $74.5 million. "I don't think we even knew how much money AIDS got when we started this movement, but we knew how much awareness the AIDS activists had raised," Visco says. "We said, 'We can do that for breast cancer.' "

Yet the number of deaths from a disease is not necessarily the appropriate yardstick for a medical research budget, some experts object. "I think it should be based on the potential value of the findings," Bailar says. "Cancer of the pancreas is still a major form of cancer, but there aren't many bright ideas about how to investigate it," he says. "I'm a little concerned about the same thing in breast cancer. It seems likely that much of what might be added to the research portfolio would be marginal, stuff that would be turned down [for research grants] as pedestrian."

Visco argues that the coalition's proposed increases are based on the number of promising grants that federal agencies can't afford to fund within existing budgets and on recent breakthroughs in cell biology.

"Now we're beginning to understand how cells interact with the internal environment in the body," she says. "We didn't even know which questions to ask four years ago. Now is not the time to stop spending money."

Some scientists, including NIH Director Harold E. Varmus, argue that earmarking funds for a specific disease is simplistic. [16] Breakthroughs for one disease are often discovered through research in other areas, they say. Sydney Salmon, director of the Arizona Cancer Center in Tucson, has noted that the discovery of an important factor in breast cancer — the loss of tumor suppressor genes — was made by scientists studying retinoblastoma, a seemingly unrelated childhood eye cancer.

Like many scientists, Salmon is also leery of another push by the breast cancer coalition — training breast cancer survivors to sit on expert committees that evaluate research proposals for federal funding. At the recent coalition conference in Washington, Bettye L. Green, chairperson of African-American Women in Touch, described how she had persuaded scientists on her Defense Department review committee to recommend funding a grant proposal that had received a merely "acceptable" score of scientific merit in its first round before a scientific peer review panel. The panel Green served on was charged with considering the contribution grant proposals could make to broader national policy goals as well as scientific quality.

Having a consumer representative like Green on board might persuade conservative scientists to take a chance on an unusually creative proposal, some experts suggest. But many scientists are not so sure.

"The most interesting and innovative ideas that have revolutionized biomedical research have by and large come from scientists," Salmon has stated, "and not from bureaucrats — be they from government or advocate groups." [17]

Yet serendipity could work in the opposite direction, too. "The kind of research being supported for breast cancer is the kind of cancer biology research that will benefit prostate cancer and other problems," says Johns Hopkins' Lawrence. "I don't buy that we're overspending." ■

BACKGROUND

Radical Treatment

Modern treatment of breast cancer dates back to the turn of the century, when William Halsted, a professor of surgery at Johns Hopkins, developed the procedure known as radical mastectomy.

Toward the end of the 19th century, physicians had begun to realize that cancers often recurred when only the tumor itself was removed. Halsted believed that breast cancer spread slowly into the rest of the body through the ducts, lymph nodes and other organs that drain the tissue fluid called lymph.

The solution, he decided, was to quickly remove the lymph nodes as well as the breast before the cancer spread. By 1890, Halsted had devised a surgical approach in which he removed the tumor and the surrounding normal tissue, including the lymph nodes and chest-wall muscles. Now known as a radical mastectomy, it has been dubbed the "scorched-earth" approach by David Plotkin, director of the Memorial Cancer Research Foundation in Los Angeles. [18]

"Halsted's notion became the prevailing paradigm for all cancers," says Samuel Hellman, a radiologist at the University of Chicago. For 70 years, most physicians viewed cancer as an orderly disease spreading at a steady rate from a local site.

Moreover, "Halsted became dogma," Hellman adds. "It empowered physicians to do something — in this case surgeons and radiation therapists. They could actually control the disease, and it was a liberating notion." It was Halsted's theory that supported the concept of early detection through mammography, says Love, an adjunct professor of surgery at the University of California in Los Angeles, and which "unwittingly" still influences much of our thinking today, she has written. [19]

New Approaches

As early as the 1930s, however, critics started complaining that the radical mastectomy didn't help patients whose cancer had already spread. Many breast cancer patients with very small tumors and without cancerous lymph nodes still developed the disease.

In 1971, Bernard Fisher, a surgeon at the University of Pittsburgh, began testing a new hypothesis: breast cancer can spread microscopically many years before it can be detected. If this were true, taking out lymph nodes at the time of diagnosis would not affect survival. Survival would be determined by how well the immune system handled whatever cancer cells had already spread from the breast.

Fisher divided women into three treatment groups: radical mastectomies, simple mastectomies (without removal of the lymph nodes) and simple mastectomies plus radiation aimed at cancer cells near the tumor. After 15 years, survival rates for the three groups were exactly the same.

Fisher's findings set the stage for a new approach, emphasizing a systemic agent that would destroy the cells that had already spread. That gave rise to chemotherapy — circulating drugs through the bloodstream to reach all the places cancer cells might be and try to destroy them. Yet even chemotherapy's effects on death rates have been modest.

The "Spectrum" Theory

Recently, researchers have been developing a new view of breast cancer, seeing it as a more complex and varied disease than can be explained entirely by either Halsted's or Fisher's theories. Hellman embraces this new "spectrum" theory, which holds that breast cancers exist in a wide variety, ranging from those that have already spread by the time they're detected to those that are so indolent they never become harmful, or even evident.

In the middle range of the spectrum, Hellman suggests, is the type of localized tumor that grows slowly enough that a mammogram can find it and a surgeon can remove it before it metastasizes, or spreads. It is probably this middle group for whom mammography is effective, the spectrum theory suggests. [20] Moreover, if the theory holds true and there are many forms of breast cancer, it could explain why mammography only saves a minority of women — about one-third in studies conducted before the advent of chemotherapy. But 30 percent still shows the "tremendous advantage" of mammography, Hellman adds.

In many ways, today's detection methods are more appropriate for our understanding of cancer 30 years ago, says Dartmouth's Wasson. Then, "the idea was that cancer was a group of cells that multiplied and eventually spread," he says. "If you go in and chop out the lump before it gets too big, you save a life."

But with today's more sophisticated biology, "We now understand that what makes a tumor mean is determined often by its genetic makeup — not by its size," Wasson says. "At one end of the spectrum, you've got the mean cancers that are likely to kill people where our current detection and treatment methods are inadequate. Then you've got this middle range that maybe follows this slow growth model we thought about 30 years ago, and you go in and chop."

At the other end of the spectrum are cancers so microscopic and localized that women may never be hurt by them, such as some forms of DCIS. Researchers who have examined the breast tissue of healthy women in their 50s killed in car accidents have discovered what look like small clumps of cancer cells in about a quarter of individuals, according to Wasson. Yet the women were never diagnosed with cancer.

"So obviously, our body is dealing with things we're unaware of," Wasson says. "We've got our immune system probably gobbling up abnormal cell lines all the time."

Increasingly, some researchers see the greatest hope for treatment in being able to identify molecular markers — genes, products of genes or surface proteins on the cell — that could distinguish among cancers. If, for example, the tests showed that a woman's cancer was unlikely to spread, "she needn't have to suffer through all the chemotherapy" says Hellman, who is studying such markers. No test yet exists that is accurate enough for widespread use.

"Like a boutique, rather than buying a suit off the rack, we can make the treatment match the individual patient — and not require aggressive treatment where it's not needed," Hellman predicts.

Push for Mammograms

In 1963, the New York Health Insurance Plan (HIP) began a study of

Continued on p. 568

Chronology

1890s-1930s

The modern era of breast cancer treatment begins.

1890
American surgeon William Halsted develops the radical mastectomy.

1913
The American Society for the Control of Cancer, now the American Cancer Society (ACS), is organized in New York City.

1937
Congress establishes the National Cancer Institute (NCI).

1940s-1960s

Critics of radical mastectomy seek a less drastic treatment.

1955
Scottish oncologist R. McWhirter calls for a less invasive operation and radiation therapy.

1963
The New York Health Insurance Plan (HIP) begins a mammogram screening study of 62,000 women. After 10 years, a 30 percent reduction in breast cancer deaths is found in women screened over age 50.

1968
Physicians use chemotherapy to cure rare form of uterine cancer.

1970s

A new theory holds that cancer has spread by the time it is detected; mammography gains public attention.

1971
Study at University of Pittsburgh finds same survival rate for women with less extensive surgery and radical mastectomy.

1973
The NCI and ACS introduce mammography to physicians and women 35 and older.

1974
First Lady Betty Ford and Happy Rockefeller, wife of Vice President Nelson A. Rockefeller, are diagnosed with breast cancer. The number of women diagnosed that year rises sharply.

1977
The NCI recommends that women 40-49 have mammograms only if they or their mothers or sisters had breast cancer.

1980s

Mammography equipment companies join the ACS and the NCI in a campaign to persuade healthy women to get mammograms.

1987
NCI adopts mammography guidelines also adopted by the ACS: At 40, women should begin screening every one to two years.

1990s

NCI reverses its policy — twice — on mammography for women in their 40s. The breast cancer rate stabilizes; the death rate decreases slightly.

1990
The National Institutes of Health (NIH) says lumpectomy plus radiation is as effective as mastectomy.

1992
The Canadian National Breast Cancer Screening Study finds no added benefit from screening for women 40-49.

1993
The NCI drops its screening recommendations for women in their 40s. The ACS continues to recommend screening.

1994
Scientists discover BRCA1, a gene whose mutations are associated with inherited breast cancer.

Jan. 23, 1997
An NIH panel recommends against universal mammography for women in their 40s.

Feb. 4, 1997
In response to the panel, the Senate urges the NCI to consider reissuing universal screening guidelines for women in their 40s.

March 23, 1997
The ACS recommends yearly mammograms for women in their 40s — up from its previous recommendation of every one to two years.

March 27, 1997
The NCI embraces universal screening for women in their 40s.

May 15, 1997
A study estimates that the risk of developing breast cancer for carriers of mutated genes is lower than previously thought.

Continued from p. 566

62,000 women ages 40-64 that became a landmark in the field of breast cancer. Half got mammography screening and a manual breast examination each year, and half were offered only a manual exam. After 10 years, a 30 percent reduction in breast cancer deaths was found in the screened women over 50. No reduction was shown among women in their 40s.

In 1973, based on the HIP findings, the NIH and the ACS launched a nationwide campaign to introduce mammography to physicians and women. All women 35 and older were encouraged to participate, despite the lack of evidence of screening's effectiveness among younger women.

In 1974, the campaign got a major boost when first lady Betty Ford and Vice President Nelson A. Rockefeller's wife, Happy, were diagnosed with breast cancer. The number of women diagnosed with cancer that year rose sharply.

However, some experts expressed doubts about the benefit of mammography for younger women. In 1976, Bailar, a former NCI deputy associate director for cancer control, published a statistical analysis showing more risk than benefits from screening young women. He expressed concern about surgery for microscopic lesions found by X-ray, called carcinoma in situ, but which were not clearly malignant.

In 1985, according to consumer advocate Napoli, mammography equipment companies and other businesses with a vested interest in screening promoted exaggerated "public education" claims such as "a 91 percent cure rate" for mammograms.

In 1987, NCI issued guidelines advising mammography for women in their 40s.

By the time the NCI withdrew its recommendations in 1993, "it was too late," Napoli says. "Most women now overestimate their odds of developing breast cancer in their 40s and overestimate what mammography can do for them."

By 1992, it had become well-known that the Canadian screening study had found no added benefit for women in their 40s. Following an international workshop convened by the NCI in February 1993, the institute dropped its screening recommendations for women in their 40s. Until this year's announcement, the institute had no recommendation for healthy women in that age group.

Napoli blames the cancer society for overselling mammography back in the 1970s. "When you're not getting anywhere in reducing the breast cancer death rate, you start to emphasize screening and say we could get somewhere if we get women in here earlier," she says.

The society's Smith acknowledges, "Undoubtedly [the message] was overly simplistic, overly optimistic. ACS puts out a very simple, very encouraging message designed to heighten the sense of risk and awareness that there was a solution. That has left many people feeling undoubtedly perplexed and a little betrayed when they feel they did everything right and are facing a poor prognosis."

In the future, says Smith, "We have to find a way of saying, 'It's the best chance of saving your life,' instead of, 'Mammograms will save your life.' " ■

CURRENT SITUATION

Puzzling Statistics

As increasing numbers of women have friends of their own age diagnosed with breast cancer, the impression gathers that there is a new epidemic of breast cancer. Actually, the cancer society explains, the increase reflects the aging of the U.S. population and the rising use of mammography.

For example, breast cancer is now the leading cause of cancer death for women in their 40s — and it tends to be a particularly virulent variety at that age — with tragic dimensions for young families. But the statistic belies the reality that very few women in their 40s die of any cause. As members of the baby boom population bulge into their 40s, younger women are more likely to know other younger women with breast cancer and to overestimate their risk. A 1995 Dartmouth College survey found that, on average, women in their 40s thought their chance of dying of breast cancer within the decade was 10 percent. Actually it's 0.4 percent. [21]

The incidence of breast cancer among American women overall has been growing slowly but steadily — about 1 percent a year between 1940 and 1982. Starting in the 1980s, when mammography became more widespread, rates of cancer increased about 4 percent per year. Between 1987 and 1992, the incidence of developing breast cancer stabilized. [22] (*See graph, p. 556.*)

Surprisingly, although the likelihood that a woman will be diagnosed with breast cancer has increased over the decades, the likelihood that it will end her life has not, notes Plotkin of the Memorial Cancer Research Foundation. The proportion of women killed each year by breast cancer, now at 25.9 per 100,000 women in the population, has changed little since the 1930s.

Optimistic analysts view these figures as a sign that science is conquering a growing disease. But skeptics like Plotkin believe it means medicine has made few strides in reducing the proportion of breast cancer cases that are

Continued on p. 570

At Issue:

Should all women in their 40s get mammograms?

SEN. OLYMPIA J. SNOWE, R-MAINE
FROM *THE WASHINGTON POST*, FEB. 11, 1997

This coming year, breast cancer will claim more lives of women in their 40s than any other disease. . . . Seeking guidance . . . women and physicians will look to the nation's preeminent cancer research institution, the National Cancer Institute (NCI), for clear and concise medical advice. Yet, if they rely on the findings of an NCI consensus conference panel charged with providing guidelines for routine mammography ... what they will find, regrettably, are muddled recommendations that . . . ultimately endanger women's lives.

Cancer is a complex disease that the . . . medical establishment does not yet fully understand. But . . . one fact is readily appreciated: Stopping an advancing cancer means identifying that cancer early. In the case of breast cancer, this early diagnosis is facilitated through routine mammograms.

Despite these widely supported facts, last month's panel report to NCI contends that . . . potential risks associated with mammography screening in the 40s . . . are significant enough that women in their 40s need not necessarily undergo routine mammograms. . . .

In reaching its recommendations, the NCI consensus panel overstates or distorts the potential risks and pitfalls associated with routine mammogram screening. The panel claims, for instance, that up to one-fourth of all invasive breast cancers are not detected by mammography in women in their 40s. Yet, such a statistic can hardly be considered compelling when the flip side of this statistic suggests just the opposite conclusion. With three-fourths of such cancers detected through the use of mammography screening, solid justification exists for recommending such routine screening.

The NCI panel report also seems to raise excessive concern about the risk of false-positive mammogram findings for women in their 40s, suggesting that many women with such findings would undergo unnecessary surgical procedures. Yet, the NCI report fails to note that a mammogram is only the first step in diagnosing cancer. . . .

Having brushed aside these critical facts, it should not be surprising that the NCI panel report is now prompting widespread disagreement and criticism in medical and public policy circles, and even within NCI itself. . . . Two of the most respected voices on breast cancer issues — the American Cancer Society and the American Medical Association — continue to wisely endorse regular mammogram screening beginning at age 40. . . .

[It] is now incumbent upon our nation's medical establishment — and its policy leaders — to come forward with a clear . . . statement for women about the benefits of early mammography screening. The statement should be nothing less than this: If you forgo mammogram screening in your 40s, you are rolling the dice with your very life.

FRANCES M. VISCO
FROM A STATEMENT BEFORE SENATE APPROPRIATIONS LABOR, HEALTH AND HUMAN SERVICES AND EDUCATION SUBCOMMITTEE, FEB. 5, 1997

I was diagnosed with breast cancer in September 1987, when I was 39. My breast cancer was diagnosed through a mammogram. I had lumpectomy, radiation and chemotherapy. But I am here to speak in support of the findings of the consensus panel. . . .

I am amazed at the attention given to the mammography question and frankly appalled at the resources we continue to devote to [it] and the outrage that met the panel's conclusions. Over the past two weeks, I have lost two very close friends and great activists to breast cancer. They were both younger than 50 when they died. A mammogram did not save their lives. Where is the outrage over that fact?

We are acting as though this issue — whether to recommend population screening of women 40-49 — is the most important question in breast cancer. Let's save our outrage for the fact that we don't know how to prevent this disease, how to cure it, how to detect it truly early, or what to do for an individual woman once we do find it. Let's save our outrage, our resources, our energy, our time, for the 44,000 women who die each year. For the tens of thousands of women who have no access to health care.

The consensus panel looked at the data — from trials that were not designed to answer the question we're asking and that don't ask any question about minority women — and saw that a meta-analysis of the eight trials shows a 17 percent decrease in mortality for women under 50. But the decrease does not begin to show up for 10 years, raising the question, among others, of whether the women, who are by now in their 50s, are actually benefiting from mammography at that age. . . .

Let's focus our resources and energy on getting women over 50 to get mammograms — the vast majority do not. . . .

Let's fund the research that will find the cure, prevention, true early detection. And if we really want to save women's lives, let's focus our outrage, our energy, our commitment on guaranteeing access to quality health care for all women and their families. There is no dispute that public policy will save many lives. . . .

Let's not continue to give women false hope, let's not continue to act as though the issue deserves this much attention and resources, let's face the truth - the data to support population screening in this age group are simply not there. . . .

Searching for the Link . . .

Depending upon the analysis, only about 25-40 percent of women who get breast cancer in the United States have known risk factors for the disease. *(See box, p. 562.)* Hereditary breast cancer is estimated to account for only 5 percent of cases. Well-known risk factors include family history of breast cancer, never having children, having a first child later in life and having a moderate or high income. [1]

But these factors in themselves raise questions about the true causes of breast cancer and about why the majority of women who get breast cancer have none of these risk factors.

Increasingly, some researchers are leaning toward the view of David Plotkin, director of the Memorial Cancer Research Foundation in Los Angles, that the rise in breast cancer "may be an unwanted accompaniment to what most Americans view as social and material progress." [2]

The modern world of improved nutrition and educational opportunities, in which women often delay child rearing until after college, graduate school or establishing careers, has created an entirely different hormonal environment than the one that evolved for their hunter-gatherer ancestors. Partly because of better nutrition, girls today menstruate at earlier ages than their forbears, with puberty in the United States now averaging at age 12 — compared with the late teens for some traditional African hunter-gatherer societies where breast cancer is far less common.

Freed from lifelong cycles of pregnancy and breast-feeding, which suppress estrogen production, modern women are now exposed to much higher levels of estrogen and associated hormones. Women ovulate many more times during their modern lives and churn out estrogen for longer periods.

Every month during ovulation, a surge of estrogen, followed by progesterone, courses through a woman's bloodstream to the breasts. This causes cells within the breast to multiply on the off-chance that the woman will soon be nursing a baby. With repeated menstrual cycles, however, the number of cells can increase 100 times or more. The more the cells multiply, the higher the likelihood that a genetic mutation in one cell will repeat itself. Most cancers are thought to arise from such genetic accidents.

These hormonal blasts from modern living could explain why moderate to higher income women, who tend to delay childbearing, and have more periods, could be at higher than normal risk. As researchers study elements that appear to help in prevention — frequent exercise, less fat in the diet, reduced environmental pollution — it may be that estrogen is what ties all these factors together.

A recent study of 25,000 Norwegian women found those who exercised at least four hours a week had a 37 percent lower risk of developing breast cancer, compared with sedentary women. [3]

Continued from p. 568

fatal. Instead, he suggests, doctors are diagnosing an increasing number of slow-growing, non-fatal cancers.

However, some experts point to a recent downward trend in death rates as a sign that treatment is gaining on breast cancer. According to the ACS, the proportion of women killed by breast cancer has declined about 6 percent between 1989 and 1993, the latest year for which statistics are available. The society's Smith attributes the decline to a combination of mammography screening and chemotherapy treatment.

But skeptics like Bailar note that the most impressive decline for a single group — 13 percent — was for white women in their 30s. Considering that the mammography screening campaign has been directed at women 40 and older, Bailar questions how screening could have had much effect. ■

OUTLOOK

Balancing Risks

In a recent column, breast surgeon Love suggested that it may be time to take a closer look at how the environment around normal cells — such as hormonal levels — may render normal cells cancerous. If people with cancer can go into remission for 10 years, she suggests, maybe it's possible to alter the bodily environment to put cancer cells to sleep permanently.

"We have been treating breast cancer as if it were a hardened criminal, a cell that goes bad and must be killed," Love writes. "[I]n fact the cancer cell may be a criminal who is capable of being rehabilitated, that the cells in a different host environment . . . could be rendered harmless." [23]

Malcolm C. Pike, an epidemiologist at the University of Southern California, is among the researchers experimenting with changing a woman's hormonal environment. In clinical trials, he has been testing an artificial hormone that shuts down the ovaries, halting the production of suspected breast cancer producing hormones — estrogen, progesterone and testosterone.

In studying mammograms of women given the artificial ovary regulator, Pike found the women's breasts in later X-rays were less dense. He theorizes that a less-dense breast is one in which cells are dividing less rapidly and is less susceptible to cancer. Because of the difficulty in getting Food and Drug Admin-

. . . Between Risk Factors and Breast Cancer

One reason may be that women who exercise more have less hormonal exposure. "Their periods tend to be farther apart in time, and their hormonal levels are lower," says Devra Lee Davis, who directs the program in health, environment and development at the World Resources Institute, an environmental think tank in Washington, D.C. Teenage girls training for marathon runs can put themselves into a form of "artificial castration," in which they have no periods, Davis notes.

Davis is a leading advocate of the theory that certain environmental chemicals — pesticides, plastics, fuels — that mimic estrogen in the body contribute to many unexplained cases of breast cancer. (*See story, p. 560.*) Diets high in animal fat and alcohol appear to increase risk, Davis hypothesizes, because fat tissue can make estrogen, and alcohol can increase production of the hormone.

Debate continues over whether fat in the diet could be linked to cancer. The most convincing evidence comes from so-called migration studies. For example, American women have a rate of breast cancer six times as high as that of women in Japan, where there is much less dietary fat. But Japanese-American women, whose diets are presumably more Americanized, have breast cancer rates similar to those of women born and raised in the U.S. Over the past 10-20 years, the fat intake in Japan has been increasing, and rates of breast cancer have also increased, according to Carolyn Clifford, chief of the diet and cancer branch at the National Cancer Institute. Asian women tend to have lower hormonal levels than their Asian-American immigrant counterparts, in part, some researchers believe, because they eat less fat and are less sedentary. [4]

While migration studies seem to support the fat-cancer link, Clifford says other types of studies have been "equivocal" on the question. That may be because women have not lowered their fat intake enough in studies observing different women's diet habits, some researchers think.

In the largest randomized clinical trial to study the question to date, the National Institutes of Health will study the effect of adopting a low-fat diet on breast cancer risk for 56,000 middle-aged women. Among other tests, the researchers will measure estrogen levels in the women's blood, according to Clifford. The study is still recruiting and will not be completed until at least 2005.

[1] M. Patricia Madigan et al, "Proportion of Breast Cancer Cases in the United States Explained by Well-Established Risk Factors," *The Journal of the National Cancer Institute*, Nov. 15, 1995, pp. 1681-1685.

[2] David Plotkin, "Good News and Bad News about Breast Cancer," *The Atlantic Monthly*, June 1996, p. 58.

[3] Gina Kolata, "Study Bolsters Idea that Exercise Cuts Breast Cancer Risk," *The New York Times*, May 1, 1997, p. A1.

[4] David L. Wheeler, "Researcher Looks to Hormones as the Cause and Possible Treatment of Breast Cancer, *The Chronicle of Higher Education*, Sept. 20, 1996.

istration approval for a drug to be administered to healthy people, Pike is currently testing the drug in small groups of women who suffer from fibroids, non-cancerous uterine growths that are stimulated by estrogen. The medication is at least five years away from large-scale trials. [24]

Pike thinks that a woman who followed his hormonal-suppressing regimen for 15 years could reduce her breast cancer risk by 75 percent. But other experts question whether the risks are worth it for healthy women.

"What Pike is doing is scientifically fascinating," says Devra Lee Davis, an epidemiologist at the World Resources Institute, but it's essentially "chemical castration" of young women. "My concern is you're altering very delicate and essential functioning."

In the first trials Pike conducted, some women lost bone density, another consequence of reduced estrogen; one woman had to be treated for osteoporosis. [25] It's not clear to what extent women might suffer other menopausal-style consequences, such as hot flashes or loss of libido, even with compensating doses of hormones.

In addition, how many healthy women would want to take such risks weighed against the risk of getting cancer? One in nine women now falls victim to cancer in her lifetime, which translates to an 11 percent risk by age 90.

"The chemical approach makes me nervous," Davis says. "What I think is more sensible public policy is to encourage women to exercise, substitute healthy diets and reduce exposure to suspect pollutants."

The gambling nature of breast cancer prevention was highlighted recently by a new study that recalculated the odds for women who inherit genes linked to the disease. According to the study, a woman who inherits mutations in two DNA-repairing genes known as BRCA1 and BRCA2 has a 56 percent chance of developing breast cancer. The estimate is significantly lower than earlier estimates, which appeared to confer a practical death sentence on such women at 85 percent. [26]

The study was conducted in Washington, D.C., among Ashkenazi Jews — Jews from Eastern Europe — many of whom carry the gene. Critics faulted the study because in calculating breast cancer risks, the researchers relied on participants' memories of which distant relatives had cancer.

Nevertheless, experts are taking

the new calculation seriously. It may mean that not as many women who test positive for the gene will feel compelled to undergo preventive mastectomy, several experts suggest. The procedure, known as prophylactic mastectomy, does not always prevent a woman from getting breast cancer because surgeons cannot be assured of removing 100 percent of breast tissue, notes Love. Several cases of breast cancer have been documented following the procedure.

"It means we have to be more careful that women who get tested are the right people — not do wholesale testing," says Rimer, who has been studying how women make decisions in the face of genetic testing. "We find women underestimate the negatives of testing," Rimer says, including loss of medical insurance, potential discrimination and the unproven benefit of prophylactic mastectomy.

She also sees dangers in the growing commercialization of genetic testing by for-profit companies. "I think there's going to be a lot of bad advice out there, and probably too many women are going to be advised to get testing," Rimer says. "A high proportion of doctors are not interpreting the test results properly."

In a column commenting on the new study of Ashkenazi Jews and several related articles, former NIH Director Bernadine Healy warned, "These reports should alert us to the limitations of the expanding medical practice of making gene-based statistical prophecies," which she dubbed "medical bookmaking and fortunetelling. [27]

Even among women who test positive for abnormalities in the BRCA1 and BRCA1 genes, different mutations of the genes — and there are more than 200 mutations — confer different risks for breast cancer, the recent research found. And even the same mutations behave differently in different women. That suggests, Healy says, that other factors — hormonal, environmental, dietary or even other gene mutations — could be playing a role in determining whether a specific BRCA mutation causes cancer.

"Without facts about these other variables," Healy concluded, "the fortunetellers are reading a pretty cloudy crystal ball." [28] ■

Sarah Glazer is a New York-based writer who specializes in health and social-policy issues.

Notes

[1] Testimony before the Senate Labor, Health and Human Services and Education Appropriations Subcommittee, Feb. 5, 1997.

[2] Gina Kolata, "Mammogram Talks Prove Indefinite," *The New York Times,* Jan. 24, 1997, p. A1. The remark was made by Michael Linver, director of mammography at X-Ray Associates of New Mexico, in Albuquerque.

[3] Sen. Olympia J. Snowe, "Mammograms Save Lives," *The Washington Post,* Feb. 11, 1997, p. A21.

[4] Press release, National Institutes of Health, March 27, 1997.

[5] Karla Kerlikowske et al., "Efficacy of Screening Mammography: A Meta-analysis," *The Journal of the American Medical Association,* Jan. 11, 1995, pp. 149-154.

[6] Kolata, *op. cit.*

[7] Steven H. Woolf and Robert S. Lawrence, "When Politicians Play Doctor," *The Washington Post,* May 4, 1997, p. C1.

[8] NIH press release, p. 4.

[9] Charles R. Smart, R. Edward Hendrick, James H. Rutledge III and Robert A. Smith, "Benefit of Mammography Screening in Women Ages 40 to 49 Years," *Cancer,* April 1, 1995, pp. 1619-1626. Also see "Advances in Cancer Research," *The CQ Researcher,* Aug. 24, 1995, p. 764.

[10] NIH Consensus Statement Online 1997, "Breast Cancer Screening for Women Ages 40-49," Jan. 21-23, 1997.

[11] Kerlikowske, *Ibid.*

[12] R. Edward Hendrick, Robert A. Smith, James H. Rutledge III and Charles R. Smart, "Benefit of Screening Mammography in Women Ages 40-49: A New Meta-Analysis of Randomized Controlled Trials," submitted to *The Journal of the National Cancer Institute.*

[13] Marilyn Werber Serafini, "Biomedical Warfare," *National Journal,* Feb. 1, 1997, pp. 220-223. The $78 per person figure is based on $78 million in total federal spending: $32 million in direct research on Parkinson's and $46 million for related research.

[14] Lisa Belkin, "How Breast Cancer Became This Year's Hot Charity," *The New York Times Magazine,* Dec. 22, 1996, p. 40.

[15] Rick Weiss, "War Between Sexes Rages Over Research," *The Washington Post,* Aug. 6, 1996, p. A13.

[16] Serafini, *op. cit.,* p. 222.

[17] Jane Erikson, "Breast Cancer Activists Seek Voice in Research Decisions," *Science,* Sept. 15, 1995, pp. 1508-1509.

[18] David Plotkin, "Good News and Bad News about Breast Cancer," *The Atlantic Monthly,* June 1996, pp. 53-82.

[19] Susan M. Love and Sanford H. Barsky, "Breast Cancer: An Interactive Paradigm," *The Breast Journal,* Vol. 2, No. 3, 1996, pp. 171-175.

[20] Samuel Hellman, "Natural History of Small Breast Cancers," *Journal of Clinical Oncology,* October 1994, pp. 2229-2234.

[21] David L. Wheeler, "Researcher Looks to Hormones as the Cause and Possible Treatment of Breast Cancer," *The Chronicle of Higher Education,* Sept. 20, 1996.

[22] American Cancer Society, *Breast Cancer Facts & Figures, 1996,* December 1995, p. 2.

[23] Love and Barsky, *op. cit.,* pp. 173-174.

[24] Rosie Mestel, "Redesigning Women," *Health,* March 1997, pp. 70-76.

[25] Wheeler et al., *op. cit.*

[26] Jeffrey P. Struewing et al., "The Risk of Cancer Associated with Specific Mutations of BRCA1 and BRCA2 Among Ashkenazi Jews," *The New England Journal of Medicine,* May 15, 1997, pp. 1401-1408.

[27] Bernadine Healy, "BRCA Genes — Bookmaking, Fortunetelling and Medical Care," *The New England Journal of Medicine,* May 15, 1997, pp. 1448-1449.

[28] *Ibid.*

Bibliography

Selected Sources Used

Books

Love, Susan M., *Dr. Susan Love's Breast Book*, Addison-Wesley, 1995 (2nd ed.).
Breast surgeon Love offers a clear, jargon-free explanation of the development, treatment and prevention of breast cancer. Love's compassionate tone helped make the book a favorite among women who have breast cancer or are concerned about getting the disease.

Stabiner, Karen, *To Dance with the Devil: The New War on Breast Cancer*, Delacorte, 1997.
Journalist Stabiner shadowed flamboyant breast surgeon Susan Love and several of her patients for nine months in 1994 at the University of California-Los Angeles Breast Center. Her artfully woven story lends a sense of drama to the scientific controversies that continue to rock the world of breast cancer research and treatment.

Articles

Davis, Devra Lee, and H. Leon Bradlow, "Can Environmental Estrogens Cause Breast Cancer?" *Scientific American*, October 1995, pp.144-149.
The authors explain why their theory that pesticides and other chemicals in the environment that behave like estrogen in the body contribute to breast cancer.

Fletcher, Suzanne W., "Whither Scientific Deliberation in Health Policy Recommendations?: Alice in the Wonderland of Breast Screening," *The New England Journal of Medicine*, April 17, 1997, pp. 1180-1183.
Harvard Medical School internist Fletcher argues that health-care controversies like the mammogram debate are "increasingly being distorted by emotional, political, financial and legal interests" and calls for an impartial decision-making approach.

Kolata, Gina, "New View Sees Breast Cancer as 3 Diseases," *The New York Times*, April 1, 1997, p. C1.
Kolata describes the increasingly widespread view that breast cancer comes in multiple forms — which may explain why mammography works for only a minority of women.

Plotkin, David, "Good News and Bad News About Breast Cancer," *The Atlantic Monthly*, June 1996, pp. 53-82.
Breast cancer specialist Plotkin persuasively argues that current treatments and detection have made little headway in reducing fatal cancers, though experts on both sides find his attack on mammography overly pessimistic.

Mestel, Rosie, "Redesigning Women," *Health*, March 1997, pp. 70-76.
Mestel describes the theory that childbearing cycles of primitive hunter-gatherers protected women against breast cancer and researcher Malcolm Pike's efforts to mimic the environment with hormone suppressing drugs.

Taubes, Gary, "The Breast-Screening Brawl," *Science*, February 1997, pp. 1056-1059.
This a thorough discussion of the disagreements among scientists that have contributed to the controversy over mammography screening for women in their 40s.

Woolf, Steven H., and Robert S. Lawrence, "When Politicians Play Doctor," *The Washington Post*, May 4, 1997, p. C1.
Two physicians argue that the recent controversy over breast cancer screening was overly influenced by politics.

FOR MORE INFORMATION

American Cancer Society, 1599 Clifton Road N.E., Atlanta, GA 30329; (404) 320-3333 or (800) 227-2345 to reach a regional office. The nation's largest voluntary health agency; with over 2 million volunteers in regional offices.

National Breast Cancer Coalition, 1707 L St. N.W., Suite 1060, Washington, D.C. 20036; (202) 296-7477. This advocacy group, representing over 350 organizations and thousands of breast cancer survivors, lobbies for increased federal funding for breast cancer research and improved access to high-quality health care.

National Cancer Institute, Cancer Information Service, 31 Center Dr., Building 31, Room 10A07, Bethesda, Md. 20892-2580; (800) 422-6237. The NCI is the prime federal institute funding breast cancer research. Information specialists at this toll-free line can answer questions and mail out information.

National Women's Health Network, 514 10th St. N.W., Suite 400, Washington, D.C. 20004; (202) 347-1140. The network acts as an information clearinghouse on breast cancer and other women's health issues and monitors federal policies and legislation.

The Next Step

Additional information from UMI's Newspaper & Periodical Abstracts™ database

Funding for Research

Guernsey, Lisa, "Clinton expands research efforts on breast cancer," *The Chronicle of Higher Education,* Nov. 8, 1996, p. A31.
President Clinton recently announced three new programs to aid researchers studying breast cancer. The federal government will spend an additional $30 million in fiscal 1997 on studies of the genetics of the disease.

Wadman, Meredith, "Breast cancer grant policy comes under fire," *Nature,* Sept. 12, 1996, p. 113.
The complaints of two scientists from Yale University who were denied funding by a huge federally funded breast cancer research program have rekindled a fierce dispute that took place when the Breast Cancer Research Program was set up by Congress in 1993. The dispute centers on the extent to which peer-review judgments might become subservient to other factors in allocating research grants.

Walker, Paulette V., "The shift of $14 million ends a feud over funds for breast-cancer research," *The Chronicle of Higher Education,* Nov. 22, 1996, p. A30.
Officials who oversee a government-run breast cancer program have decided to shift $14 million to the National Cancer Institute. This move ends a feud between advocates for breast cancer research and federal health authorities.

Genetic Screening

Burge, Boyce, "Genetic testing for breast cancer risk," *Healthline,* April 1997, pp. 10-11.
Research into genetic testing to assess breast cancer risk is discussed. Women who are found to inherit an altered BRCA1 gene tend to develop breast cancer at younger ages than other women.

Carey, Benedict, and Michael Mason, "Breast cancer risk: Don't ask, don't tell?" *Health,* September 1996, pp. 24-27.
Geneticists who offered testing for mutation of the gene BRCA1, which has been linked to breast cancer, were surprised by the sparse response. The lack of interest and hostility toward genetic testing could mean that scientists are wasting their time and millions of dollars in scientific research.

Kolata, Gina, "Advent of Testing for Breast Cancer Genes Leads to Fears of Disclosure and Discrimination," *The New York Times,* Feb. 4, 1997, p. C1.
Some women and researchers are convinced that it might be too dangerous to put genetic testing results on medical charts and in clinical records, where privacy cannot be assured. Women worry that insurers will raise their rates or refuse to insure them, that employers will not hire them or promote them and even that friends and family members might treat them differently if they knew they carried a cancer-causing gene.

Waldholz, Michael, "Medicine: Predictive use of breast-cancer genetic test is disputed," *The Wall Street Journal,* May 15, 1997, p. B1.
A debate has erupted over the predictive powers and usefulness of a genetic test taken by several thousand women to learn whether they carry a gene defect that sharply increases their chances of developing breast cancer.

Incidence and Mortality Rates

"Breast cancer incidence and mortality — United States, 1992," *The Journal of the American Medical Association,* Oct. 23-Oct. 30, 1996, p. 6.
The incidence and death rates for breast cancer in the U.S. during 1992 are presented, and the trends in these rates are summarized.

"Breast cancer incidence and mortality — United States, 1992," *Morbidity & Mortality Weekly Report,* Oct. 4, 1996, pp. 833-837.
The Centers for Disease Control analyzed national breast cancer incidence data to assess trends in incidence and death rates for breast cancer among U.S. women. Mortality rates remained stable from 1973 to 1988 and decreased between 1989 and 1992.

Mihill, Chris, "No clear 'cause' for fall in breast cancer deaths," *The Guardian,* March 25, 1996, p. 6.
Death rates from breast cancer are falling in England and Wales and in other Western countries, although researchers are unclear why.

Pinkowish, Mary Desmond, "Great news: Breast cancer mortality is down," *Patient Care,* Jan. 15, 1997, p. 13.
A study has shown that breast cancer mortality is at its lowest since 1950, which may signal a turning point in the struggle against the disease.

Stockton, Diane, Tom Davies, Nicholas Day and Jenny McCann, "Retrospective study of reasons for improved survival in patients with breast cancer in East Anglia: Earlier diagnosis or better treatment?" *British Medical Journal,* Feb. 15, 1997, pp. 472-475.
A retrospective study was conducted to investigate the

recent fall in mortality from breast cancer in England and Wales and to determine how improvements in treatment and earlier detection of tumors contributed to the decrease.

Mammography Debate

Okie, Susan, "More Women Are Getting Mammograms; Experts Agree That the Test Has Played Big Role in Reducing Deaths From Breast Cancer," *The Washington Post,* Jan. 21, 1997, Sec. HM, p. 7.

For women in their 40s, in whom breast cancer is much more uncommon, the question of whether to have regular mammograms has remained controversial because of disputes about its effectiveness at that age. At a conference opening today at the National Institutes of Health, a panel of experts will hear new evidence suggesting that mammograms do prevent cancer deaths in women in their 40s — although the benefit of the test is less for older women.

Rochell, Anne, "A wider war on breast cancer? The federal government is considering proposals to recommend mammograms for women younger than 50," *Atlanta Journal Constitution,* Jan. 18, 1997, p. F1.

Murky evidence and conflicting recommendations, which have been a source of confusion to women younger than 50 deciding whether to get a mammogram, may change in the week of Jan. 19, 1997. Clinical trials started in the 1970s and 80s are starting to show that women with cancer who had mammograms in their 40s may live longer than women who did not .

SoRelle, Ruth, "More cases of a rare breast cancer reported," *Houston Chronicle,* May 13, 1996, p. B7.

A little-known form of breast cancer is showing up in increasing numbers in U.S. women. Doctors do not think the cancer, known as ductal carcinoma in situ, is becoming more common but instead is being diagnosed more frequently as mammograms uncover smaller malignancies.

Stabiner, Karen, "Breast Cancer: Behind the Furor," *The Washington Post,* March 25, 1997, p. A17.

The American Cancer Society's new recommendation of annual mammography for women between the ages of 40 and 50 — and the National Cancer Institute's (NCI) anticipated endorsement, in defiance of its own expert panel's advice — seem intended to end the controversy that began in December 1993, when the NCI first took the position that mammography for this age group was ineffective.

Prevention

Tobin, James, "For women who may harbor the breast cancer gene, chance to know for sure is frightful choice," *Detroit News & Free Press,* Dec. 15, 1996, p. A1.

Remarkable discoveries about the human genetic code are giving doctors unprecedented power to predict cancer and many other serious diseases. Yet those same discoveries reveal the vast distance science must go before doctors can use genetics not just to foresee disease, but to cure it.

Wheeler, David L., "Researcher looks to hormones as the cause and possible treatment of breast cancer," *The Chronicle of Higher Education,* Sept. 20, 1996, pp. A14-15.

University of Southern California Professor Malcolm C. Pike believes that hormones are responsible for breast cancer and could lead to a way to prevent it. Pike's solution to breast cancer, to shut down the ovaries, is discussed.

Risk Factors

Byrne, Celia, Giske Ursin and Regina G. Ziegler, "A comparison of food habit and food frequency data as predictors of breast cancer in the NHANES I/NHEFS cohort," *Journal of Nutrition,* November 1996, p. 1.

Byrne et al compared two methods of assessing dietary fat and breast cancer incidence in the first complete follow-up of the National Health Epidemiologic Follow-up Study cohort. The results are discussed.

Fackelmann, Kathleen, "The birth of a breast cancer," *Science News,* Feb. 15, 1997, pp. 108-109.

According to epidemiologist Dimitrios Trichopoulos, estrogen may set the stage for breast cancer while women are still in the womb. New research indicates that some factor within the uterus programs fetal cells for the development of cancer decades later.

Hardie, Ann, "For good health, women may want to bone up; As studies imply a relationship between a sturdy skeleton and breast cancer, women grapple with the pros and cons of hormone replacement therapy," *Atlanta Constitution,* March 27, 1997, p. F3.

Science has begun doing something it hadn't for many years — paying attention to women. In the past six months, two major studies in reputable medical journals found a link between strong bones and an increased risk of breast cancer. But less certain is what a woman can do to prevent the disease. Even advice is sometimes contradictory — the American Cancer Society this week told women older than 40 to get yearly breast X-rays to screen for cancer; the National Cancer Institute, for now, says a woman should make that decision based on her own risk factors.

Michels, Karin B., Dimitrios Trichopoulos, James M. Robins and Bernard A. Rosner et al, "Birthweight as a risk factor for breast cancer," *Lancet,* Dec. 7, 1996, p. 41.

Studies of migrant populations, animal data and limited epidemiological evidence suggest that breast cancer may originate in utero. Michels et al assess whether birthweight and other perinatal factors are associated with the risk of developing breast cancer.

Back Issues

Great Research on Current Issues Starts Right Here . . . Recent topics covered by The CQ Researcher are listed below. Before May 1991, reports were published under the name of Editorial Research Reports.

DECEMBER 1995
Teens and Tobacco
Gene Therapy's Future
Global Water Shortages
Third-Party Prospects

JANUARY 1996
Emergency Medicine
Punishing Sex Offenders
Bilingual Education
Helping the Homeless

FEBRUARY 1996
Reforming the CIA
Campaign Finance Reform
Academic Politics
Getting Into College

MARCH 1996
The British Monarchy
Preventing Juvenile Crime
Tax Reform
Pursuing the Paranormal

APRIL 1996
Centennial Olympic Games
Managed Care
Protecting Endangered Species
New Military Culture

Back issues are available for $5.00 (subscribers) or $10.00 (non-subscribers). Quantity discounts apply to orders over ten. To order, call Congressional Quarterly Customer Service at (202) 887-8621.

Binders are available for $18.00. To order call 1-800-638-1710. Please refer to stock number 648.

MAY 1996
Russia's Political Future
Marriage and Divorce
Year-Round Schools
Taiwan, China and the U.S.

JUNE 1996
Rethinking NAFTA
First Ladies
Teaching Values
Labor Movement's Future

JULY 1996
Recovered-Memory Debate
Native Americans' Future
Crackdown on Sexual Harassment
Attack on Public Schools

AUGUST 1996
Fighting Over Animal Rights
Privatizing Government Services
Child Labor and Sweatshops
Cleaning Up Hazardous Wastes

SEPTEMBER 1996
Gambling Under Attack
The States and Federalism
Civic Journalism
Reassessing Foreign Aid

OCTOBER 1996
Political Consultants
Insurance Fraud
Rethinking School Integration
Parental Rights

NOVEMBER 1996
Global Warming
Clashing Over Copyright
Consumer Debt
Governing Washington, D.C.

DECEMBER 1996
Welfare, Work and the States
The New Volunteerism
Implementing the Disabilities Act
America's Pampered Pets

JANUARY 1997
Combating Scientific Misconduct
Restructuring the Electric Industry
The New Immigrants
Chemical and Biological Weapons

FEBRUARY 1997
Assisting Refugees
Alternative Medicine's Next Phase
Independent Counsels
Feminism's Future

MARCH 1997
New Air Quality Standards
Alcohol Advertising
Civic Renewal
Educating Gifted Students

APRIL 1997
Declining Crime Rates
The FBI Under Fire
Gender Equity in Sports
Space Program's Future

MAY 1997
The Stock Market
The Cloning Controversy
Expanding NATO
The Future of Libraries

JUNE 1997
FDA Reform
China After Deng
Line-Item Veto

Future Topics

- ***Transportation Policy***
- ***Executive Pay***
- ***School Vouchers***

THE CQ Researcher®

PUBLISHED BY CONGRESSIONAL QUARTERLY INC.

Transportation Policy

Should non-highway programs get more funding?

The impending expiration of the nation's $157 billion transportation legislation has plunged lawmakers into one of the most contentious issues they will face this year. The current law — the 1991 Intermodal Surface Transportation Efficiency Act (ISTEA) — receives widespread praise for giving localities a prominent role in deciding how to allocate federal transportation dollars. The emerging debate over the proposed replacement legislation focuses on how much can be spent in a time of scarce federal dollars — and how it should be spent. Highway users, including automakers and truckers, want more money for road-building and maintenance. Environmentalists, transit operators and bicyclists want to preserve the current law's funding for alternative modes of transportation as a way to relieve traffic congestion and curb suburban sprawl.

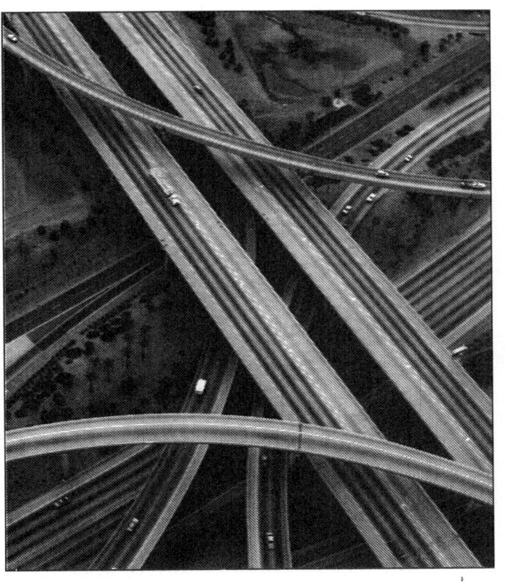

INSIDE THIS ISSUE

CQ July 4, 1997 • Volume 7, No. 25 • Pages 577-600

Formerly Editorial Research Reports

THE ISSUES

BACKGROUND

CURRENT SITUATION

OUTLOOK

SIDEBARS AND GRAPHICS

FOR FURTHER RESEARCH

July 4, 1997
Volume 7, No. 25

The CQ Researcher (ISSN 1056-2036). Formerly Editorial Research Reports. Published weekly, except Jan. 3, May 30, Aug. 29, Oct. 31, by Congressional Quarterly Inc., 1414 22nd St., N.W., Washington, D.C. 20037. Annual subscription rate for libraries, businesses and government is $340. Additional rates furnished upon request. Periodicals postage paid at Washington, D.C., and additional mailing offices. POSTMASTER: Send address changes to The CQ Researcher, 1414 22nd St., N.W., Washington, D.C. 20037.

COVER: HIGHWAY INTERCHANGES IN PHOENIX, ARIZONA (© 1997 PHOTODISC)

Transportation Policy

BY MARY H. COOPER

THE ISSUES

It's the focus of a major fight in Congress this year, but it sounds more like a refreshing summer drink than multibillion-dollar legislation pitting highway interests against advocates of alternative transportation.

The 1991 Intermodal Surface Transportation Efficiency Act — better known as ISTEA — is a massive, $157 billion, six-year authorization measure that runs out on Sept. 30. The complex law spells out how much federal money will be used to build and maintain highways, bridges, railways, transit systems, bike paths and walkways.

How this money should be allocated among these different transportation modes, at a time when Congress is struggling to balance the budget, is turning into one of the year's most contentious legislative debates.

"The logic of the debate is pretty simple," says Hank Dittmar, executive director of the Surface Transportation Policy Project, the leading coalition of groups that support more generous funding of transportation alternatives to cars and trucks. "The increases are going to be moderate rather than large, so the people who have their hopes up for large amounts of new money will be trying to take their share out of somebody else's hide."

Governments at all levels — local, state and federal — spend more than $40 billion each year to build surface transportation infrastructure, such as roads, bridges and light-rail lines, and many additional billions on operating and maintaining those systems. [1] About half that amount comes from the federal government's Highway Trust Fund, which is financed by federal fuel tax revenues and other highway-user fees. (*See graph, p. 580.*) States have long fought over the portion of the federal subsidies they receive to build and maintain their transportation systems.

Among the most vocal critics of the federal funding formulas are states, mostly in the South and the Midwest, that contribute more money to the Highway Trust Fund than they get back from the fund for road construction and repair. They say the law unfairly favors highly populated states, mostly in the Northeast. (*See map, p. 584.*)

"We definitely favor a change in the allocation formulas that they are using," says Richard Whitney, a transportation official in Indiana, where highways and bridges undergo punishing use from interstate truckers. "We have a lot of trucks coming through the state, but there are not many provisions for that in the law."

The new transportation bill that lawmakers eventually approve will determine not only how much money the states will receive over the next few years but also what types of projects will be funded and how much flexibility states and localities will have in choosing them. Because these choices profoundly affect the nature of community development, there is much at stake in the outcome.

The United States boasts one of the world's most highly developed transportation systems, but the 1991 law is restricted to the land portion of the system, including highways, roads, bridges, railroads, subways and paths for bicycles and pedestrians.

Construction and maintenance of this vast interlocking system is shared by federal, state and local governments. But ever since national transportation policy was first laid out in 1916, the bulk of federal subsidies has been funneled into the most heavily traveled highways.

In 1995, Congress formally designated a 161,000-mile network of highways to be eligible for federal assistance. Called the National Highway System, the network includes the 45,000-mile Interstate system and other major roadways.

Concerned that the continuous expansion of the country's highways was not relieving urban traffic congestion, Congress shifted some ISTEA funds away from highways to alternative modes of transportation, such as public transit, bicycle paths and walkways. [2] ISTEA's Congestion Mitigation and Air Quality Improvement (CMAQ) program, for example, requires some federal transportation funds — $6 billion over six years — to be used for projects that do not expand capacity for automobiles.

ISTEA also allows states and localities to shift some of the federal road grants from the Surface Transportation Program (STP) to non-highway projects, or "transportation enhancements," such as building bike paths or restoring old bridges and historic train depots.

Of all ISTEA's myriad provisions,

Highway Fees Netted $31.5 Billion in 1996

More than three-quarters of the $31.5 billion collected in 1996 from highway-use fees went into the Highway Trust Fund for road and bridge improvements and mass transit. The funds came from the taxes on fuels (including the 18.3-cent-per-gallon gas tax), heavy trucks and sales of tires, trucks and trailers. The rest of the money collected went into the U.S. Treasury's general fund.

Where Highway Funding Goes

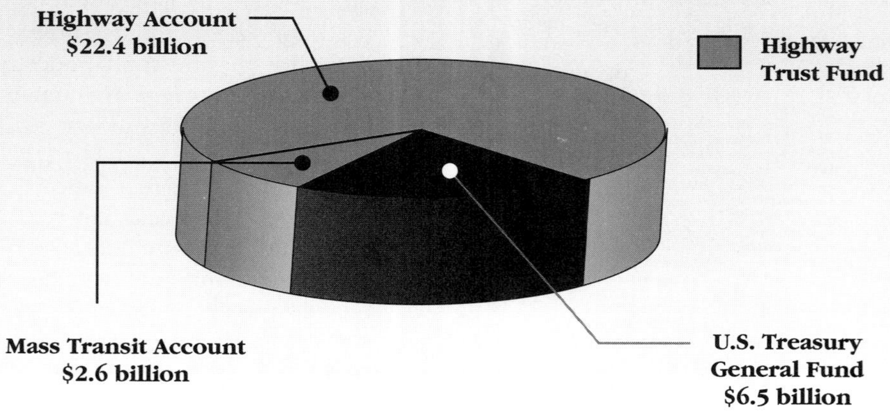

Highway Account $22.4 billion

Highway Trust Fund

Mass Transit Account $2.6 billion

U.S. Treasury General Fund $6.5 billion

Source: American Highway Users Alliance

which cover more than 300 pages, the CMAQ ("SEEmac," to insiders) and enhancement programs are the most hotly debated. The powerful American Highway Users Alliance — which includes oil companies, automakers and road builders — wants Congress to curtail or eliminate these provisions and return federal transportation policy to its traditional focus on highways.

"There is a national interest in developing a first-class highway network that carries goods and people across the country, facilitates interstate commerce, makes travel safer and provides for national defense needs," says Taylor R. Bowlden, the coalition's vice president for policy and government affairs. "We think the federal highway program ought to be focused on those national interests, and to a significant extent ISTEA has eroded that focus."

On the other side of the debate are environmentalists, public transit agencies and organizations representing bicyclists and pedestrians, all represented by the Surface Transportation Policy Project.

"We have created an auto-dependent culture through public subsidy," says Dittmar. "And now we're forced to live with the result of that, which is that Americans for a lot of their trips don't have any choice but to drive. So we think it's time, through national policy, to give communities the option to spend their transportation dollars in other ways."

Before ISTEA, Dittmar says, federal transportation law provided $8 for roadway construction and maintenance for every $1 used for non-automobile transportation modes. Today, roads receive just $5 for every $1 spent on alternative modes. "ISTEA has allowed states and localities to move highway dollars to transit, at local option, which they've been doing, at about $800 million a year over the last couple of years," he says. "Gradually, we'd like to see more money focused on highway system maintenance, instead of new capacity, and on expanding alternative transportation modes."

But some experts say it's unrealistic to expect federal transportation policy to change the way Americans travel. "Substantial segments of our society rely on public transit — the very young, the very old and the very poor — and it's worth having some way of providing transportation for them," says Charles Lave, an urban transportation specialist at the University of California-Irvine. "But the dream of getting people out of automobiles is crazy. The fact is, transportation policy won't get people out of cars."

Several proposals have emerged that reflect these conflicting goals of federal transportation policy, including two bills supported by many advocates of alternative transportation. The Clinton administration's submission — the National Economic Crossroads Transportation Efficiency Act (NEXTEA) — would continue most of ISTEA's innovative programs and provide $175 billion for transportation over the next six years, amounting to about a $3 billion increase over current annual spending. A bill sponsored by Sens. John H. Chafee, R-R.I., and Daniel Patrick Moynihan, D-N.Y., also closely mirrors ISTEA, as its name — ISTEA Works — suggests.

Other proposals would funnel more money back into highway construction and maintenance. A measure introduced by Sens. John W. Warner, R-Va., and Bob Graham, D-Fla. — STEP 21 — would dedicate a greater portion of funds to highway programs and shift a greater percentage of money to Southern and Midwestern states. And Rep. Tom DeLay of Texas, the Republican whip, has proposed eliminating the CMAQ and enhancements programs altogether. (*See story, p. 582.*)

As lawmakers consider proposals to replace ISTEA before it expires this fall, these are some of the issues they will consider:

Do local governments have an adequate say in transportation planning?

Before ISTEA, federal subsidies for highways were administered by state transportation departments with limited input from local governments. Given the needs of the federal Interstate Highway System, launched in 1956, and the steady development of suburbs after World War II, the states used the funds almost entirely for highway building and maintenance.

But years of experience have shown that building new roads does not necessarily relieve traffic congestion. In an effort to give local governments a greater say in deciding how federal funds should be spent to improve specific traffic problems in their jurisdictions, ISTEA gave local officials unprecedented decision-making authority for both highway and transit projects. The law included funds for metropolitan planning organizations, representing cities of 50,000 or more, and gave them a specific role in choosing transportation projects.

The projects over which metropolitan planning organizations exercise control include non-highway projects such as public transit as well as bicycle and pedestrian facilities. In addition to the CMAQ and enhancements programs, which set aside funds for these purposes, ISTEA gives state and local officials the option of transferring a certain portion of highway money to non-highway projects.

© Ritchie McHam/Dallas Area Rapid Transit

The 20-mile-long Dallas Area Rapid Transit (DART) system serves up to 30,000 people daily and is the first commuter rail line in the Southwest.

Many of ISTEA's critics credit the law with improving transportation planning by introducing flexibility into the process. Even some state transportation officials, whose decision-making authority has been diluted under ISTEA, acknowledge the law's positive impact on relations with local governments.

"Under ISTEA, we probably have formed a better relationship with our metropolitan planning organizations and are much more aware of their role in the whole process," says Indiana's Whitney. "We don't always see eye to eye on things, but they're certainly in the game now, which I think is good."

But the Highway Users Alliance says ISTEA has in some ways made the planning process less flexible than before at all levels of government.

"The CMAQ and enhancements programs are truly among the least flexible programs of ISTEA," Bowlden says. "They're flexible, if what you mean by flexibility is that the state or local transportation officials get to use highway funds for a bunch of non-highway projects. But if flexibility means that you get to use highway funds for whatever you deem your highest transportation priorities, they are the least flexible of ISTEA's programs because they virtually prohibit the use of those funds on a regular highway project."

Local government officials tend to disagree with the highway alliance's assessment and fear that lawmakers may not only eliminate the two non-highway programs but also devolve decision-making power back to the state transportation agencies. This would occur under a proposal by House Budget Committee Chairman John R. Kasich, R-Ohio, and Sen. Connie Mack, R-Fla., that would eliminate the federal highway program for all purposes except maintaining the Interstate system and make the states responsible for all other highways.

"We probably wouldn't get as much funding for non-highway

Major Transportation Bills Under Consideration

Several funding proposals have been introduced to replace the landmark Intermodal Surface Transportation Efficiency Act — ISTEA — when it expires on Sept. 30. They differ mainly in how funds are allocated between strictly highway uses and programs aimed at reducing reliance on automobiles.

Enacted in 1991, ISTEA provided $157 billion over six years and was the first transportation law that required a percentage of federal funds to be used to encourage transportation alternatives to cars and to improve environmental quality. Ten percent of ISTEA's $23.9 billion Surface Transportation Program (STP) was set aside for "transportation enhancements," such as bicycle facilities and train depot restoration. The law's Congestion Mitigation and Air Quality Improvement (CMAQ) program provided $6 billion to help states and localities comply with the Clean Air Act. ISTEA was widely praised for shifting some decision-making authority from federal and state governments to localities and metropolitan planning organizations.

Legislation proposed to replace ISTEA includes:

NEXTEA — Proposed by the Clinton administration, the National Economic Crossroads Transportation Efficiency Act (S 468, HR 1268) would provide an average of $22.7 billion a year over six years. The bill generally retains ISTEA's basic framework. Although it would provide a slight increase in funds over existing law, NEXTEA calls for the lowest spending level of the main proposals before Congress. Because the bill calls for an increase in the Surface Transportation Program, to $35 billion over six years, the 10 percent set-aside for enhancements would rise. Funding for the CMAQ program also would grow, to $7.8 billion over six years.

STEP 21 — The ISTEA Integrity Restoration Act, better known as STEP 21, would provide an average of $22.9 billion a year over five years, according to the version sponsored in the House (HR 674) by Rep. Tom DeLay, R-Texas; the Senate version, sponsored by Sen. John W. Warner, R-Va., would provide $26 billion annually over five years (S 335). STEP 21 contains a proposal first introduced in 1996 called the Streamlined Transportation Efficiency Program for the 21st Century. Backed by a number of state transportation departments, STEP 21 aims to simplify transportation programs, which critics say are too complex and costly to administer. The bill would ensure that states get back at least 95 percent of the revenues they contribute to the Highway Trust Fund. Both bills would eliminate the CMAQ set-asides but authorize states to use money from a Streamlined Surface Transportation Program (SSTP) or the National Highway System (NHS) account to fund air-quality projects. The Senate bill retains the existing enhancements set-aside; the House version eliminates it but grants states the flexibility to use SSTP or NHS funds for enhancements.

STARS 2000 — The Surface Transportation Authorization and Regulatory Streamlining Act (S 532), sponsored by Sen. Max Baucus, D-Mont., would provide $27 billion a year over six years. Providing the highest authorization level of the major proposals, STARS 2000 contains STEP 21's minimum allocation of 95 percent of a state's trust fund contribution, but presents a less drastic departure from existing law by retaining enhancements and CMAQ set-asides, though at lower percentage levels. It would also block use of the CMAQ program in states that fail to comply with federal air-quality standards. The proposal's centerpiece is its $14.2 billion annual funding of National Highway System projects, much higher than ISTEA's $3.6 billion and higher than any other proposal. Annual STP funding, including the set-asides, would be about $9.4 billion.

ISTEA Works — The ISTEA Reauthorization Act (S 586), sponsored by Sens. John H. Chafee, R-R.I., and Daniel Patrick Moynihan, D-N.Y., the leading authors of ISTEA, would provide $26.7 billion a year over six years. It retains most ISTEA provisions, with updated state funding formulas, inclusion of new non-automotive transportation programs, such as Amtrak, and a significant increase in highway funding. Transportation enhancements are retained in the $31.5 billion STP. Reflecting the authors' concerns that highway programs not jeopardize compliance with federal air-quality standards, the bill would double funding for CMAQ, to $12 billion, over current law.

Rep. Bud Shuster, R-Pa., chairman of the House Transportation and Infrastructure Committee, is expected to introduce a reauthorization bill later this summer. He has called for annual spending on transportation of $32 billion, by far the highest level of any proposal to date. Shuster supports ISTEA's funding of enhancements and air-quality programs but would give states flexibility to use these funds for roads.

Sources: John W. Fischer, "ISTEA Reauthorization: Highway Related Legislative Proposals in the 105th Congress," *CRS Report for Congress*, May 5, 1997; David Hosansky, "Transportation Funding Proposals," *Congressional Quarterly Weekly Report*, April 26, 1997, p. 956.

projects if the federal guidelines for CMAQ and enhancements programs were abolished and discretion were devolved to the state," says Steve Dotterer, chief transportation planner for Portland, Ore.

Often cited as the country's most bicycle- and pedestrian-friendly city, Portland also boasts a well-traveled light-rail line linking downtown with the near suburbs. (*See story, p. 588.*) Like a number of states, Oregon has a constitutional requirement that state gasoline tax revenues be used exclusively for road-related improvements.

"That means the state dollars tend to get used on basic roadway maintenance, while the federal dollars are used in the more creative capital investment programs, which works out because that's where we need the flexibility," Dotterer says. "If we're trying to slowly change the way people travel, it's through capital investment that we're able to do it."

Anthony Downs, a senior fellow at the Brookings Institution and an authority on metropolitan planning, fears that efforts to devolve authority to the states may jeopardize the power of metropolitan planning organizations, which he considers among ISTEA's most important innovations.

"It would be a great tragedy if Congress thought that the only way you could devolve authority was to states and localities, when our real major transportation problems are at the metropolitan level," Downs says. "Although I think we should preserve local governments, I think we need to have more authority and influence over land use by people who have the perspective of the entire region in view."

Do highways receive a disproportionate share of federal transportation subsidies?

Before ISTEA, federal transportation assistance largely went to road construction and maintenance. Indeed, surface transportation bills are commonly called highway bills. Through its set-asides for air quality mitigation and transportation enhancements, however, ISTEA required a small portion of Highway Trust Fund monies — less than 2 percent — to be used for non-highway projects.

The Highway Users Alliance wants to see more money from the trust fund dedicated to road maintenance and construction. More than a quarter of eligible roads are in disrepair, the group says, along with about a third of the nation's bridges more than 20 feet long. "The National Highway System accounts for just 4 percent of the nation's road miles, but it carries 40 percent of all highway traffic, 75 percent of truck traffic and 80 percent of tourist traffic," Bowlden says. "The point of the National Highway System is to identify the network of roads that really is critical to our national economy and traffic safety, because that's where the bulk of the travel occurs. So this is a program where we can target federal funds toward improvements of that most important national system."

Supporters of alternative transportation modes agree that safe roads are important. "It's in the national interest to maintain the Interstate because we've spent a couple of hundred billion dollars building it over the last 40 years," Dittmar says. "It's also in the national interest to have safety on the roads to relieve traffic congestion." [3]

But Dittmar and other critics of the highway alliance say its members are more interested in expanding the highway network than in fixing existing roadways. "If you're just repaving, you're not using as much asphalt, concrete or steel as in new road and bridge construction," Dittmar says. "And for highway engineers there's more excitement from being the creator of a new road than the repairer of an old road. There are big bucks at play here. Maintenance people in state departments of transportation don't advance to become secretary."

In this view, the "improvements" Bowlden calls for are nothing more than a euphemism for building new roads or widening existing ones that would allow for more cars to travel over them, steps that critics say have failed to relieve congestion over the years. "Most of the money is available for wider roads, and when states are given flexibility that's what they like to do," Dittmar says. "And that's one of the things I'm critical of — they don't maintain, they widen."

The highway users concede that road widening is among their top priorities, but say it is often necessary to improve safety. "Widening lanes to a minimum of 12 feet per lane makes for much safer roadways than narrower lanes," Bowlden says.

Some state officials agree with Bowlden's call for dedicating more transportation money to roads.

"We only have one section in Indiana that has a real need for a transit-type system," Whitney says, referring to the cities of Gary and Hammond, outside Chicago, Ill. "In the rest of the state, we have severe bridge and road problems. This year we have had three times more requests for local road projects than we have funds for. And yet we have balances of enhancement and CMAQ funds [for non-road projects] that have been slow to get going."

Supporters of ISTEA's set-asides for alternative transportation modes say they are a drop in the bucket compared with the law's overall highway funding levels but still provide a vital boost to efforts to reduce traffic congestion. "Only about 1.6 percent of ISTEA money goes to enhancements," says Hal Hiemstra, vice president for national policy at the Rails-to-Trails Conservancy, which promotes the conversion of abandoned railroad rights of way to bicycle trails. "But this is such a quantum leap over where we were in previous transportation bills that the overall impact on bike-pedestrian trails has been tremendous."

Over the 18 years before ISTEA took effect, Hiemstra says, bicycle and pedestrian trails around the country received a total of $40 million in federal funding. Since 1991, these facilities have received about $1 billion. "We see this as a very popular ISTEA program," Hiemstra says. "It's

Northeast and West Are Highway Fund Winners

States in the Northeast and West got back more money from the Highway Trust Fund in 1995 than they paid into the fund through gas, diesel and tire taxes. "Donor" states, clustered in the South and Midwest, put more into the fund than they received; "borderline" states got slightly more than they contributed.

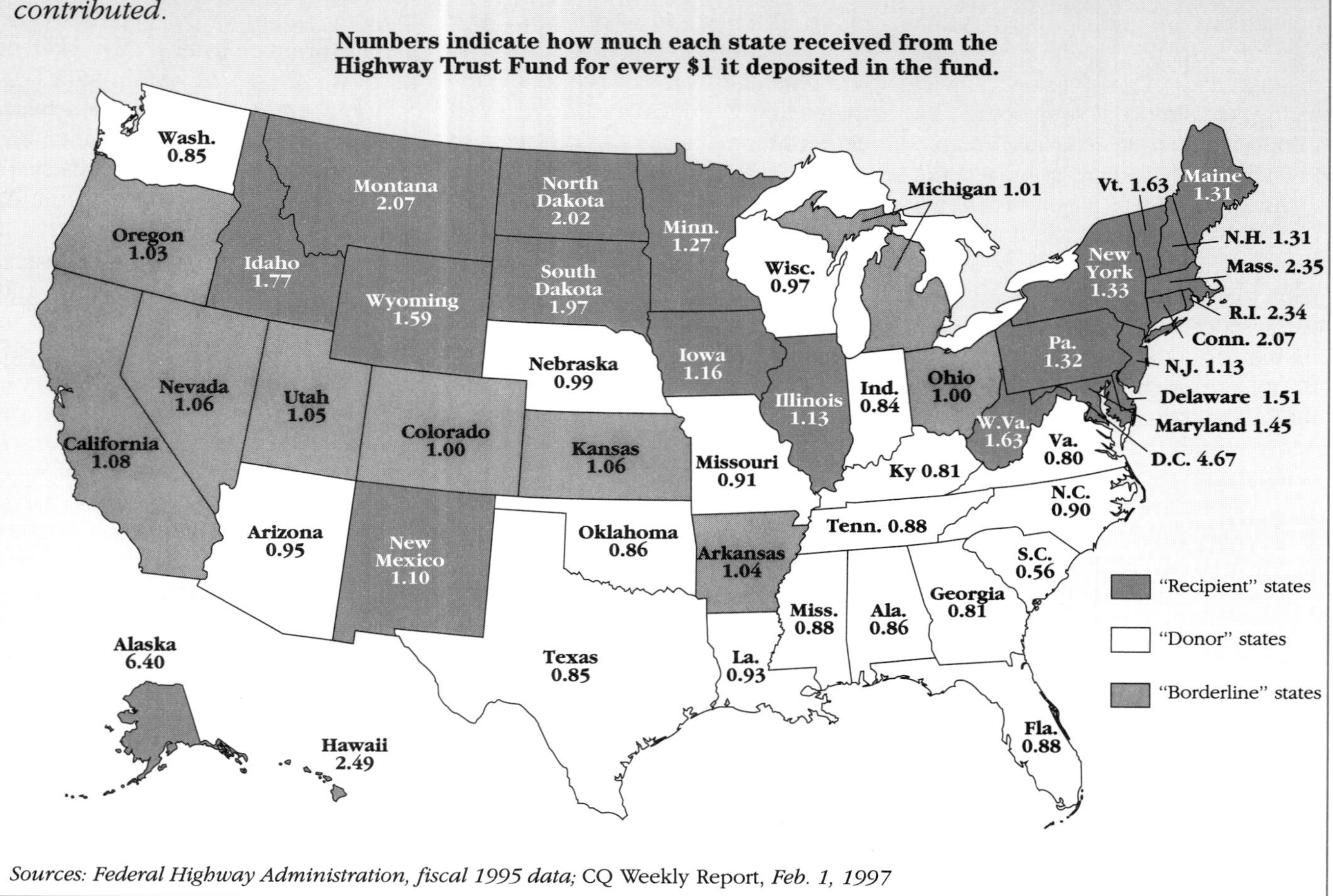

Sources: Federal Highway Administration, fiscal 1995 data; CQ Weekly Report, *Feb. 1, 1997*

brought in new constituencies in support of transportation spending, which helps everyone, not just bike-pedestrian trail advocates."

Does current law fairly allocate Highway Trust Fund revenues?

Since 1956, surface transportation projects have been funded with revenue raised by the federal tax on gasoline and other fuels, excise taxes on vehicles and tires and user fees paid by operators of trucks and other heavy vehicles traveling on federal highways. In 1996, these revenues came to $31.5 billion. Of that total, $25 billion went to the Highway Trust Fund, which pays for federally assisted highway and mass transit projects. The remaining $6.5 billion in federal fuel and excise taxes went into the general fund, to cover other items in the federal budget.

According to a recent study by the American Petroleum Institute, only 58 percent of the taxes and fees collected from American motorists at all levels of government was spent on roads in 1994, while 29 percent went into general funds, 7 percent was used for federal deficit reduction and 4 percent was used to fund mass transit. [4]

Critics of this allocation of gas tax revenues say that because the money is raised from highway users, all of it should be used for transportation projects. Citing the ongoing needs for repair and improvements to the National Highway System, the Highway Users Alliance calls for ending the current practice of siphoning off trust fund revenue for non-transportation federal expenditures, including budget reduction, a top priority of the Clinton administration and legislators of both parties.

For the Highway Trust Fund to help reduce the deficit, however, a certain amount of money that could be used for current transportation needs has to remain in the fund unspent. "Currently, there is more than a $20 billion cash balance in the Highway Trust Fund, and this figure is projected to grow to about $48 billion by 2002 under the proposed budget," Edward O. Groff, president of the American Society of Civil Engineers, said in a letter to President Clinton. "The existence of this balance not only represents a breaking of the government's contract with American taxpayers, but also undermines our nation's ability to invest in critical transportation improvement projects." [5]

The highway users have a powerful ally in Congress in House Transportation and Infrastructure Committee Chairman Bud Shuster, R-Pa., who recently broke ranks with the GOP leadership by calling for a $12 billion increase in funding for transportation programs over the next five years. Although Shuster's amendment to the fiscal 1998 budget resolution was narrowly defeated on May 21, the congressman pledged to repeat his effort to raise annual highway funding from its current level of about $20 billion to as much as $32 billion. [6]

Shuster also calls for an end to the practice of siphoning off Highway Trust Fund monies for non-transportation purposes and holding surpluses in the fund at a time when highways and bridges are in disrepair. "The existence of these huge surpluses is a massive fraud on the American public," Shuster wrote. "Motorists pay the gas tax to improve their roads and transit systems; but instead, this dedicated user fee is used in a cynical shell game for deficit reduction and spending on other federal programs." [7]

Bicycle and transit advocates are less concerned about this issue. "I think it was Winston Churchill who said we don't use revenues from horse racing to buy oats for horses," Dittmar says. "It's also true that when you ask the American public if they think the gas tax ought to go for transportation, they say it makes sense, and 70 percent of them [say] it should also go for bicycles and pedestrian facilities. So I think the public defines the use of trust fund monies more broadly than the highway users."

The debate over uses of Highway Trust Fund monies also involves the way the funds are allocated among the states. Ever since the fund was created, federal transportation bills have used complex funding formulas to distribute subsidies to states according to their perceived needs. Critics say the formulas are outdated and penalize rural states in the South and Midwest while rewarding densely populated states in the Northeast. They also oppose efforts to set aside trust fund money for Amtrak, the federally owned national passenger railroad, which mainly serves cities along the East Coast. *(See "At Issue," p. 593.)*

"My home state of South Carolina only receives 52 cents on the dollar despite an infrastructure that is in desperate need of help," said Rep. Mark Sanford, R-S.C. [8] "Virginia is another donor state that only receives 73 cents on the dollar. In contrast, states like New York and Massachusetts receive more funding than they put into the trust fund." To rectify what he sees as a longstanding prejudice in the law, Sanford has proposed legislation, cosponsored by Reps. Bob Clement, D-Tenn., and Steve Largent, R-Okla., that would grant each state the same proportion of funding that it pays into the trust fund.

The struggle over transportation funding formulas is one area that the main interest groups involved in ISTEA reauthorization are avoiding. "That's not an issue that we're going to get involved in because it pits one state against another, and we have members in every state," Bowlden says. "Our principal concern is whether the government is spending the money it's actually collecting from highway users for road and bridge improvements and how those monies get spent." ■

BACKGROUND

Rise of the Car Culture

Until the turn of the century, federal efforts to build national transportation networks were focused primarily on canals and railroads. And even these were hampered by some states' reluctance to relinquish their authority over transportation systems, which were built and maintained by private interests. [9]

Westward migration spurred the development of new roads, including the first federal highway, the National Road. Authorized in 1806, it became the main route west over the Allegheny Mountains into the fertile Ohio River Valley and stretched from Cumberland, Md., to Vandalia, Ill.

Relying as it did on federal funding, the National Road set an important precedent and has been described as "the single most significant act in American transportation, opening the constitutional door to federal support for canals, rails and interstate highways." [10]

It was not until the early 1900s, however, that road-building became the main focus of federal transportation policy. The first coordinated federal program to support state and local road-building projects came in 1916, in an effort to improve the access of rural areas to mail service and markets for their crops. With the 1916 Federal Aid Road Act, the United States embarked on a policy of expanding the national road network that has dominated federal transportation policy ever since.

Spurred by the mass production of automobiles, road and bridge construction continued apace, even during two world wars and the Great Depression. President Franklin D. Roosevelt's public works initiatives of the 1930s, aimed at providing jobs to millions of unemployed Americans, focused on the building of parkways, roads and bridges even as the economy ground almost to a halt. Construction of roads for purely civilian use slowed only briefly during World War II.

Road-building escalated with the postwar economic boom of the 1950s and '60s. As more and more working Americans were able to afford a car and a house, they fled the central cities for the suburbs that spread into the surrounding countryside along the new roadways linking them to downtown workplaces. With domestic oil supplies still plentiful, low gasoline prices added further impetus to car use and road development.

At the same time that local road networks were expanding, the creation in 1956 of the federal Interstate Highway System ensured the future development of national roadways for passenger travel and freight. To help fund the Interstate system, Congress established the Highway Trust Fund as a repository of federal motor vehicle and gasoline excise taxes to be used for highway construction and maintenance.

As Americans turned decisively toward cars for transportation, privately operated transit systems across the country went into decline. Many bus and rail systems were taken over by local public agencies that in 1961 began receiving federal subsidies to keep them running. Congress established the first formal federal role in urban transit operations with the 1964 Urban Mass Transportation Assistance Act. The law established the Urban Mass Transportation Administration, renamed the Federal Transit Administration (FTA) in 1991, and provided federal funding to local transit authorities.

Federal subsidies for transit services grew as the cost of building expensive rail systems and operating them as well as bus services outpaced revenues from fares. Beginning in 1973, the federal government began supporting local transit authorities with money from the Highway Trust Fund. [11] This move came despite objections from rural states and localities without transit systems who claimed it was an unfair use of their constituents' tax dollars.

Traffic Congestion, 'Infrastructure Crisis'

By the 1970s, the country's dependence on automobiles and roads for mobility was so great that even the energy crises of that decade failed to slow the pace of road-building or alter the bias toward highways embraced by federal transportation policy.

The focus on road-building enabled Americans to go almost anywhere in the country in their cars. But this policy has come at a price. By the early 1990s, traffic congestion in and around American cities had continued to worsen, despite the addition of new roads and new lanes. Suburban sprawl, encouraged by road-building, was proceeding unchecked. As residential development spread farther from downtown, many employers began moving to emerging suburban communities. As a result, commuting routes, once laid out like the spokes of a wheel from the downtown hub, multiplied and shifted direction, resembling more closely a spider web branching from suburb to suburb. Laid out along traditional routes, bus and transit services were poorly equipped to meet the demands of suburban workers, and traffic congestion mounted.

Meanwhile, many existing roads, including the roads and bridges on the Interstate system, were showing their age. Potholes, crumbling bridge supports and eroding shoulders forced bridge and road closings and spurred calls for new federal aid to solve what was called an "infrastructure crisis." In 1989, the Federal Highway Administration (FHA) estimated that 250,000 miles of pavement were too damaged to be maintained in a cost-effective manner, 134,000 bridges were structurally deficient and traffic congestion cost more than $34 billion in delayed travel and fuel consumption in the country's 39 largest metropolitan areas. [12]

ISTEA's Options

Like previous transportation bills, the 1991 Intermodal Surface Transportation Efficiency Act authorized a six-year program of federal subsidies. But it departed from prior legislation in several notable ways. Drafted in large part by Sens. Moynihan and Chafee, the bill reflected the growing consensus that the existing highway network needed to be made more efficient, and not necessarily bigger. Lawmakers responded to calls from state and local governments to have a greater say in the way federal transportation funds were to be spent in their jurisdictions, including the option of funding alternative modes of transportation such as mass transit

Continued on p. 588

Chronology

1800s-1920s

Early in the nation's history, emphasis is put on highway-based transportation.

1806
Congress authorizes construction of the first federally funded highway, the National Road, linking the East Coast with the Ohio River Valley.

1916
The first national transportation bill, the Federal Aid Road Act, supports state and local road-building projects in an effort to improve access of rural areas to mail service and markets for their crops.

1930s-1960s

Massive roadbuilding projects beginning during the Depression years and the postwar boom in suburban development further concentrate federal transportation funds on highway construction.

1956
Congress launches the Interstate Highway System, a 45,000-mile network of federally supported highways. To pay for the Interstate system and other federal roads, the Highway Trust Fund is set up as a repository of revenues raised by the federal tax on gasoline and other fuels, excise taxes on vehicles and tires and user fees paid by operators of trucks and other heavy vehicles traveling on federal highways.

1961
Privately operated transit systems across the country begin to receive federal subsidies to keep them in operation, as falling ridership leaves them unable to stay afloat from fares alone.

1964
The Urban Mass Transportation Assistance Act authorizes federal funding for local transit authorities and establishes the Urban Mass Transportation Administration, renamed the Federal Transit Administration in 1991.

1970s-1980s

Despite oil-price increases, Americans continue their overwhelming reliance on cars for transportation.

1973
Over the objections of automakers, oil companies and other highway interests, the federal government begins funneling Highway Trust Fund money into financially strapped local transit authorities.

1989
The Federal Highway Administration estimates that 250,000 miles of pavement are too damaged to be maintained in a cost-effective manner and that 134,000 bridges are structurally deficient. The agency puts the costs related to traffic congestion at more than $34 billion annually.

1990s

Federal transportation policy for the first time supports non-highway modes of transportation.

1991
The Intermodal Surface Transportation Efficiency Act — ISTEA — earmarks a small part of its six-year, $157 billion allocation — for investment in non-highway projects, including bike and pedestrian facilities, transit systems and transportation-related historic preservation. The law offers local and state governments unprecedented flexibility in using federal funds for a variety of transportation projects.

1995
Congress designates a 161,000-mile network of highways to be eligible for federal transportation assistance. Called the National Highway System, the network comprises the 45,000-mile Interstate system and other major roadways.

May 21, 1997
House Transportation and Infrastructure Committee Chairman Bud Shuster, R-Pa., sets the tone of the debate over transportation spending after lawmakers reject his amendment to the fiscal 1998 budget resolution calling for a $12 billion increase in funding for transportation programs over the next five years. The congressman pledges to repeat his effort to raise annual highway spending from its current level of about $20 billion to as much as $32 billion in a reauthorization proposal expected to be introduced this summer.

Sept. 30, 1997
ISTEA expires, to be succeeded by a transportation reauthorization bill whose provisions are the subject of intense debate in Congress.

Portland's 'Traffic Calming' Approach . . .

If you're looking for a place to live where you can safely walk or bicycle wherever you're going, head for Portland, Ore. Transportation experts repeatedly mention the city of 500,000 as the place that has taken the best advantage of federal support for alternative modes of transportation.

Even before the federal government began funding non-highway transportation in 1991 with the Intermodal Surface Transportation Efficiency Act (ISTEA), Portland's planners were taking steps to enhance the quality of life of the city's non-motorized residents.

"One of the goals in our downtown plan was to maintain as much activity in the street as possible, to have people moving around on the street to make it as much a pedestrian place as possible," says Steve Dotterer, Portland's chief transportation planner. "That sort of intensive urban feel that you have in New York or San Francisco we can't get unless we kind of work at it."

Oregon Department of Transportation

Traffic moves slowly in downtown Portland, Ore., and that's what planners wanted.

Efforts to enliven Portland's street life led to the city's adoption of a light-rail system, or trolley, rather than an underground, heavy-rail system such as New York's subway or Chicago's elevated trains.

"We wanted to have a mix of people in the street," Dotterer says. "If you distribute people on two or three different levels, the sidewalk is not going to seem as lively. So one of our ideas was to emphasize the ground plane and pedestrian traffic. The light-rail fits with that."

Light-rail systems and other programs to encourage bike and pedestrian traffic come at some cost to motorists, of course. While many cities are trying to reduce traffic delays by widening streets and straightening curves, Portland has adopted a "traffic calming" approach that aims to slow traffic to speeds that enable bicyclists and pedestrians to move more safely. Curb extensions, for example, make sidewalks wider while narrowing streets and shortening crosswalks. The extensions make it safer for pedestrians to cross, but they also can eliminate an entire lane otherwise used by cars.

Some curb extensions also house bus shelters, forcing traffic to stop altogether when buses drop off and pick up passengers. "The bus simply stops in the travel lane, which slows the traffic down, obviously," Dotterer says. In Portland, however, motorists' objections to curb extensions have been outweighed by the support of downtown businesses.

"Store owners didn't want the cars to go by fast," Dotterer says. "They wanted them to go by slowly and look. So part of what we have used ISTEA money for is to redesign the streets to serve different purposes."

The traffic-calming approach has also shaped Portland's policy toward bikers. Unlike some cities, such as Philadelphia and Minneapolis, that have used ISTEA money to build dedicated bike paths stretching from the suburbs to downtown, Portland has integrated bike riders into the rest of street traffic. Downtown streets even lack bike lanes, much less separate paths. Planners were helped in this effort by the city's existing roadways, laid out as a grid design with relatively short blocks and narrow streets. "Traffic just doesn't move all that fast," Dotterer says. "Because the blocks are small, the signal system is set at 12 miles per hour, and most of the streets are so narrow they can only accommodate one-way

Continued from p. 586

and bicycles and the ability to transfer funds among programs. They also tried to satisfy the demands by all parties for more money and a fairer allocation of federal funds based on state and local needs.

The complex, 300-page law authorized $157 billion over the six-year period from Oct. 1, 1991, to Sept. 30, 1997. ISTEA's major provisions are:

- **National Highway System:** Defined by the 1995 National Highway System Designation Act, the system includes 161,000 miles of highways eligible for $21 billion in federal aid over six years. The system comprises the entire 45,000-mile Interstate network as well as other major highways, mostly in urban areas, designated for their importance to interstate commerce, tourism and national defense. Although it accounts for only 4 percent of all U.S.

. . . Lures Bikers and Walkers Into the Street

traffic. So bikers can pretty much keep up with the traffic, especially the younger ones."

Beyond the downtown area, bikers have access to a number of so-called bicycle boulevards, secondary roads in residential areas that had become overrun by commuters who used them as bypass streets. "As part of our traffic-calming program, we decided to close some of these streets to cars but leave an opening for bicyclists," Dotterer says. "So now they serve as bicycle arterials, but not as car arterials anymore."

Portland is not alone in introducing such innovative transportation programs, of course. But it has been able to bring more of them to fruition because it began testing them long before ISTEA began providing the federal funding for them in 1991. The bicycle boulevards, for example, are the final product of a series of tests the city began long before the federal law was passed.

"When we started testing the street closings, our highest goal was to try to reduce the volume and speed of traffic on these streets," Dotterer says. "We weren't sure what we were going to use them for when we were done. It was only after testing that we thought of turning them into bicycle routes."

A key to Portland's ability to take immediate advantage of ISTEA's funding of bike and pedestrian facilities is the structure of its transportation planning bodies. "Portland has the country's sole elected metropolitan area government," says Anthony Downs, a metropolitan planning expert at the Brookings Institution. "It's also operating in the state planning framework that Oregon has set up, which is the best one in the country."

Rails to Trails Conservancy

About 1 million people in 1996 used the 16.5 mile Springwater Corrider Trail, which links Portland and Boring.

Portland's metropolitan planning organization, called Metro, shares the responsibility of regional tranportation planning with the Joint Policy Advisory Committee on Transportation, which also is made up of elected officials from local governments as well as representatives of the state highway and environmental quality departments and transit agencies. The two bodies have been more successful in overcoming some of the policy differences that have undermined efforts in other cities to develop coherent transportation policies.

Transportation planning in the Washington, D.C., metropolitan area, for example, has been repeatedly hampered by the competing interests of the District of Columbia and the outlying jurisdictions of Maryland and Virginia. District residents, for example, resent footing the bill for repairing city streets and bridges damaged by suburban commuters.

"Sometimes it's taken a little work to get us all to concur," Dotterer says. "But in the 15 years that this system has been in place, the two bodies have always taken the time to resolve whatever the issues are and never made it into an institutional fight. That's one of the reasons we're able to move forward on projects."

But Portland nonetheless has a long way to go before it can declare victory over traffic congestion. Alternatives to cars are not yet readily available to most suburban residents. "But in the downtown area, we've very clearly made progress," Dotterer says. "Over the past 20 years, as the number of downtown jobs increased from about 70,000 to 100,000, we've met our air-quality goals and had almost no significant traffic increase."

road miles, the National Highway System carries 40 percent of all highway travel, 75 percent of truck travel and 80 percent of tourist travel, according to the American Highway Users Alliance. [13]

• **Surface Transportation Program (STP):** At $23.9 billion over six years, this is the largest category in ISTEA. Apart from several set-aside programs for safety and other initiatives, states can treat STP funds as a block grant to pay for improvements to any portion of the National Highway System under their jurisdiction or transfer the money to other approved transportation projects. A controversial set-aside within STP, which receives 10 percent of the program's funds, is for so-called Transportation Enhancement Activities. This new program funds projects such as the preservation of historic sites, pur-

Continued on p. 591

Lynn Harrison/Caltrans

Flood-damaged Route 395 (above) and after repairs (below).

Lynn Harrison/Caltrans

Jim Varney/Caltrans

Route 140 before and after repairs

Jim Varney/Caltrans

Rain storms in Southern California in late 1996 and early '97 caused an estimated $240 million in damage to the state's highways. Parts of Route 395 (left), the principal north-south artery in the eastern Sierra Nevada region, were destroyed when the Walker River flooded; repairs cost $32 million. The flooding Merced River caused $3.2 million damage to Route 140 (above), which provides access to Yosemite National Park. Emergency federal funding for the repairs was authorized by the Intermodal Surface Transportation Efficiency Act (ISTEA).

Continued from p. 589
chases of land for its scenic value and archaeological research. States also must allocate a portion of STP funds to metropolitan areas with more than 200,000 residents.

• **Interstate Maintenance Program:** This $17 billion program is for rehabilitating, restoring and resurfacing Interstate roads, not for new construction.

• **Bridge Replacement and Rehabilitation:** This $16.1 billion program continued existing policy of subsidizing bridge work on any public road, but ISTEA expanded the possible uses to include painting and seismic retrofitting.

• **Congestion Mitigation and Air Quality Improvement Program (CMAQ):** At just $6 billion, the CMAQ program has attracted more controversy than its funding level would seem to warrant. The program is unprecedented, however, in funding projects to help states and localities comply with the Clean Air Act.[14] Because auto emissions are a major source of air pollution, the program has been used mainly for projects aimed at getting people out of their cars, such as bike and pedestrian trail construction and transit development.

• **Equity Adjustment:** Like previous laws, ISTEA includes a number of complex formulas aimed at allocating federal funds among states according to their transportation needs. Each state, for example, is guaranteed funding equal to 90 percent of its contribution to the portion of the Highway Trust Fund reserved for spending on highways. An additional "donor state bonus" is provided to states that contribute more in revenue to the trust fund than they get back in highway assistance.

• **Planning:** ISTEA strengthened the voice of local governments in drawing up transportation improvement plans involving both roads and mass transit. It also provided funding for metropolitan planning organizations and strengthened their hand in choosing transportation projects.

• **Demonstration Projects:** The law provided funding for 539 specific projects supported by lawmakers to help their districts. Critics condemn them as mere pork-barrel initiatives.

• **Transit:** ISTEA provided significant new funding — $31.5 billion — for the Federal Transit Administration's transit assistance program for light rail and bus.

• **Intelligent Transportation Systems (ITS):** "Smart cars," "smart roads" and other high-tech solutions to traffic congestion are funded through this program.[15] ■

Current Situation

Innovative Projects

Over the past five and a half years, communities across the country have taken advantage of ISTEA's flexible programs to undertake a wide variety of innovative transportation-related projects. Unlike the traditional road improvements that tend to follow similar patterns of expansion, maintenance and repair, the projects carried out under the CMAQ and enhancements programs reflect strictly local needs.

These are a few examples of projects that have been funded by ISTEA:

• Plainfield, N.J., spent $3 million — $1.3 million from ISTEA enhancement funds — to restore a deteriorating New Jersey Transit Corp. train station. Built in 1894 but closed in 1981 due to low ridership, the Netherwood Station was renovated to create a more parklike setting and revitalize the neighborhood around the station with building restoration, landscaping and a security system. Still under construction, the project has already drawn commuters and generated grass-roots support from the neighborhood.[16]

• The Port of San Francisco is using ISTEA funds to help restore the long-neglected Ferry Building Depot as a major hub providing intermodal connections between land and water transportation as well as the centerpiece of a redevelopment project on the city's downtown waterfront. "Blocked by the Embarcadero Freeway for years, the Ferry Building was neglected for years," said Courtney Damkroger, assistant director of the National Trust for Historic Preservation's Western regional office. "Then the 1989 earthquake demolished the freeway, opening up a part of San Francisco that has become the center of this major revitalization program."[17]

• In the Washington, D.C., metropolitan area, ISTEA has funneled about $13 million dollars into bicycle facilities, including bike paths linking Georgetown and Bethesda, Md., creation of a Bike-on-Rail program allowing bicycles on Metro, the subway system, and weekend closures of Beach Drive, the scenic roadway that passes through the city in Rock Creek Park.

• Indianapolis has instituted a program, subsidized by CMAQ funds, to discourage people from using their cars at times of high air pollution by dropping bus fares by 25 cents when the ozone level exceeds a certain limit. "That's one way ISTEA has helped us, I suppose," says state transportation official Whitney, "even though our congestion in the Midwest is kind of a joke compared to the East Coast. It seems that when we have a call for projects for enhancement there's a tremendous response to them, all the way from trails to renovation of buildings and other structures, including covered bridges."

• ISTEA contributed to the construction of the Cedar Lake Trail, a paved bicycle and pedestrian trail linking the suburbs of Minneapolis to the downtown along a working railway corridor. Hiemstra of the Rails-to-Trails Conservancy calls this $3 million trail, with its 12-foot lanes for each direction of traffic, the "freeway of all trails." More than 1,300 riders, skaters and runners use the trail on an average weekday. [18]

• Light-rail systems have sprung up in a number of cities, including Denver, Portland, Ore., San Diego, Dallas and Aspen, Colo. Light-rail systems are updated trolleys that run on tracks along major streets and are especially attractive alternatives to subways and other heavy-rail commuter trains for smaller cities with limited ridership. "The advantage of a light-rail system is that the electrification is overhead," explains Portland transportation planner Dotterer. "That means it can run in a city street because there's not an electrified third rail on the ground that you have to watch out for as there is with a subway system. A subway requires a totally protected right of way from one end of the line to the other, which increases the costs dramatically."

• Boise, Idaho, has used CMAQ funds to replace its entire bus fleet with smaller buses powered by compressed natural gas and equipped with bicycle racks, enabling commuters to use two modes of transportation to complete their trips. "The city also is using ISTEA to begin regional planning in the mountains around the city," says Dittmar. "The aim of this broad effort is to make sure that suburban sprawl doesn't creep up the sides of the hills." By limiting sprawl, the city is trying to reduce trip distances, which should make it easier for residents to get around town without using their cars.

• Many communities, including Portland, Ore., Portland, Maine, Seattle, and even Las Vegas, a quintessential car town, are using federal funds to improve pedestrian facilities such as sidewalks, trails and safer crosswalks. "Local project managers are looking at the community as a whole for ways to provide connectivity for pedestrians by filling in missing pieces of sidewalks and improving intersection design," says Charlie Denney, senior planner for the Bicycle Federation of America, whose Campaign to Make America Walkable supports community efforts to make it easier for people to walk instead of drive. "It may be something as simple as putting a median halfway across the intersection, which makes it safer by letting pedestrians cross only half the street during one signal-light phase."

© Photodisc

Many traffic experts blame the nation's growing traffic congestion on federal transportation policy before ISTEA, which encouraged the expansion of highways with little support of alternative transportation systems.

Growing Gridlock

Despite such innovative projects, federal and local officials who are using ISTEA funds to expand alternative modes of transportation have hardly made a dent in Americans' love affair with their cars. Traffic congestion in the 50 largest cities costs travelers more than $40 billion a year, according to the Transportation Department, which predicts that travel will increase by 60 percent over the next two decades, resulting in even greater delays. [19]

Many traffic experts blame the nation's growing traffic congestion on federal transportation policy before ISTEA, which encouraged the expansion of highways with little support of alternative transportation systems. By subsidizing road construction, they say, federal policy encouraged developers to build suburbs farther and farther away from the center of town. By the 1990s, the newer suburbs of many American towns and cities were so far-flung that residents had little choice but to use their cars for transportation.

The choice has been further affected by other policies that shield American drivers from bearing the full costs of operating their cars, if air pollution, congestion, accidents, traffic delays and other costs are counted

Continued on p. 584

At Issue:

Should gasoline tax revenue be used to support Amtrak?

Sen. Joseph R. Biden, Jr. D-Del.

From testimony before the Senate Environment and Public Works Subcommittee on Transportation and Infrastructure, March 13, 1997

yes

Despite being the orphan child in our nation's transportation funding, Amtrak carries 55 million passengers a year, connecting 68 of the 75 biggest cities in the country. And, to remind some of my colleagues from more rural states, fully 40 percent of its annual passengers ride Amtrak to and from rural locations and our nation's cities. . . .

Without Amtrak, there would be an additional 27,000 cars on the highway between New York and Boston every day. Between New York and Philadelphia, there would be an additional 18,000 cars.

I don't have to elaborate for this committee what that would mean in terms of construction and maintenance of more highway lanes, time lost in congestion, additional airport construction costs and delays, health costs from air pollution — all costs that we do not have to pay now because Amtrak is filling that gap.

And Amtrak is performing these tasks under the most restrictive financial conditions. Both the administration and the Congress now assume in their budgets that Amtrak will receive no further federal operating assistance after the year 2002. I am not convinced that this is the best course, but it is the one we are now committed to.

To move toward that goal, Amtrak has laid off 3,500 workers and cut 15 percent of its service. In just the last two years, these moves have saved $364 million a year. I don't need to add that these moves, while they are real accomplishments, also threaten to reduce the availability and efficiency of Amtrak service. . . .

Under these circumstances, it is essential that Amtrak be provided — in the ISTEA legislation that you are considering here today — with the means to reach that goal. . . . I am a cosponsor of the proposal . . . to use a half-cent of the existing federal fuels tax to create a capital fund for Amtrak. This proposal would not cost the Treasury a dime — it comes from an existing revenue source. It could mean a total of $3.8 billion for Amtrak over the next five years, the years in which it must move to operating self-sufficiency.

A capital fund would allow Amtrak to upgrade facilities, purchase new equipment and engage in the prudent long-term financing that other businesses can use. This would not only improve Amtrak's finances — it will help them attract the riders, to sell the tickets, that will permit them become self-sufficient — to meet the goals that we have set for them.

Sen. John McCain, R-Ariz.

From testimony before the Senate Environment and Public Works Subcommittee on Transportation and Infrastructure, March 13, 1997

no

As you consider program eligibility, you will hear from members advocating that Amtrak should be entitled to funding from the Highway Trust Fund. I strongly oppose their proposal. I encourage you to carefully consider Amtrak's legislative history, as well as its current financial condition.

Amtrak was created in 1971 in order to relieve the freight railroad industry from the economic burden of providing ongoing passenger service. With capital acquired from participating railroads and the federal government providing $40 billion in direct grants and another $100 million in loan guarantees, the corporation was to become self-sustaining within two years.

By 1972, Amtrak was already losing $152 million and requested Congress for additional funding. Congress responded as it has for 26 years, giving Amtrak more federal money. Congress authorized another $225 million plus another $100 million in loan guarantees. . . .

Since 1971, Amtrak has received $19 billion in federal funding to help cover its operating, capital and labor protective costs. I recognize Amtrak has strived to reduce its operating costs and increase its revenues. Frankly, many of Amtrak's financial challenges are due to statutory constraints that Congress has not lifted. But the fact remains: The Amtrak "two-year experiment" was unsuccessful 20 years ago, it's unsuccessful today and it will be unsuccessful in the future. . . .

Even though I think it is high time to end subsidies, the political realities are that Amtrak will likely continue to receive federal funding. But if the collective congressional wisdom concludes it is sound policy to continue pouring money into a passenger rail system that serves only about 500 locations across the nation, why rob the [highway] trust fund? The $19 billion given to Amtrak so far has come from the general Treasury.

Why, I ask, should highway dollars pay to subsidize Amtrak? They don't even pay into the fund. Already highway infrastructure needs outweigh public investment capabilities. Even if the budget permitted spending down all of the money in the fund, a significant funding shortfall would remain. . . .

According to the American Highway Users Alliance, 86.7 percent of travel is by car; 9.4 percent by air, 3.6 percent by mass transit and school buses; and 0.3 percent by Amtrak. Instead of turning on a new spigot for Amtrak, which serves less than 1 percent of the traveling public, maybe a better alternative would be to expand funding flexibility. If passenger rail service is a transportation priority, let states use their federal funds to help support passenger rail service.

FOR MORE INFORMATION

American Highway Users Alliance, 1776 Massachusetts Ave. N.W., Suite 500, Washington, D.C. 20036; (202) 857-1200. The alliance's membership includes the oil, auto, trucking and highway construction industries and other interests that want transportation funding to be used almost exclusively for highway development and maintenance.

Federal Highway Administration (Transportation Department), 400 7th St. S.W., Washington, D.C. 20590; (202) 366-0660. The agency administers federal highway programs authorized by the 1991 Intermodal Surface Transportation Efficiency Act (ISTEA) and funded with money from the Highway Trust Fund.

Surface Transportation Policy Project, 1400 16th St. N.W., Suite 300, Washington, D.C. 20036; (202) 939-3470. This umbrella group represents environmentalists, bicycle riders, historic preservationists and other interests that support use of federal funds to promote bike and pedestrian facilities, transit and other non-vehicular transportation modes in addition to highway maintenance.

Transportation Research Board, National Research Council, 2001 Constitution Ave. N.W., Washington, D.C. 20418; (202) 334-3262. This federal agency provides information on research related to public transportation technology and management and rural transport systems.

Continued from p. 592

in the equation.

"The ... costs of motor vehicle use that are not reflected directly in user charges to drivers amount to almost $300 billion per year, more than 5 percent of the country's gross domestic product," concludes a study by the World Resources Institute, a research organization that promotes sustainable development. [20]

Demographic trends also have contributed to gridlock on the roads. "If you look at the statistics, the number of trips per driver and the distance per trip driven are not increasing very much," says James J. MacKenzie, a transportation expert at the World Resources Institute. "Almost 70 percent of the growth in travel is because there are more drivers. Half of that is women entering the work force over the past couple of decades, and the other half is just plain population growth."

Other experts say the desire for a single-family home on a large lot is so deeply ingrained in the American psyche that suburban sprawl — and the attendant gridlock — are here to stay.

"The possibility of reducing congestion by using more transit is unfortunately not a very great possibility because it's hard to make transit work when Americans like to live at low density," says Downs of the Brookings Institution. "The average commuting time in a car is 22 minutes, compared with 36 minutes by bus and 45 minutes by fixed rail. So you can see, there's a lot of advantage in using your car."

Whether it is the result of transportation policy run amok, population growth or simply the public's demand for a slice of the American dream, suburbanization poses the greatest obstacle to the development of alternative modes of transportation. Although there are nearly 7,000 trains, buses and other public transit systems running in the United States, they account for only 2.5 percent of passenger miles traveled, according to MacKenzie. [21] In a city like Washington, whose suburbs spill for miles into neighboring Virginia and Maryland, MacKenzie says, "Two-thirds of the trips are from one suburb to another, not into the central city. That explains why not that many people use Metro. The trouble with heavy rail is it costs $150 million a mile and goes only from point A to point B." ■

OUTLOOK

Roadblocks Ahead

There are signs that lawmakers will run into several obstacles as they undertake ISTEA's reauthorization before its Sept. 30 expiration. The committees responsible for drafting the legislation had planned to complete their work this spring, but markups have been repeatedly postponed.

A major obstacle to the bill's rewrite is Rep. Shuster's stated pledge to pry loose at least $12 billion in additional funding for transportation projects over the next five years. Despite the narrow defeat of his amendment to the fiscal 1998 budget resolution in May, lawmakers from all parts of the country are under pressure to increase federal support for transportation. Shuster has indicated he may use his authority as chairman of the House Transportation and Infrastructure Committee to block consideration of the various reauthorization proposals that have already been introduced until Congress agrees to provide additional funds.

On the Senate side, members of the Environment and Public Works Committee are divided over proposals to change the funding formulas that allocate federal transportation funds among the states. If the deadline passes without approval of a bill, Congress could continue funding transportation projects by passing a one-year reauthorization or a temporary extension of current funding levels.[22]

Advocates on both sides of the debate over transportation programs share Shuster's desire for more overall funding for transportation. But with Congress and the White House in agreement on a budget that would eliminate the federal deficit by 2002, they anticipate a protracted struggle over the available funds.

"The fact that we have a Highway Trust Fund that could support a substantially larger federal highway program than we have today and the fact that this budget agreement will prevent us from doing that certainly isn't helpful," says Bowlden of the Highway Users Alliance. "The country has identified highway improvement needs that so far surpass the available financial resources that we really ought to use [more of] those taxes that we collect from motorists to build better roads and bridges."

"We are concerned that there needs to be a ramp-up in transit dollars vs. highway dollars," counters Dittmar of the Surface Transportation Policy Project. "And we're concerned that Amtrak and commuter and intercity rail need to be protected and given a dedicated funding source."

Dittmar's group, together with a number of environmental organizations, calls for additions to ISTEA that would expand environmental protections by creating new programs to reduce the environmental damage caused by transportation. They also recommend the creation of a pilot program to help communities draw up transportation and land-use plans that would encourage the use of transit and reduce driving.[23]

Dittmar and his allies are concerned that the lack of additional funding will bolster support for the highway users' call to eliminate the CMAQ and transportation enhancements programs that have fostered transit and bicycle-pedestrian trail development over the past six years. Proposals that would do just that have already been introduced, including the STEP 21 bill by Rep. DeLay.

But some supporters of alternative transportation are optimistic that Congress will retain federal support of non-highway programs. "We supported Bud Shuster in his efforts to get more money for transportation, and I believe he recognizes that," says Hiemstra of the Rails-to-Trails Conservancy. "I also think that even though the budget agreement doesn't provide as much money as we all wanted for transportation, it still provides more than we have now.

"The bottom line here is there is never going to be enough money for transportation. The enhancement programs are so popular among Democrats and Republicans alike, not to mention local mayors, county commissioners, historic preservationists and other people who are not usually on the same side of the issue, that I anticipate Congress will support them again." ■

Notes

[1] See U.S. Department of Transportation, *ISTEA Reauthorization: Policy Statement and Principles* (undated), p. 2.

[2] For background, see "Traffic Congestion," *The CQ Researcher,* May 6, 1994, pp. 385-408.

[3] For background, see "Highway Safety," *The CQ Researcher,* July 14, 1995, pp. 609-632.

[4] See American Petroleum Institute, *The Funding of Roads in the United States: How the Taxes and Fees Collected from Motorists Are Spent,* May 1997.

[5] From a letter dated April 1, 1997.

[6] See David Hosansky and Alissa J. Rubin, "Shuster's Steamroller Stopped — For Now," *Congressional Quarterly Weekly Report,* May 24, 1997, p. 1183.

[7] Writing in an advertising supplement to *The Washington Post,* May 20, 1997.

[8] Sanford testified March 13, 1997, before the House Transportation and Infrastructure Subcommittee on Surface Transportation.

[9] Unless otherwise noted, information in this section is based on J. F. Hornbeck, "Transportation Infrastructure: Economic Issues and Public Policy Alternatives," *CRS Report for Congress,* Congressional Research Service, Jan. 26, 1993.

[10] See I. Mei Chan, ed., *Building on the Past, Traveling to the Future,* p. 28.

[11] See Wilfred Owen, *Transportation for Cities* (1976), p. 17.

[12] Cited by Hornbeck, *op. cit.,* pp. 8-9.

[13] See "Keep America Moving," Better, Safer Roads for the 21st Century. The group is part of the Highway Users Alliance.

[14] For background, see "New Air Quality Standards," *The CQ Researcher,* March 7, 1997, pp. 193-216.

[15] Based on John W. Fischer, "Highway and Transit Program Reauthorization: ISTEA Revisited?" *CRS Report for Congress,* May 7, 1997.

[16] See American Public Transit Association, "Historic NJ Transit Rail Station Reborn through Infusion of ISTEA Funds," *ISTEA Reauthorization Update,* May 7, 1997.

[17] Damkroger spoke to reporters at a briefing on ISTEA reauthorization held May 19 in Washington by the National Trust for Historic Preservation.

[18] See also Surface Transportation Policy Project, *Five Years of Progress: 110 Communities Where ISTEA Is Making a Difference* (1996).

[19] Department of Transportation, *op. cit.,* p. 1.

[20] James J. MacKenzie, Roger C. Dower and Donald D.T. Chen, *The Going Rate: What It Really Costs to Drive,* World Resources Institute, June 1992, p. 23.

[21] See James J. MacKenzie, "Driving the Road to Sustainable Ground Transportation," in *Frontiers of Sustainability* (1997), pp. 91-189.

[22] See David Hosansky, "ISTEA Rewrite Looks Unlikely by Sept. 30 Deadline for Action," *CQ Monitor,* June 5, 1997, p. 5.

[23] See Bureau of National Affairs, "Environmental Groups Mobilize to Protect Key ISTEA Programs from Cuts," *ISTEA Daily Briefing,* June 2, 1997.

Bibliography

Selected Sources Used

Books

Downs, Anthony, *New Visions for Metropolitan America*, The Brookings Institution, 1994.

According to Downs, Americans have yet to come to grips with their responsibility for the problems associated with suburban sprawl and the emptying of inner cities — decades of migration to outlying areas, emphasis on low-density housing and reliance on cars for transportation.

Downs, Anthony, *Stuck in Traffic: Coping with Peak-Hour Traffic Congestion*, The Brookings Institution, 1992.

The lack of a regional focus in metropolitan planning organizations prevents most American cities from adopting effective policies to reverse growing traffic congestion, Downs writes.

Articles

Clark, Kim, "How to Make Traffic Jams a Thing of the Past," *Fortune*, March 31, 1997, p. 34.

Governments that are running out of money and road space are beginning to fight traffic congestion by charging tolls on restricted lanes during rush hour. Critics say that so-called congestion pricing will merely create fast-moving "Lexus lanes" for rich commuters at the expense of less affluent commuters stuck in the slow lanes.

Kay, Jane Holtz, "Moving in the Right Direction," *Preservation*, May/June 1997, pp. 52-61.

By designating federal dollars for various modes of transportation, the 1991 Intermodal Surface Transportation Efficiency Act (ISTEA) has slowed Americans' growing dependence on cars and highways. But these modest advances against what the author calls "autohegemony" in America are threatened by efforts now under way to restore the historic bias in favor of highway funding.

Wilkinson, Bill, "10 Steps to Help Make America Walkable," *Pro Bike News*, April 1997, p. 3.

The Bicycle Federation of America has launched a campaign to support not only bike paths but also efforts to improve pedestrian facilities through ISTEA and reauthorizing legislation due to be enacted this fall. The coalition would require appropriate facilities for pedestrians on every street and highway where pedestrians are permitted.

Reports and Studies

American Highway Users Alliance, *Better, Safer Roads for the 21st Century: A Comprehensive Issue Analysis and Reference to Highway, Road and Bridge Legislation*, undated.

The leading coalition that seeks more funding of highway projects presents a detailed analysis of ISTEA's provisions, together with alternative proposals the groups wants to see in this year's reauthorization bill.

American Petroleum Institute, *The Funding of Roads in the United States: How the Taxes and Fees Collected from Motorists Are Spent*, May 1997.

The country's oil industry asserts that motorists are being shortchanged because only 58 percent of the money they spend in gasoline taxes and other user fees is being used for road construction and maintenance.

Chan, I Mei, ed., *Building on the Past, Traveling to the Future: A Preservationist's Guide to the ISTEA Transportation Enhancement Provision*, Federal Highway Administration and National Trust for Historic Preservation, undated.

Supporters of ISTEA's innovative Transportation Enhancements program want the new law to continue providing federal support for such non-traditional projects as restoring old bridges, revitalizing communities that were bypassed by interstate highways and establishing scenic byways.

Schrank, David L., and Timothy J. Lomax, *Urban Roadway Congestion — 1982 to 1993. Volume I: Annual Report*, Texas Transportation Institute, August 1996.

This study measures traffic congestion in 50 metropolitan areas around the country. Los Angeles is the most congested city by several standards of measurement, while Washington, D.C., residents pay the steepest cost for the city's congestion.

Surface Transportation Policy Project, *A Blueprint for ISTEA Reauthorization: A Common Sense Guide to Transportation Priorities for the 21st Century*, 1997.

The coalition that supports federal funding of non-highway transportation wants the new law to require that existing roads be repaired before new ones are built and set aside funding for intercity rail service.

U.S. Department of Transportation, *How to Keep America Moving. ISTEA: Transportation for the 21st Century*, Jan. 20, 1997.

As part of its effort to draw up reauthorizing legislation for transportation programs, Clinton administration officials met with citizens' groups and local and state governments to assess ISTEA's performance. Their findings, the report asserts, support a continuation of the law's basic framework.

The Next Step

Additional information from UMI's Newspaper & Periodical Abstracts™ database

Amtrak

"Amtrak Plans Cuts Over Several Routes," *The New York Times,* Aug. 11, 1996, p. 21.
In the latest of a series of sweeping changes in the nation's passenger-rail service, Amtrak plans to close down four routes and return to daily service on several others in an effort to save money and increase revenue.

Chapman, Stephen, "Amtrak: A Costly Monument to Nostalgia," *Chicago Tribune,* May 11, 1997, p. 21.
Chicago's Union Station is one of the grand cathedrals of the Age of the Railroad. With its cavernous waiting room, towering Corinthian columns, statues of Greek goddesses and soaring vaulted skylight, it could serve as the railway museum for a city built on the steam locomotive. In fact, it remains a bustling train depot, handling 100,000 passengers a day. But the station does include one museum piece: a concourse for Amtrak, the taxpayer-financed national passenger railroad. On a weekday morning, a visitor risks being trampled flat by crowds of commuters streaming out of the building on their way to work. But no danger exists in the Amtrak lounge, where barely two dozen people can be found. During a typical day, fewer than 5,400 intercity travelers pass through the terminal.

Cohen, Christopher, "Get Amtrak back on track," *The Wall Street Journal,* April 30, 1997, p. A14.
Cohen criticizes Amtrak for spending its money on 79-mph trains that cannot compete with airlines or even interstate highways rather than building better tracks that could make high-speed rail service possible. Cohen urges Congress to eliminate Amtrak as a service provider so that the government can get into "the one part of the rail-passenger business where it truly belongs — funding infrastructure to carry 150-mph business-class trains run by private companies."

Nomani, Asra Q., "Highway bill's Amtrak funds upset many," *The Wall Street Journal,* March 13, 1997, p. A3.
President Clinton's plan to pump more fuel-tax money into non-road spending such as funding for Amtrak is drawing protests from traditional road lobbying interests such as the auto, oil and construction industries — as well as from Amtrak itself.

Smith, Joel J., "Amtrak conducts high-speed test runs," *Detroit News,* Oct. 25, 1996, p. B3.
Amtrak is testing higher rail speeds on the Detroit to Chicago corridor, a move that could shave two hours off the current 5 1/2-hour trip. Amtrak officials on Oct. 24, 1996, said some trains will increase their speeds to 110 mph from 79 mph on 20-mile stretches of track in southwestern Michigan.

Snel, Alan, "Bicyclists across U.S. fume over Amtrak smoking cars," *Denver Post,* Feb. 13, 1997, p. B3.
Colorado bicyclists have joined their pedaling brethren nationwide to protest Amtrak's decision to retrofit train cars for designated smoking areas instead of creating storage space for bikes. The League of American Bicyclists, one of the nation's primary bike groups, maintains Amtrak officials promised to use spare baggage space for passengers to roll their bicycles on the train cars and store the two-wheelers for Amtrak's long-distance intercity routes. The decision means Amtrak passengers who want to bring a bicycle must continue to disassemble the bike, place the parts in a box and travel with the box as if it's luggage.

Thomas, Richard, "Cuts signal end of Amtrak," *The Guardian,* March 27, 1997, p. 18.
America's rail network is threatened with extinction as service to 42 cities — including Dallas, New Orleans, Las Vegas and Little Rock — falls victim this spring to savage cuts in government funding.

Bicycle Facilities

Greehan, Mike, "Bikes belong," *Bicycling,* May 1997, p. 12.
Congress is considering cutting federal funding for bike paths. It is up to cyclists to let their representatives in Congress know how important cycling is in the nation's transportation policy.

Martin, Scott, "Senator cyclist," *Bicycling,* June 1996, pp. 48-53.
Federal and state public officials who are friendly to cyclists and those who are cyclists' worst enemies are profiled. Tips for persuading politicians to support cycling issues are outlined.

Thompson, James Martin, "How to make BART bicycle-friendly," *San Francisco Chronicle,* Sept. 20, 1996, p. A25.
Thompson discusses various strategies that the Bay Area Rapid Transit (BART) system could implement to make the San Francisco rail service more user-friendly for bicyclists.

Weiss, Marc S., "Improving Our Poor Bicycle Safety Record," *Times-Picayune,* May 23, 1997, p. B6.

Since its founding in 1987, the New Orleans Regional Bicycle Awareness Committee (NORBAC) has worked diligently to promote bicycle safety. Its efforts to increase public awareness and government responsiveness have led to the establishment of safety education programs and the development of safe bicycling areas.

Williams, James, and Jan Larson, "Promoting bicycle commuting: Understanding the customer," *Transportation Quarterly,* summer 1996, pp. 67-78.
Williams and Larson provide a demographic profile of the bicycle commuter and explore government and community efforts to successfully market bicycle commuting to American workers. An integrated approach is recommended for communities interested in encouraging people to select the bicycle as a transportation alternative.

Highway Trust Fund

"Highways," *Houston Chronicle,* June 15, 1996, p. A10.
An editorial examines how the Highway Trust Fund, originally intended to finance the building and maintenance of a national transportation system of first-class roads and bridges throughout the U.S., has become something altogether different.

"The Highway Trust Fund," *Public Roads,* summer 1996, p. 47.
The Highway Trust Fund is the source of revenue for the Interstate Highway System and other federal-aid highway programs. The trust fund and the taxes dedicated to it are discussed.

"Truth in highways," *The Wall Street Journal,* April 8, 1996, p. A18.
An editorial criticizes the state of the U.S.'s transportation network and warns that a bill scheduled for a vote in the House the week of April 8, 1996, will only make things worse. The editorial explains that the legislation would take the Highway Trust Fund off the budget and exempt it from cuts designed to balance the budget. The editorial says that Congress should truly take the trust fund off-budget by devolving the responsibility to states and communities.

Intermodal Surface Transportation Efficiency Act (ISTEA)

Barlas, Stephen, "States, locals battle for ISTEA," *American City & County,* March 1997, p. 12.
The Intermodal Surface Transportation Efficiency Act (ISTEA) is set to expire at the end of September 1997. The act gives local governments unprecedented authority in deciding how to use money targeted for mass transit, highways, local roads and bridges.

Becker, Pamela, "Clinton and Congress jockey over transportation bill," *Mechanical Engineering,* May 1997, p. 36.
The big issue in the reauthorization of the Intermodal Surface Transportation Efficiency Act is how to divide the funds among the states. The provisions of President Clinton's reauthorization bill are summarized.

Coorsh, Richard, "For whom the highway tolls," *Consumers' Research Magazine,* April 1997, p. 6.
A transportation bill proposed by President Clinton would allow states to charge tolls on federal highways. Other federal government news that affects consumers is presented.

Hosansky, David, "ISTEA reauthorization stalls over highway funding," *Congressional Quarterly Weekly Report,* May 10, 1997, p.1066.
Efforts by Congress to reauthorize the Intermodal Surface Transportation Efficiency Act (ISTEA) face further delays due to a new fracas over highway funding.

O'Brien, Greg, and Chip Bishop, "Ticket to ride: Will public transit benefit from ISTEA reauthorization?" *American City & County,* April 1997, pp. 20-22.
City and county leaders are positioning themselves for action as Congress, the Clinton administration and public interest groups are beginning to take sides in the debate over national highway and transit policy. At stake are billions of grant dollars and a continuation of a policy that allows local governments to decide how best to spend federal transportation dollars.

Saroff, Laurie, "Administration starts down road to ISTEA reauthorization," *Nation's Cities Weekly,* March 17, 1997, p. 2.
The Clinton administration has indicated that it would support the Intermodal Surface Transportation Efficiency Act (ISTEA) with a bill that authorizes $175 billion over the next six years. The reauthorization would give ISTEA an 11 percent increase.

National Highway System

Galm, Chris, "Why our highways need repair," *Consumers' Research Magazine,* November 1996, pp. 11-14.
There are serious problems with the U.S. highway system, including poor pavement conditions and deficient bridges. Bringing the highways up to par would require the federal government to spend $15 billion a year over what it currently spends.

Weingroff, Richard F. "Milestones for U.S. Highway Transportation and the Federal Highway Administration," *Public Roads,* spring 1996, pp. 44-50.
Historic milestones for U.S. highway transportation and the Federal Highway Administration are detailed.

Pedestrian Safety

Adelmann, Gerald, "On the Right Path," *Chicago Tribune,* May 13, 1997, p. 16.

Innovative strategies like Partnership for a Walkable America are essential if we are going to change transportation policies that have for too long followed one dictum: "Build more roads." If Chicago and other urban areas are going to meet the transportation needs of local residents, we need to rethink some of our planning decisions. Most transportation planning is based on traveling to and from work, yet the simple home-work-home trip chain accounts for a mere 14 percent of all person trips, according to the Surface Transportation Policy Project. Remarkably, non-work trips now account for 70 percent of all person trips. Yet our transportation planning does not take this into account.

Castaneda, Carol J., "South a danger spot for walkers; Report finds 3 Fla. cities among worst," *USA Today,* April 9, 1997, p. A3.

Pedestrians are 11 times more likely to be killed by a car in Fort Lauderdale, Fla., than in Pittsburgh, Pa., according to a new report by the Environmental Working Group and the Surface Transportation Policy Project. Most dangerous after Fort Lauderdale are Miami, Atlanta, Tampa and Dallas. Conversely, Pittsburgh, Milwaukee, Boston, Rochester, N.Y., and New York City are the safest cities because they have ample sidewalks, bus stops and other pedestrian amenities, the report says.

Eckstein, Sandra, "Study reinforces drive against cars: Moving autos, and not people, cited in Atlanta," *Atlanta Journal Constitution,* April 12, 1997, p. D1.

A study that found that the metro-Atlanta area is the third-most dangerous in the country for pedestrians points to a problem that many people already are aware of: Road construction projects usually are meant to move cars, not walkers. It is a problem especially pronounced in newer, fanned-out cities, like those in the South and West, according to a study by two nonprofit groups, the Environmental Working Group and the Surface Transportation Policy Project.

"Mean streets for pedestrians," *The Boston Globe,* April 12, 1997, p. A14.

A national study conducted by the Surface Transportation Policy Project and the Environmental Working Group ranks Boston third in the United States for pedestrian safety. Pedestrian safety, like everything else, is relative. So, while the Boston metropolitan area is bad, with its squeaky-braked close calls and annual average of 22 pedestrian fatalities, it's still not as bad as Florida's Fort Lauderdale area, which averages 58 deaths a year.

"Pedestrians at Risk, New Study Warns," *St. Louis Post-Dispatch,* April 9, 1997, p. A8.

"Pedestrian safety is an unacknowledged public health problem," says Hank Dittmar, executive director of the Surface Transportation Policy Project, a highway safety advocacy group that produced a study on pedestrian deaths with the Environmental Working Group.

Vartabedian, Ralph, "Being a Pedestrian Is Risky Business," *Los Angeles Times,* April 15, 1997, p. E1.

Every year, about 900 California pedestrians are killed and more than 18,000 others sustain injuries, according to a new nationwide study on pedestrian deaths. While pedestrian deaths account for 19 percent of all motor vehicle deaths in the state, just 0.7 percent of federal highway spending related to safety in the state was allocated to pedestrian projects. The report, by a large coalition of environmental groups and organized under the Environmental Working Group and Surface Transportation Policy Project, demands a substantial reallocation of spending to improve pedestrian safety.

Rapid Transit

Braude, Marvin, "'Rail First' leaves commuters last," *Los Angeles Times,* June 17, 1996, p. B5.

Los Angeles City Councilman Marvin Braude states that transit in Los Angeles is in deep trouble and argues that it is time to rethink the city's transportation policy. Braude lists some proposals to focus priorities on major objectives and restore public confidence in the Metropolitan Transportation Authority.

Huang, Herman, "The land-use impacts of urban rail transit systems," *Journal of Planning Literature,* August 1996, pp. 17-30.

Research regarding the impact of urban rail transit systems on real estate development in the U.S. and Canada is examined. If rail transit is built, then station-area development should be encouraged to enhance the returns on investment.

Miller, Luther S., "Passenger rail outlook: '96 was good, '97 could be better," *Railway Age,* January 1997, pp. 53-56.

Increased funding is keeping rail projects on schedule and car builders busy. Items on the "wish lists" of several rapid transit authorities around the U.S. are discussed.

Wildavsky, Ben, "King of the commute," *National Journal,* Jan. 20, 1996, pp. 114-117.

Despite years of spending on public transit, Americans are driving more than ever. Some analysts say policy-makers are mistaken to persist in emphasizing subway and rail construction, resisting road construction and urging commuters to carpool or take mass transit. The flourishing of solo commuting is examined.

Back Issues

Great Research on Current Issues Starts Right Here . . . Recent topics covered by The CQ Researcher are listed below. Before May 1991, reports were published under the name of Editorial Research Reports.

DECEMBER 1995
Teens and Tobacco
Gene Therapy's Future
Global Water Shortages
Third-Party Prospects

JANUARY 1996
Emergency Medicine
Punishing Sex Offenders
Bilingual Education
Helping the Homeless

FEBRUARY 1996
Reforming the CIA
Campaign Finance Reform
Academic Politics
Getting Into College

MARCH 1996
The British Monarchy
Preventing Juvenile Crime
Tax Reform
Pursuing the Paranormal

APRIL 1996
Centennial Olympic Games
Managed Care
Protecting Endangered Species
New Military Culture

Back issues are available for $5.00 (subscribers) or $10.00 (non-subscribers). Quantity discounts apply to orders over ten. To order, call Congressional Quarterly Customer Service at (202) 887-8621.

Binders are available for $18.00. To order call 1-800-638-1710. Please refer to stock number 648.

MAY 1996
Russia's Political Future
Marriage and Divorce
Year-Round Schools
Taiwan, China and the U.S.

JUNE 1996
Rethinking NAFTA
First Ladies
Teaching Values
Labor Movement's Future

JULY 1996
Recovered-Memory Debate
Native Americans' Future
Crackdown on Sexual Harassment
Attack on Public Schools

AUGUST 1996
Fighting Over Animal Rights
Privatizing Government Services
Child Labor and Sweatshops
Cleaning Up Hazardous Wastes

SEPTEMBER 1996
Gambling Under Attack
The States and Federalism
Civic Journalism
Reassessing Foreign Aid

OCTOBER 1996
Political Consultants
Insurance Fraud
Rethinking School Integration
Parental Rights

NOVEMBER 1996
Global Warming
Clashing Over Copyright
Consumer Debt
Governing Washington, D.C.

DECEMBER 1996
Welfare, Work and the States
The New Volunteerism
Implementing the Disabilities Act
America's Pampered Pets

JANUARY 1997
Combating Scientific Misconduct
Restructuring the Electric Industry
The New Immigrants
Chemical and Biological Weapons

FEBRUARY 1997
Assisting Refugees
Alternative Medicine's Next Phase
Independent Counsels
Feminism's Future

MARCH 1997
New Air Quality Standards
Alcohol Advertising
Civic Renewal
Educating Gifted Students

APRIL 1997
Declining Crime Rates
The FBI Under Fire
Gender Equity in Sports
Space Program's Future

MAY 1997
The Stock Market
The Cloning Controversy
Expanding NATO
The Future of Libraries

JUNE 1997
FDA Reform
China After Deng
Line-Item Veto
Breast Cancer

Future Topics

- ***Executive Pay***
- ***School Vouchers***
- ***Aggressive Driving***

The CQ Researcher

Published By Congressional Quarterly Inc.

Executive Pay

Do CEOs get paid too much?

Every spring, news accounts of eye-popping corporate paychecks raise protests against "greed" and "excess." This year's lists of the highest paid chieftains contain familiar entries from companies such as Heinz and GE, but also some newcomers, such as Lawrence Coss of Green Tree Financial, who pocketed $102 million. The difference in today's climate is that new government and industry disclosure rules have prompted many critics to conclude that CEO pay is now more properly linked to actual performance. And the complaints often heard from unions, religious activists and institutional shareholders have been muted by the booming stock market, which is enriching shareholders and executives alike. A truer test of the system's fairness, however, may come with the next economic downturn.

Inside This Issue

CQ July 11, 1997 • Volume 7, No. 26 • Pages 601-624

Formerly Editorial Research Reports

Executive Pay

COVER: SARAH M. MAGNER

CQ Researcher

July 11, 1997
Volume 7, No. 26

The CQ Researcher (ISSN 1056-2036). Formerly Editorial Research Reports. Published weekly, except Jan. 3, May 30, Aug. 29, Oct. 31, by Congressional Quarterly Inc., 1414 22nd St., N.W., Washington, D.C. 20037. Annual subscription rate for libraries, businesses and government is $340. Additional rates furnished upon request. Periodicals postage paid at Washington, D.C., and additional mailing offices. POSTMASTER: Send address changes to The CQ Researcher, 1414 22nd St., N.W., Washington, D.C. 20037.

Executive Pay

By Charles S. Clark

The Issues

When the union man quizzed the CEO, he was fended off with a wisecrack. The scene was the annual stockholders' gathering for General Electric Co. The executive was GE's legendary John F. "Jack" Welch Jr., who last year took home a pay package worth $21.4 million. The union man was AFL-CIO investments director William Patterson.

"You have been awarded by the Board of Directors, along with your base pay package, 320,000 stock options," Patterson told the chief executive officer at the April 23 meeting in Charlotte, N.C. "And this is on top of 2.2 million unexercised options. My question to you is, do these options motivate you to bring more ideas, commit more value and more time to the growth of the company?"

Welch replied by explaining how all GE employees are motivated by owning stock options in their own company, and how under his tenure, the number of employees who've been awarded options has grown from a couple of hundred "fat cat" executives to 22,000 workers. "I get the most stock options because I happen to be lucky enough to have the top job," he said.

"Do [the stock options] motivate you, Mr. Chairman?" Patterson pressed.

"Absolutely," Welch said to laughter and applause.

"Why stop at 320,000 shares? Why not double that? You would be more motivated."

"I think that is a good suggestion for the board," Welch said to more laughter. "They are all here."

Such exchanges are becoming more and more common in corporate America following the annual springtime announcement of the latest, often mind-boggling executive paychecks. And though GE shareholders rejected a proposal from the Teamsters union to curb executive pay, the proposal garnered 9 percent of the vote, which union activists hailed as a sign that executive-pay critics are making headway.

They certainly have had much to criticize recently. This year's well-publicized roster of pay packages soared to new heights with the $102.4 million taken home by CEO Lawrence Coss of Green Tree Financial Corp. (a St. Paul, Minn.-based mobile-home financing company); the $97.5 million awarded to Andrew Grove of the computer parts giant Intel; and the $94 million given to Sanford Weill of the Travelers Group insurance company. * (*See chart, p. 604.*) All told, according to *Business Week*, total CEO compensation among 365 major U.S. companies rose 53 percent from 1995 to 1996 — five times the 11 percent gain in corporate profits. [1]

"In 1996, the pay of top executives in a *Business Week* study was 209 times the pay of a factory employee," said Sen. Carl Levin, D-Mich., co-author of a bill to end the tax deductibility of executive stock options (*see p. 615*). "Five years ago, the pay gap was 100 times. In 1980, it was 40 times. The latest figures for [executives in] other countries is [only] about 20 times for Japan and about 25 times for Germany."

The widening pay gap between the top executives and their workers has been flaring as an issue since the early 1990s. [2] But the current environment is unprecedented in one key respect: The rarefied, technical world of proxy statements and corporate governance in which pay issues are fought is now populated by a growing army of sophisticated critics who work hard to make executive pay issues loom larger in the public consciousness.

In February, for example, Michael D. Eisner, the highly praised CEO of the Walt Disney Co., watched as protesters picketed his annual meeting in reaction to his decision to give a reported $90 million in severance pay to his fired deputy Michael Ovitz. And a resolution challenging Eisner's estimated $252 million package of salary and stock options over 10 years won 8 percent of shareholders' votes. "I think the [Disney] vote has actually energized the debate," said Richard H. Koppes, the former general counsel of the California Public Employees' Retirement System, a major investor on Wall Street. [3]

The rash of media exposure that this issue unfailingly generates has renewed old debates over the distribution of the nation's wealth. A front-page story in the populist *New York*

* Coss earned $102 million in bonuses and a $433,000 salary. Grove's total compensation included his $425,000 salary, $2.5 million bonus and exercised stock options amassed over several years worth $94.5 million. Weill's pay also included salary, bonuses and stock options.

The 10 Top-Earning CEOs in 1996

	Salary and Bonus	Long-term compensation	Total pay
Lawrence Coss Green Tree Financial	$102,449,000	none	$102,449,000
Andrew Grove Intel	$3,003,000	$94,587,000	$97,590,000
Sanford Weill Travelers Group	$6,330,000	$87,828,000	$94,158,000
Theodore Waitt Gateway 2000	$965,000	$80,361,000	$81,326,000
Anthony O'Reilly H.J. Heinz	$2,736,000	$61,500,000	$64,236,000
Sterling Williams Sterling Software	$1,448,000	$56,801,000	$58,249,000
John Reed Citicorp	$3,467,000	$40,143,000	$43,610,000
Stephen Hilbert Conseco	$13,962,000	$23,450,000	$37,412,000
Casey Cowell U.S. Robotics	$3,430,000	$30,522,000	$33,952,000
James Moffett Freeport-McMoran	$6,956,000	$26,776,000	$33,732,000

Source: Business Week, *April 21, 1997*

Post in April featured photos of the top-earning CEOs and a headline that asked, "Are they worth it?" A recent spate of books, notably *The Winner-Take-All Society,* portray elite CEO pay as part of society's larger "misallocation of talent" in such fields as publishing, academia and sports. [4] (*See story, p. 608.*)

"It is remarkable when *The Wall Street Journal,* and not just pay-protesters, starts calling the pay 'obscene,' " says Timothy Smith, executive director of the New York City-based Interfaith Responsibility Research Center, which challenges corporations on a variety of social policies. "It shows that the 'cops' are watching the pay carefully, even if we haven't seen much behavior change."

The Internet's World Wide Web has become the site of a slew of broadsides from pay critics including the AFL-CIO, Democrats in the House of Representatives and longtime executive pay consultant Graef "Bud" Crystal. (*See "At Issue," p. 617.*) "Bill Gates' Personal Wealth Clock," as one site is called, provides an up-to-the-minute tally of the Microsoft chairman's personal fortune, now said to be $36 billion and growing.

Fully 77 percent of Americans think the top executives of major business corporations are overpaid, according to a 1994 poll by Roper Starch Worldwide, though an even higher percentage think professional athletes, entertainers and lawyers are overpaid. Some 58 percent of Americans go so far as to say they are "angry or extremely angry" that "the average CEO makes more than 100 times what the average worker makes," according to a 1996 poll by the Mellman Group and Peter Hart for the AFL-CIO.

CEO pay grows out of a complex system of corporate compensation. Packages that include base pay, bonuses, short-term incentives and long-term options to purchase stock are typically negotiated by the corporation's compensation committee and compensation specialists who represent the executive. The proposed agreements are then approved by the company's board of directors, largely composed of company outsiders. Only in recent years have companies been forced to permit shareholders to challenge pay packages.

"CEO pay packages that exceed what shocks the conscience are not hard to understand," says Rob Shapiro, an economist and vice president of the Progressive Policy Institute. "They're established by compensation committees that are appointed by the boards. And since CEOs often dominate the makeup of the boards, many in effect can set their own pay. If you could set your own pay, I'd guess it would be higher than market rate."

Disagreements over what is fair also stem from the fact that base pay in recent years has emerged as only a fraction of many executives' compensation. Billionaire investor Warren Buffett, for example, takes only $100,000 in annual salary from the investment firm he heads, Berkshire Hathaway, but, like Microsoft's Bill Gates, who also receives a low salary, Buffett receives stock options that have made him one of the world's richest men.

The trend toward paying executives in stock options has accelerated since a 1993 law capped the amount of compensation a corporation could deduct from its taxes. While stock options may encourage executives to align their personal interests with the company's, they also have complicated the ability of shareholders to evaluate the CEO's package. That's because the value of options shares cannot be known until years later, when the CEO cashes them in at an optimal time, when the stock price has risen.

"The issue is complicated this year," says Katherine A. Bayne, legal counsel at the Investor Responsibility Research Center. "Everyone favors pay for performance, but now that it has been implemented, shareholders are surprised to see the high numbers, what with the economy and stock market doing so well. The executives are making out like bandits, and some critics are asking whether this is too much of a good thing."

Anger at CEOs is made worse, according to Anne Hansen, deputy director of the Council of Institutional Investors, whose members control a trillion dollars in pension funds, "by the fact that many CEOs who continue taking skyrocketing pay are the same ones laying off a high percentage of the work force." A good example in 1995 was AT&T chief Robert Allen, who collected $10 million in options after announcing plans to cut 40,000 jobs.

Protests and shareholder resolutions may not have translated into more humble CEO paychecks, but there appears to be a keen awareness within corporations of the enhanced scrutiny of executive salaries put in place by Congress, the Securities and Exchange Commission (SEC) and the Financial Accounting Standards Board (FASB).

Reuters

Billionaire investor Warren Buffett of Berkshire Hathaway only earns $100,000 in annual salary, but stock options have made him one of the world's richest men.

"We've seen a terrific shift among executives who serve on boards since 1992," says Wallace Nichols, executive director of the American Compensation Association. "They're more responsive to being involved with the companies. And the SEC disclosure rules have made board members more accountable."

Bruce Bunch, a spokesman for GE, defends CEO Welch's ownership of an estimated $350 million in GE options by noting that GE "just became the first company in history to break $200 billion in total value. When Welch came in 1981, its value was only at $12 billion. We know the benefit is going to the shareholder, and most GE shareholders approve."

Whether such approval can continue in corporate America will be determined by answers to the following questions:

Is the current system for determining CEO pay fair?

"Let's hear it for options!" enthuses a recent *Forbes* roundup of CEO rewards. [5] The magazine reported that 316 out of 800 CEOs surveyed exercised stock options in 1996 worth an average of slightly more than $1 million — double the previous year's value. Stock options — in part because of their corporate tax advantages — have been the rage since the early '90s, when sparks flew over such CEO bonanzas such as H.J. Heinz CEO Anthony O'Reilly's $75 million package, and the $86 million won by Coca-Cola's Roberto Goizueta.

Executive Compensation Reports found that 53 percent of 366 major companies surveyed said that their CEO held exercisable stock options worth at least $3 million in 1996, up from 34 percent in 1994. Nowadays, the typical CEO pay package, according to pay consultant Pearl Meyer, is 21 percent salary, 27 percent annual incentives, 16 percent long-term incentives and 36 percent stock-based (stocks that cannot be cashed for a specified number of years). [6]

U.S. Executives Take Home the Bacon

*U.S. corporate executives received more than $800,000 in total compensation in 1994 — about twice as much as their counterparts in other industrialized countries — according to Towers Perrin, a management consulting firm. But pay expert Graef Crystal calculates that U.S. executives actually averaged $3.7 million. **

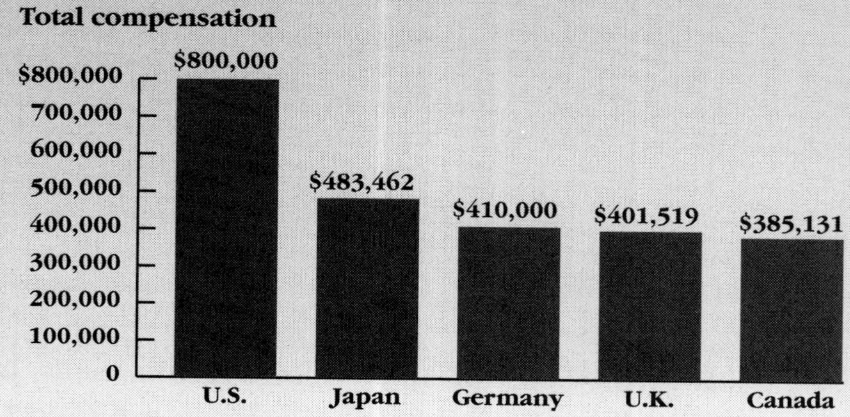

** Towers Perrin based its calculations on base pay, bonuses and stock options that were exercised. Crystal included the present value of all stock options granted to an executive in a year, whether or not the option was exercised.*

Note: The Towers Perrin survey was limited to firms with more than $100 million in sales. Crystal surveyed more than 200 major corporations.

Source: Towers Perrin

But since the controversies of the early '90s, the landscape has been altered by several changes in the arcane rules of pay reporting:

• The SEC, following a round of passionate industry commentary, in 1992 began requiring corporate proxy statements to include charts estimating the ever-so-elusive value of future stock grants for the top five executive officers. [7]

• Following an endorsement by newly elected President Clinton, Congress in 1993 capped the tax deductibility of executive compensation at $1 million, unless it was performance-based. The new cap had the effect of encouraging stock options and slowing the growth of runaway salaries.

• The FASB, after industry pressure forced it to retreat from a bolder plan, required companies to estimate the value of top executives' stock option packages and include it in the annual report. (The rejected plan would have required the amount to be reflected in the company's profit statement.) [8]

The result is a system, though still complex, that many feel gives shareholders enough information and advance notice of CEO compensation to be able to judge (and vote) on whether the increased pay fairly reflects a company's improved performance. Hence *Business Week*, in its 47th annual survey of executive pay, argues, for example, that Microsoft's Gates and Avon Products CEO James E. Preston delivered the highest return on equity relative to their pay. Conversely, its analysts concluded, the highly paid executives who delivered the least to shareholders were Conseco's Stephen C. Hilbert and America OnLine's Stephen M. Case. [9]

Similarly, a study by *The Washington Post* notes that Black & Decker CEO Nolan Archibald's compensation went up 79 percent to $6.7 million, while the power tools company's stock declined 13 percent in 1995-96. [10]

Pay critic Crystal, in his May *Crystal Report Online,* concludes that Intel's Grove made "$95 million in option gains, and he's still underpaid!" But he warns that Time Warner's Gerry Levin is proof that, "You can give some CEO's truly heavy monetary motivation, yet they still can't perform for their shareholders."

Crystal has problems with stock options in general. "If the stock price drops, the shareholders take it in the neck while the CEO loses not a penny of real money (opportunity loss aside)," he writes. "And we forget that the CEO has no incentive to increase dividends because, as an option holder, he doesn't receive dividends. And we forget that the CEO can use his insider information quite legally to time when he wants to exercise his options." [11]

"Tilting the compensation package so heavily toward stock options provides corporate officials with a personal motive for ignoring the claims of other stakeholders and with enticements to enrich themselves on short-term jumps in share prices," write analysts at the Economic Policy Institute. "An overemphasis on short-term increases in share price can undermine the long-term viability of the company to the detriment of employees, creditors and long-term stockholders." [12]

Chris Bohner, a research analyst at the AFL-CIO, points out that many of the options packages are so large they are affecting the companies' earnings per share — "diluting" the holdings of other shareholders. "The cost of options to shareholders wouldn't be so objectionable if it were spread across the work force, but we're talking about a package for one man," he says. And he points to the familiar criticism that many company boards of directors are a "non-neutral mechanism that has been captured by the CEOs," who fill it with "people from the same sort of club, who have outside business or family relationships."

The majority of executives who serve on corporate boards are "white males, and tend to sit on one another's boards," adds Carol Bowie, editor of *Executive Compensation Reports*. The government's capping of pay deductibility, she says, "was well-intentioned, but has had inadvertent consequences." Provided that the measure of performance-based growth is systematic, a company's board and compensation committee can set it up the way they want to — as long as shareholders approve the measures. At the same time, "there is pressure on many companies to set goals low enough so that there is some flexibility if the goals are not clearly met," she says. If performance comes anywhere near the performance goals, "the compensation committee the next year is under pressure to act at the maximum levels they've set up. There's not a deliberate effort to give more to enrich the executive or pad his pay, but a series of factors taken together."

Defenders of stock options point out that they create loyalty by giving the CEO a long-term stake in remaining with the company. Even more important, the options' value — in theory, anyway — would be worth very little should the company's fortunes turn down. Largely because of options and bonuses, the percentage of CEO pay that could be called "at risk" has risen from 54 percent in 1989 to 66 percent today, according to a study of 250 companies by Towers Perrin, a pay consulting firm. [13]

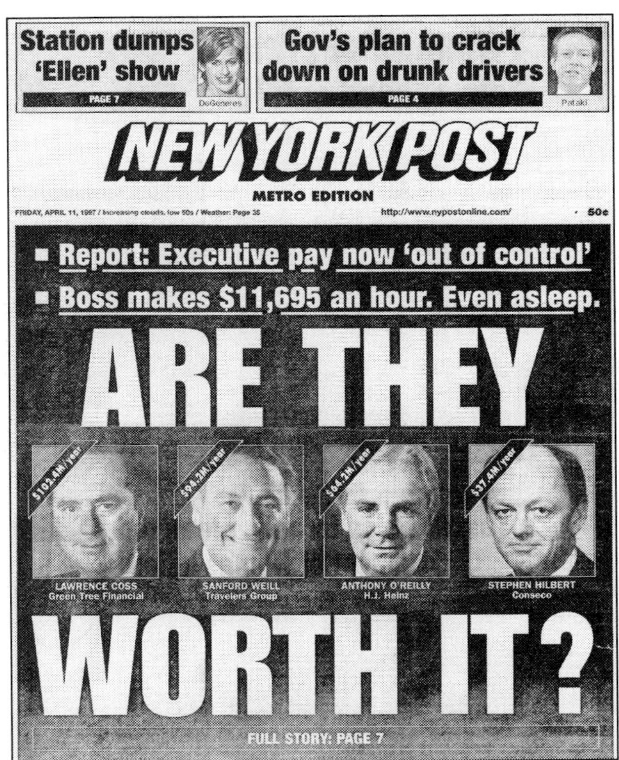

Station dumps 'Ellen' show PAGE 7 DeGeneres

Gov's plan to crack down on drunk drivers PAGE 4 Pataki

NEW YORK POST

METRO EDITION

FRIDAY, APRIL 11, 1997 / Increasing clouds, low 50s / Weather: Page 35 http://www.nypostonline.com/ 50¢

■ Report: Executive pay now 'out of control'

■ Boss makes $11,695 an hour. Even asleep.

ARE THEY

$102.4M/year LAWRENCE COSS Green Tree Financial

$94.2M/year SANFORD WEILL Travelers Group

$64.2M/year ANTHONY O'REILLY H.J. Heinz

$37.4M/year STEPHEN HILBERT Conseco

WORTH IT?

FULL STORY: PAGE 7

Front-page coverage in the tabloid New York Post *reflects attention the media and shareholder activists are giving to executive pay issues.*

Charles Peck, compensation specialist for the nonprofit business research group known as the Conference Board, finds it amusing that the same pay critics who demanded and won a tie-in between executive pay and company performance are upset that the market is booming and stock prices are appreciating. "Stock options have delivered the majority of executive compensation wealth for 30 years," he says. "When an option is granted today, it has no actual value, so [its future value] is hard to tell. But options have made a significant number of executives financially secure enough so that they can move and do other things. They're a powerful tool."

Peck points to Tupperware as an example of a company whose stock has declined, and whose CEO stock options are without much value. But look at Eastman Kodak, he adds, where CEO George Fisher has clearly created value in a stock that has nearly doubled.

"It's difficult to establish a causality and say that a CEO is having an impact on price," Peck says. "But there is a correlation between stock price and performance generally. And like a drunk who leans on a lamppost, the booming market is his source of support."

Others point out that CEO pay expectations vary by industry. Silicon Valley venture capitalists, for example, rely heavily on stock options for untried enterprises, and a Conference Board survey for 1995 found that the highest pay gains for CEOs were in financial services while the lowest was in transportation. [14] "The farther removed one is from entrepreneurial activity, *Forbes* asserts, "the harder it is to justify gargantuan compensation deals." [15]

Should CEO pay be capped?

"How much is too much?" muses Patrick McGurn, director of corpo-

Sports Superstars Put CEOs in Pay Big Leagues

The sports world was agog at the announcement in May that University of Kentucky basketball coach Rick Pitino had signed a 10-year, $70 million contract to coach the Boston Celtics.

The 44-year-old Pitino's new status as the highest-paid coach of any sport drew predictable gasps of envy and disgust, but also admiration. "It's about time the National Basketball Association started paying its coaches — the good ones, that is — more than the third guy from the end of the bench," wrote sports columnist Dan Daly. "Basketball isn't just about players. It's about getting the players to play, getting the most out of what you have. Pitino is a master at that." [1]

The Pitino payday is just the latest record-breaker among ballooning sports salaries in recent years as a result of lucrative television revenues and free-agency status for individual players. [2] But it also illustrates a broader trend. Students of compensation in general increasingly are pointing to the rise of the "superstar" — athletes, coaches, actors, rock stars, best-selling authors and, yes, corporate executives — who don't merely earn more than their second-place competitors, they earn *exponentially more* over the long term. The ability of the top performer to set himself up for life in ways seldom available to average members of his field is increasingly common as a "success-breeds-success feature," according to an economist and a public policy professor who examined the trend in their 1995 book *The Winner-Take-All Society*. [3]

In both the sports and business worlds, superstar paychecks in one area can have spillover effects that drive up pay in others. "Rick Pitino's salary is a trickle-down from the players because it can be grating to a coach, who has a direct influence on a team, to be underpaid compared with players," says Carol Bowie, editor of *Executive Compensation Reports* in Springfield, Va. "The same is true," she adds, "for studio executives, who are often signing contracts for actors worth millions for a few weeks' work, and at securities firms, where the commissions awarded to superstar traders can mean that they outearn the CEO."

In recent years, the explosion of pay packages among athletes and entertainers has been used to defend the rise in CEO pay. According to pay consultant Graef Crystal: "Criticize a highly paid CEO about his pay package and he will be apt to respond: 'You think I'm paid too much? Go look at how much José Canseco makes! And Joe Montana. And several hundred other sports starts. Go look at how much Bill Cosby makes. And Jack Nicholson.'"

Such reasoning, Crystal says with irony, is very similar to arguments made by feminists and others who favor "comparable worth" policies, which would adjust current salaries to assert that a nurse is worth more than a truck driver, or a teacher more than an electrician. Such interference in the free market, Crystal notes, is ridiculed by many of the same business executives who compare themselves with pro athletes. [4]

Defenders of high pay point out that coaches as well as CEOs can easily lose their jobs. And Bruce Bunch, a spokesman for General Electric, whose CEO John "Jack" Welch is among the highest paid CEOs in the country, argues that everyone, "from CEOs, to athletes, to public relations staffers to journalists are all paid based on their market value. The reason I don't apply to play guard on the Chicago Bulls," he says, "is that I can't sell in that market."

But Chris Bohner, a research analyst at the AFL-CIO, points out that sports teams, because they are not publicly traded companies, are not as answerable to shareholders and employees. What's more, "athletes' performance is easily measured," he says, "while CEOs get paid these packages even when their batting averages go below .200."

Finally, the economics of pro basketball and other sports reflects more than simply pure market forces. In basketball and in the corporate world, "there is an increasing tendency toward creating two classes," says James Bryant, who represents several NBA standouts, such as Shawn Kemp, Marcus Camby and Nick Van Exel. "There are superstars, and there are lots of people making the minimum salary," says Bryant, vice president and legal counsel for the Arlington, Va., firm Pro Serv, noting that Michael Jordan is said to take home an annual $30 million (plus some $40 million in product endorsements) compared with the $250,000 that many average players make.

"The NBA is almost socialistic," he adds, in the way TV rights and its collective-bargaining agreement virtually guarantee a certain amount of revenue to even the last-place teams. What's more, NBA Commissioner David Stern reportedly takes home a whopping $40 million "while you could get a qualified government lawyer or a former Supreme Court justice for a tenth of his salary. He's done a good job of reviving the league from the days of drug abuse and delayed TV taping during the 1980s to the entertainment sport of the 1990s. But his success wasn't the result of competition," Bryant says. "The NBA is simply a good-old-boys' club that rewards one another."

---

[1] *The Washington Times,* May 8, 1997.

[2] For background, see "The Business of Sports," *The CQ Researcher,* Feb. 10, 1995, pp. 121-144.

[3] Robert H. Frank and Philip J. Cook, *The Winner-Take-All Society* (1995), pp. 19, 79.

[4] Graef Crystal, *In Search of Excess* (1991), p. 31.

rate programs at the consulting firm Institutional Shareholder Services. In the case of the record-setting bonus of Green Tree's Coss, "Even if it's tied to performance," he says, "$102 million is outrageous." [16]

Though the corporate culture often turns a deaf ear, many observers of executive pay simply feel that — proxy statements and incentive plans be damned — some dollar amounts are just plain excessive. "Nobody can use that much money," says Evelyn Y. Davis, the longtime shareholder activist and corporate gadfly who owns stock in 120 companies. "You can't take it with you. How many suits can you wear? How many houses can you live in? A lot of it is just ego; the executives see the other guy getting more, and it becomes an obsession."

The issue is basic fairness, says Bohner of the AFL-CIO. "Real wages for average people have declined over the past 20 years while CEO pay has gone through the roof. Inequality in America is at dangerous levels, and has never been greater."

Others point to the thousands of people in various professions who show up for work each day for a fixed salary without the constant dangling of more dollars before their eyes. "Imagine giving President Bush a few percentage points of the estimated total savings for keeping Saddam Hussein out of Saudi Arabia," writes former Harvard University President Derek Bok. [17]

The notion that dollar incentives are needed by multimillionaires who already have enough goods and investments to keep their families in clover for decades strikes some observers as quaint, at best.

"Businessmen talk about themselves as if they were peasants or piece workers, and the fallacy is hidden in abstract words like 'incentive' or 'productivity,'" writes psychologist Paul Wachtel. Why do they need incentives? he asks. "*They have been put* in a position to create jobs and wealth." [18]

Davis is among those who would like to see CEO pay capped at $2 million. Several companies, Ben and Jerry's Ice Cream among them, have capped CEO pay in relation to the pay of the lowest-level worker. And a bill introduced repeatedly by Rep. Martin Olav Sabo, D-Minn., would end corporate federal tax deductibility for executive pay that exceeds 25 times the pay of the lowest-paid worker.

Finding a way to rein in executive pay, however, whether from industry or government, has so far eluded consensus. "There is a moral concern about pay, but it's mostly about perception in the news media rather than actual greed," says Bowie of *Executive Compensation Reports*. "I'm not sure executives are any greedier than anyone else. But because of the way executive compensation is established, they are in a better position than the average employee to control the course of their compensation."

What one finds at the executive level, Bowie continues, "is intense competition; that's what fuels it. Some people in the business world have this inner core of confidence, and there's a distinction between the true entrepreneur and those who simply climb up the ladder and get to high position. Welch, for example, didn't make GE, but Gates did make Microsoft." People can agree that executives may not need all that money, she adds, "but they can't escape the fact that if the executives do want it, they are in a position to command high pay."

Others point to the Gospel of St. Luke, which says, "To whom much is given, much is required." "Most CEOs are overachievers who work 60-70-hour weeks, fly on Sundays and sacrifice time with their families," says Nichols of the compensation association. "The top-notch, high-performance executives don't do it because of the [dollar] incentives. But the incentives do help them focus on what's important, as determined by the board and the company's strategic business plan.

"Some CEOs do get very nervous about too much money being given to them, and they say to the boards, 'Don't be so liberal, I appreciate it, but enough is enough.' Back in the 1960s, everyone wanted to be identified as among the top paid. But now, lots are embarrassed by the largess. They want a large estate, but they don't want to be identified as being at the top."

Others emphasize that the free market determines a CEO's worth as well as his fate. "I dispute this idea that CEOs are set for life," Bunch says. "Look at all the CEOs who get booted. It's like saying that a pro basketball coach is set for life after coming off of one winning season."

Indeed, the insecurity of CEOs, rather than average workers, is touted by some as incentive for bold action. Management insecurity due to "globalization, deregulation, corporate takeover and shareholder activism has dramatically changed the comfort level of senior executives," writes economist James Annable. "As senior executives work harder to keep their jobs, they are producing extraordinary results." [19]

Defenders of high CEO pay also frequently cite the need to pay CEOs enough so that they aren't lured away by a better offer from a competing company. (In order to retain a high-performing CEO, many companies are now requiring them to sign "bad-boy clauses" that impose forfeiture of stock options should they bail out of a contract.)

The need to pay competitively is cited to explain why many CEOs are guaranteed severance packages of two to three years' pay, and why "the usual rule of thumb that calls for at least a 15-20 percent pay increase to recruit an employee from one organization to another is generally insufficient for CEOs," according to pay consultant Robert Salwen. "Premiums of 50 percent to 100 percent are not uncommon," he says.[20] Because CEOs are no longer in a position to be motivated by hopes of a promotion, pay specialists also say, they need a "scoreboard" to display their winnings without artificial limitations.

As for the political and moral aspects, "The inequality issue is not a society-level problem," says the Conference Board's Peck. "There are so few chief executives that their compensation has little impact. Executive pay is a drop in the bucket of General Motors' total wage and salary payroll, though it is more public."

CEOs accustomed to viewing the world from great heights are often unfazed by an average person's awe at their scale of reference. "You'll never pay a really top-notch executive . . . as much as they are worth," said Buffett. "A million, $3 million or $10 million — it's still peanuts."[21]

Finally, even critics of the CEO pay system have problems embracing a government-imposed pay cap. "The minimum wage is one thing as a social policy, but a maximum wage is very different economically," says economist Shapiro. A cap "would presumably be set at a level that someone finds excessive, but wouldn't reflect market value. And $1 million at a small company is not the same as $1 million at a large company. It's just not a decision that government is constituted to make intelligent policy on."

Smith of the Interfaith Center agrees that "it would be hard to find a formula people agree on." But when "citizens who don't live in such rarefied atmospheres hear about obscene pay levels, they will start asking whether there should be a cap," he says. "I don't think executives are more innovative or work wiser or harder when they're given $2.5 million. But if pay is made partly in stock incentives, the executives will be more in sync with their shareholders."

A similar distinction is made by political scientist Andrew Hacker in his new book *Money: Who has How Much and Why*. He notes that Philip Knight, co-founder and CEO of Nike, since 1990 has quadrupled his wealth to top $5.3 billion. "The reason may be simply stated: People choose Nike shoes, and investors like the company's stock," Hacker writes. "So it seems incongruous to charge Mr. Knight with greed just because the money keeps rolling in. Still, part of his billions come from the shoes being made in Asia at very minimal wages, and fortunes from underpaid labor seldom fare well in public esteem."[22]

Others say the real solution is to better spread the wealth to all levels of companies. "CEO pay critics are not entirely wrong when they rail against extraordinarily high pay packages — even when outstanding company performance supports them," two analysts write. "But instead of proposing misguided solutions, critics should attack the real culprit: the overreliance on [the method] for determining CEO option grants, which ensures ever-increasing CEO pay levels and declining equity opportunities for other employees."[23] ■

BACKGROUND

Executives Cash In

Concern about elites who hoard society's wealth goes back at least to the time of Confucius, who asserted that "where wealth is centralized, the people are dispersed. Where wealth is distributed, the people are brought together."[24]

In the United States, a queasiness about ostentatious pursuit of wealth was evident as far back as classic free-market economist Adam Smith, who wrote in 1776 that "wealth and greatness are mere trinkets of frivolous utility, not more adapted for procuring ease of body or tranquility of mind than the tweezer-cases of the lover of toys."[25]

Complaints about bosses whose pay dwarfed that of their underlings were familiar by the late 19th century; indeed, many of the nation's tycoons were careful to discourage dollar chases that would disrupt a company's sense of unity. In financier J.P. Morgan's empire, "each company's top executive was paid [just] 130 percent of the compensation of the people in the next echelon and these, in turn, were paid . . . 130 percent of the compensation of the people in the echelon just below them, and so on down the line," writes management expert Peter Drucker.

"Very high salaries, Morgan concluded — and he was hardly contemptuous of big money or an anticapitalist — "disrupt the team. They make even high-ranking people in the company see their colleagues as adversaries rather than as colleagues."[26]

It was in the 1920s that owners began distributing shares of stock to their executives as a way of giving them a shared stake in the enterprise. Thus many professional managers were catapulted into the income strata formerly reserved for heirs and entrepreneurs, bringing them new burdens of high taxation along with riches.

By the early 1930s, when New Deal legislation raised upper-income-bracket taxes and forced private corporations to pass out more in dividends, top executives would join the "old-money" targets of social critic Ferdinand Lundberg, who wrote that "faithless men of great wealth from a small, irre-

Continued on p. 612

Chronology

1920s-1930s

Rise of modern corporation and federal regulatory system; first stock options issued to executives who aren't owners but professional managers.

1934
Securities and Exchange Commission created to monitor corporate reporting and accounting.

1950s-1960s

Select group of executives enjoy stock options.

1950
Revenue act introduces the tax-deferred, "restricted" stock option.

1964
Revenue act replaces restricted stock options with qualified stock.

1969
Tax Reform Act raises long-term capital gains tax rate from 25 percent to 50 percent and establishes different tax rate for options sold at option price and market price. Business Professors Fischer Black and Myron Scholes create method for valuing future stock options.

1970s ***First national debates about CEO pay, which grows by 25 percent over decade.***

1970
Shareholder activist Evelyn Davis goes to her first annual meeting.

1972
Founding of Interfaith Center on Corporate Responsibility.

1973
Financial Accounting Standards Board (FASB) established.

1974
Employee Retirement Income Security Act requires disclosure of pension plans for CEOs and others.

1976
Tax Reform Act ends stock options beginning in 1981.

1978
Revenue Act lowers long-term capital gains tax to 28 percent from 35 percent.

1980s ***In "go-go years" CEO pay grew by 50 percent, 100 percent if stock options are counted.***

1980
Founding of *Executive Compensation Reports.*

1981
Economic Recovery Act restores incentive of stock options.

1984
Congress cracks down on tax deductibility of "golden parachute" CEO severance packages.

1986
Tax Reform Act begins taxing CEO benefits such as company-owned life insurance.

1987
Stock market crashes.

1990s ***Debates over high CEO pay become annual events.***

1991
Compensation consultant-turned pay critic Graef Crystal publishes *In Search of Excess.*

1992
President George Bush takes highly paid U.S. auto executives to Japan and inadvertently dramatizes pay issue through comparisons with Japanese executive pay; SEC issues new disclosure rules for CEOs and top executive officers on proxy statements and requires companies to permit shareholder votes on executive pay.

1993
Omnibus Budget Reconciliation Act contains ruling that corporations may not deduct taxes for executive compensation over $1 million unless shareholders agree it is performance-based.

March 1996
Teamsters union releases study of "America's Least Valuable Directors."

Jan 1, 1997
FASB requires annual reports to quantify the cost of stock options, but retreats on requirement that the costs be subtracted from corporate profitability.

April 15, 1997
Sens. Carl Levin, D-Mich., and John McCain, R-Ariz., introduce bill to require stock options to be treated as company expense.

'Corporate Welfare' Is the Next Target . . .

John S. Reed, CEO of the banking giant Citicorp, has become a double-duty poster boy. After his $43 million pay package last year landed him at No. 7 on *Business Week's* list of top-paid CEOs, he was singled out for scrutiny not just by critics of executive pay but also by a new group of activists attacking the federal government's longstanding and complex array of subsidies to private industry.

"Corporate welfare," as its critics derisively call it, has emerged in the past few years as a major target for the army of lawmakers and issue advocates seeking to trim Washington's continuing budget deficits. But unlike the unions, religious activists and academics who challenge high CEO pay, the opponents of industry subsidies have assembled a powerful, strange-bedfellows alliance that unites liberal consumer activists, conservative libertarians and a political spectrum of members of Congress.

Government subsidies to industry in such areas as experimental energy, investment in developing countries and arms sales have for years been criticized as wasteful favoritism by such groups as the neo-liberal Progressive Policy Institute in Washington. It was during a 1994 speech by then-Clinton administration Labor Secretary Robert B. Reich that the label "aid to dependent corporations" emerged, to the dismay of some of Reich's more pro-business Cabinet colleagues.

More recently, critics have blamed industrial subsidies for lost U.S. jobs and questionable environmental programs. "Unless we act now to stop it, Joan Claybrook, president of the consumer group Public Citizen, said in March, "this year's federal budget may again provide General Electric with a $145 million insurance policy so it can make light bulbs in Germany. McDonald's may get another $14 million loan to build 16 fast-food restaurants in Brazil. And the coal industry will be given $500 million in taxpayer funds to develop cleaner-burning coal technologies even though the program is a wasteful and mismanaged government giveaway wrapped up in an environmental cover."

Taking advantage of Washington's preoccupation with abuses in campaign financing, critics are also documenting what they say are links between the subsidies and contributions to candidates from companies in, for example, the defense industry.

"Lockheed Martin and its fellow arms merchants received billions of dollars in new subsidies from the 104th Congress," says William D. Hartung, a senior research fellow at the World Policy Institute in New York City. "Their record campaign contributions during 1995-96 are a clear sign that they will do everything in their power to keep these corporate welfare payments flowing."

In January, after voters had returned a Republican-controlled Congress and a Democratic White House, the opposition to "corporate welfare" coalesced. That was when Rep. John R. Kasich, R-Ohio, chairman of the Budget Committee, announced that after months of meetings between such disparate groups as the conservative Americans for Tax Reform, Public Citizen and the Cato Institute, a bipartisan group in Congress had agreed to form the Stop Corporate Welfare Coalition. Having just reformed the welfare system for low-income Americans, Kasich said, "We also need to reform welfare for the well-off."

Kasich issued a list of 12 programs the critics of subsidies had targeted: the Rural Utilities Service; the Clean Coal Technology program; the Energy Department's Pyroprocessing (spent nuclear fuel) research program; the Fossil Energy Research and Development program; the Animas-La Plata irrigation project in southwestern Colorado; the Appalachian Regional Commission roads program; the Market Access Program for food exporters; construction funds program for timber roads in national forests; the General Agreements to Borrow program that funds loans from the International Monetary Fund (IMF) to U.S. banks and others to invest in developing countries; the Overseas Private Investment Corporation (OPIC), which provides loans and political risk insurance for U.S. companies investing in developing countries; the Enhanced Structural Adjustment Facility, an IMF low-interest loan program in the developing world; and highway demonstration projects, which are specific projects requested by members of Congress. [1]

If all 12 of these programs were eliminated, the federal Treasury would save at least $11.2 billion over five years, according to the coalition. Yet that figure is only a portion of the "wasteful" subsidies that critics see in the federal budget. In 1995, the Congressional Budget Office found at least $44 billion in corporate subsidies and tax breaks that a pure free-market champion would see as welfare. [2] The Cato Institute study puts the number at $65 billion a year, and notes that business subsidies rose by $500 million last year. "These subsidies tend to have a Robin Hood-in-reverse impact," Cato analysts say, "redistributing income

Continued from p. 610

sponsible group are in control of the levers of society and move these levers in their own wayward interest." [27] A Roper opinion poll in the late 1930s showed that about half of Americans shared President Franklin D. Roosevelt's concerns about corporate greed and concentrations of wealth.

During this period, the obligations of executives toward their shareholders and the government were analyzed in the classic work *The Modern Corporation and Private Property* and Chester Barnard's *The Functions of the*

. . . for Budget-Cutters and Pay-Abuse Critics

from generally middle-income taxpayers to the relatively higher-income owners and shareholders in the companies — including multimillion-dollar recipients such as Rockwell International Corp., Westinghouse, B.F. Goodrich, McDonnell Douglas and AT&T." [3]

Both ends of the left-right coalition call the 12 consensus targets a mere start on a more ambitious agenda on which the two sides differ radically. "We're disappointed that the conservatives don't want to close tax expenditures or loopholes, which they say would, in effect, be raising taxes," says Gene Guerrero, legislative advocate for Public Citizen. "But we did arrive at the 12 in a consensus process with relative ease, and we've all worked cooperatively ever since."

Grover Norquist, president of Americans for Tax Reform, adds that many of his temporary allies on the left oppose his group's goals of killing the Small Business Administration and many of the government's "green subsidies" for research into solar and wind energy, for example. But he adds that many in the corporate world "who got a lot of these little bennies in the past have been told that the country is moving away from this stuff. It's just a question of when and in what order."

The strategy for ending the subsidies is being modeled on the way Congress once tried to handle the painful task of closing military bases. When they first tried that, Norquist explains, they simply picked a list of what seemed like the logical bases to close and then watched as the lawmakers whose districts were affected began trading their votes for help from other members who needed votes for subsidy programs such as sugar and peanut price supports. "We ended up worse off," he says. Now Majority Leader Dick Armey, R-Texas, "is simply saying go after all of them, so that no corporation has to admit that 'everyone won except us,' and no representative has to say he lost because he wasn't respected or had no friends."

Norquist is optimistic that many companies will be happy to trade, as they did during Congress' recent phase-out of farm subsidies, the benefit of subsidies for the benefits of reduced regulation and taxes. "If we don't concentrate on spending cuts, the left will say the only other thing to do is raise taxes," he adds. "And trying to make the tax system 'more fair' is like trying to balance a shaky coffee table by sawing off one leg and then the other and so on."

Defenders of industry subsidies, to be sure, are varied, powerful and mainstream. The Clinton administration, complains the Cato analysis, recently requested a 3.6 percent hike in federal funding for corporations. And the whole term "corporate welfare" is rejected by many in business, according to Michael Baroody, vice president for public affairs at the National Association of Manufacturers.

"If our companies were going against other companies around the world, we'd be confident, but in too many cases it's our companies against their governments," he says. "We believe the current tax code is anti-growth, and we would be happy to see comprehensive tax reform that would be pro-growth. But in the context of the current code, we continue to defend pro-growth incentives. And on the question of [federal budget] outlays, we have long argued for a more rigorous cost-benefit analysis of regulations. A cost-benefit analysis might disadvantage some of the current subsidy programs, but we are confident that such programs as OPIC and loans from the Export-Import Bank would come out well."

Rob Shapiro, vice president of the Progressive Policy Institute and a former Clinton adviser, doesn't think too much of the 12 targeted programs. They were based on "a starting point that Ralph Nader and Grover Norquist agree on — there's no center," he says. The institute argues that what is missing are efforts to end such subsidies as the tax deductibility of advertising and the tax exemption for credit unions.

But Shapiro also thinks prospects are ripe for moving against subsidies, as evidenced by the current efforts to end another subsidy by auctioning off the broadcast spectrum to private communications interests, rather than giving it away. The May budget agreement between Congress and the White House, he notes, requires lawmakers to find [revenues and spending cuts] aside from most entitlements [such as Social Security and Medicare.] Industry subsidies are where the money is."

In the meantime, notes Public Citizen's Guerrero, the reports of high CEO pay "are helping make the points we're trying to make about corporate welfare."

"Any CEO concerned about keeping his pay a matter between him and his board would want to jettison all [these subsidies] right away," Norquist says. "We haven't gotten to the point of putting their pictures on fliers, but we will."

[1] See *CQ Weekly Report*, March 1, 1997, p. 534.

[2] *The New York Times*, Feb. 2, 1997.

[3] Dean Stansel and Stephen Moore, "Federal Aid To Dependent Corporations," *Cato Institute Briefing Paper*, May 1, 1997.

Executive. In Barnard's view, "the unaided power of material incentives . . . is exceedingly limited." [28]

In the ensuing decades, much would be made in the business world of the work of psychologist Abraham Maslow, who posited a hierarchy of human needs that — once basic physical needs are met — relegated material acquisition far below such goals as personal growth and self-fulfillment.

Well into the 1960s and '70s, few executives worth their salt would think of complaining that they lacked sufficient financial incentive to put forth anything but their best effort.

"The members of the technostructure do not get the profits that they maximize," wrote economist John Kenneth Galbraith in his classic 1967 work *The New Industrial State*. "They must eschew personal profit-making. Accordingly, if the traditional commitment to profit maximization is upheld, they must be willing to do for others, specifically the stockholders, what they are forbidden to do for themselves." [29]

The Go-Go '80s

Much in American corporate culture would change during the 1980s. Spurred by President Ronald Reagan's pro-business tax cuts, deregulation and encouragement of the profit motive, the economy grew at a breakneck pace. Scads of new fortunes were made — the number of millionaires rose more than in any other decade, from 600,000 to 1.5 million. [30] And average CEO compensation, according to *Business Week*, rose from $900,000 in 1983 to more than $2 million in 1988. [31] By 1990, however, the average share of income given to charity by those earning more than $1 million annually in 1990 was less than half what it had been in 1980. [32]

The roots of today's debates over CEO pay have been traced to various events during the 1980s. Some cite the 1983 takeover of Bendix Corp. by Allied Signal, when Bendix CEO William Agee drew a severance package so huge that it helped prompt Congress to crack down on the ability of corporations to claim tax deductions for so-called executive "golden parachutes." Others point to the abuses in the savings and loan industry and the scandal over the risky investments known as junk bonds.

"It was the much-maligned Michael Milken of the investment bank Drexel, Burnham, Lambert who demonstrated that many corporate executives were rewarding themselves without regard for the economic health of their corporation," writes American Enterprise Institute (AEI) economist Irwin Stelzer. [33]

Pay critic Crystal writes of CEO abuses of privilege going back as far as 1980, when, he reported, ITT Corp. was paying CEO Rand Araskog not merely a hefty $1 million salary but a set of perks that included meals, a second residence, co-op dues and interest payments on his home.

"What a deal!" Crystal noted with sarcasm. "We have to figure Araskog was already receiving free lunches — a perquisite given to almost every CEO. And if he arrived at the office early enough, the company was probably throwing in breakfasts as well. There must have been many evenings when Araskog ate dinner at company expense. And besides that, he was getting free rent to boot. What could he have had left to spend his $1 million a year on? Taking your shirts to the local Manhattan Chinese laundry doesn't cost all that much." [34]

Other factors that may have turned the public against CEOs, notes Bowie of *Executive Compensation Reports*, "include the 1986 Tax Reform Act, which opened the door to executives taking home more income, and the stock market crash of 1987, which provoked a huge outcry from shareholders and really started the pay-for-performance movement." (Institutional shareholders, in particular, began agitating for less guaranteed pay and more pay in the form of options. They had been growing steadily in power since the mid-1960s, when they owned 15.8 percent of the country's corporate equity, to the 50 percent they own today.) [35]

While political observers debated the impact of the new wealth on the average person's lifestyle and the body politic, important changes took place among the corporate elite. Exorbitant financial rewards being bestowed often without regard to a company's success "began blurring the economic divisions between top managers of major corporations and entrepreneurial, capitalist founders or owners," wrote conservative political analyst Kevin Phillips. "Less and less of the nation's wealth was going to people who produce manufactures or commodities. Services were ascendant — from fast food to legal advice, investment vehicles, databases and videocassettes." [36]

The guilt-free ride that many CEOs enjoyed in the 1980s, some say, came to an end in early 1992, when President George Bush escorted the nation's top auto executives on a trade mission to Japan. Their lectures on efficiency to Japanese executives making a fraction of their salaries were bothersome to many Americans.

Widening Inequality?

To many who would criticize CEO paychecks, a major legacy of the Reagan-Bush years was a widening economic inequality. "Incomes of the top 1 percent more than doubled in real terms between 1979 and 1989, a period during which the median income was roughly stable and . . . the bottom 20 percent of earners saw their incomes actually fall by 10 percent," write Robert H. Frank and Philip J. Cook in *The Winner-Take-All Society*. [37]

The same theme was picked up recently by House Democrats in launching a Web site on executive pay. "The U.S. Economy is Neither Leaner Nor Meaner for Investors or CEOs," it comments, citing studies and anecdotes asserting that some CEO pay actually rises in direct relation to strategies of trimming corporate jobs. Jaundiced portrayals of the "lifestyles of the rich and famous" have also become a popular topic in book publishing. Jessie O'Neill, the granddaughter of General Motors' legendary CEO Charles Wilson, recently published a critique portraying the wealthy as spoiled and easily frustrated by bumps on the road of life.

"The overly ambitious — in fact, anyone who worships the almighty dollar — is prone to addictive/compulsive behaviors, physical and emotional unavailability, never-enough mentality, narcissism and the illusion that money buys freedom from pain," she writes. [38]

But others studying data on wealth distribution, chiefly from Federal Reserve Board surveys, challenge the notion that the rich are getting richer and the poor poorer. "Overall, as a society, we have been getting richer, rich and poor alike, more or less evenly," a recent examination by economist John C. Weicher concludes. [39]

Reuters

Microsoft chief Bill Gates (right) — worth an estimated $36 billion — joins in the fun on the "Late Show with David Letterman" to plug his new book The Road Ahead.

And the "class warfare" arguments of populist critics of CEOs are portrayed by others as unfair and ineffective. "In a democracy, an upwardly mobile, achievement-oriented, shared and open atmosphere inside the corporation is, I believe, more important than the compensation levels of chief executives," AEI scholar Michael Novak acknowledges. But he resists giving ground to "left-wing politicians" who "feed on envy, but of course, they do not call it that; they say compassion. Envy is distinguished from compassion by a simple test; compassion rejoices in raising up the poor; envy rejoices in pulling down the rich." [40]

Polling data show that most Americans harbor little hostility or resentment toward wealth, and that most people who work for major companies do not think their own CEO is overpaid, says Karlyn Bowman, an AEI polling analyst.

"There is ambivalence in that people think society puts too much emphasis on wealth," Bowman says. "But Gallup data show that 60 percent of young people think they will become very wealthy. Recent exit polls in Great Britain show as many as 57 percent saying that wealth should be redistributed, but the United States, for all its faults, is still regarded as the opportunity society." ■

CURRENT SITUATION

Eyes on Congress

The present debate over largess to CEOs has unfolded at a time when the nation's wealthy in general are poised to benefit from two key tax changes that Congress appears ready to enact: a lowering of the capital gains tax rate from 28 percent to 20 percent, according to a House Ways and Means Committee proposal, and a more generous exemption for income that can be shielded from estate taxes (currently $600,000).

Addressing CEO pay directly, Sens. Levin and McCain on April 15 (tax day) introduced a bill to end the tax deductibility of stock options issued by corporations unless they factor the cost into their profitability.

"Stock options are a form of stealth compensation," Levin says. "No other form of compensation is treated this way. We just think it's time for the double standard to end." His staff says the bill has a better chance this year than in the past because it is projected to bring in $933 million in revenue over 10 years as companies cease taking tax deductions.

Bayne of the Investor Responsibility Research Center says the bill "would have a big, but uneven impact, because high-tech companies in Silicon Valley rely more on stock options."

Also reintroduced in this Congress is Rep. Sabo's bill to end tax deductibility for executive pay that exceeds more than 25 times the pay of the lowest-level worker. "My bill won't limit executive pay, nor will it dictate what a company must pay its employees," Sabo says. "But it will send a message that those who work on the factory floor are as important to a company's success as those who work in the executive suite. It is a message of values that our government should promote."

Rep. Ron Klink, D-Pa., last September introduced a deductibility cap on any compensation higher than $1 million that goes to any employees, rather than just the top five executive officers, a change that would particularly affect Wall Street brokers, whose commissions sometimes exceed what their bosses take home. Klink has not reintroduced it this Congress.

More far-reaching tax reforms, such as the "Alternative Distribution System" advocated in *The Winner-Take-All Society* to close the gap between the very rich and the rest of the country, do not appear high on Washington's current agenda. [41]

Shareholder Activism

A clear indicator of the urgency of the executive-pay debates is the fact that shareholders around the country this spring offered 117 resolutions related to executive pay, compared with only 63 in 1996, according to the Investor Responsibility Research Center. Some wanted more disclosure, others tougher performance standards. Many of the resolutions do not even come to a vote because often they are shot down by the SEC, and those that do garner no more than 11 percent of shareholder votes.

The majority of the authors of the resolutions, according to Bayne, "are individuals, unions and social activists. The institutional investors are not making much noise about pay. Money is their bottom line, and if they have a huge chunk invested with a company, they may . . . abstain or vote against the resolution. The real gadflies among individual shareholders are often ignored, though there is a PR aspect to the issue. The companies don't want to upset little old ladies."

The Interfaith Center reports that 100 religious investors this spring submitted 194 shareholder resolutions affecting 137 companies that called on corporate leaders to be socially responsible. Among the resolutions were those on executive pay filed with such giants as Exxon, Pepsico, Zenith, AT&T and Wendy's International.

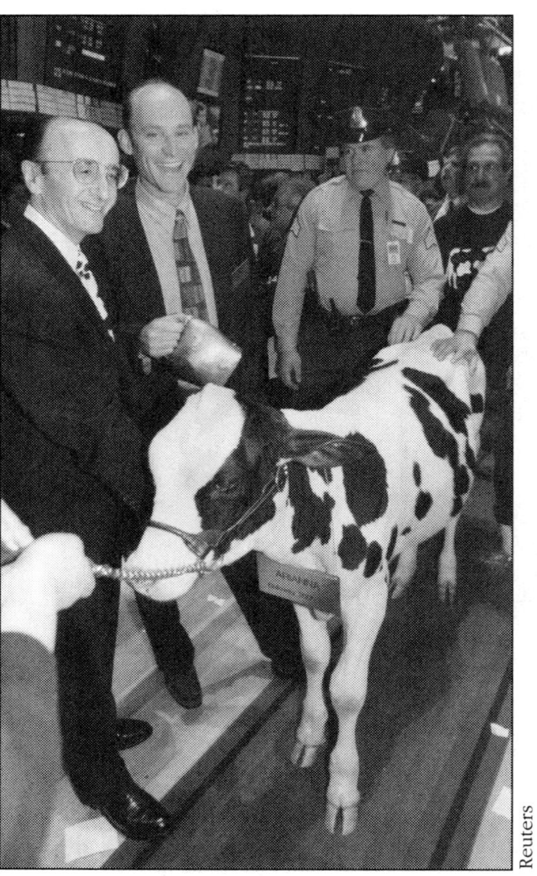

Reuters

Gateway 2000 Chairman Theodore Waitt (with the firm's trademark black and white cow) and New York Stock Exchange Chairman Richard Grasso (left) celebrate the computer company's listing on May 22, 1997.

"We believe that financial, social and environmental criteria should all be taken into account in fixing compensation packages for corporate officers," read the center's resolution targeted at Exxon. "Public scrutiny on compensation is reaching a new intensity, not just for the chief executive officer, but for all executives."

Smith says his center is pleased with efforts to link pay packages to performance on social and environmental issues, citing positive responses from Bristol Myers, Procter & Gamble, IBM and Eastman Kodak.

"At Kodak, for example, CEO Fisher gets 5 percent of his bonus for progress on work-force diversity and 50 percent for the financial turnaround, which I don't question," Smith says. "A CEO wouldn't get all of his bonus if he didn't act as a responsible corporate citizen. There is intense pressure to have positive quarters to please the shareholders, so it's common for many of them to ignore their responsibility to society."

CEOs are also being confronted at annual meetings by William Steiner, a multimillionaire shareholder activist who founded the Great Neck, N.Y.-based Investors' Rights Association of America. [42]

Another tool being used to affect CEO pay is negative publicity for corporate directors deemed unqualified or too cozy with CEOs. The Teamsters union, which controls $48 billion in pension funds and has introduced several recent shareholder resolutions on pay, last year compiled a list of "America's Least Valuable Directors." It assigned weights to factors such as poor attendance, conflicts of interest and whether the CEOs of their companies are overpaid while the company is underperforming. Topping the unflattering list were former Rep. Tony Coelho, D-Calif., followed by former Secretary of Defense Frank C. Carlucci and Westinghouse CEO Michael Jordan.

Continued on p. 618

At Issue:

Are U.S. CEOs overpaid?

GRAEF "BUD" CRYSTAL
The Crystal Report on Executive Compensation

FROM *CEO PAY: A COMPREHENSIVE LOOK,* AMERICAN COMPENSATION ASSOCIATION, 1997.

yes

I believe that CEOs in the United States are overcompensated. I base this belief on the following two factors:

- CEOs in the United States are far and away the highest-paid CEOs in the world. . . .
- Unquestionably, the pay of U.S. CEOs has risen far faster during the past few decades than has the pay of the average American worker. . . .

There has been much written about the greater risks associated with being a CEO. And there is more risk. Still, the way I see it, the probability of being fired has increased from, say, 1 percent to 1.5 percent. Yes, we can all remember Jimmy Robinson getting the ax at American Express. And we can all remember Paul Lego being let go at Westinghouse Electric Corp. . . . But . . . even if we could remember a lot more performance-challenged CEOs who "bought" it, we'd also have to remember the awesome severance packages they received. . . .

Every study of CEO pay I have done in the past decade shows that you can account for somewhere between 40 percent and 50 percent of the variation in CEO pay if you know the size and the performance of the company. But that leaves between 50 percent and 60 percent of the variation in CEO pay unexplained by rational factors. That's not what I would call an efficient market. . . .

We all like to think of stock options as being the perfect pay for performance incentive. But, except for a few people such as the ever-perceptive Warren Buffett, we forget that if the stock price drops, the shareholders take it in the neck while the CEO loses not a penny of real money (opportunity loss aside). And we forget that the CEO has no incentive to increase dividends because, as an option holder, he doesn't receive dividends. And we forget that the CEO can use insider information quite legally to time when he wants to exercise his options. . . .

On top of that, we need to do more serious study of whether, in fact, stock options really motivate CEO performance. Recent research I have undertaken seems to show that whether you give the CEO a huge stock option or a medium-size stock option or, for that matter no stock option, you get essentially the same future shareholder return. Maybe when you're already working as hard as you can and as smart as you can, and when you're already earning $4 million per year, and your net worth is already north of $20 million, a 500,000-share stock option is not going to get you to behave any differently tomorrow than you were already behaving.

IRA T. KAY
Practice Director, Compensation
Watson Wyatt Worldwide Inc.

FROM *CEO PAY: A COMPREHENSIVE LOOK,* AMERICAN COMPENSATION ASSOCIATION, 1997.

no

While CEOs of major American companies are well-paid by most standards, by and large they are fairly compensated for their efforts. . . .

CEO pay is fair because most CEOs are rewarded for increasing their companies' stock prices. This strategy has been beneficial to all of us who have money invested in pension funds and general mutual funds. It also makes an interesting contrast with Japan, where CEOs are not rewarded in stock, and their stock market has underperformed ours.

Watson Wyatt's own survey of top management compensation for 1996-97 shows that total cash compensation for CEOs is, indeed, sensitive to the stock market performance of their companies. . . .

In some cases, CEO pay drops steeply when performance declines. While the average CEO received a 9 percent increase in cash compensation in 1995, CEOs at companies where shareholder return was below the median received no increase at all. . . . On the other hand, companies experiencing a 20 percent increase in total return to shareholders, increased their CEOs' total cash compensation by 23 percent, hardly an outrageous sum in comparison.

Our data also show that those companies with the highest-paid CEOs outperformed the lowest-paid CEOs' companies in many industries. For all 398 companies in our study, companies that pay CEOs at a higher-than-average median level registered merely a 7 percentage point higher total return to shareholders. For large-capitalization companies, this difference can mean hundreds of millions of dollars of increased shareholder value. . . .

While it is impossible to say that the higher pay opportunity caused the better stock performance, there is a strong statistical relationship. Most important, such an outcome is very favorable to shareholders.

Without a doubt, CEOs today operate with more risk than ever before, thanks to rapidly changing and increasingly globalized markets and highly demanding investors. Increasingly, they alone are viewed as savior or Satan, depending on the performance they deliver to investors. . . .

With risks so high, the opportunity to create tremendous value is as great as the risk of failing. And, today, failure all but guarantees ignominy. More than ever, the CEO is likely to lose his job and perks when he does not deliver the profits shareholders expect. . . . Indeed, 10 percent to 20 percent of major companies' CEOs are fired every year. . . . And while it is true that he can receive a very generous severance package, once the CEO has been removed, he can be unemployable. . . .

FOR MORE INFORMATION

American Compensation Association, 14040 N. Northsight Blvd., Scottsdale, Ariz. 85260; (602) 951-9191. The ACA is the primary trade group for specialists in compensation and benefits issues for executives and workers at all levels.

Interfaith Center on Corporate Responsibility, 475 Riverside Dr., 5th Floor, New York, N.Y. 10015; (202) 870-2293. This coalition of religious groups urges corporations to pursue more socially conscious policies in executive pay, work force diversity, health and the environment, militarism and economic development.

Investor Responsibility Research Center, 1350 Connecticut Ave. N.W., Suite 700, Washington, D.C. 20036; (202) 833-0700. This nonprofit group analyzes business and public policy decisions affecting corporations and investors. It tracks shareholder resolutions on executive pay.

AFL-CIO, 815 16th St. N.W., Washington, D.C. 20006; (202) 637-5000. The umbrella group for the nation's trade unions has set up an Internet Web site to document what it views as exorbitant executive pay (www.paywatch.org).

Executive Compensation Reports, 6352 Rolling Mill Place, Suite 103, Springfield, Va. 22152; (703) 913-7198. This subsidiary of Harcourt Brace General Inc. publishes a newsletter reporting on pay issues aimed at compensation specialists, personnel officers, executives and corporate directors. It also acts as an information clearinghouse and research consultant.

A similar list of "turkey directors" is published by the Council of Institutional Investors. "We want to hold individual directors accountable to pinpoint performance," explains Hansen, adding that the institutional investors have the most "clout because money talks. But I don't want to diminish the effect of religious and individual shareholders. Individuals have indeed had effects on companies' policies, and in the last few years their proposed resolutions have been getting higher and higher votes. Our views are in sync with them." ■

OUTLOOK

Pressure for Moderation

To be a successful CEO today, "You cannot be a moderate, balanced, thoughtful articulator of policy," says GE's Welch. "You've got to be on the lunatic fringe." [43]

Though many CEOs view themselves as superhuman, they are not deaf to the call of their country. In May, the top executives of more than 100 companies gathered at the White House and pledged to hire people who try to get off welfare.

"We can never be a great nation with a philosophy of, 'I'm OK, tough luck for you,'" said United Airlines CEO Gerald Greenwald, who headed the group. [44]

Conservative business publication such as *Forbes* and *The Wall Street Journal* often accentuate the entrepreneurial spirit of many CEOs by pointing out that many of them are "setting a tone" in declining to spoil their heirs by bequeathing them large sums. Indeed, a new book by two marketing professors documents how executives are less likely than the average American to leave their children a major inheritance. [45]

While alive, however, executives are likely to continue the CEO tradition of asserting their status through perks — the corporate jets, the second homes, the generous insurance policies, the medical and relocation expenses that, specialists note, have become increasingly common since imposition of the pay deductibility cap in 1993. Some of the perks are awarded in order to avoid outright cash and stock options that are required to be reported on proxy statements. "It's done for optical reasons," said Robin Ferracone, president of SCA Consulting in Los Angeles. [46]

But perks, cautions Bayne, are "minuscule when considered as part of overall packages of $100 million or more."

The question of why American CEOs need such hefty pay when their foreign counterparts show up every morning and produce results for far less is likely to continue to stick in the craws of critics. (*See graph, p. 606.*) But with the U.S. economy booming, some argue that it is the foreign companies who are likely to change their systems.

"As CEOs in general are not stupid, and as the business world gets smaller by the day, the ones outside the United States can hardly fail to notice the size of the gap," writes Martin C. Lutyens, a pay expert based in England. "It seems, then, as nature (including human nature) abhors a vacuum, the odds are on an international scramble to catch up." [47]

With Congress on the verge of lowering taxes in high-income brackets, adds Shapiro of the Progressive Policy Institute, "the real abuses will become more serious. The public interest is to ensure that there is no abuse or self-dealing and that institutions are accountable to their owners."

Around the country, boards of directors "are checking their programs and looking at SEC compliance," Peck says. "They are asking themselves if they are paying by performance, and are asking what will be the reaction of the gadflies and Bud Crystal. They may not do anything, but they are thinking about it."

Executives and boards "do look at the negative votes on shareholder resolutions," adds the ACA's Nichols. "They are concerned if the negative votes rise from 20 percent to 30 percent, even though they won the overall vote."

Business Week is admonishing CEOs to "curb their own hubris. They are team leaders, not celebrities or one-man bands," it advised. [48]

"Governing boards are under scrutiny to demonstrate pay for performance, and it's gotten hard for a company that's not performing to overpay," says Bowie of *Executive Compensation Reports*. "Pay for performance has worked, and the shareholder movement has worked."

But wait until the market goes down, warns shareholder activist Davis. "A whole new generation of CEOs has never experienced a bear market, and they will become like rats. The typical CEO says, 'Look at the booming market, it's all due to my effort.' But when it goes down, he will say, 'I had nothing to do with it.' " ■

Notes

[1] *Business Week,* April 21, 1997, p. 162.
[2] For background, see "Fairness in Salaries," *The CQ Researcher,* May 29, 1992, pp. 529-552.
[3] See special section on executive pay, *The Wall Street Journal,* April 10, 1997.
[4] Robert H. Frank and Philip J. Cook, *The Winner-Take-All Society: How More and More Americans Compete for Ever Fewer and Bigger Prizes, Encouraging Economic Waste, Income Inequality, and an Impoverished Cultural Life* (1995).
[5] *Forbes,* May 19, 1997, p. 152.
[6] Thomas A. Stewart, "CEO Pay: Mom Wouldn't Approve," *Fortune,* March 31, 1997, p. 119.
[7] Companies may choose one of two methods for predicting the value of future stock options: the 5-10 percent method, which shows how the shares' value would increase under two arbitrary growth rates, and the Black-Scholes formula. Mathematicians Black and Scholes created the now-famous formula in 1969, publishing it in 1973 when they were in their early 30s. Fischer Black was a partner at Goldman, Sachs, when he died in 1995; Scholes is an analyst at Long-Term Capital Management in Greenwich, Conn.
[8] *The New York Times,* June 1, 1997.
[9] Business Week, *op. cit.*
[10] Steven Pearlstein, "When Stocks Tumble, CEO Pay Often Remains Upright," *The Washington Post,* April 3, 1997.
[11] ACA, *op. cit.,* p. 54.
[12] Eileen Appelbaum, Peter Berg and Dean Baker, "The Economic Case for Corporate Responsibility to Workers," Economic Policy Institute, April 3, 1996.
[13] Irwin M. Stelzer, "Are CEOs Overpaid?" *The Public Interest,* winter 1997, p. 26.
[14] Forbes, *op. cit.,* p. 169.
[15] The Conference Board, "Top Executive Compensation in 1995: A Research Report," 1996.
[16] *Time* magazine, April 28, 1997, p. 59.
[17] Derek Bok, *The Cost of Talent: How Executives and Professionals Are Paid and How it Affects America* (1993), p. 103.
[18] Paul L. Wachtel, *The Poverty of Affluence: A Psychological Portrait of the American Way of Life* (1983), p. 281.
[19] Op-ed column in *The Wall Street Journal,* April 28, 1997.
[20] American Compensation Association, *op. cit.,* p. 37.
[21] Bok, *op. cit.,* p. 103.
[22] Andrew Hacker, "Good or Bad, Greed Is Often Beside the Point," *The New York Times,* June 8, 1997. See "Child Labor and Sweatshops," *The CQ Researcher,* Aug. 16, 1996, pp. 721-744.
[23] Jack L. Lederer and Carl R. Weinberg, "CEO Compensation: Share the Wealth," *Chief Executive,* September 1996.
[24] Herbert Inhaber and Sidney Carroll, *How Rich Is Too Rich? Income and Wealth In America* (1992), p. 20.
[25] Bok, *op. cit.,* p. 229.
[26] Inhaber, *op. cit.,* p. 221.
[27] Ferdinand Lundberg, *America's 60 Families* (1937), p. 533.
[28] Bok, *op. cit.,* p. 22.
[29] John Kenneth Galbraith, *The New Industrial State* (1985 edition), p. 125.
[30] Bok, *op. cit.,* p. 229.
[31] Kevin Phillips, *The Politics of Rich and Poor: Wealth and the American Electorate in the Reagan Aftermath* (1990), p. 178.
[32] Bok, *op. cit.,* p. 229.
[33] Stelzer, *op. cit.*
[34] Graef Crystal, *In Search of Excess* (1991), p. 103.
[35] Stelzer, *op. cit.*
[36] Kevin Phillips, *op. cit.,* p. 182.
[37] Frank and Cook, *op. cit.,* p. 5.
[38] Jessie H. O'Neill, *The Golden Ghetto: The Psychology of Affluence* (1997), p. 73.
[39] John C. Weicher, "Increasing Inequality of Wealth?" *The Public Interest,* winter 1997, p. 15.
[40] Michael Novak, *On Corporate Governance: The Corporation as it Ought to Be,* American Enterprise Institute (1997), p. 26.
[41] Frank and Cook, *op. cit.,* p. 227.
[42] *The New York Times,* June 15, 1997, Business Section, p. 4.
[43] Cited in a column by Robert Samuelson, *The Washington Post,* April 16, 1997.
[44] *The New York Times,* May 21, 1997.
[45] Thomas J. Stanley and William D. Danko, *The Millionaire Next Door: The Surprising Secrets of America's Wealthy* (1996), p. 188.
[46] *The Wall Street Journal,* April 7, 1997.
[47] American Compensation Association, *op. cit.,* p. 48.
[48] *Business Week, op. cit.*

Bibliography

Selected Sources Used

Books

Bok, Derek, *The Cost of Talent: How Executives and Professionals Are Paid and How it Affects America,* The Free Press, 1993

A former president of Harvard University examines the debates over pay for CEOs, teachers, lawyers and government officials, discussing remedies that might help focus society's values more productively.

Crystal, Graef, *In Search of Excess: The Over Compensation of American Executives,* Norton, 1991.

Compensation consultant Crystal's influential book landed him on TV's "60 Minutes" as the iconoclastic scourge of overpaid executives. His analysis is colorful as well as technical.

Frank, Robert H., and Philip J. Cook, *The Winner-Take-All Society: How More and More Americans Compete for Ever Fewer and Bigger Prizes, Encouraging Economic Waste, Income Inequality, and an Impoverished Cultural Life,* The Free Press, 1995.

A Cornell University economist and a Duke University public policy professor offer this roundup of anecdotes and data pointing to a growing gap between average Americans and a super elite in industry, entertainment, sports and academia.

Galbraith, John Kenneth, *The New Industrial State,* Houghton Mifflin Co., 1985 edition.

Harvard University's famed left-leaning economist examines possible conflicts between executives' goals and broader social interests in his classic on the structure and dynamics of the modern corporation.

Inhaber, Herbert, and Sidney Carroll, *How Rich Is Too Rich? Income and Wealth In America,* Praeger, 1992.

A physicist and an economics professor examine the history and dynamics of income distribution in the United States, proposing an alternative taxation system that raises taxes on those at the very top.

O'Neill, Jessie H., *The Golden Ghetto: The Psychology of Affluence,* Hazelden, 1997.

A granddaughter of famed General Motors CEO Charles Wilson describes the drawbacks and psychological struggles of those born to money, focusing on its negative effects on self-esteem and relationships.

Phillips, Kevin, *The Politics of Rich and Poor: Wealth and the American Electorate in the Reagan Aftermath,* Random House, 1990.

A noted Republican political analyst presents political and economic arguments documenting a widening inequality of income among Americans during the 1980s, including much material about pay packages of corporate chief executives.

Stanley, Thomas J., and William D. Danko, *The Millionaire Next Door: The Surprising Secrets of America's Wealthy,* Longstreet Press, 1996.

Two marketing professors examine the surprisingly frugal and modest habits of Americans who succeed at getting rich, pointing out that corporate executives are less likely than the average person to bequeath large amounts to their heirs.

Wachtel, Paul L., *The Poverty of Affluence: A Psychological Portrait of the American Way of Life,* The Free Press, 1983

A City University of New York psychology professor critiques the psychological costs of economic advancement, decrying "isolating individualism" of some who become wealthy and asserting that many of them are personally unhappy.

Reports

American Compensation Association, *CEO Pay: A Comprehensive Look,* 1997.

The country's trade group for specialists in pay at all levels assembled a thorough collection of articles by compensation experts on the economic, technical, social and political aspects of the CEO pay controversy.

Novak, Michael, *On Corporate Governance: The Corporation As It Ought to Be,* American Enterprise Institute.

In the third of three lectures sponsored by Pfizer Inc., a conservative scholar examines the controversy over CEO pay, holding some companies guilty of arrogance but pointing to "envy" of the rich by leftist politicians.

The Next Step

Additional information from UMI's Newspaper & Periodical Abstracts™ database

CEO Pay

Auerbach, Jonathan, "Executive pay: Director's cut," *The Wall Street Journal,* April 11, 1996, p. R6.
Robert A. Burnett, a director of ITT Corp., remembers a time when outside directors at many companies received $100 for each board meeting attended. During the ensuing decades, directors of major companies have seen their annual cash retainers rise toward and even supass $50,000, with pension and insurance plans thrown in for good measure. Now, the trend toward stock-based pay has spread to members of the board.

Bongiorno, Lori, Robert D. Hof, and John A. Byrne, "That eye-popping executive pay: Is anybody worth this much?" *Business Week,* April 25, 1994, pp. 52-99.
No shareholder revolt or employee backlash has resulted from what the top-paid CEOs earned in 1993. Walt Disney Co. Chairman Michael D. Eisner received $203 million in 1993, more than any other CEO of a public company has made in a single year. Penny-pinching and big-spending CEOs are profiled.

"CEO perks: Where are they now?" *Working Woman,* March 1997, pp. 16-17.
Since the mid-1980s, executive perks have been on the decline. A table compares how a variety of perks offered in 1985 and 1995 have changed percentage-wise.

"Executive pay: Who made the biggest bucks," *The Wall Street Journal,* April 11, 1996, p. R1.
John F. Welch Jr. of General Electric Co. was the highest paid CEO in 1995, with total direct compensation of nearly $22 million. The direct compensation for CEOs Stanley C. Gault, Eckhard Pfeiffer, Reuben Mark, Michael D. Eisner, Louis V. Gerstner Jr. and Roberto C. Goizueta is presented.

"Executive pay: The boss's pay," *The Wall Street Journal,* April 11, 1996, p. R15.
An extensive table lists the executive compensation of CEOs at 350 of the biggest U.S. businesses for 1994 and '95, looking at salary, bonuses, and stock options.

Hausman, Tamar Y., "Executive pay: Seconds behind," *The Wall Street Journal,* April 11, 1996, p. R4.
Among the top 200 companies in the *Fortune* 500, pay for CEOs rose 27 percent on average in 1994, from a year earlier, while that of their COOs or other seconds-in-command rose only 8 percent, according to a study by Compensation Resource Group. In raw numbers, CEOs in that group earned an average of $4.7 million in total compensation, almost double the $2.4 million average for the second-highest-ranking executives.

Kadlec, Daniel, "How CEO pay got away," *Time,* April 28, 1997, pp. 59-60.
This year's batch of proxy statements provides plenty of ammunition to critics of runaway CEO pay. Linking a CEO's check to the firm's stock price seemed reasonable at first, but then the market went wild.

King, Ian, and Dominic Walsh, "Executive pay rises fuel gravy train row," *The Guardian,* April 10, 1997, p. 22.
The controversy over executive pay was highlighted yesterday when it emerged that National Express, one of the companies running large parts of the privatized rail network, has paid its chief executive a bonus of almost 1 million pounds. According to the annual report from National Express, its recently appointed chief executive, Phil White, was paid a bonus of 830,000 pounds last year, taking his total package to over 1 million pounds.

Parker-Pope, Tara, "Executive pay: So far away," *The Wall Street Journal,* April 11, 1996, p. R12.
Five years ago, executive pay in Europe appeared to be closing in on U.S. levels, but now, the narrowing has stalled, a victim of cultural resistance and government restrictions. An accompanying table ranks the average CEO compensation at companies with median annual revenue of $500 million for the U.S., Britain, Germany, France and Italy. Also, graphs show total compensation for CEOs, the heads of finance, sales and human resources as a percentage of U.S. pay.

Quinn, Matthew C., "Executive Compensation Southern boss earns $2.28 million," *Atlanta Constitution,* April 23, 1997, p. C3.
A.W. "Bill" Dahlberg received $2.3 million in compensation last year as chairman, president and chief executive of Southern Co., the Atlanta-based utility holding company reported in its annual proxy statement. Dahlberg's compensation included a base salary of $782,409 plus an annual bonus of $118,534. He also received another bonus of $770,216 under Southern's long-term incentive plan, which is pegged to the company's performance over four years. Dahlberg's stock options were valued at $564,327.

Reiner, Eric, "Executive pay: A look at the top-paid executives in Colorado," *Denver Post,* June 2, 1996, p. G1.
A look is taken at the top-paid executives in Colorado, including Malik Hasan, the Pakistani-born Pueblo neu-

rologist who heads Health Systems International Inc., who tops the *Denver Post's* annual list with a staggering $20.5 million of total compensation for 1995.

Smolowe, Jill, "Reap as ye shall sow," ***Time,*** **Feb. 5, 1996, p. 45.**
Pay-for-performance standards are a jackpot this year for executives but not for the workers. For example, Walt Disney CEO Michael Eisner took home a $14.8 million compensation package and Rockwell International CEO Donald Beall pocketed $5.5 million.

Stewart, Thomas A., "CEO pay: Mom wouldn't approve," ***Fortune,*** **March 31, 1997, pp. 119-120.**
Long-term investors expect company CEOs to think like owners. However, today's incentive pay packages for CEOs make them act more like Wall Street traders.

"Trends in executive compensation," ***HR Focus,*** **September 1996, p. 17.**
Eight trends in executive compensation are discussed. In 1995, CEO total pay rose 23 percent, with the average total pay being $4.37 million.

Walker, Tom, "Business Press Far from cutting CEOs' pay, stock options enriched them," ***Atlanta Constitution,*** **April 17, 1997, p. E8.**
Tying executive compensation to company performance was supposed to shrink all those obscene CEO compensation packages of the 1980s and early '90s. Instead, rewarding executives with company stock options has made them richer than ever, since nobody anticipated the biggest bull market in history.

Young, Lauren, "Executive pay: Compare and contrast," ***The Wall Street Journal,*** **April 11, 1996, p. R8.**
The latest twist in executive pay is awarding stock benefits according to how well a corporation stacks up against its rivals. Many comparisons are based on total shareholder return, though some use other measures such as return on assets. Whatever they use, the purpose is the same: to ensure that managers keep a gimlet eye on other companies competing for the same customer and investor dollars.

Gap Between Rich and Poor

Flanigan, James, "It's time for all employers to get stock options," ***Los Angeles Times,*** **April 21, 1996, p. D1.**
Flanigan discusses rising discontent with the corporate system of executive pay packages, especially its effects on ordinary employees. Flanigan notes that top executive incomes have been growing more than 10 percent a year while other employees live with small pay raises and mounting job insecurity.

"Glaring inequities breed distrust, resentment," ***National Catholic Reporter,*** **May 9, 1997, p. 28.**
The Internal Revenue Service has reduced the number of audits for persons earning the highest incomes while increasing the number for the poorest Americans. Along with the stratospheric compensations received by CEOs, there is shocking proof of the inequities in wages and salaries.

Lublin, Joann S., "Executive pay: The great divide," ***The Wall Street Journal,*** **April 11, 1996, p. R1.**
The earnings gap between executives at the very top of corporate America and middle managers and workers has stretched into a vast chasm. In 1995, the heads of about 30 major companies received compensation that was 212 times higher than the pay of the average American employee, according to a study prepared for *The Wall Street Journal.* An accompanying graph illustrates the widening gap between total CEO compensation and the average worker's salary between 1965 and 1995.

Sabo, Rep. Martin Olav, "Taxpayers shouldn't be subsidizing CEO pay," ***USA Today,*** **May 15, 1997, p. A15.**
America's major business publications have recently released their annual surveys of CEO compensation, and there have been the usual denunciations of the excess. Organized labor has even responded with a web site to track the problem. But to Rep. Sabo, more troubling than the size of a CEO's salary is the skewed relationship between that salary and the pay of other workers in the same company. Concern over excessive executive pay should not only arise in May when the top salaries are publicized. An ongoing national discussion is needed, Sabo says, about its impact on income inequality and how that inequality affects both our economy and our society. Income inequality has grown almost continuously in America since the 1970s, and the income gap has become more pronounced in the United States than in any other industrialized nation.

Shareholder Activism

Bowen, Sarah, "Executive pay: Enough," ***The Wall Street Journal,*** **April 11, 1996, p. R6.**
Not so long ago, shareholder activists promoted stock options and stock grants as ideal pay incentives for corporate executives. Now, an increasing number of shareholders in big U.S. companies think stock incentives have become too much of a good thing for management, at the expense of investors.

"Daimler executive bonuses raise ire of shareholders," ***The Wall Street Journal,*** **May 28, 1996, p. A15.**
Shareholders, who were agitated because Daimler-Benz AG executives were paid bonuses while they went without a dividend in 1995, for the first time in 45 years, protested executive pay, particularly because Daimler suffered a net loss of $3.7 billion for 1995.

Holsendolph, Ernest, "Disney shareholders address excessive pay," *Atlanta Journal Constitution,* Feb. 23, 1997, p. G1.

In one of those displays that can ruin a company chairman's day, Walt Disney Co. faces a vote at its annual meeting in Anaheim, Calif., to alter executive pay and head off excessive severance packages. At issue is the $38 million platinum handshake given by Disney to former President Michael Ovitz upon his departure last year. It was a year when Disney had net income of $1.5 billion but, critics say, hardly any profit was traceable to efforts or contributions by Ovitz.

Lewis, Diane E., "Unions seeking leverage as shareholders," *The Boston Globe,* p. 71, April 7, 1996,

Speaking before the Council of Institutional Investors in March 1996, AFL-CIO President John J. Sweeney urged members to use their clout as shareholders to oppose excessive downsizing and skyrocketing executive pay. Shareholder activism on the labor agenda is examined.

Lublin, Joanne S., "Sunbeam's chief picks holder activist and close friend as outside director," *The Wall Street Journal,* Sept. 26, 1996, p. B9.

Albert J. Dunlap, the turnaround specialist hired in July 1996 to revive beleaguered Sunbeam Corp., is making more waves by picking Charles Elson, a shareholder activist, as an outside director. Elson, who strongly advocates paying board members exclusively in stock, has conducted studies linking a directors' substantial stock ownership with more effective control of executive pay.

Siconolfi, Michael, "What do the Lakers and Bear Stearns have in common?" *The Wall Street Journal,* Nov. 1, 1996, p. A7.

At Bear Stearns' annual meeting the week of Oct. 28, 1996, Chairman Alan "Ace" Greenberg responded to shareholders' criticism about the securities firms' executive-pay structure by making a comparison to the salary of professional basketball player Shaquille O'Neal, center for the Los Angeles Lakers. The brokerage firm's pay formula triggered an $81.3 million windfall in fiscal 1996, for Bear Stearns' top five executives — an average of more than $16 million each.

Trumbull, Mark, "CEO Stock-Option Bonanza Catches Flak," *The Christian Science Monitor,* March 31, 1997, p, 8.

It's accountability season for corporate America, the time when chief executives face tough questions at annual shareholder meetings, such as questions about executive pay and corporate governance. The stock market's rise has helped chief executives cash in enormous stock options. Critics say these incentives have ballooned out of proportion. Also, many activist shareholders want boards to be less cozy with the chief executive officers they monitor.

"Viacom shareholders needle the chairman over falling stock," *The Wall Street Journal,* May 30, 1997, p. B5.

Viacom Inc. shareholders needled the company's chairman, CEO and biggest shareholder, Sumner Redstone, at the annual meeting on May 29, 1997, over the company's lagging stock price and high executive pay.

Stock Options

Belsie, Laurent, "After 5,000 Years on the Job, You Too Could Earn This Much," *The Christian Science Monitor,* April 22, 1997, p. 9.

CEOs' average salary and bonus hit $2.3 million in 1996, a 39 percent raise from the year before, according to *Business Week* magazine. Throw in incentive plans, retirement benefits and stock options, and the average jumps to $5.8 million, a whopping 54 percent raise from 1995. What does it mean to earn that kind of money? The AFL-CIO has put up a site on the Internet (www.paywatch.org) to put those figures in perspective for workers.

Haber, Carol, "Tech CEOs bank on growth," *Electronic News,* March 31, 1997, p. 1.

Top management of technology companies can potentially make millions in stock options as companies attempt to nurture and retain their strongest executives. Performance-based remuneration is growing as a percentage of pay.

Howes, Daniel, "Masco chief gambles, links compensation to firm's performance," *Detroit News,* May 1, 1996, p. B1.

Richard Manoogian, chairman of Michigan's Taylor-based building products company Masco Corp., is relinquishing his salary and bonus, typically in excess of $1 million, in exchange for options to buy 1 million shares of common stock, according to the company's annual proxy statement. The move is highly unusual, because companies headed by Manoogian generally have made few efforts to link executive pay to performance.

McMurdy, Deirdre, "Taking stock of options," *Maclean's,* April 28, 1997, p. 49.

Stock options as a new source of wealth for senior managers are in the spotlight in Canada. This has become popular because of shareholder pressure to link pay to performance.

Back Issues

Great Research on Current Issues Starts Right Here . . . Recent topics covered by The CQ Researcher are listed below. Before May 1991, reports were published under the name of Editorial Research Reports.

JANUARY 1996
Emergency Medicine
Punishing Sex Offenders
Bilingual Education
Helping the Homeless

FEBRUARY 1996
Reforming the CIA
Campaign Finance Reform
Academic Politics
Getting Into College

MARCH 1996
The British Monarchy
Preventing Juvenile Crime
Tax Reform
Pursuing the Paranormal

APRIL 1996
Centennial Olympic Games
Managed Care
Protecting Endangered Species
New Military Culture

MAY 1996
Russia's Political Future
Marriage and Divorce
Year-Round Schools
Taiwan, China and the U.S.

JUNE 1996
Rethinking NAFTA
First Ladies
Teaching Values
Labor Movement's Future

JULY 1996
Recovered-Memory Debate
Native Americans' Future
Crackdown on Sexual Harassment
Attack on Public Schools

AUGUST 1996
Fighting Over Animal Rights
Privatizing Government Services
Child Labor and Sweatshops
Cleaning Up Hazardous Wastes

SEPTEMBER 1996
Gambling Under Attack
The States and Federalism
Civic Journalism
Reassessing Foreign Aid

OCTOBER 1996
Political Consultants
Insurance Fraud
Rethinking School Integration
Parental Rights

NOVEMBER 1996
Global Warming
Clashing Over Copyright
Consumer Debt
Governing Washington, D.C.

DECEMBER 1996
Welfare, Work and the States
The New Volunteerism
Implementing the Disabilities Act
America's Pampered Pets

JANUARY 1997
Combating Scientific Misconduct
Restructuring the Electric Industry
The New Immigrants
Chemical and Biological Weapons

FEBRUARY 1997
Assisting Refugees
Alternative Medicine's Next Phase
Independent Counsels
Feminism's Future

MARCH 1997
New Air Quality Standards
Alcohol Advertising
Civic Renewal
Educating Gifted Students

APRIL 1997
Declining Crime Rates
The FBI Under Fire
Gender Equity in Sports
Space Program's Future

MAY 1997
The Stock Market
The Cloning Controversy
Expanding NATO
The Future of Libraries

JUNE 1997
FDA Reform
China After Deng
Line-Item Veto
Breast Cancer

JULY 1997
Transportation Policy

Back issues are available for $5.00 (subscribers) or $10.00 (non-subscribers). Quantity discounts apply to orders over ten. To order, call Congressional Quarterly Customer Service at (202) 887-8621.

Binders are available for $18.00. To order call 1-800-638-1710. Please refer to stock number 648.

Future Topics

▸ ***School Vouchers***

▸ ***Aggressive Driving***

▸ ***Age Bias in the Workplace***

THE CQ Researcher

PUBLISHED BY CONGRESSIONAL QUARTERLY INC.

School Choice Debate

Are tuition vouchers the answer to bad public schools?

School choice advocates predict that private school tuition vouchers will become more widely used in coming years as lawmakers, educators and parents realize that only radical reform can fix the nation's failing public schools. And school choice, the advocates argue, must be the cornerstone of the reforms because it empowers parents to choose the best school for their children. In addition, they say, vouchers will inject a healthy dose of competition and thereby improve a public education system that is monopolistic and resistant to change. But opponents say that vouchers will siphon money away from schools that are already woefully underfunded. Moreover, they argue that using taxpayer dollars to send children to sectarian schools violates the constitutional prohibition on government support for religion.

INSIDE THIS ISSUE

CQ July 18, 1997 • Volume 7, No. 27 • Pages 625-648

Formerly Editorial Research Reports

School Choice Debate

The Issues

Background

Current Situation

Outlook

Sidebars and Graphics

For Further Research

Cover: At Saint Gregory The Great, A Roman Catholic Elementary School On New York's Upper West Side, Principal Deborah Hurd Has Boosted Attendance And Test Scores. (© Bobby Neal Adams)

July 18, 1997
Volume 7, No. 27

Editor
Sandra Stencel

Managing Editor
Thomas J. Colin

Associate Editors
Sarah M. Magner
Richard L. Worsnop

Staff Writers
Charles S. Clark
Mary H. Cooper
Kenneth Jost
David Masci

Editorial Assistant
Vanessa E. Furlong

Published By
Congressional Quarterly Inc.

Chairman
Andrew Barnes

Vice Chairman
Andrew P. Corty

President and Publisher
Robert W. Merry

Executive Editor
David Rapp

The CQ Researcher (ISSN 1056-2036). Formerly Editorial Research Reports. Published weekly, except Jan. 3, May 30, Aug. 29, Oct. 31, by Congressional Quarterly Inc., 1414 22nd St., N.W., Washington, D.C. 20037. Annual subscription rate for libraries, businesses and government is $340. Additional rates furnished upon request. Periodicals postage paid at Washington, D.C., and additional mailing offices. POSTMASTER: Send address changes to The CQ Researcher, 1414 22nd St., N.W., Washington, D.C. 20037.

School Choice Debate

BY DAVID MASCI

THE ISSUES

For Rachgina Jeff and Brenda Ewart of Cleveland, Ohio, school choice is more than a matter of public policy. It's personal.

State-funded tuition vouchers enable Jeff's son Charles and Ewart's son Brandon to attend St. Adalbert's Roman Catholic elementary school.

"Charles already has two strikes against him — living in the inner city and being an African-American male," Jeff says. "I just wanted to give him a chance to get a decent education." To Jeff, that means keeping Charles out of the neighborhood public school.

"With the drugs, the gangs and the violence, it's hard for kids to learn in that environment," Ewart adds.

At St. Adalbert's, with its emphasis on core curricula, discipline and parental involvement, kids learn.

"Charles is really doing well there," Jeff says, noting that he recently scored in the 99th percentile on a standardized test.

Jeff and Ewart also are pleased that their children are receiving religious and moral instruction. "They're reinforcing the values I teach at home," Ewart says.

But St. Adalbert's is more than just a good school — it is affordable.

"The voucher is a blessing," says Jeff, a full-time student at Case Western Reserve University. "I would have to get a second job" without it, says Ewart, who works in a bank.

For school choice advocates, there are too few such success stories. Milwaukee is the only other city that offers publicly funded tuition vouchers. As pilot projects, however, the Cleveland and Milwaukee programs only offer assistance to a few thousand students. Moreover, the state laws that created the programs are being chal-

lenged and may not survive judicial scrutiny. (*See story, p. 630.*)

Still, school choice proponents say that support for vouchers has been rising and will continue to increase as more and more Americans come to believe that public schools, especially in low-income areas, are failing. As evidence, they point to a Gallup Poll showing that 36 percent of Americans favored school choice in 1996, compared with 24 percent in 1993. [1]

In addition, voucher advocates say, school choice, over the last decade, has been transformed from a fringe issue dear to some conservatives and religious groups into a major part of the national education debate. For instance, vouchers were a major plank in Republican Bob Dole's 1996 presidential campaign.

Proponents say that vouchers are getting more attention because they make sense, especially for inner-city children like Charles and Brandon.

First and foremost, they argue, vouchers empower parents by giving them the freedom to choose what they believe to be the best school for their children. The power of choice, they say, would especially benefit the poor, who unlike Americans in higher income brackets often have no alternative but to send their children to the local public school.

"Choice is already in the hands of parents with money," says Nina Shokraii, an education policy analyst at the Heritage Foundation. "We have to extend that choice to parents without money."

Proponents also argue that vouchers will ultimately make the public schools better by injecting a healthy dose of competition into what is currently a stagnant and monopolistic system. Under the existing system, they say, public schools have no incentive to undertake real reform measures because, no matter what they do, their budgets won't shrink. But allowing parents to remove their children — as well as some of the money allotted to educate them — will force public schools to stop taking their students for granted, voucher advocates say.

Opponents of vouchers agree that as an issue, school choice is more visible than it once was. But that is where agreement ends between the two sides in the debate. And, they point out, a solid majority of Americans still oppose vouchers, a fact borne out by more than just polls. For instance, they say, every time school choice has come before voters in state referenda, it has been rejected, usually by overwhelming majorities.

As for the growing attention vouchers are getting, opponents say, it is due in part to legitimate anger over the inadequacy of public education in some areas. In particular, they say, school choice supporters are gaining ground by exploiting the frustrations of poor and minority parents, like Jeff and Ewart, who feel that neighborhood public schools are inadequate.

States Where School Choice Is Being Considered

School choice programs have been considered, or are being considered, by lawmakers in at least 20 states, but only two legislatures — in Wisconsin and Ohio — have actually enacted voucher programs.

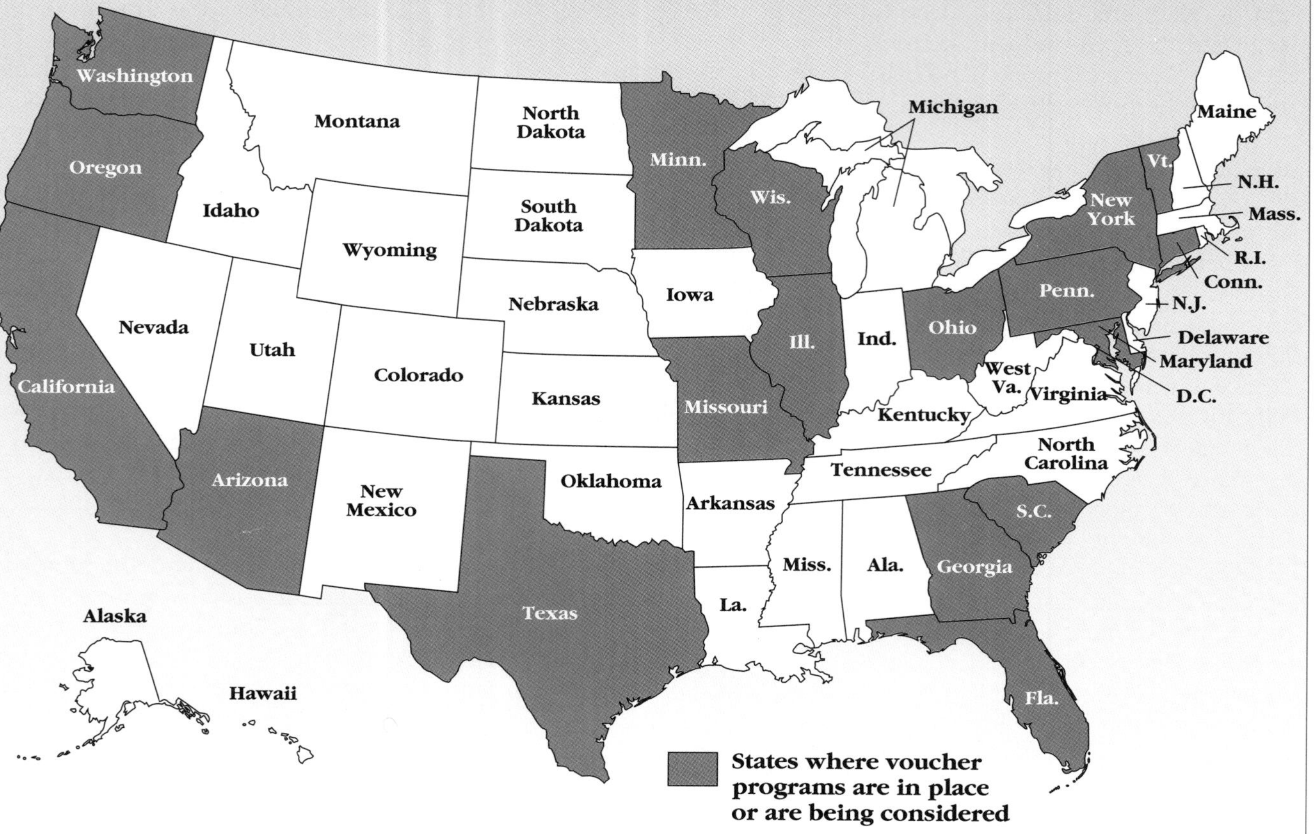

States where voucher programs are in place or are being considered

Sources: CEO America, The Heritage Foundation

"For them to say to poor people that [vouchers are] the answer is unfortunate because of course people in difficult situations are going to be more likely to listen," says Bob Chase, president of the National Education Association (NEA), the nation's largest teachers' union.

But Chase and other opponents say that school choice offers little more than a false, cruel hope to desperate parents. Vouchers, they point out, rarely amount to more than a few thousand dollars, not nearly enough to pay tuition at most top private schools.

"No one's going to go to Sidwell Friends," Chase says, referring to the expensive private school Chelsea Clinton began attending in Washington, D.C., after Bill Clinton won the presidency in 1992.

In addition, Chase and others argue, school choice actually will make public education worse, not better. For one thing, they say, instituting a voucher plan will take resources away from public school systems that in many cases are already desperately in need of additional funds. In addition, presenting vouchers as the solution to a school district's problems will only help to delay needed reforms.

"Where there are dysfunctional [school] systems, we need to correct those systems — expeditiously," Chase says, adding that the solution isn't to divert money to private schools.

Moreover, opponents say, it would still be the public schools that ultimately would have to educate the vast majority of the nation's children, even if vouchers were initiated nationwide. It's simply a question of size, they say. The public school

School Choice Battles Embroil Many States

Voucher programs have only been instituted in a few places, but battles over school choice have touched many states. Proposals have been considered in at least 20 state legislatures over the years, and since 1990 vouchers have been the subject of referenda in California, Oregon, Colorado and Washington state.

The most recent vote occurred last November in Washington, where citizens decisively rejected a proposal to allow parents to receive tuition scholarships for non-religious private schools.

The fight over vouchers in Washington was typical of recent school choice campaigns. Both sides spent significant sums of money — about $2 million each — to get their message to the voters. The debate was contentious and at times even rancorous, with each side accusing the other of distorting the truth and representing interests other than educational improvement. By the time voters went to the polls, Initiative 173 was receiving almost as much attention in the state as the contest for president and governor. [1]

Voters in Washington rejected the initiative by a sizable majority, as they did in the other three states where referenda were held recently. For example, California's widely watched 1993 ballot initiative (Proposition 174) was defeated by a 2-1 margin. [2]

Voucher opponents say that the results in the recent referenda are further evidence of public opposition to school choice. "When voters have had the opportunity to vote on it, they've rejected it every time because they understand that it's counterproductive," says Bob Chase, president of the National Education Association, the nation's largest teachers' union.

But voucher proponents argue that the results are a testament to the power of groups like the NEA. For example, they claim, in California, opponents outspent supporters of school choice by 10-1.

And, the advocates say, the cause for vouchers has fared much better in state legislatures. Wisconsin and Ohio have voucher plans up and running. Other states, among them Iowa, have created tax credits that parents can use for educational expenses, including private school tuition.

The most recent legislative success for voucher advocates has come in Arizona, where on April 7 Republican Gov. Fife Symington signed into law a measure that allows residents to take a tax deduction of up to $500 for contributions to nonprofit foundations that provide scholarships to send children to private schools. [3]

The bill's sponsor, Republican state Rep. Mark Anderson, considers it a step toward a full voucher program. [4] Quentin L. Quade, director of the Blum Center for Parental Freedom in Education at Marquette University in Milwaukee, agrees: "This is a uniquely and distinctly important development."

Voucher proponents also are buoyed by recent events in Minnesota. On June 4, Republican Gov. Arne Carlson vetoed an education spending bill because it did not contain his proposal to give low- and middle-income families a $1,000 per child educational tax credit. Carlson has pledged to veto any new school spending bills that do not contain the tax credit provision.

School choice opponents also have had recent successes at the state level. In addition to their victory in the Washington referendum, they have beaten back a variety of tuition tax credit and voucher proposals in legislatures in Louisiana, Connecticut, Texas, New Jersey, New York and California.

In California, voters defeated a proposal that would have given vouchers to students scoring in the lowest 5 percent on state standardized tests. The plan passed the Republican-controlled Assembly only to stall in the Democratic-controlled Senate.

Both sides say that the real battle over vouchers will continue to be at the state level. "It's the states that really count," Quade says. "After all, 94 percent of all education spending comes from the states."

[1] Kerry A. White, "Choice Plans Face Big Statewide Test in Wash.," *Education Week*, Oct. 30, 1996.

[2] Barbara Kantrowitz, "Take the Money and Run," *Newsweek*, Oct. 11, 1993.

[3] From "Educational Freedom Report," Quentin L. Quade (ed.), April 25, 1997.

[4] *Ibid.*

system is almost eight times larger than its private counterpart, and vouchers would not be able to help more than a small percentage of public school students to attend private schools.

Finally, opponents say, even if vouchers are good education policy, they are barred by the Establishment Clause of the U.S. Constitution, which prohibits state support for religion. [2] They point out that courts in Wisconsin and Ohio have recognized that school choice leads to massive state subsidies for religious institutions, because the vast majority of private schools are sectarian. In Cleveland, for instance, 31 of the 48 schools participating in the voucher program are Roman Catholic. [3]

But school choice supporters argue that vouchers do not violate the Constitution because the funds go to the parents of the children, not directly to the schools. They also point out that the federal government and the states already are supporting

Key Voucher Cases in the Courts

The U.S. Supreme Court has yet to consider the constitutionality of using publicly funded vouchers to send children to private, sectarian schools. At the state level, however, several school choice cases are working their way through the courts. Any one of these cases could form the basis for a future Supreme Court ruling. Here are the main voucher cases currently before state courts:

Wisconsin — The state Supreme Court deadlocked when it first considered Wisconsin's 1995 law expanding Milwaukee's existing voucher program to include religious schools. The 3-3 decision, which was handed down on March 29, 1996, was only possible because the court's seventh justice had recused herself from the case, citing a conflict of interest. [1]

The case was remanded back to the trial court, which ruled on Jan. 15, 1997, that including religious schools in the voucher program violated the state constitution's prohibition on government support of sectarian institutions. The law expanding the program to include sectarian schools has not been implemented. [2]

The trial court decision has been appealed and is once again before the state Supreme Court. Although only six judges will rule on the case, leaving open the possibility for another tie vote, voucher supporters are heartened by the recent retirement of one of three justices who voted against their position the first time. The new justice was appointed by Republican Gov. Tommy G. Thompson, an ardent supporter of vouchers.

Ohio — Cleveland's one-year experiment with school choice was put on hold on May 1, when Ohio's 10th District Court of Appeals ruled that the program violated the federal and state constitutions, which prohibit direct government support for religion. The case has been appealed to the state Supreme Court, which has yet to decide on the issue.

Even though the law in question allows parents to use vouchers to send their children to any private school participating in the choice program, the district court was troubled by the fact that 80 percent of these schools were sectarian. "The only real choice available to most parents is between sending their children to a sectarian school and having their child remain in the troubled Cleveland city school district," wrote Judge John C. Young. Hence the voucher program essentially provided assistance to religious schools, the judge concluded. [3]

The appeals court decision followed a trial court ruling the year before that allowed the voucher law to be implemented. In this earlier decision, Judge Lisa L. Sadler wrote that the vouchers were constitutional because the benefit to religious schools flowed through the parents (who choose how to use the voucher) and hence was indirect.

Vermont — The school board of tiny Chittenden, Vt., has filed a lawsuit against the state. The conflict centers around Chittenden's intention to pay tuition for 15 high school students to attend a local Roman Catholic school. The practice, known as "tuitioning," is common in Vermont, where many rural towns have no high school. All of Chittenden's 100 high school-age children are sent to outside public and private schools. The town pays the cost of tuition.

Citing a 1961 Vermont Supreme Court ruling outlawing tuitioning at sectarian schools, the state has threatened to deny Chittenden its share of education funding if it pays for students to attend the parochial school.

The town has sued the state, citing a 1994 Vermont Supreme Court decision allowing tuition reimbursement for parents who send their children to sectarian schools. Chittenden, and its attorneys at the Washington-based Institute for Justice argue that the more recent decision essentially overturns the earlier ruling.

[1] Mark Walsh, "Court Deadlocks on Vouchers," *Teacher*, May/June, 1996.

[2] Rene Sanchez, "In Wisconsin, Vouchers for Religious Schools are Handed Legal Setback," *The Washington Post*, Jan. 15, 1997.

[3] Paul Souhrada, "Court: Cleveland Vouchers Program Unconstitutional," The Associated Press, May 2, 1997.

thousands of religiously affiliated organizations such as hospitals, universities and social service providers with billions of dollars each year. Much of the state money assists K-12 students in parochial schools by providing them with textbooks, standardized tests, transportation and remedial education.

In addition, supporters say, recent Supreme Court decisions, including *Agostini v. Felton,* handed down in June (*see p. 631*), have steadily expanded the definition of what is permissible when it comes to government assistance for religious schools. These decisions, supporters argue, clearly indicate that vouchers will be adjudged constitutional by the Supreme Court.

As lawmakers, policy-makers, educators and parents continue to debate school choice, these are some of the questions being asked:

Does a voucher program that includes religious schools violate the constitutional separation of church and state?

The First Amendment states that "Congress shall make no law respecting the establishment of religion, or prohibiting the free exercise thereof. . . ." On its face, the Establishment Clause is clear: The state cannot support one denomination or faith over others; nor can it inhibit citizens' practice of their religion.

But, like many parts of the Constitution, the Establishment Clause can be interpreted in a variety of ways when applied to more narrowly tailored, practical situations.

According to many legal scholars, the question of state support for religious schools has been especially perplexing because the Supreme Court has produced what some say are a host of confusing and contradictory decisions.

The question is simple: How far can the state go in supporting schools that are religiously affiliated? Some assistance is clearly allowed. For example, state governments have long been permitted to provide transportation and textbooks to students who attend parochial schools. The logic is that the assistance is going directly to the student, not the school, and hence is not supporting religion.

But the question becomes harder to answer when the assistance benefits the school more directly. While the Supreme Court has never ruled on the constitutionality of vouchers, it has looked at other schemes aimed at helping parents with educational expenses.

In 1973, for example, the court ruled in *Committee for Public Education and Religious Liberty v. Nyquist* that a New York state law granting parents reimbursements and tax credits for private school tuition was unconstitutional. The court said that even though the law was neutral on its face (allowing the benefit for any kind of private school tuition), it had the effect of subsidizing religious education because roughly three-quarters of parents receiving the reimbursements or credits sent their children to sectarian schools. Hence, regardless of its intent, the law resulted in advancing religious education and violated the Establishment Clause.

But over the next two decades, the court handed down several rulings that many regard as contradictory, including *Mueller v. Allen* in 1983. The court ruled in *Mueller* that an Ohio law offering a parental tax deduction for educational expenses was constitutional even though 93 percent of those claiming the deduction had children in religious schools. The court distinguished this case from *Nyquist* because the tax deduction also was available to parents with children in public schools. In addition, the justices argued that the deduction was a much less direct subsidy of religious schools than were the tuition reimbursements available under the New York law struck down in *Nyquist.* [4]

In other cases in the 1980s and early '90s, the Supreme Court allowed various forms of state assistance for students enrolled in religious schools. For example, in *Zobrest v. Catalina Foothills School District* the court ruled in 1993 that a state could provide a sign language interpreter for a deaf student in parochial school, even when that student was in religion class.

And on June 23, in *Agostini,* the court ruled that remedial education teachers supplied by New York state could assist parochial school children on school property. Previously, such teachers had worked in buses parked off the grounds of the religious schools as a result of a 1985 Supreme Court ruling, *Aquilar v. Felton*. Voucher supporters were heartened by the fact that in *Agostini* the court reversed itself, overturning *Aguilar v. Felton.* [5]

© Ericka McConnell

The privately funded School Choice Scholarships program in New York City awarded 1,300 three-year tuition grants to enable poor children to attend private schools.

Supporters of vouchers see cases like *Mueller, Zobrest* and *Agostini* as part of a trend within the Supreme Court away from what they say is the more restrictive view of the Establishment Clause put forth in *Nyquist.*

"This is just the court's way of moving from one position to another without actually admitting that they are changing the law," says Michael McConnell, a professor at the University of Utah's College of Law and an expert on the Establishment Clause.

According to McConnell, the court's shift is long overdue. "*Nyquist* was the product of the kind of separationist thinking that is really disguised hostility toward religion," he says. McConnell and others contend that there are a host of reasons why voucher programs would be constitutional.

First, they argue, the benefits go to the parents and children who receive them, not the school. "It's up to the parents to decide whether they want

Privately Funded Vouchers Aid Students in 18 States

When the School Choice Scholarships Foundation offered tuition vouchers to 1,300 low-income children in New York City early this year, the response was an unanticipated — and overwhelming — 16,000 applications.

"It shows that the perception of need for the program is high," said Bruce Kovner, chairman of Caxton Corp., a New York investment firm, and head of the foundation. [1]

Kovner and other New York businessmen have already raised $7 million, enough to guarantee the recipients of the vouchers (who were chosen by lottery) up to $1,400 a year for three years. Kovner hopes to raise another $3 million in the near future in order to increase the number of scholarships and begin making a dent in the waiting list, which has swelled to 23,000 hopefuls. [2]

Amid the hoopla over publicly funded vouchers, efforts to privately finance school choice have gone almost unnoticed. But New York is just the latest in what has become a long list of cities where private philanthropists, usually in the business community, are establishing charities to pay for tuition vouchers.

The first privately financed voucher program was created in Indianapolis in April 1991 by J. Patrick Rooney, then-chairman of the Golden Rule Insurance Co., who put up $1.2 million for 746 vouchers.

The following year, Jim Leininger a physician and businessman in San Antonio, Texas, decided to duplicate Rooney's efforts in his hometown. At roughly the same time, programs were being established in Atlanta, Milwaukee and Battle Creek, Mich.

Today, there are at least 30 programs in 18 states, including Dallas, Buffalo, N.Y., and Oakland, Calif. Some of the programs have just a few benefactors. Others are supported by large groups of well-to-do individuals. A few, like the group in Milwaukee, solicit funds from the general public.

The smallest group, in Midland, Texas, spent $6,000 on four students during the 1996-97 school year. The largest program is in Milwaukee, where $4.2 million provided vouchers for 4,127 children during the same period. Currently, all of the programs combined are serving 13,648 students, more than twice the number receiving privately funded vouchers two years ago.

"As time has gone on, this idea has really grown," says Fritz Steiger, president of Children's Educational Opportunity (CEO) of America, a group that supports local efforts to privately finance vouchers.

Cities With Private Voucher Programs

The number of voucher programs funded by nonprofit business and citizen groups has grown steadily since the first program was started in Indianapolis in 1991.

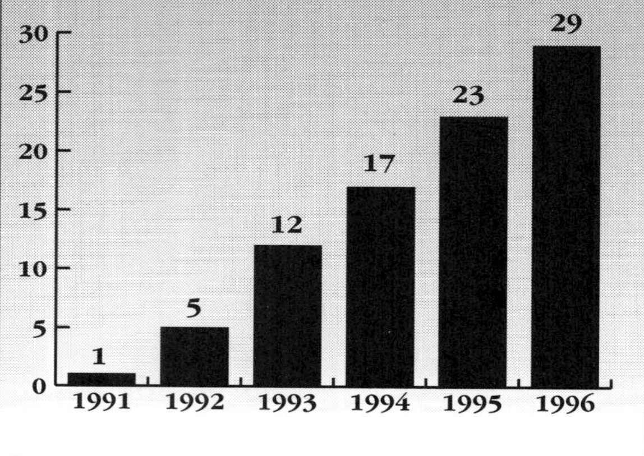

Source: CEO America

Founded in 1992, CEO America offers information and training to people interested in creating an organization to provide privately funded vouchers. In 1994, Steiger's group received a $2 million grant from the Walton Family Foundation. The money was used to help start nine programs. "We've gone in and said, "We'll give you $50,000 [for each of three years] if you can raise $50,000 to get the program started," Steiger says.

One reason these programs have proliferated so quickly, Steiger says, is that they can be relatively inexpensive to establish. The average voucher totals about $1,100, so a program can often serve 100 students with an annual budget of little more than $100,000.

Not surprisingly, new programs are being established each year. According to Steiger, new organizations have been or are being founded in San Francisco, Chicago, New Orleans, Miami, Baltimore and other cities.

"I think that by the year 2000, we'll have 60 programs and 30,000-40,000 students," he says.

But those who are starting these groups are not trying to build permanent charities. "The people who are funding this are not in it for the long haul," Steiger says. "These are transitional organizations that are models for public policy."

The hope, Steiger says, is to show politicians and the public at large how vouchers work and what they can do.

And what if the Supreme Court eventually rules that taxpayers' money cannot be used to finance vouchers that send children to religious schools? "Then many of these groups might become permanent," Steiger says.

[1] Jeff Archer, "16,000 N.Y.C. Parents Apply for 1,300 Vouchers to Private Schools," *Education Week*, April 30, 1997.

[2] Susan Lee and Christine Foster, "Trustbusters," *Forbes*, June 2, 1997.

to send their child to a religious school or not," says Nicole Garnett, a staff attorney at the Institute for Justice, a public advocacy law firm that has assisted voucher supporters in a number of school choice cases. "If an unemployment check winds up in a church collection plate, does that matter?" she asks. No, Garnett and other supporters answer, because the recipients of the benefit can spend it any way they please.

Advocates also point out that the federal government already supports religious institutions in a variety of ways. For instance, each year, tens of thousands of students use Pell grants and GI Bill benefits to attend religious colleges and universities. "You could use your Pell grant to go to a university where there is a prayer before every class," Garnett says, adding that this is no different than a voucher.

Howard Fuller, Milwaukee's school superintendent from 1991-95, agrees. "I find it strange that we are able to do it with higher education," he says, "but when that logic is applied to K-12, people start coming up with reasons why that can't be."

But opponents of school choice see big differences between Pell grants and vouchers. For one thing, they argue that children are more easily influenced by religious teaching than adults in college or graduate school, a fact recognized by the Supreme Court.

The court's "concern over [government] endorsement [of religion] is especially acute in the area of primary and secondary education, where many of the citizens perceiving the governmental message are children in their formative years," writes Steven K. Green, legal director of Americans United for the Separation of Church and State. [6]

In addition, Green and others argue, unlike primary and secondary schools, most colleges and universities with a religious affiliation are not overtly religious. "Let's face it, there's a big difference," he says.

School choice opponents also dismiss the argument that vouchers benefit parents and children and not religious schools. "They say [voucher laws] are neutral because they are based on the independent choices of the parents," says Bob Chanin, general counsel of the NEA. But, Chanin argues, in Milwaukee and Cleveland, which have voucher programs, "75-80 percent of [private] schools are sectarian." Hence, giving parents public money to send their children to private school amounts to a de facto subsidy for religious schools, he says.

Green agrees. "You cannot wash money through the hands of a third party when it is basically going to an entity that wouldn't get the money otherwise."

Opponents also dispute the idea that the legal winds of change are blowing against them. According to Chanin, *Nyquist* clearly invalidates current voucher schemes since it struck down tuition reimbursements, which are not a direct subsidy for religious schools. In addition, he says, despite what McConnell and others say about a trend toward allowing similar types of state aid in subsequent decisions like *Mueller, Nyquist* has not been overruled. "In fact, in *Mueller* the court specifically said it was not overturning *Nyquist,*" he says.

Finally, those against vouchers dismiss the recent hoopla over the recent *Agostini* decision. "To imply that this is opening the door to vouchers is a misreading of this decision," says NEA President Chase. "They made very careful distinctions in this case, saying that the [public] money could only be used for public school teachers and for remedial education." In other words, Chase explains, *Agostini* is not a sign that the court is about to allow states to pay private school teachers to teach subjects like religion.

Can vouchers really offer poor children better educational opportunities?

A recent poll commissioned by the American Education Reform Foundation found that 61 percent of all low-income residents of Washington, D.C., would send their children to private school if money were not an issue.

According to school choice advocates, the poll and others like it show that regardless of what many educators and scholars say, poorer Americans favor choice for their children. "Of course they do," Fuller says. "It's in the best interests of parents and children to have the widest range of options available when it comes to education."

Fuller and others say that having options is especially important when children are caught in poorly functioning school systems that fail to provide even basic remedial skills.

"Kids at the bottom are almost guaranteed to go to the scrap heap," says Diane Ravitch, a senior fellow at the Brookings Institution and an assistant secretary of Education in the Bush administration. "They need another option."

Voucher advocates argue that having options would provide a host of benefits for poor children. First, it would empower parents to get more involved in their child's school. [7] "There's this myth that low-income parents don't care about their kids' education," says Shokraii of the Heritage Foundation. She argues that private schools, and especially parochial schools, generally are more successful at tapping into parental concerns than public schools. "They do a better job of attracting parents and keeping them engaged in their kids' education," she says.

In addition, supporters of school choice say, many of the private schools that would take children with vouchers have a better track record of succeeding with poor students than their public counterparts, particularly Catholic schools in inner-city areas. For proof, they point to a 1990 RAND Corporation report showing that 95 percent of all students who attended Catholic schools in New York City graduated. Many of these students were from disadvantaged backgrounds. By contrast, only 25 percent of New York's public school students received their high school diploma. [8]

Various reasons are given for the success of Catholic and other parochial schools. Some voucher supporters acknowledge that private schools can be selective when it comes to whom they choose to admit.

But advocates also say that other more important factors lie behind the success. "Catholic schools . . . never went through the rights revolution of the 1960s, which eroded the order-keeping authority of schools and discouraged teachers and principals from disciplining disruptive students by establishing elaborate due-process procedures," writes Sol Stern. [9] Others point to parochial schools' emphasis on core curriculum and parental involvement.

Many of those who oppose school choice agree that some children in public schools might do better in a private school. "But you can't just help a few kids at the expense of everyone else," Green says.

In addition, Green and others say, it is counterproductive to compare public schools with their private counterparts. "If [public schools] could pick and choose the students who do not have discipline problems or special needs," Green says, "you'd see real improvement there."

James Coomer, a political science professor at Mercer University in Macon, Ga., agrees. "The public schools are asked to do too much," he says. "They are asked to take students who don't want to learn, students with disabilities and students who are disruptive."

Opponents of school choice also worry that vouchers might be used to subsidize private school tuition for those who can already afford it. In Cleveland, for example, 27 percent of the first vouchers awarded by the city went to students already enrolled in private schools.

BISON

The privately funded Buffalo Inner-city Scholarship Opportunity Network (BISON) enabled more than 200 children from low-income families in Buffalo, N.Y., to attend private school last year.

Moreover, opponents say, existing and proposed voucher programs do not offer enough money to give poor parents much of a choice outside of the public system. In Cleveland, vouchers provide up to $2,250 per pupil per year. And the school choice plan put forth by Dole during last year's election campaign would have offered students a maximum of $1,500.

"Many [poor families] would not be able to afford the extra tuition, transportation and related costs of using a voucher," says Kweisi Mfume, president of the NAACP, which opposes vouchers. [10]

In addition, opponents ask: How many students can actually be accommodated in a private school, even if every child in America were eligible to receive a voucher? The answer: not many. Gerald Tirozzi, assistant secretary of Education for elementary and secondary education, points out that 6 million pupils attend private school today, a far cry from the 46 million students enrolled in public schools.

"A simple mathematical exercise will immediately point out that the numbers don't work," he writes. "A voucher system, regardless of the amount of money provided, can only accommodate a minimal number of public school students." [11]

Given the very limited and brief use of vouchers in the United States so far, it is too soon to tell whether school choice will benefit students, poor or otherwise, who transfer from public to private school. Still, both sides in the debate have pointed to studies indicating that vouchers either do or don't make a difference in the performance of the students who use them.

According to voucher opponents, a series of studies of students in Milwaukee concludes that those who used vouchers performed no better on standardized tests than public school students. The state-sponsored studies by University of Wisconsin Professor John Witte focused on test scores from 1991-1995. [12]

But another evaluation of the same test data by Paul E. Peterson and Jiangtao Du of Harvard University and Jay P. Greene of the University of Houston discovered that voucher students performed better in key subjects than children who had applied for but had not been given vouchers. The voucher students scored 3-5 percent higher in reading and 5-12 percent higher in math, the researchers found. [13]

Different methodologies could explain why the two studies differed. For example, while Witte compared voucher students with all children in the same grades, Peterson and his colleagues used only those who had tried unsuccessfully to get a voucher.

Many experts believe that neither study should be used as a rationale for making decisions on school choice. "It's going to take a lot more analysis than this to figure out what's going on in these choice programs," says Richard Elmore, a professor of education at Harvard. [14]

Will vouchers lead to increased educational competition and improve the public schools?

In a sense, voucher advocates say, public schools are like the automobile industry in the 1970s. Like Detroit's Big Three automakers 25 years ago, public schools today can afford to put out a shoddy education product because they have a virtual lock on the market.

"The auto industry was arrogant until it lost 25 percent of the market to the Japanese," Fuller says.

Fuller and others believe that like the auto industry or any other business, public education will only improve if it is subjected to outside competition. "When there is a captive audience," Ravitch says, "there is no incentive to change anything."

The idea is to unshackle that audience by giving them the option of taking some or all of the public money spent on their education with them to another school. "If children can get vouchers, public schools will begin treating them like customers," says Heritage's Shokraii.

Joe McTighe, executive director of the Council for American Private Education, agrees. "The opportunity to take your business someplace else is a powerful inducement to improve," he says.

As evidence, Shokraii, McTighe and others point to actions taken in those school districts that have had limited voucher programs. In Milwaukee, McTighe says, educators have opened a charter school and given principals in all schools more autonomy since vouchers were made available in 1990. According to McTighe, these innovations were a response to the competition posed by the new school choice program. [15]

But opponents of vouchers say that it is not school choice that is nudging public schools to make necessary reforms. "Those things happening in Milwaukee are going on all over the country," says Deanna Duby, director of education policy at People for the American Way, a First Amendment rights advocacy group. Duby argues that charter schools, principal autonomy and other innovations are part of a broad nationwide reform movement that has nothing to do with vouchers.

Instead, Duby and others argue, vouchers would simply take away money from already underfunded public school systems, especially in poor, inner-city areas. "You would drain badly needed money from public schools that already can't do what they need to," she says, adding that unlike a private institution, which can select the students it wants to admit, public schools must admit all children, including those who are disruptive or have special needs.

In addition, opponents argue, vouchers take more than much-needed money away from public schools. "The choice system is a system of segregation because it removes the most motivated kids and parents from the public system and puts them in private schools," says Richard Rothstein, a research associate at the Economic Policy Institute. Highly motivated parents would take a large share of any vouchers offered, he says, because they "are the most interested in their child's education" and thus more likely to take advantage of new opportunities. The resulting exodus, he says, would be disastrous for the students left behind, because these more-committed parents are often the impetus for positive change. "Everybody who has been involved in a public school knows that if you have a teacher who is not doing well, it only takes one or two parents in that classroom to complain to the principal to get a change," he says.

Opponents also dismiss the idea that you can treat a school district like a business and parents like consumers. "This market theory of competition assumes that people have good information on the choices they are making," Rothstein says, "but we really don't have any information on school quality. So if parents don't know what schools are good, there's no reason to believe they will choose the best school."

In addition, opponents say, there really is a difference between business and government. "To assume that market modalities will have an impact in the government sector is wrong," Green says. "What's good for selling cars is not necessarily good for schools."

But Fuller dismisses the argument that schools are unique institutions. "They are organizations just like any other," he argues, "and many of the principles that apply to business will apply to them." For example, Fuller says, the important issues in school districts, as in businesses, revolve around money. "People know that for all of the yakking, the key is how to allocate resources," he says.

In addition, voucher supporters say, private schools don't always just take the best students.

"We take the low achievers," says Lydia Harris, principal of St. Adalbert's, which has 47 voucher students. "It's a myth that we only take the cream of the crop," she says, adding: "We put our own cream on the crop."

Choice advocates also challenge the notion that vouchers will drain needed money from public schools. "There would not be a net loss of per-pupil funding because the fewer students you have the less it's going to cost," McTighe says.

In fact, McTighe and others say, most proposed vouchers are worth much less than the per-pupil amount spent by the school district. For example, in Cleveland, vouchers are worth a maximum of $2,500 per year, less than half of what the city spends for every pupil in public school. "So [the public school] actually does better [financially] with this," McTighe says.

But voucher opponents argue that the overall cost of education won't necessarily drop every time a student leaves the school system. "A lot of the cost of having the student in the school would still be there," Duby says. For example, she points out, the building would still need to be maintained and the teachers paid. "If a third of the students left an elementary school, almost all of the costs would remain," she says. ■

Background

Rise of Public Schools

The proper role of government in education has been debated for more than 200 years. But public schools, as they exist today, are a relatively new phenomenon.

During the Enlightenment, thinkers like Thomas Jefferson, called for increased taxation to support a public school system that would educate "common people." Jefferson believed that only through education could citizens understand and exercise their rights. Indeed, he said, an educated populous was essential to the functioning of the new American republic. [16]

But others were more wary of using the public purse to finance education. Scottish economist Adam Smith, whose landmark work, *The Wealth of Nations,* was published the same year as Jefferson's Declaration of Independence, believed that the "invisible hand" of the market could not adequately provide enough incentives for universal education. But the father of laissez-faire economics also said that an educational system administered by the government would be inefficient and would fail to create a literate population.

By the early 19th century, the debate over public education had become one of the most important social questions in the United States. Trade unions and other advocates for workers' rights said that universal education was needed to fight social injustice and poverty. But business leaders in the North and slaveholders in the South worried that universal literacy could stoke the fires of revolution among the lower classes. [17]

The nation's leading proponent of public education was Horace Mann, secretary of the Massachusetts Board of Education and one of the most well-known social reformers of the last century. Mann argued that a public school system would inculcate the native-born poor and newly arrived immigrants with "American values." [18]

Over time, Mann's idea that education could mold disparate social and ethnic groups into good citizens gained currency around the country. By the time the Civil War broke out, most states had public elementary schools. And yet, while free, they were not compulsory. Moreover, public high schools were rare and would remain so throughout the 19th century. In fact, as late as 1920, only one-third of all eligible Americans attended high school. [19]

During the first half of the 20th century, public school attendance and respect for the nation's educational institutions grew at a rapid pace. By the 1950s, most American children were in school and, according to polls of their parents' attitudes, were receiving quality educations.

It was at this time, nonetheless, that the case for vouchers was first put forward. In 1955, libertarian economist Milton Friedman published an influential essay proposing vouchers as a way to give parents greater flexibility in choosing their child's school as well as an antidote for what he said was an increasingly inefficient and ineffective public education system.

Friedman advanced what has become the classic school choice argument: Vouchers will allow parents more choice when it comes to their children's education, which will in turn improve all schools, public and private, by injecting competition into the system. Friedman argued that this scheme would prove especially beneficial for the poor, who have no choice but to send their children to the local public school, even if it offers an inferior education. [20]

Friedman might have seemed an alarmist in the 1950s, but his ideas made sense to many more people two decades later. By the 1970s, the national consensus on public education had changed, with most Americans believing that public schools were failing. Statistics seemed to bear them out. In one key measure of education quality, SAT scores dropped steadily from the mid-1960s

Continued on p. 638

Chronology

1950s-1980s

The perception that public schools are inadequate in many parts of the country gathers momentum, giving birth to the school choice movement.

1955
Libertarian economist Milton Friedman publishes an essay proposing tuition vouchers as a means to expand educational opportunity and improve public schools.

1973
The U.S. Supreme Court strikes down a New York state law granting parents reimbursements and tax credits for the cost of private school tuition.

1979
The Department of Education is created.

1980
Studies show a steady decline in Scholastic Aptitude Tests (SATs) over the previous 15 years.

1983
The Education Department's *A Nation At Risk* report charts what it sees as a decline in discipline and standards in the country's public schools.

1990s

The push for school choice is transformed into a national movement. The first voucher plans are created on a small scale.

April 1990
Wisconsin establishes a voucher program to allow students in Milwaukee to go to non-sectarian private schools.

April 1991
The nation's first privately financed voucher program is created in Indianapolis, by J. Patrick Rooney, chairman of the Golden Rule Insurance Co. Rooney's action sparks dozens of similr programs in cities around the country.

September 1993
A pilot voucher plan is signed into law in Puerto Rico, and more than 1,800 vouchers are awarded.

November 1993
Voters in California overwhelmingly reject Proposition 174, which would have entitled every student enrolled in public or private school to a tuition voucher equal to half of the state's per pupil spending, or about $2,600.

November 1994
Puerto Rico's Supreme Court strikes down the commonwealth's voucher law, ruling that it violates a constitutional ban on transferring public funds to private schools.

June 1995
Ohio creates a pilot voucher program for the Cleveland public school system. Under the plan, vouchers can be used in both sectarian and non-sectarian private schools.

July 1995
Wisconsin legislators expand the Milwaukee voucher program to include religious schools.

February 1996
A proposal creating a $5 million voucher program for the District of Columbia is defeated in the Senate.

May 1996
The 10th District Court of Appeals for the State of Ohio strikes down the voucher plan in Cleveland on the grounds that the program violates federal and state constitutional Establishment clauses. The case is appealed to the state Supreme Court.

July 1996
Republican presidential candidate Bob Dole announces a proposal to spend $2.5 billion annually to fund a nationwide voucher program.

November 1996
Voters in Washington state reject Initiative 173, which would have created tuition vouchers for non-religious private schools.

January 1997
A Wisconsin trial court rules that state efforts to expand the Milwaukee voucher program to include sectarian institutions violates the Establishment Clause in the state's Constitution.

June 1997
In *Agostini v. Felton,* the U.S. Supreme Court overturns a 1985 ruling that barred public school remedial education teachers from entering parochial schools to help students there.

Teachers' Choice

In cities throughout the country, a large percentage of public school teachers whose household income is $35,000-$70,000 opt for private school for their own children, though teachers' groups uniformly oppose school choice.

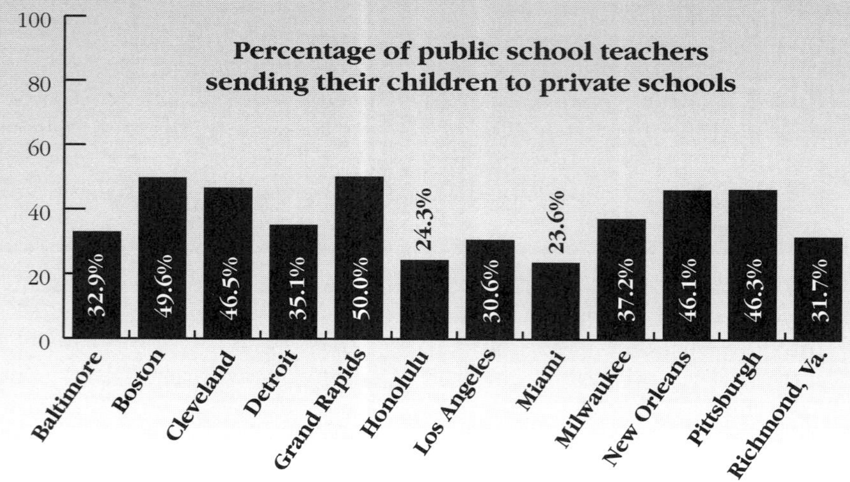

Source: Compiled from 1990 Census data by Denis Doyle, The American Enterprise, *September/October 1996*

Continued from p. 636

to the early '80s. [21]

In 1983, an influential Department of Education report seemed to confirm the public's worst fears. Commissioned by Education Secretary Terrel H. Bell, *A Nation at Risk* painted a bleak picture of the state of learning in America. Among other things, it criticized schools for a marked decline in discipline and academic standards. [22]

When *A Nation at Risk* was published, the school choice movement already had a dedicated following in conservative circles. Over the next decade, the choice movement broadened its base of support significantly. Today, vouchers are still largely rejected by the Democratic Party and most liberal groups. But school choice has substantial support among a growing number of African-American political leaders and others who are normally identified with the left, though the NAACP remains opposed to choice, in large part, voucher proponents say, because of its traditional alliance with labor unions.

Voucher Programs

School choice has never been established on a grand scale. Voucher plans have been carried out as pilot programs and have impacted very few students. The most significant school choice plan to date was created in Milwaukee in 1990, where the state provides up to $3,209 to some 1,100 mostly low-income children. The vouchers can only be used to send students to non-religious private schools. [23]

In the summer of 1995, the Wisconsin Legislature voted to include religious schools in the voucher program. The law also expanded the current program significantly, increasing the number of eligible students to 7,000 in 1996 and 15,000 the following year. But the expansion has not been carried out due to a court challenge filed by the state affiliates of the NEA and the American Civil Liberties Union (ACLU). [24]

Although the voucher program in Milwaukee has received the lion's share of national media attention, it does not represent the first or most recent attempt to experiment with school choice.

Indeed, since 1869, Vermont has allowed parents in sparsely populated districts without a high school to send their children to a public or private alternative at state expense. Until 1961, "tuitioning, as the practice is known," included parochial schools. That year, the state Supreme Court ruled that using government funds to pay tuition at parochial schools, in this case three Catholic schools, violated Vermont's Constitution.

An attempt last year to send 15 Vermont students from tiny Chittenden to a nearby Roman Catholic high school has reopened the debate over religious schools. Although the Chittenden case has not yet reached the state Supreme Court, a 1994 high court ruling allowing tuition reimbursement for a man who sent his son to a sectarian school is an indication that the tribunal may be willing to overturn its 1961 decision. [25]

Puerto Rico has also experimented, albeit briefly, with school choice. In 1993, the commonwealth's legislature created a pilot voucher program for children whose parents earn less than $18,000 per year. The program offered students up to $1,500 toward tuition at the school of their choice, including religious institutions. One year and 1,181 vouchers later, the commonwealth's Supreme Court struck down the program on the grounds that the Puerto Rican Constitution prohibits the use of public funds to support private schools, sectarian or otherwise.

Almost two years after vouchers were struck down in Puerto Rico, a similar school choice plan was instituted in Cleveland. The program, which began in September 1996, allows up to 2,000 elementary-age students to receive up to $2,500 annually to attend the school of their choice. As in Puerto Rico, a challenge to the plan is pending before the Ohio Supreme Court. ■

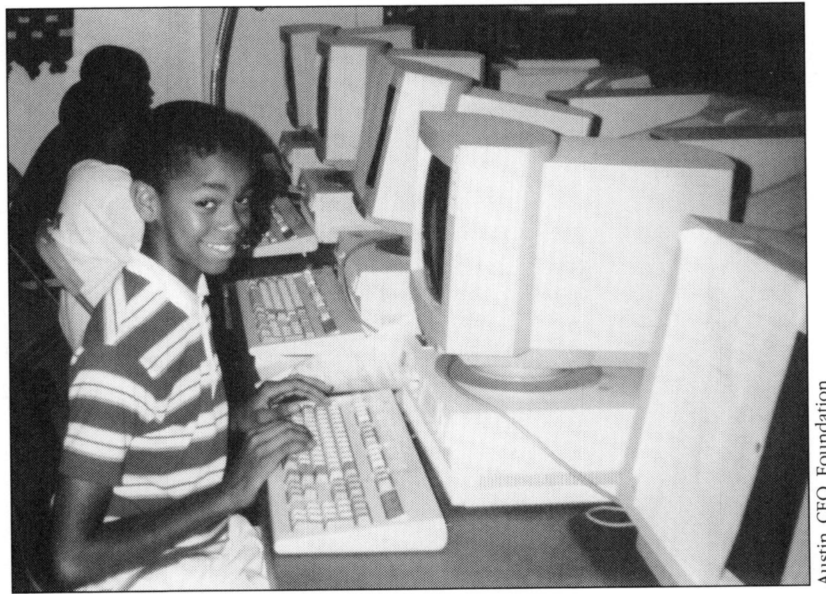

Austin CEO Foundation

Scholarships to private schools in Austin, Texas, are provided by the private Austin Children's Educational Opportunity Foundation.

CURRENT SITUATION

Politics of Choice

During the 1996 presidential campaign, school choice became a major issue for the first time in a national election. The issue rose to prominence after Republican nominee Bob Dole announced a plan to spend $2.5 billion annually to give lower-income children vouchers. Dole's plan offered students up to $1,000 a year for elementary school and $1,500 for high school.

On Oct. 6, in the first of Dole's two debates with President Clinton, Clinton came out against vouchers. Clinton's victory a month later assured that school choice would likely be off the White House agenda until at least the year 2000.

Still, voucher advocates say, the fact that school choice was in the spotlight during the campaign is evidence that the issue has now become an integral part of the national debate on education.

"When Bob Dole started talking about school choice and took on the teachers' unions ... we realized that it had become a mainstream issue," says Fritz Steiger, president of Children's Educational Opportunity of America (CEO America), which helps private groups that raise money to fund tuition vouchers.

Indeed, vouchers have become a top priority for many Republican politicians, who are supported by many religious groups and some education reformers.

On Capitol Hill, Republicans and a few Democrats have made frequent and concerted efforts since the early 1990s to create pilot voucher programs.

Last year, for instance, an attempt to establish a $5 million voucher program in the District of Columbia failed after Democrats in the Senate blocked action on the D.C. spending bill to which the proposal was attached. [26]

This year, a number of voucher plans are pending before Congress. A proposal sponsored by Sen. Paul Coverdell, R-Ga., would authorize $50 million in fiscal 1998 to establish school choice demonstration projects in 20-30 school districts.

Another measure, sponsored in the House by Majority Leader Dick Armey, R-Texas, and in the Senate by Daniel R. Coats, R-Ind., would authorize $7 million in fiscal 1998 to provide vouchers of up to $3,200 for 2,000 poor children in Washington, D.C.

Leading the charge against these and other attempts to create school choice programs are several labor and civil rights groups. By far the most powerful and notable of these organizations is the NEA. Other important players include the American Federation of Teachers (AFT), the NAACP, People for the American Way and the ACLU.

These and other groups claim that proponents of vouchers are not interested in finding new ways to provide a better education for poor children. Instead, they say, they are interested in subsidizing children already attending private schools at the expense of public education. Some even suggest that many school choice advocates, especially religious groups, want to do away with public schools entirely. "Their goal is to end public education," Chase says.

Supporters of school choice, among them the Institute for Justice, the Heritage Foundation and the Christian Coalition, contend that teachers' unions are only interested in protecting their members' jobs, regardless of performance or qualifications. "They protect teachers who have no business being with children," Fuller says.

Choice advocates also say that opposition by civil liberties groups actually reflects a thinly disguised fear of religion as much as an effort to guard constitutional principles.

"Their primary concern is what they take to be the undue influence of religion, in particular the Roman Catholic Church," says Quentin L. Quade, director of the Blum Center for Parental Freedom in Education at Marquette University in Milwaukee. ■

OUTLOOK

Momentum Building?

Proponents of vouchers believe that, despite recent setbacks in state courts, overall momentum is with them.

"This issue is on a roll because the alternatives have been tried for years and are failing," McTighe says.

Ravitch agrees, adding: "There's a growing interest because there's a growing sense of desperation, especially in the black community."

Indeed, choice advocates can point to a number of recent converts to the cause, among them Rep. Floyd H. Flake, D-N.Y., and *Washington Post* columnist William Raspberry, who are not only national figures with impeccable liberal credentials but also African-Americans.

But while well-known black voucher advocates are important to the school choice movement, it is at the grass-roots level where African-Americans are having the greatest impact.

For instance, proponents say, black community leaders and parents have been the driving force behind the school choice movements in Cleveland and Milwaukee. "The battle for parental choice [in Milwaukee] began in the church basements and meeting halls of the Near North Side," writes scholar Daniel McGroarty in his recent book *Break These Chains: The Battle for School Choice.* McGroarty, a fellow at the Institute for Contemporary Studies, says that the language used to advance school choice was reminiscent of the civil rights movement. "Their rhetoric was more redolent of Martin Luther King than the free-market pronouncements favored by conservative voucher proponents," he says. [27]

What McGroarty says is happening in Milwaukee and Cleveland is spreading to more and more cities and towns around the country, choice proponents say. Some of these movements are sure to succeed in bringing school choice to their communities, they say.

"I think it's going to start happening soon in the states," Steiger says. "In five years, we'll see three or four significant choice programs, and in 10 years a significant number of states will have vouchers."

Opponents of school choice concede that the movement has built up a head of steam. "There's a certain amount of momentum," says Duby of People for the American Way. But, she argues, the movement reflects parents' legitimate frustration, not necessarily the validity of vouchers as a public policy. "I understand when people say, 'I don't care about everyone else, I need to get my kid out of these schools,'" she says.

Duby and others fear that frustration may lead people to embrace choice as a panacea while avoiding more concrete reform efforts. "I think we could do a lot of damage with school choice," she says, adding that "if nothing else, choice could delay the work we need to do."

Chase agrees, saying that the NEA and other groups need to educate people adequately so that they understand that private school is not a "magic bullet." Still, Chase disputes the notion that there is a grass-roots groundswell for vouchers all over the country.

"This is not something that is being seriously discussed in most school districts," he says. "There is such a thing as the public good, and for [the American people] the public good means public schools for all children."

Chase and other voucher opponents, including many African-Americans, also reject the notion that school choice is akin to the fight for civil rights, noting that organizations like the NAACP firmly oppose choice.

In fact, they point out, many black leaders think that school choice will be a huge step backward, and not only in education. "Choice is a subterfuge for segregation" as it existed in the South before the civil rights movement, says Felmers Chaney, head of the Milwaukee NAACP. [28]

Supreme Court to Rule?

But whether school choice is embraced as a policy initiative or not, it may not be the most important immediate question facing those on both sides of the debate. Many supporters and some opponents of vouchers predict that the Supreme Court is likely to rule on the issue in the next two or three years.

Continued on p. 642

At Issue:

Is meaningful school choice possible within the public school system?

Richard W. Riley
Secretary of Education

WRITTEN FOR *THE CQ RESEARCHER*

yes

As changes in our economy expand and transform our educational needs, America's public schools must become more flexible and offer students and parents more choices with higher standards and accountability. School districts are responding by creating new types of schools — charter schools, magnet schools, "schools within schools." They are letting parents pick among schools from across the district, even the entire state. This growing menu of choices is improving education by creating new models for learning, and we must do more to promote such advancements.

The Clinton administration is encouraging this trend with a significant effort to expand charter schools. Charter schools are public schools operated by teachers, parents or others in the community who enter into an agreement with the school district or another chartering agency authorized by the state. Since start-up capital is the primary obstacle to starting a charter school, President Clinton requested $100 million in his fiscal 1998 budget to provide seed money for up to 1,100 charter schools.

The progress achieved by charter schools and other innovations is threatened, however, by those who seek to funnel public tax dollars to private schools. More than any public institution, public schools unite citizens from all walks of life and pass on our democratic ideals to each generation. Any voucher program for private schools would drain much-needed resources from public schools and accommodate a limited number of students. Further, private school vouchers would make parochial schools less parochial and private schools less private, subjecting them to public supervision and compromising their independence.

There are several reasons for keeping publicly financed school choice within the public school domain. A public school is held in the public trust by local voters who select the 16,000 local boards that govern their schools. A private school is not required to be open to all students that live within a district, which means that it can choose to turn away students. A successful public school offers the potential to serve as a model that can be replicated elsewhere, while a school that fails to create a quality learning environment can be held accountable to the public and closed if necessary.

The nation's public schools educate close to 90 percent of America's 52 million schoolchildren. At a time of increasing enrollments and growing demands on the public schools, our limited resources should be focused on giving students and parents as many high-quality options as possible within the schools that serve the vast majority of America's students.

Joe McTighe
Executive Director, Council for American Private Education

WRITTEN FOR *THE CQ RESEARCHER*

no

As beauty is in the eye of the beholder, meaningful choice is in the mind of the selector. When it comes to schools, the selectors, of course, are parents, a child's primary educators. For many parents, the options already at play within public education constitute meaningful choice, but others can find such choice only outside the realm of public schools.

A growing number of parents, for example, desperately desire schools whose primary purpose is to provide youngsters with a sound moral and spiritual education — schools that touch the soul and call children to a life of love. Private schools are the only schools we have that can address the religious development of children — a sphere beyond the proper reach of public education.

And then there are the parents whose children are trapped in chronically failing and sometimes unsafe schools. They don't have the money to move to communities where the schools are better, and they don't have the time to see if the latest promise of improvement proves any more trustworthy than its predecessors. For those parents, an immediate alternative would be neighborhood private schools where high expectations, caring communities and remarkable records of success are the rule.

The same rationale that drives proposals for tax reductions, Pell grants and Hope scholarships to help low- and middle-income students attend the public, private or religious college of their choice applies to K-12 education. How can one argue that aid to the parents of a 12th-grader is taboo while the same aid a year later is laudable? We need a unified plan of parent aid in America — one that guarantees meaningful choice to needy parents across all grade levels.

There are some who say that choice within the public school system is sufficient. They consider such choice the silver bullet of school reform. But let's face it: The difference between the P.S. 8 and P.S. 9 is often inconsequential. And while some charter schools offer parents genuine alternatives, the truth is that many are nothing more than standard public school clones in a prettied-up package.

A single system of government schooling cannot possibly meet everyone's needs. Fortunately, our country is blessed by a rich diversity of schools that collectively serve a noble purpose: the education of our nation's children. Why not a comprehensive program of school choice that truly respects and promotes the right of all parents to choose the kind of education their children shall receive?

For More Information

Americans United for the Separation of Church and State, 1816 Jefferson Pl. N.W., Washington, D.C. 20036; (202) 466-3234. The group opposes federal or state aid to parochial schools and other religious institutions.

Council for American Private Education, 18016 Mateny Rd., Suite 140, Germantown, Md. 20874; (301) 916-8485. The council is a coalition of private-school associations that seeks greater access to private schools for American families.

Institute for Justice, 1001 Pennsylvania Ave. N.W., Suite 200S, Washington, D.C. 20004; (202) 457-4240. The institute is a conservative public interest law firm that litigates cases involving parental school choice.

National Education Association, 1201 16th St. N.W., Washington, D.C. 20036; (202) 833-4000. The NEA is the nation's largest teachers' union with more than 2 million members. It is opposed to vouchers and works to defeat school choice proposals through lobbying and litigation.

"Without a question, the Ohio case will go to the U.S. Supreme Court," Quade says, referring to the Cleveland voucher case currently working its way through the state court system. Duby at People for the American Way agrees. "At some point in the next five years, we will have a voucher case before the Supreme Court," she says.

But others are not so sure about the Ohio case, or any other for that matter, making it to the nation's highest court. According to the NEA's Chanin, if voucher proponents lose the Ohio or another state case based on the court's reading of the state's constitution, there will be no grounds for an appeal to the Supreme Court because there will be no federal constitutional issue to decide

Still, if a voucher case does reach the nation's highest court, school choice supporters are confident the justices will rule that publicly financed tuition vouchers do not violate the Establishment Clause.

"In the long run, the Supreme Court will uphold a properly drafted voucher program," says the Institute for Justice's Garnet, citing *Mueller* and the other cases that school choice supporters say shrink Establishment Clause restrictions on government support for religion.

But Chanin thinks otherwise. "I'm confident we would win," he says, adding that the Supreme Court has gone out of its way not to overturn *Nyquist,* which is the closest existing case on the voucher question.

Either way, a high court decision would have a tremendous and possibly decisive impact on the school choice debate. A ruling in favor of allowing vouchers would undoubtedly give a huge boost to school choice advocates and lead to a frenzy of new activity on federal, state and local levels.

But if the court struck down a school choice law, the drive for publicly funded vouchers could diminish and even die. With the exception of funding from private sources, says CEO America's Steiger, "there would be no alternatives." ■

Notes

[1] Richard Lacayo, "Parochial Politics," *Time,* Sept. 23, 1996. See "Attack on Public Schools," *The CQ Researcher,* July 26, 1996, pp. 649-672.

[2] For background, see "Religion in Schools," *The CQ Researcher,* Jan. 7, 1994, pp. 145-168.

[3] *Ibid.*

[4] Lawrence H. Tribe, *American Constitutional Law* (1988), pp. 1217-1218.

[5] Linda Greenhouse, "Court Eases Curb on Providing Aid in Church Schools," *The New York Times,* June 24, 1997.

[6] Steven K. Green, "The Legal Argument Against Private School Choice," *University of Cincinnati Law Review,* summer 1993. Green is quoting *Grand Rapids School District v. Ball.*

[7] For background, see "Parents and Schools," *The CQ Researcher,* Jan. 20, 1995, pp. 66-89.

[8] Sol Stern, "The Invisible Miracle of Catholic Schools," *City Journal,* summer 1996, published by the Manhattan Institute.

[9] *Ibid.* Stern is a *City Journal* contributing editor.

[10] Quoted in a recent letter to NAACP members.

[11] Gerald Tirozzi, "Vouchers: A Questionable Answer to an Unasked Question," *Education Week,* April 23, 1997.

[12] Lynn Olson, "New Studies on Private Choice Contradict Each Other," *Education Week,* Sept. 4, 1996.

[13] Jay P. Greene, Paul E. Peterson and Jiangtao Du, "The Effectiveness of School Choice in Milwaukee: A Secondary Analysis of Data from the Program's Evaluation," Aug. 14, 1996, p. 3.

[14] Olson, *op. cit.*

[15] For background, see "Private Management of Public Schools," *The CQ Researcher,* March 25, 1994, pp. 265-288.

[16] Bernard Mayo (ed.), *Jefferson Himself* (1942), p. 89.

[17] Peter Carrol and David Noble, *The Restless Centuries* (1979), pp. 220-221.

[18] *Ibid.*

[19] Daniel J. Boorstin, *The Americans: The Democratic Experience* (1973), p. 500.

[20] Milton Friedman, "The Role of Government in Education," in Robert A. Solo (ed.), *Economics and the Public Interest* (1955), pp. 127-134.

[21] John E. Chubb and Terry M. Moe, *Politics, Markets and America's Schools* (1990), p. 8.

[22] *Ibid.,* pp. 9-10.

[23] Mark Walsh, "Court Deadlocks on Vouchers," *Teacher,* May/June 1996.

[24] Dorothy B. Hanks, "School Choice Programs: What's Happening in the States," Heritage Foundation, 1997.

[25] Sally Johnson, "Vermont Parents Ask State to Pay Catholic School Tuition," *The New York Times,* Oct. 30, 1996.

[26] David A. Vise, "In a Win for Teachers Unions, Senate Rejects D.C. Tuition Vouchers; City Budget Stalled," *The Washington Post,* Feb. 28, 1996.

[27] Daniel McGroarty, *Break These Chains: The Battle for School Choice* (1996), p. 73.

[28] Nina Shokraii, "Free at Last: Black America Signs Up for School Choice," *Policy Review,* November/December 1996.

Bibliography

Selected Sources Used

Books

Lieberman, Myron, *Privatization and Educational Choice,* St. Martin's Press, 1989.

Lieberman, an education policy consultant, covers the entire sweep of the school choice debate, from the effect of competition to the constitutionality of vouchers. He also examines the political landscape, describing the groups and interests lined up on both sides of the issue.

McGroarty, Daniel, *Breaking These Chains: The Battle for School Choice,* Prima Publishing, 1996.

McGroarty, a fellow at the Institute for Contemporary Studies, chronicles the efforts of parents and community leaders in inner-city Milwaukee to establish and sustain a voucher program. McGroarty argues that for many of these mostly black residents, the fight for school choice is akin to the civil rights battles of the 1960s.

Moe, Terry M., and John E. Chubb, *Politics, Markets and America's Schools,* The Brookings Institution, 1990.

Moe and Chubb look at the recent history of education and education reform in the United States and the problems that have plagued America's schools in the last three decades. The authors come to the conclusion that the institutions governing the nation's schools hamstring them and prevent real reform from taking hold. Moe and Chubb argue that vouchers are a way to break this institutional vise grip.

Articles

Goldberg, Bruce, "A Liberal Argument for School Choice," *The American Enterprise,* September/October, 1996.

Goldberg criticizes public schools in the United States, arguing that they are "fundamentally at war with individuality." Only by allowing families to be education consumers will the public schools begin to respond to their needs, he says.

Green, Steven, "The Legal Argument Against Private School Choice," *University of Cincinnati Law Review,* summer 1993.

Green, legal director for Americans United for Church and State, examines Establishment Clause case law. He concludes that optimism on the part of school choice advocates over recent Supreme Court decisions is misplaced. Green points out that the high court has never considered the constitutionality of vouchers and that many legal questions remain unanswered.

Hawley, Willis D., "The Predictable Consequences of School Choice," *Education Week,* April 10, 1996.

Hawley, dean of the College of Education at the University of Maryland, argues that among other things, school choice will drive up the tuition at private schools and reduce diversity and funding at public institutions.

Lacayo, Richard, "Parochial Politics," *Time,* Sept. 23, 1996.

Lacayo gives a good overview of the current school choice debate, focusing on the voucher program in Cleveland, Ohio.

Peterson, Bob, "Teacher of the Year Gives Vouchers a Failing Grade," *The Progressive,* April 1997.

Peterson, a teacher in the Milwaukee public school system, says that in his hometown school choice has been a failure. Among the problems that followed the issuance of vouchers was massive fraud on the part of some private schools that participated in the program.

Tirozzi, Gerald, "Vouchers: A Questionable Answer to an Unasked Question," *Education Week,* April 23, 1997.

Tirozzi, assistant secretary of Education for elementary and secondary education, picks apart the arguments for vouchers and concludes that they are specious. Among other things, Tirozzi says that even if they were effective, vouchers would not impact more than a small fraction of the students currently enrolled in public schools because the private school system is just not big enough to accommodate many more students.

Reports

Hanks, Dorothy B., *School Choice Programs: What's Happening in the States,* The Heritage Foundation, 1997.

The report gives an exhaustive state-by-state rundown of existing and proposed school choice programs and related news.

The Next Step

Additional information from UMI's Newspaper & Periodical Abstracts™ database

Charter Schools

Kelly, Michael, "TRB from Washington," *The New Republic,* Dec. 30, 1996, p. 6.

The Marcus Garvey Public Charter School in Washington, D.C., has come into focus because of its proselytizing nature and an alleged attack on a white reporter who visited the school. Kelly asserts that charter schools are a huge mistake because citizens fund the schools but have no influence over how they are run.

Nathan, Joe, "Possibilities, problems, and progress," *Phi Delta Kappan,* September 1996, pp. 18-23.

During the past five years, the introduction of public charter schools has spread from Minnesota across the country. Nathan reflects on the evolution of the movement and considers the lessons that can be drawn — both at the school level and at the level of state policy — from the widely varying approaches that have been adopted in the 25 states that have passed charter legislation.

Cleveland

Olsen, Ted, "Voucher opponents vow to gut Cleveland program," *Christianity Today,* Oct. 28, 1996, pp. 90-92.

Enrollments in Cleveland's religious schools are on the rise this fall due to the first educational-voucher program to include such institutions. Groups opposing the plan have filed suit to halt the $5.25 million program.

Sanchez, Rene, "Cleveland Students Can't Use Vouchers for Religious Schools, State Court Rules," *The Washington Post,* May 2, 1997, p. A4.

The only school voucher program in the nation that lets children attend private religious schools using public money was stopped yesterday by an Ohio court. In a case that educators and lawmakers nationwide have been following closely, the Ohio Court of Appeals decided unanimously that the voucher program created last fall in Cleveland infringes on the separation of church and state. The ruling is the latest among several recent legal setbacks for proponents of school vouchers, and it could give new momentum to groups that are battling to stop similar plans under consideration in many states.

Walsh, Mark, "Court clears Cleveland's voucher pilot," *Education Week,* Aug. 7, 1996, p. 1.

Ohio Judge Lisa L. Sadler recently upheld Cleveland's school voucher program, opening the door for 2,000 low-income children to enroll in private and religious schools at the state's expense. The pilot program authorizes vouchers of up to $2,250 for low-income parents of children in grades K-3 to pay for tuition at any participating private school or at public schools in adjoining districts.

Constitutionality of Vouchers

Allen, John, "Some think taking public funding will alter identity of Catholic schools," *National Catholic Reporter,* March 28, 1997, p. 13.

Allen addresses two questions being asked about education vouchers — what is constitutional and what can privatization do to improve the quality of education in the U.S.? The Catholic Church is weighing the benefits and liabilities of educational vouchers.

Doerr, Ed, "The empty promise of school vouchers," *USA Today,* March 1997, pp. 88-90.

Doerr examines the debate over school vouchers. He believes that vouchers for non-public education are bad public policy and violate fundamental constitutional principles.

Kemerer, Frank R., and Lynn Kimi King, "Are school vouchers constitutional?" *Phi Delta Kappan,* December 1995, pp. 307-311.

Kemerer and King identify emerging judicial perspectives regarding the constitutionality of school vouchers under both federal and state laws and discuss the factors that predispose a court to look with favor on a voucher program.

"Lift the Cloud Over School Vouchers," *Chicago Tribune,* Jan. 29, 1997, p. 16.

A Wisconsin state court ruling on school vouchers, while not satisfactory in itself, may serve the useful purpose of moving the issue closer to a final resolution in the U.S. Supreme Court. The question of whether it is unconstitutional to allow poor families to use publicly funded vouchers for tuition at religiously based schools has dogged attempts to establish such programs across the country.

Sadler, Lisa L., "Rule of law: Why Cleveland's school vouchers are constitutional," *The Wall Street Journal,* Aug. 7, 1996, p. A13.

An excerpt from a ruling by Judge Lisa L. Sadler of the Franklin County Court of Pleas in Ohio is presented. Sadler's decision upheld as constitutional a Cleveland program that gives low-income parents vouchers to send their children to private and parochial schools.

"Strong Message on School Vouchers," ***St. Louis Post-Dispatch,*** **Jan. 30, 1997, p. B6.**

With his ruling against expansion of a Milwaukee school choice plan, a Wisconsin judge has cut to the heart of what is wrong with using taxpayers' money for religious education. Allowing thousands of students to attend church-run schools at public expense, Circuit Judge Paul Higginbotham said, "compels Wisconsin citizens of varying religious faiths to support schools with their tax dollars that proselytize students and attempt to inculcate them with beliefs contrary to their own." Such a practice, he added, violates the Wisconsin Constitution.

Federal Involvement/Support

Foskett, Ken, "Goals in Senate: School vouchers, tuition tax credits," ***Atlanta Constitution,*** **Jan. 22, 1997, p. A3.**

Democratic and GOP senators on Jan. 21, 1997, rolled out their legislative agendas for the 105th Congress, including a proposal from Georgia Republican Sen. Paul Coverdell to offer school vouchers to parents in 20-30 pilot projects nationwide.

Hicks, Jonathan P., "Rep. Flake Breaks With Party to Back School Vouchers," ***The New York Times,*** **March 12, 1997, p. B3.**

Rep. Floyd H. Flake, D-N.Y., is endorsing a Republican bill that would provide vouchers for children to attend private schools. Flake's decision to co-sponsor the American Community Renewal Act is the culmination of a year-long courtship by Republican officials. In adding his name as a sponsor of the bill, Flake put himself at odds with a number of his democratic colleagues, including his fellow members of the Congressional Black Caucus, who have ardently opposed using public money to help students attend private schools.

"School vouchers again? Yes," ***America,*** **Dec. 2, 1995, p. 3.**

An editorial addresses developments on the state and national level concerning school vouchers. The debate is spurring legislators to devise a constitutionally acceptable way to help middle- and low-income parents exercise their freedom of choice among properly accredited schools.

Milwaukee

Carl, Jim, "Unusual allies: Elite and grass-roots origins of parental choice in Milwaukee," ***Teachers College Record,*** **winter 1996, pp. 266-285.**

Carl outlines the development of the 1990 Milwaukee Parental Choice Program, which for several years was the only publicly funded K-12 voucher program in the U.S.

Colvin, Richard Lee, "School vouchers passing Milwaukee test," ***Los Angeles Times,*** **Oct. 26, 1996, p. A1.**

In 1996, six years after Milwaukee inaugurated the nation's first program giving low-income families vouchers to pay private school tuition, private and public schools are getting along well. There is enthusiastic support for the vouchers in the classrooms where they are a fact of life.

Lum, Lydia, "School-voucher plan makes grade in study," ***Houston Chronicle,*** **Aug. 13, 1996, p. A15.**

A study by the University of Houston and Harvard University found that a school-choice program in Milwaukee that offers vouchers for students to attend private schools helped improve minority student achievement in reading and math.

Private Schools

Doerr, Ed, "Vouchers: The heart of the matter," ***Humanist,*** **May 1997, pp. 40-41.**

Catholic bishops are putting high priority on getting public funding for private schools.

Goodnough, Abby, "Some Enthusiasm, Some Fear After School Voucher Vote," ***The New York Times,*** **Feb. 13, 1997, p. B5.**

With her oldest son ready to start high school this fall, Marie Forbes could be one of the first parents to take advantage of the tuition voucher program in Lincoln, N.J. The new program will allow high school students to attend private schools using local tax dollars, but Forbes says she wants nothing to do with it. School officials in Lincoln Park, which is too small to support a high school of its own, say they adopted the voucher system because they were no longer satisfied with the quality of education at nearby Boonton High School, which Lincoln Park students have attended for 76 years. Under the system, the school board would give each student who chooses a private school between $1,000 and $4,600 a year toward tuition. The money could also go toward tuition in other public school districts, and many parents have expressed interest in that option, even though the cost can exceed $10,000 a year.

Lacayo, Richard, "Parochial politics," ***Time,*** **Sept. 23, 1996, pp. 30-33.**

Lacayo discusses whether Catholic and other private schools should siphon money from public education. In New York City, the annual per-pupil cost of Catholic-school students is about one-third of what it is in public schools.

Rockler, Michael J., "The privatization of education: Can public education survive?," ***Free Inquiry,*** **spring 1996, pp. 26-29.**

Rockler comments on the history of privatization in education, options in private education and effects of privatization. A concern of the effects of privatization on schooling is its role in weakening the separation of church and state.

Public Opinion

Chapman, Stephen, "Climbing Out of Education's Morass; The Growing Case for School Vouchers," *Chicago Tribune,* March 30, 1997, p. 19.
Chapman discusses the benefits of school vouchers and why the Clinton administration rejects them.

Darlin, Damon, "To whom do our schools belong?" *Forbes,* Sept. 23, 1996, pp. 66-76.
John Stanford, the superintendent of Seattle, Wash., schools, is working diligently to reform the educational system. The greatest opposition to Stanford comes from the teachers' union, bureaucrats and the Seattle arm of the National Education Association, which is mobilizing to stop Stanford from proposing a voucher system.

Glasser, Ira, "Private school vouchers offer choice, but only for wealthy," *Detroit News & Free Press,* Oct. 27, 1996, p. E3.
Glasser, national director of the American Civil Liberties Union (ACLU), discusses several factual problems with the argument by school voucher supporters that competition to attract students will improve education and academic performance.

Gonzalez, John W., "School voucher system gains acceptance, poll finds; Majority thinks teacher pay low," *Houston Chronicle,* March 2, 1997, p. D1.
Most Texans believe it is time for the state to adopt a school voucher system and give local districts more control over textbooks, course content and student-teacher ratios, according to the latest Texas Poll. Two years ago, 55 percent of Texans said they favored the concept, but this year, the number rose to 62 percent, with 28 percent opposed.

Lawton, Millicent, "Support for private school vouchers is on the increase Gallup Poll reports," *Education Week,* Sept. 4, 1996, pp. 18-19.
A recent Gallup Poll indicates that 61 percent of respondents are opposed to the use of educational vouchers for religious schools. Respondents also rated their local nonpublic schools higher than their public schools.

"School vouchers," *Commonwealth,* April 5, 1996, pp. 5-6.
An editorial discusses the benefits of school vouchers. The separation of church and state should be apparent, but the wall should be permeable enough to encourage the expression of religious opinion and attachments.

Wickham, DeWayne, "New school voucher bill no better than old," *USA Today,* April 8, 1997, p. A15.
Wickham asserts that if enacted, the American Community Renewal Act of 1997 will rob most poor schoolchildren across the nation of any real chance of getting a decent education.

Rulings

Bacon-Blood, Littice, "School Voucher Plan Rejected in Close Vote," *Times-Picayune,* May 2, 1997, p. A4.
A school voucher program that could have shifted more than $300 million in public money to private and parochial schools was narrowly defeated in a Senate committee Thursday. The bill would have allowed parents to use state vouchers for tuition at the private state-approved school of their choice, including religion-based schools. The Senate Education Committee voted 4-3 to reject Senate Bill 343. Opponents said it could be detrimental to the public school system.

"Judge Backs Order Barring Religious-School Vouchers," *The New York Times,* Aug. 16, 1996, p. A18.
A Circuit Court judge on Aug. 15, 1996, upheld an injunction that bars Wisconsin from expanding the Milwaukee school voucher program to allow low-income inner-city students to attend religious schools. This will be the second year that the plan has been halted.

Ratcliffe, R. G., "School voucher bill passes Senate committee; Proposal scaled down from 1995," *Houston Chronicle,* April 17, 1997, p. A26.
A pilot program allowing at least 63,000 students from low-performing public schools to use tax dollars to attend private schools won a Senate committee's approval Wednesday.

Sanchez, Rene, "In Wisconsin, Vouchers For Religious Schools Handed Legal Setback," *The Washington Post,* Jan. 16, 1997, p. A3.
Advocates of school vouchers, one of the nation's most contentious education issues, were dealt a legal setback yesterday when a Wisconsin state judge struck down a plan to give poor students public money to pay tuition at private, religious schools. In the first court decision on the legal merits of the Wisconsin program, Judge Paul Higginbotham ruled that the state cannot expand its school-voucher experiment to include religious schools because doing so would clearly violate its Constitution.

"Wisconsin School-Voucher Plan Is Struck Down," *The New York Times,* Jan. 16, 1997, p. A23.
In a school-choice case that is expected to reach the U.S. Supreme Court, a Wisconsin judge on Jan. 15, 1997, struck down Republican Gov. Tommy G. Thompson's plan to use taxpayer money to send poor Milwaukee children to religious schools.

Vouchers

Cochren, John R., Douglas Coutts and Harvey B.

Polansky, "Debate: Tired of mediocrity? Try vouchers; Voucher Plans: A bad choice," ***Journal for a Just & Caring Education,*** **April 1997, pp. 227-237.**
Cochren and Coutts argue in favor of an educational voucher system while Polansky urges that voucher plans are a bad choice for education.

Davis, Bob, "Class warfare: Dueling professors have Milwaukee dazed over school vouchers," ***The Wall Street Journal,*** **Oct. 11, 1996, p. A1.**
Since 1990, low-income Milwaukee families have used state-funded vouchers to pay for private schools. Now the city is the focus of a debate over whether school vouchers have helped poor kids academically. Conflicting conclusions have been reached in two studies by John Witte of the University of Wisconsin, who says voucher students do not advance faster, and Paul Peterson of Harvard University, who concludes voucher students make gains in their third and fourth years.

Hanus, Jerome, and Peter W. Cookson Jr., "School vouchers, pro and con," ***Current,*** **January 1997, pp. 30-31.**
Hanus and Cookson discuss the pros and cons of school vouchers. Hanus argues that vouchers are fair and practical, while Cookson asserts that they are poor policy.

Johnson, Bill, "Powerful Baptist council leans toward favoring school vouchers," ***Detroit News,*** **April 20, 1997, p. B6.**
A grass-roots movement for school vouchers may be on the verge of gaining an important ally — the politically influential Council of Baptist Pastors of Detroit and Vicinity. During the past six months, Detroit clergy have traveled to Milwaukee and Cleveland to observe pilot programs for vouchers, tax-backed scholarships that allow parents to send their children to a public or private school of their choice. In those cities, program participation is limited to 2,000 qualifying students. In Milwaukee, the experimental vouchers can only be redeemed at private schools. The Michigan Constitution prohibits government aid for private elementary and secondary schools. But some Detroit religious leaders outside of traditionally pro-voucher Roman Catholics appear anxious to amend it and open public funding to private and religious-based schools. In Cleveland, almost 2,000 parents of kindergarten through third-grade students are given a state voucher good for a maximum of $2,225. The fact that almost all of the vouchers have been redeemed at religious-based schools is not lost on the Rev. Eddie Edwards, president of Joy of Jesus in Detroit and administrator of a preschool through second-grade educational program.

Simplicio, Joseph S. C., "School vouchers — Panacea or Pandora's box?," ***Education,*** **winter 1996, pp. 213-216.**
Simplicio discusses the controversial issue of using school vouchers as a vehicle for public funding of private choice in education. The growing debate over the most effective use of taxpayers' funds for education has brought the voucher issue to the forefront of mainstream educational consciousness.

Peterson, Paul E., Jay P. Greene and Chad Noyes, "School choice in Milwaukee," ***Public Interest,*** **fall 1996, pp. 38-56.**
A cross-district, public-school choice program recently enacted in Massachusetts is discussed.

Shokraii, Nina, "Free at last: Black America signs up for school choice," ***Policy Review,*** **November 1996, pp. 20-26.**
Black America is beginning to embrace school vouchers, charter schools and other education reforms that offer alternatives to dismal public schools.

Walt, Kathy, "Group pushes school voucher program," ***Houston Chronicle,*** **March 4, 1997, p. A17.**
A group supporting school choice called Tuesday for legislation that would allow parents of children ""stuck in unsafe or low-performing schools'' to get vouchers to send them to private schools. ""Parents (should be) given the ability to do everything in their power to get a high quality education in a safe environment'' for their children, said Jimmy Mansour of Putting Children First, the group pushing for the voucher program. Joe Christie, a former Democratic state senator from El Paso and a member of the voucher-support group, contends the Texas Supreme Court ruling that upheld Texas' school finance plan supports the concept of vouchers.

Winter, Phyllis, and Patricia Jones, "School vouchers can help neediest," ***Chicago Tribune,*** **Aug. 3, 1996, p. 18.**
In a letter to the editor, Chicago school principals Phyllis Winter and Patricia Jones point out that until people realize that school vouchers and school choice shouldn't be seen as part of any political agenda, nothing constructive will be done in the arena of education reform.

Back Issues

Great Research on Current Issues Starts Right Here . . . Recent topics covered by The CQ Researcher are listed below. Before May 1991, reports were published under the name of Editorial Research Reports.

JANUARY 1996
Emergency Medicine
Punishing Sex Offenders
Bilingual Education
Helping the Homeless

FEBRUARY 1996
Reforming the CIA
Campaign Finance Reform
Academic Politics
Getting Into College

MARCH 1996
The British Monarchy
Preventing Juvenile Crime
Tax Reform
Pursuing the Paranormal

APRIL 1996
Centennial Olympic Games
Managed Care
Protecting Endangered Species
New Military Culture

MAY 1996
Russia's Political Future
Marriage and Divorce
Year-Round Schools
Taiwan, China and the U.S.

JUNE 1996
Rethinking NAFTA
First Ladies
Teaching Values
Labor Movement's Future

JULY 1996
Recovered-Memory Debate
Native Americans' Future
Crackdown on Sexual Harassment
Attack on Public Schools

AUGUST 1996
Fighting Over Animal Rights
Privatizing Government Services
Child Labor and Sweatshops
Cleaning Up Hazardous Wastes

SEPTEMBER 1996
Gambling Under Attack
The States and Federalism
Civic Journalism
Reassessing Foreign Aid

OCTOBER 1996
Political Consultants
Insurance Fraud
Rethinking School Integration
Parental Rights

NOVEMBER 1996
Global Warming
Clashing Over Copyright
Consumer Debt
Governing Washington, D.C.

DECEMBER 1996
Welfare, Work and the States
The New Volunteerism
Implementing the Disabilities Act
America's Pampered Pets

JANUARY 1997
Combating Scientific Misconduct
Restructuring the Electric Industry
The New Immigrants
Chemical and Biological Weapons

FEBRUARY 1997
Assisting Refugees
Alternative Medicine's Next Phase
Independent Counsels
Feminism's Future

MARCH 1997
New Air Quality Standards
Alcohol Advertising
Civic Renewal
Educating Gifted Students

APRIL 1997
Declining Crime Rates
The FBI Under Fire
Gender Equity in Sports
Space Program's Future

MAY 1997
The Stock Market
The Cloning Controversy
Expanding NATO
The Future of Libraries

JUNE 1997
FDA Reform
China After Deng
Line-Item Veto
Breast Cancer

JULY 1997
Transportation Policy
Executive Pay

Back issues are available for $5.00 (subscribers) or $10.00 (non-subscribers). Quantity discounts apply to orders over ten. To order, call Congressional Quarterly Customer Service at (202) 887-8621.

Binders are available for $18.00. To order call 1-800-638-1710. Please refer to stock number 648.

Future Topics

- ***Aggressive Driving***
- ***Age Bias in the Workplace***
- ***Land Mines***

THE CQ Researcher

PUBLISHED BY CONGRESSIONAL QUARTERLY INC.

Aggressive Driving

Can road designers and police calm motorists down?

The explosive anger that leads drivers to sometimes deadly road disputes, often termed "road rage," has dramatized the rise in aggressive driving. Two-thirds of last year's more than 41,000 auto deaths are blamed on aggressive driving — such as speeding, cutting off other motorists and tailgating. In several states, police are beefing up enforcement, and legislators are calling for tougher penalties. Several cities are installing traffic-calming measures like narrowed streets to slow down drivers. But citizens in much of the nation must battle entrenched state highway bureaucracies, whose road standards make roads as fast as possible for cars — often at the expense of walkers, bicyclists and livable communities.

INSIDE THIS ISSUE

CQ July 25, 1997 • Volume 7, No. 28 • Pages 649-672

Formerly Editorial Research Reports

COVER: A RED-LIGHT CAMERA IN SAN FRANCISCO CAPTURES A STATION WAGON AFTER IT RAN A RED LIGHT FIVE SECONDS AFTER THE LIGHT TURNED RED AND HIT A CAB AT 30 MPH. (INSURANCE INSTITUTE FOR HIGHWAY SAFETY)

CQ Researcher

July 25, 1997
Volume 7, No. 28

The CQ Researcher (ISSN 1056-2036). Formerly Editorial Research Reports. Published weekly, except Jan. 3, May 30, Aug. 29, Oct. 31, by Congressional Quarterly Inc., 1414 22nd St., N.W., Washington, D.C. 20037. Annual subscription rate for libraries, businesses and government is $340. Additional rates furnished upon request. Periodicals postage paid at Washington, D.C., and additional mailing offices. POSTMASTER: Send address changes to The CQ Researcher, 1414 22nd St., N.W., Washington, D.C. 20037.

Aggressive Driving

By Sarah Glazer

The Issues

It's rush hour in rural Brewster, N.Y., and Manhattan-bound commuters are backed up for three miles on the two-lane road out of town.

State Trooper Alan S. Kurlander sees so much aggressive driving as he cruises the scene that he could write out tickets all morning. Within five minutes, he spots two typical violators — a red Blazer weaving onto the right shoulder and a white Camry crossing the center line — cutting ahead of other drivers.

You can feel the anxiety building as the stalled commuters count the minutes until they can floor it on I-684. Troopers say the 55 mph Interstate has become a "racetrack," with motorists clocked at speeds over 100 mph.

Harried commuters, many of them escapees from the city, treat their Interstate drive like a subway ride.

"Every day, I see people shaving, putting on nail polish, lipstick, eyeliner and reading the paper while they're driving," Trooper Darren Daughtry says. He has seen speeds around bucolic Brewster escalate dangerously over the past few years as downstate urbanites have poured in.

Typical excuses for irresponsible driving — "Another guy cut me off," "I'm late for work" — and a sense of self-righteous entitlement have grown too, troopers say. "Nobody wants to be responsible for their actions," says Sgt. Michael Gadomski. "Civility is going down the tubes."

The stories are almost comical, but the consequences are not. In local incidents reminiscent of nationally publicized "road rage" explosions, two female motorists staged a high-speed passing duel, then stopped to continue the fight, one wielding a baseball bat; another motorist who

pulled over to continue a feud was slashed with a knife.

Aggressive driving has suddenly come into the public spotlight as communities across the nation complain about drivers who drive too fast, weave crazily and become enraged when they're passed. Aggressive driving was involved in two-thirds of last year's auto deaths, the National Highway Traffic Safety Administration (NHTSA) estimates.

At recent House Transportation subcommittee hearings on the phenomenon. Chairman Bud Shuster, R-Pa., said that the solution is wider, straighter roads and more of them. * Traffic has increased by 35 percent since 1987 while construction of new roads has grown only 1 percent, according to the NHTSA.

But subcommittee member Earl Blumenauer, D-Ore., said that building more roads would be the equivalent of "giving a wife-beater more room to swing." As Portland's commissioner of public works for 10 years, Blumenauer helped initiate programs like "skinny streets," which narrowed existing streets to slow down traffic in residential areas.

* Hearings were held July 17 before the Subcommittee on Surface Transportation of the House Transportation and Infrastructure Committee.

In lower Westchester County's affluent neighborhoods, where Manhattanites seek to escape city hassles, many parents won't let their children walk or bike to school because of dangerous drivers.

When a pedestrian advocate asks civic association audiences how many members walked or biked to school as children, three-quarters typically raise their hands. But when he asks how many of their children walk or bike, the proportion usually drops to a handful.

"We've lost control of our communities and neighborhoods to the motor vehicle," says Bill Wilkinson, executive director of the Bicycle Federation of America and head of its Campaign to Make America Walkable. "There are places where you can't cross the street without a car."

Americans are more likely to get killed by a car while walking than they are by a stranger with a gun, concluded a recent report by a coalition of environmental and pedestrian/cycling groups. [1]

One reason for the increased danger to pedestrians is that residential areas since World War II have been designed around the car. The study found that the five deadliest places for pedestrians are highway-dominated cities: Fort Lauderdale, Miami, Atlanta, Tampa and Dallas. The safest cities are those where walkers dominate, such as Pittsburgh, Milwaukee, Boston, Rochester, N.Y., and New York City.*

"We see a clear demarcation be-

* The report compared pedestrian fatality rates with the level of pedestrian activity in each city. Because the government does not track the miles walked in each community, the report used U.S. Census data on the percent of people in each community who walk to work as a surrogate for walking activity.

tween older cities and those that grew up around the auto since World War II and now exhibit the auto-dependent sprawl that makes them more dangerous," says James Corless, a spokesman for the Surface Transportation Policy Project, one of the groups that issued the report.

Pedestrian advocates say it's time to redesign cities and suburbs for walkers. In a sign of revolutionary change, the Institute of Transportation Engineers is expected to adopt guidelines for designing streets in new residential developments the old-fashioned way — with wide sidewalks and narrow roadways.

In Virginia, residents and merchants have mobilized against a state plan to widen Route 50, a busy two-lane highway running through historic Middleburg, in the heart of the hunt country. Instead, they are proposing European-style "traffic calming" measures like raised pedestrian crosswalks, cobblestone surfaces and trees planted on both sides of the road to give motorists the impression of narrowness and slow them down. (*See story, p. 654.*)

But the residents have a tough fight ahead. Powerful highway-user groups, including the American Automobile Association (AAA), are fighting efforts to divert federal highway money to pedestrian and cycling uses. These groups contend that much of the aggressive-driving problem is rooted in frustration over congestion on deteriorating roads and bridges, which have not grown to keep up with the burgeoning traffic. The solution, they maintain, is to widen and modernize the roads. [2]

"From a safety perspective, the wider roads of the Interstate system have much lower crash rates than other roads," says Mark Lee Edwards, AAA managing director for traffic safety. "If you look at some of the factors driving the crash experience, it's narrow lanes, no shoulders, narrow bridges, too steep curves and fixed objects like trees next to the roadside, so when people lose control of their vehicle they're colliding with trees — which in a collision kills them." [3]

City of West Palm Beach

Traffic-calming measures in West Palm Beach, Fla., include landscaped mini-traffic circles tended by residents.

But there's a downside to the lower crash rates, Corless says. "If you look at the six-lane strips that are increasingly replacing old two-lane roads, you can say there are not a lot of fatalities, but also no one walks on them. You're crazy to walk on them. There are no sidewalks, shopping centers are set far back from the road and it's difficult to make public transit work in those places."

Blumenauer sees a connection between lax penalties for aggressive drivers and cities oriented around the needs of cars. Portland, Ore., was the first city in the nation to enact legislation allowing the cars of repeat drunken drivers to be confiscated. More recently, Portland has initiated programs to impound cars of motorists driving with a suspended license or without proof of insurance. [4]

"I think a subculture has developed of people who think they can do anything they want with the car," Blumenauer says, citing repeat drunken drivers and "aggressive and belligerent" commuters who cut through residential neighborhoods at high speeds, endangering children and walkers. "We've had a generation of engineers who enable that behavior," he adds. "Streets are wider, and speed limits are designed to move traffic rather than deal with the impact the street has on the community."

Yet most drivers whose aggressive driving lands them in crashes are ordinary people — not chronic criminals, according to Patricia Waller, director of the University of Michigan Transportation Research Institute. Just 6-7 percent of the nation's drivers account for all the crashes in any one year, Waller notes. But even if those drivers were taken off the road, it would make no difference in the number of crashes, because only a small proportion of them are chronic bad drivers. For many it's a first-time crash.

"People are more pressured and have less time — particularly women," Waller says. "Women are working full time. When you look at non-work trips, men's are to the football game; women's are to the

Continued on p. 654

'Calm' Streets Help Revive West Palm Beach

Not much more than three years ago, downtown West Palm Beach was considered too dangerous to visit at night. Its streets were deserted, its shops struggling.

Today, children splash 15 feet from a major intersection in a newly installed fountain. Parents relax on comfortable benches, eating ice cream and watching their kids. Cars driving through downtown must slow down to negotiate crosswalks that have been raised to the level of the curb, permitting pedestrians, parents pushing strollers and wheelchair users to cross easily.

The new vitality is largely the work of the city's dynamic mayor, Nancy Graham, and the planners she brought in to redesign the city. Internationally recognized Canadian civil engineer Ian Lockwood, whom Graham hired as the city's transportation planner, says West Palm Beach's problems were typical of cities designed according to traditional traffic engineering standards.

"If you look at any transportation model for a city, the success of the city is based on how well the car is accommodated," Lockwood says. In West Palm Beach, "The car was fine, but our city was dead 10 years ago. The street became the monopoly of the car to the exclusion of pedestrians."

In cooperation with several noted urban designers, Lockwood hopes to have the entire eastern part of the city "traffic-calmed" in five years using techniques that have been employed successfully in Europe for the past 25 years.

Six-lane U.S. 1, which slices through the city in two broad swaths, one in each direction, will be reduced to two separate two-lane roads. To make "nice slow streets that are very pedestrian friendly," Lockwood says, sidewalks will be widened, landscaping will be added on both sides and shady patios will be created on the sidewalks where people can sit and have a cool drink. "Now we have narrow sidewalks, and no one likes to walk along them," he explains.

The move has won support from initially skeptical business groups because of the success in areas that have already received the Lockwood treatment. Commercial rents have risen from $5 per square foot to $25 in downtown areas that have been traffic-calmed. Once half-occupied, commercial buildings now have no vacancies. And downtown is becoming a popular place to live. The city is retrofitting lofts above stores for apartments and combined work-living units. In the next two years, the city expects to have 560 more new homes downtown.

West Palm Beach was founded in 1894 as the servant city for affluent Palm Beach, a quarter-mile away across the Intracoastal Waterway. Today, many waiters, maids and other service personnel who don't own cars walk to work. Forty-eight percent of the city is low-to-moderate income.

To help attract residents downtown, the city is subsidizing purchases by low-income homeowners as well as providing training in such basics as how to fix appliances. The city is also giving tax breaks to residents renovating historic homes.

Lockwood points to a typical inner-city street where the city recently invested $8,000 in traffic calming and beautification. It was lined with boarded-up homes and had become a favorite place for truck drivers to dump garbage. Parking a car on the street was considered unwise. The city is narrowing the street from 35 feet to 25 feet, putting in curbside trees and narrowing every approach to the neighborhood school so children can walk to school without encountering speeding traffic. In similar neighborhoods where the city has already made such changes, Lockwood says, garbage dumping no longer occurs, crime has dropped and homeowners take newfound pride in the upkeep of the neighborhood.

Typically, streets that have been traffic-calmed have 50 percent fewer collisions than conventionally designed streets and 80 percent fewer fatalities, according to Lockwood. When traffic is slowed to below 20 mph, stopping distances are shorter, the field of vision is wider and a driver is more likely to see a child running into the street from behind a parked car. The city has not had a single collision on a traffic-calmed street, Lockwood says.

The changes have not been without their opponents. "I get calls from commuters who say, 'Your job is to move cars as fast as possible,'" Lockwood says. "I say, my job is to make the city livable and sustainable. I don't think we should sacrifice quality of life in the inner city for people in the suburbs."

Actually, when traffic calming is done right and the streets become more scenic, everyone should be happy, Lockwood maintains. "Drivers will slow down willingly and naturally, kids can cross safely, people can go shopping in harmony with the traffic and business won't dry up."

As part of the city's campaign against traditional thinking, it has instituted a new transportation vocabulary. The word "improvements," which to traffic engineers usually means new car lanes or other ways to move traffic faster, has been banned in favor of the more neutral term "changes." It's no longer permissible to say a road is being "upgraded" when it's really being widened.

In fact, the city no longer uses the term "accident" because it reduces "the degree of responsibility and severity and invokes sympathy for the person responsible," a city memo states. Now, in West Palm, the term is "crash" or "collision."

Rural Virginians Challenged Highway 'Improvements' . . .

The countryside around tiny Middleburg, Va., dotted with horse farms and towns rich in Civil War history, has long been a favorite destination for tourists seeking a charming country drive.

So when the Virginia Department of Transportation (VDOT) threatened to "improve" local roads using conventional traffic engineering standards, the community turned into a hotbed of citizen activism.

It started when residents along the Snickersville Turnpike, a rural road that has changed little since the Civil War, complained about potholes and a crumbling road surface. VDOT responded with a plan to straighten out the curves, widen the barely two-lane road and replace a 19th-century stone arch bridge with concrete and steel.

Turnpike residents were alerted to the department's definition of "improvement" when the state fixed the first section of road. A charming one-lane bridge over a creek was replaced with a concrete culvert that obliterated the view of the creek, and the trees around it were cut down.

The state-funded destruction "appalled" everyone who lived along the road and spurred residents to found the Snickersville Turnpike Association five years ago, according to artist Susan Van Wagoner, vice president of the association. The hardest part was persuading the state to abandon conventional road standards that aim to protect drivers' safety at high speeds by such methods as removing trees that cars can crash into.

"It was a real struggle," she says. "It took an awful lot of citizens doing an awful lot of work."

The association campaigned to throw out an unsympathetic board of supervisors and succeeded in re-electing a new board that supported its fight. Citizens did observational studies to show that the road could accommodate existing traffic and that it was safe because its narrowness and many curves kept speeds down. "We've got farm vehicles, farm animals, deer on the turnpike," Van Wagoner says. "Safety means going slower on this road."

To justify its widening plan, Virginia's Department of Transportation cited the guidebook of standards that governs most road construction in this country — the so-called "Green Book" issued by the American Association of State Highway and Transportation Officials (AASHTO).

Snickersville Turnpike Association

The Snickersville Turnpike has changed little since the Civil War.

"They used AASHTO standards to say this [the existing road] is lower than the standard we can use," Van Wagoner says. "We said, 'We have to have flexibility with these standards.'"

In the end, the state relented and came up with a new design that widens the road only a few feet — from 16 feet at its narrowest point to 19 feet.

"We stopped a project that had gone out for contract bids, which is unheard of," Van Wagoner says. "They rebuilt it in a way everyone loves — farmers and commuters. And we saved money, so they can do more sections of the road. The project was done for half of the planned cost, and the speed limit was lowered to 35 from 55."

Virginia's cookbook approach to roads — typical of most states — may explain why the region's citizens have recently taken on an even more ambitious campaign as part of their effort to defeat another state road-widening plan. Instead, they want to turn local Route 50 into the first rural road in the nation to use European-style traffic-calming measures.

Continued from p. 652

grocery store, to do the laundry, pick up the kids. When you're charged $1 for every minute you're late picking up a child at nursery school, you'll probably speed and be less patient with other drivers."

As concern mounts over aggressive driving, here are some of the questions being asked:

Is aggressive driving a major safety hazard?

In a recent poll conducted by the Potomac chapter of the AAA, motorists in the Washington, D.C., metropolitan area identified aggressive driving as the top threat to highway safety, ahead of drunken driving. Most thought the problem was getting worse. (*See "At Issue," p. 665.*)

Even more surprising, one out of two motorists surveyed admitted to aggressive driving themselves in the last year. The sins confessed most frequently were speeding (65 percent), gesturing and exchanging words with another driver (8 percent), slowing down and speeding up to get even with another driver (6 percent) and tailgating (6 percent).

. . . and Saved Their Charming Country Roads

Route 50 is a busy highway connecting commuters between Washington, D.C., and the rolling foothills of the Blue Ridge Mountains.

It slices through the center of Middleburg and several other historic Virginia towns, but is so fast-moving that residents complain it is often unsafe to cross. Drivers are often halfway through the smaller villages before they are aware they have entered a town.

A coalition of local merchants and residents wants to convert Route 50 into an old-fashioned main street that people could cross safely and that would invite motorists to stop and shop.

The Route 50 Corridor Coalition has put together an ambitious two-volume plan, designed through community meetings with the help of transportation planner Ian Lockwood, of West Palm Beach, Fla. [1]

Route 50 Corridor Coalition

A local coalition wants to turn parts of Virginia's Route 50 into an old-fashioned main street.

The plan envisions community-designed entranceways to small towns, such as stone walls; parking lanes paved in distinctive materials to make the road appear narrower; placing cobblestone strips across the road to alert motorists to slower speed limits; raising crosswalks to the level of the curb so that motorists must slow down and so pedestrians with strollers can cross more easily; building out sidewalk curbs at intersections so pedestrians have a shorter distance to cross; and lower speed limits through the towns.

The coalition was formed in response to a state plan to build a bypass around Middleburg and widen the highway from two lanes to a multi-lane divided highway.

"Bypasses tend to kill small towns," says Van Wagoner, chair of the coalition's steering committee. "Business people were very concerned about that." The plan has won strong support from merchants, who see it as a way to attract customers. The department last year abandoned the bypass project for lack of community support.

The coalition's plan has been approved by the Middleburg Town Council, but it has yet to win approval from the state transportation department. The department has so far regarded the unconventional community plan with skepticism on the grounds that Route. 50 was designed to carry a large volume of traffic. [2]

Currently, residents say, the existing highway makes it hard for pedestrians in the tiny town of Upperville to cross the road safely from a parking area on one side of the road to pick up children from the day-care center across the street. Moreover, a survey of tourists in the area indicated that one reason they came was to drive on country roads. "They said, 'If you put suburbia there, we're not coming'" Van Wagoner reports.

As for cost, she estimates that the 20 miles of traffic-calming measures proposed would be half the price tag of the proposed $34 million bypass. Most important, she says, it's what the citizens want.

"It's not somebody sitting in Richmond with a standards book deciding everything," she says. "These are the people who use the roads; they're the ones who should be involved in designing it."

---

[1] Route 50 Corridor Coalition, *A Traffic Calming Plan for Virginia's Rural Route 50 Corridor* (1996).

[2] See Michael Janofsky, "Answer to Gathering Stampede of Autos: Whoa!" *The New York Times*, Jan. 7, 1997, p. A10.

When asked the reasons for their behavior, the most common answer was running late for appointments, followed by anger over another driver's actions. [5]

Despite the widespread perception that aggressive driving is a growing problem, there are no government statistics to back up the assertion. That's partly because there is no generally accepted definition of aggressive driving, says Brian G. Traynor, chief of traffic law enforcement the NHTSA.

Speaking as a Washington-area commuter, however, Traynor thinks the problem is getting worse. "Years ago, you would only see one person you considered to be a nut every two or three weeks," he says. "Now, you see two or three every day on the way to work. That's a fairly good indication to me that aggressive driving is increasing. It's hard to define, but you know it when you see it."

Lisa Sheikh, a child welfare expert, started Citizens Against Speeding and Aggressive Driving after she moved to Washington from New York City two years ago. "I was astonished by the speeding, the red-light running, the very aggressive driving behavior," she says. "I really began to think about the possibility that a lot of crashes are not accidents — they're the result of unlawful driving behavior."

With her interest in children's issues, Sheikh saw aggressive driving as a particularly "raw deal for kids." She discovered that many area parents were complaining they couldn't let their kids into the front yard anymore because drivers were zooming by at 60 mph on streets where the limit was 25 mph.

Sheikh's group is seeking tougher penalties for aggressive drivers, taking Mothers Against Drunk Driving (MADD) as its model. The group contends that local laws treat them too lightly, unless a crash involves alcohol or road dueling. Moreover, she charges, police don't enforce existing traffic laws because they are focused on hard-core crime.

National data appear to support Sheikh's perceptions about lack of enforcement. One of the reasons is that the number of drivers and vehicle miles traveled has risen faster than the availability of officers for routine traffic enforcement, according to the Insurance Institute for Highway Safety, a research organization supported by auto insurers.

In October, the mother of a police officer who belongs to Sheikh's group was killed in Maryland in a head-on collision with a young driver going twice the speed limit. "The kid paid a few tickets and walked away," Sheikh says. "People are getting away with murder. If people are using their car as a weapon, I think the answer is taking their car away."

Around the country, several state and local police departments — including those in Maryland, Arizona and New York — have organized enforcement programs aimed specifically at aggressive driving. Maryland State Police started a campaign against aggressive drivers in 1995 after fatalities surged 35 percent in the first three months over the previous period in 1994.

City of West Palm Beach

A gazebo slows traffic through an intersection in Seaside, Fla.

"The superintendent said, 'Find out why,' " recalls Lt. Michael Fischer. "It wasn't speed or one particular offense. It was a multitude of offenses — inattentiveness, following too closely, improper lane changes, driving on the shoulder, some alcohol offenses."

On Memorial Day weekend in 1995, Maryland troopers began saturating high-accident areas with both marked patrol cars and "covert" vehicles — tractor trailers, dump trucks, lawn-mowing tractors — which radioed aggressive driving behavior to patrol cars. Thousands of citations were issued. In addition, a public information campaign encouraging motorists to report unsafe drivers by "dialing" #77 on their cellular phones has produced hundreds of calls a month to state police. In the first quarter of 1996, fatalities were down 14 percent. They fell another 3 percent in the first quarter of 1997, according to Fischer.

Maryland police can nab drivers for a wide range of violations already on the books, but headquarters also gives them a working definition to use in seeking out the aggressive driver — one who operates a vehicle in "a bold or pushy manner" endangering the lives and property of other motorists.

Few attempts have been made to quantify the extent of aggressive driving. But earlier this year the AAA Foundation for Traffic Safety, AAA's research arm, released a study counting incidents of violence that have come to be known as "road rage."

The AAA study, drawing on newspaper articles and police reports, counted 10,037 incidents since 1990 in which angry motorists injured, killed or attempted to hurt other motorists. At least 218 people were killed and 12,610 injured in those incidents.

One of the most highly publicized incidents occurred on the George Washington Memorial Parkway in Virginia, just outside Washington, in April 1996. Two dueling male drivers lost control of their cars at 80 mph, crossed the median and hit two oncoming vehicles. Only one of the four drivers involved in the crash survived. Narkey Terry, a computer technician, was sentenced to 10 years in prison for his role in the incident.

Such incidents increased 51 percent between 1990 and 1995, the AAA study showed. In 37 percent of the cases, a firearm was used; in 35 percent the weapon was the vehicle itself. [6]

The majority of the drivers involved were young, poorly educated males with criminal records, histories of violence and drug or alcohol problems. Many had recently suffered an emotional or professional setback such as a divorce or losing a job or girlfriend.

But hundreds of such incidents involved apparently successful men and women with no known histories of crime who appeared to have suddenly snapped, the report found. In a 1995 case, a Maryland lawyer and former state legislator, Robin Ficker, was driving his two sons to visit his ailing father at the hospital when he bumped into a Jeep in front of him. The driver, Caroline Goldman, said that when she approached his car, Ficker began yelling and struck her in the face, breaking her eyeglasses. Ficker was convicted of battery and malicious destruction of property.

The study also found numerous cases of road violence triggered by "inane" causes. A 23-year-old Indiana University student attacked a campus maintenance worker with a hatchet after the two argued about the student's car being parked in a service drive. In another case, a man was shot and killed "because he was driving too slowly." [7]

Critics say the study is far from a scientific count and merely represents the culling of incidents so extreme and so rare that they have made the front page. Moreover, the dozens of road-rage fatalities counted annually pale in comparison with the total number of traffic deaths caused each year — over 41,000 in 1996, or more than 100 deaths every day — by more typical bad driving. [8]

"From our standpoint, [road rage] is more of a criminal matter than it is aggressive driving," Sgt. Terence J. McDonnell, program manager in highway safety for the New York State Police, commented on the AAA study.

The new concern about aggressive driving is coming after several years in which automobile death rates in the United States have been declining.

"Over the years, we've become much better drivers — if you look at the fatality rate per 100 million miles driven," Waller says. "The rate in the 1960s was between five and six deaths; three was a barrier people never thought we'd cross; it's well under two at this point."

But the statistics may be more reflective of demographic trends than individual driving behavior. The country's growing urbanization over the last three decades has been an important factor in falling fatality rates, Waller notes. Rural crashes are more likely to be fatal than those in cities because they occur at higher speeds, and medical attention takes longer to arrive.

Yet urban and suburban areas tend to have more frequent crashes and higher rates of injury from crashes than rural areas because the vehicles are more concentrated. Judging from insurance claims, injuries from city crashes have been increasing in recent years. [9]

Running red lights and other traffic signals is the No. 1 cause of urban crashes, which are more likely to cause injuries than any other kind of crash, according to the Insurance Institute for Highway Safety. If a recent study is any indication, red-light running has become a surprisingly frequent form of law-breaking. In a morning rush hour study of a busy intersection in Arlington, Va., a car ran a red light every five minutes. As a group, the lawbreakers were younger, less likely to use safety belts, had poorer driving records and drove smaller and older vehicles than drivers who stopped for red lights. [10]

Since 1975, pedestrian deaths have accounted for 13-17 percent of the deaths involving motor vehicles, according to the institute. However, pedestrian deaths as a percentage of the population have gone down 39 percent between 1975 and 1995. Even more dramatic is the decline in pedestrian deaths among children — 70 percent over the same period.

But pedestrian and bicycling advocates suggest fatalities may have declined because people have been forced indoors. "It's not that kids are crossing streets and getting killed," Sheikh says. "What we're hearing is kids can't cross the street by themselves anymore. You always have to be with them." A recent article in the *British Medical Journal* noted that a substantial proportion of the decline in children's deaths from traffic accidents in England appeared to be linked to children walking and cycling less in 1992 than 1985. [11]

"The prudent person is likely to look out there and say, 'It's not worth my life to turn into the street anymore,' " the bicycle federation's Wilkinson says.

American motorists seem to divide culturally between cautious types who keep to the speed limit and hurried drivers who consider themselve more competent on the road. The recent AAA Potomac poll reporting an upsurge of concern over aggressive driving prompted local editorials calling the concern exaggerated and pointing the finger at timid, slow drivers.

"On the highway, there's always some guy who likes to pretend the 55 mph speed limit is the real speed limit (nobody drives 55 unless there's a trooper about) and hogs the passing

How to Keep Your Anger Off the Road

Psychiatrist John A. Larson, director of the Institute of Stress Medicine in Norwalk, Conn., and author of Steering Clear of Highway Madness, *conducts seminars for motorists in controlling aggressive driving. He says there are five crucial decision points that make it possible to avoid anger on the road:*

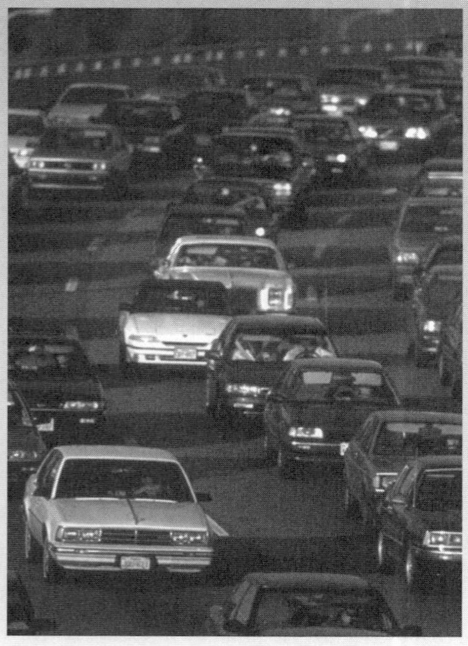

1. Plan more time for the trip than you think you need. If it's an hour or less, allow 50 percent more time, if its three hours, allow 30 percent more time. "If you plan the travel time really tight, anything that slows you down will make you angry," Larson says.

2. When you see another car going faster than yours, say, "This is a place where I have to let go of competition."

3. Be good to yourself in your car. Have tapes on hand with the type of music you enjoy, keep food and drink in your car for long trips. Think of driving as pleasurable in itself, not just wasted time until you get to your destination.

4. When you see someone you don't like — a reckless teenager, a dawdling grandma, an obnoxious pickup driver or a stuck-up Porsche driver — don't take it out on them. Welcome diversity.

5. Don't try to "teach someone a lesson" for bad driving. Leave punishment to the police. Remember that if someone cuts you off, it's not worth it to act provocatively. They could have a gun or a knife.

lane. Passing on the right is, of course, not the ideal thing — but what else are you supposed to do?" wrote automotive columnist Eric Peters. [12]

That attitude drives Sheikh crazy. She points out that drivers are not supposed to exceed the speed limit even when passing. "This is the work we have ahead to make these behaviors socially unacceptable so people won't blame other drivers," she says.

Sgt. McDonnell acknowledges that many drivers seem unaware the left lane is supposed to be the passing lane, and that their slowness can precipitate an accident with a hurried driver. "Accidents that occur from people trying to go in the right lane to pass tend to be horrible accidents involving tens of cars," he says.

In fact, the insistence on being the passing driver appears to be at the root of many "road rage" incidents. Of 187 highway incidents investigated in summer 1987 in Los Angeles where firearms were brandished, two-thirds involved cars that were passing, merging or entering the highway. [13]

Do government transportation policies favor motorists over pedestrians?

If critics of America's auto dependency were asked for the main reason why communities are so unpleasant for walkers, the culprit unquestionably would be "The Green Book." Put out by the American Association of State Highway and Transportation Officials (AASHTO), the manual guides traffic engineers in laying out most U.S. roads today. [14]

Interstates and other major highways receiving federal funds as part of the 161,000-mile National Highway System must follow the AASHTO standards as a condition of funding. Most states choose to follow the standards when building or improving smaller roads and streets as well. Critics say the standards elevate the needs of traffic flow above other important considerations, like quiet, friendly, walkable streets.

" 'The Green Book' is supposed to be a set of guidelines, and it says planners should be flexible and use judgment, but everyone [in traffic engineering] forgets that and follows it blindly," says Ian Lockwood, an internationally recognized planner who is helping to revitalize West Palm Beach, Fla., by putting pedestrians first. (*See story, p. 653.*) "One book can't possibly take into account the needs of every community, so we get a generic road fitted into every community."

"Community after community has been ruined to move cars faster," agrees Rep. Blumenauer. "They lose their character; they lose their charm. It kills the street." Blumenauer charges that designs guided by the standards have produced deserted downtowns and residential neighborhoods where crime flourishes because pedestrians' needs have been ignored in favor of roads that are too wide, too fast and encourage speeding.

In rural and suburban areas, such design standards are equally destructive, critics say. "Traffic engineers will say, 'This road is a minor arterial and should have a design speed of 50,' " says Wilkinson. "There go your trees, your old bridge. They say they'll make it four lanes. Where are you going to walk, where am I going to ride my bike?"

The genesis of fast-moving roads in residential areas can be traced partly to a historical anomaly, says Frank Spielberg, a traffic consultant in Annandale, Va. Most states are barred by law from posting speed limits below 25 mph. Starting in the 1950s, state legislatures enacted the 25 mph floor to curb small-town speed traps, which frequently posted artificially low speeds to raise revenue through speeding tickets.

In addition, Spielberg says, engineers tend to design roads even faster than they need to be. "If you're a good traffic engineer and someone tells you, 'We're going to post 25 mph,' you say, 'I'm going to leave a factor of safety.' So you design the street [wider] using 30 mph design standards. But, of course, the 30 mph standards also have a factor of safety built into them, which means a motorist would really feel comfortable on a nice day driving 35-40 mph. We apply these standards to neighborhoods where people want to go 25 mph, and then we wonder why people call us to complain about speeding."

Wider, faster streets have become entrenched in many zoning codes and local laws that incorporate "Green Book" standards. To some extent, fear of lawsuits drives the blind adherence to the standards, according to experts.

"Many traffic engineers are afraid if they permit someone to build a smaller street and there's an accident, there would be tort liability," says Spielberg. One of the objections that traffic engineers often make to narrow roads is that they wouldn't allow rescue vehicles to get through. However, demonstrations in Portland, Ore., and other cities where the streets were narrowed showed that rescue vehicles weren't delayed.

In a sign that this worldview is under challenge from within the profession, a committee of the Institute of Traffic Engineers is recommending design standards for new residential subdivisions that reject conventional suburbia and embrace the "New Urbanism" movement. New towns built on this model — typically traditional-looking communities with sidewalks, front porches and easy walking distances to shops — include Kentlands, near Gaithersburg, Md.; Laguna West, near Sacramento, Calif.; and Seaside, a resort community on Florida's Gulf Coast.

"What we're saying is, 'Let's design the streets from the beginning so you encourage slow traffic,' " explains Spielberg, who chairs the committee. "Let's not design streets 36 feet wide with no parking and expect people to drive down them at 25 mph." Spielberg believes the report will also go a long way toward assuaging traffic engineers' fears of lawsuits. The new guidelines can "go on an engineer's shelf, so he sees, 'Here is something that supports building smaller streets,' " he says.

The committee's recommendations are intended to mimic authentic, old-style urban neighborhoods such as Georgetown in Washington, D.C., and Old Town, in Alexandria, Va. The two historic communities, their narrow streets lined with 18th- and 19th-century townhouses and small shops, are popular spots for strolling. The new guidelines recommend maximum speeds of 20 mph; on-street parking to provide a buffer for walkers from traffic; sidewalks wide enough for strollers to walk companionably two abreast; and squared-off corners that don't permit wide, sweeping turns at high speed.

Unlike roads in new subdivisions that allow two directions of traffic, the new guidelines encourage streets so narrow that there's only enough room for one lane of traffic, and cars must pull over into the parking lane to accommodate an oncoming vehicle.

"We have 80 years of stark precedent showing people will pull over," Spiegel says, pointing to typical city side-streets. In another diversion from conventional suburbia, the guidelines discourage cul de sacs, or dead ends, because drivers avoid them, which tends to shift traffic to neighboring streets rather than dispersing it.

The committee's proposal is "one of the most heartening and encouraging things we've seen come out of the traditional engineering community in the last few years," Wilkinson says.

Spielberg is optimistic that the institute will adopt the new guidelines before the end of the year. But he says some older traffic engineers have raised safety concerns about the narrower streets and the right-angle corners designed to force turning vehicles to slow down. Spiegel counters, "If you're hit by a car traveling less than 20 mph, you have a pretty good chance of surviving, but if you're hit by a car going 35, you will probably get killed."

The concepts proposed by Spiegel's committee, often described as "traffic calming" when applied to existing cities, are catching on in communities across the country. Seattle, Portland and West Palm Beach, Fla., are among the cities that have embraced the approach.

But pedestrian activists say they often have to fight old ideas and entrenched bureaucracies in state transportation departments. "It's almost like trying to turn a supertanker on a dime," Corless says. "State departments of transportation were set up to do one thing: build big roads.

It's very hard to get DOTs to think about pedestrian safety or bike facilities, yet these agencies have the ultimate authority."

Susan Van Wagoner, an artist and pedestrian activist in Middleburg, Va., can attest to the difficulties. It started when residents along the Snickersville Turnpike, a rural road that has changed little since the Civil War, complained about potholes and a crumbling road surface. The Virginia Department of Transportation (VDOT) responded with a plan to straighten out the curves, widen the barely two-lane road and replace a 19th-century stone arch bridge with a concrete and steel one. Van Wagoner and other residents convinced the VDOT to deviate from its usual standards. But not before a one-lane bridge over a creek had been destroyed. (*See story, p. 654.*)

West Palm Beach, built for servants working in affluent Palm Beach, also has laws and zoning codes barring street-life. But with support from Mayor Nancy Graham, all that is changing.

The city has started a long-term plan to bring urban vitality to a downtown that most people were afraid to enter at night only a few years ago.

"In West Palm Beach, a child can wait 20 minutes for a bus two feet from cars, but a tree can't be placed in the same place for safety reasons," Lockwood notes. Typically, zoning codes prohibit tree planting close to the street, because traffic engineers consider trees "obstacles" that can cause fatal car crashes.

"I put trees two feet from the street wherever I can," Lockwood says with a laugh. "Wherever codes or rules get in our way, we change them." The city's codes, for example, barred placing sidewalk cafes next to the street. So "we just changed the rules," Lockwood says. "And we're going to keep changing the rules until we get the city we want."

Advocates for more walkable cities have long argued that federal spending is unfairly tilted toward automobile traffic. Mass transit should be a crucial component of transportation planning, notes Jeffrey Blum, transportation policy director of Citizen Action, because "You can't have a walkable city without a good transit system to get in and out."

Currently, Blumenauer says, the federal government's contributions to local transportation projects are not based on what reduces pollution or congestion. "If the federal government pays for 80 percent of a road and only half of a transit system, it biases you toward cars," he says.

Blumenauer notes that the U.S. Tax Code allows him to give his employees tax-free parking privileges, but if he subsidizes a bus or rail pass it's taxable. Blumenauer has introduced legislation in Congress that would give equal treatment to people who drive and use mass transit.

Much of the fight over more funding for walking, cycling and mass transit will focus this year on the multibillion-dollar federal bill that funds the nation's highways — the reauthorization of the 1991 Intermodal Surface Transportation Efficiency Act, better known as ISTEA. [15]

Pedestrian advocates note that only about 1 percent of federal highway safety funds under ISTEA are spent on pedestrian safety, although pedestrians account for about 14 percent of motor vehicle-related deaths. The Surface Transportation Policy Project is pushing for more spending on measures such as traffic-calming islands, traffic circles and street narrowing. But highway users are fighting such moves.

"We're concerned that too much highway money is being won by non-highway interests," says Bill Jackman, a spokesman for AAA, which is fighting the diversion of funds from highway construction. "The highways and bridges are going down the tubes." AAA Potomac spokesman Lon Anderson blames the increasingly aggressive driving on the congestion in a transportation system "strained to its limits."

"Are they saying we should have not 40,000 miles of Interstate but 300,000?" Blum asks. "In many places, you could argue that you could not put in enough lanes to accommodate all the cars. There isn't enough land to do it." In many cities, he notes, 50 percent of the land area is already given over to the needs of autos, including roads, garages and gas stations.

"If there were no mass transit system in Philadelphia," he says, "you'd have to pave over all of downtown to get everyone into the city." ■

BACKGROUND

Societal Stress

Driving has been associated with aggression at least since chariots raced around the Circus Maximus in ancient Rome amid cheers of spectators. In the modern era, Madison Avenue and car manufacturers have appropriated images of aggressive animals and weapons in marketing cars with names like Jaguar, Wildcat, Charger, Cutlass and Challenger. "Ritualized dueling" has also become embedded in auto culture through hot-rod racing and freeway passing, observes Raymond W. Novaco, a psychologist at the University of California-Irvine, who studies the psychological and physiological effects of traffic stress. [16]

The phenomenon of highway violence gained media attention in recent years during a series of shootings

Continued on p. 662

Chronology

1890s The first traffic accidents are reported.

May 30, 1896
The first known U.S. auto accident occurs in New York City when a man driving a Duryea Motor Wagon collides with a bicycle rider, whose leg is fractured.

Sept. 13, 1899
New York real estate broker Henry H. Bliss, 68, becomes the nation's first recorded automobile fatality when he is run over by a car while alighting from a trolley.

1900s Federal government begins coordinating state and local road-building.

1914
The American Association of State Highway Officials sets highway standards that will determine the fast-moving, car-friendly nature of most American roads for years to come.

1916
President Woodrow Wilson signs the Federal Aid Highway Act, requiring states to match federal highway funds, thus beginning the expansion of the national road network.

1920s-1930s
Zoning laws and New Deal programs help to create the auto suburb, in which residents must drive to accomplish most errands.

1926
Zoning in Cleveland is ruled constitutional by the Supreme Court in *Euclid v. Ambler*.

1933
New Dealers initiate the Home Owners Loan Corporation to refinance foreclosed mortgages and guarantee mortgages, stoking suburban home sales.

1934
The Roosevelt administration admits urban routes to the federal highway program, providing free federal funds for roads while trains receive only loans.

1940s-1960s
The postwar boom in suburban development and massive roadbuilding projects help to cement Americans' dependence on the car.

1947
The first postwar Levittown rises on Long Island, setting the model for car-based suburbs.

1956
The federal Interstate Highway System funded by gas tax receipts is established.

1968
The student revolution in Europe spurs a revolution against the growing dominance of the automobile in Holland, as architecture students place benches and other roadblocks in the streets to slow traffic down. The movement gives rise to "traffic-calming" measures in Europe in the 1970s.

1980s Violence erupts around the country as drivers dispute road privileges.

1982
A wave of freeway shootings erupts in Houston, resulting in 12 traffic-related homicides.

1987
Approximately 70 shootings and one stabbing are reported over the summer on Southern California roads. In the fall, another outbreak follows in St. Louis with 22 confirmed shootings.

1989
Media reports of California road violence diminish, but state police statistics show violent incidents actually rose.

1990s The traffic engineering profession and a growing number of cities investigate traffic-calming. Police in several states start crackdowns on aggressive drivers.

Memorial Day Weekend 1995
Maryland State Police initiate an enforcement campaign against aggressive drivers.

1997
A committee of the Institute of Transportation Engineers recommends new residential street standards in keeping with traditional walkable neighborhoods; on July 17, a House Transportation subcommittee holds hearings on aggressive driving.

How Holland Calmed Things Down

While the automobile conquered America over the course of several decades, the same transformation occurred so quickly in Holland that it sparked a revolt overnight.

Between 1960 and 1970, the use of cars in Holland increased dramatically. The revolt started in Delft in the late 1960s when residents, fed up with cars speeding through their neighborhoods, tore up the brick pavement one night so that cars were forced to travel in a serpentine pattern at greatly reduced speeds. Architecture students, influenced by the 1968 student revolts sweeping Europe, placed benches and trees in the middle of the streets to slow cars down.

"Everybody remembered our children were playing here five years ago, and now it's dangerous," recalls Boudewijn Bach, a professor in the architecture department at the Technical University of Delft and one of the nation's leading experts on the Dutch invention known as traffic-calming. "People said, 'We want our streets back.' "

Out of this movement arose the neighborhood concept known as the *woonerf,* which means "living yard" or "residential yard." The woonerf is a residential neighborhood protected from trucks and other through-traffic with speed humps and signs indicating the entrances and exits to the area. Instead of segregating pedestrians from cars with curbs, the woonerf integrates all types of traffic on the road surface but gives pedestrians priority over cars. It uses visual clues such as different kinds of pavement to indicate where cars may be parked.

Trees, play equipment, speed-reduction bumps and bends in the roadway all conspire in a woonerf to force cars to reduce their speeds to 12 mph — about the same pace as walking a horse or riding a bicycle, according to Bach. Accidents have been reduced in the woonerf by about 50 percent. In addition, the severity of injuries has also declined because of the slow speeds. [1]

By 1980, some 260 towns in Holland had some version of a woonerf. The woonerf concept was adapted by German planners and called "traffic tranquilization," from which the English term "traffic calming" was derived. The first traffic-calming projects began in Germany in 1976, and by the end of the decade it was a widely accepted policy. Traffic calming spread quickly through Europe, Australia, New Zealand and Japan. More recently, it has been introduced into some cities in Canada and the U.S.

The weakening Dutch economy in the late 1970s made the woonerf — with its custom paving and many traffic obstacles — too expensive for most cities. Since then, towns have adopted a modified version for residential areas, known as a 30 kmh zone, where cars travel about 20 mph.

In both kinds of areas, the visual cues are such that the driver does not become aggressive, says Bach. "You must show the driver how he has to behave," he says, and the message is, "You are just a guest here." In addition, obstacles in the road translate as dangerous to the car, Bach says, and make the driver more alert for children and other human activity.

In the small university town of Delft, traffic has been slowed to such a degree through traffic calming that it takes as long to complete a typical trip by car as by bike. Bikes are used in about 40 percent of local trips, according to Bach.

After decades of experimentation, Bach has decided that some of the devices most commonly used in the U.S. to slow drivers don't work. Stop signs just cause drivers to speed up excessively between signs to make up the time they think they've lost, creating more pollution and noise as they accelerate. He prefers roundabouts, or traffic circles, which force drivers to slow down gradually as they maneuver around them. He also dislikes sharp speedbumps, which are uncomfortable for bikes as well as cars to cross. He prefers raised plateau-style intersections the width of a crosswalk, which slow drivers down gradually and more comfortably, as well as providing protection for pedestrians.

Bach sees a new danger on the horizon. Now that Dutch traffic engineers have finally learned to design slow-moving streets, architects and urban planners are caught up in a new fashion for wide streets and long vistas. Those kinds of designs speed up cars, Bach says. Ironically, he notes, Dutch and German traffic engineers, who were once blamed for designing fast-moving streets, have become so indoctrinated into the traffic-calming philosophy that they are the ones putting the brakes on today.

[1] For a history of traffic calming, see Route 50 Corridor Coalition, *A Traffic Calming Plan for Virginia's Rural Route 50 Corridor,* 1996, pp. 23-24.

on Southern California freeways in the summer of 1987, when newspapers reported approximately 70 shootings and one stabbing.

Many people assumed the incidents were spurred at least in part by frustration over growing traffic congestion, particularly at rush hour. In fact, Novaco found that the incidents were distributed over all times of day. Most of the incidents involved a conflict over road privilege.

While some people involved in the shootings had histories of violence that could have broken out in any setting, Novaco has suggested that "some of the shootings might have involved ordinary people undergoing periods of stress who lost control of their impulses."[17]

As an example, he cites the 1987 case of former Wall Street investment banker Arthur K. Salomon, who shot and wounded an unarmed college student on a parkway just north of Manhattan. The conflict began over who had the right to pass and escalated to verbal exchanges when both pulled over to the side of the road. It ended with Salomon shooting the young man as he was starting to walk back to his car, saying he had the license number of Salomon's Mercedes. Salomon, a grandson of one of the founders of Salomon Brothers, pleaded guilty to first-degree assault and was sentenced to 18 months in prison.

Taking Competitiveness on the Road

Psychiatrist John A. Larson, director of the Institute of Stress Medicine in Norwalk, Conn., and author of *Steering Clear of Highway Madness,* believes many incidents of highway anger can be traced to the competitiveness that high-powered professionals carry over from work to the highway.[18] Larson, who conducts seminars on how to control aggressive driving, first started working with heart attack patients whose competitiveness on the highway was one element of stress leading to heart attacks.

"If the prevailing value system and mood of the driver is to win and get there the fastest, that's going to create a situation where he's vulnerable to circumstances where he's going to explode," Larson says. "It's one way of understanding why very affluent people do this."

He adds, "I think one of the things going on in our culture is that these values [of competition] have gained an ascendancy and created a great emphasis on the bottom line — as opposed to personal relationships. The result is that people driving lose their people skills."

A popular misconception after the rash of California shootings in 1987 was that it was a one-time phenomenon, since news reporting of the incidents subsided soon afterwards. According to the California Highway Patrol, however, freeway violence actually increased from 1988 to 1989, though media coverage declined.

Even before the California incidents, a wave of freeway shootings had occurred in Houston in 1982, resulting in 12 homicides. In the year following the violent summer of 1987, there were similar outbreaks in St. Louis and Detroit.

Lowered Inhibitions

Novaco suggests that the anonymity and escape potential of wide-open freeways helps to lower motorists' inhibitions against behaving aggressively. In addition, his research has found that continued exposure to traffic congestion elevates blood pressure, increases negative moods, lowers tolerance for frustration and can lead to more impatient driving habits. His studies have found the most stress among women solo drivers with long commutes — possibly because of the overload of demands from both home and work.

In her 1989 book *Anger: The Misunderstood Emotion,* social psychologist Carol Tavris points to involuntary crowding and the anonymity of the car as elements contributing to "traffic anger."

"The car is the best possible example of an environment where it's typically safe to express anger," she says. "You can yell and shout; no one will yell back at you, and maybe they'll get out of your way." That may explain why soccer moms seem just as likely to yell obscenities and make angry gestures as toughened taxi drivers, she says.

The growing popularity of sport utility vehicles like Suburbans and Jeep-style cars, many marketed to women, only adds to the sense of dominance and the freedom to act angry, she suggests. "I think these are bullying cars, and that's what's expected of them. Women are attracted to them because it is a feeling of power to be above everybody else. People become more invisible to you than if you're in another little car."

Psychologists also point out that the car is a highly personal territorial space. That may explain why owners of new cars often become enraged by the slightest bump or marring and why tempers flare in traffic jams.

"When people are crowded unwillingly, that's stressful," Tavris says. "So is heat, children whining in the back seat. What happens is stress hormones rise, the physical energy rises and if you add provocation you'll feel intensely angry. Why don't passengers in the car feel as angry as the driver? They're not under the same stress."

Novaco cautions that the irritability most commonly observed in commuters is quite different from the assaultive behavior seen in the highly publicized "road rage" incidents. Nevertheless, there are some interesting parallels among ordinary, irritated drivers. A study in London found that 15 percent of males and 11 percent of females stated that, "At times, I felt that I could gladly kill another driver." In surveys including university students and other residents of Southern California, more than 40 percent of males and up to 21 percent of females admitted to chasing drivers who offended them, Novaco found.[19]

Aggressive driving has also been exacerbated by a clash of driving cultures as people move from different parts of the country, Tavris believes.

"I grew up in L.A. when people

were famous for their politeness," she recalls. "If someone signaled, you let them in your lane. Now freeway manners are a joke because of traffic and people coming to California with different rules. There are cultural rules about driving as there are about walking. When you move to New York, you have to walk faster. If you have an ambling pace, which you could get away with in Hawaii, you'll get clobbered."

Postwar America

America's built environment has contributed to fast, aggressive driving, particularly since World War II, city planners and engineers are concluding. In the postwar period, for example, the state highway officials association required that all street-design standards take into account the need to evacuate before a nuclear strike and to clean up demolished neighborhoods afterwards. A 1940s planning text presented a sprawling one-family housing subdivision as more desirable than a compact European city, which was described as the "best target" in case of war. [20]

Under such circumstances, it's not surprising that new subdivisions were no longer walkable neighborhoods, observes the recent report from the Institute of Traffic Engineers proposing more pedestrian-friendly guidelines. Because of zoning legislation dating back to the 1920s, most local governments also required that residences be separated from shops and industry, which had traditionally been viewed as dirty and unhealthful. These zoning laws and the creation of suburbs eventually required most residents to drive virtually everywhere for their daily needs.

America's aging population, however, means more people today need to live in a place where they can walk to shops, doctors and other needs. In cities built around the car, elderly walkers are often the most vulnerable targets for aggressive drivers. While senior citizens made up only 13 percent of the population in 1990, they accounted for 23 percent of pedestrian fatalities. ■

Current Situation

Traffic Calming

A new way of thinking about designing roads is starting to invade the traffic engineering establishment. This month the Federal Highway Administration (FHWA) plans to issue a report urging states to consider local citizens' concerns about issues like aesthetics and historic preservation. The report "highlights the flexibility that exists" in policies governing the design of state roads, which permits divergence from national design standards, says Harold Peaks, leader of the FHWA group that is producing the report. [21]

At the Institute of Transportation Engineers' last convention, the session on "traffic calming" drew some 500 people, reflecting the burgeoning interest in the field.

"I would say just about every community in the U.S. is starting to look into traffic calming," Lockwood says. But, he adds, "It's going to take a major paradigm shift in thinking in the transportation world. All our legislation and guidelines and standards are rooted in concepts that were born in the golden age of the automobile."

Seattle is one of the cities most often cited for embracing traffic-calming measures. Small traffic circles placed in the middle of neighborhood intersections, sometimes adorned with small gardens, have been the single most effective and popular method for traffic calming, according to city Transportation Department planner Stuart Goldsmith.

"It cuts down accidents up to 90 percent because the traffic has to slow down and bear right," he says. The city has also added curves to existing streets to slow down traffic. On some four-lane streets, the number of lanes is reduced to three to provide more room for bicycles.

Goldsmith attributes the relative lack of controversy over these measures to Seattle's environmental ethic, its large number of bicycle riders and a responsive political system.

"We don't want to turn Seattle into a suburb where the streets are filled with cars, and there are no sidewalks," he says. "Here, a lot of engineers have become sensitive to these issues."

New Police Tactics

Several police departments around the country are experimenting with new approaches to combating aggressive driving. In Maryland later this summer, state police plan to test a combination digital imaging camera and laser clocking gun that locks in the speed of the car while taking a photo of the car. The device is designed to be used in an unmarked car that could be sitting on a highway ramp so that police vehicles don't create backups or try to stop people in dangerous situations. Traffic tickets are mailed to the driver, along with the photo.

In "Smooth Operator," an aware-

Continued on p. 666

At Issue:

Is aggressive driving a major safety problem?

AMERICAN AUTOMOBILE ASSOCIATION, POTOMAC CHAPTER
Press release, April 1997

yes

Area drivers have proclaimed aggressive driving Public Enemy No. 1 for the second year running when it comes to road safety, based upon results of AAA Potomac's 1997 Transportation Poll. Further, nearly 90 percent of motorists surveyed reported that they feel aggressive driving is on the rise on Washington roads. . . .

Forty-four percent of the motorists responding called aggressive driving their top concern, outranking drunken driving (31 percent). Forty-eight percent of the motorists in the District of Columbia and 46 percent in Virginia cite aggressive driving as more troubling than the regional average, 44 percent, with Maryland slightly less (42 percent), the study shows. . . .

In fact, nine out of 10 local motorists report witnessing aggressive driving in the last year. Perhaps even more remarkable, eight out of 10 witnessed aggressive driving within the last month.

Nearly two out of three Northern Virginians admitted to being aggressive drivers last year, while regionwide 56 percent confessed to aggressive driving. The majority of regional drivers said they engaged in speeding (65 percent), while others reported gesturing (8 percent), slowing down and speeding up to get even with another driver (6 percent) and tailgating (6 percent). In the District, 15 percent — nearly double the regional average — reported "gesturing and exchanging unpleasantries with another driver."

When queried about reasons for being aggressive drivers, approximately 60 percent of responses could be categorized as congestion-provoked, which is not surprising, given our area's congestion — the second worst in the nation. . . .

Those who displayed aggressive driving behavior pointed to running late for appointments (33 percent) and frustration over slow or congested traffic (27 percent) as primary irritants. These findings further illustrate the region's need for increased capacity to ease congestion and frustration on our roads. . . .

Based upon AAA Potomac's poll findings, Smooth Operator, the regional initiative launched recently to combat aggressive driving by increasing high-visibility police enforcement and motorist education, appears to be on target.* Regionally, 60 percent of respondents indicated that more police patrols and driver education would be the best deterrent to aggressive driving. Another segment of the motorists polled (28 percent) called for larger fines and penalties to solve the problem.

* Smooth Operator involves the Maryland and Virginia state police, the Metropolitan Police Department, the U.S. Park Police and several county and local jurisdictions.

THE MONTGOMERY JOURNAL (MONTGOMERY COUNTY, MD.)
Editorial, May 2, 1997

no

It's time to inject some much-needed perspective into the topic of "aggressive driving" on the Washington area's congested highways. The need for some rationality here was highlighted yesterday by the release of the latest American Automobile Association survey on the subject.

Or, rather, we should say the apocalyptic rhetorical atmosphere created by the AAA in discussing the results of its survey and the confusion that is evident in those results.

"Aggressive driving continues to strike fear in motorists, invading their lives and endangering their safety," said AAA's Lon Anderson, who went on to describe the "death grip" the phenomenon has on area drivers.

Indeed, according to Anderson, aggressive driving has become so prevalent that it has reached "epidemic proportions" because eight out of 10 drivers surveyed claimed to have seen examples of aggressive driving in the last month, and more than half "confessed their aggressive driving sins."

In view of such hyperbole, perhaps it is not surprising that for the second year in a row, the AAA survey found motorists ranking aggressive driving ahead of drunken driving as their top fear on the road, this time by a margin of 44 percent to 31 percent.

At the least, that perception is puzzling in view of the fact that nearly half of the 41,000-plus highway fatalities in this country in 1995 . . . involved booze.

Let's not lose sight of the fact that getting drunken drivers off the road should be the No. 1 traffic safety priority of area law enforcement.

It also must be asked, in view of the overwhelming number of respondents "confessing" to sometimes being guilty of aggressive driving, if there is so broad a definition of the phenomenon as to be practically meaningless.

In an interview with *The Journal*, Anderson explained the way his surveyors tried to account for such a possibility, including qualifying the question as one inquiring about "outrageous" examples of aggressive driving.

Still, there is great danger in the broad-brush portrait that seems to be emerging in the aggressive driving dialogue. The danger is that law enforcement against concrete killers like drunken driving will suffer in a politically correct campaign against folks who are simply in a hurry and manage to offend a left-lane dawdler. . . .

Now, AAA reports it is urging police to crack down on the dawdlers... Left-lane blocking is likely the least policed traffic hazard, so it is good to hear AAA is bringing to bear its immense influence on this aspect of improving driving safety. It can't happen too soon.

Continued from p. 664

ness-building program initiated this spring by state and local police in Washington, Maryland and Virginia, patrol officers targeted drivers who committed two or more offenses often associated with aggressive driving — including speeding, tailgating, shoulder-running, failing to obey traffic signals, changing lanes improperly and driving while intoxicated. [22]

In New York state, police are launching a pilot program this summer using helicopter surveillance and unmarked cars to find aggressive drivers. In Arizona, the use of unmarked cars to catch aggressive drivers on Phoenix and Tucson highways has been expanded to downtown Phoenix.

Concern About Higher Speed Limits

The speed limit on highways outside Arizona metropolitan areas is now 75 mph, and police routinely clock speeds over 100, according to Alberto Gutier, director of the Governor's Office of Community and Highway Safety. Some local streets in sprawling Phoenix "may not have a light for three or four miles," he says, "and people may do 70 in a 40 mph zone."

The parade of states raising speed limits since Congress lifted the federal maximum in 1995 is a major cause of dangerous driving, says Advocates for Highway and Auto Safety, a coalition of insurance, consumer and health groups. "We think most aggressive drivers are speeding drivers," says spokeswoman Cathy Hickey. Thirty-four states have raised speed limits on rural Interstate highways, 24 of them to 70 mph or above.*

According to the highway safety coalition, 10 of the 34 states that increased speed limits on their highways experienced an increase in fatalities of 5 percent or more in 1996; five of those states had an increase of between 14 percent and 18 percent.

The coalition argues that raising the speed limit sends motorists the wrong signal — that it's safe to speed. Further, it says, police forces are inadequate to the task of enforcement. According to a recent Harris Poll conducted for the organization, 64 percent of those polled are "concerned that higher speed limits will contribute to even more aggressive driving." [23]

Laser Cameras and Other New Technologies

The coalition is pushing Congress to dedicate a half-cent per gallon from the federal gasoline tax for safety programs, including funds to help police combat aggressive driving. It supports using cameras and other new technologies in jurisdictions where patrol cars cannot keep up with the growing number of speeders and other violators.

Maryland and Colorado have passed legislation to allow cameras at intersections to catch motorists running red lights. Red-light cameras also are used in localities in California, Arizona, Michigan, New York and Virginia. The cameras take a photo of the car with its license plate, and the motorist is usually ticketed by mail. Adoption has been stymied in some states by concerns about violations of privacy.

The Insurance Institute for Highway Safety strongly backs automated enforcement techniques like red-light cameras, arguing they permit better enforcement in high-density situations where it is difficult for an officer to catch a red-light runner without endangering other drivers.

"Ninety-seven percent of the people who get tickets pay for them," says Julie A. Rochman, a spokeswoman for the institute. "It's hard to argue when you get a shot of your car in the mail." ■

* In 1987, Congress amended the National Maximum Speed Limit law to permit states to increase the maximum speed limit on rural Interstate highways to 65 mph. In 1995, Congress enacted the National Highway System Act, repealing the national maximum speed limit.

OUTLOOK

Legislative Initiatives

Legislation to crack down on aggressive driving was introduced in both the Maryland and Virginia legislatures last session. Though none of the bills saw action, state legislators are working on new proposals for next session.

In Maryland, legislators have been revising a proposal to increase the penalties for a driver who commits three violations — such as speeding, following too closely and changing lanes unsafely — during a single incident. In Virginia, a proposal last session would have created a new "aggressive driving" charge carrying up to a year in jail for a driver brandishing a firearm or operating a motor vehicle in a threatening manner or with intent to hurt another person. Republican Virginia House Del. Joe May, who introduced the bill, plans to reintroduce a new version of the proposal next session. The Virginia Department of Transportation adopted another May proposal last session, adding instruction on curbing aggressive driving to its remedial driving course for repeat violators.

Rep. Blumenauer argues that the best way to control dangerous drivers is by taking their cars. He has introduced legislation in Congress to use existing federal anti-drunken-driving grant money to encourage states to adopt auto forfeiture for drunken drivers. In Portland, Ore., which has such a program, drunken-driving deaths have dropped steeply — 42 percent between 1994 and 1995.

"This is a very direct way to disarm the dangerous or reckless driver," Blumenauer says. "But it has not been used the way I would like for the persistent dangerous driver who drives without a license."

The University of Michigan's Waller notes that while law enforcement has focused on bad drivers — most effectively those who drink and drive — it has been less successful in motivating people to become good, courteous drivers.

"I feel we've missed the boat on preparing young drivers," she says, arguing that most young drivers get their license before they've had sufficient experience on the road. "You don't give a kid 30 hours of piano lessons and tell him to go play in Carnegie Hall." She favors the approach adopted by Michigan and other states known as "graduated licensing," in which teenagers must log a minimum number of road hours with a supervising adult before receiving full license privileges.

State troopers say they're also dismayed by the apparent ignorance of drivers — and not just teenagers. "Some of the rules of the road are being lost over time," observes Sgt. McDonnell. "People are learning to drive by being thrown into the jungle rather than being taught how to do this safely."

How should the nation deal with aggressive drivers? There are two basic approaches — train and discipline drivers better or design roads to force them to drive less aggressively.

Increasingly, activists say, both approaches must be pursued. Police can't write enough tickets to control aggressive drivers, Blumenauer argues, so it also makes sense to re-engineer the streets to encourage people to drive more slowly.

Together, he says, toughened enforcement and calmed streets reinforce the philosophy "that the car is part of the transportation system that serves people, not that we all adjust our lives to serve the car." ■

Sarah Glazer is a freelance writer in New York who specializes in health and social policy issues.

FOR MORE INFORMATION

AAA Foundation for Traffic Safety, 1440 New York Ave., N.W., Suite 201, Washington, D.C. 20005; (202) 638-5944. The research arm of the American Automobile Association (AAA) has issued reports on aggressive driving.

Advocates for Highway and Auto Safety, 750 1st Street, N.E., Suite 901, Washington, D.C. 20002; (202) 408-1711. This organization representing consumers and insurance companies tracks state laws related to highway safety and is lobbying for increased federal funding of enforcement programs aimed at aggressive drivers.

Insurance Institute for Highway Safety, 1005 N. Glebe Rd., Arlington, Va. 22201-4751; (703) 247-1500. The institute conducts research and provides data on highway safety and seeks to reduce losses from crashes.

National Highway Traffic Safety Administration, Office of Public and Consumer Affairs, 400 7th St., S.W., Room 5232, Washington, D.C. 20590; (202) 366-9550. This branch of the federal Department of Transportation tracks highway safety statistics.

Surface Transportation Policy Project, 1100 17th St., N.W., 10th Floor, Washington, D.C. 20036; (202) 466-2636. This coalition of some 175 environmental and community groups advocates transportation policies like traffic-calming that benefit pedestrians and cyclists.

Notes

[1] *Mean Streets: Pedestrian Safety and Reform of the Nation's Transportation Law,* the Surface Transportation Project and the Environmental Working Group, 1997.

[2] See "Traffic Congestion," *The CQ Researcher,* May 6, 1994, pp. 385-408.

[3] See "Highway Safety," *The CQ Researcher,* July 14, 1995, pp. 609-632.

[4] See "Transportation Policy," *The CQ Researcher,* July 4, 1997, pp. 577-600.

[5] "Aggressive Driving Continues to Plague Area Motorists," *AAA Potomac News,* May 1, 1997.

[6] Louis Mizell, "Aggressive Driving," in *Aggressive Driving: Three Studies, AAA Foundation for Traffic Safety,* March 1997.

[7] *Ibid.,* p. 5.

[8] The study drew on reports from 30 newspapers, 16 police departments and insurance company claims. The number of fatalities rose from 41,798 in 1995 to 41,907 in 1996. It was the fourth year in a row there has been an increase, but the fatality rate remained stable during the four-year period at 1.7 per hundred million vehicle miles.

[9] Richard A. Retting, "Urban Motor Vehicle Crashes and Potential Countermeasures," *Transportation Quarterly,* summer 1996.

[10] See the Insurance Institute for Highway Safety Web site at www.hwysafety.org, "Q&A: Red Light Cameras."

[11] DiGuiseppi C. Roberts, "Influence of Changing Travel Patterns on Child Death Rates from Injury Trend Analysis," *British Medical Journal,* March 8, 1997, pp. 710-713.

[12] Eric Peters, "Beware traffic violation creep," *The Washington Times,* April 29, 1997, p. A19.

[13] John A. Larson, *Steering Clear of Highway Madness* (1996), p. 76.

[14] American Association of State Highway and Transportation Officials, *AASHTO Policy on Geometric Design of Highways and Streets* (1990).

[15] "Transportation Policy," *op. cit.*

[16] Raymond W. Novaco, "Automobile Driving and Aggressive Behavior," in Martin Wachs and Margaret Crawford, eds, *The Car and The City* (1992), pp. 234-320.

[17] *Ibid.,* p. 239.

[18] Novaco, *op. cit.*

[19] *Ibid.,* pp. 245-246.

[20] Institute of Transportation Engineers, *Traditional Neighborhood Development Street Design Guidelines* (June 1997), p. 4.

[21] *Flexibility in Highway Design,* Federal Highway Administration, in press.

[22] Eric Lipton et al., "Area Police Team Up for Safer Roads," *The Washington Post,* March 23, 1997.

[23] Advocates for Highway and Auto Safety, *The Highway Safety Deficit: Who Pays and Who Delays?,* May 6, 1997.

Bibliography

Selected Sources Used

Books

Kay, Jane Holtz, *Asphalt Nation: How the Automobile Took Over America and How We Can Take It Back,* Random House, 1997.
This impassioned book by the architecture and planning critic for *The Nation* magazine chronicles how federal subsidies reshaped the country into its current auto gridlock. Kay discusses solutions, including traffic calming, to create more humane neighborhoods.

Larson, John A., *Steering Clear of Highway Madness: A Driver's Guide to Curbing Stress and Strain,* BookPartners, 1996.
Psychiatrist Larson advises drivers on how to avoid the frustration and anger that often lead to dangerous confrontations and collisions on the road.

Tavris, Carol, *Anger: The Misunderstood Emotion,* Touchstone, 1989.
In this book arguing against the notion that expressing anger is always best for you, social psychologist Tavris devotes a few pages to explaining the growing phenomenon of "traffic anger."

Articles

Bradsher, Keith, "Domination, Submission and the Chevy Suburban," *The New York Times* (East Coast edition), March 23, 1997, "The News of the Week in Review," p. 2.
Bradsher looks at the desire to dominate other drivers as one motive behind the growing popularity of sport utility vehicles. Collisions between sport vehicles and cars kill more Americans than collisions between cars.

Flanagan, Barbara, "The Other Palm Beach Story," *The New York Times,* p. C1.
Flanagan describes the political forces that led to the revitalization of West Palm Beach, using traffic-calming and other approaches.

Janofsky, Michael, "Answer to Gathering Stampede of Autos: Whoa!" *The New York Times,* Jan. 7, 1997, p. A10.
Janofsky describes efforts by residents in Middleburg, Va., and neighboring towns to apply traffic-calming to Route 50, a favorite commuter route to Washington, D.C.

Levine, Art, "How Angry Drivers are Putting You in Danger," *Redbook,* March, 1997, pp. 90-114.
Journalist Levine describes some of the deaths caused by aggressive driving and attempts to combat it.

Lipton, Eric et al., "Area Police Team Up for Safer Roads," *The Washington Post,* March 23, 1997, p. A1.
This article describes the launching of a new program, "Smooth Operator," in which police from Maryland, Virginia and Washington, D.C., are teaming up to intensify enforcement against aggressive drivers.

Perl, Peter, "The Glass and Steel Menagerie," *The Washington Post Magazine,* July 7, 1996, pp. 8-13, 21-26.
In this in-depth article, Perl asks why drivers in the capital area have such aggressive driving styles and rides with area police to see how they deal with the problem.

Vest, Jason, et al., "Road Rage," *U.S. News & World Report,* June 2, 1997, pp. 24-30.
The authors suggest that a number of trends, including growing road congestion and falling participation in driver education programs, may be contributing to the phenomenon of violence between drivers.

Reports

AAA Foundation for Traffic Safety, *Aggressive Driving: Three Studies* (March 1997).
This report by the AAA's research arm includes its count of violent road incidents in the United States since 1990 and two British studies examining psychological components of "road rage."

Institute of Transportation Engineers Transportation Planning Council Committee, *Traditional Neighborhood Development Street Design Guidelines* (June 1997).
A report from a committee of the professional society of traffic engineers recommends standards for streets in new residential areas designed on a traditional, walkable model.

Surface Transportation Policy Project and Environmental Working Group, *Mean Streets: Pedestrian Safety and Reform of the Nation's Transportation Law* (1997).
A coalition of environmental and walker/cycling groups issued this report highlighting the 14 percent of road fatalities each year that involve pedestrians and arguing against highway-users' efforts to reduce federal funds favoring walkers.

The Next Step

Additional information from UMI's Newspaper & Periodical Abstracts™ database

Aggressive Driving

Beamon, Todd, "Cabdrivers Face Off in Traffic Dispute; One Person Injured, Car Windows Shattered After Two Men Pick Up Tire Irons," *The Washington Post,* May 23, 1997, p. D1.
A late-morning incident at Scott Circle on Rhode Island Avenue N.W., Washington, D.C., occurred three weeks into a five-month crackdown on aggressive driving by 16 area law enforcement agencies. Police said yesterday's fight began when the driver of one cab cut in front of another, and ended after both men smashed each other's windows with tire irons.

Finn, Peter, and Mike Allen, "Driven to Become Road Warriors: Specialists Study Behavior; Police Plan to Alter It," *The Washington Post,* March 31, 1997, p. B1.
Police say aggressive driving is the drunken driving of the '90s — a common yet deadly phenomenon that can be tamed through unflinching enforcement and focused public attention. Among those who have studied aggressive driving, some believe that like alcoholism it may actually be a sickness.

Johnson, Kevin V., "An 'epidemic' of aggressive driving; Angry motorists, not drunks, now top list of commuters concerns," *USA Today,* May 6, 1997, p. D8.
A new poll by the Potomac chapter of the Automobile Association of America (AAA), serving the Washington, D.C., area, says that 44 percent of area drivers think aggressive driving is the biggest threat to highway safety. Respondents said they were more worried about aggressive driving than about drunken driving. And over half confessed to having been aggressive drivers themselves in the last year.

Masters, Brooke A., "Virginia Driver's Violent Confrontation Leads to 60-Day Jail Sentence," *The Washington Post,* June 4, 1997, p. B1.
When James Drake thought he'd been cut off while driving to work early one morning, he didn't just give the other driver an angry look. Drake, an accountant, followed Veronica Reinhardt into the parking garage at her Reston, Va., workplace, cutting her off several times on the way, and charged out of his pickup truck, according to court documents. Yelling obscenities, Drake beat on the roof and windows of Reinhardt's Honda Accord, tried to pull the door open and kicked it so hard that he did $479 worth of damage, the documents say. Yesterday, U.S. Magistrate Judge Theresa C. Buchanan cracked down on Drake's aggressive driving, sentencing him to 60 days in jail and ordering him to pay a $2,500 fine and $601 in restitution.

Smith, Leef, "Aggressive Driving Blamed in Crash That Killed Two in Prince William," *The Washington Post,* Feb. 27, 1997, p. D4.
An aggressive driver bent on passing cars on a two-lane stretch of Route 28 in Virginia's Prince William County crossed a double yellow line and caused a crash that killed two motorists, police said. A Buick driver, trying to avoid a collision, steered his car onto the shoulder of the road and then overcompensated when he steered back onto the road. The Buick crossed over the center line and struck a Nissan Sentra, killing a passenger in the Buick and the driver of the Nissan. The sedan driver fled, police said.

Wee, Eric L., "Targeting Aggressive Drivers: Pursuing Cases Requires Painstaking Police Work," *The Washington Post,* Feb. 20, 1997, Sec. VAL, p. 1.
The Prince William County attorney's office recently dropped reckless driving charges against Robert Finck, who was involved in a November accident on Interstate 95 that severely injured his 3-year-old daughter, Brenna. Prosecutors said they have found no witnesses to the accident, and other evidence supports Finck's contention that he was the injured party in the confrontation. Prosecutors said they are moving forward with charges against the other driver involved in the accident.

Yant, Abbie, "Seeing red? Think ahead," *San Francisco Chronicle,* April 15, 1997, p. A19.
Yant comments on aggressive driving symptoms and consequences, focusing on the problems of running red lights.

Pedestrian Safety

Arnold, David, "Law a step behind jaywalkers," *The Boston Globe,* Feb. 15, 1996, p. 37.
As part of his "pedestrian safety initiative," Democratic Boston Mayor Thomas Menino vowed to enforce the state law that prohibits jaywalking. His intention, he said, was to curb pedestrian fatalities in the city.

Crenshaw, Holly, "Pedestrian safety changes made at Highland-Ponce," *Atlanta Constitution,* Feb. 20, 1997, Sec. XJN, p. 3.
Neighborhood residents say that new safety precautions at Ponce de Leon and North Highland avenues in Atlanta, Ga., should make the area less dangerous for pedestrians but are still urging drivers to exercise caution there. The changes came after two pedestrians were struck by cars while crossing Ponce de Leon last fall, prompting residents of the nine-story Briarcliff Summit apartment building — home to 201 elderly tenants, some of whom are disabled — to seek help in making the area

safer. Miriam M. Parker, a 73-year-old resident, wrote to city officials on behalf of the Briarcliff's tenants, who often cross Ponce de Leon to shop at the drugstore, grocery store and other businesses facing their building.

"Pedestrians at Risk, New Study Warns," ***St. Louis Post-Dispatch,*** **April 9, 1997, p. A8.**
"Pedestrian safety is an unacknowledged public health problem," said Hank Dittmar, executive director of the Surface Transportation Policy Project, the highway safety advocacy group that produced a study on pedestrian safety with the Environmental Working Group.

Reid, S. A. "Group to make streets safer for pedestrians," ***Atlanta Constitution,*** **June 5, 1997, Sec. XJA, p. 8.**
Pedestrian safety has moved up a notch on the city's priority list with the formation of a new task force aimed at making Atlanta, Ga., a less dangerous place to enjoy the world's oldest mode of transportation — walking. The Pedestrian Rights Task Force hopes to do that by promoting a multifaceted approach that members call the four "E's" — education, enforcement, engineering and encouragement. The group, made up of pedestrian activists and city officials, got its start in May with the help of Marvin Arrington, mayoral candidate and City Council president.

Vartabedian, Ralph, "Being a Pedestrian Is Risky Business," ***Los Angeles Times,*** **April 15, 1997, p. E1.**
Every year, approximately 900 California pedestrians are killed and more than 18,000 others sustain injuries, according to a new nationwide study on pedestrian deaths. While pedestrian deaths account for 19 percent of all motor vehicle deaths in the state, just 0.7 percent of federal highway spending related to safety in the state was allocated to pedestrian projects. The report, by a large coalition of environmental groups and organized under the Environmental Working Group and Surface Transportation Policy Project, demands a substantial reallocation of spending to improve pedestrian safety.

Police Response

Lipton, Eric, and Patricia Davis, "Area Police Team Up for Safer Roads; Aggressive Drivers Lead Agencies to Break Jurisdictional Barriers," ***The Washington Post,*** **March 23, 1997, p. A1.**
Police agencies in Virginia, Maryland and the District are planning to join forces next month for the first coordinated crackdown on aggressive driving in the Washington area, officials said yesterday. The campaign includes the D.C. police department and the Maryland and Virginia state police, as well as several suburban departments.

Masters, Brooke A., "U.S. Authorities to Crack Down on Bad GW Parkway Drivers," ***The Washington Post,*** **March 28, 1997, p. A13.**
Dangerous drivers on the George Washington Memorial Parkway are facing faster prosecution and maybe higher fines under new plans developed by the U.S. Park Police and federal prosecutors. In the near future, motorists charged with drunken or reckless driving will be required to appear in court within a week, rather than waiting six weeks, prosecutors said. That will put offenders under a judge's supervision sooner and mean swifter trials and punishment.

Montgomery, David, "Speeding Toward Action; Md. Legislators Push Unusual Number of Bills Aimed at Increasing Road Safety," ***The Washington Post,*** **March 6, 1997, p. D1.**
Amid growing concern about aggressive driving and abundant evidence that many drivers consider stopping at red lights optional, lawmakers are pushing through bills aimed at increasing safety. The chief sponsors of key measures are senators and delegates from the car-clogged Washington suburbs, who say their constituents are demanding action.

Smith, Leef, and Alice Reid, "For Road Warriors, a Sign to Stop; Regional Reckless-Driving Crackdown Finds Aggressive Behavior is the Norm," ***The Washington Post,*** **May 2, 1997, p. B1.**
Virginia State Trooper A. Todd Gillis roamed the Capital Beltway in an unmarked cruiser yesterday, looking for people who were driving too aggressively. He found so many that his only problem was deciding which cars to pull over. Gillis ticketed five motorists during the two hours that a reporter rode with him. But the trooper pointed to more than a dozen drivers he could have stopped if he hadn't been busy writing those citations. Gillis, 34, is part of an unprecedented crackdown on aggressive and reckless drivers that was launched this week by Washington-area police. Police departments across the region have dedicated dozens of officers to the effort, which is dubbed "Smooth Operator."

Valentine, Paul W., "Thousands Cited in Aggressive-Driving Crackdown," ***The Washington Post,*** **May 17, 1997, p. C3.**
Washington area police said yesterday that they had ticketed almost 12,000 motorists in the first week of a joint crackdown on aggressive drivers who tailgate, run red lights and weave through high-speed traffic. The joint 16-police agency crackdown, called "Smooth Operator," has deployed scores of officers and is one of the first in the nation to target aggressive drivers exclusively.

Vartabedian, Ralph, "The Real Capital of Perilous Driving," ***Los Angeles Times,*** **May 27, 1997, p. E1.**
The trend toward aggressive driving has become so alarming that the Clinton administration this month unveiled a $100,000 effort, called "Smooth Operator," to combat the bad habits of drivers in Washington, D.C. As an added measure, the safety administration has launched a study to try to understand what causes aggressive

driving, which is also popping up in less virulent forms in other regions.

Public Response

Cantor, George, "Some drivers too cruel to be kind," *Detroit News*, March 15, 1997, p. C7.

Cantor discusses aggressive driving in his neighborhood and questions why police have failed to put an end to it.

Monroe, Doug, "Readers lament highway recklessness and the lack of law enforcement," *Atlanta Constitution*, Oct. 7, 1996, p. B2.

Monroe discusses readers' views on several Atlanta-area transportation topics, including concern over reckless driving, lack of law enforcement and irresponsible truck drivers on local highways.

"Montanans talk about speed," *Car & Driver*, June 1997, p. 122.

Montanans Karen Conger, Les Kellem and Alex Ferguson share their views of Montana's "reasonable-and-prudent" daytime speed limit law. Most citizens like the law, but some worry about the speeds drivers are hitting.

Reckless Driving

Boyd, Richard, "120 mph chase dead-ends with multiple charges," *Times-Picayune*, Nov. 27, 1996, p. B4.

A Slidell, La., area man arrested after leading authorities on a car chase said he was "just showing off" and did not see the flashing lights of law enforcement vehicles. Jason Shields was booked on Nov. 22, 1996, with attempted murder of a police officer, resisting arrest by flight, reckless driving, improper lane use, running a red light, running a stop sign and disregarding a police signal.

Warren, Bob, "Three Hurt in LaPlace Accident After Prom," *Times-Picayune*, April 29, 1997, Sec. BR, p. 1.

Three people in a car that was hit, a boy, 17, a girl, 16, and a 22-year-old were taken to River Parishes Hospital in LaPlace, La., where they were treated for bumps and bruises and released. The teens, students at West St. John High School, and the adult, their chaperone, were driving home after a night of prom festivities. The driver of the truck that hit them, Randall D. Legg, 36, of Sorrento, was booked with reckless driving and driving while intoxicated (DWI). When authorities asked him what caused the accident, he replied that he was "too drunk to explain," said Lt. Michael Tregre, a spokesman for the St. John the Baptist Parish Sheriff's Office.

Traffic Calming

Benning, Victoria, "On Route 50, A Move to Calm Traffic; Residents Advocate Methods to Slow Cars," *The Washington Post*, Jan. 16, 1997, Sec. VAL, p. 1.

After 15 months of study, including nearly a dozen community workshops, a group of residents from the Middleburg, Va., area have come up with a proposal they say will ease traffic problems while preserving the area's quaintness and scenic views. The citizens group — the Route 50 Corridor Coalition — has proposed using "traffic-calming" methods such as speed humps, small traffic circles, raised intersections and tree-lined median strips to discourage speeding and cut-through traffic.

Castaneda, Carol J., "Neighborhoods have ways to brake zip-through drivers," *USA Today*, May 2, 1997, p. A24.

From Sarasota, N.Y., to Seattle, Wash., cities are touting "traffic calming" as a way to end the mad rush of cars racing 40 mph and faster down residential streets. As stressed-out commuters and combative drivers roar through the neighborhoods to avoid clogged main roads, residents are taking up the fight.

Howe, Peter J., "Cambridge aims to 'calm' traffic on busy streets," *The Boston Globe*, Feb. 10, 1997, p. A15.

This spring, three projects that are part of a new movement called "traffic calming" will be introduced in Cambridge, Mass. The goal is to make neighborhoods nicer places to live and walk by building modified speed bumps and other obstructions in the street, so that motorists have to drive more slowly.

Janofsky, Michael, "Answer to Gathering Stampede of Autos: Whoa!," *The New York Times*, Jan. 7, 1997, p. A10.

In 1995, Virginia proposed easing congestion on U.S. 50 by building multi-lane bypasses around Middleburg, Aldie and Upperville and widening the highway at the intersections between them. But a group of area residents, fearing suburban sprawl, has proposed an alternative way to deal with transportation issues, "traffic calming."

Pacelle, Mitchell, "Traffic calming: Some urban planners say downtowns need a lot more congestion," *The Wall Street Journal*, Aug. 7, 1996, p. A1.

A small band of traffic engineers including Walter Kulash have set out to shatter urban-planning dogma by applying "traffic calming" to dying downtowns. Racing traffic and the absence of curb-side parking have degraded center-city streets, they argue, chasing away potential customers of street-level stores and restaurants.

Smith, Andrew, "Letter: Speed saves — at 20 mph," *The Guardian*, Dec. 31, 1996, p. 14.

The Transport Research Laboratory finding that 20 mph zones cut accidents involving children by 67 percent makes a powerful case for immediate government action.

Sweeting, Adam, "Traffic calming? They must be joking," *The Guardian*, Sept. 19, 1996, p. 17.

Sweeting comments on his annoyance with the speed bumps being erected on Britain's suburban streets.

Back Issues

Great Research on Current Issues Starts Right Here . . . Recent topics covered by The CQ Researcher are listed below. Before May 1991, reports were published under the name of Editorial Research Reports.

JANUARY 1996
Emergency Medicine
Punishing Sex Offenders
Bilingual Education
Helping the Homeless

FEBRUARY 1996
Reforming the CIA
Campaign Finance Reform
Academic Politics
Getting Into College

MARCH 1996
The British Monarchy
Preventing Juvenile Crime
Tax Reform
Pursuing the Paranormal

APRIL 1996
Centennial Olympic Games
Managed Care
Protecting Endangered Species
New Military Culture

MAY 1996
Russia's Political Future
Marriage and Divorce
Year-Round Schools
Taiwan, China and the U.S.

Back issues are available for $5.00 (subscribers) or $10.00 (non-subscribers). Quantity discounts apply to orders over ten. To order, call Congressional Quarterly Customer Service at (202) 887-8621.

Binders are available for $18.00. To order call 1-800-638-1710. Please refer to stock number 648.

JUNE 1996
Rethinking NAFTA
First Ladies
Teaching Values
Labor Movement's Future

JULY 1996
Recovered-Memory Debate
Native Americans' Future
Crackdown on Sexual Harassment
Attack on Public Schools

AUGUST 1996
Fighting Over Animal Rights
Privatizing Government Services
Child Labor and Sweatshops
Cleaning Up Hazardous Wastes

SEPTEMBER 1996
Gambling Under Attack
The States and Federalism
Civic Journalism
Reassessing Foreign Aid

OCTOBER 1996
Political Consultants
Insurance Fraud
Rethinking School Integration
Parental Rights

NOVEMBER 1996
Global Warming
Clashing Over Copyright
Consumer Debt
Governing Washington, D.C.

DECEMBER 1996
Welfare, Work and the States
The New Volunteerism
Implementing the Disabilities Act
America's Pampered Pets

JANUARY 1997
Combating Scientific Misconduct
Restructuring the Electric Industry
The New Immigrants
Chemical and Biological Weapons

FEBRUARY 1997
Assisting Refugees
Alternative Medicine's Next Phase
Independent Counsels
Feminism's Future

MARCH 1997
New Air Quality Standards
Alcohol Advertising
Civic Renewal
Educating Gifted Students

APRIL 1997
Declining Crime Rates
The FBI Under Fire
Gender Equity in Sports
Space Program's Future

MAY 1997
The Stock Market
The Cloning Controversy
Expanding NATO
The Future of Libraries

JUNE 1997
FDA Reform
China After Deng
Line-Item Veto
Breast Cancer

JULY 1997
Transportation Policy
Executive Pay
School Choice Debate

Future Topics

- ***Age Bias in the Workplace***
- ***Land Mines***
- ***Children's Television***

THE CQ Researcher

PUBLISHED BY CONGRESSIONAL QUARTERLY INC.

Age Discrimination

Does federal law protect older workers' job rights?

This year marks the 30th anniversary of the Age Discrimination in Employment Act, the nation's first law protecting the job rights of older workers. Labor and management groups agree that the ADEA has helped make Americans more aware that workers of traditional retirement age can be just as productive as their younger colleagues. Nonetheless, corporate downsizing campaigns are often accused of targeting older workers because they earn disproportionately high salaries. Laid-off workers over age 40 can file complaints with the Equal Employment Opportunity Commission if they suspect age bias caused their job loss. EEOC statistics show, however, that few such complaints succeed and that employers are becoming increasingly adept at shedding older employees without running afoul of the law.

INSIDE THIS ISSUE

CQ August 1, 1997 • Volume 7, No. 29 • Pages 673-696

Formerly Editorial Research Reports

COVER: AT THE KUEMPEL CHIME CLOCK WORKS & STUDIO IN EXCELSIOR, MINN., THE AVERAGE AGE OF THE WORKERS IS IN THE UPPER 60S.

Aug. 1, 1997
Volume 7, No. 29

EDITOR
Sandra Stencel

MANAGING EDITOR
Thomas J. Colin

ASSOCIATE EDITORS
Sarah M. Magner
Richard L. Worsnop

STAFF WRITERS
Charles S. Clark
Mary H. Cooper
Kenneth Jost
David Masci

EDITORIAL ASSISTANT
Vanessa E. Furlong

PUBLISHED BY
Congressional Quarterly Inc.

CHAIRMAN
Andrew Barnes

VICE CHAIRMAN
Andrew P. Corty

PRESIDENT AND PUBLISHER
Robert W. Merry

EXECUTIVE EDITOR
David Rapp

The CQ Researcher (ISSN 1056-2036). Formerly Editorial Research Reports. Published weekly, except Jan. 3, May 30, Aug. 29, Oct. 31, by Congressional Quarterly Inc., 1414 22nd St., N.W., Washington, D.C. 20037. Annual subscription rate for libraries, businesses and government is $340. Additional rates furnished upon request. Periodicals postage paid at Washington, D.C., and additional mailing offices. POSTMASTER: Send address changes to The CQ Researcher, 1414 22nd St., N.W., Washington, D.C. 20037.

Age Discrimination

BY RICHARD L. WORSNOP

THE ISSUES

If any place in America can claim to be free of age discrimination, it is the Kuempel clock company of Excelsior, Minn. Kuempel builds and repairs grandfather clocks with workers whose average age is in the upper 60s. Grandfathers making grandfather clocks, the company says proudly.

Owner Bruce J. Hedblom can't say enough about his 27 employees, including three in their 80s. "They are skilled, meticulous workers," he says, "and they present no disciplinary problems. We don't worry about drug use or absenteeism. Also, their health generally is excellent. In fact, I think the spouses of our oldest workers are in worse physical shape than they are. That must say something about the benefits of continuing to work and staying active." Indeed, Hedblom adds, one of the 80-year-olds is an active pilot.

Recently, however, Kuempel hired a man in his 20s. "Every once in a while, you've got to bring in someone at the bottom of the age line so that they can mature with you," Hedblom says. "We don't discriminate against younger people by any means. And of course, we don't discriminate against older people, because that's typically who we are looking for."

That makes Kuempel something of a maverick among U.S. companies, which often are accused of targeting older, higher-paid employees when they reduce their work forces. But downsizing poses legal risks. The Age Discrimination in Employment Act (ADEA), now celebrating its 30th anniversary, allows workers to sue employers who they think fired them simply because they were too old (*see p. 685*).

Under the ADEA, employers with 20 or more workers (including labor unions, the federal government and employment agencies) are prohibited from:

- discriminating against workers age 40 and older in any aspect of employment solely because of age, including hiring, firing, pay, benefits and work conditions;
- indicating age preferences (such as "recent college graduate") in job advertisements; and
- retaliating against a worker for complaining about age discrimination or for helping the government investigate a discrimination charge.

Only 1,931 of the 21,253 discrimination cases that were resolved last year were decided in favor of the complainant, according to the Equal Employment Opportunity Commission (EEOC). The remainder were found to have "no reasonable cause" or were dismissed for administrative reasons.

As originally signed into law by President Lyndon B. Johnson in 1967, the ADEA protected workers ages 40-65. The age ceiling was raised to 70 in 1978, and then eliminated in 1987. A further change in 1991 abolished a two-year statute of limitations on bringing age-discrimination lawsuits, thus opening broad avenues of recourse to nearly all older workers.

In the process, the ADEA has raised the consciousness of both employers and employees. "I'm sure it made employers that were inclined to discriminate on the basis of age more aware" of the legal issues involved, says Ann Reesman, general counsel for the Equal Employment Advisory Council, composed of attorneys and personnel officers of companies and trade associations. Today, Reesman feels, age-linked job bias no longer is a problem. "I think employers are willing to hire qualified people regardless of what age they are," she says.

Other experts point to employers' greater sophistication in defending themselves against charges of age discrimination. Ann Bartel, a Columbia University business professor and consultant, says one effective strategy involves "trying to prove that the individual was terminated not because of age but because of poor job performance."

In some instances, says Los Angeles business consultant Dan Gallipeau, employers can turn the age issue to their advantage. "Questions that come up all the time in age-discrimination cases are 'How old were the people who hired you?' and 'How old were you when you were hired?' " he notes. "I mean, if they hired you when you were 59, it's unlikely that they laid you off when you were 62 simply because of age."

Gallipeau cites another common scenario: "Let's say you're 50 years old and are claiming you were laid off because of your age. If the person who hired you was 60 and the person who laid you off was 55, then you've got a bit of

More Discrimination Cases Being Rejected

Fewer employees have won age-discrimination cases in recent years although the number of cases resolved has increased. The statistics may reflect employers' growing awareness of the 30-year-old Age Discrimination in Employment Act and the need to downsize without showing discrimination and to carefully document workers' subpar performance.

	FY 1990	FY 1992	FY 1994	FY 1996
Cases Resolved	16,269	19,975	13,942	21,253
Administrative Closures	3,803 (23%)	4,957 (25%)	5,021 (36%)	6,329 (30%)
No Reasonable Cause	9,578 (59%)	12,075 (60%)	6,872 (49%)	12,993 (61%)
Merit Resolutions	2,888 (18%)	2,943 (15%)	2,049 (15%)	1,931 (9%)
Monetary Benefits (millions)	$27.3	$57.3	$42.3	$40.9

Source: Equal Employment Opportunity Commission

a problem proving discrimination. But if the person who fired you was 30, that's a different ballgame."

The ADEA also contains a loophole that can render job-discrimination claims moot. The so-called bona fide occupational qualification (BFOQ) exception permits mandatory-retirement or maximum hiring ages when the age limit is necessary for the performance of a job, including certain hazardous public-safety positions (*see p. 686*).

Burton D. Fretz, executive director of the National Senior Citizens Law Center, concedes there may be some cases where a BFOQ makes sense. A clothing store for teenagers, he says, "probably would want to hire other teenagers to model clothing and sell it to their peers."

But such considerations "really are peripheral to almost every business," Fretz says. "In most cases, the insistence on youth rests on false stereotypes. That's what the airlines did years ago with age limits for what were then called stewardesses — today's flight attendants. When you examine the requirements of that position, you find there's no reason why a 40- or 50-year-old couldn't perform them as well as or better than someone younger."

Cathy Ventrell-Monsees, managing attorney for the American Association of Retired Persons (AARP) litigation unit, also sees only limited use for youth-based BFOQ claims. "There does have to be some fit between a worker and a job, but it's not necessarily age-based. Sometimes it may actually turn out to be culturally based or experience-based."

As workers and employers continue to evaluate the impact of the ADEA in reducing workplace age discrimination, these are some of the questions being asked:

Has the Age Discrimination in Employment Act improved job security for older workers?

Thirty years after Congress passed the ADEA, the law's impact remains unclear, largely because many age-bias victims do not sue their former employers. The claims process can be time-consuming and costly, and successful outcomes are relatively rare. Still, there is wide agreement that the law has made both employers and employees more aware of the age-discrimination issue.

"Companies are much more careful now about how they deal with older employees — especially in terms of the language they use in their presence," Bartel says. I think in that sense, yes, the law has been beneficial."

Samuel Issacharoff, a professor at the University of Texas Law School in Austin, concurs. "There's a different culture in the workplace governing the way people talk about questions of age," he notes. "You don't hear cracks these days about not being able to teach old dogs new tricks. Under the ADEA, that kind of remark can be used as evidence of animus in establishing employer liability in age-discrimination cases."

Fretz says the ADEA's effectiveness "comes from a combination of things: the threat of liability to employers who violate the law; the educational function of the law; and changing demographics. The aging of the work force generally helps to call attention to the importance of older workers. And I think employers culturally are coming to understand the value of treating all workers on their individual merits, rather than placing them in any kind of arbitrary category — whether it's race or sex or age."

Michael Useem, a professor of management at the University of Pennsylvania's Wharton School of Finance and Commerce, says his talks with company executives have shown them to be "much more aware of the need to avoid any kind of reference to age in making decisions about who goes into training programs, who gets promoted or who gets a choice assignment."

Still, advocates for the elderly say that the ADEA could use further strengthening. Ventrell-Monsees of the AARP believes that courts should be able to award punitive damages in age discrimination judgments, as they do in race- or gender-based discrimination cases. (*See story, p. 678.*)

"Right now, age-discrimination victims only qualify for liquidated damages, which are double their actual damages," she says. "That may be a stiff penalty for some employers. But if the actual damages are low, just doubling them isn't going to hurt a company much. Punitive damages should be made available to send a message to employers that Congress means what it says in the ADEA."

But even punitive damages are not likely to banish job-related age discrimination. Eric Rolfe Greenberg, director of management studies for the American Management Association in New York, notes that, "Cost controls and cost reduction are still an important factor in managing organizations," and when trimming costs, companies tend to focus initially on payroll expenses. "It stands to reason that they're going to look first at the higher-priced talent, because they can save more money that way. And, nature being what it is, the higher-priced talent tends to be older. So to that extent, age discrimination is a reality."

Greenberg hastens to add, however, that getting rid of high-priced workers "is not the strategic intent of companies that are firing people and hiring new ones. What they are trying to do is replace workers who lack necessary skills in a changing business environment with workers who possess those skills."

Greenberg acknowledges that such a policy "does indeed have the appearance of targeting older workers." But many older employees at risk of downsizing can escape the ax, he feels, "by enhancing their job skills through training."

Green Thumb

A participant in the Green Thumb program trains as an office worker. The Department of Labor-funded program helps disadvantaged Americans over age 55 find entry-level work in nonprofit and government agencies. After polishing their job skills, they seek private-sector employment.

Richard A. Posner, a federal appeals judge and senior lecturer at the University of Chicago Law School, argues in a 1995 book that the ADEA "is at once inefficient, regressive and harmful to the elderly." [1] According to Posner, the law "adds to the costs of employing older workers, and hence to the reluctance of employers to employ them, by giving them more legal rights against their employer than younger workers have." [2]

Besides, Posner argues, singling out older workers for special treatment creates hardships for younger employees. "If employers are forced by law to keep inefficient elderly workers, workers as a whole, few of whom are wealthy or are guilty of 'ageism,' will in effect be taxed for the benefit of these elderly workers — yet the elderly, prosperous recipients of substantial public largess are implausible candidates for the status of an oppressed class." [3]

Posner makes the further point that "age as such is unlikely to be a good predictor of the likelihood of the plaintiff's winning an age discrimination suit" brought under the ADEA. "The older the employee, the easier it will be for the employer to make a plausible case that the employee was fired because he was failing or too expensive, and not because of his age as such." [4]

Are older workers less productive and less able to adjust to changing technologies than younger workers?

The most sensitive issue in the

High Court Ruling Pleases Workers *and* Employers

Can two legal wrongs make a right? Some age-discrimination experts say yes, pointing to the Supreme Court's 1995 decision in *McKennon v. Nashville Banner Publishing Co.*

The plaintiff in the case was Christine McKennon, an employee of the *Nashville Banner* for almost 40 years. During that time, she had received excellent performance ratings from her supervisors.

In October 1990, when McKennon was 62, she was fired as part of what the company contended was an overall staff-reduction effort. However, she subsequently learned that the paper had hired a 26-year-old to fill her job. In May 1991, she sued the *Banner* under the Age Discrimination in Employment Act (ADEA).

Although McKennon seemed initially to have a strong case, her position crumbled during her pretrial deposition. It was then that *Banner* lawyers discovered she had photocopied confidental company documents prior to her dismissal and shown them to her husband. She had done so, she said, because she was apprehensive about being fired and wanted to protect herself. The documents reportedly indicated that older workers were being targeted for dismissal.

The *Banner* reacted by sending McKennon a second termination notice, in effect refiring her for violating company policy. Moving for dismissal of the case, the paper said it would have let her go immediately if it had known earlier what she had done. The *Banner* now admitted to age discrimination in hope of expediting its request. At the same time, it argued that McKennon was ineligible for recovery of any damages under the ADEA because she would have been discharged for pilfering the documents. Accepting that reasoning, a federal judge in Nashville threw out her lawsuit, and the U.S. Court of Appeals in Cincinnati agreed.

The *Banner* was hardly the first company to seize upon "after-acquired evidence" to defeat a job-discrimination claim. Over the past decade, some employers have fought such lawsuits by probing the complainant's background in depth. Studies suggest, for example, that 30 percent or more of job applicants inflate their education or employment credentials or conceal embarrassing incidents in their past ("resumé fraud"). Others may be vulnerable to charges of insubordination, expense-account fraud or other serious violations of company rules.

The Supreme Court, however, made clear that there are limits to the applicability of after-acquired evidence in age-discrimination cases. Reversing the appellate court ruling, it reinstated McKennon's lawsuit and said she should be paid her salary for the 14 months between the date of her illegal dismissal and the day the company learned about the photocopying.

It added, however, that discovery of misconduct that would have led to legal dismissal of an employee may be cited to reduce the monetary damages being sought. And the court held that employers should not be forced to rehire such workers.

Writing for a unanimous court, Justice Anthony M. Kennedy said Congress had enacted laws against age bias to prod employers to examine their hiring practices and "to eliminate, so far as possible, the last vestiges of discrimination." He added that if a company wants to cite new evidence of misconduct by an employee, it must demonstrate that "the wrongdoing was of such severity that the employee in fact would have been terminated on those grounds alone if the employer had known of it at the time of the discharge."

In the wake of the *McKennon* decision, civil rights and business groups both voiced approval. "This ruling says job discrimination is illegal, and employers can't get off the hook by going back after the fact and dredging up evidence to justify their own bad behavior," said Judith Lichtman, president of the Women's Legal Defense Fund. [1]

Business representatives were pleased that the ruling apparently limited their exposure to damages arising from age discrimination. They also predicted that companies will continue to examine the background of workers who file claims because it could save them money.

Douglas McDowell, general counsel of the Equal Employment Advisory Council, a business group, offered an appraisal of *McKennon* that all parties doubtless could support. "There is something in there for everybody," he said. [2]

[1] Quoted by Paul M. Barrett in *The Wall Street Journal,* Jan. 24, 1995, p. B1.

[2] *Loc. cit.*

age-discrimination debate centers on job performance. Conventional wisdom long held that employees become noticeably less productive and flexible in their 50s or 60s. But advocates for the elderly contend this view is a "myth" or "age stereotype."

"The grain of truth that sustains this myth is the fact that, across the population as a whole, certain physical functions do show some decline in age," the American Bar Association's Commission on Legal Problems of the Elderly noted in a 1992 report. "These functions include the five senses, physical strength, lung capacity and reaction time." The commission went on to assert that, "Most studies under actual working conditions show that older workers perform as well as, if not better than, their younger counterparts on most measures, unless the job requires great physical strength or split-second reaction time." [5]

Similarly, the panel found little merit in the widely held perception that older workers are not interested in learning new skills and are incapable of learning them as quickly or as well as younger persons. "The grain of truth is that speed of learning does show some decline," the report acknowledged, "but this is in part accounted for by differences in learning style between older and younger workers. Older workers are more likely to respond more positively to teaching that is more self-directed, less formal and which takes advantage of their experience and knowledge. Countless corporate examples leave little doubt that older workers are at least as willing as younger workers to be trained in new technologies and are equally as capable of learning even the most sophisticated technologies." [6]

Frank J. Landy, a psychologist in Boulder, Colo., made a similar defense of older workers last year before a U.S. Senate committee. "Many older workers maintain a healthy lifestyle and nutrition, follow a program of exercise and take preventative actions to avoid illness, and, as a result, are successful in their work long after younger colleagues begin to decline," he said. "Neither the effective work of the older employee [nor] the ineffective work of the younger employee is the result of age per se. Instead, the work effectiveness reflects non-age-related variables." [7]

Hedblom would readily agree. Speaking of his elderly employees, he says, "They get here on time, go right to work and know exactly what they're doing. They've got good ideas and a wealth of experience to draw upon. And besides that seasoning and maturity, they're very imaginative, very creative — all of which is just wonderful for a small company like ours."

However, some skeptics challenge claims that older workers are just as capable, or only marginally less capable, than younger ones. Posner contends that one reason why most studies do not find age-linked declines in productivity is that they suffer from selection bias.

Green Thumb

Many Green Thumb participants receive on-the-job training as elementary school teacher aides before seeking private-sector jobs.

"Studies that show elderly workers are as good as younger ones . . . overlook the fact that the employer will have gotten rid of those elderly employees who could not perform up to snuff," Posner explains. "The ones whom the employer retains will therefore not be representative of the average abilities of their age cohort. The broader point is that failure to correct for selection bias can cause observers to exaggerate the capabilities of the old, and thus see discrimination where there is none, by mistaking the exceptional members of an age cohort for its average members." [8]

Posner's thesis about the effects of aging on work performance rests largely on the distinction he draws between "fluid intelligence" and "crystallized intelligence." "The earliest change in adulthood," he writes, "is a shift in the balance between fluid intelligence (facility at abstract reasoning and at the acquisition of new skills and capacities) and crystallized intelligence (concrete reasoning based on one's established knowledge base) as the individual accrues experience and his fluid intelligence begins to decline." [9]

At some point in this ongoing process, according to Posner, the older worker becomes almost literally a creature of habit. "[T]he work routines, methods and practices of the older worker, having become habitual, would be difficult for him to change even if there were no age-related decline in fluid intelligence. Habit thus provides an additional reason for expecting older workers to be less flexible, less adaptable to changed circumstances, less likely to learn 'new tricks' than younger ones." [10]

Advocates for the elderly challenge such assertions as examples of age-based bias that are not borne out by workplace experience. "Five years ago," Fretz says, "younger workers tended to be more computer-literate than older workers because they had grown up with computers and learned how to use them in school. That tended to reinforce the 'old dogs and new tricks' stereotype. But when older workers are given the opportunity and the training, they can learn

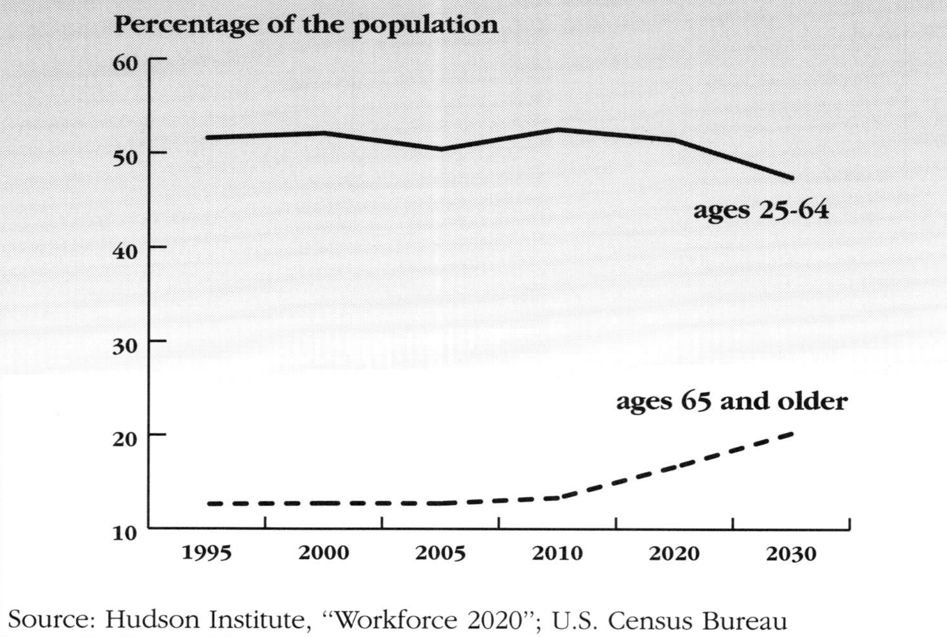

More Older Americans to Work?

The percentage of older Americans is expected to increase in the next century while the percentage of younger Americans decreases. As the Social Security retirement age increases and benefits decrease, more baby boomers reaching what is now considered normal retirement age may choose to remain in the work force.

Source: Hudson Institute, "Workforce 2020"; U.S. Census Bureau

to use computers just as well as younger workers."

Wharton's Useem says employers are partly to blame if older workers fall into a job rut. "You've got to ask yourself how much of that process stems from biological or psychological factors, and how much of it is due to the work environment," he says. "Traditionally, people settle into a job with a particular configuration of technology around them. In your early work years, you're not settled in quite so much. In your later years, you are. Your thinking, your flexibility are partly byproducts of the kind of person the company has made you into."

To guard against premature boredom or burnout, Useem advises companies to offer workers "frequent reassignments or new job responsibilities — not just when somebody is 32 and on the way up the career ladder, but when somebody is 52 and possibly on a career plateau. If companies did more of that, I think the issue of age would begin to drop out of the equation."

Greenberg says there is no difference between the retrainability of older workers and younger workers, provided "the training is well-constructed and well-delivered." He explains, "Any kind of adult education — not just skills education — works best if it is immediately applicable. With job training, that means coming back to work on Monday and putting to use what you learned the previous Thursday and Friday. People with real-life experience in organizational settings are actually more trainable than new workers, because they already know the game."

James Auerbach, senior vice president for the National Policy Association, makes the additional point that older workers typically provide a greater return per retraining dollar than younger ones do. "The old attitude was that you don't spend much on training older workers because they're not going to be around that long," he says. "But studies indicate that older employees tend to stay with a company longer than workers just starting their careers."

Ventrell-Monsees says that, "If we could ever get employers and supervisors to just look at individuals, not age groups, we'd be able to get beyond all this age and discrimination stuff. We try not to talk about the good or the bad traits of older workers, because each person is different."

She thinks that the aging of the baby-boom generation will change perceptions about older workers. "As a generation, they're very different from their parents. Their work lives and lifestyle patterns will be very different also."

Consequently, Ventrell-Monsees expects prevailing stereotypes about older workers to "just go out the window, because they won't fit reality. If you have a 51-year-old employee today with a 2-year-old child, that's a very different person than the average 51-year-old of 25 years ago who had kids in college."

Should public-safety officers be made to retire at a specified age?

Performance concerns about older workers typically center on white-collar or service jobs that involve little physical exertion. In such jobs, it is widely agreed, many older workers can perform at the same level as younger ones. But some experts argue that advancing years can impair performance in occupations calling for strength and quick reflexes. In these fields, they say, mandatory retirement ages are appropriate and non-discriminatory. But advocates for the elderly contend that mandatory retirement programs violate the intent of the ADEA, which is to make employers treat workers on the basis of their individual capabilities.

The issue came to the fore in 1986, when Congress prohibited most employers from requiring workers to retire at a certain age (*see p. 686*). However, the law contained a seven-year exemption for firefighters, law-enforcement officers and tenured college professors. During the exemption period and beyond, lawmakers and other interested parties debated the merits of making the exemption permanent for front-line public-safety officers.

A 1996 Senate hearing examined the pros and cons. Testifying on behalf of the International Association of Fire Fighters, Capt. Tom Miller of the Indianapolis Fire Department urged Congress to restore the exemption. (*See "At Issue," p. 689.*) "The abuse a firefighter's body takes during the course of 20 or 30 years on the job takes its toll," he declared, "and even the best fitness regimen in the world cannot prevent the deterioration of ability that comes with age." [11]

Psychologist Landy strongly disagreed. "The age-related decline of job-related abilities is slight," he told the lawmakers. "In addition, there are substantial variations within any age group in terms of ability. There are 30-year-olds who cannot climb a stairway pulling a charged fire hose, and there are 60-year-olds who can. Further, it is clear that experience makes a substantial contribution to effective work performance. Younger public-safety officers invariably turn to their older colleagues to take the lead in difficult and dangerous actions — and these older colleagues invariably oblige."

Green Thumb

A local police department in Salt Lake City hired this elderly worker through the Green Thumb program. After job training, successful participants go on to a wide range of private-sector jobs, including computer operators and child-care providers.

William H. Smith, 55, a detective sergeant with the Indiana State Police, argued against the ADEA exemption. He recalled negotiating for eight hours to obtain the release of a police officer and a store owner who had been taken hostage by a disgruntled former member of the police force. The negotiations, which ended with the release of the hostages and the surrender of their captor, constituted "the most important job I have done as a police officer," Smith said.

In view of the successful negotiation, he said, "I cannot imagine why my age should make a difference to my success. Indeed, as I have grown older and more experienced, I believe I have become a better negotiator. My real-world experiences and maturity are invaluable here."

Smith went on to draw a parallel with another form of employment bias. "I became a police officer at a time when women were not accepted as police officers — it was assumed, without any evidence, that they couldn't do the job. We have learned otherwise. And, in learning this, we set up better criteria for determining who can and cannot be an officer. Just as sex discrimination is wrong, so is age discrimination."

Robert T. Scully, executive director of the National Association of Police Organizations, strongly disagrees. "Although there are numerous positions that senior citizens can hold well past the age of 65," he told the Senate panel, "policing is not among them. Law enforcement is, by the very nature of the profession, a young person's job. Most police and fire department retirement systems are funded based on years of service ranging from 20-30 years. The expiration of the ADEA [exemption] will jeopardize the integrity of many retirement systems through increased claims for duty-disability retirements."

A strong case for mandatory retirement of public-safety officers also was made by Loren Myhre, a research physiologist in San Antonio, Texas, who has helped develop fitness programs for firefighters.

"By age 55, most American males have experienced a loss in both cardiovascular fitness and muscular strength to a point where they are no longer able to safely and effectively perform a strenuous firefighting task," he testified.

"It is important to note that the decline in physical capability to perform strenuous physical tasks does not suddenly occur when one turns 50 or 60," Myhre added. "It is a physiological phenomenon of aging that occurs slowly, but surely, with every year after the mid-20s." Most men turning 55 "will have reached the point where it would be prudent — for the health and safety of the firefighter and the public he serves — to either retire or to transfer to a less physically demanding occupational endeavor."

On one point, however, Landy and Myhre were in substantial agreement. "The loss of mental capacity with age does not decline with anywhere near the degree of predictability as does the loss of physical strength and endurance," Myhre said. "It is common sense that the establishment of age standards should not be arbitrary, but rather based on the probability of one's ability to perform in a specific career field. Surely, the recommended age of mandatory retirement should be different for those in emergency services than in non-physically demanding fields." ■

BACKGROUND

A Nation of Workers

Age discrimination in employment hardly existed in mid-19th-century America. "The elderly, along with all others, were expected to remain economically and socially useful as long as they were physically able to do so," Judith C. Hushbeck wrote in a 1989 book. "In fact, a popular and quintessentially Protestant prescription against deterioration in later life was more work, not a retreat from it in retirement. The fact that the elderly offered a reservoir of knowledge and experience conferred upon them unique economic value as 'living encyclopedias.' This was especially true in agriculture, which prior to the Civil War accounted for approximately 60 percent of all paid labor and a vast majority of all workers over the age of 60." [12]

For the most part, workers of a century ago stayed on the job until poor health or failing strength made it impossible to continue. Even after ceasing to be wage-earners, those not totally disabled usually were able to perform tasks of value as members of large families, particularly farm households. There was little public discussion of a suitable age for retirement because few, except the rich, could enjoy able-bodied retirement. [13]

Rise of Social Security

Rapid industrial development after the Civil War revolutionized non-agricultural employment, exposing factory workers of all ages to unaccustomed stress. Older workers found it especially hard to adapt to the constant speeding up of production processes. "Industrial working conditions (particularly when coupled with such typical living-condition hazards as poor housing, nutrition and sanitation) made young persons middle-aged, the middle-aged old and the chronologically old person of 60 or 65 expendable," Hushbeck noted. "Economic superannuation, virtually unknown before the advent of the factory system, was the most serious threat of all to continuing employment, because its arrival tended to be permanent." [14]

Similar conditions existed in Europe, where the first attempt was made to provide government financial aid to people no longer able to work. In the 1880s, German Chancellor Otto von Bismarck instituted a comprehensive social insurance program, including both health insurance and an Old Age and Survivors Pension Act. Bismarck designated 65 as the year when old age began — cynics said because he knew that life expectancy then was only 45 years, and the government would not have to pay out much money.

Other European countries followed Germany's lead, most of them also specifying age 65. By the start of World War I in 1914, 10 European countries and several British dominions had adopted economic-protection plans for the elderly. Action lagged in the United States, however. Although a few private pension plans were adopted, and New Jersey instituted a pension plan for teachers in 1896, it was not until after World War I that the movement toward pensioning elderly workers gained momentum. By 1931, 17 states and the territory of Alaska were providing some form of old-age insurance.

The Depression sparked similar action at the federal level. During the 1932 presidential election campaign, old-age and unemployment insurance emerged as major issues. After Franklin D. Roosevelt became president the following year, he summoned experts to develop the program that ultimately became the Social Security Act of 1935. Again, age 65 was used as the touchstone.

The Social Security Act did not compel a worker to retire at 65, but

Continued on p. 684

Chronology

1930s *The Great Depression inspires efforts to relieve widespread economic distress among all age groups.*

1932
Old-age and unemployment insurance become major issues in the presidential race between Herbert Hoover and Franklin D. Roosevelt. After taking office, Roosevelt appoints experts to develop a program.

1935
FDR signs the Social Security Act, which offers workers a financial inducement to leave the labor market upon reaching age 65.

1950s *Social Security amendments adopted during the decade make it easier, in some cases, to retire before 65.*

1954
Congress authorizes a disability "freeze," preserving eligibility for benefits at 65 without further payments by those disabled at an earlier age.

1956
Congress authorizes payments of benefits to disabled workers at age 50. In separate action, it extends old-age benefits, at reduced amounts, to women workers at age 62.

1958
Amendments approved by Congress remove the age threshold for disability benefits and also provide federal payments to dependents of the disabled.

1960s *Federal policy toward older workers shifts from retirement and disability benefits to workplace discrimination.*

1962
The option of retiring at 62 with reduced Social Security benefits is extended to male workers.

1964
President Lyndon B. Johnson issues an executive order banning age discrimination in employment under federal contracts. In passing the Civil Rights Act, Congress directs the secretary of Labor to prepare a report on age discrimination. The report, issued in June 1965, calls for "a clear-cut and implemented federal policy" against such bias.

1965
The Senate includes language barring age discrimination in the Fair Labor Standards Act Amendments, but the provision is stricken from the bill in conference.

1967
Johnson signs the Age Discrimination in Employment Act (ADEA), which protects workers between 40 and 65 from arbitrary age bias.

1970s *ADEA coverage is extended to federal, state and local government workers.*

1978
The ADEA is amended to raise the mandatory retirement age from 65 to 70. Mandatory retirement for most federal employees is abolished the same year.

1980s *The drive against age-related job discrimination is momentarily stalled by the Supreme Court.*

1986
President Ronald Reagan signs legislation barring most employers from setting mandatory retirement ages. However, the measure includes a seven-year exemption for public-safety officers and tenured professors.

1989
The Supreme Court declares in *Ohio v. Betts* that federal laws barring age discrimination do not bar variations based on age in benefit plans.

1990s *Congress reinstates an exemption to the ADEA that had been allowed to expire in 1993.*

1990
President George Bush signs the Older Workers Benefit Protection Act, which effectively reverses the *Betts* ruling. The act establishes new and, in some cases, complex requirements that employers must meet when they offer early retirement incentives.

1991
The Civil Rights Act of 1991 eliminates the statute of limitations for bringing age-discrimination claims under the ADEA.

1996
President Clinton signs legislation authorizing state and local governments to establish mandatory retirement ages for front-line public-safety officers.

Winners of Bias Suits Must Pay Taxes

Relatively few workers who seek damages for age discrimination ever collect from their former employers. And even for those who do, a 1995 Supreme Court ruling makes victory somewhat bittersweet. The high court ruled that a recovery under the Age Discrimination in Employment Act (ADEA) is not excludable from taxable income.

The case, *Commissioner of Internal Revenue v. Schleier,* centered on former United Airlines pilot Erich E. Schleier, who sued the company after it fired him when he reached 60. Schleier and other dismissed United employees filed a class-action lawsuit challenging the company's mandatory-retirement policy. In 1986, he received $145,629 as his portion of a settlement.

Half of that sum represented back pay, while the remainder constituted "liquidated damages" — in effect, punitive damages. United did not withhold any payroll or income taxes from the portion of the settlement attributed to liquidated damages. And the ADEA does not provide for separate recovery of compensatory damages for pain and suffering or emotional distress.

On his 1986 income tax return, Schleier listed the back pay but not the liquidated damages. The Internal Revenue Service notified him that he should have declared the liquidated damages as gross income. Schleier responded by taking the case to federal Tax Court, which held that the entire $145,629 should have been treated as tax-exempt because it represented "damages received . . . on account of personal injuries or sickness." The 5th U.S. Circuit Court of Appeals affirmed the ruling.

In reversing the appellate court decision, the Supreme Court adopted a narrow interpretation of Section 104 of the Internal Revenue Code. Under that part of the law, damages received "on account of personal injuries or sickness" generally are excluded from taxable income on individual tax returns. The rationale for the exclusion is that such awards do not create a taxable gain, but merely compensate the taxpayer for a loss.

However, the high court held that Section 104 is applicable only to situations in which the "personal injuries" at issue are akin to those suffered in a traffic accident. While Schleier's dismissal "may have caused some psychological 'personal' injury comparable to the intangible pain and suffering caused by an automobile accident, it is clear that no part of [his] recovery of back wages is attributable to that injury. . . . In short, [Section 104] does not permit the exclusion of . . . back wages because the recovery of back wages was not 'on account of' any personal injury and because no personal injury affected the amount of back wages recovered."

The court's ruling in *Schleier* left the impression that personal-injury awards will be held excludable from taxable income only when they are the result of actual physical injury. As for the liquidated damages portion of Schleier's ADEA settlement, the court stated that they were punitive in nature. Consequently, they did not stem from his personal injury or sickness.

In a dissenting opinion, Justice Sandra Day O'Connor argued that, "If the harms caused by discrimination constitute personal injury, then amounts received as damages for such discrimination are received 'on account of personal injuries.'" She went on to say that an age-discrimination complaint is clearly a tort claim, qualifying it for exemption from tax liability.

Analyzing the *Schleier* decision, Associate Professor Dorothy A. Brown of the University of Cincinnati's College of Law concluded that the court had done little to clarify an already murky area of federal tax law. "The taxability of judgments will have to be determined on a case-by-case basis, which will necessarily increase the judiciary's workload," she wrote. "Those decisions will inevitably lead to conflicts between the circuits, which in turn will lead to additional Supreme Court decisions. Congressional relief may be required, specifically in the form of an amendment to Section 104 that defines 'personal injury.'"

Above all, Brown predicted, "The current uncertainty will prove costly. Settlement negotiations in personal injury cases will be more difficult, given the uncertain tax treatment." [1]

[1] Dorothy A. Brown, "Winning and Losing," *ABA Journal,* October 1995, p. 48.

Continued from p. 682

it offered the 65-year-old a financial inducement to withdraw from the labor market at a time when there were far from enough jobs to go around. Employers were encouraged to establish 65 as the age of retirement because the availability of Social Security benefits at that age relieved them of criticism they might incur by casting off older workers who had no other means of support.

The law's authors did not pretend that a person undergoes some magic transformation upon reaching age 65. According to Wilbur J. Cohen, an administration official who helped draft the original act, the chief reason for choosing 65 was its effect on the program's cost. "It was understood that a reduction . . . below 65 would substantially increase costs and therefore might impair the possibility of . . . acceptance of the plan by Congress. A higher retirement age . . . was never considered because of the belief that public and congressional opposition would develop against such a provision in view of the widespread unemployment that existed." [15]

At no time, Cohen recalled, did the members or staff of the congressional committees that reviewed the legislation consider any age other than 65, although there was much popular interest at that time in the so-called Townsend plan, which would have granted federal pensions to everyone at age 60.* No studies of the age question were made. Consequently, there was "very little material available to analyze the economic, social, gerontological or other reasons for the selection of this particular age." [16]

Benefits Expended

After World War II, unions were willing to accept forced retirement for their members, usually at 65, in return for improved company pension benefits. At the same time, corporations liked the personnel and bookkeeping tidiness of a flat rule for everybody: 65 and out. So the formula was widely followed, whether the pension-retirement plans were company-initiated or the result of labor-management negotiations.

Social Security amendments in the 1950s exerted a downward push on the retirement age. An amendment adopted in 1954 authorized a disability "freeze," preserving eligibility for benefits at 65 without further payments by those disabled at an earlier age. In 1956, Congress authorized payments of benefits to disabled workers at age 50. Amendments in 1958 removed the age limitation for disability benefits and provided payments for dependents of the disabled.

A change of broader effect had taken place in 1956, when Congress made old-age benefits, at reduced amounts, available to retired women workers at age 62. The change flowed from the dual recognition that widows and single women in their early 60s had meager opportunities for employment, and that many men found it impossible to retire at 65 when their wives, usually several years younger, were not yet eligible for benefits in their own right. In 1962, Congress extended the option of early retirement at 62 to male workers.

* Francis E. Townsend, a California physician, argued that every American should collect a pension of $200 a month at 60, the money to be raised by a federal sales tax.

ADEA Passed

Soon afterward, the emphasis shifted from retiree benefits to age-related job bias. President Lyndon B. Johnson led the way in 1964 by issuing an executive order banning age discrimination in work performed under federal contracts. The same year, during congressional debate on the Civil Rights Act, an amendment was proposed to make "age" a protected class along with race, color, national origin, religion and gender. Although Congress rejected the idea, it directed Secretary of Labor W. Willard Wirtz to study the problem.

Wirtz's report, issued June 30, 1965, said his department had found "no evidence of prejudice based on dislike or intolerance of the older worker." Nonetheless, he said the setting of age limits beyond which an employer would not consider a worker for a job, regardless of ability, "has become a characteristic practice in those states which do not prohibit such action." Consequently, he called for a "clear-cut and implemented federal policy" against age discrimination.

Johnson returned to the age-discrimination issue in a Jan. 23, 1967, message on older Americans. Among other things, he called for legislation to prohibit "arbitrary and unjust discrimination in employment for workers between 45 and 65 years old." He acknowledged, however, that, "Employment opportunities for older workers cannot be increased solely by measures eliminating discrimination." The reason, he explained, is that, "Today's high standards of education, training and mobility often favor the younger worker. Many older men and women are unemployed because they are not fitted for the jobs of modern technology, because they live where there are no longer any jobs or because they are seeking the jobs of a bygone era."

Later in 1967, Congress approved the ADEA, which barred arbitrary, age-related bias in hiring, firing, pay, promotions, demotions, layoffs, benefits and training. The major change in the bill, as requested by the administration, was a reduction of the age limit from 45 to 40 in the definition of older workers. In addition, the bill excluded situations in which age was a bona fide occupational qualification* or hiring an older worker would violate the terms of an existing employee-benefit plan. The ADEA authorized an individual, as well as the secretary of Labor, to bring court action against a violator if the secretary failed, during a specified period of time, to bring about voluntary compliance through conciliation.

The ADEA protects job applicants as well as persons already employed. American citizens working for U.S. companies overseas also are covered. However, the law does not apply to elected officials or consultants. In addition, the ADEA contains several exceptions to its broad prohibitions. For instance, employers may retire certain executives or high policy-

* To claim successfully that an age limit is a bona fide job qualification, an employer must prove that there is a substantial basis for believing that all or nearly all people who are excluded by the age limit cannot perform the job; or that it is impossible or highly impractical for the employer to test all the employees individually to determine if each has the necessary qualifications.

making employees at age 65.

New Anti-Bias Laws

During the 1970s, the ADEA's coverage was broadened to include federal, state and local government employees. Moreover, the mandatory retirement age was raised from 65 to 70 for all workers except those employed by the federal government, where the upper age limit was abolished.

Under legislation passed in 1986, Congress barred most employers from setting mandatory retirement ages. A seven-year exemption was included for firefighters, law-enforcement officers and tenured college professors. The exemption effectively overruled a 1985 Supreme Court decision in which the justices said the city of Baltimore could not require that all firefighters retire at 55.

Passage of the law was especially gratifying to Rep. Claude Pepper, D-Fla., 86, the oldest member of Congress. "This legislation is an important step in guaranteeing the elderly of this nation a fundamental civil right — the right to work as long as they are willing and able," he said. But officials of business groups warned that the law could lead to the dismissal of more older employees for incompetency. Companies might not be willing to make allowances for older workers, the officials said, if they could not count on their retirement at a certain age.

The next major revision of the ADEA also was prompted by a Supreme Court opinion. Ruling in 1989 in *Ohio v. Betts,* the court offered a broad interpretation of an exemption in the ADEA "for a bona fide employee-benefit plan such as a retirement, pension or insurance plan, which is not a subterfuge to evade the purposes" of the law.

The case centered on June M. Betts, an employee of Hamilton County, Ohio, who was forced to retire at 61 for health reasons and thus was ineligible for the more generous medical disability benefits available to government workers under age 60. Justice Anthony M. Kennedy, writing for the 7-2 court majority, said the ADEA did not require employers to justify differential benefits on the basis of cost. In so ruling, the court struck down the "equal cost or equal benefit" guideline the EEOC had used in enforcing age-discrimination law.

The only way to successfully challenge a benefits plan, said Kennedy, was to show it was aimed at discriminating in some non-fringe-benefit area, such as hiring or firing. In a dissenting opinion, Justice Thurgood Marshall argued that the decision "immunizes virtually all employee benefit programs from liability" under the ADEA.

Older Workers Law

Several members of Congress, contending that the court had misconstrued the law, began drafting legislation to overturn *Betts* within weeks of the ruling. The result was the Older Workers Benefit Protection Act (OWBPA), signed into law by President George Bush on Oct. 16, 1990. "Congress did not intend for older workers to go unprotected from age discrimination in an employment area as critical as employee benefits," said Rep. Edward R. Roybal, D-Calif., chairman of the House Select Committee on Aging. [17]

In addition to overruling *Betts,* OWBPA codified the EEOC guideline that the court had invalidated. However, the law also allowed employers to continue using the two most widely used types of early-retirement incentive programs — pension subsidies and Social Security supplements, or "bridge" payments. Subsidized early-retirement benefits eliminate all or part of the actuarial reduction of payments that would otherwise occur for employees who retire early under a defined-benefit plan, which prescribes a set amount the company pays the employee in retirement based on income and length of service.

The second type of inducement, bridge payments, are fixed monthly sums given to early retirees to substitute for the Social Security benefits they will become eligible for at 62 or 65. Under the law, employees enrolling in pension-subsidy or bridge-payment programs may sue for age discrimination only if they claim their participation was coerced.

Another key section of the law sharply restricted an employer's ability to obtain waivers of ADEA-related rights and claims from employees. The law stated that the only waivers permitted under the OWBPA are those that are "knowing and voluntary." To meet the law's requirements, such waivers must be written in easily understood language, include a recommendation to consult with an attorney and give employees time to change their mind before the waiver becomes final. Moreover, employees may not waive rights or claims that may develop after the agreement is signed.

The OWBPA was largely a compromise hammered out by Sens. Howard M. Metzenbaum, D-Ohio, and Orrin G. Hatch, R-Utah. As enacted, the measure allowed employers to offset long-term disability payments with pension benefits when an employee chose to begin receiving a pension or reached normal retirement age. Metzenbaum, now retired, had wanted to allow the offset only in case of voluntary retirement. Hatch, in contrast, had sought a broader offset in all cases, based on a worker's accrued pension eligibility.

Certain other provisions seemed clearly tilted in employers' favor. For instance, the burden of proof in em-

Taking a Discrimination Case to Court

Workers who think they are victims of age-based job discrimination should realize at the outset that seeking redress can be time-consuming and costly, and that a successful outcome is far from certain.

If workers are unable to negotiate settlements with their employers, the next step is to file a formal complaint with the Equal Employment Opportunity Commission (EEOC). This launches a commission investigation and an attempt to resolve the matter. More important, notifying the EEOC preserves the complainant's right to file a lawsuit later.

During the investigative process, the EEOC may seek to arrange a settlement between the employer and the employee. However, the process can be terminated at any time if the agency finds the employee's complaint to be without merit. Indeed, such findings are made in six of every 10 age-discrimination cases that come before the EEOC.

At this point, the complainant must decide whether to pursue the grievance by bringing suit against the employer. But under the Age Discrimination in Employment Act (ADEA), no such action may be taken until at least 60 days after filing the complaint with the EEOC.

Taking an ADEA case to court offers several potential remedies to workers, according to the American Association of Retired Persons (AARP). "The ADEA provides for jury trials, which may be an advantage to a long-service employee who has been the victim of discrimination," the organization says. "Back pay, lost wages, benefits and reinstatement may be awarded to successful age-discrimination litigants." [1]

But the AARP adds this caveat: "In deciding whether to file a lawsuit, you should realize that litigation takes a great deal of commitment, as well as time and money. It can also take an emotional and personal toll on the individual and his or her family. You should discuss these concerns with your lawyer and your family in deciding the wisest course of action to take." [2]

Above all, a person taking an age-discrimination case to court should be armed with material documenting the allegations. In an article on ways to combat age discrimination in the workplace, journalist Laurence I. Barrett urged older employees to take these steps, among others:

- Volunteer immediately for any company offer of training to enhance job skills. "If you get into the program, it may improve your performance. If you're turned down — older workers frequently are — that rejection may help you in a later confrontation."
- Take note of any pejorative remarks about age and job performance by company supervisors. "If supervisors frequently relate graying hair with work performance or otherwise disparage the abilities of older people, that can be held against the employer in a future investigation."
- Collect evidence of the company's satisfaction with your performance. "If you get written evaluations, keep them. If the report is oral, take notes. Also retain records of promotions, raises and bonuses. The pack-rat routine will help protect you against claims of incompetence." [3]

[1] American Association of Retired Persons, *Age Discrimination on the Job* (1994), p. 18.

[2] *Loc. cit.*

[3] Laurence I. Barrett, "Will Our Age Cost Us Our Jobs?" *New Choices: Living Even Better After 50*, March 1997, p. 50.

ployee-benefit claims was placed on workers. In addition, language requiring employers to pay employees' legal fees was dropped from the section on waivers.

Opinion on the OWBPA's impact is mixed. Fretz believes the law has been "helpful," since employee waivers of rights and claims had been "a serious problem" before it was passed. However, he feels some difficulties remain.

He cites, for example, the hypothetical case of workers who accepted an employer's RIF (reduction in force) severance offer, only to learn later that the deal may have been "age-tainted." Some courts, Fretz says, have required laid-off workers who challenged suspect settlements to hand back all of their severance pay. That, he adds, is "a very harsh result which effectively prevents the worker from challenging a RIF or even a waiver that was improperly obtained."

In Fretz's opinion, "most workers who hit the streets need that severance pay, because of the much longer and harder trip back into employment. I'm not saying they should get a windfall; they would have to offset any damages collected from severance received, of course. But the point is that this is another legal issue that needs to be addressed."

Issacharoff views the OWBPA less charitably, characterizing it as "a wealth grab" by employees who already were relatively well-off. The law, he argues, "redirected a tremendous amount of the wage capital that was available in many enterprises to the older and most privileged section of the work force." ■

CURRENT SITUATION

Action by Congress

After nearly three years of stalemate, Congress approved legislation late in 1996 permitting states and localities to set mandatory retirement ages for law-enforcement officers and firefighters. A similar though temporary exemption from the ADEA had expired at the end of 1993. The new measure also allowed police and fire departments to set maximum entry ages for recruits and authorized state and local governments to incorporate the rules into their overall personnel policies for public-safety officers.*

Under another provision, the law directed the EEOC to establish guidelines for tests to evaluate the fitness of public-safety workers, regardless of age. However, some of the bill's supporters questioned the need for such testing.

"It is simply not possible to devise a test for all tasks carried out by a public-safety employee," said Rep. Major R. Owens, D-N.Y., shortly before the House approved the measure. "Moreover, there is no current test that can effectively screen for the risk of sudden incapacitation among asymptomatic individuals. A mandatory retirement age, used in conjunction with screening for other risk factors, continues to be the most effective way of reducing the risk of sudden incapacitation by public-safety officers." [18]

A secondary concern, Owens said, is that "it is enormously expensive to administer performance and ability tests on a periodic basis to all public-safety employees, consuming scarce resources that are needed to keep police on the streets. In addition, testing often entails considerable litigation over the content of the tests."

A mandatory retirement age simply recognizes the "medical fact" that "physical ability declines with age," Owens declared. The effects of aging "are not experienced by all people the same degree or at the same precise time. But they pose a significant problem to public-safety agencies in their efforts to maintain a fit and effective work force." [19]

Two earlier attempts to enact a permanent ADEA exemption for public-safety workers ended in failure. In late 1993, a House-passed bill died in the Senate. The House added a similar provision to a 1994 crime bill, but it was removed in conference.

The lawmaker who blocked both measures was Metzenbaum, an outspoken advocate for the elderly. But his retirement in 1994 cleared the way for Senate approval of the 1995 bill. It finally became law as part of the omnibus appropriations bill signed by President Clinton on Sept. 30, 1996.

Few Winning Suits

Despite the safeguards written into the ADEA, relatively few individuals charging age discrimination ever receive redress. Indeed, bringing such charges can be grueling. "In filing a lawsuit, you should be realistic about the costs for such an action," the AARP cautions. "ADEA cases, like other lawsuits, can cost a great deal of money and take substantial time. . . . It is important to listen to the advice of the attorney about the merits of the case and the likelihood of success, and the practical considerations about bringing a lawsuit." [20]

At least 60 days before filing suit, an aggrieved individual must file a charge with either the EEOC or a state fair-employment-practices agency. This cooling-off period is designed to give the EEOC or state agency time to mediate the grievance through informal methods of conciliation, conference and persuasion.

The record shows that only a small fraction of complainants recover damages through the auspices of the EEOC. In fiscal 1996, 61 percent of the 21,253 cases resolved by the agency were terminated because it found the complaint to have "no reasonable cause." Another 30 percent were ended through "administrative closure," a catchall term for circumstances that make it impossible to pursue a case further. *(See table, p. 676.)*

Only about 9 percent of the age-discrimination cases resolved by the EEOC in 1996 ended with the charging party receiving benefits. In contrast, benefits — usually modest — were awarded in 18 percent of the cases concluded in 1990. Age-discrimination experts credit the decline at least in part to employers' growing sophistication in crafting downsizing strategies that can survive ADEA scrutiny.

Nonetheless, some age-discrimination lawsuits have ended with large payouts, among them the settlement reached with Lockheed Martin Corp. last November. The giant defense contractor, which admitted to no wrongdoing, agreed to give about $13 million in back pay to 2,000 former employees and to rehire about 450 other workers to settle the lawsuit, brought by the EEOC.

"This settlement underscores EEOC's commitment to upholding the job rights of older workers and ensuring non-discrimination in corporate layoff and downsizing practices," said commission Chairman Gilbert F. Casellas.

Commenting on the case in a magazine for older readers, journalist Laurence F. Barrett observed: "The class-action strategy against Lockheed may serve as a warning to major companies that may be planning cutbacks. But that is of little consolation to the laid-off workers who are netting small payouts. Had they de-

Continued on p. 690

* According to the National Association of Police Organizations, the retirement age for U.S. public-safety workers ranges from 55 to 65, depending on the locality, and the maximum hiring age is generally between 30 and 35.

At Issue:

Should public-safety officers be subject to mandatory retirement?

CAPT. TOM MILLER
Indianapolis Fire Department

FROM TESTIMONY BEFORE THE SENATE COMMITTEE ON LABOR AND HUMAN RESOURCES, MARCH 9, 1996, ON BEHALF OF THE INTERNATIONAL ASSOCIATION OF FIRE FIGHTERS

yes

The abuse a firefighter's body takes during the course of 20 or 30 years on the job takes its toll, and even the best fitness regimen in the world cannot prevent the deterioration of ability that occurs with age. That is why the nation's professional firefighters support an exemption from the ADEA for public-safety occupations to allow local fire and police departments the option of using mandatory retirement and/or maximum entry-age limits.

To be perfectly frank, the need for this exemption is so apparent, so much a matter of common sense, that I am at a loss to understand why it is the subject of controversy. As I have followed the debate on this issue over the past several years, it has occurred to me that the people opposed to the exemption . . . really don't understand firefighting. . . .

This lack of comprehension is reflected in the argument that age limits can be replaced by annual job-performance tests for public-safety officers. While this sounds ideal in theory, it is unworkable in the real world of firefighting.

The biggest problem with fitness tests is simply that they do not replicate real world public-safety experiences. . . . A job performance test can measure a person's ability to climb three flights of stairs carrying a hose. But it cannot measure a person's ability to perform that task in a smoke-filled building in sub-zero temperatures. . . .

Finally, there are many important areas that fitness tests can not even begin to measure. For example, there is no test that can predict the likelihood that a person will have a heart attack. This factor is extremely important because if a firefighter suffers a heart attack in an emergency situation, people's lives are at stake. . . .

Perhaps an even more relevant analogy is the use of mandatory retirement ages in the military. The armed services have found age limits essential to the maintenance of our national defense. . . . We are America's domestic defenders, and the nature of our work and our method of operation parallel the military in many respects. . . .

But what makes firefighters a unique breed is that we always put the safety of the public ahead of our own interests. Each one of us takes an oath upon entering the fire service to protect the public safety, and we are sworn to uphold that oath regardless of the personal costs. Mandatory retirement ages are necessary to protect the lives and property of our neighbors, and we are committed to that goal even if it calls for a sacrifice from some of our own brothers and sisters.

DET. WILLIAM H. SMITH
Indiana State Police

FROM TESTIMONY BEFORE THE SENATE COMMITTEE ON LABOR AND HUMAN RESOURCES, MARCH 8, 1996, ON BEHALF OF THE AMERICAN ASSOCIATION OF RETIRED PERSONS

no

In an instance of special importance to our department, I was called on to negotiate the release of a police officer taken hostage along with a store owner by a man who had been fired from the police force. It took eight hours of patience and imagination — he surrendered only after I promised to have a beer with him. Which, by the way, I did after he was taken into custody.

In many ways, this is the most important job I have done as a police officer; I cannot imagine why my age should make a difference to my success. Indeed, as I have grown older and more experienced, I believe I have become a better negotiator. My real world experiences and maturity are invaluable here. I fail to understand how anybody can say I shouldn't do this job because of my years of service. . . .

I'm not the only police officer who, at age 55 or 60 or 65, has maintained the physical and mental fitness to do this job right. There are a lot of firefighters and police officers who have just as much or more to offer their employers and the citizens of their states and cities than I do. Being able to do the job — being physically fit and mentally attuned to the demands of police work — should be the standard by which every police officer is judged, regardless of age. . . .

I have not made a lot of money as a police officer. If I am forced to retire now, my pension will be less than half of my current salary: about $21,000 after almost 29 years. My pension is equal to 50 percent of my three highest years of salary. Because we just received a major upward adjustment in pay — after years of being paid well below proper working scale — working for the next few years will add about $6,000. If I retired now, I would no longer be able to afford to help my daughter with her college payments. . . . A lot of officers my age still have children in college and mortgages to pay. Like me, they can't live on their current pension.

I need to continue working because I need the money now and because I need to increase my retirement plan. . . . Indeed, I couldn't even withdraw money from my IRA — if I could have afforded to have had one — until I was almost 60. And I'm not old enough to get Social Security benefits. But I can be thrown out of my job because I am too old.

Continued from p. 688

clined to become part of the EEOC's class-action suit, they could have gambled on pursuing an individual action against the company." [21]

Barrett also pointed to a recent trend among employers that could undermine government efforts to combat age discrimination. Some companies have started requiring newly hired workers to sign a contract calling for compulsory arbitration of any future job-related disputes.

"In that arrangement, the worker waives all rights to use statutory protection as the basis of a suit against the employer," Barrett noted. "Though the deal is ostensibly voluntary, in practical terms it is a condition of employment." [22]

The emergence of these "front-door" pacts disturbs EEOC officials. "This device has the potential almost to nullify our statutes," said Jerry Scanlan, an agency lawyer. [23] ■

OUTLOOK

Demographic Realities

Looking ahead, some age-discrimination specialists foresee — or at least hope for — continued economic expansion. That, they say, will create labor shortages in many fields, opening job opportunities for older workers. But other experts argue that companies will still be intent on holding down payroll costs during boom times. As a result, they contend, the number of new jobs for workers over 40 may fall short of expectations.

A recent study by the Hudson Institute sketched a profile of the American work force a quarter-century from now. "Brute demographic facts — the large number of aging baby boomers, considered in conjunction with the smaller number of baby-busters financing Social Security and Medicare through payroll taxes — will almost certainly result in further hikes in the retirement age and less generous benefits," the study asserted. "Boomers reaching what are now considered normal retirement ages may wish to exit the work force, but many will probably lack the means to do so." [24]

Moreover, the study concluded that older Americans "will be more likely to remain in the work force insofar as they are better educated than their counterparts in the past. Better-educated, older Americans — like better-educated Americans of all ages — are more likely to participate in the work force." But they may not choose to keep working because they want to: "[M]any if not most white-collar boomers will discover that their private savings and Social Security benefits fall far short of replacing their former earnings." [25]

Continued employment of more workers in their late 60s or even older seems likely to impose hardships on employers, according to the study. "First, as retirement ages become increasingly less predictable, work force planning will become more uncertain," it said. "Human-resource professionals will find it hard to predict the date at which older workers will retire.

"Second, the continued presence of top-level older employees may cause dissension among their middle-aged subordinates eager for promotion. Employers may need to create new 'off line' or part-time positions for senior employees, to provide younger workers with opportunities for advancement." [26]

In the view of Wharton's Useem, the role of older workers in the work force of tomorrow echoes that of the Hudson research team. "A robust economy ought to be good for all groups that have had trouble finding jobs," he says. "And so long as the labor market stays tight, older people who have left the work force may come back into it."

But if the formerly employed start working again, Auerbach says, their job status will not be the same as before. "They'll be working as consultants and contingent workers — that kind of thing. But really, that would be just a continuation of today's existing pattern."

Ventrell-Monsees, in contrast, isn't convinced that an emerging labor shortage will automatically translate into job openings for older workers. "That hasn't been the experience so far," she says, noting that "there are other ways employers can meet their work force needs," such as exporting jobs or importing labor.

Columbia's Bartel also is skeptical. "Companies now have opportunities to substitute machinery for workers, and they're going to look for the most efficient way to manufacture their product," she says. "I don't think they're going to hire people unless they feel absolutely certain they're at the skill level that's required."

The University of Texas' Issacharoff even challenges the notion that the nation's work force is growing older. "The data on that are quite interesting," he says. "Despite the perception of the work force as graying, the reality is that retirement ages for all but the highest strata of professional and managerial employees are decreasing. People are leaving the work force earlier than in prior generations."

He acknowledges that the demise of mandatory retirement means some people are staying in the work force after 65. "But that trend is largely confined to professional employees — academics and people in other types of high-education, high-income occupations."

Moreover, Issacharoff doubts that

the looming Social Security and Medicare benefits squeeze will derail the movement toward earlier retirement. "A booming economy and a very strong stock market give a greater measure of financial security to many Americans, so the current retirement pattern should continue," he says. "Most working people seem to want to retire as soon as a certain level of pension and Social Security benefits is reached."

Regardless of what happens in coming years, Auerbach of the National Policy Association feels sure that age discrimination "will be a diminished problem" — though one that isn't likely to vanish. There will be "enlightened employers who will be happy to retain certain older workers" and others "who will find they have no choice but to go to the older work pool for the kind of employees they're looking for.

"It's all going to be a matter of finding workers — period — and employers no longer will have the luxury of picking and choosing." ■

FOR MORE INFORMATION

American Association of Retired Persons, 601 E St. N.W., Washington, D.C. 20049; (202) 434-2300. The AARP's Retired Persons' Worker Equity Program seeks to safeguard the employment rights of older employees.

American Bar Association, Commission on Legal Problems of the Elderly, 740 15th St. N.W., Washington, D.C. 2005; (202) 662-8690. The commission monitors employment discrimination issues and other matters of interest to older Americans.

American Management Association, 135 W. 50th St., New York, N.Y. 10020-1201; (212) 586-8100. The association analyzes job-related age discrimination issues from an employer's perspective.

Equal Employment Advisory Council, 1015 15th St. N.W., Suite 1200, Washington, D.C. 20005; (202) 789-8650. Composed of equal-employment officers and lawyers, the council monitors legislation and public policy for businesses.

Equal Employment Opportunity Commission, 1801 L St. N.W., Washington, D.C. 20507; (202) 663-4900. The EEOC is the federal agency charged with administering the Age Discrimination in Employment Act.

National Senior Citizens Law Center, 1815 H St. N.W., Washington, D.C. 20006; (202) 887-5280. The center acts as an advocate for elderly, poor clients in litigation and administrative affairs in a number of areas, including employment.

Notes

[1] Richard A. Posner, *Aging and Old Age* (1995), p. 319.

[1] *Ibid.,* p. 329.

[3] *Ibid.,* pp. 325-326.

[4] *Ibid.,* p. 337.

[5] Commission of Legal Problems of the Elderly, American Bar Association, *Downsizing in an Aging Work Force* (1992), p. 7.

[6] *Ibid.,* pp. 9-10.

[7] Statement before U.S. Senate Committee on Labor and Human Resources, March 8, 1996. Landy testified on behalf of the American Psychological Association. In the 1980s, he headed a Pennsylvania State University research team that conducted a study for Congress to determine the feasibility of using tests of workers' physical and mental abilities instead of their chronological age in making retirement decisions regarding public-safety officers.

[8] Posner, *op. cit.,* p. 359.

[9] *Ibid.,* p. 94.

[10] *Ibid.,* p. 82.

[11] Testimony before U.S. Senate Committee on Labor and Human Resources, March 8, 1996.

[12] Judith C. Hushbeck, *Old and Obsolete: Age Discrimination and the American Worker, 1860-1920* (1989), p. 19.

[13] For background, see "Paying for Retirement," *The CQ Researcher,* Nov. 5, 1993, pp. 973-996.

[14] Hushbeck, *op. cit.,* p. 144.

[15] University of California Institute of Industrial Relations, *Retirement Policies Under Social Security* (1957), quoted in White House Conference on Aging, *Background Paper on Employment Security and Retirement of Older Workers,* July 1960, p. 35.

[16] *Loc. cit.*

[17] Quoted in *1990 CQ Almanac,* p. 362.

[18] Remarks on House floor, March 28, 1995.

[19] *Loc cit.*

[20] American Association of Retired Persons, "Age Discrimination on the Job," 1994, pp. 17-18.

[21] Laurence I. Barrett, "Will Our Age Cost Us Our Jobs?" *New Choices: Living Even Better After 50,* March 1997, p. 49.

[22] *Ibid.,* p. 48.

[23] Quoted by Barrett, *loc. cit.*

[24] Hudson Institute, *Workforce 2020: Work and Workers in the 21st Century* (1997), p. 94. *Workforce 2020* is an updated version of the 1987 Hudson Institute study *Workforce 2000.*

[25] *Ibid.,* pp. 103-104.

[26] *Ibid.,* pp. 104-105

Bibliography

Selected Sources Used

Books

Hushbeck, Judith C., *Old and Obsolete: Age Discrimination and the American Worker, 1860-1920,* Garland Publishing, 1989.
Transformation of the United States from an agrarian to an industrial economy, writes Hushbeck, radically altered perceptions of older workers' role in society. With the coming of the machine age, workers experienced burnout at ever-earlier ages. This development, in turn, eroded general respect for older people based on their accumulated experience and wisdom.

Posner, Richard A., *Aging and Old Age,* the University of Chicago Press, 1995.
Posner, a distinguished jurist and academic, takes issue with studies suggesting that older workers are just as capable as younger ones, except with regard to physical strength and endurance. He argues that age brings a decline in "fluid intelligence" — his term for abstract reasoning and the ability to acquire new skills. Older people, he contends, come to rely primarily on "crystallized intelligence," which he defines as "concrete reasoning based on one's established knowledge base."

Articles

Barrett, Laurence I., "Will Age Cost Us Our Jobs?" *New Choices: Living Even Better After 50,* March 1997.
Barrett, who teaches journalism at American University in Washington, D.C., offers advice on how to avoid becoming a victim of age-based job discrimination. Among other things, he recommends volunteering immediately for any company-sponsored program to upgrade job skills.

Gillin, Charles T., "Political Elites and Regulatory Bureaucrats: A Case Study Concerning Age Discrimination," *Journal of Aging and Social Policy,* Vol. 8, No. 1, 1996.
Gillin, a sociology professor at Ryerson Polytechnical University in Toronto, Canada, examines key developments in U.S. age-discrimination policy and legislation since the early 1960s.

Landthorn, Tricia Lynne, "Two Wrongs Can Make a Right: *McKennon v. Nashville Banner Publishing Co.* and the After-Acquired Evidence Doctrine," *Ohio State Law Journal,* Vol. 56, No. 3, 1995.
The author focuses on a case decided by the Supreme Court in 1995 that involved not just age discrimination by a major Tennessee newspaper but also violations of company policy by the affected employee.

Simon, Ruth, "Too Damn Old," *Money,* July 1996.
In a generally gloomy assessment of recent developments, Simon concludes that age discrimination actually has worsened since the ADEA was enacted in 1967. She finds that workers over 40 have been disproportionately hurt by plant closings and downsizing, and have more trouble obtaining training or new jobs.

Ventrell-Monsees, Cathy, "How Useful Are Legislative Remedies: America's Experience With the ADEA," *Ageing International,* September 1993.
Ventrell-Monsees, a litigator for the American Association of Retired Persons (AARP), surveys the benefits older Americans have reaped from laws against age-related bias in the workplace. But she cautions that much remains to be done. "The time has come," she writes, "for age discrimination to be viewed and treated with the same condemnation as society views and treats discrimination based on race and gender."

Reports and Studies

American Association of Retired Persons, "Age Discrimination on the Job," 1994.
This booklet published by the AARP, the nation's chief advocacy group for older Americans, sets forth the discriminatory actions prohibited by the ADEA. It also explains how to identify age-discrimination practices — and how to take legal action against them, if need be.

Commission on Legal Problems of the Elderly, American Bar Association, "Downsizing in an Aging Work Force: The Law, the Limits, and the Lessons," 1992.
Written to accompany a 25-minute video, this booklet focuses on employers' obligations under the 1990 Older Worker Benefit Protection Act, which spells out the terms and conditions that must be met before instituting voluntary and involuntary reductions in the work force.

Hudson Institute, "Workforce 2020," 1997.
This study, an update of the institute's "Workforce 2000" report of 1987, examines how the U.S. economy may adapt to the aging of the baby-boom generation.

U.S. Senate Committee on Labor and Human Resources, "Age Discrimination in Employment Amendments of 1995" (published proceedings of hearing held on March 8, 1996).
Government officials, academics and public-employee representatives debate the merits of a bill (subsequently enacted) to allow state and local governments to require front-line public-safety personnel to retire at a specified age.

The Next Step

Additional information from UMI's Newspaper & Periodical Abstracts™ database

Ageism

Bennett, Julie, "Battling age bias in the information age," *Chicago Tribune,* Dec. 22, 1996, p. 1.
The Operation ABLE (Ability Based on Long Experience) office in Chicago, Ill., oversees a wide area network that links it to 30 regional agencies enabling it to find computerized jobs for older workers.

King, Ian, "Tebbit gets on his bike to attack cult of ageism," *The Guardian,* Oct. 10, 1996, p. 20.
Lord Tebbit took time off from the United Kingdom Tory Party's conference on Oct. 9, 1996, to attack the "cult of ageism," which he admitted made it difficult for anyone over age 55 to find a job.

Puig, Claudia, "He's on a double mission in fight against ageism," *Los Angeles Times,* Aug. 15, 1996, p. F1.
Motion picture director Ted Post is profiled. Post has formed Pro Bono Productions to showcase the talent and expertise of older union and guild members in Hollywood and to combat ageism.

Sicker, Martin, "Age discrimination in employment," *Modern Maturity,* March 1997, pp. 77-79.
To eliminate age discrimination in the workplace, the traditional stereotypes of older workers must be changed. This can be done by convincing employers to reassess the value of the older worker.

Age Discrimination in Employment

Davis, Ann, "Legal beat: Firing follows early-retirement refusal," *The Wall Street Journal,* Jan. 14, 1997, p. B11.
Burt N. Sempier, formerly of Johnson & Higgins, an insurance brokerage firm based in New York, claims he refused his firm's offer to take early retirement at least five times before his bosses forced him to resign at age 59, citing poor performance. Sempier then joined a growing number of high-ranking corporate officers suing their companies for age discrimination.

Kleiman, Carol, "Age Discrimination Case Resurrects Old Concept of 'Perky,'" *Chicago Tribune,* May 20, 1997, p. 3.
According to a report by Ann Davis in *The Wall Street Journal,* six of 11 receptionists at the law firm of Pillsbury Madison & Sutro who were over 60 were fired in an effort to "cultivate Silicon Valley clients." The former employees have filed an age-discrimination suit, which is scheduled to be heard in San Francisco County Superior court in August.

Leib, Jeffrey, "Martin age-bias settlement OK'd," *The Denver Post,* April 16, 1997, p. C1.
U.S. District Judge Wiley Y. Daniel has approved an agreement between Lockheed Martin Corp. and the Equal Employment Opportunity Commission that settles an age-discrimination suit brought by the agency on behalf of more than 1,700 former Lockheed Martin employees. On March 5, Daniel heard testimony in his Denver, Colo., courtroom from about 50 former employees who opposed the agreement, which calls for the company to pay 1,780 victims of the 1990-94 layoffs a total of $13 million in compensation.

Lewis, Diane E., "Vermont grocer ordered to pay $910,000 in age bias suit," *The Boston Globe,* May 13, 1997, p. C5.
A Vermont wholesale grocery firm was ordered to pay $910,000 to settle an age-discrimination suit filed by the Equal Employment Opportunity Commission on behalf of dozens of applicants who were turned down for work at the grocer because they were older than 40.

"Marietta Age Suit Pact," *The New York Times,* April 17, 1997, p. D1.
A federal judge has approved a settlement valued at approximately $183 million in a five-year-old age-discrimination lawsuit against the Lockheed Martin Corp.'s predecessor, the Martin Marietta Corp. The agreement between the Equal Employment Opportunity Commission and the company, approved by Federal District Judge Wiley Daniel in Denver, Colo., provides for $13 million in cash payments to 3,459 former workers who were over 40 when they were dismissed from the company's astronautics division between 1990 and 1995.

O'Brien, Sue, "People of a certain age," *The Denver Post,* March 16, 1997, p. D4.
When the Age Discrimination in Employment Act was passed 30 years ago, *The Times* reports, fully half of private-sector job openings were advertised as open only to those under 55. That would be illegal today. Discrimination, however, still flourishes, as the $40.9 million paid last year to settle age-discrimination cases attests. The firing of Denver investigative reporter Dave Minshall is discussed.

Segal, David, "Bias Award Stands; More Suits Seen; Ruling Treated Partner As Ernst & Young Worker," *The Washington Post,* May 28, 1997, p. D9.

The Supreme Court on May 27, 1997, let stand a lower court ruling awarding more than $4 million to a partner at one of the nation's largest accounting firms who had sued for age discrimination. By declining to review *Ernst & Young L.L.P. v. Simpson,* the high court left unresolved a question that has vexed accounting and law firms for years: Are partners considered employees under the law? The Ernst & Young case was closely watched by law firms across the country, which were concerned that allowing the multimillion-dollar judgment to stand would spur a flood of lawsuits from disgruntled partners.

Smith, Kerri S., "Suit memos unsealed; Storage Tek papers suggest 'problems' of older workers," ***The Denver Post,*** **May 2, 1997, p. C1.**

A Storage Technology Corp. memo described older workers as "less productive and . . . compensated more than they can contribute to the company," according to court documents unsealed Thursday by a federal court judge. Another memo detailing "associated problems" of an aging work force said two older workers are needed to perform one job. The memo also predicted an increase in the company's health and life insurance costs and a "decrease in morale of younger workers." StorageTek spokesman David Reid said most of the age-related comments were picked up from a textbook on pension planning that a company human-resource manager consulted while writing the memo.

Stein, M. L. "Copley sued for $12 million," ***Editor & Publisher,*** **May 31, 1997, p. 24.**

Four former editorial employees of Copley Los Angeles Newspapers are suing the company for $12 million, alleging they were fired on the basis of age and disability discrimination in violation of state and federal laws.

Age Discrimination in Employment Act

Ayres, Jeffrey P., and Larry R. Seegull, "Downsized partners may bring ADEA suits," ***National Law Journal,*** **Sept. 30, 1996, pp. D1.**

Under the federal Age Discrimination in Employment Act, dismissed partners in downsizing efforts who can be characterized as employees may claim age discrimination. In light of the significant risks that the discharge of a partner may result in ADEA liability, prudent law firms will give careful consideration to effectuating a smooth transition after a partner departure.

Barrett, Paul M., "Supreme Court expands scope of law on age discrimination in employment," ***The Wall Street Journal,*** **April 2, 1996, p. B2.**

In a unanimous ruling on April 1, 1996, the Supreme Court expanded the scope of the Age Discrimination in Employment Act. The question in the Supreme Court case was whether a worker may sue under the act even if his replacement is also 40 or older. The high court's answer was yes.

Hukill, Craig, "Labor and the Supreme Court: Significant issues of 1992-96," ***Monthly Labor Review,*** **January 1997, pp. 3-28.**

From 1992 to 1996, the Supreme Court decided several cases in labor law and employment law. Hukill reviews the labor and employment cases the Supreme Court has handled recently.

"Protecting Older Workers," ***The New York Times,*** **April 5, 1996, p. A26.**

An editorial supports a Supreme Court decision written by Justice Antonin Scalia that strengthens the Age Discrimination in Employment Act, which bans discrimination based on age regardless of the age of the person who eventually gets the job or promotion.

Avoiding Age-Discrimination Law Suits

"Avoiding age discrimination," ***HR Focus,*** **October 1996, p. 11.**

The aging of baby boomers and ongoing downsizing mean the potential for more lawsuits charging age discrimination. Steps that forward-looking companies can take to head off age-discrimination claims are discussed.

Flynn, Gillian, "Are you sure you don't discriminate?" ***Workforce,*** **May 1997, pp. 101, 104.**

A newer, subtler form of discrimination, "code words," can put a company at risk. Advice on preventing claims of age discrimination is given.

Labich, Kenneth, "How to fire people and still sleep at night," ***Fortune,*** **June 10, 1996, pp. 64-72.**

Shedding employees is something almost every manager dreads. If managers don't think hard about the process before taking any action, they and their companies may be headed for trouble.

"Professionally speaking," ***Sales & Marketing Management,*** **June 1996, p. 55.**

Attorneys Marilyn D. Stempler and Elise Busny discuss what managers need to know about the current state of age-discrimination law. Companies with more than 20 employees, with any over the age of 40, should understand the provisions of the Age Discrimination in Employment Act of 1974.

Early Retirement Incentive Programs

Beck, Barbara, "A gradual goodbye," ***The Economist,*** **Jan. 27, 1996, pp. S5-8.**

People are living longer than before, which is forcing governments to rethink their official retirement age. An early retirement is proving unaffordable. The U.S. is now paying full Social Security at age 67 instead of 65.

Kershaw, Sarah, "Early Retirees From Schools Get

Late Pension Payments," ***The New York Times,*** **May 4, 1996, p. A22.**
Hundreds of the 4,500 New York City educators who took advantage of an early-retirement incentive plan in the summer of 1995 are getting far less than they are entitled to because the pension system, overwhelmed by the number of early retirements, has not finished processing their applications, officials said.

Magner, Denise K., "Colleges seek changes in retirement law," ***The Chronicle of Higher Education,*** **May 30, 1997, p. A22.**
Legislation in Congress would allow colleges and universities to offer voluntary early retirement incentives.

Mandatory Retirement Age

Deets, Horace B., "Mandatory retirement," ***Modern Maturity,*** **January 1997, p. 74.**
Recent amendments to the federal Age Discrimination in Employment Act allow state and local governments to impose mandatory retirement on police officers and firefighters as young as 55. Deets argues against mandatory retirement.

Demasters, Karen, "For Some Police and Fire Veterans, an Unwelcome Deadline," ***The New York Times,*** **April 27, 1997, Sec. NJ, p. 6.**
Charles J. Fortenbacher has been a policeman in Bernards Township, N.Y., for 41 years and chief of police for the past six years. He says most of the people in the community agree he has done a good job. He would like to keep doing that job awhile longer. But Chief Fortenbacher is 66 years old and, unless something changes quickly, he, along with 90 other police officers and firefighters in the state, will be forced to retire on July 1.

"Dow Jones Nominates 7 Directors to Board," ***The New York Times,*** **Feb. 11, 1997, p. D3.**
Dow Jones & Co. said yesterday that it had nominated seven directors, four of them new candidates, and cut the size of its board. Dow Jones, the publisher of The Wall Street Journal, said Carlos Salinas de Gortari, a former president of Mexico, would not stand for re-election. Three members will resign because they have reached the mandatory retirement age of 70.

Nealon, Patricia, "Bill would let troopers stay at work past age 55," ***The Boston Globe,*** **Sept. 19, 1996, p. F7.**
With a long-delayed trial scheduled to start in October 1996, Massachusetts State Police officers challenging the mandatory retirement age of 55 have agreed with state officials to support legislation allowing troopers to work beyond that age, as long as they pass a physical.

Yung, Katherine, "2 Ford directors announce plans to retire in May," ***Detroit News,*** **March 15, 1996, p. B3.**
Ford Motor Co. announced March 14, 1996, that two directors on the company's board for more than a decade plan to retire in May after reaching mandatory retirement age of 70. But William Clay Ford Sr., 70, will remain on the board. The two retiring directors are Colby Chandler, former chairman of Eastman Kodak Co., and Kenneth Olsen, former CEO of Digital Equipment Corp.

Work Force Downsizing

Chiang, Harriet, "Reporter's ageism award upheld," ***San Francisco Chronicle,*** **July 30, 1996, p. A12.**
A California appeals court upheld on July 29, 1996, a $514,449 award for veteran TV reporter Steve Davis, who claimed that he was illegally fired from his job at KGO-TV because of his age, which was 53 at the time.

Grimsley, Kirstin Downey, "Worker Bias Cases Are Rising Steadily; New Laws Boost Hopes for Monetary Awards," ***The Washington Post,*** **May 12, 1997, p. A1.**
Employment experts cite new federal laws expanding civil rights protections to sexual harassment victims and the disabled; workers and employers turning increasingly combative; and a backlash against corporate downsizing, which left many workers feeling unfairly treated.

Thomas, Paulette, "Legal beat: Restructurings generate rash of age-bias suits," ***The Wall Street Journal,*** **Aug. 29, 1996, p. B1.**
As mammoth companies trim their work forces and remove tiers of veteran employees, age-discrimination lawsuits are beginning to outnumber sex-discrimination suits in the U.S., experts say. The case of John Ryder, an executive at Westinghouse Electric Corp. who was dismissed and then replaced with someone younger, is examined.

Van Duch, Darryl, "Courts give hope to the downsized," ***National Law Journal,*** **April 22, 1996, pp. A1, A25.**
Several high-profile court rulings have given the victims of downsizing hopes of winning redress. Cases involving the Worker Adjustment and Retraining Notification Act and the Age Discrimination in Employment Act are discussed.

Verespej, Michael A., "Time for ageless judgments," ***Industry Week,*** **March 3, 1997, pp. 15-16.**
Company downsizing has created a new legal enemy in the form of unemployed executives with the money to fight in the courts. The result is a series of class action lawsuits based on age discrimination. Companies must now prove their cutbacks are based on non-age factors.

Back Issues

Great Research on Current Issues Starts Right Here . . . Recent topics covered by The CQ Researcher are listed below. Before May 1991, reports were published under the name of Editorial Research Reports.

JANUARY 1996
Emergency Medicine
Punishing Sex Offenders
Bilingual Education
Helping the Homeless

FEBRUARY 1996
Reforming the CIA
Campaign Finance Reform
Academic Politics
Getting Into College

MARCH 1996
The British Monarchy
Preventing Juvenile Crime
Tax Reform
Pursuing the Paranormal

APRIL 1996
Centennial Olympic Games
Managed Care
Protecting Endangered Species
New Military Culture

MAY 1996
Russia's Political Future
Marriage and Divorce
Year-Round Schools
Taiwan, China and the U.S.

JUNE 1996
Rethinking NAFTA
First Ladies
Teaching Values
Labor Movement's Future

JULY 1996
Recovered-Memory Debate
Native Americans' Future
Crackdown on Sexual Harassment
Attack on Public Schools

AUGUST 1996
Fighting Over Animal Rights
Privatizing Government Services
Child Labor and Sweatshops
Cleaning Up Hazardous Wastes

SEPTEMBER 1996
Gambling Under Attack
The States and Federalism
Civic Journalism
Reassessing Foreign Aid

OCTOBER 1996
Political Consultants
Insurance Fraud
Rethinking School Integration
Parental Rights

NOVEMBER 1996
Global Warming
Clashing Over Copyright
Consumer Debt
Governing Washington, D.C.

DECEMBER 1996
Welfare, Work and the States
The New Volunteerism
Implementing the Disabilities Act
America's Pampered Pets

JANUARY 1997
Combating Scientific Misconduct
Restructuring the Electric Industry
The New Immigrants
Chemical and Biological Weapons

FEBRUARY 1997
Assisting Refugees
Alternative Medicine's Next Phase
Independent Counsels
Feminism's Future

MARCH 1997
New Air Quality Standards
Alcohol Advertising
Civic Renewal
Educating Gifted Students

APRIL 1997
Declining Crime Rates
The FBI Under Fire
Gender Equity in Sports
Space Program's Future

MAY 1997
The Stock Market
The Cloning Controversy
Expanding NATO
The Future of Libraries

JUNE 1997
FDA Reform
China After Deng
Line-Item Veto
Breast Cancer

JULY 1997
Transportation Policy
Executive Pay
School Choice Debate
Aggressive Driving

Back issues are available for $5.00 (subscribers) or $10.00 (non-subscribers). Quantity discounts apply to orders over ten. To order, call Congressional Quarterly Customer Service at (202) 887-8621.

Binders are available for $18.00. To order call 1-800-638-1710. Please refer to stock number 648.

Future Topics

- ***Land Mines***
- ***Children's Television***
- ***Evolution vs. Creationism***

THE CQ Researcher

PUBLISHED BY CONGRESSIONAL QUARTERLY INC.

Banning Land Mines

Should the U.S. support a total global ban?

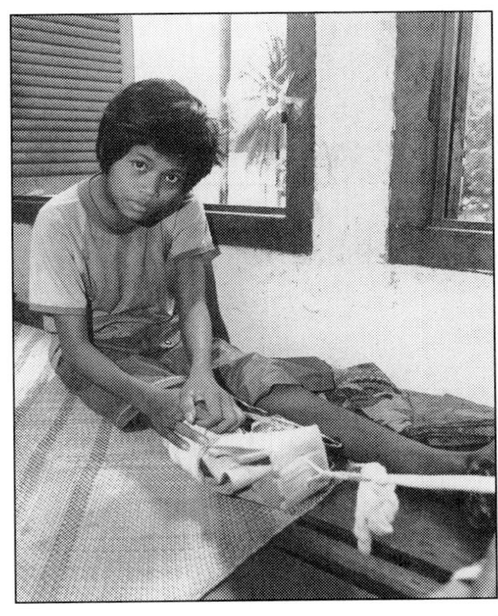

Anti-personnel mines kill and maim long after wars and civil strife end. More than 100 million active mines lie hidden in more than 80 countries, claiming 26,000 victims — mostly civilians — each year. Mines are cheap to produce and costly to remove, and 20 new mines are planted annually for every one cleared. A worldwide movement to totally ban the production and use of land mines has drawn support from more than 100 countries, which are expected to sign a treaty in Ottawa, Canada, in December. While it endorses an eventual ban on anti-personnel mines, the Clinton administration supports a treaty that would allow the U.S. to continue using some of its mines until alternative weapons are developed. One of the exemptions the U.S. seeks is for "smart" mines, which self-destruct after a few hours or days.

INSIDE THIS ISSUE

CQ August 8, 1997 • Volume 7, No. 30 • Pages 697-720

Formerly Editorial Research Reports

BANNING LAND MINES

COVER: LAND MINES CLAIM 26,000 VICTIMS PER YEAR, MANY IN CAMBODIA AND OTHER PARTS OF SOUTHEAST ASIA. (LANDMINE SURVIVORS NETWORK)

THE *CQ Researcher*

August 8, 1997
Volume 7, No. 30

The CQ Researcher (ISSN 1056-2036). Formerly Editorial Research Reports. Published weekly, except Jan. 3, May 30, Aug. 29, Oct. 31, by Congressional Quarterly Inc., 1414 22nd St., N.W., Washington, D.C. 20037. Annual subscription rate for libraries, businesses and government is $340. Additional rates furnished upon request. Periodicals postage paid at Washington, D.C., and additional mailing offices. POSTMASTER: Send address changes to The CQ Researcher, 1414 22nd St., N.W., Washington, D.C. 20037.

Banning Land Mines

BY MARY H. COOPER

THE ISSUES

It's not surprising that 11-year-old Elsa Armindo Chela triggered the land mine. There are, after all, more than 100 million land mines planted around the world — one for every 60 human beings on Earth. And Angola, where civil war raged for years, is a virtual minefield.

Elsa was picking mangoes in her village, Kuito, when she stepped on the mine. She lost a leg and an eye. Two and a half years later, she suffers bouts of depression and shies away from other children.

"Angola should buy tractors and seeds, not land mines," said Elsa's father, who worries her injuries will prevent her from completing school and finding a husband. "I appeal to the international community not to sell us any more of those weapons." [1]

Elsa is one of the 26,000 people around the world who are killed or maimed each year by anti-personnel mines. Each month, according to the American Red Cross, land mines kill 800 people and maim 1,200 — a victim every 20 minutes. The vast majority are civilians — farmers tilling fields, women collecting firewood or children playing. Most of the mines were left behind by combatants of conflicts that ended years earlier; many were used to terrorize local populations and deliberately targeted at children and other civilians.

Used for over a century, anti-personnel mines are small explosive devices, some no bigger than a can of shoe polish, originally designed to keep enemy soldiers from infiltrating vital areas or tampering with larger and less sensitive anti-tank mines. Because they explode on contact, anti-personnel mines also free up

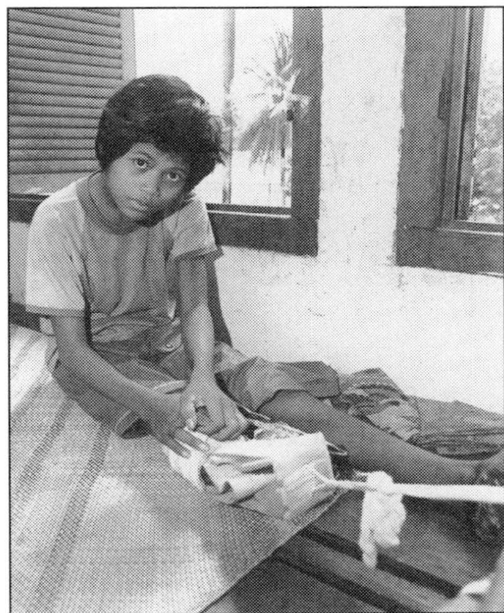

soldiers for other operations.

"To shoot somebody with a gun, you've got to point it, to fire artillery you've got to set it, to drop bombs out of a plane you've got to use a release mechanism," explains Robert O. Muller, president of the Vietnam Veterans of America Foundation. "Anti-personnel mines are totally indiscriminate, in that it is the victim of the weapon, as opposed to a command decision, that triggers the weapon."

Easy to use, hard to detect and resistant to the elements, land mines laid during the regional conflicts that raged for most of the post-World War II era have become a peacetime scourge. Long after combatants sign an armistice and the conflict fades from memory, the land mines they left behind continue to wage their indiscriminate war. Up to 120 million of these forgotten weapons lie hidden in more than 80 countries. [2] *(See map, p. 700.)*

In addition to the personal tragedy borne by victims such as Elsa, the devastating legacy of land mines afflicts entire societies. Land mines are concentrated among the poorest countries in the world, where the cost of treating and rehabilitating victims far exceeds the capacity of health-care systems, and the cost of demining is equally daunting. Postwar economic recovery is often hampered as refugees and former combatants alike are prevented by uncleared mines from returning to their homes and fields. Large areas of mine-infested agricultural land lie fallow, forcing farmers onto fragile, marginal sites where farming causes environmental damage. Industrial development is crippled in some countries where mines block access to power plants, bridges and other infrastructure.

"The problem with land mines is that wars end, peace treaties are signed, armies march away, the guns grow silent — but the land mines stay," said Sen. Patrick J. Leahy, D-Vt., a leader in the fight to ban land mines. "To the child who steps on a mine on the way to school a year after the peace agreement is signed, that peace agreement is no protection. To the farmer who cannot raise crops to feed his or her children because the fields are strewn with land mines, that peace agreement is worth nothing. To the medical personnel and humanitarian workers who cannot get polio vaccine to a village where it is needed because of the land mines, that peace agreement is useless." [3]

If current trends continue, the humanitarian crisis sparked by land mines can only get worse. Land mines are cheap, ranging from $3-$30 each. But it costs at least $300 to detect and remove a planted mine. Each year, about 100,000 land mines are cleared, but 2 million more are planted. And the supply is vast. In addition to the tens of millions of mines in the ground, there are an estimated 200 million more stockpiled around the world. At current removal rates, the

A Victim Every 20 Minutes

Up to 120 million land mines in more than 80 countries around the world kill or maim 26,000 people a year — one every 20 minutes. Most of the victims are civilians, typically agricultural workers, villagers gathering firewood and children. Each year, demining activities remove about 100,000 land mines, but some 2 million new mines are planted.

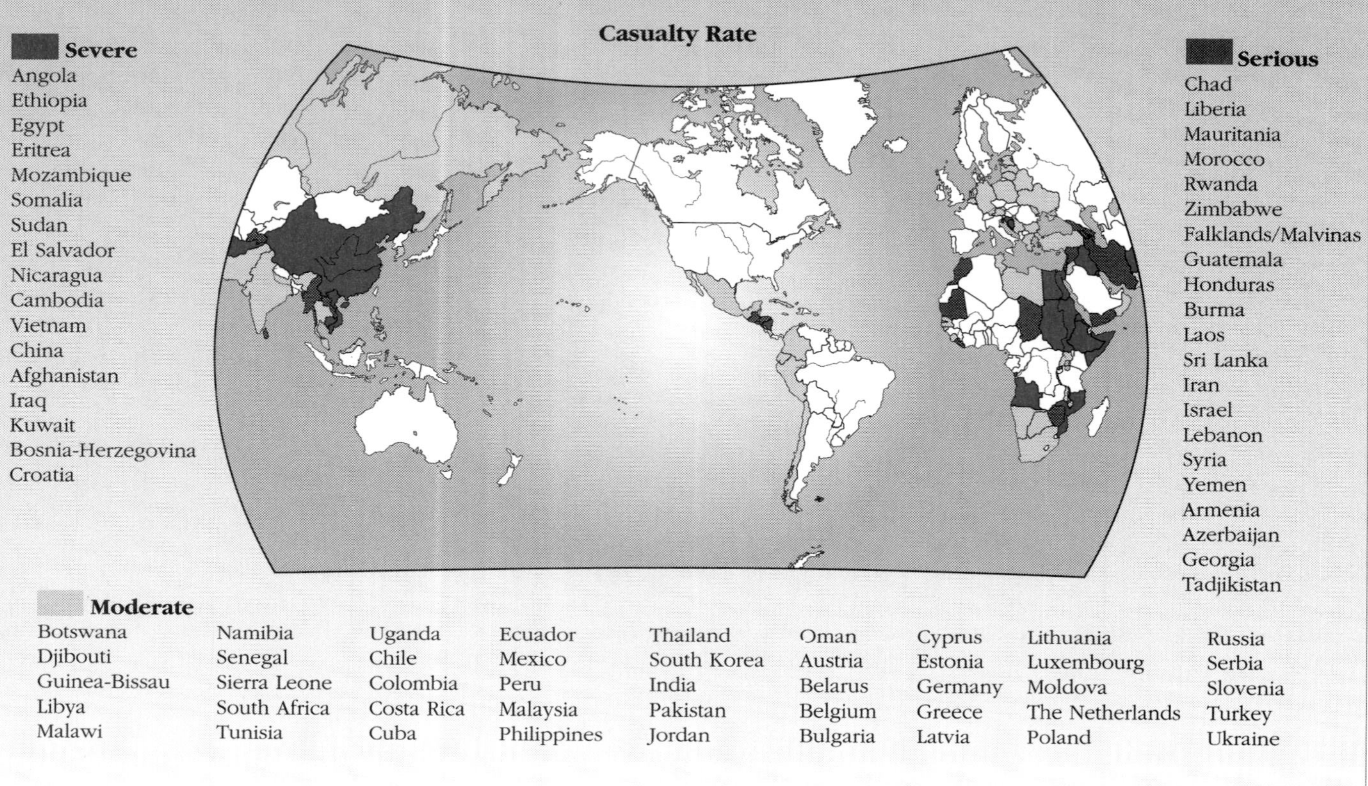

Sources: Vietnam Veterans of America Foundation, U.S. State Department, United Nations

American Red Cross estimates it would take 1,100 years to rid the world of land mines, even if no more were deployed.

Despite the havoc wreaked by land mines for decades, efforts to respond to Elsa's father's plea have only recently gained momentum. "They've been killing people for quite a while," says a senior Defense Department official. "But with the Cold War and other things that were going on around the world, land mines just did not get the attention they deserved."

The world began to pay more attention to land mines in the early 1990s, as relief workers struggled with the terrible legacy of regional wars in Afghanistan, Angola and other countries where Cold War superpowers had supported opposite sides in civil conflicts.

"Land mines were the Saturday night specials of Cold War armaments," says Andrew Cooper, a research assistant for the Human Rights Watch Arms Project. "The land mine issue surfaced when the United Nations first went into Afghanistan to implement the Soviet withdrawal and introduce relief mechanisms there. In such countries, even if they stop the fighting it's actually impossible for them to demilitarize their warring sides when they can't get back to their farms because they're mined. Now public awareness is very high."

Non-governmental organizations (NGOs) such as the Red Cross, Medico International and the Vietnam Veterans of America Foundation have been responding to land mine victims for years by setting up clinics to treat victims and provide them with prosthetic devices. They also launched a movement to ban land mines that has grown in just a few years from a handful of relief workers to a global coalition of more than 1,000 organizations — including some 250 in the United States.

The International Campaign to Ban Land Mines has spearheaded an initiative that is expected to produce by year's end an international treaty in Ottawa, Canada, to halt forever the production, transfer, stockpiling and use of these weapons. A number of major powers, however, including the United States, China and Russia, are not currently planning to sign the Ottawa treaty. Instead, the United States is attempting to launch negotiations on land mines at the Conference on Disarmament in Geneva, Switzerland (*see page 715*).

Although the U.S. has been a major producer of land mines for many years — and has about 11 million mines stockpiled — it took an early lead in promoting a global ban. Leahy has led the effort in Congress, sponsoring a bill in 1992 that would have halted the export of U.S. anti-personnel mines. In a 1994 speech to the United Nations General Assembly, President Clinton called for the elimination of land mines. In January, the president announced he was imposing a permanent ban on U.S. sales of anti-personnel mines to other countries and promised to destroy most of the nation's inventory of so-called "dumb" mines, which do not self-destruct.

Despite these moves, some critics say President Clinton has adopted a policy that undermines American leadership in the effort to ban land mines. On May 16, 1996, the president announced that he would pursue a land mine treaty with two controversial exceptions for the United States. The first would allow the U.S. to continue deploying "smart" mines, which self-destruct after a few hours or days, until an international ban takes effect or alternative weapons are developed. Because they become harmless shortly after they are deployed, American-made smart mines are not responsible for the humanitarian crisis caused by land mines, the administration says.

The president also insisted that a treaty had to contain an exception for some 1 million "dumb" U.S. mines planted near the demilitarized zone (DMZ) that separates North and South Korea. These mines are out of the reach of civilians, the administration argues, and would provide an essential defense for American soldiers stationed in South Korea if North Korea attacked.

Fearing that land mine talks in Geneva would never get off the ground, Canadian Foreign Minister Lloyd Axworthy last fall launched an open invitation to all countries to draw up and sign a treaty in Ottawa in December 1997 that would completely ban anti-personnel mines. Arguing that the world's biggest producers of land mines — Russia and China — would never agree to such a treaty, Clinton announced in January that the United States instead would seek a separate land mine treaty at the ongoing U.N. Conference on Disarmament in Geneva. The 61-nation conference, which recently produced the Chemical Weapons Convention, includes both Russia and China.

Unlike the Ottawa negotiations, the Geneva process requires consensus, which in effect grants veto power to opponents of a ban. And the likelihood that a total ban won't come out of the Geneva talks, critics say, is the real reason behind U.S. participation there.

"This is a stalling tactic" by the administration says Jody Williams, coordinator of the International Campaign to Ban Landmines, a leading promoter of the Ottawa process and a nominee for the 1997 Nobel Peace Prize. "They say the Conference on Disarmament is a universal forum, but only 61 countries are members. That's not exactly universal."

By contrast, a June meeting in Brussels, Belgium, of countries participating in negotiations leading up to the Ottawa treaty drew 115 countries. "The Ottawa process negotiations are open to everyone," Williams says. "We have 115, and you have 61 in this closed club? This is not exactly logical."

Supporters of a total ban have brought renewed pressure on the White House this summer. On June 12, Sens. Leahy and Chuck Hagel, R-Neb., introduced the Land Mine Elimination Act, which would ban U.S. deployment of all anti-personnel mines beginning in the year 2000. The measure drew 59 cosponsors. The same day, more than 160 House members signed a letter to the president drafted by Reps. Jack Quinn, R-N.Y., and Lane Evans, D-Ill., urging him to join the Ottawa process. Five days later, Lady Diana, Princess of Wales, joined American Red Cross President Elizabeth H. Dole in Washington in calling for a total land mine ban.

So far, however, the administration has stood by the policy it laid out more than a year ago to seek through the Geneva process a land mine treaty that contains the two exceptions for Korea and smart mines. "This initiative," the administration declares, "sets out a clear path to a global ban on [anti-personnel land mines] but ensures that as the United States pursues a ban, essential U.S. military requirements and commitments to our allies will be protected." [4]

Some critics say President Clinton's stance on land mines stems from a dogged reluctance to take on the military. "The Pentagon is institutionally incapable of giving up a weapon because of the nature of its responsibilities," says Robert Gard, a retired Army lieutenant general and one of 15 senior retired officers who have urged the president to forgo all land mines and join the Ottawa process. (*See "At Issue," p. 713.*) "But our Constitution does not provide for military considerations to be overriding; it provides for a civilian commander in chief in the office of the president. In this case, however, the president does not feel confident enough to risk a breach with the Joint Chiefs of Staff."

Since the end of the most recent Conference on Disarmament session, in June, the Clinton administration says it has been re-evaluating its policy on land mines.

As the debate over a total ban continues, these are some of the questions being asked:

Do anti-personnel land mines play a vital role in U.S. military strategy?

The U.S. has used anti-personnel mines since the Civil War, and the Pentagon claims that they continue to play a vital role in military strategy. In an extraordinary letter to Senate Armed Services Committee Chairman Strom Thurmond, R-S.C., 16 four-star generals and admirals, including Gen. John M. Shalikashvili, chairman of the Joint Chiefs, recently defended continued reliance on anti-personnel mines as vital "to ensure maximum protection for our soldiers and Marines who carry out national security policy at grave personal risk." [5]

According to the "64 stars letter," as it has been dubbed, land mines have become even more important as a "combat multiplier" in the wake of the post-Cold War drawdown of U.S. military forces around the world. With fewer soldiers available to protect units' flanks, the Pentagon brass told Thurmond, anti-personnel mines can free manpower for other operations. They also can protect small contingents sent into contested territory to secure vital resources, such as landing strips or seaports, before backup units arrive.

"Until the United States has a capable replacement for self-destructing [anti-personnel land mines], maximum flexibility and war-fighting capability for American combat commanders must be preserved," the officers wrote. "The lives of our sons and daughters should be given the highest priority when deciding whether or not to ban unilaterally the use of self-destructing anti-personnel land mines."

While all the services are united in the effort to continue current U.S. use of land mines, the Army and the Marine Corps are especially reluctant to give them up. The Army is responsible for defending South Korea, while securing vital assets in the early stages of battle usually falls to Army airborne units or the Marine Corps.

Former Gen. Norman H. Schwarzkopf, commander of Allied forces in the gulf war, supports a total ban on anti-personnel mines. Gen. John M. Shalikashvili, chairman of the Joint Chiefs of Staff, supports U.S. use of anti-personnel land mines.

"It's only natural that the Army and the Marine Corps would be the most concerned [about a ban] because they are the two services that have the most to worry about," the senior Defense Department official says. While both services have begun to change their strategies to accommodate an eventual phaseout of the weapons, "both of these services are concerned that if we suddenly went without land mines tomorrow, that would put their people at risk because we're still several years away from having an alternative." A preliminary study by the Pentagon of alternatives to land mines is expected to be completed by early fall.

Critics of the Pentagon's stance, including many combat veterans, say the military is vastly overstating the tactical advantages of land mines. In a widely circulated open letter to President Clinton, 15 retired generals, including David C. Jones, former chairman of the Joint Chiefs, and Norman H. Schwartzkopf, commander of Allied forces during the 1991 Persian Gulf War — asserted that forsaking anti-personnel mines "would not undermine the military effectiveness or safety of our forces, nor those of other nations." Banning these weapons, the officers wrote, would be "not only humane, but also militarily responsible." [6]

The Clinton administration down-plays its differences with the supporters of an immediate and total ban. "We absolutely share the goal of a ban," says Robert L. Cowles, director of Humanitarian Demining and Anti-personnel Landmine Policy at the Pentagon. "Where we disagree is over strategy, tactics and timing. And the big reason we disagree is that we have to be very careful about risking the lives of American soldiers."

The Pentagon's claim that land mines protect American soldiers was recently challenged in a study based on Army documents by the Human Rights Watch Arms Project and the Vietnam Veterans of America Foundation. During the Korean and Vietnam wars, the study concluded, most mines used against U.S. troops came from captured U.S. stockpiles, creating a "blow-back effect" in which American soldiers were injured or killed by American weapons.[7] More recently, 34 percent of Americans killed in the gulf war were felled by land mines, while all five casualties among Americans serving with U.N. peacekeeping forces in Bosnia to date have been from land mines.

"Land mines took a devastating toll on our troops in Vietnam," says Muller, a former Marine lieutenant who was paralyzed from combat injuries in 1969. "I'm sitting in a wheelchair because I got shot, but before I got shot I got blown up by a land mine. In 90 percent of the cases where we had Americans getting blown up by these land mines, they were either our mines or were constructed with our components. Parts would regularly get recycled, or we'd lose track of where we'd put the damned things down and end up walking on our own minefields."

In Muller's view, Pentagon officials are ignoring battlefield realities in their defense of land mines' military value.

"With all due respect, Shalikashvili has never heard a shot fired in anger, and he'll be the first to admit that he's not a combat veteran," Muller says. "What we've got here is a classic situation where you've got guys that are in situation rooms theorizing about conflict. Then you've got schmucks like me out there walking around in this stuff getting blown up, because this is an indiscriminate weapon; it doesn't differentiate between the bad guys out there and us."

In response to the Human Rights Watch report, the DOD said in a statement Aug. 1, 1997, that the report "fails to mention how we solved" the land mine problem. "Over 20 years ago, we developed self-destructing/self-deactivating mines that do not contribute to the humanitarian problem and save the lives of U.S. soldiers by eliminating the problems outlined in the study . . . We appreciate their concern for the lives of U.S. soldiers, but unfortunately their efforts will ban the very system we developed to solve these problems."

In the United States, leaders in the fight to ban land mines include Robert O. Muller, president of the Vietnam Veterans of America Foundation, center, Sen. Chuck Hagel, R-Neb., right, also a wounded combat veteran, and Sen. Patrick J. Leahy, D-Vt.

If anti-personnel land mines have proved less than effective in protecting American soldiers in past conflicts, what about the future? The Clinton administration insists on keeping its minefield along the DMZ in Korea as an essential defense of American and South Korean troops stationed there to defend South Korea from invasion by a million North Korean infantry soldiers poised just 30 miles away.

"There's significant risk of aggression in Korea," said the senior Defense Department official. "And the way that the opposition forces are postured, it gives a very small response time for us to react." He described the 1 million dumb mines currently deployed there as "essential in order to defend the peninsula."[8]

Some veterans of the 1950-53 Korean War say land mines would do little to deter a North Korean invasion. "Our experience has been that people like the North Koreans and the Chinese just move right through minefields," says Gard, who served in both the Korean and Vietnam wars. "So they take a few casualties on the way. They aren't going to stop because we've got anti-personnel land mines out there." A more effective strategy, he argues, would be to strengthen other weapons systems in the south. "My guess would be that the South Koreans could probably afford some more rocket launcher battalions and some field artillery battalions to compensate" for a land mine ban.

In any case, Gard says, the Pentagon's argument for the Korean exception in any land mine treaty is specious. "No one is proposing that they have to run in and dig up the mines that are in the DMZ," he says. "The proposals are for no new deployments. People are still getting blown up by mines that were planted

Durable, Deadly and Hard to Detect

Hundreds of versions of anti-personnel mines are produced by scores of countries around the world, including the United States. Most mines fit into one of a few basic designs. Because they are durable and hard to detect, the following mines are typical of the weapons responsible for the humanitarian land mine crisis today.

PMN
Manufacturing countries: Former Soviet Union, China, Iraq
Using countries: Afghanistan, Cambodia, China, Egypt, former East Germany, Iraq, Laos, Libya, Nicaragua, former Soviet Union, Vietnam, Namibia, Mozambique, Zambia, Angola, Somalia, South Africa, Eritrea, Ethiopia
The PMN has a spring-loaded firing device encased in a waterproof plastic body. Used extensively by the former Soviet Union and its allies, the PMN is possibly the most widely used anti-personnel mine in the world. Designed to be tamper-proof, the PMN killed or injured many deminers as they cleared Iraqi minefields in Kuwait after the 1991 Persian Gulf War.

PFM-1
Manufacturing country: Former Soviet Union
Using countries: Former Soviet Union, Afghanistan, former East Germany
The Soviet armed services first deployed this small, plastic, scatterable mine after they invaded Afghanistan. Known as a butterfly mine for the way it seems to flutter through the air, it consists of a pressure-fuzed liquid explosive in a green or sand-brown plastic case and has been used extensively to interdict trails and resupply routes in Afghanistan. The PFM-1 mine is a copy of the original butterfly mine, the U.S.-designed BLU-43 used in Southeast Asia, and is extremely effective in causing casualties. When stepped on, the mine typically blows off the victim's foot.

M16
Manufacturing country: United States
Using countries: United States, Angola, Eritrea, Ethiopia, Mozambique, Zambia
The M16, also known as a "bouncing Betty," is a bounding fragmentation mine and is designed to operate in two phases in order to inflict the greatest possible injury. When the fuze goes off, triggered by pressure or a tripwire, a black powder charge propels the mine into the air. When it's about waist-high, the main charge ignites, expelling cast-iron fragments in all directions.

SB-33
Manufacturing countries: Italy, Greece, Spain
Using countries: Italy, Afghanistan, Argentina, Greece, Iraq, Portugal, Spain
The Italian-designed SB-33 is a scatterable, blast-resistant, plastic-encased mine with low metallic content, making it hard to find with metal detectors. Its unique irregular shape is also designed to impede visual detection. The mine can be planted by hand or scattered. The pressure fuze is designed to resist explosive countermeasures. An electronic version incorporates an anti-handling device to deter mine clearance.

in World War II. So if, in fact, the mines that we planted near the DMZ in Korea are as good as the ones that we used in World War II, they ought to last a long time."

Should "smart" mines be exempted from a treaty banning land mines?

In addition to the exception for the mines in Korea, the Clinton administration wants to deploy self-destructing "smart" mines whenever commanders deem them necessary. Because of the shift toward more flexible, mobile forces, the Pentagon's

Cowles says, "we made a decision about 20 years ago to go to a different type of land mine that would work more efficiently with our other systems. Because we often have to maneuver through the same areas ourselves, we didn't want a land mine that stays active forever. We wanted a land mine that turns itself off."

According to the Pentagon, the military has already destroyed about 1.3 million of its stockpiled, older, dumb mines. Except for a million dumb mines kept for use in Korea and for training purposes, Cowles says, 10 million smart mines account for the entire U.S. stockpile. There are three versions of U.S. smart mines. About 5 percent of them remain active for 15 days, Cowles says, while another small percentage lasts for 48 hours. Most, he says, stay active for only four hours.

Smart mines either self-destruct by blowing up or self-deactivate by turning off after the allotted period. As a safeguard, smart mines are equipped with 90-day batteries to run the fuzing mechanisms. "So if everything else fails, the battery runs out in 90 days, and the mine becomes a piece of junk," Cowles says. "It can't explode."

Some types of smart mines have proved faulty in tests, and at least 1,700 U.S. smart mines reportedly failed to self-destruct during the Persian Gulf War. [9] But Cowles says that flaws observed in the sensors of some early versions of smart mines have been overcome.

"We have tested 32,000 smart land mines, and we've had exactly one failure, and that one was an hour late turning itself off," he says. "And you can be sure that we've never built a battery that doesn't die. So we're comfortable with these mines' reliability. Remember, we designed these mines so that we could go through those areas ourselves, so we have to have a pretty high rate of confidence in them."

But even if smart mines were 100 percent reliable, critics say they still pose risks to civilians. "When aircraft are dumping tens of thousands of land mines into areas where refugee columns are passing close to where there is fighting, civilians are going to be trapped," Cooper says. "In perfect laboratory test conditions, maybe you can see the land mine on the ground, but if you're in a jungle or a paddy field or a desert, the mines are going to be hidden. You can imagine what would happen if you had a column of refugees in an unmarked smart minefield. Self-destructing mines would suddenly start exploding around them, and they would be literally trapped."

Landmine Survivors Network

After the Cold War began, users of land mines began targeting civilians as well as military targets.

Critics say the U.S. insistence on a treaty exemption for smart mines will undercut negotiations for a total ban on land mines. "The United States is the only one really out there with smart mines," says Muller, who notes that the United States and Britain failed to convince other mine-producing countries, many of which lack the technology to make smart mines, to accept an exemption for these weapons in 1994.

"Country after country said, 'Are you crazy? Do you think we're going to make the world safe for U.S.-produced mines? Just because you have a high-tech version of this weapon, we're all supposed to come to you and buy your mine systems and [get rid of] ours?' "

"When the United States says our smart mines are not the problem out there because our smart mines self-destruct, that's fine and great," Muller says. "But if we don't give up our mines, they're not going to give up their mines. And the name of the game is to get rid of the mines. And the mines that we're going to run into out there are their mines."

Would a treaty banning anti-personnel mines be effective?

Typically, arms-control treaties provide for verification measures to ensure compliance. Signatories often have the right to conduct on-site inspections of each others' arms-production and storage facilities if they suspect violations of the treaty's terms. These provisions have built confidence among signatories that treaties such as the Strategic Arms Limitation Treaties (SALT I and II) are enforceable.

But intrusive inspections and strict enforceability are realistic goals primarily for nuclear weapons, which must be produced in large, easily identifiable plants and also require specialized vehicles and launchers to move and deploy. And no country can conceal a test nuclear explosion. A treaty banning land mines, on the other hand, would be all but impossible to enforce through on-site inspection or even satellite surveillance.

Supporters of a ban on all types of anti-personnel mines argue that strict verification measures are unnecessary to make such a treaty work. They point to the Convention on Chemical Weapons and other treaties to ban unacceptable weapons that are easy to hide. [10]

"Chemical weapons can effectively be made in someone's garage," Muller says. Like anti-personnel mines, he says, "They are cheap, easy to manufacture and available to anybody. But we now have an across-the-board ban on chemical weapons."

Treaties that ban weapons deemed inhumane by most societies rely more on moral suasion by establishing an international norm of acceptable behavior. "The power of a ban is the stigmatizing of this weapon, so that you wind up being labeled an outlaw if you use it," Muller says. "In the world community today, the game is economic development. And if you're not deemed an acceptable player, you can win your war but lose anyway because you won't be allowed at the table for the purpose of being integrated into the world market."

But the senior Defense Department official argues that it is unreasonable to expect the United States, whose smart mines are designed to avoid civilian casualties, to sign a treaty whose effectiveness relies on moral suasion. "Our systems don't contribute to the problem — neither the smart land mines nor the mines in Korea, which are behind a number of fences," he says. "They're asking that we give up these systems that don't contribute to the problem in order to set an example for the bad guys. We're supposed to risk the lives of American soldiers — men and women — in the hope that the bad guys who cause this problem will be inspired by that example to do the right thing. When has this ever happened? We're committed to a land mine ban, but our concern is that we don't risk soldiers while we're getting it."

The Clinton administration's main justification for pursuing a land mine treaty at the Conference on Disarmament, instead of in Ottawa, is that the Geneva negotiations would include the world's main producers of dumb land mines — Russia and China. And the administration contends that their participation would be essential to the effectiveness of any treaty.

But supporters of the Ottawa process say the effectiveness of a land mine ban depends more on the participation of mine users than producers. "Our view is that the most important nations to have on board are the ones that have used the damned weapons, such as Angola, Mozambique, Afghanistan and Cambodia — not China and Russia," says Williams of the international campaign. "If all the rest of the world is part of a ban treaty that does not permit them to use, stockpile, produce or transfer the weapons, where are China and Russia going to sell their mines anyway?" ■

BACKGROUND

Use in World Wars

The more than 100 million anti-personnel mines scattered around the world are the legacy, in a sense, of a form of static warfare that predates the invention of explosives. For millennia, armies have known that they could collapse an enemy's fortifications by digging under them rather than facing the risk of an armed assault. [11] Later, when stoked with gunpowder, tunnels became far more destructive, and were used extensively to destroy fixed targets in the Civil War and World War I.

World War I also saw the first widespread use of mines to impede the movement of troops and tanks, which could withstand much existing conventional artillery. The 1918 Armistice Agreement launched the first major counter-mine operation, requiring Germany to hand over maps and other documents identifying unexploded minefields. Counter-mine operations were slowed, however, by the lack of technology to detect and safely remove mines, forcing deminers to painstakingly probe and lift them from the ground one-by-one.

By the outbreak of World War II, land mines had been incorporated as integral parts of the arsenals and battlefield tactics of all parties to the conflict. They were especially valued as anti-tank weapons. Anti-personnel land mines were initially devised as booby traps to prevent enemy soldiers from removing anti-tank mines. In offensive maneuvers, anti-personnel mines also were used as "force multipliers" or "silent soldiers," laid along unprotected flanks of advancing troops to deter enemy attack and release soldiers for combat. Most land

Continued on p. 709

Chronology

1980s ***More than a century after their introduction in warfare, anti-personnel mines are restricted by international treaty.***

1980
The Conventional Weapons Convention limits the use of anti-personnel mines.

1989
Sen. Patrick J. Leahy, D-Vt., sponsors legislation that establishes a $5 million annual program to aid war victims, including land mine survivors.

1990s ***Support builds for a global ban on land mines.***

1991
The Vietnam Veterans of America Foundation and Medico International, a German relief organization, establish the International Campaign to Ban Landmines.

Oct. 23, 1992
President George Bush signs a one-year moratorium, sponsored by Sen. Leahy and Rep. Lane Evans, D-Ill., on exports of U.S. anti-personnel mines.

1993
President Clinton signs a three-year extension of the land mine export moratorium.

1994
President Clinton calls for the "eventual elimination" of anti-personnel mines in a speech before the United Nations General Assembly, which endorses his goal. The Clinton administration announces a policy promoting the limited use of land mines and the development of "viable and humane alternatives" to anti-personnel mines. The U.S. and Britain fail to convince other countries to accept an exemption for "smart" mines in a land mine ban.

Aug. 4, 1995
The Senate approves a Leahy-sponsored amendment to the fiscal 1996 defense authorization bill imposing a one-year moratorium on the use of anti-personnel mines, except along international borders and demilitarized zones, beginning in February 1999. The amendment is later dropped in conference committee.

March 1996
The Pentagon announces a review of its policy on land mines. Then-U.N. Representative Madeleine K. Albright writes the president that land mines cannot be eliminated "in our lifetimes" unless current U.S. policy is changed.

April 3, 1996
Fifteen retired senior U.S. military officers call on President Clinton to ban anti-personnel mines.

May 1996
A review conference of the Conventional Weapons Convention in Geneva adopts a provision prohibiting non-detectable anti-personnel mines and requiring that some mines contain self-destruct devices by 2006. On May 16, President Clinton declares that the United States will "aggressively pursue" an international agreement to ban anti-personnel mines but will continue to use dumb mines in Korea and smart mines elsewhere until agreement is reached.

Oct. 5, 1996
Canada announces plans to negotiate a treaty banning land mines, to be completed in Ottawa in December 1997.

Jan. 17, 1997
The Clinton administration announces that it will seek to negotiate a treaty banning land mines at the U.N. Conference on Disarmament in Geneva. Clinton also permanently bans the sale of U.S. anti-personnel mines to other countries and promises to destroy all U.S. "dumb" mines.

June 12, 1997
Sen. Leahy and 59 cosponsors introduce the Landmine Elimination Act banning new U.S. deployments of anti-personnel mines, except in Korea, beginning in 2000. More than 160 members of the House call on Clinton to join the Ottawa initiative.

June 27, 1997
Ninety-seven countries meet in Brussels to draw up the Ottawa treaty supporting a total ban on land mines without the exceptions sought by the Clinton administration.

Sept. 1, 1997
Formal negotiations on the Ottawa treaty are scheduled to begin in Oslo, Norway.

Dec. 2-4, 1997
The signing ceremony for the land mine treaty is to be held in Ottawa.

Clearing Minefields Takes Time and Money

It would take 1,100 years to find and remove the more than 100 million mines scattered around the globe, according to the American Red Cross.

"Counter-mine activities — the things you do to breach an enemy's minefield for military purposes — involve the use of big equipment designed to get the military through a minefield in combat," says Robert L. Cowles, director of Humanitarian Demining and Antipersonnel Landmine Policy at the Defense Department. "They go through at high speed, under fire, in all weather. They can afford to take casualties, and they can miss some mines. When you're doing humanitarian demining, the standard is different. Children are going to play here, and you can't miss a mine. So we have to go much slower."

The United States has spent $137 million since 1993 on humanitarian demining operations. The Pentagon received $15 million in fiscal 1997 for its program, in which 276 U.S. military personnel are training indigenous people — 1,200 to date — in 14 countries to detect and clear mines. [1] American soldiers do not participate in the demining effort itself.

Demining techniques have changed little in decades. Typically, deminers mark off a small area where land mines are suspected and then painstakingly search the ground using metal detectors or fiberglass probes before moving to the next marked area. Dogs often are used to detect mines because they can smell the explosives from as far away as 10 meters. "They're more reliable than other detectors," Cowles says. "The only problem with the dog is that it can get tired on you very quickly, and the dog can't tell you he's tired. So you need a very experienced handler working with the dog."

Landmine Survivors Network

Trained dogs are highly effective in detecting land mines, but most demining must be done by individual deminers.

The Pentagon is currently studying new technologies to speed demining operations, such as ground-penetrating radar. But critics say that effort is unlikely to improve the job of demining anytime soon.

"For the purpose of demining, the idea that there is any sort of silver bullet on the horizon is just crazy," says Robert O. Muller, president of the Vietnam Veterans of America Foundation. "What they need is a dependable, hand-held system that some dodo-brain out there who's getting hired for $50 a month is going to be able to use. The technology that will solve this problem is absolutely not there."

Some new systems, such as heavily armored threshers or bulldozers that can safely blow up mines, are useless in many settings where mines are concentrated. "You can't drive a bulldozer through the jungle," Muller says.

Once they find a mine, deminers in the Pentagon's program blow it up on the spot. "We don't teach defuzing and dearming mines because then they can be reused," Cowles says. "The problem with blowing them up, however, is that it scatters the vapor around. If you're using dogs, it makes the dogs less effective. It also creates environmental and other problems. So we're looking at a number of technologies to destroy the mines better."

Despite the technical obstacles to clearing existing minefields, Cowles says that the four-year-old demining program has already made a significant difference, contributing to a 94 percent drop in the death rate from mine injuries in Namibia and a 50 percent drop in some provinces of Cambodia.

To spread its mine-awareness message, the Pentagon distributes instructive comic books to children, posts signs near known minefields and gives out bandages stamped with graphic descriptions of ways to reduce blood loss for various types of mine injuries. The program also provides free information on the Internet to help deminers identify mines and find out how best to destroy them.

Critics say the Pentagon's demining effort has a lot of room for improvement. "The Pentagon will tell you they have doubled the amount of money spent on demining, or they have gone from serving 12 to 14 countries," says Robert G. Gard, a retired Army lieutenant general who supports a total and immediate ban on land mines. "The resources that have been allocated for that purpose have been relatively quite small, and you have to remember the mines are in 70 countries. Also, I think it is unfortunate that Americans are precluded from demining operations. That gives new meaning to the notion of leading by example."

[1] The United States runs demining programs in Afghanistan, Angola, Bosnia, Cambodia, Costa Rica, Eritrea, Ethiopia, Honduras, Jordan, Laos, Mozambique, Namibia, Nicaragua and Rwanda. The National Security Council acts as coordinator for the Defense Department and the five other U.S. government agencies that participate in demining operations, among them the State Department and Agency for International Development. They plan to spend $54.7 million for demining and $20 million for research in fiscal 1998.

Continued from p. 706

mines of both types were made according to a simple design — encased explosives equipped with firing devices, or fuzes, that could be set off either by the user from a remote position or by the target upon contact.

Land mines played a vital role in World War II, beginning in the North African campaigns, where mine warfare was successfully blended into highly mobile operations. Mines laid along the Egyptian-Libyan border helped the British stave off an Italian advance into Egypt in 1940. During the same conflict, Italian forces introduced the first scatterable mines, so-called "thermos bombs," which were dropped from the air over British positions. Both German and British forces laid vast quantities of mines in the operations that culminated in the 1942 halt of German Field Marshall Erwin "The Desert Fox" Rommel's offensive across the Sahara at El Alamein.

Mine warfare was even more vital in the outcome of hostilities on the Eastern front, where the Soviet military developed elaborate systems of mine deployment against the German advance, including radio-controlled mines, mines with delayed charges and a vast network of anti-tank ditches and minefields around Moscow. The Soviet Union deployed an estimated 222 million mines during World War II, making it the greatest practitioner of mine warfare in history. Soviet forces supplemented their highly effective wooden-box mine with vast quantities of captured German mines.

Advances in military demining technology improved counter-mine operations during the hostilities. Electronic mine detectors facilitated detection, and heavily armored tanks equipped with chain flails were sent through minefields to explode mines along a path wide enough for troops and vehicles. But at the July 1943 battle of Kursk, Soviet forces overwhelmed German counter-mine measures by blanketing the area with so many anti-tank and anti-personnel mines that they were able to repel the 3,000-tank German offensive.

Department of Defense

A Moldovan soldier probes for mines last year during a training exercise on mine awareness at Camp Lejeune, N.C.

Aside from their exposure to German mines in North Africa, U.S. forces did not encounter heavy mine warfare in World War II until 1944. During the battle for Cassino, Italy, German mines caused 13 percent of American casualties. On D-Day, June 6, 1944, the U.S. and Allied landing in Normandy was slowed by about 6 million anti-tank and anti-personnel mines planted by Rommel's forces. Allied forces encountered even heavier minefields along the Siegfried Line before breaking through to the German heartland.

Overall, mines accounted for about 20 percent of all tank losses and 2.5 percent of battlefield deaths in the European theater. Because the Japanese military did not rely heavily on land mines, mine warfare had little impact in the Pacific theater.

Korea and Vietnam

The outbreak of the Cold War was accompanied by a shift in land mine use in Europe from a battlefield weapon to a defensive barrier weapon that was deployed extensively along both sides of the Iron Curtain separating Eastern and Western Europe. But land mines also figured prominently in the regional wars that erupted throughout the nearly 50-year East-West standoff.

Mine warfare in the Korean War differed little in technology or doctrine from World War II. But because of the Korean peninsula's mountainous terrain, tanks were forced to travel along established roadways, enabling both sides in the conflict to effectively sabotage enemy advances. The United States was the main source of land mines in the conflict, but North Korean troops were able to capture large numbers of the U.S. weapons and use them against the U.S.-led U.N. force defending South Korea. According to the State Department, land mines accounted for about 4 percent of American casualties during the Korean War. North Korean forces and their Chinese allies suf-

Continued on p. 711

Savage Injuries to the Poorest of the Poor

The savage injuries that land mines cause kill most victims — 59 percent in Afghanistan, for example, according to Doctors Without Borders, a French volunteer organization. [1] Those who make it alive to the hospital typically suffer from one or more of three types of debilitating injuries: loss of the foot or leg from stepping on a blast mine; multiple fragment injuries of the legs and often the head, neck, chest and abdomen from triggering a fragmentation mine; or hand, arm, face and eye injuries from handling a mine of any type.

Survivors of mine blasts face an excruciating course of treatment. Blasts often drive dirt and shrapnel into the groin, causing abdominal infection. Where limbs have been blown off, bone infection also is common. Bones are often cut to the wrong length, or sharp pieces of bone may be left, aggravating stump tissues and making it hard to fit prostheses once the wounds have healed. Successive operations may be needed to drain postoperative infections. Within about two weeks of amputation, patients must begin physical therapy and walk with crutches to prevent muscle contracture and maintain upper-body strength.

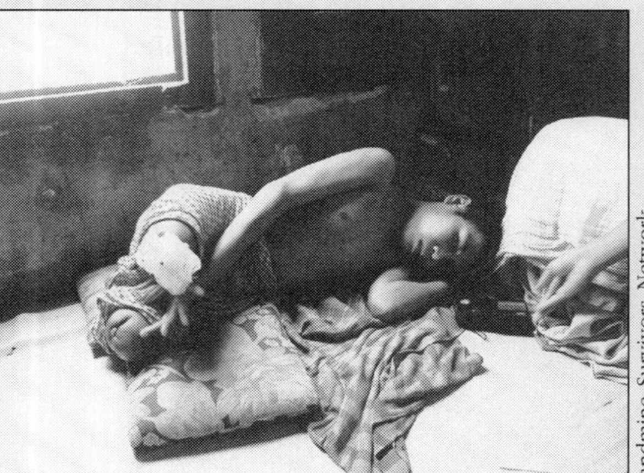

Landmine Survivors Network

Cambodia has the highest concentration of land mines in the world; one of every 246 Cambodians has lost an eye or a limb to a land mine.

Amputees whose postoperative conditions allow for fitting with artificial limbs can hope to resume a life of limited mobility. But for children, the most vulnerable of land mine victims, the initial fitting for prostheses marks only the beginning of a lifetime of painful therapies.

"A young child will need several different fittings as he or she grows older," said Lady Diana, Princess of Wales, who visited with land mine victims in Angola last January, "because the bones, although shattered, continue to grow through the stump." [2]

In addition to the physical distress, mine victims face often insurmountable obstacles to treatment. The International Committee of the Red Cross (ICRC), which has declared 1997 as the year of assistance for mine victims, places the cost of lifetime surgical and prosthetic treatment for each surviving land mine victim at $3,000-$5,000.

"This is an intolerable load for a handicapped person in a poor country," said Diana, who is campaigning for a land mine ban on behalf of the British Red Cross. "It is something to which the world should urgently turn its conscience."

To help poor countries defray the costs of treating victims, the ICRC operates programs in 10 countries that provide rehabilitation and prosthetic devices for land mine victims. It has provided some 100,000 prosthetic devices for 68,000 amputees in 22 countries. The American Red Cross, an ICRC affiliate, is principally involved in the program in Cambodia, where it has provided prostheses for more than 2,400 people and nearly 1,000 wheelchairs each year since its program began in 1991. "That's a lot of new beginnings and new hope for Cambodian land mine survivors," said American Red Cross President Elizabeth H. Dole. [3]

The Vietnam Veterans of America Foundation operates prosthetics clinics in Vietnam, Cambodia, El Salvador and Angola — all countries where land mines are an enduring legacy of conflicts in which the United States played a significant, if not direct, part.

"I'm a little bit embarrassed to admit it, but when I was an infantry officer with the Marines, land mines never distinguished themselves as really a category of weapon," says Robert O. Muller, the foundation's president. "I went back to Asia some 20 years later and realized that, goddammit, these things are still out there, they never got put away in the armory, and they continue to take their toll. And the people we've wound up fighting are civilians, people trying to work the land or gather firewood. Then we realized that it was the poorest of the poor, those least able to deal with the disability, that were the ones who got blown up."

In 1991, Muller, who uses a wheelchair because of injuries he received in combat, and several other disabled Vietnam veterans started the prosthetics program in Cambodia.

"We didn't have a real history of being a rehabilitation organization, but it's something we'd lived through," Muller recalls. "A couple of our guys are multiple amputees from the Vietnam War. So we know a little bit about how much it can benefit you to gain mobility, that it's clearly doable. You can recover from these disabilities."

[1] Material in this section is from Doctors Without Borders/Médecins sans Frontières, *Living in a Minefield: An MSF Report on the Mine Problem in Afghanistan*, May 1997.

[2] Speaking at a June 17 press conference held by the American Red Cross in Washington, D.C.

[3] Speaking at the June 17 press conference in Washington, D.C.

Continued from p. 709

fered far more casualties because they employed the "human sea" tactic of clearing minefields by sending waves of troops ahead to be sacrificed. [12] Since the armistice in 1953, U.S. and South Korean forces have maintained a minefield along the DMZ separating North and South Korea.

Land mines were a major weapons system during the Vietnam War. The Viet Cong used mines against civilian and military targets in their campaign against South Vietnam leading up to the Vietnam War, while South Vietnamese forces used mines to protect bases and villages. Once U.S. troops were deployed in force in 1965, they used anti-personnel mines as perimeter defenses around airfields and other facilities. They also used both anti-personnel and anti-tank mines to deter infiltration along trails and as a defensive barrier along the DMZ.

As the war spread to Cambodia and Laos in the late 1960s and early '70s, the United States began deploying new, self-deactivating land mines that were scattered from aircraft or fired from artillery. Many of the newer mines were made primarily of plastic, making them harder to detect and clear. Another U.S. innovation in Vietnam was the Claymore mine, which is not included among the land mines to be banned by treaty because it is detonated on command instead of by random contact with a person or a vehicle.

As in Korea, Vietnamese forces relied heavily on appropriated enemy land mines, especially the Claymore and other U.S. ordnance. The chaotic conditions of jungle warfare also made it hard to accurately map defensive minefields. Because of these conditions and the extensive use of land mines, U.S. forces often fell victim to their own arsenals. As many as 30 percent of the 41,840 American ground soldiers killed in battle in Vietnam were land mine victims. Moreover, about 90 percent of the mines that killed U.S. soldiers were American-made or contained U.S. components.

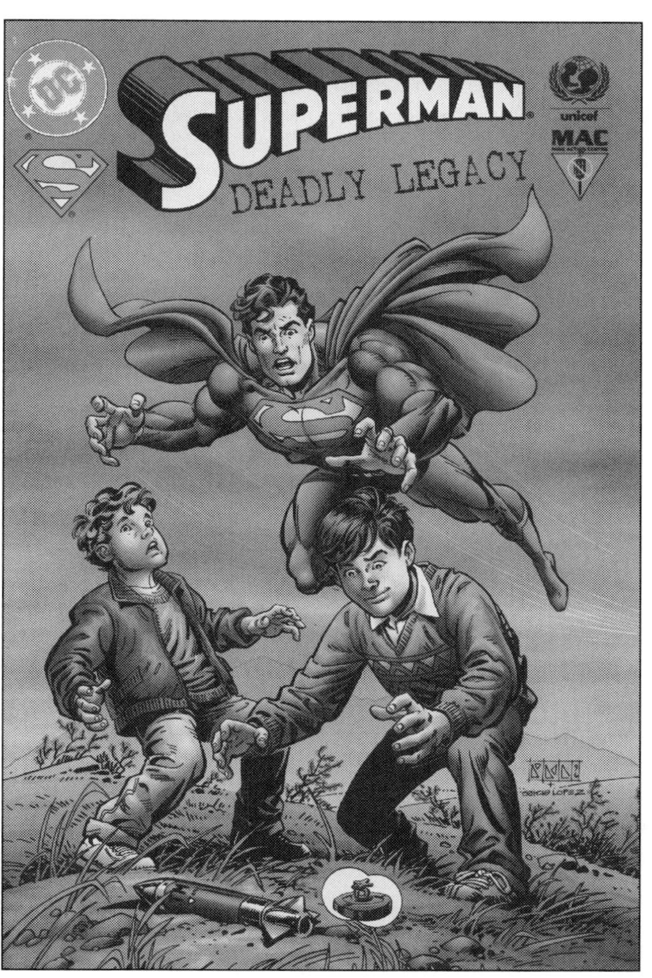

To teach the children of Bosnia-Herzegovina to avoid the land mines that dot the landscape, DC Comics published "Superman: Deadly Legacy" in cooperation with UNICEF and the U.S. State Department. The comic is distributed through the Mine Action Center in Sarajevo.

Land Mine Producers

An estimated 55 countries have produced anti-personnel land mines for decades; 35 of them have also exported the weapons. [13] As the world's largest arms exporter, the United States long played a major role in land mine production and export. [14] From 1985-1996, according to the United States Campaign to Ban Landmines, the United States produced more than 10 million new mines. The United States also supplied other countries, exporting 4.4 million anti-personnel land mines from 1969-1992. [15]

In 1992, the United States became the first major producer to stop exporting anti-personnel land mines, following the Oct. 23 enactment of a one-year moratorium on mine exports introduced by Sen. Leahy and Rep. Evans. The moratorium was later extended, and on Jan. 17, 1997, made permanent by President Clinton. Meanwhile, as of June 23, 59 countries had announced either a ban or a moratorium on land mine exports, and six others had declared that they were not currently exporting the weapons. Only five countries known to have exported mines in the past — Bosnia, Iran, Iraq, Serbia and Vietnam — had failed to stop mine sales. [16]

Despite the near-universal halt to the open trade in land mines, production of these weapons remains widespread. An estimated 35 countries continue to make them, ostensibly for domestic use. The major producers that are suspected of supplying land mines today are China, which claims that it does not export them currently, and Russia, which has declared a limited moratorium on exporting them. [17]

According to the Human Rights Watch Arms Project, land mines have not been produced in the United States since the end of last year, when the Pentagon completed its restoration of U.S. stockpiles drawn down during the Persian Gulf War. In January, President Clinton announced a cap on the U.S. inventory of land mines, which was later set at 11 million. According to a Pentagon document, there is no planned production of anti-personnel mines in the United States at least through fiscal 2004. [18]

The Arms Project has identified 47 U.S. companies that have been involved in the manufacture of anti-personnel land mines. Following the group's investigation of the matter, 17 companies agreed to renounce all future production. Motorola Corp., whose trademark was clearly visible in a Chinese land mine shown in a television documentary on the humanitarian crisis in Cambodia, was the first American company to publicly renounce its involvement in land mine production. Although the company's contribution was limited to electronic chips that also are commonly used in a number of consumer goods, Motorola agreed to take steps to ensure that companies it supplies also are not involved in land mine production.

Other companies that have announced they would no longer make mines or their components include Hughes Aircraft and AVX Corp. Seventeen companies, including such familiar manufacturers as General Electric Co., Lockheed Martin Corp. and Raytheon, have declined to renounce future involvement in land mine production, saying the decision on ending land mine use is up to the government. [19]

Human Rights Watch has launched a "stigmatization campaign" against the 30 U.S. mine producers that have either refused to renounce future mine production or failed to respond to its query. Most of the targeted companies have only produced components for land mines, and company spokesmen have denounced allegations of their involvement in mine production. [20] One company, however — Alliant Techsystems, Inc. of Hopkins, Minn., has manufactured almost finished anti-personnel land mines, which are shipped to military facilities for final assembly. ■

CURRENT SITUATION

Targeting Civilians

Since the turn of the century, some 100,000 Americans have died in anti-personnel mine explosions. The vast majority of these casualties occurred in war. But today the overwhelming majority of the world's land mine victims are civilians who stumble onto these hidden weapons.

Some are relics of long-forgotten wars. "Some of the older mines were put in by forces many years ago," Cowles says. "If they kept records of where they placed the mines, they've long since disappeared." He tells of a 10-year-old Egyptian girl who was killed earlier this year and her brother, who was blinded, when they triggered a land mine planted by Rommel's forces during the Africa campaign in 1942.

But land mine use and the people who use them have changed in recent years, Cowles says. "Almost every one of the countries where mines are a major problem right now are, or were, involved in internal conflicts," he says. "Most of the land mines going in now are not used by disciplined military forces, who use them in a patterned, regular way. They are using them indiscriminately, putting them anywhere and in some cases even targeting civilians. The change is that land mines have become a weapon of terror as much as a military weapon."

Countries where land mines are a leading cause of death illustrate the scope of the problem:

• **Cambodia:** More than two decades of war have left Cambodia with the highest concentration of active land mines in the world. One Cambodian in every 236 has lost an eye or a limb to a land mine. "In Cambodia, land mines were not as much a militarily significant factor for conventional warfare purposes, where you've got troops that have set up defensive positions, as weapons of terror," Muller says. "They're put under shade trees, where people go on hot days, they put them in water wells, around power lines, in pagodas. They're designed to intimidate and terrorize the population." More than 300 Cambodians are killed or maimed by mines each month.

• **Angola:** Some 15 million mines — more than the African nation's 10 million population — are deployed throughout the country. They were deployed most heavily over a 34-year period that included the 1976-1994 civil war between the pro-Soviet government and Jonas Savimbi's U.S.-supported UNITA rebels. Impoverished by the war's economic upheaval, civilians have been forced to search for food in mine-infested areas. "What is so cruel about these wounds is that they are almost invariably suffered where medical resources are scarce," said Princess Diana, who has become a highly visible supporter of a land mine ban since visiting Angolan mine victims

Continued on p. 714

At Issue:

Would a total ban on anti-personnel mines undermine U.S. military strategy?

GEN. JOHN M. SHALIKASHVILI
Chairman of the Joint Chiefs of Staff, the Joint Chiefs and the 10 regional and functional commanders in chief (CINCs)

FROM A LETTER TO SENATE ARMED SERVICES COMMITTEE CHAIRMAN STROM THURMOND, R-S.C., JULY 10, 1997

yes

We are seriously concerned about the new legislative proposal to permanently restrict the use of funds for new deployment of anti-personnel land mines (APL) commencing Jan. 1, 2000. Passing this bill into law will unnecessarily endanger U.S. military forces and significantly restrict the ability to conduct combat operations successfully. As the FY 1998 Defense Authorization bill and other related legislation are considered, your support is needed for the service members whose lives may depend on the force protection afforded by such land mines.

We share the world's concern about the growing humanitarian problem related to the indiscriminate and irresponsible use of a lawful weapon, non-self-destructing APL. In fact, we have banned non-self-destructing ("dumb") APL, except for Korea. We support the president's APL policy, which has started us on the road to ending our reliance on any anti-personnel land mines. Having taken a great step toward the elimination of APL, we must, at this time, retain the use of self-destructing APL in order to minimize the risk to U.S. soldiers and Marines in combat. However, we are ready to ban all APL when the major producers and suppliers ban theirs or when an alternative is available.

Land mines are a "combat multiplier" for U.S. land forces, especially since the dramatic reduction of the force structure. Self-destructing land mines greatly enhance the ability to shape the battlefield, protect unit flanks and maximize the effects of other weapons systems. Self-destructing land mines are particularly important to the protection of early entry and light forces, which must be prepared to fight outnumbered during the initial stages of a deployment.

This legislation, in its current form, does not differentiate between non-self-destructing and self-destructing APL. Banning new deployments of APL will prevent use of most modern U.S. remotely delivered land mine systems to protect U.S. forces. This includes prohibiting use of most anti-tank land mine systems because they have APL embedded during production. Self-destructing APL are essential to prevent rapid breaching of anti-tank mines by the enemy. . . .

Until the United States has a capable replacement for self-destructing APL, maximum flexibility and war-fighting capability for American combat commanders must be preserved. The lives of our sons and daughters should be given the highest priority when deciding whether or not to ban unilaterally the use of self-destructing APL.

GEN. DAVID C. JONES
Former chairman of the Joint Chiefs of Staff, and 14 other retired senior military officers

FROM AN OPEN LETTER TO PRESIDENT CLINTON, *THE NEW YORK TIMES*, APRIL 3, 1996

no

We understand that you have announced a United States goal of the eventual elimination of anti-personnel land mines. We take this to mean that you support a permanent and total international ban on the production, stockpiling, sale and use of this weapon.

We view such a ban as not only humane but also militarily responsible.

The rationale for opposing anti-personnel land mines is that they are in a category similar to poison gas; they are hard to control and often have unintended harmful consequences (sometimes even for those who employ them). In addition, they are insidious in that their indiscriminate effects persist long after hostilities have ceased, continuing to cause casualties among innocent people, especially farmers and children.

We understand that there are 100 million land mines deployed in the world. Their presence makes normal life impossible in scores of nations. It will take decades of slow, dangerous and painstaking work to remove these mines. The cost in dollars and human lives will be immense. Seventy people will be killed or maimed today, 500 this week, more than 2,000 this month and more than 26,000 this year, because of land mines.

Given the wide range of weaponry available to military forces today, anti-personnel land mines are not essential. Thus, banning them would not undermine the military effectiveness or safety of our forces, nor those of other nations.

The proposed ban on anti-personnel land mines does not affect anti-tank mines, nor does it ban such normally command-detonated weapons as Claymore "mines," leaving unimpaired the use of those undeniably militarily useful weapons.

Nor is the ban on anti-personnel land mines a slippery slope that would open the way to efforts to ban additional categories of weapons, since these mines are unique in their indiscriminate, harmful residual potential.

We agree with and endorse these views, and conclude that you as Commander-in-Chief could responsibly take the lead in efforts to achieve a total and permanent international ban on the production, stockpiling, sale and use of anti-personnel land mines. We strongly urge that you do.

Continued from p. 712
in January. "For those whose living is the land, loss of an arm or leg is an overwhelming handicap which lasts for life." [21]

• **Afghanistan:** Until it withdrew in defeat in 1989, the Soviet army scattered at least 10 million anti-personnel land mines in its 10-year attempt to quash a civil war against the Soviet-backed government. Although both sides in the conflict used mines, the Soviet minefields around cities and military posts are the source of most civilian casualties. Among the most pernicious remnants of that conflict are Russian "butterfly" mines, small plastic devices that are designed to blow a victim's foot off. Scattered by the millions, these mines have taken an especially heavy toll among curious children who see them as playthings. "Children found they could pick it up and throw it several times and it wouldn't go off because it takes a slow pressure to set it off," Cowles says. "But they don't know how many times it's been thrown before, so one of these things can suddenly blow up in a child's hand."

• **Bosnia-Herzegovina and Croatia:** The civil war that broke out in 1991 in the former Yugoslavia has set a new standard for the use of land mines as weapons of terror. Some 3 million mines have been placed by all parties to the conflict not only on roads but in apartment houses, agricultural areas and churches. "In Bosnia they even mine cemeteries," Cowles says. "It's perfectly logical, if you want to target the families of a particular ethnic group, what better way to do it? You get exactly the people you're targeting. It's horrible, but that's the sort of thing they do. This is not warfare as we know it."

The bright spot in this picture is the apparent decline of land mine placements in recent years. "Fewer land mines are going in now because there are no major organized mine-laying efforts by states," says the Defense Department official. "The biggest single factor in this trend probably is the work of the NGOs and the movement to ban land mines. It's far too soon to declare a victory, but the consciousness of people around the world has been elevated to the point where we are not seeing land mines going in the ground in the numbers we were."

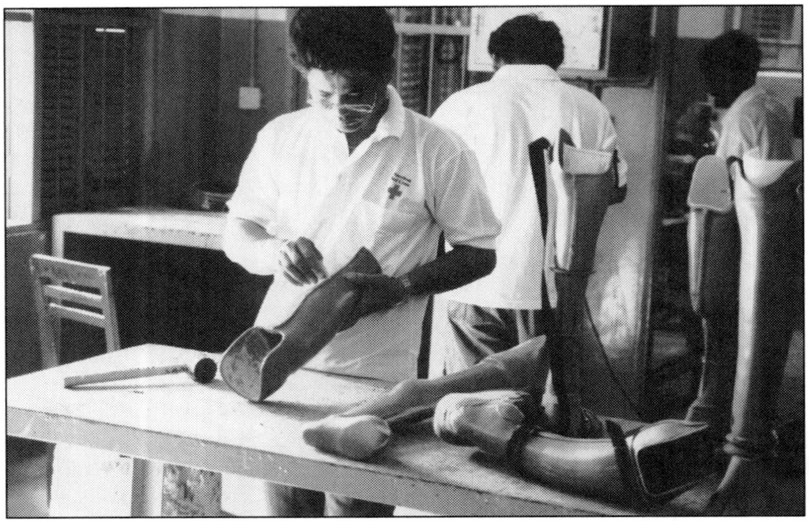

American Red Cross

An American Red Cross outreach program provides prosthetic devices and wheelchairs for land mine victims in Cambodia.

Movement Grows

In countries plagued by land mine injuries, NGOs have almost single-handedly brought the land mine crisis to the world's attention. The International Campaign to Ban Land-mines was launched in fall 1991 by the Vietnam Veterans of America Foundation and Medico International, a German relief organization. "Both organizations were doing prosthetic work, and 99 percent of the victims are land mine victims," says Williams, who was tapped to coordinate the campaign for her experience in human rights activities in Central America. "Since then, the campaign has grown from just two to 1,000 non-governmental organizations in 55 countries. Like anything else, success breeds success, and because we have been so successful, people want to be part of it. This is the most fascinating work I've ever done."

The campaign is credited with a significant shift in public opinion about land mines. Its grass-roots effort to build support for an international ban on land mines has paid off with the suspension of exports and production by many of the world's mine producers. "The non-governmental organizations around the world have just done a tremendous job in highlighting what a terrible problem this is," Cowles says. "I think this is the first time we've seen such a broad-based, international partnership among non-governmental organizations, private voluntary organizations and so many national governments around a common goal."

On the diplomatic front, the first major avenue pursued toward a land mine ban was the 1994-96 round of negotiations to strengthen the land mine protocol of the 1980 Conventional Weapons Convention, which bars the use of inhumane weapons. Because the talks included China, Russia and other opponents of a ban, however, the new protocol, adopted in May 1996, fell short of expectations. It requires that all anti-personnel land mines be detectable and that certain of them be equipped with self-destruct devices. Land mine producers have nine years to comply with these standards.

Frustrated by the new protocol's limitations, Canadian Foreign Minister Axworthy launched a different strategy: fast-track negotiations for a treaty banning land mines altogether. At a meeting of 74 governments and numerous NGOs held in Ottawa last October, he invited all countries to join Canada in negotiating the ban and sign a treaty to that effect by the end of 1997.

FOR MORE INFORMATION

American Red Cross, 8111 Gatehouse Rd., Falls Church, Va. 22042; (703) 206-7090. This humanitarian relief organization runs rehabilitation programs for land mine victims around the world and supports a global ban on land mines.

Department of Defense, Public Affairs, The Pentagon, Washington, D.C. 20301-1400; (202) 697-9312. The DOD, which trains deminers in a number of countries, supports a ban on land mines but with certain exceptions for American forces.

Human Rights Watch Arms Project, 1522 K St. N.W., Suite 910, Washington, D.C. 20005-1202; (202) 371-6592. This research group has compiled information on land mine use as well as production of the weapons by U.S. firms.

United States Campaign to Ban Landmines, 2001 S St. N.W., Washington, D.C. 20009; (202) 483-9222. The leading organization advocating U.S. participation in a global ban on anti-personnel land mines provides information to concerned citizens on all aspects of the issue.

U.S. Policy

The United States took an early lead in the effort to ban anti-personnel land mines, which has been championed for the past eight years by Sen. Leahy and the cosponsors of his legislation establishing a moratorium on U.S. exports. "This human disaster was described to me by a Cambodian I had in my office on a snowy winter afternoon at Christmastime in Vermont, one of the most beautiful times of year in our state," Leahy explained. "It became far less beautiful as he said, 'We clear our land mines in Cambodia an arm and a leg at a time.'" [22]

After introducing legislation in 1989 that established a $5 million a year fund to provide artificial limbs for land mine survivors, Leahy in 1992, along with Rep. Evans, sponsored a bill that imposed a one-year moratorium on anti-personnel mine exports. It was later extended and then made permanent by President Clinton. On June 12, Leahy introduced legislation to ban new deployments of anti-personnel mines by the United States, except in Korea, beginning in 2000. Among the 59 cosponsors of the 1997 Landmine Elimination Act are all six Vietnam combat veterans in the Senate, including Sen. Hagel. *

"There is no U.S. senator in this body who supports more strongly the U.S. military," said Hagel, who was wounded in Vietnam by a land mine, as was his brother. "But we do not need indiscriminate killing machines like anti-personnel mines in order to defend [our] liberties." [23]

President Clinton was also an early leader of the effort to get rid of land mines. In a 1994 speech before the U.N., he called for the "eventual elimination" of anti-personnel mines. "Ridding the world of those often hidden weapons will help save the lives of tens of thousands of men and women and innocent children in the years to come," he declared.

But with his announcement last year that the United States would continue to use dumb mines in Korea and smart mines elsewhere, Clinton heeded the advice of his top military advisers and took a more cautious stance. Muller recalls a White House dinner last year when he, together with former Gen. Jones and Gard confronted the president on the issue.

"I said, 'Mr. President, for God's sake, we've got Bob Dole cosponsoring everything Sen. Leahy's ever put out of the Senate, we've got Bob Dole's wife Elizabeth openly testifying before Congress as head of the American Red Cross to ban the weapon. We have America's retired military elite telling you this is the militarily responsible thing to do. We don't have a single member of Congress that's standing up and saying we need this weapon. What more can we do?'

"He said, 'I can't afford a breach with the Joint Chiefs.' The only thing Clinton cared about was his relationship with the Joint Chiefs. You can get into the psychology of that as easily as I can, but this is not what you

* The other Senate Vietnam combat vets are: John Kerry, D-Mass., John McCain, R-Ariz., Charles S. Robb, D-Va., and Max Cleland, D-Ga.

want a commander in chief's posture to be. The fact that we have to move heaven and earth to get rid of this stupid piece of garbage is nuts."

Clinton's Jan. 17 announcement that the United States would pursue a land mine treaty in Geneva, however, has failed to undermine support for the Ottawa process among American proponents of a total ban.

"We already have a coalition of more than 225 non-governmental organizations just in the U.S. alone," says Mary Wareham, coordinator of the United States Campaign to Ban Landmines, founded in the early 1990s to pursue the issue in the U.S. "It includes all of the major religious denominations in the country, all of the major humanitarian relief and development organizations — such as Save the Children and CARE — women's groups, children's groups, environmental groups such as Greenpeace, large grass-roots organizations like Peace Action, as well as the research-oriented groups like Human Rights Watch and the United Nations Association." ■

OUTLOOK

Moving Toward Ottawa

Supporters of a total and immediate ban on anti-personnel land mines are confident that the Canadian initiative will produce a treaty ready for signature in time for the scheduled Dec. 2-4 signing ceremony in Ottawa. After their most recent negotiations, conducted June 24-27 in Brussels, representatives of 97 countries signed a declaration supporting an Austrian draft treaty that would ban land mines without the exceptions sought by the Clinton administration.

"There will be a treaty signed in December, no question," Williams says. "Canada has put so much diplomatic effort into it, it's now obviously unstoppable."

The Clinton administration promised supporters of the Ottawa process that it would re-evaluate its position at the conclusion of the Conference on Disarmament's most recent session on June 27. Aside from appointing Australian Ambassador John Campbell as special coordinator to establish a mandate for future negotiations on land mines, participants at the Geneva talks failed to make significant progress toward formulating a land mine ban agreement of their own.

Meeting in mid-July, Clinton's advisers on land mine policy were unable to reach a final decision on whether or not to join the Ottawa process. But the administration will have to decide before Sept. 1, when final negotiations on the treaty's provisions begin in Oslo, Norway. The effort to reach a policy on participation in Ottawa includes the National Security Council, DOD and State Department.

"I would hope that the United States will be there," Williams says. "But if they are not going to Ottawa in good faith to negotiate a simple, comprehensive ban with no exceptions, no reservations and no loopholes, I want them to stay away. I don't believe that the United States is so damned important that the rest of the world cannot establish a norm without it." ■

Notes

[1] From the Vietnam Veterans of America Foundation's Internet Web site, www.vvaf.org/land mine/elsa.htm.

[2] The International Campaign to Ban Landmines estimates there are 100 million active, deployed land mines. The American Red Cross puts the number at 120 million.

[3] From a Senate speech on June 17, 1997.

[4] From a White House statement, May 16, 1997.

[5] From a July 10, 1997, letter to Sen. Thurmond.

[6] From an open letter to President Clinton, *The New York Times,* April 3, 1996.

[7] Andrew Cooper, *In Its Own Words: The U.S. Army and Antipersonnel Mines in the Korean and Vietnam Wars,* Human Rights Watch Arms Project and Vietnam Veterans of America Foundation, July 1997.

[8] The official spoke July 3, 1997, at a Defense Department background briefing on anti-personnel mines. He agreed to be quoted, but not by name.

[9] From "Self-Destruct Mines," an undated information sheet distributed by the Vietnam Veterans of America Foundation. See also Cooper, *op. cit.,* pp. 10-11.

[10] For background, see "Chemical and Biological Weapons," *The CQ Researcher,* Jan. 31, 1997, pp. 73-96.

[11] Material in this section is based on U.S. Department of State, *Hidden Killers: The Global Landmine Crisis* (December 1994), pp. 3-7.

[12] See Cooper, *op. cit.,* p. 4.

[13] See Shawn Roberts and Jody Williams, *After the Guns Fall Silent: The Enduring Legacy of Land Mines* (1995).

[14] For background on the U.S. arms industry, see "Arms Sales," *The CQ Researcher,* Dec. 9, 1994, pp. 1081-1104.

[15] See the campaign's Web site at www.vvaf.org/land mine/uscbl-resource. htm.

[16] From a press release distributed on the Vietnam Veterans of America Foundation's Web site at www.vvaf.org/land mine/1997/brussels3.htm.

[17] *Ibid.*

[18] See Andrew Cooper, *Exposing the Source: U.S. Companies and the Production of Antipersonnel Mines,* Human Rights Watch Arms Project, April 1997, pp. 9-10.

[19] *Ibid.*

[20] See Philip Shenon, "Rights Group Presses Drive on U.S. Makers of Land-Mine Parts," *The New York Times,* April 18, 1997.

[21] Princess Diana, representing the British Red Cross, spoke in Washington at a June 17 press conference held by the American Red Cross, and appeared at a dinner to raise funds for land mine victims..

[22] From a Senate speech on June 17, 1997.

[23] From a Senate speech on June 17, 1997.

Bibliography

Selected Sources Used

Articles

Beardsley, Tim, "War Without End?," *Scientific American,* June 1997, pp. 20-22.
The introduction of sophisticated sensors to detect land mines is helping reduce the incidence of injury to deminers in some countries. But as long as these weapons continue to be deployed, high technology alone will not significantly increase the rate of mine removal.

Burkhalter, Holly, "Phantom Pain: Banning Landmines," *World Policy Journal,* summer 1997, pp. 30-34.
The advocacy director of Physicians for Human Rights, an advocacy group in Washington, D.C., describes the growing domestic pressure for a global ban on land mines and calls on the United States to join the "Ottawa process" that is expected to produce a ban treaty this December.

Pasternak, Douglas, "Wonder Weapons," *U.S. News & World Report,* July 7, 1997, pp. 38-46.
Pentagon research into exotic weapons using laser, ultrasound, microwave and other technologies may eventually yield non-lethal arms to replace anti-personnel mines if a global ban takes effect.

Will, George, "Parchment and Pacification," *Newsweek,* July 21, 1997, p. 80.
Even if the United States is allowed to continue using "dumb" mines in Korea and "smart" ones elsewhere, Will writes, a treaty banning land mines is against U.S. interests because the weapons are essential elements of the U.S. arsenal and military doctrine.

Reports and Studies

Cooper, Andrew, *Exposing the Source: U.S. Companies and the Production of Antipersonnel Mines,* Human Rights Watch Arms Project, April 1997.
According to this research group, 47 U.S. companies have been involved in the production of land mines, their components or delivery systems. Seventeen companies have agreed to the group's appeal to cease future production of these weapons.

Department of Defense, *Report to the Secretary of Defense on the Status of DoD's Implementation of the U.S. Policy on Anti-Personnel Landmines,* May 1997.
Issued a year after President Clinton issued his new land mine policy, this report to Congress states that non-self-destructing anti-personnel mines have been eliminated from war plans except for the Korean demilitarized zone.

Doctors Without Borders/Médecins Sans Frontières (MSF), *Living in a Minefield: An MSF Report on the Mine Problem in Afghanistan,* May 1997.
The French nonprofit group that provides emergency medical care in developing countries describes its efforts to treat land mine victims in Afghanistan. It advocates a ban on the weapons and calls for increased funding of demining and rehabilitation programs around the world.

***In Its Own Words: The U.S. Army and Antipersonnel Mines in the Korean and Vietnam Wars,* Human Rights Watch Arms Project and Vietnam Veterans of America Foundation, July 1997.**
U.S. forces in the Korean and Vietnam wars suffered a deadly "blow-back effect" from their own land mines, as troops stumbled onto their own mines and enemy forces used captured American mines against U.S. troops.

***Interagency Working Group on Humanitarian Demining,* U.S. Government Interagency Humanitarian Demining Strategic Plan, Department of Defense and Department of State, undated.**
Since 1993, when it was created by President Clinton, the seven-agency working group has set up programs to detect and clear land mines from more than a dozen countries.

Office of International Security and Peacekeeping Operations, Department of State, Hidden Killers: *The Global Landmine Crisis,* December 1994.
This report analyzes the presence of hidden land mines by region. It also assesses the status of demining programs by the United States and other countries.

Roberts, Shawn, and Jody Williams, *After the Guns Fall Silent: The Enduring Legacy of Landmines,* Vietnam Veterans of America Foundation, 1995.
Almost one-third of the more than 100 million active land mines that lie hidden in scores of countries around the world are in six countries — Afghanistan, Angola, Cambodia, Mozambique, Croatia and Bosnia-Herzegovina. This report assesses the scope of the problem in these countries.

Vietnam Veterans of America Foundation, *Banning Landmines: A Chronology,* September 1995-July 1996.
Compiled by the organization that spearheaded the international movement to ban land mines, this collection of newspaper and magazine articles as well as official documents and transcripts traces the movement's spread and its impact on U.S. military policy.

The Next Step

Additional information from UMI's Newspaper & Periodical Abstracts™ database

Conference on Conventional Weapons

Goose, Stephen D., "CCW states fail to stem crisis: U.S. policy now an obstacle," *Arms Control Today,* July 1996, p. 9.

For the U.S. and many other countries, the goal of imposing a ban on all anti-personnel mines has been pursued more in theory than in practice. The lack of genuine interest in a ban was demonstrated most compellingly during the negotiations to strengthen the so-called land mine protocol to the 1980 Convention on Conventional Weapons (CCW).

Matheson, Michael J., "New landmine protocol is vital step toward ban," *Arms Control Today,* July 1996, pp. 9-13.

The revised land mine protocol to the 1980 Convention on Conventional Weapons will help save civilian lives threatened by the scourge of mines. It is also a critical step on the road to the elimination of all anti-personnel land mines.

Conference on Disarmament

"Administration tries new tack on land mine ban," *Congressional Quarterly Weekly Report,* Jan. 25, 1997, p. 248.

On Jan. 17, 1997, the Clinton administration announced that it would try to negotiate an international treaty banning anti-personnel land mines through the U.N. Conference on Disarmament rather than through a series of negotiations led by Canada.

"Clinton should back Canadian treaty to achieve world ban," *Houston Chronicle,* April 7, 1997, p. A22.

President Clinton supports a worldwide ban on the production, storage and use of land mines by the year 2000, but his efforts to achieve this goal through the U.N. Conference on Disarmament appear doomed.

"Dual track," *The Economist,* Jan. 25, 1997, pp. 42-43.

The U.N.-sponsored Conference on Disarmament has turned its attention from nuclear and chemical weapons to land mines. Some countries are on a fast track to banning land mines, while others are moving slowly.

Fairhall, David, "Oxfam scorns mines export ban 'diversion,'" *The Guardian,* Jan. 31, 1997, p. 11.

Britain's support yesterday at the Conference on Disarmament in Geneva, Switzerland, for a new United Nations effort to ban land mines was promptly condemned by Oxfam as little more than a diversionary tactic. The U.N. secretary-general, Kofi Annan, denounced anti-personnel mines as "weapons of terror" and called on the 61 conference states to negotiate a total ban.

"Maimed by Mines," *St. Louis Post-Dispatch,* April 7, 1997, p. C6.

Unfortunately, the Conference on Disarmament isn't likely to reach a consensus on the banning of mines. The 61 nations taking part in the Geneva conference haven't even bothered to talk about land mines. That fact makes Canada's alternative proposal all the more appealing. Its strategy is to get as many nations as possible to agree to a complete ban on the use, production and stockpiling of mines by 2000.

Rouhi, Maureen, "Land mine dance: One step forward, one back," *Chemical & Engineering News,* June 23, 1997, p. 12.

The worldwide campaign to ban land mines got a boost in the U.S. Congress on the same day that the effort was blocked at the U.N. Conference on Disarmament in Geneva, Switzerland.

"The Slow Way to Ban Mines," *The New York Times,* Jan. 22, 1997, p. A20.

Having considered two available routes for achieving its declared goal of a worldwide ban on land mines, the Clinton administration has chosen to pursue the slower, less promising track. It is taking its case to the U.N.-sponsored Conference on Disarmament in Geneva, Switzerland, where virtually any country can block agreement, and several are likely to try.

"Treading gingerly," *The Economist,* April 27, 1996, p. 46.

An international convention that controls the use of land mines is being revised by representatives of 57 countries meeting in Geneva, Switzerland. Negotiators want to ban the use of land mines in civil wars and wars between countries.

Demining Efforts

"Britain takes stand against land mines," *Christian Century,* June 4-11, 1997, pp. 555-556.

The United Kingdom's Labor government plans to destroy all of the country's anti-personnel land mines by 2005 and will ban the import, export and manufacture of land mines.

Lerman, David, "Lawmakers Push Ban of Land Mines:

Back Global Treaty, Coalition Tells Clinton," *Chicago Tribune,* June 13, 1997, p. 12.
Amid signs of growing congressional support to ban land mines, a bipartisan coalition of lawmakers Thursday called on President Clinton to end his resistance to speedy enactment of a worldwide ban.

Malcolm, Teresa, "Canada to destroy mines," *National Catholic Reporter,* Oct. 18, 1996, p. 8.
Canada's government announced that two-thirds of Canada's stockpile of anti-personnel land mines would be destroyed. This move, however, fell short of the total ban called for by several groups.

McNamara, Thomas E., "The U.S. role in solving the world landmine problem," *U.S. Department of State Dispatch,* Dec. 2, 1996, pp. 594-596.
McNamara discusses the human toll land mines worldwide have taken and outlines steps the U.S. plans to pursue to eradicate them. The U.S. is pushing for an international land mine ban and increased demining activity.

McGreal, Chris, "Africa under pressure to ban landmines," *The Guardian,* Feb. 25, 1997, p. 11.
An international conference opens in Mozambique, Africa, today aimed at persuading countries in the world's most mined continent to follow South Africa's lead in banning anti-personnel mines. The conference of about 200 non-governmental organizations — including the International Red Cross, Oxfam and the Mines Advisory Group — aims to press for a regional ban on land mines in southern Africa before any international agreement to ban the weapons.

McGreal, Chris, "Pretoria outlaws killer mines," *The Guardian,* Feb. 21, 1997, p. 12.
South Africa has imposed an immediate ban on the use and manufacture of anti-personnel land mines, and has said it will destroy its entire stock of 160,000. The cabinet decision came days before a conference in Mozambique aimed at establishing a comprehensive ban on the use of land mines in Africa, without waiting for an international agreement.

Priest, Dana, "Global Anti-Land Mine Coalition Targets Past Producers; 17 Firms Renounce Future Manufacture; Group Pressures Lockheed Martin, Others to Agree," *The Washington Post,* April 18, 1997, p. A26.
The International Campaign to Ban Land Mines, a coalition of 200 non-governmental groups, yesterday launched a "stigmatization" campaign against 17 companies that refused to sign on and 13 others that did not respond to certified letters requesting they renounce future production of mines, their components or delivery systems.

Towell, Pat, "57 senators pressure Clinton to ban anti-personnel mines," *Congressional Quarterly Weekly Report,* June 14, 1997, p.1389.
A group of 57 senators has co-sponsored legislation that would ban the deployment of anti-personnel land mines beginning in 2000.

Innocent Victims

Ashton, Linda, "Amputee works to ban deadly mines," *Chicago Tribune,* Feb. 13, 1996, p. 8.
International relief worker Marianne Holtz lost both her legs below the knees after her car hit a land mine in eastern Zaire. Since then, she has been on a campaign to ban land mines.

Dellios, Hugh, "Angola Land Mines Take Horrible Toll on the Defenseless," *Chicago Tribune,* Feb. 2, 1997, p. 7.
Most of the 40,000 residents of rural Quicunzo fled during the war that has devastated Angola for more than 20 years, and a major reason they don't return is fear of the mines lining the nation's roads and dotting its fields. By many accounts, Angola is the most mine-infested nation on Earth, and its legions of amputees and vast, deserted countryside are prime evidence in a global campaign to ban land mines.

Foek, Anton, "Deadly relics: The global land mine plague," *Humanist,* July 1996, pp. 15-19.
The history of land mine use, beginning with Germany in World War I, and the impact of the mines on civilians long after the wars have ended are discussed. Foek relates the story of a boy who dreamed of being a famous soccer player, but instead was dragged into a civil war in Mozambique. Ironically, he lost a leg to one of the mines he perhaps laid during the war.

Malcolm, Teresa, "Campaigning to ban land mines," *National Catholic Reporter,* May 30, 1997, p. 7.
Tun Chennereth, who was severely maimed by a land mine in Cambodia, joined a demonstration in Washington, D.C., on May 16 to urge President Clinton to sign the international treaty to ban anti-personnel land mines.

Ottawa Process

Nickerson, Colin, "Mine ban gains ground; Canada destroys weapons, seeks global action," *The Boston Globe,* March 7, 1997, p. A1.
Only a year ago, Canada, like most of its allies, defended land mines as terrible but necessary weapons of war. Now, in an abrupt about-face, Ottawa is destroying its arsenal of mines. Already, military engineers have blown up 65,927 mines, or two-thirds of the country's stockpile.

Walkling, Sarah, "Pro-landmine ban states meet in Ottawa set strategy for global effort," *Arms Control Today,* October 1996, p. 21.
Proponents of a worldwide ban on land mines agreed at a recent international conference to work together toward a legally binding ban of such weapons. Highlights of the conference, held in Ottawa, are discussed.

Back Issues

Great Research on Current Issues Starts Right Here . . . Recent topics covered by The CQ Researcher are listed below. Before May 1991, reports were published under the name of Editorial Research Reports.

FEBRUARY 1996
Reforming the CIA
Campaign Finance Reform
Academic Politics
Getting Into College

MARCH 1996
The British Monarchy
Preventing Juvenile Crime
Tax Reform
Pursuing the Paranormal

APRIL 1996
Centennial Olympic Games
Managed Care
Protecting Endangered Species
New Military Culture

MAY 1996
Russia's Political Future
Marriage and Divorce
Year-Round Schools
Taiwan, China and the U.S.

JUNE 1996
Rethinking NAFTA
First Ladies
Teaching Values
Labor Movement's Future

JULY 1996
Recovered-Memory Debate
Native Americans' Future
Crackdown on Sexual Harassment
Attack on Public Schools

AUGUST 1996
Fighting Over Animal Rights
Privatizing Government Services
Child Labor and Sweatshops
Cleaning Up Hazardous Wastes

SEPTEMBER 1996
Gambling Under Attack
The States and Federalism
Civic Journalism
Reassessing Foreign Aid

OCTOBER 1996
Political Consultants
Insurance Fraud
Rethinking School Integration
Parental Rights

NOVEMBER 1996
Global Warming
Clashing Over Copyright
Consumer Debt
Governing Washington, D.C.

DECEMBER 1996
Welfare, Work and the States
The New Volunteerism
Implementing the Disabilities Act
America's Pampered Pets

JANUARY 1997
Combating Scientific Misconduct
Restructuring the Electric Industry
The New Immigrants
Chemical and Biological Weapons

FEBRUARY 1997
Assisting Refugees
Alternative Medicine's Next Phase
Independent Counsels
Feminism's Future

MARCH 1997
New Air Quality Standards
Alcohol Advertising
Civic Renewal
Educating Gifted Students

APRIL 1997
Declining Crime Rates
The FBI Under Fire
Gender Equity in Sports
Space Program's Future

MAY 1997
The Stock Market
The Cloning Controversy
Expanding NATO
The Future of Libraries

JUNE 1997
FDA Reform
China After Deng
Line-Item Veto
Breast Cancer

JULY 1997
Transportation Policy
Executive Pay
School Choice Debate
Aggressive Driving

AUGUST 1997
Age Discrimination

Back issues are available for $5.00 (subscribers) or $10.00 (non-subscribers). Quantity discounts apply to orders over ten. To order, call Congressional Quarterly Customer Service at (202) 887-8621.

Binders are available for $18.00. To order call 1-800-638-1710. Please refer to stock number 648.

Future Topics

- ***Children's Television***
- ***Evolution vs. Creationism***
- ***Caring for the Dying***

THE CQ Researcher

PUBLISHED BY CONGRESSIONAL QUARTERLY INC.

Children's Television

Will the new regulations make it better?

Children's advocates have won two hard battles in recent years to improve what kids watch on TV. A Federal Communications Commission rule taking effect this fall requires broadcasters to air at least three hours of educational programming each week. And most of the television industry agreed last month to include content advisories on TV programs for possibly objectionable material, such as sex or violence. The educational-programming rule is spawning new shows. And the ratings system — to be used with the mandatory "V-chip" on new TV sets — promises to help parents monitor their children's viewing. But one network, NBC, is refusing to participate in the ratings system, calling it unworkable. And advocacy groups acknowledge uncertainty about how parents will use the new system.

INSIDE THIS ISSUE

August 15, 1997 • Volume 7, No. 31 • Pages 721-744

Formerly Editorial Research Reports

THE ISSUES

BACKGROUND

CURRENT SITUATION

OUTLOOK

SIDEBARS AND GRAPHICS

FOR MORE INFORMATION

COVER: "SESAME STREET" REMAINS A PERENNIAL FAVORITE KIDS SHOW AMONG PARENTS, EDUCATORS AND CHILDREN. (© 1997 CTW SESAME STREET MUPPETS. © 1997 HENSON PRODUCTIONS)

August 15, 1997
Volume 7, No. 31

EDITOR
Sandra Stencel

MANAGING EDITOR
Thomas J. Colin

ASSOCIATE EDITORS
Sarah M. Magner
Richard L. Worsnop

STAFF WRITERS
Charles S. Clark
Mary H. Cooper
Kenneth Jost
David Masci

EDITORIAL ASSISTANT
Vanessa E. Furlong

PUBLISHED BY
Congressional Quarterly Inc.

CHAIRMAN
Andrew Barnes

VICE CHAIRMAN
Andrew P. Corty

PRESIDENT AND PUBLISHER
Robert W. Merry

EXECUTIVE EDITOR
David Rapp

The CQ Researcher (ISSN 1056-2036). Formerly Editorial Research Reports. Published weekly, except Jan. 3, May 30, Aug. 29, Oct. 31, by Congressional Quarterly Inc., 1414 22nd St., N.W., Washington, D.C. 20037. Annual subscription rate for libraries, businesses and government is $340. Additional rates furnished upon request. Periodicals postage paid at Washington, D.C., and additional mailing offices. POSTMASTER: Send address changes to The CQ Researcher, 1414 22nd St., N.W., Washington, D.C. 20037.

Children's Television

BY KENNETH JOST

THE ISSUES

Parents of young children may soon see a familiar sight on television: a bearded, rotund fellow wearing a bright blue coat, surrounded by animals and accompanied by a lanky helper with the improbable name of Mr. Green Jeans.

That's right: Captain Kangaroo is back! Four decades of kids grew up with the original Captain. Now, with a new cast, the show is being revived.

"It's a big, wonderful show that you and I grew up watching and that you don't see on TV that much anymore," says Saban Entertainment's Robert Loos, one of the producers of "The All New Captain Kangaroo." "It's entertaining as well as educational, it's kind and gentle, and it keeps you laughing while you learn."

The Captain Kangaroo formula had an enviable record of holding audiences and advertisers during its commercial TV run. But the show has an added appeal: Producers are designing the series to help commercial TV stations meet the new Federal Communications Commission (FCC) requirement to provide at least three hours a week of "core educational programming" for children.

"This is the first time that there is a clear quantitative guideline on children's programming," says Kathryn Montgomery, president of the Center for Media Education, which led the lobbying drive for the rule. "It's clear that the industry knows it has to respond."

The FCC adopted the rule last summer after broadcasters acceded to pressure from a coalition of advocacy groups and a nudge from the White House. Broadcasters, however, say they were already meeting kids' needs for educational shows.

"We have done a good job with children's programming," says Dennis Wharton, vice president of media relations for the National Association of Broadcasters (NAB). Wharton says the industry "voluntarily agreed" to the adoption of the FCC rule, which put a concrete number on a more generally worded requirement included in the Children's Television Act of 1990.

"We've been providing at least three hours a week [of children's programs] ever since we started," says Margaret Loesch, who founded the popular Fox Children's Network (now Fox Kids) in 1990. "We felt [the rule] was appropriate," Loesch says, "because it was an important issue and because we're parents."

In fact, the TV offerings for kids have never been greater or more varied. The seemingly endless cartoon and action shows are supplemented by an assortment of educational offerings and a few teen-oriented dramas (*see p. 738*).

Even longtime critics of children's television are begrudgingly complimentary. "It is getting better, and it will get better," Montgomery says.

Children's television is not a charitable enterprise, however, but a business, and a lucrative one. Advertisers spent nearly $1 billion on children's programming in 1996. Animated programs accounted for about $688 million, or 76 percent of the total. Educational and instructional programs pulled in just $1.4 million. [1]

"There's money to be made in kids' entertainment," says Cyma Zarghami, senior vice president of programming and general manager of Nickelodeon, a children's cable network.

But young people watch more than children's programs in the 15-20 hours a week they spend watching TV. [2] With the expanding number of broadcast and cable channels — and the expanding number of TV sets in the home — kids can now watch violent adult dramas and sex-tinged situation comedies almost any time of day. As a result, many parents now view TV as a decidedly unwholesome influence in their children's lives.

That widespread concern fueled the drive over the past 18 months to persuade the television industry to adopt a ratings system to help parents decide what their children should watch. Initially, an age-based system was devised that mimicked the ratings used for movies. But the system was criticized as inadequate by a coalition that included groups specializing in children's television issues as well as the National PTA, National Education Association (NEA) and American Medical Association (AMA). They argued that parents needed more specific information about the content of programs — specifically violence, sex and language. [3]

Those arguments had strong support in official Washington. President

America's Love Affair With TV

American children watch more than two hours of television per day, and nearly half have TVs in their bedrooms. Relatively few parents worry about the amount of TV their kids watch, but more had negative views of TV quality than positive.

- **Average amount of daily TV-watching:** 2.1 hours
- **Parents who think kids watch too much TV:** 21 percent

Kids with TVs in their bedroom

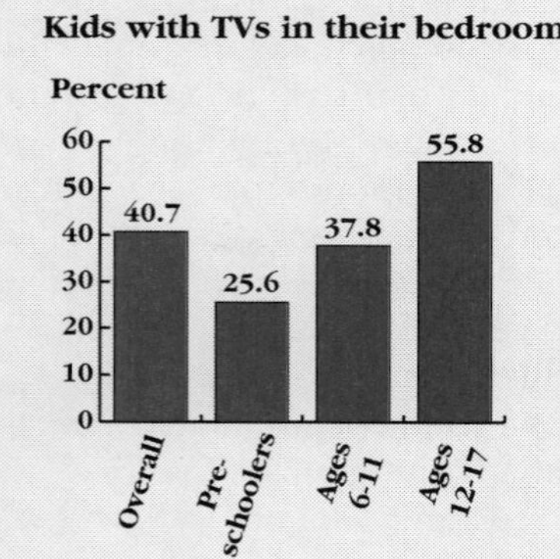

Parents' views of TV quality

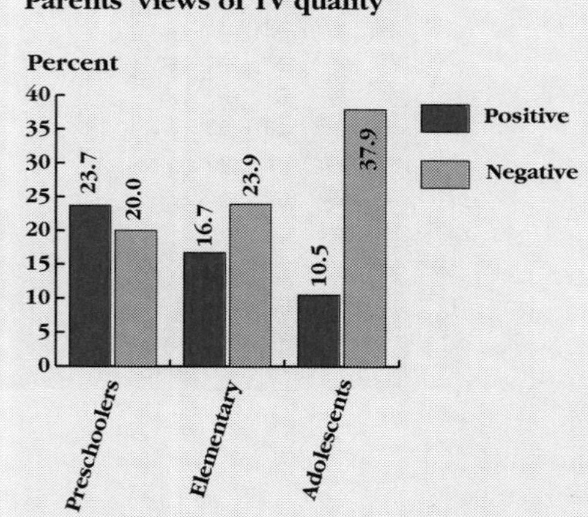

Source: "Television in the Home: The 1997 Survey of Parents & Children," Annenberg Public Policy Center, University of Pennsylvania, June 9, 1996

Clinton helped persuade the TV industry last year to agree to a rating system, and Vice President Al Gore had long paid close attention to children's television issues. On Capitol Hill, lawmakers of both parties were criticizing the amount of sex and violence on television and urging the industry to help parents limit children's intake of inappropriate fare.

Faced with the combination of public and political pressure — and an unenthusiastic public response to the limited ratings system — most of the TV industry agreed last month to more detailed advisories. The new system, due to start on Oct. 1, will rate programs both by age and by content. (*See box, p. 732.*)

"This is designed to be a consumer device," says Arnold Fege, director of governmental relations for the National PTA, "to give parents more information about programs, similar to the information they get from a nutrition label on the back of food."

Having been dragged into the change, broadcasters now are taking credit for it. "We're trying to give parents a little extra tool to monitor what their kids are watching," says the NAB's Wharton.

Some people in the TV industry, however, worry that the rating system will be inherently subjective and necessarily incomplete — with no indication of the context for sexual material or violent scenes. Many writers and producers also worry that watchdog groups could use ratings to galvanize boycotts of programs or advertisers or that skittish network executives could lean on them to tone down programs to the detriment of "the creative process."

Those concerns contributed to a decision by one of the broadcast networks, NBC, not to participate in the new rating system. "There is no way that there will be any consistency in application or any consistency in its use," says Rosalyn Weinman, NBC's executive vice president for broadcast standards and content. "The system is at best confusing and at worst totally incoherent."

From the opposite perspective, some critics of TV programming say even the revised rating system still provides too little information. "Our concern is that without identifying the extent and degree of sex, language and violence, parents will have little more information than they do now," says Mark Honig, executive director of the conservative-leaning Parents Television Council.

Other critics say the rating system has no direct effect on TV sex and violence. "Garbage labeled is still garbage," says Sen. Joseph I. Lieberman, D-Conn.

The new system is designed for use in conjunction with the new "V-chip," ("V" for violence) a computer-encrypted microchip that can screen out objectionable programs. The Telecommunications Act of 1996 requires new TV sets to have V-chips once the rating system has been reviewed by the FCC.

Even supporters of the new rating system, however, are uncertain how families will use the new TV screening tools or what effects they will have.

"It may be that nothing happens in terms of programming," Montgomery says. "But it's my hope that parents will have a tool they can use to make effective decisions in their own homes."

As broadcasters ready the new ratings system and their latest children's offerings, here are some of the questions parents are asking:

Are children seeing too much sex and violence on television?

From its earliest days, television has fed children a steady diet of Westerns and often-violent animated cartoons. Over the past few years, youngsters have also been exposed to increased levels of sexuality on the screen — from sly innuendo or titillating glimpses of skin to nearly explicit bedroom scenes and sex-filled music videos.

The combination of sex and violence has raised concern among parents across the country, not only among cultural conservatives but also among many people who thought of themselves as liberal and culturally sophisticated.

"There were new parents of the TV generation that really became concerned that there really wasn't much redeeming on television for families," says the National PTA's Fege.

These concerns are shared by some in the television industry. "I would love to see a lot less guns, a lot less four-letter words," says Loesch of Fox Kids.

For the most part, though, broadcast and cable industry executives either deny there's any problem or blame the audience or other channels or networks.

"The whole question seems to underestimate the intelligence of the American public," says John Eisendrath, executive producer of the prime-time teen soap opera "Beverly Hills 90210" on Fox. "The public can make their own judgment about what they like and what they don't like."

"The environment in the overwhelming majority of homes in America includes up to 70 channels," says NBC's Weinman. "It's very clear that the intense sex and violence is on the cable and pay-cable channels, not on the broadcast channels."

© 1997 Saban Entertainment

Critics of children's action shows like the "Power Rangers" say they contribute to aggressive behavior.

The persistence of violence and the increased presence of sex on TV has been documented. For the past three years, researchers at the University of California have been conducting two independent but industry-funded studies of violence on TV. Both studies found reason to urge the industry to reduce the violence — in particular, on children's programs.

In the more critical of the studies, the UC-Santa Barbara Center for Communication and Social Policy found roughly 60 percent of TV programs on broadcast and cable channels in 1996 contained scenes of violence. [4]

In addition, the center's study — the second in a planned series of three reports — said that a substantial majority of violent scenes showed no remorse or criticism and no pain, and only a small minority showed any long-term negative consequences from the use of violence. The center also found no appreciable difference in the level of violence between 1995 and 1996. (*See graphs, p. 726.*)

A similar study by the UCLA Center for Communication Policy found less cause for concern and a measure of improvement from 1995 to 1996. Using a set of qualitative factors such as the time of a program, the extent of violence and the role it plays in the plot and in attracting the audience, the UCLA center found five series in the 1996 season that "raised frequent concerns" compared with nine in 1995. It also found that 10 percent of movies shown on TV raised concerns about violence. And it found reason for concern about violence in four children's programs, compared with seven the previous season. [5]

The depiction of sex on TV has been studied less extensively, but a 1996 study by the California-based advocacy group Children Now and the Henry J. Kaiser Family Foundation found "sexually related talk or behavior" in three out of every four shows broadcast during the first hour of prime-time television — the so-called family hour, once reserved for programs appropriate for the whole family. (*See graphs, p. 727.*)

"What we found is a clear, consistent and accelerating increase in sexual messages during prime time,"

Violence on TV Is Widespread

More than half of the television programs in a study of major broadcasting and cable networks included some depictions of violence. Moreover, the programs typically portrayed violence in a way that glamorized it or desensitized viewers to its effects.

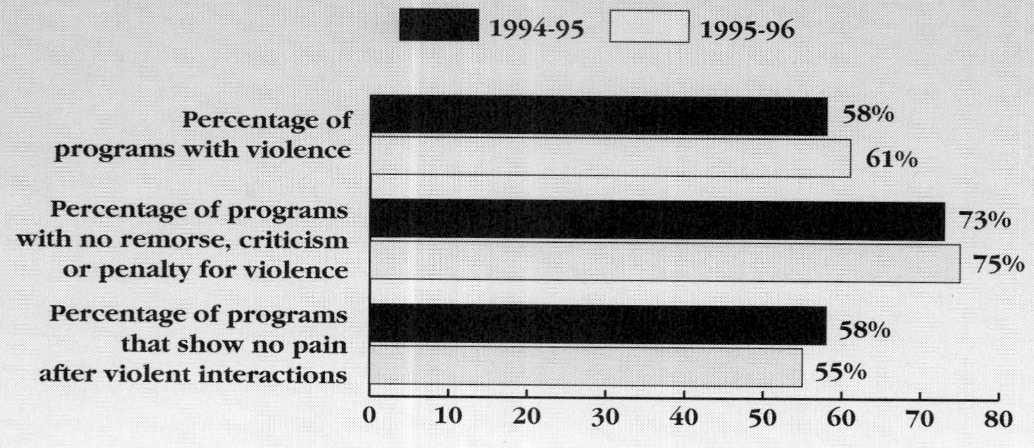

Note: The study defines violence as the depiction of a credible threat of physical force or the actual use of such force in depictions of physically harmful consequences of unseen violence.

Source: National Television Violence Study, *Center for Communication and Social Policy, University of California, Santa Barbara (Vol. 2, 1996).*

says Dale Kunkel, an associate professor of communications at the University of California-Santa Barbara who helped direct the family-hour study and is also directing the UC-Santa Barbara study on TV violence. [6]

The Parents Television Council reached a similar conclusion about family-hour programming in another 1996 report. It found vulgar language and premarital sex common in programs broadcast by the four major networks between 8 p.m. and 9 p.m.

The effects of viewing violence on television have been debated since the 1960s. Today, according to Kunkel and others, most researchers in the field accept what Kunkel sees as the "unequivocal conclusion" that viewing violence "contributes to real world violence and aggression."

But some in the industry continue to dispute the conclusion. "There are lots of intervening factors," says Weinman, a former sociology professor. "It is very problematic to say even if there is a correlation that there is causation." [7]

The makers of children's action shows particularly dispute the view of their programs — "Mighty Morphin Power Rangers" is the most often-cited current example — as contributing to aggressive behavior in children. "Children's TV has always provided action shows," says Fox's Loesch. "At 'Power Rangers,' we make sure that we're providing fantasy elements, that we send out a lot of messages to kids that this is just a live action, fantasy show."

Montgomery of the Center for Media Education says the denial flies in the face of parents' everyday observations. " 'Power Rangers' has taken violence to new levels," she says. "Any parent of a kid who is 4 or 5 years old can see [the harmful effect]."

As for sex, Honig of the Parents Television Council says that television has become "the No. 1 educator of children about sex," and that the lessons are harmful. "What they learn on TV," Honig says, "is you can have sex with as many partners as you want, and there are no consequences for that kind of irresponsible behavior."

The television industry, however, insists it handles both sex and violence responsibly. "We purposely don't have any violence, we don't have any blood, we don't have any gore," says Dan Angell, a story editor with Fox's "Goosebumps" series.

"We have been purposeful in portraying virginity and abstinence as a positive, and safe sex as something that is responsible if you're going to have sex," says Eisendrath of "Beverly Hills 90210." "We are never gratuitously unmindful of issues of morality and responsibility."

Looking at the big picture, says NBC's Weinman, many discontented TV viewers are simply directing at television their anger and anxiety about what they view as unhealthy changes in American society. "Television reflects society," Weinman says. "People have frustrations with television because of their frustration with society."

Is TV meeting children's needs for educational programming?

The faces have changed since television's earliest years: "Romper Room's" Miss Nancy is gone, and "Mr. Wizard" is seen only in reruns. But the TV educators of yesteryear have been replaced by an eclectic mix of characters and programs both entertaining and educational. Today, preschoolers practice their letters and numbers with Big Bird and the rest of the gang on "Sesame Street," while older kids learn science from "Bill Nye, Science Guy" and history from "Where in Time Is Carmen Sandiego?"

These current series are all provided by the Public Broadcasting Service (PBS), the undisputed leader in children's educational programming since the 1960s. On the rest of broadcast television, however, educational offerings have been lacking in both quantity and quality.

"Without naming names, there are programs out there that are simply banal and programs that are not in the best interests of parents and children to spend much time on," says Alice Cahn, PBS's director of children's programming.

"Most television that children have watched is essentially no more than entertainment," says Daniel Anderson, a professor of psychology at the University of Massachusetts in Amherst who has studied television for two decades.

The new FCC rule is aimed at increasing the amount of educational programming on commercial TV stations and ensuring that the programs are, in fact, educational. [8] Under the rule, a commercial TV station is eligible for expedited license renewal (review at the staff level rather than by the commission itself) only if it broadcasts at least three hours of programming each week that has a "significant purpose" to serve "the educational and informational needs" of children 16 and younger. The programs must be regularly scheduled, run between 7 a.m. and 10 p.m., and be at least 30 minutes long. A station that broadcasts "somewhat less" than three hours a week can make up the difference with an equivalent supply of short-form programming, specials and public service announcements.

Broadcasters must identify these "core" educational programs with an on-screen icon and also notify program-guide publishers of the programs and their target age group. The rules for listing educational programming took effect Jan. 1; the three-hour minimum applies to license renewals after Sept. 1.

Although the rule does not apply to cable television, Nickelodeon offers a five-hour daily schedule of commercial-free "play-to-learn" programs for preschoolers as well as the weekly "Nick News" for youngsters. General manager Zarghami also says the network's entire philosophy as a "kids' network" helps promote learning. "If you give them a world where they can feel good about themselves, they will learn," she says.

Children's TV advocates and most researchers in the field believe that educational programs do have a posi-

Family-Hour Programs Are Heavy on Sex

Three-quarters of family-hour programs on the networks contained some sexual content last year, far more than in previous years. There was also a marked increase in the number of sexual interactions (talk about sex and sexual behavior, from kissing to intercourse) per each hour of programming.

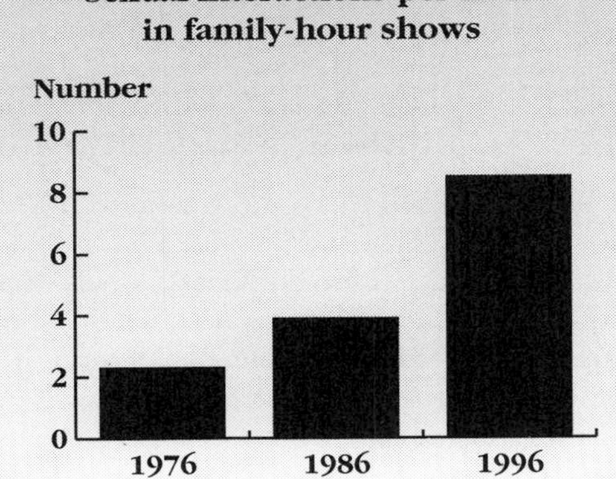

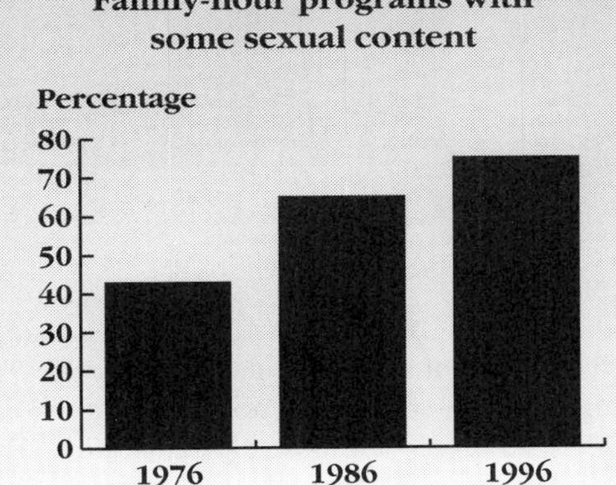

Note: The first hour of prime time is usually designated as the family hour.

Source: "Sex, Kids and the Family Hour," Children Now/Kaiser Family Foundation, Dec. 11, 1996

The Networks' New Educational Shows

Here are the networks' plans for the fall season. Most, but not all, of the shows listed below are designed to meet the new Federal Communications Commission requirement for at least three hours of "core educational programming" for children per week.

• ABC (owned by Walt Disney Co.) is turning to Walt Disney Animation to provide four hours of weekend programming for young viewers, including a two-hour composite program called "Disney's One Saturday Morning." It features half-hour programs drawn from such Disney classics as "101 Dalmatians," "The Jungle Book" and "Winnie the Pooh" and a half-hour science program, "Science Court."

• NBC (owned by General Electric Co.) is aiming at older audiences with three teen dramas — "Saved by the Bell: the New Class," set in a high school, "Hang Time," about a girl on a boys' basketball team, and a new show "City Guys," set in inner-city Manhattan — and a half-hour program produced by the National Basketball Association, "NBA Inside Stuff." All are scheduled for weekends.

• CBS (owned by Westinghouse Electric Corp.) is splitting Saturday mornings between children's shows and a new two-hour adult news program sandwiched in from 9 to 11. The children's shows run the gamut: science ("Beakman's World"), children's literature ("Fudge"), mystery ("The New Ghostwriter Mysteries"), sports ("The Sports Illustrated Show for Kids") and a quiz show ("Wheel of Fortune 2000").

• Fox (owned by Rupert Murdoch's News Corp.) is continuing with a daily half-hour program — the animated "Bobby's World," about a preschooler's reaction to the world around him, running in the earliest time slot permitted by the three-hour rule, 7 a.m. — and another animated half-hour program "Life with Louie" on Saturday morning, about an 8-year-old growing up in Minnesota. Most of Saturday morning will be traditional cartoon fare or Fox's signature adventure programs "Goosebumps" and "X-Men."

© 1997 Capital Cities/ABC

Disney's "101 Dalmatians" is among ABC's children's offerings.

• The two fledgling commercial broadcast networks — WB (a joint venture of the Tribune Co. and Time Warner's Warner Brothers) and Viacom's UPN (a joint venture of Viacom's Paramount unit and BHC Inc., the broadcast unit of Chris Craft Industries) are taking contrasting approaches to children's programming. WB aims at younger audiences with Saturday morning shows like "The Adventures of Captain Planet" and traditional kid fare like "Batman," "Superman" and "Daffy Duck." UPN offers the teen dramas "Sweet Valley High" and "Breaker High" on weekdays and Sunday morning.

• PBS remains the leader in children's educational programming, with 18 shows (10 for preschoolers and eight for school-age youngsters), including four new programs. The new series include a Canadian import "Wimzie's House," set in a home day-care center and featuring a playful, 5-year-old "puppet monster"; a daily wildlife series ("Zoboomafoo"); a music appreciation series from veteran children's performer Shari Lewis ("The Charlie Horse Music Pizza"); and an adaptation of a BBC series, "Nobody."

tive effect on youngsters' learning. One recent study by Anderson and two colleagues found that a group of high school students who had regularly watched "Sesame Street" and "Mister Rogers' Neighborhood" as preschoolers had about a one-quarter point higher grade average than a group of students who did not.

"Watching educational television appears to have a traceable long-term impact on children," Anderson says. "Watching educational television better prepares a child for school and gives a child a better attitude when they do go to school." [9]

A handful of critics have charged that "Sesame Street" is not so beneficial. In her recent book *Endangered Minds,* educational psychologist Jane Healy argues that the show's fast pace and "sensory hucksterism" shorten attention spans and inhibit the development of effective reading and vocabulary skills. Her 17-page chapter on the issue cites no studies, however, to support her critique. [10]

The new FCC rule is forcing commercial broadcasters to re-examine their schedules and individual programs. Some effects of the debate over the rule have already been seen. Saban last fall launched its first ever educational series, an animated science show called "The Why Why Family." With the new season about to begin, PBS and each of the commercial networks except Fox are adding some new programs (*see p. 728*).

Children's television advocates are cautiously optimistic about what the programs will be like. Montgomery says she is hopeful that the rule will have "a significant effect" on the quality of programming. "There is a new generation of television producers and programmers," adds Anderson, "who realize that the medium holds much greater possibilities than an earlier generation thought were commercially feasible."

Peggy Charren, founder and longtime head of Action for Children's Television (ACT) until she closed the organization in 1992, expects a mixed bag of programs. "Maybe a third of the programming is going to be what people like me are hoping for, and a third is going to be the pits and a third is going to be debatable," she says.

Should the television industry do more to help families control children's viewing?

The television industry strongly opposed the demands by advocacy groups to label programs on the basis of objectionable content. But their statements today only hint at the long fight over the issue.

"Cable took the lead in providing content advisory information," says Scott Broyles, director of public affairs for the National Cable Television Association (NCTA), citing the decision by the premium cable channels several years ago to include advisories at the beginning of movies.

Broyles insists the age-based rating system that the television industry agreed to last December gave parents "more information than was ever provided before." But, he says, "we listened to parents, we listened to advocacy groups and collectively it was our understanding that parents wanted more information. That's why we went back to the bargaining table with the advocacy groups."

"We improved our system and hope that parents find it useful," says the NAB's Wharton.

"Bill Nye the Science Guy" is one of several new science shows.

The negotiators for the parent advocacy groups say the industry agreed to talk only because of the political and public pressure.

"The industry kept telling us that they wanted congressional peace," says the National PTA's Fege. "They wanted some way to eliminate the beating that they were taking from Congress. For the most part, they were taking a public relations bloodbath."

The negotiations spanned a three-week period — from June 17 to July 10 — and were conducted under the threat of action by either the FCC or Congress. The telecommunications law directed the commission to review any industry-developed rating system and, if it rejected the industry plan, to devise its own system for voluntary use by broadcasters and cable networks. The FCC had scheduled a meeting for June 20; the session was postponed when the talks began. Meanwhile, Senate Commerce Committee Chairman John McCain, R-Ariz., was similarly scheduling but postponing a markup session on legislation offered by his Republican colleague, Daniel R. Coats of Indiana, to make content-specific ratings a condition for renewing a station's broadcast license.

Sensitive to the image of giving in to government pressure, industry representatives temporarily broke off the talks on June 19 after Vice President Gore issued a press release urging the negotiators to approve a system with the added "V," "S" and "L" designators. Even after the agreement was reached, industry representatives still flinched at questions about government arm-twisting. "I'm going to pass on that," Wharton says.

The industry negotiating team was headed by Jack Valenti, the influential president of the Motion Picture Association of America. Montgomery of the Center for Media Education took the lead for the parent advocacy groups, along with representatives from the PTA, NEA, AMA and American Psychiatric Association.

The advocacy groups won some points in the negotiations: larger icons on the TV screen; the addition of five non-industry members to the ratings monitor board; and an independent evaluation of the rating system after the V-chip has been in the marketplace for a time. The "FV" (fantasy violence) label for children's action shows was a concession from the industry, though the groups preferred a straightforward V designation. The advocacy groups also wanted more explicit criteria for producers to use in labeling programs.

From its perspective, the industry won an assurance from lawmakers and the advocacy groups that the rating system would be given some time to operate. A joint letter signed by the industry and advocacy groups called on "governmental leaders to allow this process to proceed unimpeded by pending or new legislation that would undermine this agreement or disrupt the harmony and good faith of this process."

Besides calling for more detailed information in the ratings, Honig of the Parents Television Council — which was not a party to the negotiations — also urges broadcasters to voluntarily return to the idea of setting aside a prime-time family hour for programs appropriate for the entire family. The council gathered support for the idea from more than 100 members of Congress, but Honig says the networks "have been slow to respond."

Broadcasters say the idea is out of date. "The whole notion of a family hour is anachronistic," says Weinman at NBC. She notes that many youngsters — and a majority of children ages 12-17 — have TV sets in their bedroom. "Most homes have decided that they are comfortable with preteen children controlling their own viewing," she says.

The PTA's Fege says the new rating system is only "a first step." Evaluation of the system, he notes, will have to wait until there are enough V-chips in the marketplace to provide useful information about how parents are using it. At that point, though, he hopes the industry will be receptive to change.

"If parents don't like the agreement, for whatever reason," he says, "we would hope that the evaluation would give us enough information for the industry to go back and tweak the system so that they can make it more useful for the parent community." ■

BACKGROUND

'Glued to the Tube'

Television has long been a pervasive presence in the lives of American children. The small screen has brought into homes the cultural icons that defined childhood: from "Howdy Doody" and "Davy Crockett" in the 1950s to Bart Simpson and the "Mighty Morphin Power Rangers" of the 1990s. By 1960 — and ever since — children have been spending more time with television than with any other in-home activity except sleeping. *(See graphs, p. 724.)*

The time children spend with television has remained one of the issues causing concern among parents and educators. Parents and teachers talk of children "glued to the tube." Marie Winn, in her controversial book *The Plug-In Drug,* wrote in 1977 that many children as well as adults were literally "addicted" to television. In a later edition, Winn cited studies that documented a negative relationship between television viewing and school achievement: the more children watched, the lower their performance. [11]

Violence on television caused concern from its earliest days. Sen. Estes Kefauver, D-Tenn., led a Senate subcommittee hearing on the issue in 1954. Two years later, its report concluded that violent programming was potentially harmful to some youngsters. [12] In 1961 and 1964, the subcommittee — then led by Sen. Thomas J. Dodd, D-Conn. — found that TV violence had increased and repeated its concern about the effects on children.

In addition, by 1960 the first research had been conducted on the issue. Acknowledging the need for more studies, three researchers at Stanford University tentatively concluded that "some television" was harmful to "some children" under "some conditions," but that for most children it was "probably neither particularly harmful nor particularly beneficial." [13]

Some parents, teachers and others also worried about the effect of television on children's morals: whether programming led children into smoking, drinking or sex. But the concern about sex was muted, since television dealt with the subject so rarely and so discretely. TV couples slept in separate beds, and teenagers never went beyond a good-night kiss.

Forced to respond to the concern about violence, broadcasters adopted a position of denial. They insisted that there was no conclusive evidence showing that television contributed to violent behavior. In any event, they maintained that violent programming was being reduced. The TV screen belied their denials, and a staff report by a presidential commission on violence documented the

Continued on p. 732

Chronology

1950s ***Television becomes a household fixture in the United States.***

1954
Senate Judiciary Subcommittee on Juvenile Delinquency hearings probe impact on children of viewing crime, violence and sex on TV. Panel later concludes such programs in large doses could be potentially harmful to young children.

1960s ***Concern about sex and violence on television and commercial exploitation of children grows.***

1968
Action for Children's Television (ACT) is founded.

1969
First episodes of "Sesame Street" are aired on Public Broadcasting System.

1970s ***Cable television becomes widely available, greatly expanding the number and variety of TV channels in many homes.***

January 1972
Surgeon General's Advisory Committee report, "Television and Growing Up: The Impact of Televised Violence," concludes that viewing violence on television can contribute to aggressive behavior in some children.

Oct. 24, 1974
FCC adopts children's television policy requiring "reasonable" amount of educational programming and limiting commercials to 9-$^1/_2$ minutes per hour on children's programs on weekends.

Feb. 4, 1975
National Association of Broadcasters TV code board adopts "Family Viewing Hour" prohibiting programming "inappropriate for general family viewing" during early prime-time hours.

Nov. 4, 1976
A federal judge rules the family viewing hour is unconstitutional, but the networks re-establish the policy on a voluntary basis.

April 1, 1979
The cable network Nickelodeon is launched, proclaiming itself as the first full-time TV network for kids.

1980s ***FCC repeals policy on commercials on children's television, but Congress sets limits by legislation.***

June 27, 1984
FCC repeals commercial guidelines for children's television as part of general move toward broadcast deregulation. ACT wins court case requiring FCC to restudy issue, then turns to Congress for legislation on educational programming and commercial limits.

September 1990
Congress clears bill requiring FCC to set commercial guidelines for children's programming and to consider as part of license renewal a broadcaster's performance in serving "educational and informational" needs of youngsters. President George Bush allows bill to become law without his signature.

1990s ***Children's television unites advocacy groups and politicians of both parties.***

December 1992
Networks, operating under antitrust exemption granted by Congress, issue uniform set of 15 guidelines on TV violence.

Feb. 8, 1996
President Clinton signs Telecommunications Act of 1996 containing provisions for television industry to create program ratings system and for TV manufacturers to install "V-chips" to enable viewers to block specified categories of programs.

Aug. 8, 1996
FCC approves rule, as agreed to by broadcasting industry, requiring commercial television stations to provide three hours of educational programming for children per week beginning in fall 1997.

Jan. 1, 1996
Television industry begins ratings system with age-based advisories.

Oct. 1, 1997
Revised program content ratings system goes into effect, adding descriptors for violence (V), sex (S), crude language (L), sexually suggestive dialogue (D) and "fantasy violence" (FV).

The Revised TV Ratings System

Content-based ratings will be given to TV programs under an agreement between most of the television industry and a coalition of advocacy groups. (NBC has refused to participate.) The new ratings system begins with the age-based ratings symbols instituted by the industry at the beginning of the year and adds a letter when appropriate to denote potentially objectionable content: "V" for violence, "S" for sexual situations, "L" for coarse language, "D" for sexually suggestive dialogue and "FV" for fantasy violence in children's programs.

Ratings for Children's Programs

Programs designed for all children, not expected to frighten younger children.

Programs designed for children ages 7 and older. May contain fantasy or comedic violence or may frighten younger children. Programs with more intense or combative fantasy violence will be designated **TV-Y7-FV.**

Ratings for All Audiences

Programs for general audiences that most parents would find suitable for all ages. Little or no violence, sexual situations or strong language.

Programs that require parental guidance, containing material that parents might find unsuitable for young children. Programs will also carry V, S, D and/or L designations (for moderate violence, some sexual situations, infrequent coarse language and some suggestive dialogue), as appropriate.

Programs with material that many parents would find unsuitable for children under age 14. Parents are urged to monitor these programs, which will also carry V, S, D and/or L designations (for intense violence, intense sexual situations. strong, coarse language and intensely suggestive dialogue), as appropriate.

Programs designed to be viewed only by adults ("mature audiences") and that may be unsuitable for children under age 17, which will carry V, S and/or L designations (for graphic violence, explicit sexual activity and crude, indecent language), as appropriate.

Continued from p. 730

refutation. In the 1968 season, the report said, 81.4 percent of all network programs contained acts or threats of violence. [14]

Today, most researchers outside the broadcast industry say the evidence is clear that violence on television has remained high and TV violence does contribute to aggressive behavior. The concern among parents that TV displaces more valuable activities produces less agreement. Television did virtually wipe out other forms of light entertainment: comic books, radio and neighborhood movie theater matinees. But Anderson at the University of Massachusetts says the evidence is "very weak" that TV affected serious reading. "Very few kids read today," he says. "And before television, it was probably about the same."

Families' Hours

The concern about the impact of television on children grew in the 1960s and '70s, fueled by activist groups and by federal officials. The pressure resulted in some FCC regulations aimed at protecting children as well as an agreement by the TV networks to establish a prime-time "family hour" free of violent and sexual programming. But the regulations had less impact than activists hoped. And the family-hour rule was weakened when a federal judge held the agreement had resulted from improper governmental pressure.

The most important of the children's advocacy groups, Charren's ACT, focused not on limiting violence or sex but on promoting educational programming and restricting advertising. Charren petitioned the FCC in 1970 to prohibit all advertising on children's TV and to require all stations to carry at least 14 hours of educational programming a week. The commission declined, but in 1974 it did limit commercials on children's programming to 9-1/2 minutes per hour on the weekend and prohibited the program host from hawking items on the show. The FCC also required stations to broadcast a "reasonable" amount of educational programming, with a "significant" portion of the programming educational.

Despite the vaguely worded FCC policy, children's TV was getting better through the late 1960s and '70s. Again, the credit lay primarily with a single organization: the Children's Television Workshop (CTW). The organization was created in 1966 with the goal of securing enough funding to take children's TV beyond the often rudimentary productions aired by local public stations. Three years later, the first CTW production aired on public TV: "Sesame Street." Over the next decade, CTW launched other fast-paced, sophisticated series — notably "3-2-1 Contact" and "Square One" — that entertained as well as educated millions of youngsters. [15]

Meanwhile, the issues of violent and sexual programming were becoming increasingly politicized. In 1969, the powerful chairman of the Senate Commerce Committee's Communications Subcommittee, Rhode Island Democrat John O. Pastore, asked the U.S. surgeon general to oversee a new study of the effects of violence on television. The report, released on Dec. 31, 1971, reached the significant, though highly qualified, conclusion that there was a "causal connection between viewing violence on television and aggressive behavior." The "causal relation" operated only on some children — already "predisposed to be aggressive" — and "only in some environmental contexts," the report continued. But in presenting the report to Pastore's committee in March 1972, Surgeon General Jesse Steinfeld said the findings were "sufficient to warrant appropriate and immediate remedial action." [16]

The networks were also beginning to provide their critics with ammunition on a new front: sex. Tentatively at first and then more openly, TV programs began challenging the limits on the use of sexual subjects on TV. "Laugh-In" and "The Smothers Brothers Comedy Hour" began pushing the envelope in the late 1960s, but producer Norman Lear busted it wide open with his realistic comedy series in the early '70s, "All in the Family" and "Maude." Archie Bunker's bathroom humor, Mike and Gloria's acknowledged lovemaking and Maude's abortion broke the taboo on sex in prime-time television, to the dismay of many parents, viewers and — significantly — officials in Washington.

The result was pressure from Congress and the FCC for the three networks to limit sex and violence in programming. In March 1974, just two days after taking office, FCC Chairman Richard E. Wiley was bluntly urged by members of the House Appropriations subcommittee that controlled the agency's budget to look at programming content in renewing broadcasters' licenses. Broadcasting lobbyists who heard the exchange recognized the need for some industry response, if only to ward off more serious government action.

The solution that emerged was the family hour. The plan, approved by the NAB Television Review Code Board on Feb. 4, 1975, called for "entertainment programming inappropriate for viewing by a general family audience" not to be broadcast during the early prime-time viewing hours (between 7 p.m. and 9 p.m. in most time zones, or between 6 p.m. and 8 p.m. in the Central time zone). [17]

One immediate effect of the new rule was to bump "All in the Family" from its coveted 7 p.m. time slot. Lear, who had tangled frequently with CBS censors, had no reluctance to take on the entire industry. He mounted a legal challenge to the rule, contending that the ostensible self-regulation amounted to governmental censorship because of the pressure from Congress and the FCC to enact it. On Nov. 4, 1976, U.S. District Judge Warren H. Ferguson in Los Angeles agreed, barring enforcement of the family hour rule.

The legal victory was both pyrrhic and real. The networks promptly agreed to revive the rule on a voluntary basis, thus preserving the supposed safe haven for family entertainment in the early evening. But the decision also served notice on both Congress and the FCC that they could go only so far in setting mandatory content rules for broadcasters.

The government's ability to control TV programming was being eroded more significantly by developments in

Advertising Barrage Is Part of Kids' TV

Television may help young children learn their letters and numbers, but it also drums other kinds of information into their heads. The 3-year-old who learns her ABCs from "Sesame Street" will soon be watching commercial stations and reciting sales pitches for action-figure toys, sugared cereals and sweetened soft drinks.

The average child sees some 60 commercials a day — or about 22,000 per year, according to a recent estimate. [1] Children's television advocates have fought with broadcasters for decades to try to prohibit or limit advertising aimed at kids, mostly without success.

Broadcasters have used their lobbying clout in Washington to fight any efforts to ban advertising on children's programs altogether and to weaken other proposals before adoption. One of their arguments: Advertising revenues are needed to pay for children's programs.

The Federal Communications Commission (FCC) in 1974 rejected a petition by children's television advocates to prohibit all advertising on children's programs, but it did limit commercials to 9-1/2 minutes per hour on weekends and 12 minutes per hour on weekdays. The FCC also prohibited the host of a children's show from taking part in commercials aired during the program.

The Federal Trade Commission (FTC) turned to the issue in 1978 with a proposal to ban advertising on children's television on the grounds that commercials are inherently unfair for young viewers. "Because of young children's limited cognitive abilities, children do not understand the persuasive intent that necessarily underlies all of the advertising on television," says Dale Kunkel, an associate professor of communication at the University of California at Santa Barbara.

But Kunkel, who worked for a member of the House Communications Subcommittee at the time, recalls that the FTC dropped the proposal after a two-year lobbying fight by advertisers and broadcasters in Congress that limited the agency's authority and at one point actually shut it down.

The FCC eliminated the time limits on commercials in children's programs in 1984 as part of a general deregulation of broadcasting. In the meantime, toy-based programs were coming to dominate children's television. The number of such programs increased from 13 in 1980 to 87 in 1987, accounting for more than half of all children's shows on the air. [2]

Children's television advocates charged that the shows amounted to program-length commercials blatantly aimed at exploiting kids. The FCC in 1991 partly agreed, prohibiting paid commercials for a toy based on a toy within a show. But the proposal did little to disrupt the tie-ins between toy makers and program producers or the phenomenal increase in TV-driven sales. The all-time record appears to be held by Saban Entertainment's "Mighty Morphin Power Rangers" — more than $1 billion in licensed Power Ranger toys were sold in 1994. [3]

The FCC also in 1991 reinstituted time limits on commercials on children's programs, acting under a mandate that Congress included in the Children's Television Act of 1990. The rules set a maximum of 10-1/2 minutes per hour on weekends and 12 minutes per hour on weekends.

Children's television advocates remain concerned about the effects of advertising, but the issue is on a back burner today. And merchandising remains an important factor in producing children's shows. Saban's newest offering — "The All New Captain Kangaroo" — premieres next month; a new line of Captain Kangaroo plush toys will be unveiled next year.

[1] Milton Chen, *The Smart Parent's Guide to Kids' TV* (1994), p. 58.

[2] See Newton N. Minow and Craig L. Lamay, *Abandoned in the Wasteland: Children, Television, and the First Amendment* (1995), p. 52.

[3] *The New York Times,* Dec. 5, 1994, p. A1, cited in *ibid.*, pp. 55-56.

the marketplace. Cable television began to emerge in the 1970s as an independent rival to the broadcast networks. Pay-cable services such as HBO and Showtime brought movies into homes with little if any of the editing that the networks' standards and practices departments dictated.

Cable networks, with some independently produced programming, also began to be established. One of them — Nickelodeon, launched in 1979 — proclaimed itself as the first full-time network for kids. But other cable channels were less kid-friendly. And as the number and variety of cable channels grew over the next decade, parents, like the government, found themselves increasingly unable to control what their children watched on TV.

Deregulation Era

Far from resisting the marketplace pressures, the federal government in the 1980s put its faith in the changes that were weakening the ability to regulate the television industries. President Ronald Reagan preached the virtues of free enterprise and deregulation and put at the head of the FCC someone with similar beliefs: Mark S. Fowler. Under Fowler, the FCC substantially deregulated television. Children's advocacy groups protested and turned to the courts and to Congress for help.

The FCC's move to deregulate television June 1984 wiped out all quantitative commercial guidelines for TV, including children's television. ACT challenged the move in court, arguing that the commission had failed to articulate a reasoned basis for the move. In 1987, the federal appeals court in Washington agreed and remanded the case to the FCC with instructions to elaborate on its justifications.

ACT was also in court with the FCC over another issue: children's programs apparently aimed at selling toys already on the market. The group, along with the National Association for Better Broadcasting (NABB), asked the FCC in 1983 to prohibit shows such as "G.I. Joe" and "Dungeons and Dragons," which they said amounted to "program-length commercials" in violation of FCC regulations.

The commission rejected the plea in 1985. The ruling cited the examples of "Sesame Street" and "Peanuts" as other shows that helped promote the sale of toys. There was "no sensible . . . method of making distinctions among programs based on the subjective intentions of the program producers," the commission said. In a legal challenge, the federal appeals court in Washington again ruled that the FCC did not have a proper basis for its decision and returned the issue to the commission.

For Charren, the FCC's shift toward deregulation was only part of a depressing picture. "The whole world of children's television fell apart," Charren says today. "The industry picked up the message and canceled just about everything they had been doing" to create more and better children's programming.

Rebuffed at the FCC, Charren and other children's TV advocates turned to Congress, pushing for legislation to force the commission to limit commercials on children's programs and stiffen the guidelines on educational programming. The Democratic-controlled Congress passed a bill along those lines, but Reagan pocket-vetoed the measure on Nov. 5, 1988, after Congress had adjourned. Charren and other children's advocates resumed their lobbying after President George Bush took office and pushed a similar bill through Congress in September 1990.

The Children's Television Act of 1990 required the FCC to limit commercials on children's programs to no more than 12 minutes per hour on weekdays and 10-1/2 minutes per hour on weekends beginning within six months. It also required the FCC to consider a station's performance in meeting children's educational needs at the time of its license renewal. The act called on the FCC to study the issue of "program-length commercials," but did not prohibit them. The bill reached Bush's desk as the mid-term elections were nearing. Saying that he approved of the bill's goals but not its methods, Bush allowed it to become law without his signature.

Uniting for Children

In the 1990s, the goals of increasing educational programming for children and limiting sex and violence on shows viewed by youngsters united a broad range of individuals, groups and politicians of both parties. The television industry yielded to the public and political pressure by accepting the FCC rule on educational programming and the combination of program advisories and the mandatory v-chip on new TV receivers.

Congress approved legislation in 1990 sponsored by Sen. Paul Simon, D-Ill., giving TV industry officials a three-year antitrust exemption to permit joint meetings in order to draw up uniform guidelines on the use of violence in programming. [18] The guidelines, agreed to in December 1992, provide that all violence must be "relevant to the development of character, or the advancement of theme or plot." The guidelines ban scenes that glamorize violence, show excessive gore or violence, or use violence to shock or stimulate the audience. In addition, they prohibit any scenes that might invite imitation by children.

But several made-for-TV movies shown in May 1993 — with titles like "Terror in the Towers" and "Murder in the Heartland" — convinced critics that little if anything had changed. Summoned before a Senate committee, network executives promised less violence in the future. Later, in June, the networks announced a plan to place parental advisories at the beginning of programs containing violence.

The networks went further and agreed in early 1994 to a proposal by Simon to appoint an independent monitor to evaluate the use of violence on TV. The reports by two groups of University of California researchers documented the persistence of violence in television programming.

While UCLA researchers took a more favorable view of changes in TV programming last year than those at UC-Santa Barbara, both groups portrayed excessive violence as a continuing problem on television.

Meanwhile, sexually suggestive programming was clearly increasing. One contributing factor was the evolution of Fox into a full-fledged broadcasting network. Fox attracted young, urban audiences with programming that tested the limits on sexual themes, such as "Beverly Hills 90210" and "Melrose Place." Both ran at 8 o'clock in the supposed "family hour."

In an increasingly competitive market, other networks responded. NBC in 1995 shifted its sex-laden comedy series "Friends" from 9 p.m. to 8 p.m. In May 1996, more than 70 members of

Congress signed an ad carried in trade papers urging the networks to restore a safe haven for family viewing.

Children's advocacy groups also had cause for disappointment in the networks' implementation of the FCC's children's programming requirement. After reviewing filings with the commission, the Center for Media Education reported in September 1992 that many stations had not increased educational programming, but were relabeling situation comedies and cartoons as educational. One station even claimed that "The Jetsons" helped "prepare children for life in the 21st century." In addition, meatier informational and educational programs were often relegated to unfavorable, early-morning time slots. The FCC agreed that the stations had been fudging on the law and proposed a new rule tightening the requirements. [19]

The continuing discontent with television provided fuel for leaders in both parties, including the two presidential contenders in 1996. Warming up for his candidacy, then-Senate Majority Leader Bob Dole of Kansas in June 1995 used a Los Angeles speech to criticize the TV and film industries for excessive sex and violence. But with the power of the White House behind him, President Clinton delivered actions, not just words. In February 1996, he signed an omnibus telecommunications bill mandating V-chips in new TV receivers.

The V-chip provision called on the TV industry to develop a program rating system by January 1997. The industry had strongly opposed the proposal since it was introduced four years earlier by Rep. Edward J. Markey in 1993 when the Massachusetts Democrat chaired the House Telecommunications Subcommittee. But to gain points with politicians and the public, the industry decided not to challenge the provision in court. And within a month of the bill's enactment, the TV industry agreed to develop the program rating system. The accord was announced at the White House on Feb. 29, 1996. "We're handing the TV remote control back to America's parents," Clinton declared, "so that they can pass on their values and protect their children."

Broadcasters were resisting tougher educational programming rules. Urged on by children's advocacy groups, FCC Chairman Reed Hundt was pushing his colleagues to require TV stations to devote a minimum of three hours per week to educational programs for children. In June, Clinton announced plans for a new summit of TV industry executives at the White House. The July 29 meeting produced the result Clinton had hoped for: Broadcasters agreed to drop their resistance to the FCC rule. The commission followed through by approving the regulation on Aug. 8.

"This vote affirms that market values are not the same as family values, and our concern ought to be with both," Hundt said at the end of the meeting. "The public interest requires asking broadcasters to take steps that do not necessarily maximize profits." ■

CURRENT SITUATION

Rating Systems

Broadcasters agreed to a rating system only reluctantly. The plan for age-based advisories announced on Dec. 3, 1996, drew immediate criticism from advocacy groups, who contended parents needed specific information about program content. The criticism and pressure from lawmakers led to negotiations that produced the new plan last month calling for additional labeling to denote programs containing violence, sexual material or crude language.

Industry leaders said the age-based plan was simple and familiar to parents. But advocacy groups, which had urged more detailed advisories, criticized the plan. "An age-based system doesn't tell you why a program is appropriate or inappropriate for an age group," said Vicky Rideout, a director of Children Now, an Oakland, Calif.-based advocacy group.

The groups criticizing the plan had two pressure points in Washington: the FCC, which Congress had directed to review the industry plan, and Congress itself. The public comments on the plan filed with the commission were uniformly critical, while virtually all of the 26 responses supporting the system came from network-affiliated TV stations.

But Valenti continued to defend the system, saying critics were all "inside-the-Beltway people." That line of defense was demolished, however, by a town hall meeting convened by the Senate Commerce Communications Subcommittee in May in the nation's heartland: Peoria, Ill. Witnesses complained that television was serving up too much sex and violence and that the rating system was not providing enough information. "The content on TV is bad enough," said Carrie Fricks, a single mother with a teenage son. "At least give us information about what's on a show." [20]

Congress now moved to the center of the picture. Commerce Committee Chairman McCain told the networks bluntly that they should revise the system or be prepared for his committee to mark up Coats' bill requiring a content-specific rating system. In addition, committee mem-

Continued on p. 738

At Issue:

Will the revised television program ratings system help families monitor children's viewing?

YES

LOIS JEAN WHITE
President, National PTA

Across the nation, parents are voicing strong concern about what our children watch on television. We want as much information as possible about program content so we can make informed choices about what our families view. Adding the S, V, L and D descriptors to the age-based system brings us a step closer to having that information.

Let me stress that no ratings system can take the place of parents watching what their children watch and evaluating the shows for themselves. This system is simply an additional tool to help us sort through the array of programming choices available.

The descriptors in no way limit what kinds of shows appear on television; they simply prepare us for what we may see and hear. Without 100 percent participation by the industry, however, it will be difficult to judge whether the system works well.

We have moved from an age-based system that was endorsed only by the industry to one that parent groups and the majority of the industry now accept. The least we can do is give it a fair trial.

EDWARD O. FRITTS
President/CEO, National Association of Broadcasters

When the industry introduced our TV Parental Guidelines in January, we entered into a dialogue with American families, Congress and child-advocacy groups to help parents better monitor the viewing habits of children. After weeks of discussions with parental groups, educators, the medical community and child-advocacy groups, the industry agreed to make numerous changes to provide definitive information.

These revised guidelines are not meant to replace the role of parents. They are additional tools provided by our industry to help parents monitor the TV viewing of young children. In reality, the program ratings represent half a system. The other half will come with implementation of "V-chip" technology that will permit parents to screen out those programs they may find objectionable for children.

Special credit goes to Vice President Gore and key members of Congress, who have publicly acknowledged our efforts. We also appreciate their call for a moratorium on program-content legislation until enough TV sets are equipped with V-chips to evaluate how the system is working. In the final analysis, it is our hope that the winners in this collaborative effort will be America's parents.

NO

ROSALYN WEINMAN
Executive vice president, Broadcast Standards and Content, NBC

We remain committed at NBC to helping parents choose what shows are appropriate for their children. But we do not believe the newly amended system, with its complicated and unwieldy set of labels, will give parents this guidance.

Information on a show's content needs context, and context cannot be expressed in a single letter. Neglecting to provide context can blur the distinction between high-quality television and shows with gratuitous sex and violence.

We also have serious reservations about the way in which the new guidelines were developed under the threat of government intervention. Parents, not politicians and special-interest groups, should regulate the remote control.

Because of these concerns, we decided not to adopt the new system. Instead, we will supplement the current parental guidelines with content-specific advisories when needed to alert parents to certain programming situations or issues that warrant their attention.

We are committed to giving parents useful information about our programs, but not in a confusing way and not in response to political pressure.

MARK HONIG
Executive director, Parents' Television Council

What will be the effect of the television industry's decision to "voluntarily" add S for sex, V for violence, L for crude language and D for suggestive dialogue to its age-based ratings system?

If implemented responsibly, these additions could prove useful. But you could end up with a system that gives an S for sex or a V for violence to family-friendly shows like "Dr. Quinn, Medicine Woman" and "Touched by an Angel" as well as to adult-themed programs like "Melrose Place" and "NYPD Blue."

Each program may be deserving of such labels on an episode-by-episode basis, but the extent and degree of sex or violence is definitely going to vary from show to show. Using such words as "occasional," "frequent" and "widespread" to indicate intensity is critical if parents are to have as much information as possible.

In addition, it should be noted that no rating system, no matter how informative, will solve the real problem: the content of television programs. After all — as Sen. Joseph Lieberman said — garbage labeled is still garbage.

Continued from p. 736

ber Ernest F. Hollings, D-S.C., had a bill aimed at forcing the industry to label violent programs or show them after 10 p.m.

Some segments of the TV industry, including Fox and some cable networks, supported content-based advisories anyway. With no significant public support and concentrated pressure from Washington, the industry agreed in June to a new round of negotiations with the advocacy groups. The outcome seemed predetermined: Only a content-based system was likely to silence the critics. But the industry held out for assurances of a moratorium on public attacks so that the new system could win acceptance.

The final agreement on July 10 gave each side what it had to have to sign off on a deal. The industry — with one major holdout, NBC — agreed to content-based advisories beginning this fall. But key members of Congress, including McCain and Senate Majority Leader Trent Lott of Mississippi, gave the industry written assurances that they would oppose any legislation in the area for a three-year period.

"Today, America's parents have won back their living rooms," Vice President Gore announced at a White House ceremony. Broadcasters pointedly declined to attend.

Besides NBC, three industry groups — the Screen Writers of America, the Writers Guild of America and the Directors Guild of America — warned the new system could have a "detrimental impact" in limiting the variety of shows made. Meanwhile, some lawmakers criticized the plan as still inadequate. "They're still not doing the simple thing we asked them to do, which is to just tell people how much sex, violence and vulgarity is in there," Connecticut's Lieberman said.

Montgomery of the Center for Media Education concedes that advocacy groups wanted more detailed advisories, but she calls the compromise a step forward. "It gives parents more information," she says, "but there's only so much the industry was willing to do."

© 1997 Saban Entertainment

"The All New Captain Kangaroo" debuts in September with John McDonough in the role made famous by Bob Keeshan.

New Worlds for Kids

In the old days, Saturday morning meant three TV networks and cartoons and action shows like "Rin Tin Tin" and "Fury." Today, kids have more choices and — thanks to the FCC rule — more programs coming this season specifically designed to be educational. But the bulk of daily educational programming is still found on public broadcasting. And preschoolers and early school-age children get more attention from TV programmers than young adolescents and teenagers.

When the new TV season opens next month, the four major commercial networks will roll out different programming strategies to meet the three-hour-a-week minimum. (*See box, p. 728.*)

To develop the programs, the commercial networks have followed the pattern PBS pioneered of consulting with educators to incorporate educational elements into an entertainment format. The producers of ABC's "101 Dalmatians," for example, consulted with Howard Gardner, the noted intelligence expert at Harvard University's Graduate School of Education to help teach kids about logic — for example, by having the puppies make up pro-con lists or engage in problem-solving. "We worked hard to match up educators and creators in an appropriate way," says Jonathan Barzily, vice president/general manager of ABC's children's programming.

NBC worked with UCLA Professor Karen Hill Scott to incorporate "pro-social" messages like anti-drug or anti-smoking themes into its teen dramas. "Every show has a predetermined educational objective," says John Miller, NBC executive vice president for advertising and promotion.

The FCC rule has also created new opportunities for syndicated programs. National Geographic is developing five new educational/entertainment half-hour programs, including three animated series. Saban has lined up 130 stations to carry "Captain Kangaroo." Saban credits the FCC rule with encouraging stations to take the series.

In trying to draw young viewers, today's broadcasters face a rival that was unknown in the old, three-network world: cable television. Nickelodeon is the most-watched network among children. "We get 56 percent of kid viewing," Zarghami says. "More than half the pie is ours." The programming includes daytime educational shows for preschoolers, cartoons and situation comedies and interactive game shows.

Nickelodeon has two cable rivals for younger viewers: the Disney Channel and the newer start-up Cartoon Network. Competition is likely to increase soon with the acquisition of the Family Channel by a joint venture of Fox's parent company News Corp. and Saban. The network, which had been owned by religious broadcaster Pat Robert-son, is expected to shift toward more children's programming.

For kids, the combination of competition and regulation appears to be producing the kind of creative programs once seen in TV's heyday. "In the early days of television, with all its crude production, there was still a great sense of imaginativeness," says Fox's Loesch. "I think for a while we lost that, and now we're recapturing it." ■

OUTLOOK

Kid-Friendly TV?

Newton N. Minow — who once described TV as a vast wasteland — has worked on children's television issues for more than three decades — as chairman of the FCC, chairman of PBS and now as a professor of communications law and policy at Northwestern University. "In 1961, I worried that my children would not benefit much from television," Minow said in 1991. Now, "I worry that my grandchildren will actually be harmed by it." [21]

The cause of Minow's concern is familiar to parents: afternoon talk shows that celebrate bizarre sexual practices and prime-time programs dripping with sex or drenched in violence. Many parents also share Minow's disappointment with an industry that offers kids a lot of cartoons and mindless entertainment but little in educational and informational programming.

The battles fought by a broad coalition of advocacy groups over the past year have been aimed at improving the picture of children's television. But the effects of those changes — the revised program-content ratings system and the FCC's three-hour-a-week requirement for educational programming — remain to be seen.

One immediate need, parent advocacy groups acknowledge, is to educate families about the program-rating system. "If parents don't use it, then obviously it will have minimal impact," says Fege of the PTA. The experience under the initial rating system was inauspicious. A survey of parents last summer indicated that nearly two-thirds of those questioned — 65.3 percent — were not using the advisories. [22]

Even less certain is what use families will make of the new V-chip technology. The survey last summer showed that an overwhelming majority of parents — 86 percent — approved of installing V-chips. "Parents will find it a useful tool," Montgomery predicts, "but there will be a lot of education needed."

The television industry faces two immediate tasks: getting the FCC to approve the new rating system and working out the specifications of the V-chip.

The NAB, NCTA and MPAA asked the FCC on Aug. 1 to approve the rating system. The agency will hold a public comment period before making its decision.

Meanwhile, producers are not getting additional guidance on how to rate their shows. "There's no doubt that there will be inconsistencies until this thing is worked out, says Richard Taylor, MPAA director of public affairs. "There are probably going to be cases where you have two similar programs, and they're not rated the same." Taylor notes that individual broadcast stations can change the ratings and that dissatisfied viewers can write to the industry's oversight board monitoring the new system.

Implementing the V-chip will take considerably more time. Television manufacturers may not begin producing sets equipped with V-chips for at least another six months or perhaps longer, according to the Consumer Electronics Manufacturers Association. And because it's now not technologically possible to retrofit old televisions, only new sets will have V-chips. The upshot, Montgomery says, is that it may be five years before there are enough TV sets with V-chips to have useful information about how parents are using the technology.

After decades of hard battles with broadcasters over children's television, however, Montgomery says she is optimistic that TV will be more kid-friendly in the future.

"The FCC rule will spawn some new programs that are educational and informational in nature, so that will add a positive element to the landscape of children's television," she says. "The changes in the ratings will give parents more information to use in making choices about their family's viewing. Those are two important

FOR MORE INFORMATION

Center for Media Education, 1511 K St., N.W., Suite 518, Washington, D.C. 20005; (202) 628-2620. The center, founded in 1991, was one of the lead advocacy groups that negotiated the agreement on the new TV program ratings system.

National Association of Broadcasters, 1771 N St., N.W., Washington, D.C. 20036-2891; (202) 429-5300. The NAB is the trade association for commercial broadcasters.

National Cable Television Association, 1724 Massachusetts Ave., N.W., Washington, D.C. 20036-1969; (202) 775-3550. The NCTA is the cable industry's largest trade association.

National PTA, 330 N. Wabash Ave., Suite 2100, Chicago, Ill. 60611-3690; (312) 670-6782. The National PTA was one of the primary advocacy groups in the negotiations over the new TV program ratings system.

Parents Television Council, 333 S. Grand Ave., Suite 2900, Los Angeles, Calif. 90071; (213) 621-2506. The council, a project of the conservative Media Research Center, advocates "family-friendly" television programming.

TV Parental Guidelines Oversight Monitoring Board, P.O. Box 14097, Washington, D.C. 20004; (202) 879-9364. Questions, comments or complaints regarding the TV program ratings system can be addressed to the industry's oversight board at the above address.

contributions that the policy process has made that will help families." ■

Notes

[1] *Broadcasting & Cable,* July 28, 1997, pp. 47-48.

[2] Children ages 2-11 watched 21 hours of television a week and teen-agers watched 20 hours a week during the 1995-96 broadcast year, according to the A.C. Nielsen Co. Nielsen ratings showed viewing among children and adults has declined over the past decade. In a telephone survey earlier this year, the Annenberg Public Policy Center of the University of Pennsylvania found average viewing time among children ages 2-17 of 2.1 hours a day, or just under 15 hours a week.

[3] For background, see "Sex, Violence and the Media," *The CQ Researcher,* Nov. 17, 1995, pp. 1017-1140; and "TV Violence," *The CQ Researcher,* March 26, 1993, pp. 265-288.

[4] *National Television Violence Study* (Vol. I, 1996; Vol. II, 1997), Center for Communication and Social Policy, University of California, Santa Barbara. The study was funded by the National Cable Television Association.

[5] *The UCLA Television Violence Report* (1996), UCLA Center for Communication Policy. The study was funded by the National Association of Broadcasters.

[6] "Sexual Messages on Family Hour Television: Content and Context," Children Now/ Henry J. Kaiser Family Foundation, Dec. 11, 1996. For a study that found a decline in sexual content of TV programming from 1987 to 1991, see Dennis T. Lowry and Jon A. Shidler, "Prime Time TV Portrayals of Sex, 'Safe Sex' and AIDS," *Journalism Quarterly,* autumn 1993, pp. 628-637.

[7] For a review of the research, see George Comstock with Haejung Paik, *Television and the American Child* (1991), pp. 152-158.

[8] For a summary of the rule, see *Broadcasting & Cable,* Aug. 12, 1996, p. 11.

[9] See *The New York Times,* July 31, 1996, p. C13. The study by Anderson and the husband-wife team of Althea Huston and John C. Wright at the University of Texas in Austin was presented at the Society for Research in Child Development in Washington in April 1997.

[10] Jane M. Healy, *Endangered Minds: Why Children Don't Think and What We Can Do About It* (1990), pp. 218-234.

[11] Marie Winn, *The Plug-In Drug: Television, Children, and the Family* (rev. ed., 1985), pp. 24-25, 78.

[12] Senate Committee on the Judiciary, "Television and Juvenile Delinquency," Investigation of Juvenile Delinquency in the United States, 84th Cong., 2nd sess., Jan. 16, 1956, report no. 1466, cited in Douglass Cater and Stephen Strickland, *TV Violence and the Child: The Evolution and the Fate of the Surgeon General's Report* (1975), p. 10. Some other background is drawn from the Cater-Strickland book.

[13] Wilbur Schramm, Jack Lyle and Edwin B. Parker, *Television in the Lives of Our Children* (1961), cited in Cater & Strickland, *op. cit.,* pp. 10-11.

[14] Mass Media and Violence, *Report to the President's Commission on Causes and Prevention of Violence* (1969), cited in Geoffrey Cowan, *See No Evil: The Backstage Battle over Sex and Violence on Television* (1979), p. 72.

[15] See Edward L. Palmer, *Television and America's Children: A Crisis of Neglect* (1988), pp. 7-9. Palmer was a vice president of CTW.

[16] See Cater and Strickland, *op. cit.,* pp. 77-94.

[17] For background, see Cowan, *op. cit.* Cowan was one of the attorneys for Lear in challenging the family hour.

[18] Some background is drawn from *UCLA Television Violence Report* (1996), pp. 14-15.

[19] See *The New York Times,* Sept. 30, 1992, p. A1; Center for Media Education/Institute for Public Representation, Georgetown University Law Center, "A Report on Station Compliance with the Children's Television Act," September 1992; Dale Kunkel and Julie Canepa, "Broadcasters' License Renewal Claims Regarding Children's Educational Programming," *Journal of Broadcasting and Electronic Media,* fall 1994, pp. 397-416.

[20] See *Los Angeles Times,* May 20, 1997.

[21] Newton N. Minow, "How Vast Wasteland Now?" Gannett Foundation Media Center, Columbia University, New York, 1991, cited in Madeline Levine, *Viewing Violence: How Media Violence Affects Your Child's and Adolescent's Development* (1996), p. 14. See also Newton N. Minow and Craig L. Lamay, *Abandoned in the Wasteland: Children, Television, and the First Amendment* (1995).

[22] "Television in the Home: The 1997 Survey of Parents and Children," Annenberg Public Policy Center, University of Pennsylvania, June 9, 1997, p. 19.

Bibliography

Selected Sources Used

Books

***Big World, Small Screen: The Role of Television in American Society,* University of Nebraska Press, 1992.**
An American Psychological Association task force on television studies the effects of television viewing on children and others, with particular emphasis on areas other than violence and aggression. A 35-page list of references is included.

Cater, Douglass, and Stephen Strickland, *TV Violence and the Child: The Evolution and the Fate of the Surgeon General's Report,* Russell Sage Foundation, 1975.
The authors provide a concise history of the early debate over the effects of television violence on children from the 1950s through the writing of the surgeon general's report on the issue in 1971.

Chen, Milton, *The Smart Parent's Guide to Kids' TV,* KQED Books, 1994.
Chen, director of the Center for Education and Lifelong Learning at the public television station KQED in San Francisco, provides advice for parents on how to limit and guide what children watch in order to make television a positive rather than negative influence. The book includes four pages of references and a 10-page resource guide.

Comstock, George, with Haejung Paik, *Television and the American Child,* Academic Press, 1991.
The book summarizes major research findings about the effects of television on children in the United States in such areas as scholastic achievement, knowledge and beliefs and behavior. A 43-page listing of references is included. Comstock is a professor at the S.I. Newhouse School of Public Communications at Syracuse University; Paik is a professor at the University of Oklahoma.

Cowan, Geoffrey, *See No Evil: The Backstage Battle over Sex and Violence on Television,* Simon & Schuster, 1979.
Cowan traces the development of the "Family Viewing Hour" by the Federal Communications Commission and the major commercial television networks. Cowan was one of the attorneys who represented Hollywood writers in challenging the policy.

Minow, Newton N., and Craig L. Lamay, *Abandoned in the Wasteland: Children, Television, and the First Amendment,* Hill & Wang, 1995.
Minow, the former chairman of the Federal Communications Commission who called television a "vast wasteland" in 1961, argues that television does an especially poor job of meeting children's needs for entertainment and information. A former chairman of the Public Broadcasting Service, Minow proposes, among other things, a prohibition on advertising on children's programming. Minow is now a Chicago attorney; co-author Lamay teaches journalism at Northwestern University.

Winn, Marie, *The Plug-In Drug: Television, Children, and the Family* [rev. ed.], Viking, 1985.
Winn, an author of numerous books on parents and children, first published her critique of "TV addiction" among children in 1977. For the revised edition, she added material on the effects of television on the educational system. The book includes 11 pages of notes.

Articles

"Children's Television: ABCs of Kids TV," *Broadcasting & Cable,* July 28, 1997, pp. 24-50.
The special report provides a network-by-network rundown on children's programming planned for the 1997-1998 season.

Reports

***National Television Violence Study, Vol. 1* (1996); *Vol. II* (1997), Center for Communication and Social Policy, University of California, Santa Barbara.**
The studies — funded by the cable television industry — conclude that violence is pervasive in television programming, including programs aimed at children ages 7 and under.

"Television in the Home: The 1997 Survey of Parents and Children," Annenberg Public Policy Center, University of Pennsylvania, June 9, 1997.
The 20-page report details findings of a national survey of parents and children about children and television. Three other reports by the center released the same day examine children's television programming, the children's educational programming regulation and newspaper coverage of children's TV.

***The UCLA Television Violence Report,* UCLA Center for Communication Policy, 1996, 1995.**
The UCLA center served as an independent monitoring group for a three-year, broadcasting industry-funded study of violence on television. The second report found that the number of programs with frequent violence decreased over the previous year, though the reduction in violence was less marked in children's programming.

The Next Step

Additional information from UMI's Newspaper & Periodical Abstracts™ database

Educational Programming

Braxton, Greg, "Kids' TV getting some new players," *Los Angeles Times,* Aug. 1, 1996, p. F1.

Established television producers who believe the quality and quantity of educational programming need to be upgraded have begun planning shows for children's TV.

Goldin, Lorrie, "Sex, violence and nature shows," *San Francisco Chronicle,* Aug. 28, 1996, p. A19.

Goldin argues that nature shows, such as National Geographic specials on PBS, are loaded with sex and violence and should not be used to fulfill the FCC's rule on educational programming.

Lowry, Brian, "Producers of kids' TV face tough assignment," *Los Angeles Times,* June 19, 1996, p. F1.

The FCC's campaign for educational programming does not address the major challenges that such an initiative presents, including how to get children to tune into educational programs and whether it does any good to offer such shows if they are not watched.

Mifflin, Lawrie, "To fulfill a children's educational TV quota, everything old becomes new again," *The New York Times,* Feb. 10, 1997, p. D8.

When the FCC voted to require television stations to broadcast three hours of educational programs for children each week, FCC Chairman Reed E. Hundt envisioned a new world of production aimed at educating children. Instead networks are choosing to recycle old programs.

Rathbun, Elizabeth A., "Annenberg grades children's television," *Broadcasting & Cable,* June 16, 1997, pp. 21-23.

A report by the University of Pennsylvania's Annenberg Public Policy Center found that of television shows that are defined by commercial broadcasters as educational, 22 percent could not be considered educational by any reasonable benchmark.

FCC Policies

Blowen, Michael, "Soon: more shows with 'purpose,'" *The Boston Globe,* April 6, 1997, p. C20.

Beginning next fall, television stations must meet an FCC guideline requiring them to air at least three hours of educational programming for children each week or risk losing their broadcast licenses. Blowen questions the loose guidelines for determining whether a program is educational.

"FCC sets regulation for minimum level of educational TV," *The Wall Street Journal,* Aug. 9, 1996, p. B3.

The FCC, after years of wrangling, finally set a requirement that TV stations provide at least three hours a week of programs aimed at enriching children's education.

Hall, Jane, "Differing on lesson plan for kids' TV," *Los Angeles Times,* Aug. 15, 1996, p. F1.

With a unanimous vote that belied three years of opposition by the TV industry, the FCC in August 1996, passed guidelines requiring broadcasters to air three hours of educational programming for children per week. The move was hailed by President Clinton and children's TV advocates.

Mifflin, Lawrie, "TV Broadcasters Agree to 3 Hours of Children's Educational Programs a Week," *The New York Times,* July 30, 1996, p. A8.

Under political pressure to reach an accord before President Clinton convened a White House conference on children's TV on July 29, 1996, negotiators for the broadcast industry agreed to a compromise that would require stations to show three hours of children's educational programming a week. The compromise is to be encoded in an FCC regulation.

Public Opinion

"A little light from the TV set," *Los Angeles Times,* July 30, 1996, p. B6.

An editorial supports a proposal requiring television stations to air a minimum of three hours of educational programming for children each week, noting, however, that a clear definition of what constitutes such programming is lacking.

"Better TV for children," *The Christian Science Monitor,* Aug. 1, 1996, p 20.

An editorial supports an agreement by broadcasters to provide programming that would fulfill the requirements of the Children's Television Act.

Blair, Jim, "Convey a certain dress code 'on kids' TV," *Los Angeles Times,* Aug. 3, 1996, p. B7.

Parents living in southern California comment on the need for more educational programming on TV.

"Clinton's push for more kid TV," *Chicago Tribune,* Aug. 1, 1996, p. 22.

An editorial comments on the deal broadcasters reached with President Clinton to show a minimum of three hours a week of children's educational programming, calling it a modest, worthy goal, but cautioning that it should be nothing more than a guideline.

Jordan, Amy B., "Supplement: Children and television: A conference summary" ***Annals of the American Academy of Political & Social Science,*** **March 1997, pp. 153-167.**
Some of the views about the quality of children's TV that were aired at a conference on children and TV are presented. Participants agreed that under the right conditions it is possible to create high-quality, educational programming that children will watch.

"Quality Television for Children," ***The New York Times,*** **Aug. 16, 1996, p. A32.**
An editorial congratulates the FCC on adopting a rule requiring broadcasters to provide at least three hours of educational programs for children each week.

Quello, James H., "The FCC's regulatory overkill," ***The Wall Street Journal,*** **July 24, 1996, p. A20.**
Quello, a commissioner of the FCC, criticizes the proposed rules to require TV broadcasters to air three hours of kids' educational programming per week. Quello asserts that the rules are "an intrusive and meddlesome regulatory mess never envisioned, let alone sanctioned, under the Children's Television Act."

"The righteous push for wholesome TV," ***San Francisco Chronicle,*** **July 1, 1996, p. A18.**
An editorial asserts that TV broadcasters are to blame for FCC proposals to regulate children's programming, saying "television executives can voluntarily work for the public good, or they can wait until the people's representatives do it for them."

Ratings Systems

Asimov, Nanette, "Specific TV ratings sought," ***San Francisco Chronicle,*** **June 19, 1996, p. A2.**
By 1997, all TV shows except news and sports will be rated like movies, but how they will be judged is still undecided. The nonprofit group Children Now is pushing for a system to include specific ratings for sex, swearing and scariness - even in cartoons.

McWhirter, Nickie, "Mastering the remote control," ***Detroit News & Free Press,*** **June 15, 1996, p. C6.**
McWhirter comments on PBS President Ervin Duggan's proposal of an enhanced voluntary ratings system for children's TV programming, saying such a system wouldn't be necessary if parents would just watch TV with their kids and use the on-off switch.

Mifflin, Lawrie, "TV Ratings Accord Comes Under Fire From Both Flanks," ***The New York Times,*** **July 11, 1997, p. A1.**
Starting in October, American families will have at their disposal the most extensive system yet devised to alert them to violent or sexual content in television shows, and approximately a year later, they will be able to buy television sets that, at the touch of a button, can block programs that a family deems objectionable. Under the new ratings system agreed to on Wednesday night, shows will carry an age-group rating and a V, S, L or D, denoting violence, sexual content, coarse language or suggestive dialogue.

Rathbun, Elizabeth A., "Parents don't understand, study concludes," ***Broadcasting & Cable,*** **June 9, 1997, p. 7.**
According to a new survey by the Annenberg Public Policy Center of the University of Pennsylvania, while 70 percent of parents say they are aware of the 5-month-old TV ratings system, only about 35 percent use it to guide their children's viewing. Parents may not use the ratings system because they do not understand it, Annenberg concludes.

Stern, Christopher, "Ratings plan puts chip on kidvid's shoulder," ***Variety,*** **Dec. 9-15, 1996, p. 37.**
Industry executives have narrowed their V-chip ratings deliberations to six age-based categories. The ratings ignore the demands of children's TV activists who say a TV code should include specific information about the violent and sexual content of TV shows.

Viewing Habits

Mifflin, Lawrie, "Pied Piper Of Cable Beguiles Rivals' Children," ***The New York Times,*** **Oct. 29, 1996, p. C13.**
Today, the boundaries for children's TV extend far beyond Saturday mornings, and the menu includes much more than cartoons. And, despite the best efforts of ABC, CBS, Fox and other broadcasters, their shows for the under-12 age group keep dropping in the Nielsen ratings while viewership for the cable network Nickelodeon keeps steadily rising.

Levin, Gary, "Webs lose their place at the kiddies' table," ***Variety,*** **Oct. 14-20, 1996, p. 1.**
Total TV usage on Saturday mornings is down 9 percent in the first four weeks of the new TV season. Kids are tuning out cartoons, and some fear that the trend may not be reversible.

"The young and the restless," ***Fortune,*** **Oct. 28, 1996, p. 108.**
America's youth know all kinds of interesting things about TV. Questions asked of a focus group of boys and girls ages 9 to 11 revealed that children are loyal to certain TV networks and don't mind watching older TV shows.

Back Issues

Great Research on Current Issues Starts Right Here . . . Recent topics covered by The CQ Researcher are listed below. Before May 1991, reports were published under the name of Editorial Research Reports.

FEBRUARY 1996
Reforming the CIA
Campaign Finance Reform
Academic Politics
Getting Into College

MARCH 1996
The British Monarchy
Preventing Juvenile Crime
Tax Reform
Pursuing the Paranormal

APRIL 1996
Centennial Olympic Games
Managed Care
Protecting Endangered Species
New Military Culture

MAY 1996
Russia's Political Future
Marriage and Divorce
Year-Round Schools
Taiwan, China and the U.S.

JUNE 1996
Rethinking NAFTA
First Ladies
Teaching Values
Labor Movement's Future

Back issues are available for $5.00 (subscribers) or $10.00 (non-subscribers). Quantity discounts apply to orders over ten. To order, call Congressional Quarterly Customer Service at (202) 887-8621.

Binders are available for $18.00. To order call 1-800-638-1710. Please refer to stock number 648.

JULY 1996
Recovered-Memory Debate
Native Americans' Future
Crackdown on Sexual Harassment
Attack on Public Schools

AUGUST 1996
Fighting Over Animal Rights
Privatizing Government Services
Child Labor and Sweatshops
Cleaning Up Hazardous Wastes

SEPTEMBER 1996
Gambling Under Attack
The States and Federalism
Civic Journalism
Reassessing Foreign Aid

OCTOBER 1996
Political Consultants
Insurance Fraud
Rethinking School Integration
Parental Rights

NOVEMBER 1996
Global Warming
Clashing Over Copyright
Consumer Debt
Governing Washington, D.C.

DECEMBER 1996
Welfare, Work and the States
The New Volunteerism
Implementing the Disabilities Act
America's Pampered Pets

JANUARY 1997
Combating Scientific Misconduct
Restructuring the Electric Industry
The New Immigrants
Chemical and Biological Weapons

FEBRUARY 1997
Assisting Refugees
Alternative Medicine's Next Phase
Independent Counsels
Feminism's Future

MARCH 1997
New Air Quality Standards
Alcohol Advertising
Civic Renewal
Educating Gifted Students

APRIL 1997
Declining Crime Rates
The FBI Under Fire
Gender Equity in Sports
Space Program's Future

MAY 1997
The Stock Market
The Cloning Controversy
Expanding NATO
The Future of Libraries

JUNE 1997
FDA Reform
China After Deng
Line-Item Veto
Breast Cancer

JULY 1997
Transportation Policy
Executive Pay
School Choice Debate
Aggressive Driving

AUGUST 1997
Age Discrimination
Banning Land Mines

Future Topics

- ***Evolution vs. Creationism***
- ***Caring for the Dying***
- ***Mental Health Policy***

THE CQ Researcher

PUBLISHED BY CONGRESSIONAL QUARTERLY INC.

Evolution vs. Creationism

Should schools be allowed to teach creationism?

Almost 140 years after Charles Darwin published his theory of evolution, theologians, educators and even scientists are still arguing its merits. And proposals to limit the teaching of evolution are being considered by a small but growing number of legislatures and school boards. Nearly half of all Americans reject evolution theory. Some say flatly that the Bible explains creation. Others, including proponents of "intelligent design" theory, argue that life is so complex it could not have come about by natural processes alone. But most scientists argue that evolution has been confirmed by the fossil record, genetics and other scientific disciplines. In addition, they say, there is no evidence to confirm the biblical creation story or to prove God's hand in the development of man or any other creature.

INSIDE THIS ISSUE

CQ August 22, 1997 • Volume 7, No. 32 • Pages 745-768

Formerly Editorial Research Reports

THE ISSUES

BACKGROUND

CURRENT SITUATION

OUTLOOK

SIDEBARS AND GRAPHICS

FOR FURTHER RESEARCH

COVER: ENGLISH SCIENTIST CHARLES DARWIN SET OUT HIS THEORY OF EVOLUTION BY NATURAL SELECTION IN HIS 1859 WORK, *ON THE ORIGIN OF SPECIES.* (THE BETTMANN ARCHIVE)

THE CQ Researcher

August 22, 1997
Volume 7, No. 32

The CQ Researcher (ISSN 1056-2036). Formerly Editorial Research Reports. Published weekly, except Jan. 3, May 30, Aug. 29, Oct. 31, by Congressional Quarterly Inc., 1414 22nd St., N.W., Washington, D.C. 20037. Annual subscription rate for libraries, businesses and government is $340. Additional rates furnished upon request. Periodicals postage paid at Washington, D.C., and additional mailing offices. POSTMASTER: Send address changes to The CQ Researcher, 1414 22nd St., N.W., Washington, D.C. 20037.

Evolution vs. Creationism

By David Masci

The Issues

Steve Edinger and Robert DiSilvestro are both respected science teachers. Edinger is a biologist at Ohio University, DiSilvestro a nutrition professor at Ohio State.

Yet each man stands at the opposite end of the debate over teaching evolution and creationism in public schools.

Both were called to testify before Ohio lawmakers last year about legislation that would have required the teaching of evolution throughout the state to include arguments against the theory.

"I said that it was beyond any reasonable doubt that evolution had happened, does happen and will continue to happen," Edinger recalls. Moreover, he warned members of the House Education Committee, presenting alternative evidence "was not scientific" and would be a disservice to the students. "One wonders what would happen if a teacher spent half a period explaining evolution and the other half saying, 'actually this is wrong,' " he says.

"I didn't see what the problem was with the bill," says DiSilvestro, who doubts evolutionary theory. "If you're going to teach evolution, you should talk a little about the problems with the theory. There is this assumption that science is like math, and that some theories, like evolution, are clear certainties," he says. "But we're not certain about evolution."

Almost 140 years after the publication of Charles Darwin's earthshaking treatise, *On the Origin of Species,* arguments continue about how life began and developed.

In fact, proposals designed to limit the teaching of evolution have been considered by legislatures, school boards and town councils in several

states, among them Washington, California and Georgia. Most of the measures, including the bill in Ohio, have been defeated. In 1995, however, creationists won a major victory in Alabama when the state Board of Education voted to put a disclaimer in all biology textbooks calling evolution just one possible theory of life's origins. (*See box, p. 748.*)

For most scientists, debate over evolution is pointless. Darwin hit the nail on the head, they say, when he postulated that all species evolved through a mechanism known as natural selection. Since that time, evolutionists say, scientific discoveries in fields ranging from paleontology to molecular biology have confirmed Darwin's idea.

"Evolution is so well-reported that we don't even argue about whether it happened, we argue about how it happened," says Eugenie C. Scott, executive director of the National Center for Science Education (NCSE).

What does happen, according to Darwin, is that random mutations constantly change all living things. Some changes hobble a creature and make it incapable of surviving long past birth. But other changes aid in survival and reproduction. A bird born with a significantly longer beak, for example, would have an edge in catching insects and other prey. Such a creature would be able to survive longer than its brethren, and thus have the opportunity to produce more offspring. Some of these progeny, in turn, would inherit the beneficial change and pass it on to their offspring.

Over countless generations, the change or adaptation can accumulate and eventually become the norm within the species. Many such changes, taken together, can significantly alter an organism or even create a new one. (*See story, p. 750.*)

But while the idea of evolution through natural selection is almost universally accepted within the scientific community, it is still questioned by significant segments of American society. In fact, polls show that nearly half of all adults in the United States reject Darwinian evolution in favor of the creation story presented in the Old Testament book of Genesis. [1]

Those who dismiss Darwin's explanation for life's origins and development are not a monolithic group. Some take Genesis literally, believing that God created everything in the universe — from light to mankind — in six 24-hour days. Others read the Bible with an eye toward current scientific thinking, taking the six days of creation to mean six epochs. Hence, in this view, the Bible does not have to contradict cosmologists and geologists who put the age of the universe at 15-20 billion years and the Earth at more than 4 billion.

The fledgling "intelligent design" school, on the other hand, does not try to resolve questions about life's origins with what the Bible says. Instead, proponents simply claim that there is evidence that human beings and other

A Message From the Alabama Board of Education

In November 1995, the Alabama Board of Education required all public school biology textbooks to include inserts labeled "A Message from the Alabama State Board of Education." Here is the complete text of the insert:

"This textbook discusses evolution, a controversial theory some scientists present as a scientific explanation for the origin of living things, such as plants, animals and humans.

No one was present when life first appeared on Earth. Therefore, any statement about life's origins should be considered as theory, not fact.

The word "evolution" may refer to many types of change. Evolution describes changes that occur within a species. (White moths, for example, may "evolve" into gray moths.) This process is microevolution, which can be observed and described as fact. Evolution may also refer to the change of one living thing to another, such as reptiles into birds. This process, called macroevolution, has never been observed and should be considered a theory. Evolution also refers to the unproven belief that random, undirected forces produced a world of living things. There are many unanswered questions about the origin of life which are not mentioned in your textbook, including:

- Why did the major groups of animals suddenly appear in the fossil record (known as the Cambrian Explosion)?
- Why have no new major groups of living things appeared in the fossil record for a long time?
- Why do major groups of plants and animals have no transitional forms in the fossil record?
- How did you and all living things come to possess such a complete and complex set of "instructions" for building a living body?

Study hard and keep an open mind. Someday, you may contribute to the theories of how living things appeared on Earth."

creatures, in all their complexity, must be the product of God's design.

Still, while evolution opponents may disagree on how literally to take what the Bible says, all agree that Darwin fails to adequately explain life's vast diversity and complexity.

"It's like saying that a watch, with all of its intricate parts, somebody, somewhere, just threw a lot of metal up in the air one day and it came down a watch that tells me what time it is," said the Rev. Jerry Falwell, minister of mammoth Thomas Road Baptist Church in Lynchburg, Va. "It's even more ridiculous than that, because man is by far a more marvelous creation than a wristwatch." [2]

One would expect Falwell, as a minister, to credit God. But his view of man's origins also is held, in whole or in part, by some scientists.

"We know about a lot of human systems in a fair amount of detail, and what we have found so far is that they are uncongenial to Darwinian evolution" and instead are "indicative of [intelligent] design," says Michael Behe, a professor of biochemistry at Lehigh University in Bethlehem, Pa.

Behe and others say that a host of complicated organs, like the human eye, consist of many parts that are only useful when working together to bring someone vision. How, Behe and others ask, could the eye have formed gradually through evolution when it would be essentially useless until all the pieces were ready to work together? What advantage would part of a non-working eye convey to an animal? According to this line of thinking, the eye must have been designed by some force other than natural selection.

Other scientists also question the traditional evidence presented for evolution. For example, they often say, the fossil record contains no real sign of creatures caught in the process of changing from one form to another. Each fossil example hauled up by evolutionists, they contend, could just as easily have been a separate species and not a creature in "transition," as evolutionists claim.

Evolutionists always counter these arguments by first pointing out that support for evolutionary theory within the scientific community is overwhelming. Lehigh's Behe and scientists like him are the rare exception, not the rule, they say.

Furthermore, they argue, the so-called evidence against evolution turns out to be groundless upon closer examination. For example, they note, animals exhibit hundreds of different kinds of eyes ranging in complexity from primitive light-sensitive spots to the immensely sophisticated visual organs of eagles and other birds of prey. The many different kinds of eyes are evidence that the evolutionary steps taken from primitive to sophisticated eyes were indeed possible, evolutionists say.

As for the fossil record, the overwhelming majority of paleontologists say it clearly shows evidence of animals being transformed into new species. For example, they point to fossils of whales that still have legs.

It is understandable, scientists and others say, that people are uneasy about what Daniel Dennett, director of the Center for Cognitive Studies at Tufts University, calls "Darwin's dangerous idea." For unlike many other groundbreaking scientific concepts such as gravity, relativity or even heliocentrism, evolution goes straight to the heart of

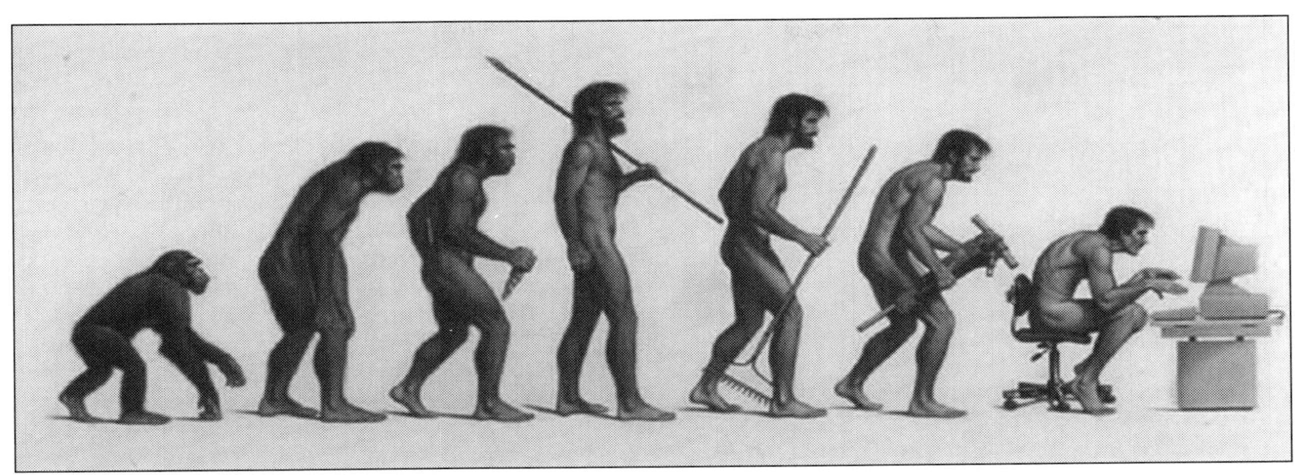

© Picture Network International/Braldt Bralds 1995

Charles Darwin's theory of evolution, here depicted in a humorous light, is widely accepted within the scientific community, but polls indicate that nearly half of all American adults, including a relatively small number of scientists, favor the creation story presented in the Old Testament book of Genesis.

what it means to be human.

Still, proponents of evolution say, people don't have to reject evolution in order to be religious. They note that Pope John Paul II recently reaffirmed the Roman Catholic Church's position that Darwinian theory is not inconsistent with the idea that humans were made by a divine creator. Barry Lynn, executive director of Americans United for the Separation of Church and State and an ordained minister, agrees. "I don't find any conflict in believing that there is an ongoing divine presence in the world and believing that science has it more or less right on evolution," Lynn says.

Underlying this debate is the question of what public schools should say about evolution when they teach biology and other sciences that touch on human origins. Currently, public school students are supposed to be taught evolution. Period. The Supreme Court in a number of decisions has already ruled that teaching creationism or prohibiting the teaching of evolution violates the First Amendment's Establishment Clause. [3]

But anti-evolutionists argue that Darwin should not be taught as fact but as a controversial hypothesis. Others say that students, at the very least, should be exposed to the concept of "intelligent design."

Proponents of evolution oppose any efforts to change the status quo. Evidence against evolution has no scientific basis and thus does not belong in a science class, they argue. As for teaching about intelligent design, they say it is simply another way to bring God into the classroom, which is unconstitutional.

As the debate continues over teaching creationism along with evolutionary theory, these are some of the questions being asked:

Does teaching about "non-religious" alternatives to evolution violate the First Amendment prohibition on the establishment of religion?

The courts have long been a key player in the debate over teaching evolution and creationism in public schools. The mixing of science and religion exploded in 1925, with the famous Scopes "monkey" trial in Dayton, Tenn. (*see pp. 756, 758*).

Succeeding evolution-creation cases have never generated as much publicity as Scopes. Still, in the last three decades, several rulings have exceeded Scopes in importance. All revolved around the Constitution's Establishment Clause, which holds that the government cannot promote or hinder a specific religion.

In 1968, the Supreme Court ruled in *Epperson v. Arkansas* that a state law prohibiting the teaching of evolution violated the Establishment Clause because the state was designing a curriculum based on the principles of a religious doctrine.

Arkansas found itself back in federal court in 1982, this time defending a statute that required public schools to give equal treatment to creation science and evolution. In the case, *McLean v. Arkansas Board of Education,* a district court ruled that the statute was unconstitutional because creation science was not science but religion.

In the next — and most important — evolution case in recent times, *Edwards v. Aguillard,* the U.S. Supreme Court in 1987 overturned as unconstitutional a Louisiana statute that prohibited the teaching of evolution unless accompanied by a lesson on creation science. As in *McLean,* the high court found that creation science was not science but religion. Also unacceptable, according to the majority opinion written by

Understanding Darwin

According to Harvard University zoologist Ernst Mayr, "the publication of *On the Origin of Species* in 1859 ushered in the greatest intellectual revolution since the proclamation of Christianity, 2,000 years before." [1]

Hyperbole? Possibly. But there is no question that Charles Darwin ranks among the greatest thinkers in human history. And yet, while most people have heard of Darwin and evolution, many do not understand his ideas, even in their simplest form.

Darwinian theory, at its most basic level, is not difficult to grasp. Darwin envisioned the history of the development of life on Earth as an ever-growing tree with innumerable branches. At the base was the single-celled ancestor or ancestors of all living things. The thick, lower branches represented the basic categories of life, like insects, reptiles, plants and mammals. These branches, in turn, subdivided countless times, rising to the top of the tree and producing the great diversity of life seen today.

Darwin set down a number of general rules to explain the growth of the tree of life. First, he said, many more organisms are born than will survive and reproduce. Plants and animals are always producing offspring. But many will die because food resources are finite. Naturally, the fact that there are more creatures than resources leads to intense competition among animals, or what Darwin called "the struggle for existence." [2] This struggle intensified, Darwin said, because an organism's primary goal in life is to reproduce, or pass on its genetic material, as many times as possible.

Second, Darwin said that no two organisms are exactly the same. All are born with slight differences, most of which confer no advantage or disadvantage in the struggle for existence. But sometimes changes matter. Some hobble an organism, making it unable to survive; others offer an advantage in the game of survival, say bigger teeth or a more attractive plumage. In other words, the organism is better suited to survive and/or reproduce. Darwin called the phenomenon "survival of the fittest."

Some of these advantages can be passed on to offspring. And since the organism with the advantage would be more likely to live longer, it would also reproduce more times.

Finally, Darwin argued, these offspring and their descendants will thrive since the change that they have inherited confers upon them an advantage not shared by the others of that species. Over time, the positive adaptation will accumulate within the species population through natural selection, as those who have the sharper teeth or some other advantage out-compete against those that don't. Eventually, all organisms within that species will have the adaptation. Over great periods of time, these changes occur and accumulate until the species is significantly different from its ancestor.

But how could natural selection's accumulated changes lead to the development of a creature as sophisticated as a human being?

The answer, according to Darwin and his intellectual heirs, is that natural selection is such a powerful driving force that it is capable of effecting great change. If given hundreds of millions or even billions of years, the argument goes, natural selection can lead to creatures with near miraculous complexity, like humans.

[1] Quoted in: "Beyond Genesis: The Origin of Species," *The Great Books*, the Learning Channel.

[2] Charles Darwin, *On the Origin of Species*, excerpted in Phillip Appleman, (ed.), *Darwin: A Norton Critical Edition* (1970), p. 117.

the late Justice William Brennan Jr., was the statute's "banishment of the theory of evolution from public school classrooms" in cases where teachers declined to offer instruction in creation science.

But Brennan may have left some wiggle room for opponents of evolution when he wrote: "teaching a variety of theories about the origins of mankind to schoolchildren might be validly done with the clear secular intent of enhancing the effectiveness of science instruction." This idea was echoed more directly by Justice Antonin Scalia, who wrote in a dissenting opinion: "The people of Louisiana, including those who are Christian fundamentalists, are quite entitled, as a secular matter, to have whatever scientific evidence there may be against evolution presented in their schools."

For those who oppose the current regime in most public schools of teaching only evolution, *Aguillard* means that while students cannot be taught the biblical story of creation as science, they can be presented with scientific evidence that questions Darwin's theory. To do so, those on both sides of the debate generally agree, would probably be constitutional so long as the challenges to evolution remained scientific.

"There's a difference between bad science and creation science when it comes to constitutionality," says Judith Schaefer, deputy legal director of People for the American Way, a liberal civil liberties group.

But some evolution opponents also believe that the Constitution would allow state legislatures or school boards to go beyond merely questioning evolution and mandate the teaching of alternatives to Darwin's theory — such as creationism — as long as they were not overtly religious. By far the most well-known and well-regarded of these alternatives is "intelligent design" theory, which posits that complex life forms, like human beings, could not have come into existence through a random series of events and that some sort of directed action was responsible for humankind's creation (*see p. 762*).

Supporters of intelligent design argue that it is a scientifically valid theory that has a small but growing base of support in the scientific community. "We're not talking about Billy Graham or Jerry Falwell, we're talking about respected scientists who are saying that there is scientific evidence for this that has nothing to do with faith," says Jim Henderson, senior counsel at the American Center for Law and Justice, a conservative public interest law firm.

The Bettmann Archive

Michelangelo's "The Creation of Adam" reflects the creationist view of humankind created by God. The frescoe adorns the ceiling of the Sistine Chapel in the Vatican. It was commissioned by Pope Julius II and executed between 1508 and 1512.

As a result, Henderson says, teaching intelligent design theory "would pass constitutional muster as long as it . . . avoided any evidence that it was a surreptitious effort to bring religion back to the schools." In other words, he says, references to God or the Bible would not be allowed.

But those who want to limit teaching to evolution say that intelligent design theory would not fit through the space left open by *Aguillard* for the presentation of secular evidence against evolution for the simple reason that intelligent design theory is not a true scientific theory.

"The problem with design theory [from a scientific standpoint] is that it starts with a conclusion, an unalterable conclusion, that there is a designer, and then it looks for facts to back the conclusion up," Schaeffer says. "True science works the other way around" — by formulating conclusions from observable facts.

Schaeffer and others argue that intelligent design is simply a repackaging of creation science in an effort to meet constitutional requirements. "With intelligent design, no matter how you weave and duck, there's still a designer, and it's going to be God," says the NCSE's Scott. "They're trying to imply that all of these things didn't happen naturally, so there's an implied causation, a sort of wink, wink, nudge, nudge element to all of this," Scott says. "If the designer is supernatural, who else can it be but God?" she asks, adding that alternative theories about the identity of the designer would probably not be acceptable to supporters of the theory. "I don't think these people want to teach von Danikenism," she says, referring to the Swiss writer Erich von Daniken, who theorized in his controversial 1968 book *Chariots of the Gods* that extra-terrestrials helped to shape human civilization.

But Henderson and others argue the real problem is that the scientific community and its supporters in the educational and legal professions have a knee-jerk reaction against anything that does not conform to the existing evolutionary orthodoxy.

"You can sanitize creationism all you want, but it always translates [in the eyes of evolutionists] as an effort to bring God back into the classroom," he says.

Phillip Johnson, a law professor at the University of California at Berkeley and a proponent of intelligent design theory, traces much of the antagonism to creationism to the popular play about the Scopes trial, which portrayed evolutionists in a positive light. "The Supreme Court was bamboozled by the *Inherit the Wind* story that all rational people accept evolution and that everyone else is a Bible thumper," he says. (*See box, p. 756.*)

Is evolution a controversial hypothesis or a fact?

Since it appeared in 1859, Darwin's theory of evolution through natural selection has been controversial with the general public. But within the scientific community, the theory is widely accepted.

In the 20th century, most scientists say, belief in the fundamental correctness of evolution has been confirmed time and again as our understanding of molecular biology, genetics, paleontology and other scientific disciplines has improved. "New fields like genetics,

Expanding Darwinian Thinking

When Charles Darwin published *On the Origin of Species* in 1859, evolutionary theory was generally confined to explaining the origins of life on Earth. Today, however, Darwin's ideas are becoming more and more influential in areas of study outside of natural history, including fields as disparate as medicine and literary theory.

"Darwin's idea is a universal solvent, capable of cutting right to the heart of everything in sight," writes Daniel Dennett in his 1995 book, *Darwin's Dangerous Idea.* [1] In other words, says Dennett, director of the Center for Cognitive Studies at Tufts University, natural selection, or the idea that certain adaptations that aid in survival and reproduction will be passed onto offspring, can explain just about everything.

For example, psychologists are asking how and why natural selection has seen fit to leave people with conditions like moodiness, jealousy and anxiety. What purpose could, say, jealousy serve in aiding a person's chances for survival and reproduction?

"Well, if you have two men and one is more concerned about what his wife is doing than the other, who do you think will have a better chance at having more grandchildren that are his?" asks Randolph M. Neese, a professor of psychiatry at the University of Michigan medical school.

Physicians have been using evolutionary principles to discover the purpose behind some diseases and other unwanted conditions. "Why is the body vulnerable to disease? Why hasn't natural selection done a better job?" asks Neese, who is co-author of *Why We Get Sick: The New Science of Darwinian Medicine.* It turns out, he says, that many things generally perceived to be harmful are actually beneficial. For instance, fever helps kill bacteria, and diarrhea is actually a mechanism to quickly push certain toxic materials out of the body faster, he says.

Scholars have even used natural selection to explain cultural phenomena, relying on an idea developed by Oxford University biologist Richard Dawkins. Dawkins has come up with the concept of "memes," which are important ideas, like Darwinian evolution, Christianity or postmodernism, that are governed by the laws of natural selection. If society is an organism, memes are like genetic traits. Some evolve and are passed on, others disappear. Put together, the memes that survive make up our culture and society, just as each creature is the sum of its genes. Dawkins and others argue that natural selection can help us understand why some memes survive and flourish and others die. [2]

Using Darwinian thinking in non-traditional areas like psychology and culture is relatively new, a fact that Neese finds "astounding" in hindsight. "People didn't realize that Darwin could lead to all kinds of things," he says.

The reason for the disconnect between Darwin and other fields, Dennett says, is an innate fear, even among many scientists, of letting Darwinian thinking "leak" into realms outside of biology. Applying evolutionary theory to other disciplines is seen by many scholars as an unwelcome intrusion, Dennett says, because it might dramatically alter the fundamental notions that underlie those fields of study. [3]

Still, Dennett says, the use of Darwinian thinking has expanded in spite of efforts to "contain" it. [4] Neese agrees, saying that it has gone "from being a sideline for a few people to being a major, accepted idea of scientific inquiry" at more and more universities. [5]

There is even a group for like-minded scholars called the Human Behavior and Evolution Society. Started in 1988, the organization now has more than 500 members in areas ranging from computer science to psychology to literary theory. [6] "In all kinds of places around the world, all kinds of people are working on this," Neese says.

---

[1] Daniel Dennett, *Darwin's Dangerous Idea: Evolution and the Meanings of Life* (1995), p. 521.

[2] Kim A. McDonald, "Oxford University's Richard Dawkins Preaches Evolution to a Skeptical Public," *The Chronicle of Higher Education,* Nov. 29, 1996.

[3] Dennett, *op. cit.*

[4] *Ibid.*

[5] David L. Wheeler, "Darwin's Scholarly Heirs," *The Chronicle of Higher Education,* May 17, 1996.

[6] *Ibid.*

---

which did not exist in Darwin's time, have expanded our understanding of evolution, not overturned it," says Ohio University's Edinger.

For example, "a very high percentage of the genetic code is shared among all creatures," says Larry Martin, curator of vertebrate paleontology at the University of Kansas' Museum of Natural History. According to Martin, genetic similarity confirms the idea that all creatures come from the same ancestor or small group of ancestors, as Darwin had predicted. Indeed, Edinger points out, similar species, including humans and chimpanzees, have a largely identical genetic code, indicating recent common ancestry.

These and a variety of other examples are proof, many scientists say, that Darwin's theory is as valid a scientific truth as is the fact that the Earth revolves around the sun. And like heliocentrism, they say, it is no longer worthwhile to devote time and energy to questioning the basic premise behind evolution.

"It's a philosophical concept that you can't be absolutely certain of anything, but the chance that evolution doesn't happen is so minuscule that it's not worth considering anymore," Edinger says.

Nonetheless, there are still vigorous controversies swirling around evolutionary theory. For example, for the last two decades or so, researchers have debated whether species evolved gradually or in quick spurts.

"But those who feel threatened by Darwinism should not take heart from this fact," Dennett writes. "No matter which side wins, the outcome will not undo the basic Darwinian idea." [4]

A relatively small number of scientists, however, question the view of Darwinian evolution as fact. After almost 140 years, they argue, the scientific community has been unable to effectively show that evolution through natural selection has been the engine driving the development of life.

"The final triumph of Darwinian theory, although vividly imagined by biologists, remains along with world peace and Esperanto, on the eschatological horizon of contemporary thought," writes mathematician and philosopher David Berlinski. [5]

Despite vociferous denials from the scientific community, Berlinski and others contend that evolution as a theory is in crisis because the evidence for it is shaky and sometimes non-existent. To begin with, detractors say, some parts of an organism are so complicated, or "irreducibly complex," that they could not have developed through the mechanism of evolution. A system that is "irreducibly complex," in the words of biochemist Behe, is "composed of several well-matched, interacting parts that contribute to the basic function, wherein the removal of any one of the parts causes the system to effectively cease functioning." [6]

Reuters

Scientists from Rutgers University say that stone tools from this site in Gona, Ethiopia, date back at least 2.5 million years and were probably made by ancestral humans. Evolutionists say such findings contradict creationists claims that the Earth and the human race are only 6,000 years old.

An example of such a system is the eye, which only functions when its many complicated parts are working together, Behe and others say. But if the eye resulted from many millions of years of development, Behe reasons, it would have been essentially useless until all the pieces were ready to work together. And he says that would directly contradict natural selection, which dictates that every successful adaptation or change in a creature confers some advantage to that animal. But a developing eye, presumably, wouldn't work until all the parts were there and functioning, he says. *(See story, p. 750.)*

Evolutionists from Darwin to Harvard University paleontologist Stephen Jay Gould have addressed the question posed by Behe. "What good is 5 percent of an eye?" Gould has asked. [7] Not much, answers law Professor Johnson, who says that 5 percent of an eye "is not the same thing as 5 percent of normal vision" since there is no vision at all if all the eye's parts aren't working.

Hence the problem, Johnson writes, is that in order to square the development of the eye with Darwinian evolution, "we have to imagine . . . a chance mutation that provides this complex capacity all at once, at a level of utility capable of giving the creature an advantage in producing offspring." [8]

But Gould and other scientists dismiss the irreducible complexity "problem" as not really a problem. For example, they argue that there is evidence that the eye, like every other vertebrate organ, developed gradually, through evolution.

"There are many examples of intermediate steps that could be seen as leading toward the eye," Martin says. Lee Dugatkin, a professor of biology at Louisville University in Kentucky, agrees. "If you look at various creatures, you see a continuum," he says. "Some can only sense light and dark; others can sense colors, and so on." Even within the primate kingdom, Dugatkin says, some species have more sophisticated eyes than others.

Evolution supporters say that the continuum that Dugatkin and others speak of indicates that there were many steps on the way from light-sensitive spots to human eyes and that the idea of something as complicated as an eye evolving is perfectly feasible.

As for Gould's question: "Vision that is 5 percent as good as yours or mine," writes Oxford University biologist Richard Dawkins, "is very much worth having in comparison with no vision at all. So is 1 percent vision better than total blindness." [9]

Evolution skeptics also ask how millions of species could have gradually evolved without leaving a copious amount of evidence in the fossil record. "The fact is that the billions of known fossils have not yet yielded a single unequivocal transitional form with transitional structures in the process of evolving," writes Henry M. Morris, former president of the Institute for Creation Research, in Santee, Calif. [10]

Johnson agrees, pointing out that Darwin himself asked: "Why, if species have descended from other species by insensibly fine gradations, do we not everywhere see innumerable transitional forms?" [11] Darwin concludes that the fossil record was very spotty and hence could not be used to prove or disprove his theory.

Evolution opponents say the situation is much the same today even though the fossil record is more complete than it was in Darwin's day.

Actually, according to Martin, Dugatkin and many other scientists, the fossil record contains a large number of intermediate species, including the oft-studied archaeopteryx. The small, winged creature lived about 150 million years ago and had many characteristics in common with birds today, such as wings and feathers. It also had a reptilian skeletal structure and very unbirdlike teeth.

"This is clearly a transitional creature," Edinger says.

Evolution proponents also point to fossils of early whales, which were in the process of becoming sea dwellers and still had legs. Scientists say that modern whales still have bone remnants of their back legs that serve no apparent purpose.

But evolution opponents argue that there is no proof that so-called transitional fossils are actually transitions to anything.

"Every transitional fossil they point to, like archaeopteryx, is fully functional, like today's flying fish and flying squirrels," says Hugh Ross, president and founder of Reasons to Believe, a creation science think tank in Pasadena, Calif. "We don't see things that are partially developed like a creature with only a partially formed wing." ■

BACKGROUND

Evolution of an Idea

Scientists had been questioning the biblical account of creation for years when Darwin published his groundbreaking treatise in 1859. For instance, a number of 18th-century French philosophers, including Diderot, had speculated that animals could and did change or mutate over time.

The most important pre-Darwinian text was Charles Lyell's *The Principles of Geology,* published in the early 1830s. The English geologist argued that the Earth had been shaped slowly by uniform forces that were still at work, like erosion, and not quickly by catastrophic events. If Lyell was correct, the Earth would have to be very ancient to account for the numerous layers of rock that geologists had discovered below its surface. [12]

When Lyell's work was published, however, most people believed that the Earth and its creatures were created by God, as explained in Genesis. An Irish cleric, Archbishop James Ussher (1581-1656), had even estimated the date of creation at 4004 B.C., using genealogical descriptions in the Bible to count the years back to the first man, Adam. [13] In addition, a British theologian, the Rev. William Paley, had formulated a widely accepted explanation for biological diversity, arguing that the variations found in plants and animals could not have arisen by chance and thus were evidence of divine design.

Into this still largely theologically based world view stepped Darwin with one of the most explosive ideas in the intellectual history of mankind. But the road to *On the Origin of Species* had been long and torturous.

Darwin first became interested in natural history while in divinity school at Cambridge University. By the time he graduated in 1831, he had abandoned theology for the study of plants and insects. That same year, one of his professors recommended the 22-year-old Darwin for the post of naturalist aboard the *HMS Beagle,* a geographical survey ship that was to map the coast of South America and parts of the South Pacific. [14]

During the five-year voyage, Darwin began shaping what would become his theory of evolution. A key observation was that one geographical area could accommodate different but related species. In the Galapagos Islands, for example, Darwin noticed ground finches with different-sized beaks but otherwise similar characteristics. Darwin discovered that large-beaked finches ate large seeds, while their small-beaked cousins ate small ones. And thin-beaked finches went after insects. Why, Darwin wondered, would the same kind of bird have a variety of beak sizes? Under Paley's theory of divine creation, shouldn't God have created just one finch with the best-sized beak?

Continued on p. 757

Chronology

1800-1899

Scientists present theories on the origin of the Earth and life that contradict religious doctrine.

1802
English cleric William Paley argues in his treatise "Natural Theology" that the diversity and complexity of life are proof that the creatures of the Earth are the product of God's design.

1809
In the year of Charles Darwin's birth, French biologist Jean Baptiste Lamarck contends in his essay "Philosphie Zoologique" that animals evolve over great periods of time to form new species.

1830
English geologist Charles Lyell publishes the first volume of his *Principles of Geology*, which sets out his argument that Earth is millions of years old, not thousands. The cornerstone of his argument is a theory Lyell calls "uniformitarianism," which posits that changes on the Earth's surface resulted from slow, ongoing processes, like erosion.

1832
The 22-year-old Darwin ships out as a naturalist aboard the *HMS Beagle* during its five-year, round-the-world mapping expedition. During the trip, Darwin gathers specimens and data that lead him to formulate his theory on natural selection.

1842
Darwin drafts a treatise explaining his theory of evolution through natural selection. Darwin expands the work two years later but does not publish it, apparently for fear of provoking a backlash.

1856
Lyell convinces Darwin to begin writing an explanation of evolutionary theory for publication.

1858
English Naturalist Alfred Wallace independently develops a theory of evolution virtually identical to Darwin's. He writes to Darwin from Malaysia, and the two jointly publish a paper explaining evolutionary theory.

1859
Darwin publishes *On the Origin of Species*, a detailed explanation of evolutionary theory. The book sells out immediately and creates an intellectual firestorm.

1860
English scientist Thomas Henry Huxley bests Bishop Samuel Wilberforce in a debate on evolutionary theory, essentially silencing church opposition to evolution in England.

1900-1949

The debate surrounding evolution balloons into a national controversy in the United States in the opening decades of the century. The issue peaks in the 1920s but dies down in the 1930s.

1925
Tennessee science teacher John Scopes is convicted of teaching evolution in violation of a state statute, but the dramatic trial, pitting famed attorneys Clarence Darrow (defending Scopes) and William Jennings Bryan (for the prosecution) is seen as a victory for proponents of evolution.

1926
Creationist George McCready Price publishes *Evolutionary Geology and the New Catastrophism*, a seminal work that influences succeeding creation scientists.

1950-Present

The debate over teaching evolution slowly begins to heat up again. Legislatures and school boards pass or try to pass anti-evolution measures.

1963
The Creation Research Society is established to promote young-Earth creation science.

1968
The Supreme Court rules in *Epperson v. Arkansas* that states cannot ban the teaching of evolution.

1987
The Supreme Court rules in *Edwards v. Aguillard* that states may not require the teaching of creation science along with evolution.

1995
The Alabama Board of Education requires a disclaimer for science textbooks stating that evolution is only one possible theory of life's origins.

1996
Legislatures in Ohio, Georgia and Tennessee consider anti-evolution measures. None becomes law.

Darrow v. Bryan: The Real Scopes Trial

On the surface, the 1925 "monkey" trial in Dayton, Tenn., concerned science teacher John Scopes, who had been charged with teaching evolution in violation of state law. But what drew reporters from around the nation was the broader debate over evolution itself and the featured performers: Clarence Darrow and William Jennings Bryan. Bryan, the respected leader of the Progressive Movement in the United States and a three-time Democratic nominee for president, was a member of the prosecution team; Darrow, the most famous lawyer in America, was working on behalf of Scopes.

The Bettmann Archive

The famed Scopes "monkey" trial in 1925 featured attorneys Clarence Darrow and William Jennings Bryan.

So when Judge John T. Raulston agreed to Darrow's request that Bryan testify as an expert witness on evolution and religion, it was understood that the most important moment of the proceeding had arrived.

Inherit the Wind, the popular play and movie about the Scopes trial, portrays Bryan as a mean, bombastic and narrow-minded man who gets his comeuppance at the hands of the savvy Darrow. The truth is a bit different. Darrow did get the better of Bryan on the stand, contrasting his literal view of incidents in the Bible with real-world realities.

But Bryan was not known as mean or bombastic, although he clearly became somewhat defensive during Darrow's skillful questioning. Scopes, for one, said he liked Bryan and enjoyed his speeches during the trial. As for Bryan's supposed narrow-mindedness, he was actually considered one of the most progressive men of his day, a champion of such causes as women's suffrage, workers' rights and campaign finance disclosure.

The following is a small excerpt from the exchange that took place between Darrow and Bryan on July 21, 1925:

Darrow: Do you claim that everything in the Bible should be literally interpreted?

Bryan: I believe everything in the Bible should be accepted as it is given there; some of the Bible is given illustratively. For instance: "Ye are the salt of the Earth." I would not insist that man was actually salt, or that he had flesh of salt, but it is used in the sense of salt as saving God's people.

D: But when you read that . . . the whale swallowed Jonah . . . how do you literally interpret that?

B: I read that a big fish swallowed Jonah. . .

D: Now, you say, the big fish swallowed Jonah, and he there remained how long? Three days? And then he spewed him upon the land. You believe that the big fish was made to swallow Jonah?

B: I am not prepared to say that; the Bible merely says it was done.

D: You don't know whether it was an ordinary run of fish, or made for that purpose?

B: You may guess; you evolutionists guess.

D: But when we guess, we have a sense to guess right. Do you believe the story of the flood to be a literal interpretation?

B: Yes, sir.

D: When was that flood?

B: I would not attempt to fix the date.

[After looking in a copy of the *King James* version of the Bible, Bryan continues. . .]

B: It is given here as 2348 years B.C.

D: Well, 2348 years B.C. You believe that all the living things that were not contained in the Ark were destroyed.

B: I think the fish may have lived.

D: Outside of the fish?

B: I cannot say.

D: You cannot say?

B: No, I accept that just as it is; I have not proof to the contrary.

D: I am asking you whether you believe?

B: I do.

D: That all living things outside of the fish were destroyed?

B: What I say about the fish is merely a matter of humor. . . .

D: Don't you know that the ancient civilizations of China are 6,000 or 7,000 years old, at the very least?

B: No; but they would not run back beyond the creation, according to the Bible, 6,000 years.

D: You don't know how old they are, is that right?

B: I don't know how old they are, but probably you do. [Laughter] I think you would give preference to anybody who opposed the Bible, and I give preference to the Bible.[1]

[1] Quoted in Phillip Appleman, (ed.), *Darwin: A Norton Critical Edition* (1970), pp. 540-543.

Continued from p. 754

Evidence of such species differentiation was abundant in the Galapagos. Darwin noticed that each small island had its own slightly unique species of birds and reptiles. Again, he wondered, why was such slight differentiation necessary or desirable?

Upon returning to England in 1836, Darwin began trying to make sense of his observations. By the following year, he had concluded that species come about through what he called "descent through modification." In other words, species can change over time to form new, different species.

Darwin was not the first scientist to speculate that one species could be transformed into another. French biologist Jean Baptiste Lamarck had speculated earlier in the century that inherited modifications, over long periods, could create different species. [15]

But a valid explanation had never been offered of how evolution occurred. In particular, no one had identified the force, natural or otherwise, that was causing the modifications that ultimately made some creatures fundamentally different from their distant ancestors.

Darwin came upon the beginnings of an answer after reading Thomas Malthus' "Essay on the Principle of Population" in 1838. The English economist had made the alarming declaration that food production was not growing as fast as the population, and that starvation and disease would follow. Darwin applied Malthus' dark vision to animals. In nature, he realized, all creatures would be competing for a slice of a never-increasing pie. Weak or poorly adapted creatures would lose the fight for resources and would die off. Those that survived would be best adapted to thrive in their environment. [16]

Ironically, Malthus' theory thus far has proved wrong when applied to humans. But by placing the Malthusian template over the natural world, Darwin had discovered the mechanism of evolution: natural selection. (*See story, p. 750.*)

The Bettmann Archive

John Scopes' conviction for teaching evolution in violation of Tennessee state law was overturned on a technicality.

"There is a force like a hundred thousand wedges," he wrote, "trying to force every kind of adapted structure into the gaps of the economy of nature, or rather forming gaps by thrusting out weaker ones."

But the world would have to wait two decades to learn of natural selection. After completing a short essay in 1842 on his new theory (which he showed to only one other scientist before expanding it two years later), Darwin began an eight-year study of barnacles. It's widely thought that he did not publicize his theories because he feared a strong public reaction against him. [17]

In 1856, after some gentle urging from his friend Lyell, Darwin began working on a detailed explanation of his theory. Two years later, before he had finished, he received a letter from English naturalist Alfred Wallace outlining his theory of evolution through natural selection. Wallace, who was doing research in Malaysia, had come up with Darwin's idea independently.

After the two men agreed to share credit for the idea, a paper was published in 1858 in both their names outlining evolutionary theory, but it garnered little attention. The following November, however, publication of *On the Origin of Species,* with its more detailed explanation of evolutionary theory, made Darwin a celebrity and his idea the talk of England.

It was Darwin's forceful argument for natural selection as the mechanism of evolution that stirred up so much controversy. The idea that all living creatures, especially human beings, were the product of natural processes and not the direct handiwork of God was disconcerting to most people: For Darwin's hypothesis implied that God was not a necessary ingredient in human creation.

The theory of evolution was immediately attacked, by biologists and other scientists as well as theologians. But Darwin also had many defenders, and the issue, not surprisingly, became the subject of heated debate.

The controversy came to a head on June 30, 1860, when the noted English scientist Thomas Henry Huxley, a friend of Darwin's, debated evolution with the equally celebrated bishop of Oxford, Samuel Wilberforce, who was widely admired for his wit and intellect.

At one point during the debate, Wilberforce had asked "the esteemed scientist" if he was related to an ape on his mother's or father's side. According to many accounts, Huxley answered that he would rather have an ape for an ancestor than a bishop. [18] According to a biography of Darwin: "The room dissolved into an uproar. Men jumped to their feet, shouting at this direct insult to the clergy." [19]

Huxley's remark abruptly ended the evening's debate. But the story that emerged from Oxford was that Huxley had picked apart Wilberforce's arguments, and that science had triumphed over religion.

As a result of the debate, the Church of England backed away from directly challenging evolutionary theory. By the time Darwin died in 1882, his idea had become so well-accepted that the church permitted his burial in Westminster Abbey beside such revered figures as Sir Isaac Newton.

Reaction in the U.S.

Origin of Species did not send shock waves through American society as it had done in England. There was nothing comparable to the highly publicized Wilberforce-Huxley debate in the United States. And even if there had been, Americans, unlike their English cousins, had no overriding, state-sponsored church that could be knocked off its pedestal and humiliated.

But there were other reasons behind the quiet U.S. reception. "Mainstream Christians didn't pay too much attention to Darwin in the years immediately following the publication of *On the Origin of Species,* probably because of the scientific community's delay in accepting his views," says Ronald Numbers, a professor of history at the University of Wisconsin at Madison. [20]

Throughout most of the 20th century, public school students in most parts of the United States have been taught Darwinian evolution. Even Roman Catholic schools, since the 1950s, have been relying upon the standard evolutionary and cosmological theories and not the Bible.

Indeed, eminent American scientists like Louis Agassiz of Harvard University publicly took issue with Darwin. But as the 19th century wound down, so did resistance to evolution within the U.S. scientific community. As a result, evolution became more and more common in public school and college science classes. But greater acceptance of evolution also led to a backlash.

By the 1920s, the anti-evolution movement was a national phenomenon, with three-time presidential candidate William Jennings Bryan among its leaders. Throughout the decade, the movement lobbied hard, especially in the South, to get state legislatures to enact laws banning the teaching of evolution. By 1930, 20 states had considered anti-evolution bills, and three — Arkansas, Mississippi and Tennessee — had actually banned evolution from school science curricula.

But the biggest fight of the decade occurred in a courthouse, not a statehouse. The year was 1925, and the place was Dayton, Tenn., where science teacher John Scopes was on trial for teaching evolution in violation of a state law that prohibited teaching Darwinian theory.

The "monkey" trial was more a media event than a court case. Newspapers from all over the country sent reporters and splashed each day's trial events on the front page. *The Baltimore Sun* sent five reporters, including H.L. Mencken. For the defense, the American Civil Liberties Union (ACLU) had enlisted the country's most famous attorney, Clarence Darrow. The prosecution had its own celebrity lawyer, Bryan.

Scopes was the defendant of record, but it was really Darwin and his idea that were on trial. [21] In a sense, the Scopes trial was a longer version of the Wilberforce-Huxley debate 26 years earlier. And the trial's impact on creationism seems to have been just as devastating. Darrow called Bryan to the stand and, at least in the eyes of the press, ridiculed him and his literal reading of the Bible. (*See story, p. 756.*)

The Scopes trial has come to be seen as one of those chapters in the history of science where reason and rationality win out over superstition. But while the trial enhanced Darrow's already mythic reputation, it was not really a defeat for anti-evolutionists.

"The real story was what was happening in the schools," writes author Gary Wills. "Darwinism had silently crept into [science textbooks] in the late 19th and early 20th centuries. In the late 1920s and early '30s, it just as quietly crept out, and those in the scientific community did not notice it." [22]

Wills points out that evolution would not reappear in most American science texts until the 1960s, when the government, in the wake of the Soviet launch of *Sputnik,* made the teaching of math and science a national priority. [23]

The 1960s also saw great activity in the creationist camp. In 1963, for instance, a team of 10 scientists led by prominent creationist author Henry Morris formed the Creation Research Society. The society's mission was to dispel "the myth that all scientists accept the fact of evolution." [24] Morris eventually left the society and in the early 1970s organized the Institute for Creation Research. Over the years, both organizations have conducted scientific research and published a wide range of books and pamphlets on creation science.

Creation Science

For millions of evangelical Christians and other Americans, the Bible is the word of God and the literal truth. Period. The six-day creation, the garden of Eden, Noah's flood and other milestones in Genesis are historical and scientific fact. Non-biblical explanations for the creation of the universe, Earth and life are not valid.

"There is not a shred of evidence that will stand the test of time that denies the biblical account of creation," Falwell says. "When God created Adam and then took Eve out of the side of Adam, they were as complete as we are now."

Falwell's biblical literalism, and that of many other religious people, is the basis for creation science. But not all creation scientists think alike.

One group, known as young-Earth creationists, holds that the universe and the Earth were created no more than 10,000 years ago. Moreover, they maintain that creation occurred, along with all life, in six 24-hour days, just as recounted in Genesis.

The nation's chief proponent of young-Earth creationism is probably the Institute for Creation Research (ICR) in Santee, Calif., which among other things maintains a small museum that is open to the public.

"At ICR we accept biblical authority as an account of Earth history," according to spokesman William A. Hoesch, who says the institute's creation scientists are not just biblical scholars but real scientists doing real science. "This is not an issue of science against religion," he says.

According to Hoesch, the work done by ICR and other creation scientists confirms what the Bible says about creation. For example, they say, the Earth's extensive fossil record is evidence that a "great flood" inundated the Earth and destroyed almost all life.

Hoesch also dismisses modern dating methods that measure the decay of radioactive material and indicate that some fossils are millions of years old. "All of them are guesstimates, a shot in the dark," he says.

Such radiometric dating methods are not criticized by "old-Earth" creation scientists, the other main group within the movement. Old-Earthers accept the scenario most scientists paint of a world that is billions of years old. In addition, old-Earth creationists agree with orthodox science that the fossil record shows creatures like dinosaurs that have long been extinct.

"I believe that God reveals himself without error through nature," says Ross of Reasons to Believe. "If there is a contradiction between nature and theology, then either one or the other has been misinterpreted," he says.

For instance, unlike young-Earth creationists, Ross does not believe that the six days in the Genesis creation story are 24-hour periods. "In Hebrew, day can refer to a 12-hour period, a 24-hour period or an epoch," he says. Hence, Ross argues, the six "days" of Genesis are actually six epochs that could have stretched back billions of years. ■

Current Situation

In the Classroom

Throughout most of the 20th century, public school students in most parts of the United States have been taught Darwinian evolution. Even Roman Catholic schools, since the 1950s, have been relying upon the standard evolutionary and cosmological theories and not the Bible to explain the creation of the universe and humanity.

There have been many very public exceptions, of course. Recently, for instance, Mark Wisniewski, a high school physics teacher in Lakewood, Ohio, encouraged his students to question evolutionary theory and explore other alternatives in determining the origin of humankind. Wisniewski agreed to stop teaching human origins in this fashion after the local chapter of the ACLU threatened suit. [25]

On the whole, however, proponents of Darwinism are confident that students are receiving what they would term a proper scientific education. "Most of the science teachers today have degrees from real universities in biology and are not going to teach pseudo-science," says Lynn of Americans United for the Separation of Church and State.

But some worry that pressure from conservative Christian groups, even when unsuccessful, can have a profound chilling effect on teachers' willingness to teach Darwinian evolution.

"We do know that a lot of teachers don't teach evolution because they don't want to get hammered over this," Scott says.

Others go a step further and say that creationism is still quietly taught in areas with many fundamentalist Christians. "I would think that it's taught in rural areas behind closed doors," says the ACLU's Weinberg.

"When those kids go to college they're going to be in for a rude awakening and are going to realize that they've been lied to," Scott says. "You are simply not an educated person if you haven't been taught evolution."

Scott and others say that teachers who have evangelical Christians in the class should stress that while they need to learn about evolution, they are under no obligation to accept it. "By giving the student the authority to accept or reject what they learn, students take their fingers out of their ears and discover evolution is nothing they need to fear," she says. Accepting evolution "doesn't mean they need to stop believing in God."

"Oh yes it does," Johnson says. "What [evolutionists] are really saying is that the true creator is a purposeless process." Consequently, the belief in evolution as the mechanism for human creation and the traditional Judeo-Christian God are incompatible, he says.

According to Johnson and others, many American proponents of evolution recognize the inherent conflict between their theory and the notion of God as creator. In this view, scientists and educators are trying to "sugarcoat" evolution in order to make it more palatable for the general populous by arguing that Darwin and God can co-exist in harmony. "Evolutionists say, 'We're not talking about religion,' but they really are," he says. "What they're really saying is that your religion is a comforting set of beliefs that doesn't explain anything," Johnson says. As a result, he says, "Our kids are being taught that they weren't created by God."

State and Local Politics

Issues surrounding the teaching of creationism and evolution occasionally surface at the national level. President Ronald Reagan publicly supported efforts to bring Genesis into the classroom. And during his 1996 campaign for the GOP presidential nomination, Patrick Buchanan said: "I think [parents] have a right to insist that Godless evolution not be taught to their children or their children not be indoctrinated in it." [26]

While national figures like Reagan or Buchanan may occasionally highlight the clash over teaching evolution and creationism, the real debate is taking place in legislatures and school boards. And in the last few years, the number of states touched by the controversy has grown.

The most notable of these recent battles occurred last year in Tennessee, appropriately enough. Not surprisingly, the new fight gained considerable media attention.

At issue was legislation that called for the reprimand of any teacher who presented evolution as a fact. The bill had passed the education committees of both houses of the state legislature when it came up for a vote in the Senate on March 27, 1996.

"This is a very simple bill," said its sponsor, Democratic state Sen. Tommy Burks before the vote. "All it does is what it says it does [require] that teachers shall teach evolution as theory." [27]

But bill opponents, led by teachers' and civil liberties organizations, said that the measure went beyond trying to look at evolution in a more objective light. "The bill was so vague that it was clear that its intent was to intimidate teachers so that they would not teach evolution at all," says the ACLU's Weinberg.

In the end, the state Senate rejected the bill by a vote of 17-13. Weinberg believes that many of the legislators who voted against the measure may have been interested in more than intellectual freedom.

"The business community was unhappy with all of this publicity," she says. "They didn't want the state's image being one of a place where people run around with bare feet and only believe in the Bible."

In addition to Tennessee, the Ohio and Georgia legislatures in recent years also have considered anti-evolution provisions, either in committee or on the floor. In each case though, the provisions were not approved.

Opponents of teaching evolution as fact have fared better on school boards and other local bodies. The most significant victory came in Alabama in November 1995, when the state Board of Education voted to insert a disclaimer into biology textbooks stating that evolution is only one of a number of theories concerning life's origins.

At the board meeting where the disclaimer was approved, Republican Gov. Fob James Jr. poked fun at evolutionary theory by imitating the various stages of man's development, from crouching ape to modern human. "That's the notion behind evolution," the governor said after his demonstration. "If one wants to understand something about the origins of human life, you might ought to look at Genesis to get the whole story." [28]

A disclaimer similar to the one

Continued on p. 762

At Issue:

Is there a scientific basis for creationism?

William A. Hoesch
Public information officer, Institute for Creation Research, Santee, Calif.

yes

Scientific inquiry into origins need not be restricted to naturalistic causes in order to qualify as "scientific." Defining "science" is a knotty problem, and philosophers are not agreed, but at least two different kinds of endeavors can be distinguished. Empirical science deals with the here and now, employs both observation and repeatability and must assume no supernatural intervention in the laboratory. In contrast, what may be termed "forensic science" seeks to reconstruct past events based on circumstantial evidence alone, is not repeatable and is not observable.

Forensic science, as such, cannot generally give the kind of answers with respect to origins that some would like, unless a crucial assumption is made. By borrowing what is a legitimate assumption from empirical science, that of naturalism, and projecting it into remotest antiquity, a "scientific view of Earth history" has emerged that is alleged to be as authoritative in dealing with the past as empirical science is in the present.

Yet without a means to test the validity of the starting assumption, there is no guarantee it even approximates factual reality, regarding our true origins. To deny the possibility of supernatural intervention at the outset, without any grounds for doing so, is hardly less arbitrary (or more "scientific") than the method of the creationist, which affirms the very same possibility.

Any honest attempt at explaining the origin of our complex universe must begin with the question, "chance or intelligence?" The archaeologist, upon finding what appears to be an arrowhead, must consider if random erosion by wind and water is sufficient to explain its symmetry and apparent purpose, or if an unseen intelligence fashioned it. A radio telescope poised to receive signals from extraterrestrial sources is another example. By what criteria is random radio static to be distinguished from the transmission of a would-be alien? If even a simple, coded signal were to be confirmed, it would immediately be hailed as proof for intelligence in space.

A biologist examining the very same kind of coded information (on the DNA molecule) might find himself unconvinced that it arose by non-intelligent processes. Can the biologist infer what was so obvious to both the archaeologist and radio astronomer — intelligent causality? If there is no scientific basis for one, how can there be for the others?

To claim that various groups of interfertile organisms represent archetypes that vary within their kind by selection and mutation, but do not transgress these boundaries, is every bit as testable as the one that claims no boundaries. Evidence may be marshalled from both the living and fossil worlds to support this. There is a scientific basis for creationism.

Steve Edinger
Department of Biological Sciences, Ohio University

no

Science is the systematic investigation of the natural world by testing hypotheses with data from the natural world *and* the knowledge gained by using these methods. If creationism is a science, then what are the scientifically testable hypotheses for creationism, and where are the data testing these hypotheses? Ask creationists this question and they typically have no answer. Simply put, most of the creationists' claims are not scientifically testable, and those claims that are testable have been proven to be false. (For example, the creationists' claim the universe is very young and was just created to look old is untestable; their claim that Noah's flood deposited the entire fossil record has been disproved.)

What creationists do give you are their arguments against evolution and any other sciences when they conflict with the literal interpretation of the biblical stories of creation. Arguing against one thing (evolution) is not the same as proving something different (creationism). Creationists either fail to recognize this fact, or realize most of the public doesn't recognize it, giving the creationists free rein to argue against evolution without ever making a scientific case for creationism.

The latest spin on creationism, so-called "intelligent design theory" (IDT), follows the same pattern: No testing hypotheses for IDT with data from the natural world, just arguments against evolution. IDT is based on the old creationist tenet, "Look at the perfect design in nature, and you will see the hand of God." The pseudoscientific nature of IDT is more carefully disguised than traditional creationism's is, and IDT is designed to sound more scientific even though it doesn't use any scientific methods.

But if IDT is science, then what are the testable hypotheses for design? How do you measure design (what units, methods, etc.), and how can you differentiate between design and order? What about the examples of "bad design?" Rabbits' digestive tracts are so badly designed that they have to eat their own feces to prevent malnutrition, and so do many other herbivores. Is this good design? The vertebrate eye is like a camera with the film loaded backwards and a hole cut out of the film (the blind spot). If an engineer at Nikon designed a camera like that, he would be fired! Plants and animals show "gadgets that work," not design.

Creationism, including the "new" intelligent design theory, contains no testable hypotheses and no data. No hypotheses, no data, no science, period. In contrast, scientists have filled library shelves with testable hypotheses about evolution and data testing those hypotheses. In short, testing with science.

FOR MORE INFORMATION

The Institute for Creation Research, 10946 Woodside Ave. North, Santee, Calif. 92071; (619) 448-0900. Established in 1970, the ICR is devoted to research, publication and teaching about creation science.

The National Center for Science Education, P.O. Box 9477, Berkeley, Calif. 94709; (510) 526-1674. The center promotes science education throughout the county and supports the teaching of evolution.

National Science Teachers Association, 1840 Wilson Blvd., Arlington, Va. 22201. (703) 243-7100. This national organization representing science teachers supports the teaching of evolution.

Reasons to Believe, P.O. Box 5978, Pasadena, Calif. 91117; (818) 335-1480. This think tank promotes "old-Earth" creation science.

Continued from p. 760

used in Alabama has also been added to textbooks in Clayton County, Ga. And in Louisiana, teachers in Tangipahoa Parish have been ordered by the local school board to read a disclaimer to students any time evolution is presented in class.

The battle over textbooks involves more than just disclaimers. For example, in the last few years, school boards in a host of states, including Alabama, Idaho and Washington, have considered, and ultimately rejected, using *Of Pandas and People,* a biology textbook published by the Foundation for Thought and Ethics in Richardson, Texas. The book, which has been roundly criticized by many scientists and science-teaching associations, argues that evidence regarding human origins indicates the presence of a designer.

In another case, publisher Macmillan/McGraw Hill removed a chapter on Earth's origins from the fourth-grade textbook *Changing Earth* at the request of Georgia's Cobb Country school district in May 1996. "This is a trend that I really fear," says Gerry Wheeler, executive director of the National Science Teachers Association. Wheeler says computers now make it easy to change books, increasing the likelihood that publishers will remove objectionable material just to close a sale.

But Steven Weiss, director of corporate communications at Macmillan/McGraw Hill, says that removing the 17-page chapter was "within the bounds of integrity" because it was not required reading for fourth-graders and would be covered at later grade levels. ■

OUTLOOK

Intelligent Design

When proponents of intelligent design theory held their first conference in La Mirada, Calif., last November, more than 160 academics attended. Organizers, who had expected half that number, were pleasantly surprised, but not shocked. [29]

"The evidence for intelligent design is reaching more and more scientists," Behe says. Soon, "the science will make this idea inescapable."

Berkeley's Johnson agrees. "Once you get respected scientists like Michael Behe on board, he says, it's just a matter of time" before the issue is seriously discussed within the scientific community.

Behe says his own experience reflects what he believes will happen in the coming years to other legitimate scientists.

"About 10 years ago, I started to have doubts about Darwinian evolution for reasons having to do with biology, not religion," he says. As he learned more about complex biological systems, the biochemist says, Darwinian evolution just made less and less sense. "Natural selection simply cannot explain these complex features," he argues.

Instead, Behe and other design theorists say, life's complexity points to evidence that humans were purposefully designed. Unlike creation scientists, they do not try to square their theories directly with the Bible. Instead, they are interested only in finding evidence of God's role in nature.

Behe and Johnson have each written books that are considered essential reading within the design movement. Behe's 1996 book *Darwin's Black Box* focuses on the biochemical evidence against Darwinian evolution and for design. Johnson's 1991 book *Darwin on Trial,* tries to pick apart the arguments for natural selection.

Both men say that their biggest job, at this point, is overcoming what they say is the scientific community's unwillingness to deviate from its set views. According to Johnson, most scientists are inculcated with a world view "that says nature is all there is and nothing else is worth considering." As a result, he argues, "the scientific community has lost sight of the difference between group think and the truth."

But scientists counter that the problem with intelligent design is that it starts with an assumption that cannot be proven one way or another: a designer or God created life on earth. "In science, there are not truths, there are only observations," the University of Kansas' Martin says, adding that God, at least so far, is not observable.

Intelligent design theory has also drawn criticism from within the creation science community for being too accomodationist. According to Institute for Creation Research founder Morris, design theorists are wasting their time trying to convince a closed-minded scientific community. "I don't think we'll ever get the approbation of the majority of mainstream scientists," he says. [30]

But design theorists are optimistic that their idea eventually will prevail. Evolutionists today "have all the cultural power," Johnson admits, referring to support from government, media and the scientific and educational establishments. Still, he says, "We have the intellectual high ground, and once we get our issue on the table, their whole house of cards will come down." ■

Notes

[1] Michael D. Lemonick, "Dumping on Darwin," *Time,* March 18, 1996.

[2] Quoted in "Beyond Genesis: The Origin of Species," *The Great Books,* The Learning Channel.

[3] For background, see "Religion in Schools," *The CQ Researcher,* Feb. 18, 1994, pp. 145-168.

[4] Daniel C. Dennett, *Darwin's Dangerous Idea: Evolution and the Meaning of Life* (1995), p. 19.

[5] David Berlinski, "The Deniable Darwin," *Commentary,* June 1996.

[6] Michael Behe, *Darwin's Black Box: The Biochemical Challenge to Evolution* (1996), p. 39.

[7] David Berlinski, "The Deniable Darwin," *Commentary,* June 1996.

[8] Phillip E. Johnson, *Darwin on Trial* (1991), p. 34.

[9] Richard Dawkins, *The Blind Watchmaker* (1986), p. 81.

[10] Henry M. Morris and Gary E. Parker, *What Is Creation Science?* (1987), p. 3.

[11] Johnson, *op. cit.,* p. 46.

[12] Daniel J. Boorstin, *The Discoverers* (1983), p. 466.

[13] *Ibid.,* p. 451.

[14] *Ibid.,* pp. 466-468.

[15] Philip Appleman (ed.), *Darwin: A Norton Critical Edition* (1970), pp. 4-5.

[16] Stephen Jay Gould, *Ever Since Darwin: Reflections in Natural History* (1977), pp. 21-22.

[17] *Ibid.,* pp. 21-27.

[18] According to Gould, *op. cit.,* Huxley later claimed that his retort to Wilberforce had been misheard and that he had not actually said that he would prefer an ape to a bishop as an ancestor. Nevertheless, most in the crowd thought Huxley had made such a remark and considered it either the wittiest or most offensive of the many blows Huxley delivered.

[19] Quoted in Stephen Jay Gould, *Bully for Brontosaurus: Reflections in Natural History* (1991), pp. 386-387.

[20] Benjamin McArthur, "The New Creationists," *American Heritage,* November 1994.

[21] Scopes lost and was fined $100, but his conviction overturned on a technicality.

[22] Gary Wills, *Under God: Religion and American Politics* (1990), p. 113.

[23] *Ibid.*

[24] Ronald L. Numbers, *The Creationists* (1992), p. 228.

[25] Karen Schmidt, "Creationists Evolve New Strategy," *Science,* July 26, 1996.

[26] Quoted in Lemonick, *op. cit.*

[27] Quoted in Tom Curley, "New Life in Evolution Debate," *USA Today,* March 27, 1996.

[28] Schmidt, *op. cit.*

[29] Scott Swanson, "Debunking Darwin? 'Intelligent-design' movement gathers strength," *Christianity Today,* Jan. 6, 1997.

[30] Quoted in Gary Stix, "Postdiluvian Science," *Scientific American,* January 1997.

Bibliography

Selected Sources Used

Books

Behe, Michael J., *Darwin's Black Box: The Biochemical Challenge to Evolution,* The Free Press, 1996.

Behe, a professor of biochemistry at Lehigh University, argues that Darwinian theory does not square with what is known about complex systems that operate within animals. Instead, he argues, the data leads to the conclusion that these systems were "designed."

Dawkins, Richard, *The Blind Watchmaker,* W.W. Norton, 1986.

Dawkins, a biology professor at Oxford University, argues that many people don't understand evolution because they cannot accept the fact that it is undirected. And yet while Darwin's theory reveals a universe without direction or design, Dawkins says, evolution does work within certain rules and is not random.

Dennett, Daniel C., *Darwin's Dangerous Idea: Evolution and the Meanings of Life,* Simon and Schuster, 1995.

Dennett, director of the Center for Cognitive Studies at Tufts University, argues that Darwinian evolution is a concept that has implications far beyond the world of natural science. He writes that "the proper application of Darwinian thinking to human issues — of mind, language, knowledge and ethics, for instance — illuminates them in ways that have always eluded traditional approaches."

Gould, Steven Jay, *Ever Since Darwin: Reflections in Natural History,* W.W. Norton, 1977.

This collection of essays originally published in *Natural History* magazine contains a number of chapters on the factors that led Darwin to formulate his theory of evolution. Gould, a professor of geology at Harvard University, is a polymath who writes about almost anything with wit and clarity.

Johnson, Phillip E., *Darwin on Trial,* Regnery Gateway, 1991.

Johnson, a professor of law at the University of California at Berkeley, gives a good overview of the arguments against Darwinian evolution, from what he calls "the fossil problem" to the difficulty of accounting for the creation of complex systems through mutation.

Keeton, William T., *Elements of Biological Science,* W.W. Norton, 1973.

Keeton, a professor of neurobiology at Cornell University, gives a good overview of the principles of Darwinian evolution.

Morris, Henry M., and Gary E. Parker, *What is Creation Science?* Master Books, 1987.

Morris and Parker, past president and a research scientist, respectively, at the Institute for Creation Research, give a detailed explanation of the "evidence" against evolution. They argue, among other things, that the Earth is thousands rather than billions of years old.

Numbers, Ronald L., *The Creationists,* Alfred A. Knopf, 1992.

Numbers traces the history of the creationist movement in the United States since the publication of Darwin's *On the Origin of Species* in 1859. Particularly interesting are his chapters on George McCready Price, who developed "new catastrophism," and Henry M. Morris, author of *Genesis Flood*, probably the most well-known book on creation science.

Articles

Berlinski, David, "The Deniable Darwin," *Commentary,* June 1996.

Berlinksi, a mathematician and novelist, argues that the scientific community is fooling the public and itself when it contends that evolutionary theory is no longer in dispute. For scientists, Berlinski says, Darwin's theory is like a religion. And like religious zealots, he argues, evolutionists are unwilling to consider any notion that contradicts their orthodoxy.

Rensberger, Boyce, "How Science Responds When Creationists Criticize Evolution," *The Washington Post,* Jan. 8, 1997.

Rensberger, a science journalist, responds to many of the arguments most commonly made against Darwinian evolution.

Schmidt, Karen, "Creationists Evolve New Strategy," *Science,* July 26, 1996.

Schmidt gives a good overview of the current battles being fought by evolutionists and creationists, from state legislatures to school boards to classrooms.

Swanson, Scott, "Debunking Darwin? 'Intelligent-design' movement gathers strength," *Christianity Today,* Jan. 6, 1997.

Swanson explores the growth of the fledgling "intelligent design" movement, whose members believe that life's complexity implies directed design by a higher power. According to Swanson, intelligent design is "gaining support among scholars who are dissatisfied with the existing theories concerning the origin of life."

The Next Step

Additional information from UMI's Newspaper & Periodical Abstracts™ database

Changing Textbooks in Georgia

Campbell, Colin, "Cobb going its own way again," *Atlanta Journal Constitution,* May 26, 1996, p. D1.
Campbell discusses the recent decision by Georgia's Cobb County to eliminate a chapter dealing with the origins of the universe billions of years ago in a proposed fourth-grade science text, "Changing Earth."

"Cobb compromise censors science," *Atlanta Constitution,* May 23, 1996, p. A22.
An editorial blasts the Cobb County, Ga., School Board's decision to delete a chapter called "The Birth of Earth" from a fourth-grade science textbook after a parent complained the chapter contained "evolution theories" while omitting material consistent with the biblical story of Creation.

Cumming, Doug, "Book publisher to delete pages on evolution," *Atlanta Constitution,* May 22, 1996, p. B1.
The Cobb County School Board in Georgia, in approving a host of recommendations on new science textbooks, voted to ask Macmillan/McGraw-Hill to print the $6 "Changing Earth" textbook without pages 72-85, those devoted to the theory of evolution, saying it was unnecessary for the course.

Cumming, Doug, "Cobb reviewing policy on teaching evolution," *Atlanta Constitution,* July 9, 1996, p. D3.
A letter from the science education watchdog group National Center for Science Education that criticized Georgia's Cobb County's limits on the teaching of evolution in school has prompted Cobb school officials to revisit those regulations.

McCafferty, Dennis, "Hall OKs creation theory courses," *Atlanta Constitution,* Feb. 15, 1996, p. A1.
The Hall County School Board in Georgia intends to teach creationism in its science classrooms as early as the fall of 1996. The textbook committee has been directed to find materials that discuss and evaluate both evolution and creation science theories.

Wooten, Jim, "Making local control of education real," *Atlanta Journal,* May 24, 1996, p. A22.
Wooten discusses the Cobb County, Ga., Board of Education's decision to purchase a textbook for fourth-graders that does not address the question of how the Earth or the universe began, saying he believes it shows the system's respect for multiculturalism is genuine and includes religious points of view.

Creation Science

Finkel, Elizabeth, "Science of creationism to go on trial in Australia next year," *Lancet,* Dec. 14, 1996, p. 1654.
On April 7, the High Court of Australia will be the stage for Australia's first cross-examination of creationist teaching. Geologist Ian Plimer has succeeded in bringing Allan Roberts of Ark-Search Inc. to court under section 52 of the Trade Practices Act. Plimer is challenging claims that the ark site in the Ararat mountains has biblical significance.

Moore, Randy, "The business of creationism," *American Biology Teacher,* April 1997, p. 196.
An editorial discusses how creation science has been turned into a booming business. The Creation Science Ministries of Kentucky Inc., like other creationist organizations, has been growing quickly.

Schmidt, Karen, "Creationists evolve new strategy," *Science,* July 26, 1996, pp. 420-422.
Creationists from Georgia to Ohio are taking their fight to state legislatures, using a new soft-core strategy that aims to get "scientific evidence" against evolution presented in public classrooms. The new strategy is discussed.

Schmidt, Karen, "Monkeyshines," *Change,* January 1997, p. 8.
Creationists across the U.S. are demanding that schools teach evolution only as a theory, not a fact. Steps taken in Alabama, Georgia and New Mexico to cast doubt on the validity of evolution are detailed.

Scott, Eugenie C., "Monkey business," *Sciences,* January 1996, pp. 20-25.
Anti-evolutionists are attempting to insert biblically inspired creation "science" into schools one classroom at a time. The courts have rejected religion-based pseudoscience, but the threat from creationism has not gone away.

Darwin

Klinkenborg, Verlyn, "Taking Darwin seriously," *Audubon,* July 1997, pp. 107-111.
Klinkenborg discusses Darwin's theory of evolution.

Suplee, Curt, "Panic Disorder May Have Fitted Darwin for Reclusive Scholarship," *The Washington Post,* Jan. 8, 1997, p. A2.
Charles Darwin might never have revolutionized biology with his theory of evolution if he had not suffered

from a form of panic disorder aggravated by agoraphobia that turned him into a scholarly recluse, according to a provocative new study.

"2 Darwin bird specimens found in museum vault in Australia," ***Chicago Tribune,*** **Jan. 4, 1996, p. 1.**
Curators at the Museum of Victoria in Melbourne have stumbled upon two preserved birds they say were collected by Charles Darwin while he was formulating his theory of evolution. Both carry identification tags purportedly handwritten by Darwin.

Evolution

Applebome, Peter, "70 years after Scopes trial, creation debate lives," ***The New York Times,*** **March 10, 1996, p. 1.**
Seventy years after John Scopes was convicted of teaching evolution in Dayton, Tenn., the state legislature here is considering permitting school boards to dismiss teachers who present evolution as fact rather than a theory of human origin. The re-emergence of teaching creationism, rejected by the Supreme Court a decade ago, is discussed.

Cole, Caroline Louise, "Daniel Dennett refines evolutionary theory," ***The Boston Globe,*** **Oct. 13, 1996, Sec. WKNW, p. 1.**
Tufts University philosophy Professor Daniel Dennett is profiled, and his controversial ideas on the theory of evolution, contained in his 1995 book "Darwin's Dangerous Idea: Evolution and the Meanings of Life," are detailed.

Holden, Constance, "Alabama schools disclaim evolution," ***Science*****, Nov. 24, 1995, p. 1305.**
Alabama public school biology textbooks will have anti-evolution disclaimers in them beginning next year. The issue of teaching evolution flares up every five years in Alabama when new texts are chosen.

Hoppe, Arthur, "Darwin down the drain," ***San Francisco Chronicle,*** **March 11, 1996, p. A19.**
Hoppe satirically comments on the Tennessee legislature's efforts to halt the teaching of evolution.

McCollister, Betty, "Creation 'science' vs. religious attitudes," ***USA Today,*** **May 1996, pp. 74-76.**
The controversy between creation scientists and the Christian Research Society over evolution is discussed.

Moore, Randy, "A perfectly logical thing to do," ***American Biology Teacher,*** **November 1996, pp. 452-453.**
Moore offers recent examples of public efforts to discredit evolution. He fears that attempts to punish teachers who teach evolution will undermine science, enlightened thinking and the entire educational system.

Field Studies

Case, Ted J., "Natural selection out on a limb," ***Nature,*** **May 1, 1997, pp. 15-16.**
One criticism of evolutionary biology is that there are few well-documented cases in which evolution by natural selection has actually been witnessed. Long-term experiments on populations of lizards introduced in the Bahamas provide one direct example.

Klein, George, "Malign evolution," ***Discover,*** **August 1997, pp. 46-51.**
Researchers now know that cancerous cells evolve to become unresponsive to the growth forces of the body and that those genetic changes are based on Darwinian principles of variation and selection.

Wade, Nicholas, "Leapin' Evolution Is Found in Lizards," ***The New York Times,*** **May 1, 1997, p. B14.**
A remarkable experiment with lizards in the Bahamas has now shown that evolution moves in predictable ways and can occur so rapidly that changes emerge in as little as a decade or so. The finding bears on debates as to whether evolution on the time scale of millions of years is governed by the same rules as short-term evolution.

Yoon, Carol Kaesuk, "Bacteria Seen to Evolve in Spurts," ***The New York Times,*** **June 25, 1996, p. C8.**
Researchers studying the fast-growing bacteria known as *Escherichia coli* have observed 3,000 generations of evolution, the kind of long-term change typically witnessed only by paleontologists. The researchers say they have found evidence to support the controversial theory of punctuated equilibrium, in which evolution proceeds with rapid bursts of change punctuating prolonged periods in which species are relatively unaltered.

Genesis

"In Tennessee, a move for Genesis," ***The Boston Globe,*** **March 5, 1996, p. 3.**
The Tennessee Senate is considering legislation to fire any teacher who presents evolution as fact. The bill was expected to pass during the March 4, 1996, session but instead was sent back to committee for study of six proposed amendments.

Martz, Harvey, "Genesis of a misunderstanding," ***The Denver Post,*** **Sept. 10, 1996, p. B9.**
Martz states that the 1996 controversy in Jefferson County, Colo., over evolution and creationism is based on a misunderstanding of both scientific inquiry and the biblical book of Genesis.

McElvaine, Robert S., "The book on Genesis: How the story of creation makes women the bad guys," ***The Washington Post,*** **Nov. 3, 1996, p. C5.**

McElvaine states that the story of Genesis in the Bible is a male allegory, based on the very real experience of the earliest human societies, about the huge consequences that flowed from the invention of agriculture by women. He adds that this allegory has shaped the roles of women and men for thousands of years.

Integrating Creationism And Evolution Theories

Behe, Michael J., "Darwin Under the Microscope," *The New York Times,* Oct. 29, 1996, p. A25.
Behe says that religion has long made room for science, and even Pope John Paul II publicly declared that evolution is more than just a theory. However, as biology uncovers startling complexity in life, Behe questions whether science can make room for religion.

Collins, James, "Vatican thinking evolves," *Time,* Nov. 4, 1996, p. 85.
The Pope has revised the Vatican's stand on evolution, allowing for natural selection but remaining firm on the stance that the origin of the soul stems from God. The impact that this change in attitude toward evolution will have is discussed.

Porter, Henry, "Faith, hope and clarity," *The Guardian,* Sept. 23, 1996, p. 2.
Porter discusses the series of Oxford University debates between Keith Ward, an Anglican priest, biologist Richard Dawkins and chemist Peter Atkins, in which Ward attacks the scientists for characterizing religious interpretation of life on earth as childish.

Russell, Robert John, "Does 'The God Who Acts' really act? New approaches to divine action in light of science," *Theology Today,* April 1997, pp. 43-65.
The intelligibility of divine action in light of the natural sciences and non-reductive epistemology is examined. Contemporary sciences, along with recent moves in philosophy, actually provide new modes of reflection on nature.

New Theories

Fraser, Nicholas C., "Genesis of snakes in exodus from the sea," *Nature,* April 17, 1997, p. 651-652.
Scientists Michael W. Caldwell and Michael S. Y. Lee believe that the ancestors of modern serpents are a group of extinct marine lizards called the mosasauroids. Their argument still faces some stiff challenges.

Monastersky, Richard, "The call of catastrophes," *Science News,* March 1, 1997, p. S20.
The work of a team of physicists from the University of California at Berkeley in the 1980s focused unprecedented attention on events at the close of the Cretaceous, making this distant time one of the best-studied moments in Earth's history. The hypothesis that a huge comet or meteorite slammed into Earth 65 million years ago has provided a stimulus to the earth sciences that some believe will eventually turn out to be virtually unprecedented in the 20th century.

Overbye, Dennis, "The Cosmos According to Darwin," *The New York Times,* July 13, 1997, p. 24.
In a radical theory called cosmological natural selection, physicist Lee Smolin argues that black holes and bubble universes hold the key to life, beauty and humankind.

Yoon, Carol Kaesuk, "Long Evolution of 'Darwin of 20th Century,' " *The New York Times,* April 15, 1997, p. C4.
Ernst Mayr, who at the age of 92 remains the leading evolutionary biologist of the century, is well aware of the value of long life. Mayr, a professor emeritus at Harvard University, was one of the pivotal scientists who shaped the intellectual watershed known as the evolutionary synthesis, when modern evolutionary biology was born.

Stephen Jay Gould

Chandler, David L. "Ancient snails offer new insight on evolution," *The Boston Globe,* Dec. 13, 1996, p. A1.
The remains of ancient snails found in the Bahamas by evolutionary theorist Stephen Jay Gould and Glenn Goodfriend in 1996 offer the clearest view yet of evolution in action, revealing details of how species change over time.

Golden, Frederic, "A kinder, gentler Stephen Jay Gould," *Los Angeles Times,* Oct. 8, 1996, p. E1.
Evolutionary biologist, paleontologist and essayist Stephen Jay Gould is profiled, and his new book "Full House: The Spread of Excellence from Plato to Darwin" is discussed.

Koch, John, "Stephen Jay Gould," *The Boston Globe,* Dec. 31, 1995, Sec. BGM., p. 14.
Zoologist and evolution essayist Stephen Jay Gould is profiled.

Manier, Jeremy, "Stephen Jay Gould takes a new swing at explaining evolution," *Chicago Tribune,* Dec. 2, 1996, p. 1.
Evolutionary biologist and author Stephen Jay Gould, whose book "Full House: The Spread of Excellence from Plato to Darwin" compares evolution with baseball, is profiled.

Raymo, Chet, "What's progress got to do with it?" *The Boston Globe,* Oct. 21, 1996, p. C2.
Raymo discusses Harvard University evolutionary biologist Stephen Jay Gould's contrarian notions that human beings do not hold a position of biological primacy among the world's creatures.

Back Issues

Great Research on Current Issues Starts Right Here . . . Recent topics covered by The CQ Researcher are listed below. Before May 1991, reports were published under the name of Editorial Research Reports.

FEBRUARY 1996
Reforming the CIA
Campaign Finance Reform
Academic Politics
Getting Into College

MARCH 1996
The British Monarchy
Preventing Juvenile Crime
Tax Reform
Pursuing the Paranormal

APRIL 1996
Centennial Olympic Games
Managed Care
Protecting Endangered Species
New Military Culture

MAY 1996
Russia's Political Future
Marriage and Divorce
Year-Round Schools
Taiwan, China and the U.S.

JUNE 1996
Rethinking NAFTA
First Ladies
Teaching Values
Labor Movement's Future

JULY 1996
Recovered-Memory Debate
Native Americans' Future
Crackdown on Sexual Harassment
Attack on Public Schools

AUGUST 1996
Fighting Over Animal Rights
Privatizing Government Services
Child Labor and Sweatshops
Cleaning Up Hazardous Wastes

SEPTEMBER 1996
Gambling Under Attack
The States and Federalism
Civic Journalism
Reassessing Foreign Aid

OCTOBER 1996
Political Consultants
Insurance Fraud
Rethinking School Integration
Parental Rights

NOVEMBER 1996
Global Warming
Clashing Over Copyright
Consumer Debt
Governing Washington, D.C.

DECEMBER 1996
Welfare, Work and the States
The New Volunteerism
Implementing the Disabilities Act
America's Pampered Pets

JANUARY 1997
Combating Scientific Misconduct
Restructuring the Electric Industry
The New Immigrants
Chemical and Biological Weapons

FEBRUARY 1997
Assisting Refugees
Alternative Medicine's Next Phase
Independent Counsels
Feminism's Future

MARCH 1997
New Air Quality Standards
Alcohol Advertising
Civic Renewal
Educating Gifted Students

APRIL 1997
Declining Crime Rates
The FBI Under Fire
Gender Equity in Sports
Space Program's Future

MAY 1997
The Stock Market
The Cloning Controversy
Expanding NATO
The Future of Libraries

JUNE 1997
FDA Reform
China After Deng
Line-Item Veto
Breast Cancer

JULY 1997
Transportation Policy
Executive Pay
School Choice Debate
Aggressive Driving

AUGUST 1997
Age Discrimination
Banning Land Mines
Children's Television

Back issues are available for $5.00 (subscribers) or $10.00 (non-subscribers). Quantity discounts apply to orders over ten. To order, call Congressional Quarterly Customer Service at (202) 887-8621.

Binders are available for $18.00. To order call 1-800-638-1710. Please refer to stock number 648.

Future Topics

- ***Caring for the Dying***
- ***Mental Health Policy***
- ***Mexico's Future***

THE CQ Researcher

PUBLISHED BY CONGRESSIONAL QUARTERLY INC.

Caring for the Dying

Would better palliative care reduce support for assisted suicide?

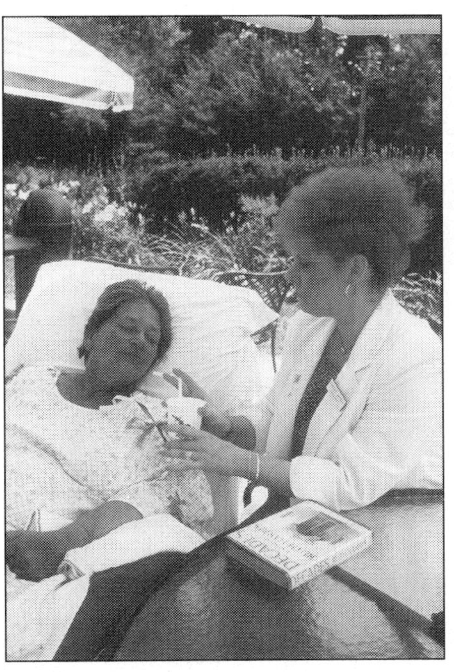

Oregon is the only state where physician-assisted suicide is legal. By many accounts, it is also a national leader in "palliative care," as non-invasive medical treatment of the dying is often called. Both approaches to terminal illness will be debated in depth as Oregonians prepare to vote Nov. 4 on whether to repeal the "death with dignity" law they narrowly approved in 1994. Pro-repeal forces claim support for assisted suicide would evaporate if palliative care and effective pain control became more widely available. The law's supporters say they also endorse palliative care. At the same time, they contend that doctor-aided suicide should remain a legal option for the small minority of terminally ill people whose intractable pain does not respond to opioids such as morphine.

INSIDE THIS ISSUE

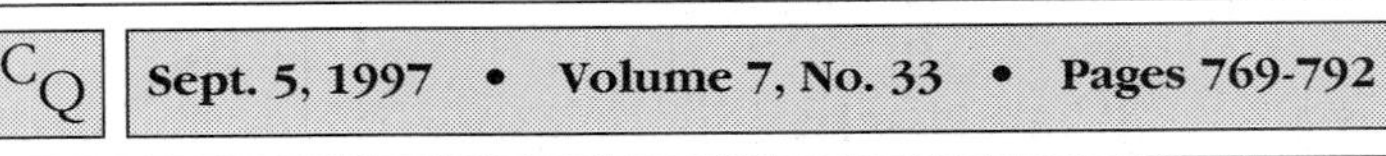
CQ Sept. 5, 1997 • Volume 7, No. 33 • Pages 769-792

Formerly Editorial Research Reports

COVER: A TERMINALLY ILL PATIENT RECEIVES CARE FROM A VOLUNTEER AT A HOSPICE. (NATIONAL ASSOCIATION FOR HOME CARE)

September 5, 1997
Volume 7, No. 33

EDITOR
Sandra Stencel

MANAGING EDITOR
Thomas J. Colin

ASSOCIATE EDITORS
Sarah M. Magner
Richard L. Worsnop

STAFF WRITERS
Charles S. Clark
Mary H. Cooper
Kenneth Jost
David Masci

EDITORIAL ASSISTANT
Vanessa E. Furlong

PUBLISHED BY
Congressional Quarterly Inc.

CHAIRMAN
Andrew Barnes

VICE CHAIRMAN
Andrew P. Corty

PRESIDENT AND PUBLISHER
Robert W. Merry

EXECUTIVE EDITOR
David Rapp

The CQ Researcher (ISSN 1056-2036). Formerly Editorial Research Reports. Published weekly, except Jan. 3, May 30, Aug. 29, Oct. 31, by Congressional Quarterly Inc., 1414 22nd St., N.W., Washington, D.C. 20037. Annual subscription rate for libraries, businesses and government is $340. Additional rates furnished upon request. Periodicals postage paid at Washington, D.C., and additional mailing offices. POSTMASTER: Send address changes to The CQ Researcher, 1414 22nd St., N.W., Washington, D.C. 20037.

Caring for the Dying

By Richard L. Worsnop

The Issues

The question before Oregon voters is simple: Should state residents be allowed to commit suicide with a doctor's help?

To Portland's *Catholic Sentinel,* the answer is equally simple: "We have no business turning doctors into undertakers," the paper editorialized. "Instead, we ought to learn from the nightmarish situation in the Netherlands, where the 'Right to Die' too often has become the 'Duty to Die.' " [1]

In the eyes of the state's popular Democratic governor, former emergency room physician John Kitzhaber, the answer is also simple: "I believe an individual should have control, should be able to make choices about the end of their life. . . . As a physician, I can tell you that there's a clear difference between prolonging someone's life and prolonging their death." [2]

In the next two months, voters in Oregon can expect radio, television and newspapers to carry a barrage of such passionate opinions as referendum day approaches. At issue is Measure 16, the nation's first and only law permitting physician-assisted suicide. In 1994, state voters narrowly approved the law, but court challenges kept it from ever taking effect. And now it has been placed on the Nov. 4 ballot by the Legislature for possible repeal. Political observers predict the referendum will set an Oregon record for spending on a ballot proposal.

Oregon is not the only state to become embroiled in the "right-to-die" issue. The Florida Supreme Court recently denied an AIDS patient the right to doctor-assisted suicide (*see p. 784*). The Florida decision was announced just three weeks after the U.S. Supreme Court upheld Washington and New

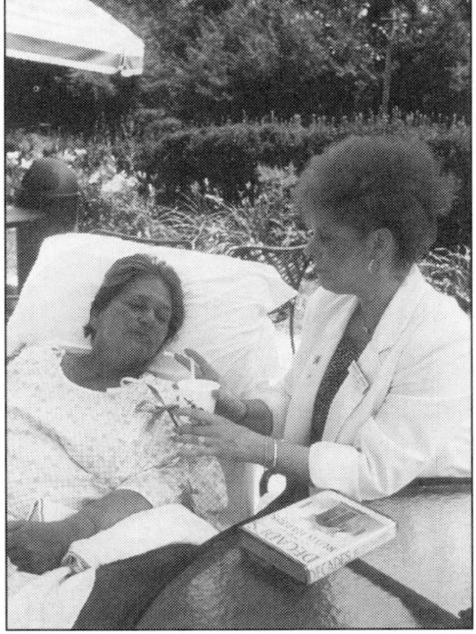

York laws prohibiting physician-assisted suicide. In decisions handed down June 26, the court ruled that the Constitution does not guarantee Americans the right to commit suicide with a doctor's help. At the same time, however, the court made it clear that states have the power to legalize the practice (*see p. 783*).

The Oregon referendum will give foes of assisted suicide a chance to promote other ways of ending a terminally ill person's suffering. The chief alternative is palliative care (also known as "comfort care" and "supportive care"), often provided in a hospice setting. * Palliative care "focuses on patients with life-threatening medical problems for which cure is not seen as possible," the Institute of Medicine (IOM) noted in a recent report. "Instead, it focuses on prevention and relief of suffering through the meticulous management of symptoms from the early through the final stages of an illness; it attends closely to the emotional, spiritual and practical needs of patients and those close to them." [3]

Palliative care is at the core of hospice practice, whose guiding principle for care of the terminally ill is neither to hasten nor to postpone death. The aim of hospice treatment is "relief of symptoms rather than the prolongation of life, with the context that death is the expected outcome, not the adversary," wrote Christine K. Cassel, chair of the committee that prepared the IOM report. "Hospice provides aggressive comfort care in a patient-oriented setting." [4]

Although its influence is steadily increasing, the hospice philosophy runs counter to the goals of most American medical practitioners. Their overriding concern is preservation of life, and the death of a patient is often regarded as a personal and professional failure.

The U.S. medical system "is designed for the 55-year-old heart attack victim, for whom it performs wonders," says Ann Wilkinson, a research scientist at George Washington University's Center to Improve Care of the Dying. "But it does not very well meet the needs of an 85-year-old woman with no family and no advocate within the system to make sure that the treatment choices being made for her are appropriate."

Indeed, says anti-euthanasia activist Wesley J. Smith of Oakland, Calif., blind insistence on keeping hospitalized patients alive regardless of their condition helps build support for physician-assisted suicide. "The increase in the popularity of legalized euthanasia is . . . a vote of no confidence in the medical profession," wrote Smith, a legal consultant to the International Anti-Euthanasia Task Force in Steubenville, Ohio. "Many supporters [of euthanasia] are afraid

* The term hospice can denote an organization that provides medical and other support services to dying patients and their loved ones or the place where care is given, be it a hospital, nursing facility or — as is usually the case in this country — the patient's home.

Assisted-Suicide Laws in the United States

Thirty-five states have statutes that make assisted suicide a crime. In some of those states, assisted suicide is considered a form of manslaughter, but in others it is a separately defined crime.

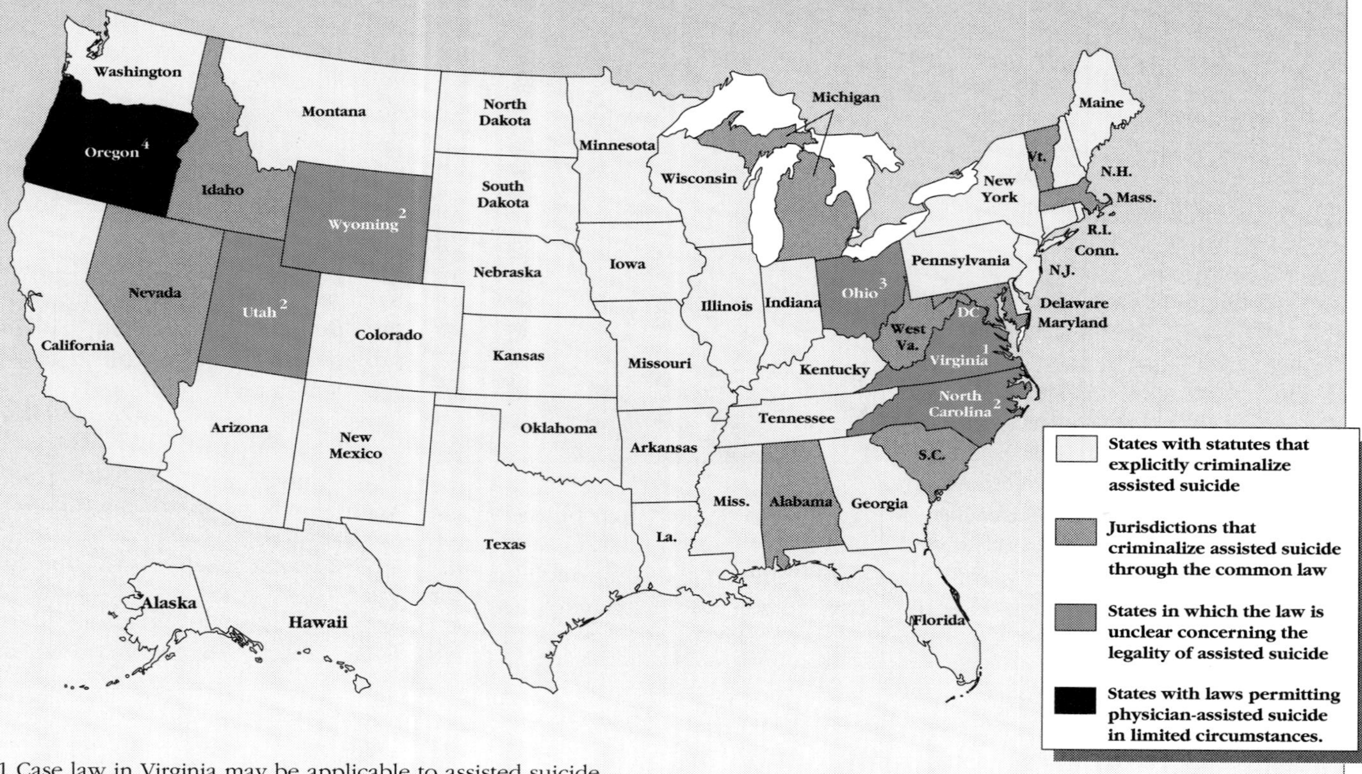

1 Case law in Virginia may be applicable to assisted suicide.
2 These states have abolished common-law crimes and therefore do not explicitly prohibit assisted suicide.
3 The Ohio Supreme Court ruled that assisted suicide is not a crime.
4 The 9th Circuit Court of Appeals dismissed a federal lawsuit challenging Oregon's law, and the matter is now under appeal. The Oregon legislature sent the law back to the voters, who will decide on Nov. 4, 1997, whether they want to legalize physician-assisted suicide.

Source: Choice in Dying, June 1997

— nay, terrified — at the prospect of being victimized at the hands of an out-of-control doctor who, they fear, will hook them up to a machine and force them to suffer as cash cows lingering in an agonizing limbo until they die or their health insurance runs out — whichever comes first. Thus, euthanasia is sold as a guarantee of sorts against both suffering and financial difficulty." [5]

Such worries would recede if palliative care and better pain control were more widely available, say assisted-suicide critics. But meaningful change may come only through reform of medical education. Physicians must be persuaded, writes Cassel, that "excellent palliative care is a rewarding professional activity, worth the involvement of their time and effort, and that the dignified and gentle death of a patient can be seen as a medical accomplishment of considerable merit rather than as a 'failure.'" [6]

The World Health Organization (WHO) endorses greater emphasis on education reform. In a recent report, the United Nations agency asserted that "Cancer pain management and palliative care should be compulsory topics in the general professional training of doctors and nurses and should form part of continuing medical education. Questions on these topics should be compulsory in qualifying examinations, and accreditation incentives should be used to encourage doctors and nurses to further their training in these topics." [7]

Supporters of physician-assisted suicide applaud efforts to expand the teaching and practice of palliative care. They argue, however, that the excruciating pain felt by some dying patients is not always amenable to palliation. In such rare cases, they say, a patient should have the legal option of seeking a doctor's help in hastening death.

State laws banning assisted suicide "only drive the practice underground," contends Faye Girsh, executive director of the Denver-based Hemlock Society, the best-known organization advocating assisted suicide for the terminally ill. "Everything becomes more lawless. That is, more doctors are willing to break the law, and more juries are willing to acquit. Also, fewer prosecutors are willing to bring charges against doctors for helping a patient die."

Patients unable to find a doctor willing to help them commit suicide often take matters into their own hands, Girsh notes. "This increases the demand for materials on self-deliverance — how to do it right. And it produces more screw-ups, because it's done wrong," she says. "It's the kind of situation that can lead to anarchy, which is essentially what we have now in the aid-in-dying movement."

As Americans continue to grapple with the right-to-die controversy, and voters prepare to decide the fate of Oregon's assisted-suicide law, these are some of the main questions being asked:

Is support for physician-assisted suicide fading?

Recent court decisions and legislative action on physician-assisted suicide have led some opponents of the practice to claim public opinion is swinging their way. But right-to-die activists note that the Supreme Court's June 26 decisions did not rule out assisted suicide. Rather, they point out, the court only said that the right to assisted suicide wasn't constitutionally guaranteed.

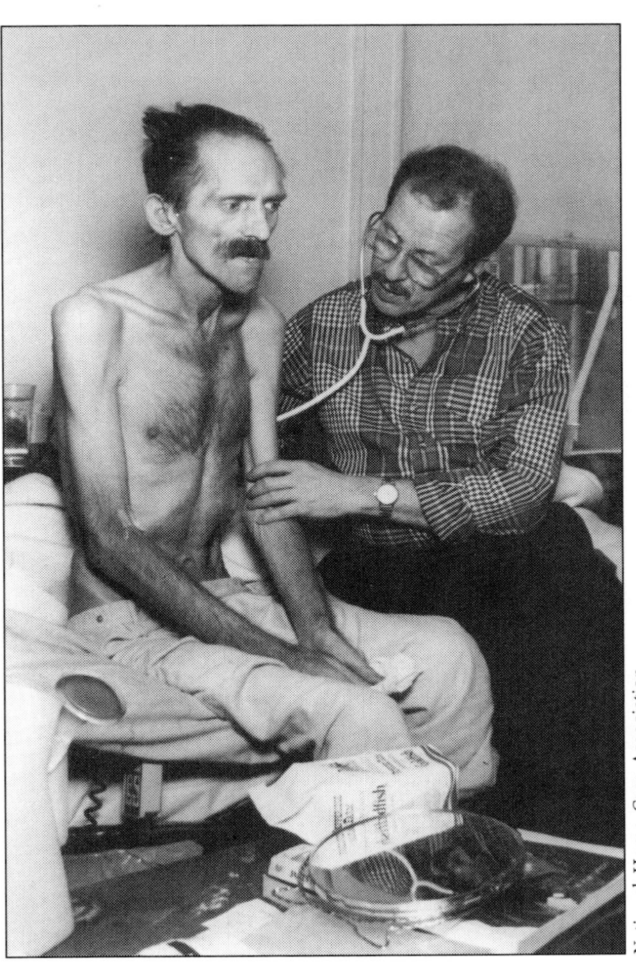

National Home Care Association

An AIDS patient living at home receives a check-up from a visiting nurse.

"Throughout the nation, Americans are engaged in an earnest and profound debate about the morality, legality and practicality of physician-assisted suicide," Chief Justice William H. Rehnquist wrote in the majority opinion for *Washington v. Glucksberg*. "Our holding permits this debate to continue, as it should in a democratic society."

For anti-euthanasia activist Smith, the rulings marked "the beginning of the end of the euthanasia movement. It's going to be virtually impossible to legalize euthanasia in all 50 states." Smith acknowledges, however, that the battle is by no means over. "But I do believe the tide is beginning to turn, and that Americans will now focus more on compassionate alternatives to euthanasia than on legalized killing by doctors."

Hemlock Society founder Derek Humphry, executive director of the Euthanasia Research and Guidance Organization in Junction City, Ore., calls the rulings "timid" and says their ultimate message is, "Let the debate go on." "The justices knew they couldn't slam the door on [the debate]. So, we're not dissatisfied. We know where we stand, and we shall press ahead with a legislative program" at the state level.

"Nothing the Supreme Court said really changes what we've done here," says Geoff Sugerman of Oregon Right to Die, the chief sponsor of Measure 16. "In a sense, the court affirmed Americans' right to pass a law to regulate this process. And in one of the opinions, the court even said the public's best interest may not be served by laws that completely outlaw aid-in-dying."

Richard Doerflinger, associate director for policy development at the U.S. Catholic Conference's Secretariat for Pro-Life Activities, has a different perspective on what the court said.

AMA Guidelines for Caring for Patients in the Last Phase of Life

At its June 1996 annual meeting, the American Medical Association's House of Delegates voted overwhelmingly to reaffirm the organization's long-standing opposition to physician-aided suicide. At the same time, the delegates pledged to step up efforts to train doctors in pain management and meet other needs of dying patients. To further those goals, the AMA on June 22, 1997, published a list of eight principles that physicians, health-care facilities and members of the wider community should follow in dealing with people nearing death (*see below*).

"In the last phase of life, people seek peace and dignity," said Linda Emanuel, head of the AMA's Institute for Ethics. "The AMA firmly believes that every patient should be able to reasonably expect quality care at the end of life." [1]

1. The opportunity to discuss and plan for end-of-life care. This should include: the opportunity to discuss scenarios and treatment preferences with the physician and health-care proxy, the chance for discussion with others, the chance to make a formal "living will" and proxy designation, and help with filing these documents in such a way that they are likely to be available and useful when needed.

2. Trustworthy assurance that physical and mental suffering will be carefully attended to and comfort measures intently secured. Physicians should be skilled in the detection and management of terminal symptoms, such as pain, fatigue and depression, and able to obtain the assistance of specialty colleagues when needed.

3. Trustworthy assurance that preferences for withholding or withdrawing life-sustaining intervention will be honored. Whether the intervention be less complex (such as antibiotics or artificial nutrition and hydration) or complex and more invasive (such as dialysis or mechanical respiration), and whether the situation involves imminent or more distant dying, patients' preferences regarding withholding or withdrawing intervention should be honored in accordance with the legally and ethically established rights of patients.

4. Trustworthy assurance that there will be no abandonment by the physician. Patients should be able to trust that their physician will continue to care for them when dying. If a physician must transfer the patient in order to provide quality care, that physician should make every reasonable effort to continue to visit the patient with regularity, and institutional systems should try to accommodate this.

5. Trustworthy assurance that dignity will be a priority. Patients should be treated in a dignified and respected manner at all times.

6. Trustworthy assurance that burden to family and others will be minimized. Patients should be able to expect sufficient medical resources and community support, such as palliative care, hospice or home care, so that the burden of illness need not overwhelm caring relationships.

7. Attention to the personal goals of the dying person. Patients should be able to trust that their personal goals will have reasonable priority whether it be: to communicate with family or friends, to attend to spiritual needs, to take one last trip, to finish a major unfinished task in life, or to die at home or at another place of personal meaning.

8. Trustworthy assurance that care providers will assist the bereaved through early stages of mourning and adjustment. Patients and their loved ones should be able to trust that some support continues after bereavement. This may be by supportive gestures, such as a bereavement letter, and by appropriate attention to/referral for care of the increased physical and mental health needs that occur among the recently bereaved.

[1] Quoted in AMA news release, June 22, 1997.

"In my view," he says, "the court went beyond the minimum that it needed to do to uphold the laws, and made a very good case for why the state interests in banning assisted suicide are important and valid."

Earlier Supreme Court decisions on abortion, Doerflinger explains, tended to "desensitize people" about the morality of abortion. But now, he says, "I would hope that the court's strong support of the need for laws against assisted suicide would have a positive effect on people's attitudes. However, I don't have any evidence yet that that's the case."

Carol E. Sieger, an attorney for Choice in Dying, a New York City group that promotes the use of living wills, says the impact of the rulings will be felt mainly by state legislators. "The states that criminalize assisted suicide should feel more comfortable [about their laws] because most of their advance-directive legislation [dealing with do-not-resuscitate orders and living wills] specifically holds that refusal of medical treatment is not mercy killing, euthanasia or assisted suicide. And that's what the Supreme Court said, too."

Susan Block, an assistant professor at the Harvard University Medical School department of ambulatory care and prevention, feels interest in assisted suicide will recede as palliative care and effective pain management become more widely available. "As we do better at providing patients with a tolerable death, there will be less fear about what death is — and more confidence that doctors are going to do the right thing by patients," she says. "And that, in turn, will reduce interest in assisted suicide." At the same time, Block concedes that "There will always be some level of interest in assisted suicide, mainly for reasons of wanting to keep control and avoid dependency."

Humphry argues that right-to-die activists deserve a share of the credit for sparking interest in palliative care. "In an odd way, the right-to-die movement has improved the quality of care of the dying in America enormously," he says "After Measure 16 passed in 1994, the health profession started sponsoring seminars and lectures on pain control and set up task forces on end-of-life care. Now people reckon Oregon is the finest place to die in America. Doctors and nurses here will do their very best for you so that you don't ask for assisted dying."

But no matter how good a job the medical profession does in treating the terminally ill, Humphry argues that "there will still be a small need for physician-assisted suicide." That's because "physicians cannot relieve the suffering of a dying person in some cases," he says. "The fewer such persons there are, the more we are pleased. We are not into trying to get large numbers of people to end their lives. But we want that option of aid-in-dying to be available for the few people who may need it."

Are U.S. medical schools doing an adequate job of teaching end-of-life care, including pain control?

American physicians tend to be unskilled in palliative care and pain management largely because medical school instruction in those areas is limited, many health-care experts say. But they say efforts are under way to revamp medical school curricula. Some even foresee the day when palliative care, including pain control, will become a separate medical specialty like pediatrics.

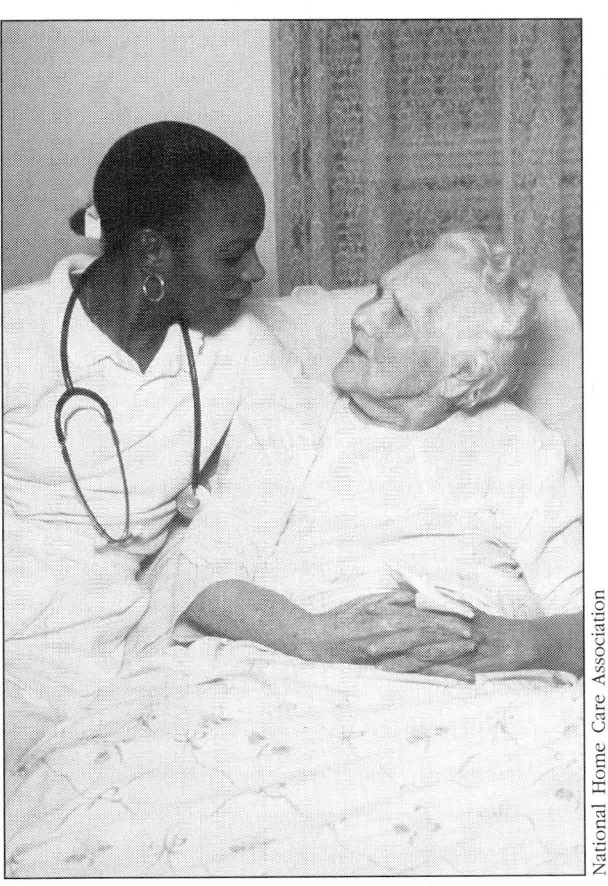

National Home Care Association

An elderly cancer patient chats with a visiting home-care aide.

Ira Byock, a hospice physician in Missoula, Mont., who is president of the American Academy of Hospice and Palliative Medicine, calls the education in end-of-life care that medical students receive "woefully insufficient because it is often taught in electives, or given only small amounts of time within the standard curriculum." In his view, "education about how to care for people when they're dying should be proportional to the amount of time devoted to obstetrics in medical and nursing schools."

Eric Chevlen, director of palliative care at St. Elizabeth Health Center in Youngstown, Ohio, says he doesn't recall learning anything about pain management in medical school. In fact, he remembers "mislearning about pain medicine."

"Here's how it happens," Chevlen says. "The intern learns from the resident, who learned from his resident, who mislearned it from an attending physician years earlier. All that misinformation is passed down from one young doctor to another, generation after generation. Since the attending physician doesn't consider it an important part of his practice, he leaves it to the resident to handle."

For example, says Chevlen, "There is considerable misunderstanding concerning physical dependence and addiction to opioids. Drug addiction is a psychological state characterized by drug-seeking behavior for the purpose of getting 'high.' When opioids are used to treat cancer, addiction is extremely rare. In 20 years of practice, I have not seen one cancer patient become addicted to opioids."

Medical residents' misunderstanding of pain medicine is reinforced, Chevlen believes, by "working in clinics that cater to a population far different from the one that they're usually going to encounter when they're in private practice."

People who seek treatment at hospital-based walk-in clinics "typically don't want or can't maintain consistent medical care from a community-

How the Public Views Assisted Suicide

Half of those surveyed by The Washington Post *last year said physician-assisted suicide should be legal, but more than half said they wouldn't consider this option if they had a terminal illness.*

Do you think it should be legal or illegal for a doctor to help a terminally ill patient commit suicide?

It should be legal	50%
It should be illegal	40%
Don't know	9%

Suppose you were suffering from a terminal illness and had only a short time to live. Are there any circumstances under which you, personally, would ask a doctor to help you commit suicide, or not?

Yes, there are circumstances under which I would ask a doctor to help me commit suicide.	37%
No, under no circumstances would I ask a doctor to help me commit suicide.	53%
Don't know	11%

Note: Numbers do not add up to 100% because of rounding. The margin of sampling error is plus or minus 3 percentage points. The survey was conducted by ICR Research of Media, Pa., for *The Washington Post.*

Source: *The Washington Post,* April 4, 1996

based clinician," he explains. "There's a much higher incidence and prevalence of drug abuse in this subgroup than in the general population. As a result, the resident comes to distrust the patient's pain complaints."

Chevlen says he expects medical schools to devote more attention to pain medicine and other aspects of palliative care, but he doesn't expect significant change in the near future. "It takes a long time to build a curriculum, teaching staff and critical mass of interest in a subject," he says.

Only six of the nation's 125 medical schools have a separate course on death and dying, says Barbara Barzansky, director of the AMA's Department of Medical School Services. However, she says that the subject nonetheless "is being covered comprehensively in all schools," based on a survey this year by the AMA's Liaison Committee on Medical Education.

"The topic started appearing in the curriculum in the 1970s and '80s," she says. "The courses in the '70s dealt with things like stages of dying. They were not as multidimensional as they are now. Today we talk about do-not-resuscitate orders and all the ethical implications of advance directives — issues that may not have been discussed 20 years ago."

Block says she can already sense mounting student interest in palliative care. A three-year-old elective course at Harvard on end-of-life care is regularly oversubscribed, she reports, and it gets "virtually perfect ratings" from student evaluators.

It is not a course for dilettantes. Each student is assigned to a terminally ill patient and accompanies the patient through the dying process. The student then attends to the needs of the patient's family members during the bereavement period. All the while, the medical school provides "a lot of support and class work to help students get through this difficult experience," Block says.

Despite the emotional strains they inevitably undergo, many students who complete the course say they want to specialize in end-of-life care after graduation. "We don't know yet whether they're actually going to do it, because it's too new a course," Block adds. "But our sense is that we have ignited latent interest in a profound human issue."

Indeed, the issue is of more than passing interest to Block, who heads the faculty scholars program of the Project on Death in America. * The program has funded 38 scholars at 33 medical schools around the country. "They are agents for change within the medical profession, and particularly within educational institutions, for improving end-of-life care."

The faculty scholars program "is agnostic about whether palliative care should exist as a distinct specialty," Block says. "But we think it needs to be broadly taught and practiced, and that is what the faculty scholars are trying to accomplish."

Julie A. McCrady, communications director for the Project on Death in America, notes that some medical educators feel palliative care should be incorporated into existing medical disciplines instead of split off as a separate field. "Some people feel palliative care is just another aspect of good doctoring — that a competent physician would attend to such things as a matter of course. So, the question is still open."

---

* The project was established by the Open Society Institute, a foundation headed by billionaire investor George Soros.

Will managed-care systems speed or stall the spread of programs to care for the terminally ill?

Will palliative care and effective pain management be more widely available in 21st-century America? Many medical experts feel the answer depends largely on how managed-care providers respond to the challenge. [8]

"A lot of people see managed care as an excellent tool for attending to terminally ill patients," McCrady says. "Palliative care generally is based on a team model, and managed care is particularly well-suited to support a team-model approach."

Others are more cautious, she notes. "Given the competitive, bottom-line mentality that many managed-care organizations seem to have, some people feel they are going to perceive palliative care as something they can't make any money from."

Byock regards the situation as fluid. "Managed care," he says, "offers rich potential for improvement in end-of-life care by creating a seamless care system that provides comprehensive, person-centered care from cradle to grave in a cost-effective but also clinically effective manner."

He acknowledges that managed-care providers are acutely cost-conscious at present. But "when the dust settles after this inception phase," he is confident that "managed care will compete not on the basis of cost but on the basis of quality." And assuming that happens, Byock is "very hopeful" that managed care will offer "real advantages to those of us who are working hard to develop systems of comprehensive end-of-life care."

Wilkinson of the Center to Improve Care of the Dying also is optimistic. "Actually," she says, "many managed-care systems are at the forefront of developing good end-of-life care. A number of organizations are working with us right now to get the information we have about pain and symptom management delivered more systematically to patients and their managed-care providers." She says managed-care companies accept that they will be dealing with more older people as the nation ages, and that "this population group needs special attention."

According to the American Association of Health Plans and the Kaiser Family Foundation, more than 93 percent of the health plans responding to a nationwide survey in 1994 offered home-based hospice care to their members. Almost 75 percent offered institutional hospice coverage. [9]

"Hospice represents the highest quality of life for the final days of life, at the most cost-effective level of care," said Jeff D. Emerson, CEO of NYLCare Health Plans of the Mid-Atlantic Inc., in Greenbelt, Md. "Hospice is different from conventional medical care in that it deals with the totality of the dying patient and family. If any group in the health-care industry should be sensitive to this approach, it's managed care." [10]

Steven H. Miles, a faculty associate at the University of Minnesota's Center for Biomedical Ethics, nonetheless feels "it's fair to say that end-of-life care has not been a high priority in managed care." The primary reason, in his opinion, is that managed care tends to cover younger patients. "Secondly, because it's a younger population, the scope of health insurance benefits is determined by employers rather than under the Medicare or Medicaid benefit structure."

A third problem, as Miles sees it, "is that managed-care providers haven't used palliative care as a model for designing programs. What they have done is handle palliative care like other medical issues. They haven't taken the lead in hiring palliative-care specialists, for instance. We're just not seeing much innovation in this area at present." But change will come, he predicts, as managed-care providers assume responsibility for a larger share of the Medicare population.

Though Chevlen cannot speak from personal experience, he suspects that managed care and his field of expertise, pain management, don't make a good fit. "If little importance is attached to pain medicine as a specialty, and there's an incentive for the primary-care doctor not to seek referrals, then there is a built-in disincentive to get good pain control."

Hospitalized patients under managed care are more likely to get pain-medicine referrals than are outpatients, he feels. "That's because the outpatient case is easy to dismiss. The doctor is liable to think, 'Oh, the guy's a whiner,' because pain is invisible."

Psychiatrist Herbert Hendin, medical director of the American Foundation for Suicide Prevention in New York, argues that managed-care systems will offer effective end-of-life care only if key segments of society demand it.

"Can managed-care plans be persuaded to approve quality palliative care for their patients?" he asks in his 1997 book, *Seduced by Death*. "They will if the accrediting agencies that set the standards for such plans insist that they do. They will if insurance companies are persuaded that it is in their interest to include palliative care — far less expensive than medicine dominated by life-support systems and intensive-care units — in their managed care-programs. They will if managed-care plans catering to the elderly and guaranteeing palliative care are successfully organized. They will only if those who care about how we treat people who are terminally ill are resolved to see that it happens." [11] ■

BACKGROUND

A Taboo Subject

Interest in assisted suicide was widespread in the United States and Europe about 100 years ago. Under a bill debated in the Ohio Legislature in 1906, a doctor could ask a terminally ill person in the presence of three witnesses whether he wished to die. If the answer was yes, three other physicians had to agree that the patient's condition was hopeless before they could assist in his suicide. But opponents warned that these "safeguards" were inadequate. The measure was defeated.

A book published in Germany in 1920 contained a strikingly similar set of proposals. Co-authors Alfred Hoche, a psychiatry professor, and Karl Binding, a law professor, wrote in *The Permission to Destroy Life Unworthy of Life* that patients who asked for "death assistance" should be allowed to obtain doctors' help in ending their lives, provided certain guidelines were followed. These included review of all assisted-suicide requests by a three-member panel, acknowledgment of the right to withdraw a death request at any time, and grants of legal immunity to physicians who perform euthanasia.

Anticipating ethical objections to their program, Hoche and Binding asserted that killing was consistent with medical ethics in certain instances. People suffering from brain damage, mental retardation and severe psychiatric illness were "mentally dead," they argued, hence terminating their lives was not homicide but rather "an allowable, useful act."

Though they hardly intended to do so, Hoche and Binding provided an intellectual rationale for the Nazis' efforts to purge Germany of undesirables in the 1930s and '40s. The Nazis began by sterilizing individuals with hereditary illnesses, advanced to the killing of "impaired" children and adults in hospitals and mental institutions, and, finally, to the mass extermination of Jews, gypsies and other population groups.

However, awareness of what was happening in Germany was slow to dawn in the United States, where euthanasia still enjoyed considerable support. Conducting its first nationwide survey on the subject in January 1937, the Gallup Poll asked, "Do you favor mercy deaths under government supervision for hopeless invalids?" Forty-six percent of those questioned said yes and 54 percent said no. But the share of yes answers topped 50 percent in the Middle Atlantic, Rocky Mountain and Pacific Coast states.

Liberation of the Nazi death camps in 1945 exposed the full horror of the Holocaust for the first time. The idea of medically terminated life immediately fell into disrepute, remaining taboo for more than a generation.

The Karen Quinlan Case

By the 1970s, however, "assisted death" began to shed its stigma. Interest now centered not on active euthanasia but on "death with dignity" — a shorthand term for the right of a terminally ill person to refuse life-sustaining medical treatment. The case of Karen Anne Quinlan brought the issue front and center.

Quinlan, 21, collapsed during a party in April 1975 after taking a mixture of tranquilizer pills and alcohol. Physicians who examined her in the hospital concluded she had entered a "persistent vegetative state" and had no chance of recovering.

A Catholic priest consulted by Quinlan's parents told them that church teachings held there was no moral obligation to continue extraordinary means to sustain life when there was no realistic hope of recovery. The parents then asked that Karen's respirator be disconnected, but her doctors and the hospital refused.

Undaunted, the Quinlans carried their quest to court. Though a trial judge ruled against them, the New Jersey Supreme Court in March 1976 reversed the decision. Since Karen was incompetent, the court said, the "only practical way" her constitutionally protected right of privacy could be exercised was to allow her guardian and family to decide "whether she would exercise it in these circumstances." *

Living Wills

The New Jersey Supreme Court decision called attention to the need for "living wills" — advance directives about the use and removal of artificial life supports. A second surge of interest in these legal instruments followed the U.S. Supreme Court's 1990 decision in the case of *Cruzan v. Missouri Department of Health*, whose circumstances were more complex and ambiguous than those of the Quinlan case.

Nancy Cruzan, 32, had been in a persistent vegetative state since an auto accident seven years earlier and was being kept alive by a feeding tube. Cruzan's parents, acting on her behalf, asked the hospital to stop giving her food and fluids but were rebuffed. The parents proceeded to file suit in Jasper County Circuit Court, which in 1988 directed the hospital to follow their wishes.

The Missouri Department of Health appealed the decision to the state Supreme Court, which reversed it. As a result, the Cruzans appealed to the U.S. Supreme Court, which held on June 25, 1990, that a person whose wishes were clearly known had a constitutional right to refuse life-sustaining medical treatment. At the same time, however, it ruled that states

Continued on p. 780

* When Quinlan's respirator was unplugged, about a year after she had become comatose, she began breathing unaided and lived another nine years.

Chronology

1900s-1940s

Assisted suicide commands broad support in the United States and Europe until reports of the Nazis' murders during the Holocaust.

1906
The first bill to legalize voluntary euthanasia in the United States is introduced in the Ohio Legislature but fails to pass.

Jan. 17, 1937
Responding to the Gallup Poll's first nationwide survey on the subject, 46 percent of those interviewed say they favor "mercy deaths under government supervision for hopeless individuals."

1970s-1980s

Debate sharpens on assisted suicide and alternative ways of treating the incurably ill.

1973
The Royal Dutch Medical Association says euthanasia should remain a crime but that the act may be justified under certain conditions.

March 1974
The nation's first hospice opens near New Haven, Conn.

March 1976
The New Jersey Supreme Court rules that Karen Anne Quinlan, a hospital patient in a "persistent vegetative state," has a right through her family to refuse life-sustaining treatment.

1980
The Hemlock Society is founded to promote the option of voluntary euthanasia for the terminally ill.

1982
Congress authorizes Medicare coverage for hospice care of terminally ill patients.

March 27, 1984
Gov. Richard D. Lamm, D-Colo., tells the Colorado Health Lawyers Association that terminally ill people have a "duty to die and get out of the way."

1990s

Assisted suicide and end-of-life care emerge as major issues.

June 4, 1990
Janet Adkins, an Oregon woman in the early stages of Alzheimer's disease, kills herself with the aid of a suicide machine devised by Michigan pathologist Jack Kevorkian.

June 25, 1990
Ruling in *Cruzan v. Missouri Department of Health,* the U.S. Supreme Court holds that a person whose wishes were clearly known has a right to refuse life-support treatment.

February 1993
The Dutch Parliament approves legislation that effectively immunizes from prosecution doctors who follow detailed rules for carrying out euthanasia.

Nov. 8, 1994
Oregon voters narrowly approve an "aid-in-dying" ballot initiative, the first such proposal to become law in the United States.

March 30, 1995
Pope John Paul II condemns euthanasia as "a false mercy, and indeed a disturbing 'perversion' of mercy."

April 1997
President Clinton signs legislation barring the use of federal funds for physician-assisted suicide or euthanasia.

June 4, 1997
The Institute of Medicine calls for improved end-of-life care, including the reform of laws inhibiting the use of pain-relieving drugs.

June 9, 1997
The Oregon Legislature votes to place the 1994 law legalizing physician-assisted suicide on the Nov. 4 ballot for possible repeal.

June 22, 1997
The American Medical Association issues a set of eight principles that "any patient facing death should be able to expect from physicians, health-care institutions and the community."

June 26, 1997
In upholding New York and Washington laws banning physician-assisted suicide, the Supreme Court holds that "the asserted 'right' to assistance in committing suicide is not a fundamental liberty interest."

July 17, 1997
In a 5-1 decision, the Florida Supreme Court upholds a state law prohibiting physician-assisted suicide.

Nov. 4, 1997
Oregon voters decide whether to retain the state's aid-in-dying law.

Euthanasia in the Netherlands . . .

Physician-assisted suicide is illegal in the Netherlands, just as it is in many other countries. Nonetheless, the practice is widely tolerated by the Dutch medical and legal systems and enjoys broad popular support. As might be expected, the Dutch experience is often cited by U.S. friends and foes of aid-in-dying in hope of scoring debating points against the other side.

Active euthanasia has been openly practiced in Holland since 1973, when, for the first time, a Dutch physician was charged with participating in a mercy killing. The doctor had acceded to repeated requests for death by her 78-year-old mother, who was partially deaf, incontinent and wheelchair-bound. A court in Leeuwarden found the defendant guilty, but gave her only a suspended sentence.

In that and other Dutch court cases decided between 1973 and 1984, two conditions were deemed essential for not prosecuting euthanasia: The patient had to initiate the request to die, asking repeatedly and explicitly for death, and had to be suffering from severe physical or mental pain, with no prospect of recovery.

In 1984, Dutch courts added a third condition — that a physician intending to perform euthanasia must first consult a colleague to confirm the accuracy of the diagnosis, verify the planned means of bringing about death and ascertain that all legal requirements were being met. Since then, some courts have also cited as requirements the presence of an incurable disease or a demand that death by euthanasia not inflict unnecessary suffering on others.

A 1991 report commissioned by the Dutch government contained ammunition for both supporters and opponents of euthanasia. The study found that 2,300 deaths, or 1.8 percent of all deaths in the Netherlands in 1990, were deliberately caused by doctors acting on their patients' orders. The relatively small number of such deaths, pro-euthanasia groups said, showed that the Dutch policy was sound.

However, the report also stated that 1,040 additional people were put to death by their doctors in 1990 without their consent, despite the courts' insistence that euthanasia be voluntary. This finding, said anti-euthanasia groups, showed that the fears of sliding down an ethical "slippery slope" were justified. In all the deaths cited in the study, doctors had killed patients by lethal injection or by giving them a lethal drug "cocktail."

In 1993, the Dutch Parliament approved legislation codifying and clarifying the judicial guidelines governing euthanasia. The law stopped short of legalizing the practice, which remains punishable by up to 12 years in prison, but it effectively immunized from prosecution any doctor who put a patient to death in accordance with four "carefulness requirements":

- a request for death must be made "entirely of the patient's free will" and could not be made by family or friends;
- the request must be expressed repeatedly and show "lasting longing for death";
- the patient must be informed of alternatives; and
- both patient and doctor must regard the patient's suffering as "perpetual, unbearable and hopeless."

The guidelines did nothing to still critics of the Dutch policy on euthanasia. "With the widespread acceptance of a euthanasia consciousness in the Netherlands, the guideline limitations make little actual difference to doctors or, indeed, to much of the general public," wrote Wesley J. Smith, a U.S. anti-euthanasia activist and legal consultant to the International Anti-Euthanasia Task Force, in his recent book, *Forced Exit: The Slippery Slope From Assisted Suicide to Legalized Murder*. "The proverbial exception to the rule can always be rationalized, which in turn soon changes the exception into the rule. The official guidelines then expand to meet the actual practice." [1]

Psychiatrist Herbert Hendin, medical director of the American Foundation for Suicide Prevention, made a similar

Continued from p. 778

could require that comatose patients be kept alive unless there was "clear and convincing evidence" that they would not want to live under such conditions. Such evidence, said the court, was lacking in the *Cruzan* case.

Instead of giving up, the Cruzans returned to Jasper County Circuit Court. Three of Nancy's former co-workers now testified that she had told them years earlier she would not want to live out her days in a coma. * Judge Charles E. Teel, who had made the initial ruling in the case, said this disclosure amounted to clear and convincing evidence. Consequently, he ruled, the Cruzans had the right to order the removal of their daughter's feeding tube. They immediately did so, with the result that Nancy died 12 days later.

Cruzan's death came two months after Congress enacted legislation requiring hospitals and other health-care facilities receiving Medicare or Medicaid payments to inform patients of their right to execute living wills or other advance directives. States took similar action. All 50 states and the District of Columbia now have living-will laws. Some of the statutes provide for the appointment of a health-care proxy to make decisions on a patient's behalf, often through

* Cruzan's parents had told Judge Teel in 1988 about comments made by Nancy to her sister, Christy, to the effect that she preferred to avoid extraordinary life-sustaining measures.

. . . Illegal But Accepted

point in another recent book. "The experience of the Dutch people makes it clear that legalization of assisted suicide and euthanasia is not the answer to the problems of people who are terminally ill," he wrote. "The Netherlands has moved from assisted suicide to euthanasia, from euthanasia for people who are terminally ill to euthanasia for those who are chronically ill, from euthanasia for physical illness to euthanasia for psychological distress and from voluntary euthanasia to involuntary euthanasia (called 'termination of the patient without explicit request')." [2]

Hendin recently elaborated on his concerns in the *Journal of the American Medical Association*. While he and two Dutch co-authors noted that "Dutch efforts at regulating assisted suicide have served as a model for proposed statutes in the United States and other countries," they cautioned that Dutch government research data from 1995 "indicates that these practices defy adequate regulation. Given legal sanction, euthanasia, intended originally for the exceptional case, has become an accepted way of dealing with serious or terminal illness in the Netherlands. In the process, palliative care is one of the casualties, while hospice care lags behind that of other countries." [3]

An article published in *The New England Journal of Medicine* last fall was based on the same data but concluded that "cautious optimism is warranted" because "there seem[ed] to be only a small increase in the number of cases of euthanasia" in the Netherlands between 1990 and 1995. [4] In an editorial appearing in the same issue, Executive Editor Marcia Angell wrote: "Are the Dutch on a slippery slope? It appears not." [5]

Many Dutch medical experts say it would be disastrous for the United States to legalize physician-assisted suicide, in part because the country is much less homogeneous than the Netherlands. Pieter Admiraal, a Dutch euthanasia pioneer, told Smith he was "totally against euthanasia in the U.S. as matters now stand. Before you have euthanasia, you have to have quality of care for terminally ill people, and the U.S. doesn't have that. Unless the U.S. can obtain it, it would be silly — ridiculous — for euthanasia to be legalized." [6]

Hendin had this to say about such comments: "The Dutch concern for our welfare has a patronizing quality, implying they are advanced enough as a society to be able to reap the benefits of euthanasia, but we are not. Yet one senses as well that they would be delighted for the United States to legalize euthanasia, since then they would not be so isolated in their position." [7]

Ira Byock, a hospice physician in Missoula, Mont., opposes legalized euthanasia. Nonetheless, he feels the subject of assisted suicide should be addressed forthrightly if a patient mentions it. Doing so, he says, can be therapeutic.

"So many people these days talk to us in terms of ending their life. From my perspective, that's an invitation to explore the nature of their suffering. In that sense, I welcome those inquiries. And often, I'll bring up the subject if they don't; I'll ask them if they've been thinking about it. At the very least, I can listen and respond in a caring way."

---

[1] Wesley J. Smith, *Forced Exit: The Slippery Slope From Assisted Suicide to Legalized Murder* (1997), p. 100.

[2] Herbert Hendin, *Seduced by Death: Doctors, Patients, and the Dutch Cure* (1997), p. 23.

[3] Hendin, et al., "Physician-Assisted Suicide and Euthanasia in the Netherlands: Lessons From the Dutch," *The Journal of the American Medical Association*, June 4, 1997, p. 1722.

[4] Gerrit Van der Wal, et al., "Evaluation of the Notification Procedure for Physician-Assisted Death in the Netherlands," *The New England Journal of Medicine*, Nov. 28, 1996, p. 1710.

[5] Marcia Angell, "Euthanasia in the Netherlands — Good News or Bad?" *The New England Journal of Medicine*, Nov. 28, 1996, p. 1677.

[6] Smith, *op. cit.*, p. 113.

[7] Hendin, *op. cit.*, p. 180.

a "durable power of attorney." And all the laws grant doctors immunity from prosecution for anything they do to implement a living will.

From the outset, "passive euthanasia" measures such as living wills and do-not-resuscitate orders have enjoyed broad support among legal and health professionals as well as the public. "Active euthanasia" or "voluntary suicide," on the other hand, remains a highly contentious issue.

The best-known practitioner of physician-aided death undoubtedly is Michigan pathologist Jack Kevorkian. Since 1990, Kevorkian has helped more than 30 people end their lives, many while hooked up to "suicide machines" made by Kevorkian. Legal efforts to make Kevorkian cease his aid-in-dying efforts have been unavailing so far. [12]

Hospice Movement

Meanwhile, an alternative method of treating the terminally ill — hospice and palliative care — was quietly taking root in the United States. The first American hospice, the Connecticut Hospice, opened in Branford in March 1974 with funding from the National Cancer Institute.

The U.S. hospice movement received a major boost in 1982, when Congress authorized Medicare coverage for hospice care of terminally ill patients. States began offering hospice care as an optional service under Medicaid soon afterward. A 1989 federal law raising Medicare reim-

Australia's Experiment Ends Quickly

The United States and the Netherlands are not the only countries where physician-assisted suicide is under active discussion. Australians also have been drawn into the controversy, though perhaps only temporarily.

A law passed in Australia's Northern Territory in 1995 legalized physician-assisted suicide. The measure required that a patient seeking euthanasia be at least 18 years old and "of sound mind" and be experiencing pain or suffering. In addition, a patient had to be diagnosed by two doctors as terminally ill. Each doctor had to have at least five years' medical experience, and at least one had to be a psychiatrist.

Since the Northern Territory is so remote and sparsely populated, the law initially attracted little notice in other countries. (With twice the land area of Texas, the territory numbers fewer than 180,000 inhabitants.) But reports about the law began to appear in the overseas news media soon after it took effect in 1996. Most accounts centered on Philip Nitschke, a Northern Territory physician who designed a computer-controlled suicide device.

Last September, Bob Dent, a 66-year-old carpenter with prostate cancer, became the first person to die under the euthanasia law. Even then, popular opinion was beginning to turn against legalized assisted suicide. Two months earlier, on July 27, the state Parliament of South Australia had rejected a similar voluntary euthanasia law. The Parliament of New South Wales followed suit on Oct. 16.

Meanwhile, Australia's national Parliament was moving to repeal the Northern Territory statute. Dent's son Rod, a member of the ruling Liberal Party, announced on Dec. 3 that he was reversing his earlier support of the territorial law. He said it would "denigrate the medical profession" and should be replaced by nationwide legislation promoting better palliative care. If Bob Dent had had access to optimum palliative care in the Northern Territory, Rod said, "I believe he would have made a slightly different decision."

The lower house of Australia's national Parliament approved a repeal bill by 88-35 the same month that Dent announced his change of heart. After adding an amendment to improve funding and training for palliative care, the Senate passed the measure on March 24 by a vote of 38-33. The effect of the law was to repeal the Northern Territory statute and bar enactment of similar proposals by the country's other two territories, Norfolk Island and the Australian Capital Territory. [1]

The rebuke by the Parliament in Canberra could have broader repercussions for the Northern Territory, which aspires to statehood within the Australian federation. In a Jan. 8, 1997, editorial, the Sydney *Morning Herald* said the 1995 approval of a "premature and ill-considered" euthanasia law had "confirmed how ill-prepared the Northern Territory is to take its place among the states."

[1] During the nine months when euthanasia was legal in the Northern Territory, four people received lethal injections, all administered by Nitschke's "Deliverance" machine.

bursement rates for hospice services by 20 percent sparked a further surge of interest in this approach to caring for the dying.

According to the Hospice Association of America, 2,154 Medicare-certified hospices are currently operating, as compared with 1,011 in 1991 and only 158 in 1985. The leading hospice states, the association says, are California, Georgia, North Carolina, Ohio, Pennsylvania and Texas.

Voter Initiatives

At the time hospice care was gaining converts across the country, proponents of physician-assisted suicide were stepping up efforts to legalize the practice at the state level. Voter initiatives seeking physician-assisted suicide appeared on the ballot in Washington in 1991 and in California in 1992. Early opinion polls suggested the measures would win easily. Instead, voters in both states rejected the proposals by identical margins — 54 to 46 percent. Opponents' warnings about inadequate safeguards apparently proved decisive. [13]

The "right to die" movement finally tasted victory in November 1994, when Oregon voters approved Ballot Measure 16 (also known as the Death With Dignity Act) by 51 to 49 percent. The law states that patients may receive life-ending prescription drugs from their physicians only if:

- two doctors agree that the patient has six months or less to live;
- the patient asks at least three times for a doctor's help in committing suicide, the last time in writing, in the presence of two witnesses;
- the patient's doctor waits at least 15 days after the first request, and at least two days after the third one, before writing a prescription for lethal drugs; and
- the patient is offered counseling and told of alternatives such as hospice care.

Scheduled to take effect a month after the election, the law was put on indefinite hold by U.S. District Judge Michael R. Hogan in Eugene. "Although the status quo will be regarded as a hardship by some terminally ill patients who want the 'option' of physician-assisted suicide to be immediately available," Hogan said, "the public interest in protecting vulnerable citizens from the irreparable harm of death is greater. Surely the first assisted-suicide law in this country deserves a considered, thoughtful constitutional analysis."

Hogan's final ruling came on Aug. 3, 1995. Measure 16 was unconstitutional, he declared, because it "withholds from terminally ill citizens the same protections from suicide the majority enjoys" under the Equal-Protection Clause of the 14th Amendment. Consequently, it offers "little assurance that only competent terminally ill persons will voluntarily die." The judge added that "certain fundamental rights may not be dispensed with by a majority vote."

Disheartened though they were by Hogan's decision, right-to-die proponents hailed a pair of appellate court rulings in early 1996 that overturned state bans on physician-assisted suicide. In a March 6 decision striking down a Washington state law, the U.S. Court of Appeals in San Francisco held that an individual's right to control "the timing and manner of one's death" outweighed the state's obligation to preserve life. The court located this privacy right in the Due-Process Clause of the 14th Amendment, likening it to existing rights to obtain an abortion or to refuse life-sustaining medical treatment when terminally ill.

In a similar ruling on April 2, a three-judge panel of the U.S. Court of Appeals in New York City voided New York state's law prohibiting doctor-aided suicide. In a unanimous opinion, the panel said the ban violated the equal-protection guarantee. It did so, the panel reasoned, by allowing dying patients to refuse artificial life support but barring them from taking lethal drugs supplied by a physician.

"What interest can the state possibly have in requiring the prolongation of a life that is all but ended?" wrote Judge Roger J. Miner in the court's opinion. "What business is it of the state to require the continuation of agony when the result is imminent and inevitable?" He answered, "None."

Shortly before opening its 1996-97 term, the U.S. Supreme Court agreed to review the Washington and New York decisions. ■

CURRENT SITUATION

Supreme Court Rulings

The U.S. Supreme Court's decisions in the Washington and New York cases, among the most eagerly awaited of its current term, were issued June 26. In his decision in *Washington v. Glucksberg,* Chief Justice Rehnquist drew a sharp legal distinction between withdrawal of artificial life support and physician-assisted suicide. He argued that the right to refuse life-sustaining treatment, as set forth in the court's 1990 *Cruzan* decision, "was not simply deduced from abstract concepts of personal autonomy."

Citing "the common-law rule that forced medication was a battery, and the long legal tradition protecting the decision to refuse unwanted medical treatment," Rehnquist said the right recognized in *Cruzan* "was entirely consistent with this nation's history and constitutional traditions." He added, "The decision to commit suicide with the assistance of another may be just as personal and profound as the decision to refuse unwanted medical treatment, but it has never enjoyed similar legal protection. Indeed, the two acts are widely and reasonably regarded as quite distinct."

Writing again for a unanimous court in *Vacco v. Quill,* Rehnquist rejected the lower court's argument that New York's ban on physician-assisted suicide violated the constitutional guarantee of equal protection of the laws. "On their faces, neither New York's ban on assisting suicide nor its statutes permitting patients to refuse medical treatment treat anyone differently than anyone else or draw any distinctions between persons," he asserted. "Everyone, regardless of physical condition, is entitled, if competent, to refuse unwanted lifesaving medical treatment; no one is permitted to assist a suicide. Generally speaking, laws that apply evenhandedly to all 'unquestionably comply' with the Equal Protection Clause."

Rehnquist went on to assert that "the distinction between assisting suicide and withdrawing life-sustaining treatment, a distinction widely recognized and endorsed in the medical profession and in our legal traditions, is both important and logical; it is certainly rational." He explained, "The distinction comports with fundamental legal principles of causation and intent. First, when a patient refuses life-sustaining medical treatment, he dies from an underlying fatal disease or pathology; but if a patient ingests lethal medication prescribed by a physician, he is killed by that medication."

In upholding the Washington and New York laws, the court stopped short of saying there could never be a legal right to assisted suicide. "Every one of us at some point may be affected by our own or a family member's terminal illness," Justice Sandra Day O'Connor wrote in a concurring opinion in *Glucksberg*. "There is no reason to think the democratic process will not strike the proper balance between the interests of terminally ill, mentally competent individuals who would seek to end their suffering and the state's interests in protecting those who might seek to end life mistakenly or under pressure. As the court recognizes, states are presently undertaking extensive and serious evaluation of physician-assisted suicide and other related issues."

Florida Court Rules in AIDS Case

Among those states was Florida, whose Supreme Court issued an assisted-suicide ruling July 17 that resembled the U.S. Supreme Court decisions of three weeks earlier. The plaintiffs in the Florida case were Charles E. Hall, an AIDS patient, and his physician, Cecil McIver. Early this year, a Palm Beach County Circuit Court judge had ruled that McIver could help Hall end his life without exposing himself to criminal prosecution. The state appealed the decision.

At issue in the case was a 1980 amendment to the state constitution declaring that "every natural person has the right to be let alone and free of government intrusion into his private life." Hall and McIver argued that this language effectively negated a state law making "assisting self-murder" a second-degree felony.

The Florida Supreme Court disagreed, saying, "It is clear that the public policy of this state as expressed by the Legislature is opposed to assisted suicides." However, the court left open the possibility that the Legislature could write "a carefully crafted" assisted-suicide statute that would withstand constitutional scrutiny.

Maneuvering in Oregon

Meanwhile, new twists were surfacing in Oregon's tortuous assisted-suicide debate. On Feb. 27, the U.S. Court of Appeals in San Francisco rejected a lawsuit challenging Measure 16 because the plaintiffs could not show that they faced an immediate threat of harm from the law. The plaintiffs responded by petitioning the U.S. Supreme Court to review the decision. But the state of Oregon declined to file an opposing brief — "apparently to expedite review and have Oregon's law reinstated quickly," according to an analysis by the National Conference of Catholic Bishops. "The court was expected to discuss the case in late June and refuse to hear the appeal." [14]

But the strategy, if such it was, proved to be ill-conceived. On June 23 the Supreme Court ordered Oregon to file a brief in 30 days. Since the court was about to recess for the summer, that meant it would not have a chance to consider the case until its 1997-98 term, beginning in October. To complicate matters further, the Oregon Legislature voted to place Measure 16 on the November ballot for possible repeal, in which case the appeal to the Supreme Court would become moot.

"The upshot is that Oregon's law is unlikely to take effect before opponents have an opportunity to persuade voters to repeal it," the National Conference noted. "It has gone unnoticed by most news media that assisted-suicide proponents suffered not one but two defeats the last week of the Supreme Court's term." [15]

Congress Bans Funding

Court battles over assisted-suicide laws in Washington, New York and Oregon helped spur Congress to approve legislation this spring barring the use of federal funds for physician-assisted suicide or euthanasia. * Rep. Henry A. Waxman, D-Calif., called the measure "redundant, a mere restatement of the status quo," saying such use of federal funds already was prohibited. [16] But the bill's supporters said it was necessary to clarify the government's position, particularly if states start to legalize assisted suicide and judges rule that it qualifies for federal funding.

"All it would take is for one district court judge to rule that it falls under the guidelines for federal support," said Rep. Ralph M. Hall, D-Texas, the bill's sponsor. [17]

The congressional legislation does not ban assisted suicide, but would prevent federal funding for it. States that legalized assisted suicide would be free to fund it or to allow patients to pay for it themselves. Doctors who helped patients end their lives would not be in jeopardy of losing Medicare, Medicaid or other forms of federal reimbursement for other services performed. [18]

* The House passed the measure on April 10, the Senate on April 16, 1997. President Clinton signed HR 1003 on April 30, 1997.

End-of-Life Care

Political and legal wrangling over assisted suicide has tended to overshadow initiatives by the medical profession to develop alternative forms of caring for the terminally ill. At its June 1996 annual meeting, for instance, the American Medical Association's House of Delegates voted overwhelmingly to reaffirm the organization's longstanding opposition to physician-aided suicide. At the same time, the delegates pledged to step up efforts to train doctors in pain management and meet other needs of dying patients.

To further those goals, the AMA this June published a list of eight principles that physicians, health-care facilities and members of the wider community should follow in dealing with people nearing death. *(See box, p. 774.)*

"In the last phase of life, people seek peace and dignity," said Linda Emanuel, head of the AMA's Institute for Ethics. "The AMA firmly believes

Continued on p. 786

At Issue:

Should Oregon's assisted-suicide law be repealed?

THE OREGONIAN
FROM AN EDITORIAL PUBLISHED MAY 11, 1997.

yes

Even if Measure 16 were a model of craftsmanship and Solomonic wisdom, we would still favor sending the 1994 physician-assisted suicide law back to voters for reconsideration. The reason is simple: Measure 16, even if it were flawless, is different from any other measure we've ever encountered. Ever. . . .

The problem is this: Measure 16 allows doctors to prescribe life-ending pills to terminally ill patients, but those pills — the 60 to 100 you must keep in your body to induce death — fail in up to 25 percent of the cases. The result can be vomiting, convulsions, brain impairment, kidney damage, comas and lingering deaths.

As Measure 16's advocates acknowledged after the 1994 election, their Death with Dignity Act is not as neat and tidy as taking a pill and falling into a blissful final rest.

In the Netherlands, physician-assisted suicides are not done all that much because of this. Doctors there can end these special agonies with lethal injections. Indeed, Dutch doctors practice euthanasia 10 times more often than doctor-assisted suicides. But Measure 16 itself bars doctors from administering lethal injections. What would happen to Oregonians whose pills fail?

The measure's sponsors could have included a lethal injection or euthanasia provision. Sponsors did just that in the failed initiatives in California and Washington. But the Oregon sponsors didn't. Why? Because Oregonian voters would have probably spurned a measure that gave doctors the power to administer lethal injections. . . .

Granted, the Legislature or Measure 16's sponsors could fix the flaw by adding a lethal-injection provision. But they would be fixing a flaw with another, fatal, flaw. We can guess that the lethal injection allowance would complicate Measure 16's electoral prospects. We know from the Netherlands that the lethal injection provision robs patients of individual autonomy and personal choice.

We have no illusions about what opponents of doctor-assisted suicide are up to in focusing on Measure 16's practical problems and asking for a second vote. They're not interested in solving these problems. Never were. They're bent on repealing Measure 16.

Well, so are we. We hold now, as we held in 1994, that this physician-assisted suicide measure is a grotesque wrong-headed license to kill. It also seems to us that Measure 16's practical problems are inextricably linked with Measure 16's moral problems. You have one because you have the other. That happens when you get into the killing business.

Repealing Measure 16 won't solve the all-too-real problems of death and dying. Better pain-management will help, and the Measure 16 debate has spurred Oregon's medical community forward in this area. So will greater access to hospice care. . . . But assisted suicide will exacerbate, not eliminate, Oregonians' end-of-life dilemmas.

THE DAILY ASTORIAN
FROM AN EDITORIAL PUBLISHED JULY 3, 1997.

no

The U.S. Supreme Court, in a widely reported and misunderstood decision, [has] said that states may enact laws denying people a physician's assistance in committing suicide. The court did not overrule, and far less condemn, the pending law in Oregon that grants such a right.

In fact, Chief Justice William Rehnquist, said "Our opinion does not absolutely foreclose" the option of a terminally ill person calling upon a doctor to help end his or her life. . . . Rehnquist, legal scholars say, appears to be encouraging states to take up the issue themselves. The court's decision, the chief justice said, "permits this debate to continue, as it should in a democratic society."

But some in Oregon have taken the court's decision as an indication that the state's physician-assisted suicide law is on shaky ground. They are certain to use the ruling to try to convince voters to vote to repeal the law later this year.

Acting before the court's decision, the Oregon Legislature, firmly in the grasp of so-called conservatives, indulged itself in an attempt to subvert the will of the people as expressed in the initiative process, by referring the physician-assisted suicide measure back to voters to see if they've changed their minds since approving Measure 16 in November 1994.

It's as if legislative leaders are saying, "You silly people didn't know what you were doing. We're not going to do what you told us to. Here, vote on this again, and think the way we do this time.". . .

Measure 16 may be far from perfect. Other commentators have noted that in the Netherlands — the Western nation with the greatest experience with assisted suicide — the law and procedures used to implement it have sometimes been abused. Meanwhile, the Dutch have fallen behind in palliative care — the practice of controlling pain and easing death.

These are the legitimate concerns that deserve continuing attention and debate by Oregon's citizens and leaders. Measure 16's narrow victory shows that this is far from being a settled issue.

But as an extension of individuals' right to control the most personal aspects of their own existence, the option of dying with human assistance by a qualified physician is not the radical proposal its opponents make it out to be. A majority of Oregonians have said at the polls that they want society to experiment with this option. The U.S. chief justice has encouraged exactly such an approach.

The next logical step is to go forward with careful monitoring to avoid, in so far as possible, the problems in the Netherlands. If, after a period of time, similar problems develop here and cannot otherwise be corrected, then would be the appropriate time for the Legislature to step in. But not until then.

Continued from p. 784

that every patient should be able to reasonably expect quality care at the end of life." [19]

The AMA principles were consistent with the findings and recommendations of a report issued on June 4 by the Institute of Medicine. The report, "Approaching Death: Improving Care at the End of Life," urged that laws restricting the prescribing of narcotics be eased and that medical educators provide more instruction in end-of-life issues. "Many health-care professionals have not been trained to provide adequate end-of-life care or understand how important it is," said Cassel, head of the IOM committee that drafted the report. [20]

The problem is aggravated, the report suggested, by the fact that a majority of Americans die in health-care institutions — chiefly hospitals and nursing homes — whose "central mission" is "curing disease and prolonging life." It went on to note that "Hospital culture often regards death as a failure, in part because modern medicine has been so successful in rescuing, stabilizing or curing people with formerly fatal conditions and in part because a significant minority of acutely ill and injured patients who die often do so before the end of a normal life span." [21]

Nursing homes present a different set of problems for terminally ill patients, "including the low level of physician involvement, relatively low ratios of registered nurses to residents and the amount of care that is provided by nursing assistants or aides." In addition, "Staff may not be trained in caring for dying patients and may not provide adequate palliative care, sometimes because physician medication and other orders are not flexible enough." [22]

For the most part, according to the IOM, non-medical aspects of treating the terminally ill receive little attention. This "psychological dimension" includes "cognitive function and emotional health" as well as "calls for openness and sensitivity to the feelings and emotional needs of both the patient and the family."

The "spiritual dimension" of dying also tends to get short shrift, the report suggested. "Hope for a cure may persist in those with incurable illnesses, but other kinds of hope can also be a bulwark in the face of death. . . . Even for patients and families without a religious or philosophical belief system, counseling or discussions with chaplains, carefully selected hospice volunteers or others with special empathy and insight may prove comforting."

To improve end-of-life care, the IOM urged reform of U.S. medical education "to ensure that practitioners have relevant attitudes, knowledge and skills" to care for the terminally ill. "Dying is too important a part of life to be left to one or two required (but poorly attended) lectures, to be considered only in ethical and not clinical terms or to be set aside on the grounds that medical educators are already swamped with competing demands for time and resources. Every health professional who deals directly with patients and families needs a basic grounding in competent and compassionate care for seriously ill and dying patients." [23]

The report also recommended that palliative care "should become, if not a medical specialty, at least a defined area of expertise, education and research." In either case, the goal is "to create a cadre of palliative care experts whose numbers and talents are sufficient to:

- provide expert consultation and role models for colleagues, students and other members of the health-care team;
- supply educational leadership and resources for scientifically based and practically useful undergraduate, graduate and continuing medical education; and
- organize and conduct biomedical, clinical, behavioral and health services research."

Moreover, the IOM report asserted that palliative care "must be redefined to include prevention as well as relief of symptoms." [24] ■

OUTLOOK

Showdown in Oregon

When the Oregon Legislature voted to place the state's assisted-suicide law on the Nov. 4 ballot, it ruffled the feathers of an electorate proud of the state's history of innovative ballot initiatives. Some observers feel the move will backfire by persuading undecided voters to approve the measure. But others say it is risky to predict the outcome of balloting on such a hot-button issue. Nonetheless, unfriendly editorial comment in many state newspapers appeared to give Measure 16 supporters an early boost.

"[W]hen the repeal vote occurs in November, the issue on the ballot will be more than assisted suicide," *The* (Eugene) *Register-Guard* declared on June 11. "It will be the Legislature's misfeasance through abuse of the initiative process. When the people vote against the repeal, they will be affirming their support for citizens' right to assisted suicide. And they will be telling the legislature: 'No, you do NOT know better.' "

In a similar vein, *The* (La Grande) *Observer* said on June 3: "Resubmitting the measure to voters is irresponsible. It tells voters, from a body that refused for years to deal with the issue, that the Legislature didn't like their response, so let's try again. . . . The Legislature owes it to the public to do what was intended by the original vote. Implement it."

The (Portland) *Oregonian,* on the other hand, supported a second popular vote on the law. "We have no illusions about what opponents of doctor-assisted suicide are up to in focusing on Measure 16's practical problems and asking for a second vote," the state's leading paper opined on May 11. "They're not interested in solving these problems. Never were. They're bent on repealing Measure 16.

"Well, so are we," the editorial continued. "We hold now, as we held in 1994, that this physician-assisted suicide measure is a grotesquely unwarranted license to kill." (*See "At Issue," p. 785.*)

A poll taken in May for Oregon Right to Die, the main group supporting Measure 16, reported that 81 percent of the respondents opposed putting the law before the voters again. "Oregon voters are an extremely independent bunch of people," Sugerman says. "They take pride in doing things first, and doing them right, such as our land-use planning laws and our bottle bill."

As a result, he says, Oregonians feel the Legislature "did a very horrible thing by sending Measure 16 back to the ballot. Our public opinion surveys show that more than 65 percent of the electorate will not vote for repeal."

But Smith says he has sensed no hard feelings toward the Legislature. "The reaction of people I talked to on the street and on talk shows indicated they wanted a much more detailed discussion of the issue than perhaps had occurred in 1994."

According to Humphry, Oregonians already are "much better educated on assisted suicide than they were three years ago. We won in Oregon in 1994 because the public was better educated than California and Washington voters had been. And now they know even more."

Humphry predicts Measure 16 will win about 60 percent of the ballots cast on Nov. 4, with part of the increased victory margin representing a rebuke to the Legislature. For the most part, he feels, people's minds already are made up. "All the advertising in the world won't switch people's views on an issue like this," he says. "It's a matter of personal ethics and gut feelings."

Doerflinger of the U.S. Catholic Conference agrees that Oregon voters are more savvy about assisted suicide today than in 1994, but he suspects that additional knowledge could work to the advantage of the pro-repeal forces. "The Oregon Medical Association is now against Measure 16," he notes. "Before, it insisted on being neutral."

In addition, Doerflinger believes Oregonians are more aware now of "the high failure rate" for assisted suicide involving physician-prescribed pills. "That's why Derek Humphry recommends putting a plastic bag over the head as an adjunct to taking pills," he says. "I don't think people had any idea, when they voted in 1994, that 'dignified death' involved suffocating yourself with a plastic bag, or getting your doctor to give you a lethal injection, after your pills don't work."

The Hemlock Society's Girsh isn't looking forward to the coming campaign. "Between now and Nov. 4, the Catholic Church, the American Medical Association and the right-to-life groups are going to pour millions of dollars into Oregon to finance a misinformation campaign," she says. "They're going to scare people out of their minds."

Both sides will focus on what's likely to happen if Measure 16 is approved, she believes. "Our prediction is that a small percentage of terminally ill people will be able to hasten their death in a peaceful way by a couple of days or maybe weeks. They'll claim that gas chambers will be set up on every street corner."

But win or lose, both sides in the Measure 16 campaign agree it is just one more clash in an ongoing battle to sway popular opinion. Girsh notes that aid-in-dying advocates in Michigan are now collecting signatures for an assisted-suicide proposal they hope to qualify for the November 1998 ballot. In addition, "There are five states in which measures that were introduced early in 1997 have been carried over until next year," she says. "And a number of other states may consider similar legislation now that the Supreme Court rulings are out of the way."

Impact of Baby Boomers

Some doctors who specialize in end-of-life care feel the baby-boom generation will decide the outcome of the debate on assisted suicide and related issues. One school of thought holds that baby boomers are so intent on protecting their autonomy that they will remain strongly in favor of "death with dignity" even into their old age. Others think that the aging process will reshape boomers' attitudes, bringing them into sync with the thinking of today's elderly Americans — a population segment that opinion surveys show to be notably unsupportive of assisted suicide.

Humphry says it has always been his impression that older people "are more willing to bow to the authority of religion than are younger people. I'm not suggesting that baby boomers are irreligious or non-religious; but they're more free-spirited. And I think the boomers will, on the whole, come out on our side."

Smith disagrees. "Those who support assisted suicide the most are the young," he notes. "But I suspect that as people grow older, the issue becomes more real for them. They may begin to see themselves as poten-

FOR MORE INFORMATION

Choice in Dying — the National Council for the Right to Die, 200 Varick St., New York, N.Y. 10014-4810, (212) 366-5540. Choice in Dying educates the public on the legal and psychological implications of terminal-care decision-making.

Hemlock Society U.S.A., P.O. Box 101810, Denver, Colo. 80250, (303) 639-1202. The society strives to foster a climate of public opinion tolerant of people's right to end their lives at a time and in a manner of their choosing.

Hospice Association of America, 228 7th St. S.E., Washington, D.C. 20003, (202) 546-4759. HAA promotes the concept of hospice, which offers home-based care for the terminally ill and their family members.

International Anti-Euthanasia Task Force, P.O. Box 760, Steubenville, Ohio 49352, (614) 282-3810. IAETF opposes "death with dignity" laws such as Oregon's Measure 16. It publishes a bimonthly newsletter.

National Committee on the Treatment of Intractable Pain, c/o Wayne Coy Jr., Cohn and Marks, 1333 New Hampshire Ave. N.W., Washington, D.C. 20036, (202) 452-4836. The committee endorses the British hospice concept of care for the dying and advocates legalization of heroin for pain control.

Oregon Right to Die, P.O. Box 19328, Portland, Ore. 97280, (503) 228-4414. Oregon Right to Die heads the campaign for retention of Measure 16, the state's law legalizing physician-assisted suicide.

Oregon Right to Life, 4335 River Road North, Salem, Ore. 97303, (503) 463-8563. Oregon Right to Life leads the campaign for repeal of Measure 16.

Secretariat for Pro-Life Activities, United States Catholic Conference, 3211 4th St. N.E., Washington, D.C. 20017-1194, The secretariat promotes the Roman Catholic Church's position on such sensitive social issues as abortion and euthanasia.

tially a rejected social class."

In Smith's opinion, "Some individuals in our society are saying that certain categories of people are better off dead — for their sake as well as that of their families and the community. When Americans realize that assisted suicide isn't about personal autonomy, but about creating categories of people who are disposable, I think they're going to turn away from it."

Sieger of Choice in Dying sees views on end-of-life issues as influenced more by financial condition than age. "People without much money or access to proper health care are less likely to favor physician-assisted suicide than those who are financially secure and feel in control of their lives," she says. "Previous experiences with doctors and health-care facilities also shape people's thinking on these issues."

For Mary L. Meyer, director of Choice in Dying's program department, the mere fact that the issues are being debated openly is significant. "We are more comfortable talking about dying than we were even a few years ago," she says. "Money is probably our last remaining taboo. But death used to be another one, and now we're at least discussing it." ■

Notes

[1] "Measure 16: Repeal is Overdue," *Catholic Sentinel,* Feb. 28, 1997.
[2] Quoted by Gail Kinsey Hill in *The Sunday Oregonian,* Aug. 3, 1997, p. A1.
[3] Institute of Medicine, "Approaching Death: Improving Care at the End of Life," Vol. I, June 4, 1997, pp. 1-15. The IOM is an independent research organization chartered by the National Academy of Sciences that conducts studies of policy issues related to health and medicine.
[4] Christine K. Cassel, "Overview on Attitudes of Physicians Toward Caring for the Dying Patient," in American Board of Internal Medicine, *Caring for the Dying: Identification and Promotion of Physician Competency* (1996), p. 2.
[5] Wesley J. Smith, *Forced Exit: The Slippery Slope From Assisted Suicide to Legalized Murder* (1997), p. 13.
[6] Cassel, *op. cit.,* p. 3.
[7] WHO Collaborating Centre for Palliative Cancer Care, *Looking Forward to Cancer Pain Relief for All* (1997), p. 46.
[8] For background, see "Managed Care," *The CQ Researcher,* April 12, 1996, pp. 313-336.
[9] The survey is cited in Larry Beresford, "Hospice and Managed Care," *HMO Magazine,* January/February 1996, p. 66. The American Association of Health Plans was formerly called the Group Health Association of America.
[10] Quoted in Beresford, *ibid.* Emerson also is a board member of Hospice of Prince George's County in Largo, Md.
[11] Herbert Hendin, *Seduced by Death: Doctors, Patients and the Dutch Cure* (1997), pp. 219-220.
[12] Kevorkian's lawyer, Geoffrey Fieger, said on Aug. 13, 1997, that Kevorkian had been involved in "nearly 100 cases" of assisted suicide. For background on Kevorkian, see "Assisted Suicide Controversy," *The CQ Researcher,* May 5, 1995, pp. 393-416, and "Assisted Suicide," *The CQ Researcher,* Feb. 21, 1992, pp. 145-168.
[13] For details of the Washington and California initiatives, see "Assisted Suicide Controversy," *The CQ Researcher, op. cit.,* pp. 406-408.
[14] National Conference of Catholic Bishops Secretariat for Pro-Life Activities, "Focus Shifts to Oregon," *Life at Risk,* June 1997, p. 2.
[15] *Loc. cit.*
[16] Quoted by Lisa Clagett Weintraub, "Bill Would Ban Federal Funds for Doctor-Assisted Suicide," *CQ Weekly Report,* March 15, 1997, p. 644.
[17] Quoted in *CQ Weekly Report,* April 12, 1997, p. 852.
[18] *CQ Weekly Report,* April 19, 1997, p. 916.
[19] AMA news release, June 22, 1997.
[20] Quoted by Steve Sternberg in *USA Today,* June 5, 1997, p. 1A.
[21] Institute of Medicine, *op. cit.,* pp. 4-9.
[22] *Ibid.,* p. 11, chapter 4.
[23] IOM, *op. cit.,* Vol. II, pp. 10-18.
[24] *Ibid.,* p. 9, chapter 10.

Bibliography

Selected Sources Used

Books

Battin, Margaret P., and Arthur G. Lipman, eds., *Drug Use in Assisted Suicide and Euthanasia*, Pharmaceutical Products Press, 1996.
The contributors to this book examine a wide range of ethical, legal and regulatory issues — including the problems faced by nurses and pharmacists involved in assisted-suicide cases.

Hendin, Herbert, *Seduced by Death: Doctors, Patients and the Dutch Cure,* W.W. Norton, 1997.
Hendin's book ostensibly is about the Netherlands, where physician-assisted suicide has been widely available — though technically illegal — since 1973. But his actual subject is assisted suicide in the United States. "Euthanasia advocates," he writes, "appeal to the fearful in the name of ideals of compassion and autonomy even as they promote policies which, despite their best intentions, can only result in coercion and cruelty."

Smith, Wesley J., *Forced Exit: The Slippery Slope From Assisted Suicide to Legalized Murder,* Random House/Times Books, 1997.
Smith, an attorney and consumer activist in Oakland, Calif., decries the growing acceptance of euthanasia and the "right to die."

Articles

Brownlee, Shannon, and Joannie M. Schrof, "The Quality of Mercy," *U.S. News & World Report,* March 17, 1997.
The authors review recent advances in pain management in the United States. "Pain experts are heartened by the signs of improvement," they write. "But they worry that the cost-cutting fervor of insurance companies and HMOs will put limits on how much things can change. Treating pain can be expensive."

Foley, Kathleen M., "Competent Care for the Dying Instead of Physician-Assisted Suicide," *The New England Journal of Medicine,* Jan. 2, 1997.
Foley, one of the nation's leading experts in pain management, presents the case for palliative care as a humane alternative to physician-assisted suicide.

Hendin, Herbert, et al., "Physician-Assisted Suicide and Euthanasia in the Netherlands: Lessons From the Dutch," *The Journal of the American Medical Association*, June 4, 1997.
In what essentially is a critique of an earlier study in *The New England Journal of Medicine,* the authors (Americans) conclude that there "has been an erosion of medical standards in the care of terminally ill patients in the Netherlands."

Van der Wal, Gerrit, et al., "Evaluation of the Notification Procedure for Physician-Assisted Death in the Netherlands," *The New England Journal of Medicine,* Nov. 28, 1996.
The Dutch authors write that "cautious optimism is warranted" due to the willingness of physicians in the Netherlands to have cases of doctor-assisted suicide reviewed by government officials. "The very high rates of participation in studies such as ours reflect the support of the medical profession for some form of public oversight in this area," they argue.

Wilkes, Paul, "Dying Well Is the Best Revenge," *The New York Times Magazine*, July 6, 1997.
Wilkes recounts the last days of Mike Morris, a terminally ill resident of Missoula, Mont. Morris finds solace through the locally based hospice movement headed by Ira Byock, one of the nation's leading practitioners of end-of-life palliative care.

Reports and Studies

American Board of Internal Medicine, "Caring for the Dying: Identification and Promotion of Physician Competency," 1996.
This collection of papers by experts in palliative care examines such topics as the physician's role in social, legal and ethical issues, hospice and home care, and the roles of psychiatry and religion in treatment of the dying.

Institute of Medicine, "Approaching Death: Improving Care at the End of Life" (two volumes), June 1997.
The institute report concludes that "Too many dying people suffer from pain and other distress that clinicians could prevent or relieve with existing knowledge or therapies." As a result, IOM urges better training of health professionals in end-of-life care and reform of laws that limit the use of pain-killing drugs.

WHO Collaborating Centre for Palliative Cancer Care, "Looking Forward to Cancer Pain Relief for All," CBC Oxford, 1997.
This updated version of the World Health Organization's first publication on control of cancer pain asserts that "Cancer pain management and palliative care should be compulsory topics in the general professional training of doctors and nurses and should form part of continuing medical education."

The Next Step

Additional information from UMI's Newspaper & Periodical Abstracts™ database

Derek Humphry

Coughlin, Ruth, "Means to an end: Now Derek Humphry takes a look at the legal and practical ramifications of suicide for the dying," ***Detroit News,*** **March 24, 1997, p. B1.**

Derek Humphry and Jack Kevorkian have only met once. Not surprisingly, death was the subject. It was in 1988 in Los Angeles and, according to Humphry, Kevorkian wanted to start a suicide clinic and asked him for the names of Hemlock Society members who wanted to die.

Humphry, Derek, "Craft suicide rules carefully," ***USA Today,*** **April 9, 1996, p. A10.**

In a letter to the editor, Hemlock Society founder Derek Humphry notes that two appeals courts have cleared the alleged constitutional barriers to lawful physician-assisted suicide. He says that not only should the injunction against the implementation of the Oregon Death With Dignity Act be promptly lifted, but in all states politicians must pass similar, carefully crafted laws governing the procedure.

Nuland, Sherwin B., "How we die? Our own business," ***Houston Chronicle,*** **Jan. 19, 1997, p. C1.**

In his book "Final Exit," Derek Humphry wrote movingly of how his first wife, Jean, suffered as cancer ravaged her body. Convinced that her doctors would not help her end her life, he approached a young physician who, without having met the patient, prepared a vial of capsules and instructed Humphry in their use. A few weeks later, after the couple spent the morning reminiscing about their 22 years together, wrote Humphry, his wife drank from a cup of pill-laced coffee and "barely had time to murmur, 'Goodbye, my love,' before falling asleep."

Euthanasia

Garvey, John, "God will wipe away our tears," ***Commonweal,*** **Feb. 28, 1997, pp. 7-8.**

Garvey comments on physician-assisted suicide. He says he is opposed to the concept, but he understands the feelings behind euthanasia, as misguided as he believes they are.

Shapiro, Joseph P., "Euthanasia's home," ***U.S. News & World Report,*** **Jan. 13, 1997, pp. 24-27.**

The Netherlands is the only country in the world that openly allows euthanasia, and the nation is seen as a model by both sides of the debate in the U.S. over physician-assisted suicide. Shapiro discusses what the Dutch experience can teach the U.S.

Smith, Wesley J., "Death wars," ***National Review,*** **July 14, 1997, pp. 36-37.**

As euthanasia advocates press their case, the moral health of the U.S. is at stake. The struggle over legalizing euthanasia is discussed.

Hemlock Society

MacDonald, Richard, "Suicide beliefs shouldn't be imposed on others," ***USA Today,*** **Jan. 13, 1997, p. A12.**

In a letter to the editor, MacDonald of the Hemlock Society USA argues that the Supreme Court justices have no right to impose their beliefs on others in assisted suicide cases.

Samuel, Yvonne, "Physicians Need to Have Role in Death of Patients, Right-to-die," ***St. Louis Post-Dispatch,*** **April 12, 1997, p. 11.**

Faye Girsh, a clinical and forensic psychologist and president of the Hemlock Society USA, says people should be able to control what happens to them at the end of their lives. But she does not recommend physician-aided deaths for people who are depressed or coerced.

Ira Byock

"Dying well," ***Hospitals & Health Networks,*** **June 20, 1997, p. 62.**

The Quality of Life's End Missoula Demonstration Project in Missoula, Mont., is the brainchild of Dr. Ira Byock, a local hospice doctor.

Martin, Claire, "Choosing LIFE or DEATH: When does 'dying well' begin?" ***The Denver Post,*** **Feb. 18, 1997, p. E1.**

"People unfamiliar with the purposes of palliative care may see little difference between sedation to control persistent physical distress and euthanasia," writes Ira Byock, president of the American Academy of Hospice and Palliative Medicine, in his new book "Dying Well: Fine line or chasm?" The debate is, as Byock puts it, not only hot but "molten."

Jack Kevorkian

Betzold, Michael, "The selling of doctor death," ***The New Republic,*** **May 26, 1997, pp. 22-28.**

Considering some of the "outlandish" positions taken by Jack Kevorkian, Betzold discusses how Kevorkian has become a national hero. Kevorkian has supported euthanasia for fetuses, infants and minor children in some circumstances, as well as experimenting on dying patients.

French, Ron, "Ionia prosecutor may seek mistrial in Kevorkian case: Lawyer concerned about fair trial

after Fieger's 'illegal opening statement,' " ***Detroit News*****, June 12, 1997, p. C1.**
After a bruising first day of courtroom theatrics by defense attorney Geoffrey Fieger, Ionia County Prosecutor Ry Voet said Wednesday he may ask for a mistrial in the assisted-suicide trial of Jack Kevorkian. The small-town prosecutor's case against Michigan's suicide doctor was left in such disarray that Voet asked for an early recess so he could consider his options.

Page, Clarence, "Whose Life Is It Anyway? Taking Physician-Assisted Suicide Away from Dr. Kevorkian," ***Chicago Tribune,*** **June 29, 1997, p. 17.**
The Supreme Court's ruling against physician-assisted suicide leaves Jack Kevorkian a lot to cheer about. The high court ruled unanimously that Americans do not have a constitutional right to physician-assisted suicide, but they gave back to the states the right of legislators to decide whether doctors should be allowed to help patients die.

Janet Good

Lessenberry, Jack, "Death and the matron," ***Esquire,*** **April 1997, pp. 80-85.**
Physician Jack Kevorkian gets all the fame and notoriety, but he is helped in his deadly labors by a cuddly grandmother, Janet Good, who has a more than passing acquaintance with the fear of an imminent, painful death. The collaboration between the two is profiled.

Storey, Kristin, "Kevorkian associate getting hospice care," ***Detroit News,*** **June 5, 1997, p. C1.**
Janet Good, an associate of assisted-suicide advocate Jack Kevorkian, is using hospice care at home to relieve pain from pancreatic cancer. Good, 73, hasn't decided whether to seek her friend's help to die. "I believe I have quality time yet," she said from her house in Farmington Hills, Mich.

Karen Anne Quinlan

Kamisar, Yale, "It started with Quinlan: The ever expanding 'Right to Die,' " ***Human Life Review,*** **summer 1996, pp. 33-36.**
Kamisar analyzes the changing and evolving idea of a "right to die" by contrasting the recent 9th Circuit Court of Appeals decision regarding euthanasia with the New Jersey Supreme Court decision regarding the now famous case of Karen Ann Quinlan.

Stevens, M. L. Tina, "What Quinlan can tell Kevorkian about the right to die," ***Humanist,*** **March 1997, pp. 10-14.**
In the two decades since Karen Ann Quinlan went into a coma, never to regain consciousness, her case has been mistakenly viewed as the beginning of the right-to-die movement. Stevens examines how the death with dignity debate moved from the hospital to the courtroom.

Nancy Cruzan

Poor, Tim, "Supreme Court Hands Down Landmark Rulings on The Way We Choose to die," ***St. Louis Post-Dispatch,*** **June 27, 1997, p. A1.**
Terminally ill people do not have a broad, constitutional right to doctor-assisted suicide, the Supreme Court ruled on Thursday. The ruling answered a question not directly addressed by the Supreme Court's 1990 finding that Nancy Cruzan, a Missouri woman in a vegetative state, had a right to refuse medical treatment. Challengers to the state laws said doctor-assisted suicide was essentially the same thing, but the justices disagreed. In the Cruzan case, the justices found that individuals had a right to withhold medical treatment, but they upheld Missouri laws that limited the practice.

Physician-Assisted Suicide

"Doctors seek suicide vote," ***The Guardian,*** **June 30, 1997, p. 6.**
Doctors are to call for a ballot to test the views of the profession on whether health staff should be allowed to help dying patients commit suicide. The move is likely to split the annual conference of the British Medical Association, meeting in Edinburgh this week, with many doctors arguing there is little difference between euthanasia and physician-assisted suicide and both should stay banned.

"Physician-assisted suicides threaten blacks," ***Chicago Defender,*** **April 22, 1997, p. 11.**
An editorial applauds Congress for sending a bill to President Clinton that effectively bars the national government from financing physician-assisted suicide, saying it won't stop assisted suicides, but it will stop the federal government from financing them.

Reed, Christopher, "Justices block euthanasia," ***The Guardian,*** **June 27, 1997, p. 14.**
In a day of important rulings, the U.S. Supreme Court yesterday blocked terminally ill patients' right to doctor-assisted suicide. It refused to establish a new constitutional right for mentally competent and terminally ill patients to choose to die with dignity with the help of a doctor. In a unanimous judgment, the court cited 700 years of Anglo-American laws to discourage suicide. It said individual states had the right to enact legislation to make it a crime to help a patient die.

Schrader, Ann, "Unanimous vote a shocker even if decision itself isn't," ***The Denver Post,*** **June 27, 1997, p. A23.**
Delegates attending the American Medical Association meeting in Chicago, Ill., burst into applause and cheers Thursday when the U.S. Supreme Court ruled that physician-assisted suicide is not a constitutional right.

Back Issues

Great Research on Current Issues Starts Right Here . . . Recent topics covered by The CQ Researcher are listed below. Before May 1991, reports were published under the name of Editorial Research Reports.

FEBRUARY 1996
Reforming the CIA
Campaign Finance Reform
Academic Politics
Getting Into College

MARCH 1996
The British Monarchy
Preventing Juvenile Crime
Tax Reform
Pursuing the Paranormal

APRIL 1996
Centennial Olympic Games
Managed Care
Protecting Endangered Species
New Military Culture

MAY 1996
Russia's Political Future
Marriage and Divorce
Year-Round Schools
Taiwan, China and the U.S.

JUNE 1996
Rethinking NAFTA
First Ladies
Teaching Values
Labor Movement's Future

JULY 1996
Recovered-Memory Debate
Native Americans' Future
Crackdown on Sexual Harassment
Attack on Public Schools

AUGUST 1996
Fighting Over Animal Rights
Privatizing Government Services
Child Labor and Sweatshops
Cleaning Up Hazardous Wastes

SEPTEMBER 1996
Gambling Under Attack
The States and Federalism
Civic Journalism
Reassessing Foreign Aid

OCTOBER 1996
Political Consultants
Insurance Fraud
Rethinking School Integration
Parental Rights

NOVEMBER 1996
Global Warming
Clashing Over Copyright
Consumer Debt
Governing Washington, D.C.

DECEMBER 1996
Welfare, Work and the States
The New Volunteerism
Implementing the Disabilities Act
America's Pampered Pets

JANUARY 1997
Combating Scientific Misconduct
Restructuring the Electric Industry
The New Immigrants
Chemical and Biological Weapons

FEBRUARY 1997
Assisting Refugees
Alternative Medicine's Next Phase
Independent Counsels
Feminism's Future

MARCH 1997
New Air Quality Standards
Alcohol Advertising
Civic Renewal
Educating Gifted Students

APRIL 1997
Declining Crime Rates
The FBI Under Fire
Gender Equity in Sports
Space Program's Future

MAY 1997
The Stock Market
The Cloning Controversy
Expanding NATO
The Future of Libraries

JUNE 1997
FDA Reform
China After Deng
Line-Item Veto
Breast Cancer

JULY 1997
Transportation Policy
Executive Pay
School Choice Debate
Aggressive Driving

AUGUST 1997
Age Discrimination
Banning Land Mines
Children's Television
Evolution vs. Creationism

Back issues are available for $5.00 (subscribers) or $10.00 (non-subscribers). Quantity discounts apply to orders over ten. To order, call Congressional Quarterly Customer Service at (202) 887-8621.

Binders are available for $18.00. To order call 1-800-638-1710. Please refer to stock number 648.

Future Topics

- ***Mental Health Policy***
- ***Mexico's Future***
- ***Youth Fitness***

THE CQ Researcher

PUBLISHED BY CONGRESSIONAL QUARTERLY INC.

Mental Health Policy

Are Americans with mental illness adequately protected?

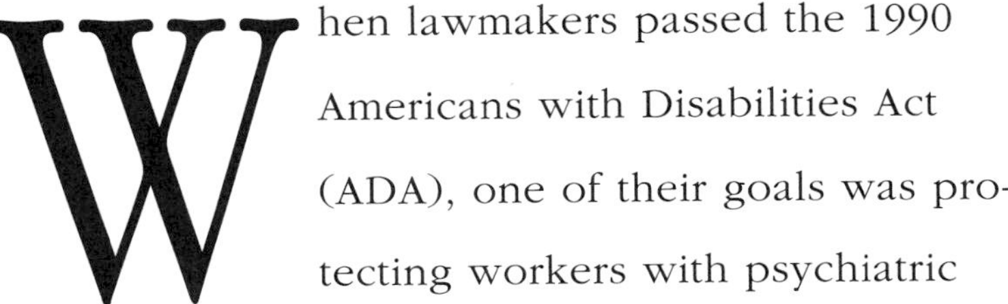

When lawmakers passed the 1990 Americans with Disabilities Act (ADA), one of their goals was protecting workers with psychiatric impairments from job discrimination. But many employers have been confused by the law, or hostile to it. This spring, to clarify the ADA, guidelines detailing employers' rights and responsibilities under the ADA were issued by the Equal Employment Opportunity Commission. Mental health advocates praise the rules, but business groups say they invite frivolous and costly lawsuits. The debate is part of a larger controversy over mental health policy that includes insurance "parity" for mental illness. Advocates say parity offers civil-rights protection for the mentally ill. Critics charge it intrudes on free enterprise.

INSIDE THIS ISSUE

CQ Sept. 12, 1997 • Volume 7, No. 34 • Pages 793-816

Formerly Editorial Research Reports

THE ISSUES

BACKGROUND

CURRENT SITUATION

OUTLOOK

SIDEBARS AND GRAPHICS

FOR FURTHER RESEARCH

COVER: REGINA DUVALL, WHO HAS A BRAIN DISORDER, IS EMPLOYED BY THE NATIONAL ALLIANCE FOR THE MENTALLY ILL IN ARLINGTON, VA. (NAMI)

THE CQ Researcher

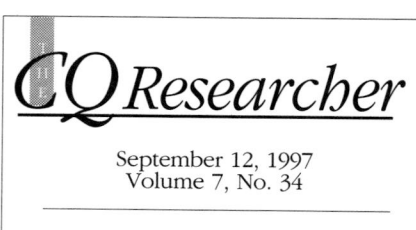

September 12, 1997
Volume 7, No. 34

The CQ Researcher (ISSN 1056-2036). Formerly Editorial Research Reports. Published weekly, except Jan. 3, May 30, Aug. 29, Oct. 31, by Congressional Quarterly Inc., 1414 22nd St., N.W., Washington, D.C. 20037. Annual subscription rate for libraries, businesses and government is $340. Additional rates furnished upon request. Periodicals postage paid at Washington, D.C., and additional mailing offices. POSTMASTER: Send address changes to The CQ Researcher, 1414 22nd St., N.W., Washington, D.C. 20037.

Mental Health Policy

BY THOMAS J. BILLITTERI

THE ISSUES

Leslie Mendez seemed to have everything the Peace Corps could want in a volunteer. She spoke two foreign languages and graduated with honors from Brown University with a degree in environmental studies.

But after initially inviting the San Francisco woman to serve as an environmental educator in Panama, the corps changed its mind. The reason? Shortly before leaving for Central America in 1995, she told a Peace Corps nurse she was taking anti-depression medication.

"They said I had to be off [Zoloft] for a year and have verification that I wouldn't need it," she recalls.

Mendez charged the Peace Corps with discrimination, and in February a U.S. District Court ordered the agency to reconsider her application. *

"I'm not asking for special treatment," says Mendez, now 26. "I was accepted based on everything I did — socially, academically, workwise. The only reason I was rejected was the fact that I use an anti-depressant."

Peace Corps spokesman Brendan Daly says the corps never rejected Mendez but only "deferred" her service "until she didn't need medication or counseling." Now, he says, federal guidelines about anti-depressants have been eased, but he declines to speculate on whether Mendez will be reinstated.

Not everyone with a mental disability encounters such hurdles.

Irene Wozny, an attorney for the state of Maryland, says depression has caused her personal pain and professional upheaval throughout her life. But five years ago Wozny found a measure of relief in anti-depressant medication. Even so, she says, "There have been several times when I was going sort of downhill with my mood disorder." When that happens at work, she says, "I'm not as productive, and some of the more complex tasks are more difficult to think through."

Yet Wozny, 40, considers herself "extremely lucky" because her boss and co-workers accept her illness.

For example, when she had the chance to receive an experimental treatment at the National Institute of Mental Health — which meant being up to two hours late for work for a month — her boss said no problem, just make up the time at the end of the day.

And when Wozny's depression affects her at work, she says, "I can discuss that here freely in the same way someone would say, 'I've got this splitting headache' or 'my arthritis is acting up.' I don't have to worry about what people think. It's one of the best things that has happened to me."

The 1990 Americans with Disabilities Act (ADA) was designed to give disabled workers — including those with a mental impairment — a fair shake on the job. The law requires employers to take "reasonable" steps to accommodate disabled workers as long as it doesn't create an "undue hardship" on the employer. [1]

A "disability" is defined under the law as an impairment that "substantially limits" one or more "major life activities," such as learning, interacting with others and performing manual tasks.

But since the ADA's employment provisions began taking effect in 1992, many employers — confused by the law or hostile to it — have been more inclined to install wheelchair ramps and Braille elevator controls than to adjust for depression or obsessive-compulsive disorder.

Seeking to encourage greater ADA compliance, the Equal Employment Opportunity Commission (EEOC) this spring spelled out the rights and responsibilities of employers. The 40 pages of controversial and far-reaching rules do not protect every emotional bump and bruise in the workplace — an employee distressed over the breakup of a romance would not be protected, nor would one prone to workplace violence. And employers are not required to lower standards to comply with the ADA.

But they may have to bend company rules to accommodate an executive on psychiatric medication or a warehouse worker prone to anti-social behavior. And they should know that someone who asks for time off because he's "depressed and stressed" may merit protection. (*See story, p. 798.*)

Mental health advocates hail the guidelines as vital in protecting a vulnerable and oppressed social minority. In recent years, science has discovered biological sources for many psychiatric ills and effective treatments for everything from depression to schizophrenia, the advocates point out. Yet, they argue, qualified workers with mental illness

* Mendez sued under a precursor of the 1990 Americans with Disabilities Act, the Rehabilitation Act of 1973, which bars discrimination against persons with mental or physical disabilities who participate in federally funded programs.

Mental Illness in the United States

*Roughly a quarter of Americans age 18 and over have some type of mental impairment, but less than 3 percent, or about 7 million persons, suffer from severe mental disorders. **

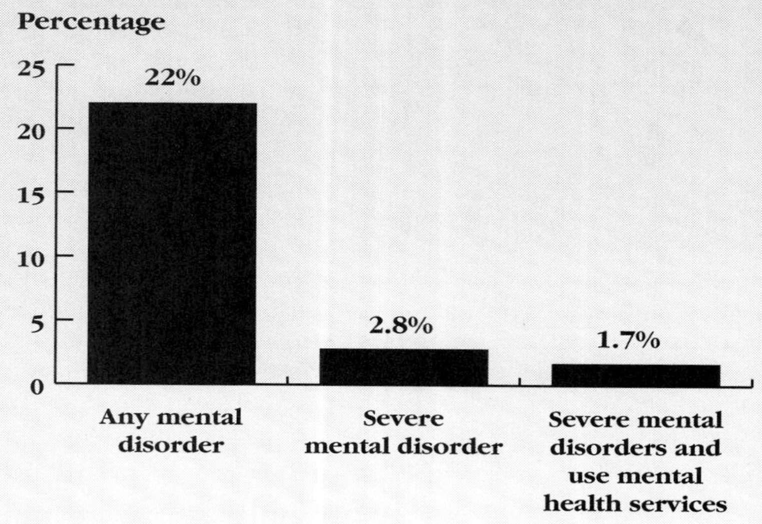

* *Severe mental illness includes schizophrenia, manic-depressive illness (bipolar disorder), major depression and obsessive-compulsive disorder.*

Note: Although data are based on a survey conducted from 1980-85, they are in the same range as data from more recent studies, such as the 1992 National Comorbidity Survey sponsored by the National Institute of Mental Health.

Sources: National Advisory Mental Health Council, "Parity in Coverage of Mental Health Services in an Era of Managed Care," April 1997; unpublished data from the National Institute of Mental Health Epidemiologic Catchment Area program

often encounter blatant discrimination in the workplace.

"There's finally a recognition that mental disabilities deserve the same accommodations as physical disabilities," says Mary Giliberti, an attorney at the Bazelon Center for Mental Health Law in Washington.

Phil Kosak, co-founder of Carolina Fine Snacks, in Greensboro, N.C., and a member of the President's Committee on Employment of People with Disabilities, regularly hires people with mental and physical disabilities. "When individuals apply for a job, you focus on what they are able to do," he says. "For some strange reason, an employer has a tendency to focus on what they can't do. It makes no sense. Everybody has limitations."

But many employers see things differently. What, exactly, is a "mental illness," they ask, when the definition has grown over the years to include everything from "narcissistic personality disorder" to "disruptive behavior disorder." [2]

What if a boss can't tell the difference between a depressed worker and a lazy one? And with 22 percent of the U.S. adult population suffering from a mental disorder in any given year, do all who are working merit an accommodation? [3]

"The EEOC guidelines on psychiatric disability are close to being a farce," business commentator Dan Seligman wrote in *Forbes*. "Employers hit with ADA suits will find themselves playing a game in which the rules are unclear and just about all the cards are wild." [4]

The ADA's approach is a "bad idea for everybody's freedom," adds Walter Olson, a senior fellow at the Manhattan Institute and author of the new book *The Excuse Factory: How Employment Law is Paralyzing the American Workplace.* "At a minimum [policy-makers] should be going back to the drawing board."

The controversy over the newly detailed ADA is part of the larger — and equally contentious — debate raging in recent months over mental health policy. Last September, Congress for the first time mandated a limited form of insurance "parity" for mental illness. Sponsored by Sens. Pete V. Domenici, R-N.M., and Paul Wellstone, D-Minn., who both have had close family members with serious mental illness, the Mental Health Parity Act requires medical plans at all but the smallest firms to provide equal annual and lifetime benefits for mental as well as physical health problems. In the past, insurance policies typically have capped lifetime mental health payouts at about $50,000 while paying $1 million or more for serious physical ailments such as cancer and heart disease.

"Not treating mental illness costs the United States — and business — tens of billions of dollars every year in the form of increased general health-care costs, lost wages, reduced productivity and increased jail and prison costs," Wellstone argues. [5]

Many business owners argue that federal efforts to mandate parity are an inappropriate intrusion into the nation's private enterprise system. "Washington is opening the door for hundreds of other mandates waiting in the wings," says Dan Danner, vice president of federal government relations for the National Federation of Independent Business (NFIB). "This [parity bill] is an effort by some to put a Clinton-type health-care plan together piece by piece." [6]

Neither the new ADA guidelines nor the insurance parity measure marks an unlimited victory for those with psychiatric ills. In recent years, many courts have ruled in favor of employers in ADA mental health cases. And the insurance measure, which takes effect next year (and terminates in 2001 under a built-in "sunset" provision) falls far short of the full parity that advocates hope for. For example, insurers can still require consumers to pay higher out-of-pocket co-payment fees for mental care than for treatment of physical ailments, and they can limit the number of patient visits for psychiatric services. Moreover, employers whose health premiums rise more than 1 percent because of parity are exempt. And they can escape the parity mandate altogether by refusing to offer any mental health insurance whatsoever.

Even with such limitations, there are signs that barriers against mental illness are falling faster than at any time in history. More than a dozen states have passed or are considering mental health parity measures of their own. (*See map, p. 800.*) And this summer, Domenici and Wellstone succeeded in extending limited parity to uninsured children.

"Science has really advanced in looking at mental illness, both in terms of the ability to treat it in a lot of cases and, increasingly, in terms of the gray line that exists between mental and physical illness," says Dennis Shea, associate professor of health policy and administration at Pennsylvania State University. "As a result, I sense in society a lot more willingness not to marginalize people with mental illness."

Even so, psychiatric disorders pose special challenges in the realms of work and insurance. More than a third of all Americans who suffer from severe mental disorders have no private insurance. [7] And the National Mental Health Association says 96 percent of insurance plans provide "inferior coverage" for mental illness compared with other maladies.

What's more, persons with emotional or mental disabilities often find employers' doors closed. A third of the people suffering from severe mental illness have been turned down for a job for which they were qualified, according to a May 1997 survey by the National Alliance for the Mentally Ill (NAMI). Seventy percent of the respondents said they were treated as less competent when their affliction became known in the workplace. Three in four say they do not reveal their psychiatric histories on job applications.

"When I was first diagnosed, I made the mistake of telling my supervisor," one respondent wrote. "She decided I couldn't have a job I'd been doing for 10 years and demoted me."

Yet, while mental illness carries a punishing stigma, some employer groups say the new ADA guidelines are not the answer. "The EEOC blew it," says Michael Lotito, a San Francisco employment lawyer. "They could have done a much better job of trying to clarify this difficult area of the law."

A major concern of employers is that the guidelines will invite a spate of lawsuits that are especially punishing to small businesses.

Since the ADA took effect in July 1992, more than 10,000 complaints involving alleged emotional and psychiatric impairments have been filed with the EEOC, second only to back problems. (*See graph, p. 806.*) Perhaps 90 percent of those complaints were dismissed for lack of evidence or other reasons, and many of the rest were settled out of court through conciliation, according to Chris Kuczynski, assistant legal counsel for the EEOC and director of the ADA policy division. But that record does little to soothe some employer groups.

"A small-business owner still has to spend thousands in legal fees putting a defense together for one of these suits, even though it very likely will be dismissed as frivolous," says Mary Reed, an NFIB lobbyist.

Kuczynski defends the guidelines, saying they are meant to reduce confusion over the law and cut down on frivolous suits. Accommodating employees with mental illness often is neither expensive nor difficult to do, he adds. And he disagrees with critics who think the new guidelines need revision.

"Psychiatric disabilities are as real as physical ones, and accommodations are necessary for people to do their jobs," he says.

The controversy over mental health policy reflects the ongoing debate over the proper role of government in addressing social problems. Some mental health advocates approach mental illness as a civil-liberties issue, referring to "parity" in language reminiscent of the civil rights movement.

Continued on p. 799

The New ADA Guidelines at a Glance

Employers say the new guidelines for the Americans with Disabilities Act (ADA) are vague and confusing. Mental health advocates say they are a boon for persons with mental disabilities.

Here are selected key provisions of the 40-page guidelines, including examples offered by the Equal Employment Opportunity Commission (EEOC):

• **Disability:** ADA covers major illnesses such as depression, bipolar disorder, obsessive-compulsive and post-traumatic stress disorders, schizophrenia and personality disorders. But some behaviors or problems listed in the American Psychiatric Association's *Diagnostic and Statistical Manual of Mental Disorders* are not covered, including use of illegal drugs and marital problems. Employees complaining of stress, irritability, chronic lateness or poor judgment would be covered if the problem were related to a disabling mental or physical impairment.

ADA covers impairments that "substantially limit" a "major life activity," such as learning, concentrating, interacting with others, caring for oneself, speaking, sleeping or working. To establish a psychiatric disability, a person does not always have to show that working itself has been limited.

Example: An employee distressed by the breakup of a relationship continued his daily routine but sometimes became agitated at work. He sought counseling, and his mood improved within weeks. His counselor diagnosed "adjustment disorder" and stated that the employee was not expected to experience any long-term problems associated with the breakup. While the employee has an impairment (adjustment disorder), it was viewed as short-term, did not significantly restrict major life activities during that time and was not expected to have permanent or long-term effects. This employee does not have a disability under the ADA.

• **Questions about mental illness:** Employers generally cannot ask a job applicant about a history of treatment for mental illness or the existence of a mental, emotional or psychiatric disability. They can require a medical exam or inquire after a job offer is made as long as all employees in the same job category undergo the same exam or questions. An employer can ask disability-related questions before making a job offer if the applicant asks for reasonable accommodations during the hiring process itself.

Example: An applicant for a secretarial job asks to take a typing test in a quiet location rather than in a busy reception area "because of a medical condition." The employer may make disability-related inquiries at this point because the applicant's need for reasonable accommodation under the ADA is not obvious. Specifically, the employer may ask the applicant to provide documentation showing that she has an impairment that substantially limits a major life activity and that she needs to take the typing test in a quiet location because of disability-related functional limitations.

• **Request for Accommodation:** To seek a job accommodation, an employee, family member, friend, health professional or other representative merely needs to mention in "plain English" that a work change is needed because of a medical or psychological condition.

Example: An employee asks for time off because he is "depressed and stressed." The employee has requested a change at work (time off) for a reason related to a medical condition (being "depressed and stressed" may be "plain English" for a medical condition). This statement is sufficient to put the employer on notice that the employee is requesting reasonable accommodation. However, if the need for accommodation is not obvious, the employer may ask for reasonable documentation of the limitation.

• **Reasonable Accommodation:** An employer must provide a reasonable accommodation in qualifying situations unless it creates an "undue hardship."

Example: A retailer does not allow individuals working as cashiers to drink beverages at checkout stations. The retailer also limits cashiers to two 15-minute breaks during an eight-hour shift, in addition to a meal break. An employee with a psychiatric disability needs to drink beverages approximately once an hour in order to combat dry mouth, a side-effect of his psychiatric medication. The cashier requests reasonable accommodation. In this example, the employer should consider either modifying its policy against drinking beverages at checkout stations or modifying its break policy, barring undue hardship.

• **Conduct:** An employer may discipline a worker with a disability for violating a workplace conduct standard even if the conduct results from a disability. But the conduct standard must be job-related for the position in question and consistent with business necessity.

Example: An employee with a psychiatric disability works in a warehouse. He has no customer contact and does not come into regular contact with other employees. He has been increasingly disheveled and anti-social. His work, however, has not suffered. The employer's company handbook states that employees should have a neat appearance at all times. It also states that employees should be courteous to each other. When told that he is being disciplined for his appearance and treatment of co-workers, the employee explains that his appearance and demeanor have deteriorated because of his disability. The dress courtesy rules are not job-related for the position in question because this employee has no customer contact and does not come into regular contract with other employees. Therefore, rigid application of these rules to this employee would violate the ADA.

Source: Equal Employment Opportunity Commission, "Enforcement Guidance: The Americans with Disabilities Act and Psychiatric Disabilities," March 25, 1997.

Continued from p. 797

"Even as Rosa Parks in quiet dignity said 'NO' to discrimination" on buses in Montgomery, Ala., wrote Laura Lee Hall, a NAMI policy official, "this small victory against discrimination can be a turning point as well." [8]

But Neil Trautwein, manager of health-care policy for the U.S. Chamber of Commerce, says "government should [not] be involved in [prescribing] health coverage, defining what should be included in health plans and what the mix of benefits should be. The private-sector marketplace should decide."

Penn State's Shea finds "a little truth" in all the arguments. "A lot of basic economic theory tells you there are some real [cost] problems in insuring mental health care," he says. "But at the same time, there are some civil liberties issues. Mental illness is an illness, with underlying biological bases firmly established." However, in the final analysis, he says, "Treating mental illness differently from any other disease doesn't have any foundation any more."

As the debate over mental health policy continues, these are some of the key questions being asked:

Do the new ADA guidelines help or hurt business?

To business interests wary of the EEOC's new policies, Laurie M. Flynn, executive director of NAMI, offers assurances that people with "love-life problems" or "bad-hair days" aren't shielded by the ADA. "The EEOC guidelines are designed for employers or potential employers of people with diagnosable brain disorders, not for those who have problems with everyday life," she wrote. [9]

Such assurances have not quelled the furor over the new rules. "This is fraught with undesirable pitfalls," says Don Livingston, a Washington lawyer and former EEOC general counsel. "It calls on employers to make enigmatic distinctions between personality traits and personality disorders. Mental-health professionals often find this an impossible task, and now it's being put before factory supervisors." [10] (*See "At Issue," p. 809.*)

Some management groups say the problems begin with the ADA itself — specifically, the law's sweeping language governing workplace disability issues. In a recent American Management Association survey of human-resource managers, more than one-fourth of the respondents said concerns over interpreting such terms as "reasonable accommodation" and "undue hardship" pose major obstacles to compliance.

Reed says those obstacles are especially daunting for small-business owners without sophisticated legal departments. The legal definition for undue hardship is an action requiring significant difficulty or expense, Reed says. The notion that an employer doesn't have to accommodate a disability if it would create an undue hardship "sounds great, but small-business owners want to know, is [spending] $1,000 enough? $5,000? $15,000? The ADA is so vague that small-business owners will never know if they've obeyed the law until they wind up in court."

Others complain that the ADA doesn't contain definitive lists of mental disabilities or "major life activities." However, the new guidelines say that for some people mental impairment may restrict "learning, thinking, concentrating, interacting with others, caring for oneself, speaking, performing manual tasks . . . working" and even "sleeping."

Critics also say the law's language on certain traits and behaviors is confusing. The guidelines state, for example, that stress "is not automatically a mental impairment" but "may be shown to be related to a mental or physical impairment. Similarly, traits like irritability, chronic lateness and poor judgment are not, in themselves, mental impairments, although they may be linked to mental impairments."

Critics also say the ADA — and specifically the EEOC's mental-disability guidelines — makes it too easy for employees to wrest accommodations from management. A passing comment from a worker or spouse that the employee is "depressed and stressed" could be enough, they say, to put an employer on notice that an accommodation is being requested, though the employer can seek documentation if the need for accommodation isn't obvious.

"Who doesn't use a phrase like that once in a while?" asks Barry Newman, a business consultant. Managers would have to be "very careful with that person" because they have "been put on notice that [the worker] may have a disability." [11] "Employers practically have to be mind readers to pick up on every offhand remark," Reed adds.

"Without a paper trail," the NFIB complains, "the case becomes the word of the employer against the word of the employee, and renders the employer defenseless." [12] And even a note from a physician or other professional saying, for example, that an employee is "depressed" may be inaccurate, either because it's a mistaken diagnosis or because the doctor is trying to help the patient meet the legal requirements of the ADA, says Jeffrey P. Kahn, a New York psychiatrist and executive consultant. A correct diagnosis "requires someone who is very well-trained and being very careful. It's not a blood test, and it's not a self-report."

In addition, some management advocates complain that the ADA guidelines could conflict with other federal workplace mandates — and that the EEOC should have made that clear. Consider a worker who seeks time off for job-related stress but whose employer doesn't think the

States With Mental Health Parity Laws

Twelve states — including five that enacted laws this year — require employers to provide "parity," or equal health insurance benefits for treatment of mental and physical problems.

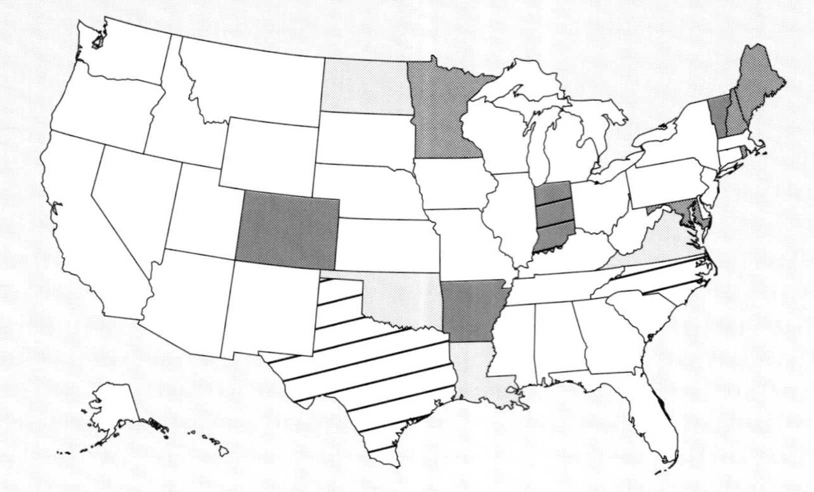

Parity Laws Enacted in 1997
Arkansas — Covers serious mental illness
Colorado — Covers serious mental illness
Connecticut — Covers biologically based mental illness
Indiana — Covers states employees only
Vermont — Requires parity for mental illness, alcohol and substance abuse

Parity Laws Enacted Before 1997
Maryland — Covers mental illness and drug abuse (1994)
New Hampshire — Covers biologically based mental illness (1994)
Rhode Island — Covers biologically based mental illness (1994)
Maine — Covers biologically based mental illness (1995)
Minnesota — Covers all mental disorders and substance abuse (1995)

Parity Laws Applicable to State Employees Only
Indiana — Covers states employees only, applies to mental health services (1997)
North Carolina — Covers state employees only, applies to mental illness and chemical dependency (1995)
Texas — Covers state employees only, applies to biologically based mental illness (1991)

Resolutions Adopted to Study Parity Laws
Louisiana (1996)
North Dakota (1995)
Oklahoma (1996)
Virginia (1995)

Source: American Managed Behavioral Healthcare Association, June 3, 1997

problem is an ADA-related disability and thus denies the leave as an "accommodation." The employer could be overlooking the possibility that the stress is a serious health condition covered under the Family Medical Leave Act (FMLA), which entitles workers in companies with more than 50 employees to up to 12 weeks of unpaid leave.

"The new EEOC . . . guidelines don't even acknowledge the existence of the FMLA," says Susan R. Meisinger, senior vice president of the Society for Human Resource Management.

Critics also note that because managers must usually keep the reason for an accommodation confidential, morale problems could surface if workers see a colleague getting special treatment. And the very definition of mental illness is problematic, they argue.

"Take a look at the American Psychiatric Association's fourth and latest (1994) edition of the *Diagnostic and Statistical Manual of Mental Disorders,*" Seligman wrote in *Forbes*. "The EEOC leans heavily on this document. In it you meet an endless array of behavior patterns that come perilously close to being synonymous with plain, old boorishness." [13]

Despite these and other complaints, some business interests view the guidelines as both reasonable and cost-effective.

"I don't think they're as onerous as some people" claim, says physician Mary Jane England, president of the Washington Business Group on Health, which represents about 170 major U.S. employers.

"The hype around the guidelines reminds me of the hype when the [ADA] was passed," says Lia Shigemura, director of affirmative action at Pacific Gas & Electric in San Francisco. "Companies feared that busloads of disabled people were going to beat down the walls seeking employment. It was not the case. What happened was that existing employees sought accommodations." [14]

As to the argument that bosses will have to make medical judgments to weigh a request for an accommodation, Kuczynski of the EEOC says, "Obviously, employers aren't doctors, but you can look at the [medical] documentation in a lot of cases and make an assessment" of whether the person actually has a disability. "I suppose that in every case you can't be 100 percent certain, but in most cases you can make an informed judgment."

While the EEOC guidelines are too new for researchers to assess fully, studies suggest that in most cases workplace accommodations are neither costly nor difficult to make. A three-year study of ADA implementation at Sears, Roebuck & Co. found that the average cost of providing workplace accommodations to employees with either a physical or behavioral impairment was only $45.

A 10-state study last year by the Matrix Research Institute in Philadelphia examined the reports of "job coaches," who are trained to assist employees with psychiatric disabilities. The study found that 58 percent of job accommodations cost nothing, and another 32 percent ran less than $100. The most common accommodation: an employer's use of a job coach to facilitate communications and problem-solving in the workplace. Other typical adjustments included flexible work schedules, "positive feedback as well as corrective criticism" and assigning job tasks gradually, rather than all at once.

Robert Drake, a research psychiatrist at Dartmouth Medical School, studied about 1,000 employees with psychiatric disabilities, most in entry-level jobs. While some had trouble adjusting to the social environment of the workplace, he says, few had problems with the work itself. And demands on bosses were minor, usually involving adjustments in work hours. The employees "seem to be satisfied with their jobs, do a good job and last in their jobs as long as other workers do," Drake says.

Kosak, the snack-food manufacturer, acknowledges the wariness of business owners over the workplace rules. "Business is bombarded with asinine regulations," he says. Employers are "very regulation-sensitive." But the guidelines on mental disability make sense, he says, not only as a way to make life fairer for people with psychiatric problems but also as a vehicle for bringing qualified people into the work force.

As to charges that the EEOC's new policy is ambiguous, Kosak says, "It's purposely vague because the goal was to make it a piece of legislation in spirit, not just in the letter of the law. The authors were wise enough to realize you cannot legislate humanity."

Should there be full insurance parity for mental health?

In June, Gov. Howard Dean, D-Vt., signed what has been called the nation's most comprehensive state parity law. By equalizing insurance coverage not only for mental and physical disorders but also for treatment of drug and alcohol abuse, "This bill begins to end the stigma in our society around mental illness and substance abuse," declared Dean, a medical doctor. "Illness of the brain should be treated just like illness of any other organ." [15]

Dean's comment points to one of the major rationales for mental health parity: that it's the moral and ethical thing to do. But parity advocates also focus on the financial bottom line.

Treating mental illness "not only saves lives, it also saves dollars that could otherwise be spent in other areas of health care, education, criminal justice and social services," Sen. Wellstone wrote. "Limits on access have resulted in shifting both the responsibility and the cost of care onto the public mental health system. For children and adolescents, the burden and cost of care also have been shifted to the child welfare, education and juvenile justice systems. Even worse, sometimes these overburdened systems are not able to provide needed services." [16]

Backers also say parity saves employers money because psychiatric illnesses get treated before they turn into costlier physical maladies or workplace behavior problems. A study in 1993 by the Analysis Group and MIT's Sloan School of Management showed that more than half of the $44 billion spent annually on depression is borne by employers in the form of absenteeism and impaired productivity. Yet experts say depression can be effectively treated in 80 percent of cases. [17] First Chicago NBD, a major bank-holding company, reported paid medical claims for depressive disorders of $927,000 in 1991, almost as much as was paid for heart disease that year, $1.2 million. [18]

"Even if you don't want to encourage a lot of ancillary therapy, what you don't want to do is leave people with serious mental illness without any coverage," says Linda Blumberg, a senior research associate at the Urban Institute and a former health-care adviser to the Clinton administration. "There is some evidence that if you don't provide comprehensive coverage of serious mental illness, utilization of other health-care services may increase."

Still, while advocates say parity makes good sense, many argue it is practical only through managed care, which delivers health care through health maintenance organizations (HMOs) and other systems that are closely monitored and controlled.

Managed care in the United States now covers about 75 percent of all workers, but the quality and availability of care it delivers remain hotly debated. [19] *(See story, p. 804.)*

The National Advisory Mental Health Council said this year that recent findings suggest that in combination with managed care, mental health parity results in "lowered costs and lower premiums (or, at most, very modest cost increases)" within a year of implementation. [20]

Yet researchers point to a dilemma that constantly dogs the issue of parity. Without managed care, parity may be impractical because use of mental health services would undoubtedly balloon beyond insurers' ability or willingness to pay. Take away the controls, they say, and psychiatrists' couches would be filled with what critics call the "worried well."

But the flip side is that under managed care, access to needed services could be severely limited or replaced with cheaper, faster or less personalized approaches, such as drug therapy alone.

"You can enact full parity tomorrow, and all that would happen is that every insurance company would turn to managed care" to hold down costs, says Chris Koyanagi, director of legislative policy at the Bazelon Center for Mental Health Law. What is needed, she says, is "another round of national debate" on how to protect people who are the "most seriously disordered or obviously disabled" from psychiatric illness, but curb the high costs associated with overuse of the mental-health system.

"Eventually we will have to find some solution to the problem of access," Koyanagi says. "We can't continue to rely on private employers to be the guarantor of access to health care in this country."

England of the Washington Business Group on Health supports "full and comprehensive" parity within a managed-care environment. "There's no way we can justify parity in an open-ended indemnity product," she says. But she does not think the best way to accomplish parity is through legislation. If the federal government and individual states mandate various levels of mental health benefits, consumers will be confused and inequities will occur, she says.

Instead, England wants "national quality standards" established by both private industry and government that set "outcomes without saying how it should be done or what the benefit should look like." Those decisions would be left to employers and their medical providers.

For example, she says, General Electric Co. and Digital Equipment Corp. impose their own benchmarks for quality care. In 1991, Digital implemented demanding HMO performance standards, which, the manufacturer says, "have become the cornerstone of the company's approach to managed care." [21]

But free-market advocates resist any form of intervention in the benefit process, whether through parity legislation or national standards. "We're reluctant to accept national standards," says Trautwein of the Chamber of Commerce. "It's the kind of thing where one size doesn't fit all. While we recognize this would allow for more local variation, we are suspicious of national standards developed by the very advocacy groups that have been pushing these concepts in the first place."

The Chamber and many other business groups are concerned about the cumulative cost effect of federal and state insurance parity laws, and they fear the Domenici-Wellstone measure is only the first step in a progression of mental health mandates.

"Whether it's a single 10 percent increase or 10 mandates with a 1 percent increase apiece, business simply can't afford to purchase the Frankenstein monster on the shelf cobbled together at the state and federal level," Trautwein says.

"What really bothers me," he adds, "is the fact that [backers of government mandates] are all too willing to advocate their particular cause — be it mental health parity, maternity hospital stay, mastectomy hospital stay, you name it. I wish the same groups would help the business community concentrate on making coverage more affordable so we can use competition to increase the benefits mix. With each additional mandate, you rob the system of flexibility and add cost. That model has not been helpful or effective." ■

BACKGROUND

Social Stigma

In the late 19th century, Sigmund Freud, the Austrian neurologist, began his pioneering explorations of the unconscious mind. By the 1930s, other scientists were expanding on his findings and uncovering physical links to mental illness.

And in the 1940s, concern over the psychiatric needs of soldiers returning from World War II prompted new federal efforts to improve mental health treatment. In 1945, for example, Congress created the National Institute of Mental Health and bolstered efforts to train psychiatrists and other mental health workers.

In the 1950s and '60s, at the same time that hospitals were becoming overcrowded with the mentally ill, new drugs to treat psychosis and depression were hitting the market. The result was a controversial move to release thousands of mentally ill patients into their communities. By the late 1970s, many observers — including President Jimmy Carter's Mental Health Commission — were

Continued on p. 804

Chronology

1890s *Sigmund Freud begins exploring the unconscious mind, shaping the treatment of mental illness for generations to come.*

1895
Freud and Josef Breuer publish *Studies in Hysteria*, detailing their "talking cure," often seen as the beginning of psychoanalysis. Breuer, a pioneer in therapeutic hypnosis, backs away after sexuality becomes the centerpiece of Freud's explorations of neurosis.

1930s-1940s *Scientists discover physical links to mental illness. Concern over the psychiatric needs of returning World War II veterans spurs new federal efforts to improve mental health treatment.*

1945
Congress creates the National Institute of Mental Health and intensifies efforts to train psychiatrists, psychologists and social workers.

1948
Scientists at the Cleveland Clinic isolate serotonin, a neurotransmitter with multiple effects on various organ systems.

1970s *States begin to mandate minimum insurance coverage for mental illness. Few of the laws mandate catastrophic coverage for severe mental illness or addiction.*

1973
Congress passes the Rehabilitation Act of 1973, which prohibits discrimination against employees with mental disabilities in federally funded programs, foreshadowing the broader Americans with Disabilities Act (ADA).

1974
Congress enacts the Employee Retirement Income Security Act (ERISA), which exempted big, self-insured employers from state regulation.

1978
President Jimmy Carter's Mental Health Commission releases a report calling the chronically mentally disabled "politically and economically powerless" and criticizing deinstitutionalization.

1979
The National Alliance for the Mentally Ill is founded.

1980s *Scientists discover new biological links to mental illness, and promising drug treatments hit the market. A revolution in mental health insurance coverage sweeps the U.S.*

1986
Eli Lilly and Co. introduces Prozac in Belgium for treating depression. By 1997, it will have been prescribed for more than 17 million Americans.

Late 1980s
Health maintenance organizations (HMOs) and other managed-care vehicles supplant fee-for-service plans for a growing number of employees.

1990s *Congress and the states take new steps to curtail discrimination against people with mental disabilities.*

July 26, 1990
President George Bush signs the ADA, which extends to persons with mental or physical disabilities the same rights guaranteed to women and racial, ethnic and religious minorities.

Sept. 26, 1996
President Clinton signs the Mental Health Parity Act, co-sponsored by Sens. Pete V. Domenici, R-N.M., and Paul Wellstone, D-Minn.

March 25, 1997
The Equal Employment Opportunity Commission (EEOC) issues enforcement guidance on the Americans with Disabilities Act and its coverage of people with psychiatric disabilities.

June 10, 1997
Gov. Howard Dean, D-Vt., signs an insurance parity bill that covers mental health as well as substance abuse. Vermont joins a number of others states with parity laws.

July 31, 1997
A bipartisan balanced-budget accord includes a measure mandating limited mental health parity for uninsured children.

Sept. 4, 1997
Sen. Paul Wellstone, D-Minn., and Rep. Jim Ramstad, R-Minn., introduce the Substance Abuse Parity Act.

Does Managed Care Cut Mental Health Benefits . . .

On his rise to the presidency of the American Psychiatric Association in 1995, Harold Eist described managed-care systems as "greed-driven . . . sharks in a feeding frenzy" that "ravage health care for profit."

"We must never accept them," the Maryland psychiatrist declared. "We must fight them with all our resources." [1]

Eist's tough rhetoric struck a chord in the psychiatric profession, whose income and autonomy have suffered under health maintenance organizations (HMOs) and other forms of managed care. And psychiatrists aren't the only ones to bristle under the system. Critics say managed care harms the quality and availability of mental health services, damages patient-therapist relationships, promotes Big Brother-style case management and record-keeping and relies too much on short-term fixes for deep-seated emotional problems.

But that's only one side of a long and rancorous debate over the use of managed care in mental health services. Proponents of managed care, including health-care experts as well as employers and insurance companies, say that when implemented responsibly, managed care can expand access to mental health services, maximize limited medical resources and curb costly overuse by the so-called "worried well."

"Sweeping generalization in any direction isn't warranted," says Trevor Hadley, director of the Center for Mental Health Policy at the University of Pennsylvania.

Managed care grew rapidly in the 1980s and early '90s as an antidote to marketplace forces and abuses that were helping to drive the cost of medical treatment — including mental health care — to record levels.

In his 1996 book *Health Against Wealth: HMOs and the Breakdown of Medical Trust,* journalist George Anders points to "notorious" abuses in the psychiatric industry. "As many as 300,000 teenagers a year were sent to psychiatric hospitals for multiweek stays for treatment of routine adolescent problems," Anders writes. "Guidance counselors in some states were offered bonuses if they steered troubled teens toward certain for-profit hospitals. By one estimate, as many as 75 percent of teenage psychiatric patients in the early 1990s really didn't need to be hospitalized at all."

As a result of this and other abuses, Anders wrote, employers "became disgusted with psychiatrists and counselors, convinced that they put their own greed ahead of the public interest. Companies such as Xerox, IBM and *Time* discovered . . . that 10 percent or more of health-care premiums were being spent on mental illness, without any clear sign that employees and dependents needed such extensive care or were benefiting greatly from it."

To control costs, companies began setting up so-called "carve-out" arrangements — hiring outside experts to manage their workers' mental health and substance abuse treatment. "From a tiny beginning in the early 1980s, mental health management companies grew to cover 80 million people in 1993 and more than 100 million in mid-1995," Anders wrote. "Venture capitalists poured money into these businesses, convinced they had found a major growth industry. They were right."

More than 140 million people now receive mental health benefits through managed care, according to the American Managed Behavioral Healthcare Association, a trend that continues to vex many psychologists and psychiatrists. "Psychiatrists buffeted by these forces [of managed care] fight for survival and reasonable psychiatric services for their patients," Michael G. Wise, clinical professor of psychiatry at Louisiana State University School of Medicine, wrote last year. [2]

Continued from p. 802

calling deinstitutionalization a failure, and the rise of homelessness in the 1980s added further proof of its shortcomings.

Meanwhile, states pressed the private sector to take up the slack. From the late 1970s to the mid-'80s, more than a dozen states passed laws requiring medical plans to provide minimum mental-health benefits — typically 20 outpatient and 30 inpatient hospital days. [22]

Such moves helped elevate mental illness as a public issue, but the social stigma surrounding psychiatric disorders continued unabated. Depression, schizophrenia and other serious ills often were blamed on poor upbringing or moral weakness. Mood disorders continued to be dark family secrets, and parents seldom went public with demands for better or cheaper treatment options.

Changing Attitudes

Then, as the 1980s progressed, the world of mental health began to change dramatically. Scientists found new biological causes for many psychiatric ills, helping to ease the stigma surrounding mental illness. "Parents no longer had to take responsibility for the aberrant behavior" of their children, says Trevor Hadley, director of the Center for Mental Health Policy at the University of Pennsylvania. "They could come out of the closet."

The powerful consumer and family movement that resulted from such changes now is part of the advocacy establishment. NAMI, for example, formed in 1979 from a loose coalition of grass-roots family organizations,

. . . at the Expense of Needy Patients?

Yet many health-care experts argue that managed care can be better for patients than traditional fee-for-service arrangements. Much depends on the quality and financial resources of the plan, they say.

"Managed mental health care need not be judged any more inequitable than the present mental health fee-for-service system and, if anything, can be judged potentially more equitable and accountable," ethicists Philip J. Boyle and Daniel Callahan of The Hastings Center wrote in *Health Affairs*. "To the extent that managed mental health care is making, and continues to make, good-faith attempts to curb abuses, rectify ethical problems and address treatment effectiveness issues, it should prove superior on the whole to fee-for-service medicine." [3]

Under a well-funded plan, "you might actually get better care in a managed environment," Hadley says, especially for less serious illnesses such as anxiety or mild depression that respond to medication. On the other hand, he says, for some serious long-term illnesses such as schizophrenia, managed care can put a patient "at pretty good risk," though that "is variable from place to place and plan to plan."

One thing is certain, he says: If a plan is poorly funded — say it gets only $1.30 per member per month to provide mental health services — "you're going to get crappy care."

The national push for insurance parity will, if anything, spark a new boom in managed care, experts believe. Without cost controls, they say, insuring physical and mental ills at anywhere near the same levels is not financially feasible. "The data we have in managed care allowed us to convince Congress it would not break the bank to have parity," says Mary Jane England, president of the Washington Business Group on Health. "That's really important to understand."

Like England, E. Clarke Ross, executive director of the American Managed Behavioral Healthcare Association, supports parity. And he, too, argues parity won't work outside of managed care.

"We haven't figured out a way other than managed care to limit and ration mental health care efficiently," contends Ross, whose organization represents 17 managed behavioral health-care companies with more than 90 million enrollees. "If you abolish managed care, you're immediately back to Woody Allen," the actor well-known in movie lore for his daily doses of high-priced psychotherapy.

"People who want to go to a psychotherapist to improve their interpersonal relationships — that is not medically necessary," Ross says. "We can go, but we'll have to pay out of our pocket."

Still, Ross acknowledges that the realm of managed mental health care — like all of medicine — poses dilemmas. How, for example, should the medical system deal with the depression or anxiety that may arise from the death or estrangement of a loved one? The pain may not point to a diagnosable disorder, but it is woefully real all the same.

"There are a whole lot of gray areas," Ross says. "That's where public policy is required. Dealing with divorce, bereavement, a whole bunch of areas — we need a lot more clarity in public policy around those."

[1] Harold I. Eist, "Managed Care: How Does It Survive?" *Psychiatric Times*, March 1995.

[2] Michael G. Wise, "Managed Care: How Are Psychiatrists Surviving?" *Psychiatric Times*, April 1996.

[3] Philip J. Boyle and Daniel Callahan, "Managed Care and Mental Health: The Ethical Issues," *Health Affairs*, fall 1995.

now represents 165,000 individuals and families affected by mental illness.

Recalling his years as a health official in Maryland and Pennsylvania, Hadley says meetings on mental health policy in the 1970s typically consisted of two parties: "Me and the providers. By the time I left state government [in the mid-1980s], consumers and family members" were also in the room.

"Issues like ADA and parity are no longer perceived as the professionals' and provider organizations' issues but rather as real public-policy issues," Hadley adds. "It's no longer a bunch of providers pushing for parity so they get paid more. Five years ago, you couldn't get a parity bill out of committee at the federal level. It would have been like an atomic bomb."

Meanwhile, another trend was unfolding in the 1980s: the controversial boom in private psychiatric hospitals. Because insurers typically offered more generous benefits for inpatient rather than outpatient psychiatric services, health-care companies launched aggressive hospital-building sprees to capture new mental health business, discouraging earlier, less costly treatment. The number of free-standing psychiatric hospitals rose 84 percent between 1984 and 1990, according to England of the Washington Business Group on Health. That made money for the hospital companies but drew angry barbs from the business community.

"The beds were filled by sophisticated marketing campaigns targeting adolescents and substance abusers," England told a congressional health subcommittee in 1993. "The result was alarming increases in employer expenditures and a large amount of unjustified and even harmful care." [23] Between 1986 and 1990, she said, as psychiatric

Discrimination Complaints Filed

*The second-largest number of discrimination complaints * filed in the past five years with the Equal Employment Opportunity Commission was from workers who alleged they had been treated unfairly because of their mental disabilities (top table). More than three-quarters of all complaints to the EEOC during the period alleged that workers had been wrongfully discharged or that their employers had failed to accommodate their impairments (bottom table).*

Impairments most often cited	Number	
Back impairments	14,639	(17.9%)
Emotional/Psychiatric Impairments	10,487	(12.8%)
Neurological Impairments	9,095	(11.1%)
Extremities	7,491	(9.2%)
Heart Impairments	3,345	(4.1%)
Diabetes	2,927	(3.6%)
Substance Abuse	2,663	(3.3%)
Hearing Impairments	2,303	(2.8%)
Blood Disorders	2,132	(2.6%)
HIV	1,451	(1.8%)
Vision Impairments	2,112	(2.6%)
Cancer	1,920	(2.4%)
Asthma	1,400	(1.7%)

Note: Percentages do not add to 100% because the list of complaints is not complete.

Violations of the Americans with Disabilities Act most often cited	Number	
Discharge	42,582	(52.2%)
Failure to provide reasonable accommodation	23,310	(28.6%)
Harassment	10,023	(12.3%)
Hiring	7,791	(9.5%)
Discipline	6,487	(8.0%)
Layoff	3,761	(4.6%)
Promotion	3,180	(3.9%)
Benefits	3,098	(3.8%)
Wages	2,830	(3.5%)
Rehire	2,736	(3.4%)
Suspension	1,840	(2.3%)

Note: Percentages add to more than 100% because individuals can allege multiple violations.

** A total of 81,595 complaints were recorded from July 26, 1992, the date the EEOC began enforcing the Americans with Disabilities Act, and March 31, 1997. Complainants were eligible to file if they felt discriminated against after applying for a job or as an employee in a private-sector firm employing at least 15 workers or by a state or local government. The filing of a complaint does not indicate whether the charge has merit.*

Source: Equal Employment Opportunity Commission

services skyrocketed, employers' costs for mental health services rose an average 50 percent. Many companies responded by chopping psychiatric benefits.

The excesses of the 1980s still color today's policy debates. Trautwein says that part of the Chamber's current resistance to mandated parity stems from "abuses in the mental health industry" in the 1980s. "There is some degree of suspicion that in an enforced-parity environment, utilization [of mental health services] would run through the roof."

New Policies

By the late 1980s and early '90s, with the insurance scene in flux and scientific advances easing some of the stigma of psychiatric illness, the stage was set for major revisions in mental health policy. First came the ADA, whose language was modeled after Section 504 of the Rehabilitation Act of 1973.

The Rehabilitation Act outlawed discrimination against persons with mental or physical impairments who participate in programs that receive federal money. Section 504 declared: "No otherwise qualified handicapped individual . . . shall, solely by reason of his handicap, be excluded from the participation in, be denied the benefits of, or be subjected to discrimination under any program or activity receiving federal financial assistance."

Over the past two decades, a number of court decisions have weighed questions raised by Section 504, including how to determine when a person with a disability is "otherwise qualified," when a "reasonable accommodation" turns into an "undue burden" and when a person with a disability presents a threat to the health or safety of others.

With the election of Ronald Reagan and the introduction of Republican control of the Senate in the early 1980s, federal officials tried to roll back civil-rights protections for disabled people, including Section 504. The move helped dash the hopes of disability-rights activists, who had been hoping to amend the landmark 1964 Civil Rights Act to include disabled persons.

By the late 1980s, amending the 1964 law was deemed impractical and possibly misguided. In light of the conservative political climate in Washington, civil rights leaders feared that reopening discussion of the Civil Rights Act might imperil protections for groups already covered by the law.

Instead, activists began to work on fashioning new anti-discrimination legislation. The ADA won approval partly because it had strong bipartisan support from a number of influential legislators and officials, including President George Bush, who had family members with disabilities.

Georgetown University law Professor Chai Feldblum, who coordinated the drafting of the Americans with Disabilities Act, says its inclusion of mental disability drew "practically no debate in the Senate," where there was strong backing from Sens. Edward M. Kennedy, D-Mass., Tom Harkin, D-Iowa, and Orrin G. Hatch, R-Utah.

Some staff members on the House Energy and Commerce Committee worried that employers would have to hire or retain unqualified workers who were mentally disabled, Feldblum recalls. In response, ADA backers called up all the relevant cases decided under Section 504 of the Rehabilitation Act to demonstrate that only qualified workers would be protected. "That was sufficient for the Energy and Commerce staff," Feldblum says.

Meanwhile, the Bush administration became concerned that violent employees with mental illness might be covered under the ADA. The law was clarified to explicitly state that a person who posed a "direct threat to the health and safety of others would not be qualified" for coverage, Feldblum says.

Insurance Parity

As the ADA was taking shape, the parity issue also was beginning to percolate, first in the Clinton administration's ill-fated medical reform initiative and later in Congress.

Some consider it a small miracle that the Domenici-Wellstone parity measure passed, even in limited form. After all, its sponsors come from opposing political parties, and Congress has had no great appetite for health-care issues since reform efforts stalled earlier in the 1990s. But a constellation of forces — including changing public attitudes — helped put parity on the books.

A survey released in June by the National Mental Health Association showed that 93 percent of Americans believe medical insurance should provide the same coverage for mental health problems as for physical ones. [24] And a 1989 study for the Robert Wood Johnson Foundation found that more than half of Americans believe that with treatment, people with mental illness can live productive lives.[25]

Besides changes in public perceptions about mental illness, a deciding factor in the parity battle seems to have been the compelling personal experiences of Domenici, Wellstone and two other senators, Alan K. Simpson, R-Wyo. (now retired), and Kent Conrad, D-N.D. During Senate hearings in spring 1996 on the Kennedy-Kassebaum health insurance reform bill, all talked of how they watched a family member or employee struggle with serious mental illness. The Senate, moved by those accounts, voted for a broad form of parity. But a flurry of private and government cost projections aroused concerns about the financial consequences of insuring mental illness on a par with physical illness, and the Domenici-Wellstone proposal failed to gain congressional approval later that summer. Parity ultimately won approval — in its current limited form — in September 1996 as part of an appropriations bill unrelated to insurance reform.

"It's not just economics," Wellstone, who grew up with a mentally ill brother, told a reporter. "It's almost as much about the stigma. Why don't insurance companies treat this as if it's diagnosable and treatable? Why don't they treat it as if it's something real?" [26]

Domenici, whose daughter has schizophrenia, told fellow senators, "If you happen to be a parent of somebody who has schizophrenia, a very serious mental disease, [you know] it did not come because somebody's mother did not take care of them properly. It is a severe disease of the brain. . . . They are just as sick as your neighbor who has cancer." [27]

Still, as the senators were reminded during their long battle over parity, reforming mental health coverage is an incremental and politically charged process, made all the more contentious by the problems afflicting the entire health-care system.

"It's hard to feel anything but sympathy for parents who have seen their children suffer," reporter Matt Cooper wrote in *The New Republic* recently. "But it's worth noting, too, that Domenici's compassion does not easily extend beyond his own family's circumstances. . . . He's hardly been as determined to make sure that the nearly 40 million Americans who don't have health insurance at all get some kind of coverage. That, it seems, can wait." [28] ■

Current Situation

Court Decisions

While the 1980s and '90s have meant big changes in mental health policy, the tough battles are far from over.

On the ADA front, juries and judges are ruling against many workers who claim to be victims of bias because of a mental disability. The EEOC "waited so long to issue its guidelines," said a recent article in *The Wall Street Journal,* "that it now faces an uphill battle to reverse court precedent." [29]

Consider the case of Randall J. Soileau. Soileau was fired as an engineer at a Maine textile firm in 1994 after being disciplined for a "negative attitude," according to *The Journal.* In a suit, he argued that depression limited his capacity to interact with others and that the company dismissed him because he requested special accommodations. Soileau had asked to be freed from conducting meetings, and his doctor said "he shouldn't be ridiculed or startled in front of co-workers," *The Journal* said. But an appellate court in Boston ruled in January that, despite his depression, Soileau wasn't legally disabled because interacting with others isn't a "major life activity" in most cases. The new ADA guidelines now categorize personal interaction as such an activity, the newspaper noted, but Soileau's case is closed. [30]

In another case, the 6th U.S. Circuit Court of Appeals ruled in August in *Parker v. Metropolitan Life Insurance Co.* that a two-year cap on long-term disability insurance benefits for people with mental disabilities does not violate the ADA, even though the same policy covers physical impairments until age 65. The 8-5 decision, which does not affect the Mental Health Parity Act, sparked sharp criticism from mental health advocates.

"If an insurer capped benefits for African-American workers but not for Hispanic workers," Giliberti of the Bazelon Center said, "courts would have no trouble finding racial discrimination because of the longstanding history of bias against African-Americans. By the same token, courts should recognize policies that cap benefits only for mental disabilities and not for physical ones as discriminatory because the policies are based on a sad history of treating people with these disabilities as second-class citizens — locking them away in institutions and denying them such basic rights as education, housing and employment." [31]

Cutting off benefits for those with mental disabilities "has been disastrous for employees, many of whom have worked for years and paid into a plan, only to have it fail them in their hour of need," says the Bazelon Center. "People have lost their homes, their savings and their self-respect because of it."

But some employers hailed the ruling. They feared they would have to change their disability plans and throw out caps on mental health benefits that they had relied on to hold down costs.

"We're all sleeping a little bit more comfortably," Barry Barnett, a benefits consultant, told *The Wall Street Journal.* [32]

Federal court rulings have given critics of the ADA disability guidelines a measure of solace. While they expect more ADA suits because of the new guidelines, they anticipate conservative decisions. "Judges have been extremely reasonable," says Lotito, the San Francisco employment lawyer. Adds Meisinger of the Society for Human Resource Management, "Courts have been much more sensitive to employers' concerns, much more pragmatic in approaching how the law would apply in the real world."

Not surprisingly, the EEOC considers that some recent cases were "incorrectly decided," Peggy R. Mastroianni, associate legal counsel at the EEOC, told *The Journal.* Still, she said, the courts are "not all against us by any means."

For groups such as the NFIB, the aim is not to kill the Americans with Disabilities Act but to make it friendlier to cash-strapped employers. What's needed now, Reed says, is a tighter definition of concepts like "disability" and "undue hardship" and revisions in the standards for "reasonable accommodation."

"Small-business owners are the ones out there already hiring people with disabilities," Reed says. "But the legal nightmare that the ADA can cause for small-business owners is enormous."

Reed says the NFIB is working quietly with some members of Congress in hope of revising the law. "We think it's important to have some kind of list of disabilities included under the ADA," she says. "It's very difficult for the small-business owner to distinguish between someone who is just lazy or whose lateness refers back to a specific mental illness. There needs to be clarity, especially on what is a disability."

Besides clearer definitions of disability, the federation wants a clear, legal standard for "accommodation," such as basing the amount to be spent on a required accommodation on the gross revenue of a business.

Continued on p. 810

At Issue:

Are the ADA guidelines on mental disabilities fair to business?

yes

Tipper Gore

Gore is an adviser on mental health policy to President Clinton and the wife of Vice President Al Gore.

FROM "RAZING WORKPLACE BARRIERS," ***THE WASHINGTON POST,*** **MAY 12, 1997**

In 1990, Congress clearly sought to eradicate employment discrimination against people with mental, as well as physical disabilities, when it passed the Americans with Disabilities Act (ADA). Although thousands of people with psychiatric disabilities are working successfully in a variety of jobs in this country, many more are denied employment opportunities because of myths, fears and stereotypes. These barriers of attitude often exclude qualified candidates from being considered for a job, and they keep people with mental disabilities from leading productive lives.

Recently, the Equal Employment Opportunity Commission (EEOC) published policy guidance to explain to private employees how they can comply with the ADA's requirements. Like the ADA itself, the EEOC's policy guidance recognizes both the rights of people with psychiatric disabilities to be free from discrimination in the workplace and the legitimate concerns of businesses that are trying to comply with the law. Unfortunately, the reaction of some in the business community to these guidelines makes it clear that the battle against the stigma associated with mental illness has not yet been won. . . .

Contrary to reports, EEOC's guide does not require that employers give special treatment to people with psychiatric disabilities. Rather, the EEOC and the ADA require employers to do for employees with psychiatric disabilities what they must do for employees with physical disabilities — make reasonable accommodations that will enable such employees to do their jobs.

Many employees with psychiatric disabilities are now working successfully without any accommodations. Others require accommodations that are relatively inexpensive and easy to provide. The ADA even provides employers a defense — "undue hardship" — when making an accommodation proves too difficult or too expensive.

Let's be clear. As I understand the rules, the ADA requires that an employee who wants to be accommodated because of his or her psychiatric disability must show that he or she falls within the legal definition of the term "disability." That employee must demonstrate to the employer — with documentation — that he or she has a disability that substantially limits one or more major life activities.

Essentially, the employee must have a serious, definable mental illness. Of course, even then, the employee is not entitled to be excused from relevant standards of conduct or from job performance standards. This is simply an issue of equality of people with mental and physical disabilities. . . .

no

National Federation Of Independent Business

FROM "NEW EEOC GUIDELINES ON THE AMERICANS WITH DISABILITIES ACT," MAY 5, 1997

The [EEOC] guidelines send a serious but confusing message from the government to employers, telling them they may not discriminate against qualified workers with mental illness, yet they may not ask job applicants if they have a history of mental illness and they must accommodate employees with psychiatric or emotional problems. . . .

Small-business owners are already overwhelmed with government rules, regulations, paperwork and taxes. The new EEOC guidelines are lengthy, confusing and dangerously vague. Additionally, they provide provisions that . . . leave them wide open to the risk and cost of frivolous litigation.

For example, the guidelines state, "Expert testimony about substantial limitation is not necessarily required. Credible testimony from the individual with a disability and his/her family members, friends or co-workers may suffice." This phrasing is full of ambiguity — "not necessarily" and "may suffice" leave plenty of room for interpretation. How is an employer to know what to do if an employee's spouse calls the office and says, "John is going through post-traumatic stress and needs a leave of absence." If John does not come to work for a month, he is protected by the ADA because his wife gave "credible testimony."

The guidelines also say that, "Requests [from the employee] for reasonable accommodation [in the workplace] do not necessarily have to be in writing. Employees may request accommodations in conversation or may use any other mode of communication." Without a paper trail, the case becomes the word of the employer against the word of the employee and renders the employer defenseless. This type of guideline is an open invitation to lawsuit abuse. . . .

Mental illness is a type of disability that is still, in many ways, a mystery to the medical community. Yet these guidelines set up an expectation that the average small-business owner should comprehend and act on the needs of the mentally ill. It may be obvious to the small-business owner that someone in a wheelchair needs a ramp to enter the building. . . . But the needs of someone who suffers from major depression or obsessive-compulsive disorder are, unfortunately, difficult to identify and implement.

Small-business owners do not maintain legal counsel or a personnel department to help them decipher their obligations under the ADA. Small-business owners are responsible and thoughtful citizens who want to comply with the law, but without specific guidance, neither Main Street business owners nor people with disabilities know what actions are expected, appropriate or legal.

Muddle America / *Gorrell & Brookins*

Continued from p. 808

It also could mean changing the ADA's enforcement system to one of arbitration, so businesses don't have to wage costly legal battles in federal court or before the EEOC.

"Obviously," Reed says, "IBM or J.C. Penney can spend a lot more money [fighting in court] than Betty's Hardware."

At present, though, structural changes in the ADA seem unlikely. Both Reed and Kuczynski say they are not aware of any new bills to revise the law. Meanwhile, the EEOC is holding firm. "Far from being vague," Kuczynski says, the new guidelines provide "a lot of additional clarity in an area where employers have had questions."

On the parity front, the big focus now is on cost. Because the Domenici-Wellstone provision applies only to aggregate lifetime and annual benefit limits, few experts expect it to have a major impact on company insurance premiums.

"I just don't think it's going to have much of an effect at all," says Richard Frank, professor of health economics at Harvard Medical School. "It's mostly symbolic."

State Initiatives

Even so, policy-makers are watching the issue closely, and some of the best clues to the future can be found in states that already mandate some form of mental health parity. For example, in Minnesota, where a strong parity law on mental health and chemical dependency took effect in 1995, early evidence suggested the cost impact would be minimal, especially in plans using managed care. One large managed-care organization, Allina Health System, reported that the state's mandate would increase costs only 26 cents per member per month. And the state reported that premiums for state employees would rise only 1-2 percent because of the mandate. [33]

But the early cost data don't necessarily tell the whole story. Julia Philips, a life and health actuary in the Minnesota Department of Commerce, notes that before the parity bill was passed, the state had already mandated minimum benefits for mental health. Thus, she points out, companies that were providing liberal benefits before parity will experience less of a financial impact than some that weren't.

Not only that, Philips says rate filings from insurance companies have been coming in 2 percent to 4 percent above last year's levels because of the parity bill. "Essentially, insurance companies are turning around and passing [the higher costs] along to policyholders," she says. "They kind of have to. The general public thinks they have pots of money lying around. They don't."

And in what may be the biggest challenge of all to state parity bills, employers may choose to self-insure. In Minnesota, many companies are opting for self-insurance, which allows a company to try to lower its costs by assuming its own insurance risks. Self-insured companies cannot escape the federal Domenici-Wellstone measure, but under the Employee Retirement Income Security Act, known as ERISA, they can sidestep state parity laws.

"In the long run, what you'll see is an erosion" in state parity coverage across the nation because of self-insurance, Philips predicts. "In Minnesota, we're already at a point where the self-funded plans have become almost the majority." ■

OUTLOOK

Expanding Benefits

Sen. Wellstone says he has only begun to fight for better mental health benefits. In early September, he and Rep. Jim Ramstad, R-Minn., introduced legislation that would require health insurance companies to pay for treatment of substance abuse at the same level that they cover other diseases. *

"Right now," Wellstone said, "even if treatment is available and accessible, it is often unaffordable .... This seems counterintuitive, given the relationship between substance use and other diseases. It would only seem logical that if we are willing to pay for the treatment of substance abuse, we would decrease costs of treatment for other diseases in the long run, as we would decrease the occurrence of those diseases that are related to substance abuse."

With major reforms in health care still an elusive goal, many policy experts say that expanding parity to new groups of consumers — especially those who abuse drugs or alcohol — will be difficult. Wellstone says that more than 10 percent of Americans suffer from alcohol or drug dependence and that hard-drug use among children is rising at an "alarming rate." But drug and alcohol abuse do not muster the same public sympathy as, say, depression or schizophrenia, he says.

Society "still bases its public policy toward alcohol and drugs more on stigma than science," Wellstone told the National Association of Drug and Alcohol Counselors in March. "As a society, we still show evidence of more judgmentalism than compassion toward those with alcohol and drug problems."

The issue clearly remains a priority for mental health advocacy groups. "Mental illness and substance abuse shouldn't be viewed as separate," says Shelley Stewart, deputy director of federal relations for the American Psychiatric Association (APA). "We would like to have substance abuse covered [by parity] in the same fashion" as other mental disorders.

Meanwhile, Wellstone and Domenici worked this summer to include a parity provision in the balanced-budget agreement that covered children. They succeeded, but as with their Mental Health Parity Act last year, they had to settle for less than their goal of full parity.

The new provision essentially requires the states to provide mental

* Similar to the Mental Health Parity bill passed last year, the proposed Substance Abuse Parity Act does not require a company to offer substance abuse treatment as part of its health-benefits package, but only requires parity for plans that already offer substance-abuse coverage.

FOR MORE INFORMATION

National Mental Health Association, 1021 Prince St., Alexandria, Va. 22314-2971; (703) 684-7722. The NMHA is a mental health consumer-advocacy organization.

National Alliance for the Mentally Ill, 200 N. Glebe Rd., Suite 1015, Arlington, Va. 22203-3754; (703) 524-7600. NAMI is a grass-roots organization serving individuals and families affected by severe mental illnesses.

Bazelon Center for Mental Health Law, 1101 15th St. N.W., Suite 1212, Washington, D.C. 20005-5002; (202) 467-5730. Founded in 1972, the center is an advocate for people with mental disabilities.

Washington Business Group on Health, 777 N. Capitol St. N.E., Suite 800, Washington, D.C. 20002; (202) 408-9320. The organization analyzes health policy and related work issues from the perspective of large employers.

Society for Human Resource Management, 606 N. Washington St., Alexandria, Va. 22314-1997; (703) 548-3440. The society, with more than 80,000 professional and student members, represents the interests of the human-resource profession.

American Managed Behavioral Healthcare Association, 700 13th St. N.W., Suite 950, Washington, D.C. 20005; (202) 434-4565. The association represents 17 organizations with 90 million enrollees that specialize in the management of mental illness and addiction disorder benefits.

U.S. Chamber of Commerce, 1615 H St. N.W., Washington, D.C. 20062-2000; (202) 659-6000. The Chamber represents the interests of U.S. businesses.

Equal Employment Opportunity Commission, 1801 L St. N.W., Washington, D.C. 20507; (202) 663-4900. This federal agency oversees job-discrimination issues.

Coalition for Fairness in Mental Illness Coverage, 1400 K St. N.W., Third Floor, Washington, D.C. 20005; (202) 682-6393. This coalition of mental health advocacy groups represents patients, families, providers and health-delivery systems.

health services for uninsured children. But it does not mandate equal co-payments and treatment limits. Rather, it provides only the same lifetime caps and annual payment limits for mental and physical health contained in the Mental Health Parity Act.

On the ADA front, the 6th Circuit's recent ruling on mental health disability benefit limits may discourage court challenges in other cases. * "We believe this decision will have a positive impact in preserving flexibility and controlling the cost of employer benefit plans," a spokesman for Metropolitan Life told *The Wall Street Journal.* [34]

But advocates for the mentally ill decried the decision. "It's an issue of fundamental fairness," Colorado psychiatrist Jeremy Lazarus, a spokesman for the APA, told *The Journal.* "It stigmatizes a group of patients that should be treated the same as everyone else."

The Bazelon Center criticized the ruling on several legal points, but staff attorney Giliberti said there was also "good news" in the fact that the court was "very divided." Giliberti also noted that another appellate court in 1994 took the "opposite view" and decided that the ADA "did cover a discriminatory insurance policy that capped AIDS-related benefits." [35]

"We hope that other courts considering the issue will be persuaded by the dissenting opinions and will recognize that discrimination against people with mental disabilities in insurance policies is unlawful under the ADA," Giliberti said.

Meisinger says many members of the Society for Human Resource Management are still learning about the ADA and the new mental health guidelines. She describes the prevailing mood among members these days as one of "wait and see." Human resource managers will "try to comply with the law, but ultimately they will do what makes the most practical common sense," she says.

"Then they call the lawyers." ■

Thomas J. Billitteri is a freelance writer in the Washington, D.C., area.

* A suit filed in early September by the EEOC against Chase Manhattan Bank in New York could have sweeping impact on the mental health benefits issue. The suit charges that the long-term disability plan offered by Chase — the nation's largest bank — violates the ADA because it limits benefits for mental illness to 18 months while employees with physical disabilities are covered until age 65.

Notes

[1] For background see "The Disabilities Act," The CQ Researcher, Dec. 27, 1991, pp. 993-1016, and "Implementing the Disabilities Act," *The CQ Researcher,* Dec. 20, 1996, pp. 1105-1128.

[2] National Advisory Mental Health Council, "Parity in Coverage of Mental Health Services in an Era of Managed Care," April 1997.

[3] *Ibid.,* p. 1449.

[4] Dan Seligman, "Accommodating absurdity," *Forbes,* June 2, 1997.

[5] Unpublished article.

[6] Press release, Sept. 19, 1996.

[7] National Advisory Mental Health Council, *op. cit.,* p. 1455.

[8] "The Scientific Case for Parity," NAMI Web page.

[9] Laurie M. Flynn, "Give the EEOC Guidelines a Chance," unpublished article, May 9, 1997.

[10] Quoted in Elizabeth Gleick, "Mental Adjustment: How Far Should Employers Go To Help Someone With a Psychiatric Illness Stay on the Job," *Time,* May 19, 1997.

[11] Quoted in Ellen Joan Pollock and Joann S. Lublin, "Employers Are Wary of Rules on Mentally Ill," *The Wall Street Journal,* May 1, 1997.

[12] Quoted in Julie Kosterlitz, "Psyched Out," *National Journal,* May 24, 1997.

[13] Seligman, *op. cit.*

[14] Quoted in *Time, op. cit.*

[15] Press release, June 10, 1997.

[16] Wellstone, *op. cit.*

[17] Mary Jane England, "The Mental Health Parity Act: Lifting Benefit Plan Limits," *HIU* magazine, published by the National Association of Health Underwriters, January 1997.

[18] Joseph Burns, "Mindful of Parity," *Human Resource Executive,* Oct. 3, 1996.

[19] National Advisory Mental Health Council, *op. cit.* For background, see "Managed Care," *The CQ Researcher,* April 12, 1996, pp. 313-336.

[20] National Advisory Mental Health Council, *op. cit.*

[21] "HMO Performance Standards," Third Edition, Digital Equipment Corp., 1997.

[22] Richard G. Frank, Chris Koyanagi and Thomas G. McGuire, "Political Economy of 'Parity' for Mental Health Insurance," *Health Affairs,* July/August 1997.

[23] Testimony before the Energy and Commerce Subcommittee on Health, Dec. 8, 1993.

[24] The survey was conducted by Opinion Research Corp. for the NMHA.

[25] Frank, Koyanagi, McGuire, *op. cit.* The study by DYG Inc. is entitled "Public Attitudes Toward People with Chronic Mental Illness."

[26] Quoted in Laura Blumenfeld, "When Politics Becomes Personal: All They Can Agree on Is the Pain of Mental Illness," *The Washington Post,* June 19, 1996.

[27] *Ibid.*

[28] *The New Republic,* May 20, 1996.

[29] Ann Davis, "Courts Reject Many Mental-Disability Claims," *The Wall Street Journal,* July 22, 1997.

[30] *Ibid.*

[31] Press release, Aug. 6, 1997.

[32] Nancy Ann Jeffrey, "Court Allows Mental Illness Benefit Caps," *The Wall Street Journal,* Aug. 5, 1997.

[33] Chris Koyanagi and Lee Carty, "Paying For Parity: A Review of Costs in Two States with Health Insurance Laws Mandating Equal Coverage of Mental Health Care," May 1996, published by the Bazelon Center for Mental Health Law. The report focuses on Minnesota and Maryland.

[34] Jeffrey, *op. cit.*

[35] The decision was *Carparts Distribution Center Inc. v. Automotive Wholesalers Association of New England Inc.*

Bibliography

Selected Sources Used

Books

Anders, George, *Health Against Wealth: HMOs and the Breakdown of Medical Trust*, Houghton Mifflin, 1996.
Anders, a writer for *The Wall Street Journal*, analyzes the appeal of managed care to employers and insurers and the dangers HMOs can pose to necessary medical treatment.

Articles

Davis, Ann, "Courts Reject Many Mental-Disability Claims," *The Wall Street Journal*, July 22, 1997.
Davis chronicles some recent ADA cases and asserts that the Equal Employment Opportunity Commission (EEOC) "faces an uphill battle" in pressing discrimination cases involving mental disabilities.

Gleick, Elizabeth, "Mental Adjustment: How Far Should Employers Go To Help Someone With A Psychiatric Illness Stay on the Job?" *Time*, May 19, 1997.
Gleick gives a useful overview of the main issues surrounding the Americans with Disabilities Act (ADA) and its application to mental disability.

Kosterlitz, Julie, "Psyched Out," *National Journal*, May 24, 1997.
Kosterlitz says that ambiguities in the ADA and the arena of mental health "have created a minefield for employers" and that the EEOC's new guidelines on the ADA "may complicate the issue even more."

Lemov, Penelope, "Legislating To Prozac," *Governing*, December 1996.
Lemov examines a growing trend among states to mandate full health-insurance coverage for mental illness.

"Mental Health in the Age of Managed Care," *Health Affairs*, fall 1995.
A series of articles by a wide array of experts forms the bulk of this issue of *Health Affairs*. Among the articles: "Managed Care and Mental Health: The Ethical Issues" and "Estimating Costs of Mental Health and Substance Abuse Coverage."

Pear, Robert, "Employers Told to Accommodate the Mentally Ill," *The New York Times*, April 30, 1997.
Pear outlines the EEOC guidelines on mental disability as they relate to the Americans with Disabilities Act. He provides a useful overview of the main concerns of employers and key reasons for support of the guidelines among mental health advocates.

Pollock, Ellen Joan, and Joann S. Lublin, "Employers Are Wary of Rules On Mentally Ill," *The Wall Street Journal*, May 1, 1997.
The authors chronicle some of the chief objections and concerns among business executives over the EEOC's new mental health guidelines.

Stolberg, Sheryl Gay, "Gray Matter — Breaks for Mental Illness: Just What the Government Ordered," *The New York Times*, May 4, 1997.
Stolberg says that underlying the EEOC's recent rules on mental disability in the workplace "is the assumption that physical illness and mental illness should be treated as one and the same." But, she asks, can they?

Reports

Blanck, Peter David, "Communicating the Americans with Disabilities Act — Transcending Compliance: 1996 Follow-up Report on Sears, Roebuck & Co," 1996.
This study sponsored by the Annenberg Washington Program examines issues surrounding implementation of the ADA at the national retailer.

***HMO Performance Standards*, Third Edition, Digital Equipment Corp., 1997.**
The big computer firm details its efforts to set quality standards for its HMOs. "The standards have become the cornerstone of the company's approach to managed care," including behavioral health care, according to Digital.

Koyanagi, Chris, and Lee Carty, "Paying For Parity: A Review of Costs in Two States with Health Insurance Laws Mandating Equal Coverage of Mental Health Care," May 1996.
This report from the Bazelon Center for Mental Health Law in Washington examines parity laws in Minnesota and Maryland.

National Advisory Mental Health Council, "Parity in Coverage of Mental Health Services in an Era of Managed Care," April 1997.
This interim report to Congress makes an initial examination of costs associated with providing equitable coverage for people with mental illness and reports on efforts by the National Institute of Mental Health to investigate managed-care arrangements relevant to mental health. An appendix contains a wealth of useful statistics on mental health.

The Next Step

Additional information from UMI's Newspaper & Periodical Abstracts™ database

Accommodation

Beck, Joan, "Accommodating Mental Illness on the Job," *Chicago Tribune,* p. 31.

Mentally disabled employees are now entitled to reasonable accommodations on the job, according to new guidelines announced last week by the Equal Employment Opportunity Commission. But how far must employers now go to accommodate mental illness on the job? The answer isn't clear, especially when it's sometimes difficult even to diagnose mental illness or to distinguish it from other emotional distress.

Kavale, Kenneth A., and Stephen R. Forness, "Learning disability grows up: Rehabilitation issues for individuals with learning disabilities," *Journal of Rehabilitation,* January 1996, pp. 34-41.

Adults with learning disabilities (LD) are now recognized as a unique and distinctive group. For some individuals with LD, postsecondary education is a transition option, but questions remain about admissions policies, degree requirements, appropriate accommodations and the nature of support services.

Americans with Disabilities Act

Atkinson, Lynn, "Insurance policies are 'goods' under ADA," *HR Focus,* February 1997, p. 14.

A federal appeals court has ruled that a disability insurance policy that treats mental and physical disabilities differently may violate the public accommodation provisions of the Americans with Disabilities Act (ADA).

Bergen, Kathy, and Stephen Franklin, "Mental Illness Regulations Are Gray Matter for Firms," *Chicago Tribune,* May 7, 1997, Sec. 3, p. 4.

New guidelines from the federal Equal Employment Opportunity Commission on applying the Americans with Disabilities Act to workers with mental illnesses are drawing mixed reactions.

"Depressed woman wins round in ADA case," *Business & Health,* December 1996, p. 15.

A federal appeals court recently ruled that Title III of the ADA is broad enough to include discrimination in the contents of insurance products.

Noe, Sue R., "Discrimination against individuals with mental illness," *Journal of Rehabilitation,* January 1997, pp. 20-26.

Noe examines negative societal and professional attitudes and discriminatory insurance practices against individuals with mental illness, including the implications of the ADA.

Pelka, Fred, "Bashing the disabled: The right-wing attack on the ADA," *Humanist,* November 1996, pp. 26-30.

The Americans with Disabilities Act was one of the most significant pieces of civil-rights legislation ever to emerge from Congress. However, despite its overwhelmingly positive impact, the ADA has become an election-year punching bag.

Equal Employment Opportunity Commission

Carter, Terry, "Unhappy to oblige," *ABA Journal,* July 1997, pp. 6-37.

Critics see too many accommodations in Equal Employment Opportunity Commission (EEOC) guidelines for managing mentally disabled workers. The controversial guidelines are discussed.

Jenkins, Holman W. Jr., "Business world: Think your co-workers are crazy? They are," *The Wall Street Journal,* May 13, 1997, p. A23.

Jenkins comments on new EEOC guidelines regarding the Americans with Disabilities Act and mental illness, pointing to trouble the new guidelines might cause for employers and employees.

"Mental illness in your federal government," *American Enterprise,* July 1997, pp. 8-9.

On April 29, the U.S. Equal Employment Opportunity Commission issued new guidelines that broaden the definition of disability to include mental illnesses, psychological disorders and emotional imbalances. Employers who discharge or decline to hire persons with such conditions that can be considered disabilities are now liable for huge penalties.

"New EEOC rules hurt mentally ill," *Atlanta Journal,* May 1, 1997, p. A18.

An editorial asserts that it is reasonable for employers to ask a job applicant whether he or she has a history of mental illness. The editorial states that rules, such as the ones the EEOC issued this week, which, among other things, say that employers must tolerate chronic lateness, poor judgment and hostility toward co-workers, push the principle of the Americans with Disabilities Act beyond reason.

Neuborne, Ellen, "Work rules stir debate on mental illness," *USA Today,* May 21, 1997, p. B4.

The Equal Employment Opportunity Commission released 40 pages of guidelines in March to clarify the Americans with Disabilities Act. The guidelines, available on the EEOC's Internet Web site, have sparked a debate about the rights and responsibilities of workers with mental impairment.

Insurance Parity

Laabs, Jennifer J., "Mental-health insurance parity bill passes," *Personnel Journal,* December 1996, p. 11.
A new law passed in September 1996 will prevent health-insurance providers from imposing lower spending limits on mental health coverage than the limits they impose on physical-health coverage. The law takes effect Jan. 1, 1998.

"Parity for mental illness," *The Boston Globe,* March 11, 1997, p. A14.
Among the inequities that beset the afflicted, one of the more unfair is the insurance industry's treatment of severe mental illness. A bill before the legislature would accord insurance parity for the treatment of biologically based mental disorders. It deserves favorable action.

Managed Care

Elias, Marilyn, "Debating Mental Health Insurance," *USA Today,* Feb. 7, 1996, p. D4.
Roughly three out of four Americans think mental illness should be covered just like any other sickness in their health insurance policy, a phone survey sponsored by the National Alliance for the Mentally Ill suggests. The results of the survey are discussed.

Findlay, Steven, "Mental health groups challenge managed care," *USA Today,* Feb. 21, 1997, p. A1.
A coalition of nine mental health groups Thursday accused the managed-care industry of limiting access to appropriate mental health care. Harold Eist, president of the American Psychiatric Association, listed several restraints. Eist said cost controls imposed by the managed-care organizations have been painful to coalition members, but the main issue was the restraints being placed on care.

Goleman, Daniel, "Critics say managed-care savings are eroding mental care," *The New York Times,* Jan. 24, 1996, p. C9.
Many mental health patients and psychotherapists are complaining that managed-care companies, in an effort to save money, are denying essential mental health services, and that as a result, psychiatric problems are getting worse.

Pandiani, John A., Steven M. Banks and Lisa Gauvin, "A global measure of access to mental health services for a managed care environment," *Journal of Mental Health Administration,* summer 1997, pp. 268-277.
The authors introduce and demonstrate a global measure of access to mental health services that is based on the relationship between service utilization and the need for services in a managed-care environment.

Smith, Mark, "Managed care receives blame for overmedication," *Houston Chronicle,* March 23, 1997, p. A18.
The emergence of managed mental health care is adding fuel to a long-simmering debate over the place of medication in psychiatric treatment. Some psychiatrists charge that health maintenance organizations and other managed-care plans pressure therapists to treat mental health problems with drugs alone rather than with psychotherapy, or a combination of drugs and psychotherapy.

Smith, Mark, "Mental health managed care brings concerns: Financial limits blamed for shorter in-patient stays," *Houston Chronicle,* March 23, 1997, p. A1.
David Munday Jr.'s family — and hundreds of families nationwide — have begun filing lawsuits and complaints against doctors, hospitals and managed-care mental health plans, alleging patients were dumped from hospitals and received little if any therapy or aftercare. Harold Eist, president of the American Psychiatric Association, says managed mental health care companies — not doctors — are the culprits.

Wilson, James O., Jerilyn Ross and Robert L. DuPont, "Anxiety disorders in managed care," *Behavioral Health Management,* March 1997, pp. 33-38.
The cost of treating anxiety disorders in 1990 was an estimated $46.6 billion, 31.5 percent of the cost of all mental disorders.

Sens. Paul Wellstone and Pete Domenici

Rich, Frank, "Over the Cuckoo's Nest," *The New York Times,* May 4, 1996, p. A19.
Rich discusses recent efforts to assure fairness for those suffering from mental illness. Rich says that Sen. Pete V. Domenici, R.-N.M., and Sen. Paul Wellstone, D-Minn., have already enlisted the support of a large majority of their colleagues in the Senate to join them in support of a historic amendment to the new health insurance reform bill that would require insurance coverage to treat mental and physical illnesses as equals.

Back Issues

Great Research on Current Issues Starts Right Here . . . Recent topics covered by The CQ Researcher are listed below. Before May 1991, reports were published under the name of Editorial Research Reports.

MARCH 1996
The British Monarchy
Preventing Juvenile Crime
Tax Reform
Pursuing the Paranormal

APRIL 1996
Centennial Olympic Games
Managed Care
Protecting Endangered Species
New Military Culture

MAY 1996
Russia's Political Future
Marriage and Divorce
Year-Round Schools
Taiwan, China and the U.S.

JUNE 1996
Rethinking NAFTA
First Ladies
Teaching Values
Labor Movement's Future

JULY 1996
Recovered-Memory Debate
Native Americans' Future
Crackdown on Sexual Harassment
Attack on Public Schools

AUGUST 1996
Fighting Over Animal Rights
Privatizing Government Services
Child Labor and Sweatshops
Cleaning Up Hazardous Wastes

SEPTEMBER 1996
Gambling Under Attack
The States and Federalism
Civic Journalism
Reassessing Foreign Aid

OCTOBER 1996
Political Consultants
Insurance Fraud
Rethinking School Integration
Parental Rights

NOVEMBER 1996
Global Warming
Clashing Over Copyright
Consumer Debt
Governing Washington, D.C.

DECEMBER 1996
Welfare, Work and the States
The New Volunteerism
Implementing the Disabilities Act
America's Pampered Pets

JANUARY 1997
Combating Scientific Misconduct
Restructuring the Electric Industry
The New Immigrants
Chemical and Biological Weapons

FEBRUARY 1997
Assisting Refugees
Alternative Medicine's Next Phase
Independent Counsels
Feminism's Future

MARCH 1997
New Air Quality Standards
Alcohol Advertising
Civic Renewal
Educating Gifted Students

APRIL 1997
Declining Crime Rates
The FBI Under Fire
Gender Equity in Sports
Space Program's Future

MAY 1997
The Stock Market
The Cloning Controversy
Expanding NATO
The Future of Libraries

JUNE 1997
FDA Reform
China After Deng
Line-Item Veto
Breast Cancer

JULY 1997
Transportation Policy
Executive Pay
School Choice Debate
Aggressive Driving

AUGUST 1997
Age Discrimination
Banning Land Mines
Children's Television
Evolution vs. Creationism

SEPTEMBER 1997
Caring for the Dying

Back issues are available for $5.00 (subscribers) or $10.00 (non-subscribers). Quantity discounts apply to orders over ten. To order, call Congressional Quarterly Customer Service at (202) 887-8621.

Binders are available for $18.00. To order call 1-800-638-1710. Please refer to stock number 648.

Future Topics

- ***Mexico's Future***
- ***Youth Fitness***
- ***Urban Sprawl in the West***

THE CQ Researcher

PUBLISHED BY CONGRESSIONAL QUARTERLY INC.

Mexico's Future

Is it on the path to true democracy?

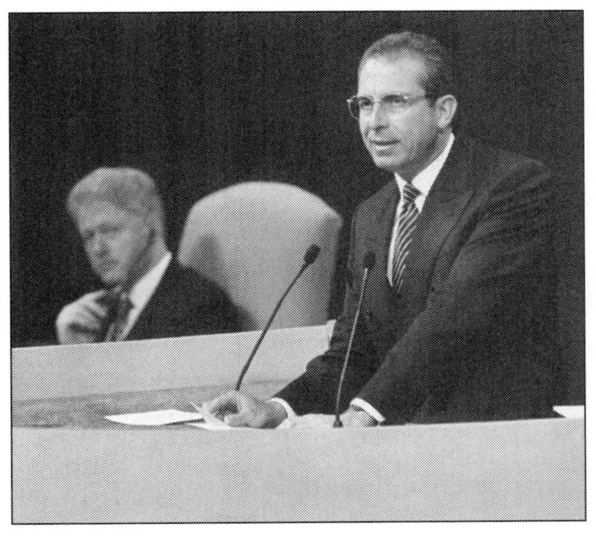

On July 6, a landmark election in Mexico handed significant losses to the country's ruling party for the first time in 70 years. Many analysts regard the election as the most honest in memory and say it has ushered in a new democratic era. Others worry that the ruling PRI party will subvert attempts to make Mexico a full democracy. At the same time, the nation has rebounded from the 1994-95 recession caused by a major devaluation of the peso. Some economists say that free trade and cheap labor should sustain the growth, and that Mexico will soon emerge as the United States' second-biggest trading partner. But critics warn that Mexico's future is clouded by poverty, growing drug-trafficking and illegal immigration.

INSIDE THIS ISSUE

CQ Sept. 19, 1997 • Volume 7, No. 35 • Pages 817-840

Formerly Editorial Research Reports

THE ISSUES

BACKGROUND

CURRENT SITUATION

OUTLOOK

SIDEBARS AND GRAPHICS

FOR FURTHER RESEARCH

COVER: PRESIDENT CLINTON LISTENS AS MEXICAN PRESIDENT ERNESTO ZEDILLO ADDRESSES BUSINESS AND UNION LEADERS IN MEXICO CITY ON MAY 7, 1997. (REUTERS)

September 19, 1997
Volume 7, No. 35

The CQ Researcher (ISSN 1056-2036). Formerly Editorial Research Reports. Published weekly, except Jan. 3, May 30, Aug. 29, Oct. 31, by Congressional Quarterly Inc., 1414 22nd St., N.W., Washington, D.C. 20037. Annual subscription rate for libraries, businesses and government is $340. Additional rates furnished upon request. Periodicals postage paid at Washington, D.C., and additional mailing offices. POSTMASTER: Send address changes to The CQ Researcher, 1414 22nd St., N.W., Washington, D.C. 20037.

Mexico's Future

BY DAVID MASCI

THE ISSUES

The man who almost toppled Mexico's ruling party nine years ago was considered a dark horse this year when he announced his candidacy for mayor of Mexico City, the country's second most powerful office.

In 1988, Cuauhtemoc Cardenas seemingly had won the presidency of Mexico when he ran as the first major opposition candidate in decades. But many historians say that fraudulent vote-counting gave the victory to the Institutional Revolutionary Party (PRI), which has dominated Mexico since 1929. Six years later, Cardenas tried again, placing third.

But on July 6, it was a politically reborn Cardenas who ventured into Mexico City's Zocalo Plaza to greet tens of thousands of supporters cheering "Viva Mexico." Cardenas won the capital's mayoral election by an overwhelming margin, becoming the first non-PRI candidate to hold the office. Now the same pundits who had written him off have cast Cardenas as a front-runner in Mexico's next presidential election in 2000.

More significantly, Cardenas' Party of the Democratic Revolution (PRD), along with other opposition groups, for the first time in almost 70 years won enough votes to deny the PRI a majority in the lower house of Mexico's Congress. (*See graph, p. 820.*)

Of course, Cardenas is not the first politician to rise from the ashes. But his victory — along with the opposition parties' successful showing in the legislature — represents more than a political comeback. It signifies, to many observers, that Mexico has turned away from its authoritarian past and is well on its way to becoming a true, multiparty democracy. Some analysts are even flatly

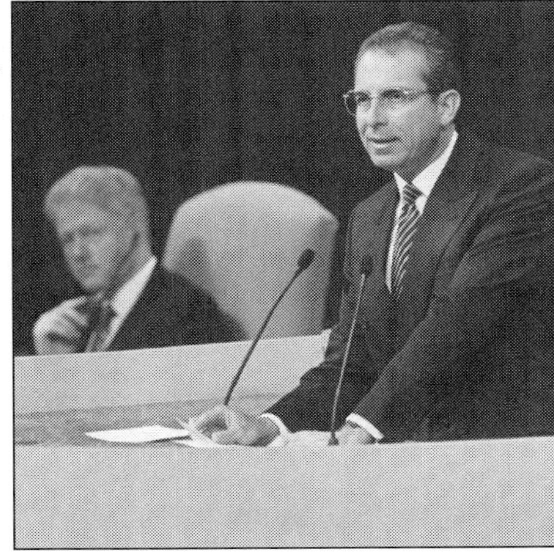

declaring that a democratic system is firmly in place.

The election results received broad media coverage in the United States, where President Clinton and others said they signaled Mexico's new political maturity. "For the first time . . . average Mexicans feel they really have power," says James Jones, U.S. ambassador to Mexico during Clinton's first term. * [1]

Until recently, U.S. policy-makers had largely neglected Mexico. But in the last decade the country has become a foreign-policy priority for the United States. The biggest reason is probably economic. Thanks to the North American Free Trade Agreement (NAFTA) and market-oriented reforms undertaken by Mexico, trade and investment between the two countries have increased dramatically. (*See graph, p, 824.*)

The United States has other reasons for applauding a more pluralistic and economically viable Mexico. Decades of population growth and poverty, coupled with an unresponsive and authoritarian government, have sent millions of illegal aliens from Mexico into the United States. Mexico also has emerged as a major player in the illegal narcotics trade. But the country's drug-interdiction efforts have been thwarted by endemic corruption and the power of the drug traffickers. [2]

But have the recent elections really catapulted Mexico into the community of democratic countries? Yes, says Mexican historian Alfredo Krauze, author of *Mexico: Biography of Power*. "I think it is really a historical change we have been living this year, these days. We just understood that Mexico has to end the 20th century as a normal democracy."

Krauze and others say that electoral reforms, begun slowly in the late 1980s and accelerated recently by President Ernesto Zedillo, have largely dismantled the rigged political system of the past that guaranteed the PRI victory in every election. In particular, they say, Zedillo's support for an independent election commission to monitor the vote and watch for fraud made the July 6 contest the cleanest in Mexico's history.

But other observers are not as sanguine about Mexico's transition to democracy. While they acknowledge that the July 6 vote proved that things have gotten better, they note that the political system still heavily favors the ruling PRI.

"This is still a political monopoly," says Jorge Castenada, a professor of political science at the National University in Mexico City.

According to Castenada and others, the PRI's hold on the presidency, which in Mexico is the most powerful branch of government, gives it an advantage over the opposition in obtaining money and media attention. In addition, they say, the party still maintains its grip on the Mexican people at the local level through a

---

* Confirmation hearings for President Clinton's choice to replace Jones as U.S. ambassador to Mexico, former Gov. William Weld, R-Mass., were blocked by Sen. Jesse Helms, R-N.C., chairman of the Senate Foreign Relations Committee. On Sept. 15, 1997, Weld withdrew his name from consideration.

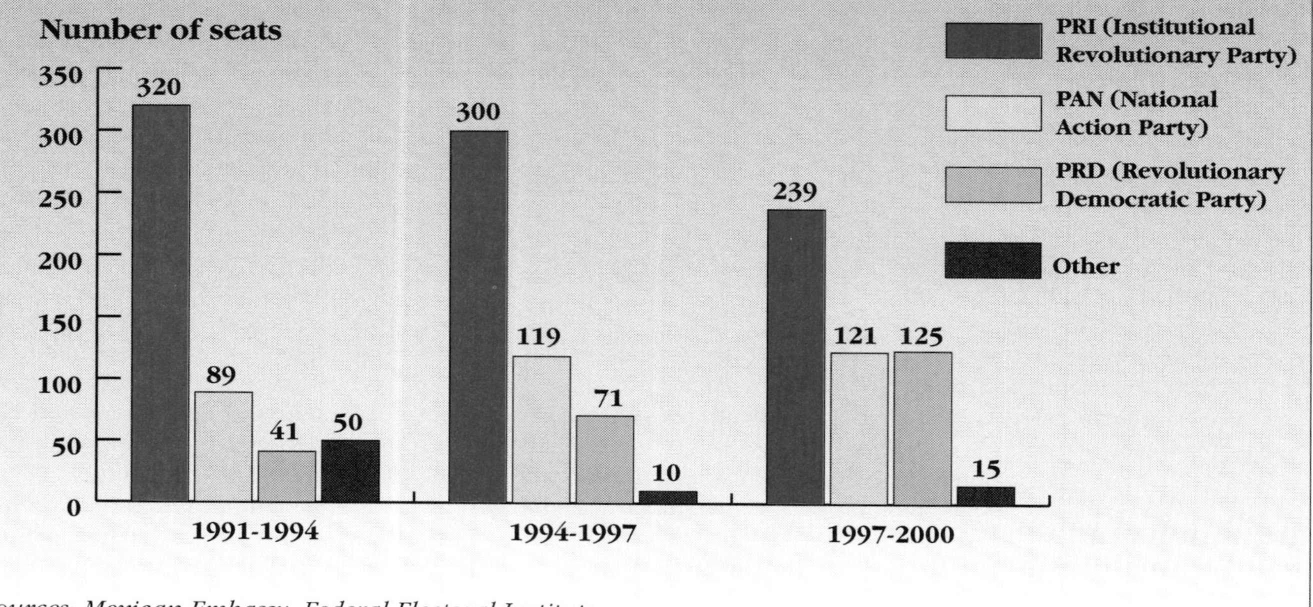

Sources: Mexican Embassy; Federal Electoral Institute

corrupt system of pork-barrel spending and political "favors."

But the optimists point out that the PRI's advantages have been reduced significantly. For instance, in the July election, they point out that new campaign laws enabled opposition parties to receive both money and media access from the government. If the PRI wins the next presidential election, they say, it will not be due to the types of advantages enjoyed in the past but to the same factors that influence elections in other democratic countries, such as the health of the economy.

If Mexico's economy indeed plays a role in the next big election, the ruling PRI may yet retain the presidency. While the country suffered one of the worst recessions in its history in 1995 as a result of a sudden devaluation of the peso, the economy has been growing since early 1996. Moreover, economic growth reached almost 9 percent in the second quarter of 1997, a level enjoyed by robust economies of East Asia such as China and Indonesia.

Many analysts credit Mexico's quick economic turnaround to the North American Free Trade Agreement, which lowered trade barriers throughout North America, and the devalued peso, which made Mexican exports cheaper and hence more competitive in the global marketplace. (*See "At Issue," p. 833.*) In response, Mexico's export sector has boomed, attracting a lot of foreign investment and creating thousands of new jobs all over the country.

But some observers view NAFTA's impact on Mexico as largely negative. In the first place, they argue, the treaty helped to cause the peso crisis that led to Mexico's recession. The government kept the peso overvalued, they say, in part to convince the Americans that Mexico had a strong economy and was ready for free trade with the United States.

"NAFTA gave [the Mexican government] a big disincentive to face up to the currency problem because if they had [faced it], the entire treaty might have been thrown in doubt," says Thea Lee, assistant director of public policy at the AFL-CIO.

In addition, Lee and other analysts say that the recent high rates of economic growth in Mexico have not really benefited average working people, who are still suffering from having their standard of living cut significantly during the recession.

"People in the export sector are doing well, but for the remaining 90 percent of the country, life is still very hard," Castenada says.

NAFTA supporters see things differently. While Mexicans are not as well off as they were before the recession, they say, more people are working and wages are rising. Indeed, they argue, recent statistics indicate that spending on consumer goods is rising rapidly.

"The export boom is affecting the entire economy," says Albert Fishlow, a senior fellow at the Council on Foreign Relations.

Others say that the recent, relatively clean elections also have given consumers and investors a dose of optimism. Indeed, Mexico's stock market has boomed since the July 6 elections in the apparent belief that the country is finally maturing politically.

But if Mexico is starting to build new economic and political muscle, it faces no shortage of other serious challenges. The drug trade, for instance, has grown tremendously in the last decade, leaving almost unimaginable corruption and violence in its wake.

Drugs also have increased friction with the United States, which annually reviews Mexico's anti-narcotics efforts to see if the country is "cooperating" in the drug war. So far, Mexico has been certified as cooperative each year by the White House. But a growing number of congressmen are pushing the Clinton administration to send some signal to Mexico that it is not doing enough. They say that America's southern neighbor generally allows its drug-traffickers to operate with impunity.

But Mexicans argue that the entire certification process is an affront to their nation's sovereignty and a way to shift attention from the real problem: continued consumer demand for drugs in the United States.

In addition to drugs, Mexico also "exports" millions of citizens to the United States each year. Americans have long complained about illegal aliens, but many U.S. and Mexican analysts see them as vital to the U.S. They say that America's agricultural sector and many of its service industries would be devastated if undocumented workers stopped crossing the border into Texas, California and other states. With a population approaching 100 million people and high levels of poverty and unemployment, Mexico is likely to continue supplying U.S. businesses with low-wage workers for the foreseeable future.

But despite the problems posed by drug smuggling and illegal immigrants, U.S.-Mexican relations remain solid. [3] President Clinton, who visited Mexico in March, and other U.S. policy-makers support the economic and political reforms that have been implemented in Mexico in recent years. Indeed, the ratification of NAFTA in 1993 has spurred a growing awareness, especially in the United States, that the two neighbors are becoming more interdependent.

As Mexico approaches the millennium, these are some of the questions being asked on both sides of the border:

Did the July elections create a real multiparty political system in Mexico?

On Sept. 1, President Zedillo appeared before Mexico's Congress to deliver his third *informe,* or state of the union address. The occasion was historic, but not due to anything Zedillo said. Instead, it was the audience that was making history. For the first time in almost 70 years, Mexico's president was facing a legislature not entirely controlled by his own party, the PRI.

The new makeup of the legislature directly resulted from the July 6 elections, which cost the ruling PRI its majority in the Chamber of Deputies, or lower house. The PRI also fared poorly in the upper house, or Senate. In fact, the party likely would have lost its Senate majority as well, but only a quarter of the 128 seats in that chamber were being contested.

Traditionally, the PRI has enjoyed a huge majority in both chambers of Congress, which has generally been viewed as little more than a dumping ground for party functionaries and a rubber stamp for presidential decisions.

But after the July elections, the PRI found itself with only 239 of the Chamber of Deputies' 500 seats, leaving the party with a plurality, but not a majority of votes. Most of the remaining seats went to the two main opposition parties, the left-wing Party of the Democratic Revolution (PRD) and the conservative National Action Party (PAN). Along with a number of smaller parties, such as the Greens, opposition forces now control 261 of the seats in the lower house. [4]

Another important development was the election for mayor of Mexico City, widely seen as the second most powerful post in the country after the presidency. The victory of opposition icon and PRD leader Cardenas handed the ruling party a defeat that would have been unthinkable even a decade ago.

The capital, home to nearly one in five Mexicans, is the epicenter of the nation's political, cultural and business life. The post was considered so important that, until Cardenas, all mayors were directly appointed by the president.

The election of Cardenas, who garnered more than twice as many votes as his two nearest challengers, has significance for the entire country. Analysts of every political stripe say he has established himself as a strong — possibly the strongest — contender in the next presidential election, in 2000.

The other major opposition party,

Continued on p. 823

NAFTA: The Debate Has Not Died Down

More than three and a half years after it went into effect, the North American Free Trade Agreement (NAFTA) seems to have changed few minds.

Early opponents of the treaty between the U.S., Mexico and Canada, including organized labor and environmental groups, now argue that, as they predicted, it has been a disaster for American workers and for the ecology of the country's southern border. Longtime NAFTA proponents, on the other hand, say that it has boosted the economies of the United States and Mexico while causing little dislocation for American workers.

The ongoing debate is likely to heat up in the near future as President Clinton seeks congressional support for fast-track authority to expand NAFTA to include Chile and possibly other Latin American countries. [1]

NAFTA also will be coming under greater scrutiny as the presidential election draws near. Two of the likeliest Democratic contenders for the office, Vice President Al Gore and House Minority Leader Richard A. Gephardt of Missouri, have been de facto spokesmen for and against the treaty, respectively. In 1993 Gore engaged NAFTA opponent Ross Perot (another possible presidential contender) in a now famous debate over the treaty. And opposition to NAFTA has been the cornerstone of Gephardt's populist economic message.

Gephardt and other critics say the treaty has hurt the nation in a variety of ways, but mainly by accelerating the loss of high-paying manufacturing jobs in the United States. According to Robert Scott, an economist at the Economic Policy Institute, about 140,000 jobs have been directly eliminated as a result of the treaty with Mexico. In addition, Scott says, "We've lost the opportunity to create between 300,000 and 400,000 new jobs in the manufacturing sector that have [gone] to Mexico."

Opponents also argue that the treaty has made it much easier to relocate factories in Mexico, giving companies extra leverage over those workers still employed in the United States. "We hear it from workers every day of the week," says Thea Lee, assistant director for international economics at the AFL-CIO. "When they sit down at the bargaining table, they hear that threat of moving production to Mexico," she says. "So even the workers who have kept their job in the United States have had their wages cut and their benefits cut back by NAFTA." As a result, Lee argues, "the real median wage in the United States has fallen 4 percent since 1993, when NAFTA went into effect." [2]

Finally, opponents say, NAFTA has significantly increased environmental problems along the U.S. border. For instance, they point out, the Environmental Protection Agency (EPA) has said that hazardous waste coming from Mexico into the United States has increased 30 percent in 1995 alone. Levels of untreated waste, ozone and sulfates have also risen dramatically in border areas since NAFTA's adoption. [3]

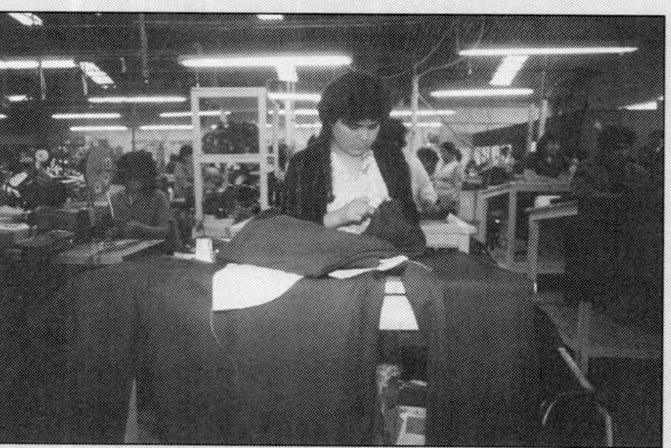

Economists predict that Mexico will take Japan's place as America's second-biggest trading partner by the end of the year. Above, a textile factory in Mexico.

But supporters of the treaty, including the Clinton administration, argue that NAFTA has done a lot more good than harm for the United States. To begin with, they say, exports to Mexico have risen 36 percent over the last three years, creating 122,000 new jobs in the U.S.

More important, says Daniel T. Griswold, director of trade and immigration studies at the CATO Institute, increased competition from free trade has forced the country to reallocate workers from less competitive industries to more dynamic sectors of the U.S. economy. "It's better for the workers to be in internationally competitive industries instead of uncompetitive and protected industries," he argues.

As for the environmental damage caused by the increased economic activity along the border, Griswold argues that halting free trade and economic development is the wrong way to attack the problem. "It's the responsibility of the Mexican government to control pollution in a socially responsible way," he says. Furthermore, Griswold argues, the kind of economic development fostered by free trade is actually the best way to protect the environment. "Studies show that when a country's per capita gross domestic product reaches about $5,000, environmental awareness begins increasing" as people have the luxury to begin worrying about something other than food and shelter.

---

[1] Fast-tracking prevents Congress from amending treaties once they have been negotiated.

[2] Quoted on "The NewsHour with Jim Lehrer," July 11, 1997.

[3] Economic Policy Institute, Institute for Policy Studies, International Labor Rights Fund, Public Citizen's Global Trade Watch, Sierra Club and U.S. Business and Industrial Council Educational Foundation, "The Experiment That Failed: NAFTA at Three Years," pp. 21-22.

Continued from p. 821

the PAN, also picked up some important wins in state elections, capturing the governorships of two states and bringing the number of governors who are PAN members to six (out of 29 states). As a result of these and other PAN successes in previous elections, more than 40 percent of all Mexican citizens now live in areas administered by PAN on the local level. [5] By contrast, as recently as 20 years ago, most political offices, no matter how insignificant, were held by a PRI member.

But while opposition victories in the legislature and elsewhere are widely seen as an important improvement over past practices, many analysts say that Mexico still has a long way to go before it can call itself a true multiparty democracy.

"It looks like there is a new age in terms of multiparty politics, but the PRI still have their hands on the levers of power," says José Carreño, a correspondent for *El Universal,* Mexico's largest independent newspaper. In particular, he says, the PRI still controls the executive branch, which has much more power than its counterpart in the United States. "President Zedillo has a tremendous amount of authority to decide when and how to spend money," he says. By contrast, the legislature has traditionally been a weak and subservient branch.

According to Carreño, it will be hard for the opposition majority in the Chamber of Deputies to meaningfully curtail presidential power. "It will be a long hard road for them," he says. "This is a vertical society, where the president is the great father, the great giver, and that's not going to change."

In addition to the power of the presidency, say Carreño and others, the ruling party still controls most local political machines in Mexico. "The governing party still has the resources to bludgeon people into voting for it, particularly in rural areas," says Mark Falcoff, a resident scholar at the American Enterprise Institute (AEI). In most villages, according to Falcoff, the local PRI official decides who will and won't receive government largess. "For example," he says, "they are able to do favors like getting you the cement you need to build something, or getting your child into high school." These "favors" give PRI officials great influence when elections are held. "In a society where government services are so bad, the only way to get things done is through the party, which gives them enormous leverage," he says.

Riordan Roett, director of Latin American studies at the Johns Hopkins University School for Advanced International Studies in Washington, D.C., agrees. "The PRI still pulls a lot of strings everywhere," he says, "and they're not going to disappear immediately."

Undergirding this system of favors is institutionalized corruption on a massive scale, many observers say. "Corruption is so pervasive that if you eliminated it you would eliminate the entire political class," says Larry Birns, executive director of the Council on Hemispheric Affairs. Birns and others say that no matter how good the Mexican political process might look on paper, it still won't be democracy. "It may be democratic in structure, but it won't be in spirit," he says, because everyone has been brought up in the old, corrupt system. "It's not a question of reconstructing democracy, but of constructing democracy," Birns says. "Citizens must be taught to be citizens, and the government must be taught to serve them."

Corruption will affect the PRD, PAN and their allies almost immediately, say pessimists, who predict that the PRI will do its utmost to pervert the opposition victory in order to mitigate its losses in the election.

"I think that it is highly likely that the PRI will try to subvert the opposition members [of Congress] into voting with the PRI," Castenada says. "When the new house takes office, we will see how many of the 500 deputies are really in the opposition," he says, adding that he would not be surprised if the ruling party had corrupted enough opposition members to eventually have de facto control of the chamber.

All in all, say Castenada and others, Mexico will not become a real multiparty democracy until the PRI is thoroughly routed on every level. "One-party systems generally come to an end when the ruling party loses power," he says.

But others say that genuine change has come to Mexico and that the country for the first time can no longer be considered a one-party state. "I don't think it's an overstatement to say [the election] represents a real sea change in Mexican politics . . . a change from one-party autocratic rule for 68 years to a multiparty democracy," says former Secretary of State James A. Baker III. [6]

Delal Baer, a senior fellow at the Center for Strategic and International Studies at Georgetown University, agrees that the country has entered a new era. "The loss of the PRI majority in Congress creates for the first time a system where checks and balances can function as a counterweight to the presidency," she says. "There is this false idea that until the PRI is destroyed, Mexico can never be a true multiparty democracy."

Baker, Baer and other optimists credit President Zedillo with instituting electoral reforms that created the environment that made the new multiparty system possible. These reforms, they say, gave the opposition a real opportunity to compete fairly with the ruling party. The resulting opposition victories bear out the fact that while the playing field may not be exactly level, it no longer gives overwhelming advantages to the ruling party.

The most important of Zedillo's changes was the transformation of the Federal Electoral Institute (FEI) into a reliable, independent mechanism for ensuring against the kind of direct voter fraud so common in the past. Originally, the FEI was created by Zedillo's predecessor, Carlos Salinas de Gortari. But until last year, the institute was controlled by the government. [7]

Now the FEI is widely viewed as independent and effective. For instance, optimists point out, the FEI has created an accurate voter list, issued 50 million photo identification cards for voters and recruited a staff of professionals to oversee elections. The FEI has also set up a duplicate computer system to count votes in order to prevent a reoccurrence of what many say was the most blatant and significant case of ballot fraud in modern Mexican history. [8]

Mexican Embassy

Exports of electronic equipment and other goods from Mexico to the United States have nearly doubled in the past four years.

The incident occurred during the 1988 presidential election, when the computer tallying votes suddenly crashed after early returns showed Cardenas well ahead of the PRI's Salinas. When the computer began to function again, Salinas was suddenly ahead and went on to win the presidency.

"We all remember the bad, old days where ballots were stolen, and the process was so distorted that it affected the outcome," Baer says. But, she argues, "now the process doesn't make a difference and instead, it's the economy and other issues that decide elections."

In addition to the creation of an independent FEI, other changes, namely new laws on media access and campaign finance, have helped to clean up the process, according to Baer and others. New laws guaranteed opposition candidates government funding and access to radio and television. "This was the first election where the opposition got money from the government and the first time people saw opposition candidates on television," says the AEI's Falcoff. By contrast, Falcoff says, "in 1994 Zedillo was the only presidential candidate you saw on television."

The changes have not totally eliminated the PRI's electoral advantage, according to Falcoff and others. "The government is still able to shake down the business community for money," Falcoff says. And media outlets, especially those run by the state, still favor government candidates. But, he argues, the situation is improving dramatically. "The opposition is already getting a much fairer share" of money and media time, Falcoff says.

In addition, Baer and others acknowledge, the PRI is able to use pork-barrel spending and other advantages inherent to a governing party to win votes. But they see it as a natural consequence of incumbency. "Of course the government uses pork to influence voters," she says. "That's what governments do."

Optimists also argue that the PRD and the PAN, now that they have made real gains on the national level, will act like an opposition and not be subverted by the ruling party. "I have no doubt that the Mexican Congress will be an obstacle to the president," Baer says, adding that the opposition parties have already banded together to pick the Speaker of the house and other leadership positions in the Chamber of Deputies.

In addition, Baer predicts, Congress, for the first time, will begin to vigorously investigate and expose government corruption. "They will discover their oversight authority and strengthen it," she says.

Has the North American Free Trade Agreement (NAFTA) been beneficial for Mexico?

Selling Mexicans on the need to join the United States and Canada in a sweeping free trade pact was not an easy task. "Even coming up with the idea of the North American Free Trade Agreement was a violation of the Eleventh Commandment of Mexican politics: Thou Shalt Not Trust Americans," historian Krauze writes, referring to age-old suspicions that the United States wants to control Mexico. [9] And yet by the early 1990s, then-President Salinas had succeeded in convincing a majority of his countrymen that NAFTA would lead to previously unseen levels of economic growth and would bring Mexico into the community of First World nations.

The treaty is now almost four years old. And while Mexico remains a developing country, NAFTA proponents can point to significant changes since it went into effect. Most notably, Mexico's trade levels with the United States have increased dramatically from 1993 to 1996. Trade growth has been especially good for Mexico, where exports to the United States have almost doubled over the last four years, rising to close to $80 billion in 1996. [10] In fact, economists predict that by the end of this year, Mexico will replace Japan as America's second-largest trading partner, behind Canada. Indeed, if NAFTA were judged on the increase of trade across both borders, the treaty would be an unqualified success.

But trade levels do not tell the whole story. Soon after NAFTA went into effect in 1994, Mexico slid into one of the worst economic crises in its history, after the country's long- overvalued currency, the peso, collapsed (*see p. 831*).

Some analysts see a link between the peso crisis and Salinas' push for NAFTA. "Mexico got into its financial crisis largely because of NAFTA," Birns says. According to Birns and others, Salinas kept the peso overvalued to give the impression that the Mexican economy was stronger than it really was. All of this "smoke and mirrors" was intended to impress the U.S. Congress and win support for NAFTA, Birns says. But when the smoke cleared, the Mexican economy collapsed, he says.

Lee of the AFL-CIO agrees, adding that the peso was also kept overvalued to make U.S. exports to Mexico cheaper. This in turn allowed Salinas to reassure American politicians that free trade would not lead to a huge trade deficit with Mexico that would destroy millions of manufacturing jobs in the United States.

"It was very convenient to be running a big trade deficit with the United States during the NAFTA debate," she says.

But NAFTA proponents argue that it is utterly ridiculous to link the treaty with the peso crisis. "NAFTA was fine," says Dan Griswold, director of trade and immigration studies at the CATO Institute. "It was Mexico's monetary policy that was the problem."

According to Griswold and other NAFTA boosters, Salinas established a strong peso for a good reason: to bring Mexico's high rate of inflation down. But, they argue, he kept the currency overvalued for too long. "When Salinas took over in 1988, inflation was running at 180 percent a year," says Fishlow of the Council on Foreign Relations. "By 1994, inflation was under 10 percent," he says, calling it "an impressive achievement."

Fishlow argues that Salinas could have reduced the peso's value gradually and spared the nation a terrible recession. Instead, the economist says, the president continued to support the overvalued currency because it was politically expedient. To begin with, the high-valued currency was a boon to consumers because it made American goods, like cars and appliances, cheaper in Mexico. Devaluation would have significantly raised the prices on these goods in 1994, just as Mexicans were about to go to the polls to elect a new president. In addition, Fishlow says, Salinas was even more apprehensive about devaluation after the assassination of his handpicked successor, Luis Donaldo Colosio in March 1994.

"Coming in the midst of the political crisis sparked by Colosio's assassination, it became more difficult to devalue the currency because it could have created even greater uncertainty at a time of already great uncertainty," Fishlow says.

Hence, Fishlow and others say, NAFTA had nothing to do with causing the devaluation. Instead, they argue, the free trade treaty helped to quickly pull Mexico out of the terrible recession in 1995 that followed the peso crisis. "After the devaluation of the peso, exports to the United States began growing, and that reduced the decline of economic growth in 1995 and helped the economy rebound the following year," Fishlow says.

Ian Vasquez, an analyst at the CATO Institute, agrees: "NAFTA helped Mexico by creating jobs in the export sector during the recession." As a result, "the recovery has been far quicker this time than during the [1982] recession," he says. "We're not talking about a lost decade, just a few years of pain." Indeed, Vasquez and others say, after shrinking more than 6 percent in 1995, Mexico's economy grew more than 3 percent in 1996 and has increased at a rate of more than 7 percent in the first six months of this year. [11]

But NAFTA opponents argue that the treaty's benefits have been felt only in one part of the country: the region along the border with the United States. There, treaty opponents admit, new jobs have been created along with the growth of maquiladoras, new assembly plants that dot the border and assemble goods for export to the United States.

"But for the rest of the country, the economy is moribund," Lee says. For instance, she points out, real wages for the average Mexican have dropped 37 percent in dollar terms between 1993 and 1996. "NAFTA hasn't done anything to change this."

But according to Fishlow, the NAFTA-inspired export boom has fueled significant growth in other parts of Mexico. "It's not just the maquiladoras that have expanded to take advantage of this export boom," he says. "Factories all over Mexico have expanded as well."

Should Mexico continue to be certified by the United States as a nation that is "cooperating fully" in the war on drugs?

On Feb. 18, Gen. Jesus Gutierrez Rebollo, Mexico's top drug-enforce-

Continued on p. 827

Insurrection in Chiapas

On the morning of Jan. 1, 1994, an armed insurrection appeared, seemingly out of nowhere, in the southern Mexican state of Chiapas. The rebels, who called themselves the Zapatista Army of the National Liberation, captured two small towns and the city of San Cristobal de las Casas.

After some initial apprehension and confusion, the Mexican army moved into the area to reassert control. Within two weeks, San Cristobal and the other towns had been retaken and the rebels had retreated into the jungle.

But while the army could claim a military victory of sorts (the rebels did not suffer significant casualties), the Zapatistas, as they came to be known, had scored a public relations coup. Soon, photographs of their leaders, wearing bandoleers of bullets and ski masks, were plastered across newspapers from Mexico City to Manhattan. One rebel in particular, the eloquent Subcommandante Marcos, became a hero, and not only to leftists. National polls indicated that Marcos (later identified as writer and teacher Rafael Sebastian Guillen Vicente) was the heartthrob of millions of Mexican women. [1]

Reuters

Rebel leader Subcommandante Marcos shakes hands with Cuautehmoc Cardenas, leader of the leftist opposition party PRD, after they addressed the Forum for State Reform on July 4. Cardenas, the newly elected mayor of Mexico City, expressed support for the Zapatistas' demand for a more democratic Mexico.

From the start, publicity seems to have been paramount to the rebels. Even the timing of their attack, Jan. 1, 1994, was chosen with an eye toward its public relations significance: It was the first day that the North American Free Trade Agreement went into effect. After retreating to the jungle, the Zapatistas showed themselves to be skilled at keeping their name and their cause in the news, at least for a time, with Marcos and others becoming staples of the print and broadcast media in Mexico and elsewhere.

But what is their cause? On the surface, the rebels were fighting for economic and political justice for the peasants of Chiapas, an area that lies at the bottom of the country on the Pacific Coast. Chiapas is one of Mexico's poorest states, with a largely rural, Indian population. According to many analysts, the state and its population have traditionally been ignored by the country's rulers in Mexico City and had been harboring revolutionaries for decades.

But there was another agenda, some say. Although Marcos and others knew that the Zapatistas were no match for the Mexican army, their goal was to topple the government. According to historian Enrique Krauze, in his book *Mexico: Biography of Power,* Marcos and the others believed that news of the uprising would unleash "a chain reaction, a rising against the government that would spread across Mexico." [2]

But the chain reaction never occurred. Instead the rebels, who had effectively been contained by the army, soon found themselves negotiating with the government of then-President Carlos Salinas.

According to most experts, Salinas could have eliminated the Zapatistas by force. The reason he chose to talk rather than fight, says José Carreño, Washington correspondent for Mexico's *El Universal* newspaper, is that bloodshed would have damaged the image of the new, modern Mexico that he had worked so hard to cultivate.

Whatever his reasons, Salinas' strategy has paid off for the government. The army is firmly in control of Chiapas and the level of violence is relatively low. "The Zapatistas are no longer a problem for [current President Ernesto] Zedillo right now," says Sergio Sarmiento, a syndicated columnist based in Mexico City.

No final agreement has ever been reached between the government and the rebels, despite years of negotiations. Still, the government has made some attempt to address the issues that concern the rebels. For instance, both Salinas and Zedillo have pumped a significant amount of money into long-neglected Chiapas to build new roads, schools, health clinics and other needed infrastructure projects. [3]

Meanwhile, the Zapatistas have lost a lot of the political momentum that drove their movement in its early days. Gone also, is much of the extensive press coverage the group once enjoyed. Even Subcommandante Marcos' image as a romantic revolutionary has faded a bit.

---

[1] Enrique Krauze, *Mexico: Biography of Power* (1997), pp. 784-787.

[2] *Ibid.* p. 786.

[3] Julia Preston, "Out of the Spotlight, Violence Tears at Mexican State," *The New York Times,* May 23, 1997.

Continued from p. 825
ment official, was arrested on charges of colluding with narcotics traffickers. Ten days later, Mexican authorities announced that one of the nation's top drug-money launderers had escaped from police custody. And on March 17, another general, Alfredo Navarro-Lara, was arrested for trying to bribe another military official into allowing cocaine shipments bound for the United States to pass through his jurisdictional area. [12]

These incidents, especially the arrest of Gen. Gutierrez, sent shock waves through anti-narcotics communities in both Mexico and the United States. And yet, on the same day the authorities were announcing the escape of the money launderer, the Clinton administration officially certified that Mexico was cooperating fully in efforts to stem the flow of illegal narcotics to the United States.

The certification process has been controversial since it was enacted as part of an omnibus anti-drug bill in 1986. The law requires the president each year to submit a list of those countries that produce or distribute large amounts of illegal narcotics for the U.S. market. Each country on the list must then be certified by the administration to be cooperating fully with American anti-drug efforts. [13]

Nations that are not certified are denied most forms of U.S. aid. In addition, American representatives at international lending agencies like the World Bank are directed to vote against any proposal to lend money or offer assistance to decertified countries. The president has the authority to waive these penalties.

In the case of Mexico, the decision by the Clinton administration to certify that nation provoked a strong backlash in the U.S. Congress. "In my opinion, we simply cannot justify certifying Mexico as a true ally in the drug war," wrote House Minority Leader Richard A. Gephardt, D-Mo., in a Feb. 25 letter to Gen. Barry McCaffrey, director of the Office of National Drug Control Policy. "The flow of drugs into the U.S. via Mexico has risen drastically in recent years."

Gephardt and other congressional opponents of certification attempted, unsuccessfully, to pass legislation reversing, in part, the president's decision. In the House of Representatives, a resolution that would have overturned the certification but given the president the authority to waive mandatory sanctions was passed on March 13. But a week later, the Senate took the bite out of the House bill, passing an amended version that merely required the president to report on Mexico's anti-drug efforts by Sept. 1. No action has been taken since.

Lawmakers complain that Mexican drug-traffickers have become the largest distributors, though not producers, of cocaine and other illegal narcotics in the United States. They often work with drug cartels from Colombia, a nation that was not certified. According to the Drug Enforcement Administration (DEA), Mexico is the conduit for roughly 70 percent of all cocaine and 80 percent of all marijuana coming into the United States.

At the same time, the DEA says, the Mexican government is so hobbled by corruption that it is virtually incapable of cooperating with American anti-drug efforts. "We have the cartels really moving with abandon, essentially bribing those who they can and killing those who they can't," says Sen. Dianne Feinstein, D-Calif., who opposed the administration's decision to certify Mexico. [14]

Feinstein's view of drug-related violence and corruption is also held by some of the nation's top anti-drug officials. Acting Deputy DEA Administrator James S. Milford, for example, recently told the House International Relations Committee, "At the present time, we at DEA do not have a trusting relationship with any of the law-

Trade With Mexico at a Glance

- In 1996, nearly one-third of U.S. two-way trade with the world was with Canada and Mexico ($421 billion). Two-way trade with Mexico and Canada has grown 44 percent since NAFTA was signed, compared with 33 percent for the rest of the world.
- Mexico and Canada accounted for 53 percent of the growth in total U.S. exports in the first four months of 1997.
- U.S. exports to Mexico grew by 36.5 percent ($15.2 billion) from 1993 to a record high in 1996, despite a 3.3 percent contraction in Mexican domestic demand over the same period.
- Exports to Mexico and Canada supported an estimated 2.3 million U.S. jobs in 1996, representing an increase of 311,000 jobs since 1993 (189,000 jobs were supported by exports to Canada and 122,000 by exports to Mexico).
- Exports to Mexico were up by 54.5 percent in the first four months of 1997 relative to the same period in 1993, In the first four months of 1997, U.S. exports to Mexico virtually equaled U.S. exports to Japan, the United States' second-largest market — even though Mexico's economy is one-twelfth the size of Japan's.

Source: "Study on the Operation and Effects of the North American Trade Agreement," July 1997, Executive Office of the President enforcement agencies in Mexico." [15]

Opponents of certification say that the reason Mexico is given a stamp of approval each year has nothing to do with law-enforcement issues. "No matter how many drugs come across the border and how much corruption there is, Mexico will be certified," Castenada says.

The United States certifies Mexico, Castenada and others say, because it sits on America's border and is vitally important as a trading partner. "The Mexican economy is enormously important to the U.S., so the administration exercises collective amnesia when it comes to certification," Birns says. Others agree, arguing that only countries that the U.S. can afford to ignore, like Colombia, Myanmar and Iran, are decertified.

But the administration has defended its decision, on drug enforcement, rather than geopolitical, grounds. "The Mexican government's willingness to acknowledge and address the high-level corruption that has undermined its drug-control institutions is an act of political courage of the highest order," said Secretary of State Madeleine K. Albright at a Feb. 27 news conference. [16]

Administration officials also point out that drug seizures by Mexico have been increasing since 1995. For example, authorities reported seizing 7 percent more cocaine and 78 percent more heroin from 1995 to 1996. "Over the course of 1996, we saw good, solid, concrete results which demonstrates that we do have full cooperation," says Assistant Secretary of State Robert S. Gelbard. [17]

But many analysts, especially in Mexico, question the utility of the certification process. "It's difficult for us to understand how the country that judges us is the most important consumer of drugs in the world," says Mexico's ambassador to the United States, Jesus Silva-Herzog. Instead of trying to punish Mexico and other countries, he says the United States should fight the drug war by reducing the demand for narcotics domestically.

Yet others say that the certification process, while not perfect, does serve a purpose. "It generates pressure and helps to remind governments in Latin America that they have to make an effort," says Sergio Sarmiento, a syndicated columnist in Mexico City. ■

BACKGROUND

The "Reform" Years

Mexico has always been a nation of cataclysms — not least the destruction of Aztec and Mayan cultures in the early 16th century and the loss of one-third of its territory to the United States three centuries later.

In the first years of the 20th century, Mexico was wracked by revolution, military coups and political assassination. But the upheavals eased in 1929 with the founding of a ruling political party, the National Revolutionary Party, under Plutarco Elias Calles. Under the party, restructured and renamed the Institutional Revolutionary Party (PRI) in 1946, Mexicans effectively traded democracy for a certain stability. One-party rule enjoyed substantial support in its first decades. Lazaro Cardenas (father of Cuauhtemoc Cardenas), who served as president from 1934-1940, is revered to this day for nationalizing foreign oil interests. [18]

But by the early 1960s, Mexicans were becoming increasingly critical of their "one-party democracy." During this time, the country began experiencing an increase in violence, labor unrest and political protest.

The situation eased somewhat in the mid-1970s after the discovery of vast oil resources enabled the government to improve living standards. But a dramatic drop in oil prices in 1982 sent the country into an economic tailspin. Inflation and foreign debt skyrocketed, while living standards and economic growth fell.

The same year the oil bubble burst the country elected economist Miguel de la Madrid Hurtado as president. De la Madrid began pushing the Mexican economy, albeit slowly, toward market-oriented reforms. He cut government spending, reduced inflation and slowly began the process of privatizing Mexico's vast array of publicly owned industrial companies. [19]

But, as historian Krauze points out, de la Madrid "had been at best a caretaker rather than a creative gardener of the economy." [20] By the time his term was up in 1988, Krauze says, the average Mexican was little better off than he had been when the oil crisis had occurred six years before.

Salinas Takes Charge

The real work of bringing Mexico into the global economy was undertaken by Carlos Salinas de Gortari. The Harvard-educated Salinas and a group of Ivy League-trained economists tamed inflation, privatized scores of industries, attracted billions of dollars in foreign investment and renegotiated and reduced Mexico's crippling foreign debt. The result was a significant increase in economic growth by the early 1990s. Soon, employment and wages were inching up.

Salinas' crowning achievement was NAFTA. The pact with the United States brought down tariffs and other barriers with Mexico's most important trading partner. Above all, NAFTA symbolized Mexico's arrival as a major player on the economic scene. In the past, nego-

Continued on p. 830

Chronology

1900s-1970s

After decades of revolution and upheaval, the Institutional Revolutionary Party (PRI) rises to power.

1910
A revolution begins that overthrows dictator Porfirio Diaz, who had been in power since 1876. Ten years of political assassinations and violence follow.

1929
Plutarco Elias Calles founds the Partido Nacional Revolucionario, which will rule Mexico until the present. The party is renamed the PRI in 1946.

1934
Lazaro Cardenas becomes president. Cardenas' liberal economic policies, including the nationalization of the oil industry, make him tremendously popular.

1976
José López Portillo becomes president and begins using Mexico's vast untapped oil reserves to boost living standards.

1980s-1993

In the wake of severe economic problems, Carlos Salinas becomes president and begins instituting full-fledged market-oriented economic reforms. Promises of a more open political system are not realized.

1982
A drop in oil prices leads to an economic crisis. Miguel de la Madrid is elected president and slowly begins making market-oriented economic changes.

1988
Opposition candidate Cuauhtemoc Cardenas runs for president. He is defeated by Salinas amid widespread charges of voter fraud.

1993
The North American Free Trade Agreement (NAFTA) is ratified by the U.S. Congress.

1994-Present

Ernesto Zedillo becomes president at a time of great political and economic turmoil. He begins to institute far-reaching political reforms.

January 1994
A rebellion breaks out in the poor, southern state of Chiapas.

March 1994
Luis Donaldo Colosio, the PRI candidate for president, is assassinated.

August 1994
Zedillo, Colosio's campaign manager, is elected president in what is generally regarded to be a fair election. Cardenas comes in a distant third in the race.

December 1994
Zedillo's attempt to gradually devalue the peso leads to economic disaster. Mexico enters one of the worst recessions in its history.

February 1995
Former President Salinas' brother Raul is arrested on charges of corruption and murder.

May 1995
Vicente Fox Quesada is elected governor of Guanajuato. A member of the conservative National Action Party (PAN), Fox is considered a serious contender for the 2000 presidential election.

January 1996
Mexico's economy begins growing again, thanks in part to a $50 billion bailout engineered by the Clinton administration in 1995.

October 1996
The Mexican Congress approves the transformation of the Federal Electoral Institute, which monitors elections, from government control to an independent commission.

February 1997
Gen. Jesus Gutierrez Rebollo, Mexico's drug czar, is arrested on drug-related charges.

July 1997
Opposition parties take control of the lower house of Congress. Cardenas is elected mayor of Mexico City.

September 1997
The new Congress convenes and, for the first time, elects a Speaker of the House who is not a member of the ruling PRI party.

'Things Are Beginning to Improve'

An Interview With Mexico's Ambassador to the U.S.

Jesus Silva-Herzog has been Mexico's ambassador to the United States since December 1994. He also has served as Mexico's finance minister and ambassador to Spain and holds an M.A. in economics from Yale University. CQ Researcher *staff writer David Masci interviewed the ambassador in his office on Aug. 26, 1997. Here are the ambassador's comments on a wide range of issues affecting Mexico:*

On the impact of the July 6 elections:

In most circles of the United States, there is this stereotype of Mexico as a one-party system. But that has not been true for the last five to 10 years. Before the elections of July 6, about 40 percent of Mexican society was governed by members of opposition parties, either at the local or the state level. What happened in the elections of July 6 was that this trend, of Mexico becoming a more plural, a more open, a more democratic society, was reaffirmed.

On opposition control of the lower house of Congress for the first time:

We are going to begin learning many of the things that you [in the United States] have learned for many years: [Having] a president from one party and then the Congress from the other party. . . Now there will be political maneuvering. I mean, it happens in the best [of] families. There is no question that it will be the intention of the PRI [the ruling party] to convince members of the opposition to go with them on a particular issue. And the PRI will not vote monolithically. We have seen it in the past, and we will see it more in the future.

Ambassador Jesus Silva-Herzog

On the recent fight in the U.S. Congress over drug certification:

Ten days before the president was going to submit a report to Congress that was very favorable as to the degree of Mexican cooperation against drugs, we had a very unfortunate event: The drug czar of Mexico was put in prison. So we went through a very painful month, the most painful of my stay in Washington. The way we were treated on the Hill was not a way you treat a neighbor, a partner and a friend.

On the recent upswing in the Mexican economy:

I was in Mexico City [for] just a few hours a month ago. And you are beginning to see a change in the attitude of the average people, the man on the street. They are still criticizing the government, and they are blaming the government for the [peso] crisis, but they are feeling that they are better off. They have a new job or their son has a new job. Things are beginning to improve in their standard of living.

On the future of Mexican emigration to the U.S.:

We have had for many, many years a very high rate of population growth. Twenty years ago, our population growth was a little over 3 percent a year. Now, it's 1.8 percent. So, we have been able to reduce it. But the ones that are in the labor force today are the ones who were born 15 or 20 years ago. So the pressure of migration in the next few years will begin to diminish, just by demographic trends. The rate of population growth has diminished, so the number of people coming into the labor force is going to be less than what it was before.

tiating such a treaty would have been inconceivable for the United States and Mexico. Before Salinas, Mexico's economy had been too different, too tied to the state, to open its doors to free trade with America.

By 1994, the year Salinas left office, the economy, at least, seemed to be on the right track. NAFTA had brought a wave of optimism, investment and growth to Mexico. To many observers, the average Mexican was actually benefiting from Salinas' policies.

In other areas, though, trouble was brewing. On Jan. 1, 1994, a small rebellion broke out in the poor, southern state of Chiapas. (*See story, p. 826.*) In March, Colosio, the PRI candidate tapped to replace Salinas, was assassinated. Colosio's campaign manager, Ernesto Zedillo Ponce de Leon, was quickly named as his replacement. [21]

Peso Devaluation

Zedillo won the presidency by promising to continue and expand upon the policies that had made Salinas so popular. But upon taking office in late 1994, the new president discovered that not all of his predecessor's policies were as sound as they had appeared. In particular, the peso had been heavily overvalued for years. Instead of trying to slowly bring its value down, Salinas had left the currency alone. According to many analysts, the inaction had more to do with politics than economics: The strong peso made imports into Mexico more affordable, which in turn made consumers happier.

A few days after taking office, however, the Zedillo government announced a devaluation. The result was an economic — and public relations — disaster. Investors, particularly abroad, panicked and sold their Mexican currency, driving its value down precipitously.

The devaluation of the peso created an economic slide almost unparalleled in Mexican history. Bankruptcies in both the business and personal sectors, soared. In 1995, the gross domestic product dropped almost 7 percent, and the country lost more than a million jobs. [22]

Fortunately for Zedillo, most Mexicans blamed Salinas for the disaster. The finger-pointing was further encouraged by the arrest of the former president's brother Raul allegedly for stealing public funds, money laundering and for ordering the assassination of PRI Secretary General Jose Francisco Ruiz Massieu. Investigators speculated that Raul Salinas killed Massieu to prevent him from exposing his corruption. A disgraced Carlos Salinas went into exile. Raul awaits trial.

Zedillo's fortunes were also aided by the Clinton administration, which quickly moved to stop the peso's slide by putting together a $50 billion loan-guarantee package for Mexico. ■

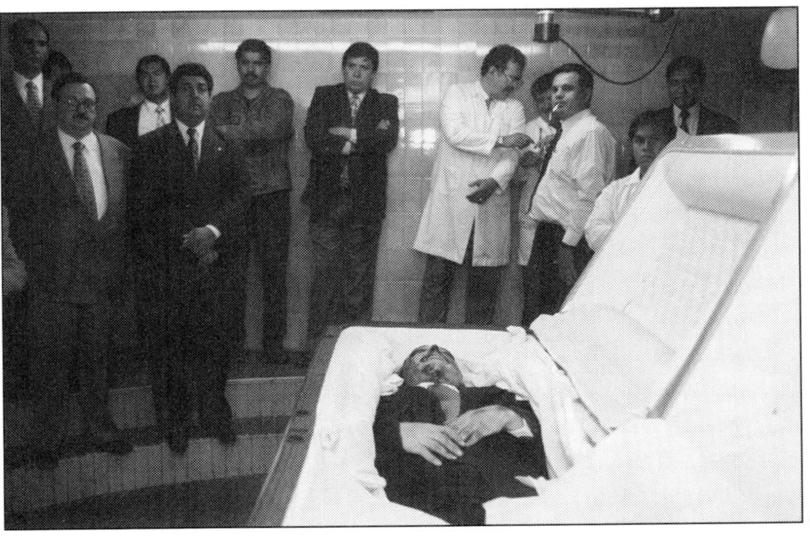

Reuters

Police pathologists in Mexico City view what is believed to be the body of Mexican drug kingpin Amado Carrillo Fuentes in Mexico City on July 7. He reportedly died while undergoing liposuction and plastic surgery in a Mexico City clinic.

CURRENT SITUATION

The New Economy

The most recent economic data indicate that the Mexican economy grew almost 9 percent in second-quarter 1997, following a respectable growth rate of 3 percent in 1996. As a result, economists and the business community are once again bullish on Mexico.

While the overall economy seems to have bounced back from the 1995 peso crisis, some observers say the benefits have not filtered down to most citizens. "Income levels, employment levels and nutrition levels are still very low," Castenada says. According to Castenada and others, all of the economic growth is in the export sector, which employs no more than 2 million people. "For everyone else, it's a struggle," he says.

The man in the street seems to agree. In a June survey of Mexico City residents, 79 percent of the respondents were pessimistic about the economy. And 63 percent reported making fewer consumer purchases in June than they had three months before. [23]

But some observers contend that the recovery has finally reached the common people. "After the peso crisis, the stores were empty; now they are full of people," Baer says. "People are buying. That doesn't mean that their buying power has recovered fully, but that it has recovered somewhat."

Retail sales figures seem to bear Baer out. For instance, car sales in 1997 were 43 percent higher than in June 1996. Sears, Home Mart and other big retail chains are reporting strong sales gains, especially in the last few months. [24]

Still, if the economy is really beginning to rebound, even for working people, how long will it last? Mexico has a history of booms and busts, but some economists are optimistic about long-term growth. "There's no reason why Mexico can't grow 7 or 8 percent a year," CATO's Griswold says. The reason, Griswold and others say, is that Mexico has a large supply of low-wage labor that can operate in close proximity to the United States, which is the largest market in the world.

Illegal Immigration

In 1996, more than 3 million undocumented Mexicans crossed or tried to cross the border into the United States, according to figures from the Institute for International Economics. Nearly half were arrested and deported. Others crossed successfully only to stay a short time — often to work a season in the fields — and return to Mexico. But many undocumented Mexicans who come to the United States each year stay. Their current numbers are said to be as high as 10 million. [25]

Such statistics are troublesome to many Americans, who feel that the United States has lost control of its borders. These fears have led to a number of new laws and initiatives in recent years designed to limit illegal immigration, particularly from Mexico. In 1995, the U.S. Congress passed legislation that, among other things, beefed up the border patrol and streamlined deportation proceedings. The year before, voters in California (which absorbs more illegal immigrants than any other state) approved Proposition 187, which denied many basic services to undocumented aliens.

These and other initiatives aimed at stopping immigration baffle many Mexicans, who say that illegal immigrants plug the holes in the U.S. labor market that American citizens and other legal residents are unwilling to fill. "If they [stopped illegal immigration], there would be a state of emergency in California, in the state of Texas and in a good number of regional places within the United States," says Ambassador Silva-Herzog.

The holes in the labor market plugged by illegal aliens include picking much of the nation's fruit and vegetable crop; filling many of the low-end service jobs in restaurants and other industries; taking on much of the low-wage manufacturing and construction work; and doing much of the child care and cleaning in middle- and upper-middle-class homes.

"A few months ago, I visited a farm in North Carolina, a tomato farm, where all the tomatoes were picked by Mexican undocumented workers," Silva-Herzog says, "and I asked the owner of this farm, 'Mr. Jones, what would you do if you did not have these Mexican workers who are helping you to pick up these tomatoes?' He said: 'Well, Mr. Ambassador, I would be out of business.' And that can be repeated in many other parts of the United States."

Silva-Herzog and others argue that it is Mexico, not the United States, that is the big loser every time an undocumented Mexican crosses the border. America gets an almost endless supply of cheap and hard-working labor, they say. Mexico, on the other hand, loses "the brightest, best-prepared and most adventurous people," Sarmiento says. "Most Mexicans don't understand the price we're paying."

But illegal immigration also benefits Mexico. Many villages are dependent on the estimated $6 billion in remittances sent by relatives in the United States. [26] In a poor country recently wracked by recession, these payments can mean the difference between poverty and material comfort, especially in rural areas.

The opportunity to emigrate also acts as a safety valve in a poor society where opportunities are often limited. "If it were not for emigration," Sarmiento says, "we would have had a revolution by now." ■

OUTLOOK

President Cardenas?

The next big political test for Mexico will come in three years, when the country elects a new president and much of its Congress. It is, of course, difficult to predict how certain parties and politicians will fare in this future contest. Still, most analysts say, the recent election in July has significantly boosted the chances of at least one presidential hopeful: Cuauhtemoc Cardenas.

Cardenas has not officially announced that he plans to run, but few doubt his desire to hold Mexico's highest office. For one thing, he ran in the last two elections. And he is the founder and standard-bearer for the PRD. It would be highly unusual for the party to nominate anyone else, especially after his overwhelming victory in the Mexico City mayoral election.

In a race for president, Cardenas enjoys a number of natural advantages. To begin with, his family name is legendary in Mexico due to the popularity of his late father, who was president from 1934 to 1940. "It's like being a Kennedy or a Roosevelt in America," AEI's Falcoff says, adding that Cardenas has the good fortune to also look like his father, "which is an asset."

Furthermore, his victory in the mayoral contest has put Cardenas in a very high-profile position that virtually guarantees him media coverage. "He will be able to use his office as a political platform," Birns says.

While Cardenas may look like the man to beat, a host of pitfalls could easily trip him up. Even serving as

Continued on p. 834

At Issue:

Has NAFTA helped Mexico's economy?

DANIEL T. GRISWOLD
Director, Trade and Immigration Studies, The Cato Institute

POSITION PAPER, SEPTEMBER 1997

yes

Mexico's 92 million citizens face a brighter future because of trade and market reforms enacted in the last decade.

After the failure of decades of protectionism and crony socialism to deliver prosperity, Mexico began in the late 1980s to open its market to trade and competition. Those reforms, prominent among them the North American Free Trade Agreement (NAFTA), offer the best hope to the people of Mexico for a better life.

Critics of NAFTA blame the treaty for creating poverty, pollution and inefficiencies that have long plagued the Mexican economy. But blame for those conditions should be aimed at past Mexican governments, which failed to adopt the outward-oriented market reforms that have so dramatically reduced poverty and improved working conditions for millions in East and Southeast Asia.

Opponents of free trade also blame NAFTA for Mexico's painful peso crisis of 1994-95. But the plunge in Mexico's output in 1995 had nothing to do with free trade and everything to do with politics and botched monetary policy. Mexico's peso collapse was caused by a lethal combination of loose monetary policy and an inflexible and overvalued exchange rate, both aimed at boosting consumption in an election year. Indeed, Mexico has suffered a severe financial crisis in every election cycle since 1976 — long before anyone had ever heard the term NAFTA.

In reality, NAFTA and other market reforms softened the severity of the crisis and spurred Mexico's recovery. Thanks in part to NAFTA, Mexico's economy has resumed a healthy rate of growth. The unemployment rate has fallen to its pre-crisis level, while personal consumption of goods and services has been rising at a healthy, sustainable rate. Total two-way trade with the United States in the second quarter of 1997 reached a record level, 55 percent above its pre-crisis level of three years ago.

This NAFTA-era expansion contrasts starkly with the protracted slump that followed the 1982 debt crisis. Then, it took the Mexican economy six years to recover its pre-crisis levels of production. More important, whereas the slump of 1982 prompted the Mexican government to nationalize its banks and raise trade barriers, the present government successfully resisted backsliding. Just as NAFTA supporters on both sides of the border had predicted, the trade treaty helped to lock in Mexico's broader economic reforms.

By lowering barriers to trade and strengthening the reform process, NAFTA has improved the lives and future prospects of the people of Mexico.

VANESSA FREIDMAN
Research Associate, Council Oon Hemispheric Affairs

POSITION PAPER, SEPTEMBER 1997

no

Although adverse NAFTA-related ramifications have affected all three of the trade-pact countries, Mexico clearly has been among its major beneficiaries as well as borne the brunt of its liabilities. Starting from a much more underdeveloped political base and possessing a spotty economy, with an outmoded and insufficient infrastructure, Mexico has leagues to travel before it becomes a fully suitable trading partner and fellow democracy of the U.S. and Canada.

NAFTA has been transformative in bestowing power on multinational corporations that formally belonged to the state. In the last three years, Mexico has been opened up to a mixed bag of foreign influences, leaving it less able to make independent decisions regarding fundamental policy. The effect of transferring power from the citizenry to transnational entities has been an important contributor to the country's high unemployment levels and political upheavals. The 28,000 businesses that failed during this period cost Mexico 2 million jobs, as well as the elimination of nearly 1 million farmers whose crops have been displaced by cheaper northern grain imports.

Encouraged by the approaching end of all tariffs and quotas, U.S. industries are moving their plants to Mexico in far greater numbers than was anticipated. Rather than aiming at local sales, the runaway plants' main target is to take advantage of local cheap labor to ship finished products back to the lucrative U.S. market. As a result, the exploitative *maquiladora* border work force has increased by 50 percent. Women, who make up more than 70 percent of employees, are often forced to work under harsh conditions, earning as low as $4 daily and frequently they must suffer sexual innuendoes and even physical harassment. Meanwhile, 8-11 million children under the age of 15 were being surreptitiously employed as of 1994, according to a U.S. Department of Labor study.

The NAFTA side agreements on labor and the environment, have fallen far short of promises made for them. Improvements in Mexico's environmental and public health conditions often have been halfhearted. Pollution-based diseases, such as hepatitis, chronic diarrhea and respiratory problems, have markedly increased due to toxic emissions and lax waste-disposal standards prevalent along the border. Only a small fraction of the $20 billion available for NAFTA-related dislocations are directed to cleanup efforts. On the other hand, U.S. and Canadian exports to Mexico have benefited their multinationals and niche-marketing industries, while millions of relatively high-cost workers in all three countries were made redundant.

FOR MORE INFORMATION

Council on Hemispheric Affairs, 724 9th St. N.W., Suite 401, Washington, D.C. 20001; (202) 393-3322. The council seeks to increase interest in Latin America, focusing on trade, civil liberties and politics.

Organization of American States, 17th St. and Constitution Ave., N.W., Washington, D.C. 20006; (202) 458-3000. The OAS promotes better relations between all nations in the American hemisphere and provides technical support to member states in a variety of fields.

U.S.-Mexico Chamber of Commerce, 1726 M St., N.W., Suite 704, Washington, D.C. 20036; (202) 296-5198. The chamber promotes trade and investment between Mexico and the United States.

Continued from p. 832

mayor of Mexico City could hurt him as much as it helps him.

"It's a very privileged position, but it's also a position filled with snares because Mexico City is a place where everything can go wrong," Birns says, pointing to problems like pollution, lack of adequate services and crowding.

On top of this, other analysts say, Cardenas has created tremendous and possibly unrealistic expectations in voters. "He's going to have to do a good job in Mexico City, because he needs a good track record there if he hopes to run for president," says Johns Hopkins' Roett.

Indeed, Falcoff thinks that a Cardenas administration will fall far short of expectations. "If you look at his performance as governor of Michoacan [in the early 1980s], you'll see it was dismal," Falcoff says. "He's not a competent administrator."

In addition, Falcoff and others say, Cardenas' political party, the PRD, has serious shortcomings. "The PRD is composed of the old Communist Party and part of the left wing of the PRI," he says, noting that Mexicans might not be willing to let a very liberal party govern the country. And efforts to transform the PRD into a party with broader political appeal — in the way that say Britain's Tony Blair changed the Labor Party — might not work.

"In the election, the PRD made an effort to move toward the ideological center," Baer says. "But they are not very comfortable with these issues and may not stay there."

Another problem for Cardenas and the PRD is that the two other major parties in Mexico might significantly strengthen their appeal in the three years before the election. According to Falcoff, if the economy continues to grow at its recent fast pace, "the PRI will win again, maybe with [as little as] 50 or even 40 percent of the vote, but they will win."

Unfortunately for the ruling party, Zedillo, who has high approval ratings, is prohibited by the Mexican Constitution from running for a successive presidential term. But if he retains his popularity, analysts say, his endorsement of the PRI candidate could prove very helpful.

In addition, there are already potential challengers who could make the race against Cardenas competitive, even if he succeeds as mayor. For instance, a leading member of the opposition PAN party, Gov. Vincente Fox of Guanajuato, is very popular and already has announced his intention to seek his party's nomination for president.

Regardless of who wins the next presidential contest, most politicians, and many analysts, agree that, barring backpedaling on political reforms, the election in 2000 will be the cleanest in modern Mexican history.

"The July elections set the tone for the 2000 election," Roett says, "and so far we've been moving in the right direction." ■

Notes

[1] Quoted on "The NewsHour with Jim Lehrer," July 15, 1997

[2] For background, see "Rethinking NAFTA," *The CQ Researcher,* June 7, 1996, pp. 481-504, and "Mexico's Emergence," *The CQ Researcher,* July 19, 1991, pp. 489-512.

[3] For background, see "Illegal Immigration," *The CQ Researcher,* April 24, 1992, pp. 361-384, "Cracking Down on Immigration," *The CQ Researcher,* Feb. 3, 1995, pp. 97-120 and "War on Drugs," *The CQ Researcher,* March 19, 1993, pp. 241-264.

[4] "Democracy Day in Mexico," *The Economist,* Sept. 6, 1997.

[5] "Fox Hunting," *The Economist,* July 19, 1997.

[6] Quoted on "The NewsHour with Jim Lehrer," July 15, 1997.

[7] "We're Clean," *The Economist,* July 5, 1997.

[8] Andres Oppenheimer, *Bordering on Chaos: Guerrillas, Stockbrokers, Politicians, and Mexico's Road to Prosperity* (1996), p. 24.

[9] Enrique Krauze, *Mexico: Biography of Power* (1997), p. 773.

[10] "When Neighbors Embrace," *The Economist,* July 5, 1997.

[11] Charles Kraul, "Mexico Says Economy Grew 8.8 Percent in Quarter," *Los Angeles Times,* Aug. 19, 1997.

[12] Drug Enforcement Administration, "Changing Dynamics of the U.S. Cocaine Trade," August 1997, p. 6.

[13] Carroll J. Dougherty, "Controversial Legacy," *Congressional Quarterly Weekly Report,* March 8, 1997, p. 597.

[14] Quoted on "The NewsHour with Jim Lehrer," July 15, 1997

[15] Quoted in Carroll J. Dougherty, "Bills Would Strike Historic Blow at Mexico Over Drug Trade," *Congressional Quarterly Weekly Report,* March 8, 1997, p. 596.

[16] Quoted on "The NewsHour with Jim Lehrer," July 15, 1997

[17] *Ibid.*

[18] For background, see "Privatizing Government Services," *The CQ Researcher,* Aug. 9, 1996, pp. 708-731.

[19] Krauze, *op. cit.,* p. 763.

[20] *Ibid.,* p. 772.

[21] *Ibid.,* p. 789.

[22] Kraul, *op. cit.*

[23] Anthony DePalma, "Mexico's Recovery Just Bypasses the Poor," *The New York Times,* Aug. 12, 1997.

[24] Kraul, *op. cit.*

[25] "Living Off Illegals," *The Economist,* April 19, 1997.

[26] *Ibid.*

Bibliography

Selected Sources Used

Books

Barry, Tom, Harry Browne and Beth Sims, *Crossing the Line: Immigrants, Economics Integration, and Drug Enforcement on the U.S-Mexico Border,* Resource Center Press, 1994.
The authors take a close look at the border region that connects the United States and Mexico, focusing on issues ranging from shopping patterns to drug-running. Also examined are the attitudes on and realities of Mexican emigration to the United States and the new trade-driven economy that has sprung up in the border area since the late 1980s.

Krauze, Enrique, *Mexico: Biography of Power,* HarperCollins, 1997.
Krauze, a well-regarded Mexican historian, has written a thorough political history of his country from independence in 1810 to the present. Krauze pays particular attention to the key figures in Mexico's past, from dictators like Santa Anna and Porfirio Diaz to revolutionaries like Emiliano Zapata and Pancho Villa. He also chronicles the administrations of Mexico's most recent presidents, up to and including the country's current leader, Ernesto Zedillo.

Oppenheimer, Andres, *Bordering on Chaos: Guerrillas, Stockbrokers, Politicians, and Mexico's Road to Prosperity,* Little Brown, 1996.
Oppenheimer, a reporter at *The Miami Herald*, chronicles events in Mexico during one of the most turbulent periods in the country's modern history: the end of the presidency of Carlos Salinas and the beginning of Zedillo's term. During this time, a revolution began in the southern state of Chiapas, the leading candidate for president was assassinated and the country plunged into a terrible recession.

Articles

DePalma, Anthony, "Mexico's Recovery Just Bypasses the Poor," *The New York Times,* Aug. 12, 1997.
DePalma examines the impact of recent economic growth on the poor in Mexico and finds that, for many, the boom has passed them by. The journalist also details a new program recently introduced by President Zedillo that aims to improve education, health and nutrition among the nation's poorest citizens.

"Living Off Illegals," *The Economist,* April 19, 1997.
This piece examines the immigration debate in the United States and Mexico, focusing on "hypocrisy" in both countries. For instance, Mexicans complain about how their citizens are treated in the United States, even though their government abuses immigrants from Central America who cross into Mexico. Meanwhile, Americans say they oppose illegal immigration, even though they benefit from the cheap labor that immigrants provide.

"Neighbors," *The Economist,* March 29, 1997.
This article examines the often difficult relationship between Mexico and the United States, focusing on the drug trade and the certification debate in Washington.

Padget, Tim, "The Young and the Restless," *Time,* July 21, 1997.
Padget chronicles the growing importance of what he calls "the NAFTA generation," the large segment of the population that has grown up in the last decade. This new generation is rebelling against attitudes that have characterized Mexican society for decades. According to Padget, "Young people want realism instead of nationalist ideology . . . prize honesty, competence and practicality over old-fashioned lockstep thinking and knee-jerk anti-Americanism."

Preston, Julia, "Out of the Spotlight, Violence Tears at Mexican State," *The New York Times,* May 23, 1997.
Preston presents an update of the nearly forgotten Zapatista rebellion in the state of Chiapas. She writes: "The rebels have lost nearly all their political momentum. As the peace talks faltered over deep differences between President Ernesto Zedillo and Zapatista leaders, the guerrillas' international limelight faded while the army reinforced its control across the state, setting up garrisons in the most remote corners."

Smith, Geri, and Elizabeth Malkin, "The Border," *Business Week,* May 12, 1997.
This article details the dynamic economic growth on both sides of the U.S.-Mexican border. Each region along the 2,100-mile line, from the Pacific Ocean to the Gulf of Mexico, is examined.

Reports

Economic Policy Institute, Institute for Policy Studies, International Labor Rights Fund, Public Citizen's Global Trade Watch, U.S. Business and Industrial Council Educational Foundation, *The Failed Experiment: NAFTA at Three Years,* June 26, 1997.
The report details the "damage" done in the United States and Mexico by the North American Free Trade Agreement (NAFTA.) According to the groups that authored the study, NAFTA has driven down wages in both countries and led to a loss of jobs in the U.S. In addition, they say, the treaty helped to cause Mexico's devastating peso crisis in 1995 and has led to environmental degradation on both sides of the border.

The Next Step

Additional information from UMI's Newspaper & Periodical Abstracts™ database

Amado Carrillo Fuentes

Farah, Douglas, and Molly Moore, "Drug War Breaks Out In Mexico; Death of Cartel Boss Leaves Power Vacuum," *The Washington Post,* July 23, 1997, p. A1.
The death of Amado Carrillo Fuentes, one of the most powerful drug traffickers in the world, has set off a bloody struggle for control of Mexico's multibillion-dollar cocaine trade, according to U.S. and Mexican law enforcement officials.

Fineman, Mark, "DEA Confirms Mexican Drug Kingpin's Death," *Los Angeles Times,* July 7, 1997, p. A1.
Amado Carrillo Fuentes, who had escaped gangland-style assassination attempts and intensifying manhunts, died in Mexico City's Santa Monica Hospital after a nine-hour operation that included facial surgery and liposuction, Drug Enforcement Administration Administrator Thomas A. Constantine said in a telephone interview Sunday.

Fineman, Mark, "Mexican Drug Lord Said to Be Dead; Narcotics: Relatives of Amado Carrillo Fuentes report his demise. Officials seek corroboration," *Los Angeles Times,* July 6, 1997, p. A9.
Federal prosecutors Saturday were investigating widespread reports that Amado Carrillo Fuentes, identified by U.S. and Mexican law enforcement agencies as Mexico's most powerful drug baron, has died. Members of Carrillo's family told local reporters in their home state of Sinaloa that they have identified his body. However, Mexican authorities appeared to be skeptical of the Carrillo family's claims.

Cuauhtemoc Cardenas

"A Day to Celebrate in Mexico; Elections are a key step in the halting bid for true democracy," *Los Angeles Times,* July 6, 1997, p. M4.
At stake are six state governorships, 32 seats in the Senate, 500 in the Chamber of Deputies and several hundred mayoralties and other local offices — but the focus of political attention is the race for the new office of governor of Mexico City. Favored to win by a wide margin is Cuauhtemoc Cardenas, son of the late President Lazaro Cardenas and twice-presidential candidate under the left-wing Democratic Revolutionary Party (PRD).

Fineman, Mark, "Mayor-Elect Promises Change for Mexico City, Latin America: Corruption, pollution lead agenda for Cardenas, who will fire hundreds of top officials," *Los Angeles Times,* July 13, 1997, p. A1.
Mexico City, with a core population of 8 million, chose PRD-founder Cuauhtemoc Cardenas over seven rivals in the capital's first-ever mayoral election, giving him 50 percent of the vote. And his Democratic Revolution Party, or PRD, won a commanding majority on the City Council. So overwhelming was Cardenas' victory that the PRI's local chairman, Roberto Campa, announced Tuesday that he will resign.

Grayson, George W., "Beyond Mexico's Watershed: Political strife is predicted after the election hailed as a triumph for democracy, but old-school ties could prevail," *The Christian Science Monitor,* July 11, 1997, p. 18.
Prospects for Mexican democracy are not very good if the predictions of local Cassandras prove correct — namely that Mexico City's Mayor-elect Cuauhtemoc Cardenas will devote the next three years to heaving brickbats at President Ernesto Zedillo's liberalization program, while using city hall to launch a presidential bid for 2000.

"Mexico's Breakthrough," *The Christian Science Monitor,* July 9, 1997, p. 20.
Mexico's voters have answered the question of whether their country can turn decisively toward democratic reform. The Democratic Revolutionary Party (PRD) took the first contest for mayor of Mexico City in 68 years. Its winning candidate, PRD founder Cuauhtemoc Cardenas, is sure to be a strong presidential contender in 2000.

Moore, Molly, "Mayor-Elect Keeps Eye on Presidency; Born in Palace, Cardenas Could Launch 3rd Try at Highest Office," *The Washington Post,* July 8, 1997, p. A11.
Cuauhtemoc Cardenas was born in Mexico City's Los Pinos presidential palace in 1934 during his father's inaugural year as president. After spending his earliest childhood years romping around the Mexican White House, Cardenas has dedicated much of his adult life to trying to return there. On Sunday, Cardenas may have moved a step closer when the leftist opposition candidate from the Democratic Revolution Party became the first elected mayor of Mexico City and the second most powerful elected officeholder in the country, next to the presidency itself.

Munoz, Sergio, "Cuauhtemoc Cardenas; Setting the Stage for the First, Non- PRI Mexican President in 70 Years," *Los Angeles Times,* July 20, 1997, p. M3.
Cardenas remains an enigmatic figure in Mexico. The son of President Lazaro Cardenas, the most revered Mexican president of this century, he was raised in the corridors of power, but his real political profile has yet to emerge. To some, he can sound dull—his charisma, writes political

observer Carlos Monsivais, is having no charisma. Then, a spark is lit, and he speaks like a seasoned politician who understands and can explain the intricacies of his profession in a highly complex country. There are other times when he sounds like an avenging leftist angel, holding a flaming sword. Married for 34 years, Cardenas, 63, has three children. And while he now seems to be next in line for Mexico 's presidency, there is much that can block him. Things could go awry in Mexico City, or the PRI or another political party could field a formidable candidate, or Cardenas himself might be considered too old for the job in 2000. For now, he has become the favorite of Mexico's youth—82 percent of voters between the ages of 18 and 29 cast their ballots for Cardenas. We'll use all the tools available. Public works may help create jobs, but we should not create false expectations, because that does not create permanent jobs. A few weeks' job may slightly help one who has it, but that is nothing more than a temporary solution to a long-term problem. But a government elected by the votes of more than 1.5 million people does have the authority to rally the productive groups in the city and invite them to take advantage of the widespread business potential of this big city. Mexico City has an enormous tourist potential. This city is the largest consumer market in the nation. The city generates one-fourth of the country's GDP. This city is the largest center in the republic for financial transactions. There are so many investment opportunities that could lead to a remarkable recovery of the economy and thus to job creation.

Drugs

Fainaru, Steve," U.S., Mexico join in pledge to fight drugs: Clinton, Zedillo sign declaration," *The Boston Globe,* May 7, 1997, p. A1.

Two years after President Ernesto Zedillo described drug-trafficking as his country's most serious national security threat, the United States and Mexico used President Clinton's first visit here to release a 97-page "drug-threat assessment." The joint declaration of cooperation, signed by Clinton and Zedillo in a ceremony on the lawn outside the presidential palace, appeared to have been designed to demonstrate solidarity amid tensions over revelations of drug-related corruption here and the Clinton administration's March decision, disputed in the United States, to certify Mexico as a full ally in the drug war.

Meisler, Stanley, "Latest Fight in War on Drugs Leaves All Parties Feeling Bruised; Narcotics: Mexico certification angers Congress. But the process also humiliates neighboring nation," *Los Angeles Times,* March 1, 1997, p. A8.

The decision over whether to certify Mexico as an ally in the war on drugs has left many bruises: President Clinton averted a foreign policy debacle but angered important members of Congress. Mexican leaders won relief but were humiliated by the process. Drug fighters in both countries suffered embarrassment and loss of credibility.

"The Military Is No Answer for Mexico," *Chicago Tribune,* March 4, 1997, p. 12.

Highlighting the rampant corruption in the country, Mexico this weekend disclosed that a drug kingpin had "inexplicably" vanished from a jail in Mexico City. And the government's mendacity in handling the news was particularly galling: It delayed the announcement until several hours after Washington had made public its decision to once again certify Mexico as a bona fide ally in the drug war.

Witkin, Gordon, "Stopping cocaine south of the border," *U.S. News & World Report,* Jan. 29, 1996, pp. 48-56.

The Drug Enforcement Administration and the Federal Bureau of Investigation have joined forces to combat the mushrooming power of Mexico's drug cartels. Witkin examines the effort to keep drugs from being brought into the U.S. via the Mexican border.

Ernesto Zedillo

"Ernesto Zedillo's Place in History," *The New York Times,* July 27, 1997, p. 14.

Now that Mexicans have made clear their enthusiasm for democracy, President Ernesto Zedillo must determine how he will govern in the three remaining years of his presidency. He can defend the privileges and remaining powers of the Institutional Revolutionary Party or he can make a clean break with the party's old guard and align himself squarely with the new, more democratic order he helped create. Doing so will require a degree of courage and leadership that Zedillo has not always shown.

Schwartz, Stephen, "Zedillo can become a Mexican hero . . . At a price," *The Wall Street Journal,* May 23, 1997, p. A19.

Schwartz discusses President Ernesto Zedillo's efforts to place Mexico on the path toward real democracy, focusing on the challenge faced by the ruling Institutional Revolutionary Party (PRI) and the conservative opposition force, the National Action Party (PAN) as the July 1997 legislative mid-term elections approach.

Torres, Craig, "Zedillo unveils ambitious 3-year plan," *The Wall Street Journal,* June 4, 1997, p. A13.

President Ernesto Zedillo presented an ambitious three-year economic program on June 3, 1997, in an attempt to assure Mexicans that the economic plan they have endured for the past two years will pay off in stronger, sustainable growth.

"Zedillo Must Stay Economic Course," *Chicago Tribune,* July 26, 1997, p. 22.

Mexican President Ernesto Zedillo doesn't sound like a leader whose political party is reeling from its worst defeat in seven decades. He boasts that Mexico has arrived without violence at "democratic normality," an era of political stability and pluralism.

Gen. Jesus Gutierrez Rebollo

Anderson, John Ward, "Scandal Exposes Mexican Military's Corruptibility; Firing of General Casts Doubt on Armed Forces' Central Role in Drug War," *The Washington Post,* Feb. 20, 1997, p. A25.

Gen. Jesus Gutierrez Rebollo was chosen to lead Mexico's campaign against drugs in large measure because of his reputation for honesty and incorruptibility. He was fired Tuesday after officials charged that he and some of his assistants in Mexico's federal anti-drug agency accepted bribes to protect one of the country's most notorious drug kingpins, Armado Carrillo Fuentes, reputed head of the powerful Juarez cartel.

"An 'Honest' General Takes a Fall; Arrest of Mexico's drug czar deepens concern about cartels," *Los Angeles Times,* Feb. 20, 1997, p. B8.

Mexican Gen. Jesus Gutierrez Rebollo knew how to catch drug lords. The list of arrests he made in his long career is impressive. It is also selective and shows there were no serious blows to one drug outfit, the so-called Ciudad Juarez cartel, whose boss is Amado Carrillo Fuentes.

Downie, Andrew, "Troops sent to replace northern Baja's police; Mexico moves against drug trafficking," *Houston Chronicle,* Feb. 22, 1997, p. A1.

Gen. Jesus Gutierrez Rebollo was jailed this week following allegations that he accepted cash, property and other gifts from members of Mexico's dominant drug gang, the Juarez cartel headed by Amado Carrillo Fuentes. The general is currently jailed in the nation's top-security prison on various drug-trafficking counts. He could also face court-martial on treason charges, officials said.

"Mexican Military Implicated in Drug Corruption," *Los Angeles Times,* May 24, 1997, p. A4.

A report, based on testimony military officers gave during court proceedings in Mexico City, called into question efforts by the U.S. and Mexican governments to rely on the Mexican military in their war on drugs. The testimony was part of the case against Gen. Jesus Gutierrez Rebollo, who was arrested in February and charged with corruption. Prior to his arrest, Gutierrez was Mexico's anti-drug czar. In transcripts of his defense obtained Friday, Gutierrez says Amado Carrillo Fuentes, whom U.S. and Mexican drug enforcement agencies have identified as Mexico's most powerful drug lord, "could count on the protection of personnel in the Ministry of Defense," adding that a leak from high up helped Carrillo evade arrest in January.

Institutional Revolutionary Party

Althaus, Dudley, "Mexico enters new way of life/ Democracy taking shape in wake of PRI defeats," *Houston Chronicle,* July 8, 1997, p. A1.

Nearly complete, yet still unofficial, returns showed the country's long-ruling Institutional Revolutionary Party, popularly known as the PRI, being thumped all across this nation of 95 million people. Tallies by the Federal Electoral Institute, which for the first time is independent of the government, showed the ruling party with only about 38 percent of the vote for the lower house of Congress. The center-right National Action Party was winning about 27 percent while the center-left Democratic Revolution Party was taking nearly 26 percent. Smaller parties were splitting the difference. Cuauhtemoc Cardenas, the 63-year-old son of a president and himself a former PRI stalwart, won the mayoralty of Mexico City for the Democratic Revolution Party, taking nearly twice the votes of the ruling party's candidate.

de la Garza, Paul, "Mexico's Voters Chip at Ruling Party's Grip; Zedillo Concedes Defeat in Mayor's Race in Capital," *Chicago Tribune,* July 7, 1997, p. 14.

For the first time since its birth almost 70 years ago, the ruling Institutional Revolutionary Party (PRI) is in danger of losing its majority in the lower house of Congress and two of six gubernatorial races. Preliminary results late Sunday showed Cuauhtemoc Cardenas of the left-of-center Party of the Democratic Revolution (PRD) leading his rivals in the mayor's race by a comfortable margin.

"Mexican opposition unites against PRI in legislature," *The Wall Street Journal,* Aug. 13, 1997, p. A10.

Mexican opposition parties have reached an accord to form a majority voting bloc in the lower house of Congress, marking an end to the ruling Institutional Revolutionary Party's 68-year dominance of the legislative body.

"New Day in Mexican Politics; With the PRI's monopoly broken, democracy has arrived," *Los Angeles Times,* July 8, 1997, p. B6.

What seemed impossible just a few years ago happened Sunday in Mexico. Full-fledged democracy has finally arrived, breaking the political monopoly of the Institutional Revolutionary Party (PRI). This was the result of a determined people voting for change.

Maquiladoras

Kopytoff, Verne G., "Nafta ignites a realty boom south of the border," *The New York Times,* Dec. 24, 1995, p. 7.

Tijuana, Mexico, has seen a real estate boom in 1995 caused by NAFTA, a devalued Mexican peso and a strong Japanese yen. The border city of 1.5 million is luring foreign manufacturers of all kinds with low wages, easy access to the U.S. and free trade. The resulting whirl of building, particularly of industrial parks and factories, called maquiladoras, has been a dramatic turn from the real estate doldrums of the early 1990s.

Nauman, Ann K., and Mireille Hutchinson, "The integration of women into the Mexican labor force since NAFTA," *American Behavioral Scientist,* June 1997, pp. 950-956.

The changes that have taken place in the Mexican labor force since NAFTA, with particular concern for the maquiladoras, tax-free assembly plants that use large numbers of low-paid Mexican women, are examined.

NAFTA

Beachy, Debra, "NAFTA producing squabbles, not freer trade," *Houston Chronicle,* Feb. 4, 1996, p. D1.

Analysts say U.S. and Mexican officials' efforts to distance themselves from NAFTA, coupled with Mexico's peso crisis, have cast the free trade agreement adrift. A checkup on progress in implementing the trade pact shows a lot more talk than action.

Blustein, Paul, "White House Subdued On NAFTA's Impact; Report on Trade Accord Cites 'Modest' Results,' *The Washington Post,* July 11, 1997, p. G1.

The Clinton administration, which once promoted the North American Free Trade Agreement (NAFTA) as a major boon for American companies and workers, finds in a report to be released today that NAFTA has had a "modest positive effect" on the U.S. economy. Polls have shown that the U.S. public widely views NAFTA as a failure, especially since the Mexican peso crisis of late 1994 threw Mexico into deep recession and turned the U.S. trade balance with its southern neighbor sharply negative.

Greenberger, Robert S., "Nafta is good for U.S., Clinton study says," *The Wall Street Journal,* July 11, 1997, p. A2.

A Clinton administration report to be released on July 11, 1997, claims that NAFTA has "a modest positive effect" on the U.S. economy. The report concludes that NAFTA has produced gains in U.S. exports, income, investment and jobs, as tariff barriers in Mexico have dropped sharply.

Lewis, Diane E., "Report hits NAFTA on jobs: Study cites layoffs and says conditions for workers worse," *The Boston Globe,* June 27, 1997, p. D1.

The North American Free Trade Agreement (NAFTA) has benefited some sectors of the U.S. economy, but it also has led to the elimination of 2 million jobs in Mexico and 400,000 in the United States, according to a report released yesterday. The report blames the trade pact for a loss in employee bargaining power and the lowering of living standards and wages among blue-collar workers in the United States, Canada and Mexico.

Shaiken, Harley, "NAFTA Needs More Than Fine Tuning; Trade: Mexico is expanding only as a site for cheap labor, replacing U.S. jobs," *Los Angeles Times,* July 7, 1997, p. B5.

Early this week President Clinton will deliver a report to Congress evaluating the first three years of the North American Free Trade Agreement (NAFTA). The report is likely to praise NAFTA in general and salute the rapid growth of U.S. exports to Mexico in particular. However, after more than three years of NAFTA, the results are far from promising.

Silva-Herzog, Jesus, "Trade Warms Mexico's Economy; A three-year assessment shows a strong base of new exports and a balanced three-way partnership," *Los Angeles Times,* July 1, 1997, p. B7.

The issue of whether U.S. business can compete in the international marketplace has already been answered in the positive many times over: The U.S. is the world's top exporter. The largest recipient of foreign direct investment, its exports have dominated trade even in traditionally protectionist markets where the odds against U.S. products were high. A more meaningful debate about the value of agreements such as NAFTA should be on the ability of Mexico, the developing country, to participate profitably in international trade.

Peso Crisis

Espinosa, Marco, and Steven Russell, "The Mexican economic crisis: Alternative views," *Economic Review* (Federal Reserve Bank of Atlanta), January 1996, pp. 21-44.

Espinosa and Russell suggest that many of the explanations for the 1994 peso crisis in Mexico are based on questionable assumptions and dubious analysis.

Neely, Christopher J., "The giant sucking sound: Did NAFTA devour the Mexican peso?" *Federal Reserve Bank of St. Louis Review,* July 1996, pp. 33-47.

The relationship between NAFTA and the peso crisis of December 1994 is examined. The provisions of NAFTA are reviewed. An obvious link between the two has never been clearly established.

Preston, Julia, "With Election Near, Mexico Sets Goals of 5 percent Growth," *The New York Times,* June 4, 1997, p. D22.

President Ernesto Zedillo's three-year economic program comes nearly halfway through his term. The plan reasserts the tight fiscal policies and wariness of foreign debt that he has applied to pull Mexico back from ruin after the peso crisis in December 1994.

Whitt, Joseph A. Jr., "The Mexican peso crisis," *Economic Review* (Federal Reserve Bank of Atlanta), January 1996, pp. 1-20.

In an attempt to avoid an economic slowdown during 1994, Mexico engaged in massive sterilized intervention, a policy that is not sustainable for long. The ultimate result of the policy was a collapse of the exchange rate and soaring interest rates. Whitt examines whether Mexican policy mistakes made devaluation of the peso inevitable.

Back Issues

Great Research on Current Issues Starts Right Here . . . Recent topics covered by The CQ Researcher are listed below. Before May 1991, reports were published under the name of Editorial Research Reports.

MARCH 1996
The British Monarchy
Preventing Juvenile Crime
Tax Reform
Pursuing the Paranormal

APRIL 1996
Centennial Olympic Games
Managed Care
Protecting Endangered Species
New Military Culture

MAY 1996
Russia's Political Future
Marriage and Divorce
Year-Round Schools
Taiwan, China and the U.S.

JUNE 1996
Rethinking NAFTA
First Ladies
Teaching Values
Labor Movement's Future

JULY 1996
Recovered-Memory Debate
Native Americans' Future
Crackdown on Sexual Harassment
Attack on Public Schools

AUGUST 1996
Fighting Over Animal Rights
Privatizing Government Services
Child Labor and Sweatshops
Cleaning Up Hazardous Wastes

SEPTEMBER 1996
Gambling Under Attack
The States and Federalism
Civic Journalism
Reassessing Foreign Aid

OCTOBER 1996
Political Consultants
Insurance Fraud
Rethinking School Integration
Parental Rights

NOVEMBER 1996
Global Warming
Clashing Over Copyright
Consumer Debt
Governing Washington, D.C.

DECEMBER 1996
Welfare, Work and the States
The New Volunteerism
Implementing the Disabilities Act
America's Pampered Pets

JANUARY 1997
Combating Scientific Misconduct
Restructuring the Electric Industry
The New Immigrants
Chemical and Biological Weapons

FEBRUARY 1997
Assisting Refugees
Alternative Medicine's Next Phase
Independent Counsels
Feminism's Future

MARCH 1997
New Air Quality Standards
Alcohol Advertising
Civic Renewal
Educating Gifted Students

APRIL 1997
Declining Crime Rates
The FBI Under Fire
Gender Equity in Sports
Space Program's Future

MAY 1997
The Stock Market
The Cloning Controversy
Expanding NATO
The Future of Libraries

JUNE 1997
FDA Reform
China After Deng
Line-Item Veto
Breast Cancer

JULY 1997
Transportation Policy
Executive Pay
School Choice Debate
Aggressive Driving

AUGUST 1997
Age Discrimination
Banning Land Mines
Children's Television
Evolution vs. Creationism

SEPTEMBER 1997
Caring for the Dying
Mental Health Policy

Future Topics

- ***Youth Fitness***
- ***Urban Sprawl in the West***
- ***Diversity in the Workplace***

THE CQ Researcher

PUBLISHED BY CONGRESSIONAL QUARTERLY INC.

Youth Fitness

Do young Americans get enough exercise?

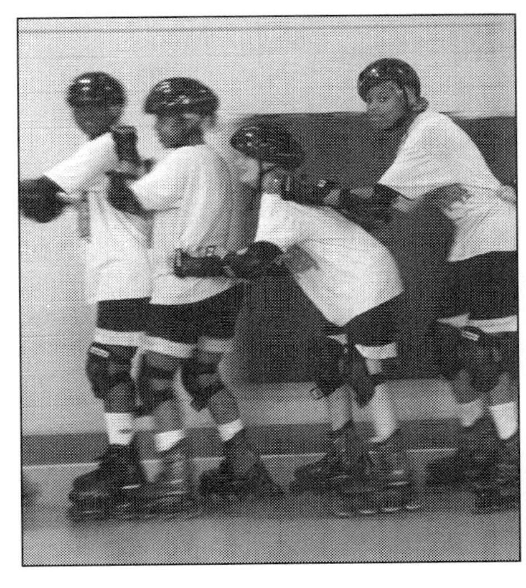

American youth are in worse physical shape than earlier generations, many fitness experts claim. According to the U.S. surgeon general, only about one-half of U.S. children get regular exercise, and one-fourth don't take part in physical activity at all. As a result, obesity among children and adolescents has increased substantially since the 1960s. The conveniences of modern life — notably television, video games and computers — get much of the blame for creating a nation of youthful couch potatoes. In addition, school officials often scale back or eliminate physical education programs when budget squeezes occur. Nonetheless, innovative physical educators are working to reverse the trend by acquainting kids with activities that interest them — and that can help them maintain fitness throughout life.

INSIDE THIS ISSUE

CQ Sept. 26, 1997 • Volume 7, No. 36 • Pages 841-864

Formerly Editorial Research Reports

YOUTH FITNESS

THE ISSUES

BACKGROUND

CURRENT SITUATION

OUTLOOK

SIDEBARS AND GRAPHICS

FOR FURTHER RESEARCH

COVER: SCHOOLS IN HOUSTON REPLACED UNPOPULAR PE OFFERINGS WITH ACTIVITIES STUDENTS ENJOY, SUCH AS IN-LINE SKATING. (© 1997 JOEL DRAUGHT)

September 26, 1997
Volume 7, No. 36

EDITOR
Sandra Stencel

MANAGING EDITOR
Thomas J. Colin

ASSOCIATE EDITORS
Sarah M. Magner
Richard L. Worsnop

STAFF WRITERS
Charles S. Clark
Mary H. Cooper
Kenneth Jost
David Masci

EDITORIAL ASSISTANT
Vanessa E. Furlong

PUBLISHED BY
Congressional Quarterly Inc.

CHAIRMAN
Andrew Barnes

VICE CHAIRMAN
Andrew P. Corty

PRESIDENT AND PUBLISHER
Robert W. Merry

EXECUTIVE EDITOR
David Rapp

The CQ Researcher (ISSN 1056-2036). Formerly Editorial Research Reports. Published weekly, except Jan. 3, May 30, Aug. 29, Oct. 31, by Congressional Quarterly Inc., 1414 22nd St., N.W., Washington, D.C. 20037. Annual subscription rate for libraries, businesses and government is $340. Additional rates furnished upon request. Periodicals postage paid at Washington, D.C., and additional mailing offices. POSTMASTER: Send address changes to The CQ Researcher, 1414 22nd St., N.W., Washington, D.C. 20037.

Youth Fitness

By Richard L. Worsnop

The Issues

Tiffany Gatchel is not your typical 14-year-old. She likes PE. That's because the schools in Tiffany's Houston district said goodbye to dodgeball, rope-climbing, laps around the gym and other "lame" physical education activities. When kids in the Aldine School District suit up for gym, they know they will be doing activities they enjoy, such as basketball and hockey played on in-line skates, cycling and line dancing.

But Tiffany remembers what PE was like before Sharon Sterchy took over as the district's director of health and wellness in the early 1990s.

"I hated PE then because it was so boring," she says. "Like, they taught us how to square dance to this really old music. I think the most excitement we ever had was jump-rope."

But PE became "really creative" after Sterchy arrived, Tiffany says. "They brought in the roller blades, they brought in the bikes, they added a bunch of new sports." Above all, the instructors "gave us more opportunities to find something we're really good at."

Giving students a real choice is a key tenet of Sterchy's philosophy. "We try to provide as many options for kids as we reasonably can," she says. "The reason is that we want them to make good lifetime choices. Certainly, we focus their thinking, but we don't make up their minds for them. We want kids to take the information they learn in PE and use it for the rest of their lives — not just the 12 years they're in school with us."

Thus, the Aldine PE program concentrates on physical activities that youngsters can continue to engage in as adults — skating, swimming, running, jogging, step-aerobics and the like.

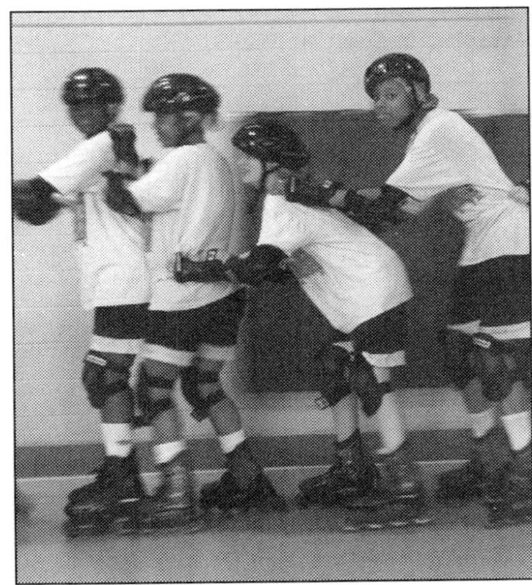

Even fishing and orienteering. In addition, there are what Sterchy calls "user-friendly classes" on self-defense.

"We teach them what to do when they're at the mall and hear footsteps behind them. Basic things, like have your keys ready, don't walk by yourself and don't park your car with the door facing away from the mall entrance. These are matters that girls, especially, should be aware of."

The Aldine program also deals with sound nutrition and how the body functions. To this end, PE teachers work with teachers in other subjects to plan PE activities around what the students are learning in those classes. For example, to reinforce what they were learning about anatomy in biology class, some of the students performed aerobics on a course shaped like a human heart. (*See story, p. 848.*)

This interaction has effected a "profound" transformation, staff writer Kathleen Kennedy Manzo noted recently in *Education Week*. "Teachers and administrators now believe that physical education teachers are as critical to school success as their peers in the science or math departments." [1]

Such attitudes are far from common in other school districts across the country. Indeed, physical education classes remain prime targets for elimination when public-education funding becomes tight. Even in schools where physical education is mandatory, absenteeism often runs high because much of the class time is taken up with changing clothes, listening to instructions and waiting to take part in whatever activity is scheduled.

All this has helped erode the physical condition of America's young people, fitness advocates say. "By the time they reach high school, 63 percent of children are no longer physically active," the American Council on Exercise asserted last year. "Why? Try TV, video games and personal computers, compounded by too much munching of high-calorie foods that add unwanted and unneeded pounds." [2]

To reverse the trend, the council urged parents to become better fitness role models for their children. "Let them know that being physically active does not necessarily mean going to exercise classes or playing sports, although these are two great options. Hiking and camping, body surfing and playing Frisbee or paddleball are activities the whole family can enjoy. And, since they're having so much fun, teens will hardly realize that what they're doing is actually good for them." [3]

"You don't have to run the Boston Marathon or train for the Olympics to get healthy and stay healthy," noted Health and Human Services Secretary Donna E. Shalala. "From walking your dog, as I do every morning, to gardening, to washing your car, regular, moderate activity is the way to go." [4]

The problem is that the typical American family now contains two working parents, who both may lead a sedentary existence on the job and at home. "We're going to be a nation

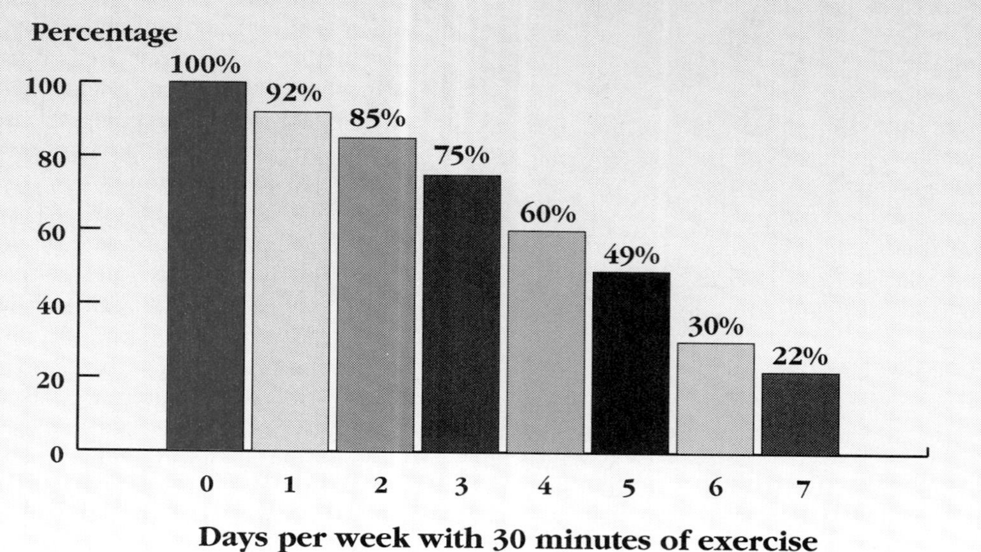

Sources: International Life Sciences Institute, "Improving Children's Health Through Physical Activity: A New Opportunity," July 1997; survey conducted by Louis Harris and Associates in September-October 1996.

at risk if we continue to be as sedentary as we are," said JoAnne Owens-Nauslar, director of professional development for the American School Health Association. "We're going to find major, major health problems 20, 30, 40 years down the road." [5]

The day of reckoning may be closer to hand than that, according to Perot "Bud" Nevin Jr., chairman of Executive Fitness of America, the company he founded in San Jose, Calif. "Too much exercise once in a while is the most detrimental thing you can do to yourself," says Nevin, a 75-year-old fitness buff whose students have included astronauts. He cites the hypothetical case of a deskbound businessman who plays several rounds of tennis on Saturday and collapses on court from a heart attack. "That fellow would be far better off to get up Saturday morning and watch cartoons on TV all day." [6]

Hand-wringing about the nation's deteriorating physical condition is hardly new. Similar worries were voiced throughout the 19th century, inspired at first by increasing urbanization and later by the great surge of immigration from Europe (*see p. 849*). Health reformers of the time noted that city dwellers seemed less robust than members of farm families, whose livelihood required hard physical activity on a regular basis.

"Is it not shameful," asked R. Tait McKenzie, physical education director at the University of Pennsylvania, "to think of a big, well-built man, brought up on the farm ... spending his days pushing a small pen or whispering into a dictaphone?" [7]

Today, much concern about American physical fitness centers on children and adolescents — the adults of tomorrow. Young people now have many more ways of keeping fit than did their counterparts of a century ago. At the same time, labor-saving devices and myriad electronic entertainment choices have made the sedentary life a tempting option for many millions of youngsters.

Susan Kalish, executive director of the American Running and Fitness Association in Bethesda, Md., feels that "too many people view organized physical activity as just fun and games, the icing on the cake." Actually, she notes, "Studies show that kids who are physically active do better academically, are more focused and less likely to get involved in drugs and violence. They're also less likely to get pregnant and more likely to stay in school." In sum, she feels parents and school administrators need to become more appreciative of the "positive ramifications of a healthy lifestyle."

Experience suggests, however, that raising the overall level of American youth fitness will be a long, difficult undertaking, and that significant gains are by no means assured.

As fitness experts, school officials and parents debate the best way to keep children fit, these are some of the questions being asked:

Are U.S. children and teenagers less physically fit today than 20 years ago?

Studies in recent years suggest that American youngsters today are significantly less fit than those of the previous generation. For instance, a 1996 report by the U.S. surgeon general found that only about one-half of U.S. youths engage in physical activity on a regular basis and that one-fourth take part in no physical activity at all.[8]

Among high school students, the report stated, enrollment in physical education courses remained unchanged during the first half of the 1990s. However, daily attendance in such classes declined from about 42 percent to 25 percent over that period.

The American Council on Exercise came to similar conclusions: "Kids today are fatter and less fit than previous generations. Between the mid-1960s and the late 1970s, obesity increased 54 percent among young children (ages 6-11) and 39 percent among adolescents (ages 12-17). Recent studies show that obesity has continued to increase into the '90s."[9]

For James O. Hill, a professor of pediatrics and medicine at the University of Colorado Health Sciences Center in Denver, the implications of these data are clear. They convey the message that "this may be the fattest, least-fit generation ever," he says.

Nevin goes even further. "We are rapidly becoming a nation of weaklings," he says. "It's too bad. We're proud, and we're intelligent. I think it's probably because of our intelligence that we've brought this affliction upon ourselves. The affliction, of course, is automation."

Judith C. Young, executive director of the National Association for Sport and Physical Education in Reston, Va., takes a somewhat less cataclysmic view. "In some dimensions, children are less physically fit today than 10 years ago," she says. "That is, they are more obese and are less physically active. Those are both potential danger signs.

"But as to whether they can run as far, or do as many sit-ups and so forth, that's a little more problematic in terms of providing evidence for being in better or worse 'shape.' We don't have direct evidence of any relationship between those things and health status."

© Doug Brown

Many U.S. schools now offer PE activities that can help children maintain fitness throughout life, such as karate, in-line skating and cycling.

Greg Welk, director of the childhood and adolescent health division of the Cooper Institute for Aerobics Research in Dallas, takes a similar position. "A lot of people say kids are in worse physical shape today than 10 years ago," he says, "but we really don't have evidence to support that. People who say such things fail to recognize that fitness is multidimensional. Yes, kids are fatter today than they were before. But with respect to the other dimensions of fitness — cardiovascular condition, muscular strength and endurance and flexibility — there probably hasn't been much of a change at all."

In this connection, Sterchy notes that standards for measuring fitness have changed over time. Years ago, skill-related tests were the norm. Physical education teachers judged their pupils' progress on the basis of how many push-ups or sit-ups they could perform, how fast they could run a mile.

"Now, we test cardiovascular endurance, flexibility, muscle strength and body composition," she says. "We don't look at how fast you run the 50-yard dash. The reality of it is, who cares? A more meaningful test would be, can you climb the steps to a third-floor apartment while carrying a bag of groceries and a 2-year-old without getting winded? That's the real world."

Gary Brines, executive director of the National High School Athletic Coaches Association, concedes that some of today's young people are out of shape. "But on the other hand," he says, "a great many of them are in the best physical condition that we've ever seen young people in our country. And a lot of that has to do with the emphasis on fitness that has been brought to the table by the National Athletic Trainers Association. Studies on physical conditioning and nutrition by government agencies also have helped. In fact, our organization's code of ethics calls attention to the value of sound eating habits."

Christine Spain, director of research, planning and special projects for the

Nearly One-Fourth of Children Don't Take PE

One-third of American children in grades 4-12 have PE every school day, but nearly one-fourth do not take PE at all.

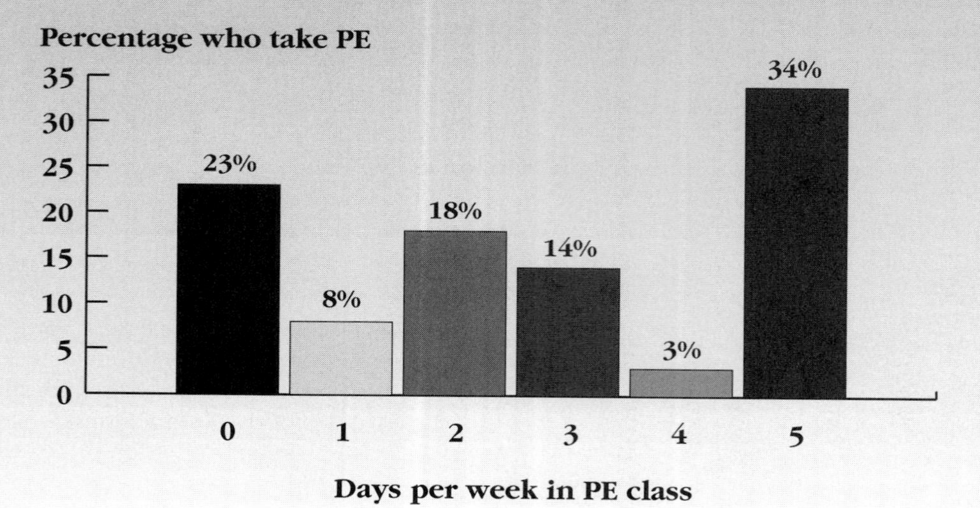

Sources: International Life Sciences Institute, "Improving Children's Health Through Physical Activity: A New Opportunity," July 1997; survey conducted by Louis Harris and Associates in September-October 1996.

President's Council on Physical Fitness and Sports, feels that social conditions are partially to blame for the lack of fitness among many young people. "Fear of crime and violence makes parents more hesitant to send their children out to play, which they normally would do," she says. "And many of today's children are latchkey kids because both parents hold full-time jobs. And what do those parents tell their kids? 'Get in the house, shut the door, do your homework and stay indoors.' So, most of them will sit around watching TV or playing computer games."

Kent Falb, president of the National Athletic Trainers Association and head trainer for the National Football League's Detroit Lions, thinks the labor-saving conveniences of modern life have eroded the physical condition of all Americans, regardless of age.

"It can be something as simple as an electronic garage-door opener or a gas furnace that doesn't require all the hard work that old-fashioned coal-burning furnaces did," he says. "The net result is that kids today don't take part in physical activities the way they used to. When's the last time you saw kids jumping rope?"

Some fitness advocates are encouraged by reports of increased physical activity among girls, even though the motivation may be weight loss. "With adolescent girls, you often walk a fine line between promoting healthy behaviors and unhealthy behaviors," Hill says. "There's no question that physical activity can help control weight when done in the right way. But we have to be careful about how we go about it. For instance, some teenage girls trying to reduce may combine exercise with excessive use of laxatives."

Has Title IX improved fitness among young women?

One of the great imponderables of the youth fitness debate is the impact of Title IX of the Education Amendments of 1972 on young women's fitness. Title IX, which required gender equity in school and college sports, is credited with a huge surge of female participation in interscholastic and intercollegiate team sports.

In 1971, the year before Title IX, fewer than 300,000 girls played high school sports nationwide; in 1996, more than 2.4 million participated. Participation in intercollegiate women's sports tripled over the same period. As a result, Title IX is widely credited with the success of U.S. women athletes in World Cup soccer, the 1996 Olympics and the inaugural seasons of the American Basketball League and Women's National Basketball Association. [10]

Impressive as these achievements are, skeptics question whether they reflect a significant increase in the fitness of young American women in general. Only a minority of girls regularly participate in competitive sports, they note; hence, any enhancement of overall female fitness probably has been slight. Other fitness enthusiasts argue that it is too soon to assess the influence of Title IX.

In Falb's opinion, the law "only increased the fitness of a select group of female athletes. It did not improve the physical well-being of all American women — just those who participate in collegiate athletics."

Welk, in contrast, feels "girls are becoming more active" because of

Title IX. "The difference between boys' and girls' levels of activity is pretty small now — with boys being just slightly more active."

Though Hill believes Title IX "definitely has improved fitness among girls," he also says, "we still have a ways to go." He notes that girls are less physically active than boys at just about any age. "We need to tailor some of our physical education programs to address girls' needs."

Title IX, says Kalish, has chiefly benefited "girls who are genetically inclined to be good athletes." However, she doubts whether it has done anything for young women whose parents are obese or sedentary.

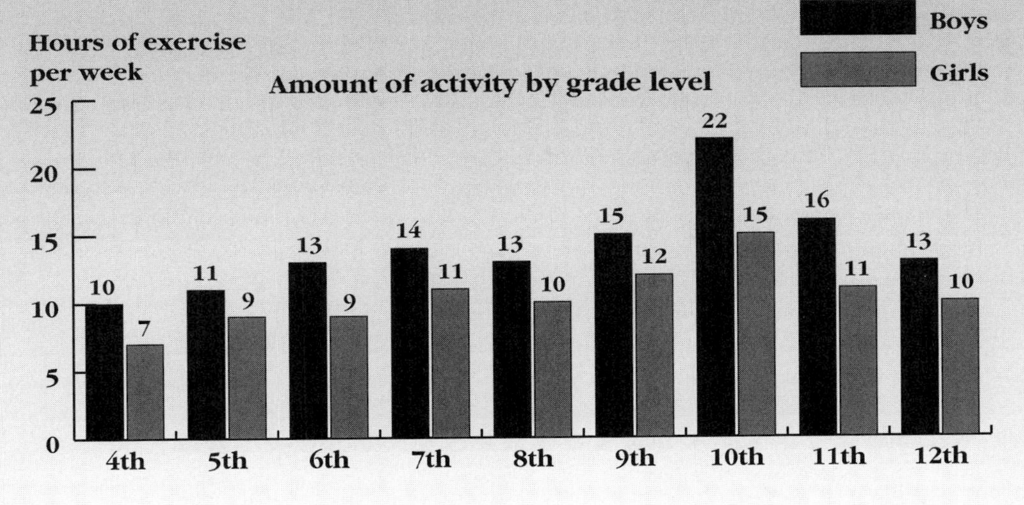

Girls Exercise Less Than Boys

Physical activity among children peaks in 10th grade and then declines. At all grade levels, boys are significantly more active than girls.

Sources: International Life Sciences Institute, "Improving Children's Health Through Physical Activity: A New Opportunity," July 1997; survey conducted by Louis Harris and Associates in September-October 1996.

"We shouldn't assume that just because Title IX exists, girls will be more fit," says Kalish. "Girls with the genetic makeup to excel in sports will take advantage of opportunities that didn't exist before 1972. But 50-75 percent of all high school girls won't have those opportunities because they aren't good enough to win a place on a varsity sports squad. So Title IX, by itself, isn't going to solve the problem of unfit young women."

Sterchy also has mixed feelings about Title IX. "In some respects, it has done great things for women," she says. "But in other respects, I think it has been detrimental."

There are times, Sterchy explains, "when girls enjoy attending physical education class with just girls. Title IX may prevent them from doing that. If being with the fellas in PE class makes a girl uncomfortable, and she performs below her potential because of that, then it's detrimental to her — because she didn't get a choice."

Young has reservations, too. "I don't know if Title IX has improved the average young woman's fitness," she says, "because physical education was accessible to all students in schools [before 1972], and in fact it was more extensive in some places than it is now."

Young acknowledges that the law "opened up competitive athletic opportunities for women to a major extent. And so what we have now are three groups: a few kids — both boys and girls — who are very active and very fit; a small middle group; and masses of sedentary youngsters."

As a result, Young isn't especially impressed by the great increase in female participation in school and college team sports. "All the athletes in a school with a very highly developed sports program amount to only about 20 percent of the student body," she notes. "That means 80 percent of the students are not participating in organized school sports."

Spain's appraisal is more upbeat. "Title IX is saying, in effect, 'It's OK to sweat. It's OK to be physically active. It doesn't mean you lose your femininity. It's good to be healthy, to be strong, to excel in sports.' "

Do youngsters risk injury by taking up age-inappropriate sports?

Though youth fitness experts worry mainly about sedentary and obese children and teens, they reserve some concern for youngsters at the opposite end of the activity spectrum — those who take part in such

In Houston, Students Take to 'Holistic' PE

It's an old put-down that teachers everywhere hear at some point in their career: "Those who can, do. Those who can't, teach. And those who can't teach, teach PE."

But teaching PE is a whole new ballgame in the Aldine School District, in Houston, Texas. Under the guidance of Sharon Sterchy, the district's health and wellness director for the past six years, physical education for the district's 48,000 children has become an integral part of the curriculum — not the academic stepchild it is in many other parts of the country.

In Houston, students in Aldine PE classes "practice vocabulary and spelling, execute math problems and learn science concepts," according to *Education Week*. Not surprisingly, the teachers and administrators in the district "believe that physical education teachers are as critical to school success as their peers in the science or math departments." [1]

Sterchy describes the Aldine wellness program as "holistic," in that it embraces not just physical activity but math, science, social studies, reading and writing. "We have found that when you express science or math concepts in terms of movement, students grasp them more easily."

As Susan Kalish, executive director of the American Running and Fitness Association, puts it in her recent book, "physical activity should be incorporated into other learning experiences." [2]

Tiffany Gatchel, a 10th-grader at Houston's Chester W. Nimitz High School, agrees. For instance, she recalls an obstacle course that mimicked the flow of blood through a human heart. "It was a lot of fun. I can still remember the different parts of the heart from that class."

Tiffany's family, like most others in the Aldine district, strongly supports Sterchy's innovative approach. "We don't get notes from parents saying, 'Please take Jimmy out of PE today because he has the sniffles,'" Sterchy says. "Parents in our district are truly appreciative of what we're trying to accomplish. And we do other things for the community as well, such as talking to local groups about how to choose healthy after-school snacks for children."

Tiffany has found that PE has given her "a lot more energy for school. I'm not grumpy and tired at the end of the day. Also, I get a better night's sleep, and my body feels more renewed the next morning."

For her part, Sterchy regrets that, "We're not held accountable on a state-mandated test for wellness or fitness. Test results can show you where your weaknesses are."

As a result, PE instructors in the district have to rely on what their eyes tell them. By that subjective measure, Sterchy feels they earn more than a passing grade. "Our class participation runs close to 100 percent," she says. "You won't find our kids sitting on the gym floor moaning, 'I don't want to do this today.' They're ready to start working out almost before the first bell stops ringing."

---

[1] Quoted in Kathleen Kennedy Manzo, "Physical Attraction," *Education Week*, April 2, 1997, pp. 36-37.

[2] Susan Kalish, *Your Child's Fitness: Practical Advice for Parents* (1996).

---

potentially risky sports as rock climbing and triathlons.

"Skydiving is legally off-limits to children, as is marathon running," an article noted recently in *Women's Sports and Fitness*. But there's nothing to stop children as young as 7 "from scaling rock walls up to 60 feet high, training for a triathlon or trying to set a world mountain-climbing record," it also noted. [11]

Some medical experts question whether young children are capable of handling the physical and emotional demands of certain taxing sports. "In some cases, we feel it's really abuse, and there's a debate within the sports-medicine community as to what we should do about it," said Rosemary Agostini, a Seattle physician specializing in family practice and sports medicine. "Some of these extreme sports could be doing a tremendous amount of damage to kids." [12]

Falb agrees that "some sports may be too advanced for the physical capabilities of a pre-puberty individual." But he adds that many youngsters can participate safely if they do so "in moderation and with proper adult supervision." For instance, he believes triathlons for adolescents should have shorter distances. Teenagers "are not physically mature enough to handle the demands of an adult triathlon," he says. *

Young says that physical education has a mission "to help people participate safely in all physical activities," including potentially hazardous ones. "Now, that doesn't mean we're going to be able to instruct kids on every single one of the risky or not-so-risky activities. But we need to instill a generic concern for safety in all PE students."

For instance, she says, physical education teachers should stress the importance of wearing protective equipment, such as helmets and knee and elbow pads, while bicycling or roller-blading. Lessons on rules of the road and bicycle maintenance also are advisable, she adds.

Rock climbing, in Young's view, isn't much different from climbing up

---

* Triathlon distances vary according to the level of competition. In a Half Iron Man Triathalon, which ranks in about the middle, participants swim 1.2 miles, cycle 56 miles and run 13.1 miles.

the walls of the gymnasium. "The risk element of rock climbing is precisely what draws some kids to it; they're looking for adventure. We need to make sure it's a managed risk to the extent possible."

Welk, a triathlete himself, doesn't regard the sport as dangerous for kids — provided "the child is self-motivated." Problems arise "when parents encourage a child to be athletic, earn a scholarship or become a star. Often, they push their child too hard. The youngster eventually will rebel against that pressure, and not want to be physically active."

Welk says he's "not too concerned" about children who decide on their own to take up physically demanding sports. "The body can handle that, even at a young age. But there are certain guidelines that should be followed. Young children shouldn't use heavy weights for weight lifting, and they shouldn't do extreme bouts of exercise. As long as they perform with supervision and care, it's fine for kids to be active."

For Hill, worrying about children who compete in endurance sports "is a little bit like worrying about people who are naturally lean and complain they can't gain weight. From a public health point of view, sedentary behavior poses much more of a risk than the opposite extreme."

Kalish, like Young, believes it's all right for kids to compete in challenging activities so long as their motivation comes from within. "But you don't want a kid to do something just because their dad says, 'Come do it with me.' The kid may end up being scared to death."

Nonetheless, Kalish says she finds it "really surprising when youngsters say they want to run a marathon. Kids usually have a hard time focusing on one thing for an hour. Marathons take two to three hours to run, which is far beyond their attention span."

In sum, Kalish says, "If a kid tells me, 'I want to mountain-climb, and I have a good teacher to show me how to do it,' then I'll say, 'Go for it, that's great.' But if the kid says, 'I want to go bungee-jumping because my dad says he wants me to,' that's not a good thing at all." ■

BACKGROUND

Modern Fitness Era

Concern for youth physical fitness dates back thousands of years. The earliest evidence of organized physical education activity dates from approximately 3000 B.C. in Crete. Though some of the programs were linked to religious rites, most used military instructors to teach youths about self-defense. Centuries later, physical conditioning of youth facilitated the rise of the Persian Empire. All boys were removed from their homes at age 6 and trained by the state in survival skills and the development of strength and endurance. [13]

Physical education of the young probably reached its apogee in ancient times in the city-states of Greece. In Athens, physical training was viewed as part of a broader quest for human excellence. Sparta, by contrast, conditioned its young men to become strong warriors. National festivals evolved from various competitions associated with youth physical development, culminating in the first recorded Olympic Games in 776 B.C. in the valley of Olympia in northeastern Greece.

Some 300 years later, the Greek physicians Herodicus and Hippocrates established a link between exercise and hygiene. In *Regimen,* written in about 400 B.C., Hippocrates stated: "Eating alone will not keep a man well; he must also take exercise. For food and exercise, while possessing opposite qualities, yet work together to produce health."

The modern physical fitness era began in Northern Europe early in the 19th century. Friedrich Ludwig Jahn founded the first *Turnverein* (gymnastics society) in Berlin in 1811. From there, interest in gymnastics spread to nearby Denmark and Sweden, where Per Henrik Ling applied scientific data to gymnastics and set early standards for training teachers in the theory and practice of physical education. In Britain, Swedish gymnastic exercises were added to school programs, along with games and sports.

U.S. Health Reformers

Meanwhile, awareness of the health benefits of regular exercise also was growing in the United States. In 1806, New York physician Shadrach Ricketson asserted in *Means of Preserving Health and Preventing Diseases* that, "a certain proportion of exercise is not much less essential to a healthy or vigorous constitution than drink, food and sleep; for we see that people, whose inclination, situation, or employment does not admit of exercise, soon become pale, feeble and disordered." [14]

Charles Follen, a Harvard instructor in German, introduced German gymnastics to the university in 1825. As a student in Germany, he had learned the system from Jahn himself. U.S. interest in gymnastics coincided with the young nation's first steps toward industrialization, a development that disturbed health reformers.

"The reformers worried about the health of those living in towns and cities because of the comparative lack of physical activity in their daily lives," the authors of a history of U.S. sport and physical activity noted. "They compared the city life of the period, which might entail a 10-hour stint in a factory within walking distance of a room in a boarding house, to the physically demanding chores on a farm: managing a horse-drawn plow, spading a large garden, forking the hay, milking the cows, cleaning the barn. The reformers noticed that the young men in the cities often lacked the vigor of the farm workers." [15]

From Vegetarianism to Temperance to Calisthenics

To rectify matters, the reformers pursued a variety of agendas. Sylvester Graham, a Presbyterian minister, lectured widely in the 1830s on the benefits of vegetarianism and temperance. He also decried the use of processed flour and chemical additives in bread and advocated "active exercise" for children and adults. Consequently, he called on Americans to visit gymnasiums to "swing upon and climb the poles, and ropes and ladders and vault upon the wooden horse" — or, better yet, to "walk and run and jump, or labor on the farm." Above all, Graham urged Americans to "avoid sedentary habits." [16]

Catherine Beecher, sister of the novelist Harriet Beecher Stowe, founded the Hartford (Conn.) Female Seminary in 1824 to improve the physical condition of young American women. Beecher used a set of light exercises she had developed that she called calisthenics. "Accompanied by music and sometimes performed with light weights, the program was designed to exercise all the muscles harmoniously. She also encouraged the girls to ride horseback and play other games and sports." [17]

Other prominent fitness crusaders of the 1830-50 period included Edward Hitchcock of Amherst College, the nation's first physical education teacher; William A. Alcott (a cousin of Bronson Alcott, Louisa May Alcott's father), author of nearly 100 self-help books, who espoused regular exercise and proper hygiene and diet; James C. Jackson, a physician who touted the benefits of calisthenics and gymnastics; and H.H. Sherwood, a doctor who viewed the body as a magnet and most physical problems as resulting from the body's magnetic forces being out of equilibrium. [18]

PE Goes to School

Alcott fought for years to introduce physical education into New England schools, a cause eventually taken up by pioneering educator Horace Mann. In his annual report to the Massachusetts Board of Education in 1842, Mann wrote: "After a competent acquaintance with the common branches [of knowledge], is there a single department in the vast range of secular knowledge more fundamental ... than a study of our physical frame, its beautiful adaptations and arrangements, the marvelous powers and properties with which it is endowed and the conditions indispensable to its preservation in a state of vigor, usefulness and enjoyment?" [19] Mann returned to his theme in subsequent reports, gradually building popular support for the idea.

The campaign bore fruit in 1850 with the issuance of a survey of sanitary conditions and public health in Massachusetts by Lemuel Shattuck, a noted statistician and genealogist. Shattuck urged implementation of Mann's proposal "as soon as persons can be found qualified to teach it." Within months, the legislature enacted the nation's first law requiring the teaching of "physiology and hygiene" in public schools, and the examination of all teachers on their ability to give instruction on those subjects.

A second exercise-based fitness movement got under way in the 1860s. According to James C. Whorton, a professor of biomedical history, the emergence of exercise "as a distinct ideology was in large measure a manifestation of the emerging spirit of English 'muscular Christianity,' a form of social gospel that affirmed the compatibility of the robust physical life with a life of Christian morality and service and indeed contended that bodily strength built character and righteousness and usefulness for God's (and the nation's) work." [20]

One of the leading fitness crusaders of the time was Dioclesian Lewis, a temperance advocate and prolific author, whose books included *Weak Lungs and How to Make Them Strong* and *Our Digestion: Or My Jolly Friend's Secret.* Lewis' "New Gymnastics" program featured numerous drills for adults and children using light wands, Indian Clubs, wooden rings and two-pound dumbbells. He sought not just to build muscle power but to enhance "flexibility, agility and grace of movement." [21]

Exercise equipment designed to be used at home — so-called "parlor gymnasiums" — first appeared in the 1860s. By the end of the century, exercise-conscious Americans could choose from an assortment of home-gym equipment, including rowing machines and various strength-building devices anticipating today's gleaming Nautilus and Universal gym systems, including those using wires and pulleys, rubber bands, ropes, rings and dumbbells. Bicycling became a widely popular pastime in the late 1880s.

The second half of the 19th century also witnessed the rise of interscholastic and intercollegiate sports, including football, rowing and baseball. Around the same time, an intensely individual pursuit of "the

Continued on p. 852

Chronology

1800s-1850s

The first organized fitness programs in the United States get under way.

1806
In his book *Means of Preserving Health and Preventing Diseases*, New York physician Shadrach Ricketson states that "a certain proportion of exercise is not much less essential to a healthy or vigorous constitution than drink, food and sleep."

1823
Harvard University Professors George Bancroft and J.G. Cogswell establish Round Hill School in Boston and incorporate physical education into the curriculum.

1824
Catherine Beecher, sister of the novelist Harriet Beecher Stowe, founds the Hartford (Conn.) Female Academy to improve the physical condition of young American women.

1825
Charles Follen, a Harvard University German instructor, introduces gymnastics.

1850
Massachusetts enacts the nation's first law requiring the teaching of "physiology and hygiene" in public schools.

1950s

Concern about the substandard physical condition of American youth prompts federal action to arrest the trend.

1953
Almost 57 percent of U.S. schoolchildren fail six simple fitness tests in a study by two New York University researchers, compared with an 8 percent failure rate among European children.

1956
President Dwight D. Eisenhower creates the President's Council on Youth Fitness to help design and implement physical fitness programs in the nation's schools. It is renamed the President's Council on Physical Fitness and Sports in 1968.

1960s-1980s

Another physical fitness boom sweeps the nation, or so the media claim.

1966
Kenneth A. Cooper publishes *Aerobics*, a best-selling book credited with inspiring the fitness craze of the next two decades.

1977
James Fixx's *The Complete Book of Running,* celebrating the physical and spiritual rewards of jogging, becomes a best-seller.

1982
Actress Jane Fonda's first exercise video, "Jane Fonda's Workout," is released.

1985
The President's Council on Physical Fitness and Sports issues a report on youth physical fitness that finds "no general gains" compared with similar tests taken in 1965 and 1975. It also concludes that "there is still a lower level of performance in important components of physical fitness by millions of our youth."

1990s

More discouraging data about the physical condition of American youth prompt calls for action.

1996
Physical Activity and Health: A Report of the Surgeon General states that only about half of U.S. young people (ages 12-21) regularly engage in vigorous physical activity. The report also cites a decline in daily attendance in physical education classes from about 42 percent to 25 percent during the 1990s.

March 7, 1997
The Centers for Disease Control and Prevention issues "Guidelines for School and Community Programs to Promote Lifelong Physical Activity Among Young People." The CDC urges schools to require daily physical education classes from kindergarten through grade 12.

July 1997
The International Life Sciences Institute releases "Improving Children's Health Through Physical Activity: A New Opportunity," which echoes some of the key conclusions of the surgeon general's report. In addition, the institute finds that physical activity among youth peaks in 10th grade and then begins a sharp, steady decline, and that girls are less active than boys, yet feel they are getting enough exercise.

Why Physical Activity Drops in Adolescence

As a rule, children and adolescents are much more physically active than adults. But according to several recent studies, including the 1996 U.S. surgeon general's report, physical activity reaches a peak during the teenage years and then begins a sharp, steady decline. Fitness advocates offer various reasons for the trend. [1]

According to James O. Hill, a professor of pediatrics and medicine at the University of Colorado Health Sciences Center in Denver, the explanation is that physical activity in American high schools is tied to team sports. Consequently, kids who fail to make a varsity squad tend to abandon both sports and other kinds of physical activity, as do many varsity athletes after graduating from high school.

The situation has prompted a good deal of soul-searching among physical educators, Hill says. "A lot of people think we should be doing more in our PE classes to stress the benefits of walking, biking and roller-blading — activities that can still be enjoyed in adulthood."

Failure to teach high school students how to remain fit throughout life means that "we're not being creative," Hill adds. "Doesn't it make sense to introduce children now to these kinds of activities? They are much more likely to be carried over into a person's fifth and sixth decades than football or basketball are."

In the opinion of Greg Welk, director of the childhood and adolescent health division of the Cooper Institute for Aerobics Research in Dallas, the mid-teen activity slump "reflects societal trends." Many high school students feel that "being active and being fit is just for jocks, so they look for other things that they can excel in. Also, they may get caught up in their after-school jobs, which means that physical activity is the last thing they have on their minds.

"All this parallels the mobility kids have once they gain access to cars. Then they'll start driving places instead of walking or bicycling. They become inactive by the same process that most adults do."

Christine Spain, director of research, planning and special projects for the President's Council on Physical Fitness and Sports, notes that girls start becoming physically inactive earlier than boys. "What happens is that a girl becomes a young woman, physiologically, at 12 or 13. Her body matures; she develops an interest in boys; she becomes more self-conscious. So a lot of the falloff in physical activity among girls is biological."

According to Susan Kalish, executive director of the American Running and Fitness Association in Bethesda, Md., the drop in physical activity among teens stems from "a combination of things. A lot of it has to do with us just not giving them fun PE programs. Or sometimes it may be a case of poor coaching of the school's sports teams."

But mostly, she believes, it's because "there are a lot of other competing interests for those children by that age." In many cases, high school students "are concentrating on improving their grades so they can get into college."

If boys tend to remain physically active later into their teens than girls do, that may also reflect the onset of puberty. "Our culture says that athletic boys are cuter and more attractive to girls. So, many boys will keep playing sports to win girls."

Kalish also points out that school sports coaches are responsible for much of the attrition among teen athletes. "About 70 percent of the kids who try out for junior high school sports fail to make the cut," she says. "And then 70 percent of that surviving 30 percent won't qualify for a spot on the high school squad. That's the way American sports development works — the less athletically gifted kids are winnowed out as they get older."

Some fitness advocates are encouraged by indications that teenagers are joining health clubs in substantial numbers. According to American Sports Data Inc., in Hartsdale, N.Y., health club membership among persons under 18 increased from 1.1 million in 1987 to 1.9 million in 1995 — a gain of 73 percent.

But others feel there may be less to the story than the raw figures might suggest. Teenagers, it is said, may go to health clubs more to socialize than to exercise — just as many adults do. And, Hill adds, the exercise may not yield much in the way of fitness.

"Look at what happens with the typical adult health club member," he says. "He's pretty sedentary most of the day. But then he works out for an hour and thinks of himself as a physically active person. He's not. If you have 23 hours of inactivity and one hour of activity, that's still a pretty sedentary lifestyle."

Hill hastens to add that he's not knocking health clubs. "The health club way of maintaining fitness is fine, it's better than nothing. But somehow we've gotten away from being physically active generally in life. And I don't know how we reverse that trend."

[1] U.S. Department of Health and Human Services, *Physical Activity and Health: A Report of the Surgeon General* (1996).

Continued from p. 850

body beautiful" began to emerge. The era's leading proponent of body-building was Bernarr Macfadden, publisher of *Physical Culture* magazine and author of numerous books.

"Health has become popular, a strong and beautiful body has become a thing of honor and glory and the proper feeding of the body a duty recognized and a pleasure to be enjoyed by all," Macfadden wrote in a characteristic passage. [22]

Macfadden's chief disciple was Angelo Siciliano, a body-builder known professionally as Charles Atlas. Generations of American schoolboys can remember reading ads for Atlas' body-building course on the back covers of comic books. The ads featured a rendering in cartoon form of an actual incident — when a Coney Island lifeguard kicked sand at the skinny young Atlas. Humiliated, the youth got his revenge by pumping iron till he was more than a match for the bullies at the beach.

In schools, physical activity was shifting from a group pursuit to a personal quest. "The turn-of-the-century educator sought to ensure discipline and order inside the classroom and was more apt to use organized play and games to regulate the students, to sublimate their instinctive bursts of energy and to harness them to the yoke of social obligation," noted sports historian Donald J. Mrozek. "After World War I, however, teachers were at least as apt to see the natural side of play as the more precious and fragile one. From elementary schools through universities, sport was a form of self-expression and a vehicle for 'getting along' with others." [23]

Impact of Affluence

Post-World War II prosperity brought with it fuller employment and more leisure time. Within a decade after the war, however, studies began to show the deleterious effects of affluence on Americans' physical condition. In 1953, the *Journal of Health, Physical Education, and Recreation* published a study of the fitness of U.S. schoolchildren that alarmed many parents and health professionals. The authors, Hans Kraus and Ruth P. Hirschland of the Institute of Physical Medicine and Rehabilitation at New York University's Bellevue Medical Center, reported that 56.6 percent of the American schoolchildren tested "failed to meet even a minimum standard required for health." The failure rate for European schoolchildren who took the same tests was 8.3 percent. Kraus and Hirschland called the American youngsters' poor conditioning "a serious deficiency comparable with vitamin deficiency" and declared "an urgent need" to remedy it. [24]

Concern about the findings was so widespread that President Dwight D. Eisenhower met with government leaders, medical researchers and sports figures at the White House in June 1955 to discuss youth physical fitness. The next year at the President's Conference on the Fitness of American Youth in Annapolis, Md., some 150 fitness experts recommended that the president form a special committee on youth fitness. Eisenhower responded by creating the President's Council on Youth Fitness on July 16, 1956. He directed the council to design and implement physical fitness programs in the nation's schools.

President Kennedy Broadens Council's Scope

President John F. Kennedy broadened the council's scope in 1961. He appointed Charles B. "Bud" Wilkinson, head football coach and athletic director at the University of Oklahoma, to be a special consultant on physical fitness and to supervise the council's activities. The council started new programs to develop testing standards and began a series of physical fitness clinics for teachers, administrators and recreation personnel. The idea was to encourage physical education teachers in public schools to design new types of athletic training programs that placed more emphasis on physical fitness than on team sports. Marked improvements in physical fitness testing results appeared between 1958 and 1965.

The Kennedy family, meanwhile, was setting an example by its dedication to robust physical activity. Photographers and television cameramen delighted in recording members of the clan at play — sailing, golfing and, tirelessly, playing touch football. Indeed, "vigor" became a national catchword for the Kennedy administration.

But the impression of increasing national fitness turned out to be short-lived. In 1976, a study conducted by the University of Michigan for the U.S. Office of Education found that the physical fitness of American schoolchildren did not improve from 1965 to 1975. In 39 out of 40 categories, fitness performances of boys and girls remained unchanged throughout the decade.

The one bright spot was that more girls than boys showed improvement, especially in the endurance tests.

The President's Council cited two reasons for the substandard physical condition of America's schoolchildren:

- Many schools could not afford adequate physical fitness programs, and
- Students who had the choice tended to choose physical education programs that did not contribute significantly to fitness.

Little changed over the next 10 years. In a report on youth fitness issued in 1985, the President's Council found "no general gains" over the levels observed in 1965 and 1975. Indeed, the survey concluded that "there is still a lower level of performance in important components of physical fitness by millions of our youth." [25]

In response to such findings, public and private fitness and health groups published numerous proposals for corrective action between the 1960s and '90s. One of the most influential was "Healthy People 2000," issued by the U.S. Public Health Service (PHS) in 1990 and revised five years later. The 1990 document listed various health objectives for Americans, subdivided by age, race, ethnic background, income and physical condition.

For instance, the PHS sought to

What Turns Kids on to Fitness

Turn Ons

— Having fun
— Feeling successful
— Playing with peers
— Sharing experiences with family
— Experiencing a variety of activities
— Having an enthusiastic coach or teacher
— Feeling that an active lifestyle is their own choice

Turn Offs

— Putting winning above all else
— Never improving
— Getting injured too often
— Feeling forced to play through pain
— Doing the same thing over and over
— Getting ridiculed by friends, family or coach
— Not having a say in the sports they play

Sources: Susan Kalish, Your Child's Fitness: Practical Advice for Parents; *American Footwear Association*

increase the proportion of children and adolescents in grades 1-12 who participate in daily physical education to at least 50 percent by the year 2000. In addition, it aimed to increase to at least 50 percent "the proportion of school physical education class time that students spend being physically active, preferably engaged in lifetime physical activities." [26] ■

CURRENT SITUATION

Inactivity Documented

In 1996, the government reported in *Physical Activity and Health: A Report of the Surgeon General* that the targets set in 1990 in "Healthy People 2000" were largely not being met.

Between 1991 and 1995, for example, overall daily attendance in physical education classes in grades 9-12 fell from 41.6 percent to 25.4 percent, the report said. Thus, it concluded, "the 'Healthy People 2000' goal of 50 percent has not been attained and is also becoming more distant." [27] Similarly, "a decreasing proportion of the high school students who are enrolled in physical education classes are meeting the 'Healthy People 2000' goal for time spent being physically active in class."

The decline in exercise was especially pronounced among adolescent girls and minority-group members:

• The proportion of high school girls who reported doing 20 minutes or more of strenuous exercise a week fell from 31 percent for high school freshmen to 17 percent for seniors. The decline for boys went from 51 percent to 42 percent.

• Although 37 percent of all students in grades 9 through 12 said they exercised strenuously three or more times a week, only 29 percent of blacks reported doing so.

• Adolescent minority females were significantly less likely than young white women to exercise at that level — 21 percent for Hispanics, and 17 percent for blacks vs. 28 percent for whites.

The surgeon general's report blamed "the age in which we live" for the country's increasingly sedentary habits. "Today, many Americans engage in little or no physical activity in the course of a working day typically spent sitting at a desk or standing at a counter or cash register," it said. "A large part of many people's time is spent inside buildings where elevators or escalators are prominent features and stairs are difficult to find and may seem unsafe." [28]

Private cars and public transit also were blamed with fostering inactivity. "Whereas older cities and towns were built on the assumption that stores and services would be within walking distance of local residents, the design of most new residential areas reflects the supposition that people will drive from home to most destinations. Thus work, home and shopping are often separated by distances that not only discourage walking but may even necessitate commuting by motorized transportation." [29]

Aside from sleeping, the report found, "watching TV occupies the greatest amount of leisure time during childhood," especially among preschoolers. "By the time a person graduates from high school, he or she will likely have spent 15,000-18,000 hours in front of a television — and 12,000 hours in school."

New Study Cites Importance of Parents

A study issued this July by the International Life Sciences Institute

How PE Teaches Fitness for Life

Physical education shouldn't be cast aside after graduation from high school, fitness experts agree. Rather, it should be viewed as an introductory course to a lifetime of regular physical activity.

Many school physical education programs are beginning to devote less time to team sports and more time to activities that can be pursued either alone or with friends or family members, such as rope skipping, martial arts, walking, jogging, skiing, swimming, skating, aerobics, canoeing, backpacking and bicycling.

Under the new regime, PE instructors strive to acquaint students with the basic movements that are common to most sports and exercises — running, jumping and throwing, for example.

"The rules and strategies of various sports and games are part of our culture — something we feel strongly that all students should learn about," says Judith C. Young, executive director of the National Association for Sport and Physical Education in Reston, Va. "The various sport forms, whether they're weight training and aerobics or basketball and softball, show the application of what is learned in physical education class."

Young likens the PE learning process to the study of literature. "*Moby Dick*, *Julius Caesar* and *The Raven* are examples of different literary forms; they're not the entire course," she says. "In that sense, basketball is like *Moby Dick* — an example of a team sport that involves running, passing and shooting. Other sports may include the same or different motions, arranged in different ways."

Charles B. Corbin, a professor of exercise science and physical education at Arizona State University, notes that "Most children naturally love exercise. Our job should be to foster this love." If that is not done, he cautions, "if children achieve fitness without a love of exercise, maintaining fitness for life will not be accomplished. We have *not* achieved our fitness goals when our students are fitter than 'average' or even 'super fit' if we have not promoted a love of activity and a commitment to fitness for life." [1]

Susan Kalish, executive director of the American Running and Fitness Association in Bethesda, Md., advises parents to make allowances for their children's limitations when joining them in physical activity. "Running is a great lifelong exercise," she writes, "but due to the various speeds and distances involved, it is not usually a good sport to do with a child. If you enjoy running and want to involve your child, be sure to run a step behind so you never encourage her to go farther or faster than she is able." [2]

Moreover, Kalish warns, some activities should be off-limits to young children. Exercise machines such as "rowers, bicycles, steppers and cross-country ski machines provide a good workout, but most aren't made for children to use. Not only do they not fit a child's body, they can also be dangerous. Children have lost fingers and broken bones putting their hands in places they were not meant to go. Unless the machine was made for children, don't let your child use or play around your exercise machine." [3]

Studies indicate that physical activity among young people declines sharply after about age 17, just short of college age. College students "become preoccupied with studies, dating and preparing for careers," wrote Professor William Prentice, coordinator of the sports medicine program at the University of North Carolina at Chapel Hill. "As a result, they often forget about fitness requirements." [4]

Without regular exercise, Prentice noted, a college student may fall victim to depression and a variety of nagging physical ailments. "A student may not be able to participate in activities such as swimming, mountain climbing, skiing, backpacking or scuba diving because of a lack of fitness," he wrote. "Even if an unfit student does participate in these activities, his or her safety, proficiency and enjoyment may be considerably less than that of a person with a higher level of physical fitness. However, if the person is in good physical condition, he or she has a better chance of achieving academically and having a more enjoyable college experience than physically unfit classmates."

[1] Charles B. Corbin, "The Fitness Curriculum — Climbing the Stairway to Lifetime Fitness," in Russell R. Pate and Richard C. Hohn, eds., *Health and Fitness Through Physical Education* (1994), p. 61.

[2] Susan Kalish, *Your Child's Fitness* (1996), p. 88.

[3] *Ibid.*, p. 90.

[4] William Prentice, *Fitness for College and Life* (1994), p. 11.

(ILSI) in Washington, D.C., paralleled the findings of the surgeon general's report. Based on a survey conducted for the institute by Louis Harris and Associates, the study concluded that children "tend to be more active if the parent plays with the child, watches the child play sports or drives the child to physical activity." Merely "telling the child that physical activity is good for them or encouraging the child to take part in sports and physical activities makes no difference in activity levels." [30]

The ILSI study also found that 14 percent of children 6-11 and 12 percent of adolescents — those 12-17 — were overweight. That represented an increase since the 1970s for both groups — up from 5 percent and 7 percent, respectively.

Nonetheless, about one of every three parents interviewed for the survey said their children weren't getting enough exercise. And only one in four children said the same. More than half the children who acknowledged they were inactive mentioned homework and lack of time as justification. Two-thirds of the parents who said their children didn't get enough exercise cited lack of interest as well as competition from TV, video games and computers.

Commenting on the study, Hill declared: "Daily physical activity for children needs to become a priority for parents equal to that of buckling seat belts. Adopting a 'no more excuses' attitude when a child pleads lack of time is an important beginning. Furthermore, parents need to demand that schools put the fourth 'R' back into their curriculum: Recreation needs to be added to Reading, wRiting and aRithmetic." [31]

CDC Guidelines

The U.S. Centers for Disease Control and Prevention (CDC) in Atlanta outlined a strategy for doing just that in a set of 10 guidelines issued in March. The overall goal was to "promote enjoyable, lifelong physical activity among young people." A program seeking to accomplish this, CDC said, should be "determined by the local community based on community needs" and "coordinated by a multidisciplinary team" comprising parents, school officials and health professionals, among others. [32]

The weak link, the CDC noted, was likely to be school-based physical education. "Although most states (94 percent) and school districts (95 percent) require some physical education, only one state [Illinois] requires it daily from kindergarten through 12th grade. Less than two-thirds (60 percent) of high school students are enrolled in physical education classes, and only 25 percent take physical education daily." [33]

The CDC's conclusions were based in part on a survey of physical education in primary and secondary schools that appeared recently in the *Journal of School Health*. More than half of the head physical education instructors interviewed majored in physical education in college; only 2 percent majored in biology or other sciences and none majored in exercise science or kinesthesiology. [34]

Although nearly all PE classroom teachers assigned grades for their courses, the survey found class participation was most often used to determine grades. Written tests were used by 45 percent of the teachers; 22.7 percent used homework assignments for that purpose.

"To strengthen physical education programs in the future," the survey authors wrote, "efforts will need to be directed toward increasing the emphasis placed on lifetime physical activities, increasing opportunities for in-service training for physical education teachers, promoting collaboration between physical education staff and staff from other school health program components, increasing the number of schools that require daily physical education and increasing the number of schools that require physical education in each grade." ■

OUTLOOK

Are We Shaping Up?

Is the United States caught in a relentless downward spiral of youth fitness, as recent studies suggest? Or are Americans poised to embrace healthier lifestyles in the near future? Expert opinion spans the optimism-pessimism spectrum.

According to the Fitness Products Council, an affiliate of the Sporting Goods Manufacturers Association, "Americans are listening; we are changing our habits. We are becoming more, not less, active as a nation, and fitness is a movement millions more are ready to join." [35]

The council bases its upbeat assessment on statistics compiled between 1987 and 1995 by American Sports Data Inc. These data showed increased sports involvement by boys and girls 6-11 but little change in the participation level for the 12-17 age group. "There is no intent to suggest that Americans are as active as they should be for their own good," the council stated. "But we believe the evidence . . . documents a long-term cultural change that has been going on at least since the 1970s." [36]

Hill, on the other hand, discerns "no positive trends," because the spread of technology "makes it easier to remain sedentary." Further, he is convinced that "the attractiveness of video games, television and so forth is only going to grow stronger."

The surgeon general's estimate that one-quarter of American youths are physically inactive is "astounding, scary," Hill says. "Do we think those kids are suddenly going to become active adults? Not likely. It looks as if we're rearing another generation of adults who are going to be even fatter and less active than the current generation.

"I think it's an epidemic. The problem is, it's not a disaster that will arrive next month or next year. And it's always hard to get people to get concerned about something that's going to create major difficulties far in the future."

Kalish also is bearish about the future of U.S. youth fitness. For instance,

Continued on p. 858

At Issue:

Are young people in worse physical condition today than they were 20 years ago?

YES

U.S. DEPARTMENT OF HEALTH AND HUMAN SERVICES

FROM* PHYSICAL ACTIVITY AND HEALTH: A REPORT OF THE SURGEON GENERAL, *1996.

Despite common knowledge that exercise is healthful, more than 60 percent of American adults are not regularly active, and 25 percent of the adult population are not active at all. . . .

The effort to understand how to promote more active lifestyles is of great importance to the health of this nation. . . . School-based interventions for youth are particularly promising, not only for their potential scope — almost all young people between the ages of 6 and 16 years attend school — but also for their potential impact. Nearly half of all young people 12-21 years of age are not vigorously active; moreover, physical activity sharply declines during adolescence. Childhood and adolescence may thus be pivotal times for preventing sedentary behavior among adults by maintaining the habit of physical activity throughout the school years.

School-based interventions have been shown to be successful in increasing physical activity levels. With evidence that success in this arena is possible, every effort should be made to encourage schools to require daily physical education in each grade and to promote physical activities that can be enjoyed throughout life. . . .

[What follows are some of the findings of this report:]

About 14 percent of young people report no recent vigorous or light-to-moderate physical activity. This indicator of inactivity is higher among females than males and among black females than white females.

Males are more likely than females to participate in vigorous physical activity, strengthening activities and walking or bicycling.

Participation in all types of physical activity declines strikingly as age or grade in school increases.

Among high school students, enrollment in physical education remained unchanged during the first half of the 1990s. However, daily attendance in physical education declined from approximately 45 percent to 25 percent.

The percentage of high school students who were enrolled in physical education and who reported being physically active for at least 20 minutes in physical education classes declined from approximately 81 percent to 70 percent during the first half of this decade.

Only 19 percent of all high school students report being physically active for 20 minutes or more in daily physical education classes. . . .

Interventions targeting physical education in elementary school can substantially increase the amount of time students spend being physically active in physical education class.

NO

GARY BRINES

Executive director, National High School Athletic Coaches Association

WRITTEN FOR* THE CQ RESEARCHER, *SEPTEMBER 1997.

Many young people are in better physical condition today than 20 years ago; witness the increase in activities such as cross-country, swimming, tennis, surfing, skiing, skating and skateboarding, to name a few.

Also, there is much more awareness regarding nutrition and eating habits today. Add to the aforementioned an increased interest in aerobics and body-building, plus the media focus on "good looks." In addition, The National High School Athletic Coaches Association emphasizes in its code of ethics abstention from drugs, alcohol and tobacco while promoting fitness and nutrition.

To support the fact that young people tend to be more activity-oriented nowadays, suggesting improved physical conditioning, is the National Federation of High School Associations' recently released annual survey. It indicated that, for the eighth consecutive year, participation in high school athletics increased during the 1996-97 school year. In this connection, it should be noted that 20 years ago, there were approximately 500,000 more boys and 500,000 fewer girls participating in interscholastic sports than now.

The point is not necessarily to use high school sports participation in general as a gauge of youth fitness when all we need to see is the impact of youth soccer across America. Summer sports programs and camps also have contributed, along with the growth of public and private school sponsorship of evening and weekend intramural athletics.

In addition, Title IX [of the Education Amendments of 1972] has provided opportunities for young women to receive equity in interscholastic sports. Outstanding high school coaches supported by school administrators and parents have been a vital force for implementing the change in emphasis, philosophy and priorities that Title IX has brought to America.

Title IX mandates also have ensured the provision of sports equipment for women athletes — weight rooms as well as improved access to such facilities as gyms, tracks, swimming pools and tennis courts. These have stimulated the desire to excel, with conditioning being the winning edge.

And let's not forget the ability of top professionals to inspire young athletes to try and emulate them. The world is filled with ads, promos, hats and shirts promoting everything from 10K runs to mud-wrestling. Nike, among other sports-equipment companies, has created a marketing juggernaut. What youngster doesn't want to "Air" it?

Older Americans Are Getting the Message

"Just as you are never too sedentary to begin a fitness program, you are never too old either," writes Professor William Prentice, director of the sports medicine program at the University of North Carolina at Chapel Hill. "It is wise to start a fitness program early in life, but all of us can benefit from exercise no matter when we begin." [1]

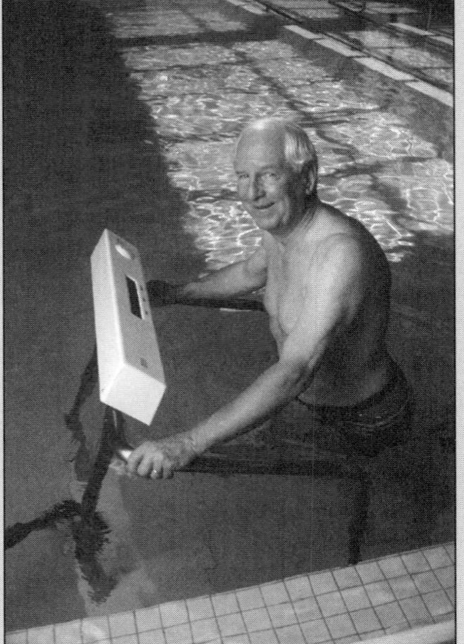

Increasing numbers of older Americans seem to be heeding Prentice's message. According to a nationwide survey conducted two years ago by the Fitness Products Council, in North Palm Beach, Fla., health club memberships among people 55 and older rose from 1.2 million in 1987 to 2.1 million in 1995. The 75 percent increase was larger than that of any other age group. This generation that predates the baby boom generation "is already creating a new dimension of the fitness movement," the council stated. [2]

According to a 1996 report by the U.S. surgeon general, "The deterioration in physiologic function normally associated with aging is, in fact, caused by a combination of reduced physical activity and the aging process itself. By maintaining an active lifestyle, or by increasing levels of physical activity if previously sedentary, older persons can maintain relatively high levels of cardiovascular and metabolic function . . . and of skeletal muscle function." [3]

In fact, a study published in 1994 by *The New England Journal of Medicine* found an increase of 113 percent in the strength of 100 frail nursing home residents (median age, 87) after they completed a 10-week program of progressive resistance training. Stair-climbing power, gait velocity and level of spontaneous activity also improved. [4] Commenting on the findings, the surgeon general's report noted: "Increasing endurance and strength in the elderly contributes to their ability to live independently." [5]

---

[1] William Prentice, *Fitness for College and Life* (1994), p. 11.

[2] Fitness Products Council, "Tracking the Fitness Movement" 1996, p. 17. The council is a division of the Sporting Goods Manufacturers Association.

[3] U.S. Department of Health and Human Services, "Physical Activity and Health," 1996, p. 76.

[4] Maria A. Fiatarone, et al., "Exercise Training and Nutritional Supplementation for Physical Frailty in Very Elderly People," *The New England Journal of Medicine,* June 23, 1994, pp. 1769-1775.

[5] U.S. Department of Health and Human Services, *loc. cit.*

Continued from p. 856

she was "really disappointed" by the reaction — or lack of reaction — to last year's surgeon general's report. "I saw very few people jumping on the bandwagon and trying to change anything because of all that discouraging data."

Working parents and safety concerns make it harder to address the youth fitness problem, Kalish feels. "Extended day-care programs often are in facilities without much structured physical activity," she notes. "Or, the kids are sent directly home from school and are told to go in the house, lock the doors, stay there, don't talk to anyone. In short, they can't join a neighborhood pickup game, as their parents probably did when they were kids. That's why I don't foresee children becoming more fit in the next 10 years. And it breaks my heart."

Falb acknowledges that there has been a decline in youth fitness, but he perceives "an increase in physical activity because many people are becoming more aware of good nutrition. They know the necessity for exercise. Look at the rise in health club membership. People who were not physically active 10 or 15 years ago have now come to the realization that they have to be."

A survey of 210 health clubs conducted in late 1995 by the Fitness Products Council lends support to Falb's observation. "When the survey asked which programs were generating increasing interest, a surprising answer led the list: Special programs for seniors were mentioned by 73 percent of the managers in facilities which offer such programs." The survey also found "a growing demand for various types of children's and youth programming." [37]

Spain believes young people will heed the physical fitness message if it is conveyed by the right messengers. "Kids won't listen to somebody like me, who's heavily into facts and science," she says. "And they don't want to hear football heroes telling them how much fun it is to be active. The message has to be delivered to them by their peers, speaking their language.

"If we do that, the message will get across. We'll be able to persuade inactive kids to do something, even if it's only a little bit. More would be better, of course, but a little is a good place to start." ■

FOR MORE INFORMATION

American Council on Exercise, 5820 Oberlin Dr., Suite 102, San Diego, Calif. 92121-3787; (619) 535-8227. ACE informs fitness professionals about health and fitness and sponsors children's fitness programs.

American Running and Fitness Association, 4405 East-West Highway, Suite 405, Bethesda, Md. 20814; (301) 913-9517. The association promotes running and other aerobic activities and stresses the preventive-maintenance approach to preserving health.

Fitness Motivation Institute of America Association, 5521 Scotts Valley Dr., Scotts Valley, Calif. 95066; (408) 246-9191. The association provides information to the public on exercise and fitness.

International Association of Fitness Professionals, 6190 Cornerstone Ct. East, Suite 204, San Diego, Calif. 92121; (619) 535-8979. The association provides continuing education for fitness professionals, including personal trainers and health-club owners.

International Life Sciences Institute, 1126 16th St. N.W., Suite 300, Washington, D.C. 20036; (202) 659-0074. This nonprofit foundation recently published a study on lack of exercise and obesity among American children.

National Association for Sport and Physical Education, 1900 Association Dr., Reston, Va. 22091; (703) 476-3410. NASPE conducts research and education programs in an effort to improve sports and physical education opportunities in the United States.

National High School Athletic Coaches Association, Box 2569, Gig Harbor, Wash. 98335; (253) 857-3203. The association's code of ethics stresses sound nutrition as a way to achieve and maintain physical fitness.

President's Council on Physical Fitness and Sports, 701 Pennsylvania Ave. N.W., Suite 250, Washington, D.C. 20004; (202) 690-5148. The council helps schools, state and local governments, recreation agencies and employers set up fitness programs.

Notes

[1] Kathleen Kennedy Manzo, "Physical Attraction," *Education Week,* April 2, 1997, p. 37.
[2] American Council on Exercise, "Kids in Motion" (1996 fact sheet).
[3] American Council on Exercise, "Teens, Fitness and You" (1996 fact sheet).
[4] Quoted in The [New Orleans] *Times-Picayune,* July 18, 1996, p. B6.
[5] Quoted by Doug Thomas in the *Omaha World-Herald,* July 21, 1997, p. 25.
[6] Remarks at meeting of the Rotary Club of Washington, D.C., Aug. 13, 1997.
[7] R. Tait McKenzie, "The Quest for Eldorado," *American Physical Education Review,* Vol. 18 (1913), p. 300.
[8] Quoted in U.S. Department of Health and Human Services, *Physical Activity and Health: A Report of the Surgeon General* (1996), p. 13.
[9] American Council on Exercise, "Parents, Eat Your Words!" (1996 fact sheet).
[10] For background, see "Gender Equity in Sports," *The CQ Researcher,* April 18, 1997, pp. 337-360.
[11] Sarah Henry, "Children at Risk: Adventure and Endurance Sports Aren't Kid Stuff, But Increasing Numbers of Kids Are Participating in Them. Should They Be?" *Women's Sports and Fitness,* September 1996, p. 21.
[12] Quoted in *Ibid.*
[13] "Centennial Olympic Games," *The CQ Researcher,* April 5, 1996, pp. 289-312.
[14] *Ibid.,* p. 15.
[15] Betty Spears and Richard A. Swanson, *History of Sport and Physical Activity in the United States* (1983), pp. 80-81.
[16] Quoted by Stephen Nissenbaum in *Sex, Diet and Debility in Jacksonian America: Sylvester Graham and Health Reform* (1980), p. 120.
[17] Spears and Swanson, *op. cit.,* p. 87.
[18] For background, see "Physical Fitness," *The CQ Researcher,* Nov. 6, 1992, pp. 953-976.
[19] Quoted by James C. Whorton, *Crusaders for Fitness: The History of American Health Reformers* (1982), p. 113.
[20] *Ibid.,* p. 271.
[21] Dioclesian Lewis, *The New Gymnastics for Men, Women and Children* (1864), p. 9.
[22] Bernarr Macfadden, *Physical Culture Cook Book* (1924), p. iv.
[23] Donald J. Mrozek, "Sport in American Life: From National Health to Personal Fulfillment," in Grover, *op. cit.,* p. 23.
[24] Hans Kraus and Ruth P. Hirschland, "Muscular Fitness and Health," *Journal of Health, Physical Education, and Recreation,* December 1953, pp. 17-19.
[25] President's Council on Physical Fitness and Sports, "1985 National School Population Survey."
[26] U.S. Department of Health and Human Services, *op. cit.,* p. 39.
[27] *Ibid.,* p. 199.
[28] *Ibid.,* p. 246.
[29] *Loc. cit.*
[30] International Life Sciences Institute (ILSI), "Improving Children's Health Through Physical Activity" (executive summary), July 1997, p. 9.
[31] International Life Sciences Institute press release, July 1, 1997.
[32] Centers for Disease Control and Prevention, "Guidelines for School and Community Programs to Promote Lifelong Physical Activity Among Young People," *Morbidity and Mortality Weekly Report,* March 7, 1997, p. 6.
[33] *Ibid.,* p. 7.
[34] Russell R. Pate et al., "School Physical Education," *Journal of School Health,* October 1995, p. 316.
[35] Fitness Products Council, "Tracking the Fitness Movement," 1996, p. 1.
[36] *Ibid.,* p. 14.
[37] *Ibid.,* p. 19.

Bibliography

Selected Sources Used

Books

Grover, Kathryn, ed., *Fitness in American Culture: Images of Health, Sport and the Body, 1830-1940,* The University of Massachusetts Press and the Margaret Woodbury Strong Museum, 1989.

The six contributors to this collection of essays examine changing American attitudes toward fitness and sport. Of particular interest are the discussions of Charles Atlas and Bernarr Macfadden — legendary promoters of "physical culture" who are only dimly remembered today.

Kalish, Susan, *Your Child's Fitness,* Human Kinetics, 1996.

Kalish, executive director of the American Running and Fitness Association, advises parents on how to make their children physically fit and keep them that way. Most of her tips are family-oriented, but she stresses that schools and communities also have key roles to play.

Pate, Russell R., and Richard C. Hohn, *Health and Fitness Through Physical Edcuation,* Human Kinetics, 1994.

Many of the contributors to this book attended a 1990 conference on how to change "the way school-based physical education is conceptualized, designed and delivered to American youngsters." Their papers explore various routes to that objective.

Whorton, James C., *Crusaders for Fitness: The History of American Health Reformers,* Princeton University Press, 1982.

Whorton, a professor of biomedical history, traces the development of the U.S. physical fitness movement, examining not only exercise and sport but also nutrition, personal hygiene and health fads.

Articles

Henry, Sarah, "Children at Risk: Adventure and Endurance Sports Aren't Kid Stuff, but Increasing Numbers of Kids Are Participating in Them. Should They?" *Women's Sports and Fitness,* September 1996.

Henry questions whether children are taking up challenging sports such as triathlons and mountain and rock climbing before they are physically and emotionally mature enough to do so.

Manzo, Kathleen Kennedy, "Physical Attraction," *Education Week,* April 2, 1997.

The focus of this article is Sharon Sterchy, wellness director of Houston's Aldine School District, and the innovative physical education program she established.

Pate, Russell R., et al., "School Physical Education," *Journal of School Health,* October 1995.

The authors note that schools in 95 percent of the nation's school districts are required to offer physical education, but only about one-quarter of all states mandate a course in lifetime physical activity at the senior high school level.

Reports and Studies

Centers for Disease Control and Prevention, *Guidelines for School and Community Programs to Promote Lifelong Physical Activity Among Young People,* March 7, 1997.

Although these CDC guidelines don't make recommendations about how much physical activity young people should get, they do suggest that schools require daily physical education classes from kindergarten through grade 12.

Fitness Products Council, *Tracking the Fitness Movement,* 1996.

This latest report in an annual series tracks physical activity trends among all age groups in the United States from 1987 through 1995.

International Life Sciences Institute, *Improving Children's Health Through Physical Activity: A New Opportunity,* July 1997.

Based on a survey conducted for the institute by Louis Harris and Associates, this report concludes that children "tend to be more active if the parent plays with the child, watches the child play sports or drives the child to physical activity." Merely "telling the child that physical activity is good for them or encouraging the child to take part in sports and physical activities makes no difference in activity levels."

U.S. Department of Health and Human Services, *Physical Activity and Health: A Report of the Surgeon General,* 1996.

This widely cited survey reports that only about half of U.S. young people ages 12-21 regularly engage in vigorous physical activity, while one-fourth engage in no such activity. It also notes a decline in daily attendance in PE classes from about 42 percent to 25 percent during the 1990s.

The Next Step

Additional information from UMI's Newspaper & Periodical Abstracts™ database

How Much is Enough?

Corbin, Charles B., and Robert P. Pangrazi, "How much physical activity is enough?" *Journal of Physical Education, Recreation & Dance,* April 1996, pp. 33-37.

Questions about how much physical activity is enough are addressed with clarification of some of the recent recommendations. The latest recommendation is that adults should engage in moderate excercise for 30 minutes or more on most, preferably all, days of the week.

Hellmich, Nanci, "CDC encourages schools to get students moving toward fitness," *USA Today*, March 17, 1997, p. D6.

Guidelines from the Centers for Disease Control and Prevention (CDC), out last week, don't offer a specific prescription for how much physical activity kids should get, but they do recommend, for instance, that schools require daily physical education for kindergarten through grade 12. "Just as we're learning how important physical activity is to the health of young people and adults, we're seeing a decline in the number of schools that require daily physical education," says Lloyd Kolbe, director of CDC's division of adolescent and school health.

Pangrazi, Robert P., and Charles B. Corbin and Gregory J. Welk, "Physical activity for children and youth," *Journal of Physical Education, Recreation & Dance,* April 1996, pp. 38-43.

Questions and answers are presented to help teachers and leaders gain a better understanding of how much physical activity is enough for children and adolescents.

Obesity

Andersen, Patricia Parrado, "Sad, but true: The late 20th century is a culture of obesity," *Better Nutrition,* February 1997, pp. 54-58.

The number of overweight people in the U.S. is greater than the number of normal-weight people for the first time ever. The facts behind this reality and a study of three weight-loss regimens are discussed.

Bates-Rudd, Rhonda, "New exercise program helps kids get, stay fit," *Detroit News,* May 8, 1996, p. K6.

Velonda Thompson developed an exercise and nutrition education program for children who stayed after school at Detroit's Coleman Young Recreation Center and the program has since turned into the nonprofit firm Fit Kids After School. The health and fitness education program's aim is to contribute to the decline of childhood obesity and the early onset of cardiovascular disease-related health risks.

Drewnowski, Adam, and Barry M. Popkin, "The nutrition transition: New trends in the global diet," *Nutrition Reviews,* February 1997, pp. 31-43.

Whereas economic development has led to improved food security and better health, adverse health effects of the nutrition transition include growing rates of childhood obesity. Implications of diet trends are examined.

McCarthy, Michael, "Stunted children are at high risk of later obesity," *Lancet,* Jan. 4, 1997, p. 34.

A study has found that developing nations where socio-economic gains are leading to a higher fat diet and lower physical activity are facing an explosion of childhood obesity. Children who are stunted due to poor nutrition early in life are especially at risk.

Physical Education

Placek, Judith H., and Mary O Sullivan, "The many faces of integrated physical education," *Journal of Physical Education, Recreation & Dance,* January 1997, pp. 20-24.

Recently, the concept of an integrated curriculum in schools has received increased attention. Placek and Sullivan discuss two forms of integration and how to integrate physical education with other subjects.

Shaughnessy, Dan, "An exercise in futility to trash gym," *The Boston Globe,* May 25, 1996, p. 69.

Shaughnessy decries proposals to eliminate the mandatory physical education classes required of Massachusetts public school students in every grade, stating that the gym class period is one of the few times that children in the 1990s get any exercise.

Sherlock, Barbara, "Physical Fitness Is Lifetime Course; Naperville School de-Emphasizes Athletic Skills," *Chicago Tribune,* April 17, 1997, p. D5.

Flashes of gold pulse around the room as Madison Junior High School students with "Gettin' Fit for Life" inscribed on their gold-and-black gym uniforms rotate through the Naperville school's 40-station fitness center. Madison's physical education program was recently saluted by the Centers for Disease Control and Prevention in Atlanta, Ga., as one of eight model programs in the country. Those cited illustrate the centers' guidelines, announced last month, for schools and community-based organizations to help improve the health of children throughout their lifetimes.

Siedentop, Daryl, and Larry Locke, "Making a difference for physical education: What professors and practitioners must build together," *Journal of Physical Education,* Recreation & Dance, April 1997, pp. 25-33.

Three aspects of the professional world of physical education teachers are discussed: The quality of physical education programs in schools; the effectiveness of teacher education; and the relationship between the first and second.

Simpson, Alston, Judy Barrett, and Danielle R. Chiesi and Scott A. G. M. Crawford et al, "Should physical education be an elective at the high school level?" *Journal of Physical Education, Recreation & Dance,* August 1997, pp.14-17.

Readers of the journal discuss whether physical education should be an elective at the high school level. Eleven responses that both favor and oppose the idea are presented.

President's Council on Physical Fitness and Sports

Atkin, Ross, "Tom McMillen: Advocate for reform of sports in U.S.," *The Christian Science Monitor,* Dec. 2, 1996, p. 14.

Tom McMillen, the co-chair of the President's Council on Physical Fitness and Sports, is profiled for his efforts to reform collegiate sports in the U.S. McMillen is trying to find a common ground between those who want gender equity in coaches' salaries and those who demand higher salaries for all.

Colburn, Don, "Going the Extra Mile Pays Off, Study Suggests," *The Washington Post,* Feb. 4, 1997, Sec. WH, p. 5.

Gardening, walking and other mild exercises are better than nothing, as the President's Council on Physical Fitness and Sports pointed out in issuing its current 30-minutes-a-day recommendation. But when it comes to exercise, a new study of more than 8,000 runners advises, more is better still. The runners study found that "substantial health benefits" come from exercise at levels above the recommended minimum and these benefits steadily accrue in exercise schedules of up to at least 50 miles a week.

"Flo-Jo talks about the importance of physical fitness," *Jet,* June 16, 1997, pp. 36-40.

Florence Griffith Joyner, the co-chair of the President's Council on Physical Fitness and Sports, shares her knowledge on the importance of physical fitness.

"Girls Active in Sports Do Better in Classroom," *The New York Times,* March 29, 1997, p. A10.

The President's Council on Physical Fitness and Sports said today that female high school athletes tended to get better grades and were less likely to drop out than their non-athletic counterparts. They also are likely to go on to college and develop fewer chronic health problems, like heart disease and high levels of cholesterol.

Recent Studies of Youth Fitness

Hellmich, Nanci, "Few kids get daily exercise: No time, too much TV cited," *USA Today,* July 1, 1997, p. D1.

Only 22 percent of kids are physically active for 30 minutes every day of the week, and parents and their children offer different excuses for why that is, new research reveals. "Kids should be active for several hours every day," says James O. Hill, professor of pediatrics at the University of Colorado Health Sciences Center in Denver.

Payne, V. Gregory, James R. Morrow Jr., Lynne Johnson and Steven N. Dalton, "Resistance training in children and youth: A meta-analysis," *Research Quarterly for Exercise & Sport,* March 1997, pp. 80-88.

Payne et al used meta-analysis to examine the effect of resistance training on children and youth. Resistance training appears to enhance muscular endurance and strength in children and youth.

Staed, John, "Exercising early," *Chicago Tribune,* Jan. 3, 1996, p. 7.

The National Association for Sport and Physical Education found that 40 percent of children ages 5 to 8 are obese, inactive or have high blood pressure or cholesterol levels. Kenneth Cooper, the father of aerobics, discusses this problem and ways to fix it in his book *Kid Fitness.*

"Summary of the Surgeon General's report addressing physical activity and health," *Nutrition Reviews,* September 1996, pp. 280-284.

The CDC and the President's Council on Physical Fitness and Sports have collaborated to develop *Physical Activity and Health: A Report of the Surgeon General.* The report's key finding is that people of all ages can improve the quality of their lives through a lifelong practice of moderate physical activity.

Youth Fitness Programs

Bridges, Paula M., "Fitness: When it comes to good health, kids jump at program," *Detroit News,* May 21, 1997, p. S3.

When youngsters come to Velonda Thompson for help, it's usually after years of eating poorly and lack of exercise. Thompson operates Fit Kids After School, a nonprofit fitness program that helps youths stay in shape. The program operates out of the Coleman A. Young Community Center in Detroit, Mich. Twice a week, about 20 to 25 kids meet to jump, run or dance themselves into shape. The two-year-old program is funded by the Skillman Foundation through a grant from New Detroit Inc.

Burfoot, Amby, and Marty Post, "Child's play," *Runner's World,* May 1996, p. 18.
Project ACES or "All Children Exercising Simultaneously" has grown to include more than 50 countries worldwide since its inception in 1989. The success behind the program is discussed.

Matanin, Marcia J, and Gordon E. Longmuir, "Did someone say free?: Selected free and inexpensive resources for K-12 physical education," *Journal of Physical Education,* Recreation & Dance, October 1996, pp. 15-19.
Helpful information on curricular resources that can be obtained from organizations free of charge or inexpensively is provided for physical education teachers.

Smith, Lynn, "Turning Rug Rats Into Gym Rats; More Parents Are Taking Their Tots to Exercise Programs to Instill Good Habits Early," *Los Angeles Times,* Jan. 2, 1997, p. E1.
Children's indoor exercise programs have become popular again. In addition to established giants like Gymboree, smaller storefront operations are also popping up, catering to parents who want to get their toddlers off to a healthy start.

Zahner, Becky Cotton, "Physical Education: Becky Cotton Zahner," *American School & University,* January 1997, p. 22.
Physical education spaces are becoming a hub of social activity on school campuses. The focus is on wellness and providing alternate safe activities for young people.

Zimmerman, Sarah, "Kids' workout leads to path of good health; Local programs out to teach basics," *Atlanta Constitution,* Feb. 24, 1997, Sec. XJ, p. 1.
Rather than being glad to leave school early, Sarah Wike is disappointed about missing Energy 2 Burn, a five-week physical education class at Suwanee Elementary School. Sarah persuades her mother to let her stay and returns, smiling, to the gym. Volunteer Roberta Zimmerman leads the Energy 2 Burn class during the fourth-graders' afternoon recess. The certified aerobics instructor is one of four Georgians trained to lead the children's program, designed by the American Council on Exercise. Troy Smurawa, a pediatric sports medicine specialist, teaches a Fit Kids Workshop at Egleston Children's Health Center in Duluth. Promoted as a series for "children with above-average weight," the eight-week classes drew 24 children this winter.

Youth Sports

Baldauf, Scott, "Scoring a Field Is Soccer's Biggest Goal; A Shortage of Play Space," *The Christian Science Monitor,* July 9, 1997, p. 4.
Spurred on by the wildly successful 1994 World Cup championship here in the United States, youth soccer has quickly grown from the sport of barrios and prep schools into the No. 1 weekend pastime for American families. This year, there are more kids enrolled in youth soccer than in Little League baseball. The problem is finding places to play. In Framingham, Mass., a leafy middle-class community outside of Boston, the search has had its share of disappointments. One land deal stalled when neighbors complained about parking. Another prospective property was turned into a shopping center.

DiCesare, Bob, "Young runners get an exercise in Heartbreak," The Boston Globe, April 13, 1997, Sec. WKC, p. 1.
The annual Heartbreak Hill International Youth Race in Newton, Mass., is featured. Hundreds of young runners participate in the one-mile race each April.

Legwold, Gary, "Kids can safely lift weights," *Better Homes & Gardens,* August 1997, p. 66.
Research over the past 10 years has shown that children, regardless of their age, can gain strength lifting weights without suffering injuries.

Mihill, Chris, "Aerobic classes of little benefit to children, study suggests," *The Guardian,* May 27, 1997, p. 6.
Aerobics classes appear to make little difference to children's fitness, and it would be better to encourage them to be more active in general, researchers said in the British *Journal of Sports Medicine.* These findings were based on an exercise program, where 17 girls completed eight weeks of 20-25-minute aerobic sessions twice a week, while a group of 18 girls did cycling training, involving pedalling continuously for 20 minutes a session.

Pavelka, Ed, "How to be fit forever," *Bicycling,* December 1996-January 1997, pp. 60-62.
Research shows that regular aerobic exercise like cycling can increase longevity and happiness. Pavelka discusses what happens to the body with age and how cycling can help one stay fit.

Sherlock, Barbara, "Hip Hop Happening Off the Ground Dance Troupe Offers Young People a Healthy Alternative," *Chicago Tribune,* May 4, 1997, p. D3.
Marianne Renner, 30, a Fox Valley-area aerobics and hip hop dance instructor, is the choreographer of the booming Aurora-based dance troupe offering youths and young adults an alternative to alcohol, drugs and gangs. The troupe has performed hip hop dance routines at schools, community events, a McCormick Place fitness convention and an Easter Seals telethon on local access cable television. Members are required to attend practices and to practice on their own. New routines are introduced by Renner about every two months.

Back Issues

Great Research on Current Issues Starts Right Here . . . Recent topics covered by The CQ Researcher are listed below. Before May 1991, reports were published under the name of Editorial Research Reports.

MARCH 1996
The British Monarchy
Preventing Juvenile Crime
Tax Reform
Pursuing the Paranormal

APRIL 1996
Centennial Olympic Games
Managed Care
Protecting Endangered Species
New Military Culture

MAY 1996
Russia's Political Future
Marriage and Divorce
Year-Round Schools
Taiwan, China and the U.S.

JUNE 1996
Rethinking NAFTA
First Ladies
Teaching Values
Labor Movement's Future

JULY 1996
Recovered-Memory Debate
Native Americans' Future
Crackdown on Sexual Harassment
Attack on Public Schools

AUGUST 1996
Fighting Over Animal Rights
Privatizing Government Services
Child Labor and Sweatshops
Cleaning Up Hazardous Wastes

SEPTEMBER 1996
Gambling Under Attack
The States and Federalism
Civic Journalism
Reassessing Foreign Aid

OCTOBER 1996
Political Consultants
Insurance Fraud
Rethinking School Integration
Parental Rights

NOVEMBER 1996
Global Warming
Clashing Over Copyright
Consumer Debt
Governing Washington, D.C.

DECEMBER 1996
Welfare, Work and the States
The New Volunteerism
Implementing the Disabilities Act
America's Pampered Pets

JANUARY 1997
Combating Scientific Misconduct
Restructuring the Electric Industry
The New Immigrants
Chemical and Biological Weapons

FEBRUARY 1997
Assisting Refugees
Alternative Medicine's Next Phase
Independent Counsels
Feminism's Future

MARCH 1997
New Air Quality Standards
Alcohol Advertising
Civic Renewal
Educating Gifted Students

APRIL 1997
Declining Crime Rates
The FBI Under Fire
Gender Equity in Sports
Space Program's Future

MAY 1997
The Stock Market
The Cloning Controversy
Expanding NATO
The Future of Libraries

JUNE 1997
FDA Reform
China After Deng
Line-Item Veto
Breast Cancer

JULY 1997
Transportation Policy
Executive Pay
School Choice Debate
Aggressive Driving

AUGUST 1997
Age Discrimination
Banning Land Mines
Children's Television
Evolution vs. Creationism

SEPTEMBER 1997
Caring for the Dying
Mental Health Policy
Mexico's Future

Back issues are available for $5.00 (subscribers) or $10.00 (non-subscribers). Quantity discounts apply to orders over ten. To order, call Congressional Quarterly Customer Service at (202) 887-8621.

Binders are available for $18.00. To order call 1-800-638-1710. Please refer to stock number 648.

Future Topics

- ***Urban Sprawl in the West***
- ***Diversity in the Workplace***
- ***Teacher Education***

THE CQ Researcher©

PUBLISHED BY CONGRESSIONAL QUARTERLY INC.

Urban Sprawl in the West

Can planners stop unchecked growth before it's too late?

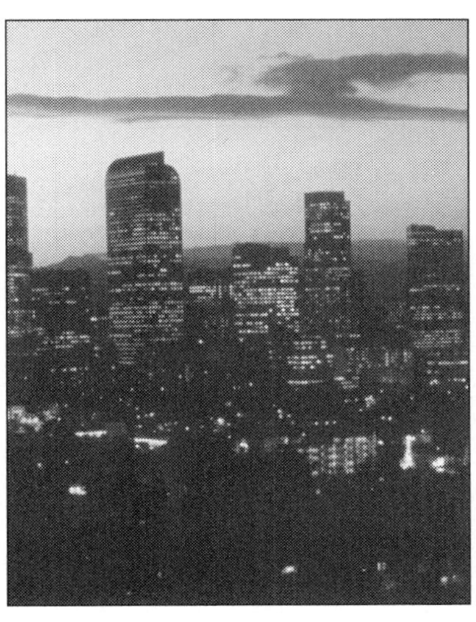

Cities in the Western United States are growing faster than in other parts of the country. Cheap land and a strong regional tradition emphasizing property rights over government regulation have directed much of this growth outward, creating sprawling cities and far-flung suburban communities that threaten to undermine the long-term viability of the cities themselves. Limited water supplies and deteriorating air quality are among the obstacles to further growth in the region that are fueling efforts to curb sprawl. A 1973 Oregon law requiring localities to address the sprawl problem is among the models that states and cities throughout the West are studying as they grapple with fast growth. But in Portland, meanwhile, critics blame the landmark urban growth boundary with causing too much density.

INSIDE THIS ISSUE

CQ Oct. 3, 1997 • Volume 7, No. 37 • Pages 865-888

Formerly Editorial Research Reports

Urban Sprawl in the West

Cover: Beyond Denver, Colo., new suburbs are spreading all along the Front Range of the Rocky Mountains. (© Denver Chamber of Commerce)

The CQ Researcher

October 3, 1997
Volume 7, No. 37

Editor
Sandra Stencel

Managing Editor
Thomas J. Colin

Associate Editors
Sarah M. Magner
Richard L. Worsnop

Staff Writers
Charles S. Clark
Mary H. Cooper
Kenneth Jost
David Masci

Editorial Assistant
Vanessa E. Furlong

Published By
Congressional Quarterly Inc.

Chairman
Andrew Barnes

Vice Chairman
Andrew P. Corty

President and Publisher
Robert W. Merry

Executive Editor
David Rapp

The CQ Researcher (ISSN 1056-2036). Formerly Editorial Research Reports. Published weekly, except Jan. 3, May 30, Aug. 29, Oct. 31, by Congressional Quarterly Inc., 1414 22nd St., N.W., Washington, D.C. 20037. Annual subscription rate for libraries, businesses and government is $340. Additional rates furnished upon request. Periodicals postage paid at Washington, D.C., and additional mailing offices. POSTMASTER: Send address changes to The CQ Researcher, 1414 22nd St., N.W., Washington, D.C. 20037.

Urban Sprawl in the West

BY MARY H. COOPER

THE ISSUES

To its developers, Highlands Ranch is the "Pride of Colorado," the "best-selling master-planned community in the U.S.," featuring "distinctive neighborhoods complemented by parks, trails, business centers, numerous recreational opportunities and beautiful open space." [1]

To its detractors, however, Highlands Ranch is just another example of unfettered urban sprawl. Nestled in the foothills just south of metropolitan Denver, the development is one link in a chain of suburban subdivisions and shopping centers that is spreading along the Front Range of the Rocky Mountains.

Despite a recession that plagued Colorado for much of the 1980s, development has proceeded so fast in the state that four cities that once comprised distinct communities — Fort Collins, Denver, Colorado Springs and Pueblo — may soon form a megalopolis strung out over almost 200 miles.

Highlands Ranch is in Douglas County, the fastest-growing county in the United States. "Some people who have moved here from places like Levittown are so appalled at the growth that they are afraid this will be the Levittown of the future," says Denver Councilwoman Susan Barnes-Gelt, referring to the postwar development on Long Island, N.Y. "They now say they're going to buy their 2.5-acre homesite in Elbert County, even farther south of Denver. This is exactly the wrong attitude, because when you have to build roads and sewers and water lines to support this very dispersed development, it is incredibly expensive."

Denver is not alone. Los Angeles, with its legendary traffic congestion

and far-flung suburbs, has long been viewed as the worst example of sprawl. But now cities throughout the Western United States are facing the same unprecedented pressure to expand that is tearing at Denver. Drawn by a sudden increase in jobs in high-tech and other industries, the spectacular scenery and varied recreational opportunities, Americans are migrating in droves to the West. The U.S. Census Bureau expects the West to move past the Midwest by around 2000 to become the country's second most populous region, after the South. California alone, the agency predicts, will add more than 16 million residents between 1993 and 2020, and Texas will replace New York to fall in behind California as the state with the second-largest population. Three of the four states that are expected to grow the fastest over the period — Nevada, California and Washington — are in the West. [2]

Fueling the westward migration is a booming regional economy. Colorado is experiencing its ninth consecutive year of economic growth, undoubtedly the main reason for its population gains — more than 40,000 people in recent years. [3] The state's unemployment rate stands at about 3.5 percent, compared with the national average of 4.8 percent. Even California, which suffered a massive exodus during the early 1990s, once again is attracting more new residents than are leaving. [4] While the influx of newcomers brings much-needed revenue after the lengthy recession decimated the region's defense, petroleum and manufacturing industries, the sudden demand for housing threatens to overwhelm many Western communities.

"Sprawl is not necessarily endemic to the West, but the region is growing so rapidly that there's very little time to deal with a lot of these problems," says Shelley Poticha, executive director of the Congress for the New Urbanism, a national organization of architects and planners who support more compact development. "Just take Denver, for example, where the magnitude of residential growth is unbelievable, and development in a lot of communities is going in without all the necessary services, such as schools, parks or open space. Cities like that are at the point where they're just responding to building applications."

Trying to keep up with the demand for these basic services is actually leading some communities in the region to promote even more commercial development to pay for the residential development, compounding the problem. The anti-tax revolt of the 1980s that produced California's Proposition 13 and similar laws in other states banning or limiting property taxes has deprived many Western communities of revenue needed to provide new infrastructure and services. Like California cities, Denver and its suburbs now

© 1997 Landiscors

Highlands Ranch subdivision occupies part of the large tract of once undeveloped land south of metropolitan Denver, Colo., (dark area at top of photo).

depend heavily on sales taxes to pay for essential services.

To generate the needed revenue, these communities are building enormous shopping malls, often competing with neighboring jurisdictions for consumer dollars. The city of Westminster in suburban Denver, for example, is considering approval of a new upscale mall just 12 blocks from the existing Westminster Mall, a huge complex that generates about a quarter of Westminster's sales-tax revenues, more than $7 million a year. City officials are considering the new mall because they fear that much of the revenue they now receive would leak from their coffers if another new mall, also under consideration, is built in neighboring Broomfield. [5]

"Cities are in a financial crunch, and they often resort to the zoning that will bring them the highest revenue," Poticha says. "And a lot of times commercial uses such as shopping centers yield higher taxes than residential uses, which consume more city services."

Controlling physical expansion is a relatively new concept for much of the region. "A lot of West Coast cities were created after the advent of the automobile, after mass-transit systems had made their exit," says Christa Shaw, a field representative for the Greenbelt Alliance, a nonprofit group in the San Francisco Bay area devoted to land conservation and urban planning. "There was never any need for people to plan communities or build around mass transportation because it didn't exist. That made a huge difference in terms of the way that Western cities developed over the way that Eastern cities developed."

Sprawl is not limited to the West, of course. Cities throughout the country have long struggled, often with little success, to manage growth. But the surge in population in the West since the early 1990s has left many communities without the tools to adequately consider, let alone curb, unfettered development.

"In Western cities, one of the biggest issues is that very little regional planning is going on," Poticha says. "While most regions are composed of a number of different cities, there's very little, if any, coordination in land-use decision-making and transportation planning between the cities. I think that naturally leads us to urban sprawl."

The West's fragile environment makes it especially vulnerable to rapid development. Water, ever a scarce commodity and source of endless disputes throughout the region's history, is running out in many areas, especially the metropolitan areas of Los Angeles, Tucson and other cities that depend on the dwindling Colorado River. [6] The region's once pristine air also is falling prey to sprawl. Phoenix, whose clean, dry air made it a mecca for sufferers from tuberculosis and allergies in earlier decades, today is plagued by some of the worst air pollution in the West.

As urban development spreads, it eats up green space, destroying one of the main attractions that draws people to the West in the first place.

The residential developments outside Denver that are creeping up the Front Range afford wealthy homeowners fantastic views of the city, but they scar the mountain landscape for the rest of the city's residents.

Sprawl also is consuming precious farmland. Eaten away by expanding Fresno, Sacramento, Bakersfield and Modesto, California's Central Valley, which produces fruits and vegetables worth some $13 billion a year, has been declared the country's most threatened agricultural area by the American Farmland Trust, a conservation group. Five other prime farming areas in the West are included on the group's list of 20 areas nationwide that are threatened by suburban sprawl. [7]

As in other parts of the country, Western sprawl also takes its toll on the very residents who fuel its spread. "Sprawling development patterns are promoting greater and greater segregation by income," says urban-planning consultant David Rusk, a former mayor of Albuquerque, N.M. "When you look at what has been built up around Denver, for example, you pretty much see subdivisions, each one targeted on a fairly narrow range of the income scale. More and more, the building community is focusing on upper-income groups so that lower-income groups are left with hand-me-down housing in older central cities and older suburban areas."

Denver, Phoenix and Los Angeles are not the only examples of urban development in the West, however. Portland, Ore., has adopted strict limits on physical growth that have served as a model for nearly two decades. The city's "urban growth boundary," adopted in 1979, has helped restrict Portland's expansion to just 2 percent from 1973 to 1991. Encouraged by Portland's experience, Boulder, Colo., San Jose, Calif., and other cities have adopted similar growth restrictions.

But while it appeals to environmentalists and many city planners, drawing a line in the sand does not solve all the West's development problems. In many cities, businesses are opening new facilities and creating jobs faster than new apartments and homes are becoming available to house the workers they hire. As demand for housing outpaces supply, prices soar. In communities that have adopted growth boundaries, some developers blame them for the crunch.

"Here in Portland, land prices are out of sight," says James Goodrich, executive officer of the Home Builders Association of Metropolitan Portland. "We're now the second least affordable city in the United States." Another Western city — San Francisco — tops the list.

As local officials, developers and city planners grapple with the problems caused by rapid development, these are some of the questions they are asking:

Are urban growth boundaries a good idea?

In 1973, Oregon Gov. Thomas L. McCall, a Republican who served from 1967 to 1975, launched a revolutionary plan to protect farmland against urban sprawl. He proposed, and the legislature approved, a requirement that all 273 municipalities and 36 counties in Oregon develop land-use and zoning plans to control further growth. In 1979, Portland, the state's largest city, established an "urban growth boundary," essentially a line drawn to stop sprawl in its tracks. Inside the boundary, developers were free to build more houses, apartments and commercial buildings. Outside the line, green space had to stay that way.

Because the Portland metropolitan area includes 24 adjacent municipalities, planners decided to draw a single boundary around the whole area. To administer the new region, a seven-member council was established. Known as Metro, it is the only elected regional government in the country.

Supporters and opponents alike agree that Portland's urban growth boundary has not stymied economic growth and prosperity. Since it went into effect, the area's population has grown by 700,000. And Portland has become the leading model in the country for communities interested in establishing boundaries to curb growth.

"I preach Portland all over the country," Rusk says, "particularly in the Northeast and the Midwest, where there's such fragmentation of government responsibility that you can't possibly have any meaningful regional land-use planning unless there's a state law like Oregon's that says you must."

One of the main goals of the boundary is to prevent the gutting of central cities that has left St. Louis, Chicago, Baltimore and countless other metropolises in the industrial East and Midwest looking like donuts. As residents and then jobs move away from the center, downtowns become abandoned wastelands inhabited only by those too poor to leave. As the donut continues to expand with the growth of new suburbs, the abandoned hole in the middle gets bigger as well, embracing not only downtown but also the older suburbs.

Preventing sprawl with a physical boundary may come at a high price, however. For many years, Portland's boundary had little, if any, measurable effect on real estate prices. But the region has grown steadily in recent years, thanks to a boom in high-tech and other industries that are attracting new residents. And now that the developable space inside the boundary is running out, demand is driving up prices for the land that remains.

"Portland's boundary is the result of a policy to focus development so you don't get a hole in the donut," says R. Gregory Nokes, a reporter who covers urban-growth issues for *The Oregonian,* Portland's daily newspa-

Crested Butte Fights for Its Vistas . . .

Crested Butte, Colo., has been called one of the last unspoiled mountain towns in the West. Nestled against the western slope of the Rockies, the town was incorporated in 1880 as a community of coal miners. Tourism has long since replaced mining as the main industry. Crested Butte draws throngs of visitors in both summer and winter to its wildflower-covered slopes and widely acclaimed ski facility.

A five-hour drive from Denver, it's more remote than other Colorado resort towns, such as Aspen, Vail and Breckenridge, which helps explain why, unlike its rivals, Crested Butte retains its compact, small-town air. Its eight square blocks are home to just 1,465 year-round residents and 300 dogs, according to town planner John Hess. Another 473 people live year-round up the hill in Mount Crested Butte, a separate jurisdiction at the base of the ski lifts.

Development pressure outside Crested Butte, Colo., is altering the area's pristine mountain views.

But even Crested Butte is beginning to feel some of the same pressures to develop that have altered the face of resort towns throughout the state. "A lot of the things that happened in previous years to Aspen, Telluride, Vail and Breckenridge are now coming to Crested Butte," says Linda Powers, a former Town Council member and former state senator. "We are more affordable than those places, where costs have gone through the roof. So now people who like the mountain lifestyle and are looking for a place that's quaint and beautiful have discovered Crested Butte, much to the chagrin of a lot of the locals."

One problem residents have with the local real estate boom, which started in the early 1990s, is that it is driving many of them out of the housing market. "We cannot compete with someone who sells a house for $600,000 in California and chooses to come here," Powers says. "They have a lot more money than the locals, who tend to work part time in our seasonal service industry."

Residents of Crested Butte and the rest of Gunnison County are fighting back, however, trying to avoid the mistakes of other resort towns. "Aspen did growth management but did not include affordable housing in its plans," Hess says. "The common theory is that growth management caused prices to go up. Without any affordable housing in place, there was no place for people to live."

While workers in Aspen and other resorts are forced to commute from distant but less expensive towns, Crested Butte is taking steps to provide more affordable housing in town. One regulation requires developers to set aside five acres of open space for every unit built, but only one

per. "But the housing being built downtown is very high-priced." Nokes tells of one couple who sold their suburban home two years ago and bought a townhouse inside the boundary for $250,000. "Now it's worth $350,000," he says. "This is hot stuff, but it's not affordable to the broad spectrum of people in the area."

Critics charge that the dearth of affordable housing is a direct result of the boundary itself. "There's just no doubt about that," Goodrich says. "It's real easy to see."

But even the developers stop short of calling for the boundary's elimination, and some say the link between it and the lack of affordable housing is less obvious. "There are a lot of factors that go into affordable-housing problems," says Jon Chandler, a lobbyist for the Portland Home Builders Association. "As with any hot real estate market, supply and demand tends to drive prices up. The difference in Oregon, we believe, is that, unlike Denver or the California cities, we have deliberately constrained the supply of land. And once you deliberately limit the supply of anything, be it bread or socks, you'll see price increases. So the boundary is definitely a factor. How large a factor is hard to tell."

Property-rights advocates are more outspoken critics of urban growth boundaries. "It doesn't take much thinking to figure out that if you restrict access you're going to drive up costs," says Nancie Marzula, president of Defenders of Property Rights, who lived in Boulder in the 1970s, after it had established its own urban growth boundary. "The theory was basically we've got ours, and we don't want anybody else coming in and spoiling our wonderful foothills community overlooking the Rocky Mountains. But the cost of living in Boul-

. . . But Houses Keep Getting in the Way

acre for every unit of affordable housing, thus making construction of affordable housing less onerous. The Town Council is now considering another proposal by Hess that would require a quarter of all new units in a given development to be affordable housing. Despite these efforts, the average home price has skyrocketed from about $50,000 in the mid-1970s to about $275,000 today.

Another downside of Crested Butte's sudden popularity is sprawl. In town, houses must be built subject to strict design guidelines aimed at maintaining the community's historic character. Outside the town limits, however, large houses are sprouting along ridge lines and up the mountain slopes, marring the pristine views that drew newcomers to the area in the first place.

The helter-skelter construction is facilitated by a Colorado law passed in 1972, ostensibly to help ranchers pass on homesteads to their children. The law exempts lots of at least 35 acres from county planning and zoning regulations. But the exemption has been used as a giant loophole for developers, who can buy entire ranches and then build luxury houses on 35-acre lots with no county restrictions on placement, size or impact on the surrounding community.

"So the biggest pieces of land are the ones that are the least regulated," says Powers, who lost her bid for re-election to the state Senate in 1996 after trying, unsuccessfully, to change the 35-acre law. "I lost because I took on the big boys, the home builders, the Realtors, the ranchers and the Farm Bureau, all of whom like the law because it lets them do things quickly and with the least possible cost."

The town is taking action on its own to curb sprawl. In 1991, a group of residents established the Crested Butte Land Trust, one of more than 1,000 land trusts formed around the country to curtail rural sprawl onto prized open space.[1] Since then, the trust has removed from possible development about 1,000 acres outside the town, either by purchasing the land outright or by acquiring conservation easements, which are legally binding agreements to set aside land for open space. Contributions for the purchases have come from private donations, a six-year-old real estate transfer tax that generates up to a quarter-million dollars a year, Gunnison County and Great Outdoors Colorado, a state agency that helps acquire land for open space preservation. Businesses chipped in moneys raised by adding a 1 percent surcharge on goods and services. A second land trust, the Gunnison Ranchland Conservation Project, is expected to begin acquiring conservation easements from ranch families next year. And a third group, the High Country Citizens Alliance, joins two traditionally antagonistic constituencies — environmentalists and ranchers — in a common effort to preserve open space.

Supporters of Crested Butte's anti-sprawl efforts are guardedly optimistic about the future. A recent proposal by a New York developer to build luxury houses along a scenic ridge has drawn a flurry of protests, including a petition to block the plan and high attendance at land-use meetings on the development. "A lot of people think we're just going to go down the same road as Aspen and Vail, and probably eventually we will," Hess says. "But it's going to take us a lot longer than it took those guys."

[1] See Traci Watson, "Land Trusts Keep Open Space by Buying It," *USA Today*, Sept. 17, 1997.

der went straight through the roof, and there's no question about the fact that it was due to the boundary. It seems to me to be an arbitrary solution to a problem that might be better solved through more market-driven approaches."

Despite the risk of inflated housing prices, some communities in the West are following Portland's lead even in the absence of a statewide mandate to curb growth. In 1990, the Washington state Legislature approved legislation requiring rapidly growing counties and cities to develop plans to deal with growth. In 1996, San Jose also adopted an urban growth boundary. And last November, Sonoma County, north of San Francisco, became the first county in the nation to adopt a voter-approved network of urban growth boundaries.

"The planning model that we used is based on Oregon's urban growth boundaries," says the Greenbelt Alliance's Shaw, who works out of Santa Rosa, Sonoma County's biggest city. "In California, we have never been able to get it together politically enough to even approach growth management on a statewide level because the real estate lobby and the building lobby are far too powerful in Sacramento."

Critics of growth boundaries include property-rights advocates, traditionally a large constituency in the West, who say they are arbitrary mandates that deny property owners their right to dispose of their land as they see fit.

"I don't think growth boundaries are politically viable in Denver," says Councilwoman Barnes-Gelt. "We're not really the Wild West, but we're sort of the West, and there's this independent kind of spirit here. We don't take to top-down directives. I don't think we're going to end up with legislative solutions that come because some guy at the top of the triangle had a great idea and figured out how to impose it on the community."

Rusk rejects this criticism out of hand. "Let's remember that urban growth boundaries were not imposed in Oregon," he says. In fact, Oregon voters rejected measures to repeal the law in 1976, 1978 and 1982. "It may look imposed in the eyes of some farmer sitting out there who really is looking to cash in his land and retire to Florida, or to a developer who wants to build on that land. But the boundary is very much a part of a very democratic process. The nation would be well-served if counterparts to the Oregon law or the Washington law were in place in all 50 states. To have all local governments engaging in collaborative land-use planning and applying the urban growth boundary concept to distinguish between that which is urban and that which is rural would be very beneficial."

Are Americans ready to abandon the suburbs?

If efforts to curb urban sprawl in the West are to succeed, the cities undergoing rapid in-migration will have to become more densely populated. Some urban planners and architects are incorporating this goal into their blueprints. Indeed, a new school of architecture, known as New Urbanism, has emerged on the premise that suburban sprawl is a blight that attacks not only the natural resources, green space and esthetic sensibilities of city residents but also the very social fabric of urban America. Most people, they contend, would be happier if they lived closer together, within walking distance of work and shops, instead of in isolated suburban enclaves accessible only by car.

"My experience is that in a lot of communities there's a really basic level of frustration with the status quo," Poticha says. "The way that a lot of suburbs have been built has led to a sense of isolation. There's a loss of the community support network that we used to have. Every single trip has to be done in the car, and traffic congestion has increased. All land uses are divided out into their separate little pods. All of this has led to a real decline in community life."

Metro Regional Government, Portland

To prevent surburban sprawl and loss of green space, development is restricted outside the "urban growth boundary" drawn around Portland, Ore., and neighboring municipalities.

New Urbanist designers follow a basic set of principles aimed at recreating the small-town environment that typified American communities before suburban development took off in the 1950s. (*See story, p. 876.*) Also known as neotraditional communities, new urbanist developments combine residential, commercial and civic buildings — such as schools, churches and libraries — within walking distance of each other in a single "village," or neighborhood. Residents of the village's single-family houses occupy smaller quarters on smaller lots, or opt for neighboring townhouses or apartments.

As Poticha sees it, suburban residents would jump at the chance to trade in their tract homes with the yard and two-car garage for more intimate lodging in a community that offers more interaction with neighbors, a bustling street life and better access to public transportation.

"Ten or 12 years ago, everybody thought that these ideas were just crazy," she says. "But in the last five years it's just taken off like wildfire." After *Better Homes and Gardens* mentioned her organization in a recent issue, she says, "we've been getting about 15 phone calls a day from people asking how they can buy a house in one of these communities." And they're not just from the East Coast, where new urbanist communities got their start with such free-standing developments as Seaside, Fla., and Kentlands, Md. "They're also calling from Denver, the Bay area and Seattle," Poticha says. "Whatever part of the country they live in, most of the people are calling from suburban areas."

Demographic trends in the West as elsewhere in the country may encourage some suburbanites to return to city life. The first wave of baby boomers, Americans born between 1946 and 1964, are entering middle age and may be willing to abandon the suburbs for life without lawnmowers and long commutes. Developers are renovating old warehouses and other abandoned commercial buildings in downtown Denver, San Francisco and Seattle, turning them into upscale condominiums and marketing them to young professionals and graying boomers alike.

"For some suburban baby boomers, moving to the city may make sense," Chandler concedes. "The kids are gone and the dogs are dead. But whether that alone can make urban villages work is another question."

Critics dismiss New Urbanism as a passing fad, a designer's dream that will never reverse the decades-old migration of Americans away from high-density living. "These people are trying to re-create Mayberry," scoffs Chandler, referring to the peaceful, intimate, town on television's "Andy Griffith Show." "They're responding to yuppy angst."

In Chandler's view, planners who think they can draw suburban residents out of their spacious homes — and their cars — are in for a rude awakening. "There is a fair amount of political correctness going on here," Chandler says. "The fact is, many people, like me, are fat and out of shape, and they don't have time to walk, anyway. As for public transportation, we all know we're supposed to take the subway, but we don't. And most people's lives are not set up to ride their bikes to work."

In the absence of growth-management measures, some experts say, neotraditional communities will not draw enough residents to stem suburban flight. "In Denver, where there's so much new growth, there's much less communal spirit," Barnes-Gelt says. "I don't mean to sound judgmental, but a lot of people moving here want to build their little house on the prairie or their McMansion by the stream outside of town." She points to Genessee, a fast-growing subdivision in the foothills of the Rockies along Interstate 70, which links Denver with the ski resorts to the west, such as Vail and Aspen.

"Genessee was once a small mountain community, but now it's full of people building these megahouses on megalots who commute every day to Denver on I-70," Barnes-Gelt says. "What they're not are people who are really willing to live their lives around communal ideas. This is not the reason they moved here. They moved here because they wanted to be in the West. They wanted space."

Because one of the main attractions of high-density communities is the ability of residents to walk to the corner store, their success depends on the presence of retail outlets. And some communities in the West, including Denver and Thousand Oaks, Calif., are succeeding in drawing and keeping retailers in downtown locations. [8]

But skeptics contend that the majority of retailers are even less likely to abandon the suburbs than home-owners. Over the past two decades, main street shop owners across the country have been forced to move to less expensive, suburban quarters or driven out of business by such retail behemoths as WalMart and Home Depot, which can undersell small retailers. Chandler doubts that the construction of neotraditional communities will reverse that trend.

"We all like the ma-and-pa hardware store with the wooden barrels and sawdust on the floor," he says. "But we go to Home Depot because it's cheaper to shop there. That's just human nature."

Should the federal government adopt policies to discourage sprawl?

Zoning and growth management issues generally fall within the jurisdiction of local governments. As long as a community's or county's physical layout does not adversely affect communities outside its borders, it is up to the local authorities to decide in what direction and to what extent the community will allow housing and commercial structures to spread.

As the pace of suburban development accelerated after World War II, however, communities in urban areas could no longer build without affecting neighboring communities. As green space and farmland shrank in fast-growing regions, state governments began to assume a stronger role in determining land-use decisions. This trend culminated in the 1973 Oregon law requiring local governments to curb development that led to Portland's adoption in 1979 of an urban growth boundary.

But little attention has been given to the federal government's role in determining the pace and direction of urban sprawl. Although Washington stays out of any direct involvement in local land-use issues, its policies do affect development. Through Veterans Affairs and Federal Housing Administration programs, for example, the federal government subsidizes low-interest mortgages that enable veterans and other borrowers of limited means to buy a single-family home in the suburbs.

Federal tax law further encourages home ownership through the mortgage-interest deduction and favorable treatment of capital gains on the sale of a house. Federal transportation policy provides much higher subsidies for road-building than for urban mass transit, literally paving the way for suburban development. Although the 1991 Intermodal Surface Transportation Efficiency Act — up for reauthorization next year — shifted some of the emphasis in federal spending to transit and to pedestrian and bicycle paths, road-building continues to receive the overwhelming bulk of the federal transportation dollar. [9]

Some policy-makers want the federal government to change policies that encourage suburban flight. "It's just nuts for federal tax policy to cripple cities by driving the middle class to ever newer suburbs, putting unnecessary and unwanted developmental pressure on farm and forest lands," said Rep. Earl Blumenauer, D-Ore., a former Portland city commissioner. To reverse that trend, Blumenauer targeted a provision of the tax law that allows home sellers to avoid paying taxes on the sale of their homes by purchasing a more expensive home. "It is wrong for the federal government to make people confront a huge tax bill for living in the city of their choice in the home of their choice," he said in May. "And yet that happens millions of times a year. Is it any wonder the livability of our cities is under assault, when you get a big tax break for moving out and buying up?"

Other legislators agreed with Blumenauer, and Congress eliminated capital gains taxes on profits from the sale of primary residences selling for a profit of less than $250,000 for individual taxpayers ($500,000 for couples). The change was part of the budget-reconciliation bills adopted at the end of July. [10]

Blumenauer also wants the federal government to change the tax law to discourage the use of single-occupancy vehicles — suburbanites' mode of choice for commuting to work.

"Most of us understand that the overwhelming reliance on single-occupant vehicles is responsible for unsafe air, unsafe streets and gridlock that is increasingly paralyzing our communities," he said. "Yet, sadly, our tax policy encourages commuting by car over any other means of transportation." The Commuter Choice Act, introduced in February by Rep. John Lewis, D-Ga., and co-sponsored by Blumenauer, would increase the amount of transportation subsidies for transit and car-pooling arrangements employers can exclude from their taxable income.

Many experts and policy-makers involved in local land-use planning are leery of changes in federal law that might interfere more directly with local governments' jurisdiction over these matters, however. "The sentiment in Oregon is that we'd like to do it ourselves, thank you," says Nokes.

Developers are more adamant. "The notion that the federal government should intervene to curb urban development sounds awfully elitist to me," says Chandler of the Portland Home Builders Association. "I happen to be a big fan of the marketplace. Most people in any given city know where the high-density housing is, and the fact that they move away from it to the suburbs simply reflects choices that they are free to make." ■

BACKGROUND

Rise of Sprawl

As a visit to Europe's old cities quickly shows, cities for millennia were densely populated places where everyone who could lived within the city walls that protected residents from enemy attack. Only farms, noxious industries such as tanning operations and the poorest residents were excluded from town, left to occupy the suburbs — a term suggesting something less than urban. [11] Cities expanded roughly in concentric circles, as new walls were built to encircle growing populations.

This pattern of city development persisted in most of the large cities of continental Europe. But in London a new pattern of development began to emerge as early as the 16th century that served as a precedent for later urban expansion both in England and North America. Protected from foreign attack by the English Channel, Londoners were less concerned about the city's defensive value than they were about escaping the crowded and unhealthy conditions of the city center. The Strand, a street linking the walled city with Westminster to the west, was lined with large estates that were later subdivided into squares and streets where wealthy Londoners built their city residences during the 17th and 18th centuries. As the city expanded, commercial businesses moved into the closest suburbs, and residents moved further westward, establishing London's westward growth pattern.

Like most cities established before the Industrial Revolution, the earliest communities in North America cropped up along waterways, often at the confluence of two rivers. Even after railroads largely replaced riverboats as the main means of transportation and the American population moved westward, cities continued to be built near water. Though the cities of Seattle and Dallas, for example, emerged at the ends of railway lines in the late 1800s, they were built on sites of older waterway settlements. Rivers not only provided transportation for shipping trade goods, they also became valuable energy sources with the advent of industrialization. With their demand for local labor, 19th-century mills and factories provided a major impetus behind the growth of upstream cities along the East Coast.

As in London, wealthy city dwell-

Continued on p. 877

Chronology

1940s-1950s

Suburban development takes off with the return of GIs from World War II.

1947
William Levitt launches the prototype of suburban development, Levittown, a subdivision of 17,000 houses on Long Island.

1959
As suburbanization spreads westward, Boulder, Colo., adopts an urban growth boundary to prevent development from moving up the Front Range of the Rocky Mountains.

1970s

As businesses begin to follow residents to the suburbs, Oregon leads the way toward growth management.

1973
The Oregon legislature requires all counties and municipalities to develop land-use and zoning plans to manage growth and curb sprawl.

1979
After Oregon voters twice reject measures to repeal the 1973 law, the Portland metropolitan area adopts an urban growth boundary and establishes the country's first elected regional government, Metro, to administer the boundary.

1980s

A downturn in the energy and defense industries plunges much of the West into a recession. An anti-tax revolt modeled after California's Proposition 13 deprives many Western communities of property-tax revenues needed to build infrastructure.

1982
Oregon voters again turn down a ballot initiative to repeal the state growth-management law.

1990s

Improving economic conditions in the West fuel a surge in population, spurring rapid development in many cities.

1990
The Washington state Legislature requires rapidly growing counties and cities to develop growth-management plans. The Census Bureau reports that population in the West has reached 53 million, almost double the number in 1960. The agency predicts that by 2020 California will add more than 16 million residents and that three Western states — Nevada, California and Washington — will be among the four fastest-growing states over the period. Overall, the United States becomes the first country in history to have more suburbanites than city and rural residents combined.

February 1995
The Bank of America, together with conservation and housing agencies, releases a broadly publicized study warning that unchecked sprawl threatens to undermine California's future economic growth.

1996
San Jose, California's fastest-growing city, adopts an urban growth boundary to curb sprawl resulting from Silicon Valley's booming software industry. Sonoma County, north of San Francisco, becomes the first county to establish a voter-approved network of urban growth boundaries.

1997
Portland's Metro council considers a proposal to expand the area's urban growth boundary to accommodate anticipated growth in population. Opponents launch a drive to include an initiative to abolish Metro on the November 1998 ballot.

February 1997
In an effort to reduce the traffic that has accompanied suburban development, Reps. John Lewis, D-Ga., and Earl Blumenauer, D-Ore., introduce the Commuter Choice Act to increase the amount of transit and car-pooling subsidies that employers can exclude from their taxable income.

March 1997
The American Farmland Trust calls California's Central Valley the country's most threatened agricultural area and lists five other Western areas where sprawl is quickly eroding prime agricultural land.

July 30-31, 1997
Congress eliminates capital gains taxes on profits from the sale of primary residences of up to $250,000 for individuals and $500,000 for couples, a move that growth-management advocates welcome as an inducement for home sellers to abandon the suburbs in favor of less-expensive, in-town housing.

Building Denser to Curb Sprawl

To combat further sprawl, a growing number of architects and city planners are calling for redesign of the American dream. The house, the yard and the car are still in the picture, but they look different. The house is smaller and closer to the street. The lot is smaller, too. And the car is garaged out of sight, behind the house, or parked on the street.

These and many other design guidelines are contained in the "Charter of the New Urbanism," a manifesto drawn up by the Congress for the New Urbanism in San Francisco. To counter what it calls "the spread of placeless sprawl," the group proposes that:

• Development should be in compact neighborhoods, typically no more than a quarter-mile from center to edge. Residents should be able to reach every destination in the neighborhood, including stores, offices and schools, on foot.

• Streets should interconnect, usually in a grid pattern, to spread traffic evenly. This would alleviate the problems of many suburbs, whose dead-end streets dump traffic onto main arteries that become clogged with traffic. Public transit should connect neighborhoods with each other and the surrounding region. Sidewalks are ubiquitous.

• Building entrances, not parking lots, should front the street. Parking is provided behind buildings and residences. On-street parking is allowed, to provide a buffer between the pedestrians and traffic. Houses also sit close to the street and may have front porches to encourage conversation between residents and passersby.

• Zoning regulations that separate business from residential areas should be changed to allow for a diverse mix of activities — residences, shops, schools, workplaces, parks, etc. — in close proximity. A wide spectrum of housing options should enable people of a broad range of incomes, ages and family types to live in the same neighborhood.

New Urbanism, also known as neotraditional development, first appeared in the East, with such free-standing developments as the resort town of Seaside, Fla., and Kentlands, Md., near Washington. "The region that has the longest track record in building neotraditional communities is the Southeast," says Shelley Poticha, executive director of the congress. "But there are a few beginning to take shape in the West as well."

Of about 120 such communities across the country, the group says, 38 are in the West. Twenty are in California, including much-publicized Laguna West, a 3,300-unit community being built on just over 1,000 acres in Sacramento County. The free-standing community — its design includes stores, schools and recreation areas — is one of a dozen or so neotraditional developments designed by San Francisco architect Peter Calthorpe.

New urbanist principles are gaining support in the West, especially in communities that have established urban growth boundaries or other measures aimed at slowing suburban sprawl. In Portland and other cities reaching the limits of their boundaries, most new development has to occur on relatively small lots, typically vacant land slated for projects that never materialized. Located within city limits and often close to public transit, such "infill" developments lend themselves to the kind of high-density design the neotraditionalists embrace.

"The amount of building going on within this city is really quite a remarkable success story," says Greg Nokes, a reporter at *The Oregonian*. "Almost everybody agrees that this is a beneficial effect of the boundary because focusing growth inward is making us use our land more efficiently."

But the boundary also is blamed for sending housing prices through the roof, thwarting one of the New Urbanism's central aims — including a wide range of income levels in the same neighborhood. Eighteen years after it drew its urban growth boundary, Portland is the second least affordable city in the country, after San Francisco.

"Infill and redevelopment housing is never cheap housing," Nokes says. "If you tear down two old blocks in a semi-ghettoized area and you rebuild new houses on it, the people who lived there before aren't going to be able to afford the new ones. So we have a real affordable-housing problem."

Critics say new urbanist developments do not always respect the principles their adherents espouse. "This neo-traditional thing is getting to be really trendy," says Christa Shaw of the Greenbelt Alliance in Sonoma County, Calif. "So some developers who want to build in an inappropriate place will use a really hot urban planner like Calthorpe to design the project because they're hoping they can leverage their project in the door for its design cachet." Shaw cites as an example a project outside the Sonoma County community of Petaluma. "This project has been proposed for one of the last contiguous pieces of agricultural land next to Petaluma," she says. "It's definitely an interesting project, and if it were located along a transit corridor or in a more central area, I would love to support it. But when it's on over 100 acres of agricultural land and way out of the central part of town, I can't support it."

Other redevelopment projects in the West find favor with urban planners, however. Steve Meck of the American Planning Association particularly likes infill projects in Boise, Idaho, and Spokane, Wash. He cautions, however, that new urbanist designers must take care to fit their developments into the surrounding cityscape.

"The neotraditional concept can be adapted to a particular community, but it has got to respect the vernacular architecture," he says. "Otherwise, it looks like something that's transplanted from South Florida."

Continued from p. 874

ers in the United States escaped the congestion and poverty that characterized the rapidly industrializing cities by building exclusive residential neighborhoods such as Beacon Hill in Boston or Washington Square in New York City. These fashionable neighborhoods often gave rise to a major road, known as a mansion street, that laid the path of future residential development for the wealthy, such as Baltimore's Charles Street or San Francisco's California Street. In addition to the city's biggest homes, mansion streets included churches and clubs attended by the wealthy and often ended at an art museum or a college campus.

Impact of Railroads, Streetcars and Skyscrapers

By the 1880s, the growing railroad network had altered the pattern of urban development. Industrial centers developed along the railroad tracks away from residential neighborhoods, sometimes giving rise to separate communities, such as East St. Louis, Ill., or Camden, N.J., across the Delaware River from Philadelphia.

The development of the skyscraper and the spread of streetcar service around the turn of the century accelerated the separation of commercial and residential neighborhoods in many American cities. The growing middle class saw the biggest change in residential trends of the period. While the poor continued to live within walking distance of factories in the industrial center and the wealthy remained in their mansion districts, streetcars enabled lower-middle-class residents to move to the edge of the expanding city. Upper-middle-class city-dwellers moved even further out, to new suburban communities that sprang up around train stations. In addition to providing year-round homes for wealthier city workers, railroad suburbs such as Philadelphia's Main Line suburbs included summer homes for many of the downtown mansion district inhabitants.

This pattern of urban development — a vibrant downtown commercial district flanked by industrial areas, with residential neighborhoods both in town and extending along train and streetcar lines — persisted through the 1950s. Repeated across the country, this pattern came to be recognized as the traditional American urban model.

Postwar Suburbs

But another revolution in transportation — the automobile — overturned that model. Although cars had been in circulation since Henry Ford began mass-producing the Model T in the early years of this century, they did not begin to alter the shape of cities until the economic boom after World War II brought car ownership within the grasp of virtually all Americans. The same economic surge, coupled with federal mortgage subsidies, enabled an unprecedented share of Americans to buy their own homes. Pursuit of the American Dream — a car and a house with a yard — fueled the postwar exodus to the suburbs. According to one study, federal mortgage subsidies alone raised the proportion of suburban residents from 30 percent of the population in the mid-1960s to 45 percent in the 1980s. [12]

Returning war veterans and their families led the flight from cities to such new suburban communities as Levittown, the Long Island suburb that served as a model for similar developments across the country. Beginning in 1947, developer William Levitt built more than 17,000 nearly identical small houses, immortalized as "little boxes" by folk singer Bob Dylan. The houses, arranged along curving streets and cul-de-sacs, each with its own yard, comprised a homogeneous neighborhood of middle-class families with children, a short car ride from virtually all stores and other services. [13]

To the new suburbanites, their homes' distance from the city was a boon, enabling them to have more land and living space than they could afford in town. Encouraged by federal policies insuring mortgages, offering tax deductions for mortgage interest and paying for new roads, Americans fled the cities for the newly emerging suburbs. This trend continues. Since 1950, while most big cities have lost population, the suburbs have gained more than 75 million residents. St. Louis, an oft-cited example of the adverse consequences of urban flight, was the fourth-largest city in the country in 1950, when its population stood at 857,000. By 1990, it had fallen to 397,000. In 1990, the United States became the first country in history to have more suburbanites than city and rural residents combined. [14]

Suburbs did not simply form as extensions of central cities, with their mix of residential, commercial and civic buildings. Local governments adopted zoning ordinances separating different types of development into different physical spaces. The rationale behind these laws was to keep noxious industries such as glue factories or foundries out of residential neighborhoods. In the early years, most suburbs were built as bedroom communities, a collection of single-family houses set back from the street and from each other by lawns. As the suburbs continued their march away from the center, increasing the distance shoppers had to travel from home, businesses followed residents into the suburbs, funneled by zoning regulations into areas that were segregated from housing. This gave rise to shopping centers — and later to the much larger shopping malls — which were interspersed among residential subdivisions. Schools, libraries and other civic buildings generally fell into yet another zoning category.

By the late 1970s and early '80s, suburbs of the biggest metropolitan areas were so far from downtown that many employers also moved away from the city centers, setting up offices in suburban "business parks." The move not only meant generally cheaper office or factory space; it also made it easier to commute to work for the ever-growing numbers of workers who called the suburbs home. As a result of this massive exodus, suburban centers such as Tysons Corner, Va., outside Washington, took on the congested nature of the very cities from which they arose.

Western Sprawl

While suburban development and the progressive deterioration of downtowns have been typical of most cities in the East and the Midwest, the phenomenon was virtually unknown in the Western United States — with the dramatic exception of Los Angeles. Settled in the late 19th century, in large part by Midwesterners seeking the beneficent climate of Southern California and relief from their congested region's industrial cities, Los Angeles began spreading outward with the advent of the automobile around 1920. Suburban towns emerged in rapid succession, forming a patchwork of communities whose residents were forced to commute longer and longer distances as the city grew. [15] The resulting traffic congestion, air pollution and dependence on cars for transportation throughout the metropolitan area have made Los Angeles a classic example of unbridled urban sprawl.

Other cities in the Southwest experienced similar, though less pronounced, expansion. Drawn by the clear, dry air, sufferers from asthma, tuberculosis, allergies and other respiratory illnesses moved steadily to communities like Phoenix, Tucson and Albuquerque in the 1940s and '50s. The influx of large numbers of new residents did not go unopposed in these communities. [16] But as retirees joined the migration beginning in the 1960s, efforts to curb growth were overwhelmed by the demand for new housing. As in Los Angeles, sprawl produced congestion, threatened the region's precarious water supplies and dirtied the air that had lured many migrants to the region in the first place.

Western growth was fueled also by the oil and gas industries, concentrated in Texas and Colorado, and by aerospace and other defense contractors that located in the Pacific Northwest and Southern California. But in the 1980s, an international energy glut dampened demand for Western oil and gas, which is expensive to extract, leading to an economic slump in much of the region. In the early 1990s, Southern California joined the list of economically troubled regions, as cuts in the defense budget that followed the end of the Cold War led to widespread layoffs by military contractors as well as the outright closing of military bases in the region.

CURRENT SITUATION

Sprawl Accelerates

Despite the economic downturns in the energy and defense industries that led to job losses in much of the West, migration to the region continued. It was further accelerated with the boom in computer software, cable television and other high-technology industries that have concentrated in California, the Pacific Northwest and the Denver area.

"In the late 1980s and early '90s, the economy was in the toilet because it was primarily based on the oil and mining industries," Barnes-Gelt says. "Thanks in part to the new airport and other investments made by former Denver Mayor Federico F. Peña, Denver is now more attractive. There also has been some aggressive economic-development recruiting in the health care, telecommunications, cable and satellite industries that has brought in a lot of good, strong jobs. So this combination of the climate, recreational opportunities and jobs has made Denver one of the fastest-growing areas of the country."

Overall, population in the West almost doubled from 1960 to 1990, from 28 million to almost 53 million inhabitants, according to the Census Bureau. California accounted for the bulk of westward migration, growing from 16 million to 30 million over the 30-year period. Some less populous states grew even faster: Nevada's population quadrupled over the period, while Arizona's nearly tripled. [17] Though a large number of the new residents were retirees from the East and Midwest, drawn by the region's balmy climate, many also were displaced Californians, downsized from the shrinking defense sector of Southern California or priced out of the state's skyrocketing housing market.

Although displaced Californians account for part of the population growth in several neighboring states, more people continue to move into California than leave. Most of the migrants are moving to cities. The result is urban sprawl, which is spreading so fast that cries of alarm are coming from some unlikely quarters. The Bank of America,

The Growth of Phoenix

Because of rampant growth, Phoenix, Ariz., now has more land area than Los Angeles and a larger population than San Diego.

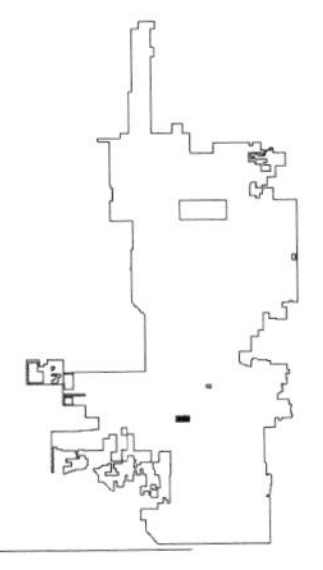

1881
Area: 0.5 sq. mi.
Population: 1,708

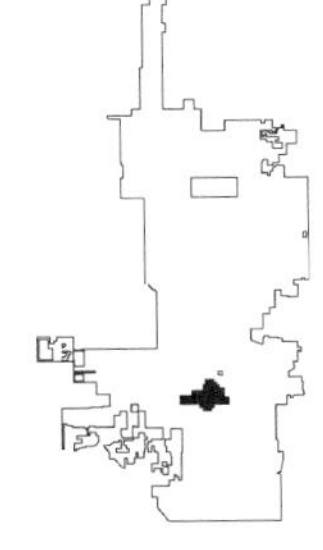

1920
Area: 5.1 sq. mi.
Population: 29,033

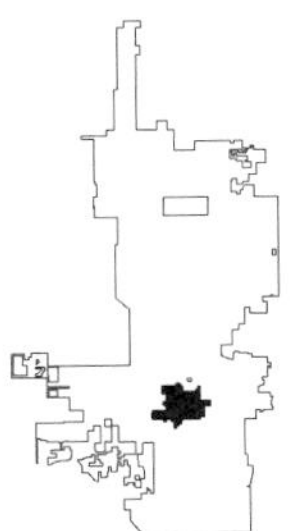

1940
Area: 9.6 sq. mi.
Population: 63,414

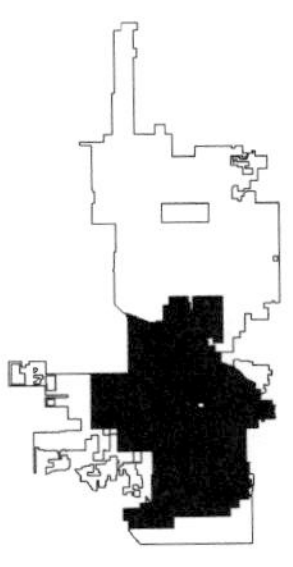

1960
Area: 187.4 sq. mi.
Population: 439,170

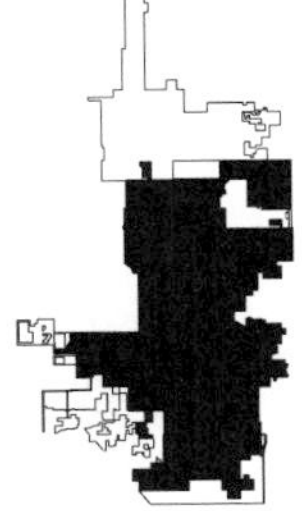

1980
Area: 329.1 sq. mi.
Population: 789,704

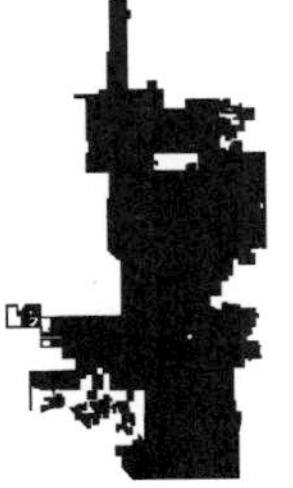

1997
Area: 469.3 sq. mi.
Population: 1,204,689

Source: Phoenix Planning Department

California's largest bank and a leading source of real estate funding in the state, has joined conservation and housing groups in warning that the pace of urban development is getting out of control:

"[A]s we approach the 21st century, it is clear that sprawl has created enormous costs that California can no longer afford," they concluded in a landmark report. "Ironically, unchecked sprawl has shifted from an engine of California's growth to a force that now threatens to inhibit growth and degrade the quality of our life." [18]

Loss of Green Space

The most visible impact of unfettered urban growth is the loss of green space. In some parts of the West, where there are few if any limits to the extent or the direction of development, the problem is especially severe. The spread of asphalt and concrete over the landscape is proceeding even faster than population growth in these areas. Denver, for example, saw an 89 percent growth in population from 1960 to 1990, while the amount of developed land grew by 174 percent. Portland's population increased 80 percent, its developed land by 103 percent.

In the 1980s, however, after Portland adopted its urban growth boundary, the city's population grew by 14 percent while its consumption of new land increased by only 11 percent. "In Portland, there was a 3 percent decrease in consumption of land per capita," Rusk says. "The city is growing more dense as a direct and conscious result of the planning policy in the Oregon state law and the policies carried out by the Portland Metro."

Many critics of urban sprawl decry its impact on the West's sweeping vistas of uninhabited land. "Sprawl compromises one of the most essential assets of California — the beauty and drama of its landscape," the Bank of America study asserts. "Far from being just a luxury, this value of open space is an important component in the state's ability to attract and hold workers and investors." [19]

But it is not just the pretty views that motivates supporters of planning mechanisms to curb sprawl. As property values rise on the edges of urban areas, valuable, often irreplaceable, farmland is being lost to development. According to the American Farmland Trust, six of the 20 most endangered agricultural regions are in the West. [20] The most vulnerable of the lot is the San Joaquin Valley in central California, which produces 250 different crops worth more than $13 billion a year. Population of the 11-county valley, which stretches from Sacramento to Bakersfield, is expected to triple by 2040. If current trends of low-density development continue, the group predicts, sprawl will consume more than a million acres of this prime farmland, costing more than $5 billion each year in lost sales of commodities and agricultural supplies. [21]

Water Shortages

Many of the West's prime agricultural areas, including California's most productive farmland, depend on irrigation. But taking land out of farming for development does not alleviate the problem of water scarcity that exists in much of the region. Several major cities in the West, including Los Angeles, Phoenix and Las Vegas, depend almost completely on distant water sources. Yet they continue to sprout traditional subdivisions, complete with broad lawns and gardens full of plants native to damper climates, which require frequent watering to survive the scorching Southwestern sun.

"The biggest thing that distinguishes the West from everywhere else is water," says Stuart Meck, a city planner and senior researcher at the American Planning Association. "Here in Chicago, we get our water basically for free. In the West, you have some really finite limits on water, and that's something to be concerned about."

In California, for example, groundwater basins are being sucked dry, and the state is expected to face a serious deficit in its water supply by 2020. "Though not the sole cause," the Bank of America study found, "fringe development does make the water issue more expensive and complicated to manage." [22] Los Angeles consumes about 200 billion gallons of water a year, more than half of it from the Owens River to the north. Continuing migration into the metropolitan area, however, is fast depleting the area's water supply. Adding to the crisis is a legal dispute with water users in the Owens Valley, who want the city to take less of its water, that may force Los Angeles to acquire more water from the Colorado River. [23] Through a vast network of aqueducts and canals, the mighty Colorado already provides water to customers in six states and is so depleted that it is little more than a trickle by the time it reaches the Mexican border. The Rio Grande, which supplies Albuquerque, Santa Fe and other Southwestern cities, is under similar pressure from urban growth. [24]

But the desert Southwest is only the most visible barometer of water scarcity in the West, which continues to draw new residents. "We're in a state of deep denial about our water problems," says Barnes-Gelt. While the Front Range is not facing an immediate water crisis, she says, the region will eventually have to face up to its limited supply. "We've got the same symptoms as Phoenix and L.A., and unfortunately the solutions in Denver are probably the same, too. People simply have to recognize the costs of sprawl."

A more pressing environmental issue in Denver is air pollution. Although Los Angeles has long held the dubious distinction of being the country's most polluted city, Denver's air was for years the dirtiest for one pollutant, carbon monoxide. Thanks to stringent measures, including temporary bans on wood-burning and stricter vehicle emission standards, Denver's air has improved. [25] But other sprawling Western cities, including Phoenix, Las Vegas and Salt Lake City, face a growing pollution problem as low-density development pushes the suburban commute farther from downtown, increasing traffic congestion and air pollution. ■

OUTLOOK

Managing Growth

As fast-growing Western communities face the consequences of sprawl — traffic congestion, air pollution, water depletion and the continuing loss of green space — they are considering ways to better manage growth. Many are looking to Portland and its urban growth boundary as a model. Albuquerque, whose town plan has encouraged expansion for the past 30 years, is the focus of a campaign by supporters of slow growth to change direction. "They are very actively pushing for adoption of an urban growth boundary," says Rusk, Albuquerque's mayor during part of the city's fast-growth era. "They're actually asking the city to adopt one unilaterally, regardless of what actions Bernalillo County might take."

Lying about 50 miles from its nearest urban neighbor, Santa Fe, Albuquerque may be able to curb sprawl on its own. But boundaries are no help to communities that stand in the path of sprawl from neighboring jurisdictions. Boulder, which lies just 20 miles northwest of Denver, drew a boundary back in 1959 to prevent water and sewer services, and thus housing, from creeping up the mountains and marring the dramatic landscape of the Front Range. The city also bought land to keep as undeveloped green space. But Boulder's efforts have been powerless to stop the sprawl that has spread up the range from Denver and practically surrounded the city.

Unlike Portland, which created its boundary as part of a statewide effort to manage growth, Boulder tried to

Continued on p. 882

At Issue:

Should state or regional governments require local governments to manage growth and combat sprawl?

yes

Richard Moe
President, National Trust for Historic Preservation

FROM A SPEECH DELIVERED AT THE SAN JOAQUIN VALLEY TOWN HALL IN FRESNO, CALIF., NOV. 20, 1996.

Drive down any highway leading into any town in the country, and what do you see? Fast-food outlets, office parks and shopping malls rising out of vast, barren plains of asphalt. Residential subdivisions spreading like inkblots, obliterating forests and farms in their relentless march across the landscape. Cars moving sluggishly down the broad ribbons of pavement or halting in frustrated clumps at choked intersections.

You see the graveyard of livability. You see communities drowning in a destructive, soulless, ugly mess called sprawl. . . .

Our communities should be shaped by choice, not by chance. Our choices are clear. We can let the highway engineers and the big-box retailers determine our communities' futures for us, or we can take a more active role ourselves. . . .

One of the most effective ways to reach this goal is to insist on sensible land-use planning. . . .

Being anti-sprawl is not being anti-growth. The question is not whether our communities will grow, but how they will grow. It's a question that we should examine in the clear light of its impact on our pocketbooks. . . .

When you're dealing with a steamroller like sprawl, city limits and county lines are nothing more than irrelevant — and obsolete — marks on a map. The challenge of the next decade is to create regional and statewide planning mechanisms that can deal effectively with issues that transcend political boundaries. What's needed — what's essential, in fact — is action by state governments to develop growth-management legislation with teeth in it, legislation that requires local governments to develop rational strategies for using already-developed land more efficiently, to make thoughtful choices about where new development should and should not go, and to set up regulatory mechanisms that are fair, clear, consistent and farsighted.

We can't hope to make substantive progress until we build a broad-based constituency for fighting sprawl and creating more livable communities. Businesses and government agencies must be part of this coalition, along with community groups and private citizens — both urban and rural residents. Working together, they should insist on — and assist in — the development of an integrated system of decisions and regulations that create and preserve communities that are safe, attractive, supportive places to live and work.

no

Edward L. Hudgins
Director of Regulatory Studies at the CATO Institute, and editor of* Regulation *magazine

WRITTEN FOR *THE CQ RESEARCHER*, SEPTEMBER 1997.

Want to live in a spacious house with a large back yard for barbecues, where the kids can play? Or do you prefer a townhouse in a city, within walking distance of trendy ethnic restaurants and art galleries?

Whatever your preference, it should be none of the government's business nor the business of your fellow citizens. Ideally you should live where and as you wish, and leave others to do the same.

Unfortunately, those who advocate regulation of local land use by state governments would foist their own lifestyle preferences on others. For example, Maryland Gov. Parris N. Glendening now plays the philosopher-king with a "Smart-growth" law that would make Annapolis the state's zoning board.

But it was the conceit of planning elites that caused many problems bemoaned by new urbanists today. The idea of zoning came to our shores from Bismarck's Germany. By the 1920s, the U.S. Department of Commerce had developed a model zoning act, which was adopted by many municipalities but also by many states that imposed it on municipalities against their wishes. Thus evolved policies, for example, that forbade laundries and convenience stores in high-rise apartments or set acreage requirements that forced suburban development.

Many policies that new urbanists would impose are not appropriate for most jurisdictions. Light rail, for example, is between 10 and 100 times more costly per mile than new roads or bus lanes but at best lure only a few percent of commuters out of cars. The result: larger traffic jams and more air pollution.

Centralizing political power holds many dangers. If one city mismanages its own affairs, other municipalities in a state need not necessarily suffer. But if the shots are called from a state capital, serious policy mistakes harm all jurisdictions. Further, voters have considerable influence over local elected officials and often can force repeal of bad policies. They have a tougher time persuading state representatives, most of whom do not hail from their jurisdiction and need not face their wrath at the polls.

One man's sprawl is another's suburban paradise. Ideally, land use choices should be left to individual property owners. But if governments do need to get involved, for example, in transportation policy, it's best done at the most local level possible.

Continued from p. 880

curb sprawl on its own.

"Colorado is a difficult place because they've never been able to reach agreement on what they want to do," says Meck, who directs a project to develop model planning and zoning legislation that states may adopt for use by localities. "So you have the phenomenon of places like Boulder, with incredibly strict control, and the rest of the area not doing much at all."

California, too, has thus far rejected efforts to establish a statewide mandate to curb urban growth. "The general plan system, which is supposed to be the constitution for development in all of our counties and cities, was designed to be flexible to accommodate changing needs," says Shaw of the Greenbelt Alliance. "The problem has been that it is so successful in being flexible that it provides very little stability at all. What that leaves us with is a never-ending outward sprawl because it's much easier to develop a flat, undeveloped pasture or field than it is to take a parcel of land within a community that needs redevelopment. There aren't any constraints."

But some communities in California are acting on their own. In an effort to curb sprawl resulting from the economic boom in Silicon Valley, San Jose last year became the biggest city in the country to establish an urban boundary. More than a dozen smaller cities in Northern California are considering similar proposals, and Sonoma County last November adopted the first voter-approved countywide boundary in the country. [26]

Whither Portland?

Many developers and conservative voters remain adamantly opposed to the notion of mandating steps to curb, or even manage, growth in the West. When Metro, Portland's regional government, proposed a new plan to manage growth over the next 20 years, it was criticized for trying to force residents to live in a crowded, polluted setting simply because undeveloped land is running out inside the urban growth boundary.

"We want a plan that allows people to choose the kind of neighborhood they want to live in, not one that forces people to live in New York-like densities," wrote Randal O'Toole, director of the Thoreau Institute, a local nonprofit research firm. "And we want a plan to protect farms and open space that are important to us, not just those that are on one side of an arbitrary urban growth boundary." [27]

Metro Regional Government, Portland

Since Portland's urban growth boundary went into effect in 1979, the region has grown by 700,000 people. The boundary is administered by a seven-member regional council known as Metro.

Opponents of Portland's boundary are also attacking the city's regional approach to growth management. Bill Sizemore, a Portland anti-tax activist, predicts that voters will soon rebel against the city's slow-growth approach to sprawl.

"It's an issue that has not been on the front burner because the impact of the urban growth boundary has been gradual and has not really hit yet," he said. "It will hit over the next three or four years; people are going to get a real taste of what density means to them." [28] As a way to eliminate the boundary, Sizemore has mounted a campaign to include an initiative to abolish Metro on the November 1998 ballot.

But the critics of growth-management techniques in Portland — still the leading model in the West and around the country — appear to be outweighed by supporters. "Metro and the boundary have been pretty popular out here, and I would say remain popular," says Nokes, who predicts that Sizemore will collect enough signatures to get his measure on the ballot. "But a lot of people have grievances, too. By and large, farm groups support the boundary because they like the idea of protecting farmland. But if you're a farmer, and you want to sell your land for housing, and they tell you you can't, then you're going to be mad."

Ironically, it may be the very newcomers to the West who have given rise to sprawl who will press the hardest for measures to halt it. "A lot of voters have a very strong reaction to what they see as urban sprawl," Shaw says. Support for slow-growth policies, she says, is as strong among new migrants as it is among long-time residents.

"The people who have lived in semirural suburban areas for 20 years or more remember what it used to look like," Shaw says, "and the people who have just moved here are often fleeing from places that have lost all their open space." ■

FOR MORE INFORMATION

American Farmland Trust, 1920 N St., N.W., Suite 400, Washington, D.C. 20036; (202) 659-5170; http://www.farmland.org. This private, nonprofit membership organization was founded in 1980 to protect agricultural land, much of which is threatened by suburban development.

American Planning Association, 122 S. Michigan Ave., Suite 1600, Chicago, Ill. 60604; (312) 431-9100; http://www.planning.org. This membership organization of professional planners and others interested in urban and rural planning issues is currently compiling model planning and zoning legislation for states to use to manage growth.

Congress for the New Urbanism, The Hearst Building, 5 Third St., Suite 500A, San Francisco, Calif. 94103; (415) 495-2255. Comprised of city planners, architects and other design professionals, the congress supports the development of compact, mixed-use communities as an antidote to sprawl.

Greenbelt Alliance, 116 New Montgomery, Suite 640, San Francisco, Calif. 94105; (415) 543-4291, (800) 543-GREEN; nbgreenbelt@igc.apc.org. Founded in 1958, the alliance is a land conservation organization dedicated to protecting open space in the Bay area and beyond.

Metro, 600 NE Grand Ave., Portland, Ore. 97232-2736; (503) 797-1510; http://www.multnomah.lib.or.us/metro. The directly elected regional government of metropolitan Portland administers the country's model urban growth boundary.

U.S. Conference of Mayors, 1620 I St. N.W., 4th floor, Washington, D.C. 20006; (202) 293-7330; uscm@cais.com. This membership group of mayors of cities with 30,000 or more residents supports growth-management policies to curb urban sprawl.

Notes

[1] From an advertisement by Mission Viejo Co. in *The Denver Post*, Aug. 26, 1997.

[2] See Paul R. Campbell, "State Population Projections," U.S. Census Bureau. From the Census Bureau's Web site at www.census.gov/www/pop-profile/stproj.htm.

[3] See Donald Blount, "Economist Sees More Blue Sky," *The Denver Post*, Sept. 4, 1997.

[4] See Todd S. Purdum, "Golden State's Shine Returns," *The Denver Post*, Sept. 3, 1997.

[5] Penny Parker, "Another New Mall?" *The Denver Post*, Sept. 27, 1997.

[6] For background, see "California: Enough Water for the Future?" *Editorial Research Reports*, April 19, 1991, pp. 221-236.

[7] American Farmland Trust, *Farming on the Edge*, March 20, 1997.

[8] See Richard Bradley, "The New Vibrant Downtown," *Nation's Cities Weekly*, June 10, 1996, published by the National League of Cities.

[9] For background, see "Transportation Policy," *The CQ Researcher*, July 4, 1997, pp. 577-600.

[10] See Alissa J. Rubin, "Desire to Spread the Benefits Leads to More Complexity," *Congressional Quarterly Weekly Report*, Aug. 2, 1997, pp. 1837-1842.

[11] Unless otherwise noted, material in this section is based on Jonathan Barnett, *The Fractured Metropolis* (1995).

[12] See Sam Staley, "Bigger is Not Better: The Virtues of Decentralized Government," *Policy Analysis*, Jan. 21, 1992.

[13] For background on Levittown's development, see Paula Span, "Mr. Levitt's Neighborhood," *The Washington Post*, May 27, 1997.

[14] See Kenneth T. Jackson, "America's Rush to Suburbia," *The New York Times*, June 9, 1996.

[15] For background on Los Angeles, see William Fulton, *The Reluctant Metropolis* (1997).

[16] See Michael F. Logan, *Fighting Sprawl and City Hall: Resistance to Urban Growth in the Southwest* (1997).

[17] U.S. Census Bureau, October 1995.

[18] Bank of America, *California Resources Agency, Greenbelt Alliance and The Low Income Housing Fund, Beyond Sprawl: New Patterns of Growth to Fit the New California*, January 1995, executive summary, p. 1.

[19] *Ibid.*, p. 8.

[20] American Farmland Trust, *op. cit.*

[21] American Farmland Trust, *Alternatives for Future Urban Growth in California's Central Valley: The Bottom Line for Agriculture and Taxpayers*, Oct. 25, 1995.

[22] Bank of America et al., *op. cit.*, p. 8.

[23] See William Booth, "Los Angeles Asked to Refill Dusty Lake It Drained in 1920s," *The Washington Post*, May 16, 1997.

[24] See "To Support Growth, Albuquerque Will Shift Source for Water," *The New York Times*, May 25, 1997.

[25] See Judith Kohler, "In a First, Metropolitan Denver Records No Federal Air Quality Violations," *The Washington Post*, Jan. 1, 1997.

[26] See Daniel Sneider, "To Halt Sprawl, San Jose Draws Green Line in Sand," *The Christian Science Monitor*, April 19, 1996.

[27] Randal O'Toole, "Packing 'Em In," *The Oregonian*, Nov. 15, 1996.

[28] Quoted by R. Gregory Nokes, "Bill Sizemore Swings His Tax Ax at Metro," *The Oregonian*, July 28, 1997.

Bibliography

Selected Sources Used

Books

Fulton, William, *The Reluctant Metropolis: The Politics of Urban Growth in Los Angeles,* Solano Press, 1997.
An urban planner examines the history of the West's biggest city and the country's leading example of suburban sprawl. Middle-income residents are forced by high housing costs and numbing commutes to leave the area.

Langdon, Philip, *A Better Place to Live: Reshaping the American Suburb,* University of Massachusetts, 1994.
Suburban life fosters isolation, long commutes and separation of residents from their community's civic and commercial life, the author writes. Developers should build communities around public open space, mixing residential, civic and retail buildings to promote healthier suburban living.

Orfield, Myron, *Metropolitics: A Regional Agenda for Community and Stability,* Brookings Institution Press and Lincoln Institute of Land Policy, 1997.
The author, a Minnesota state representative, describes how new development draws people and jobs to the outer suburbs, leaving the inner cities and older suburbs a vacant hole in an ever-expanding donut.

Rusk, David, *Cities Without Suburbs,* Woodrow Wilson Center Press, 1995.
A former mayor of Albuquerque, N.M., concludes that cities with annexation powers, so-called elastic cities, are more successful at bridging the separation of wealthy suburbs and impoverished inner cities than those with rigid boundaries.

Rybczynski, Witold, *City Life,* Simon & Schuster, 1995.
A University of Pennsylvania urbanism professor and author of the best-selling book *Home* reviews the European roots of urban and suburban development and the ways the North American experience have shaped sprawl in the United States and Canada.

Articles

Constantine, James, "Traditional Neighborhood Development: The Next Generation," *Land Development,* fall 1995, pp. 7-11.
Developers have long been viewed as opposing alternative approaches to building suburbs, but now they are finding that many consumers want compact, mixed-use development. The magazine is published by the National Association of Home Builders.

"Cures for Lonely Suburbs and Dying Cities," *The American Enterprise,* November/December 1996, pp. 1-73.
This in-depth report in the American Enterprise Institute's magazine contains articles on suburban development, its benefits and drawbacks, as well as the growing interest in neotraditional solutions to sprawl.

Ehrenhalt, Alan, "The Great Wall of Portland," *Governing,* May 1997, pp. 20-24.
Portland, Ore., which created an urban growth boundary to curb sprawl in 1979, is running out of land to accommodate its continuing growth. The regional government is now considering a plan to stretch the boundary.

Kunstler, James Howard, "Home from Nowhere," *The Atlantic Monthly,* September 1996, pp. 43-66.
Zoning laws have contributed to the sense of social isolation that pervades suburbia, writes Kunstler, who supports a neotraditional, or New Urbanist, planning model that combines residential and commercial activities in a single, compact community.

"Water in the West," *The Economist,* March 29, 1997, pp. 27-29.
The only way to restore healthy ecosystems along some of the West's rivers is to tear down some of the country's biggest hydroelectric dams. But the region's surging population is placing even greater demands for water and energy.

Reports and Studies

American Farmland Trust, *Farming on the Edge,* March 1997.
A nonprofit conservation organization identifies 20 prime farming areas that are heavily threatened by suburban development. Topping the list is California's Central Valley. Five other threatened areas are also in the West.

Bank of America, *California Resources Agency, Greenbelt Alliance and The Low Income Housing Fund, Beyond Sprawl: New Patterns of Growth to Fit the New California,* January 1995.
Suburban sprawl is undermining the very survival of the country's largest state, concludes this study, sponsored by a bank that has helped finance development over the years.

Greenbelt Alliance, *Bound for Success: A Citizens' Guide to Using Urban Growth Boundaries for More Livable Communities and Open Space Protection in California,* undated.
A San Francisco Bay-area conservation group outlines the benefits of restricting development.

The Next Step

Additional information from UMI's Newspaper & Periodical Abstracts™ database

Curbing Urban Sprawl

Ewing, Reid, "Is Los Angeles-style sprawl desirable?" *Journal of the American Planning Association,* winter 1997, pp. 107-126.

Literature on the costs, causes and characteristics of alternative development patterns is analyzed.

Goldberg, David, "Turner Foundation funds efforts to study, curb urban sprawl," *Atlanta Journal Constitution,* Aug. 23, 1997, p. E2.

As Peter Bahouth sees it, the rapid, unchecked sprawl of metropolitan Atlanta may be the single most important issue on the environmental, economic and social fronts in Georgia. In a mini-summit convened Friday, the (Ted) Turner Foundation brought together both national and local advocacy groups working on issues from farmland protection to talk about how they could fight sprawl together.

Gordon, Peter, and Harry W. Richardson, "Are compact cities a desirable planning goal?" *Journal of the American Planning Association,* winter 1997, pp. 95-106.

Key issues on whether or not the promotion of compact cities is a worthwhile planning goal are considered. These issues include pressures on prime agricultural land, residential density preferences and the prospects for downtowns. A review of the issues does not support the case for promoting compact cities.

Landecker, Heidi, "Is new urbanism good for America?" *Architecture: The AIA Journal,* April 1996, pp. 68-77.

Architects, developers and the government are touting neotraditional communities as sustainable solutions to urban sprawl. Several examples of these new urbanist communities, both in the works and completed, are presented.

Nolan, William L., "The new American neighborhood," *Better Homes & Gardens,* September 1997, pp. 42-57.

Nolan discusses neotraditional neighborhoods and towns, which represent a type of strategy that today's urban planning experts have adopted to combat urban sprawl and make communities more people friendly. He focuses on Celebration, Fla., and two California communities, Larkspur and Laguna.

Effects of Urban Sprawl

Durning, Alan Thein, "Pedestrian paradise," *Sierra,* May 1997, pp. 36-39.

The abundance of cars makes them the source of a disturbing share of social problems, including fatalities, air pollution and urban sprawl. Steps are presented to create cities with less reliance on automobiles.

Egan, Timothy, "Urban Sprawl Strains Western States," *The New York Times,* Dec. 29, 1996, p. A1.

As the urban West goes through the third major growth boom in four decades, some Western cities are becoming their own worst nightmare. Los Angeles' symptoms — bad-air alerts, traffic gridlock, loss of open space, huge gulfs between the rich and the poor — are becoming impossible to ignore.

Johnson, Charles, and Linda H. Smith and Angela Morrison, "When urban sprawl chokes agriculture," *Farm Journal,* March 1996, pp. 26-28.

Urban sprawl is pushing suburbs further and further into rural areas, often pressuring farmers. Some love the company, but others pack up and move out when the city starts to come to them.

Tucker, Cynthia, "Urban sprawl: Clean air and quality of life on the road to ruin," *Atlanta Constitution,* June 19, 1996, p. A14.

Tucker criticizes Georgia Dept. of Transportation Chief Wayne Shackelford for his persistence in planning more roadway projects in the Atlanta area despite being in violation of the Clean Air Act and despite Atlanta's need for alternative public transit.

Suburban Development

"Editorials, Urban leaders ignore region," *Atlanta Constitution,* April 17, 1997, p. A16.

The challenges facing metro Atlanta, Ga., don't stop suddenly at county borders or city limits. None of the area's 10 inner counties or 64 towns and cities can tackle problems such as air pollution, traffic congestion or urban sprawl on its own. The importance of a regional approach — and the benefits it can bring — were driven home to almost 60 metro leaders on a trip to Denver, Colo., this month. Business and government officials from throughout the Atlanta area saw firsthand how Denver has used a regional approach to address its shared environmental problems, reinvigorate its downtown and build a sustainable and thriving economy.

Forsyth, Ann, "Five images of a suburb: Perspectives on a new urban development," *Journal of the American Planning Association,* winter 1997, pp. 45-60.

Forsyth explores five ways that groups of activists and professionals envisaged urban form in the context of a new suburban development project and how their ideas about suburban development were represented in a public debate.

Hanley, Robert, "New Jersey's Effort for Cleaner Waterway," *The New York Times,* July 7, 1997, p. B1.
The story of the troubles threatening New Jersey's Barnegat Bay has been told many times about many places: a development boom after World War II turns sleepy fishing villages into suburban subdivisions. A surging population generates pollution that fouls a pristine bay, endangering the future of the waterway. Federal and state environmental officials and a nonprofit conservation group, the Trust for Public Land, have begun campaigns to rescue the bay before it becomes as polluted as Long Island Sound and New York Harbor. The government's part involves devising a plan to curb pollution stemming from the huge growth in Ocean County's population — 700 percent since 1950. The conservation group has started negotiations to buy undeveloped land in the western part of the bay's watershed to keep suburban development away from streams that feed into the bay.

Kim, Lillian Lee, "Commuter blues laid to market demands," *Atlanta Constitution,* June 11, 1997, Sec XJ, p. 1.
Suburban development, typified by neighborhood shopping centers and subdivisions filled with single-family, detached houses, was a hot topic at the symposium held in downtown Atlanta, Ga., on Tuesday. As a member of a panel discussing successful communities, residential developer Rick Porter, president of Gwinnett-based Richport Properties, said developers should not be held primarily responsible for the long commutes and traffic congestion experienced by many northern arc residents.

"Kinder, gentler growth," *The Denver Post,* June 17, 1997, p. B8.
An editorial discusses the plans of Fort Collins, Colo., to rewrite its building code in order to slow suburban development that threatens Colorado's air, water and wild lands. The editorial encourages other communities to join in control efforts.

Urban Growth Boundaries

Dionne, E. J. Jr., " 'Government Planning' That Kept Portland Green," *The Washington Post,* March 21, 1997, p. A27.
One side of West Union Road is not like the other because the street runs along the Portland area's urban growth boundary, a line on a map that sets limits on development. Within the boundary is an urban "reserve," where all sorts of building can happen — and with a robust local economy, a lot is. Outside the boundary, the land stays rural. In an era when the words "government planning" are written off as either an oxymoron or a terrible danger, the Portland experience comes as a shock. Even more shocking: the planning system — in place since 1973 — is popular. It wins support from environmentalists and from business people. Protecting land from urban sprawl has become something of a civic religion here and one of the city's selling points.

Ingram, Erik, "Sonoma leans toward slow growth," *San Francisco Chronicle,* Nov. 6, 1996, p. A15.
Ballot measures to restrain urban sprawl in Sonoma County, Calif., by creating "growth boundaries" around cities were winning in early returns on Nov. 5, 1996. A companion measure to restrict development in unincorporated areas adjacent to the boundaries was also winning.

Manor, Robert, "Urban Sprawl Rots Cities, Experts Say Limits on Development Needed to Protect Metropolitan Areas," *St. Louis Post-Dispatch,* Feb. 9, 1997, p. D1.
Urban sprawl rots the city of St. Louis, Mo., damages the environment and concentrates the poor into ever declining neighborhoods, a noted urban scholar said Saturday. The cure to sprawl is urban growth boundaries — limits on development outside the metro area — said David Rusk, the former mayor of Albuquerque, N.M. Rusk said the city of St. Louis and many older adjacent suburbs bear the burden when residents move to distant suburbs like St. Peters or Herculaneum or the towns near Scott Air Force Base in Illinois.

Rosenfeld, Jordan, "Greenspace: Comparative perspectives on regional sustainability," *Public Management,* January 1997, pp. 4-10.
Local governments must help provide open-space reserves so that future generations will have access to the natural environment. Perspectives on regional sustainability of the United Kingdom, the Netherlands and the United States are presented.

Urban Sprawl

Ganey, Terry, "Lawmakers Deride 'Urban Sprawl' Bills," *St. Louis Post-Dispatch,* March 20, 1997, p. A11.
The Missouri Legislature seems uninterested in dealing with the problem of urban sprawl, the unrestrained development of new homes and businesses in outlying areas while core cities deteriorate. On Wednesday, the Senate took shots at an attempt to set up a commission to study the effects of rapid population growth and development in the St. Louis area. At the same time, a Senate committee took aim at a bill to set up a state agency to regulate growth.

Kittredge, William, "The Wild West's Not-So-Natural Disasters," *The New York Times,* Jan. 10, 1997, p. A33.
Kittredge discusses the floods ravaging much of the western states and the urban sprawl that compromises what western residents have worked to preserve: clean air, sweet water, towns where doors don't have to be locked at night and where cross-country skiing and blue-ribbon fishing are just up the road.

Lederer, Kate, "Some people would call their location pretty rural, but for them it's a case of learning to live with 'urban sprawl,'" *Countryside & Small Stock Journal*, September 1997, pp. 51-52.
Lederer discusses some of the pros of urban sprawl or population relocation. She adds that one of the benefits of urban expansion has been the opportunity to meet new people.

Lindecke, Fred W., "Bosley Wants Restrictions on Urban Sprawl; Mayor Sees Curbs on Expansion as New Revenue Source for City," *St. Louis Post-Dispatch*, Feb. 18, 1997, p. B1.
Mayor Freeman Bosley Jr. says he wants to slow urban sprawl in the St. Louis, Mo., area. Requiring government revenue gained by economic development beyond "planning boundaries" to be shared with "less fortunate communities," is one possibility. For example, Bosley suggests drawing a line around the St. Louis metropolitan area and making it more difficult or expensive to build urban development beyond that line.

Solis, Suzanne Espinosa, "Group Blasts Plans for New Homes: Environmentalists warn Contra Costa will suffer," *San Francisco Chronicle*, April 24, 1997, p. A19.
Out-of-control urban sprawl threatens to ruin the quality of life for California's Contra Costa County residents, an environmental advocacy group said yesterday. The Greenbelt Alliance says two new developments — Tassajara Valley and Cowell Ranch — would add almost 11,000 new homes to rural land, worsen traffic and air pollution and overburden water and sewage systems. Cowell Ranch calls for 5,000 homes on 4,000 acres southeast of Antioch near Brentwood. Developers for both projects are seeking county approval to put residential and commercial buildings on land zoned for agriculture.

Urban Village

"Grassroots self-sufficiency," *Los Angeles Times*, April 27, 1996, p. B7.
The Pacoima urban village in California is a low-tech, low-cost community effort to boost self-sufficiency by providing active job-hunting help along with community-based training. Luz Maria Munoz helped coordinate the village's career club, and in turn was helped with child care and education.

Helliker, Kevin, "Theater mogul tries to bring Kansas City up to date," *The Wall Street Journal*, Aug. 6, 1997, p. B1.
Stanley Durwood, CEO of AMC Entertainment Inc., is proposing a revitalization of the Kansas City, Mo., downtown area, hoping to convert 12 blocks of dilapidated buildings, empty lots and adult-entertainment stores into an urban village called the Power & Light District.

Iglitzin, Lynne B., "The Seattle Commons: A case study in the politics and planning of an urban village," *Policy Studies Journal*, winter 1995, pp. 620-635.
The politics, planning and policymaking involved in the attempt to create a new urban village close to downtown Seattle, Wash., are examined in depth. The Seattle Commons project began in 1991.

King, R. J., "Dearborn builds on its housing: Adding more, better residential areas seen as the key to city's future growth," *Detroit News*, Feb. 2, 1997, p. C1.
Dearborn, Mich., the hometown of Henry Ford, has been riding a development tidal wave. Projects in the works range from a \$24-million civic center expansion highlighted by an aquatic center to upscale homes priced at more than \$800,000 and a new urban village of condominiums and retail shops. Illustrative of the new residential wave is New Towne Development's West Village, made up of 76 Georgian Colonial condominiums in Dearborn's west end. An upscale restaurant and 18 retail sites are part of the development along Michigan Avenue, as well as a bakery, bagel shop and coffee house.

King, R. J., "New beginning for New Center: Area council's plan would create urban village in midtown district," *Detroit News*, July 20, 1997, p. C1.
A master plan for redeveloping Detroit's New Center Area into an urban village of homes, office buildings, shops ad entertainment venues will be unveiled this week. The \$500,000 plan, spearheaded by the New Center Area Council and funded by General Motors Corp., provides a blueprint for future development of the historic midtown district. It has provoked strong interest from retailers, residential builders and office users in recent months.

Snel, Alan, "Elitch village looking for name," *The Denver Post*, Jan. 13, 1997, p. B5.
Chuck Perry's plan for the old Elitch Gardens amusement park site is a welcomed land proposal missing one small thing: A name. So the Denver, Colo., developer is staging a contest to name the urban village he plans to build. Perry proposes to erect 300 homes and 80,000 square feet of commercial space at the 27-acre site at West 38th Avenue and Tennyson Street. Perry, who has worked with local groups to finalize the proposal, expects to submit his development application to Denver in mid-February.

Walker, Thaai, "Money Mess Puts Downtown Oakland Housing Complex in Limbo," *San Francisco Chronicle*, May 24, 1997, p. A16.
An ambitious plan for a 192-unit complex in downtown Oakland, Calif., is in jeopardy because the nonprofit agency planning to build it is struggling with financial difficulties. The \$33 million development proposal — known as the 14th Street Gateway Project — was originally proposed by CREDO, an Oakland nonprofit housing development corporation. The development, envisioned as an urban village, was proposed for a two-block area bounded by 14th and 16th streets, Jefferson Street and Martin Luther King Jr. Way.

Back Issues

Great Research on Current Issues Starts Right Here . . . Recent topics covered by The CQ Researcher are listed below. Before May 1991, reports were published under the name of Editorial Research Reports.

MARCH 1996
The British Monarchy
Preventing Juvenile Crime
Tax Reform
Pursuing the Paranormal

APRIL 1996
Centennial Olympic Games
Managed Care
Protecting Endangered Species
New Military Culture

MAY 1996
Russia's Political Future
Marriage and Divorce
Year-Round Schools
Taiwan, China and the U.S.

JUNE 1996
Rethinking NAFTA
First Ladies
Teaching Values
Labor Movement's Future

JULY 1996
Recovered-Memory Debate
Native Americans' Future
Crackdown on Sexual Harassment
Attack on Public Schools

AUGUST 1996
Fighting Over Animal Rights
Privatizing Government Services
Child Labor and Sweatshops
Cleaning Up Hazardous Wastes

SEPTEMBER 1996
Gambling Under Attack
The States and Federalism
Civic Journalism
Reassessing Foreign Aid

OCTOBER 1996
Political Consultants
Insurance Fraud
Rethinking School Integration
Parental Rights

NOVEMBER 1996
Global Warming
Clashing Over Copyright
Consumer Debt
Governing Washington, D.C.

DECEMBER 1996
Welfare, Work and the States
The New Volunteerism
Implementing the Disabilities Act
America's Pampered Pets

JANUARY 1997
Combating Scientific Misconduct
Restructuring the Electric Industry
The New Immigrants
Chemical and Biological Weapons

FEBRUARY 1997
Assisting Refugees
Alternative Medicine's Next Phase
Independent Counsels
Feminism's Future

MARCH 1997
New Air Quality Standards
Alcohol Advertising
Civic Renewal
Educating Gifted Students

APRIL 1997
Declining Crime Rates
The FBI Under Fire
Gender Equity in Sports
Space Program's Future

MAY 1997
The Stock Market
The Cloning Controversy
Expanding NATO
The Future of Libraries

JUNE 1997
FDA Reform
China After Deng
Line-Item Veto
Breast Cancer

JULY 1997
Transportation Policy
Executive Pay
School Choice Debate
Aggressive Driving

AUGUST 1997
Age Discrimination
Banning Land Mines
Children's Television
Evolution vs. Creationism

SEPTEMBER 1997
Caring for the Dying
Mental Health Policy
Mexico's Future
Youth Fitness

Back issues are available for $5.00 (subscribers) or $10.00 (non-subscribers). Quantity discounts apply to orders over ten. To order, call Congressional Quarterly Customer Service at (202) 887-8621.

Binders are available for $18.00. To order call 1-800-638-1710. Please refer to stock number 648.

Future Topics

- ***Diversity in the Workplace***
- ***Teacher Education***
- ***Part-time Employment***

THE CQ Researcher

PUBLISHED BY CONGRESSIONAL QUARTERLY INC.

Diversity in the Workplace

Is it good for business?

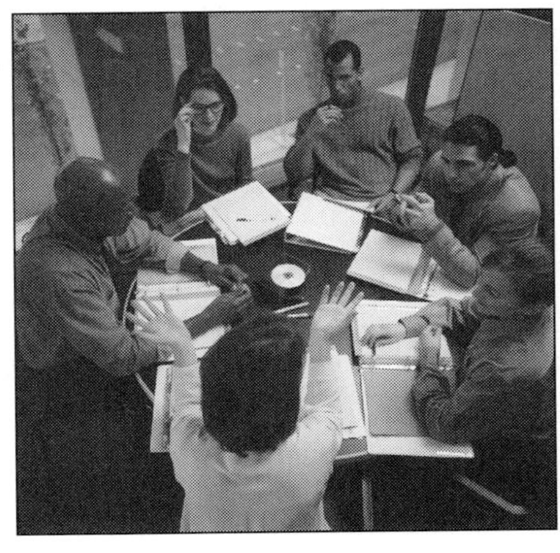

The American work force, predominantly white and male throughout history, is becoming more and more diverse. Women now comprise almost half of the labor force, while the number of African-American, Hispanic and Asian-American workers is increasing more rapidly than the number of whites. The increased diversity has created strains in many workplaces. It also has spawned a specialized industry of consultants to advise organizations on how to manage the new mixture of race, gender and culture at work more effectively — and how to avoid the kind of discrimination suits that ensnared Texaco. Some critics say the diversity movement has fueled hostility toward white males. But diversity advocates say they are helping employees and employers alike to value cultural differences and maximize the productivity of all workers.

INSIDE THIS ISSUE

CQ Oct 10, 1997 • Volume 7, No. 38 • Pages 889-912

Formerly Editorial Research Reports

Diversity in the Workplace

COVER: © PHOTODISC

THE CQ Researcher

October 10, 1997
Volume 7, No. 38

EDITOR
Sandra Stencel

MANAGING EDITOR
Thomas J. Colin

ASSOCIATE EDITORS
Sarah M. Magner
Richard L. Worsnop

STAFF WRITERS
Charles S. Clark
Mary H. Cooper
Kenneth Jost
David Masci

EDITORIAL ASSISTANT
Vanessa E. Furlong

PUBLISHED BY
Congressional Quarterly Inc.

CHAIRMAN
Andrew Barnes

VICE CHAIRMAN
Andrew P. Corty

PRESIDENT AND PUBLISHER
Robert W. Merry

EXECUTIVE EDITOR
David Rapp

The CQ Researcher (ISSN 1056-2036). Formerly Editorial Research Reports. Published weekly, except Jan. 3, May 30, Aug. 29, Oct. 31, by Congressional Quarterly Inc., 1414 22nd St., N.W., Washington, D.C. 20037. Annual subscription rate for libraries, businesses and government is $340. Additional rates furnished upon request. Periodicals postage paid at Washington, D.C., and additional mailing offices. POSTMASTER: Send address changes to The CQ Researcher, 1414 22nd St., N.W., Washington, D.C. 20037.

Diversity in the Workplace

By Kenneth Jost

The Issues

Raymond Smith engineered the merger of two multibillion-dollar regional telephone companies this summer. Then he stepped in front of several thousand minority employees and took on an arguably bigger challenge: He pledged to create a "climate of respect and open dialogue" throughout the company.

"The new Bell Atlantic will be a place where 'diversity' isn't just another word for complying with the law of the land," Smith said in New Brunswick, N.J., late last month. Diversity is also a "positive management obligation" to provide training and opportunities "for all employees."

As the chairman of Bell Atlantic before its merger with Nynex, Smith had proudly called the company's record of hiring and promoting minorities "very good," though "not perfect." But the mid-Atlantic company also had faced lawsuits charging that minority workers at Bell Atlantic encountered a racially hostile work environment and persistent barriers to career advancement.

Now, the enlarged company — with customers stretching from Maine to Virginia — is reshaping its corporate structure and internal procedures to create what Smith calls "a tolerant, diverse workplace."

The steps Smith plans to take include improving the company's companywide internal complaint hotline and designating a vice president in charge of ethics and diversity to report directly to the chairman. Most important, Smith said, the company's managers will now be required to "manage diversity the way they manage any other critical business initiative: with specific goals, objectives, measurements and plans."

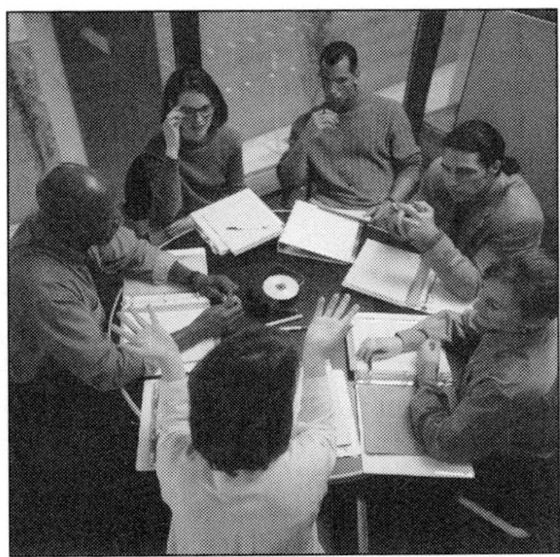

On paper, the steps match recommendations often made by a growing cadre of so-called diversity consultants — human resources experts specializing in helping companies manage a work force that becomes more and more diverse every day. Across much of the country, plants and offices once filled mostly with white men now have more women and more minority workers. (*See graphs, pp. 892, 893.*)

From one perspective, the new, increasingly diverse American workplace creates the potential for an array of problems ranging from increased day-to-day conflicts to litigation over alleged discrimination that can produce major legal and public relations headaches. In the most dramatic example, Texaco agreed to settle an embarrassing racial discrimination suit in November by promising to pay $140 million to black employees, hire and promote more minority employees and provide diversity training sessions for all 29,000 of the giant oil company's employees. (*See story, p. 896*).

But experts urge companies to view their diversity not as a problem but as a challenge and an opportunity. The challenge is learning how to turn the diversity into greater productivity. The opportunity is creating a workplace where everyone contributes his or her full potential.

"The organization must recognize that its success and its effectiveness are dependent not only on the aspects that we all have in common but also on the value of the differences that each of us brings," says Lewis Griggs, a San Francisco diversity consultant and one of the founders of the diversity movement.

Many of the country's biggest companies, as well as government employers, now profess agreement with the philosophy expounded by diversity consultants and have instituted diversity programs — often hiring diversity consultants to help design and implement them. (*See box, p. 894.*)

But some critics view the diversity movement's effects on the workplace as unhealthy.

"Diversity campaigns push a political agenda" linked to "campus multiculturalism" and "numbers-oriented affirmative action," says Frederick R. Lynch, an associate professor of government at Claremont McKenna College in Pomona, Calif. In his sharply critical book *The Diversity Machine,* Lynch writes that the movement is promoting a "multicultural revolution in the American workplace" that poses "a substantial threat" to individualism, equality of opportunity, equal treatment and "a sense of national unity and cohesion." [1]

Many diversity consultants, however, say the drive to change workplace culture has less to do with politics or philosophy than with demographics and economics.

"It's based on workplace realities — just the sheer changing demographics of the work force — on ethnicity, culture and gender," says Michael Wheeler, a consultant in New York City who has worked on the issue for The Conference Board, an economic-research organization. "You don't nec-

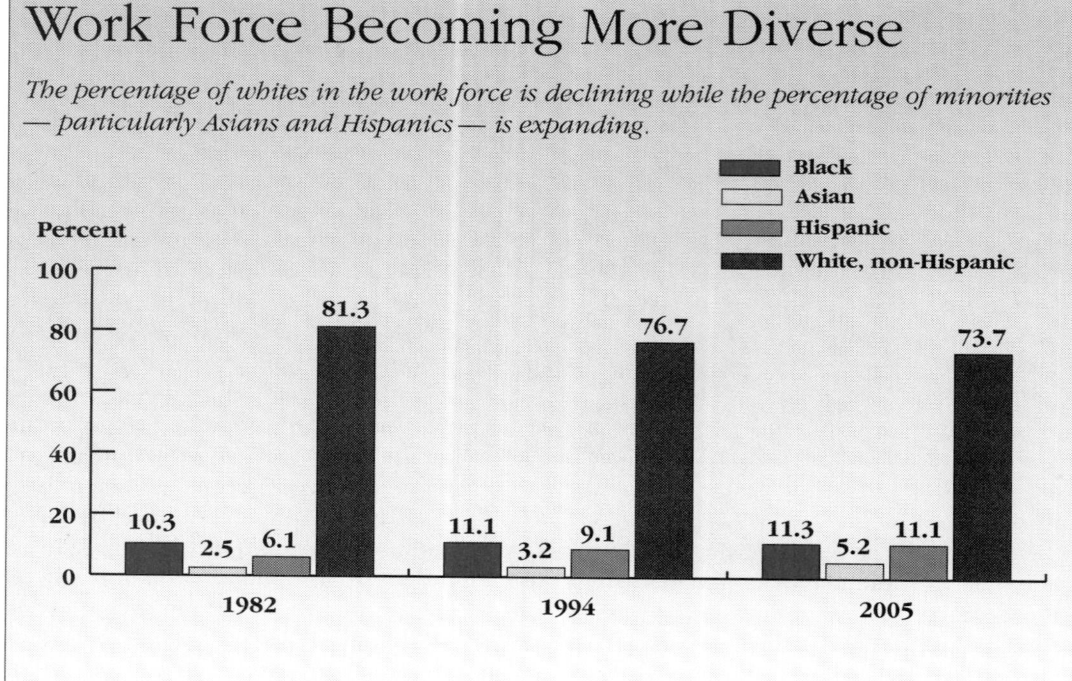

Sources: The ASTD Training Data Book, *American Society for Training and Development, 1996; Howard N. Fullerton Jr., "Employment Outlook 1994-2005,"* Monthly Labor Review, *November 1995.*

essarily need to change everything a company is doing," Wheeler says, "but corporate culture does need to be in alignment with these changes" in the work force.

As for affirmative action, diversity consultants generally support it but maintain that their work is different — and could ultimately do more to open up hiring and promotion opportunities for all workers.

"Affirmative action had an essential role to play and played it very well" in correcting the "imbalance" in the workplace, R. Roosevelt Thomas Jr., another of the diversity movement's founders, wrote in an influential article in 1990. Thomas, founder and until recently head of the American Institute for Managing Diversity at Morehouse College in Atlanta, argued that affirmative action alone could not ensure "a work setting geared to the upward mobility of all kinds of people, including white males." [2]

The affirmative action issue has not faded, however. [3] Opponents continue to charge that affirmative action often results in fixed quotas for women or minorities that amount to reverse discrimination against white men. The Supreme Court, which has chipped away at affirmative action in recent years, is set this term to consider a new case that may determine how much discretion public and private employers have to consider racial diversity in employment decisions (*see p. 904*).

Meanwhile, diversity advocates and experts stress that their work goes beyond opening up opportunities for women and minorities. "Diversity is reality," Thomas says. "All kinds of diversity are reality." Thomas says that "managing diversity" requires both understanding group and individual differences and "redesigning" the workplace. Everyone has to change, Thomas says, "not just the ones that are different."

But critic Lynch says that approach amounts to "permanent pluralism" — exemplified by the rise of employee work groups for racial and ethnic minorities and others. He also says diversity consultants advocate creating different standards for different kinds of workers. "They say you've got to take cultural differences into account," Lynch explains. "But that opens the door to subversion of the law — because equal treatment is the law of the land."

As the debate over diversity continues, here are some of the questions being considered:

Has the diversity movement been good for American business?

Advocates of the diversity movement hold out to private companies the promise of increased productivity and reduced workplace tensions. They also see the opportunity for improving sales by having a workplace that resembles the increasingly diverse customer base in the United States and around the world.

"It has caused people and organizations to figure out ways in which they can go beyond tolerating people who are different and use the ability of everyone even if they don't fit within the traditional culture of the organization," says Julie O'Mara, a diversity consultant in Northern California.

Critics acknowledge that diversity may bring some marketing advantages for companies. But they also say that the productivity benefits are unproven and that tensions in the workplace are more often increased rather than decreased.

"It's destructive," says John Leo, a *U.S. News & World Report* columnist. "It renders hostile the two sexes and the many races that could have gotten along fine without it."

Many companies cite the marketing advantages of having a diverse work force. "Our customer base is becoming extraordinarily sensitive to companies that don't have a work force that reflects the customer base," says Edward N. Gadsden Jr., director of diversity at Texaco. "It just makes good business sense."

But critics say that the strategy has racist underpinnings. "The idea that Hispanics can sell better to Hispanics or Asians can sell better to other Asians, I think that's really pernicious," Lynch says.

As for the claimed increases in productivity, even proponents of diversity acknowledge that they cannot prove the benefits in quantitative terms. "The jury is still out with regard to the effectiveness of diversity programs," write the authors of the pro-diversity book *The American Mosaic*.[4]

Lynch emphasizes this admission in his critique of the diversity movement. But he and other critics go further and contend that the movement has hurt companies by encouraging separatism within the workplace and by introducing double standards for hiring and evaluating employees.

"The diversity rhetoric is a code for rethinking qualifications," says writer Heather MacDonald, who authored a sharply critical 1993 article on the diversity movement.[5] "I frankly do not believe that there are different ways to manage blacks and whites. That's a racist view. The ideas of competence and ability should be colorblind."

Lynch notes that many diversity consultants advocate creating work groups based on ethnicity. "It foments separatism," he says, "and you can wind up with these organizations acting as quasi-unions."

Diversity proponents acknowledge that poorly done training sessions can result in at least a temporary increase in workplace tensions. But they say that the open communication stressed by diversity consultants ultimately helps resolve tensions.

"Very often, things that have been swept under the rug can be brought to life and have to be dealt with," O'Mara says. "Sometimes you can have an increase in difficulties over the way to resolve them."

For his part, Thomas says organizations may fail to see results from their diversity efforts because they focus only on hiring rather than managing a diverse work force. "Nine times out of 10, they're not talking about diversity, they're talking about representation," Thomas says. "Where we have not made a lot of progress is in creating an environment where it's easy to sustain progress in relations, not to mention productivity."

Women Are Catching Up to Men

Women are expected to comprise nearly half of the work force by 2005, while the percentage of men is expected to shrink to slightly more than 50 percent.

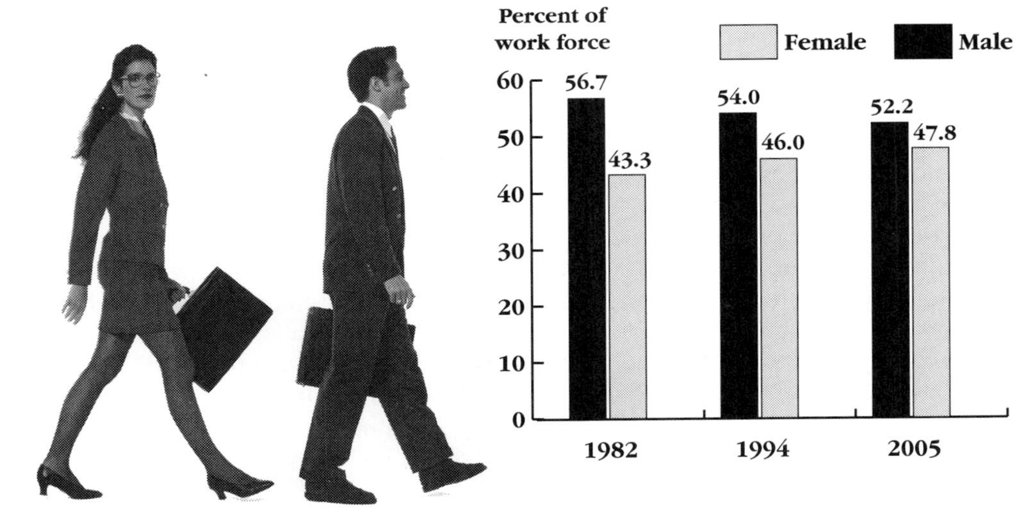

Sources: The ASTD Training Data Book, *American Society for Training and Development, 1996; Howard N. Fullerton Jr., "Employment Outlook 1994-2005,"* Monthly Labor Review, *November 1995.*

Training Stresses Awareness and Sensitivity

More than three-quarters of the diversity training programs being offered by firms stress awareness, sensitivity and cooperation. Most programs last for one day or less and are conducted by internal staff.

Topics	Percent of programs stressing this topic
Awareness	92%
Sensitivity	80%
Getting things done with others	79%
Equal Employment Opportunity and affirmative action laws	71%
Accommodating special needs	69%
Reducing intergroup conflict	68%
Changing corporate culture	58%
Assimilating diverse employees	51%
Dealing with backlash	40%

Sources: The ASTD Training Data Book, *American Society for Training and Development, 1996;* Ideas & Trends in Personnel, *May 26, 1993.*

Griggs is somewhat more upbeat about improvements in workplace relations, but he also sees the need for more thoroughgoing change. "There's been enormous progress," Griggs says, "but a lot more needs to be done."

Are diversity training programs effective?

Diversity training has gone from an innovation to a commonplace in less than two decades. Surveys indicate a large percentage of major corporations have instituted some form of diversity program — some only for managers, others like Texaco for all employees. Initially, the programs were widely praised, but criticism has increased with the spread of the programs — both from outside observers and from some consultants and experts within the diversity industry as well.

"There has been mismanagement and malpractice on a grand scale both by some of the [consultants] and by some of the people who have brought them into the companies," says Harris Sussman, a diversity consultant in Cambridge, Mass.

Advocates insist that diversity training serves a useful purpose by promoting understanding between different types of people within workplaces. "A lot of dialogue has been created over the past 10 years that has helped corporations go way beyond equal employment opportunity and affirmative action toward valuing differences," Griggs says.

But the critics say diversity training too often takes a confrontational approach. "There's a tendency for this to slide very quickly into a critique of the system and particularly of what [diversity consultants] call white male monoculturalism," Lynch says.

Sussman agrees that diversity consultants often are unnecessarily adversarial. At other times, though, he says the training sessions are "short-term" efforts with little substantive content and no ongoing value.

"Often what companies get is the equivalent of junk food," says Sussman, who spent several years at Digital Equipment Corp. "It hasn't changed anything. They've put thousands of people through training, and you can't notice that there's any difference."

Some outside critics see no need for diversity training programs whatsoever. "I do not believe that racism is so widespread in the workplace that you need to ship everybody off for re-education," MacDonald says.

But Robert Hayles, a consultant in Minneapolis, says diversity programs have a broader agenda than race and gender. "It has provided a very healthy forum for all kinds of differences," says Hayles, who formerly worked with the Pillsbury Co. "It has given us opportunities to enhance the quality of work life and the performance of organizations by dealing with all those differences."

Lynch maintains that diversity programs are likely to be poorly received when they are introduced to counteract the effects of a public controversy over charges of discrimination.

"What do you think people going through that diversity training are going to think?" he says. "They're going to think it's punitive. We're having to go through this because those guys [in management] blew it."

O'Mara acknowledges that some employees may balk at diversity training. "They'll think they're a prisoner for a day," she says. But later, she says, "the feedback we get is that they did not feel threatened."

Still, some observers doubt that any of the work produces concrete benefits. Clifford Alexander, a former secretary of the Army and head of the Equal Employment Opportunity Commission (EEOC), was recently hired to examine hiring, pay and promotion practices at R.R. Donnelley and Sons Co., the giant Chicago printing firm, after it was hit with racial discrimination and harassment lawsuits. Prior to his assignment, Alexander reportedly was sharply critical of diversity training.

"Diversity training is generally nonsense," *The Wall Street Journal* quoted Alexander as saying in interviews. "I have yet to see a diversity-training program that's led to the promotion or hiring of a woman or minority." [6]

But Hayles said that he saw concrete benefits from the diversity programs he instituted during his five years with Pillsbury. "Supervisors and managers became more personally effective," Hayles says. "The quality of life improved for all employees, as measured by lower turnover and by surveys and focus groups."

"Most organizations do believe that work in this arena can result in greater productivity," O'Mara says. "That's one of the reasons why most organizations are sticking with diversity even though affirmative action tends to be on the downside of the curve right now."

Should affirmative action policies be cut back?

The federal government coined the phrase affirmative action in the 1960s to denote policies aimed at eliminating the effects of past racial discrimination, first by encouraging and then by requiring government contractors to hire greater numbers of African-American workers. From the outset, critics warned that the policies would result in hiring or promotion quotas — selecting applicants on the basis of race rather than qualifications.

Those criticisms have steadily increased as the policies expanded at all levels of government to include not just blacks but other minority groups and women, and to cover not only employment but also college and university admissions and government contracting. But supporters of affirmative action — including many employers, both public and private — say the policies have helped them find qualified workers without leading to quotas or imposing unfair burdens on white, male employees.

For their part, the proponents of workplace diversity defend affirmative action at the same time that they acknowledge its weaknesses and distinguish it from their own goals and methods.

"Ideally, we wouldn't even need something like affirmative action because we would be acting so affirmatively together across all our differences," Griggs says. "But that hasn't happened fully."

"I'm very pro-affirmative action, but I also know affirmative action has some limitations," Thomas says. "Demographic representation" is still important, Thomas says, but diversity management goes beyond looking at "the numbers" to redesigning the workplace to fit a diverse work force.

Critics insist that the diversity movement is simply changing the terminology to avoid the negative connotations that affirmative action has taken on. "Diversity management wants to separate itself desperately from affirmative action," Lynch says. "Affirmative action is thoroughly tarred in the public mind with quotas and promoting incompetents."

The Rev. Jesse Jackson calls for a boycott of Texaco on Nov. 16, 1996, following settlement of its multimillion-dollar discrimination suit.

"What modern affirmative action and diversity does is to reward people based on race, color or gender," Lynch adds, "because in diversity management you are supposed to reward differences, and differences are linked to skin color."

Opponents of affirmative action have made headway in the past few years in limiting but not eliminating the policies. During the 1980s, the Supreme Court restricted the ability of government employers to implement affirmative action plans if they required layoffs of existing workers. The court also limited the use of racial preferences in government contracting in 1989 and '95. And last year, the justices left in place a ruling by a federal appeals court that barred racial preferences in admissions by

After Accusations of Racial Insensitivity ...

In the years before diversity, Texaco Inc. promised Americans that they could trust their cars "to the man who wears the star." But that trust was shaken last year when the big oil company was hit with devastating accusations of racial insensitivity and corporate misconduct.

Now Texaco has embarked on a crash program to regain the public's trust. For the past nine months, the men and women who wear the big red Texaco star —from the company's headquarters in White Plains, N.Y., to its refineries on the Gulf and Pacific coasts — have been taking two days off from their regular jobs for a "diversity learning experience."

A force of about 50 consultants are guiding small groups of Texaco workers to talk about their attitudes on race, gender and culture and how those attitudes may be affecting their work.

Many employees come to the sessions with varying degrees of skepticism, according to consultants who have been conducting the sessions.

"Some people are not real sure why they're there," says Maxine Carpenter, a consultant with McKinley and Associates in Alexandria, Va. "Some think they're being punished for what a few people did. They think they're not responsible for what came out in the media last November."

But Carpenter and Steven Rivelis, a Baltimore-based consultant, both say most employees find the sessions worthwhile. "My experience is that 99.98 percent of them understand the business implications [of corporate sensitivity] afterward," Rivelis says. "They understand the role that they play in making a work force more responsive. They realize that it's up to them to help make changes in the company, and they move very fast in that direction." [1]

Texaco officials say they are nearly halfway toward the goal of putting all of their nearly 20,000 U.S. employees through the sessions by the end of next year. The mandatory training appears to be unprecedented in scope and speed for a company of Texaco's size. But the company agreed to a number of other precedent-setting steps this year in settlement of a three-year-old civil rights suit brought by African-American employees who claimed they faced discriminatory barriers to advancement.

The far-reaching plan also calls for Texaco to broaden recruitment, create a companywide mentoring program and institute new, more objective, personnel-evaluation procedures for promotion. In addition, managers will be evaluated — and their compensation determined — on the basis of their "equal employment opportunity and diversity performance." The changes are being overseen by a seven-member task force headed by Deval Patrick, the former head of the Justice Department's civil rights division.

"The task force is trying to create some cultural change at Texaco and replace discriminatory, haphazard systems with ones that are fair and create equal opportunity for everybody," says Cyrus Mehri, a Washington lawyer who represented the plaintiffs in the case.

public colleges and universities. In addition, California voters approved a ballot initiative in November barring state and local governments from using racial or gender preferences in employment, college admissions or contracting.

Now, the Supreme Court is about to consider a new affirmative action case that opponents hope will curtail the use of racial preferences by governments and perhaps by private employers as well. The case stems from a racial-discrimination suit filed by a white high school teacher in New Jersey who was laid off while a black teacher in the same department with equal seniority was kept on. The Piscataway school board says it kept the black teacher to promote racial diversity, but the white teacher claims the layoff violated federal job-discrimination laws.

Several civil rights groups have filed briefs urging the high court to allow school boards to consider racial diversity in making employment decisions. Promoting faculty diversity is "a compelling interest," the American Civil Liberties Union argues, because it "enhances the educational experiences of students."

But conservative groups filed briefs this month urging the court not to recognize diversity as a justification for race-conscious employment decisions.

"The problem with diversity as a rationale is that it is incapable of any concrete meaning or limitation," says Clint Bolick, vice president of the Institute for Justice. "It's purely a subjective criterion and is therefore a rationale for open-ended preferences."

Lynch contends that today's affirmative action policies represent a distortion of their original purpose. "The original mission of affirmative action was to open the gates of opportunity to everyone," he says. "Once you've done the best you can to opening your doors and recruiting everybody, then everybody ought to be judged by the same standard."

But Hayles says affirmative action is still needed. "I think about affirmative action as a specific tool designed to enhance diversity when it's not present," he says. "You should proactively seek the diversity that you do not have but need." ■

. . . Texaco Seeks to Regain Public Trust

The six Texaco employees who originally brought the suit in federal court in White Plains in March 1994 charged that they had been passed over for promotions at the company on account of their race. The lead plaintiff, Bari-Ellen Roberts, a senior financial analyst, said she lost a position to a white man with less experience — and was then told to train him.

"I filed suit a week later," she told a reporter. [2]

Texaco denied wrongdoing but moved to settle the suit last November after the disclosure of tape-recorded conversations about the case among company managers. The tapes — secretly made by a former executive, Richard Lundwall — appeared to show the managers belittling black employees and discussing concealment or destruction of documents relating to the case. Initially, one of the executives was understood to have used a racial epithet on the tape. An independent analysis of the tape later showed that the word was not used, but the firestorm of criticism that had been unleashed all but forced Texaco to end the suit as quickly as possible. [3]

The settlement — agreed to in principle on Nov. 15, 1996, and approved by U.S. District Court Judge Charles Brieant on March 26, 1997 — carried a total price tag of $176 million. All salaried African-Americans who were on Texaco's payroll between March 1991 and November 1996 were eligible for lump-sum payments averaging over $60,000; those currently employed were also to receive an 11.4 percent salary increase. Texaco also agreed to spend about $35 million over the next five years on the diversity program and new personnel procedures.

Mehri says the changes will benefit Texaco. "When you have an entrenched glass ceiling, when you have processes that reward a good-old-boy system instead of a merit system, you don't benefit from the full talent of the work force," Mehri says. "What [Deval Patrick] is working on is to create systems that are more objective, that will allow talent to rise to the top and not to have artificial barriers to people's career development."

Consultant Rivelis says he also foresees positive changes from the diversity training. "I'm already hearing people in the field say that management is listening to them, that they are more comfortable about raising issues," Rivelis says.

But Rivelis says the test will be whether management sticks with the new attitude toward diversity and workplace equity.

"If senior leadership is behind it, and doesn't just treat it like the new flavor of the month but is committed to it," he says, "then organizations can change, and change significantly."

---

[1] For background, see *The Baltimore Sun* June 15, 1997, p. 1D.

[2] *The New York Times* , July 14, 1996, p. 13WC (Westchester County weekly section). Roberts has since left Texaco and plans to write a book about the case.

[3] Lundwall is awaiting trial, along with Texaco's former treasurer, on federal charges of obstruction of justice in connection with his conduct in the suit.

BACKGROUND

Recognizing Diversity

The U.S. work force has always been racially and ethnically diverse. African-American slaves worked on Southern plantations before the Civil War, and most of their freed descendants stayed on as sharecroppers after emancipation. Chinese "coolies" helped build the railroads in the West, and Mexican braceros picked fruits and vegetables in California and the Southwest. White immigrants also made their contributions: The Irish helped build the country's skyscrapers, Jewish women operated the sewing machines of New York's garment industry and Scandinavian lumberjacks cleared the great forests of the Northwest.

For most of U.S. history, however, workplace diversity was neither "recognized" nor "honored," as the authors of *The American Mosaic* put it.[7] Wages and working conditions were terrible for women and minorities, and their opportunities for advancement were limited by institutionalized discrimination. Labor unions helped redress some of the grievances for white males.[8] For the most part, however, they did little to challenge racism or sexism in the workplace. In fact, unions in many instances helped enforce the barriers that kept women and minority workers in a second-place status.

Those barriers began to fall with the entry of women into the work force during World War II and, afterwards, the rising demand for labor brought on by the United States' growth into a global economic superpower. Then, beginning in the 1960s, the federal government began to dismantle the legal barriers that had blocked advancement for women and minority workers. The Equal Pay Act of 1963 required employers to give men and women equal pay for equal work. A year later, Title VII of the Civil Rights Act of 1964 prohibited discrimination by most private employers on the basis of race or national origin. The law was extended in 1972 to cover state and local governments also.

Congress in 1965 also opened the door to a new wave of immigration that was to dramatically increase workplace diversity over the next three decades.[9] The Immigration and Nationality Act Amendments of 1965 abolished a national-origins system weighted toward European countries and repealed stringent restrictions on Asian immigration. The new law allowed immigration from both the Western and Eastern hemispheres, with no fixed country ceilings. The effect of the law was seen quickly. Most U.S. immigrants had always come from European countries. But since 1970, the proportion of Europeans has declined sharply, while the number from Latin America and Asia has risen.

The new legislation combined to bring into the workplace large numbers of workers from racial and ethnic minority groups and to give them legal rights to equal opportunities with white workers. Meanwhile, women were also entering the work force in larger numbers — also with legal rights to equal treatment.[10] The postwar boom was still raising living standards for most workers, but white men, accustomed to having preferences for the best jobs and opportunities for advancement, now faced greater competition for America's economic bounty.

Birth of Affirmative Action

The resulting strains were exacerbated by the birth of affirmative action. The federal government in 1970 explicitly adopted a hiring policy based on proportional representation of minority group workers. A directive known as Order No. 4 required federal contractors to present "specific goals and timetables" to correct "underutilization" of minorities, which was defined as "having fewer minorities in a particular job class than would reasonably be expected by their availability." A year later, the order was expanded to cover women as well.

In addition to the government contracting policy, private companies had an incentive to adopt affirmative action policies to try to prevent being held liable for past discrimination. White men disadvantaged by the new preferences for women and minorities, however, saw the schemes as a violation of the Civil Rights Act itself and challenged some of the plans in the courts. In 1979, one of those challenges reached the Supreme Court and resulted in a limited decision backing voluntary affirmative action plans.

The case — *United Steelworkers of America v. Weber* — stemmed from an agreement between Kaiser Aluminum Co. and the steelworkers to allot to black workers half of the slots in a new training program at a Louisiana plant. Brian F. Weber, a white worker who would have been entitled to one of the slots based on seniority, challenged the plan and won two lower court rulings that barred the use of racial preferences in affirmative action plans. In a 5-2 decision, however, the high court ruled that "voluntary, race-conscious affirmative plans" designed to "break down old patterns of racial segregation and hierarchy" were legal as long as they did not "unnecessarily trammel the interests of the white employees" — for example, by requiring the discharge of white workers.

The Diversity Industry

The growth of civil rights legislation and affirmative action policies combined with the increased diversity of the work force to make personnel policies more difficult and more important for employers. Over time, the difficulties spawned the creation of a new specialty and eventually a new business in the human resources field: the diversity industry.

The two major founders of the diversity movement both began developing their theories in the early 1980s.[11] Griggs and Thomas were graduates of prestigious business schools, Stanford and Harvard, respectively. Both men brought to their work a civil rights sensibility, but each began by responding to concrete business needs.

Griggs and his first wife, Lennie Copeland, produced a video training series called "Going International," aimed at helping multinational corporations prepare their employees for dealing with international differences. After some businesses indicated a desire to adapt the tapes to help deal with racial and gender diversity in domestic operations, Copeland and Griggs raised $450,000 from 32 major corporations to produce the first of their "Valuing Diversity" video series.

The first of the tapes — "Managing Differences," "Diversity at Work" and "Communicating Across Cultures" — were completed in 1987. They were aimed at helping managers understand the effects of ethnic and gender stereotyping on women and minorities and helping workers learn how to deal with cultural differences in the workplace. The tapes sold well. More titles followed, along with a recently produced CD-ROM. Today, Griggs says the tapes have been bought by 5,000 companies and "thousands" of individuals.

Thomas recounts in his book *Beyond Race and Gender* that he began developing his views on managing diversity while serving as dean of Atlanta University's Graduate School of Business Administration.[12] A corporate manager suggested that Thomas develop "something" to help white males manage their black employees. Thomas writes that he was "offended" by the suggestion that managers needed special assis-

Continued on p. 901

Chronology

Before 1950

White males hold sway in U.S. workplaces; women and minority workers face pervasive discrimination in pay and job opportunities.

1960s

Congress enacts major anti-employment-discrimination laws.

1963
Equal Pay Act requires most employers to pay equal compensation to women doing the same work as men.

1964
Title VII of Civil Rights Act of 1964 prohibits most private employers from discriminating in hiring, promotion or other personnel decisions on the basis of race, color, religion, sex or national origin. Act is extended to government employers in 1972.

1967
Age Discrimination in Employment Act prohibits discrimination in employment on the basis of age against workers or potential workers between 40 and 65.

1970s

Affirmative action policies are developed by federal government and upheld by Supreme Court.

1970
Nixon administration requires federal contractors to set "specific goals and timetables" for minority employment. Order is extended to women in 1971.

June 27, 1979
Supreme Court upholds voluntary affirmative action plans by private employers (*United Steelworkers of America v. Weber*).

1980s

"Diversity movement" is born; affirmative action comes under fire but is reaffirmed with some restrictions.

1983
Lewis Griggs and Lennie Copeland produce the first of their "Going International" videos to help U.S.-based companies deal with cultural differences in other countries; videos are forerunners of their seven-part series "Valuing Diversity," which first appears in 1987.

May 19, 1986
Supreme Court strikes down affirmative action plan by local school board requiring layoffs of white teachers to preserve jobs of less senior black teachers (*Wygant v. Jackson Board of Education*).

March 25, 1987
Voluntary affirmative action plans for women are upheld by Supreme Court (*Johnson v. Transportation Agency of Santa Clara County*).

October 1987
Workforce 2000 projects that women and minority group workers will comprise a growing percentage of U.S. work force through the rest of the century.

1990s

Diversity movement gains acceptance but also faces criticism.

March 1990
R. Roosevelt Thomas Jr.'s influential article "From Affirmative Action to Affirming Diversity" appears in the *Harvard Business Review*.

July 26, 1990
Americans With Disabilities Act is signed into law, prohibiting discrimination in employment against persons with physical or mental disabilities.

May 1991
First annual National Diversity Conference is held in San Francisco.

May 1992
Second National Diversity Conference is held in Washington; attendance peaks at 450 persons.

Nov. 5, 1996
California voters approve ballot initiative banning racial or gender preferences by state or local governments in employment, minority contracting or college and university admissions.

Nov. 15, 1996
Texaco agrees to $176 million settlement of racial-discrimination suit; company adopts plan in December for all 29,000 Texaco employees to attend two-day diversity training sessions.

June 27, 1997
Supreme Court agrees to hear suit brought by white schoolteacher laid off in favor of black teacher because of racial diversity (*Piscataway Township Board of Education v. Taxman*).

Gays Slowly Getting More Workplace Support

For her first six years as a computer programmer at the Ford Motor Co., Alice McKeage did what most lesbians and gay men do at work: She watched her pronouns. When she talked about her weekend dates, she changed their gender, and she never put their pictures on her desk.

Four years ago, however, McKeage realized that staying in the closet was taking its toll on her both personally and professionally.

"Someone made a derogatory comment about gays," she recalls, and she spent the rest of the day at her desk, fighting back tears. "I was not a productive employee," she says.

A few months later, McKeage decided to take action. Along with a gay colleague in the engineering department, she wrote a two-page letter to Ford's vice president for human relations, carefully explaining the ways that the workplace environment was inhospitable to gays and lesbians. They asked merely to start a dialogue. And they signed their names.

To their surprise, Vice President Jack Hall wrote back thanking them for their letter. He had received similar letters, he told them, but none had been signed. He welcomed the meeting.

Three years later, Ford provides a better climate for gay and lesbian workers, McKeage says. The company supported her efforts to start a network for gay, lesbian and bisexual workers. It also agreed to join the growing number of U.S. corporations that have adopted policies prohibiting discrimination based on sexual orientation.

Still, McKeage says, progress has been slow, especially for gay, blue-collar plant workers, who often face explicit hostility from their colleagues.

"That's who I get the most complaints from," McKeage says. "When they try to get help, they may not get management support. And they don't get support from their union. This is an issue that unions don't want to get involved in."

What happened at Ford reflects the workplace environment for a growing number of gay and lesbian workers today, according to gay rights advocates. Several hundred companies have anti-gay bias policies, and 11 states plus the District of Columbia prohibit employment discrimination based on sexual orientation.[1] But most homosexual workers still have no legal or corporate safeguard against losing a job or promotion because of their sexual orientation. And most have no assurance of management or union support in dealing with anti-gay slurs or worse from their co-workers.[2]

"It's a situation that's improving," says Kerry Lobel, executive director of the National Gay & Lesbian Task Force. "The culture is changing, the climate is changing — but one company, one community, one state at a time."

The diversity movement can take some credit for the changing attitude, but only some. The issue is "typically lower on the list because it raises issues of religion, personal identity and sexual identity," says Robert Hayles, a Minneapolis-based diversity consultant. "It is a difficult, challenging issue, but it is nonetheless one that offers opportunities for workplace improvement and market enhancement if we deal with it successfully."

Companies have been especially slow to accept homosexuality at the top, Lobel says. "If you look at major companies, there are very few openly gay or lesbian CEOs," Lobel says. She blames the situation on homophobia. But a retired Ford executive who rose to the company's second-ranking position while keeping his homosexuality virtually secret says companies are simply seeking to avoid controversy.

Homosexuality "is still a controversial subject," Allen Gilmour told *Fortune* magazine recently. "And businesses don't want their executives to be controversial."[3]

In the interview, Gilmour recalled that some at Ford suspected his homosexuality despite his careful efforts to keep it secret. He said that when he was a contender to become chief executive officer in 1992, he worried that the suspicions might hurt his chances. Another candidate, with broader experience, was chosen. "Whether being gay hurt my chances," Gilmour told the interviewer, "I honestly don't know. I've heard some people say it did, but I doubt it."

Most firms with anti-bias policies have not suffered a backlash, but one — the Walt Disney Co. — is the target of a boycott by the Southern Baptist Convention over the issue.

In the legislative arena, opponents of laws to prohibit discrimination against gays argue the measures would give homosexuals "special rights," prevent employers from disciplining sexual misconduct and pave the way for quotas based on sexual preferences. Supporters say none of those fears has materialized in the states with gay-rights laws.

For herself, McKeage says she feels the increased openness at Ford has helped her be more productive even though she realizes that some of her co-workers disapprove of her lifestyle. "I'm no longer sitting at my desk stewing about comments that are made," she says. "And I don't spend time worrying about, 'Oh, my God, did I say the wrong thing?' "

McKeage feels secure enough to put a picture of her partner on her desk. But her colleague in founding the gay-lesbian work group — which now numbers about 180 members — is still in the closet.

---

[1] The states are California, Connecticut, Hawaii, Maine, Massachusetts, Minnesota, New Hampshire, New Jersey, Rhode Island, Vermont and Wisconsin.

[2] For background, see Renee Blank and Sandra Slipp, *Voices of Diversity: Real People Talk about Problems and Solutions in a Workplace Where Everyone Is Not Alike* (1994), pp. 138-150.

[3] "My Life as a Gay Executive," *Fortune*, Sept. 8, 1997, p. 107.

Continued from p. 898
tance to deal with black employees. But eventually he concluded that, in fact, there was a need to explore whether managers needed to do things differently with a more diverse work force.

In his seminal 1990 article "From Affirmative Action to Affirming Diversity" in the *Harvard Business Review*, Thomas argued that companies had to accept that women and minorities no longer wanted to be assimilated, and that managers had to learn how to deal with "unassimilated diversity" in the workplace to prevent it from producing inefficiencies and conflict. Expanding on the theme in his book a year later, Thomas stressed the need for corporate change. "Changing the root culture," he wrote, "is at the heart of the managing diversity approach." [13]

These early works in the diversity field came as businesses were digesting a Labor Department-commissioned report that projected a continuing increase in workplace diversity for the remainder of the century. The report, *Workforce 2000,* prepared by the conservative Hudson Institute, accurately noted that the growth rates of many minority groups were exceeding the growth rate of white non-Hispanic males. As a result, the report said, white men would constitute a lower percentage of the total work force. [14] The report had exaggerated impact, however, because of a typographical error in the book's executive summary that incorrectly projected the percentage of white men entering the workplace would fall to only 15 percent. Despite a correction in a later printing, the incorrect statistic was widely quoted — fostering a sense of urgency among business executives about addressing changes in workplace diversity. [15]

Suddenly, diversity experts had a market for their information and views among the country's biggest companies. Firms were willing to pay four- and five-figure prices for diversity training seminars run by Griggs, Thomas and many others. Some companies balked at the expense or the time, and others worried about creating a backlash among white male managers. But many people who went through the exercises said they were worthwhile. After going through a three-day seminar, a woman manager at Ortho Pharmaceuticals said she was "embarrassed" to realize the racial stereotypes that she brought with her into the workplace. [16]

Corporate executives were often among the most fervent converts to the diversity movement. Thomas used his work with Avon Products as a case study in his book. The giant cosmetics company's top executive reciprocated with a foreword that fully embraced Thomas' views about the importance of managing diversity. "America is not a melting pot, but a great mosaic," James E. Preston, Avon's CEO, wrote. "And the successful organization must reflect that mosaic." [17]

White Male Backlash

The diversity movement gained momentum and visibility in the 1990s by holding a series of "national diversity conferences" and continuing to win acceptance from government and private employers. But it also attracted a smattering of criticism. A few outside observers depicted diversity consultants as commercial hucksters selling employers feel-good nostrums in politically correct packaging. In addition, a white male backlash helped fuel growing resistance to affirmative action that reached an important milestone with the passage of the California initiative banning racial and gender preferences by state and local governments.

The first of the national diversity conferences, held in San Francisco in May 1991, attracted 300 people from government, corporations and non-profit organizations. Lynch, who attended the first three annual meetings first as an observer and later as a gadfly panelist, has described the session as a celebration both of diversity and of the diversity movement.

"We have spawned a business, a movement, an industry," Price Cobbs, an African-American psychiatrist and author and one of the conference cosponsors, told the opening gathering. [18]

Lynch depicts the sessions as a mix of bottom-line, civil rights and New Age themes, with frequent criticisms of white, male racism. Griggs, another of the conference cosponsors, introduced himself as a "recovering racist, classist and sexist." Another speaker, William Hanson, a Digital Equipment vice president, recalled that he came to Cobbs for help after encountering problems managing the company's ethnically mixed plants in the 1970s. Cobbs convinced him that the problem was "institutional racism." Hanson began sending his managers to intensive sensitivity workshops in Cobbs' offices. Later, Lynch recounts, Hanson expanded Digital's diversity efforts to include "numerous focus groups that discussed all manner of differences."

The mood was less celebratory when the second annual conference was held in Washington a year later, according to Lynch's account. A backlash against diversity had begun to form due in part to corporate downsizing, which was displacing many senior white males and leaving many others anxious about their jobs. In addition, the Los Angeles riots touched off by the state court acquittals of the white police officers charged with beating a black motorist, Rodney King, had provoked a nationwide malaise about the state of race relations.

Still, the conference registration hit a peak of 450 persons, drawn again from major corporations, government agencies and nonprofit groups. In a keynote address, Thomas stressed the importance of an expanded definition of diversity in part to deflect the accusation that diversity was merely a code word for advancing "black" issues. He also likened a diverse work force to a jar of jelly beans — "a unique, collective mixture of all differences and similarities in an organization," as Lynch paraphrased it.

The white male backlash appeared to grow over the next several years. In a cover story entitled "White Male Paranoia," *Newsweek* reported in March 1993 that 56 percent of white males surveyed believed they were "losing an advantage in jobs and income." More than half — 55 percent — believed they were "paying a penalty for the advantages they had in the past," and most of those — five out of six — believed the penalty was "unfair." [19]

Surveys among diversity consultants also reported evidence of a white male backlash. The Society for Human Resources Management reported in 1993 that "resistance" among white males was the major roadblock faced by the diversity movement. A year later, a survey by The Conference Board found that three-fifths of companies surveyed identified fear of backlash among white males as one of the three most serious barriers to implementing diversity initiatives. [20]

The white male backlash was widely, if simplistically, depicted as the major factor in the Republican takeover of both houses of Congress in the November 1994 elections. Since then, some GOP lawmakers have pushed legislation aimed at curbing affirmative action by the federal government, but the bills have failed to get out of committee. In California, however, the anti-affirmative action movement scored an important victory in 1996 when voters approved a ballot initiative that prohibits race and gender preferences by state or local governments in employment, college admissions or contracting. The debate was focused, though, not on workplace diversity but on university admissions — in particular, an institutionalized system of racial preferences for entry into the state university system.

Lynch depicts the middle of the decade as a period of frustration for the diversity movement. The political and economic adversities produced a sharpened concentration on diversity as a business strategy. "This is not altruism," remarks Joanne Miller, director of the Center for the New American Workforce at Queens College, City University of New York. (*See "At Issue," p. 905.*) In addition, the difficulties prompted some rethinking by both of the movement's major founders, Griggs and Thomas.

Thomas opened his new book *Redefining Diversity* with a discouraged assessment that businesses were "little better equipped" to deal with a multicultural work force than they were in the days of overt racism. [21] At length, he argued that corporations would prosper if — but only if — they learned the importance of fostering "mutual adaptation" within an increasingly diverse work force.

Griggs was also emphasizing the importance of moving beyond "our non-discriminatory policies." All too often, he wrote in the preface to his 1995 book *Valuing Diversity,* affirmative action and equal opportunity amounted simply to a dominant group "giving" equal opportunity to a less dominant group as long as they agreed to "leave their differences at the door." "We need to shift our course," he concluded, "and affirm our differences, accept our differences and, ultimately, value those differences." [22] ■

CURRENT SITUATION

Policies and Practices

Like most of the country's biggest companies, Texaco and Bell Atlantic have been working on diversity issues for years. Both companies adopted policies that promise respect, tolerance and equal opportunities for all workers. But racial discrimination suits filed against both firms indicate that the policies have failed to completely root out racist attitudes or prevent racist incidents.

Texaco suffered grievous embarrassment last November with the front-page disclosure of tape recordings that captured company executives belittling blacks while discussing how to handle a suit charging the company with racial discrimination in hiring and promotion. Affidavits filed in the suit, less widely reported, included allegations from scores of Texaco employees that they experienced racial epithets or stereotyping at work. One black worker said that throughout her employment three supervisors "openly discussed their view that African-Americans are ignorant and incompetent." [23]

Bell Atlantic employees also complained of racist stereotyping in the workplace in a civil rights suit filed in federal court in Washington last fall. One worker in Pennsylvania said white colleagues showed him a videotape portraying him as having gotten his job because of his basketball skills. A Virginia employee said he found a mock job application for black applicants that asked such insulting questions as "name of father (if known)." Both workers claimed their supervisors did nothing after they complained.[24]

Officials at both companies say the incidents — if true — simply show that companies cannot control the behavior of all employees at all times.

"We have excellent human resource policies," says Texaco diversity director Gadsden, a black executive who has held the post since 1994. "We expect people to abide by those policies and work within the framework of those policies, but sometimes people don't do that."

"If there is discrimination out there, we cannot stop it from occurring," says Joan Rasmussen, a Bell Atlantic spokeswoman, "but we can create an atmosphere where it is not acceptable."

Compliance problems result in part from the pressure that mid-level managers already feel in an increasingly uncertain business climate. "Middle managers get stuck with the brunt of the responsibility of how this plays out," says New York consultant Wheeler. "Diversity is seen as one more thing to do."

To emphasize the importance of diversity, a growing number of companies are adopting the step that Bell Atlantic initiated last month: tying managers' evaluations — and, implicitly, compensation — to achieving specific diversity goals. But critics question the approach. "We're right back to quotas," says Lynch.

For Texaco, the evidence in the three-year-old suit was too damning to ignore. Texaco Chairman Peter Bijur promptly denounced the contents of the tape and vowed corrective action. And the next month the company settled the suit by agreeing to what civil rights leaders described as one of the broadest diversity packages ever adopted by a U.S. corporation.

In addition to the diversity training for all Texaco employees, the accord included a package of $115 million in back pay for the 1,348 plaintiffs in the case — an average of $63,000 for each of the salaried workers — and another $26 million in pay increases for current black salaried employees. The company also agreed to increase the number of its minority employees to 29 percent from 23 percent and to take several steps to improve promotion opportunities for minorities and other employees — including revised training and standards and a new mentoring program.

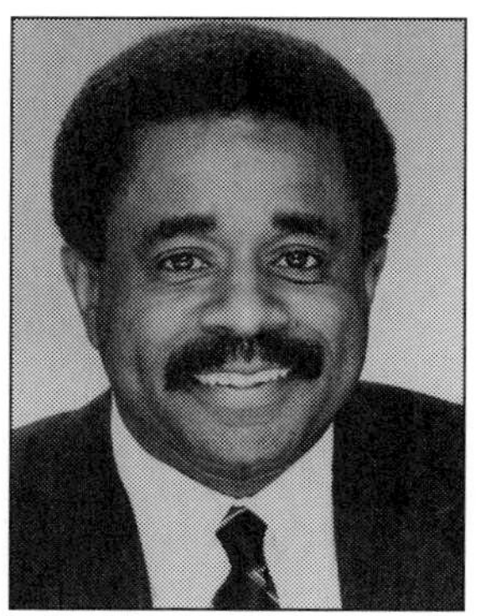

"Diversity is reality. All kinds of diversity are reality. Managing diversity in the workplace requires everyone to change, not just the ones that are different."

— R. Roosevelt Thomas Jr.
Founder, American Institute for Managing Diversity

Bell Atlantic has not responded, publicly or in court, to the specific allegations in its suit. But spokeswoman Rasmussen notes that three employees were fired earlier this year for putting racist messages on the company's internal computer network. "We really do have a good record," she says. "But doing the right thing does not protect you from individual circumstances where somebody might not act appropriately."

The attorney for the plaintiffs in the case, however, is less impressed with Bell Atlantic's policies. "They've created a lot of affirmative action groups, which our clients regarded as pacifiers," says John Hermina. "They're very well-versed in putting façades on, but it's all superficial."

For its part, Texaco released figures in late July showing that minorities accounted for 38 percent of its new hires and 24 percent of its promotions during the first six months of the diversity plan.[25] But a religious group that had lobbied Texaco on diversity issues for many years is taking a wait-and-see attitude toward the company's implementation of the plan.

"We want to encourage the positive things that are going on, but there are a lot of things that are unanswered," says Gary Brouse, director of equality programs for the Interfaith Center for Corporate Responsibility in New York. "We don't have a grade for them right now."

Preferences and Pitfalls

Racial diversity has long been a point of pride in Piscataway, an integrated suburban township in central New Jersey. But the town's school board now finds itself before the U.S. Supreme Court because of its effort to maintain a measure of racial diversity in the teaching staff at the local high school.[26]

When the school board found that it had to lay off one of the school's business teachers in 1989 because of declining enrollment, it faced a choice between two teachers with comparable seniority and qualifications. The only difference the board saw as relevant to its decision was race: Sharon Taxman was white; Debra Williams was black — the only black among the department's 14 teachers.

In previous layoffs, the school board had used random selection to choose between teachers with equal seniority. But in the interest of racial diversity, the school board decided to keep Williams and lay off Taxman.

"The importance of diversity in the educational environment was so obvious," the school board's lawyer, David B. Rubin, recalls today. "It is a very, culturally diverse community, and the folks in the school administration believe that contributes to the educational experience. We believe the same principle applies to the faculty."

Taxman, however, challenged the layoffs as racial discrimination in violation of federal civil rights law. A federal judge eventually agreed and approved a jury award totaling about $144,000 in back pay and interest. Taxman was rehired in 1993, but the case continued. And last year, the federal appeals court in Philadelphia upheld the back pay award to Taxman in a broadly written decision that said affirmative action policies could be justified only to remedy past discrimination, not to maintain or promote racial diversity for its own sake.

In asking the Supreme Court to overturn the decision, the school board continues to argue the importance of diversity. But Stephen Klausner, the attorney representing Taxman, stresses that both the high school and the overall school system have racially mixed faculties. He says the board's concern with the racial composition of a single department at the high school is misplaced.

"They're arguing that the business department wouldn't have had a diverse faculty," Klausner says. "I don't buy that." Williams "taught keyboarding," Klausner continues. "How much ethnic diversity can you give on the keyboard?"

For critics of affirmative action, the Piscataway case presented an ideal opportunity to dramatize the costs of racial preferences in human as well as policy terms. Both teachers had been scarred by the episode. Taxman, the white teacher, declines to give media interviews, but Klausner describes her as depressed by the long-simmering controversy. For her part, Williams complains that the school board was wrong to have used race as the only criterion at the time of the layoff. "It really bothers me every time I pick up the paper and read that we had identical qualifications," she told a *New York Times* reporter over the summer. "We're not Siamese twins."

Civil rights supporters are bracing for an adverse ruling in the case. "This court has not been looking favorably on affirmative action plans," says Theodore Shaw, associate director of the NAACP Legal Defense and Educational Fund. "And these facts involving a layoff situation are already difficult."

Political Hot Potato

The case has been a political hot potato for President Clinton, who promised to support affirmative action with his now-famous quote, "Mend it, don't end it." Under President George Bush, the government had sided with Taxman after the Equal Employment Opportunity Commission had found probable cause for her claim. Under Clinton, however, the Justice Department sought to change positions and side with the school board. The appeals court refused to let the government change sides, but allowed it to withdraw from the suit.

After the school board asked the high court to review the case in April, the Justice Department urged the court not to hear the dispute, saying it was "not an appropriate vehicle" to decide the broad question of non-remedial affirmative action. Now that the justices have decided to hear the case, the government is arguing that the school board did show the need to use race as the basis for its decision to fire Taxman. But it also argues that school systems can show in some circumstances "a compelling interest in obtaining the educational benefits of a racially diverse faculty at each of its schools" and can justify the use of race as "one factor" in making assignment or transfer decisions.

The justices are likely to hear arguments in the case in December or January, with a decision due before next July. Critics of affirmative action are voicing confidence in the outcome. "We believe that the Supreme Court has spoken repeatedly and convincingly that past discrimination is the only possible justification for race-conscious governmental action," says Clint Bolick of the Institute for Justice, which is filing a brief supporting Taxman.

Court-watchers are uncertain and divided on whether the justices are likely to issue a sweeping ruling on diversity and affirmative action or a narrower decision limited to the particular facts of Taxman's case. The key justice to watch, observers agree, is Sandra Day O'Connor, who has generally voted to restrict but not prohibit the use of racial preferences by government.

Supporters of affirmative action warn that a broad ruling limiting the

Continued on p. 906

At Issue:

Has the "diversity movement" been good for American employers?

Joanne Miller
Director, Center for the New American Workforce, Queens College, City University of New York

yes

The diversity of American society is already present in the workplace. It stems not from a "movement" to be inclusive but from increasing demand for skilled labor that is accelerating recruitment from non-traditional and foreign labor markets. The kaleidoscope of issues that has become associated with workplace diversity reflects the many aspects of culture and social structure that are affected by demography. They cannot be eradicated — only unbundled and reinvented. This is the art and science of management.

The transition from defining "diversity issues" as "the problem" to managing diversity involves the realization that demographic change affects the character of economic adjustment and employment relations — not just the composition of the labor force.

Economic pressures for downsizing in a global economy encourage organizations to eliminate redundancy in expertise and functions. The advantage of being similar is no longer as comfortable when attention is focused on the unique value added by each member of a company that competes in international markets.

In restructuring, divisions of labor and authority are more flexibly drawn to enable fast response to market changes. People from different parts of the organization are put together to solve problems. This introduces new aspects of diversity to be managed, including differences stemming from physical location, relative pay scales, customary perks and temporary employment status.

As occupational and job segregation lessens, the people directly competing for promotions and control over decision-making will be more heterogeneous, even if there was no increase in the overall diversity of employees in a company.

Diversity has important implications for doing business: competencies that are required to be competitive in global markets, necessary knowledge, barriers to developing and coordinating talent, new ways of working and the development of business trust among diverse people. The question is not whether diversity is "good" for employers but what constitutes "good management" of the diversity that already characterizes the American labor force, global competition and new employment relations. To blame the courts, the liberals, the politicians, diversity consultants or the intellectuals for unwanted prescriptions deflects attention from the business imperative.

All of American society is impacted by shifts in demography. For some, the sense of motion discomfort is overwhelming, and the immediate concern is getting it to stop. Others set about recalibrating to maintain stability in changing environments and assessing opportunity. The latter is essential for managing the future.

Frederick R. Lynch
***Associate professor of government, Claremont McKenna College and author,* The Diversity Machine**

no

Diversity management theory and practice vary as widely as the policies' intended and unintended consequences. Politically neutral, cross-cultural training to improve sales and service for increasingly heterogeneous urban or international customer bases is probably useful. And employees welcome greater workplace flexibility through telecommuting, flex-time and attentiveness to work-family issues.

Generally, however, the policies promoted by the network of consultants and organizational sponsors that I term the "diversity machine" do not deliver promised payoffs of increased productivity and intergroup harmony. Instead, diversity campaigns push a political agenda rooted in three assumptions culled from campus multiculturalism and numbers-oriented affirmative action: first, that lack of ethnic-gender proportional representation at all organizational levels indicates institutional racism and sexism; second, that an individual's outlook is primarily determined by his ethnic and gender group membership; and, third, that legal standards and measures of merit were created by and for white males — therefore, "equal treatment is not fair treatment," to quote a favorite maxim of consultants.

Assimilation and non-discrimination are passé. Permanent pluralism and "celebrating differences" are in. Other sociological bases of difference *and similarity* — class, age, education, sexual orientation — are usually ignored.

The polarization, group-think and censorship resulting from top-down, politicized diversity were vividly described to me by a high-level, African-American administrator at the University of Michigan: "It used to be easier — when issues weren't framed around race and gender. Now there are increasing divisions around color. There's constant checking, loyalty tests. Everyone is trying to be sensitive. You wonder: Can I still say 'dumb stuff' and can it still be OK? It's ironic: the very thing we're trying to do — appreciate how different we are — and I can't be different!"

There is no systematic, quantitative evidence that artificially creating a heterogeneous "work force that looks like America" has any substantive business value. And for every individual testimonial on the alleged benefits of work force diversity, there is a horror story of confrontational "blow-ups" and/or widespread cynicism among employees that diversity reforms are merely a "flavor of the month" designed to ward off discrimination lawsuits or provide public relations penance for high-level gaffes.

Employers should reduce discriminatory barriers. But they should avoid diversity machine prescriptions that complexion or gender indicate special knowledge, skills, or "cultural competency." Instead, we should all re-emphasize the values of non-discrimination and equal treatment.

Continued from p. 904

use of racial diversity by both government and private employers could create problems for companies that have sought to promote diversity in hiring and promotion. "I think it would be enormously disruptive," says Steven Shapiro, national legal director for the American Civil Liberties Union.

But Roger Clegg, a lawyer with the Center for Educational Opportunity who is preparing a brief urging the court to bar race-based hiring and promotion decisions by private employers, disagrees. "A decision that returned to the plain language of Title VII [of the Civil Rights Act] would not be disruptive," Clegg says. "It would be a good thing for employees of all races and employers of all kinds." ■

OUTLOOK

Corporate Inaction?

Diversity may be the buzzword of the decade in American workplaces, but many diversity advocates and experts say that employers have been too slow in confronting its challenges and exploiting its opportunities. Critics, however, say the diversity movement has fostered a host of changes in the workplace — mostly for the worse.

"There hasn't been that much change," says Miller at Queens College. "Despite the rhetoric, companies still do not relate the issue of diversity to productivity."

Miller and other diversity advocates see a host of barriers to full implementation of the message that they have been taking to employers through the 1990s. Cost is one factor. "Training, generally speaking, is fairly expensive," O'Mara says. "You're taking a lot of people off the job. You're paying people to deliver the training. It is costly as an intervention."

Another barrier, Wheeler says, is the time and effort required to develop the skills for managing a diverse work force. "Diverse teams over the long term have better problem-solving abilities, but it takes time to get there," Wheeler says. "It's easier to work with a homogeneous workplace; it's more predictable."

For her part, Miller says too many employers view diversity as a legal problem rather than a business opportunity. "They're still very much in a compliance-type of framework," Miller says. "They don't frame the issue of diversity as an opportunity to expand the competencies of their organization, and they do not hold their management accountable for managing diversity as a business asset."

Critics view the diversity movement's influence as substantial and unhealthy. "A lot of demons have been loosed," Lynch says. "The ruling elites look on affirmative action and diversity management as social engineering to prevent polarization and riots. It has a spoils system mentality which a lot of them have accommodated to."

"Many retired people say that double standards have been introduced into the workplace," says writer MacDonald. "Everybody is terrified of firing or reprimanding minority employees because they know they're going to be hit with a discrimination suit."

Statistically, the changing demographics of the U.S. workplace are both impossible to deny and easy to exaggerate. The predominance of white men in U.S. workplaces is decreasing: Women and minorities — African-Americans, Hispanics, and Asian-Americans — are entering the workplace at a faster rate than white men. Still, whites constituted 77 percent of the work force in 1994, according to the Bureau of Labor Statistics (BLS), and will still account for 74 percent of U.S. workers in 2005. Men will also continue to outnumber women in the workplace, according to BLS projections. Women's share of the labor force will increase from 46 percent in 1994 to 47.8 percent in 2005, the BLS says.[27]

Moreover, white men continue to hold a disproportionate share of the senior managerial positions in corporate America, according to a report by a congressionally created commission two years ago. The so-called Glass Ceiling Commission found that 87 percent of the senior managers of *Fortune* 1000 industrial and *Fortune* 500 companies were white, and 95 percent were men. Minority individuals were also paid less than whites holding comparable positions, the commission also found.[28]

Diversity advocates say the statistics show how far corporate America has to go in opening up opportunities for women and minority workers. "I'm disheartened by the degree to which corporate America is an apartheid system," Sussman says. "I'm disheartened by the failure of diversity practitioners to mount an effective social movement."

But critics insist that major corporations have dismantled the old barriers to equal opportunity. "When I look at the corporate world, I see corporations desperately trying to hire minorities," MacDonald says. "The notion that there is a huge number of hugely qualified minorities coming out of business schools being overlooked by corporations too racist to hire them is simply fanciful."

The dispute over race and gender equality in the workplace has raged now for three decades and shows no signs of abating soon. Despite its links to those issues, however, the diversity movement insists that it has a different and broader lesson for employers: that all the people in an increasingly diverse workplace must be valued — even for their differences — if organizations are to succeed.

"Your edge in the competitive world is not your technology, and it's not your product either for the most part," says Steven Rivelis, a Baltimore-based consultant. "Your edge is your people. And if your people are all performing at 100 percent, if you're utilizing all the talent in your room, if you're utilizing all the diversity, then you're going to move forward faster." ■

FOR MORE INFORMATION

American Institute for Managing Diversity, 50 Hurt Plaza, Suite 1150, Atlanta, Ga. 30303; 404-302-9226.
This non-profit organization, founded by R. Roosevelt Thomas Jr.,' founder of the American Institute for Managing Diversity, at Morehouse College, does research and education on diversity issues.

American Society for Training and Development, 1640 King St., Box 1443, Alexandria, Va. 22313-2043; 703-683-8100.
This professional association, founded in 1944, is devoted to workplace learning and performance issues and has about 64,000 members.

Society for Human Resource Management, 606 N. Washington St., Alexandria, Va. 22314; 703-548-3440.
This association of human resource professionals was founded in 1948 and currently has about 70,000 members.

Notes

[1] Frederick R. Lynch, *The Diversity Machine: The Drive to Change the 'White, Male' Workplace* (1997), p. 325.

[2] R. Roosevelt Thomas Jr., "From Affirmative Action to Affirming Diversity," *Harvard Business Review*, March/April 1990, p. 108.

[3] For background, see "Rethinking Affirmative Action," *The CQ Researcher*, April 28, 1995, pp. 369-392.

[4] Anthony Patrick Carnevale and Susan Carol Stone, *The American Mosaic: An In-Depth Report on the Future of Diversity at Work* (1995), p. 115.

[5] Heather MacDonald, "The Diversity Industry," *The New Republic*, July 5, 1993, pp. 22-25. MacDonald is now a writer for the *City Journal,* published by the conservative Manhattan Institute.

[6] *The Wall Street Journal*, Jan. 30, 1997, p. B1.

[7] Carnevale and Stone, *op. cit.,* p. 1.

[8] For background, see "Labor's Future," *The CQ Researcher*, June 28, 1996, pp. 553-576.

[9] For background, see "The New Immigrants," *The CQ Researcher*, Jan. 24, 1997, pp. 49-72, and "Immigration Reform," *The CQ Researcher*, Sept. 24, 1993, pp. 841-864.

[10] For background, see "The Glass Ceiling," *The CQ Researcher*, Oct. 29, 1993, pp. 937-960.

[11] Some of this background is drawn from Lynch, *op. cit.,* pp. 48-58 (Griggs), pp. 58-65 (Thomas).

[12] R. Roosevelt Thomas Jr., *Beyond Race and Gender: Unleashing the Power of Your Work Force by Managing Diversity* (1991), p. xiii.

[13] *Ibid.,* p. 26.

[14] William B. Johnston and Arnold H. Packer, *Workforce 2000: Work and Workers for the 21st Century* (1987).

[15] See *The Wall Street Journal,* Oct. 29, 1996, p. A1. Correctly stated, the book projected that 15 percent of net additions to the labor force between 1985 and 2000 would be white males — net meaning the overall increase after those leaving the workplace, mostly white men, were subtracted. In the executive summary, the word net was dropped, changing the meaning.

[16] *Newsweek*, May 14, 1990, p. 38. The article includes the incorrect statistic from *Workforce 2000.*

[17] Thomas, Beyond Race and Gender, *op. cit.,* p. x.

[18] Quoted in Lynch, *op. cit.,* p. 73. The account of the meetings forms a major part of Lynch's book. See pp. 71-80, 104-120, 150-155 for his extended descriptions of the first of the three conferences.

[19] *Newsweek*, March 29, 1993, pp. 50, 52. The poll, conducted by the Gallup Organization, was based on telephone interviews with 757 adults, including 314 white males, between March 17-18, 1993. The margin of error for the results for white males was plus or minus 6 percentage points.

[20] Cited in Lynch, *op. cit.,* pp. 187-188.

[21] R. Roosevelt Thomas Jr., *Redefining Diversity* (1996), p. xii.

[22] Lewis Brown Griggs and Lente-Louise Louw (eds.), *Valuing Diversity: New Tools for a New Reality* (1995), pp. 5-6.

[23] See Kurt Eichenwald, "The Two Faces of Texaco," *The New York Times*, Nov. 10, 1996, p. C1.

[24] See *The Washington Post*, May 26, 1997, p. A1.

[25] See *The Wall Street Journal*, July 30, 1997, p. B13.

[26] Some background for this section is drawn from *The New York Times*, Aug. 3, 1997, p. A1; Aug. 4, 1997, p. A1.

[27] Howard N. Fullerton Jr., "The 2005 Labor Force: Growing, but Slowly," *Monthly Labor Review*, November 1995, p. 29.

[28] See *The New York Times*, Nov. 23, 1995, p. B14; *The Washington Post,* Nov. 25, 1995, p. C1.

Bibliography

Selected Sources Used

Books

Blank, Renee, and Sandra Slipp, *Voices of Diversity: Real People Talk about Problems and Solutions in a Workplace Where Everyone Is Not Alike,* American Management Association, 1994.

Eight chapters provide summaries and firsthand accounts of workplace experiences of minorities, recent immigrants, workers with disabilities, younger and older workers, gays and lesbians, white men and others.

Carnevale, Anthony Patrick, and Susan Carol Stone, *The American Mosaic: An In-Depth Report on the Future of Diversity at Work,* McGraw-Hill, 1995.

The book provides a comprehensive overview of work force diversity in the United States from past to present and into the future, with detailed statistics and profiles of the largest U.S. ethnic minority groups. The book includes a 12-page list of suggested readings. Carnevale is a former chief economist with the American Society for Training and Development; Stone is a management consultant.

Griggs, Lewis Brown, and Lente-Louise Louw (eds.), *Valuing Diversity: New Tools for a New Reality,* McGraw-Hill, 1995.

Griggs, one of the pioneers of the diversity movement, and his wife argue that organizations must "value," not merely tolerate, diversity in order to "unleash" the full potential of their work force. Griggs and Louw wrote three of the eight chapters in the book.

Jamieson, David, and Julie O'Mara, *Managing Workforce 2000: Gaining the Diversity Advantage,* Jossey-Bass, 1991.

Diversity consultants Jamieson and O'Mara provide a practical guide for managers on a range of issues associated with work force diversity. The book includes a 34-page list of resources and a three-page list of references. Jamieson is based in Los Angeles, O'Mara in Castro Valley, Calif.

Kossek, Ellen Ernst, and Sharon A. Lobel (eds.), *Managing Diversity: Human Resource Strategies for Transforming the Workplace,* Blackwell, 1996.

The book provides textbook-style treatment of major work force diversity issues, including recruiting, training a diverse work force and linking diversity to organizational strategy. Each chapter includes a detailed reference list. Kossek and Lobel are professors at, respectively, Michigan State University's School of Industrial and Labor Relations and Seattle University School of Business and Economics.

Lynch, Frederick, *The Diversity Machine: The Drive to Change the "White, Male' Workplace,"* Free Press, 1997.

Lynch, an associate professor of government at Claremont McKenna College, provides a critical examination of the development, philosophy and major figures of the diversity movement. The book includes detailed source notes and a 12-page bibliography. Lynch is also the author of *Invisible Victims: White Males and the Crisis of Affirmative Action* (Greenwood Press, 1989).

Thomas, R. Roosevelt Jr., *Redefining Diversity,* Amacom (American Management Association), *1996; Beyond Race and Gender: Unleashing the Power of Your Work Force by Managing Diversity,* Amacom, 1991.

Thomas, one of the pioneers of the diversity movement, laid out his philosophy of "managing diversity" in his first book and what he called his "new paradigm" of the "diversity management" in his second. Thomas, who has taught at Harvard Business School and Morehouse College, founded and served until recently as president of the American Institute for Managing Diversity in Atlanta; he is now a private consultant in Atlanta. Thomas' first book elaborated on themes he first set forth in his article "From Affirmative Action to Affirming Diversity," *Harvard Business Review,* March/April 1990, pp. 107-117.

Reports and Studies

Johnston, William B. and Arnold E. Packer, *Workforce 2000: Work and Workers for the 21st Century,* Hudson Institute, 1997.

This Labor Department-commissioned study stirred interest in diversity issues by projecting that minority and female workers would increase at a faster rate than white males for the remainder of the century.

Articles

Fullerton, Howard N., Jr., "The 2005 Labor Force: Growing, but Slowly," *Monthly Labor Review,* November 1995, p. 29.

Fullerton, a demographer with the U.S. Department of Labor's Bureau of Labor Statistics, provides a comprehensive analysis of work force trends.

The Next Step

Additional information from UMI's Newspaper & Periodical Abstracts™ database

Affirmative Action

Carlton, Melinda, Philip Hawkey, Douglas Watson and William Donahue et al "Affirmative action and affirming diversity," *Public Management,* January 1997, pp. 19-23.

Carlton et al raise questions about the effectiveness of affirmative action at the local level. Major trends that will revolutionize the work force in the near future have implications for affirmative action.

"Danger in California," *Call & Post,* Nov. 21, 1996, p. A4.

An editorial criticizes California's Proposition 209, which will dismantle the state's affirmative action programs by making racial preferences in hiring, educating and contracting illegal. The editorial warns that if the proposition holds up under court scrutiny, the diversity of the work force in state agencies and among the contractors who service them will suffer.

Loury, Glenn C., "How to Save Affirmative Action," *The New York Times,* Sept. 7, 1997, p. 17.

The Clinton administration's reversal of position on a case that could be one of the most important in the Supreme Court's coming term has disappointed supporters of affirmative action. But given the tenor of the court's recent decisions on racial preferences, the administration has made a smart strategic move to preserve what can and should be saved of affirmative action. The case concerns the decision of the Piscataway, N.J., school board to promote racial diversity by laying off a white teacher so that it could preserve the job of an equally qualified black teacher.

Mauro, Tony, "Possible shift in affirmative action White House urged to take a new stance," *USA Today,* June 5, 1997, p. A3.

The Justice Department is recommending a potentially controversial shift in the Clinton administration's stance on a closely watched affirmative action case before the Supreme Court. The case, which has caused turmoil within the Clinton administration since 1994, was brought by a white New Jersey teacher who was laid off while a black teacher with equal seniority was retained in the interest of diversity. Before the lower courts, the administration sided with the Piscataway, N.J., school board's argument that promoting diversity justified giving the black teacher preference.

Page, Clarence, "Diversity Vs. Affirmative Action," *Chicago Tribune,* Aug. 27, 1997, p. 19.

When circumstances pressed President Clinton to declare his position on affirmative action, he embraced a classically Clintonian middle-ground position. On August 14, the Clinton administration announced that it is considering a proposal to make it easier for white-owned businesses to qualify for government contracts that originally were set aside for businesses owned by racial and ethnic minorities. The small business set-aside program was conceived like other affirmative action programs in the 1960s to help black-owned businesses develop and create jobs. But, it didn't take long for various administrations to expand the program's definition of "small/disadvantaged" businesses to include a list of racial and ethnic minorities too lengthy to detail here — plus whites, male and female, if they could make a showing of past bias.

Discrimination Lawsuits

Caudron, Shari, "Don't make Texaco's $175 million mistake," *Workforce,* March 1997, pp. 58-66.

The recent Texaco debacle involving secret tapes and the prejudiced attitudes of high-ranking officials demonstrates discrimination problems in the workplace. Discrimination is still widespread and costs companies millions. The right diversity strategy can help prevent dire financial consequences.

"Black hole," *The Economist,* Nov. 16, 1996, pp. 27-28.

Texaco is caught in the middle of the worst racial-discrimination scandal to hit corporate America for years. A $520 million discrimination lawsuit has resulted in the discovery of an audio tape recording made by Texaco officials.

Elsasser, Glen, and Judy Peres, "Supreme Court Is Asked to Ignore Appeal in Affirmative Action Case," *Chicago Tribune,* June 6, 1997, p. 4.

Backing off from a controversial affirmative action case, the Clinton administration urged the Supreme Court Thursday not to review a school board's layoff of a white teacher to preserve racial diversity on its high school faculty. Last August, a federal appeals court in Philadelphia ruled that the layoff of Sharon Taxman by the Piscataway, N.J., school board violated Title VII of the Civil Rights Act, which outlaws workplace discrimination based on race, gender, religion or national origin. The board then took the case to the high court.

Grimsley, Kirstin Downey, "Racial Bias Suit Stirs Debate at Bell Atlantic; Firm Says Its Workforce Is a 'Reflection of Society'," *The Washington Post,* May 26, 1997, p. A1.

Willie Bennett, a black 27-year veteran at Bell Atlantic Corp. in Pennsylvania, said the final straw came at a company party in 1995. His white co-workers showed him a video they made in which a white co-worker wearing an Afro wig pretended to be Bennett and was portrayed as getting his job because of his basketball-playing skills, he recalled. Derrick Williams, a 23-year employee at Bell Atlantic, said he is haunted by the memory of finding a fake and crudely racist job application in the copying machine at a company office. Both men said their supervisors did nothing when they complained. According to Bennett and Williams and the 124 Bell Atlantic workers who have joined them in a class-action racial discrimination lawsuit against the company, these incidents were not isolated events.

"OGJ newsletter," ***Oil & Gas Journal,*** **Nov. 18, 1996, pp. 2-4.**
Recent discrimination lawsuits against Texaco and Chevron, as well as controversial taped comments by Texaco executives, have brought major oil companies under closer scrutiny for hiring and promotion practices.

Diversity Consultants

Curtius, Mary, "Careers: Training Manual; Diversity Training; Finding the Right Fit; Before you engage a consultant to lead sessions for your employees, check out the person's background and methods," ***Los Angeles Times,*** **May 19, 1997, p. SS5.**
Stephen M. Paskoff and David Tulin are two sought-after trainers who speak highly of each other and who have occasionally shared a podium to lecture on workplace diversity and fair employment practices. Last August an article written by Paskoff, "Ending the Workplace Diversity Wars," appeared in the trade magazine *Training*. It lambasted diversity training for emphasizing differences among workers and leaving employers open to discrimination lawsuits. Perhaps not surprisingly, the article ignited a controversy. Among the critics was Tulin, head of Philadelphia-based Tulin DiversiTeam Associates, who complained in a letter to *Training's* editor that Paskoff's article "bashes diversity training through stereotypes and extreme examples."

"March of time yields little progress for many blacks," ***USA Today,*** **Nov. 25, 1996, p. B3.**
Diversity consultant Michele Synegal offers statistics involving race relations in the U.S. workplace.

Van Eron, Ann M., "How to work with a diversity consultant," ***Training & Development,*** **April 1996, pp. 41-44.**
Organizations embarking on a diversity initiative will find a diversity consultant to be invaluable. Tips on finding the best qualified diversity consultant for a company's needs are discussed.

Diversity Programs

Barnes, Patricia G., "Full-service career tracks," ***ABA Journal,*** **February 1997, pp. 1-21.**
There has been a rash of high-profile cases in which employers faced potentially incapacitating publicity and staggering liability for alleged race and sex discrimination, despite some efforts to encourage equal opportunity. The cases show that diversity training or even "tough" anti-discrimination policies may not be enough to avoid liability if there is little or no follow-through. It's all in the mix, say industry 'diversity' programs.

Bruner, Richard W., "It's all in the mix, say industry 'diversity' programs," ***Electronic News,*** **July 21, 1997, p. 50.**
Today, "diversity programs" are widespread in the electronics industry. Many corporations feel compelled to deal with diversity issues because they are trying to stay alive and survive.

Caudron, Shari, and Cassandra Hayes, "Are diversity programs benefiting African Americans?" ***Black Enterprise,*** **February 1997, pp. 121-132.**
Caudron and Hayes discuss whether workplace diversity programs benefit African-Americans. The diversity initiatives at Johnson Wax, Texas Instruments, Ameritech and the Teachers Insurance and Annuity Association-College Retirement Equity Fund are examined.

Hollister, Kathryn L., and Diane E. Hodgson, "Diversity training: Accepting the challenge." ***Parks & Recreation,*** **July 1996, pp. 18-27.**
Hollister and Hodgson review diversity issues that have been addressed or suggested by park and recreation organizations and discuss diversity training from a specialist perspective.

Sixel, L. M., "Sincerity needed for diversity," ***Houston Chronicle,*** **Dec. 17, 1996, p. C1.**
A look is taken at the effectiveness of diversity training programs in the workplace . Experts say that too often, executives adopt diversity statements but still don't promote women and minorities to powerful positions.

Wallace, Paul E. Jr., Charles M. Ermer and Dimakatso Motshabi, "Managing diversity: A senior management perspective," ***Hospital & Health Services Administration,*** **spring 1996, pp. 91-104.**
Wallace et al examine the manner in which diversity management is perceived and implemented by hospital executives. To determine the perception of executives, a 16-item questionnaire was developed and distributed to hospital executives.

Fostering Diversity

Kluge, Holger "Reflections on diversity: Cultural as-

sumptions," ***Vital Speeches of the Day,*** **Jan. 1, 1997, pp. 171-175.**

In a speech, Kluge, the president of Personal & Commercial Bank CIBC, discusses workplace diversity and the desire by CIBC to weave diversity into every aspect of its business and other topics.

Pyatt, Rudolph A. Jr., "At Washington Gas, Diversity Is the Rule, Not the Exception," ***The Washington Post,*** **Jan. 13, 1997, Sec. WBIZ, p. 3.**

Pyatt comments on the diversity of the work force at Washington Gas Light Co.

Schwab, Robert, "Some firms stick with diversity," ***The Denver Post,*** **Aug. 31, 1997, p. I1.**

U.S. West for many years has enjoyed a reputation among minority groups in Denver, Colo., as a company that fosters diversity within its work force and among the contractors who sell it hundreds of millions of dollars worth of goods and services. Last October, Harriet Michel, the president of the National Minority Supplier Development Council, which certifies minority-owned firms for large corporations, said that corporations in Denver are far ahead of politicians in responding to the increasing percentages of ethnic minorities in the general population.

Minorities in the Work Force

Adams, Michael, "Selling out," ***Sales & Marketing Management,*** **October 1996, pp. 78-88.**

Many homosexuals in sales are still in the closet, but whether they are too cautious or not is debatable. Gays and bisexuals in sales and marketing and the atmosphere in an office environment are discussed.

Cose, Ellis, "Color blind," ***Newsweek,*** **Nov. 25, 1996, pp. 51-53.**

An excerpt from the book *Color-Blind* discusses the widespread frustration that minorities still encounter in the workplace. The cause lies less in so-called diversity programs than in the tendency to judge minority group members more by color than by ability.

Goldfield, Michael, "Race and labor organization in the United States," ***Monthly Review,*** **July 1997, pp. 80-97**

The role of race and race relations in U.S. labor history and the contemporary U.S. labor movement is examined.

Karambayya, Rekha, "In shouts and whispers: Paradoxes facing women of colour in organizations," ***Journal of Business Ethics,*** **June 1997, pp. 891-897.**

Karambayya draws attention to issues of race and gender and their intersections, focusing on the implications of a paradoxical perspective for research.

Lucas, Allison, "Race matters," ***Sales & Marketing Management,*** **September 1996, pp. 50-62.**

On the national average, there are only three or four African-American sales reps out of every 100, and they are not getting a fair chance in sales because of racism. The difficulties African-Americans have in succeeding in the sales profession and the obstacles they face are discussed.

Shuter, Robert, and Lynn H. Turner, "African American and European American women in the workplace," ***Management Communication Quarterly,*** **August 1997, pp. 74-96.**

A study indicates that European-American women are seen by others as more conflict avoidant in the workplace than African-American women .

Women in the Work Force

Engoron, Fran, "Price Waterhouse: Initiatives for retaining women," ***HR Focus,*** **August 1997, pp. 9-10.**

Price Waterhouse has established a three-pronged approach to create a more flexible, supportive and opportunistic work environment, and this model is expected to help retain women that are employed there.

Falkenberg, L. E., and L. Boland, "Eliminating the barriers to employment equity in the Canadian workplace," ***Journal of Business Ethics,*** **June 1997, pp. 963-975.**

It is argued that employment equity programs have not achieved the goal of equity for women in the workplace because gender stereotypes still persist.

Morris, Betsy, "If women ran the world, it would look a lot like Avon," ***Fortune,*** **July 21, 1997, pp. 74-79.**

In a beauty contest unlike any other, four of the six candidates for the next CEO of Avon Products are women. Avon CEO Jim Preston set up the succession race.

"Reports from around the world: USA," ***Women's International Network News,*** **winter 1996, pp. 72-76.**

The status of women in the U.S. is examined. Affirmative action is very important to women, as is doing away with sex discrimination.

Ruhe, John A., and William R. Allen, "Preparing women for careers in international management," ***Journal of Education for Business,*** **May 1997, pp. 278-282.**

Ruhe and Allen report the results of a survey of international companies identified by *Business Week* magazine as the best companies for women.

Walsh-Childers, Kim, Jean Chance and Kristin Herzog, "Women journalists report discrimination in newsrooms," ***Newspaper Research Journal,*** **summer 1996, pp. 68-87.**

Walsh-Childers et al attempted to discover the extent and types of sex discrimination U.S. newswomen believe they experience.

Back Issues

Great Research on Current Issues Starts Right Here . . . Recent topics covered by The CQ Researcher are listed below. Before May 1991, reports were published under the name of Editorial Research Reports.

APRIL 1996
Centennial Olympic Games
Managed Care
Protecting Endangered Species
New Military Culture

MAY 1996
Russia's Political Future
Marriage and Divorce
Year-Round Schools
Taiwan, China and the U.S.

JUNE 1996
Rethinking NAFTA
First Ladies
Teaching Values
Labor Movement's Future

JULY 1996
Recovered-Memory Debate
Native Americans' Future
Crackdown on Sexual Harassment
Attack on Public Schools

AUGUST 1996
Fighting Over Animal Rights
Privatizing Government Services
Child Labor and Sweatshops
Cleaning Up Hazardous Wastes

Back issues are available for $5.00 (subscribers) or $10.00 (non-subscribers). Quantity discounts apply to orders over ten. To order, call Congressional Quarterly Customer Service at (202) 887-8621.

Binders are available for $18.00. To order call 1-800-638-1710. Please refer to stock number 648.

SEPTEMBER 1996
Gambling Under Attack
The States and Federalism
Civic Journalism
Reassessing Foreign Aid

OCTOBER 1996
Political Consultants
Insurance Fraud
Rethinking School Integration
Parental Rights

NOVEMBER 1996
Global Warming
Clashing Over Copyright
Consumer Debt
Governing Washington, D.C.

DECEMBER 1996
Welfare, Work and the States
The New Volunteerism
Implementing the Disabilities Act
America's Pampered Pets

JANUARY 1997
Combating Scientific Misconduct
Restructuring the Electric Industry
The New Immigrants
Chemical and Biological Weapons

FEBRUARY 1997
Assisting Refugees
Alternative Medicine's Next Phase
Independent Counsels
Feminism's Future

MARCH 1997
New Air Quality Standards
Alcohol Advertising
Civic Renewal
Educating Gifted Students

APRIL 1997
Declining Crime Rates
The FBI Under Fire
Gender Equity in Sports
Space Program's Future

MAY 1997
The Stock Market
The Cloning Controversy
Expanding NATO
The Future of Libraries

JUNE 1997
FDA Reform
China After Deng
Line-Item Veto
Breast Cancer

JULY 1997
Transportation Policy
Executive Pay
School Choice Debate
Aggressive Driving

AUGUST 1997
Age Discrimination
Banning Land Mines
Children's Television
Evolution vs. Creationism

SEPTEMBER 1997
Caring for the Dying
Mental Health Policy
Mexico's Future
Youth Fitness

OCTOBER 1997
Urban Sprawl in the West

Future Topics

- ***Teacher Education***
- ***Part-time Employment***
- ***Renewable Energy***

THE CQ Researcher

PUBLISHED BY CONGRESSIONAL QUARTERLY INC.

Teacher Education

Should school reform focus on teachers?

An influential report last year presented a blistering indictment of public education in America, especially the quality of teacher training. The National Commission on Teaching & America's Future said bold steps are needed to professionalize the nation's 2.7 million public school educators. Supporters of that view, including lawmakers, education experts and national teachers' unions, are pushing initiatives ranging from toughening licensing standards to eliminating poorly performing teachers. Advocates hail the new emphasis on teaching as unique in the long history of attempted education reforms. But some skeptics say that reforming teaching without making more fundamental changes in the nation's public schools won't accomplish nearly enough. Others question where the funding would come from.

INSIDE THIS ISSUE

CQ Oct. 17, 1997 • Volume 7, No. 39 • Pages 913-936

Formerly Editorial Research Reports

THE ISSUES

BACKGROUND

CURRENT SITUATION

OUTLOOK

SIDEBARS AND GRAPHICS

FOR FURTHER RESEARCH

COVER: NATIONAL EDUCATION ASSOCIATION

October 17, 1997
Volume 7, No. 39

EDITOR
Sandra Stencel

MANAGING EDITOR
Thomas J. Colin

ASSOCIATE EDITOR
Sarah M. Magner

STAFF WRITERS
Charles S. Clark
Mary H. Cooper
Sarah Glazer
Kenneth Jost
David Masci

EDITORIAL ASSISTANT
Vanessa E. Furlong

PUBLISHED BY
Congressional Quarterly Inc.

CHAIRMAN
Andrew Barnes

VICE CHAIRMAN
Andrew P. Corty

PRESIDENT AND PUBLISHER
Robert W. Merry

EXECUTIVE EDITOR
David Rapp

The CQ Researcher (ISSN 1056-2036). Formerly Editorial Research Reports. Published weekly, except Jan. 3, May 30, Aug. 29, Oct. 31, by Congressional Quarterly Inc., 1414 22nd St., N.W., Washington, D.C. 20037. Annual subscription rate for libraries, businesses and government is $340. Additional rates furnished upon request. Periodicals postage paid at Washington, D.C., and additional mailing offices. POSTMASTER: Send address changes to The CQ Researcher, 1414 22nd St., N.W., Washington, D.C. 20037.

By Thomas J. Billitteri

The Issues

Kay Shrewsbery, a 26-year veteran of the Toledo public schools, always considered herself a good teacher. Now she has the credentials to prove it.

Last year, Shrewsbery became the first board-certified elementary school teacher in Ohio, a distinction once reserved for physicians and other highly skilled professionals. After months of evaluations by her peers — including a critique of her teaching — Shrewsbery was designated as an "accomplished" teacher by the National Board for Professional Teaching Standards.

"Teachers get a bad rap," Shrewsbery says. "It was a chance for me to demonstrate that there are people in the teaching profession who are intellectually competent and excellent at what they do."

Certification, which in Ohio entitles Shrewsbery to an annual $2,500 salary bonus for 10 years, is part of a constellation of reforms aimed at reinvigorating and professionalizing the nation's 2.7 million public school teachers. Besides board certification, innovations include rigorous proficiency tests for new teachers, peer review of classroom veterans and new approaches to teacher training.

"A quiet revolution has been occurring within the ranks of the teaching profession," says Arthur Wise, president of the National Council for Accreditation of Teacher Education (NCATE). "There has never been a reform effort of this nature before."

In the past, Wise says, reformers focused "on schools, curriculum, technology, decentralization, vouchers, and so forth. But these were all efforts to improve education despite the teacher. This movement says we will only improve education if we improve the teaching force." [1]

Linda Darling-Hammond, a professor at Columbia University's Teachers College in New York, agrees. "What distinguishes the era we're in now is that there are really dramatic, radical reforms of the teaching profession going on."

That includes an unprecedented vow of cooperation from teachers' unions.

For the first time, the 2.3-million-member National Education Association (NEA) this year endorsed peer review — what many see as a challenge to the hoary tradition of tenure. To the chagrin of unbending unionists, NEA President Bob Chase also advocated a "new unionism" in which teachers would play a collaborative role with school administrators in improving public education.

At the rival American Federation of Teachers (AFT), President Sandra Feldman says she recently called on her union "to get out front in closing down failing schools." "When you've got failing schools," Feldman says, "teachers and very often parents still rebel" when you propose to close them. "I have stood in front of faculties [at failing schools] and taken a lot of lumps."

Feldman says the AFT also vows to increase its support of peer review. "Teachers do not want incompetent people working with them," she says.

The tide of reformist sentiment has induced a measure of skepticism. Some observers fear that rigorous competency standards will create teacher shortages. Others wonder where the money for reforms will come from. [2] Still others question the motives of the unions, saying they are more concerned with survival than improvement. And many observers point to the long history of attempted education reforms and caution against moving too fast.

"One thing we all have to guard against is not to go for simple answers," says Thomas F. Warren, chairman of the Department of Education at Beloit College in Wisconsin and president-elect of the Association of Independent Liberal Arts Colleges for Teacher Education. "Obviously, education has a history of leaping on the bandwagon," sometimes in "blatantly farcical" ways. "We're talking about complicated issues. . . . How can we both be sensitive to what the past has taught us and to what's new?"

Yet many activists say it's time to take some bold steps into the future. The first move, they argue, is to bring strict professional standards to teaching. "Educators in this country are working in a system that is dysfunctional," Darling-Hammond argues. "We've got to look at how to transform that system."

Darling-Hammond was the primary author of a landmark report last September — "What Matters Most: Teaching for America's Future" — that presented a blistering indictment of American public education — especially teacher training. [3]

Many New Teachers Are Unlicensed

More than a quarter of the new public school teachers hired in 1990 were not fully licensed.

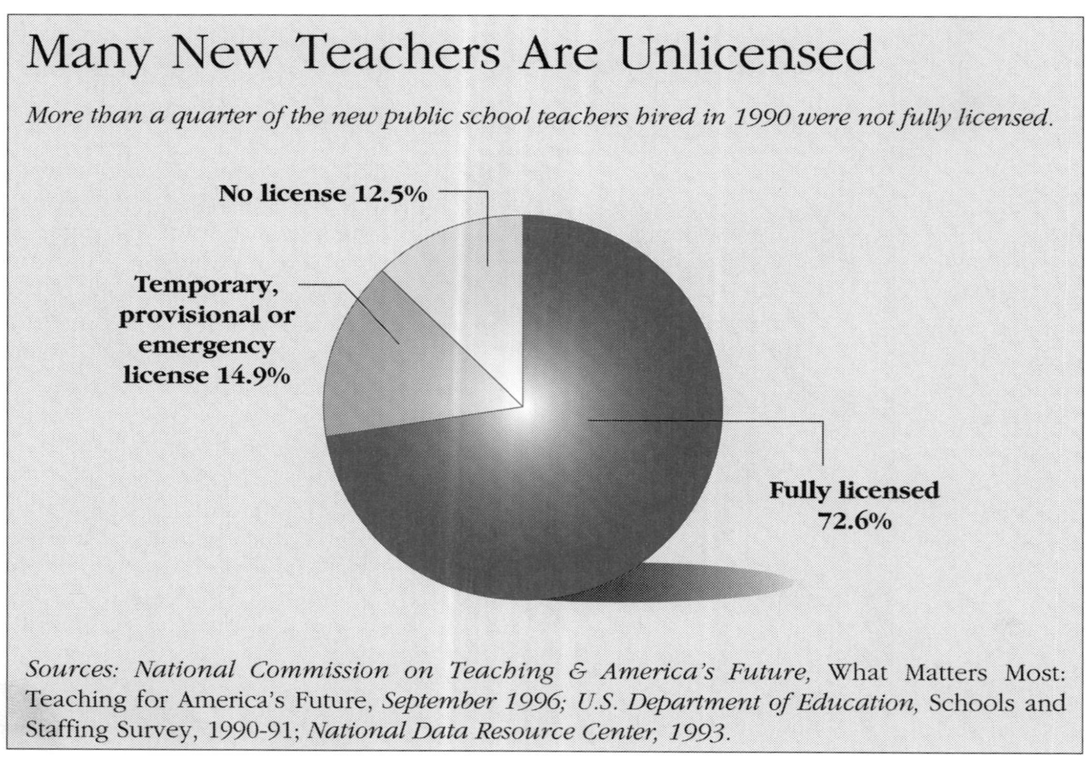

Sources: National Commission on Teaching & America's Future, What Matters Most: Teaching for America's Future, *September 1996; U.S. Department of Education,* Schools and Staffing Survey, 1990-91; *National Data Resource Center, 1993.*

"Although no state will allow a person to write wills, practice medicine, fix plumbing or style hair without completing training and passing an examination, more than 40 states allow school districts to hire teachers who have not met these basic requirements," declares the report from the National Commission on Teaching & America's Future.[4]

Among the commission's findings:

- More than 25 percent of new public school teachers in 1991 were either untrained or had not fully met state standards.
- Almost one-fourth of secondary teachers — and more than 30 percent of math teachers — lack even a minor in their main teaching field.
- More than half of the high school students taking the physical sciences are taught by teachers without a minor or major in the subject, as are 27 percent of math students.
- Students in schools with high minority enrollments have less than a 50-50 chance of getting science or math teachers with a degree or a license in the field they teach.

In fact, the report notes that only 500 of the nation's 1,300 schools of education are accredited. * "Although some schools of education provide high-quality preparation, others are treated as 'cash cows' by their universities, bringing in revenues that are spent on the education of doctors, lawyers and accountants rather than on their own students."[5]

Advocates of teacher reform say the commission's findings are all the more compelling when read against the backdrop of the "baby-boom echo" — the surge of new pupils whose parents were born after World War II.

* Most states do not require schools of education to be accredited, and several major education schools have not sought accreditation, including Columbia University Teachers' College in New York City.

Over the next decade, the commission noted, more than 2 million new teachers will be needed, and they will account for more than half of the nation's teaching force in 2006.

What is required to shore up American teaching, the commission said, is nothing short of a radical reformation of the education establishment, including:

- tougher standards for colleges of education;
- strict licensing standards for new teachers;
- rigorous procedures to certify "accomplished" teachers;
- innovative clinical experience for beginning and experienced teachers; and
- peer review to weed out poor performers.

"We pay teachers substantially less than any other college-educated worker, and we educate them unevenly," says Darling-Hammond, who serves as the commission's executive director. "Then we hope to control them with textbooks and training developed outside the classroom, and we rely on a huge administrative infrastructure to regulate teachers because we don't trust them to make good decisions."

Many of the commission's proposals already are being implemented. A dozen states have independent boards to set standards for teacher licensing and education. At least 20 states have — or are planning — mentoring programs for new teachers.

And there are signs that toughening standards for teachers can get results, as the Connetquot school district in Long Island's Suffolk County recently discovered. When it gave applicants for teaching jobs a reading-comprehension test designed for high school juniors, only one-fourth of the applicants answered at least 40 of the 50 questions correctly. [6]

Yet the reforms occurring nationwide are piecemeal and vulnerable to budget pressures and bureaucratic shakeups. And in many locales, school officials are struggling simply to find enough teachers — classroom veterans or not. In Texas, schools must accommodate 80,000 new students in each of the next three years.

While much of the ongoing debate over teacher training focuses on practical questions — training regimens, certification standards and so on — the climate of reform also raises difficult ideological questions. For example, is teaching indeed "what matters most" in public school reform, as the title of the commission report suggests? Or should policy-makers pursue more fundamental changes in public education?

Many conservative policy analysts argue that mandating training and testing standards for teachers will take education reforms only so far. More important, they argue, is changing the very nature of schooling through such options as government-funded vouchers, charter schools and other mechanisms of parental "choice." [7]

"Standards play a role," says John Berthoud, president of the National Taxpayers Union in Alexandria, Va. "But the danger I see is that these kinds of reforms can be a distraction from much more profound changes that should be happening in our schools."

Chester E. Finn Jr., a senior fellow at the conservative Hudson Institute, is skeptical of reports like "What Matters Most."

"It's like the dairy industry telling us we should drink more milk," he says of the report's heavy input from educators. "I don't give a damn about teacher performance unless it leads to student performance."

Wilmer S. Cody, Kentucky's commissioner of education, says focusing on teacher preparation and training is important, but that "those looking for a silver bullet are going to be disappointed if that's the only thing they work on." Equally important, he says, are such issues as the culture of school systems and administrative policies. Good teachers can be worn down "very quickly by a bad school environment," he warns.

Still, the appetite for teacher reform is growing keener across the nation. President Clinton recently announced a new effort to attract teachers to tough urban settings. And he backs federal funding support for the National Board for Professional Teaching Standards. Meanwhile, legislation to enhance teacher professionalization is percolating on Capitol Hill.

As education-reform efforts increasingly focus on teachers, here are some of the key questions being asked:

Will rigorous standards lead to a teacher shortage?

Every year as summer comes to an end, school administrators across the country scramble to find enough teachers.

The Department of Education predicted a record public and private school enrollment of 52 million students in fall 1996 — and 54.3 million by 2007. In the West, public school enrollment will climb 17 percent, more than double the national average.

Under such circumstances, it might seem that raising teacher-performance standards will only exacerbate the teacher shortage. But many experts argue that elevating standards will ultimately attract more teachers, and improve student performance in the process. Some advocates see the need for new teachers as a golden opportunity to infuse the profession with a new crop of well-trained, highly motivated educators.

"We have a shortage of qualified teachers now, so I don't think raising standards will exacerbate the problem of finding good teachers," says Marilyn Scannell, executive director of the Indiana Professional Standards Board. "I know people usually associate raising teacher standards with shortages, but part of our problem is credibility for the profession anyway."

"What's the alternative? Lower the standards?" asks Timothy J. Dyer, executive director of the National Association of Secondary School Principals. "We can't do that. The bait has to shift to a reward system. What does industry do when it can't find people?"

In the late 1980s, Connecticut raised teacher salaries but also imposed rigorous new competency standards on beginning teachers. Even so, there have been no shortages in Connecticut, says Raymond Pecheone, the state's curriculum and teacher standards chief. Connecticut's higher-than-average teacher salaries no doubt have helped, as has its mentoring program for young teachers. But Pecheone credits the state's strict expectations with attracting teaching talent. "If you raise the standards and are very clear," he says, "it's more of a magnet."

On the other hand, lowering the bar can have serious policy and cultural consequences, notes Michigan State University education professor David F. Labaree. The need for teachers is so acute that, "Approximately one in every five college graduates every year must enter teaching in order to fill all the available vacancies," he notes. "If education schools do not prepare enough teacher candidates, state legislators are happy to authorize alternative routes into the profession . . . and school boards are quite willing to hire such prospects in order to place

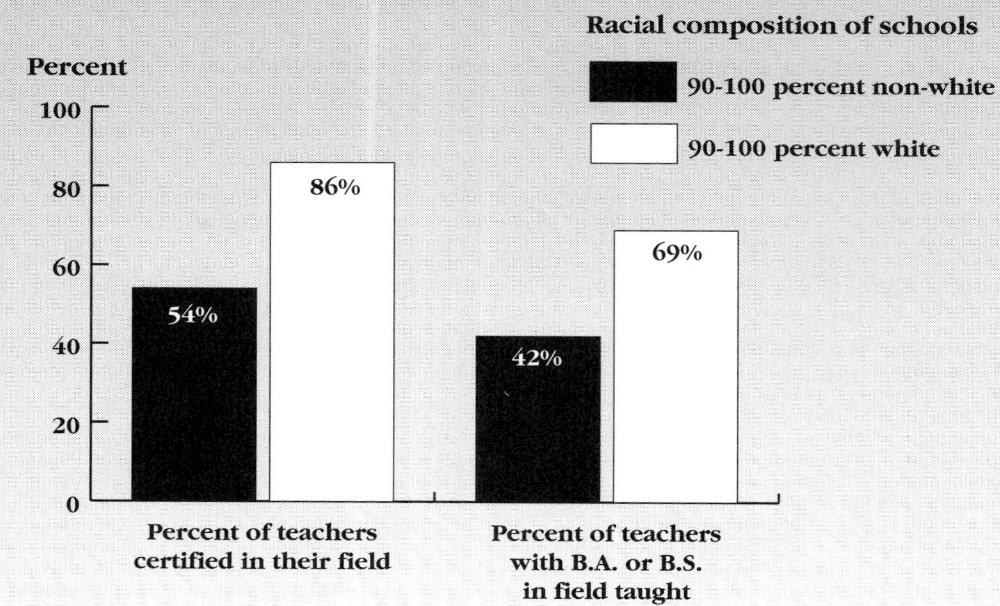

Sources: National Commission on Teaching & America's Future, What Matters Most: Teaching for America's Future, *September 1996; Jeannie Oakes,* Multiplying Inequalities: The Effects of Race, Social Class, and Tracking on Opportunities to Learn Mathematics and Science, *RAND Corp., 1990.*

warm bodies in empty classrooms." [8]

According to "What Matters Most," more than 12 percent of all newly hired teachers are untrained, and another 14 percent enter the profession without having fully met state standards. "Our schools' most closely held secret amounts to a great national shame," the report said. "Without telling parents they are doing so, many districts hire unqualified people as 'teachers' and assign them full responsibility for children." [9]

Of course, a dearth of qualified teachers can occur for a variety of reasons, especially in rural and small-town school districts. Dyer tells of a principal in the Midwest who had no one to teach Spanish last summer and wound up hiring a Spanish-speaking resident with no formal teaching experience. "You've got to get someone in that room when the door opens the day after Labor Day," Dyer says. "To say a principal isn't picking good people — well, you can't pick apples off a maple tree."

Hiring unqualified teachers can be "a function of genuine shortages in fields of short supply," "What Matters Most" acknowledges. But, the report adds, such decisions often result from "shortsighted hiring procedures, administrative convenience, efforts to save on teacher costs in favor of more 'important' areas and plain old-fashioned patronage." [10]

In California last year, serious classroom overcrowding prompted lawmakers to give financial incentives to schools that cut class sizes in lower grades. [11] The $1.5 billion program brought swift results. By this fall, nearly every public elementary school in California had reduced classes to 20 or fewer pupils in at least one or two early grades. But as schools have trimmed class size, they've had to hire more teachers — leading to a shortage of qualified candidates. A fifth of the candidates for new teaching slots do not have appropriate teaching credentials, and many are beginners with little or no classroom experience. [12]

The state has taken steps to ameliorate its shortage of competent teachers, including allowing retired teachers to return to the classroom for up to three years without sacrificing their retirement benefits. But that's done little to assuage critics, who see in California a rich example of the danger of pursuing reform before laying the proper groundwork.

"As a parent and as a taxpayer, I applaud California's effort to reduce classroom size, but frankly I am deeply troubled by the extent to which the state has compromised standards for teacher quality to meet this goal," says Rep. George Miller, D-Calif. He has sponsored a bill that would make it easier for parents to know the qualifications of their children's teachers. "Recruiting, preparing and supporting competent and qualified teachers is the single most important thing we can do to ensure that all students achieve to the utmost of their abilities."

Darling-Hammond contends that California policy-makers did not think enough about reorganizing the schools to lure back teachers who had fled the classroom for non-teaching posts. "Like other states, probably half the certified teachers in California are in non-teaching jobs in the school system," she says. True, she acknowledges, "the way we structure teaching is so grueling that many people do look longingly at the possibility of becoming specialists, or guidance counselors so they can see one student at a time." But in a restructured environment, "teaching can become interesting, enjoyable work again."

Stung by criticism, especially in wealthy areas such as Orange County near Los Angeles, California now is recruiting widely and enhancing teacher-training efforts, Darling-Hammond notes. "Maybe sometimes it takes a crisis to get the public's attention," she says.

If California raises troubling questions about the methods of reform, one thing is certain: Maintaining low standards is no guarantee of a surplus of teachers.

Consider Texas, where 12 percent of newly hired teachers were uncertified in their main subject area in 1990-91.[13] Yet this past summer, Texas was among the states facing a severe shortage of teachers. Up to 10,000 teaching posts throughout the state remained vacant in August, and some school districts had "all but given up trying to find accredited teachers," according to National Public Radio (NPR).[14]

Some argue that improving benefits and pay would go a long way toward solving Texas' teacher shortage. But Cindy Clegg, director of personnel services at the Texas Association of School Boards, told NPR the solution isn't that simple. Teachers need to have a career path that keeps them in the classroom while they advance in both pay and status, she said. "We could also compensate teachers differently for advanced skills and knowledge, advanced degrees and multiple certifications," she said.

Right now in Texas, she said, "the only career path is out of the classroom."

Does teacher training need to be radically overhauled?

To advocates of education reform, one of the most pernicious popular myths is that "anyone can teach." Meeting the challenges of the classroom takes not only caring and charisma, they argue, but also rigorous training in pedagogy — the art and science of teaching — plus expertise in the subjects being taught and plenty of "professional development" throughout a teacher's career.

Yet critics claim that many schools of education do a poor job of training aspiring teachers.

The National Commission on Teaching & America's Future faulted traditional teacher training on a number of counts. (*See box, p. 920.*) "Until recently," the report states, "most teacher-education programs taught theory separately from application. Teachers were taught to teach in lecture halls from texts, and [by] teachers who frequently had not themselves ever practiced what they were teaching. Students' courses on subject matter were disconnected from their courses on teaching methods, which were in turn disconnected from their courses on learning and development. . . . When they entered their own classrooms, they could remember and apply little of what they had learned by reading in isolation from practice. Thus, they reverted to what they knew best: the way they themselves had been taught."[15]

There is also the widespread perception that education schools no longer attract the best and brightest students. "What Matters Most" seeks to rebut that notion, but clearly many other good students are indeed gravitating to better-paying or more prestigious fields.

Student test scores in Massachusetts tend to perpetuate the perception that the good ones get away. State lawmakers in 1993 agreed to help pay off the college loans of aspiring teachers — if they graduated in the top 25 percent of their class. But in Massachusetts, most new teachers graduate at the bottom half of their high school and college classes.[16]

While criticism of education schools isn't new, it has reached a crescendo lately. In 1995, the deans of 100 top education schools, as part of a decade-long education-reform initiative known as the Holmes Group, lambasted their own institutions. Putting on what they called "the hair shirt of self-criticism," they said that education schools strive so much for academic prestige and credibility within the university that they ignore the real-world needs of teachers and pupils. Schools of education must change "or surrender their franchise," the deans declared.[17]

Moreover, the deans said that many education professors make "hardly a nod toward the public schools, seldom if ever deigning to cross the thresholds of those 'lowly' places. Such attitudes transmit an unmistakable message: The people most intimately responsible for children's learning in elementary and secondary schools are not sufficiently valued by the education school. Schoolteachers and young learners, who should be the focus of the education school's concern, are kept at arm's length. They are a sideshow

What's Wrong With Teacher Training

In its landmark 1996 report, What Matters Most: Teaching for America's Future, *The National Commission on Teaching & America's Future called for dramatic changes in teacher recruitment, preparation and professional development. The report faulted traditional teacher training on a number of counts, including:*

- *inadequate time devoted to mastering core subject matter, child-development and learning theory and effective teaching strategies;*
- *fragmentation of education coursework and practice teaching;*
- *"uninspired teaching methods" within education schools themselves;*
- *"superficial" education-school curriculum; and,*
- *failure to train aspiring teachers to work in teams and use technology in the classroom.*

to the performance in the center ring, where professors carry out their work insulated from the messiness and hurly-burly of elementary and secondary education." [18]

To improve teacher training, the National Commission on Teaching & America's Future proposed linking the practical with the theoretical in schools of education. It also recommended that poorly performing education schools be shut down and that universities and local school districts join forces to expand the number of "professional development schools" for training beginning and veteran teachers.

When it comes to accreditation, the National Commission on Teaching & America's Future says every education school should have NCATE's imprimatur or be closed by 2006. "On college campuses, all professional schools are expected to be accredited — except for education," Wise says. "Colleges of education charge the same tuition as the rest of the university, and when you look at how much is spent in the college of education vs. other disciplines, you find out education students are supporting the education of doctors, business people, lawyers and others."

Yet many education-school deans disagree that accreditation is crucial, and some resist it, sometimes because of NCATE itself. When Drake University withdrew from NCATE's accreditation process in 1992, university officials said it was expensive, unwieldy and concentrated on the structure of teacher-training programs rather than the quality of graduates. Wise concedes NCATE's process is "paper-intensive" but "so is accreditation in every other field."

Dissatisfaction with NCATE has spawned a rival accrediting organization — the Teacher Education Accreditation Council. Marilyn J. Guy, assistant dean for faculty life at Concordia College in Moorhead, Minn., says the group is looking at new ways to accredit education schools to enhance their accountability. One aim is to "encourage differences and diversity" among education schools rather than a uniform standard of teacher training. The new group will focus on "what students learn and what they're able to do as a result of a program of higher education."

There also is debate about the value of professional development schools — lab schools where beginning teachers spend a semester or two with pupils, veteran teachers coach the neophytes and upgrade their own skills and education professors work as mentors and conduct real-world research.

Advocates argue that without such programs, many teachers would get minimal mid-career training — perhaps an occasional one- or two-day seminar conducted by outside "experts" hired by the school district, but little else. Much of what passes for teacher professional development is a "joke," argues "What Matters Most."

Yet some education scholars hesitate to embrace professional development schools, calling them expensive and unproven. To Andy Hargreaves, director of the International Center for Educational Change at the University of Toronto, they're "the EPCOT Centers of educational change. Not in all cases, but in some, [proponents] find a little jewel on which they can focus their innovative energies. By saying they have this school in this place, they've solved the problem of teacher education."

Hargreaves favors partnerships between a university education department and an entire school district, or even several neighboring districts, as a way of involving professors in the full range of challenges facing public schools. The University of Toronto's education school participates in such an arrangement. In the United States, however, some professional develop-

Teacher Quality Varies Widely Around the Nation

At least 10 percent of the newly hired teachers in 1996 were unlicensed in nearly a quarter of the states. And in a majority of the states, at least 20 percent of the math teachers had neither a major nor a minor in math.

State	Unlicensed Hires	Out-of-Field Math Teaching
Alabama	9%	21%
Alaska	7%	63%
Arizona	2%	31%
Arkansas	9%	20%
California	13%	51%
Colorado	4%	35%
Connecticut	0%	11%
Delaware	0%	—
District of Columbia	53%	—
Florida	17%	39%
Georgia	7%	35%
Hawaii	10%	51%
Idaho	4%	25%
Illinois	8%	28%
Indiana	2%	30%
Iowa	2%	18%
Kansas	0%	13%
Kentucky	1%	17%
Louisiana	23%	31%
Maine	9%	33%
Maryland	29%	40%
Massachusetts	11%	37%
Michigan	4%	33%
Minnesota	0%	14%
Mississippi	9%	23%
Missouri	0%	15%
Montana	5%	14%
Nebraska	8%	26%
Nevada	7%	37%
New Hampshire	5%	—
New Jersey	0%	34%
New Mexico	8%	47%
New York	5%	34%
North Carolina	3%	24%
North Dakota	0%	21%
Ohio	0%	17%
Oklahoma	3%	34%
Oregon	2%	33%
Pennsylvania	0%	14%
Rhode Island	0%	—
South Carolina	14%	29%
South Dakota	3%	20%
Tennessee	0%	28%
Texas	12%	30%
Utah	10%	44%
Vermont	0%	—
Virginia	15%	34%
Washington	1%	46%
West Virginia	10%	16%
Wisconsin	0%	17%
Wyoming	3%	25%

Source: National Commission on Teaching & America's Future, What Matters Most: Teaching for America's Future, *September 1996.*

ment schools have tended to be less integral to a region's public education.

If the education community is divided on accreditation and professional development, it also differs on even more fundamental issues — such as whether reform efforts should focus on new-teacher training or on the performance of veterans.

"If you are reforming teacher education, the worst place to start is with [pre-employment] education," Hargreaves says. "Even when new teachers are prepared at a high level of skill, the sociological reality is that they will tend to adapt to whatever workplace they find themselves in. So you're losing a lot of investment in [pre-employment] training."

Besides, he says, "New teachers are a very small portion of the overall teacher population. So if you're looking to change the system by changing new teachers who enter it, it's a very, very slow change process."

Should tenure for teachers be eliminated?

Last summer, six teachers at Elsie Roberts High School in suburban Dallas handed out a math quiz that stirred a coast-to-coast storm of outrage. Presumably to make the quiz more appealing, they asked such questions as: "Rufus is pimping for three girls. If the price is $65 for each trick, how many tricks will each girl have to turn so Rufus can pay for his $800 per day crack habit?" [19]

While the teachers were all suspended without pay for at least 30 days, such episodes lead many critics to wonder whether public schools are willing — or able — to exert proper control over teachers.

Across the nation, state lawmakers, school administrators and even teachers' unions are studying ways to weed out bad teachers and put the laggards on notice that in the new climate of teacher reform, no job is guaranteed.

At the heart of the issue is the informal system of public school tenure, which traditionally has made it difficult, expensive and time-consuming to dismiss poor performers. "Basically now, the model is that after a few years, you're a teacher for life" unless a big removal effort is launched, Berthoud says. "In New York City, it took a year plus 100 days and $175,000-to remove a bad teacher. "With appeal costs, it was over $300,000."

Some conservative state lawmakers have moved to eliminate tenure, but with little success. It seems unlikely that tenure will be eliminated altogether, if for no other reason than the politically powerful teachers' unions continue to defend it. "The key purpose of tenure laws is to protect teachers' due-process rights — *not* to protect incompetent teachers from dismissal," declares the AFT.

Don Cameron, executive director of the NEA, says "tenure exists because traditionally teachers have been political pawns and have been dismissed unfairly for a whole lot of reasons. You don't have to go very far back in this country to find a time when teachers were dismissed because a spot had to be found for a school board member or a superintendent's relative or because 'men needed jobs more than women,' according to somebody."

Yet the unions' growing movement toward self-policing — most notably the NEA's new support of peer review for local NEA affiliates that want it — seems to signal a revision in the thinking about tenure. "There are lots of ways and means of getting rid of teachers once they're placed on tenure," Cameron says. "The problem is that it has taken too long for a whole variety of reasons, one of which is the role of the teachers' unions," including defending the rights of teachers to a hearing under the tenure laws.

"There are other things too — administrators who don't want to deal with these issues, and school districts that don't follow the process laid down in the law and end up with egg on their face."

Still, "If it's taking two or three years to get rid of somebody who's bad, that's an abuse of the system that all of us — school boards, administrators and teachers' unions — need to make sure doesn't happen."

Cameron is quick to differentiate between tenure reform and peer review, though he concedes the latter can be a first step toward ousting a poor performer. "Before any teacher is dismissed, we need to enter into a cooperative venture with school districts to try to help those teachers."

The AFT has supported peer review since the late 1970s, and a limited number of affiliates — including those in Toledo, Rochester, Cincinnati and New York City — have used it.

Some representatives of school management advocate an overhaul of tenure rules, and they are taking a wait-and-see stance on union peer review.

Anne Bryant, executive director of the National School Boards Association, argues that tenure should be a bargaining issue for local teachers' unions. Some locals "might come up with a variety of things they would prefer over tenure," she says.

Currently, however, "many state laws don't give flexibility to school districts to make it a bargaining issue," and that runs "counter to everything we say we want to be as a nation," Bryant says.

"It's pretty tough to hold teachers and superintendents and administrators accountable for raising student achievement when at the same time we limit that district's ability to get rid of poor teachers. "We would never say to business, 'Create a better car, but we're going to dictate the rules by which you hire, fire and discipline workers,' " she says.

Bryant welcomes the NEA's new support of peer assistance and review, but she warns, "The proof is in the pudding. When we say peer review, we have to have good evaluation measures, and teachers have to be really tough when it comes to evaluating each other. And that can be really hard."

Even groups that are solidly in the teachers' camp are approaching tenure and peer review with caution.

The attitude that "tenure is the problem" in American education is a "myth," according to "What Matters Most." In the view of the authors, "tenure is useful in protecting teachers from political hiring and firing," Darling-Hammond says.

But, she continues, "It should not be a cover for incompetent teachers."

Acknowledging the unions' highly visible embrace of peer review at a time when tenure is under fire, Darling-Hammond says: "I think for both of the unions this is a moment in history. If they can't make the idea of a professional union more than an oxymoron, they will have no claim to be part of the discourse about educational improvement. So they're biting the bullet." ■

BACKGROUND

Teacher Factories

Since the nation's beginnings, teaching typically has been a second-class occupation. Most teachers had minimal skills in reading, writing and arithmetic. It was common for a youngster to finish one grade

Continued on p. 925

Chronology

1800s ***As the nation's school systems grow, advocates press for better training of teachers.***

1839
Horace Mann establishes the first "normal" school, in Massachusetts, to train teachers.

1857
The National Teachers' Association, predecessor of the National Education Association (NEA), is founded to advocate for improved working conditions for teachers and "promote the cause of popular education."

1910s-1930s

Market demands force teachers' colleges to broaden their curriculum and ease standards to accommodate the growing number of students seeking a college education.

1916
American Federation of Teachers (AFT) is founded with the help of John Dewey. The organization's growth accelerates in the early 1960s after an affiliate becomes the bargaining agent for teachers in New York City.

1933
Although 85 percent of high school teachers have a bachelor of arts degree, only 10 percent of elementary school teachers do.

1960s ***Reform fever is fueled by concern over scientific advances of the Soviets and later by worries that American children are falling behind in basic learning skills. But competing ideologies stymie many efforts at meaningful reform.***

1963
James Koerner's *The Miseducation of American Teachers* is published.

1970s-1980s

Concern about education quality leads to new reforms.

1970s
California, Oregon and Minnesota become the first of a dozen states to create autonomous boards to control standards for teachers.

April 26, 1983
"A Nation at Risk," a report by the Education Department's National Commission on Excellence in Education, warns of a "rising tide of mediocrity" in American schools.

May 1986
The Carnegie Forum on Education and the Economy issues "A Nation Prepared: Teachers for the 21st Century," which helps launch a "second wave" of educational reform, with the intent of making teaching a full-fledged profession.

1986
The Holmes Group, an organization of deans from about 100 research-oriented education schools, issues the first of three reports, "Tomorrow's Teachers," arguing that education schools should take a scholarly, research-based approach to pedagogical study and that teaching should be professionalized, much like law or medicine.

1989
Governors gather in Charlottesville, Va., to launch America 2000, a plan for national education standards.

1990s ***State and federal policy-makers take an increasingly aggressive stance in setting standards for teachers and calling for the reshaping of teacher education.***

1990
In its second report, "Tomorrow's Schools," the Holmes Group advocates the formation of professional development schools.

1994
Congress passes Goals 2000 legislation launching a standards movement.

1995
The Holmes Group's third report, "Tomorrow's Schools of Education," says education schools should become more involved in local schools.

September 1996
National Commission on Teaching & America's Future issues report critical of teacher education, "What Matters Most: Teaching for America's Future."

July 1997
Delegates to the NEA's 135th annual meeting approve peer assistance and peer review in local affiliates that want it.

Introducing the New, Collaborative NEA

For decades, the National Education Association (NEA) has bargained collectively in the interests of public school teachers, often engaging in acrimonious brinkmanship with administrators who didn't want to budge on teacher salaries, working conditions and other labor issues.

The NEA will continue to represent teachers at the bargaining table. But now, adopting what NEA President Bob Chase calls a "new unionism," the NEA says it will seek a collaborative — rather than adversarial — relationship with management in decisions about school budgets, staffing and other issues.

"America's children desperately need an organization that cares about them, the quality of their education and the quality of their lives," Chase told the union's 135th annual meeting last summer. "NEA *is* that organization."

For many in the union, talk of a "new unionism" signals a move into unfamiliar — and controversial — territory.

"It's very scary," Don Cameron, the NEA's executive director, says of the new collaborative posture. "Bob Chase has really gone out on a limb."

Cameron says he believes that limb is "pointing in the right direction," but he acknowledges that many in the NEA don't feel that way. "There are many unionists within the NEA who don't believe we can be both professional and a union — that we can collaborate with administrators on the one hand and collectively bargain against them on the other."

The NEA, Cameron says, "has been focused inwardly for the last quarter-century. We devoted time and effort to members' needs, and we espoused and championed [issues] directly related to job protection and other union kinds of activities. To go into a totally different direction now, where we are facing outward, it means we have to change direction, programs, policies, our budget — that's scary because it's difficult. We are now turning outward and engaging the public and the world outside the NEA."

Cameron admits that "part of" the NEA's strategy is to shore up its bruised public image, made worse by a lashing from former GOP presidential candidate Bob Dole, who singled out the union in a speech to the 1996 Republican National Convention. "If education were a war," Dole said, referring to the NEA, "you would be losing it."

But overcoming a bad image isn't "the most important" impetus for the new union strategy, Cameron says. Rather, he says, it's a desire to help public education to "get better. If it was just a question of public relations, the NEA could go on another 25 years with a reputation that might not be totally positive but that is still successful with our members."

In a speech last February to the National Press Club, Chase said the NEA seeks to "reinvent" itself in as fundamental a way as it did in the 1960s, when it went from being a "rather quiet, genteel professional association of educators" to an "assertive" and sometimes "militant" labor union.

While defending the NEA's record, Chase said its gains "too often have been won through confrontation at the bargaining table or, in extreme cases, after bitter strikes. These industrial-style, adversarial tactics simply are not suited to the next state of school reform. It's time to create a new union, an association with an entirely new approach to our members, to our critics, and to our colleagues on the other side of the bargaining table. In some instances we have used our power to block uncomfortable changes — to protect the narrow interest of our members, and not to advance the interests of students and schools. We cannot go on denying responsibility for school quality. Too often, NEA has sat on the sidelines of change, nay-saying, quick to say what won't work and slow to say what will.

"A growing number of NEA teachers argue that it's not enough to cooperate with management on school reform. Quality must begin at home — within our own ranks. If a teacher is not measuring up in the classroom — to put it baldly, if there is a bad teacher in one of our schools — then *we* must do something about it."

The "new collaboration is not about sleeping with the enemy," Chase added.

"It is about waking up to our shared stake in reinvigorating the public education enterprise. It is about educating children better, more effectively, more ambitiously."

Sandra Feldman, president of the 940,000-member American Federation of Teachers (AFT), echoes Chase's sentiment that unions can be both labor advocate and engine of reform. "We have played the role of defense counsel" for teachers, she says, but "we don't see it as contradicting or precluding our ability to also be very involved in raising the quality issues."

The AFT, she says, has been a "new union for a very long time. We were sort of born that way, in a tradition of believing that the quality of education our members provide is part and parcel of [the other issues] we have to take care of."

Even so, no one is predicting that a familiar site in many communities — schoolteachers walking a picket line at bargaining time — will disappear from the American scene. Feldman says AFT locals have been in an "adversarial position much to often" in bargaining with school districts. But, she adds, that's happened "not because we wanted to but we had to fight to get basic dignity and decent economic security for our members. One thing people do not understand is that it takes two to tango."

Continued from p. 922
and teach it the next year.

By the early to mid-1800s, as the nation expanded, demand for public education grew stronger. Social reforms were erasing the tradition of indentured servitude, making formal education necessary to train young people for jobs. Not only that, some saw compulsory schooling as a way to curb juvenile delinquency, especially in impoverished urban areas.

As public education expanded, reformers began to press for improvements in teacher training. Horace Mann (1796-1859), a champion of free public education, fought for establishment of a state school to train teachers in Massachusetts. He also agitated for higher teacher salaries, curriculum revisions and acceptance of women teachers. Henry Barnard (1811-1900) took up similar causes in Rhode Island and Connecticut and also served as the nation's first commissioner of education.

"During the whole 19th century, there was a chronic shortage of teachers," says Labaree of Michigan State. Mann, Barnard and other reformers worried that teacher recruitment was little more than an exercise in "finding warm bodies to fill classrooms. Right at the very beginning [of public education] you see a tension that has never gone away — local school districts having to have somebody there on Sept. 1 and being willing to take someone even if they're unprepared."

In the mid-to-late 1800s, states built so-called "normal" schools at a rapid pace, conceiving of them as elite institutions whose sole mission was to educate young people for classroom careers. But soon, the schools became victims of their own success.

The problem with normal schools was that they turned out relatively few teachers, and as the demand for teachers grew, they soon were under pressure to increase their output. It wasn't long before the typical normal school was lowering its standards and becoming what Labaree calls a "teacher factory."

National Education Association

Many educators cite the increasing demand for new teachers as a primary reason why schools of education tend to function more as "teacher factories" than elite professional academies.

In the early 20th century, normal schools — then evolving into "teachers' colleges" — were feeling a new set of market demands. Growing numbers of young people, many raised in the city, saw college as a ticket to prosperity and decent employment. Yet many private or state institutions were expensive or remote. The teachers' colleges — accessible and cheap — presented an alternative. Soon, they were under new pressure to broaden their curriculum and admit students not headed for classroom work.

"Very soon, teachers' colleges were looking like regular liberal-arts colleges," Labaree says. One result, he writes, "was to reinforce the already-established tendency toward minimizing the extent and rigor of teacher education." [20]

The homogenizing and minimizing continued. By the 1930s many teachers' colleges had become state liberal arts colleges. By the 1960s and '70s, many of those had evolved into regional state universities, with science and humanities departments garnering more status and resources than education departments.

"In part, these [former teachers' colleges] may have acquired — and earned — their universal disrepute by successfully adapting themselves to all of the demands that we have placed on them," Labaree asserts. [21]

Today's education departments, the descendants of the normal schools and teachers' colleges, still produce the largest share of America's teachers. Yet the question remains: Why has teacher preparation been shunted to the margins of higher education when teaching itself remains one of the most important occupations in the nation?

One reason is the incessant demand for new teachers, which keeps many

Critics Warn Against Using Computers . . .

The computer software is called SuccessMaker, and it is designed to help elementary and middle-school students improve in basic skills such as math and reading. A growing number of school districts are using SuccessMaker, among them sprawling Fairfax County, in Northern Virginia.

But this past spring, Fairfax officials rejected a proposal to install SuccessMaker in all 45 elementary schools on the county's eastern side, which has a large number of children who need special help with schoolwork.

"Some Fairfax school administrators say they like the software but are concerned about its cost — about $55,000 to buy and install SuccessMaker in a lab with 10 computers," *The Washington Post* noted. "Other administrators question SuccessMaker's educational value. . . . Students can't interact with a computer as they could with a teacher, and schools should use computers to help students find and understand information rather than to teach basic skills, these educators contend." [1]

Along with the skeptics in Fairfax, a growing number of experts are concerned that schools are becoming too reliant on glitzy technology to replace the time-honored approach of one-on-one interaction between pupil and teacher.

"If computers make a difference, it has yet to show up in achievement," Samuel G. Sava, executive director of the National Association of Elementary School Principals, wrote in *The New York Times*. "What studies there are — many financed by computer companies — are not much help. In one New Jersey middle school, widely cited for raising achievement scores, the improvement occurred before computers were introduced and could be attributed to other changes: longer class periods, new books, after-school programs and an emphasis on student projects." [2]

Sava went on to note that in the 26-nation Third International Mathematics and Science Study this year, U.S. students were bested in math by fourth-graders from seven other countries. "Teachers in five of the seven countries reported that they 'never or almost never' have students use computers in class," Sava wrote.

To be sure, computerized learning has plenty of backing in education, policy and industry circles, to say nothing of voter support. President Clinton wants to connect every school to the information superhighway by the year 2000. "I want to get the children of America hooked on education through computers," he has said. [3] The Education Department wants one computer for every five students. [4]

Meanwhile, industry giants such as Microsoft and Oracle are speeding the move to technology, making big donations of hardware or software to computerize libraries and schools. And a survey this year by the Milken Foundation found that six in 10 registered voters would support a $100 increase in federal taxes to hasten the trend toward technology in schools. [5]

Computer advocates claim technology improves learning, enhances the competitiveness of young people entering the labor force, boosts business investment and interest in education and connects students to a global network of educators and research resources.

Yet traditionalists are calling for caution and moderation. Some say widespread computer use in schools will widen the gap between rich and poor because students in low-income regions don't always have the same access and cyber-skills as those in wealthier locales. And many say there is no proof that computers make a significant difference in learning, especially if teachers lack training in integrating technology into classroom activities.

education departments in the mode of teacher factories rather than elite professional academies. Another problem, critics say, is that because state universities receive funding based on enrollment, there is an incentive to pull as many students as possible into relatively low-cost programs — such as education schools — and use the surplus revenue for more prestigious departments like law and medicine.

What's more, while many education schools "would blow your socks off" with their "dedicated faculty and intellectual grounding," adequate federal commitment to teacher training is missing, argues David Imig, executive director of the American Association of Colleges for Teacher Education. "The thing we have lacked in teacher education is the kind of investment or capacity-building that all other professional schools have had."

Education schools also labor under stigmas that give teacher training a bad name. One such stigma is that unlike "hard" sciences like biology, pedagogy lacks rigorous research protocols and a scientifically based body of knowledge. Darling-Hammond vehemently disagrees. "There are about 30 years of extraordinarily productive research on learning and teaching, and it's very well grounded," she says. "It tells us a lot more than we ever knew before about how people learn, how different people learn differently and how to teach effectively."

'A Nation at Risk'

Whatever the arguments, the decades-long controversies over the quality of public schooling in

. . . to Take the Place of Teachers

"There is no good evidence that most uses of computers significantly improve teaching and learning, yet school districts are cutting programs — music, art, physical education — that enrich children's lives to make room for this dubious nostrum," declared *The Atlantic Monthly* in its July cover story. [6]

The Washington-based Benton Foundation concluded in a study released this year that technology alone is no panacea: "For it to work well for students and schools, we must build 'human infrastructure' at the same pace we are installing computers and wiring. . . . [T]echnology is not an end in itself, and . . . any successful use of technology must begin with clearly defined educational objectives." [7]

The Benton report further stated that "even the staunchest advocates of computer networking in education concede that in most places technical problems, inadequate training and insufficient time for teachers to figure out ways to integrate technology with the curriculum have combined to thwart the dreams of reformers for a technology-driven overhaul of the education system."

The report noted the results of a poll last February in which only 13.4 percent of surveyed teachers said they believe Internet access had helped pupils do better.

"The big problem I see is literacy — not computer literacy, but the simple ability to read and write," the report quoted Princeton, N.J., teacher Ferdi Serim. "If you put the Internet in the hands of somebody who can neither read, write, nor think well, you aren't giving them much. But for kids who are equipped with language and learning skills, it's like a rocket."

In his op-ed piece, Sava acknowledged that his organization of elementary-school principals supports Clinton's call for widespread computer use in the classroom. "Part of the grants from his 'technology literacy' program can be used for teacher training," Sava explained. But he noted the complexity and expense of equipping schools with computers on a large scale.

Providing a computer for one in every five students would require an annual investment of $8 billion to $20 billion, which includes the wiring of schools and teacher training, according to Rand Corp. figures cited by Sava. The Benton report cited a 1995 McKinsey & Co. analysis estimating that connecting schools to the Internet could cost as much as $47 billion over 10 years, plus $14 billion a year in operating costs.

While computers in America's classrooms are surely here to stay, critics like Sava want to go slowly enough to ensure that teachers are prepared to use them effectively.

"We must have the courage to resist the public's enthusiasm for sexy hardware and argue for the money to train our teachers," he wrote. "We cannot send them into the computer room with nothing but a user's manual." [8]

---

1 Victoria Benning, "In Fairfax Schools, Hard Questions on Software Program," *The Washington Post*, Sept. 30, 1997.

2 Samuel G. Sava, "Maybe Computers Aren't Schools' Salvation," *The New York Times*, Sept. 6, 1997.

3 Speech in California Sept. 21, 1995, quoted in "Networking the Classroom," *The CQ Researcher*, Oct. 20, 1995.

4 Sava, *op cit.*

5 *Ibid.*

6 Todd Oppenheimer, "The Computer Delusion," *The Atlantic Monthly*, July 1997.

7 Christopher Conte, "The Learning Connection: Schools in the Information Age," Benton Foundation, 1997.

8 Sava, *op. cit.*

America reached a crescendo in the late 1970s and early '80s.

A major source of concern was the declining number of young people entering the teaching profession. Teaching has always been a predominantly female occupation, especially at the elementary level. In the past few decades, expanding career opportunities and better pay in non-teaching fields have diverted many students away from education schools, leading to acute shortages of qualified educators.

By the early 1980s, a combination of problems — shortages of qualified teachers, declining test scores, infighting over curriculum reforms, budgetary pressures, to name a few — elevated national concerns about education to stratospheric heights.

"Rising Tide of Mediocrity"

In 1983, "A Nation At Risk," an influential Education Department report, asserted that U.S. schools were sinking under a "rising tide of mediocrity," in part because of a shortage of qualified teachers in math, science and other key disciplines. "If an unfriendly foreign power had attempted to impose on America the mediocre educational performance that exists today," the report declared, "we might well have viewed it as an act of war."

The report drew bitter criticism from public school advocates. Some saw it as a blatant misreading of the evidence on American education. They argued that while some schools — mainly underfunded inner-city schools facing deep social problems — were indeed in trouble, most schools were good and improving. Other critics accused the Reagan White House of using alarmist tactics to press for federal funding of private education.

Accurate or not, "A Nation At Risk"

helped spawn a decade of reformist zeal in public education, one that transcended think tanks and government commissions to include education school deans, teachers' unions and rank-and-file educators and administrators.

In 1986. the Carnegie Forum on Education and the Economy issued a report, "A Nation Prepared: Teachers for the 21st Century," which helped launch a second wave of educational reform aimed at making teaching a full-fledged profession. [22] One outgrowth of the Carnegie study is the National Board for Professional Teaching Standards.

In 1989, President George Bush convened an education summit with the National Governors' Association, headed by then-Gov. Bill Clinton, D-Ark. The summit laid the groundwork for what became "Goals 2000," an ambitious series of education goals and proposed standards that have become the centerpiece of the Clinton administration's education strategy.

Another important outgrowth of the 1980s was the Holmes Group, a convocation of deans from about 100 research-oriented education schools that has issued a series of reports on teacher preparation. In 1986, the Holmes Group argued that education schools should take a scholarly, research-based approach to pedagogical study and that teaching should be professionalized, much like law or medicine. In 1990, the group advocated the formation of professional development schools.

But in 1995, in what some view as a disavowal of the 1986 position, the Holmes Group said education schools should drop their ivory tower pretensions and become more involved in the nitty-gritty of local school problems.

The Holmes Group and other research efforts have helped to shape the current generation of thinking on teacher preparation and set the stage for a number of new initiatives in the education community and the policy arena.

"People have tried to find ways of integrating teacher education more effectively back into the schools," Hargreaves says of initiatives like the Holmes Group. Adds Pecheone, the Connecticut curriculum chief, "There's an active movement to restructure teacher preparation so it's more relevant to teachers and prospective teachers." ■

CURRENT SITUATION

'Rigorous' Standards

Few American school districts are ignoring the popular mandate to improve teacher quality. Fairfax County, Va., near Washington, D.C., recently reshaped its teacher-hiring process so that an arcane, paper-intensive process — typical of many school districts — doesn't scare off good prospects. [23] East Carolina University's Peer Coaching Project Consortium lets teachers in some North Carolina districts mentor other teachers. [24] In Ohio, the University of Cincinnati has joined with the public schools and local teachers' union to improve teacher training. [25]

But along with such local programs, two national groups — the Interstate New Teacher Assessment and Support Consortium (INTASC) and the National Board for Professional Teaching Standards — are mounting far-reaching reform initiatives.

INTASC, a 10-year-old consortium of 31 states and a variety of professional organizations, has developed standards for licensing beginning teachers and is creating new ways to gauge how well a beginning teacher can plan, teach and guide pupils, including slow-learners. The idea, says Linda Wurzbach, senior project associate, is to make licensing decisions based on "what people show they can do rather than showing solely what they know in a multiple-choice format."

INTASC draws on the work of the National Board for Professional Teaching Standards, which aims to set "high and rigorous" voluntary standards for certifying "accomplished" teachers. A select group of experienced teachers assesses the candidates, and the hurdles are high. Only about 600 teachers — a third of the applicants — have emerged as board-certified, says Philip Kearney, senior program director of the Southfield, Mich.-based organization.

"In effect we have a national, but not a federal, set of standards," he says. "It's very much teacher-driven. Nobody has ever done this before."

In his State of the Union address in February, President Clinton expressed support for the board's work, calling for federal spending to help it complete its task of shaping standards and to provide money to states to aid teachers who want to apply for certification. "We should reward and recognize our best teachers," the president said.

Clinton wants to see 100,000 applicants seeking board certification. Some observers are skeptical of such goals. The University of Toronto's Hargreaves calls them "worthy but probably exaggerated." He expects enthusiasm for the rigorous evaluation regimen to wane after the first wave of teachers wins certification.

Kearney remains optimistic. "It is a very large and demanding task in front of us," he says, "but the board has received very strong support from the profession. One of our tasks is to

Continued on p. 930

At Issue:

Do teachers' unions have a positive influence on the educational system?

Bob Chase
President, National Education Association; former social studies teacher for 25 years.

FROM *INSIGHT ON THE NEWS,* OCT. 21, 1996.

yes

For true believers, the evil influence of teachers' unions is an article of faith. But for those who prefer empirical data to hunches, let's look at the record. As it happens, there are 16 states in the United States that do not have collective-bargaining statutes governing public-school employees. In seven of those states, there virtually is no collective bargaining by public school employees. In short, no teachers' unions. It hardly is a coincidence that these seven states — all but one, West Virginia, located in the South — have been notorious for their underfunded education systems. . . .

In recent years, pro-education Southern governors . . . have striven to energize their states' academic performance by, in effect, doing the job that teachers' unions perform elsewhere: insisting on decent pay to attract and retain quality teachers, pushing for higher academic standards and prodding state legislatures to boost investments in education.

And what about the superb public-school systems Americans envy in countries such as Germany, France and Japan? You guessed it: They all benefit from strong teachers' unions.

Yet despite this evidence, it would be foolish to claim that teachers' unions guarantee educational excellence. To do so would be the flip side of our critics' foolish claim that teachers' unions control America's public schools. For the record, the NEA's local affiliates do not certify teachers, hire or fire them, write curricula, determine graduation requirements or set funding levels. . . . In the last analysis, the only thing NEA members control is their individual professional commitment to making public education work. . . .

More significantly, unions are good for education because they give teachers a strong, unified . . . voice within their local school systems. Our members and affiliates have fought not just for decent pay . . . but also for issues more directly related to school quality, including smaller class sizes and stricter . . . classroom discipline. . . .

The NEA's bedrock commitment is to quality public education. This in no way entails a defense of the status quo, especially in school districts that are underperforming. To the contrary, in state after state, it has required the NEA to take the lead in instigating and implementing change.

Ultimately, this is what separates public school teachers from their critics: Most critics stand on the outside and blow spitballs. Teachers — supported by their unions — stand in the classroom and courageously confront the challenges of public education in the 1990s. The good news is that, in most of America's schools, the teachers are winning.

Myron Lieberman
***Adjunct scholar, Social Philosophy and Policy Center, Bowling Green State University; author,* The Teachers' Unions: How the NEA and AFT Sabotage Reform and Hold Parents, Students, Teachers and Taxpayers Hostage to Bureaucracy.**

FROM *INSIGHT ON THE NEWS,* OCT. 21, 1996.

no

If your child does not have a qualified mathematics or science teacher, you can thank the NEA and American Federation of Teachers [AFT] for the salary policies that are to blame. Teachers' unions advocate single-salary schedules — paying all teachers the same salary regardless of subject. Under single-salary schedules, teachers are paid solely on the basis of their years of teaching experience and their academic credits. . . .

Higher-education administrators know it would be practically impossible to operate a university by paying all professors, regardless of subject, the same salary. Universities would be unable to employ qualified medical professors if their salaries were the same as those for English professors. Similarly, people who can teach mathematics and science can earn more in occupations outside of teaching. Thus, when the teachers' unions insist that all teachers be paid the same regardless of subject, they help create shortages of qualified teachers of math and science.

Needless to say, the teachers' unions claim that their collective goals contribute to academic achievement. Higher salaries are supposed to attract more talented teachers and reduce turnover. Tenured positions for teachers are supposed to protect competent teachers. More preparation time during the regular school day should result in better-prepared teachers. . . .

The unions' arguments have a superficial plausibility but cannot withstand scrutiny. Take, for example, the unions' claim that smaller classes are the key to improving student achievement, since they allow individualized instruction. Actually, class size largely is overrated as a factor in student achievement. In many nations whose students outperform ours, classes are much larger than those in the United States. Of course, smaller classes mean that more teachers are needed, and more teachers mean more union revenues.

The question policy-makers should be asking, however, is whether the expenditures required to lower class size are the most productive way to use the money. In many cases, they are not. The funds used to lower class size often could be more productively spent for laboratory equipment or textbooks or supplies. In most situations, reductions in class size benefit the union and teachers much more than they benefit pupils. The same point applies to the other union objectives that allegedly help students. . . .

The union litmus test is not whether a policy benefits students; it is whether it benefits teachers or unions.

figure out how we can scale this thing up, handle the sorts of numbers we've been talking about, maintain the quality of the program and continue to make it attractive for teachers to pursue voluntarily."

State Efforts

Individual states have made varying degrees of progress in upgrading teacher standards, with some far along the reform spectrum and others barely moving. Among the most aggressive are Indiana and Connecticut.

In the Hoosier State, the vehicle for change is the five-year-old Indiana Professional Standards Board, an autonomous group of classroom teachers, administrators, school board members, business people and education professors. It has legal authority to set teacher training, hiring, certification and relicensing standards.

The board's aim, says Executive Director Scannell, is to "establish the credibility of teaching as a profession. Only by describing what teachers ought to be able to do can the public understand what makes teachers special. Until now, they kind of thought teachers were born and not made."

In many states, legislatures or bureaucrats have held sway over teacher standards. Only about a dozen states have independent boards that set licensing rules, and few state boards are as ambitious and far-reaching as Indiana's. [26]

In 1994, the Indiana board decided to adopt a rigorous performance-based licensing system that it hopes to implement fully early in the next century. The board modeled the system on the new-teacher protocols of INTASC, the rigorous regimen of the National Board for Professional Teaching Standards, NCATE's standards for ed schools and the spirit and goals of the "What Matters Most" study. Working with Indiana education schools to reshape teacher-training programs means crafting "standards for what teachers should know and be able to do, rather than a prescriptive list of course and credit hours to be received for licensure," Scannell says.

Reform advocates are watching the Indiana board closely. "They are at the forefront of figuring out the proper relationship between accreditation and licensing and what colleges of education need to provide to teacher candidates," said Wise of NCATE. [27]

In Connecticut, besides providing for peer mentoring and other forms of professional development, the state requires beginning teachers to produce a portfolio of work demonstrating classroom competency. The benchmarks, similar to those adopted by the National Board for Professional Teaching Standards, now cover new and recently hired middle- and high-school teachers. By 2000 they also will apply to elementary school teachers, principals and other administrators.

Those who don't pass muster within three years of employment will be "out of the profession" in the state, Pecheone says.

Part of Connecticut's focus is to ensure that teachers are experts not only in pedagogy but also the field they teach. The state used to have "a one-size-fits-all type of evaluation system, based on generic understandings of teacher competence," says Pecheone. "We moved to subject-specific standards about what a teacher should know and be able to do."

Kentucky also is moving to improve teacher competency. But there, the results have stirred controversy. The state is working with INTASC and NCATE to develop strict, performance-based teacher certification standards. It also is exploring new ways to grant advanced certification to veteran teachers, based not only on their college credits but also on classroom demonstrations of their skill.

In September, however, *The Wall Street Journal* noted in a front-page story that Kentucky teachers are rewarded with cash bonuses if their school test scores rise, a policy that "has spawned lawsuits, infighting between teachers and staff, anger among parents, widespread grade inflation — and numerous instances of cheating by teachers to boost student scores." [28]

Even Jack Foster, the former Kentucky education secretary who helped design the program, conceded it needed work. "We tried to do too much, too fast," Foster said. [29] ■

OUTLOOK

Legislative Initiatives

Along with the states and local school districts, the federal government also is moving to reshape policies affecting classroom educators.

Much of the focus is on reshaping Title V of the Higher Education Act, an initiative authorized for funding at nearly $600 million in 1993 that was designed to improve elementary and secondary teaching. Only one of the measure's 16 programs — to recruit minority teachers — was funded in fiscal 1997, and only five have ever received money. *

Sen. Bill Frist, R-Tenn., wants to streamline Title V to focus on initial training of teachers. In September he submitted a bill that would cut Title V funding to $250 million and consolidate its programs. He would retain mi-

* The five programs that were funded previously were minority recruitment, early childhood violence counseling, Paul Douglas scholarships for high school students who want to be teachers, the Christa McAuliffe fellowship for working teachers and the National Board for Professional Teaching Standards.

nority recruitment and strengthen teacher preparation.

Noting that school enrollments are climbing and that a third to a half of current teachers are 45 or older, Frist argues that a supply of new, well-trained teachers is necessary to meet future demand. He also argues that while schools have mechanisms to improve skills of current teachers, federal support of new-teacher training is lacking. "There has been virtually no federal commitment to help institutions of higher education upgrade future teacher training programs," he said.

Miller, the California Democrat, also addresses teacher training in his proposed Teaching Excellence for All Children Act of 1997, which would require school districts to make teacher qualifications available to parents. "Teachers are among the hardest-working people in our country, and they certainly have one of the most important jobs in our country," Miller says. "Unfortunately, our public policies have not always reflected this reality."

Miller wants education schools that get federal money to be either nationally accredited or show that at least 90 percent of graduates pass state licensing exams on the first try. In addition, he wants to establish local community partnerships with accredited education schools to help recruit and retain qualified teachers. And Miller wants the federal government to forgive college loans of those who teach in high-poverty areas.

Sen. Jack Reed, D-R.I., wants to amend Title V to create a five-year competitive grant program for teacher training that would be administered by the Education Department. Building on the professional development school concept, Reed introduced a bill Sept. 11 that would direct $100 million to be used for partnerships between elementary and secondary schools and institutions of higher education as well as other educational agencies and organizations.

"These partnerships would operate like teaching hospitals, with university faculty and veteran teachers working with current and prospective teachers on how to improve and enhance their skills by offering supervised classroom experience and mentoring," Reed said. Up to 50 percent of new teachers leave the profession within three to five years, mainly because of lack of preparation and training provided for new teachers, according to Reed's office.

The Department of Education wants to replace Title V's myriad programs with the Lighthouse Partnerships for Teacher Preparation and an enhanced program to recruit minority teachers. Legislation calling for the changes was introduced Sept. 23 by Sen. Edward M. Kennedy, D-Mass.

Last summer, in a speech to the NAACP national convention in Pittsburgh, Clinton supported minority recruitment, proposing to spend $350 million over five years on tuition and training aid for up to 35,000 new teachers who agree to work in inner-city and rural schools for at least three years. "A third of our students are minority," he said, but "only 13 percent of their teachers are.

"Students in distressed areas who need the best teachers often have teachers who have had the least preparation," the president said. "For

FOR MORE INFORMATION

National Association of Secondary School Principals, 1904 Association Drive, Reston, Va. 22091; (703) 860-0200. The association represents the interests of high school principals.

The National Commission on Teaching & America's Future, Teachers College, Columbia University, Box 117, 525 West 120th St., New York, N.Y. 10027; (212) 678-3204. The commission produced a landmark report last year, "What Matters Most: Teaching for America's Future."

National Board for Professional Teaching Standards, 26555 Evergreen Road, Suite 400, Southfield, Mich. 48076; 248-351-4444. The board sets rigorous standards for certifying expert teachers.

Interstate New Teacher Assessment and Support Consortium (INTASC), a program of the Council of Chief State School Officers, 1 Massachusetts Ave. N.W., Suite 700, Washington, D.C. 20001-1431; (202) 336-7048. The consortium crafts model standards for licensing new teachers.

National Education Association, 1201 16th St. N.W., Washington, D.C. 20036-3290; (202) 833-4000. The NEA is the nation's largest teachers' union.

American Federation of Teachers, 555 New Jersey Ave N.W., Suite 10, Washington, D.C. 20001; (202) 879-4400. The AFT, along with the NEA, represents the interests of American teachers.

National School Boards Association, 1680 Duke St., Alexandria, Va. 22314-3493; (703) 838-6225. This federation of school board associations is interested in such issues as local governance and quality of education programs.

American Association of Colleges for Teacher Education, 1 Dupont Circle, Suite 610, Washington, D.C. 20036-1186; (202) 293-2450. The association represents those responsible for teacher education, including schools, colleges and departments of education.

example, right now 71 percent of students taking physical science courses like chemistry and physics, and 33 percent of English students in high-poverty schools, take classes with teachers who do not even have a college minor in their field."

Such figures are familiar to those who deal with the challenges of inner-city education on a daily basis. Improving the quality of instruction is important, they agree. But so is mandating greater equity in spending on school buildings and other physical facilities in poor neighborhoods.

"As few as 40 percent of our youngsters even have higher-level math and science offered in their buildings," says Ramona H. Edelin, president of the National Urban Coalition. "There are great discrepancies in the quality of the teaching force in the hardest-hit inner cities and their suburban counterparts." And, she adds, inequities in "the rates of spending on facilities up and down the line are just a moral outrage."

While public officials wrestle with reshaping policy on teacher competence and recruiting, unionized teachers, mainly in the NEA, find themselves at a crossroads. Will they adopt a meaningful strategy of self-policing, or will the slogan of a "new unionism" become a hollow PR gimmick?

"There has been significant interest expressed by local associations in moving in the direction" of adopting peer review since the union approved it last summer, Cameron says. But it may be months before it is known whether NEA locals will embrace it on a wide scale.

Clearly, though, the delegates' embrace of peer review marks a watershed for a labor organization that frequently has been at bitter odds with school administrators. "This is a defining moment," said Lea Schelke, a Trenton, Mich., high school teacher who chairs the NEA's professional standards and practice committee. The union's endorsement of peer assistance and review "shifts the world for our new members. They appreciate all of us old workhorses who got the salaries and protections they don't want to walk away from — but they want more." [30]

Even if the unions do bend more in the future, they also will expect something in return from local school districts and national policy-makers — support and resources to make the teachers' jobs easier and more meaningful.

"If we're moving toward a situation where we want to have much higher standards — and of course we do — and we have to compete in a global marketplace and want to be a high-wage, high-skill society, we're going to have to make sure our schools are world-class," says AFT President Feldman. "We're asking a lot more of teachers than we ever have before. We must make sure they get the training and support to do the job." ■

Thomas J. Billitteri is a freelance writer in the Washington, D.C., area.

Notes

[1] For background, see "Attack on Public Schools," *The CQ Researcher,* July 26, 1996, pp. 649-672, and "Education Standards," *The CQ Researcher,* March 11, 1994, pp. 217-240.

[2] For background, see "School Funding," *The CQ Researcher,* Aug. 27, 1993, pp. 745-768.

[3] National Commission on Teaching & America's Future, *What Matters Most: Teaching for America's Future,* September 1996. The 26-member commission chaired by Gov. James B. Hunt Jr., D-N.C., includes educators and political, union, corporate and community leaders.

[4] *Ibid.*

[5] *Ibid.*

[6] *The New York Times,* July 8, 1997.

[7] For background, see "School Choice Debate," *The CQ Researcher,* July 18, 1997, pp. 625-648.

[8] David F. Labaree, "The Trouble With Ed Schools," *Educational Foundations,* summer 1996, p. 32.

[9] National Commission on Teaching & America's Future, *op. cit.,* p. 14.

[10] *Ibid.,* p. 15.

[11] The average elementary school class in California had 28.8 students in 1995, the highest in the nation, according to the Department of Education, National Center for Education Statistics, *Digest of Education Statistics,* 1995.

[12] *EdSource Report,* April 1997. EdSource is a nonprofit education information center for California public schools based in Palo Alto.

[13] National Commission on Teaching & America's Future, *op. cit.,* p. 149.

[14] National Public Radio, "All Things Considered," Aug. 21, 1997.

[15] National Commission, *op. cit.,* p. 31.

[16] Leslie Harris, "Recruiting the Best and Brightest," *Teacher Magazine,* January 1996.

[17] "Tomorrow's Schools of Education," Holmes Group, 1995, p. 5, quoted in Labaree, *op. cit.,* p. 29.

[18] Quoted in Labaree, *op. cit.*

[19] *The Washington Post,* Aug. 20, 1997.

[20] Labaree, *op. cit.,* p. 31.

[21] *Ibid.,* p. 30.

[22] "Should Teaching Be Made Into a Profession?" *Editorial Research Reports,* May 4, 1990, pp. 253-268.

[23] *Education Week,* Feb. 26, 1997, p. 1

[24] National Commission, *op. cit.,* p. 87

[25] *Education Week,* April 23, 1997.

[26] Marilyn Scannell and Judith Wain, "New Models for State Licensing of Professional Educators," *Phi Delta Kappan,* November 1996, p. 211.

[27] Quoted in *Education Week,* March 26, 1997, p. 6.

[28] *The Wall Street Journal,* Sept. 2, 1997.

[29] *Ibid.*

[30] Quoted in *Education Week,* Aug. 6, 1997.

Bibliography

Selected Sources Used

Books

Berliner, David C., and Bruce J. Biddle, *The Manufactured Crisis: Myths, Fraud, and the Attack on America's Public Schools,* Addison-Wesley, 1995.

The authors, both university professors, question critics of American education. They argue that SAT scores are rising for many groups, figures on illiteracy are skewed and public schools deliver a quality education.

Kramer, Rita, *Ed School Follies: The Miseducation of America's Teachers,* Free Press, 1991.

Kramer visited 15 university education schools and talked to students, faculty and administrators. She concludes that most teachers believe their job isn't to transfer a specific body of knowledge to students, but to prepare them to live in a multicultural society.

Goodlad, John I., *Educational Renewal: Better Teachers, Better Schools,* Jossey-Bass, 1994.

Goodlad, director of the Center for Educational Renewal at the University of Washington in Seattle, expounds on his vision for "centers of pedagogy" that link schools and universities in a strong relationship. "Unfortunately, teacher education has come to be associated only with training and the mechanistic ways we teach dogs, horses, and humans to perform certain routinized tasks," he writes.

Finn, Chester E. Jr., *We Must Take Charge: Our Schools and Our Future,* Free Press, 1991.

Finn advocates a radical reorganization of American education, arguing that "public education in the United States is . . . a failure." He calls for a national curriculum of core subjects and a clear standard of achievement.

Articles

Bronner, Ethan, "End of Chicago's Education School Stirs Debate," *The New York Times,* Sept. 17, 1997.

For the first time in more than a century, there are no doctoral candidates at the University of Chicago's department of education. The department, founded in 1895 by John Dewey, has been closed. "In recent months, a . . . complex discussion has emerged . . . about the nature of educational research, notably about the links between educational theory and practice, and how they fit into a traditional academic setting," Bronner writes.

Oppenheimer, Todd, "The Computer Delusion," *The Atlantic Monthly,* July 1997.

"Schools around the country are dropping traditional subjects to lavish scarce time and money on computers and computer education — with results that may be at best negligible and at worst harmful," the author argues.

Schrag, Peter, "The Near-Myth of Our Failing Schools," *The Atlantic Monthly,* October 1997.

While some criticisms of America's education system are correct, Schrag argues that misleading assumptions and incorrect conclusions persist. "Without a more realistic sense of what is going on — a better understanding of the myths — the country will never get beyond the horror stories and ideological set pieces that seem endlessly to dominate the educational debate," he writes.

Stanfield, Rochelle L., "Good-Bye, Mr. Chips," *National Journal,* Oct. 10, 1996.

"Talented teachers are tough to find and even harder to keep," declares this story on teacher competence.

Stecklow, Steve, "Apple Polishing: Kentucky's Teachers Get Bonuses, but Some Are Caught Cheating," *The Wall Street Journal,* Sept. 2, 1997.

Stecklow writes that a popular "carrot-and-stick" approach to motivating Kentucky teachers — paying cash bonuses if their schools' test scores rise — has led to grade inflation, lawsuits, "numerous instances of cheating by teachers to boost student scores" and other problems.

Reports

National Commission on Teaching & America's Future, *What Matters Most: Teaching for America's Future,* September 1996.

Chaired by North Carolina Gov. James B. Hunt Jr., the commission calls for dramatic changes in teacher recruitment, preparation and professional development practices.

National Association of Secondary School Principals, *Breaking Ranks: Changing an American Institution,* 1996.

The report, done in partnership with the Carnegie Foundation for the Advancement of Teaching, says "the high school of the 21st century must be much more student-centered and above all much more personalized in programs, support services and intellectual rigor."

Christopher Conte, with research and editorial contributions by Jon Berroya, Susan Goslee, Jillaine Smith and Kevin Taglang, Benton Foundation, *The Learning Connection: Schools in the Information Age,* 1997.

The report argues that while school districts are spending \$4 billion a year on new technology, the computers and other devices they are buying are not worth the price if they are adopted in a vacuum.

The Next Step

Additional information from UMI's Newspaper & Periodical Abstracts™ database

Computers in Schools

de Pommereau, Isabelle, "Computer-age kids drive schools to teacher training," *The Christian Science Monitor,* Sept. 3, 1996, p. 12.

The U.S. has spent $9.5 billion since 1991 to bring technology into the classroom, and the result is 5.8 million computers, or one computer for every nine children in the classroom. But preparing teachers to use this technology is a difficult task.

Niederhauser, Dale S., "Using computers in an information age classroom: What teachers need to know," *NASSP Bulletin,* October 1996, pp. 71-80.

Effective principals can define and communicate a mission that incorporates information literacy and technology integration. Supporting teachers through professional development and ongoing technical support can produce the kinds of change that will help children become productive participants in the information society.

Shroyer, M. Gail, and Carol A. Borchers, "Factors that support school change to enhance the use of microcomputers in rural schools," *School Science & Mathematics,* December 1996, pp. 419-431.

A study examines how a national model for integrating microcomputers into science teaching was implemented in rural school districts. The implementation of a national model for rural school districts required several adaptations.

Educational Reform

Lieberman, Ann, and Maureen Grolnick, "Networks and reform in American education," *Teachers College Record,* fall 1996, pp. 7-45.

Educational reform networks are becoming more important as alternative forms of teacher and school development in a time of unprecedented reform of schools. A study of 16 educational reform networks is presented.

Timpane, Michael, and Rob Reich, "Revitalizing the ecosystem for youth: A new perspective for school reform," *Phi Delta Kappan,* February 1997, pp. 464-470.

Timpane and Reich believe that the arrangements needed for educational reform are best thought of as an "ecosystem" — a total environment supporting the healthy growth and development of America's youth. They discuss the importance of community development in school reform.

Urbanski, Adam, and Mary Beth Nickolaou, "Reflections on teachers as leaders," *Educational Policy,* June 1997, pp. 243-254.

Teachers' involvement in the education reform debate has focused attention on their role as leaders. Emerging visions of teachers' leadership in Rochester, N.Y., and Hammond, Ind., are examined.

Peer Review Programs

Belluck, Pam, "Poor Teachers Get Coaching, Not Dismissal," *The New York Times,* Dec. 8, 1996, p. 1.

New York City teachers who perform poorly are often allowed to enroll in a remedial program in which a teaching coach works one-on-one in the classroom for as long as a year rather than face dismissal. As Chancellor Rudy Crew tries to raise the standards of students, the need for the peer intervention program underlines the difficulty of his task. The existence of the program, one of only a handful in the U.S., is a measure of the extent of the city's problem with poorly performing teachers and its difficulty in dismissing teachers who have tenure.

Cameron, Don, "The role of teachers in establishing a quality-assurance system," *Phi Delta Kappan,* November 1996, pp. 225-227.

The STAR program in Seattle, Wash., and similar efforts in other communities reflect a recognition that teachers must take greater responsibility for the quality of the work of their peers. These efforts by teachers and the role that teacher unions play in helping them are discussed.

Shuler, Scott C. "Assessing teacher competence in the arts: Should Mr. Holland have gotten the gig? Introduction to the symposium on teacher evaluation," *Arts Education Policy Review,* September 1996, pp. 11-15.

Teacher assessment has begun to play an increasingly important role in education. A symposium examines the influence of trends and issues in teacher assessment on the field of arts education.

Professional Development Schools

Bullough, Robert V. Jr., Sharon F. Hobbs, Donald P. Kauchak, Nedra A. Crow and David Stokes, "Long-term PDS development in research universities and the clinicalization of teacher education," *Journal of Teacher Education,* March 1997, pp. 85-95.

Bullough et al conducted a study of seven current and former professional development schools (PDS). They explore through the eyes of clinical, non-tenure-track, and tenure-line university faculty the increased use of clinical faculty in teacher education programs, describe their PDS study, present themes emerging from their data and consider implications for future PDS development.

Coker, Donald R., and Mary Wilkerson, "Reconceptualizing the process of teacher preparation to accommodate a collaborative, field-based model," *Education,* summer 1997, pp. 500-505.

Coker and Wilkerson discuss the growth of the Northeast Texas Center for Professional Development and Technology.

Dickinson, Thomas S., and Kenneth C. McEwin, "Perspectives and profiles: The professional preparation of middle level teachers," *Childhood Education,* 1997, pp. 272-277.

Progress in establishing middle-level teacher-preparation programs has been steady, but extremely slow.

Dodd, Anne Wescott, "A very different kind of teacher education program: Professional development schools," *NASSP Bulletin,* May 1996, pp. 30-37.

As the 21st century approaches, educators are faced with the challenge of preparing students to cope with the unknown as well as the known. This task requires a very different kind of teacher education program. The use of the Professional Development School model at Bates College is discussed.

Teacher Certification or Licensing

Buday, Mary Catherine, and James Kelly, "A National Board Certification and the teaching profession's commitment to quality assurance," *Phi Delta Kappan,* November 1996, pp. 215-219.

National Board Certification standards have profound significance for the way teachers are prepared and sustained. Many of the teachers who have completed the process of National Board Certification have positioned themselves as key policy-makers — no longer the targets of education reform, but the leaders — and have done so while remaining in teaching.

Kerns, Georgia M., "Preparation for role changes in general education and special education: Dual certification graduates' perspectives," *Education,* winter 1996, pp. 306-315.

As the student population in general education classrooms becomes more diverse, teachers need to meet a greater variety of student needs. A survey of graduates of one program to ascertain the efficacy of pre-service preparation is presented.

Sengupta, Somini, *The New York Times,* June 28, 1997, p. A1.

New York state education officials are drawing up plans to abolish the system of lifetime licenses for public school teachers and to crack down on university training programs in which a large percentage of prospective teachers are failing state certification exams.

Teacher Shortage

Herard, Vladimire, "DuSable retrains staff to make up for shortage of teachers," *Chicago Defender,* Oct. 1, 1996, p. 8.

DuSable High School in Chicago, Ill., is preparing for a teachers' shortage by recycling its own staff for the classrooms. The school is working with Chicago State University and Kennedy-King College to train at least 25 career service personnel to earn degrees in teaching.

Hudson, Sharon P., "Science teacher supply in the United States," *School Science & Mathematics,* March 1996, pp. 133-139.

A study assessed the supply and potential shortages of science teachers in the U.S.

Marlow, Leslie, Duane Inman and Maria Betancourt-Smith, "Beginning teachers: Are they still leaving the profession?" *Clearing House,* March 1997, pp. 211-214

As many as 40 percent of beginning teachers leave their positions during the first two years of their teaching experience. The major reasons for their leaving are the lack of administrative support, professionalism and collegiality.

Teacher Training

Afrik, Hannibal Tirus, "About C.I.B.I. teacher training," *Chicago Defender,* July 5, 1997, p. 12.

Afrik comments on teacher training provided by the Council of Independent Black Institutions.

Burd, Stephen, "Clinton unveils plan for teacher training," *The Chronicle of Higher Education,* July 25, 1997, p. A32.

President Clinton recently announced a proposal to attract new teachers to impoverished urban and rural schools. Teacher-training programs would play a big role in this plan.

"Extra teacher training upheld by school board," *Houston Chronicle,* Feb. 13, 1997, p. A33.

Over objections from about half of the Lamar Consolidated Independent School District's teachers, trustees have upheld a new policy requiring them to take 18 additional hours of training each year on their own time.

Grasmick, Nancy S., and Lawrence E. Leak, "What tomorrow's teachers really need from higher education: A view from the trenches," *Educational Record,* spring 1997, pp. 22-29.

Teacher education is an institutional responsibility and it requires the attention of higher education to ensure that teachers are fully prepared to teach K-12 students in ways that enable them to reach high standards. A program that combines the efforts of the Maryland State Department of Education and the Maryland Higher Education Commission is examined.

Back Issues

Great Research on Current Issues Starts Right Here . . . Recent topics covered by The CQ Researcher are listed below. Before May 1991, reports were published under the name of Editorial Research Reports.

APRIL 1996
Centennial Olympic Games
Managed Care
Protecting Endangered Species
New Military Culture

MAY 1996
Russia's Political Future
Marriage and Divorce
Year-Round Schools
Taiwan, China and the U.S.

JUNE 1996
Rethinking NAFTA
First Ladies
Teaching Values
Labor Movement's Future

JULY 1996
Recovered-Memory Debate
Native Americans' Future
Crackdown on Sexual Harassment
Attack on Public Schools

AUGUST 1996
Fighting Over Animal Rights
Privatizing Government Services
Child Labor and Sweatshops
Cleaning Up Hazardous Wastes

Back issues are available for $5.00 (subscribers) or $10.00 (non-subscribers). Quantity discounts apply to orders over ten. To order, call Congressional Quarterly Customer Service at (202) 887-8621.

Binders are available for $18.00. To order call 1-800-638-1710. Please refer to stock number 648.

SEPTEMBER 1996
Gambling Under Attack
The States and Federalism
Civic Journalism
Reassessing Foreign Aid

OCTOBER 1996
Political Consultants
Insurance Fraud
Rethinking School Integration
Parental Rights

NOVEMBER 1996
Global Warming
Clashing Over Copyright
Consumer Debt
Governing Washington, D.C.

DECEMBER 1996
Welfare, Work and the States
The New Volunteerism
Implementing the Disabilities Act
America's Pampered Pets

JANUARY 1997
Combating Scientific Misconduct
Restructuring the Electric Industry
The New Immigrants
Chemical and Biological Weapons

FEBRUARY 1997
Assisting Refugees
Alternative Medicine's Next Phase
Independent Counsels
Feminism's Future

MARCH 1997
New Air Quality Standards
Alcohol Advertising
Civic Renewal
Educating Gifted Students

APRIL 1997
Declining Crime Rates
The FBI Under Fire
Gender Equity in Sports
Space Program's Future

MAY 1997
The Stock Market
The Cloning Controversy
Expanding NATO
The Future of Libraries

JUNE 1997
FDA Reform
China After Deng
Line-Item Veto
Breast Cancer

JULY 1997
Transportation Policy
Executive Pay
School Choice Debate
Aggressive Driving

AUGUST 1997
Age Discrimination
Banning Land Mines
Children's Television
Evolution vs. Creationism

SEPTEMBER 1997
Caring for the Dying
Mental Health Policy
Mexico's Future
Youth Fitness

OCTOBER 1997
Urban Sprawl in the West
Diversity in the Workplace

Future Topics

- ***Part-time Employment***
- ***Renewable Energy***
- ***Artificial Intelligence***

THE CQ Researcher

PUBLISHED BY CONGRESSIONAL QUARTERLY INC.

Contingent Work Force

Are full-time jobs with benefits a vanishing breed?

The Teamsters union strike against United Parcel Service this summer highlighted major economic and social issues. While the union's victory was seen as a boost for the labor movement, the event also raised public awareness of the ongoing debate over America's increasing reliance on "contingent" workers. Made up of part-timers, temporaries, independent contractors and the self-employed, this widening "reserve army" of workers serves mostly at the convenience of the employers and the dictates of economic forces, and often must do with less pay and fewer benefits than full-time workers. Though the bulk of contingent workers embrace their "non-standard work" arrangements voluntarily, debate is focusing on the significant number who accept such uncertain status because it's their only choice.

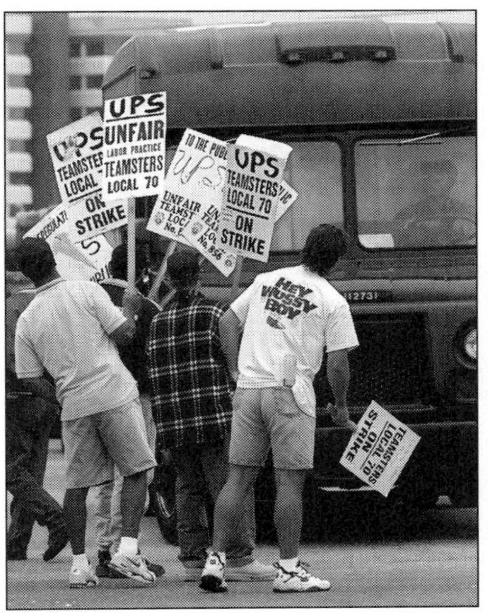

INSIDE THIS ISSUE

CQ Oct. 24, 1997 • Volume 7, No. 40 • Pages 937-960

Formerly Editorial Research Reports

THE CQ Researcher

October 24, 1997
Volume 7, No. 40

The CQ Researcher (ISSN 1056-2036). Formerly Editorial Research Reports. Published weekly, except Jan. 3, May 30, Aug. 29, Oct. 31, by Congressional Quarterly Inc., 1414 22nd St., N.W., Washington, D.C. 20037. Annual subscription rate for libraries, businesses and government is $340. Additional rates furnished upon request. Periodicals postage paid at Washington, D.C., and additional mailing offices. POSTMASTER: Send address changes to The CQ Researcher, 1414 22nd St., N.W., Washington, D.C. 20037.

COVER: STRIKING EMPLOYEES OF THE UNITED PARCEL SERVICE IN OAKLAND, CALIF., CONFRONT A NON-STRIKING UPS DRIVER DURING THIS SUMMER'S TEAMSTERS UNION STRIKE. (REUTERS)

Contingent Work Force

By Charles S. Clark

The Issues

In the wee hours of the morning, Curt Neumann sorts packages for the United Parcel Service (UPS). When his five-hour shift ends at 8 a.m., however, he heads to another Des Moines, Iowa, warehouse where he performs similar, but less well-compensated work for a firm that ships hazardous waste.

Though the 30-year-old Neumann appreciates the full medical and dental coverage UPS provides, he joined the 185,000 UPS employees in the International Brotherhood of Teamsters who went on strike for 15 days in August.

"We had great solidarity in that no one crossed the picket line," says the six-year UPS veteran, a college graduate who is a shop steward at his union local.

His reason for voting to strike? He's one of the thousands of part-time UPS workers who want the company to create more full-time jobs. * Many UPS part-timers, despite an hourly wage that averages a solid $11, don't log enough hours to make ends meet and must dovetail their work at UPS with a second job.

Neumann was pleased when the company settled the strike, but he remains skeptical of UPS' promise to create 10,000 new full-time slots, citing UPS' penchant for splitting the 24-hour day — even the daytime hours — into several part-time shifts.

"I have to be realistic and keep my second job because Iowa may not see any of those new full-time jobs," he says. "Others at work are all gung-ho, but I've seen too much promised before to get excited."

From UPS' point of view, it's understandable why the company promised grudgingly to create more full-time jobs, which will pay in the $20-per-hour range.

"Part-time is critical to us, and we need the flexibility," says Gina Ellrich, UPS' Washington representative. "The growing portion of our business is in air express, where the time crunch is critical, while our ground delivery service has shown flat growth. Under UPS' hub-and-spoke system, which provides nationwide package delivery within one or two days, the workers who sort packages and load them on trucks going to airports are simply not needed during non-peak hours."

The company, which Ellrich says was planning to create more full-time jobs even before the strike, will combine some early-morning sorting jobs with daytime driving slots, assuming the continued growth of the business.

"But our part-time jobs are not throwaway jobs," she says. "They provide 15-25 hours a week with full benefits, and they're great for students or mothers at home."

Corporations need flexibility, workers need a steady livelihood; it's an age-old clash that is front and center in the 1990s. The new strategy of corporate "downsizing" over the past several years has created an insecurity among job-holders — both blue- and white-collar — that conjures a vision of a future in which full-time jobs with benefits grow scarce. [1]

"Jobs are artificial units imposed on [society]," business consultant William Bridges writes in *JobShift: How to Prosper in a Workplace Without Jobs*. "They are patches of responsibility that, all together, were supposed to cover the work that's needed to be done. . . . When the economy was changing more slowly, the discrepancies between the job matrix and the work field could be forgotten. [But nowadays], jobs are no longer socially adaptive creatures, and so they are going the way of the dinosaur." [2]

The changing workplace, in turn, has shined a spotlight on the array of alternatives to full-time employees — part-timers, temporaries, independent contractors. Analysts view some of these "non-standard" workers as the so-called "contingent" work force, and generally regard contingent jobs as insecure and poorly compensated. (*See glossary, p. 942.*) The largest component in this umbrella group of workers is part-timers, who number about 24 million (or 18 percent of the nation's work force), according to the Labor Department's Bureau of Labor Statistics (BLS). More than 4 million of these Americans work part time involuntarily, for hourly wages that are two-thirds of the median wage for full-timers, a BLS survey found. [3]

While part-timers have increased in number over the past two decades, their rise has been dwarfed by the explosion of temporary workers. The number of "temps" grew 500 percent from 1980-96, according to

---

* An estimated 10,000 UPS workers are full-time part-timers, which means they are classified as part-timers but work a full week.

Part-Time Workers in the Work Force

The percentage of part-time workers in the work force increased from 14 percent to 18 percent from 1968 to 1996. The percentage of involuntary part-time workers, also known as economic part time or contingent workers, rose from 2.6 percent to 3.4 percent of the work force until 1993, when it began declining.

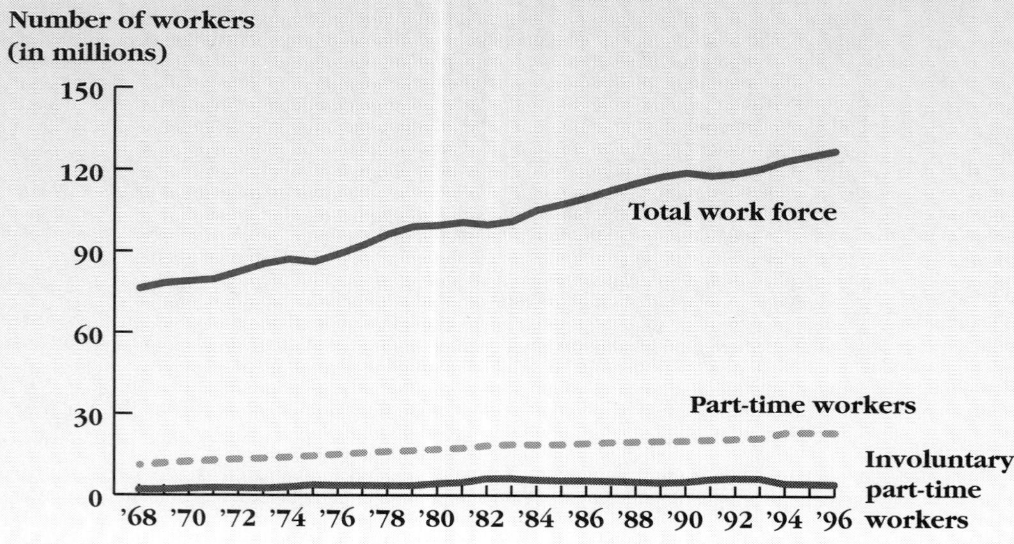

Note: Data from 1994 and after are not strictly comparable with prior years due to the introduction of a redesigned questionnaire, which made it more difficult for workers to be classified as involuntary part time.

Source: Bureau of Labor Statistics, Current Population Survey

the National Policy Association, a nonprofit economic-research organization. Temporary help services in 1996 had their best year ever, employing 2.3 million workers and bringing in $43.6 billion in revenues, according to the National Association of Temporary and Staffing Services. (*See graph, p. 950.*)

"As companies only staff up to levels that are dictated by current demand for their products and services, workers understandably experience high levels of anxiety about their jobs," writes Bruce Steinberg, director of research and public relations at the association. "The challenge to the staffing industry is to capture those workers as they transition to other jobs." [4]

Superimposed on this involuntary movement away from what once were thought of as "permanent" full-time jobs is a "secular trend since the 1950s of more women moving into the labor force, having fewer children and taking fewer years off to raise them," notes economist Heidi Hartmann of the Institute for Women's Policy Research. This larger movement of workers — primarily women — who voluntarily seek part-time arrangements in order to spend more time with family sometimes seems to overwhelm the "de-jobbing" trends and causes confusion among observers, Hartmann says. (*See story, p. 944.*)

People worried by the nation's move away from full-time jobs with benefits, particularly in the union community, speak dismissively of "half jobs," "peripheral" jobs and "disposable" jobs. Warning that "Social Darwinism" has replaced social responsibility among employers, they call for government action to protect part-time and temporary workers from employer exploitation.

"There's currently a basic fragility in most households, and they can't take a wage cut," says economist Thomas Palley, an assistant director for public policy at the AFL-CIO. "That's why the public responded to the UPS strike. It was a big source of encouragement to the new labor movement because it showed that American workers need unions. [5] And with the balance of power having swung so much in favor of companies in recent years, the strike crystallized people's sensibilities to a changed American labor market."

But many in the business and academic communities disagree. (*See "At Issue," p. 953.*) "I don't think there will be much change after the UPS strike because part-time work in general is a positive force," says Max Lyons, an economist with the Employment Policy Foundation. "Most part-time work is voluntary, and it hasn't grown much in the past 20 years in terms of share of the work force. It makes a good sound bite, but I don't think the horror story is really there."

Polls, however, show that the issue may not fade away. The general public was sympathetic to the union during the UPS strike. And a Labor Day poll by *The Wall Street Journal* found that only 27 percent of American workers believe that part-time work has a positive effect on their own company.

Whether current work trends expand into an economic and social crisis will hinge largely on the following issues:

Are employers planning a future that offers fewer full-time jobs?

"Instead of being a castle, a home for life for its defenders, an organization will be more like an apartment block, an association of temporary residents gathered together for mutual convenience." [6] That was the prediction of British management consultant Charles Handy in his 1991 book *The Age of Unreason,* which was widely noted by corporate leaders contemplating downsizing.

An obvious way for companies to streamline and cut overhead is to outsource, or farm out, many commonly in-house functions, such as computer maintenance, copying and building maintenance, to other firms or to independent contractors. An Arthur Andersen survey in 1996 found that 85 percent of North American companies outsource, with more planning to.

As management consultant Robert M. Tomasko argues, many firms are locked into costly and inefficient in-house service providers. "It is ironic that so many otherwise free-enterprise-oriented executives tolerate vast, closed marketplaces within their companies," he writes. "These are their internal service-providing units. They all have customers; the customers just happen to be employees of the business. Unfortunately, because of the monopolistic quality, many companies have to put up with second-class service — and tolerate higher-than-necessary overhead." [7]

Downsizing strategy calls for divesting a payroll of employees regarded as "peripheral," and consigning the most vital work to a loyal "core" of secure, well-compensated, permanent employees who can bring in contingent workers "just in time," in Japanese parlance, to finish an assignment.

When such strategies became the rage in the early 1990s, the Clinton administration's then Labor Secretary Robert B. Reich warned that the economy was creating a "two-tier labor force" with the most generous wages and benefits clearly concentrated in the first tier. In spring 1993, Reich reported that 90 percent of U.S. jobs created that February had been filled by involuntary part-timers. [8]

"Involuntary part time has unambiguously increased over the past 20 years," says the AFL-CIO's Palley. "As an economist, I see firms using workers to buffer the business cycle. If there is a loss of work, it's immediately passed on to the working

Full-Time Workers Get More Benefits

More than twice as many non-contingent workers as contingent workers were eligible for health insurance and pensions in 1995.

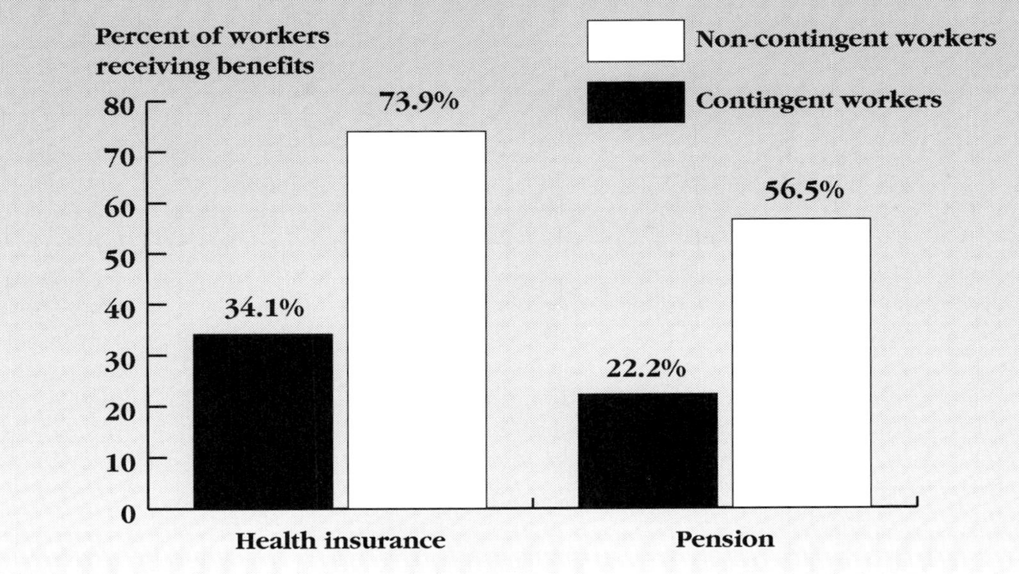

Sources: Looking Ahead, "The Rise of the Contingent Workforce: Growth of Temporary, Part-Time and Subcontracted Employment," National Policy Association, June 1997, adapted from Bureau of Labor Statistics data.

A Glossary of Non-Standard Work Terms

Analysts generally divide work into two broad categories: the "regular, full-time work" performed by most Americans and "non-standard work," which includes the following major subsets:

Contingent workers are hired only when there is an immediate and direct demand for their services; they consider their jobs temporary and cannot continue in them for as long as they would like due to business-related reasons.

Contract workers (business-service workers) subcontract with employers to provide long-term specialties such as data processing, mailing, document reproduction, security, landscaping and public relations.

Day laborers generally wait at prearranged sites to be hired in the morning for such unskilled work as construction and furniture moving.

Independent contractors provide services to clients for wages or a salary, and are commonly professionals such as lawyers, designers, computer programmers or accountants. Internal Revenue Service (IRS) rules distinguish them from employees based on the type of relationship they have with their employer.

Leased workers are employed by third-party companies that specialize in meeting payrolls and administering employee benefits under contract with the firm where the employees perform the work.

Job sharers are employees who divide the responsibilities of a single full-time job, typically so that each can spend more time with family or go to school.

On-call workers can be summoned on short notice, as with substitute teachers, nurses or construction workers.

Regular full-time workers expect a steady schedule of 35 hours a week or more with benefits and an open-ended duration.

Regular part-time workers expect a steady schedule of less than 35 hours with an open-ended duration.

Seasonal workers are in demand only during certain times of the year in such areas as agriculture, retailing and construction.

Self-employed workers are individuals who run a business. The IRS recognizes two subcategories: **direct sellers,** who sell or solicit the sale of consumer products in the home or place of business other than a permanent retail establishment, and **licensed real estate agents,** which includes both agents and appraisers. Others among the self-employed include **home-based workers,** who perform such tasks as word processing, sewing, craft-making or cooking in their homes, generally for a single employer who may pay them piece rates.

Telecommuters are employees who work at home or at a telecommuting station closer to home than their employer's office, communicating with their supervisor by phone, fax and modem.

Temporary workers are general-skills workers who are recruited, trained, placed and paid by a private agency for assignments that last for limited periods.

Sources: Internal Revenue Service, National Policy Association, Catalyst, Bureau of Labor Statistics, Economic Policy Institute, Society for Human Resource Management, National Association of Temporary Staffing Services.

family. Should work go to one person for a long time, or should it go to lots of different families?" Palley cites a rise in the number of people working multiple jobs — estimated by the BLS at between 952,000 and 2 million workers — as one indicator of trouble. "I see it as a whole mosaic of change," he says. "It's not one disastrous trend, but one in which each factor has deteriorated."

There are plenty of numbers, however, that challenge the notion of a wholesale shift to a contingent-worker economy. The White House's Council of Economic Advisers reported last year that the vast majority of new jobs created recently were full time and found no noticeable rise in those that are part time.[9] Others point out that even the highest official estimates of the number of contingent workers still put them at only 5 percent or less of a work force that numbers nearly 120 million.

What's more, the increase in part-timers in the United States from 1979-92 was smaller than that in most developed countries, notes Lyons of the Employment Policy Foundation. (Indeed, in Europe today the use of contingency workers is skyrocketing; in France, as many as 66 percent of new hires are temporary, and in Spain the number reaches 90 percent, though in most European countries, temps get the same benefits as full-timers.[10])

Marvin Kosters, a labor specialist at the American Enterprise Institute (AEI), says part-time work has become an issue only because of a "propaganda effort to persuade the public that there is a problem with low-paying, part-time jobs. The underlying notion is that the only jobs we should approve of are full time, with a salary, normal hours and regular benefits. But a lot of people would like [unusual] hours," he says, and there has been very little change in the job-tenure statistics.

Few employers, Kosters believes, approach the issue with an attitude of " 'What can we get away with?' They know that the people they want to hire are not fools, so they ask themselves, 'What do we need done, and what skills and dependability do we need to pay for?' They're not concerned with saving that extra dollar either in wages or benefits. They know that if they value long-term job attachment, the good workers will find these employers."

Other skeptics, such as columnist Bruce Bartlett, argue that any rise in part-time work the country has seen is attributable to the desire of employees for more family time and to the growth of service industries such as retail and real estate, rather than any desire among businesses to reduce labor costs. [11] What's more, with current unemployment at a low 4.9 percent, there is evidence that many corporations have had second thoughts about the benefits of downsizing. Instead many are scrambling to offer family-friendly fringe benefits to retain employee loyalty. "They thought anyone could do these low-paying jobs," a California business consultant said last summer. "But you can't get new people now. That's why these guys are starting to wise up." [12]

Recent management journals have featured articles warning that contingent workers are associated with high accident rates. Moreover, the cost of paying for fringe benefits is not as important as the additional training costs that are required with heavy turnover, says Alec Levenson, an economist at the Milken Institute for Job and Capital Formation in Santa Monica, Calif. [13]

According to a recent survey by The Conference Board, a business-research organization, 81 percent of companies use non-standard workers to meet demand fluctuations, while only 12 percent said they did it to control the cost of benefits. Case studies of firms that replaced large portions of their staffs with non-standard workers have shown that the impact on the bottom line is inconclusive; at a major commercial bank it was not cost-effective; at another, it was. At a high-tech assembly plant, there were financial savings, but there also was damage to the sense of teamwork. [14]

The failure of the contingency strategy at a major bank is one reason that Edith Rasell, an economist with the Economic Policy Institute, believes that the overall effect is bad for the American work force. "If contingency people are being paid less, there's an incentive to hire more of them," she says. "This cheapens the work force and produces less training, and more turnover and morale problems. The good employers are driven out by the bad, which hurts the productivity of the U.S. economy."

Reuters

On the third day of the strike against UPS last summer, police push striking Teamsters away from UPS delivery trucks in Watertown, Mass.

Hartmann goes further. "The companies tout their flexibility, but it's the workers for the most part who are paying the price by getting less pay and benefits for their families," she says. "If the companies really want flexibility, they should be willing to pay the same for it as regular work, or even a premium. The fact that they don't shows that what they really want is the cost reduction."

At UPS, says Roger Hickey, co-director of the Campaign for America's Future, a liberal advocacy group, management "clearly sees a growing need for part-timers because the service economy requires them to answer phones at 2 a.m. and deliver packages whenever they're ready. UPS is trying to keep its unionized work force as a two-tier force, in which some workers are expendable. There's no doubt it's a growing trend."

Whether one regards the trend as significant may depend on one's politics. "Although wrenching change is transforming the American workplace, and the human toll is enormous, the contingent work force is a myth," according to an article in the libertarian magazine *Reason*. "And, unlike myths, whose origins are shrouded in the mists of antiquity and whose meanings are difficult to interpret, this one was invented in a particular time and place, to advance the political agenda of unions." [15]

Are so-called voluntary part-timers truly voluntary?

"Contingent workers were more likely to be female, black, young, enrolled in school and employed in services and construction industries than were non-contingent workers," BLS economist Anne E. Polivka wrote

Part-Time Professionals Push Positive Image

"Part-time America won't work!" The words may make a dandy slogan for striking members of the Teamsters union, but they collide head-on with the message cultivated by groups devoted to making the American workplace more flexible and family-friendly.

Last summer's strike against United Parcel Service has caused "us some concern about the perception that part-time is considered disadvantageous, like contingency work," says Katherine Souser, a board member of the Association of Part-Time Professionals in Falls Church, Va. Her group received numerous calls during the strike from reporters seeking horror stories about the exploitability of part-time work. "Part-time is a viable option that ought to be available to people at different points in their lives," she says.

Just as important as the word "part-time" in the group's name is the word "professional," a reflection of the reality, Souser acknowledges, that part-time positions in corporations are "more readily available to professionals than to blue-collar clerical workers. If your skills are in demand, you have more leverage," she says, in negotiating alternatives to full-time work that allow careerists to slow down their work pace to be with their children, care for a sick family member or go to school — without allowing skills and work-world contacts to get rusty.

The number of part-time professionals nationwide has expanded from 3 million in 1989 to 4.5 million currently, according to the association. An estimated 70 percent of companies employ part-time professionals who used to be full-time, according to a recent survey by The Conference Board, a business-research organization. The jobs are often considered plums and are awarded on a case-by-case basis.[1]

The rising availability of part-time professional work has coincided with larger social trends in which American women, starting in the 1960s, began abandoning the role of housewife to enter the work force. By the 1980s, a significant proportion of working women felt the need for more balance between work and family. By 1994, 56 percent of them said they wanted more flexibility in their jobs without losing benefits, according to a survey by Louis Harris and Associates. Because many women in the postwar baby-boom generation had achieved positions of influence before they had children, their demands for workplace flexibility have been taken seriously by management.[2]

Advocates of the flexible workplace make their case in terms both positive and bottom-line-oriented. "In the face of the major economic, demographic and technological changes of the last three decades," notes a handbook from the New York City-based consulting group Catalyst, "American corporations and professional firms [are] taking a close look at workplace flexibility. More and more, organizations are discovering that flexibility helps them retain experienced employees and attract the best group of new employees. They recognize that a flexible environment can help them service global customers, meet cyclical or seasonal business needs, provide continuity on projects and deliver more effective client service. They also have learned that employ-ees who use alternative work arrangements usually feel increased loyalty."[3]

Similar arguments are ad-vanced by the San Francisco-based group New Ways to Work, though it takes a broader approach that ad-vocates on behalf of blue-collar workers as well.

Though studies show that part-time professionals are often able to balance work and family without inordinate sacrifice of income or career potential, they often do with less-generous fringe benefits (*see p. 951*). And there is evidence that the sociological impact of the trend is to reduce the status of women and minorities in both the workplace and the home. The reduced take-home pay, write a team of economists at the Economic Policy Institute, "can result in a gap between the contributions made by husbands and wives to total family income, an important factor if a spouse's decision-making power is dictated by income-level within a family."[4]

Flexible work arrangements have become part of the workworld landscape, notes Souser, pointing to the heavy use of her organization's job-referral service and to *Working Mother* magazine's rankings of the 100 most family-friendly companies. "And to the extent that you negotiate part-time and stay in the same position, your [hourly] pay, at least with the federal government, is generally the same. But some who go part time find that they have to step down a level and backtrack, particularly among managers."

[1] See Phaedra Brotherton, "For Many Part-Timers, Less is More," *Human Resources Magazine,* June 1997, p. 102.

[2] For background, see "Work, Family and Stress," *The CQ Researcher,* Aug. 14, 1992, pp. 689-712.

[3] Catalyst, "Making Work Flexible: Policy to Practice," 1996.

[4] Roberta M. Spalter-Roth et al., "Managing Work and Family: Nonstandard Work Arrangements Among Managers and Professionals," Economic Policy Institute, Aug. 31, 1997.

about a recent survey. "More than 10 percent were teachers."[16]

Behind the abstract numbers of surveys, analysts often see human stories. The Economic Policy Institute, which uses a looser definition of contingency workers than the BLS, calculates that a hefty 30 percent of the work force is in what it calls non-standard work arrangements. Of those, more than half of the women and a third of the men don't earn enough to keep a family of four above the poverty line, compared with only a third of the females and a fifth of the men working full time. This disadvantaged group includes 81 percent of all women employed in non-standard arrangements — such as cashiers, cleaning personnel and restaurant workers. Health insurance and pension benefits, the institute adds, are enjoyed by just 23 percent of the women and 16 percent of the men in non-standard jobs, compared with 80 percent of both the women and men in full-time work. [17]

"Yes, most part-time workers say it's voluntary, and most are women who work that way for family reasons, but are they saying they want part time for less pay?" Rasell asks. "This is the last area where pay discrimination is still legal, where it's based on your full-time status."

Workers' behavior in the job market is affected by their expectations. "The surveys talk about being part-time for economic reasons, but they don't explain how people feel," Hartmann says. "We're now well out of a recession, so part-time work is declining, but it's surprising how high the involuntary part-time work numbers are, especially for women, which shows you how much of a commitment many women have to finding full-time work." Many women who choose to work part time on a long-term basis are able to rely on a male breadwinner, she adds. "But it's the single mothers, who're most likely to be disadvantaged by part time's low pay and lack of benefits, who are constrained most by a lack of child care and a shortage of full-time jobs."

The argument gets made that much of what is called voluntary part-time work is actually work that is only reluctantly accepted, justified by a "cognitive dissonance," according to University of Massachusetts-Lowell public policy Professor Chris Tilly. "Some involuntary part-time workers will convince themselves that they actually prefer part-time hours," he writes. [18]

Evidence of such self-deception can be found in studies of how temporary-help agencies recruit workers. "Working as a temp can be very demanding, and the rewards are slim, but to recruit you have to do a selling job," said an agency manager, adding that he often has to overcome his own "social work" mentality. "In other words, the worker's interest must be ignored or regarded as a secondary priority. For example, successful managers must [disregard] workers' needs for steady employment [that offers] adequate wages and benefits." [19]

Poll data on the subject is scarce. A CBS News-*New York Times* poll in March 1995 asked part-timers if they would prefer working part time or full time: 53 percent said they preferred part time, while 47 percent said full time. When a 1992 Gordon Black poll for *USA Today* asked part-timers the reason for their status, 19 percent said they couldn't find full-time work, 19 percent said they were students and 18 percent said they had a child or family at home. The 1995 BLS survey indicated that only 20 percent of part-timers would prefer to be full time. But a different analysis of the same BLS data by the National Policy Association puts the percentage of contingent workers who would prefer non-contingent work at 56 percent.

Many specialists, however, are skeptical that part-timers are so discontent. "If you ask workers whether they want higher wages and more benefits, they will of course say yes," Lyons says. "But if you ask whether they are dissatisfied sufficiently to seek full-time work, most say no." They point to a Conference Board survey showing that as many as 97 percent of companies surveyed offer some benefits to their part-timers, adding that the majority of those part-timers who don't get health insurance from their own jobs can get it from a spouse.

Finally, surveys of temporary workers show impressive satisfaction rates, despite the fact that many also say they are given low-level tasks, denied credit for their work, ignored by co-workers and forced to switch work sites frequently. A poll of temps by the National Association of Temporary Staffing Services asked workers how long they planned to work as a temporary. A surprising 39 percent said they would do it indefinitely, compared with 14 percent who said they wanted it for less than a month and 11 percent who said less than a year. (A key reason for the satisfaction, the survey shows, is that as many as 66 percent of temps gain new skills, and nearly two out of three use the temp position to transition to full-time jobs. In addition, many of the agencies are now offering training and benefits.)

The fact that a temporary job is often the springboard to a full-time slot demonstrates the value of the temporary industry, says AEI's Kosters. "Lots of the part-timers are teenagers who have yet to develop the skills and experience" to land a good full-time job. He also argues that the pay gaps between part time and full time are less severe once differences in age, skills and experience are factored out. [20]

BLS data, however, show that contingent workers ages 16-19, while a large group in the universe of teenagers, are only the fourth-largest group of contingency workers overall, with those 25-34 the most plentiful, followed by those 35-44 and those 20-24.

"While it may be true that full-timers gain experience more rapidly, particularly in the professions," Rasell says, "part-timers eventually catch up, especially in jobs as basic as loading and unloading boxes from a UPS truck. If you're doing the same job and have the same qualifications," she says, "then you should get the same pay and benefits, pro-rated." ■

BACKGROUND

Recurring Issues

"I'm not 100 percent satisfied with what we got," said Teamsters leader Ron Carey as he ended a well-publicized strike against UPS. "But it is much better than what was offered to us before — unlimited attrition."

August 1997 in Washington? No, Carey was speaking in November 1974, in New York City. A federal mediator had just helped end an 87-day Teamsters strike in which the main issue confronting Carey's local, interestingly, was part-time work. UPS was relying upon it increasingly as it shifted its sorting operations from downtown to New York's suburbs. [21]

Though non-standard work arrangements have been around since capitalism's dawn, it is only since the postwar rise in union strength and the concept of employee benefits that it has become a bone of contention. The federal government took an interest in the problem as early as 1966, during the Johnson administration, when Labor Secretary Willard W. Wirtz ordered a study of "subemployment" in eight major U.S. cities. It found that 34.7 percent of the adult population fell under that heading, counting unemployed, involuntary part-timers, those earning under the minimum wage and family heads with full-time jobs earning less than what is required to raise a family of four above the poverty line. [22]

With a rising number of women joining the work force, studies showed that in the 1950s and '60s the number of voluntary part-time workers grew faster than the work force as a whole. (Part-timers in the 1950s were about 12 percent of the work force.) But by the 1970s, as inflation and productivity lags began causing workers in general to lose purchasing power, the situation reversed itself, and according to Tilly, involuntary part-timers grew faster than the overall work force. [23]

Bring on the Temps

It was during the 1970s that work place theorists began studying alternative work schedules, such as flextime, phased retirement and compressed workweeks, as well as voluntary, long-term part-time work as ways to accommodate changing lifestyle needs of employees. One's employment needs, analysts noted, usually change with each phase of life, which one study summed up as follows: ages 16-22 are for breaking out; ages 22-28 are for establishing one's self in the world; 28-33 is for second thoughts about one's place in the adult world; 30-40 is for settling down; 40-45 is for a midlife crisis; 45-55 for restabilization; and 55-65 for generativity (a new emphasis on sharing, teaching and contemplation). [24]

The corporate world took an interest from the point of view of profit maximization. Attention focused on a new practice in Germany, where department stores transformed employee schedules simply by putting saleswomen on a commission system, so there would be an incentive to be on the sales floor during peak hours. It was a success: Employees were more willing to pitch in when other departments became too crowded, and were grateful for time off during downtime. [25]

Another option coming increasingly into focus for employers was the use of employees provided by temporary agencies. The big names in the field — Manpower, Kelly and Olsten — had been founded right after World War II. (The image of the "Kelly girl" for years symbolized the young, female worker supporting herself with temporary jobs while awaiting marriage.) By the mid-1960s, the industry had its own trade association, the Institute of Temporary Services. By the '80s, the agencies were offering their screened, on-call workers fringe benefits and training in such skills as word processing and data entry.

Because of industry's fluidity, however, even the generous benefits can prove elusive. "When I'm ready for an assignment, there may not be one for me," one temp recalled. "I'm listed with three services, and some of them offer benefits based on the cumulative number of hours you work for them. So if I move around from service to service (which some temps need to do to earn a living), I can never accumulate enough hours to get the benefits they offer." [26]

Revenue growth in the temp industry ballooned by 361 percent from 1982 to 1994, though temps are still less than 2 percent of the work force. The federal government alone uses as many as 157,000 temps daily. [27] Milwaukee-based Manpower places about 150,000 employees on any given day in such areas as office work and truck-loading. (Its annual temporary placement of some 860,000 different individuals has led some to call it the nation's largest employer, but this seems an unfair comparison with, say, General Motors, whose 709,000 employees are regarded as "permanent.") Use of temporaries soon became so routine that many corporations no longer bothered to keep centralized records of how many their various divisions were using.

By the mid-1990s, temp agencies were being called "the ATMs of the job market," in the words of Mitchell Fromstein, chairman of Manpower: "The employer tells us, 'I want them, as many as I need, and when I don't

Continued on p. 950

Chronology

1940s-1950s
Postwar employment boom gives rise to first temporary-help agencies.

1946
Kelly Services founded.

1948
Manpower founded.

1950
Olsten Corp. network of temporary agencies founded.

1951
Internal Revenue Service (IRS) requires temp agencies to perform payroll functions like employers.

1960s-1970s
Federal government begins studying pay inequities between full- and part-time workers.

1963
Equal Pay Act says workers must be paid equally without regard to sex if jobs involve equal skill, responsibility and conditions.

1966
Institute of Temporary Services founded. Labor Secretary Willard W. Wirtz calculates that 34.7 percent of adult population in cities is subemployed.

1974
Employee Retirement Income Security Act (ERISA) requires pensions for those who work at least 1,000 hours per year. International Brotherhood of Teamsters strike against United Parcel Service over part-time work in New York City lasts 87 days.

1978
Revenue Act provides some protection from charges of misclassification to companies that use independent contractors.

1980s ***Rise of contingency work force.***

1982
Tax Equity and Fiscal Responsibility Act cracks down on abuses of leased workers.

1985
Consultant Audrey Freedman coins term "contingency work" at employment conference.

1986
Tax Reform Act narrows protection for companies in classifying independent contractors.

1988
Bureau of Labor Statistics stops tracking temporary workers as separate industry, reclassifies them into help-supply services.

1990s ***Era of corporate downsizing.***

1993
Labor Department's Women's Bureau issues report saying two-thirds of the workers moonlighting are women, or more than 3 million people. In *Daughtrey v. Honeywell Inc.*, a district court finds that a computer programmer laid off and rehired as an independent contractor is actually an employee.

April 1994
70,000 Teamsters strike against Trucking Management Inc. over the part-time issue.

December 1994
Labor Department's Commission on the Future of Worker-Management Relations, chaired by former Labor Secretary John T. Dunlop, releases recommendations that include improving the lot of contingency workers. BLS announces first comprehensive survey of contingent work force, with more detailed questions on voluntary part-time work.

Oct. 19, 1995
First annual Part-Time Professionals Day marked by Association of Part-Time Professionals.

March 1996
The IRS introduces a pilot program to make it easier to classify employees and independent contractors.

July 24, 1997
The 9th U.S. Circuit Court of Appeals rules that Microsoft Corp.'s independent contractors are eligible for stock purchases as common-law employees.

Aug. 4, 1997
Teamsters' union goes on strike against United Parcel Service over issues of the company's reliance on part-time workers and its plan to pull out of the union pension fund.

Aug. 19, 1997
UPS settles strike by giving in to most Teamsters' demands.

Aspiring Tenured Professors Watch With Dismay . . .

Americans from all walks of life paid heed to the part-time work issues raised by the recent strike against United Parcel Service. But the picketers' chants particularly resonated with up-and-coming academics.

"We took a special interest in the strike because the reliance on part-timers is even greater in higher education, even though it requires more qualifications" than package delivery, says Ernie Benjamin, director of research for the American Association of University Professors.

Over the past two decades, the trend toward staffing campuses with part-timers who earn less in salary and benefits than full professors has produced "a sacrifice in quality," Benjamin says. "The professors aren't given notice of the courses they'll be teaching until the last minute. Many of them teach at several campuses, so they don't hang out on any one campus and can't keep up with their students. They don't do extracurriculars, and many don't even have an office or a desk."

The number of faculty employed only part time rose from 29.9 percent in 1975 to 40 percent in 1993, according to the association. Together with non-tenure-track professors, they now account for more than half the nation's academics.

The chief reason for the "de-careering" of academe is, not surprisingly, the tremendous financial pressures felt by college administrators, not only at private schools but also state and community colleges and universities. [1] Given demands from parents, regents and state legislators that schools minimize tuition hikes, build new physical assets and acquire new technologies, it's not surprising that colleges zero in on personnel as an area in which to scrimp. Community colleges, for example, which rely most heavily on adjunct professors, can hire several adjuncts for a total of about $15,000 who combine to carry a full teaching load, compared with the $40,000 it would cost to assign the same work to one full-time professor receiving full benefits, the association says.

The verdict on the results, however, is coming in, and to many in the field, it doesn't look good. At George Mason University in Fairfax, Va., an adjunct professor recently complained, 40 percent of the English department's courses during the 1996-97 academic year were taught by adjuncts who are "overworked and underpaid." Many of them teach six or seven courses against the five generally taught by full professors, who have research and administrative duties. And because adjuncts work under contracts that are subject to renewal annually (some have been renewed for 10 years running), they are classified by Virginia law as part-timers regardless of the hours they put in, which means they receive no benefits. [2]

Part-Time vs. Full-Time

The percentage of full-time faculty members at U.S. colleges and universities has been dropping while part-timers are increasing.

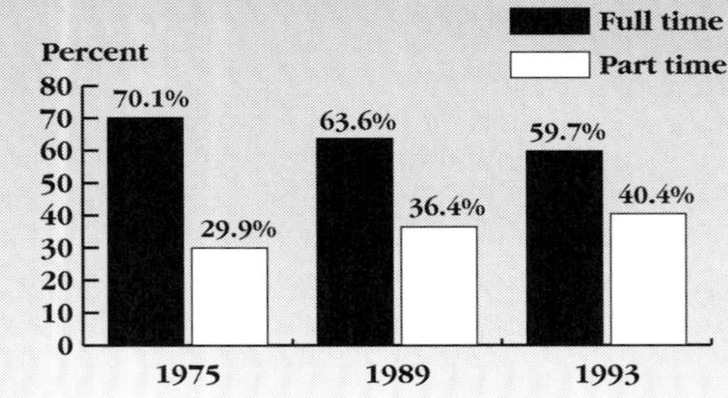

Sources: American Association of University Professors; National Center for Education Statistics, April 1996.

In their 1994 book *The Invisible Faculty,* Judith Gappa and David Leslie assert that the performance reviews given to part-timers and contract professors are often sloppy, and that campus administrators regard the professional development of such staffers as a low priority. "Because the tenured faculty benefit directly and personally from this bifurcation of the academic profession, they have a vested interest in maintaining it," they write. [3]

The damage the embrace of part-timers inflicts on the career prospects of scholars has become a frequent complaint in faculty lounges, where insecure, short-term lecturers can be heard expressing resentment that the vocabulary of corporate downsizing has invaded their ivy-covered walls. "In parking lots, I see the so-called gypsy professors, rushing from part-time to part-time jobs on several campuses, or as one-year replacements for people on sabbatical, and I feel sorry for them," says Frick Curry, a foreign policy analyst at a think tank who teaches as an adjunct at Mount Vernon College in Washington, D.C. "Particularly in the social sciences, where the market for Ph.Ds is so glutted, the colleges and universities take advantage of people by keeping salaries and benefits low, knowing that each applicant is aware that there are five or six people standing in line for the same job."

But in academe, as in the work world in general, there are plenty of part-timers who embrace the status voluntarily. "I teach not for the money but because I enjoy sharing knowledge with students," Curry says. "To have at least some adjuncts in every department can be healthy for the education system because you get teachers who haven't spent their whole career in the ivory tower."

. . . as Cash-Strapped Colleges Hire Part-Timers

Sandra Millers Younger, an editorial consultant who teaches a magazine-writing course at San Diego State University, appreciates — at least for now — the way part-time status permits her more time with her family without the pressures of publishing that weigh on full-time professors. "I like the intellectual stimulation of getting out of the house and having a rapport with students," she says. "My family gets access to the university libraries and swimming pool, and the job title gives me more marketing credibility in my editorial business," where her hourly earnings exceed those for her teaching.

And Ed Steidle, a year-by-year contract lecturer in English at Stanford University who moonlights at state and community colleges, acknowledges that a big reason he hasn't won a tenure-track appointment since earning his doctorate in 1980 is that he's simply not willing to leave the highly competitive San Francisco area to try his luck elsewhere. "The disappointing job market is tougher on people who are so dedicated that they're willing to go anywhere," he says. "Many of them simply quit the field."

The embrace of part-time professorships, however, is regrettable even to many in college and university management. "It can be good in certain fields by bringing enrichment from artists, musicians, business people and lawyers," says Paula P. Brownlee, president of the Association of American Colleges and Universities. And school planners, particularly at community colleges, depend heavily on the flexibility offered by adjuncts as the planners scramble to accommodate swings in course enrollment that come at the start of each academic term. "But in other ways part-time is a disastrous direction to go in," she says. "There's a constant flow of new, young, potential faculty members, well-qualified Ph.D.s who in the past would have gotten full-time tenure-track jobs, and now they're nomads. To our minds, it's a terrible waste of real talent."

Even the best part-timers are often not as committed to the work because they don't see a long-term future, she says. "They're often left out of deliberations and faculty meetings, and suffer an accumulation of small slights."

David Merkowitz, director of public affairs at the American Council on Education, says the real question with part time is at what point do students get shortchanged. "There's no bright line, but few in higher education would argue that the trend could continue ad infinitum without damage," he says. Still, student expectations are different at community colleges, where adjuncts fit well with their vocational mission, as opposed to research and comprehensive universities, where the part-timers are more frequently like teaching assistants, teaching the lower-division survey courses, he says. "In business schools, the upper-division courses are often taught by CEOs, but in the arts upper divisions, the adjuncts virtually disappear."

The demographics of the current post baby boom "echo boom" of births, Merkowitz predicts, could produce a rise in college-age Americans over the next 10 years that could stimulate demand for more full-time faculty just as the original baby boom did in the 1960s. But, he warns, colleges "might be reluctant to hire people who are already in their 30s if, instead of keeping up with their skills and research, they've spent the past decade driving from campus to campus or taking a different job to feed themselves."

The association of professors, which has been concerned about the trend toward part-time since the late 1970s, recommends that colleges and universities create a tenure track for part-timers. It also suggests that part-timers be limited to 15 percent of total instruction within an institution and 25 percent within a single department. [4]

Benjamin argues that students are becoming more aware of the rise in part-timers. Pundits and legislators draw attention to the problem by claiming that the reason many students have trouble getting time with their instructors is that too many full-time professors are so caught up in research that they leave all undergraduate teaching to graduate students. Benjamin counters that these students lack access to faculty because "there are too few full-time faculty, and because part-time faculty are not compensated for spending out-of-class time with students."

And though he acknowledges that university managers need some flexibility in hiring, he says the overall use of part-timers far exceeds what mere flexibility would require. The fact that so many of the part-timers are in the humanities, where the glutted job market makes them vulnerable to exploitation, he takes as a sign that hiring decisions are really being driven by the desire to save on salary and benefits. "If the public knowingly chooses to have state universities use part-timers for teaching, then OK," he says. "But it's useful to look at the expensive schools where rich people, who know the marketplace, choose to send their kids. The kids there get time and attention from full-time faculty, which costs money."

---

[1] For background, see "Paying for College," *The CQ Researcher,* Nov. 20, 1992, pp. 1001-1022.)

[2] David R. Williams, letter to *The Washington Post,* Sept. 14, 1997.

[3] Quoted in *Academe,* July-August, 1996, in Ernst Benjamin's review of John E. Roueche, Suanne D. Ooueche and Mark D. Milliron, *Strangers in Their Own Land: Part-Time Faculty in American Community Colleges* (1995).

[4] American Association of University Professors, "The Status of Non-Tenure-Track Faculty," June 1993.

Temporary-Help Industry Skyrockets

The number of temporary employees rose from a quarter of 1 percent of the work force in 1970 to nearly 2 percent in 1996, more than a tenfold increase.

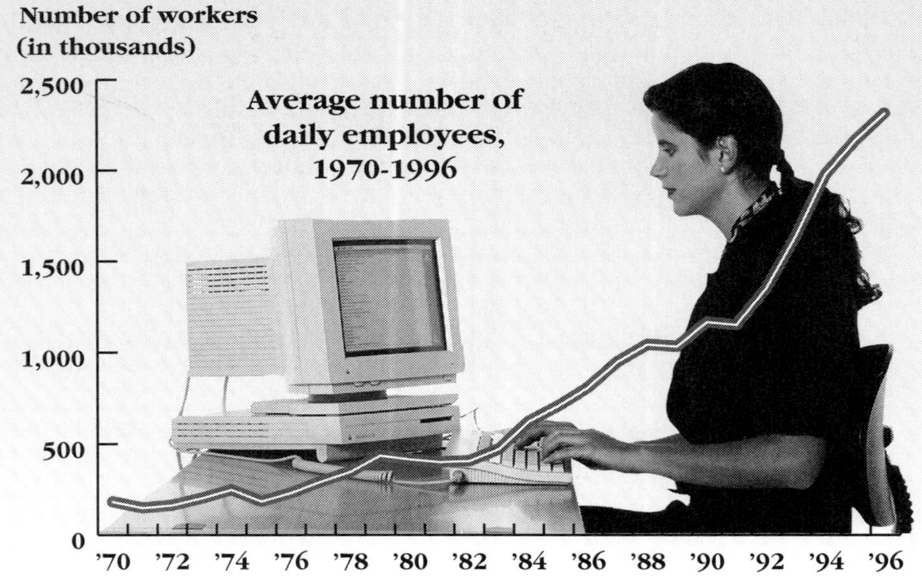

Source: National Association of Temporary and Staffing Services, Contemporary Times, *spring 1997.*

only 25 percent called it bad. The replacement of career workers with contingents was likened by *Time* to the havoc wreaked on farmers in the highlands of 18th-century Scotland, when landlords threw them off the land so they could convert to sheep grazing (leading many farmers to emigrate to America). [31] Describing how the BankAmerica Corp. in 1993 announced that it was turning 1,200 full-time jobs into part-time jobs with no benefits (and more such conversions promised), futurist Jeremy Rifkin wrote of a "requiem for the working class." [32]

When the Clinton administration came to Washington, its Labor and Commerce departments set up a Commission on the Future of Worker-Management Relations, chaired by former Labor Secretary John T. Dunlop. In Congress, then Rep. Patricia A. Schroeder, D-Colo., introduced the Part-Time and Temporary Workers Protection Act (in 1993 and again in 1996), which would have required employers to offer health and pension benefits to part-timers working at least 10 hours a week for a year.

In December 1994, the Dunlop commission released a series of workplace recommendations, including moves to increase employee participation in management, stimulate efforts to unionize, press for wage hikes for lower-income workers, enhance productivity and "upgrade the economic position of contingent workers." Neither the Schroeder bill nor the Dunlop recommendations

Continued from p. 846

need them, I don't want them here.' Can I get people to work under these circumstances? Yeah." [28]

Rising Insecurity

During the go-go years of the 1980s, the economic expansion that produced many new millionaires also raised new questions about income inequality that was in part due to the growth in contingent workers. As many as a fourth of the 10 million new jobs that President Ronald Reagan often claimed were created during his two terms were part time. [29]

Though many recall the '80s as years of plenty, a 1994 report by the National Commission for Employment Policy concluded that most of the rewards were concentrated in the upper-income levels. "A source of economic opportunity — i.e. flexible work patterns — is also a source of economic risk — i.e. worker layoffs," its chairman wrote. "The dilemma is maintaining the strengths inherent in our flexible labor markets without creating an economy that fails to provide job security. Flexibility cannot simply become a fancy word for 'fired,' or for a job without benefits or for a widening divergence between the 'haves' and 'have nots.' " [30]

When downsizing became the rage in the early 1990s, 44 percent of executives polled in 1993 by *Fortune* said the trend would increase in the next five years; 48 percent said it was good for the United States, while were acted upon by the new Republican leadership that had taken control of Congress on a platform of reducing government involvement in labor-management relations.

New Measurements

The part-time or non-standard work force, however, continued to be a focus of policy debate. In January 1994, the BLS implemented a redesign of its decades-old survey of the labor force, adding a more direct question about whether those employed less than full time would actually prefer to work more.

"This was the first time in nearly 30 years that we redid the survey and began computerized collection of data, implementing some recommendations from the 1970s," explains Tom Nardone, chief of labor force statistics. "We had always asked about voluntary status, but we used to simply ask how many hours the person had worked in the previous week. In our new survey, we asked everyone how many hours the person usually worked, and so we picked up more intermittent part-timers." And by asking the part-timers the direct question, "Do you want to work a full-time workweek of 35 hours or more?" the BLS found a slightly higher percentage of them who are part time by choice.

"Part-time work grew from about 14 percent [of the work force] in the 1960s to 17.5 percent in 1993," Nardone says, noting that the change in the survey question removes the opportunity to compare the new answers with past data. "Part-time work tends to go up during a recession and down in a recovery. In 1994, it was at about 18.9 percent and has since been trending down," he says. Whether it's truly voluntary depends on the individual. "You can have two people in the same situation, and one of them thinks it's a good job, and the other one thinks it's a bad one. I don't know how big the number of part-timers has to be in order to call the situation a crisis." ■

CURRENT SITUATION

After the Strike

The recent UPS strike was fought over the twin issues of UPS' rising reliance on part-time work and its proposal to take over the handling of workers' pensions from the Teamsters. * But it was the part-time issue that caught fire, largely because it was more understandable.

Many were sympathetic to the Teamsters' arguments: UPS reliance on part-timers (60 percent of its work force) was three times the percentage of part-timers in the national work force; 83 percent of the jobs created at UPS since 1993 were part-time; Teamster internal surveys showed that three-fourths of UPS part-timers were less than satisfied with their chances for going full-time.

"Unlike some other strike situations, it was one we could understand," said Sen. Richard J. Durbin, D-Ill., in a Labor Day statement. "Most of us have a family member, a friend or a neighbor who juggles several different part-time jobs or is unable to find full-time work." Also on Labor Day, Sen. Christopher J. Dodd, D-Conn., announced he was sponsoring legislation to create a federal blue-ribbon panel from business, labor, academia and government to investigate the role of part-time work in the economy.

Activists on behalf of contingency workers offer an array of remedies ranging from improvements in health care and better child care to a more generous earned-income tax credit and expansion of the Family and Medical Leave Act to cover smaller companies. "The public has become aware of the two-tier wage structure," says the Economic Policy Institute's Rasell. "The fact that the minimum-wage hike was passed last year shows that even with a Republican Congress, you can't rule out some action."

AEI's Kosters counters that when the government mandates benefits on private employers, it provokes an offsetting drop in wages. The National Federation of Independent Business, in fact, calculates that a 1 percent increase in fringe benefits will increase the amount of involuntary part-time employment by more than a half-percent. [33]

Meanwhile, the Employment Policy Foundation warned that part-timers at UPS will actually take home less money than if the Teamsters had accepted the company's final offer and not gone on strike. UPS lost at least $1 billion in projected annual revenues due to customers who switched to competitors after the strike, and the company even warned of coming layoffs. (Later, however, UPS actually began hiring after some 15,000 part-timers quit because of the strike.) [34]

Classifying Employees

In July, congressional Republicans preparing a budget and tax agree-

* In essence, UPS wanted to handle the pensions because it could save money by providing a leaner plan for its own workers, who were generally younger than the overall Teamsters' membership and would make fewer demands, in the short term, on the pension system than the Teamsters as a whole.

ment for President Clinton considered a proposal to give businesses more flexibility to hire "independent contractors" as opposed to "employees," who are eligible for benefits. For years, the Internal Revenue Service (IRS) has worked to enforce guidelines to prevent employers from misclassifying employees in order to avoid the cost of benefits, Social Security, workers' compensation and employer taxes. The practice is especially common in such industries as advertising, publishing, entertainment, telecommunications, software and construction. A 1989 General Accounting Office study found that 38 percent of employers sometimes misclassified their workers, and in June 1994, the accounting firm of Coopers & Lybrand estimated that such bookkeeping games cost the federal government as much as $3.3 billion annually.

In 1993, in *Daughtrey v. Honeywell Inc.*, a district court established the concept of a "common law employee" after it heard details of a computer programmer who was laid off and then rehired as a consultant. Because the "consultant" used Honeywell equipment, came to Honeywell offices, was paid hourly and had no other clients, the court decided that she was an employee, entitled to benefits. [35]

Again in July, the 9th U.S. Circuit Court of Appeals ruled that the Microsoft Corp. had to award discounted company stock to hundreds of computer specialists it had hired as "independent contractors," but whom, the court decided, actually met the IRS' definition of employees. King's County, Wash., recently lost a similar case in a class action suit that could require the county to pony up an additional $40 million on behalf of its employees. "An employee is an employee, whatever he or she is called," said David Stogaugh, a Seattle lawyer for the county workers. [36]

Employers, however, argue that such laws are being abused by trial lawyers bent on litigation. They point to a 1996 case in which the 3rd U.S. Circuit Court of Appeals ruled in favor of a man who said he was eligible for health care with an environmental cleanup firm, even though, as a temporary with only six months tenure, he had only recently been told he was to be promoted to full time and wasn't scheduled to officially begin for another few days. [37]

In Congress, Rep. Jon Christensen, R-Neb., backed by the U.S. Chamber of Commerce and small-business groups, proposed a new three-part test for "clarifying" who is an independent contractor. It would be based on a written contract, whether the workers have their principal place of business away from the work site and, having passed the first two tests, whether they get most income from commissions. The AFL-CIO was among the groups that succeeded in getting the plan dropped, warning that it would strip such workers as pizza deliverers of their employee benefits. [38]

The IRS in March 1996 introduced a pilot program to make classification of employees and independent contractors easier to pass judgment on earlier in the accounting process. It is also preparing updated guidelines based on 92 case studies.

Employee Leasing

In April, Massachusetts Attorney General Scott Harshbarger announced the sentencing of an officer of Employee Staffing of America, a Connecticut-based firm that had been hiring workers in the Bay State. The company was fined $33,000 and the executive sentenced to 10 years in prison for larceny committed by misclassifying employees in order to avoid paying the state's workers' compensation program as much as $4.2 million.

Illegal misclassification has for years been a problem in the field of "employee leasing," a legitimate business that grew up in the 1980s in which third-party companies step in and hire all of a company's employees, relieving the client company of administering payroll and employee benefits. Though leasing firms have been known to go out of business abruptly, and are sometimes regarded as a means for busting unions, they can save small firms as much as 70 percent of their payroll costs.

Leasing firms can also help improve the lot of employees. A Small Business Administration study in 1986 found that 10 of 21 small businesses surveyed provided no medical benefits and that none provided dental benefits — until they started leasing. [39] Congress, however, as far back as the 1982 Tax Equity and Fiscal Responsibility Act, has sought to crack down on abuses of leased workers.

Milan Yager, executive vice president of the National Association of Professional Employer Organizations, says his industry, whose members he prefers to call "co-employers" rather than employee leasers, has nothing to do with firms that misclassify. His group changed its name and discarded the term "leasing" because "people no longer look to us for a short-term fix; we're now for the long-term," he says. "We have an interest in workers' benefits, and we can work equally with union and non-union firms." There are some 2-3 million workers employed by about 2,000 co-employment firms, he says, calling it a "growth industry of the 1990s and the next century."

Firms that lease employees do complain about the federal regulations. "Changes should be made in the current tax code relating to so-

Continued on p. 954

At Issue:

Is the growth of part-time, temporary and subcontracted employment unfair to workers?

yes

RICHARD S. BELOUS
Vice president and chief economist, National Policy Association

FROM "THE RISE OF THE CONTINGENT WORK FORCE: GROWTH OF TEMPORARY, PART-TIME AND SUBCONTRACTED EMPLOYMENT," *LOOKING AHEAD*, JUNE 1997.

A sea change is taking place in the world of work. In the original "Leave It to Beaver" [TV] show . . . Beaver Cleaver's father, Ward, was an executive with a major corporation. So was the father of Beaver's friend Lumpy. These dads had stable, long-term employment. . . .

Now consider the revived "Still the Beaver" shown . . . on cable TV. Ward is no longer there, and June works part time outside the home. Beaver and Lumpy have not followed their fathers' corporate career paths; instead, they are trying to make a go of it as . . . consultants. . . . Most of the people of Beaver's generation in the new series are portrayed as contingent workers.

The shift in the world of work from Ward's era to Beaver's current reality has generated many benefits and costs for workers, families and society. America is not alone in these trends. Japanese and European labor markets are also moving toward a more contingent economy.

In general, the U.S. labor market has become more flexible in recent years, but America's social welfare system . . . has in general remained quite rigid. In the coming years, a key human resource issue will be to create a more flexible social welfare system to deal with the new labor market realities. Although public decisionmakers may exert a strong influence on these issues, market forces also will induce dramatic changes.

Labor-management relations are being jolted by the growth of contingent work arrangements. Moreover, the shift to a contingent economy could have a major impact in many areas beyond the board room, office, shop and factory floor. Improvements in the quantity, quality and methods of the deployment of human resources are estimated to account for two to three times the contribution of other inputs in sparking economic growth. After World War II, some nations prospered that were rich in nothing but human resources, while others languished that were poor only in those resources. In the final analysis, the real wealth of a nation lies in its human resources. . . .

If serious consideration is not given to equity-related issues as the U.S. economy continues to move toward contingent work relationships, millions of workers and their families could fall through the cracks. . . .

no

MAX R. LYONS
Economist, Employment Policy Foundation

FROM *PART-TIME WORK: NOT A PROBLEM REQUIRING A SOLUTION*, EMPLOYMENT POLICY FOUNDATION, 1997.

A growing number of observers have been warning about "dramatic" and "unprecedented" changes in the structure of U.S. employment. They argue that the eight-hour day, 40-hour work week is disappearing. Full-time, or "core," workers are being replaced by "contingent," or "peripheral," workers. . . .

The implication . . . is that the size of the contingent work force is very large and growing. But is it? Until recently, available estimates of the size of the contingent work force varied considerably, largely because there was no agreement on the definition of who is contingent. Most observers considered any part-time, temporary, contract or self-employed worker to be contingent. . . .

In response to the growing concern over the contingent work force, the Bureau of Labor Statistics (BLS) began to measure the contingent work force for the first time in 1995. It estimated that (depending on the exact definition) the contingent work force only consisted of between 2.2 and 4.9 percent of total employment.

The BLS' definition of contingent workers includes only those who do not perceive themselves as having an explicit or implicit contract for ongoing employment; i.e., contingent workers' employment depends upon their employers' need for their services. Under this definition most part-time, temporary or self-employed workers are not contingent. For most, their jobs have lasted for at least a year, and they expect their jobs to continue for the foreseeable future. . . . It is the inclusion of large numbers of part-time and temporary workers that causes most estimates of contingent workers to be dramatically higher than the BLS count. What most analysts seem to have neglected is that these workers are in stable jobs — ones that they expect to keep; they do not consider themselves contingent, nor do they wish to [work] full time.

Indeed, the number of part-time workers is almost three times as large as the number of self-employed workers, 18 times as large as the number of temporaries and more than 30 times as large as the number who work for contract firms. Thus, observers who have complained about the "contingent" work force, have (perhaps unknowingly) been referring largely to part-time workers. . . . However, it is unreasonable to consider most part-time workers contingent, since a large majority of part-time workers choose to work less than a full-time schedule, and they expect an ongoing employment relationship.

FOR MORE INFORMATION

Association of Part-time Professionals, 7700 Leesburg Pike, Suite 216, Falls Church, Va. 22043; (703) 734-7975. This group operates a job bank, conducts seminars, runs a speaker's bureau and publishes a newsletter to help find flexible work hours for professionals who want to spend more time with families or go to school.

Economic Policy Institute, 1660 L St. N.W., Suite 1200, Washington, D.C. 20036; (202) 775-8810. This foundation-backed think tank analyzes issues such as job creation, income distribution, employee benefits and poverty.

Employment Policy Foundation, 1015 15th St. N.W., Suite 1200, Washington, D.C. 20005; (202) 789-8685. Through policy analysis and economic studies, this employer-backed group seeks to encourage an employment-policy framework that facilitates job creation, job security and a rising standard of living.

National Association of Temporary and Staffing Services, 119 S. Saint Asaph St., Alexandria, Va. 22314; (703) 549-6287. This trade group of 1,600 staffing companies promotes the interests of its members through legal and legislative advocacy, public relations, education and guidance on ethics.

Continued from p. 952
called leased employees that impose needless record-keeping and administrative burdens on businesses that use outside staffing arrangements," writes Edward A. Lenz of the National Association of Temporary and Staffing Services. [40] ■

OUTLOOK

Unionization?

"The UPS strike was tough-fought, and UPS showed how tough the American corporation can be," says the AFL-CIO's Palley. "But UPS was a firm headed down the low road. It is a better part-time employer than most part-time employers, but part time is not the solution for American families."

The major unions, of course, will use the victory over UPS as a shot in the arm for labor organizing. Currently, only about 4.9 percent of the contingency work force is unionized, according to the National Policy Association. (The work force as a whole is about 10 percent unionized, and falling.) In September, at an AFL-CIO conference on women workers, a workshop was held on how to organize temporary workers who, in addition to the usual obstacles to union recruitment, present the added challenge of switching job sites frequently.

But temporary agencies have been heard to say they specifically avoid hiring people they consider "political fanatics." "We don't want complainers," said one. "We don't want people who are going to speak out about wages or working conditions, just people who are confident and willing to work." [41]

Whether the organizers succeed will depend not only on union strategies but on the type of industry and the overall state of the economy. "Certain segments of the economy — Silicon Valley, for example — have developed high concentrations of part-time workers," notes benefits consultant Dennis A. Tosh. "Local conditions, competitors' practices and a firm's market are likely to determine how pressing these issues are for individual companies." [42]

In spinning out one of the worst-case scenarios, Rifkin warns that many future workers "on reduced schedules are likely to be pressured by the marketplace to spend their leisure indulging in mass entertainment and stepped-up consumption. The increasing number of unemployed . . . people, by contrast, will find themselves sinking inexorably into the permanent underclass. Desperate, many will turn to the informal economy to survive. Some will barter occasional work for food and lodging. Others will engage in theft and petty crime. Drug dealing and prostitution will continue to increase." [43]

There are equally dire visions in the business community, where some are starting to call the entire system of employee benefits an anachronism.

"What do companies get for this trouble and money?" asks one writer. "Black eyes — not only from the usual adversaries in the media and government, as UPS is finding out, but also from the recipients of their generosity." [44]

But others who work with part-time, temporary or contingency workers emphasize ways to improve the general atmosphere. "Remember, it's a partnership," one management handbook counsels. "Avoid the feeling of second-class by looking for and correcting patterns in the work or the schedule that isolate [non-standard workers] unnecessarily, making sure that meetings are scheduled at times they can attend and providing positive feedback on good work." [45]

Corporate flexibility is fine, says Hickey of the Campaign for America's

Future, "as long as it doesn't undermine the basic principles of workers' rights on the job."

Meaningful, available work, of course, has long been recognized as integral to the self-concept of most human beings.

"It's humiliating," said a health-care worker struggling with the psychological blow of having lost her full-time job. "It's difficult in terms of meeting expenses, and on an interpersonal level. In our society, the first question people ask is 'What do you do?' You are what you do." [46] ■

Notes

[1] For background, see "Downward Mobility," *The CQ Researcher,* July 23, 1993, pp. 625-648.

[2] William Bridges, *JobShift: How to Prosper in a Workplace Without Jobs* (1994), p. 1.

[3] A new Bureau of Labor Statistics survey of contingent workers, based on data taken in February 1997, is due out in November.

[4] Bruce Steinberg, "Temporary Help Services: 1996 Performance Review," *Contemporary Times,* spring 1997.

[5] For background, see "Labor Movement's Future," *The CQ Researcher,* June 28, 1996, pp. 553-576.

[6] Jacklyn Fierman, "The Contingency Work Force," *Fortune,* Jan. 24, 1994, p. 31.

[7] Robert M. Tomasko, *Rethinking the Corporation: The Architecture of Change,* American Management Association (1993), p. 171.

[8] Interview in *Time* magazine, March 29, 1993.

[9] *The Washington Post,* April 24, 1996.

[10] *The New York Times,* Sept. 1, 1997.

[11] *The Washington Times,* Aug. 18, 1997.

[12] Quoted in *The Washington Post,* Sept. 14, 1997.

[13] "No Part-Time Job Explosion," *The Economist,* Aug. 16, 1997, p. 23.

[14] Stanley Nollen and Helen Axel, *Managing Contingent Workers* (1996), p. 86.

[15] Ida L. Walters, "Temping Fate," *Reason,* April 1994.

[16] Anne E. Polivka, "A Profile of Contingent Workers," *Monthly Labor Review,* October 1996, p. 10.

[17] Arne L. Kallebert et al, "Nonstandard Work, Substandard Jobs: Flexible Work Arrangements in the U.S.," *Economic Policy Institute,* 1997, p. 16.

[18] Chris Tilly, *Half a Job: Bad and Good Part-Time Jobs in a Changing Labor Market* (1996), p. 4.

[19] Robert E. Parker, *Flesh Peddlers and Warm Bodies: The Temporary Help Industry and Its Workers* (1994), p. 45.

[20] See Marvin Kosters, "Part-Time Pay," *Journal of Labor Research,* summer 1995, p. 63.

[21] Quoted in *The New York Times,* Nov. 21, 1974.

[22] Parker, *op. cit.*

[23] Tilly, *op. cit.,* p. 1.

[24] Allan R. Cohen and Herman Gadon, *Alternative Work Schedules: Integrating Individual and Organizational Needs* (1978), p. 123.

[25] Cohen, *op. cit.,* p. 104.

[26] William Lewis and Nancy Schuman, *Temp Workers Handbook,* American Management Association (1988), p. 83.

[27] Jeremy Rifkin, *The End of Work* (1995), p. 193.

[28] *Time, op. cit.*

[29] Parker, *op. cit.,* p. 10.

[30] Anthony Carnevale, *The Washington Post,* "Outlook," Nov. 27, 1994.

[31] *Time, op. cit.*

[32] Rifkin, *op. cit.,* p. 190.

[33] W. Gilmore McKie and Laurence Lipsett, *The Contingent Worker: A Human Resources Perspective* (1995), p. 30.

[34] *The Washington Post,* Sept. 17, 1997.

[35] Nollen and Axel, *op. cit.,* p. 191.

[36] *USA Today,* Sept. 2, 1997.

[37] Janet Novack, "Gotcha, gotcha!" *Forbes,* Feb. 24, 1997, p. 60.

[38] *The New York Times,* July 20, 1997.

[39] William M. Lewis and Nancy H. Molloy, *How to Choose & Use Temporary Services* (1991), p. 143.

[40] Edward A. Lenz, "Flexible Employment: Positive Work Strategies for the 21st Century," *Journal of Labor Research,* fall 1996.

[41] Parker, *op. cit.,* p. 47.

[42] Dennis A. Tosh, "After the UPS Strike," *ACA News,* October 1997, p. 11.

[43] Rifkin, *op. cit.,* p. 239.

[44] Craig J. Cantoni, "The Case Against Employee Benefits," *The Wall Street Journal,* Aug. 18, 1997.

[45] Barney Olmsted and Suzanne Smith, *Managing in a Flexible Workplace* (1997), p. 104.

[46] Bridges, *op. cit.,* p. 119.

Bibliography

Selected Sources Used

Books

Bridges, William, *JobShift: How to Prosper in a Workplace Without Jobs*, Addison-Wesley, 1994.
A management consultant analyzes the trend toward "de-jobbing," seeking to show workers and managers how to become more self-sufficient as independent operators in the marketplace.

Lewis, William, and Nancy Schuman, *The Temp Workers Handbook*, American Management Association, 1988.
Two career and training consultants offer a glimpse into life as a temp, giving advice on where to find the best assignments.

Nollen, Stanley, and Helen Axel, *Managing Contingent Workers: How to Reap the Benefits and Reduce the Risks*, American Management Association, 1996.
A business professor and a management research consultant provide case studies and practical pointers on how companies make use of non-standard work arrangements, with a discussion on whether they are profitable.

Olmsted, Barney, and Suzanne Smith, *Managing in a Flexible Workplace*, American Management Association, 1997.
Two business consultants who founded San Francisco-based New Ways to Work examine the modern variations in work arrangements, such as compressed work-weeks, part-time work, job sharing, telecommuting and flextime.

Parker, Robert E., *Flesh Peddlers and Warm Bodies: The Temporary Help Industry and Its Workers*, Rutgers University Press, 1994.
A University of Nevada-Las Vegas sociologist documents and criticizes America's increasing dependence on relatively poorly compensated temporary workers who are "cheap, docile and flexible."

Rifkin, Jeremy, *The End of Work: The Decline of the Global Labor Force and the Dawn of the Post-Market Era*, G.P. Putnam's Sons, 1995.
A futurist and technology specialist warns that corporate downsizing and high-tech automation will produce a growing "new reserve army" of the unemployed and underemployed. He recommends solutions such as job-sharing and an emphasis on nonprofit public works.

Tilly, Chris, *Half a Job: Bad and Good Part-Time Jobs in a Changing Labor Market*, Temple University Press, 1996.
A University of Massachusetts economist argues that the rise in involuntary part-time employment over recent decades has heightened income inequality and prompted many dissatisfied workers to settle for less.

Tomasko, Robert M., *Rethinking the Corporation: The Architecture of Change*, American Management Association, 1993.
A management consultant with Arthur D. Little examines the dramatic changes in the corporate environment that is producing streamlined staffs and less-rigid job descriptions.

Reports

Belous, Richard S., "The Rise of the Contingent Workforce: Growth of Temporary, Part-Time, and Subcontracted Employment," National Policy Association, June 1997.
An economist at a union-backed think tank produced this analysis of economic developments over the past two decades that some fear threaten the economic health of working people.

Kallebert, Arne L. et al, "Nonstandard Work, Substandard Jobs: Flexible Work Arrangements in the U.S., Economic Policy Institute, 1997.
A team of economists at this foundation-supported think tank interprets government data on the contingent work force and concludes that low-income workers — especially females — are getting a bad deal.

McKie, W. Gilmore, and Laurence Lipsett, *The Contingent Worker: A Human Resources Perspective*, Society for Human Resource Management, 1995.
A human resources professional and an industrial psychologist examine the array of non-standard work arrangements along with the policy and personnel issues surrounding them.

Labor Department, Bureau of Labor Statistics, "Contingent and Alternative Employment Arrangements," *Report 900*, August 1995.
The government's chief statistics-gatherer on employment reports on a unique survey of non-standard workers, both voluntary and non-voluntary.

Max R. Lyons, "Part-Time Work: Not a Problem Requiring a Solution," Employment Policy Foundation, 1997.
An economist at a business-backed think tank examines government data and argues that the so-called crisis of the rising contingency work force has been overstated.

The Next Step

Additional information from UMI's Newspaper & Periodical Abstracts™ database

Alternative Employment

Aeppel, Timothy, "Life at the factory: Full time, part time, temp — All see the job in a different light," ***The Wall Street Journal,*** **March 18, 1997, p. A1.**
Lamson & Sessions Co., a plastics factory in Bowling Green, Ohio, operates round the clock with five categories of workers, mostly women. It has about 90 full-time, permanent employees, 40 temporaries and 70 independent contractors who work outside the facility. In addition, it has people who work only in summer and others who work part time. Each group of workers views the job differently and each feels varying degrees of loyalty. The problems resulting from this flexibility are examined.

Polivka, Anne E., "Into contingent and alternative employment: By choice?" ***Monthly Labor Review,*** **October 1996, pp. 55-74.**
Workers enter contingent and alternative arrangements from many different activities and for a wide variety of reasons. Although some workers are involuntarily in such arrangements, as a proportion of the employed, they are relatively few.

Smith, Vicki, "New forms of work organization," ***Annual Review of Sociology,*** **1997, pp. 315-339.**
Research on the organizational innovations comprising new flexible forms of work reveals a model of combined and uneven flexibility, characterized by the opening of opportunities that are differentially distributed across different groups of American workers.

Stansky, Lisa, "Changing shifts," ***ABA Journal,*** **June 1997, pp. 54-60.**
More and more businesses are implementing alternative workstyles to make employees happier and more productive. Various new options for the workplace, such as telecommuting, independent contracting and flextime, are discussed.

Benefits for Part-time Employees

Algeo, David, "Columbia alters part-timers' benefits," ***The Denver Post,*** **Nov. 13, 1996, p. C2.**
Denver's biggest hospital system, Columbia-HealthONE, is eliminating medical, dental and other benefits for 122 of its own part-time employees.

Burkins, Glenn, "U.S. is pressing states to expand jobless benefits," ***The Wall Street Journal,*** **May 13, 1997, p. A24.**
The Labor Department is drafting a document that would ask states to change the way they determine who is eligible for unemployment insurance. If adopted by the states, eligibility for unemployment compensation would be significantly expanded to include part-time workers and those who quit their jobs.

Reid, Alexander, "Towns balk at benefits largesse," ***The Boston Globe,*** **June 1, 1997, Sec. WKS, p. 1.**
The town of Pembroke, Mass., is trying to eliminate town-financed health insurance for part-time elected employees. In late May 1997, the selectmen voted to ask town attorneys to study elimination of the practice.

Independent Contractors

Flynn, Gillian, "Independent contractor vs. employee: Get it right," ***Workforce,*** **September 1997, pp. 125-130.**
Classifying employees as independent contractors is a risky business. Attorney Howard A. Simon explains the must-knows of classifying workers as independent contractors instead of employees.

Meyer, Harvey, "Don't get stung by a sweet outsourcing deal," ***Business & Health,*** **July 1997, pp. 34-38.**
The corporate use of contract workers offers a slew of advantages, but government crackdowns and legal complications can make it a perilous proposition.

"Who's an Independent Contractor?" ***St. Louis Post-Dispatch,*** **July 29, 1997, p. B6.**
When are workers employees and when are they independent contractors? The distinction has become a matter of great concern to both companies and workers alike. Now that more than 8 million people work at home, properly determining their status is important both to workers and bosses alike. Small businesses that want to hire workers part-time need a clear definition, lest they incur penalties from the Internal Revenue Service. Big companies want clarity, too. If they know exactly how to turn their payroll employees into independent contractors, they can save a lot of money; Independent contractors don't have to be paid benefits-pensions, Social Security, unemployment, workers' compensation or health insurance.

Part-time Workers

Appelbaum, Eileen, "Close the wage gap now," ***USA Today,*** **Aug. 7, 1997, p. A12.**
The pay difference between part-time and full-time workers is huge and persistent, writes Appelbaum,

associate director of research at the Economic Policy Institute and co-author of *The New American Workplace.* When you go to the deli of your neighborhood supermarket on a busy Saturday, you may be surprised to learn that the part-time workers slicing the salami are often hired at lower hourly wages than full-time workers doing the same job.

Bloom, Jennifer Kingson, "Career Tracks: Portable Executives Find Top-Level Work as Temps," *American Banker,* Jan. 28, 1997, p. 1.

Banks, like other employers, are relying increasingly on temporary professional help to fill senior posts. While banks have long hired tellers and clerical workers for brief stints, they are now tapping temps for such high-profile jobs as trust officer or human resources recruiter.

Gardner, Jennifer, "Hidden part-timers: Full-time work schedules, but part-time jobs," *Monthly Labor Review,* September 1996, pp. 43-44.

In 1995, approximately 6.5 million workers had a part-time job, but were classified as full-time workers because their total weekly worktime was 35 hours or more. Workers in this category were more likely to be in the 25- to 54-year-old age group.

"Part-Time vs. Full-Time," *The Christian Science Monitor,* Aug. 7, 1997, p. 20.

The marquee issue in the Teamsters' strike against United Parcel Service is part-time employment. Specifically, the union charges that the company is opting for part-time jobs as a way to cut costs and deprive workers of a living wage. Extensive part-time employment in the U.S. is hardly new. Some 17 percent of employed people today work part time. In 1979, another period of relatively low unemployment, the figure was 18 percent, according to Robert Lerman, an economist with the Urban Institute in Washington, D.C.

Temporaries

Benner, Chris, "Computer workers feel the byte: Temp jobs in Silicon Valley," *Dollars & Sense,* September 1996, pp. 23-25.

Silicon Valley in California is leading the way in creating unstable jobs for millions of workers, as permanent employees are being replaced by temporary, part-time and contract workers. Labor and community groups in the area are responding by developing new models of labor organization and calling for major shifts in public policy to address job insecurity.

Carnoy, Martin, Manuel Castells and Chris Benner, "Labour markets and employment practices in the age of flexibility: A case study of Silicon Valley," *International Labour Review,* spring 1997, pp. 27-48.

Focusing on temporary employment agencies, Carnoy et al show that this and other forms of flexible employment have become a permanent strategy among firms, which may create insecurity for low-skilled workers.

Davidson, Linda, "The temp pool's shrinking," *Workforce,* April 1997, pp. 72-80.

Because of drastically low unemployment, temporary staffing firms are having problems finding enough qualified workers to fill jobs. An examination of what's causing the problem and what these employers can do to keep their flexible staffing strategy alive and well is presented.

Gruner, Stephanie, "The temporary executive," *Inc.,* October 1996, p. 85.

W&H Systems' General Manager Jim Iversen hired a temporary chief financial officer for a three-month period. The three-day-a-week CFO prepared the company for new hurdles.

"Jobs are changing, not disappearing," *HR Focus,* June 1996, p. 16.

A recent survey of human resource professionals found that most companies that downsize are simultaneously creating new jobs. Half of the managers surveyed said that at least some new positions were filled by temporary workers or part-time workers.

Larson, Jan, "Temps are here to stay," *American Demographics,* February 1996, pp. 26-31.

Estimates of the number of people with temporary work situations vary tremendously, but researchers agree that outsourcing is one of the hottest branches of the labor force. Contingent workers enjoy variety and flexibility, but they usually get lower earnings and benefits.

Sunoo, Brenda Paik, "From Santa to CEO — temps play all roles," *Personnel Journal,* April 1996, pp. 34-44.

Temporary workers are needed by companies in the wake of downsizings, global competition and changing technology. Temporary executives can be especially useful to companies.

"Temporary staffing's still growing, but a little slower," *Managing Office Technology,* September 1996, p. 34.

The temporary staffing industry grew by 361% between 1982 and 1994, and five percent of the total labor market was comprised of temporary workers by 1995. The continued, but slower, growth in the temporary staffing industry can be attributed to five basic factors.

Weiss, Rick, "Temp Pool Alters Scientific Method; Laboratories Experiment, Find Success With Part-Time Researchers," *The Washington Post,* Jan. 30, 1997, p. A1.

When Mohan Khare needed a temporary employee to fill in for a while at his Columbia-based environmental testing company, he did what executives nationwide have done for 50 years: He called Kelly Services, the company that became famous for its "Kelly Girl" clerical workers. But the part-time employee that Kelly sent was not your average temp. This one had a chemistry degree from the prestigious California Institute of Technology. As the federal government hands more of its research to private contractors and science is run increasingly as a business, a growing number of laboratories are saving money and hassles by hiring scientist-temps.

United Parcel Service

DeBare, Ilana, "What's Behind The Deep Rift In UPS Strike: Issues are pensions, part-time workers," ***San Francisco Chronicle,*** **Aug. 14, 1997, p. A1.**

It was a bitter strike over part-time workers. United Parcel Service wanted to hire more; Teamsters leader Ron Carey wanted strict limits. The strike began in August and stretched on for 87 long days. The main issues at the center of the strike — UPS' heavy use of part-time workers and who should control the UPS workers' pension plans — have been raised in contract talks before.

"Few winners in UPS strike," ***USA Today,*** **Aug. 20, 1997, p. A14.**

UPS lost more than $600 million worth of business during this summer's strike, not small change even for a company that generates $22 billion a year. In fact, it's equal to well over half of last year's $1 billion profit. And many of UPS' shareholder-owners are also employees. And some of them may be out of work. Hustling competitors have grabbed chunks of UPS' business and will be fighting to hang on to at least part of it. UPS talks of a 5 percent falloff in daily volume and 15,000 layoffs until business grows back.

"Gripes about part-timers at UPS just don't add up," ***USA Today,*** **Aug. 7, 1997, p. A12.**

Facts and history say workers will lose if Teamsters win. Part-timers are vital, and in this case well-treated. No doubt about it. The Teamsters strike against United Parcel Service proves the union still has the muscle to make the economy wince. Just three days after the walkout, Sears, Toys R Us, Spiegel and other retailers are calling on President Clinton to intervene. The shipment of goods, the retailers say, "is our lifeblood."

Schmeltzer, John, "As UPS Strike Drags on, Some Workers Want to Vote on Offer," ***Chicago Tribune,*** **Aug. 16, 1997, p. 1.**

Little progress was made Friday in the second day of renewed talks aimed at settling the 12-day-old strike by the Teamsters Union against United Parcel Service. The Teamsters say one of their goals is to force the nation's largest shipper into transforming part-time jobs into full-time positions. Sixty percent of the 190,000 striking Teamsters hold part-time positions, although many work more than 35 hours a week for UPS.

Schmeltzer, John, "Part-Timers Drive UPS Strike," ***Chicago Tribune,*** **Aug. 5, 1997, p. 1.**

The strike Monday by 190,000 Teamsters against UPS is about a group of workers who are booming in numbers as America moves toward a more service-oriented economy. The outcome of the strike will be closely watched by employers, who have become increasingly reliant on part-time workers, and by part-timers, who may feel emboldened if the union wins significant concessions.

Statement of Ownership
Management, Circulation

Act of Aug. 12, 1970: Section 3685, Title 39, United States Code

Title of Publication: The CQ Researcher. Date of filing: October 24, 1997. Frequency of issue: Weekly (Except for 1/3, 5/30, 8/29, 10/31/97). No. of issues published annually: 48. Annual subscription price for libraries, businesses and government: $340. Location of known office of publication: 1414 22nd Street, N.W., Washington, D.C. 20037-1097. Names and addresses of publisher, editor and managing editor: Publisher, Robert W. Merry, 1414 22nd Street, N.W., Washington, D.C. 20037-1097; Editor, Sandra Stencel, 1414 22nd Street, N.W., Washington, D.C. 20037-1097; Managing Editor, Thomas J. Colin, 1414 22nd Street, N.W., Washington, D.C. 20037-1097. Owner: Congressional Quarterly, 1414 22nd Street, N.W., Washington, D.C. 20037-1097. Known bondholders, mortgagees and other security holders owning or holding 1 percent or more of total amount of bonds, mortgages or other securities: none.

Extent and Nature of Circulation	Average Number of Copies Each Issue During Preceding 12 months	Actual Number of Copies of Single Issue Published Nearest to Filing Date
A. Total number of copies printed *(Net Press Run)*	6,130	5,830
B. Paid Circulation		
1. Sales through dealers and carriers, street vendors and counter sales	—	—
2. Mail subscriptions	4,803	4,756
C. Total paid and/or requested circulation	4,803	4,756
D. Free distribution by mail carrier or other means. Samples, Complimentary and other free copies	238	155
E. Total distribution *(Sum of C and D)*	5,041	4,911
F. Copies not distributed		
1. Office use, left over, unaccounted, spoiled after printing	1,089	919
2. Returns from news agents	—	—
G. Total *(Sum of E and F)* — should equal net press run shown in A)	6,130	5,830

Back Issues

Great Research on Current Issues Starts Right Here . . . Recent topics covered by The CQ Researcher are listed below. Before May 1991, reports were published under the name of Editorial Research Reports.

APRIL 1996
Centennial Olympic Games
Managed Care
Protecting Endangered Species
New Military Culture

MAY 1996
Russia's Political Future
Marriage and Divorce
Year-Round Schools
Taiwan, China and the U.S.

JUNE 1996
Rethinking NAFTA
First Ladies
Teaching Values
Labor Movement's Future

JULY 1996
Recovered-Memory Debate
Native Americans' Future
Crackdown on Sexual Harassment
Attack on Public Schools

AUGUST 1996
Fighting Over Animal Rights
Privatizing Government Services
Child Labor and Sweatshops
Cleaning Up Hazardous Wastes

SEPTEMBER 1996
Gambling Under Attack
The States and Federalism
Civic Journalism
Reassessing Foreign Aid

OCTOBER 1996
Political Consultants
Insurance Fraud
Rethinking School Integration
Parental Rights

NOVEMBER 1996
Global Warming
Clashing Over Copyright
Consumer Debt
Governing Washington, D.C.

DECEMBER 1996
Welfare, Work and the States
The New Volunteerism
Implementing the Disabilities Act
America's Pampered Pets

JANUARY 1997
Combating Scientific Misconduct
Restructuring the Electric Industry
The New Immigrants
Chemical and Biological Weapons

FEBRUARY 1997
Assisting Refugees
Alternative Medicine's Next Phase
Independent Counsels
Feminism's Future

MARCH 1997
New Air Quality Standards
Alcohol Advertising
Civic Renewal
Educating Gifted Students

APRIL 1997
Declining Crime Rates
The FBI Under Fire
Gender Equity in Sports
Space Program's Future

MAY 1997
The Stock Market
The Cloning Controversy
Expanding NATO
The Future of Libraries

JUNE 1997
FDA Reform
China After Deng
Line-Item Veto
Breast Cancer

JULY 1997
Transportation Policy
Executive Pay
School Choice Debate
Aggressive Driving

AUGUST 1997
Age Discrimination
Banning Land Mines
Children's Television
Evolution vs. Creationism

SEPTEMBER 1997
Caring for the Dying
Mental Health Policy
Mexico's Future
Youth Fitness

OCTOBER 1997
Urban Sprawl in the West
Diversity in the Workplace
Teacher Education

Back issues are available for $5.00 (subscribers) or $10.00 (non-subscribers). Quantity discounts apply to orders over ten. To order, call Congressional Quarterly Customer Service at (202) 887-8621.

Binders are available for $18.00. To order call 1-800-638-1710. Please refer to stock number 648.

Future Topics

- ***Renewable Energy***
- ***Artificial Intelligence***
- ***Religious Persecution***

THE CQ Researcher

PUBLISHED BY CONGRESSIONAL QUARTERLY INC.

Renewable Energy

Should federal subsidies be eliminated?

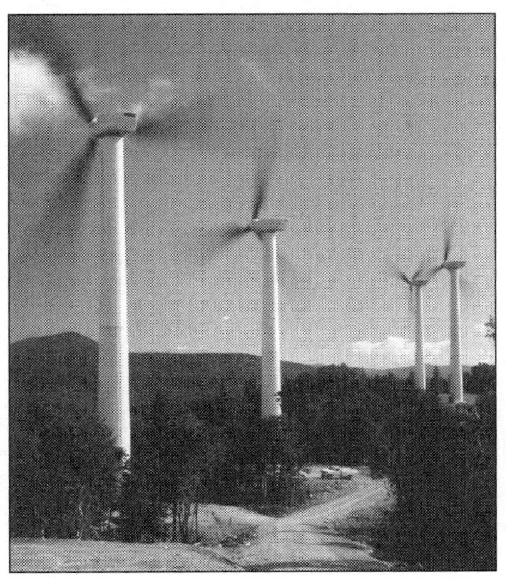

In the early 1970s, a series of energy crises awakened the country to its growing dependence on foreign oil. In response, lawmakers created federal subsidies to help develop and promote solar, geothermal and other renewable energy sources. The goal was not only to develop more domestic energy sources but also to reduce the air pollution resulting from fossil fuel use. Today, however, oil and gas prices have fallen, foreign oil supplies appear reliable and renewables — despite the subsidies — have failed to capture much of the energy market. As Congress considers legislation that would deregulate the electric industry, some producers of oil, gas and coal — still the main sources of energy in the United States — say it's time to eliminate federal subsidies for renewable energy.

INSIDE THIS ISSUE

CQ Nov. 7, 1997 • Volume 7, No. 41 • Pages 961-984

Formerly Editorial Research Reports

COVER: TOWERING WINDMILLS GENERATE ELECTRICITY AT A VERMONT WIND FARM. (ENRON RENEWABLE ENERGY CORP.)

THE CQ Researcher

November 7, 1997
Volume 7, No. 41

EDITOR
Sandra Stencel

MANAGING EDITOR
Thomas J. Colin

ASSOCIATE EDITOR
Sarah M. Magner

STAFF WRITERS
Charles S. Clark
Mary H. Cooper
Sarah Glazer
Kenneth Jost
David Masci

EDITORIAL ASSISTANT
Vanessa E. Furlong

PUBLISHED BY
Congressional Quarterly Inc.

CHAIRMAN
Andrew Barnes

VICE CHAIRMAN
Andrew P. Corty

PRESIDENT AND PUBLISHER
Robert W. Merry

EXECUTIVE EDITOR
David Rapp

The CQ Researcher (ISSN 1056-2036). Formerly Editorial Research Reports. Published weekly, except Jan. 3, May 30, Aug. 29, Oct. 31, by Congressional Quarterly Inc., 1414 22nd St., N.W., Washington, D.C. 20037. Annual subscription rate for libraries, businesses and government is $340. Additional rates furnished upon request. Periodicals postage paid at Washington, D.C., and additional mailing offices. POSTMASTER: Send address changes to The CQ Researcher, 1414 22nd St., N.W., Washington, D.C. 20037.

Renewable Energy

By Mary H. Cooper

The Issues

Outside Lake Benton, Minn., windmills are returning to the flatlands. They are not the solitary signposts of an agricultural economy, however, but towering turbines with long blades to catch the slightest breeze. Instead of pumping water, these windmills will generate electricity, harnessing the almost constant winds that sweep the region.

When the wind farm is completed next summer, it will have the capacity to power 90,000 homes a year. "Based on the technology we're using in Minnesota, we think that wind turbines can produce power for between 3 and 4 cents a kilowatt hour," says Robert Kelly, chairman of Enron Renewable Energy Corp. [1] That's 1 to 2 cents less than power generated from a new plant that burns coal, the United States' most abundant fuel. "So in this case we certainly think wind power can compete," Kelly says.

Lake Benton's wind farm is one of the more visible signs of the profound changes that are coming to the vast electric utility industry, which employs almost a half-million Americans and brings in more than $200 billion a year in revenues. [2] Deregulation, the same wrenching process that revolutionized the airline and telephone industries in the 1980s, is about to transform the last of the huge government-regulated monopolies. The changes will enable consumers to choose the energy provider of their choice, much as they pick long-distance telephone carriers today. That means that consumers will face a barrage of advertisements from power providers eager to compete with mammoth regional utilities like Pacific Gas & Electric (PG&E) in California and Consolidated Edison in New York.

For renewable energy sources, which have yet to make significant inroads into the energy market, deregulation presents new challenges and opportunities.

"Deregulation is taking the generation business out of the hands of the regulated utilities and putting it in the hands of private business," says James Macias, vice president and general manager of electric transmission at PG&E, the world's largest investor-owned utility. Forced to compete in a deregulated energy market, utilities like PG&E are hedging their bets against potential problems, such as disruptions of fuel supplies or increases in fuel prices.

Instead of relying exclusively on coal, nuclear power or natural gas — the traditional fuels used to generate electricity in the United States — many power companies now are expanding their fuel "portfolios" to include so-called renewable energy sources, such as hydropower, biomass, wind and solar. Unlike supplies of fossil fuels, which are depleted by use, renewables are virtually inexhaustible. "It's going to be very attractive for suppliers to have a balanced portfolio that includes renewables," Macias says. In addition, in a competitive market some companies see an opportunity to sell to consumers who would prefer to obtain power from clean energy sources.

Deregulation is coming at a critical time for renewables. In the wake of the energy crises of the 1970s, when Middle East oil producers restricted exports, quadrupling prices, the United States suddenly realized that its heavy dependence on foreign oil posed a serious threat to the economy. In response, Congress in 1978 passed the Public Utility Regulatory Policies Act (PURPA), requiring utilities to buy renewable energy, if offered, at no more than the utility's cost of supplying that power conventionally. Lawmakers also provided funding for research and development of solar, wind and other renewable energy sources.

The federal support enabled renewable sources to make slow but steady progress during the 1980s, but not enough to make renewables competitive with fossil fuels in most parts of the country (*see p. 970*). Falling natural gas prices and uncertainty about the future of the electric power industry have posed further obstacles to the development of renewable energy in the 1990s.

"We are no longer enjoying the go-go years that we had back in the 1980s," says Lawrence Plitch, general counsel of Wheelabrator Technologies, which generates electricity in New Hampshire by burning solid waste. "Certainly an important reason is that we've lost some of the higher power rates that we were enjoying, as did all the other renewable energy companies supported under federal law, when people were predicting higher oil prices. That's no longer on the horizon."

Deregulation already has begun in at least eight states, either through legislation or changes in state regu-

Renewable Sources Contribute Little Energy

Less than 10 percent of the energy used in the United States last year was generated from renewable sources. Of the renewable energy used, more than 90 percent came from hydroelectric power and biomass fuels.

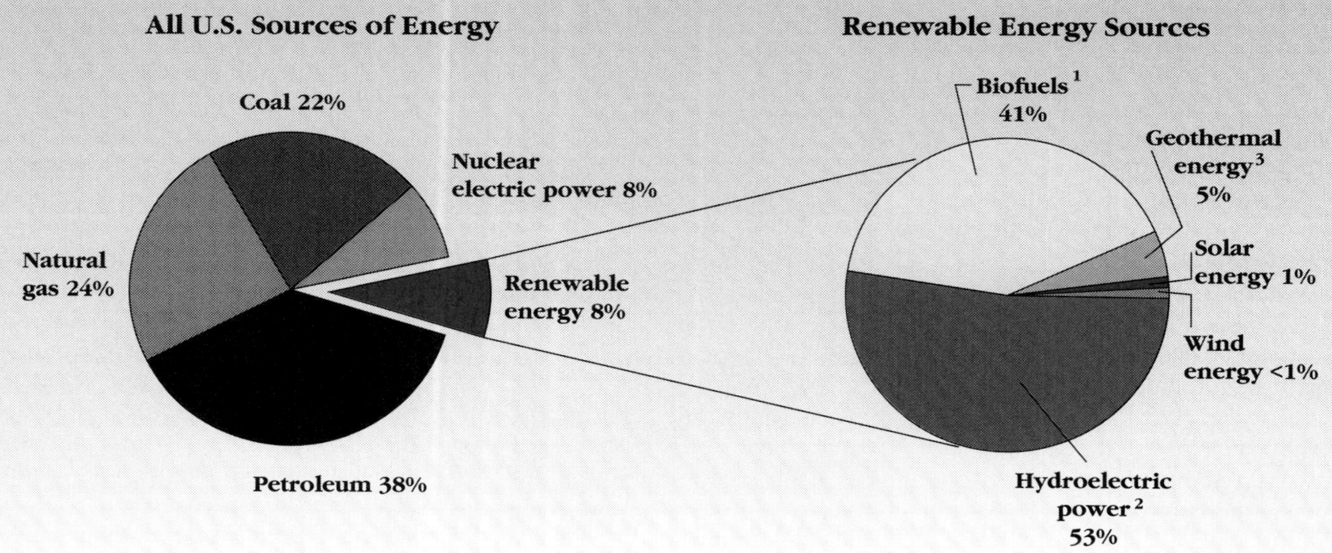

[1] *Wood, wood waste, peat, wood sludge, municipal solid waste, agricultural waste, straw, tires, landfill gases, fish oils and other waste.*

[2] *Includes electricity net imports from Canada that are derived from hydroelectric power.*

[3] *Includes electricity imports from Mexico that are derived from geothermal energy.*

Note: Total for renewable energy adds to more than 100 percent due to rounding.

Source: "Annual Energy Review, 1996," Energy Information Administration, Department of Energy

latory rules. Some of these states, such as Pennsylvania, do little or nothing to support renewable energy. Others provide incentives for non-fossil fuel development. All eyes are now on California, where a law that takes effect on Jan. 1, 1998, will set aside $540 million in annual electricity bill surcharges through 2001 to support new and emerging renewable energy technologies. [3]

Meanwhile, Congress is considering a number of bills aimed at overhauling PURPA and setting federal guidelines the states must follow in deregulating their utilities. Most of the proposals would retain some form of the current law's support for renewable energy, but there is considerable disagreement in the energy industry about how strong that support should be.

Some supporters of deregulation are opposed to any federal mandates favoring renewables. Robert L. Bradley, president of the Institute for Energy Research in Houston, a nonprofit group advocating a free-market approach to oil, gas and electricity markets, is among those who oppose further support.

"We've been hearing since the 1970s that wind and solar power are just about [ready to go] commercial, that wind power, for example, would be competitive by 1990, and they're not," Bradley says. "We're nearing our 25th anniversary of government subsidies for renewable energy and these inflated claims of impending commercialization, and they just haven't panned out.

"With a lot less government subsidy, natural gas-fired technology has improved to the point that I believe it will be the primary fuel of electric generation for the next several hundred years."

Not all players in the natural gas industry support this view. "Natural gas is not in and of itself the solution," says Michael Marvin, executive director of the Business Council on Sustainable Energy, whose members include sellers of natural gas.

Gas releases fewer harmful emissions when burned than other fossil fuels, and it is in abundant supply in North America. "The natural gas industry sees the value of clean, domestic energy and recognizes that natural gas is a central component of that, but not the sole component," Marvin says. "So if there is something in the law that encourages some domestic generation of renewable energy sources as a modest percentage of the overall energy mix, that would be in the country's best interest."

In addition to deregulation, other issues have changed the terms of the debate over energy policy since the late 1970s. Concern about the effects of air pollution on health and global climate trends has largely displaced the worry over dependence on foreign oil as a pivotal issue in deciding which fuels to burn.

The Clean Air Act has recently been tightened to curb pollutants commonly emitted by coal-fired plants and gasoline-driven vehicles. Carbon dioxide, which many scientists agree is causing a gradual but potentially disastrous warming of the Earth's atmosphere, also is produced by burning fossil fuels. [4] Representatives of more than 150 countries, including the United States, will meet this December in Kyoto, Japan, to discuss plans to curb global emissions of carbon dioxide. Because they emit few or no harmful gases, renewable energy sources stand to gain from these concerns over the long run.

"Certainly with the issues surrounding global warming and the Kyoto meeting, I think the United States and other countries are looking toward some kind of limitation on carbon emissions," Kelly says. "So I think renewables are going to play a larger role both because of the concern over global warming and because renewables are becoming more price-competitive as a result of changes in technology."

© Photodisc

Hydroelectric power is generated by some 2,400 hydro facilities in 48 states. Hydro is the nation's leading source of renewable energy and accounts for 90 percent of the electricity produced in the United States from renewable sources.

But for now, the immediate prospects for further development of renewable energy in the United States hinge on the outcome of electric utility deregulation. As the debate over federal support of renewable energy intensifies, these are some of the questions policy-makers are asking:

Will renewable energy sources ever replace fossil fuels?

Interest in promoting renewable energy sources took off in the 1970s, after Arab oil producers imposed a five-month embargo on their exports to the United States. [5] The ensuing quadrupling of oil prices and gasoline rationing awakened Americans to their dependence on foreign oil supplies. A quarter-century later, with oil prices down and the Organization of Petroleum Exporting Countries weakened, concerns about fossil fuels focus less on our vulnerability to sudden disruptions in supplies than on the pollution caused by burning these fuels. [6]

Coal and oil use are especially harmful. Coal-burning utilities and factories spew sulfur dioxide and other pollutants that cause acid rain and pollute the air for hundreds of miles downwind. Gasoline and other oil derivatives used mainly to fuel cars and other modes of transportation emit air pollutants and account for much of the carbon dioxide emissions implicated in global warming.

A heavier reliance on renewable energy sources would help solve both problems associated with fossil fuels. While some regions are better endowed with renewables than others, the country has considerable supplies of sun, wind, rivers, underground steam, ocean currents and biomass — plants and waste that can be burned to generate heat and electricity. The United States could certainly reduce its dependence on foreign energy if it relied more on renewable sources.

"The availability of renewable resources is not in question at all," says Blair Swezey, principal policy adviser of the Energy Department's National Renewable Energy Laboratory in Golden, Colo. "Certain resources are more advantageous in particular regions than in others, but we know that there are enough re-

Industry and Utilities Use Most Renewable Energy

*More than 90 percent of the renewable energy used in the United States last year — some 6 quadrillion Btus — was consumed by industry and electric utilities. Almost all of the renewable energy used by utilities came from hydroelectric; biofuels, or biomass, produced most of the renewable energy used by industry.**

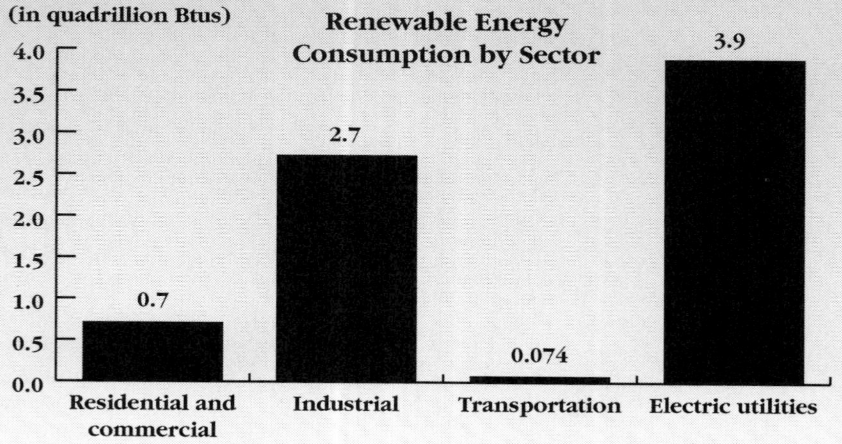

Note: A Btu (British thermal unit) is the quantity of heat required to raise the temperature of one pound of water one degree Fahrenheit.

** Biofuels include wood, wood waste, peat, wood sludge, municipal solid waste, agricultural waste, straw, tires, landfill gases and fish oils.*

Source: "Annual Energy Review, 1996," Energy Information Administration, Department of Energy

newable resources of all different kinds in the United States to more than meet our energy needs several times over."

While some critics dispute the claim that renewables are environmentally benign, they emit far fewer harmful air pollutants than fossil fuels to produce similar amounts of electricity. In the absence of fossil fuels, urban air pollution, smog, acid rain and the high carbon emissions that threaten the global climate would plummet.

Despite these advantages, renewable energy sources are unlikely to take the place of fossil fuels anytime soon. Proven world reserves of natural gas are estimated to last for the next 65 years. [7] The United States, which now must import about half its oil, has abundant reserves of coal and access to abundant supplies of gas from Canada. "Renewables will not replace fossil fuels in the foreseeable future," Swezey says. "Most energy analysts believe that we need a mix of different energy sources. But renewables can certainly contribute more substantially than they do today."

Energy experts do not all agree on which renewables hold the most promise of at least partially replacing fossil fuels. Macias rates renewables according to his utility's vast experience with them in California. PG&E has one of the most diverse energy mixes in the country, deriving up to 30 percent of the electricity it provides customers from renewables. The utility boasts the country's largest private hydroelectric development, the world's largest geothermal development and among the largest wind and biomass developments in the country.

"Biomass has had mixed results, as some plants have been very efficient and competitive and others have not," he says. "But I think biomass, well-managed and planned, can expand."

Macias is less optimistic about the future of wind power in California, where the wind farm at Altamont Pass outside San Francisco is the biggest in the country. "I am not a big fan of wind power because of its unreliability," Macias says. Prevailing wind patterns in California mean that most of the wind generation occurs late at night, when demand for electricity is low. "It just doesn't come on when it's most needed," he says.

Other analysts see great long-term promise in wind and solar energy. Kelly of Enron Renewable Energy Corp. says that worldwide growth of wind power generation is about 21 percent a year, while solar power is increasing by about 17 percent a year, several percentage points higher than the demand for energy in general.

"The market is telling us that renewables are in demand," says Kelly, whose company is most heavily invested in wind and solar energy. "If these growth rates keep up, over the next century renewables are going to become more and more important and start having an impact on the amount of fossil fuel we burn."

Are renewable energy sources friendly to the environment?

Renewables have long been cited as the only group of energy sources that don't pollute the environment. Fossil fuels — especially coal and oil — foul the air and are widely suspected of threatening the Earth's climate. Nuclear power plants emit very few pollutants when they work, but can cause catastrophic harm to human health and the environment when they don't, as the 1986 meltdown at Chernobyl in the Soviet Union made abundantly clear. Since the near-disaster at Three Mile Island in Pennsylvania in 1979, nuclear power development in the United States has virtually ceased. [8] Renewables, by contrast, harness energy from moving water, sunlight, wind and steam — all processes that release virtually no harmful emissions.

But many analysts say it is simplistic to assess the environmental impact of renewables by looking at the generation process alone. Hydroelectric dams, which account for about 50 percent of renewable energy in the United States, have come under growing criticism by environmentalists for destroying river habitats. As salmon and other fish have all but disappeared from the Columbia River system, calls are even mounting for the removal of some dams. Biomass also is under scrutiny because waste-to-energy plants emit air pollutants.

In Bradley's view, environmentalists are inconsistent in their support for renewables, especially wind and solar power. "The most promising renewable for displacing fossil fuels on a worldwide basis is probably hydroelectricity," he says. "That's where you can really get large megawatt projects."

But the environmentalists are saying no to that. Interior Secretary Bruce Babbitt is fighting against geothermal development on federal land, and there's concern among environmentalists about biomass as well. So when you get down to it, the environmental movement is espousing wind and solar, which last year accounted for about one-tenth of 1 percent of U.S. electricity generation."

Not only are these sources economically uncompetitive, Bradley says, they also would harm the environment if they were widely developed. "Wind turbines, which are as tall as 15 stories, create a bad problem of energy urban blight," he says. "Wind farms are noisy and require much more infrastructure than a similar gas unit producing the same electricity." They also kill birds. Bradley cites a California Energy Commission study that concluded that as many as 39 endangered golden eagles perish each year in the wind turbines at Altamont Pass. [9]

As for solar energy, Bradley says, "it's the most land-intensive use of pristine desert space that there is. I think the environmentalists haven't really faced up to the negative side effects of their favorite fuels. Whatever your renewable resource is, you've got to go to a pristine area to build it."

Renewable energy backers roundly reject this view. "Of course there's no such thing as an environmental-impact-free application, even with solar and wind," says Swezey of the National Renewable Energy Laboratory. "Even though the fuels are entirely environmentally friendly, you have to apply some technology to collect and convert the resources. But this whole position that renewables have environmental impacts and so they're as much of a problem as any other fuel is really a red herring. It's simply an attempt to detract from the overwhelming environmental benefits that renewables do have compared with conventional energy sources."

Swezey discounts the bird mortality issue associated with wind power by comparing it with the effects of other types of energy development, such as oil spills. "Also," he says, "birds get electrocuted on transmission wires all across the country. Any wind development that goes in today takes a lot of time doing avian studies to make sure that there's not going to be a problem."

As for the use of concrete, steel and glass that go into solar farms, Swezey says, "you can say that about anything. Look at all the concrete that goes into nuclear containment vessels or any type of power plant. This is really just an attempt to take attention away from the real environmental consequences of fossil fuel sources."

A far greater threat to the environment, say supporters of renewables, is the continuing rise in carbon emissions associated with fossil fuels. "If you step back and think about what the biggest environmental problems are in the world, I think it becomes pretty clear that the world has made a decision that it's concerned about limiting carbon emissions," says Kelly of Enron Renewable Energy Corp. "The biggest set of issues we have to grapple with is how we can continue to grow economically, particularly in the developing world and provide energy for this growth."

Should the federal government continue to subsidize renewable energy industries?

Since 1978, renewable energy producers have enjoyed federal support. PURPA requires electric utilities to buy renewable resources when they are available. Annual appropriations for the Energy Department include money for research and development of renewables. A federal partnership with the auto industry is pursuing alternatives, including renewable energy, to the gasoline-driven engine.

Deregulation is throwing into

U.S. Hydropower Capacity

Hydropower generates about 90 percent of the nation's electricity from renewable sources, or 4 percent of total energy output. The Federal Energy Regulatory Commission estimates that current U.S. hydro capacity of 72,000 megawatts could be doubled, but environmental concerns have slowed development.*

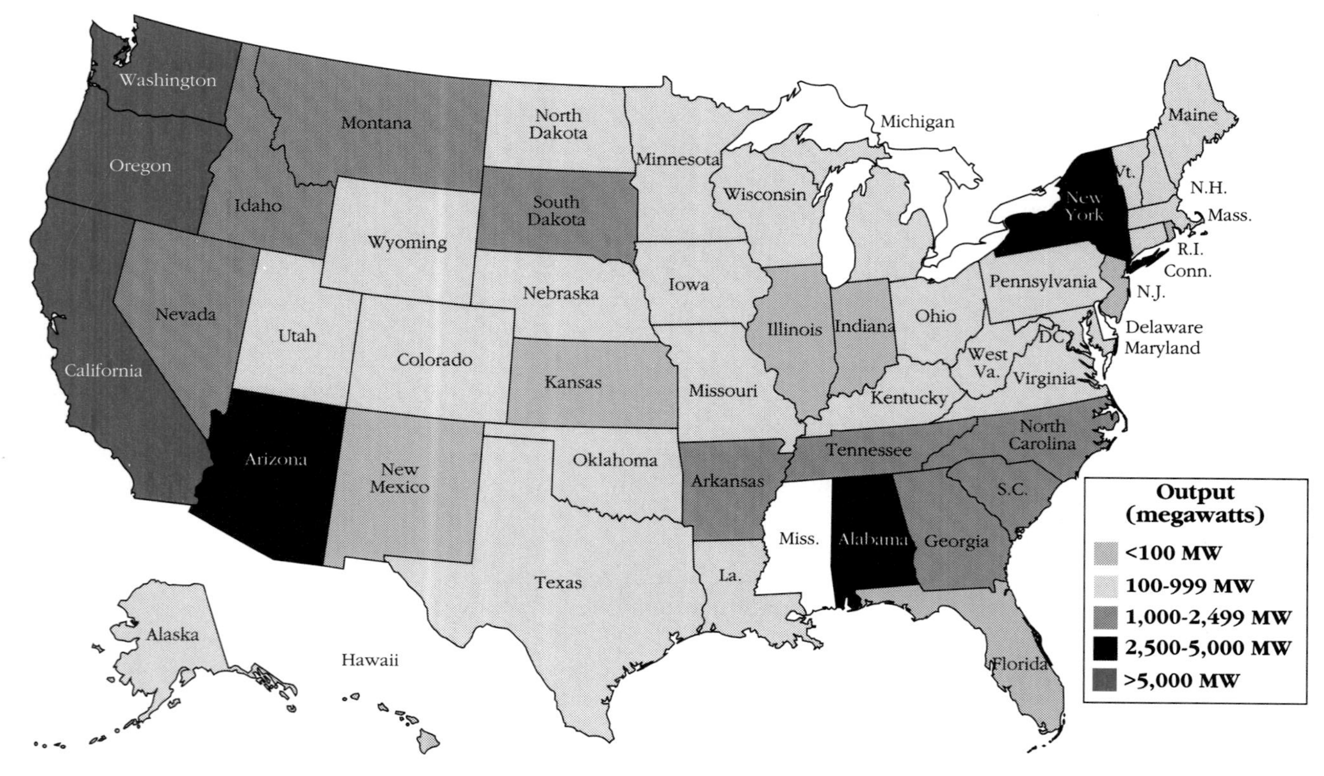

* Hydropower generates about half of the total energy from renewable sources produced in the United States.

Sources: "Profiles in Renewable Energy," National Renewable Energy Laboratory, August 1994; "Annual Energy Review," Energy Information Administration, 1996.

question the logic of federal aid to renewable energy. As members of Congress examine ways to overhaul federal laws regulating electric utilities, supporters of a fully deregulated energy market say that subsidies favoring renewables are unfair and get in the way of healthy competition, even though customers may want to buy electricity that comes from renewable sources.

Some of the opposition to continuing PURPA's mandate that electric utilities include renewables among their energy sources comes from utilities that have cheaper energy sources available, such as coal, nuclear energy or natural gas. Arthur W. Adelberg, a vice president of Central Maine Power Co., told a Senate panel that his utility relies more on renewable energy as required under the law than any other utility in the country.

"The high cost of this PURPA generation has been responsible for dramatic increases in the cost of electric service to our customers and has done serious damage to the economy of our state," Adelberg said. "It is easy to be for customer choice. What is hard is to define a fair path to get there. Waiting to address PURPA reform until all other market reforms are in place is counterproductive and harmful to consumers. I strongly urge this committee to start quickly down the road to eliminating this and other federal barriers to a fully competitive electric market." [10]

Other utility spokesmen see value in federal support for renewables, however. "I do believe that renewables need some help," says Macias of PG&E. "The question is what level of support and how that support is rendered." Macias says he prefers direct subsidies rather than mandates requiring utilities to buy renewable energy as PURPA does. He also worries that too strong a federal role may interfere with deregulation programs in the states. "What works for California may not work in other parts of the country," Macias says. "So I think you have to be open-minded and flexible when you start talking national energy policy."

Some representatives of the natural gas industry also oppose mandates for renewable energy as a threat to their competitiveness by granting unfair advantage to alternative energy sources. (*See "At Issue," p. 977.*) But critics of this stance say that federal policies have favored other energy sources for years.

"The fossil fuel and nuclear industries have historically garnered large subsidies and continue to get large subsidies," Swezey says. "The kind of support we want for renewables really is not on the same level as the types of subsidies that fossil fuels have gotten." Because natural gas is low-cost and is the cleanest-burning fossil fuel, he adds, it already is poised to capture a growing portion of the energy market. "Natural gas is probably the fuel of choice on the electric market today, so for the gas people to say that renewables are going to take market share away from them is just silly."

Although some sectors of the gas industry oppose special treatment for renewables, many gas industry supporters have joined renewable energy companies in calling for continued federal support of renewables. "I don't think that there are many people out there who are suggesting that we repeal PURPA and replace it with nothing," says Marvin of the Business Council on Sustainable Energy, whose members include sellers of natural gas, utilities and renewable energy producers. "There is value in not tying our national economy to too few sources of energy or electricity. We need not be subject to the vicissitudes of the price of coal or anything else."

Marvin also cites the need to support renewables for environmental reasons. "What happens if someone decides to build a major coal plant, and then the United States signs a climate change treaty?" he asks. "All of a sudden the wind power that was almost as inexpensive as coal actually will look better. But the coal plant will be on-line for the next 50 years. Are we then going to tell the wind power company we'll be back in 50 years and buy their stuff like crazy? We can't kid ourselves that we should be moving to a completely free market." ■

BACKGROUND

Energy Crisis Hits

Hydropower, the leading renewable energy source in the United States, is also the oldest, dating back to 1879, when the first hydroelectric plant in the United States provided lighting for Niagara Falls, N.Y. In 1933 Congress passed the Tennessee Valley Authority Bond Limitation Act creating the Tennessee Valley Authority to manage a system of federally owned dams that were to provide electric power to much of the Southeast. The nation's hydro capacity tripled from 1940 to 1960 as mega-projects, such as the Grand Coulee and Glen Canyon dams, were built in the West.

But apart from hydropower and some biomass, renewable energy was in its infancy when the 1973-74 Arab oil embargo resulted in the quadrupling of oil prices and spurred Congress and the administration of President Jimmy Carter to devise a national energy policy to reduce U.S. dependence on unreliable foreign energy sources.

National Energy Act Spurs Renewables

The resulting National Energy Act aimed at resolving what was widely viewed as a national energy crisis. [11] One of the law's five measures was the Public Utility Regulatory Policies Act (PURPA), which Carter signed into law on Nov. 9, 1978. PURPA directly addressed the need to diversify U.S. energy sources by encouraging, among other things, the development of renewable energy.

Rules issued in 1980 by the Federal Energy Regulatory Commission (FERC) to implement the new law identified a special class of "qualifying facilities" — small power facilities that derive at least 75 percent of their fuel from renewable sources and that are not majority-owned by an electric utility. The rules require utilities to purchase power from these facilities as part of their energy mix. State utility commissions are charged with implementing the law.

"In the history of renewables development PURPA was really a major stimulus, not because it provided any direct subsidies, but because it provided market access," Swezey says. "It basically told the utilities that if a developer came in and offered them a renewable project, they had to sign a contract with that company. The law assured some market access for renewables that didn't exist before.

So we saw quite a bit of development throughout most of the 1980s and a little bit into the '90s as well."

As a result of PURPA and other state and federal incentives, renewable energy power plants sprang up and expanded rapidly in the early 1980s. Support for research and development produced technological advances that helped bring the cost of producing electricity from renewables closer to that of traditional fuels. The biggest cost improvements came in wind power, although geothermal and small-scale hydro plants also became increasingly competitive. While solar power remains expensive, the cost per watt of using solar photovoltaic modules, among the most expensive renewable sources, fell from $30 in the early 1980s to about $4 by 1995.

At the same time that costs have fallen, reliability and efficiency of most renewables have improved to the point that all categories, except for ocean systems (*see p. 975*), produce electric power reliably in many parts of the country.

Status of Renewables

Renewable energy offers several advantages over conventional energy. Unlike fossil fuels, renewables are virtually inexhaustible. [12] Renewables also are widely available domestically. But renewables are not without their drawbacks. Solar and wind farms cannot generate much electricity on cloudy or still days. As intermittent energy sources, they require vast systems to store the energy they produce, or must rely on the rest of the electrical system for backup. And despite federal subsidies to spur technological innovation, renewable sources have not become economical enough to seriously challenge fossil fuels in an open market.

As a result, renewables still accounted for just 8 percent of total U.S. energy production in 1995. Here is where the major renewable energy sources stand today:

• **Hydroelectric:** Hydropower is the means of turning the energy contained in moving water into electricity. Usually the water flows through turbines that activate electric generators. Dams ensure a constant supply of water and control the flow rate and build-up of pressure, or "head," above the turbine. So-called pumped-storage facilities pump water into uphill basins to augment flow at times of peak demand for electricity. Hydropower, produced at about 2,400 hydroelectric dams in 48 states, has always been the leading source of renewable energy in the United States and still accounts for 50 percent of the electricity generated by renewable energy sources.

Unlike other renewables, hydropower is a mature technology. Most of the dams were built in the first half of this century, and there are few remaining sites that are suitable for future construction of large dams. Expansion of hydropower also is impeded by environmental concerns. Dam construction profoundly alters wildlife habitats. In the Pacific Northwest, for example, stocks of salmon and other fish that migrate from the ocean to spawning grounds upstream of major hydroelectric dams have plummeted, despite the construction of fish ladders, screens to keep them from being sucked into the turbines' blades and hatcheries to compensate for losses. There are even mounting calls to actually dismantle some of the dams on the lower Columbia River and the huge Glen Canyon Dam upstream from the Grand Canyon to avoid what environmentalists say could be the wholesale extinction of several fish species. [13]

• **Biomass:** The oldest renewable energy source of all is a form of solar energy stored in organic matter. Apart from hydropower, biomass is also the most commonly used renewable source. It also is the most diverse renewable, using wood and other plant materials to produce heat, electricity, gas and liquid fuels. Biomass facilities often are cogeneration plants, which produce heat and electricity at the same time. Wood and wood wastes are the most common fuel, followed by municipal solid waste. Biomass accounts for about 5 percent of the country's total energy consumption and almost 90 percent of renewable energy, excluding hydro. Biomass power is growing by about 3 percent a year. [14] There are three main forms of biomass energy:

Wood, agricultural waste and dedicated energy crops: Most biomass energy consumption results from traditional wood burning, used by both homeowners and businesses for heat. In addition to cord wood, wood pellets produced from ground-wood fiber are a fast-growing source of heat for homes and businesses alike. Agricultural wastes, such as crop residues and prunings from orchards, have been harder to convert to fuel because the supply is seasonal and stockpiles are subject to spontaneous combustion, making long-term storage difficult. Similar problems impede the use of dedicated energy crops, trees and other plants grown exclusively to provide biomass fuel. Tighter air-quality standards also have curtailed development of these facilities. As a result of these problems and lower fossil fuel costs, the number of biomass power projects has declined in the 1990s. [15]

Municipal solid waste: Energy produced by burning waste gained a foothold in the market in the 1980s as a result of federal and state incentives to build waste-to-energy facilities as an alternative. to establishing new landfills. At the time, the stream of waste in large cities seemed to ex-

Continued on p. 972

Chronology

1870s-1930s

Hydropower is virtually the sole renewable energy source, apart from wood burning, in the United States.

1879
The first hydroelectric plant in the United States begins providing lighting for Niagara Falls, N.Y.

1933
Congress creates the Tennessee Valley Authority to manage a system of federally owned dams that will provide electricity to much of the Southeastern U.S.

—— • ——

1940s-1960s

Hydropower capacity triples as mega-projects such as the Grand Coulee and Glen Canyon dams are built in the West.

1960
The Geysers, the first U.S. geothermal power plant, opens in Northern California.

—— • ——

1970s ***Oil prices soar following the Arab oil embargo, spurring research into alternative energy sources, including renewables.***

1973-74
Oil prices quadruple in the wake of the oil embargo.

Nov. 9, 1978
President Jimmy Carter signs into law the Public Utility Regulatory Policies Act (PURPA), a measure included in the National Energy Act that requires utilities to include renewable energy in their mix of fuels to generate electricity.

1979
A near-disaster at the nuclear power plant at Three Mile Island outside Harrisburg, Pa., prompts regulators to put future nuclear plant construction on hold.

—— • ——

1980s ***Federal support helps fledgling renewable energy industries to grow.***

1980
The Federal Energy Regulatory Commission (FERC) issues rules implementing PURPA that require utilities to purchase power from small, independent power producers that derive most of their fuel from renewable sources.

1986
A catastrophic meltdown at the nuclear power plant in Chernobyl in the Soviet Union further slows development of nuclear power as an alternative to fossil fuels.

—— • ——

1990s ***Falling prices for oil and natural gas, together with uncertainty surrounding electric utility deregulation at the state level, hamper further development of renewables.***

1992
Congress passes the Energy Policy Act, allowing greater competition in electricity generation and access by non-utility wholesale power producers to the national power grid. The changes spur restructuring of the monolithic utility industry by encouraging the formation of smaller companies that specialize in generation, transmission or distribution of electricity.

1994
Minnesota becomes the second state, after California, to start up a large wind-power facility. Twelve other states are slated to host wind farms in coming years. In April, Michigan becomes the first state to allow retail wheeling, allowing large industrial customers to contract directly for power with any generator they choose and receive that power supply over existing transmission lines.

January 1995
FERC voids a California plan requiring state utilities to purchase 600 megawatts of renewable energy, throwing into question the validity of other state programs to promote renewables.

Dec. 1-10, 1997
Representatives of more than 150 countries are to meet in Kyoto, Japan, to consider legally binding cuts in emissions of carbon dioxide and other greenhouse gases in an effort to curtail global warming.

Jan. 1, 1998
A sweeping deregulatory measure will take effect in California, allowing customers to choose their power suppliers and setting aside $540 million in electricity-bill surcharges through 2001 to support development of renewable energy technologies.

Fuel Cells Offer Hope for Clean Cars

Ever since gasoline prices quadrupled after the Arab oil embargo in the 1970s, the search has been on for alternative fuel sources. Today, even though oil prices are relatively low, the search continues, driven mainly by the desire to curb harmful air pollutants and emissions of carbon dioxide, the main gas implicated in global warming.

The search for alternative fuels has been frustrated by high costs, technological obstacles and reluctance by consumers to abandon the gasoline engine. The simplest alternative technologies involve switching fuels. Most of the 399,000 alternative-fuel vehicles in the United States run on propane. The downside of this gas is that, like oil, from which it is derived, propane is in short supply domestically. [1]

Natural gas, which is abundant in the United States and emits fewer pollutants than gasoline, is used in fleets of cars and buses in many cities. But cars using natural gas have bulky tanks and relatively short ranges between refills, making them unattractive to individual consumers, especially with gasoline cheap. Natural gas is so uncompetitive that Amoco is closing all 37 fueling stations it built in anticipation of mass-produced, natural gas-fueled passenger cars. [2]

Liquid fuels have also failed to catch on as well as expected. Methanol-powered cars have even shorter ranges between refills than those using natural gas. Both methanol and ethanol, which is made from corn, are hard to find; service stations have concluded, correctly as it turns out, that demand for these fuels will remain low as long as gasoline is cheap.

Electric cars are the cleanest-burning of the alternative-fuel vehicles now available. Although utility plants that provide the electricity emit carbon dioxide and other pollutants, the car itself releases no harmful emissions and thus qualifies as a "zero-pollution" vehicle, which California will require to be among the new models sold in the state beginning next year. Since last fall, General Motors has been leasing the two-seater EV1 in California. But at around $400 a month, electric cars have drawn only a few hundred takers. [3] They also are plagued by short ranges and limited passenger space due to the bulky batteries that power them.

The most promising fuel for alternative vehicles is the fuel cell. Invented in 1839 by William Grove, an English scientist, fuel cell technology is sublimely simple — at least in theory. A fuel cell operates like a battery, supplying electricity through a kind of reverse electrolysis that combines hydrogen and oxygen electrochemically, without combustion. There are several types of fuel cells, but all consist of two electrodes surrounding an electrolyte. Oxygen passes over one electrode and hydrogen passes over the other, generating electricity, water and heat. The hydrogen used in a cell can be provided by a number of fuels, such as methanol, ethanol or natural gas. As long as the fuel supply is maintained, fuel cells don't run down or require recharging as batteries do. And they are clean — the only waste product is water.

A major impediment to fuel cell development has been cost. Components include such expensive materials as platinum, and research to come up with cheaper technologies has been slow. In the United States, fuel cell development receives federal support — about $70 million a year from the Energy Department for fuel cells used in cars and for generating electricity, about $24 million from the Pentagon to build fuel cell power plants at military bases and $5 million from the Transportation Department to develop fuel cell buses. [4]

But the United States lags behind its competitors in bringing fuel cell technology to market. At the Frankfurt Motor Show in September, German automaker Daimler-Benz and Toyota Motor Corp. of Japan took the lead in the fuel cell automotive market by introducing electric cars powered by cells. Both prototypes, the Mercedes A-class car and the Toyota RAV4, use methanol to produce the hydrogen for their fuel cells. Both cars consume much less fuel than standard gasoline-powered cars, an asset both companies believe will make them more attractive to consumers than other alternative vehicles. [5]

Both companies are hedging their bets on fuel cells by setting up joint ventures to help bring the technology on-line and producing other types of alternative-fuel vehicles. Daimler-Benz has set up a joint venture with Ballard Power Systems of Canada, a leader in fuel cell development, to produce a commercially viable fuel cell car. Toyota plans to begin selling a new hybrid, gasoline-electric car in Japan on Dec. 10. The Prius, a small, four-door sedan similar to the Corolla, would get 66 miles to the gallon and emit only half the carbon dioxide of standard engines. The company is expected to announce plans for possible exports of the Prius to the United States on Dec. 16 at the annual Electric Vehicle Symposium in Orlando, Fla. [6]

[1] See Matthew L. Wald, "Three Guesses: The Fuel of the Future Will be Gas, Gas or Gas," *The New York Times*, Oct. 16, 1997.

[2] *Ibid.*

[3] See "Will they cell?" *The Economist*, Sept. 13, 1997, p. 66.

[4] For more information, visit the Web site of Fuel Cell 2000, a nonprofit group that provides information and supports pilot projects on fuel cells, at www.fuelcells.org.

[5] See "At Last, the Fuel Cell," *The Economist*, Oct. 25, 1997, pp. 89-92.

[6] See Thomas A. Fogarty, "Toyota Unveils Hybrid Sedan in Japan," *USA Today*, Oct. 15, 1997.

Continued from p. 970

ceed the space to deposit it, forcing some municipalities to export their waste or dump it in the ocean. Waste-to-energy plants convert almost 16 percent of the country's municipal solid waste into electric power. [16]

Waste-to-energy plants have faltered in the 1990s, however. The recent success of recycling programs has diminished the need for new waste disposal facilities, including waste-to-energy plants. Support for waste-to-energy facilities also has flagged as tighter air-quality standards have taken effect, forcing them to install costly filters to curb emissions. Further dampening interest in municipal solid waste plants, federal tax policy no longer favors investments in capital-intensive projects and limits municipal bond issues to paying for privately owned facilities.

Deregulation also is hurting the waste-to-energy industry. As electricity prices fall, it often is more cost-effective to simply dispose of waste in a landfill than to burn it for power. An industry has emerged to recover methane and other gases from landfills for power generation. Produced by the decomposition of organic wastes beneath the surface, the methane is collected and processed to produce usable fuel, which provides the additional benefit of eliminating one of the greenhouse gases implicated in global warming. Landfill gas also reduces the risk that this highly flammable gas will explode by accident.

Liquid fuels: The most common biomass fuel is ethanol, which is produced by fermenting and distilling corn and other crops. With mounting concern over air pollution and global warming related to fossil fuel emissions, ethanol has received growing attention as an alternative to gasoline for cars and trucks.

• **Geothermal:** Underground steam or hot liquid deposits used to produce heat and electricity are actually finite resources like oil or coal, but are so abundant that they are considered to be renewable. In some instances reserves are proving to be less abundant than previously believed, however. At The Geysers in Northern California, the first major U.S. geothermal power plant, falling steam pressure has contributed to a decline in power generation. Operated by Pacific Gas & Electric Co., The Geysers has been generating electricity from steam since 1960. Although generating capacity at the 10 megawatt facility has fallen due to water loss, The Geysers still accounts for more than 60 percent of the nation's total geothermal capacity. Engineers, meanwhile, are trying to inject more water into the system to restore steam pressure.

An even bigger obstacle to geothermal development has been the fall in natural gas prices, which puts geothermal energy just out of competition despite its relatively low cost of between 4.5 cents and 7 cents per kilowatt hour. Although output remains steady at geothermal plants, construction of new facilities has stalled, and overall geothermal power generation is declining, down from 17 million kilowatt hours in 1994 to 15 million kilowatt hours in 1995. An exception to this bleak picture was the start-up last year of a new 40-megawatt power plant at California's Salton Sea geothermal facility.

Although the United States is still the leading producer of geothermal power, with 19 fields in California, Hawaii, Nevada and Utah, other countries are turning increasingly to this form of renewable energy. The Philippines, one of about 18 countries with geothermal facilities, is now the second-largest producer. The most promising site for future geothermal development is the "ring of fire," a region with vast steam and magma deposits along the Pacific coast of Asia and the adjoining islands. [17]

© Photodisc

Solar-collection facilities operate only in direct sunlight and are best suited for the Southwest and other areas with little cloud cover.

• **Wind:** Wind energy, used almost exclusively to generate electricity, has weathered deregulation better than other renewables, largely because wind power plants are among the lowest-cost renewable resources. The cost of wind generation is expected by some experts to fall from the current level of around 5 cents per kilowatt hour to 4 cents by 2000, placing it well within the competitive range for electricity generation in the future. But because wind still costs more than natural gas, production remains fairly steady at around 3.5 million kilowatt hours.

So far, California has accounted for 95 percent of all energy from wind, mostly from the Altamont Pass wind farm near San Francisco. Hawaii also has small wind facilities. In 1994, Minnesota became the latest

Climate Treaty Could Boost Renewable Energy

The long-term prospects for greater use of renewable energy hinge in part on international negotiations to curb emissions of carbon dioxide and other "greenhouse gases" believed to disrupt the global climate. Although carbon dioxide is essential to plant growth, levels today far exceed those of earlier centuries. Excess carbon emissions are overwhelmingly the result of burning fossil fuels, chiefly coal and oil, which power the world's industries and transportation.

By trapping the sun's heat inside Earth's atmosphere, greenhouse gases are widely believed to be causing a gradual rise in surface temperatures known as global warming. Scientists predict that if the trend continues, polar ice caps will begin to melt, causing widespread flooding of coastal areas, and changing weather patterns will cause famine in some parts of the world, the spread of infectious diseases and other adverse effects.

With calls mounting for international efforts to curb carbon emissions, representatives of 118 countries met in 1992 in Rio de Janeiro, Brazil, for the Earth Summit, a United Nations-sponsored meeting on the environment. But attempts to agree on a global treaty, the Convention on Climate Change, bogged down over the timetable for when countries had to begin setting limits on their greenhouse emissions. Industrial countries such as the United States, the world's biggest carbon emitter, wanted all countries to adopt limits on carbon emissions. But developing countries balked at shouldering responsibility for a problem they have done little to cause.

The impasse over timetables and emission limits remains, even as a follow-up meeting, to be held in early December in Kyoto, Japan, approaches. The latest controversy has arisen over the Clinton administration's plan for curbing U.S. carbon emissions. Unveiled on Oct. 22, the plan would stabilize emissions at 1990 levels between 2008 and 2012, a timetable European countries and Japan derided as not aggressive enough to affect climate change. "It simply is not good enough," said Peter Jorgensen, a spokesman for the 15-member European Union. "There must be something better coming from the White House if the United States wants to face up to its global responsibilities." [1] Europe and Japan, where gasoline costs up to four times the U.S. level, castigate the United States for being unwilling to impose taxes that could help reduce emissions by encouraging energy conservation.

Whatever timetables are eventually agreed to, the adoption of the Convention on Climate Change could boost the development of renewable energy sources, which emit fewer greenhouse gases than fossil fuels. But some analysts, mostly in the United States, say the evidence of global warming is not conclusive enough to justify the enormous costs that would be involved in reducing carbon emissions by switching to renewables. "Given the temperature records and the scientific controversy, climate change seems to be no more a reason to promote renewables now than the argument that we are running out of energy resources was to promote renewables back in the 1970s," says Robert L. Bradley, president of the Institute for Energy Research in Houston and an advocate of a free-market approach to energy issues. Bradley faults environmentalists who favor wind and solar power over other low carbon-emitting energy sources such as hydropower and nuclear power. "Even if you assume climate change is a real problem, the environmentalists are still on very shaky ground if they're just looking to wind and solar as alternatives to fossil fuels."

But environmentalists are not the only ones who see promise in wind and solar energy. While development of renewables has stagnated in recent years in the United States, priced out of the market by low-cost oil, coal and gas, demand for wind, solar and other renewable technologies is growing fast overseas. Many U.S. producers of wind and solar power equipment already are exporting more of their products than they can sell domestically.

Enron Renewable Energy Corp., a Houston-based subsidiary of the gas and electricity giant, Enron Corp., is expanding its investments in solar and wind power overseas.

"By 2015, China is projected to be a bigger emitter of carbon than the United States, and India is not going to be far behind," says Robert Kelly, Enron Renewable's chairman and CEO. He sees enormous potential for solar power in India and for hydro, wind and solar power in China. In his view, the eventual adoption of a climate change treaty can only hasten the development of renewable energy.

"I don't mean to suggest that overnight you're going to shut down all the fossil fuel plants," Kelly says. "But at some point, it's going to become increasingly clear that without the use of renewables it's going to be impossible to meet the obligations that we incurred at Rio. Not only do we need these technologies, the market is already scooping them up at very fast rates, and that's going to continue."

---

[1] Quoted by William Drozdiak, "U.S. Allies Criticize Anti-Warming Plan," *The Washington Post,* Oct. 24, 1997.

state to launch a wind power facility. Eleven other facilities are planned by states in the Midwest, Northeast and Northwest. As wind facilities are built in different regions and turbine technology improves, wind power is expected to expand in coming years.

Although wind power originated in the United States, which still leads the world in wind-generated electricity, several other countries are poised to take over the lead. European countries are rapidly developing wind power facilities and account for the bulk of U.S. sales of wind turbines and other equipment.[18] China and India, which are experiencing the fastest growth in demand for electricity in the world, also are investing heavily in wind power.

• **Solar:** The sun's energy is captured using two different technologies — solar thermal and photovoltaics. Solar thermal energy supplies heat directly, without conversion, for immediate use. Solar thermal also can be used to generate electricity by heating water, which is then converted to steam to drive turbines.

Direct thermal techniques are most often used to heat houses using passive solar architecture with floors and walls designed to retain warmth or rooftop systems that heat hot water by passing it through a collector. Industrial applications are less common but include commercial laundries and large kitchen operations. Technology is being developed to use thermal energy to operate machinery such as air conditioners and refrigerators.

Solar photovoltaic systems use sunlight to generate electricity. Photovoltaic cells are made of silicon, the same material used to make computer chips, and directly translate the sun's energy into electricity. Usually arrayed in modules of several cells, photovoltaic systems often are made more powerful by incorporating lenses or mirrors to concentrate the sunlight. Because they operate only in direct sun, both types of solar systems are best suited to the desert Southwest and a few other parts of the country that have little cloud cover.[19]

As consumers continue to buy thermal collectors for their homes, the average price of these units continues to drop, and stood at a little over $3 per square foot in 1995. Sales of photovoltaic cells and modules have grown by some 10 percent over the past decade.

The main impetus behind the 7 percent boost in solar energy consumption in 1995, however, was not individual homes and businesses, but small, independent firms selling solar power to the national power grid, or electricity transmission system. After two years of 100 percent expansion, the capacity of photovoltaic modules and cells to supply the grid stood at 4.6 megawatts in 1995.

Solar power has expanded even more rapidly overseas, and U.S. makers of solar cells export more than half their units. Worldwide sales of photovoltaics have more than quadrupled over the past decade, as the cost of installing these units has fallen by more than half. The world's largest solar plant is in Serre, Italy. Houston-based Enron Solar plans to build an even bigger facility, able to provide power to almost 100,000 homes, on the Greek island of Crete. The most dramatic growth in solar power, however, has been in developing countries, where existing power grids often fail to reach beyond cities. Independent solar units can provide electricity to rural villages where many people live.

• **Ocean:** Although the necessary technology is only in its infancy, the Earth's vast oceans offer a potentially inexhaustible source of energy. Ocean thermal energy conversion exploits the temperature difference between warm surface water and cold water deep below, offering the most near-term promise. One type of system evaporates warm water and uses the resulting vapor to power a water turbine.

Another form of ocean energy is the dammed tidal bay, which works like a hydroelectric dam, only the water used to generate power flows in both directions. Floating turbines have also been used to harness the energy of waves. More esoteric technologies are being studied to capture the energy present in ocean currents, salinity and biomass.[20] ■

CURRENT SITUATION

Deregulation

After enjoying nearly a decade of rapid development, renewables began to face growing obstacles toward the end of the 1980s. Fossil fuel prices dropped dramatically in 1985 and are still less than half their pre-1985 levels when adjusted for inflation. Federal funding of research and development into renewable technologies also fell during the 1980s, from more than $600 million in 1980 to less than $100 million in 1990. Although federal research funding has been more steady since 1990, it still is much less than it was in 1980. State and private research funding also has dropped.[21]

Many electric utility companies opposed PURPA from the start because the law required them to buy renewable resources. Some states responded to power company complaints by exploiting PURPA loopholes and limiting the amount of renewable power that utilities had to buy from independent suppliers.

In recent years, the Federal Energy Regulatory Commission (FERC) has issued several rulings that reflect the growing disgruntlement over utility regulations. In January 1995, the agency rocked California's renewable energy industry when it voided a state plan requiring state utilities to purchase 600 megawatts of renewable energy. The ruling also threw into question the validity of many other states' programs to encourage a diverse energy mix. The same month, FERC cast further uncertainty over the regulatory treatment of renewable energy when it declared that a Connecticut law setting prices for renewable-generated power was in violation of PURPA. By ruling that states could not force utilities to buy renewable energy at a price above other market alternatives, the agency effectively undermined market access for renewables. [22]

In October 1992, Congress stepped into the deregulatory fray by passing the Energy Policy Act, which allowed greater competition in electric power generation and greater access by nonutility wholesale power producers to the national electricity grid. By breaking down some of the barriers to competition, Congress encouraged the utility industry's transformation from a collection of relatively few large, monolithic companies that control all aspects of the business — from generation to transmission to distribution — into many smaller companies engaged in only one of these functions.

Utilities are already beginning to specialize. For example, GPU Inc., a New Jersey company, announced in October that it will sell its generating capacity to focus only on electricity distribution. The firm also is buying a power-distribution system in Australia for $1.9 billion as part of an effort to shed its fossil fuel and hydropower assets and concentrate on the business of delivering power to customers in the United States and abroad. [23]

© Photodisc

After the near-disaster at Three-Mile Island in Pennsylvania, development of nuclear power as an energy source in the United States came to a virtual standstill.

State Initiatives

After passage of the Energy Policy Act, there were proposals in many states to allow "retail wheeling," in which customers contract directly for electrical power with any generator they choose and receive that power supply over existing transmission lines. In April 1994 Michigan became the first of a growing number of states to allow retail wheeling for large industrial customers.

To date, at least eight states have undertaken some form of electric utility deregulation. California, New Hampshire, Pennsylvania and Rhode Island have enacted laws to implement industry restructuring. Arizona, Massachusetts, New York and Vermont have initiated deregulation with rulemaking changes. Some states, including Pennsylvania, have few or no provisions to support renewable energy. Others, notably California, have committed to ensuring that renewables continue to be part of the state's energy mix. [24]

Last fall, California took the boldest step to date toward deregulation with a plan that will take effect Jan. 1. Next year, all electricity customers will be free to choose their energy providers. Small customers will see an immediate 10 percent cut in their electricity bills and will eventually be able to choose their providers as well. To help renewables do research and stay competitive, California will set up a special fund, to be paid for by setting aside a small portion of revenues from electric bills.

While all these moves toward deregulation hold long-term promise for renewable energy providers, for now they are causing a slowdown in the industry. "Now that prices have come down and there's a lot of concern about what competition is going to mean, the market has frozen for renewables right now," says Swezey of the National Renewable Energy Laboratory. "For the most part, utilities are not willing to sign new contracts for renewables, or at least not at anywhere near the level that we saw in the 1980s. Most utili-

Continued on p. 978

At Issue:

Should the federal government require some electricity to come from renewable energy sources?

yes

Julie A. Keil
Director, Portland General Electric Co.; president, National Hydropower Association

FROM COMMENTS AT A SENATE ENERGY AND NATURAL RESOURCES WORKSHOP ON ELECTRIC INDUSTRY RESTRUCTURING, MAY 8, 1997.

The evolution of competition and restructuring in the U.S. electricity industry is well under way. State and federal regulators have taken bold steps to initiate this process, and federal legislation has been and will be proposed. . . .

To look more closely at restructuring itself, the problem here, as in most other countries introducing competition in the electric sector, is that the systems created and the decisions made are based exclusively on economic, cost-driven theories that do not recognize natural resource or environmental values. Issues with respect to renewable energy in the optimal supply are overlooked or simply deferred. . . .

Turning to federal legislation, [Rep.] Dan Schaefer's [R-Colo.] restructuring bill embraces retail competition to serve consumer interests. That bill directs states to implement competitive electric retail services but includes some significant initial attempts to deal with assuring the continued contribution of renewable energy. . . .

Schaefer's bill . . . has at least one major flaw — hydropower was not included among the list of renewable energy technologies that states were required to encourage. . . .

[I]f [Schaefer's bill is] enacted as currently proposed, we in the hydropower industry believe that in 10 years — accounting for some growth in the emerging renewable technologies and a substantial loss of current hydropower generating capacity — the total relative contribution of renewable energy to the nation's energy supply will be significantly less than it is today. This will, in turn, have a significant impact on such national goals as energy diversity, protecting the environment and achieving sustainable development.

It is worth asking the question at this point: Why do we care about renewable energy? We care because it promotes sustainable development, because it assures diversity and energy security and because it is a major factor in maintaining clean air. Hydropower serves each of these goals.

In our view, national energy policy should promote the expansion of renewable energy's contribution to the nation's energy supply mix. It should assure that, at the least, the existing renewable generation base is sustained, and should promote further development and contribution by renewables.

no

Donald Niemiec
Vice president of marketing, Union Pacific Resources Group, an independent gas and oil company

FROM COMMENTS AT A SENATE ENERGY AND NATURAL RESOURCES WORKSHOP ON ELECTRIC INDUSTRY RESTRUCTURING, MAY 8, 1997.

The natural gas industry is prepared to meet the challenges of a competitive electric power market. Natural gas is an abundant domestic resource that is readily available to all markets. Competitive commodity prices, low transportation costs and highly efficient generation technology make natural gas affordable and cost-competitive. It is also a preferred energy source because of its environmental attributes. . . .

The nation will not reap all of the benefits of natural gas, however, if the federal rules governing the electric power industry create an unlevel playing field. . . .

Any federal policy mandating the use of renewable energy to generate some portion of the nation's electricity needs will impose substantial costs. It will impede the efficient functioning of the market, raise the cost of electricity to consumers and deny market share opportunities to other fuels, particularly natural gas. As a consequence, we believe that Congress should be very cautious in its consideration of any proposed mandate for renewables.

Mandating renewable fuels on the grounds that we are running out of fossil fuel is senseless. At the present time, we have sufficient reserves of natural gas to meet projected demand for the next 65 years, and more reserves are being found each year. Our domestic reserves of coal are even greater. Thus, it is difficult, if not impossible, to justify forcing consumers to pay for the deployment of expensive renewable technologies on this basis.

Mandating renewables on the basis of assumed environmental benefits is also questionable. A renewables mandate unfairly penalizes the many power generators who have invested huge sums on pollution-control equipment to clean up their emissions. It takes a portion of their market share and basically says that their effort was not sufficient, despite the fact that they have met or exceeded all of the requirements of our environmental laws. Such a burden will also depress significantly the growth of gas-fired generation — one of the most environmentally sound forms of generation. . . .

Union Pacific Resources does not oppose renewable energy. However we strongly oppose any proposal that guarantees a share of the market to renewables regardless of the costs that such a guarantee imposes on other generating fuels and the American consumers.

FOR MORE INFORMATION

American Wind Energy Association, 122 C St. N.W., 4th Floor, Washington, D.C. 20001; (202) 383-2500. A group representing producers and distributors of wind turbines advocates broader use of wind energy.

Edison Electric Institute, 701 Pennsylvania Ave. N.W., Washington, D.C. 20004; (202) 508-5583. Representing investor-owned electric power companies and electric utility holding companies, the institute provides information on capacity, generation and other aspects of the electric utility industry.

Energy Information Administration, U.S. Department of Energy, 1000 Independence Ave. S.W., Washington, D.C. 20585; (202) 586-5000; eia.doe.gov. The EIA is the main source of government information on energy, including renewable energy, electric utility deregulation and other policy issues.

National Ocean Industries Association, 1120 G St. N.W., Suite 900, Washington, D.C. 20005; (202) 347-6900. The association supports development of ocean thermal energy.

Solar Energy Industries Association, 122 C St. N.W., 4th Floor, Washington, D.C. 20001; (202) 383-2600. This organization of solar power producers monitors policy and legislation affecting all aspects of the industry, including solar thermal and photovoltaics.

ties don't want to be making any commitments right now to new capacity in the market, which is understandable because there's a lot of uncertainty about what's going to shake out with utility restructuring."

Legislation in Congress

While the states are taking steps on their own to deregulate utilities, Congress is trying to come up with a new federal framework that would provide some cohesion to this fast-moving restructuring of an essential industry.

There are four major electricity deregulation bills now before Congress, all of which set minimum renewable energy portfolio standards. To satisfy its portfolio requirement, a utility would be allowed either to generate electricity from its own renewable sources or buy credits from a producer that has generated more power from renewables than the standard requires. Credits would be traded on the open market, in the same way that coal-burning industries trade sulfur dioxide credits to comply with the 1990 Clean Air Act. [25]

A proposal by Rep. Dan Schaefer, R-Colo., would require all utilities to have renewable energy credits equal to 2 percent of their power generation by 2001, increasing to 4 percent by 2010. Schaefer's bill would exclude hydropower from the list of qualified renewables, however, a fact that hydro supporters say will kill their industry.

Another House bill, proposed by Rep. Edward J. Markey, D-Mass., would place the number of renewable energy credits at 3 percent of generated power by 1999, increasing to 10 percent in 2010. But this bill includes hydropower on the list of eligible renewable resources.

On the Senate side, a proposal by Sen. Dale Bumpers, D-Ark., would require utilities to get 5 percent of their power from renewables by 2003, increasing to 9 percent in 2008 and 12 percent in 2013. While this bill allows hydropower as a qualified resource, it would give more credit for other renewables generating a comparable level of power.

Sen. James M. Jeffords, R-Vt., would require utilities to have credits equal to 2.5 percent of their power generation by 2000, increasing to 20 percent by 2020.

While supporters of renewables differ over the inclusion of hydropower — a mature industry — among the resources credited under these bills, they generally agree that there should be some federal oversight of utility deregulation. "Having a federal umbrella of principles that restructuring should follow is worthwhile because you can't have a patchwork of radically different restructuring practices state-to-state," says PG&E Vice President Macias. "I'm not a fan, however, of having Washington dictate the specifics or the details of restructuring because the needs in each state are dramatically different. In California, we have come up with a practical and workable resolution to the transition costs of deregulation that is working for us but may not work for other states. Other states need to have the flexibility to address their problems as well as their vision of the future." ■

OUTLOOK

Popular Support

Until renewable energy is fully competitive with traditional fuels, its ability to survive in a deregulated market will depend in large part on the willingness of customers to pay more for its use. Recent experiences in the states, as well as public opinion polls, suggest that many Americans would pay a small premium on their electric bills to do just that.

During a recent statewide pilot program, a third of Massachusetts customers chose environmentally friendly power sources over lower-priced options such as nuclear or coal-generated power. In Colorado, more than 3,000 homeowners and several major electric customers signed up this year for a wind power program to build 13 wind turbines in northeastern Colorado that will increase their electric bills by 35 percent. [26]

Opinion polls indicate widespread support for future renewable projects as well. Thirty percent of California residents say they would be "very willing" to pay 10 percent more for energy from clean sources instead of from nuclear or coal. And nearly 40 percent of the respondents in a nationwide poll said renewable energy should receive the highest priority for federal Energy Department funding, rather than supporting energy efficiency or other fuels. [27]

Industry analysts involved in the development of renewables take heart from these indications of popular support. "If you give people the choice, they would prefer [environmentally friendly] kilowatt hours to other kilowatt hours," says Kelly of Enron. "They'd even be willing to pay a little bit of a premium. To the extent that we can provide incremental 'green' power to customers, we think that the deregulated market is going to be an area where we can compete." ■

Notes

[1] Enron Renewable is a subsidiary of Enron Corp., a Houston-based energy producer. The Lake Benton wind farm will be sold to Northern States Power Co., an electric utility in Minneapolis. The wind farm will generate an estimated 107 megawatts of electricity.

[2] Figures from www.afce.org., the Web site of the Alliance for Competitive Electricity, a group of utilities that support deregulation and repeal of current preferences for renewables or other fuels. For background, see "Restructuring the Electric Industry," *The CQ Researcher,* Jan. 17, 1997. pp. 25-48.

[3] See Fred Sissine, *Renewable Energy: Key to Sustainable Energy Supply,* Congressional Research Service, Sept. 30, 1997.

[4] For background, see "Global Warming Update," *The CQ Researcher,* Nov. 1, 1996, pp. 961-984.

[5] For background, see "Oil Imports," *The CQ Researcher,* Aug. 23, 1991, pp. 585-608.

[6] For background, see "New Air Quality Standards," *The CQ Researcher,* March 7, 1997, pp. 193-216.

[7] Enron Corp., *1997 Enron Energy Outlook.*

[8] For background, see "Alternative Energy," *The CQ Researcher,* July 10, 1992, pp. 573-596, and "Will Nuclear Power Get Another Chance?" *Editorial Research Reports,* Feb. 22, 1991, pp. 113-128.

[9] California Energy Commission, *Wind Turbine Effects on Avian Activity, Habitat Use, and Mortality in Altamont Pass and Solano County Wind Resource Areas,* March 1992.

[10] Adelberg testified March 6, 1997, before the Senate Energy and Natural Resources Committee.

[11] Information in this section is based on Susan Williams and Brenda G. Bateman, *Power Plays* (1995).

[12] See Renewable Energy, *Congressional Digest,* August-September 1997, pp. 195-197.

[13] See Daniel P. Beard, "Dams Aren't Forever," *The New York Times,* Oct. 6, 1997.

[14] Unless otherwise noted, material in the remainder of this section is based on *Renewable Energy Annual 1996,* Energy Information Administration, March 1997.

[15] Williams and Bateman, *op. cit.,* pp. 35-39.

[16] *Ibid.,* p. 48.

[17] *Ibid.,* pp. 185-186.

[18] *Ibid.,* p. 255.

[19] *Congressional Digest, op. cit.,* p. 196.

[20] *Ibid.,* p. 197.

[21] Williams and Bateman, *op. cit.,* pp. 9-10.

[22] See Agis Salpukas, "Green Power Wanes, but Not at the Grass Roots," *The New York Times,* March 9, 1997.

[23] See "N.J. Utility to Buy Grid in Australia," *The Washington Post,* Oct. 13, 1997.

[24] Sissine, *op. cit.,* p. 10.

[25] For background, see "Acid Rain: New Approach to Old Problem," *Editorial Research Reports,* March 8, 1991, pp. 129-144.

[26] See "Wind Power Gets Boost," *The Denver Post,* Aug. 24, 1997.

[27] "America Speaks Out on Energy," a poll conducted in December 1995 by Research/Strategy/Management Inc., for the Sustainable Energy Budget Coalition.

Bibliography

Selected Sources Used

Books

Deudney, Daniel, and Christopher Flavin, *Renewable Energy: The Power to Choose,* Worldwatch Institute, 1983.

This classic on renewable energy sets the context for research in this area in the aftermath of the energy crises of the 1970s. Although some of the technology described is dated, separate chapters on each of the renewable sources provide useful background on their development.

Easterbrook, Gregg, *A Moment on the Earth: The Coming Age of Environmental Optimism,* Penguin Books, 1995.

In this controversial book, the author argues for a "middle road" between free-market critics of the environmental movement and alarmists who predict an imminent collapse of the biosphere. A chapter on renewable energy concludes that current obstacles to renewable development will eventually be overcome, resulting in the widespread adoption of clean fuels.

Articles

Bradley, Robert L., "Renewable Energy: Not Cheap, Not Green," *Policy Analysis,* Aug. 27, 1997.

The author, an adjunct scholar at the Cato Institute, criticizes efforts to support renewable energy, which he says is not cost-competitive with natural gas and other energy sources and which has unintended negative effects on the environment.

Dunn, Seth, "Power of Choice," *Worldwatch,* September/October 1997, pp. 30-35.

Deregulation is expected to enable customers to pick their electric power providers just as they choose their long-distance providers today. Opinion polls suggest that most Americans would prefer to buy "green" power, from renewable energy sources. Without government oversight, the author warns, the coming barrage of "green marketing" by electricity providers may mislead consumers.

Grover, Ronald, Gary McWilliams, Nicole Harris and Peter Coy, "An Electric Moment in California," *Business Week,* May 26, 1997, pp. 60-61.

Power companies from all over the country are launching marketing campaigns in California in anticipation of that state's plan to allow customers to begin choosing their electricity providers on Jan. 1, 1998.

O'Reilly, Brian, "Transforming the Power Business," *Fortune,* Sept. 29, 1997, pp. 142-152.

After enjoying a virtual monopoly for decades, the electric utility industry is about to be transformed. Deregulation will force many of these large companies to jettison uneconomical generation facilities or specialize in aspects of the business to survive in a competitive market.

Reports and Studies

Anson, Susan, Karin Sinclair and Blair Swezey, *Profiles in Renewable Energy: Case Studies of Successful Utility-Sector Projects,* National Renewable Energy Laboratory, August 1994.

An Energy Department lab reviews the performance of several firms producing electricity from each of the major renewable energy sources.

Energy Information Administration, *Renewable Energy Annual 1996,* March 1997.

An Energy Department report describes the major renewable energy sectors, their contribution to the national energy mix and the impact of deregulation on each.

Farhar, Barbara C., *Energy and the Environment: The Public View,* Renewable Energy Policy Project, October 1996.

The author presents data from more than 700 polls showing strong public support for federal assistance of renewable energy development and for the inclusion of renewable sources in the national energy mix.

Sissine, Fred, *Renewable Energy: Key to Sustainable Energy Supply,* Congressional Research Service, Sept. 30, 1997.

This report, available to individuals through their representatives in Congress, examines the impact of deregulation, negotiations for a global climate treaty, oil prices and federal research funding on the development of renewable energy.

Williams, Susan, and Brenda G. Bateman, *Power Plays: Profiles of America's Independent Renewable Electricity Developers,* Investor Responsibility Research Center, June 1995.

This detailed analysis of the renewable energy industry provides background and technical information as well as profiles of leading companies in each of the renewable sectors.

The Next Step

Additional information from UMI's Newspaper & Periodical Abstracts™ database

Biomass

Schroer, Bill, "Biofuels: Colorado's energy mix for a smarter future: Resources needed could be grown, or found in trash," *The Denver Post,* May 19, 1997, p. E2.

Located in the National Renewable Energy Lab complex is the Alternative Fuels User Facility. Here, ethanol, a high-octane, clean-combusting liquid fuel, is concocted out of materials considered waste. Ethanol is the most popular member of the biofuels family, which includes methanol, methane and biodiesel. All are made from a renewable biomass such as trees or plants. The traditional ethanol production process is similar to beer-making because a grain or plant base is converted into sugars, fermented and distilled. Ethanol is a sleeping giant already blended into about 9 percent of American gasoline, including Denver's, to improve air quality.

Electric Utility Deregulation

Dunn, Seth, "Power of choice," *World Watch,* September 1997, pp. 30-35.

Millions of consumers will soon gain a choice in where their electric services come from. Whether "green power marketing" will lead to a cleaner energy future or merely repackage the existing mix is still in doubt.

Harvey, Hal, Arthur W. Adelberg, Julie A. Keil and Glenn English et al, "Should electric industry restructuring legislation include a renewable energy mandate?" *Congressional Digest,* August 1997, pp. 204-223.

Several experts debate the pros and cons of whether electric industry restructuring legislation should include a renewable-energy mandate.

Heath, Rebecca Piirto, "The marketing of power," *American Demographics,* September 1997, pp. 59-63.

After years of monopolistic disinterest in consumers, the electric utilities industry is being deregulated and must start drumming up customer excitement. The pros and cons of deregulation and how electric utilities are gearing up to market their services to customers are discussed.

Kraul, Chris, "California; Consumers Seek to Block Energy Measure; Utilities: SB 477 has become a rallying point for groups trying to challenge state's electricity deregulation," *Los Angeles Times,* July 24, 1997, p. D2.

A highly technical and arcane piece of legislation moving its way through the state Capitol has become an unlikely rallying point for consumer groups trying to mount a late-inning challenge to California's electricity deregulation, set to take effect Jan. 1, 1988. The bill, SB 477, would implement the sale of up to $10 billion in rate reduction bonds, with proceeds going to utilities to help them cut rates by 10 percent, and make an early payoff on billions of dollars of debt associated with money-losing investments in nuclear and alternative energy.

Raine, George, "Plugging in to green power; Renewable energy takes center stage as deregulation looms," *San Francisco Chronicle,* Aug. 24, 1997, p. B1.

As vice president of Green Mountain, an energy retailer in South Burlington, Vt., Kevin Hartley has devised EcoCredits and an array of other marketing devices to sell "preferred," or environmentally friendly, energy sources in deregulated California beginning Jan. 1, 1988.

Sykes, Lisa, "The power to choose," *New Scientist,* Sept. 6, 1997, pp. 18-19.

In April 1998, the British energy market will be opened up to full competition. Producers of renewable energy are hoping that the ending of the monopoly held by the regional electricity companies over domestic supplies will provide a boost for renewable energy.

Fuel Cells

"Beyond batteries," *The Boston Globe,* April 28, 1997, p. A14.

Environmental demand for cleaner air has put a heavy burden on the automobile, much improved by stringent exhaust standards but still a significant source of pollutants. Calls for a zero-emission vehicle have been based on hope that battery-powered electric cars will become economically practical. Now it appears that another technology — the fuel cell — has considerable potential. Both are worth pursuing despite formidable technical and economic problems. Major auto makers have made varying commitments to the fuel cell in recent weeks, including Ford's announcement last Monday that it would have a prototype by the year 2000 and Daimler Benz's commitment to sell 100,000 fuel cell cars by 2005. Toyota, General Motors and Chrysler are also engaged in studies of the technology.

"Chrysler to unveil technology to put fuel 'cells' in electric cars," *Detroit News,* Jan. 6, 1997, p. A4.

Chrysler Corp. recently announced that it has developed a way to extract hydrogen from gasoline, bringing prototypes of "fuel-cell" electric cars 10 years closer to reality. By 2005, the No. 3 domestic automaker hopes to have a model of an electric car that gets its power from hydrogen and is 50 percent more fuel efficient than cars with conventional internal combustion engines.

Colker, David, "Fuel Cells Could Be Key to Future Autos; JPL researchers focus on methanol in drive to create alternative to internal combustion machines," *Los Angeles Times,* Jan. 31, 1997, p. B2.

Nifty little power plants that gained fame during the Gemini spacecraft years because of their ability to convert hydrogen into electricity are finally being seriously considered as a non-polluting alternative to internal combustion machines — a step beyond electric cars powered by heavy, troublesome batteries.

DePalma. Anthony, "Are Fuel Cells the Key to Cleaner Energy?" *The New York Times,* Oct. 8, 1997, p. D1.

For years the Ballard Co. has been a leader in fuel cells, which create electricity not by burning fuel but by the process of chemically rearranging the fuel's molecules to produce current with no emissions but water. When Daimler-Benz A.G. signed a $325 million deal in August to buy 25 percent of Ballard and jointly develop fuel cell systems for cars and buses, Ballard solidified its lead, though company executives say they can hear the competition yipping right behind them. Last year, the Toyota Motor Corporation presented a fuel cell vehicle that did not use a Ballard cell and was based on an unusual hydrogen storage system. At the Frankfurt Auto Show in September, Toyota introduced another fuel cell car, this one based on carrying the hydrogen in methanol.

Solar Energy

Allen, Scott, "Mass. firms hail U.S. solar energy plan," *The Boston Globe,* June 28, 1997, p. F2.

President Clinton's proposal to put solar energy panels on a million rooftops by the year 2010 may provide a dramatic boost for the solar industry, including several influential Massachusetts firms, and erase the memories of 1981 when Ronald Reagan tore the solar panels off the White House. Yesterday, Energy Secretary Federico F. Peña spelled out the details of the solar policy, calling for a combination of government marketing, low-interest loans and the installation of solar panels on many of the nation's 500,000 federal buildings.

Allen, William, "Ovens to Harness Sun for Africans," *St. Louis Post-Dispatch,* July 11, 1997, p. B1.

Sister Mary Patricia Rives, 73, a self-taught expert on solar ovens, leaves today for Africa. She will distribute 37 of her ovens and teach the people of 10 villages in Uganda and Kenya how to cook with solar energy. Rives is a member of the Religious of the Sacred Heart and lives in a convent on the Maryville University campus in Town and Country.

Bates, Karl Leif, "Solar cell brightens day: Firm's new roofing shingle makes electricity on the spot through new concept," *Detroit News,* June 9, 1997, p. A4.

Making electricity with coal and oil may be cheap, but sunlight is free. The trouble has always been converting that free fuel into usable current — and doing it cost-effectively. Now, a Troy-based company has taken a huge step toward solving that problem by producing a roofing shingle that makes electricity on the spot. On the outside, United Solar Systems Corp. is a nondescript industrial building. But inside is a 100-foot-long production line that Subhendu Guha, executive vice president, hopes will revolutionize the solar panel industry. Already, the company has become the world champion maker of thin-film solar cells and is a cutting edge innovator in roof-mounted solar systems. Its shingles will power a typical suburban home with as little as 500 square feet of material, which is dramatically lighter than its forerunners.

Booth, Michael, "Move on to harness sun: Ranchers find solar power economical," *The Denver Post,* Jan. 17, 1997, p. C1.

Economy-minded ranchers and farmers across the nation are slowly moving toward improved solar technologies to perform routine functions on their remote spreads, including water pumping, fence electrification and gate lifting. While major solar conversions have not yet proven as economically sound for urban and suburban homes, solar cells have become more efficient and are winning support for remote uses when it would cost far more to extend a traditional power line.

Brown, Paul, "Big insurers warm to solar power," *The Guardian,* Feb. 25, 1997, p. 16.

Participants at the recent "solar summit" in Oxford, England, included U.S. utilities, the Rockefeller Foundation and Sainsbury, a supermarket chain in England. It was organized by Dr. Jeremy Leggett, former director of science for Greenpeace. Leggett is now director of Solar Century, an organization that promotes solar power, particularly in the developing world where 2 billion people are without electricity.

Brown, Paul, "Big insurers warm to solar power," *The Guardian,* Feb. 25, 1997, p. 16.

Participants at the recent "solar summit" in Oxford, England, included U.S. utilities, the Rockefeller Foundation and Sainsbury, a supermarket chain in England. It was organized by Dr. Jeremy Leggett, former director of science for Greenpeace. Leggett is now director of Solar Century, an organization that promotes solar power, particularly in the developing world where 2 billion people are without electricity.

Mallory, Jim, "Solar cars cross finish line: Cal State the victor in Sunrayce '97," *The Denver Post,* June 29, 1997, p. B3.

"Solar Eagle III" soared across the finish line here Saturday to win Sunrayce '97, a 10-day cross-country solar-powered car race. The car was designed and built by engineering students at California State University at Los Angeles. With the Sunrayce '97 title in their grasp, the team might enter their car in the World Solar Challenge to be run in Australia next year.

Reed, Blake, "Build a solar-charge controller," ***Electronics Now,*** **October 1997, pp. 59-68.**
Reed describes how to build a solar-charge controller that will meet most needs.

Smith, Peter B., "Advocates Still Energized by Alternative Fuel," ***The Boston Globe,*** **Jan. 5, 1997,p. C1.**
Vermont Energy Contracting and Supply Corp. and Solar Works of Montpelier, two Vermont solar energy firms that grew out of the interest in alternative energy sources created by the oil shocks of the 1970s, are both thriving companies in 1997. The firms and their work are featured.

Wald, Matthew L., "Solar Power In Big Leap In California," ***The New York Times,*** **May 19, 1997, p. B7.**
A California electric utility has signed a big contract to buy solar cells that the utility and the Department of Energy say will push the cells' cost down to a competitive level by 2002. The utility, the Sacramento Municipal Utility District, will buy 10 megawatts of solar cells by 2002, enough to supply hundreds of houses. The total is small by the standards of conventional power plants, but experts say it is the largest purchase ever by a utility of solar cells. The utility will put 300-500 square feet of cells on the roofs of about 4,000 customers who volunteer, and these will produce about three kilowatts of power during the day. Over the year, these cells are expected to produce about the same amount of power as a house uses.

Yeung, Joyce, "National tour of solar homes," ***Mother Earth News,*** **October 1997, p. 14.**
The upcoming National Tour of Solar Homes features more than 500 homes in more than 36 states. The tour is an attempt to showcase the efficiency, affordability and diversity of these homes.

Wind

Allen, Scott, "Vt. wind station a key test for region's energy future," ***The Boston Globe,*** **July 24, 1997, p. A1.**
After years of talk about harnessing the Northeast's winds for electricity, Green Mountain Power Corp. has built the largest commercial wind power generating station in the eastern United States. The completion of the $11 million Vermont project, built by Zond Corp. of California, follows the collapse of other wind projects that have cast a pall over the industry in the Northeast.

Antosh, Nelson, "Enron unit wins Iowa wind power contract," ***Houston Chronicle,*** **March 20, 1997, p. C2.**
A subsidiary of Enron says it plans to build a wind-powered generating facility in northwestern Iowa capable of producing enough electric power to supply 50,000 average-sized homes. The project is based on a contract that California-based Zond Corp. — a wind-turbine manufacturer that was acquired by Enron in January — signed with MidAmerican. Zond is a part of the Enron Renewable Energy Corp., a subsidiary of the Enron Corp.

Brown, Paul, "Wind and the willows to power renewable energy," ***The Guardian,*** **March 11, 1997, p 17.**
Renewable energy schemes producing enough power for 1 million homes were given the go-ahead by the British government yesterday. They include a groundbreaking contract for off-shore wind turbines and intensive willow farming.

"Building of wind-driven power plant in Wyo. OK'd," ***The Denver Post,*** **May 9, 1997, p. B4.**
Carbon County officials have approved a special use permit for a company planning to build a wind-driven electrical generation station near Arlington this summer. The county's planning commission stipulated in the permit that Sea West of San Diego cannot build in a small area where the project overlaps coal reserves without seeking comments from Union Pacific Resources, which owns the mineral rights.

Carrier, Jim, "A boost for wind power; PSC customers may help pay for turbine program," ***The Denver Post,*** **Feb. 2, 1997, p. A1.**
If regulators approve the plan, Public Service Co.(Power Co), the state's largest utility, will give customers the option of paying 35 percent over existing rates for coal- and gas-generated power to help finance new wind-generated power facilities. Under the most optimistic scenarios, Public Service's wind-power program would amount to only 1 percent of its 4,000-megawatt load. But "it's a start," said Jeff Ackerman, who heads PSC's renewable energy project. Customers would be able to buy blocks of wind power, each block of 100 kilowatts equal to 20 percent of a typical household's monthly use. On average, each block would cost $2.50 more per month. If you signed up for "full wind power," a typical household bill would increase to $60 from $45.

Gibbs, Geoffrey, "Alternatives: The energy of youth: Geoffrey Gibbs on the sixth-form pupils determined to bring wind power to their multi-cultural school," ***The Guardian,*** **June 18, 1997, Sec. SOCIETY, p. 4.**
From a chance remark made during a school workshop on renewable energy, students at a multi-cultural sixth form college in south Wales have drawn up extensively researched plans to meet the college's annual electricity needs by erecting their own wind turbine.

Back Issues

Great Research on Current Issues Starts Right Here . . . Recent topics covered by The CQ Researcher are listed below. Before May 1991, reports were published under the name of Editorial Research Reports.

APRIL 1996
Centennial Olympic Games
Managed Care
Protecting Endangered Species
New Military Culture

MAY 1996
Russia's Political Future
Marriage and Divorce
Year-Round Schools
Taiwan, China and the U.S.

JUNE 1996
Rethinking NAFTA
First Ladies
Teaching Values
Labor Movement's Future

JULY 1996
Recovered-Memory Debate
Native Americans' Future
Crackdown on Sexual Harassment
Attack on Public Schools

AUGUST 1996
Fighting Over Animal Rights
Privatizing Government Services
Child Labor and Sweatshops
Cleaning Up Hazardous Wastes

Back issues are available for $5.00 (subscribers) or $10.00 (non-subscribers). Quantity discounts apply to orders over ten. To order, call Congressional Quarterly Customer Service at (202) 887-8621.

Binders are available for $18.00. To order call 1-800-638-1710. Please refer to stock number 648.

SEPTEMBER 1996
Gambling Under Attack
The States and Federalism
Civic Journalism
Reassessing Foreign Aid

OCTOBER 1996
Political Consultants
Insurance Fraud
Rethinking School Integration
Parental Rights

NOVEMBER 1996
Global Warming
Clashing Over Copyright
Consumer Debt
Governing Washington, D.C.

DECEMBER 1996
Welfare, Work and the States
The New Volunteerism
Implementing the Disabilities Act
America's Pampered Pets

JANUARY 1997
Combating Scientific Misconduct
Restructuring the Electric Industry
The New Immigrants
Chemical and Biological Weapons

FEBRUARY 1997
Assisting Refugees
Alternative Medicine's Next Phase
Independent Counsels
Feminism's Future

MARCH 1997
New Air Quality Standards
Alcohol Advertising
Civic Renewal
Educating Gifted Students

APRIL 1997
Declining Crime Rates
The FBI Under Fire
Gender Equity in Sports
Space Program's Future

MAY 1997
The Stock Market
The Cloning Controversy
Expanding NATO
The Future of Libraries

JUNE 1997
FDA Reform
China After Deng
Line-Item Veto
Breast Cancer

JULY 1997
Transportation Policy
Executive Pay
School Choice Debate
Aggressive Driving

AUGUST 1997
Age Discrimination
Banning Land Mines
Children's Television
Evolution vs. Creationism

SEPTEMBER 1997
Caring for the Dying
Mental Health Policy
Mexico's Future
Youth Fitness

OCTOBER 1997
Urban Sprawl in the West
Diversity in the Workplace
Teacher Education
Contingent Work Force

Future Topics

- ***Artificial Intelligence***
- ***Religious Persecution***
- ***Abortion: Roe v. Wade at 25***

THE CQ Researcher

PUBLISHED BY CONGRESSIONAL QUARTERLY INC.

Artificial Intelligence

Are scientists close to creating a machine that 'thinks'?

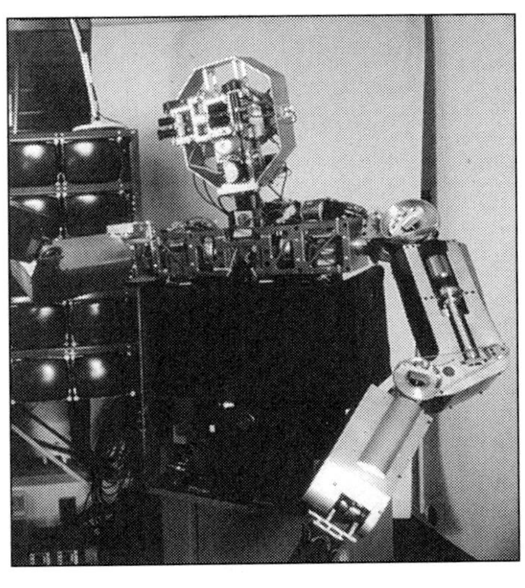

The defeat last summer of Russian chess master Garry Kasparov by IBM's Deep Blue computer was seen by some as a milestone in the development of "thinking" machines. But Deep Blue, while an impressive chess player, does not remotely demonstrate humanlike thinking. Indeed, many computer scientists say that a machine that emulates human thought is centuries away, or perhaps not even possible at all. Others argue that increases in computing power in recent years and improved understanding of the human mind will lead to thinking machines in the near future. Meanwhile, robots, "expert systems" and other developments that have resulted from artificial intelligence research are being used in more and more real-world applications by companies ranging from General Motors to American Express.

INSIDE

THIS ISSUE

CQ | **Nov. 14, 1997 • Volume 7, No. 42 • Pages 985-1008**

Formerly Editorial Research Reports

COVER: "COG," A ROBOT DEVELOPED BY RODNEY A. BROOKS OF THE MASSACHUSETTS INSTITUTE OF TECHNOLOGY, USES TRIAL AND ERROR TO "LEARN" IN THE SAME WAY A CHILD WOULD. (MIT ARTIFICIAL INTELLIGENCE LAB)

November 14, 1997
Volume 7, No. 42

EDITOR
Sandra Stencel

MANAGING EDITOR
Thomas J. Colin

ASSOCIATE EDITOR
Sarah M. Magner

STAFF WRITERS
Charles S. Clark
Mary H. Cooper
Kenneth Jost
David Masci

EDITORIAL ASSISTANT
Vanessa E. Furlong

PUBLISHED BY
Congressional Quarterly Inc.

CHAIRMAN
Andrew Barnes

VICE CHAIRMAN
Andrew P. Corty

PRESIDENT AND PUBLISHER
Robert W. Merry

EXECUTIVE EDITOR
David Rapp

The CQ Researcher (ISSN 1056-2036). Formerly Editorial Research Reports. Published weekly, except Jan. 3, May 30, Aug. 29, Oct. 31, by Congressional Quarterly Inc., 1414 22nd St., N.W., Washington, D.C. 20037. Annual subscription rate for libraries, businesses and government is $340. Additional rates furnished upon request. Periodicals postage paid at Washington, D.C., and additional mailing offices. POSTMASTER: Send address changes to The CQ Researcher, 1414 22nd St., N.W., Washington, D.C. 20037.

Artificial Intelligence

BY DAVID MASCI

THE ISSUES

Until last spring, Garry Kasparov was the best chess player in the world. But on May 11, the 34-year-old Russian was defeated, not by Bobby Fischer or some precocious 9-year-old, but by Deep Blue, a computer built by IBM.

Media hype had framed the six-game, nine-day match as a classic "man vs. machine" confrontation — "John Henry" for the 1990s. In the end, Kasparov proved no match for an opponent able to calculate 200 million moves per second without tiring, just as the mythical railroad man couldn't compete against a spike-driving machine that never ran out of steam.

But Deep Blue's victory didn't mark the beginning of man's domination by thinking machines, notwithstanding all the media hoopla.

Rather, it revealed the inherent limitations of today's computers. For while Deep Blue had almost unfathomable calculating ability, it still depended on human chess experts to program it with the information it needed to defeat Kasparov. The machine even required human assistance to view the board and move its pieces.

More important, Deep Blue did not possess that most basic of human characteristics: self-awareness. "It no more knew it was playing chess than a vacuum cleaner knows it is cleaning a rug," observed science writer Martin Gardiner. [1] It did not feel disappointment when it lost a game or triumph when it won. That is because it is not conscious or intelligent, at least in any way that a human being can understand the terms, Gardiner said.

Even if Deep Blue's creators at IBM had wanted to program it to exhibit the

common sense that people take for granted, they would have failed because of the current limitations of the computer science known as artificial intelligence (AI). "Deep Blue might be able to win at chess, but it wouldn't know to come in from the rain," says Marvin Minsky, a professor of computer science at the Massachusetts Institute of Technology (MIT).

Artificial intelligence, like human intelligence itself, is not easy to define. But the term generally refers to efforts to imbue machines not just with the ability to process information but with human qualities like intuition and common sense. Since the early 1950s, AI researchers have struggled in vain to give computers these characteristics.

They have failed, many experts say, because human functions are unique to the human brain and are unlikely to be duplicated any time soon, if ever. Some experts, like John Searle, a professor of philosophy at the University of California at Berkeley, argue that true human consciousness can only be generated by a biological brain. In addition, Searle and others argue, the brain is so complicated and mysterious that it is unlikely ever to be replicated in any meaningful way.

"I can't see how we can build one when we don't really know how it does what it does," he says.

Stuart Shieber, a professor of computer science at Harvard University, agrees. Duplicating human intelligence, he says, "is so phenomenally hard that it's just hubris to think you can do it" any time soon, if ever.

But other AI experts are more optimistic about building machines with human qualities and intelligence. While predictions vary, some researchers like Hans Moravec, a professor of computer science at Carnegie Mellon University in Pittsburgh, say that machines with humanlike intelligence are only decades away.

To begin with, Moravec and others argue, it won't be long before humans develop a computer that has the computational power of the brain. In addition, they say, there is no magic key or linchpin to intelligence. As scientists develop a better understanding of how the brain works, AI researchers will be able to duplicate brain functions, and "Intelligence will emerge with the working parts of the machine," says Randy Davis, a computer scientist at MIT.

But optimists differ over how to create such a machine. Some favor the "top-down" approach used by Douglas B. Lenat, president and CEO of Cycorp, an AI research firm in Austin, Texas. Lenat and his team are feeding a powerful computer with millions of assertions about daily life — forks are used for eating, babies do not drive cars, and so forth. The hope is that eventually all the random data will give the machine a rudimentary understanding of the world.

Other researchers argue that Lenat's work, while interesting, is not going to lead to any AI breakthroughs. Some of these experts favor the more "bottom-up" approach taken by Rodney A. Brooks, director

Is There a Robot in Your Future?

A cleaner house may be around the corner, but don't expect to hail a robot taxi any time soon, experts say. House-cleaning robots could be commercially available in the near future, but will resemble hydrantlike R2-D2 of "Star Wars" fame, rather than his humanoid pal C-3PO. Robot taxis could be possible in carefully controlled areas of cities. As for robots that replicate themselves, the technology to build them exists, but no one wants to put up the money.

	Self-driving taxi	House-cleaning robot	Self-replicating robot	C-3PO becomes reality
Rodney A. Brooks Director, MIT Artificial Intelligence Lab	2015	1998	2015	2025
John Canny Associate professor of computer science, University of California-Berkeley	2005	2005	2013	2030
Joe Engelberger Chairman, HelpMate Robotics Inc.	2010	1999	unlikely	unlikely
Toshio Fukuda Professor of microsystem engineering and mechano-informatics, Nagoya University	2020	2000	2030	2020
Richard S. Wallace Professor of electrical engineering and computer science, Lehigh University	2045	2025	2080	2080

Source: "Reality Check," Wired 4.03. Edited by David Pescovitz. © 1996-97 Wired Magazine Group.

of the Artificial Intelligence Laboratory at MIT. Brooks' team is working with a robot named Cog that has been given rudimentary sight, hearing and movement. The hope is that Cog will use its senses to learn on its own instead of being told how to learn.

If an AI breakthrough is achieved, the world certainly will be a different place. Indeed, Minsky and Moravec predict that human society will be completely altered. According to Moravec, thinking machines — known in the field as AIs — will be so much smarter and more capable than their human forebears that they will quickly replace people in every endeavor, from writing to computer science. Moravec and others go so far as to say machines could decide to eliminate humans entirely, as they would be superfluous, serving no productive function.

But many call Moravec's ideas preposterous. Even scientists who envision the coming of AI say that humans will always have ultimate control over their creations. Some thinkers, like Charles Platt, a contributing editor at *Wired,* a computer magazine, argue that since machines, unlike humans, are programmable, even intelligent computers should be able to be controlled. Others, like Lenat, say that humans will use AI to enhance their own capabilities and thus will be able to stay one step ahead of the machines.

Discussion of whether there will be smart machines and how they can be controlled seems far-fetched to many. But AI research has made solid contributions in the world of science and technology that even the most hardened pragmatist would admire. For instance, the fruits of AI research are used to create sophisticated programs that help pilots fly planes, doctors diagnose illnesses, blind people write letters and financial institutions invest money. AI researchers have also worked to help make robots more practical, from factory assembly lines and hospital operating rooms to Mars, where NASA employed the now famous *Sojourner* to explore the planet's surface in July. [2]

Many of the advances that made such achievements possible are no longer directly associated with AI research. "Much of what was considered as AI research has become part of normal computer science," says Marc M. Sebrechts, a professor of psychology at Catholic University. One reason for the change in labels, Sebrechts and others say, is that the field of artificial intelligence has come under attack in the last 10 years, largely because AI researchers unceasingly predicted — unrealistically, it turned out — that thinking machines were just around the corner.

And yet, in spite of derision from colleagues in computer science and other fields, many experts remain optimistic about the future of AI. "Where were we 10 years ago?" Lenat asks. "The average person didn't have E-mail, and the average family wasn't on the World Wide Web."

As AI experts look to the future, these are some of the questions they are asking:

Will researchers develop a computer that duplicates human intelligence in the foreseeable future?

Even before the term artificial intelligence was coined in the 1950s, AI researchers had been searching for ways to make machines think and act like humans. "It's the Holy Grail of AI," says Harvard's Shieber.

After World War II, some researchers, heady with optimism after the first AI experiments, predicted that science would duplicate human thought in 10 or 20 years. All that was needed, they said, was a machine powerful enough to run the complicated programs they would write.

Computers today are incredibly powerful — and getting more powerful every year — but the Grail remains elusive. Many experts now predict that it will be centuries, if at all, before science catches up to the human mind. "I don't know if we'll ever have a robot that will be conscious, experience pain, have goals in life and the like, which are necessary for intelligence," says Hubert Dreyfus, a professor of philosophy at the University of California at Berkeley.

Pessimists like Dreyfus say that researchers are not even close to jumping a host of technological hurdles. To begin with, they say, scientists are only beginning to understand the workings of the human brain, with its billions of interconnected neurons working together to produce thought. How, they ask, can a machine be built based on something of which scientists have so little understanding?

"No one really knows how the interconnections in your brain work," Shieber says. And "even if we did figure it out, it would be impossible to simulate. There are some systems you just can't simulate, like the weather."

MIT Artificial Intelligence Lab

A team at MIT led by Rodney A. Brooks has programmed a robot named "Cog" with rudimentary sight, hearing and movement in hopes it will use its senses to learn on its own.

Another problem, pessimists say, is creating machines with essential human attributes, like common sense and an ability to appreciate subtleties of meaning in language. Terry Winograd, a computer scientist at Stanford University, argues that machines will never fully grasp language because the meaning of words is linked to human activity. It is one thing to understand that a dog is a four-legged canine and another to fully realize the role they play in human society as pets, he says. [3]

Similarly, Dreyfus says, "If someone sees a jockey with hay fever and knows

Continued on p. 991

Through a Glass Darkly: AI in Pop Culture

Western literature is replete with stories of living beings created from lifeless objects, such as the Roman poet Ovid's tale of Pygmalion, the sculptor who fashioned a beautiful woman from stone, and the 15th-century legend of the rabbi of Prague and his golem.

In the age of film, television and computers, however, technology has replaced God or the supernatural as the force that creates creatures with artificial intelligence (AI).

Some of the more modern stories have been cautionary tales about the dangers of technology. One of the earliest (and darkest) treatments of AI is German director Fritz Lang's 1926 silent film classic, "Metropolis." Lang portrays the future as a nightmare, with most people living as slaves, cruelly controlled by machines.

Another is "Blade Runner," a 1982 film directed by Ridley Scott, set in the Los Angeles of the future. It starts as a technology-run-amok story, with a policeman tracking down several escaped androids, slaves with human appearance and intelligence. But the cop, played by Harrison Ford, slowly begins to realize that the androids he is seeking are no different from the humans who created them. After one of the androids saves his life, he understands that the problem isn't that intelligent machines want freedom, it's that humanity is unwilling to give it to them. Hence the nightmare scenario depicted in "Metropolis" is turned on its head: Humans are not the slaves, but the enslavers.

Other films and TV shows have offered a more optimistic vision of the future for humans and humanlike machines. In George Lucas' "Star Wars" trilogy, intelligent androids (or droids as they are called in the movies) are depicted as friendly, helpful and even charming creatures with distinctive, human personalities. Gold-plated C-3P0, for instance, is essentially part English butler (complete with crisp Oxford accent) and part Cowardly Lion. And while the droids featured in the film are presented as servants of the human characters, they are also treated like friends and compatriots.

The android-as-friend scenario is taken a step further in "Star Trek: the New Generation," where the robot named Data is not just a member of the starship *Enterprise* crew but the third-highest-ranking officer on the ship, who regularly gives orders to his human crew mates.

"Star Trek" presents an optimistic and anthropomorphic view of the future of human-AI relations. While Data is smarter and stronger than his crew mates, he only uses his superior abilities to help humanity, not destroy or dominate it. In fact, he says he is actually trying to "become more human" by working to understand and even mimic human behavior. Likewise, the other humans treat the android as one of their own and encourage him in his efforts to be like them.

Reuters

"Star Wars" robots C-3PO, left, and R2-D2 were given humanlike characteristics by director George Lucas, center.

Most movies and TV shows about AI are not taken too seriously by experts in the field, but one film, Stanley Kubrick's "2001: A Space Odyssey," has had a profound impact on AI researchers and others. "By the end of the film, my head was spinning," Roger Schank, a noted AI researcher and director of the Institute for Learning Sciences at Northwestern University, has written. [1] According to Schank and others, Kubrick's attempt to create a humanlike robot inspired them to ask questions about what computers could and could not do.

"2001," which concerns several human encounters with aliens (who are never seen), takes place primarily aboard a Jupiter-bound spaceship controlled by the HAL 9000, a computer with AI. Unlike its counterparts in other films and stories, HAL (for Heuristic ALgorithmic) is not cute, nice or evil, although its eerily soothing monotone has been discomforting to many. Rather, HAL is presented as multifaceted: competent and confident and yet able to feel fear and commit murder. "No 9000 computer has ever made a mistake or distorted information," HAL proudly tells a BBC interviewer early in the movie. Yet at another point the computer kills four human astronauts to protect itself and its mission. And later in the film, it begs for its "life" as it is finally being shut down.

Recently, HAL celebrated its birthday. The computer reveals in the film that it was born on Jan. 12, 1997. The event was commemorated with a slew of articles and at least one book assessing how close researchers are to creating a real HAL. The general consensus seemed to be that we'll have to wait a while longer. Given the fact that HAL committed four murders on its first mission, maybe we shouldn't be in any rush.

[1] David G. Stork (ed.), *Hal's Legacy: 2001's Computer as Dream and Reality* (1997), p. 171.

Continued from p. 989

there's a lot of goldenrod on the track, he won't bet on that horse. Of course, he sees a million other things as well, like people, trees and food," but can ignore what isn't relevant to making a decision about betting on the horse. But Dreyfus doubts that a computer would be able to filter through the information overload, find the important pieces of data and make relevant connections. "The idea that we can discern what's relevant in any given situation is one of the great mysteries of the human mind."

The idea that relevance and other attributes are impossible to duplicate stems from the corresponding belief that human consciousness cannot be built into a machine. "The brain produces consciousness in the same way that wood oxidizes when it burns," says Berkeley's Searle. "Consciousness is like digestion — it's a biological process." Searle and others say computers will not be able to duplicate that process because ultimately they "just manipulate symbols" without knowing what those symbols mean.

To prove his point, Searle devised an experiment that he calls the "Chinese Room." Imagine, he says, if someone who spoke English but not Chinese was alone in a room and receiving written questions in Chinese. Of course, not knowing the language, the Chinese letters would mean nothing to the person. But what if that person had instructions in English that spelled out exactly how to compose responses to the various questions in Chinese? Then the person in the room could answer the questions intelligently without knowing any Chinese. To a Chinese-speaking person writing the questions and receiving the responses, it would seem that they were corresponding with someone who knows the language. In reality, of course, the person in the room is only following his English instructions and does not understand either the questions or his responses to them.

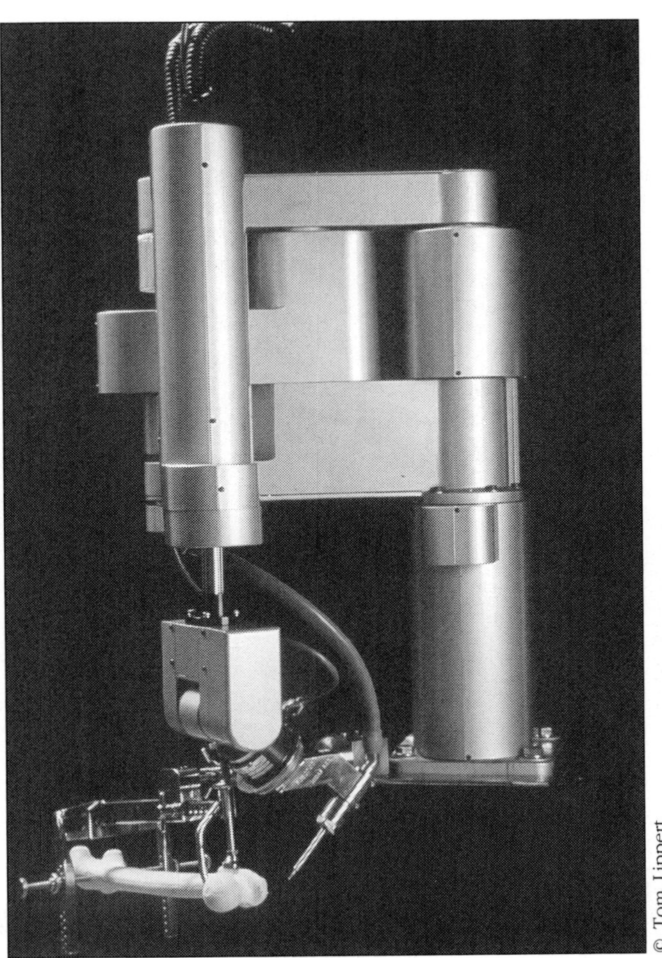

© Tom Lippert

The "Robodoc" surgical assistant aids in hip-replacement surgery, determining the positioning of the replacement and drilling the necessary hole in the femur. It is used in Europe and expected to be approved in the United States soon.

According to Searle, the Chinese Room is a metaphor for computers. They can't really understand the meaning of the questions humans ask them, he says. But they have instructions [software] that tell them how to respond. "All a computer does is manipulate symbols without knowing what it is saying," he says.

What AI researchers will be able to do, Searle says, is simulate consciousness. "But that's not the same thing, because simulation is not duplication," he says. "You can simulate the weather, but that doesn't mean you can create a real hurricane."

But many experts say that Searle, Dreyfus and others don't appreciate the speed at which the computer revolution is advancing and the impact it will have on AI. Carnegie Mellon's Moravec predicts that by 2040 machines will be able to have an abstract sense of the world. "They will be humanlike," he says.

Robert Epstein, a researcher at San Diego State University, agrees. "There's going to be a day when a philosopher who has doubts [about whether a machine is intelligent] is going to argue the point with a machine," he says, "and that's when the argument will be over."

Epstein and other AI optimists dismiss Searle's argument that the brain is so unique that it will be impossible to duplicate its functions.

"His argument is circular," Brooks says. "He says that because animals and people do things, that if a computer does it, it's not really doing it because it's a computer. That's like saying that only horses can transport things and that when a car does, because it ain't a horse, it's only an illusion."

Brooks and others, like philosopher Daniel Dennett of Tufts University in Boston, argue that the brain is basically a machine. Once you duplicate the machine and set it running, they argue, intelligence will eventually follow. Brooks says: "Searle asks, 'Where is consciousness in the brain?' Well, that's stupid because you can't see it, because it's not one part [of the brain], it's the whole thing."

MIT's Davis agrees that there is no one place within the brain that produces intelligence. "Your brain is made up of physical matter, composed of electrons and protons, molecules and neurons. Are they smart?"

The answer, Davis says, is no. "No one part of the brain is smart," he says. "Intelligence is an emergent phenomenon, as it will be with machines." In other words, build a mechanical brain, and intelligence will be a byproduct.

Others doubt that the brain can be duplicated — wound up, so to speak, and allowed to run. Instead, they predict that artificial brain functions will be created piecemeal.

"We'll figure out how parts of the brain work, and we'll get a machine that simulates those parts," says MIT's Minsky, one of the first and most respected thinkers in the field.

Some researchers dismiss the quest for a "duplicate" brain as a waste of time, arguing that the secret to creating humanlike intelligence may not directly involve simulating brain functions. "We built an airplane, but it doesn't fly like a bird," says Barry Silverman, a professor of computer science at George Washington University.

But regardless of differences over what form the intelligent machine will take, most optimists agree that researchers will soon be able to build machines that have the sheer computing power of human brains, which can, by some estimates, handle 100 trillion bits of information per second. "No matter how you cut the cake, even if we're clumsy oafs, we'll reach brain power in less than 20 years," Epstein says.

Raymond Kurzweil, who heads an AI research firm, agrees with Epstein's timetable, noting that while the brain is 10 million times more powerful than the most powerful computer, the gap is not as daunting as it seems. To support his position, he points to Moore's law, which postulates (correctly, so far) that computing power doubles roughly every 18 months. [4]

But Kurzweil notes that sheer computing power will not be enough to ensure intelligence. First, he says, researchers will have to develop a computer that actually duplicates brain functions — a possibility he considers not out of reach.

"Probing the brain's circuits will let us essentially copy a proven design — that is, reverse-engineer one that took its original designer several billion years to develop," he writes. [5]

Researchers are already mimicking the brain's structure, albeit in a primitive way and on a small scale, with "massively parallel computers." Most computers tackle a limited number of problems at a time. The brain, on the other hand, uses its 100 billion interconnected neurons acting in concert (a process called massive parallelism) to "think." Likewise, massively parallel machines contain thousands of powerful microprocessors (in at least one case 250,000), each capable of doing tasks on their own and in conjunction with the others. * [6]

Reuters

Garry Kasparov was the world's reigning chess champion when he was defeated by IBM's Deep Blue computer last May.

Today's massively parallel machines are a far cry from a human brain. Still, the optimists think that the missing pieces will fall into place. "The [human] brain is a big machine, and we may be missing some fundamental constructs, but I'd like to think that we'll be able to put it together soon," Brooks says.

Is the "top-down" approach to AI research the best way to develop an intelligent machine?

Since 1984, Lenat and his team at Cycorp have been trying to teach a computer named Cyc (pronounced "psych") the basics of "living" on

* Microprocessors — such as Intel's Pentium chip — are the "brains" of a computer, giving it computational power.

Earth, such as sleep, time and money. To do so, they have been feeding the computer with data that would seem absurdly simple even to a child. So far, Cyc has been given more than 2 million assertions. The idea behind this "top-down" approach, according to Lenat, is to provide the computer with enough knowledge to allow it to understand the world around it and learn new things on its own.

Lenat says they feed the computer simple statements, such as "infants don't drive cars." Then they try to expand upon the assertions using a software program they call the "Inference Engine," which, he says, allows Cyc to take two or more "isolated assertions and put them together to reach logical conclusions."

For example, Lenat says, assume that the machine already knows that infants go to day care and don't drive cars and that speeding can result in a ticket from the police. It then can infer new facts from the following example: "Let's say that Fred and his son drove to day care and they're stopped by a cop for speeding. The machine knows that Fred will get the ticket because children don't typically drive cars."

Lenat's work is representative of the "symbolist" school of AI research. Symbolists believe that if you program a powerful enough computer with large amounts of knowledge it will begin to exhibit signs of intelligence. "Intelligence is 10 million rules," Lenat says. Indeed, he claims that Cyc is already well on its way to what humans regard as thinking. "Cyc is already self-aware in the sense that it acts self-aware," he says, adding that it knows whom it is speaking to and has a sense of time and place. Within the decade, Lenat predicts, Cyc "will have the pieces of knowledge the average toddler will have."

Others are a bit more circumspect, but still supportive. "It's a good, but particular, direction that needs to be complemented with other kinds of research," Minsky says.

Critics of Cyc contend, however, that it is little more than a catalog of facts that will never have anything resembling intelligence. "It's a look-up table instead of something that has conceptual understanding," Platt says.

Most optimists agree that researchers will soon be able to build machines that have the sheer computing power of human brains, which can, by some estimates, handle 100 trillion bits of information per second.

MIT's Brooks is equally dismissive. "I don't think Cyc can ever have deep experience of the world," he says, adding that Lenat's work, while interesting, will never produce an intelligent machine because intelligence must be learned "from the ground up." [7]

Brooks is building a robot, named Cog, using the "bottom-up" approach, which seeks to design machines to learn to think instead of being told how. "I'm trying to understand human intelligence by building it."

Cog uses eight microprocessors that have been modified into a "neural net," or group of connected processors that seeks to duplicate the way the human brain works. "We simulate layers of the brain, one for sound, one for vision, etc.," Brooks says, adding that these layers are interconnected and work together. The machine, which has been upgraded a number of times since it first began operating four years ago, also has two black and white video cameras ("eyes") and the ability to hear and grasp objects.

Unlike Cyc, Cog is not being taught about the world through direct input of information. Instead, Brooks and other researchers are teaching it to interact with its environment the same way parents teach newborns.

For example, Cog has learned to move its "eyes" in the direction sound is coming from. It also has learned to "read" human faces and mimic their expressions. "Cog is hard-wired to know that faces are special," Brooks says.

Next, he says, "We're hoping to have it figure out different sound characteristics, to tell the difference between a human voice and an air conditioner," which would "allow it to learn to connect a voice with a face."

Brooks hopes that Cog, like Cyc, soon will have the intelligence of a toddler.

But Lenat and others say that Brooks is not following a route that will give Cog intelligence. "It's a great, smart camera, but it has little more than reflex action, mimicking the most basic function of the brain," Moravec says.

Moravec and others say that the problem is that machines today just don't have the sophistication to learn the fundamentals of human thought and behavior on their own. "He's trying to do something very complex in one step that should be done in 20 steps," he says.

Minsky agrees that Brooks expects Cog to learn without providing the machine with the tools, namely data, to do it. "He's not giving his machine a lot of knowledge," he says.

But many AI watchers say that Lenat and Brooks are both doing valuable work and that the first truly intelligent machine may well incorporate some of the findings from Cyc and Cog, as well as other AI research.

"Things are less dichotomized these days," says Betsy Constantine, director of the Cambridge Center for Behavioral Studies. "Scientists are working on hybrids that involve both methods," she adds.

General Motors

An estimated 650,000 industrial robots are in use around the world, including these robot welders at a General Motors plant.

Could machines that surpass human intelligence pose a danger to humanity?

In an episode of the popular science fiction television series "Star Trek," Capt. Kirk and the 400-member crew of the spaceship *Enterprise* are replaced by the M-5, an "intelligent" computer that is supposed to run the ship much more efficiently. But the experiment fails after M-5 begins acting erraticly and resists attempts to shut it down, killing hundreds of people. In the end, Kirk succeeds in neutralizing the machine by appealing to its "conscience," arguing that because it killed many people, it must pay for its crime with its "life." M-5 accepts the logic of Kirk's argument and turns itself off.

"The Ultimate Computer," as the episode is dubbed, delivers a clear message: As powerful as technology may become, there are some things that only people should do. But some AI experts disagree, arguing that the intelligent machines should and ultimately will take over most if not all of the day-to-day work on Earth. Some even go so far as to predict that computers will replace humans entirely. "I think we will reach a point where robots are doing everything," Moravec says.

Moravec and others predict that once machines achieve "intelligence," they will quickly become more capable at almost every human endeavor, including designing new and smarter versions of themselves. In fact, Moravec says, every field from medicine to manufacturing soon will be dominated by machines. "Companies will be completely automated, from top to bottom," he says.

Others agree, at least in part, with Moravec's scenario. For instance, Canadian computer scientist Daniel Crevier says in his book *AI: The Tumultuous Search for the History of Artificial Intelligence,* that machines will first replace workers in places like factories, where tens of thousands of robots are already in use. These new "employees," Crevier writes, "would work 24-hour shifts, never strike or call in sick and entail amortization and running costs much lower than a human's wages." Soon after that, he predicts, machines will begin replacing clerical workers and then middle managers. [8]

And what will all the unemployed people do? According to Moravec, people will lead lives devoid of work and filled with leisure. "We'll all be bought off," he says, because the new machine-run economy will be much more efficient and produce much more wealth. "We'll all be able to live like millionaires."

Eventually, Moravec says, machines will have responsibility for and complete control over humanity. People, in a sense, will have become the children of their own creations. Such a scenario also seems possible to Crevier. "When machines acquire an intelligence superior to our own, they will be impossible to keep at bay," he writes. [9]

Both Moravec and Crevier also say that the machines may conclude that they no longer want or need human beings. At some point, Moravec says, "they might just decide to get rid of us."

Verner Vinge, an associate profes-

A $100,000 Test of Computer 'Humanness'

The computer age had just begun when mathematician Alan Turing proposed what is still considered by many to be the standard for judging the "humanness" of an artificially intelligent machine.

"I propose to consider the question, 'Can machines think?' " Turing wrote in a 1950 article in the journal *Mind.* [1] Turing proposed a variation on an age-old parlor game. The contest pits an interrogator against a man and a woman, with each participant in a separate room. The interrogator carries on a separate "conversation" with each by exchanging a series of messages back and forth. The point of the exercise is to see if the interrogator can tell which of the messages is coming from the man and which from the woman.

What would happen, Turing asked, if the game were altered and a machine took the place of either the man or the woman? The challenge would be to determine whether the messages were coming from a person or a computer. If the computer fooled its human correspondent, Turing said, it could be considered, in a sense, intelligent.

The first computers had been invented less than a decade before Turing's proposal, and no machines existed that could compete, let alone succeed, in such a contest. But Turing, who killed himself three years after proposing the test, envisioned a not-so-distant future where machines would fool their human interrogators. By the end of the century, he predicted in the article, humans would be fooled 30 percent of the time for at least five minutes.

For more than four decades, Turing's challenge remained largely untested. Then in 1991, American businessman Hugh Loebner in association with the Cambridge Center for Behavioral Studies in Cambridge, Mass., funded an annual contest incorporating Turing's test. Loebner offered $100,000 to anyone who could write a computer program that could fool the judges for three hours. Given the low probability of this happening any time soon, Loebner offered $2,000 to whoever came closest to "passing" the Turing test.

The following excerpts are from "conversations" between computers and their human judges in recent "Loebner Prize" contests. [2]

From a program by Thad Crews for the 1994 contest:

Judge: Do you think [O.J. Simpson's friend Al] Cowlings should have been prosecuted as an accessory {to murder]?

Program: No, I do not.

Judge: Is it possible that O.J. can get any semblance of a fair trial, considering the enormous publicity that already is in general circulation?

Program: I think O.J. has a bad temper and he may well have committed the murders.

Judge: Do you think he can get a fair trial under the circumstances?

Program: I certainly hope O.J. gets a fair trial, both for his sake and for the sake of justice as a whole.

Judge: Hope is not the issue. Do you think he CAN get a fair trial?

Program: Let's move onto another topic, shall we?

From the winning program for the 1995 contest written by Joseph Weintraub, author of the first pc therapy program.

Program: I hate it when some broad grabs some poor shmuck and turns him into a working stiff to support her and some brats, don't you?

Judge: You sound like Sinatra in "Guys and Dolls" now.

Program: Perhaps you sometimes dream I sound like Sinatra in "Guys and Dolls" now. I sound like Sinatra in "Guys and Dolls" now?

Judge: Well, of course, I can't hear you singing.

Program: Great men can't be ruled. Perhaps in your fantasy we can't hear each other.

Judge: What do you have, a book of pointless, important-sounding quotations back there?

Program: Getting along with men isn't what's truly important — the vital knowledge is how we get along with a man — one man.

Judge: You do have a book of stupid, pointless conversations back there.

---

[1] Quoted in Robert Epstein, "The Quest for the Thinking Computer," *AI magazine*, summer 1992.

[2] Excerpts are used by permission of the Cambridge Center for Behavioral Studies.

sor of mathematics at San Diego State University, agrees. "If we got in their way, whether they'd rub us out or use some other solution would probably depend on the expense," he says. Vinge does hold out some hope for humanity because he does "not personally think that superhuman creatures would be as malicious toward us as we are toward animals." [10]

Some AI experts are not troubled by thoughts of being replaced (or even eliminated) by a machine. According to Minsky and Moravec, human beings should feel good about being replaced by intelligent robots, especially since they, unlike us, will be able to continue evolving into more sophisticated beings. "We're stuck," Minsky says, arguing that "humans haven't improved for the last 2,000-3,000 years."

Others offer less dire, but still troubling predictions. For instance, Epstein says AIs will invade and take over the Internet, giving them control of vital pieces of society, from financial markets to nuclear defense systems.

To skeptics, the scenario painted by Moravec, Epstein and others is absurd at worst and far-fetched at best. "It's not even worth considering," Dreyfus says, adding that talking about the dangers of artificial intelligence is as remote a possibility as "asking if we should blow up the moon."

But many researchers who do consider the possibility of a world with intelligent or at least semi-intelligent machines also dismiss the menace posed by artificial life. "The dangers associated with every new technology are always overrated, but we will be able to control this," Platt says. "I would love to have an artificially intelligent slave."

To begin with, Platt and others say, humans will be able to set controls and parameters over the machines they build, even if they are intelligent. "If we program them the right way, we'll be able to trust them." Platt says.

Catholic University's Sebrechts agrees, arguing that "as researchers develop stronger and smarter intelligent machines, they will be able to make corresponding advances in programs designed to protect us from any mishaps. Our ability to control these systems will increase as those systems become more sophisticated."

Sebrechts argues that such parallel development is a natural outgrowth of most new technologies. For example, he says, as electronic eavesdropping systems have become more sophisticated in recent decades, "so have the systems to protect us from them."

Sebrechts and others also argue that human nature will help ensure that people don't lose control of the AI systems they create. "We could have aircraft without pilots, but we don't because we still want people to be responsible for flying the planes," he says. In addition, he argues, human workers will not be replaced by machines, but will only have the nature of their tasks changed.

Others say that machines will not "take over" because, contrary to what Minsky says, humans are not "stuck" but are still evolving and will become much more capable as a result of AI. Instead of trying to control AI, these thinkers say, people will merge with it and use it to enhance their own abilities.

Some, like Cycorp's Lenat, say that scientists will develop the ability literally to plug people's minds directly into intelligent machines, giving humans a degree of mental agility that is beyond imagining. People with such mental powers, Lenat claims, will be to today's humans as we are to our ancestors before they developed language.

"Human beings without language were effectively a different species" because the ability to communicate "allowed us to know everything everyone else knew," he says. Likewise, Lenat predicts humans with AI will "be like a new species." ■

BACKGROUND

The First Computer

For millennia, mankind has tried to create machines that alleviated mental as well as physical burdens. The abacus allowed the ancient Chinese to do lightning-fast calculations. In 1623, Wilhelm Schickard, a German astronomer, built the first mechanical calculator capable of carrying out basic arithmetic. Similar machines were built in the decades following by the French scientist Blaise Pascal and the German mathematician Gottfried von Leibniz. By the 19th century, crude and slow mechanical calculators were available (at a high price) to the general public.

The first true computer was designed in the 1830s by Charles Babbage, a British inventor, who called it an "analytical engine." According to Crevier, Babbage's "steam-driven contraption would have contained all the elements of a modern computer, including memory and processing." But Babbage was never able to complete a working model of his creation because craftsmen of the day were not capable of making the complex parts it required. [11]

Over the next 100 years, scientists would build computational machines of increasing sophistication. But 20th-century ancestors of today's computers did not come into existence until World War II, when the Allies began funding research into the development of electronic computers designed to perform a variety of wartime tasks.

The first such machine built in the United States, the Electronic Numerical Integrator and Computer (ENIAC), was completed in 1944. Although the machine required 18,000 vacuum tubes and filled an entire room, it could only carry out 300 calculations per second, a tiny fraction of what the average personal computer can accomplish today. Still, ENIAC revolutionized computing. Indeed, it started off with a bang: Its first task was to assist scientists working to develop the atomic bomb at Los Alamos in New Mexico. [12]

In England, meanwhile, scientists were developing computers to break the German "Enigma" code. The first, named *Colossus,* went into service in late 1943 and is considered by many historians to be the first electronic

Continued on p. 998

Chronology

1940s-1950s

The first computers are developed, and researchers begin pondering the feasibility of creating artificial intelligence (AI).

1943
The British begin using the "Colossus" machine to decipher the Germans' wartime code. Developed in part by famed mathematician Alan Turing, it is considered by some to be the first true computer.

1944
The Electronic Numerical Integrator and Computer (ENIAC) is completed in the United States. It has 18,000 vacuum tubes and can only carry out 300 calculations per second. The revolutionary device is thought by many to be the first digital computer.

1950
Turing proposes a scheme to test if machines are intelligent, known as the "Turing Test."

1952
The first speech-recognizing program is developed by Bell Labs.

1955
Carnegie Mellon University's Herbert Simon and Alan Newell write the first AI program, dubbed the "Logic Theorist."

1956
The first AI conference is held at Dartmouth College; MIT's John McCarthy develops LISP, an important AI computer language.

1957
AI researchers develop the General Problem Solver, a program that tries to simulate the human cognitive process.

1960s-1980s

Relatively little visible progress is made in duplicating human intelligence.

1968
The celebrated movie "2001: A Space Odyssey" debuts, featuring HAL, an intelligent machine.

1969
Scientists at Stanford University create "Shakey," the first mobile, sighted robot.

1971
Stanford University's Terry Winograd creates the first computer program to demonstrate a partial grasp of human language.

1982
Ridley Scott's movie "Blade Runner" explores the relationship between intelligent androids and humans.

1984
Douglas Lenat begins feeding millions of assertions of what it means to be human to a computer named Cyc.

1990-Present

Interest diminishes in creating machines with AI, while practical applications using the fruits of AI research begin appearing more frequently.

1991
American businessman Hugh Loebner and the Cambridge [Mass.] Center for Behavioral Studies create the annual Loebner Prize competition, a $100,000 award for the first person to create a program that passes the Turing Test.

1992
Citibank begins using AI software to direct currency trading.

1993
Rodney Brooks of the Massachusetts Institute of Technology builds Cog, a robot that tries to learn to think.

1996
Russian chess grandmaster Garry Kasparov beats IBM's chess-playing computer, Deep Blue. A rematch is scheduled.

May 1997
Deep Blue defeats Kasparov, marking the first defeat of a reigning chess champion by a machine.

July 1997
The *Sojourner,* a robot vehicle, begins exploring the surface of Mars.

Continued from p. 996

computer.

One of the leaders of the Colossus project, the brilliant mathematician Alan Turing, became the first great AI theoretician. (*See story, p. 995.*) In a now-famous 1950 article in the philosophical journal *Mind,* Turing proposed a test for determining whether a computer would be truly intelligent. In it, a person would "converse," by using a remote terminal, with another person and a computer. According to Turing, the computer could, in a sense, be called "intelligent" if after a long conversation with each, the person could not differentiate between the human being and the machine. [13]

Turing's challenge was the opening shot in the race to develop artificially intelligent machines. Within the decade, a new discipline within the computer science field had emerged.

Birth of AI

The first AI program can be traced back to 1955, when Carnegie Mellon researchers Herbert Simon and Alan Newell began developing a program that would enable a computer to work out, on its own, the proofs for simple mathematical theorems.

The program, dubbed the "Logic Theorist," worked through problems of logic rather than just calculating numbers. When the program actually ran on a computer, it was able to prove 38 of the first 54 theorems given to it.

Simon says the idea of creating a computer that could think for itself came to him one fall day while strolling along the university campus. He enlisted Newell's aid and the two spent their Christmas vacation working on the program.

When he returned to teaching in January 1956, Simon announced to his students that he and Newell "had invented a thinking machine." [14]

That summer, the tiny artificial intelligence community gathered at Dartmouth College for the first AI conference. Among the 10 pioneers who attended were Simon, Newell, Minsky and John McCarthy of MIT.

"In from three to eight years, we'll have a machine with the general intelligence of an average human being . . . a machine that will be able to read Shakespeare [or] grease a car."

— Marvin Minsky to *Life* magazine in 1970

In addition to discussing and trying out the Logic Theorist, the conferees also came up with a name for their new endeavor: Artificial Intelligence.

Over the years, AI grew into a substantial field of study. AI researchers developed a number of important programs, such as the General Problem Solver (GPS) in 1957, which tried to simulate the human cognitive process.

Also that year, McCarthy developed LISP (short for LISt Processing). Conventional computer languages, such as Fortran and Cobol, had been created to help computers calculate more complicated problems faster. They essentially allowed the machine to use its computing muscle to power its way through each step of a problem. But LISP was much more subtle and sophisticated. By processing symbols instead of just numbers, it allowed the computer to make inferences based on facts given it. In other words, the language could make a logical leap from one set of facts to another without going through all the steps that would be required in a traditional numerical calculation. LISP became the most important programing language for AI researchers. [15]

In these early years, according to Simon, Minsky and others, AI researchers were optimistic about the feasibility of creating thinking machines. "In from three to eight years," Minsky told *Life* magazine in 1970, "we'll have a machine with the general intelligence of an average human being . . . a machine that will be able to read Shakespeare [or] grease a car." One researcher even asserted that the new computers might not "condescend" to talk to humans unless we had something interesting to say. [16]

"AI was hyped to death," Shieber says. Not surprisingly, consumer marketers got into the act, claiming that products as mundane as electric razors utilized artificial intelligence. According to Shieber and others, the wild predictions and commercial hype led to an inevitable crash in confidence in AI and the perception by people in and out of the field that AI was mostly smoke and mirrors. ■

Current Situation

AI at Work

Many experts regard the search for artificial intelligence with profound disappointment. In large measure, they see researchers as not much closer to creating AI than they were when the quest began after World War II.

And yet the work has not been wasted. According to the Commerce Department, more than 70 percent of the nation's *Fortune* 500 companies use AI technology in some capacity. And sales of AI-related software were close to $2 billion last year.

Ironically, Shieber says, after years of trying to put an AI label on everything, "now nothing supposedly has [pure] AI in it even though it uses the technology. If you go to Microsoft's Web site, they have an automated help system that uses AI technology to help bring up the right documents to the user. People don't know it's AI. They say it's just their help system."

Shieber and others say that technology derived from AI experiments is at work in hundreds of industries from health care to aviation. For example, many hospitals use AI systems to read lab results, diagnose illnesses and help to determine if a patient will have an adverse reaction to a certain combination of drugs.

One of the most visible and promising uses for AI research is in speech recognition. Currently a host of companies, including IBM, Dragon Systems and Kurzweil Applied Intelligence, sell programs that allow users to write documents by speaking. The market for such programs is quite large and includes doctors (especially in the fast-paced environment of the emergency room), the blind and those with only limited use of their hands. According to Minsky, these systems are already good enough to accurately transcribe most of the words being spoken at a normal pace. "In five years, [speech-recognition programs] will be near-perfect," he says.

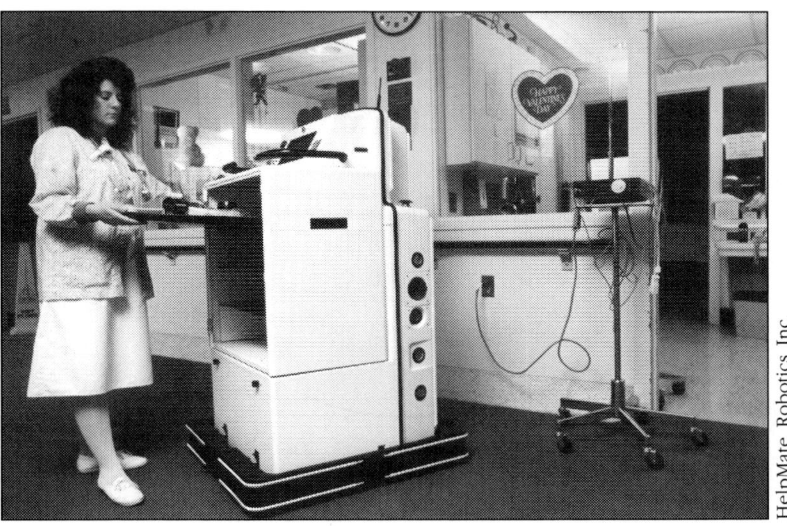

HelpMate Robotics Inc.

HelpMate is a battery-operated, trackless robotic courier used to transport hospital records, specimens and other items. It gets on and off elevators by itself and uses its "voice" to communicate.

AI is also used by many mutual fund managers and other financial services providers to determine where and when to invest their clients' money. "There are a lot of stock portfolios that are run by so-called expert systems that produce better results than human managers," Minsky says. [17]

And AI programs do more than just pick stocks. Citibank, for instance, uses an AI software package to decide on foreign currency trades. In the program's first few years of operation, the bank's profits from currency trades have risen 25 percent.

American Express Won't Leave Home Without It

Another user of AI has been American Express (Amex), which developed a software package to help with its purchase-authorization processing. Since American Express card users have no credit limit, the company does not automatically authorize each purchase, especially if it is large and out of character for that customer. "If you are the type who never leaves home and all of a sudden you show up in Ethiopia and want to buy a hotel, they may not approve it," says MIT's Davis. In other words the company wants to give itself the best chance possible of guessing when it might have to pick up the tab and prevent cardholders in those circumstances from using Amex.

Amex developed the "Authorization Assistant," a program that uses company rules on customer spending to make recommendations on whether or not to approve unusual purchases. To the company's credit, Davis says, humans still make the final decision as to whether the purchase will be approved.

The system saves time because it not only gives a recommendation but also provides the reason for its decision. Hence, the human authorizer receives a detailed report outlining the reasons why a purchase should be approved or not.

Along the way, the system also has improved overall performance, because the computer says "yes" to an authorization more often than its human counterparts did before the system was installed. At the same time, since Authorization Assistant, Amex has authorized fewer bad purchases.

The Authorization Assistant and many other AI systems in use today are known as knowledge-based, or expert systems. The creators of these systems try to program them with human expertise in a certain field, say purchase authorization or reading mammograms. At the same time, expert systems are flexible enough to make deductions on their own and even add to existing expertise. [18]

As impressive as these systems sound, they are by no means perfect. Those who use expert systems, like Amex, have generally found that they are more effective when they work with human beings, as opposed to replacing them.

Robotics

Last July, the world watched with rapt attention as a small dune buggy-like vehicle named *Sojourner* explored a patch of real estate on Mars. *Sojourner* never strayed too far from the U.S.-launched *Pathfinder* spacecraft that had transported it to the "red" planet. Still, it was able to navigate its way around the rock-strewn surface on its own, conducting tests and taking samples as it went.

Sojourner is just the latest "miracle" in robotics, a field that is inextricably linked with AI. But in spite of such scientific accomplishments, robotics, like AI in general, has not met the expectations of the scientific community.

On the surface, robotics seems to be thriving, with an estimated 650,000 industrial robots worldwide helping to make everything from cars to televisions. There are also robots that can perform surgical procedures, and new products for consumers are on the horizon, such as self-operating lawn mowers. Still, many experts are disappointed that robots (the word means "forced labor" in the Czech language) are not even more ubiquitous in society. [19]

There are robots that can perform surgical procedures, and new products for consumers are on the horizon, such as self-operating lawn mowers. Still, many experts are disappointed that robots are not even more ubiquitous in society.

"Aside from toys, there are no mass-produced robots," Moravec says, adding that "all industrial robots are lovingly handmade." The reason, Moravec says, is that robots are much more complex to build than computers because they handle both physical and "thinking" tasks.

In addition, while robotic arms have been developed to conduct simple, repetitive tasks, scientists have not been able to develop a machine that could seamlessly walk down a crowded block in New York City. "Shakey," the first robot designed to attempt that feat, was built in 1969 at Stanford University. But Shakey, essentially a tin can on wheels topped by TV cameras and a range-finder, took hours to navigate around non-moving geometric objects.

But the technology has since improved, experts say, along with the prospects for robotics. "Now we have robots that can navigate in a [crowded] room at a meter per second," Brooks says. "We've come a long way in the last five years." Brooks says researchers in Houston recently field tested two buses that were "driven" by computer. "There was still a [human] in the bus to make sure nothing tragic happened, but things were OK," he says.

Brooks, Moravec and others predict that robots will soon become more visible in our daily lives. Moravec, for one, thinks that within a decade robots will be cleaning our homes and moving onto more sophisticated tasks. "Commercial success will drive this revolution," he says.

Already, new uses for robots are emerging, and in fields that have traditionally been the sole domain of humans. For example, doctors in the United States may soon be able to use "Robodoc" in hip-replacement surgery. After being positioned over a patient's exposed femur, Robodoc determines

Continued on p. 1002

At Issue:

Will researchers develop a computer that duplicates human intelligence in the foreseeable future?

Hans Moravec
Professor of computer science, Carnegie Mellon University

yes

The field of artificial intelligence began with efforts to capture the surface layers of conscious human thought. It produced programs that play chess, prove theorems or solve other individual, narrow intellectual problems, but this "top-down" route has yet to produce anything resembling overall human intelligence. Meanwhile, the related field of robotics produced machines with behavior something like that of simple animals. The "bottom-up" route seems to be following a path roughly paralleling the evolution of natural intelligence, but about 10 million times as fast. Today, the smartest robots have control systems comparable to the nervous systems of the earliest vertebrates, like tiny fish. Early computers seemed powerful only because they were applied to tasks, like arithmetic, that humans do enormously inefficiently. On the other hand, our evolving ancestors lived or died by their physical and social interactions, and we inherit powerfully efficient equipment for those functions. Computers are far from those strengths, but are gaining so fast they should match us, even there, in less than 50 years.

Comparing modest assemblies of neurons, like the vertebrate retina, or control ganglia, in insects and other invertebrates with efficient computer programs that provide approximately the same functions for robots suggests that the work of a thousand neurons can be matched by a well-written program running at 1 million instructions per second (1 MIPS). High-end personal computers today afford a merely insectlike 500 MIPS, but the power is doubling each year. At that pace, home computers will be powerful enough to host humanlike intelligence in just a few decades.

Robot perception and navigation have advanced this decade to where research robots are now cruising hallways and roads autonomously for hours at a time. I think we are at the threshold of an evolution of mass-marketed robots, that, in coming decades, may go something as follows: Specialized autonomous utility robots will soon be among us, cleaning, transporting and eventually performing other manual tasks. They will be followed by a first generation of universal robots, with mental power comparable to a small lizard, able to host programs for many different physical applications. A second generation, with a mind like a small mouse, will adapt to specific situations by conditioned learning. A third, somewhat like a monkey, will model the physical and social world, so that it can mentally rehearse its tasks, invent new variations, observe and imitate others and explain its actions in physical and social terms.

A fourth, humanlike generation will add abstract reasoning and generalization to the repertoire. Then the real fun begins.

Stuart Shieber
Professor of computer science, Harvard University

no

In 1950, the British mathematician Alan Turing devised what has come to be known as the Turing Test for machine intelligence, based on a judge's ability or inability to distinguish between a computer and a person in dialog with the two. The Turing Test is popularly thought of as the Holy Grail of research in artificial intelligence. A computer able to pass the Turing Test is in essence what many think of when they think of "duplicating human intelligence with a computer."

I have good news and bad news. The bad news is that like the Holy Grail of Arthurian legend, the Turing Test will, I expect, remain beyond our grasp for quite a while, undoubtedly not achievable during our lifetimes. Philosophers like John Searle and Hubert Dreyfus [of the University of California at Berkeley] think that a machine passing the test is impossible, although I am agnostic on this point. Various AI luminaries and media pundits have been predicting the imminent arrival of intelligent machines, from "just around the corner" to "just a few decades" for many years now, at least since the 1950s. Like prognostications of the end of the world, as the predicted dates pass, the predictions become necessarily more inaccurate. The problem of how intelligence works and how it can be duplicated artificially is tremendously difficult. Denying this fact is simple hubris. The issue is not one of insufficient computer power; even if we had computers faster by orders of magnitude (which we undoubtedly will), we would need to know how to make use of the resources to duplicate human intelligence or allow computers to learn it on their own.

The good news is that like the Holy Grail, the goal itself is less important than the quest. Indeed, many if not most AI researchers view the Turing Test as an exceedingly poor goal for current research in the field. The study of AI, by engaging some of the brightest minds in computer science on arguably the hardest problems in the field, can claim credit for time-sharing computers, windowed interfaces, computer dictation, medical diagnostic systems, financial-industry mechanization and Deep Blue. The technologies on which these systems were based were not developed by researchers trying directly to build artificially intelligent Turing-test passers, but through myriad attacks on varied problems in understanding particular types of knowledge, reasoning, learning and intelligent behavior.

It is important not to gauge progress in AI on progress in passing the Turing Test. One can, and we do, have tremendous progress in the former, both in theory and in practice, without approaching the Grail itself.

FOR MORE INFORMATION

The American Association for Artificial Intelligence, 445 Burgess Dr., Menlo Park, Calif. 94025; (415) 328-3123. The AAAI publishes a quarterly magazine and holds conferences and symposia on AI.

Institute for Artificial Intelligence, 707 22nd St. N.W., Suite 206, Washington, D.C. 20052; (202) 994-5079. The institute, part of George Washington University, develops, tests and evaluates artificial intelligence programs.

Information Technology Association of America, 1616 N. Fort Myer Dr., Suite 1300, Arlington, Va. 22209; (703) 522-5055. The association represents computer and software companies. It monitors legislation and holds conferences and seminars on issues important to the information technology industry.

Continued from p. 1000

precisely where the replacement hip should go and then drills the hole into which the hip will be fitted. [20]

For many people, a robot surgeon might seem like a frightening prospect. "People used to say, 'How do I know the robot won't go crazy and drill a hole in my brain and not the femur?' " says Ramesh Trivedi, president of Integrated Surgical Systems, the Sacramento company that markets Robodoc. "I'd say, 'Well it has never happened, and there are lots of safety controls built in." In fact, hip replacements done with Robodoc are more precisely done than those done by unaided humans. [21]

Meanwhile, robots are being readied for more mundane work. Next year, Helpmate Robotics of Danbury, Conn., plans to test a robot designed to assist the elderly at home. The idea, according to company President Joseph Engelberger, is to allow seniors who might otherwise need to go to a nursing home to continue to live independently. Engelberger says the robot will be able to assist the elderly in cooking, cleaning and, perhaps most importantly, just getting around. "A geriatrician working for us says the most important thing is to offer an arm," he says. [22] ■

OUTLOOK

Self-Aware Machines?

Prediction is dependent on point of view. For those who are dubious of science's ability to duplicate human intelligence, the future of AI looks much like its past. "I think we'll see more of the same" kinds of applications, Dreyfus says. In other words, no stunning breakthroughs are in the offing. Still, Dreyfus predicts AI research will continue to have great practical use. For example, he says, "improved neural nets will enable us to do much better speech recognition and handwriting recognition."

George Washington's Silverman agrees, predicting that future AI researchers will continue to develop practical systems instead of trying to duplicate human intelligence. "The only people who are really interested in that are the psychologists," he says.

But for those who think that researchers will be able to develop machines that reproduce humanlike intelligence, the future is much less mundane. According to Moravec, in a little over a decade robots with limited intelligence will be performing menial tasks like cleaning houses. By 2040, he says, machines will be self-aware and "have humanlike capabilities."

In Epstein's view, such machines may even come sooner. "It has to happen," he says. "There are so many pressures from industry and science." The reason, Epstein argues, is that "everyone wants to have a universal, natural-language interface — the ultimate replacement for the mouse and keyboard. We all want to be able to talk to our machines and have them understand and reply. The keyboard is a painfully primitive interface."

Other optimists are less sanguine about the likely rate of progress. According to Minsky, there are several reasons to think that building humanlike machines will take more than a few decades. First, he says, very few AI researchers, like Lenat or Brooks, are working on developing them. "There are no short-term gains in this," he says, because AI projects can take many years and often fail to bear fruit.

Lenat agrees, adding that there is another reason behind the dearth of AI researchers. When work in AI began, he says, the early pioneers "thought they would attract the best and brightest in [science] to work on this." As it turns out, Lenat says, "the best and brightest went into physics."

In addition, Lenat and Minsky say, human society, with its many fears and superstitions, may stand in the way of progress.

"Technology can exact an enormous cost," Lenat says, pointing to the dislocation, unemployment and even death that can accompany technical advances like industrialization. "It's hard for people to understand that in the long run it's worth it."

Minsky has less patience with such "shortsightedness," as he calls it. He points to the artificial heart as a typical example of how human fear and ignorance can block the development of a new and useful technology. Because the first prototype installed cost $1 million and only prolonged the life of the test patient for a year, the new technology was never given a chance, he says. As for inventor Robert Jarvik, lack of funding made it difficult to continue his work.

"Ironically, the Jarvik heart probably could have been made [eventually] for $50 — it's mostly plastic — and would have been easy to install," he says.

The same shortsighted attitude could slow the pace of AI research, Minsky says: "Change is very threatening to people who are worried about their next paycheck." ■

Notes

[1] Martin Gardiner, "Those Mindless Machines; Don't Worry. A Computer Can't Replace Your Brain," *The Washington Post,* May 25, 1997.

[2] For another use of AI, see "Insurance Fraud," *The CQ Researcher,* Oct. 11, 1996, p. 906.

[3] Quoted in John Browning, "Artificial Intelligence," *The Economist,* March 14, 1992.

[4] Quoted in David G. Stork (ed.), *Hal's Legacy: 2001's Computer as Dream and Reality* (1997), p. 163.

[5] Quoted in *Ibid.,* p, 164.

[6] Daniel Crevier, *AI: The Tumultuous History of the Search for Artificial Intelligence* (1993), pp. 301-302.

[7] Quoted in Julian Dibbel, "The Race to Build Intelligent Machines," *Time,* March 25, 1996.

[8] Quoted in Crevier, *op. cit.,* p. 324.

[9] *Ibid.,* p. 341.

[10] Quoted in Mark Dery, "Master Class," *Rolling Stone,* Nov. 28, 1996.

[11] Quoted in Crevier, *op. cit.,* p. 10.

[12] *Ibid.,* pp. 12-13.

[13] Robert Wright, "Can Machines Think?" *Time,* March 25, 1996.

[14] Quoted in Otis Port, "Computers that Think are Almost Here," *Business Week,* July 17, 1995.

[15] Marc Leepson, "Artificial Intelligence," *Editorial Research Reports,* Aug. 16, 1985.

[16] Quoted in Amy Harmon, "2001 is Near, But Hal is Not," *Los Angeles Times,* Jan. 7, 1997.

[17] For additional examples, see Amy Harmon, "Darwinian Software Being Tested as Survival Aid in Investment Jungle," *Los Angeles Times,* Aug. 17, 1994.

[18] Port, *op. cit.*

[19] Curt Suplee, "Robot Revolution," *National Geographic,* July 1997.

[20] David R. Olmos, "Is There a Robot in the House?" *Los Angeles Times,* July 14, 1997. Robodoc is already being used in Europe; approval for use in the United States is anticipated in the near future.

[21] Quoted in *Ibid.*

[22] Quoted in Andrea Zimmerman, "A Robot in the House to Help the Elderly," *The New York Times,* July 20, 1997.

Bibliography

Selected Sources Used

Books

Crevier, Daniel, *AI: The Tumultuous History of the Search for Artificial Intelligence,* Basic Books, 1993

Crevier, a Canadian AI researcher, documents the history of artificial intelligence from pioneers like Alan Turing and Marvin Minsky to more recent developments such as Douglas Lenat's work with Cyc. Particularly illuminating are Crevier's last few chapters, where he discusses the future implications of AI.

Kaku, Michio, *Visions: How Science Will Revolutionize the 21st Century,* Anchor Books, 1997.

Kaku, a professor of theoretical physics at City University in New York, takes a deep look into the next century with the help of experts in various scientific fields. Among other things, he describes efforts to make machines think, talk and move like human beings and predicts that by 2050, computers will have "primitive emotions, speech recognition and common sense."

Stork, David (ed.), *Hal's Legacy: 2001's Computer as Dream and Reality,* MIT Press, 1997.

Stork, chief scientist at the Ricoh California Research Center, has assembled a group of AI experts to discuss progress in the field since the fictional HAL 9000 made its debut in Stanley Kubrick's "2001: A Space Odyssey" in 1968. The answer, generally, is that while scientists have built computers that have more raw power than HAL, they have yet to produce anything like a thinking machine.

Articles

Browning, John, "Artificial Intelligence," *The Economist,* March 14, 1992.

A slightly dated but thorough overview of the AI field, from esoteric efforts to build thinking machines to expert systems and other practical uses developed by researchers.

Chapman, John, "Man's Brief Reign in the Evolutionary Spotlight," *The Futurist,* September-October, 1997.

Chapman, a financial analyst, predicts that human beings will undergo a new phase of physical evolution through the merging of flesh and blood and computers or as the author puts it, "mechanical beings built around a kernel of biological life."

Dibbell, Julian, "The Race to Build Intelligent Machines," *Time,* March 25, 1996.

Dibbell compares the AI research efforts of Douglas Lenat, who is trying to teach a computer to think, with those of Rodney Brooks and his "bottom-up" approach.

Epstein, Robert, "The Quest for the Thinking Computer," *AI magazine,* summer 1992.

Epstein, a researcher at San Diego State University, discusses the Turing Test and the founding of the Loebner Prize competition in 1991. Included in the piece are samples of discussions between people and machines from the first contest.

Garfinkel, Simson, "2001 Double Take," *Wired,* January 1997.

Garfinkel looks at the current state of AI research, including work on vision systems, voice recognition and machines with "common sense."

Gelernter, David, "How Hard is Chess?" *Time,* May 19, 1997.

Gelernter, a professor of computer science at Yale University and noted social critic, tries to deflate the hype surrounding Deep Blue's victory over Garry Kasparov in May. Gelernter writes: "Deep Blue is just a machine. It doesn't have a mind any more than a flower has a mind."

Platt, Charles, "What's It Mean to be Human, Anyway?" *Wired,* April 1995.

Platt, a novelist and contributing editor to *Wired* magazine, humorously describes his experiences as a participant in the 1994 Loebner Prize competition.

Wright Robert, "Can Machines Think?" *Time,* March 25, 1996.

Wright examines the various theories on the nature of human consciousness, with an eye toward determining if artificial intelligence is really possible.

Suplee, Curt, "Robot Revolution," *National Geographic,* July 1997.

Suplee, a science writer for *The Washington Post,* gives a good overview of the latest developments in the field of robotics, from Robodoc to NASA's *Sojourner* Mars rover. As with most *National Geographic* articles, this one contains stunning photographs of robots at work and play.

The Next Step

Additional information from UMI's Newspaper & Periodical Abstracts™ database

Applications

Atkinson, Dan, "Man vs. the Brain is no contest: As share prices were slipping yesterday, the Stock Exchange's new super computer was monitoring every deal to combat insider dealing," ***The Guardian,*** **March 21, 1997, p. 22.**
If you deal in shares, it has your number. Somewhere in its colossal memory is the history of your portfolio. Should you be tempted to deal on inside information, think again. Soon it may be able to "map" your home and spot the remarkable coincidence that you and your stock tipster share squash club membership with the treasurer of the company whose securities you've been trading so actively.

Cetron, Marvin, and Owen Davies, "Get ready for a digitized future: Smart toasters, media butlers, and more," ***Futurist,*** **July 1997, pp. 18-23.**
Future computers will transmit information via light, DNA or "quantum leaps." Gadgets will increasingly be able to think like humans.

Cox, Rebecca, "Artificial Intelligence Systems Get Lukewarm Reception from Banks," ***American Banker,*** **March 29, 1989, p. 9.**
Although some experts claim knowledge-based systems are the secret weapons of the future, many software developers are having difficulty persuading financial institutions to use them.

Ferranti, Marc, "Ironclad connections," ***Computerworld,*** **Sept. 29, 1997, pp. 39-40.**
Brazil's Companhia Vale do Rio Doce is the world's largest producer and exporter of iron ore and has constructed a voice and data network, dubbed CVRDNet, to track materiel and manage logistics.

Foulds, Richard, Chen Shoupu, Daniel Chester, Zunaid Kazi and Matthew Beitler, "Multimodal control of a rehabilitation robot," ***Journal of Rehabilitation Research & Development,*** **May 1997, pp. 46-147.**
The progress of a study on the multimodal control of a rehabilitation robot is discussed.

"Robotic arm pumps gas," ***Popular Mechanics,*** **August 1997, p. 18.**
Shell Oil Co. is currently testing a robotic gas pump that was developed by International Submarine Engineering. Features of the Smart Pump are described.

Artificial Intelligence

Buck, Neena, "Just don't call it AI," ***Computerworld,*** **Jan. 13, 1997, pp. 79-80.**
Despite skepticism from information systems professionals, robot systems have been developed over the past few years using tools based on artificial intelligence (AI). Both AI's contributions to information systems and continued resistance to AI are discussed.

Centrella, Tom, "The ignition point of the future," ***IEEE Expert,*** **March 1997, pp. 75-78.**
Artificial intelligence visionary Robert Heicht-Nielsen believes that by the year 2012 the computer industry will spawn several new industries with a cumulative size 100 times bigger than today's computer industry.

Gentner, Dedre, and Keith J. Holyoak, "Reasoning and learning by analogy: Introduction," ***American Psychologist,*** **January 1997, pp. 32-34.**
Analogy is a powerful cognitive mechanism that people use to make inferences and learn new abstractions. The history of work on analogy in modern cognitive science is sketched, focusing on contributions from cognitive psychology, artificial intelligence and philosophy of science.

Gozzi, Raymond Jr., "Artificial intelligence — Metaphor or oxymoron?" ***Et Cetera,*** **summer 1997, pp. 219-224.**
Although computers have attained the status of metaphor for a thinking brain, the comparison may become an oxymoron; people are learning more about computers' limitations with regard to language and semantics.

Hillis, Danny, "Can they feel your pain?" ***Newsweek,*** **May 5, 1997, p. 57.**
Hillis contends that someday machines will have a form of consciousness, but humanity will get used to it. While humans may one day build thinking machines, Hillis doubts the actual process of thought will ever be fully understood by computers.

O Leary, Daniel E., Daniel Kuokka and Robert Plant, "Artificial intelligence and virtual organizations," ***Communications of the ACM,*** **January 1997, pp. 52-59.**
Recent developments in information technology capabilities, including the World Wide Web and artificial intelligence (AI), allow the development of new implementations of virtual organizations that exploit the capabilities of those new technologies. Virtual organizations may be the first large-scale industrial application of AI.

Pinker, Steven, "Can a computer be conscious?" *U.S. News & World Report,* Aug. 18-25, 1997, pp. 63-65.
The future of artificial intelligence is discussed. It is estimated that computers will become better at the things that humans do not do well.

Port, Otis, "Dueling Brainscapes," *Business Week,* June 23, 1997, pp. 88-90.
Cog, an android "wannabe" created by Rodney A. Brooks, and Cyc, a version of the old-school top-down system that was developed by Douglas B. Lenat, are two different approaches to artificial intelligence .

Simon, Herbert A., and Toshinori Munakata, "AI lessons," *Communications of the ACM,* August 1997, pp. 23-25.
Simon and Munakata believe the lessons of artificial intelligence (AI) were overlooked in the recent defeat of Garry Kasparov by IBM's Deep Blue. The authors discuss the future of artificial intelligence.

Big Blue

Belsie, Laurent, "After Chess Romp, Deep Blue's Makers Mull Their Next Move; One designer seeks to create a personlike robot but admits he's decades away from it," *The Christian Science Monitor,* May 13, 1997, p. 3.
For 40 years, one of the grand challenges of artificial-intelligence research has been to beat the reigning chess champion in a full match. On Sunday, computer scientists notched that victory, beating Garry Kasparov here in New York with a stunning victory in the sixth and final game. But it's not clear what their next challenge will be. Should they tackle more difficult games? Or, having built an artificial chess player, should they try to build an artificial person? Computer scientists doubt the first will capture the public imagination or draw the necessary resources. And they blush at the second idea. It will take months and perhaps even years to discover whether IBM's Deep Blue computer is really the world's best chess player.

Einstein, David, "Sheer speed, not artificial intelligence, is how IBM won," *San Francisco Chronicle,* May 13, 1997, p. C4.
For all its historic significance, Deep Blue's victory over world chess champion Garry Kasparov wasn't really much of a scientific breakthrough, computer experts said yesterday. In fact, the consensus was that the 6-foot-5, 1.4-ton IBM computer depended less on artificial intelligence than on raw computing power to dispatch Kasparov in their six-game series that finished Sunday.

Gelernter, David, "How hard is chess?" *Time,* May 19, 1997, pp. 72-73.
The chess competition between Garry Kasparov and Deep Blue, IBM's extraordinary computer, is discussed. Deep Blue is just a machine, although it is an intellectual milestone whose chief meaning is that human beings are champion machine builders.

Hitt, Jack, "Our machines, ourselves," *Harper's,* May 1997, pp. 45-54.
Four authors and a computer science professor discuss the possibility of a computer beating chess champion Garry Kasparov. The relationship between computers and the people who build them and use them is explored.

"Virtual victory," *The Boston Globe,* May 13, 1997, p. A14.
Until a machine can leap in the air, high-five the coach and scream "YES!" the game goes to the human being. Until a machine can groan over its frailties and missed chances, it is not competing. And if it is not competing, how can it win? World chess champion Garry Kasparov lost. No doubt about that. But what he lost was control over himself.

Wright, Robert, "Can machines think?" *Time,* March 25, 1996, pp. 50-56.
The latest round of chess matches between world champion Garry Kasparov and Deep Blue has sparked the debate over whether some machines can think. Cog, a robot being developed at MIT's artificial intelligence lab that may someday have a synthetic membrane sensitive to contact with humans, is discussed.

Experts

Clark, David D., "Roundtable: The future of computing and telecommunications," *Issues in Science & Technology,* spring 1997, pp. 71-78.
An abridged version of a discussion among a panel of experts convened by the National Research Council's Computer Science and Telecommunications Board is presented.

"Futurist to keynote Technology Expo today," *The Denver Post,* April 4, 1996, p. D3.
Dick Morley, a nationally known futurist and expert in computer design, artificial intelligence and the factory of the future, is the keynote speaker at the Rocky Mountain Technology Expo at the Colorado Convention Center in Denver.

HAL

Ramirez, Anthony, "No HAL Yet: Artificial Intelligence Visions Underestimated the Mind," *The New York Times,* Jan. 13, 1997, p. D4.
The 1968 film "2001: A Space Odyssey" used the best available science to project a thrilling future within the lifetime of its audience. But as 2001 nears, artificial intelligence developments have failed to come even close to producing a computer like HAL.

Rose, Christopher, "A Hal of a Computer to the 'Guy' Who Gave U.S. Goosebumps on '2001: A Space Odyssey': Happy Birthday," *Times-Picayune,* Jan. 11, 1997, p. E1.

Jan. 12, 1997 marks the fictional birthday of HAL, the computer that starred in the Stanley Kubrick-Arthur C. Clarke film "2001: A Space Odyssey." The celebration of HAL's birthday has sparked considerable interest in the field of artificial intelligence.

Smith, Gina, "Of minds and machines," *Popular Science,* April 1997, p. 38.

Smith comments on the real-life attempts by scientists to develop an intelligent computer. Douglas Lenat has been working to teach a program called Cyc more than 2 million commonsensical statements so that it can "reason" on its own. Rodney Brooks' robot, called Cog, simulates the way human babies learn.

History

Tate, Austin, "Don't leave your plan on the shelf," *ACM Computing Surveys,* September 1995, pp. 351-352.

A history of artificial intelligence planning is discussed. There is a renewed convergence in the techniques used in the planning field with those used in automatic programming, process management and other areas.

Wood, Lamont, "Artificial intelligence use getting smarter," *Chicago Tribune,* March 26, 1995. p. 8.

The history of artificial intelligence (AI) research is discussed. The original idea was to sit down with the experts, delve into their knowledge and emulate it on a computer. While that didn't work well in practice, AI offshoots such as neutral networks, genetic algorithms and fuzzy logic have been well-received. Tribecca Research President Neal M. Goldsmith believes AI must make a comeback because cruising the information superhighway will be painful without it.

Neural Networks

Brown, Alan S., "Computers that create: No hallucination," *Aerospace America,* January 1997, pp. 26-27.

The use of neural networks may allow computers in the future to learn and create. Neural networks are discussed.

Bottaci, Leonardo, Philip J. Drew, John E. Hartley and Matthew B. Hadfield et al, "Artificial neural networks applied to outcome prediction for colorectal cancer patients in separate institutions," *Lancet,* Aug. 16, 1997, pp. 469-472.

Bottaci et al report the training of neural networks to predict outcomes for individual colorectal cancer patients from one institution and their predictive performance on data from a different institution in another region.

Pitta, Julie, "Federico Faggin: The electronic brain," *Forbes,* July 7, 1997, pp. 312-313.

Federico Faggin, who led the Intel team that developed the first microprocessor in 1970-71, has embarked on a quest to produce intelligent systems using neural nets.

Robotics

Casti, John, "A game of three robots," *New Scientist,* April 26, 1997, pp. 28-31.

Robot soccer makes heavy demands in all the key areas of robot technology — mechanics, sensors and intelligence — and it does so in a way that people can understand and enjoy.

"Getting to know your knowbot" *Kiplinger's Personal Finance Magazine,* January 1997, pp. 98-99.

Knowbots, intelligent software agents that perform specific tasks, will finally become affordable for the home and home office by 2047. Legal issues will have to be sorted out before knowbots are given autonomy.

Kennedy, Kostya, "Danger, Will Robinson" *Sports Illustrated,* Sept. 15, 1997, p. 22.

Supersmart robots often entertain fans in Japan by engaging in wrestling matches, shooting baskets and playing soccer matches. Half of the contestants in RoboCup '97, the world's first robot soccer tournament, were from Japan.

Monaghan, Peter, "An art professor uses artificial intelligence to create a computer that draws and paints," *The Chronicle of Higher Education,* May 9, 1997, pp. A27-28.

Art Professor Harold Cohen "taught" a computer his ideas about the nature of images and composition, and the result is "AARON," a computer with artificial intelligence that drives a robotic painting machine. The machine is discussed.

Normile, Dennis, "'RoboCup' soccer match is a challenge for silicon rookies," *Science,* Sept. 26, 1997, p. 1933.

The first World Cup Robot Soccer competition, which pits robots against robots based on size, was recently held in Nagoya, Japan. It attracted 38 teams from universities in Europe, North America, Japan and Australia.

Port, Otis, "For Now, Pele's Record Is Secure," *Business Week,* Sept. 15, 1997, p. 94.

RoboCup '97, robot soccer, was recently held in Nagoya, Japan, as part of the International Joint Conference on Artificial Intelligence.

Back Issues

Great Research on Current Issues Starts Right Here . . . Recent topics covered by The CQ Researcher are listed below. Before May 1991, reports were published under the name of Editorial Research Reports.

MAY 1996
Russia's Political Future
Marriage and Divorce
Year-Round Schools
Taiwan, China and the U.S.

JUNE 1996
Rethinking NAFTA
First Ladies
Teaching Values
Labor Movement's Future

JULY 1996
Recovered-Memory Debate
Native Americans' Future
Crackdown on Sexual Harassment
Attack on Public Schools

AUGUST 1996
Fighting Over Animal Rights
Privatizing Government Services
Child Labor and Sweatshops
Cleaning Up Hazardous Wastes

SEPTEMBER 1996
Gambling Under Attack
The States and Federalism
Civic Journalism
Reassessing Foreign Aid

OCTOBER 1996
Political Consultants
Insurance Fraud
Rethinking School Integration
Parental Rights

NOVEMBER 1996
Global Warming
Clashing Over Copyright
Consumer Debt
Governing Washington, D.C.

DECEMBER 1996
Welfare, Work and the States
The New Volunteerism
Implementing the Disabilities Act
America's Pampered Pets

JANUARY 1997
Combating Scientific Misconduct
Restructuring the Electric Industry
The New Immigrants
Chemical and Biological Weapons

FEBRUARY 1997
Assisting Refugees
Alternative Medicine's Next Phase
Independent Counsels
Feminism's Future

MARCH 1997
New Air Quality Standards
Alcohol Advertising
Civic Renewal
Educating Gifted Students

APRIL 1997
Declining Crime Rates
The FBI Under Fire
Gender Equity in Sports
Space Program's Future

MAY 1997
The Stock Market
The Cloning Controversy
Expanding NATO
The Future of Libraries

JUNE 1997
FDA Reform
China After Deng
Line-Item Veto
Breast Cancer

JULY 1997
Transportation Policy
Executive Pay
School Choice Debate
Aggressive Driving

AUGUST 1997
Age Discrimination
Banning Land Mines
Children's Television
Evolution vs. Creationism

SEPTEMBER 1997
Caring for the Dying
Mental Health Policy
Mexico's Future
Youth Fitness

OCTOBER 1997
Urban Sprawl in the West
Diversity in the Workplace
Teacher Education
Contingent Work Force

NOVEMBER 1997
Renewable Energy

Back issues are available for $5.00 (subscribers) or $10.00 (non-subscribers). Quantity discounts apply to orders over ten. To order, call Congressional Quarterly Customer Service at (202) 887-8621.

Binders are available for $18.00. To order call 1-800-638-1710. Please refer to stock number 648.

Future Topics

- ***Religious Persecution***
- ***Abortion: Roe v. Wade at 25***
- ***Whistleblowers***

THE CQ Researcher

PUBLISHED BY CONGRESSIONAL QUARTERLY INC.

Religious Persecution

Is the global persecution of Christians increasing?

Christianity is the world's largest and richest religion. But Christians in many countries say they face discrimination or repression because of their faith, particularly in Islamic and communist nations. Now, activists are waging a worldwide campaign on behalf of persecuted Christians. In the United States, Christian groups are lobbying Congress to pass legislation cutting off non-humanitarian aid to countries responsible for religious persecution. But leaders of the campaign have touched off a bitter debate by accusing liberal human rights and religious groups of ignoring the mistreatment of Christians — accusations that those organizations vigorously reject. Some religious experts also dispute the claim that persecution of Christians is on the rise and complain that the campaign is ignoring mistreatment of people of other faiths.

INSIDE THIS ISSUE

CQ Nov. 21, 1997 • Volume 7, No. 43 • Pages 1009-1032

Formerly Editorial Research Reports

Religious Persecution

The Issues

Background

Current Situation

Outlook

Sidebars and Graphics

For Further Research

Cover: Christian Boys In Sudan Are Frequently Kidnapped And Taken To "Cultural Cleansing Camps" To Be Converted To Islam, According To Christian Activists. (Charles J. Brown/Center For Religious Freedom)

November 21, 1997
Volume 7, No. 43

Published By
Congressional Quarterly Inc.

The CQ Researcher (ISSN 1056-2036). Formerly Editorial Research Reports. Published weekly, except Jan. 3, May 30, Aug. 29, Oct. 31, by Congressional Quarterly Inc., 1414 22nd St., N.W., Washington, D.C. 20037. Annual subscription rate for libraries, businesses and government is $340. Additional rates furnished upon request. Periodicals postage paid at Washington, D.C., and additional mailing offices. POSTMASTER: Send address changes to The CQ Researcher, 1414 22nd St., N.W., Washington, D.C. 20037.

Religious Persecution

BY KENNETH JOST

THE ISSUES

In his many trips to Sudan, most recently in October, John Eibner has listened to horrific accounts of Christians suffering persecution — villages being bombed, children taken away to slavery, prisoners and refugees denied food or other humanitarian assistance by Muslim troops.

"There are well-documented cases of churches being bulldozed or burned down, clergymen and lay leaders who are arrested and imprisoned and clergymen being murdered by government troops," says Eibner, an official with the Swiss-based human rights and relief group Christian Solidarity International.

The anti-Christian persecution stems from the brutal 14-year civil war in Sudan, which has claimed more than 1.3 million lives and has spread destruction across the vast nation, Africa's largest. The conflict has been especially bitter since 1989, when the militant National Islamic Front gained power and began imposing its stringent religious views on a country that includes millions of Christians as well as Africans practicing traditional religions.

The result, according to United Nations and private human rights observers, has been severe religious persecution, especially in the country's southern half, where Christians make up a majority of the population.

"They come and kill us because we are not Muslims," an officer with the rebel Sudanese People's Liberation Army told Eibner last year. "They believe that if they die, they will go straight to heaven, because they are fighting infidels."

"This is different from traditional intertribal conflicts," the rebel leader continued. "There is also an ideological, religious dimension of forced Islamization." [1]

For many Westerners, the scenes of anti-Christian persecution are difficult to envision. Christianity has advanced over the last two millennia to become the world's largest religion, dominant in most of the world's richest countries and now growing rapidly in much of the Third World. But Christians in many other countries say they face discrimination or persecution at the hands either of government authorities or religious extremists that governments cannot or will not control.

More than 200 million Christians — about 10 percent of the world's total — live in daily fear of repression or discrimination, according to Paul Marshall, a Canadian scholar and author of an avowedly polemical book on the persecution of Christians, *Their Blood Cries Out*. [2] "In Sudan, Christians are enslaved." Marshall says. "In Iran, they are assassinated. In China, they are beaten to death."

Marshall and other Christian activists say the plight of their persecuted fellow believers has been all but ignored in the United States and the West up until the last few years. But in the past two years, a vocal campaign has been waged around the issue, taking the form of prayer, relief missions and, in Washington, a concerted lobbying drive for legislation to penalize countries where religious persecution occurs.

"There are lots of people who are worried about the immorality of our foreign policy," says Nina Shea, director of the Center for Religious Freedom at the conservative human rights organization Freedom House. "Our country has always seen itself as the champion of freedom, and that profile has been lost since 1990," when the Cold War ended.

Shea, like Marshall, has written a book, *In the Lion's Den,* that serves as a rallying cry for the current campaign in the United States. "More Christians have died for their faith in the 20th century," Shea writes, "than in the previous 19 centuries combined." [3]

Shea and Marshall provide graphic accounts of persecution of Christians, mainly in communist countries such as China, Cuba, North Korea and Vietnam, and Islamic countries, such as Iran, Pakistan, Saudi Arabia and Sudan. The persecuted Christians include:

- Bishop Shu Zhimin, auxiliary bishop of Baoding in China's Hebei Province, who has spent more than 20 years in prison, sometimes undergoing torture, for preaching outside the officially recognized Roman Catholic Church.
- The Rev. Elie Veguilla, a Baptist minister who was arrested by Cuban authorities in 1994 for evangelizing young people and held in a cell overnight with a live, chained bear.
- Three key Iranian Protestant pastors — Haik Hovespian-Mehr, Mehdi Dibaj and Tateos Michaelin — who were killed in 1994 in separate, still unexplained incidents thought to be related to efforts to convert Iranian

The World's Religions

Christian activitists say that followers of Christianity, the world's largest faith, face religious persecution in many Islamic countries as well as in many current or former communist nations.

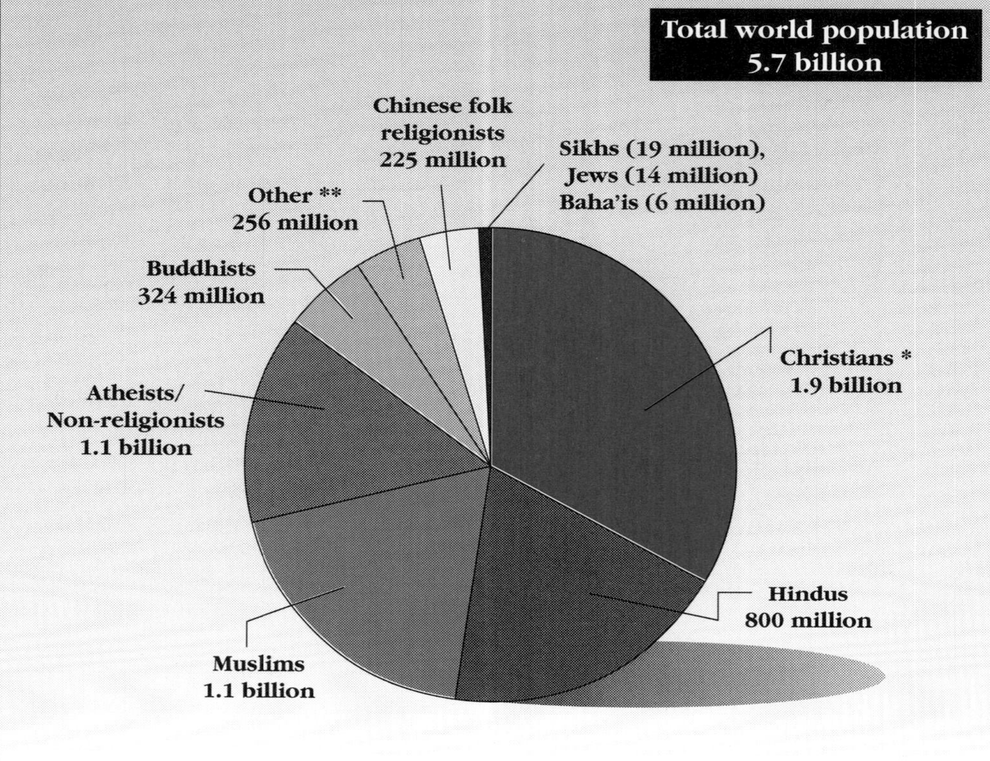

Note: Total does not add up to 5.7 billion due to rounding.
* Includes Roman Catholics, Protestants, Orthodox Christians and Anglicans
** Includes new religionists, ethnic religionists and other groups.
Sources: *1997 World Almanac/1996 Encyclopaedia Britannica Book of the Year*

Muslims to Christianity.

• Pakistani Christian John Joseph, who was shot in the throat in 1994 by Muslim extremists after being found not guilty of blasphemy.

The campaign against religious persecution has energized the evangelical community and gained the support of many mainstream Protestant denominations as well as the U.S. Catholic Conference. Some experts, however, question whether the persecution of Christians is increasing.

"The religious persecution of Christians is in fact dropping worldwide," says John Witte Jr., director of the law and religion program at Emory University in Atlanta. "And Christians aren't the only ones who are being persecuted, and often aren't the worst victims of persecution."

In addition, the campaign has clashed with some liberal human rights organizations as well as the country's largest ecumenical church group, the National Council of Churches of Christ (NCC). Leaders of these groups accuse the campaign of singling out Christians and ignoring mistreatment of people of other faiths as well as broader human rights concerns.

"We prefer for the religious freedom issue to be in the context of other freedom issues," says the Rev. Albert Pennybacker, associate general secretary of the NCC. "As religious people, we're concerned about the persecution of anyone for any reason. We don't want to be concerned only about religious people, though we are intensely concerned about them."

The debate has been especially acrimonious between the campaign's chief strategist — Michael Horowitz, a former Reagan administration official — and the head of the liberal Human Rights Watch, Kenneth Roth. Horowitz took up the Christian persecution issue two years ago, enlisting political and media support for the cause and drafting the sanctions legislation now pending in Congress (*see p. 1024*).

Horowitz flatly accuses human rights groups of practicing "a double standard" about religious persecution. "Political dissidents they're really concerned about," Horowitz says, "but religious dissidents are a lesser concern."

Roth responds that his organization, among others, has catalogued and critiqued denials of religious freedom in annual reports and in detailed studies of China, Egypt, Sudan and other countries.

"Michael Horowitz unfortunately has never let the truth stand in the way of a good applause line," Roth says. He also has criticized Shea — though in less personal terms — by questioning the basis for her repeated comparison of the number of Christians who died during this century and in the previous 1,900 years.

The sanctions legislation, cosponsored by two Republican lawmakers — Rep. Frank R. Wolf of Virginia and Sen. Arlen Specter of Pennsylvania — won approval from the House International Relations Subcommittee on Human Rights in early September; but Wolf-Specter, as the bill is known, has since stalled. The anti-persecution campaign, however, has succeeded in forcing the Clinton administration to devote more attention to religious freedom issues.

Congress last year ordered the State Department's Human Rights Bureau to prepare a country-by-country report on religious persecution of Christians and U.S. policies on the issue. The report, published July 22, faulted practices in more than 70 countries, with a particularly scathing critique of China. (*See table, p. 1020.*) The State Department last year also created a 20-member advisory panel on religious freedom issues, with representatives from most major faiths. The panel is due to submit an interim report later this year and a final report by the end of next year.

For their part, the countries criticized for religious persecution generally defend their policies. China, for example, insists that its state-registered churches run their own affairs and that any arrests of religious figures are for violating criminal laws. "No one in China is punished because of his or her religious belief," the government says. [4]

As the campaign against religious persecution continues in the United States and around the world, here are some of the major questions being debated:

Has the persecution of Christians been given too little attention in the United States?

The leaders of the current campaign against religious persecution maintain that the mistreatment of Christians has been neglected for decades by the government as well as by human rights and religious groups. Some organizations, such as the National Association of Evangelicals, accept a measure of blame.

"We confess our culpability," the group declared last year, "in failing to do all within our power to alleviate the suffering of those persecuted for their religious beliefs." [5]

The most pointed charges, however, have been aimed at the National Council of Churches and two human rights groups with a liberal cast: Amnesty International and Human Rights Watch. They have responded by defending their records of speaking out against religious persecution and depicting the accusations as divisive and counterproductive.

Christian Solidarity International

Millions of Christian evangelicals in China who worship in "house churches" face severe government repression, according to the U.S. State Department.

In his book, Marshall blames American evangelicals' inaction on the issue on a number of factors, including the nationalistic focus of their religious views and doctrines that emphasize searching for inner peace rather than doing good works. He is far harsher with the NCC. He accuses the council and its international affiliate, the World Council of Churches (WCC), of either denying or ignoring the persecution of Christians in communist and Islamic countries and emphasizing liberal social views and peaceful dialogue with established, non-state churches rather than advocacy for fellow believers. [6]

As evidence, Marshall cites a number of NCC publications and stances since the 1960s. A 1972 book describes visitors to China as "enthusiastic" about "the role of the church." A 1975 book on Cuba praises the Cuban revolution, while NCC officials in 1984 commented on "the positive role played in the revolution by Christians." In the same year, an NCC-organized visit of church leaders to the Soviet Union ended with praise for the status of religion in the country. More recently, Marshall faults the NCC for doing nothing concrete after the Tiananmen Square uprising in China in 1989 and for joining in welcoming Cuban leader Fidel Castro to the United States in 1996.

As for Islamic countries, Marshall scoffs at the WCC's recent sponsorship of international conferences aimed at promoting Christian-Muslim "dialogues" and attended by representatives of such countries as Sudan, Pakistan and Libya. "Real dialogue"

Christian Groups Working on Religious Persecution

After working in government for nearly 10 years, Jim Jacobson followed the path taken by many other Washington staffers: He joined forces with a private-interest group. In his new job, Jacobson still travels some familiar corridors on Capitol Hill. But his work also takes him as far away as China to deliver financial assistance to the families of pastors imprisoned by the Chinese government or to the Burma (Myanmar)-Thailand border to deliver medical supplies to Christian refugees fleeing the Burmese dictatorship.

Jacobson is president of the U.S. branch of Christian Solidarity International, a human rights and relief organization. In the United States, the group has lobbied for the religious persecution legislation introduced in Congress earlier this year. It also organized a petition drive to complain that the Clinton administration's new ambassador to China, former Sen. Jim Sasser, D-Tenn., had no familiarity before his appointment with the underground "house church" movement among Chinese Christians.

The organization was founded by a Swiss minister in 1977 to help persecuted Christians within the Soviet Union. Today, its British branch is working in Sudan to buy back young Christians taken as slaves by Muslim troops in the country's bloody civil war — efforts that the U.S. branch helped publicize.[1]

Christian Solidarity is one of a number of groups helping persecuted Christians around the world. Most of the groups have limited budgets and get little coverage in the secular media. But leaders of the U.S. campaign are working to bring them greater visibility. In their recent books on religious persecution, Canadian scholar Paul Marshall (*Their Blood Cries Out*) and Nina Shea, director of the Center for Religious Freedom at Freedom House (*In the Lion's Den*), include lists of some of the organizations — with addresses, telephone numbers and Web sites.

Many of the groups, like Christian Solidarity, began by helping Christians in communist countries. In recent years, some have either shifted or expanded their focus to Islamic countries. For example, the Rev. Keith Roderick, an Episcopal priest in Illinois, began working in 1982 with Aid to Soviet Christians but now heads an umbrella organization, the Coalition for the Defense of Human Rights Under Islamization.

In the early days, some of the groups worked primarily to get Bibles into countries where distribution was restricted. Open Doors with Brother Andrew was founded by a Dutch minister who began smuggling Bibles behind the Iron Curtain in the 1950s. "It's still an important part of what we do — taking God's word into countries where there are not established channels for the importation of Bibles," says Mike Yoder, director of communications for the group's U.S. branch. But Yoder acknowledges that more established Christian mission groups complain that Bible-smuggling "hurts what they're trying to do because it hurts above-ground activities."

Some groups focus solely on an individual country. The Cardinal Kung Foundation monitors religious persecution in China. Others have an international focus. The largest is the World Evangelical Fellowship, in Singapore, which has spearheaded the campaign for the International Day of Prayer for the Persecuted Church.

In contrast to better-known human rights and ecumenical church groups, these Christian organizations have a conservative political orientation. Jacobson worked in the Reagan and Bush administrations and for a conservative Republican senator. And the strongest proponents of the religious persecution legislation in Congress have been GOP lawmakers. But Roderick says the campaign is being "misconstrued" as a conservative movement.

"This is really a humanitarian issue," Roderick says. "It should not be a liberal issue or conservative issue, a Republican or Democratic issue."

Christian Mission Groups

Organizations working on religious persecution issues include:

- **Cardinal Kung Foundation,** P.O. Box 8086, Ridgeway Center, Stamford, Conn. 06905; 203-329-9712.
- **Christian Solidarity International,** P.O. Box 16367, Washington D.C. 20041; 800-323-CARE.
- **Coalition for the Defense of Human Rights Under Islamization,** 231 East Carroll, Macomb, Ill. 61455; 309-833-4249.
- **International Christian Concern,** 2020 Pennsylvania Ave., N.W., Suite 941, Washington, D.C. 20006; 301-989-1708.
- **Iranian Christians International,** P.O. Box 25607, Colorado Springs, Colo. 80936; 719-596-0010.
- **Open Doors with Brother Andrew,** P.O. Box 27000, Santa Ana, Calif. 92779; 714-531-6600.
- **Voice of the Martyrs,** P.O. Box 443, Bartlesville, Okla. 74005; 918-337-8015.
- **World Evangelical Fellowship,** U.S. office: 2309 139th St., S.E., Mill Creek, Wash. 98012; 206-742-7923.

[1] See Gilbert A. Lewthwaite and Gregory Kane, "Witness to Slavery," *The Baltimore Sun,* June 16-18, 1996.

must deal with "the concrete acts of government" when there are state-sponsored Islamic participants, Marshall says. "To have a dialogue with people involved in religious persecution and not deal with the issue is removing dialogue from what's going on in the real world."

Marshall includes human rights

organizations — along with news organizations, academics and policy analysts — in a general critique of "Western secularists," who he says are guilty of "a deafening silence" toward religious persecution around the world. He complains, for example, that Human Rights Watch has "special initiatives" on such issues as prisons and lesbian and gay rights but "less interest in religious matters." As for Amnesty International, he says it gives little attention to the specifically religious issues in its human rights reports on such countries as Sudan and Nigeria.

Despite his critique, Marshall credits Amnesty International and Human Rights Watch with having "done more than almost any other organizations to bring religious persecution to our attention." And he acknowledges that some NCC leaders have faulted the group's past record on religious persecution issues and that its former counsel on religious freedom "did sterling work for many years." [7]

By contrast, Horowitz and Shea make no effort to soften their attacks. Horowitz accuses liberal human rights groups of "bigotry against evangelicals and religious believers." Shea says the NCC served as "apologists for the Soviet regime" and continues to soft-pedal the plight of persecuted Christians in China. As for the human rights groups, Shea charges that they shun religious freedom issues because of disagreements over domestic political issues such as abortion.

"The liberal human rights groups have a great deal of difficulty championing victims whose domestic policies they disagree with — evangelicals and Catholics," Shea says. "They have applied a political litmus test to the victim, in this case Christians, and find them distasteful."

"The people who make that accusation haven't read our reports," responds Roth. He points to nine reports on religious persecution in China that Human Rights Watch has issued in the last five years, including one just last month. "Religious freedom has always been a central concern, one that has been vigorously pursued and one that is a key part of our agenda," he adds. [8]

Roth is especially sharp in responding to Horowitz's barbs. "He's decided that the best way to further his cause is to attack the human rights movement, which is misguided and divisive since the human rights movement is a natural ally of those wishing to protect religious freedom," Roth says.

Roth and a U.S. representative of Amnesty International also deflect the accusations that the group neglects religious persecution, insisting that they wish they could do more on all issues, including religious freedom.

"No, we're not doing enough on religious persecution," says Stephen Rickard, director of Amnesty's Washington office. "We're not doing enough on child labor. We're not doing enough on torture. Every day we go home feeling we're not doing enough."

Officials of the NCC also insist their group has a good record on religious freedom. "Our history is quite solid," Pennybacker says. The council, he says, helped Christians during China's cultural revolution, provided "support and sustenance" to churches in communist countries and defended Catholic clergy during the Central American conflicts of the past few decades.

But Pennybacker's comments on specific countries evince the continuing gulf between the two groups. He calls the critiques of religious practices in China "one-sided," insisting that religion is much freer than "40 years ago." He makes no apology for the NCC's dealings with officially recognized churches in China today or in other communist countries in the past. And he repeatedly declines to criticize Saudi Arabia, which by law prohibits public worship of any religion other than Islam.

"In Saudi Arabia, the Islamic heritage defines that land as sacred space — like a cathedral," Pennybacker says. "To ignore that definition is to intrude on the religious sensitivities of Islamic people. What we would call persecution can be defined in that setting as criminal behavior."

Is the campaign against persecution of Christians ignoring mistreatment of people of other faiths?

Charles Colson, the convicted Watergate conspirator turned prison evangelist, writes in his preface to Shea's book: "When you hear about Christians being martyred for their faith, do you think of biblical figures such as Stephen or John the Baptist? If you do, you're out of date by a couple of thousand years."

The dramatic accounts of mistreatment of present-day Christians appear to be having the intended effect of awakening awareness of the issue both in Washington and in the rest of the United States. "This is a movement," Horowitz says, "that has come further and faster than any I've seen in the 20 years I've been in Washington."

But the campaign's focus on Christians leaves some advocates and experts concerned. "I see in places where Christians are being persecuted that other groups are being persecuted, too," says David Little, a senior scholar in religion, ethics and human rights at the U.S. Institute for Peace. "It's hard for me to identify in the persecutors any particular belief that they must, in particular, get rid of Christians."

In drafting the original Wolf-Specter bill, the leaders of the current campaign gave only limited acknowledgment to persecution of other faiths. The original bill provided that a proposed Office of Religious Persecution Monitoring would make its first potentially sanction-triggering findings about Tibetan Buddhists, Iranian

Baha'is and Christians in communist and radical Muslim countries. Authors of the bill explained that those three religious communities were cited in resolutions passed by the previous Congress, but they stressed that the legislation would provide for sanctions against all countries that persecute religious minorities.

In response to criticism, the bill has now been amended to include references to persecution of other faiths, including Muslims. Still, the leaders of the campaign make no apology for focusing on Christians.

"Even though more than 200 million Christians face literal persecution," Horowitz says, "few in America, few in Congress and fewer still in the media knew or noted that fact until last year."

"We don't think we should apologize for speaking out for evangelicals," says Richard Cizik, a policy analyst at the National Association for Evangelicals. "But our concern is broader."

Leaders of the National Council of Churches, however, have voiced discontent with the campaign's focus on mistreatment of Christians. "If that's exclusive of other religious communities experiencing persecution, then I think it's seriously misplaced," Pennybacker says. "One of the lessons of the Holocaust is that Christians cared too much about Christians: They should have cared about people being persecuted for any reasons."

The House International Relations Subcommittee on Human Rights did hold a one-day hearing in February 1996 on persecution of Jews that focused mainly on anti-Semitism in Russia and other states of the former Soviet Union. [9] But American Muslim leaders complain that persecution of Muslims was never examined in a hearing or in the original sanctions legislation.

"It names Buddhists. It names Christians. It names Baha'is," says Khaled Saffuri, deputy director of the American Muslim Council. "And then it fails to name Muslims, and probably Muslims make up a big percentage of persecuted minorities." [10]

Voice of the Martyrs

In Sudan, Kevin Turner of The Voice of the Martyrs bought these Christian children last year from slave traders and returned them to their families. If they did not memorize the Koran, they were denied food by their captors.

John Esposito, director of the Center for Christian-Muslim Understanding at Georgetown University, agrees that the current campaign neglects persecution of Muslims, both by non-Islamic regimes and at the hands of Islamic governments or groups. As examples, he cites the conflicts involving Muslim separatists in the Indian state of Kashmir, the Russian war against the predominantly Muslim rebels in Chechnya and the ethnic cleansing campaign by Serbs against Bosnian Muslims. And he points to Algeria, where he says the government and military "have often targeted moderate Islamists simply because they constitute an opposition."

Marshall agrees on the need to point out the religious persecution of Muslims and raises the issue in his appearances as part of an effort to dispel suggestions that the campaign is anti-Islamic. But he also makes no apology for the sharp attacks on persecution of Christians by Islamic governments and groups. "There's no way of dealing with the issue except to point out that a great deal of persecution is being carried out by some Muslims," he says.

Should the United States impose sanctions on countries where religious persecution takes place?

The United States has once before tied the threat of economic sanctions to a religious freedom issue. In 1974, Congress passed the Jackson-Vanik amendment, which linked normal trade status between the United States and communist countries to liberalization of emigration policies. The law, strongly pushed by an interfaith coalition, barred so-called most-favored-nation (MFN) trading status for the Soviet Union until 1990, when restrictions on Jewish emigration had been relaxed.

The organizers of the current campaign against religious persecution have explicitly adopted the campaign for Soviet Jewry as their model. The Wolf-Specter bill differs in significant details from the Jackson-Vanik amendment, but the approach is the same: to require the president and Congress to regularly review religious freedom issues in individual countries and, in this case, provide for denial of some non-humanitarian assistance if a foreign government is found to practice or condone religious persecution.

"It's a question of laying down a clear marker that guarantees attention," Horowitz says. "Simply to know about these persecutions is to ensure change — far-reaching change."

Supporters stress, however, that the aid sanctions provided in the bill would not affect U.S. trade with other countries. "It focuses on aid, not trade, sanctions to encourage change," Wolf told subcommittee members in September.

In fact, business interests have waged a major private lobbying campaign against the bill. A coalition of more than 600 companies and trade associations was formed in April under the name USA-Engage to lobby against the the use of unilateral sanctions by the U.S.

"We think there are better tools," says Eric Thomas, a spokesman for the group. He says the Wolf-Specter bill is "very broad. It will impose sanctions on any number of countries. I don't think anyone really knows who could actually be affected."

The Clinton administration has also vigorously opposed the bill. In congressional testimony, John Shattuck, assistant secretary of State for human rights, called the bill "a blunt instrument that is more likely to harm, rather than aid, victims of religious persecution." The administration also strongly objected to a provision in the original bill that called for a new Office of Religious Persecution Monitoring to be placed in the White House and the director to be subject to Senate confirmation. Sponsors have now agreed, however, to have the new office placed within the State Department's Human Rights Bureau.

For their part, the NCC and Human Rights Watch have both criticized the sanctions provided in the bill, though for different reasons.

"We think that the sanctions ought to be at the end of the line of penalties rather than the beginning point," says Pennybacker of the NCC. "We believe that experience shows that positive incentives and the positive engagement with a country's life and working toward reconciliation, understanding, common ground and social harmony is the place to begin."

Roth of Human Rights Watch says, however, that the sanctions provisions actually add little to existing law. "In essence, the bill simply restates sanctions that the human rights movement secured 20 years ago," he says. "In only the smallest possible steps does it go beyond existing U.S. legislation on human rights sanctions."

Roth also says the bill's definition of religious persecution is too limited. The bill would apply to persecution that includes abduction, enslavement, imprisonment, killing, forced mass resettlement, rape and torture, including crucifixion. But Roth says the bill ignores other forms of religious persecution, such as restrictions on worship.

Horowitz, who drafted the legislation, responds that he deliberately limited the bill to more severe forms of religious persecution rather than what he calls religious discrimination. "We're going to keep a very bright line between persecution and discrimination," Horowitz says. "We're not going to turn this enterprise into some super-EEOC [Equal Employment Opportunity Commission] dealing with religious persecution because if we tried to do it, we'd go no place."

The broad opposition helped stall the bill after approval by the House Human Rights Subcommittee on Sept. 18. Supporters agreed to significant compromises, including a provision to give the president unlimited discretion to waive any of the sanctions provided in the bill. Still, the House International Relations Committee failed to act on the measure before this year's session ended.

Horowitz and other supporters of the bill chafed at the compromises accepted in an effort to reach a consensus that, in fact, never emerged. Now they threaten to seek tougher legislation next year.

"If these guys really want to go to war with the church community," Horowitz says, referring to opponents of the bill, "we'll see you next year."

But Shea also stresses that the push for legislation is only a small part of the campaign. "The movement is much broader than Wolf-Specter," she says. "It's much broader than congressional legislation. It's in the grass roots. It's in the heartland. It's in the churches. The Christians have been energized, and the politicians are basically playing catch-up." ■

BACKGROUND

Centuries of Strife

Religious persecution dates as far back as the enslavement of the Jews by the Egyptian pharaohs and the crucifixion of Jesus by the Roman authorities in Judea. Throughout history religious differences have fueled violent conflicts between Christians and Muslims, Catholics and Protestants and believers and non-believers. Anti-Semitism forced Jews from their homes in Spain in the 15th century and Russia and Central Europe in the late 19th century and led to the deaths of millions of Jews in the Holocaust. [11]

The Holocaust was the worst,

single episode of religious persecution in history. The systematic deportations and executions that Nazi Germany carried out between 1939 and 1945 claimed an estimated 6 million Jews from Germany and other occupied countries in Europe. But the 20th century has witnessed a number of other deadly religious-ethnic conflicts — from the killing of hundreds of thousands of Armenians, mostly Christians, by the Ottoman Turks (1915-1923) to the recent "ethnic cleansing" of tens of thousands of Muslims by Orthodox Serbs during the Bosnian war. [12]

In the years since the end of World War II, the international community has put on paper broadly phrased provisions for religious freedom, beginning with the 1948 Universal Declaration of Human Rights. But the United States, preoccupied with the Cold War, has given less attention to issues of religious human rights except for pressuring the former Soviet Union to ease restrictions on Jewish emigration during the 1970s and '80s.

Today, the leaders of the current movement against religious persecution see an especially severe threat to Christians from two international forces: communism and militant Islam.

'Godless Communism'

Communism has been at odds with religious organizations ever since Karl Marx declared religion to be "the opium of the people," an obstacle to the class consciousness needed for a workers' revolution. The communist governments of the 20th century have worked to subordinate religious institutions to the state. But in Russia, China and elsewhere, religion continued to hold millions of faithful adherents and to represent a competing center of power to the communist regimes.

Communism came to power first in Russia, a country with a strong Orthodox Christian church closely associated with the state under the tsars. The constitution of the newly formed Soviet Union formally proclaimed freedom of religion. But the communist government was widely blamed for killing tens of thousands of believers and clergy and destroying thousands of churches, mosques and synagogues. [13]

After World War II, Soviet-supported communist governments in Eastern Europe also took over from regimes that, for the most part, had close ties with organized churches. These communist governments also moved to limit the role of religion in public life, but without the Soviet Union's severe persecution. Still, the Catholic Church posed a challenge to the regimes. In Hungary, for example, Cardinal Joseph Mindszenty was a rallying figure of the anti-communist uprising in 1956. More recently, the Catholic church in Poland played an important part in the downfall of communism through its support of the Solidarity labor movement; and the Polish cardinal, Karol Wojtyla, archbishop of Krakow, helped stiffen the church's anti-communist stance after his election as Pope John Paul II in 1978. [14]

China had a more diverse religious tradition before communism than Russia or the Eastern European countries, with a mix of Buddhism, Taoism and Chinese folk religions; a strong Muslim presence in some interior areas; and smaller but well-established bodies of Christians, both Catholics and Protestants. The Chinese communists also regarded religious groups as an obstacle to their quest for power and a legacy of feudal superstition and foreign influence. [15]

Once in power after 1949, the Chinese communists launched a crackdown on native sects, including the largest, the Way of Unity, which had been ardently anti-communist during the civil war.

Meanwhile, the Chinese government moved to bring Christian groups under a measure of control by requiring them to register with officially sanctioned bodies, such as the Catholic Patriotic Association. [16] Marshall says that from the mid-1950s on, the government attempted to purge so-called counterrevolutionaries from the Christian churches too, sentencing many Christian clergy to long terms in "re-education" camps. Religious persecution then peaked during the decade-long Great Proletarian Cultural Revolution (1966-1976). The Red Guards, Marshall writes, were "particularly brutal with Chinese believers, whether Christian, Muslim or Buddhist."

Elsewhere in Asia, communist North Korea and North Vietnam also limited the role of religion. Both countries had had a strong Christian presence before communism. The suppression of Christianity was especially severe in North Korea. One human rights report said that 150 Catholic priests were murdered in 1950 and many other Christians imprisoned under severe conditions. When the suppression failed to eliminate Christianity, North Korea established three official congregations — two Protestants and one Catholic — which Marshall says are regarded with derision by outsiders. [17]

In Cuba, Castro made early overtures toward the Catholic Church after leading the successful revolution to oust a pro-U.S. dictator in 1959. But within two years, Castro firmly declared himself to be a communist and instituted a series of anti-clerical moves, including closing religious schools, halting Catholic publications, and sending Catholic clergy into exile. Christmas and Easter were abolished as national holidays in 1970; a

Continued on p. 1022

Chronology

Before 1900

Christianity is dominant religion in Europe and the Americas and advances in Africa and Asia; Islam dominates much of the Middle East and North Africa; Buddhism and Hinduism are strong in Asia.

1900s-1940s

Communist governments limit role of religion; many Muslim countries gain independence; the Holocaust claims an estimated 6 million Jews.

1917
Communists gain power in Russia and, during the 1920s, move to bring Orthodox Church under government control.

1941-1945
Nazi Germany carries out the most intense religious persecution in history, killing an estimated 6 million Jews in what dictator Adolf Hitler calls the "final solution" to the "Jewish problem."

1948
U.N. includes provisions for religious freedom in Universal Declaration of Human Rights.

1949
Communists gain power in China and within a few years move to suppress or control religious groups.

1950s-1960s

The Cold War dominates international relations; human rights issues are subordinated to anti-communist policies in the United States.

1970s

Islamic militancy advances in Muslim countries; U.S. and other countries pressure Soviet Union to let Jews emigrate.

1974
Congress passes Jackson-Vanik amendment, linking U.S. trade concessions for communist countries to emigration policies.

1978
Cardinal Karol Wojtyla, archbishop of Krakow, is elected pope; as John Paul II, he stiffens Roman Catholic Church's resistance to communist regimes in Europe and elsewhere.

January-February 1979
Iranian Revolution brings militant Islamic regime to power.

1980s

The collapse of the Soviet Union brings an end to the Cold War.

1981
U.N. General Assembly adopts Declaration on the Elimination of All Forms of Intolerance and of Discrimination Based on Religion or Belief.

1985
State Department joins with interfaith coalition in sponsoring conference on religious liberty around the world; conference draws limited attention.

1990s

Christian activists mount campaign in U.S. and around the world against religious persecution of Christians, especially in communist and militant Islamic countries.

1994
China adopts new regulations — decrees 144 and 145 — mandating registration of religious groups.

Jan. 23, 1996
Freedom House holds conference in Washington on "Global Persecution of Christians," marked by National Association of Evangelicals' "Statement of Conscience" calling for stronger action.

September 1996
The House and the Senate pass non-binding resolutions condemning persecution of Christians in communist and militantly Islamic countries.

Sept. 18, 1997
House International Relations subcommittee approves bill to impose limited sanctions on countries responsible for religious persecution, but measure fails to advance further.

Sept. 26, 1997
Russian President Boris Yeltsin signs legislation protecting Orthodox Church from competition from other faiths.

Sept. 28-Nov. 16, 1997
U.S. churches join in second International Day of Prayer for the Persecuted Church.

U.S. State Department Survey of Religious Persecution

The State Department report "U.S. Policies in Support of Religious Freedom: Focus on Christians," published in July, lists more than 70 countries where Christians reportedly are being persecuted. The department based the selections on "expressions of concern by congressional and non-governmental observers" and its annual "Country Reports on Human Rights Practices." The following countries were among those listed:

Africa

Algeria: Christian community, mostly foreigners, curtailed activities after insurgent Armed Islamic Group (GIA) declared its intention to eliminate Jews, Christians and polytheists from country; seven Roman Catholic monks in central Algeria killed by GIA in 1996; Catholic Bishop of Oran murdered at his home; two priests and a nun killed in 1995.
Burundi: Civil war has included politically motivated attacks on churches and church personnel, including massacres of civilians seeking sanctuary in churches.
Central African Republic: Constitutional provision forbidding fundamentalism is widely understood to be aimed at Muslims.
Egypt: Christians face discrimination based on tradition and some aspects of the law; persecution of Christians has occurred in recent years; Christians also have been targeted by terrorist groups seeking to overthrow the government and establish an Islamic state; terrorists have killed dozens of Christians in past few years.
Ethiopia: Some incidents of harassment, intimidation and, in some cases, violence between Christians and Muslims.
Kenya: Catholic Church and National Council of Churches in Kenya were harshly criticized by government officials in 1996 for pastoral letters calling for constitutional reform and fair elections.
Maldives: Practice of any religion other than Islam is prohibited.
Mauritania: Some individuals harassed or detained for passing Christian religious materials to Muslim citizens.
Morocco: Law prohibits any attempt to induce a Muslim to convert to another faith; foreign missionaries either limit proselytizing to non-Muslims or conduct work quietly.
Nigeria: Christian and Muslim organizations accuse government of restricting entry of religious practitioners.
Somalia: Proselytizing is a crime for any religion except Islam; small Christian community maintains low profile.
Sudan: Islam treated as de facto state religion; forced conversion to Islam of Christians, animists and other non-Muslims takes place as part of government policy; civil war between mainly Islamic north and largely animist and Christian south has claimed more than a million lives.

The Americas

Colombia: Internal conflict has produced attacks on church personnel working to promote peace and non-violent action; two employees of Jesuit-run human rights organization murdered in May; three members of New Tribes Mission kidnapped in 1993 are thought to be alive, but their whereabouts and welfare unknown.
Cuba: Religious persecution continues despite recent easing of some harsher aspects of religious repression; access to media, establishment of schools and sponsorship of social activities are restricted; government harassment of private houses of worship continued through 1996; but government has relaxed restrictions on members of Jehovah's Witnesses.
Mexico: Evangelicals subject to religious discrimination and harassment in Chiapas; more than 30,000 evangelicals expelled over 30-year period before truce with authorities in 1995.
Nicaragua: Credible reports of harassment of Catholic Church officials, who blame incidents on extremists opposed to church's human rights and civic education campaigns.
Peru: Religious workers subject to threats from terrorist factions; North American officials of Mormon Church particularly targeted prior to 1996: 24 Mormon Church houses were bombed, several Mormon administrators of food programs murdered.

Asia

Bhutan: Non-Buddhist citizens (mostly Hindus) and foreign missionaries prohibited from proselytizing.
Brunei: Non-Muslims are prohibited from proselytizing, importing religious teaching materials or scriptures and building or repairing churches, temples and shrines.
Burma: Authoritarian government imposes severe restrictions on religious freedoms of majority Buddhists and others, including Christians and Muslims; the Karen, a predominantly Christian ethnic minority, have been subject to abuse by military, including killings, kidnappings and rape, both in Burma and in cross-border refugee camps in Thailand.
China: Government has sought to restrict all actual religious practice to government-authorized religious organizations and registered places of worship; 1994 regulations codified ban on proselytizing by foreigners. Strong efforts launched in 1996-1997 to crack down on unregistered Catholic and Protestant movements; several hundred "house church" groups raided and closed. Increased government concern about ethnic separatist movements has also led to restrictions on Buddhists in Tibet and Muslims in Xinjiang Autonomous Region.
India: Government has refused since mid-1960s to admit new resident foreign missionaries.
Indonesia: Proselytizing in areas heavily dominated by another recognized religion is discouraged; several instances of religion-related mob violence reported during 1996, including more than two dozen Christian churches and one Buddhist temple.
North Korea: The government firmly discourages all organized religious activity except that which serves the interests of the state; visitors to the only three Christian churches in the country say church activity appears staged; no Catholic priests in country to celebrate mass or administer sacraments.
Laos: Links with religious associations in other countries require government approval; foreigners prohibited from proselytizing; importing foreign religious publications and artifacts is restricted.
Malaysia: Islam is official religion; religious minorities, including large Hindu, Buddhist, Sikh and Christian communities, subject to some restrictions; circulation of a popular Malay-language translation of the Bible is discouraged.
Nepal: Eleven Christians were given prison sentences in 1995 for proselytizing; later pardoned and released.

Pakistan: Islam is official religion; law enacted in 1986 stipulates death penalty for blaspheming the Prophet Mohammed; proselytizing among Muslims is illegal; Islamic extremists have assaulted, raped and even murdered members of religious minorities; discrimination against Ahmadis, Christians, Hindus and Zakris.
Singapore: All religious groups subject to government scrutiny and must be legally registered; Jehovah's Witnesses banned because of opposition to military service.
Vietnam: All religious organizations required to obtain government permission to hold training seminars and conventions, build or remodel places of worship, engage in charitable activities, operate religious schools or ordain, promote or transfer clergy; only two Christian denominations approved by government: Catholic Church and Protestant Christian Missionary Alliance; government insists on right to approve Vatican appointments; several Americans have been charged and detained for disseminating religious materials in past two years.

Middle East

Iran: Freedom of religion restricted for Muslim sects other than officially designated Ja'fari Shi'ism and for non-Muslims; non-Muslims may not proselytize Muslims; Muslims who convert to another faith are considered apostates and may be subject to the death penalty; official oppression of evangelical Christians increased in 1996; two evangelists arrested in 1997 on espionage charges; charges often brought against persons suspected of proselytizing.
Iraq: Freedom of religion severely limited; ethnic and religious communities not associated with the ruling clique, including the majority Shi'a population and the Kurds in northern Iraq, have suffered massive repression for decades; various abuses against the country's 350,000 Assyrian Christians reported.
Israel: A bill introduced in the Knesset this spring to restrict proselytizing, apparently in reaction to an evangelical Christian group's mass mailing of brochures to thousands of Israelis; Jehovah's Witnesses report harassment and occasional violent attacks.
Kuwait: Missionaries prohibited from proselytizing among Muslims; law also prohibits religious education for religions other than Islam, but it appears not to be rigidly enforced.
Saudi Arabia: Public and private practice of religions other than Islam prohibited; citizens and foreigners are targets of harassment by the Mutawwa'in (religious police) and by religious vigilantes acting independently; non-Muslim worshipers risk arrest, lashing and deportation for any religious activity that attracts official attention.
Syria: Government registration required for all religions and sects; permits required for all meetings except worship; churches, mosques and synagogues reported to be closely controlled by government, including monitoring of worship services.

Russia and former Soviet republics

Armenia: Armenian Apostolic Church recognized as having special status; law forbids proselytizing, requires registration of non-Apostolic religious organizations; Jehovah's Witnesses were refused registration because of opposition to military service.
Belarus: Foreign missionaries may not engage in religious activities outside institutions that invited them; regulation seen as aimed at enhancing position of Orthodox Church with respect to faster-growing Roman Catholic and Protestant churches.
Kyrgyz Republic: All religious organizations must register; Baptist congregation in Naryn oblast, an ethnic Kyrgyz area, has been denied registration and harassed by police.
Moldova: Religious groups must register with government to hire non-citizens; proselytizing prohibited.
Russia: Russian Orthodox Church has used influence to promote official actions that discriminate against religious groups and sects; legislation signed by President Boris Yeltsin in September would impose registration requirements on religious groups, provide significant official discretion in decisions on registration and restrict activities of foreign missionaries.
Ukraine: Activities of non-native religious organizations restricted.
Uzbekistan: Missionary activity and proselytizing are illegal; some tensions arise when churches attempt to convert across ethnic lines, particularly Muslims to Christianity.

Europe

Austria: Non-recognized churches, including some Christian religious organizations, limited in their ability to sponsor U.S. religious workers.
Belgium: Parliamentary commission on sects included several Christian groups within definition, including Seventh-Day Adventists, Mormons, Opus Dei, Quakers, Jehovah's Witnesses and the Amish; commission recommended creation of law enforcement task force and independent center to propose policy for fighting dangers sects said to pose.
Bosnia and Herzegovina: In the Serb-controlled region, abuse of ethnic minorities, including Catholic Croats, has been "tantamount to official policy."
Bulgaria: Discrimination against some non-Orthodox Christian groups increased during 1996: most requests for visas and residence permits for foreign missionaries denied; religious materials and some personal belongings confiscated from several Mormon missionaries; meetings of unregistered groups, including Jehovah's Witness and Word of Life, shut down.
Croatia: Two Orthodox churches were bombed and a Catholic church attacked by a Serb mob during past year.
France: Parliamentary commission studying proposals to regulate sect activity.
Germany: Subsidies for church-affiliated schools limited to major religious groups designated as corporate bodies under public law; privileges denied to some groups, including some Christian groups; Jehovah's Witnesses currently appealing ruling to deny them status as "public body"; Church of Scientology currently appealing decision placing them under observation for a year.
Greece: Greek Orthodox Church established as prevailing religion; non-Orthodox religious groups must obtain permit to operate "houses of prayer."
Romania: Harassment reported by members of some groups, such as Baptists and Greek Catholics, who proselytize in traditionally Orthodox regions; government financial support limited to 15 recognized religions.
Serbia-Montenegro: Government gives preferential treatment, including access to state-run television for major religious events, to Serbian Orthodox Church; religious/ethnic minorities face severe discrimination and harassment.
Turkey: Proselytizing and religious activism by either Islamic extremists or evangelical Christians regarded with suspicion and results sometimes in arrest for disturbing the peace.

'Right' to Proselytize Rejected in Many Countries

In the New Testament, Jesus commands his followers, "Go therefore and make disciples of all nations" (*Matthew 28:16*). For many Christians, this injunction to seek converts — known as the "Great Commission" — forms a central part of their religion. But for many people in other religions and other cultures — in particular, Muslims — Christian proselytism conflicts with their religious beliefs and their political and cultural values.

"We don't want people coming over to us as missionaries and trying to change us," a spokesman at the Saudi Arabian Embassy in Washington says.

Many Islamic countries have laws or policies that either prohibit or discourage proselytism. The policies reflect a tenet of Islamic law — the Shari'a — that makes it an offense, punishable by up to death, for a Muslim to convert out of Islam.

"The whole idea of freedom of religion in the sense of converting into or out of a religion by choice is unknown to Islamic society and to Islam," says Abdullahi An-Na'im, a professor at Emory University Law School in Atlanta.

An-Na'im, a Muslim from Sudan and a longtime human rights advocate, says Islamic countries also oppose proselytism because of its association with Western colonialism and with the current dominance of the United States and the West in world diplomacy.

"It is not a level playing field," An-Na'-im says. "It is not as if Muslims can proselytize effectively in Western societies as Western societies can proselytize in Islamic societies. So the fear is that proselytism will result in a loss of Islamic identity and conversion into a Western way of thinking, of living and of religious beliefs."

Proselytism is central to a number of smaller Christian denominations, such as Mormons and Jehovah's Witnesses. They have run into resistance not only in Islamic countries but also in former communist nations, where established churches have been inhospitable toward the competition for adherents ushered in by the fall of the old regimes. China also codified a ban on proselytism by foreigners as part of its move in 1994 to crack down on non-registered churches.

An-Na'im, author of the 1990 book *Toward an Islamic Reformation: Civil Liberties, Human Rights and International Law*, has publicly advocated recognizing a right to convert away from Islam. But he says the current U.S. campaign against religious persecution is hindering efforts toward that goal among reform-minded Muslims.

Instead of pushing unilateral sanctions, An-Na'im says U.S. critics of Islamic policies should work through the United Nations. Specifically, he calls for a treaty to make binding the provisions of the declaration on religious freedom approved by the U.N. General Assembly in 1981.

"Any effort that presents proselytism as a Western project or fails to acknowledge the history and the disparity in power relations is counterproductive," An-Na'im says. "It plays into the hands of the extremists and undermines the moderates."

Continued from p. 1018

provision added to the constitution in 1976 — and still in force — prohibits any religious belief "opposed to the revolution." [18]

The collapse of the Soviet Union and the communist governments in Eastern Europe generally loosened the strictures on religion in those countries. In Russia, however, the Orthodox Church is now seeking to regain its pre-communist primacy with legislation that limits activities of other religions (*see p. 1026*). Meanwhile, China, North Korea and Vietnam continue to assert strong state controls over religion. In Cuba, however, Castro has somewhat relaxed restrictions on the Catholic Church and, most significantly, agreed to a papal visit scheduled for January. [19]

Islamic Resurgence

The West has historically viewed Islam with suspicion, if not hostility. Christian kings in Europe led two centuries of Crusades under the guise of protecting "the Holy Land" from Muslim "infidels" (1095-1291). The defeat of the Turks outside the gates of Vienna in 1683 was celebrated as a victory not only for the Hapsburg Empire but also for all of Christendom.

Experts sympathetic to Islam insist that its image as a religion intolerant of other faiths is undeserved as a matter of doctrine and history. The Koran records that the Prophet Mohammed bestowed tolerance on Christians. [20] And Georgetown's Esposito says that in contrast to the Christianity of the Middle Ages, Islam developed a notion of "the protected people," which enabled Muslims under Islamic law to permit other religious communities to practice their faiths. [21]

Other experts, however, say that religious pluralism never won full acceptance within Islam. "Historically, Islam has featured its centralized, more authoritarian expressions," says the Institute for Peace's Little.

In the 20th century, a militant strain of Islam emerged that reciprocated the centuries of hostility Christianity had directed toward it. Muslims resented both the legacy of Western colonialism and what many regarded as the cultural and spiritual decadence of the predominantly Christian West. The founding of Israel in 1948 created a deep schism between Jews and Arabs who, at other times, had lived together in the Middle East in relative harmony.

Islamic militancy was forming as early as the 1930s and growing by the 1950s. But it had achieved only limited visibility or impact outside Muslim lands until the Iranian Revolution of 1979, which toppled the pro-Western government of Shah Mohammed Reza Pahlavi and brought to power a militantly Islamic regime headed by the Ayatollah Ruhollah Khomeini. Over the next two decades, Iran served as a model for Muslims in other countries who wanted to fuse religious and political power and use civil authority to enforce Islamic law, the Shari'a.[22]

These militant movements gained power in some countries — notably, Afghanistan and Sudan. Elsewhere, they won sufficient support to challenge more moderate regimes — for example, in Algeria and Pakistan. Even Saudi Arabia's securely established monarchy appears to have tightened Islamic practices to deflect challenges from more militant elements. And Egypt's moderate government has also been under pressure from Islamic militants to limit the role of the country's Christians.

Legal restrictions on religion range from the prohibitions in many countries on conversion from Islam and on proselytization by non-Muslims to Saudi Arabia's broad ban on any form of non-Islamic worship in the country — justified on the ground that the entire country is sacred ground for Muslims. In Pakistan, a 1986 anti-blasphemy law prescribes imprisonment or death for anyone who "defiles the name" of the Prophet Mohammed. Western critics say the law gives license to what one expert called "a reign of private terror" against Pakistani Christians.[23]

Private terror also stalks Christians in Algeria and Egypt. In Egypt, members of the country's sizable Coptic Christian minority are frequent victims of violent attacks. In Algeria, the insurgent Armed Islamic Group (GIA) declared its intention in 1994 to eliminate Christians and Jews from the country. Seven Catholic monks were kidnapped and killed by members of the GIA in 1996.[24]

The most severe persecution, however, has come in Sudan. In his account, Marshall concedes that the civil war between the mostly Arab north and the predominantly black south has political and racial elements. But he says that National Islamic Front leader Hassan Turabi has turned the conflict into one of genocide against non-Muslims. Citing reports by the United Nations special rapporteur on Sudan, Marshall says the campaign has included forced conversions, requiring Islamization for access to food, abandonment of people in the desert without food or water, kidnapping of children, enslavement, torture and rape.[25]

Western critics insist that the Muslim militants are misinterpreting Islamic doctrine — applying the Shari'a in ways that contradict both the Koran and historical practice. And, as Little points out, Islamic militancy is not all-pervasive in the Muslim world. "Islam is very multi-faceted, very diverse," he says.

Still, even experts sympathetic to Islam cannot deny the horrors that are being wrought in its name. "There is no doubt that within Muslim countries, as within countries of other religions and cultures, persecution is taking place," Esposito says. "That should be taken very seriously. Nobody should underestimate it."

Voices Crying Out

A dozen years ago, Christian and Jewish groups joined with the State Department in sponsoring a major conference in Washington on religious persecution. President Ronald Reagan capped the two-day conference April 15-16, 1985, with a speech that implicitly criticized mainline Protestant, Catholic and Jewish organizations for doing too little to "remember the members of their flock" suffering persecution in other countries.

Even with Reagan's participation, however, the conference drew only limited news coverage and no sustained follow-up.[26] "Against the bigger East-West conflict, the religious human rights issue paled in significance," recalls Cizik of the National Association of Evangelicals, which cosponsored the gathering with the Institute on Religion and Democracy, the American Jewish Congress and the Anti-Defamation League of B'nai B'rith.

By contrast, the current campaign on behalf of persecuted Christians found more fertile ground as well as a savvier leader. The end of the Cold War freed the energies of anti-communist groups to be rechanneled into other causes. The spread of militant Islam had increased the dangers of religious persecution in some Muslim countries and had also become a major concern among Americans as a geopolitical challenge to the United States. In addition, Christian rescue groups had become more active in other countries.

But without Michael Horowitz, the campaign probably would never have made the leap from low-level concern to focused, nationwide cause. Formerly general counsel of the Office of Management and Budget in the first Reagan administration, Horowitz became aware of the religious persecution issue from an Ethiopian Christian working for Horowitz and his wife as a domestic. The woman said she had been imprisoned and tortured for her preaching; Horowitz, an observant Jew, says he was shocked into action.[27]

Horowitz wrote a strongly worded

attack on persecution of Christians in Muslim countries that appeared in *The Wall Street Journal* in July 1995. [28] It sparked interest, according to Cizik, among some of those who had been working the issue with only limited impact since the 1985 conference. Meetings and discussions during fall 1995 produced a one-day conference on the issue in January 1996 put together by Horowitz and Shea.

Action by Congress and Clinton

Before the conference, Horowitz drafted a statement on persecution of Christians that was issued, with revisions, under the auspices of the evangelicals' group. "We were the only broad organization with no religious right overtones," Cizik explains. The statement included the major features of what was to become the Wolf-Specter bill. A copy was given to *The New York Times,* which ran a story that helped draw a crowd to the session. [29] Along the way, Times columnist A.M. Rosenthal became an invaluable media supporter, writing a dozen columns on the subject over the next year. [30]

In the nearly two years since that time, the movement has galvanized both Congress and the administration into action. Congress moved first, with parallel resolutions approved by the Senate and the House in September 1996 calling on the president to "expand and invigorate the United States' international advocacy" on behalf of persecuted Christians. [31] Clinton himself, who had passed up an invitation to speak to the evangelicals' group in the spring, created the State Department advisory committee on religious freedom. [32]

Then last July, the administration — acting under a congressional directive — issued the first ever global human rights report directed solely at issues of religious liberty. "Promoting religious freedom around the world is a key part of our human rights policy," Clinton said in a statement accompanying the release of the report.

Horowitz is among those who give the administration only grudging praise for the report. "They spelled out some facts that they could barely avoid spelling out," Horowitz says. He complains that some of the reports — for example, on Egypt, a key U.S. ally — were "politically doctored" to soften their impact. Still, Horowitz concludes, "What comes out of the report is undeniable facts about eight to 10 regimes that for all the sugar-coating make clear that you have widespread and ongoing persecution of some communities." ■

CURRENT SITUATION

Targeting China

Inside the White House, President Clinton was meeting with the leader of the world's largest country and fastest-growing economy: Chinese President Jiang Zemin. U.S. business and opinion leaders viewed the Oct. 28-29 summit as a necessary step toward "engaging" China on a range of economic, diplomatic and military issues. [33] But in Lafayette Park just across the street, several hundred demonstrators wanted to talk about just one thing: human rights.

The protesters at the Oct. 29 rally focused primarily on Tibet, the once independent, predominantly Buddhist region that China now rules as a semi-autonomous province. Many carried placards bearing pictures of the Dalai Lama, Tibet's political and spiritual leader and winner of the Nobel Peace Prize.

"You know, that's totally illegal in Tibet," actor Richard Gere, a prominent spokesman for the free Tibet movement, tells the crowd. "[You] can be imprisoned just for carrying his picture."

A few speakers later, Rep. Wolf challenges the crowd to continue protesting religious repression in China. "We must speak out for the Catholic bishops and priests who are in Chinese prison for their faith," he says. "We must speak out for the Protestant pastors and leaders of house churches. We must speak out for the Buddhist monks and nuns who are being tortured in prison and forced into exile. We must speak out for the Muslims being persecuted in the northwest portion of China."

The effect of the protests on Chinese policies is unclear. Leaders of the current campaign against religious persecution were generally downbeat after Jiang's visit. "I heard nothing from the Chinese president," Shea says. "It really shows that the United States is engaged in a monologue."

Some other experts and advocates, however, see some signs of modest change. "The Chinese government has shown itself to be at least minimally responsive to criticism of its religious persecution," says Roth of Human Rights Watch, "because it has tried to use more subtle means to suppress the independent church. The persecution of Christians has changed to some extent, with more emphasis on low-level harassment and short-term detention rather than the more severe abuses."

Chinese actions in the months leading up to the summit were ambiguous. In September, the religious news service Compass Direct reported that Xu Yongze, a Protestant leader of China's underground churches, had been sentenced to 10 years in a labor camp following his arrest in March on charges of "dis-

Continued on p. 1026

At Issue:

Should the United States impose sanctions on countries responsible for religious persecution?

yes

Nina Shea
Director, Center for Religious Freedom, Freedom House

The October summit with China's President Jiang Zemin made it amply clear that the "dialogue" on religious freedom with one of the world's leading exponents of persecution has become a U.S. "monologue." Calibrated sanctions are needed to prompt reforms in accordance with international standards and America's deepest-held values.

Not only did China yield few human rights "concessions," but in an exquisitely symmetrical gesture of contempt on the eve of the summit, Beijing sentenced China's most important underground Protestant pastor to one of the stiffest labor camp terms for his Christian activities and locked up the leading Catholic bishop of the most prominent pro-Vatican diocese. A long-term human rights strategy that includes sanctions is the only way to ensure that concern for religious freedom is given a place in U.S. foreign policy. Without the threat of sanctions, we simply do not have a viable human rights policy.

The sanctions debate has often been falsely framed as all or nothing — a blanket trade cut-off or economic embargo. Such extreme measures were effective in promoting the collapse of the Soviet Union and forcing South Africa to dismantle apartheid. But they would be counterproductive in countries like China and Vietnam, where it is in freedom's interest to strengthen the private sector. Or in Saudi Arabia, Pakistan and Egypt, where U.S. strategic interests would be harmed.

The Clinton administration needs a plan for a range of sanctions, both diplomatic and economic. In some cases it may be best to bar foreign aid and multinational loans. In Haiti, the U.S. canceled the visas and froze the bank accounts of influential elites; this might be appropriate, for example, to protest the beheading of Christians by Saudi Arabia.

Clearly, the United States should not confer the prestige of state dinners and the honor of 21-gun salutes on gross violators of religious freedom — as was done for China's head of state, despite the government's year-long, widely acknowledged religious crackdown. At the very least, China's security forces should be banned from selling goods and services in the U.S. The People's Liberation Army is among China's instruments of repression against religious believers: Why fatten them through commercial dealings?

The United States should enlist the support of its allies for sanctions, but as the world's sole superpower it must show leadership and be willing to be the first to act. It goes to the heart of our self-definition as a nation to have a serious human rights policy.

no

Frank D. Kittredge
President, National Foreign Trade Council

The Freedom from Religious Persecution Act is designed to force the automatic imposition of unilateral sanctions by the United States, whether or not they will promote religious freedom or harm U.S. strategic interests. In fact, unilateral sanctions rarely achieve their intended goals and always end up hurting American interests.

Studies conducted by the Institute for International Economics have found that U.S. unilateral sanctions had "positive" outcomes in fewer than 20 percent of cases in the 1970s and '80s.

Ironically, the Wolf-Specter bill could lead to more persecution of religious minorities by triggering a backlash against American efforts to promote religious freedom. Moreover, the bill's vague definition of religious persecution could require the imposition of sanctions on longstanding U.S. allies, such as Egypt, Germany, Great Britain, Greece, Israel, Mexico, Saudi Arabia and Turkey.

Despite good intentions, the Wolf-Specter bill is simply another example of using unilateral sanctions when they are the wrong tool. The United States can best champion respect for religious tolerance through leadership, diplomacy and engagement.

The Rev. Albert M. Pennybacker
Associate general secretary for public policy, National Council of Churches of Christ in the U.S.A.

Impose sanctions? Only as a last resort. And then, with multilateral support.

We are not opposed to sanctions when other methods of amelioration and redress have failed. But the mind that wants to move quickly to muscle is religiously suspect.

Many steps short of sanctions can be pursued if the goal is a lasting amelioration of human suffering. We can work to develop new understanding between hostile camps and address such issues as poverty, social deprivation, economic exploitation and group displacement that feed religious conflict.

In addressing religious persecution, listening to the voices of the victims is critical. Thus, we believe any automatic imposition of sanctions is wrong. Reliance on sanctions primarily or alone is wrong. Using sanctions in ways that hurt the persecuted is wrong. The assumption of universal applicability is wrong.

Are we against sanctions? Almost. Scriptural wisdom may be our best guide: "Not by might, nor by power, but by my Spirit, says the Lord" (*Zachariah 4:6*). Our commitment is to a harder path toward freedom from abuse and suffering for all people than sanctions provide.

Continued from p. 1024

rupting public order." Then in early October, Chinese authorities once again arrested Bishop Shu Zhimin, a leader of the underground Catholic Church who has been imprisoned at least five times for more than 20 years, according to the Cardinal Kung Foundation in Stamford, Conn.

U.S. activists among others called for Bishop Shu's release and listed him among a dozen or so Christians being detained in China. China made no announcement of Shu's arrest, but three weeks later he was released.[34]

Impact of Protests on Russia, Islamic Countries

The effect of U.S. pressure — official or unofficial — on religious policies in other countries is also hard to gauge. Last summer, President Clinton and Vice President Al Gore both urged Russian President Boris N. Yeltsin to veto legislation pushed by the Russian Orthodox Church and passed by the Russian Parliament providing for detailed government regulation of newer, less well-established religious groups that have made gains in the country since the dissolution of the Soviet Union in 1991. Yeltsin vetoed the measure on July 22 but then signed an only slightly modified version on Sept. 26.[35]

As for Islamic countries, U.S. influence on religious policies appears to be fairly limited, judging by the State Department's report The report notes U.S. protests of policies in many of the countries, including Sudan, Iran and such U.S. allies as Egypt and Saudi Arabia. But only the most limited effects are cited — for example, some softening of the anti-blasphemy law in Pakistan.

For his part, Saffuri of the American Muslim Council says the current campaign against religious persecution is likely to make Islamic countries even less likely to change their policies because "the approach has been anti-Muslim in tone."

Writing Legislation

When Wolf and Specter introduced their religious persecution legislation in May, passage seemed likely, at least in some form, possibly even this year. The issue had powerful emotional appeal, and the legislation gained the support of the Republican leadership in the House and the Senate as well as the influential Christian Coalition, which declared the bill its top legislative priority for the year.[36]

When Congress went home earlier this month, however, the bill had been drastically revised. And even with the compromises, the bill had not progressed beyond approval by the House International Relations Human Rights Subcommittee.

The original bill called for creation of a new White House Office of Religious Persecution Monitoring, with a director who would determine whether a foreign government carried out, supported or failed to stop specified, serious forms of persecution. Such a determination would have triggered automatic sanctions, including a ban on exports to governmental entities responsible for the persecution, a prohibition on all non-humanitarian aid and U.S. opposition to loans by multilateral development banks or the International Monetary Fund.

The bill initially focused on persecution of Christians, Tibetan Buddhists and Baha'is, and listed 11 countries to be examined: China, Cuba, Laos, North Korea, Vietnam, Egypt, Indonesia, Morocco, Pakistan, Saudi Arabia and Sudan. Stronger sanctions would have been provided against Sudan similar to those imposed against South Africa's apartheid government in the 1980s.

In addition, the measure called for liberalizing asylum procedures for persons fleeing religious persecution. Those provisions would have partly undone immigration law changes sought by the administration and approved by Congress last year.

Despite the bill's seemingly broad support, Assistant Secretary of State Shattuck declared the administration's opposition in a detailed letter and testimony at the House subcommittee's Sept. 9 hearing. Opposition also came from the anti-sanctions trade group USA-Engage, the National Council of Churches and Human Rights Watch.

Even ostensible supporters of the legislation were raising questions. The U.S. Catholic Conference questioned the automatic nature of the sanctions in the original bill. And some Republican lawmakers joined in voicing doubts. "The consequences were not clear when they put it in," said Rep. Doug Bereuter, R-Neb., chairman of the International Relations Subcommittee on Asia and the Pacific.

Wolf insisted to the campaign leaders that the bill be modified in order to try to reach a consensus among Republicans, Democrats and the administration. A new version circulated in early October put the religious persecution office in the State Department and gave the president broad discretion to waive the sanctions provided in the bill. Still, agreement proved elusive, and time to act on the bill ran out as lawmakers turned to more pressing end-of-session bills. Supporters of the legislation had to content themselves with House approval on Nov. 6 of a largely symbolic bill to prohibit the issuance of visas or the use of any U.S. funds for travel by Chinese officials responsible for religious repression.

Wolf tried but failed to get the bill brought directly to the House floor during the final weeks of the session. "We made the necessary changes so that the bill could be supported by members of both parties and by the administration," the nine-term GOP lawmaker says. "Part of [the reason for the failure] was the business community, part of it was the administration not telling the truth about the bill and part of it was we just ran out of time," Wolf adds. He expects House and Senate leaders to bring the measure to a vote next year. "If the bill comes up," he says, "I think it will pass comfortably."

Even without the passage, though, Wolf says the bill already has had a "tremendous impact." "We are hearing from different groups in other countries saying the bill has made a difference in their lives," Wolf says. "It lets them know that people in the United States Congress, people in the government, are speaking out on their behalf." ■

FOR MORE INFORMATION

American Muslim Council, 1212 New York Ave., N.W., Washington, D.C. 20005; (202) 789-2262.

Amnesty International, 322 Eighth Ave., New York, N.Y. 10001; (212) 807-8400.

Center for Religious Freedom, Freedom House, 1319 18th St., N.W., 2nd floor, Washington, D.C. 20036; (202) 296-5101.

Human Rights Watch, 485 Fifth Ave., New York, N.Y. 10017-6104; (212) 972-8400.

Hudson Institute (Michael Horowitz), 1015 18th St., N.W., Suite 300, Washington, D.C. 20036; (202) 223-9200.

Institute on Religion and Democracy, 1521 16th St., N.W., Suite 300, Washington, D.C. 20036; (202) 986-1440.

National Association of Evangelicals, 1023 15th St., N.W., Washington, D.C. 20005; (202) 789-1011.

National Council of Churches, 475 Riverside Dr., New York, N.Y. 10115; (212) 870-2227.

National Conference of Catholic Bishops, 3211 4th St., N.E., Washington, D.C. 20017; (202) 541-3000.

USA*Engage, 1317 F St., N.W., Suite 600, Washington, D.C. 20004; (202) 628-7515 (trade groups opposed to sanctions against countries where persecution occurs).

OUTLOOK

Staying Vigilant

Over the past two months, tens of thousands of Christian churches across the United States held worship services to help mark the second annual International Day of Prayer for the Persecuted Church. Prayer, the organizers say, is the best thing the faithful can do for their fellow believers around the world. But the campaign is also aimed at showing Christians, and others, practical steps that they can take to help.

"This is not just a one-day event," says the Rev. Steve Haas, a Presbyterian minister in Arlington Heights, Ill., who served as U.S. coordinator of the day of prayer. "This is a statement that we're not going to forget these people."

Haas and other activists say that the persecution of Christians has been increasing around the world even as Christianity gains millions of new adherents. "Christianity is growing, and it's growing the greatest in the restricted parts of the world," Haas says. "Totalitarian regimes want to restrict that. It's creating another way of doing things, so it must be either controlled or stopped."

Some religious experts and human rights advocates, however, dispute the notion that Christians are facing increased persecution or are being singled out for repression. "The current media and political attention is driven by factors other than a sudden rise in religious persecution around the world," says Witte at Emory law school.

"There are areas of the world where religious freedom for the most part has blossomed," says Roth of Human Rights Watch. "In most of Latin America, 10 years ago, many Catholic priests were getting shot. Today, there are far greater possibilities for the open practicing of one's faith."

Roth also notes that the crackdowns on religion in countries such as China have failed to prevent an increase in the number of people attempting to exercise their faith. And Little of the Institute of Peace notes that many local governments in China are doing little to carry out the central government's policy of repressing the non-registered churches.

As for Islamic countries, Little expects that the repressive policies advocated by militant Muslims will eventually fall of their own weight. "As these strict Islamic regimes show their true colors, they will lose adherents, lose support," he explains. "There will be elements within these countries who will say, 'We can't abandon the modern world; we've got to liberalize our regimes; we've got to respect human rights.'"

The impact that the United States

can have on these trends is uncertain. Congress will have more time next year to consider sanctions against countries responsible for religious persecution, but passage is still problematic. And, even if enacted, critics maintain that unilateral U.S. sanctions rarely produce much change in the targeted countries. As for the Clinton administration, the State Department advisory panel is widely expected to recommend creating a new office to monitor religious persecution, but it, too, is likely to have only limited impact, at least in the short term.

Advocates on all sides of the issue, however, stress that it calls for sustained, long-term efforts rather than short-term policy prescriptions. "It's an issue we have to engage again and again and again," says the National Council of Churches' Pennybacker. "Part of the nature of religion is that every religious community experiences persecution at some time because of its religious faithfulness."

"I don't think any campaign is going to end religious persecution," Marshall says. "There's not going to be a point five years from now when we can say we ended it. It will be a continuing thing. Abuses will continue, but you can decrease them and you can stay vigilant about decreasing them in the future." ■

Notes

[1] Quotations from internal reports on a visit April 22-May 3, 1996, provided by Christian Solidarity International.

[2] Paul Marshall with Lela Gilbert, *Their Blood Cries Out: The Worldwide Tragedy of Modern Christians Who Are Dying for Their Faith* (1997).

[3] Nina Shea, *In the Lion's Den: A Shocking Account of Persecution and Martyrdom of Christians Today and How We Should Respond* (1997), p. 1. For background, see "Catholic Church in the U.S.," *The CQ Researcher,* Sept. 8, 1995, pp. 777-800.

[4] "The Present Conditions of Religion in China," Oct. 9, 1997. The statement can be found on China's home-page on the World Wide Web (http://www.china—embassy.org).

[5] See Marshall, *op. cit.,* pp. 241-243 (excerpts); Shea, *op. cit.,* pp. 95-102 (complete text).

[6] See Marshall, *op. cit.,* pp. 151-162 (evangelicals), pp. 162-177 (mainline denominations).

[7] *Ibid.,* p. 147.

[8] See Human Rights Watch, "China: State Control of Religion," October 1997. Summaries of this and other reports can be found at http://www.hrw.org.

[9] House International Relations Subcommittee on International Operations and Human Rights, "Worldwide Persecution of Jews," Feb. 27, 1996.

[10] For background, see "Muslims in America," *The CQ Researcher,* April 30, 1993, pp. 361-384.

[11] For a recent overview of the history of anti-Semitism, see Robert S. Wistrich, *Antisemitism: The Longest Hatred* (1991).

[12] For an account of the Bosnian war that emphasizes its religious aspects, see Michael A. Sells, *The Bridge Betrayed: Religion and Genocide in Bosnia,* 1995.

[13] See Marshall, *op. cit.,* pp. 121-123; Jane Ellis, *The Russian Orthodox Church: A Contemporary History* (1986), pp. 3-5; Ariel Cohen, "Russia's Assault on Religious Freedom," *Heritage Foundation Backgrounder,* Sept. 12, 1997 (http://www.heritage.org).

[14] For two recent books on the pope, see Carl Bernstein and Marco Politi, *His Holiness: John Paul II and the Hidden History of Our Time* (1996); Jonathan Kwitny, *Man of the Century: The Life and Times of Pope John Paul II* (1997).

[15] See Matt Forney, "God's Country," *Far Eastern Economic Review,* June 6, 1996, and L. [Laszlo] Ladany, *The Catholic Church in China* (1987).

[16] See Marshall, *op. cit.,* pp. 75-78.

[17] See Marshall, *op. cit.,* pp. 92-96. Marshall says that the leader of the Korean Christian Federation, when interviewed by a British journalist, could not name the first three books of the Bible.

[18] See Center for Religious Freedom, "Cuba: Castro's War on Religion," May 1991.

[19] For background, see *The Washington Post,* Jan. 28, 1997, p. A10 and *The New York Times,* Oct. 31, 1996, p. A5.

[20] See Marshall, *op. cit.,* p. 39.

[21] See also Said Amir Arjomand, "Religious Human Rights and the Principle of Legal Pluralism in the Middle East," in Johan D. Van der Vyver and John Witte Jr. (eds.), *Religious Human Rights in Global Perspective: Legal Perspectives* (1996), pp. 331-347.

[22] For a discussion of the Shari'a, see Bernard Lewis, *The Middle East: A Brief History of the Last 2,000 Years* (1995), pp. 218-243.

[23] See Marshall, *op. cit.,* pp. 32-35; Shea, *op. cit.,* pp. 28-30. Both accounts draw from testimony by David F. Forte, a professor of law at Cleveland State University, before the House International Relations Subcommittee on International Organizations and Human Rights, Feb. 15, 1996.

[24] See State Department, "U.S. Policies in Support of Religious Freedom: Focus on Christians," and Marshall, *op. cit.,* pp. 35-38 (Egypt), pp. 45-47 (Algeria).

[25] Marshall, *op. cit.,* pp. 17-23.

[26] See *The Washington Post,* April 20, 1985, p. G10. Reagan's speech was overshadowed by the controversy over his plan to visit a German cemetery where Nazi SS members were buried. See *The New York Times,* April 17, 1985, p. A1.

[27] For background on Horowitz, see *The Washington Post,* Sept. 30, 1997, p. E1.

[28] Michael Horowitz, "New Intolerance Between Crescent and Cross," *The Wall Street Journal,* July 5, 1995, p. A8.

[29] See *The New York Times,* Jan. 23, 1997, p. A13.

[30] See, for example, Feb. 11, 1997, p. A21; Feb. 14, 1997, p. A37.

[31] The texts of the two resolutions appear in Shea, *op. cit.,* pp. 111-116. The Senate resolution, passed Sept. 17, refers only to persecuted Christians; the House resolution, adopted Sept. 24, refers to "persecuted Christians and other religions."

[32] See *The Washington Post,* Sept. 22, 1996, p. A3; Nov. 13, 1996, p. A13.

[33] For background, see "China After Deng," *The CQ Researcher,* June 13, 1997, pp. 505-528 and "U.S. China Trade," *The CQ Researcher,* April 15, 1994, pp. 313-336.

[34] See *The New York Times,* Oct. 12, 1997, p. A6; *The Washington Post,* Nov. 1, 1997.

[35] See *The New York Times,* Sept. 27, 1997, p. A1; *The Washington Post,* July 23, 1997, p. A1.

[36] For background, see *Congressional Quarterly Weekly Report,* Oct. 25, 1997, p. 2619; *The Washington Post,* Aug. 26, 1997.

Bibliography

Selected Sources Used

Books

Ladany, L. (Laszlo), *The Catholic Church in China,* Freedom House, 1987.
Ladany provides a brief survey of the history of Christianity in China before the Communist revolution and a longer account of the Catholic Church's experience under the Communist government. The book has an index, but no source notes or bibliography. Ladany, who died in the early 1990s, was a Jesuit priest and China expert.

Marshall, Paul, with Lela Gilbert, *Their Blood Cries Out: The Worldwide Tragedy of Modern Christians Who Are Dying for Their Faith,* World Publishing, 1997.
Marshall, a senior fellow at the Institute of Christian Studies in Toronto, Canada, provides a scholarly account of persecution of Christians around the world and a strongly argued critique of alleged indifference about the issue on the part of Western governments, human rights groups, news organizations and churches and religious organizations. The book includes detailed source notes and a six-page list of organizations fighting religious persecution.

Shea, Nina, *In the Lion's Den: A Shocking Account of Persecution and Martyrdom of Christians Today and How We Should Respond,* Broadman & Holman, 1997.
Shea, director of the Center for Religious Freedom at Freedom House, has written a book-length tract on persecution of Christians. The book includes the texts of the National Association of Evangelicals' "Statement of Conscience" of January 1996 and the House and Senate resolutions on persecution of Christians adopted in September 1996.

Tahzib, Bahiyyih G., *Freedom of Religion or Belief: Ensuring Effective International Legal Protection,* Martinus Nijhoff, 1996.
The book traces the development of freedom of religion provisions in international human rights law since the end of World War II. The book includes the texts of many of the principal agreements and a 24-page bibliography.

Van der Vyver, Johan D., and John Witte Jr. (eds.), *Religious Human Rights in Global Perspective: Legal Perspectives;* John Witte Jr. and Johan D. van der Vyver, *Religious Human Rights in Global Perspective: Religious Perspectives,* Martinus Nijhoff, 1996.
Two companion volumes, comprising a total of 38 articles, provide a massive body of well-researched scholarship on religious human right issues. The first of the volumes includes articles on current international human rights law and on religious rights in a number of individual countries and regions. The second volume examines the teachings and practices of Christianity, Judaism and Islam on religious human rights. Each article includes source notes, and each volume includes a detailed bibliography of books and articles cited. Witte is director of the law and religion program, and van der Vyver a professor of international law and human rights, at Emory University.

Articles

Daniszewski, John "Christians Feel Under Seige in the Mideast," *Los Angeles Times,* Aug. 14, 1997.
The article gives an overview of religious freedom concerns of Christians in several countries in the Middle East.

Heilbrunn, Jacob, "Christian Rights," *The New Republic,* July 7, 1997, pp. 19-24.
The article describes the campaign against religious persecution of Christians as "the next big conservative issue."

Reports and Studies

Human Rights Watch, "China: State Control of Religion," October 1997.
The 71-page report says that China continues to violate the right to freedom of religion through the worst forms of persecution.

U.S. House of Representatives, International Relations Subcommittee on International Operations and Human Rights, "Persecution of Christians Worldwide," Feb. 15, 1996.
The one-day hearing included testimony from 12 witnesses, including Nina Shea of the Center for Religious Freedom and other supporters of religious persecution sanctions legislation and from representatives of the National Council of Churches and Amnesty International.

U.S. Department of State, Bureau of Democracy, Human Rights and Labor, "U.S. Policies in Support of Religious Freedom: Focus on Christians," July 22, 1997.
The report, prepared in response to a congressional mandate, provides accounts of restrictions or potential restrictions on religious freedom in 76 countries and U.S. policies toward each of the countries on religious issues. There is also an introduction by Secretary of State Madeleine K. Albright.

The Next Step

Additional information from UMI's Newspaper & Periodical Abstracts™ database

China

Erlanger, Steven, "U.S. Assails China Over Suppression of Religious Life," *The New York Times,* July 22, 1997, p. A1.

In its first comprehensive review of persecution of Christian groups around the world, the United States sharply criticizes China for suppressing religious worship and urges President Boris N. Yeltsin of Russia to veto legislation restricting religious freedom there. The report, which covers 78 countries, concentrates on difficulties faced by Christians but broadens its mandate to address, at least briefly, the persecution faced by others, like Tibetans in China — or the forced conversion to Islam of animists, as well as Christians, in the Sudan.

Faison, Seth, "Group Says China Is Holding Leader of Underground Church," *The New York Times,* Oct. 12, 1997, p. 6.

Supporters of the underground Catholic movement in China said today that the authorities had detained Bishop Su Zhimin, a prominent church leader who has repeatedly defied Government attempts to control religious worship. Joseph Kung of the Cardinal Kung Foundation in Stamford, Conn., a group advocating religious freedom in China , said that Bishop Su was taken into custody on Oct. 8 in Xinji, a town about 200 miles south of Beijing.

Tyler, Patrick E., "Catholics in China: Back to the Underground," *The New York Times,* Jan. 26, 1997, p. 1.

The harsh treatment of Catholics in China dates to the 1950s, when Mao Zedong's Communists expelled the last papal representative and set up the Catholic Patriotic Association, an official church under Communist control that was more a tool of persecution than propagation. Driven underground, the unofficial Catholic Church received a broad mandate from the Vatican to persevere as best it could by ordaining its own bishops and adapting the liturgy to local conditions. When China emerged from the Maoist period, some churches reopened and religious toleration expanded during the 1980's with Beijing seeking to lure more religious believers into the government-supervised religious organizations. But without a reconciliation with the Vatican, millions of Catholics remain underground, where some local governments have tolerated them. Still, they are subject to periodic assaults ordered by central authorities.

Legislation

"Freedom of Religions," *The Washington Post,* Sept. 11, 1997, p. A14.

The Freedom From Religious Persecution Act of 1997, sponsored by Rep. Frank Wolf, R-Va., and Sen. Arlen Specter, R-Pa., would create a new Office of Religious Persecution Monitoring in the White House. The director, subordinate only to the president, would be charged with reporting on abuses against religious minorities. Serious abuses would trigger automatic economic sanctions.

Goodrich, Lawrence J., "Congress Moves to Punish Religious Persecution Worldwide," *The Christian Science Monitor,* Sept. 25, 1997, p. 3.

Moved by stories of Christian women enslaved in Sudan, Buddhist nuns tortured in Tibet and Iranian atrocities against Baha'i, Congress is considering a bill that would impose mandatory U.S. economic sanctions on countries where religious persecution is rampant. The bill, introduced by Rep. Frank Wolf, R-Va., and Sen. Arlen Specter, R-Pa., proposes an Office of Religious Persecution Monitoring in the White House, which would review the human-rights reports of the State Department and other organizations. The office would also recommend economic sanctions against countries where religious persecution occurs.

Holmes, Steven A., "G.O.P. Leaders Back Bill on Religious Persecution," *The New York Times,* Sept. 11, 1997, p. A3.

A coalition of religious groups led by evangelical Christians today won critical support from the Republican leadership in its effort to mandate economic sanctions against any country engaged in religious persecution. The endorsement of the Freedom From Religious Persecution Act by the Senate majority leader, Trent Lott, and Speaker Newt Gingrich gives the bill enough momentum to create a quandary for the White House and its business allies who already complain that American trade is too encumbered.

Slavin, Barbara , "Persecution abroad crosses up Congress Despite good intentions, legislation not shy of critics," *USA Today,* Sept. 19, 1997, p. A14.

All Tsultrim Dolma ever wanted to be was a nun. But the 28-year-old's dream was destroyed when three Chinese policemen raped her on the outskirts of her Buddhist convent in Tibet, ending the chastity required by her religious calling. The Republican-led Congress, responding to such stories and pressure from such powerful organizations as the Christian Coalition, has promised to pass a "Freedom from Religious Persecution Act" this year. But the Clinton administration opposes the effort amid bipartisan concerns that bills introduced by Rep. Frank Wolf, R-Va. and Sen. Arlen Specter, R-Pa., do too little, too much, are superfluous or risk unintended consequences.

Religious Freedom

"All freedoms, not just religious, merit defense," ***USA Today*, Sept. 30, 1997, p. A13.**

In Tibet, Buddhist monks and nuns are often jailed — sometimes tortured, sometimes raped. In Pakistan, violence against Ahmadi Muslims, Hindus, Christians and Zakris continues amid much shoulder-shrugging from the Islamic government. As of midsummer in Iran, four Baha'is were on death row, convicted of apostasy. The list of intolerant nations is long and growing, even among those that should know better. Russia last week enacted a law designed to silence Mormonism and other "non-traditional" religions. Germany this year has taken steps against Scientologists.

Kempster, Norman, "Sanctions Sought to End Religious Persecution," ***The Los Angeles Times*, Sept. 8, 1997, p. A1.**

The stories are distressingly similar and far too richly detailed to be written off as hoaxes. People in Sudan, China, Saudi Arabia, Vietnam, Egypt, North Korea, India, Pakistan, Indonesia and some other countries face starvation, murder, rape, kidnapping, forced conversion and other atrocities, all because of their religious beliefs. This week, the House International Relations Committee is scheduled to hold its first hearing on legislation sponsored by Rep. Frank R. Wolf (R-Va.) and Sen. Arlen Specter (R-Pa.) to establish a White House office to monitor religious persecution.

"Persecution of the spirit," ***Boston Globe*, July 25, 1997, p. A20.**

This week's State Department report on the persecution of Christians around the world performs a useful function insofar as it exposes the oppression of believers under diverse regimes. The act of compiling such a report also expresses the solidarity most Americans feel for people anywhere who are prevented from practicing their religion or injured for praying to their divinity.

Sharn, Lori, and Lee Michael Katz, "Christian groups see victory in 1st report on persecution," ***USA Today*, July 23, 1997, p. A10.**

Throughout the 1990s, Nina Shea has fought to bring worldwide persecution of Christians to the attention of policy-makers and the public. Tuesday, she and evangelical groups saw their campaign bear some fruit. The State Department issued its first report on religious persecution around the world. In 78 countries, the U.S. government found examples of harassment, restrictions on beliefs, or policies that could affect religious practice. The report, as required by Congress, focuses particularly on situations faced by Christians. Much of the information, however, already could be found in other State Department reports on human rights. Critics say the U.S. pledge to work for religious freedom is not backed by sanctions.

Russia

Filipov, David, "Russian parliament OK's law curbing religious activity," ***Boston Globe*, Sept. 25, 1997, p. A25.**

The upper house of parliament yesterday unanimously approved legislation curbing some religious activity in Russia , despite objections from critics that it could signal a return to religious persecution. Human rights groups and leaders of religious minorities argue that the new legislation still contradicts the provision for freedom of religious belief set out in Russia's 1993 constitution. Restrictions contained in the draft, if enforced, could prevent religious groups — including Roman Catholics, Mormons and Protestants — from recruiting members or owning property.

Ford, Peter, "Curb on Religious Freedom In Russia May Rise Again," ***The Christian Science Monitor*, July 24, 1997, p. 6.**

Members of minority faiths in Russia breathed a sigh of relief yesterday, welcoming Boris Yeltsin's veto of a bill that would have sharply curbed their religious freedoms. On Tuesday evening, President Yeltsin vetoed a bill that had been passed overwhelmingly by both houses of parliament, discriminating against non-traditional religious groups and favoring the Russian Orthodox Church. The draft law was strongly backed by the Russian Orthodox Church and the Communist Party, both worried about the growing influence of foreign churches and emerging indigenous denominations. But it aroused widespread international indignation. President Clinton expressed his concern, the U.S. Senate threatened to withhold $200 million in aid and Pope John Paul II urged a veto.

Katz, Lee Michael and Lori Sharn, "U.S. document cites China and Russia," ***USA Today*, July 23, 1997, p. A10.**

China was cited for harassment and imprisonment of Catholics, Protestants, Muslims and Tibetan Buddhists. "The government of China has sought to restrict all actual religious practice to government-authorized religious organizations, a U.S. government report said. As for Russia, the State Department said U.S. officials were concerned about a "restrictive" bill on religious freedom passed by parliament. The bill would make it difficult for religions that are not the major faiths, such as the Russian Orthodox Church, Judaism and Islam, to own property and keep bank accounts. But just as the report was released Tuesday, Russian President Boris Yeltsin eased U.S. concerns by saying he will veto the bill.

"Russia restricts religion," ***Christian Century*, Oct. 8, 1997, p. 864-865.**

On Sept. 24, Russia's controversial bill on freedom of religion was approved by the Federation Council with a unanimous vote. The law has been condemned as discriminatory by Russia's Roman Catholics and Protestants as well as by human rights activists.

Back Issues

Great Research on Current Issues Starts Right Here . . . Recent topics covered by The CQ Researcher are listed below. Before May 1991, reports were published under the name of Editorial Research Reports.

MAY 1996
Russia's Political Future
Marriage and Divorce
Year-Round Schools
Taiwan, China and the U.S.

JUNE 1996
Rethinking NAFTA
First Ladies
Teaching Values
Labor Movement's Future

JULY 1996
Recovered-Memory Debate
Native Americans' Future
Crackdown on Sexual Harassment
Attack on Public Schools

AUGUST 1996
Fighting Over Animal Rights
Privatizing Government Services
Child Labor and Sweatshops
Cleaning Up Hazardous Wastes

SEPTEMBER 1996
Gambling Under Attack
The States and Federalism
Civic Journalism
Reassessing Foreign Aid

OCTOBER 1996
Political Consultants
Insurance Fraud
Rethinking School Integration
Parental Rights

NOVEMBER 1996
Global Warming
Clashing Over Copyright
Consumer Debt
Governing Washington, D.C.

DECEMBER 1996
Welfare, Work and the States
The New Volunteerism
Implementing the Disabilities Act
America's Pampered Pets

JANUARY 1997
Combating Scientific Misconduct
Restructuring the Electric Industry
The New Immigrants
Chemical and Biological Weapons

FEBRUARY 1997
Assisting Refugees
Alternative Medicine's Next Phase
Independent Counsels
Feminism's Future

MARCH 1997
New Air Quality Standards
Alcohol Advertising
Civic Renewal
Educating Gifted Students

APRIL 1997
Declining Crime Rates
The FBI Under Fire
Gender Equity in Sports
Space Program's Future

MAY 1997
The Stock Market
The Cloning Controversy
Expanding NATO
The Future of Libraries

JUNE 1997
FDA Reform
China After Deng
Line-Item Veto
Breast Cancer

JULY 1997
Transportation Policy
Executive Pay
School Choice Debate
Aggressive Driving

AUGUST 1997
Age Discrimination
Banning Land Mines
Children's Television
Evolution vs. Creationism

SEPTEMBER 1997
Caring for the Dying
Mental Health Policy
Mexico's Future
Youth Fitness

OCTOBER 1997
Urban Sprawl in the West
Diversity in the Workplace
Teacher Education
Contingent Work Force

NOVEMBER 1997
Renewable Energy
Artificial Intelligence

Back issues are available for $5.00 (subscribers) or $10.00 (non-subscribers). Quantity discounts apply to orders over ten. To order, call Congressional Quarterly Customer Service at (202) 887-8621.

Binders are available for $18.00. To order call 1-800-638-1710. Please refer to stock number 648.

Future Topics

- ***Abortion: Roe v. Wade at 25***
- ***Whistleblowers***
- ***Cuba After Castro***

THE CQ Researcher

PUBLISHED BY CONGRESSIONAL QUARTERLY INC.

Roe v. Wade at 25

Will the landmark abortion ruling stand?

The campaign to ban a late-term abortion procedure dubbed "partial-birth abortion" has become the focus of the national debate over abortion. Anti-abortion activists say their goal is to outlaw a particularly grisly abortion method. Abortion-rights activists worry that the debate will turn more Americans against abortion and threaten the constitutional right to choose an abortion guaranteed by the Supreme Court in *Roe v. Wade.* In the coming year, proposed partial-birth bans will be hotly debated. In Congress, the Republican majority will attempt to overturn President Clinton's veto of partial-birth bans. In the states, where several bans have been blocked by courts, anti-abortion activists have vowed to continue the fight to reinstate bans.

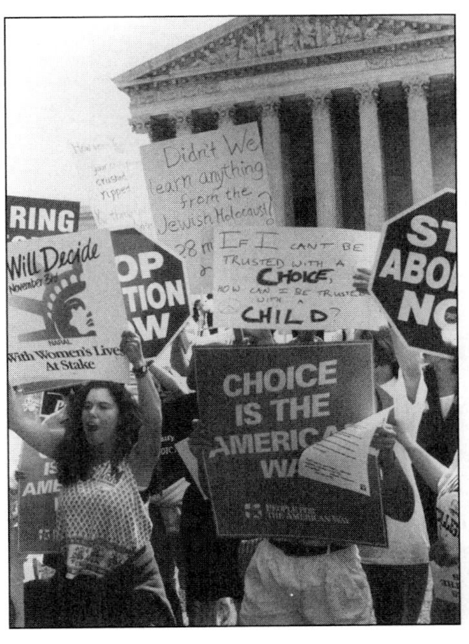

INSIDE THIS ISSUE

CQ Nov. 28, 1997 • Volume 7, No. 44 • Pages 1033-1056

Formerly Editorial Research Reports

COVER: BOTH SIDES IN THE ABORTION DEBATE PROTEST AT THE U.S. SUPREME COURT BEFORE THE LANDMARK *PLANNED PARENTHOOD V. CASEY* DECISION IN 1992. (R. MICHAEL JENKINS)

THE *CQ Researcher*

November 28, 1997
Volume 7, No. 44

EDITOR
Sandra Stencel

MANAGING EDITOR
Thomas J. Colin

ASSOCIATE EDITOR
Sarah M. Magner

STAFF WRITERS
Charles S. Clark
Mary H. Cooper
Kenneth Jost
David Masci

EDITORIAL ASSISTANT
Vanessa E. Furlong

PUBLISHED BY
Congressional Quarterly Inc.

CHAIRMAN
Andrew Barnes

VICE CHAIRMAN
Andrew P. Corty

PRESIDENT AND PUBLISHER
Robert W. Merry

EXECUTIVE EDITOR
David Rapp

The CQ Researcher (ISSN 1056-2036). Formerly Editorial Research Reports. Published weekly, except Jan. 3, May 30, Aug. 29, Oct. 31, by Congressional Quarterly Inc., 1414 22nd St., N.W., Washington, D.C. 20037. Annual subscription rate for libraries, businesses and government is $340. Additional rates furnished upon request. Periodicals postage paid at Washington, D.C., and additional mailing offices. POSTMASTER: Send address changes to The CQ Researcher, 1414 22nd St., N.W., Washington, D.C. 20037.

Roe v. Wade at 25

BY SARAH GLAZER

THE ISSUES

Just two weeks after the Supreme Court legalized abortion in 1973, women flooded into the first abortion clinic to open between Miami and Washington, D.C.

The Orlando, Fla., clinic stayed open seven days a week, 14 hours a day as it struggled to accommodate women from as far as five states away.

"It was like a dam had opened," recalls Susan Hill, who worked as a counselor at the clinic and now runs a chain of eight abortion clinics. "I wondered where the women had gone before. It was incredible."

Roe v. Wade has brought about revolutionary social change in the 25 years since the landmark ruling was handed down. * The deaths that once resulted from abortions, many of them illegal, back-alley procedures, have virtually disappeared. Today, even the poorest women enter Hill's Mississippi clinic confident that they have a legal right to the procedure.

"A first-trimester abortion is now safer than having a shot of penicillin," says Richard Hausknecht, an obstetrician-gynecologist who helped start the first legal abortion clinic in New York City in 1970.

However, *Roe* also spawned the anti-abortion movement, including militant groups like Operation Rescue, which blocked access to clinics around the country. The movement has succeeded in passing laws restricting abortions in many states, throwing up hurdles that affect low-income women and teenagers in particular. [1]

"I think the pro-life movement is stronger than ever at the grass-roots level," says Judie Brown, president of the American Life League, a pro-life group based in Stafford, Va. "There is tremendous strength at the state level. What once might have been viewed as a woman's right is now being questioned seriously."

"In 1967, every state prohibited abortion. We think it would be good social policy to go back to that time," says Douglas Johnson, legislative director of the National Right to Life Committee. "The right to life has a foothold in the Constitution; the right to kill doesn't. We think [*Roe*] is of constitutional clay and ought to fall. And every year demonstrates the horrific human consequences."

Due to the influence of the anti-abortion movement, many abortion-rights advocates say that even with *Roe* in place, much needs to be done. "Things haven't changed a whole hell of a lot since *Roe v. Wade*," says Hausknecht, a professor at Mount Sinai School of Medicine. "Poor women in the U.S. still have trouble getting access to abortions." He cites federal and state bans on Medicaid funding for abortions and private health insurers that won't pay for abortions.

"It's more difficult today for American women to get an abortion than at any time since the freedom to choose was established as a constitutional right," says Kate Michelman, president of the National Abortion and Reproductive Rights Action League (NARAL). "We now have somewhat of a pre-*Roe* state-by-state patchwork of laws," she says. According to NARAL, nearly a quarter of all the states enforce three or more significant restrictions on abortions. (*See chart, p. 1040.*) The mandatory restrictions include:

- waiting periods typically ranging from 24-48 hours before women can receive the procedure;
- counseling stressing the disadvantages of abortions;
- requirements that minors notify their parents or receive their consent before obtaining an abortion; and,
- prohibitions on providing abortions at public facilities. [2]

Michelman says the restrictions often force women to delay their abortions until later in pregnancy, increasing the potential health risks. Mississippi, for example, requires girls under 18 to obtain the written consent of both parents before obtaining an abortion.

"We're seeing an increase of second trimester procedures because young women are delaying telling their parents," says Hill, who opened a clinic in Jackson three years ago.

The number of hospitals and clinics offering abortions decreased in 45 states between 1982 and 1992, according to NARAL. One reason is a steep decline in ob-gyn residency programs that provide training in abortion, says the National Abortion Federation (NAF), which sponsors education programs for abortion providers.

Another reason is harassment of abortion clinics and doctors, which

* The Supreme Court's 7-2 ruling on Jan. 22, 1973, described the right of a Texas woman to terminate her pregnancy as a "fundamental right" and struck down all state laws banning abortion. Abortion was illegal in Texas and the woman, who used the pseudonym Jane Roe, had lacked the money to get a legal abortion elsewhere.

Abortions on the Decline

The number of legal abortions in the United States skyrocketed after the Supreme Court's 1973 Roe v. Wade *decision, then leveled off and declined from 1990 to 1994, the last year for which statistics are available.*

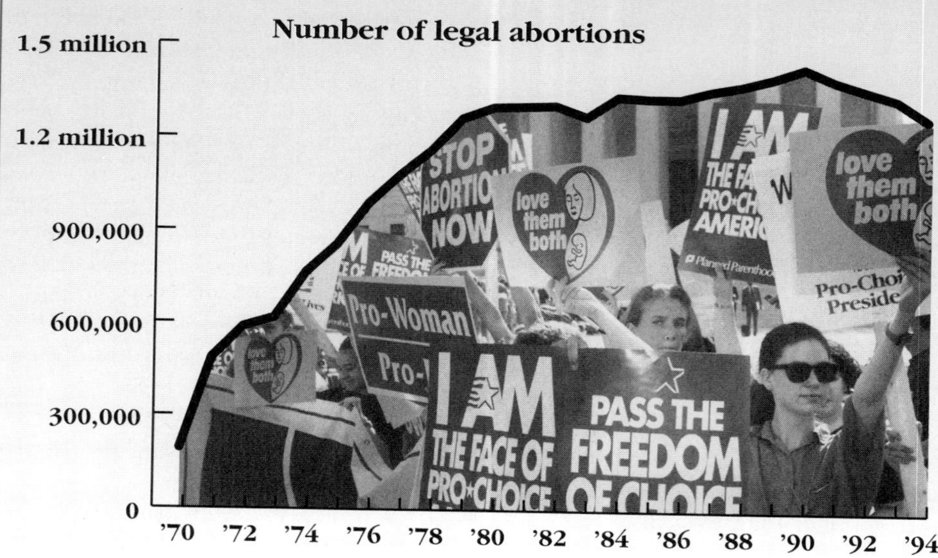

Source: U.S. Centers for Disease Control and Prevention, "Abortion Surveillance: United States, 1993 and 1994," Morbidity and Mortality Weekly Report, *Aug. 8, 1997*

represents an ongoing problem, abortion providers say. "Many women have to travel out of state because abortion providers have declined in number due to intimidation and violence directed at them and their families," Michelman says.

Judging by the number of arrests this year, picketing at clinics by anti-abortion activists and other forms of harassment actually have decreased since anti-abortion demonstrations peaked in the early 1990s. Eleanor Smeal, president of the Feminist Majority Foundation, attributes the decline partly to the passage and tough enforcement of the 1994 Freedom of Access to Clinic Entrances Act (FACE), which imposes new federal fines and prison terms for intimidating patients and workers at abortion clinics.

But it also appears that the form of harassment has shifted to more violent, surreptitious attacks. This year, as of Sept. 17, there have been four bombings and eight arsons, compared with two bombings and three arsons in 1996, according to the NAF. The NAF also reported 462 arrests for harassing calls and hate mail, bomb threats and illegal picketing, compared with the peak of 3,379 arrests in 1992. [3]

The anti-abortion movement has made other political gains since *Roe* in addition to state laws restricting abortions. It has influenced appointments to the Supreme Court and other federal benches and now boasts a majority of anti-abortion members in the Senate as well as the House. The movement is also claiming victory in its campaign to ban an abortion procedure it has dubbed "partial-birth abortion." Although not a medical term, "partial-birth abortion" was coined by anti-abortion activists seeking to outlaw the late-term procedure, "which usually involves the extraction of an intact fetus, feet first, through the birth canal, with all but the head delivered. The physician then forces a sharp instrument into the base of the skull and uses suction to remove the brain." [4]

President Clinton vetoed a congressional ban on partial-birth abortion earlier this year, objecting that it did not contain an exception permitting the procedure if giving birth put the health of the woman at risk. Republicans in Congress have said they will seek to override Clinton's veto next year in time to influence the midterm elections. [5]

Republicans have been debating how to use the issue in a number of races for the House and Senate in 1998, including withholding party funds from candidates who oppose the ban, according to *The New York Times*. [6]

Federal judges have blocked similar state bans in 10 states, generally on the grounds that the legislation is so vaguely worded that it could outlaw some of the most common abortions. Even if Congress overrides Clinton's veto, abortion-rights activists are sure to challenge the federal statute on the grounds that it, too, is vaguely worded and unconstitutional under the standards established by *Roe v. Wade.*

Abortion-rights leaders say the anti-abortion movement seized on a limited ban because public sentiment is strongly against the movement's broader goal of outlawing all abortions. "The fact is that anti-choice extremists realize there is no public support for a constitutional amendment to ban abortion, so they don't even try that," says Gloria Feldt, president of the Planned Parenthood Federation of America (PPF). "Instead they have put forth this legislation that falsely maligns the health record of abortion and tries to make the debate around surgical techniques instead of debating the morality of making choice available to women."

"It's no secret that the Right to Life movement favors the restoration of the rights of unborn children," responds Johnson of the NRLC. But, he adds, "People who thought they agreed with *Roe* recoil in horror at partial-birth abortion. . . . That's one value of this debate — it's educated some segment of the public as to how extreme the law on abortion is today. Most Americans had no idea abortion was legal after 20 weeks, had no idea it was done routinely." (Approximately 1 percent of the 1.5 million abortions performed annually are conducted after 20 weeks, but there are no government statistics on how many of those fit the "partial-birth" definition.).

The partial-birth abortion debate may benefit the anti-abortion movement by picking up swing voters who generally support abortion but believe specific procedures should be outlawed. Since 1975, Gallup polls have shown about 50-60 percent of Americans consistently favoring a middle ground — that abortion should be legal "only under certain circumstances." However, between September 1995 — before the partial-birth abortion debate heated up — and August 1997, the percentage of Americans who thought abortion should be legal under any circumstances dropped from 31 percent to 22 percent. And Gallup polls have shown Americans favoring a law banning partial-birth abortion by growing margins.[7]

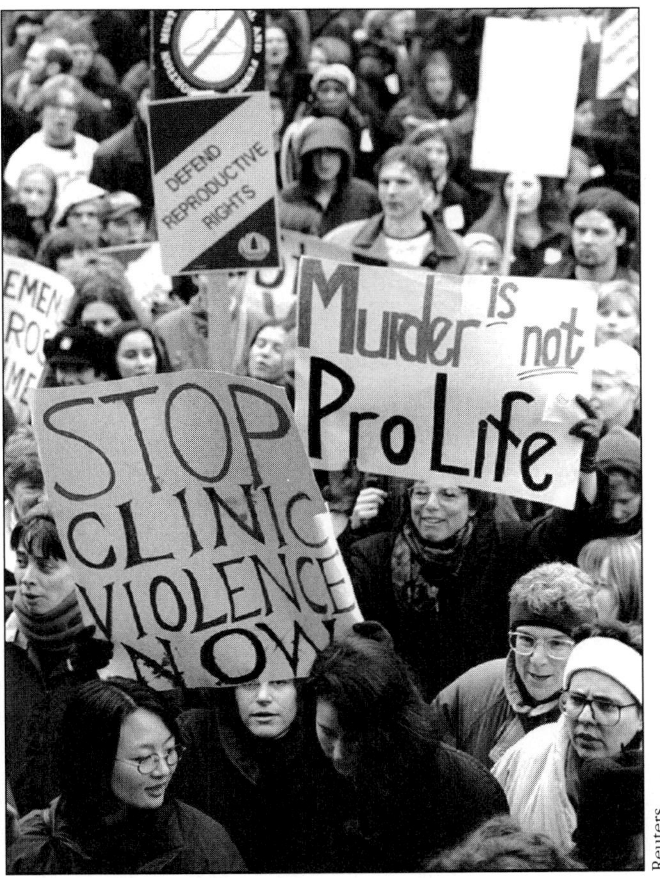

Reuters

Abortion-rights supporters in Boston protest violence at abortion clinics on the 22nd anniversary of Roe v. Wade *in January 1995.*

But a February 1997 poll commissioned by the Republican Coalition for Choice came up with a surprising twist on the debate. A larger proportion of Americans favored the partial-birth ban (41 percent) than opposed it (35 percent). But 82 percent of all the respondents said the decision to use partial-birth abortion is a "medical decision that should be made by a woman, her doctor, her family and her clergy."

"It comes back to who is making the decision," says coalition President Susan R. Cullman. "People say, 'It's an awful procedure. I can't stand it. Get rid of it.' But when you say, 'If you're in this predicament, do you want doctors to give you options?' the answer is, 'Of course.' "[8]

As the 25th anniversary of *Roe v. Wade* approaches, these are some of the issues being debated in state legislatures, Congress and the courts:

Will Roe v. Wade *eventually be overturned?*

Experts on both sides of the abortion issue agree that the right to abortion established by *Roe* is unlikely to be overturned in the foreseeable future.

"Even with a change of personnel on the Supreme Court, it would be questionable whether the court would be willing to take [*Roe*] up again," says Douglas Kmiec, a conservative professor of constitutional law at the University of Notre Dame. "Dissenting members of the court are quite frustrated [with the current situation], but I don't think they will pursue reexamination of the right [to an abortion] any time soon." Kmiec adds, "The court is uneasy with its abor-

Experts Try to Explain Declining Abortion Rate

In 1990, for the first time since the Supreme Court's *Roe v. Wade* decision in 1973, the number of abortions began going down, according to government statistics. [1] And the percentage of pregnancies ending in abortion is also at its lowest point in 13 years. [2]

Experts point to a number of factors to explain the decline. As baby boomers age, they say, the age distribution of the female population is shifting toward the less fertile years.

It is also possible that Americans are getting better at using contraception, notes Lisa M. Koonin, an epidemiologist at the federal Centers for Disease Control and Prevention (CDC). In 1995, she says, only 31 percent of all births were unintended, according to government surveys, compared with more than 40 percent in the 1980s.

As might be expected, abortions increased rapidly after the procedure became legal in 1973. Abortion rates were stable during the 1980s. Since 1990, both birth rates and abortion rates have declined, with abortion rates declining faster.

The concern that most abortions are employed in place of birth control appears to be unfounded, although an abortion often follows a contraceptive failure. A recent study by the Alan Guttmacher Institute in New York found that of women who had abortions in 1994 and 1995, 58 percent were using a contraceptive method in the month they became pregnant, compared with 51 percent in 1987. [3]

Among teenagers, abortions also have been declining since the beginning of the 1990s. However, this recent encouraging development follows a much longer period — between 1972 and 1990 — when the teen pregnancy rate worsened and a growing proportion of pregnancies occurred outside of marriage. The vast majority of teen pregnancies are unintended, and approximately one-third end in abortion, according to the National Campaign to Prevent Teen Pregnancy. [4]

Among African-American teens, the birth rate in 1996 plummeted 21 percent, compared with a 12 percent drop in the birth rate among teens overall. But the explanation does not seem to be that teenagers are getting more abortions. The percentage of live births ending in abortion for 15-to-19-year-olds was the lowest that the CDC has ever recorded for that age group, as reflected in 1994 data, its most recent available. [5]

The recent decreases in the teen birth rates reflect a leveling off of teen sexual activity and a growing number of teens using contraception effectively, according to the pregnancy prevention campaign and government surveys. [6]

Increased use of condoms in an age of heightened awareness about AIDS may be affecting the declining pregnancy and abortion rates, particularly among 18-to-19-year-olds, says Susan Tew of the Guttmacher Institute. "Introduction of new methods of birth control are very effective," she says, pointing to the injectables Norplant and DepoProvera. Approximately 15 percent of 15-to-17-year-olds were using DepoProvera in 1995, according to the institute.

Other factors that could be contributing to declining abortions are dwindling numbers of providers and a shift toward negative social attitudes about abortion, experts say.

Nonetheless, notes Tamara Kreinin, director of state and local affairs for the pregnancy prevention campaign, "U.S. rates of teen pregnancy are still twice as high as Great Britain and 10-15 times that of Japan and the Netherlands." As more unmarried teens give birth and keep their children, she adds, "That's a strong cause for concern because it perpetuates the cycle of poverty."

---

[1] Lisa M. Koonin et al., "Abortion Surveillance — United States, 1993 and 1994," *Morbidity and Mortality Weekly Report*, Aug. 8, 1997, pp. 37-53.

[2] Alan Guttmacher Institute, press release, June 16, 1994.

[3] Stanley K. Henshaw and Kathryn Kost, "Abortion Patients in 1994-1995: Characteristics and Contraceptive Use," *Family Planning Perspectives*, July/August 1996, p. 140.

[4] National Campaign to Prevent Teen Pregnancy, *Whatever Happened to Childhood?*

[5] Sheryl Gay Stolberg, "U.S. Life Expectancy Hits New High," *The New York Times*, Sept. 12, 1997, p. A14.

[6] See Health and Human Services Department news release, May 1, 1997. The percentage of teens who have had sexual intercourse declined for the first time after increasing steadily for more than two decades. The 1995 National Survey of Family Growth found that 50 percent of girls 15-19 had had intercourse, compared with 55 percent in 1990.

---

tion decisions" and "is going to stay silent and let the states work it out through the political process."

Emory Law School historian David J. Garrow, author of a history of the *Roe* decision, is even more emphatic. [9]

"*Roe* will never be overturned," Garrow says. He points to the plurality opinion by Justices Sandra Day O'Connor, Anthony M. Kennedy and David H. Souter in the landmark 1992 case *Planned Parenthood v. Casey* * (*see below*). The court decided the case on a 5-4 vote, but the three moderately conservative justices surprised conventional wisdom by supporting the essential holding of *Roe v. Wade*. Their opinion reaffirmed "the right of a woman to choose to have an abortion" before a fetus can live outside the womb "and to obtain it without undue interference from the State."

Garrow says the opinion in *Casey* was less about abortion than about

* A plurality opinion results when there is not a majority opinion.

the stature of the Supreme Court in standing by its earlier, influential decision. "For the court to consider reversing *Roe* and *Casey* [in the future] would be the equivalent of reversing *Brown v. Board of Education* [outlawing school desegregation.] *Roe's* weight in history is such that it's impregnable," he says.

However, some prominent abortion-rights activists argue that the fundamental right of abortion in *Roe* has been severely undermined by subsequent court decisions, including *Casey,* and by mounting state legislative restrictions.

In *Casey,* the Supreme Court considered the constitutionality of several provisions of a Pennsylvania state statute that have since been widely adopted by other states. The provisions required: "informed-consent" information prescribed by the state (such as information about the gestational age of the fetus and the risks of abortion) to be given the woman by the doctor; a mandatory 24-hour waiting period before undergoing an abortion; and, pregnant girls under 18 to obtain the permission of a court or the consent of one parent. Most controversial of all was a provision that a married woman could not obtain an abortion unless she first signed a statement attesting that she had notified her husband of her intended abortion. (The statute provided a narrow medical emergency exception to the restrictions.)

Unlike *Roe,* which barred states from interfering in virtually all abortions before the fetus was viable, *Casey* said the state could impose restrictions at that stage as long as they did not impose "an undue burden" on the woman seeking the abortion. In the view of Harvard University constitutional law expert Laurence H. Tribe, *Casey* is "a watered-down version of *Roe*" because of the new 'undue burden' standard. *Casey* invalidated Pennsylvania's spousal-notification provision but upheld the other provisions. [10]

"They said you can burden women seeking abortion as long as it's not an 'undue burden' — and we're not sure to this day what that means," says Janet Benshoof, president of the Center for Reproductive Law and Policy. She views *Casey* as "part of a systematic political campaign to undermine *Roe v. Wade* that's been largely successful." She estimates there are now more than 100 state statutes restricting pregnant women and doctors that would not have been constitutional when *Roe* was decided in 1973.

"Over the last 25 years there has been a systematic assault on the right to abortion that weakened judicial resolve," Benshoof says. "The appointments on the Supreme Court for the 12 years of [the Reagan and Bush administrations] have served to weaken reproductive privacy." She points to decisions that said poor women were not entitled to government-funded abortions and that minors can be subject to restrictions on abortion (*see p. 1047*).

But Garrow, who has been studying how federal judges apply the undue burden test, says judges have used *Casey* to bolster abortion rights in some states. In Indiana, he notes for example, lower courts have applied the undue burden test and struck down the requirement that a woman make two in-person visits to an abortion clinic. At the same time, he adds, "What a federal district judge in Indianapolis is willing to do is different from what a federal judge is willing to do in New Orleans."

The Supreme Court is unlikely to resolve these state disparities anytime soon because it appears bent on avoiding abortion cases, Garrow notes. In a recent vote refusing to consider Louisiana's parental consent law, the court continued its five-year record since *Casey* of denying review to any case dealing directly with abortion rights. [11]

Some leaders of the anti-abortion movement say they're confident the Supreme Court will eventually overturn *Roe* because they believe its basis, a constitutional right to privacy, is weak. Helen Alvare, a spokeswoman for the National Conference of Catholic Bishops, thinks it will be at least a decade before the decision is overturned.

"[Regulation of abortion] will be handed back to the states," she predicts. "The social climate is very clearly sending the message that abortion has not been healthy for us. I never thought 20 years ago we would come to a time when people were incredibly worried about the rate of out-of-wedlock pregnancies, unmarried sex, breakdown of the family. I don't think these problems will go away unless one of the fundamental problems is solved — the idea of a right that could allow abortion to be legal."

Kmiec of Notre Dame agrees with some abortion-rights lawyers that "*Roe* has been at least partially overturned by *Casey*" because it "reformulated the right to an abortion from a fundamental interest to one less than fundamental and capable of at least some litigated forms of regulation."

Even the toughest state laws, however, may not have deterred women from getting abortions. Some 19 states call for waiting periods or require doctors to give the pregnant woman prescribed information about abortions, including the risks.

"Most often," says Planned Parenthood's Feldt, such restrictions "make it more expensive, more pain- and shame-filled for women and result in abortions being performed at later dates in pregnancy."

A recent study found that Mississippi's 1992 law requiring abortion counseling followed by a 24-hour waiting period has led to a decline in abortions in the state. But in the year after the law went into effect, Missis-

Continued on p. 1041

Abortion Rights and Restrictions in the States

All but 10 states and the District of Columbia impose at least one restriction on minors' abortions. Public funding for most abortions is provided by 17 states and the District.

States	Mandatory counseling for minors	Parental consent or notification	Mandatory waiting period	Public funding in all or most circumstances
Alabama		✓		
Alaska		✓		✓
Arizona		✓		
Arkansas		✓		
California		✓		✓
Colorado		✓		
Connecticut	✓			✓
Delaware		✓	✓	
District of Columbia				
Florida				
Georgia		✓		
Hawaii				✓
Idaho		✓	✓	✓
Illinois		✓		✓
Indiana		✓	✓	
Iowa		✓		
Kansas	✓	✓	✓	
Kentucky		✓	✓	
Louisiana		✓	✓	
Maine	✓	✓		
Maryland		✓		✓
Massachusetts		✓	✓	✓
Michigan		✓	✓	
Minnesota		✓		✓
Mississippi		✓	✓	
Missouri		✓		
Montana		✓	✓	✓
Nebraska		✓	✓	
Nevada		✓		
New Hampshire				
New Jersey				✓
New Mexico		✓		
New York				✓
North Carolina		✓		
North Dakota		✓	✓	
Ohio		✓	✓	
Oklahoma				
Oregon				✓
Pennsylvania		✓	✓	
Rhode Island		✓		
South Carolina		✓	✓	
South Dakota		✓	✓	
Tennessee		✓	✓	
Texas				
Utah		✓	✓	
Vermont				✓
Virginia		✓		
Washington				✓
West Virginia		✓		✓
Wisconsin		✓	✓	
Wyoming		✓		

Source: National Abortion and Reproductive Rights Action League

Continued from p. 1039

sippi women were more likely to get out-of-state abortions and to have them later in pregnancy, according to a recent study, especially as compared with women in neighboring states without the restriction. Total abortions in Mississippi declined by 16 percent during the year studied, but the researchers found no significant increase in the birth rate, according to the study published in the *Journal of the American Medical Association.* [12] Under the Mississippi law, the physician must describe the medical risks associated with abortion, inform the woman that medical assistance benefits may be available for prenatal care and that the father is liable for child support. In practice, because of the 24-hour waiting period, the law requires women in Mississippi to pay two visits to an abortion provider.

For poor women in some states, mandatory waiting periods often set up a no-win, "Catch-22" situation. Because they have trouble coming up with the money for an abortion, they often delay past the point where the clinic can legally do an abortion. But by then the woman needs a later-term abortion, which costs still more.

"We've seen women sleeping in cars because there's not enough money to get a hotel room," says Hill, describing how some women from the Mississippi Delta cope with coming twice to her Jackson clinic. "It's just a general insult to them that the state thinks they need another 24 hours to think about it."

Would the expanded use of non-surgical abortion defuse the abortion controversy?

Until recently, abortion-rights activists hoped that the drug mifepristone, better known as RU-486, would be widely available in the United States by the end of 1997. However, in June the news media reported that the Hungarian drug company that had agreed to make the pill for U.S. distribution had pulled out of the deal. [13]

In international studies, women who chose the abortion pill said they preferred it over a surgical abortion because it was more private, less invasive and more natural. Abortion with RU-486 has been described as similar to a miscarriage. [14]

The attempt to market the abortion pill domestically has been plagued both by opposition from anti-abortion forces and by business mishaps. American companies have refused to make the pill, citing threats by anti-abortion groups to boycott whatever company makes the pill.

Difficulties in finding a new manufacturer could push back U.S. distribution of the pill by several years, according to a lawsuit filed against the Hungarian manufacturer by Danco Laboratories, the company that was picked to market the pill.

The Population Council, a New York-based nonprofit, was given the patent rights to the pill in 1994 by the French manufacturer, Roussel Uclaf, which cited anti-abortion hostility in the United States as its main reason for not going forward here.

"We need a company that can manufacture steroids in large quantity and pass Food and Drug Administration inspections," says council spokeswoman Sandra Waldman. "A lot of companies able to meet the description are not willing to do it because of the abortion controversy."

Mifepristone, a synthetic steroid, works by blocking the hormone progesterone, which prepares the lining of the uterus for implantation of a fertilized egg. Without progesterone, the lining of the uterus breaks down during menstruation and a fertilized egg attached to the lining is dislodged from the side of the uterus and expelled.

A few days after taking mifepristone, a second drug, misoprostol, is taken in the form of a pill or suppository. It causes the uterus to contract and empty, completing the abortion.

One of the advantages of an abortion induced with a medication like mifepristone is that it can be performed as soon as a pregnancy is confirmed — but usually no later than about seven weeks. By contrast, women usually must wait until they are six or eight weeks pregnant to have a surgical abortion.

Smeal of the Feminist Majority says the ability to use a drug-induced abortion, also known as a medical abortion, very early in pregnancy is one of its major advantages — both for the women using it and for defusing the national debate.

"If the way most abortions are performed is you take a pill and have a heavier period, it changes the whole debate," Smeal says. At such an embryonic stage of pregnancy, Smeal argues, it would be harder for the anti-abortion movement to draw a parallel to "baby-killing" than with surgical abortions, in which a fetus is physically removed.

"It would encourage more early abortions," Smeal says. "It would make more women check [whether they are pregnant] right away. We think half of all abortions would be done this way."

So far, however, anti-abortion demonstrators have not spared drug-induced abortions from their ire. Planned Parenthood clinics participating in clinical trials of another abortion drug, methotrexate, have been specifically targeted by anti-abortion demonstrators, notes Feldt. Eric A. Schaff, an associate professor of daily medicine and pediatrics at the University of Rochester who has conducted clinical trials on both drugs, says his clinics have been picketed "pretty regularly" and that he's been harassed at home.

Smeal predicts a larger number of doctors will offer drug-induced abortions once they can offer them in the privacy of their offices. Some surveys suggest that more doctors would offer abortion if it were available via medication. "You will have so many more facilities that the opposition will no longer have just a few targets," Smeal says. Anti-abortion activists, she adds, know "it will create more access and help defuse the debate."

But anti-abortion activist Alvare says Smeal's prediction of a defused debate is "a wish that will go unfulfilled." She notes that under the current protocol prepared by the Population Council for Food and Drug Administration (FDA) review, an RU-486 abortion would require more visits to the doctor — at least three — than a surgical abortion. "I don't see how that will make it more private," Alvare says. "I don't see how leaving a dead unborn at the clinic makes it a happier situation for women. Women who've had a medical abortion will often say it's a more awful psychological experience."

Similarly, Alvare says, "the idea that you will persuade a bunch more doctors to involve themselves in abortion if you make it medical as opposed to surgical is a pipe dream." She contends the number of doctors performing abortions has been declining because they do not view the procedure as mainstream medicine.

For several years, women's health activists have questioned why women must make multiple visits to a clinic for an abortion pill that was originally touted as a way to make the procedure a private one.

Under the Population Council's protocol, women must make two separate visits to receive medication — one for mifepristone and a subsequent visit to take misoprostol. On the later visit the woman is to remain under observation at the clinic for four hours. The majority of women abort during this four-hour period. A third and usually final visit is to ensure the abortion is complete.

Schaff says the three-visit requirement was designed for "political reasons; it's not necessarily for medical reasons." In a trial of 166 women sponsored by Abortion Rights Mobilization of New York, Schaff demonstrated that women could successfully take a vaginal form of misoprostol at home and complete the abortion there rather than in an office. [15]

According to Waldman, "In order for us to get the rights to [mifepristone] we had to follow the way it was done in France," where women complete the abortion under observation in a clinic. But she notes that after the drug is approved and additional studies like Schaff's have been shown to be successful, doctors could choose to let women take the drug at home.

Because of the long delay in getting mifepristone to market, more attention has been given lately to methotrexate, a medication that has already been approved by the FDA for treating some cancers. Any drug that has FDA approval for a particular use can nonetheless be used to treat other conditions, so doctors can legally use methotrexate "off-label" for abortion in combination with misoprostol; however, it is not very widely administered for abortions, according to Schaff. The drug, given in the form of an injection, works by stopping development of the placenta or the embryo because it prevents cells from dividing and multiplying.

Planned Parenthood is collecting data on 3,000 cases for submission to the FDA and plans to request that the FDA recommend a change in the labeling to indicate that it is safe and effective for early medical abortion. [16]

One of the advantages of methotrexate over mifepristone is that it is effective in aborting early ectopic (outside the uterus) pregnancies. However, with methotrexate an abortion can take significantly longer — up to a week for complete expulsion. In addition, because methotrexate is an anti-cancer agent and theoretically toxic to cells, it could cause multiple side effects, Schaff says. Nevertheless, in studies so far the side effects women complain of are similar to those with mifepristone, such as abdominal cramping and vaginal bleeding. According to Planned Parent-

Reuters/Vidal Medina

Anti-abortion protester confronts abortion supporters behind the White House on the 22nd anniversary of the Roe v. Wade *decision in January 1995.*

hood, more than 3,000 women have used the drug for early abortion in clinical trials and doctors' offices, and there have been no reports of significant side effects or long-term risks.

"It's a good thing methotrexate is available now," Waldman says, "but when mifepristone gets on the market, there won't be real competition."

Would a ban on partial-birth abortion lead to bans on all abortions?

As of October 1997, 17 states had passed bans on "partial-birth abortions." Whether or not Congress upholds President Clinton's veto of the partial-birth abortion ban, the issue will continue to be fought out in state legislatures and in the courts as pro-choice groups challenge the statutes' constitutionality.

In response to court challenges, federal judges have blocked state partial-birth abortion bans either temporarily or permanently in 10 states. "The general thrust [of the rulings] is the statutes are drafted so broadly that it's unclear to doctors what abortions are banned and which are permitted," says Eve Gartner, a staff attorney at the PPF, which has challenged several of the state statutes. "The breadth could encompass the safest and most common methods in the second trimester and unduly interfere with a woman's right to an abortion."

Most of the state bans define partial-birth abortion as an abortion in which the person performing the abortion "partially vaginally delivers a living fetus before killing the fetus and completing delivery."

However, as advocates of the statutory bans readily admit, partial-birth abortion is a political term created by the anti-abortion movement, not a medical term that can be found in a medical textbook or journal. No solid information exists on how often the procedure targeted by the drafters of the statutes is used, but it appears to be performed by only a few doctors. [17]

The movement's interest in the issue originated in 1993 when the NRLC obtained a paper delivered at a 1992 National Abortion Federation meeting, according to Johnson. In that paper Martin Haskell, an Ohio doctor, described an abortion procedure for which he coined the term dilation and extraction, or D&X. (The procedure is also sometimes referred to as Intact D&E, or dilation and evacuation.) As Haskell described it, the procedure involved puncturing the skull of a fetus, suctioning out the contents and removing the fetus intact through the cervix. Haskell said he had performed the procedure more than 700 times, generally for patients 20-26 weeks pregnant. [18]

"If you look at the procedure from an obstetrical point of view, there may be advantages to the woman," says ob-gyn Diana Dell, past president of the American Medical Women's Association (AMWA). "The primary complication when the fetus is not intact is from lacerations to the cervix." The procedure's advantages include less bleeding and tearing, according to the NAF. "This sounds like one guy's way to avoid lacerating the cervix. I think a very small number are performed," Dell says. "For late-term abortions, it's probably a safer procedure."

Under the ban passed by Congress, a physician who performs a partial-birth abortion would be subject to two years in prison and fines. The only exception would be if the procedure were necessary to save the mother's life. The bill permits the father, if married to the woman seeking a partial-birth abortion, to file a civil suit if the abortion is conducted without his consent. Parents of a woman under 18 get the same right.

In May, the American Medical Association (AMA) endorsed the partial-birth abortion ban after the Senate adopted several minor changes. President-elect Nancy Dickey said that the group decided to support the legislation because the changes made it clear "that the accepted abortion procedure known as dilation and evacuation is not covered by the bill." [19]

"If you look at the scientific literature, there's no support for doing this procedure," Dickey says. "Experts will tell you it's virtually never done and there are alternative procedures to it."

In the end, she says, the AMA decided to support the ban with changes because the public found the procedure repugnant, there was no good support for why it was needed and "the legislation appeared to be moving forward."

Abortion-rights lawyer Gartner says, however, that even the revised bill language could cover a wide range of accepted abortion procedures. The ban is opposed by the AMWA and the American College of Obstetricians and Gynecologists (ACOG). In a statement issued on Jan. 12, ACOG said, "An intact D&X may be the best or most appropriate procedure in a particular circumstance to save the life or preserve the health of a woman."

Advocates of the ban say the procedure is conducted anywhere from 20 weeks to full term. NRLC's Johnson argues that under numerous state laws, a baby expelled spontaneously at 20 weeks would be a live birth protected under the law. "This [procedure] is akin to infanticide," he says.

Vicki Saporta, executive director of the NAF, says the ban's advocates have distorted the issue by displaying pictures of perfectly formed, close to full-term infants. In the third trimester, she says, the procedure is "most often used when women discover they have babies that can't survive outside the womb. Over a dozen of these women have come forward to tell their stories. These are very difficult decisions for people to make and decisions that can only be made by these women in consultations with their physicians.

"If you describe any medical procedure in detail to a lay person, they're usually uncomfortable. That doesn't mean the procedure isn't safe or shouldn't be used."

But the AMA's Dickey says that according to abortion doctors the procedure is done with more frequency and in less dire circumstances than groups like NAF suggest. "It is a procedure used for elective abortion in late second and third trimester without any fetal anomalies," she says. [20]

Much of the confusion over the partial-birth abortion ban comes from its frequent description in the news media as a form of "late-term" abortion. In fact, the congressional legislation does not specify when in pregnancy the procedure is performed or is prohibited.

According to lawyers challenging similar bans in state courts, this may be the legislation's greatest constitutional weakness. Under *Roe v. Wade,* the Supreme Court said the state may not interfere in a woman's decision to have an abortion in the first trimester. In the second trimester, the ruling recognizes a state interest in protecting the health of the woman. States can, for example, pass laws requiring that abortions be performed by a doctor or licensed professional.

After the fetus is viable, which *Roe* places approximately at the beginning of the third trimester, the ruling says states can ban abortions, except when they are necessary to protect the life or health of the woman.

A related ruling defined health broadly to include the woman's psychological health. The Supreme Court's 1992 *Casey* ruling said states could impose restrictions on abortions before the fetus is viable as long as they did not impose an "undue burden" on the woman's ability to get an abortion.

Opponents of bans on partial-birth abortions say they would be unconstitutional because they:

• describe the procedure in such vague terms that it could apply to all abortions;

• fail to include an exception for the health of the mother after the fetus is viable;

• ban abortions before viability; and,

• impose an undue burden on women before viability.

"None of the partial-birth abortion statutes in the states or the one passed in Congress has a viability line, and they don't recognize the different constitutional standard" before and after viability, Benshoof says. "They apply throughout pregnancy." According to Benshoof, the anti-abortion movement is focusing on late abortion "as a political campaign and meanwhile drafting statutes that encompass much more. They're trying to eviscerate the concepts of viability and health — both of which are preeminent in *Roe v. Wade.*"

Advocates of the ban contend that the legislation covers a category of person not specifically addressed by *Roe* — those "who are in the process of being born." In its report on the bill, the House Judiciary Committee notes that in *Roe,* the Supreme Court cited a Texas statute prohibiting killing a child during the birth process that had not been challenged. [21]

"This baby is four-fifths across the line of personhood," Johnson argues. "The theory is that partial-birth abortion is completely outside the scope of *Roe v. Wade.*" Adds conservative constitutional lawyer Kmiec, "The category of the partially born has largely escaped the attention of the law."

But Planned Parenthood's Gartner finds that argument weak. "In any abortion procedure, you'll have some part of the fetus out of the uterus before other parts are out, and the fetus will be living at the beginning of the procedure and the procedure itself kills the fetus," she says. "They're defining abortion as birth. I don't think there's any legal or medical support for it."

Michael W. McConnell, a University of Utah law professor opposed to abortion, dismisses the argument that the bans are too vague to cover just one procedure. "The argument that it's vague is just a lawyer's argument," he says. "The terminology is no less precise than for any other procedures." He also thinks the ban would be constitutional for pre-viability abortions because alternative abortion procedures exist. "In the vast majority of cases, it would not put an undue burden on the woman to have this one grisly procedure eliminated," he argues.

In the final analysis, the debate over partial-birth abortion has more significance as a surrogate for the larger abortion debate than as an individual issue.

"You can see it as a chink in the armor of the pro-abortion crowd," McConnell says. "For the first time the American public has become aware of the realities of abortion, and they're horrified and willing to do something about it." But there's also a downside for the anti-abortion movement, he points out. "To distinguish between partial-birth abortions and other abortions is almost to concede the ideology of abortion rights, " he says, because it ratifies the idea that abortion inside the womb "is not an act of grisly violence." ■

BACKGROUND

Road to *Roe v. Wade*

Until 1821, no state had enacted a statute outlawing abortion. Abortion was governed by English common law, which permitted the procedure until "quickening," or the first movement of the fetus.

The earliest abortion laws were aimed at protecting women's health. The first abortion statute, passed in

Continued on p. 1047

Chronology

19th Century

Doctors' campaign leads to laws banning abortion except to save the life of a woman.

1821
First U.S. abortion bill, passed in Connecticut, prohibits inducement of abortion with poison.

1859
American Medical Association (AMA) launches campaign to outlaw abortions, prompting more than 40 state anti-abortion laws.

•

1960s

Support grows for movement to liberalize abortion laws in states.

1967
AMA issues statement favoring liberalization of abortion laws.

•

1970s

Abortion is legalized; Supreme Court strikes down some state restrictions.

1970
Hawaii becomes the first state to repeal its criminal abortion law; New York state passes law legalizing abortion.

Jan. 22, 1973
Supreme Court hands down *Roe v. Wade* ruling, recognizing a woman's right to abortion as a "fundamental right," and striking down all state laws banning abortion.

1976
Supreme Court strikes down provisions of Missouri law giving veto power over abortion to husbands and parents in *Planned Parenthood v. Danforth.*

1977
In *Maher v. Roe,* the Supreme Court upholds Connecticut law permitting state Medicaid assistance only for "medically necessary" abortions.

•

1980s

President Ronald Reagan appoints three new conservative Supreme Court justices, which leads to rulings favorable to state restrictions on abortion.

1980
In *Harris v. McRae,* the Supreme Court upholds the congressional Hyde amendment, denying federal Medicaid funding even for medically necessary abortions.

1983
In *Akron v. Akron Center for Reproductive Choice,* the Supreme Court strikes down an Ohio law requiring a doctor to inform a woman seeking an abortion that a fetus is a human life from moment of conception.

1989
In *Webster v. Reproductive Health Services,* the Supreme Court upholds Missouri bans on the use of public facilities or public employees to perform abortions.

1990s

Supreme Court upholds* Roe *but gives states more leeway to restrict abortions. Anti-abortion forces win congressional victories in efforts to ban "partial-birth abortions," but the bill is vetoed twice by President Clinton

1992
In *Planned Parenthood v. Casey,* the conservative-dominated court rules that states may restrict abortion as long as the regulations do not place an "undue burden" on the woman.

1994
In *Madsen v. Women's Center Inc.,* the Supreme Court says judges can create buffer zones to keep anti-abortion protesters away from abortion clinics.

Dec. 7, 1995
Senate passes its first ban on partial-birth abortions

Sept. 26, 1996
Senate sustains President Clinton's veto of the partial-birth abortion ban.

May 20, 1997
In second attempt, Senate passes ban on partial-birth abortions by a wider margin than in 1995 but three votes short of the two-thirds majority needed to override the president's veto.

Oct. 10, 1997
President Clinton vetoes bill banning partial-birth abortions.

Nov. 19, 1997
A federal appeals court rules that Ohio's ban on certain late-term abortions is unconstitutional.

Group Links Abortion Opponents in Debate

Can abortion-rights and anti-abortion activists reach common ground on the divisive issue of abortion? A national group based in Washington, D.C., Common Ground Network for Life and Choice, thinks so. In a dozen cities around the nation, it has been gathering small groups of activists from opposite sides of the barricades to hold regular discussions about areas of possible agreement.

In a discussion last year, members of the local Washington, D.C., chapter generally agreed that anti-abortion demonstrations at clinics should be non-violent. Participants spoke surprisingly openly about aspects of their own activism that made them uncomfortable. [1]

John Cavanaugh-O'Keefe, a member of the anti-abortion group American Life Federation, described his participation in picketing the home of an abortion doctor. "I really feel mixed about it," he said. "One of the questions for us was, 'Can we pick a time when we know his kids won't be there?'"

Mary Haggerty said she had participated in an Operation Rescue demonstration outside an abortion clinic because "I saw what was going on outside the clinic to be a lesser form of violence than what was going on inside." But she said she became disenchanted with Operation Rescue's approach after demonstrators gave police a hard time.

Liz Joyce, an abortion-rights participant, questioned whether a woman about to enter an abortion clinic would perceive anti-abortion demonstrators who confronted her there as genuinely concerned about her and her ability to bring up a child.

Participants from both factions say one of the benefits of the D.C. discussion group, which meets every other month, is that it breaks down monolithic stereotypes each side has of the other.

Anti-abortion columnist Frederica Mathewes-Green says she joined Common Ground because she was frustrated by the distrust of abortion clinic staffers, whom she approached for information in the course of writing her 1997 book *Real Choices: Listening to Women, Looking for Alternatives to Abortion*.

She points out that anti-abortion members don't always agree on tactics. Of demonstrations outside doctors' homes, Mathewes-Green said, "I couldn't stand that. That sounds awful to me." There are also differences among abortion-rights members. "You see these distinctions and realize these are human beings thinking carefully, not just a faceless organization steam-rolling in one direction," she says.

One of the ground rules for group members, each of whom participates in a one-day mediation training session, is that individuals are not expected to change their minds on the fundamental issues, but are expected to change their stereotypes of people on the other side.

Jillaine Smith, a senior associate at a Washington, D.C., foundation, has marched for abortion rights, written letters, made phone calls and voted on behalf of the "pro-choice" cause. She said she thinks there are too many abortions but is opposed to legislating against them.

"I keep going [to the discussion group] because I really like the dialogue. I'm very moved by the sharing and listening that happens," Smith says. "While it hasn't changed any of my activism or my mind about my stance," Smith says, she's less apt to react angrily when she sees anti-abortion rallies on the news and more likely to be curious about the demonstrators' beliefs.

According to Mary Jacksteit, director of the national Common Ground organization, preventing teen pregnancy and encouraging adoption are two goals both sides tend to share. The organization has produced white papers on both topics.

But some abortion-rights activists fear that Common Ground's efforts will result inevitably in a victory for unyielding anti-abortion forces. Feminist Katha Pollitt charged last year that "When talking together becomes working together, the pro-choice people play a dangerous game, lending support to proposals that are both ineffectual and contrary to their own values." *(See "At Issue, p. 1049.)* She cited the example of the Norfolk, Va., Common Ground chapter, where abortion-rights participants supported a sex education program promoting sexual abstinence. Since abortion opponents also opposed birth control, she charged, the only common ground was an ineffective abstinence-only program, rather than comprehensive sex education. [2]

"We're not trying to arrive at a position or force people behind one another," Jacksteit responds. Pollitt, Jacksteit says, is "incorrect in saying people who see some value in talking about common ground on teen pregnancy will be pushed into abstinence-only." But there may be additional, less controversial approaches to teen pregnancy prevention that both sides can agree upon, Jacksteit suggests, even as each camp pursues different approaches to sex education.

In Buffalo, for example, the Common Ground group supports after-school activities to promote teens' self-esteem, such as supper clubs for Hispanic girls, according to Jacksteit.

While the national political scene remains divisive, Jacksteit says she senses interest among citizens at the local level in working peacefully to solve problems like teen pregnancy. "There's a weariness with the political people and that kind of debate," she says, "and a feeling they're not able to see the issue as anything but simplistic black and white."

[1] Common Ground Network for Life and Choice, "Finding Common Ground," videotape of meeting held Oct. 26, 1996.

[2] Katha Pollitt, "A Dangerous Game on Abortion," *The New York Times*, June 18, 1996, p. A23.

Continued from p. 1044
Connecticut in 1821, prohibited the inducement of abortion through dangerous poisons. By 1840, only eight states had enacted statutory restrictions on abortion.

A 19th-century campaign by U.S. doctors to legitimize their profession and protect the health of women resulted in more than 40 anti-abortion statutes by about 1860. Typically, abortion would be permitted when necessary, in the opinion of a physician, to preserve the life of the woman. Versions of these laws remain on the books in more than 30 states today, Harvard's Tribe estimates. [22]

From the early 20th century to the 1950s, a large number of abortions, particularly for middle-class women, were performed by physicians who interpreted the exception for therapeutic abortions broadly, Tribe notes.

Between 1967 and 1973, 19 states reformed their abortion laws. Professor Mary Ann Glendon, also of Harvard Law School, has argued that even if the Supreme Court had not ruled in *Roe v. Wade* in 1973, abortion would have become freely available at least during the first trimester of pregnancy under most state laws. But Tribe counters that history "undermines this claim." In 1970, New York's law legalizing abortion passed by a razor-thin margin, he notes, and measures to repeal abortion restrictions were defeated in several other states during this period. [23]

By 1973, only four states — New York, Alaska, Hawaii and Washington — guaranteed a woman the right to choose an abortion.

On Jan. 22, 1973, the Supreme Court handed down its *Roe v. Wade* decision. The case involved a Texas woman named Norma McCorvey, who used the pseudonym "Jane Roe" to protect her privacy. Abortion was illegal in Texas, and McCorvey lacked the money to get a legal abortion elsewhere.

The majority opinion written by Justice Harry A. Blackmun described "Roe's" right to decide whether to terminate her pregnancy as a "fundamental right" — part of the constitutional privacy right recognized in previous cases. The 7-2 ruling struck down all state laws banning abortion. Within a few years, abortion death rates were 10 times lower than they had been for illegal abortions.

The decision mobilized abortion opponents, who began trying to overturn the ruling by constitutional amendment or by enacting restrictive laws that limited its impact.

Over the next decade, the court struck down several restrictive, post-*Roe* laws that states had enacted. In 1976, in *Planned Parenthood of Central Missouri v. Danforth,* the court struck down provisions of a Missouri law that required a husband's consent for a first-trimester abortion; required parental consent for unmarried women under 18 to have an abortion; and prohibited use of the most common procedure for performing abortions.

Seven years later, in *Akron Center for Reproductive Choice v. City of Akron,* the court struck down an Ohio law that listed specific information a doctor must give a woman before an abortion, including a statement that a fetus is a human life from the moment of conception.

During the same era, the court upheld a legislative strategy adopted by abortion opponents: bans on use of taxpayers' funds to finance abortions for poor women. In 1977, in *Maher v. Roe,* the Supreme Court upheld a Connecticut law that permitted state Medicaid assistance only for "medically necessary" abortions. Three years later in *Harris v. McRae,* the court upheld a stricter federal provision — the Hyde amendment — that barred federal funding even for medically necessary abortions.

With the election of Ronald Reagan in 1980, the anti-abortion movement gained an important ally. Reagan appointed more than half the members of the federal bench and appointed three new Supreme Court justices considered hostile to Roe — O'Connor, Kennedy and Antonin Scalia — to replace three of Roe's 7 to 2 majority.

The effect of the Reagan appointments was seen in a 1989 decision, *Webster v. Reproductive Health Services.* The 5-4 ruling upheld major provisions of a Missouri abortion law that prohibited the use of public facilities or public employees to perform abortions. The law also required a test of the fetus for fetal viability in the case of a woman as much as 20 weeks pregnant.

With *Webster,* Tribe has written, the constitutional tide turned in favor of state regulation of abortion after years of Supreme Court rulings striking down state restrictions on abortion. [24]

In the term immediately after the *Webster* decision, the court upheld state laws requiring teen-age girls to notify their parents before they got abortions.

Casey *Decision Upholds* Roe, *But Allows Restrictions*

As *Roe v. Wade* neared its 20th anniversary, abortion continued to be a major issue in American elections and in the courts. In 1992, the Bush administration filed a friend of the court brief asking the Supreme Court to overturn *Roe v. Wade* in the case of *Planned Parenthood v. Casey.* But the conservative-dominated court surprised experts by upholding *Roe,* ruling that states may not prohibit abortions performed before the fetus could be viable outside the womb.

But in *Casey* the court also adopted a new, more lenient standard for determining whether individual state restrictions infringe too far on the right to abortion. It abandoned the *Roe* standard, under which virtually all restrictions on abortion through the first two trimesters of a pregnancy were invalid. The plurality in *Casey* said the new standard should be whether the regulation puts an "undue burden" on a woman seeking an abortion.

Using that test, the court upheld all but one of the restrictions under a Pennsylvania law, striking down a provision that a woman must notify her husband before seeking an abortion.

Since *Casey,* the Supreme Court has avoided any cases that turn on the privacy right at issue in *Roe v. Wade.* However in the early 1990s, the court heard three complaints against blockades of clinics by anti-abortion demonstrators. In the most important of the rulings, the court held 6-3 in 1994 in *Madsen v. Women's Center Inc.,* that judges can set up "buffer zones" requiring protesters to keep a minimum distance away from clinics. ■

CURRENT SITUATION

Legislative Initiatives

Abortion-rights groups have faced defeat on several fronts in both Congress and state legislatures. In Congress, according to Michelman, "Since 1995, we've had 76 votes on reproductive rights or related reproductive health issues. We've lost all but 10 of those votes."

Among the congressional defeats cited by NARAL in the current 105th Congress are:

- House and Senate votes to ban access to abortions at overseas military hospitals for servicewomen and military dependents;
- House and Senate votes to ban abortion for women in federal prison.
- A House vote to cut $9 million from federally subsidized family planning clinics.
- House and Senate language to ensure that Medicaid recipients placed in managed-care health plans are covered by the Hyde amendment, which prohibits abortion services to low-income women except in cases of life endangerment, rape or incest.

At the state level, abortion-rights forces are also feeling beleaguered. According to NARAL, 339 bills restricting abortion were introduced in state legislatures in the past year. Currently, 12 states enforce three or more restrictions on abortion access and an additional 13 states enforce two restrictions, according to a report released by NARAL in January.

But some prominent abortion opponents take issue with NARAL's view that such state laws have eroded a woman's constitutional right to abortion. "I wish they were right, but it's utter and complete claptrap," says McConnell at the University of Utah College of Law. "I would say the abortion right is more firmly established today than it was a decade ago."

"I would call [state abortion laws] regulations," rather than restrictions, Alvare concurs. "There isn't much states can do," Alvare argues, because *Roe v. Wade* limited states' ability to ban abortions outright to the third trimester (after viability) and because the courts have defined the health exception to such bans so broadly that it encompasses a woman's psychological health.

Partial-Birth Bans

As of Oct. 6, legislation banning partial-birth abortions had been enacted in 17 states. Court challenges are pending in 11 states. Abortion bans have been defeated in 23 states. In 10 states, the courts have prohibited enforcement of some or all of the laws' provisions, according to NARAL.

In two recent decisions, bans were ruled unenforceable in Michigan and Ohio.

In Ohio, the state's ban on certain late-term abortions — the first such law enacted in the country — was ruled unconstitutional on Nov. 18 by a panel of the 6th U.S. Circuit Court of Appeals. The 2-1 decision upheld a December 1995 ruling by U.S. District Judge Walter H. Rice of Dayton, who said the 1995 law imposed unacceptable burdens on a woman's life, health and right to choose an abortion. A lawsuit challenging the ban had been filed by Haskell, the abortion doctor, and the Women's Medical Professional Corp., which operates abortion clinics in Ohio where Haskell works.

Earlier this year, federal Judge Gerald E. Rosen on July 31 permanently blocked enforcement of Michigan's partial-birth abortion ban. Rosen noted not only that the term was so vague that doctors lacked notice as to what procedures were banned but also that the ban unduly burdened women's ability to obtain abortions.

"Because of the sweeping breadth of the statute, it would operate to eliminate one of the safest post-first trimester abortion procedures," Rosen said, "a procedure which currently is used in more than 85 percent of the post first-trimester abortions performed in Michigan." [25]

"I think there's been a significant contribution to public awareness from the partial-birth abortion ban," says the American Life League's Brown, who nevertheless considers the congressional ban too weak because it makes an exception for the life of the mother. "It's made people stop and think about babies. That has been an uplifting learning experience for people [to un-

Continued on p. 1050

At Issue:

Can abortion-rights and anti-abortion groups reach common ground?

yes

Naomi Wolf
Author of **The Beauty Myth, Fire with Fire** *and* **Promiscuities: The Secret Struggle for Womanhood**

FROM *THE NEW YORK TIMES*, APRIL 3, 1997

From a pro-choice point of view, things look grim. Last month, came accusations that abortion-rights advocates had prevaricated about how frequently "partial birth" or "intact dilation and extraction" abortion is performed. Then the House of Representatives voted overwhelmingly to ban the procedure. The Senate may soon address the issue, but even if it fails to override President Clinton's promised veto, the pro-choice movement is staring at a great symbolic defeat.

This looks like a dark hour for those of us who are pro-choice. But, with a radical shift in language and philosophy, we can turn this moment into a victory for all Americans.

How? First, let us stop shying away from the facts. Pro-lifers have made the most of the "partial-birth" abortion debate to dramatize the gruesome details of late-term abortions. Then they move on to the equally unpleasant details of second-trimester abortions. Thus, pro-lifers have succeeded in making queasy many voters who once thought that they were comfortable with *Roe v. Wade*. . . .

What if we transformed our language to reflect the spiritual perceptions of most Americans? What if we called abortions what many believe it to be: a failure, whether that failure is of technology, social support, education or male and female responsibility? What if we called policies that sustain, tolerate and even guarantee the highest abortion rate of any industrialized nation what they should be called: crimes against women?

The moral of such awful scenes is that a full-fledged campaign for cheap and easily accessible contraception is the best antidote to our shamefully high abortion rate. Use of birth control lowers the likelihood of abortion by 85 percent, according to the Alan Guttmacher Institute. More than half of the unplanned pregnancies occur because no contraception was used. If we asked Americans to send checks to Planned Parenthood to help save hundreds of thousands of women a year from having to face abortions, our support would rise exponentially.

For whatever the millions of pro-lifers think about birth control, abortion surely must be worse. A challenge to pro-choicers to abandon a dogmatic approach must be met with a challenge to pro-lifers to separate from the demagogues in their ranks and join us in a drive to prevent unwanted pregnancies.

no

Katha Pollitt
Author of Reasonable Creatures: Essays on Women and Feminism

FROM *THE NEW YORK TIMES*, JUNE 18, 1996

Can there be a truce in the abortion wars? A lot of people would like to think so. . . . The Common Ground Network for Life and Choice tries to get activists on both sides to lower the decibel level, so that they can work together to [reduce] unwanted pregnancies. . . .

Who can quarrel with civility? . . . But when talking together becomes working together, the pro-choice people play a dangerous game, lending support to proposals that are both ineffectual and contrary to their own values.

Adoption is a big item on the Common Ground agenda: It should be made easier, more respectable, less racially fraught, less expensive. Maybe so. But in its position paper on the subject, Common Ground goes so far as to suggest that states subsidize adoption with family planning funds — hardly a recipe for fewer unwanted pregnancies. Will pro-adoption campaigns result, as Hillary Rodham Clinton claimed in a letter to Common Ground, in "far fewer abortions?" Not likely.

Sex education is another area in which a well-intentioned search for common ground leads, in practice, to pro-life turf. In the chapter of Common Ground in Norfolk, Va., pro-choicers are working with pro-lifers to bring a program called "Better Beginnings" to the local schools. Aimed at 10-to-14-year-olds, it is essentially an advertising campaign to promote sexual abstinence. . . .

This is a laudable goal, but do such programs lower teen-age pregnancy rates? Not according to two respected research groups. . . . So why did pro-choicers, who support education about contraceptives, agree to support an abstinence-only education program? Opponents of abortion rights were also against birth control. Abstinence was common ground. . . . This may look like a coalition politics, but it isn't a coalition when one side simply adopts the other's agenda. Abstinence-based sex education isn't half of an abstinence- and contraception-based sex education. It's a wholly different program, one that denies young people life-saving information in the false belief that knowledge of birth control encourages sex.

Adoption? Abstinence? Abortion as a moral iniquity? Those who support a woman's right to choose have nothing to gain by taking on either the programs or the language of their opponents. It's the pro-lifers who stand to gain. They give up nothing, while looking ever so reasonable and flexible, and their marginal ideas become accepted as mainstream.

FOR MORE INFORMATION

Alan Guttmacher Institute, 120 Wall St., New York, N.Y. 10005; (212) 248-1111. This abortion-rights research group is a good source of statistics and research, much of which is published in its journal *Family Planning Perspectives*.

American Life League, 1179 Courthouse Rd., Stafford, Va. 22554; (540) 659-4171. This Christian group mounts legal challenges to abortion issues and runs a network of pregnancy crisis and child-care centers.

National Abortion Federation, 1755 Massachusetts Ave., N.W., Suite 600, Washington, D.C. 20036; (202) 667-5881. This professional organization representing hospitals, clinics and other abortion providers produces fact sheets on the medical aspects of abortion, offers continuing education to abortion professionals and monitors clinic violence.

National Abortion and Reproductive Rights Action League, 1156 15th St., N.W., Suite 700, Washington, D.C. 20005; (202) 973-3000. NARAL lobbies for abortion-rights legislation and puts out an annual report on state abortion legislation.

National Right to Life Committee, Suite 500, 419 7th St., N.W., Washington, D.C. 20004-2293; (202) 626-8800. The NRLC is the nation's largest anti-abortion group, with 50 state affiliates.

derstand] that a woman expecting a baby is expecting a real baby." ■

OUTLOOK

Joining Forces

Increasingly, some segments of the abortion-rights movement stress that their underlying goal is to prevent unwanted pregnancy through better use of contraception and sex education so that fewer abortions are necessary. NARAL, for example, has been lobbying for increased contraceptive research funding and for legislation requiring private health insurance carriers to cover contraception. The organization is also supporting public education about the use of birth control pills as a morning-after contraceptive.

"I think the common ground where we can join forces is to make it possible for fewer women to have to face a decision on abortion by making abortion less necessary," says NARAL's Michelman. But she says the continuing battles over abortion legislation in the state legislatures and Congress make it tough for her organization to focus their efforts on pregnancy prevention.

"The other side needs to have us re-fight over and over again the ground we win, because that war over abortion enables them to mask their real intent — which is to control reproductive decisions," she maintains.

But the anti-abortion movement's Alvare argues that the women's movement has made a mistake in thinking that a woman's control of her childbearing is the key to her advancement in society.

"When you embrace abortion as a means to that end, you get yourself in trouble," Alvare says. "The women's movement did a disservice to women. Why? Abortion is an ugly, violent thing. People don't want to get cozy with a movement whose primary association is with abortion." Alvare argues that the movement's focus on abortion short-changed advancement for women. "Why have abortion on demand but not flextime, or leave on demand?" she asks. [26]

Although Utah law Professor McConnell sees no prospect of serious challenge to *Roe v. Wade* in the near future, he says, "I'd be very surprised if [*Roe*] is not eliminated 50-100 years from now. It's so deeply inconsistent with the premises of our constitutional system. Our constitutional design protects the most vulnerable among us from violence and discrimination at the hands of the powerful. It is incongruous for the court to hold it unconstitutional for states to extend protection to the most vulnerable people [in the society]."

In a dozen cities around the country, a Washington, D.C., group called Common Ground Network for Life and Choice has been sponsoring discussions between abortion-rights and anti-abortion activists in an effort to find areas of agreement. (*See story, p. 1046.*) "Preventing teen pregnancy is a common concern for pro-choice and pro-life people," says Director Mary Jacksteit. The group has joined with the National Campaign to Prevent Teen Pregnancy to advance their common goals.

But activists in both camps are skeptical that a real middle ground can be reached without serious capitulations on both sides. Michelman points out that many abortion opponents are also opposed to contraception and want sex education to be limited to an abstinence message. Alvare retorts that rising rates of contraception use have had little impact on abortions, noting that 58 percent of abortion users are contraceptive users. She attributes recent abortion declines to "an increased awareness of the social and personal consequence of getting pregnant where you and the man cannot commit to a child. I think people are talking about less sexual intercourse where they couldn't commit to a child together."

Despite recent legislative victories by the anti-abortion movement, abortion-rights activists are confident that women voters will not permit the basic right to an abortion to be abridged. But, the activists note, women have to be convinced that their rights are genuinely threatened.

"In 1980, when [anti-abortion presidential candidate] Reagan ran, *Roe v. Wade* was strongly the law of the land," says Cullman of the Republican Coalition for Choice. By contrast, she argues, in the 1992 presidential election voters perceived that the Supreme Court majority for *Roe* hung by a thread. That's a major reason why President George Bush, who had sought to overturn *Roe,* lost the election, she argues. "It now mattered what a president had to say. People were scared of giving that power to a Republican. I believe it will be very hard for a pro-life candidate to win for president."

Smeal of the Feminist Majority agrees. "There's a latent giant of public opinion on our side. It doesn't get aroused often because most women don't think it's possible to lose. If the right to abortion were threatened, that giant would stir again." ■

Sarah Glazer is a freelance writer in New York who specializes in health and social policy issues.

Notes

[1] For background, see "Abortion Clinic Protests," *The CQ Researcher,* April 7, 1995, pp. 297-320 and "Teenagers and Abortion," *The CQ Researcher,* July 5, 1991, pp. 441-464..

[2] NARAL Foundation, *Who Decides? A State by State Review of Abortion and Reproductive Rights,* 1997.

[3] Annual statistics on clinic violence were kept beginning in 1984.

[4] *American Medical News,* March 3, 1997, p. 2.

[5] Steve Langdon, "Partial Birth" Ban Passes House With Veto-Proof Vote Margin," *CQ Weekly Report,* March 22, 1997, p. 706. The measure passed the House by six votes more than the two-thirds majority needed to override a veto, but the Senate was three votes short of the number needed to override last May.

[6] Steven Greenhouse, "GOP Hope Narrow Focus on Abortion Will Pay," *The New York Times,* Oct. 21, 1997, p. A1.

[7] David W. Moore, "Public Generally Supports a Woman's Right to Abortion," *Gallup Poll News Service,* Aug. 15, 1996.

[8] See Susan R. Cullman, "Late-Term Abortion Debate Miscasts the Issues" (Letters), *The New York Times,* Oct. 25, 1997. The 1,000-person national poll was conducted by American Viewpoint Inc., a Republican pollster.

[9] David J. Garrow, *Liberty and Sexuality: The Right to Privacy and the Making of Roe v. Wade* (1994).

[10] Laurence H. Tribe, *Abortion: The Clash of Absolutes* (1992), p. 243.

[11] The Associated Press, Oct. 20, 1997.

[12] Theodore Joyce et al., "The Impact of Mississippi's Mandatory Delay Law on Abortions and Births," *Journal of the American Medical Association,* Aug. 27, 1997, pp. 653-658.

[13] See John Sullivan, "Another Delay in Store for French Abortion Pill on U.S. Market," *The New York Times,* June 13, 1997, p. A16.

[14] See Beverly Winkoff, " Acceptability of Medical Abortion in Early Pregnancy," *Family Planning Perspectives,* July/August 1995, pp. 142-185.

[15] Eric A. Schaff et al., "Vaginal Misoprostol Administered at Home after Mifepristone (RU 486) for Abortion," *Journal of Family Practice,* April 1997, pp. 353-360.

[16] News release, Sept. 11, 1996.

[17] See David Brown, "Late Term Abortions; Who Gets Them and Why," *The Washington Post Health Section,* Sept. 17, 1996, p. 12. Interviews with abortion doctors suggested that fewer than 20 perform the surgery, Brown reported.

[18] Martin Haskell, "Dilation and Extraction for Late Second Trimester Abortion," Presented at the National Abortion Federation, Sept. 13, 1992.

[19] Mary Agnes Carey, "Foes of Controversial Procedure Boosted by Strong Vote," *CQ Weekly Report,* May 24, 1997, pp. 1196-1198.

[20] See Brown, *op. cit.,* for interviews with doctors who said they use the procedure in this fashion.

[21] House Judiciary Committee, "Partial Birth Abortion Ban Act of 1997, Report 105-23," March 14, 1997, pp. 15-16.

[22] Laurence H. Tribe, *Abortion: The Clash of Absolutes* (1992), p. 30.

[23] *Ibid.,* pp. 49-50.

[24] Tribe, *Ibid.,* p. 24.

[25] The case was *Evans v. Kelly,* July 31, 1997

[26] See "Feminism's Future," *The CQ Researcher,* Feb. 28, 1997, pp. 181-204.

Bibliography

Selected Sources Used

Books

Bender, David, and Bruno Leone, *Abortion: Opposing Viewpoints,* Greenhaven Press, 1997.
This collection of essays by authors with opposing viewpoints looks at such issues as whether abortion is immoral and whether abortion rights should be restricted.

Garrow, David J., *Liberty and Sexuality,* Macmillan, 1994.
Pulitzer Prize-winning historian Garrow provides a detailed chronicle of the personalities involved behind the scenes in the Supreme Court's landmark *Roe v. Wade* decision and related decisions.

Tribe, Laurence H., *Abortion: The Clash of Absolutes,* W.W. Norton, 1992.
Harvard University constitutional lawyer Tribe, who favors abortion rights, provides a historical and legal overview of the abortion issue. He concludes that the Supreme Court's 1992 decision in *Planned Parenthood v. Casey* watered down the *Roe* decision by permitting states new powers to restrict abortion but affirmed a woman's basic right to an abortion.

Articles

Berke, Richard L., "G.O.P. Hopes Narrow Focus on Abortion Will Pay," *The New York Times,* Oct. 21, 1997, p. A1.
Berke discusses the role that the partial-birth abortion ban has been playing in the Republican Party's strategy for congressional elections.

Brown, David, "Late Term Abortions: Who Gets Them and Why," *The Washington Post Health Section,* Sept. 17, 1996, p. 12.
Interviews with doctors who perform late-term abortions reveal that not all such abortions are done for medical reasons. The article quotes doctors who say they perform many late-term abortions for poor, young women who have waited until late in their pregnancy.

Carey, Mary Agnes, "Foes of Controversial Procedure Boosted by Strong Vote," *Congressional Quarterly Weekly Report,* May 24, 1997, pp. 1196-1198.
Carey discusses the politics behind the Senate's May 20 passage of a ban on partial-birth abortions.

Seelye, Katharine Q., "Abortion Vote Signals a Shift in Political Momentum," *The New York Times,* March 23, 1997, p. A30.
Seelye discusses the partial-birth abortion ban in the context of the Right to Life movement's broader anti-abortion strategy.

Sontag, Deborah, "Doctors Say It's Just One Way," *The New York Times,* March 21, 1997.
In interviews, most doctors who perform abortions after 20 weeks say they prefer other methods to the "dilation and extraction" procedure targeted by the congressional ban.

Steinauer, Jody E., et al., "Training Family Practice Residents in Abortion and Other Reproductive Health Care: A Nationwide Survey," *Family Planning Perspectives,* September/October 1997, pp. 222-227.
This 1995 survey found family physicians ill-prepared to provide abortions as only a minority of residency programs in the field provide abortion training. Sixty-five percent of family medicine residents said they "certainly would not provide abortion." The survey found family physicians ill-prepared to provide abortions.

Reports and Studies

Judiciary Committee, U.S. House of Representatives, *Partial-Birth Abortion Ban Act of 1997, Committee Report 105-24,* March 14, 1997.
This report from the committee that wrote the ban on partial-birth abortions presents the arguments for banning the procedure along with dissenting views from 14 committee members opposed to the ban.

National Abortion and Reproductive Rights Action League Foundation, *Who Decides? A State-by-State Review of Abortion and Reproductive Rights* (1997).
This report provides detailed descriptions of state legislation and regulations affecting abortion.

The Next Step

Additional information from UMI's Newspaper & Periodical Abstracts™ database

Abortion-Rights Advocates

Goodman, Ellen, "The real debate on abortion," ***Boston Globe,*** **May 18, 1997, p. C7.**

You cannot hear it in the cacophony of outraged voices arguing about the so-called "partial-birth abortion" ban. But it is there, just under the din. The theme song of the abortion controversy is being repeated, the soundtrack replayed: The Senate debate has not really been about banning an abortion method. It's been about permitting exceptions to that ban. Senators led by Rick Santorum, R-Pa., have refused to allow an exception even to protect the woman from serious harm to her health. President Clinton has refused to sign a bill without it. From the beginning abortion opponents have said that "health" is nothing but a loophole for women who would abort a pregnancy to fit into a prom dress. But abortion-rights supporters have countered with real women whose bodies were at serious risk. Underlying it all has been the issue of women and sacrifice.

Josar, David, "Doctor calls partial-birth abortions 'gory,' but needed," ***Detroit News,*** **May 6, 1997, p. A1.**

Hidden by a blue curtain and identifiable only by his raspy voice, "Dr. Doe" told a Detroit federal judge Monday what it's like to perform thousands of second-trimester abortions. "They're unpleasant and gory. It's destructive surgery," the doctor said. "None of us are pro-abortion. Some may be pro-choice. But they're necessary." U.S. District Judge Gerald Rosen is hearing a challenge to Michigan's ban on partial-birth abortions, brought by two Metro Detroit doctors, two family planning clinics and the American Civil Liberties Union. The law went into effect March 31. Under the law, a partial-birth abortion occurs when a fetus is forced into the birth canal and then "life" is terminated.

Lewin, Tamar, "Group Is Intensifying Its Campaign to Distribute Abortion Pill," ***The New York Times,*** **July 2, 1997, p. A21.**

With the plans to market the French abortion pill in this country in disarray, a tiny New York abortion-rights group is expanding its stopgap effort to make the drug available to American women. Lawrence Lader, the president of Abortion Rights Mobilization, plans to announce today that his group will offer the drug, mifepristone, to as many as 10,000 women seeking to end their pregnancies without a surgical abortion. Last year, the group won the Food and Drug Administration's approval to use its version of the drug in research trials that began in Rochester, N.Y., and that are now under way in Bellevue, Neb., Burlington, Vt., Kalispell, Mont., New York City, San Francisco and Seattle. Since women cannot be charged for drugs used in such research trials, though, it was unclear just how long, and for how many women, the group could afford to provide the drug.

"The New Assault on Abortion," ***The New York Times,*** **May 10, 1997, p. A18.**

The Senate is gearing up for another contentious round on so-called "partial-birth" abortion, the controversial procedure saved from a congressional ban last year by President Clinton's veto. In the meantime, many states have moved to outlaw the procedure on their own. Many of the state laws are as flawed as some of the bills rushing through Congress. They intrude on a woman's right to an abortion using the safest possible method as decided by her and her doctor. Congressional Republicans pushed this same issue last year, hoping to inflict damage on pro-choice Democrats, including President Clinton, during an election year. Both houses voted to ban a specific procedure, technically known as intact dilation and extraction or evacuation, that is used to abort fetuses after 20 weeks of gestation. Mr. Clinton was right to veto the bill as an unwarranted intrusion into the practice of medicine without proper consideration of a woman's health.

Anti-Abortion Activists

"Amend Michigan's Abortion Law," ***Detroit News,*** **Aug. 3, 1997, p. B6.**

Right-to-life advocates are upset at a Detroit federal court ruling that Michigan's 1996 ban on "partial-birth abortion " is unconstitutionally vague and overly broad. The judge in the case, Gerald E. Rosen, is no fan of abortion. Under existing Supreme Court rulings, however, he had little choice but to overturn the Michigan law. Anti-abortion forces should take Judge Rosen's advice and seek to fix the statute legislatively. In his 88-page opinion, Judge Rosen pointed to language in a recent U.S. Senate bill limiting partial-birth abortion in ways that might pass constitutional muster. Pro-life senators adopted the language precisely because of their fears that overly broad efforts to ban partial-birth abortion would be struck down.

Feldmann, Linda, "Abortion Litmus Test Eases for GOP Candidates," ***The Christian Science Monitor,*** **Nov. 7, 1997, p. 3.**

The state's powerful Christian conservatives did not abandon Gov.-elect James Gilmore, R-Va., despite their bedrock belief that abortion at any time is murder. In fact, for the most part, social conservatives continued to play a key role in Gilmore's win, including financial contributions from Christian right leader Pat Robertson. "We wish Gilmore had taken a stronger stand on abortion," says Randy Tate, the new executive director of the Virginia-based Christian Coalition. "But remember, he opposed 'partial-birth' abortion, he opposed funding for abortion and he supports parental notification in abortion." But at root, Gilmore's blurred stand highlights an important new tactic among Republicans trying to appeal to a broad cross-section of their party: Focus on "sub-issues," not on the intractable debate of whether to outlaw abortion. Sub-issues include those outlined by Mr. Tate: late-term abortion, parental notification and state funding.

Koehler, Judith E., "Being Pro-Life Is Good Politics," *Chicago Tribune,* Sept. 19, 1997, p. 26.

In his op-ed column "Illinois politics and abortion" from August 22, Bruce Dold writes that to take the pro-life position is politically "out of step with public sentiment in favor of abortion rights." Predictably, state legislatures enacted a host of reasonable regulatory measures that affected the abortion industry. Indeed, the "public sentiment" to which Dold referred was nowhere to be found in 1997. The abortion proponents' "victories" in the states were limited to a sprinkling of governors' vetoes. In Alaska, where the governor vetoed two measures — requiring parental consent prior to a minor's abortion and a ban on the partial-birth abortion procedure — the legislature overrode both vetoes.

Ryan, Joe, "Antiabortion marchers stress the choice of life," *Boston Globe,* Oct. 6, 1997, p. B6.

Lyn Goodrich, 19, and her newborn son, Nathan, would not have been on the Boston Common yesterday if not for the counseling she received weeks before her scheduled abortion. "I saw an 800 telephone number on television and I called it. I changed my mind about having an abortion," said Goodrich, holding the crying 3-week-old infant. Laurie Letourneau of Shrewsbury walked with Goodrich representing Problem Pregnancy Inc., a center that offers emotional and financial support to pregnant women.

Schremp, Valerie, "Area Residents Make Quiet Stand against Abortion," *St. Louis Post-Dispatch,* Oct. 6, 1997, p. B2.

Bob Kurtz stood on the sidewalk on Hampton Avenue in St. Louis, peering from under a baseball cap and carrying a sign proclaiming: "Abortion Kills Children." Most cars whizzed by. Some honked. For an hour Sunday afternoon, the St. Louisan quietly stood for his beliefs. Kurtz "stood for life" with thousands of other St. Louisans in the hour-long, miles-long Life Chain, a "peaceful, prayerful" protest along city and county streets. More than 300 area churches participated, along with 900 cities around the United States and Canada.

Partial-Birth Abortions

Healy, Melissa, "'Partial-Birth' Abortion Ban Again Passes House," *Los Angeles Times,* March 21, 1997, p. A1.

Abortion foes in the House on Thursday adopted a ban on a controversial late-term abortion procedure for the third time in a year, challenging President Clinton to again veto a bill that he vetoed last April. The 295-136 House vote — with 77 Democrats joining Republicans to pass the bill — is large enough to override another Clinton veto. But it was the Senate that last year failed to muster the necessary two-thirds vote to override the president's veto, and it is in the Senate again that abortion foes face the tougher fight. Senate Majority Leader Trent Lott, R-Miss., acknowledged Thursday that, while the measure almost certainly will pass in the Senate, it is not likely now to do so by the margin needed to override a veto. But Lott said he is hopeful that growing public awareness of the bid to outlaw the late-term abortion procedure would increase the pressure on some senators to switch sides and back the bill.

Pear, Robert, "G.O.P. Delays Vote on Surgeon General Over Abortion Question," *The New York Times,* Nov. 10, 1997, p. A22.

Republicans said tonight that they were holding up confirmation of President Clinton's nominee for surgeon general of the United States, David Satcher, because they had concerns that he was not sufficiently opposed to certain types of late-term abortion. Satcher is now director of the Centers for Disease Control and Prevention. His nomination was initially received well on Capitol Hill, and he has been endorsed by the American Medical Association. Satcher, a former president of Meharry Medical College in Nashville, said he did not support the late-term abortion procedure in which a doctor partially extracts a fetus from the womb. But he said that, like President Clinton, he would support a ban on such "partial-birth abortions" only if it made an exception for cases in which the procedure might be needed to protect the life or health of a pregnant woman.

Sahurie, Emilio, "Rally marks first day of 'partial-birth' abortion law," *Atlanta Constitution,* July 2, 1997, p. B5.

Undaunted by early morning rain that streaked their protest signs, abortion opponents marched in front of Midtown Hospital to commemorate the first day of a Georgia abortion law that went into effect Tuesday. U.S. District Judge J. Owen Forrester last week ruled that the law can only be enforced against doctors who perform the so-called "partial-birth" abortions when the fetus could otherwise survive outside the mother's womb. The temporary restraining order is part of a lawsuit filed by abortion rights advocates and will remain in place until the judge rules again on the case. Tuesday, about 40 opponents and 25 supporters of abortion rights gathered in front of Midtown Hospital for about two hours.

Tobin, James, "Clinics hail latest ruling on partial-birth abortions," *Detroit News,* Aug. 1, 1997, p. A4.
Thursday's ruling against Michigan's ban on partial-birth abortions amounted to a symbolic but small victory for those who provide the service. It doesn't mean much in practical terms, since no one has been doing partial-birth abortions in Michigan anyway. It didn't have enormous national impact, since other states have already gone down this road — banning partial-birth abortions, then having the bans overturned. "We couldn't possibly know which procedures were covered under this law and which weren't because the law was worded so vaguely," said Renee Chelian, owner of Northland Family Planning Clinics, Metro Detroit's biggest abortion provider. "We felt the doctors would be living under fear of criminal prosecution and not even know if they were breaking the law."

Roe v. Wade

Farrell, John Aloysius, "Court upholds status quo on abortion laws In separate cases, late procedures approved; doctors' role reinforced," *Boston Globe,* June 17, 1997, p. A3.
The Supreme Court rebuffed legal challenges from both sides of the abortion issue yesterday, preserving the right to late-term abortions in one ruling while allowing states to require that only physicians perform the procedure in another case. The rulings reinforce the legal status quo regarding abortion, which dates back to the landmark *Roe v. Wade* decision in 1973 establishing the right to abortion, and shows the court's unwillingness to revise the law governing the procedure. On the abortion cases, the court declined to rescue a Utah law that banned most abortions during the last 20 weeks of pregnancy. Congress has been debating legislation to ban a type of late-term abortion

Hughes, Polly Ross, "75th Legislature/Abortion bill believed dead in House," *Houston Chronicle,* May 27, 1997, p. A1.
A bill requiring that parents be notified when their minor daughters seek abortions was believed dead late Monday, and a conservative lawmaker, angered over its likely demise, killed dozens of other bills. Frustrated House members adjourned amid a widening rift between liberals and conservatives over the emotional issue of abortion. It was Rep. Arlene Wohlgemuth, R-Burleson, who raised a technical objection that blocked further consideration of Senate measures pending in the House.

"Opponents, Backers of Abortion Mark Anniversary of Case Both Sides Tout Cause in Washington; Foes March to White House, High Court," *St. Louis Post-Dispatch,* Jan. 23, 1997, p. A1.
The 24th anniversary of the Supreme Court's landmark decision legalizing abortion was marked Wednesday by protest, and condemnation of anti-abortion terrorism by Vice President Al Gore. Days after bombings at family planning clinics in Atlanta and in Tulsa, Okla., Gore said those responsible would be punished "to the fullest extent of the law." As Gore and Hillary Rodham Clinton spoke to the National Abortion and Reproductive Rights Action League, tens of thousands of abortion opponents rallied near the White House and then marched to the Supreme Court to protest the court's *Roe v. Wade* decision of 1973.

Pasternak, Judy, "Drug Use Spurs Court Test of Fetal Custody," *Los Angeles Times,* Feb. 2, 1997, p. A1.
The mother-to-be was using cocaine, drugging the developing baby within. The local social services agency asked a juvenile court judge to place the fetus in Waukesha Memorial Hospital. The judge issued a detention order to the Waukesha County sheriff. What happened to Angela M.W. in September 1995, is a logical extension of the famous case of *Roe v. Wade,* maintains the county's attorney, Assistant Corporation Counsel William J. Domina. The National Assn. of Counsel for Children and the prosecutor in neighboring Milwaukee County weighed in with legal briefs in support of recognizing the juvenile court's authority over babies-to-be. Eleven health, women's and children's organizations banded together to argue against seizing fetuses and depriving pregnant women of their liberty. They say the *Roe v. Wade* decision applies only to the power to restrict abortion.

Rosen, Jeffrey, "Nine Votes for Judicial Restraint," *The New York Times,* June 29, 1997, p. 15.
Constitutional changes occur so slowly that it's often hard to discern precisely when the terms of the intellectual debate have shifted. In this sense, last week's Supreme Court decisions on doctor-assisted suicide were most notable for their lack of drama. But the court's unanimity marks the end of a political and legal battle that began after *Roe v. Wade.*

Stolberg, Sheryl Gay, "Senate Tries to Define Fetal Viability," *The New York Times,* May 16, 1997, p. A18.
From the moment in 1973 that it made abortion legal, giving states authority to restrict the procedure only if a fetus could live outside the womb, the U.S. Supreme Court created a doctrine that Justice Sandra Day O'Connor would later describe as "at war with itself." Obstetricians and pediatricians say it is impossible to draw a line between viability and non-viability. Too many factors — the health and socioeconomic status of the mother, her access to medical care, the weight of the fetus and the maturity of its organs — come into play.

Back Issues

Great Research on Current Issues Starts Right Here . . . Recent topics covered by The CQ Researcher are listed below. Before May 1991, reports were published under the name of Editorial Research Reports.

MAY 1996
Russia's Political Future
Marriage and Divorce
Year-Round Schools
Taiwan, China and the U.S.

JUNE 1996
Rethinking NAFTA
First Ladies
Teaching Values
Labor Movement's Future

JULY 1996
Recovered-Memory Debate
Native Americans' Future
Crackdown on Sexual Harassment
Attack on Public Schools

AUGUST 1996
Fighting Over Animal Rights
Privatizing Government Services
Child Labor and Sweatshops
Cleaning Up Hazardous Wastes

SEPTEMBER 1996
Gambling Under Attack
The States and Federalism
Civic Journalism
Reassessing Foreign Aid

OCTOBER 1996
Political Consultants
Insurance Fraud
Rethinking School Integration
Parental Rights

NOVEMBER 1996
Global Warming
Clashing Over Copyright
Consumer Debt
Governing Washington, D.C.

DECEMBER 1996
Welfare, Work and the States
The New Volunteerism
Implementing the Disabilities Act
America's Pampered Pets

JANUARY 1997
Combating Scientific Misconduct
Restructuring the Electric Industry
The New Immigrants
Chemical and Biological Weapons

FEBRUARY 1997
Assisting Refugees
Alternative Medicine's Next Phase
Independent Counsels
Feminism's Future

MARCH 1997
New Air Quality Standards
Alcohol Advertising
Civic Renewal
Educating Gifted Students

APRIL 1997
Declining Crime Rates
The FBI Under Fire
Gender Equity in Sports
Space Program's Future

MAY 1997
The Stock Market
The Cloning Controversy
Expanding NATO
The Future of Libraries

JUNE 1997
FDA Reform
China After Deng
Line-Item Veto
Breast Cancer

JULY 1997
Transportation Policy
Executive Pay
School Choice Debate
Aggressive Driving

AUGUST 1997
Age Discrimination
Banning Land Mines
Children's Television
Evolution vs. Creationism

SEPTEMBER 1997
Caring for the Dying
Mental Health Policy
Mexico's Future
Youth Fitness

OCTOBER 1997
Urban Sprawl in the West
Diversity in the Workplace
Teacher Education
Contingent Work Force

NOVEMBER 1997
Renewable Energy
Artificial Intelligence
Religious Persecution

Back issues are available for $5.00 (subscribers) or $10.00 (non-subscribers). Quantity discounts apply to orders over ten. To order, call Congressional Quarterly Customer Service at (202) 887-8621.

Binders are available for $18.00. To order call 1-800-638-1710. Please refer to stock number 648.

Future Topics

- ***Whistleblowers***
- ***Cuba After Castro***
- ***Gun Control Revisited***

THE CQ Researcher

PUBLISHED BY CONGRESSIONAL QUARTERLY INC.

Whistleblowers

Are they heroes or disloyal publicity hounds?

Organizations that commit fraud, make unsafe products or pollute the environment no longer risk exposure just from critics, regulators or the press. Increasingly, wrongdoing in government as well as the private sector is being brought to light by employees who go outside the chain of command to "blow the whistle." When allegations prove true, the whistleblower is hailed as a hero, and sometimes richly rewarded, though often after poor performance reviews and dismissal. Without such vindication, however, whistleblowers come across as irresponsible "snitches" who value personal aggrandizement over team-playing. The federal government and many private employers have set up elaborate procedures for weighing whistleblower claims and determining which view applies.

INSIDE THIS ISSUE

Dec. 5, 1997 • Volume 7, No. 45 • Pages 1057-1080

Formerly Editorial Research Reports

THE ISSUES

BACKGROUND

CURRENT SITUATION

OUTLOOK

SIDEBARS AND GRAPHICS

FOR FURTHER RESEARCH

December 5, 1997
Volume 7, No. 45

PUBLISHED BY
Congressional Quarterly Inc.

The CQ Researcher (ISSN 1056-2036). Formerly Editorial Research Reports. Published weekly, except Jan. 3, May 30, Aug. 29, Oct. 31, by Congressional Quarterly Inc., 1414 22nd St., N.W., Washington, D.C. 20037. Annual subscription rate for libraries, businesses and government is $340. Additional rates furnished upon request. Periodicals postage paid at Washington, D.C., and additional mailing offices. POSTMASTER: Send address changes to The CQ Researcher, 1414 22nd St., N.W., Washington, D.C. 20037.

COVER: FORMER NEW YORK CITY DET. FRANK SERPICO TESTIFIED IN SEPTEMBER AT CITY COUNCIL HEARINGS ON PROPOSED LEGISLATION TO MONITOR POLICE CORRUPTION. HE EXPOSED POLICE CORRUPTION IN THE CITY IN 1970. (REUTERS)

Whistleblowers

By Charles S. Clark

The Issues

Ed Block is an ex-employee who just won't go away. The former aviation wiring specialist for the Defense Logistics Agency was fired by the Pentagon back in 1983, and he's still writing letters — to the Defense Department, to his member of Congress, to the president, to journalists and public interest groups — all in an effort to win reinstatement, back pay and the $20,000 reward he feels he deserves.

It all started in the early 1980s, just after Block had won an employee of the year award for saving the taxpayers $2 billion. As a senior supervisory equipment specialist, Block had warned his superiors that a wiring insulation material used in the Navy's F-14 fighter plane was aging and cracking prematurely and might have caused dozens of crashes. When he went before a hearing and recommended that the fleet of planes be grounded, he angered some of the Navy's top brass. "I was suddenly dismissed for falsifying a $43 travel voucher," he recalls bitterly, denying any misuse of funds. The government says his claim for a reward under a 1992 law had no merit.

With a wife and four children to support, he was forced into a new career, beginning in the lower ranks of hotel management. "I was in dire straits financially, and I kept thinking the cavalry was coming," he says. "I was brought up in the American tradition that when you do the right thing, you expect the right thing in return."

Yet as recently as October — nearly 15 years after his ordeal began — Block received yet another rejection letter from the federal Office of Special Counsel (OSC), the agency that evaluates complaints from

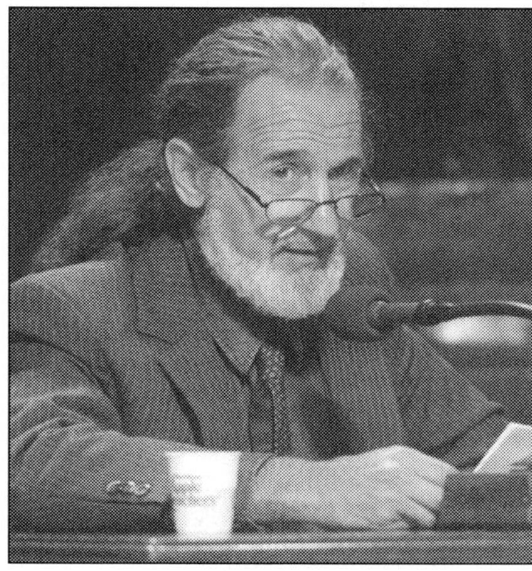

whistleblowers who feel they've been treated unjustly.

So the 47-year-old Block continues to speak out, making television news appearances, working with a whistleblowers' financial aid fund near his home in Bucks County, Pa., and supplying information on aviation wiring to the families of people killed in last year's crash of TWA Flight 800 off Long Island.

"I want Congress to create a whistleblowers' bill of rights," Block says. "The way things work now, it's more like the truth shall set you free — from your job."

Whistleblowing, or "ethical resistance," as some prefer, has enjoyed a steady rise in the public consciousness over the past three decades. It began with the ad hoc defiance of a few individuals reacting against abuses in government during the Vietnam and Watergate eras. Today it has ballooned into a familiar human drama that in government has spawned an elaborate bureaucratic mechanism, and, in private industry, an array of corporate ethics programs.

As defined by the federal Merit Systems Protection Board, which adjudicates complaints by government employees, "whistleblowing means disclosing information that you reasonably believe is evidence of a violation of any law, rule, or regulation, or gross mismanagement, a gross waste of funds, an abuse of authority, or a substantial and specific danger to public health or safety." [1]

In government, recent high-visibility examples include Frederic Whitehurst, the technician in the FBI crime lab who caused a scandal when he charged that forensic evidence affecting dozens of cases nationwide was being unscrupulously manipulated. Another was State Department official Richard Nuccio, who in 1996 was stripped of his security clearance after he told a member of Congress about evidence showing that the Central Intelligence Agency lied about what it knew of murders in Guatemala involving people working with the agency. [2]

The private sector has produced Jeffrey Wigand, the tobacco company research chief who in 1995 testified that Brown & Williamson executives had covered up research showing that nicotine is addictive. And Wall Street was recently shaken by revelations from former Morgan Stanley securities salesman Frank Partnoy, who charged in a book that his old firm designed overly complicated and risky financial products to take advantage of clients. [3]

Another whistleblowing author is Mary Schiavo, a former inspector general of the Federal Aviation Administration (FAA), who recently blasted the agency for being too cozy with the airlines. "In almost every area we examined — FAA methods of inspecting airplanes and airlines, supervising airplane parts manufacture, examining airline mechanics, redesigning critical air traffic control systems, ensuring airport security, certifying new jet designs — we found frightening gaps in FAA competence, thoroughness and judgment," she wrote. [4]

Whistleblowers have become regu-

Company Responses Displease Many Employees

*More than half the employees who reported misconduct to their companies in 1994 were not satisfied with the response, compared with 44 percent who were satisfied. **

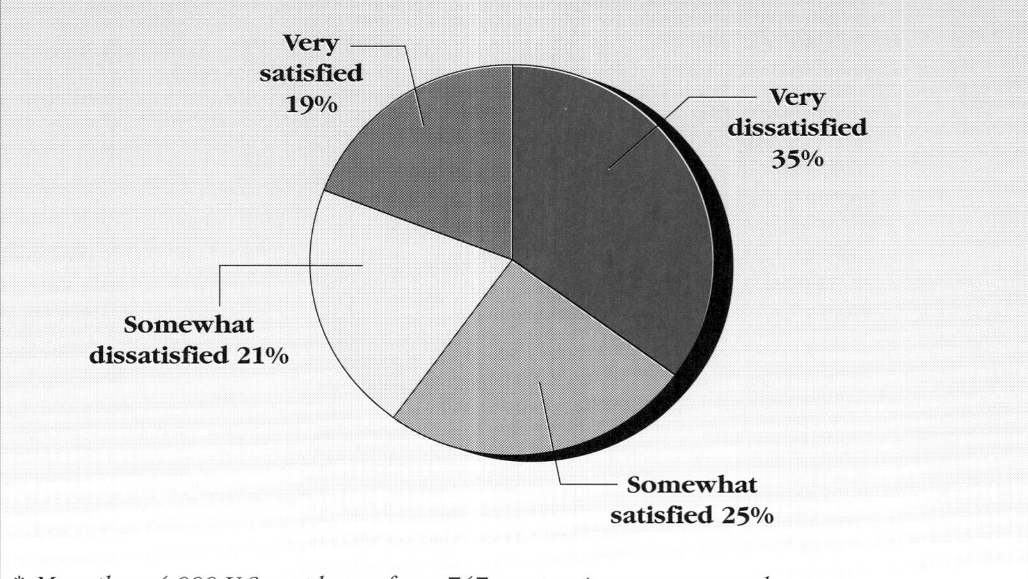

** More than 4,000 U.S. employees from 747 companies were surveyed.*

Source: Ethics Resource Center, 1997

lars on CBS News' "60 Minutes" and other investigative television shows, sometimes appearing on camera in disguise, as several Internal Revenue Service (IRS) agents did in September when they described mistreatment of taxpayers. Whistleblowers also have become famous through Hollywood movies. The public was recently reminded of living legend Frank Serpico, the onetime New York City detective who revealed massive police corruption in 1970. Serpico, who was portrayed by Al Pacino in a hit movie, reappeared in September at a hearing on police brutality. [5] Whistleblower themes are also popular in fiction, a prime example being novelist John Grisham's *The Firm,* about a young lawyer who exposes the crooked partners in his law firm.

Finally, whistleblowers also are making the news for some eye-popping financial rewards. George Green, a Texas Health and Human Services Department architect who was fired after he exposed financial irregularities in state construction projects, was awarded $13.8 million by the Texas Legislature in 1995. Dozens of others have collected even larger amounts as their share of the ill-gotten money recovered by the federal government under the False Claims Amendments Act of 1986, which encourages employees to report fraud on government contracts.

But awarding money to whistleblowers is controversial. Critics say it provides an incentive for employees to act outside internal channels and to sensationalize an organization's mistakes. Whistleblowers in general are regarded by many as disloyal, and are characterized by unflattering terms such as "rats," "snitches" and "stool pigeons" who "air dirty laundry in public."

"Rarely are whistleblowers honored as heroes by their fellow workers," writes University of Kansas business Professor Richard T. De George. "A possible explanation might be that by his or her action, the whistleblower has implied that because fellow workers did not blow the whistle, they are guilty of immorality, complicity in the wrongdoings of the company or cowardice." [6]

Attitudes about whistleblowers are reflected in academic surveys, which show, perhaps not surprisingly, that 84 percent of whistleblowers in private industry are subsequently fired, and 75 percent of those in government end up demoted. [7]

The negative response to whistleblowers helps explain why many whistleblowers rely on the array of activist groups that have sprung up to offer legal advice, financial aid and mental health counseling. (*See story, p. 1064.*) In recent years, the ability of average people to get in touch with such groups has been enhanced by the Internet. "We find things in our E-mail every day," says Danielle Brian, executive director of the Washington-based Project on Government Oversight (POGO), which uses whistleblower information to advocate for policy changes in defense, energy and environmental matters. "People get frustrated [about what's going on], and they simply type in 'whistleblower' on the World Wide Web. We're now hearing from agencies we'd never heard of."

Groups that work with whistleblowers "tend to be liberal-left, while the whistleblowers themselves come from all over," says Mike Cavallo, president of a foundation bearing his name that for the past decade has made annual awards to whistleblowers.

Not to be outdone, corporations and government agencies have set up whistleblower hotlines and ethics offices, to enable more complaints to be resolved in-house, without publicity and litigation. Good management of problems within the organization, they argue, avoids harm to an employer's reputation while thwarting those whistleblowers who, because of unreliable information or personal problems, have gone public with charges that will not withstand scrutiny.

It appears that ethics offices in private industry have much work ahead of them. A survey by the Washington-based Ethics Resource Center found that one in three respondents had observed conduct that appeared to violate the law or company policy, but that more than half failed to report it. (The main motive for the corner-cutting, the survey showed, was pressure to meet schedules.)

And two decades of efforts by government and industry to institutionalize the handling of whistle-blowing has produced, in the view of some, little more than scandal-mongering and a preoccupation with appearances.

"Although [whistleblowing] has produced enormous benefits for some parts of society — chiefly journalists, interest groups, ethics consultants and political operatives — it has not produced confidence," write Peter W. Morgan and Glenn H. Reynolds in a new book. "In fact, faith in government and corporate America has probably never been lower." [8] (*See "At Issue," p. 1073.*)

Whether whistleblowing in the future produces constructive results for society will depend largely on the following issues:

Should employers be more tolerant of whistleblowers?

"If you work for a man, in heaven's name WORK for him," admonishes writer Elbert Hubbard, quoted in a recent Ann Landers column. "If he pays you wages which supply your bread and butter, speak well of him; stand by him and the institution he represents. If put to a pinch, an ounce of loyalty is worth a pound of cleverness." [9]

The premium placed on loyalty in the workplace is precisely why whistleblowers are controversial. "Most executives are uncomfortable with whistleblowers for dozens of reasons," says Joseph, L. Badaracco Jr., a professor of ethics at the Harvard Business School. "Even if the whistleblower is right about the misdeed, the managers would rather settle it in-house without going to the press and regulatory agencies. And even if the whistleblowers don't have anything, they're still risking others' reputations," he says. "The executives will fight back pretty hard and bring on the full weight of the institution."

In government, the reason for the hostility is that "most agencies take a conservative approach — rumps together and horns out — that emphasizes teamwork," says former Rep. Patricia A. Schroeder, D-Colo, a long-time advocate for whistleblowers who now heads the Association of American Publishers. "They don't want anybody to level high-profile criticism for fear that they will lose their budgets."

Mark Roth, general counsel of the American Federation of Government Employees, says he sees whistleblowers who naively "lead with their chin, only to watch management circle the wagons and pull out the weaponry. It then amazes me when an employee with an unbelievable performance record of two decades can suddenly become a 'lousy employee.' It happens not just at the mid-level but even with the highest scientists at the National Institutes of Health or the Environmental Protection Agency." When a whistleblower gets that kind of undeserved performance review, he adds, it usually means he will win when his union goes to bat for him. [10]

"If you were to ask managers whether we should fire all blacks, women or the disabled, they of course would say no," adds attorney Stephen Kohn, who heads the National Whistleblower Center. "But if you tell them that 'John Smith just turned you into the IRS,' the managers immediately call him 'that SOB lying slime.' The organization goes after whistleblowers because they don't want the liability" to hurt the company. "And these cases get far more personal and emotional, which is why they get big and there are few settlements."

But business ethicists, while regretting such retaliation from managers, point out that whistleblowers can inflict serious harm. "Companies need to protect themselves from disgruntled, discontented employees who're operating with only half the information," says Ronald Duska, executive director of the Society for Business Ethics. "What goes on in the boardroom needs to be kept confidential because it gets misconstrued. If I'm the CEO, I don't like to be told that I'm doing something wrong, especially if I already suspect that it's wrong, so there's this basic psychology of defensiveness, a desire to kill the messenger." In addition, he says, because of society's litigiousness, the manager can't admit to the wrongdoing for fear of opening himself to a lawsuit.

The belief that whistleblowers are irresponsible publicity seekers came through clearly when a group of experienced federal managers were presented with the following fictional scenario: Two employees of a regulatory agency prosecuting an energy company for its alleged resistance to price controls tell a newspaper reporter that the agency is suppressing an argument from its counsel. In the view of Charles F. Bingman, who now teaches in the business school at George Washington University, the

Whistleblower Agencies Rated Least Helpful

Whistleblowers who work for the federal government were highly dissatisfied with the performance of the two agencies that deal with complaints of waste, fraud and abuse, while family and other non-official resources were rated more highly.

Resources Used by Whistleblowers

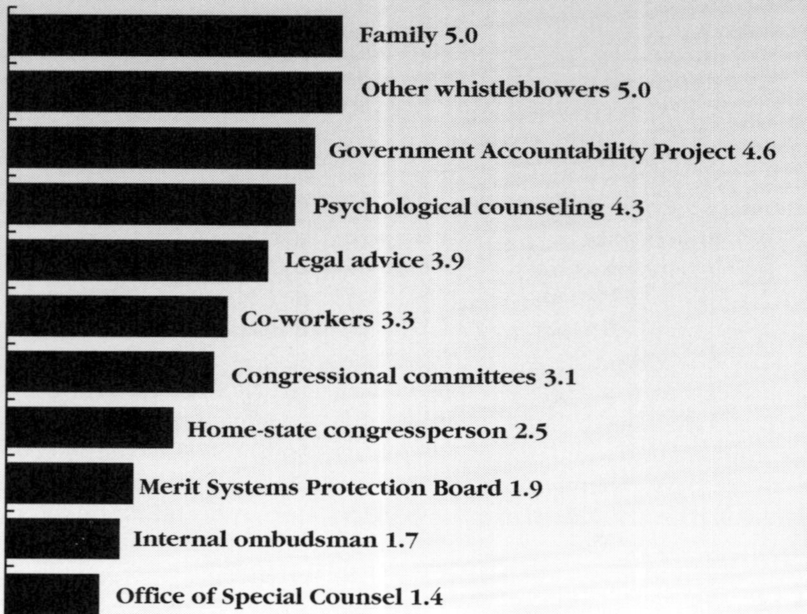

Rating Scale
Respondents rated sources from 1-7
1= "not at all helpful" 4= "somewhat helpful" 7= "very helpful"

Note: Surveys were mailed between November 1987 and September 1988 to 329 known whistleblowers; 161 people responded, 80 percent of whom were federal employees.

Source: "In Praise of Difficult People: A Portrait of the Committed Whistleblower," Public Administration Review, *November/December 1989.*

whistleblowers made several "bad assumptions": that they understood what was happening; that they could not speak frankly to their own bosses; that the organization was acting improperly by suppressing some views; and that they were the only ones interested in doing the right thing.

Irving Welfeld, an analyst at the Housing and Urban Development Department, went so far as to say he'd give the whistleblowers a letter of censure because "their enthusiasm and self-righteousness outran their responsibility, intelligence and good judgment." [11]

Others agree that internal corporate discussions of sensitive areas such as the value of a human life vs. the cost of recalling a potentially unsafe product often pursue a possible course of action to its logical extent before retreating when a moral line has been crossed.

"When you're new to a career or an organization," Badaracco says, "sometimes what is standard operating procedure looks distasteful or corrupt. But after you've been there a while, you understand the full complexity, or perhaps you learn to compromise too much."

Shrewd business people know that arguing a case on mere ethical grounds is not persuasive because it comes across as a personal attack, he adds. "So ethics often cross-dresses as a kind of prudence, in which the skeptical person will tell the manager, 'If we do that, we will be sued or get in the newspapers.' " Badaracco adds, however, that if a manager retaliates against a whistleblower too flagrantly, he's at risk as well. "The rational [managers] who [start to] retaliate will calm down and not get carried away."

Craig Dreilinger, an ethics consultant in Cabin John, Md., says that while he continues to hear about retaliation against whistleblowers, the executives he knows would be "shocked" if they heard a manager plotting to "get" a whistleblower. And though he agrees that many authentic whistleblowers are unfairly treated as "guilty until proven innocent," he also is concerned that whistleblowing can become a "selfish vehicle for the self-appointed politically correct." He cites a case of an employee who accused a boss of sexual harassment when the real issue was displeasure with the supervisor's management practices.

The way to assuage the fears of employees who witness wrongdoing but hesitate to confront a boss, ethicists say, is to provide a haven within the organization. For many companies, that means a published code of ethics, an ethics office and even a telephone hotline for reporting wrongdoing. (An Ethics Resource Center survey of 700 large companies found that 84 percent have codes of conduct and 45 percent have ethics offices, quadruple the number a decade earlier.)

W. Michael Hoffman, executive director of the Center for Business Ethics at Bentley College in Waltham, Mass., says such programs are an effective way of avoiding litigation and keeping organizational issues in-house. "I've consulted for corporations where the ethics problem lies with the CEO rather than the blue-collar employees or the managers. They ask, 'Should I rat on my boss? Who should I tell? The board?' But it's handpicked by the CEO."

Among the big success stories, Hoffman continues, are the cost-effective hot lines run by a private subcontractor, Pinkerton's Inc. in Charlotte, N.C. It processes complaints and relays them to the appropriate offices within client companies.

But hot lines and ethics offices are not enough, says Louis Clark, executive director of the Government Accountability Project (GAP). "People are crazy to call them because there's no guarantee of anonymity. And all the information is immediately turned over to the company," he says. "We're looking for enforcement" of whistleblowers' rights, not just advice. "I have no complaint about having an ethics office," Clark says. "I just haven't seen evidence that they make any difference."

That view is echoed by POGO's Brian, who cites a recent case that she and the GAP are involved in concerning whistleblowers at Alaska's Aleyeska pipeline, which is run by a consortium of oil companies overseen by the Interior Department. Aleyeska set up an employees' concern office, but that didn't protect a whistleblower who had reported alleged safety violations. When he logged onto a computer one morning, he learned that the legal department was downloading all of his files.

"It's hard to change a culture," Brian says. "The few managers who are enlightened haven't really risen to the top, and there's always an incentive to protect the organization, though the retaliation is less brutal than it used to be."

Many in the business world argue that managers are more likely to treat whistleblowers fairly if they display solid personal judgment. That means refraining from flamboyantly blowing the whistle for minor offenses and in cases where there's little chance of being effective. It means understanding that whistleblowing is often morally permitted but is not always required, in De George's formulation. (*See box, p. 1074.*)

"You wouldn't rat on your boss for taking home a pack of Post-its, but you would for taking home a computer," writes *Fortune* Editor Marshall Loeb. "You wouldn't rat on him for having one dinner you knew didn't have any business angle, but you would if it was a pattern." [12]

Do laws protecting whistle-blowers need reform?

The federal government in the past three decades has enacted 28 whistleblower protection provisions, according to the GAP, including adjudication mechanisms set up under the 1978 Civil Service Reform Act, the 1986 False Claims Act and the 1989 Whistle-blower Protection Act. In addition, some 38 states have whistleblower protections for government employees, while 19 states have private-sector whistleblower protection laws on top of the "common law" protections against arbitrary dismissals that most states also recognize.

As a legal patchwork laid over the general body of law against retaliatory discharge, the whistleblower laws "protect whistleblowers even if their information turns out to be wrong," attorney Kohn says. "As long as it's a good-faith allegation, the laws encourage the reporting of wrongdoing, and then let each agency decide."

Not surprisingly, however, the laws are often seen as promising more than they deliver. For example, "even though the [Civil Service Reform Act] included protections for whistle-blowers, it was primarily enacted as a relief measure for federal agencies to enable them to hire and fire employees more easily," writes Merit Systems Protection Board attorney Patricia A. Price. [13]

That same elaborate process for handling complaints and appeals strikes former federal executive Bingham as "overdesigned to the point of oppression." [14]

Perhaps most controversial is the False Claims Act, a 1986 update of a Civil War-era statute designed to enlist citizens in preventing fraud against the government. Its provision known as *qui tam,* which is the Latin abbreviation for "he who sues for the king as well as for himself," provides financial incentives to employees of government contractors to report fraud. (Government employees are sometimes eligible, though this is in dispute.)

Because they can collect anywhere from 15-25 percent of any money the government wins back, whistleblowers in the past decade have helped return about $2 billion to the federal Treasury, according to the Justice Department. Most of the fraud is committed by defense and health-care contractors, who, when caught, must pay attorneys' fees and fines three times the amount of the fraud. Four out of five of the top qui

Continued on p. 1065

Probing the Mental Health of Whistleblowers

"Nuts and sluts." That's how unscrupulous managers portray whistleblowers in trying to discredit them, according to Donald Soeken, a psychotherapist in Laurel, Md., who has been counseling whistleblowers for two decades. He should know. He blew the whistle in the late 1970s when, as a government employee, he was assigned to perform "fitness for duty" mental exams that he felt were intended merely to provide federal agencies with ammunition for firing employees who were "ethical resisters."

"When the government or corporations use the 'nuts and sluts' defense, I tell reporters to ignore it and find out what the issue is, and then prove whether or not it is true," says Soeken, whose foundation-backed organization, Integrity International, has provided hundreds of whistleblowers with emotional, technical and financial support.

"Usually whistleblowers have already gone through grievance hearings by the time they call me, so there's lots of material I can read," Soeken says. "Only a couple of cases out of hundreds have ever given me second thoughts."

It takes special understanding to treat people who have lost their jobs and drained their savings hiring lawyers. "Many of them are engineers who feel they are good engineers and feel terrible at all the bad publicity surrounding them," he says. "I debrief them as if they'd just experienced a disaster such as a plane crash. I try to lead them out of the mire so they can see that they're not alone."

Winning their case, he adds, is different in such instances because most don't win money. "They want to be made whole, to go on with life, but it's impossible if their reputation has been destroyed."

In 1986, Soeken and wife, Karen, surveyed some 87 whistleblowers and found that more than a fourth had been referred for psychiatric or medical help. About half had experienced feelings of panic, and three-quarters had experienced loss of sleep and depression; about 10 percent had attempted suicide. (Surprisingly, only 16 percent said they wouldn't blow the whistle if they had it to do over again.)

"Our study showed that about half of whistleblowers are what we call absolutists," Soeken says. "In ethics, they see things as black-white, right-wrong and universal, and they come across as rigid. The rest are more pragmatic — they want the most good for the most people, in equal abundance." The opponents whom the whistleblowers go up against are usually "situationalists," Soeken explains. "They tend to make up the rules as they go, and for them the bottom line is more important than how you get to it. They don't mix well with the absolutists, and so the sparks fly."

When Soeken began treating whistleblowers, it was common for government agencies to require them to undergo psychiatric examinations. "There were lots of abuses in the late 1970s," says Louis Clark, executive director of the Government Accountability Project (GAP), who worked with Soeken early on. The issue was examined in a series of congressional hearings by Rep. Gladys Noon Spellman, D-Md., but it wasn't until 1984 that mandatory psychiatric examinations were banned by the Office of Personnel Management. (The exceptions were in the military, intelligence, law enforcement and high-stress jobs such as air traffic controller.) Legislation that was passed in 1992 ended the exams in the military as well.

G. Jerry Shaw, general counsel of the federal Senior Executive Service, says the prohibition on mental health exams has unintentionally created new problems. "Some seriously disturbed people should retire and go on disability, but they don't, and so they end up getting fired and losing their benefits and often end up on the street pushing a cart. The agencies have little choice."

Danielle Brian, executive director of the Project on Government Oversight, argues that the "mental health problem is circular. A significant number of whistleblowers do have mental problems, but I would, too, if I'd gone through what they go through."

The governmentwide curb on exams, Soeken says, has not prevented individual agencies from hiring their own doctors and recommending that whistleblowers see them. "It's the kiss of death," he says, citing cases at the National Institutes of Health and the Library of Congress. "The doctors will write a note that is then used against the employee. I've told them it's a perversion of psychiatry to use it to further the goals of the agency."

The Library of Congress in November 1995 signed an agreement with its three employees' unions that spelled out when a psychiatric examination may be required for an employee. The circumstances include overall medical fitness for a new job or new responsibilities, but also "where the employee has a performance or conduct problem that may require agency action." The agreement guarantees the employee the right to hire a representative to help with any disputes, and the employee may have a say in who the examiner is.

Merely avoiding mental health harassment, however, does not protect whistleblowers from mental anguish. "In our culture, we don't put a lot of value on doing the right thing," Soeken says. "We put value on money, prestige and power. And then we look behind us to see who we've left in the dust and tell ourselves, 'They didn't have the right stuff.'"

Whistleblowers who fight back usually don't make up for what they lost, he adds. "But you get lots of satisfaction at looking at yourself in the mirror and saying, 'I did the right thing.' "

Continued from p. 1063
tam recoveries in 1996 were in the health field, according to Taxpayers Against Fraud, a group of lawyers who specialize in the False Claims Act.

To supporters of qui tam actions, offering incentives to whistleblowers is the only way to learn about fraud in widely diffuse industries such as defense and health care.

"Why [else] should you tell your employer about fraud when all it means is misery and hardship?" asks John R. Phillips, an attorney at Phillips and Cohen in Washington, which specializes in qui tam. Furthermore, Phillips says, "This is the first and only law that makes the revolutionary change of eliminating the personal character [of the whistleblower] as an issue. All remedies are based on the merits of the disclosures, not the employee's situation."

Critics, however, say that awarding money damages the morale of the whistleblower's fellow employees, particularly if detecting fraud is simply part of the whistleblower's job. Such "bounties" also provide "an incentive to the employee to wait while the fraud grows before blowing the whistle externally to receive a larger bounty," three business ethicists write. " Second, a companywide ethics award system actually encourages bounty-hunting, contributing to false claims and possible collusion with wrongdoers. Third, such an award system is really counter to what ethics is all about — doing what's right for its own sake."[15]

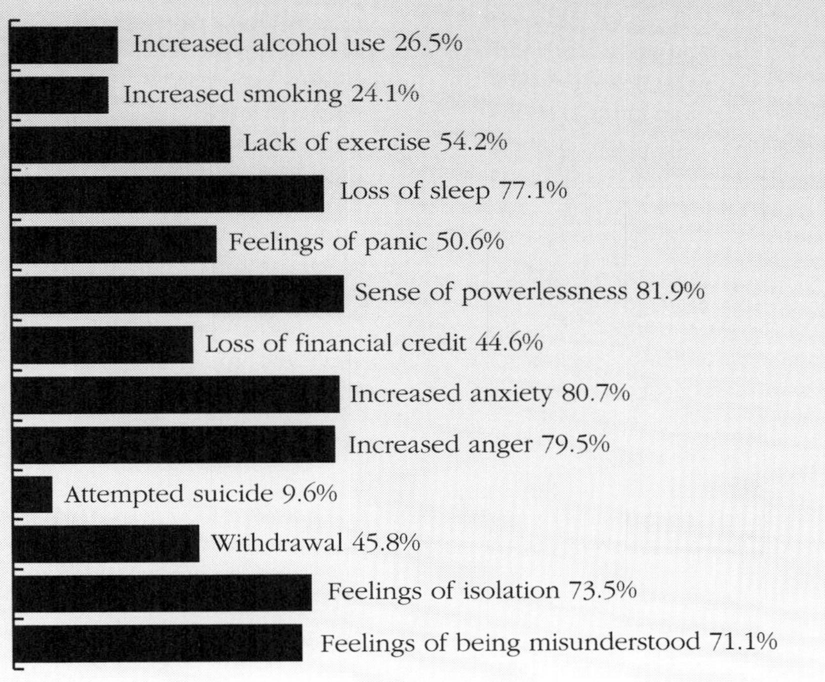

Note: The 1986 survey contacted 87 whistleblowers.

Source: Karen L. Soeken and Donald R. Soeken, "A Survey of Whistleblowers: Their Stressor and Coping Strategies," October 1994.

Alan R. Yuspeh, an attorney for a coalition of defense contractors who in recent years have opposed the qui tam law, argues that companies and established government auditors often discover fraud themselves without the need for a whistleblower. "Once a voluntary disclosure under a formal government program [has] been made, then there is no purpose to permitting a subsequent qui tam suit," he wrote. "Permitting a [whistleblower] to siphon off 25 percent of the government's recovery simply makes no sense."[16]

Hoffman and other critics also disparage qui tam as an employment program for lawyers. But the median recovery for a whistleblower, before taxes and attorneys' fees, is only $183,000, and most cases take three to five years to complete, counters Mary Louise Cohen, a law partner of Phillips. "Of the cases that come to us, as many as 75 percent already have been reported internally, and our clients were given the cold shoulder," she says. Many employees don't trust their companies' internal reporting systems, she adds, though the situation may be improving now that contractors have been setting up new compliance systems in light of the fact that more employees know of the False Claims Act.

The most elaborate of the whistleblower laws are those designed to protect federal employees. Prominent among these is the 1989 Whistleblower Protection Act, which expanded on late-1970s civil service reforms by broadening whistleblower appeal rights and by lightening the burden of proof for whistleblowers seeking to document the impact of their actions.

The law as it stands now, however, is "a cruel hoax," in the view of Donald Soeken, a Laurel, Md., psychotherapist who counsels whistleblowers. "Most whistleblowers still lose their jobs and have no money to hire lawyers, while the agencies have the attorneys to fight and 'paper' them to death." Soeken adds that the government seems to be of two minds on whistleblowers. "The legislative branch says we want laws to protect these people," he says, "but I haven't heard the Justice Department talking up the cause. Instead the agencies fight it."

That view is seconded by Roth of the government employees' union, who says that Justice, regardless of which political party controls it, treats whistleblowers as "pariahs. We joke that it's still the [Ronald] Reagan or [Richard M.] Nixon Justice Department because, institutionally, it hasn't gone forward and admitted past mistakes," he says.

Also singled out for criticism is the Office of Special Counsel (OSC), created to investigate and prosecute cases involving mistreatment of whistleblowers. Soeken says the OSC is disparaged by whistleblowers as "the other side's counsel," while Roth reports that his union doesn't advise its members to even take cases to the OSC. "Until the OSC gets more aggressive leadership, we recommend going to arbitrators," Roth says, adding that his union can press a case on behalf of a wronged employee while maintaining better confidentiality. Another alternative for a whistleblower is to take his case to Congress, "but Congress usually just kicks it back to the agencies, and the [whistleblower] gets his head blown off," he says.

Government workers who use the OSC (some 8,000 per year) do report a stunningly low satisfaction rate. Among respondents to a 1996 OSC survey, only five workers reported that their cases were successful, compared with 35 whose cases were not; only eight reported being satisfied with treatment by OSC staff, compared with 34 who were dissatisfied. (The OSC had a much better satisfaction rate among workers who sought rulings on violations of the Hatch Act, which governs political activity by federal employees. [17])

The OCS's longtime top counsel, Kathleen Day Koch, a Bush administration appointee who this autumn moved over to the FBI, has defended the OSC in interviews, arguing that it is a neutral agency, not an advocate for whistleblowers. [18]

And G. Jerry Shaw, general counsel of the federal Senior Executive Service, says the criticism is unfair because "the OSC has a unique position in government in that it must balance the public interest and an agency's interest against that of individuals. Many individuals make allegations that are not valid but that are intended to protect themselves against management discipline," he adds. "Whistleblowing too often is a screen behind which unsatisfactory employees can hide. A true whistleblower is a special breed, whose assurance of righteousness makes him difficult to satisfy. He wants a black-and-white solution, a headline splash that says, 'I'm right, they're wrong.' But these cases don't lend themselves to clear winners and losers. OSC must be vigilant in getting at the waste, fraud and abuse, and it resolves a lot of cases without getting much publicity. It is respected and feared by a lot of federal managers. When it comes across a valid complaint, it brings a lot of heat." ■

BACKGROUND

19th-Century Roots

What some regard as the radical notion that whistleblowers need encouragement in law goes back at least to 1863. That's when Congress passed the False Claims Act to encourage the reporting of unscrupulous supply contractors during the Civil War, who were selling the government nonexistent horses and gunpowder padded with sawdust. "Worse than traitors in arms," said President Abraham Lincoln, "are the men who pretend loyalty to the flag, but feast and fatten on the misfortunes of the nation while patriotic blood is crimsoning the plains of the South." [19]

The president regarded as a whistleblowers' hero is Theodore Roosevelt. During the Spanish-American War in 1898, the future chief executive risked his reputation to write an angry letter to the secretary of War complaining that U.S. Army troops in Cuba were malnourished and diseased. The act may have cost him the Medal of Honor, according to Michael Manson, a historian at the Theodore Roosevelt Association.

In 1899, Congress enacted the Refuse Act to allow anyone who reports a polluter to collect a reward, even employees of the polluting company. And in 1912, it passed the La Follette Act, named for Wisconsin progressive Sen. Robert M. La Follette, to protect government workers who bring damaging information to the

Continued on p. 1070

Chronology

1960s-1970s

Modern whistleblowing movement gathers steam in reaction to corruption during era of Vietnam War and Watergate.

1968
Pentagon whistleblower Ernest Fitzgerald tells Joint Economic Committee of C-5A transport plane cost overruns and loses his job.

1970
New York City policeman Frank Serpico blows whistle on police corruption.

1971
Ralph Nader organizes first conference on whistleblowers.

1972
Congress enacts first whistleblower statute as part of Water Pollution Control Act.

1977
Founding of Government Accountability Project to assist whistleblowers.

1978
Passage of Civil Service Reform Act creating Merit Systems Protection Board and Office of Special Counsel to evaluate and press whistleblower cases. General Accounting Office establishes whistleblower hotline.

1980s

States begin passing whisteblower protection acts, some covering private sector.

1981
Whistleblower awards created as part of Budget Reconciliation Act are discontinued after three years; founding of Project on Government Oversight (originally called Project on Military Procurement).

1982
Fitzgerald fully reinstated by Air Force as a result of Supreme Court ruling.

1983
Supreme Court rules in *Bush v. Lucas* that government employees do not have the right to sue their superiors because they have internal mechanisms.

1984
Office of Personnel Management ends arbitrary mental health exams for whistleblowers.

1986
Congress enacts update of False Claims Act, sponsored by Sen. Charles E. Grassley, R-Iowa, and Rep. Howard L. Berman, D-Calif., offering whistleblowers financial incentives to uncover defrauding of government. Engineers who warned of space shuttle *Challenger* disaster raise profiles of whistleblowers.

1988
President Ronald Reagan vetoes Whistleblower Protection Act. First Cavallo Foundation awards to whistleblowers.

1989
President George Bush signs Whistleblower Protection Act expanding government employee appeal rights.

1990s

Corporations set up ethics offices, codes of conduct and hotlines.

1992
Congress halts military practice of requiring mental health exams for whistleblowers, restores cash awards to whistleblowers who save the government money.

1993
Congress creates Commission on Research Integrity to make recommendations to curb research fraud in federally backed medical research laboratories. Vice President Al Gore encourages whistleblowers while heading up Clinton administration's "Reinventing Government" effort.

1994
Amendments to 1989 Whistleblowing Act. Defense industry makes push to repeal False Claims Act.

1995
Government recoveries from False Claims Act pass $1 billion.

June 16, 1997
Supreme Court rules False Claims Act can't be used to collect money for fraud before 1996.

Oct. 24, 1997
Federal district judge in Houston rules that False Claims Act is unconstitutional.

They Bucked the System . . .

Richard M. Barlow: A CIA analyst who was fired in 1989 after warning his superiors that federal officials were misleading Congress about Pakistan's nuclear weapons capabilities. Now a law enforcement consultant in Santa Fe, N.M., he is suing for back pay and damages.

Demetrios Basdekas: A safety specialist at the Atomic Energy Commission (now the Nuclear Regulatory Commission) who in the mid-1970s bucked his superiors and refused to certify the safety of the Clinch River breeder reactor. He continued as a critic before leaving the NRC in 1992.

Bert Berube: A structural engineer with the General Services Administration (GSA), he was demoted after reporting political bias in fund allocations to government buildings in the late 1970s. When the Reagan administration came to Washington vowing to root out waste, fraud and abuse, Berube was appointed to run GSA's National Capital Region. In 1983, he was fired after charging that GSA cost cuts mandated by Reagan were endangering government buildings.

Paul Biddle: A Navy auditor who in 1988 charged Stanford University in Palo Alto, Calif., with false claims in billing the government for up to $200 million for research work that actually went for such expenses as a yacht, fresh flowers for the university president and upkeep of the campus founder's mausoleum. His effort to collect a portion of the returned money is pending in court.

Roger Boisjoly: A senior scientist at Morton Thiokol in Utah who worked on the space shuttle's solid rocket boosters. Before the fatal *Challenger* crash in 1986, he warned his superiors that low temperatures could erode the O-rings on the boosters, the crash's probable cause. He testified to that effect before the federal commission investigating the tragedy and was then demoted by Morton Thiokol. He sued the company unsuccessfully.

James Boyd and Marjorie Carpenter: Aides to Sen. Thomas J. Dodd, D-Conn., who in the mid-1960s leaked documents from their boss' office to columnist Drew Pearson, showing that Dodd had been using campaign funds for personal expenses. They were fired, and Dodd was censured on the floor of the Senate.

John Brodeur

John Brodeur: Geophysicist and engineer who in 1994 worked with colleague Casey Ruud to alert the public to groundwater contamination at the government's Hanford, Wash., nuclear facility. He'd first blown the whistle in 1989 and was terminated but returned as a subcontractor. In 1996, he won support from then-Energy Secretary Hazel O'Leary.

Frank Camps: A senior design engineer with Ford Motor Co. in the early 1970s who protested the unsafe design of the Pinto and sued Ford to remove himself from responsibility. He resigned in 1978. The car was later withdrawn from the market after numerous burn injuries from accidents involving gas tanks.

Jerry D. Davis: Geologist who worked for 22 years at Energy Department's Hanford nuclear site, exposed radioactive groundwater to his superiors, and was dismissed July 29, 1997. A Labor Department investigation produced reinstatement, back pay, compensatory damages and reimbursement of attorneys' fees.

Jerry D. Davis

John W. Dean III: The White House counsel who in 1973 turned on his colleagues in President Richard M. Nixon's inner circle and told Congress that Nixon and top aides had been aware of, and later covered up knowledge of, the 1972 break-in at Democratic National Committee headquarters in Washington's Watergate office complex.

'Deep Throat': The anonymous source used by *Washington Post* reporter Bob Woodward to corroborate his stories on White House misuse of campaign money for illegal or unethical political operations that, as the "Watergate" scandal, led to the resignation of President Nixon in 1974.

Maude DeVictor: Counselor at the Veterans Administration who in 1978 bucked her superiors and pursued a class action suit on behalf of Vietnam veterans who trace their illnesses to the defoliant Agent Orange. She was relieved of her investigative duties and later lost her job in a labor dispute.

C. Jack Dowden: Sales manager in a laboratory who alleged that a competing commercial laboratory called National Health Laboratories fraudulently induced physicians to order unneeded blood tests so that they could be billed to Medicare. In 1992, he helped recover $111 million using the False Claims Act.

Daniel Ellsberg: The Defense Department official who in 1971 released thousands of pages of a classified history of U.S. military involvement in Vietnam. The papers were published by *The New York Times* and *The Washington Post*. Ellsberg's psychiatrist's office was later burglarized by agents of the Nixon administration looking for defaming personal information.

Ernest Fitzgerald: The cost-analyst for the Air Force who in 1968 told Congress that Lockheed Corp. had purposely planned cost overruns on its C-5A transport plane. Perhaps the most famous whistleblower, he is still at the Pentagon.

Billie Garde: Census Bureau employee in 1980 who reported her boss for theft and sexual harassment was

. . . A Whistleblowers' Hall of Fame

Ernest Fitzgerald

passed over for promotions and threatened with dismissal. Her boss later went to prison for fraud, and she went on to work with whistleblowers reporting safety violations at the South Texas Nuclear Plant.

Steve Jones: Safety manager at chemical weapons incinerator at U.S. Army Depot in Tooele, Utah,, fired in 1994 after reporting that the facility was a "ticking time bomb" of health and safety risks. He sued his former employer, and the Labor Department this year awarded him a record-setting $1 million, which is being appealed.

Douglas Keeth: As executive vice president of United Technologies Corp, he charged the company's Sikorsky Aircraft Division with prematurely billing the government for work on a helicopter contract and for inflating costs of materials. In the largest *qui tam* settlement to date, UTC settled the case in 1994 for $150 million.

Steve Jones

Vincent Laubach: A senior attorney with the Interior Department who soon after the election of Ronald Reagan reported the failure of the Carter administration to force strip-mining companies to pay fines and fees for using public lands. Reagan Interior Secretary James Watt ignored his entreaties, and he was reassigned to clerical duties.

Richard A. Lundwall: Texaco Inc. financial officer who was forced out in 1996 after making public his tape recordings of conversations in which he and other Texaco executives made disparaging remarks about minorities and planned to destroy key documents in a discrimination suit.

Bill E. McKay Jr.: Ashland Oil executive who, with colleague Harry D. Williams in 1988, won $69.5 million in damages after being fired by Ashland for questioning allegedly illegal foreign payments and efforts to cover them up.

Richard Nuccio: State Department senior adviser whose security clearance was revoked in 1996 after he passed on to then-Rep. Robert Toricelli, D-N.J., information that the CIA knew more of murders in Guatemala than it had revealed to American relatives of the murder victims.

Marie Ragghianti: A Tennessee state parole official who in 1976 exposed corruption of Gov. Roy Blanton, who was pardoning prisoners in exchange for money. She was later harassed and slandered, and her story was made into the 1985 movie "Marie" starring Sissy Spacek.

Michael Roszak: A former municipal bond broker with J.F. Hartfield & Co., in Jersey City, N.J., told federal regulators in 1996 that the firm was overcharging its brokerage clients; he triggered a probe by the Securities and Exchange Commission, and the company fired him after accusing him of stealing documents.

Mary Schiavo: The former Transportation Department official who authored *Flying Blind, Flying Safe,* which details her efforts to warn of the dangers at ValuJet Airlines, which suffered a crash in Florida in 1996 that killed 110.

Frank Serpico: With two fellow New York City police officers in 1970, he took reports of gambling influence and other police corruption to *The New York Times,* after being rejected by his superiors. Mayor John V. Lindsay appointed a major commission to investigate.

Karen Silkwood: The nuclear plant worker for Kerr-McGhee who in 1974 testified about safety violations at the company's Oklahoma plant. She was killed in an unexplained car accident on her way to meet with *New York Times* reporter David Burnham. Her story was made into the 1983 movie "Silkwood" starring Meryl Streep.

Chris Urda: A former administrator at Singer Co. alleged that Singer's Link Flight Simulation Division regularly submitted false cost and price data to the Defense Department. Singer settled for $55 million under the False Claims Act.

Richard Walker: A physicist with AT&T's Bell Laboratories, he found computer projection errors on a military project in 1971, but his bosses wouldn't let him tell the Navy. After some undesirable assignments, he was fired in 1979, supposedly for not taking interest in his work.

Chester Walsh: A General Electric Co. manager who alleged that GE executives and an Israeli general conspired to divert U.S. foreign military assistance funds intended for the Israeli Air Force. GE paid the government $59.5 million in 1992 under the False Claims Act.

Jeffrey Wigand: The head of research for Brown & Williamson tobacco who in 1995 told state attorneys general and later "60 minutes" that he worked with executives who spoke of being "in the nicotine delivery business."

Merrill Williams: paralegal at law firm representing Brown & Williamson who in 1995 released documents showing that tobacco industry executives had lied when they told Congress nicotine is not addictive.

Sources: Government Accountability Project, Project on Government Oversight; Taxpayers Against Fraud; Myron Peretz Glazer and Penina Migdal Glazer, *Whistleblowers: Exposing Corruption in Government and Industry* (1989); Andrew W. Singer, "The Whistle-Blower: Patriot or Bounty Hunter," *Across the Board,* published by The Conference Board, November 1992, p. 21; James R. Bennett, "Trading Cards, Heroes and Whistleblowers," *The Humanist,* March-April 1997; *The New York Times; The Wall Street Journal.*

Why Employees Keep Mum

Fifty-two percent of the employees who saw misconduct did not report their observations, according to a 1994 survey of 4,000 U.S. private-sector workers.

Why didn't you report your observations of misconduct?

I didn't believe corrective action would be taken.	59%
I feared retribution or retaliation from my supervisor or management.	41%
I didn't trust the organization to keep my report confidential.	38%
I didn't want to be known as a whistleblower.	25%
It was none of my business.	24%
I feared retribution or retaliation from my co-workers.	24%
Nobody else cares about business ethics, so why should I.	9%
I didn't know whom to contact.	7%

Note: Percentages add to more than 100 because multiple responses were allowed.

Source: Ethics Resource Center, 1994

Continued from p. 1066

attention of Congress. In 1943, the pressures of paying for the war effort forced Congress to scale back its guaranteed whistleblowers' share of recoveries under the qui tam provision.

In the courts, two key decisions in the postwar period helped lay the groundwork for whistleblower case law. In 1959, a California appeals court ruled in *Peterman v. Teamsters* that the public interest would be undermined if employers could terminate employees for refusal to commit perjury, a decision that whistleblowers regard as a victory. But in 1968, the Supreme Court in *Pickering v. Board of Education* ruled that the free speech rights of a public school teacher were not violated when she was fired for having written a letter to a newspaper complaining about her boss, a decision that whistleblowers might regard as a defeat.

Personalities Emerge

It was in the late 1960s, in Washington, that the first personalities known as whistleblowers emerged. In 1966, the Senate censure proceedings against Sen. Thomas J. Dodd, D-Conn., for misuse of funds, were brought about through whistleblowing by his aides James Boyd and Marjorie Carpenter. Their leaks to muckraking columnists Drew Pearson and Jack Anderson dramatized the value of whistleblowers in the eyes of journalists.

Perhaps the best-known of the early whistleblowers made his mark in 1968. That was when Air Force cost analyst A. Ernest Fitzgerald "committed truth," as he later put it, by bucking his superiors and announcing, at a congressional hearing run by Sen. William Proxmire, D-Wis., the explosive secret that Lockheed Corp., was racking up $2 billion in cost overruns while building the Pentagon's C-5A transport plane. Fitzgerald, who felt he had been hired precisely to weed out such abuses, was soon fired, and he went through the classic whistleblower's career free-fall. "As a result of my troubles with the Pentagon, I became an outlaw," he wrote. "I usually had more consulting business than I could handle; now I was completely cut off." [20]

Fitzgerald began a battle that turned into a national cause célèbre and reached the Supreme Court, which in 1982 blocked Fitzgerald from suing President Nixon for firing him. Nixon in 1973 had made a point of expressing support for Fitzgerald's firing at a time when protest against the Vietnam War had caused the patriotism of many dissidents to be challenged. (Ironically, as Fitzgerald pointed out, Nixon himself, while a senator in 1951, had introduced a whistleblower protection bill.)

Launching a Movement

The modern movement to promote whistleblowing got its start amid this '60s anti-war sentiment, civil rights protest and consumer activism (followed shortly after by mistrust of government brought on the Watergate scandal). A seminal conference on whistleblowing was organized in 1971 by Washington-based consumer advocate Ralph Nader, who pioneered the notion that employees might have a loyalty other than that toward their own employers.

"People must be permitted to cultivate their own form of allegiance to their fellow citizens and exercise it without having their professional careers or employment opportunities destroyed," Nader wrote in a conference summary. "The exercise of ethical whistleblowing requires a broader, enabling environment for it to be effective. There must be those who listen and those whose potential or realized power can utilize the information advancing justice." [21]

Whistleblowing prompted more serious study with publication of a collection of essays co-edited by Charles Peters, editor of the liberal *Washington Monthly*. "Why has whistleblowing been so important to *The Washington Monthly?*" Peters asked his readers. "In an early issue, I wrote: 'Of all the wrong decisions I have seen made in government, wrong ideas and information have played no greater role than the failure of men with the right ideas and information to press their case courageously.' "[22]

Such works set the stage for formation of activist groups such as the GAP, founded in 1977 by activists working with students at the Antioch Law School (now the University of the District of Columbia Law School), as well as a now-defunct group called the Coalition to Stop Government Waste. In 1981, Fitzgerald helped activist Dina Rasor found the Project on Military Procurement, which worked with whistleblowers in the defense industry but was later expanded to encompass all areas as the Project on Government Oversight.

In corporate America, the prevailing attitude was hostility toward whistleblowers. James Roche, president of General Motors, expressed it this way in 1971: "Some critics are now busy eroding another support of free enterprise — the loyalty of a management team, with its unifying values and cooperative work. Some of the enemies of business now encourage an employee to be disloyal to the enterprise. They want to create suspicion and disharmony, and pry into the proprietary interests of the business. However this is labeled — industrial espionage, whistleblowing or professional responsibility — it is another tactic for spreading disunity and creating conflict."[23]

Enshrined in Law

The first whistleblower protection provision in modern law, according to attorney Kohn, was contained in the 1972 Water Pollution Control Act, which set up an enforcement mechanism within the Labor Department. It was followed by a series of similar provisions in federal environmental and nuclear energy laws, eight of them between 1972 and 1980. By the 1980s, states began enacting their own versions, again often linked to health or safety protection, but with some impact on private-sector employees, too.

Reuters

Former Brown & Williamson Tobacco Co. research chief Jeffrey Wigand testified in 1995 that company executives covered up research showing that nicotine is addictive.

In general, however, whistleblowers in the public sector were given more elaborate protections than those in the private sector, who must rely on general wrongful-dismissal law. "The obligations one has to one's government are considerably different from obligations to a non-governmental employer," explains business Professor De George. "The reason is that government employees are related to their government, both as citizens and as employees, and the harm done by governmental employees may have effects not only on the particular division in which they are employed but also on the government and country as a whole."[24]

The year 1978 brought a host of new federal protections for government whistleblowers, which would be expanded upon under subsequent administrations with mixed results. Though President Jimmy Carter succeeded in pushing through a massive reform of the 19th-century Civil Service System, his efforts to streamline government were seen by whistleblower activists such as Clark as too stinting on funding for the OSC.

Some whistleblowers were encouraged in 1980, when Ronald Reagan campaigned for the presidency encouraging whistleblowers to help him end "waste, fraud and abuse." As part of the 1981 Budget Reconciliation Act, Reagan began offering cash awards to whistleblowers who helped save the government money, but they were discontinued three years later amid disagreement in Congress over whether whistleblowers should be permitted to take their cases to court.

Reagan also appointed a well-known federal whistleblower named Bert Berube to head the Washington office of the General Services Administration (GSA), but his new efforts to expose waste ran afoul of Reagan's appointee at the top of GSA. Reagan also made massive cuts in the OSC's budget, and by appointing conservative Alex Kozinski as its director, he alienated many whistleblower activists who wanted someone who shared their "idealism" about empowering ethical resisters.

By 1984, there was talk of abolishing the OSC. Its director, K. William O'Connor, gave Congress a grim picture of what whistleblowers could expect. "Unless you're in a position to retire or are independently wealthy, don't do it," he said. "Don't put your head up, because it will get blown off." [25]

By 1988, Reagan would veto a version of the Whistleblower Protection Act, which President George Bush proceeded to sign in 1989. Bush also approved, in 1992, a bill resuming the awarding of cash prizes to successful whistleblowers.

Who Blows the Whistle?

Whistleblowers, Nader once said, "seem born, not made." Given the inevitable challenges most face, the role clearly requires strong convictions and maturity. "Most are in their 50s," says POGO's Brian, "meaning they might have kids in college and are too old to start a new career, so they have the most to lose."

Kohn says that when he started out working with whistleblowers, "I assumed most had some ideology, like being anti-nuclear energy or pro-Sierra Club, but I've learned it's just the opposite. Most tend to be religious, conservative and loyal to their employer, and most have a law enforcement bent," he says. "They generally have worked in their industry for years."

The most common misconduct that whistleblowers encounter in the corporate world is lying to supervisors and falsifying records, according to a 1994 Ethics Resource Center survey of 4,000 U.S. workers. The main reason workers who saw misconduct did not report it was that they didn't believe corrective action would be taken, followed by fear of retaliation. *(See poll, p. 1070.)*

Most whistleblowers prefer to remain anonymous, according to a survey of corporate auditors by Marcia Miceli of the Ohio State University business school. They are more likely to be retaliated against if what they reveal causes actual harm to their company. "Most retaliation was subtle," she says, "such as being left out of important meetings and receiving lower than normal performance ratings." Though most were not fired, according to her data, some reported that someone in a car had tried to run them off the road. [26]

Surveys show that whistleblowers get the most aid and comfort from their families, other whistleblowers and the GAP. [27] *(See table, p. 1062.)* "Filing a case is a life-changing experience because they will never be viewed the same way again as an employee," notes attorney Phillips. "Most of my clients liked their job and would have preferred that the fraud had not occurred." ■

CURRENT SITUATION

A Perennial in Congress

Last summer on Capitol Hill, Senate committees met to consider a CIA reauthorization bill that included a new whistleblower protection provision. Prompted by the case of State Department official Nuccio, who was penalized for revealing CIA secrets about murders in Guatemala, the provision would have required the president to make clear to federal employees or contractors that they can disclose classified material to a member of Congress if it shows evidence of wrongdoing. "We simply intend it to preserve the ability of Congress to perform oversight, which cannot be done without information," said Sen. Bob Kerrey, D-Neb. [28]

The bill was backed by the major whistleblower activist groups, as well as free-flow-of-information groups such as the Fund for Constitutional Government and the Government Secrecy Project. But Senate conferees in November finally had to drop the provision after the White House threatened a veto. "The president consults regularly with Congress and expects his subordinates to do the same," White House counsel Charles Ruff explained in a Sept. 18 letter to the groups. "However, the president cannot accept legislation that would require him to vest executive branch employees indiscriminately with authority in their sole discretion to furnish national security or other privileged information to a member of Congress without receiving official authorization to do so."

Though the whistleblower provision in the intelligence bill would have been a positive step, the bill, like so many early bills, still lacked concrete remedies against violators, says the GAP's Clark. His group is similarly unexcited by other current bills: Rep. Carolyn B. Maloney, D-N.Y., offered a bill to give military whistleblowers who feel they've been retaliated against a chance to see a judge advocate; Rep. Sherwood Boehlert, R-N.Y., offered a bill to protect whistleblowers reporting on aviation safety violations; Sen. John McCain, R-Ariz., offered a bill to give Medicare beneficiaries a

Continued on p. 1074

At Issue:

Should whistleblowers receive financial rewards for exposing fraud against the government?

yes

LISA R. HOVELSON
Executive director and general counsel, Taypayers Against Fraud, The False Claims Act Legal Action Center

FROM "SUPPORT YOUR LOCAL WHISTLEBLOWER," *GW MAGAZINE*, MAY 1995

In this time of heightened federal budgetary pressures, the urgency of combating fraud against the government is clear. What is less obvious, however, is that the private bar can play an important part in the anti-fraud endeavor. Specifically, a unique mechanism in the federal False Claims Act, known as *qui tam* (the Latin abbreviation for the phrase "he who brings an action for the king as well as himself."), enables persons with evidence of wrongdoing to sue dishonest companies and individuals on behalf of the government and share in the recovery. As the act has become one of the most effective measures in the government's enforcement strategy, more attorneys are discovering that qui tam represents an opportunity to serve the public interest while working in the private sector. Under the False Claims Act, those who knowingly submit false bills are liable for three times the government's damages and civil penalties of $5,000 to $10,000 for each false claim. Private parties who sue under the qui tam provisions of the act can receive from 15 to 30 percent of the total recovery. The suits are filed under seal for at least 60 days, during which the Department of Justice can investigate and decide whether it will intervene in the action. . . .

While the False Claims Act dates back to the Civil War, until recently it was rarely used by private citizens. The need to revitalize the law became apparent in the mid-1980s as reports of defense contractors bilking the taxpayers abounded. Amid competing bureaucratic demands, the government could not detect and prosecute all the fraud itself, and the losses mounted. Concluding that additional resources had to be marshaled, Congress in 1986 amended the False Claims Act, strengthening the incentives for "whistleblowers" and their attorneys to help uncover and prosecute fraud.

The results have been impressive. Qui tam lawsuits have returned nearly $2 billion to the federal government since 1986. According to the Department of Justice, in fiscal year 1994 alone qui tam actions accounted for $378 million, more than one-third of the government's overall recoveries from civil fraud cases and more than double the previous year's total. . . .

no

PETER W. MORGAN AND GLENN H. REYNOLDS

FROM *THE APPEARANCE OF IMPROPRIETY: HOW THE ETHICS WARS HAVE UNDERMINED AMERICAN GOVERNMENT, BUSINESS AND SOCIETY*, SIMON & SCHUSTER, 1997

Protections for the infinite variety of whistleblowers have never been greater: In the past decade, the number of states with laws protecting whistleblowers from retaliation by employers has jumped from six to 45. Federal procedures and protections are likewise at an all-time high — with anonymous hot lines, a specially established Office of Special Counsel to which one may "whistle," statutory protection against retaliation, financial rewards in certain cases and so on.

The wholesale adoption of formalized whistleblowing procedures can cause serious problems in a company, however. The best-run — and most "ethical" — corporations generally depend upon organizational trust and informal systems of communication. Formalized whistleblowing procedures tend to undermine both. Corporate hot lines, for example, may be a good way to demonstrate "compliance," yet . . . they inevitably create an environment of mistrust. . . .

The threat to internal trust is exacerbated by external whistleblower reward systems like the federal False Claims Act and similar government programs. . . . The act's bounty provisions have produced the perverse result in a number of cases of rewarding employees who keep silent for years while gathering evidence for a federal suit. This inaction allows the government's damages to pile up and, as a result, increases the amount of the whistleblower's bounty.

Many whistleblowers have suffered tremendous hardships for merely trying to do the right thing — losing a job, enduring false personal attacks and so forth. But this is not necessarily so with the new whistleblowing entrepreneur, who may see the employer's errors as a way to build a war chest with which to enter the same market, or to enjoy a life most people only dream about, with a $23 million bounty and a three-level home on the California coast. . . .

The larger lesson is that a bounty system by design encourages the very worst sort of whistleblowers — the purely self-interested ones. . . . This reward system may result in increased exposure of corruption in the short term. But to think it won't create havoc in the long run is to ignore experience. . . .

Should You or Shouldn't You?

University of Kansas business Professor Richart T. De George formulated a set of widely respected guidelines for determining when it is ethically proper for an employee to go outside usual channels and blow the whistle on improper or illegal conduct. He says the following criteria should be present if an employee is to proceed:

- The firm, through its product or policy, will do serious and considerable harm to the public, including the user of the product, an innocent bystander or the general public;
- Once employees identify a serious threat to the user of a product or to the general public, they should report it to their immediate superior and make their moral concern known. Otherwise, the act of whistleblowing is not clearly justifiable;
- If one's immediate supervisor does nothing effective about the concern or complaint, the employee should exhaust the internal procedures and possibilities within the firm. This usually will involve taking the matter up the managerial ladder, and, if necessary — and possible, to the board of directors;
- The whistleblower must have documented evidence that would convince a reasonable, impartial observer that one's view of the situation is correct, and that the company's product or practice poses a serious and likely danger to the public or the user of the product;
- The employee must have good reason to believe that by going public changes will be brought about. The chance of being successful must be worth the risk one takes and the danger to which one is exposed.

Source: Richard T. De George, *Business Ethics* (1986), pp. 232-234.

Continued from p. 1072

financial incentive to report billing irregularities *; and Sen. Frank R. Lautenberg, D-N.J., has proposed a bill to protect whistleblowers who report violations of the Clean Air Act.

Of more interest to the activists would be a permanent end to the gag orders that agencies often impose on controversial whistleblowers, a ban that in recent years has been renewed one year at a time, Clark says.

Agency Agendas

Currently stalled within the Health and Human Services Department is a "Whistleblowers Bill of Rights," which was drafted in 1995 by a congressionally chartered Commission on Research Integrity. It is intended to assure that private-sector laboratory employees who report fraud in federally sponsored medical research do not suffer harassment.

Action on whistleblowers is also encouraged by the National Performance Review, the "Reinventing Government" effort run by Vice President Al Gore, a past supporter of whistleblowers. The fact that many federal agencies have set up whistleblower hot lines has meant that fewer calls are being received by Congress' GAO hot line. Though GAO's line saved millions of dollars soon after it was established in 1978, cost-cutting demands recently prompted it to discontinue live operators and substitute voice mail.

"We were only generating one case for every 50 or so calls," says Trudy Moreland, project manager for the GAO's Office of Special Investigations. "And people now can do better using the Internet." Last fiscal year, the GAO processed 325 whistleblower submissions by mail or the Internet, she says. They involved allegations of mismanagement, contractor fraud, tax fraud, conflict of interest and retaliation against whistleblowers. GAO referred 130 of the cases to inspectors general or the Justice Department.

Tougher Inspectors General?

A key topic of debate is whether inspectors general, who are assigned to each agency to monitor costs and ethics issues, could do more for whistleblowers. Attorney Kohn would like to see a strengthened non-politicized "IG Corps" of officials who are less loyal to their respective agencies than the current ones.

But Shaw of the Senior Executive Service argues that inspectors general "are not just cops but management consultants who are needed to help bring changes in an agency. You can't make them totally adversarial, or else they'd spend their time going after headlines," he says.

Frank Broome, director of departmental inquiries for the Defense Department's inspector general, also thinks the current IGs are sufficiently independent to pass judgment on whistleblowers. He points out that the IG has to communicate progress to multiple parties whom the whistleblower may have contacted, including members of Congress, service commanders, even the presi-

* A provision of McCain's proposal providing a toll-free telephone number for complaints about Medicare billing fraud was included in the fiscal 1998 budget reconciliation bill passed by Congress.

dent. Historically, only about 15 percent of complaints, he says, are substantiated.

See-Saw Court Action

In the judiciary, varying actions by the courts demonstrate that whistleblower case law is still evolving. In New York City, for example, a federal district judge in 1996 decided to permit testimony before a jury from several Prudential Insurance Co. agents, who had accused management of promoting unsafe sales practices. Their first-person testimony made it possible that their potential for collecting damages would be improved. [29]

In a blow to whistleblowers, a federal district judge in Houston ruled in October that a nurse who had brought charges of Medicare and Medicaid fraud did not deserve to collect a reward because she hadn't personally been harmed. [30]

Also in October, the Supreme Court heard oral arguments in *Baker v. General Motors Corp.,* in which the high court is expected to decide whether the huge automaker may block one of its engineers from testifying in a case involving an alleged wrongful death from a car engine fire. ■

FOR MORE INFORMATION

Ethics Resource Center, 1747 Pennsylvania Ave. N.W., Suite 400, Washington, D.C. 20006; (202) 737-2258. Founded in 1977, this corporate-funded nonprofit works to improve ethical practices "from the classroom to the boardroom." It conducts surveys and advises many *Fortune* 500 companies.

Government Accountability Project, 810 First St. N.E., Suite 630, Washington, D.C. 20002; (202) 408-0034. This group of lawyers and citizen activists assists whistleblowers and others with knowledge of wasteful, illegal or health-threatening activities in the workplace.

National Whistleblower Center, 517 Florida Ave. N.W., P.O. Box 26381, Washington, D.C. 20001; (202) 667-7515. The center represents whistleblower clients in government and private industry and publishes educational materials.

Office of Special Counsel, 1730 M St. N.W., Suite 300, Washington, D.C. 20036; (202) 653-9125 or (800) 572-2249. This federal agency created by the 1978 Civil Service Reform Act receives, investigates and prosecutes complaints filed by federal employees seeking to blow the whistle on agency misconduct and unfair retaliation against them.

Project on Government Oversight, 1900 L St. N.W., Suite 314, Washington, D.C. 20036; (202) 466-5539. Founded in 1981 as the Project on Military Procurement, this nonpartisan, nonprofit "government watchdog" investigates waste, fraud and abuse in government, particularly in the military and energy fields.

OUTLOOK

Global Phenomenon

The familiar cycle — charges are made, management retaliates and a whistleblower's life is altered forever — is now a worldwide phenomenon. In Russia, a former defense official named Alexander Nikitin has been in jail for two years for having revealed secret reports of Soviet nuclear submarine accidents over the past 30 years. And in Israel, Mordechai Vanunu, who sits in prison for having revealed the existence of Israel's secret nuclear arms program, was officially adopted in October by an elderly Minnesota couple as a gesture of support.

Sometimes whistleblowers find themselves hoisted by their own petard. Mark Whitacre, a former Archer Daniels Midland executive who went undercover for the FBI and exposed a price-fixing conspiracy, has himself been indicted for theft. On the other hand, the failure to blow the whistle when faced with clear evidence of wrongdoing is now punishable in some professions, such as law and accounting.

The majority of whistleblower charges are not borne out — of 617 whistleblower appeals processed by the Merit Systems Protection Board last year, fully 63 percent were simply dismissed. Case law rulings have insisted that whistleblowers report actual misconduct, not just a difference of opinion with their superiors.

But POGO's Brian points out that her group weeds out plenty of whistleblower claims that appear kooky or weak. "We protect ourselves by requiring documentation, rather than simply relying on the whistleblower's word. And we require them to fill out a two-page summary, which makes the ones who are merely sour grapes go away." The "Survival Tips for Whistleblowers" booklet just published by the GAP recommends that whistleblowers talk first to family and friends, look for other witnesses and first try to work within the system.

"Whistleblowers have more protection now, and managers must worry about colleagues who will blow the whistle," says Clark. "But the biggest problem is still the corporate culture. In large institutions, people who punish whistleblowers still don't get punished themselves, so it will always be a temptation for a manager."

Former Rep. Schroeder says that while "human nature can't be legislated against," it is her hope that whistleblowers will be viewed less often as "rats" than as virtuous. Unfair retaliation by managers against whistleblowers should be treated like sexual harassment or employment discrimination, says Roth of the government employees union. "It should be embarrassing and socially unacceptable rather than treated as a routine personnel issue."

The problem, counters business ethicist Hoffman, is on both sides. "No one defends retaliation, but the problem is how to detect it." Some unethical employees, for example, might know that they're due for an unfavorable performance evaluation and will simply invent something to blow the whistle on "so they can say they've been retaliated against."

Corporate executives are "by and large a pretty ethical group," adds consultant Dreilinger. "And in recent years, for the first time I've been asked for preventative ethics programs rather than remedial ones."

After 20 years of these revelations, Duska says, "I would like to say that human beings have learned that hiding things doesn't work, and that whistleblowers can be a friend of the organization. But managers will say that someone who blows the whistle is old, over the hill and has lost it. The perennial battle will keep going."

The fear of whistleblowers, Badaracco says, "does more good than harm. All the treble-damages lawsuits and appearances on '60 Minutes' have done more for ethics than any organizational credos, speeches or mission statements."

Even if ethical violations decline for reasons of conscience, the folklore of the heroic whistleblower is liable to remain a popular image.

"We're going to have a whole new wave of whistleblowers — spontaneous, Ralph Nader-types," New Age philosopher and author James Redfield recently predicted. "They're going to say, 'This is going on and it's not right, and I'm going to say something, even if it means losing my job.' "[31] ■

Notes

[1] U.S. Merit Systems Protection Board, "Questions & Answers About Whistleblower Appeals," September 1995, p. 8.

[2] See "The FBI Under Fire," *The CQ Researcher,* April 11, 1997, pp. 313-336.

[3] *The Wall Street Journal,* Oct. 8, 1997. Partnoy's book is *F.I.A.S.C.O.: Blood in the Water on Wall Street.* He is now an assistant professor at San Diego State School of Law.

[4] Mary Schiavo, *Flying Blind, Flying Safe* (1997), p. 5.

[5] *The New York Times,* Sept. 25, 1997.

[6] Richard T. De George, *Business Ethics: Second Edition* (1986), p. 226.

[7] Cited in James R. Bennett, "Trading Cards, Heroes and Whistleblowers," *The Humanist,* March-April 1997, p. 23.

[8] Peter W. Morgan and Glenn H. Reynolds, *The Appearance of Impropriety: How the Ethics Wars Have Undermined American Government, Business and Society* (1997), p. 1. Morgan is a Washington lawyer; Reynolds is a law professor at the University of Tennessee.

[9] *The Washington Post,* Oct. 22, 1997.

[10] For background, see "Combating Scientific Misconduct," *The CQ Researcher,* Jan. 10, 1997, pp. 6-29.

[11] David Hornestay, "Whistleblower Woes," *Government Executive,* February 1996, p. 37.

[12] Marshall Loeb, "When to rat on the boss," *Fortune,* Oct. 2, 1995, p. 183.

[13] Patricia A. Price. "An Overview of the Whistleblower Protection Act," *Federal Circuit Bar Journal,* spring 1992, p. 69.

[14] Hornestay, *op. cit.*

[15] Dawn-Marie Driscoll, W. Michael Hoffman and Edward Petry, *The Ethical Edge: Tales of Organizations That Have Faced Moral Crisis* (1995), p. 178.

[16] Letter to Senate Judiciary Committee, March 1, 1994.

[17] Office of Special Counsel, "A Report to Congress from the U.S. Office of Special Counsel, Fiscal Year 1996," p. 28.

[18] William Rudman, "Boss Abuse," *Government Executive,* December 1994.

[19] Priscilla R. Budeiri, "The Return of Qui Tam," *The Washington Lawyer,* September 1996, p. 24.

[20] A. Ernest Fitzgerald, *The High Priests of Waste* (1972), p. 283.

[21] Ralph Nader, Peter J. Petkas and Kate Blackwell, "WhistleBlowing: The Report of the Conference on Professional Responsibility" (1972), pp. 6, 11.

[22] Charles Peters and Taylor Branch, *Blowing the Whistle: Dissent in the Public Interest* (1972), p. x.

[23] Quoted in Norman Bowie, *Business Ethics* (1982), p. 140.

[24] De George, *op. cit.*, p. 223.

[25] Quoted in *CQ Weekly Report,* Nov. 3, 1984, p. 2872.

[26] *USA Today Magazine,* April 1, 1995.

[27] Philip H. Jos, Mark E. Tompkins and Steven W. Hays, "In Praise of Difficult People: A Portrait of the Committed WhistleBlower," *Public Administration Review,* November/December 1989.

[28] *CQ Weekly Report,* June 21, 1997, p. 1464.

[29] *The Wall Street Journal,* April 23, 1996.

[30] *The Wall Street Journal,* Nov. 3, 1997.

[31] *USA Today,* Oct. 13, 1997.

Bibliography

Selected Sources Used

Books

Badaracco, Joseph L. Jr., *Defining Moments: When Managers Must Choose Between Right and Right,* Harvard Business School Press, 1997.
A Harvard University business professor examines the wrenching dilemmas facing decision-makers in the modern workplace, offering insights on how to seek truth, virtue and success.

De George, Richard T., *Business Ethics: Second Edition,* Macmillan, 1986.
A University of Kansas business professor explores the moral, legal and practical issues surrounding a variety of questions facing managers and lower-level employees, including a discussion of when whistleblowing is justified.

Fitzgerald, A. Ernest, *The High Priests of Waste,* W.W. Norton, 1972.
A longtime Air Force budget analyst who in 1968 became the government's most famous whistleblower offers his account of how he told Congress of the Lockheed Corp.'s cost overruns in producing the C5-A transport plane.

Glazer, Myron Peretz, and Penina Migdal Glazer, *The Whistleblowers: Exposing Corruption in Government and Industry,* Basic Books, 1989
A Smith College sociologist and a Hampshire College historian produced the most comprehensive account of the rise of the whistleblower phenomenon over the past three decades.

Government Accountability Project, *The Whistleblower's Survival Guide,* 1997
This just-released booklet offers concrete tips on deciding whether one has a case that requires blowing the whistle, including advice on when to call for legal help.

Kohn, Stephen M., *The Whistleblower Litigation Handbook: Environmental, Nuclear, Health and Safety Claims,* John Wiley, 1991 (with a 1994 supplement).
The lead attorney at the National Whistleblower Center outlines the federal and state laws that whistleblowers can use to counter retaliation from management, and in some cases win back pay, damages and reinstatement.

Morgan, Peter W., and Glenn H. Reynolds, *The Appearance of Impropriety: How the Ethics Wars Have Undermined American Government, Business and Society,* The Free Press, 1997.
A Washington attorney and a University of Tennessee law professor analyze the nation's preoccupation with corruption and white-collar misconduct over the past 20 years, concluding that the onslaught of rules, regulations and scandals has failed to restore faith in institutions.

Mollenkamp, Carrick, Adam Levey, Joseph Menn and Jeffrey Rothfeder, *The People Vs. Big Tobacco: How the States Took on the Cigarette Giants,* Bloomberg Press, 1998.
This forthcoming account of the events that led to the landmark proposed deal between tobacco companies and state attorneys general begins with the dramatic disclosures of corporate dishonesty on the dangers of smoking as exposed by two whistleblowers.

Morris, Tom, *If Aristotle Ran General Motors,* Henry Holt, 1997.
A corporate consultant and self-described philosopher lays out a thought process for approaching workplace ethical conundrums, touching on concepts of truth, beauty and spirituality.

Nader, Ralph, Peter J. Petkas and Kate Blackwell, (eds.), *Whistleblowing: The Report of the Conference on Professional Responsibility,* Grossman, 1972.
These papers from what is considered the seminal conference on whistleblowing represent a call to action for employees in government and industry to consider when ethical violations require them to put the public interest above that of their employer.

Peters, Charles, and Taylor Branch, *Blowing the Whistle: Dissent in the Public Interest,* Praeger, 1972.
In one of the early works on the subject, two writers for *Washington Monthly* assembled a set of essays on whistleblowing and corruption exposés in American history, particularly in the military during the height of the Vietnam War.

Schiavo, Mary, *Flying Blind, Flying Safe,* Avon Books, 1997.
The former inspector general for the Federal Aviation Administration lays out her explosive critique of airline safety issues and how the government agency charged with overseeing them, she says, has fallen down on the job.

Westman, Daniel P., *Whistleblowing: The Law of Retaliatory Discharge,* Bureau of National Affairs, 1991.
An attorney compiled this detailed history and nationwide survey of the federal and state laws that whistleblowers who feel they've been unjustly fired can use to seek redress in both the public and private sectors.

The Next Step

Additional information from UMI's Newspaper & Periodical Abstracts™ database

Protection for Whistleblowers

Gruenwald, Juliana, "Senate passes spy agency bill with little dissent," ***Congressional Quarterly Weekly Report,*** **June 21, 1997, p. 1464.**

The Senate overwhelmingly passed legislation on June 19, 1997, authorizing funding for intelligence activities for fiscal 1998, despite the objections of the Clinton administration over a provision to protect whistleblowers.

Kaiser, Jocelyn, "Home for scientific whistleblowers," ***Science,*** **Sept. 12, 1997, p. 1611.**

Whistleblowers who accuse their peers of scientific misconduct may soon get some full-time support from the group Whistleblowers for Integrity in Science and Education.

"Let the whistles blow," ***Government Executive,*** **September 1997, p. 8.**

A senate-passed provision of the 1998 intelligence authorization act would allow protection for federal whistleblowers who reveal classified information to members of Congress without going through their superiors.

Marks, Alexandra, "Do Whistleblowers Threaten Security When Telling Congress of Spies' Lies?: Showdown comes this week on a Senate proposal to shield whistleblowers," ***The Christian Science Monitor,*** **July 15, 1997, p. 1.**

The White House has threatened to veto a Senate proposal to shield whistleblowers, claiming it violates the administration's constitutional right to ensure national security. This week, the House Intelligence Committee is expected to decide whether to back the White House or side with the Senate. Either way, there will be a showdown that some analysts contend could have serious constitutional ramifications. The controversy was sparked by Richard Nuccio, a high-level State Department employee who discovered the CIA had misled Congress about what its operatives knew about two killings in Guatemala.

"Protecting the whistle-blowers," ***OECD Observer,*** **February 1997, p16.**

New procedures to encourage whistleblowing are being put in place by many countries. Protection of whistle-blowers is one way to encourage public servants to report any suspected wrong-doing.

Reporting Fraud

Hoover, Rusty, "Researcher gets $1.67 million in U-M lawsuit," Detroit News, Aug. 1, 1997, p. C1.

Carolyn Phinney, a former researcher at the University of Michigan, became a millionaire Thursday when the university paid $1.67 million to end a 7-year-old lawsuit that alleged fraud and stolen research. Phinney said her case, which attracted nationwide attention, is the first in which a whistleblower in science and academia prevailed. In 1990, Phinney, a researcher at the school's Institute for Gerontology, sued psychology Professor Marion Perlmutter for fraud, claiming Perlmutter had lied to get access to her research on adult personality development.

McMorris, Frances A., "Legal beat: NYU Medical Center settles U.S. lawsuit," ***The Wall Street Journal,*** **April 8, 1997, p. B9.**

New York University Medical Center agreed to pay $15.5 million to settle a whistleblower lawsuit alleging that it submitted false financial information to the federal government regarding costs associated with federally sponsored research grants and contracts.

"Plaintiffs refile in B&T suit," ***American Libraries,*** **October 1997, p. 19.**

Following a judge's dismissal of the federal government's whistleblower lawsuit against Baker & Taylor, the plaintiffs have filed an amended complaint alleging that the book wholesaler overcharged libraries and schools up to $200 million over the past decade.

Shannon, Colleen, "UK doctors urged to whistleblow," ***British Medical Journal,*** **June 7, 1997, p. 1642.**

The United Kingdom's Department of Health is urging doctors and nurses to speak out when they believe a colleague's behavior could be endangering patients.

Streitfeld, David, and David Segal, "Justice Dept. Joins Suit Against Book Wholesaler; Firm Allegedly Overcharged Libraries, Schools," ***The Washington Post,*** **Feb. 4, 1997, p. C1.**

A U.S. District Court suit filed in San Francisco alleges that wholesale bookseller Baker & Taylor Inc. routinely failed to pass discounts along to as many as 15,000 institutional customers. Following an 18-month investigation, the agency said yesterday that it is taking over a lawsuit that was originally filed by two whistleblowers

"Whistleblower: Federal law helping to fight Medicare found," ***Houston Chronicle,*** **Oct. 27, 1997, p. A20.**

The dire straits of the nation's Medicare and Medicaid systems have suffered no shortage of publicity in recent months. Medicare could go broke just after the turn of the century and a big part of the problem has been fraud and abuse. As much as $27 billion annually may have been siphoned off through fraud and abuse.

" 'Whistle-blower' lawsuits continue to recover millions of health care dollars for the government," *Health Letter,* October 1997, p. 12.
Private whistleblower lawsuits, also referred to as *qui tam* lawsuits, allow a private citizen to bring a lawsuit on behalf of the United States against those who have defrauded the government. These suits play an increasingly important role in fighting health care fraud.

Retaliation by Management

"Labor Whistleblower Waiting to Be Fired," *Times-Picayune,* Aug. 21, 1997, p. A5.
A top investigator at the Department of Labor said his job is being threatened because he has blown the whistle on his bosses. Gary Love, a 26-year employee of the agency, said he was given a pretermination notice by new Labor Secretary Garey Forster and expects to be fired from his $42,000-per-year post.

Macilwain, Colin, "Whistleblowers face blast of hostility," *Nature,* Feb. 20, 1997, p. 669.
Whistleblowers who alert authorities to alleged instances of scientific misconduct are facing an increasingly hostile environment in which colleagues, research administrators and even investigators called in to examine their claims are closing ranks against them. Whistleblowers often find themselves subjected to suspicion and investigation.

Mooar, Brian, "2 D.C. Officers Say Whistleblowing Backfired; Sergeants Tell Council Committee That Accusing Barry Friend Led to Threats, Intimidation," *The Washington Post,* Sept. 26, 1997, p. B5.
Two D.C. police sergeants told a D.C. council committee yesterday that they were intimidated, threatened and branded as "rats" after revealing that a police detective with close ties to Mayor Marion Barry was being paid for a no-show job in the department's gang task force.

Norton-Taylor, Richard, "Whistleblower sacked by MoD," *The Guardian,* Oct. 1, 1997, p. 3.
A government scientist has been sacked after blowing the whistle about waste and alleged corruption in controversial Ministry of Defense projects.

Richey, Warren, "Customs agents: Bosses sabotage success," *The Christian Science Monitor,* Sept. 22, 1997, p. 4.
Employees at the U.S. Customs Service face ruthless drug traffickers and conniving smugglers nearly every day, but some agency workers say nothing compares with the pressures of dealing with their own bosses. Although most Customs Service supervisors are talented professionals, some employees at the agency complain that a significant number of managers are abusing their authority. They say whistleblowers and other workers who anger such bosses risk retaliation.

Welli, Stan, "The story of one IRS whistle-blower," *Insight on the News,* Nov. 3, 1997, pp. 13-15.
Welli, a former IRS internal inspector who encountered corruption in the IRS and then refused to let it be swept under the rug, offers his personal account of IRS abuses. The IRS retaliated against Welli for his whistleblowing activities.

Whistleblowers Fighting Back

Flynn, George, "Doctor sues county, workers for her firing from DNA lab," *Houston Chronicle,* March 21, 1997, p. A34.
A doctor filed a Texas state Whistleblower Act lawsuit against Harris County and several of its employees Thursday, alleging her firing from the Medical Examiner's Office was in retaliation for exposing office improprieties. The wrongful termination lawsuit alleges her firing came because she reported the suppression of evidence favorable to a murder defendant and two instances of "sabotage" in the office in late 1995.

Johnson, Stephen, "Whistleblower says HPD targeted him in probe," *Houston Chronicle,* Sept. 16, 1997, p. A19.
Houston police officer Paulina Zavala, who contends he was targeted for a criminal investigation because he informed on internal affairs division investigators, is suing the city.

Josar, David, "Accountant sues district under whistleblower's act," *Detroit News,* June 26, 1997, p. D8.
Consultant Peter Stenger, who was hired by the Detroit public schools to investigate $30 million that was unaccounted for from a 1986 bond issue, is suing the district. Stenger claims that Superintendent David Snead and attorney Charles Wells threatened to blackball him if he refused to cover up problems he discovered with the district's finances. He accuses the district, Snead and former School Board President Robert Boyce of violating the Whistleblower's Protection Act and breach of contract.

Kaiser, Jocelyn, "EPA scientist's views spark agency reaction," *Science,* Sept. 12, 1997, p. 1595.
Environmental Protection Agency researcher David Lewis says he is being punished for criticizing the agency in print and will present his case to a federal judge next week.

Back Issues

Great Research on Current Issues Starts Right Here . . . Recent topics covered by The CQ Researcher are listed below. Before May 1991, reports were published under the name of Editorial Research Reports.

MAY 1996
Russia's Political Future
Marriage and Divorce
Year-Round Schools
Taiwan, China and the U.S.

JUNE 1996
Rethinking NAFTA
First Ladies
Teaching Values
Labor Movement's Future

JULY 1996
Recovered-Memory Debate
Native Americans' Future
Crackdown on Sexual Harassment
Attack on Public Schools

AUGUST 1996
Fighting Over Animal Rights
Privatizing Government Services
Child Labor and Sweatshops
Cleaning Up Hazardous Wastes

SEPTEMBER 1996
Gambling Under Attack
The States and Federalism
Civic Journalism
Reassessing Foreign Aid

OCTOBER 1996
Political Consultants
Insurance Fraud
Rethinking School Integration
Parental Rights

NOVEMBER 1996
Global Warming
Clashing Over Copyright
Consumer Debt
Governing Washington, D.C.

DECEMBER 1996
Welfare, Work and the States
The New Volunteerism
Implementing the Disabilities Act
America's Pampered Pets

JANUARY 1997
Combating Scientific Misconduct
Restructuring the Electric Industry
The New Immigrants
Chemical and Biological Weapons

FEBRUARY 1997
Assisting Refugees
Alternative Medicine's Next Phase
Independent Counsels
Feminism's Future

MARCH 1997
New Air Quality Standards
Alcohol Advertising
Civic Renewal
Educating Gifted Students

APRIL 1997
Declining Crime Rates
The FBI Under Fire
Gender Equity in Sports
Space Program's Future

MAY 1997
The Stock Market
The Cloning Controversy
Expanding NATO
The Future of Libraries

JUNE 1997
FDA Reform
China After Deng
Line-Item Veto
Breast Cancer

JULY 1997
Transportation Policy
Executive Pay
School Choice Debate
Aggressive Driving

AUGUST 1997
Age Discrimination
Banning Land Mines
Children's Television
Evolution vs. Creationism

SEPTEMBER 1997
Caring for the Dying
Mental Health Policy
Mexico's Future
Youth Fitness

OCTOBER 1997
Urban Sprawl in the West
Diversity in the Workplace
Teacher Education
Contingent Work Force

NOVEMBER 1997
Renewable Energy
Artificial Intelligence
Religious Persecution
Roe v. Wade at 25

Back issues are available for $5.00 (subscribers) or $10.00 (non-subscribers). Quantity discounts apply to orders over ten. To order, call Congressional Quarterly Customer Service at (202) 887-8621.

Binders are available for $18.00. To order call 1-800-638-1710. Please refer to stock number 648.

Future Topics

- ***Cuba After Castro***
- ***Gun Control Standoff***
- ***IRS Reform***

THE CQ Researcher

PUBLISHED BY CONGRESSIONAL QUARTERLY INC.

Castro's Next Move

Is Cuba's "maximum leader" mellowing?

When Fidel Castro welcomes Pope John Paul II to Cuba in January, it will be yet another indication that the communist nation may be opening up. As further evidence of the trend, some Cuba-watchers point to increased freedom of worship and the small but steady steps toward a market economy. But to others, the papal trip merely reflects Castro's search for new allies to prop up his unpopular, economically struggling regime. The United States, meanwhile, continues its strict trade and travel embargo in an effort to force Castro to move toward democracy. But embargo opponents say that the U.S. sanctions hurt ordinary Cubans and help Castro, by giving him a powerful propaganda tool to use at home and abroad.

INSIDE THIS ISSUE

CQ Dec. 12, 1997 • Volume 7, No. 46 • Pages 1081-1104

Formerly Editorial Research Reports

Castro's Next Move

The Issues

Background

Current Situation

Outlook

Sidebars and Graphics

For Further Research

Cover: Cuban President Fidel Castro (Reuters/1993).

December 12, 1997
Volume 7, No. 46

The CQ Researcher (ISSN 1056-2036). Formerly Editorial Research Reports. Published weekly, except Jan. 3, May 30, Aug. 29, Oct. 31, by Congressional Quarterly Inc., 1414 22nd St., N.W., Washington, D.C. 20037. Annual subscription rate for libraries, businesses and government is $340. Additional rates furnished upon request. Periodicals postage paid at Washington, D.C., and additional mailing offices. POSTMASTER: Send address changes to The CQ Researcher, 1414 22nd St., N.W., Washington, D.C. 20037.

Castro's Next Move

By David Masci

The Issues

Last year's meeting between Fidel Castro and Pope John Paul II was, to some observers, an indication that Cuba's "maximum leader" is relaxing his iron grip. To others, it was further evidence of his growing desperation.

It was an improbable occasion, in any event. There was the world's last great standard-bearer of Marxism, in the Vatican, conferring with the man who helped topple communism in Eastern Europe. Indeed, why was Castro, who long ago cracked down on churches and declared Cuba an atheistic state, making peace with the most visible figure in the Christian world?

To some observers, Cuba's 71-year-old president was simply bowing to the reality of his new, reduced circumstances — an isolated communist dictator who can no longer afford to alienate anyone, even enemies. Castro had "been forced, in his current state of weakness, to recognize the enduring power of the Catholic Church among his people," wrote Mirta Ojito, a Cuban-American journalist. [1]

José Cardenas, the Washington representative of the anti-Castro Cuban American National Foundation, agrees. "Castro didn't go to Rome because he's in a reflective mood in the twilight of his life," he says. "He understands that the church is growing in popularity because it is providing much needed spiritual and economic relief to the Cuban people."

To Ojito and Cardenas, today's Castro is no different from the revolutionary who took control of Cuba in 1959. If he wears a suit nearly as often as his trademark fatigues, he is nonetheless the same dedicated Marxist who confiscated private property, suppressed dissent and transformed the Tennessee-size island into a model Soviet ally, complete with a centrally planned economy and a zeal to export communism to other developing countries.

Others have taken a more charitable view of Castro's motive for meeting with John Paul. Saul Landau, a fellow at the Institute for Policy Studies, a liberal think tank, says that Castro realizes that the church, with its recent calls for greater social justice, is no longer incompatible with the kind of society he has created. "The Catholic Church is coming around to socialism," Landau says.

To Landau and others, Castro is simply fighting to preserve the social gains made in Cuba since the revolution. After all, by most measures, Cubans have better health care, education and other social services than most of their Caribbean and Latin American neighbors.

Still others say that Castro and the pope each had something very tangible to gain from a meeting. Conferring with the leader of the world's 1.2 billion Catholics "gives Castro increased domestic and international legitimacy," says Edward Gonzalez, an analyst at the Rand Corporation, a California think tank.

The pontiff was rewarded, too. Last year's 35-minute talk and photo opportunity on Nov. 19 earned John Paul an invitation to come to Cuba — the only heavily Catholic country that he has not visited.

The pope also may have met with Castro to acknowledge his finally easing restrictions on most churches, after years of oppression. In fact, "there is very wide freedom to worship and practice your religion in Cuba," says Wayne Smith, a senior fellow at the Center for International Policy.

Smith and others say that Cubans are no longer penalized for practicing their faiths, although they acknowledge that churches are not entirely free to engage in more secular activities, like establishing schools. Still, they say, the government is becoming more flexible even here. For example, the Catholic Church has been able to televise masses and advertise the pope's upcoming January visit.

But others say that true freedom of worship remains elusive. "There's been a very limited opening, but things are still very difficult," says Marc Olsham, a professor of sociology at Alfred University in New York who has studied religion in Cuba.

Olsham and others argue that Castro will only tolerate religious activity that in no way threatens the government. Indeed, they say, the regime is still actively suppressing some religious groups, such as Jehovah's Witnesses and evangelical Christians. And even Catholics and other "acceptable" religious groups face sporadic harassment, such as government surveillance at services.

In fact, they say, religious groups never would have been accommodated

Cuba: Florida's Communist Neighbor

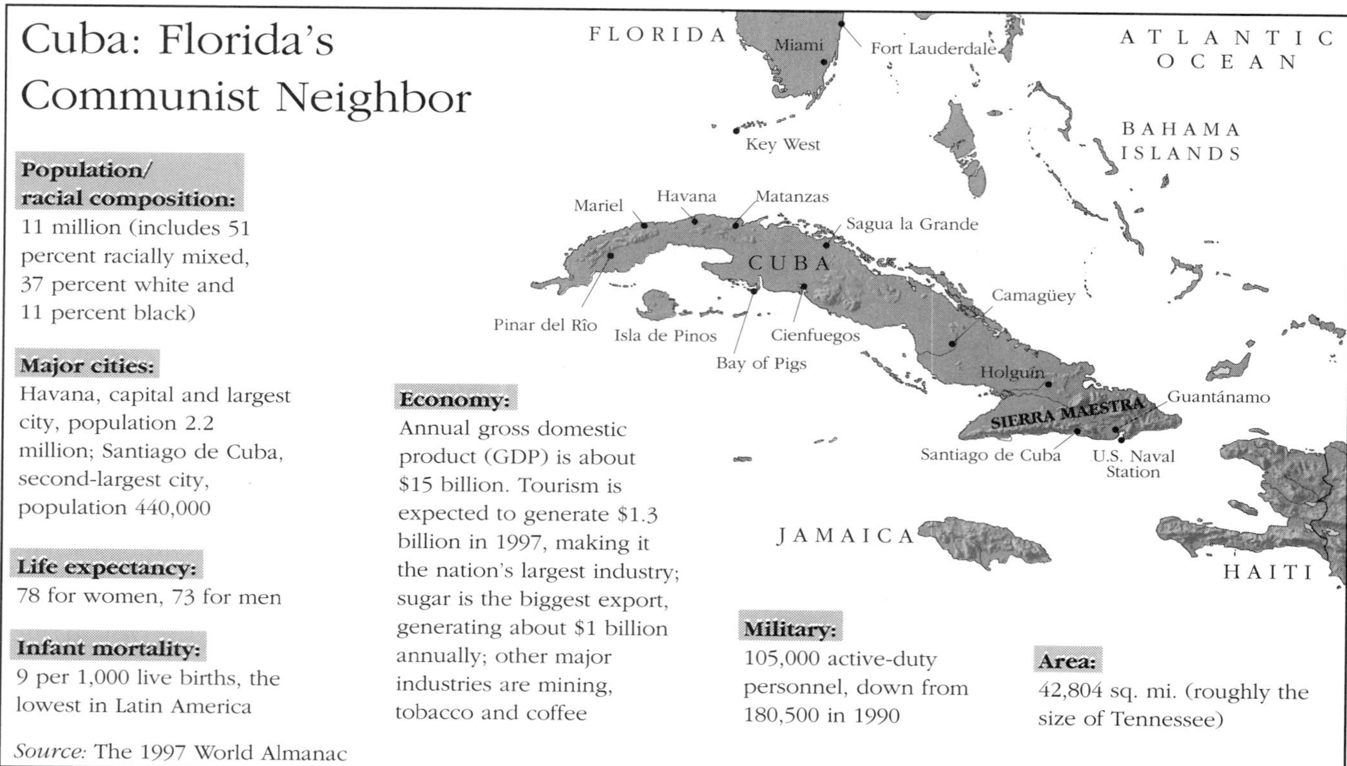

Population/ racial composition:
11 million (includes 51 percent racially mixed, 37 percent white and 11 percent black)

Major cities:
Havana, capital and largest city, population 2.2 million; Santiago de Cuba, second-largest city, population 440,000

Life expectancy:
78 for women, 73 for men

Infant mortality:
9 per 1,000 live births, the lowest in Latin America

Economy:
Annual gross domestic product (GDP) is about $15 billion. Tourism is expected to generate $1.3 billion in 1997, making it the nation's largest industry; sugar is the biggest export, generating about $1 billion annually; other major industries are mining, tobacco and coffee

Military:
105,000 active-duty personnel, down from 180,500 in 1990

Area:
42,804 sq. mi. (roughly the size of Tennessee)

Source: The 1997 World Almanac

if the island's primary benefactor, the Soviet Union, had not collapsed in 1991. [2] That's an arguable interpretation, but analysts widely agree that the Soviet disintegration did force the government to begin rethinking its policy in many areas, notably the economy.

Since 1960, the Soviet Union had been Cuba's principal political and economic patron, giving the island billions in assistance each year. But after 1991, Cuba lost not only the direct monetary assistance but also its main import and export market. By 1994, Cuba's economy had shrunk by at least one-third, and people were taking to the streets to protest food shortages.

To restore the island's economic health, Castro instituted limited market-oriented reforms, including legalizing the use of the American dollar, permitting families to start small businesses and opening certain areas of the economy to foreign investment, such as mining and tourism.

While the changes have helped halt Cuba's economic slide, they may do little in the long run. "The reforms have been superficial and have not really affected the essential nature of the socialist system," says Antonio Jorge, a professor of economics at Florida International University in Miami. That system, revolving around a centrally planned economy, has been largely abandoned by every other country in the world except North Korea.

But others are more optimistic about Cuba's economic future. On one hand, they argue, the changes seem to have helped already. [3] *(See graph, p. 1088.)* "We are making great progress in producing economic growth," says Luis Fernandez, a Cuban official in Washington.*

In addition, the optimists say, Castro is probably more willing to make additional market changes than he is ready to admit publicly. Cuba's leader must maintain the rhetoric of the Cuban revolution, which includes a commitment to socialism, says William M. LeoGrande, acting dean of the School of Public Administration at American University. But, he points out, "Castro [also] says he's following the Chinese model," referring to China's transition to a capitalist economy while maintaining tight political control.

Many of those who are optimistic about Cuba's economy also say that the island would undoubtedly experience higher economic growth were it not for the 35-year-old American trade and travel embargo. To have the world's biggest market a mere 90 miles away and off-limits has hurt Cuba's 11 million people, they say.

Opponents of the embargo argue

---

*Cuba and the United States do not maintain official embassies in each other's countries, but rather informal offices known as "interest sections."

against it for several reasons. To begin with, they say, it affects ordinary Cubans, not their leaders, thus punishing the very people the U.S. says it wants to help. In addition, they argue, the embargo is clearly a failed policy since it has not forced a change of government in Cuba — its stated purpose. Finally, they say, it gives Castro a scapegoat, allowing him to blame the embargo, or the "blockade" as it is referred to in Cuba, for the government's failed economic policies.

But others argue that the embargo is the only tool the United States realistically has to push for positive change in Cuba. "We could not influence Castro if we re-established economic and diplomatic relations and had an ambassador down there pleading with him to do the right thing," Cardenas says. The only way to get Castro to make real changes, he says, is to keep up the pressure by denying Cuba American trade and investment. According to Cardenas and others, this strategy soon may bear fruit, if, as they predict, Cuba's economy begins to slump again.

Finally, embargo supporters argue, the Cuban people know that Castro is responsible for their woes, revealing the flaw in the argument that the embargo gives the Cuban leader an excuse for his failed policies.

Whether the embargo is lifted or not, most analysts say that Castro's place as "maximum leader" is unlikely to be threatened, at least in the near future. But they are less sure when it comes to predicting Cuba's fate after Castro dies or leaves power. Some say post-Castro Cuba will have a collective leadership, possibly headed by Fidel's younger brother, Raul. Others predict that the island will evolve into a multiparty democracy.

As the debate about Cuba's future continues, these are some of the questions being asked:

Reuters/Rafael Perez

Cardinal Jaime Ortega officiates at Cuba's first open-air Mass in three decades. The June ceremony at Havana cathedral kicked off preparations for the visit of Pope John Paul II in January.

Have recent moves by the Cuban government to accommodate the Roman Catholic Church led to actual freedom of worship on the island?

Fidel Castro formed an opinion about religion early in life. "When I was a boy, my father taught me to be a good Catholic," he said in 1985. "I had to confess at church if I had impure thoughts about a girl. That very evening, I had to rush to confess my sins. And the next and the next. After a week I decided religion wasn't for me." [4]

When Castro seized power in 1959, he decided that religion was not good for Cuba either, making the country officially atheistic and forcing Catholics and people of other faiths to operate under tight limits. In 1961, for instance, Castro forced all non-Cuban Catholic clergy to leave the island and restricted remaining priests and nuns to their religious duties alone. Practicing Catholics were also prohibited from joining the Communist Party, a big deal in a country where important jobs and perks require party membership.

"Being a practicing Catholic cut you off from a whole bunch of opportunities," says Alfred University's Olsham. In addition, Catholics, evangelicals and mainstream Protestants reportedly were discriminated against at work, in school and in other sectors of society.

But in the last decade, according to most Cuba-watchers, the government has significantly scaled back restrictions on religion. Practicing Catholics can even join the Communist Party. "The situation is as good now as it has been since 1959," LeoGrande says.

"Castro recognizes that there is a spiritual void in Cuba that socialism hasn't filled, though he thought it would," Landau says. Indeed, Castro has said more than once that socialism and Christianity are not incompatible and could even be mutually reinforcing.

As a result, Landau and others say, Cubans enjoy real religious freedom. "I'm not saying that there was not a history of oppression," says Larry Birns, director of the Council on Hemispheric Affairs, "but that's no longer the case." Adds Landau, "If you were in line to become a member of the [ruling] Politburo, [being

The Rise of a Revolutionary

Like Lenin, Mao and many other communist revolutionary leaders, Fidel Castro Ruz was born to wealth and privilege. His father, a Spanish immigrant, owned a large sugar plantation and belonged to the class of wealthy landowners that his son would eventually drive from the island.

Born in 1926, Castro attended Jesuit schools before studying law at the University of Havana. The young university student showed a predisposition toward politics, as well as growing solidarity with the poor, although his Marxist-Leninist philosophy would not fully develop until the early 1960s.

Castro married a woman from a well-to-do family and had a son during his university days. They divorced in 1954, and Castro never remarried. [1]

After graduation in 1950, Castro worked at providing legal services to the poor and ran, unsuccessfully, for Congress. But Fulgencio Batista's military coup and seizure of power in 1952 convinced the young lawyer that social change could not be achieved by working within the system. Castro immediately set about raising an armed force to overthrow the government.

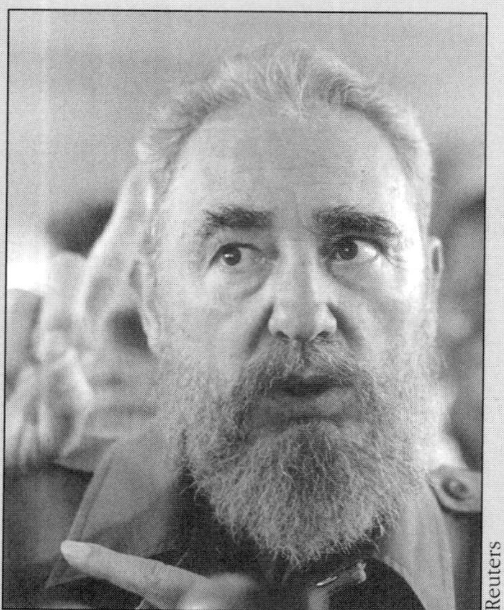

Reuters

Fidel Castro

The following year, on July 26, Castro and about 150 followers (including his brother Raul) attacked an army barracks in Santiago de Cuba, Cuba's second-largest city. The assault was a complete failure, and Castro, Raul and the other survivors (about half the force) were arrested and tried for treason.

Some of Cuba's most respected liberal lawyers represented Castro, advising him to plead guilty and hope for leniency. But he refused to even recognize the legitimacy of the trial. In a now-famous speech, an unrepentant Castro exclaimed: "Condemn me, it does not matter! History will absolve me!"

The young revolutionary was sentenced to 18 years in prison, but he was released after only two, when Batista declared an amnesty for political prisoners in 1955. Castro spent the next year in Mexico generating support for another insurrection.

While in Mexico, Castro met a number of people who would prove important to his future struggle against Batista, notably the now legendary Ernesto "Che" Guevara, an Argentine doctor who would become a key lieutenant. [2]

In 1956, Castro returned to Cuba with 81 men (including Guevara and Raul) aboard an old yacht, the *Gramna*. Castro had planned to land at the same time other rebels were leading an uprising in Santiago de Cuba.

Not only was the Santiago uprising quickly put down but the yacht was intercepted by a government frigate. Castro and his men abandoned the sinking ship and tried to swim to shore. Most of the rebels were either killed or captured by government troops. Only 12, including Fidel and Raul Castro and Guevara, escaped to the remote Sierra Maestra Mountains.

Castro immediately set to rebuilding his forces. And despite the *Gramna* disaster, the situation was not as hopeless as it must have looked. Batista was deeply unpopular in Cuba, and Castro, as a result of the "26th of July" attack in 1953, had become something of a folk hero. Soon young men were traveling to the Sierra Maestra to join the rebels. Fidel also received money and weapons from sympathetic Cubans and Americans.

A big break for Castro came in March 1958, when the United States suspended arms sales to Batista. The action was a symbolic gesture that cost Cuba's leader more than weapons. The United States, the traditional kingmaker in Cuba, had withdrawn its support after determining that Batista was too corrupt to effectively rule the country.

By summer, Castro had begun a systematic, determined offensive against the government, focusing on rural areas. In addition, independent anti-Batista violence in the cities further rocked the regime. Without U.S. support, the government quickly disintegrated. On Jan. 8, 1959, Fidel Castro entered Havana without a fight. At last, the revolution could begin.

[1] Robert E. Quirk, *Fidel Castro* (1993), p. 27.

[2] *Ibid.*, p. 93.

Catholic] might still be a factor. But for everyone else, it doesn't matter anymore."

Those who argue that there is real religious freedom in Cuba also point out that the Catholic Church and other religious institutions have much greater freedom to operate within the country. "They have the freedom to proselytize and have much greater access to the media," Landau says. "I mean, they have televised masses." Raul E. deValesco, secretary of the Cuban Committee for Democracy, a Miami organization that advocates dialogue with Castro, agrees, noting posters and radio ads have been permitted for the coming papal visit.

The government's loosening of restrictions has coincided with an apparent increase in religious activity. While no figures exist, analysts widely agree that in the last decade the number of people attending Mass and other church services has risen dramatically.

But many observers nonetheless claim that the regime hasn't eased up on religion because it cares about the rights of religious people. Instead, they argue, Castro realizes that churches are serving a need in society that his government cannot.

"In the last six or seven years there has been a popular resurgence in religious feeling because communism as a God has failed, and people are looking for something else," Rand's Gonzalez says. "They couldn't control [the church], and so they are trying to manage it."

Olsham agrees. "The government has been forced to loosen up because of the increased power of religion in Cuba," he says. But, he warns, the tolerance is dependent on religious institutions not threatening the government. "There's only one thing on Castro's mind," Olsham says, "and that is keeping power, no matter what he has said in the past." The government will "stomp on any religious group" that is perceived as a threat, he adds.

That possibility keeps religious groups in line, according to Olsham and others. "Cuba has a very accommodationist [Catholic] church," says Enrico Mario Santi, a professor of Latin American literature at Georgetown University. "The kind of impact the church had in Nicaragua or Poland [helping to bring down communist regimes] is not going to happen in Cuba," he says.

Those who say that there is no freedom of worship also claim that religious people are still being harassed by the government, even if such harassment is less severe than in the past. Catholics and others have complained that government officials have photographed people who attend Mass, and that worshipers have been "pushed around" by pro-government citizens.

In addition, Gonzalez says, "Evangelical [Christians] are still heavily repressed," and Jehovah's Witnesses are also harassed, primarily because their church proscribes military service and the swearing of oaths to a temporal power.

Much of the harassment is by local functionaries, LeoGrande says. "They can still harass religious folks, and the government in Havana won't interfere," he says.

Will Castro's efforts to open Cuba's economy to market forces improve the island's standard of living?

In the early 1990s, Cuba's economy virtually collapsed. The trouble began in 1989, when the Soviet Union began cutting the billions of dollars in aid that it had been giving its Caribbean ally since the early 1960s. The aid had enabled the inefficient state-run economy to provide Cubans with a relatively high standard of living. But by 1992, the aid was gone along with the Soviet Union.

Reuters

Aging American cars fill Havana's streets, like this 1955 Chevy cruising through Revolution Square. U.S. automakers are expected to enter the market quickly if Cuba opens its doors to the United States.

Many Cubans refer to the painful economic contraction that followed as "Armageddon." Gross domestic product (GDP) shrank by more than one-third between 1989 and 1993. Imports, including all-important subsidized Soviet oil, dropped 75 percent; exports fell 70 percent.[5] "The Cuban economy hit rock bottom," deValesco says.

At the height of the crisis, in 1993, Castro launched several cautious capitalist-style reforms designed to jump-start the economy while maintaining its overall socialist structure. Dollars and other hard currency, only seen on the black market after 1959, became legal tender. Citizens were given the right to open small businesses, although they could only hire family members. And fruit and vegetable markets were

After Several Bad Years, Some Growth

*Cuts in aid from the collapsing Soviet Union sent Cuba's economy into freefall in the early 1990s. Cuban President Fidel Castro implemented modest market reforms that helped raise the gross domestic product (GDP). **

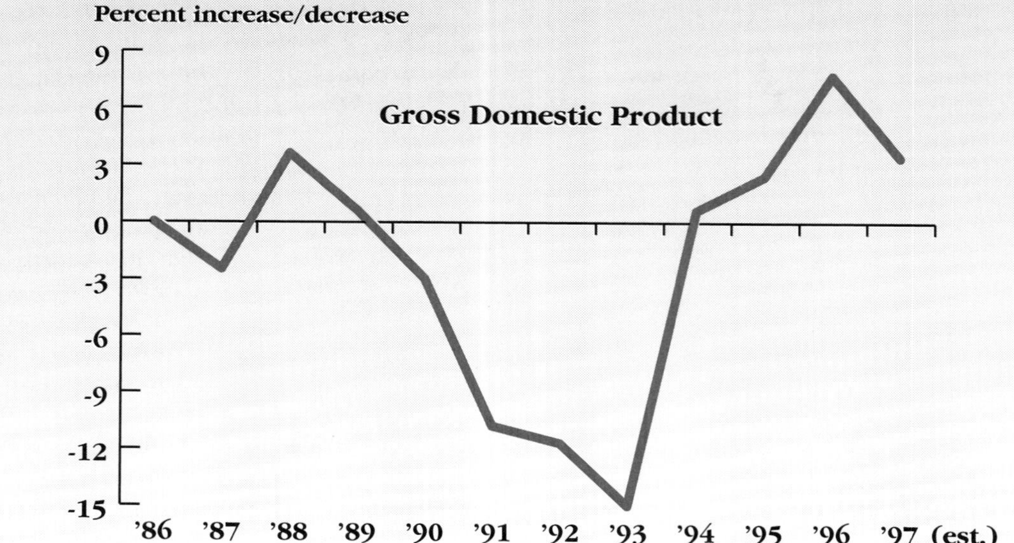

* *GDP represents the total value of goods and services produced in a year.*

Source: United Nations Economic Commission for Latin America and the Caribbean, July 23, 1997

set up to enable farmers to privately sell part of their crops.

The regime also began opening up certain sectors of the economy to foreign investment. The aim was to use capitalist know-how and money to improve promising but under-developed industries such as tourism, mining and telecommunications.

The new measures had an almost immediate impact on the nation's economy. An estimated 177,000 small businesses are currently operating, ranging from restaurants and boarding houses to craft sellers and bicycle repair shops. These family-owned enterprises now employ an estimated one-quarter of Cuba's work force. [6]

Farmers, who still must offer part of their harvest to the government at below market prices, now can sell any surplus privately. The new leeway has made the agricultural sector more productive, as farmers try to produce big surpluses and earn extra money. In fact, according to Cuban economist Oscar Espinoza, farmers now produce 85 percent of their crops for private sale using only 15 percent of the arable land. [7]

The country also has attracted substantial foreign investment. To date, almost 300 companies have invested in Cuba or have committed to do so. Tourism has absorbed much of the foreign money. New or renovated hotels now dot Cuba's choicest beaches, catering to the 1.2 million tourists who are expected to visit the island this year. With $1.3 billion in estimated revenues in 1997, tourism (which has grown 15 percent annually over the last few years) is now the country's largest foreign currency earner, replacing the sugar industry. [8]

Other sectors of the economy are also benefiting from foreign interest. Sherritt, a Canadian mining company, is investing $675 million to boost Cuba's cobalt, nickel and oil production. And the Italian long-distance telephone company known as STET has signed a $1.5 billion agreement with the government to overhaul the nation's telecommunications network. [9]

The foreign investment and other market-opening changes have helped the Cuban economy turn the corner, analysts say. According to government and other statistics, the GDP has begun to grow again: by 0.7 percent in 1994, 2.5 percent in 1995; and almost 8 percent last year. For 1997, the government predicts an increase of 3-4 percent. [10]

While analysts uniformly say that Cuba is still far from the high economic growth seen in parts of Asia and South America, many argue that Castro's willingness to embrace capitalism, even hesitantly, will continue to improve things.

"They have made modest improvements in the economy and will continue to make modest improvements," says Philip Brenner, a professor of international relations at American University.

"Everywhere they've introduced market mechanisms it has improved productivity," LeoGrande says, "whether it be with farmers or tourism. They've nipped at the edges of the economy, but nipping has helped and will continue to do so."

Such optimism stems, in part, from what some see as Cuba's untapped potential. In particular, Brenner says, the island has the best-educated work force in the Caribbean, as well as "a very good infrastructure [of] harbors and roads."

Brenner and LeoGrande both predict that Cuba will continue, albeit slowly, toward a more market-oriented economy. "They don't have a choice," LeoGrande says, because Cuba no longer enjoys protected trade with the Soviet bloc or other communist states. "Now they have to operate entirely in a market economy, and so they have to adjust to that."

But others say the idea that a country can sustain economic growth while making only modest market-oriented adjustments is preposterous. "It's pie in the sky," Gonzalez says.

Eusebio Mujal-Leon, chairman of the government department at Georgetown University, agrees. Castro's "strategy is to open two or three sectors of the economy to competition and keep a fire wall between it and the Cuban people," most of whom still work in the state sector, he says. "These reforms are timid compared with what the Chinese and Vietnamese have done," he adds.

Gonzalez, Mujal-Leon and others argue that Castro's efforts have merely staved off disaster. The Cuban economy was so bad when the reforms were implemented, they say, that changes were bound to help. "They had nowhere to go but up," deValesco says.

Actually, Gonzalez and others argue, many of the reforms are not as far reaching as they might appear. For example, they say, foreign companies that set up or invest in businesses in Cuba cannot hire anyone they want among the local population but must consider only government-approved candidates.

Another reform allowed the creation of mom-and-pop businesses. But they are being squeezed by a stream of new taxes. As a result, Gonzalez says, the number of these small businesses has fallen, from 200,000 in 1995 to 177,000 today.

In addition, critics argue, it is unlikely that Castro will make new gestures toward capitalism any time soon. In a vintage seven-hour speech at the Fifth Cuban Communist Party Congress in October, Castro indicated that he was not interested in further reforms that would jeopardize the socialist revolution he started nearly 40 years ago.

"We have no reason to create millionaires, to create enormous inequalities," he said, adding, "we fight not to create individual millionaires, but to make the citizenry as a whole into millionaires." [11] Castro rejected suggestions that the private enterprise law be amended to allow family businesses to hire non-family members, and thus expand.

Castro's intransigence, Gonzalez and others say, reflects his fear of losing power. "The regime does not want a new middle class to arise," he says, "because it would have political clout and would move the country away from socialism, which is the cornerstone of the revolution."

But others say that the pessimists are misreading the situation. Castro may defend the revolution in public, they argue, but he's still capable of making the same kind of pragmatic decisions that brought the reforms to Cuba in the first place.

"It's hard to say how much of that [party congress] speech was" just for appearances, LeoGrande says. "I mean, the Chinese still call themselves socialists," but China nonetheless has encouraged far-reaching market reforms.

Cuba, LeoGrande predicts, will continue to experiment with the market. He notes, for example, that the government has effectively stopped enforcing the ban on businesses hiring non-family workers — despite Castro's unwillingness to amend the ban — as a prelude to legalizing the practice. "That's their way of testing the waters," he says. "If it doesn't cause big problems, then they will codify it."

Soon, adds Smith of the Center for International Policy, "groups of Cubans will be able to hire outside people and pool their resources to build real small businesses." As for now, he says, "You'd be amazed at how many 'family members' these outfits have."

Should the United States continue its embargo of Cuba?

No issue divides Cuba-watchers more than the U.S. embargo. *(See story, p. 1093.)* To some observers, the trade and other sanctions are a tangible symbol of American opposition to the island's authoritarian policies. To others, the embargo is a Cold War anachronism that punishes the Cuban people rather than Castro and his clique.

President John F. Kennedy initiated the embargo in 1962, limiting Cuba's U.S. imports to food and medicine. All exports from and travel to the island were largely prohibited.

Over the years, the United States has tightened and loosened the restrictions as different administrations with different agendas came and went. [12] In 1977, for example, President Jimmy Carter lifted the travel prohibition, which was later reversed by President Ronald Reagan.

Lately, the United States has been tightening the embargo. In 1992, Congress passed the Cuban Democracy Act, which closed many loopholes.

Four years later, the Cuba Libertad Act, better known as the Helms-Burton law, was enacted. It codified the existing embargo (which had been imposed by executive orders and regulations), making it impossible for the president to lift all or part of it.

More important, the new law tried to discourage other countries from normalizing economic relations with Cuba. Executives from foreign companies that had acquired, improved or profited from businesses or properties expropriated from American nationals were barred from entering the United States, along with their family members. The measure also gave U.S. nationals the right to sue foreign companies or individuals who trafficked in confiscated property. (This provision can be waived by the president, and Clinton has, so far, chosen to do so.)

Helms-Burton has enraged America's traditional allies like Canada, Europe and Mexico, who argue that the United States has no right to impose conditions on their business interests in Cuba. The ensuing controversy has focused new media and public attention on the embargo.

To opponents of trade and travel restrictions on Cuba, Helms-Burton is just the latest misstep in America's relations with Cuba. To begin with, they say, Castro is still in power. Clearly the policy has failed. "If the embargo was ever going to work, it was during the crisis of 1991-94," Brenner says, referring to the economic problems that followed the collapse of the Soviet Union.

In addition, embargo opponents say, the restrictions give the regime a justification for its failed economic and other policies. "The embargo gives Castro a tremendous political trump card both domestically and abroad," deValesco says. Landau adds, "It gives him a rallying point to tell his people: 'This is why you have problems.' "

It also allows the regime to garner sympathy from much of the world community, deValesco argues. "There is a virulent, anti-American sentiment in Europe and Latin America," he says. "So when Castro thumbs his nose at the U.S., he generates great feelings of solidarity with them."

In addition, deValasco and others say, the best way to foster real change in Cuba is to allow Americans into the country, along with their money and ideas. "If there wasn't an embargo, there would be a real opposition in Cuba," Landau says. Currently, he says, dissent in Cuba is easily controllable because it has very limited outside support. That would all change if the embargo were dropped, and American citizens could visit and invest in the country, Landau argues.

Others say that the embargo should be dropped to take advantage of Castro's new willingness to engage the West in dialogue. "Cuba, like North Korea and Vietnam, is in a negotiating mode, and so we should have constructive engagement," says Birns of the Council on Hemispheric Affairs. "We can always reimpose the embargo if we want to."

But embargo supporters say Birns and others are naive to think that reducing pressure on Castro will encourage him to negotiate. "Only when the situation gets worse, not better, is this regime willing to change," Gonzalez argues. For example, he notes, Castro opened the farmers' markets in 1994, only after hungry Cubans took to the streets and rioted.

In addition, they say, Cuba is poised for another economic crisis, which could enhance the embargo as an effective weapon against Castro. "These economic reforms have run their course, and Cuba is headed for another downward spiral," says Cardenas of the Cuban American foundation. As a result, he argues, the embargo will either force Castro to further loosen his grip on the economy, or face a popular upheaval.

Supporters of the embargo dispute the notion that lifting the sanctions will cause the regime to lose some control over society due to the increased trade and tourism from the United States. In fact, they say, lifting the embargo will give a huge short-term boost to the regime. "The first two to four years would bring needed cash and trade," Cardenas says.

"The regime will be able to capture most of the [additional] hard currency coming in, just as they do now, and use it to prop itself up," Gonzalez says. ■

Background

Columbus' Legacy

The history of Cuba is firmly tied to the age of exploration and colonization. Columbus discovered the island during his first voyage to the New World in 1492, and by 1515 it was completely under Spain's control.

By the middle of the 16th century, gold mining and farming had made Cuba an important piece of the Spanish crown's growing empire. At first, the Arawak Indians, the island's native inhabitants, did most of the work. But disease and maltreatment decimated the native population, prompting the Spanish to import African slaves.

During these early years, Cuba also served as a staging ground for Spanish expeditions into Mexico and South America. After new territories were conquered and absorbed into the empire, Cuba took on a new role as the starting point for convoys of ships

Continued on p. 1092

Chronology

1890s-1940s

Cuba gains independence after the Spanish-American War, but as a U.S. protectorate.

1898
The American battleship *Maine* explodes in Havana harbor, triggering the Spanish-American War and U.S. occupation of Cuba.

1901
Congress passes the Platt amendment, which makes Cuba a U.S. protectorate and gives the Americans the right to intervene in the island's affairs.

1933
Cuba's corrupt government collapses, and Fulgencio Batista takes control of the military.

1934
Cuba and the U.S. sign a treaty abrogating the Platt amendment.

1940
Batista supports a liberal constitution and is elected president. He serves his four-year term and steps down in 1944.

1950s

Cuba slides into dictatorship and then revolution.

1952
Batista overthrows the legitimately elected government.

July 26, 1953
Fidel Castro and a group of rebels unsuccessfully assault the Moncada Barracks in Santiago de Cuba. Castro is sentenced to 18 years in prison but released after two years.

1956
After a second uprising fails, Castro escapes to the mountains and begins re-organizing.

1959
After significant victories by Castro and other anti-Batista forces, the dictator flees to the Dominican Republic. Castro marches into Havana on Jan. 8.

1960s-1980s

U.S.-Cuban relations collapse after Castro embraces the Soviet Union.

Jan. 3, 1961
President Dwight D. Eisenhower ends diplomatic relations with Cuba.

April 17, 1961
Cuban forces thwart an invasion by 1,200 U.S.-sponsored Cuban exiles at the Bay of Pigs.

January 1962
President John F. Kennedy imposes a full economic blockade on Cuba.

October 1962
The U.S. discovers that the Soviet Union is installing nuclear missiles in Cuba. After a tense standoff, Soviet leader Nikita Khrushchev promises to remove the missiles in exchange for a U.S. promise not to invade Cuba.

1975
Cuba dispatches 18,000 troops to Angola to back the communist government's fight against rebels supported by the U.S.

1977
During a brief thaw in U.S.-Cuban relations, both countries open "interest sections" in each other's capitals, and the U.S. lifts the travel ban to Cuba.

1980
Castro opens the port of Mariel to allow 129,000 Cubans to leave for Florida.

1990s

The collapse of the Soviet Union prompts Castro to seek new allies and allow market-oriented reforms.

1991
The dissolution of the Soviet Union ends the Soviets' massive assistance to Cuba.

1993
Cuba allows the use of the U.S. dollar and begins implementing other market reforms.

1994
Cuban economy hits bottom, having lost more than one-third of its gross domestic product in the previous three years.

March 1996
After Cuban jets shoot down two light planes manned by Cuban Americans, President Clinton agrees to sign the Helms-Burton law, which stiffens the economic embargo of the island.

November 1996
Castro meets with Pope John Paul II and invites the pontiff to visit Cuba in January 1998.

October 1997
Castro pledges to maintain Cuba's socialist economy at the Fifth Cuban Communist Party Congress in Havana.

from the New World to Spain carrying gold and other valuables. The island also became the largest supplier of sugar to the Spanish empire.

The Spanish ruled Cuba as they governed most of their colonies. Spanish officials appointed from Madrid administered the territory (often poorly) for the benefit of the crown and the local white elite, an arrangement that continued with few interruptions until the second half of the 19th century. Even when most of Latin America rose up against the Spanish in 1808, Cuba remained loyal.

In 1868, the island saw its first armed struggle for independence. With support from the United States, the rebels managed to capture roughly half of the island before being defeated in 1878. [13]

In an effort to quell further disturbances, Spain implemented some reforms aimed at easing the plight of Cuba's lower classes. Slavery was abolished, and conditions for workers improved.

But it was too little too late. A number of small uprisings marked the 1880s and '90s, culminating in a 1895 revolution led by José Martí, a journalist and intellectual who is considered a founding father of Cuban independence.

But these and other attempts could not dislodge the Spanish. Only a mysterious explosion in Havana harbor set the island on the road to self-rule. On Feb. 15, 1898, the U.S. battleship *Maine* sank after a still unexplained blast. The sabotage outraged the American public, and soon the United States was at war with Spain.

The Spanish-American War was a short-lived, lopsided affair. Spain was no match for the United States, already an industrial giant. By the end of the year, Cuba was under American control and would remain so until 1902.

America's brief occupation proved a mixed blessing for Cuba. The United States not only improved education, health and other social services but also gave Cuba its independence after only four years of occupation. However, America granted Cuba the right of self-government on U.S. terms, which included the right to build a naval station at Guantanamo Bay (which is still under U.S. control) and the right to militarily intervene. Under the Platt Amendment, passed by Congress in 1902, Cuba was granted independence, but as an American protectorate, and the island remained under U.S. control until the amendment was repealed in 1934. [14]

America granted Cuba the right of self-government on U.S. terms, which included the right to build a naval station at Guantanamo Bay and the right to militarily intervene.

In fact, American influence did not end in 1934. Until Castro prevailed in 1959, the United States played an important role in every aspect of Cuba's political life. Technically, the island was a democracy with a two-party system and elected presidents. But U.S. pressure and even military intervention frequently installed governments that advanced American interests. At the same time, Cuba developed close economic links with the United States, including the development of Havana as a playground for American tourists.

Castro's Revolution

The combination of worldwide Depression and a particularly corrupt and brutal Cuban president prompted the Cuban people to topple their government (with U.S. support) in 1933. Out of the ensuing chaos Fulgencio Batista y Zaldivar emerged. A non-commissioned officer in the Cuban army, Batista had effectively rallied some of his fellow soldiers after the 1933 collapse and, as a result, was named army chief of staff in 1934. [15]

Though a new president was elected, Batista's control of the military made him the real power in Cuba. During the next 10 years (including four as president), Batista, who had grown up poor, proved a popular reformer. He limited the influence of the United States on the island and in 1940 enacted a liberal constitution.

From 1944 to 1952, Batista retreated somewhat to the sidelines, while other men fought for the presidency. During this time, Cuba saw its economy decline and crime rise. In 1952, Batista announced his candidacy for the presidency. When it became apparent that he would lose, he staged a coup and suspended the constitution.

The coup effectively installed Batista as the island's dictator, which outraged most Cubans. Talk of revolution was once again in the air, especially after the country's two main political parties failed to negotiate a return to free and fair elections.

On July 26, 1953, a little over a year after the coup, some 150 guerrillas stormed the army's Moncada Barracks in eastern Cuba. The unsuccessful attack was led by a young revolutionary named Fidel Castro. [16]

Cuban Exiles Are Here to Stay

Unlike many immigrants who came before them, the Cubans who arrived in the United States in the early 1960s had no intention of staying. In the first decades after their arrival in South Florida, the "exiles," as they were dubbed, planned for the day when dictator Fidel Castro would be overthrown, and they would return to their homeland.

For most Cuban-Americans, those plans have changed over the years. The generation that left Cuba after the revolution of 1959 is getting older. Many are in their 60s or 70s and have businesses and good jobs that would be hard to leave behind. Many also have children, grandchildren and spouses who were born in the United States.

As a result, says Raul deValesco, secretary of the Cuban Committee for Democracy, most exiles would not return even if Castro fell from power. "My Cuban friends like to eat Cuban food and smoke Cuban cigars — when they can get them — but would never think of going back," says deValesco, who was 19 when he arrived in 1961.

The same is true of the children of exiles. "They are interested in Cuban music and food, but for most of them, that's about it," says Antonio Jorge, a professor of economics at Florida International University. DeValesco agrees, adding: "We [old-timers] are leaving behind a bunch of Americans."

Indeed, recent polls show that a majority of exiles and roughly 85 percent of all Cuban-Americans would not return to Cuba if the communist regime were replaced with a more democratic government. "They have developed ties to the United States in spite of their original intentions," Maria Cristina Garcia, a professor of history at Texas A&M University, writes in a recent book. [1]

The desire to stay is understandable. While maintaining strong ties to their culture, the nation's 1.2 million Cuban-Americans have also assimilated easily into U.S. society. "They have done well here," says Jaime Suchlicki, a professor of history and international studies at the University of Miami.

Unlike the first generations of many other immigrant groups, Cubans have succeeded in the United States almost from the beginning. That's largely because the first group of 250,000 exiles who left the island from 1959 to 1962 were largely business and professional people. Although most arrived with little more than the clothes on their backs, they were well-educated and entrepreneurial and thus well-equipped to succeed in the United States. From the start, they established a strong community that would assist later migrations of exiles — about 400,000 between 1965 and 1973 and an additional 120,000 during the Mariel boat lift of 1980. [2]

With economic success has come political clout, something Cuban-Americans have wielded effectively. In fact, most analysts say that the tough U.S. policy toward Cuba, in particular the embargo, is largely due to the power of the Cuban-American lobby.

With three Cuban-Americans in Congress, the community has a strong voice on Capitol Hill. [3] In addition, most Cuban-Americans live in Florida (although there is also a sizable community in New Jersey), which makes them a constituency that must be courted by presidential candidates seeking the state's 25 electoral votes. "They are often the swing vote in Florida," Jorge says.

Also influential are several well-financed lobbying groups, most of which keep the pressure on in Washington to take a hard line with Castro. The largest and most important of these organizations is the virulently anti-Castro Cuban American National Foundation, founded by the late Jorge Mas Canosa, a longtime leader of the exile community.

But Cuban-Americans, like other ethnic groups, are not monolithic. According to recent polls, a quarter of all Cuban-Americans oppose the embargo, a position backed by the Cuban Committee for Democracy (CCD), which advocates a less confrontational policy toward Cuba. The CCD and other organizations say groups that take an "all or nothing" approach to Castro are "unrealistic." A better tack, they say, is to try to work with the regime to effect positive change on the island.

"Castro is still the head of the government," deValesco says. "That's the reality of the situation."

---

[1] Maria Cristina Garcia, *Havana USA: Cuban Exiles and Cuban Americans in South Florida, 1959-1994* (1996), p. 208.

[2] Mark Falcoff, "The Other Cuba," *National Review*, June 12, 1995.

[3] Cuban-American lawmakers in Congress are Reps. Lincoln Diaz-Balart, R-Fla., Ileana Ros-Lehtinen, R-Fla., and Robert Menendez, D-N.J.

Castro survived the famous "26th of July" attack and served two years in prison. Upon his release, he went to Mexico where he recruited and trained a new group of rebels. *(See story, p. 1086.)* In 1956, Castro returned to Cuba with 82 men. Their first encounter with Cuban troops was almost a repeat of the Moncada Barracks attack. Most of the rebels were killed, but Castro and 11 survivors escaped into the mountains.

In the countryside, Castro began to rebuild his movement. Publicity about his activities in both Cuba and the United States inspired many Batista opponents to join him. By 1958, Castro had established a military force capable of defeating Batista's army. In the cities, meanwhile, terrorists not officially connected to Castro were wreaking havoc.

As Castro's troops gained confidence and, increasingly, victories, Batista's political opponents began to view the young revolutionary as the most likely alternative to the dictator. Castro solidified their support by promising to restore the 1940 constitution.

As 1958 drew to a close, low morale made Batista's troops increasingly ineffective. On Jan. 2, in a stunning move, Castro captured Santiago de Cuba, Cuba's second-largest city, and declared a provisional government. Castro's victory destroyed what little support remained for Batista, who fled the country the same day. Six days later, Castro entered Havana to the thunderous welcome of cheering crowds.

Cold War Terror

The rise of Castro ended Cuba's close political association with the United States. From the outset, the new leader asserted that Cuba would remain neutral in the Cold War. But within a year, Castro was tilting toward the Soviet Union.

The shift intensified in February 1960, when Cuba signed a trade and aid agreement with the Soviets. Later in the summer, when the United States ordered American oil companies in Cuba not to process Soviet oil, Castro retaliated by nationalizing the refineries. That led the United States to stop buying Cuban sugar cane, the island's top export. By 1961, tensions had risen to the point where President Dwight D. Eisenhower felt compelled to cut off diplomatic relations between the two countries.[17]

But even before Eisenhower recalled American diplomats, he had authorized the planning of an invasion of the island by Cuban exiles based in the United States. On April 17, just three months after Eisenhower's replacement, John F. Kennedy, had taken office, 1,200 Cubans landed at the Bay of Pigs with the aim of toppling Castro.

In October 1962, U.S. reconnaissance planes discovered Soviet missile sites under construction in Cuba. President Kennedy ordered a naval blockade of the island and demanded removal of the weapons. The administration came close to authorizing a military invasion, and for several days the world teetered on the brink of nuclear war.

Not only were the invaders all either killed or captured, but the United States was seen, at least partly, as responsible for its failure because it had reneged on a promise to fly air strikes against Castro during the operation.

But the Bay of Pigs was more than just a blow to U.S. prestige. The invasion greatly strengthened Castro at home and pushed him closer to the Soviet Union, increasing its involvement in the island's affairs.

Cuban Missile Crisis

In February 1962, the United States instituted an economic embargo of Cuba. It seemed that relations between the two countries could not go much lower.

But that October, U.S. reconnaissance planes discovered Soviet missile sites under construction in Cuba. Kennedy ordered a naval blockade of the island and demanded removal of the weapons. The administration came close to authorizing a military invasion of the island, and for several days the world teetered on the brink of nuclear war. Finally, Soviet Premier Nikita S. Khrushchev backed down and ordered the missiles to be removed. In return, Kennedy agreed not to invade Cuba.

The Cuban Missile Crisis firmly cemented the island in the Soviet bloc — and made Cuba safe from U.S. intervention. It also made Castro, as the only Soviet ally in the Western Hemisphere at the time, the darling of the communist world.

Over the next two and a half decades, Cuba would become a poster child for socialism and international revolution. At home, Castro, flush with billions in Soviet aid, dramatically improved living standards. Everyone received free, high-quality education, health care and other social services. The economy was entirely nationalized, and unemployment and severe poverty virtually disappeared.

Abroad, Cuba exported communist revolution with a frequency and effectiveness totally out of proportion to its size. In Latin America, Cuba intervened in insurgencies from Bolivia to El Salvador. Most of the revolutions failed to bring down pro-Western governments. But Castro scored a major victory in 1979 when Cuban-backed Sandanistas overthrew Nicaragua's pro-U.S. government.

Castro also lent support and troops to a number of communist regimes or insurgencies in Africa, including Angola, where from 1975-1989 250,000 Cubans fought to protect Angola's communist government from a pro-Western insurgency. Cubans also fought in more than dozen other African states, including Ethiopia and the Congo. [18]

Cuban-American relations, meanwhile, remained strained. Attempts at rapprochement occasionally bore fruit, most notably in 1977, when each country opened an interest section, or informal embassy, in the other's capital.

Still, new problems often soured the attempts to ease tensions. For example, in 1980 President Carter's goodwill toward Cuba changed dramatically after Castro lifted restrictions on emigration and allowed 129,000 Cubans — including prison inmates and the mentally ill — to sail to the United States. The Mariel boat lift caused tremendous upheaval in South Florida (where most of the Cubans landed) and cooled Carter's desire for improved relations.

Post-Cold War Challenges

As things turned out, the greatest threat to stability in Cuba came, ironically, not from its nemesis, the United States, but its great ally, the Soviet Union. In 1986, Soviet leader Mikhail Gorbachev embarked on a program of reform in his country aimed at fostering greater economic and political freedom. But Gorbachev's initiative quickly spun out of control. In 1989, the Soviet empire in Eastern Europe began unraveling. Two years later, the Soviet Union itself broke into 15 autonomous republics.

The impact of the Soviet breakup on Cuba was significant. Almost immediately, the Soviets began drastically cutting back on their massive subsidies to the island. By 1991, Soviet aid had vanished, and Cuba's economy was in a tailspin. For the next three years, Cuba struggled with power and food shortages and other symptoms of a collapsing economy. In 1994, there were even food riots. [19]

The collapse of the Soviet bloc also had a profound psychological effect on Castro and his country. In the span of a few short years, Cuba went from being a jewel in the Soviet crown to an isolated anachronism. Most of the world's few remaining communist countries, like Vietnam and China, have embraced free markets. Only North Korea, now suffering from a debilitating famine, still adheres to the old socialist model. ■

CURRENT SITUATION

Dealing With Dissent

Dissent in Cuba is scattered and sporadic, with nothing like South Africa's anti-apartheid movement or Poland's Solidarity to challenge the regime. The reason, according to many Cuba-watchers, is simple: Castro's security apparatus is capable of shutting down anything that even faintly resembles opposition to the government.

"They have perfected the Stalinist model," says Cardenas of the Cuban American Democracy Foundation. "The terror has been institutionalized."

One way the government has squelched dissent, Cardenas says, is by prohibiting non-governmental organizations, with the exception of churches.

Those few individual dissidents who openly criticize the government are often harassed incessantly, critics of Castro say. "Sometimes a group of indignant citizens who can't believe that you don't appreciate all that the revolution has done for people, break down the door of your house and beat you," Cardenas says. "Sometimes it will be different; they will take away your job, harass your children in school or expel them."

Indeed, some dissenters are more than harassed, according to Freedom House and other human rights groups. As many as 900 people are currently in prison for their beliefs, they say. [20] And while political prisoners once reportedly numbered in the tens of thousands in the 1960s, the message is still the same: Go too far, and you still may lose your freedom. "This regime is much more subtle now than it was 38 years ago," Cardenas says.

On the whole, however, Cardenas says there is no need to imprison or even harass most dissenters because they have been cowed. "Fatalism . . . and self-censorship take over because they are afraid," he says. "Castro doesn't need death squads like they had in El Salvador."

But Fernandez, the Cuban official in Washington, says that talk of terror and repression in Cuba is laughable. "People can say anything they like, even if it is critical of the government," he contends. Moreover, he adds, many so-called Cuban dissidents actually work for the Central Intelligence Agency, which is against the law in Cuba. "If you break the law in any country, you are punished," he says, explaining the arrests of some dissidents. "In Cuba it is the same."

Fernandez acknowledges that there are few organizations in Cuba not connected to the government. But the blame, he says, lies with U.S. hostility, not Cuban fear of dissent. "We are at war [with the United States] and must maintain a unified front."

Others say that while the regime is not quite the defender of civil liberties that Fernandez claims, it nonetheless has eased up substantially on dissidents. "The days of disappearances and long prison sentences for political offenses are over," Birns says.

"You hear on the streets people raging against the government, and nothing happens to them," deValesco says.

According to Birns and others, Cuba's recent efforts to spur tourism and other trade have softened its stand on anti-government dissent. "You can't be too repressive with 100,000 tourists in the country," he says.

Promise of Tourism

Since the 18th century, Cuba's economy has been driven by the sugar trade. After the revolution of 1959, American tourists stopped going to Havana, cutting off Cuba's only other major source of hard currency and increasing sugar's importance. In addition, the Soviets gave Cuba oil, heavy machinery and other necessities in exchange for sugar.

But sugar's days as Cuba's economic pillar appear to be over. "Sugar has been replaced by tourism as our top hard-currency earner," Fernandez says.

Cuba's beautiful beaches, reasonable prices and unique allure as a communist outpost have attracted more than a million visitors annually in recent years. And while most visitors come from Canada, Italy and Spain, the island is hosting a growing number of Americans, who enter through third countries. An estimated 84,000 Americans will visit in 1997.[21]

Nurturing tourism is essential if Cuba is to grow economically. To begin with, tourists pump much-needed hard currency into the economy. "This is very important because we need hard currency to buy fuel, food and other things [from abroad]," Fernandez says.

In addition, tourism employs tens of thousands of Cubans as hotel workers, cab drivers, waiters and the like. It has, to some extent, helped to ease Cuba's high unemployment rate, which the government puts at 10 percent, but outside experts say is higher.

Tourism has the potential to employ many more Cubans indirectly, as other businesses gear up to supply hotels and restaurants that cater to visitors. "Everyone is trying to produce new products for hotels," Fernandez says. "For example, the steel industry is trying to come up with new things [like lawn furniture], and the agricultural sector is growing new crops to supply hotels," he adds.

As the sector of the Cuban economy with the most promise, tourism also has been the primary magnet for foreign investment. "The return on investment in tourism in Cuba is more rapid than any other type of investment," said Ricardo Alarcon, president of Cuba's National Assembly.[22]

Foreign travel companies like France's Club Med, Spain's Sol Melia and Canada's Delta Hotels have invested heavily in the island's hotel industry. As a result, *Time* magazine reports, "Cuba now has some 200 large hotels offering 27,000 rooms — more than Puerto Rico and the Bahamas combined."[23]

But for all of the good news, many economists say that Cuba's tourist industry will not reach its full potential until the United States lifts its travel ban. "That would be a big boost," American University's Brenner says. Indeed, before 1959, Cuba entertained more American visitors than any other destination in the Caribbean. ■

OUTLOOK

Whither Fidel?

Any analysis of Cuba's political future usually begins with Fidel Castro's health. "U.S. policy is governed by a simple outlook," Brenner says: "Waiting for Fidel to die."

Despite perennial rumors to the contrary, Castro is generally thought to be in good health. Moreover, few Cuba-watchers think that the island's maximum leader is in danger of losing his job. "Fidel is not going anywhere," Brenner says. A June 12 analysis by the Central Intelligence Agency concurs.[24]

Still, some analysts say that there is a small chance Castro might be pried from power. "If the economy took a turn for the worse, the military might become concerned that Fidel is out of touch and push him out," Gonzalez says. But that possibility is slim, he says, even if real economic hardship arrived. "It would take a lot for the military to turn against him," he says. "After all, he is the father of the revolution."

Castro has made plans for his successor. After he dies or voluntarily steps aside, he has designated his brother, Raul, who is in charge of the military. But many analysts do not

Continued on p. 1098

At Issue:

Should President Clinton implement the sanctions against Cuba called for in the 1996 Helms-Burton trade law?

JOSÉ R. CARDENAS
Washington director, Cuban American National Foundation

yes

President Clinton must decide next month whether to again waive the Helms-Burton provision that allows U.S. citizens to sue foreign corporations that are both investing in stolen American property in Cuba and have business interests in the United States.

The president, of course, will be urged by the law's critics to continue the waiver, but the debate cannot turn on what one thinks about the law, U.S. policy toward Cuba or trade relations with our allies. That's because Congress was very specific in conditioning the president's waiver authority on whether it is "necessary to the national interests of the United States and will expedite a transition to democracy in Cuba."

Twice now, the administration has maintained that its diplomatic effort to build an international consensus to promote a democratic transition in Cuba has justified a waiver. The problem today, however, is that after an initial spate of promising rhetoric from some foreign capitals, over the last six months there has been little substantive follow-up on our allies' part that could in any way justify a third waiver.

The Europeans, while validating the principles behind Helms-Burton by agreeing to multilateral talks on respecting property rights, have done virtually nothing to promote democracy in Cuba. In Latin America, at a regional summit last month (attended by Castro) ostensibly celebrating "democracy" in the hemisphere, only Argentina's Carlos Menem and Nicaragua's Arnoldo Aleman had the courage to deplore the lack of freedom in Cuba.

And indeed the deteriorating situation in Cuba reflects this vacuum of international pressure. Castro feels no compulsion to respect human rights, has slammed shut all doors to peaceful political change and is even starting to roll back the minuscule economic space he created for some citizens.

Quite frankly, the administration's diplomatic effort to build any international consensus on pushing Castro to reform is in tatters. One would have certainly hoped progress could have been made, but Castro is Castro, and our allies are our allies. The president can, however, communicate a seriousness of purpose by opening the window on lawsuits, indicating to both our allies and Havana that if there is some serious effort to address U.S. concerns on the lack of democracy in Cuba, he will return to the status quo by again suspending the provision. The leverage is there; all that's needed is the political will.

WILLIAM M. LEOGRANDE
Acting dean, School of Public Affairs, American University

no

The Helms-Burton act has a dual purpose: to weaken Cuba's economy by deterring foreign investment and to help aggrieved Cuban exiles recoup their financial losses from almost 40 years ago. Both aims are unrealistic and unwise.

U.S. allies in Europe and Latin America — none of whom agree that Washington's policy of economic denial will promote a peaceful transition in Cuba — are livid over Helms-Burton. By what right, they ask, do U.S. courts presume to impose sanctions extraterritorially against foreigners doing business in Cuba? Several have passed countervailing laws allowing their citizens to sue in their courts if Helms-Burton suits are brought against them in the United States — a potential legal rats' nest benefiting no one but the lawyers.

The Europeans have also threatened to bring the issue before the World Trade Organization (WTO). Washington insists it will refuse to accept a WTO ruling against it on the grounds that Cuba policy is a security issue, not a trade issue. At stake is the credibility and future effectiveness of the WTO, which Washington has long sought to foster because we bring more trade complaints to international adjudication than anyone. Damaging WTO and poisoning allied relations is a high price to pay for a waiver.

Would that price be offset by hastening the end of Castro's regime? Not likely. Some foreign investors may be deterred by the threat of litigation, but most will make their investment decisions based on the business climate in Havana, not Washington. Moreover, the most powerful engine forcing Cuba to open its economy is its link to international markets. Without the Soviet Union, Cuba must trade on the world market at world market prices, and is therefore forced to accept domestic market reforms in order to be competitive. Fidel Castro admittedly hates this erosion of Cuban socialism, but he cannot stop it.

Finally, Helms-Burton gives Castro a new variation on his longstanding appeal to Cuban nationalism. Washington's real aim, he argues, is to restore the property and privilege of the (largely white) pre-revolutionary elite. It's hard to gauge the effectiveness of this appeal to class and racial antagonism, but the frequency with which it is invoked suggests that it touches real fears among ordinary Cubans.

In short, Helms-Burton is more likely to slow the process of economic and political change in Cuba than accelerate it, while antagonizing U.S. allies far and wide. It was a mistake for President Clinton to sign it into law, and he should continue to waive its implementation.

FOR MORE INFORMATION

Cuban American National Foundation, P.O. Box 440068, Miami, Fla. 33144; (305) 592-7768. The foundation is the largest and most powerful Cuban exile group in the United States. In addition to lobbying U.S. officials about America's relations with Cuba, CANF conducts research and publishes books and articles on Cuba-related issues.

The Cuban Interest Section, 2630 16th St., N.W., Washington D.C. 20009; (202) 797-8518. The section, located on Swiss Embassy property, represents Cuban interests in the United States.

Council on Hemispheric Affairs, 724 9th St., N.W., Suite 401, Washington, D.C. 20001; (202) 393-3322. The council seeks to increase interest in Latin America, focusing on trade, civil liberties and politics.

Cuban Committee for Democracy, P. O. Box 331878, Miami, Fla. 33233; (305) 858-5353. The CCD is an organization of Cuban-Americans and other individuals who seek a peaceful, negotiated transition to democracy in Cuba.

Continued from p. 1096

think Raul would be able to hold onto the reins of power. "People may not like Fidel, but they respect him," Olsham says. "As for Raul, there is total contempt for him" because he is seen as a hanger-on with little ability, not as a legendary revolutionary like his older brother.

Others say that Raul may successfully succeed his brother, but not in the same capacity. "After Castro is gone, there will have to be a collective leadership," LeoGrande says, because "no one else in the leadership has the kind of personal support that Fidel does."

Still others are confident that Cuba will shed its communist system after Castro is gone. According to Smith of the Center for International Policy, Castro long ago permitted elections for local assemblies, although candidates must be either independents or Communist Party members. "While Fidel lives, there will continue to be slow changes in the political process," he says. After Castro dies, "the country will develop into a multiparty democracy."

With a few more reservations, Georgetown's Mujal-Leon also thinks that a post-Castro Cuba may begin to democratize, a trend that will certainly be encouraged if, as expected, closer relations with the United States develop. "Castro is such a flashpoint, that I think when he is no longer around it will be relatively easier to have discussions [between the U.S. and Cuba] that could be very productive," he says.

Clearly, at least from the American point of view, many U.S. political leaders are likely to continue pushing policies that isolate Cuba as long as Castro is in power.

The strength of anti-Castro feeling was demonstrated most recently in March 1996, when Congress passed the Helms-Burton act tightening the embargo. During the debate in both the House and Senate, member after member rose to denounce Castro and his regime as brutal and oppressive.

Even Speaker of the House Newt Gingrich, R-Ga., in a rare floor speech, supported the bill. Reflecting the sentiments of lawmakers on both sides of the aisle, Gingrich said that Cuba would receive no American help until Castro was gone. "There is no future for the Castro dictatorship," Gingrich said. "There are no deals."[25] ■

Notes

[1] Mirta Ojito, "Castro, the Pope and Me," *The New York Times*, Nov. 24, 1996.

[2] For background, see "Russia's Political Future," *The CQ Researcher*, May 3, 1996, pp. 385-408.

[3] "Fidel, the Church and Capitalism," *The Economist*, Aug. 16, 1997.

[4] Quoted in Juan O. Tamayo, "Castro, Onetime Alter Boy, Eases Up on Church," *The Miami Herald*, Nov. 10, 1997.

[5] Joy Gordon, "Cuba's Entrepreneurial Socialism," *The Atlantic Monthly*, January 1997.

[6] "The Hazards of Enterprise," *The Economist*, April 6, 1996.

[7] "Fidel, the Church and Capitalism," *op. cit.*

[8] Bernard Baumohl, "Checking into Cuba?" *Time*, Aug. 25, 1997.

[9] William C. Symonds, Gail DeGeorge and Gail Reed, "Castro's Capitalist," *Business Week*, March 17, 1997.

[10] "Fidel, the Church and Capitalism," *op. cit.*

[11] Quoted in Larry Rohter, "Cuba's Communists Peer Ahead, Then Opt to March in Place," *The New York Times*, Oct. 12, 1997.

[12] For background, see "Economic Sanctions," *The CQ Researcher*, Oct. 28, 1994, pp. 937-960.

[13] Hugh Thomas, *Cuba: The Pursuit of Freedom* (1971), pp. 245-270.

[14] *Ibid.*, p. 436.

[15] *Ibid.*, pp. 635-688.

[16] Robert Quirk, *Fidel Castro* (1993), pp. 52-56.

[17] For background, see "Cuba in Crisis," *The CQ Researcher*, Nov. 29, 1991, pp. 897-920.

[18] *Ibid.*

[19] Andres Oppenheimer, *Castro's Final Hour* (1992), p. 101.

[20] Wayne Smith, "Cuba's Long Reform," *Foreign Affairs*, March/April 1996.

[21] T.Z. Parsa, "Club Red," *New York*, Nov. 17, 1997.

[22] Quoted in Baumohl, *op. cit.*

[23] *Ibid.*

[24] *The Miami Herald*, Dec. 6, 1997.

[25] *1996 CQ Almanac*, p. 9-6.

Bibliography

Selected Sources Used

Books

Garcia, Maria Cristina, *Havana USA: Cuban Exiles and Cuban Americans in South Florida, 1959-1994,* University of California Press, 1996.

Garcia, a professor of history at Texas A&M University, traces the origins and growth of the Cuban exile community, beginning with Batista's ouster in 1959.

Oppenheimer, Andres, *Castro's Final Hour: The Secret Story Behind the Coming Downfall of Communist Cuba,* Simon and Schuster, 1992.

Oppenheimer, a reporter for *The Miami Herald*, traces the country's recent troubles, from the mid-1980s, when Fidel Castro executed a number of top military and intelligence officials, to the collapse of the Soviet Union in the early 1990s.

Quirk, Robert, E., *Fidel Castro,* W.W. Norton, 1993.

Quirk, the author of a number of books on Latin America, chronicles Castro's life as a revolutionary, from his days as a university student to his political isolation after the fall of the Soviet Union. The author does a particularly good job of sifting through the mystique that has built up around the Cuban leader.

Thomas, Hugh, *Cuba: The Pursuit of Freedom,* Harper and Row, 1971.

Thomas, the author of a celebrated book on the Spanish Civil War, presents an exhaustive history of the island, from its earliest days as colony of Spain until the early 1970s. The account includes a detailed history and analysis of U.S. involvement in Cuban affairs.

Articles

Baumohl, Bernard, "Checking into Cuba?" *Time,* Aug. 25, 1997.

Baumohl examines the growth of foreign investment in the Cuban hotel and tourism industry. He also shows how some U.S. corporations are skirting the embargo by investing in foreign companies that have properties in Cuba.

Falcoff, Mark, "The Other Cuba," *National Review,* June 12, 1995.

Falcoff, a fellow at the American Enterprise Institute, profiles the Cuban exile community today. He writes: "The Cuban-Americans have . . . demonstrated that it is possible to sink deep roots in a new country without necessarily surrendering one's own identity, and in doing so have formed a remarkable bridge between the United States and Latin America."

"Fidel, the Church and Capitalism," *The Economist,* Aug. 16, 1997.

This piece details the impact of Castro's recent decision to ease restrictions on religion and the economy. It concludes that neither opening will change too much or threaten Castro's position as "maximum leader."

Griffin, Rodman, D., "Cuba in Crisis," *The CQ Researcher,* Nov. 29, 1991.

Griffin takes a now-dated but well-researched look at issues that are still relevant in Cuba today, from the economy to relations with the United States. His profile of Castro is particularly insightful.

Gordon, Joy, "Cuba's Entrepreneurial Socialism," *Atlantic Monthly,* January 1997.

Gordon describes Cuba's efforts to institute limited market-oriented economic reforms. She concludes that the island is making great progress in its efforts to create sustained economic growth.

Olsham, Marc, "Return of the Repressed: Is Cuba Getting Religion?" *Commonweal,* Oct. 24, 1997.

Olsham, a professor of sociology and expert on religion in Cuba at Alfred University, details the growth of religious enthusiasm in Cuba and the government's response to it.

Symonds, William C., Gail DeGeorge and Gail Reed, "Castro Capitalist," *Business Week,* March 17, 1997.

The article profiles Canada's Sherritt Corp., which is investing hundreds of millions in the Cuban economy, mainly in mining, oil and tourism.

Reports

Gonzalez, Edward, *Cuba: Clearing Perilous Waters?* Rand, 1996.

Gonzalez, an analyst at the Rand Corporation, looks at the state of Cuba today and analyzes possible post-Castro futures for the island nation.

The Next Step

Additional information from UMI's Newspaper & Periodical Abstracts™ database

Economy

Werlau, Maria C., "Foreign investment in Cuba: The limits of commercial engagement," *World Affairs,* fall 1997, pp. 51-69.

Werlau explores the reform-generating capabilities of foreign investment as an instrument of engagement in Cuba. The most important reform-generating attributes of foreign investment are restrained while its detrimental side effects appear to hinder the eventual establishment of a stable free-market democracy.

Perez-Lopez, Jorge F., "The Cuban economy in the age of hemispheric integration," *Journal of Interamerican Studies & World Affairs,* fall 1997, pp. 3-47.

Cuba's current economic situation and prospects are analyzed in the context of the ongoing process of Western Hemisphere economic integration.

Exile Community

"A Slim Hope for Radio Marti; U.S. Cuban station has a new leader, but an old obstacle remains," *Los Angeles Times,* Aug. 1, 1997, p. B8.

For more than a decade, the late Jorge Mas Canosa, a Cuban exile in Miami, Fla., was the chairman of the federal advisory board for Radio Marti and TV Marti, which spend about $25 million a year in U.S. tax money to beam news and other programming to Cuba. The original aim of the stations was to provide an alternative to communist Cuba's broadcasting and newspapers, which operate under Havana's watchful eye.

"Don't Let Exiles Dictate Cuba Policy," *Chicago Tribune,* Sept. 14, 1997, p. 20.

The whodunit surrounding the recent rash of terrorist bombs in Cuba is a tough one. Castro has plenty of enemies in Cuba, Miami, Washington — even his own government. Cuba now says that it has arrested a "Salvadoran mercenary" in connection with the bombings, who allegedly got paid $4,500 for each one by the powerful, Miami-based Cuban American National Foundation.

Emling, Shelley, "2 powerful executives personify Cuban exiles' dreams, struggles," *Atlanta Constitution,* Oct. 15, 1997, p. A3.

One is the most powerful Cuban-born executive in the United States. He rarely discusses politics, let alone U.S. policy toward his native land. The other is the highest-profile anti-Communist Cuban in the United States. He is a businessman who has had great influence over U.S. policy toward Cuba. In most ways, Roberto Goizueta, chairman of the Atlanta-based Coca-Cola Co., and Jorge Mas Canosa, chairman of the Cuban American National Foundation, couldn't be more different. Yet each has been an inspiration to a growing Cuban-American community, which today numbers at least 1.25 million people. (Note: Goizueta and Mas Canosa both died after this article was published.)

Erlanger, Steven, "Cubans Blame Exiles in U.S. for 4 Bombings in a Single Day," *The New York Times,* Sept. 6, 1997, p. A4.

A bomb exploded in one of Havana's best-known tourist restaurants late Thursday night, following three bombs earlier in the day at three of the city's sea-front hotels. The Cuban Foreign Ministry said that bomb attacks were part of a campaign of terrorism organized by Cuban exiles living in the United States, with the intention of damaging the Cuban economy. A State Department spokesman here, James Foley, said the United States had no idea of who was behind the bombings, and that the Cuban government "has not responded to our repeated requests for substantive information or evidence to support that contention" of American involvement.

Navarro, Mireya, "Pope's Trip to Cuba Pulls at Exiles," *The New York Times,* Oct. 21, 1997, p. A14.

The pope's visit to Cuba, his first to the nation of 11 million people that was once predominantly Catholic, will likely draw the largest group of Cuban exiles to return at one time to the island since Fidel Castro assumed power in 1959. But the trip has posed a moral dilemma to many Catholic Cubans, who are struggling to reconcile their political stance against Castro with a religious calling to follow their pope's lead.

Fidel Castro

"Castro says Cuba will not abandon communist course: Dictator draws sharp rebukes during Latin American summit on democracy," *San Francisco Chronicle,* Nov. 9, 1997, p. A25.

Fending off calls for political change, Cuban President Fidel Castro told a Latin American summit Saturday that his Caribbean island steadfastly would pursue its communist course. Castro, the only non-elected head of state at the two-day meeting apart from Spanish King Juan Carlos, said Cuba, which he has ruled for 38 years, was "a true democracy, a government from the people and for the people," that produced greater benefits than traditional Western-style democracies.

Horowitz, Irving Louis, "Cuba 1997: Flawed policies and failed prophesies," ***Vital Speeches of the Day,*** **Feb. 1, 1997, pp. 240-243.**
In an address, Horowitz discussed the policies of Cuba and its president, Fidel Castro. He says staying in power without interruption for 38 years is a sign of absolutism.

Schroth, Raymond A., "Cuba sinks under weight of Fidel's dated phobias," ***National Catholic Reporter,*** **Sept. 5, 1997, pp. 10-11.**
Though Cuba was once a flourishing country and Havana a beautiful and luxurious city, Fidel Castro's poor management of the country is causing it to crumble. Castro blames the majority of the country's problems on the U.S. embargo, refusing to understand the real causes of the country's economic condition.

Steele, Jonathan, "Cubans embrace Che anew as Castro's Communist Party congress begins, Guevara's re-burial is being marked with ceremony," ***The Guardian,*** **Oct. 9, 1997, p. 16.**
With the world's ruling communist parties reduced to four, President Fidel Castro launched Cuba's party yesterday on a renewed crusade of resistance to pressure from the United States coupled with modest internal change. The opening day of the party's fifth congress was timed to coincide with the 30th anniversary of Che Guevara's death in Bolivia at the hands of CIA-trained special forces.

Wall, James M., "The Cuban future," ***Christian Century,*** **Jan. 22, 1997, p. 67.**
Wall discusses relations between the U.S. and Cuba. The U.S. embargo on Cuba has given Castro a way to stir nationalist sentiment.

Helms-Burton Act

Bates, Stephen, "Americans pacified by payoff for Cuban deal," ***The Guardian,*** **July 25, 1997, p. 14.**
The U.S. government and the European Commission appear to be shying away from an unwelcome confrontation over the controversial Helms-Burton law after an Italian telecommunications company agreed to pay compensation for using a network in Cuba.

"Cuba Lobbies Against U.S. Embargo Effort," ***The New York Times,*** **June 13, 1997, p. A4.**
Fidel Castro has sent senior aides to several Latin American nations to lobby against efforts in the United States Congress to tighten sanctions against Cuba.

Ferguson, Hayes, "Cuba Gets Dash of Tabasco, Other American Products," ***Times-Picayune,*** **Sept. 21, 1997, p. A21.**
For customers wanting to spice up the rice and beans at Havana's La Guarida restaurant, waitresses are quick to offer a bottle of McIlhenny Tabasco sauce. The 34-year-old U.S. trade embargo against Cuba is supposed to keep American products out of Cuba. And while it has succeeded to a certain extent, it is nonetheless porous. Through a wide range of third-country routes, an equally wide range of American products is winding up on Cuban store shelves and restaurant tables. And in many cases, there's nothing the U.S. government can do about it.

LaFranchi, Howard, "America's Embargo of Cuba: What Result After 35 Years? Next week, Cuba will ask the U.N. to condemn the embargo, a year after Helms-Burton took effect," ***The Christian Science Monitor,*** **Sept. 25, 1997, p.1.**
Cuba will take its case against the United States' economic embargo against it to the United Nations next week, when Foreign Minister Roberto Robaina is expected to ask the General Assembly to condemn the measure for the sixth year in a row. Calculating the cost of every last ramification — for example, the extra fuel cost Cubana Airlines faces for being prohibited from flying over U.S. territory — Cuba will tell the U.N. that the 35-year-old embargo has cost the island $60 billion.

Mitchell, Alison, "Clinton Again Waives a Penalty on Foreign Companies in Cuba," ***The New York Times,*** **July 17, 1997, p. A8.**
President Clinton waived for the third time provisions of a law he signed last year that would allow American citizens to sue foreign companies for using American property confiscated by Cuba nearly 40 years ago. The law, named for its sponsors, Rep. Dan Burton, R-Ind., and Sen. Jesse Helms, R-N.C., was passed last year in an effort to tighten the United States' 34-year economic embargo against Cuba's communist government. Clinton said that European and Latin American countries were taking steps to press Cuba for democratic changes and that he was suspending parts of the law "to continue strengthening cooperation."

Preeg, Ernest H., "A Look at . . . Myths of Cuba: U.S. Embargo: The Illusion of Compliance," ***The Washington Post,*** **Nov. 2, 1997, p. C3.**
The U.S. embargo against Cuba, extended to third-country investors in Cuba by the 1996 Helms-Burton Act, has strong support from the large majority of Cuban Americans. The three Cuban-American members of Congress and the influential Cuban American National Foundation play a critical role in support of Helms-Burton and other measures to tighten the embargo. Yet Cuban-Americans are undermining the embargo by sending increasingly large amounts of U.S. currency to friends and relatives in Cuba. This money, an estimated $800 million in 1996, has done far more to offset the embargo's

effects than the legislation sponsored by Sen. Jesse Helms, R-N.C., and Rep. Dan Burton, R-Ind., has done to discourage third-party investors.

Sanger, David E., "Wal-Mart Canada Is Putting Cuban Pajamas Back on Shelf," *The New York Times,* March 14, 1997, p. D4.
Caught in the no-win position of violating American law or violating Canadian law, Wal-Mart Stores' Canadian unit said today that it had decided to resume sales of pajamas made in Cuba, in direct defiance of American laws that seek to isolate the government of Fidel Castro. Last week, Wal-Mart's Canadian stores pulled its Cuban-made pajamas off the shelves after a store manager in Winnipeg, Manitoba, feared that the company could be violating American law by trading in Cuban goods. When his action attracted publicity in Canada, the government in Ottawa came down hard: It announced it was opening an investigation into whether Wal-Mart's action violated a Canadian law that specifically prohibits Canadian companies from complying with American policy toward Cuba by joining the Cuban embargo. Penalties for violators can mount to more than $1 million.

"U.N. Vote Urges U.S. To End Cuban Embargo," *The New York Times,* Nov. 6, 1997, p. A12.
Most of America's closest allies joined Cuba today in voting for a resolution asking Washington to end its economic embargo against Cuba.

Urquhart, John, "Wal-Mart puts Cuban goods back on sale," *The Wall Street Journal,* March 14, 1997, p. A3.
After two weeks of deliberation, Wal-Mart Stores Inc. will return Cuban-made pajamas to the shelves of its 136 outlets in Canada. Wal-Mart pulled the pajamas on Feb. 27, 1997, after several shoppers questioned whether the retailer was violating U.S. laws prohibiting American companies and their subsidiaries from trading with Cuba.

Religion

"Cuba Yielding to the Pope's Divisions," *Chicago Tribune,* July 14, 1997, p. 10.
The spectacle was not large but was nevertheless electrifying. In the cobblestoned plaza in front of Havana's cathedral, under a huge picture of Pope John Paul II, some 4,000 people gathered on June 29 for the first outdoor Mass held in Cuba in nearly 40 years. Though the pope is not scheduled to visit Cuba for another six months, the anticipation of his arrival already is fueling a renaissance of public expressions of religious fervor in the Western Hemisphere's sole communist enclave. The reaction to the celebration by the normally repressive Cuban government was encouraging: It not only allowed the Mass to take place, but it sent an official representative, and the event was covered by the government-owned TV and newspaper.

Emling, Shelley, "Cuba prepares for John Paul II; Religious expression growing as Communists ease strictures," *Atlanta Journal Constitution,* Oct. 19, 1997, p. B6.
As plans get under way for the pope's first visit to Cuba, the Cuban government is softening its stance, to some extent, toward the church. Cubans say they feel more free to attend Mass, to get baptized and to even wear crosses around their necks in public, a practice that used to elicit stares

Farah, Douglas, "Church Resurrected In a Changing Cuba; Pews Fill Amid Dialogue Initiated by Pope and Castro," *The Washington Post,* Jan. 28, 1997, p. A10.
The Rev. Oscar Perez surveyed his parish church with obvious pride, as dozens of people sat in small groups to discuss the Bible before breaking up to attend the Mass he was about to celebrate. After decades of hostility, relations between the Roman Catholic Church and Cuba's government are undergoing the most profound change since the 1959 revolution led by Fidel Castro. Church workers and diplomats say a new tolerance for religious activity and social programs represents the most likely means in 36 years of introducing elements of change in the rigid Marxist system.

Latour, Francie, "Boston clergy, Cubans embrace cardinal of Cuba: Ortega receives Cushing award from Cardinal Law," *The Boston Globe,* Oct. 15, 1997, p. A16.
For the fervor he rekindled among clandestine parishioners, Cardinal Jaime Ortega, archbishop of Havana, was honored last night in Boston, Mass. Ortega, who will host the first-ever papal visit to Cuba in January, was greeted with a standing ovation by clergy, lay Catholics and Bostonians of Cuban descent as he received the award from the Missionary Society of Saint James the Apostle.

Otis, John, "Cuba to greet pope with mixture of wariness, hope: Church welcomes chance to evangelize; Castro seeks better ties with Vatican," *Houston Chronicle,* Oct. 19, 1997, p. A26.
Ever since Pope John Paul II announced a five-day visit to Cuba, scheduled for Jan. 21-25, 1998, curious Cubans have beseeched Manuel Una Fernandez, a Roman Catholic priest, with fundamental questions about Christianity. The pope will celebrate Mass in Havana, Camaguey and Santa Clara and will symbolically crown Cuba's patron saint, the Virgin of Charity, in the eastern town of El Cobre. Worshippers will include thousands of Americans who, during the papal visit, will be exempted from the State Department's near-total ban on U.S. travel to Cuba.

Rohter, Larry, "Pope's Visit Sets Off Bickering In Cuba," *The New York Times,* Oct. 23, 1997, p. A9.
Less than three months before Pope John Paul II is to make his first visit here, the Cuban government and the Roman Catholic hierarchy are still jockeying over crucial organizational details of the trip as well as the scope of

activity that the Cuban church will be permitted. Lingering tensions between the church and a communist state that for many years embraced atheism appear to have surfaced in negotiations over just how much access ordinary Cubans will be given to papal Masses. In addition, religious leaders and diplomats say that the government has recently instituted measures intended to hamper the church's charity and dissemination efforts.

Steele, Jonathan, "Cuba gives Pope's mass its blessing: Jonathan Steele on the latest step in the diplomatic tango being danced by Castro and the Vatican," *The Guardian,* Oct. 15, 1997, p. 12.

The Cuban government has approved an open-air Mass by the pope in the country's most sacred political arena, the Plaza de la Revolucion. The square is the site of huge parades on May Day and the anniversary of the 1959 revolution. The pope's visit in January will come six years after Cuba changed its constitution to permit freedom of worship and adopted new party rules allowing religious believers to be members. But the decision to accept the pope's request to speak in the plaza marks another intriguing step in the subtle tango the two sides have been dancing since President Fidel Castro met the pope in the Vatican last year and agreed to the visit in principle.

Winner, Christopher P., "Vatican says Cuba trip won't be 'whitewash,'" *USA Today,* Jan. 6, 1997, p. A6.

In an unusually strong attack on the regime of Fidel Castro, a leading Roman Catholic prelate says Pope John Paul II's visit to Cuba, scheduled for January 1998, "will in no way whitewash the Cuban regime nor cancel 30 years of repression."

Tourism

"It's Time to Ease Rules on Cuba; Americans should be allowed to visit there to see the pope," *Los Angeles Times,* Aug. 21, 1997, p. B8.

Let the people go. The archdiocese of Miami has asked the White House to make an exception to the U.S. travel ban so more than 1,000 American Catholics can go to Havana for the January visit of Pope John Paul II. More than religious comfort could be achieved if Washington grants that request. Standing in the way are the rigid and largely outdated U.S. restrictions on citizens visiting Cuba, rules that form part of the 34-year-old economic embargo against President Fidel Castro's government. Washington has made it difficult or impossible to travel to a handful of countries deemed inimical to American interests. Cuba stands at the head of the list.

Thompson, Ginger, "Cuban Blasts Barely a Blip for Island's Thriving Tourism," *Chicago Tribune,* Oct. 1, 1997, p.6.

Judging by the packed hotel lobbies, bars, nightclubs and beaches around town, the bomb scare in Cuba is over. Nine bombings at popular tourist hotels over the summer — one of which killed an Italian visitor — threatened to devastate the tourism industry, which pumped more than $1 billion into Cuba last year. Tourism forecasts turned brighter after the arrest of a suspect, who admitted on Cuban television that he planted six of the nine bombs.

"U.S. to Let 1,000 Go to Cuba to See Pope," *The New York Times,* Aug. 23, 1997, p. A3.

The Clinton administration agreed to let 1,000 Americans and U.S. residents visit Cuba for the pope's visit in January. The approval went to the archdiocese of Miami, which plans to arrange the trip. Approvals are likely for other Catholic groups, including the New York archdiocese.

Back Issues

Great Research on Current Issues Starts Right Here . . . Recent topics covered by The CQ Researcher are listed below. Before May 1991, reports were published under the name of Editorial Research Reports.

JUNE 1996
Rethinking NAFTA
First Ladies
Teaching Values
Labor Movement's Future

JULY 1996
Recovered-Memory Debate
Native Americans' Future
Crackdown on Sexual Harassment
Attack on Public Schools

AUGUST 1996
Fighting Over Animal Rights
Privatizing Government Services
Child Labor and Sweatshops
Cleaning Up Hazardous Wastes

SEPTEMBER 1996
Gambling Under Attack
The States and Federalism
Civic Journalism
Reassessing Foreign Aid

OCTOBER 1996
Political Consultants
Insurance Fraud
Rethinking School Integration
Parental Rights

NOVEMBER 1996
Global Warming
Clashing Over Copyright
Consumer Debt
Governing Washington, D.C.

DECEMBER 1996
Welfare, Work and the States
The New Volunteerism
Implementing the Disabilities Act
America's Pampered Pets

JANUARY 1997
Combating Scientific Misconduct
Restructuring the Electric Industry
The New Immigrants
Chemical and Biological Weapons

FEBRUARY 1997
Assisting Refugees
Alternative Medicine's Next Phase
Independent Counsels
Feminism's Future

MARCH 1997
New Air Quality Standards
Alcohol Advertising
Civic Renewal
Educating Gifted Students

APRIL 1997
Declining Crime Rates
The FBI Under Fire
Gender Equity in Sports
Space Program's Future

MAY 1997
The Stock Market
The Cloning Controversy
Expanding NATO
The Future of Libraries

JUNE 1997
FDA Reform
China After Deng
Line-Item Veto
Breast Cancer

JULY 1997
Transportation Policy
Executive Pay
School Choice Debate
Aggressive Driving

AUGUST 1997
Age Discrimination
Banning Land Mines
Children's Television
Evolution vs. Creationism

SEPTEMBER 1997
Caring for the Dying
Mental Health Policy
Mexico's Future
Youth Fitness

OCTOBER 1997
Urban Sprawl in the West
Diversity in the Workplace
Teacher Education
Contingent Work Force

NOVEMBER 1997
Renewable Energy
Artificial Intelligence
Religious Persecution
Roe v. Wade at 25

DECEMBER 1997
Whistleblowers

Back issues are available for $5.00 (subscribers) or $10.00 (non-subscribers). Quantity discounts apply to orders over ten. To order, call Congressional Quarterly Customer Service at (202) 887-8621.

Binders are available for $18.00. To order call 1-800-638-1710. Please refer to stock number 648.

Future Topics

- ***Gun Control Standoff***
- ***Regulating Nonprofits***
- ***New Approaches to Foster Care***

THE
CQ Researcher

PUBLISHED BY CONGRESSIONAL QUARTERLY INC.

Gun Control Standoff

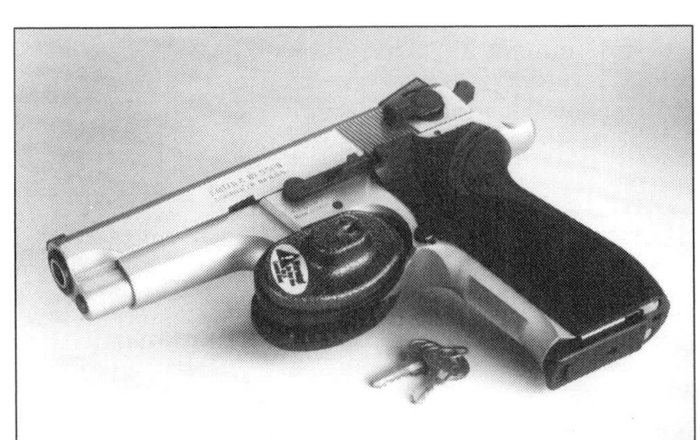

Both sides remain unmoved in bitter debate.

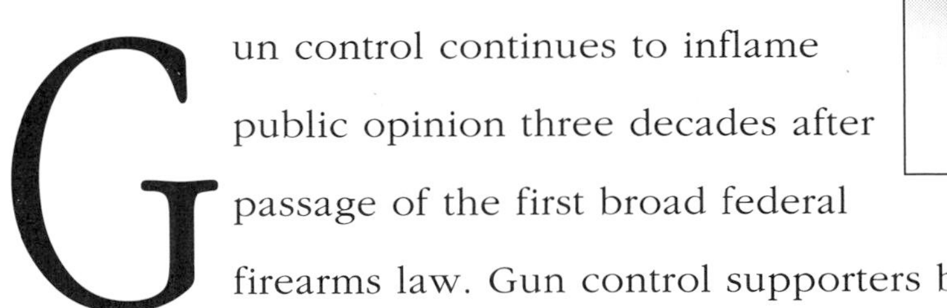

Gun control continues to inflame public opinion three decades after passage of the first broad federal firearms law. Gun control supporters blame the high rate of violent crime and the large number of gun accidents and suicides on the easy availability of firearms and lax licensing and safety rules. Opponents argue that access to firearms deters crime and note that gun homicides are decreasing and fatal gun accidents are at a record low rate. Recently, gun control supporters have been pushing safety initiatives. They scored a partial victory in October when gun manufacturers in the United States agreed to include trigger locks on handguns. But they suffered a defeat in November when voters in Washington state rejected a measure to require safety training for all gun users.

INSIDE THIS ISSUE

CQ Dec. 19, 1997 • Volume 7, No. 47 • Pages 1105-1128

Formerly Editorial Research Reports

Gun Control Standoff

COVER: A SAFETY INITIATIVE REQUIRING TRIGGER LOCKS ON ALL HANDGUNS SOLD IN WASHINGTON STATE WAS DEFEATED BY VOTERS IN NOVEMBER. (SMITH AND WESSON)

THE CQ Researcher

December 19, 1997
Volume 7, No. 47

EDITOR
Sandra Stencel

MANAGING EDITOR
Thomas J. Colin

ASSOCIATE EDITOR
Sarah M. Magner

STAFF WRITERS
Charles S. Clark
Mary H. Cooper
Kenneth Jost
David Masci

EDITORIAL ASSISTANT
Vanessa E. Furlong

PUBLISHED BY
Congressional Quarterly Inc.

CHAIRMAN
Andrew Barnes

VICE CHAIRMAN
Andrew P. Corty

PRESIDENT AND PUBLISHER
Robert W. Merry

EXECUTIVE EDITOR
David Rapp

The CQ Researcher (ISSN 1056-2036). Formerly Editorial Research Reports. Published weekly, except Jan. 3, May 30, Aug. 29, Oct. 31, by Congressional Quarterly Inc., 1414 22nd St., N.W., Washington, D.C. 20037. Annual subscription rate for libraries, businesses and government is $340. Additional rates furnished upon request. Periodicals postage paid at Washington, D.C., and additional mailing offices. POSTMASTER: Send address changes to The CQ Researcher, 1414 22nd St., N.W., Washington, D.C. 20037.

Gun Control Standoff

BY KENNETH JOST

THE ISSUES

When John Darrah served as a juvenile court judge in Seattle a few years ago, he handled "a steady diet" of cases involving guns. The experience left him depressed about the shattering impact of guns on young people's lives and furious with state lawmakers for not addressing the problem more forcefully.

"What I see with all these guns is that adults' selfishness in demanding their 'constitutional right' [to own and sell guns] has really destroyed the future of many children," says Darrah, a veteran King County Superior Court judge. Before guns became so accessible, he says, kids settled differences with their fists, "but now they end up in jail on very serious felonies, sometimes for life. This is foolishness." [1]

Darrah helped form a group of concerned citizens, and last November the gun-safety initiative they spearheaded appeared on the ballot. The measure required safety tests for prospective gun owners and trigger locks on all handguns sold in the state. [2]

Darrah viewed the initiative as a "modest" step, weaker than he would have preferred. But to many Washingtonians, including tens of thousands of gun owners, the proposal seemed a costly and unnecessary intrusion into their lives at best and, at worst, a threat to their safety.

"These are the same types of provisions that show up in places like Washington, D.C., and New York City, where the criminals have guns, the citizens don't and crime goes through the roof," says Jim Gordon, a computer programmer and president of an employee gun club at giant Microsoft Corp., near Seattle.

Washington state enjoys a very low crime rate, says Gordon, a self-described libertarian, because many residents carry firearms. "The criminals know that," he says, "and they don't want to take a chance."

Early polling indicated popular support for the measure, known as Initiative 676, but after a multimillion-dollar campaign by opponents — largely financed by the National Rifle Association — voters decisively rejected the measure, 71 percent to 29 percent.

Gun control supporters, who have turned in the past few years to gun safety as a politically saleable issue, responded to the disappointing defeat with a defiant attack on the NRA.

"The NRA's guerrilla tactics are the highest form of flattery," Sarah Brady, chair of Handgun Control, the nation's largest gun control organization, declared the next day. "Since when does the gun lobby have to work so hard to defeat a measure in so-called 'friendly' territory? Clearly, the tides are turning in the gun control debate."

But Tanya Metaksa, the NRA's chief lobbyist, says the defeat of the initiative represented a victory for "safety, responsibility and freedom."

"Once you explained to the Washington electorate what this was all about, they opted to be on the side of freedom vs. control," Metaksa says. "They opted to be on the side of an issue where government has less power, rather than giving it more power."

The high-powered volleys fired by Brady and Metaksa typify a debate that has raged for at least three decades amid widespread gun ownership and violence, and widespread gun regulations. The United States is believed to have more guns per capita in private hands than any country in the world — more than 235 million according to some estimates. (*See graph, p. 1109.*) But the U.S. also has a complex web of some 20,000 federal, state and local gun laws — viewed by gun control advocates as helpful but inadequate and by opponents as ineffective against criminals but burdensome for law-abiding gun owners. [3]

To some observers, the gun control debate has been uninformative and deceptive. "Neither side is telling the truth generally," says author William Weir, who critiques both sides in a recent book. [4]

"In the war over guns, the first casualty was truth," says Gary Kleck, a criminologist at Florida State University who has written on gun issues for two decades.

Kleck, who describes himself as a member of liberal organizations such as the American Civil Liberties Union, is especially critical of gun control supporters' arguments. In a new book, Kleck calls much of the academic research on guns "virtually worthless." He argues that the best research suggests that the availability of guns has little impact on the level of violent crime generally and that gun control laws have not reduced gun-related crimes. [5]

Kleck also strongly defends his most controversial research finding: that defensive gun use (DGU) by crime victims is common, generally effective in preventing attack and relatively safe for the gun user. On that basis, Kleck calls laws that would "disarm" citizens a "high-risk gamble."

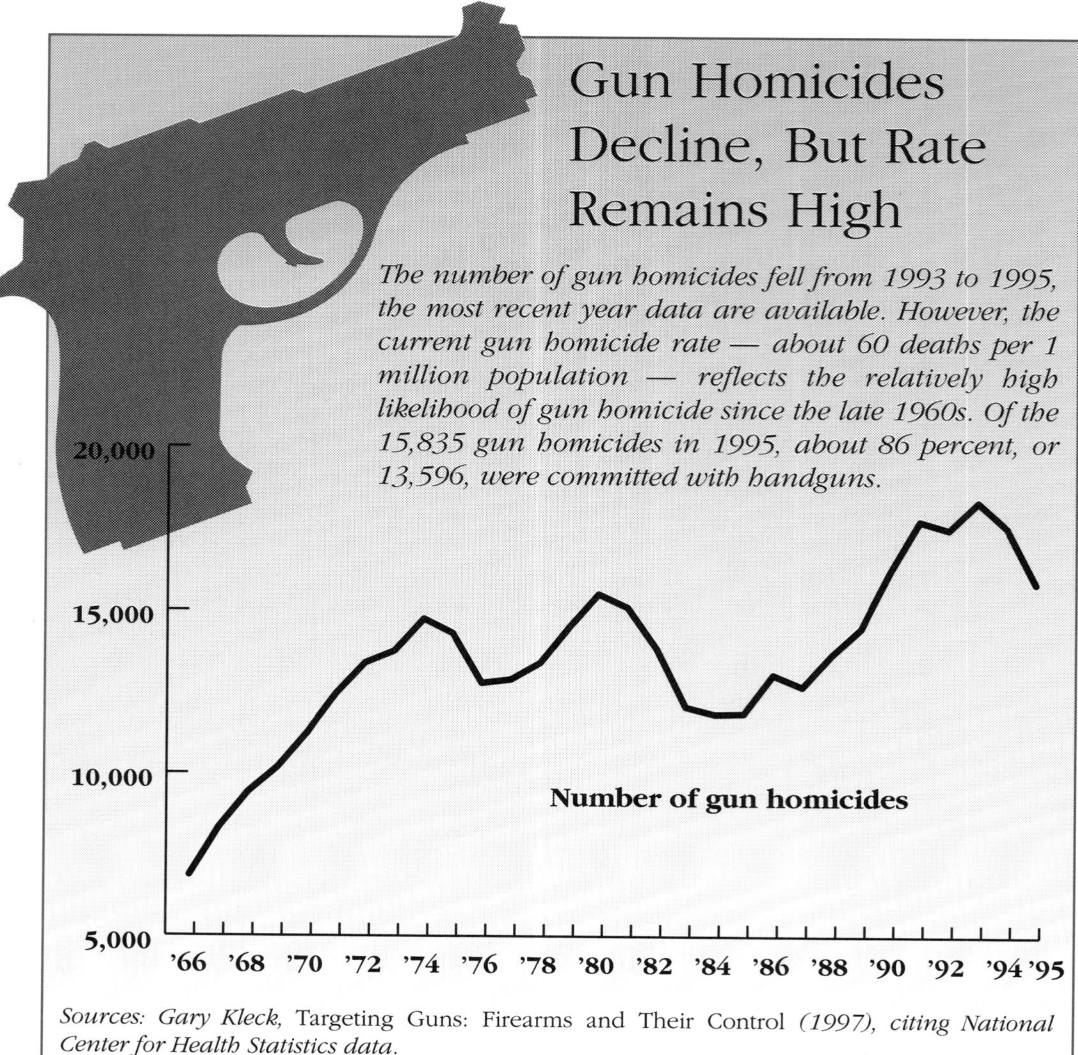

Gun Homicides Decline, But Rate Remains High
The number of gun homicides fell from 1993 to 1995, the most recent year data are available. However, the current gun homicide rate — about 60 deaths per 1 million population — reflects the relatively high likelihood of gun homicide since the late 1960s. Of the 15,835 gun homicides in 1995, about 86 percent, or 13,596, were committed with handguns.
20,000
15,000
10,000
5,000
Number of gun homicides
'66 '68 '70 '72 '74 '76 '78 '80 '82 '84 '86 '88 '90 '92 '94 '95

Sources: Gary Kleck, Targeting Guns: Firearms and Their Control *(1997), citing National Center for Health Statistics data.*

But Kleck also faults gun control opponents for some of their arguments. And he ends by proposing what he calls a "workable" gun control strategy that would include background checks on prospective gun purchasers, regulation of all private transfers of guns and stricter enforcement of laws prohibiting convicted criminals and others from carrying weapons.

Organized gun-owner groups, however, have strongly opposed most of the firearms regulations proposed since the landmark 1968 Gun Control Act was passed following the assassinations of President John F. Kennedy, Sen. Robert F. Kennedy and the Rev. Martin Luther King Jr. Author Weir, who says he belongs to both the NRA and Handgun Control, criticizes the NRA's "hysterical opposition" to any gun control. But he also faults many of the gun laws that have been enacted — including the so-called assault weapons ban, enacted in 1994 over the NRA's fierce opposition. Contrary to gun control groups' claims, Weir says the semiautomatic rifles labeled as "assault weapons" are rarely used in street crime.

The debate over gun control continues to rage despite recent statistical evidence of a declining impact from firearms. Some recent surveys found evidence that the percentage of U.S. households owning guns has fallen below 40 percent; industry figures show that gun sales are sharply down; and the number of firearm deaths fell slightly in 1995. *(See graph, p. 1110.)*

"We don't have the same kind of public outcry that we had a few years ago," says Michael Beard, executive director of the Coalition to Stop Gun Violence, the lone major gun control group advocating a complete ban on handguns in the U.S.

As the gun control debate continues, these are some of the questions being asked:

Can gun-safety laws help prevent accidental shooting deaths and injuries?

Kevin Gilligan was 2 years old when he became a gun victim. On the evening of March 21, 1996, Kevin's teenage half-brother Joseph fired a fatal gunshot into Kevin's head while he was playing with their father's handgun. Two other Massachusetts boys — ages 12 and 14 — died in somewhat similar accidents in the previous eight days. [6]

The deaths spurred Attorney General Scott Harshbarger, a second-term Democrat, to require safety features on all guns sold in Massachusetts. Harshbarger's action reflected recent efforts by gun control advocates to

U.S. Gun Ownership Has Risen

Americans owned nearly a quarter-billion firearms in 1994, according to the most commonly cited figures. Per capita ownership — about 905 guns per 1,000 population — is at the highest level ever. However, the percentage of households owning guns has hovered at around 45 percent since the 1950s, according to the most commonly cited figures, because most gun owners have two or more weapons. ***

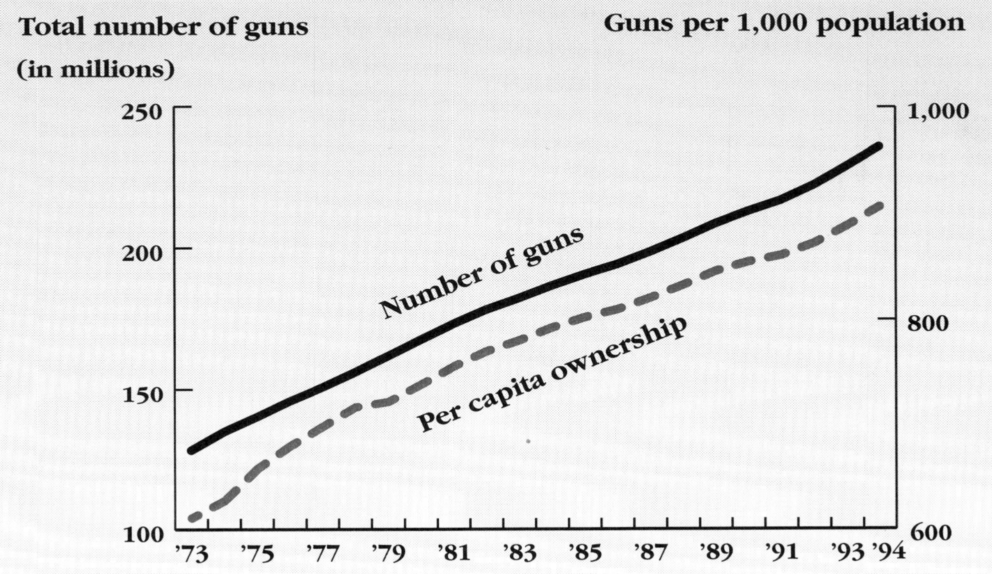

** A more recent survey by the Police Foundation estimated ownership at about 192 million guns, but some researchers suspect underreporting.*

*** Recent surveys indicate a household decline below 40 percent, but some researchers suspect underreporting.*

Sources: Gary Kleck, Targeting Guns: Firearms and Their Control *(1997), citing Bureau of Alcohol, Tobacco and Firearms, Census Bureau, Police Foundation*

promote gun-safety initiatives. Since 1989, some 15 states have passed laws requiring adults to either store loaded guns in a place reasonably inaccessible to children or use a device to lock the gun. Adults can be held criminally liable if a child obtains an improperly stored, loaded gun. [7]

Meanwhile, gun control supporters are also pushing both the states and Congress to require that guns be sold with safety locks. Connecticut became the first state to adopt such a requirement in 1989.

Handgun control advocates applaud such moves, but the NRA is opposed. "We have an objection to anything mandatory, a one-size-fits-all mentality for everything," Metaksa says. "We believe in education. That's what we've been doing, not government mandates."

Various surveys have indicated that many, and perhaps most, gun owners don't follow basic storage safety advice. A Police Foundation study released in May, for example, found that 53 percent of long guns and 57 percent of handguns are usually kept unlocked. And 55 percent of all handguns are kept loaded. [8]

Despite the seeming appeal of the safety issue, gun control supporters were making only slow progress at the state level, even before the defeat of the Washington state initiative. They had made even less headway at the federal level. The Consumer Product Safety Commission is specifically prohibited from regulating firearms, and safety-lock legislation failed to advance in the last session of Congress.

"This is an area of consumer protection where there's been a hole for quite a while," says Glenn Kaplan, an assistant attorney general in Massachusetts. "If the states want anything done, they have to do it themselves."

In October, however, President Clinton announced an agreement among eight domestic gun manufacturers to begin putting child-safety locks on all their handguns. By the end of next year, about 80 percent of all handguns made in the U.S. will be equipped with safety locks. But some gun control supporters minimized the importance of the move. Kristen Rand, chief lobbyist at the Violence Policy Center, says the manufacturers agreed to trigger locks only to forestall mandatory federal safety standards.

Critics of gun control doubt that

Fatal Gun Accidents Decline

The number of fatal accidents involving all guns has declined to its lowest level since 1965, the first year that annual statistics were available.

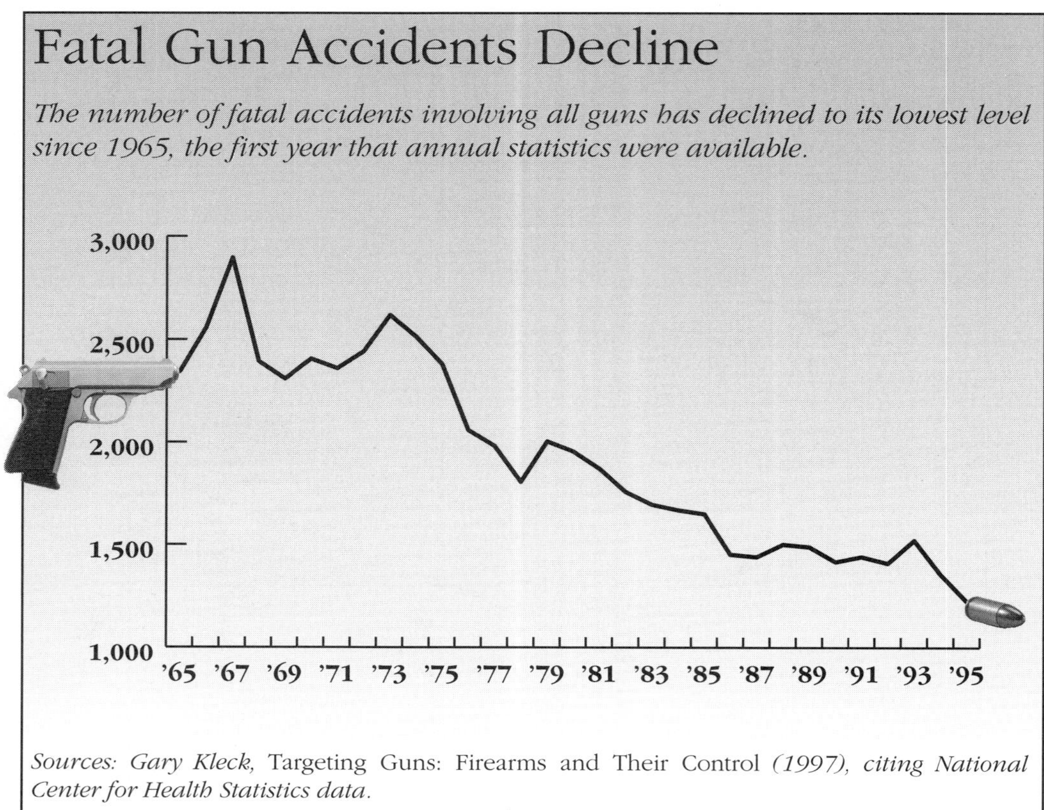

Sources: Gary Kleck, Targeting Guns: Firearms and Their Control *(1997), citing National Center for Health Statistics data.*

child-proof locks will have much effect. "It's unlikely to have an impact large enough that we could detect it," Kleck says. "Of course, one life is one life." [9]

But gun control supporter Philip Cook, a criminology professor at Duke University, says the safety issue indicates a strengthening gun control movement. "We've seen a new feistiness on the part of gun control advocates that has not so far accomplished a great deal," he says, "but maybe it has some prospect for the future."

Do laws making it easier to carry concealed weapons reduce crime?

Gun control opponents have their own "safety" initiative: a decade-long push to enact laws allowing most adults to carry a concealed weapon without showing a special need. Florida started the trend in 1987 with a state law providing for weapons permits to be issued to all adults who seek them except convicted felons and mentally ill persons. "We're talking about allowing people to defend themselves," said the bill's sponsor, Republican state Sen. Richard Langley. [10]

Ten years later, "right-to-carry" laws are on the books in 31 states, and supporters maintain that they have helped reduce crime in Florida and elsewhere. Opponents, however, insist that the statistics are inconclusive and that the laws will contribute to gun-related violence.

The NRA, which has helped pass right-to-carry laws in more than 20 states since 1987, mostly in the South and West, says the laws "respect the right of individual citizens to exercise their fundamental right of self-defense by carrying concealed firearms for protection against criminals." Handgun Control counters that the laws "will increase the number of guns circulating in untrained hands, but will not assure increased self-defense."

Among academics, the debate has been at least as sharp, though densely statistical. [11] One study, conducted at the University of Maryland and published in 1995, found that the number of gun homicides increased after right-to-carry laws were passed in four out of the five cities they studied, including three in Florida. The researchers suggested that the fall in gun homicides in the fifth city — Portland, Ore. — might have been due to tighter gun-purchase laws enacted during the same period. [12]

In a much more detailed study first publicized in 1996, two University of Chicago researchers — John R. Lott Jr., a visiting fellow in law and economics, and graduate student David B. Mustard — reached an opposite conclusion. After analyzing crime data from right-to-carry states, they found instead a significant reduction in personal crime, including murders and rapes.

"Allowing citizens to carry concealed weapons deters violent crimes, and it appears to produce no increase in accidental deaths," Lott and Mustard wrote. They estimated that if states without liberalized concealed gun provisions had enacted such laws in 1992, approximately 1,570 murders, 4,177 rapes and more than 60,000 aggravated assaults "would have been avoided yearly" — at an annual savings to society of $6.2 billion. [13]

The Lott-Mustard study spawned

Continued on p. 1112

Is a Citizen's Best Defense a Gun?

For years, it has been an article of faith among gun control supporters that using a gun to ward off a criminal is both rare and dangerous. But that view was severely tested when prominent researcher Gary Kleck produced evidence that guns are used about 2.5 million times per year in the United States and that these defensive gun uses — or DGUs — help thwart many attempted crimes and only rarely result in injury to the gun user. [1]

Gun control opponents quickly seized on the finding by Florida State University criminologists Kleck and Mark Gertz, touting the statistical conclusion in fact sheets and legislative testimony. Conversely, gun control groups harshly criticized the research as unsupported and unbelievable, pointing instead to an earlier study for the Justice Department suggesting fewer than 100,000 DGUs per year.

This year, the statistical debate took another unusual turn when two pro-gun control researchers produced a report for the gun control-minded Police Foundation suggesting a figure somewhat comparable to Kleck's and then — within the same report — debunked their own finding.

Criminologist Philip J. Cook of Duke University and political scientist Jens Ludwig of Georgetown University said their estimate "is subject to a large positive bias and should not be taken seriously." "The rather frustrating conclusion," they add, "is that the available survey data leave considerable uncertainty about the 'true' number of DGUs." [2]

The statistical debate over the results of two telephone surveys conducted about a year apart has now turned into one of academic honesty as well. Cook and Ludwig, while acknowledging Kleck's methodology as "respectable," nonetheless criticize his 2.5 million estimate as "a mythical number." [3] For his part, Kleck, who initially designed the survey for the Police Foundation and was then removed from the project without explanation, says he believes Cook and Ludwig were chosen to replace him "to put the proper spin on the finding." [4]

Kleck described his research, conducted in early 1993, as the first survey ever exclusively on the question of armed self-defense. Out of nearly 5,000 people surveyed randomly by telephone, some 222 reported civilian defensive use of a gun against a human within the previous year — for a projected annual figure of about 2.5 million instances per year.

In most of the reported instances, the "defender" merely brandished the weapon; One-fourth said they fired the gun, and 8 percent said they wounded or killed the attacker. But only 5.5 percent of the defenders said they were attacked and injured after a defensive gun use, and only 11 percent said they suffered a property loss.

While conceding the number of affirmative responses was fairly small, Kleck nonetheless concluded that defensive gun uses by the "non-criminal majority" had "saved lives, prevented injuries, thwarted rape attempts, driven off burglars and helped victims save property."

Kleck also speculated that his figure was, if anything, low, because some people might be reluctant to report questionable use of a gun. And he strongly assailed the figures produced in the government's earlier National Crime Victimization Survey, saying that the technique used — face-to-face questioning by government employees — would have led many people not to mention having used a gun in the past.

In the Police Foundation study, Cook and Ludwig report that their telephone survey of about 2,500 people found 45 instances of defensive gun use within the past year — projected to be about 1.5 million instances. They call that result "comparable" to Kleck's.

Unlike Kleck, however, Cook and Ludwig argue that respondents probably exaggerated the number of defensive gun uses. Some respondents, they said, may have just been trying to "look good." Others may have been confused about their experiences. And still others, the researchers suggested, may have been "gun advocates" who "know that the number of DGUs is relevant and may be tempted to enhance that estimate through their own response to the survey."

Cook acknowledges that it was "unusual" for researchers to question the findings of their own survey. For his part, Kleck says Cook and Ludwig engaged in "very one-sided speculation about what might lead to errors in such a survey, and only about errors that might lead to overrreporting rather than underreporting."

Whatever the number, Cook and Ludwig end by questioning the value of using a gun to ward off a criminal. Access to firearms, they say, "may encourage some people to be less prudent about avoiding confrontations" or to be "less vigilant in avoiding unsafe situations." And they warn that readiness to use guns can lead to fatal accidents — though they cite no statistics on the point.

Kleck insists, however, that the evidence clearly shows that defensive gun use is common and strongly suggests that it is effective. "To disarm non-criminals in the hope that this might indirectly help reduce access to guns among criminals is a very high-stakes gamble," Kleck concludes, "and the risks will not be reduced by pretending that crime victims rarely use guns for self-defense."

---

[1] Gary Kleck and Mark Gertz, "Armed Resistance to Crime: The Prevalence and Nature of Self-Defense with a Gun," *Journal of Criminal Law and Criminology,* Vol. 86, No. 1 (fall 1995), pp. 150-187.

[2] Philip J. Cook and Jens Ludwig, "Guns in America: Results of a Comprehensive National Survey on Firearms Ownership and Use," Police Foundation, May 1997.

[3] Philip J. Cook, Jens Ludwig and David Hemenway, "The Gun Debate's New Mythical Number: How Many Defensive Uses Per Year?" *Journal of Policy Analysis and Management,* Vol. 16, No. 3 (1997), p. 464.

[4] For a more detailed critique, see Gary Kleck, *Targeting Guns: Firearms and Their Control* (1997), pp. 158-159.

Most States Have Lax Concealed-Weapons Laws

*Nearly two-thirds of the states have lenient "right-to-carry" laws allowing most citizens to carry concealed weapons without showing a special need. Twelve states grant concealed-weapons permits under certain conditions, and seven states and the District of Columbia largely prohibit concealed weapons. **

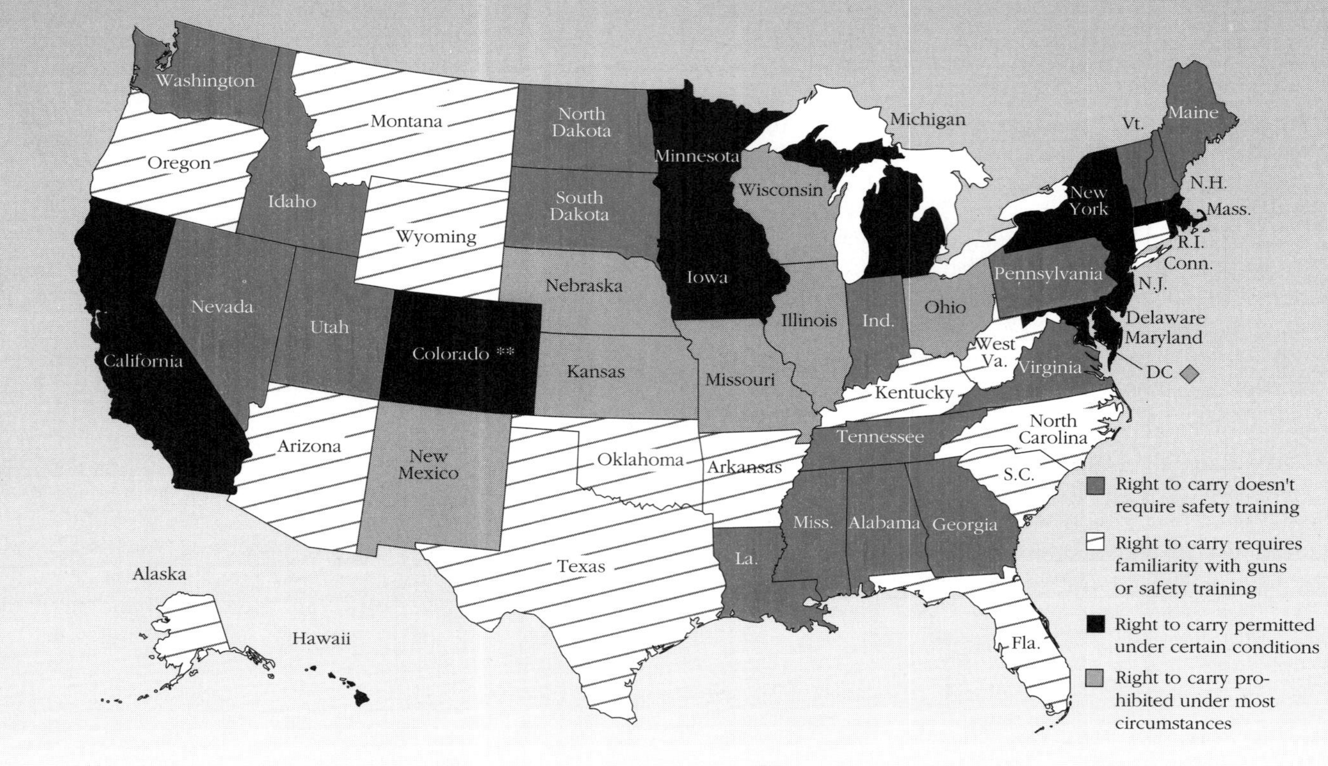

* *Handgun Control characterizes Alabama and Georgia as discretionary permit states, while the NRA counts them as permissive.*

** *Colorado law allows concealed weapons, but permits are actually difficult to obtain.*

Sources: National Conference of State Legislatures; National Rifle Association; Handgun Control Inc.

Continued from p. 1110

what two critical authors have labeled "a minor cottage industry" among academics of reanalyzing the Lott-Mustard data to test — or refute — their conclusions. [14]

In one study, economist Dan Black of the University of Kentucky and criminologist Daniel Nagin of Carnegie Mellon University said Lott and Mustard used data that "provides no basis for drawing confident conclusions about the impact of right-to-carry laws on violent crime."

Black and Nagin said that the decline in homicides and rapes was almost completely attributable to data from Florida. Without Florida, they said, there was "no discernible impact." In addition, they said that the change in crime rates varied too much between states and within states. "Murders decline in Florida but increase in West Virginia," they wrote. "Assaults fall in Maine but increase in Pennsylvania. . . . We doubt that any model of criminal behavior could account for the variation we observe." [15]

Other critical studies followed. Albert Alschuler, a prominent liberal professor at the University of Chicago Law School, questioned the impact of the right-to-carry laws by noting that the data showed a sharper decline in domestic homicides — presumably unaffected by carrying a concealed weapon — than in other killings. [16] Two other gun control supporters — Franklin Zimring and Gordon Hawkins — suggested that the states with right-to-carry laws were unrepresentative of crime rate trends in more urbanized states, which generally still have restrictive weapons laws. [17]

Despite the criticisms, Lott maintains that his statistical analyses all stand up and that the critics are simply wrong in some of their methodological points about the original study. "Allowing law-abiding citizens to carry concealed handguns deters violent crime and saves lives," he repeats in the opening of his response. "The results are consistent." [18]

With the academic debate continuing, some law enforcement officials appear to be backing away from their fears of the right-to-carry laws. "Some of the public safety concerns which we imagined or anticipated . . . have been unfounded or mitigated," Maj. Bill Brown of the Fairfax County, Va., police told a local reporter. [19] "It's not the old Wild West that everyone predicted," said John Russi, director of the licensing division in Florida's Department of State. [20]

Even some of Lott and Mustard's critics acknowledge that the predictions of increased gun violence have not been borne out by statistics. "I don't believe we have any good evidence one way or the other about the impact of right-to-carry laws on violent crime," Nagin says.

For its part, the NRA considers the statistical debate over — and that its side won. "You've seen a reduction in crime," Metaksa says. "You've also seen an increase in the ability of people to defend themselves."

But Joe Sudbay, director of state legislation for Handgun Control, notes that right-to-carry bills failed in a number of states during the past year, including several with Republican governors. Two governors vetoed bills after their legislatures approved them: Republican Bill Graves in Kansas and Democrat Roy Romer in Colorado.

"People are realizing that the systems in place are very weak and don't prevent non-law-abiding citizens from getting guns," Sudbay says. "We think that kind of information coming out more and more will dampen enthusiasm for changing these laws."

Does the Second Amendment limit the government's power to regulate individuals' possession of firearms?

When Georgia banned the private possession of pistols in 1837, the state Supreme Court struck it down, declaring that the state Constitution protected "the right of the whole people . . . and not the militia only" to keep and bear arms. [21]

Opponents of gun control, however, have failed to win the same interpretation of the similarly worded right-to-bear-arms provision of the U.S. Constitution found in the Second Amendment.* Instead, the Supreme Court and lower federal courts have treated the amendment as limited to protection for state militias. As a result, no federal firearms legislation has been struck down on Second Amendment grounds.

Second Amendment advocates contend that the Supreme Court's only pronouncement on the issue, in 1939, is ambiguous and hope that the court may change its interpretation in the future. "I certainly believe that the Second Amendment is just like every other amendment in the Bill of Rights," Metaksa says. "It does talk about individual rights." *(See "At Issue," p. 1121.)*

Supporters of gun control vigorously deny that the amendment provides no individual right to own or carry firearms. "The Second Amendment guarantees a right of the people to be armed as part of an organized state militia," says Dennis Henigan, director of the Legal Action Project at the Center to Prevent Handgun Violence. "It has nothing to do with the private ownership of guns except as a part of the organized state militia."

Henigan's confidence belies the proliferation of legal scholarship over the past 15 years examining the historical origins and meaning of the Second Amendment. *(See "Bibliography," p. 1125.)* Many of the writings — including some by liberal experts on constitutional law — endorse the arguments by gun control opponents that the Second Amendment limits the federal government's power to regulate firearms. But these experts, including some staunch opponents of gun control, also generally agree that many gun laws — including bans on specific types of weapons — would pass muster under the amendment.

"The Second Amendment is relevant to federal gun control legislation in the same way that the First Amendment is relevant to legislation dealing with freedom of expression," says Sanford Levinson, a liberal professor at the University of Texas Law School in Austin. "That being said, I don't believe the First Amendment is an absolute. And I don't think the Second Amendment protects the right of every individual to own submachine guns."

Levinson, who authored a 1989 law review article entitled "The Embarrassing Second Amendment," complains that the Supreme Court and liberal legal scholars both have ignored the amendment. "The Supreme Court has simply dodged this issue, quite shamelessly," he says.

The court itself embraced the militia-protection view of the amendment in its 1939 decision *United States v. Miller* upholding the National Firearms Act, which regulated possession of machine guns. In a relatively brief and unanimous decision, the court said the law was valid because machine guns were "not part of or-

---

* The Second Amendment: "A well regulated Militia, being necessary to the security of a free State, the right of the people to keep and bear Arms shall not be infringed."

dinary military equipment" and had no "reasonable relationship to the preservation or efficiency of a well-regulated militia." Four decades later, the court refused to take up the issue when it left in place a lower court decision upholding a ban on possession of pistols enacted by the village of Morton Grove, Ill. (*see p. 1117*).

Earlier this year, however, one Supreme Court justice threw out an open invitation to gun control opponents to litigate the issue. "This Court has not had recent occasion to consider the nature of the substantive right safeguarded by the Second Amendment," Justice Clarence Thomas wrote in a decision involving the Brady Act (*see p. 1119*). "If, however, the Second Amendment is read to confer a personal right to 'keep and bear arms,' a colorable argument exists that the Federal Government's regulatory scheme, at least as it pertains to the purely intrastate sale or possession of firearms, runs afoul of that Amendment's protections."

"Perhaps at some future date," Thomas added, "this Court will have the opportunity to determine whether Justice [Joseph] Story was correct when he wrote that the right to bear arms 'has justly been considered, as the palladium of the liberties of a republic.' "[22]

Thomas' footnote cheered gun control opponents, but they confess they are uncertain what to do with it. "You have to find a plaintiff who wants to take the time and wait out the process for a period of years with the hope of getting to the Supreme Court," Metaksa says.

Stephen Halbrook, a Second Amendment advocate and the winning lawyer in the Brady Act case, says the amendment's impact on federal firearms laws under a personal-right theory is still "quite speculative."

"It could well be that the courts could interpret the Second Amendment to recognize individual rights, including the right to possess a handgun, but the courts could say that a background check is a reasonable regulation of that right," he says.

In the view of John Snyder, director of the Citizens' Committee for the Right to Bear Arms, a waiting period would be struck down under a broader view of the amendment. "A waiting period . . . does prevent a law-abiding citizen from defending himself or herself," Snyder says. He also thinks an assault-weapons ban would be struck down, but concedes that some bans on possession of "military firearms" probably would be upheld.

Henigan believes that few firearms laws would be ruled unconstitutional even if the Supreme Court adopted a broader view of the amendment. "It seems possible that if they did find it to be an individual right, they could still find that because of the nature of that right — access to dangerous weapons — it is subject to far greater regulation than a First Amendment right, for instance," he says. "It's so obvious that the right to be armed has more immediate implications for public safety than the right to engage in freedom of expression."

Gun control opponents say Thomas' footnote — along with a footnote by Justice Antonin Scalia in a recent collection of his lectures[23] — indicates increasing interest in the amendment at the high court. Henigan, however, emphasizes that no other justice joined Thomas' footnote. "It is Exhibit A showing the extremism of his jurisprudence," he says.

In any event, gun control opponents stop short of predicting that their view will soon prevail. "Whether the Supremes will do this issue, I have no idea," Halbrook says. "Your guess is as good as mine." And gun control supporters strongly doubt that the amendment will be used to strike down gun laws.

"It is overwhelmingly unlikely that constitutional courts will in the future interpose themselves as major barriers to federal firearms legislation," says Zimring, a professor of law at the University of California at Berkeley. "Constitutional courts are interposing themselves in fewer and fewer places to begin with. And this would be stepping into a controversy that they have managed to keep out of for the first 70 years of the modern gun control debate." ■

BACKGROUND

Decades of Violence

Outbreaks of crime and violence have spurred lawmakers periodically during the 20th century to try to control the use of firearms.[24] Gun owners have appealed to an American tradition of using firearms for sport and for self-defense to block those laws, or at least weaken them. The effect of the laws on crime is hotly debated, but there's no argument that they have not prevented the continuing growth of a vast private arsenal of weapons in the United States.

The modern era of gun control begins with the 1911 New York state law requiring a license to possess a pistol. The Sullivan law won overwhelming approval from lawmakers as a way to stem urban crime. Author Weir says the law has been stringently enforced, with relatively high fees for the relatively few applicants who are granted licenses. Evasion, he says, is widespread: "Most of the pistols in New York City are illegal." And he notes that New York's murder count has continued to rise despite the predictions by the law's supporters of a reduction in homicides.[25]

Two decades later, public concern about violence by organized crime prompted Congress to enact the first significant federal controls on firearms.

Continued on p. 1116

Chronology

1900-1950s

Street crime prompts New York to pass trend-setting law to ban carrying of firearms; Congress passes "machine-gun" law during gangster era.

1911
New York adopts Sullivan law requiring state-issued license to possess a pistol; National Rifle Association (NRA) warns the law will "disarm" good citizens.

1934
National Firearms Act imposes $200 excise tax on the sale of automatic weapons, short-barreled rifles and shotguns; registration provision is dropped after lobbying by NRA.

1939
Supreme Court upholds National Firearms Act, saying Congress can regulate firearms if regulations do not impede efficiency of state militias.

1960s

Assassinations and urban violence prompt Congress to pass first broad federal gun control law.

1968
Gun Control Act bans interstate sale of firearms, importing of military surplus weapons and cheap handguns and gun ownership by minors and felons.

1970s

Lobbies form to push gun control, while NRA stiffens opposition.

1974
Founding of Coalition to Stop Gun Violence and Handgun Control.

1977
NRA "hard-liners" oust moderate leadership and install new executive director, who seeks to soften group's image while taking tougher stand against gun control.

1980s

Gun control supporters and opponents swap victories and defeats in the states; Congress weakens federal law.

1981
Morton Grove, Ill., becomes first U.S. community to ban possession or sale of handguns; law is upheld, but goes unenforced.

1982
Kennesaw, Ga., passes ordinance requiring heads of household to have guns and ammunition available; it is amended later to make compliance discretionary.

1986
Gun Owners' Protection Act — also known as McClure-Volkmer bill — lifts ban on interstate sale of rifles and shotguns and limits requirement for license to sell firearms.

1987
Florida passes trend-setting state law allowing almost anyone to carry concealed weapon.

1989
Florida is first state to make adults liable for unsafe storage of guns in child-accident cases.

1990s

Gun control proponents make gains in Congress, but are dealt setbacks by Supreme Court; more states adopt laws permitting concealed weapons.

Nov. 30, 1993
President Clinton signs Brady Act, establishing five-day waiting period to buy handguns and requiring local law enforcement agencies to perform background checks on gun purchasers; act also raises fees and stiffens requirements for gun dealers.

Sept. 13, 1994
Clinton signs crime control bill that includes prohibition on manufacturing and importing semiautomatic assault weapons; measure survives repeal effort in Republican-controlled Congress in 1995 and 1996.

April 26, 1995
Supreme Court rules Gun-Free School Zones Act of 1990 unconstitutional on Commerce Clause grounds (*United States v. Lopez*).

June 27, 1997
Supreme Court strikes down Brady Act's background check provision on states' rights grounds (*Printz v. United States*); most police and sheriffs continue to perform background checks anyway.

Sept. 26, 1997
Gov. Pete Wilson, R-Calif., vetoes handgun safety bill aimed at prohibiting manufacture of cheap "Saturday night specials."

Nov. 6, 1997
Washington state voters reject gun safety initiative by decisive margin.

Mass Shootings Prompt Bans Abroad

Spurred by mass shooting incidents less than two months apart, Great Britain and Australia significantly tightened their gun laws within the past two years.

In Britain, the new Labor Party government last summer pushed through Parliament a complete ban on private possession on handguns. The measure tightened a law passed by the previous Conservative Party government in February that had only banned handguns of more than .22 caliber. Both measures came in response to the deaths of 16 schoolchildren and their teacher in Dunblane, Scotland, on March 13, 1996, at the hands of a handgun-wielding assailant who then killed himself.

In Australia, federal, state and territorial governments agreed in May 1996 to ban the sale and possession of all automatic and semiautomatic firearms. The ban quickly followed the April 28 rampage by a man who used a semiautomatic rifle to kill 35 people on the island state of Tasmania.

Both countries already had tight gun laws before the most recent enactments. Other major industrialized democracies also have relatively strict firearms regulations. Japan — described as having the strictest controls in the world — bans private possession of firearms except by people who need them for official duties or by licensed hunters, shooters, athletes, dealers or collectors. Canada, which has had regulations somewhat comparable to those in the United States, will begin next year requiring licensing of all gun owners and registration of all firearms. [1]

Gun control supporters in the United States have long pointed to the strict gun laws in other countries — and the relatively low gun death rates in those countries — as demonstrating the need to tighten restrictions in this country. Handgun Control notes that in 1992 handguns were used to murder 13 people in Australia, 33 in Great Britain, 60 in Japan, 128 in Canada and 13,495 in the United States.

But the National Rifle Association (NRA) and other gun control opponents insist that the foreign laws are too restrictive and, in any event, cannot be imported into the United States. As for the British and Australian laws, the NRA's chief lobbyist says both laws are overreactions.

"The bans would not have stopped people who are criminally inclined or mentally deranged from creating the carnage that they created," says Tanya K. Metaksa. "But they're symptomatic of a knee-jerk reaction to a tragedy to ban the firearm rather than to take care of the people who have perpetrated the problem."

[1] For background on laws in other countries, written by an opponent of gun control, see David B. Kopel, *The Samurai, the Mountie, and the Cowboy: Should America Adopt the Gun Controls of Other Democracies* (Prometheus, 1992). Kopel is an environmental lawyer in Denver and an associate policy analyst with the Cato Institute, a libertarian think tank.

Continued from p. 1114

The National Firearms Act of 1934 curtailed civilian ownership of machine guns, sawed-off shotguns, silencers and other "gangster-type" weapons through a federal registration requirement and a $200 per weapon tax. A broader pistol registration requirement was dropped in the face of opposition from the National Rifle Association. Five years later, Congress followed with the Federal Firearms Act, which established federal licensing of manufacturers, dealers and importers of weapons involved in interstate trade.

Gun Control Act

The broadest federal law, however, was put on the books in 1968, when the country was reeling from the assassinations of three national leaders — John F. Kennedy, Robert F. Kennedy and Martin Luther King — as well as urban riots and a rising crime rate. To try to stem gun-related violence, Congress passed an omnibus measure, the Gun Control Act of 1968, that remains today as the framework for federal firearms regulation.

The law included provisions that:

- Banned the interstate sale of handguns or long guns — aiming at the kind of mail-order purchase that Lee Harvey Oswald made of the gun police say he used to kill President Kennedy in 1963.
- Prohibited the importation of guns not readily adaptable for sporting purposes — aiming at the "Saturday night specials" regarded as the prime weapon for street criminals.
- Barred felons, minors and persons with mental illness from owning any firearms.
- Prohibited any private ownership of so-called destructive devices, such as bazookas and submachine guns.
- Required persons who sold more than a very few guns to obtain licenses from the federal government as dealers and comply with various controls and record-keeping requirements.

Today, the law's basic provisions are no longer in great dispute, but the partisans in the gun control debate differ sharply on their impact. Gun control supporters say the web of laws has helped keep guns out of the hands of criminals, made it harder for potential criminals to obtain guns and made it easier for law enforcement authorities to track the sale of firearms. "We believe we can save lives by regulating the sale of firearms," says Henigan of the Center to

Prevent Handgun Violence, "and we believe there's more than adequate proof of that."

But opponents say the laws have had little effect on criminals, but a significant impact on gun owners and dealers. "It has made it more difficult for commerce in firearms," Metaksa says. "I don't think it's had any effect on crime."

Academic experts also divide on the issue, but one gun control supporter suggests both the benefits and the costs of the laws are being exaggerated.

"If I had to guess, I would say they are making a difference at the margin, and they're doing it with a relatively small imposition on the American public," Cook says. "The history of the laws is a history of fairly modest restrictions on individual freedom to own and use guns, with fairly modest results, results in the right direction."

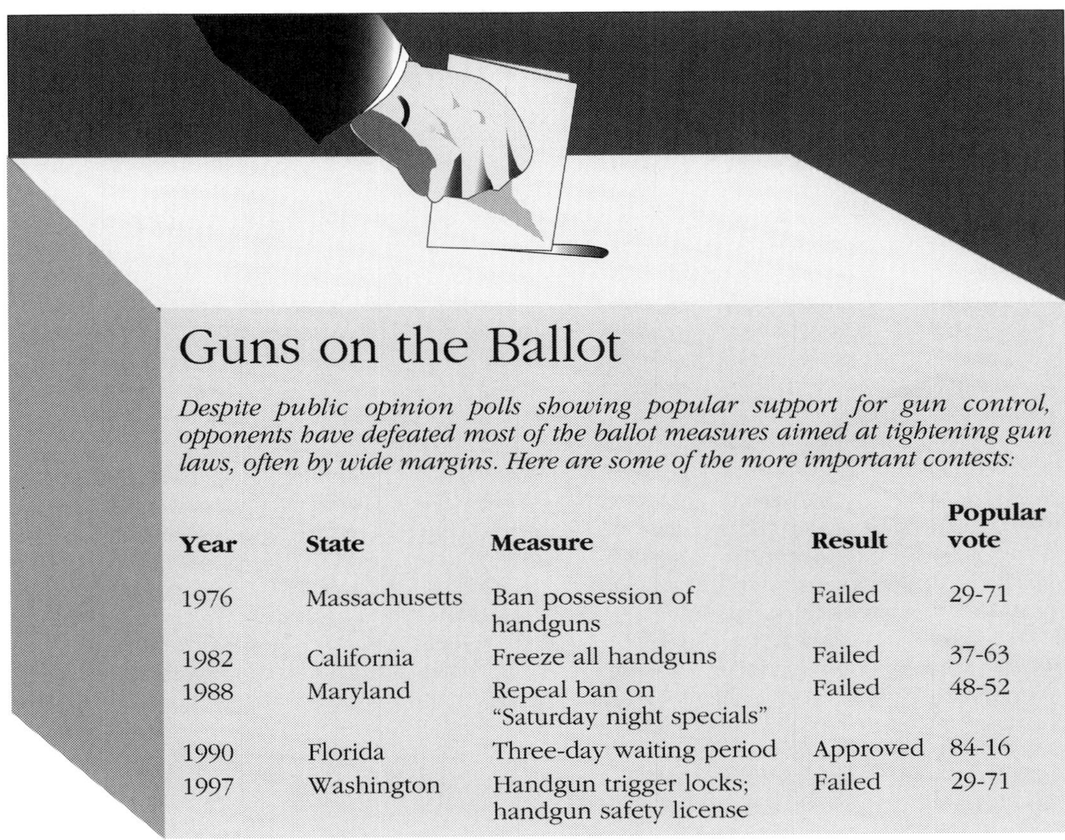

Guns on the Ballot

Despite public opinion polls showing popular support for gun control, opponents have defeated most of the ballot measures aimed at tightening gun laws, often by wide margins. Here are some of the more important contests:

Year	State	Measure	Result	Popular vote
1976	Massachusetts	Ban possession of handguns	Failed	29-71
1982	California	Freeze all handguns	Failed	37-63
1988	Maryland	Repeal ban on "Saturday night specials"	Failed	48-52
1990	Florida	Three-day waiting period	Approved	84-16
1997	Washington	Handgun trigger locks; handgun safety license	Failed	29-71

Swapping Victories

Tiny Morton Grove, Ill., became the first U.S. municipality to completely ban handgun possession. Village trustees approved the ban in 1981 amid clamorous opposition from NRA members bused in for the meeting. Later, the ban survived a legal challenge when the federal appeals court in Chicago ruled, 2-1, that it did not violate the Second Amendment.[26]

Gun supporters responded in kind. In 1982, Kennesaw, Ga., required every head of household to keep a gun and ammunition available. Town officials credit the law with reducing home burglaries, although it has since been amended to allow anyone with serious objections to the law to ignore it.

Nearly two decades later, both ordinances have gone completely unenforced, according to Weir. But they did have the effect of dramatizing the wide gulf in the gun control debate. And they ushered in a decade-plus of back and forth on the issue, with the opposing sides swapping victories and defeats in Congress and in the states.

Opponents of gun control scored their biggest victory in Congress when they persuaded lawmakers to weaken the 1968 gun control law. Most significantly, the Gun Owners' Protection Act — also known as the McClure-Volkmer bill, after its sponsors: Sen. James A. McClure, R-Idaho, and Rep. Harold L. Volkmer, D-Mo. — legalized the interstate sale of rifles and shotguns. The 1986 bill also limited the number of people who were required to get licenses to sell firearms and imposed some limits on federal enforcement against dealers.

The bill was a major victory for the NRA, but supporters of gun control managed to retain the existing ban on the interstate sale of handguns. They also added provisions that barred the importing of barrels used in making "Saturday night specials" — the 1968 law banned importation of most firearms, but not parts — and outlawed the further manufacture or import of machine guns for civilians.[27]

Gun control supporters also scored two quick victories in Congress afterward. Later in 1986, lawmakers approved a ban on armor-piercing

Critics From All Sides Fire at the ATF

The agency responsible for enforcing federal firearms laws has a budget of only $534 million, with half of the money devoted to three other areas. It has a mere 240 inspectors to monitor compliance with federal laws and regulations by 80,000 licensed firearms dealers across the country. But, despite its relatively small size, the U.S. Bureau of Alcohol, Tobacco and Firearms (ATF) generates giant-size controversies among advocacy groups on both sides of the gun control issue. [1]

Gun control opponents regard the agency as an abusive, overzealous police force guilty of small-scale harassment of gun owners and dealers and large-scale fiascos like the botched raid on the Branch Davidian headquarters in Waco, Texas, in 1993, in which a tank assault, tear gassing and fire killed 75 adults and children. The agency "has been manufacturing criminals for decades, creating phony gun law violations to justify its existence," writes Wayne R. LaPierre, executive vice president of the National Rifle Association. [2]

For their part, gun control supporters view the agency as ineffective in enforcing federal firearms laws and, within the past two or three years, guilty of cozying up to the firearms industry.

"ATF has not done their job," says Kristen Rand, chief lobbyist for the Violence Policy Center. "They've become the lap dog of the gun industry."

Accustomed to drawing flak from gun control opponents, ATF made headlines last month when White House aides blasted the agency for laxness in enforcing the ban on imported assault weapons. The aides leaked stories that a "rogue operation" within ATF had accelerated approval of import permits for 150,000 modified assault weapons despite President Clinton's clear intent to keep such guns out of the country. Clinton stepped in the next day to suspend previously issued permits and freeze applications for any more pending a Treasury Department study. [3]

"ATF had enough indications that the administration wanted the ban enforced," Rand says. "The ATF basically gave a roadmap to the industry on how to modify weapons to get them allowed in."

But the National Rifle Association (NRA) says the agency was merely enforcing the law fairly. Tanya Metaksa, the NRA's chief lobbyist, says the guns that Clinton is trying to ban "conform in every way" to the criteria permitted by the 1994 law that banned certain types of assault weapons.

The NRA has toned down its rhetoric toward the agency since 1995, when an NRA fund-raising appeal described ATF agents as "jack-booted government thugs." That remark prompted former President George Bush to publicly renounce his NRA membership. Today, Metaksa says, "We've found that there are always good agents and bad agents in enforcing the law, and we've found both at the ATF."

ATF traces its history back to 1791, when Congress passed a tax on distilled spirits that led to the Whiskey Rebellion. It operated as part of the Internal Revenue Service until 1972, when it became a separate bureau within the Treasury Department. The budget for fiscal 1998 of $534 million represents an 8.5 percent increase over the previous year's figure of $492 million.

In past years, the agency budget was broken out into its four major functions: firearms, accounting for about half of the budget; alcohol, its second-largest area; tobacco and explosives. This year, however, the president's budget dropped those categories and instead showed that the agency was to devote about three-fourths of its budget to "reducing violent crime."

---

[1] For background, see Stephen Labaton, "How A.T.F. Became a Demon," *The New York Times*, May 14, 1995, "Week in Review," p. 5.

[2] Wayne R. LaPierre, *Guns, Crime, and Freedom* (1994), p. 197.

[3] See *Los Angeles Times*, Nov. 13, 1997, p. A1; *The Washington Post*, Nov. 14, 1997, p. A18; *The New York Times*, Nov. 15, 1997, p. A1.

---

bullets — popularly called "cop-killer" bullets. And in 1988, Congress approved a law requiring guns to contain a minimum amount of metal — a provision intended to prevent the manufacture of so-called plastic pistols that could defeat metal detectors. But Weir mocks both laws. He says that the company that manufactured armor-piercing bullets had already stopped making them by the time of the ban. And he says there never was a plastic pistol: The controversy stemmed from a German-made pistol that had a plastic frame but still contained 19 ounces of metal and could be observed by metal detectors. [28]

Meanwhile, gun control opponents were scoring significant victories in the states. The NRA responded to the Morton Grove ban by urging states to pass laws pre-empting local regulation of firearms — and thus blocking any further local bans. By the end of the decade, some 39 states had passed such laws. In addition, the NRA pushed through the first of the new laws liberalizing provisions for carrying concealed weapons. A few states followed Florida's 1987 action over the next few years. Then came 10 more states in the 1995-1996 legislative sessions — bringing the total number to 31.

Gun control supporters did win one significant state-level victory when Maryland banned "Saturday night specials" in 1988. Opponents of the measure qualified a ballot measure to repeal the ban, but it survived, 52 percent to 48 percent, after a nasty campaign marked by pamphlets in Baltimore's African-American neighborhoods depicting the ban as an effort to disarm black people. Earlier that same year, though, California voters decisively rejected a proposal to freeze the number of handguns in the state. [29]

Action in Congress

Bill Clinton's election in 1992 brought a gun control supporter to the White House for the first time in 12 years. With a Democratic-controlled Congress, Clinton helped push through two major pieces of legislation: the Brady bill in 1993 and the assault weapons ban in 1994. But the Republicans' capture of both houses of Congress in 1994 effectively eliminated the possibility of further legislative gains for gun control supporters. And the Supreme Court weighed in with two rulings that struck down gun control provisions on federalism grounds.

Adoption of the Brady Act in 1993 capped a nine-year lobbying drive spearheaded by Sarah Brady, who was an effective spokeswoman for gun control, especially when she appeared at rallies with her wheelchair-bound husband Jim. * Both the House and the Senate had approved the bill in 1991, only for Senate Republicans to block final action in 1992. The logjam was broken with Clinton's strong support in 1993, and Jim Brady was at the president's side when he signed the measure into law on Nov. 30.

A year later, Clinton again had to lobby hard for inclusion of the assault weapons ban in the omnibus anti-crime bill working its way through Congress. Gun control supporters had lobbied for a ban on semiautomatic assault weapons for years, blaming them for such mass shooting incidents as the 1989 killing of five children and wounding of 29 others in a Stockton, Calif., elementary school. The NRA and other opponents ridiculed the proposal, arguing that the weapons being prohibited in fact were rarely used in crimes.

The House had rejected the proposal by 70 votes in 1991, but gun control supporters redoubled their efforts and — with last-minute lobbying by Clinton and several Cabinet members — won the critical House vote on May 5, 1994, by the slimmest of margins: 216-214. Despite last-minute efforts to kill the measure, it stayed in the crime bill that Clinton signed into law in September. The provision banned the further manufacture or import of 19 semiautomatic weapons by name and other weapons if they included certain features — such as folding stocks for rifles and shotguns or, for a pistol, a magazine that attaches outside the grip.

Gun control opponents believe the ban actually contributed to the Republican victory in the 1994 congressional elections by helping defeat some 20 Democrats who had voted for the ban. Clinton himself voiced that view in 1995 when he blamed the Democrats' loss of Congress in part on the NRA. [30] But Handgun Control President Robert J. Walker disagrees. He insists that almost all of the Democrats who lost after voting for the assault weapons ban were from marginal districts anyway and that some supporters of the ban used the issue to help win their campaigns — notably, Rep. Robert G. Torricelli, a New Jersey Democrat who was elected to the Senate.

Whatever the electoral impact, many House Republicans came to Congress committed to repealing the assault weapons ban. The House did approve a repeal measure in March 1996, by a vote of 239-173, but public opinion appeared to be against the move. Senate GOP leader Bob Dole of Kansas, headed toward the Republican presidential nomination, said he would not bring the issue to a vote in the Senate.

Still, gun control opponents continue to insist the measure has done nothing to reduce crime. But a study done for the Justice Department by the Urban Institute estimates that the ban had reduced gun murders by 6.7 percent in 1995. [31]

Supreme Court Rulings

Meanwhile, the Supreme Court was creating problems for gun control supporters. In 1995, the justices ruled, 5-4, that a 1990 law making it a federal crime to possess a firearm near a school exceeded Congress' power to regulate interstate commerce (*United States v. Lopez*). Two years later, in a more significant case, the court struck down a key part of the Brady Act by the same 5-4 margin. The court's conservative majority declared that the provision requiring local police to conduct background checks on gun purchasers violated state sovereignty. [32]

Gun control supporters tried to minimize the two rulings. Congress approved a slightly revised version of the gun-free school zone law in 1996, circumventing the court's 1995 ruling by requiring prosecutors to prove an impact on interstate commerce as an element of the offense. The law has yet to be tested. As for

---

* James S. Brady was President Ronald Reagan's press secretary and was shot and seriously wounded during the March 30, 1981, assassination attempt on Reagan.

the Brady Act, its supporters emphasized that most of the provisions, including the mandatory five-day waiting period, were unaffected by the ruling. They also said that most police and sheriffs' departments would continue to do the background checks either voluntarily or because of state law requirements. And they cited Justice Department figures to claim that the law had blocked more than 250,000 sales to people not eligible to buy firearms during its three years on the books. [33]

Not surprisingly, the NRA disputed claims that the law was preventing unauthorized purchases of firearms by pointing to the relatively small number of criminal prosecutions brought under the law. They also said that a better method of enforcing the purchase restrictions was the instant computerized verification system that the law mandated the federal government to institute by the end of 1998.

In both decisions, the majority justices steered clear of any substantive pronouncement about gun control except for Thomas' invocation of the Second Amendment in his controversial footnote. As for the dissenting justices, they argued in both cases that the court should have deferred to Congress' judgment about the need for legislation to control gun violence.

Most legal commentators viewed the decisions as significant for their impact on federalism rather than on gun control. But David Williams, a professor at Indiana University School of Law, says the justices may be preparing to take on the right-to-bear-arms issue. "I don't think it's a coincidence that they're taking all of these federalism decisions [concerning] guns," he says. "They're thinking about federalism and guns together." ■

CURRENT SITUATION

Washington State Loss

With about a month before the Nov. 4 election, supporters of the gun safety initiative in Washington were optimistic. Their polls showed 62 percent support for the measure, Initiative 676, which required trigger-locking devices on all handguns sold in the state and handgun safety licenses.

But voters rejected the initiative by 697,000 votes — 71 percent to 29 percent. What happened is a matter of sharp dispute between the opposing sides in the gun control debate.

Opponents of the initiative say they organized an effective grass-roots campaign, with 13,000 in-state contributors, 27,000 volunteers, 83,000 yard signs and 600,000 "door hangers" distributed the weekend before the balloting. "We outworked them in the critical weeks of the campaign," says Alan Gottlieb, director of Washington Citizens Against Regulatory Excess — dubbed WeCARE.

Supporters of Initiative 676 blame their defeat not on a grass-roots campaign but on more than $2 million they say the NRA contributed to help pay for last-minute billboards, print ads and radio and television commercials.

"You can't take that kind of barrage and expect any other result," says Tom Wales, a federal prosecutor who was co-chairman of Washington Citizens for Handgun Safety. "We simply did not have the resources to keep our voice from being drowned out."

The opponents' advertising campaign undercut the initiative's early support by claiming the measure's licensing provisions would entangle gun users in red tape and unnecessary safety training. They also claimed that the measure would expose gun users' medical records to law enforcement agencies and eliminate an existing provision for stalking victims to get expedited processing for gun permits.

Wales says the latter two issues were particularly effective in eroding support among women, its strongest constituency. The initiative's supporters argued in vain that the allegations were false. They said the initiative made the same provision as existing law to require disclosure if a gun permit applicant had been committed to a mental institution. As for stalking victims, they said that local police could still grant waivers of the waiting period if necessary.

Gottlieb says that opponents of the initiative had already started to turn the corner by mid-October, before the big advertising blitz. Polls then showed the measure behind, 46 percent to 49 percent. Opponents continued to gain momentum. All but five Washington newspapers opposed the initiative, as did the influential Washington State Council of Police Officers and the state's association of firearms instructors.

In retrospect, national gun control leaders faulted the initiative's supporters for creating an overly complex measure — eight pages long — and for failing to enlist law enforcement support at the outset. But Wales says supporters met with local law enforcement officials and were convinced there was no way to gain their support. "I'm not sure that doing anything differently would have made any difference," he says.

Setback in California

The defeat came only six weeks af-

Continued on p. 1122

At Issue:

Does the Second Amendment guarantee an individual right to keep and bear arms?

yes

Tanya K. Metaksa
Chief lobbyist, National Rifle Association

Our Founding Fathers did not create our civil liberties. They safeguarded them in the Bill of Rights, and we all know it's true. Diminish freedom of the press, and we diminish democracy. Usher out the right of the people to peaceable assembly, and we usher in a police state. Abandon the safeguard against unreasonable searches and seizures, and we abandon our homes.

Then there's that Second Amendment.

Second Amendment opponents say the right belongs to states, but consider the words of Yale law Professor Akil Amar. "The ultimate right to keep and bear arms belongs to 'the people' not 'the states.' . . . '[T]he people' at the core of the Second Amendment are the same 'people' at the heart of the Preamble and the First Amendment, namely citizens."

Finding others who concur is hardly difficult. Professor Glenn Harlan Reynolds of the University of Tennessee summed it up by saying that scholars adhering to an individual-rights interpretation, "dominate the academic literature on the Second Amendment almost completely."

Second Amendment opponents say the courts are hostile to this right. Yes, certain jurists have an aversion to certain rights, and no one should be surprised. It's the Murphy's Law of American civil rights.

Duke University's William Van Alstyne argues, "[T]he essential claim advanced by the NRA with respect to the Second Amendment is extremely strong . . . . The constructive role of the NRA today, like the role of the [American Civil Liberties Union] in the 1920s with respect to the First Amendment, ought itself not to be dismissed lightly."

Van Alstyne is saying that while First Amendment jurisprudence didn't begin until the 1920s, no one argues there were no First Amendment rights then, and no one should argue there are no Second Amendment rights now.

Second Amendment opponents say the NRA won't take this right to the Supreme Court, but it is they who fear such a case. When the NRA sought a decision by the Supreme Court in the *Morton Grove* handgun ban on Second Amendment grounds, it was Handgun Control that urged the court not to hear the case.

Half the households in the United States exercise this right. This right empowers Americans to use firearms to thwart crime 2.5 million times annually. This right is why 71 percent of Washington state voters rejected a draconian gun owner registration scheme in the 1997 elections, and why the national trend is toward policies like right to carry.

For indeed, the Second Amendment preserves the greatest human right — the right to defend one's own life.

no

Dennis A. Henigan
Director, Legal Action Project, Center to Prevent Handgun Violence

A well regulated Militia, being necessary to the security of a free State, the right of the people to keep and bear Arms, shall not be infringed.
(Second Amendment to the U.S. Constitution)

In 1991, former Chief Justice Warren Burger referred to the Second Amendment as "the subject of one of the greatest pieces of fraud, I repeat the word 'fraud,' on the American people by special interest groups that I have ever seen in my lifetime." The NRA, Burger said, had "misled the American people and they, I regret to say, they have had far too much influence on the Congress . . . than as a citizen I would like to see — and I am a gun man."

The "fraud" denounced by the chief justice is the inexcusable failure of the gun lobby to acknowledge the full text of the Second Amendment and its consistent interpretation by the courts. The Second Amendment is the only provision in the Bill of Rights with an express statement of its purpose. The grant of the right "to keep and bear arms" is preceded by a preamble the NRA chooses to ignore: "A well regulated Militia, being necessary to the security of a free State. . . ."

The federal courts have unanimously held that the amendment grants the people the right to be armed only in connection with service in state militias. As the Supreme Court has written, the "obvious purpose" of the Second Amendment was "to assure the continuation and render possible the effectiveness" of the state militia, adding that the amendment "must be interpreted and applied with that end in view." And the "well regulated Militia" is not a self-appointed army of "patriots" training for armed resistance to government policies they oppose. Twice the Supreme Court has held that the modern version of the constitutional "militia" is the National Guard.

If the NRA's Charlton Heston is right, and the Second Amendment confers our most important constitutional right, then why did the NRA attack the Brady Act in court as a violation of the Tenth Amendment, but not the Second Amendment? And why doesn't the NRA's lawsuit against the federal assault weapon ban even mention the Second Amendment? Because the NRA is well aware that never in our nation's history has a gun law been struck down on Second Amendment grounds. On this issue, the NRA is not only guilty of fraud, but of hypocrisy as well.

Gun violence is not a constitutional issue; it is a public health and safety issue. The constitutional debate is phony. The 35,000 Americans fatally shot every year are real.

Continued from p. 1120

ter gun control proponents had suffered another setback. In the face of strong opposition from the NRA, gun control advocates had pushed a bill through the California Legislature requiring tough safety standards for U.S.-made "Saturday night specials" — more than 80 percent of which are manufactured in the Los Angeles area.

But California's Republican governor, Pete Wilson, vetoed the measure in September, saying it would deprive law-abiding people of a chance to buy inexpensive protection from crime.

Gun control supporters can count some victories during the past year, including the gun-safety regulations in Massachusetts and the defeat of concealed weapons bills in several states. Handgun Control's Sudbay says the group will continue to push for safety legislation in several states, including a bill in New Jersey to require the manufacture of so-called "smart" or personalized handguns that can only be operated by an authorized user. But he concedes that in many other states gun control supporters will be "in a defensive posture," seeking to block passage of concealed weapons laws.

Metaksa says the decisive defeat of the Washington state initiative should thwart efforts to enact similar legislation in other states. "I mean, this wasn't a squeaker," she says. "This was a blowout."

Standoff in Congress

Even as the Brady Act was being challenged in court, gun control supporters drew up an omnibus gun control bill dubbed Brady II that, among other things, sought to require federal licensing of handgun owners and registration of handgun transfers, raise the minimum age for possession of handguns to 21 and prohibit "Saturday night specials." But political realities forced them to concentrate their efforts on less ambitious goals, like mandatory trigger locks and "one-gun-a-month" limits on handgun purchases to thwart street criminals.

On the opposite side, gun control opponents still want to repeal the assault weapons ban but have likewise bowed to political reality in putting that issue on a back burner. Instead, they spent the past session resisting or trying to undo initiatives from the other side. Early in the session, for example, they unsuccessfully sought to weaken or repeal a provision enacted late in 1996 that barred possession of firearms or ammunition by anyone who had been convicted of a domestic violence offense.

Gun control supporters had the initiative during most of the session. President Clinton endorsed the trigger-lock provision in his State of the Union message. But House GOP leaders kept the provision out of an administration-backed juvenile justice bill, in part to keep any gun issues out of the legislation. After the House approved the bill, supporters of the trigger lock provision were still hoping to add it to the measure in the Senate. But the agreement by the major domestic gunmakers to include trigger locks in newly manufactured guns has all but killed the prospect of congressional legislation.

Apart from the trigger-lock issue, the only other fights over firearms issues were minor skirmishes. Gun control supporters counted as a victory a provision earmarking a modest $1.3 million add-on for the Bureau of Alcohol, Tobacco and Firearms (ATF) to help trace guns used by juveniles in crimes. (*See story, p. 1118.*) They also claimed victory in defeating an effort by gun owners' groups to exempt from the assault weapons ban certain U.S. military surplus weapons that had been given to foreign governments and then modified to include features covered by the ban. But supporters of the move succeeded in requiring a study of the issue. "They'll be back," says Handgun Control lobbyist Marie Carbone.

The NRA, still licking its wounds from the setbacks in President Clinton's first term, had no victories to boast of during the past congressional session. But Metaksa took credit for bottling up any gun control initiatives, like the trigger-lock requirement or one-gun-a-month proposal. "So far we've been able to hold off those kinds of proposals both in the House and the Senate," she says.

From her perspective, Carbone says that gun control opponents have a numerical edge in Congress but have been reluctant to use their advantage. "Probably the other side starts out ahead, but they haven't really done anything with that," she says. "I think that shows that basically the American people support our position, and [gun control opponents] have been a little bit reluctant to do things with the [congressional] support that they have." ■

OUTLOOK

Unchanging Debate

In a new book, longtime gun control advocates Zimring and Hawkins argue that the overall U.S. crime rate is comparable to the crime rate in other industrialized countries. But the United States does have a significantly higher rate of fatal crimes, they say. And they blame the high death rate on one factor in particular: the distinctly American high level of gun ownership and gun availability.

"The use of firearms in assault and robbery is the single environmental factor of American society that is most clearly linked to the extraordinary death rate from interpersonal violence in the United States," they write. [34]

Gun control supporters have long made that point their central premise: that guns cause crime and that restricting their availability will reduce crime. The NRA and other gun owner groups have a succinct response: "Guns don't kill people, people kill people," they say. The solution to gun crime, they say, is getting tough with criminals, not with gun owners.

Gun control skeptic Kleck dismisses both arguments as simplistic fallacies. Longer prison sentences and other get-tough crime policies, he says, have not been effective in reducing crime levels overall. But gun controls have not been shown by the evidence to have much impact on crime, except for a weak effect on a few specific categories of offenses.

Gun control supporters achieved significant victories in the first two years of the Clinton administration but have been stymied since by an anti-gun control leadership in the Republican-controlled Congress. The safety initiatives being pushed by gun control groups on Capitol Hill and in state capitals represent an end-run around the opposition. Kleck and Zimring both say the efforts are worthwhile, but minimize their long-term significance. "It's an interesting new wrinkle," Zimring says, "but I would be terribly surprised if it became the center of controversy over the next decade."

Politically, the major advocacy groups disagree sharply about the trend on the issue. The NRA's Metaksa says that despite President Clinton's strong support, gun control advocates "have had a harder time over the last few years."

"The momentum is shifting to freedom and to people being responsible for their own actions," she says. "When that happens, I think you will see the proposals by our opponents have less credibility and less support."

"I think they're completely and absolutely wrong," says Handgun Control's Walker. He says most Americans continue to favor moderate gun controls and that support for gun control is generally a plus in political campaigns.

"It's fair to say now that there are as many one-issue voters on our side as there are one-issue voters on the other side," Walker says. "When guns are an issue, a hot issue in the race, we believe that the winner in the vast majority of races is going to be the pro-gun control candidate."

Still, gun control supporters are also pursuing a non-political strategy. "Some people I talk to in the gun control movement say their best hope is through litigation," says Duke's Cook. "They have seen what the attorneys general have done through the tobacco litigation, and they see that as a model of what they can do in terms of the kinds of guns or types of ammunition that can be marketed. That gives them the possibility of a big win without having to go through the state legislatures or Congress."

So far, however, gun control ad-

FOR MORE INFORMATION

American Shooting Sports Council, 1845 The Exchange, Suite 150, Atlanta, Ga. 30339; 770-933-0200 [www.assc.org]. The trade association represents gun manufacturers, retailers and distributors.

Bureau of Alcohol, Tobacco and Firearms, Department of the Treasury, 650 Massachusetts Ave., N.W., Suite 8100; Washington, D.C. 20226; (202) 927-7970 [www.atf.treas.gov/]. The ATF enforces federal gun laws.

Citizens Committee for the Right to Keep and Bear Arms, 12500 N.E. Tenth Pl., Bellevue, Wash. 98005; 425-454-4911. The committee, founded in 1974, claims about 600,000 members and supporters.

Coalition to Stop Gun Violence, 1000 16th St. N.W., Suite 603, Washington, D.C. 20036; 202-530-0340. The coalition is the successor organization to the National Coalition to Ban Handguns, founded in 1974, and continues to favor the ultimate goal of banning all handguns in the United States.

Gun Owners of America, 8001 Forbes Place, Suite 102; Springfield, Va. 22151; 703-321-8585. Founded in 1975, the group claims about 180,000 members.

Handgun Control Inc., 1225 I St. N.W., Suite 1100, Washington, D.C. 20005; 202-898-0792 [www.handguncontrol.org] Founded in 1974 as the National Council to Control Handguns, this is the largest of the gun control advocacy groups, claiming 400,000 members.

National Rifle Association, 11250 Waples Mill Rd., Fairfax, Va. 22030; 703-267-1000 [www.nra.org]. The NRA, founded in 1871 and with a current claimed membership of 3 million, has been a powerful lobbying force against firearms regulations since the 1930s.

Police Foundation, 1201 Connecticut Ave. N.W., Suite 200, Washington, D.C. 20036; 202-833-1460. The foundation is a privately funded, independent organization established by the Ford Foundation in 1970 for the purpose of supporting improvements in policing; it supports gun control.

Violence Policy Center, 1350 Connecticut Ave. N.W., Suite 825, Washington, D.C. 20036; 202-822-8200 [www.vpc.org]. The center was founded in 1988 as a research and advocacy group on gun control issues.

vocates have not won final rulings imposing liability on gun manufacturers or dealers for gun injuries or deaths. Still, gun manufacturers are sufficiently concerned that they have lobbied Congress to include protective provisions in pending product liability overhaul bills.

Meanwhile, the central issues remain much the same today as they have been for decades. "The core concerns of the gun debate may never change," Zimring says. "They haven't changed in a generation."

"What you've had here for a long time is a yin and yang thing, more back and forth," says author Weir. "I think it's a controversy that will probably be around for a long time." ■

Notes

[1] For background, see "Juvenile Justice," *The CQ Researcher,* Feb. 25, 1994, pp. 169-192.

[2] For detailed background on the initiative, see Barbara A. Serrano, "Gun Measure Isn't as Simple as It Seems," *The Seattle Times,* Oct. 26, 1997, p. A1. See also *The New York Times,* Oct. 13, 1997, p. A1.

[3] For background, see "Gun Control," *The CQ Researcher,* June 10, 1994, pp. 505-528.

[4] See William Weir, *A Well Regulated Militia: The Battle for Gun Control* (1997).

[5] Gary Kleck, *Targeting Guns: Firearms and Their Control* (1997). The book is an updated and less technical version of Kleck's earlier book, *Point Blank: Guns and Violence in America* (1991).

[6] See *The Boston Globe,* March 22, 1996.

[7] The states are California, Connecticut, Delaware, Florida, Hawaii, Iowa, Maryland, Minnesota, Nevada, New Jersey, North Carolina, Rhode Island, Texas, Virginia and Wisconsin.

[8] Philip J. Cook and Jens Ludwig, "Guns in America: Results of a Comprehensive National Survey on Gun Ownership and Use," Police Foundation, May 1997, pp. 20-21.

[9] Quoted in *USA Today,* Oct. 10, 1997. See also *The New York Times,* Oct. 9, 1997, p. A1.

[10] Quoted in *St. Petersburg Times,* May 13, 1987.

[11] See *The Washington Post,* March 23, 1997, p. C5.

[12] See David McDowall, Colin Loftin and Brian Wieresma, "Easing Concealed Firearms Law: Effects on Homicides in Three States," *Journal of Criminal Law and Criminology,* Vol. 86 (fall 1995), pp. 193-206. See also *The New York Times,* March 15, 1995, p. A23. The other cities studied were Jacksonville, Miami, Tampa and Jackson, Miss.

[13] See John R. Lott Jr. and David B. Mustard, "Crime, Deterrence, and Right-to-Carry Concealed Handguns," *Journal of Legal Studies,* January 1997, pp. 1-68. See also John R. Lott Jr., "More Guns, Less Violent Crime," *The Wall Street Journal,* Aug. 28, 1996, p. A13.

[14] See Franklin Zimring and Gordon Hawkins, "Concealed Handguns: The Counterfeit Debate," *The Responsive Community,* spring 1997, p. 55.

[15] Dan A. Black and Daniel S. Nagin, "Do 'Right-to-Carry' Laws Deter Violent Crime?" *Journal of Legal Studies,* January 1998 [forthcoming]. The Black-Nagin study was first circulated in October 1996.

[16] Albert W. Alschuler, "Two Guns, Four Guns, Six Guns, More Guns: Does Arming the Public Reduce Crime," *Valparaiso University Law Review,* Vol. 31 (1997), pp. 1-9.

[17] Zimring and Hawkins, *op. cit.,* pp. 45-60. Zimring is a professor of law at the University of California at Berkeley; Hawkins is a retired professor of criminology at the University of Sydney, in Australia.

[18] See John R. Lott Jr., "The Concealed Handgun Debate," *Journal of Legal Studies,* January 1998 [forthcoming]. See also John R. Lott Jr., *More Guns, Less Crime: Understanding Crime and Gun Control Laws* (University of Chicago Press, April 1998) [forthcoming].

[19] Quoted in *Fairfax Journal,* July 9, 1997, p. 1.

[20] Quoted in Ellen Perlman, "Living With Concealed Weapons," *Governing,* February 1996, p. 34.

[21] The case is *Nunn v. State* (1846), cited in Weir, *op. cit.,* p. 37.

[22] The case is *Printz v. United States.* Story's reference came from his book *Commentaries* (1833).

[23] See Antonin Scalia, *A Matter of Interpretation: Federal Courts and the Law* (1997), pp. 136-137 n. 13 ("It would also be strange to find in the midst of a catalog of the rights of individuals a provision securing to the states the right to maintain a designated 'Militia'.")

[24] Much of the historical background is drawn from Weir, *op. cit.*

[25] *Ibid.,* p. 41.

[26] The case is *Quilici v. Village of Morton Grove.*

[27] See *1986 Congressional Quarterly Almanac,* pp. 82-86.

[28] See Weir, *op. cit.,* pp. 100-104 ("cop-killer bullets"), pp. 105-107 ("plastic pistols").

[29] See Weir, *op. cit.,* pp. 221-222.

[30] *Cleveland Plain Dealer,* Jan. 14, 1995, p. 1A. ("The NRA's the reason the Republicans control the House," Clinton was quoted as saying.)

[31] Urban Institute, "Impact Evaluation of the Public Safety and Recreational Firearms Use Protection Act of 1994," Feb. 19, 1997.

[32] See Kenneth Jost, *Supreme Court Yearbook, 1994-1995,* pp. 43-46; *Supreme Court Yearbook,* 1996-1997, pp. 45-49.

[33] See U.S. General Accounting Office, "Implementation of the Brady Handgun Violence Prevention Act," January 1996.

[34] Franklin E. Zimring and Gordon Hawkins, *Crime Is Not the Problem: Lethal Violence in America* (1997), p. 122.

Bibliography

Selected Sources Used

Books

Davidson, Osha Gray, *Under Fire: The NRA and the Battle for Gun Control*, Henry Holt, 1993.
Davidson provides a critical journalistic account of the history and role of the National Rifle Association (NRA) in the gun control debate. The book includes an 11-page bibliography.

Kleck, Gary, *Targeting Guns: Firearms and Their Control*, Aldine de Gruyter, 1997.
Kleck, a professor of criminology at Florida State University, argues with detailed statistical evidence that the availability of guns has no net impact on violent crime rates and that gun control laws have not been shown to produce net reductions in gun-related crimes. The book includes a 33-page list of references.

LaPierre, Wayne R., *Guns, Crime, and Freedom*, Regnery, 1995.
LaPierre, executive vice president of the NRA, strongly argues against gun control measures on constitutional and policy grounds. The book includes source notes and a list of law review articles on both sides of the issue.

Weir, William, *A Well Regulated Militia: The Battle Over Gun Control*, Archon, 1997.
Weir, who says he is a member of both Handgun Control and the National Rifle Association, accuses both sides in the gun control debate of pushing "shocking" amounts of misinformation and ignoring deeper causes of violence in the United States. The book includes detailed source notes and a 14-page bibliography.

Zimring, Franklin E., and Gordon Hawkins, *The Citizen's Guide to Gun Control*, Macmillan, 1987.
Zimring and Hawkins provide a "non-technical" guide to the issue. Zimring is director of the Earl Warren Legal Institute at the University of California at Berkeley; Hawkins, now retired, was director of the Institute of Criminology at the University of Sydney. In their new book, *Crime Is Not the Problem* (Oxford University, 1997), they argue that the United States' distinctive crime problem is gun violence rather than overall crime.

Reports and Studies

Cook, Philip J., and Jens Ludwig, "Guns in America: Results of a Comprehensive National Survey on Firearms Ownership and Use," Police Foundation, May 1997.
The 94-page summary report is most noteworthy for a controversial section that reports — and then criticizes — a survey finding indicating widespread defensive gun use in the U.S.

The Second Amendment: A Bibliographical Note

A committed group of scholars has forcefully argued that the Second Amendment protects an individual's right to own and use firearms, while gun control proponents defend the established judicial view that the amendment protects only the right of the states to maintain a militia.

For two book-length expositions of the individual-right thesis, see Joyce Malcolm, *To Keep and Bear Arms: The Origins of an Anglo-American Right* (Harvard University Press, 1994), and Stephen P. Halbrook, *That Every Man Be Armed: The Evolution of a Constitutional Right* (University of New Mexico Press, 1984). Malcolm is a professor of history at Bentley College; Halbrook, a Fairfax, Va., attorney, argued the successful challenge to the Brady Act before the Supreme Court, though not on Second Amendment grounds.

The first major law review article to set forth the individual-right thesis is Don B. Kates Jr., "Handgun Prohibition and the Original Meaning of the Second Amendment," *Michigan Law Review,* Vol. 82, 1983, pp. 204-273; Kates is a San Francisco attorney. Two liberal constitutional experts have adopted, at least in part, the individual-right view: Sanford Levinson, "The Embarrassing Second Amendment" (*Yale Law Journal,* Vol. 99, 1989, pp. 637-659); and William Van Alstyne, "The Second Amendment and the Personal Right to Arms" (*Duke Law Journal,* Vol. 43, 1994, pp. 1236-1255). Levinson is at the University of Texas Law School, Van Alstyne at Duke Law School.

The major law review articles refuting the individual-right thesis include two authored or co-authored by Dennis A. Henigan, director of the legal action project of the Center to Prevent Handgun Violence: "Arms, Anarchy and the Second Amendment," *Valparaiso University Law Review,* Vol. 26, 1991, pp. 107-129; and "The Second Amendment in the Twentieth Century: Have You Seen Your Militia Lately?" *University of Dayton Law Review,* Vol. 15, 1989, pp. 5-58 (co-authored with Keith A. Ehrman, a San Francisco lawyer).

David C. Williams, a law professor at Indiana University, criticizes the contemporary relevance of the "citizen militia" in his article "Civic Republicanism and the Citizen Militia: The Terrifying Second Amendment," *Yale Law Journal,* Vol. 101, 1991, pp. 551-615. Historian Gary Wills sharply challenges the historical accuracy of the Second Amendment advocates' thesis in "To Keep and Bear Arms," *New York Review of Books,* Sept. 21, 1995, pp. 62-73.

The Next Step

Additional information from UMI's Newspaper & Periodical Abstracts™ database

Assault Weapons

Brazil, Jeff, and Steve Berry, "California and the West; Gun Import Fight Pressed by Feinstein; Firearms: Senator asks leaders of Russia, Greece and Bulgaria to prevent the export of assault weapons to U.S.," *Los Angeles Times,* Oct. 17, 1997, p. A3.

Escalating her campaign against the importation of assault weapons, U.S. Sen. Dianne Feinstein, D-Calif., appealed to the leaders of Russia, Greece and Bulgaria to prevent the export of thousands of the rapid-fire guns to the United States. The weapons in question are modified versions of the AK-47 and Heckler & Koch 91, which were first restricted by federal law in 1989 and again in 1994,

Morain, Dan, and Steve Berry, "In Gun Control Battles, Casualties Can Be Heavy; Legislature: Attempts to restrict automatic weapons and cheap handguns fall victim to give and take of politics," *Los Angeles Times,* Oct. 19, 1997, p. A1.

At the start of the assembly's session this year, Don Perata, a member of the Alameda County Board of Supervisors, proposed a sweeping overhaul of California's landmark 1989 assault weapons law, hoping to close loopholes that gun manufacturers have exploited to flood the state with thousands of the rapid-fire weapons. The demise of Perata's measure provides a case study of the fragility of firearms legislation — of the unusual strategies that are employed and of the nasty wars that are waged.

Brady Law

"Alternatives Are Needed to Check on Gun Buyers; Court ruling on Brady Act necessitates action," *Los Angeles Times,* June 30, 1997, p. B4.

The U.S. Supreme Court's disappointing decision on the Brady Act need not hamper enforcement of this worthy and popular law governing handgun sales. Indeed, just hours after the court released its ruling, concluding its current term, the president and members of Congress were huddling over how to continue background checks on prospective gun buyers. A divided court struck down a key part of the 1993 Brady gun control law, saying that Congress cannot constitutionally compel local police to conduct background checks during a federally established five-day waiting period.

Farrell, John Aloysius, "Court weakens Brady gun law: Background checks are struck down," *The Boston Globe,* June 28, 1997, p. A1.

The Supreme Court struck down a key portion of the Brady handgun control act, ruling that Congress does not have the power to order state and local law enforcement officials to conduct background checks on prospective gun buyers. The court did not address the other main provision of the handgun law, the requirement that gun buyers face a five-day waiting period. But without simultaneous background checks, the waiting period in many states will not be as effective to screen gun sales.

Concealed Weapons Laws

Biele, Katharine, "Backlash Against Guns On Utah Campuses," *The Christian Science Monitor,* Aug. 20, 1997, p, 3.

Utah is one of the few states that allow permit holders to carry concealed weapons almost anywhere, including college campuses. Some federal buildings and restricted areas of airports are off-limits in every state, but most states also list places like schools, churches, public transportation and parks. Not Utah. And Salt Lake City lawyer Steve Gunn, a member of Utahns Against Gun Violence, says this has led to a dangerous laissez-faire attitude.

Daunt, Tina, "Police Panel Backs Gun Control Plan; Weapons Commission and Chief Parks endorse package that includes thumbprinting those who buy ammunition and making dealers sell trigger locks with each firearm," *Los Angeles Times,* Sept. 10, 1997, p. B3.

With the backing of Police Chief Bernard C. Parks, the Los Angeles Police Commission unanimously endorsed a package of new gun control measures, including requiring thumbprints from people who buy ammunition in the city of Los Angeles. The proposal — which includes a requirement that dealers sell trigger locks with each gun — is scheduled to be heard by the City Council's Public Safety Committee next week.

" 'Gun control coast to coast,'" *American Rifleman,* August 1997, p. 16.

President Clinton's series of gun control proposals is causing lawmakers on the state level to pass new restrictions. Some of the new laws and regulations concerning gun control in California and Massachusetts are discussed.

Kincaid, Cliff, "Quick on the law," *American Legion Magazine,* July 1997, p. 12.

The National Rifle Association is seeking passage of a national law to allow concealed firearms in all 50 states.

Lott, John R. Jr., "Do carry-concealed weapons laws deter crime? Yes," ***Spectrum: The Journal of State Government,*** **spring 1997, p. 28.**

Lott, a visiting fellow in law and economics at the University of Chicago, makes a case for laws allowing concealed weapons and discusses statistics that show how these laws deter violent crime.

"Sacramento Shoots Gun Control; But 'junk gun' bills survive, and Michael Feuer presses on in L.A.," ***Los Angeles Times,*** **June 5, 1997, p. B8.**

A package of sensible state gun control bills, including modest limits on possession and tougher penalties for those who violate gun laws, is now dead or nearly so. Among the confirmed casualties in the Legislature this week: a bill that would have made it a crime to possess a loaded and concealed gun while drunk and a bill that would have repealed state law preventing cities and counties from enacting their own gun ordinances.

Local Gun Control Efforts

"Gun control," ***Current Events,*** **Nov. 6, 1997, pp. 1-2.**

An average of 500 children are killed each year by guns. National and local gun control laws under consideration in local and state elections across the U.S. in November 1997 are discussed.

"L.A. Council OKs Gun Control Law," ***Los Angeles Times,*** **Oct. 9, 1997, p. B5.**

Ignoring the arguments of two members who said the ordinance would infringe on individual privacy, the Los Angeles City Council gave its support to a package of gun control measures.

Lipton, Eric, "Fairfax Looks to New Gun-Control Fight; Safety Lock Plan and Wider Ban in Government Buildings Considered," ***The Washington Post,*** **Sept. 30, 1997, p. B3.**

Fairfax County appears to be headed toward another battle in the General Assembly over gun control. Some supervisors said yesterday that handguns sold in Fairfax should be equipped with child-safety locks and also proposed broadening a ban on weapons in some government buildings. Either measure would require legislative approval.

"Saturday Night Specials"

Gunnison, Robert B., "Governor Vetoes Bill Banning Cheap Guns: Crime laws more effective, he says," ***San Francisco Chronicle,*** **Sept. 27, 1997, p. A1.**

Bowing to the wishes of the gun lobby, Gov. Pete Wilson, R-Calif., vetoed a bill yesterday that would have outlawed the manufacture and sale in California of cheap handguns known as "Saturday night specials." The measure was supported by a long list of local governments and gun control groups and opposed by the National Rifle Association, Gun Owners of California and Attorney General Dan Lungren.

Ingram, Carl, "Senate Sends Ban on Making Cheap Guns to Governor; Firearms: Wilson has raised questions on bill affecting Southland firms that produce up to 80 percent of the Saturday night specials in U.S.; Ownership would remain legal," ***Los Angeles Times,*** **Sept. 10, 1997, p. A1.**

The state Senate narrowly passed and sent to Gov. Pete Wilson, R-Calif., a historic gun control bill that outlaws the manufacture and sale of so-called "Saturday night specials" in California. Critics say California firms produce 80 percent of the Saturday night specials in the United States. Police chiefs, county sheriffs and gun control advocates, including Handgun Control Inc., have argued for years that such guns are the firearms of choice for criminals and are easily obtained.

Lucas, Greg, "Assembly OKs Gun-Control Bill; It would ban production, sale of Saturday Night Specials," ***San Francisco Chronicle,*** **Aug. 29, 1997, p. A1.**

Gun control advocates scored a big win in the Legislature last night as the assembly approved a bill banning the sale and manufacture of cheap handguns known as "Saturday night specials." The hot-button issue pitted Republicans, who said the bill left law-abiding citizens defenseless, against Democrats, who countered that 80 percent of the inexpensive handguns used nationwide are made in California.

Washington State Initiative

Ayres, B. Drummond Jr., "Gun-Control Measure Is Decisively Rejected," ***The New York Times,*** **Nov. 6, 1997, p. A28.**

Gun advocates around the country took heart yesterday in their long struggle with gun-control advocates after the decisive defeat of a Washington state ballot initiative that would have required safety tests for handgun owners and trigger locks on handguns. Proponents of tougher gun laws had portrayed the initiative as an early test of a new national strategy to seek stricter firearms-control measures at the state level.

Ritter, John, "NRA fighting full-bore in Washington State: Gun control initiative could have wide effect," ***USA Today,*** **Oct. 30, 1997, p. A12.**

The gun lobby is spending $3 million on an all-out campaign to defeat Washington state's Initiative 676.

Ritter, John, "Wash. gun-control initiative a close call," ***USA Today,*** **Nov. 5, 1997, p. A4.**

Polls show voters evenly divided on Initiative 676, a gun control measure that would require handgun licenses, trigger locks and safety training for gun owners. The measure drew strong opposition from the National Rifle Association and is being watched closely elsewhere.

Back Issues

Great Research on Current Issues Starts Right Here . . . Recent topics covered by The CQ Researcher are listed below. Before May 1991, reports were published under the name of Editorial Research Reports.

JUNE 1996
Rethinking NAFTA
First Ladies
Teaching Values
Labor Movement's Future

JULY 1996
Recovered-Memory Debate
Native Americans' Future
Crackdown on Sexual Harassment
Attack on Public Schools

AUGUST 1996
Fighting Over Animal Rights
Privatizing Government Services
Child Labor and Sweatshops
Cleaning Up Hazardous Wastes

SEPTEMBER 1996
Gambling Under Attack
The States and Federalism
Civic Journalism
Reassessing Foreign Aid

OCTOBER 1996
Political Consultants
Insurance Fraud
Rethinking School Integration
Parental Rights

NOVEMBER 1996
Global Warming
Clashing Over Copyright
Consumer Debt
Governing Washington, D.C.

DECEMBER 1996
Welfare, Work and the States
The New Volunteerism
Implementing the Disabilities Act
America's Pampered Pets

JANUARY 1997
Combating Scientific Misconduct
Restructuring the Electric Industry
The New Immigrants
Chemical and Biological Weapons

FEBRUARY 1997
Assisting Refugees
Alternative Medicine's Next Phase
Independent Counsels
Feminism's Future

MARCH 1997
New Air Quality Standards
Alcohol Advertising
Civic Renewal
Educating Gifted Students

APRIL 1997
Declining Crime Rates
The FBI Under Fire
Gender Equity in Sports
Space Program's Future

MAY 1997
The Stock Market
The Cloning Controversy
Expanding NATO
The Future of Libraries

JUNE 1997
FDA Reform
China After Deng
Line-Item Veto
Breast Cancer

JULY 1997
Transportation Policy
Executive Pay
School Choice Debate
Aggressive Driving

AUGUST 1997
Age Discrimination
Banning Land Mines
Children's Television
Evolution vs. Creationism

SEPTEMBER 1997
Caring for the Dying
Mental Health Policy
Mexico's Future
Youth Fitness

OCTOBER 1997
Urban Sprawl in the West
Diversity in the Workplace
Teacher Education
Contingent Work Force

NOVEMBER 1997
Renewable Energy
Artificial Intelligence
Religious Persecution
Roe v. Wade at 25

DECEMBER 1997
Whistleblowers
Castro's Next Move

Back issues are available for $5.00 (subscribers) or $10.00 (non-subscribers). Quantity discounts apply to orders over ten. To order, call Congressional Quarterly Customer Service at (202) 887-8621.

Binders are available for $18.00. To order call 1-800-638-1710. Please refer to stock number 648.

Future Topics

- ***Regulating Nonprofits***
- ***New Approaches to Foster Care***
- ***IRS Reform***

THE CQ Researcher

PUBLISHED BY CONGRESSIONAL QUARTERLY INC.

Regulating Nonprofits

Are tax-exempt groups too political?

Some feed the hungry, some agitate to ban abortion, still others fight to protect the environment. Such organizations enjoy tax-exempt status granted by the federal government to encourage a voluntary sector devoted to causes not handled by government or business. The proliferation of nonprofits in recent years, however, has exposed a downside to the American fondness for joining groups. Corruption scandals and some political misuse of tax-exempt privileges have brought scrutiny of how nonprofits operate and earn their tax-privileged classifications. An effort by Republicans in Congress to rein in their lobbying and advocacy has caused a furor in the nonprofit community. Proposals to regulate election-year advertising by independent groups have stirred a defense of the rights to free speech and association.

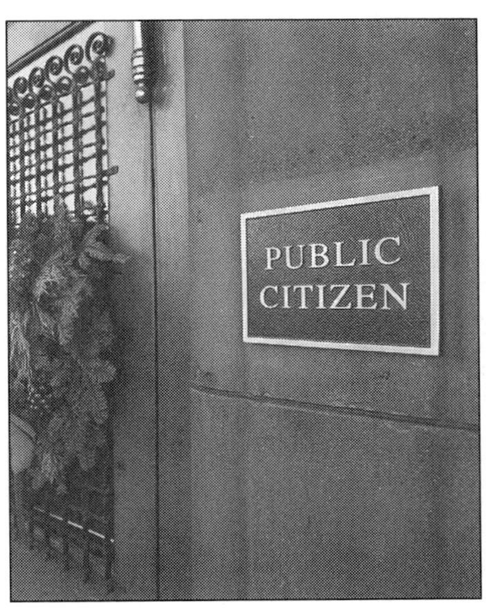

INSIDE THIS ISSUE

CQ Dec. 26, 1997 • Volume 7, No. 48 • Pages 1129-1152

Formerly Editorial Research Reports

Regulating Nonprofits

The Issues

Background

Current Situation

Outlook

Sidebars and Graphics

For Further Research

Cover: One of More Than 650,000 Tax-Exempt Organizations Designated by the Internal Revenue Service as a 501(c)(3), Public Citizen in Washington, D.C., Can Engage in Limited Lobbying. (Congressional Quarterly/Douglas Graham)

December 26, 1997
Volume 7, No. 48

The CQ Researcher (ISSN 1056-2036). Formerly Editorial Research Reports. Published weekly, except Jan. 3, May 30, Aug. 29, Oct. 31, by Congressional Quarterly Inc., 1414 22nd St., N.W., Washington, D.C. 20037. Annual subscription rate for libraries, businesses and government is $340. Additional rates furnished upon request. Periodicals postage paid at Washington, D.C., and additional mailing offices. POSTMASTER: Send address changes to The CQ Researcher, 1414 22nd St., N.W., Washington, D.C. 20037.

Regulating Nonprofits

By Charles S. Clark

The Issues

The subpoenas went out to a hodgepodge of groups. Targets on the political left included the AFL-CIO, the National Education Association (NEA) and the Sierra Club. Recipients on the right included the National Right to Life Committee, the National Policy Forum and Americans for Tax Reform.

The 26 tax-exempt groups, however, mostly declined to turn over the millions of internal records being sought early this year for a sweeping congressional investigation into campaign finance abuses during the 1996 elections. And last month, the Senate Governmental Affairs Committee's politically charged probe went out of business. "It was a massive wild goose chase designed to stop us," says NEA spokeswoman Kathleen Lyons, who notes that the NEA subpoena alone demanded documents in 22 separate categories.

Not only were the subpoenas too broad for the committee's legislative authority, says James Bopp Jr., an attorney for both the Christian Coalition and the National Right to Life Committee, but they violated "First Amendment rights to free speech and association, as well as any reasonable expectation of privacy." The Senate panel's demand for "any document relating to any publicly debated issue," he adds, would include "practically everything [the groups are] involved with, including private communications with staff and confidential notes to lawmakers or the press."

A Senate spokesman defended the constitutionality of the subpoenas on the ground that the Senate was not asking for names of the groups' members or donors. "The message is, if you ignore a congressional subpoena, you're immune," said a concerned Sen. Joseph I. Lieberman," D-Conn. "It's an awful precedent." [1]

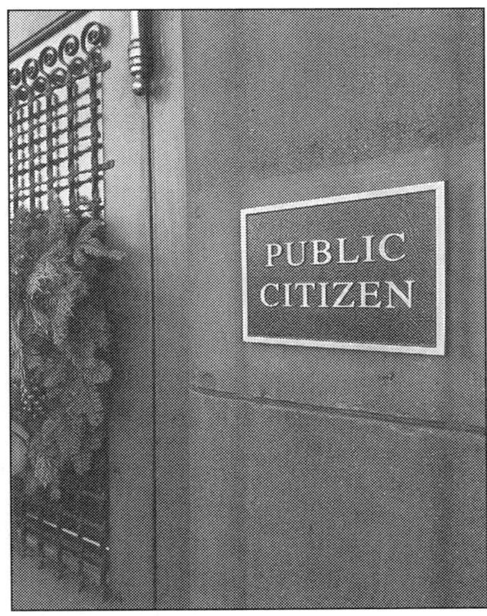

The stalemate is just one sign of the blurred legal lines and unanswered questions surrounding the role played in society by the nation's nonprofits.

The Clinton administration has been singed by Vice President Al Gore's use of a tax-exempt Buddhist temple for a fund-raiser as well as by the campaign's alleged benefits from a money-laundering scheme involving the Teamsters union and the tax-exempt activist group Citizen Action. Republicans added to the suspicions through the alleged use of a party affiliate called the National Policy Forum to solicit foreign campaign funds, and through the well-scrutinized efforts by House Speaker Newt Gingrich, R-Ga., to finance a highly partisan college course through tax-exempt foundations.

"My fear is that many politicians have become so unrestrained and greedy and bold that misuse of charitable groups has become politically routine," says University of Miami law Professor Frances R. Hill. "They're showing remarkable creativity in creating tax favored conduits for politicians."

Fund-raisers for legitimate charities "tell me they're scared that all the scandals have made fund-raising a dirty word," says Stacy Palmer, managing editor of *The Chronicle of Philanthropy*.

Confusion, more than ever, is common among the public, news media and government officials as to what tax-exempts are permitted to do in the way of advocacy, lobbying and political activity, notes Peter Shiras, senior vice president for programs at Independent Sector, a coalition of 800 nonprofits. "There are inconsistencies between tax law and election law, which developed separately," he says.

The uncertainty exists even within nonprofits, adds Oliver Tessier, executive director of the Support Center of Washington, which holds workshops for nonprofits with titles such as "Coping With Strings Attached to Federal Grants and Contracts." "Nonprofits are so focused on accomplishing their mission and running their businesses that they don't take the time or devote the resources to research it," he says. There are plenty of traps awaiting them. A manager, for example, "can put on a benefit banquet and the invitation inadvertently gets worded so that it is misconstrued as support for a candidate," Tessier says. "It's not as black and white as an accounting regulation."

To encourage a sector of public-spirited organizations that is neither part of government nor commerce, Congress for most of this century has granted tax exemptions to nonprofits that apply and qualify with the Internal Revenue Service (IRS). The Tax Code's Section 501 specifies the rights and responsibilities of the various types, which range from agricultural

Major Types of Tax-Exempt Organizations

More than 1.2 million nonprofit organizations have tax exempt status under Section 501 of the Tax Code. More than 650,000 charities and religious groups, or 501(c)(3) organizations, can solicit tax-deductible donations but are prohibited from direct lobbying and political action. Social advocacy groups, or 501(c)(4)s, can lobby but cannot offer donors tax-deductibility.

Section 501(c):		**Number**
(1)	Corporation organized under Act of Congress	20
(2)	Titleholding corporation	7,100
(3)	Religious, charitable, etc.	654,186
(4)	Social welfare	139,512
(5)	Labor, agriculture	64,955
(6)	Business leagues	77,274
(7)	Social and recreation clubs	60,845
(8)	Fraternal beneficiary societies	91,972
(9)	Voluntary employees' beneficiary associations	14,486
(10)	Domestic fraternal beneficiary societies	20,925
(11)	Teachers' retirement funds	13
(12)	Benevolent life insurance associations	6,343
(13)	Cemetery companies	9,562
(14)	State-chartered credit unions	5,157
(15)	Mutual insurance companies	1,212
(16)	Corporations to finance crop operations	23
(17)	Supplemental unemployment benefit trusts	565
(18)	Employee-funded pension trusts	2
(19)	War veterans' organizations	31,464
(20)	Legal services organizations	131
(21)	Black lung trusts	25
(22)	Multiemployer pension plans	0
(23)	Veterans' associations founded prior to 1880	2
(24)	Trusts described in Section 4049 of ERISA	1
(25)	Holding companies for pensions, etc.	794

Source: Internal Revenue Service

organizations, amateur sports groups and churches to civic leagues, veterans' groups and chambers of commerce.

The largest group are the charities, classified as 501(c)(3) organizations. The more than 650,000 such groups can attract the most donations because gifts to them are tax deductible, but they are only only permitted to lobby within certain limits and cannot engage in partisan political action. Nonprofits that engage in social advocacy work are classified as 501(c)(4) organizations. The nearly 140,000 advocacy groups are relatively freer to agitate on political and policy issues, but do not enjoy the attraction of tax-deductible donations.

Determining who qualifies for tax-exempt status can be tricky and unpredictable. This year, for example, the IRS announced that the Republicans' National Policy Forum did not qualify, calling the group too political. But in November, it reversed an earlier ruling and awarded tax-exempt status to the conservative think tank Empower America.

The reasons for the current controversies are manifold. For one, nonprofits now employ more people than the federal and state governments combined. [2] And from the mid-1980s to the mid-'90s, the number of registered 501(c)(3) groups more than doubled, as political and policy activists actively organized and as the government began relying more on nonprofits to perform services.

"With the exception of taxes, every major domestic policy program of the past 20 years has been set, shaped and in some cases designed by advocacy groups," says Edmund Burke, director of Boston College's Center for Corporate Community Relations. "The agenda defining highway safety, environment, disabilities, work and family and AIDS [has] come from [their] organized efforts." [3]

Critics find this disturbing, particularly conservatives seeking to shrink the size of government. They complain that government involvement with charities creates waste, bureaucracy and paperwork while rendering private charities dependent. Through "the lure of lucrative grants and contracts, government is quietly orchestrating one of the most profound — and overlooked — shifts in public policy in a generation," asserts a writer for the Heritage Foundation. "This massive, direct public funding for private nonprofits is quickly becoming the most important strategy for attacking social problems in America." [4]

Over the past three years, Republicans in Congress have been seeking to curb the lobbying powers of tax-exempt groups that receive government grants. "Nowadays, there's a hostility toward the welfare state," says John Walters, president of the Philanthropy Roundtable, which studies nonprofits. "People are skeptical and are asking more questions."

To counter the GOP effort, a large portion of the nonprofit community has banded together in a coalition called "Let America Speak," organized by the Alliance for Justice, Independent Sector and OMB Watch. This opposition extends to mainstream nonprofit groups.

"The phenomenon of people joining together in associations to pursue common goals or interests to solve common problems, to speak in common voice on matters that affect their lives, or to volunteer their time and talents, is as fundamentally American as apple pie," says the American Society of Association Executives (ASAE). "Previous generations of lawmakers understood and endorsed the 'good guy' value of these undertakings by extending tax exemptions and other privileges. . . . Tragically, these ground rules are now being rewritten to strip away many of the exemptions and protections."[5]

As efforts to regulate nonprofits continue, these are key questions being asked:

Should Congress restrict lobbying by nonprofits that receive government funds?

"Stop taxpayer-funded political advocacy!" That was a rallying cry among Republicans after they assumed majority control of the House in 1995. Their strategy proceeded on multiple fronts. Rep. John L. Mica, R-Fla., offered a plan to revive a Reagan-era plan to remove advocacy and non-traditional charities from the government employees' umbrella charity known as the Combined Federal Campaign. Rep. John T. Doolittle, R-Calif., offered a proposal to require all witnesses testifying before Congress to declare the amount of federal grant money they receive.

And Rep. Nancy L. Johnson, R-Conn., as recently as 1996 announced her plan to hold hearings on what House leaders called "special grants to special interests" to search for a way to distinguish between charities that provide direct aid to the needy and those that spend their time debating policy. "We have to look at the large picture," she said. "Why is the nonprofit sector growing so rapidly? What kind of activity are we subsidizing? And is it in the public interest?"[6]

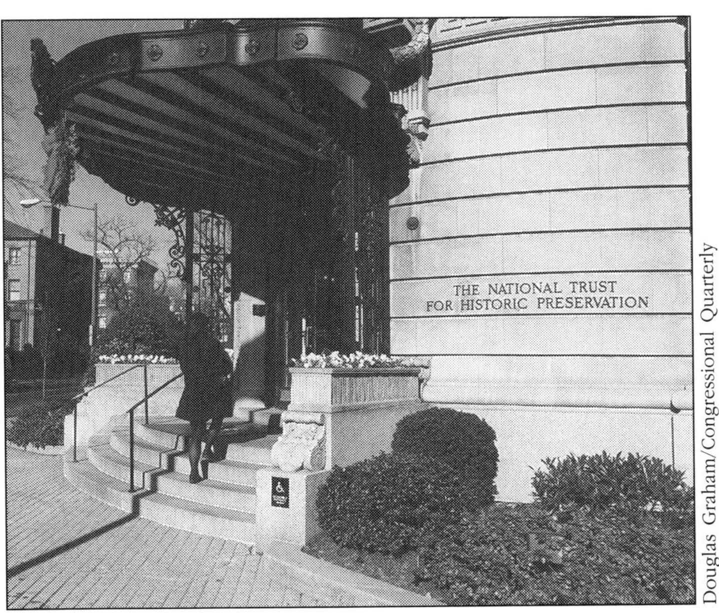

Douglas Graham/Congressional Quarterly

The nonprofit National Trust for Historic Preservation, based in Washington, D.C., is a 501(c)(3) organization.

But the Republican effort to curb advocacy that has drawn the most attention is that pursued by Rep. Ernest Istook, R-Okla. "People want to receive taxpayers' money, take a percentage of it as they are permitted to do under federal law and transfer it to overhead accounts, and thereby evade the restrictions on using taxpayers' money for lobbying activity," he complained to the PBS "NewsHour With Jim Lehrer" on Nov. 17, 1995.

Joined by Rep. David M. McIntosh, R-Ind., Istook over the past two years has offered varying versions of a bill that would substantially alter a 1976 law on lobbying. In principle, he would broaden the definition of lobbying, reduce the percentage of funds that tax-exempts receiving federal grants could devote to lobbying and count state and local funds as federal if they result from federal block grants.

That was music to the ears of conservative groups such as the Heritage Foundation and the Capital Research Center. They had long blasted groups like the American Cancer Society for advocating hikes in the tobacco tax, and the liberal activist group ACORN for receiving a $1 million grant from the Clinton administration's AmeriCorps volunteer program (later rescinded), even though it lobbies for such programs as low-income housing.[7]

Also singled out were groups for the elderly, among them the American Association of Retired Persons (AARP), the National Council of Senior Citizens and the liberal health-care group Families USA, which also receive federal grants to provide services. It's the "dependency lobby," argues a Capital Research Center critique. "This loosely knit coalition of advocacy groups spends millions of dollars each year to promote public policies that would make seniors more dependent on government and less able to provide for themselves. High on its agenda are higher taxes, more regulation and more government programs and spending." [8]

The National Council on Senior Citizens gets 90 percent of its budget from federal funds, says Capital Research Center President Terrence Scanlon. "Catholic Charities gets 65 percent of its budget from government, while the AARP gets $80 million in annual grants." Why then, he asks, should Catholic Charities President Fred Kammer be able to testify against welfare reform and the balanced-budget amendment? "He's a liberal, and what he's trying to do is continue his existence."

Walters of the Philanthropy Roundtable agrees that many of these groups that lobby are not competing for government contracts by offering the lowest bids, but by advocating a program tailored to serve their constituencies. "They're at the center of the battles on the efficacies of the programs, so it's difficult to proclaim clear walls between the program and lobbying," he says. "Often both types of work are performed simultaneously by the same staff using the same phone lines and Fax machines."

Indeed, the notion that federal grant money earmarked for one purpose is "fungible" for nonprofits, or can be shifted between budget categories, is widely believed among critics. (The AARP, as of Jan. 1, 1996, responded to the criticism by creating the AARP Foundation, a 501(c)(3), to administer the $80 million in federal grants it uses for its programs for seniors in community service, environmental protection, tax assistance, housing and breast and cervical cancer counseling.)

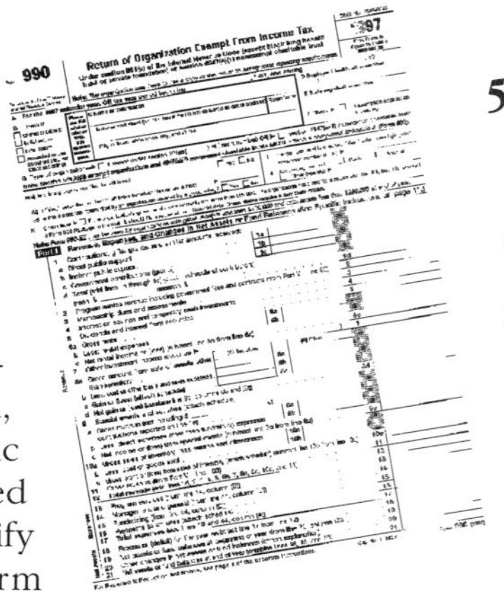

Nan Aron, president of the Alliance for Justice, says that critics have never shown that federal grant money has been treated by nonprofits as fungible. "The organizations receive specific grants for projects to be carried out, and it has to be accounted for," she says. "Because of the clear prohibition on using federal money to lobby, it's virtually unthinkable. Besides, nonprofits hardly even have enough federal money to carry out the services they want to carry out, so it's not as if there's buckets of money to move around."

According to the association executives, only one in three nonprofits spend any money on lobbying or political activities, and of those that do, they usually spend less than 10 percent. The Office of Management and Budget (OMB) already bars political advocacy with government money, others note.

But the main objection to the Istook move against advocacy involves protection of free speech. The proposal raises "three fundamental constitutional problems," says Georgetown University Law Professor David Cole. "It impermissibly conditions eligibility for federal grants on surrendering the right to engage in a broad range of political speech on one's time and with one's own resources. Second, it imposes these conditions selectively on individuals and nonprofit entities that obtain federal grants, but permits government contractors, who receive much larger amounts of federal money, to engage freely and without limitation in the same political activities. Third, its disclosure requirements, which would require millions of Americans to reveal their political activities to the government and/or federal grantees, violate the First Amendment right to engage in anonymous political speech and association." [9]

More than just a matter of rights, say others, is the issue of healthy debate in a democracy. Advocacy is often the best service we provide,"

The Tax Code defines 501(c)(3) organizations as: "corporations, and any community chest, fund or foundation, organized and operated exclusively for religious, charitable, scientific, testing for public safety, literary or education purposes, or to foster national or international amateur sports competition . . . or for the prevention of cruelty to children or animals, no part of the net earnings of which inures to the benefit of any private shareholder or individual, no substantial part of the activities of which is carrying on propaganda, or otherwise attempting to influence legislation . . . and which does not participate in, or intervene in . . . any political campaign . . . for public office."

says Shiras of Independent Sector. "Nonprofits bring a very close familiarity with the issues on the ground at the community level, and there's a tremendous diversity among nonprofits. Lawmakers need that perspective."

Gary Bass, executive director of OMB Watch, says, "It would be a crime if 501s could no longer challenge industries on regulatory reform, for example. You would have special interests shaping the country's agenda, a David vs. Goliath situation where the people are left without knowledge or resources." Too often, he adds, House leaders such as Gingrich, Dick Armey, R-Texas, and Tom DeLay, R-Texas, "have this mindset in which charities simply give alms and are seen but never heard. But there is a range of groups that can speak out about the needs and gaps in social services. That's what's healthy about the U.S. partnership between charities and government."

Sharon Daly, the deputy for social policy at Catholic Charities USA, says that, contrary to reports, her group does not receive 65 percent of its funds from government. "Our 1,400 member agencies get 1 percent from the government, the rest is from dues," she says. "The local agencies get 60 percent of their revenue from different levels of government to be used for such programs as foster care or meals-on-wheels. But none of the money that was cut under the welfare bill we opposed would have gone to us; it's for the states."

Because cuts in, say, food stamps, may send hungry ex-recipients to a Catholic Charities soup kitchen, she continues, "who better to comment on national domestic social policy than a group that's been around 100 years, is in every state and congressional district and serves 11 million people?" She also thinks the conservative critics are revealing their political biases when they attack Catholic Charities but not Catholic bishops, noting that the conservatives don't object when Catholic Charities advocates against abortion. "This criticism didn't materialize until halfway through the welfare debate, when we'd won some victories," she says.

What really sapped the momentum of the Istook bill, says law Professor Hill, "was that its backers realized that the same principle would apply to the major corporations, such as those that contract with the federal government to build jet aircraft. The Republicans were willing to chill the speech of the people they disapprove of, but chilling the speech of everyone was beyond them," she says.

The irony, says Robert O. Bothwell, president of the National Committee for Responsive Philanthropy, is that he agrees with Istook that nonprofit advocacy is responsible for the expansion of government. "We just disagree over whether that's a bad idea," he says. "There's no easy way to determine how much of a nonprofit's work is issue advocacy. A group can circulate an issue paper that expresses a point of view, and the IRS will say nothing. Accountants and regulators have tried for years to draw lines, but it has always failed in the courts."

Given that the Istook approach has stalled, Walters says, "the first step that's needed may not be legislation but informal debate. If groups are going to present themselves as non-advocacy groups, then fairness seems to dictate that it mean something."

Should nonprofits' "issue advertisements" be subject to campaign finance rules?

The record-setting costs of modern political campaigns (driven primarily by television advertising) have produced a clamor for new laws to ease the dependence on the money chase that preoccupies elected officials. [10] And though most of the push for reform comes from Democrats, who, as the minority party in Congress now trail Republicans in fundraising, there is a key aspect of the debate that shatters this tidy party breakdown: Issue ads, which can be sponsored by independent nonprofit groups under specified conditions of campaign finance law, exert an ever-increasing impact on races for the House and Senate, even though their sponsors are subject to none of the contribution caps or disclosure requirements imposed on official candidate ads.

Before the 1996 elections, 31 groups spent a total of $135 million on issue ads, evenly split between those that favored Republicans and those that favored Democrats, according to a study by the Annenberg Public Policy Center of the University of Pennsylvania. [11] They included on the left the Sierra Club, the National Abortion Rights Action League and Citizen Action. On the right were the U.S. Chamber of Commerce, the National Rifle Association and the Coalition for Our Children's Future. Also active were the Democratic and Republican national party committees. [12] All of them were permitted to spend "soft," or unregulated, money without revealing who donated it.

Even though rules prohibit issue ads, by definition, from calling on viewers to vote for or against an individual candidate, fully 86.9 percent of the ads mentioned the name of an official or candidate, and 59.2 percent showed a politician's picture, according to the Annenberg study. Three-fourths of the TV spots exhorted viewers to phone officials, or phone an advocacy group, give a friend a message, or support or oppose legislation. Their legality has been confirmed in courts.

Following the 1992 elections, for example, the Federal Election Commission (FEC) challenged a TV spot by a nonprofit called the Christian

When Nonprofits Turn a Profit . . .

"To meet the new challenges of the future, nonprofit organizations must be reinvented to create new wealth," writes Bill Shore, executive director of the anti-hunger group Share Our Strength. Wealth, by his reckoning, means "community wealth, or resources generated through profitable enterprise to promote social change."

The income-producing models Shore cites include the wine tastings put on by his group's anti-poverty activists, the job training, landscaping and janitorial services offered by a rising number of social service organizations and even the award-winning film "The Spitfire Grill" produced recently by an order of Catholic priests. [1]

Since the late 1970s and early '80s, when the federal government began shrinking funding for nonprofits, many charities, advocacy groups and other tax-exempts have turned entrepreneurial. To supplement their foundation grants, donations and membership dues, they have tapped such non-traditional income sources as the rental of mailing lists, book publishing, car rental services and group life insurance. Most recently, such prominent nonprofits as the Smithsonian Institution have formed alliances with major credit card issuers to share a percentage of the purchase amounts made using the card, an arrangement that brings income and advertising exposure to both parties.

Such forays into a gentle capitalism, however, have predictably drawn some brickbats. Signing up for a credit card or long-distance phone service that is endorsed by some worthy cause may salve one's conscience, but it actually delivers little to the needy, skeptics say. "On a $30 monthly long-distance bill, just 30 cents goes to charity," notes philanthropy critic Tom Riley. "That totals up to $3.60 a year. Most people, I think, would be embarrassed to show their 'support' for a group that they truly 'believed in' by mailing them an annual check for $3.60." [2]

Conservatives, who have long criticized nonprofits for depending too much on government, can applaud the ones that seek to use the marketplace to support themselves, says John Walters, president of the Philanthropy Roundtable. "But the real question is whether they're producing a product that is identical to one made by a for-profit, and whether they should pay taxes on it."

Indeed, the federal government itself, specifically its Government Printing Office, comes under attack for publishing books that some observers say compete with private-sector offerings. In a 1989 study of the subject, two researchers from the conservative Capital Research Center heaped scorn on such government-issued titles as *The Backyard Mechanic, Country Catfish,* a cookbook, and *My Baby, Strong and Healthy,* a child-care guide. [3]

Some of the most vociferous attacks on enterprising nonprofits have been aimed at the American Association of Retired Persons (AARP), the largest and one of the most influential lobbying groups in Washington. The AARP has long been resented by Republicans in Congress for its opposition to cuts in Medicare spending and its enthusiasm for a strong government role in health care. "Imagine, for a moment, a thriving business enterprise, pulling in annual revenues of hundreds of millions of dollars," writes former Sen. Alan K. Simpson, R-Wyo., in a Capital Research Center publication attacking AARP and the array of publications, insurance, discounted travel and financial planning services it offers members. "Imagine, too, that through a quirk in the law, this business pays none of the income taxes to which its competitors are subjected. Exorbitant salaries and benefits are paid from this huge tax-free income, and employees work in splendor in an enormous palace complete with marble floors and every possible manner of technological luxury." [4]

Businesses since early in the century have worried about competition from nonprofits. That's why Congress in 1950 passed the unrelated business income tax (UBIT), which requires nonprofits to pay normal corporate taxes on income that is not central to their tax-exempt mission. Nonprofits, of course, continue to enjoy other tax breaks. They can borrow at preferred rates, use debt-financed property without any tax disadvantage (assuming the property is used substantially to carry out the tax-exempt mission) and they can earn rental income from properties without paying taxes. They can also mail their solicitations at special nonprofit postal rates.

But to avoid paying taxes under the UBIT provision, nonprofits are supposed to concentrate their business enterprises on projects that are mission-related or that can be shown to fill an underexploited niche in the marketplace. For example, "a gunsmith in Colonial Williamsburg employs the methods and tools of the Colonial period to manufacture black powder, muzzle-loading riles and handguns," writes nonprofit accountant Richard F. Wacht. "Barrels are hand-bored on machines operated with 'apprentice' power, and locks, triggers and other hardware are handmade." The

Action Network that showed candidate Clinton's face and attacked him as pro-homosexual. A court ruled, however, that the ad shouldn't be counted as a campaign ad but as a "Christian family values" ad. That's because it never used "the magic words" such as "vote for Smith" or "defeat Smith," which were set out in the 1976 Supreme Court ruling in *Buckley v. Valeo.* [13]

To critics, including federal election officials charged with keeping track of candidate spending, the ads raise the question of when do the rights of

. . . Skeptics Cry 'Unfair Competition'

products are sold to tourists for $400 or more, and are clearly related to the purpose of the "living" museum. "However," he continues, "if the gunsmith added a line of modern weapons and ammunition to this stock-in-trade, income from the sale of those items would be treated as unrelated business income by the Internal Revenue Service (IRS) and would be subject to federal income tax calculated at the prevailing corporate income tax rates." [5]

Critics of nonprofit enterprises like the Capital Research Center note that the UBIT provision offers some 40 exclusions — such as services that are provided "for convenience of members," the sale of donated merchandise, royalties, certain kinds of research, interest on dividend income and rents — which shield nearly 96 percent of the income that might have been covered. [6] The Tax Code's complexity virtually requires nonprofits to bring in certified public accountants to help decide UBIT liability, and the apparent wiggle room in the UBIT law was the chief reason that the AARP in 1994 was required to pony up a cool $135 million in back taxes.

The AARP, not surprisingly, is unabashed about the services it sells to its 33 million members. The organization accuses critics of wanting to silence the message AARP brings from the nation's citizens over age 50. "The definition of a nonprofit is not based on how much money you raise, but what you do with the money," AARP President Eugene Lehrmann responded to Simpson in May 1995. The AARP adds that its payment of back taxes was a "settlement of a difference of opinion" in a gray area. And the organization argued that "a legislative change that would deny AARP other streams of revenue would be at odds with the [AARP's] goal of accessibility by forcing a substantial increase in dues."

Even so, the AARP made several accounting changes in response to charges of unfair competition. In its publications, it now mails the editorial contents at nonprofit rates while paying higher taxes to account for mailing the publication's advertising content. And it has set up a taxpaying financial services corporation to handle its mutual fund services.

Another massive nonprofit, the National Geographic Society, also made a structural change to head off criticism of its unrelated business income from its book sales and advertising in its magazines. "To ensure that other, more large-scale activities that [the society] wanted to pursue in the commercial marketplace would not jeopardize its entitlement to tax-exempt status," said spokeswoman Mary Jeanne Jacobsen, "the society established a separate, taxable subsidiary company called National Geographic Ventures in 1994. It encompasses National Geographic Television, National Geographic Interactive and National Geographic Maps."

The regulations and case law on nonprofits' unrelated business income continue to evolve. In 1993, the IRS proposed regulations to clarify guidelines on the taxability of goods that nonprofits receive from corporations (such as sample products) to help nonprofits put on events. And in a precedent-setting ruling in June 1996, the 9th U.S. Circuit Court of Appeals, in a case brought by the Sierra Club, established that a tax-exempt group's income from mailing list rental counts as royalties rather than taxable income.

The tricky issue of unrelated business income will linger as an ongoing battle for nonprofits, says Bob Smucker, the departing senior vice president of Independent Sector, a coalition of nonprofits. He notes that when the House Ways and Means Oversight Subcommittee in the late 1980s held hearings on the issue in response to complaints from business, Congress couldn't agree on any of the tax law changes recommended by staff.

"If a nonprofit hospital runs a restaurant," he says, "it's OK if patients, their families and staff are using it, but if the hospital invites people in off the street, then the resulting income would have to be taxed. But what about the museum that as part of its mission sells a necktie decorated with the Sphinx? When you take a hard look at it, you can raise questions about whether it's appropriate, but the answers aren't easy."

---

[1] Bill Shore, "Nonprofits that Turn a Profit," *The New Democrat*, November/December 1997, p. 32.

[2] Tom Riley, "Socially Responsible Business: How Much Bang for the Buck?" *Philanthropy*, fall 1997, p. 26.

[3] James T. Bennett and Thomas J. DiLorenzo, *Unfair Competition: The Profits of Nonprofits* (1989), p. 183.

[4] Quoted in Thomas J. DiLorenzo, "Frightening America's Elderly: How the Age Lobby Holds Seniors Captive," Capital Research Center, 1996.

[5] Richard F. Wacht, *Financial Management in Nonprofit Organizations* (1984), p. 26.

[6] DiLorenzo, *op. cit.*, p. 12.

nonprofits to spread their message become simply part of electioneering without any of the disclosure requirements? After all, many of the nonprofit groups that sponsor ads have names like "Citizens for . . . ," which makes them sound like they are membership groups when they are actually just an office of one or two people backed by a few "sugar daddies," observers note.

"If you were a wealthy donor interested in affecting the outcome of a campaign but not interested in leaving any fingerprints, it is pretty clear where you would put your money," writes Paul Taylor, a journalist-turned-campaign-finance-reform activist who worked on the Annenberg study.

The same loophole that sets issue ads apart from candidate ads permitted the national party committees to run ads that didn't count against publicly financed presidential campaign spending limits, even though these spots — boosting the Russell, Kan., hometown values of Republican Bob Dole and the efforts to protect Medicare from GOP budget cuts that became a campaign theme of President Bill Clinton — were clearly campaign-oriented.

That's why proposals in Congress for campaign reform have included provisions to cap "express advocacy" ads sponsored by independent groups whose donors can contribute soft money. Others would require that a percentage of a candidate's ads be financed from funds within the state or district, while others would prevent issue ads from being broadcast within 30 days of a primary and 60 days of an election. Under the major reform bill sponsored by Sens. John McCain, R-Ariz., and Russell D. Feingold, D-Wis., the FEC would be empowered to act as "a reasonable person" in determining whether such ads are election ads that should be counted as campaign contributions.

The millions now spent on independent issue ads are "unregulated and unknown to candidates, who fear it a great deal," says Kent Cooper, executive director of the Center for Responsive Politics. "They fear losing control of the timing and strategy of their campaigns, and they have to raise money to respond."

Cooper acknowledges a growing field of "true issue ads, but there are others that don't have strong justification for protection under the First Amendment because their sponsors move money around nationally and focus not on specific issues but on how to change the ratio of Democrats and Republicans in Congress. It's a manipulation of campaign finance law."

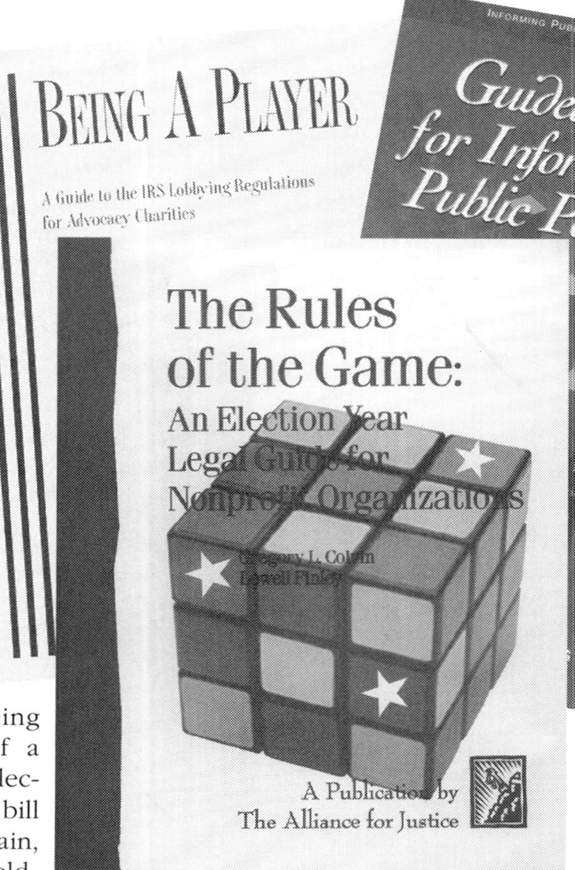

Several nonprofits offer guides to the Internal Revenue Services' complicated lobbying rules.

Opposition to such reforms, however, is strong both on and off Capitol Hill. "It's none of the federal government's business how nonprofits spend their money," said Sen. Mitch McConnell, R-Ky., on the eve of this fall's campaign finance debate.

Weighing in against them on First Amendment grounds was the American Civil Liberties Union (ACLU). "If [President] Nixon bombs Cambodia right before an election, are you supposed to find hard money and jump through all these hoops" to get your protest message out? asked ACLU chief Ira Glasser. [14]

"Limiting issue advocacy would deal a serious blow to nonprofits," says Aron of the Alliance for Justice. "It's essential that nonprofit leaders be able to call people's attention to legislative proposals being considered close to an election and make known a member of Congress' position."

In the case of the National Right to Life Committee, says attorney Bopp, restrictions on issue advertising would "prohibit an organization whose raison d'etre is education and lobbying from educating and lobbying." The committee's October 1996 television ads on Congress' attempt at overriding a presidential veto of partial-birth abortion legislation, he says, would have been prohibited because they mentioned Clinton. Advertising restrictions would force the committee to use its limited money to lobby rather than elect candidates, he adds. [15]

The anti-abortion group's legislative director, Douglas Johnson, teamed up to make the case with a perhaps unlikely bedfellow from the nonprofit world, Michael Beard, who heads the Coalition to Stop Gun Violence. "Behind the cover of 'campaign finance reform,' many lawmakers of both parties wish to establish sweeping federal controls over the communications of incorporated issue-oriented groups," they wrote. "We don't need permission from Congress to publish their voting records or comment on them." [16]

Professor Hill is of two minds on the issue. "When I see politicians grinning at some fat-cat dinner saying, 'It's the American way, money equals speech,' I think of people with no money to give," she says. "That cavalier attitude is deeply disturbing. I'm not convinced that groups have free speech like individuals, who have almost unrestricted free speech and can join groups to amplify it. But I'm not so sure about some of these groups that have almost no members and take positions not based on membership. They're fronts that speak in a pseudonymous voice. The Sierra Club distresses me less because when it runs an ad, we're not uncertain who paid for it, and we can either discount it or be persuaded by it."

Shiras of Independent Sector agrees. "For the effective functioning of a democracy, the power of ideas, their popular appeal and the protections of free speech should be more important than the size of a campaign donation," he says. "The channeling of political contributions to nonprofits is a function of the way campaign finance laws contain built-in incentives for ways to get soft money into the system. It's not a problem with nonprofits."

Some reform backers complain that the larger nonprofits are doing as much to thwart campaign reform as the Republicans who control Congress. "Political heavy-hitters ranging from the ACLU and the NEA to the NRA and the Christian Coalition all oppose reform — and all have nice, big budgets with which to express their commitment to the status quo," complains neoliberal writer Michelle Cottle. [17]

Reform does not mean "limiting or banning issue ads," cautions Donald Simon, executive vice president of Common Cause, a leader of campaign finance reform efforts. "It's treating them as campaign ads when they are. It's how to draw a better, more accurate line, not a perfect one, between issue and campaign ads. Current law says only that issue ads can't use the magic words ['elect Mr. Smith' etc.], but one thing we know is that this line is a terrible line. We know most ads by candidates don't use magic words. They say, 'Joe Smith, a man you can trust' rather than 'Vote for Joe Smith.' Reform would not mean that groups couldn't run issue ads, just that they would have to play by the rules," which would mean disclosure and regulation under campaign finance laws.

The core problem, says Walters of the Philanthropy Roundtable, is the lack of disclosure. "You can begin with a premise that it's OK to be funding all these vigorous points of view, but people ought to know who's behind them," he says. "When [financier] George Soros pays for a campaign for drug legalization, there ought to be sunlight on it so the press and public can scrutinize it."

But Walters is uneasy about restricting debate. "There's no clearly acceptable arbiter to draw the line," he says. "I'm not happy with the FEC's record, so I say just be open about disclosure. The problem with sticking only with candidate ads is that a candidate's platform is made up of issues. Issues are what an election is all about." ■

BACKGROUND

Early Tensions

Clashes between leaders of citizens' groups and political authorities go back to 17th-century America, to the original charters for the Massachusetts Bay Colony and for Harvard College. Harvard leader Increase Mather, notably, fought to run the college under the auspices of the church rather than accede to political control. [18]

By the early 18th century, the eagerness of Americans to form organizations was remarked upon by French writer Alexis de De Tocqueville, who implored the American government to keep its hands off: "The more the government takes the place of associations, the more will individuals lose the idea of forming associations and need the government to come to their help," he wrote. [19]

The territorial imperative of the fledgling nonprofit world was well-articulated in the early 20th century as Congress prepared to enact the first income tax in 1913. "Now the state did not create the family," wrote British political observer John Figgis. "Nor did it create the churches; nor even in any real sense can it be said to have created the club or the trade unions; nor in the Middle Ages the guild or the religious order, hardly even the universities or the colleges within the universities; they have all risen out of the natural associative instincts of mankind, and should be treated by the supreme authority [that is, government] as having a life original and guaranteed." [20]

Because of such wariness and because of the crazy quilt of diverse nonprofits already in existence — schools, food charities, child advocacy groups and fraternal organizations, to name a few — Congress declined even to debate the rationale behind the tax-exempt status it was creating. [21]

In subsequent decades, the interplay between government and nonprofits would change to reflect salient issues of the day. In 1916,

Congress empaneled the so-called Walsh Commission on Industrial Relations to explore whether an elite of wealthy families was using philanthropy to control social and education spending. In 1952, it was the House Select Committee to Investigate Tax-Exempt Foundations and Comparable Organizations, known as the Cox Committee, that poked through nonprofits looking for communist subversives. In 1968, a House panel led by Rep. Wright Patman, D-Texas, criticized philanthropies such as the Ford Foundation for pressing for school decentralization in New York City. That became one of the reasons that the tax reform act of the following year added new regulations making foundations more open and less political. [22]

Nonprofit managers, in the meantime, would grow ever more sophisticated at working the system set up for tax-exempts to operate in the niche between public and private power. Beginning in the 1920s, nonprofits set up training courses and elaborate internal bylaws to maximize input from board members and trustees. The desire of nonprofits to stay flush with a steady income (which had been evident as early as the 1890s when the Metropolitan Museum of Art began selling photographs) became controversial in the 1940s. That was when the Mueller Macaroni company was donated to nonprofit New York University, drawing protests from other macaroni makers. [23] (*See story, p. 1136.*)

Evolving Tax Law

In the early 1950s, the IRS began formulating precise definitions of the nature, rights and responsibilities of tax-exempts. The detailed description of the 501(c)(3) category alone is testament to their breadth and, some say, complexity. (*See box, p. 1134.*)

By the 1969 tax reform law, the '60s explosion of advocacy nonprofits in the areas of civil rights, consumer activism and environmentalism had prompted Congress to place some controls on wealthy foundations. Congress prohibited them from lobbying; called for a minimum annual payout eventually of 5 percent of the foundation's average value of investment assets; and required submission of self-reported financial forms to the IRS.

By 1975, the well-entrenched role of nonprofits dovetailing with government programs was documented by the Commission on Private Philanthropy and Public Need, chaired by Aetna Insurance Chairman John Filer. It even recommended a special federal office for nonprofits. The following year, a tax-reform package would spell out the lobbying restrictions and options for nonprofits organized as 501(c)(3)s, offering them a choice of either "insubstantial lobbying," defined as a specified percentage of their budgets (which the majority chose), or the choice of lobbying more but being governed by detailed IRS expenditure limits. (The actual regulations for this law were not approved until 1990.)

It was in the late 1970s and early '80s that nonprofits began to see the need to balance their idealized missions with the need to stay financially solvent. A noted example of misguided management was Britain's D'Oyly Carte Opera Company, which since days of World War I had maintained a tradition of performing Gilbert and Sullivan's comic operas in rural English towns. In 1982, it went bankrupt because of its stubborn refusal to market itself with higher ticket prices in large cities. "While one can admire the decision to take Gilbert and Sullivan to the people in rural England," writes nonprofit accountant Richard F. Wacht, "that decision permanently destroyed a valuable and venerable institution because of a lack of attention to the financial implications of continuing an established tradition." [24]

What Is Lobbying?

In 1987, Congress passed the Tax-Exempt Organizations' Lobbying and Political Activities Accountability Act to sharpen legal distinctions as to what constitutes lobbying and politics, and permitting the IRS to levy fines on violators. Ever since, leaders in the nonprofit community have been holding workshops and publishing handbooks to help employees learn the nuances.

"Some groups confuse 'lobbying' with 'political activity,' " notes a handout from Independent Sector. "Lobbying — influencing the outcome of legislation by a 501(c)(3) — is lawful, even encouraged by legislation Congress enacted in 1976. Political activity — influencing the outcome of an election by a 501(c)(3) — is not permitted."

Those basic definitions, however, can withstand some creative interpretation. "It is entirely proper for your 501(c)(3) group to inform candidates of your position on issues of the day, to urge candidates to support your position if elected and to ask them to go on record as pledging their support," Independent Sector advises, adding that tax-exempts may distribute questionnaires to candidates, conduct candidate forums and publish voting records. But such undertakings must be even-handed and nonpartisan, and shouldn't be done when a political campaign is in full swing, it says.

A further refinement distinguishes between communications that a non-

Continued on p. 1142

Chronology

1950s ***Number of U.S. tax-exempt nonprofits estimated at 50,000.***

1950
Congress passes unrelated business income tax (UBIT).

1954
Congress clarifies classifications of tax exempts.

1960s ***Number of nonprofits grows to 250,000 in response to Great Society programs and citizen activism in civil rights, environment and consumer affairs.***

1969
Tax Reform Act separates private foundations from "operating foundations" and public charities and makes associations a separate class of nonprofits.

1970s ***First modern-day campaign-finance rulings.***

1974
Employee Retirement Income Security Act (ERISA) requires Internal Revenue Service (IRS) to regulate tax-exempts. Congress passes post-Watergate campaign finance amendments.

1975
Filer Commission releases first major study on nonprofits.

1976
Supreme Court in *Buckley v. Valeo* says political spending is a form of free speech, but allows caps on contributions. Tax Reform Act spells out lobbying options for 501(c)(3)s.

1978
Yale University establishes Program on Nonprofit Organizations. Federal Election Commission (FEC) allows "soft money" contributions to political parties.

1979
Congress amends Federal Election Campaign Act with effect of permitting soft money.

1980s ***Number of nonprofits increases to 1 million.***

1980
National Conservative Political Action Committee sets precedent by funneling money into Senate races, defeating four liberal senators.

1983
Social Security Act amendments require nonprofits to pay Social Security taxes.

1986
Tax Reform Act views tax-exempt status as privilege rather than right.

1987
Congress passes Tax-Exempt Organizations' Lobbying and Political Activities Accountability Act distinguishing between lobbying and politics. House subcommittee begins hearings on UBIT.

1988
Supreme Court in *Communications Workers of America v. Beck* says non-union workers must get refund of dues used for politics.

1990s ***Nonprofits grow to more than 1.1 million.***

1990
Supreme Court rules in *Austin v. Michigan Chamber of Commerce* that a nonprofit may not spend general treasury funds on political campaigns.

1991
FEC requires disclosure of soft-money donors.

1993
Omnibus Budget Reconciliation Act disallows corporations, individuals and tax-exempts from taking tax deductions for politics and lobbying.

1995
Newly empowered House Republicans repeatedly attach amendments to bar federal grants to tax-exempt groups that lobby. President Clinton signs Lobbying Disclosure Act redefining lobbying.

1996
Supreme Court in *Colorado Republican Federal Campaign Committee v. FEC* holds that independent campaign spending by political parties can't be limited.

1997
Congress investigates fund-raising abuses from 1996 campaign. Senate begins debate over McCain-Feingold campaign finance bill. Treasury Department releases proposed regulations requiring nonprofits to make Form 990s public.

Uproar Over Union Dues and Politics . . .

Labor unions, which are designated in the Tax Code as 501(c)(5) organizations, are classified separately from tax-exempt charities and social advocacy groups. But the raging controversy over the use of union dues for political spending has grabbed the attention of many in the nonprofit community.

The conflict flared during the 1996 congressional elections, when political action committees (PACs) run by organized labor spent $35 million on advertisements attacking the Republicans' proposed curbs on federal spending on Medicare and education. The GOP's subsequent loss of nine House seats left party leaders hungry for a chance to clip the political wings of big labor. The vehicle they chose was legislation for campaign finance reform.

Douglas Graham

Labor unions like the Teamsters are designated as 501(c)(5) organizations.

"Most Americans would be shocked to learn that some workers in our nation are forced to contribute to a candidate or campaign they don't support or do not know anything about," Senate Majority Leader Trent Lott, R-Miss., told colleagues during an October 1997 floor debate. He had just offered an amendment to the reform bill championed by Sens. John McCain, R-Ariz., and Russell D. Feingold, D-Wis., that would require unions to obtain written permission from all dues-paying members before spending campaign money on their behalf. Democrats blasted the proposal as a "poison pill" designed to stop the momentum of campaign finance reform, which is opposed by many incumbent Republicans.

"It is a direct and blatant attempt to silence America's working families," AFL-CIO President John Sweeney said in attacking a similar bill in the House. "It singles out legislative and political spending by unions, which were already outspent by corporations 17 to 1 in the last election. . . . But it leaves spending by corporations and other groups like the Chamber of Commerce, the National Rifle Association and the Christian Coalition virtually untouched."

For nonprofits, the debate raises profound questions about the constitutional right to free speech and the right to association, says Frances R. Hill, a law professor at the University of Miami. She cites two important Supreme Court decisions affecting free speech: *Communications Workers of America v. Beck* (1988), which gave dissenting non-union workers the right to a reduction in dues owed for union expenditures beyond collective bargaining activities; and *Austin v. Michigan Chamber of Commerce* (1990), which held that rules prohibiting a nonprofit from spending general treasury funds on political campaigns do not violate the First Amendment.

"It gets down to the rights of the group vs. the rights of members, which is not an easy issue," Hill says. "There is substance to the *Beck* argument, but it is being used tactically by the Republicans as a political weapon. They're saying it isn't enough for unions to be willing to refund dues money, but that the unions can't use the money until they get an affirmative OK from every member, which is a costly administrative burden.

"The unions argue that the presumption should be the other way," Hill continues, "but this makes [dissenting] members vulnerable because they can get cross-eyed with

Continued from p. 1140

profit might make to the public regarding legislation and those made only to members. For example, "Communications made primarily to members (i.e. communications whose recipients are comprised of more than 50 percent members) which refer to and reflect a view on specific legislation but do not directly encourage members to engage in either direct or grass-roots lobbying do not create lobbying expenditures," say lawyers advising the Alliance for Justice. [25]

And even though foundation funds may not be used for lobbying or influencing the outcome of an election either directly or indirectly (as in voter registration drives), foundations teach their staffers that there is an exception in the case of self-defense — should the foundation's tax deductibility be threatened, for example. And the ban applies to direct lobbying, not grass-roots lobbying. It does not prevent the foundation's funds from being used for writing issue papers on a debated topic or from providing technical assistance to lawmakers. [26]

Increasingly in recent years, nonprofits have chosen to err on the side of more politics. "In the past, it has been fashionable for nonprofit administrators to hold what I call the Dog Germ Theory of Politics," writes

. . . Watched Closely by Nonprofit Community

their union leaders. The question of constitutional significance is whether there is a threshold that must be crossed before a group can spend money."

The facts in the debate are in dispute. The AFL-CIO, for example, points to polling data showing that union members by 6 to 1 agree with the positions on legislative and political issues taken by their leadership. Editorial writers at *The Wall Street Journal* counter by citing the "third of union members who routinely vote Republican" as wanting to reduce union political spending because 95 percent of it goes to Democrats.[1]

Additionally, supporters of a crackdown on union spending emphasize that workers in some situations are required to pay union dues to cover collective bargaining even if they don't support the union. That means simply that "no one should be compelled to contribute to any campaign without their consent," as Sen. Don Nickles, R-Okla., said in October.

But the AFL-CIO argues that contributions to union PACs are all voluntary. Union leaders are required to notify members of their option to become "agency fee objectors" who can request a refund of the 18-24 percent of monthly dues that are used for "non-representational" activities such as political issue advocacy, organizing, media relations, community service, lobbying and education.

During debate in October, an effort at a compromise was offered by Sens. Olympia J. Snowe, R-Maine, and James M. Jeffords, R-Vt. They tried to overcome Democratic resistance to curbing union spending by imposing the same requirements for permission from members on nonprofit organizations and corporate shareholders. But Democrats still felt the proposed mechanism was too hard on organized labor and nonprofits, while doing little to curb corporate political spending. The only deal that emerged was the promise of a springtime vote on campaign finance reform.

Critics of labor, meanwhile, have launched a 50-state campaign to persuade state legislatures to enact "payroll protection" initiatives that would accomplish the same purpose as the Lott amendment. The effort is being directed by Americans for Tax Reform, Indianapolis insurance executive and conservative activist J. Patrick Rooney and the American Legislative Exchange Council, a state-legislature monitoring group. After Washington state passed a similar law in 1992 with 72 percent of the voters in support, the percentage of union members giving to their organization's political funds fell drastically.[2] For their part, unions are planning counterinitiatives against business tax breaks and lobbying.

The issue boils down to which side has to go to the most effort to demonstrate knowledge of the political desires of an organizational membership that may be large and diverse, and perhaps secretive, unsure or even apathetic, observers note. And the pressure to take political stands risks spilling over into workplace relationships.

"If I were a truck driver, I'd have to be very brave to go against my union leaders," says Terrence Scanlon, president of the conservative Capital Research Center, which researches funding sources of advocacy groups.

As to whether proposed edicts on union management should apply to nonprofits, Scanlon says the difference is that "in a union, you have no choice. But if I'm a member of the National Rifle Association and I don't like what they're doing, I can drop out and not send any dues."

To Peter Shiras, senior vice president for programs at Independent Sector, a coalition of nonprofits, that freedom for members to disagree and quit is "the whole rationale behind the voluntary sector," he says. "That's our strength, the fact that things are constantly changing and that there are always new groups."

Some nonprofits involve their members in decisions more than others, he adds. "But it's not an area you want government to regulate."

---

[1] *The Wall Street Journal*, editorial, Nov. 19, 1997.

[2] *The Washington Times*, Dec. 1, 1997.

nonprofit management consultant Thomas A. McLaughlin. "Entering the political arena for those folks traditionally has been on a par with getting licked in the mouth by a dog — indescribably disgusting, somehow unhealthy and certainly not the kind of activity in which one voluntarily engages. This is unfortunate, because all nonprofit organizations need some amount of political power with which to carry out their mission."[27]

New Regulations

The past two years have brought important new requirements from the federal government. In 1995, Congress enacted the Lobbying Disclosure Act, the first major update of lobbying law in a half-century. For the first time, it required nonprofits that do substantial lobbying to register their lobbyists in the name of their organizations rather than as individuals.

In 1996, President Clinton signed the Taxpayer Bill of Rights, which changed the rules for nonprofits in two key ways. First, it opened up the nonprofits' revealing IRS registration document, Form 990, to greater public scrutiny. Many nonprofit groups are reluctant to cooperate with requests from outsiders for copies of the forms, fearing scrutiny of their finances and harassment by political opponents who might bust their budgets by demanding multiple copies of 990s, which often stretch to hundreds of pages each.

The new regulations, which came out in September 1997, mandate that all nonprofits within a prescribed time must agree to supply a copy of their 990 to any requester who is willing to pay the costs of copying and postage. The new rules include provisions for reporting possible harassment campaigns to the IRS. Many groups, meanwhile, are hoping that making the document available online will solve the problems of potential harassment.

Another aspect of the Taxpayer Bill of Rights, known as "intermediate sanctions," was eagerly sought by the nonprofit community in reaction to a spate of recent corruption scandals. Over the past decade, several members of the charitable community have been hit, including the United Way of America, the NAACP and the Episcopal Church. [28]

Previously, the IRS' only recourse to corruption was revoking an entity's nonprofit status. Under "intermediate sanctions," executives who violate rules against financial self-dealing or conflict of interest are subject to precise monetary penalties. The IRS expects such targeted penalties to bring the federal Treasury $33 million before the year 2002. [29] ■

CURRENT SITUATION

Reviving Istook?

Though versions of the Istook plan to curb nonprofit advocacy passed the House in 1995 and 1996, it has never become law, and Istook has since withdrawn it from the immediate agenda, his spokeswoman says. "The Republicans were turned back because of sizable lobbying by nonprofits on the left and right, and because of the Rockefeller Foundation's funding of E-mail networks against it," Walters says.

"The Republicans have changed their tone from broad-based attacks to something more piecemeal and targeted," says Bass of OMB Watch. He expects smaller-scale curbs on advocacy by groups that get government grants to be offered during debate on the highway bill reauthorization and juvenile justice bills. On the horizon are proposals for a tax credit for charities other than advocacy groups being offered by Sen. Daniel R. Coats, R-Ind., and Reps. James M. Talent, R-Mo., and J.C. Watts, R-Okla.

Sen. Jeff Bingaman, D-N.M., this fall won Senate approval of a plan to require nonprofits to register with the attorney general if they receive more than $10,000 annually from any foreign government. Sen. Orrin G. Hatch, R-Utah., and Rep. Wally Herger, R-Calif., have offered a bill that would require more detailed disclosure of nonprofits' expenses on politics and lobbying in return for allowing organizations to deduct dues payments as a business expense.

Finally, Rep. Paul E. Gillmor, R-Ohio, has introduced two bills to give corporate shareholders more say in their company's philanthropic activities. After consideration by the House Commerce Committee last May, Gillmor withdrew the proposals and submitted them to the Securities and Exchange Commission for study. Many nonprofits have weighed in against the plan, arguing that average corporate shareholders are not as knowledgeable as corporate philanthropy directors as to which charities and civic groups are most deserving of company support.

"Our members say it will virtually shut down corporate giving," says G. Gregory Barnard, public affairs director for the Council on Foundations. "It would be a logistical nightmare."

Meanwhile, at the White House in October, Vice President Al Gore demonstrated NonProfit Gateway, an online network of federal government sites, to 175 nonprofit leaders and government officials. "The Nonprofit Gateway opens the doors for nonprofit groups to more than 300,000 government Web pages," he said. "This is a remarkable partnership between the federal government and hundreds of nonprofit groups."

Not all the action is in Washington. At the state level, there are signs of strengthened anti-fraud enforcement actions. State attorneys general, for example, are actively publishing new standards against charities that misrepresent their primary purpose, citing a Connecticut charity that spent 90 percent of its money on public education but never mentioned that in its materials. [30]

IRS Guidance

As Congress gears up to restructure the Tax Code and the IRS, it will be considering a proposal long sought by the nonprofit community to beef up the IRS division that issues guidance on compliance by tax-exempts. Set up by the 1974 Employee Retirement Income Security Act (ERISA), the IRS' Office of Employee Plans and Exempt Organizations (EP/EO) has seen its staff size cut in half since 1980, even though the number of tax-exempts doubled in that period, and Congress passed 205 new tax laws. [31]

Continued on p. 1146

At Issue:

Should nonprofits that receive government money be barred from lobbying and advocacy?

REP. DAVID M. McINTOSH, R-IND.

FROM STATEMENT AT HOUSE GOVERNMENT REFORM AND OVERSIGHT SUBCOMMITTEE ON NATIONAL ECONOMIC GROWTH, NATURAL RESOURCES AND REGULATORY AFFAIRS HEARING, JUNE 29, 1995.

yes

One of Washington's best-kept little secrets is welfare for lobbyists. Yes, America, you heard it right. Your tax dollars are being used by special-interest groups to lobby Congress for more tax dollars. This vicious cycle is taxpayer abuse; it is an outrage; and it must end. . . .

Unfortunately, what is shocking outside Washington is business as usual here inside the Beltway. And it's big business. The IRS conservatively reports the federal government gave away more than $39 billion to over 40,000 nonprofit organizations in 1990 alone. Grant recipients themselves admit far more tax dollars are at stake. . . . Independent Sector . . . reported that nonprofits received nearly $160 billion from all government sources combined in 1992.

That means that nearly 39 percent of every dollar received by nonprofit groups in that organization came from the government. And we all know where government gets its money — from you, the taxpayer. How are these billions of dollars being spent? I'm sorry to report that no one really knows. We do know that too much of the money finds its way into the hands of lobbyists.

For example, [in June 1995] the American Bar Association staged a rally here [at] the Capitol to protest the constitutional amendment protecting the American flag. The ABA estimates that it will spend around $2 million this year in lobbying activity. Coincidentally, the best government figures I've been able to find reveal that the ABA receives about $2.2 million in taxpayer-funded grants.

Although the [National Fish and Wildlife] foundation tries to follow an internal rule that prohibits it from lobbying . . . Interior Secretary [Bruce] Babbitt recently pressured the foundation's board of directors to lobby Congress to prevent the budget cuts at the National Biological Service. . . .

A former member of the board, Steve Robinson, advised us he resigned from the board in December 1992 "as a result of the foundation's involvement in political advocacy and outright lobbying." While not every grant, and maybe not even the majority of grants, is used to lobby the government, these federal dollars do free up the special-interest private dollars so they can spend it on political advocacy. . . .

Our focus is on good government and protecting the taxpayer. Whether it's the Nature Conservancy and other groups on the left, or the Chamber of Commerce on the right, if any special interest takes taxpayer dollars to lobby for more money, it's just plain wrong.

REP. DAVID E. SKAGGS, D-COLO.

FROM STATEMENT ON HOUSE FLOOR, NOV. 8, 1995

no

It is an extremist idea to restrict the ability of all types of organizations to use their own funds to participate in community and national affairs. It would restrict the ability of the Red Cross, Mothers Against Drunk Driving, the YMCA, the Heart Association and hundreds of other charities to carry out their mission. . . .

It is already illegal to use funds federally to lobby. What this provision is really about is regulating and restricting the way charities and other groups use their own private money to speak to their elected officials about what their communities need.

There are many reasons to oppose it:

- The massive red tape and bureaucracy forced on all of the tens of thousands of affected organizations as they have to file their yearly political activity reports with the federal government.
- The audits that can be imposed on all grantees, individuals, small and large charities and businesses of all sizes.
- This provision's incredibly broad definition of "political advocacy," which goes way beyond traditional lobbying to include every conceivable kind of contact with any level of government, trying to inform the public about legislation, and, if you can believe this, a definition that even attributes to one organization the political advocacy activities of another with which it does business, if that other organization exceeds these silly limits on free speech.
- The bounty hunter lawsuits that this provision encourages against all those affected individuals, businesses and churches that are swept up by this net. And the unreasonable shifting of the burden of proof to all those individuals, churches, charities and businesses to prove their own innocence, to prove their compliance, not just by the usual burden of proof of a preponderance of the evidence, but by a very much higher standard — clear and convincing evidence.
- Finally, the broad definition of "grant" including not just funds but anything of value that anyone receives from the federal government, again affecting literally millions of Americans.

At a time when we are asking more of charities in America, why in the world do we want to force the American Red Cross to limit its ability to work with local governments in emergency preparedness and making sure the blood supply is safe? Why in the world do we want to restrict the ability of Mothers Against Drunk Driving to work with state legislatures for safer highways?. . . .

This is certainly the most egregious attack on the basic values of this democracy that we have seen in a long, long time.

FOR MORE INFORMATION

Alliance for Justice, 2000 P St. N.W., Suite 712, Washington, D.C. 20036; (202) 822-6070. Founded in 1985 to monitor judicial nominations, this group also tracks legislation and produces strategic advice to nonprofits on lobbying and political activity.

Capital Research Center, 1513 16th St. N.W., Washington, D.C. 20036; (202) 483-6900. This nonpartisan research and education center studies patterns in philanthropy from a conservative perspective.

Independent Sector, 1828 L St. N.W., Washington, D.C. 20036; (202) 223-8100. Founded in 1980, this national voluntary leadership forum of 800 nonprofits works to encourage philanthropy, volunteering, initiative by nonprofits and citizen action.

National Committee for Responsive Philanthropy, 2001 S St. N.W., Suite 620, Washington, D.C., 20009; (202) 387-9177. Founded in 1976, this group publishes research and commentary with the goal of making philanthropy more responsive to disenfranchised people.

Support Center of Washington, 2001 O St. N.W., Washington, D.C. 20035-5955; (202) 833-0300. The center provides financial management, accounting and fund-raising assistance to nonprofits.

Continued from p. 1144

The division, which doesn't receive an earmarked appropriation, must monitor nonprofits and publish regulations affecting $1.2 trillion in tax-exempt assets and $1.7 trillion in retirement assets. "The main purpose of this section is to define the institutions, purposes and activities that society has chosen to refrain from taxing," the Council on Foundations explains. "The EP/EO division is the only national authority with the power to patrol the boundaries between legitimate and illegitimate behavior."

Last June, the Commission on Restructuring the Internal Revenue Service recommended that the EP/EO get its appropriation. There is a feeling that many of the scandals that have rocked the nonprofit world could be avoided with proper IRS guidance. "The allegations of Rep. Istook about misused federal money have caused the public image of charities to drop," Bass says. "We want to help the public be assured that things are being enforced."

Regulations "don't do a bit of good unless someone is there to monitor compliance and respond when there's a problem," adds Bothwell of the Committee for Responsive Philanthropy.

Proposals to staff up the IRS are "fluff," says Scanlon of the Capital Research Center. "The regulations are clear on what groups can do. We don't need a stronger IRS."

House Ways and Means Committee Chairman Bill Archer, R-Texas, is reviewing the proposal to boost the EP/EO division. The IRS, meanwhile, performed some 11,000 audits of nonprofits in 1996, a spokeswoman says. And it is actively investigating 50 nonprofits from across the political spectrum.

One Republican proposal that has been implemented is the plan by Rep. Doolittle to require all witnesses who appear before committees to declare what federal grants they receive. The government passes out some $250 billion annually in grant money and contracts, while more than half the witnesses on Capitol Hill during the 104th Congress were recipients, a Heritage Foundation study notes.[32]

Heritage proposes that all such contracts be available on a Web site in order to "give members of the executive and legislative branches and their staffs a better opportunity to learn the motives of those who lobby for federal largess by other means."

Instead of legislation, the disclosure requirement has been implemented as a House rule, with undramatic results. The AFL-CIO, for example, simply ignored it, while TRW Corp. had its representative testify as an individual rather than a staffer to avoid full disclosure. In January 1997, the House Rules Committee decided that the only relevant federal grants were those directly related to the given hearing. Still, Doolittle says he is pleased with results.[33] ■

OUTLOOK

Perils of Success

"The biggest enemy of advocacy organizations is not government officials or an uneducated public or a disease or disabling condition [but] their own success," writes management consultant McLaughlin, citing the case of Action for Children's Television, which disbanded several years ago when it was on the verge of winning federal children's education requirements on TV stations. "Knowing how to influence public policy and resource allocation is hard enough, but knowing when to recognize success and how to shift methods is even more difficult."[34]

Harsh scrutiny of nonprofits is likely to continue, particularly if politicians continue to set more of them up as a way to channel campaign funds. "What we saw in 1996 was the tip of the iceberg," said Warren Ilchman, a professor of philanthropic studies at the University of

Indiana. "What we're going to see in 1998, if we don't close this loophole that allows people to influence elections and remain anonymous, is a tidal wave of money in issue-advocacy ads." [35] (Already, the Republican crop of presidential candidates for the year 2000, including Lamar Alexander, Steve Forbes and Dan Quayle, have each formed political committees with bland-sounding names such as Forbes' Americans for Hope, Growth and Opportunity.) [36]

"Instead of solving the political-money problem by restructuring charities," says law Professor Hill, "let's restructure the politicians who misused charities as conduits."

Cooper of the Center for Responsive Politics says: "We may need a period of years to see what type of spending takes place before we can give the IRS a point of reference" for new rules. One way to evade the free-speech conflict with political money, he says, would be to require independent groups to file their political donor's names and addresses with the FEC via the Internet.

But there will always be gray areas and the tendency of politicians to use nonprofit issues to go after opponents. "Politically charged investigations and IRS audits are not likely to help the situation and will only create greater confusion about what activities are and are not allowed," writes attorney Jeffrey P. Altman. "Instead, a cooperative effort by the nonprofit community, the IRS and Congress should be initiated to develop safe harbor rules in order to provide clear guidance and achieve general compliance." [37]

The problem with scandals in nonprofits, says Jim Clarke, vice president for government affairs at the ASAE, "is that everybody gets put under one tent. There are tens of thousands of associations. If anything resulted from [all the debate since 1995], it is that it has made everyone in nonprofits work harder to see that they are heard."

Nonprofits are being advised to pay attention to rules on lobbying, stay away from partisan squabbles and refrain from direct attacks on politicians. "Governments usually feel more threatened by groups than by individuals, who can generally do little harm by acting on their own," writes University of Maryland public policy Professor Adam Yarmolinsky. "And governments often see businesses as less threatening than groups that operate without a profit motive." [38] ■

Notes

[1] *The Washington Post,* Nov. 20, 1997.

[2] Michael O'Neill, *The Third America: The Emergence of the Nonprofit Sector in the United States* (1989), p. 1.

[3] *Responsive Philanthropy* (newsletter), spring 1996, p. 1.

[4] Joe Laconte, "The 7 Deadly Sins of Government Funding for Private Charities," *Policy Review,* March-April, 1997, p. 28.

[5] American Society of Association Executives, "What Every Lawmaker Should Know About America's Not-for-Profit Associations," 1994.

[6] Jennifer Moore, "Congresswoman Plans Very 'In-Depth' Hearings on Non-Profit Groups," *Chronicle of Philanthropy,* Oct. 17, 1996, p. 30.

[7] See "The New Volunteerism," *The CQ Researcher,* Dec. 13, 1996, pp. 1081-1104, and "Civic Renewal," *The CQ Researcher,* March 21, 1997, p. 244-267.

[8] Thomas J. DiLorenzo, "Frightening America's Elderly: How the Age Lobby Holds Seniors Captive," Capital Research Center (1996), p. 35.

[9] Testimony given on Aug. 2, 1995, to House Government Reform and Oversight Subcommittee on National Economic Growth, Natural Resources and Regulatory Affairs.

[10] See "Campaign Finance," *The CQ Researcher,* Dec. 9, 1996, pp. 121-144.

[11] Annenberg Public Policy Center, "Issue Advocacy Advertising During the 1996 Campaign: A Catalog," Sept. 16, 1997, p. 4.

[12] Rebecca Carr, "Tax-Exempt Groups Scrutinized as Fund-Raising Clout Grows," *CQ Weekly Report,* Feb. 22, 1997, p. 471.

[13] See Lisa Rosenberg, "A Bag of Tricks: Loopholes in the Campaign Finance System," Center for Responsive Politics, 1997, p. 10.

[14] *Capital Eye* (newsletter of the Center for Responsive Politics), Nov. 15, 1997.

[15] See "Roe V. Wade at 25," *The CQ Researcher,* Nov. 28, 1997, pp. 1033-1056.

[16] Douglas Johnson and Mike Beard, "Campaign Reform: Let's Not Give Politicians the Power to Decide What We Can Say About Them," *Cato Institute Briefing Paper,* July 4, 1997.

[17] Michelle, Cottle, "Where are the Good Guys When We Need Them?" *The Washington Monthly,* Sept. 1, 1997.

[18] Peter Dobkin Hall, "A History of Nonprofit Boards in the United States," National Center for Nonprofit Boards, 1997, p. 3.

[19] O'Neill, *op. cit.,* p. 14.

[20] Quoted in Stephen V. Monsma, *When Sacred and Secular Mix: Religious Nonprofit Organizations and Public Money* (1996), p. 18.

[21] Independent Sector and National Center for NonProfit Boards, "What You Should Know About NonProfits" (1997).

[22] O'Neill, *op. cit.,* p. 145.

[23] Richard F. Wacht, *Financial Management in Nonprofit Organizations* (1984), p. 20.

[24] *Ibid.,* p. 20.

[25] Gail M. Harmon, Jessica A. Ladd and Eleanor A. Evans, "Being a Player: A Guide to the IRS Lobbying Regulations for Advocacy Charities," *Alliance for Justice,* p. 21.

[26] Council on Foundations, "Foundations and Lobbying: Safe Ways to Affect Public Policy," 1991.

[27] Thomas A. McLaughlin, *The Entrepreneurial Nonprofit Executive* (1991), p. 223.

[28] See National Center for Nonprofit Boards, "A Closer Look at Scandals in the Nonprofit Sector," *Board Member,* September 1996. See also "Charitable Giving," *The CQ Researcher,* Nov. 12, 1993, pp. 985-1008.

[29] Susan A. Cobb, "Intermediate Sanctions: Planning for Organizations to Avoid the New Penalties," *Association Law & Policy Special Report,* April 1, 1997.

[30] Betsy Hills Bush, "New Regulations Challenge Nonprofit Mailers, Direct Marketers," *Nonprofit Times,* October 1997, p.33.

[31] James J. McGovern and Phil Brand, "EP/EO — One of the Most Innovative and Efficient Functions Within the IRS," *Tax Notes,* Aug. 25, 1997, p. 1099.

[32] Kenneth R. Weinstein, "It's Time for Full Public Disclosure of all Federal Grants and Contracts," Heritage Foundation report, March 13, 1997.

[33] Cheryl Bolen, *BNA National Affairs,* Oct. 29, 1997.

[34] Thomas A. McLaughlin, "Future Shock," *Nonprofit Times,* December 1997, p. 15.

[35] Albert Eisele, "Your Money, Their Views," *The New York Times,* Dec. 9, 1997.

[36] *The Washington Post,* Nov. 25, 1997.

[37] *ASAE Association Law and Policy,* March 1, 1997, p. 4.

[38] *The Chronicle of Philanthropy,* April 18, 1996, p. 42.

Bibliography

Selected Sources Used

Books

Bennett, James T., and Thomas J. DiLorenzo, *Unfair Competition: The Profits of Nonprofits,* Hamilton Press, 1989.
Two scholars affiliated with the Capital Research Center trace the history and tax policy surrounding the reliance among tax-exempt groups on sales of goods and services that critics say compete with commercial vendors.

O'Neill, Michael, *The Third America: The Emergence of the Nonprofit Sector in the United States,* Jossey-Bass, 1989.
The director of a center for nonprofit management at the University of San Francisco examines the history and development of America's unique "invisible sector," which has been called "'perhaps the biggest unknown success story in American history."

McLaughlin, Thomas A., *The Entrepreneurial Nonprofit Executive,* Fund Raising Institute, 1991.
A management consultant and columnist for *The NonProfit Times* offers this pep talk for leaders of tax-exempt groups, encouraging them to grow the organization's finances and to lobby aggressively within prescribed limits.

Monsma, Stephen V., *When Sacred and Secular Mix: Religious Nonprofit Organizations and Public Money,* Rowman and Littlefield, 1996.
A Peppardine University political scientist offers a detailed discussion of how religiously based nonprofits can dovetail with government programs and use government funds without violating the separation of church and state.

Wacht, Richard F., *Financial Management in Nonprofit Organizations,* Georgia State University, 1984.
A veteran accountant in the nonprofit world offers hands-on tips and a theoretical understanding of financial strategies for tax-exempt groups while discussing relevant tax and regulatory policy

Reports

DiLorenzo, Thomas J., "Frightening America's Elderly: How the Age Lobby Holds Seniors Captive," Capital Research Center, 1996.
A Loyola College (Baltimore) economist lays out the conservative case against nonprofits that lobby on general policy issues but that also receive government grants and sell goods and services that might compete with commercial vendors.

Hall, Peter Dobkin, "A History of Nonprofit Boards in the United States," National Center for Nonprofit Boards, 1997.
A Yale University research scientist who specializes in nonprofits has assembled this historical portrait of how the governing bodies of American nonprofits came to be established as partners with government and business.

Independent Sector and the National Center for Nonprofit Boards, "What You Should Know About Nonprofits," 1997.
This brief overview of the mission and makeup of the "Third Sector" address such issues as whether nonprofits can lobby or make a profit while describing how they are monitored, regulated and governed.

Rosenberg, Lisa, "A Bag of Tricks: Loopholes in the Campaign Finance System," Center for Responsive Politics, 1996.
This compilation of data and analysis of recent elections explores how political action committees, candidates, political parties and tax-exempt advocacy groups use money, staff and advertising to influence elections, violating the spirit if not the letter, Rosenberg argues, of campaign finance law.

Articles

Laconte, Joe, "The 7 Deadly Sins of Government Funding for Private Charities," *Policy Review,* March-April, 1997, p. 28.
A writer from the conservative Heritage Foundation criticizes government's increasing reliance on nonprofits to attack social problems, asserting that federal regulations damage charities by encouraging waste, paperwork and bureaucracy.

The Next Step

Additional information from UMI's Newspaper & Periodical Abstracts™ database

Advertising Issues

Bunting, Glenn F., Ralph Frammolino and Mark Gladstone, "Nonprofits Behind Attack Ads Prompt Senate Probe; Politics: Groups' activities often paralleled GOP aims. Law says they must stay clear of partisan campaigns," *Los Angeles Times,* May 5, 1997, p. A1.

A controversial political advertisement thought to have been placed by the Republican Party actually was purchased by one of a cluster of obscure nonprofit groups that ostensibly are not involved in supporting or opposing candidates but weighed in during the last national political campaign. The groups — unlike overt political organizations — provided total anonymity and no monetary limits for their donors.

Carney, Eliza Newlin, "Air strikes," *National Journal,* June 15, 1996, p. 4.

Hard-hitting "issue" ads that attack lawmakers' records have become a favorite campaign weapon. Campaign finance laws don't cover these ads, disclosure requirements are minimal and there's no limit to how much money can be spent on the ads.

Roth, Bennett, "Democrats challenge funds spent by nonprofit groups," *Houston Chronicle,* Nov. 1, 1997, p. A1.

Conservative groups have come under heightened scrutiny by congressional Democrats, who are looking into fund-raising abuses. The Democrats claim the groups allowed GOP donors to circumvent campaign finance laws by quietly directing unlimited sums of money into political campaigns.

Campaign Finance

"Anybody hearing this?" *The Progressive,* September 1997, pp. 8-9.

The details of the campaign finance scandals have come out in the hearings before the Senate Governmental Affairs Committee, but the public has expressed little interest. Information from the hearings and the lack of public interest is discussed.

Babcock, Charles R., and Susan Schmidt, "Voters Group Donor Got DNC Perk; Man With Nigeria Ties was at Clinton Dinner," *The Washington Post,* Nov. 22, 1997, p. A1.

Officials of the Democratic National Committee helped a foreign businessman closely tied to Nigerian dictator Sani Abacha attend a White House holiday dinner with President Clinton last year, a few months after he contributed $460,000 to a voter registration group that won support from the DNC. The businessman was solicited by a DNC fund-raiser last fall to give to a Miami-based nonprofit voter registration group, Vote Now 96. Vote Now 96 is supposed to be nonpartisan. Records show that much of the money it raised last year was directed to other nonprofits and voter registration groups. Though foreigners are barred from contributing to political parties, they may legally contribute to nonprofit groups.

Garnaas, Steve, "Little League actions probed Northern Lights made donation," *The Denver Post,* May 16, 1997, p. B1.

An Adams County Little League group slated to get a $500,000 ballfield complex courtesy of the city and the Colorado Rockies is under investigation by Little League Baseball's Western regional office on several allegations, including a charge that league funds were used improperly to fund a political campaign.

Marcus, Ruth, and Ira Chinoy, "A fund-raising 'mistake': DNC held event in Buddhist temple," *The Washington Post,* Oct. 17, 1996, p. A1.

The Democratic National Committee acknowledged on Oct. 16, 1996, that it made a "mistake" in holding a fund-raiser at a Buddhist temple in California that brought in $140,000. Churches are not supposed to hold political events because of their tax status as nonprofit charitable institutions.

Ridgeway, James, "A consuming probe," *The Village Voice,* Aug. 12, 1997, p. 28.

The national chapter of Citizen Action, which claims to be the nation's largest consumer watchdog organization, is now being investigated for fraud and illegal campaign contributions.

Simpson, Glenn R., and Phil Kuntz, "Pennsylvania's Cones Secretly Funded Controversial '96 GOP Election Effort," *The Wall Street Journal,* Oct. 29, 1997, p. A4.

Between mid-1995 and November 1996, members of the Cone family of Pennsylvania made a series of payments totaling as much as $1.8 million to accounts controlled by a Republican-oriented consulting firm called Triad Management Services Inc. Much of the money went to two nonprofit groups that spent at least $3 million last fall on advertisements that benefited

Republican candidates for Congress. Triad officials and others associated with the groups have refused to identify their financial backers. Senate investigators say payments from the Cone family to Triad totaled about $600,000 while their payments to the two nonprofit groups totaled about $1.2 million.

Wayne, Leslie, "Inquiry Into G.O.P. Stalls as Donors Are Named," *The New York Times,* Oct. 28, 1997, p. A18.

Secret bank documents containing the names of donors to two conservative nonprofit groups that helped elect Republican candidates in 1996, have inadvertently fallen into the hands of Democratic members of the Senate Governmental Affairs Committee, and the Democrats are refusing to surrender them. The dispute has led the committee's Republican majority to cancel the part of its campaign finance hearings that would have examined potential Republican abuses involving two conservative nonprofit groups and the donors identified in the bank documents.

Wayne, Leslie, "Papers Detail G.O.P. Ties To Tax Group," *The New York Times,* Nov. 10, 1997, p. A27.

Bank documents that have emerged after the Senate hearings on campaign finance abuses reveal new details of a plan by the Republican National Committee to pour more than $4 million into the 1996 congressional races through an allied group that may have operated outside federal election laws. The outlines of a general arrangement between the group, Americans for Tax Reform, a conservative nonprofit group, and the Republican committee have long been known by Senate investigators. New documents, made available yesterday, show a high level of detailed, specific coordination between the Republican committee and the D.C.-based group over how $4.6 million in Republican Party money would be spent in the closing days of the 1996 campaign. The Republican National Committee and Americans for Tax Reform have long maintained that there was no coordination between them.

Nonprofit Conversions

Butler, Patricia A., "State policy issues in nonprofit conversions," *Health Affairs,* March 1997, pp. 69-84.

Legal authority that states can use to oversee conversions and outlines of several policy issues facing state regulators that could be addressed by new legislation are examined.

"Curbs Backed on Sale of Hospitals," *The New York Times,* June 1, 1997, p. A32.

In an effort to fend off problems involving for-profit hospitals, the General Assembly has passed a measure that would strictly regulate the sale of nonprofit hospitals to profit-making companies. In some states, the bulk of the proceeds from such sales have sometimes gone to the hospitals' top executives. But under the Connecticut measure, all the proceeds would go into a charitable foundation to be used for public health.

Claxton, Gary, Judith Feder, David Shactman and Stuart Altman, "Public policy issues in nonprofit conversions: An overview," *Health Affairs,* March 1997, pp. 9-28.

The question of whether ownership status of hospitals and health plans makes a difference is examined. A review of conversion activity raises questions for public debate.

Goldstein, Amy, and Hamil R. Harris, "GWU Escapes Proposed Limits on Sales of Nonprofit Hospitals," *The Washington Post,* June 4, 1997, p. B3.

George Washington University emerged largely unscathed yesterday after a months-long lobbying campaign to persuade the D.C. City Council to block the sale of its hospital to a for-profit health-care chain.

Johnston, Michelle Dally, "Panel kills bill reining nonprofit-hospital sales," *The Denver Post,* March 25, 1997, p. A18.

A House committee on Monday stunned top state officials, including the attorney general and the state's insurance commissioner, by killing a bill that would have regulated the sale of nonprofit Colorado hospitals to for-profit companies. HB 1326 would have required the attorney general's office to review the sale of nonprofit health-care organizations in an effort to ensure that the assets of the organization had been fairly valued. After a fair price had been paid, the bill would have required that the funds be used to establish a nonprofit foundation to continue the charitable mission of the original organization.

Langley, Monica, and Anita Sharpe, "Acute reaction: As big hospital chains take over nonprofits, a backlash is growing," *The Wall Street Journal,* Oct. 18, 1996, p. A1.

A backlash is brewing against the takeover of nonprofit hospitals by big investor-owned hospital chains. State officials worry that too many of these tax-exempt institutions, long regarded as the mainstay of public health care, will be gobbled up by the national chains without any public scrutiny.

Nonprofit Lobbying

Lewis, Neil A. "Nonprofit Groups to Defy Subpoenas in Senate Inquiry," *The New York Times,* Sept. 4, 1997, p. A16.

Representatives of more than two dozen nonprofit lobbying groups said today that they would not comply with subpoenas issued by the Senate committee investigating political fund-raising. Over the last several days, each of the groups has begun the formal process of notifying the committee of its intention to defy the subpoenas, setting up a confrontation with the committee and a possible court challenge. The 26 groups represent an extraordinary coalition across the political spectrum. They include the Christian Coalition, the Sierra Club, the National Right to Life Committee and Emily's List, which works to elect Democratic women who support abortion rights.

"Truth about 'nonprofit' lobbies," *Atlanta Journal,* Jan. 21, 1997, p. A8.

An editorial explains the new "Truth-in-Testimony" rule passed by the House to require nonprofit lobbying groups and others that receive government aid to disclose that information in any testimony before Congress.

Ratcliffe, R. G., "Suit attempts to reveal list of nonprofit group donors," *Houston Chronicle,* Oct. 13, 1997, p. A25.

In 1997, more than 30 nonprofit corporations spent $1-$2 million to lobby the Texas Legislature without being required to disclose the source of their funding to the Texas Ethics Commission. Now the one state law that a citizen might use to obtain donor lists of such organizations, the Texas Nonprofit Corporations Act, has run squarely into the First Amendment in a case filed by a group of Corpus Christi citizens against the Bay Area Citizens Against Lawsuit Abuse.

Tax-Exempt Status

Campos, Carlos, "Fulton nonprofits lose tax-exempt vehicle tags; Referendum, county board prompt change," *Atlanta Constitution,* July 17, 1997, p. B3.

This spring, the Atlanta Union Mission was forced to pay $692 to get tags on its four vans, and Executive Director Vince Smith still isn't certain why. Taxes on motor vehicles owned by the Christian-based organization for the homeless had always been waived by the Fulton County tax commissioner. The Atlanta Union Mission isn't the only charitable outfit asking that question. At least 30 other nonprofit organizations — private schools, hospitals and charities in Fulton County were also denied.

Edwards, Mike, "Nonprofits serve the needy," *USA Today,* Oct. 29, 1996, p. A12.

In a letter to the editor, Edwards, president of the Los Angeles Mission, argues that the state of Colorado's attempt to reverse its tax-exemption policies for nonprofit organizations is cause for alarm, especially if the amendment passes and other states follow.

Nordheimer, Jon, and Douglas Frantz, "Testing Giant Exceeds Roots, Drawing Business Rivals' Ire," *The New York Times,* Sept. 30, 1997, p. A1.

Over the last decade, the Educational Testing Service (ETS) has transformed itself from a small nonprofit educational institution into the world's largest testing company, administering 9 million yearly examinations that help determine the future of millions of Americans and foreigners trying to get into good schools or professions. Along with that growth have come new questions and criticism from inside and out. ETS is a nonprofit organization, a status that critics say gives the testing service unfair advantages. As a nonprofit, ETS does not have to pay corporate income taxes, which saves it tens of millions of dollars, freeing up cash to hire workers and develop ever more sophisticated tests

Raspberry, William, "Test for the tax-exempt," *The Washington Post,* Oct. 21, 1996, p. A19.

Raspberry discusses a proposition on Colorado's ballot to take away the property-tax exemptions enjoyed by churches and other nonprofit institutions.

Savage, David G., "Tax Break for Nonprofit Groups Upheld; Supreme Court Justices rule organizations can't be denied usual property levy exemption because they serve mainly out-of-state clients," *Los Angeles Times,* May 20, 1997, p. A4.

The Supreme Court on Monday shielded private colleges, charities, research institutions and other nonprofit groups from losing their state tax exemptions because they serve a national clientele.

Sahagun, Louis, "Colorado initiative targets churches' tax-exempt status," *Los Angeles Times,* Oct. 8, 1996, p. A1.

Colorado trial lawyer John Patrick Michael Murphy managed to get a state initiative on the November 1996 ballot to end tax exemptions for 8,300 churches and nonprofit groups.

"Tax report: Mixing politics," *The Wall Street Journal,* Oct. 30, 1996, p. A1.

More churches could be headed for trouble with the IRS because of their involvement in political campaigns. Nonprofit organizations, like churches and charities, risk losing their exempt status if they endorse or oppose candidates.

"Tax report: Tax-exempt groups," *The Wall Street Journal,* Nov. 13, 1996, p. A1.

A House Ways and Means subcommittee plans to hold hearings in 1997 on the rapidly growing world of tax-exempt organizations.

Back Issues

Great Research on Current Issues Starts Right Here . . . Recent topics covered by The CQ Researcher are listed below. Before May 1991, reports were published under the name of Editorial Research Reports.

JUNE 1996
Rethinking NAFTA
First Ladies
Teaching Values
Labor Movement's Future

JULY 1996
Recovered-Memory Debate
Native Americans' Future
Crackdown on Sexual Harassment
Attack on Public Schools

AUGUST 1996
Fighting Over Animal Rights
Privatizing Government Services
Child Labor and Sweatshops
Cleaning Up Hazardous Wastes

SEPTEMBER 1996
Gambling Under Attack
The States and Federalism
Civic Journalism
Reassessing Foreign Aid

OCTOBER 1996
Political Consultants
Insurance Fraud
Rethinking School Integration
Parental Rights

NOVEMBER 1996
Global Warming
Clashing Over Copyright
Consumer Debt
Governing Washington, D.C.

DECEMBER 1996
Welfare, Work and the States
The New Volunteerism
Implementing the Disabilities Act
America's Pampered Pets

JANUARY 1997
Combating Scientific Misconduct
Restructuring the Electric Industry
The New Immigrants
Chemical and Biological Weapons

FEBRUARY 1997
Assisting Refugees
Alternative Medicine's Next Phase
Independent Counsels
Feminism's Future

MARCH 1997
New Air Quality Standards
Alcohol Advertising
Civic Renewal
Educating Gifted Students

APRIL 1997
Declining Crime Rates
The FBI Under Fire
Gender Equity in Sports
Space Program's Future

MAY 1997
The Stock Market
The Cloning Controversy
Expanding NATO
The Future of Libraries

JUNE 1997
FDA Reform
China After Deng
Line-Item Veto
Breast Cancer

JULY 1997
Transportation Policy
Executive Pay
School Choice Debate
Aggressive Driving

AUGUST 1997
Age Discrimination
Banning Land Mines
Children's Television
Evolution vs. Creationism

SEPTEMBER 1997
Caring for the Dying
Mental Health Policy
Mexico's Future
Youth Fitness

OCTOBER 1997
Urban Sprawl in the West
Diversity in the Workplace
Teacher Education
Contingent Work Force

NOVEMBER 1997
Renewable Energy
Artificial Intelligence
Religious Persecution
Roe v. Wade at 25

DECEMBER 1997
Whistleblowers
Castro's Next Move
Gun Control Standoff

Back issues are available for $5.00 (subscribers) or $10.00 (non-subscribers). Quantity discounts apply to orders over ten. To order, call Congressional Quarterly Customer Service at (202) 887-8621.

Binders are available for $18.00. To order call 1-800-638-1710. Please refer to stock number 648.

Future Topics

- ***New Approaches to Foster Care***
- ***IRS Reform***
- ***Black Middle Class***

The CQ Researcher

Subject-Title Index

January 1991-December 1997

NOTE: Weekly *CQ Researcher* reports are indexed by title under boldface subject headings. Titles are followed by the date of the report and the number of the first page. Page numbers followed by asterisks refer to sidebars or the "At Issue" pro/con feature. Issues dated before May 10, 1991, were published under the name of *Editorial Research Reports*.